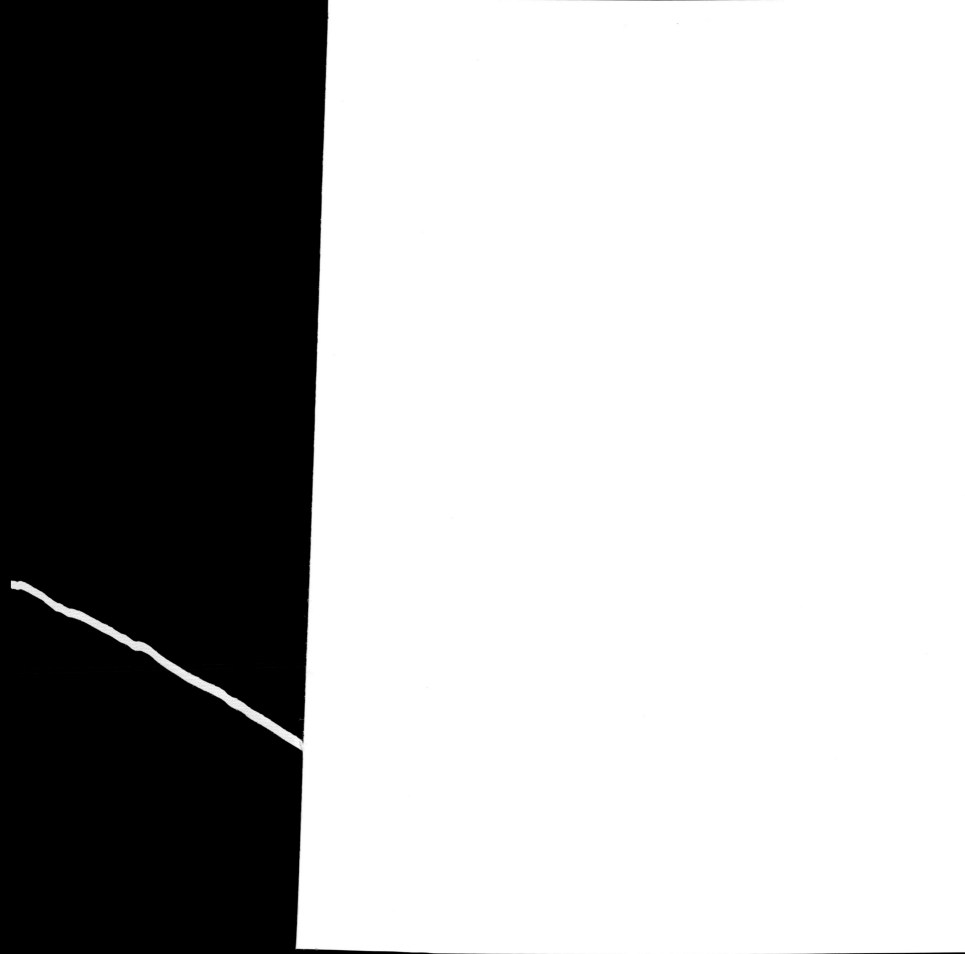

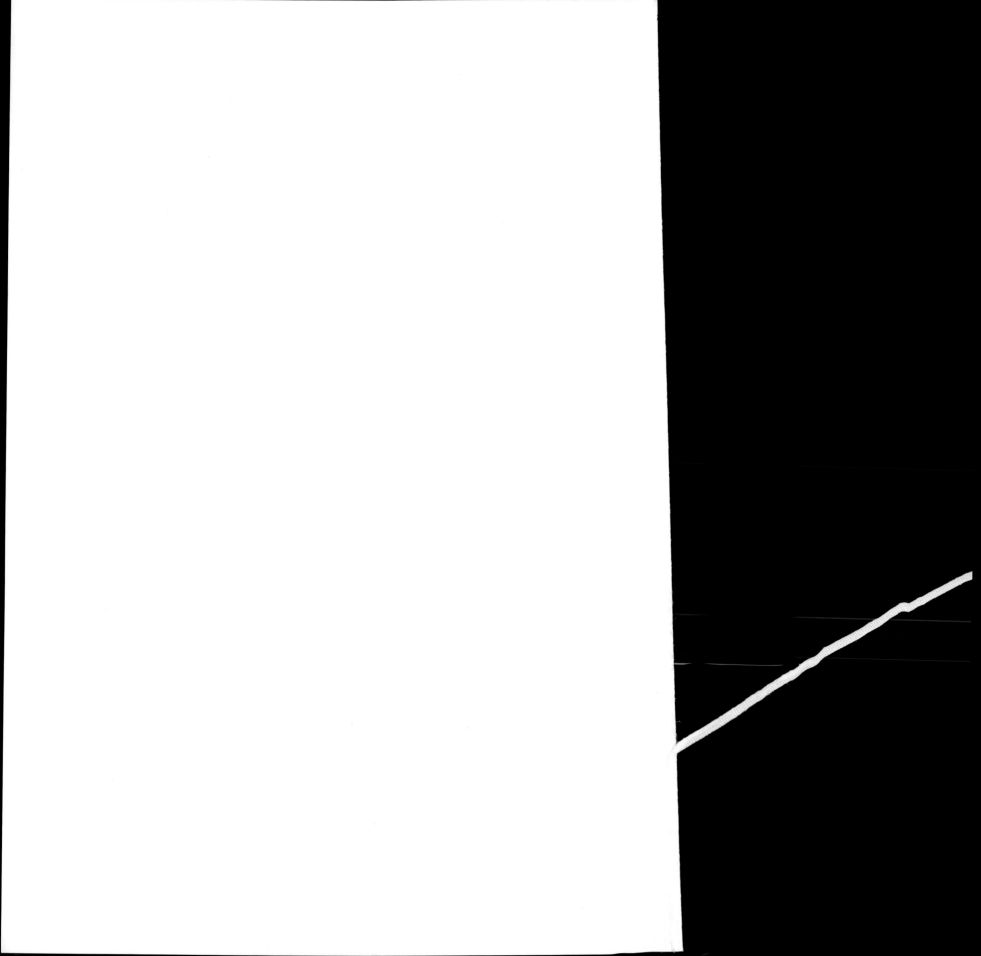

CASES AND MATERIALS

CRIMINAL LAW AND PROCEDURE

ELEVENTH EDITION

by

RONALD N. BOYCE
Professor of Law, The University of Utah

DONALD A. DRIPPS
Professor of Law
University of San Diego School of Law

ROLLIN M. PERKINS
Connell Professor of Law Emeritus, UCLA
Professor Emeritus, University of California
Hastings College of the Law

FOUNDATION PRESS
2010

THOMSON REUTERS™

© 1952, 1959, 1966, 1972, 1977, 1984, 1989, 1999, 2004 FOUNDATION PRESS

© 2007 THOMSON REUTERS/FOUNDATION PRESS

© 2010 By THOMSON REUTERS/FOUNDATION PRESS

      195 Broadway, 9th Floor

      New York, NY 10007

      Phone Toll Free 1–877–888–1330

      Fax (212) 367–6799

      foundation–press.com

Printed in the United States of America

ISBN 978–1–59941–592–5

Mat #40775059

INTRODUCTION TO THE
ELEVENTH EDITION

Three years have passed since the task of composing the introduction to a new edition last fell to me. I have found it sounder to teach complicity before teaching conspiracy, and the new edition reflects that judgment. I have also modified the materials on the intoxication defense in an effort to make that particularly puzzling body of doctrine as accessible as the topic allows. For the first time since I assumed editorship of the materials, however, the new edition's primary revisions are the conventional ones reflecting doctrinal changes emanating from the Supreme Court of the United States.

Twenty years ago, new rulings by the Court could be counted on to alter the law of criminal procedure significantly, but to modify the substantive criminal law little if at all. Today the line between substance and procedure has grown harder to discern, and the significance of federal criminal law has grown steadily. The new edition incorporates a state-of-the art Supreme Court statutory interpretation case (*Flores–Figueroa v. United States*), a decision extending the scope of jury-trial rights at sentencing (*Kimbrough v. United States*), and a decision rejecting a federal constitutional challenge to a narrow version of the insanity defense (*Clark v. Arizona*). New Supreme Court decisions respecting procedural developments under the Fourth and Sixth amendments have been noted in the footnotes. The one such development signal enough to be dealt with in text is the change in the search-incident-to-arrest rules worked by *Arizona v. Gant*, discussed in the new edition in the Eighth Circuit's opinion in *United States v. Davis*.

I have omitted the Court's Second Amendment decision, *District of Columbia v. Heller*, because it remains to be seen whether that decision works major changes in the criminal law. The question of whether the robust right to bear arms there recognized applies to the states is still in the bosom of time, and it is not clear how many prosecutions actually take place under statutes that might plausibly be challenged under *Heller*.

Soon enough, further changes will make the current volume obsolete. At this writing, for example, we await the Court's decision in *United States v. Comstock*, a case testing the federal government's power to civilly commit sexually-violent persons who have served their sentences or been deemed incompetent to stand trial. Whatever comes from the Court, moreover, this seems to be a season of rapid economic and political change.

The precise content of the changes to come, let alone a reasoned judgment about whether they turn out for good or for ill, is of course impossible now. There is nonetheless nothing impossible about predicting change as such. My hope is that the materials continue to offer the most comprehensive introduction available to basic principles—the things that don't change—in criminal law and procedure. Guided by that compass, the young lawyers destined to cope with the evolving ecology of criminal justice have as good a chance as we can give them of keeping their bearings.

DONALD A. DRIPPS

San Diego, California
March 22, 2010

SUMMARY OF CONTENTS

PART 2. PROCEDURE AND ENFORCEMENT

TABLE OF CONTENTS

PART 2. PROCEDURE AND ENFORCEMENT

TABLE OF CASES

Principal cases are in bold type. Non-principal cases are in roman type. References are to Pages.

CASES AND MATERIALS

CRIMINAL LAW AND PROCEDURE

PART 1

THE SUBSTANTIVE CRIMINAL LAW

CHAPTER 1

CRIMINALIZATION, DEFINITION AND CLASSIFICATION

SECTION 1. NATURE AND PURPOSES OF THE CRIMINAL LAW

Defining criminal law is notoriously challenging. The definition suggested by Blackstone is as follows: "A crime or misdemeanour is an act committed or omitted, in violation of a public law either forbidding or commanding it."[1] As pointed out in the Eighth Edition, this focus on conduct overlooks the fact that many acts may or may not be crimes, depending on their results and the attending circumstances.

Suppose, for example, **D** stabbed **X** unlawfully, inflicting a serious injury that resulted in **X's** death six weeks thereafter. Under the theory of the common law of crimes, unchanged by statute, **D** should be punished for the unlawful killing of **X**, but **X's** death was the result of **D's** act rather than the act itself, which was thrusting the knife.[2] If, quite by accident, a surgeon should have come upon **X** so soon after the wounding as to be able to save his life this would not in any way change **D's** act. The knife thrust by **D** would be unaltered by this fortuitous occurrence although the difference in the consequences would be tremendous. And although **D's** act would be the same in either case his crime would be entirely different because under the first assumption he is to be punished for an unlawful killing whereas under the second, there would be no killing and the punishment would be for unlawful wounding. In other words it is more accurate to define crime in terms of the social harm caused rather than the act committed.[3]

---

1. 4 Bl.Comm. * 5.

2. "The word 'act' is used throughout the Restatement of this Subject to denote an external manifestation of the actor's will and does not include any of its results even the most direct, immediate and intended." Restatement, Second, Torts § 2 (1965).

3. For this reason Bishop defined crime in terms of the "wrong" done. "A crime is any wrong which the government deems injurious to the public at large, and punishes through a judicial proceeding in its own name." 1 Bishop, New Criminal Law § 32 (8th ed. 1892).

If **A** and **B** perform the same physical act of setting off a fire alarm, **A** is not guilty of a crime if the purpose was to report a fire. However, if **B** set off the alarm as a joke, the act of **B** would be a crime. The social harm proscribed by the conduct is the essence of the crime, not the physical act.

These considerations led Professors Perkins and Boyce to conclude that that a crime is any social harm defined and made punishable by law.[4] Criminologists and sociologists have sometimes given the concept of crime a broader definition.[5] Whatever benefit that may have for such purposes, from the standpoint of the law a crime is not such until it is recognized as a crime by law.[6] Although some civil remedies may involve sanctions similar to those normally imposed by criminal courts, i.e., fines, loss of rights, the degree of sanction[7] imposed by the criminal law is usually much more severe and the opprobrium associated with the criminal sanction is, except for minor offenses, usually more extreme.[8]

This is sensible, so far as it goes; but it leaves open the question of what counts as "social harm," and of when the legislature has decided to make harm-causing conduct punishable as a crime. Ordinarily the legislature declares conduct to be criminal, and willingly shoulders the burden of the criminal law's procedural safeguards. In the two cases that follow, however, the legislature purported to be imposing civil, as distinct from criminal, liability. Why might a legislature choose to invoke the criminal process rather than civil sanctions? To what extent does the Constitution *require* the legislature to proceed through the criminal process? What distinctive procedures do tradition and the Constitution require in criminal cases? Condensed to two short but very difficult questions, what is the nature, and what are the purposes, of the criminal law?

---

4. There were witnesses to a murder who were well acquainted with the killer. But since he was one of identical twins and no witness could be sure which of the twins committed the crime, there could be no conviction. Usually a person can be held criminally responsible only for that person's own misconduct and the person need not show noninvolvement. People v. Lopez, 72 Ill.App.3d 713, 28 Ill.Dec. 906, 391 N.E.2d 105 (1979).

5. Bottomley, Criminology in Focus 1–38 (1979); Rob White and Fiona Haines, Crime and Criminology 5 (1996).

6. "No relevant statutory provision makes punishable as a crime a person's disobedience of an order closing a body of water ... In the absence of such an express penal provision, the statute cannot be a basis for criminal prosecution...." People v. Boyd, 642 P.2d 1, 3 (Colo.1982).

A statute defining domestic violence did not create a substantive crime but was a procedural statute applicable to other offenses. It was error to impose a separate sentence under the domestic violence statute. State v. Schackart, 153 Ariz. 422, 737 P.2d 398 (App.1987).

A crime is made up of two parts, forbidden conduct and prescribed penalty; the former without the latter is no crime. Cook v. Commonwealth, 20 Va.App. 510, 458 S.E.2d 317, 319 (1995).

The purpose of codification of all criminal offenses is to advise the public as to what conduct is criminal. State v. Boyd, 925 S.W.2d 237 (Tenn.Cr.App.1995).

7. A civil contempt may result in confinement to coerce a person to take some action. Matter of Thornton, 560 F.Supp. 183 (S.D.N.Y.1983). The purpose is not a punitive sanction, but to obtain compliance with a court order.

8. Hart, The Aims of the Criminal Law, 23 Law and Contemp.Prob. 401, 404–406 (1958); Robinson, The Criminal–Civil Distinction and Dangerous Blameless Offenders, 83 J.Crim.L. & Crim. 693, 694 (1993).

Kansas v. Crane

Supreme Court of the United States, 2002.
534 U.S. 407, 122 S.Ct. 867, 151 L.Ed.2d 856.

[According to Justice Scalia's dissent, otherwise omitted, "Respondent was convicted of lewd and lascivious behavior and pleaded guilty to aggravated sexual battery for two incidents that took place on the same day in 1993. In the first, respondent exposed himself to a tanning salon attendant. In the second, 30 minutes later, respondent entered a video store, waited until he was the only customer present, and then exposed himself to the clerk. Not stopping there, he grabbed the clerk by the neck, demanded she perform oral sex on him, and threatened to rape her, before running out of the store. Following respondent's plea to aggravated sexual battery, the State filed a petition in State District Court to have respondent evaluated and adjudicated a sexual predator under the SVPA. That Act permits the civil detention of a person convicted of any of several enumerated sexual offenses, if it is proven beyond a reasonable doubt that he suffers from a 'mental abnormality'—a disorder affecting his 'emotional or volitional capacity which predisposes the person to commit sexually violent offenses'—or a 'personality disorder,' either of 'which makes the person likely to engage in repeat acts of sexual violence.' " Kan. Stat. Ann. §§ 59–29a02(a), (b) (2000 Cum.Supp.).

Several psychologists examined respondent and determined he suffers from exhibitionism and antisocial personality disorder. Though exhibitionism alone would not support classification as a sexual predator, a psychologist concluded that the two in combination did place respondent's condition within the range of disorders covered by the SVPA, "cit[ing] the increasing frequency of incidents involving [respondent], increasing intensity of the incidents, [respondent's] increasing disregard for the rights of others, and his increasing daring and aggressiveness." *In re Crane*, 269 Kan. 578, 579, 7 P.3d 285, 287 (2000). Another psychologist testified that respondent's behavior was marked by "impulsivity or failure to plan ahead," indicating his unlawfulness "was a combination of willful and uncontrollable behavior," *id.*, at 584–585, 7 P.3d, at 290. The State's experts agreed, however, that " '[r]espondent's mental disorder does not impair his volitional control to the degree he cannot control his dangerous behavior.' " *Id.*, at 581, 7 P.3d, at 288.

Respondent moved for summary judgment, arguing "that for his detention to comport with substantive due process the State was required to prove not merely what the statute requires—that by reason of his mental disorder he is 'likely to engage in repeat acts of sexual violence'—but also that he is unable to control his violent behavior. The trial court denied this motion, and instructed the jury pursuant to the terms of the statute. *Id.*, at 581, 7 P.3d, at 287–288. The jury found, beyond a reasonable doubt, that respondent was a sexual predator as defined by the SVPA. The Kansas Supreme Court reversed, holding the SVPA unconstitutional as applied to someone, like respondent, who has only an emotional or personality disorder within the meaning of the Act, rather than a volitional impairment. For such a person, it held, the State must show not merely a likelihood that the defendant would engage in repeat acts of sexual violence, but also an inability to control violent behavior."]

■ JUSTICE BREYER delivered the opinion of the Court.

This case concerns the constitutional requirements substantively limiting the civil commitment of a dangerous sexual offender—a matter that this Court considered in Kansas v. Hendricks, 521 U.S. 346, 117 S.Ct. 2072, 138 L.Ed.2d 501 (1997). The State of Kansas argues that the Kansas Supreme Court has interpreted our decision in *Hendricks* in an overly restrictive manner. We agree and vacate the Kansas court's judgment.

I

In *Hendricks,* this Court upheld the Kansas Sexually Violent Predator Act, Kan. Stat. Ann. § 59–29a01 *et seq.* (1994), against constitutional challenge. 521 U.S., at 371, 117 S.Ct. 2072. In doing so, the Court characterized the confinement at issue as civil, not criminal, confinement. *Id.,* at 369, 117 S.Ct. 2072. And it held that the statutory criterion for confinement embodied in the statute's words "mental abnormality or personality disorder" satisfied " 'substantive' due process requirements." *Id.,* at 356, 360, 117 S.Ct. 2072.

In reaching its conclusion, the Court's opinion pointed out that "States have in certain narrow circumstances provided for the forcible civil detainment of people who are unable to control their behavior and who thereby pose a danger to the public health and safety." *Id.,* at 357, 117 S.Ct. 2072. It said that "[w]e have consistently upheld such involuntary commitment statutes" when (1) "the confinement takes place pursuant to proper procedures and evidentiary standards," (2) there is a finding of "dangerousness either to one's self or to others," and (3) proof of dangerousness is "coupled ... with the proof of some additional factor, such as a 'mental illness' or 'mental abnormality.' " *Id.,* at 357–358, 117 S.Ct. 2072. It noted that the Kansas "Act unambiguously requires a finding of dangerousness either to one's self or to others," *id.,* at 357, 117 S.Ct. 2072, and then "links that finding to the existence of a 'mental abnormality' or 'personality disorder' that makes it difficult, if not impossible, for the person to control his dangerous behavior," *id.,* at 358, 117 S.Ct. 2072 (citing Kan. Stat. Ann. § 59–29a02(b) (1994)). And the Court ultimately determined that the statute's "requirement of a 'mental abnormality' or 'personality disorder' is consistent with the requirements of ... other statutes that we have upheld in that it narrows the class of persons eligible for confinement to those who are unable to control their dangerousness." 521 U.S., at 358, 117 S.Ct. 2072.

The Court went on to respond to Hendricks' claim that earlier cases had required a finding, not of "mental abnormality" or "personality disorder," but of "mental illness." *Id.,* at 358–359, 117 S.Ct. 2072. In doing so, the Court pointed out that we "have traditionally left to legislators the task of defining [such] terms." *Id.,* at 359, 117 S.Ct. 2072. It then held that, to "the extent that the civil commitment statutes we have considered set forth criteria relating to an individual's inability to control his dangerousness, the Kansas Act sets forth comparable criteria." *Id.,* at 360, 117 S.Ct. 2072. It added that Hendricks' own condition "doubtless satisfies those criteria," for (1) he suffers from pedophilia, (2) "the psychiatric profession itself classifies" that condition "as a serious mental disorder," and (3) Hendricks conceded that he cannot " 'control the urge' " to molest children. And it concluded that this "admitted lack of volitional control, coupled with a prediction of future dangerousness, adequately distinguishes Hendricks from other dangerous persons who are perhaps more properly dealt with exclusively through criminal proceedings." *Ibid.*

II

In the present case the State of Kansas asks us to review the Kansas Supreme Court's application of *Hendricks.* The State here seeks the civil commitment of Michael Crane, a previously convicted sexual offender who, according to at least one of the State's psychiatric witnesses, suffers from both exhibitionism and antisocial personality disorder. *In re Crane,* 269 Kan. 578, 580–581, 7 P.3d 285, 287 (2000); *cf. also* American Psychiatric Association, Diagnostic and Statistical Manual of Mental Disorders 569 (rev. 4th ed. 2000) (DSM–IV) (detailing exhibitionism), 701–706 (detailing antisocial personality disorder). After a jury trial, the Kansas District Court ordered Crane's civil commitment. 269 Kan., at 579–584, 7 P.3d, at 286–288. But the Kansas Supreme Court reversed. *Id.,* at 586, 7 P.3d, at 290. In that court's view, the Federal Constitution as interpreted in *Hendricks* insists upon "a finding that the defendant cannot control his dangerous behavior"—even if (as provided by Kansas law) problems of "emotional capacity" and not "volitional capacity" prove the "source of bad behavior" warranting commitment. 269 Kan., at 586, 7 P.3d, at 290; *see also* Kan. Stat. Ann. § 59–29a02(b) (2000 Cum.Supp.) (defining "[m]ental abnormality" as a condition that affects an individual's emotional *or* volitional capacity). And the trial court had made no such finding.

Kansas now argues that the Kansas Supreme Court wrongly read *Hendricks* as requiring the State *always* to prove that a dangerous individual is *completely* unable to control his behavior. That reading, says Kansas, is far too rigid.

III

We agree with Kansas insofar as it argues that *Hendricks* set forth no requirement of *total* or *complete* lack of control. *Hendricks* referred to the Kansas Act as requiring a "mental abnormality" or "personality disorder" that makes it "*difficult,* if not impossible, for the [dangerous] person to control his dangerous behavior." 521 U.S., at 358, 117 S.Ct. 2072 (emphasis added). The word "difficult" indicates that the lack of control to which this Court referred was not absolute. Indeed, as different *amici* on opposite sides of this case agree, an absolutist approach is unworkable. Brief for Association for the Treatment of Sexual Abusers as *Amicus Curiae* 3; *cf.* Brief for American Psychiatric Association et al. as *Amici Curiae* 10; *cf. also* American Psychiatric Association, Statement on the Insanity Defense 11 (1982), reprinted in G. Melton, J. Petrila, N. Poythress, & C. Slobogin, Psychological Evaluations for the Courts 200 (2d ed. 1997) (" 'The line between an irresistible impulse and an impulse not resisted is probably no sharper than that between twilight and dusk' "). Moreover, most severely ill people—even those commonly termed "psychopaths"—retain some ability to control their behavior. *See* Morse, *Culpability and Control, 142 U. Pa. L.Rev. 1587, 1634–1635 (1994);* cf. Winick, *Sex Offender Law in the 1990s: A Therapeutic Jurisprudence Analysis*, 4 Psychol. Pub. Pol'y & L. 505, 520–525 (1998). Insistence upon absolute lack of control would risk barring the civil commitment of highly dangerous persons suffering severe mental abnormalities.

We do not agree with the State, however, insofar as it seeks to claim that the Constitution permits commitment of the type of dangerous sexual offender considered in *Hendricks* without *any* lack-of-control determination. *See* Brief for Petitioner 17; Tr. of Oral Arg. 22, 30–31. *Hendricks* underscored the constitutional importance of distinguishing a dangerous sexual offender subject to civil commitment "from other dangerous persons who are perhaps more properly dealt with exclusively through criminal proceedings." 521 U.S., at 360, 117 S.Ct. 2072. That distinction is necessary lest "civil commitment" become a "mechanism for retribution or general deterrence"—functions properly those of criminal law, not civil commitment. *Id.,* at 372–373, 117 S.Ct. 2072 (KENNEDY, J., concurring); *cf. also Moran,* The Epidemiology of Antisocial Personality Disorder, 34 Social Psychiatry & Psychiatric Epidemiology 231, 234 (1999) (noting that 40%–60% of the male prison population is diagnosable with antisocial personality disorder). The presence of what the "psychiatric profession itself classifie[d] ... as a serious mental disorder" helped to make that distinction in *Hendricks.* And a critical distinguishing feature of that "serious ... disorder" there consisted of a special and serious lack of ability to control behavior.

In recognizing that fact, we did not give to the phrase "lack of control" a particularly narrow or technical meaning. And we recognize that in cases where lack of control is at issue, "inability to control behavior" will not be demonstrable with mathematical precision. It is enough to say that there must be proof of serious difficulty in controlling behavior. And this, when viewed in light of such features of the case as the nature of the psychiatric diagnosis, and the severity of the mental abnormality itself, must be sufficient to distinguish the dangerous sexual offender whose serious mental illness, abnormality, or disorder subjects him to civil commitment from the dangerous but typical recidivist convicted in an ordinary criminal case. 521 U.S., at 357–358, 117 S.Ct. 2072; *see also* Foucha v. Louisiana, 504 U.S. 71, 82–83, 112 S.Ct. 1780, 118 L.Ed.2d 437 (1992) (rejecting an approach to civil commitment that would permit the indefinite confinement "of any convicted criminal" after completion of a prison term).

We recognize that *Hendricks* as so read provides a less precise constitutional standard than would those more definite rules for which the parties have argued. But the Constitution's safeguards of human liberty in the area of mental illness and the law are not always best enforced through precise bright-line rules. For one thing, the States retain considerable leeway in defining the mental abnormalities and personality disorders that make an individual eligible for commitment. *Hendricks,* 521 U.S., at 359, 117 S.Ct. 2072; *id.,* at 374–375, 117 S.Ct. 2072 (BREYER, J., dissenting). For another, the science of psychiatry, which informs but does not control ultimate legal determinations, is an ever-advancing science, whose distinctions do not seek precisely to mirror those of the law. *See id.,* at 359, 117 S.Ct. 2072. *See also, e.g.,* Ake v. Oklahoma, 470 U.S. 68, 81, 105 S.Ct. 1087, 84 L.Ed.2d 53 (1985) (psychiatry not "an exact science"); DSM–IV xxx ("concept of mental disorder ... lacks a consistent operational definition"); *id.,* at xxxii-xxxiii (noting the "imperfect fit between the questions of ultimate concern to the law and the information contained in [the DSM's] clinical diagnosis"). Consequently, we have sought to provide constitutional guidance in this area by proceeding deliberately and contextually, elaborating generally stated constitutional standards and objectives as specific circumstances require. *Hendricks* embodied that approach.

IV

The State also questions how often a volitional problem lies at the heart of a dangerous sexual offender's serious mental abnormality or disorder. It points out that the Kansas Supreme Court characterized its state statute as permitting commitment of dangerous sexual offenders who (1) suffered from a mental abnormality properly characterized by an "emotional" impairment and (2) suffered no "volitional" impairment. 269 Kan., at 583, 7 P.3d, at 289. It adds that, in the Kansas court's view, *Hendricks* absolutely forbids the commitment of any such person. 269 Kan., at 585–586, 7 P.3d, at 290. And the State argues that it was wrong to read *Hendricks* in this way. Brief for Petitioner 11; Tr. of Oral Arg. 5.

We agree that *Hendricks* limited its discussion to volitional disabilities. And that fact is not surprising. The case involved an individual suffering from pedophilia—a mental abnormality that critically involves what a lay person might describe as a lack of control. DSM–IV 571–572 (listing as a diagnostic criterion for pedophilia that an individual have acted on, or been affected by, "sexual urges" toward children). Hendricks himself stated that he could not " 'control the urge' " to molest children. 521 U.S., at 360, 117 S.Ct. 2072. In addition, our cases suggest that civil commitment of dangerous sexual offenders will normally involve individuals who find it particularly difficult to control their behavior—in the general sense described above. *Cf.* Seling v. Young, 531 U.S. 250, 256, 121 S.Ct. 727, 148 L.Ed.2d 734 (2001); *cf. also* Abel & Rouleau, Male Sex Offenders, in Handbook of Outpatient Treatment of Adults: Nonpsychotic Mental Disorders 271 (M. Thase, B. Edelstein, & M. Hersen eds.1990) (sex offenders' "compulsive, repetitive, driven behavior ... appears to fit the criteria of an emotional or psychiatric illness"). And it is often appropriate to say of such individuals, in ordinary English, that they are "unable to control their dangerousness." *Hendricks, supra,* at 358, 117 S.Ct. 2072.

Regardless, *Hendricks* must be read in context. The Court did not draw a clear distinction between the purely "emotional" sexually related mental abnormality and the "volitional." Here, as in other areas of psychiatry, there may be "considerable overlap between a ... defective understanding or appreciation and ... [an] ability to control ... behavior." American Psychiatric Association Statement on the Insanity Defense, 140 Am. J. Psychiatry 681, 685 (1983) (discussing "psychotic" individuals). Nor, when considering civil commitment, have we ordinarily distinguished for constitutional purposes among volitional, emotional, and cognitive impairments.

See, e.g., Jones v. United States, 463 U.S. 354, 103 S.Ct. 3043, 77 L.Ed.2d 694 (1983); Addington v. Texas, 441 U.S. 418, 99 S.Ct. 1804, 60 L.Ed.2d 323 (1979). The Court in *Hendricks* had no occasion to consider whether confinement based solely on "emotional" abnormality would be constitutional, and we likewise have no occasion to do so in the present case.

* * *

For these reasons, the judgment of the Kansas Supreme Court is vacated, and the case is remanded for further proceedings not inconsistent with this opinion.

In re Winship

Supreme Court of the United States, 1970.
397 U.S. 358, 90 S.Ct. 1068, 25 L.Ed.2d 368.

■ MR. JUSTICE BRENNAN delivered the opinion of the Court.

Constitutional questions decided by this Court concerning the juvenile process have centered on the adjudicatory stage at "which a determination is made as to whether a juvenile is a 'delinquent' as a result of alleged misconduct on his part, with the consequence that he may be committed to a state institution." In re Gault, 387 U.S. 1, 13, 87 S.Ct. 1428, 1436, 18 L.Ed.2d 527 (1967). Gault decided that, although the Fourteenth Amendment does not require that the hearing at this stage conform with all the requirements of a criminal trial or even of the usual administrative proceeding, the Due Process Clause does require application during the adjudicatory hearing of "the essentials of due process and fair treatment." *Id., at 30, 87 S.Ct. at 1445.* This case presents the single, narrow question whether proof beyond a reasonable doubt is among the "essentials of due process and fair treatment" required during the adjudicatory stage when a juvenile is charged with an act which would constitute a crime if committed by an adult.[9]

Section 712 of the New York Family Court Act defines a juvenile delinquent as "a person over seven and less than sixteen years of age who does any act which, if done by an adult, would constitute a crime." During a 1967 adjudicatory hearing, conducted pursuant to § 742 of the Act, a judge in New York Family Court found that appellant, then a 12–year-old boy, had entered a locker and stolen $112 from a woman's pocketbook. The

---

9. Thus, we do not see how it can be said in dissent that this opinion "rests entirely on the assumption that all juvenile proceedings are 'criminal prosecutions,' hence subject to constitutional limitations." As in Gault, "we are not here concerned with * * * the prejudicial stages of the juvenile process, nor do we direct our attention to the post-adjudicative or dispositional process." 387 U.S., at 13, 87 S.Ct., at 1436. In New York, the adjudicatory stage of a delinquency proceeding is clearly distinct from both the preliminary phase of the juvenile process and from its dispositional stage. *See* N.Y. Family Court Act §§ 731–749. Similarly, we intimate no view concerning the constitutionality of the New York procedures governing children "in need of supervision." *See id.,* at §§ 711, 712, 742–745. nor Do we consider whether there are other "essentials of due process and fair treatment" required during the adjudicatory hearing of a delinquency proceeding. Finally, we have no occasion to consider appellant's argument that § 744(b) is a violation of the Equal Protection Clause, as well as a denial of due process.

petition which charged appellant with delinquency alleged that his act, "if done by an adult, would constitute the crime or crimes of Larceny." The judge acknowledged that the proof might not establish guilt beyond a reasonable doubt, but rejected appellant's contention that such proof was required by the Fourteenth Amendment. The judge relied instead on § 744(b) of the New York Family Court Act which provides that "(a)ny determination at the conclusion of (an adjudicatory) hearing that a (juvenile) did an act or acts must be based on a preponderance of the evidence."[10] During a subsequent dispositional hearing, appellant was ordered placed in a training school for an initial period of 18 months, subject to annual extensions of his commitment until his 18th birthday—six years in appellant's case. The Appellate Division of the New York Supreme Court, First Judicial Department, affirmed without opinion, 30 A.D.2d 781, 291 N.Y.S.2d 1005 (1968). The New York Court of Appeals then affirmed by a four-to-three vote, expressly sustaining the constitutionality of § 744(b), 24 N.Y.2d 196, 299 N.Y.S.2d 414, 247 N.W.2d 253 (1969). We noted probable jurisdiction 396 U.S. 885, 90 S.Ct. 179, 24 L.Ed.2d 160 (1969). We reverse.

I

The requirement that guilt of a criminal charge be established by proof beyond a reasonable doubt dates at least from our early years as a Nation. The "demand for a higher degree of persuasion in criminal cases was recurrently expressed from ancient times, (though) its crystallization into the formula 'beyond a reasonable doubt' seems to have occurred as late as 1798. It is now accepted in common law jurisdictions as the measure of persuasion by which the prosecution must convince the trier of all the essential elements of guilt." C. McCormick, Evidence § 321, pp. 681–682 (1954); *see also* 9 J. Wigmore, Evidence, § 2497 (3d ed. 1940). Although virtually unanimous adherence to the reasonable-doubt standard in common-law jurisdictions may not conclusively establish it as a requirement of due process, such adherence does "reflect a profound judgment about the way in which law should be enforced and justice administered." Duncan v. Louisiana, 391 U.S. 145, 155, 88 S.Ct. 1444, 1451, 20 L.Ed.2d 491 (1968).

Expressions in many opinions of this Court indicate that it has long been assumed that proof of a criminal charge beyond a reasonable doubt is constitutionally required. Mr. Justice Frankfurter stated that "(i)t the duty of the Government to establish * * * guilt beyond a reasonable doubt. This notion—basic in our law and rightly one of the boasts of a free society—is a requirement and a safeguard of due process of law in the historic, procedural content of 'due process.' " Leland v. Oregon, *supra*, 343 U.S., at 802–803, 72 S.Ct., at 1009 (dissenting opinion). In a similar vein, the Court said in Brinegar v. United States, *supra*, 338 U.S., at 174, 69 S.Ct., at 1310, that "(g)uilt in a criminal case must be proved beyond a reasonable doubt and by evidence confined to that which long experience in the common-law

---

10. The ruling appears in the following portion of the hearing transcript:

Counsel: "Your Honor is making a finding by the preponderance of the evidence."

Court: "Well, it convinces me."

Counsel: "It's not beyond a reasonable doubt, Your Honor."

Court: "That is true * * * Our statute says a preponderance and a preponderance it is."

tradition, to some extent embodied in the Constitution, has crystallized into rules of evidence consistent with that standard. These rules are historically grounded rights of our system, developed to safeguard men from dubious and unjust convictions, with resulting forfeitures of life, liberty and property." Davis v. United States, *supra*, 160 U.S., at 488, 16 S.Ct., at 358 stated that the requirement is implicit in "constitutions * * * (which) recognize the fundamental principles that are deemed essential for the protection of life and liberty." In Davis a murder conviction was reversed because the trial judge instructed the jury that it was their duty to convict when the evidence was equally balanced regarding the sanity of the accused. This Court said: "On the contrary, he is entitled to an acquittal of the specific crime charged, if upon all the evidence, there is reasonable doubt whether he was capable in law of committing crime. * * * No man should be deprived of his life under the forms of law unless the jurors who try him are able, upon their consciences, to say that the evidence before them * * * is sufficient to show beyond a reasonable doubt the existence of every fact necessary to constitute the crime charged." *Id.*, at 484, 493, 16 S.Ct., at 357, 360.

The reasonable-doubt standard plays a vital role in the American scheme of criminal procedure. It is a prime instrument for reducing the risk of convictions resting on factual error. The standard provides concrete substance for the presumption of innocence—that bedrock "axiomatic and elementary" principle whose "enforcement lies at the foundation of the administration of our criminal law." Coffin v. United States, *supra*, 156 U.S., at 453, 15 S.Ct., at 403. As the dissenters in the New York Court of Appeals observed, and we agree, "a person accused of a crime * * * would be at a severe disadvantage, a disadvantage amounting to a lack of fundamental fairness, if he could be adjudged guilty and imprisoned for years on the strength of the same evidence as would suffice in a civil case." 24 N.Y.2d, at 205, 299 N.Y.S.2d, at 422, 247 N.E.2d, at 259.

The requirement of proof beyond a reasonable doubt has this vital role in our criminal procedure for cogent reasons. The accused during a criminal prosecution has at stake interest of immense importance, both because of the possibility that he may lose his liberty upon conviction and because of the certainty that he would be stigmatized by the conviction. Accordingly, a society that values the good name and freedom of every individual should not condemn a man for commission of a crime when there is reasonable doubt about his guilt. As we said in Speiser v. Randall, *supra*, 357 U.S., at 525–526, 78 S.Ct., at 1342: "There is always in litigation a margin of error, representing error in factfinding, which both parties must take into account. Where one party has at stake an interest of transcending value—as a criminal defendant his liberty—this margin of error is reduced as to him by the process of placing on the other party the burden of * * * persuading the factfinder at the conclusion of the trial of his guilt beyond a reasonable doubt. Due process commands that no man shall lose his liberty unless the Government has borne the burden of * * * convincing the factfinder of his guilt." To this end, the reasonable-doubt standard is indispensable, for it "impresses on the trier of fact the necessity of reaching a subjective state of certitude of the facts in issue." Dorsen & Reznick, In

Re Gault and the Future of Juvenile Law, 1 Family Law Quarterly, No. 4, pp. 1, 26 (1967).

Moreover, use of the reasonable-doubt standard is indispensable to command the respect and confidence of the community in applications of the criminal law. It is critical that the moral force of the criminal law not be diluted by a standard of proof that leaves people in doubt whether innocent men are being condemned. It is also important in our free society that every individual going about his ordinary affairs have confidence that his government cannot adjudge him guilty of a criminal offense without convincing a proper factfinder of his guilt with utmost certainty.

Lest there remain any doubt about the constitutional stature of the reasonable-doubt standard, we explicitly hold that the Due Process Clause protects the accused against conviction except upon proof beyond a reasonable doubt of every fact necessary to constitute the crime with which he is charged.

II

We turn to the question whether juveniles, like adults, are constitutionally entitled to proof beyond a reasonable doubt when they are charged with violation of a criminal law. The same considerations that demand extreme caution in factfinding to protect the innocent adult apply as well to the innocent child. We do not find convincing the contrary arguments of the New York Court of Appeals, Gault rendered untenable much of the reasoning relied upon by that court to sustain the constitutionality of § 744(b). The Court of Appeals indicated that a delinquency adjudication "is not a 'conviction'" (§ 781); that it affects no right or privilege, including the right to hold public office or to obtain a license (§ 782); and a cloak of protective confidentiality is thrown around all the proceedings (§§ 783–784).' 24 N.Y.2d at 200, 299 N.Y.S.2d, at 417–418, 247 N.E.2d, at 255–256. The court said further: "The delinquency status is not made a crime; and the proceedings are not criminal. There is, hence, no deprivation of due process in the statutory provision (challenged by appellant) * * *." 24 N.Y.2d, at 203, 299 N.Y.S.2d, at 420, 247 N.E.2d, at 257. In effect the Court of Appeals distinguished the proceedings in question here from a criminal prosecution by use of what Gault called the "civil label-of-convenience which has been attached to juvenile proceedings." 387 U.S., at 50, 87 S.Ct., at 1455. But Gault expressly rejected that distinction as a reason for holding the Due Process Clause inapplicable to a juvenile proceeding. 387 U.S., at 50–51, 87 S.Ct., at 1455, 1456. The Court of Appeals also attempted to justify the preponderance standard on the related ground that juvenile proceedings are designed "not to punish, but to save the child." 24 N.Y.2d, at 197, 299 N.Y.S.2d, at 415, 247 N.E.2d, at 254. Again, however, Gault expressly rejected this justification. 387 U.S., at 27, 87 S.Ct., at 1443. We made clear in that decision that civil labels and good intentions do not themselves obviate the need for criminal due process safeguards in juvenile courts, for "(a) proceeding where the issue is whether the child will be found to be 'delinquent' and subjected to the loss of his liberty for years is comparable in seriousness to a felony prosecution." *Id.*, at 36, 87 S.Ct., at 1448.

Nor do we perceive any merit in the argument that to afford juveniles the protection of proof beyond a reasonable doubt would risk destruction of beneficial aspects of the juvenile process. Use of the reasonable-doubt standard during the adjudicatory hearing will not disturb New York's policies that a finding that a child has violated a criminal law does not constitute a criminal conviction, that such a finding does not deprive the child of his civil rights, and that juvenile proceedings are confidential. Nor will there be any effect on the informality, flexibility, or speed of the hearing at which the factfinding takes place. And the opportunity during the post-adjudicatory or dispositional hearing for a wide-ranging review of the child's social history and for his individualized treatment will remain unimpaired. Similarly, there will be no effect on the procedures distinctive to juvenile proceedings that are employed prior to the adjudicatory hearing.

The Court of Appeals observed that "a child's best interest is not necessarily, or even probably, promoted if he wins in the particular inquiry which may bring him to the juvenile court." 24 N.Y.2d, at 199, 299 N.Y.S.2d, at 417, 247 N.E.2d, at 255. It is true, of course, that the juvenile may be engaging in a general course of conduct inimical to his welfare that calls for judicial intervention. But that intervention cannot take the form of subjecting the child to the stigma of a finding that he violated a criminal law[11] and to the possibility of institutional confinement on proof insufficient to convict him were he an adult.

We conclude, as we concluded regarding the essential due process safeguards applied in Gault, that the observance of the standard of proof beyond a reasonable doubt "will not compel the States to abandon or displace any of the substantive benefits of the juvenile process." *Gault, supra*, at 21, 87 S.Ct., at 1440.

Finally, we reject the Court of Appeals' suggestion that there is, in any event, only a "tenuous difference" between the reasonable-doubt and preponderance standards. The suggestion is singularly unpersuasive. In this very case, the trial judge's ability to distinguish between the two standards enabled him to make a finding of guilt that he conceded he might not have made under the standard of proof beyond a reasonable doubt. Indeed, the trial judge's action evidences the accuracy of the observation of commentators that "the preponderance test is susceptible to the misinterpretation that it calls on the trier of fact merely to perform an abstract weighing of the evidence in order to determine which side has produced the greater quantum, without regard to its effect in convincing his mind of the truth of the proposition asserted." *Dorsen & Rezneck,* supra, at 26–27.

III

In sum, the constitutional safeguard of proof beyond a reasonable doubt is as much required during the adjudicatory stage of a delinquency proceeding as are those constitutional safeguards applied in Gault—notice of charges, right to counsel, the rights of confrontation and examination,

---

11. The more comprehensive and effective the procedures used to prevent public disclosure of the finding, the less the danger of stigma. As we indicated in Gault, however, often the "claim of secrecy * * * is more rhetoric than reality." 387 U.S., at 24, 87 S.Ct., at 1442.

and the privilege against self-incrimination. We therefore hold, in agreement with Chief Judge Fuld in dissent in the Court of Appeals, "that, where a 12–year-old child is charged with an act of stealing which renders him liable to confinement for as long as six years, then, as a matter of due process * * * the case against him must be proved beyond a reasonable doubt." 24 N.Y.2d, at 207, 299 N.Y.S.2d, at 423, 247 N.E.2d, at 260.

Reversed.

■ Mr. Justice Harlan, concurring.

No one, I daresay, would contend that state juvenile court trials are subject to no federal constitutional limitations. Differences have existed, however, among the members of this Court as to what constitutional protections do apply. *See In re Gault*, 387 U.S. 1, 87 S.Ct. 1428, 18 L.Ed.2d 527 (1967).

The present case draws in question the validity of a New York statute that permits a determination of juvenile delinquency, founded on a charge of criminal conduct, to be made on a standard of proof that is less rigorous than that which would obtain had the accused been tried for the same conduct in an ordinary criminal case. While I am in full agreement that this statutory provision offends the requirement of fundamental fairness embodied in the Due Process Clause of the Fourteenth Amendment, I am constrained to add something to what my Brother BRENNAN has written for the Court, lest the true nature of the constitutional problem presented become obscured or the impact on state juvenile court systems of what the Court holds today be exaggerated.

I

[E]ven though the labels used for alternative standards of proof are vague and not a very sure guide to decisionmaking, the choice of the standard for a particular variety of adjudication does, I think, reflect a very fundamental assessment of the comparative social costs of erroneous factual determinations.

To explain why I think this so, I begin by stating two propositions, neither of which I believe can be fairly disputed. First, in a judicial proceeding in which there is a dispute about the facts of some earlier event, the factfinder cannot acquire unassailably accurate knowledge of what happened. Instead, all the fact-finder can acquire is a belief of what probably happened. The intensity of this belief—the degree to which a factfinder is convinced that a given act actually occurred—can, of course, vary. In this regard, a standard of proof represents an attempt to instruct the fact-finder concerning the degree of confidence our society thinks he should have in the correctness of factual conclusions for a particular type of adjudication. Although the phrases "preponderance of the evidence" and "proof beyond a reasonable doubt" are quantitatively imprecise, they do communicate to the finder of fact different notions concerning the degree of confidence he is expected to have in the correctness of his factual conclusions.

A second proposition, which is really nothing more than a corollary of the first, is that the trier of fact will sometimes, despite his best efforts, be wrong in his factual conclusions. In a lawsuit between two parties, a factual error can make a difference in one of two ways. First, it can result in a judgment in favor of the plaintiff when the true facts warrant a judgment for the defendant. The analogue in a criminal case would be the conviction of an innocent man. On the other hand, an erroneous factual determination can result in a judgment for the defendant when the true facts justify a judgment in plaintiff's favor. The criminal analogue would be the acquittal of a guilty man.

The standard of proof influences the relative frequency of these two types of erroneous outcomes. If, for example, the standard of proof for a criminal trial were a preponderance of the evidence rather than proof beyond a reasonable doubt, there would be a smaller risk of factual errors that result in freeing guilty persons, but a far greater risk of factual errors that result in convicting the innocent. Because the standard of proof affects the comparative frequency of these two types of erroneous outcomes, the choice of the standard to be applied in a particular kind of litigation should, in a rational world, reflect an assessment of the comparative social disutility of each.

When one makes such an assessment, the reason for different standards of proof in civil as opposed to criminal litigation becomes apparent. In a civil suit between two private parties for money damages, for example, we view it as no more serious in general for there to be an erroneous verdict in the defendant's favor than for there to be an erroneous verdict in the plaintiff's favor. A preponderance of the evidence standard therefore seems peculiarly appropriate for, as explained most sensibly, it simply requires the trier of fact "to believe that the existence of a fact is more probable than its nonexistence before (he) may find in favor of the party who has the burden to persuade the (judge) of the fact's existence."

In a criminal case, on the other hand, we do not view the social disutility of convicting an innocent man as equivalent to the disutility of acquitting someone who is guilty. As Mr. Justice Brennan wrote for the Court in Speiser v. Randall, 357 U.S. 513, 525–526, 78 S.Ct. 1332, 1341–1342, 2 L.Ed.2d 1460 (1958):

"There is always in litigation a margin of error, representing error in factfinding, which both parties must take into account. Where one party has at stake an interest of transcending value—as a criminal defendant his liberty—this margin of error is reduced as to him by the process of placing on the other party the burden * * * of persuading the fact-finder at the conclusion of the trial of his guilt beyond a reasonable doubt."

In this context, I view the requirement of proof beyond a reasonable doubt in a criminal case as bottomed on a fundamental value determination of our society that it is far worse to convict an innocent man than to let a guilty man go free. It is only because of the nearly complete and long-standing acceptance of the reasonable-doubt standard by the States in criminal trials that the Court has not before today had to hold explicitly that due process, as an expression of fundamental procedural fairness, requires a more stringent standard for criminal trials than for ordinary civil litigation.

II

When one assesses the consequences of an erroneous factual determination in a juvenile delinquency proceeding in which a youth is accused of a crime, I think it must be concluded that, while the consequences are not identical to those in a criminal case, the differences will not support a distinction in the standard of proof. First, and of paramount importance, a factual error here, as in a criminal case, exposes the accused to a complete loss of his personal liberty through a state-imposed confinement away from his home, family, and friends. And, second, a delinquency determination, to some extent at least, stigmatizes a youth in that it is by definition bottomed on a finding that the accused committed a crime. Although there are no doubt costs to society (and possibly even to the youth himself) in letting a guilty youth go free, I think here, as in a criminal case, it is far worse to declare an innocent youth a delinquent. I therefore agree that a juvenile court judge should be no less convinced of the factual conclusion that the accused committed the criminal act with which he is charged than would be required in a criminal trial.

III

I wish to emphasize, as I did in my separate opinion in *Gault*, 387 U.S. 1, 65, 87 S.Ct. 1428, 1463, that there is no automatic congruence between the procedural requirements imposed by due process in a criminal case, and those imposed by due process in juvenile cases. . . . [12]

[The dissenting opinions of Chief Justice Burger and Justice Black, are omitted].

SECTION 2. MORAL AND CONSTITUTIONAL LIMITS ON THE CRIMINAL SANCTION

The standard theoretical accounts of punishment, whether retributive or utilitarian, recognize a widely-accepted set of limits or side-constraints. For retributivists, side-constraints exclude punishment even when punishment is deserved; for utilitarians, side-constraints exclude punishment even when it is useful, or at least when it appears to be useful in the short-run. Indeed, one of the important purposes of administering punishment through law is to respect and enforce these constraints.

Legislators take heed of these moral side-constraints when they decide what to prohibit and how severely to punish offenses. In the United States, the moral side-constraints are also expressed in constitutional provisions, and the courts have the authority to invalidate legislation that conflicts with these provisions. In the cases that follow, ask yourself what side-

---

12. In Gault, for example, I agreed with the majority that due process required (1) adequate notice of the "nature and terms" of the proceedings; (2) notice of the right to retain counsel, and an obligation on the State to provide counsel for indigents "in cases in which the child may be confined"; and (3) a written record "adequate to permit effective review." 387 U.S., at 72, 87 S.Ct., at 1467. Unlike the majority, however, I thought it unnecessary at the time of Gault to impose the additional requirements of the privilege against self-incrimination, confrontation, and cross-examination.

constraint is at issue, whether you agree with the prosecution or the defense as a matter of legislative policy, and, finally, whether violations of the moral side-constraint are also violations of the Constitution.

(A) LEGALITY

Keeler v. Superior Court of Amador County

Supreme Court of California, In Bank, 1970.
2 Cal.3d 619, 87 Cal.Rptr. 481, 470 P.2d 617.

■ MOSK, JUSTICE. In this proceeding for writ of prohibition we are called upon to decide whether an unborn but viable fetus is a "human being" within the meaning of the California statute defining murder (Pen.Code, § 187). We conclude that the Legislature did not intend such a meaning, and that for us to construe the statute to the contrary and apply it to this petitioner would exceed our judicial power and deny petitioner due process of law.

The evidence received at the preliminary examination may be summarized as follows: Petitioner and Teresa Keeler obtained an interlocutory decree of divorce on September 27, 1968. They had been married for 16 years. Unknown to petitioner, Mrs. Keeler was then pregnant by one Ernest Vogt, whom she had met earlier that summer. She subsequently began living with Vogt in Stockton, but concealed the fact from petitioner. Petitioner was given custody of their two daughters, aged 12 and 13 years, and under the decree Mrs. Keeler had the right to take the girls on alternate weekends.

On February 23, 1969, Mrs. Keeler was driving on a narrow mountain road in Amador County after delivering the girls to their home. She met petitioner driving in the opposite direction; he blocked the road with his car, and she pulled over to the side. He walked to her vehicle and began speaking to her. He seemed calm, and she rolled down her window to hear him. He said, "I hear you're pregnant. If you are you had better stay away from the girls and from here." She did not reply, and he opened the car door; as she later testified, "He assisted me out of the car.... [I]t wasn't roughly at this time." Petitioner then looked at her abdomen and became "extremely upset." He said, "You sure are. I'm going to stomp it out of you." He pushed her against the car, shoved his knee into her abdomen, and struck her in the face with several blows. She fainted, and when she regained consciousness petitioner had departed.

Mrs. Keeler drove back to Stockton, and the police and medical assistance were summoned. She had suffered substantial facial injuries, as well as extensive bruising of the abdominal wall. A Caesarian section was performed and the fetus was examined *in utero*. Its head was found to be severely fractured, and it was delivered stillborn. The pathologist gave as his opinion that the cause of death was skull fracture with consequent cerebral hemorrhaging, that death would have been immediate, and that the injury could have been the result of force applied to the mother's abdomen. There was no air in the fetus' lungs, and the umbilical cord was intact.

Upon delivery the fetus weighed five pounds and was 18 inches in length. Both Mrs. Keeler and her obstetrician testified that fetal movements had been observed prior to February 23, 1969. The evidence was in conflict as to the estimated age of the fetus;[13] the expert testimony on the point, however, concluded "with reasonable medical certainty" that the fetus had developed to the stage of viability, i.e., that in the event of premature birth on the date in question it would have had a 75 percent to 96 percent chance of survival.

An information was filed charging petitioner, in Count I, with committing the crime of murder (Pen.Code, § 187) in that he did "unlawfully kill a human being, to wit Baby Girl VOGT, with malice aforethought." In Count II petitioner was charged with wilful infliction of traumatic injury upon his wife (Pen.Code, § 273d), and in Count III, with assault on Mrs. Keeler by means of force likely to produce great bodily injury (Pen.Code, § 245). His motion to set aside the information for lack of probable cause (Pen.Code, § 995) was denied, and he now seeks a writ of prohibition; as will appear, only the murder count is actually in issue. Pending our disposition of the matter, petitioner is free on bail.

I

Penal Code section 187 provides: "Murder is the unlawful killing of a human being, with malice aforethought." The dispositive question is whether the fetus which petitioner is accused of killing was, on February 23, 1969, a "human being" within the meaning of this statute. If it was not, petitioner cannot be charged with its "murder" and prohibition will lie.

Section 187 was enacted as part of the Penal Code of 1872. Inasmuch as the provision has not been amended since that date, we must determine the intent of the Legislature at the time of its enactment. But section 187 was, in turn, taken verbatim from the first California statute defining murder, part of the Crimes and Punishments Act of 1850. (Stats.1850, ch. 99, § 19, p. 231.)[14] Penal Code section 5 (also enacted in 1872) declares: "The provisions of this Code, so far as they are substantially the same as existing statutes, must be construed as continuations thereof, and not as new enactments." We begin, accordingly, by inquiring into the intent of the Legislature in 1850 when it first defined murder as the unlawful and malicious killing of a "human being."

---

13. Mrs. Keeler testified, in effect, that she had no sexual intercourse with Vogt prior to August 1968, which would have made the fetus some 28 weeks old. She stated that the pregnancy had reached the end of the seventh month and the projected delivery date was April 25, 1969. The obstetrician, however, first estimated she was at least 31½ weeks pregnant, then raised the figure to 35 weeks in the light of the autopsy report of the size and weight of the fetus. Finally, on similar evidence an attending pediatrician estimated the gestation period to have been between 34½ and 36 weeks. The average full-term pregnancy is 40 weeks.

14. "Murder is the unlawful killing of a human being, with malice aforethought, either express or implied. The unlawful killing may be effected by any of the various means by which death may be occasioned." The revisers of 1872 did no more than transpose the "express or implied malice" language of this provision to the following section (§ 188), and delete the second sentence as surplusage. (Code Commissioners' Note, Pen.Code of Cal. (1st ed. 1872), p. 80.)

It will be presumed, of course, that in enacting a statute the Legislature was familiar with the relevant rules of the common law, and, when it couches its enactment in common law language, that its intent was to continue those rules in statutory form. (Baker v. Baker (1859) 13 Cal. 87, 95–96; Morris v. Oney (1963) 217 Cal.App.2d 864, 870, 32 Cal.Rptr. 88.) This is particularly appropriate in considering the work of the first session of our Legislature: its precedents were necessarily drawn from the common law, as modified in certain respects by the Constitution and by legislation of our sister states.

We therefore undertake a brief review of the origins and development of the common law of abortional homicide. (For a more detailed treatment, *see* Means, The Law of New York concerning Abortion and the Status of the Foetus, 1664–1968: A Case of Cessation of Constitutionality (1968) 14 N.Y.L.F. 411 [hereinafter cited as Means]; Stern, Abortion: Reform and the Law (1968) 59 J.Crim.L., C. & P.S. 84; Quay, Justifiable Abortion—Medical and Legal Foundations II (1961) 49 Geo.L.J. 395.) From that inquiry it appears that by the year 1850—the date with which we are concerned—an infant could not be the subject of homicide at common law *unless it had been born alive.* Perhaps the most influential statement of the "born alive" rule is that of Coke, in mid–17th century: "If a woman be quick with childe, and by a potion or otherwise killeth it in her wombe, or if a man beat her, whereby the child dyeth in her body, and she is delivered of a dead childe, this is a great misprision [i.e., misdemeanor], and no murder; but if the child be born alive and dyeth of the potion, battery, or other cause, this is murder; for in law it is accounted a reasonable creature, *in rerum natura,* when it is born alive." (3 Coke, Institutes *58 (1648).) In short, "By Coke's time, the common law regarded abortion as murder only if the foetus is (1) quickened, (2) born alive, (3) lives for a brief interval, and (4) then dies." (Means, at p. 420.) Whatever intrinsic defects there may have been in Coke's work (see 3 Stephen, A History of the Criminal Law of England (1883) pp. 52–60), the common law accepted his views as authoritative. In the 18th century, for example, Coke's requirement that an infant be born alive in order to be the subject of homicide was reiterated and expanded by both Blackstone and Hale. . . .

We conclude that in declaring murder to be the unlawful and malicious killing of a "human being" the Legislature of 1850 intended that term to have the settled common law meaning of a person who had been born alive, and did not intend the act of feticide—as distinguished from abortion—to be an offense under the laws of California. . . .

Properly understood, the often cited case of People v. Chavez (1947) 77 Cal.App.2d 621, 176 P.2d 92, does not derogate from this rule. There the defendant was charged with the murder of her newborn child, and convicted of manslaughter. She testified that the baby dropped from her womb into the toilet bowl; that she picked it up two or three minutes later, and cut but did not tie the umbilical cord; that the baby was limp and made no cry; and that after 15 minutes she wrapped it in a newspaper and concealed it, where it was found dead the next day. The autopsy surgeon testified that the baby was a full-term, nine-month child, weighing six and one-half pounds and appearing normal in every respect; that the body had very little blood in it, indicating the child had bled to death through the untied umbilical cord; that such a process would have taken about an hour; and that in his opinion "the child was born alive, based on conditions he found and the fact that the lungs contained air and the blood was extravasated or pushed back into the tissues, indicating heart action." (Id. at p. 624, 176 P.2d at p. 93.)

On appeal, the defendant emphasized that a doctor called by the defense had suggested other tests which the autopsy surgeon could have performed to determine the matter of live birth; on this basis, it was contended that the question of whether the infant was born alive "rests entirely on pure speculation." (Id. at p. 624, 176 P.2d 92.) The Court of Appeal found only an insignificant conflict in that regard (Id. at p. 627, 176 P.2d 92), and focused its attention instead on testimony of the autopsy surgeon admitting the possibility that the evidence of heart and lung action could have resulted from the child's breathing "after presentation of the head but before the birth was completed" (Id. at p. 624, 176 P.2d at p. 93).

The court cited the mid–19th century English infanticide cases mentioned hereinabove, and noted that the decisions had not reached uniformity on whether breathing, heart action, severance of the umbilical cord, or some combination of these or other factors established the status of "human being" for purposes of the law of homicide. (Id. at pp. 624–625, 176 P.2d 92.) The court then adverted to the state of modern medical knowledge, discussed the phenomenon of viability, and held that "a viable child *in the process of being born* is a human being within the meaning of the homicide statutes, whether or not the process has been fully completed. It should at least be considered a human being where it is a living baby and where in the natural course of events *a birth which is already started* would naturally be successfully completed." (Italics added.) (Id. at p. 626, 176 P.2d at p. 94.) Since the testimony of the autopsy surgeon left no doubt in that case that a live birth had at least begun, the court found "the evidence is sufficient here to support the implied finding of the jury that this child *was born alive and became a human being within the meaning of the homicide statutes.*" (Italics added.) (Id. at p. 627, 176 P.2d at p. 95.)[15]

Chavez thus stands for the proposition—to which we adhere—that a viable fetus "in the process of being born" is a human being within the meaning of the homicide statutes. But it stands for no more; in particular it does not hold that a fetus, however viable, which is *not* "in the process of being born" is nevertheless a "human being in the law of homicide." On the contrary, the opinion is replete with references to the common law requirement that the child be "born alive," however that term is defined, and must accordingly be deemed to reaffirm that requirement as part of the law of California.[16] ... And the text writers of the same period are no

---

15. Penal Code section 192, which the defendant in *Chavez* was convicted of violating, defines manslaughter as "the unlawful killing of a human being without malice."

16. In People v. Belous (1969) 71 Cal.2d 954, 968, 80 Cal.Rptr. 354, 458 P.2d 194, a majority of this court recognized "there are major and decisive areas where the embryo and fetus are not treated as equivalent to the born child.... The intentional destruction of the born child is murder or manslaughter. The intentional destruction of the embryo or fetus is never treated as murder, and only rarely as manslaughter but rather as the lesser offense of

less unanimous on the point. (Perkins on Criminal Law, *supra*, pp. 29–30, 176 P.2d 92; Clark & Marshall, Crimes (6th ed. 1958) § 10.00, pp. 534–536; 1 Wharton, Criminal Law and Procedure (Anderson ed. 1957) § 189; 2 Burdick, Law of Crime (1946) § 445; 40 Am.Jur.2d, Homicide, §§ 9, 434; 40 C.J.S. Homicide § 2b.)

We conclude that the judicial enlargement of section 187 now urged upon us by the People would not have been foreseeable to this petitioner, and hence that its adoption at this time would deny him due process of law.

Let a peremptory writ of prohibition issue restraining respondent court from taking any further proceedings on Count I of the information, charging petitioner with the crime of murder.[17]

■ McComb, Peters, and Tobriner, JJ., and Peek, J. pro tem.,[18] concur.

■ Burke, Acting Chief Justice (dissenting).…

■ Sullivan, J., concurs.

City of Chicago v. Morales

Supreme Court of the United States, 1999.
527 U.S. 41, 119 S.Ct. 1849, 144 L.Ed.2d 67.

■ Justice Stevens announced the judgment of the Court and delivered the opinion of the Court with respect to Parts I, II, and V, and an opinion with respect to Parts III, IV, and VI, in which Justice Souter and Justice Ginsburg join.

In 1992, the Chicago City Council enacted the Gang Congregation Ordinance, which prohibits "criminal street gang members" from "loitering" with one another or with other persons in any public place. The question presented is whether the Supreme Court of Illinois correctly held that the ordinance violates the Due Process Clause of the Fourteenth Amendment to the Federal Constitution.

I

Before the ordinance was adopted, the city council's Committee on Police and Fire conducted hearings to explore the problems created by the city's street gangs, and more particularly, the consequences of public loitering by gang members. Witnesses included residents of the neighbor-

---

abortion." While the case was decided after the occurrence of the acts with which petitioner is charged, it nonetheless indicates that *Chavez* did not change California law on this point. Indeed, in footnote 13 we proceeded to distinguish *Chavez* as a case holding that "for purposes of the manslaughter and murder statutes, human life may exist where childbirth has commenced but has not been fully completed." (Accord, Perkins on Criminal Law (2d ed. 1969), p. 30.) In the case at bar, of course, the record is devoid of evidence that "childbirth" had commenced at the time of the acts charged.

17. [Added by the Compiler.] Aftermath, Cal.Pen.Code § 187. "Murder is the unlawful killing of a human being, *or a fetus,* with malice aforethought.…" The words in italics were added by amendment in 1970, "triggered" by *Keeler.* Legal abortions are excluded from the current California statute. *See* People v. Smith, 188 Cal.App.3d 1495, 234 Cal.Rptr. 142 (1987).

18. Retired Associate Justice of the Supreme Court sitting under assignment by the Acting Chairman of the Judicial Council.

hoods where gang members are most active, as well as some of the aldermen who represent those areas. Based on that evidence, the council made a series of findings that are included in the text of the ordinance and explain the reasons for its enactment.

The council found that a continuing increase in criminal street gang activity was largely responsible for the city's rising murder rate, as well as an escalation of violent and drug related crimes. It noted that in many neighborhoods throughout the city, " 'the burgeoning presence of street gang members in public places has intimidated many law abiding citizens.' " 177 Ill.2d 440, 445, 227 Ill.Dec. 130, 687 N.E.2d 53, 58 (1997). Furthermore, the council stated that gang members " 'establish control over identifiable areas ... by loitering in those areas and intimidating others from entering those areas; and ... [m]embers of criminal street gangs avoid arrest by committing no offense punishable under existing laws when they know the police are present....' " *Ibid.* It further found that " 'loitering in public places by criminal street gang members creates a justifiable fear for the safety of persons and property in the area' " and that " '[a]ggressive action is necessary to preserve the city's streets and other public places so that the public may use such places without fear.' " Moreover, the council concluded that the city " 'has an interest in discouraging all persons from loitering in public places with criminal gang members.' " *Ibid.*

The ordinance creates a criminal offense punishable by a fine of up to $500, imprisonment for not more than six months, and a requirement to perform up to 120 hours of community service. Commission of the offense involves four predicates. First, the police officer must reasonably believe that at least one of the two or more persons present in a " 'public place' " is a " 'criminal street gang membe[r].' " Second, the persons must be " 'loitering,' " which the ordinance defines as "remain[ing] in any one place with no apparent purpose." Third, the officer must then order " 'all' " of the persons to disperse and remove themselves " 'from the area.' " Fourth, a person must disobey the officer's order. If any person, whether a gang member or not, disobeys the officer's order, that person is guilty of violating the ordinance. *Ibid.*[19]

---

19.   The ordinance states in pertinent part:

Whenever a police officer observes a person whom he reasonably believes to be a criminal street gang member loitering in any public place with one or more other persons, he shall order all such persons to disperse and remove themselves from the area. Any person who does not promptly obey such an order is in violation of this section.

"(b) It shall be an affirmative defense to an alleged violation of this section that no person who was observed loitering was in fact a member of a criminal street gang.

"(c) As used in this Section:

"(1) 'Loiter' means to remain in any one place with no apparent purpose.

"(2) 'Criminal street gang' means any ongoing organization, association in fact or group of three or more persons, whether formal or informal, having as one of its substantial activities the commission of one or more of the criminal acts enumerated in paragraph (3), and whose members individually or collectively engage in or have engaged in a pattern of criminal gang activity.

. . .

"(5) 'Public place' means the public way and any other location open to the public, whether publicly or privately owned."

Two months after the ordinance was adopted, the Chicago Police Department promulgated General Order 92–4 to provide guidelines to govern its enforcement. That order purported to establish limitations on the enforcement discretion of police officers "to ensure that the anti-gang loitering ordinance is not enforced in an arbitrary or discriminatory way." Chicago Police Department, General Order 92–4, reprinted in App. to Pet. for Cert. 65a. The limitations confine the authority to arrest gang members who violate the ordinance to sworn "members of the Gang Crime Section" and certain other designated officers, and establish detailed criteria for defining street gangs and membership in such gangs. *Id.,* at 66a–67a. In addition, the order directs district commanders to "designate areas in which the presence of gang members has a demonstrable effect on the activities of law abiding persons in the surrounding community," and provides that the ordinance "will be enforced only within the designated areas." *Id.,* at 68a–69 a. The city, however, does not release the locations of these "designated areas" to the public.

II

During the three years of its enforcement, the police issued over 89,000 dispersal orders and arrested over 42,000 people for violating the ordinance.[20] In the ensuing enforcement proceedings, 2 trial judges upheld the constitutionality of the ordinance, but 11 others ruled that it was invalid. In respondent Youkhana's case, the trial judge held that the "ordinance fails to notify individuals what conduct is prohibited, and it encourages arbitrary and capricious enforcement by police."

The Illinois Appellate Court affirmed the trial court's ruling in the *Youkhana* case, consolidated and affirmed other pending appeals in accordance with *Youkhana,* and reversed the convictions of respondents Gutierrez, Morales, and others. The Appellate Court was persuaded that the ordinance impaired the freedom of assembly of nongang members in violation of the First Amendment to the Federal Constitution and Article I of the Illinois Constitution, that it was unconstitutionally vague, that it

---

(e) Any person who violates this Section is subject to a fine of not less than $100 and not more than $500 for each offense, or imprisonment for not more than six months, or both.

"In addition to or instead of the above penalties, any person who violates this section may be required to perform up to 120 hours of community service pursuant to section 1–4–120 of this Code." Chicago Municipal Code § 8–4–015 (added June 17, 1992), reprinted in App. to Pet. for Cert. 61a–63a.

20. Brief for Petitioner 16. There were 5,251 arrests under the ordinance in 1993, 15,660 in 1994, and 22,056 in 1995. City of Chicago, R. Daley & T. Hillard, Gang and Narcotic Related Violent Crime: 1993–1997, p. 7 (June 1998). The city believes that the ordinance resulted in a significant decline in gang-related homicides. It notes that in 1995, the last year the ordinance was enforced, the gang-related homicide rate fell by 26%. In 1996, after the ordinance had been held invalid, the gang-related homicide rate rose 11%. Pet. for Cert. 9, n. 5. However, gang-related homicides fell by 19% in 1997, over a year after the suspension of the ordinance. Daley & Hillard, at 5. Given the myriad factors that influence levels of violence, it is difficult to evaluate the probative value of this statistical evidence, or to reach any firm conclusion about the ordinance's efficacy. *Cf.* Harcourt, *Reflecting on the Subject: A Critique of the Social Influence Conception of Deterrence, the Broken Windows Theory, and Order-Maintenance Policing New York Style,* 97 Mich. L.Rev. 291, 296 (1998) (describing the "hotly contested debate raging among ... experts over the causes of the decline in crime in New York City and nationally").

improperly criminalized status rather than conduct, and that it jeopardized rights guaranteed under the Fourth Amendment.

The Illinois Supreme Court affirmed. It held "that the gang loitering ordinance violates due process of law in that it is impermissibly vague on its face and an arbitrary restriction on personal liberties." 177 Ill.2d, at 447, 227 Ill.Dec. 130, 687 N.E.2d, at 59. The court did not reach the contentions that the ordinance "creates a status offense, permits arrests without probable cause or is overbroad." *Ibid.*

In support of its vagueness holding, the court pointed out that the definition of "loitering" in the ordinance drew no distinction between innocent conduct and conduct calculated to cause harm. "Moreover, the definition of 'loiter' provided by the ordinance does not assist in clearly articulating the proscriptions of the ordinance." *Id.*, at 451–452, 227 Ill.Dec. 130, 687 N.E.2d, at 60–61. Furthermore, it concluded that the ordinance was "not reasonably susceptible to a limiting construction which would affirm its validity."

We granted certiorari, and now affirm. Like the Illinois Supreme Court, we conclude that the ordinance enacted by the city of Chicago is unconstitutionally vague.

III

The basic factual predicate for the city's ordinance is not in dispute. As the city argues in its brief, "the very presence of a large collection of obviously brazen, insistent, and lawless gang members and hangers-on on the public ways intimidates residents, who become afraid even to leave their homes and go about their business. That, in turn, imperils community residents' sense of safety and security, detracts from property values, and can ultimately destabilize entire neighborhoods." The findings in the ordinance explain that it was motivated by these concerns. We have no doubt that a law that directly prohibited such intimidating conduct would be constitutional,[21] but this ordinance broadly covers a significant amount of additional activity. Uncertainty about the scope of that additional coverage provides the basis for respondents' claim that the ordinance is too vague.

We are confronted at the outset with the city's claim that it was improper for the state courts to conclude that the ordinance is invalid on its face. The city correctly points out that imprecise laws can be attacked on their face under two different doctrines. First, the overbreadth doctrine permits the facial invalidation of laws that inhibit the exercise of First Amendment rights if the impermissible applications of the law are substan-

---

21. In fact the city already has several laws that serve this purpose. *See*, e.g., Ill. Comp. Stat., ch. 720 §§ 5/12–6 (1998) (intimidation); 570/405.2 (streetgang criminal drug conspiracy); 147/1 *et seq.* (Illinois Streetgang Terrorism Omnibus Prevention Act); 5/25–1 (mob action). Deputy Superintendent Cooper, the only representative of the police department at the Committee on Police and Fire hearing on the ordinance, testified that, of the kinds of behavior people had discussed at the hearing, "90 percent of those instances are actually criminal offenses where people, in fact, can be arrested." Record, Appendix II to plaintiff's Memorandum in Opposition to Motion to Dismiss 182 (Tr. of Proceedings, Chicago City Council Committee on Police and Fire, May 18, 1992).

tial when "judged in relation to the statute's plainly legitimate sweep." Broadrick v. Oklahoma, 413 U.S. 601, 612–615, 93 S.Ct. 2908, 37 L.Ed.2d 830 (1973). Second, even if an enactment does not reach a substantial amount of constitutionally protected conduct, it may be impermissibly vague because it fails to establish standards for the police and public that are sufficient to guard against the arbitrary deprivation of liberty interests. Kolender v. Lawson, 461 U.S. 352, 358, 103 S.Ct. 1855, 75 L.Ed.2d 903 (1983).

While we, like the Illinois courts, conclude that the ordinance is invalid on its face, we do not rely on the overbreadth doctrine. We agree with the city's submission that the law does not have a sufficiently substantial impact on conduct protected by the First Amendment to render it unconstitutional. The ordinance does not prohibit speech. Because the term "loiter" is defined as remaining in one place "with no apparent purpose," it is also clear that it does not prohibit any form of conduct that is apparently intended to convey a message. By its terms, the ordinance is inapplicable to assemblies that are designed to demonstrate a group's support of, or opposition to, a particular point of view. *Cf.* Clark v. Community for Creative Non–Violence, 468 U.S. 288, 104 S.Ct. 3065, 82 L.Ed.2d 221 (1984); Gregory v. Chicago, 394 U.S. 111, 89 S.Ct. 946, 22 L.Ed.2d 134 (1969). Its impact on the social contact between gang members and others does not impair the First Amendment "right of association" that our cases have recognized. *See* Dallas v. Stanglin, 490 U.S. 19, 23–25, 109 S.Ct. 1591, 104 L.Ed.2d 18 (1989).

On the other hand, as the United States recognizes, the freedom to loiter for innocent purposes is part of the "liberty" protected by the Due Process Clause of the Fourteenth Amendment.[22] We have expressly identified this "right to remove from one place to another according to inclination" as "an attribute of personal liberty" protected by the Constitution. Williams v. Fears, 179 U.S. 270, 274, 21 S.Ct. 128, 45 L.Ed. 186 (1900); *see also* Papachristou v. Jacksonville, 405 U.S. 156, 164, 92 S.Ct. 839, 31 L.Ed.2d 110 (1972).[23] Indeed, it is apparent that an individual's decision to

---

22. See Brief for United States as *Amicus Curiae* 23: "We do not doubt that, under the Due Process Clause, individuals in this country have significant liberty interests in standing on sidewalks and in other public places, and in traveling, moving, and associating with others." The city appears to agree, at least to the extent that such activities include "social gatherings." Brief for Petitioner 21, n. 13. Both Justice SCALIA, *post,* at 1872–1874 (dissenting opinion), and Justice THOMAS, *post,* at 1881–1883 (dissenting opinion), not only disagree with this proposition, but also incorrectly assume (as the city does not, see Brief for Petitioner 44) that identification of an obvious liberty interest that is impacted by a statute is equivalent to finding a violation of substantive due process. *See* n. 35, *infra.*

23. Petitioner cites historical precedent against recognizing what it describes as the "fundamental right to loiter." Brief for Petitioner 12. While antiloitering ordinances have long existed in this country, their pedigree does not ensure their constitutionality. In 16th-century England, for example, the " 'Slavery acts' " provided for a 2–year enslavement period for anyone who " 'liveth idly and loiteringly, by the space of three days.' " Note, Homelessness in a Modern Urban Setting, 10 Ford. Urb. L.J. 749, 754, n. 17 (1982). In *Papachristou* we noted that many American vagrancy laws were patterned on these "Elizabethan poor laws." 405 U.S., at 161–162, 92 S.Ct. 839. These laws went virtually unchallenged in this country until attorneys became widely available to the indigent following our decision in Gideon v. Wainwright, 372 U.S. 335, 83 S.Ct. 792, 9 L.Ed.2d 799 (1963). *See* Recent Developments, Constitutional Attacks on Vagrancy Laws, 20 Stan. L.Rev. 782, 783 (1968). In addition,

remain in a public place of his choice is as much a part of his liberty as the freedom of movement inside frontiers that is "a part of our heritage" Kent v. Dulles, 357 U.S. 116, 126, 78 S.Ct. 1113, 2 L.Ed.2d 1204 (1958), or the right to move "to whatsoever place one's own inclination may direct" identified in Blackstone's Commentaries. 1 W. Blackstone, Commentaries on the Laws of England 130 (1765).

There is no need, however, to decide whether the impact of the Chicago ordinance on constitutionally protected liberty alone would suffice to support a facial challenge under the overbreadth doctrine. *Cf.* Aptheker v. Secretary of State, 378 U.S. 500, 515–517, 84 S.Ct. 1659, 12 L.Ed.2d 992 (1964) (right to travel); Planned Parenthood of Central Mo. v. Danforth, 428 U.S. 52, 82–83, 96 S.Ct. 2831, 49 L.Ed.2d 788 (1976) (abortion); Kolender v. Lawson, 461 U.S., at 355, n. 3, 358–360, and n. 9, 103 S.Ct. 1610. For it is clear that the vagueness of this enactment makes a facial challenge appropriate. This is not an ordinance that "simply regulates business behavior and contains a scienter requirement." *See* Hoffman Estates v. Flipside, Hoffman Estates, Inc., 455 U.S. 489, 499, 102 S.Ct. 1186, 71 L.Ed.2d 362 (1982). It is a criminal law that contains no *mens rea* requirement, *see* Colautti v. Franklin, 439 U.S. 379, 395, 99 S.Ct. 675, 58 L.Ed.2d 596 (1979), and infringes on constitutionally protected rights, *see id.,* at 391, 99 S.Ct. 675. When vagueness permeates the text of such a law, it is subject to facial attack.[24]

---

vagrancy laws were used after the Civil War to keep former slaves in a state of quasi slavery. In 1865, for example, Alabama broadened its vagrancy statute to include " 'any runaway, stubborn servant or child' " and " 'a laborer or servant who loiters away his time, or refuses to comply with any contract for a term of service without just cause.' " T. Wilson, Black Codes of the South 76 (1965). The Reconstruction-era vagrancy laws had especially harsh consequences on African–American women and children. L. Kerber, No Constitutional Right to be Ladies: Women and the Obligations of Citizenship 50–69 (1998). Neither this history nor the scholarly compendia in Justice THOMAS' dissent, *post,* at 1881–1883, persuades us that the right to engage in loitering that is entirely harmless in both purpose and effect is not a part of the liberty protected by the Due Process Clause.

24. The burden of the first portion of Justice SCALIA's dissent is virtually a facial challenge to the facial challenge doctrine. *See post,* at 1867–1872. He first lauds the "clarity of our general jurisprudence" in the method for assessing facial challenges and then states that the clear import of our cases is that, in order to mount a successful facial challenge, a plaintiff must "establish that no set of circumstances exists under which the Act would be valid." *See post,* at 1870 (emphasis deleted); United States v. Salerno, 481 U.S. 739, 745, 107 S.Ct. 2095, 95 L.Ed.2d 697 (1987). To the extent we have consistently articulated a clear standard for facial challenges, it is not the *Salerno* formulation, which has never been the decisive factor in any decision of this Court, including *Salerno* itself (even though the defendants in that case did not claim that the statute was unconstitutional as applied to them, *see id.,* at 745, n. 3, 107 S.Ct. 2095, the Court nevertheless entertained their facial challenge). Since we, like the Illinois Supreme Court, conclude that vagueness permeates the ordinance, a facial challenge is appropriate.

We need not, however, resolve the viability of *Salerno's* dictum, because this case comes to us from a state—not a federal—court. When asserting a facial challenge, a party seeks to vindicate not only his own rights, but those of others who may also be adversely impacted by the statute in question. In this sense, the threshold for facial challenges is a species of third party *(jus tertii)* standing, which we have recognized as a prudential doctrine and not one mandated by Article III of the Constitution. *See* Secretary of State of Md. v. Joseph H. Munson Co., 467 U.S. 947, 955, 104 S.Ct. 2839, 81 L.Ed.2d 786 (1984). When a state court has reached the merits of a constitutional claim, "invoking prudential limitations on [the respondent's] assertion of *jus tertii* would serve no functional purpose." City of Revere v. Massachu-

Vagueness may invalidate a criminal law for either of two independent reasons. First, it may fail to provide the kind of notice that will enable ordinary people to understand what conduct it prohibits; second, it may authorize and even encourage arbitrary and discriminatory enforcement. *See* Kolender v. Lawson, 461 U.S., at 357, 103 S.Ct. 1855. Accordingly, we first consider whether the ordinance provides fair notice to the citizen and then discuss its potential for arbitrary enforcement.

IV

"It is established that a law fails to meet the requirements of the Due Process Clause if it is so vague and standardless that it leaves the public uncertain as to the conduct it prohibits...." Giaccio v. Pennsylvania, 382 U.S. 399, 402–403, 86 S.Ct. 518, 15 L.Ed.2d 447 (1966). The Illinois Supreme Court recognized that the term "loiter" may have a common and accepted meaning, 177 Ill.2d, at 451, 227 Ill.Dec. 130, 687 N.E.2d, at 61, but the definition of that term in this ordinance—"to remain in any one place with no apparent purpose"—does not. It is difficult to imagine how any citizen of the city of Chicago standing in a public place with a group of people would know if he or she had an "apparent purpose." If she were talking to another person, would she have an apparent purpose? If she were frequently checking her watch and looking expectantly down the street, would she have an apparent purpose?[25]

Since the city cannot conceivably have meant to criminalize each instance a citizen stands in public with a gang member, the vagueness that dooms this ordinance is not the product of uncertainty about the normal meaning of "loitering," but rather about what loitering is covered by the ordinance and what is not. The Illinois Supreme Court emphasized the law's failure to distinguish between innocent conduct and conduct threatening harm. Its decision followed the precedent set by a number of state courts that have upheld ordinances that criminalize loitering combined with some other overt act or evidence of criminal intent.[26] However, state

---

setts Gen. Hospital, 463 U.S. 239, 243, 103 S.Ct. 2979, 77 L.Ed.2d 605 (1983) (internal quotation marks omitted).

Whether or not it would be appropriate for federal courts to apply the *Salerno* standard in some cases—a proposition which is doubtful—state courts need not apply prudential notions of standing created by this Court. See ASARCO Inc. v. Kadish, 490 U.S. 605, 618, 109 S.Ct. 2037, 104 L.Ed.2d 696 (1989). Justice SCALIA's assumption that state courts must apply the restrictive *Salerno* test is incorrect as a matter of law; moreover it contradicts "essential principles of federalism." *See* Dorf, *Facial Challenges to State and Federal Statutes*, 46 Stan. L.Rev. 235, 284 (1994).

25. The Solicitor General, while supporting the city's argument that the ordinance is constitutional, appears to recognize that the ordinance cannot be read literally without invoking intractable vagueness concerns. "[T]he purpose simply to stand on a corner cannot be an 'apparent purpose' under the ordinance; if it were, the ordinance would prohibit nothing at all." Brief for United States as *Amicus Curiae* 12–13.

26. See, *e.g.,* Tacoma v. Luvene, 118 Wash.2d 826, 827 P.2d 1374 (1992) (upholding ordinance criminalizing loitering with purpose to engage in drug-related activities); People v. Superior Court, 46 Cal.3d 381, 394–395, 250 Cal.Rptr. 515, 758 P.2d 1046, 1052 (1988) (upholding ordinance criminalizing loitering for the purpose of engaging in or soliciting lewd act).

courts have uniformly invalidated laws that do not join the term "loitering" with a second specific element of the crime.[27]

The city's principal response to this concern about adequate notice is that loiterers are not subject to sanction until after they have failed to comply with an officer's order to disperse. "[W]hatever problem is created by a law that criminalizes conduct people normally believe to be innocent is solved when persons receive actual notice from a police order of what they are expected to do." We find this response unpersuasive for at least two reasons.

First, the purpose of the fair notice requirement is to enable the ordinary citizen to conform his or her conduct to the law. "No one may be required at peril of life, liberty or property to speculate as to the meaning of penal statutes." Lanzetta v. New Jersey, 306 U.S. 451, 453, 59 S.Ct. 618, 83 L.Ed. 888 (1939). Although it is true that a loiterer is not subject to criminal sanctions unless he or she disobeys a dispersal order, the loitering is the conduct that the ordinance is designed to prohibit. If the loitering is in fact harmless and innocent, the dispersal order itself is an unjustified impairment of liberty. If the police are able to decide arbitrarily which members of the public they will order to disperse, then the Chicago ordinance becomes indistinguishable from the law we held invalid in Shuttlesworth v. Birmingham, 382 U.S. 87, 90, 86 S.Ct. 211, 15 L.Ed.2d 176 (1965).[28] Because an officer may issue an order only after prohibited conduct has already occurred, it cannot provide the kind of advance notice that will protect the putative loiterer from being ordered to disperse. Such an order cannot retroactively give adequate warning of the boundary between the permissible and the impermissible applications of the law.[29]

Second, the terms of the dispersal order compound the inadequacy of the notice afforded by the ordinance. It provides that the officer "shall order all such persons to disperse and remove themselves from the area." App. to Pet. for Cert. 61a. This vague phrasing raises a host of questions. After such an order issues, how long must the loiterers remain apart? How far must they move? If each loiterer walks around the block and they meet again at the same location, are they subject to arrest or merely to being ordered to disperse again? As we do here, we have found vagueness in a criminal statute exacerbated by the use of the standards of "neighborhood" and "locality." Connally v. General Constr. Co., 269 U.S. 385, 46 S.Ct. 126, 70 L.Ed. 322 (1926). We remarked in *Connally* that "[b]oth terms are

---

27. See, *e.g.,* State v. Richard, 108 Nev. 626, 627, n. 2, 836 P.2d 622, 623, n. 2 (1992) (striking down statute that made it unlawful "for any person to loiter or prowl upon the property of another without lawful business with the owner or occupant thereof").

28. "Literally read . . . this ordinance says that a person may stand on a public sidewalk in Birmingham only at the whim of any police officer of that city. The constitutional vice of so broad a provision needs no demonstration." 382 U.S., at 90, 86 S.Ct. 211.

29. As we have noted in a similar context: "If petitioners were held guilty of violating the Georgia statute because they disobeyed the officers, this case falls within the rule that a generally worded statute which is construed to punish conduct which cannot constitutionally be punished is unconstitutionally vague to the extent that it fails to give adequate warning of the boundary between the constitutionally permissible and constitutionally impermissible applications of the statute." Wright v. Georgia, 373 U.S. 284, 292, 83 S.Ct. 1240, 10 L.Ed.2d 349 (1963).

elastic and, dependent upon circumstances, may be equally satisfied by areas measured by rods or by miles." *Id.,* at 395, 46 S.Ct. 126.

Lack of clarity in the description of the loiterer's duty to obey a dispersal order might not render the ordinance unconstitutionally vague if the definition of the forbidden conduct were clear, but it does buttress our conclusion that the entire ordinance fails to give the ordinary citizen adequate notice of what is forbidden and what is permitted. The Constitution does not permit a legislature to "set a net large enough to catch all possible offenders, and leave it to the courts to step inside and say who could be rightfully detained, and who should be set at large." United States v. Reese, 92 U.S. 214, 221, 23 L.Ed. 563 (1876). This ordinance is therefore vague "not in the sense that it requires a person to conform his conduct to an imprecise but comprehensible normative standard, but rather in the sense that no standard of conduct is specified at all." Coates v. Cincinnati, 402 U.S. 611, 614, 91 S.Ct. 1686, 29 L.Ed.2d 214 (1971).

V

The broad sweep of the ordinance also violates " 'the requirement that a legislature establish minimal guidelines to govern law enforcement.' " Kolender v. Lawson, 461 U.S., at 358, 103 S.Ct. 1855. There are no such guidelines in the ordinance. In any public place in the city of Chicago, persons who stand or sit in the company of a gang member may be ordered to disperse unless their purpose is apparent. The mandatory language in the enactment directs the police to issue an order without first making any inquiry about their possible purposes. It matters not whether the reason that a gang member and his father, for example, might loiter near Wrigley Field is to rob an unsuspecting fan or just to get a glimpse of Sammy Sosa leaving the ballpark; in either event, if their purpose is not apparent to a nearby police officer, she may—indeed, she "shall"—order them to disperse.

Recognizing that the ordinance does reach a substantial amount of innocent conduct, we turn, then, to its language to determine if it "necessarily entrusts lawmaking to the moment-to-moment judgment of the policeman on his beat." Kolender v. Lawson, 461 U.S., at 360, 103 S.Ct. 1855 (internal quotation marks omitted). As we discussed in the context of fair notice, *see* supra, at 1859–1860, this page, the principal source of the vast discretion conferred on the police in this case is the definition of loitering as "to remain in any one place with no apparent purpose."

As the Illinois Supreme Court interprets that definition, it "provides absolute discretion to police officers to decide what activities constitute loitering." 177 Ill.2d, at 457, 227 Ill.Dec. 130, 687 N.E.2d, at 63. We have no authority to construe the language of a state statute more narrowly than the construction given by that State's highest court."The power to determine the meaning of a statute carries with it the power to prescribe its extent and limitations as well as the method by which they shall be determined." Smiley v. Kansas, 196 U.S. 447, 455, 25 S.Ct. 289, 49 L.Ed. 546 (1905).

Nevertheless, the city disputes the Illinois Supreme Court's interpretation, arguing that the text of the ordinance limits the officer's discretion in three ways. First, it does not permit the officer to issue a dispersal order to anyone who is moving along or who has an apparent purpose. Second, it does not permit an arrest if individuals obey a dispersal order. Third, no order can issue unless the officer reasonably believes that one of the loiterers is a member of a criminal street gang.

Even putting to one side our duty to defer to a state court's construction of the scope of a local enactment, we find each of these limitations insufficient. That the ordinance does not apply to people who are moving— that is, to activity that would not constitute loitering under any possible definition of the term—does not even address the question of how much discretion the police enjoy in deciding which stationary persons to disperse under the ordinance. Similarly, that the ordinance does not permit an arrest until after a dispersal order has been disobeyed does not provide any guidance to the officer deciding whether such an order should issue. The "no apparent purpose" standard for making that decision is inherently subjective because its application depends on whether some purpose is "apparent" to the officer on the scene.

Presumably an officer would have discretion to treat some purposes— perhaps a purpose to engage in idle conversation or simply to enjoy a cool breeze on a warm evening—as too frivolous to be apparent if he suspected a different ulterior motive. Moreover, an officer conscious of the city council's reasons for enacting the ordinance might well ignore its text and issue a dispersal order, even though an illicit purpose is actually apparent.

It is true, as the city argues, that the requirement that the officer reasonably believe that a group of loiterers contains a gang member does place a limit on the authority to order dispersal. That limitation would no doubt be sufficient if the ordinance only applied to loitering that had an apparently harmful purpose or effect or possibly if it only applied to loitering by persons reasonably believed to be criminal gang members. But this ordinance, for reasons that are not explained in the findings of the city council, requires no harmful purpose and applies to nongang members as well as suspected gang members.[30] It applies to everyone in the city who may remain in one place with one suspected gang member as long as their purpose is not apparent to an officer observing them. Friends, relatives, teachers, counselors, or even total strangers might unwittingly engage in forbidden loitering if they happen to engage in idle conversation with a gang member.

Ironically, the definition of loitering in the Chicago ordinance not only extends its scope to encompass harmless conduct, but also has the perverse consequence of excluding from its coverage much of the intimidating conduct that motivated its enactment. As the city council's findings demonstrate, the most harmful gang loitering is motivated either by an apparent purpose to publicize the gang's dominance of certain territory, thereby

---

30. Not all of the respondents in this case, for example, are gang members. The city admits that it was unable to prove that Morales is a gang member but justifies his arrest and conviction by the fact that Morales admitted "that he knew he was with criminal street gang members." Reply Brief for Petitioner 23, n. 14. In fact, 34 of the 66 respondents in this case were charged in a document that only accused them of being in the presence of a gang member. Tr. of Oral Arg. 34, 58.

intimidating nonmembers, or by an equally apparent purpose to conceal ongoing commerce in illegal drugs. As the Illinois Supreme Court has not placed any limiting construction on the language in the ordinance, we must assume that the ordinance means what it says and that it has no application to loiterers whose purpose is apparent. The relative importance of its application to harmless loitering is magnified by its inapplicability to loitering that has an obviously threatening or illicit purpose.

Finally, in its opinion striking down the ordinance, the Illinois Supreme Court refused to accept the general order issued by the police department as a sufficient limitation on the "vast amount of discretion" granted to the police in its enforcement. We agree. *See* Smith v. Goguen, 415 U.S. 566, 575, 94 S.Ct. 1242, 39 L.Ed.2d 605 (1974). That the police have adopted internal rules limiting their enforcement to certain designated areas in the city would not provide a defense to a loiterer who might be arrested elsewhere. Nor could a person who knowingly loitered with a well-known gang member anywhere in the city safely assume that they would not be ordered to disperse no matter how innocent and harmless their loitering might be.

VI

In our judgment, the Illinois Supreme Court correctly concluded that the ordinance does not provide sufficiently specific limits on the enforcement discretion of the police "to meet constitutional standards for definiteness and clarity."[31] 177 Ill.2d, at 459, 227 Ill.Dec. 130, 687 N.E.2d, at 64. We recognize the serious and difficult problems testified to by the citizens of Chicago that led to the enactment of this ordinance. "We are mindful that the preservation of liberty depends in part on the maintenance of social order." Houston v. Hill, 482 U.S. 451, 471–472, 107 S.Ct. 2502, 96 L.Ed.2d 398 (1987). However, in this instance the city has enacted an ordinance that affords too much discretion to the police and too little notice to citizens who wish to use the public streets.

Accordingly, the judgment of the Supreme Court of Illinois is

Affirmed.

■ JUSTICE O'CONNOR, with whom JUSTICE BREYER joins, concurring in part and concurring in the judgment.

I agree with the Court that Chicago's Gang Congregation Ordinance, Chicago Municipal Code § 8–4–015 (1992) (gang loitering ordinance or ordinance) is unconstitutionally vague. A penal law is void for vagueness if it fails to "define the criminal offense with sufficient definiteness that ordinary people can understand what conduct is prohibited" or fails to establish guidelines to prevent "arbitrary and discriminatory enforcement" of the law. Kolender v. Lawson, 461 U.S. 352, 357, 103 S.Ct. 1855, 75

---

31. This conclusion makes it unnecessary to reach the question whether the Illinois Supreme Court correctly decided that the ordinance is invalid as a deprivation of substantive due process. For this reason, Justice THOMAS, *see post,* at 1881–1883, and Justice SCALIA, *see post,* at 1873, are mistaken when they assert that our decision must be analyzed under the framework for substantive due process set out in Washington v. Glucksberg, 521 U.S. 702, 117 S.Ct. 2258, 138 L.Ed.2d 772 (1997).

L.Ed.2d 903 (1983). Of these, "the more important aspect of the vagueness doctrine 'is ... the requirement that a legislature establish minimal guidelines to govern law enforcement.' " *Id.*, at 358, 103 S.Ct. 1855 (quoting Smith v. Goguen, 415 U.S. 566, 574–575, 94 S.Ct. 1242, 39 L.Ed.2d 605 (1974)). I share Justice THOMAS' concern about the consequences of gang violence, and I agree that some degree of police discretion is necessary to allow the police "to perform their peacekeeping responsibilities satisfactorily." *Post,* at 1885 (dissenting opinion). A criminal law, however, must not permit policemen, prosecutors, and juries to conduct " 'a standardless sweep ... to pursue their personal predilections.' " Kolender v. Lawson, *supra,* at 358, 103 S.Ct. 1855 (quoting Smith v. Goguen, *supra,* at 575, 94 S.Ct. 1242). . . .

As it has been construed by the Illinois court, Chicago's gang loitering ordinance is unconstitutionally vague because it lacks sufficient minimal standards to guide law enforcement officers. . . .

This vagueness consideration alone provides a sufficient ground for affirming the Illinois court's decision, and I agree with Part V of the Court's opinion, which discusses this consideration. . . . Accordingly, there is no need to consider the other issues briefed by the parties and addressed by the plurality. I express no opinion about them.

It is important to courts and legislatures alike that we characterize more clearly the narrow scope of today's holding. As the ordinance comes to this Court, it is unconstitutionally vague. Nevertheless, there remain open to Chicago reasonable alternatives to combat the very real threat posed by gang intimidation and violence. For example, the Court properly and expressly distinguishes the ordinance from laws that require loiterers to have a "harmful purpose," *see ibid.,* from laws that target only gang members, see *ibid.,* and from laws that incorporate limits on the area and manner in which the laws may be enforced, *see ibid.* In addition, the ordinance here is unlike a law that "directly prohibit[s]" the " 'presence of a large collection of obviously brazen, insistent, and lawless gang members and hangers-on on the public ways,' " that " 'intimidates residents.' " *Ante,* at 1856 (quoting Brief for Petitioner 14). Indeed, as the plurality notes, the city of Chicago has several laws that do exactly this. *See ante,* at 1857, n. 17. Chicago has even enacted a provision that "enables police officers to fulfill ... their traditional functions," including "preserving the public peace." *See post,* at 1883 (THOMAS, J., dissenting). Specifically, Chicago's general disorderly conduct provision allows the police to arrest those who knowingly "provoke, make or aid in making a breach of peace." *See* Chicago Municipal Code § 8–4–010 (1992).

In my view, the gang loitering ordinance could have been construed more narrowly. The term "loiter" might possibly be construed in a more limited fashion to mean "to remain in any one place with no apparent purpose other than to establish control over identifiable areas, to intimidate others from entering those areas, or to conceal illegal activities." Such a definition would be consistent with the Chicago City Council's findings and would avoid the vagueness problems of the ordinance as construed by the Illinois Supreme Court. See App. to Pet. for Cert. 60a–61a. As noted above, so would limitations that restricted the ordinance's criminal penalties to gang members or that more carefully delineated the circumstances in which those penalties would apply to nongang members.

The Illinois Supreme Court did not choose to give a limiting construction to Chicago's ordinance.... Nevertheless, we cannot impose a limiting construction that a state supreme court has declined to adopt.... Accordingly, I join Parts I, II, and V of the Court's opinion and concur in the judgment.

■ JUSTICE KENNEDY, concurring in part and concurring in the judgment.

I join Parts I, II, and V of the Court's opinion and concur in the judgment.

I also share many of the concerns Justice STEVENS expresses in Part IV with respect to the sufficiency of notice under the ordinance. As interpreted by the Illinois Supreme Court, the Chicago ordinance would reach a broad range of innocent conduct. For this reason it is not necessarily saved by the requirement that the citizen must disobey a police order to disperse before there is a violation.

We have not often examined these types of orders. *Cf.* Shuttlesworth v. Birmingham, 382 U.S. 87, 86 S.Ct. 211, 15 L.Ed.2d 176 (1965). It can be assumed, however, that some police commands will subject a citizen to prosecution for disobeying whether or not the citizen knows why the order is given. Illustrative examples include when the police tell a pedestrian not to enter a building and the reason is to avoid impeding a rescue team, or to protect a crime scene, or to secure an area for the protection of a public official. It does not follow, however, that any unexplained police order must be obeyed without notice of the lawfulness of the order. The predicate of an order to disperse is not, in my view, sufficient to eliminate doubts regarding the adequacy of notice under this ordinance. A citizen, while engaging in a wide array of innocent conduct, is not likely to know when he may be subject to a dispersal order based on the officer's own knowledge of the identity or affiliations of other persons with whom the citizen is congregating; nor may the citizen be able to assess what an officer might conceive to be the citizen's lack of an apparent purpose.

■ JUSTICE THOMAS, with whom THE CHIEF JUSTICE and JUSTICE SCALIA join, dissenting.

The duly elected members of the Chicago City Council enacted the ordinance at issue as part of a larger effort to prevent gangs from establishing dominion over the public streets. By invalidating Chicago's ordinance, I fear that the Court has unnecessarily sentenced law-abiding citizens to lives of terror and misery. The ordinance is not vague. "[A]ny fool would know that a particular category of conduct would be within [its] reach." Kolender v. Lawson, 461 U.S. 352, 370, 103 S.Ct. 1855, 75 L.Ed.2d 903 (1983) (White, J., dissenting). Nor does it violate the Due Process Clause. The asserted "freedom to loiter for innocent purposes," *ante,* at 1857 (plurality opinion), is in no way " 'deeply rooted in this Nation's history and tradition,' " Washington v. Glucksberg, 521 U.S. 702, 721, 117 S.Ct. 2258, 138 L.Ed.2d 772 (1997) (citation omitted). I dissent.

I

The human costs exacted by criminal street gangs are inestimable. In many of our Nation's cities, gangs have "[v]irtually overtak[en] certain neighborhoods, contributing to the economic and social decline of these areas and causing fear and lifestyle changes among law-abiding residents." U.S. Dept. of Justice, Office of Justice Programs, Bureau of Justice Assistance, Monograph: Urban Street Gang Enforcement 3 (1997). Gangs fill the daily lives of many of our poorest and most vulnerable citizens with a terror that the Court does not give sufficient consideration, often relegating them to the status of prisoners in their own homes.

The city of Chicago has suffered the devastation wrought by this national tragedy. Last year, in an effort to curb plummeting attendance, the Chicago Public Schools hired dozens of adults to escort children to school. The youngsters had become too terrified of gang violence to leave their homes alone. Martinez, Parents Paid to Walk Line Between Gangs and School, Chicago Tribune, Jan. 21, 1998, p. 1. The children's fears were not unfounded. In 1996, the Chicago Police Department estimated that there were 132 criminal street gangs in the city. Illinois Criminal Justice Information Authority, Research Bulletin: Street Gangs and Crime 4 (Sept. 1996). Between 1987 and 1994, these gangs were involved in 63,141 criminal incidents, including 21,689 nonlethal violent crimes and 894 homicides. *Id.*, at 4–5.

Before enacting its ordinance, the Chicago City Council held extensive hearings on the problems of gang loitering. Concerned citizens appeared to testify poignantly as to how gangs disrupt their daily lives. Ordinary citizens like Ms. D'Ivory Gordon explained that she struggled just to walk to work:

"When I walk out my door, these guys are out there. . . .

. . .

"They watch you. . . . They know where you live. They know what time you leave, what time you come home. I am afraid of them. I have even come to the point now that I carry a meat cleaver to work with me. . . .

". . . I don't want to hurt anyone, and I don't want to be hurt. We need to clean these corners up. Clean these communities up and take it back from them." Transcript of Proceedings before the City Council of Chicago, Committee on Police and Fire 66–67 (May 15, 1992) (hereinafter Transcript).

Eighty-eight-year-old Susan Mary Jackson echoed her sentiments, testifying: "We used to have a nice neighborhood. We don't have it anymore. . . . I am scared to go out in the daytime. . . . [Y]ou can't pass because they are standing. I am afraid to go to the store. I don't go to the store because I am afraid. At my age if they look at me real hard, I be ready to holler." *Id.*, at 93–95. Another long-time resident testified:

"I have never had the terror that I feel everyday when I walk down the streets of Chicago. . . .

"I have had my windows broken out. I have had guns pulled on me. I have been threatened. I get intimidated on a daily basis, and it's come to the point where I say, well, do I go out today. Do I put my ax in my briefcase. Do I walk around dressed like a bum so I am not looking rich or got any money or anything like that." *Id.,* at 124–125.

Following these hearings, the council found that "criminal street gangs establish control over identifiable areas ... by loitering in those areas and intimidating others from entering those areas." App. to Pet. for Cert. 60a. It further found that the mere presence of gang members "intimidate[s] many law abiding citizens" and "creates a justifiable fear for the safety of persons and property in the area." *Ibid.* It is the product of this democratic process—the council's attempt to address these social ills—that we are asked to pass judgment upon today.

II

... The plurality ... concludes that the city's commonsense effort to combat gang loitering fails constitutional scrutiny for two separate reasons—because it infringes upon gang members' constitutional right to "loiter for innocent purposes," *ante,* at 1857, and because it is vague on its face, *ante,* at 1858. A majority of the Court endorses the latter conclusion. I respectfully disagree.

A

We recently reconfirmed that "[o]ur Nation's history, legal traditions, and practices ... provide the crucial 'guideposts for responsible decision-making' ... that direct and restrain our exposition of the Due Process Clause." *Glucksberg,* 521 U.S., at 721, 117 S.Ct. 2258 (quoting Moore v. East Cleveland, 431 U.S. 494, 503, 97 S.Ct. 1932, 52 L.Ed.2d 531 (1977) (plurality opinion)).

Only laws that infringe "those fundamental rights and liberties which are, objectively, 'deeply rooted in this Nation's history and tradition'" offend the Due Process Clause. *Glucksberg, supra,* at 720–721, 117 S.Ct. 2258....

Tellingly, the plurality cites only three cases in support of the asserted right to "loiter for innocent purposes." *See ante,* at 1857–1858. Of those, only one—decided more than 100 years after the ratification of the Fourteenth Amendment—actually addressed the validity of a vagrancy ordinance. That case, *Papachristou, supra,* contains some dicta that can be read to support the fundamental right that the plurality asserts.[32] However, the

---

32. The other cases upon which the plurality relies concern the entirely distinct right to interstate and international travel. *See* Williams v. Fears, 179 U.S. 270, 274–275, 21 S.Ct. 128, 45 L.Ed. 186 (1900); Kent v. Dulles, 357 U.S. 116, 78 S.Ct. 1113, 2 L.Ed.2d 1204 (1958). The plurality claims that dicta in those cases articulating a right of free movement, *see Williams, supra,* at 274, 21 S.Ct. 128; *Kent, supra,* at 125, 78 S.Ct. 1113, also supports an individual's right to "remain in a public place of his choice." Ironically, *Williams* rejected the argument that a tax on persons engaged in the business of importing out-of-state labor impeded the freedom of transit, so the precise holding in that case does not support, but undermines, the plurality's view. Similarly, the precise holding in *Kent* did not bear on a constitutional right to travel; instead, the Court held only that Congress had not authorized the Secretary of State to deny certain passports. Furthermore, the plurality's approach distorts the principle articulated in those cases, stretching it to a level of generality that permits the Court to disregard the

Court in *Papachristou* did not undertake the now-accepted analysis applied in substantive due process cases—it did not look to tradition to define the rights protected by the Due Process Clause. In any event, a careful reading of the opinion reveals that the Court never said anything about a constitutional right. The Court's holding was that the antiquarian language employed in the vagrancy ordinance at issue was unconstitutionally vague. *See id.,* at 162–163, 92 S.Ct. 839. Even assuming, then, that *Papachristou* was correctly decided as an original matter—a doubtful proposition—it does not compel the conclusion that the Constitution protects the right to loiter for innocent purposes. The plurality's contrary assertion calls to mind the warning that "[t]he Judiciary, including this Court, is the most vulnerable and comes nearest to illegitimacy when it deals with judge-made constitutional law having little or no cognizable roots in the language or even the design of the Constitution. . . . [We] should be extremely reluctant to breathe still further substantive content into the Due Process Clause so as to strike down legislation adopted by a State or city to promote its welfare." *Moore,* 431 U.S., at 544, 97 S.Ct. 1932 (White, J., dissenting). When "the Judiciary does so, it unavoidably pre-empts for itself another part of the governance of the country without express constitutional authority." *Ibid.*

B

The Court concludes that the ordinance is also unconstitutionally vague because it fails to provide adequate standards to guide police discretion and because, in the plurality's view, it does not give residents adequate notice of how to conform their conduct to the confines of the law. I disagree on both counts.

1

At the outset, it is important to note that the ordinance does not criminalize loitering *per se.* Rather, it penalizes loiterers' failure to obey a police officer's order to move along. A majority of the Court believes that this scheme vests too much discretion in police officers. Nothing could be further from the truth. Far from according officers too much discretion, the ordinance merely enables police officers to fulfill one of their traditional functions. Police officers are not, and have never been, simply enforcers of the criminal law. They wear other hats—importantly, they have long been vested with the responsibility for preserving the public peace. . . .

In order to perform their peacekeeping responsibilities satisfactorily, the police inevitably must exercise discretion. Indeed, by empowering them to act as peace officers, the law assumes that the police will exercise that discretion responsibly and with sound judgment. That is not to say that the law should not provide objective guidelines for the police, but simply that it cannot rigidly constrain their every action. By directing a police officer not to issue a dispersal order unless he "observes a person whom he reasonably believes to be a criminal street gang member loitering in any public place," App. to Pet. for Cert. 61a, Chicago's ordinance strikes an appropriate

---

relevant historical evidence that should guide the analysis. Michael H. v. Gerald D., 491 U.S. 110, 127, n. 6, 109 S.Ct. 2333, 105 L.Ed.2d 91 (1989) (plurality opinion).

balance between those two extremes. Just as we trust officers to rely on their experience and expertise in order to make spur-of-the-moment determinations about amorphous legal standards such as "probable cause" and "reasonable suspicion," so we must trust them to determine whether a group of loiterers contains individuals (in this case members of criminal street gangs) whom the city has determined threaten the public peace. . . .

In concluding that the ordinance adequately channels police discretion, I do not suggest that a police officer enforcing the Gang Congregation Ordinance will never make a mistake. Nor do I overlook the *possibility* that a police officer, acting in bad faith, might enforce the ordinance in an arbitrary or discriminatory way. But our decisions should not turn on the proposition that such an event will be anything but rare. Instances of arbitrary or discriminatory enforcement of the ordinance, like any other law, are best addressed when (and if) they arise, rather than prophylactically through the disfavored mechanism of a facial challenge on vagueness grounds. *See* United States v. Salerno, 481 U.S. 739, 745, 107 S.Ct. 2095, 95 L.Ed.2d 697 (1987) ("A facial challenge to a legislative Act is, of course, the most difficult challenge to mount successfully, since the challenger must establish that no set of circumstances exists under which the Act would be valid").

. 2

The plurality's conclusion that the ordinance "fails to give the ordinary citizen adequate notice of what is forbidden and what is permitted," *ante,* at 1861, is similarly untenable. There is nothing "vague" about an order to disperse. . . .

The plurality also concludes that the definition of the term loiter—"to remain in any one place with no apparent purpose," *see* 177 Ill.2d, at 445, 227 Ill.Dec. 130, 687 N.E.2d, at 58—fails to provide adequate notice.[33] "It is difficult to imagine," the plurality posits, "how any citizen of the city of Chicago standing in a public place . . . would know if he or she had an 'apparent purpose.' " *Ante,* at 1859. The plurality underestimates the intellectual capacity of the citizens of Chicago. Persons of ordinary intelligence are perfectly capable of evaluating how outsiders perceive their conduct, and here "[i]t is self-evident that there is a whole range of conduct that anyone with at least a semblance of common sense would know is [loitering] and that would be covered by the statute." *See* Smith v. Goguen, 415 U.S. 566, 584, 94 S.Ct. 1242, 39 L.Ed.2d 605 (1974) (White, J., concurring in judgment). Members of a group standing on the corner staring blankly into space, for example, are likely well aware that passersby would conclude that they have "no apparent purpose." In any event, because this is a facial challenge, the plurality's ability to hypothesize that

---

33. The Court asserts that we cannot second-guess the Illinois Supreme Court's conclusion that the definition " 'provides absolute discretion to police officers to decide what activities constitute loitering,' " *ante,* at 1861 (quoting 177 Ill.2d, at 440, 457, 227 Ill.Dec., at 140, 687 N.E.2d, at 63). While we are bound by a state court's construction of a statute, the Illinois court "did not, strictly speaking, construe the [ordinance] in the sense of defining the meaning of a particular statutory word or phrase. Rather, it merely characterized [its] 'practical effect'. . . . This assessment does not bind us." Wisconsin v. Mitchell, 508 U.S. 476, 484, 113 S.Ct. 2194, 124 L.Ed.2d 436 (1993).

some individuals, in some circumstances, may be unable to ascertain how their actions appear to outsiders is irrelevant to our analysis. Here, we are asked to determine whether the ordinance is "vague in all of its applications." *Hoffman Estates, supra,* at 497, 102 S.Ct. 1186. The answer is unquestionably no.

* * *

Today, the Court focuses extensively on the "rights" of gang members and their companions. It can safely do so—the people who will have to live with the consequences of today's opinion do not live in our neighborhoods. Rather, the people who will suffer from our lofty pronouncements are people like Ms. Susan Mary Jackson; people who have seen their neighborhoods literally destroyed by gangs and violence and drugs. They are good, decent people who must struggle to overcome their desperate situation, against all odds, in order to raise their families, earn a living, and remain good citizens. As one resident described: "There is only about maybe one or two percent of the people in the city causing these problems maybe, but it's keeping 98 percent of us in our houses and off the streets and afraid to shop." Transcript 126.

By focusing exclusively on the imagined "rights" of the two percent, the Court today has denied our most vulnerable citizens the very thing that Justice STEVENS, *ante,* at 1858, elevates above all else—the " 'freedom of movement.' " And that is a shame. I respectfully dissent.

(B) CONDUCT VERSUS STATUS

Robinson v. California

Supreme Court of the United States, 1962.
370 U.S. 660, 82 S.Ct. 1417, 8 L.Ed.2d 758.

■ JUSTICE STEWART delivered the opinion of the Court.

A California statute makes it a criminal offense for a person to "be addicted to the use of narcotics."[34] This appeal draws into question the constitutionality of that provision of the state law, as construed by the California courts in the present case.

The appellant was convicted after a jury trial in the Municipal Court of Los Angeles. The evidence against him was given by two Los Angeles police officers. Officer Brown testified that he had had occasion to examine the appellant's arms one evening on a street in Los Angeles some four months

---

34. The statute is § 11721 of the California Health and Safety Code. It provides: "No person shall use, or be under the influence of, or be addicted to the use of narcotics, excepting when administered by or under the direction of a person licensed by the State to prescribe and administer narcotics. It shall be the burden of the defense to show that it comes within the exception. Any person convicted of violating any provision of this section is guilty of a misdemeanor and shall be sentenced to serve a term of not less than 90 days nor more than one year in the county jail. The court may place a person convicted hereunder on probation for a period not to exceed five years and shall in all cases in which probation in granted require as a condition thereof that such person be confined in the county jail for at least 90 days. In no event does the court have the power to absolve a person who violates this section from the obligation of spending at least 90 days in confinement in the county jail."

before the trial.[35] The officer testified that at that time he had observed "scar tissue and discoloration on the inside" of the appellant's right arm, and "what appeared to be numerous needle marks and a scab which was approximately three inches below the crook of the elbow" on the appellant's left arm. The officer also testified that the appellant under questioning had admitted to the occasional use of narcotics.

Officer Lindquist testified that he had examined the appellant the follow morning in the Central Jail in Los Angeles. The officer stated that at that time he had observed discolorations and scabs on the appellant's arms, and he identified photographs which had been taken of the appellant's arms shortly after his arrest the night before. Based upon more than ten years of experience as a member of the Narcotic Division of the Los Angeles Police Department, the witness gave his opinion that "these marks and the discoloration were the result of the injection of hypodermic needles into the tissue into the vein that was not sterile." He stated that the scabs were several days old at the time of his examination, and that the appellant was neither under the influence of narcotics nor suffering withdrawal symptoms at the time he saw him. This witness also testified that the appellant had admitted using narcotics in the past.

The appellant testified in his own behalf, denying the alleged conversations with the police officers and denying that he had ever used narcotics or been addicted to their use. He explained the marks on his arms as resulting from an allergic condition contracted during his military service. His testimony was corroborated by two witnesses.

The trial judge instructed the jury that the statute made it a misdemeanor for a person 'either to use narcotics, or to be addicted to the use of narcotics."[36] That portion of the statute referring to the "use" of narcotics is based upon the "act" of using. That portion of the statute referring to "addicted to the use" of narcotics is based upon a condition or status. They are not identical. * * * To be addicted to the use of narcotics is said to be a status or condition and not an act. It is a continuing offense and differs from most other offenses in the fact that (it) is chronic rather than acute; that it continues after it is complete and subjects the offender to arrest at any time before he reforms. The existence of such a chronic condition may be ascertained from a single examination, if the characteristic reactions of that condition be found present.

The judge further instructed the jury that the appellant could be convicted under a general verdict if the jury agreed either that he was of

---

35. At the trial the appellant, claiming that he had been the victim of an unconstitutional search and seizure, unsuccessfully objected to the admission of Officer Brown's testimony. That claim is also pressed here, but since we do not reach it there is no need to detail the circumstances which led to Officer Brown's examination of the appellant's person. Suffice it to say, that at the time the police first accosted the appellant, he was not engaging in illegal or irregular conduct of any kind, and the police had no reason to believe he had done so in the past.

36. The judge did not instruct the jury as to the meaning of the term "under the influence of" narcotics, having previously ruled that there was no evidence of a violation of that provision of the statute. *See* note 1, *supra.*

the "status" or had committed the "act" denounced by the statute.[37] "All that the People must show is either that the defendant did use a narcotic in Los Angeles County, or that while in the City of Los Angeles he was addicted to the use of narcotics * * *."[38]

Under these instructions the jury returned a verdict finding the appellant "guilty of the offense charged." An appeal was taken to the Appellate Department of the Los Angeles County Superior Court, "the highest court of a State in which a decision could be had' in this case." 28 U.S.C. § 1257, 28 U.S.C.A. § 1257. *See* Smith v. California, 361 U.S. 147, 149, 80 S.Ct. 215, 216, 4 L.Ed.2d 205; Edwards v. California, 314 U.S. 160, 171, 62 S.Ct. 164, 165, 86 L.Ed. 119. Although expressing some doubt as to the constitutionality of "the crime of being a narcotic addict," the reviewing court in an unreported opinion affirmed the judgment of conviction, citing two of its own previous unreported decisions which had upheld the constitutionality of the statute.[39] We noted probable jurisdiction of this appeal, 368 U.S. 918, 82 S.Ct. 244, 7 L.Ed.2d 133, because it squarely presents the issue whether the statute as construed by the California courts in this case is repugnant to the Fourteenth Amendment of the Constitution.

The broad power of a State to regulate the narcotic drugs traffic within its borders is not here in issue. More than forty years ago, in Whipple v. Martinson, 256 U.S. 41, 41 S.Ct. 425, 65 L.Ed. 819, this Court explicitly recognized the validity of that power: "There can be no question of the authority of the state in the exercise of its police power to regulate the administration, sale, prescription and use of dangerous and habitforming drugs * * *. The right to exercise this power is so manifest in the interest of the public health and welfare, that it is unnecessary to enter upon a discussion of it beyond saying that it is too firmly established to be successfully called in question." 256 U.S. at 45, 41 S.Ct. at 426.

Such regulation, it can be assumed, could take a variety of valid forms. A State might impose criminal sanctions, for example, against the unauthorized manufacture, prescription, sale, purchase, or possession of narcotics within its borders. In the interest of discouraging the violation of such laws, or in the interest of the general health or welfare of its inhabitants, a State might establish a program of compulsory treatment for those addict-

---

37. "Where a statute such as that which defines the crime charged in this case denounces an act and a status or condition, either of which separately as well as collectively, constitute the criminal offense charged, an accusatory pleading which accuses the defendant of having committed the act and of being of the status or condition so denounced by the statute, is deemed supported if the proof shows that the defendant is guilty of any one or more of the offenses thus specified. However, it is important for you to keep in mind that, in order to convict a defendant in such a case, it is necessary that all of you agree as to the same particular act or status or condition found to have been committed or found to exist. It is not necessary that the particular act or status or condition so agreed upon be stated in the verdict."

38. The instructions continued "and it is then up to the defendant to prove that the use, or of being addicted to the use of narcotics was administered by or under the direction of a person licensed by the State of California to prescribe and administer narcotics or at least to raise a reasonable doubt concerning the matter." No evidence, of course, had been offered in support of this affirmative defense, since the appellant had denied that he had used narcotics or been addicted to their use.

39. The appellant tried unsuccessfully to secure habeas corpus relief in the District Court of Appeal and the California Supreme Court.

ed to narcotics.[40] Such a program of treatment might require periods of involuntary confinement. And penal sanctions might be imposed for failure to comply with established compulsory treatment procedures. *Cf.* Jacobson v. Massachusetts, 197 U.S. 11, 25 S.Ct. 358, 49 L.Ed. 643. Or a State might choose to attack the evils of narcotics traffic on broader fronts also— through public health education, for example, or by efforts to ameliorate the economic and social conditions under which those evils might be thought to flourish. In short, the range of valid choice which a State might make in this area is undoubtedly a wide one, and the wisdom of any particular choice within the allowable spectrum is not for us to decide. Upon that premise we turn to the California law in issue here.

It would be possible to construe the statute under which the appellant was convicted as one which is operative only upon proof of the actual use of narcotics within the State's jurisdiction. But the California courts have not so construed this law. Although there was evidence in the present case that the appellant had used narcotics in Los Angeles, the jury were instructed that they could convict him even if they disbelieved that evidence. The appellant could be convicted, they were told, if they found simply that the appellant's "status" or "chronic condition" was that of being "addicted to the use of narcotics." And it is impossible to know from the jury's verdict that the defendant was not convicted upon precisely such a finding.

The instructions of the trial court, implicitly approved on appeal, amounted to "a ruling on a question of state law that is as binding on us as though the precise words had been written" into the statute. Terminiello v. Chicago, 337 U.S. 1, 4, 69 S.Ct. 894, 895, 93 L.Ed. 1131. "We can only take the statute as the state courts read it." *Id.*, at 6, 69 S.Ct. at 896 Indeed, in their brief in this Court counsel for the State have emphasized that it is "the proof of addiction by circumstantial evidence * * * by the tell-tale track of needle marks and scabs over the veins of his arms, that remains the gist of the section."

This statute, therefore, is not one which punishes a person for the use of narcotics, for their purchase, sale or possession, or for antisocial or disorderly behavior resulting from their administration. It is not a law which even purports to provide or require medical treatment. Rather, we deal with a statute which makes the "status" of narcotic addiction a criminal offense, for which the offender may be prosecuted "at any time before he reforms." California has said that a person can be continuously guilty of this offense, whether or not he has ever used or possessed any narcotics within the State, and whether or not he has been guilty of any antisocial behavior there.

It is unlikely that any State at this moment in history would attempt to make it a criminal offense for a person to be mentally ill, or a leper, or to be afflicted with a venereal disease. A State might determine that the general health and welfare require that the victims of these and other human afflictions be dealt with by compulsory treatment, involving quaran-

40. California appears to have established just such a program in §§ 5350–5361 of its Welfare and Institutions Code. The record contains no explanation of why the civil procedures authorized by this legislation were not utilized in the present case.

tine, confinement, or sequestration. But, in the light of contemporary human knowledge, a law which made a criminal offense of such a disease would doubtless be universally thought to be an infliction of cruel and unusual punishment in violation of the Eighth and Fourteenth Amendments. *See* State of Louisiana ex rel. Francis v. Resweber, 329 U.S. 459, 67 S.Ct. 374, 91 L.Ed. 422.

We cannot but consider the statute before us as of the same category. In this Court counsel for the State recognized that narcotic addiction is an illness.[41] Indeed, it is apparently an illness which may be contracted innocently or involuntarily.[42] We hold that a state law which imprisons a person thus afflicted as a criminal, even though he has never touched any narcotic drug within the State or been guilty of any irregular behavior there, inflicts a cruel and unusual punishment in violation of the Fourteenth Amendment. To be sure, imprisonment for ninety days is not, in the abstract, a punishment which is either cruel or unusual. But the question cannot be considered in the abstract. Even one day in prison would be a cruel and unusual punishment for the "crime" of having a common cold.

We are not unmindful that the vicious evils of the narcotics traffic have occasioned the grave concern of government. There are, as we have said, countless fronts on which those evils may be legitimately attacked. We deal in this case only with an individual provision of a particularized local law as it has so far been interpreted by the California courts.

Reversed.

■ JUSTICE FRANKFURTER took no part in the consideration or decision of this case.

■ JUSTICE HARLAN, concurring.

I am not prepared to hold that on the present state of medical knowledge it is completely irrational and hence unconstitutional for a State to conclude that narcotics addiction is something other than an illness nor that it amounts to cruel and unusual punishment for the State to subject narcotics addicts to its criminal law. Insofar as addiction may be identified with the use or possession of narcotics within the State (or, I would suppose, without the State), in violation of local statutes prohibiting such acts, it may surely be reached by the State's criminal law. But in this case the trial court's instructions permitted the jury to find the appellant guilty

---

41. In its brief the appellee stated: "Of course it is generally conceded that a narcotic addict, particularly one addicted to the use of heroin, is in a state of mental and physical illness. So is an alcoholic." Thirty-seven years ago this Court recognized that persons addicted to narcotics "are diseased and proper subjects for (medical) treatment." Linder v. United States, 268 U.S. 5, 18, 45 S.Ct. 446, 449, 69 L.Ed. 819.

42. Not only may addiction innocently result from the use of medically prescribed narcotics, but a person may even be a narcotics addict from the moment of his birth. *See* Schneck, Narcotic Withdrawal Symptoms in the Newborn Infant Resulting from Maternal Addiction, 52 Journal of Pediatrics, 584 (1958); Roman and Middelkamp, Narcotic Addiction in a Newborn Infant, 53 Journal of Pediatrics 231 (1958); Kunstadter, Klein, Lundeen, Witz, and Morrison, Narcotic Withdrawal Symptoms in Newborn Infants, 168 Journal of the American Medical Association, 1008, (1958); Slobody and Cobrinik, Neonatal Narcotic Addiction, 14 Quarterly Review of Pediatrics, 169 (1959); Vincow and Hackel, Neonatal Narcotic Addiction, 22 General Practitioner 90 (1960); Dikshit, Narcotic Withdrawal Syndrome in Newborns, 28 Indian Journal of Pediatrics 11 (1961).

on no more proof than that he was present in California while he was addicted to narcotics.[43] Since addiction alone cannot reasonably be thought to amount to more than a compelling propensity to use narcotics, the effect of this instruction was to authorize criminal punishment for a bare desire to commit a criminal act.

If the California statute reaches this type of conduct, and for present purposes we must accept the trial court's construction as binding, Terminiello v. Chicago, 337 U.S. 1, 4, 69 S.Ct. 894, 895, 93 L.Ed. 1131, it is an arbitrary imposition which exceeds the power that a State may exercise in enacting its criminal law. Accordingly, I agree that the application of the California statute was unconstitutional in this case and join the judgment of reversal.

[The concurring opinion of Justice Douglas, and the dissenting opinions of Justice Clark and Justice White, are omitted.]

(C) LIBERTY

(1) Liberty Protected by the Specific Constitutional Provisions

R.A.V. v. City of St. Paul, Minnesota

Supreme Court of the United States, 1992.
505 U.S. 377, 112 S.Ct. 2538, 120 L.Ed.2d 305.

■ JUSTICE SCALIA delivered the opinion of the Court.

In the predawn hours of June 21, 1990, petitioner and several other teenagers allegedly assembled a crudely-made cross by taping together broken chair legs. They then allegedly burned the cross inside the fenced yard of a black family that lived across the street from the house where petitioner was staying. Although this conduct could have been punished under any of a number of laws,[44] one of the two provisions under which respondent city of St. Paul chose to charge petitioner (then a juvenile) was the St. Paul Bias–Motivated Crime Ordinance, St. Paul, Minn.Legis.Code § 292.02 (1990), which provides:

"Whoever places on public or private property a symbol, object, appellation, characterization or graffiti, including, but not limited to, a burning cross or Nazi swastika, which one knows or has reasonable grounds to

---

43. The jury was instructed that "it is not incumbent upon the People to prove the unlawfulness of defendant's use of narcotics. All that the People must show is either that the defendant did use a narcotic in Los Angeles County, or that while in the City of Los Angeles he was addicted to the use of narcotics." (Emphasis added.) Although the jury was told that it should acquit if the appellant proved that his "being addicted to the use of narcotics was administered (sic) by or under the direction of a person licensed by the State of California to prescribe and administer narcotics," this part of the instruction did not cover other possible lawful uses which could have produced the appellant's addiction.

44. The conduct might have violated Minnesota statutes carrying significant penalties. *See, e.g.*, Minn.Stat. § 609.713(1) (1987) (providing for up to five years in prison for terroristic threats); § 609.563 (arson) (providing for up to five years and a $10,000 fine, depending on the value of the property intended to be damaged); § 609.595 (Supp.1992) (criminal damage to property) (providing for up to one year and a $3,000 fine, depending upon the extent of the damage to the property).

know arouses anger, alarm or resentment in others on the basis of race, color, creed, religion or gender commits disorderly conduct and shall be guilty of a misdemeanor."

Petitioner moved to dismiss this count on the ground that the St. Paul ordinance was substantially overbroad and impermissibly content-based and therefore facially invalid under the First Amendment. The trial court granted this motion, but the Minnesota Supreme Court reversed. That court rejected petitioner's overbreadth claim because ... the modifying phrase "arouses anger, alarm or resentment in others" limited the reach of the ordinance to conduct that amounts to "fighting words," *i.e.*, "conduct that itself inflicts injury or tends to incite immediate violence ...," and therefore the ordinance reached only expression "that the first amendment does not protect." The court also concluded that the ordinance was not impermissibly content-based because, in its view, "the ordinance is a narrowly tailored means toward accomplishing the compelling governmental interest in protecting the community against bias-motivated threats to public safety and order."

<h3 style="text-align:center">I</h3>

In construing the St. Paul ordinance, we are bound by the construction given to it by the Minnesota court. Accordingly, we accept the Minnesota Supreme Court's authoritative statement that the ordinance reaches only those expressions that constitute "fighting words"....

The First Amendment generally prevents government from proscribing speech, see, *e.g.*, Cantwell v. Connecticut, 310 U.S. 296, 309–311, 60 S.Ct. 900, 905–906, 84 L.Ed. 1213 (1940), or even expressive conduct, *see, e.g.*, Texas v. Johnson, 491 U.S. 397, 406, 109 S.Ct. 2533, 2540, 105 L.Ed.2d 342 (1989), because of disapproval of the ideas expressed. Content-based regulations are presumptively invalid. From 1791 to the present, however, our society, like other free but civilized societies, has permitted restrictions upon the content of speech in a few limited areas, which are "of such slight social value as a step to truth that any benefit that may be derived from them is clearly outweighed by the social interest in order and morality." We have recognized that "the freedom of speech" referred to by the First Amendment does not include a freedom to disregard these traditional limitations. Beauharnais v. Illinois, 343 U.S. 250, 72 S.Ct. 725, 96 L.Ed. 919 (1952) (defamation); Chaplinsky v. New Hampshire, *supra*, ("fighting words") ... [B]ut a limited categorical approach has remained an important part of our First Amendment jurisprudence.

... What they mean is that these areas of speech can, consistently with the First Amendment, be regulated *because of their constitutionally proscribable content* (obscenity, defamation, etc.)—not that they are categories of speech entirely invisible to the Constitution, so that they may be made the vehicles for content discrimination unrelated to their distinctively proscribable content. Thus, the government may proscribe libel; but it may not make the further content discrimination of proscribing *only* libel critical of the government....

Our cases surely do not establish the proposition that the First Amendment imposes no obstacle whatsoever to regulation of particular instances of such proscribable expression, so that the government "may regulate [them] freely," ... That would mean that a city council could enact an ordinance prohibiting only those legally obscene works that contain criticism of the city government or, indeed, that do not include endorsement of the city government. Such a simplistic, all-or-nothing-at-all approach to First Amendment protection is at odds with common sense and with our jurisprudence as well. It is not true that "fighting words" have at most a *"de minimis"* expressive content, or that their content is *in all respects* "worthless and undeserving of constitutional protection"; sometimes they are quite expressive indeed. We have not said that they constitute *"no* part of the expression of ideas," but only that they constitute "no *essential* part of any exposition of ideas."

... We have long held, for example, that nonverbal expressive activity can be banned because of the action it entails, but not because of the ideas it expresses—so that burning a flag in violation of an ordinance against outdoor fires could be punishable, whereas burning a flag in violation of an ordinance against dishonoring the flag is not. Similarly, we have upheld reasonable "time, place, or manner" restrictions, but only if they are "justified without reference to the content of the regulated speech." And just as the power to proscribe particular speech on the basis of a noncontent element (*e.g.*, noise) does not entail the power to proscribe the same speech on the basis of a content element; so also, the power to proscribe it on the basis of one content element (*e.g.*, obscenity) does not entail the power to proscribe it on the basis of *other* content elements.

In other words, the exclusion of "fighting words" from the scope of the First Amendment simply means that, for purposes of that Amendment, the unprotected features of the words are, despite their verbal character, essentially a "nonspeech" element of communication. Fighting words are thus analogous to a noisy sound truck: ...

... In our view, the First Amendment imposes not an "underinclusiveness" limitation but a "content discrimination" limitation upon a State's prohibition of proscribable speech....

Even the prohibition against content discrimination that we assert the First Amendment requires is not absolute. It applies differently in the context of proscribable speech than in the area of fully protected speech. The rationale of the general prohibition, after all, is that content discrimination "rais[es] the specter that the Government may effectively drive certain ideas or viewpoints from the marketplace." But content discrimination among various instances of a class of proscribable speech often does not pose this threat.

When the basis for the content discrimination consists entirely of the very reason the entire class of speech at issue is proscribable, no significant danger of idea or viewpoint discrimination exists. Such a reason, having been adjudged neutral enough to support exclusion of the entire class of speech from First Amendment protection, is also neutral enough to form the basis of distinction within the class.... And the Federal Government can criminalize only those threats of violence that are directed against the President, *see* 18 U.S.C. § 871—since the reasons why threats of violence are outside the First Amendment (protecting individuals from the fear of violence, from the disruption that fear engenders, and from the possibility that the threatened violence will occur) have special force when applied to the person of the President. But the Federal Government may not criminalize only those threats against the President that mention his policy on aid to inner cities. . . .

Another valid basis for according differential treatment to even a content-defined subclass of proscribable speech is that the subclass happens to be associated with particular "secondary effects" of the speech, so that the regulation is "*justified* without reference to the content of the . . . speech." A State could, for example, permit all obscene live performances except those involving minors. Moreover, since words can in some circumstances violate laws directed not against speech but against conduct (a law against treason, for example, is violated by telling the enemy the nation's defense secrets), a particular content-based subcategory of a proscribable class of speech can be swept up incidentally within the reach of a statute directed at conduct rather than speech. Thus, for example, sexually derogatory "fighting words," among other words, may produce a violation of Title VII's general prohibition against sexual discrimination in employment practices, 42 U.S.C. § 2000e–2; 29 CFR § 1604.11 (1991). Where the government does not target conduct on the basis of its expressive content, acts are not shielded from regulation merely because they express a discriminatory idea or philosophy.

. . .

II

Applying these principles to the St. Paul ordinance, we conclude that, even as narrowly construed by the Minnesota Supreme Court, the ordinance is facially unconstitutional. . . .

In its practical operation, moreover, the ordinance goes even beyond mere content discrimination, to actual viewpoint discrimination. Displays containing some words—odious racial epithets, for example—would be prohibited to proponents of all views. But "fighting words" that do not themselves invoke race, color, creed, religion, or gender—aspersions upon a person's mother, for example—would seemingly be usable *ad libitum* in the placards of those arguing *in favor* of racial, color, etc. tolerance and equality, but could not be used by that speaker's opponents. One could hold up a sign saying, for example, that all "anti-Catholic bigots" are misbegotten; but not that all "papists" are, for that would insult and provoke violence "on the basis of religion." St. Paul has no such authority to license one side of a debate to fight freestyle, while requiring the other to follow Marquis of Queensbury Rules.

What we have here, it must be emphasized, is not a prohibition of fighting words that are directed at certain persons or groups (which would be *facially* valid if it met the requirements of the Equal Protection Clause); but rather, a prohibition of fighting words that contain (as the Minnesota Supreme Court repeatedly emphasized) messages of "bias-motivated" hatred and in particular, as applied to this case, messages "based on virulent notions of racial supremacy." One must wholeheartedly agree with the Minnesota Supreme Court that "[i]t is the responsibility, even the obligation, of diverse communities to confront such notions in whatever form they appear," but the manner of that confrontation cannot consist of selective limitations upon speech. St. Paul's brief asserts that a general "fighting words" law would not meet the city's needs because only a content-specific measure can communicate to minority groups that the "group hatred" aspect of such speech "is not condoned by the majority."

. . .

The content-based discrimination reflected in the St. Paul ordinance comes within neither any of the specific exceptions to the First Amendment prohibition we discussed earlier, nor within a more general exception for content discrimination that does not threaten censorship of ideas. It assuredly does not fall within the exception for content discrimination based on the very reasons why the particular class of speech at issue (here, fighting words) is proscribable. As explained earlier, the reason why fighting words are categorically excluded from the protection of the First Amendment is not that their content communicates any particular idea, but that their content embodies a particularly intolerable (and socially unnecessary) *mode* of expressing *whatever* idea the speaker wishes to convey. St. Paul has not singled out an especially offensive mode of expression—it has not, for example, selected for prohibition only those fighting words that communicate ideas in a threatening (as opposed to a merely obnoxious) manner. Rather, it has proscribed fighting words of whatever manner that communicate messages of racial, gender, or religious intolerance. Selectivity of this sort creates the possibility that the city is seeking to handicap the expression of particular ideas. That possibility would alone be enough to render the ordinance presumptively invalid, but St. Paul's comments and concessions in this case elevate the possibility to a certainty.

St. Paul argues that the ordinance comes within another of the specific exceptions we mentioned, the one that allows content discrimination aimed only at the "secondary effects" of the speech. According to St. Paul, the ordinance is intended, "not to impact on [*sic*] the right of free expression of the accused," but rather to "protect against the victimization of a person or persons who are particularly vulnerable because of their membership in a group that historically has been discriminated against." Even assuming that an ordinance that completely proscribes, rather than merely regulates, a specified category of speech can ever be considered to be directed only to the secondary effects of such speech, it is clear that the St. Paul ordinance is not directed to secondary effects. . . .

It hardly needs discussion that the ordinance does not fall within some more general exception permitting *all* selectivity that for any reason is beyond the suspicion of official suppression of ideas. The statements of St. Paul in this very case afford ample basis for, if not full confirmation of, that suspicion.

Finally, St. Paul and its *amici* defend the conclusion of the Minnesota Supreme Court that, even if the ordinance regulates expression based on hostility towards its protected ideological content, this discrimination is nonetheless justified because it is narrowly tailored to serve compelling state interests. Specifically, they assert that the ordinance helps to ensure the basic human rights of members of groups that have historically been subjected to discrimination, including the right of such group members to live in peace where they wish. We do not doubt that these interests are compelling, and that the ordinance can be said to promote them. But the "danger of censorship" presented by a facially content-based statute, requires that that weapon be employed only where it is "*necessary* to serve the asserted [compelling] interest." The existence of adequate content-neutral alternatives thus "undercut[s] significantly" any defense of such a statute, casting considerable doubt on the government's protestations that "the asserted justification is in fact an accurate description of the purpose and effect of the law." The dispositive question in this case, therefore, is whether content discrimination is reasonably necessary to achieve St. Paul's compelling interests; it plainly is not. . . .

The judgment of the Minnesota Supreme Court is reversed, and the case is remanded for proceedings not inconsistent with this opinion.

It is so ordered.[45]

■ JUSTICE WHITE, with whom JUSTICE BLACKMUN and JUSTICE O'CONNOR join, and with whom JUSTICE STEVENS joins except as to Part I(A), concurring in the judgment.

I agree with the majority that the judgment of the Minnesota Supreme Court should be reversed. However, our agreement ends there.

This case could easily be decided within the contours of established First Amendment law by holding, as petitioner argues, that the St. Paul ordinance is fatally overbroad because it criminalizes not only unprotected expression but expression protected by the First Amendment.

(2) Unenumerated Rights

Lawrence v. Texas

Supreme Court of the United States, 2003. *CASE DECIDED*
539 U.S. 558, 123 S.Ct. 2472, 156 L.Ed.2d 508.

■ JUSTICE KENNEDY delivered the opinion of the Court.

Liberty protects the person from unwarranted government intrusions into a dwelling or other private places. In our tradition the State is not omnipresent in the home. And there are other spheres of our lives and existence, outside the home, where the State should not be a dominant presence. Freedom extends beyond spatial bounds. Liberty presumes an autonomy of self that includes freedom of thought, belief, expression, and certain intimate conduct. The instant case involves liberty of the person both in its spatial and more transcendent dimensions.

---

45. A statute enhancing the penalty when the victim is selected on the basis of race, religion, color, etc., does not offend the First Amendment. That statute does not punish thought. Wisconsin v. Mitchell, 508 U.S. 476 (1993). *See also,* In re M.S., 10 Cal.4th 698, 42 Cal.Rptr.2d 355, 896 P.2d 1365 (1995).

I

The question before the Court is the validity of a Texas statute making it a crime for two persons of the same sex to engage in certain intimate sexual conduct.

In Houston, Texas, officers of the Harris County Police Department were dispatched to a private residence in response to a reported weapons disturbance. They entered an apartment where one of the petitioners, John Geddes Lawrence, resided. The right of the police to enter does not seem to have been questioned. The officers observed Lawrence and another man, Tyron Garner, engaging in a sexual act. The two petitioners were arrested, held in custody over night, and charged and convicted before a Justice of the Peace.

The complaints described their crime as "deviate sexual intercourse, namely anal sex, with a member of the same sex (man)." App. to Pet. for Cert. 127a, 139a. The applicable state law is Tex. Penal Code Ann. § 21.06(a) (2003). It provides: "A person commits an offense if he engages in deviate sexual intercourse with another individual of the same sex." The statute defines "[d]eviate sexual intercourse" as follows:

"(A) any contact between any part of the genitals of one person and the mouth or anus of another person; or

"(B) the penetration of the genitals or the anus of another person with an object." § 21.01(1).

The petitioners exercised their right to a trial *de novo* in Harris County Criminal Court. They challenged the statute as a violation of the Equal Protection Clause of the Fourteenth Amendment and of a like provision of the Texas Constitution. Tex. Const., Art. 1, § 3a. Those contentions were rejected. The petitioners, having entered a plea of *nolo contendere,* were each fined $200 and assessed court costs of $141.25. App. to Pet. for Cert. 107a–110a.

The Court of Appeals for the Texas Fourteenth District considered the petitioners' federal constitutional arguments under both the Equal Protection and Due Process Clauses of the Fourteenth Amendment. After hearing the case en banc the court, in a divided opinion, rejected the constitutional arguments and affirmed the convictions. 41 S.W.3d 349 (Tex.App.2001). The majority opinion indicates that the Court of Appeals considered our decision in Bowers v. Hardwick, 478 U.S. 186, 106 S.Ct. 2841, 92 L.Ed.2d 140 (1986), to be controlling on the federal due process aspect of the case. *Bowers* then being authoritative, this was proper.

We granted certiorari, 537 U.S. 1044, 123 S.Ct. 661, 154 L.Ed.2d 514 (2002), to consider three questions:

"1. Whether Petitioners' criminal convictions under the Texas 'Homosexual Conduct' law—which criminalizes sexual intimacy by same-sex couples, but not identical behavior by different-sex couples—violate the Fourteenth Amendment guarantee of equal protection of laws?

"2. Whether Petitioners' criminal convictions for adult consensual sexual intimacy in the home violate their vital interests in liberty and privacy protected by the Due Process Clause of the Fourteenth Amendment?

"3. Whether Bowers v. Hardwick, 478 U.S. 186, 106 S.Ct. 2841, 92 L.Ed.2d 140 (1986), should be overruled?" Pet. for Cert. i.

The petitioners were adults at the time of the alleged offense. Their conduct was in private and consensual.

II

We conclude the case should be resolved by determining whether the petitioners were free as adults to engage in the private conduct in the exercise of their liberty under the Due Process Clause of the Fourteenth Amendment to the Constitution. For this inquiry we deem it necessary to reconsider the Court's holding in *Bowers*.

There are broad statements of the substantive reach of liberty under the Due Process Clause in earlier cases, including Pierce v. Society of Sisters, 268 U.S. 510, 45 S.Ct. 571, 69 L.Ed. 1070 (1925), and Meyer v. Nebraska, 262 U.S. 390, 43 S.Ct. 625, 67 L.Ed. 1042 (1923); but the most pertinent beginning point is our decision in Griswold v. Connecticut, 381 U.S. 479, 85 S.Ct. 1678, 14 L.Ed.2d 510 (1965).

In *Griswold* the Court invalidated a state law prohibiting the use of drugs or devices of contraception and counseling or aiding and abetting the use of contraceptives. The Court described the protected interest as a right to privacy and placed emphasis on the marriage relation and the protected space of the marital bedroom. *Id.,* at 485, 85 S.Ct. 1678.

After *Griswold* it was established that the right to make certain decisions regarding sexual conduct extends beyond the marital relationship. In Eisenstadt v. Baird, 405 U.S. 438, 92 S.Ct. 1029, 31 L.Ed.2d 349 (1972), the Court invalidated a law prohibiting the distribution of contraceptives to unmarried persons. The case was decided under the Equal Protection Clause, *id.,* at 454, 92 S.Ct. 1029; but with respect to unmarried persons, the Court went on to state the fundamental proposition that the law impaired the exercise of their personal rights, *ibid.* It quoted from the statement of the Court of Appeals finding the law to be in conflict with fundamental human rights, and it followed with this statement of its own:

"It is true that in *Griswold* the right of privacy in question inhered in the marital relationship. . . . If the right of privacy means anything, it is the right of the *individual,* married or single, to be free from unwarranted governmental intrusion into matters so fundamentally affecting a person as the decision whether to bear or beget a child." *Id.,* at 453, 92 S.Ct. 1029.

The opinions in *Griswold* and *Eisenstadt* were part of the background for the decision in Roe v. Wade, 410 U.S. 113, 93 S.Ct. 705, 35 L.Ed.2d 147 (1973). As is well known, the case involved a challenge to the Texas law prohibiting abortions, but the laws of other States were affected as well. Although the Court held the woman's rights were not absolute, her right to elect an abortion did have real and substantial protection as an exercise of her liberty under the Due Process Clause. The Court cited cases that protect spatial freedom and cases that go well beyond it. *Roe* recognized the right of a woman to make certain fundamental decisions affecting her destiny and confirmed once more that the protection of liberty under the Due Process Clause has a substantive dimension of fundamental significance in defining the rights of the person.

In Carey v. Population Services Int'l, 431 U.S. 678, 97 S.Ct. 2010, 52 L.Ed.2d 675 (1977), the Court confronted a New York law forbidding sale or distribution of contraceptive devices to persons under 16 years of age. Although there was no single opinion for the Court, the law was invalidated. Both *Eisenstadt* and *Carey,* as well as the holding and rationale in *Roe,* confirmed that the reasoning of *Griswold* could not be confined to the protection of rights of married adults. This was the state of the law with respect to some of the most relevant cases when the Court considered *Bowers v. Hardwick.*

The facts in *Bowers* had some similarities to the instant case. A police officer, whose right to enter seems not to have been in question, observed Hardwick, in his own bedroom, engaging in intimate sexual conduct with another adult male. The conduct was in violation of a Georgia statute making it a criminal offense to engage in sodomy. One difference between the two cases is that the Georgia statute prohibited the conduct whether or not the participants were of the same sex, while the Texas statute, as we have seen, applies only to participants of the same sex. Hardwick was not prosecuted, but he brought an action in federal court to declare the state statute invalid. He alleged he was a practicing homosexual and that the criminal prohibition violated rights guaranteed to him by the Constitution. The Court, in an opinion by Justice White, sustained the Georgia law. Chief Justice Burger and Justice Powell joined the opinion of the Court and filed separate, concurring opinions. Four Justices dissented. 478 U.S., at 199, 106 S.Ct. 2841 (opinion of Blackmun, J., joined by Brennan, Marshall, and STEVENS, JJ.); *id.,* at 214, 106 S.Ct. 2841 (opinion of STEVENS, J., joined by Brennan and Marshall, JJ.).

The Court began its substantive discussion in *Bowers* as follows: "The issue presented is whether the Federal Constitution confers a fundamental right upon homosexuals to engage in sodomy and hence invalidates the laws of the many States that still make such conduct illegal and have done so for a very long time." *Id.,* at 190, 106 S.Ct. 2841. That statement, we now conclude, discloses the Court's own failure to appreciate the extent of the liberty at stake. To say that the issue in *Bowers* was simply the right to engage in certain sexual conduct demeans the claim the individual put forward, just as it would demean a married couple were it to be said marriage is simply about the right to have sexual intercourse. The laws involved in *Bowers* and here are, to be sure, statutes that purport to do no more than prohibit a particular sexual act. Their penalties and purposes, though, have more far-reaching consequences, touching upon the most private human conduct, sexual behavior, and in the most private of places, the home. The statutes do seek to control a personal relationship that, whether or not entitled to formal recognition in the law, is within the liberty of persons to choose without being punished as criminals.

This, as a general rule, should counsel against attempts by the State, or a court, to define the meaning of the relationship or to set its boundaries absent injury to a person or abuse of an institution the law protects. It suffices for us to acknowledge that adults may choose to enter upon this relationship in the confines of their homes and their own private lives and still retain their dignity as free persons. When sexuality finds overt expression in intimate conduct with another person, the conduct can be but one element in a personal bond that is more enduring. The liberty protected by the Constitution allows homosexual persons the right to make this choice.

Having misapprehended the claim of liberty there presented to it, and thus stating the claim to be whether there is a fundamental right to engage in consensual sodomy, the *Bowers* Court said: "Proscriptions against that conduct have ancient roots." *Id.*, at 192, 106 S.Ct. 2841. In academic writings, and in many of the scholarly *amicus* briefs filed to assist the Court in this case, there are fundamental criticisms of the historical premises relied upon by the majority and concurring opinions in *Bowers*. Brief for Cato Institute as *Amicus Curiae* 16–17; Brief for American Civil Liberties Union et al. as *Amici Curiae* 15–21; Brief for Professors of History et al. as *Amici Curiae* 3–10. We need not enter this debate in the attempt to reach a definitive historical judgment, but the following considerations counsel against adopting the definitive conclusions upon which *Bowers* placed such reliance.

At the outset it should be noted that there is no longstanding history in this country of laws directed at homosexual conduct as a distinct matter. Beginning in colonial times there were prohibitions of sodomy derived from the English criminal laws passed in the first instance by the Reformation Parliament of 1533. The English prohibition was understood to include relations between men and women as well as relations between men and men. *See, e.g.,* King v. Wiseman, 92 Eng. Rep. 774, 775 (K.B.1718) (interpreting "mankind" in Act of 1533 as including women and girls). Nineteenth-century commentators similarly read American sodomy, buggery, and crime-against-nature statutes as criminalizing certain relations between men and women and between men and men. See, *e.g.,* 2 J. Bishop, Criminal Law § 1028 (1858); 2 J. Chitty, Criminal Law 47–50 (5th Am. ed. 1847); R. Desty, A Compendium of American Criminal Law 143 (1882); J. May, The Law of Crimes § 203 (2d ed. 1893). The absence of legal prohibitions focusing on homosexual conduct may be explained in part by noting that according to some scholars the concept of the homosexual as a distinct category of person did not emerge until the late 19th century. *See, e.g.,* J. Katz, The Invention of Heterosexuality 10 (1995); J. D'Emilio & E. Freedman, Intimate Matters: A History of Sexuality in America 121 (2d ed. 1997) ("The modern terms *homosexuality* and *heterosexuality* do not apply to an era that had not yet articulated these distinctions"). Thus early American sodomy laws were not directed at homosexuals as such but instead sought to prohibit nonprocreative sexual activity more generally. This does not suggest approval of homosexual conduct. It does tend to show that this particular form of conduct was not thought of as a separate category from like conduct between heterosexual persons.

Laws prohibiting sodomy do not seem to have been enforced against consenting adults acting in private. A substantial number of sodomy prosecutions and convictions for which there are surviving records were for predatory acts against those who could not or did not consent, as in the case of a minor or the victim of an assault. As to these, one purpose for the prohibitions was to ensure there would be no lack of coverage if a predator committed a sexual assault that did not constitute rape as defined by the criminal law. Thus the model sodomy indictments presented in a 19th-century treatise, see 2 Chitty, *supra,* at 49, addressed the predatory acts of an adult man against a minor girl or minor boy. Instead of targeting relations between consenting adults in private, 19th-century sodomy prosecutions typically involved relations between men and minor girls or minor boys, relations between adults involving force, relations between adults implicating disparity in status, or relations between men and animals.

To the extent that there were any prosecutions for the acts in question, 19th-century evidence rules imposed a burden that would make a conviction more difficult to obtain even taking into account the problems always inherent in prosecuting consensual acts committed in private. Under then-prevailing standards, a man could not be convicted of sodomy based upon testimony of a consenting partner, because the partner was considered an accomplice. A partner's testimony, however, was admissible if he or she had not consented to the act or was a minor, and therefore incapable of consent. *See, e.g.,* F. Wharton, Criminal Law 443 (2d ed. 1852); 1 F. Wharton, Criminal Law 512 (8th ed. 1880). The rule may explain in part the infrequency of these prosecutions. In all events that infrequency makes it difficult to say that society approved of a rigorous and systematic punishment of the consensual acts committed in private and by adults. The longstanding criminal prohibition of homosexual sodomy upon which the *Bowers* decision placed such reliance is as consistent with a general condemnation of nonprocreative sex as it is with an established tradition of prosecuting acts because of their homosexual character.

The policy of punishing consenting adults for private acts was not much discussed in the early legal literature. We can infer that one reason for this was the very private nature of the conduct. Despite the absence of prosecutions, there may have been periods in which there was public criticism of homosexuals as such and an insistence that the criminal laws be enforced to discourage their practices. But far from possessing "ancient roots," *Bowers,* 478 U.S., at 192, 106 S.Ct. 2841, American laws targeting same-sex couples did not develop until the last third of the 20th century. The reported decisions concerning the prosecution of consensual, homosexual sodomy between adults for the years 1880–1995 are not always clear in the details, but a significant number involved conduct in a public place. *See* Brief for American Civil Liberties Union et al. as *Amici Curiae* 14–15, and n. 18.

It was not until the 1970's that any State singled out same-sex relations for criminal prosecution, and only nine States have done so. *See* 1977 Ark. Gen. Acts no. 828; 1983 Kan. Sess. Laws p. 652; 1974 Ky. Acts p. 847; 1977 Mo. Laws p. 687; 1973 Mont. Laws p. 1339; 1977 Nev. Stats. p. 1632; 1989 Tenn. Pub. Acts ch. 591; 1973 Tex. Gen. Laws ch. 399; *see also* Post v. State, 715 P.2d 1105 (Okla.Crim.App.1986) (sodomy law invalidated as applied to different-sex couples). Post-*Bowers* even some of these States did not adhere to the policy of suppressing homosexual conduct. Over the course of the last decades, States with same-sex prohibitions have moved toward abolishing them. *See,* e.g., Jegley v. Picado, 349 Ark. 600, 80 S.W.3d 332 (2002); Gryczan v. State, 283 Mont. 433, 942 P.2d 112 (1997); Campbell v. Sundquist, 926 S.W.2d 250 (Tenn.App.1996); Commonwealth v. Wasson, 842 S.W.2d 487 (Ky.1992); *see also* 1993 Nev. Stats. p. 518 (repealing Nev.Rev.Stat. § 201.193).

In summary, the historical grounds relied upon in *Bowers* are more complex than the majority opinion and the concurring opinion by Chief Justice Burger indicate. Their historical premises are not without doubt and, at the very least, are overstated.

It must be acknowledged, of course, that the Court in *Bowers* was making the broader point that for centuries there have been powerful voices to condemn homosexual conduct as immoral. The condemnation has been shaped by religious beliefs, conceptions of right and acceptable behavior, and respect for the traditional family. For many persons these are not trivial concerns but profound and deep convictions accepted as ethical and moral principles to which they aspire and which thus determine the course of their lives. These considerations do not answer the question before us, however. The issue is whether the majority may use the power of the State to enforce these views on the whole society through operation of the criminal law. "Our obligation is to define the liberty of all, not to mandate our own moral code." Planned Parenthood of Southeastern Pa. v. Casey, 505 U.S. 833, 850, 112 S.Ct. 2791, 120 L.Ed.2d 674 (1992).

Chief Justice Burger joined the opinion for the Court in *Bowers* and further explained his views as follows: "Decisions of individuals relating to homosexual conduct have been subject to state intervention throughout the history of Western civilization. Condemnation of those practices is firmly rooted in Judeao–Christian moral and ethical standards." 478 U.S., at 196, 106 S.Ct. 2841. As with Justice White's assumptions about history, scholarship casts some doubt on the sweeping nature of the statement by Chief Justice Burger as it pertains to private homosexual conduct between consenting adults. See, *e.g.,* Eskridge, *Hardwick and Historiography*, 1999 U. Ill. L.Rev. 631, 656. In all events we think that our laws and traditions in the past half century are of most relevance here. These references show an emerging awareness that liberty gives substantial protection to adult persons in deciding how to conduct their private lives in matters pertaining to sex. "[H]istory and tradition are the starting point but not in all cases the ending point of the substantive due process inquiry." County of Sacramento v. Lewis, 523 U.S. 833, 857, 118 S.Ct. 1708, 140 L.Ed.2d 1043 (1998) (KENNEDY, J., concurring).

This emerging recognition should have been apparent when *Bowers* was decided. In 1955 the American Law Institute promulgated the Model Penal Code and made clear that it did not recommend or provide for "criminal penalties for consensual sexual relations conducted in private." ALI, Model Penal Code § 213.2, Comment 2, p. 372 (1980). It justified its decision on three grounds: (1) The prohibitions undermined respect for the law by penalizing conduct many people engaged in; (2) the statutes regulated private conduct not harmful to others; and (3) the laws were arbitrarily enforced and thus invited the danger of blackmail. ALI, Model Penal Code, Commentary 277–280 (Tent. Draft No. 4, 1955). In 1961 Illinois changed its laws to conform to the Model Penal Code. Other States soon followed. Brief for Cato Institute as *Amicus Curiae* 15–16.

In *Bowers* the Court referred to the fact that before 1961 all 50 States had outlawed sodomy, and that at the time of the Court's decision 24 States and the District of Columbia had sodomy laws. 478 U.S., at 192–193, 106 S.Ct. 2841. Justice Powell pointed out that these prohibitions often were being ignored, however. Georgia, for instance, had not sought to enforce its law for decades. *Id.,* at 197–198, n. 2, 106 S.Ct. 2841 ("The history of nonenforcement suggests the moribund character today of laws criminalizing this type of private, consensual conduct").

The sweeping references by Chief Justice Burger to the history of Western civilization and to Judeo–Christian moral and ethical standards did not take account of other authorities pointing in an opposite direction. A committee advising the British Parliament recommended in 1957 repeal of laws punishing homosexual conduct. The Wolfenden Report: Report of the Committee on Homosexual Offenses and Prostitution (1963). Parliament enacted the substance of those recommendations 10 years later. Sexual Offences Act 1967, § 1.

Of even more importance, almost five years before *Bowers* was decided the European Court of Human Rights considered a case with parallels to *Bowers* and to today's case. An adult male resident in Northern Ireland alleged he was a practicing homosexual who desired to engage in consensual homosexual conduct. The laws of Northern Ireland forbade him that right. He alleged that he had been questioned, his home had been searched, and he feared criminal prosecution. The court held that the laws proscribing the conduct were invalid under the European Convention on Human Rights. Dudgeon v. United Kingdom, 45 Eur. Ct. H.R. (1981) & ¶ 52. Authoritative in all countries that are members of the Council of Europe (21 nations then, 45 nations now), the decision is at odds with the premise in *Bowers* that the claim put forward was insubstantial in our Western civilization.

In our own constitutional system the deficiencies in *Bowers* became even more apparent in the years following its announcement. The 25 States with laws prohibiting the relevant conduct referenced in the *Bowers* decision are reduced now to 13, of which 4 enforce their laws only against homosexual conduct. In those States where sodomy is still proscribed, whether for same-sex or heterosexual conduct, there is a pattern of nonenforcement with respect to consenting adults acting in private. The State of Texas admitted in 1994 that as of that date it had not prosecuted anyone under those circumstances. State v. Morales, 869 S.W.2d 941, 943.

Two principal cases decided after *Bowers* cast its holding into even more doubt. In Planned Parenthood of Southeastern Pa. v. Casey, 505 U.S. 833, 112 S.Ct. 2791, 120 L.Ed.2d 674 (1992), the Court reaffirmed the substantive force of the liberty protected by the Due Process Clause. The *Casey* decision again confirmed that our laws and tradition afford constitutional protection to personal decisions relating to marriage, procreation, contraception, family relationships, child rearing, and education. *Id.,* at 851, 112 S.Ct. 2791. In explaining the respect the Constitution demands for the autonomy of the person in making these choices, we stated as follows:

"These matters, involving the most intimate and personal choices a person may make in a lifetime, choices central to personal dignity and autonomy, are central to the liberty protected by the Fourteenth Amendment. At the heart of liberty is the right to define one's own concept of existence, of meaning, of the universe, and of the mystery of human life. Beliefs about these matters could not define the attributes of personhood were they formed under compulsion of the State." *Ibid.*

Persons in a homosexual relationship may seek autonomy for these purposes, just as heterosexual persons do. The decision in *Bowers* would deny them this right.

The second post-*Bowers* case of principal relevance is Romer v. Evans, 517 U.S. 620, 116 S.Ct. 1620, 134 L.Ed.2d 855 (1996). There the Court struck down class-based legislation directed at homosexuals as a violation of the Equal Protection Clause. *Romer* invalidated an amendment to Colorado's constitution which named as a solitary class persons who were homosexuals, lesbians, or bisexual either by "orientation, conduct, practices or relationships," *id.,* at 624, 116 S.Ct. 1620 (internal quotation marks omitted), and deprived them of protection under state antidiscrimination laws. We concluded that the provision was "born of animosity toward the class of persons affected" and further that it had no rational relation to a legitimate governmental purpose. *Id.,* at 634, 116 S.Ct. 1620.

As an alternative argument in this case, counsel for the petitioners and some *amici* contend that *Romer* provides the basis for declaring the Texas statute invalid under the Equal Protection Clause. That is a tenable argument, but we conclude the instant case requires us to address whether *Bowers* itself has continuing validity. Were we to hold the statute invalid under the Equal Protection Clause some might question whether a prohibition would be valid if drawn differently, say, to prohibit the conduct both between same-sex and different-sex participants.

Equality of treatment and the due process right to demand respect for conduct protected by the substantive guarantee of liberty are linked in important respects, and a decision on the latter point advances both interests. If protected conduct is made criminal and the law which does so remains unexamined for its substantive validity, its stigma might remain even if it were not enforceable as drawn for equal protection reasons. When homosexual conduct is made criminal by the law of the State, that declaration in and of itself is an invitation to subject homosexual persons to discrimination both in the public and in the private spheres. The central holding of *Bowers* has been brought in question by this case, and it should be addressed. Its continuance as precedent demeans the lives of homosexual persons.

The stigma this criminal statute imposes, moreover, is not trivial. The offense, to be sure, is but a class C misdemeanor, a minor offense in the Texas legal system. Still, it remains a criminal offense with all that imports for the dignity of the persons charged. The petitioners will bear on their record the history of their criminal convictions. Just this Term we rejected various challenges to state laws requiring the registration of sex offenders. Smith v. Doe, 538 U.S. 84, 123 S.Ct. 1140, 155 L.Ed.2d 164 (2003); Connecticut Dept. of Public Safety v. Doe, 538 U.S. 1, 123 S.Ct. 1160, 155

L.Ed.2d 98 (2003). We are advised that if Texas convicted an adult for private, consensual homosexual conduct under the statute here in question the convicted person would come within the registration laws of a least four States were he or she to be subject to their jurisdiction. Pet. for Cert. 13, and n. 12 (citing Idaho Code §§ 18–8301 to 18–8326 (Cum.Supp.2002); La.Code Crim. Proc. Ann., §§ 15:540–15:549 (West 2003); Miss.Code Ann. §§ 45–33–21 to 45–33–57 (Lexis 2003); S.C.Code Ann. §§ 23–3–400 to 23–3–490 (West 2002)). This underscores the consequential nature of the punishment and the state-sponsored condemnation attendant to the criminal prohibition. Furthermore, the Texas criminal conviction carries with it the other collateral consequences always following a conviction, such as notations on job application forms, to mention but one example.

The foundations of *Bowers* have sustained serious erosion from our recent decisions in *Casey* and *Romer*. When our precedent has been thus weakened, criticism from other sources is of greater significance. In the United States criticism of *Bowers* has been substantial and continuing, disapproving of its reasoning in all respects, not just as to its historical assumptions. *See, e.g.,* C. Fried, Order and Law: Arguing the Reagan Revolution—A Firsthand Account 81–84 (1991); R. Posner, Sex and Reason 341–350 (1992). The courts of five different States have declined to follow it in interpreting provisions in their own state constitutions parallel to the Due Process Clause of the Fourteenth Amendment, *see* Jegley v. Picado, 349 Ark. 600, 80 S.W.3d 332 (2002); Powell v. State, 270 Ga. 327, 510 S.E.2d 18, 24 (1998); Gryczan v. State, 283 Mont. 433, 942 P.2d 112 (1997); Campbell v. Sundquist, 926 S.W.2d 250 (Tenn.App.1996); Commonwealth v. Wasson, 842 S.W.2d 487 (Ky.1992).

To the extent *Bowers* relied on values we share with a wider civilization, it should be noted that the reasoning and holding in *Bowers* have been rejected elsewhere. The European Court of Human Rights has followed not *Bowers* but its own decision in Dudgeon v. United Kingdom. *See* P.G. & J.H. v. United Kingdom, App. No. 00044787/98, & ¶ 56 (Eur.Ct.H. R., Sept. 25, 2001); Modinos v. Cyprus, 259 Eur. Ct. H.R. (1993); Norris v. Ireland, 142 Eur. Ct. H.R. (1988). Other nations, too, have taken action consistent with an affirmation of the protected right of homosexual adults to engage in intimate, consensual conduct. *See* Brief for Mary Robinson et al. as *Amici Curiae* 11–12. The right the petitioners seek in this case has been accepted as an integral part of human freedom in many other countries. There has been no showing that in this country the governmental interest in circumscribing personal choice is somehow more legitimate or urgent.

The doctrine of *stare decisis* is essential to the respect accorded to the judgments of the Court and to the stability of the law. It is not, however, an inexorable command. Payne v. Tennessee, 501 U.S. 808, 828, 111 S.Ct. 2597, 115 L.Ed.2d 720 (1991) ("*Stare decisis* is not an inexorable command; rather, it 'is a principle of policy and not a mechanical formula of adherence to the latest decision' ") (quoting Helvering v. Hallock, 309 U.S. 106, 119, 60 S.Ct. 444, 84 L.Ed. 604 (1940)). In *Casey* we noted that when a Court is asked to overrule a precedent recognizing a constitutional liberty interest, individual or societal reliance on the existence of that liberty cautions with particular strength against reversing course. 505 U.S., at

855–856, 112 S.Ct. 2791; *see also id.,* at 844, 112 S.Ct. 2791 ("Liberty finds no refuge in a jurisprudence of doubt"). The holding in *Bowers,* however, has not induced detrimental reliance comparable to some instances where recognized individual rights are involved. Indeed, there has been no individual or societal reliance on *Bowers* of the sort that could counsel against overturning its holding once there are compelling reasons to do so. *Bowers* itself causes uncertainty, for the precedents before and after its issuance contradict its central holding.

The rationale of *Bowers* does not withstand careful analysis. In his dissenting opinion in Bowers Justice STEVENS came to these conclusions:

"Our prior cases make two propositions abundantly clear. First, the fact that the governing majority in a State has traditionally viewed a particular practice as immoral is not a sufficient reason for upholding a law prohibiting the practice; neither history nor tradition could save a law prohibiting miscegenation from constitutional attack. Second, individual decisions by married persons, concerning the intimacies of their physical relationship, even when not intended to produce offspring, are a form of 'liberty' protected by the Due Process Clause of the Fourteenth Amendment. Moreover, this protection extends to intimate choices by unmarried as well as married persons." 478 U.S., at 216, 106 S.Ct. 2841 (footnotes and citations omitted).

■ JUSTICE STEVENS' analysis, in our view, should have been controlling in *Bowers* and should control here.

Bowers was not correct when it was decided, and it is not correct today. It ought not to remain binding precedent. *Bowers v. Hardwick* should be and now is overruled.

The present case does not involve minors. It does not involve persons who might be injured or coerced or who are situated in relationships where consent might not easily be refused. It does not involve public conduct or prostitution. It does not involve whether the government must give formal recognition to any relationship that homosexual persons seek to enter. The case does involve two adults who, with full and mutual consent from each other, engaged in sexual practices common to a homosexual lifestyle. The petitioners are entitled to respect for their private lives. The State cannot demean their existence or control their destiny by making their private sexual conduct a crime. Their right to liberty under the Due Process Clause gives them the full right to engage in their conduct without intervention of the government. "It is a promise of the Constitution that there is a realm of personal liberty which the government may not enter." *Casey, supra,* at 847, 112 S.Ct. 2791. The Texas statute furthers no legitimate state interest which can justify its intrusion into the personal and private life of the individual.

Had those who drew and ratified the Due Process Clauses of the Fifth Amendment or the Fourteenth Amendment known the components of liberty in its manifold possibilities, they might have been more specific. They did not presume to have this insight. They knew times can blind us to certain truths and later generations can see that laws once thought necessary and proper in fact serve only to oppress. As the Constitution endures, persons in every generation can invoke its principles in their own search for greater freedom.

The judgment of the Court of Appeals for the Texas Fourteenth District is reversed, and the case is remanded for further proceedings not inconsistent with this opinion.

It is so ordered.

■ JUSTICE O'CONNOR, concurring in the judgment.

The Court today overrules Bowers v. Hardwick, 478 U.S. 186, 106 S.Ct. 2841, 92 L.Ed.2d 140 (1986). I joined *Bowers,* and do not join the Court in overruling it. Nevertheless, I agree with the Court that Texas' statute banning same-sex sodomy is unconstitutional. *See* Tex. Penal Code Ann. § 21.06 (2003). Rather than relying on the substantive component of the Fourteenth Amendment's Due Process Clause, as the Court does, I base my conclusion on the Fourteenth Amendment's Equal Protection Clause.

The Equal Protection Clause of the Fourteenth Amendment "is essentially a direction that all persons similarly situated should be treated alike." Cleburne v. Cleburne Living Center, Inc., 473 U.S. 432, 439, 105 S.Ct. 3249, 87 L.Ed.2d 313 (1985); *see also* Plyler v. Doe, 457 U.S. 202, 216, 102 S.Ct. 2382, 72 L.Ed.2d 786 (1982). Under our rational basis standard of review, "legislation is presumed to be valid and will be sustained if the classification drawn by the statute is rationally related to a legitimate state interest." Cleburne v. Cleburne Living Center, *supra*, at 440, 105 S.Ct. 3249; *see also* Department of Agriculture v. Moreno, 413 U.S. 528, 534, 93 S.Ct. 2821, 37 L.Ed.2d 782 (1973); Romer v. Evans, 517 U.S. 620, 632–633, 116 S.Ct. 1620, 134 L.Ed.2d 855 (1996); Nordlinger v. Hahn, 505 U.S. 1, 11–12, 112 S.Ct. 2326, 120 L.Ed.2d 1 (1992).

Laws such as economic or tax legislation that are scrutinized under rational basis review normally pass constitutional muster, since "the Constitution presumes that even improvident decisions will eventually be rectified by the democratic processes." Cleburne v. Cleburne Living Center, *supra*, at 440, 105 S.Ct. 3249; *see also* Fitzgerald v. Racing Assn. of Central Iowa, 539 U.S. 103, 123 S.Ct. 2156, 156 L.Ed.2d 97 (2003); Williamson v. Lee Optical of Okla., Inc., 348 U.S. 483, 75 S.Ct. 461, 99 L.Ed. 563 (1955). We have consistently held, however, that some objectives, such as "a bare ... desire to harm a politically unpopular group," are not legitimate state interests. Department of Agriculture v. Moreno, *supra*, at 534, 93 S.Ct. 2821. *See also* Cleburne v. Cleburne Living Center, *supra*, at 446–447, 105 S.Ct. 3249; Romer v. Evans, *supra*, at 632, 116 S.Ct. 1620. When a law exhibits such a desire to harm a politically unpopular group, we have applied a more searching form of rational basis review to strike down such laws under the Equal Protection Clause....

The statute at issue here makes sodomy a crime only if a person "engages in deviate sexual intercourse with another individual of the same sex." Tex. Penal Code Ann. § 21.06(a) (2003). Sodomy between opposite-sex partners, however, is not a crime in Texas. That is, Texas treats the same conduct differently based solely on the participants. Those harmed by this law are people who have a same-sex sexual orientation and thus are more likely to engage in behavior prohibited by § 21.06....

Texas attempts to justify its law, and the effects of the law, by arguing that the statute satisfies rational basis review because it furthers the legitimate governmental interest of the promotion of morality. In *Bowers,* we held that a state law criminalizing sodomy as applied to homosexual couples did not violate substantive due process. We rejected the argument that no rational basis existed to justify the law, pointing to the government's interest in promoting morality. 478 U.S., at 196, 106 S.Ct. 2841. The only question in front of the Court in *Bowers* was whether the substantive component of the Due Process Clause protected a right to engage in homosexual sodomy. *Id.,* at 188, n. 2. *Bowers* did not hold that moral disapproval of a group is a rational basis under the Equal Protection Clause to criminalize homosexual sodomy when heterosexual sodomy is not punished.

This case raises a different issue than *Bowers:* whether, under the Equal Protection Clause, moral disapproval is a legitimate state interest to justify by itself a statute that bans homosexual sodomy, but not heterosexual sodomy. It is not. Moral disapproval of this group, like a bare desire to harm the group, is an interest that is insufficient to satisfy rational basis review under the Equal Protection Clause. *See, e.g.*, Department of Agriculture v. Moreno, *supra,* at 534, 93 S.Ct. 2821; Romer v. Evans, 517 U.S., at 634–635, 116 S.Ct. 1620. Indeed, we have never held that moral disapproval, without any other asserted state interest, is a sufficient rationale under the Equal Protection Clause to justify a law that discriminates among groups of persons.

Moral disapproval of a group cannot be a legitimate governmental interest under the Equal Protection Clause because legal classifications must not be "drawn for the purpose of disadvantaging the group burdened by the law." *Id.,* at 633, 116 S.Ct. 1620. Texas' invocation of moral disapproval as a legitimate state interest proves nothing more than Texas' desire to criminalize homosexual sodomy. But the Equal Protection Clause prevents a State from creating "a classification of persons undertaken for its own sake." *Id.,* at 635, 116 S.Ct. 1620. And because Texas so rarely enforces its sodomy law as applied to private, consensual acts, the law serves more as a statement of dislike and disapproval against homosexuals than as a tool to stop criminal behavior. The Texas sodomy law "raise[s] the inevitable inference that the disadvantage imposed is born of animosity toward the class of persons affected." *Id.,* at 634, 116 S.Ct. 1620.

Texas argues, however, that the sodomy law does not discriminate against homosexual persons. Instead, the State maintains that the law discriminates only against homosexual conduct. While it is true that the law applies only to conduct, the conduct targeted by this law is conduct that is closely correlated with being homosexual. Under such circumstances, Texas' sodomy law is targeted at more than conduct. It is instead directed toward gay persons as a class. "After all, there can hardly be more palpable discrimination against a class than making the conduct that defines the class criminal." *Id.,* at 641, 116 S.Ct. 1620 (SCALIA, J., dissenting) (internal quotation marks omitted). When a State makes homosexual conduct criminal, and not "deviate sexual intercourse" committed by persons of different sexes, "that declaration in and of itself is an invitation to subject homosexual persons to discrimination both in the public and in the private spheres." *Ante,* at 2482. . . .

Whether a sodomy law that is neutral both in effect and application, see Yick Wo v. Hopkins, 118 U.S. 356, 6 S.Ct. 1064, 30 L.Ed. 220 (1886), would violate the substantive component of the Due Process Clause is an issue that need not be decided today. I am confident, however, that so long as the Equal Protection Clause requires a sodomy law to apply equally to the private consensual conduct of homosexuals and heterosexuals alike, such a law would not long stand in our democratic society. . . .

■ JUSTICE SCALIA, with whom THE CHIEF JUSTICE and JUSTICE THOMAS join, dissenting.

"Liberty finds no refuge in a jurisprudence of doubt." Planned Parenthood of Southeastern Pa. v. Casey, 505 U.S. 833, 844, 112 S.Ct. 2791, 120 L.Ed.2d 674 (1992). That was the Court's sententious response, barely more than a decade ago, to those seeking to overrule Roe v. Wade, 410 U.S. 113, 93 S.Ct. 705, 35 L.Ed.2d 147 (1973). The Court's response today, to those who have engaged in a 17–year crusade to overrule Bowers v. Hardwick, 478 U.S. 186, 106 S.Ct. 2841, 92 L.Ed.2d 140 (1986), is very different. The need for stability and certainty presents no barrier.

Most of the rest of today's opinion has no relevance to its actual holding—that the Texas statute "furthers no legitimate state interest which can justify" its application to petitioners under rational-basis review. *Ante,* at 2484 (overruling *Bowers* to the extent it sustained Georgia's anti-sodomy statute under the rational-basis test). Though there is discussion of "fundamental proposition[s]," *ante,* at 2477, and "fundamental decisions," *ibid.* nowhere does the Court's opinion declare that homosexual sodomy is a "fundamental right" under the Due Process Clause; nor does it subject the Texas law to the standard of review that would be appropriate (strict scrutiny) if homosexual sodomy *were* a "fundamental right." Thus, while overruling the *outcome* of *Bowers,* the Court leaves strangely untouched its central legal conclusion: "[R]espondent would have us announce . . . a fundamental right to engage in homosexual sodomy. This we are quite unwilling to do." 478 U.S., at 191, 106 S.Ct. 2841. Instead the Court simply describes petitioners' conduct as "an exercise of their liberty"—which it undoubtedly is—and proceeds to apply an unheard-of form of rational-basis review that will have far-reaching implications beyond this case. *Ante,* at 2476.

I

I begin with the Court's surprising readiness to reconsider a decision rendered a mere 17 years ago in *Bowers v. Hardwick.* I do not myself believe in rigid adherence to *stare decisis* in constitutional cases; but I do believe that we should be consistent rather than manipulative in invoking the doctrine. Today's opinions in support of reversal do not bother to distinguish—or indeed, even bother to mention—the paean to *stare decisis* coauthored by three Members of today's majority in *Planned Parenthood v. Casey.* There, when *stare decisis* meant preservation of judicially invented abortion rights, the widespread criticism of *Roe* was strong reason to *reaffirm* it:

"Where, in the performance of its judicial duties, the Court decides a case in such a way as to resolve the sort of intensely divisive controversy reflected in *Roe* [,] ... its decision has a dimension that the resolution of the normal case does not carry.... [T]o overrule under fire in the absence of the most compelling reason ... would subvert the Court's legitimacy beyond any serious question." 505 U.S., at 866–867, 112 S.Ct. 2791.

Today, however, the widespread opposition to *Bowers,* a decision resolving an issue as "intensely divisive" as the issue in *Roe,* is offered as a reason in favor of *overruling* it. *See ante,* at 2482–2483. Gone, too, is any "enquiry" (of the sort conducted in *Casey*) into whether the decision sought to be overruled has "proven 'unworkable,' " *Casey, supra,* at 855, 112 S.Ct. 2791. ...

I do not quarrel with the Court's claim that Romer v. Evans, 517 U.S. 620, 116 S.Ct. 1620, 134 L.Ed.2d 855 (1996), "eroded" the "foundations" of *Bowers'* rational-basis holding. *See Romer, supra,* at 640–643, 116 S.Ct. 1620 (SCALIA, J., dissenting). *But Roe* and *Casey* have been equally "eroded" by Washington v. Glucksberg, 521 U.S. 702, 721, 117 S.Ct. 2258, 138 L.Ed.2d 772 (1997), which held that *only* fundamental rights which are " 'deeply rooted in this Nation's history and tradition' " qualify for anything other than rational basis scrutiny under the doctrine of "substantive due process." *Roe* and *Casey,* of course, subjected the restriction of abortion to heightened scrutiny without even attempting to establish that the freedom to abort *was* rooted in this Nation's tradition....

To tell the truth, it does not surprise me, and should surprise no one, that the Court has chosen today to revise the standards of *stare decisis* set forth in *Casey.* It has thereby exposed *Casey*'s extraordinary deference to precedent for the result-oriented expedient that it is.

II

Having decided that it need not adhere to *stare decisis,* the Court still must establish that *Bowers* was wrongly decided and that the Texas statute, as applied to petitioners, is unconstitutional.

Texas Penal Code Ann. § 21.06(a) (2003) undoubtedly imposes constraints on liberty. So do laws prohibiting prostitution, recreational use of heroin, and, for that matter, working more than 60 hours per week in a bakery. But there is no right to "liberty" under the Due Process Clause, though today's opinion repeatedly makes that claim. *Ante,* at 2478 ("The liberty protected by the Constitution allows homosexual persons the right to make this choice"); *ante,* at 2481 (" 'These matters ... are central to the liberty protected by the Fourteenth Amendment' "); *ante,* at 2483 ("Their right to liberty under the Due Process Clause gives them the full right to engage in their conduct without intervention of the government"). The Fourteenth Amendment *expressly allows* States to deprive their citizens of "liberty," *so long as "due process of law" is provided:*

"No state shall ... deprive any person of life, liberty, or property, *without due process of law*." Amdt. 14 (emphasis added).

Our opinions applying the doctrine known as "substantive due process" hold that the Due Process Clause prohibits States from infringing *fundamental* liberty interests, unless the infringement is narrowly tailored to serve a compelling state interest. Washington v. Glucksberg, 521 U.S., at 721, 117 S.Ct. 2258. We have held repeatedly, in cases the Court today does not overrule, that *only* fundamental rights qualify for this so-called "heightened scrutiny" protection—that is, rights which are " 'deeply rooted in this Nation's history and tradition,' " *ibid. See* Reno v. Flores, 507 U.S. 292, 303, 113 S.Ct. 1439, 123 L.Ed.2d 1 (1993) (fundamental liberty interests must be "so rooted in the traditions and conscience of our people as to be ranked as fundamental" (internal quotation marks and citations omitted)); United States v. Salerno, 481 U.S. 739, 751, 107 S.Ct. 2095, 95 L.Ed.2d 697 (1987) (same). *See also* Michael H. v. Gerald D., 491 U.S. 110, 122, 109 S.Ct. 2333, 105 L.Ed.2d 91 (1989) ("[W]e have insisted not merely that the interest denominated as a 'liberty' be 'fundamental' ... but also that it be an interest traditionally protected by our society"); Moore v. East Cleveland, 431 U.S. 494, 503, 97 S.Ct. 1932, 52 L.Ed.2d 531 (1977) (plurality opinion); Meyer v. Nebraska, 262 U.S. 390, 399, 43 S.Ct. 625, 67 L.Ed. 1042 (1923) (Fourteenth Amendment protects "those privileges *long recognized at common law* as essential to the orderly pursuit of happiness by free men" (emphasis added)).[46] All other liberty interests may be abridged or abrogated pursuant to a validly enacted state law if that law is rationally related to a legitimate state interest.

Bowers held, first, that criminal prohibitions of homosexual sodomy are not subject to heightened scrutiny because they do not implicate a "fundamental right" under the Due Process Clause, 478 U.S., at 191–194, 106 S.Ct. 2841. Noting that "[p]roscriptions against that conduct have ancient roots," *id.,* at 192, 106 S.Ct. 2841, that "[s]odomy was a criminal offense at common law and was forbidden by the laws of the original 13 States when they ratified the Bill of Rights," *ibid.,* and that many States had retained their bans on sodomy, *id.,* at 193, *Bowers* concluded that a right to engage in homosexual sodomy was not " 'deeply rooted in this Nation's history and tradition,' " *id.,* at 192, 106 S.Ct. 2841.

The Court today does not overrule this holding. Not once does it describe homosexual sodomy as a "fundamental right" or a "fundamental liberty interest," nor does it subject the Texas statute to strict scrutiny. Instead, having failed to establish that the right to homosexual sodomy is " 'deeply rooted in this Nation's history and tradition,' " the Court concludes that the application of Texas's statute to petitioners' conduct fails the rational-basis test, and overrules *Bowers*' holding to the contrary, *see id.,* at 196, 106 S.Ct. 2841. "The Texas statute furthers no legitimate state interest which can justify its intrusion into the personal and private life of the individual." *Ante,* at 2484.

---

46. The Court is quite right that "history and tradition are the starting point but not in all cases the ending point of the substantive due process inquiry," *ante,* at 2480. An asserted "fundamental liberty interest" must not only be "deeply rooted in this Nation's history and tradition," Washington v. Glucksberg, 521 U.S. 702, 721, 117 S.Ct. 2258 (1997), but it must *also* be "implicit in the concept of ordered liberty," so that "neither liberty nor justice would exist if [it] were sacrificed," *ibid.* Moreover, liberty interests unsupported by history and tradition, though not deserving of "heightened scrutiny," are *still* protected from state laws that are not rationally related to any legitimate state interest. *Id.,* at 722, 117 S.Ct. 2258. As I proceed to discuss, it is this latter principle that the Court applies in the present case.

I shall address that rational-basis holding presently. First, however, I address some aspersions that the Court casts upon *Bowers'* conclusion that homosexual sodomy is not a "fundamental right"—even though, as I have said, the Court does not have the boldness to reverse that conclusion.

III

* * *

After discussing the history of antisodomy laws, *ante,* at 2478–2480, the Court proclaims that, "it should be noted that there is no longstanding history in this country of laws directed at homosexual conduct as a distinct matter," *ante,* at 2478. This observation in no way casts into doubt the "definitive [historical] conclusion," *id.,* on which *Bowers* relied: that our Nation has a longstanding history of laws prohibiting *sodomy in general*—regardless of whether it was performed by same-sex or opposite-sex couples. . . .

IV

I turn now to the ground on which the Court squarely rests its holding: the contention that there is no rational basis for the law here under attack. This proposition is so out of accord with our jurisprudence—indeed, with the jurisprudence of *any* society we know—that it requires little discussion.

The Texas statute undeniably seeks to further the belief of its citizens that certain forms of sexual behavior are "immoral and unacceptable," *Bowers, supra,* at 196, 106 S.Ct. 2841—the same interest furthered by criminal laws against fornication, bigamy, adultery, adult incest, bestiality, and obscenity. *Bowers* held that this *was* a legitimate state interest. The Court today reaches the opposite conclusion. The Texas statute, it says, "furthers *no legitimate state interest* which can justify its intrusion into the personal and private life of the individual," *ante,* at 2484 (emphasis added). The Court embraces instead Justice STEVENS' declaration in his *Bowers* dissent, that "the fact that the governing majority in a State has traditionally viewed a particular practice as immoral is not a sufficient reason for upholding a law prohibiting the practice," *ante,* at 2483. This effectively decrees the end of all morals legislation. If, as the Court asserts, the promotion of majoritarian sexual morality is not even a *legitimate* state interest, none of the above-mentioned laws can survive rational-basis review.

* * *

Today's opinion is the product of a Court, which is the product of a law-profession culture, that has largely signed on to the so-called homosexual agenda, by which I mean the agenda promoted by some homosexual activists directed at eliminating the moral opprobrium that has traditionally attached to homosexual conduct. I noted in an earlier opinion the fact that the American Association of Law Schools (to which any reputable law school *must* seek to belong) excludes from membership any school that refuses to ban from its job-interview facilities a law firm (no matter how small) that does not wish to hire as a prospective partner a person who openly engages in homosexual conduct. *See Romer, supra,* at 653, 116 S.Ct. 1620.

One of the most revealing statements in today's opinion is the Court's grim warning that the criminalization of homosexual conduct is "an invitation to subject homosexual persons to discrimination both in the public and in the private spheres." *Ante,* at 2482. It is clear from this that the Court has taken sides in the culture war, departing from its role of assuring, as neutral observer, that the democratic rules of engagement are observed. Many Americans do not want persons who openly engage in homosexual conduct as partners in their business, as scoutmasters for their children, as teachers in their children's schools, or as boarders in their home. They view this as protecting themselves and their families from a lifestyle that they believe to be immoral and destructive. The Court views it as "discrimination" which it is the function of our judgments to deter. So imbued is the Court with the law profession's anti-anti-homosexual culture, that it is seemingly unaware that the attitudes of that culture are not obviously "mainstream"; that in most States what the Court calls "discrimination" against those who engage in homosexual acts is perfectly legal; that proposals to ban such "discrimination" under Title VII have repeatedly been rejected by Congress, see Employment Non–Discrimination Act of 1994, S. 2238, 103d Cong., 2d Sess. (1994); Civil Rights Amendments, H.R. 5452, 94th Cong., 1st Sess. (1975); that in some cases such "discrimination" is *mandated* by federal statute, *see* 10 U.S.C. § 654(b)(1) (mandating discharge from the armed forces of any service member who engages in or intends to engage in homosexual acts); and that in some cases such "discrimination" is a constitutional right, *see* Boy Scouts of America v. Dale, 530 U.S. 640, 120 S.Ct. 2446, 147 L.Ed.2d 554 (2000).

Let me be clear that I have nothing against homosexuals, or any other group, promoting their agenda through normal democratic means. Social perceptions of sexual and other morality change over time, and every group has the right to persuade its fellow citizens that its view of such matters is the best. That homosexuals have achieved some success in that enterprise is attested to by the fact that Texas is one of the few remaining States that criminalize private, consensual homosexual acts. But persuading one's fellow citizens is one thing, and imposing one's views in absence of democratic majority will is something else. I would no more *require* a State to criminalize homosexual acts—or, for that matter, display *any* moral disapprobation of them—than I would *forbid* it to do so. What Texas has chosen to do is well within the range of traditional democratic action, and its hand should not be stayed through the invention of a brand-new "constitutional right" by a Court that is impatient of democratic change. It is indeed true that "later generations can see that laws once thought necessary and proper in fact serve only to oppress," *ante,* at 2484; and when that happens, later generations can repeal those laws. But it is the premise of our system that those judgments are to be made by the people, and not imposed by a governing caste that knows best.

One of the benefits of leaving regulation of this matter to the people rather than to the courts is that the people, unlike judges, need not carry things to their logical conclusion. The people may feel that their disapprobation of homosexual conduct is strong enough to disallow homosexual marriage, but not strong enough to criminalize private homosexual acts— and may legislate accordingly. The Court today pretends that it possesses a similar freedom of action, so that that we need not fear judicial imposition of homosexual marriage, as has recently occurred in Canada (in a decision that the Canadian Government has chosen not to appeal). *See* Halpern v. Toronto, 2003 WL 34950 (Ontario Ct.App.); Cohen, Dozens in Canada Follow Gay Couple's Lead, Washington Post, June 12, 2003, p. A25. At the end of its opinion—after having laid waste the foundations of our rational-basis jurisprudence—the Court says that the present case "does not involve whether the government must give formal recognition to any relationship that homosexual persons seek to enter." *Ante,* at 2484. Do not believe it. More illuminating than this bald, unreasoned disclaimer is the progression of thought displayed by an earlier passage in the Court's opinion, which notes the constitutional protections afforded to "personal decisions relating to *marriage,* procreation, contraception, family relationships, child rearing, and education," and then declares that "[p]ersons in a homosexual relationship may seek autonomy for these purposes, just as heterosexual persons do." *Ante,* at 2482 (emphasis added). Today's opinion dismantles the structure of constitutional law that has permitted a distinction to be made between heterosexual and homosexual unions, insofar as formal recognition in marriage is concerned. If moral disapprobation of homosexual conduct is "no legitimate state interest" for purposes of proscribing that conduct, *ante,* at 2484; and if, as the Court coos (casting aside all pretense of neutrality), "[w]hen sexuality finds overt expression in intimate conduct with another person, the conduct can be but one element in a personal bond that is more enduring," *ante,* at 2478; what justification could there possibly be for denying the benefits of marriage to homosexual couples exercising "[t]he liberty protected by the Constitution," *ibid.*? Surely not the encouragement of procreation, since the sterile and the elderly are allowed to marry. This case "does not involve" the issue of homosexual marriage only if one entertains the belief that principle and logic have nothing to do with the decisions of this Court. Many will hope that, as the Court comfortingly assures us, this is so.

The matters appropriate for this Court's resolution are only three: Texas's prohibition of sodomy neither infringes a "fundamental right" (which the Court does not dispute), nor is unsupported by a rational relation to what the Constitution considers a legitimate state interest, nor denies the equal protection of the laws. I dissent.

■ JUSTICE THOMAS, dissenting.

I join Justice SCALIA's dissenting opinion. I write separately to note that the law before the Court today "is . . . uncommonly silly." Griswold v. Connecticut, 381 U.S. 479, 527, 85 S.Ct. 1678, 14 L.Ed.2d 510 (1965) (Stewart, J., dissenting). If I were a member of the Texas Legislature, I would vote to repeal it. Punishing someone for expressing his sexual preference through noncommercial consensual conduct with another adult does not appear to be a worthy way to expend valuable law enforcement resources.

Notwithstanding this, I recognize that as a member of this Court I am not empowered to help petitioners and others similarly situated. My duty, rather, is to "decide cases 'agreeably to the Constitution and laws of the United States.' " *Id.,* at 530, 85 S.Ct. 1678. And, just like Justice Stewart, I "can find [neither in the Bill of Rights nor any other part of the Constitution a] general right of privacy," *ibid.,* or as the Court terms it today, the "liberty of the person both in its spatial and more transcendent dimensions," *ante,* at 2475.

(D) EQUALITY

United States v. Armstrong

Supreme Court of the United States, 1996.
517 U.S. 456, 116 S.Ct. 1480, 134 L.Ed.2d 687.

■ CHIEF JUSTICE REHNQUIST delivered the opinion of the Court.

In this case, we consider the showing necessary for a defendant to be entitled to discovery on a claim that the prosecuting attorney singled him out for prosecution on the basis of his race. We conclude that respondents failed to satisfy the threshold showing: They failed to show that the Government declined to prosecute similarly situated suspects of other races.

In April 1992, respondents were indicted in the United States District Court for the Central District of California on charges of conspiring to possess with intent to distribute more than 50 grams of cocaine base (crack) and conspiring to distribute the same, in violation of 21 U.S.C. §§ 841 and 846 (1988 ed. and Supp. IV), and federal firearms offenses. For three months prior to the indictment, agents of the Federal Bureau of Alcohol, Tobacco, and Firearms and the Narcotics Division of the Inglewood, California, Police Department had infiltrated a suspected crack distribution ring by using three confidential informants. On seven separate occasions during this period, the informants had bought a total of 124.3 grams of crack from respondents and witnessed respondents carrying firearms during the sales. The agents searched the hotel room in which the sales were transacted, arrested respondents Armstrong and Hampton in the room, and found more crack and a loaded gun. The agents later arrested the other respondents as part of the ring.

In response to the indictment, respondents filed a motion for discovery or for dismissal of the indictment, alleging that they were selected for federal prosecution because they are black. In support of their motion, they offered only an affidavit by a "Paralegal Specialist," employed by the Office of the Federal Public Defender representing one of the respondents. The only allegation in the affidavit was that, in every one of the 24 § 841 or § 846 cases closed by the office during 1991, the defendant was black. Accompanying the affidavit was a "study" listing the 24 defendants, their race, whether they were prosecuted for dealing cocaine as well as crack, and the status of each case.

The Government opposed the discovery motion, arguing, among other things, that there was no evidence or allegation "that the Government has acted unfairly or has prosecuted non-black defendants or failed to prosecute them." App. 150. The District Court granted the motion. It ordered the Government (1) to provide a list of all cases from the last three years in which the Government charged both cocaine and firearms offenses, (2) to identify the race of the defendants in those cases, (3) to identify what levels of law enforcement were involved in the investigations of those cases, and (4) to explain its criteria for deciding to prosecute those defendants for federal cocaine offenses. *Id.,* at 161–162.

The Government moved for reconsideration of the District Court's discovery order. With this motion it submitted affidavits and other evidence to explain why it had chosen to prosecute respondents and why respondents' study did not support the inference that the Government was singling out blacks for cocaine prosecution. The federal and local agents participating in the case alleged in affidavits that race played no role in their investigation. An Assistant United States Attorney explained in an affidavit that the decision to prosecute met the general criteria for prosecution, because

"there was over 100 grams of cocaine base involved, over twice the threshold necessary for a ten year mandatory minimum sentence; there were multiple sales involving multiple defendants, thereby indicating a fairly substantial crack cocaine ring; ... there were multiple federal firearms violations intertwined with the narcotics trafficking; the overall evidence in the case was extremely strong, including audio and videotapes of defendants; ... and several of the defendants had criminal histories including narcotics and firearms violations." *Id.,* at 81.

The Government also submitted sections of a published 1989 Drug Enforcement Administration report which concluded that "[l]arge-scale, interstate trafficking networks controlled by Jamaicans, Haitians and Black street gangs dominate the manufacture and distribution of crack." J. Featherly & E. Hill, Crack Cocaine Overview 1989; App. 103.

In response, one of respondents' attorneys submitted an affidavit alleging that an intake coordinator at a drug treatment center had told her that there are "an equal number of caucasian users and dealers to minority users and dealers." *Id.,* at 138. Respondents also submitted an affidavit from a criminal defense attorney alleging that in his experience many nonblacks are prosecuted in state court for crack offenses, *id.,* at 141, and a newspaper article reporting that federal "crack criminals ... are being punished far more severely than if they had been caught with powder cocaine, and almost every single one of them is black," Newton, Harsher Crack Sentences Criticized as Racial Inequity, Los Angeles Times, Nov. 23, 1992, p. 1; App. 208–210.

The District Court denied the motion for reconsideration. When the Government indicated it would not comply with the court's discovery order, the court dismissed the case.[47]

---

47. We have never determined whether dismissal of the indictment, or some other sanction, is the proper remedy if a court determines that a defendant has been the victim of prosecution on the basis of his race. Here, "it was the government itself that suggested

A divided three-judge panel of the Court of Appeals for the Ninth Circuit reversed, holding that, because of the proof requirements for a selective-prosecution claim, defendants must "provide a colorable basis for believing that 'others similarly situated have not been prosecuted' " to obtain discovery. 21 F.3d 1431, 1436 (1994) (quoting United States v. Wayte, 710 F.2d 1385, 1387 (C.A.9 1983), aff'd, 470 U.S. 598, 105 S.Ct. 1524, 84 L.Ed.2d 547 (1985)). The Court of Appeals voted to rehear the case en banc, and the en banc panel affirmed the District Court's order of dismissal, holding that "a defendant is not required to demonstrate that the government has failed to prosecute others who are similarly situated." 48 F.3d 1508, 1516 (1995) (emphasis deleted). We granted certiorari to determine the appropriate standard for discovery for a selective-prosecution claim. 516 U.S. 942, 116 S.Ct. 377, 133 L.Ed.2d 301 (1995)....

A selective-prosecution claim asks a court to exercise judicial power over a "special province" of the Executive. Heckler v. Chaney, 470 U.S. 821, 832, 105 S.Ct. 1649, 1656, 84 L.Ed.2d 714 (1985). The Attorney General and United States Attorneys retain " 'broad discretion' " to enforce the Nation's criminal laws. Wayte v. United States, 470 U.S. 598, 607, 105 S.Ct. 1524, 1530–1531, 84 L.Ed.2d 547 (1985) (quoting United States v. Goodwin, 457 U.S. 368, 380, n. 11, 102 S.Ct. 2485, 2492, n. 11, 73 L.Ed.2d 74 (1982)). They have this latitude because they are designated by statute as the President's delegates to help him discharge his constitutional responsibility to "take Care that the Laws be faithfully executed." U.S. Const., Art. II, § 3; *see* 28 U.S.C. §§ 516, 547. As a result, "[t]he presumption of regularity supports" their prosecutorial decisions and, "in the absence of clear evidence to the contrary, courts presume that they have properly discharged their official duties." United States v. Chemical Foundation, Inc., 272 U.S. 1, 14–15, 47 S.Ct. 1, 6, 71 L.Ed. 131 (1926). In the ordinary case, "so long as the prosecutor has probable cause to believe that the accused committed an offense defined by statute, the decision whether or not to prosecute, and what charge to file or bring before a grand jury, generally rests entirely in his discretion." Bordenkircher v. Hayes, 434 U.S. 357, 364, 98 S.Ct. 663, 668, 54 L.Ed.2d 604 (1978).

Of course, a prosecutor's discretion is "subject to constitutional constraints." United States v. Batchelder, 442 U.S. 114, 125, 99 S.Ct. 2198, 2204–2205, 60 L.Ed.2d 755 (1979). One of these constraints, imposed by the equal protection component of the Due Process Clause of the Fifth Amendment, Bolling v. Sharpe, 347 U.S. 497, 500, 74 S.Ct. 693, 694–695, 98 L.Ed. 884 (1954), is that the decision whether to prosecute may not be based on "an unjustifiable standard such as race, religion, or other arbitrary classification," Oyler v. Boles, 368 U.S. 448, 456, 82 S.Ct. 501, 506, 7 L.Ed.2d 446 (1962). A defendant may demonstrate that the administration of a criminal law is "directed so exclusively against a particular class of persons . . . with a mind so unequal and oppressive" that the system of prosecution amounts to "a practical denial" of equal protection of the law. Yick Wo v. Hopkins, 118 U.S. 356, 373, 6 S.Ct. 1064, 1073, 30 L.Ed. 220 (1886).

---

dismissal of the indictments to the district court so that an appeal might lie." 48 F.3d 1508, 1510 (C.A.9 1995).

In order to dispel the presumption that a prosecutor has not violated equal protection, a criminal defendant must present "clear evidence to the contrary." *Chemical Foundation, supra,* at 14–15, 47 S.Ct., at 6. We explained in *Wayte* why courts are "properly hesitant to examine the decision whether to prosecute." 470 U.S., at 608, 105 S.Ct., at 1531. Judicial deference to the decisions of these executive officers rests in part on an assessment of the relative competence of prosecutors and courts. "Such factors as the strength of the case, the prosecution's general deterrence value, the Government's enforcement priorities, and the case's relationship to the Government's overall enforcement plan are not readily susceptible to the kind of analysis the courts are competent to undertake." *Id.,* at 607, 105 S.Ct., at 1530. It also stems from a concern not to unnecessarily impair the performance of a core executive constitutional function. "Examining the basis of a prosecution delays the criminal proceeding, threatens to chill law enforcement by subjecting the prosecutor's motives and decisionmaking to outside inquiry, and may undermine prosecutorial effectiveness by revealing the Government's enforcement policy." *Ibid.*

The requirements for a selective-prosecution claim draw on "ordinary equal protection standards." *Id.,* at 608, 105 S.Ct., at 1531. The claimant must demonstrate that the federal prosecutorial policy "had a discriminatory effect and that it was motivated by a discriminatory purpose." *Ibid.;* accord, *Oyler, supra,* at 456, 82 S.Ct., at 506. To establish a discriminatory effect in a race case, the claimant must show that similarly situated individuals of a different race were not prosecuted. This requirement has been established in our case law since Ah Sin v. Wittman, 198 U.S. 500, 25 S.Ct. 756, 49 L.Ed. 1142 (1905). Ah Sin, a subject of China, petitioned a California state court for a writ of habeas corpus, seeking discharge from imprisonment under a San Francisco County ordinance prohibiting persons from setting up gambling tables in rooms barricaded to stop police from entering. *Id.,* at 503, 25 S.Ct., at 757. He alleged in his habeas petition "that the ordinance is enforced 'solely and exclusively against persons of the Chinese race and not otherwise.' " *Id.,* at 507, 25 S.Ct., at 758–759. We rejected his contention that this averment made out a claim under the Equal Protection Clause, because it did not allege "that the conditions and practices to which the ordinance was directed did not exist exclusively among the Chinese, or that there were other offenders against the ordinance than the Chinese as to whom it was not enforced." *Id.,* at 507–508, 25 S.Ct., at 758–759.

The similarly situated requirement does not make a selective-prosecution claim impossible to prove. Twenty years before *Ah Sin,* we invalidated an ordinance, also adopted by San Francisco, that prohibited the operation of laundries in wooden buildings. *Yick Wo,* 118 U.S., at 374, 6 S.Ct., at 1073. The plaintiff in error successfully demonstrated that the ordinance was applied against Chinese nationals but not against other laundry-shop operators. The authorities had denied the applications of 200 Chinese subjects for permits to operate shops in wooden buildings, but granted the applications of 80 individuals who were not Chinese subjects to operate laundries in wooden buildings "under similar conditions." *Ibid.* We explained in *Ah Sin* why the similarly situated requirement is necessary:

"No latitude of intention should be indulged in a case like this. There should be certainty to every intent. Plaintiff in error seeks to set aside a criminal law of the State, not on the ground that it is unconstitutional on its face, not that it is discriminatory in tendency and ultimate actual operation as the ordinance was which was passed on in the *Yick Wo case,* but that it was made so by the manner of its administration. This is a matter of proof, and *no fact should be omitted to make it out completely,* when the power of a Federal court is invoked to interfere with the course of criminal justice of a State." 198 U.S., at 508, 25 S.Ct., at 759 (emphasis added).

Although *Ah Sin* involved federal review of a state conviction, we think a similar rule applies where the power of a federal court is invoked to challenge an exercise of one of the core powers of the Executive Branch of the Federal Government, the power to prosecute.

Respondents urge that cases such as Batson v. Kentucky, 476 U.S. 79, 106 S.Ct. 1712, 90 L.Ed.2d 69 (1986), and Hunter v. Underwood, 471 U.S. 222, 105 S.Ct. 1916, 85 L.Ed.2d 222 (1985), cut against any absolute requirement that there be a showing of failure to prosecute similarly situated individuals. We disagree. In *Hunter,* we invalidated a state law disfranchising persons convicted of crimes involving moral turpitude. *Id.,* at 233, 105 S.Ct., at 1922–1923. Our holding was consistent with ordinary equal protection principles, including the similarly situated requirement. There was convincing direct evidence that the State had enacted the provision for the purpose of disfranchising blacks, *id.,* at 229–231, 105 S.Ct., at 1920–1922, and indisputable evidence that the state law had a discriminatory effect on blacks as compared to similarly situated whites: Blacks were " 'by even the most modest estimates at least 1.7 times as likely as whites to suffer disfranchisement under' " the law in question, *id.,* at 227, 105 S.Ct., at 1919–1920 (quoting Underwood v. Hunter, 730 F.2d 614, 620 (C.A.11 1984)). *Hunter* thus affords no support for respondents' position.

In *Batson,* we considered "[t]he standards for assessing a prima facie case in the context of discriminatory selection of the venire" in a criminal trial. 476 U.S., at 96, 106 S.Ct., at 1723. We required a criminal defendant to show "that the prosecutor has exercised peremptory challenges to remove from the venire members of the defendant's race" and that this fact, the potential for abuse inherent in a peremptory strike, and "any other relevant circumstances raise an inference that the prosecutor used that practice to exclude the veniremen from the petit jury on account of their race." *Ibid.* During jury selection, the entire *res gestae* take place in front of the trial judge. Because the judge has before him the entire venire, he is well situated to detect whether a challenge to the seating of one juror is part of a "pattern" of singling out members of a single race for peremptory challenges. *See id.,* at 97, 106 S.Ct., at 1723. He is in a position to discern whether a challenge to a black juror has evidentiary significance; the significance may differ if the venire consists mostly of blacks or of whites. Similarly, if the defendant makes out a prima facie case, the prosecutor is called upon to justify only decisions made in the very case then before the court. *See id.,* at 97–98, 106 S.Ct., at 1723–1724. The trial judge need not review prosecutorial conduct in relation to other venires in other cases.

Having reviewed the requirements to prove a selective-prosecution claim, we turn to the showing necessary to obtain discovery in support of such a claim. If discovery is ordered, the Government must assemble from its own files documents which might corroborate or refute the defendant's claim. Discovery thus imposes many of the costs present when the Government must respond to a prima facie case of selective prosecution. It will divert prosecutors' resources and may disclose the Government's prosecutorial strategy. The justifications for a rigorous standard for the elements of a selective-prosecution claim thus require a correspondingly rigorous standard for discovery in aid of such a claim.

The parties, and the Courts of Appeals which have considered the requisite showing to establish entitlement to discovery, describe this showing with a variety of phrases, like "colorable basis," "substantial threshold showing," Tr. of Oral Arg. 5, "substantial and concrete basis," or "reasonable likelihood," Brief for Respondents Martin et al. 30. However, the many labels for this showing conceal the degree of consensus about the evidence necessary to meet it. The Courts of Appeals "require some evidence tending to show the existence of the essential elements of the defense," discriminatory effect and discriminatory intent. United States v. Berrios, 501 F.2d 1207, 1211 (C.A.2 1974).

In this case we consider what evidence constitutes "some evidence tending to show the existence" of the discriminatory effect element. The Court of Appeals held that a defendant may establish a colorable basis for discriminatory effect without evidence that the Government has failed to prosecute others who are similarly situated to the defendant. 48 F.3d, at 1516. We think it was mistaken in this view. The vast majority of the Courts of Appeals require the defendant to produce some evidence that similarly situated defendants of other races could have been prosecuted, but were not, and this requirement is consistent with our equal protection case law. United States v. Parham, 16 F.3d 844, 846–847 (C.A.8 1994); United States v. Fares, 978 F.2d 52, 59–60 (C.A.2 1992); United States v. Peete, 919 F.2d 1168, 1176 (C.A.6 1990); C.E. Carlson, Inc. v. SEC, 859 F.2d 1429, 1437–1438 (C.A.10 1988); United States v. Greenwood, 796 F.2d 49, 52–53 (C.A.4 1986); United States v. Mitchell, 778 F.2d 1271, 1277 (C.A.7 1985). As the three-judge panel explained, " '[s]elective prosecution' implies that a selection has taken place." 21 F.3d, at 1436.[48]

The Court of Appeals reached its decision in part because it started "with the presumption that people of *all* races commit *all* types of crimes— not with the premise that any type of crime is the exclusive province of any particular racial or ethnic group." 48 F.3d, at 1516–1517. It cited no authority for this proposition, which seems contradicted by the most recent statistics of the United States Sentencing Commission. Those statistics show: More than 90% of the persons sentenced in 1994 for crack cocaine

---

48. We reserve the question whether a defendant must satisfy the similarly situated requirement in a case "involving direct admissions by [prosecutors] of discriminatory purpose." Brief for United States 15.

trafficking were black, United States Sentencing Comm'n, 1994 Annual Report 107 (Table 45); 93.4% of convicted LSD dealers were white, *ibid.;* and 91% of those convicted for pornography or prostitution were white, *id.,* at 41 (Table 13). Presumptions at war with presumably reliable statistics have no proper place in the analysis of this issue.

The Court of Appeals also expressed concern about the "evidentiary obstacles defendants face." 48 F.3d, at 1514. But all of its sister Circuits that have confronted the issue have required that defendants produce some evidence of differential treatment of similarly situated members of other races or protected classes. In the present case, if the claim of selective prosecution were well founded, it should not have been an insuperable task to prove that persons of other races were being treated differently than respondents. For instance, respondents could have investigated whether similarly situated persons of other races were prosecuted by the State of California and were known to federal law enforcement officers, but were not prosecuted in federal court. We think the required threshold—a credible showing of different treatment of similarly situated persons—adequately balances the Government's interest in vigorous prosecution and the defendant's interest in avoiding selective prosecution.

In the case before us, respondents' "study" did not constitute "some evidence tending to show the existence of the essential elements of" a selective-prosecution claim. *Berrios, supra,* at 1211. The study failed to identify individuals who were not black and could have been prosecuted for the offenses for which respondents were charged, but were not so prosecuted. This omission was not remedied by respondents' evidence in opposition to the Government's motion for reconsideration. The newspaper article, which discussed the discriminatory effect of federal drug sentencing laws, was not relevant to an allegation of discrimination in decisions to prosecute. Respondents' affidavits, which recounted one attorney's conversation with a drug treatment center employee and the experience of another attorney defending drug prosecutions in state court, recounted hearsay and reported personal conclusions based on anecdotal evidence. The judgment of the Court of Appeals is therefore reversed, and the case is remanded for proceedings consistent with this opinion.

It is so ordered.

[The concurring opinions of Justice Souter, Justice Ginsburg, and Justice Breyer, are omitted]

■ JUSTICE STEVENS, dissenting.

The Court correctly concludes that in this case the facts presented to the District Court in support of respondents' claim that they had been singled out for prosecution because of their race were not sufficient to prove that defense. Moreover, I agree with the Court that their showing was not strong enough to give them a *right* to discovery, either under Rule 16 or under the District Court's inherent power to order discovery in appropriate circumstances. Like Chief Judge Wallace of the Court of Appeals, however, I am persuaded that the District Judge did not abuse her discretion when she concluded that the factual showing was sufficiently disturbing to require some response from the United States Attorney's

Office. *See* 48 F.3d 1508, 1520–1521 (C.A.9 1995). Perhaps the discovery order was broader than necessary, but I cannot agree with the Court's apparent conclusion that no inquiry was permissible.

The District Judge's order should be evaluated in light of three circumstances that underscore the need for judicial vigilance over certain types of drug prosecutions. First, the Anti–Drug Abuse Act of 1986 and subsequent legislation established a regime of extremely high penalties for the possession and distribution of so-called "crack" cocaine. Those provisions treat one gram of crack as the equivalent of 100 grams of powder cocaine. The distribution of 50 grams of crack is thus punishable by the same mandatory minimum sentence of 10 years in prison that applies to the distribution of 5,000 grams of powder cocaine.[49] The Sentencing Guidelines extend this ratio to penalty levels above the mandatory minimums: For any given quantity of crack, the guideline range is the same as if the offense had involved 100 times that amount in powder cocaine. These penalties result in sentences for crack offenders that average three to eight times longer than sentences for comparable powder offenders.[50] United States Sentencing Commission, Special Report to Congress: Cocaine and Federal Sentencing Policy 145 (Feb.1995) (hereinafter Special Report).

Second, the disparity between the treatment of crack cocaine and powder cocaine is matched by the disparity between the severity of the punishment imposed by federal law and that imposed by state law for the same conduct. For a variety of reasons, often including the absence of mandatory minimums, the existence of parole, and lower baseline penalties, terms of imprisonment for drug offenses tend to be substantially lower in state systems than in the federal system. The difference is especially marked in the case of crack offenses. The majority of States draw no distinction between types of cocaine in their penalty schemes; of those that do, none has established as stark a differential as the Federal Government. *See id.,* at x, 129–138. For example, if respondent Hampton is found guilty, his federal sentence might be as long as a mandatory life term. Had he been tried in state court, his sentence could have been as short as 12 years, less worktime credits of half that amount. 11370.2. Thus, with three priors and the possibility of worktime reductions, *see* Cal.Penal Code Ann. § 2933 (West Supp.1996), Hampton could have served as little as six years under California law. Since the time of the offenses, California has raised several of these penalties, but the new punishments could not be applied to respondents.

---

49. Compare 21 U.S.C. § 841(b)(1)(A)(iii) with § 841(b)(1)(A)(ii). Similarly, a mandatory 5–year sentence is prescribed for distribution of 500 grams of cocaine or 5 grams of crack. Compare § 841(b)(1)(B)(ii) with § 841(b)(1)(B)(iii). Simple possession of 5 grams of crack also produces a mandatory 5–year sentence. The maximum sentence for possession of *any* quantity of other drugs is one year. § 844(a). With one prior felony drug offense, the sentence for distribution of 50 grams of crack is a mandatory 20 years to life. § 841(b)(1)(A). With two prior felony drug offenses, the sentence is a mandatory life term without parole. *Ibid.*

50. Under the Guidelines, penalties increase at a slower rate than drug quantities. For example, 5 grams of heroin result in a base offense level of 14 (15–21 months) while 10 grams of heroin (double the amount) result in an offense level of 16 (21–27 months). USSG §§ 2D1.1(c)(13), (12). Thus, the 100–to–1 ratio does not translate into sentences that are 100 times as long.

Finally, it is undisputed that the brunt of the elevated federal penalties falls heavily on blacks. While 65% of the persons who have used crack are white, in 1993 they represented only 4% of the federal offenders convicted of trafficking in crack. Eighty-eight percent of such defendants were black. *Id.*, at 39, 161. During the first 18 months of full guideline implementation, the sentencing disparity between black and white defendants grew from preguideline levels: Blacks on average received sentences over 40% longer than whites. *See* Bureau of Justice Statistics, Sentencing in the Federal Courts: Does Race Matter? 6–7 (Dec.1993). Those figures represent a major threat to the integrity of federal sentencing reform, whose main purpose was the elimination of disparity (especially racial) in sentencing. The Sentencing Commission acknowledges that the heightened crack penalties are a "primary cause of the growing disparity between sentences for Black and White federal defendants." Special Report 163.

The extraordinary severity of the imposed penalties and the troubling racial patterns of enforcement give rise to a special concern about the fairness of charging practices for crack offenses. Evidence tending to prove that black defendants charged with distribution of crack in the Central District of California are prosecuted in federal court, whereas members of other races charged with similar offenses are prosecuted in state court, warrants close scrutiny by the federal judges in that district. In my view, the District Judge, who has sat on both the federal and the state benches in Los Angeles, acted well within her discretion to call for the development of facts that would demonstrate what standards, if any, governed the choice of forum where similarly situated offenders are prosecuted.

Respondents submitted a study showing that of all cases involving crack offenses that were closed by the Federal Public Defender's Office in 1991, 24 out of 24 involved black defendants. To supplement this evidence, they submitted affidavits from two of the attorneys in the defense team. The first reported a statement from an intake coordinator at a local drug treatment center that, in his experience, an equal number of crack users and dealers were caucasian as belonged to minorities. App. 138. The second was from David R. Reed, counsel for respondent Armstrong. Reed was both an active court-appointed attorney in the Central District of California and one of the directors of the leading association of criminal defense lawyers who practice before the Los Angeles County courts. Reed stated that he did not recall "ever handling a [crack] cocaine case involving non-black defendants" in federal court, nor had he even heard of one. *Id.*, at 140. He further stated that "[t]here are many crack cocaine sales cases prosecuted in state court that *do* involve racial groups other than blacks." *Id.*, at 141 (emphasis in original).

The majority discounts the probative value of the affidavits, claiming that they recounted "hearsay" and reported "personal conclusions based on anecdotal evidence." *Ante,* at 1489. But the Reed affidavit plainly contained more than mere hearsay; Reed offered information based on his own extensive experience in both federal and state courts. Given the breadth of his background, he was well qualified to compare the practices of federal and state prosecutors. In any event, the Government never objected to the admission of either affidavit on hearsay or any other grounds. *See* 48

F.3d, at 1518, n. 8. It was certainly within the District Court's discretion to credit the affidavits of two members of the bar of that Court, at least one of whom had presumably acquired a reputation by his frequent appearances there, and both of whose statements were made on pains of perjury.

The criticism that the affidavits were based on "anecdotal evidence" is also unpersuasive. I thought it was agreed that defendants do not need to prepare sophisticated statistical studies in order to receive mere discovery in cases like this one. Certainly evidence based on a drug counselor's personal observations or on an attorney's practice in two sets of courts, state and federal, can " 'ten[d] to show the existence' " of a selective prosecution. *Ante,* at 1488.

Even if respondents failed to carry their burden of showing that there were individuals who were not black but who could have been prosecuted in federal court for the same offenses, it does not follow that the District Court abused its discretion in ordering discovery. There can be no doubt that such individuals exist, and indeed the Government has never denied the same. In those circumstances, I fail to see why the District Court was unable to take judicial notice of this obvious fact and demand information from the Government's files to support or refute respondents' evidence. The presumption that some whites are prosecuted in state court is not "contradicted" by the statistics the majority cites, which show only that high percentages of blacks are *convicted* of certain federal crimes, while high percentages of whites are convicted of other federal crimes. *See ante,* at 1488–1489. Those figures are entirely consistent with the allegation of selective prosecution. The relevant comparison, rather, would be with the percentages of blacks and whites who *commit* those crimes. But, as discussed above, in the case of crack far greater numbers of whites are believed guilty of using the substance. The District Court, therefore, was entitled to find the evidence before it significant and to require some explanation from the Government[51]. . . .

(E) PROPORTIONALITY

Ewing v. California

Supreme Court of the United States, 2003.
538 U.S. 11, 123 S.Ct. 1179, 155 L.Ed.2d 108.

■ JUSTICE O'CONNOR announced the judgment of the Court and delivered an opinion in which THE CHIEF JUSTICE and JUSTICE KENNEDY join.

---

51. Also telling was the Government's response to respondents' evidentiary showing. It submitted a list of more than 3,500 defendants who had been charged with federal narcotics violations over the previous three years. It also offered the names of 11 nonblack defendants whom it had prosecuted for crack offenses. All 11, however, were members of other racial or ethnic minorities. *See* 48 F.3d 1508, 1511 (CA9 1995). The District Court was authorized to draw adverse inferences from the Government's inability to produce a single example of a white defendant, especially when the very purpose of its exercise was to allay the court's concerns about the evidence of racially selective prosecutions.

As another court has said: "Statistics are not, of course, the whole answer, but nothing is as emphatic as zero. . . ." United States v. Hinds County School Bd., 417 F.2d 852, 858 (C.A.5 1969) *(per curiam).*

In this case, we decide whether the Eighth Amendment prohibits the State of California from sentencing a repeat felon to a prison term of 25 years to life under the State's "Three Strikes and You're Out" law.

I

A

California's three strikes law reflects a shift in the State's sentencing policies toward incapacitating and deterring repeat offenders who threaten the public safety. The law was designed "to ensure longer prison sentences and greater punishment for those who commit a felony and have been previously convicted of serious and/or violent felony offenses." Cal.Penal Code Ann. § 667(b) (West 1999). On March 3, 1993, California Assemblymen Bill Jones and Jim Costa introduced Assembly Bill 971, the legislative version of what would later become the three strikes law. The Assembly Committee on Public Safety defeated the bill only weeks later. Public outrage over the defeat sparked a voter initiative to add Proposition 184, based loosely on the bill, to the ballot in the November 1994 general election.

On October 1, 1993, while Proposition 184 was circulating, 12–year-old Polly Klaas was kidnaped from her home in Petaluma, California. Her admitted killer, Richard Allen Davis, had a long criminal history that included two prior kidnaping convictions. Davis had served only half of his most recent sentence (16 years for kidnaping, assault, and burglary). Had Davis served his entire sentence, he would still have been in prison on the day that Polly Klaas was kidnaped.

Polly Klaas' murder galvanized support for the three strikes initiative. Within days, Proposition 184 was on its way to becoming the fastest qualifying initiative in California history. On January 3, 1994, the sponsors of Assembly Bill 971 resubmitted an amended version of the bill that conformed to Proposition 184. On January 31, 1994, Assembly Bill 971 passed the Assembly by a 63 to 9 margin. The Senate passed it by a 29 to 7 margin on March 3, 1994. Governor Pete Wilson signed the bill into law on March 7, 1994. California voters approved Proposition 184 by a margin of 72 to 28 percent on November 8, 1994.

California thus became the second State to enact a three strikes law. In November 1993, the voters of Washington State approved their own three strikes law, Initiative 593, by a margin of 3 to 1. U.S. Dept. of Justice, National Institute of Justice, J. Clark, J. Austin, & D. Henry, "Three Strikes and You're Out": A Review of State Legislation 1 (Sept.1997) (hereinafter Review of State Legislation). Between 1993 and 1995, 24 States and the Federal Government enacted three strikes laws. *Ibid.* Though the three strikes laws vary from State to State, they share a common goal of protecting the public safety by providing lengthy prison terms for habitual felons.

B

California's current three strikes law consists of two virtually identical statutory schemes "designed to increase the prison terms of repeat felons." People v. Superior Court of San Diego Cty. ex rel. Romero, 13 Cal.4th 497,

504, 53 Cal.Rptr.2d 789, 917 P.2d 628, 630 (1996) *(Romero)*. When a defendant is convicted of a felony, and he has previously been convicted of one or more prior felonies defined as "serious" or "violent" in Cal.Penal Code Ann. §§ 667.5 and 1192.7 (West Supp.2002), sentencing is conducted pursuant to the three strikes law. Prior convictions must be alleged in the charging document, and the defendant has a right to a jury determination that the prosecution has proved the prior convictions beyond a reasonable doubt. § 1025; § 1158 (West 1985).

If the defendant has one prior "serious" or "violent" felony conviction, he must be sentenced to "twice the term otherwise provided as punishment for the current felony conviction." § 667(e)(1) (West 1999); § 1170.12(c)(1) (West Supp.2002). If the defendant has two or more prior "serious" or "violent" felony convictions, he must receive "an indeterminate term of life imprisonment." § 667(e)(2)(A) (West 1999); § 1170.12(c)(2)(A) (West Supp. 2002). Defendants sentenced to life under the three strikes law become eligible for parole on a date calculated by reference to a "minimum term," which is the greater of (a) three times the term otherwise provided for the current conviction, (b) 25 years, or (c) the term determined by the court pursuant to § 1170 for the underlying conviction, including any enhancements. §§ 667(e)(2)(A)(i–iii) (West 1999); §§ 1170.12(c)(2)(A)(i–iii) (West Supp.2002).

Under California law, certain offenses may be classified as either felonies or misdemeanors. These crimes are known as "wobblers." Some crimes that would otherwise be misdemeanors become "wobblers" because of the defendant's prior record. For example, petty theft, a misdemeanor, becomes a "wobbler" when the defendant has previously served a prison term for committing specified theft-related crimes. § 490 (West 1999); § 666 (West Supp.2002). Other crimes, such as grand theft, are "wobblers" regardless of the defendant's prior record. *See* § 489(b) (West 1999). Both types of "wobblers" are triggering offenses under the three strikes law only when they are treated as felonies. Under California law, a "wobbler" is presumptively a felony and "remains a felony except when the discretion is actually exercised" to make the crime a misdemeanor. People v. Williams, 27 Cal.2d 220, 229, 163 P.2d 692, 696 (1945) (emphasis deleted and internal quotation marks omitted).

In California, prosecutors may exercise their discretion to charge a "wobbler" as either a felony or a misdemeanor. Likewise, California trial courts have discretion to reduce a "wobbler" charged as a felony to a misdemeanor either before preliminary examination or at sentencing to avoid imposing a three strikes sentence. Cal.Penal Code Ann. §§ 17(b)(5), 17(b)(1) (West 1999); People v. Superior Court of Los Angeles Cty. ex rel. Alvarez, 14 Cal.4th 968, 978, 60 Cal.Rptr.2d 93, 928 P.2d 1171, 1177–1178 (1997). In exercising this discretion, the court may consider "those factors that direct similar sentencing decisions," such as "the nature and circumstances of the offense, the defendant's appreciation of and attitude toward the offense, . . . [and] the general objectives of sentencing." *Ibid.* (internal quotation marks and citations omitted).

California trial courts can also vacate allegations of prior "serious" or "violent" felony convictions, either on motion by the prosecution or *sua sponte. Romero, supra,* at 529–530, 53 Cal.Rptr.2d 789, 917 P.2d, at 647–648. In ruling whether to vacate allegations of prior felony convictions, courts consider whether, "in light of the nature and circumstances of [the defendant's] present felonies and prior serious and/or violent felony convictions, and the particulars of his background, character, and prospects, the defendant may be deemed outside the [three strikes'] scheme's spirit, in whole or in part." *People v. Williams,* 17 Cal.4th 148, 161, 69 Cal.Rptr.2d 917, 948 P.2d 429, 437 (1998). Thus, trial courts may avoid imposing a three strikes sentence in two ways: first, by reducing "wobblers" to misdemeanors (which do not qualify as triggering offenses), and second, by vacating allegations of prior "serious" or "violent" felony convictions.

C

On parole from a 9–year prison term, petitioner Gary Ewing walked into the pro shop of the El Segundo Golf Course in Los Angeles County on March 12, 2000. He walked out with three golf clubs, priced at $399 apiece, concealed in his pants leg. A shop employee, whose suspicions were aroused when he observed Ewing limp out of the pro shop, telephoned the police. The police apprehended Ewing in the parking lot.

Ewing is no stranger to the criminal justice system. In 1984, at the age of 22, he pleaded guilty to theft. The court sentenced him to six months in jail (suspended), three years' probation, and a $300 fine. In 1988, he was convicted of felony grand theft auto and sentenced to one year in jail and three years' probation. After Ewing completed probation, however, the sentencing court reduced the crime to a misdemeanor, permitted Ewing to withdraw his guilty plea, and dismissed the case. In 1990, he was convicted of petty theft with a prior and sentenced to 60 days in the county jail and three years' probation. In 1992, Ewing was convicted of battery and sentenced to 30 days in the county jail and two years' summary probation. One month later, he was convicted of theft and sentenced to 10 days in the county jail and 12 months' probation. In January 1993, Ewing was convicted of burglary and sentenced to 60 days in the county jail and one year's summary probation. In February 1993, he was convicted of possessing drug paraphernalia and sentenced to six months in the county jail and three years' probation. In July 1993, he was convicted of appropriating lost property and sentenced to 10 days in the county jail and two years' summary probation. In September 1993, he was convicted of unlawfully possessing a firearm and trespassing and sentenced to 30 days in the county jail and one year's probation.

In October and November 1993, Ewing committed three burglaries and one robbery at a Long Beach, California, apartment complex over a 5–week period. He awakened one of his victims, asleep on her living room sofa, as he tried to disconnect her video cassette recorder from the television in that room. When she screamed, Ewing ran out the front door. On another occasion, Ewing accosted a victim in the mailroom of the apartment complex. Ewing claimed to have a gun and ordered the victim to hand over his wallet. When the victim resisted, Ewing produced a knife and forced the victim back to the apartment itself. While Ewing rifled through the bedroom, the victim fled the apartment screaming for help. Ewing absconded with the victim's money and credit cards.

On December 9, 1993, Ewing was arrested on the premises of the apartment complex for trespassing and lying to a police officer. The knife used in the robbery and a glass cocaine pipe were later found in the back seat of the patrol car used to transport Ewing to the police station. A jury convicted Ewing of first-degree robbery and three counts of residential burglary. Sentenced to nine years and eight months in prison, Ewing was paroled in 1999.

Only 10 months later, Ewing stole the golf clubs at issue in this case. He was charged with, and ultimately convicted of, one count of felony grand theft of personal property in excess of $400. *See* Cal.Penal Code Ann., § 484 (West Supp.2002); § 489 (West 1999). As required by the three strikes law, the prosecutor formally alleged, and the trial court later found, that Ewing had been convicted previously of four serious or violent felonies for the three burglaries and the robbery in the Long Beach apartment complex. *See* § 667(g) (West 1999); § 1170.12(e) (West Supp.2002).

At the sentencing hearing, Ewing asked the court to reduce the conviction for grand theft, a "wobbler" under California law, to a misdemeanor so as to avoid a three strikes sentence. *See* § 17(b) (West 1999); § 667(d)(1); § 1170.12(b)(1) (West Supp.2002). Ewing also asked the trial court to exercise its discretion to dismiss the allegations of some or all of his prior serious or violent felony convictions, again for purposes of avoiding a three strikes sentence. *See Romero,* 13 Cal.4th, at 529–531, 53 Cal.Rptr.2d 789, 917 P.2d, at 647–648. Before sentencing Ewing, the trial court took note of his entire criminal history, including the fact that he was on parole when he committed his latest offense. The court also heard arguments from defense counsel and a plea from Ewing himself.

In the end, the trial judge determined that the grand theft should remain a felony. The court also ruled that the four prior strikes for the three burglaries and the robbery in Long Beach should stand. As a newly convicted felon with two or more "serious" or "violent" felony convictions in his past, Ewing was sentenced under the three strikes law to 25 years to life.

The California Court of Appeal affirmed in an unpublished opinion.... The Supreme Court of California denied Ewing's petition for review, and we granted certiorari, 535 U.S. 969, 122 S.Ct. 1434, 152 L.Ed.2d 379 (2002). We now affirm.

II

A

The Eighth Amendment, which forbids cruel and unusual punishments, contains a "narrow proportionality principle" that "applies to noncapital sentences." Harmelin v. Michigan, 501 U.S. 957, 996–997, 111 S.Ct. 2680, 115 L.Ed.2d 836 (1991) (KENNEDY, J., concurring in part and concurring in judgment); *cf.* Weems v. United States, 217 U.S. 349, 371, 30 S.Ct. 544, 54 L.Ed. 793 (1910); Robinson v. California, 370 U.S. 660, 667, 82 S.Ct. 1417, 8 L.Ed.2d 758 (1962) (applying the Eighth Amendment to the States via the Fourteenth Amendment). We have most recently addressed the proportionality principle as applied to terms of years in a series of cases beginning with *Rummel v. Estelle, supra.*

In *Rummel,* we held that it did not violate the Eighth Amendment for a State to sentence a three-time offender to life in prison with the possibility of parole. *Id.,* at 284–285, 100 S.Ct. 1133. Like Ewing, Rummel was sentenced to a lengthy prison term under a recidivism statute. Rummel's two prior offenses were a 1964 felony for "fraudulent use of a credit card to obtain $80 worth of goods or services," and a 1969 felony conviction for "passing a forged check in the amount of $28.36." *Id.,* at 265, 100 S.Ct. 1133. His triggering offense was a conviction for felony theft—"obtaining $120.75 by false pretenses." *Id.,* at 266, 100 S.Ct. 1133.

This Court ruled that "[h]aving twice imprisoned him for felonies, Texas was entitled to place upon Rummel the onus of one who is simply unable to bring his conduct within the social norms prescribed by the criminal law of the State." *Id.,* at 284, 100 S.Ct. 1133. The recidivism statute "is nothing more than a societal decision that when such a person commits yet another felony, he should be subjected to the admittedly serious penalty of incarceration for life, subject only to the State's judgment as to whether to grant him parole." *Id.,* at 278, 100 S.Ct. 1133. We noted that this Court "has on occasion stated that the Eighth Amendment prohibits imposition of a sentence that is grossly disproportionate to the severity of the crime." *Id.,* at 271, 100 S.Ct. 1133. But "[o]utside the context of capital punishment, successful challenges to the proportionality of particular sentences have been exceedingly rare." *Id.,* at 272, 100 S.Ct. 1133. Although we stated that the proportionality principle "would . . . come into play in the extreme example . . . if a legislature made overtime parking a felony punishable by life imprisonment," *id.,* at 274, n. 11, 100 S.Ct. 1133, we held that "the mandatory life sentence imposed upon this petitioner does not constitute cruel and unusual punishment under the Eighth and Fourteenth Amendments" *id.,* at 285, 100 S.Ct. 1133.

In Hutto v. Davis, 454 U.S. 370, 102 S.Ct. 703, 70 L.Ed.2d 556 (1982) *(per curiam),* the defendant was sentenced to two consecutive terms of 20 years in prison for possession with intent to distribute nine ounces of marijuana and distribution of marijuana. We held that such a sentence was constitutional: "In short, *Rummel* stands for the proposition that federal courts should be reluctant to review legislatively mandated terms of imprisonment, and that successful challenges to the proportionality of particular sentences should be exceedingly rare." *Id.,* at 374, 102 S.Ct. 703 (citations and internal quotation marks omitted).

Three years after *Rummel,* in Solem v. Helm, 463 U.S. 277, 279, 103 S.Ct. 3001, 77 L.Ed.2d 637 (1983), we held that the Eighth Amendment prohibited "a life sentence without possibility of parole for a seventh nonviolent felony." The triggering offense in *Solem* was "uttering a 'no account' check for $100." *Id.,* at 281, 103 S.Ct. 3001. We specifically stated that the Eighth Amendment's ban on cruel and unusual punishments "prohibits . . . sentences that are disproportionate to the crime committed," and that the "constitutional principle of proportionality has been recognized explicitly in this Court for almost a century." *Id.,* at 284, 286,

103 S.Ct. 3001. The *Solem* Court then explained that three factors may be relevant to a determination of whether a sentence is so disproportionate that it violates the Eighth Amendment: "(i) the gravity of the offense and the harshness of the penalty; (ii) the sentences imposed on other criminals in the same jurisdiction; and (iii) the sentences imposed for commission of the same crime in other jurisdictions." *Id.*, at 292, 103 S.Ct. 3001.

Applying these factors in *Solem*, we struck down the defendant's sentence of life without parole. We specifically noted the contrast between that sentence and the sentence in *Rummel*, pursuant to which the defendant was eligible for parole. 463 U.S., at 297, 103 S.Ct. 3001; *see also id.*, at 300, 103 S.Ct. 3001 ("[T]he South Dakota commutation system is fundamentally different from the parole system that was before us in *Rummel*"). Indeed, we explicitly declined to overrule *Rummel*: "[O]ur conclusion today is not inconsistent with *Rummel v. Estelle*." 463 U.S., at 303, n. 32, 103 S.Ct. 3001; *see also id.*, at 288, n. 13, 103 S.Ct. 3001 ("[O]ur decision is entirely consistent with this Court's prior cases—including *Rummel v. Estelle*").

Eight years after *Solem*, we grappled with the proportionality issue again in *Harmelin, supra. Harmelin* was not a recidivism case, but rather involved a first-time offender convicted of possessing 672 grams of cocaine. He was sentenced to life in prison without possibility of parole. A majority of the Court rejected Harmelin's claim that his sentence was so grossly disproportionate that it violated the Eighth Amendment. The Court, however, could not agree on why his proportionality argument failed. Justice SCALIA, joined by THE CHIEF JUSTICE, wrote that the proportionality principle was "an aspect of our death penalty jurisprudence, rather than a generalizable aspect of Eighth Amendment law." *Id.*, at 994, 111 S.Ct. 2680. He would thus have declined to apply gross disproportionality principles except in reviewing capital sentences. *Ibid.*

Justice KENNEDY, joined by two other Members of the Court, concurred in part and concurred in the judgment. Justice KENNEDY specifically recognized that "[t]he Eighth Amendment proportionality principle also applies to noncapital sentences." *Id.*, at 997, 111 S.Ct. 2680. He then identified four principles of proportionality review—"the primacy of the legislature, the variety of legitimate penological schemes, the nature of our federal system, and the requirement that proportionality review be guided by objective factors"—that "inform the final one: The Eighth Amendment does not require strict proportionality between crime and sentence. Rather, it forbids only extreme sentences that are 'grossly disproportionate' to the crime." *Id.*, at 1001, 111 S.Ct. 2680 (citing *Solem, supra*, at 288, 103 S.Ct. 3001). Justice KENNEDY's concurrence also stated that *Solem* "did not mandate" comparative analysis "within and between jurisdictions." 501 U.S., at 1004–1005, 111 S.Ct. 2680.

The proportionality principles in our cases distilled in Justice KENNEDY's concurrence guide our application of the Eighth Amendment in the new context that we are called upon to consider.

B

For many years, most States have had laws providing for enhanced sentencing of repeat offenders. *See, e.g.*, U.S. Dept. of Justice, Bureau of

Justice Assistance, National Assessment of Structured Sentencing (1996). Yet between 1993 and 1995, three strikes laws effected a sea change in criminal sentencing throughout the Nation.[52] These laws responded to widespread public concerns about crime by targeting the class of offenders who pose the greatest threat to public safety: career criminals. As one of the chief architects of California's three strikes law has explained: "Three Strikes was intended to go beyond simply making sentences tougher. It was intended to be a focused effort to create a sentencing policy that would use the judicial system to reduce serious and violent crime." Ardaiz, California's Three Strikes Law: History, Expectations, Consequences 32 McGeorge L.Rev. 1, 12 (2000) (hereinafter Ardaiz).

Throughout the States, legislatures enacting three strikes laws made a deliberate policy choice that individuals who have repeatedly engaged in serious or violent criminal behavior, and whose conduct has not been deterred by more conventional approaches to punishment, must be isolated from society in order to protect the public safety. Though three strikes laws may be relatively new, our tradition of deferring to state legislatures in making and implementing such important policy decisions is longstanding. *Weems,* 217 U.S., at 379, 30 S.Ct. 544; Gore v. United States, 357 U.S. 386, 393, 78 S.Ct. 1280, 2 L.Ed.2d 1405 (1958); Payne v. Tennessee, 501 U.S. 808, 824, 111 S.Ct. 2597, 115 L.Ed.2d 720 (1991); *Rummel,* U.S., at 274; *Solem,* 463 U.S., at 290, 103 S.Ct. 3001; *Harmelin,* 501 U.S., at 998, 111 S.Ct. 2680 (KENNEDY, J., concurring in part and concurring in judgment).

Our traditional deference to legislative policy choices finds a corollary in the principle that the Constitution "does not mandate adoption of any one penological theory." *Id.,* at 999, 111 S.Ct. 2680 (KENNEDY, J., concurring in part and concurring in judgment). A sentence can have a variety of justifications, such as incapacitation, deterrence, retribution, or rehabilitation. *See* 1 W. LaFave & A. Scott, Substantive Criminal Law § 1.5, pp. 30–36 (1986) (explaining theories of punishment). Some or all of these justifications may play a role in a State's sentencing scheme. Selecting the sentencing rationales is generally a policy choice to be made by state legislatures, not federal courts.

When the California Legislature enacted the three strikes law, it made a judgment that protecting the public safety requires incapacitating criminals who have already been convicted of at least one serious or violent crime. Nothing in the Eighth Amendment prohibits California from making that choice. To the contrary, our cases establish that "States have a valid interest in deterring and segregating habitual criminals." Parke v. Raley, 506 U.S. 20, 27, 113 S.Ct. 517, 121 L.Ed.2d 391 1992); Oyler v. Boles, 368 U.S. 448, 451, 82 S.Ct. 501, 7 L.Ed.2d 446 (1962) ("[T]he constitutionality of the practice of inflicting severer criminal penalties upon habitual offenders is no longer open to serious challenge"). Recidivism has long been recognized as a legitimate basis for increased punishment. *See* Almendarez–

---

52. It is hardly surprising that the statistics relied upon by Justice BREYER show that prior to the enactment of the three strikes law, "*no* one like Ewing could have served more than *10* years in prison." *Post,* at 1197 (dissenting opinion). Profound disappointment with the perceived lenity of criminal sentencing (especially for repeat felons) led to passage of three strikes laws in the first place. *See, e.g.,* Review of State Legislation 1.

Torres v. United States, 523 U.S. 224, 230, 118 S.Ct. 1219, 140 L.Ed.2d 350 (1998) (recidivism "is as typical a sentencing factor as one might imagine"); Witte v. United States, 515 U.S. 389, 399, 115 S.Ct. 2199, 132 L.Ed.2d 351 (1995) ("In repeatedly upholding such recidivism statutes, we have rejected double jeopardy challenges because the enhanced punishment imposed for the later offense ... [is] 'a stiffened penalty for the latest crime, which is considered to be an aggravated offense because a repetitive one' " (quoting Gryger v. Burke, 334 U.S. 728, 732, 68 S.Ct. 1256, 92 L.Ed. 1683 (1948))).

California's justification is no pretext. Recidivism is a serious public safety concern in California and throughout the Nation. According to a recent report, approximately 67 percent of former inmates released from state prisons were charged with at least one "serious" new crime within three years of their release. *See* U.S. Dept. of Justice, Bureau of Justice Statistics, P. Langan & D. Levin, Special Report: Recidivism of Prisoners Released in 1994, p. 1 (June 2002). In particular, released property offenders like Ewing had higher recidivism rates than those released after committing violent, drug, or public-order offenses. *Id.,* at 8. Approximately 73 percent of the property offenders released in 1994 were arrested again within three years, compared to approximately 61 percent of the violent offenders, 62 percent of the public-order offenders, and 66 percent of the drug offenders. *Ibid.*

In 1996, when the Sacramento Bee studied 233 three strikes offenders in California, it found that they had an aggregate of 1,165 prior felony convictions, an average of 5 apiece. *See* Furillo, Three Strikes—The Verdict's In: Most Offenders Have Long Criminal Histories, Sacramento Bee, Mar. 31, 1996, p. A1. The prior convictions included 322 robberies and 262 burglaries. *Ibid.* About 84 percent of the 233 three strikes offenders had been convicted of at least one violent crime. *Ibid.* In all, they were responsible for 17 homicides, 7 attempted slayings, and 91 sexual assaults and child molestations. *Ibid.* The Sacramento Bee concluded, based on its investigation, that "[i]n the vast majority of the cases, regardless of the third strike, the [three strikes] law is snaring [the] long-term habitual offenders with multiple felony convictions...." *Ibid.*

The State's interest in deterring crime also lends some support to the three strikes law. We have long viewed both incapacitation and deterrence as rationales for recidivism statutes: "[A] recidivist statute['s] ... primary goals are to deter repeat offenders and, at some point in the life of one who repeatedly commits criminal offenses serious enough to be punished as felonies, to segregate that person from the rest of society for an extended period of time." *Rummel, supra,* at 284, 100 S.Ct. 1133. Four years after the passage of California's three strikes law, the recidivism rate of parolees returned to prison for the commission of a new crime dropped by nearly 25 percent. California Dept. of Justice, Office of the Attorney General, "Three Strikes and You're Out"—Its Impact on the California Criminal Justice System After Four Years 10 (1998). Even more dramatically:

"[a]n unintended but positive consequence of 'Three Strikes' has been the impact on parolees leaving the state. More California parolees are now leaving the state than parolees from other jurisdictions entering California.

This striking turnaround started in 1994. It was the first time more parolees left the state than entered since 1976. This trend has continued and in 1997 more than 1,000 net parolees left California." *Ibid.*

See also Janiskee & Erler, Crime, Punishment, and Romero: An Analysis of the Case Against California's Three Strikes Law, 39 Duquesne L.Rev. 43, 45–46 ("Prosecutors in Los Angeles routinely report that 'felons tell them they are moving out of the state because they fear getting a second or third strike for a nonviolent offense.' ") (quoting Sanchez, A Movement Builds Against "Three Strikes" Law, Washington Post, Feb. 18, 2000, p. A3).

To be sure, California's three strikes law has sparked controversy. Critics have doubted the law's wisdom, cost-efficiency, and effectiveness in reaching its goals. *See, e.g.,* Zimring, Hawkins, & Kamin, Punishment and Democracy: Three Strikes and You're Out in California (2001); Vitiello, Three Strikes: Can We Return to Rationality?, 87 J.Crim. L. & C. 395, 423 (1997). This criticism is appropriately directed at the legislature, which has primary responsibility for making the difficult policy choices that underlie any criminal sentencing scheme. We do not sit as a "superlegislature" to second-guess these policy choices. It is enough that the State of California has a reasonable basis for believing that dramatically enhanced sentences for habitual felons "advance[s] the goals of [its] criminal justice system in any substantial way." *See Solem,* 463 U.S., at 297, n. 22, 103 S.Ct. 3001.

III

Against this backdrop, we consider Ewing's claim that his three strikes sentence of 25 years to life is unconstitutionally disproportionate to his offense of "shoplifting three golf clubs." Brief for Petitioner 6. We first address the gravity of the offense compared to the harshness of the penalty. At the threshold, we note that Ewing incorrectly frames the issue. The gravity of his offense was not merely "shoplifting three golf clubs." Rather, Ewing was convicted of felony grand theft for stealing nearly $1,200 worth of merchandise after previously having been convicted of at least two "violent" or "serious" felonies. Even standing alone, Ewing's theft should not be taken lightly. His crime was certainly not "one of the most passive felonies a person could commit." *Solem, supra,* at 296, 103 S.Ct. 3001 (internal quotation marks omitted). To the contrary, the Supreme Court of California has noted the "seriousness" of grand theft in the context of proportionality review. *See In re Lynch,* 8 Cal.3d 410, 432, n. 20, 105 Cal.Rptr. 217, 503 P.2d 921, 936, n. 20 (1972). Theft of $1,200 in property is a felony under federal law, 18 U.S.C. § 641, and in the vast majority of States. *See* App. B to Brief for Petitioner 21a.

That grand theft is a "wobbler" under California law is of no moment. Though California courts have discretion to reduce a felony grand theft charge to a misdemeanor, it remains a felony for all purposes "unless and until the trial court imposes a misdemeanor sentence." *In re Anderson,* 69 Cal.2d 613, 626, 73 Cal.Rptr. 21, 447 P.2d 117, 152 (1968) (Tobriner, J., concurring); *see generally* 1 B. Witkin & N. Epstein, California Criminal Law § 73 (3d ed.2000). "The purpose of the trial judge's sentencing discretion" to downgrade certain felonies is to "impose a misdemeanor sentence in those cases in which the rehabilitation of the convicted defendant either does not require or would be adversely affected by, incarceration in a state prison as a felon." *Anderson, supra,* at 664–665, 73 Cal.Rptr. 21, 447 P.2d, at 152 (Tobriner, J., concurring). Under California law, the reduction is not based on the notion that a "wobbler" is "conceptually a misdemeanor." Necochea v. Superior Court, 23 Cal.App.3d 1012, 1016, 100 Cal.Rptr. 693, 695 (1972). Rather, it is "intended to extend misdemeanant treatment to a potential felon." *Ibid.* In Ewing's case, however, the trial judge justifiably exercised her discretion not to extend such lenient treatment given Ewing's long criminal history.

In weighing the gravity of Ewing's offense, we must place on the scales not only his current felony, but also his long history of felony recidivism. Any other approach would fail to accord proper deference to the policy judgments that find expression in the legislature's choice of sanctions. In imposing a three strikes sentence, the State's interest is not merely punishing the offense of conviction, or the "triggering" offense: "[I]t is in addition the interest . . . in dealing in a harsher manner with those who by repeated criminal acts have shown that they are simply incapable of conforming to the norms of society as established by its criminal law." *See Rummel,* 445 U.S., at 276, 100 S.Ct. 1133; *Solem, supra,* at 296, 103 S.Ct. 3001. To give full effect to the State's choice of this legitimate penological goal, our proportionality review of Ewing's sentence must take that goal into account.

Ewing's sentence is justified by the State's public-safety interest in incapacitating and deterring recidivist felons, and amply supported by his own long, serious criminal record. Ewing has been convicted of numerous misdemeanor and felony offenses, served nine separate terms of incarceration, and committed most of his crimes while on probation or parole. His prior "strikes" were serious felonies including robbery and three residential burglaries. To be sure, Ewing's sentence is a long one. But it reflects a rational legislative judgment, entitled to deference, that offenders who have committed serious or violent felonies and who continue to commit felonies must be incapacitated. The State of California "was entitled to place upon [Ewing] the onus of one who is simply unable to bring his conduct within the social norms prescribed by the criminal law of the State." *Rummel, supra,* at 284, 100 S.Ct. 1133. Ewing's is not "the rare case in which a threshold comparison of the crime committed and the sentence imposed leads to an inference of gross disproportionality." *Harmelin,* 501 U.S., at 1005, 111 S.Ct. 2680 (KENNEDY, J., concurring in part and concurring in judgment).

We hold that Ewing's sentence of 25 years to life in prison, imposed for the offense of felony grand theft under the three strikes law, is not grossly disproportionate and therefore does not violate the Eighth Amendment's prohibition on cruel and unusual punishments. The judgment of the California Court of Appeal is affirmed.

It is so ordered.

■ JUSTICE SCALIA, concurring in the judgment.

In my concurring opinion in Harmelin v. Michigan, 501 U.S. 957, 984, 985, 111 S.Ct. 2680, 115 L.Ed.2d 836 (1991), I concluded that the Eighth

Amendment's prohibition of "cruel and unusual punishments" was aimed at excluding only certain *modes* of punishment, and was not a "guarantee against disproportionate sentences." Out of respect for the principle of *stare decisis,* I might nonetheless accept the contrary holding of Solem v. Helm, 463 U.S. 277, 103 S.Ct. 3001, 77 L.Ed.2d 637 (1983)—that the Eighth Amendment contains a narrow proportionality principle—if I felt I could intelligently apply it. This case demonstrates why I cannot.

Proportionality—the notion that the punishment should fit the crime—is inherently a concept tied to the penological goal of retribution. "[I]t becomes difficult even to speak intelligently of 'proportionality,' once deterrence and rehabilitation are given significant weight," *Harmelin, supra,* at 989, 111 S.Ct. 2680—not to mention giving weight to the purpose of California's three strikes law: incapacitation. In the present case, the game is up once the plurality has acknowledged that "the Constitution does not mandate adoption of any one penological theory," and that a "sentence can have a variety of justifications, such as incapacitation, deterrence, retribution, or rehabilitation." *Ante,* at 1187 (internal quotation marks omitted). That acknowledgment having been made, it no longer suffices merely to assess "the gravity of the offense compared to the harshness of the penalty," *ante,* at 1189; that classic description of the proportionality principle (alone and in itself quite resistant to policy-free, legal analysis) now becomes merely the "first" step of the inquiry, *ibid.* Having completed that step (by a discussion which, in all fairness, does not convincingly establish that 25–years-to-life is a "proportionate" punishment for stealing three golf clubs), the plurality must then *add* an analysis to show that "Ewing's sentence is justified by the State's public-safety interest in incapacitating and deterring recidivist felons." *Ante,* at 1190.

Which indeed it is—though why that has anything to do with the principle of proportionality is a mystery. Perhaps the plurality should revise its terminology, so that what it reads into the Eighth Amendment is not the unstated proposition that all punishment should be reasonably proportionate to the gravity of the offense, but rather the unstated proposition that all punishment should reasonably pursue the multiple purposes of the criminal law. That formulation would make it clearer than ever, of course, that the plurality is not applying law but evaluating policy.

Because I agree that petitioner's sentence does not violate the Eighth Amendment's prohibition against cruel and unusual punishments, I concur in the judgment.

■ JUSTICE THOMAS, concurring in the judgment.

I agree with Justice SCALIA's view that the proportionality test announced in Solem v. Helm, 463 U.S. 277, 103 S.Ct. 3001, 77 L.Ed.2d 637 (1983), is incapable of judicial application. Even were *Solem*'s test perfectly clear, however, I would not feel compelled by *stare decisis* to apply it. In my view, the Cruel and Unusual Punishments Clause of the Eighth Amendment contains no proportionality principle. *See* Harmelin v. Michigan, 501 U.S. 957, 967–985, 111 S.Ct. 2680, 115 L.Ed.2d 836 (1991) (opinion of SCALIA, J.).

Because the plurality concludes that petitioner's sentence does not violate the Eighth Amendment's prohibition on cruel and unusual punishments, I concur in the judgment.

■ JUSTICE STEVENS, with whom JUSTICE SOUTER, JUSTICE GINSBURG and JUSTICE BREYER join, dissenting.

JUSTICE BREYER has cogently explained why the sentence imposed in this case is both cruel and unusual.[53] The concurrences prompt this separate writing to emphasize that proportionality review is not only capable of judicial application but also required by the Eighth Amendment.

"The Eighth Amendment succinctly prohibits 'excessive' sanctions." Atkins v. Virginia, 536 U.S. 304, 311, 122 S.Ct. 2242, 153 L.Ed.2d 335 (2002); see also U.S. Const., Amdt. 8 ("Excessive bail shall not be required, nor excessive fines imposed, nor cruel and unusual punishments inflicted"). Faithful to the Amendment's text, this Court has held that the Constitution directs judges to apply their best judgment in determining the proportionality of fines, see, e.g., United States v. Bajakajian, 524 U.S. 321, 334–336, 118 S.Ct. 2028, 141 L.Ed.2d 314 (1998), bail, see, e.g., Stack v. Boyle, 342 U.S. 1, 5, 72 S.Ct. 1, 96 L.Ed. 3 (1951), and other forms of punishment, including the imposition of a death sentence, see, e.g., Coker v. Georgia, 433 U.S. 584, 592, 97 S.Ct. 2861, 53 L.Ed.2d 982 (1977). It "would be anomalous indeed" to suggest that the Eighth Amendment makes proportionality review applicable in the context of bail and fines but not in the context of other forms of punishment, such as imprisonment. Solem v. Helm, 463 U.S. 277, 289, 103 S.Ct. 3001, 77 L.Ed.2d 637 (1983). Rather, by broadly prohibiting excessive sanctions, the Eighth Amendment directs judges to exercise their wise judgment in assessing the proportionality of all forms of punishment.

The absence of a black-letter rule does not disable judges from exercising their discretion in construing the outer limits on sentencing authority that the Eighth Amendment imposes. After all, judges are "constantly called upon to draw ... lines in a variety of contexts," id., at 294, 103 S.Ct. 3001, and to exercise their judgment to give meaning to the Constitution's broadly phrased protections. For example, the Due Process Clause directs judges to employ proportionality review in assessing the constitutionality of punitive damages awards on a case-by-case basis. See, e.g., BMW of North America, Inc. v. Gore, 517 U.S. 559, 562, 116 S.Ct. 1589, 134 L.Ed.2d 809 (1996). Also, although the Sixth Amendment guarantees criminal defendants the right to a speedy trial, the courts often are asked to determine on a case-by-case basis whether a particular delay is constitutionally permissi-

---

53. For "present purposes," *post* at 1194, 1202 (dissenting opinion), Justice BREYER applies the framework established by Harmelin v. Michigan, 501 U.S. 957, 1004–1005, 111 S.Ct. 2680, 115 L.Ed.2d 836 (1991), in analyzing Ewing's Eighth Amendment claim. I agree with Justice BREYER that Ewing's sentence is grossly disproportionate even under *Harmelin*'s narrow proportionality framework. However, it is not clear that this case is controlled by *Harmelin*, which considered the proportionality of a life sentence imposed on a drug offender who had *no* prior felony convictions. Rather, the three-factor analysis established in Solem v. Helm, 463 U.S. 277, 290–291, 103 S.Ct. 3001, 77 L.Ed.2d 637 (1983), which specifically addressed recidivist sentencing, seems more directly on point.

ble or not. *See, e.g.,* Doggett v. United States, 505 U.S. 647, 112 S.Ct. 2686, 120 L.Ed.2d 520 (1992).

Throughout most of the Nation's history—before guideline sentencing became so prevalent—federal and state trial judges imposed specific sentences pursuant to grants of authority that gave them uncabined discretion within broad ranges. *See* K. Stith & J. Cabranes, Fear of Judging: Sentencing Guidelines in the Federal Courts 9 (1998) (hereinafter Stith & Cabranes) ("From the beginning of the Republic, federal judges were entrusted with wide sentencing discretion"); *see also* Mistretta v. United States, 488 U.S. 361, 364, 109 S.Ct. 647, 102 L.Ed.2d 714 (1989). It was not unheard of for a statute to authorize a sentence ranging from one year to life, for example. *See,* e.g., State v. Perley, 86 Me. 427, 30 A. 74, 75 (1894) (citing Maine statute that made robbery punishable by imprisonment for life or any term of years); In re Southard, 298 Mich. 75, 77, 298 N.W. 457 (1941) ("The offense of 'robbery armed' is punishable by imprisonment for life or any term of years"). In exercising their discretion, sentencing judges wisely employed a proportionality principle that took into account all of the justifications for punishment—namely, deterrence, incapacitation, retribution and rehabilitation. See Stith & Cabranes 14. Likewise, I think it clear that the Eighth Amendment's prohibition of "cruel and unusual punishments" expresses a broad and basic proportionality principle that takes into account all of the justifications for penal sanctions. It is this broad proportionality principle that would preclude reliance on any of the justifications for punishment to support, for example, a life sentence for overtime parking. *See* Rummel v. Estelle, 445 U.S. 263, 274, n. 11, 100 S.Ct. 1133, 63 L.Ed.2d 382 (1980).

Accordingly, I respectfully dissent.

■ Justice Breyer, with whom Justice Stevens, Justice Souter, and Justice Ginsburg join, dissenting.

The constitutional question is whether the "three strikes" sentence imposed by California upon repeat-offender Gary Ewing is "grossly disproportionate" to his crime. *Ante,* at 1185, 1190 (plurality opinion). The sentence amounts to a real prison term of at least 25 years. The sentence-triggering criminal conduct consists of the theft of three golf clubs priced at a total of $1,197. *See ante,* at 1184. The offender has a criminal history that includes four felony convictions arising out of three separate burglaries (one armed). *Ante,* at 1184. In Solem v. Helm, 463 U.S. 277, 103 S.Ct. 3001, 77 L.Ed.2d 637 (1983), the Court found grossly disproportionate a somewhat longer sentence imposed on a recidivist offender for triggering criminal conduct that was somewhat less severe. In my view, the differences are not determinative, and the Court should reach the same ultimate conclusion here.

I

This Court's precedent sets forth a framework for analyzing Ewing's Eighth Amendment claim ...

The plurality applies Justice KENNEDY's analytical framework in *Harmelin, supra,* at 1004–1005, 111 S.Ct. 2680 (opinion concurring in part and concurring in judgment). *Ante,* at 1186–1187. And, for present purposes, I will consider Ewing's Eighth Amendment claim on those terms. *But see ante,* at 1191, n. 1 (STEVENS, J., dissenting). To implement this approach, courts faced with a "gross disproportionality" claim must first make "a threshold comparison of the crime committed and the sentence imposed." *Harmelin, supra,* at 1005, 111 S.Ct. 2680 (KENNEDY, J., concurring in part and concurring in judgment). If a claim crosses that threshold—itself a *rare* occurrence—then the court should compare the sentence at issue to other sentences "imposed on other criminals" in the same, or in other, jurisdictions. *Solem, supra,* at 290–291, 103 S.Ct. 3001; *Harmelin, supra,* at 1005, 111 S.Ct. 2680 (KENNEDY, J., concurring in part and concurring in judgment). The comparative analysis will "validate" or invalidate "an initial judgment that a sentence is grossly disproportionate to a crime." *Ibid.*

I recognize the warnings implicit in the Court's frequent repetition of words such as "rare." Nonetheless I believe that the case before us is a "rare" case—one in which a court can say with reasonable confidence that the punishment is "grossly disproportionate" to the crime.

II

Ewing's claim crosses the gross disproportionality "threshold." First, precedent makes clear that Ewing's sentence raises a serious disproportionality question. Ewing is a recidivist. Hence the two cases most directly in point are those in which the Court considered the constitutionality of recidivist sentencing: *Rummel* and *Solem.* Ewing's claim falls between these two cases. It is stronger than the claim presented in *Rummel,* where the Court upheld a recidivist's sentence as constitutional. It is weaker than the claim presented in *Solem,* where the Court struck down a recidivist sentence as unconstitutional.

Three kinds of sentence-related characteristics define the relevant comparative spectrum: (a) the length of the prison term in real time, *i.e.,* the time that the offender is likely actually to spend in prison; (b) the sentence-triggering criminal conduct, *i.e.,* the offender's actual behavior or other offense-related circumstances; and (c) the offender's criminal history. *See Rummel, supra,* at 265–266, 269, 276, 278, 280–281, 100 S.Ct. 1133 (using these factors); *Solem, supra,* at 290–303, 103 S.Ct. 3001 (same). *Cf.* United States Sentencing Commission, Guidelines Manual ch. 1, pt. A, intro., n. 5 (Nov.1987) (USSG) (empirical study of "summary reports of some 40,000 convictions [and] a sample of 10,000 augmented presentence reports" leads to sentences based primarily upon (a) offense characteristics and (b) offender's criminal record); *see id.,* p. s. 3.

In *Rummel,* the Court held constitutional (a) a sentence of life imprisonment *with parole available within 10 to 12 years,* (b) for the offense of obtaining $120 by false pretenses, (c) committed by an offender with two prior felony convictions (involving small amounts of money). 445 U.S., at 263, 100 S.Ct. 1133; *ante,* at 1185–1186. In *Solem,* the Court held unconstitutional (a) a sentence of life imprisonment *without parole,* (b) for the crime of writing a $100 check on a nonexistent bank account, (c) committed by an offender with six prior felony convictions (including three for burglary). 463 U.S., at 277, 103 S.Ct. 3001; *ante,* at 1186. Which of the three pertinent comparative factors made the constitutional difference?

The third factor, prior record, cannot explain the difference. The offender's prior record was *worse* in *Solem,* where the Court found the sentence too long, than in *Rummel,* where the Court upheld the sentence. The second factor, offense conduct, cannot explain the difference. The nature of the triggering offense—viewed in terms of the actual monetary loss—in the two cases was about the same. The one critical factor that explains the difference in the outcome is the length of the likely prison term measured in real time. In *Rummel,* where the Court upheld the sentence, the state sentencing statute authorized parole for the offender, Rummel, after 10 or 12 years. 445 U.S., at 280, 100 S.Ct. 1133; *id.,* at 293, 100 S.Ct. 1133 (Powell, J., dissenting). In *Solem,* where the Court struck down the sentence, the sentence required the offender, Helm, to spend the rest of his life in prison.

Now consider the present case. The third factor, *offender characteristics—i.e.,* prior record—does not differ significantly here from that in *Solem.* Ewing's prior record consists of four prior felony convictions (involving three burglaries, one with a knife) contrasted with Helm's six prior felony convictions (including three burglaries, though none with weapons). The second factor, *offense behavior,* is worse than that in *Solem,* but only to a degree. It would be difficult to say that the actual behavior itself here (shoplifting) differs significantly from that at issue in *Solem* (passing a bad check) or in *Rummel* (obtaining money through false pretenses). Rather the difference lies in the *value* of the goods obtained. That difference, measured in terms of the most relevant feature (loss to the victim, *i.e.,* wholesale value) and adjusted for the irrelevant feature of inflation, comes down (in 1979 values) to about \$379 here compared with \$100 in *Solem,* or (in 1973 values) to \$232 here compared with \$120.75 in *Rummel. See* USSG § 2B1.1, comment., n. 2(A)(i) (Nov.2002) (loss to victim properly measures value of goods unlawfully taken); U.S. Dept. of Labor, Bureau of Labor Statistics, Inflation and Consumer Spending, Inflation Calculator (Jan. 23, 2003), http://www.bls.gov. Alternatively, if one measures the inflation-adjusted value difference in terms of the golf clubs' sticker price, it comes down to \$505 here compared to \$100 in *Solem,* or \$309 here compared to \$120.75 in *Rummel. See ibid.*

The difference in *length* of the real prison term—the first, and critical, factor in *Solem* and *Rummel*—is considerably more important. Ewing's sentence here amounts, in real terms, to at least 25 years without parole or good-time credits. That sentence is considerably shorter than Helm's sentence in *Solem,* which amounted, in real terms, to life in prison. Nonetheless Ewing's real prison term is more than twice as long as the term at issue in *Rummel,* which amounted, in real terms, to at least 10 or 12 years. And, Ewing's sentence, unlike Rummel's (but like Helm's sentence in *Solem*), is long enough to consume the productive remainder of almost any offender's life. (It means that Ewing himself, seriously ill when sentenced at age 38, will likely die in prison.)

The upshot is that the length of the real prison term—the factor that explains the *Solem/Rummel* difference in outcome—places Ewing closer to

Solem than to *Rummel,* though the greater value of the golf clubs that Ewing stole moves Ewing's case back slightly in *Rummel*'s direction. Overall, the comparison places Ewing's sentence well within the twilight zone between *Solem* and *Rummel*—a zone where the argument for unconstitutionality is substantial, where the cases themselves cannot determine the constitutional outcome.

Second, Ewing's sentence on its face imposes one of the most severe punishments available upon a recidivist who subsequently engaged in one of the less serious forms of criminal conduct. *See infra,* at 1198–1199. I do not deny the seriousness of shoplifting, which an *amicus curiae* tells us costs retailers in the range of $30 billion annually. Brief for California District Attorneys Association as *Amicus Curiae* 27. But consider that conduct in terms of the factors that this Court mentioned in *Solem*—the "harm caused or threatened to the victim or society," the "absolute magnitude of the crime," and the offender's "culpability." 463 U.S., at 292–293, 103 S.Ct. 3001. In respect to all three criteria, the sentence-triggering behavior here....

Ewing's "gross disproportionality" argument is a strong one. That being so, his claim *must* pass the "threshold" test. If it did not, what would be the function of the test? A threshold test must permit *arguably* unconstitutional sentences, not only *actually* unconstitutional sentences, to pass the threshold—at least where the arguments for unconstitutionality are unusually strong ones. A threshold test that blocked every ultimately invalid constitutional claim—even strong ones—would not be a *threshold* test but a *determinative* test. And, it would be a *determinative* test that failed to take account of highly pertinent sentencing information, namely, comparison with other sentences, *Solem, supra,* at 291–292, 298–300, 103 S.Ct. 3001. Sentencing comparisons are particularly important because they provide proportionality review with *objective* content. By way of contrast, a threshold test makes the assessment of constitutionality highly subjective. And, of course, so to transform that *threshold* test would violate this Court's earlier precedent. *See* 463 U.S., at 290, 291–292, 103 S.Ct. 3001; *Harmelin, supra,* at 1000, 1005, 111 S.Ct. 2680 (KENNEDY, J., concurring in part and concurring in judgment).

III

Believing Ewing's argument a strong one, sufficient to pass the threshold, I turn to the comparative analysis. A comparison of Ewing's sentence with other sentences requires answers to two questions. First, how would other jurisdictions (or California at other times, *i.e.,* without the three strikes penalty) punish the *same offense conduct?* Second, upon what other conduct would other jurisdictions (or California) impose the *same prison term?* Moreover, since hypothetical punishment is beside the point, the relevant prison time, for comparative purposes, is *real* prison time, *i.e.,* the time that an offender must *actually serve.*

Sentencing statutes often shed little light upon real prison time. That is because sentencing laws normally set *maximum* sentences, giving the sentencing judge discretion to choose an actual sentence within a broad range, and because many States provide good-time credits and parole, often permitting release after, say, one-third of the sentence has been served, *see, e.g.,* Alaska Stat. § 33.20.010(a) (2000); Conn. Gen.Stat. § 18–7a (1998). Thus, the statutory maximum is rarely the sentence imposed, and the sentence imposed is rarely the sentence that is served. For the most part, the parties' briefs discuss sentencing statutes. Nonetheless, that discussion, along with other readily available information, validates my initial belief that Ewing's sentence, comparatively speaking, is extreme.

As to California itself, we know the following: First, between the end of World War II and 1994 (when California enacted the three strikes law, *ante,* at 1182), *no one* like Ewing could have served more than *10* years in prison. We know that for certain because the maximum sentence for Ewing's crime of conviction, grand theft, was for most of that period 10 years. Cal.Penal Code Ann. §§ 484, 489 (West 1970); *see* Cal. Dept. of Corrections, Offender Information Services, Administrative Services Division, Historical Data for Time Served by Male Felons Paroled from Institutions: 1945 Through 1981, p. 11 (1982) (Table 10) (hereinafter Historical Data for Time Served by California Felons), Lodging of Petitioner. From 1976 to 1994 (and currently, absent application of the three strikes penalty), a Ewing-type offender would have received a maximum sentence of 4 years. Cal.Penal Code Ann. § 489 (West 1999), § 667.5(b) (West Supp. 2002). And we know that California's "habitual offender" laws did not apply to grand theft. §§ 644(a), (b) (West 1970) (repealed 1977). We also know that the time that any offender actually served was likely far less than 10 years. This is because statistical data shows that the median time actually served for grand theft (other than auto theft) was about two years, and 90 percent of all those convicted of that crime served less than three or four years. Historical Data for Time Served by California Felons 11 (Table 10).

Second, statistics suggest that recidivists *of all sorts* convicted during that same time period in California served a small fraction of Ewing's real-time sentence. On average, recidivists served three to four additional (recidivist-related) years in prison, with 90 percent serving less than an additional real seven to eight years. *Id.,* at 22 (Table 21).

Third, we know that California has reserved, and still reserves, Ewing-type prison time, *i.e.,* at least 25 real years in prison, for criminals convicted of crimes far worse than was Ewing's. Statistics for the years 1945 to 1981, for example, indicate that typical (nonrecidivist) male first-degree murderers served between 10 and 15 real years in prison, with 90 percent of all such murderers serving less than 20 real years. *Id.,* at 3 (Table 2). Moreover, California, which has moved toward a real-time sentencing system (where the statutory punishment approximates the time served), still punishes far less harshly those who have engaged in far more serious conduct. It imposes, for example, upon nonrecidivists guilty of arson causing great bodily injury a maximum sentence of nine years in prison, Cal.Penal Code Ann. § 451(a) (West 1999) (prison term of 5, 7, or 9 years for arson that causes great bodily injury); it imposes upon those guilty of voluntary manslaughter a maximum sentence of 11 years, § 193 (prison term of 3, 6, or 11 years for voluntary manslaughter). It reserves the sentence that it here imposes upon (former-burglar-now-golf-club-thief)

Ewing, for nonrecidivist, first-degree murderers. *See* § 190(a) (West Supp. 2003) (sentence of 25 years to life for first-degree murder).

As to other jurisdictions, we know the following: The United States, bound by the federal Sentencing Guidelines, would impose upon a recidivist, such as Ewing, a sentence that, in any ordinary case, would not exceed 18 months in prison. USSG § 2B1.1(a) (Nov.1999) (assuming a base offense level of 6, a criminal history of VI, and no mitigating or aggravating adjustments); *id.,* ch. 5, pt. A, Sentencing Table. The Guidelines, based in part upon a study of some 40,000 actual federal sentences, *see supra,* at 1182, 1185, reserve a Ewing-type sentence for Ewing-type *recidivists* who currently commit such crimes as murder, § 2A1.2; air piracy, § 2A5.1; robbery (involving the discharge of a firearm, serious bodily injury, and about $1 million), § 2B3.1; drug offenses involving more than, for example, 20 pounds of heroin, § 2D1.1; aggravated theft of more than $100 million, § 2B1.1; and other similar offenses. The Guidelines reserve 10 years of real prison time (with good time)—less than 40 percent of Ewing's sentence— for Ewing-type *recidivists* who go on to commit, for instance, voluntary manslaughter, § 2A1.3; aggravated assault with a firearm (causing serious bodily injury and motivated by money), § 2A2.2; kidnaping, § 2A4.1; residential burglary involving more than $5 million, § 2B2.1; drug offenses involving at least one pound of cocaine, § 2D1.1; and other similar offenses. Ewing also would not have been subject to the federal "three strikes" law, 18 U.S.C. § 3559(c), for which grand theft is not a triggering offense.

With three exceptions, *see infra* this page and 1199, we do not have before us information about actual time served by Ewing-type offenders in other States. We do know, however, that the law would make it legally impossible for a Ewing-type offender to serve more than 10 years in prison in 33 jurisdictions, as well as the federal courts, *see* Appendix, Part A, *infra,* more than 15 years in 4 other States, *see* Appendix, Part B, *infra,* and more than 20 years in 4 additional States, *see* Appendix, Part C, *infra.* In nine other States, the law *might* make it legally possible to impose a sentence of 25 years or more, *see* Appendix, Part D, *infra*—though that fact by itself, of course, does not mean that judges have actually done so. *But see infra* this page. I say "might" because the law in five of the nine last-mentioned States restricts the sentencing judge's ability to impose a term so long that, with parole, it would amount to at least 25 years of actual imprisonment. *See* Appendix, Part D, *infra.*

We also know that California, the United States, and other States supporting California in this case, despite every incentive to find someone else like Ewing who will have to serve, or who has actually served, a real prison term anywhere approaching that imposed upon Ewing, have come up with precisely three examples. Brief for United States as *Amicus Curiae* 28–29, n. 13. The Solicitor General points to *Ex parte Howington,* 622 So.2d 896 (Ala.1993), where an Alabama court sentenced an offender with three prior burglary convictions and two prior grand theft convictions to "life" for the theft of a tractor-trailer. The Solicitor General also points to State v. Heftel, 513 N.W.2d 397 (S.D.1994), where a South Dakota court sentenced an offender with seven prior felony convictions to 50 years' imprisonment for theft. And the Solicitor General cites Sims v. State, 107 Nev.

438, 814 P.2d 63 (1991), where a Nevada court sentenced a defendant with three prior felony convictions (including armed robbery) and nine misdemeanor convictions to life without parole for the theft of a purse and wallet containing $476.

The first of these cases, *Howington,* is beside the point, for the offender was eligible for parole after 10 years (as in *Rummel*), not 25 years (as here). Ala.Code § 15–22–28(e) (West 1982). The second case, *Heftel,* is factually on point, but it is not legally on point, for the South Dakota courts did not consider the constitutionality of the sentence. 513 N.W.2d, at 401. The third case, *Sims,* is on point both factually and legally, for the Nevada Supreme Court (by a vote of 3 to 2) found the sentence constitutional. I concede that example—a single instance of a similar sentence imposed outside the context of California's three strikes law, out of a prison population now approaching two million individuals. U.S. Dept. of Justice, Office of Justice Programs, Bureau of Justice Statistics, Prison Statistics (Jan. 8, 2003), http://www.ojp.usdoj.gov/bjs/prisons.htm (available in Clerk of Court's case file).

The upshot is that comparison of other sentencing practices, both in other jurisdictions and in California at other times (or in respect to other crimes), validates what an initial threshold examination suggested. Given the information available, given the state and federal parties' ability to provide additional contrary data, and given their failure to do so, we can assume for constitutional purposes that the following statement is true: Outside the California three strikes context, Ewing's recidivist sentence is virtually unique in its harshness for his offense of conviction, and by a considerable degree....

SECTION 3.　CLASSIFICATION

The common law divided crime into three major groups: (1) treason, (2) felony and (3) misdemeanor. To remove the uncertainty which had developed in the ancient law, the Statute of Treasons enacted in 1350[54] specified exactly what should constitute this offense including, among certain other wrongs, a manifested intent to kill the king, queen or prince, levying war against the king, adhering to his enemies, giving them aid and comfort. The original determinant of felony was forfeiture of lands and goods, although three influences tended to obscure this fact: (1) under the English common law all felonies carried also the death penalty except mayhem for which mutilation was substituted,[55] (2) misdemeanors were never punished capitally and (3) early statutes creating new felonies regularly imposed and emphasized the penalty of death. Because of these facts there has been a tendency to say that under the common-law plan all offenses punished by death were felonies whereas those punished only by

---

54.　25 Edw. 111, c. 2.

55.　Whipping was substituted for death as the penalty for petit larceny, but this was a change from the common law resulting from an early statute. Statute of Westminster, 1, c. 15 (1275).

some milder penalty were misdemeanors. This is very nearly accurate but it is well to bear in mind that the actual determinant was forfeiture.[56]

What has been said shows the common-law classification to be unsound because one category was determined by the nature of the wrong perpetrated and the other two by the penalty provided. In fact, since treason was punished by forfeiture of lands and goods (and by death) it was strictly speaking a felony, although it was convenient to deal with it as a separate category for procedural reasons. Statutes in this country commonly divide offenses into two classes: (1) felony and (2) misdemeanor. The determinant is usually the penalty imposed although the exact nature of the penalty employed for this purpose is not uniform and nowhere has any resemblance to the common law[57] in this regard except that a capital offense is a felony. Very few felonies are capital today and the other type of penalty used to distinguish felony from misdemeanor usually follows one of two patterns. It is based upon either: (1) the type of institution in which the offender may be incarcerated (such as the state prison), or (2) the length of term which may be imposed (as, for example, a term exceeding one year).

Some jurisdictions have provided for a different classification than just felonies and misdemeanors and have classified some minor offenses as infractions or petty offenses. The United States Code, 18 U.S.C.A. § 1, divides federal crimes into felonies, an offense punishable by death or imprisonment in excess of one year, misdemeanors and petty offenses. A petty offense is a misdemeanor punishable by not more than six months imprisonment. 18 U.S.C.A. § 3559 divides felonies into classes A through E and misdemeanors into classes A through C. An offense called an infraction is punishable by imprisonment for not more than five days and a fine of up to $5,000 and is also a petty offense.

The California Penal Code § 16 divides crimes into felonies, misdemeanors and infractions. A felony is a crime punishable by death or by imprisonment in the state prison. Other crimes are misdemeanors or infractions.[58]

It is expressly provided (in § 19.b) that an infraction is not punishable by imprisonment, and that one charged with an infraction is not entitled to a jury trial, nor to assigned counsel if indigent.

For certain purposes quite a different classification may be employed. For a consideration of the specific offenses, for example, it is common to have categories dependent upon the particular type of social harm involved,

---

56. In the words of Blackstone, "the true criterion of felony is forfeiture". 4 Bl.Comm. * 97.

57. "The common law of England has been by statute adopted as a rule of decision in this state, § 8–17, W.S.1957; and statutes are to be construed in harmony with existing law and their meaning determined in the light of the common law." Goldsmith v. Cheney, 468 P.2d 813, 816 (Wyo.1970).

"The English common law, so far as it is reasonable in itself, suitable to the condition and business of our people, and consistent with the letter and spirit of our federal and state constitutions and statutes, has been and is followed by our courts, and may be said to constitute a part of the common law of Ohio." Bloom v. Richards, 2 Ohio St. 387, 390 (1853); State v. McElhinney, 88 Ohio App. 431, 433, 100 N.E.2d 273, 275 (1950).

58. West's Cal.Penal Code § 17 (1987).

such as (1) offenses against the person, (2) offenses against property, (3) offenses against habitation and occupancy, and so forth, as indicated in the following chapter.

One very important classification scheme divides offenses into (1) capital crimes and (2) noncapital crimes. Under modern statutes a capital crime is one which *may* be punished by death; the customary provision being that one convicted of such an offense "shall be punished by death or by imprisonment for life." Both policy questions and issues of constitutional law are discussed in *Kansas v. Marsh, infra* Chapter 12.

Another special dichotomy in crime classification is based upon the concept of infamy, and divides the field into (1) infamous crimes and (2) noninfamous crimes. Like the distinction between felonies and misdemeanors, this distinction is important because of the collateral civil disabilities that may attend conviction. A wide variety of legal rights, such as the right to possess a firearm, to vote, to hold office, to enter or remain in the United States as an alien, and to hold certain public posts, are denied to those convicted of serious crimes, sometimes on the basis of the felony/misdemeanor distinction, and sometimes on the basis of the infamous/noninfamous distinction.[59]

The sex-offender registration statutes offer a new variation on this theme, as conviction for designated sex offenses subjects the offender to extensive affirmative obligations to avoid certain areas or persons and to keep the authorities informed about his whereabouts. The registration laws may also subject the offender to public notice of his record and current address. The Supreme Court has, so far, rejected constitutional challenges to these laws. *See* Connecticut Dept. of Public Safety v. Doe, 538 U.S. 1, 123 S.Ct. 1160, 155 L.Ed.2d 98 (2003) (no constitutional violation in posting offenders name and address on the internet); Smith v. Doe, 538 U.S. 84, 123 S.Ct. 1140, 155 L.Ed.2d 164 (2003) (registration laws are nonpunitive and may be enforced *ex post facto*).

Courts generally hold that the accused need not be admonished about the collateral civil consequences of a conviction before pleading guilty. It therefore bears emphasis that counsel carries an important responsibility to advise the defendant of the possible ramifications of pleading to an offense within one classification or another, bearing in mind that different clients may place different values on the various legal entitlements at risk from conviction, such as immigration status, the right to vote, or to possess a rifle in deer season.

---

59. [Added by compiler] New York law provides for automatic disbarment of an attorney convicted of a felony in New York or other state, if the offense were committed in New York it would constitute a felony. A Texas conviction for first degree manslaughter by vehicle was not essentially similar to that of New York to constitute a "felony" for purposes of automatic disbarment. Matter of Johnston, 75 N.Y.2d 403, 553 N.E.2d 566 (1990).

A physician's license was properly revoked in Colorado based on a Kentucky assault conviction. The crime was punishable by imprisonment in a penitentiary in Kentucky and was therefore a felony under Colorado law for purposes of license revocation. Colorado State Bd. of Medical Examiners v. Boyle, 924 P.2d 1113 (Colo.App.1996). See Burton, Cullen & Travis, The Collateral Consequences of a Felony Conviction: A National Study of State Statutes, 51 Federal Probation, no. 3 p. 61 (1987); The Collateral Consequences of a Criminal Conviction, 23 Vanderbilt L.Rev. 924 (1970).

MODEL PENAL CODE[60]

Section 1.04   Classes of Crimes; Violations.

(1) An offense defined by this Code or by any other statute of this State, for which a sentence of [death or of][61] imprisonment is authorized, constitutes a crime. Crimes are classified as felonies, misdemeanors or petty misdemeanors.

(2) A crime is a felony if it is so designated in this Code or if persons convicted thereof may be sentenced [to death or] to imprisonment for a term which, apart from an extended term, is in excess of one year.[62]

(3) A crime is a misdemeanor if it is so designated in this Code or in a statute other than this Code enacted subsequent thereto.

(4) A crime is a petty misdemeanor if it is so designated in this Code or in a statute other than this Code enacted subsequent thereto or if it is defined by a statute other than this Code which now provides that persons convicted thereof may be sentenced to imprisonment for a term of which the maximum is less than one year.

(5) An offense defined by this Code or by any other statute of this State constitutes a violation if it is so designated in this Code or in the law defining the offense or if no other sentence than a fine, or fine and forfeiture or other civil penalty is authorized upon conviction or if it is defined by a statute other than this Code which now provides that the offense shall not constitute a crime. A violation does not constitute a crime and conviction of a violation shall not give rise to any disability or legal disadvantage based on conviction of a criminal offense.

(6) Any offense declared by law to constitute a crime, without specification of the grade thereof or of the sentence authorized upon conviction, is a misdemeanor.

(7) An offense defined by any statute of this State other than this Code shall be classified as provided in this Section and the sentence that may be imposed upon conviction thereof shall hereafter be governed by this Code:

Section 6.08   Sentence of Imprisonment for Misdemeanors and Petty Misdemeanors; Ordinary Terms.

A person who has been convicted of a misdemeanor or a petty misdemeanor may be sentenced to imprisonment for a definite term which shall be fixed by the Court and shall not exceed one year in the case of a misdemeanor or thirty days in the case of a petty misdemeanor.

---

60. Prepared by the American Law Institute. All references to the Model Penal Code herein, unless otherwise indicated, are to the Proposed Official Draft, 1962. Such quotations have been expressly authorized by the American Law Institute.

Copyright© 1962 by the American Law Institute.

61. Since a few jurisdictions do not have capital punishment all references to the death sentence are bracketed in the Code.

62. A felony punished by death is a separate category. Aside from this, felonies are divided into three degrees. For a felony of the first degree the maximum penalty is life imprisonment; for a felony of the second degree the maximum is ten years; and for a felony of the third degree the maximum is five years.

CHAPTER 2

OFFENSES AGAINST THE PERSON

SECTION 1.   HOMICIDE

Patterson v. New York

Supreme Court of the United States, 1977.
432 U.S. 197, 97 S.Ct. 2319, 53 L.Ed.2d 281.

■ MR. JUSTICE WHITE delivered the opinion of the Court.

The question here is the constitutionality under the Fourteenth Amendment's Due Process Clause of burdening the defendant in a New York State murder trial with proving the affirmative defense of extreme emotional disturbance as defined by New York law.

After a brief and unstable marriage, the appellant, Gordon Patterson, became estranged from his wife, Roberta. Roberta resumed an association with John Northrup, a neighbor to whom she had been engaged prior to her marriage to appellant. On December 27, 1970, Patterson borrowed a rifle from an acquaintance and went to the residence of his father-in-law. There, he observed his wife through a window in a state of semiundress in the presence of John Northrup.

He entered the house and killed Northrup by shooting him twice in the head.

Patterson was charged with second-degree murder. In New York there are two elements of this crime: (1) "intent to cause the death of another person"; and (2) "caus[ing] the death of such person or of a third person." N.Y. Penal Law § 125.25 (McKinney 1975). Malice aforethought is not an element of the crime. In addition, the State permits a person accused of murder to raise an affirmative defense that he "acted under the influence of extreme emotional disturbance for which there was a reasonable explanation or excuse."

New York also recognizes the crime of manslaughter. A person is guilty of manslaughter if he intentionally kills another person "under circumstances which do not constitute murder because he acts under the influence of extreme emotional disturbance." Appellant confessed before trial to killing Northrup, but at trial he raised the defense of extreme emotional disturbance.

The jury was instructed as to the elements of the crime of murder. Focusing on the element of intent, the trial court charged,

"Before you, considering all of the evidence, can convict this defendant or any one of murder, you must believe and decide that the People have established beyond a reasonable doubt that he intended, in firing the gun, to kill either the victim himself or some other human being.... Always remember that you must not expect or require the defendant to prove to your satisfaction that his acts were done without the intent to kill. Whatever proof he may have attempted, however far he may have gone in an effort to convince you of his innocence or guiltlessness, he is not obliged, he is not obligated to prove anything. It is always the People's burden to prove his guilt, and to prove that he intended to kill in this instance beyond a reasonable doubt." . . .

The jury was further instructed, consistently with New York law, that the defendant had the burden of proving his affirmative defense by a preponderance of the evidence. The jury was told that if it found beyond a reasonable doubt that appellant had intentionally killed Northrup but that appellant had demonstrated by a preponderance of the evidence that he had acted under the influence of extreme emotional disturbance, it must find appellant guilty of manslaughter instead of murder.

The jury found appellant guilty of murder. . . . While appeal to the New York Court of Appeals was pending, this Court decided Mullaney v. Wilbur, 421 U.S. 684, 95 S.Ct. 1881, 44 L.Ed.2d 508 (1975), in which the Court declared Maine's murder statute unconstitutional. Under the Maine statute, a person accused of murder could rebut the statutory presumption that he committed the offense with "malice aforethought" by proving that he acted in the heat of passion on sudden provocation. The Court held that this scheme improperly shifted the burden of persuasion from the prosecutor to the defendant and was therefore a violation of due process. In the Court of Appeals appellant urged that New York's murder statute is functionally equivalent to the one struck down in Mullaney and that therefore his conviction should be reversed.

The Court of Appeals rejected appellant's argument, holding that the New York murder statute is consistent with due process. . . .

In determining whether New York's allocation to the defendant of proving the mitigating circumstances of severe emotional disturbance is consistent with due process, it is therefore relevant to note that this defense is a considerably expanded version of the common law defense of heat of passion on sudden provocation and that at common law the burden of proving the latter, as well as other affirmative defenses—indeed, "all . . . circumstances of justification, excuse or alleviation"—rested on the defendant. 4 W. Blackstone, Commentaries *201; M. Foster, Crown Law 255 (1762); Mullaney v. Wilbur, *supra,* 421 U.S., at 693–694, 95 S.Ct., at 1886–1887. This was the rule when the Fifth Amendment was adopted, and it was the American rule when the Fourteenth Amendment was ratified.

In 1895 the common law view was abandoned with respect to the insanity defense in federal prosecutions. This ruling had wide impact on the practice in the federal courts with respect to the burden of proving various affirmative defenses, and the prosecution in a majority of jurisdictions in this country sooner or later came to shoulder the burden of proving the sanity of the accused and of disproving the facts constituting other affirmative defenses, including provocation. . . .

[In Leland v. Oregon, 343 U.S. 790, 72 S.Ct. 1002 (1952), the Supreme Court upheld the constitutionality of requiring a defendant to prove his insanity beyond a reasonable doubt.]

In 1970, the court declared that the Due Process Clause "protects the accused against conviction except upon proof beyond a reasonable doubt of every fact necessary to constitute the crime with which he is charged." . . . [T]he Court further announced that under the Maine law of homicide, the burden could not constitutionally be placed on the defendant of proving by a preponderance of the evidence that the killing had occurred in the heat of passion on sudden provocation. . . .

Subsequently, the Court confirmed that it remained constitutional to burden the defendant with proving his insanity defense when it dismissed, as not raising a substantial federal question, a case to which the appellant specifically challenged the continuing validity of Leland v. Oregon. . . .

We cannot conclude that Patterson's conviction under the New York law deprived him of due process of law. The crime of murder is defined by the statute, which represents a recent revision of the State criminal code, as causing the death of another person with intent to do so. The death, the intent to kill, and causation are the facts that the State is required to prove beyond reasonable doubt if a person is convicted of murder. No further facts are either presumed or inferred in order to constitute the crime. The statute does provide an affirmative defense—that the defendant acted under the influence of extreme emotional disturbance for which there was a reasonable explanation—which, if proved by a preponderance of the evidence, would reduce the crime to manslaughter, an offense defined in a separate section of the statute. It is plain enough that if the intentional killing is shown, the State intends to deal with the defendant as a murderer unless he demonstrates the mitigating circumstances.

Here, the jury was instructed in accordance with the statute, and the guilty verdict confirms that the State successfully carried its burden of proving the facts of the crime beyond reasonable doubt. Nothing in the evidence, including any evidence that might have been offered with respect to Patterson's mental state at the time of the crime, raised a reasonable doubt about his guilt as a murderer; and clearly the evidence failed to convince the jury that Patterson's affirmative defense had been made out.

In convicting Patterson under its murder statute, New York did no more than Leland and Rivera permitted it to do without violating the Due Process Clause. Under those cases, once the facts constituting a crime are established beyond reasonable doubt, based on all the evidence including the evidence of the defendant's mental state, the State may refuse to sustain the affirmative defense of insanity unless demonstrated by a preponderance of the evidence.

The New York law on extreme emotional disturbance follows this pattern. . . . Here, in revising its criminal code, New York provided the affirmative defense of extreme emotional disturbance, a substantially expanded version of the older heat of passion concept; but it was willing to do so only if the facts making out the defense were established by the defendant with sufficient certainty. The State was itself unwilling to undertake to establish the absence of those facts beyond reasonable doubt, perhaps fearing that proof would be too difficult and that too many persons deserving treatment as murderers would escape that punishment if the evidence need merely raise a reasonable doubt about the defendant's emotional state. It has been said that the new criminal code of New York contains some 25 affirmative defenses which exculpate or mitigate but which must be established by the defendant to be operative.[1] The Due Process Clause, as we see it, does not put New York to the choice of abandoning those defenses or undertaking to disprove their existence in order to convict for a crime which otherwise is within its constitutional powers to sanction by substantial punishment.

The requirement of proof beyond reasonable doubt in a criminal case is "bottomed on a fundamental value determination of our society that it is far worse to convict an innocent man than to let a guilty man go free." The social cost of placing the burden on the prosecution to prove guilt beyond a reasonable doubt is thus an increased risk that the guilty will go free. While it is clear that our society has willingly chosen to bear a substantial burden in order to protect the innocent, it is equally clear that the risk it must bear is not without limits; and Justice Harlan's aphorism provides little guidance for determining what those limits are. . . .

It is said that the common law rule permits a State to punish one as a murderer when it is as likely as not that he acted in the heat of passion or under severe emotional distress and when, if he did, he is guilty only of manslaughter. But this has always been the case in those jurisdictions adhering to the traditional rule. It is also very likely true that fewer convictions for murder would occur if New York were required to negative the affirmative defense at issue here. But in each instance of a murder conviction under the present law, New York will have proved beyond reasonable doubt that the defendant has intentionally killed another person, an act which it is not disputed the State may constitutionally criminalize and punish. If the State nevertheless chooses to recognize a factor that mitigates the degree of criminality or punishment, we think the State may assure itself that the fact has been established with reasonable certainty. To recognize at all a mitigating circumstance does not require the State to prove its nonexistence in each case in which the fact is put in issue, if in its judgment this would be too cumbersome, too expensive, and too inaccurate.[2]

---

1.   The State of New York is not alone in this result:

"Since the Model Penal Code was completed in 1962, some 22 states have codified and reformed their criminal laws. At least 12 of these jurisdictions have used the concept of an 'affirmative defense' and have defined that phrase to require that the defendant prove the existence of an 'affirmative defense' by a preponderance of the evidence. Additionally, at least six proposed state codes and each of the four successive versions of a revised federal code use the same procedural device. Finally, many jurisdictions that do not generally employ this concept of 'affirmative defense' nevertheless shift the burden of proof to the defendant on particular issues." . . .

2.   The drafters of the Model Penal Code would, as a matter of policy, place the burden of proving the nonexistence of most affirmative defenses, including the defense involved in this case, on the prosecution once the defendant has come forward with some evidence that the defense is present. The drafters recognize the need for flexibility, however, and would, in

We thus decline to adopt as a constitutional imperative, operative country-wide, that a State must disprove beyond reasonable doubt every fact constituting any and all affirmative defenses related to the culpability of an accused. Traditionally, due process has required that only the most basic procedural safeguards be observed; more subtle balancing of society's interests against those of the accused have been left to the legislative branch. We therefore will not disturb the balance struck in previous cases holding that the Due Process Clause requires the prosecution to prove beyond reasonable doubt all of the elements included in the definition of the offense of which the defendant is charged. Proof of the nonexistence of all affirmative defenses has never been constitutionally required; and we perceive no reason to fashion such a rule in this case and apply it to the statutory defense at issue here.

This view may seem to permit state legislatures to reallocate burdens of proof by labeling as affirmative defenses at least some elements of the crimes now defined in their statutes. But there are obviously constitutional limits beyond which the States may not go in this regard. "[I]t is not within the province of a legislature to declare an individual guilty or presumptively guilty of a crime." ... The legislature cannot "validly command that the finding of an indictment, or mere proof of the identity of the accused, should create a presumption of the existence of all the facts essential to guilt." ...

It is urged that Mullaney v. Wilbur necessarily invalidates Patterson's conviction. In Mullaney the charge was murder, which the Maine statute defined as the unlawful killing of a human being "with malice aforethought either express or implied." The trial court instructed the jury that the words "malice aforethought" were most important "because malice aforethought is an essential and indispensable element of the crime of murder." Malice, as the statute indicated and as the court instructed, could be implied and was to be implied from "any deliberate, cruel act committed by one person against another suddenly or without a considerable provocation," in which event an intentional killing was murder unless by a preponderance of the evidence it was shown that the act was committed "in the heat of passion upon sudden provocation." The instructions emphasized that " 'malice aforethought and heat of passion on sudden provocation are two inconsistent things'; thus, by proving the latter the defendant would negate the former." ...

Mullaney's holding, it is argued, is that the State may not permit the blameworthiness of an act or the severity of punishment authorized for its commission to depend on the presence or absence of an identified fact without assuming the burden of proving the presence or absence of that

---

"some exceptional situations," place the burden of persuasion on the accused. "Characteristically these are situations where the defense does not obtain at all under existing law and the Code seeks to introduce a mitigation. Resistance to the mitigation, based upon the prosecution's difficulty in obtaining evidence, ought to be lowered if the burden of persuasion is imposed on the defendant. Where that difficulty appears genuine and there is something to be said against allowing the defense at all, we consider it defensible to shift the burden in this way." ALI, Model Penal Code § 1.13, Comment, p. 113 (Tentative Draft No. 4, 1955).

fact, as the case may be, beyond reasonable doubt. In our view, the Mullaney holding should not be so broadly read. . . .

Mullaney surely held that a State must prove every ingredient of an offense beyond a reasonable doubt, and that it may not shift the burden of proof to the defendant by presuming that ingredient upon proof of the other elements of the offense. This is true even though the State's practice, as in Maine, had been traditionally to the contrary. Such shifting of the burden of persuasion with respect to a fact which the State deems so important that it must be either proved or presumed is impermissible under the Due Process Clause.

It was unnecessary to go further in Mullaney. The Maine Supreme Court made it clear that malice aforethought, which was mentioned in the statutory definition of the crime, was not equivalent to premeditation and that the presumption of malice traditionally arising in intentional homicide cases carried no factual meaning insofar as premeditation was concerned. Even so, a killing became murder in Maine when it resulted from a deliberate, cruel act committed by one person against another, "suddenly, and without any, or without considerable, provocation." Premeditation was not within the definition of murder; but malice, in the sense of the absence of provocation, was part of the definition of that crime. Yet malice, i.e., lack of provocation, was presumed and could be rebutted by the defendant only by proving a preponderance of the evidence that he acted with heat of passion upon sudden provocation. In Mullaney we held that however traditional this mode of proceeding might have been, it is contrary to the Due Process Clause as construed in Winship.

As we have explained, nothing was presumed or implied against Patterson; and his conviction is not invalid under any of our prior cases. The judgment of the New York Court of Appeals is affirmed.[3]

---

3. It is not a violation of due process to place the burden of proving self-defense on a defendant charged with aggravated murder. Martin v. Ohio, 480 U.S. 228, 107 S.Ct. 1098 (1987).

Where under Montana's deliberate homicide law the jury was instructed that "the law presumes that a person intends the ordinary consequences of his lawful acts", it was held the instruction denied the defendant due process by shifting the burden of proof on the issue of purpose or knowledge. "Because David Sandstrom's jury may have interpreted the judge's instruction as constituting either a burden-shifting presumption . . . or a conclusive presumption . . . and because either interpretation would have deprived defendant of his right to the due process of law, we hold the instruction given in this case unconstitutional." Sandstrom v. Montana, 442 U.S. 510, 524, 99 S.Ct. 2450 (1979).

In a murder prosecution an instruction to the jury that, "The acts of a person of sound mind and discretion are presumed to be the product of a person's will, but the presumption may be rebutted. A person of sound mind and discretion is presumed to intend the natural and probable consequences of his acts, but the presumption may be rebutted. A person will not be presumed to act with criminal intention but the trier of facts . . . may find criminal intention upon a consideration of the words, conduct, demeanor, motive and all the circumstances . . . " violated due process. The instruction could be read as creating a mandatory presumption that shifted the burden of proof to the defendant or that the jury was required to make such inference unless rebutted. Other instructions did not cure the error. Francis v. Franklin, 471 U.S. 307, 105 S.Ct. 1965 (1985).

Advising jury in a murder case that "malice" is implied or presumed from a "willful, deliberate or intentional act" and "from the use of a deadly weapon" shifted the burden of

Errington and Others' Case

Newcastle Assizes, 1838.
2 Lewin C.C. 217, 168 Eng.Rep. 1133.

. . .

facts

The case against the prisoners was a very serious one. It appeared, that the deceased, being in liquor, had gone at night into a glass-house, and laid himself down upon a chest: and that while he was there asleep the prisoners covered and surrounded him with straw, and threw a shovel of hot cinders upon his belly; the consequence of which was, that the straw ignited, and he was burnt to death.

issue

There was no evidence in the case of express malice; but the conduct of the prisoners indicated an entire recklessness of consequences, hardly consistent with anything short of design.

■ PATTESON, J., cited from the text books the law applicable to the case, and pointed the attention of the jury to the distinctions which characterise murder and manslaughter. He then adverted to the fact of there being no evidence of express malice; but told them, that if they believed the prisoners really intended to do any serious injury to the deceased, although not to kill him, it was murder; but if they believed their intention to have been only to frighten him in sport, it was manslaughter.

The jury took a merciful view of the case, and returned a verdict of manslaughter only.[4]

R. v. Vickers

Court of Criminal Appeal, 1957.
2 All E.R. 741.

Appeal.

This was an appeal by John Willson Vickers, the appellant, against his conviction of capital murder under § 5 (1) (a) of the Homicide Act, 1957, viz., of murder done in the course or furtherance of theft. . . . The appellant was sentenced to death. In the early hours of Sunday morning, Apr. 14,

---

proof and violated constitutional standards. Yates v. Evatt, 500 U.S. 391, 111 S.Ct. 1884 (1991).

4. "Murder is when a man . . . unlawfully killeth . . . any reasonable creature . . . with malice forethought, either expressed by the party, or implied by law, so as the party . . . die . . . within a year and a day after the same." Coke, 3 Institutes 47.

"Following the common law trend, this court has recognized that malice aforethought . . . 'denotes four types of murder, each accompanied by distinct mental states.' . . .

First, . . . where the perpetrator acts with the specific intent to kill. . . . Second, . . . where the perpetrator has the specific intent to inflict serious bodily harm. . . . Third, . . . disregard of an unreasonable human risk. . . . [Fourth] . . . in the course of the intentional commission of a felony." Comber v. United States, 584 A.2d 26, 38–39 (D.C.App.1990).

See Wechsler and Michael, A Rationale of the Law of Homicide I & II, 37 Col.L.Rev. 701, 1261 (1937).

Malice may consist of the intent to kill, to cause great bodily harm, or to do an act in wanton and willful disregard of the likelihood that the natural tendency of such behavior is to cause death or great bodily harm. People v. Woods, 416 Mich. 581, 331 N.W.2d 707 (1982).

1957, the appellant, who was a labourer aged twenty-two, broke into the cellar of a shop which was occupied by an old woman of seventh-three, a Miss Duckett, intending to steal money. At the shop Miss Duckett carried on a prosperous business of grocer and tobacconist, and she lived alone on the same premises in two rooms above the shop; she was a small woman and the appellant, who lived in lodgings a short distance away, knew that she was deaf. While the appellant was in the cellar Miss Duckett came down the stairs leading to it and saw the appellant. She asked him what he was doing and came towards him, whereupon the appellant attacked her with his fists and struck her several blows; she fell down. The medical evidence was that Miss Duckett was struck by ten to fifteen blows and was kicked in the face by the appellant, and that death was caused by shock due to general injuries; the medical evidence was also that the degree of force necessary to inflict the injuries sustained by Miss Duckett would be moderately severe to quite slight force.

The appellant now appealed against his conviction inter alia on the ground that the judge misdirected the jury when he told them that malice aforethought could be implied if the victim was killed by a voluntary act done with the intention of causing grievous bodily harm.

■ LORD GODDARD, C.J., ... The point that has been raised on the appellant's behalf turns entirely on § 1 (1) of the Homicide Act, 1957, which came into force this year[5]. ...

The point that is raised is this: § 1 (1) of the Act of 1957 says:

"Where a person kills another in the course or furtherance of some other offence, the killing shall not amount to murder unless done with the same malice aforethought (express or implied) as is required for a killing to amount to murder when not done in the course or furtherance of another offence."

The marginal note of § 1, which of course is not part of the section, but may be looked at as some indication of the purpose, is: "Abolition of 'constructive malice'."

"Constructive malice" is an expression that has crept into the law—I do not think that it will be found in any particular decision but it is to be found in the text-books—and is something different from implied malice. The expression "constructive malice" is generally used and the best illustration of constructive malice which is generally given is that if a person caused death during the course of his carrying out a felony which involved violence, that always amounted to murder. There were cases in which a man was not intending to cause death, as for instance where a mere push was given which would never have been considered in the ordinary way as one which would cause death, but the person pushed fell down and most unfortunately struck his dead or fell down the stairs and broke his neck, yet if the act were done, for example, in the course of burglary, it amounted to murder. ... Murder is, of course, killing with malice aforethought and "malice aforethought" is a term of art. Malice aforethought has always been defined in English law as either an express intention to kill such as

---

5.   The Homicide Act, 1957, came into force on Mar. 21, 1957.

could be inferred when a person, having uttered threats against another, produced a lethal weapon and used it on him, or an implied intention to kill, as where the prisoner inflicted grievous bodily harm, that is to say, harmed the victim by a voluntary act intended to harm him and the victim died as the result of that grievous bodily harm. If a person does an act on another which amounts to the infliction of grievous bodily harm he cannot say that he did not intend to go so far. It is put as malum in se in the old case and he must take the consequences. If he intends to inflict grievous bodily harm and that person dies, that has always been held in English law, and was at the time when the Act of 1957 was passed, sufficient to imply the malice aforethought which is a necessary constituent of murder.

. . .

I will now briefly refer to the summing-up of HINCHCLIFFE, J., which the court thinks is quite impeccable. He put it, I think, exceedingly well. He said to the jury:

"If you are not satisfied that the charge of capital murder has been proved, that is to say, if you are in doubt whether the accused man had the intention to inflict grievous bodily harm on Miss Duckett, it is right that, in those circumstances the accused would be guilty of manslaughter, if you were satisfied that the accused had brought about the old lady's death without any malice, without any intention to do her grievous bodily harm."

. . .

"Murder is with the intention to kill or to do grievous bodily harm; manslaughter is an unlawful killing, but without any intention."

Finally, he gave this direction to the jury:

"Malice will be implied, if the victim was killed by a voluntary act of the accused—and here is the importance of what I am going to say—done with the intention either to kill or to do some grievous bodily harm. The grievous bodily harm need not be permanent, but it must be serious, and it is serious or grievous if it is such as seriously and grievously to interfere with the health or comfort of the victim ... Ask yourselves: Is it proved that the accused man killed Miss Duckett with malice, that is, when he struck the blows he intended to do her serious bodily harm?"

The court desires to say quite firmly that in considering the construction of s. 1 (1), it is impossible to say that the doing of grievous bodily harm is the other offence which is referred t in the first line and a half of the sub-section. It must be shown that independently of the fact that the accused is committing another offence, that the act which caused the death was done with malice aforethought as implied by law. The existence of express or implied malice is expressly preserved by the Act of 1957 and, in our opinion, a perfectly proper direction was given by HINCHCLIFFE, J., to the jury, and accordingly this appeal fails and is dismissed.

Appeal dismissed.[6]

---

6. Several state codes expressly provide for the crime of murder where defendant acts with intent to inflict serious bodily injury. LaFave & Scott, Substantive Criminal Law, § 7.3 (1988). *See also* Comber v. United States, 584 A.2d 26, 38 n. 10 (D.C.App.1990).

Commonwealth v. McLaughlin

Supreme Court of Pennsylvania, 1928.
293 Pa. 218, 142 A. 213.

■ Opinion by Mr. JUSTICE SCHAFFER, May 7, 1928.

Defendant, a young man, twenty years of age at the time of the occurrence we are to deal with, appeals from his conviction and sentence for murder of the second degree, contending that the evidence produced against him did not establish this crime.

With two companions he was driving his father's automobile about half past ten o'clock at night along Northampton Street in Wilkes–Barre Township in the County of Luzerne. His progress was down grade and was at the rate of twenty or twenty-five miles an hour. The highway was well lighted. Frank Ravitt and his wife were walking in the cartway of the street ahead of and in the same direction as the automobile, their presence within the street limits and not on the sidewalk being due to the pavement's bad condition. They were at the right-hand side of the center of the cartway, the wife in or near the street car track, the husband on her right. He was pushing a baby coach in which was their infant child. Defendant so drove his automobile that it struck the group in the cartway, killing the husband and the baby and seriously injuring the wife. The impact was with such force as to knock the bodies of the man and woman a distance of from twenty-five to fifty feet and the child out of the coach and over onto the pavement. There was a dispute in the testimony as to whether the lights on the automobile were lit and as to whether defendant sounded his horn as he approached the stricken people; whether he was intoxicated was likewise a controverted fact.

One of the Commonwealth's most material witnesses, Lawrence Brosinski, the only person except defendant and the two others who were in the car with him who actually saw the tragedy, testified that if defendant "had swung his machine toward the side instead of the middle of the road he would never have struck these people." Defendant's story in amplification of this was that he blew his horn and noticed the two persons walking in the center of the road, that he had ample room to pass them to the right, that when he blew his horn "they seemed to be going to the left, and all of a sudden they veered to the right, and as they did I applied my brakes, but it was too late. I had already struck them—he [the husband] seemed to dart to the right quicker than I could get the machine stopped." In this recital he was corroborated by the two young men who were in the car with him. The automobile ran some distance, perhaps 200 feet beyond the point of the collision. Defendant and his companions ascribed this to the circumstance that in his excitement he took his foot off the brake. It appeared in the prosecution's case by the testimony of more than one witness that the brakes were applied, as they heard their screeching before the crash. Immediately after the automobile stopped, defendant ran back, picked up the woman and aided in placing her and the husband in automobiles, one of them in his own, to convey them to the hospital. Upon this evidence the

---

"As the common law developed, the definition of malice expanded to include an intent to cause serious bodily injury.... " State v. Johnson, 158 Vt. 508, 515, 615 A.2d 132, 136 (1992).

Issue

jury found defendant guilty of murder of the second degree and the question to be decided is whether that finding can be sustained.

Murder, as defined by the common law, consists of the unlawful killing of a human being with malice aforethought, express or implied: Com. v. Harman, 4 Pa. 269, 271. Malice is a legal term which comprehends not only a particular ill will, but every case where there is wickedness of disposition, hardness of heart, cruelty, recklessness of consequences, or a mind regardless of social duty: Com. v. Drum, 58 Pa. 9, 15. In this State the legislature has divided the common law crime of murder into two degrees. The statute defines murder of the first degree, and then provides that "all other kinds of murder shall be deemed murder of the second degree": Act of March 31, 1860, P.L. 332, section 74. Thus murder of the second degree is common law murder, but the killing is not accompanied by the distinguishing features of murder of the first degree. The crime includes every element which enters into murder of the first degree except the intention to kill. "Premeditation is essential as in other cases of murder". It is apparent, therefore, that malice is a necessary element of the crime of murder of the second degree, and it was with this in view that we recently said "it is rarely that the facts in a motor vehicle accident will sustain a charge of murder. The element of malice is usually missing. There must be a consciousness of peril or probable peril to human life imputed to the operator of a car before he can be held for murder". In the present case one of the things which seems to have been given much weight by the court below in its opinion sustaining the conviction was defendant's failure to see the people on the road in time to avoid striking them. This negatives any specific intent to injure them. Unless he intended to strike them, which we think it manifest from the evidence he did not, or was recklessly disregardful of their safety, which the testimony does not establish, he could not legally be convicted of murder. Malice may be inferred from the wanton and reckless conduct of one who kills another from wicked disregard of the consequences of his acts, but here defendant's actions after the collision negative the idea of wickedness of disposition or hardness of heart. He endeavored as best he knew how to care for those he had injured. Moreover, it cannot be implied from the circumstances of the accident that defendant was driving his car with wanton disregard of the rights and safety of others upon the highway. The mere fact that he was intoxicated (conceding this to have been proved), without more being shown, would not sustain the conviction. Consequently, we are of the opinion that it could not properly be found, upon the evidence presented, that defendant either purposely, intentionally, recklessly, or wantonly drove his car upon the deceased, and therefore that he should not have been convicted of murder.

If defendant was guilty of any crime, it was that of involuntary manslaughter, which consists in "the killing of another without malice and unintentionally, but in doing some unlawful act not amounting to a felony nor naturally tending to cause death or great bodily harm, or in negligently doing some act lawful in itself, or by the negligent omission to perform a legal duty."

Defendant may still be tried on the indictment charging involuntary manslaughter, notwithstanding that the district attorney entered a nolle prosequi on the indictment. A nolle prosequi is a voluntary withdrawal by the prosecuting attorney of present proceedings on a particular bill. At common law it might at any time be retracted, and was not a bar to a subsequent prosecution on another indictment, but it might be so far cancelled as to permit a revival of the proceedings on the original bill. Whatever the rule may be elsewhere, such action in this jurisdiction is not a bar to a subsequent indictment for the same offense, or may be so far cancelled as to permit a revival of proceedings on the original bill.

The first assignment of error is sustained and the judgment of sentence is reversed without prejudice to the Commonwealth's right to proceed against defendant for the crime of involuntary manslaughter.[7]

■ Dissenting Opinion by Mr. Justice Simpson:

The majority opinion states that defendant, while driving his father's automobile struck three persons who were travelling in front of him and going in the same direction he was, killing two of them and greatly injuring the third; that the car then ran some 200 feet further, after which he returned and helped convey two of the three to the hospital, and from this concludes that "defendant's actions after the collision negative the idea of wickedness of disposition or hardness of heart." With all due respect, the jury and trial judge who saw the witnesses when they testified, and the colleagues of the latter who obtained from him a clear picture of their conduct on the witness stand, were far better able to draw the true inferences, than the judges of this court who must rely upon what appears in cold type only. At least as possible an inference from the facts above stated is that the defendant, while running the 200 feet beyond the place of the accident, concluded he would be better off if he came back than if he fled further, and hence the fact of his return did not negative the conclusion, which the jury drew from all the evidence, that defendant's "wanton and reckless conduct ... [*at the time of the accident* shows his] wicked disregard of the consequences of his acts," and this, if found to be true, as it was, the majority agree would be sufficient to sustain the verdict and sentence. For this reason I dissent.

■ The Chief Justice concurred in this dissent.

King v. State

Court of Criminal Appeals of Alabama, 1987.
505 So.2d 403.

■ Patterson, Judge.

Appellant, Christopher Doyle King, was indicted by a two-count indictment for murder in violation of § 13A–6–2, Code of Alabama 1975. Count one charged that appellant

---

7. "Implied malice may be found when a defendant, knowing that his conduct endangers life and acting with conscious disregard of danger, commits an act the natural consequences of which are dangerous to life." People v. Roberts, 2 Cal.4th 271, 6 Cal.Rptr.2d 276, 826 P.2d 274, 298 (1992).

" ... did recklessly engage in conduct which manifested extreme indifference to human life and created a grave risk of death to a person other than the said Christopher Doyle King, and did thereby cause the death of Dwight Lee Reeves by shooting into an automobile in which the said Dwight Lee Reeves was a passenger and shooting the said Dwight Lee Reeves with a pistol, ... "

Count two charged that appellant

" ... did intentionally cause the death of another person, Dwight Lee Reeves, by shooting him with a pistol, ... "

The case was tried to a jury, and ... the jury returned a verdict of guilty of murder, as charged in count one. ...

King appeals, raising one issue: "Whether or not the State of Alabama failed to prove that the appellant manifested extreme indifference to human life in general as required by Section 13A–6–2(a)(2) of the Alabama Code so as to support a conviction for reckless murder." ...

The evidence presented by the State disclosed that on the evening of November 22, 1984, Dwight Lee Reeves and his cousin, Rodney Dunnaway, traveled from Fultondale to Birmingham to visit Trader Johns, a nightclub in east Birmingham. They traveled in Dunnaway's automobile. That same evening, appellant and a friend, Bobby Knight, visited the same club. ... While at the club, appellant and Reeves apparently "bumped" into each other and exchanged words. Both were apparently upset by the encounter. Dunnaway and Reeves left the club around 1:30 a.m. to go home. Appellant and Knight left shortly before Dunnaway and Reeves. As Dunnaway and Reeves were pulling out of the parking lot of the club, a blue pickup truck pulled up closely behind Dunnaway's automobile and stopped for a short period. Dunnaway was driving, and Reeves was sitting on the passenger's side in the front seat of the automobile. Dunnaway drove away from the club, entered the interstate highway, ... Appellant and Knight left the parking lot of the club in the pickup truck, which appellant was driving, and after entering the interstate highway, proceeded westward in the same direction as Dunnaway was proceeding, and in the opposite direction from appellant's home. Appellant observed Dunnaway's automobile and recognized the passenger, Reeves, as the person with whom he had had the altercation at the club. Appellant drove his truck closely behind Dunnaway's automobile and, while blinking his truck's lights, "tailgated" it for several miles. Dunnaway reduced his speed several times to let the truck pass, but it continued closely behind him. As the vehicles approached the 31st Street exit, appellant pulled a .38–caliber pistol from under the seat of his truck, pulled up beside Dunnaway's automobile on the right side, fired two or three shots at the vehicle, and turned right on the off-ramp, leaving the interstate highway. Bullets struck the rear tires of Dunnaway's vehicle, causing them to immediately go flat, and the vehicle came to a halt some distance beyond the 31st Street exit. One bullet pierced the window on the passenger's side and struck Reeves in the head. He fell over into Dunnaway's lap. Reeves died from the head wound several hours later. Reeves and Dunnaway were unarmed and did nothing to provoke the shooting. ... Appellant gave conflicting stories to several persons about the incident, and when arrested, falsely stated that he had no knowledge of the incident. He disposed of the pistol in a "dumpster," and it was never recovered. The State's case was primarily based upon the testimony of Dunnaway and Knight, and the testimony of each was essentially consistent with the other's.

Knight, testifying for the State, stated that, just before the incident, appellant stated that he was going to "mess with them and shoot the tires out." He further testified that, just after the shooting, appellant stated that he "might have messed up or he shot the window out." In substance, Knight testified that there was no provocation or excuse for appellant's actions.

This court interpreted the meaning of reckless homicide ... in Northington v. State, 413 So.2d 1169 (Ala.Cr.App.1981). Therein, we stated the following:

"Reckless homicide manifesting extreme indifference to human life (13A–6–2(a)(2)) must be distinguished from purposeful or knowing murder (13A–6–2(a)(1)). *See* American Law Institute, Model Penal Code and Commentaries, Part II, Section 210.2 (1980). Under whatever name, the doctrine of universal malice, depraved heart murder, or reckless homicide manifesting extreme indifference to human life is intended to embrace those cases where a person has no deliberate intent to kill or injure any particular individual. 'The element of "extreme indifference to human life," by definition, does not address itself to the life of the victim, but to human life generally.' "

We also stated,

"The function of this section is to embrace those homicides caused by such acts as driving an automobile in a grossly wanton manner, shooting a firearm into a crowd or moving train, and throwing a timber from a roof onto a crowded street".

The Supreme Court of Alabama subsequently adopted this interpretation.

In Ex parte Weems, 463 So.2d 170, 172 (Ala.1984), the Supreme Court, in an opinion by Justice Faulkner, stated the following:

"Alabama's homicide statutes were derived from the Model Penal Code. In providing that homicide committed 'recklessly under circumstances manifesting extreme indifference to human life' constitutes murder, the drafters of the model code were attempting to define a degree of recklessness 'that cannot be fairly distinguished from homicides committed purposely or knowingly.' Model Penal Code and Commentaries, § 210.02, Comment, 4 (1980). That standard was designed to encompass the category of murder traditionally referred to as 'depraved heart' or 'universal malice' killings. Examples of such acts include shooting into an occupied house or into a moving automobile or piloting a speedboat through a group of swimmers."

We find in a discussion of "depraved heart murder" in LaFave & Scott, Criminal Law, § 70 (1972), the following:

"For murder the degree of risk of death or serious bodily injury must be more than a mere unreasonable risk, more even than a high degree of risk. Perhaps the required danger may be designated a 'very high degree' of risk to distinguish it from those lesser degrees of risk which will suffice for other crimes. Such a designation of conduct at all events is more accurately descriptive than that flowery expression found in the old cases and occasionally incorporated into some modern statutes—i.e., conduct 'evincing a depraved heart, devoid of social duty, and fatally bent on mischief.' Although 'very high degree of risk' means something quite substantial, it is still something less than certainty or substantial certainty. The distinctions between an unreasonable risk and a high degree of risk and a very high degree of risk are, of course, matters of degree, and there is no exact boundary line between each category; they shade gradually like a spectrum from one group to another.

"It should be noted, however, that for depraved-heart murder it is not a great amount of risk in the abstract which is decisive. The risk is exactly the same when one fires his rifle into a window of what appears to be an abandoned cabin in a deserted mining town as when one shoots the same bullet into the window of a well-kept city home, when in fact in each case one person occupies the room into which the shot is fired. In the deserted cabin situation it may not be, while in the occupied home situation it may be, murder when the occupant is killed. This illustrates that it is what the defendant should realize to be the degree of risk, in the light of the surrounding circumstances which he knows, which is important, rather than the amount of risk as an abstract proposition of the mathematics of chance.

"Another matter to be noted is that the risk must not only be very high, as the defendant ought to realize in the light of what he knows, it must also under the circumstances be unjustifiable for him to take the risk. The motives for the defendant's risky conduct thus become relevant; or, to express the thought in another way, the social utility of his conduct is a factor to be considered.... Since the amount of risk which will do for depraved-heart murder varies with these two variable factors—the extent of the defendant's knowledge of the surrounding circumstances and the social utility of his conduct—the mathematical chances of producing death required for murder cannot be measured in terms of percentages.

"The following types of conduct have been held, under the circumstances, to involve the very high degree of unjustifiable homicidal danger which will do for depraved-heart murder: firing a bullet into a room occupied, as the defendant knows, by several people; shooting into the caboose of a passing train or into a moving automobile, necessarily occupied by human beings; ... driving a car at very high speeds along a main street.... Other sorts of extremely risky conduct may be imagined: throwing stones from the roof of a tall building onto the busy street below; piloting a speedboat through a group of swimmers; swooping an airplane as to risk the decapitation of the motorist. In any such case, if death actually results to an endangered person and occurs in a foreseeable way, the defendant's conduct makes him an eligible candidate for a murder conviction."

In Hill v. Commonwealth, 239 Ky. 646, 40 S.W.2d 261 (1931), the court held that one who intentionally fires into an automobile which he knows is occupied and who kills someone therein is guilty of murder....

In Washington v. State, 60 Ala. 10, 15, 31 Am.Rep. 28 (1877) (quoting Code of 1876, § 4295), in affirming a murder conviction where the defendant had fired a pistol into a room occupied by several people, the Alabama Supreme Court stated:

"Every homicide ... perpetrated by any act greatly dangerous to the lives of others, and evidencing a depraved mind regardless of human life, although without any perceived purpose to deprive any particular person of life, is murder in the first degree."

. . .

In the instant case, appellant questions the sufficiency of the State's evidence that he manifested extreme indifference to human life in general, an element of the offense charged which must be found to exist in order to sustain a conviction for reckless murder under § 13A–6–2(a)(2).

. . .

Section 13A–6–2(a)(2) requires the prosecution to prove conduct which manifests an extreme indifference to human life, and not to a particular person only. Its gravamen is the act of reckless by engaging in conduct which creates a grave or very great risk of death under circumstances "manifesting extreme indifference to human life." What amounts to "extreme indifference" depends on the circumstances of each case, but some shocking, outrageous, or special heinousness must be shown. A person acts recklessly when he is aware of and consciously disregards a substantial and unjustifiable risk. "The risk must be of such nature and degree that disregard thereof constitutes a gross deviation from the standard of conduct that a reasonable person would observe in the situation." To bring appellant's conduct within the murder statute, the State is required to establish that his act was imminently dangerous and presented a very high or grave risk of death to others and that it was committed under circumstances which evidenced or manifested extreme indifference to human life. The conduct must manifest extreme indifference to human life generally. The crime charged here differs from intentional murder in that it results not from a specific, conscious intent to cause the death of any particular person, but from an indifference to or disregard of the risks attending appellant's conduct.

The State's evidence of appellant's conduct in firing his pistol at the Dunnaway vehicle on the interstate highway without excuse or provocation, under the circumstances enumerated above, was sufficient for the jury to conclude that appellant was aware of a very great risk of death to others and consciously disregarded it. . . . There was sufficient evidence presented for the jury to conclude that appellant's conduct manifested an extreme indifference to human life generally. The firing at the vehicle under the circumstances created a very great risk of death to Dunnaway, the driver, as well as his passenger, Reeves, and to anyone else who might have been using that portion of the interstate highway on that occasion.

. . .

Affirmed.

All Judges concur.[8]

---

8. Cf. State v. Capps, 134 N.C. 622, 46 S.E. 730 (1904); Banks v. State, 85 Tex.Cr.R. 165, 211 S.W. 217 (1919). Firing weapon into a packed barroom constituted depraved indifference

State v. Hokenson

Supreme Court of Idaho, 1974.
96 Idaho 283, 527 P.2d 487.

■ Donaldson, Justice.

Appellant Fred W. Hokenson, armed with a homemade bomb and a knife, entered Dean's Drug Center, Lewiston, on the evening of January 13, 1972 with the intent to commit robbery. The resulting course of events ended with the death of Officer Ross D. Flavel. In June, 1972, trial was held in the Second Judicial District Court for Nez Perce County and a jury found the appellant guilty of murder in the first degree. Judgment of conviction was entered and sentence of life imprisonment was imposed. This appeal is from that judgment.

On the evening of January 13, 1972, Kent Dean, owner and manager of Dean's Drug Center, Lewiston, received a call from an individual (later identified as appellant Fred W. Hokenson) asking him to return to the store and fill a prescription which was urgently needed. Upon agreeing to do so, Mr. Dean, accompanied by his wife and two small sons, returned to the store arriving shortly after 7:00 p.m. After a short wait, appellant Fred W. Hokenson entered the rear of the Drug Center wearing a gas mask and carrying a sack close to his shoulder in his right hand. He stated, "Nobody moves, nobody gets hurt."

Kent Dean immediately raced over to the appellant and grabbed him in a bear hug. The two men struggled, rolled against the counter, and Dean obtained a headlock on Hokenson. Hokenson then stated that he had a bomb. Mr. Dean asked his wife to call the police and to get his gun. While she was doing so, the two men fell to the ground and the appellant again mentioned the bomb. Dean managed to grasp the sack the appellant was holding and to slide it approximately ten feet away. Upon coming to rest, cylindrical rods could be seen protruding from the sack's top.

While both men were still on the floor, Dean heard the appellant say, "Okay, I have a knife and this is it." Dean felt the knife at the back of his neck but changed his position and managed to wrestle it away.

Mrs. Dean called the police and returned to the rear of the store. She was holding a gun on the appellant and Mr. Dean was still grasping Hokenson in a headlock when the police arrived. Officer Ross D. Flavel entered the store through the rear door and upon learning the facts started handcuffing Hokenson. After securing appellant's left wrist, he told Mrs. Dean that another officer, Tom Saleen, was at the front of the store. Mrs. Dean promptly let him in and the two officers along with Mr. Dean completed the task of handcuffing Hokenson.

to human life murder. People v. Register, 60 N.Y.2d 270, 469 N.Y.S.2d 599, 457 N.E.2d 704 (1983); see also Ishmael v. State, 688 S.W.2d 252 (Tex.App.1985).

Officer Flavel then left the store and backed the patrol car to the rear door. Upon his return Mrs. Dean mentioned the bomb. Officer Flavel approached the device, picked it up and identified it as being a bomb. Some conflict then exists in the testimony concerning the following events. Officer Saleen testified that Officer Flavel began pulling wires out of the device and that Hokenson stated that it would make no difference since they only had thirty seconds to live.[9] The Deans testified that Officer Flavel merely had his hands on the sack at the time of Hokenson's statement and subsequent explosion. Nonetheless, the device did explode killing Officer Flavel and injuring Officer Tom Saleen and Kent Dean.

The following morning two handwritten notes were found near the rear of the store. One established drugs as being the object of the robbery and the other contained a threat against Dean's family....

Appellant pleaded not guilty to murder under I.C. § 18–603 applicable at the time.[10] It reads as follows:

§ 18–603. *Murder.*—(1) Except as provided in section 18–604(1)(b) of this code, criminal homicide constitutes murder when:

"(a) it is committed purposely or knowingly; or

(b) it is committed recklessly under circumstances manifesting extreme indifference to the value of human life. Such recklessness and indifference are presumed if the actor is engaged or is an accomplice in the commission of, or an attempt to commit, or flight after committing or attempting to commit robbery, rape, or deviate sexual intercourse by force or threat of force, arson, burglary, kidnaping or felonious escape.

(2) Murder is a felony of the first degree, but a person convicted of murder may be sentenced to death, as provided in section 18–607 of this code." ...

Asserted error in denying appellant's motion for acquittal, or in the alternative, the verdict is contrary to the evidence.

Appellant argues that since he was under arrest and in custody at the time of the explosion, the attempted crime had been fully terminated and therefore he was not liable for the death under I.C. § 18–603.

Idaho Code § 18–603 provides that a criminal homicide is murder if it is committed recklessly under circumstances manifesting extreme indifference to the value of human life. This recklessness and indifference is presumed if the actor is engaged in the commission of, attempt to commit, or flight after committing or attempting to commit robbery. The state argues that the evidence presented showed beyond a reasonable doubt that the homicide was committed recklessly under circumstances manifesting extreme disregard to human life. As such, the state argues their case was established without the aid of the felony-murder presumption. We agree.

---

9. The remains of the device were sent for F.B.I. analysis and no evidence of a timing device was found.

10. Former I.C. § 18–603 (S.L.1971, Ch. 143, Sec. 1, p. 676) was repealed effective April 1, 1972.

The statute requires no showing that the homicide took place during the attempted robbery. The appellant's act of carrying an active bomb into the store, knowing it to be extremely dangerous as shown by his handling, manifests extreme indifference to the value of human life. This act, coupled with the ensuing explosion and death, suffices without the presumption to establish murder under I.C. § 18–603(1)(b).

Further, this Court cannot accept the appellant's contention that he should escape liability under the felony-murder rationale. The record shows that the appellant entered the store armed with a homemade bomb and a knife with the intent to commit robbery. His handling of the bomb illustrated his full cognizance of its characteristics. The fact he was met by resistance on the part of his intended victim, and in fact placed under arrest, does not release him from the final consequence of his act.

In the case of People v. Welch, 8 Cal.3d 106, 104 Cal.Rptr. 217, 501 P.2d 225 (1972) the California Supreme Court stated:

" ... homicide is committed in perpetration of the felony if the killing and the felony are parts of one continuous transaction.... The person killed need not be the object of the felony." 104 Cal.Rptr. at 225, 501 P.2d at 233.

In Commonwealth v. Banks, 454 Pa. 401, 311 A.2d 576, 578 (1973) the court stated that liability would be imposed where the conduct causing the death was done in furtherance of the design to commit the felony.

The explosion causing the death of Officer Flavel clearly falls within the above two definitions. A person is criminally liable for the natural and probable consequences of his unlawful acts as well as unlawful forces set in motion during the commission of an unlawful act. The appellant voluntarily set in motion an instrumentality which carried a very real probability of causing great bodily harm. Death ensued, and the fact appellant was under arrest does not erase criminal liability....

Judgment affirmed.

■ SHEPARD, C.J., and McQUADE, McFADDEN and BAKES, JJ., concur.[11]

---

11. [Added by Compiler]. The Idaho statute in the above case is based on the Model Penal Code § 210.2. Idaho repealed its adoption of the M.P.C. Most states that have adopted the M.P.C. have not adopted the full scheme of the Code's suggestion on murder. The Code did away with malice aforethought and defines murder by a standard of the significance of the mens rea, i.e., purposely, knowingly, recklessly manifesting extreme indifference. *See* Zimring & Hawkins, Murder, The Model Code and The Multiple Agendas of Reform, 19 Rutgers L.Jnl. 773 (1988).

Felony murder does not create an unconstitutional presumption of malice. People v. Leach, 41 Cal.3d 92, 221 Cal.Rptr. 826, 710 P.2d 893 (1985). However, *see* Regina v. Vaillancourt, [1987] 2 S.C.R. 636, holding the Canadian constructive murder statute to violate the Canadian Charter of Rights provision on the presumption of innocence. *See also*, Regina v. Sit, 66 CCC 3d 449 (S.C.C. 1991).

The fact that a defendant in a felony murder prosecution may not rely on defenses such as accident, self-defense, etc., applicable to other forms of murder, does not deny due process. State v. Walker, 893 S.W.2d 429 (Tenn.1995).

New Mexico "has a distinct version of the felony murder doctrine" and requires a mens rea which is satisfied by proof of an intent to kill, knowledge that one's actions create a strong probability of death or great bodily harm, or an action greatly dangerous to the lives of others.

People v. Patterson

Supreme Court of California, 1989.
49 Cal.3d 615, 262 Cal.Rptr. 195, 778 P.2d 549.

■ KENNARD, JUSTICE.

The issue before us is whether the second degree felony-murder doctrine applies to a defendant who, in violation of Health and Safety Code section 11352, furnishes cocaine to a person who dies as a result of ingesting it. We reaffirm the rule that, in determining whether a felony is inherently dangerous to human life under the second degree felony-murder doctrine, we must consider "the elements of the felony in the abstract, not the particular 'facts' of the case." (People v. Williams (1965) 63 Cal.2d 452, 458, fn. 5, 47 Cal.Rptr. 7, 406 P.2d 647.) While Health and Safety Code section 11352 includes drug offenses other than the crime of furnishing cocaine, which formed the basis for the prosecution's theory of second degree felony murder here, we conclude that the inquiry into inherent dangerousness must focus on the felony of furnishing cocaine, and not on section 11352 as a whole. We further hold that—consistent with the established definition of the term "inherently dangerous to life" in the context of implied malice as an element of second degree murder—a felony is inherently dangerous to life when there is a high probability that its commission will result in death.

We reverse the decision of the Court of Appeal affirming the trial court's ruling that, as a matter of law, the second degree felony-murder doctrine was inapplicable to this case. We direct the Court of Appeal to remand the matter to the trial court.

FACTUAL AND PROCEDURAL BACKGROUND

According to the testimony at the preliminary hearing, the victim Jennie Licerio and her friend Carmen Lopez had been using cocaine on a daily basis in the months preceding Licerio's death. On the night of November 25, 1985, the two women were with defendant in his motel room. There, all three drank "wine coolers," inhaled "lines" of cocaine, and smoked "coco puffs" (hand-rolled cigarettes containing a mixture of tobacco and cocaine). Defendant furnished the cocaine. When Licerio became ill, Lopez called an ambulance. Defendant stayed with the two women until the paramedics and the police arrived. The paramedics were unable to revive Licerio, who died of acute cocaine intoxication.

The People filed an information charging defendant with one count each of murder (Pen.Code, § 187), possession of cocaine (Health & Saf. Code, § 11350), and possession of cocaine for sale (Health & Saf.Code, § 11351). Defendant was also charged with three counts of violating Health and Safety Code section 11352, in that he "did willfully, unlawfully and feloniously transport, import into the State of California, sell, furnish, administer, and give away, and attempt to import into the State of California and transport a controlled substance, to-wit: cocaine."

The felony must be in the first degree, and an inherently dangerous felony. State v. McGruder, 123 N.M. 302, 940 P.2d 150 (1997).

Defendant moved under Penal Code section 995 to set aside that portion of the information charging him with murder, contending the evidence presented at the preliminary hearing did not establish probable cause to believe he had committed murder. In opposing the motion, the People did not suggest the murder charge was based on a theory of implied malice. Instead, they relied solely on the second degree felony-murder doctrine. They argued that by furnishing cocaine defendant committed an inherently dangerous felony, thus justifying application of the rule. The trial court denied the motion. However, when the case was reassigned for trial, the court dismissed the murder charge under Penal Code section 1385. . . .

Following the dismissal, defendant entered a negotiated plea of guilty to the three counts of violating Health and Safety Code section 11352. In his written plea form, defendant specifically admitted he had "furnished a controlled substance, to wit: cocaine, knowing it was cocaine." The remaining charges were dismissed, and defendant was placed on probation for three years, with credit for the time he had already spent in custody. The People appealed the dismissal of the murder charge.

The Court of Appeal affirmed the dismissal of the murder count. . . .

As we shall explain, the Court of Appeal has interpreted our previous decisions in this area too broadly. In determining whether defendant had committed an inherently dangerous felony, the court should have considered only the particular crime at issue, namely, furnishing cocaine, and not the entire group of offenses included in the statute but not involved here. Thus, it is the offense of furnishing cocaine, not the statute as a whole, which must be examined "in the abstract."

DISCUSSION

1. Second degree felony-murder doctrine

There is no precise statutory definition for the second degree felony-murder rule.[12] In People v. Ford (1964) 60 Cal.2d 772, 795, 36 Cal.Rptr. 620, 388 P.2d 892, we defined the doctrine as follows: "A homicide that is a direct causal result of the commission of a felony inherently dangerous to human life (other than the six felonies enumerated in Pen.Code, § 189) constitutes at least second degree murder. [Citations.]" In determining whether the felony is inherently dangerous, "we look to the elements of the felony in the abstract, not the particular 'facts' of the case." (People v. Phillips (1966) 64 Cal.2d 574, 582, 51 Cal.Rptr. 225, 414 P.2d 353).[13]

. . .

12. Penal Code section 189 provides in relevant part: "All murder which is perpetrated by means of a destructive device or explosive, knowing use of ammunition designed primarily to penetrate metal or armor, poison, lying in wait, torture, or by any other kind of willful, deliberate, and premeditated killing, or which is committed in the perpetration of, or attempt to perpetrate, arson, rape, robbery, burglary, mayhem, or any act punishable under Section 288, is murder of the first degree; and all other kinds of murders are of the second degree."

13. [Added by the compiler.]. In People v. Phillips, 64 Cal.2d 574, 51 Cal.Rptr. 225, 414 P.2d 353 (1966) cited by the court, the defendant had fraudulently obtained money from the parents of a child that was afflicted with cancer. Defendant represented a cure for the child's cancer. The child died. The defendant was charged with second degree felony murder for death

The second degree felony-murder doctrine has been a part of California's criminal law for many decades. Pike, Second Degree Murder in California (1936) 9 So.Cal.L.Rev. 112, 118–119. In recent years, we have characterized the rule as "anachronistic" and "disfavored", based on the view of many legal scholars that the doctrine incorporates an artificial concept of strict criminal liability that "erodes the relationship between criminal liability and moral culpability." (People v. Washington (1965) 62 Cal.2d 777, 783, 44 Cal.Rptr. 442, 402 P.2d 130; People v. Satchell (1971) 6 Cal.3d 28, 33, 98 Cal.Rptr. 33, 489 P.2d 1361.) The Legislature, however, has taken no action to alter this judicially created rule, and has declined our more recent suggestion in People v. Dillon (1983) 34 Cal.3d 441, 472, fn. 19, 194 Cal.Rptr. 390, 668 P.2d 697, that it reconsider the rules on first and second degree felony murder and misdemeanor manslaughter. In this case, our limited purpose in granting the People's petition for review was to determine the applicability of the second degree felony-murder doctrine to the crime of furnishing cocaine. We decline defendant's invitation that we determine the continued vitality of the rule.

We also turn down the People's invitation that we expand the second degree felony-murder doctrine by eliminating the requirement of People v. Williams, supra, 63 Cal.2d 452, 47 Cal.Rptr. 7, 406 P.2d 647, that the elements of the offense be viewed "in the abstract," and by adopting a new standard focusing instead on the actual conduct of a defendant in determining whether the felony is inherently dangerous.

In People v. Williams, *supra*, 63 Cal.2d 452, 47 Cal.Rptr. 7, 406 P.2d 647, the defendants argued with their drug dealer and stabbed him to death, assertedly in self-defense. We reversed the convictions for second degree murder because of the trial court's improper instruction to the jury that the defendants were guilty of second degree murder if the jury found the killing had occurred in the perpetration of the felony of conspiracy to possess Methedrine without a prescription. We explained that, in evaluating the inherent dangerousness of a particular felony, "we look to the elements of the felony in the abstract, not the particular 'facts' of the case." (Id., at p. 458, fn. 5, 47 Cal.Rptr. 7, 406 P.2d 647.) We concluded that under this analysis the conspiracy involved in Williams was not a felony inherently dangerous to human life. (Id., at p. 458, 47 Cal.Rptr. 7, 406 P.2d 647.)

Sound reasons support the Williams rule. As we observed in People v. Burroughs, *supra*, 35 Cal.3d at page 830, 201 Cal.Rptr. 319, 678 P.2d 894: "This form of [viewed-in-the-abstract] analysis is compelled because there is a killing in every case where the rule might potentially be applied. If in such circumstances a court were to examine the particular facts of the case prior to establishing whether the underlying felony is inherently dangerous, the court might well be led to conclude the rule applicable despite any unfairness which might redound to so broad an application: the existence of the dead victim might appear to lead inexorably to the conclusion that the underlying felony is exceptionally hazardous."

during the offense of grand theft. The California Supreme Court set aside the conviction. Defendant was retried under an implied malice theory and again convicted.

For the reasons set forth above, we are reluctant to significantly expand the scope of the second degree felony-murder rule, as the People have urged us to do. We have repeatedly said that the felony-murder rule "deserves no extension beyond its required application." (People v. Phillips, *supra*, 64 Cal.2d at p. 582, 51 Cal.Rptr. 225, 414 P.2d 353; People v. Dillon, *supra*, 34 Cal.3d at pp. 462–463, 194 Cal.Rptr. 390, 668 P.2d 697; People v. Burroughs, supra, 35 Cal.3d at p. 829, 201 Cal.Rptr. 319, 678 P.2d 894.) Both the People's suggestion that we expand the second degree felony-murder doctrine and defendant's suggestion that we abolish it are matters appropriately left to the Legislature.

2.   Determining "inherent dangerousness" of the felony of furnishing cocaine

As discussed earlier, in determining whether defendant committed an inherently dangerous felony, we must consider the elements of the felony "in the abstract." (People v. Williams, *supra*, 63 Cal.2d 452, 458, fn. 5, 47 Cal.Rptr. 7, 406 P.2d 647.) Because Health and Safety Code section 11352 also proscribes conduct other than that involved here (furnishing cocaine), the issue still to be resolved is whether we must consider only the specific offense of furnishing cocaine or the entire scope of conduct prohibited by the statute.

.   .   .

In *Lopez, supra*, 6 Cal.3d 45, 98 Cal.Rptr. 44, 489 P.2d 1372, the defendant and another inmate engaged in what initially was a nonviolent escape, but which culminated in a fatal assault perpetrated by the other escaping inmate. We held the crime of escape (Pen.Code, § 4532) not to be an inherently dangerous felony for purposes of applying the second degree felony-murder rule. . . .

In *Henderson, supra*, 19 Cal.3d 86, 137 Cal.Rptr. 1, 560 P.2d 1180, the defendant was accused of murder based on a death that had occurred in the course of aggravated false imprisonment. (Pen.Code, § 236.) The crime was a felony because it had been "effected by violence, menace, fraud or deceit." (Pen.Code, § 237.)[14] After analyzing the statutory scheme as a whole, we concluded: "While the elements of violence or menace by which false imprisonment is elevated to a felony may involve danger to human life, the felony offense viewed as a whole in the abstract is not inherently dangerous to human life." (19 Cal.3d at p. 94, 137 Cal.Rptr. 1, 560 P.2d 1180.) In rejecting the People's contention that, instead of examining the statute as a whole, we consider whether the felony of false imprisonment by violence or menace was inherently dangerous, we said: "The Legislature has not drawn any relevant distinctions between violence, menace, fraud, or deceit. These types of conduct are specified only as a basis for distinguishing between false imprisonment punishable as a misdemeanor and

---

14. Code section 236 reads: "False imprisonment is the unlawful violation of the personal liberty of another." When we decided Henderson, Penal Code section 237 provided: "False imprisonment is punishable by fine not exceeding five hundred dollars, or by imprisonment in the county jail not more than one year, or by both. If such false imprisonment be effected by violence, menace, fraud, or deceit, it shall be punishable by imprisonment in the state prison for not less than one nor more than ten years."

false imprisonment punishable as a felony." (Id., at p. 95, 137 Cal.Rptr. 1, 560 P.2d 1180.)

Finally, in *Burroughs, supra*, 35 Cal.3d 824, 201 Cal.Rptr. 319, 678 P.2d 894, we held that a violation of Business and Professions Code section 2053, which prohibits the practice of medicine without a license "under circumstances or conditions which cause or create a risk of great bodily harm, serious physical or mental illness, or death," was not a felony inherently dangerous to human life. We explained: "In this examination we are required to view the statutory definition of the offense as a whole, taking into account even nonhazardous ways of violating the provisions of the law which do not necessarily pose a threat to human life. [¶] The primary element of the offense in question here is the practice of medicine without a license. The statute defines such practice as 'treating the sick or afflicted.' One can certainly conceive of treatment of the sick or afflicted which has quite innocuous results—the affliction at stake could be a common cold, or a sprained finger, and the form of treatment an admonition to rest in bed and drink fluids or the application of ice to mild swelling. Thus, we do not find inherent dangerousness at this stage. . . . "

. . .

The determination whether a defendant who furnishes cocaine commits an inherently dangerous felony should not turn on the dangerousness of other drugs included in the same statute, such as heroin and peyote; nor should it turn on the danger to life, if any, inherent in the transportation or administering of cocaine. Rather, each offense set forth in the statute should be examined separately to determine its inherent dangerousness.

For the reasons discussed above, we hold the Court of Appeal and the trial court erred in concluding that Health and Safety Code section 11352 should be analyzed in its entirety to determine whether, in furnishing cocaine, defendant committed an inherently dangerous felony. Defendant, however, argues that even the more narrow offense of furnishing cocaine is not an inherently dangerous felony and therefore the trial court acted correctly in dismissing the murder charge, despite its faulty analysis. In countering that argument, the People have asked us to take judicial notice of various medical articles and reports that assertedly demonstrate that the offense of furnishing cocaine is sufficiently dangerous to life to constitute an inherently dangerous felony.

The task of evaluating the evidence on this issue is most appropriately entrusted to the trial court, subject, of course, to appellate review. We therefore direct the Court of Appeals to remand the matter to the trial court for further proceedings in light of this opinion. This remand does not foreclose a finding by the trial court that the crime of furnishing cocaine is not a felony inherently dangerous to life, thus justifying a dismissal of the murder charge. If, however, the trial court concludes the offense of furnishing cocaine is inherently dangerous and therefore the murder charge should not be dismissed, defendant must be allowed to withdraw his guilty plea to the charges of violating Health and Safety Code section 11352, with credit for any interim time served.

3. *Meaning of the term "inherently dangerous to human life"*

For the guidance of the trial court on remand, we shall elaborate on the meaning of the term "inherently dangerous to life" for purposes of the second degree felony-murder doctrine.

The felony-murder rule generally acts as a substitute for the *mental state* ordinarily required for the offense of murder. We observed in People v. Satchell, *supra*, 6 Cal.3d at page 43, 98 Cal.Rptr. 33, 489 P.2d 1361: "Under well-settled principles of criminal liability a person who kills—whether or not he is engaged in an independent felony at the time—is guilty of murder *if he acts with malice aforethought*. The felony-murder doctrine, whose ostensible purpose is to deter those engaged in felonies from killing negligently or accidentally, operates to posit the existence of that crucial mental state—and thereby to render irrelevant evidence of actual malice or the lack thereof—when the killer is engaged in a felony whose inherent danger to human life renders logical an imputation of malice on the part of all who commit it." Ordinarily, when a defendant commits an unintentional killing, a murder conviction requires a showing that he acted with implied malice. (Pen.Code, § 188.) With the felony-murder rule, however, such malice need not be shown.

Implied malice, for which the second degree felony-murder doctrine acts as a substitute,[15] has both a physical and a mental component. The physical component is satisfied by the performance of "an act, the natural consequences of which are dangerous to life." The mental component is the requirement that the defendant "knows that his conduct endangers the life of another and . . . acts with a conscious disregard for life."

The second degree felony-murder rule eliminates the need for the prosecution to establish the *mental* component. The justification therefor is that, when society has declared certain inherently dangerous conduct to be felonious, a defendant should not be allowed to excuse himself by saying he was unaware of the danger to life because, by declaring the conduct to be felonious, society has warned him of the risk involved. The *physical* requirement, however, remains the same; by committing a felony inherently dangerous to life, the defendant has committed "an act, the natural consequences of which are dangerous to life" (*Watson, supra*, 30 Cal.3d at p. 300, 179 Cal.Rptr. 43, 637 P.2d 279), thus satisfying the physical component of implied malice.

The definition of "inherently dangerous to life" in the context of the implied malice element of second degree murder is well established. An act is inherently dangerous to human life when there is "a *high probability* that it will result in death."

---

15. Although the second degree felony-murder doctrine operates as a substitute for implied malice, this does not mean that the doctrine results in a "conclusive presumption" of malice. (*See* People v. Dillon, *supra*, 34 Cal.3d at p. 475, 194 Cal.Rptr. 390, 668 P.2d 697.) Nevertheless, in determining the proper scope of the second degree felony-murder doctrine, it is appropriate for the courts, in recognition of the Legislature's authority to define criminal offenses, to attempt to minimize the disparity between the legislatively created and the judicially recognized categories of second degree murder.

We therefore conclude—by analogy to the established definition of the term "dangerous to life" in the context of the implied malice element of second degree murder—that, for purposes of the second degree felony-murder doctrine, an "inherently dangerous felony" is an offense carrying "a high probability" that death will result. A less stringent standard would inappropriately expand the scope of the second degree felony-murder rule reducing the seriousness of the act which a defendant must commit in order to be charged with murder.

. . .

DISPOSITION

We reverse the decision of the Court of Appeal, and direct that court to remand the matter to the trial court for further proceedings consistent with this opinion.

State v. Mayle

Supreme Court of Appeals of West Virginia, 1987.
178 W.Va. 26, 357 S.E.2d 219.

■ BROTHERTON, JUSTICE:

This is an appeal from a judgment of felony murder by the Circuit Court of Cabell County in December, 1982. . . .

On December 14, 1981, at 1:15 a.m. two men entered a McDonald's restaurant in Chesapeake, Ohio. One was a tall, white man, the other was a shorter, black man. They wore dark blue or black ski masks over their faces. The pair demanded that the employees give them the combination to the safe. The employees did not know the combination, so the robbers took the keys to one of the employee's cars, a 1972 Matador, and left in the stolen car. . . .

Approximately one-half hour after the Ohio robbery, Officer Byard of the Huntington Police Department observed a possible breaking and entering by two men at a gasoline station. He notified Officer Harman, a few blocks away. Harman indicated over the radio "I've got 'em over here." A few minutes later, Officer Byard heard a gunshot and started running to Harman's aid. He heard more gunshots, and saw two men running west down Jefferson Street in Huntington. Officer Harman had been fatally wounded by several hard blows to the head and five gunshot wounds from his service revolver. Officer Byard observed the men getting into a green Buick and leaving the scene.

One witness, Ted Norman, looked out the window of his home and saw Officer Harman on the ground with a man on top of him trying to take something from the officer. The man raised up and shot Harman several times. Mr. Norman turned on his porch light and clearly saw the man's face at a distance of between eight and ten feet. He later identified the man as Bobby Stacy. Other witnesses saw two men running from the area, one white and the other a shorter, fair-skinned black man.

. . .

Kathy Pearson, a resident of Columbus, Ohio, had been a friend of Bobby Stacy for several years and was acquainted with Wilbert Mayle. Pearson was told by Stacy at 6:00 p.m. on the night of the shooting that "he had to go meet Jackie and pick him up and go to the hills and take care of business." Jackie was Wilbert Mayle's nickname. It is undisputed that Stacy and Mayle were good friends and had been for a long time.

The automobile found on Sycamore Street was registered in the name of Bobby Stacy and contained a tape deck and tapes stolen from the Matador in Ohio, a black ski mask, and Officer Harman's gun. Wilbert Mayle's fingerprints were found on the steering wheel. An analysis of hair samples found in two ski masks (the one found in the car and another found near the car) revealed that one mask had hair consistent with Mayle's hair and the other had hair consistent with Bobby Stacy's and Mayle's.

. . .

At the end of the evidence, the jury found Wilbert Mayle guilty of first degree murder, with a recommendation of mercy. He appeals to this Court, citing numerous errors which we now address.

. . .

Mr. Mayle claims that the State failed to meet its burden in proving felony murder under W.Va.Code § 61–2–1 (1984), which provides: "Murder by poison, lying in wait, imprisonment, starving, or by any willful, deliberate and premeditated killing, or in the commission of, or attempt to commit, arson, rape, robbery or burglary, is murder of the first degree." The State is not required in a felony murder case to prove any specific intent to kill, premeditation, or malice. *See* syl. pt. 7, State v. Sims, 162 W.Va. 212, 248 S.E.2d 834 (1978). Instead, "the elements which the State is required to prove to obtain a conviction of felony murder are: (1) The commission of, or attempt to commit, one or more of the enumerated felonies; (2) the defendant's participation in such commission or attempt; and (3) the death of the victim as a result of injuries received during the course of such commission or attempt."

We will look at each of the three elements individually, starting with the commission or attempt to commit a felony. A felony was unquestionably committed in this case. A robbery, which is one of the enumerated felonies in § 61–2–1, was committed when the two men took car keys at gunpoint from an employee of a McDonald's restaurant in Chesapeake, Ohio.

The defendant's participation in such commission or attempt was also satisfactorily proved. In this case, one of the robbers was a short, black man who fit Mayle's general description. He was wearing a ski mask. A ski mask similar to the one used in the robbery was found in Bobby Stacy's car, and another was found near the car. Both had hair similar to Mayle's hair in them. The car, which Mayle was seen driving shortly after the robbery, was quickly abandoned when a police officer came to investigate, and contained articles stolen from a car which was taken during the McDonald's robbery. While individually each item of evidence presented above would be quite weak evidence, taken together it is strong evidence pointing toward Mayle's guilt from which a jury could easily conclude that there was no reasonable hypothesis of innocence.

Finally, there was sufficient evidence to support the jury's determination that Officer Harman was killed during the commission of the felony. The act of robbing had been completed several minutes earlier, but the incident was not complete. The robbers had yet to return home to a place of safety. The distance from the McDonald's in Chesapeake to the scene of the shooting was only 2.1 miles. The loot had not been distributed, but remained in the trunk of Stacy's car. Whether the robbers were conducting their escape or were moving on to another crime, their activities were a part of "one continuous transaction."

In State v. Wayne, 169 W.Va. 785, 289 S.E.2d 480 (1982), the defendant was convicted of first degree murder in a felony murder situation. His claim of error to this Court was that the underlying felony of the robbery had been completed prior to the murder. After an examination of the law of several other jurisdictions, we concluded that the felony murder statute does apply where the robbery was complete but the defendants were still in the act of escape. We noted with approval the case of State v. Squire, 292 N.C. 494, 234 S.E.2d 563 (1977), where a car containing bank robbers was stopped by a state policeman for a traffic violation ten miles from the scene of the robbery. As the state policeman approached the car, he was killed. Despite the distance from the scene, the North Carolina court found that the robbers were still in the act of escape and applied the felony murder rule. In the present case, the escape was not complete. Wilbert Mayle and Bobby Stacy were still "in the hills taking care of business." They were still involved in the chain of events surrounding the robbery. Therefore the felony murder rule was properly applied.

. . .

Affirmed.[16]

---

16. "The res gestae embraces not only the actual facts of the transaction and the circumstances surrounding it, but the matters immediately antecedent to and having a direct causal connection with it, as well as acts immediately following it and so closely connected with it as to form in reality a part of the occurrence." State v. Fouquette, 67 Nev. 505, 221 P.2d 404, 417 (1950).

Defendant lost control of his vehicle thirty minutes after fleeing from a robbery, struck another vehicle and killed the occupant. Whether defendant had reached a place of temporary safety was an objective standard. Defendant had not reached such a position. The felony murder rule was applicable. People v. Johnson, 5 Cal.App.4th 552, 7 Cal.Rptr.2d 23 (1992). *See also*, People v. Johnson, 15 Cal.App.4th 169, 18 Cal.Rptr.2d 650 (1993).

Contra: After the burglar has left the building empty-handed he is no longer in the perpetration or attempted perpetration of burglary and hence a killing by him 25 or 30 feet from the house and on another lot, in his effort to resist arrest was not first-degree murder under the felony-murder rule. It might have been first-degree murder but the conviction is reversed because of an improper instruction on the felony-murder rule. People v. Huter, 184 N.Y. 237, 77 N.E. 6 (1906).

Under the circumstances of this case the jury might find that killing a trooper 45 minutes after the robbery and 37.75 miles from the situs, was a killing during immediate flight after the offense. People v. Donovan, 385 N.Y.S.2d 385 (App.Div.1976).

People v. Hansen

Supreme Court of California, In Bank, 1994.
9 Cal.4th 300, 36 Cal.Rptr.2d 609, 885 P.2d 1022.

■ GEORGE, JUSTICE.

In this case we must determine whether the offense of discharging a firearm at an inhabited dwelling house is a felony "inherently dangerous to human life" for purposes of the second degree felony-murder doctrine, and, if so, whether that doctrine nonetheless is inapplicable in the present case under the so-called "merger" doctrine applied in People v. Ireland (1969) 70 Cal.2d 522, 75 Cal.Rptr. 188, 450 P.2d 580, and its progeny. For the reasons explained hereafter, we conclude that this offense, for such purposes, is a felony inherently dangerous to human life and does not "merge" with a resulting homicide so as to preclude application of the felony-murder doctrine. Because the Court of Appeal reached a similar conclusion, we affirm the judgment of that court upholding defendant's conviction of second degree murder.

On September 19, 1991, defendant Michael Hansen, together with Rudolfo Andrade and Alexander Maycott, planned to purchase $40 worth of methamphetamine. With that purpose, defendant, accompanied by his girlfriend Kimberly Geldon and Maycott, drove in defendant's Camaro to an apartment duplex located in the City of San Diego. Upon arriving at the duplex, defendant pounded on the door of the upstairs apartment where Christina Almenar resided with her two children. When he received no response, defendant proceeded to return to his automobile and was approached by Michael Echaves.

Echaves resided in the downstairs apartment with Martha Almenar (Christina's sister) and Martha's two children, Diane Rosalez, thirteen years of age, and Louie Miranda, five years of age. At the time, Diane and Louie were outside with Echaves helping him with yard work. In response to a question from Echaves, defendant said he was looking for Christina. When Echaves stated he had not seen her, defendant asked whether Echaves would be able to obtain some crystal methamphetamine (speed). After making a telephone call, Echaves informed defendant that he would be able to do so. Defendant said he would attempt to purchase the drug elsewhere but, if unsuccessful, would return.

Defendant and his companions departed but returned approximately 20 minutes later. Defendant, accompanied by Echaves, Maycott, and Geldon, then drove a short distance to another apartment complex. Defendant parked his vehicle, gave Echaves two $20 bills, and told Echaves he would wait while Echaves obtained the methamphetamine. Echaves said he would be back shortly.

When Echaves failed to return, defendant and his companions proceeded to Echaves's apartment. Defendant knocked on the door and the

"We have held that escape from the scene of the underlying felony is part of the *res gestae* of a crime so that a murder committed to facilitate the flight can be felony murder." People v. McCrary, 190 Colo. 538, 549 P.2d 1320, 1331 (1976).

Contra: Escape is not a part of the offense of burglary for felony murder rule. In re D.C., 259 Ill.App.3d 637, 197 Ill.Dec. 661, 631 N.E.2d 883 (1994).

windows. Diane and Louie were inside the apartment alone but did not respond. Their mother, Martha, had left the apartment to meet Echaves, who had telephoned her after eluding defendant. After meeting Echaves at a hardware store, Martha telephoned her children from a public telephone booth. Diane answered and told her mother that the "guys in the Camaro" had returned, pounded on the door, and then had left.

Meanwhile, defendant, Maycott, and Geldon returned to the location where Andrade was waiting for them, acquiring en route a handgun from an acquaintance. The three men then decided to return to Echaves's apartment with the objective either of recovering their money or physically assaulting Echaves. At approximately 7:30 p.m., defendant approached the apartment building in his automobile with the lights turned off, and then from the vehicle fired the handgun repeatedly at the dwelling. At the time, Diane was inside the apartment, in the living room with her brother. The kitchen and living room lights were on. Diane was struck fatally in the head by one of the bullets fired by defendant.

. . .

Five bullet holes were found at the scene of the homicide inside the apartment. It later was determined that shell casings and three bullets recovered at that location had been fired from the handgun found inside the trunk of defendant's vehicle.

. . . [D]efendant was advised of his *Miranda* rights and waived them. He then confessed to having fired several shots from a handgun aimed at the apartment building. He stated that he had been waiting for someone whom he believed "took off with forty bucks" belonging to him, that he was shooting at "[j]ust the house," and that he would not have engaged in this conduct had he known "those kids were in there."

. . .

The trial court instructed the jury on several theories of murder, including second degree felony murder as an unlawful killing that occurs during the commission or attempted commission of a felony inherently dangerous to human life, further instructing that the felony of shooting at an inhabited dwelling is inherently dangerous to human life. The jury returned a verdict finding defendant guilty of second degree murder (without specifying the theory upon which the conviction was based), and found true the allegation that he personally used a firearm during the commission of that offense (§ 12022.5, subd. (a)). The jury also found defendant guilty of discharging a firearm at an inhabited dwelling. . . .

On appeal, defendant asserted, among other contentions, that the trial court erred in instructing the jury on second degree felony murder based upon the underlying felony of discharging a firearm at an inhabited dwelling, because the latter offense merged with the resulting homicide within the meaning of *Ireland, supra,* 70 Cal.2d 522, 75 Cal.Rptr. 188, 450 P.2d 580. Defendant relied upon People v. Wesley (1970) 10 Cal.App.3d 902, 905–910, 89 Cal.Rptr. 377, a decision holding that the offense proscribed by section 246 was an integral part of the resulting homicide and therefore could not support a second degree felony-murder conviction. . . . Concluding the underlying felony proscribed by section 246 did not merge with the homicide, the Court of Appeal affirmed the conviction of second degree murder but struck the section 12022.5 firearm-use enhancement.

Murder is the unlawful killing of a human being, or a fetus, with malice aforethought. Second degree murder is the unlawful killing of a human being with malice, but without the additional elements (i.e., willfulness, premeditation, and deliberation) that would support a conviction of first degree murder.

. . .

The felony-murder rule imputes the requisite malice for a murder conviction to those who commit a homicide during the perpetration of a felony inherently dangerous to human life. "Under well-settled principles of criminal liability a person who kills—whether or not he is engaged in an independent felony at the time—is guilty of murder *if he acts with malice aforethought*. The felony-murder doctrine, whose ostensible purpose is to deter those engaged in felonies from killing negligently or accidentally, operates to posit the existence of that crucial mental state—and thereby to render irrelevant evidence of actual malice or the lack thereof—when the killer is engaged in a felony whose inherent danger to human life renders logical an imputation of malice on the part of all who commit it."

The felony-murder rule applies to both first and second degree murder. . . .

In determining whether a felony is inherently dangerous, the court looks to the elements of the felony *in the abstract*, "not the 'particular' facts of the case," i.e., not to the defendant's specific conduct.

. . .

. . . [W]e hold that the offense of discharging a firearm at an inhabited dwelling is an "inherently dangerous felony" for purposes of the second degree felony-murder rule.

Defendant contends that, even if the section 246 felony of discharging a firearm is inherently dangerous to human life, the commission of that felony in the present case "merged" with the resulting homicide, within the meaning of People v. Ireland, *supra*, 70 Cal.2d 522, 75 Cal.Rptr. 188, 450 P.2d 580, thereby precluding application of the second degree felony-murder rule.

As we shall explain, defendant's contention rests upon an unduly expansive view of the scope of the "merger" doctrine applied in *Ireland*. Prior to our decision in *Ireland*, the "merger" doctrine had been developed in other jurisdictions as a shorthand explanation for the conclusion that the felony-murder rule should not be applied in circumstances where the only underlying (or "predicate") felony committed by the defendant was *assault*. The name of the doctrine derived from the characterization of the assault as an offense that "merged" with the resulting homicide. In explaining the basis for the merger doctrine, courts and legal commentators reasoned that, because a homicide generally results from the commission of an assault, every felonious assault ending in death automatically would be elevated to murder in the event a felonious assault could serve as the predicate felony for purposes of the felony-murder doctrine. Consequently, application of the felony-murder rule to felonious assaults would usurp most of the law of homicide, relieve the prosecution in the great majority of homicide cases of the burden of having to prove malice in order to obtain a murder conviction, and thereby frustrate the Legislature's intent to punish certain felonious assaults resulting in death (those committed with malice aforethought, and therefore punishable as murder) more harshly than other felonious assaults that happened to result in death (those committed without malice aforethought, and therefore punishable as manslaughter).

In *Ireland, supra*, we adopted the merger rule in a case involving the underlying felony of assault with a deadly weapon, where the defendant had shot and killed his wife. The jury was instructed that it could return a second degree felony-murder verdict based upon the underlying felony of assault with a deadly weapon, and the defendant was convicted of second degree murder.

On appeal, this court reversed, reasoning that "[t]o allow such use of the felony-murder rule would effectively preclude the jury from considering the issue of malice aforethought in all cases wherein homicide has been committed as a result of a felonious assault—a category which includes the great majority of all homicides. This kind of bootstrapping finds support neither in logic nor in law." The court therefore concluded that the offense of assault with a deadly weapon, which was "an integral part of" and "included in fact" within the homicide, could not support a second degree felony-murder instruction.

Subsequent decisions have applied the *Ireland* rule to other felonies involving assault or assault with a deadly weapon. (See People v. Smith (1984) 35 Cal.3d 798, 201 Cal.Rptr. 311, 678 P.2d 886 [felony child abuse of the assaultive category]; People v. Wilson (1969) 1 Cal.3d 431, 440, 82 Cal.Rptr. 494, 462 P.2d 22 [burglary with intent to commit the felony of assault with a deadly weapon]; People v. Landry (1989) 212 Cal.App.3d 1428, 1437–1439, 261 Cal.Rptr. 254 [assault with a deadly weapon].)

Our court, however, has not extended the *Ireland* doctrine beyond the context of assault, even under circumstances in which the underlying felony plausibly could be characterized as "an integral part of" and "included in fact within" the resulting homicide....

We agree with [the] definition of the scope of the *Ireland* rule and its rejection of the premise that *Ireland*'s "integral part of the homicide" language constitutes the crucial test in determining the existence of merger. Such a test would be inconsistent with the underlying rule that only felonies "inherently dangerous to human life" are sufficiently indicative of a defendant's culpable mens rea to warrant application of the felony-murder rule. The more dangerous the felony, the more likely it is that a death may result directly from the commission of the felony, but resort to the "integral part of the homicide" language would preclude application of the felony-murder rule for those felonies that are most likely to result in death and that are, consequently, the felonies as to which the felony-murder doctrine is most likely to act as a deterrent (because the perpetrator could foresee the great likelihood that death may result, negligently or accidentally).

We decline, however, to adopt as the critical test determinative of merger in all cases the following language ... that the rationale for the merger doctrine does not encompass a felony "committed with a collateral and independent felonious design.'' Under such a test, a felon who acts with a purpose other than specifically to inflict injury upon someone—for example, with the intent to sell narcotics for financial gain, or to discharge a firearm at a building solely to intimidate the occupants—is subject to greater criminal liability for an act resulting in death than a person who actually intends to injure the person of the victim. Rather than rely upon a somewhat artificial test that may lead to an anomalous result, we focus upon the principles and rationale underlying the foregoing language ... , namely, that with respect to certain inherently dangerous felonies, their use as the predicate felony supporting application of the felony-murder rule will not elevate all felonious assaults to murder or otherwise subvert the legislative intent.

In the present case, ... application of the second degree felony-murder rule would not result in the subversion of legislative intent.... [A]pplication of the felony-murder doctrine in the case before us would not frustrate the Legislature's deliberate calibration of punishment for assaultive conduct resulting in death, based upon the presence or absence of malice aforethought. As in Taylor, this is not a situation in which the Legislature has demanded a showing of actual malice (apart from the statutory requirement that the firearm be discharged ''maliciously and willfully'') in order to support a second degree murder conviction. Indeed, ... application of the felony-murder rule, when a violation of section 246 results in the death of a person, clearly is consistent with the traditionally recognized purpose of the second degree felony-murder doctrine—namely the deterrence of negligent or accidental killings that occur in the course of the commission of dangerous felonies.

. . .

For the foregoing reasons, we conclude that the offense of discharging a firearm at an inhabited dwelling house does not ''merge'' with a resulting homicide within the meaning of the *Ireland* doctrine, and therefore that this offense will support a conviction of second degree felony murder. Accordingly, the trial court did not err in instructing the jury on a second degree felony-murder theory based upon the underlying felony of discharging a firearm at an inhabited dwelling house.

Affirmed.[17]

Commonwealth v. Drum

Supreme Court of Pennsylvania, 1868.
58 Pa. 9.

William Drum was charged in the Court of Quarter Sessions of Westmoreland County for the murder of David Mohigan. A true bill having

---

17. [Compiler's note.] Entering home for sole purpose of killing precludes use of burglary for capital murder. Parker v. State, 292 Ark. 421, 731 S.W.2d 756 (1987). The merger doctrine was rejected in the case of a killing occurring during a robbery. People v. Burton, 6 Cal.3d 375, 99 Cal.Rptr. 1, 491 P.2d 793 (1971). The merger doctrine is inapplicable to felony-murder during the commission of child abuse. State v. O'Blasney, 297 N.W.2d 797 (S.D.1980). Single assaultive incident of abuse of a child which resulted in the death of the child merged with the killing and a felony murder charge was improper. State v. Lucas, 243 Kan. 462, 759 P.2d 90 (1988).

been found by the grand jury of that court, it was certified into the Court of Oyer and Terminer of the same county. . . .

■ JUSTICE AGNEW charged the jury as follows: . . .

A life has been taken. The unfortunate David Mohigan has fallen into an untimely grave; struck down by the hand of violence; and it is for you to determine whose was that hand, and what its guilt. The prisoner is in the morning of life; as yet so fresh and fair. As you sat and gazed into his youthful face, you have thought, no doubt, most anxiously thought, is his that hand? Can he, indeed, be a murderer? This, gentlemen, is the solemn question you must determine upon the law and the evidence.

At the common law murder is described to be, when a person of sound memory and discretion unlawfully kills any reasonable creature in being and under the peace of the Commonwealth, with malice aforethought, express or implied. The distinguishing criterion of murder is malice afore-thought. But it is not malice in its ordinary understanding alone, a particular ill-will, a spite or a grudge. Malice is a legal term, implying much more. It comprehends not only a particular ill-will, but every case where there is wickedness of disposition, hardness of heart, cruelty, recklessness of consequences, and a mind regardless of social duty, although a particular person may not be intended to be injured. Murder, therefore, at common law embraces cases where no intent to kill existed, but where the state or frame of mind termed malice, in its legal sense, prevailed.

In Pennsylvania, the legislature, considering that there is a manifest difference in the degree of guilt, where a deliberate intention to kill exists, and where none appears, distinguished murder into two grades—murder of the first and murder of the second degree; and provided that the jury before whom any person indicted for murder should be tried, shall, if they find him guilty thereof, ascertain in their verdict whether it be murder of the first or murder of the second degree. By the Act of 31st March 1860, "all murder which shall be perpetrated by means of poison,[18] or by lying in wait, or by any other kind of wilful, deliberate and premeditated killing, or which shall be committed in the perpetration of, or attempt to perpetrate any arson, rape, robbery or burglary, shall be deemed murder of the first degree; and all other kinds of murder shall be deemed murder of the second degree."[19]

In this case we have to deal only with that kind of murder in the first degree described as "wilful, deliberate, and premeditated." Many cases have been decided under this clause, in all of which it has been held that

---

18. Some statutes have added by means of torture. This does not require an intent to kill, but it does require a wilful, deliberate and premeditated intent to inflict extreme and prolonged pain. People v. Steger, 16 Cal.3d 539, 128 Cal.Rptr. 161, 546 P.2d 665 (1976). Murder by torture requires acts involving a high probability of death. Givens v. Housewright, 786 F.2d 1378 (9th Cir.1986).

California provides that it is murder in the first degree if perpetrated by means of a "destructive device or explosive, knowing use of ammunition designed primarily to penetrate metal or armor. . . . " West's Ann.Cal.Pen.Code § 189 (1982).

19. This is essentially the same as the first statute which divided murder into degrees, enacted in Pennsylvania in 1794. It was adopted, sometimes with minor variations, in over two-thirds of the states.

the *intention* to kill is the essence of the offence. Therefore, if an intention to kill exists, it is wilful; if this intention be accompanied by such circumstances as evidence a mind fully conscious of its own purpose and design, it is deliberate; and if sufficient time be afforded to enable the mind fully to frame the design to kill, and to select the instrument, or to frame the plan to carry this design into execution, it is premeditated. The law fixes upon no length of time as necessary to form the intention to kill, but leaves the existence of a fully formed intent as a fact to be determined by the jury, from all the facts and circumstances in the evidence.... [20]

The proof of the intention to kill, and of the disposition of mind constituting murder in the first degree, under the Act of Assembly, lies on the Commonwealth. But this proof need not be express or positive. It may be inferred from the circumstances. If, from all the facts attending the killing, the jury can fully, reasonably, and satisfactorily infer the existence of the intention to kill, and the malice of heart with which it was done, they will be warranted in so doing. He who uses upon the body of another, at some vital part, with a manifest intention to use it upon him, a deadly weapon, as an axe, a gun, a knife or a pistol, must, in the absence of qualifying facts, be presumed to know that his blow is likely to kill; and, knowing this, must be presumed to intend the death which is the probable and ordinary consequence of such an act. He who so uses a deadly weapon without a sufficient cause of provocation, must be presumed to do it wickedly, or from a bad heart. Therefore, he who takes the life of another with a deadly weapon, and with a manifest design thus to use it upon him, with sufficient time to deliberate, and fully to form the conscious purpose of killing, and without any sufficient reason or cause of extenuation, is guilty of murder in the first degree.

All murder not of the first degree, is necessarily of the second degree, and includes all unlawful killing under circumstances of depravity of heart, and a disposition of mind regardless of social duty; but where no intention to kill exists or can be reasonably and fully inferred. Therefore, in all cases of murder, if no intention to kill can be inferred or collected from the circumstances, the verdict must be murder in the second degree.

Manslaughter is defined to be the unlawful killing of another without malice expressed or implied; which may be voluntarily in a sudden heat, or involuntarily, but in the commission of an unlawful act....

---

20. "No specific period of time is required but if the time is sufficient to fully and clearly conceive the design to kill and purposely and deliberately execute it, the requirements of the statute are satisfied." State v. Pierce, 4 N.J. 252, 267–8, 72 A.2d 305, 313 (1950). Accord, Clozza v. Commonwealth, 228 Va. 124, 321 S.E.2d 273 (1984). The time involved may be a space of a few seconds, Watson v. United States, 501 A.2d 791 (D.C.App.1985). Instruction permitting design to be formed at the moment of the fatal act was error. Windham v. State, 520 So.2d 123 (Miss.1987).

" 'When a design to kill another person is once formed, the haste with which it is put into execution in no way affects or modifies the degree of guilt incurred.' " State v. Gregory, 66 Nev. 423, 427, 212 P.2d 701, 703–4 (1949).

"To prove deliberate premeditation the Commonwealth must show that a defendant's resolution to kill was a result of reflection which 'is not so much a matter of time as logical sequence. First the deliberation and premeditation, then the resolution to kill, and lastly the killing in pursuance of the resolution; and all this may occur in a few seconds.' " Commonwealth v. Soares, 377 Mass. 461, 387 N.E.2d 499, 506 (1979).

You will now take the case and render such a verdict as the evidence warrants; one which will do justice to the Commonwealth and to the prisoner.

People v. Perez

Supreme Court of California, In Bank, 1992.
2 Cal.4th 1117, 9 Cal.Rptr.2d 577, 831 P.2d 1159.

■ PANELLI, JUSTICE.

We granted review in this case after a divided Court of Appeal reduced defendant's first degree murder conviction to second degree murder for insufficient evidence of premeditation and deliberation. As explained here-after, we conclude that the judgment of the Court of Appeal should be reversed.

FACTS

Defendant killed Victoria Mesa in her home in Garden Grove on the morning of September 30, 1988. There is no question that he was the perpetrator. . . .

Victoria's employer called Michael about 9:45 a.m. to tell him that Victoria had not come to work. Michael called a neighbor to ask her to check on Victoria. The neighbor enlisted the aid of a gas company meter reader who, upon approaching the house, found the front door slightly ajar; he entered, found Victoria's body, and immediately left to call the police.

Police officers arrived about 9:50 a.m. and found Victoria's fully clothed body lying face down with her arms under her head in the bathroom and her legs extending into the hallway. A broken dish and dog food were lying near the body. A six-inch blade of a serrated steak knife was found under Victoria's head. A broken piece of knife handle was near her feet. The wood appeared to be the same as the handles of knives in the kitchen drawer. There was no sign of a forced entry, and the only unlocked door was the front door.

. . . .

The entire kitchen was peppered with blood spots. There were drops of blood on the refrigerator and counter top and smeared blood around the handles of cupboards and drawers. Many of the cupboards and drawers were open. There were drops of blood inside some of the drawers, including one containing knives.

Victoria's purse was on top of a table in the kitchen. The contents of the purse were lying on the table. A removable car stereo was also on the table. All of the items had drops of blood on them.

The victim's husband found nothing missing from the house except for one of his dress shirts.

According to the pathologist who performed the autopsy, Victoria bled to death. She had sustained blunt force trauma to her eyes, nose and lips, probably from a fist. There were about 38 knife wounds, including 26 stab and slash wounds and 12 puncture wounds. . . . Two different knives were used. Most of the wounds were inflicted by a single-blade knife consistent with the one found under the victim's body. Three wounds in the back were inflicted by a double-edged knife. These wounds appeared to have been inflicted after the victim was dead.

The only connection between defendant and the victim and her husband was that they had attended the same high school some 10 years earlier. Defendant had played sports with Michael Mesa. Defendant lived about two and a quarter miles away and would drive by the Mesa house about twice a week in the early evening and wave to Michael as the latter was working in the yard. Defendant's fingerprint was found on the wall in the hallway near the victim's body and on a bloody Band–Aid wrapper found in the master bathroom. Analysis of blood scrapings from the master bedroom, wall phone, kitchen floor, blood-soaked towel on the water cooler, and blood-soaked Band–Aid from the master bedroom revealed that they were consistent with 1 percent of the population, which includes defendant. To Michael Mesa's knowledge, defendant had never been in his house before.

Defendant's sister testified that he arrived home about 9 a.m. on the day of the murder. His hand was cut, and he was sweaty and pale. . . .

At 9:20 a.m. the same day, defendant was treated at a hospital emergency room for severe cuts on his right hand and smaller cuts on his left hand. Defendant told the nurse that he had cut himself with a Skil Saw. Based on her experience, the nurse did not believe that defendant's injury was the result of having been cut by a Skil Saw.

. . .

Defendant's father produced for officers the shirt that Michael Mesa identified as the one missing from his house.

Defendant did not testify, and he made no statements about the offense. In argument, defense counsel challenged the sufficiency of the evidence of first degree murder and suggested that whoever killed Victoria had acted in a rage. The jury returned a verdict of guilty of first degree, premeditated and deliberate murder. As previously mentioned, a divided Court of Appeal reduced the conviction to second degree murder.

DISCUSSION

Sufficiency of Evidence of Premeditation and Deliberation

The People contend that the Court of Appeal erred in finding the evidence of premeditation and deliberation insufficient to support the judgment. Before proceeding to that question, we find it helpful to review the definition of premeditation and deliberation that was given to the jury, CALJIC No. 8.20, which we have found to be a correct statement of the law. (People v. Lucero (1988) 44 Cal.3d 1006, 1021, 245 Cal.Rptr. 185, 750 P.2d 1342.) CALJIC No. 8.20 defines premeditated and deliberate murder as follows:

> "All murder which is perpetrated by any kind of willful, deliberate and premeditated killing with express malice aforethought is murder of the first degree.

"The word 'willful' as used in this instruction, means intentional.

"The word 'deliberate' means formed or arrived at or determined upon as a result of careful thought and weighing of considerations for and against the proposed course of action. The word 'premeditated' means considered beforehand.

"If you find that the killing was preceded and accompanied by a clear, deliberate intent on the part of the defendant to kill, which was the result of deliberation and premeditation, so that it must have been formed upon pre-existing reflection and not under a sudden heat of passion or other condition precluding the idea of deliberation, it is murder of the first degree.

"The law does not undertake to measure in units of time the length of the period during which the thought must be pondered before it can ripen into an intent to kill which is truly deliberate and premeditated. The time will vary with different individuals and under varying circumstances.

"The true test is not the duration of time, but rather the extent of the reflection. A cold, calculated judgment and decision may be arrived at in a short period of time, but a mere unconsidered and rash impulse, even though it included an intent to kill, is not such deliberation and premeditation as will fix an unlawful killing as murder of the first degree.

"To constitute a deliberate and premeditated killing, the slayer must weigh and consider the question of killing and the reasons for and against such a choice and, having in mind the consequences, he decides to and does kill."

. . .

In challenging the Court of Appeal's reversal of the first degree murder conviction, the People argue that there is sufficient evidence to support the jury's verdict of premeditated and deliberate murder under traditional standards of review and that the Court of Appeal majority misapplied People v. Anderson (1968) 70 Cal.2d 15, 73 Cal.Rptr. 550, 447 P.2d 942 in reaching a contrary determination. We agree.

In People v. Anderson, *supra*, 70 Cal.2d 15, 73 Cal.Rptr. 550, 447 P.2d 942, this court surveyed a number of prior cases involving the sufficiency of the evidence to support findings of premeditation and deliberation. (Id. at p. 26, 73 Cal.Rptr. 550, 447 P.2d 942.) From the cases surveyed, the court distilled certain guidelines to aid reviewing courts in analyzing the sufficiency of the evidence to sustain findings of premeditation and deliberation. The Anderson analysis was intended only as a framework to aid in appellate review; it did not propose to define the elements of first degree murder or alter the substantive law of murder in any way. Nor did Anderson change the traditional standards of appellate review that we have set forth above. The Anderson guidelines are descriptive, not normative. The goal of Anderson was to aid reviewing courts in assessing whether the evidence is supportive of an inference that the killing was the result of preexisting reflection and weighing of considerations rather than mere unconsidered or rash impulse. (People v. Anderson, *supra*, 70 Cal.2d at p. 27, 73 Cal.Rptr. 550, 447 P.2d 942.)

In identifying categories of evidence bearing on premeditation and deliberation, Anderson did not purport to establish an exhaustive list that would exclude all other types and combinations of evidence that could support a finding of premeditation and deliberation. From the cases surveyed, the Anderson court identified three categories of evidence pertinent to the determination of premeditation and deliberation: (1) planning activity, (2) motive, and (3) manner of killing. Regarding these categories, Anderson stated: "Analysis of the cases will show that this court sustains verdicts of first degree murder typically when there is evidence of all three types and otherwise requires at least extremely strong evidence of (1) or evidence of (2) in conjunction with either (1) or (3)." (Ibid.) It is thus evident from the court's own words that it was attempting to do no more than catalog common factors that had occurred in prior cases. The Anderson factors, while helpful for purposes of review, are not a sine qua non to finding first degree premeditated murder, nor are they exclusive.

. . .

... From the evidence presented, the jury reasonably could have inferred the following: Defendant surreptitiously entered the house while Victoria was warming up her car; there were no signs of forced entry or of the presence of an additional car. Defendant surprised her as she was carrying the dog food; the broken dog dish and dog food were strewn about the floor. Defendant first beat Victoria about the head and neck with his fists. Then he stabbed her with a steak knife obtained from the victim's kitchen; the handle and blade were consistent with knives in the kitchen drawer. When that knife broke, cutting him, defendant went in search of another knife; drippings of defendant's blood were found all over the kitchen, including a drawer containing knives. Regardless of defendant's motive for entering the house, once confronted by Victoria, who knew him and could identify him, he determined to kill her to avoid identification.

As so viewed, the evidence is sufficient to support the jury's findings of premeditation and deliberation. Evidence of planning activity is shown by the fact that defendant did not park his car in the victim's driveway, he surreptitiously entered the house, and he obtained a knife from the kitchen. As to motive, regardless of what inspired the initial entry and attack, it is reasonable to infer that defendant determined it was necessary to kill Victoria to prevent her from identifying him. She was acquainted with him from high school and obviously would have been able to identify him. The manner of killing is also indicative of premeditation and deliberation. The evidence of blood in the kitchen knife drawer supports an inference that defendant went to the kitchen in search of another knife after the steak knife broke. This action bears similarity to reloading a gun or using another gun when the first one has run out of ammunition.

Thus, though the evidence is admittedly not overwhelming, it is sufficient to sustain the jury's finding. As we have stated, the relevant question on appeal is not whether we are convinced beyond a reasonable doubt, but whether *any* rational trier of fact could have been persuaded beyond a reasonable doubt that defendant premeditated the murder. We have previously observed that premeditation can occur in a brief period of time. "The true test is not the duration of time as much as it is the extent of the reflection. Thoughts may follow each other with great rapidity and cold, calculated judgment may be arrived at quickly. . . ."

Defendant challenges the strength of the inferences we have set forth, claiming that they are speculative and insubstantial. He asserts that it is speculative that the steak knife came from the kitchen. We disagree. Although one might think of other possibilities, the most reasonable inference is that the knife came from the kitchen, because it matched the kitchen knives and the victim's husband testified that he and Victoria were well-organized and kept everything in its place. Defendant dismisses reliance on the use of the second knife by noting that the coroner's testimony indicated that the wounds inflicted by it were post-mortem and in nonvital areas. There is no indication, however, that it would have been readily apparent, at the time of the assault, that the victim was already dead. She was knocked to the ground and lay bleeding to death; defendant would not have known the precise moment of death or which wound would cause it. Moreover, the jury could reasonably infer that the post-mortem wounds were inflicted to make certain the victim was dead. Given that the post-mortem wounds were inflicted after defendant had broken the first knife and used a second knife to inflict these wounds, it is difficult to characterize defendant's conduct as "mere rash and unconsidered impulse." Some period of time necessarily must have elapsed between the first and second set of wounds. While this conduct, in itself, may not necessarily support a finding of premeditation, in conjunction with the manner of killing, it could easily have led the jury to infer premeditation and deliberation.

Additionally, the conduct of defendant *after* the stabbing, such as the search of dresser drawers, jewelry boxes, kitchen drawers and the changing of a Band–Aid on his bloody hand, would appear to be inconsistent with a state of mind that would have produced a rash, impulsive killing. Here, defendant did not immediately flee the scene. Again, while not sufficient in themselves to establish premeditation and deliberation, these are facts which a jury could reasonably consider in relation to the manner of killing.

. . .

. . . Defendant's obtaining of the steak knife from the kitchen is indicative of planning activity. A plausible motive is evident from the fact that the victim was acquainted with defendant. After defendant initially surprised and attacked Victoria, he then decided it was necessary to silence her to prevent her from identifying him. Finally, the manner of the killing is indicative of premeditation. Defendant went searching for another knife after the first knife broke. Even if the initial knifing was spontaneous, defendant had time to reflect upon his actions when the knife broke. That he went searching for another knife is indicative of a reasoned decision to kill. Thus, the evidence here is actually stronger than that in Wharton.

Accordingly, we conclude that the evidence is sufficient to sustain the jury's finding of premeditation and deliberation and that the judgment of the Court of Appeal should be reversed.

. . .

CONCLUSION

The judgment of the Court of Appeal is reversed.

■ LUCAS, C.J., and ARABIAN, BAXTER, and GEORGE, JJ., concur.

■ MOSK, JUSTICE, dissents.[21]

Callins v. Collins

Supreme Court of the United States, 1994.   DEATH PENALTY
510 U.S. 1141, 114 S.Ct. 1127, 127 L.Ed.2d 435.

On writ of certiorari to the United States Court of Appeals for the Fifth Circuit.

The petition for a writ of certiorari is denied.

■ JUSTICE BLACKMUN, dissenting.

On February 23, 1994, at approximately 1:00 a.m., Bruce Edwin Callins will be executed by the State of Texas. Intravenous tubes attached to his arms will carry the instrument of death, a toxic fluid designed specifically for the purpose of killing human beings. The witnesses, standing a few feet away, will behold Callins, no longer a defendant, an appellant, or a petitioner, but a man, strapped to a gurney, and seconds away from extinction.

Within days, or perhaps hours, the memory of Callins will begin to fade. The wheels of justice will churn again, and somewhere, another jury or another judge will have the unenviable task of determining whether some human being is to live or die. We hope, of course, that the defendant whose life is at risk will be represented by competent counsel—someone

---

21. For guilt of first-degree murder under the willful, deliberate and premeditated clause of the statute there must have been time for reflection—for a "second look"—between the formation of homicidal intent and the fatal act. People v. Hoffmeister, 394 Mich. 155, 229 N.W.2d 305 (1975). To prove deliberate premeditation the prosecution must prove "that the defendant's resolution to kill was a product of cool reflection." Commonwealth v. Stewart, 398 Mass. 535, 499 N.E.2d 822, 826 (1986).

Intent alone is insufficient for premeditated murder. The accused must, with a cool mind reflect before killing. The accused who shot victim three times at close range must have reflected prior to the fatal shot in order to be convicted of premeditated murder. The evidence was held to be insufficient to show premeditation. United States v. Hoskins, 36 M.J. 343 (CMA 1993).

In People v. Anderson, 70 Cal.2d 15, 73 Cal.Rptr. 550, 447 P.2d 942 (1968), the court said "the legislative classification of murder into two degrees would be meaningless if 'deliberation' and 'premeditation' were construed as requiring no more reflection than may be involved in the mere formation of a specific intent to kill".

"The achievement of a mental state contemplated in a statute such as ours can immediately precede the act of killing. Hence what is really meant by the language 'willful, deliberate and premeditated' in W.Va.Code 61–2–1 (1923) is that the killing be intentional." State v. Schrader, 172 W.Va. 1, 302 S.E.2d 70, 75 (1982). (Note, this takes us back to the original theory of *Drum* and gives no meaning to deliberate and premeditated.)

Under the Model Penal Code, premeditation is not a required factor. Murder may be based on intentional or knowing conduct as well as reckless indifference; however, some states following the Model Penal Code format divide murder into degrees and an intentional or knowing killing will frequently suffice for the highest degree of murder. State v. Lavers, 168 Ariz. 376, 814 P.2d 333 (1991).

who is inspired by the awareness that a less than vigorous defense truly could have fatal consequences for the defendant. We hope that the attorney will investigate all aspects of the case, follow all evidentiary and procedural rules, and appear before a judge who is still committed to the protection of defendants' rights—even now, as the prospect of meaningful judicial oversight has diminished. In the same vein, we hope that the prosecution, in urging the penalty of death, will have exercised its discretion wisely, free from bias, prejudice, or political motive, and will be humbled, rather than emboldened, by the awesome authority conferred by the State.

But even if we can feel confident that these actors will fulfill their roles to the best of their human ability, our collective conscience will remain uneasy. Twenty years have passed since this Court declared that the death penalty must be imposed fairly, and with reasonable consistency, or not at all, *see* Furman v. Georgia, 408 U.S. 238, 92 S.Ct. 2726, 33 L.Ed.2d 346 (1972), and, despite the effort of the States and courts to devise legal formulas and procedural rules to meet this daunting challenge, the death penalty remains fraught with arbitrariness, discrimination, caprice, and mistake. This is not to say that the problems with the death penalty today are identical to those that were present 20 years ago. Rather, the problems that were pursued down one hole with procedural rules and verbal formulas have come to the surface somewhere else, just as virulent and pernicious as they were in their original form. . . .

To be fair, a capital sentencing scheme must treat each person convicted of a capital offense with that "degree of respect due the uniqueness of the individual." Lockett v. Ohio, 438 U.S., at 605, 98 S.Ct., at 2964 (plurality opinion). That means affording the sentencer the power and discretion to grant mercy in a particular case, and providing avenues for the consideration of any and all relevant mitigating evidence that would justify a sentence less than death. Reasonable consistency, on the other hand, requires that the death penalty be inflicted evenhandedly, in accordance with reason and objective standards, rather than by whim, caprice, or prejudice. Finally, because human error is inevitable, and because our criminal justice system is less than perfect, searching appellate review of death sentences and their underlying convictions is a prerequisite to a constitutional death penalty scheme.

On their face, these goals of individual fairness, reasonable consistency, and absence of error appear to be attainable: Courts are in the very business of erecting procedural devices from which fair, equitable, and reliable outcomes are presumed to flow. Yet, in the death penalty area, this Court, in my view, has engaged in a futile effort to balance these constitutional demands, and now is retreating not only from the *Furman* promise of consistency and rationality, but from the requirement of individualized sentencing as well. Having virtually conceded that both fairness and rationality cannot be achieved in the administration of the death penalty, *see* McCleskey v. Kemp, 481 U.S. 279, 313, n. 37, 107 S.Ct. 1756, 1778, n. 37, 95 L.Ed.2d 262 (1987), the Court has chosen to deregulate the entire enterprise, replacing, it would seem, substantive constitutional requirements with mere esthetics, and abdicating its statutorily and constitutionally imposed duty to provide meaningful judicial oversight to the administration of death by the States.

From this day forward, I no longer shall tinker with the machinery of death. For more than 20 years I have endeavored—indeed, I have struggled—along with a majority of this Court, to develop procedural and substantive rules that would lend more than the mere appearance of fairness to the death penalty endeavor. Rather than continue to coddle the Court's delusion that the desired level of fairness has been achieved and the need for regulation eviscerated, I feel morally and intellectually obligated simply to concede that the death penalty experiment has failed. . . .

I

In 1971, in an opinion which has proved partly prophetic, the second Justice Harlan, writing for the Court, observed:

"Those who have come to grips with the hard task of actually attempting to draft means of channeling capital sentencing discretion have confirmed the lesson taught by the history recounted above. To identify before the fact those characteristics of criminal homicides and their perpetrators which call for the death penalty, and to express these characteristics in language which can be fairly understood and applied by the sentencing authority, appear to be tasks which are beyond present human ability. . . . For a court to attempt to catalog the appropriate factors in this elusive area could inhibit rather than expand the scope of consideration, for no list of circumstances would ever be really complete." McGautha v. California, 402 U.S. 183, 204, 208, 91 S.Ct. 1454, 1466, 1467, 28 L.Ed.2d 711.

In *McGautha,* the petitioner argued that a statute which left the penalty of death entirely in the jury's discretion, without any standards to govern its imposition, violated the Fourteenth Amendment. Although the Court did not deny that serious risks were associated with a sentencer's unbounded discretion, the Court found no remedy in the Constitution for the inevitable failings of human judgment.

A year later, the Court reversed its course completely in Furman v. Georgia, 408 U.S. 238, 92 S.Ct. 2726, 33 L.Ed.2d 346 (1972) (*per curiam,* with each of the nine Justices writing separately). The concurring Justices argued that the glaring inequities in the administration of death, the standardless discretion wielded by judges and juries, and the pervasive racial and economic discrimination rendered the death penalty, at least as administered, "cruel and unusual" within the meaning of the Eighth Amendment. Justice White explained that, out of the hundreds of people convicted of murder every year, only a handful were sent to their deaths, and that there was "no meaningful basis for distinguishing the few cases in which [the death penalty] is imposed from the many cases in which it is not." *Id.,* at 313, 92 S.Ct., at 2764. If any discernible basis could be identified for the selection of those few who were chosen to die, it was "the constitutionally impermissible basis of race." *Id.,* at 310, 92 S.Ct., at 2762 (Stewart, J., concurring).

I dissented in *Furman.* Despite my intellectual, moral, and personal objections to the death penalty, I refrained from joining the majority because I found objectionable the Court's abrupt change of position in the single year that had passed since *McGautha*. ...

A

There is little doubt now that *Furman's* essential holding was correct....

Delivering on the *Furman* promise, however, has proved to be another matter.... In the years following *Furman,* serious efforts were made to comply with its mandate. State legislatures and appellate courts struggled to provide judges and juries with sensible and objective guidelines for determining who should live and who should die. Some States attempted to define who is "deserving" of the death penalty through the use of carefully chosen adjectives, reserving the death penalty for those who commit crimes that are "especially heinous, atrocious, or cruel," *see* Fla.Stat. § 921.141(5)(h) (1977), or "wantonly vile, horrible or inhuman," *see* Ga. Code Ann. § 27–2534.1(b)(7) (1978). Other States enacted mandatory death penalty statutes, reading *Furman* as an invitation to eliminate sentencer discretion altogether. *See, e.g.,* N.C.Gen.Stat. § 14–17 (Supp.1975). *But see* Woodson v. North Carolina, 428 U.S. 280, 96 S.Ct. 2978, 49 L.Ed.2d 944 (1976) (invalidating mandatory death penalty statutes). Still other States specified aggravating and mitigating factors that were to be considered by the sentencer and weighed against one another in a calculated and rational manner. See, *e.g.,* Ga.Code Ann. § 17–10–30(c) (1982); *cf.* Tex.Code Crim. Proc.Ann., Art. 37.071(c)–(e) (Vernon 1981 and Supp.1989) (identifying "special issues" to be considered by the sentencer when determining the appropriate sentence).

Unfortunately, all this experimentation and ingenuity yielded little of what *Furman* demanded. It soon became apparent that discretion could not be eliminated from capital sentencing without threatening the fundamental fairness due a defendant when life is at stake. Just as contemporary society was no longer tolerant of the random or discriminatory infliction of the penalty of death, *see Furman, supra,* evolving standards of decency required due consideration of the uniqueness of each individual defendant when imposing society's ultimate penalty. *See Woodson,* 428 U.S., at 301, 96 S.Ct., at 2989 (opinion of Stewart, Powell, and STEVENS, JJ.), referring to Trop v. Dulles, 356 U.S. 86, 101, 78 S.Ct. 590, 598, 2 L.Ed.2d 630 (1958) (plurality opinion).

This development in the American conscience would have presented no constitutional dilemma if fairness to the individual could be achieved without sacrificing the consistency and rationality promised in *Furman.* But over the past two decades, efforts to balance these competing constitutional commands have been to no avail. Experience has shown that the consistency and rationality promised in *Furman* are inversely related to the fairness owed the individual when considering a sentence of death. A step toward consistency is a step away from fairness.

B

There is a heightened need for fairness in the administration of death. This unique level of fairness is born of the appreciation that death truly is different from all other punishments a society inflicts upon its citizens.... In *Woodson,* a decision striking down mandatory death penalty statutes as unconstitutional, a plurality of the Court explained: "A process that accords no significance to relevant facets of the character and record of the individual offender or the circumstances of the particular offense excludes from consideration in fixing the ultimate punishment of death the possibility of compassionate or mitigating factors stemming from the diverse frailties of humankind." *Id.,* at 304, 96 S.Ct., at 2991.

While the risk of mistake in the determination of the appropriate penalty may be tolerated in other areas of the criminal law, "in capital cases the fundamental respect for humanity underlying the Eighth Amendment ... requires consideration of the character and record of the individual offender and the circumstances of the particular offense as a constitutionally indispensable part of the process of inflicting the penalty of death." *Ibid.* Thus, although individualized sentencing in capital cases was not considered essential at the time the Constitution was adopted, *Woodson* recognized that American standards of decency could no longer tolerate a capital sentencing process that failed to afford a defendant individualized consideration in the determination whether he or she should live or die. *Id.,* at 301, 96 S.Ct., at 2989.

The Court elaborated on the principle of individualized sentencing in Lockett v. Ohio, 438 U.S. 586, 98 S.Ct. 2954, 57 L.Ed.2d 973 (1978). In that case, a plurality acknowledged that strict restraints on sentencer discretion are necessary to achieve the consistency and rationality promised in *Furman,* but held that, in the end, the sentencer must retain unbridled discretion to afford mercy. Any process or procedure that prevents the sentencer from considering *"as a mitigating factor,* any aspect of a defendant's character or record and any of the circumstances of the offense that the defendant proffers as a basis for a sentence less than death" creates the constitutionally intolerable risk that "the death penalty will be imposed in spite of factors which may call for a less severe penalty." *Id.,* at 604–605, 98 S.Ct., at 2964–2965 (emphasis in original). *See also* Sumner v. Shuman, 483 U.S. 66, 107 S.Ct. 2716, 97 L.Ed.2d 56 (1987) (invalidating a mandatory death penalty statute reserving the death penalty for life-term inmates convicted of murder). The Court's duty under the Constitution therefore is to "develop a system of capital punishment at once consistent and principled but also humane and sensible to the uniqueness of the individual." Eddings v. Oklahoma, 455 U.S., at 110, 102 S.Ct., at 874.

C

I believe the *Woodson–Lockett* line of cases to be fundamentally sound and rooted in American standards of decency that have evolved over time. The notion of prohibiting a sentencer from exercising its discretion "to dispense mercy on the basis of factors too intangible to write into a statute," *Gregg,* 428 U.S., at 222, 96 S.Ct., at 2947 (White, J., concurring), is offensive to our sense of fundamental fairness and respect for the uniqueness of the individual.... Yet, as several Members of the Court have recognized, there is real "tension" between the need for fairness to the individual and the consistency promised in *Furman.* ... The power to consider mitigating evidence that would warrant a sentence less than death is meaningless unless the sentencer has the discretion and authority to dispense mercy based on that evidence. Thus, the Constitution, by requiring a heightened degree of fairness to the individual, and also a greater degree of equality and rationality in the administration of death, demands sentencer discretion that is at once generously expanded and severely restricted.

This dilemma was laid bare in Penry v. Lynaugh, 492 U.S. 302, 109 S.Ct. 2934, 106 L.Ed.2d 256 (1989). The defendant in *Penry* challenged the Texas death penalty statute, arguing that it failed to allow the sentencing jury to give full mitigating effect to his evidence of mental retardation and history of child abuse. The Texas statute required the jury, during the penalty phase, to answer three "special issues"; if the jury unanimously answered "yes" to each issue, the trial court was obligated to sentence the defendant to death. Tex.Code Crim.Proc.Ann., Art. 37.071(c)–(e) (Vernon 1981 and Supp.1989). Only one of the three issues—whether the defendant posed a "continuing threat to society"—was related to the evidence Penry offered in mitigation. But Penry's evidence of mental retardation and child abuse was a two-edged sword as it related to that special issue: "[I]t diminish[ed] his blameworthiness for his crime even as it indicate[d] that there [was] a probability that he [would] be dangerous in the future." 492 U.S., at 324, 109 S.Ct., at 2949. The Court therefore reversed Penry's death sentence, explaining that a reasonable juror could have believed that the statute prohibited a sentence less than death based upon his mitigating evidence. *Id.,* at 326, 109 S.Ct., at 2950.

After *Penry,* the paradox underlying the Court's post-*Furman* jurisprudence was undeniable. Texas had complied with *Furman* by severely limiting the sentencer's discretion, but those very limitations rendered Penry's death sentence unconstitutional.

D

The theory underlying *Penry* and *Lockett* is that an appropriate balance can be struck between the *Furman* promise of consistency and the *Lockett* requirement of individualized sentencing if the death penalty is conceptualized as consisting of two distinct stages.[22] In the first stage of capital sentencing, the demands of *Furman* are met by "narrowing" the class of death-eligible offenders according to objective, fact-bound characteristics of the defendant or the circumstances of the offense. Once the pool of death-eligible defendants has been reduced, the sentencer retains the discretion to consider whatever relevant mitigating evidence the defendant chooses to offer. *See* Graham v. Collins, 506 U.S., at 503–504, 113 S.Ct., at 917 (STEVENS, J., dissenting) (arguing that providing full discretion to the sentencer is not inconsistent with *Furman* and may actually help to protect against arbitrary and capricious sentencing).

Over time, I have come to conclude that even this approach is unacceptable: It simply reduces, rather than eliminates, the number of people

---

22. See Sundby, The *Lockett* Paradox: Reconciling Guided Discretion and Unguided Mitigation in Capital Sentencing, 38 UCLA L.Rev. 1147, 1162 (1991).

subject to arbitrary sentencing.[23] It is the decision to sentence a defendant to death—not merely the decision to make a defendant eligible for death—that may not be arbitrary. While one might hope that providing the sentencer with as much relevant mitigating evidence as possible will lead to more rational and consistent sentences, experience has taught otherwise. It seems that the decision whether a human being should live or die is so inherently subjective—rife with all of life's understandings, experiences, prejudices, and passions—that it inevitably defies the rationality and consistency required by the Constitution.

E

The arbitrariness inherent in the sentencer's discretion to afford mercy is exacerbated by the problem of race. Even under the most sophisticated death penalty statutes, race continues to play a major role in determining who shall live and who shall die. Perhaps it should not be surprising that the biases and prejudices that infect society generally would influence the determination of who is sentenced to death, even within the narrower pool of death-eligible defendants selected according to objective standards. No matter how narrowly the pool of death-eligible defendants is drawn according to objective standards, *Furman*'s promise still will go unfulfilled so long as the sentencer is free to exercise unbridled discretion within the smaller group and thereby to discriminate. " '[T]he power to be lenient [also] is the power to discriminate.' "McCleskey v. Kemp, 481 U.S., at 312, 107 S.Ct., at 1778 quoting K. Davis, Discretionary Justice 170 (1973).

A renowned example of racism infecting a capital sentencing scheme is documented in McCleskey v. Kemp, 481 U.S. 279, 107 S.Ct. 1756, 95 L.Ed.2d 262 (1987). Warren McCleskey, an African–American, argued that the Georgia capital sentencing scheme was administered in a racially discriminatory manner, in violation of the Eighth and Fourteenth Amendments. In support of his claim, he proffered a highly reliable statistical study (the Baldus study) which indicated that, "after taking into account some 230 nonracial factors that might legitimately influence a sentencer, the jury *more likely than not* would have spared McCleskey's life had his victim been black." *Id.*, at 325, 107 S.Ct., at 1784 (emphasis in original) (Brennan, J., dissenting). The Baldus study further demonstrated that blacks who kill whites are sentenced to death "at nearly *22 times* the rate of blacks who kill blacks, and more than *7 times* the rate of whites who kill blacks." *Id.*, at 327, 107 S.Ct., at 1785 (emphasis in original).

Despite this staggering evidence of racial prejudice infecting Georgia's capital sentencing scheme, the majority turned its back on McCleskey's claims, apparently troubled by the fact that Georgia had instituted more procedural and substantive safeguards than most other States since *Furman*, but was still unable to stamp out the virus of racism. Faced with the apparent failure of traditional legal devices to cure the evils identified in

---

23. The narrowing of death-eligible defendants into a smaller subgroup coupled with the unbridled discretion to pick among them arguably emphasizes rather than ameliorates the inherent arbitrariness of the death penalty. Gillers, Deciding Who Dies, 129 U.Pa.L.Rev. 1, 27–28 (1980) (arguing that the inherent arbitrariness of the death penalty is only magnified by post-*Furman* statutes that allow the jury to choose among similarly situated defendants).

Furman, the majority wondered aloud whether the consistency and rationality demanded by the dissent could ever be achieved without sacrificing the discretion which is essential to fair treatment of individual defendants:

"[I]t is difficult to imagine guidelines that would produce the predictability sought by the dissent without sacrificing the discretion essential to a humane and fair system of criminal justice.... The dissent repeatedly emphasizes the need for 'a uniquely high degree of rationality in imposing the death penalty'.... Again, no suggestion is made as to how greater 'rationality' could be achieved under any type of statute that authorizes capital punishment.... Given these safeguards already inherent in the imposition and review of capital sentences, the dissent's call for greater rationality is no less than a claim that a capital punishment system cannot be administered in accord with the Constitution." *Id.,* at 314–315, n. 37, 107 S.Ct., at 1778, n. 37.

I joined most of Justice Brennan's significant dissent which expounded McCleskey's Eighth Amendment claim, and I wrote separately, *id.,* at 345, 107 S.Ct., at 1795, to explain that McCleskey also had a solid equal protection argument under the Fourteenth Amendment. I still adhere to the views set forth in both dissents, and, as far as I know, there has been no serious effort to impeach the Baldus study. Nor, for that matter, have proponents of capital punishment provided any reason to believe that the findings of that study are unique to Georgia.

The fact that we may not be capable of devising procedural or substantive rules to prevent the more subtle and often unconscious forms of racism from creeping into the system does not justify the wholesale abandonment of the *Furman* promise. To the contrary, where a morally irrelevant—indeed, a repugnant—consideration plays a major role in the determination of who shall live and who shall die, it suggests that the continued enforcement of the death penalty in light of its clear and admitted defects is deserving of a "sober second thought." Justice Brennan explained:

"Those whom we would banish from society or from the human community itself often speak in too faint a voice to be heard above society's demand for punishment. It is the particular role of courts to hear these voices, for the Constitution declares that the majoritarian chorus may not alone dictate the conditions of social life. The Court thus fulfills, rather than disrupts, the scheme of separation of powers by closely scrutinizing the imposition of the death penalty, for no decision of a society is more deserving of 'sober second thought.' Stone, The Common Law in the United States, 50 Harv.L.Rev. 4, 25 (1936)." *Id.,* at 343, 107 S.Ct., at 1793–1794.

F

... But even if the constitutional requirements of consistency and fairness are theoretically reconcilable in the context of capital punishment, it is clear that this Court is not prepared to meet the challenge. In apparent frustration over its inability to strike an appropriate balance between the *Furman* promise of consistency and the *Lockett* requirement of individualized sentencing, the Court has retreated from the field, allowing relevant mitigating evidence to be discarded, vague aggravating circumstances to be employed, and providing no indication that the problem of race in the administration of death will ever be addressed. In fact some Members of the Court openly have acknowledged a willingness simply to pick one of the competing constitutional commands and sacrifice the other. *See Graham,* 506 U.S., at 478, 113 S.Ct., at 903 (THOMAS, J., concurring) (calling for the reversal of *Penry*); Walton v. Arizona, 497 U.S. 639, 673, 110 S.Ct. 3047, 3067–3068, 111 L.Ed.2d 511 (1990) (SCALIA, J., concurring in part and concurring in judgment) (announcing that he will no longer enforce the requirement of individualized sentencing, and reasoning that either *Furman* or *Lockett* is wrong and a choice must be made between the two). These developments are troubling, as they ensure that death will continue to be meted out in this country arbitrarily and discriminatorily, and without that "degree of respect due the uniqueness of the individual." *Lockett,* 438 U.S., at 605, 98 S.Ct., at 2965. In my view, the proper course when faced with irreconcilable constitutional commands is not to ignore one or the other, nor to pretend that the dilemma does not exist, but to admit the futility of the effort to harmonize them. This means accepting the fact that the death penalty cannot be administered in accord with our Constitution....

III

Perhaps one day this Court will develop procedural rules or verbal formulas that actually will provide consistency, fairness, and reliability in a capital sentencing scheme. I am not optimistic that such a day will come. I am more optimistic, though, that this Court eventually will conclude that the effort to eliminate arbitrariness while preserving fairness "in the infliction of [death] is so plainly doomed to failure that it—and the death penalty—must be abandoned altogether." Godfrey v. Georgia, 446 U.S. 420, 442, 100 S.Ct. 1759, 1772, 64 L.Ed.2d 398 (1980) (Marshall, J., concurring in judgment). I may not live to see that day, but I have faith that eventually it will arrive. The path the Court has chosen lessens us all. I dissent.

■ JUSTICE SCALIA, concurring.

Justice BLACKMUN dissents from the denial of certiorari in this case with a statement explaining why the death penalty "as currently administered," *post,* at 22, is contrary to the Constitution of the United States. That explanation often refers to "intellectual, moral and personal" perceptions, but never to the text and tradition of the Constitution. It is the latter rather than the former that ought to control. The Fifth Amendment provides that "[n]o person shall be held to answer for a capital ... crime, unless on a presentment or indictment of a Grand Jury, ... nor be deprived of life, ... without due process of law." This clearly permits the death penalty to be imposed, and establishes beyond doubt that the death penalty is not one of the "cruel and unusual punishments" prohibited by the Eighth Amendment.

As Justice BLACKMUN describes, however, over the years since 1972 this Court has attached to the imposition of the death penalty two quite incompatible sets of commands: The sentencer's discretion to impose death must be closely confined, *see* Furman v. Georgia, 408 U.S. 238, 92 S.Ct.

2726, 33 L.Ed.2d 346 (1972) (*per curiam*), but the sentencer's discretion *not* to impose death (to extend mercy) must be unlimited, *see* Eddings v. Oklahoma, 455 U.S. 104, 102 S.Ct. 869, 71 L.Ed.2d 1 (1982); Lockett v. Ohio, 438 U.S. 586, 98 S.Ct. 2954, 57 L.Ed.2d 973 (1978) (plurality opinion). These commands were invented without benefit of any textual or historical support; they are the product of just such "intellectual, moral, and personal" perceptions as Justice BLACKMUN expresses today, some of which (viz., those that have been "perceived" simultaneously by five Members of the Court) have been made part of what is called "the Court's Eighth Amendment jurisprudence," *post*, at 1131.

Though Justice BLACKMUN joins those of us who have acknowledged the incompatibility of the Court's *Furman* and *Lockett–Eddings* lines of jurisprudence, *see* Graham v. Collins, 506 U.S. 461, 478, 113 S.Ct. 892, 903, 122 L.Ed.2d 260 (1993) (THOMAS, J., concurring); Walton v. Arizona, 497 U.S. 639, 656–673, 110 S.Ct. 3047, 3058–68, 111 L.Ed.2d 511 (1990) (SCALIA, J., concurring in part and concurring in judgment), he unfortunately draws the wrong conclusion from the acknowledgment. He says:

"[T]he proper course when faced with irreconcilable constitutional commands is not to ignore one or the other, nor to pretend that the dilemma does not exist, but to admit the futility of the effort to harmonize them. This means accepting the fact that the death penalty cannot be administered in accord with our Constitution." *Post*, at 1137.

Surely a different conclusion commends itself—to wit, that at least one of these judicially announced irreconcilable commands which cause the Constitution to prohibit what its text explicitly permits must be wrong.

Convictions in opposition to the death penalty are often passionate and deeply held. That would be no excuse for reading them into a Constitution that does not contain them, even if they represented the convictions of a majority of Americans. Much less is there any excuse for using that course to thrust a minority's views upon the people. Justice BLACKMUN begins his statement by describing with poignancy the death of a convicted murderer by lethal injection. He chooses, as the case in which to make that statement, one of the less brutal of the murders that regularly come before us—the murder of a man ripped by a bullet suddenly and unexpectedly, with no opportunity to prepare himself and his affairs, and left to bleed to death on the floor of a tavern. The death-by-injection which Justice BLACKMUN describes looks pretty desirable next to that. It looks even better next to some of the other cases currently before us which Justice BLACKMUN did not select as the vehicle for his announcement that the death penalty is always unconstitutional—for example, the case of the 11-year-old girl raped by four men and then killed by stuffing her panties down her throat. *See McCollum v. North Carolina*, cert. pending, No. 93–7200. How enviable a quiet death by lethal injection compared with that! If the people conclude that such more brutal deaths may be deterred by capital punishment; indeed, if they merely conclude that justice requires such brutal deaths to be avenged by capital punishment; the creation of false, untextual, and unhistorical contradictions within "the Court's Eighth Amendment jurisprudence" should not prevent them.

State v. Guebara

Supreme Court of Kansas, 1985.
236 Kan. 791, 696 P.2d 381.

■ PRAGER, JUSTICE:

This is a direct appeal in a criminal action in which the defendant-appellant, Paul Guebara, was convicted of murder in the first degree. It was undisputed that the defendant shot and killed his wife, Genny Guebara. The defendant admitted the homicide in his testimony at the trial. The only issue raised on the appeal is that the trial court erred by failing to instruct the jury on the lesser included offense of voluntary manslaughter.

At the trial, the factual circumstances were not greatly in dispute and essentially were as follows: Defendant Paul Guebara and Genny Guebara were common-law husband and wife, having declared themselves married in 1980. There were two children living with the couple: Sylvia Dawn Guebara, the natural child of the defendant, and Candice Ann Virgil, the natural child of Genny. Their marital relationship was characterized by frequent arguments and occasional violence. In February 1983, Genny filed for divorce. About the same time she also filed criminal charges against the defendant alleging misdemeanor battery and misdemeanor theft. On February 15, 1983, the defendant was served with a misdemeanor warrant by Ms. Anna Gallardo, a Finney County deputy sheriff who is related to the Guebara family by marriage. She testified that she had a conversation with defendant at the sheriff's office on the day before the shooting. She first saw him in the morning when he came to inquire where his divorce hearing was going to be held. She showed him a copy of the warrant and told him what the misdemeanor charges were. She told him to come back to the office at 2:30 p.m. to take care of the warrant and appear before the court.

He returned and appeared before the magistrate at 2:30 p.m. that afternoon. Following the hearing, she had a conversation with him in the sheriff's conference room. They discussed the divorce, and defendant told her he was very upset that the divorce was going on. He said that it made him very angry. He told her at different points in the conversation that he was going to kill Genny and that, if he did, he was not going to fight it—that he was going to turn himself in to the sheriff. He told her that he did not want to kill Genny but, when she made him angry, he could not hold back. Following the conversation, Ms. Gallardo concluded that he was not serious and was not really going to do anything. She did not report the conversation to anyone.

On February 16, 1983, the date of the shooting, Sylvia Dawn Guebara was staying with defendant at defendant's parents' house in accordance with an agreed visitation schedule. Genny and two of her friends arrived at the house to pick Sylvia up. Genny and another woman left the pickup truck and approached defendant, who was standing on the porch. At that point, defendant handed Genny the criminal process papers. According to defendant's testimony, when he handed Genny the papers, she stated that she tried to drop the charges but the assistant county attorney would not let her. The defendant testified that he immediately became angry, pulled out his gun, and started shooting her. According to defendant, he did not think about the act; it was a sudden impulse to shoot without reflection. A prosecution witness testified that Genny attempted to walk past defendant to the house after defendant refused to accept back the process papers. He grabbed her arm and turned her around towards him, displaying a gun. Genny turned her head and defendant fired the gun at her. Genny then stepped back, brought her hands up, and defendant fired the gun again. Then Genny turned and ran or stumbled toward the pickup truck. Defendant followed her into the street firing several additional shots. As Genny was lying in the street, defendant ran toward the house, throwing the gun at the house and immediately ran to the Finney County Law Enforcement Center where he turned himself in to a sheriff's employee.

... Defendant stated that he was depressed and upset. [An] officer asked defendant if he had shot his wife, and defendant admitted it. Defendant stated to the officer that he had thought about shooting her the day before and that he had thought about shooting her just prior to her arrival at the house. The officer asked defendant whether he intended to shoot her, and defendant replied that he had planned to shoot her.

On cross-examination the police officer testified that defendant told him defendant had smoked one and one-half joints of marijuana just before his wife arrived on the scene. Defendant informed him that, when he first pulled the gun out, he did not intend to shoot his wife and did not intend to shoot her with the first shot. The evidence presented by the defense at the trial sought to prove that the defendant was a person who, when put into pressure situations, was likely to respond in a violent, impulsive, quick manner. Defendant was characterized as a person who showed indications of gross thought disorder which might lead to an inability to assess reality accurately and respond to it accordingly. Defendant was described as an action-oriented person who could act in an assaultive manner.

The defense called to the witness stand a staff psychiatrist at Larned State Security Hospital who diagnosed defendant to have an anti-social personality disorder. She testified that, when a person with an anti-social personality disorder uses drugs such as marijuana, it is possible for the individual to have altered judgment and maladaptive behavior. The use of marijuana by such a person would have a tendency to worsen the individual's judgment, and if the individual had an aggressive personality, the use of the drugs would probably make the person more aggressive. Although defendant testified he had smoked marijuana shortly before the shooting, there was no evidence he was under the influence of drugs.

. . .

At the close of the evidence, the defendant's counsel requested the trial court to instruct the jury on the lesser included offense of voluntary manslaughter. The trial court instructed the jury on murder in the first and second degree but refused to give the requested instruction on voluntary manslaughter. In making its ruling, the trial court reasoned that two elements must exist to prove voluntary manslaughter: First, there must be evidence of an emotional state constituting heat of passion and, second, there must be a sufficient provocation. The trial court concluded that the refusal of a person to dismiss misdemeanor criminal charges arising from a domestic squabble was not a sufficient legal provocation to kill. The case was submitted to the jury and defendant was convicted of murder in the first degree.... [T]he sole issue is whether the trial court erred in failing to instruct the jury on the lesser included offense of voluntary manslaughter.

. . .

The basic issue before us is whether there was sufficient evidence presented in the case to support the defendant's theory that the killing was committed in the heat of passion under such circumstances as to require the requested instruction on voluntary manslaughter....

(1) Voluntary manslaughter is the intentional killing in the heat of passion as a result of severe provocation. As a concession to human frailty, a killing, which would otherwise constitute murder, is mitigated to voluntary manslaughter.

(2) "Heat of passion" means any intense or vehement emotional excitement of the kind prompting violent and aggressive action, such as rage, anger, hatred, furious resentment, fright, or terror. Such emotional state of mind must be of such a degree as would cause an ordinary man to act on impulse without reflection.

(3) In order to reduce a homicide from murder to voluntary manslaughter, there must be provocation, and such provocation must be recognized by the law as adequate. A provocation is adequate if it is calculated to deprive a reasonable man of self-control and to cause him to act out of passion rather than reason. In order for a defendant to be entitled to a reduced charge because he acted in the heat of passion, his emotional state of mind must exist at the time of the act and it must have arisen from circumstances constituting *sufficient provocation*.

(4) The test of the sufficiency of the provocation is objective, not subjective. The provocation, whether it be "sudden quarrel" or some other form of provocation, must be sufficient to cause an ordinary man to lose control of his actions and his reason. In applying the objective standard for measuring the sufficiency of the provocation, the standard precludes consideration of the innate peculiarities of the individual defendant. The fact that his intelligence is not high and his passion is easily aroused will not be considered in this connection.

(5) Mere words or gestures, however insulting, do not constitute adequate provocation, but insulting words when accompanied by other conduct, such as assault, may be considered. In State v. Buffington, 71 Kan. 804, 81 P. 465 (1905), it was held that the trial court properly instructed the jury that no words, however abusive and insulting, will justify an assault or will justify a sufficient provocation to reduce to manslaughter what otherwise would be murder.

(6) An assault or battery resulting in a reasonable belief that the defendant is in imminent danger of losing his life or suffering great bodily harm may be of sufficient provocation to reduce the killing to voluntary manslaughter.

(7) If two persons engage in mutual combat, the blows given by each are adequate provocation to the other; thus, if one kills the other, the homicide may be reduced to voluntary manslaughter.

With these basic principles in mind, we now turn to a consideration of the factual circumstances of this case as set forth above in detail. We have concluded that the trial court did not err in refusing to give the defendant's requested instruction on voluntary manslaughter. We agree with the trial court that, although the requisite emotional state necessary to constitute heat of passion was present, the evidence in the record does not show that the defendant's emotional state of mind arose from circumstances constituting sufficient provocation. . . .

In State v. Stafford, 213 Kan. 152, 515 P.2d 769 (1973), modified 213 Kan. 585, 518 P.2d 136 (1974), the defendant was convicted of shooting her husband. She and her husband got into an argument because of his remarks about her son-in-law and a friend. As she was standing in the kitchen preparing to make coffee he struck her behind the left ear, knocking her glasses off. The blow did not bruise or hurt her. She then squirted him in the face with a paralyzer spray from a pressurized can. This dazed him and, as he was trying to rub the spray out of his eyes, she wrapped the cord from the electric tea kettle around his neck and choked him with it. She grabbed him by what little hair he had on his bald head and threw him against the wall. She then threw him down on the floor and got astraddle of him with her knees on his arms. She picked up a hammer and hit him with it three or four times. The husband's death was caused by strangulation. This court held that, although there was some evidence of prior quarreling or even a blow on occasions, insufficient provocation existed to reduce the charge to voluntary manslaughter.

In State v. Coop, 223 Kan. at 304, 573 P.2d 1017, both the defendant and his deceased wife were alcoholics and were extremely intoxicated at the time of the homicide. The undisputed evidence showed that a violent fight occurred which was characterized as a drunken brawl. There were signs of a struggle in the house. The defendant's hair was found under his wife's ring on her finger. In spite of this evidence of a violent drunken quarrel, this court held that the evidence was not sufficient to require an instruction on voluntary manslaughter as a lesser included offense of the charge of murder.

As this court has held many times before, a court must apply an objective standard for measuring the sufficiency of the provocation. In doing so, the court should not consider the innate peculiarities of the individual defendant. We hold that the trial court did not err in refusing to instruct on voluntary manslaughter.

The judgment of the district court is affirmed.[24]

---

24. Defendant, a Vietnamese immigrant, asserted that he killed his wife because her alleged infidelity caused him to lose face and honor and that his Vietnamese culture ought to be considered in determining whether there was killing under provocation that would reduce murder to manslaughter. The trial judge instructed that the provocation assessment was to be made as against an ordinary person standard. The cultural background of the accused was held not to be relevant to the issue of the reasonableness of the provocation but a factor to be considered on whether the defendant actually acted under the provocation before the time for

People v. Chevalier

Supreme Court of Illinois, 1989.
131 Ill.2d 66, 136 Ill.Dec. 167, 544 N.E.2d 942.

■ JUSTICE STAMOS delivered the opinion of the court:

In each of these consolidated cases, the defendant shot and killed his wife and was convicted of murder. Defendants do not dispute that they committed the killings or that the killings were not legally justified. They contend that the evidence was sufficient to warrant giving the jury an instruction on the offense of voluntary manslaughter (Ill.Rev.Stat.1983, ch. 38, par. 9–2). The issue common to both appeals is whether the provocation on the part of the victim was legally adequate to reduce the homicide from murder to voluntary manslaughter. . . .

In each case, the appellate court reversed the conviction and remanded the case for a new trial. We granted the petitions for leave to appeal filed by the State in both cases (107 Ill.2d R. 315), and the actions were consolidated for purposes of review. We reverse the judgments of the appellate court and reinstate the convictions of murder.

The facts of each case are fully set forth in the appellate court opinions and need not be repeated here. Although the details differ, the circumstances surrounding the killings are similar. In each, defendant suspected his wife of marital infidelity. Just prior to the killing, the defendant and the victim had an argument, during which the victim admitted committing adultery and either disparaged the defendant's sexual abilities (*People v. Chevalier*) or flaunted the fact that she slept with her lover in the marital bed (*People v. Flores*). The victims were shot during these arguments. Defendant Chevalier concealed the shooting, eventually driving from Illinois to Michigan to deposit the body along a highway. Chevalier told a police officer that he took the body to Michigan because the grass along the roadway there is left uncut all summer. . . .

In *People v. Flores,* the trial court refused to give defendant's tendered jury instruction on the offense of voluntary manslaughter. In *People v. Chevalier,* although the trial court instructed the jury on voluntary manslaughter, defendant contends that the instruction was erroneous; the appellate court agreed. We need not address the accuracy of the jury instruction, however, unless Chevalier was entitled to a voluntary manslaughter instruction. As Chevalier appears to concede, if the evidence did not support such an instruction, then an erroneous instruction on the

his passion to cool had occurred. Reg. v. Ly, 33 CCC3d 32 (B.C.Ct.App.1987). Contrast, Reg. v. Hill, [1986] 1 SCR 313, 27 D.L.R. 4th 187, 25 CCC3d 322 (S.C.C.1986).

The repeated humiliation of defendant by his wife did not support the extreme emotional disturbance standard, under the Model Penal Code language, for the killing of defendant's wife weeks later. Passage of time does not preclude the defense, but the evidence must show proof that a temporarily remote provocative act affected the defendant at the time of the homicide to the extent that it could be concluded the defendant acted under extreme emotional disturbance. People v. White, 79 N.Y.2d 900, 590 N.E.2d 236 (1992).

Forty minutes after an initial confrontation, where defendant had calmed down and was no longer visibly angry, defendant, on finding victim, threatened and shot victim numerous times knowing victim was unarmed. Defendant had an adequate cooling off time and was properly convicted of murder. Isom v. State, 501 N.E.2d 1074 (Ind.1986).

offense could not have prejudiced defendant. Accordingly, we turn to a consideration of whether defendants were entitled to a voluntary manslaughter instruction.

Issue

VOLUNTARY MANSLAUGHTER

At the time of the offenses, section 9–2 of the Criminal Code of 1961 provided as follows:

"A person who kills an individual without lawful justification commits voluntary manslaughter if at the time of the killing he is acting under a sudden and intense passion resulting from serious provocation by:

(1) The individual killed[.]

* * *

Serious provocation is conduct sufficient to excite an intense passion in a reasonable person." Ill.Rev.Stat.1983, ch. 38, par. 9–2.

The principles governing voluntary manslaughter based on serious provocation are well established. "The only categories of serious provocation which have been recognized are: 'substantial physical injury or assault, mutual quarrel or combat, illegal arrest, and adultery with the offender's spouse; but not mere words or gestures or trespass to property.' (S.H.A., chap. 38, par. 9–2, Committee Comments * * *.)" (People v. Crews (1967), 38 Ill.2d 331, 335, 231 N.E.2d 451.) The rule that mere words are insufficient provocation applies no matter how aggravated, abusive, opprobrious or indecent the language.

In Illinois, adultery with a spouse as provocation generally has been limited to those instances where the parties are discovered in the act of adultery or immediately before or after such an act, and the killing immediately follows such discovery. (People v. Harris (1984), 123 Ill.App.3d 899, 904, 79 Ill.Dec. 476, 463 N.E.2d 1030; People v. Middleswart (1984), 124 Ill.App.3d 35, 39, 79 Ill.Dec. 496, 463 N.E.2d 1050; People v. Wax (1966), 75 Ill.App.2d 163, 182, 220 N.E.2d 600.) A verbal communication that adultery has occurred or will occur falls within the rule that mere words are insufficient provocation. *Middleswart,* 124 Ill.App.3d at 40, 79 Ill.Dec. 496, 463 N.E.2d 1050; *see also* People v. Arnold (1974), 17 Ill. App.3d 1043, 1047, 309 N.E.2d 89 (defendant's long-held belief that his wife had committed adultery was not a basis for a voluntary manslaughter instruction); contra Commonwealth v. Schnopps (1981), 383 Mass. 178, 181, 417 N.E.2d 1213, 1215 (a sudden admission of adultery is equivalent to a discovery of the act itself, and is sufficient evidence of provocation).

The appellate court decisions in the cases at bar, in concluding that defendants were entitled to the requested instruction, followed People v. Ambro (1987), 153 Ill.App.3d 1, 106 Ill.Dec. 75, 505 N.E.2d 381, which in turn relied on People v. Ahlberg (1973), 13 Ill.App.3d 1038, 301 N.E.2d 608, and People v. Carr (1980), 91 Ill.App.3d 512, 46 Ill.Dec. 955, 414 N.E.2d 1108. These cases recognize an exception to the general rule that a verbal communication of adultery is insufficient provocation.

Ahlberg was an appeal from a conviction of voluntary manslaughter. In the days preceding the homicide, defendant's wife left the couple's home and told defendant she had filed for divorce. Just before the killing, defendant's wife told him that he had never satisfied her sexually, that she had found an older man, and that she was going to get a divorce. Defendant then dragged his wife from their home and beat, kicked and stomped her, causing injuries from which she later died.

Defendant appealed, contending that he was guilty of murder or of nothing. The court disagreed, stating:

"To follow unequivocally the rule that 'mere words['] are insufficient to cause the provocation necessary to support a finding of guilt of voluntary manslaughter would be in keeping with precedent and an established rule; however, it would be a direct refutation of logic and a miscarriage of justice. We reach this conclusion for it is not incumbent on us to determine what could or did provoke the defendant into a state of intense passion,, for by his testimony he made such determination." *Ahlberg,* 13 Ill.App.3d at 1041, 301 N.E.2d 608.

In the first place, the court in *Ahlberg* was simply incorrect in its view that it need not inquire into the nature of the provocation which allegedly caused a state of passion. To the contrary, as we have stated, the law recognizes only certain categories of provocation. Under the appellate court's view in *Ahlberg,* even the slightest provocation would suffice, as long as the defendant testified that the deceased's conduct provoked intense passion. As the appellate court correctly stated in People v. Neal (1983), 112 Ill.App.3d 964, 969, 68 Ill.Dec. 536, 446 N.E.2d 270: "Passion on the part of the slayer, no matter how violent will not relieve him from liability for murder unless it is engendered by a serious provocation which the law recognizes as being reasonably adequate. If the provocation is inadequate, the crime is murder. People v. Matthews (1974), 21 Ill.App.3d [249], 253 [314 N.E.2d 15]."

Moreover, it is obvious from the *Ahlberg* opinion that the court was loath to reverse the voluntary manslaughter conviction. Defendant in that case had been acquitted of murder; therefore, reversal of the voluntary manslaughter conviction likely would mean that defendant would escape any punishment for the crime. (See People v. Thompson (1973), 11 Ill. App.3d 752, 297 N.E.2d 592 (a defendant charged with murder may properly be found guilty of the lesser offense of voluntary manslaughter, but only if the evidence establishes the necessary elements of that offense; voluntary manslaughter conviction reversed); People v. Delaney (1978), 63 Ill.App.3d 47, 50, 19 Ill.Dec. 957, 379 N.E.2d 829 (Linn, J., dissenting).) The court in *Ahlberg* stated: "Having escaped a guilty of murder conviction [defendant] now asks that we set aside a voluntary manslaughter conviction even though by his own testimony the words of his wife were such as to cause him to lose all control of himself * * *. To grant the request of the defendant would make a mockery of the law." (*Ahlberg,* 13 Ill.App.3d at 1041, 301 N.E.2d 608.) The court candidly stated that its holding ignored precedent and established rules. The court's ruling in the *Ahlberg* case proves the old adage, "Hard cases make bad law."

People v. Carr (1980), 91 Ill.App.3d 512, 46 Ill.Dec. 955, 414 N.E.2d 1108, was also an appeal from a conviction for voluntary manslaughter. On facts similar to those in *Ahlberg,* the court in *Carr* followed *Ahlberg* and affirmed the conviction.

People v. Ambro (1987), 153 Ill.App.3d 1, 106 Ill.Dec. 75, 505 N.E.2d 381, unlike *Ahlberg* and *Carr,* was an appeal from a murder conviction in which defendant contended that the trial court erred in refusing to instruct the jury on the offense of voluntary manslaughter. The majority acknowledged the general rules we have set out, but thought that *Ahlberg* and *Carr* created "[a]n apparent exception to these general rules, based on verbal revelations of infidelity and other conduct." (153 Ill.App.3d at 5, 106 Ill.Dec. 75, 505 N.E.2d 381.) Since the circumstances in *Ambro* were similar to those in *Ahlberg* and *Carr* (a history of ongoing marital discord, a wife who evidenced an intent to permanently leave her husband, insulting remarks concerning the husband's masculinity, and an announcement of adultery by the wife), the court applied the exception created by *Ahlberg* and held it was reversible error to refuse defendant's voluntary manslaughter instruction. *Ambro,* 153 Ill.App.3d at 6–7, 106 Ill.Dec. 75, 505 N.E.2d 381.

Parenthetically, we fail to understand why a history of marital discord should be a factor favoring a voluntary manslaughter instruction. The appellate court's opinions in *Ahlberg, Carr, Ambro, Chevalier* and *Flores,* without explanation, all list this factor as one favoring a voluntary manslaughter instruction. Since voluntary manslaughter requires evidence of a *sudden* passion, a history of marital discord, particularly suspicions of adultery, if relevant at all, would undermine, not support, a defendant's claim that the evidence supports a voluntary manslaughter instruction.

Justice Lindberg dissented from that portion of the *Ambro* opinion which held that defendant presented sufficient evidence to warrant giving a voluntary manslaughter instruction. He pointed out that "serious provocation" is a legal standard that has been defined by this court to include adultery with the offender's spouse. (People v. Crews (1967), 38 Ill.2d 331, 335, 231 N.E.2d 451.) In his view, " 'words alone [even those that carry messages of adultery] are insufficient evidence of provocation.' " *(Ambro,* 153 Ill.App.3d at 9, 106 Ill.Dec. 75, 505 N.E.2d 381, quoting People v. Arnold (1974), 17 Ill.App.3d 1043, 309 N.E.2d 89 (bracketed language in *Ambro*).) He concluded that the evidence in *Ambro* did not meet the legal standard of provocation. Therefore, the evidence did not authorize or mandate the giving of a voluntary manslaughter instruction, and the conviction of murder should have been affirmed.

Justice Lindberg wrote the opinion for the court in *Chevalier.* He referred to his dissent in *Ambro,* but stated that he felt bound by *stare decisis* to follow the majority opinion in *Ambro. Chevalier,* 167 Ill.App.3d at 797 n. 1, 118 Ill.Dec. 563, 521 N.E.2d 1256.

We conclude that the "exception" to the general rule created by the *Ahlberg* line of cases is an incorrect statement of Illinois law. *A fortiori,* the appellate court's reliance on those cases in *Chevalier* and *Flores* is misplaced. Further, we decline defendant Flores' invitation to change the law by holding that a confession of adultery by a spouse is legally adequate provocation.

Given our rejection of the *Ahlberg* line of cases, defendants' positions are unsupportable; defendants appear to concede as much. Whatever may be the outer limits of the general rule that only the discovery of the parties in the act of adultery, or immediately before or after the act, will suffice as provocation, neither case falls within the rule. In *People v. Chevalier,* during the course of the marriage, the victim left the defendant three times to live with defendant's best friend. The night before the murder, defendant discovered his wife's soiled panties in his car but said nothing to his wife.

The next evening, he confronted his wife and said more than once that he knew she was "messing around" again. Similarly, in *People v. Flores,* defendant testified that he suspected his wife of having an affair for approximately eight months prior to the murder. Thus, neither case can possibly come within the rule. As for the insulting remarks made by the victims, the *Ahlberg* line of cases simply ignores the rule that no matter how insulting, mere words are insufficient provocation.

For these reasons, we hold that in each of the cases before us, the provocation claimed was, as a matter of law, insufficient to constitute the serious provocation necessary to reduce the homicide from murder to voluntary manslaughter. . . .

Commonwealth v. Troila

Supreme Judicial Court of Massachusetts, Suffolk, 1991.
410 Mass. 203, 571 N.E.2d 391.

■ NOLAN, JUSTICE.

The defendant appeals from his conviction of murder in the first degree. . . .

At approximately 10 A.M., on May 2, 1987, two children discovered a body in a lot behind their home in the Roxbury section of Boston. The victim had been stabbed several times. A medical examiner testified that two of the stab wounds to the heart were fatal and that a third, to the neck, was potentially fatal. Time of death was set sometime within twenty-four hours of the body's discovery.

The defendant, Matthew Troila, was indicted for murder in the first degree and brought to trial. Several witnesses testified to having seen the defendant and the victim together on the evening of May 1, 1987, the night before the body was discovered. The jury heard a tape recording of the defendant being interrogated by Boston police in connection with the murder. In addition, three witnesses testified that the defendant had, on separate occasions, admitted to the killing.

One witness, Margaret Wilson, testified that she was with both the defendant and the victim on May 1 and into the early morning hours of May 2. She testified that, at that time, she was dating the defendant's brother, Joseph Troila. According to Wilson, she, Joseph, the defendant, and the victim traveled in her automobile to and from various gathering places. At one point, Wilson testified, she was directed to drive to the place where the body was subsequently found. Wilson was told to stay in her automobile while the three men went off in search of drugs. Approximately fifteen minutes later, Joseph returned, followed shortly by the defendant. Wilson testified that she then asked where the victim was, to which the defendant replied that he had killed him because the victim had "made a pass" at him. . . .

Another witness, Debra Miele, with whom the defendant was living at the time of the murder, testified at trial that, on the morning of May 2, 1987, the defendant told her, "I think I killed somebody last night." When asked why, the defendant allegedly said that the victim was a homosexual and "had tried something on him sexually." The defendant's sister also testified that, about one week after the murder, the defendant said to her that he thought he killed somebody but was not sure.

There was corroboration of aspects of this testimony. The victim's sister testified that the victim was a homosexual. Several witnesses testified that they saw the victim in the company of the defendant, Joseph, and Wilson.

The jury convicted the defendant of murder in the first degree on the theory of extreme atrocity or cruelty. The defendant now appeals from that conviction. . . .

The defendant next contends that the judge erred by failing to instruct the jury that, if they found that the defendant had been provoked by the victim and committed the crime in the heat of passion, they could find him guilty of manslaughter rather than murder. The defendant contends that the jury could find that, because the victim allegedly made homosexual overtures to him, the defendant was reasonably provoked such that the severity of the crime ought to be reduced. We disagree.

"Voluntary manslaughter is 'a killing from a sudden transport of passion or heat of blood, upon a reasonable provocation and without malice, or upon sudden combat.' "Commonwealth v. Zukoski, 370 Mass. 23, 28, 345 N.E.2d 690 (1976), quoting Commonwealth v. Soaris, 275 Mass. 291, 299, 175 N.E. 491 (1931). The only evidence of provocation was the defendant's alleged statement that the victim "made a pass" at him. No jury could find on the basis of this evidence that reasonable provocation existed. On this record, no manslaughter instruction was necessary.

Judgment affirmed.

People v. Borchers

Supreme Court of California, In Bank, 1958.
50 Cal.2d 321, 325 P.2d 97.

■ SCHAUER, JUSTICE. The People appeal "from an Order of the Superior Court . . . modifying the verdict in the above entitled cause by reducing the punishment imposed." (Pen.Code, § 1238(6).) Defendant does not appeal. A jury found defendant guilty of murder of the second degree and found that he was sane at the time of the commission of the offense. The trial judge denied defendant's motion for a new trial on the issue of sanity and ordered that "Defendant's motion for new trial on the case in chief is ruled upon as follows: In lieu of granting a new trial, the verdict of second degree Murder is reduced to Voluntary Manslaughter.'' The People argue that the evidence was sufficient to justify the implied finding of malice aforethought, that the evidence did not show that defendant was guilty of voluntary manslaughter, and that the trial court erred in reducing the class of crime found by the jury. We have concluded that no ground for reversal is shown.

Defendant, a Pasadena insurance broker, aged 45, met deceased, referred to throughout the testimony as ''Dotty,'' aged 29, at a zoo on May 13, 1956. With Dotty was Tony, an illegitimate child of four whom Dotty had cared for since 16 days after his birth. Defendant was attracted by the ''warmth,'' ''kindness,'' and ''sweetness'' with which Dotty spoke to the child. Defendant spoke to the boy and thus became acquainted with Dotty. They had dinner together that night and thereafter, according to defendant's testimony, ''went together steadily from then on'' until he killed her on October 9, 1956. From May 13 until October 9 ''excepting the days that I was away on a business trip to Mexico and one other day ... there was not a day that went by but what Tony and Dotty and I saw each other''. . . .

[Although defendant was married (divorce proceedings had been started) he and Dotty became ''engaged'' nine days after they first met. He provided an apartment for her and Tony, and took her on a trip to Las Vegas. There they recited a ''common-law marriage ceremony''. After they returned to Pasadena he learned that Marvin Prestidge and another man were ''hanging around'' Dotty and using her automobile. As these men had criminal records, defendant employed Fagg, a private detective, to investigate. Fagg reported that Prestidge had a police record as a pimp, that he was having sexual relations with Dotty, and that she was taking money from defendant and giving it to Prestidge. Defendant believed she was acting because of fear of Prestidge although Fagg assured him that fear was not the reason.

On October 5, 1956, while returning from a trip to San Diego, she said she wished she were dead and tried to jump from the moving car. A few nights later, while they were riding, she repeatedly suggested suicide. She took a pistol from the glove compartment, saying she was going to shoot him, but permitted him to take the weapon. She said he should kill her, Tony and himself. Then she turned to him and said: ''Go ahead and shoot. What is the matter,—are you chicken?'' And as defendant told it, ''he heard the explosion of the gun as he shot Dotty in the back of the head.'']

Section 1181, paragraph 6 of the Penal Code provides that the trial court may grant a new trial ''When the verdict is contrary to law or evidence, but if the evidence shows the defendant to be not guilty of the degree of the crime of which he was convicted, but guilty of a lesser degree thereof, or of a lesser crime included therein, the court may modify the verdict, finding or judgment accordingly without granting or ordering a new trial ...''

The trial court in ruling on the question of reducing the class of the crime stated that in its opinion there was ''a duty fixed on the trial court to independently weigh and consider the testimony and all of the ramifications of it and determine in his own mind if he is satisfied that the evidence beyond a reasonable doubt shows guilt of second degree murder. Tested in that light and tested further in the light of the evidence of the psychiatrists on the mental condition of this defendant, I am not satisfied that the evidence is sufficient to sustain the finding of malice to make this second degree murder; hence, the Court in lieu of granting a new trial will reduce the degree to that of voluntary manslaughter.''

Rule

In passing on a motion for new trial it is not only the power but also the duty of the trial court to consider the weight of the evidence. The power and duty of the trial court in considering the question of the reduction of the class or degree of the crime are the same.

In a criminal trial the burden is upon the prosecution to prove beyond any reasonable doubt every essential element of the crime of which a defendant is to be convicted. Here, from the evidence viewed as a whole, the trial judge was amply justified in concluding that defendant did not possess the state of mind known as "malice aforethought" which is an essential ingredient of murder. (Pen.Code, § 187.) "Such malice may be express or implied. It is express when there is manifested a deliberate intention unlawfully to take away the life of a fellow-creature. It is implied, when no considerable provocation appears, or when the circumstances attending the killing show an abandoned and malignant heart." (Pen.Code, § 188.) Voluntary manslaughter is "the unlawful killing of a human being, without malice . . . upon a sudden quarrel or heat of passion." (Pen.Code, § 192.)

From the evidence viewed as a whole the trial judge could well have concluded that defendant was roused to a heat of "passion" by a series of events over a considerable period of time: Dotty's admitted infidelity, her statements that she wished she were dead, her attempt to jump from the car on the trip to San Diego, her repeated urging that defendant shoot her, Tony, and himself on the night of the homicide, and her taunt, "are you chicken." As defendant argues persuasively, "passion" need not mean "rage" or "anger". According to dictionary definition, "passion" may be any "violent, intense, highwrought, or enthusiastic emotion." (Webster's New International Dictionary, 2d ed.) As stated in People v. Logan (1917), 175 Cal. 45, 49, 164 P. 1121, "the fundamental of the inquiry (in determining whether a homicide is voluntary manslaughter) is whether or not the defendant's reason was, at the time of his act, so disturbed or obscured by some passion—not necessarily fear and never, of course, the passion for revenge—to such an extent as would render ordinary men of average disposition liable to act rashly or without due deliberation and reflection, and from this passion rather than from judgment." It may fairly be concluded that the evidence on the issue of not guilty supports a finding that defendant killed in wild desperation induced by Dotty's long continued provocatory conduct. . . .

The trial judge here is to be commended for his diligent alertness to the power and duty, reposed *only in trial courts,* to reappraise the weight of the evidence on motion for new trial. He very properly showed no hesitance in reducing the class of the homicide in the light of his determination, supported by a reasonable view of the evidence, that there was no sufficient showing of malice aforethought. Such unhesitant exercise of this power by the trial judge, when he is satisfied that the action is indicated by the evidence, not only makes for justice in the individual case but tends also to lighten the burden of reviewing courts and to expedite the finality of judgments.

For the reasons above stated the order appealed from is affirmed.[25]

■ GIBSON, C.J., and SHENK, CARTER, TRAYNOR, SPENCE and McCOMB, JJ., concur.

State v. Dumlao

Intermediate Court of Appeals of Hawaii, 1986.
6 Hawaii App. 173, 715 P.2d 822.

■ HEEN, JUDGE.

Issue

Defendant Vidado B. Dumlao appeals from his conviction of murder. He argues on appeal that the trial court erred in refusing to give his requested manslaughter instruction.... [H]e contends there was sufficient evidence that he shot his mother-in-law, Pacita M. Reyes (Pacita), while "under the influence of extreme mental or emotional disturbance for which there [was] a reasonable explanation" to support an instruction under HRS § 707–702(2) (1976).[26] We agree and reverse.

Facts

The trial court instructed the jury that they could find Dumlao guilty of manslaughter if they concluded that he had recklessly shot Pacita to death, HRS § 707–702(1)(a) (1976), but refused to give the instruction Dumlao had requested.

After a jury trial, Dumlao was convicted of murder for shooting Pacita, and of reckless endangering in the first degree, for shooting and injuring his brother-in-law, Pedrito Reyes (Pedrito)....

... The language of § 707–702(2) does not comport with the historical test for reducing a charge of murder to manslaughter, and we cannot determine from the language alone whether the legislature intended to

---

25. "We agree with defendant's initial point that provocation sufficient to reduce murder to manslaughter need not occur instantaneously, but may occur over a period of time...."

"By contrast, the court erred in refusing to instruct the jury, at defendant's request, that legally adequate provocation could occur over a considerable period of time." People v. Wharton, 53 Cal.3d 522, 280 Cal.Rptr. 631, 809 P.2d 290, 318 (1991).

26. HRS § 707–702(2) reads as follows:

Manslaughter....

(2) In a prosecution for murder it is a defense, which reduces the offense to manslaughter, that the defendant was, at the time he caused the death of the other person, under the influence of extreme mental or emotional disturbance for which there is a reasonable explanation. The reasonableness of the explanation shall be determined from the view-point of a person in the defendant's situation under the circumstances as he believed them to be.

Although the statute refers to the mental state of a defendant as a defense, it is really a mitigating factor. "Intentionally killing while under the influence of extreme emotional disturbance does not present a true 'defense,' for the punishment is merely reduced through the mechanism of denominating the crime as 'manslaughter' rather than 'murder.' It could be considered a 'partial defense' in the sense that an acquittal of the charge of murder occurs when the jury finds that the defendant is guilty only of manslaughter." State v. Ott, 297 Or. 375, 377 n. 2, 686 P.2d 1001, 1003 n. 2 (1984).

effect a change in that test. Consequently, we must seek assistance from other sources.

The legislative history of § 707–702(2) is of no assistance, and we must look to the history of the offense of manslaughter generally and under Hawaii law, and to materials construing the pertinent provision of the Model Penal Code (MPC), upon which our penal code is based.

HISTORY OF THE MITIGATING FACTOR IN MANSLAUGHTER

The principle that the presence of an extreme mental or emotional disturbance will reduce the offense of murder to manslaughter is a modification of the ancient distinction between slaying in cold blood and slaying in the heat of passion existing in Anglo–Saxon criminal law prior to the Norman conquest of 1066. The "Doctrine of Provocation" became firmly established in the common law in 1628 and the distinction between murder and manslaughter turned on the presence of heat of passion caused by adequate provocation.

In the United States mutual combat, assault and adultery were gradually recognized as having been legally adequate provocation at common law to reduce murder to manslaughter. In some jurisdictions illegal arrest, injuries to third parties, and even words tending to give rise to heat of passion are sufficient provocation.

The determination of the adequacy of the provocation gradually became a jury prerogative in marginal cases, and the reasonable person test was devised to assist the jury. Today the test has four elements: (1) provocation that would rouse a reasonable person to the heat of passion; (2) actual provocation of the defendant; (3) a reasonable person would not have cooled off in the time between the provocation and the offense; and (4) the defendant did not cool off. The reasonable person yardstick is strictly objective; neither the mental nor physical peculiarities of the accused are evaluated in determining whether the loss of self-control was "reasonable."

CRITICISM OF THE "REASONABLE PERSON" TEST

As originally developed the provocation defense focused on the mental state of the accused as the test for moral culpability; however, under the objective or "reasonable person" test the individual's mental state is not the determinative factor. State v. Ott, 297 Or. 375, 381, 686 P.2d 1001, 1005 (1984).

Some commentators have remarked on the inconsistency of the reasonable person test.

The reasonable man test, being objective in nature, is antithetical to the concept of mens rea. Like all objective standards, it is an external standard of general application that does not focus on an individual accused's mental state. Thus, from the point of view of traditional Anglo–American jurisprudence, a paradox is inherent in the use of the reasonable man standard to test criminal responsibility: the presence or absence of criminal intent is determined by a standard which ignores the mental state of the individual accused.

The objective test placed the jury in the conceptually awkward, almost impossible, position of having to determine when it is reasonable for a reasonable person to act unreasonably.

. . .

Surely the true view of provocation is that it is a concession to "the frailty of human nature" in those exceptional cases where the legal prohibition fails of effect. It is a compromise, neither conceding the propriety of the act nor exacting the full penalty for it. This being so, how can it be that that paragon of virtue, the reasonable man, gives way to provocation?

Williams, Provocation and the Reasonable Man, 1954 Crim.L.Rev. 740, 742.

The MPC's response to this criticism is discussed below.

HAWAII LAW PRIOR TO THE PENAL CODE

Prior to the effective date of the Hawaii Penal Code (HPC) in 1973, Hawaii statutorily defined manslaughter as any killing "without malice aforethought, and without authority, justification, or extenuation." HRS § 748–6 (1968). Hawaii case law at that time adhered to the historical common-law principle of reducing murder in the first or second degree to manslaughter when mitigating mental or emotional disturbances were present. Hawaii case law employed the concept of "heat of passion," The King v. Greenwell, 1 Haw. 146 (1853), and recognized a more general approach, acknowledging extenuations attributable to individual mental and emotional weakness under the circumstances. See The King v. Sherman, 1 Haw. 150 (1853); *Greenwell, supra*. However, the latter, more liberal approach, was limited by the additional requirement that the killing be without malice and that the assailant had been provoked by the victim.

Under HRS § 707–702(2), the two principal elements of the extenuating factor are established: (1) extreme mental or emotional disturbance and (2) an objective/subjective test of the reasonableness of the explanation for the disturbance. However, the nature of those elements are not clear from the language of the statute, and neither the *Commentary* nor the legislative history indicates what considerations go into making up those elements.

Since HRS § 707–702(2) is derived from MPC § 210.3,[27] we may look to the commentaries and cases from other jurisdictions explaining and construing that section for insight into the meaning of the language of our statute. We will examine the first element of § 707–702 first.

"Extreme mental or emotional disturbance" sometimes is, but should not be, confused with the "insanity" defense. The point of the extreme

---

27. Section 210.3 states in pertinent part as follows:

Manslaughter

(1) Criminal homicide constitutes manslaughter when:

. . .

(b) a homicide which would otherwise be murder is committed under the influence of extreme mental or emotional disturbance for which there is reasonable explanation or excuse. The reasonableness of such explanation or excuse shall be determined from the viewpoint of a person in the actor's situation under the circumstances as he believes them to be.

emotional disturbance defense is to provide a basis for mitigation that differs from a finding of mental defect or disease precluding criminal responsibility. The disturbance was meant to be understood in relative terms as referring to a loss of self-control due to intense feelings.

The extreme mental or emotional disturbance concept of the MPC must also be distinguished from the so-called "diminished capacity" defense.

The doctrine of diminished capacity provides that evidence of an abnormal mental condition not amounting to legal insanity but tending to prove that the defendant could not or did not entertain the specific intent or state of mind essential to the offense should be considered for the purpose of determining whether the crime charged or a lesser degree thereof was in fact committed.

Although the MPC does *not* recognize diminished capacity as a distinct category of mitigation, II Model Penal Code and Commentaries § 210.3 at 72 (Official Draft and Revised Comments 1980), by placing more emphasis than does the common law on the actor's subjective mental state, it also may allow inquiry into areas which have traditionally been treated as part of the law of diminished responsibility or the insanity defense.

Thus, the MPC is said to have in fact adopted an expanded concept of diminished capacity to reduce murder to manslaughter. People v. Spurlin, 156 Cal.App.3d 119, 127 n. 4, 202 Cal.Rptr. 663, 668 n. 4 (1984).

Diminished capacity involves a mental disturbance which peculiarly involves the killer. Heat of passion is a concession to human weakness, to a universal human condition. *Diminished capacity is an effort to reduce punishment because the actor is not like all humans, whereas heat of passion reduces punishment because the actor is, unfortunately, like most humans.* (Footnotes omitted and emphasis added.)

Dressler, Rethinking Heat of Passion: A Defense in Search of a Rationale, 73 J.Crim.L. and Criminology 421, 459–60 (1982).

The MPC merges the two concepts of heat of passion and diminished capacity.

It is enough if the killing occurs while the defendant's capacity to form an intent to murder is diminished by an extreme mental or emotional disturbance deemed to have a reasonable explanation or excuse from the defendant's standpoint.

An explanation of the term "extreme emotional disturbance" which reflects the situational or relative character of the concept was given in People v. Shelton, 88 Misc.2d 136, 149, 385 N.Y.S.2d 708, 717 (1976), as follows:

> [T]hat extreme emotional disturbance is the emotional state of an individual, who: (a) has no mental disease or defect that rises to the level established by Section 30.05 of the Penal Law;[28] and (b) is exposed to an extremely unusual and overwhelming stress; and (c) has

---

28. At that time, N.Y. Penal Law § 30.05 (McKinney 1975) set forth New York's insanity defense. . . .

an extreme emotional reaction to it, as a result of which there is a loss of self-control and reason is overborne by intense feelings, such as passion, anger, distress, grief, excessive agitation or other similar emotions.[29]

It is clear that in adopting the "extreme mental or emotional disturbance" concept, the MPC intended to define the provocation element of manslaughter in broader terms than had previously been done. It is equally clear that our legislature also intended the same result when it adopted the language of the MPC.[30]

We turn then to the second prong of our analysis, the test to determine the reasonableness of the explanation for the mental or emotional disturbance. It is here that the most significant change has been made in the law of manslaughter.

The anomaly of the reasonable person test was corrected by the drafters of the MPC through the development of an objective/subjective test of reasonableness.

It makes the test more, although not entirely, subjective, by requiring the jury to test the reasonableness of the actor's conduct, "from the viewpoint of a person in the actor's situation." Thus, the actor's sex, sexual preference, pregnancy, physical deformities, and similar characteristics are apt to be taken into consideration in evaluating the reasonableness of the defendant's behavior.

This more subjective version of the provocation defense goes substantially beyond the common law by abandoning preconceptions of what constitutes adequate provocation, and giving the jury wider scope.

Under the prior law of provocation, personal characteristics of the defendant were not to be considered. Under the MPC a change from the old

---

29. The extreme emotional disturbance defense is also broader than the heat of passion doctrine which it replaced, in that a cooling off period intervening between the fatal act and the disturbance does not negate the defense. People v. Parmes, 114 Misc.2d 503, 505, 451 N.Y.S.2d 1015, 1017 (1982). "A spontaneous explosion is not required." Id. Rather, "a significant mental trauma" could have "affected a defendant's mind for a substantial period of time, simmering in the unknown subconscious and then inexplicably coming to the fore." People v. Shelton, 88 Misc.2d 136, 144, 385 N.Y.S.2d 708, 715 (1976). *See also People v. Parmes, supra.*

The drafters of the Model Penal Code (MPC) found it "shocking" that the common law disregarded the fact that the passage of time sometimes served only to increase rather than diminish outrage. MPC § 201.3 at 48, Comments (Tent.Draft No. 9, 1959). They said:

Though it is difficult to state a middle ground between a standard which ignores all individual peculiarities and one which makes emotional distress decisive regardless of the nature of its cause, we think that such a statement is essential. For surely if the actor had just suffered a traumatic injury, if he were blind or were distraught with grief, if he were experiencing an unanticipated reaction to a therapeutic drug, it would be deemed atrocious to appraise his crime for purposes of sentence without reference to any of these matters. They are material because they bear upon the inference as to the actor's character that it is fair to draw upon the basis of his act. So too . . . where lapse of time increased rather than diminished the extent of the outrage perpetrated on the actor, . . . it was shocking in our view to hold this vital fact to be irrelevant.

30. As noted in II Model Penal Code and Commentaries § 210.3 at 64–65 (Official Draft and Revised Comments 1980), however, it is implicit that extreme emotional disturbance will not reduce murder to manslaughter, if the actor has intentionally, knowingly, recklessly, or negligently brought about his own mental disturbance, such as by involving himself in a crime.

provocation law and the reasonable person standard has been effected by requiring the factfinder to focus on a person in the defendant's situation. Thus, the MPC, while requiring that the explanation for the disturbance must be reasonable, provides that the reasonableness is determined from the defendant's viewpoint. The phrase "actor's situation," as used in § 210.3(b) of the MPC, is designedly ambiguous and is plainly flexible enough to allow the law to grow in the direction of taking account of mental abnormalities that have been recognized in the developing law of diminished responsibility.

Moreover, the MPC does not require the provocation to emanate from the victim as was argued by the State here. *Spurlin,* 156 Cal.App.3d at 127 n. 4, 202 Cal.Rptr. at 668 n. 4; 1980 MPC Commentary, *supra,* at 60–61.

In light of the foregoing discussion and the necessity of articulating the defense in comprehensible terms, we adopt the test enunciated by the New York Court of Appeals in People v. Casassa, 49 N.Y.2d 668, 427 N.Y.S.2d 769, 775, 404 N.E.2d 1310, 1316, cert. denied, 449 U.S. 842, 101 S.Ct. 122, 66 L.Ed.2d 50 (1980):

[W]e conclude that the determination whether there was reasonable explanation or excuse for a particular emotional disturbance should be made by viewing the subjective, internal situation in which the defendant found himself and the external circumstances as he perceived them at the time, however inaccurate that perception may have been, and assessing from that standpoint whether the explanation ... for his emotional disturbance was reasonable, so as to entitle him to a reduction of the crime charged from murder ... to manslaughter.... (Footnote omitted.)

Thus, we hold in the instant case that the trial court was required to instruct the jury as requested by Dumlao, if there was any evidence to support a finding that at the time of the offense he suffered an "extreme mental or emotional disturbance" for which there was a "reasonable explanation" when the totality of circumstances was judged from his personal viewpoint.

. . .

In the instant case, there was evidence of the following:

Arthur Golden, M.D., Dumlao's expert witness, stated at trial that his diagnosis of Dumlao was one of "paranoid personality disorder," which is a "long range, almost lifetime or certainly over many, many years, emotional or mental disorder. It is almost a way of functioning."

Dr. Golden diagnosed Dumlao as having unwarranted suspiciousness, one of the basic indicators of the "paranoid personality disorder." That unwarranted suspiciousness included pathological jealousy, which Dumlao suffered throughout his ten-year marriage. Dumlao harbored the belief that other males, including his wife's relatives, were somehow sexually involved with her. He could never figure out exactly who or where or how, yet this extreme suspiciousness persisted.

Dr. Golden described the second major sign of Dumlao's paranoid personality disorder as hypersensitivity, characterized by being easily slighted or quick to take offense, and a readiness to counterattack when a threat was perceived. . . .

Dumlao's extreme and irrational jealousy concerning his wife was known to all the family members. According to Agapito, they couldn't even talk to their sister in Dumlao's presence. "If we have to talk to her, we have to talk from a distance because he suspects us." Furthermore, Dumlao "never allowed us to talk in a group."

Dumlao's testimony, describing his own perceptions of the night in question, further confirms the nature of his extreme jealousy. . . .

Reviewing the evidence within the context of the meaning of HRS § 707–702(2), we conclude that it was sufficient to require the trial court to give Dumlao's requested instruction on manslaughter. . . .

Reversed and remanded for new trial.[31]

Murray v. State

Supreme Court of Wyoming, 1993.
855 P.2d 350.

■ MACY, CHIEF JUSTICE.

Appellant Donald Murray appeals from his conviction for involuntary manslaughter in violation of Wyo.Stat. § 6–2–105(a)(ii) and (b) (1988).

We affirm as modified.

Appellant presents the following issues for our consideration:

. . .

II.   Whether the evidence was sufficient to sustain a conviction for involuntary manslaughter?

. . .

Appellant and the victim worked together on an oil rig located near Granger, Wyoming. The men were good friends who had known each other since 1983. On September 30, 1991, they completed their shift on the oil rig at approximately 6:30 p.m. They began drinking shortly thereafter, and eventually went to the Cowboy Bar in Mountain View. While they were at the Cowboy Bar, the victim and Appellant started arguing about one of their co-workers. Appellant left the bar before the argument could escalate into a physical confrontation. He proceeded by himself to Pete's Bar where he ate pizza and continued drinking. At about 10:30 p.m., Appellant drove home.

At eleven o'clock that same evening, the victim had his cousin drive him to Appellant's house so that he could retrieve his work clothes which were in the back of Appellant's truck. As the victim's cousin drove down

---

31. Repeated humiliation of defendant by his wife did not support the affirmative defense of extreme emotional disturbance for the killing of the wife weeks later. Passage of time does not preclude the defense, but evidence must show proof that a temporarily remote provocative act affected the defendant at the time of the homicide to the extent that it could be concluded the defendant acted under extreme emotional disturbance. People v. White, 79 N.Y.2d 900, 590 N.E.2d 236 (1992).

Appellant's driveway, she observed a flash from a gun barrel. While continuing on down the driveway, she saw and heard additional shots being fired and noticed Appellant standing on his porch holding a handgun. The victim exited the vehicle, identified himself, and explained to Appellant that he just wanted to get his work clothes. Appellant yelled " '[g]et off of my property' " to the victim. He fired three additional shots from his porch, two of which landed near the victim's feet. The victim again identified himself and started walking toward Appellant's truck. Appellant left his porch and walked toward the victim until they were approximately six feet apart. The victim said: " 'Just let me get my work clothes and we'll leave.' " Appellant repeated the command to get off his property. The victim said, " 'Okay. I'm leaving,' " turned around, and had started walking back towards the car when Appellant fired three or four additional shots. One of the bullets ricocheted off a rock and passed through the victim's right thigh, severing his femoral artery and femoral vein. The victim also suffered a relatively minor bullet wound to his right buttock. The doctor who performed the autopsy was unable to determine whether the two wounds were the result of a single gunshot or multiple gunshots.

The victim hopped back to the car after being shot. His cousin drove him to Pete's Bar which was located approximately two miles from Appellant's house. The victim's cousin and one of the bartenders placed the victim on the pavement in the bar's parking lot and elevated his leg with a stool. Another bartender telephoned 911. The ambulance arrived about half an hour after the 911 call had been placed. When the ambulance arrived, the victim's vital signs were normal, and his level of consciousness indicated that he was in "great shape." The emergency medical technicians thought that the victim had lost only a minimal amount of blood. In reality, he had lost a massive quantity of blood during the time that it took to drive from Appellant's house to Pete's Bar. The victim lost consciousness shortly before reaching the hospital, his breathing became difficult, and his pupils dilated. The EMTs and the emergency room physicians were unable to resuscitate him.

Appellant was arrested and initially charged with second-degree murder. The deputy county and prosecuting attorney subsequently reduced the charge to involuntary manslaughter. A jury found Appellant guilty of involuntary manslaughter,....

Sufficiency of the Evidence

Appellant claims that the prosecution did not present sufficient evidence to sustain a conviction for involuntary manslaughter. He argues that, at most, the evidence supported a conviction for criminally negligent homicide. ...

Our involuntary manslaughter statute, § 6–2–105(a)(ii), provides: "A person is guilty of manslaughter if he unlawfully kills any human being without malice, expressed or implied, ... [i]nvoluntarily, but recklessly." According to Wyo.Stat. § 6–1–104(a)(ix) (1988) (emphasis added):

A person acts recklessly when he *consciously disregards* a substantial and unjustifiable risk that the harm he is accused of causing will occur, and the harm results. The risk shall be of such nature and degree that disregarding it constitutes a gross deviation from the standard of conduct that a reasonable person would observe in the situation[.]

The principal distinction between criminally negligent homicide[32] and involuntary manslaughter is whether the defendant consciously disregarded a substantial and unjustifiable risk or whether he failed, through criminal negligence, to perceive that risk. The Utah Supreme Court succinctly explained this distinction in State v. Howard, 597 P.2d 878, 881 (Utah 1979) (emphasis in original):

The difference between the minimum required *mens rea* of recklessness for manslaughter and criminal negligence for negligent homicide is simply whether the defendant was *aware, but consciously disregarded* a substantial risk the result would happen, or was *unaware but ought to have been aware* of a substantial risk the result would happen.

Appellant testified in this case that he had served an extended tour of duty with the United States army in Vietnam, where he was a rifleman and a machine gunner. The army rated Appellant as being a sharpshooter. Both the army and Appellant's father instructed him not to point a gun at anyone because someone could get hurt. His father also told him not to use guns when he had been drinking. Appellant admitted that, whenever someone discharges a gun, it is a terribly dangerous activity. Appellant was also an avid hunter who hunted with a wide variety of guns. A reasonable jury could infer from Appellant's extensive experience with weapons that he was aware of, but consciously disregarded, the substantial and unjustifiable risk that the victim could be injured by a ricocheting bullet.

In his brief, Appellant repeats his trial testimony that, on the night of the shooting, he did not realize he was engaged in a dangerous activity because he aimed the gun away from the victim. The victim's cousin contradicted this assertion with her testimony that some of the bullets raised the dirt near the victim's feet. Even Appellant testified that one of the bullets hit the dirt three or four feet from the victim's feet. In Wyoming, where rocks are plentiful, it is reasonable to infer that shooting at someone's feet creates a substantial and unjustifiable risk of injury resulting from a ricocheting bullet.[33]

. . .

---

32.   Wyo.Stat. § 6–2–107(a) (1988) provides:

(a) Except under circumstances constituting a violation of W.S. § 6–2–106 [homicide by vehicle], a person is guilty of criminally negligent homicide if he causes the death of another person by conduct amounting to criminal negligence.

Wyo.Stat. § 6–1–104(a)(iii) (1988) provides in pertinent part:

A person acts with criminal negligence when, through a gross deviation from the standard of care that a reasonable person would exercise, he fails to perceive a substantial and unjustifiable risk that the harm he is accused of causing will occur, and the harm results. The risk shall be of such nature and degree that the failure to perceive it constitutes a gross deviation from the standard of care that a reasonable person would observe in the situation[.]

33.   Appellant argues that People v. Post, 39 Ill.2d 101, 233 N.E.2d 565 (1968), mandates a contrary result. In Post, the defendant fired a single shot into the ground to scare off an intruder. The shot apparently ricocheted and killed the intruder. The Illinois Supreme Court held:

Affirmed as modified.[34]

People v. Rodriguez

District Court of Appeal, Second District, Division 3, California, 1960.
186 Cal.App.2d 433, 8 Cal.Rptr. 863.

■ VALÉE, JUSTICE. By information defendant was accused of manslaughter in that on November 8, 1959 she did wilfully, unlawfully, feloniously, and without malice kill Carlos Quinones. In a nonjury trial she was found guilty of involuntary manslaughter. A new trial was denied. She appeals from the judgment and the order denying a new trial.

In November 1959 defendant was living with her four children in a single-family residence at 130 South Clarence Street, Los Angeles. The oldest child was 6 years of age. Carlos Quinones was the youngest, either 2 or 3 years of age.

Olive Faison lived across the street from defendant. About 10:45 p.m. on November 8, 1959 Miss Faison heard some children calling, "Mommy, mommy." For about 15 or 20 minutes she did not "pay too much attention." She noticed the cries became more shrill. She went to the front window and saw smoke coming from defendant's house. She "ran across

---

The shooting of a .22 caliber pistol toward the ground is not per se reckless and is not such an act as would likely cause death or bodily harm to a person some distance away. Firing into the ground or into the air to frighten a marauder in order to keep him from returning is not, in our opinion, such a reckless act as to justify conviction of involuntary manslaughter.

233 N.E.2d at 567. Obviously, several distinctions exist between Post and the present facts; e.g., Appellant fired several shots at the victim's feet, as opposed to firing a single warning shot; and the victim was a known friend as opposed to being a "marauder." We decline to follow Post to the extent, if any, our holding in the present case is inconsistent with the Post opinion.

34. Accord: State v. Hardie, 47 Iowa 647 (1878) pointing supposedly inoperable weapon at victim was gross negligence.

Evidence that the defendant took a loaded revolver from his belt area, with his finger on the trigger and pointed it in the direction of the deceased a short distance away and the weapon discharged justified a conviction for manslaughter in the second degree. "... there was ample evidence demonstrating defendant's subjective awareness and conscious disregard of the risk." People v. Licitra, 47 N.Y.2d 554, 419 N.Y.S.2d 461, 393 N.E.2d 456, 459 (1979).

Two friends had a revolver. There was one cartridge in the chamber, so placed that they thought it would not fire until the trigger had been pulled about five times. One playfully put the weapon against the side of the other and pulled the trigger three times. The third pull resulted in a fatal shot. A conviction of second-degree murder was affirmed. Commonwealth v. Malone, 354 Pa. 180, 47 A.2d 445 (1946).

Evidence that defendant did not know if shotgun was loaded and pulled the trigger while the gun was pointed in the direction of the victim to show the victim the gun would shoot was reckless conduct constituting culpable negligence for manslaughter conviction. State v. Davis, 691 S.W.2d 333 (Mo.App.1985).

Manslaughter conviction was proper against a defendant for improperly keeping pit bulls which amounted to reckless conduct. Pit bulls attacked and killed a child. Turnipseed v. State, 186 Ga.App. 278, 367 S.E.2d 259 (1988).

Defendant's conviction for involuntary manslaughter was established by evidence that defendant held a rifle pointed towards a tavern when the safety was in such a position that the rifle could be fired. The rifle discharged killing a patron in the tavern. State v. Miller, 772 S.W.2d 782 (Mo.App.1989).

the street and commenced to knock the door in and started pulling the children out." There was a screen door on the outside and a wooden door inside the screen door. The screen door was padlocked on the outside. The other door was open. She broke the screen door and with the help of neighbors pulled three of the children out of the house. She tried to get into the house through the front door but could not because of the flames. A neighbor entered through the back door but could not go far because of the flames. Miss Faison took the three children to her apartment and shortly thereafter returned to the scene of the fire. . . .

Maria Lucero, defendant's sister, went to defendant's home about 12 p.m. on November 8, 1959. She went looking for defendant. She found her about 2 or 2:30 a.m. in the same block as "Johnny's Place." Defendant was nervous and frightened, said she knew about the fire and that she went over to tell Johnny Powers about it. Defendant had not been drinking.

Carlos Quinones died from "thermal burns, second and third degree involving 50 to 60 per cent of the body surface." Defendant did not testify. . . .

"Manslaughter is the unlawful killing of a human being without malice. It is of three kinds: . . . 2. Involuntary—in the commission of an unlawful act, not amounting to felony; or in the commission of a lawful act which might produce death, in an unlawful manner, or without due caution and circumspection. . . ." Pen.Code, § 192. "In every crime or public offense there must exist a union, or joint operation of act and intent, or criminal negligence." Pen.Code, § 20. Section 20 of the Penal Code makes the union of act and wrongful intent or criminal negligence an invariable element of every crime unless it is excluded expressly or by necessary implication. Section 26 of the Penal Code lists, among the persons incapable of committing crimes, "[p]ersons who committed the act or made the omission charged through misfortune or by accident, when it appears that there was no evil design, intention, or culpable negligence." Thus the question is: Was there any evidence of criminal intent or criminal negligence? . . .

It appears from the record that guilt was predicated on the alleged "commission of a lawful act which might produce death, in an unlawful manner, or without due caution and circumspection." Pen.Code, § 192.

In People v. Penny, 44 Cal.2d 861, 285 P.2d 926, the defendant was convicted of involuntary manslaughter. While engaged in the practice of "face rejuvenation" she applied a formula containing phenol to the skin. Death was caused by phenol poisoning. The trial court charged the jury that ordinary negligence was sufficient to constitute lack of "due caution and circumspection" under Penal Code, § 192. The court said (44 Cal.2d at page 869, 285 P.2d at page 931): "It has been held that without 'due caution and circumspection' is the equivalent of 'criminal negligence.' "[35]

---

35. "To constitute involuntary manslaughter, the homicide must have resulted from the defendant's failure to exercise due caution and circumspection, which has been held to be the equivalent of 'criminal negligence' or 'culpable negligence.' " State v. Sorensen, 104 Ariz. 503, 507, 455 P.2d 981, 985 (1969).

After reviewing numerous California authorities, the court continued (44 Cal.2d at page 876, 285 P.2d at page 935):

"So far as the latest cases are concerned, it appears that mere negligence is sufficient to constitute a lack of due caution and circumspection under the manslaughter statute. Pen.Code, § 192, subd. 2. This does not appear to be a correct rule. Something more, in our opinion, is needed to constitute the criminal negligence required for a conviction of manslaughter." . . .

"We hold, therefore, that the general rule just quoted, sets forth the standard to be used in California for negligent homicide, Pen.Code § 192, subd. 2, in other than vehicle cases. Defendant here was charged with a violation of section 192, subdivision 2, of the Penal Code."

It is generally held that an act is criminally negligent when a man of ordinary prudence would foresee that the act would cause a high degree of risk of death or great bodily harm. The risk of death or great bodily harm must be great. Whether the conduct of defendant was wanton or reckless so as to warrant conviction of manslaughter must be determined from the conduct itself and not from the resultant harm. Criminal liability cannot be predicated on every careless act merely because its carelessness results in injury to another. The act must be one which has knowable and apparent potentialities for resulting in death. Mere inattention or mistake in judgment resulting even in death of another is not criminal unless the quality of the act makes it so. The fundamental requirement fixing criminal responsibility is knowledge, actual or imputed, that the act of the accused tended to endanger life.

In a case of involuntary manslaughter the criminal negligence of the accused must be the proximate cause of the death. . . .

It clearly appears from the definition of criminal negligence stated in People v. Penny, *supra* 44 Cal.2d 861, 285 P.2d 926, that knowledge, actual or imputed, that the act of the slayer tended to endanger life and that the fatal consequences of the negligent act could reasonably have been foreseen are necessary for negligence to be criminal at all. Must a parent never leave a young child alone in the house on risk of being adjudged guilty of manslaughter if some unforeseeable occurrence causes the death of the child? The only reasonable view of the evidence is that the death of Carlos was the result of misadventure and not the natural and probable result of a criminally negligent act. There was no evidence from which it can be inferred that defendant realized her conduct would in all probability produce death. There was no evidence as to the cause of the fire, as to how or where it started. There was no evidence connecting defendant in any way with the fire. There was no evidence that defendant could reasonably have foreseen there was a probability that fire would ignite in the house and that Carlos would be burned to death. The most that can be said is that defendant may have been negligent; but mere negligence is not sufficient to authorize a conviction of involuntary manslaughter. . . .

The judgment and order denying a new trial are reversed.[36]

---

36. In a case in which the mother locked the children in the house and went to join her paramour in his apartment it was held that the jury could find culpable negligence. Delay v. Brainard, 182 Neb. 509, 156 N.W.2d 14 (1968).

■ SHINN, P.J., concurs.

■ FORD, J., did not participate.

State v. Bier

Supreme Court of Montana, 1979.
181 Mont. 27, 591 P.2d 1115.

■ SHEA, JUSTICE. Defendant appeals from a conviction of negligent homicide, section 95–4–104, R.C.M.1947, now section 45–5–104 MCA, following a jury trial in the Cascade County District Court.

The facts show that in the early morning of June 25, 1977, Deputy Sheriff Donovan responded to a call concerning a possible suicide at the Red Wheel Trailer Court in Great Falls. He arrived at about 1:30 a.m. and noticed defendant Richard Bier wave and holler at him to hurry. Donovan entered the trailer and saw defendant's wife, Sharon Bier, on the floor in the doorway between the bedroom and hall of the trailer. She was bleeding from a neck wound. Defendant told Donovan that his wife shot herself. A .357 Magnum revolver lay on the bed in the bedroom. Moments later, an ambulance arrived. Temporary aid was administered and Sharon Bier was transported to the hospital accompanied by the defendant. Deputy Donovan stayed behind. He washed his hands in the trailer's bathroom and noticed blood in the basin and on a cabinet. He photographed the interior of the trailer, identified and took custody of the gun, bullets and spent casing, and saw that the two minor children present were cared for before proceeding to the hospital.

When Deputy Donovan arrived at the hospital, he placed each of Mrs. Bier's hands in plastic bags and taped them shut to preserve any evidence of gun powder. He then located defendant for questioning. After being read his rights, defendant related the events leading up to the shooting.

Defendant stated he and his wife had been at the stock car races all evening and consumed a total of three six-packs of beer. Mrs. Bier, normally a mild social drinker, finished two six-packs. When the couple returned home, an argument ensued. Intent on leaving and avoiding further quarrel, defendant went into the bedroom to ready his departure. Mrs. Bier stood in the bedroom doorway, apparently to block his exit. Defendant reached into the closet, pulled a gun from its holster, cocked it and cast it on the bed stating words to the effect that to stop him she'd have to shoot him. Defendant turned away and his wife picked up the gun, held it with both thumbs on the trigger and pointed it at her head. Defendant shouted "that damn thing's loaded" and either grabbed or slapped at the gun to avert its aim. It discharged and Mrs. Bier collapsed on the floor.

Pursuant to police procedure, Deputy Donovan took hand swabs of defendant and his wife for analysis of possible gun powder residue by the proper authorities. The test results showed no appreciable level of residue

---

Manslaughter was a proper verdict where the evidence showed defendant was aware that a substantial and unjustified risk would occur at the time defendant improperly wired a heater resulting in the death of a child. State v. Salz, 226 Conn. 20, 627 A.2d 862 (1993).

from which to conclude either Mr. or Mrs. Bier was holding the gun when it discharged. Defendant had washed his hands while his wife was being administered medical aid at the trailer. Mrs. Bier never regained consciousness and died six days after the shooting.

About a month after the incident, defendant was questioned at the Cascade County Sheriff's Office. He essentially recounted the statement previously given except that he thought maybe he'd grabbed rather than slapped at the gun when it discharged, and that perhaps this had caused the gun to fire.

On October 17, defendant was charged with negligent homicide and on October 19, he entered a plea of not guilty.

The State's case consisted of Deputy Donovan, two expert witnesses from Washington, D.C., and the ambulance attendant who answered the emergency call at the Bier residence. One of the experts testified to the slight force necessary to discharge a cocked .357 Magnum revolver and that the handgun fired at a distance of one foot produced a powder dispersal pattern of four to five inches in diameter. Exhibits revealed a four-inch dispersal pattern on Mrs. Bier's neck. The other expert witness reported the results of the hand swab analysis conducted in Washington, D.C. He could not determine who held the gun when it fired.

Defendant testified on his own behalf. He was a career Air Force Sergeant and the father of three minor children by Mrs. Bier. He stated on direct examination, "I don't know if I made her hands squeeze the trigger or if she squeezed the trigger, or how it happened." On cross-examination he admitted that he was aware of his wife's intoxicated condition and should have realized the danger involved.

During defendant's testimony, defense counsel attempted to show through defendant's testimony and diagrams that the angle of the bullet's path was such as to preclude any possibility that defendant held the gun when it discharged. The County Attorney objected to this line of questioning on the ground that evidence relating to the bullet's angle was a technical subject requiring the testimony of an expert. Following an intense exchange between court and counsel, the court ruled that all evidence relating to bullet's angle would be excluded as a technical subject admissible only through expert testimony.

Defendant raises five issues for our review:

(1) Whether the facts presented preclude a finding of negligent homicide as a matter of law.

(2) Whether the District Court abused its discretion by denying defendant's motion for a jury view of the mobile home in which the shooting occurred....

Defendant contends the State failed to prove the required mental state and causation elements for a prima facie case of negligent homicide. Concerning the mental element, defendant argues that his conduct did not evidence a conscious disregard for his wife's life. Negligent homicide is defined by statute as follows:

"(1) Criminal homicide constitutes negligent homicide when it is committed negligently.

"(2) A person convicted of negligent homicide shall be imprisoned in the state prison for any term not to exceed ten (10) years." Section 95–4–104, R.C.M.1947, now section 45–5–104 MCA.

Negligence is defined as follows:

"... [A] person acts negligently with respect to a result or to a circumstance described by a statute defining an offense when he consciously disregards a risk that the result will occur or that the circumstance exists *or if he disregards a risk of which he should be aware* that the result will occur or that the circumstance exists. The risk must be of such a nature and degree that to disregard it involves *a gross deviation* from the standard of conduct that a reasonable person would observe in the actor's situation. Gross deviation means a deviation that is *considerably greater than lack of ordinary care*. Relevant terms such as 'negligent' and 'with negligence' have the same meaning." (Emphasis added.) Section 94–2–101(31), R.C.M. 1947, now section 45–2–101(31) MCA.

In State v. Kirkaldie (1978), Mont., 587 P.2d 1298, 1304, 35 St.Rep. 1532, 1538, this Court explained that "[u]nlike deliberate homicide, which requires that the offense be committed purposely or knowingly, negligent homicide does not require such purpose or knowledge. Negligent homicide only requires a gross deviation from a reasonable standard of care." A gross deviation under the statutory definition is analogous to gross negligence in the law of torts. Although somewhat nebulous in concept, gross negligence is generally considered to fall short of a reckless disregard for consequences and is said to differ from ordinary negligence only in degree, not in kind. *See*, Prosser, Law of Torts, 183–84 (4th Ed.1971). Here, defendant's conduct in pulling out, cocking and throwing a loaded gun within reach of his intoxicated wife clearly qualifies as a gross deviation giving rise to criminal culpability.

Defendant also contends he should not be held responsible to have foreseen his wife's alleged suicide attempt. Generally, where a crime is based on some form of negligence the State must show not only that defendant's negligent conduct was the "cause in fact" of the victim's death, but also that the victim was foreseeably endangered, in a manner which was foreseeable and to a degree of harm which was foreseeable. Clearly, the risk created by defendant's conduct under the circumstances (that in a highly intoxicated state his wife would shoot either the defendant or herself), was a foreseeable risk. Indeed, he challenged her to use the gun. Affirmed.

People v. Watkins

Supreme Court of Colorado, En Banc, 1978.
196 Colo. 377, 586 P.2d 43.

■ PRINGLE, JUSTICE. Defendant Henry Lee Watkins was convicted of second-degree murder of Walter McDonald and of first-degree assault upon David Buckner. He contends that the trial court's refusal to give instructions to the jury relating to lesser included offenses under the circumstances of this *issue* case was error. We agree and reverse.

A rather full recital of the evidence in this case is necessary to put the legal issues in perspective. Eddie Watkins and the deceased, Walter Mc-Donald, argued over access to the pool table at New Joe's Bar where they *facts* were drinking. Eddie and Walter apparently resolved the dispute between them, but the argument flared again between Walter and a friend of Eddie's. This latter dispute was left unresolved.

Walter McDonald and his brother Byron then went to another bar where they met David Buckner. Evidently there was some discussion that they should return to New Joe's and "settle the score." They did, in fact, return to New Joe's but walked past the defendant and Eddie and into the bar. The defendant testified, however, that one of them pointed out his brother Eddie and said, "That's our man." Later the two McDonald brothers, Buckner and Eddie went outside to play craps.

During the dice game the shooting occurred. The defendant testified that he saw David Buckner pull a knife on his brother when Eddie bent down to throw the dice and that Walter McDonald had yelled to Buckner, "Cut that nigger's throat." When the defendant tried to warn his brother, Buckner turned toward him with the knife. The defendant fired his gun at Buckner. The defendant testified that Walter McDonald had started toward him with a gun and that he had shot him in self-defense.

An open knife was later found in the bar but no other evidence was presented to support the defendant's testimony. The trial judge instructed the jury on first and second-degree murder but refused the defendant's request that the jury be instructed on criminally negligent homicide. The trial court based its refusal on the grounds that there was *no evidence* that Walter McDonald's death was negligently rather than intentionally caused. The jury was also instructed on the affirmative defense of self-defense.

I

Error which requires reversal stems from the trial court's refusal to give defendant's tendered instruction on criminally negligent homicide. We held in Read v. People, 119 Colo. 506, 205 P.2d 233 (1949), and reiterated in People v. Miller, 187 Colo. 239, 529 P.2d 648 (1974), that "when there is any evidence, however improbable, unreasonable or slight, which tends to reduce the homicide to [a lesser grade], the defendant is entitled to an instruction thereon upon the hypothesis that the same is true, and that it is for the jury, under proper instructions, and not the trial judge, to weigh and consider the evidence and determine therefrom what grade of crime, if any, was committed; and that the court's refusal to instruct thereon is reversible error."

During the trial, the defendant testified that he believed, in good faith, that his brother Eddie's, and then his own, life was threatened. Such a belief, even if unreasonable, presents a case for criminally negligent homicide. Section 18–3–105, C.R.S.1973.

The People cite People v. Shannon, 189 Colo. 287, 539 P.2d 480 (1975), and People v. Rivera, 186 Colo. 24, 525 P.2d 431 (1974), to buttress their position that there was no "rational basis" to justify a criminally negligent homicide instruction. In *Shannon,* the victims suffered grievous gunshot wounds at the hands of the defendant and there was absolutely no evidence given to support a lesser charge of third-degree assault. In *Rivera,* we specifically held that the defendant is entitled to have the court instruct the jury on the defense theory of the case as revealed by the evidence. The mere fact that the evidence in this case was supplied by the defendant who took the stand in his own defense does not preclude it from the jury's consideration.

As in People v. Miller, *supra,* we quote with approval from Crawford v. People, 12 Colo. 290, 20 P. 769 (1888):

"We do not say that . . . the jury would have found differently had they been properly instructed. What we do say is that there was not an entire absence of evidence tending to establish the crime of manslaughter, and that defendant was entitled to an instruction with reference thereto. It is obviously impossible for us to hold that the error thus committed was without prejudice."

There is no doubt that the defendant shot Walter McDonald and David Buckner. However, while a jury might not believe that a reasonable man would be in fear of his life under the circumstances of this case, they might in fact believe that the defendant held a good faith belief, though an unreasonable one, that he feared for his life. Such a belief by the jury would entitle him to a verdict of criminally negligent homicide rather than second-degree murder under the legislative definitions which appear in our statutes.

II

We recently decided that where a jury determined that the defendant committed the assault in the good faith but unreasonable belief that his actions were justified, the sentence imposed can be no greater than that which could be imposed upon a defendant under the criminally negligent homicide statute. Since, in this case, there was evidence to support a jury instruction based on the defendant's good faith but unreasonable fear of serious harm, and since the assault charge and the homicide arose out of the same incident, on remand, the trial judge should provide such an instruction as to the assault charge to the jury and, if the defendant is again found guilty of first-degree assault, sentence the defendant in accordance with *Bramlett.*

III

We find the defendant's argument that there was insufficient evidence to support the jury's finding that the defendant caused "serious bodily injury" as required for first-degree assault, Section 18–3–202, C.R.S.1973 (1977 Supp.), to be without merit. The evidence presented at trial indicated that Buckner had been shot and wounded by the defendant. It is within the province of the jury to determine the degree of the injury and we find that there was sufficient evidence for them to determine in this case that the injury was serious.

The judgment is reversed and the cause remanded to the district court for a new trial.[37]

Harris v. State

Court of Appeals of Georgia, 1937.
55 Ga.App. 189, 189 S.E. 680.

■ MacIntyre, J. W.J. Harris was convicted of voluntary manslaughter, and his punishment was fixed by the verdict at not less than ten nor more than fifteen years. His motion for a new trial was overruled, and he excepted.

1.   Taking the view of the evidence which is most unfavorable to the accused, which we do in passing on a motion for new trial, it in effect shows that the defendant, who was somewhat drawn with rheumatism, was smaller in size than the deceased; that, after an argument about a certain jug which had been left with the defendant at his place of business by the deceased, the defendant not only called the deceased a liar, but also a God damn liar; that the deceased, an able-bodied, strong, and robust man, thereupon struck the defendant two hard blows with his fists, and that the defendant killed the deceased by shooting him three times, once in the thigh, once in the stomach above the navel, and once in the shoulder. A witness testified: "The first shot hit him in the leg. I know, 'cause I seen him give. He just kept right on going down. The second shot missed him. I seen it dig dirt up by him. Harris [the defendant] was shooting somewhere' bout his legs along about here" (indicating). On the other hand, the effect of the defendant's statement and one of his witness's testimony was that the deceased, after hitting the defendant twice with his fists, hit him a third time over the head with the stick, which knocked him down, and that the deceased thereupon picked up his small goat-cart, or wagon, and was trying to advance on the defendant with that weapon when the defendant shot him. The wagon, or goat-cart, and stick were introduced in evidence by the defendant, without objection. We think the jury were authorized to render a verdict of voluntary manslaughter....

3.   The defendant assigns error on the failure of the court to charge the law on involuntary manslaughter. This assignment is based on the evidence of two witnesses, one of whom testified as follows: "Mr. Harris [the defendant] was not shooting up in the body. He was shooting down in his legs, shooting at his feet, yes." The other testified, "Mr. Harris was shooting somewhere about his legs along here" (indicating). The defendant contends that this evidence shows conclusively "that Harris in shooting Pittman down in his legs, at his feet, somewhere about his legs along here (indicating), was the act of a man trying to keep Pittman from unmercifully

---

37.   "[A] homicide is reduced from murder to voluntary manslaughter if the defendant subjectively believed the circumstances justifying the killing existed, but objective reality negates that existence. Logically, the defendant's belief, sincere though unreasonable, negates malice." Commonwealth v. Carter, 502 Pa. 433, 466 A.2d 1328, 1332 (1983).

Amendments to the California Penal Code did not abolish the doctrine of imperfect self-defense. Imperfect self-defense is not rooted in a notion of capacity or awareness of the need to act but is based on an unreasonable belief of defendant in the need for self-defense. The unreasonable belief may be based on defendant's erroneous conclusion that he was in imminent danger of death or great bodily injury. In such a situation, the defendant acts without malice. In re Christian S., 7 Cal.4th 768, 30 Cal. Rptr.2d 33, 872 P.2d 574 (1994).

beating him, and disproves clearly that Harris had any intention at the time to kill Pittman.'' We can not agree to this contention of the defendant. ''Where one voluntarily fires a loaded pistol at another, without excuse and not under circumstances of justification, and kills the person at whom he shot, the law will hold the slayer responsible for the consequences of his act. It conclusively presumes malice on the part of the slayer; and the grade of the homicide, so committed, will not be reduced to involuntary manslaughter, even if the intent of the slayer, under such circumstances, was to wound or cripple the deceased, and not to kill.'' . . . [38]

State v. Sety

Court of Appeals of Arizona, Division 1, Department A, 1979.
121 Ariz. 354, 590 P.2d 470.

■ Schroeder, Judge. In the morning hours of March 19, 1976, Donald Cue died as the result of injuries inflicted by the appellant, David Sety, during a bizarre series of confrontations at an isolated campground. Appellant was tried on an open charge of murder. During trial the court granted a directed verdict of acquittal as to first degree murder, and the jury convicted the appellant of second degree murder. On post trial motions, the trial court reduced the charge to voluntary manslaughter and sentenced Sety to serve not less than nine nor more than ten years in the Arizona State Prison.

Appellant Sety appeals from the judgment and sentence, and the State appeals from the trial court's reduction of the conviction from second degree murder to voluntary manslaughter. We affirm the conviction and modify the sentence.

SUFFICIENCY OF THE EVIDENCE SUPPORTING VOLUNTARY MANSLAUGHTER AND SECOND DEGREE MURDER

Sety initially contends that the court should have directed a verdict of acquittal with respect to all charges. In its appeal the State urges that the

---

38. ''We think, however, that an instruction should have been given whereunder Vires could have been found guilty of voluntary manslaughter if the jury believe that the shooting was the result of reckless, wanton and felonious disregard of the safety of human life. Also there should have been an instruction authorizing the jury to find Vires guilty of involuntary manslaughter if he was found to be guilty of the reckless use of firearms, though the shooting was not done wantonly and feloniously.'' Vires v. Commonwealth, 308 Ky. 707, 215 S.W.2d 837 (1948).

Involuntary manslaughter is distinguished from voluntary manslaughter by lack of an intent to kill. State v. Childers, 217 Kan. 410, 536 P.2d 1349 (1975).

An assailant who commits an unlawful assault and battery on another without malice, resulting in death, is guilty of manslaughter although the death was not intended and the assault was not of a character likely to result fatally. State v. Black, 360 Mo. 261, 227 S.W.2d 1006 (1950).

To sustain a charge of involuntary manslaughter the state must prove an unintentional killing and that D was at the time of the killing either engaged in the commission of a misdemeanor or committing a lawful act in a wanton manner. State v. Betts, 214 Kan. 271, 519 P.2d 655 (1974).

For an historical analysis of the development of voluntary and involuntary manslaughter, see Comber v. United States, 584 A.2d 26, 35–40 (D.C.App.1990).

trial court abused its discretion when, following the trial, it reduced the conviction from second degree murder to voluntary manslaughter. Resolution of both issues turns upon the unusual facts developed at trial.

On the day in question, the appellant was camping alone in an area below Bartlett Lake Dam in Maricopa County, Arizona. Sety testified that at approximately 6:00 a.m., the obviously intoxicated victim, Mr. Cue, awakened him and engaged him in a rambling discussion, primarily about weapons. Cue admired the appellant's hunting knife, asked Sety to sharpen Cue's own knife and then boasted of having killed eight people with that knife. Sety testified that he was shaken by this talk and that he crawled into his camper to get a pistol. Sety stated that as he emerged from the camper Cue was pointing a gun directly at his head and laughing in a threatening manner.

Cue continued to talk about weapons, pulled a number of them from his car, and then began firing a large caliber rifle across the river. Thereafter, Cue loaded his weapon, repeatedly pointed it at Sety and joked about how afraid Sety was of him. Finally, Sety grabbed his own pistol and told Cue to "freeze." The armed Cue continued to approach, prompting Sety to fire two warning shots and to take Cue's rifle from him. Sety testified that Cue then reached into his jacket as if to take a gun from his belt. The appellant fired, striking Cue in the side, told Cue he was making a citizen's arrest and ordered him to begin walking toward the dam keeper's house. The two men then left the site near the camper, referred to at trial as site A, and proceeded toward the house. The physical evidence and Sety's testimony up to that point are not in dispute. The State does not contend that Sety was guilty of any culpable conduct prior to the time that the men left site A.

The two men then headed in the direction of the dam keeper's house, with Sety constantly prodding the resistant Cue. According to Sety's testimony, when Cue attempted to flee back toward the arsenal of weapons at site A, Sety fired first one or more warning shots and then two shots which struck Cue in the back. The victim fell on his back and lay motionless, apparently dead. As Sety approached him, however, Cue grabbed him and pulled him to the ground. Sety stated that he choked the victim into unconsciousness, went back to the camper to reload his pistol and then returned to where Cue was lying, designated during trial as site B. Sety then cut off part of the victim's clothing explaining at various times that he did so in order to make it harder for Cue to flee, to search for weapons or to determine the extent of the victim's wounds. Physical evidence found at site B, including the outer shirt worn by Cue, shell casings and evidence of a struggle corroborated Sety's version of the events.

At this point, however, the physical evidence and Sety's version of the incident diverge somewhat. Sety testified that as he again began prodding Cue in the direction of the dam keeper's house, Cue knocked the rifle from Sety's grasp and ran. Sety fired several pistol shots from what he claimed was a distance of roughly 75 feet. Cue fell and, by Sety's account, pretended to be dead. Sety testified, however, that as he looked more closely Cue reached up suddenly to grab him. As he jerked away, Sety claimed that his gun discharged striking Cue in the head. Certain at last that Cue was dead

Sety continued to the dam keeper's house and reported the homicide to the Sheriff's Department.

Thus, according to Sety, the wounds which he inflicted upon Cue after they left site B were all either in self defense or in justified furtherance of a citizen's arrest. He argues that, based upon his testimony, he should have been acquitted of all charges.

The physical evidence, however, does not fully support Sety's version of what transpired after Cue and Sety left site B. Although Sety testified that Cue had bolted from scene B and had been shot at a distance of approximately 75 feet, Cue's undershirt, which he was wearing at the time the final shots were fired, showed evidence of powder burns indicating shots fired at a very close range. Shell casings were found fairly close to the corpse rather than at the greater distance indicated by Sety's testimony. The State also presented evidence of the trajectory of the bullets which could be interpreted as rebutting Sety's claim that he fired these shots from a distance at the fleeing Cue. The State's evidence suggests that Sety fired at least two final shots, in addition to the shot which struck Cue in the head, at very close range, and not, as he asserted, while Cue was in flight. The State thus presented evidence from which the jury could have concluded that the victim was shot repeatedly in circumstances which no longer justified deadly force. This evidence contradicted Sety's proffered defenses. We conclude that the evidence presented was sufficient to find criminal culpability.

Having rejected the appellant's argument that he was entitled to a judgment of acquittal of all charges we now consider the State's contention that the trial court erred in reducing the conviction to voluntary manslaughter from second degree murder.

The presence of malice distinguishes murder from manslaughter under the statutes in effect at the time of this incident. A.R.S. § 13–451(A) provided that "murder is the unlawful killing of a human being with malice aforethought." A.R.S. § 13–455 defined manslaughter as "the unlawful killing of a human being without malice." Malice has been defined as the absence of justification, excuse or mitigation. The trial court properly reduced the conviction to manslaughter only if the evidence was not sufficient to show an absence of justification, excuse or mitigation.

The State's principal argument in its appeal is that Sety's use of a deadly weapon supplies the element of malice. This is, however, only a presumption and may be rebutted by evidence of mitigation, justification or excuse sufficient to raise a reasonable doubt as to the existence of malice. We find it difficult to conceive of a case in which this presumption is rebutted by stronger evidence of mitigation. In its briefs and at trial the State has conceded that Sety's initial use of force was fully justified and not culpable. There is no doubt that the provocation and terror which precipitated this killing were instigated by the intrusion of the seemingly crazed Cue into the pre-dawn solitude of the appellant's campground. In our view, this is a classic illustration of manslaughter resulting from mitigating circumstances.

... As a matter of juridical science, any circumstance of substantial mitigation should be sufficient to reduce to manslaughter a killing that would otherwise be murder. Suppose, for example, the defendant thought he was in imminent danger of death and must kill to save himself from being murdered, and that he did kill for that reason. Suppose, also, there was no actual danger to his life at the moment, and the facts fell a little short of reasonable grounds for a belief in such danger. His homicide is not excused; but if the circumstances came rather close to such as would constitute an excuse his guilt is of manslaughter rather than murder, ... Perkins, Criminal Law (1st ed. 1957), at 40. (footnote omitted).

The real factual issue presented in this case was whether the amount of force used by Sety was excessive under the circumstances. We believe that there was sufficient evidence for the jury to reject Sety's defenses and to convict him of manslaughter, but that the evidence did not support a murder conviction. At most, appellant was guilty of excessive retaliation constituting manslaughter rather than murder.

Rule

Accordingly, we conclude that the trial court's reduction of the conviction from second degree murder to voluntary manslaughter was mandated by the evidence. Conviction affirmed, sentenced modified.[39]

People v. Ochoa

Supreme Court of California, In Bank, 1993.
6 Cal.4th 1199, 26 Cal.Rptr.2d 23, 864 P.2d 103.

■ LUCAS, CHIEF JUSTICE.

Alberto Ochoa was convicted of two counts of gross vehicular manslaughter while intoxicated (Pen.Code, § 191.5, subd. (a)) and one count of hit-and-run driving (Veh.Code, § 20001). He argued on appeal, among other contentions, ... that there was insufficient evidence of his gross negligence. The Court of Appeal, by a two-to-one vote, agreed with defendant, reversed defendant's gross vehicular manslaughter convictions and remanded for resentencing for the less serious offense of vehicular manslaughter (Pen.Code, § 192, subd. (c)(3)). We disagree....

Facts

The following facts, with minor modifications, are adopted from the Court of Appeal opinion in this case. On Sunday, September 2, 1990, defendant and his family attended a barbecue at his sister-in-law's house in Corona. They brought three 12–packs of beer, which were consumed by four adults during the course of the afternoon and evening. Defendant himself drank around 17 to 22 beers. When he and his wife went to bed at 11:30 p.m., at his sister-in-law's house, he was intoxicated.

Sometime no later than 1:50 a.m. on Monday, defendant awoke, entered his Ford Bronco alone, and headed for his home. He was driving west on the Garden Grove Freeway at 60 to 65 miles per hour. Traffic was light. Around this time, Brian Doan was also driving home, using the

---

39. "A defendant may be guilty of voluntary manslaughter if he kills in self defense, but uses excessive force." State v. Owens, 60 N.C.App. 434, 299 S.E.2d 258 (1983).

middle of three lanes, at a speed of 50 to 55 miles per hour. He saw a Bronco pass him on the left and abruptly start to move into the lane in front of him, then move back into its original lane without completing the lane change. Doan applied his brakes and slowed to 40 miles per hour. As the Bronco passed by, Doan saw its right front and rear tires cross over the lane dividing-line and then back again.

A short distance ahead of Doan's car, Brian Simurda was driving his Chevrolet pickup in the middle lane at a speed of 55 to 60 miles per hour. For the last two or three miles he had been trailing a red Honda. The Honda was travelling at 45 to 50 miles per hour, and its taillights were lighted and visible. Simurda saw the Bronco pass him in the left lane and estimated its speed at 65 to 70 miles per hour. When the Bronco was only one car length ahead of him, it changed lanes without signaling, crossing to the right side of the lane, then back to the left. Defendant continued at the same speed, heading for the Honda. Soon thereafter, without first applying his brakes, defendant hit the left rear portion of the Honda, which spun into a ravine and hit a tree, killing the two occupants. The accident occurred no later than 1:50 a.m.

. . .

Eventually, after failing a series of field coordination tests, defendant was arrested for driving under the influence of alcohol. He claimed he saw neither the Honda nor its taillights until the collision. A blood sample taken about two hours later showed his blood-alcohol level to be .128 percent. A criminalist testified that, at the time of the accident, defendant's blood-alcohol level may have been as high as .15 percent, a level sufficient to render a driver incapable of safely operating a motor vehicle.

. . .

Based on the foregoing facts, the Court of Appeal majority ruled the evidence insufficient to sustain a finding that defendant exercised gross negligence under Penal Code section 191.5, subdivision (a). (Further statutory references are to this code.) In the majority's view, the evidence showed at most that defendant drove at high speeds while intoxicated, conduct amounting to simple negligence. Accordingly, the majority ordered defendant's gross negligence conviction set aside and remanded the case for resentencing under section 192, subdivision (c)(3) (vehicular manslaughter without gross negligence). . . .

The Court of Appeal majority reasoned that because defendant's probable blood-alcohol level (.15 percent) was "not excessive," because he slept for two hours before attempting to drive, because his driving involved "relatively minor speeding" in light traffic conditions, and because his lane changing evidenced "some prudent driving," no gross negligence was proved. The dissenting opinion strongly disagreed, accusing the majority of reweighing the evidence to favor defendant, contrary to the deferential standard of review ordinarily applicable in resolving evidentiary challenges to criminal convictions. As will appear, we agree with the dissent.

. . .

Discussion

1. *Gross negligence*—As previously indicated, defendant was convicted of gross vehicular manslaughter while intoxicated. (§ 191.5, subd. (a).) That provision states in pertinent part: "Gross vehicular manslaughter while intoxicated is the unlawful killing of a human being without malice aforethought, in the driving of a vehicle, where the driving was in violation of Section 23152 or 23153 of the Vehicle Code, and the killing was either the proximate result of the commission of an unlawful act, not amounting to a felony, and with gross negligence, or the proximate result of the commission of a lawful act which might produce death, in an unlawful manner, and with gross negligence." On appeal, defendant disputed the sufficiency of the evidence regarding the requisite element of gross negligence.

We have previously explained that "[g]ross negligence is the exercise of so slight a degree of care as to raise a presumption of conscious indifference to the consequences. [Citation.] 'The state of mind of a person who acts with conscious indifferences to the consequences is simply, "I don't care what happens." ' [Citation.] The test is objective: whether a reasonable person in the defendant's position would have been aware of the risk involved. [Citation.]" (People v. Bennett (1991) 54 Cal.3d 1032, 1036, 2 Cal.Rptr.2d 8, 819 P.2d 849 [hereafter *Bennett*].)

. . .

... In determining whether a reasonable person *in defendant's position* would have been aware of the risks, the jury should be given relevant facts as to what defendant knew, including his actual awareness of those risks. True, as the majority observed, the defendant's *lack* of such awareness would not preclude a finding of gross negligence if a reasonable person would have been so aware. But the converse proposition does not logically follow, for if the evidence showed that defendant *actually appreciated the risks* involved in a given enterprise, *and nonetheless proceeded* with it, a finding of gross negligence (as opposed to simple negligence) would be appropriate whether or not a reasonable person in defendant's position would have recognized the risk.

Our *Bennett* decision acknowledged that, although the test for gross negligence was an objective one, "[t]he jury should therefore consider all relevant circumstances ... *to determine if the defendant acted with a conscious disregard of the consequences rather than with mere inadvertence.* [Citations.]" (*Bennett, supra,* 54 Cal.3d at p. 1038, 2 Cal.Rptr.2d 8, 819 P.2d 849....)

. . .

3. *Sufficiency of evidence*—Thus, we turn to the primary issue before us, namely, whether the Court of Appeal erred in concluding there was insufficient evidence of gross negligence to sustain a conviction under section 191.5, subdivision (a).

. . .

As the dissenting opinion below observes, the Court of Appeal's majority opinion does not view the evidence in the light most favorable to the People, nor does it accord due deference to the findings of the trier of fact.

First, the Court of Appeal majority characterized defendant's probable .15 percent intoxication as "not excessive," a characterization finding no support in the record. As the People observe, this percentage was nearly twice the legally permitted level for drivers of motor vehicles, and one and one-half times the level at which one is presumed intoxicated and impaired. Second, the majority labeled defendant's speeding as "relatively minor," but as the People note, defendant's speed near the time of the accident was estimated by one witness to be as high as 15 miles per hour faster than the legal speed limit.

Third, the majority's belief that defendant's initial aborted lane change after passing the Doan vehicle evidenced "prudent driving," is entirely speculative and inappropriate, drawing an inference favorable to defendant rather than in support of the judgment of conviction. Under the evidence, it was just as likely that defendant's failure to complete the lane change evidenced an inebriated and confused driving pattern, rather than reflective behavior.

Finally, the Court of Appeal majority improperly focused on evidence indicating that defendant went to bed at 11:30 p.m. and slept for about two hours before attempting to drive. As the People explain, other evidence in the record rebuts the possibility that defendant could have slept for two hours (presumably from 11:30 p.m. to 1:30 a.m.) and still have travelled 45 miles to encounter his victims at approximately 1:50 a.m. According to the People's calculations, defendant would have had to average approximately 120 miles per hour, while intoxicated, to accomplish that feat.

Thus, in deciding that no gross negligence existed in this case, the Court of Appeal majority largely ignored established review standards and reweighed the evidence. The Court of Appeal majority additionally relied on cases indicating that gross negligence is not established merely by showing that the defendant violated some traffic laws while intoxicated. As stated ... gross negligence cannot be shown by the *mere fact* of driving under the influence and violating the traffic laws. Otherwise, gross and simple vehicular manslaughter while intoxicated would be identical crimes with different punishments which would create obvious due process problems.

But this case involves no "mere" traffic violation while intoxicated. As we pointed out in *Bennett, supra,* 54 Cal.3d at pages 1038–1039, 2 Cal. Rptr.2d 8, 819 P.2d 849, gross negligence may be shown from all the relevant circumstances, including the manner in which the defendant operated his vehicle, the level of his intoxication, and any other relevant aspects of his conduct. The record herein contains facts from which the trier of fact reasonably could infer that defendant, (a) having suffered a prior conviction for driving under the influence of alcohol, (b) having been placed on probation, (c) having attended traffic school, including an alcohol-awareness class, and (d) being fully aware of the risks of such activity, nonetheless (e) drove while highly intoxicated, (f) at high, unsafe and illegal speeds, (g) weaving in and out of adjoining lanes, (h) making abrupt and dangerous lane changes (i) without signaling, and (j) without braking to avoid colliding with his victims' vehicle.

In short, the trier of fact could conclude from defendant's course of conduct and preexisting knowledge of the risks that he exercised so slight a degree of care as to exhibit a conscious indifference or "I don't care attitude" concerning the ultimate consequences of his actions. Applying the objective test for gross negligence, any reasonable person in defendant's position would have been aware of the risks presented by his conduct. As *Bennett* states, "the finding of gross negligence ... may be based *on the overall circumstances surrounding the fatality*. Intoxication is one of those circumstances and its effect on the defendant's driving may show gross negligence."

A finding of gross negligence in this case is consistent with prior case law. In *Bennett, supra*, the defendant, driving while intoxicated, wove in and out of traffic, passed three cars on a blind curve, exceeded the speed limit, and ultimately lost control of his car at the bottom of a hill. The car rolled several times, killing one passenger. We upheld a finding of gross negligence based on those facts. In *Von Staden, supra*, the defendant drove while highly intoxicated (.22 percent blood-alcohol level) on a foggy night, travelling 30 miles per hour over the speed limit. A serious accident ensued. The Court of Appeal held that defendant's excessive intoxication and driving speed were sufficient to sustain a finding of gross negligence. As previously explained, facts comparable to Bennett and Von Staden exist in this case.

Conclusion

Viewing the facts in a light favorable to the judgment, we conclude that the trial court's finding of gross negligence should be sustained. The judgment of the Court of Appeal is reversed with directions to determine defendant's remaining unresolved appellate issues.

■ KENNARD, ARABIAN, BAXTER and GEORGE, JJ., concur.

■ PANELLI, JUSTICE, concurs and dissents.[40]

MODEL PENAL CODE

Article 210. Criminal Homicide

Section 210.0 Definitions.

In Articles 210–213, unless a different meaning plainly is required:

(1) "human being" means a person who has been born and is alive;

(2) "bodily injury" means physical pain, illness or any impairment of physical condition;

(3) "serious bodily injury" means bodily injury which creates a substantial risk of death or which causes serious, permanent disfigurement, or protracted loss or impairment of the function of any bodily member or organ;

---

40. Vehicular homicide under a Washington statute, RCW 46.61.520, may be committed by (1) driving a vehicle while under the influence of liquor or drugs; (2) operating a vehicle in a reckless manner; or (3) operating a vehicle with disregard for the safety of others. State v. Tang, 75 Wash.App. 473, 878 P.2d 487 (1994).

(4) "deadly weapon" means any firearm, or other weapon, device, instrument, material or substance, whether animate or inanimate, which in the manner it is used or is intended to be used is known to be capable of producing death or serious bodily injury.

Section 210.1 Criminal Homicide.

(1) A person is guilty of criminal homicide if he purposely, knowingly, reckless-ly[41] or negligently[42] causes the death of another human being.

(2) Criminal homicide is murder, manslaughter or negligent homicide.

Section 210.2 Murder.

(1) Except as provided in Section 210.3(1)(b), criminal homicide constitutes murder when:

(a) it is committed purposely or knowingly; or

(b) it is committed recklessly under circumstances manifesting extreme indifference to the value of human life. Such recklessness and indifference are presumed if the actor is engaged or is an accomplice in the commission of, or an attempt to commit, or flight after committing or attempting to commit robbery, rape or deviate sexual intercourse by force or threat of force, arson, burglary, kidnapping or felonious escape.

(2) Murder is a felony of the first degree [but a person convicted of murder may be sentenced to death, as provided in Section 210.6].

Section 210.3 Manslaughter.

(1) Criminal homicide constitutes manslaughter when:

(a) it is committed recklessly; or

(b) a homicide which would otherwise be murder is committed under the influence of extreme mental or emotional disturbance for which there is reasonable explanation or excuse. The reasonableness of such explanation or excuse shall be determined from the viewpoint of a person in the actor's situation under the circumstances as he believes them to be.

(2) Manslaughter is a felony of the second degree.

Section 210.4 Negligent Homicide.

(1) Criminal homicide constitutes negligent homicide when it is committed negligently.

(2) Negligent homicide is a felony of the third degree.

Section 210.5 Causing or Aiding Suicide.

(1) Causing Suicide as Criminal Homicide. A person may be convicted of criminal homicide for causing another to commit suicide only if he purposely causes such suicide by force, duress or deception.

(2) Aiding or Soliciting Suicide as an Independent Offense. A person who purposely aids or solicits another to commit suicide is guilty of a felony of the

---

41. "Recklessly" is defined elsewhere in the Code to mean that the actor consciously disregards a substantial and unjustifiable risk amounting to a "gross deviation" from due care. Section 2.02(2)(c).

42. "Negligently" is defined elsewhere in the Code in terms equivalent to "inadvertent criminal negligence". Section 2.02(2)(d).

second degree if his conduct causes such suicide or an attempted suicide, and otherwise of a misdemeanor.

(Since a few states do not have capital punishment, provisions for such a penalty in the Code are bracketed, since they would not be needed in such states. A sentence for a felony of the first degree would mean that the maximum would be life imprisonment.)

Section 210.6 Sentence of Death for Murder; Further Proceedings to Determine Sentence.

(1) Death Sentence Excluded. When a defendant is found guilty of murder, the Court shall impose sentence for a felony of the first degree if it is satisfied that:

(a) none of the aggravating circumstances enumerated in Subsection (3) of this Section was established by the evidence at the trial or will be established if further proceedings are initiated under Subsection (2) of this Section; or

(b) substantial mitigating circumstances, established by the evidence at the trial, call for leniency; or

(c) the defendant, with the consent of the prosecuting attorney and the approval of the Court, pleaded guilty to murder as a felony of the first degree; or

(d) the defendant was under 18 years of age at the time of the commission of the crime; or

(e) the defendant's physical or mental condition calls for leniency; or

(f) although the evidence suffices to sustain the verdict, it does not foreclose all doubts respecting the defendant's guilt.

. . .

(If the penalty may be death the Code provides that this shall be determined in a separate proceeding after guilt has been established. The sentence may not be death unless (a) there is found one of the aggravating circumstances enumerated in subsections (3) *and* (b) *no* "mitigating circumstances sufficient to call for leniency".)

(3) Aggravating Circumstances.

(a) The murder was committed by a convict under sentence of imprisonment.

(b) The defendant was previously convicted of another murder or of a felony involving the use or threat of violence to the person.

(c) At the time the murder was committed the defendant also committed another murder.

(d) The defendant knowingly created a great risk of death to many persons.

(e) The murder was committed while the defendant was engaged or was an accomplice in the commission of, or an attempt to commit, or flight after committing or attempting to commit robbery, rape or deviate sexual intercourse by force or threat of force, arson, burglary or kidnapping.

(f) The murder was committed for the purpose of avoiding or preventing a lawful arrest or effecting an escape from lawful custody.

(g) The murder was committed for pecuniary gain.

(h) The murder was especially heinous, atrocious or cruel, manifesting exceptional depravity.

(4) Mitigating Circumstances.

(a) The defendant has no significant history of prior criminal activity.

(b) The murder was committed while the defendant was under the influence of extreme mental or emotional disturbance.

(c) The victim was a participant in the defendant's homicidal conduct or consented to the homicidal act.

(d) The murder was committed under circumstances which the defendant believed to provide a moral justification or extenuation for his conduct.

(e) The defendant was an accomplice in a murder committed by another person and his participation in the homicidal act was relatively minor.

(f) The defendant acted under duress or under the domination of another person.

(g) At the time of the murder, the capacity of the defendant to appreciate the criminality [wrongfulness] of his conduct or to conform his conduct to the requirements of law was impaired as a result of mental disease or defect or intoxication.

(h) The youth of the defendant at the time of the crime.[43]

California Penal Code

§ 187.   Murder defined

(a) Murder is the unlawful killing of a human being, or a fetus, with malice aforethought.

(b) This section shall not apply to any person who commits an act that results in the death of a fetus if any of the following apply: *3yrs + 1 day*

(1) The act complied with the Therapeutic Abortion Act, Article 2 (commencing with Section 123400) of Chapter 2 of Part 2 of Division 106 of the Health and Safety Code.

(2) The act was committed by a holder of a physician's and surgeon's certificate, as defined in the Business and Professions Code, in a case where, to a medical certainty, the result of childbirth would be death of the mother of the fetus or where her death from childbirth, although not medically certain, would be substantially certain or more likely than not.

(3) The act was solicited, aided, abetted, or consented to by the mother of the fetus.

(c) Subdivision (b) shall not be construed to prohibit the prosecution of any person under any other provision of law.

§ 188.   Malice, express malice, and implied malice defined

Such malice may be express or implied. It is express when there is manifested a deliberate intention unlawfully to take away the life of a fellow creature. It is implied, when no considerable provocation appears, or when the circumstances attending the killing show an abandoned and malignant heart.

When it is shown that the killing resulted from the intentional doing of an act with express or implied malice as defined above, no other mental state need be shown to establish the mental state of malice aforethought. Neither an awareness of

---

43. Copyright © 1962 by the American Law Institute. Reprinted with the permission of the American Law Institute.

the obligation to act within the general body of laws regulating society nor acting despite such awareness is included within the definition of malice.

§ 189. Murder; degrees

All murder which is perpetrated by means of a destructive device or explosive, a weapon of mass destruction, knowing use of ammunition designed primarily to penetrate metal or armor, poison, lying in wait, torture, or by any other kind of willful, deliberate, and premeditated killing, or which is committed in the perpetration of, or attempt to perpetrate, arson, rape, carjacking, robbery, burglary, mayhem, kidnapping, train wrecking, or any act punishable under Section 206, 286, 288, 288a, or 289, or any murder which is perpetrated by means of discharging a firearm from a motor vehicle, intentionally at another person outside of the vehicle with the intent to inflict death, is murder of the first degree. All other kinds of murders are of the second degree.

206 – TORTURE
286 –
288 –
288a –
289 –

As used in this section, "destructive device" means any destructive device as defined in Section 12301, and "explosive" means any explosive as defined in Section 12000 of the Health and Safety Code.

As used in this section, "weapon of mass destruction" means any item defined in Section 11417.

To prove the killing was "deliberate and premeditated," it shall not be necessary to prove the defendant maturely and meaningfully reflected upon the gravity of his or her act.

§ 191.5. Gross vehicular manslaughter while intoxicated

(a) Gross vehicular manslaughter while intoxicated is the unlawful killing of a human being without malice aforethought, in the driving of a vehicle, where the driving was in violation of Section 23140, 23152, or 23153 of the Vehicle Code, and the killing was either the proximate result of the commission of an unlawful act, not amounting to a felony, and with gross negligence, or the proximate result of the commission of a lawful act which might produce death, in an unlawful manner, and with gross negligence.

(b) Gross vehicular manslaughter while intoxicated also includes operating a vessel in violation of subdivision (b), (c), (d), (e), or (f) of Section 655 of the Harbors and Navigation Code, and in the commission of an unlawful act, not amounting to felony, and with gross negligence; or operating a vessel in violation of subdivision (b), (c), (d), (e), or (f) of Section 655 of the Harbors and Navigation Code, and in the commission of a lawful act which might produce death, in an unlawful manner, and with gross negligence.

(c) Except as provided in subdivision (d), gross vehicular manslaughter while intoxicated is punishable by imprisonment in the state prison for 4, 6, or 10 years.

(d) Any person convicted of violating this section who has one or more prior convictions of this section or of paragraph (1) or (3) of subdivision (c) of Section 192, subdivision (a) or (c) of Section 192.5 of this code, or of violating Section 23152 punishable under Sections 23540, 23542, 23546, 23548, 23550, or 23552 of, or convicted of Section 23153 of, the Vehicle Code, shall be punished by imprisonment in the state prison for a term of 15 years to life. Article 2.5 (commencing with Section 2930) of Chapter 7 of Title 1 of Part 3 shall apply to reduce the term imposed pursuant to this subdivision.

(e) This section shall not be construed as prohibiting or precluding a charge of murder under Section 188 upon facts exhibiting wantonness and a conscious disregard for life to support a finding of implied malice, or upon facts showing malice consistent with the holding of the California Supreme Court in People v. Watson, 30 Cal.3d 290.

(f) This section shall not be construed as making any homicide in the driving of a vehicle or the operation of a vessel punishable which is not a proximate result of the commission of an unlawful act, not amounting to felony, or of the commission of a lawful act which might produce death, in an unlawful manner.

(g) For the penalties in subdivision (d) to apply, the existence of any fact required under subdivision (d) shall be alleged in the information or indictment and either admitted by the defendant in open court or found to be true by the trier of fact.

§ 192. Manslaughter; voluntary, involuntary, and vehicular

Manslaughter is the unlawful killing of a human being without malice. It is of three kinds:

(a) Voluntary—upon a sudden quarrel or heat of passion.

(b) Involuntary—in the commission of an unlawful act, not amounting to felony; or in the commission of a lawful act which might produce death, in an unlawful manner, or without due caution and circumspection. This subdivision shall not apply to acts committed in the driving of a vehicle.

(c) Vehicular—N32(1) Except as provided in Section 191.5, driving a vehicle in the commission of an unlawful act, not amounting to felony, and with gross negligence; or driving a vehicle in the commission of a lawful act which might produce death, in an unlawful manner, and with gross negligence.

(2) Except as provided in paragraph (3), driving a vehicle in the commission of an unlawful act, not amounting to felony, but without gross negligence; or driving a vehicle in the commission of a lawful act which might produce death, in an unlawful manner, but without gross negligence.

(3) Driving a vehicle in violation of Section 23140, 23152, or 23153 of the Vehicle Code and in the commission of an unlawful act, not amounting to felony, but without gross negligence; or driving a vehicle in violation of Section 23140, 23152, or 23153 of the Vehicle Code and in the commission of a lawful act which might produce death, in an unlawful manner, but without gross negligence.

(4) Driving a vehicle in connection with a violation of paragraph (3) of subdivision (a) of Section 550, where the vehicular collision or vehicular accident was knowingly caused for financial gain and proximately resulted in the death of any person. This provision shall not be construed to prevent prosecution of a defendant for the crime of murder.

This section shall not be construed as making any homicide in the driving of a vehicle punishable which is not a proximate result of the commission of an unlawful act, not amounting to felony, or of the commission of a lawful act which might produce death, in an unlawful manner.

"Gross negligence," as used in this section, shall not be construed as prohibiting or precluding a charge of murder under Section 188 upon facts exhibiting wantonness and a conscious disregard for life to support a finding of implied malice, or upon facts showing malice, consistent with the holding of the California Supreme Court in People v. Watson, 30 Cal. 3d 290.

NEW YORK PENAL LAW

ARTICLE 125. HOMICIDE, ABORTION AND RELATED OFFENSES

Section 125.00 Homicide defined.

125.05   Homicide, abortion and related offenses; definitions of terms.

125.10   Criminally negligent homicide.

125.12   Vehicular manslaughter in the second degree.

125.13   Vehicular manslaughter in the first degree.

125.15   Manslaughter in the second degree.

125.20   Manslaughter in the first degree.

125.25   Murder in the second degree.

125.27   Murder in the first degree.

§ 125.00 Homicide defined.

Homicide means conduct which causes the death of a person or an unborn child with which a female has been pregnant for more than twenty-four weeks under circumstances constituting murder, manslaughter in the first degree, manslaughter in the second degree, criminally negligent homicide, abortion in the first degree or self-abortion in the first degree.

§ 125.05   Homicide, abortion and related offenses; definitions of terms.

The following definitions are applicable to this article:

1.   "Person," when referring to the victim of a homicide, means a human being who has been born and is alive. . . .

§ 125.10   Criminally negligent homicide.

A person is guilty of criminally negligent homicide when, with criminal negligence, he causes the death of another person. Criminally negligent homicide is a class E felony.

§ 125.12   Vehicular manslaughter in the second degree.

A person is guilty of vehicular manslaughter in the second degree when he:

(1) commits the crime of criminally negligent homicide as defined in section 125.10, and either

(2) causes the death of such other person by operation of a vehicle in violation of subdivision two, three or four of section eleven hundred ninety-two of the vehicle and traffic law or by operation of a vessel or public vessel in violation of paragraph (b), (c), (d) or (e) of subdivision two of section forty-nine-a of the navigation law, or

(3) causes the death of such other person by operation of a motor vehicle with a gross vehicle weight rating of more than eighteen thousand pounds which contains flammable gas, radioactive materials or explosives in violation of subdivision one of section eleven hundred ninety-two of the vehicle and traffic law, and such flammable gas, radioactive materials or explosives is the cause of such death, by operation of a snowmobile in violation of paragraph (b), (c) or (d) of subdivision one of section 25.24 of the parks, recreation and historic preservation law or by operation of an all terrain vehicle as defined in paragraph (a) of subdivision one of section twenty-two hundred eighty-one of the vehicle and traffic law in violation of subdivision two, three, or four of section eleven hundred ninety-two of the vehicle and traffic law. Vehicular manslaughter in the second degree is a class D felony.

§ 125.13   Vehicular manslaughter in the first degree.

A person is guilty of vehicular manslaughter in the first degree when he:

(1) commits the crime of vehicular manslaughter in the second degree as defined in section 125.12, and

(2) commits such crime while knowing or having reason to know that:

(a) his license or his privilege of operating a motor vehicle in another state or his privilege of obtaining a license to operate a motor vehicle in another state is suspended or revoked and such suspension or revocation is based upon a conviction in such other state for an offense which would, if committed in this state, constitute a violation of any of the provisions of section eleven hundred ninety-two of the vehicle and traffic law; or (b) his license or his privilege of operating a motor vehicle in the state or his privilege of obtaining a license issued by the commissioner of motor vehicles is suspended or revoked and such suspension or revocation is based upon either a refusal to submit to a chemical test pursuant to section eleven hundred ninety-four of the vehicle and traffic law or following a conviction for a violation of any of the provisions of section eleven hundred ninety-two of the vehicle and traffic law. Vehicular manslaughter in the first degree is a class C felony.

§ 125.15   Manslaughter in the second degree.

A person is guilty of manslaughter in the second degree when:

1.   He recklessly causes the death of another person; or

2.   He commits upon a female an abortional act which causes her death, unless such abortional act is justifiable pursuant to subdivision three of section 125.05; or

3.   He intentionally causes or aids another person to commit suicide.

Manslaughter in the second degree is a class C felony.

§ 125.20   Manslaughter in the first degree.

A person is guilty of manslaughter in the first degree when:

1.   With intent to cause serious physical injury to another person, he causes the death of such person or of a third person; or

2.   With intent to cause the death of another person, he causes the death of such person or of a third person under circumstances which do not constitute murder because he acts under the influence of extreme emotional disturbance, as defined in paragraph (a) of subdivision one of section 125.25. The fact that homicide was committed under the influence of extreme emotional disturbance constitutes a mitigating circumstance reducing murder to manslaughter in the first degree and need not be proved in any prosecution initiated under this subdivision; or

3.   He commits upon a female pregnant for more than twenty-four weeks an abortional act which causes her death, unless such abortional act is justifiable pursuant to subdivision three of section 125.05; or

4.   Being eighteen years old or more and with intent to cause physical injury to a person less than eleven years old, the defendant recklessly engages in conduct which creates a grave risk of serious physical injury to such person and thereby causes the death of such person.

Manslaughter in the first degree is a class B felony.

§ 125.25   Murder in the second degree.

A person is guilty of murder in the second degree when:

1.   With intent to cause the death of another person, he causes the death of such person or of a third person; except that in any prosecution under this subdivision, it is an affirmative defense that:

(a) The defendant acted under the influence of extreme emotional disturbance for which there was a reasonable explanation or excuse, the reasonableness of which is to be determined from the viewpoint of a person in the defendant's situation under the circumstances as the defendant believed them to be. Nothing contained in this paragraph shall constitute a defense to a prosecution for, or preclude a conviction of, manslaughter in the first degree or any other crime; or

(b) The defendant's conduct consisted of causing or aiding, without the use of duress or deception, another person to commit suicide. Nothing contained in this paragraph shall constitute a defense to a prosecution for, or preclude a conviction of, manslaughter in the second degree or any other crime; or

2. Under circumstances evincing a depraved indifference to human life, he recklessly engages in conduct which creates a grave risk of death to another person, and thereby causes the death of another person; or

3. Acting either alone or with one or more other persons, he commits or attempts to commit robbery, burglary, kidnapping, arson, rape in the first degree, sodomy in the first degree, sexual abuse in the first degree, aggravated sexual abuse, escape in the first degree, or escape in the second degree, and, in the course of and in furtherance of such crime or of immediate flight therefrom, he, or another participant, if there be any, causes the death of a person other than one of the participants; except that in any prosecution under this subdivision, in which the defendant was not the only participant in the underlying crime, it is an affirmative defense that the defendant:

(a) Did not commit the homicidal act or in any way solicit, request, command, importune, cause or aid the commission thereof; and

(b) Was not armed with a deadly weapon, or any instrument, article or substance readily capable of causing death or serious physical injury and of a sort not ordinarily carried in public places by law-abiding persons; and

(c) Had no reasonable ground to believe that any other participant was armed with such a weapon, instrument, article or substance; and

(d) Had no reasonable ground to believe that any other participant intended to engage in conduct likely to result in death or serious physical injury; or

4. Under circumstances evincing a depraved indifference to human life, and being eighteen years old or more the defendant recklessly engages in conduct which creates a grave risk of serious physical injury or death to another person less than eleven years old and thereby causes the death of such person.

Murder in the second degree is a class A–I felony.

§ 125.27   Murder in the first degree.

A person is guilty of murder in the first degree when:

1. With intent to cause the death of another person, he causes the death of such person or of a third person; and

(a) Either:

(i) the intended victim was a police officer as defined in subdivision 34 of section 1.20 of the criminal procedure law who was at the time of the killing engaged in the course of performing his official duties, and the defendant knew or reasonably should have known that the intended victim was a police officer; or

(ii) the intended victim was a peace officer as defined in paragraph a of subdivision twenty-one, subdivision twenty-three, twenty-four or sixty-two (employees of the division for youth) of section 2.10 of the criminal procedure law who was at the time of the killing engaged in the course of performing his official duties, and the defendant knew or reasonably should have known that the intended victim was such a uniformed court officer, parole officer, probation officer, or employee of the division for youth; or

(iii) the intended victim was an employee of a state correctional institution or was an employee of a local correctional facility as defined in subdivision two of section forty of the correction law, who was at the time of the killing engaged in the course of performing his official duties, and the defendant knew or reasonably should have known that the intended victim was an employee of a state correctional institution or a local correctional facility; or

(iv) at the time of the commission of the killing, the defendant was confined in a state correctional institution or was otherwise in custody upon a sentence for the term of his natural life, or upon a sentence commuted to one of natural life, or upon a sentence for an indeterminate term the minimum of which was at least fifteen years and the maximum of which was natural life, or at the time of the commission of the killing, the defendant had escaped from such confinement or custody while serving such a sentence and had not yet been returned to such confinement or custody; or

(v) the intended victim was a witness to a crime committed on a prior occasion and the death was caused for the purpose of preventing the intended victim's testimony in any criminal action or proceeding whether or not such action or proceeding had been commenced, or the intended victim had previously testified in a criminal action or proceeding and the killing was committed for the purpose of exacting retribution for such prior testimony, or the intended victim was an immediate family member of a witness to a crime committed on a prior occasion and the killing was committed for the purpose of preventing or influencing the testimony of such witness, or the intended victim was an immediate family member of a witness who had previously testified in a criminal action or proceeding and the killing was committed for the purpose of exacting retribution upon such witness for such prior testimony. As used in this subparagraph "immediate family member" means a husband, wife, father, mother, daughter, son, brother, sister, stepparent, grandparent, stepchild or grandchild; or

(vi) the defendant committed the killing or procured commission of the killing pursuant to an agreement with a person other than the intended victim to commit the same for the receipt, or in expectation of the receipt, of anything of pecuniary value from a party to the agreement or from a person other than the intended victim acting at the direction of a party to such agreement; or

(vii) the victim was killed while the defendant was in the course of committing or attempting to commit and in furtherance of robbery, burglary in the first degree or second degree, kidnapping in the first degree, arson in the first degree or second degree, rape in the first degree, sodomy in the first degree, sexual abuse in the first degree, aggravated sexual abuse in the first degree or escape in the first degree, or in the course of and furtherance of immediate flight after committing or attempting to commit any such crime or in the course of and furtherance of immediate flight after attempting to commit the crime of murder in the second degree; provided however, the victim is not a participant in one of the aforementioned crimes and, provided further that, unless the defendant's criminal liability under this subparagraph is based upon the defendant having commanded another person to cause the death of the victim or intended victim pursuant to section 20.00 of this chapter, this subparagraph shall not apply where the defendant's criminal liability is based upon the conduct of another pursuant to section 20.00 of this chapter; or

(viii) as part of the same criminal transaction, the defendant, with intent to cause serious physical injury to or the death of an additional person or persons, causes the death of an additional person or persons; provided, however, the victim is not a participant in the criminal transaction; or

(ix) prior to committing the killing, the defendant had been convicted of murder as defined in this section or section 125.25 of this article, or had been convicted in another jurisdiction of an offense which, if committed in this state, would constitute a violation of either of such sections; or

(x) the defendant acted in an especially cruel and wanton manner pursuant to a course of conduct intended to inflict and inflicting torture upon the victim prior to the victim's death. As used in this subparagraph, "torture" means the intentional and depraved infliction of extreme physical pain; "depraved" means the defendant relished the infliction of extreme physical pain upon the victim evidencing debasement or perversion or that the defendant evidenced a sense of pleasure in the infliction of extreme physical pain; or

(xi) the defendant intentionally caused the death of two or more additional persons within the state in separate criminal transactions within a period of twenty-four months when committed in a similar fashion or pursuant to a common scheme or plan; or

(xii) the intended victim was a judge as defined in subdivision twenty-three of section 1.20 of the criminal procedure law and the defendant killed such victim because such victim was, at the time of the killing, a judge; or

(xiii) the victim was killed in furtherance of an act of terrorism, as defined in paragraph (b) of subdivision one of section 490.05 of this chapter; and

(b) The defendant was more than eighteen years old at the time of the commission of the crime.

2. In any prosecution under subdivision one, it is an affirmative defense that:

(a) The defendant acted under the influence of extreme emotional disturbance for which there was a reasonable explanation or excuse, the reasonableness of which is to be determined from the viewpoint of a person in the defendant's situation under the circumstances as the defendant believed them to be. Nothing contained in this paragraph shall constitute a defense to a prosecution for, or preclude a conviction of, manslaughter in the first degree or any other crime except murder in the second degree; or

(b) The defendant's conduct consisted of causing or aiding, without the use of duress or deception, another person to commit suicide. Nothing contained in this paragraph shall constitute a defense to a prosecution for, or preclude a conviction of, manslaughter in the second degree or any other crime except murder in the second degree.

Murder in the first degree is a class A–I felony.

SECTION 2. ASSAULT AND BATTERY[44]

State v. Jimerson

Court of Appeals of Washington, Division 3, Panel Three, 1980.
27 Wn.App. 415, 618 P.2d 1027.

■ MUNSON, JUDGE. Raymond Arthur Jimerson, Jr., appeals his conviction on two counts of second-degree assault. We reverse for failure to give an instruction on simple assault.

On December 22, 1978, Jimerson was driving his car and was accompanied by several friends. The car spun out on ice and snow near two off-duty policemen walking to a Christmas party. The policemen went over to the car to suggest that Jimerson drive more carefully. Jimerson and party responded by hurling epithets; Jimerson started to get out of the car, apparently prepared to fight. What then ensued is in question, but it appears the policemen identified themselves and forced Jimerson back into the car by pushing or possibly by grabbing his hair. Jimerson then drove away in one direction while the police proceeded in another. However, Jimerson turned around and accelerated rapidly toward the policemen on the other side of the street. The two officers tried to evade the car by climbing an embankment. One of them pulled his service revolver and fired at the oncoming car, putting a hole in a door; no occupant was injured. The car swerved toward the officers, but missed them. Jimerson then drove away and went home. Both he and his wife later called the police to report this incident; an investigation resulted in Jimerson's arrest and eventual conviction.

Jimerson testified that he had no intention of running down the officers, but merely intended to drive by, splashing them with slush. A jury

---

44. "An assault is an unlawful attempt coupled with a present ability to commit a violent injury on the person of another." West's Cal. Penal Code § 240.

"A battery is any willful and unlawful use of force or violence upon the person of another." West's Cal. Penal Code § 242.

"Assault is an incipient or inchoate battery, and 'battery' is a consummated assault." People v. Colantuono, 7 Cal.4th 206, 26 Cal.Rptr.2d 908, 865 P.2d 704, 710 (1994).

"An assault is an unlawful attempt, coupled with a present ability, to commit a violent injury on the person of another, or in other words it is an attempt to commit a battery." People v. Rocha, 3 Cal.3d 893, 92 Cal.Rptr. 172, 176, 479 P.2d 372, 376 (1971).

An assault is an offer or attempt to do a battery and every battery includes an assault. Commonwealth v. Burke, 390 Mass. 480, 457 N.E.2d 622 (1983).

Under statutes providing different penalties for battery and for assault it was held that where the victim suffered no physical contact, directly or indirectly, there was no battery and the charge was reduced from assault and battery to a simple assault. Reese v. State, 3 Tenn.Cr. App. 97, 457 S.W.2d 877 (1970).

Under RCW 9A:36.041(1): "Three common-law definitions of assault are recognized: (1) an attempt with unlawful force to inflict bodily injury upon another, (2) an unlawful touching with criminal intent, and (3) putting another in apprehension of harm whether or not the actor intends to inflict or is capable of inflicting harm." State v. Frohs, 83 Wash.App. 803, 924 P.2d 384, 390 (1996).

nevertheless found him guilty of second-degree assault. He asserts two grounds of appeal.

Jimerson first argues that he should have been allowed a jury instruction as to the lesser included offense of simple assault. Jimerson was charged with assault in the first degree under RCW 9A.36.010,[45] and an instruction was given as to the lesser included offense of assault in the second degree pursuant to RCW 9A.36.020.[46] Jimerson's proposed instruction on simple assault was denied because the court believed there was insufficient evidence.

In State v. Workman, 90 Wash.2d 443, 447–48, 584 P.2d 382 (1978), the court held:

> Under the Washington rule, a defendant is entitled to an instruction on a lesser included offense if two conditions are met. First, each of the elements of the lesser offense must be a necessary element of the offense charged.... Second, the evidence ... must support an inference that the lesser crime was committed.

(Citations omitted.)

Neither the present nor the former criminal codes defined the word "assault." We presume this is because it has been firmly established in this state that an assault is an attempt, with unlawful force, to inflict bodily injury upon another, accompanied with apparent present ability to give effect to the attempt if not prevented. Thus, simple assault as defined by the legislature[47] concerns an assault which involves neither the intent nor the result denoted in the definition of assault in the first, second or third

---

45. RCW 9A.36.010:

"(1) Every person, who with intent to kill a human being, or to commit a felony upon the person or property of the one assaulted, or of another, shall be guilty of assault in the first degree when he:

"(a) Shall assault another with a firearm or any deadly weapon or by any force or means likely to produce death; or

"(b) Shall administer to or cause to be taken by another, poison or any other destructive or noxious thing so as to endanger the life of another person.

"(2) Assault in the first degree is a class A felony."

46. RCW 9A.36.020:

"(1) Every person who, under circumstances not amounting to assault in the first degree shall be guilty of assault in the second degree when he:

"(a) With intent to injure, shall unlawfully administer to or cause to be taken by another, poison or any other destructive or noxious thing, or any drug or medicine the use of which is dangerous to life or health; or

"(b) Shall knowingly inflict grievous bodily harm upon another with or without a weapon; or

"(c) Shall knowingly assault another with a weapon or other instrument or thing likely to produce bodily harm; or

"(d) Shall knowingly assault another with intent to commit a felony.

"(2) Assault in the second degree is a class B felony."

47. RCW 9A.36.040 states:

"(1) Every person who shall commit an assault or an assault and battery not amounting to assault in either the first, second, or third degree shall be guilty of simple assault.

"(2) Simple assault is a gross misdemeanor."

degree.[48] The first condition of lesser included offenses has been met. State v. Johnson, 184 Wash. 493, 496, 52 P.2d 317 (1935).

As to the second element, whether the evidence supports the inference that the lesser crime was committed, the facts determine whether a lesser-included-offense instruction should be given. State v. Johnson, *supra* at 496, 52 P.2d 317, quoting from State v. Reynolds, 94 Wash. 270, 276, 162 P. 358 (1917), states:

> "In law, assault in the third degree [under the previous criminal code assault in the third degree was defined in the same manner as is simple assault now] is included within a charge of assault in the second degree, but where a defendant is charged with assault in the second degree, the question whether he is guilty of assault in the third degree should not be submitted to the jury unless the facts of the particular case are such that they will sustain a conviction of assault in the third degree."

In *Johnson*, there is no statement of facts and so it is impossible for this court to determine how the assault was committed. However, in State v. Emerson, 19 Wash.2d 700, 144 P.2d 262 (1943), the evidence supported an allegation that an assault had been committed with a knife. There, the court held that the defendant was guilty of assault in the second degree or not guilty of any degree of assault. Similarly, in State v. Snider, 70 Wash.2d 326, 422 P.2d 816 (1967), on the charge of robbery, Snider had pleaded guilty to grand larceny resulting from his taking a wristwatch off the victim's arm after an affray had ceased. Snider also testified that a codefendant, Olson, had been engaged in the fight and had some money and a wallet in his hands. The court there held that as to Olson there was no error in failing to give a lesser-included-offense instruction because he was either guilty of the robbery or nothing. Here, the state argues that a simple assault is not to be carried out by the car but rather the car is to be used to put some other nondeadly force into motion which amounts to an assault, such as slush or water from a mud puddle, then the car could be used to commit a simple assault. Here, Jimerson testified his intention was not to hit the officers with his car, but only to spray them with slush from the icy and wet road. He also testified that he drove the car up the bank and then swerved away as a reflex action upon seeing one of the officers draw his gun. The trial court apparently weighed this testimony and found it wanting.[49]

---

48. RCW 9A.36.030 states:

"(1) Every person who, under circumstances not amounting to assault in either the first or second degree, shall be guilty of assault in the third degree when he:

"(a) With intent to prevent or resist the execution of any lawful process or mandate of any court officer or the lawful apprehension or detention of himself or another person shall assault another; or

"(b) With criminal negligence, shall cause physical injury to another person by means of a weapon or other instrument or thing likely to produce bodily harm.

"(2) Assault in the third degree is a class C felony."

49. The court in chambers stated:

"I examined that question and concluded that it would be improper for me to give instructions as to simple assault, not being supported by the evidence, that is, the only evidence one could find of simple assault was disputed and denied by the defendant. The police

Jimerson is entitled to a jury instruction on a lesser included offense if any evidence was produced which would justify a reasonable person in concluding that the lesser included offense had been committed. The credibility of Jimerson's testimony was for the jury to decide. We find the instruction on the lesser included offense of simple assault should have been given and the failure to do so was prejudicial error. . . .

Reversed and remanded for new trial.[50]

■ McInturff, Acting C.J., and Roe, J., concur.

---

officers did not allege that the door opening incident constituted any part of the assault, and other than that, I couldn't find any evidence that I could warrant the giving of that Instruction to the jury.

"As you say, the defendant has indicated that his intent was to splash these parties. I didn't hear any evidence that it was possible to splash the parties by way of their location and by way of road conditions. In addition, the evidence was that the automobile went up on whatever we call it, the knoll or embankment or whatever word you are prepared to accept.

" . . .

" . . . And it just didn't in any way cause me to believe a charge of simple assault for the actions alleged would apply. As a consequence, I denied that."

50. "It has long been established, both in tort and criminal law, that 'the least touching' may constitute a battery. In other words, *force* against the person is enough, it need not be violent or severe, it need not cause bodily harm or even pain, and it need not leave any mark." People v. Rocha, 3 Cal.3d 893, 92 Cal.Rptr. 172, 479 P.2d 372, footnote 12 (1971).

A kick is a battery if unlawful, even if the kick was with a bare foot against the booted leg of the other. People v. Martinez, 3 Cal.App.3d 886, 83 Cal.Rptr. 914 (1970).

"[We] hold that only the slightest touching is necessary to constitute the 'force or violence' element of battery." Steele v. State, 778 P.2d 929, 931 (Okl.Cr.1989).

It is a battery to spit in another's face, Regina v. Cotesworth, 6 Mod. 172, 87 Eng.Rep. 928 (1705), or to cut the clothes he is wearing. Regina v. Day, 1 Cox C.C. 207 (1845). It is also a battery for a man to kiss a woman against her will, or to lay hands on her for this purpose. Moreland v. State, 125 Ark. 24, 188 S.W. 1 (1916). But it is not an assault (battery) for a man to kiss an intimate friend when he has good reason to believe this will be agreeable to her. Weaver v. State, 66 Tex.Cr.R. 366, 146 S.W. 927 (1912).

Squeezing and pinching prosecutrix while she was standing in line at a restaurant constituted "simple battery" in violation of Georgia Code § 26–1304(b) which provides that simple battery is committed when one intentionally causes physical harm to another. As she was "firmly grabbed" and "squeezed" some pain may be presumed to have resulted. Mize v. State, 135 Ga.App. 561, 218 S.E.2d 450 (1975).

Throwing a cup of urine in a person's face is a battery. People v. Pinholster, 1 Cal.4th 865, 4 Cal.Rptr.2d 765, 824 P.2d 571 (1992).

Throwing an egg and striking at Congressman with it constitutes an assault on a member of Congress under 18 U.S.C.A. § 351(e). United States v. Guerrero, 667 F.2d 862 (10th Cir.1981).

Defendants who were located seventy feet from the alleged victim, who was inside a store, had no present ability to inflict injury and could not commit the offense of assault. Hamby v. State, 173 Ga.App. 750, 328 S.E.2d 224 (1985).

The fact that the victim was behind a bulletproof glass which made it impossible for bullets to strike the victim did not negate the present ability element of assault. People v. Valdez, 175 Cal.App.3d 103, 220 Cal.Rptr. 538 (1985).

United States v. Bell

United States Court of Appeals, Seventh Circuit, 1974.
505 F.2d 539.

■ Before FAIRCHILD, SPRECHER and TONE, CIRCUIT JUDGES.

■ TONE, CIRCUIT JUDGE.

The defendant Tommie Bell was convicted in a bench trial of assault with intent to commit rape at a place within the special territorial jurisdiction of the United States, in violation of 18 U.S.C. § 113(a). On appeal he raises only one question, *viz.*, whether it is necessary to the offense of assault that the victim have a reasonable apprehension of bodily harm. We answer this question in the negative and affirm the conviction.

It is conceded that while defendant was a patient in the detoxification ward for alcoholic and drug addiction patients in the Veterans Administration Hospital, Downey, Illinois, he attempted to rape a female geriatric patient. It is also undisputed that the victim was suffering from a mental disease which made her unable to comprehend what was going on. Defendant's only asserted defense in the trial court and here is that, because the victim was incapable of forming a reasonable apprehension of bodily harm, there was no assault.

Defendant's contention is squarely contradicted by this court's statement in United States v. Rizzo, 409 F.2d 400, 403 (7th Cir.1969), cert. denied, 396 U.S. 911, 90 S.Ct. 226, 24 L.Ed.2d 187 (1969). There, in sustaining a jury instruction defining assault (taken from W. Mathes and E. Devitt, Federal Jury Practice and Instructions § 43.07 (1965)), the court recognized that there are two concepts of assault in criminal law, the first being an attempt to commit a battery and the second an act putting another in reasonable apprehension of bodily harm. While the second concept was applicable in that case, the court, said with respect to the first:

"There may be an attempt to commit a battery, and hence an assault, under circumstances where the intended victim is unaware of danger. Apprehension on the part of the victim is not an essential element of that type of assault." (Footnotes omitted.)

We adhere to that statement of the law. When a federal criminal statute uses a common law term without defining it, the term is given its common law meaning. A criminal assault at common law was originally an attempt to commit a battery. 1 W. Hawkins, Pleas of the Crown c. 62, § 1 (6th ed. 1788) states:

"It seems that an assault is an attempt or offer, with force and violence, to do a corporal hurt to another.... [E]very battery includes an assault...."

See also 3 S. Greenleaf, Evidence § 59 (16th ed. Harriman 1899); R. Perkins, Criminal Law 114 et seq. (2d ed. 1969). This is the definition given the term in the federal cases. The second concept of assault referred to in *Rizzo*, an act putting another in reasonable apprehension of bodily harm, originated in the law of torts. R. Perkins, id. at 114. Most jurisdictions recognize both concepts of criminal assault.

The notion that a reasonable apprehension on the part of the victim is an essential element of criminal assault probably originated with Bishop, who confused the two concepts in a single definition of the offense and included the element of creating a reasonable apprehension of immediate physical injury in that definition. 2 J. Bishop, Criminal Law § 23 (9th ed. 1923).... [51]

Since an attempted battery is an assault, it is irrelevant that the victim is incapable of forming a reasonable apprehension. Occasions for so holding seem rarely to have been presented. Alderson, B., in The Queen v. Camplin, 1 Cox C.C. 220, 221 (1845), reports that there was such a case in his experience. Regina v. March, 1 Car. & K. 496 (1844), was a conviction for assault against a newborn infant. There are many statements to the effect that an attempt upon an unconscious or otherwise insensitive victim is an assault....

Defendant's attempt to rape an insensitive victim was an assault under 18 U.S.C. § 113(a). His conviction is affirmed.

Affirmed.[52]

---

51. By statute in Illinois assault is defined as the reasonable-apprehension offense (Ill.Rev.Stat., Ch. 38, § 12–1 (1973)) and the attempted-battery offense is covered by the general attempt section (Id. § 8–4). A similar approach is adopted in the proposed bill to revise the Federal Criminal Code. See Revised Committee Print of Amended S. 1, 93d Cong., 2d Sess. §§ 1001, 1613, 1614 (Oct. 15, 1974). In the statutes of other states assault is defined as an attempted battery, but most state statutes, like the federal, do not define the term assault. *See* Comments to § 201.10, ALI, Model Penal Code, Tentative Draft No. 9, p. 83 (1959). Appendix H to the Comments lists and classifies the state statutes. Id. at 141. ALI, Proposed Official Draft of the Model Penal Code (1962), p. 134, with some refinements not relevant here, recognizes both the attempted-battery and reasonable-apprehension types of assault as offenses.

52. [Added by the Compiler.] An apprehension of immediate bodily harm is required under the Kansas statute of aggravated assault. State v. Warbritton, 215 Kan. 534, 527 P.2d 1050 (1974).

An assault was committed by defendant against victims by threatening to have his dog attack the victims. Garrett v. State, 619 S.W.2d 172 (Tex.Cr.App. 1981).

Defendant could not be convicted of an attempted battery type of assault if the victim suffered no harm and was not aware of the alleged assault. Harrod v. State, 65 Md.App. 128, 499 A.2d 959 (1985).

Under Arizona law an attempt to commit a physical injury is not a necessary element of assault. Hence one may be guilty of assault with a deadly weapon by pointing a gun at another even if he did not intend to cause bodily harm. State v. Gary, 112 Ariz. 470, 543 P.2d 782 (1975), cert. denied 425 U.S. 916, 96 S.Ct. 1517.

For a discussion of the two theories of assault *see* State v. Frazier, 81 Wash.2d 628, 503 P.2d 1073 (1972).

May a criminal assault be committed by pointing an unloaded firearm at another within shooting distance but not within striking distance (as a club)?

It was held "yes" under a statute defining assault as a wilful and unlawful attempt or offer, with force or violence, to do a corporal hurt to another. State v. Wiley, 52 S.D. 110, 216 N.W. 866 (1927).

It was held "no" under a statute defining assault as an unlawful attempt, coupled with present ability, to commit violent injury. Klein v. State, 9 Ind.App. 365, 36 N.E. 763 (1894).

Without basing the decision on the wording of the statute it was held that while such a menace is sufficient for a civil action it does not constitute a criminal assault. Chapman v.

United States v. Jacobs

United States Court of Appeals, Seventh Circuit, 1980.
632 F.2d 695.

■ DUMBAULD, SENIOR DISTRICT JUDGE.[53]

The jury found appellant Isaac Jacobs guilty, under Count I of the indictment, of assault resulting in serious bodily injury in violation of 18 U.S.C. § 113(f).[54] He was acquitted of assault with a dangerous weapon, with intent to commit bodily harm, an offense charged in Count II of the indictment as a violation of 18 U.S.C. § 113(c).[55] Defendant and his victim were both Indians, and the offense took place "within the Indian country."[56]

The evidence disclosed that because of a family quarrel defendant planned to evict the victim Earl Bodoh and his family from their home on the disputed premises. He blocked the driveway with his car while the Bodohs were away. But when they returned, Earl Bodoh drove around the obstacle, and proceeded to enter the house. As he reached for the door with his left hand he could feel an unusual condition, and upon looking at his arm saw that he had been shot. Not until then did he see defendant with his gun about eight or ten feet away. He did not see defendant until after he was shot and was not aware that defendant had aimed the gun at him, although other witnesses testified to that fact. Earl Bodoh, after seeing defendant, hurried into the house fearing further gunfire. Defendant followed him in and struck him and others with the gun. Defendant insisted that the gun was discharged accidently.

Defendant now constructs an ingenious argument designed to show that because the victim Bodoh did not see his assailant before being shot

---

State, 78 Ala. 463 (1885). A contrary view was expressed in State v. Deso, 110 Vt. 1, 1 A.2d 710 (1938).

D thrust his hand against X, said "stick 'em up", and began to go through X's pockets until X noticed that D did not have a gun and pushed him away. This was held to be an assault with intent to rob. People v. Rockwood, 358 Ill. 422, 193 N.E. 449 (1934).

Exposing a child to the weather was held not to constitute an assault where the child was rescued before suffering any injury. Regina v. Renshaw, 2 Cox C.C. 285 (1847).

53. The Honorable Edward Dumbauld, United States District Judge from the Western District of Pennsylvania, sitting by designation.

54. "Whoever, within the special maritime and territorial jurisdiction of the United States, is guilty of an assault, shall be punished as follows: ... (f) Assault resulting in serious bodily injury, by fine of not more than $10,000 or imprisonment for not more than ten years, or both."

55. "Whoever, within the special maritime and territorial jurisdiction of the United States, is guilty of an assault, shall be punished as follows: ... (c) Assault with a dangerous weapon, with intent to do bodily harm, and without just cause or excuse, by fine of not more than $1,000 or imprisonment for not more than five years, or both."

56. Accordingly, both 18 U.S.C. §§ 113(c) and 113(f) were made applicable by 18 U.S.C. § 1153, which provides:

"Any Indian who commits against the person or property of another Indian or other person any of the following offenses, namely ... assault with a dangerous weapon, assault resulting in serious bodily injury ... within the Indian country, shall be subject to the same laws and penalties as all other persons committing any of the above offenses, within the exclusive jurisdiction of the United States."

there can be no violation of § 113(f). That provision must be construed, according to defendant, as requiring the assault to occur before the "serious bodily injury" is inflicted, because it makes punishable only an "assault *resulting* in serious bodily injury." This causal relationship requires that the assault take place before the bodily injury is produced as an effect. The Government, on the other hand, contends that the "apprehension" contemplated by the standard definition of simple assault[57] suffices if it occurs *after* the bodily harm is inflicted. (Brief, p. 12).

On this point defendant has the better of the argument. While clearly Bodoh's fear of a second shot while standing in the line of fire after seeing defendant with his gun pointed towards Bodoh would constitute an assault, it would be a subsequent assault and would not constitute the assault "resulting in serious bodily injury" for which defendant was convicted, for such injury had already been received before the subsequent simple assault occurred. In response to the Government's contention the words used by the venerable Virginia jurist George Wythe in argument against his illustrious pupil Thomas Jefferson are pertinent: "it would not be less preposterous than that an effect should be prior to its cause, or than that a thing should act before it exists."[58]

But this does not exonerate the defendant. Another established rule is that when an actual battery is committed it includes an assault.[59] In the case at bar the actual battery was clearly proved,[60] and such proof will support a conviction for the included offense of assault.

Finally, it should be noted that defendant's attempt to invalidate his conviction under Count I of the indictment by reason of his acquittal under Count II is unprofitable. Even if defendant's refined course of reasoning succeeded in demonstrating logical inconsistency in the implications derivable from the separate determinations reached by the jury, it would avail him nothing. For it is a settled rule that inconsistent or compromise verdicts are permissible and legitimate.

But Judge Warren states very persuasively in denying defendant's motion for new trial that the verdict in the case at bar is not inconsistent.

The jury in this case, based upon the evidence presented, could well have found that defendant Isaac Jacobs intended to commit an assault by placing the Bodohs in fear through a display of force, but that Mr. Jacobs

---

57. "Any act of such a nature as to excite an apprehension of a battery may constitute an assault." Prosser, Handbook of the Law of Torts (3d ed. 1964) 38; Restatement, Torts 2d, § 21. The instruction given, taken from Devitt and Blackmar, Federal Jury Practice and Instructions (3d ed. 1977) § 42.04 states that "any intentional display of force such as would give the victim reason to fear or expect immediate bodily harm, constitutes an assault." App.Ex. H–1. The testimony of other witnesses shows that defendant's action "would give" the victim reason to fear harm *if he had seen it* or if an objective rather than subjective standard is applicable. Is an assault upon a blind or deaf person legally impossible when the victim is unaware of the impending danger?

58. Dumbauld, Thomas Jefferson and the Law, 118 (1978).

59. Prosser disagrees. "It is not accurate to say that 'every battery includes an assault.'" Handbook (3d ed. 1964) 41.

60. Battery may be inflicted by means of a gun, just as well as by fists, a club, knife, bow and arrow, or any other "substance put in motion" by an aggressor. 563 F.2d at 323.

did not intend to do the bodily injury that resulted. The evidence clearly supports such a factual finding. Such a factual determination would make Jacobs guilty of violating section 113(f) but not guilty of section 113(c), because the specific intent to do bodily harm was absent.

For the foregoing reasons, the judgment of the District Court is affirmed.

State v. Capwell

Court of Appeals of Oregon, 1981.
52 Or.App. 43, 627 P.2d 905.

■ GILLETTE, PRESIDING JUDGE. This is a criminal case in which defendant seeks reversal of his conviction for Assault in The Fourth Degree. ORS 163.160. Defendant contends that the trial court erred in denying his motion for acquittal on the basis of insufficient evidence. We agree and reverse his conviction.

ORS 163.160 provides, in pertinent part, that a person commits the crime of Assault in the Fourth Degree if he "intentionally, knowingly or recklessly causes physical injury to another...." "Physical injury" is defined as "impairment of physical condition or substantial pain." ORS 161.015(6). Defendant claims that there is no evidence that the alleged victim suffered any impairment of his physical condition or substantial pain.

At approximately 3 a.m. on June 1, 1980, the victim's wife noticed a man, later identified as the defendant, standing in front of their house and carrying a gas can. She awakened her husband, Tenderella, who is an Oregon State Police officer. After dressing he picked up his nightstick and went outside to investigate the matter. He told the defendant to stop where he was. The defendant, who appeared startled, swung the gas can at Tenderella but did not hit him. Tenderella identified himself as a police officer and began to question the defendant about his activities. At that point, he noticed a bulge underneath the defendant's coat and attempted to pat him down for weapons. The defendant pulled back and swung the gas can at Tenderella again, this time hitting him in the arm. Tenderella testified that he felt pain, a stinging sensation, when the defendant hit him.

Tenderella told the defendant that he was under arrest. The defendant attempted to leave and Tenderella tried "to put him down" by hitting him around the knee area with his nightstick. The defendant reacted by swinging the gas can and kicking out at Tenderella. At one point the defendant kicked him in the arm, knocking the nightstick out of his hand. The victim testified that this "hurt." He could not recall, however, whether the defendant was wearing soft or hard shoes.[61]

The officer did not know exactly how many times he was hit with the gas can. He stated that it was a "couple of times" and that each time he stopped the blow with his arm. He reported no sensation other than it

---

61. These facts are presented in a light most favorable to the state. The defendant claimed that Officer Tenderella hit him first and that he, the defendant, was acting in self-defense.

"hurt" and was painful. There is no indication of bruising or any other injury to the victim. He stated that he did not seek medical treatment after the scuffle and did not miss any work.

The question to be answered in determining the sufficiency of the evidence in this case is

" . . . whether, after viewing the evidence in the light most favorable to the prosecution, any rational trier of fact could have found the essential elements of the crime beyond a reasonable doubt."

There is no evidence that the victim suffered any impairment of his physical condition as a result of defendant's blows. The question is whether there is sufficient evidence to allow the jury to find, beyond a reasonable doubt, guilt according to the alternative statutory requirement, *viz.,* that the victim suffered substantial pain. We conclude that there is not.

"Substantial" is defined as

"(1) That is or exists as a substance; having a real existence, subsisting by itself; (2) of ample or considerable amount, quantity or dimensions, (3) having substance, not imaginary, unreal or apparent only; true, solid real." Oxford English Dictionary, Compact Edition (1971).

Substantial pain means considerable pain. In this case, the victim testified that he had pain and that it hurt when the defendant struck him. There is no other evidence of the degree of the pain or that it was anything more than a fleeting sensation.[62] The state was required to prove that the defendant's blows caused either physical impairment or substantial pain to the victim. We conclude that there was insufficient evidence to support such a finding in this case.

Having stated that the evidence is insufficient to convict defendant of the offense of Assault in the Fourth Degree, the question remains: what disposition must be made of this case?

Assault in the Fourth Degree is a Class A misdemeanor. ORS 163.160. ORS 161.405 provides, in pertinent part:

"(1) A person is guilty of an attempt to commit a crime when he intentionally engages in conduct which constitutes a substantial step toward commission of the crime.

"(2) An attempt is a:

" . . .

"(e) Class B misdemeanor if the offense attempted is a Class A misdemeanor.

" . . ."

The Oregon Constitution, Amend. Art. VII, § 3 directs:

---

62. The legislative history reveals that criminal assault, in whatever degree, requires the infliction of actual physical injury. Petty batteries not producing injury do not constitute criminal assault. *See* Criminal Law Revision Commission, Proposed Criminal Code, Final Draft, 123, Commentary to § 94 and 219 Commentary to § 223. The term "physical injury" recognizes that the cause of such an injury is some form of external violence that produces a harmful effect upon the body. *See* Criminal Law Revision Commission, Proposed Criminal Code, Final Draft, 3, Commentary to § 3.

" ... if, in any respect, the judgment appealed from should be changed, and the [appellate court] shall be of the opinion that it can determine what judgment should have been entered in the court below, it shall direct such judgment to be entered...."

In the present case, the trier of fact necessarily found that defendant had taken a "substantial step" toward commission of the assault offense. Entry of a judgment for Attempted Assault in the Fourth Degree is appropriate.[63]

Reversed and remanded for entry of a new judgment and for resentencing.

People v. Santiago

Supreme Court, New York County, 2003.
2003 WL 21507176.

■ JEFFREY M. ATLAS, J.

The defendant is charged with Aggravated Criminal Contempt and two counts of Criminal Contempt in the First Degree based on Angela R.'s allegations that he violated an Order of Protection which was issued to protect her. She and the defendant have lived together for many years, and as happens frequently in cases of this kind, prior to trial, Angela R. declared that she no longer wished to press charges, that she would decline to testify at trial, and that if she were made to testify she would declare that all the allegations she previously made to the police, prosecutor, and Grand Jury were fabricated by the police and the District Attorney. In view of that, the People moved for an order permitting them to use Angela R.'s Grand Jury testimony and her other out of court statements during the presentation of their direct case against the defendant. The People's theory is that the defendant's longstanding pattern of physical and emotional abuse toward Angela R. effectively forced her to become unavailable as a witness for the People at trial. The defendant opposes this motion, arguing that Angela R. is available and willing to testify at trial, and that her credibility is a matter for the jury. For the reasons which follow, the People's motion is granted.

As a general rule, the Grand Jury testimony and out of court statements of an unavailable witness are inadmissible as evidence in chief. However, our courts have adopted certain exceptions to this rule when the People can prove, by clear and convincing evidence, that the defendant procured the witness's unavailability through violence, threats or chicanery. (Matter of Holtzman v. Hellenbrand, 92 A.D.2d 405, 460 N.Y.S.2d 591 [2d Dep't.1983]). If the defendant's misconduct is proved, sound public policy demands the defendant forfeit the assertion of his constitutional right of confrontation and the protection of such evidentiary rules which would otherwise preclude the admission of hearsay declarations. (People v. Cotto, 92 N.Y.2d 68 [1998], denial of Habeus Corpus rev'd on other grounds

---

63. ORS 163.160 provides that Assault in the Fourth Degree may be committed "intentionally, knowingly *or recklessly*." However, our disposition of this case is permissible because the trial court, in instructing the jury, instructed the jury that they must find that the defendant acted intentionally. No mention was made of recklessness.

sub nom. Cotto v. Herbert, 331 F.3d 217, 2003 WL 1989700 (2nd Cir. May 1, 2003); People v. Geraci, 85 N.Y.2d 359 [1995]). This rule is invoked to "[protect] the integrity of the adversary process by deterring litigants from acting on strong incentives to prevent the testimony of an adverse witness." (People v. Geraci, *supra*, quoting Steele v. Taylor, 684 F.2d 1193, 1202 [6th Cir.1982]).

In this case, the People's papers demonstrated a distinct possibility that the defendant engaged in witness tampering. Such a showing mandated a Sirois[64] hearing. . . .

At the Sirois hearing I heard testimony from the People's witnesses: the complainant Angela R., the Grand Jury stenographer in this case, Domestic Violence Counselor Nelida Vasquez, Police Officer Geneva Eleutice, Assistant District Attorney Christopher Hill, and Dr. Ann Wolbert Burgess, who is an expert in domestic violence and Battered Women's Syndrome. The defendant, Victor Santiago, also testified. Much of what the complainant and the defendant said during their testimony was patently incredible. On the other hand, the testimony of the remaining witnesses was believable and, in some instances, beyond dispute.

Domestic Violence and Battered Women's Syndrome

Dr. Ann Wolbert Burgess is an expert in the field of relationship violence and domestic violence. She has testified many times in State and Federal courts, in criminal and civil matters, as an expert in domestic violence and "Battered Women's Syndrome." At the Sirois hearing, Dr. Burgess's testimony was based upon her own experiences in counseling battered women, as well as widely accepted studies on domestic violence which support her conclusions. Dr. Burgess testified that domestic violence is an intentional injurious act committed by one partner against the other within an intimate relationship. The act of abuse can be physical, sexual, financial, emotional, or psychological. According to Dr. Burgess, Battered Women's Syndrome describes the behavioral pattern of an abused person and explains the actions of the abused person. Dr. Burgess testified that domestic violence is part of the effort by one partner to dominate and control the other so that the dominant partner can experience a sense of power. In approximately 90% of the reported cases the batterer is male and the battered person is female. Domestic violence is characterized by the three phases of behavior which are commonly referred to as the "cycle of violence." These are (1) the tension building phase, (2) the violent phase, and (3) the honeymoon phase.

The tension building phase is one of conflict, often arising from an aggravating situation or a simple disagreement. It is followed by the violent phase which consists of either physically abusive acts, or other acts designed to hurt the woman in indirect ways. The violent phase is followed by the honeymoon phase, which is characterized by acts of contrition by the abuser, his requests for forgiveness and his declarations of love. The

---

64. The so-called Sirois hearing is named for Mrs. Sirois, a witness in the Murder trial of her once estranged husband, who recanted her testimony after reconciling with the defendant. (*Matter of Holtzman v. Hellenbrand, supra*).

duration, intensity and frequency of these cycles can vary, and are sometimes dependent on external aggravating factors. . . .

Dr. Burgess's experiences and studies of battered women show that it is very common for women to tolerate abuse and not seek help because they are too ashamed and humiliated to reveal their plight and accept assistance. Often, battered women simply do not want their friends or family to know what they have endured. Dr. Burgess noted that the presence of children in the home becomes another complicating factor in these relationships. The child becomes a means of leverage used by the batterer as he seeks to convince the battered partner that she cannot maintain a home for the child without the batterer's presence and assistance. Studies also show that it is common for battered women, fearful that their children may be abused, to take further abuse simply to shield their children. . . .

Angela R. and Victor Santiago's Relationship

At the hearing, Angela R. testified that she and the defendant are married by common-law and by love, and have been living together, as she put it, for "ten beautiful years." During her testimony, Angela R. professed to being a religious person with a deep faith in God. When confronted with the many reports of abuse she filed against the defendant she testified that all of them were false, notwithstanding the fact that she admitted to having written and/or signed them. Throughout the course of her brief testimony, when challenged about these discrepancies, Angela R. answered the prosecutor's questions: "I don't remember," "I don't recall," "No, I did not," "I do not understand," and "I do not know" over 100 times. As the record bears out, she often responded so inconsistently as to be virtually irrational, all the while nervously watching the defendant for his approval, as he blew kisses to her from his seat at counsel table. . . . [The court then reviews a evidence of a long record of physical violence by the defendant against Angela R., including repeated violations of civil protection orders.]

The Instant Indictment

Assistant District Attorney Hill next heard from Angela R. a few months later on May 3, 2002, when she called and left another message for him. In it she requested information about how to contact a woman who had helped her in the past but whose number she no longer had because the defendant had taken all of her papers. Her message continued: "I need to go to the 24th Precinct and make a report because . . . again he put his hands on me—he just 'went off' this morning and he's been doing this for a couple of days and I don't call the cops because I don't have the Order of Protection in my hand." At the end of the message, she choked back tears while trying to say "Thank-you."

On May 5, 2002, Angela filed another Domestic Incident Report at the 24th Precinct. It lists her relationship to the defendant as "child in common" and the signed statement in Angela R.'s handwriting reads: "I Angel R. ask Victor Santiago to please leave my room he said no then hit me." (Sic.)

When Assistant District Attorney Hill returned Angela R.'s phone call of May 3, 2002, he discovered that since they last spoke in December 2001, the defendant had been arrested yet again for violating an Order of Protection by assaulting Angela R. That case had been assigned to another Assistant and, again, Angela R. refused to testify against the defendant and the case was dismissed. In their phone conversation, Angela R. told Mr. Hill that she had to do something about the defendant, that nothing had worked before, that all her cases had just gone away, but that now she had to get him out of the house and get on with her life.

Assistant District Attorney Hill testified that Angela R. came to his office on May 7, 2002, and cataloged for him the defendant's recent behavior toward her, all of which violated her outstanding Order of Protection against him. She recounted incidents of slapping her, throwing her against a dresser, bending her fingers back so as to cause her pain, and punching her. Hill told her that he wanted her to testify before the Grand Jury, but she expressed reluctance. She said that she was ashamed to tell her story in front of other people, she didn't want them to judge her, and she was concerned that the defendant would be there. The Assistant reassured her, explaining that he must ask certain questions to establish the defendant's course of conduct, but Angela R. insisted that she could not talk about certain incidents in front of other people. The Assistant and she determined what she could bring herself to discuss, and they went down the hall to the Grand Jury. When the case was called, Angela went to the door of the Grand Jury, but froze and did not want to enter. Mr. Hill and another Assistant District Attorney spoke to her, and she eventually agreed to go in and testify. In general, she testified that the defendant physically abused her in violation of the specific terms of the Order of Protection. As a consequence of her testimony, the instant indictment was voted charging the defendant with Aggravated Criminal Contempt and two counts of Criminal Contempt in the First Degree. The defendant was arrested on May 14, 2002.

In the weeks that followed, Angela left three messages for the Assistant which he saved and played at the hearing. Those messages are:

(1) "Hi Chris–Christopher Hill, this is Angela R. I was informed that they, umm, arrested Victor on Friday and I know tomorrow morning is his court date and Chris, umm, I mean, umm, he got arrested but please don't ... work something out so that he won't be in jail for so long. Okay Chris? Thank-you. Bye, bye."

(2) "Good Morning Christopher Hill, this is Angela R., umm, sorry to bother you again, umm, but, umm, I been doing a lot of thinking and, umm, things are very hard for me as a single parent right now Chris and, ummm, again I'm asking you, umm, lets try to work this out, umm, so Victor, umm, he won't do the jail time, umm, I really ... I really need, umm, for you to help me on this. I know you're just doing your job, and you protected me and I appreciate the fact that you did help me when I needed you, so, umm, umm, we need to work something out Chris, umm, because, umm, I'm having a hard time just me with my daughter. I cannot work full time because I have no one to take care of her. It's getting a little rough and this was not my intention for Victor. I'm sure he learned his lesson, so let's try to work something out Chris, umm, if you need to get back to me, My number is: xxx-xxx.... Thank-you and have a good day Chris. Bye".

(3) "Good afternoon, Christopher Hill, this is Angela R., again, umm, I don't want to be a pest, I don't want to seem like I'm calling you to bother you constantly, but I'm seriously asking you to, umm, reconsider. I want to drop all the charges against Victor Santiago. We wanted to punish him, we did, alright. He doesn't deserve jail time, so, he went into himself to think, he already has. I can feel it. I haven't had any contact with him, and, umm, things got exaggerated and I'm asking you ... let's drop the charges, and I thank-you and have a good day. Thank-you very much. Bye, bye."

Thereafter, Assistant District Attorney Hill spoke to Angela R. a number of times about the importance of her going forward with the prosecution but she adamantly refused to do so. Instead she accused him of betraying her by putting her in the Grand Jury. . . .

The defendant's instant case was adjourned to September 10, 2002, for trial. However, realizing that Angela R. would resist testifying or if forced to testify she intended to perjure herself, the People requested the Sirios hearing which is the subject of this decision. . . .

Dr. Burgess testified that, in her expert opinion, the relationship between Angela R. and the defendant is a classic example of a domestic violence relationship and that Angela R. is an abused woman whose current behavior is explained by Battered Women's Syndrome. In support of her opinion, Dr. Burgess noted that over a period of years, in a relationship marked by episodes of violence, Angela R. regularly called the police when attacked, obtained orders of protection from the court, then recanted her allegations and refused to prosecute. Dr. Burgess also noted evidence of the defendant's use of psychological abuse to control the complainant. He threatened to kill her, he blamed her for things that she had not done, he took things that were precious to her, he destroyed things that were important to her, and he acted in ways that enhanced her dependance upon him. While noting that their domestic violence cycle has entered the so-called honeymoon phase, Dr. Burgess also observed that while the defendant is in prison, Angela R. has been placed under tremendous pressure to not testify against him. Dr. Burgess testified that, given the amount of recent contact between the defendant and Angela R., the defendant has played a major role in her recantation and willingness to perjure herself. Dr. Burgess concluded that Angela R.'s behavior as a reluctant witness, her willingness to tell patent lies in court, to rationalize the defendant's behavior, and to accept blame for her current predicament reflects her imposed lack of self esteem and her level of desperation. This, according to the expert, can only be attributed to the coercion inherent in the honeymoon phase of the cycle of violence and the tremendous pressure that the defendant has placed on Angela R. to relieve him of his current confinement.

I am convinced that Angela R. has been physically and emotionally abused by the defendant for many years, and her suffering has gone unchecked and untreated since, at least, 1996. The credible evidence at this hearing makes very clear that Angela R.'s current attitude toward testifying is a classic example of a battered woman's reaction to what has been described as the honeymoon phase of the abusive relationship. . . .

The record also shows Angela R.'s repeated withdrawal of her complaints to law enforcement. In every case that she initiates, she eventually recants and she takes the blame for incidents in which she has been the wounded party. Indeed, the hearing evidence establishes in this case the defendant's contribution toward the complainant's sense of guilt for the predicament she currently finds herself in. Over time, the defendant has violated one court Order of Protection after another with impunity because, as he testified, the complainant never testifies against him.

Once again, Angela R. has declined to testify against the defendant. However, in this instance there is clear and convincing evidence that her unwillingness to continue with the prosecution comes after persistent efforts by the defendant to reconcile with the complainant and convince her to do what is necessary to get him out of jail. The defendant, in over 100 conversations with her (each of which seems to have constituted another violation of an Order of Protection), has used the complainant's desires for a normal and loving relationship to his own end. Angela R. fears that continued prosecution will make the defendant suffer in prison, hurt their relationship and likely lead to additional acts of violence. Obviously, the avoidance of any jail time is a tremendous incentive for the defendant to place extraordinary pressure upon the complainant. Indeed, the defendant testified that he has regularly discussed with Angela R. his urgent desire to be out of jail, and his view that it is up to her to get him out of jail and home to her.

Conclusions

Nonetheless, the defense contends that the defendant did not explicitly threaten the complaining witness during those 100 phone calls and that the complainant's current reluctance to testify is not as a result of any misconduct committed by him since the inception of this case. The defendant argues that this distinguishes this case from others in which a witness's prior statements were properly admitted because the defendant's misconduct, committed between the inception of the case and the date of trial, was found sufficiently threatening to have caused the witness's unavailability (*See, People v. Geraci, supra; People v. Cotto, supra.*) Moreover, implicit in the defendant's argument is the notion that I should treat the complainant's current effort to withdraw the charge with no greater concern than I might have toward efforts to withdraw in other kinds of cases. The defense argument in this case suggests that no matter how frustrating, I should simply accept this as a failed prosecution. In this respect the defense argument implies that I view the withdrawal of complaints in domestic violence cases in the same way that I have viewed the occasional attempts to withdraw prosecutions in other kinds of cases where the complainant and defendant were strangers to each other. Except where proof existed that the witness became unavailable because of the wrongdoing of the defendant, in other kinds of cases we have often taken for granted that a complainant's desire to withdraw from the prosecution was based on the simple unwillingness to get involved in the process, or give up the time it takes to follow through on the complaint, or because of the witness's unsubstantiated fears of reprisal from some unspecified source. We have frequently not looked beyond those excuses in such cases where no proof was immediately available that a particular and recent act of misconduct by the defendant had brought about the witness's unavailability.

However, I do not believe domestic violence cases are of the same character as other kinds of cases and I am unable to be indifferent about the effort of this complainant to withdraw her complaint. Moreover, I do not believe that the cases admitting prior testimony of an unavailable witness should be read to hold that prior evidence given by an unavailable witness is admissible only when the defendant's misconduct causing the unavailability occurs between the defendant's arrest and the date of trial. While that may occur in the usual case, domestic violence matters are of such a different character as to justify a broader application of the rule.

Expert studies and our experience in the criminal process has taught us that there is a difference between the dynamics of domestic violence and other types of assault cases adjudicated by our courts. Countless Judges have presided in courts through which the devastated victims of domestic violence have come, first to seek protection but later to withdraw their complaints even though it was clear from prior experience that they were likely to be the victims of violence again at the hands of their partners. There was a time when domestic violence cases were taken less seriously than other cases because of the routine withdrawal of such complaints and the frequent inability to prosecute these cases notwithstanding the serious injuries suffered by the complainants. Over the years we threw up our hands in surrender and tolerated domestic violence because we did not have a method by which these cases could be prosecuted over the complainants' objections.

Frustrated by this recurring sequence of events, police policy and the law evolved in ways designed to circumvent the inevitable recantation of the domestic violence victim. The Police Department implemented a "must arrest" policy in domestic violence cases many years ago. The legislature both amended P.L. § 215.51, Criminal Contempt in the First Degree, (amended by L.1994, c.222 and c. 224; L.1996, c.353; L.1998, c.597) and later redefined a section of that statute to create a new statute, P.L. § 215.52, Aggravated Criminal Contempt, (Added L.1996, c.353; amended L.1998, c.597) in an effort at more effective intervention in domestic violence cases. While these efforts have proved effective in getting the abusers to court, the prosecution nonetheless still runs into real obstacles at trial when the complainants refuse to testify. Attempts to hold complainants in contempt as a means of compelling their testimony are notably unsuccessful and serve only to abuse the complainants further. Efforts to call the complainants as witnesses and cross-examine them with their prior testimony are of limited usefulness since impeached disclaimers cannot serve as proof of the abuse on the people's direct case. (CPL 60.35(2)). Attempts to simply persuade the complainants to testify fail, as they did in this case, because the negative pressures upon the battered complainants far outweigh any thoughts they might entertain of gaining relief from the abuse by prosecuting the defendant.

We are now aware that domestic violence cases brought by complainants with a long standing history of abuse are to be viewed differently from other crimes of violence which come through our courts. We are accustomed to injured victims seeking retribution, punishment and protection from society. That, without a doubt, is the norm. It is fair to say that we now recognize that in domestic violence cases repeated abuse followed by repeated withdrawal of prosecution and the repeated grant of forgiveness to the abuser make such cases very different from the norm.

What is evident is that domestic violence cases are different because of the complainant's desire for a stable relationship and the exploitation of that desire by the defendant. The hallmark of such cases is the hope for a brighter future with the abuser held by the complainant who is weakened by past abuse and seduced by untrustworthy gestures of love but, whose expectations are eventually met with repeated abuse to the perverse satisfaction of the abuser. In other kinds of cases there has been little, if any, intimate interaction between the parties and generally there is no expectation of a future relationship. As I have noted, in the vast majority of cases victims pursue their complaints seeking retribution and safety from the process provided by the police and courts. Such complainants, although sometimes apprehensive, follow through because they have the strength, the will and the need to do so. Victims of domestic violence do not have the will to follow through. They lack the self esteem and strength to seek retribution or permanent safety from their attackers. This is so not only because of the psychological damage done by repeated abuse but, also because there lurks in the mind of such complainants the fear of physical retaliation to themselves and their children at the hands of an offender whose past behavior toward the complainant makes it highly probable that such abuse will occur again. In short, the defendant's pattern of behavior causes the victim of domestic abuse to succumb to the offender's importuning in ways that others might not. Thus, attempts to become unavailable as a prosecuting witness cannot be viewed as we might see voluntary withdrawal in a case where the complainant and the defendant are strangers to one another. Nor, can such withdrawal be viewed as having been made without the misconduct of the defendant when it is attempted during the honeymoon phase of a cycle of violence filled, as it is here, with a mix of fear, false hope, a sense of guilt and weakness of will all resulting from the defendants prior behavior.

Clearly, the nature of this syndrome and the cost to the families involved, the police, medical professionals, the courts and society in general cry out for a solution. It is simply unacceptable for our process to turn a blind eye to the dangers of such abuse by shrugging our shoulders and saying that nothing can be done within the framework of existing law.

In fact, such a prosecution may continue even without the complainant's cooperation, so long as the prosecution can show by clear and convincing evidence, either direct or circumstantial, that the witness's unavailability was procured by violence, threats, chicanery or other acts of misconduct on the part of the defendant. No class of cases seem more worthy of the protections afforded by the public policy which dictated this evidentiary rule than matters involving domestic violence. Moreover, given the purpose of the rule it is hard to conceive that it should be limited to situations in which the misconduct occurred between the date of the charge and the date of the trial and, indeed, no language contained in any of the cases on this subject suggests that it should.

In this case the conclusion is inescapable that this abused complainant seeks to make herself unavailable as a witness because of the pattern of misconduct directed toward her by the defendant. The defense notes that in recent weeks the defendant has not threatened the witness but has spoken to her only in terms of endearment, seeking her forgiveness and expressing his desire to return to a harmonious relationship with her. While that claim may be true to some extent, it is clear that the defendant's promises are not to be trusted and, in any event, always contain the implicit threat that the complainant's unwillingness to cooperate with him will result in dire consequences for her. The complainant's decision not to cooperate with this prosecution is, without a doubt, strongly, if not totally influenced by the long history of domestic abuse that appears to affect all the decisions made by the complainant with respect to this defendant. It is true that the evidentiary consequences would be different in this case if the complainant's choice not to go forward were premised exclusively on feelings of love and loyalty to the defendant. However, the violent domestic history of these two people, and defendant's recent persistent importuning of the complainant to withdraw from this prosecution, have made clear that Angela R.'s choice with respect to continuing this prosecution was not made without fear of the defendant and the complex mix of emotions one might expect to find in a person suffering from Battered Women's Syndrome. Indeed, abuse of the complainant by the defendant is the recurrent theme in the relationship between these two parties. Thus, in my view, there is clear and convincing evidence that the defendant's misconduct procured the complainant's unavailability as a witness in this prosecution and, as a fitting consequence, the People should be allowed to present evidence of the complainant's prior statements and Grand Jury testimony regarding this incident to the trial jury.

Commonwealth v. Matsos

Supreme Judicial Court of Massachusetts, Essex, 1995.
421 Mass. 391, 657 N.E.2d 467.

■ GREANEY, JUSTICE.

The defendant challenges his conviction by a jury of six in the District Court under the so-called stalking statute, G.L. c. 265, § 43, inserted by St.1992, c. 31. The defendant argues that his motion for a required finding of not guilty, see Mass.R.Crim.P. 25(a), 378 Mass. 896 (1979), should have been allowed because the Commonwealth's evidence was insufficient to prove that he had made a threat with the intent to place the victim in imminent fear of death or serious bodily injury.... We affirm the defendant's conviction.

The evidence in the Commonwealth's case would have warranted the jury in finding the following facts. The defendant and the victim, a black officer with the Salem police department, first met in early 1991. On May 18, 1992, the victim was walking to work when she was confronted by the defendant.[65] The victim asked the defendant what he was doing there and told him to stop following her around. On May 21, 1992, the victim received the first in a series of letters from the defendant. From May 21, 1992, until March 16, 1993, he sent approximately forty letters to the victim. The letters repeatedly lamented the victim's perceived indifference toward the defendant, and were filled with sexual references. Several of the letters described in explicit detail the defendant's sexual fantasies about the victim. Many of the letters admitted in evidence expressed the defendant's anger with the victim, sometimes couched in racial terms. There were references to the defendant's dangerous acquaintances (including one old friend whom the United States Attorney said was responsible for five murders) and to guns.[66] The letters also established that the defendant was following the victim during the relevant period, spying on her and her friends, and attempting to acquire information about her private life.

The victim first had initiated a complaint against the defendant for stalking in June, 1992. On July 17, 1992, the victim learned that the defendant had signed documents and forwarded them to her employer, the Salem police department, claiming that the victim had used drugs with him. The allegations prompted an extensive internal affairs investigation, including drug testing for the victim. The police department ultimately concluded the allegations were unfounded.

The victim testified that, at first, the letters made her feel uncomfortable. Later she became fearful, ceased opening the letters, and changed her residence. There was also testimony that she had obtained a special telephone service that permitted her to screen her telephone calls to ensure that incoming calls were not from the defendant.

1. Following the close of the Commonwealth's case, the defendant moved for a required finding of not guilty. He argues that this motion was improperly denied because the Commonwealth's proof was insufficient to show that he had made threats with the intent to place the victim in imminent fear of death or serious bodily injury. We reject the defendant's argument.

... To obtain a conviction under G.L. c. 265, § 43, the prosecution must prove that the defendant made a threat with the intent to place the victim in imminent fear of death or bodily injury. This element closely approximates the common law definition of the crime of assault, and we may presume that the Legislature was aware of this when it enacted the statute. Accordingly, we turn to the common law treatment of assault for purposes of examining the legislation. *See* Commonwealth v. Gordon, 407 Mass. 340, 349, 553 N.E.2d 915 (1990) (discussing definition of "abuse" in G.L. c. 209A, § 1, by reference to decisions defining criminal assault).

... [T]his court [has] summarized the common law definition of criminal assault, as follows. "Under the common law, 'it is well established ... that an act placing another in reasonable apprehension that force may

---

65. On the same day, the stalking statute went into effect.

66. In one letter, the defendant, who, according to the victim, was Greek, referred to himself as a Greek with a gun, and wrote: "Silencers are quite often [sic] found in Europe than they are in this country. The reason there [sic] good is they don't wake up the children."

be used is sufficient for the offense of criminal assault.' Commonwealth v. Delgado, 367 Mass. 432, 437 [326 N.E.2d 716] (1975), and cases cited. In determining whether an apprehension of anticipated physical force is reasonable, a court will look to the actions and words of the defendant in light of the attendant circumstances." In a case of simple criminal assault, the Commonwealth need not prove that the defendant actually intended to harm the victim, it need only prove that the defendant's threats were reasonably calculated to place the victim in imminent fear of bodily injury.

The defendant sent the victim more than forty letters during a ten-month period. These letters, which amounted to hundreds of pages, revealed the defendant's intense obsession with the victim and his anger at her rejection of him,[67] and the letters chronicle a campaign of harassment mounted by him,[68] which included a malicious attempt to interfere with the victim's employment. We disagree with the defendant's contention that the evidence did not provide a basis for a reasonable juror to conclude that the defendant had intentionally placed the victim in imminent fear of death or serious bodily injury. The defendant identified himself as "The Stalker" in a return address. Among other quite explicit threats, he warned the victim, "There is [going to come] a day when you are [going to] want to come and see me. . . . But you will never see me, your eyes will alway[s] be closed."[69] He made references to guns and silencers, to dangerous friends, and to his own involvement in illegal activity. He made it clear that he was following the victim and would be able to find her,[70] and his accusation against her of drug use demonstrated that he was prepared to act on his threats of harassment and violence. On the basis of the Commonwealth's evidence, the jury could have found that the defendant intended to place the victim in fear of imminent bodily injury, and that she was afraid of him. The judge correctly denied the defendant's motion for a required finding.

2.   Nearly one year after the defendant was convicted, this court issued its decision in Commonwealth v. Kwiatkowski, *supra*, which held the stalking statute, as enacted, to be unconstitutionally vague. Id. at 546–547, 637 N.E.2d 854. We noted, in the Kwiatkowski decision, that the statute set forth the crime of stalking with reasonable clarity: "Whoever willfully,

---

67.   The defendant referred to the victim as a "black bitch," and wrote that the victim's "mother should have aborted her." He wrote, "I just hope that when I see you I won't want to give you a beating."

68.   In one letter, the defendant expressed his deliberate intent to harass the victim: "I will put so much [pressure] on you at work, home and at play. The heat is on you to stop doing the shit. All I want you to do is make that little sacrifice. For your fellow workers, your family and son. And for me."

69.   Another letter contained the following postscript: "You know what would be funny, if you took all the letters I wrote did not read them and threw them in the trash like junk mail. And you are a very lucky girl. The day you made threats to me on Essex St. were you reading my mind? How very easy it is. Its [sic] very easy isn't it. It may be to [sic] easy."

70.   A number of the letters refer to specific activities of the victim that had been observed by the defendant. He wrote of seeing her automobile, and suggested that she take an alternate route. He wrote of observing a brief visit she made to the apartment where she was no longer living, and commented on the attire of her companion. On another occasion, the defendant wrote that he saw the victim carrying cookies into work. At least one other communication also strongly supports the inference that the defendant was constantly following the victim.

maliciously, and repeatedly follows or harasses another person and who makes a threat with the intent to place that person in imminent fear of death or serious bodily injury shall be guilty of the crime of stalking." The definition of "harasses" appearing in G.L. c. 265, § 43(d), however, left it unclear whether, to be guilty under the "harassment" aspect of § 43(a), one must engage repeatedly in a pattern of conduct or series of acts over a period of time. Id. at 546, 637 N.E.2d 854. Because the Legislature did not state with sufficient clarity its presumed intent that a single pattern of conduct or a single series of acts satisfied the harassment aspect of the crime of stalking, we held the statute to be unconstitutionally vague. Id. at 547, 637 N.E.2d 854. The defendant argues that, in view of this decision, his conviction must be reversed.

. . .

Moreover, the defendant's actions clearly fall within the scope of the conduct prohibited by the "harassment" portion of the statute, even if the statute is interpreted as requiring that the defendant engage repeatedly in patterns of conduct or series of acts that would cause a reasonable person to suffer substantial emotional distress. The jury heard of more than forty letters sent by the defendant to the victim over a ten-month period. The twenty-three letters admitted in evidence were replete with vulgar language, sexual fantasies about the victim, and threats of various kinds. The jury also heard evidence that the defendant followed the victim to work on at least one occasion, and his letters provided ample evidence that he continued to follow her as she changed residences and phone numbers in an attempt to avoid him. The jury were also informed that the defendant had made an unfounded accusation to the Salem police department that he and the victim had used drugs together which caused the victim considerable difficulty at work. Measured by any standard, these facts establish that the defendant's campaign of harassment involved distinctive, but equally disturbing, patterns of conduct in which the defendant engaged more than once. The statute gave the defendant fair notice that his repeated, obsessive behavior, which poisoned the victim's personal and professional lives, was prohibited. It cannot be said that prosecuting the defendant under the stalking statute, and the jury's conviction of the defendant, constituted an affront to due process or created a substantial risk of a miscarriage of justice.

Judgment affirmed.

MODEL PENAL CODE

Article 211. Assault; Reckless Endangering; Threats

Section 211.0 Definitions.

In this Article, the definitions given in Section 210.0 apply unless a different meaning plainly is required.

Section 211.1 Assault.

(1) Simple Assault. A person is guilty of assault if he:

(a) attempts to cause or purposely, knowingly or recklessly causes bodily injury to another; or

(b) negligently causes bodily injury to another with a deadly weapon; or

(c) attempts by physical menace to put another in fear of imminent serious bodily injury.

Simple assault is a misdemeanor unless committed in a fight or scuffle entered into by mutual consent, in which case it is a petty misdemeanor.

(2) Aggravated Assault. A person is guilty of aggravated assault if he:

(a) attempts to cause serious bodily injury to another, or causes such injury purposely, knowingly or recklessly under circumstances manifesting extreme indifference to the value of human life: or

(b) attempts to cause or purposely or knowingly causes bodily injury to another with a deadly weapon.

Aggravated assault under paragraph (a) is a felony of the second degree; aggravated assault under paragraph (b) is a felony of the third degree.

Section 211.2 Recklessly Endangering Another Person.

A person commits a misdemeanor if he recklessly engages in conduct which places or may place another person in danger of death or serious bodily injury. Recklessness and danger shall be presumed where a person knowingly points a firearm at or in the direction of another, whether or not the actor believed the firearm to be loaded.

Section 211.3 Terroristic Threats.

A person is guilty of a felony of the third degree if he threatens to commit any crime of violence with purpose to terrorize another or to cause evacuation of a building, place of assembly, or facility of public transportation, or otherwise to cause serious public inconvenience, or in reckless disregard of the risk of causing such terror or inconvenience.[71]

SECTION 3. OTHER OFFENSES AGAINST THE PERSON

(A) ABDUCTION — KIDNAPPING

The social interest in the personal security of the individual member of the community goes far beyond the effort to safeguard his life and to protect him against an ordinary attack. Viewed in the most primitive light, the state must undertake to deal with various other types of personal harm in order to have any adequate check upon violent acts of private retaliation. It must do so, furthermore, if the organized group is to continue to strive for an ever higher level of cultural development, and "a more abundant" life, intellectually and morally, as well as physically.

There was no such crime as abduction known to the English common law, but a statute, passed a few years before Columbus discovered America, created a felony which is the forerunner of all the present statutes on abduction. This early statute was designed primarily to protect young heiresses from designing fortune hunters, although its wording was not so limited. It provided in substance that if any person should take any woman

---

71. Copyright © 1962 by the American Law Institute. Reprinted with the permission of the American Law Institute.

("maid, widow or wife") against her will, unlawfully, and such woman had substance in the form of lands or goods or was the heir apparent of her ancestor, such person should be guilty of felony. It was stated in an introduction to the statute that a woman, so taken, was often thereafter married to or defiled by the misdoer, or to or by another with his consent, but this was not made an element of the original crime itself. This element, however, has been included in some of the modern statutes. Today only a few jurisdictions also have statutes making it a crime for any person to take or entice any unmarried female under a certain age for the purpose of prostitution (or for the purpose of sexual intercourse, concubinage or prostitution). This general field, often involving two or more statutes which may be in different parts of the code, has come to be referred to as *abduction.*

Some statutes prohibit the unlawful taking (perhaps adding enticing or detaining) a child under a specified age from a parent or guardian for the purpose of depriving the parent or guardian of his lawful custody, § 280 Can. Cr. Code (1986). However, today abduction is not frequently found as an offense in most criminal codes. The word "abduction," meaning literally a taking or drawing away, was employed by Blackstone in his definition of kidnaping, and "child stealing" is frequently included as a special form of that offense.

Many of the earlier statutes have been superseded by gender neutral statutes on kidnapping or sexual assault on a child. Other statutes prohibit child stealing and various abuses against children.

(B) ABORTION

Abortion literally means miscarriage. It was a misdemeanor at common law to cause the miscarriage of a woman after the foetus had quickened unless necessary or reasonably believed to be necessary to save her life, and the word "abortion" came to be applied to this offense. Most of the statutes in this country have no requirement that the foetus must have quickened, and do not make actual miscarriage essential to guilt. A few jurisdictions define an offense that is frequently, and more properly, called "attempt to procure an abortion," and consists of the administration of a drug, use of an instrument, or employment of other means with intent to cause a miscarriage not necessary, or reasonably supposed to be necessary, to save the life of the woman. And in at least a dozen states the crime of manslaughter has been extended, by statute, to include certain types of foeticide.

A medicine or means for producing a miscarriage is known as an abortifacient and statutes exist that punish the sale of restricted items to persons not authorized to perform abortions.

Therapeutic abortion is, literally, a miscarriage induced for medical reasons. It was generally understood to refer to one for the purpose of saving the mother's life since justifiable abortion was commonly thus restricted in this country, England and Canada. Abortions are still proper for therapeutic purposes, but are constitutionally available in the early stages of pregnancy based on the choice of the woman. The recent position has been to leave the matter of abortion entirely to the discretion of the woman and her doctor, and some statutes go almost that far. In Roe v. Wade, 410 U.S. 113, 93 S.Ct. 705, 35 L.Ed.2d 147 (1973), the Court held that during the first trimester of pregnancy the abortion decision must be left entirely to the decision of the woman and her physician without interference by the state. After the first stage the state could, if it chose, reasonably regulate abortion procedure to preserve and protect maternal health. Subsequent to viability the state could regulate an abortion to protect the life of the fetus and may even proscribe abortion except where necessary for the preservation of the life or health of the mother. As discussed in *Lawrence v. Texas,* Chapter 1 *supra*, the Court declined to overrule *Roe v. Wade* in Planned Parenthood of Southeastern Pennsylvania v. Casey, 505 U.S. 833, 112 S.Ct. 2791, 120 L.Ed.2d 674 (1992), and indeed the *Casey* plurality in one sense went further, by discarding the trimester approach. The Court recently struck down a state statute prohibiting so-called "late-term" or "partial-birth" abortions. Stenberg v. Carhart, 530 U.S. 914, 120 S.Ct. 2597, 147 L.Ed.2d 743 (2000).

(C) RAPE

Rape, at common law, is unlawful carnal knowledge of a woman without her consent.[72] Any sexual penetration, however slight, is sufficient to complete the crime if the other elements are present.[73]

"By force and against her will" is the phrase often used in the definitions, but as unlawful carnal knowledge of a woman who is insensibly drunk or unconscious at the time is held to be rape unless she had consented in advance, it is obvious that no more is required than that the deed be done without her consent. Until recently sexual intercourse by a man with his lawful wife was not unlawful and hence is not rape even if she did not consent.[74] But while at common law a husband could not rape[75]

---

72. Russell, On Crime (Tuner, 12th ed.) p. 706, Vol. I (1964). American courts often took a more severe attitude in the actual application. See, Susan Estrich, Real Rape (1987).

English law recognizes the offense of rape of a male victim, Criminal Justice and Public Order Act 1994, S. 142(1) & (2).

73. State v. Anderson, 499 So.2d 1252 (La.App.1986); Kackley v. State, 63 Md.App. 532, 493 A.2d 364 (1985).

74. "Rape is an act of sexual intercourse committed by a man with a woman not his wife without her consent and when the woman's resistance has been overcome by force or fear." State v. Clark, 218 Kan. 726–728, 544 P.2d 1372, 1375 (1976).

75. Most states have modified the traditional rule by statute either abrogating the limitation on rape by a spouse, or by modifying it to cover situations where the parties are separated or living apart. Comment, Spousal Exemption to Rape, 65 Marq.L.Rev. 120 (1981).

Note, The Marital Rape Exemption: Evolution to Extinction, 43 Clev. St. L. Rev. 351 (1995).

From a wider social perspective see Raquel Kennedy Bergen, Wife Rape (1996).

Comment, 72 N.C.L.Rev. 261 (1993). *See also*, West Cal. Penal Code § 262 (1995).

Several states have abolished the marital exemption altogether. *See* Nev.Rev.Stat. § 200.373 (1987). The New York "marital exemption" provision was held to violate equal protection. People v. Liberta, 64 N.Y.2d 152, 485 N.Y.S.2d 207, 474 N.E.2d 567 (1984); *see also*, Warren v. State, 255 Ga. 151, 336 S.E.2d 221 (1985).

English, Scots and Australian courts have also eliminated or significantly modified the previous marital exemption. R. v. L., 103 ALR 577 (H.Ct. Aust. 1991); S. v. H.M. Advocate,

his wife he can be guilty of the crime of rape committed upon her. That is, if A should aid B in having sexual intercourse with A's wife without her consent, both A and B would be guilty of rape.

Rape may be committed by fraud, such as under the guise of a medical examination[76] or when the victim lacks capacity to consent.[77]

Statutory rape. It is commonly provided by statute that unlawful carnal knowledge is a crime committed upon a girl under a certain age (called the age of consent) even if she consents. To distinguish between this and the other type of rape, the first is often called "statutory rape," "carnal knowledge of a child" or "sexual abuse of a child" and "common-law rape."[78]

Commonwealth v. Mlinarich

Supreme Court of Pennsylvania, 1988.
518 Pa. 247, 542 A.2d 1335.

■ Nix, Chief Justice.

In the instant appeal we have agreed to consider the Commonwealth's contention that the threats made by an adult guardian to a fourteen year old girl to cause her to be recommitted to a juvenile detention facility supplies the "forcible compulsion" element of the crime of rape. For the reasons that follow, we are constrained to conclude that they do not and that the appellee's convictions of rape and attempted rape may not be permitted to stand.

The facts of the instant matter are no longer open to dispute. Immediately prior to the events which culminated in the rape and attempted rape charges under consideration herein, the complainant was living with her brother Gary and his wife and child in one-half of a double house in Vintondale, Cambria County. The complainant's father and her other siblings resided in the other half of the house; her mother was apparently institutionalized during the time of the relevant occurrences in this matter. When a diamond ring belonging to his wife disappeared, Gary asked the

---

[1989] SLT 4679, 473 (H.Ct. Scot); R. v. R. [1991] 3 W.L.R. 767 (H.L.). *See also*, § 278 Can. Cr. Code; 35 Rape Act 1990 (Ireland).

76. McNair v. State, 108 Nev. 53, 825 P.2d 571 (1992).

77. A person is incapable of appreciating or understanding the nature and consequences of an act of sexual penetration, for the purposes of determining whether that person is "mentally incapable" of consenting to such act under the sexual assault statute, where the person does not have capacity to understand the full range of ordinary and foreseeable social, medical, and practical consequences that the act entails. Jackson v. State, 890 P.2d 587 (Alaska App.1995).

In Nebraska, a statute which provides that sexual penetration of a person who is mentally or physically incapable of resisting is first degree sexual assault is not limited to only those victims who suffer from a mental handicap or deficiency. A person otherwise competent can be sexually assaulted if physically or mentally incapable of resisting. Outrageous and continued sexual activity with young girls that continued into years 16 and 17 where defendant started "grooming" victim at a young age precluded a finding of consent. State v. Collins, 7 Neb.App. 187, 583 N.W.2d 341 (1998).

78. Michael M. v. Superior Court, 450 U.S. 464, 101 S.Ct. 1200, 67 L.Ed.2d 437 (1981).

complainant if she had taken it, which she admitted. She asserted, however, that she had "lost" the ring, which prompted Gary to file criminal charges against her to teach her a lesson, apparently believing that the experience would lead to the recovery of the ring. As a result, the complainant was committed by court order to the custody of the Cambria County Detention Home.

Appellee, Joseph Mlinarich, lived with his wife, mother and sister two doors from the home of the complainant's father. Appellee was sixty-three years old and suffered from emphysema and heart trouble. He was retired but his wife, who was considerably younger, worked as a nurse's aide. Appellee and his wife had known the complainant's family for approximately six years, and the complainant had done housework for appellee's wife. After the complainant was committed to the detention home, appellee's wife suggested that the complainant live with her and appellee. The complainant's father considered this to be an acceptable arrangement, and, after a juvenile hearing, the complainant was released into the custody of appellee's wife pending further proceedings.

On May 28, 1981, the complainant's fourteenth birthday, she and appellee were watching television in the living room. Appellee told her to remove her outer garments and sit on his lap. She complied, and appellee fondled her for approximately four minutes, during which time the victim "told him he shouldn't do that...." RR. 145. Appellee engaged in similar conduct towards the complainant "[a] couple times a week," RR. 147, over her protestations, desisting only if she began to cry. Appellant's wife was always out of the house during these and subsequent episodes.

In mid and late June of 1981, the perverse character of appellee's unwanted attentions escalated. During one incident, which led to a charge of attempted rape, appellee asked the victim to disrobe and, when she did not remove her bra and under garments, he ordered her to undress completely. When she refused, appellee threatened to send her back to the detention home if she did not comply. The complainant obeyed, and appellee removed his clothing. When she insisted that she "did not want to do anything," RR. 154, appellee repeated his threat to "send [her] back." RR. 155. Appellee then proceeded with an unsuccessful attempt at penetration, during which the complainant experienced pain and "scream[ed], holler[ed]" and cried. RR. 157. A similar encounter on June 19, 1981, resulted in a second charge of attempted rape. Appellee, in yet another attempt to achieve penetration, finally succeeded on June 26, 1981.

Appellee also successfully engaged the complainant in oral intercourse on June 29 and July 1, 1981. The same threat was repeated on those occasions. Finally, on July 2, 1981, when appellee "asked [her] to do that again, and [she] wouldn't," RR. 171, appellee engaged in verbal abuse of the victim which convinced her to leave appellee's home and report his reprehensible conduct to her father.

Appellee was subsequently arrested and charged with rape as well as multiple counts of attempted rape, involuntary deviate sexual intercourse, corruption of a minor, indecent exposure, and endangering the welfare of a minor. After a jury trial in the Court of Common Pleas of Cambria County appellee was convicted of all charges. His post-verdict motions were denied with the exception of his challenge to the counts of endangering the welfare of a minor, which were subsequently vacated. Appellee was sentenced to an aggregate term of three to eight years' imprisonment in the county jail.[79]

Appellee took a direct appeal to the Superior Court, which, after considering *en banc* the issues raised, reversed the rape and attempted rape convictions, affirmed the involuntary deviate sexual intercourse and corrupting the morals of a minor convictions, and vacated the sentences imposed on the indecent exposure convictions.[80] Commonwealth v. Mlinarich, 345 Pa.Super. 269, 498 A.2d 395 (1985). Four members of the nine-judge panel dissented and would have affirmed the rape and attempted rape convictions. *Id.* at 288, 498 A.2d at 404 (Spaeth, P.J., dissenting, joined by Wickersham, J.), 345 Pa.Super. at 320, 498 A.2d at 421 (Johnson, J., dissenting); 345 Pa.Super. at 288, 498 A.2d at 404 (Popovitch, J., concurring and dissenting). Both the Commonwealth and appellee responded by filing petitions for allowance of appeal in this Court. After full consideration, appellee's petition was denied; the Commonwealth's petition for allowance of appeal was granted. 512 Pa. 115, 516 A.2d 299 (1986). The prosecution's appeal having been allowed, the matter has been ably briefed and argued and is now ripe for resolution.

I.

Much of the confusion in this matter has resulted from the attempt to focus upon the words "forcible compulsion" out of the context in which it was used by the legislature. When viewed in proper context, the meaning of the phrase at issue becomes clear and the legislative scheme readily apparent. For the reasons that follow, we conclude that the term "forcible compulsion" includes both physical force as well as psychological duress. We are constrained to reject the contention that "forcible compulsion" was intended by the General Assembly, in this context, to be extended to embrace appeals to the intellect or the morals of the victim.

Section 3121 of the Crimes Code has made it a felony of the first degree where:

Rape

A person commits a felony of the first degree when he engages in sexual intercourse with another person not his spouse:

(1) by forcible compulsion;

(2) by threat of forcible compulsion that would prevent resistance by a person of reasonable resolution;

---

79. Appellee was sentenced to consecutive one to three year terms on one count each of rape and involuntary deviate sexual intercourse, and to a one to two year consecutive term on one count of corruption of a minor. Separate one to three year terms on two counts of attempted rape were to be served concurrently with the rape sentence. Sentence was suspended on the remaining convictions. The sentencing court designated the county jail as the place of incarceration in view of appellee's age and health and to permit regular treatment by appellee's personal physician.

80. As a result of the Superior Court's ruling, the term of imprisonment was reduced from the three (3) to eight (8) years imposed by the trial court to a term of two (2) to five (5) years imprisonment. The decision entered this day leaves the latter sentence undisturbed.

(3) who is unconscious; or

(4) who is so mentally deranged or deficient that such person is incapable of consent.

18 Pa.C.S. § 3121.

The General Assembly has also established under section 3123 a felony of the first degree where one engages in involuntary deviate sexual intercourse under these circumstances:

Involuntary deviate sexual intercourse

A person commits a felony of the first degree when he engages in deviate sexual intercourse with another person:

(1) by forcible compulsion;

(2) by threat of forcible compulsion that would prevent resistance by a person of reasonable resolution;

(3) who is unconscious;

(4) who is so mentally deranged or deficient that such person is incapable of consent; or

(5) who is less than 16 years of age.

18 Pa.C.S. § 3123.

Instantly apparent is that the treatment of the two types of conduct were intended to be treated identically with the exception that section 3123 has the addition of subsection (5) which addresses the minority of the victim. However, the complete picture is furnished by section 3122.

Statutory Rape

A person who is 18 years of age or older commits statutory rape, a felony of the second degree, when he engages in sexual intercourse with another person not his spouse who is less than 14 years of age.

18 Pa.C.S. § 3122.[81]

Section 3122 supplies to the scheme of punishment for forcible sexual intercourse that facet which is provided for in involuntary deviate sexual intercourse under subsection (5) of section 3123. It is clear that the

---

81. At common law the age of consent was ten years. Engaging in intercourse with a female child under that age was conclusively presumed to be nonconsensual and against her will. *E.g.,* Commonwealth v. Exler, 243 Pa. 155, 89 A. 968 (1914); Commonwealth v. Stephens, 143 Pa.Super. 394, 17 A.2d 919 (1941); Commonwealth ex rel. Case v. Smith, 134 Pa.Super. 183, 3 A.2d 1007 (1939); 3 Co. Inst. 60. *See generally* R. Perkins, Criminal Law 111 (1957). Under our Penal Code of 1939 the presumptive level was raised to the age of sixteen years. Act of 1939, P.L. 872, § 721, 18 P.S. § 4721. Intercourse with a female child between the ages of 10 and 16 years was presumed nonconsensual unless it could be established that the "woman child" was not of good repute, in which event the defendant would be acquitted of the crime of rape and convicted of fornication. *Id.*; Commonwealth v. Bonomo, 396 Pa. 222, 151 A.2d 441 (1959); Commonwealth v. Kester, 58 Pa.Super. 509 (1914); Commonwealth v. Howe, 35 Pa.Super. 554 (1908). In considering the importance of the minority of the victim to the legislative scheme incorporated in our present Crimes Code it is to be noted that the present act reduced the presumptive age rather than maintain or increase the former age of 16 years for sexual intercourse. Where the sexual contact is deviate sexual contact, the General Assembly has conclusively presumed a lack of consent where the victim is under the age of 16 years.

legislature did consider the impact that should be given the minority of these victims of sexual assaults and specifically provided for it. Thus the arguments raised by the Commonwealth based upon the age of the victim in this appeal can only be considered as provided for under the statutory provisions in question. The courts may not through judicial gloss attempt to either enhance or diminish the consequences the legislature has expressly established for that factor.

The legislative intent to treat assault involving sexual intercourse whether deviate or not in the same fashion except for the minority of the victim is clear. Having made a judgment that deviate sexual intercourse is more offensive when committed upon a minor victim, that concern was addressed by providing that the offense would be a felony of the first degree, without regard to whether submission was compelled or consented to, if the victim was under the age of sixteen. In contrast, a sexual assault under section 3121 does not reflect an intent to accommodate the minority of the victim. Rather, the General Assembly deemed it appropriate to protect this societal interest under section 3122 by defining a felony of the second degree for engaging in sexual intercourse even though consensual if that victim was under the age of fourteen and was not the spouse of the actor at the time.

The General Assembly expressly set forth the purpose it sought to achieve in passing the Crimes Code. 18 Pa.C.S. § 104. It expressed one of its objectives as being "[t]o differentiate on reasonable grounds between serious and minor offenses, and to differentiate among offenders with a view to a just individualization in their treatment." *Id.* In these sections instantly under consideration the legislature has articulated with clarity when the age of the victim is to be relevant and in those instances the extent to which the age should impact upon the seriousness of the act. To give any further consideration to the age of the victim beyond the legislative directive would intrude upon the authority of that body's right to differentiate between the varying degrees of criminal behavior. It would also offend the express direction that "[t]he provisions of this title shall be construed according to the fair import of their terms...." 18 Pa.C.S. § 105.

It is also helpful in bringing into focus the issues raised herein to recognize that the convictions under section 3121 can be sustained only if the provisions of subsection (2) of that section have been established. Under the theory of the Commonwealth's case submission to sexual intercourse was accomplished by the *threat of,* rather than by actual "forcible compulsion." To attempt to argue that "forcible compulsion" can be expanded to include threats would render subsection (2) redundant. We may not assume that the legislature intended any of its statutory language to be mere surplusage. 1 Pa.C.S. § 1922(2); Colodonato v. Consolidated Rail Corporation, 504 Pa. 80, 470 A.2d 475 (1983); Consumers Education and Protective Association v. Nolan, 470 Pa. 372, 368 A.2d 675 (1977); Commonwealth v. Mack Brothers Motor Car Company, 359 Pa. 636, 59 A.2d 923 (1948). It is also of significance to our decision to note that subsection (2) of section 3121 qualifies the "threat" as being one that "would prevent resistance by a person of reasonable resolution." Thus there is a clear legislative expression that the offense requires not only some degree of compulsion but that the compulsion must reach a prescribed level of intensity designed to have an effect upon the will of the victim. An "objective" test has been established to determine whether the pressure generated upon the victim by the threat would be such as to overcome the resolve and prevent further resistance of a person of reasonable resolution. Thus any uniqueness in the emotional makeup of the victim is irrelevant in determining whether the threat possessed the requisite force to satisfy this element of the offense. What is germane is its impact on a person of reasonable resolve.

II.

In this setting we will now undertake to ascertain the legislative intent in its use of the term "forcible compulsion." Webster's Third New International Dictionary gives the following as a primary meaning of the noun "compulsion": "an act of compelling: a driving by force, power, pressure or necessity...." The legislative use of the adjective "forcible" was obviously an effort to describe the particular type of compulsion required. The same source instructs us that the adjective "forcible" may be employed to convey that something is "effected by force used against opposition or resistance...." Unlike the preceding discussion, isolating the words utilized by the legislature to convey the intended thought does not provide the precision that would justify an invocation of the "fair import" approach mandated by the Crimes Code. The term "forcible compulsion" does not describe either the intensity of the force nor does it tell us the source of the opposition or resistance that must be overcome. Fortunately, the impact of the force has been described as one sufficient to overcome the "resistance by a person of reasonable resolution." The meaning of that clause has already been discussed. Thus the only question remaining is the source of the opposition or resistance, *i.e.,* the will or the intellect. A clarification of this issue is best assisted by the historical development of the underlying offense of rape in this Commonwealth.

At common law rape was defined as "carnal knowledge of a woman forcibly and against her will." 4 W. Blackstone, *Commentaries on the Laws of England* 209 (G. Sharswood ed. 1890). Prior to the enactment of our present Crimes Code, Pennsylvania's rape statutes merely codified this common law formulation. *See* Act of June 24, 1939, P.L. 872, § 721; Act of March 31, 1860, P.L. 382. "Force and absence of consent [were] essential elements of the crime of rape, both at common law and under the [1939 Penal Code]." Commonwealth v. Shrodes, 354 Pa. 70, 72, 46 A.2d 483, 484 (1946).

Under the traditional formulation of the crime of rape, the element of lack of consent, as manifested by the extent of the victim's resistance to her assailant's advances, became paramount in rape prosecutions. *See* Estrich, *Rape,* 95 Yale L.J. 1087 (1986). This, of course, focused attention on the actions of the victim rather than those of the defendant. Because of the emphasis on the victim's resistance, compulsion by threat was recognized only to a limited degree.

Because coercion may be effected by threat as well as by physical force, the common law punished intercourse achieved by certain forms of intimidation as rape. This version of the offense, however, was subject to strict construction. At common law and under derivative statutes, the actor's threats were significant chiefly to show that the woman was excused from the duty of "utmost resistance." In line with the traditional focus on victim behavior, courts often defined the kind of threat that might constitute rape in terms of the character and intensity of fear induced in the victim. The standard was demanding. Thus, one court held that a woman must resist to the utmost unless the actor's threats or behavior put her in " 'fear of death or great bodily harm,' a 'fear of great personal injury' or 'serious personal injury,' a fear that 'so overpowers her that she dares not resist,' a 'fear and terror so extreme as to preclude resistance.' " In addition to emphasizing that the woman's fear must encompass harm of extreme gravity, the courts often required that her reaction be reasonable or, in indirect statement of the same idea, that the actor have present capacity to inflict the harm feared. Thus, proof that the actor compelled submission to intercourse by intimidating his victim did not necessarily make him guilty of rape. His threat had to induce in her a not unreasonable and virtually incapacitating fear of imminent harm—usually bodily injury. Otherwise, liability of the male depended upon the manifestation of non-consent by resistance to force.

Model Penal Code § 213.1 Comment 4(b), at 308–309 (Official Draft 1980) (footnotes omitted).

The gravamen of common law rape was the non-volitional participation of the woman in the act, either because of being overpowered by force or being confronted with imminent threat of serious bodily injury or both. In either of these instances the victim's submission was deemed not to be the product of her will and the nonconsensual quality of her participation was established.

There has never been a question that the gravamen of the crimes of rape and the later statutory offense of involuntary deviate sexual intercourse was their non-volitional quality. Indeed, the title of the statutory offense defined under section 3123 (involuntary deviate sexual intercourse) clearly expresses the intention of retaining the non-volitional aspect of the crime. The departure from the common law formulation was to direct the focus upon the conduct of the alleged offender rather than upon the response of the victim. Thus the degree of compulsion created by the conduct was measured against an objective standard rather than attempting to evaluate the resistance of the particular victim in each instance. The degree of resistance, by that objective standard, was modified to remove the requirement that the victim continue the struggle when struggle would be useless and dangerous. This is reflected in our present standard requiring only that the conduct by the actor "would prevent resistance by a person of reasonable resolution."

III.

This historical review of the offense of rape provides no support for the position that there has been any discontent with the essence of that crime being an *involuntary* submission to sexual intercourse. The changes in the language in the formulation set forth under the 1939 Crimes Code and the present statute were merely to accommodate the complaints that had been articulated. The focus of the inquiry has been removed from the victim's actions to a scrutiny of the conduct of the offender. Moreover, the test of the degree of compulsion is now judged on an objective standard as opposed to a subjective one. However, the conclusion that the will was overborne is still critical to a finding that the offense has been committed. We are therefore satisfied that the adjective "forceful" was employed to establish that the assault must be upon the will. Nor does the modification of the former requirement appearing in some of our earlier cases requiring that the victim resist "to the utmost" in any way undercut this conclusion. As previously noted, the compulsion to submit is still the requirement although we no longer require that involuntariness must be demonstrated by useless resistance which would further imperil the victim's safety.

The critical distinction is where the compulsion overwhelms the will of the victim in contrast to a situation where the victim can make a deliberate choice to avoid the encounter even though the alternative may be an undesirable one. Indeed, the victim in this instance apparently found the prospect of being returned to the detention home a repugnant one. Notwithstanding, she was left with a choice and therefore the submission was a result of a deliberate choice and was not an involuntary act. This is not in any way to deny the despicable nature of appellee's conduct or even to suggest that it was not criminal. We are merely constrained to recognize that it does not meet the test of "forcible compulsion" set forth in subsections (1) and (2) of sections 3121 and 3123.[82]

Any lingering question as to the accuracy of our interpretation of the legislative intent in using the term "forcible compulsion" to require a non-volitional submission evaporates in view of the legislative decision to define the new offense set forth under section 3123 as *involuntary* deviate sexual intercourse. Under the rules of statutory construction we are instructed that "[t]he headings prefixed to ... sections ... shall not be considered to control but may be used to aid in the construction thereof." 1 Pa.C.S. § 1924. It would be highly improbable that the General Assembly would employ the term "involuntary" to describe a crime intended to embrace willful submission by the victim. The legislature has clearly indicated its awareness of the distinction between "involuntary" and "voluntary" in its entitling section 3124 as the offense of voluntary deviate sexual intercourse. 18 Pa.C.S. § 3124. In that subsections (1) and (2) of sections 3121 and 3123 are identical, it would be absurd to argue that the latter section's use of the language intended to convey involuntary submission and that the former did not.[83] 1 Pa.C.S. § 1922(1).

---

82. These conclusions compel us, with equal force, to conclude that this conduct would not establish the offense of involuntary sexual deviate intercourse as defined under § 3123(1) and (2). However, the conviction for this offense can stand under § 3123(5) since the victim had not reached the age of 16 and was not the spouse of appellee.

83. Section 3124 provides:

Voluntary deviate sexual intercourse

A person who engages in deviate sexual intercourse under circumstances not covered by section 3123 of this title (related to involuntary deviate sexual intercourse) is guilty of a misdemeanor of the second degree.

18 Pa.C.S. § 3124.

In reaching its conclusion that the charges of rape and attempted rape were not established, the majority of the Superior Court erroneously inferred that the term "forcible compulsion" required physical violence. As we have indicated, the term "forcible compulsion" was employed to convey that the result produced must be non-voluntary rather than to describe the character of force itself. Certainly, psychological coercion can be applied with such intensity that it may overpower the will to resist as effectively as physical force. *See e.g.*, Commonwealth v. Rhodes, 510 Pa. 537, 510 A.2d 1217 (1986). The purpose of the term was to distinguish between assault upon the will and the forcing of the victim to make a choice regardless how repugnant. Certainly difficult choices have a coercive effect but the result is the product of the reason, albeit unpleasant and reluctantly made. The fact cannot be escaped that the victim has made the choice and the act is not involuntary.

Accordingly, for the reasons set forth herein, the order of the Superior Court is affirmed.

■ HUTCHINSON, former J., did not participate in the consideration or decision of this case.

■ FLAHERTY and ZAPPALA, JJ., join in this Opinion in Support of Affirmance.

■ LARSEN, J., files an Opinion in Support of Reversal in which PAPADAKOS, J., joins.

■ MCDERMOTT, J., files an Opinion in Support of Reversal.

OPINION IN SUPPORT OF REVERSAL

■ LARSEN, JUSTICE.

Threatening to have her placed in physical confinement unless she complied with his demands, Joseph Mlinarich, at sixty-three years of age, engaged in sustained, systematic sexual abuse of a fourteen year old child with low mental abilities, despite her continual crying, her pain and her pleading with him to stop. Those members of the Court in support of affirmance find in this neither "forcible compulsion," nor the "threat of forcible compulsion that would prevent resistance by a person of reasonable resolution," 18 Pa.C.S.A. § 3121(1) and (2), and would rule as a matter of law that the child-victim *voluntarily* agreed to have sexual intercourse with her sixty-three year old custodial supervisor of her own free will. Thus, as the Superior Court's decision is affirmed because this Court is equally divided, the injustice and manifest error of that decision is perpetuated. I would reverse.

The victim in this case was placed in a juvenile detention center by her brother "to teach her a lesson" for having taken a ring of his which she lost. She has indeed been "taught a lesson," a cruel and traumatic one about the depravity of some men, and now about the unresponsiveness, unfairness and failure of the criminal "justice" system when it comes to the victims of crimes.

After several frightening days in the detention center, the victim was released on May 26, 1981 in the custody of her neighbors, Mr. and Mrs. Mlinarich, for whom the victim had done housework. Mrs. Mlinarich, a nurse at a local hospital, was never in the house when her husband sexually abused the child. Joseph Mlinarich held the power to deprive this child of her liberty, and he threatened to exercise this power and have her placed back under lock and key in the detention center if she did not comply with his sexual requests or if she told anyone about his sexual activity.

Waiting until the very day on which he could no longer face prosecution for statutory rape (18 Pa.C.S.A. § 3122), namely May 28, 1981, the child's fourteenth birthday, Mlinarich began a six week ordeal of escalating sexual assaults on this victim, which started with compelling her to remove most of her clothing and fondling her, escalated to attempted sexual intercourse and sexual intercourse, and further degenerated to involuntary occasion, including the two attempts at sexual intercourse (which failed only because Mlinarich could not achieve penetration) and deviate sexual intercourse (oral, or "per os"). On *each* occasion, including the two attempts at sexual intercourse (which failed only because Mlinarich could not achieve penetration) and one act of sexual intercourse, the victim refused Mlinarich's requests, but she offered no physical resistance after he threatened to have her physically confined in the detention center. On the three occasions of sexual intercourse and attempts, the victim told Mlinarich she did not want to "do anything" with him, but nevertheless he persisted, despite her pain, her continual crying, her "screaming and hollering" and her pleas to stop. The jury called these acts rape and attempted rape. The Opinion in Support of Affirmance says the jury was wrong because a person of reasonable resolution would have withstood Mlinarich's threats and advances, and would hold that this fourteen year old child voluntarily consented to have sexual intercourse with the sixty-three year old Mlinarich of her own free will and volition.

To the affirming members of this Court, the victim "was left with a choice and therefore the submission was as a result of a deliberate choice and was not an involuntary act." Slip op. at 15. The Opinion in Support of Affirmance acknowledges that hers was a "difficult" choice, but states that the sexual intercourse was "the product of the reason, albeit unpleasant and reluctantly made. The fact cannot be escaped that the victim has made the choice and the act is not involuntary." Slip op. at 17. Has civilization fallen so far, have our values become so distorted and misplaced, as to leave a fourteen year old child without protection when she is forced to make such an awful "choice"? Thus does the criminal "justice" system, once again, place the blame of sexual abuse upon the victim of that abuse. Thus does the criminal "justice" system take a giant step backward towards the universally condemned state of the law where the rape victim was put on trial and blamed for seducing her assailant by "asking for it" and by not putting up enough resistance.

There are certain points on which I agree with the Opinion in Support of Affirmance. The first is that "the term 'forcible compulsion' includes both physical force as well as psychological duress." Slip op. at 1338. Indeed, this was the primary thrust of our recent decision in Commonwealth v. Rhodes, 510 Pa. 537, 510 A.2d 1217 (1986). The second point is that section 3121(1) and (2) remains concerned, as at common law and under the Penal Code of 1939, with conduct of the defendant which overbears the will of the victim. Slip op. at 1341–1342. However, I part company with the application of these two points. Initially, I believe that Mlinarich's threats to deprive this child of her liberty and to have her physically confined constituted threats of *physical force and violence.* Moreover, *if Mlinarich's conduct here did not constitute "psychological duress" which overwhelmed the will of the victim, then I doubt that any conduct could.*

One wonders what is the "prescribed level of intensity designed to have an effect upon the will of the victim," slip op. at 10, that will satisfy the criteria of those who would affirm Superior Court and prove to their satisfaction that the victim's will was overborn and that her participation in sexual intercourse was "non-volitional." If a man threatens to lock a woman (say a utility company meter reader) in his basement, and tells her he will keep her there until she has intercourse with him, and she then complies, would such compulsion reach the "prescribed level of intensity"? If a policeman, or someone posing as a policeman, pulls a female motorist to the side of the road at night and threatens to throw her in jail until morning unless she has intercourse with him, and she complies, would such compulsion satisfy the majority's "prescribed level of intensity"? If a male judge calls a female litigant into his chambers, and tells her he will find her in contempt of court and have her thrown in jail unless she has intercourse with him, and she complies, would such compulsion reach the majority's "prescribed level of intensity"?

I would find, under all of these hypothetical circumstances, sufficient evidence *to allow the jury to decide* whether sexual intercourse was accomplished by "forcible compulsion" or by the "threat of forcible compulsion that would prevent resistance by a person of reasonable resolution." The members of this Court in support of affirmance would, no doubt, remove this decision from the jury's consideration, and would hold as a matter of law that these victims were "left with choices, albeit difficult and unpleasant ones," and since they chose of their own "free will" to engage in sexual intercourse rather than the "unpleasant" alternatives, their choices were "deliberate" and were "the product of reason" and were merely, therefore, consensual acts of intercourse.

In a recent novel by William Styron, "Sophie's Choice," the principle character was forced by a Nazi gestapo officer to make a horrifying choice. She was ordered to either choose one of her two children to remain with her while the other was sent to a German concentration camp possibly to die, or to watch both of them be sent away. By no conceivable stretch of the imagination could it be said that "Sophie's Choice" was a voluntary, consensual choice, although, in the reasoning and language of the majority, she was "left with choices, albeit difficult and unpleasant ones," and her choice was a "deliberate" exercise of her "free will" and the "product of reason."

The Opinion in Support of Affirmance recognizes the pernicious feature of the common law of rape and derivative statutes which focused attention on the conduct of the victim and ended up putting her on trial, which focus resulted in the various "resistance" requirements. Quoting the comments to section 213.1 of the Model Penal Code, that opinion observes:

> At common law and under derivative statutes, the actor's threats were significant chiefly to show that the woman was excused from the duty of "utmost resistance." In line with the traditional focus on victim behavior, courts often defined the kind of threat that might constitute rape in terms of the character and intensity of fear induced in the victim. The standard was demanding.... *In addition to emphasizing that the woman's fear must encompass harm of extreme gravity, the courts often required that her reaction be reasonable or, in indirect statement of the same idea, that the actor have present capacity to inflict the harm feared.* Thus, proof that the actor compelled submission to intercourse by intimidating his victim did not necessarily make him guilty of rape. *His threat had to induce in her a not unreasonable and virtually incapacitating fear of imminent harm*—usually bodily injury.

Slip op. at 1340–1341 (emphasis added).

Purporting to appreciate the injustice in this exaggerated focus on the victim's fear (was it reasonable?) and her resistance (was it enough?), the Opinion in Support of Affirmance indicates in one breath that the modern law has changed all that, stating that the Crimes Code has shifted the focus from the conduct of the victim to the conduct of the actor, stating:

> Thus the degree of compulsion created by the conduct [under the Crimes Code] was *measured against an objective standard rather than attempting to evaluate the resistance of the particular victim in each instance. The degree of resistance, by that objective standard, was modified* to remove the requirement that the victim continue the struggle when struggle would be useless and dangerous. This is reflected in our present standard requiring *only that* the conduct by the actor "*would prevent* resistance by a person of reasonable resolution."

Slip op. at 1341 (emphasis added).

Yet in the next breath, the Opinion in Support of Affirmance turns around and places the focus of attention in a rape prosecution squarely *back on the victim,* only this time that focus is achieved in a more subtle, but no less pernicious, manner. Instead of requiring the victim to resist "to the utmost," she is now required to satisfy the court that she withstood a "prescribed level" of compulsion. Under this formulation, the court is able to overrule the jury's determination and make its own determination as to "whether the pressure generated upon the victim by the threat" was of sufficient intensity "as to overcome the resolve and prevent *further* resistance of a person of reasonable resolution." Slip op. at 1340 (emphasis added). Hence, the Opinion in Support of Affirmance finds this child-victim's resolve lacking, because she should have been able to further resist Mlinarich's sexual commands—it was not enough that the fourteen year old child initially refused her sixty-three year old custodial supervisor, screamed, hollered, and cried continually, begged him to stop and ceased further resistance when he threatened to put her back in the detention center; no, this victim was, to the affirming members of this Court, not a person of reasonable resolution (although she was such a person to the jury).

The Opinion in Support of Affirmance maintains the notion that we are able to devine some *purely objective* standard to measure the "prescribed level of intensity" of the actor's conduct, which will in turn lead us to a *purely objective* measurement of the victim's resolve, which will thus allow us to answer whether the actor's threat of forcible compulsion actually was of sufficient "pressure" to prevent resistance by a person of reasonable resolution. Under such a purely "objective test," the actual resolve of the actual victim is measured against that of the proverbial "Reasonable Man" (or rather, the "reasonable victim") without regard to the actual victim's age, mental abilities, status vis a vis the defendant, or any individual characteristics or circumstances—indeed, *"any uniqueness in the emotional makeup of the victim is irrelevant* in determining whether the threat possessed the requisite force to satisfy this element of the offense." Slip op. at 1340.

This perceived legislative intent to create a purely objective measurement of the victim's resolution is arrived at as follows: 1) the legislature split the crime of rape into four categories of rape, 18 Pa.C.S.A. § 3121(1)–(4), and the crime of statutory rape of a person under the age of fourteen, 18 Pa.C.S.A. § 3122; 2) the legislature created a single crime of involuntary deviate sexual intercourse[84] containing four categories identical to the four rape categories and an additional age-related category where the victim is "less than 16 years of age," 18 Pa.C.S.A. § 3123(1)–(5); 3) since the legislature has concerned itself with age of the victim in these sections, it "would intrude upon the authority of that" body for a court or jury "to give any further consideration to the age of the victim;" 4) and since the legislature has *therefore* precluded consideration of the victim's age in all contexts other than the aforementioned sections of Chapter 31 ("Sexual Offenses"), it has *also* precluded consideration of *any other* subjective factors and renders *"any uniqueness* in the emotional makeup of the victim . . . irrelevant." Slip op. at 1338–1340.

This "logic" requires quantum leaps of faith from step two to step three, and again from step three to step four. More importantly, this stilted reasoning defies real logic and common sense, ignores recent precedent of this Court and ignores explicit language of the legislature contained in other relevant provisions of the Crimes Code.

First, the age of the victim as dealt with in the separate provisions for rape, statutory rape and involuntary deviate sexual intercourse are directed at different evils, *see* Commonwealth v. Walker, 468 Pa. 323, 362 A.2d 227 (1976) and Commonwealth v. Norris, 498 Pa. 308, 446 A.2d 246 (1982), and

---

84. "Deviate sexual intercourse" is defined as "Sexual intercourse per os or per anus between human beings who are not husband and wife, and any form of sexual intercourse with an animal." 18 Pa.C.S.A. § 3101.

the differing treatment of age within these provisions does not preclude a court from taking age into account in other contexts such as the equation of whether sexual intercourse was achieved by forcible compulsion or the threat of forcible compulsion that would prevent resistance by a person of reasonable resolution.

Second, this reasoning and conclusion are *flatly contradicted by other provisions of the Crimes Code.* The Opinion in Support of Affirmance reasons that, with section 3121(2) ("threat of forcible compulsion that would prevent resistance by a person of reasonable resolution") the legislature "modified ... the requirement that the victim continue the struggle when struggle would be useless and dangerous," and in 1972 adopted a purely objective requirement that the victim resist as much as a court determines that a person of reasonable resolution should have resisted without regard to any of the peculiar characteristics of the victim such as age. The legislature, however, amended Chapter 31 of the Crimes Code four years later to provide:

§ 3107.   Resistance not required

The alleged victim need not resist the actor in prosecutions under this chapter: *Provided, however, that nothing in this section shall be construed to prohibit a defendant from introducing evidence that the alleged victim consented* to the conduct in question.

18 Pa.C.S.A. § 3107 (emphasis added).

This section does not merely "modify" the "degree of resistance requirement in sexual assault cases," it makes it clear that *there is no such requirement*—period! By the same token, it maintains the *defense* of consent of an alleged victim.

There is *some* objective measurement in the language "threat of forcible compulsion that would prevent resistance by a person of reasonable resolution," but section 3107 clarifies that this is not a requirement that *the victim* must have put forth some minimum level of actual resistance. This language does ensure that the threat must meet some minimum level of forcible compulsion, so that mere seduction or persuasion will not suffice; however, the language is not meant to require some minimum level of actual resistance or to preclude the jury from considering the emotional makeup of the victim in determining whether the actor used forcible compulsion to overbear her will.

Section 311 of the Crimes Code, 18 Pa.C.S.A. § 311 *Consent,* provides, in relevant part:

(a) General rule.—*The consent of the victim* to conduct charged to constitute an offense or to the result thereof *is a defense if such consent negatives an element of the offense* or precludes the infliction of the harm or evil sought to be prevented by the law defining the offense.

* * *

(c) Ineffective consent.—Unless otherwise provided by this title or by the law defining the offense, *assent does not constitute consent if:*

(1) *it is given by a person who is legally incompetent* to authorize the conduct charged to constitute the offense;

(2) *it is given by a person who by reason of youth, mental disease or defect or intoxication is manifestly unable or known by the actor to be unable to make a reasonable judgment as to the nature or harmfulness of the conduct charged to constitute the offense;*

(3) it is given by a person whose improvident consent is sought to be prevented by the law defining the offense; or

(4) *it is induced by force, duress or deception* of a kind sought to be prevented by the law defining the offense. (emphasis added)

(The official comments to subsection (c) (Purdon's supp. 1987) state that this is in accord with existing law, citing authority wherein it was held that "consent" to intercourse by a woman who is insane is not a defense if the actor knew her to be insane, and that "consent" obtained through fraud or deception is no defense.) As this provision makes clear, *assent* to the defendant's conduct does not constitute *consent* if that assent is procured by "force, duress or deception" or is given by an incompetent or by a person who by reason of her youth, mental condition or intoxication cannot make a reasonable judgment. These are *subjective* factors which the legislature has provided *must* be taken into account. With the interplay of sections 3121(1), 3107 and 311, therefore, we can see the legislative intent and scheme to establish some objective standard regarding a minimum level of forcible compulsion sufficient "to prevent resistance by a person of reasonable resolution;" however, that standard does not make the unique characteristics of the victim "irrelevant," as the Opinion in Support of Affirmance states, for sections 3107 and 311 establish that "resistance" and "assent" and "consent" are to be viewed from the perspective of a person of reasonable resolution in the victim's peculiar situation, considering subjective factors.

Finally, the historical overview of the common law of rape and the extended analysis of the interpretation of section 3121(1) and (2) set forth in the Opinion in Support of Affirmance assumes the posture of examining an issue of "first impression." The interpretation of section 3121(1) and (2) is not, however, an issue of first impression for in Commonwealth v. Rhodes, 510 Pa. 537, 510 A.2d 1217 (1986), this Court dealt at length with precisely this issue. . . .

In *Rhodes,* the twenty year old defendant lured the eight year old victim into an abandoned building near a playground and had sexual intercourse with the victim although she "told him to stop." The Superior Court held inter alia, that there was no evidence of forcible compulsion or threat of forcible compulsion under section 3121(1) or (2) in that case because there was no evidence of physical force or violence. In reversing the Superior Court, we found the evidence sufficient to establish beyond a reasonable doubt that the crime of rape had been committed by forcible compulsion and by threat of forcible compulsion.

Rhodes analyzed at some length the adoption of section 3121 as part of the Pennsylvania Crimes Code of 1972, reviewed its predecessors at common law and under the Penal Code of 1939, compared these with the corresponding provisions of the Model Penal Code, reviewed the common understanding and definitions of the principal terms, and rejected the Superior Court's determination that the "forcible compulsion" or threat thereof needed to overcome a victim's will and prevent resistance under section 3121(1) and (2) meant *only* physical force or violence or threat thereof. 510 Pa. at 543–44, 510 A.2d at 1220–26. We held:

From all of the foregoing, therefore, we hold that "forcible compulsion" as used in section 3121(1) includes not only physical force or violence but also *moral, psychological or intellectual force used to compel a person to engage in sexual intercourse against that person's will.*

Closely related to section 3121(1) is section 3121(2) which applies to the situation where "forcible compulsion" is not actually used but is threatened. That section uses the phrase "by threat of forcible compulsion that would prevent resistance by a person of reasonable resolution." ... By use of the phrase "person of reasonable resolution," *the legislature introduced an objective standard regarding the use of threats* of forcible compulsion to prevent resistance (as opposed to actual application of "forcible compulsion.")

The determination of whether there is sufficient evidence to demonstrate beyond a reasonable doubt that an accused engaged in sexual intercourse by forcible compulsion.... or by the threat of such forcible compulsion that would prevent resistance by a person of reasonable resolution is, of course, *a determination that will be made in each case based upon the totality of the circumstances that have been presented to the fact finder. Significant factors to be weighed in that determination would include the respective ages of the victim and the accused, the respective mental and physical conditions of the victim and the accused, the atmosphere and physical setting in which the incident was alleged to have taken place, the extent to which the accused may have been in a position of authority, domination or custodial control over the victim, and whether the victim was under duress.* This list of possible factors is by no means exclusive. 510 Pa. at 555–56, 510 A.2d at 1226 (emphasis added).

Thus, in *Rhodes* we recognized that threat of forcible compulsion that would prevent resistance by a person of reasonable resolution was an "objective standard" but one applied in light of the circumstances which actually existed, not in the abstract. Chief Justice Nix, author of the Opinion in Support of Affirmance, strongly supported this view when he stated in his concurring opinion in *Rhodes:* "the force necessary to constitute that crime [of rape] has been described as force sufficient to overcome the will of the victim.... *This test has a subjective aspect which takes into account the immaturity of the victim as well as all other factors bearing upon the will of the victim to resist."* 510 Pa. 565, 510 A.2d 1231 (Nix, C.J., concurring; emphasis added).

As former Justice Hutchinson noted in his concurring opinion in *Rhodes,* this objective/subjective standard is not unlike that applied in the context of confessions challenged by a defendant as involuntary. 510 Pa. at 566, 510 A.2d at 1232 (Hutchinson, J., concurring). The task of the fact finder in each case will be essentially the same: based on the totality of the circumstances, including age, did the victim agree to sexual intercourse or did the defendant confess to a crime voluntarily and of her/his own free will? Former Justice Hutchinson stated:

> Certainly, if a grown man can be coerced or compelled to confess to a crime by the questioning of an arresting officer, *see* Culombe v. Connecticut, 367 U.S. 568, 602, 81 S.Ct. 1860, 1879, 6 L.Ed.2d 1037 (1961), an eight year old victim of a sexual assault is no less likely to have had her will forcibly overcome by an adult male in the dirty, bare and unfamiliar place in which this crime took place. *It is, indeed, time for us to apply to the victims of crime the same protective standards that we give criminal defendants.*

Id. (emphasis added).

So too in the instant case, a fourteen year old child who had just spent several days in a detention center and was living under the "care" and supervision of a temporary foster family had her will overborn by the sixty-three year old adult male of this custodial family, who threatened her with loss of liberty when she refused to accede to his perverted requests, as the jury in this case determined. These threats of forcible compulsion, i.e., physical confinement, were threats of physical force *as well as* psychological duress and were clearly sufficient, as the jury determined, to "prevent resistance by a person of reasonable resolution" considering the totality of the circumstances. Those circumstances show that this victim actually resisted, but that her will was overcome by the psychological coercion and duress. This child-victim did not deliberately and voluntarily choose to engage in sexual intercourse with Joseph Mlinarich of her own free will, as the Opinion in Support of Affirmance would hold.

Rhodes is the law of this Commonwealth, and is unquestionably dispositive in this case; *Rhodes* compels the conclusion that Mlinarich engaged in sexual intercourse with the child victim without her consent and by forcible compulsion or its threat. The Opinion in Support of Affirmance does not attempt to distinguish *Rhodes,* nor does it attempt to explain in any way why it is not controlling. Instead, the three members of this Court in support of affirmance simply ignore *Rhodes* and pretend that it does not exist. *Rhodes* does exist, however, and remains the law of this Commonwealth.

For all of the foregoing reasons, I enter this Opinion in Support of Reversal, and I implore the legislature to correct this misreading of its intention and the injustice it will cause. Sadly, it is too late for the legislature to correct the injustice done to this child-victim.

■ PAPADAKOS, J., joins in this Opinion in Support of Reversal.

OPINION IN SUPPORT OF REVERSAL

■ McDERMOTT, JUSTICE.

The crime of rape is accomplished when a person "engages in sexual intercourse with another person not his spouse ... by threat of forcible compulsion that would prevent resistance by a person of reasonable resolution." 18 Pa.C.S. § 3121(2).

The gravamen of rape is to take what would not be given except for "forcible compulsion", or "threats" of forcible compulsion.

That all threats, however compelling in the mind of the actor, leave a choice in the victim is not to be denied. If one yields their bodily integrity for small reason the law may imply their consent. What reasons are small and what sufficient to compel assent are subject to interpretation under the circumstances of the occasion. Not every threat is necessarily such that it presents an illegal choice to persons of reasonable resolution.

The question here is whether the return of a person to confinement qualifies as a threat of forcible compulsion sufficient to overcome reasonable resolve. If it is such, then whether fact finders could find that it in fact overcame reasonable resolution, given the circumstances, remains for them to decide.

Three members of this Court have decided, however, that the question cannot be put, because to their minds the victim had choices that could be exercised, choices that would have obviated the occasion. To my mind, under the circumstances here, that view is an arcane quibble.

A person may well believe that one who secured her release could return her to confinement. Confinement in a detention facility is, among other things, a *punishment* provided by law, which by its very nature is a serious loss in the life of a person: a condition only imposed, as a last resort, by proper judicial officers. Its purposes and unpleasantness were not designed as an adjunct for would-be rapists.

Here the threats were employed to deprive the victim of her freedom; to institutionalize her if she did not yield. The size of the dread imposed upon her is certainly a question for fact finders to determine, and not a question of law that implies there could be no forcible compulsion in such a threat. The question is not whether she could make a choice to yield or be confined, but whether the law should allow such a choice at all. The purpose of law is to narrow the choices that may be offered to compel others in order to gain an end of one's own. Certainly, we should be spared, where possible, choices imposed by others that require surrender or certain punishment. *See* generally Commonwealth v. Plank, 329 Pa.Super. 446, 453, 478 A.2d 872, 876 (1984).

The threat of confinement, that a victim could believe possible, is objectively a threat of forcible compulsion that could, as here, overcome a person's reasonable resolve. It ought not be a choice one may legally impose upon another. The actor believed it sufficient to gain his end and so did the jury. Under any standard we ought not to countenance, as a game of choices, so clear and deliberate a threat.

Commonwealth v. Berkowitz

Supreme Court of Pennsylvania, 1994.
537 Pa. 143, 641 A.2d 1161.

OPINION OF THE COURT

■ CAPPY, JUSTICE.

We granted allocatur in this case to address the question of the precise degree of force necessary to prove the "forcible compulsion" element of the crime of rape. In addition, our disposition of this case further defines the scope of the Rape Shield Law.

The Commonwealth appeals from an order of the Superior Court which overturned the conviction by a jury of Appellee, Robert A. Berkowitz, of one count of rape and one count of indecent assault. The judgment of the Superior Court discharged Appellee as to the charge of rape and reversed and remanded for a new trial on the charge of indecent assault because it found that evidence was improperly excluded under the Rape Shield Law. For the reasons that follow, we affirm the Superior Court's reversal of the conviction for rape, vacate its decision reversing and remanding the charge of indecent assault for a new trial, and reinstate the verdict of the jury as to indecent assault.

The relevant facts of this case are as follows. The complainant, a female college student, left her class, went to her dormitory room where she drank a martini, and then went to a lounge to await her boyfriend. When her boyfriend failed to appear, she went to another dormitory to find a friend, Earl Hassel. She knocked on the door, but received no answer. She tried the doorknob and, finding it unlocked, entered the room and discovered a man sleeping on the bed. The complainant originally believed the man to be Hassel, but it turned out to be Hassel's roommate, Appellee. Appellee asked her to stay for a while and she agreed. He requested a back-rub and she declined. He suggested that she sit on the bed, but she declined and sat on the floor.

Appellee then moved to the floor beside her, lifted up her shirt and bra and massaged her breasts. He then unfastened his pants and unsuccessfully attempted to put his penis in her mouth. They both stood up, and he locked the door. He returned to push her onto the bed, and removed her undergarments from one leg. He then penetrated her vagina with his penis. After withdrawing and ejaculating on her stomach, he stated, "Wow, I guess we just got carried away," to which she responded, "No, we didn't get carried away, you got carried away."

In reviewing the sufficiency of the evidence, this Court must view the evidence in the light most favorable to the Commonwealth as verdict winner, and accept as true all evidence and reasonable inferences that may be reasonably drawn therefrom, upon which, if believed, the jury could have relied in reaching its verdict. Commonwealth v. Davis, 491 Pa. 363, 421 A.2d 179 (1980) If, upon such review, the Court concludes that the jury could not have determined from the evidence adduced that all of the necessary elements of the crime were established, then the evidence will be deemed insufficient to support the verdict. Commonwealth v. Bryant, 524 Pa. 564, 567, 574 A.2d 590, 592 (1990) (citing Commonwealth v. Strong, 522 Pa. 445, 563 A.2d 479 (1989)); Commonwealth v. Hughes, 521 Pa. 423, 430, 555 A.2d 1264, 1267 (1989) (citing Commonwealth v. Harper, 485 Pa. 572, 576–77, 403 A.2d 536, 538–39 (1979)); Commonwealth v. Chambers, 528 Pa. 558, 599 A.2d 630, 633 (1991).

The crime of rape is defined as follows:

§ 3121.   Rape

A person commits a felony of the first degree when he engages in sexual intercourse with another person not one's spouse:

(1) by forcible compulsion;

(2) by threat of forcible compulsion that would prevent resistance by a person of reasonable resolution;

(3) who is unconscious; or

(4) who is so mentally deranged or deficient that such person is incapable of consent.

18 Pa.C.S.A. § 3121. The victim of a rape need not resist. 18 Pa.C.S.A. § 3107. "The force necessary to support a conviction of rape ... need only be such as to establish lack of consent and to induce the [victim] to submit without additional resistance.... The degree of force required to constitute rape is relative and depends on the facts and particular circumstance of the case." Commonwealth v. Rhodes, 510 Pa. 537, 554, 510 A.2d 1217 (1986) (citations omitted.)

In regard to the critical issue of forcible compulsion, the complainant's testimony is devoid of any statement which clearly or adequately describes the use of force or the threat of force against her. In response to defense counsel's question, "Is it possible that [when Appellee lifted your bra and shirt] you took no physical action to discourage him," the complainant replied, "It's possible." When asked, "Is it possible that [Appellee] was not making any physical contact with you ... aside from attempting to untie the knot [in the drawstrings of complainant's sweatpants]," she answered, "It's possible." She testified that "He put me down on the bed. It was kind of like—He didn't throw me on the bed. It's hard to explain. It was kind of like a push but not—I can't explain what I'm trying to say." She concluded that "it wasn't much" in reference to whether she bounced on the bed, and further detailed that their movement to the bed "wasn't slow like a romantic kind of thing, but it wasn't a fast shove either. It was kind of in the middle." She agreed that Appellee's hands were not restraining her in any manner during the actual penetration, and that the weight of his body on top of her was the only force applied. She testified that at no time did Appellee verbally threaten her. The complainant did testify that she sought to leave the room, and said "no" throughout the encounter. As to the complainant's desire to leave the room, the record clearly demonstrates that the door could be unlocked easily from the inside, that she was aware of this fact, but that she never attempted to go to the door or unlock it.

As to the complainant's testimony that she stated "no" throughout the encounter with Appellee, we point out that, while such an allegation of fact would be relevant to the issue of consent, it is not relevant to the issue of force. In Commonwealth v. Mlinarich, 518 Pa. 247, 542 A.2d 1335 (1988) (plurality opinion), this Court sustained the reversal of a defendant's conviction of rape where the alleged victim, a minor, repeatedly stated that she did not want to engage in sexual intercourse, but offered no physical resistance and was compelled to engage in sexual intercourse under threat of being recommitted to a juvenile detention center. The Opinion in Support of Affirmance acknowledged that physical force, a threat of force, or psychological coercion may be sufficient to support the element of "forcible compulsion", if found to be enough to "prevent resistance by a person of reasonable resolution." However, under the facts of *Mlinarich,* neither physical force, the threat of physical force, nor psychological coercion were found to have been proven, and this Court held that the conviction was properly reversed by the Superior Court. Accordingly, the ruling in *Mlinarich* implicitly dictates that where there is a lack of consent, but no showing of either physical force, a threat of physical force, or psychological coercion, the "forcible compulsion" requirement under 18 Pa.C.S. § 3121 is not met.[85]

Moreover, we find it instructive that in defining the related but distinct crime of "indecent assault" under 18 Pa.C.S. § 3126, the Legislature did not employ the phrase "forcible compulsion" but rather chose to define indecent assault as "indecent contact with another ... *without the consent of the other person.*" (Emphasis added.) The phrase "forcible compulsion" is explicitly set forth in the definition of rape under 18 Pa.C.S. § 3121, but the phrase *"without the consent of the other person,"* is conspicuously absent. The choice by the Legislature to define the crime of indecent assault utilizing the phrase "without the consent of the other" and to not so define the crime of rape indicates a legislative intent that the term "forcible compulsion" under 18 Pa.C.S. § 3121, be interpreted as something more than a lack of consent. Moreover, we note that penal statutes must be strictly construed to provide fair warning to the defendant of the nature of the proscribed conduct. 1 Pa.C.S.A. § 1928; 18 Pa.C.S.A. § 104.

Reviewed in light of the above described standard, the complainant's testimony simply fails to establish that the Appellee forcibly compelled her to engage in sexual intercourse as required under 18 Pa.C.S. § 3121. Thus, even if all of the complainant's testimony was believed, the jury, as a matter of law, could not have found Appellee guilty of rape. Accordingly, we hold that the Superior Court did not err in reversing Appellee's conviction of rape.

As to the indecent assault charge, the Superior Court reversed the trial court's judgment of sentence and remanded for a new trial, holding that the trial court had erred by excluding evidence proffered by Appellee. Defense counsel attempted to admit evidence of the jealous nature of the victim's boyfriend. Defense counsel wanted to argue before the jury that the boyfriend was jealous because he believed that the victim had been unfaithful to him, that the victim and her boyfriend had argued over the

---

85. The Opinion in Support of Reversal in *Mlinarich* did not take issue with the implicit holding of the Opinion in Support of Affirmance that something more than a lack of consent is required to prove "forcible compulsion." The Opinion in Support of Reversal acknowledged a general legislative intent to introduce an objective standard regarding the degree of physical force, threat of physical force, or psychological coercion required under 18 Pa.C.S. § 3121, in that it must be sufficient to "prevent resistance by a person of reasonable resolution," but argued that the "peculiar situation" of the victim and other subjective factors should be considered by the court in determining "resistance," "assent," and "consent," and that under the specific circumstances in *Mlinarich* sufficient facts were set forth to allow a finding of the requisite degree of psychological coercion to support the forcible compulsion element of 18 Pa.C.S. § 3121. *Mlinarich,* 518 Pa. at 270, 542 A.2d at 1347.

issue of her alleged infidelity, and that it was the victim's fear of her boyfriend's jealousy which motivated her to accuse Appellee of rape. The trial court allowed defense counsel to offer evidence of frequent fights between the victim and her boyfriend, but excluded any mention that the content or subject matter of these fights involved the victim's alleged infidelity, citing the Rape Shield Law.

The Superior Court held that the trial court had erred in its application of the Rape–Shield Law, finding that because the proffered evidence was *not that the victim had, in fact, been unfaithful,* but rather only that the victim and her boyfriend had argued over *whether or not she had been unfaithful,* the Rape–Shield Law was not seriously implicated. In this Court's view, the Rape Shield Law does not recognize such a distinction.

The Rape–Shield Law provides in pertinent part as follows:

§ 3104.   Evidence of victim's sexual conduct

(a) General rule.—Evidence of specific instances of the alleged victim's past sexual conduct, opinion evidence of the alleged victim's past sexual conduct, and reputation evidence of the alleged victims's past sexual conduct shall not be admissible in prosecutions under this chapter except evidence of the alleged victim's past sexual conduct with the defendant where consent of the alleged victim is at issue and such evidence is otherwise admissible pursuant to the rules of evidence.

18 Pa.C.S. § 3104(a). The purpose of the Rape Shield Law is to prevent a sexual assault trial from degenerating into an attack upon the victim's reputation for chastity. *See* Commonwealth v. Johnson, 536 Pa. 153, 638 A.2d 940 (1994); Commonwealth v. Majorana, 503 Pa. 602, 470 A.2d 80 (1983). The allegation that the victim and her boyfriend had argued over the issue of her infidelity is so closely tied to the issue of the victim's fidelity itself that, for the purposes of the Rape Shield Law, they are one and the same. This is precisely the type of allegation regarding past sexual conduct from which the Rape–Shield Law is specifically designed to protect victims.

Furthermore, the evidence presented at trial was sufficient to support Appellee's conviction of indecent assault. The crime of indecent assault is defined as follows:

§ 3126.   Indecent Assault

A person who has indecent contact with another not his spouse, or causes such other to have indecent contact with him is guilty of indecent assault, a misdemeanor of the second degree, if:

(1) He does so without the consent of the other person;

(2) He knows that the other person suffers from a mental disease or defect which renders him or her incapable of appraising the nature of his or her conduct;

(3) He knows that the other person is unaware that a indecent contact is being committed;

(4) He has substantially impaired the other person's power to appraise or control his or her conduct, by administering or employing without

knowledge of the other drugs, intoxicants or other means for the purpose of preventing resistance; or

(5) The other person is in custody of law or detained in a hospital or other institution and the actor has supervisory or disciplinary authority over him.

18 Pa.C.S. § 3126.

As discussed earlier, the crime of indecent assault does not include the element of "forcible compulsion" as does the crime of rape. The evidence described above is clearly sufficient to support the jury's conviction of indecent assault. "Indecent contact" is defined as "[a]ny touching of the sexual or other intimate parts of the person for the purpose of arousing or gratifying sexual desire, in either person." 18 Pa.C.S. § 3101. Appellee himself testified to the "indecent contact." The victim testified that she repeatedly said "no" throughout the encounter. Viewing that testimony in the light most favorable to the Commonwealth as verdict winner, the jury reasonably could have inferred that the victim did not consent to the indecent contact. Thus, the evidence was sufficient to support the jury's verdict finding Appellee guilty of indecent assault.

We hold that the trial court's application of the Rape–Shield Law, excluding the proffered evidence under the instant facts, was not error, that the evidence was sufficient to support a conviction of indecent assault, and that the Superior Court's reversal of the trial court's order with regard to the indecent assault charge was error.

Accordingly, the order of the Superior Court reversing the rape conviction is affirmed. The order of the Superior Court reversing Appellee's conviction of indecent assault and remanding for a new trial is vacated. The conviction and the trial court's sentence on the indecent assault charge are reinstated.

PENNSYLVANIA CONSOLIDATED STATUTES, TITLE 18, SECTION 8

Except as provided in section 3121 [relating to rape] or 3123 [relating to involuntary deviate sexual intercourse], a person commits a felony of the second degree when that person engages in sexual intercourse or deviate sexual intercourse with a complainant without the complainant's consent.

1995, March 31, P.L. 985, No. 10 (Spec. Sess. No. 1), section 8, effective in 60 days.

CALIFORNIA PENAL CODE

§ 261.   Rape defined

(a) Rape is an act of sexual intercourse accomplished with a person not the spouse of the perpetrator, under any of the following circumstances:

(1) Where a person is incapable, because of a mental disorder or developmental or physical disability, of giving legal consent, and this is known or reasonably should be known to the person committing the act. Notwithstanding the existence of a conservatorship pursuant to the provisions of the Lanterman–Petris–Short Act (Part 1 (commencing with Section 5000) of Division 5 of the Welfare and Institutions Code), the prosecuting attorney shall prove, as an element of the crime, that a mental disorder or developmental or physical disability rendered the alleged victim incapable of giving consent.

(2) Where it is accomplished against a person's will by means of force, violence, duress, menace, or fear of immediate and unlawful bodily injury on the person or another.

(3) Where a person is prevented from resisting by any intoxicating or anesthetic substance, or any controlled substance, and this condition was known, or reasonably should have been known by the accused.

(4) Where a person is at the time unconscious of the nature of the act, and this is known to the accused. As used in this paragraph, "unconscious of the nature of the act" means incapable of resisting because the victim meets one of the following conditions:

(A) Was unconscious or asleep.

(B) Was not aware, knowing, perceiving, or cognizant that the act occurred.

(C) Was not aware, knowing, perceiving, or cognizant of the essential characteristics of the act due to the perpetrator's fraud in fact.

(D) Was not aware, knowing, perceiving, or cognizant of the essential characteristics of the act due to the perpetrator's fraudulent representation that the sexual penetration served a professional purpose when it served no professional purpose.

(5) Where a person submits under the belief that the person committing the act is the victim's spouse, and this belief is induced by any artifice, pretense, or concealment practiced by the accused, with intent to induce the belief.

(6) Where the act is accomplished against the victim's will by threatening to retaliate in the future against the victim or any other person, and there is a reasonable possibility that the perpetrator will execute the threat. As used in this paragraph, "threatening to retaliate" means a threat to kidnap or falsely imprison, or to inflict extreme pain, serious bodily injury, or death.

(7) Where the act is accomplished against the victim's will by threatening to use the authority of a public official to incarcerate, arrest, or deport the victim or another, and the victim has a reasonable belief that the perpetrator is a public official. As used in this paragraph, "public official" means a person employed by a governmental agency who has the authority, as part of that position, to incarcerate, arrest, or deport another. The perpetrator does not actually have to be a public official.

(b) As used in this section, "duress" means a direct or implied threat of force, violence, danger, or retribution sufficient to coerce a reasonable person of ordinary susceptibilities to perform an act which otherwise would not have been performed, or acquiesce in an act to which one otherwise would not have submitted. The total circumstances, including the age of the victim, and his or her relationship to the defendant, are factors to consider in appraising the existence of duress.

(c) As used in this section, "menace" means any threat, declaration, or act which shows an intention to inflict an injury upon another.

People v. Galvarino–Gonzalez

Court of Appeal, Fourth District, Division 3.

2003 WL 21214264, Nonpublished/Noncitable, (Cal. Rules of Court, Rules 976, 977), Cal.App. 4 Dist., May 27, 2003.

■ O'LEARY, J.

Hector Galvarino–Gonzalez (Gonzalez) appeals from his conviction of forcible rape and false imprisonment. He argues the court erred in allowing the "unsworn" testimony of the mentally disabled adult victim. Gonzalez also asserts the forcible rape conviction lacks sufficient evidentiary support and the court erred in failing to give a unanimity instruction. None of these claims has merit.

FACTS

Myrna A. is mentally disabled. Though no expert testified concerning her mental abilities, at the trial her family members described 25–year-old Myrna as childlike and "slow." An emergency room physician who examined her for evidence of sexual trauma thought she appeared to be mentally retarded. Myrna attended special education classes from the age of eight until she was 23, where she learned things "like crossing streets, how to shop, how to behave [.]" At the prosecution's request, the court did not require Myrna to take the standard oath but rather allowed her to testify after simply promising to tell the truth.

Myrna lives with her mother and three younger siblings in their Costa Mesa apartment. On a "very warm" night in November 1999, Myrna left the apartment at around 8:00 p.m. and went to wait for her brothers in a nearby alley where it was cooler. Her mother went to check on her an hour later and could not find her.

Myrna testified that while she was in the alley Gonzalez drove by in a truck with a male friend. She waved at Gonzalez and he stopped. Gonzalez told her to get in the truck. She said "no," but he "hugged" her and lifted her into the truck. He put a seat belt on her and locked the truck door. Gonzalez dropped off his friend and drove Myrna to a local motel. During the drive he touched her arms and chest and told her he wanted to have sexual intercourse with her. She told him, "Don't touch me," about five times and he then stopped touching her.

At the motel, Gonzalez bought Myrna a soda from a machine and then led her into the motel room. He double-locked the door. Once inside the room, he touched Myrna's breasts and vaginal area. He helped her lay down on the bed and touched her "everywhere." She told him to stop, but he did not listen. He tried to pull down her pants but she resisted, holding on to them "tight" with both hands. Despite Myrna's efforts and protestations (she said, "Don't do it," but "he was not listening to me, to directions"), Gonzalez succeeded in pulling off her pants.

Gonzalez unsuccessfully attempted oral copulation and anal intercourse with Myrna, and then raped her. She told him, "Don't do it." It was painful and she cried. When Gonzalez was finished raping Myrna, he went into the bathroom. She hid inside the closet. At some point Myrna left the motel room, but Gonzalez brought her back inside. She stated, "[H]e pushed me in. And he locked the door. He won't let me go out there."

Gonzalez and Myrna watched television together for a while. He told her he wanted to see her again but she said "no." Myrna told him she did not like what had happened. Gonzalez said he liked her and they were "friends." He told her to sit on the bed, but she did not want to. He pushed her onto the bed and "helped" her lay down. He touched her "everywhere" and then raped her again. She testified, "[H]e hurt me a lot." After the second rape, Gonzalez drove Myrna home and gave her $5.75. Her mother found her walking toward their apartment around 1:00 a.m.

A jury convicted Gonzalez of one count of false imprisonment by violence or menace (a lesser included offense in the charged count of kidnapping to commit rape), and one count of forcible rape. The court sentenced Gonzalez to six years in state prison for the forcible rape, and to a two-year prison term, to be served concurrently, for the false imprisonment. . . .

2. *Sufficient evidence supports the forcible rape conviction.*

Forcible rape requires proof beyond a reasonable doubt that the victim's will was overcome by "force, violence, duress, menace, or fear of immediate and unlawful bodily injury." (§ 261, subd. (a)(2)). Gonzalez argues there is insufficient evidence Myrna's will was overcome by any of these means. We disagree. The evidence is sufficient to support the jury's finding Myrna's will was overcome by force.

In People v. Mom (2000) 80 Cal.App.4th 1217, the court described the force required for a forcible rape conviction as follows: "Force, within the meaning of section 261, subdivision (a)(2), is that level of force substantially different from or substantially greater than that necessary to accomplish the rape itself. [Citations.] This is not a heavy burden. For example, in [People v.] Bergschneider [(1989) 211 Cal.App.3d 144, 153], the court found there was sufficient force in the defendant's act of pushing aside the victim's hands. [Citation.]" (People v. Mom, *supra,* 80 Cal.App.4th at pp. 1224–1225.) . . .

The record reveals the difficulty the prosecution faced in this case: Myrna's mental disability made her a poor witness. Her initial hesitancy in reporting the rape, and her inarticulacy in recounting its details, give Gonzalez plenty of room to argue that the evidence against him is weak. He emphasizes all that is *missing* from her testimony: He says Myrna "did not testify she struggled during the intercourse nor did she resist or try to close her legs to prevent the act." Gonzalez further trumpets the fact that he "did not use any weapons, did not hit her, . . . did not tie her up, did not t[h]reaten her, bite her, choke her or hurt her in any way." But the absence of brutality does not equal the absence of force. Myrna's testimony, though simple and at times faltering, provided sufficient evidence Gonzalez used force in raping her.

The factual context in which the rape occurred is significant. Myrna, a "childlike," mentally retarded woman, had been forcibly taken from the alley outside her apartment, touched repeatedly by Gonzalez during the drive to the motel despite her demands he stop, and then locked inside the motel room with Gonzalez. He touched her "everywhere" though she told him to stop. His show of control and domination over her culminated in a physical struggle: Myrna fought his attempt to take off her pants by holding on to them "tight" with both hands, and telling him "Don't do it." He physically overcame her resistance and took off her pants. He tried oral copulation and anal intercourse, and then raped her though she said, "Don't do it." She cried during the rape.

Though Gonzalez's actions were not violent or especially brutal, they nonetheless forced Gonzalez's will on a very unwilling, vulnerable victim. Given Myrna's childlike, compliant nature, neither substantial nor violent force was necessary to overcome her will. We conclude the cumulative effect of Gonzalez's persistent touching, false imprisonment, and domination of Myrna, and his physical overpowering of her in the struggle over her pants, constituted force sufficient for conviction under section 261, subdivision (a)(2).

Rule

Gonzalez argues his act of pulling down Myrna's pants cannot constitute "force" because that act was merely "prepatory" to the sexual intercourse. Moreover, he asserts that because rape cannot be accomplished without the removal of the victim's pants, "the removal of the pants cannot be considered a level of force different from, or in excess of that required for the act" of rape. Neither argument has merit.

Gonzalez's characterization of his forceful removal of Myrna's pants as "prepatory" to the rape is irrelevant. Gonzalez cites no authority holding that "prepatory" acts cannot constitute the force required for forcible rape. In fact, case law suggests otherwise. In People v. Bolander (1994) 23 Cal.App.4th 155, the court held there was sufficient evidence of "force" in the commission of a lewd act on a child where the defendant pulled down the victim's shorts, stopped the victim from pulling them up, bent the victim over, put his hand on the victim's waist and pulled the victim towards him. (*Id.* at p. 159.) Each of these acts specified by the court as constituting "force" was obviously "prepatory" to the lewd act that followed, in the same way Gonzalez's removal of Myrna's pants was "prepatory" to the rape.

We are likewise unpersuaded by Gonzalez's argument that because removal of Myrna's pants was necessary for accomplishing the rape, the struggle over the pants could not constitute "that level of force substantially different from or substantially greater than that necessary to accomplish the rape itself. [Citations.]" (People v. Mom, *supra,* 80 Cal.App.4th at pp. 1224–1225.) In sex offense cases, it is not unusual for the element of force to be supplied by acts "necessary" to accomplishing the sex offense. For example, in People v. Bergschneider, *supra,* 211 Cal.App.3d 144, the 14–year-old victim attempted to resist her stepfather's advances by placing her hands in front of her vagina but "her resistance was physically overcome" by his act of pushing her hands aside. (*Id.* at pp. 150, 153.) The court found the stepfather's "acts in pushing aside [the victim's] hands constituted force greater than that necessary to accomplish the act of intercourse itself." (*Id.* at p. 153.) Of course, pushing aside the victim's hands—and thus removing a barrier to intercourse—was *necessary* to accomplishing the rape. Yet the necessity of that act did not disqualify it from constituting force.

Finally, we note that People v. Kusumoto (1985) 169 Cal.App.3d 487 clarified even further the sort of force required for forcible rape. " '*The force to which reference is made* [in the rape statute] *is not the force inherent in the act of penetration but the force used or threatened to overcome or prevent resistance by the female.*' [Citation.]'' (*Id.* at p. 493.) Myrna's effort to keep her pants on was an act of '' '*resistance by the female.*' '' Gonzalez's act of forcibly removing her pants was indisputably '' '*force used . . . to overcome*' '' that resistance. (*Ibid.*)

We conclude the force Gonzalez used against Myrna, particularly his conduct in physically overcoming her efforts to keep her pants on and prevent the unwanted intercourse, is sufficient force within the meaning of section 261, subdivision (a)(2).

[handwritten: Pure]

People v. Iniguez

Supreme Court of California, in Bank, 1994.
7 Cal.4th 847, 30 Cal.Rptr.2d 258, 872 P.2d 1183.

■ ARABIAN, JUSTICE.

[handwritten: Facts]

Defendant Hector Guillermo Iniguez admitted that on the night before Mercy P.'s wedding, he approached her as she slept on the living room floor, removed her pants, fondled her buttocks, and had sexual intercourse with her. He further conceded that he had met Mercy for the first time that night, and that Mercy did not consent to any sexual contact or intercourse. The Court of Appeal reversed defendant's conviction for rape on the grounds that the evidence of force or fear of immediate and unlawful bodily injury was insufficient. We granted review to determine whether there was sufficient evidence to support the verdict, and to delineate the relationship between evidence of fear and the requirement under Penal Code section 261, subdivision (a)(2), that the sexual intercourse be "accomplished against a person's will," in a case where lack of consent is not disputed. We reverse the Court of Appeal.

I.   FACTS AND PROCEDURAL BACKGROUND

On June 15, 1990, the eve of her wedding, at approximately 8:30 p.m., 22–year-old Mercy P. arrived at the home of Sandra S., a close family friend whom Mercy had known for at least 12 years and considered an aunt. Sandra had sewn Mercy's wedding dress, and was to stand in at the wedding the next day for Mercy's mother who was unable to attend. Mercy was planning to spend the night at her home.

Mercy met defendant, Sandra's fiance, for the first time that evening. Defendant was scheduled to stand in for Mercy's father during the wedding.

Mercy noticed that defendant was somewhat "tipsy" when he arrived. He had consumed a couple of beers and a pint of Southern Comfort before arriving at Sandra's. Mercy, Sandra, and defendant celebrated Mercy's impending wedding by having dinner and drinking some wine. There was no flirtation or any remarks of a sexual nature between defendant and Mercy at any time during the evening.

Around 11:30 p.m., Mercy went to bed in the living room. She slept on top of her sleeping bag. She was wearing pants with an attached skirt, and a shirt. She fell asleep at approximately midnight.

Mercy was awakened between 1:00 and 2:00 a.m. when she heard some movements behind her. She was lying on her stomach, and saw defendant, who was naked, approach her from behind. Without saying anything, defendant pulled down her pants, fondled her buttocks, and inserted his penis inside her. Mercy weighed 105 pounds. Defendant weighed approximately 205 pounds. Mercy "was afraid, so I just laid there." "You didn't try to resist or escape or anything of that nature because of your fear?" "Right." Mercy further explained that she "didn't know how it was at first, and just want[ed] to get on with my wedding plans the next day." Less than a minute later, defendant ejaculated, got off her, and walked back to the bedroom. Mercy had not consented to any sexual contact.

Officer Fragoso, who interviewed Mercy several days after the attack, testified that she told him she had not resisted defendant's sexual assault because, "She said she knew that the man had been drinking. She hadn't met him before; he was a complete stranger to her. When she realized what was going on, she said she panicked, she froze. She was afraid that if she said or did anything, his reaction could be of a violent nature. So she decided just to lay still, wait until it was over with and then get out of the house as quickly as she could and get to her fiancee [sic] and tell him what happened."

Mercy immediately telephoned her fiance Gary and left a message for him. She then telephoned her best friend Pam, who testified that Mercy was so distraught she was barely comprehensible. Mercy asked Pam to pick her up, grabbed her purse and shoes, and ran out of the apartment. Mercy hid in the bushes outside the house for approximately half an hour while waiting for Pam because she was terrified defendant would look for her.

Pam arrived about 30 minutes later, and drove Mercy to Pam's house. Mercy sat on Pam's kitchen floor, her back to the wall, and asked Pam, "Do I look like the word 'rape' [is] written on [my] face?" Mercy wanted to take a shower because she "felt dirty," but was dissuaded by Pam. Pam telephoned Gary, who called the police.

Gary and his best man then drove Mercy to the hospital, where a "rape examination" was performed. Patricia Aiko Lawson, a blood typing and serology expert, testified that there was a large amount of semen present in Mercy's vagina and on the crotch area of her underpants. A deep vaginal swab revealed that many sperm were whole, indicating intercourse had occurred within a few hours prior to the rape examination. ABO blood group, blood type B, which was consistent with defendant's, but not Gary's or Mercy's blood type, was found on the internal and external vaginal swabs and on the underpants.

The following day, Mercy and Gary married. Gary picked up the wedding dress from Sandra while Mercy waited in the car. Neither Sandra nor defendant participated in the wedding.

Defendant was arrested the same day. When asked by the arresting officer if he had had sexual intercourse with Mercy, defendant replied, "I guess I did, yes."

Dr. Charles Nelson, a psychologist, testified as an expert on "rape trauma syndrome." He stated that victims respond in a variety of ways to the trauma of being raped. Some try to flee, and others are paralyzed by fear. This latter response he termed "frozen fright."

Defendant conceded at trial that the sexual intercourse was nonconsensual. Defendant testified that he fondled Mercy without her consent, pulled down her pants, had sexual intercourse, and thereafter ejaculated. However, defense counsel argued that the element of force or fear was absent. "So if he was doing anything, it wasn't force or fear. . . . It's a situation where it looks to him like he can get away with it and a situation where his judgment is flown out the window. . . . He keeps doing it, probably without giving much thought to it, but certainly there is nothing there to indicate using fear ever entered his mind. What he was doing was taking advantage, in a drunken way, of a situation where somebody appeared to be out of it."

The jury was instructed on both rape pursuant to then Penal Code section 261, subdivision (2), and sexual battery.[86] Upon the jury's request for further instruction on the definition of fear of immediate and unlawful bodily injury, the court instructed in relevant part, " '[F]ear' means, a feeling of alarm or disquiet caused by the expectation of danger, pain, disaster or the like." "Verbal threats are not critical to a finding of fear of unlawful injury, threats can be implied from the circumstances or inferred from the assailant's conduct. A victim may entertain a reasonable fear even where the assailant does not threaten by words or deed."

The jury found defendant guilty of rape. He was sentenced to state prison for the midterm of six years.

The Court of Appeal reversed, concluding that there was insufficient evidence that the act of sexual intercourse was accomplished by means of force or fear of immediate and unlawful bodily injury. On the issue of fear, the court stated: "While the [defendant] was admittedly much larger than the small victim, he did nothing to suggest that he intended to injure her. No coarse or sexually suggestive conversation had taken place. Nothing of an abusive or threatening nature had occurred. The victim was sleeping in her aunt's house, in which screams presumably would have raised the aunt and interrupted the intercourse. Although the assailant was a stranger to the victim, she knew nothing about him which would suggest that he was violent. [The] event of intercourse is singularly unusual in terms of its ease of facilitation, causing no struggle, no injury, no abrasions or other marks, and lasting, as the victim testified, 'maybe a minute.' " The court modified the judgment, reducing defendant's conviction of rape under section 261, former subdivision 2, to the offense of sexual battery under section 243.4, subdivision (a), and remanded for resentencing.

---

86. Sexual battery is defined in section 243.4, which at the time of the crime provided in relevant part:

"(a) Any person who touches an intimate part of another person while that person is unlawfully restrained by the accused or an accomplice, and if the touching is against the will of the person touched and is for the purpose of sexual arousal, sexual gratification, or sexual abuse, is guilty of sexual battery. . . .

" . . .

"(f)(2) 'Sexual battery' does not include the crimes defined in Section 261. . . ."

We granted the Attorney General's petition for review.

II. DISCUSSION

The test on appeal for determining if substantial evidence supports a conviction is whether " 'a reasonable trier of fact could have found the prosecution sustained its burden of proving the defendant guilty beyond a reasonable doubt.' " (People v. Johnson (1980) 26 Cal.3d 557, 576, 162 Cal.Rptr. 431, 606 P.2d 738.) In making this determination, we " 'must view the evidence in a light most favorable to respondent and presume in support of the judgment the existence of every fact the trier could reasonably deduce from the evidence.' " (*Ibid.*)

Prior to 1980, section 261, subdivisions 2 and 3 "defined rape as an act of sexual intercourse under circumstances where the person resists, but where 'resistance is overcome by force or violence' or where 'a person is prevented from resisting by threats of great and immediate bodily harm, accompanied by apparent power of execution.... ' " (People v. Barnes (1986) 42 Cal.3d 284, 292, 228 Cal.Rptr. 228, 721 P.2d 110 [*Barnes*]; Stats.1979, ch. 994, § 1, p. 3383.) Under the former law, a person was required to either resist or be prevented from resisting because of threats. (*Barnes, supra,* 42 Cal.3d at p. 295, 228 Cal.Rptr. 228, 721 P.2d 110.)

Section 261 was amended in 1980 to eliminate both the resistance requirement and the requirement that the threat of immediate bodily harm be accompanied by an apparent power to inflict the harm. (*See Barnes, supra,* 42 Cal.3d at p.302, 228 Cal.Rptr.228, 721 P.2d 110; Enrolled Bill Rep., Youth and Adult Correctional Agency, 3d reading analysis of Assem. Bill No. 2899 (1979–1980 Reg. Sess.) July 9, 1980 [Enrolled Bill Rep.].) As the legislative history explains, "threat is eliminated and the victim need only fear harm. The standard for injury is reduced from great and immediate bodily harm to immediate and unlawful bodily injury." (Enrolled Bill Rep., *supra,* at p. 2.)

In discussing the significance of the 1980 amendments in *Barnes,* we noted that "studies have demonstrated that while some women respond to sexual assault with active resistance, others 'freeze,' " and "become helpless from panic and numbing fear." (*Barnes, supra,* 42 Cal.3d at p. 299, 228 Cal.Rptr. 228, 721 P.2d 110.) In response to this information, "For the first time, the Legislature has assigned the decision as to whether a sexual assault should be resisted to the realm of personal choice." (*Id.* at p. 301, 228 Cal.Rptr. 228, 721 P.2d 110.) "By removing resistance as a prerequisite to a rape conviction, the Legislature has brought the law of rape into conformity with other crimes such as robbery, kidnapping and assault, which require force, fear, and nonconsent to convict. In these crimes, the law does not expect falsity from the complainant who alleges their commission and thus demand resistance as a corroboration and predicate to conviction." (*Id.* at p. 302, 228 Cal.Rptr. 228, 721 P.2d 110.)

At the time of the crime in this case, section 261, subdivision (2), provided, "Rape is an act of sexual intercourse accomplished with a person not the spouse of the perpetrator, under any of the following circumstances:.... [¶] (2) Where it is accomplished against a person's will by means of force, violence, or fear of immediate and unlawful bodily injury on the person or another." The deletion of the resistance language from section 261 by the 1980 amendments thus effected a change in the purpose of evidence of fear of immediate and unlawful injury. Prior to 1980, evidence of fear was directly linked to resistance; the prosecution was required to demonstrate that a person's *resistance* had been overcome by force, or that a person was prevented from resisting by threats of great and immediate bodily harm. (*See Barnes, supra,* 42 Cal.3d at p. 297, 228 Cal.Rptr. 228, 721 P.2d 110 ["In our state, it had long been the rule that the resistance required by former section 261, subdivision 2, was only that which would reasonably manifest refusal to consent to the act of sexual intercourse."]; *see* People v. Newlan (1959) 173 Cal.App.2d 579, 581, 343 P.2d 618.) As a result of the amendments, evidence of fear is now directly linked to the overbearing of a victim's will; the prosecution is required to demonstrate that the act of sexual intercourse was accomplished against the person's *will* by means of force, violence, or fear of immediate and unlawful bodily injury.

In *Barnes,* we then addressed the question of the role of force or fear of immediate and unlawful bodily injury in the absence of a resistance requirement. We stated that "[a]lthough resistance is no longer the touchstone of the element of force, the reviewing court still looks to the circumstances of the case, including the presence of verbal or nonverbal threats, or the kind of force that might reasonably induce fear in the mind of the victim, to ascertain sufficiency of the evidence of a conviction under section 261, subdivision (2)." (*Barnes, supra,* 42 Cal.3d at p. 304, 228 Cal.Rptr. 228, 721 P.2d 110.) "Additionally, the complainant's conduct must be measured against the degree of force manifested or in light of whether her fears were genuine and reasonably grounded." (*Ibid.*) "In some circumstances, even a complainant's unreasonable fear of immediate and unlawful bodily injury may suffice to sustain a conviction under section 261, subdivision (2), if the accused knowingly takes advantage of that fear in order to accomplish sexual intercourse." (*Id.* at p. 304, fn. 20, 228 Cal.Rptr. 228, 721 P.2d 110.) "[T]he trier of fact 'should be permitted to measure consent by weighing both the acts of the alleged attacker and the response of the alleged victim, rather than being required to focus on one or the other.'" (*Id.* at p. 304, 228 Cal.Rptr. 228, 721 P.2d 110.) We concluded that "[i]n light of the totality of [the] circumstances" in that case, "a reasonable juror could have found that [the victim's] subsequent compliance with" defendant's insistence on sexual intercourse "was induced either by force, fear, or both, and, in any case, fell short of a consensual act."[87] (*Id.* at p. 305, 228 Cal.Rptr. 228, 721 P.2d 110.)

Thus, the element of fear of immediate and unlawful bodily injury has two components, one subjective and one objective. The subjective component asks whether a victim genuinely entertained a fear of immediate and unlawful bodily injury sufficient to induce her to submit to sexual intercourse against her will. In order to satisfy this component, the extent or

---

87. "Consent" currently is, and was at the time of the crime, defined for purposes of rape prosecutions as "positive cooperation in act or attitude pursuant to an exercise of free will. The person must act freely and voluntarily and have knowledge of the nature of the act or transaction involved." (§ 261.6.)

seriousness of the injury feared is immaterial. (*See* People v. Harris (1951) 108 Cal.App.2d 84, 89, 238 P.2d 158, cited with approval in *Barnes, supra,* 42 Cal.3d at p. 304, 228 Cal.Rptr. 228, 721 P.2d 110 ["[t]he kind of physical force that may induce fear in the mind of a woman is immaterial ... it may consist in the taking of indecent liberties or of embracing and kissing her against her will"].)

In addition, the prosecution must satisfy the objective component, which asks whether the victim's fear was reasonable under the circumstances, or, if unreasonable, whether the perpetrator knew of the victim's subjective fear and took advantage of it. (*See Barnes, supra,* 42 Cal.3d at p. 304, & fn. 20, 228 Cal.Rptr. 228, 721 P.2d 110.) The particular means by which fear is imparted is not an element of rape. (*Cf. In re Michael L.* (1985) 39 Cal.3d 81, 88, 216 Cal.Rptr. 140, 702 P.2d 222 [robbery].)

Applying these principles, we conclude that the evidence that the sexual intercourse was accomplished against Mercy's will by means of fear of immediate and unlawful bodily injury was sufficient to support the verdict in this case. First, there was substantial evidence that Mercy genuinely feared immediate and unlawful bodily injury. Mercy testified that she froze because she was afraid, and the investigating police officer testified that she told him she did not move because she feared defendant would do something violent.

The Court of Appeal stated, however, "But most importantly, the victim was unable to articulate an experience of fear of immediate and unlawful bodily injury." This statement ignores the officer's testimony as to Mercy's state of mind. Moreover, even absent the officer's testimony, the prosecution was not required to elicit from Mercy testimony regarding what precisely she feared. "Fear" may be inferred from the circumstances despite even superficially *contrary* testimony of the victim. (*See* People v. Renteria (1964) 61 Cal.2d 497, 499, 39 Cal.Rptr. 213, 393 P.2d 413 [in robbery prosecution, People not bound by clerk's testimony that he was not in fear, since there was other evidence to support conclusion "that he acted in fear and would not have disgorged the contents of his employer's till except in fear of the harm which might come to him or his employer if he failed to comply with defendant's demands"]; People v. Borra (1932) 123 Cal.App. 482, 484–485, 11 P.2d 403 [not necessary that there be proof of actual fear, as fear may be presumed where there is just cause for it, and thus "In spite of the bravado of the merchant in declaring that he was not much afraid, we are inclined to believe he meant he was not afraid of receiving bodily harm so long as he complied with the demands of the robber"]; *see also* People v. Brew (1991) 2 Cal.App.4th 99, 104, 2 Cal. Rptr.2d 851 [cashier in retail store robbed when defendant, considerably larger than she, with alcohol on his breath, stood close to her, without barrier or counter between them, causing cashier to step back from cash register drawer in fear]; People v. Franklin (1962) 200 Cal.App.2d 797, 798, 19 Cal.Rptr. 645 [although no testimony by checker that she handed over money because she was afraid, evidence sufficient to show that taking was by means of force or fear].)

In addition, immediately after the attack, Mercy was so distraught her friend Pam could barely understand her. Mercy hid in the bushes outside the house waiting for Pam to pick her up because she was terrified defendant would find her; she subsequently asked Pam if the word "rape" was written on her forehead, and had to be dissuaded from bathing prior to going to the hospital. (*See* People v. Bledsoe (1984) 36 Cal.3d 236, 251, 203 Cal.Rptr. 450, 681 P.2d 291.)

Second, there was substantial evidence that Mercy's fear of immediate and unlawful bodily injury was reasonable. The Court of Appeal's statements that defendant "did nothing to suggest that he intended to injure" Mercy, and that "[a]lthough the assailant was a stranger to the victim, she knew nothing about him which would suggest that he was violent" ignores the import of the undisputed facts. Defendant, who weighed twice as much as Mercy, accosted her while she slept in the home of a close friend, thus violating the victim's enhanced level of security and privacy. (Cf. People v. Jackson (1992) 6 Cal.App.4th 1185, 1190, 8 Cal.Rptr.2d 239 ["A person inside a private residence, whether it be their own or that of an acquaintance, feels a sense of privacy and security not felt when outside or in a semipublic structure.... providing the [attacker] with the advantages of shock and surprise which may incapacitate the victim(s)."].)

Defendant, who was naked, then removed Mercy's pants, fondled her buttocks, and inserted his penis into her vagina for approximately one minute, without warning, without her consent, and without a reasonable belief of consent. Any man or woman awakening to find himself or herself in this situation could reasonably react with fear of immediate and unlawful bodily injury. Sudden, unconsented-to groping, disrobing, and ensuing sexual intercourse while one appears to lie sleeping is an appalling and intolerable invasion of one's personal autonomy that, in and of itself, would reasonably cause one to react with fear. (*See* People v. Bermudez (1984) 157 Cal.App.3d 619, 624–625, 203 Cal.Rptr. 728 [evidence of fear sufficient where victim assaulted in her own home by a stranger]; *cf.* § 263 ["The essential guilt of rape consists in the outrage to the person and feelings of the victim of the rape."].)

The Court of Appeal's suggestion that Mercy could have stopped the sexual assault by screaming and thus eliciting Sandra S.'s help, disregards both the Legislature's 1980 elimination of the resistance requirement and our express language in *Barnes* upholding that amendment. (*Barnes, supra,* 42 Cal.3d at p. 302, 228 Cal.Rptr. 228, 721 P.2d 110.) It effectively guarantees an attacker freedom to intimidate his victim and exploit any resulting reasonable fear so long as she neither struggles nor cries out. *See* People v. Bermudez, *supra,* 157 Cal.App.3d at p. 622, 203 Cal.Rptr. 728 [a criminal invasion of sexual privacy does not become a nonrape merely because the victim is too fearful or hesitant to say, "I guess you know I don't want you to do this."]. Moreover, it is sheer speculation that Mercy's assailant would have responded to screams by desisting the attack, and not by causing her further injury or death.

The jury could reasonably have concluded that under the totality of the circumstances, this scenario, instigated and choreographed by defendant, created a situation in which Mercy genuinely and reasonably responded with fear of immediate and unlawful bodily injury, and that such fear allowed him to accomplish sexual intercourse with Mercy against her will.[88]

Jones v. State

Supreme Court of Indiana, 1992.
589 N.E.2d 241.

■ SHEPARD, CHIEF JUSTICE.

After a bench trial, Jerry L. Jones was convicted of rape, a class B felony. Ind.Code § 35–42–4–1 (West Supp.1991). He was sentenced to twenty years in prison. The Court of Appeals affirmed his conviction in a memorandum decision. Jones v. State, 581 N.E.2d 471 (Ind.App.1991) (Barteau, J., dissenting). We grant transfer.

Jones contends that there was insufficient evidence to support his rape conviction. Specifically, he argues there was insufficient evidence to prove he compelled C.L. to have sexual intercourse by force or imminent threat of force. . . .

The evidence most favorable to the verdict follows. The victim, twenty-six year old C.L., lived in the same home with Jones, Jones' wife and child, and C.L.'s foster mother. One night in July 1989 when Jones had been drinking, he came into C.L.'s bedroom and asked her to have sex with him. She said no, and asked him why he did not have intercourse with his wife. He again asked her to have intercourse, and again she refused because it would not be fair to his wife and child. He asked her a third time and C.L. testified she "just let him have it, you know." She was laying on her side, and he turned her over and had sexual intercourse with her. She testified he told her not to tell anyone, particularly not to tell his wife. She said she did not give him permission to have sexual intercourse with her. She did not yell out or cry for help because she was afraid. She testified on cross-examination that she was afraid of Jones, his wife and her own foster mother. She stated it was difficult to tell her foster mother. She testified Jones did not have a weapon, and she did not think to hit him.

Jones was charged with rape pursuant to Indiana Code § 35–42–4–1(1) which states, "A person who knowingly or intentionally has sexual intercourse with a member of the opposite sex when the other person is compelled by force or imminent threat of force commits rape, a Class B felony."[89] The force necessary to sustain a rape conviction need not be physical; it may be constructive or implied from the circumstances. Smith v. State (1986), Ind., 500 N.E.2d 190. "Force or threat of force may be shown even without evidence of the attacker's oral statement of intent or willingness to use a weapon and cause injury, if from the circumstances it

---

88. In light of our disposition on the issue of the sufficiency of the evidence of fear of immediate and unlawful bodily injury, it is unnecessary for us to address the issue of whether the evidence of force was also sufficient to support the verdict.

89. Although there were statements at trial to the effect that C.L. was somewhat mentally deficient, the State did not charge Jones under that portion of the rape statute which prohibits sexual intercourse with a member of the opposite sex when the other person is so mentally disabled or deficient that consent to sexual intercourse cannot be given. Ind.Code § 35–42–4–1(3).

is reasonable to infer the attacker was willing to do so." Lewis v. State (1982), Ind., 440 N.E.2d 1125, 1127, *cert. denied,* 461 U.S. 915, 103 S.Ct. 1895, 77 L.Ed.2d 284 (1983).

We conclude that the evidence recited above does not constitute substantial evidence of probative value showing that Jones had sexual intercourse with C.L. by *force or imminent threat of force.* There was no evidence that Jones used any force or threats to encourage C.L. to engage in sexual intercourse. He asked her three times, and on the third time she "just let him have it." There was no evidence of any previous threats or force against C.L. from which the trier of fact could infer a fear of force or threats on this occasion. The circumstances do not lead to an inference of constructive or implied force. C.L. stated she was afraid to yell for help, but there was no evidence she was afraid because Jones had forced her to do anything or threatened her. There are reasons a person might be afraid to attract attention other than fear of forced activity.

We have upheld rape convictions where the force or threat was conveyed through something other than menacing words. *See, e.g.,* Ives v. State (1981), 275 Ind. 535, 418 N.E.2d 220 (sufficient evidence of force when rape victim told defendant to stop, he pinned her down, she cried and screamed and tried to prevent him from removing her clothing); Jenkins v. State (1978), 267 Ind. 543, 372 N.E.2d 166 (sufficient evidence of force when defendant broke into rape victim's home, demanded her money, and pushed her onto the bed); *Lewis,* 440 N.E.2d 1125 (sufficient evidence of force when rape victim honked horn to attract attention and told defendant to stop; he pointed a pocketknife at her). In all of these cases, however, there was some evidence of force or threats, either actual or implied from the surrounding circumstances. In this case, there is no evidence that Jones forced or threatened force against C.L. to induce her to have sexual intercourse with him. By her own testimony, C.L. "just let him have it" after he had made three requests for sexual intercourse.[90]

Because there is insufficient evidence to prove force or imminent threat of force, we reverse Jones' rape conviction.

■ DEBRULER, GIVAN, DICKSON and KRAHULIK, JJ., concur.

Commonwealth v. Lopez

Supreme Judicial Court of Massachusetts, Hampden, 2001.
433 Mass. 722, 745 N.E.2d 961.

■ SPINA, J.

The defendant, Kenny Lopez, was convicted on two indictments charging rape and one indictment charging indecent assault and battery on a person over the age of fourteen years. We granted his application for direct appellate review. The defendant claims error in the judge's refusal to give a

---

90. *Compare* Indiana Code § 35–42–5–1 (West 1986), the robbery statute, which prohibits a person from knowingly or intentionally taking property from another by using or threatening the use of force *or by putting any person in fear.* The rape statute specifies that force or imminent threat of force is necessary; it does not state that putting a person in fear without force or threats is sufficient for a rape conviction.

mistake of fact instruction to the jury. He asks us to recognize a defendant's honest and reasonable belief as to a complainant's consent as a defense to the crime of rape, and to reverse his convictions and grant him a new trial. Based on the record presented, we decline to do so, and affirm the convictions.

1. *Background.* We summarize facts that the jury could have found. On May 8, 1998, the victim, a seventeen year old girl, was living in a foster home in Springfield. At approximately 3 P.M., she started walking to a restaurant where she had planned to meet her biological mother. On the way, she encountered the defendant. He introduced himself, asked where she was going, and offered to walk with her. The victim met her mother and introduced the defendant as her friend. The defendant said that he lived in the same foster home as the victim and that "they knew each other from school." Sometime later, the defendant left to make a telephone call. When the victim left the restaurant, the defendant was waiting outside and offered to walk her home. She agreed.

The two walked to a park across the street from the victim's foster home and talked for approximately twenty to thirty minutes. The victim's foster sisters were within earshot, and the victim feared that she would be caught violating her foster mother's rules against bringing "a guy near the house." The defendant suggested that they take a walk in the woods nearby. At one point, deep in the woods, the victim said that she wanted to go home. The defendant said, "trust me," and assured her that nothing would happen and that he would not hurt her. The defendant led the victim down a path to a secluded area.

The defendant asked the victim why she was so distant and said that he wanted to start a relationship with her. She said that she did not want to "get into any relationship." The defendant began making sexual innuendos to which the victim did not respond. He grabbed her by her wrist and began kissing her on the lips. She pulled away and said, "No, I don't want to do this." The defendant then told the victim that if she "had sex with him, [she] would love him more." She repeated, "No, I don't want to. I don't want to do this." He raised her shirt and touched her breasts. She immediately pulled her shirt down and pushed him away.

The defendant then pushed the victim against a slate slab, unbuttoned her pants, and pulled them down. Using his legs to pin down her legs, he produced a condom and asked her to put it on him. The victim said, "No." The defendant put the condom on and told the victim that he wanted her to put his penis inside her. She said, "No." He then raped her, and she began to cry. A few minutes later, the victim made a "jerking move" to her left. The defendant became angry, turned her around, pushed her face into the slate, and raped her again. The treating physician described the bruising to the victim's knees as "significant." The physician opined that there had been "excessive force and trauma to the [vaginal] area" based on his observation that there was "a lot of swelling" in her external vaginal area and her hymen had been torn and was "still oozing." The doctor noted that in his experience it was "fairly rare" to see that much swelling and trauma.

The defendant told the victim that she "would get in a lot of trouble" if she said anything. He then grabbed her by the arm, kissed her, and said, "I'll see you later." The victim went home and showered. She told her foster mother, who immediately dialed 911. The victim cried hysterically as she spoke to the 911 operator.

The defendant's version of the encounter was diametrically opposed to that of the victim. He testified that the victim had been a willing and active partner in consensual sexual intercourse. Specifically, the defendant claimed that the victim initiated intimate activity, and never once told him to stop. Additionally, the defendant testified that the victim invited him to a party that evening so that he could meet her friends. The defendant further claimed that when he told her that he would be unable to attend, the victim appeared "mildly upset."

Before the jury retired, defense counsel requested a mistake of fact instruction as to consent. The judge declined to give the instruction, saying that, based "both on the law, as well as on the facts, that instruction is not warranted." Because the defendant's theory at trial was that the victim actually consented and not that the defendant was "confused, misled, or mistaken" as to the victim's willingness to engage in sexual intercourse, the judge concluded that the ultimate question for the jury was simply whether they believed the victim's or the defendant's version of the encounter. The decision not to give the instruction provides the basis for this appeal.[91]

2. *Mistake of fact instruction.* The defendant claims that the judge erred in failing to give his proposed mistake of fact instruction. The defendant, however, was not entitled to this instruction. In Commonwealth v. Ascolillo, 405 Mass. 456, 541 N.E.2d 570 (1989), we held that the defendant was not entitled to a mistake of fact instruction, and declined to adopt a rule that "in order to establish the crime of rape the Commonwealth must prove *in every case* not only that the defendant intended intercourse but also that he did not act pursuant to an honest and reasonable belief that the victim consented" (emphasis added). *Id.* at 463, 541 N.E.2d 570, quoting Commonwealth v. Grant, 391 Mass. 645, 651, 464 N.E.2d 33 (1984). Neither the plain language of our rape statute nor this court's decisions prior to the *Ascolillo* decision warrant a different result.

A fundamental tenet of criminal law is that culpability requires a showing that the prohibited conduct (actus reus) was committed with the concomitant mental state (mens rea) prescribed for the offense. *See, e.g.,* Morissette v. United States, 342 U.S. 246, 250, 72 S.Ct. 240, 96 L.Ed. 288 (1952) ("The contention that an injury can amount to a crime only when inflicted by intention is no provincial or transient notion"). The mistake of fact "defense" is available where the mistake negates the existence of a mental state essential to a material element of the offense. *See* Model Penal Code § 2.04(1)(a) (1985) ("Ignorance or mistake as to a matter of fact or law is a defense if: ... the ignorance or mistake negatives the purpose,

---

91. The defendant proposed the following instruction: "If the Commonwealth has not proved beyond a reasonable doubt that the defendant was not motivated by a reasonable and honest belief that the complaining witness consented to sexual intercourse, you must find the defendant not guilty."

knowledge, belief, recklessness or negligence required to establish a material element of the offense"). In determining whether the defendant's honest and reasonable belief as to the victim's consent would relieve him of culpability, it is necessary to review the required elements of the crime of rape.[92]

At common law, rape was defined as "the carnal knowledge of a woman forcibly and against her will." 4 W. Blackstone, Commentaries 210. *See* Commonwealth v. Chretien, 383 Mass. 123, 127, 417 N.E.2d 1203 (1981). Since 1642, rape has been proscribed by statute in this Commonwealth. *See* Commonwealth v. Burke, 105 Mass. 376, 380 (1870) (citing first rape statute codified at 2 Mass. Col. Rec. 21). While there have been several revisions to this statute, the definition and the required elements of the crime have remained essentially unchanged since its original enactment. The current rape statute, G.L. c. 265, § 22(*b*), provides in pertinent part:

"Whoever has sexual intercourse or unnatural sexual intercourse with a person and compels such person to submit by force and against his will, or compels such person to submit by threat of bodily injury, shall be punished by imprisonment in the state prison for not more than twenty years."

This statute follows the common-law definition of rape, and requires the Commonwealth to prove beyond a reasonable doubt that the defendant committed (1) sexual intercourse (2) by force or threat of force and against the will of the victim. *See* Commonwealth v. Sherry, 386 Mass. 682, 687, 437 N.E.2d 224 (1982) ("The essence of the crime of rape, whether aggravated or unaggravated, is sexual intercourse with another compelled by force and against the victim's will or compelled by threat of bodily injury").

As to the first element, there has been very little disagreement. Sexual intercourse is defined as penetration of the victim, regardless of degree. The second element has proven to be more complicated. We have construed the element, "by force and against his will," as truly encompassing two separate elements each of which must independently be satisfied. *See generally* Commonwealth v. Caracciola, 409 Mass. 648, 653–654, 569 N.E.2d 774 (1991) (stating elements of "force" and "against his will" not superfluous, but instead must be read together). Therefore, the Commonwealth must demonstrate beyond a reasonable doubt that the defendant committed sexual intercourse (1) by means of physical force, Commonwealth v. Sherry, *supra* at 696, 437 N.E.2d 224; nonphysical, constructive force, Commonwealth v. Caracciola, *supra* at 653–655, 569 N.E.2d 774; or

---

92. Thus understood, a mistake of fact is not truly a defense, but rather a means of demonstrating that the prosecution has failed to prove beyond a reasonable doubt the essential elements of the crime. See Keedy, Ignorance and Mistake in the Criminal Law, 22 Harv. L.Rev. 75, 86 n. 4 (1908) ("Such defenses as mistake and alibi, each of which denies one of the elements of guilt, must not in this connection be confounded with defenses of an affirmative character under which the defendant admits the commission of the crime but claims exemption from punishment because of some excusing fact, such as self-defense"). *See also* W.R. LaFave & A.W. Scott, Jr., Substantive Criminal Law § 5.1(a), at 406 (2d ed.1986) ("[i]nstead of speaking of ignorance or mistake of fact, it would be just as easy to note simply that the defendant cannot be convicted when it is shown that he does not have the mental state required by law for commission of that particular offense").

threats of bodily harm, either explicit or implicit, *Commonwealth v. Sherry, supra* ("threats of bodily harm, inferred or expressed"); and (2) at the time of penetration, there was no consent.

Although the Commonwealth must prove lack of consent, the "elements necessary for rape do not require that the defendant intend the intercourse be without consent." Commonwealth v. Grant, 391 Mass. 645, 650, 464 N.E.2d 33 (1984). See Commonwealth v. Cordeiro, 401 Mass. 843, 851 n. 11, 519 N.E.2d 1328 (1988) ("The Commonwealth is not required to prove either that the defendant intended the sexual intercourse be without consent or that he had actual knowledge of the victim's lack of consent"); Commonwealth v. Lefkowitz, 20 Mass.App.Ct. 513, 518, 481 N.E.2d 227 (1985) ("As the Supreme Judicial Court made clear in Commonwealth v. Grant, [*supra* at 649, 464 N.E.2d 33,] the crime of rape ... does not require for conviction proof that the defendant harbored a 'specific intent that the intercourse be without consent' "). Historically, the relevant inquiry has been limited to consent in fact, and no mens rea or knowledge as to the lack of consent has ever been required. *See* Commonwealth v. Burke, *supra* at 377 ("The simple question, expressed in the briefest form, is, Was the [victim] willing or unwilling?"). *See also* Commonwealth v. Lefkowitz, *supra* at 519, 481 N.E.2d 227 ("the prosecution has proved rape if the jury concludes that the intercourse was in fact nonconsensual [that is, effectuated by force or by threat of bodily injury], without any special emphasis on the defendant's state of mind").

A mistake of fact as to consent, therefore, has very little application to our rape statute. Because G.L. c. 265, § 22, does not require proof of a defendant's knowledge of the victim's lack of consent or intent to engage in nonconsensual intercourse as a material element of the offense, a mistake as to that consent cannot, therefore, negate a mental state required for commission of the prohibited conduct. Any perception (reasonable, honest, or otherwise) of the defendant as to the victim's consent is consequently not relevant to a rape prosecution. *See* Cavallaro, Big Mistake: Eroding the Defense of Mistake of Fact About Consent in Rape, 86 J.Crim. L. & Criminology 815, 818 (1996) (mistake of fact instruction is "available as a defense to a particular charge only where the definition of the offense makes a defendant's mental state as to a particular element material").

This is not to say, contrary to the defendant's suggestion, that the absence of any mens rea as to the consent element transforms rape into a strict liability crime. It does not. *See* Commonwealth v. Cordeiro, 401 Mass. 843, 850–851 n. 11, 519 N.E.2d 1328 (1988); Commonwealth v. Grant, *supra* at 649–651, 464 N.E.2d 33. Rape, at common law and pursuant to G.L. c. 265, § 22, is a general intent crime, Commonwealth v. Troy, 405 Mass. 253, 260, 540 N.E.2d 162 (1989), citing Commonwealth v. Grant, *supra* at 649–650, 464 N.E.2d 33, and proof that a defendant intended sexual intercourse by force coupled with proof that the victim did not in fact consent is sufficient to maintain a conviction. *See* Bryden, Redefining Rape, 3 Buff.Crim. L.Rev. 317, 325 (2000) ("At common law, rape was a 'general intent' crime: The requisite intention was merely to perform the sexual act, rather than have nonconsensual intercourse").

Other jurisdictions have held that a mistake of fact instruction is necessary to prevent injustice. New Jersey, for instance, does not require the force necessary for rape to be anything more than what is needed to accomplish penetration. *See* In re M.T.S., 129 N.J. 422, 444, 609 A.2d 1266 (1992) ("physical force in excess of that inherent in the act of sexual penetration is not required for such penetration to be unlawful"). Thus, an instruction as to a defendant's honest and reasonable belief as to consent is available in New Jersey to mitigate the undesirable and unforeseen consequences that may flow from this construction. By contrast, in this Commonwealth, unless the putative victim has been rendered incapable of consent, the prosecution must prove that the defendant compelled the victim's submission by use of physical force; nonphysical, constructive force; or threat of force. *See* Commonwealth v. Caracciola, 409 Mass. 648, 653, 569 N.E.2d 774 (1991). *See also* Commonwealth v. Helfant, 398 Mass. 214, 220–222, 496 N.E.2d 433 (1986) ("Because the victim there was 'so drunk as to be utterly senseless and incapable of consenting,' the court upheld the conviction based on proof only of 'such force as was necessary to effect the [penetration]' ") (citation omitted). Proof of the element of force, therefore, should negate any possible mistake as to consent.[93] *See* Johnson v. State, 204 Ga.App. 369, 419 S.E.2d 96 (1992). *See also* Estrich, Rape, 95 Yale L.J. 1087, 1098–1099 (1986) ("The requirement that sexual intercourse be accompanied by force or threat of force to constitute rape provides a [defendant] with some protection against mistakes as to consent").

We also have concerns that the mistake of fact defense would tend to eviscerate the long-standing rule in this Commonwealth that victims need not use any force to resist an attack. *See* Commonwealth v. Sherry, *supra* at 688, 437 N.E.2d 224, citing Commonwealth v. McDonald, 110 Mass. 405, 406 (1872). A shift in focus from the victim's to the defendant's state of mind might require victims to use physical force in order to communicate an unqualified lack of consent to defeat any honest and reasonable belief as to consent. The mistake of fact defense is incompatible with the evolution of our jurisprudence with respect to the crime of rape.

We are cognizant that our interpretation is not shared by the majority of other jurisdictions. States that recognize a mistake of fact as to consent generally have done so by legislation. Some State statutes expressly require a showing of a defendant's intent as to nonconsent. Alaska, for example, requires proof of a culpable state of mind. "Lack of consent is a 'surrounding circumstance' which under the Revised Code, requires a complementary mental state as well as conduct to constitute a crime." Reynolds v. State,

---

93. In the case before us, the Commonwealth's evidence of force consisted of physical force, as described by the victim and corroborated by medical examination. The trial judge properly instructed as to the amount of force necessary to support a conviction. The judge, in essence, gave the model jury instruction as to the required element of force. We quote the model instruction, in pertinent part:

"The second element the Commonwealth must prove beyond a reasonable doubt is that the natural or unnatural sexual intercourse was accomplished by force or by threat of bodily injury and against the complainant's will. The force needed for rape may, depending on the circumstances, be constructive force, as well as physical force, violence or threat of bodily harm."

664 P.2d 621, 625 (Alaska App.1983). Because no specific mental state is mentioned in Alaska's statute governing sexual assault in the first degree, the State "must prove that the defendant acted 'recklessly' regarding his putative victim's lack of consent." *Id.* So understood, an honest and reasonable mistake as to consent would negate the culpability requirement attached to the element of consent. *See* Colo.Rev.Stat. § 18–3–402(1) (1999) ("Any actor who knowingly inflicts sexual intrusion or sexual penetration on a victim commits sexual assault . . ."); Or.Rev.Stat. §§ 161.115(2) (1999) ("Except as provided in [Or.Rev.Stat. §] 161.105, if a statute defining an offense does not prescribe a culpable mental state, culpability is nonetheless required and is established only if a person acts intentionally, knowingly, recklessly or with criminal negligence"); Tex.Penal Code § 22.021(a)(1)(A)(i) (West Supp.2001) ("A person commits an offense if the person . . . intentionally or knowingly . . . causes the penetration of the anus or female sexual organ of another person by any means, without that person's consent").

The New Jersey statute defines sexual assault (rape) as "any act of sexual penetration engaged in by the defendant without the affirmative and freely-given permission of the victim to the specific act of penetration." In re M.T.S., *supra* at 444, 609 A.2d 1266. A defendant, by claiming that he had permission to engage in sexual intercourse, places his state of mind directly in issue. The jury must then determine "whether the defendant's belief that the alleged victim had freely given affirmative permission was reasonable." *Id.* at 448, 609 A.2d 1266.

The mistake of fact "defense" has been recognized by judicial decision in some States. In 1975, the Supreme Court of California became the first State court to recognize a mistake of fact defense in rape cases. *See* People v. Mayberry, 15 Cal.3d 143, 125 Cal.Rptr. 745, 542 P.2d 1337 (1975) (en banc). Although the court did not make a specific determination that intent was required as to the element of consent, it did conclude that, "[i]f a defendant entertains a reasonable and bona fide belief that a prosecutrix [*sic*] voluntarily consented . . . to engage in sexual intercourse, it is apparent he does not possess the wrongful intent that is a prerequisite under Penal Code section 20 to a conviction of . . . rape by means of force or threat." *Id.* at 153, 125 Cal.Rptr. 745, 542 P.2d 1337. Thus, the intent required is an intent to engage in nonconsensual sexual intercourse, and the State must prove that a defendant intentionally engaged in intercourse and was at least negligent regarding consent.[94]

---

94. Since that time, the Supreme Court of California has retreated from its original holding and steadily has eroded the defense. Today, the defense is available only if there is "substantial evidence of equivocal conduct that would have led a defendant to reasonably and in good faith believe consent existed where it did not." People v. Williams, 4 Cal.4th 354, 362, 14 Cal.Rptr.2d 441, 841 P.2d 961 (1992). Thus, as a threshold matter, the judge, not the jury, must find that the evidence with respect to consent is equivocal. Unless this showing is made, the "jury will be foreclosed from considering evidence that the defendant honestly and reasonably believed that there was consent, even if that jury would have credited such evidence." Cavallaro, *supra* at 852. This requirement, in effect, virtually eliminates the mistake of fact doctrine because "[t]hose defendants who, as a factual matter, would present the strongest mistake case, by testifying to conduct that could be characterized as 'unequivocal,' are precluded by the rule of *Williams* from presenting that defense to the jury." *Id.* at 838. On the other hand, a "defendant who describes an encounter in which the complainant's

In the present case, there was no evidence of equivocal conduct. The complaining witness testified that she had told the defendant, repeatedly and explicitly, that she did not want any form of sexual contact; that she tried to get away from the defendant; and that she cried during the forced intercourse. The defendant testified that the complaining witness was the one to initiate intimate contact; that she participated actively; and

Rule

Other State courts have employed a variety of different constructions in adopting the mistake of fact defense. *See* State v. Smith, 210 Conn. 132, 142, 554 A.2d 713 (1989) ("We arrive at that result, however, not on the basis of our penal code provision relating to a mistake of fact ... but on the ground that whether a complainant should be found to have consented depends upon how her behavior would have been viewed by a reasonable person under the surrounding circumstances"); State v. Koonce, 731 S.W.2d 431, 437 n. 2 (Mo.Ct.App.1987) (construing rape statute to require defendant acted at least recklessly as to consent).

However, the minority of States sharing our view is significant. *See* People v. Witte, 115 Ill.App.3d 20, 26 n. 2, 70 Ill.Dec. 619, 449 N.E.2d 966 (1983) ("whether the defendant intended to commit the offense[s] without the victim's consent is not relevant, the critical question being whether the victim did, in fact, consent. This involves her mental state, not the defendant's"); State v. Christensen, 414 N.W.2d 843, 845–846 (Iowa App. 1987) ("[D]efendant's awareness of a putative sexual abuse victim's lack of consent is not an element of third-degree sexual abuse.... [I]t follows from this premise that a defendant's mistake of fact as to that consent would not negate an element of the offense"); State v. Reed, 479 A.2d 1291, 1296 (Me.1984) ("The legislature, by carefully defining the sex offenses in the criminal code, and by making no reference to a culpable state of mind for rape, clearly indicated that rape compelled by force or threat requires no culpable state of mind"); State v. Ayer, 136 N.H. 191, 195, 612 A.2d 923 (1992); Commonwealth v. Williams, 294 Pa.Super. 93, 100, 439 A.2d 765 (1982) ("The crux of the offense of rape is force and lack of [the] victim's consent.... When one individual uses force or the threat thereof to have sexual relations with a person ... and without the person's consent he has committed the crime of rape"). *See also* People v. Hale, 142 Mich.App. 451, 453, 370 N.W.2d 382 (1985); State v. Elmore, 54 Wash.App. 54, 56, 771 P.2d 1192 (1989); Brown v. State, 59 Wis.2d 200, 213–214, 207 N.W.2d 602 (1973). This case does not persuade us that we should recognize a mistake of fact as to consent as a defense to rape in *all* cases. *See* Commonwealth v. Ascolillo, *supra* at 463, 541 N.E.2d 570. Whether such a defense might, in some circumstances, be appropriate is a difficult question that we may consider on a future case where a defendant's claim of reasonable mistake of fact is at least arguably supported by the evidence. This is not such a case.

Judgments affirmed.

Sexual Offences Act

United Kingdom, Act of Parliament (2003)

Section 1: Rape

---

conduct was admittedly equivocal as to consent essentially concedes that point and is doomed to almost certain conviction." *Id.* at 838–839.

(1) A person (A) commits an offence if—

(a) he intentionally penetrates the vagina, anus or mouth of another person (B) with his penis,

(b) B does not consent to the penetration, and

(c) A does not reasonably believe that B consents.

(2) Whether a belief is reasonable is to be determined having regard to all the circumstances, including any steps A has taken to ascertain whether B consents.

(3) Sections 75 and 76 apply to an offence under this section.

(4) A person guilty of an offence under this section is liable, on conviction on indictment, to imprisonment for life.

* * *

Section 74 "Consent"

For the purposes of this Part, a person consents if he agrees by choice, and has the freedom and capacity to make that choice.

Section 75 Evidential presumptions about consent

(1) If in proceedings for an offence to which this section applies it is proved—

(a) that the defendant did the relevant act,

(b) that any of the circumstances specified in subsection (2) existed, and

(c) that the defendant knew that those circumstances existed,

the complainant is to be taken not to have consented to the relevant act unless sufficient evidence is adduced to raise an issue as to whether he consented, and the defendant is to be taken not to have reasonably believed that the complainant consented unless sufficient evidence is adduced to raise an issue as to whether he reasonably believed it.

(2) The circumstances are that—

(a) any person was, at the time of the relevant act or immediately before it began, using violence against the complainant or causing the complainant to fear that immediate violence would be used against him;

(b) any person was, at the time of the relevant act or immediately before it began, causing the complainant to fear that violence was being used, or that immediate violence would be used, against another person;

(c) the complainant was, and the defendant was not, unlawfully detained at the time of the relevant act;

(d) the complainant was asleep or otherwise unconscious at the time of the relevant act;

(e) because of the complainant's physical disability, the complainant would not have been able at the time of the relevant act to communicate to the defendant whether the complainant consented;

(f) any person had administered to or caused to be taken by the complainant, without the complainant's consent, a substance which, having regard to when it was administered or taken, was capable of causing or enabling the complainant to be stupefied or overpowered at the time of the relevant act.

(3) In subsection (2)(a) and (b), the reference to the time immediately before the relevant act began is, in the case of an act which is one of a continuous series of sexual activities, a reference to the time immediately before the first sexual activity began.

Section 76 Conclusive presumptions about consent

(1) If in proceedings for an offence to which this section applies it is proved that the defendant did the relevant act and that any of the circumstances specified in subsection (2) existed, it is to be conclusively presumed—

(a) that the complainant did not consent to the relevant act, and

(b) that the defendant did not believe that the complainant consented to the relevant act.

(2) The circumstances are that—

(a) the defendant intentionally deceived the complainant as to the nature or purpose of the relevant act;

(b) the defendant intentionally induced the complainant to consent to the relevant act by impersonating a person known personally to the complainant.

* * *

(D) KIDNAPING

Kidnaping is aggravated false imprisonment.

(i) Simple Kidnaping

There is some disagreement among the different jurisdictions as to the exact ingredients needed to place this type of misconduct in the category of the graver crime. At common law kidnaping was defined as the forcible abduction or stealing away of a man, woman or child from his or her own country and sending the person into another. In other words it was false imprisonment aggravated by conveying the victim out of the country. This would be kidnaping anywhere today but the statutes go beyond this, the most common addition being false imprisonment with intent to cause the victim to be imprisoned secretly within the state.[95] Some enactments go further, such as including within the offense the forcible or fraudulent taking of a person from his place of residence without authority of law.[96]

---

95. One type of statute includes imprisonment with intent, (1) to send the victim out of the state, or (2) to confine him secretly within the state. Vandiver v. State, 97 Okl.Cr. 217, 261 P.2d 617 (1953).

96. Where hitchhikers consented to be driven to their homes, but instead, over their objections and under threats of death, were driven to a far distant and remote place where one was raped; they were kidnaped. Matter of Appeal in Maricopa Cty. J.A. No. J–72472 S, 25 Ariz.App. 377, 543 P.2d 806 (1975). There are three elements of "restraint" for purposes of a kidnapping conviction: without consent; without legal authority; and, in a manner that substantially interferes with a victim's liberty. State v. Styers, 177 Ariz. 104, 865 P.2d 765 (1993).

Kidnaping is not an offense in many states if it is only incidental to another crime.[97]

(ii) Kidnaping for Ransom or Injury to Victim

Kidnaping was a misdemeanor at common law, punished by fine, imprisonment and pillory. Under modern statutes it is a felony, and the special form of the offense known as "kidnaping for ransom" is regarded as one of the gravest of crimes, not infrequently made a capital offense. A wrongdoer is guilty of kidnaping for ransom if the person participates in any of the three elements of the offense,—(1) unlawful seizure, (2) secret confinement, or (3) extortion of ransom.[98] This includes one who acts as a go-between to collect the ransom for the actual abductors. Kidnaping for extortion or other gain is also recognized by some statutes.

Many jurisdictions punish kidnapping more severely where the victim is seriously injured or harmed.[99]

(iii) Child Stealing

The "child-stealing" statutes commonly provide a penalty for anyone who shall lead, take, entice or detain a child under a specified age with intent to keep or conceal it from its parent, guardian, or other person having lawful care or control thereof.[100] Great variation is found in the age used for this purpose, such as any child under the age of 12, 14 or 16,—or any minor child. Recently Congress enacted legislation to assist in locating one parent who has stolen a child from the custody of another parent.[101]

(iv) Consent

There has been no kidnaping if the person who was confined or transported freely consented thereto, without being under any legal, physical or mental disability at the time, or being subjected to any coercion, threats or fraud. A child under the age specified in a child-stealing statute is incapable of giving a legally-recognized consent.

(v) The Federal Kidnaping Act (The Lindbergh Law)

It is a federal felony to take a kidnaped person from one state to another or in foreign commerce if the captive was "held for ransom or reward or otherwise," and the punishment may be for any term of years or

---

97. See Apodaca v. People, 712 P.2d 467 (Colo.1985); State v. Fisher, 257 Kan. 65, 891 P.2d 1065 (1995).

98. " ... to be found guilty of first-degree kidnapping a defendant must be shown either to have secretly confined or imprisoned another, *or* to have held another person to service in any way with the intent to extort or obtain money or reward for his release or disposition." State v. Quinlivan, 81 Wn.2d 124, 499 P.2d 1268 (1972).

99. State v. Grissom, 251 Kan. 851, 840 P.2d 1142 (1992).

100. Custodial interference statutes are intended to prohibit parents from abducting their children as a means of settling a custody dispute. Strother v. State, 891 P.2d 214 (Alaska App. 1995).

101. Parental Kidnapping Prevention Act of 1980, 18 U.S.C.A. § 1073, note.

for life. 18 U.S.C. § 1201. Federal law also punishes international parental kidnapping. 18 U.S.C. § 1204.

(E) MAYHEM

Mayhem, according to the English common law, is maliciously depriving another of the use of such of his members as may render him less able, in fighting, either to defend himself or to annoy his adversary. To cut off a hand or a finger or to put out an eye or knock out a front tooth were all mayhems at common law, if done maliciously, because they rendered the victim less efficient as a fighting man (for the king's army). But to cut off an ear or to slit the nose was not mayhem because it merely disfigured the person. This distinction whereby the penalty for maiming was much more severe than for disfiguring (a mere battery), may have seemed quite appropriate in very ancient times but was not viewed with approval in the seventeenth century when malefactors intentionally slit the nose of a member of Parliament. A statute in 1670, prompted by the facts of that atrocity, provided the death penalty for maliciously intentional disfigurement,—and since such an injury should not be punished more severely than that of the other type the same penalty was provided for mayhem if intentionally perpetrated. This statutory offense, known as mayhem, did not displace the common-law crime of that name but was in addition to it. Thus the definition in terms of English law of the time was required to be in some such form as this: Mayhem is maliciously maiming or maliciously and intentionally disfiguring another,—with the explanation that the penalty for maiming was more severe if it was intentional as well as malicious than if malicious but not actually intentional (such as a wrongful act done in wanton and wilful disregard of the likelihood of maiming but without a specific intent to maim).

This distinction between the two types of injury, traceable to historical accident, has not met with general approval here. Our statutes commonly include both but whereas some follow the common law otherwise and say only "maliciously," others adopt the addition of the English statute and require the injury to be inflicted maliciously and intentionally. Hence mayhem under American statutes is maliciously maiming or disfiguring another, except that in a number of states a specific intent to maim or disfigure is required.

The Model Penal Code does not provide for the offense of mayhem and several states have replaced the offense with aggravated assault statutes. Some jurisdictions that have revised their criminal codes using the Model Penal Code have elected to keep a mayhem statute.

(F) DUELING

Dueling is fighting by previous agreement with deadly weapons. It is usually under a so-called "code of honor" which establishes rules for the conduct of the fight as well as for the preliminary arrangements.

The social interest in the life and security of the individual member of the community is too great to permit the settlement of private disputes and grudges by deadly combat. Hence the law does not permit persons to consent to such an encounter, and no justification or excuse can be established by the fact that such consent was given. Furthermore, since the combat is deliberately arranged the law does not even take notice of whatever provocation there may have been, and which might have been recognized as a mitigating circumstance had the conflict flared up in the heat of passion on the spur of the moment. Because of these facts, one who kills another in a duel is guilty of murder. And since the duel probably would not have been fought if no persons had been found willing to serve as seconds, the seconds are held to have aided and abetted in the killing and hence are also guilty of the murder. This applies to the second for the deceased as well as to the second for the victor. If the duel does not result in death, the participants are guilty of an attempt to commit murder at common law (and usually of some aggravated assault under modern statutes,—such as assault with intent to murder, or assault with a deadly weapon).

The duel is itself a common-law misdemeanor; and parties may be guilty of a misdemeanor even if the duel does not actually take place. One is guilty who challenges another to fight a duel, whether the challenge is accepted or not. One is guilty who is knowingly the bearer of such a challenge, whether it is accepted or not. One is guilty who intentionally provokes such a challenge. In this case, while guilt does not depend upon the actual fighting of the duel, it is necessary that the intentional provocation actually result in the issuance of a challenge.

Dueling does not present a present-day problem and has been omitted from most of the new penal codes. Some states have a form of statute prohibiting challenges to fight.[102]

---

102.   Wilmeth v. State, 96 Nev. 403, 610 P.2d 735 (1980).

CHAPTER 3

OFFENSES AGAINST THE HABITATION AND OTHER PROTECTED ENTITIES

SECTION 1. BURGLARY

Woods v. State

Supreme Court of Mississippi, Division A, 1939.
186 Miss. 463, 191 So. 283.

■ GRIFFITH, J., delivered the opinion of the court.

Appellant was indicted and convicted under the charge of the burglary of a dwelling house. The undisputed proof showed that the house in question, although intended for a dwelling house, had been only recently erected and had not yet been occupied as a dwelling. It was vacant.

Appellant relies on Haynes v. State, 180 Miss. 291, 177 So. 360, wherein the court held that a house from which the occupants had permanently removed on the day before the night of the burglary was not a dwelling at the time of the commission of the alleged crime; and that proof of the burglary of such a house would not sustain the conviction under an indictment charging the burglary of a dwelling. Appellant submits that if a house from which the occupants have permanently removed is not a dwelling house within the statutes on burglary, then, upon the same reasoning, a house into which no dwellers have ever yet moved is not a dwelling house; and in this contention appellant is clearly correct....

Reversed and remanded.[1]

---

1. The room of a transient guest at an inn should be laid as the dwelling house of the innkeeper, not of the guest, whether the innkeeper lives in the inn or elsewhere. Rodgers v. People, 86 N.Y. 360 (1881). *Cf.* Russell v. State, 36 Ala.App. 19, 52 So.2d 230 (1951), *certiorari denied* 255 Ala. 581, 52 So.2d 237.

However, a dwelling house has been defined as a "place where a man lives with his family. Thus, it is possible for a mobile home to be a dwelling house." (citations omitted.) People v. Winhoven, 65 Mich.App. 522, 526, 237 N.W.2d 540, 542 (1975).

Although the dweller had not lived in the building for a year and a half, during which time it had been used for storage, as he still regarded it as his home it had not lost its character as a "dwelling." Hamilton v. State, 354 So.2d 27 (Ala.Crim.App.1977).

Apartment of a recently deceased tenant who had been murdered and her body put in a closet was still a dwelling. State v. Edwards, 589 N.W.2d 807 (Minn.App.1999).

Entry of an attached garage constituted entry into an "inhabited dwelling". People v. Moreno, 158 Cal.App.3d 109, 204 Cal.Rptr. 17 (1984); accord Gaunt v. State, 457 N.E.2d 211 (Ind.1983); State v. Otto, 529 N.W.2d 193 (S.D.1995).

State v. Neff

Supreme Court of Appeals of West Virginia, 1940.
122 W.Va. 549, 11 S.E.2d 171.

■ HATCHER, JUDGE. The two Neffs were charged with burglariously breaking and entering in the night time a chicken house, an outhouse adjoining the dwelling house of J.A. Trent and belonging to him, and stealing from the chicken house his chickens valued at $30.00. The Neffs were found guilty of burglary and sentenced to the penitentiary.

The evidence is incomplete as to the size of the alleged chicken house and its proximity to the Trent dwelling. The former is described as a "small house", having a floor space of four and a half by five feet; but neither its height, nor evidence from which the height might be estimated, is shown. It had a hinged door fastened by a chain drawn through holes bored in the door and "the building face", respectively. The dwelling "sets back about" seventy-five feet from a public road; the chicken house is "out across" the road somewhere, but its distance from the road or the dwelling is not shown.

At common law burglary was "an offense against the habitation not against the property." But burglary could be committed on uninhabited structures, provided they were "parcel of" and within the same common fence as the mansion-house, though not contiguous to it. The Virginia Assembly, Acts 1847–8, Ch. IV, Sec. 13, modified the common law by restricting the burglary of a building other than the dwelling house to "an outhouse adjoining thereto and occupied therewith." That restriction remained in the Virginia statute until this state was formed and then we adopted it. West Virginia Acts, 1882, Ch. 148, Sec. 11, substituted the alternative "or" for the connective "and", so that the phrase read "outhouse adjoining thereto (the dwelling-house) or occupied therewith." There has been no further change.

All the words in the phrase are plain and well understood. No reason appears for not holding that they are used in their ordinary sense. We held in State v. Crites, 110 W.Va. 36, 156 S.E. 847, that the word "outhouse" was so used, and, in effect, that it meant a building constructed at least large enough for an adult to enter erect and to turn around comfortably within. The State, failing to show the height of the structure in question, did not prove it to be a house at all. But if we should concede that because the Trents called it a house, it should be taken as such, the State has still failed to make a case because the so-called house, being across the public road one hundred feet or more from the dwelling house, can not, under any fair construction, be said to adjoin it. Since the statute limits the burglary

---

An unsold mobile home on a sales lot was "designed" to be occupied and was a dwelling. The definition is expanded over the common law. State v. Bennett, 565 So.2d 803 (Fla.App. 1990).

Fishing boat designed to sleep crew members was a "dwelling" under burglary statute. Shoemaker v. State, 716 P.2d 391 (Alaska App.1986).

Entry by an inmate into the cellblock of other inmates to engage in riot was burglary. The block satisfied the definition of "occupied structure" defining the offense of burglary. State v. Gollehon, 864 P.2d 1257 (Mont.1993).

of an outhouse not occupied in connection with the dwelling house, to one "adjoining" it, such contiguity must be proven. We are not advised of any decision on a statute like ours. But the statute, as amended in 1882, differs from the common law more in words than substance. And under the common law an outhouse across a public road from its owner's dwelling house is held to be not parcel thereof and not the subject of burglary.

The judgment is reversed, the verdict set aside and a new trial awarded defendants.

Reversed and remanded.

State v. Mann

Court of Appeals of Arizona, Division 2, 1981.
129 Ariz. 24, 628 P.2d 61.

OPINION

■ HOWARD, JUDGE. Is the Salvation Army collection box a "structure" within the meaning of A.R.S. Sec. 13–1506(A) and Sec. 13–1501(8)? We hold that it is and affirm appellants' conviction of burglary, third-degree.

Appellants were caught by the police while they were removing used clothing from a Salvation Army collection box. The box in question was located on a corner of the intersection of Ft. Lowell Road and Dodge Boulevard in Tucson. It was approximately six feet high and four feet deep by four feet wide, made of tin metal. About four feet from the bottom of one side it had an unlockable chute-like door for depositing items. The items in the box were regularly collected about every 36 hours. The Salvation Army removed the articles through a locked trap door located near the bottom of another side. Mary Lou Mann removed the clothing by reaching into the unlocked chute.

A.R.S. Sec. 13–1506 provides in part:

"A. A person commits burglary in the third degree by entering or remaining unlawfully in a non-residential structure ... with the intent to commit any theft ... therein."

The word structure is defined in A.R.S. Sec. 13–1501(8):

" 'Structure' means any building, object, vehicle, railroad car or place with sides and a floor, separately securable from any other structure attached to it and used for lodging, business, transportation, recreation or storage."

Appellants contend that the trial court erred when it instructed the jury that the Salvation Army collection box was a nonresidential structure as a matter of law. They claim that this was a question of fact for the jury. We do not agree. The box had sides and a floor and it was used for storage. There were no facts in dispute and its nature was a question of law for the court. The trial court did not err in its instruction.

Appellants next contend the trial court erred in refusing to give their Instruction No. 14 which stated that abandoned property cannot be the subject of a theft. Appellants' contention that the clothing inside the Salvation Army collection box was abandoned, however, is without merit.

The property was not abandoned but was donated to the Salvation Army and in its possession.

Appellants also argue that the trial court erred in the giving of an aiding and abetting instruction to the jury. We note, first of all, that no objection was ever made at trial to the giving of this instruction. In any event, if there were any error, it was harmless beyond a reasonable doubt since appellants were caught "red-handed" and when they took the witness stand at trial, they admitted they took the clothing from the box in order to sell it at a swap meet.

Affirmed.[2]

Davis v. Commonwealth

Supreme Court of Appeals of Virginia, 1922.
132 Va. 521, 110 S.E. 356.

■ KELLY, P., delivered the opinion of the court.

The defendant, Annie Davis, under indictment for burglary was convicted and sentenced to confinement in the penitentiary for a term of five years.

The indictment charged that in the nighttime she broke and entered the dwelling house of one E.P. Fowlkes, and "feloniously and burglariously" stole and carried away therefrom the sum of $412.50 belonging to one Dolly Wingfield.

The case is before us for review, and the sole assignment of error is that the court refused to set aside the verdict as being contrary to the law and the evidence.

It is insisted that the evidence failed to show that the alleged theft was committed in a house owned by E.P. Fowlkes, and also failed to show that the defendant was the thief. As to this contention we express no opinion, because the judgment will have to be reversed and a new trial awarded upon another ground, namely, that there was no "breaking" within the meaning of the familiar definition of burglary.

The evidence tends to show that, as contended by the Commonwealth, the theft was committed in a house owned by Fowlkes, and in a room therein occupied and controlled by Dolly Wingfield, the owner of the stolen money. The testimony of Fowlkes and Dolly Wingfield conclusively shows that the defendant was and long had been their intimate associate and friend, and that with their consent and encouragement she carried a key to the house, was "just the same as at home there," was "over there day and night, and anything she wanted there she came and got it." She was not in any sense a servant or employee of the owners, nor a care keeper or custodian of the property. Her relationship was that of a companion and friend, her right to enter the premises up to the time of the alleged theft

---

2. Defendant committed burglary when he opened the hood of a car, reached inside and removed a battery. People v. Dail, 139 Ill.App.3d 941, 94 Ill.Dec. 460, 488 N.E.2d 286 (1985).

Removal of mail from a post office box was an unauthorized entry of a "structure" where the boxes opened into a mail sorting area. State v. Gregory, 117 N.M. 104, 869 P.2d 292 (N.M.App. 1993).

being as free and unlimited as that of Dolly Wingfield herself. She came
and went at will; she ate and slept there whenever she pleased; and, in
short, as expressed by Fowlkes she was "treated the same as homefolks."

Breaking, as an element of the crime of burglary, may be either actual
or constructive. There is a constructive breaking when an entrance has
been obtained by threat of violence, by fraud, or by conspiracy. The
entrance to the premises in the instant case was not obtained by either of
these means, and cannot be classed as a constructive breaking.[3]

Actual breaking involves the application of some force, slight though it
may be, whereby the entrance is effected. Merely pushing open a door,
turning the key, lifting the latch, or resort to other slight physical force is
sufficient to constitute this element of the crime.[4] See the authorities cited,
supra. But a breaking, either actual or constructive, to support a conviction
of burglary, must have resulted in an entrance contrary to the will of the
occupier of the house.

But in the instant case the right of the defendant to enter the premises
as freely and unrestrictedly as either Fowlkes or Dolly Wingfield is undisputed, and it follows that she did not "break" and enter the house, and
therefore cannot be convicted of the alleged burglary.

The following language of Judge Moncure, who delivered the opinion of
the court in Clarke's Case, *supra*, may well be applied here:

"We have seen no case, and think there has been none, in which the
entry was by the voluntary act and consent of the owner or occupier of the
house, which has been held to be burglary. And were we to affirm the
judgment in this case, we would establish a doctrine of constructive
burglary which would not only be new, but contrary to the well known
definition of that offense. While the legislature might make such a change,
we think it would be judicial legislation in us to do so. If the question, upon
principle, were more doubtful than it is, we would be inclined *in favorem
vitae*, not to apply the doctrine of constructive burglary to this new case.
The offense of burglary may be punished with death."

It is only fair and proper to say that the point upon which we are
reversing the judgment does not seem to have been raised in the lower
court. The point is one, however, which goes to the substance of the
Commonwealth's case, and the failure to raise it at an earlier stage does
not deprive the accused of the right to take advantage of it here.

Reversed.[5]

---

3. Where victim who was awakened by loud pounding on his door, opened the door and
was confronted by the defendant who was armed and forced victim into home there was a
constructive breaking. State v. Edwards, 75 N.C.App. 588, 331 S.E.2d 183 (1985).

4. "However, the breaking necessary to constitute the crime of burglary may be by any
act of physical force, however slight, by which obstructions to entering are forcibly removed,
and the opening of a closed door in order to enter a building may constitute a breaking."
Luker v. State, 552 P.2d 715, 718 (Okl.Cr.1976).

"It is not necessary that splinters fly to have a breaking. Opening a closed door, effecting
an entrance thereby, is a breaking". United States v. Evans, 415 F.2d 340, 342 (5th Cir.1969).

5. Under Arizona statute that defines burglary as entry to commit a felony "and nothing
more", defendant's entry into a dwelling, where defendant had lived on occasion, to commit a
felony is burglary. State v. Van Dyke, 127 Ariz. 335, 621 P.2d 22 (1980).

People v. Gauze

Supreme Court of California, In Bank, 1975.
15 Cal.3d 709, 125 Cal.Rptr. 773, 542 P.2d 1365.

■ MOSK, JUSTICE.

Can a person burglarize his own home? That is the quandary which emerges in the case of James Matthew Gauze, who appeals from a judgment of conviction of assault with a deadly weapon (Pen.Code, § 245, subd. (a)) and burglary (Pen.Code, § 459).

Defendant shared an apartment with Richard Miller and a third person and thus had the right to enter the premises at all times. While visiting a friend one afternoon, defendant and Miller engaged in a furious quarrel. Defendant directed Miller to "Get your gun because I am going to get mine." While Miller went to their mutual home, defendant borrowed a shotgun from a neighbor. He returned to his apartment, walked into the living room, pointed the gun at Miller and fired, hitting him in the side and arm. Defendant was convicted of assault with a deadly weapon and burglary; the latter charge was predicated on his entry into his own apartment with the intent to commit the assault.

Common law burglary was generally defined as "the breaking and entering of the dwelling *of another* in the nighttime with intent to commit a felony." (Italics added.) (Perkins on Criminal Law (2d ed. 1969) p. 192.) The present burglary statute, Penal Code section 459, provides in relevant part that "Every person who enters *any* house, room, apartment . . . with intent to commit grand or petit larceny or any felony is guilty of burglary." (Italics added.)

Facially the statute is susceptible of two rational interpretations. On the one hand, it could be argued that the Legislature deliberately revoked the common law rule that burglary requires entry into the building of another.[6] On the other hand, the Legislature may have impliedly incorporated the common law requirement by failing to enumerate one's own home as a possible object of burglary. (Comment, Burglary: Punishment Without Justification, 1970 Ill.L.Rev. 391, 397.) No cases directly on point have been found.[7] Therefore, in determining which statutory interpretation should be adopted, it is necessary to examine the purposes underlying common law burglary and how they may have been affected by the enactment of the Penal Code.

Common law burglary was essentially an offense "against habitation and occupancy." (Perkins, op. cit. *supra*, p. 192.) By proscribing felonious nighttime entry into a dwelling house, the common law clearly sought to protect the right to peacefully enjoy one's own home free of invasion. In the law of burglary, in short, a person's home was truly his castle. (2 Blackstone, Commentaries (Jones ed. 1916) § 258, p. 2430.) It was clear under

---

6. The term "building" is used throughout this opinion for literary convenience; section 459 actually encompasses entry into a variety of structures, not all of them buildings.

7. Several early cases involving pleading problems appear to have assumed one cannot be charged with burglarizing his own premises. *See, e.g.*, People v. Price (1904) 143 Cal. 351, 353, 77 P. 73; People v. LaMarr (1942) 51 Cal.App.2d 24, 28, 124 P.2d 77; People v. Redman (1919) 39 Cal.App. 566, 568, 179 P. 725.

common law that one could not be convicted of burglary for entering his *own* home with felonious intent. This rule applied not only to sole owners of homes, but also to joint occupants. (Clarke v. Commonwealth (1874) 66 Va. 908; *Perkins*, op. cit. *supra*, p. 206.) The important factor was occupancy, rather than ownership.

California codified the law of burglary in 1850. (Stats.1850, ch. 99, § 58, p. 235.) That statute and subsequent revisions and amendments preserved the spirit of the common law, while making two major changes. First, the statute greatly expanded the type of buildings protected by burglary sanctions. Not only is a person's home his castle under the statute, but so, inter alia, are his shop, tent, airplane, and outhouse. (See fn. 1, ante.) This evolution, combined with elimination of the requirement that the crime be committed at night, signifies that the law is no longer limited to safeguarding occupancy rights. However, by carefully delineating the type of structures encompassed under section 459, the Legislature has preserved the concept that burglary law is designed to protect a possessory right in property, rather than broadly to preserve any place from all crime.

The second major change effected by codification of the burglary law was the elimination of the requirement of a "breaking": under the statute, every person who *enters* with felonious intent is a burglar. This means, at a minimum, that it no longer matters whether a person entering a house with larcenous or felonious intent does so through a closed door, an open door or a window. The entry with the requisite intent constitutes the burglary.

The elimination of the breaking requirement was further interpreted in People v. Barry (1892) 94 Cal. 481, 29 P. 1026, to mean that trespassory entry was no longer a necessary element of burglary. In *Barry,* this court held a person could be convicted of burglary of a store even though he entered during regular business hours.[8] A long line of cases has followed the *Barry* holding.

Barry and its progeny should not be read, however, to hold that a defendant's right to enter the premises is irrelevant. Indeed, the court in *Barry,* by negative implication, substantiated the importance of determining the right of an accused to enter premises. When the defendant thief in *Barry* argued he had a right to be in the store, the court could have replied that his right to enter the store was immaterial. Instead the court declared,

---

8. [Inserted by the Compiler.] A burglary can occur of premises open during regular business hours where a defendant has the intent to commit a felony at the time of entry. Defendant took property from a retail store open for business. People v. Smith, 264 Ill.App.3d 82, 202 Ill.Dec. 392, 637 N.E.2d 1128 (1994). Compare Macias v. People, 161 Colo. 233, 421 P.2d 116 (1966) (Where the public is invited to enter the entry cannot be trespassory and hence cannot constitute burglary). Accord, State v. Starkweather, 89 Mont. 381, 297 P. 497 (1931); People v. Peery, 180 Colo. 161, 503 P.2d 350 (1972).

Having been caught shoplifting, D was served with a written notice prohibiting him from entering the store again at any time without written consent of a corporate officer of the store. Some months later, without such consent and with intent to steal, he entered the store while it was open for business. His conviction of second-degree burglary was affirmed. The notice given under these circumstances was valid. And since he was expressly prohibited to enter, he was not one of the general public who was entitled to enter whenever the store was open for business. State v. Ocean, 24 Or.App. 289, 546 P.2d 150 (1976).

"To this reasoning, we can only say a party who enters with the intention to commit a felony enters without an invitation. He is not one of the public invited, nor is he entitled, to enter. Such a party could be refused admission at the threshold, or ejected from the premises after the entry was accomplished." (Id., 94 Cal. at p. 483, 29 P. at p. 1027.) Thus, the underlying principle of the *Barry* case is that a person has an implied invitation to enter a store during business hours for legal purposes only. The cases have preserved the common law principle that in order for burglary to occur, "The entry must be *without consent*. If the possessor actually invites the defendant, or actively assists in the entrance, e.g., by opening a door, there is no burglary." (1 Witkin, Cal.Crimes (1963) Crimes Against Property, § 457, p. 420.) (Italics in original.)

Thus, section 459, while substantially changing common law burglary, has retained two important aspects of that crime. A burglary remains an entry which invades a possessory right in a building. And it still must be committed by a person who has no right to be in the building.

Applying the foregoing reasoning, we conclude that defendant cannot be guilty of burglarizing his own home. His entry into the apartment, even for a felonious purpose, invaded no possessory right of habitation; only the entry of an intruder could have done so. More importantly defendant had an absolute right to enter the apartment. This right, unlike that of the store thief in *Barry*, did not derive from an implied invitation to the public to enter for legal purposes. It was a personal right that could not be conditioned on the consent of defendant's roommates. Defendant could not be "refused admission at the threshold" of his apartment, or be "ejected from the premises after the entry was accomplished." (People v. Barry (1892) *supra*, 94 Cal. 481, 483, 29 P. 1026, 1027.) He could not, accordingly, commit a burglary in his own home.

. . . .

To hold otherwise could lead to potentially absurd results. If a person can be convicted for burglarizing his own home, he could violate section 459 by calmly entering his house with intent to forge a check. A narcotics addict could be convicted of burglary for walking into his home with intent to administer a dose of heroin to himself. Since a burglary is committed upon entry, both could be convicted even if they changed their minds and did not commit the intended crimes.

In positing such hypotheticals, we indulge in no idle academic exercise. The differing consequences are significant, for the punishment for burglary is severe. First degree burglary is punishable by imprisonment for five years to life,[9] while a second degree burglar is subject to imprisonment in the county jail for a one-year maximum or in state prison for one to fifteen years. (Pen.Code, § 461.) In contrast, the punishment for assault with a deadly weapon, the underlying crime committed in this case, is less severe: imprisonment in state prison for six months to life or in county jail for a maximum of one year, or a fine. (Pen.Code, § 245, subd. (a).)[10]

---

9. First degree burglary, the crime charged in the present case, includes nighttime burglaries of dwellings and armed burglaries. (Pen.Code, § 460.)

10. The penalties for both burglary and assault with a deadly weapon are substantially increased when a firearm is used in commission of the crime. (Pen.Code, § 12022.5.)

For the foregoing reasons, we conclude defendant cannot be guilty of burglarizing his own home, and the judgment of conviction for burglary must therefore be reversed.....

The judgment is reversed on count I (burglary) and affirmed on count II (assault with a deadly weapon).

■ WRIGHT, C.J., and McCOMB, TOBRINER, SULLIVAN, CLARK and RICHARDSON, JJ., concur.[11]

Stowell v. People[12]

Supreme Court of Colorado, en Banc, 1939.
104 Colo. 255, 90 P.2d 520.

■ BURKE, JUSTICE.... Defendant was a freight conductor employed by the Rock Island railway. As such he was furnished with a "switch key" which he used in his work. It opened all switches and all depot and freight room doors on his division. There were no regulations governing its use. By means of it he entered the company's freight warehouse at Genoa and had taken therefrom two parcels of the value of $10, when he was arrested. The question here presented was raised by an instruction tendered and refused and by motion for a directed verdict at the close of all the evidence.

Had the switch key not been furnished defendant by the company, nor any authority given him under the terms of his employment to enter the building at the time and place in question, the evidence would have supported a conviction of burglary under the statute. For present purposes we assume, without deciding, that it would also have supported a conviction under this information. From the record it appears that defendant had

---

[Added by Compilers.]

R was convicted of first-degree burglary under a statute speaking in terms, inter alia, of burglary by one armed with a burglar's tool. R had effected entry by breaking the glass of a window with a beer bottle. It was held that a beer bottle is not a burglar's tool within the meaning of the statute. This provision was aimed at the professional burglar, and picking up the first thing available to break a window does not indicate a professional. Conviction was reduced to second-degree burglary. State v. Reid, 36 Or.App. 417, 585 P.2d 411 (1978).

11. Since each spouse had a legal right to be on the premises so long as the marriage existed entry onto the premises could not be a burglary. Vazquez v. State, 350 So.2d 1094 (Fla.App.1977).

California statute that provided that neither husband nor wife can be excluded from other's dwelling did not give husband the right to enter estranged wife's dwelling and a burglary conviction was proper. People v. Davenport, 219 Cal.App.3d 885, 268 Cal.Rptr. 501 (1990).

Even in the absence of a restraining order, estranged spouse is not privileged or licensed to enter the separate residence of the other spouse even if the property was leased before the estrangement. People v. Johnson, 906 P.2d 122 (Colo.1995).

The owner of property can be guilty of burglarizing the same property that is leased to a tenant. State v. Schneider, 36 Wash.App. 237, 673 P.2d 200 (1983).

A person who enters a building for a felonious purpose may be found guilty of burglary even if the person enters with the occupant's consent. Entry need not be a trespass. Invitation by murder victim to enter cabin did not preclude burglary conviction. *People v. Gauze, supra,* distinguished. People v. Frye, 18 Cal.4th 894, 77 Cal. Rptr.2d 25, 959 P.2d 183, 212 (1998).

12. Cited with approval, People v. Woods, 182 Colo. 3, 510 P.2d 435 (1973).

Rule

a right to enter this warehouse at the time and in the manner he did, provided his intent in so doing was lawful. Hence this offense, if burglary, is raised to that grade solely by his unlawful intent. But intent alone is not always sufficient for that purpose. There is "no burglary, if the person entering has a right so to do, although he may intend to commit, and may actually commit, a felony, and although he may enter in such a way that there would be a breaking if he had no right to enter." Considering the history of the crime of burglary, and its evolution, this rule appears reasonable and necessary. The common law crime was an offense against habitation. Its purpose was to give security to the home when it was presumably least protected. Essential elements thereof were an actual *breaking,* in the *night time,* with intent to commit a *felony.* It has been extended by statute in most states to entry in any way, into any kind of building, at any time, for any unlawful purpose. Under the rule of strict construction of statutes in derogation of the common law courts must necessarily be careful not to extend such acts beyond the clear intent of the Legislature. For instance, among the buildings enumerated in our statute are "schoolhouses". Hence, but for the rule above stated, a school teacher, using the key furnished her by the district to re-open the schoolhouse door immediately after locking it in the evening, for the purpose of taking (but not finding) a pencil belonging to one of her pupils, could be sent to the penitentiary. . . .

The judgment is accordingly reversed.[13]

People v. Dupree

Supreme Court of Michigan, 1893.
98 Mich. 26, 56 N.W. 1046.

■ GRANT, J. The respondent was convicted of burglary under section 9132, How.St. The evidence on the part of the people tended to show that the owner of the dwelling house occupied the front room for a shoe shop, and the rear and overhead part as a dwelling. The shop was upon the ground floor, and had two windows, each about four feet from the ground. These windows had double sash; were without pulley weights; were fastened when raised, and bolted when down, by stops operated by springs. When the windows were closed, the springs threw the bolts into the slots in the cases, so that the window could not be raised without drawing the bolt. One of these windows was opened during the night of October 8th, and three pairs of shoes were stolen. The owner closed the shades on the night of the 6th, and did not notice that the window was raised even an eighth of an inch. On the morning of the 9th, on opening his shop, he found the window raised about 1½ feet. The respondent called at the house on October 6th,

---

13. Permission to enter when the dweller is present is not permission to enter when he is absent. And entry when he is absent is trespassory. State v. McKinney, 535 P.2d 1392 (Or.App.1975).

University policeman's entry into a building for which he had been given a key did not preclude conviction for burglary where the policeman's duties did not require his entry and he did not enter for the purpose of performing his duty. People v. Powers, 138 A.D.2d 806, 525 N.Y.S.2d 727 (1988).

between noon and 2 P.M., and asked for dinner. He asked permission to step into the shoe shop for the purpose of changing his pantaloons. This request was granted. The window was not broken. If the bolt was in the slot, the window could have been raised from the inside only. On Monday following the burglary, respondent had in his possession, and offered for sale, a pair of shoes alleged to have been taken upon the night of October 8th. On the following Wednesday, he sold a pair of shoes which were identified as one of the three pairs stolen on October 8th. The complaining witness testified that he believed that the window was unfastened and raised on October 6th from the inside, and something placed under the sash so as to keep the bolt from entering the slot. The owner left the shop about the time it was necessary to light the lamps to see, and did not return to it till the next morning. No testimony was introduced on the part of the respondent. His counsel moved the court to discharge the respondent for the reason that the crime was not established against him. This the court refused.

FACTS

It is contended on behalf of the respondent (1) that no breaking or entering in the nighttime was established; (2) that this shop was not a part of the dwelling house; (3) that if the window was partially raised on October 6th, and was further raised on the night of the 8th, the crime was not established. We think the motion was properly overruled, and the case properly submitted to the jury. . . .

3. The theory of the prosecution was that the respondent, when in the shop, either on the 6th or 7th of October, (the court, in its charge, referred to the date as Friday, October 7th,) raised the window just enough to prevent the bolt from entering the slot, and there was evidence to sustain it. It is insisted that even if this was so, and the respondent raised the window on the following night, it did not establish the crime of burglary. We cannot agree with this contention. It is said in Dennis v. People, 27 Mich. 151: "If an entry is effected by raising a trapdoor which is kept down merely by its own weight, or by raising a window kept in its place only by pulley weight, instead of its own, or by descending an open chimney, it is admitted to be enough to support the charge of breaking; and I am unable to see any substantial distinction between such cases and one where an entry is effected through a hanging window over a shop door, and which is only designed for light above, and for ventilation, and is down, and kept down by its own weight, and so firmly as to be opened only by the use of some force, and so situated as to make a ladder, or something of the kind, necessary to reach it for the purpose of passing through it." We think the doctrine there enunciated covers the present case. If there had been no bolt, and respondent had raised the window and entered in the nighttime, under all the authorities, he would have been guilty of burglary. Upon what reason can it be said that his removal of the bolt, or his raising the window a fraction of an inch, in the daytime, changes the character of his offense? If the owner had failed to see that the bolts were in place, or if something had been accidentally placed upon the window sill, which was of slight thickness, but sufficient to prevent the bolts from entering the slots, the raising of the window would have been sufficient breaking to support the charge. How can the act be relieved of criminality by secretly fixing the window in the daytime so that the bolt or lock will not be effective, and

ISSUE

thus render the perpetration of the crime more easy and certain? There is no reason in such a rule. In Lyons v. People, the door was left unlocked, and the court was requested to instruct the jury that, in order to constitute the crime, it must appear that the door was secured in the ordinary way. The supreme court, in determining the question, said: "We are not aware of any authority which goes to the extent of these instructions. To hold that the carelessness of the owner in securing and guarding his property shall be a justification to the burglar or thief would leave communities very much to the mercy of this class of felons. It would in effect be a premium offered for their depredations, by the removal of the apprehension of punishment. Whether property is guarded or not, it is larceny in the thief who steals it. When a door is closed, it is burglary for any one, with a felonious intent, to open it, and enter the house, in the nighttime, without the owner's consent; and it makes no difference how many bolts and bars might have been used to secure it, but which were neglected." The language of the court was perhaps too broad, in stating that if the window was raised any distance, but was not sufficient to permit the defendant to enter, and he raised it further, it would be breaking, in the meaning of the law;[14] but the entire evidence was to the effect that it was raised so little as not to attract the notice of the occupant. We therefore think that the jury could not have been misled by the language . . . .

Conviction affirmed. The other justices concurred.[15]

Nichols v. State

Supreme Court of Wisconsin, 1887.
68 Wis. 416, 32 N.W. 543.

■ CASSODAY, J. There is undisputed testimony on the part of the state to the effect that Saturday, July 25, 1885, the plaintiff in error was stopping at a hotel in Black River Falls, having his name registered as W.H. Eldredge, and a room assigned him opposite thereto. He had then been there about three days. In the afternoon of the day named he had a box or chest taken from the depot to his room, weighing about 150 pounds. No evidence was

---

14. If a door is partly open, but insufficient for entrance, the further opening of the door constitutes a breaking. Jones v. State, 537 P.2d 431 (Okl.Cr.1975).

After victim opens a door one or two feet, defendant's further pushing open the door was a forcible breaking for burglary. Pack v. State, 819 P.2d 280 (Okl.Cr.1991).

15. Defendant used force to enter whether door was locked or not. "Any effort, however slight, such as the turning of a door knob to enter, constitutes a breaking . . ."

Penetration of a window screen that was an outer barrier of the structure was an entry within the meaning of the burglary statute. It was not necessary for the defendant to penetrate the window itself. People v. Nible, 200 Cal.App.3d 838, 247 Cal.Rptr. 396 (1988).

In a prosecution for burglary it was error to instruct that entry through an open window constitutes a "breaking". People v. Williams, 29 A.D.2d 780, 287 N.Y.S.2d 797 (1968).

In Stehl v. State, 283 Ala. 22, 214 So.2d 299 (1968), it was held reversible error to refuse to charge, in a trial for burglary, that D "would not be guilty, even though he were in the house, if he entered through an open door or window without further opening such door or window."

Opening a door constitutes a breaking although another door was open through which entry could have been effected. State v. Campbell, 190 Neb. 394, 208 N.W.2d 670 (1973).

given as to what was in it. About three o'clock in the afternoon of the same day he arranged with the local express agent for the sending of a box to Chicago, then at the hotel, and represented by him as weighing about 225 pounds. By his prearrangement, the box was brought to the depot just in time for the 7:50 P.M. Chicago train, and was shipped in the express car thereon by the local agent, as directed. Soon after the starting of the train, there seems to have been a suspicion as to the contents of the box. This suspicion was increased as telegrams were received at different stations from Black River Falls respecting the box. Finally, being convinced by such dispatches that there was a man in the box, the train-men telegraphed forward to Elroy to secure the presence of an officer on the approach of the train to make the arrest. On reaching Elroy, in the night, this box in the express car was opened, and the plaintiff in error was found therein, with a revolver, billy, razor, knife, rope, gimlet, and a bottle of chloroform. There was also evidence tending to show that there were packages of money in the custody of the express agent on the car; that such agent had an assistant as far as Elroy; that from there to Chicago such car was usually in charge of only one man; that after the arrest, and when asked his object in being thus shipped in the box, the prisoner voluntarily admitted, in effect, that he had considered his chances carefully; that he went into the thing as a matter of speculation; that he needed money, and needed it quickly; that he expected to get fully $50,000; that had he passed out of Elroy he would have got off with the money; that, in a case of that kind, if a human life stood in his way, it did not amount to a snap of the finger. . . .

2.   The question recurs whether the proofs show that there was a breaking in fact, within the meaning of the statute. Certainly not in the sense of picking a lock, or opening it with a key, or lifting a latch, or severing or mutilating the door, or doing violence to any portion of the car. On the contrary, the box was placed in the express car with the knowledge, and even by the assistance, of those in charge of the car. But it was not a passenger car, and the plaintiff in error was in no sense a passenger. The railroad company was a common carrier of passengers as well as freight. But the express company was exclusively a common carrier of freight, that is to say, goods, wares and merchandise. As such carrier, it may have at times transported animals, birds, etc., but it may be safely assumed that it never knowingly undertook to transport men in packages or boxes for special delivery. True, the plaintiff in error contracted with the local express agent for the carriage and delivery of such box, but neither he nor any one connected with the express car or the train had any knowledge or expectation of a man being concealed within it. On the contrary, they each and all had the right to assume that the box contained nothing but inanimate substance,—goods, wares, or merchandise of some description. The plaintiff in error knew that he had no right to enter the express car at all without the consent of those in charge. The evidence was sufficient to justify the conclusion that he unlawfully gained an entrance without the knowledge or consent of those in charge of the car, by false pretenses, fraud, gross imposition, and circumvention, with intent to commit the crime of robbery or larceny, and, in doing so, if necessary, the crime of murder. This would seem to have been sufficient to constitute a constructive breaking at common law, as defined by Blackstone, thus: "To come

down a chimney is held a burglarious entry; for that is as much closed as the nature of things will permit. So, also, to knock at the door, and, upon opening it, to rush in with a felonious intent; or, under pretense of taking lodgings, to fall upon the landlord and rob him; or to procure a constable to gain admittance in order to search for traitors, and then to bind the constable and rob the house. All these entries have been adjudged burglarious, though there was no actual breaking, for the law will not suffer itself to be trifled with by such evasions, especially under the cloak of legal process. And so, if a servant opens and enters his master's chamber door with a felonious design; or if any other person, lodging in the same house or in a public inn, opens and enters another's door with such evil intent, it is burglary. Nay, if the servant conspires with a robber and lets him into the house by night, this is burglary in both; for the servant is doing an unlawful act, and the opportunity afforded him of doing it with greater ease rather aggravates than extenuates the guilt." 4 Bl.Comm. 226, 227.

So it has frequently been held in this country that, "to obtain admission to a dwelling-house at night, with the intent to commit a felony, by means of artifice or fraud or upon a pretense of business or social intercourse, is a constructive breaking, and will sustain an indictment charging a burglary by breaking and entering." The same was held in Ohio under a statute against "forcible" breaking and entering. But it is claimed that in this state the common-law doctrine of constructive breaking has no application to a case of this kind, and in fact is superseded by statute, except in so far as it is re-affirmed. Thus: "*Any unlawful entry of* a dwelling-house or other building with intent to commit a felony, shall *be deemed* a breaking and entering of such dwelling-house or other building, within the meaning of the last four sections." Sec. 4411, R.S. This section merely establishes a rule of evidence whereby the scope of constructive breaking is enlarged so as to take in "*any* unlawful entry of a dwelling-house or other building with intent to commit a felony." It in no way narrows the scope of constructive breaking, as understood at common law, but merely enlarges it in the particulars named. In all other respects such constructive breaking signifies the same as at common law. It necessarily follows that as the word "break," used in sec. 4410, had obtained a fixed and definite meaning at common law when applied to a dwelling-house proper or other buildings within the curtilage, the legislature must be presumed to have used it in the same sense when therein applied to other statutory breakings. That is to say, they must be deemed to have used the word as understood at common law in relation to the same or a like subject matter. We must hold the evidence sufficient to support the charge of breaking. . . .

By the Court. The judgment of the circuit court is affirmed.[16]

---

16. One who enters a store while it is open for business, secretes himself therein and is apprehended after closing hours under circumstances which indicate an intent to steal, can be convicted of storehouse breaking Code Article 27, § 32. His failure to leave when the store closed for business made his original entrance an illegal breaking and entering *ab initio*. Brooks v. State, 25 Md.App. 194, 333 A.2d 352 (1975).

Modern burglary statutes cover the circumstance where a defendant remains on premises to commit a felony. Defendant was guilty of burglary where he was possibly admitted to premises but intentionally remained with intent to commit rape. People v. DeLarosa, 172 A.D.2d 156, 568 N.Y.S.2d 47 (N.Y.App. 1991),

Hebron v. State

Court of Special Appeals of Maryland, 1992.
92 Md.App. 508, 608 A.2d 1291.

■ WILNER, CHIEF JUDGE.

A jury in the Circuit Court for Montgomery County convicted appellant of breaking and entering a dwelling house, attempted breaking and entering a dwelling house, and malicious destruction of property.

These convictions stemmed from an incident that occurred on May 21, 1991 at the home of Dr. Hilary Weiner, located in the Tanglewood development. When she left in the morning to go to work, Dr. Weiner secured the house, presumably meaning that she closed and locked the front door. When she returned later in the afternoon, she found the door frame "splintered" and "broken apart." As a result, "you could just push the door open and could not secure the door afterwards." Evidence from a neighbor established that, about 11:00 that morning, appellant, driving a gray car with what turned out to be stolen plates, parked near Dr. Weiner's home and proceeded to walk between two buildings in the direction of the home. The neighbor lost sight of him but shortly heard "a loud, really loud, bang noise. Not a pop bang, but a bash bang." About 20 seconds later, she saw appellant emerge from between the two buildings, get into his car, and drive away.

Appellant makes three complaints in this appeal: ... that the evidence was legally insufficient to sustain his conviction for breaking and entering, ...

Sufficiency of Evidence

Appellant's argument as to evidentiary sufficiency goes only to the conviction for breaking and entering and indeed only to the question of whether the State adequately proved an entry into Dr. Weiner's home. He does not contest that the evidence sufficed to show a breaking.

It is true, as he posits, that no one saw him enter Dr. Weiner's home; nor was anything taken from the house. The only evidence indicating an entry came from the condition of the door frame and the fact that, when she returned home, Dr. Weiner found her cats "spooked."

Although there are many cases in which the Maryland courts have discussed and defined what constitutes a "breaking" for purpose of our various burglary and trespass statutes, we seem not yet to have addressed

---

N.B. Many cases have held that there is no doctrine of trespass *ab initio* in the criminal law.

The Montana statute reads: "A person commits the offense of burglary if he knowingly enters or remains unlawfully in an occupied structure with the purpose to commit an offense therein." Mont. Code Ann. 1995 § 45–6–204(1). Under this statute remaining in a store after closing hours constituted a trespass. State v. Watkins, 163 Mont. 491, 518 P.2d 259 (1974).

Although the English common law required a "breaking into" the building, a prohibited entry followed by a breaking out is sufficient under the Kentucky statute. Lawson v. Commonwealth, 160 Ky. 180, 169 S.W. 587 (1914).

the requisites of an entry. The law on that elsewhere, stemming from the English common law, is well established, however. Wharton states the law this way:

"There is an entry when any part of the defendant's person passes the line of the threshold.

Thus, there is an entry when the defendant, after opening a closed door, steps across the threshold; when, after breaking the glass of a door or window, he reaches inside to unlock the door or window or to steal property; when, in the course of breaking the glass of a door or window, his finger, hand, or foot happens to pass through the opening; or when, in the course of pushing open a closed door or raising a closed window, his finger or hand happens to pass the line of the threshold."

(Emphasis added). 3 Wharton's Criminal Law, 14th Ed., § 332. *See also* LaFave and Scott, Criminal Law, p. 710; R. Perkins, Criminal Law, pp. 155–56; Clark and Marshall, A Treatise on the Law of Crimes, 7th ed., § 13.04. We see no reason not to adopt that view.

Apart from the splintering of the door frame, Dr. Weiner stated that she observed splintered wood on a mat inside the house. Officer Hall also noticed splinters or chips on the inside floor. That evidence, coupled with the loud bang heard by the neighbor and the fact that the frame was so damaged as to make it impossible to close and latch the door, could lead a rational trier of fact reasonably to find that appellant used his body to batter the door with such force as to defeat the lock and open the door. From that, the trier of fact could further reasonably infer that, with the application of that kind of body pressure to the door, some part of appellant's body must necessarily have crossed the threshold when the door opened. We therefore conclude that the evidence was sufficient to sustain the charge.

. . .

Judgments Affirmed; Appellant to Pay the Costs.[17]

---

17. A defendant who pushed in a window to a shop and whose finger extended into the shop committed a sufficient entry to constitute burglary. Rex v. Davis, 168 Eng.Rep. 917, Crown Case R'vd. 1823.

The putting of a hand through the window would constitute an entry. People v. Lamica, 274 Cal.App.2d 640, 79 Cal.Rptr. 491 (1969).

Defendant made entry by placing part of his body and boot inside an apartment. State v. Falls, 508 So.2d 1021 (La.App.1987).

"Here it is undisputed that defendant invaded the space between the outer storm window and the inner window. We hold under the circumstances there was sufficient evidence of entry to the house to support the aggravated burglary conviction under Count 13." State v. Crease, 230 Kan. 541, 638 P.2d 939, 940 (1982).

In California an entry need not constitute a trespass to support a burglary conviction. People v. Pendleton, 25 Cal.3d 371, 158 Cal.Rptr. 343, 599 P.2d 649 (1979).

Placing a forged check in a chute in the walk-up window of a check cashing facility, or inserting stolen ATM card into an ATM is not an entry for purposes of burglary. People v. Davis, 18 Cal.4th 712, 76 Cal.Rptr.2d 770, 958 P.2d 1083 (1998).

Walker v. State

Supreme Court of Alabama, 1879.
63 Ala. 49.

■ BRICKELL, C.J. The statute (Code of 1876, § 4343) provides, that "any person, who, either in the night or day time, with intent to steal, or to commit a felony, breaks into and enters a dwelling-house, or any building, structure or inclosure within the curtilage of a dwelling-house, though not forming a part thereof, or into any shop, store, warehouse, or other building, structure or inclosure in which any goods, merchandise, or other valuable thing is kept for use, sale, or deposit, *provided* such structure, other than a shop, store, warehouse or building, is specially constructed or made to keep such goods, merchandise or other valuable thing, is guilty of burglary," etc.

The defendant was indicted for breaking into and entering "a corncrib of Noadiah Woodruff and Robert R. Peeples, a building in which corn, a thing of value, was at the time kept for use, sale, or deposit, with intent to steal," & c. He was convicted; and the case is now presented on exceptions taken to instructions given, and the refusal of instructions requested, as to what facts will constitute a breaking into and entry, material constituents of the offense charged in the indictment. The facts, on which the instructions were founded, are: that in the crib was a quantity of shelled corn, piled on the floor; in April, or May, 1878, the crib had been broken into, and corn taken therefrom, without the consent of the owners, who had the crib watched; and thereafter the defendant was caught under it, and, on coming out, voluntarily confessed that, about three weeks before, he had taken a large auger, and, going under the crib, had bored a hole through the floor, from which the corn, being shelled, ran into a sack he held under it; that he then got about three pecks of corn, and with a cob closed the hole. On these facts, the City Court was of opinion, and so instructed the jury, that there was such a breaking and entry of the crib, as would constitute the offense, and refused instructions requested asserting the converse of the proposition. . . .

The boring of the hole through the floor of the crib, was a sufficient breaking; but with it there must have been an entry. Proof of a breaking, though it may be with an intent to steal, or the intent to commit a felony, is proof of one only of the facts making up the offense, and is as insufficient as proof of an entry through an open door, without breaking. If the hand, or any part of the body, is intruded within the house, the entry is complete. The entry may also be completed by the intrusion of a tool, or instrument, within the house, though no part of the body be introduced. Thus, if A. breaks into the house of B. in the night time, with intent to steal goods, and breaks the window, and puts his hand, or puts in a hook, or other engine, to reach out goods; or puts a pistol in at the window, with an intent to kill, though his hand be not within the window, this is burglary.—1 Hale, 555. When no part of the body is introduced "when the only entry is of a tool, or instrument, introduced by the force and agency of the party accused, the inquiry is, whether the tool or instrument was employed solely for the purpose of *breaking,* and thereby effecting an *entry;* or whether it was employed not only to *break and enter,* but also to aid in the consummation of the criminal intent, and its capacity to aid in such consummation. Until there is a *breaking* and *entry,* the offense is not consummated. The offense rests largely in intention; and though there may be sufficient evidence of an attempt to commit it, which, of itself, is a crime, the attempt may be abandoned" of if there may be repentance, before the consummation of the offense intended. The *breaking* may be complete, and yet an *entry* never effected. From whatever cause an *entry* is not effected, burglary has not been committed. When one instrument is employed to *break,* and is without capacity to aid otherwise than by opening a way of *entry,* and another instrument must be used, or the instrument used in the breaking must be used in some other way or manner to consummate the criminal intent, the intrusion of the instrument is not, of itself, an *entry.* But when, as in this case, the instrument is employed not only to *break,* but to effect the only *entry* contemplated, and necessary to the consummation of the criminal intent; when it is intruded within the house, *breaking* it, effecting an *entry,* enabling the person introducing it to consummate his intent, the offense is complete. The instrument was employed, not only for the purpose of *breaking* into the house, but to effect the larceny intended. When it was intruded into the crib, the burglar acquired dominion over the corn intended to be stolen. Such dominion did not require any other act on his part. When the auger was withdrawn from the aperture made with it, the corn ran into the sack he used in its asportation. There was a *breaking* and *entry,* enabling him to effect his criminal intent, without the use of any other means, and this satisfies the requirements of the law.

Let the judgment be affirmed.

Gray v. State

Supreme Court of Wisconsin, 1943.
243 Wis. 57, 9 N.W.2d 68.

■ MARTIN, J. The dwelling of Edmund Feldner, located on Highway 38, about three fourths of a mile west of the village of Rosendale in the town of Fond du Lac, Fond du Lac county, Wisconsin, was burglarized on the night of June 19, 1941. Mr. Feldner and members of his family retired at about 8:30 p.m. When he retired his overalls and two suits of clothing were hanging on a hook in his bedroom. His winter overcoat was in a room next to his bedroom. When Mr. Feldner arose at 5:30 a.m. the following morning he noticed that his overalls, his two suits, and overcoat were missing and that some of the rooms of his residence had been ransacked. He found his overalls and the vest and coat of one suit lying outside. One suit, the overcoat, and trousers of the other suit were missing.

At about 1 a.m., on June 20, 1941, George Habeck, a truck driver, left the city of Fond du Lac for Ripon and Berlin via Highway 38. When he reached a point on said highway about three fourths of a mile west of Rosendale, in the immediate vicinity of the Feldner residence he saw three Negroes, whom he later identified as the defendants, with their car parked alongside the road. Defendants followed Habeck to Ripon. At Ripon they inquired of Habeck as to the direction to Fond du Lac. He gave them the proper direction, whereupon defendants left but did not go in the direction which had been given them. The facts here related took place between 1 and 2:30 a.m. on June 20th. . . .

To the information charging burglary of a dwelling in the nighttime with intent to commit larceny, defendants entered a plea of not guilty. The jury found defendants guilty in the manner and form as charged in the information. Defendants contend that the evidence did not establish beyond a reasonable doubt that the Feldner dwelling was burglarized in the nighttime. Sec. 352.32, Stats., defines the term "nighttime" as follows:

"The term 'nighttime,' when used in any statute, ordinance, indictment or information shall be construed to mean the time between one hour after the setting of the sun on one day and one hour before the rising of the same on the following day; and the time of sunset and sunrise shall be ascertained according to the mean solar time of the ninetieth meridian west from Greenwich, commonly known as central time, as given in any published almanac."

Sunset on the evening of June 19th was at 7:39 p.m., and sunrise on the morning of June 20th was at 4:23 a.m. Thus, nighttime, within the meaning of the statute, on the night in question, was from 8:39 p.m., June 19th, to 3:23 a.m., June 20th. Defendants argue that since Feldner testified that he retired about 8:30 p.m. on June 19th, and that he arose at about 5:30 a.m. the following morning, his dwelling may have been burglarized either in the daytime or in the nighttime, and that therefore the state failed to establish that the crime had been committed in the nighttime as alleged in the information. It is definitely established that the crime was committed sometime between 8:30 p.m., June 19th, and 5:30 a.m., June 20th. The witness Habeck testified that he left the city of Fond du Lac at about 1 a.m. on June 20th. Rosendale is about eleven miles west of the city of Fond du Lac. According to Habeck's testimony, he would, with normal driving, have arrived at the place where he saw the three defendants and their parked car in the immediate vicinity of the Feldner residence at about 1:30 a.m. The circumstance of defendants having been seen in the immediate vicinity of the burglarized residence at the time fixed by Habeck, well warranted the jury in concluding that the burglary had been committed in the nighttime. *See* Simon v. State, 125 Wis. 439, 103 N.W. 1100; Winsky v. State, 126 Wis. 99, 102, 105 N.W. 480. In the latter case, referring to State v. Bancroft, 10 N.H. 105, it is said:

"There was no direct proof that the burglary was committed in the nighttime, other than the fact that the property was in the house after dark and was missing the next morning when the witness arose; and the court said that this evidence 'led very strongly to the conclusion that it was taken in the course of the night, although the precise hour when the witness called it dark did not appear, and the time when she arose in the morning was not stated. At whatever time in the morning the loss was discovered, the jury might well weigh the probability whether the article would have been taken from the house in the daytime, in connection with the other evidence. It was sufficient that, upon the whole case, they had no reasonable doubt that the act was done in the nighttime.' Sufficient appears from the evidence in the case before us to warrant the jury in finding that the entry was made in the nighttime. Simon v. State, supra." . . .

By the Court—Judgment affirmed.[18]

State v. Bowen

262 Kan. 705, 942 P.2d 7 (1997).

■ McFARLAND, CHIEF JUSTICE:

Travis W. Bowen, in a trial by jury, was convicted of aggravated burglary (K.S.A. 21–3716), a severity level 5 person felony; possession of methamphetamine (K.S.A.1994 Supp. 65–4160), a severity level 4 drug felony; and possession of marijuana (K.S.A.1994 Supp. 65–4162), a misdemeanor. He was sentenced to 41 months' imprisonment, 15 months' imprisonment, and 30 days' in the county jail, respectively. These terms were ordered to run concurrently for a controlling term of 41 months. Defendant appeals only his aggravated burglary conviction, contending that the evidence is insufficient to support his conviction. . . .

K.S.A. 21–3716 defines aggravated burglary as follows:

"Aggravated burglary is knowingly and without authority entering into or remaining within any building, manufactured home, mobile home, tent or other structure, or any motor vehicle, aircraft, watercraft, railroad car or other means of conveyance of persons or property in which there is a human being, *with intent to commit a felony,* theft or sexual battery *therein.*" (Emphasis supplied.)

Specifically, defendant challenges the sufficiency of the evidence as to his intent to commit a felony in the residence.

The State alternatively charged the aggravated burglary intended felony element, and the jury was instructed on the elements of each intended felony in the following format:

Theft (Instruction 6–A)

Possession of methamphetamine (Instruction 6–B)

Aggravated Battery (Instruction 6–C)

Aggravated Assault (Instruction 6–D)

The verdict form submitted as to the aggravated burglary count was completed as follows:

"Count 3

_____☑_____ Guilty of Aggravated Burglary pursuant to Instruction Number:

---

18. Where the uncontradicted evidence showed that if D committed the burglary he did so at night it was proper to instruct the jury that they must either find the defendant not guilty or guilty of the offense charged. There was no need to instruct the jury in regard to the lesser included offense of burglary in the daytime. People v. White, 218 Cal.App.2d 267, 32 Cal.Rptr. 322 (1963).

But where there was conflicting evidence as to the time it was error not to submit this issue to the jury. State v. Miller, 104 Ariz. 335, 452 P.2d 509 (1969).

Nighttime under the Iowa statutes is the same as at common law, "a period between sunset and sunrise during which there is not enough daylight to discern a man's face." State v. Billings, 242 N.W.2d 726 (Iowa 1976).

___ 6–A (Theft)

___ ☑ ___ 6–B (Possession of Methamphetamine)

___ 6–C (Aggravated Battery)

___ ☑ ___ 6–D (Aggravated Assault)

___ Not Guilty of Aggravated Burglary—

Thus, we need not speculate as to which of the alternative felonious intents the jury found. Further, possession of methamphetamine and aggravated assault are the only two with which we are concerned.

The physical facts relative to the crime were not seriously controverted, nor was there any question of identity.

As the facts are crucial to the determination of the issue raised, they must be set forth in considerable detail.

During the early morning hours of December 7, 1994, Layne and Ruth White were asleep in a second floor bedroom of their rural home. They were awakened by a loud impact sound on the side of the house, which was followed by the sound of footsteps on the first floor. Mr. White's parents live about 1 1/2 miles away. Pursuant to a sort of mutual protection agreement, the parents were called and requested to seek help. Layne White had his wife take their young child and hide in a closet. Meanwhile, the senior Whites arrived and illuminated the house with their headlights. Reno County Sheriff's officers then arrived.

Defendant was found on the first floor of the residence on his knees beside a wood stove. He had a knife in each hand. He told officers he had placed a pressure-activated bomb in the home's basement beams. Defendant put down the pocket knife but refused to push it out of his reach. The long butcher knife was held and moved in a threatening manner toward the officers. It took approximately 30 minutes to disarm and arrest defendant. Marijuana and methamphetamine were found on defendant.

Defendant testified that he was on methamphetamine at all pertinent times. He had been at his uncle's home located some unspecified distance down the road from the Whites' home. He started walking up the road in the direction of Nickerson to meet up with some friends. It was a very cold and icy night and defendant became chilled. He walked to the Whites' home in order to get warm. He took his pocket knife out for protection. He kicked the door open and went to the kitchen to get a knife better suited "[t]o protect myself if need be." Officer Flynn testified that defendant told him after his arrest that he had opened the pocket knife before entering the residence. In further recounting defendant's statements, the officer testified:

> "[H]e stated to me he was going to defend him, himself if someone tried to hurt him or bother him or jump him while he was asleep. I asked him why he had the knife before he entered the house in his hand as he kicked the door. He stated to me for the same reason. I asked him what he would have done if he was approached by someone, and he said he would have to cut them because he was going to defend himself, whatever it took."

We shall first consider the sufficiency of the evidence relative to the intent to commit the felony of possession of methamphetamine.

It is undisputed that defendant's possession of methamphetamine was wholly incidental to his entry of the Whites' home. The drug was on defendant's person but played no role in his decision to enter the residence by force or otherwise or in his decision as to what he intended to do after entering. The State does not argue otherwise. Rather, the State contends that as possession of a narcotic has been held to be a continuing offense, its mere possession by defendant is sufficient to support the aggravated burglary conviction. In support of this contention, the State cites State v. Chapman, 252 Kan. 606, 847 P.2d 1247 (1993).

The question in *Chapman* was venue. Three individuals were involved in drug transactions which by travel occurred in multiple counties.... Thus, *Chapman* is concerned with where a crime may be charged, a question wholly unrelated to the issue before us. The State cites no authority for the proposition that the mere happenstance of methamphetamine being on Chapman's person with no showing or inference that its possession was in any manner related to defendant's unlawful entry into the residence is legally sufficient to support a conviction of aggravated burglary based upon entering with the intent to commit the felony of possession of methamphetamine. Our research has yielded no authority for this contention.

Although the precise issue before us was not present in State v. Mogenson, 10 Kan.App.2d 470, 701 P.2d 1339, *rev. denied* 238 Kan. 878 (1985), the case is helpful by analogy. In *Mogenson*, defendant had entered a residence with authority, and then became embroiled in an argument therein, which resulted in the withdrawal of the authority to be there. Defendant remained and committed battery. He was convicted of aggravated burglary. On appeal, defendant argued that the intent to commit battery had to be present at the time of the entering. The Court of Appeals disagreed, holding that the formation of intent to commit the ulterior felony must have existed either at the time defendant entered the house or after defendant remained in the house without authorization. The intent and the entering or remaining without authority must at some time be concurrent. 10 Kan.App.2d at 472–76, 701 P.2d 1339.

The specific intent in an aggravated burglary, where one is charged with entering into the dwelling without authority, must exist at the time of the unauthorized entry. State v. Brown, 6 Kan.App.2d 556, 560, 630 P.2d 731 (1981). Although defendant's methamphetamine possession in the case before us was wilful and wanton, he did not enter the residence with the purpose of possessing the drugs therein. We must conclude that there was insufficient evidence to support the conviction of aggravated burglary based upon entry with the intent to possess methamphetamine.

We turn now to the sufficiency of the evidence relative to aggravated burglary based upon the intent to commit an aggravated assault. The jury was instructed:

"The elements of aggravated assault are as follows:

1.   That the defendant intentionally placed another person in reasonable apprehension of immediate bodily harm;

2.   That the defendant used a deadly weapon;

3.   That this act occurred on or about the 7th day of December, 1994, in Reno County, Kansas.

"No bodily contact is necessary."

There was evidence defendant kicked in the door and entered the residence armed with a knife in his hand to use against any occupant who approached him. Additionally, upon entry, he immediately searched for and acquired a much larger knife. He had a knife in each hand when first seen by the officers. We conclude that the evidence of aggravated burglary, based upon the intended felony of aggravated assault, is sufficient to support the conviction.

The final question to be determined is whether the insufficiency of the evidence as to the intended felony of possession of methamphetamine requires reversal of the aggravated burglary conviction even though the evidence was legally sufficient as to the intended felony of aggravated assault.

In this case, we are not dealing with a general verdict on an aggravated burglary charge which set forth multiple theories as to the element of felonious intent in entering a building, such as was present in State v. Skelton, 247 Kan. 34, 795 P.2d 349 (1990), nor are we dealing with a general verdict on a felony-murder charge which alleged multiple underlying felonies, as in State v. Garcia, 243 Kan. 662, 763 P.2d 585 (1988). Likewise, we need not discuss State v. Grissom, 251 Kan. 851, 840 P.2d 1142 (1992), which disapproved some of the language quoted in *Garcia*. The case herein does not involve a general verdict. The jury specifically found defendant had two felonious intents when he entered the residence—the possession of methamphetamine and the commission of an aggravated assault. We have held the evidence was insufficient as to the former, but sufficient as to the latter. Thus, there is no opportunity to even speculate that the jury may have convicted defendant of aggravated burglary based upon a felonious intent which was not supported by the evidence. The State was not required to prove more than one of the alternatively charged felonious intents.

The judgment is affirmed.

Taylor v. United States

Supreme Court of the United States, 1990.
495 U.S. 575, 110 S.Ct. 2143, 109 L.Ed.2d 607.

■ JUSTICE BLACKMUN delivered the opinion of the Court.

In this case we are called upon to determine the meaning of the word "burglary" as it is used in § 1402 of Subtitle I (the Career Criminals Amendment Act of 1986) of the Anti–Drug Abuse Act of 1986, 18 U.S.C. § 924(e). This statute provides a sentence enhancement for a defendant who is convicted under 18 U.S.C. § 922(g) (unlawful possession of a firearm) and who has three prior convictions for specified types of offenses, including "burglary."

I

Under 18 U.S.C. § 922(g)(1), it is unlawful for a person who has been convicted previously for a felony to possess a firearm. A defendant convicted for a violation of § 922(g)(1) is subject to the sentence-enhancement provision at issue, § 924(e):

> "(1) In the case of a person who violates section 922(g) of this title and has three previous convictions by any court . . . for a violent felony or a serious drug offense, or both . . . such person shall be fined not more than $25,000 and imprisoned not less than fifteen years. . . .

> "(2) As used in this subsection"

> . . .

> "(B) the term 'violent felony' means any crime punishable by imprisonment for a term exceeding one year . . . that"

> "(i) has as an element the use, attempted use, or threatened use of physical force against the person of another; or

> "(ii) is burglary, arson, or extortion, involves use of explosives, or otherwise involves conduct that presents a serious potential risk of physical injury to another."

In January 1988, in the United States District Court for the Eastern District of Missouri, petitioner Arthur Lajuane Taylor pleaded guilty to one count of possession of a firearm by a convicted felon, in violation of § 922(g)(1). At the time of his plea, Taylor had four prior convictions. One was for robbery, one was for assault, and the other two were for second-degree burglary under Missouri law.

The Government sought sentence enhancement under § 924(e). Taylor conceded that his robbery and assault convictions properly could be counted as two of the three prior convictions required for enhancement, because they involved the use of physical force against persons, under § 924(e)(2)(B)(i). Taylor contended, however, that his burglary convictions should not count for enhancement, because they did not involve "conduct that presents a serious potential risk of physical injury to another," under § 924(e)(2)(B)(ii). His guilty plea was conditioned on the right to appeal this issue. . . .

The word "burglary" has not been given a single accepted meaning by the state courts; the criminal codes of the States define burglary in many different ways. *See* United States v. Hill, 863 F.2d 1575, 1582, and n. 5 (C.A.11 1989) (surveying a number of burglary statutes). On the face of the federal enhancement provision, it is not readily apparent whether Congress intended "burglary" to mean whatever the State of the defendant's prior conviction defines as burglary, or whether it intended that some uniform definition of burglary be applied to all cases in which the Government seeks a § 924(e) enhancement. And if Congress intended that a uniform definition of burglary be applied, was that definition to be the traditional common-law definition,[19] or one of the broader "generic" definitions articulated in the Model Penal Code and in a predecessor statute to § 924(e), or some other definition specifically tailored to the purposes of the enhancement statute?

III

These observations about the purpose and general approach of the enhancement provision enable us to narrow the range of possible meanings of the term "burglary."

A

First, we are led to reject the view of the Court of Appeals in this case. It seems to us to be implausible that Congress intended the meaning of "burglary" for purposes of § 924(e) to depend on the definition adopted by the State of conviction. That would mean that a person convicted of unlawful possession of a firearm would, or would not, receive a sentence enhancement based on exactly the same conduct, depending on whether the State of his prior conviction happened to call that conduct "burglary."

. . .

We think that "burglary" in § 924(e) must have some uniform definition independent of the labels employed by the various States' criminal codes.

B

Some Courts of Appeals, have ruled that § 924(e) incorporates the common-law definition of burglary, relying on the maxim that a statutory term is generally presumed to have its common-law meaning. *See* Morissette v. United States, 342 U.S. 246, 263 (1952). This view has some appeal, in that common-law burglary is the core, or common denominator, of the contemporary usage of the term. Almost all States include a breaking and entering of a dwelling at night, with intent to commit a felony, among their definitions of burglary. Whatever else the Members of Congress might have been thinking of, they presumably had in mind at least the "classic" common-law definition when they considered the inclusion of burglary as a predicate offense.

The problem with this view is that the contemporary understanding of "burglary" has diverged a long way from its commonlaw roots. Only a few States retain the common-law definition, or something closely resembling it. Most other States have expanded this definition to include entry without a "breaking," structures other than dwellings, offenses committed in the daytime, entry with intent to commit a crime other than a felony, etc. This statutory development, "when viewed in totality, has resulted in a modern crime which has little in common with its common-law ancestor except for the title of burglary."

---

19. "Burglary was defined by the common law to be the breaking and entering of the dwelling house of another in the nighttime with the intent to commit a felony." W. LaFave & A. Scott, Substantive Criminal Law § 8.13, p. 464 (1986) (LaFave & Scott). *See* 4 W. Blackstone, Commentaries * 224.

Also, interpreting "burglary" in § 924(e) to mean common-law burglary would not comport with the purposes of the enhancement statute. The arcane distinctions embedded in the common-law definition have little relevance to modern law enforcement concerns.[20] It seems unlikely that the Members of Congress, immersed in the intensely practical concerns of controlling violent crime, would have decided to abandon their modern, generic 1984 definition of burglary and revert to a definition developed in the ancient English law—a definition mentioned nowhere in the legislative history. Moreover, construing "burglary" to mean common-law burglary would come close to nullifying that term's effect in the statute, because few of the crimes now generally recognized as burglaries would fall within the common-law definition.

This Court has declined to follow any rule that a statutory term is to be given its common-law meaning, when that meaning is obsolete or inconsistent with the statute's purpose. . . .

Petitioner argues that the narrow common-law definition of burglary would comport with the rule of lenity—that criminal statutes, including sentencing provisions, are to be construed in favor of the accused. This maxim of statutory construction, however, cannot dictate an implausible interpretation of a statute, nor one at odds with the generally accepted contemporary meaning of a term.

. . .

D

We therefore reject petitioner's view that Congress meant to include only a special subclass of burglaries, either those that would have been burglaries at common law, or those that involve especially dangerous conduct. These limiting constructions are not dictated by the rule of lenity. We believe that Congress meant by "burglary" the generic sense in which the term is now used in the criminal codes of most States.

Although the exact formulations vary, the generic, contemporary meaning of burglary contains at least the following elements: an unlawful or unprivileged entry into, or remaining in, a building or other structure, with intent to commit a crime.[21]

---

20. Consider Blackstone's exposition of one of the elements of burglary:

"The time must be by night, and not by day: for in the day *time* there is no burglary. We have seen, in the case of justifiable homicide, how much more heinous all laws made an attack by night, rather than by day; allowing the party attacked by night to kill the assailant with impunity. As to what is reckoned night, and what day, for this purpose: anciently the day was accounted to begin only at sun-rising, and to end immediately upon sun-set; but the better opinion seems to be, that if there be daylight or *crepusculum* enough, begun or left, to discern a man's face withal, it is no burglary. But this does not extend to moonlight; for then many midnight burglaries would go unpunished: and besides, the malignity of the offence does not so properly arise from its being done in the dark, as at the dead of night; when all the creation, except beasts of prey, are at rest; when sleep has disarmed the owner, and rendered his castle defenceless." 4 W. Blackstone, Commentaries *224. *See also id.*, at *224–*228 (burglary must be of a "*mansion*-house," must involve a breaking and entering, and must be with intent to commit a felony).

21. This usage approximates that adopted by the drafters of the Model Penal Code:

We conclude that a person has been convicted of burglary for purposes of a § 924(e) enhancement if he is convicted of any crime, regardless of its exact definition or label, having the basic elements of unlawful or unprivileged entry into, or remaining in, a building or structure, with intent to commit a crime.

IV

... We therefore hold that an offense constitutes "burglary" for purposes of a § 924(e) sentence enhancement if either its statutory definition substantially corresponds to "generic" burglary, or the charging paper and jury instructions actually required the jury to find all the elements of generic burglary in order to convict the defendant.

In Taylor's case, most but not all the former Missouri statutes defining second-degree burglary include all the elements of generic burglary. Despite the Government's argument to the contrary, it is not apparent to us from the sparse record before us which of those statutes were the bases for Taylor's prior convictions. We therefore vacate the judgment of the Court of Appeals and remand the case for further proceedings consistent with this opinion.

It is so ordered.

MODEL PENAL CODE

Article 221. Burglary and Other Criminal Intrusion

Section 221.0 Definitions.

In this Article, unless a different meaning plainly is required:

(1) "occupied structure" means any structure, vehicle or place adapted for overnight accommodation of persons, or for carrying on business therein, whether or not a person is actually present.

(2) "night" means the period between thirty minutes past sunset and thirty minutes before sunrise.

Section 221.1 Burglary.

(1) Burglary Defined. A person is guilty of burglary if he enters a building or occupied structure, or separately secured or occupied portion thereof, with purpose to commit a crime therein, unless the premises are at the time open to the public or the actor is licensed or privileged to enter. It is an affirmative defense to prosecution for burglary that the building or structure was abandoned.

(2) Grading. Burglary is a felony of the second degree if it is perpetrated in the dwelling of another at night, or if, in the course of committing the offense, the actor:

    (a) purposely, knowingly or recklessly inflicts or attempts to inflict bodily injury on anyone; or

    (b) is armed with explosives or a deadly weapon. Otherwise, burglary is a felony of the third degree. An act shall be deemed "in the course of commit-

---

"A person is guilty of burglary if he enters a building or occupied structure, or separately secured or occupied portion thereof, with purpose to commit a crime therein, unless the premises are at the time open to the public or the actor is licensed or privileged to enter." American Law Institute, Model Penal Code § 221.1 (1980).

ting'' an offense if it occurs in an attempt to commit the offense or in flight after the attempt or commission.

(3) Multiple Convictions. A person may not be convicted both for burglary and for the offense which it was his purpose to commit after the burglarious entry or for an attempt to commit that offense, unless the additional offense constitutes a felony of the first or second degree.

Section 221.2 Criminal Trespass.

(1) Buildings and Occupied Structures. A person commits an offense if, knowing that he is not licensed or privileged to do so, he enters or surreptitiously remains in any building or occupied structure, or separately secured or occupied portion thereof. An offense under this Subsection is a misdemeanor if it is committed in a dwelling at night. Otherwise it is a petty misdemeanor.

(2) Defiant Trespasser. A person commits an offense if, knowing that he is not licensed or privileged to do so, he enters or remains in any place as to which notice against trespass is given by:

(a) actual communication to the actor; or

(b) posting in a manner prescribed by law or reasonably likely to come to the attention of intruders; or

(c) fencing or other enclosure manifestly designed to exclude intruders.

An offense under this Subsection constitutes a petty misdemeanor if the offender defies an order to leave personally communicated to him by the owner of the premises or other authorized person. Otherwise it is a violation.

(3) Defenses. It is an affirmative defense to prosecution under this Section that:

(a) a building or occupied structure involved in an offense under Subsection (1) was abandoned; or

(b) the premises were at the time open to members of the public and the actor complied with all lawful conditions imposed on access to or remaining in the premises; or

(c) the actor reasonably believed that the owner of the premises, or other person empowered to license access thereto, would have licensed him to enter or remain.[22]

SECTION 2. ARSON[23]

Common-law arson is the malicious burning of the dwelling house of another.

This crime is usually the result of a deliberate intent and this may anciently have been assumed to be requisite. It has been rather common, for example, to give the definition in this form: Arson is the wilful (or voluntary) and malicious burning of the dwelling house of another. The addition of either word, however, lost all meaning when it became estab-

---

22. Copyright © 1962 by the American Law Institute. Reprinted with the permission of the American Law Institute.

23. For a careful consideration of this subject, *see* Poulos, The Metamorphosis of the Law of Arson, 51 Mo.L.Rev. 295 (1986).

lished that an intent to burn might be implied by law when it did not exist in fact. Thus, if without justification, excuse or mitigation, one sets a fire which obviously creates an unreasonable fire hazard for another's dwelling, which is actually burned thereby, the result is common-law arson even if this was not an intended consequence but there was hope that it would not happen. The ancient explanation that an intent to burn is implied under such circumstances is quite outmoded. The true explanation is that the law does not require the burning to be intentional but only that it be malicious, and that such a burning of the dwelling house of another *is malicious.*

Common-law arson was a felony and in point of gravity ranked only a little less than the crime of murder. It was very distinctly not regarded as a mere violation of property rights. The harm done to the habitation was the primary consideration. Every man's house was his "castle" no matter how humble it might be, and the essence of this crime was the violation of the "castle." Hence one might be guilty of arson for burning a building which he himself *owned,* if someone else was the actual dweller therein; but he could not commit this offense (at common law) by burning his own habitation, if he did not also burn the habitation of another, even if another held the title and hence would suffer the financial loss. The terror caused by seeing one's abode in flames, and the grave risk to human life, were also taken into consideration. This was not only a capital crime at common law, but in the reign of Edward the First the execution was by burning.

Arson had four requisites at common law:

1. There must be some actual burning (but the requirement does not include a destruction of the building or of any substantial part of the building).

2. The burning must be malicious.

3. The object burned must be a dwelling house[24] (but as in burglary any out-house "within the curtilage," was regarded as "parcel of the dwelling house").

4. The house burned must be the habitation of another.

An actual burning of some part of the house is essential but it is not necessary that the building should be destroyed. A blackening by smoke or blistering of the paint by heat is not enough. On the other hand, if any of fiber of the wood is actually consumed by fire, this is a *burning* even if it does not actually burst into flame.[25]

A negligent burning of the dwelling of another does not constitute arson. The burning must be malicious. An intentional burning of such a building will be malicious unless there is some justification, excuse or

---

24. A structure "unoccupied for several months, in a dilapidated condition, not habitable without renovation, and boarded up to prevent ingress and egress" does not constitute a "dwelling" as that word is used in the arson statute. People v. Reed, 13 Mich.App. 75, 163 N.W.2d 704 (1968).

Defendant could not be convicted of arson of an inhabited structure where the tenants had been evicted before the fire, had removed most of their possessions, and no one slept in the premises, even though some items of clothing and furniture remained. People v. Jones, 199 Cal.App.3d 543, 245 Cal.Rptr. 85 (1988).

25. Accord, State v. Nielson, 25 Utah 2d 11, 474 P.2d 725 (1970).

mitigation for the deed. In fact, as mentioned above, an obvious fire hazard may be created under circumstances which will amount to a malicious burning if fire does result, even without an actual intent to cause the particular harm which ensues. One, for example, who set fire to his own dwelling to defraud the insurer was held guilty of arson for the burning of his neighbor's house because he had wantonly and wilfully exposed the other building to this hazard, even though he hoped the fire would not spread to the other building. In some states, and the Model Penal Code, the statutory offense of reckless burning would cover like conduct.

Although it is not common-law arson for one to burn his own dwelling if no other is burned by this fire, it is a common-law misdemeanor if the burning is intentional and the house is situated in a city or town, or is beyond those limits but so near to other houses as to create a danger to them. Most statutes on arson have eliminated the requirement that the building be the dwelling "of another," thereby including under this offense the wilful burning of one's own dwelling (for the purpose of collecting insurance or otherwise).[26] Other enactments have expressly prohibited this very type of burning—sometimes without using the label "arson." Burning personal property to defraud the insurer has also been made a statutory crime. It is common today for arson statutes to include the use of explosives or incendiary devices.[27]

It has also been common for statutes to provide a penalty (under the name of arson or otherwise) for the malicious burning of buildings other than dwellings, such as stores, shops, warehouses and so forth. The term "statutory arson" is employed to designate the entire area of statutory proscription which is analogous to, but not included in common-law arson.

MODEL PENAL CODE
OFFENSES AGAINST PROPERTY

Article 220.   Arson, Criminal Mischief and other Property Destruction

Section 220.1   Arson and Related Offenses.

(1) Arson. A person is guilty of arson, a felony of the second degree, if he starts a fire or causes an explosion with the purpose of:

(a) destroying a building or occupied structure of another; or

(b) destroying or damaging any property, whether his own or another's, to collect insurance for such loss. It shall be an affirmative defense to prosecution under this paragraph that the actor's conduct did not recklessly endanger any building or occupied structure of another or place any other person in danger of death or bodily injury.

---

26.   An arson statute which makes it a felony intentionally to set fire to any building or other structure, so drawn as to include the intentional burning of one's own property for a proper purpose, is unconstitutional. State v. Dennis, 80 N.M. 262, 454 P.2d 276 (1969).

An owner who caused a person to burn his home for reasons other than to get insurance may be convicted of arson. State v. Durant, 674 P.2d 638 (Utah 1983).

Although the wilful and malicious burning of another's automobile is a felony, and is in the chapter on "arson", it is not "arson" within the special clause of the first degree murder statute. People v. Nichols, 3 Cal.3d 150, 89 Cal.Rptr. 721, 474 P.2d 673 (1970).

27.   18 U.S.C. § 844; United States v. Ramsey, 726 F.2d 601 (10th Cir.1984).

(2) Reckless Burning or Exploding. A person commits a felony of the third degree if he purposely starts a fire or causes an explosion, whether on his own property or another's, and thereby recklessly:

(a) places another person in danger of death or bodily injury; or

(b) places a building or occupied structure of another in danger of damage or destruction.

(3) Failure to Control or Report Dangerous Fire. A person who knows that a fire is endangering life or a substantial amount of property of another and fails to take reasonable measures to put out or control the fire, when he can do so without substantial risk to himself, or to give a prompt fire alarm, commits a misdemeanor if:

(a) he knows that he is under an official, contractual, or other legal duty to prevent or combat the fire; or

(b) the fire was started, albeit lawfully, by him or with his assent, or on property in his custody or control.

(4) Definitions. "Occupied structure" means any structure, vehicle, or place adapted for overnight accommodation of persons or for carrying on business therein, whether or not a person is actually present. Property is that of another, for the purposes of this section, if anyone other than the actor has a possessory or proprietary interest therein. If a building or structure is divided into separately occupied units, any unit not occupied by the actor is an occupied structure of another.

Section 220.2   Causing or Risking Catastrophe.

(1) Causing Catastrophe. A person who causes a catastrophe by explosion, fire, flood, avalanche, collapse of building, release of poison gas, radioactive material or other harmful or destructive force or substance, or by any other means of causing potentially widespread injury or damage, commits a felony of the second degree if he does so purposely or knowingly, or a felony of the third degree if he does so recklessly.

(2) Risking Catastrophe. A person is guilty of a misdemeanor if he recklessly creates a risk of catastrophe in the employment of fire, explosives or other dangerous means listed in Subsection (1).

(3) Failure to Prevent Catastrophe. A person who knowingly or recklessly fails to take reasonable measures to prevent or mitigate a catastrophe commits a misdemeanor if:

(a) he knows that he is under an official, contractual or other legal duty to take such measures; or

(b) he did or assented to the act causing or threatening the catastrophe.

Section 220.3   Criminal Mischief.

(1) Offense Defined. A person is guilty of criminal mischief if he:

(a) damages tangible property of another purposely, recklessly, or by negligence in the employment of fire, explosives, or other dangerous means listed in Section 220.2(1); or

(b) purposely or recklessly tampers with tangible property of another so as to endanger person or property; or

(c) purposely or recklessly causes another to suffer pecuniary loss by deception or threat.

(2) Grading. Criminal mischief is a felony of the third degree if the actor purposely causes pecuniary loss in excess of $5,000, or a substantial interruption or impairment of public communication, transportation, supply of water, gas or power, or other public service. It is a misdemeanor if the actor purposely causes pecuniary loss in excess of $100, or a petty misdemeanor if he purposely or recklessly causes pecuniary loss in excess of $25. Otherwise criminal mischief is a violation.[28]

---

28. Copyright © 1962 by the American Law Institute. Reprinted with the permission of the American Law Institute.

CHAPTER 4

OFFENSES AGAINST PROPERTY

SECTION 1. LARCENY[1]

(A) PERSONAL PROPERTY

Larceny was one of the common-law felonies, punishable anciently by total forfeiture—the loss of life and lands and goods.[2] Had it not been for this drastic penalty the courts would probably have recognized, as a possible subject of larceny, any property capable of being taken into possession and removed to another place. As it was, many such things were held not to be the subject of larceny. This applied to animals of a "base nature". Thus it was larceny to steal a horse, cow, pig or chicken, but not to steal a cat, monkey or fox. Many instruments or documents were excluded. The paper or parchment was no longer the subject of larceny, as such, because it was deemed to have been completely merged in the legal instrument or document written upon it. The latter, in turn, was deemed to be merged in whatever was represented by it. As real estate was not the subject of larceny, so neither was a deed to land. A contract represented an intangible right which could not be stolen and hence the wrongful taking of the written evidence of a contract was not larceny. Even negotiable notes and bills were held to be outside the larceny field. A pawn ticket, on the other hand, was the subject of larceny because it represented a specific chattel which could be stolen. Natural gas was the subject of larceny because it can be taken and carried away although not so easily handled as many other things. Electric current, by the prevailing view, was not, on the theory that it is not a substance but comparable to water power which may be used but not "taken and carried away".

These arbitrary exclusions from the scope of larceny have been almost entirely eliminated today, to a considerable extent as a result of legislation.[3]

---

1. There being no statutory definition of larceny in Michigan, all the elements of common-law larceny are required. People v. Anderson, 7 Mich.App. 513, 152 N.W.2d 40 (1967).

2. A.T.H. Smith, Property Offenses, § 1–09 (1994).

3. The wrongful use of another's machinery to spin 20,000 pounds of raw wool into yarn does not constitute larceny. People v. Ashworth, 220 App.Div. 498, 222 N.Y.S. 24 (1927). The court said:

"Personal property has been variously defined. That which may be the subject of larceny is well comprehended in the following statement (36 Corpus Juris, 737): It 'should have corporeal existence, that is, be something the physical presence, quantity, or quality of which is detectable or measurable by the senses or by some mechanical contrivance; for a naked right existing merely in contemplation of law, although it may be very valuable to the person who is entitled to exercise it, is not a subject of larceny.' "

People v. Caridis

Court of Appeals of California, First Appellate District, 1915.
29 Cal.App. 166, 154 P. 1061.

■ LENNON, P.J. The defendant in this case was, by an information filed in the superior court of the city and county of San Francisco, charged with the crime of grand larceny, alleged to have been committed as follows:

"The said Antonio Caridis on the 29th day of July, A.D.1914, at the said City and County of San Francisco, State of California, did then and there willfully, unlawfully and feloniously steal, take and carry away one lottery ticket of the Original Nacional Company, No. 16235, that theretofore and on the 27th day of July, 1914, the said ticket was, after a drawing held by said Original Nacional Company, and its officers, representatives and agents, declared by said Original Nacional Company and its officers, representatives and agents, to be one of the winning tickets of the said Original Nacional Company, and its officers, representatives and agents, after said drawing aforesaid, did become liable for and did promise to pay to the holder of said ticket the sum of twelve hundred and fifty ($1250.00) dollars in gold coin of the United States of America and did then and there promise to pay to the holder of said ticket the sum of twelve hundred and fifty ($1250.00) dollars in gold coin of the United States of America;

"That thereafter, and on the 30th day of July, 1914, the said Antonio Caridis did present said ticket to said Original Nacional Company and to its officers, representatives and agents, and did receive from said Original Nacional Company, and its officers, representatives and agents, the sum of twelve hundred and fifty ($1250) dollars in gold coin of the United States of America therefor;

"That at all of said times the said lottery ticket was the personal property of Jim Papas and was of the value of twelve hundred and fifty ($1250.00) dollars in gold coin of the United States of America."

A demurrer to the information was allowed upon the ground that the facts stated did not constitute a public offense, in the particular that it affirmatively appeared that the subject matter of the alleged larceny had no legitimate value. The action was thereupon dismissed and the people have appealed from the order allowing the demurrer.

The ruling of the court below was correct. It is essential to the commission of the crime of larceny that the property alleged to have been

---

Defendant making unauthorized phone calls created an obligation to the owner of the service to pay for the calls made but did not deprive the owner of "property," even intangible property for purposes of theft. Akbulut v. Grimshaw, 96 Aust. Crim. Rep. 599 (Vict.1997).

Use of computer services could not support a theft conviction where there was no interference with the owner's use or added cost. State v. McGraw, 480 N.E.2d 552 (Ind.1985). Some jurisdictions now cover this problem by special statute. Rev.Code Wash.Ann. 9A.52.110–130 (1988).

Intellectual property is not property that could justify a larceny prosecution at common law, nor within statutory coverage, and therefore cannot be the subject of theft. Commonwealth v. Yourawski, 384 Mass. 386, 425 N.E.2d 298 (1981).

Theft of services is now covered in many statutes. Taking a cab ride can be theft of transportation services. Rodriguez v. State, 889 S.W.2d 559 (Tex.App.1994).

stolen have some value—intrinsic or relative—which, where grand larceny is charged and the property was not taken from the person of another, must exceed the sum of fifty dollars.

Evidently the information in the present case was framed to fit the requirements of section 492 of the Penal Code, which fixes the value in cases of the larceny of written instruments by providing that "If the thing stolen consists of any evidence of debt, or other written instrument, the amount of money due thereupon, or secured to be paid thereby and remaining unsatisfied, or which in any contingency might be collected thereon or the value of the property the title to which is shown thereby, or the sum which might be recovered in the absence thereof, is the value of the thing stolen." Clearly this section contemplates and controls the value to be placed only upon written instruments which create some legal right and constitute a subsisting and an enforceable evidence of a debt.

The lottery ticket which was the subject matter of the larceny charged in the present case had no relative value save, as affirmatively alleged in the information, as the evidence of a debt due from an enterprise which was denounced by law and which apparently existed and was conducted by its promoters in defiance of the law. (Pen.Code, sec. 319 et seq.) It is a well-settled principle that an obligation which exists in defiance of a law which denounces it has, in the eye of the law, neither validity nor value. An instance of the application of this principle is to be found in the analogous case of Culp v. State, 1 Port. (Ala.) 33, 26 Am.Dec. 357, where the court held that an indictment charging the larceny of several "bills of credit of the United States Bank," which were alleged to be of the aggregate value of $310, could not be sustained because each of the bills was for a sum less than the bank was authorized by its charter to issue, and consequently could not, in contemplation of law, be the subject matter of a larceny.

The fact as alleged in the information, that the drawing had taken place prior to the alleged larceny of the ticket, and that the defendant ultimately collected thereon the sum of $1,250 from the lottery company, added nothing to the validity or value of the ticket. Being a void and valueless obligation in the eye of the law from its very inception, it could not be transformed into a legitimate and valuable thing by a voluntary payment, which in itself was a contravention of the law. Moreover, the sufficiency of the information must be determined by the facts as they existed at the time of the alleged taking, and not by anything that may have occurred subsequently.

Considered as a mere piece of paper, the lottery ticket in question possessed perhaps some slight intrinsic value, which, however small, would have sufficed to make the wrongful taking of it petit larceny, and if that had been the charge preferred against the defendant, it doubtless would have stood the test of demurrer.

The order appealed from is affirmed.[4]

---

4. Thirty money orders with figure $200 printed on them, but otherwise blank, were worth the value indicated and not just the value of the paper. Regina v. Zinck, 32 CCC3d 150 (N.B.Ct.App.1986).

People ex rel. Koons v. Elling, Sheriff

Supreme Court, Special Term, Ontario County, New York, 1948.
190 Misc. 998, 77 N.Y.S.2d 103.

■ CRIBB, JUSTICE. The relator, Walter Koons, by this habeas corpus proceeding, seeks his release from the sentence of imprisonment under which he is confined in the Ontario County jail. . . .

It is conceded that the money with the larceny of which relator was charged was removed by him and his confederates from slot machines, commonly referred to as "one armed bandits", located in a room of the Moose Club, by the drilling of a small hole in the machine, through which, by means of an inserted wire, the mechanism was tripped allowing moneys inside to drop down into an exposed receptacle in the same manner as if the machine had been operated in the usual way and had paid out in some amount. The information charged the relator with committing the crime of petit larceny against the property of the named club; the relator plead guilty to the charge. However, if the moneys could not be the subject of larceny, and, as he contends, he therefore committed no crime, his plea of guilty was a nullity. A plea of guilty may not be substituted for the crime itself. Relator maintains that his plea of guilty was a nullity because the moneys were taken from unlawful slot machines in which, as well as in their contents, no person had or could have any title or possessory rights, and that therefore there was no larceny from the "true owner" as contemplated by section 1290 of the Penal Law. The question is therefore presented as to whether money in an unlawful slot machine may be the subject of larceny. Counsel have cited no cases, and the independent search of this Court has discovered none, determinative of the question.

In this case relator was not convicted of stealing the slot machines, which concededly were gambling devices and unlawful under the provisions of section 982 of the Penal Law but rather of stealing moneys contained in them. He was convicted of petit larceny. It is the opinion of this Court that the reasoning adopted by the Court in People v. Otis, 235 N.Y. 421, 139 N.E. 562, is equally applicable in the instant case. In that case the defendant having been indicted for stealing a quantity of whiskey, was convicted of petit larceny. The whiskey was unlawfully possessed under the provisions of the National Prohibition Act, 27 U.S.C.A. § 1 et seq. The question presented was whether the conviction could be sustained under such circumstances. The Court said: "The possessor not being able to make any legal use of it, it is said the liquor itself has no value. This is, however, to make the value of a chattel to its possessor the test as to whether it is the subject of larceny. Such is not the rule. It is enough if the object taken has inherent value. No one can doubt that whiskey has such value. It may be sold by the government and the proceeds covered into the treasury. It

A dog may be the subject of larceny and receiving stolen property. State v. Hernandez, 121 Ariz. 544, 592 P.2d 378 (App.1979).

Fraudulent efforts to avoid payment of a lawful debt do not constitute larceny of the debt. United States v. Mervine, 26 M.J. 482 (CMA 1988).

The value of checks defendant stole was their face value where the checks were not worthless, even though not endorsed or stamped for deposit. Gallegos v. State, 113 N.M. 339, 825 P.2d 1249 (1992).

may be sold by druggists. That it is held illegally is immaterial."[5] Although the statute, 27 U.S.C.A. § 39, under discussion in that case specifically provided that "no property rights shall exist" in liquor illegally possessed, the Court held that such liquor could be the subject of larceny, and after referring to the statutory provisions for the issuance of search warrants, the seizure and final disposition by the courts of liquor so illegally possessed, and the prohibitory provision as to property rights in such liquor, the Court further said: "Property rights in such liquor are not forever ended. They pass to the government." . . .

An order may be issued dismissing the writ of habeas corpus heretofore granted in this proceeding and remanding relator to the custody of the sheriff of Ontario County to serve the remainder of his sentence in accordance with the provisions of law applicable thereto.[6]

Bell v. State

Supreme Court of Tennessee, 1874.
63 Tenn. 426.

■ DEADERICK, J., delivered the opinion of the Court.

The plaintiff in error was convicted at the November Term, 1874, of the Criminal Court of Montgomery County, of petit larceny, for stealing as charged, cabbage and sweet potatoes, the goods and chattels of G.B. White, the prosecutor, and sentenced to the penitentiary for one year.

It is insisted that the charge of the Judge was erroneous in its definition of the offense charged.

In the beginning of his charge the Judge gives a full and accurate definition of the offence, and correctly instructs the jury as to the difference between grand and petit larceny, and the punishment annexed to each.

It is true, in a subsequent part of his instructions, as introductory to the definition of "personal property," he says: "The jury will observe that larceny is the felonious taking away of personal property." He then proceeds to state to the jury when vegetables, etc., growing in or upon the ground, may become "personal property," and the subject of larceny, and uses this language: "If defendant went at night into the garden of another, intending to steal, and dug a lot of sweet potatoes, laying them on the

5. Accord, People v. Odenwald, 104 Cal.App. 203, 285 P. 406 (1930), overruling People v. Spencer, 54 Cal.App. 54, 201 P. 130 (1921), which had held such liquor was not the subject of larceny, because the statute provided that "no property right shall exist in any such liquor".

There is no such defense to theft known as *de minimis non curat lex*. Regina v. Li, 16 CCC3d 382 (Ont.H.C.1984); $180 dollar bill is "property" subject to theft for robbery. State v. Gomez, 234 Kan. 447, 673 P.2d 1160 (1983).

One who larcenously takes the stolen object from a thief may be convicted of larceny despite the criminality of the possession of the latter. Commonwealth v. Rourke, 64 Mass. 397 (1852).

6. Theft under 18 U.S.C.A. § 641 is established by the taking of any "thing of value;" and the selling of information from a government computer is prohibited by the statute. United States v. Lambert, 446 F.Supp. 890 (D.C.Conn.1978), affirmed United States v. Girard, 601 F.2d 69 (2d Cir.1979).

ground, or cut a lot of cabbage, severing them from the earth, and afterwards picked up the vegetables, put them in a bag, and carried them off, that would be larceny.''

This latter part of the charge is not strictly accurate, according to the rule of the common law. In 3 Greenleaf on Ev., § 163, it is said: "If the severance and asportation were one continued act of the prisoner, it is only a trespass; but if the severance were the act of another person, or if, after the severance by the prisoner, any interval of time elapsed, after which he returned and took the article away, the severance and asportation being two distinct acts, it is larceny," citing 1 E. Hale P.C., 510; 2 East P.C., 587. . . .

The principle is, that when the severance and asportation constitute one continuous act, then it is a trespass only, but if the severance is a distinct act, and not immediately connected with or followed by the asportation it is a larceny.

To dig potatoes, whereby they are cast upon the surface of the earth, and then immediately to pick them up, and put them in a bag, and carry them away, would be one continuous act, although the picking up, necessarily, was after the digging, and after they had lain upon the ground. The act would be continuous, without cessation, until the asportation, as well as the severance, was completed, and thus a trespass only. And so, also, of cutting a "lot of cabbages," "severing them from the earth," the "severing" necessarily preceded the taking away, yet, when the taking away immediately follows, it is a "continuous act," and is trespass only.

It is argued by the Attorney–General, that the taking of vegetables severed from the ground, and the carrying of stolen goods into another county, seem to stand upon the same footing, although it is conceded that the authorities hold, as to the first mentioned, that the possession is not in the owner as personalty, and in the latter, that the legal possession still remains in him.

The trespasser holds the severed property, as personalty, but he cannot be convicted of a larceny, for he did not obtain that possession feloniously. No felony was committed in the taking and carrying away from the owner, but a trespass only.

In the case of an original felonious taking and carrying away, every moment's continuance of the trespass and felony amounts to a new caption and asportation, (2 Arch.Cr.Pr. & Pl., 343, note 1,) and the offence is considered as committed in every county or jurisdiction into which the thief carries the goods. Ibid. It is difficult to see any difference in the moral guilt of one who takes and carries away immediately upon the severance from the freehold and one who severs at one time and takes away at another, but the Legislature has not altered the distinction made by the common law, and it is still in force in Tennessee.[7]

---

7. The legislature made the change later. Williams v. State, 186 Tenn. 252, 257, 209 S.W.2d 29, 31 (1948).

Copper wire taken from poles was realty not personalty and could not be the subject of larceny. Parker v. State, 352 So.2d 1386 (Ala.Crim.App.1977).

The judgment of the Criminal Court will be reversed.[8]

The Queen v. Townley

Court for Crown Cases Reserved, 1871.
L.R. 1 C.C. 315, 12 Cox C.C. 59.

■ BOVILL, C.J. The prisoner in this case has been convicted of felony in stealing rabbits, and the question is, whether he has been properly convicted. The facts are, that the rabbits, 126 in number, were taken and killed upon land the property of the Crown. The rabbits were then, together with 400 yards of net, placed in a ditch on the same land on which they had been taken; some of them being in bags, and some in bundles strapped together by the legs. They were placed there by the poachers, who in so placing them had no intention to abandon the wrongful possession which they had acquired by taking them, but placed them in the ditch as a place of deposit till they could conveniently remove them. Here they were found by the keepers at about eight in the morning. At about a quarter to eleven the prisoner arrived, went straight to the place where the rabbits were concealed, and began to remove them.

Now, the first question is as to the nature of the property in these rabbits. In animals ferae naturae there is no absolute property. There is only a special or qualified right of property—a right ratione soli to take and kill them. When killed upon the soil they become the absolute property of the owner of the soil. This was decided in the case of rabbits by the House of Lords in Blade v. Higgs.[9] And the same principle was applied in the case of grouse in Lord Lonsdale v. Rigg.[10] In this case therefore the rabbits, being started and killed on land belonging to the Crown, might, if there were no other circumstance in the case, become the property of the Crown. But before there can be a conviction for larceny for taking anything not capable in its original state of being the subject of larceny, as for instance, things fixed to the soil, it is necessary that the act of taking away should not be one continuous act with the act of severance or other act by which the thing becomes a chattel, and so is brought within the law of larceny. This doctrine has been applied to stripping lead from the roof of a church, and in other cases of things affixed to the soil. And the present case must be governed by the same principle. It is not stated in the case whether or not the prisoner was one of the poachers who killed the rabbits. But my Brother Blackburn says that such must be taken to be the fact. Under all the circumstances of the case I think a jury ought to have found that the

---

8. Since the *statutory* offense of "theft" includes the taking of anything of value the fact that what was taken was severed from the realty is unimportant. State v. Mills, 214 La. 979, 39 So.2d 439 (1949). Some courts reached a similar result in regard to larceny without the aid of statute. Ex parte Willke, 34 Tex. 155 (1870); Stephens v. Commonwealth, 304 Ky. 38, 199 S.W.2d 719 (1947). The wrongful severance of a part of the realty and its appropriation is expressly made larceny in some of the statutes. More frequently it is punished as some other offense, such as malicious mischief and trespass.

9. [Footnotes by the Court.] 11 H.L.C. 621; 34 L.J.(C.P.) 286.

10. 1 H. & N. 923; 26 L.J.(Ex.) 196.

whole transaction was a continuous one; and the conviction must be quashed. . . .

■ (MARTIN, B., BRAMWELL, B., BYLES, J., and BLACKBURN, J., were of the same opinion, and the conviction was quashed.)[11]

(B) "OF ANOTHER"

(i) In General

State v. Cohen

Supreme Court of Minnesota, 1935.
196 Minn. 39, 263 N.W. 922.

(The defendant, having had her fur coat repaired by a furrier, regained control of it by the pretense of trying it on, after which she concealed it and refused either to return it or to pay for the work done. She appealed from a conviction of the crime of grand larceny in the second degree.)

■ HOLT, JUSTICE. . . . The verdict is not contrary to law. A person may be guilty of larceny of his own property if taken from the possession of one who has a lien thereon under which possession may lawfully be retained until the lien is discharged. Sections 8507 and 8508, 2 Mason Minn.St.1927, gave a possessory lien to Mellon, and the way defendant procured the coat to see how it looked on her person does not, as a matter of law, bring her within the protection of 2 Mason Minn.St.1927, § 10372. On the contrary, the jury had warrant for finding that defendant's scheme of trying on the coat and disappearing with it was with the felonious intent of depriving Mellon of his lien and his right of possession until the lien was discharged. An owner of personal property may be found guilty of larceny thereof when he wrongfully takes it from a pledgee or from one whom he has given possession for the purpose of having it cared for or repaired under statutes such as ours giving a lien therefor and the right to retain possession until the lien is paid. State v. Hubbard, 126 Kan. 129, 266 P. 939, annotated in 58 A.L.R. 327, 330, 331, where the authorities are cited and this conclusion therefrom is stated:

"If personal property in the possession of one other than the general owner by virtue of some special right or title is taken from him by the general owner, such taking is larceny if it is done with the felonious intent of depriving such person of his rights, or of charging him with the value of the property." . . .

Defendant complains of the ruling excluding evidence of an expert that the material and labor which Mellon expended in making the agreed alterations and repairs on the coat did not enhance its value. We think the ruling right. Defendant was permitted to testify as to her opinion of Mellon's work; that it ruined the coat instead of enhancing its value; that she thought he had substituted inferior fur for that which was in the coat

---

11.   See A.T.H. Smith, Property Offenses § 3–51–54 (1994).

Animal theft statute does not apply when proof shows that the animal was dead when the larceny occurred; however, if the animal is killed as a means of making the theft, it is the same as stealing a live animal. Knowles v. State, 410 So.2d 380 (Miss.1982).

when delivered to him; and that she took possession because she was afraid the value of the coat would be utterly destroyed. All this properly went to disprove felonious intent. But we think the amount of Mellon's lien was not an issue that could be litigated in this case. It was not between the proper parties. The quantum of proof is not the same in this criminal case as it would be in an action between Mellon and defendant either to establish or defeat a lien. We take it that in this prosecution the only value in issue was the value of the coat which defendant feloniously took and concealed.[12] Mellon was entitled to the possession of the entire coat until his lien was determined in a lawful manner. And defendant was not entitled to have the amount of Mellon's possessory lien determined in this criminal case. It was conceded that possession of the coat had been given by her to Mellon in order that he might alter and repair it at an agreed price.

Other assignments of error are made. They had been examined, but we do not consider them of sufficient merit to note in this opinion.

The conviction is affirmed.[13]

(ii) Distinction Between Custody and Possession

There was no common-law crime known as "embezzlement", which is a statutory crime enacted to fill certain gaps that appeared during the development of the crime of larceny. These gaps (there were others) grew out of the holding that no appropriation by one having lawful possession could constitute the felony of larceny. One of the refinements of this development was the distinction between custody and possession, because

---

12. If the thief gave consideration for, or had a legal interest in, the stolen property, the amount of such consideration or value shall be deducted from the total value of the property. W.S.A. 943.20.

13. It was held not to be larceny for a wife to appropriate money belonging to 30 people, one of whom was her husband. Rex v. Willis, 1 Moody 375, 168 Eng.Rep. 1309 (1833). It was held otherwise under a statute authorizing a married woman to acquire, hold and transfer property as freely as if she were single. Fugate v. Commonwealth, 308 Ky. 815, 215 S.W.2d 1004 (1948).

Defendant could not be charged with stealing property from an estate, since an estate is not capable of possession or ownership of property. State v. S.E., 675 S.W.2d 86 (Mo.App. 1984). Contra, Smith v. State, 664 N.E.2d 758 (Ind.App.1996). Decedent's estate is a "person" for theft offense.

One partner does not commit larceny by wrongfully appropriating partnership property since each partner has an individual interest therein. State v. Elsbury, 63 Nev. 463, 175 P.2d 430 (1946); People v. Clayton, 728 P.2d 723 (Colo.1986).

A joint tenant may not be convicted of the crime of theft for taking funds from a joint account. State v. Haack, 220 Mont. 141, 713 P.2d 1001 (1986).

"Proof of a greater right to possession than the thief is always sufficient proof of 'ownership.' " State v. Lemon, 203 Kan. 464, 454 P.2d 718 (1969).

To constitute "property of another" it is not necessarily that title be in the other person. It is sufficient if the other person has an interest in the property and the defendant has no interest without the other's consent. State v. Joy, 121 Wash.2d 333, 851 P.2d 654 (1993).

It is no defense to a charge of robbery or larceny that the victim is not the true owner of the property because larceny can be committed against one who is himself a thief. People v. Moore, 4 Cal.App.3d 668, 84 Cal.Rptr. 771 (1970).

A partner may be convicted of theft of partnership property. State v. Larsen, 834 P.2d 586 (Utah App.1992).

the rule came to be that if the one having control of the property had custody only, and not possession, his conversion of the property could result in larceny. And because the statutory offense was intended to fill "gaps" in the law of larceny it was held there was no overlapping. The result was a mutually-exclusive area, and in this area a holding that the appropriation constituted embezzlement was a holding that it did not constitute larceny, and vice versa. The problem is now only of historical interest in most jurisdictions and has been remedied by statute.

People v. Walker

Colorado Court of Appeals, Div. II, 1980.
44 Colo.App. 249, 615 P.2d 57.

■ ENOCH, CHIEF JUDGE. Defendant was convicted by a jury of theft in violation of § 18–4–401(4), C.R.S.1973 (1978 Repl.Vol. 8). He contends that the trial court erred in failing to grant a judgment of acquittal and improperly refused to give certain jury instructions. We affirm.

These facts are undisputed: A team of six Denver police officers, including one who was posing as a drunk, were positioned near the intersection of 15th and Welton Streets in downtown Denver around 10 p.m. on September 22, 1977. The policeman pretending to be drunk was lying face down in the entryway to a "hock" shop and carried a wallet containing marked bills. He testified that someone approached him, that he was asked, "What's the matter, brother?" but that he remained silent. He said his wallet was taken.

Others on the police team testified that defendant was apprehended less than a block away. The marked money—two one-hundred-dollar bills and two twenty-dollar bills—was found in his pocket.

Defendant testified on his own behalf that he first approached the decoy officer in the belief that he was injured, but that he saw no signs of violence and noted that the body of the prone officer was stiff. Defendant concluded that he had encountered a dead man. He then admitted taking the money from a wallet on the officer's person.

Defendant contends first that the evidence does not sufficiently establish that he had the specific intent required to support a conviction of theft. The argument in support of this contention is not clear; however, from the record we interpret it to be that defendant could not have had the specific intent, as required by the statute, to permanently deprive another of a thing of value because he took the money from what he thought to be a dead body. Thus, he did not intend to "deprive another." We disagree.

Even if defendant in good faith believed that he was taking money from a dead man's wallet, he was not entitled to possession of that property. From the moment of death, the heirs or devisees become the rightful possessors of property until the estate of the deceased has passed through probate or administration. See § 15–11–101 et seq., and § 15–12–101 et seq., C.R.S.1973. Therefore, it makes no difference whether the money was taken from a living person or a dead body. Affirmed.[14]

The King v. Bazeley

Court for Crown Cases Reserved, 1799.
2 Leach 835, 168 Eng.Rep. 517.

At the Old Bailey in February Session 1799, Joseph Bazeley was tried before John Silvester, Esq. Common Serjeant of the city of London, for feloniously stealing on the 18th January preceding, a Bank-note of the value of one hundred pounds, the property of Peter Esdaile, Sir Benjamin Hammett, William Esdaile, and John Hammett.

The following facts appeared in evidence. The prisoner, Joseph Bazeley, was the principal teller at the house of Messrs. Esdaile's and Hammett's bankers, in Lombard-street, at the salary of £100 a year, and his duty was to receive and pay money, notes, and bills, at the counter. The manner of conducting the business of this banking-house is as follows: There are four tellers, each of whom has a separate money-book, a separate money-drawer, and a separate bag. The prisoner being the chief teller, the total of the receipts and payments of all the other money-books were every evening copied into his, and the total balance or rest, as it is technically called, struck in his book, and the balances of the other money-books paid, by the other tellers, over to him. When any monies, whether in cash or notes, are brought by customers to the counter to be paid in, the teller who receives it counts it over, then enters the Bank-notes or drafts, and afterwards the cash, under the customer's name, in his book; and then, after casting up the total, it is entered in the customer's book. The money is then put into the teller's bag, and the Bank-notes or other papers, if any, put into a box which stands on a desk behind the counter, directly before another clerk, who is called the cash bookkeeper, who makes an entry of it in the received cash-book in the name of the person who has paid it in, and which he finds written by the receiving teller on the back of the bill or note so placed in the drawer. The prisoner was treasurer to an association called "The Ding Dong Mining Company"; and in the course of the year had many bills drawn on him by the Company, and many bills drawn on other persons remitted to him by the Company. In the month of January 1799, the prisoner had accepted bills on account of the Company, to the amount of £112, 4s. 1d. and had in his possession a bill of £166, 7s. 3d. belonging to the Company, but which was not due until the 9th February. One of the bills, amounting to £100, which the prisoner had accepted, became due on 18th January. Mr. William Gilbert, a grocer, in the surry-road, Black-friars, kept his cash at the banking-house of the prosecutors, and on the 18th January 1799, he sent his servant, George Cock, to pay in £137. This sum consisted of £122 in Bank-notes, and the rest in cash. One of these Bank-notes was the note which the prisoner was indicted for stealing. The prisoner received this money from George Cock, and after entering the £137 in Mr. Gilbert's Bank-book, entered the £15 cash in his own money-

---

14. Taking money from a police decoy who appeared to be drunk was not excused on a theory that the decoy consented to the taking. State v. Woodard, 378 N.W.2d 32 (Minn.App. 1985).

book, and put over the £22 in Bank-notes into the drawer behind him, keeping back the £100 Bank-note, which he put into his pocket, and afterwards paid to a banker's clerk the same day at a clearing-house in Lombard-street, in discharge of the £100 bill which he had accepted on account of the Ding Dong Mining Company. To make the sum in Mr. Gilbert's Bank-book, and the sum in the book of the banking-house agree, it appeared that a unit had been added to the entry of £37 to the credit of Mr. Gilbert, in the book of the banking-house, but it did not appear by any direct proof that this alteration had been made by the prisoner; it appeared however that he had made a confession, but the confession having been obtained under a promise of favour it was not given in evidence.

Const and Jackson, the prisoner's Counsel, submitted to the Court, that to constitute a larceny, it was necessary in point of law that the property should be taken from the possession of the prosecutor, but that it was clear from the evidence in this case, that the Bank-note charged to have been stolen, never was either in the actual or the constructive possession of Esdaile and Hammett, and that even if it had been in their possession, yet that from the manner in which it had been secreted by the prisoner, it amounted only to a breach of trust.

The Court left the facts of the case to the consideration of the Jury, and on their finding the prisoner Guilty, the case was reserved for the opinion of the Twelve Judges on a question, whether under the circumstances above stated, the taking of the Bank-note was in law a felonious taking, or only a fraudulent breach of trust.

The case was accordingly argued before nine of the Judges (Lord Kenyon, L.C.J.; C.J. Eyre, C.B. Macdonald, Mr. Baron Hotham, Mr. B. Perryn, Mr. Baron Thompson, Mr. J. Grose, Mr. J. Lawrence, Mr. J. Rooke) in the Exchequer Chamber, on Saturday, 27th April 1799, by Const for the prisoner, and by Fielding for the Crown. . . .

The Judges, it is said, were of opinion, upon the authority of Rex v. Waite, that this Bank-note never was in the legal custody or possession of the prosecutors, Messrs. Esdailes and Hammett; but no opinion was ever publicly delivered[15]; and the prisoner was included in the Secretary of State's letter as a proper object for a pardon.

(In consequence of this case the statute 39 Geo. III, c. 85 was passed, entitled: "An Act to protect Masters and others against Embezzlement, by

---

15. On consultation among the Judges, some doubt was at first entertained but at last all assembled agreed that it was not felony, inasmuch as the note was never in the possession of the bankers, distinct from the possession of the prisoner: though it would have been otherwise if the prisoner had deposited it in the drawer, and had afterwards taken it. (Vide Chipchase's case, ante, p. 699.) And they thought that this was not to be differed from the cases of Rex v. Waite, ante, p. 28, and Rex v. Bull, ante, p. 841, which turned on this consideration, that the thing was not taken by the prisoner out of the possession of the owner: and here it was delivered into the possession of the prisoner. That although to many purposes the note was in the actual possession of the masters, yet it was also in the actual possession of the servant, and that possession not to be impeached; for it was a lawful one. Eyre, C.J. also observed that the cases ran into one another very much, and were hardly to be distinguished: That in the case of Rex v. Spears, ante, p. 825, the corn was in the possession of the master under the care of the servant: and Lord Kenyon said that he relied much on the Act of Parliament respecting the Bank not going further than to protect the Bank. 2 East, C.L. 574.

their Clerks or Servants." The scope of embezzlement has been greatly enlarged by subsequent enactments—both in England and in this country.)

Rex v. Sullens

Court for Crown Cases Reserved, 1826.
1 Moody 129, 168 Eng.Rep. 1212.

■ The prisoner was tried before ALEXANDER C.B., at the Spring Assizes for the county of Essex, in the year 1826, on an indictment at common law: the first count of which charged the prisoner with stealing at Doddinghurst, on the 25th September, 1825, one promissory note, value $5, the property of Thomas Nevill and George Nevill, his master; the second count with stealing silver coin, the property of Thomas Nevill and George Nevill.

It appeared in evidence that Thomas Nevill, the prisoner's master, gave him a £5 country note, to get change, on the said 25th of September; that he got change, all in silver, and on his obtaining the change he said it was for his master, and that his master sent him. The prisoner never returned.

The jury found the prisoner not guilty on the first count, but guilty on the second count.

The question reserved for the consideration of the Judges was, whether the conviction was proper, or whether the indictment should not have been on the statute 39 Geo. III. c. 85, for embezzlement?

In Easter Term, 1826, the Judges met and considered this case, and held that the conviction was wrong, because as the masters never had possession of the change, except by the hands of the prisoner, he was only amenable under the statute 39 Geo. III. c. 85. (Rex v. Headge, Russ & Ry. C.C.R. 160; Rex v. Walsh, ib. 215.)

State v. Brooks

Court of Appeals of New Mexico, 1993.
116 N.M. 309, 862 P.2d 57, certiorari granted, reversed other grounds 117 N.M. 751, 877 P.2d 557 (1994).

■ ALARID, JUDGE.

I. INTRODUCTION

Defendant appeals his conviction of, and sentence on, seven counts of embezzlement. He raises six issues on appeal: (1) whether the single larceny doctrine applies in this case; ... We affirm.

II. FACTS

Defendant was the bookkeeper for RMS, a property management service. He shared an office and desk with the president of the company. His responsibilities included keeping track of receipts, checking credit, making deposits, balancing check books, and other general financial matters. In particular, it was Defendant's responsibility to make out deposit slips and reconcile the deposits with the accounts receivable ledger. Rental payments were sometimes made by cash, check, or money order. When rent was paid in cash, a receipt was given and the money was placed in an envelope, which was sealed, and stored in a desk drawer. The money was logged in on a worksheet and also in an accounts receivable book.

Sometime in August of 1989, the president of RMS discovered over $3000 missing from rental monies. He hired a private investigator to look into the matter. The private investigator began his inquiries with Defendant. Defendant was given a polygraph test and acknowledged taking the money. In addition, Defendant wrote a confession admitting that he took the money.

. . .

D.   Entrustment

Defendant argues that his motion for directed verdict should have been granted because the State failed to prove that he was entrusted with tenants' rent money. A motion for directed verdict tests the sufficiency of the evidence. In reviewing for sufficiency of the evidence, the question is whether substantial evidence exists of either a direct or circumstantial nature to support a verdict of guilty beyond a reasonable doubt with respect to each element of the crime. The evidence is viewed in the light most favorable to the verdict, resolving all conflicts therein, and indulging all reasonable inferences therefrom in the light most favorable to the judgment.

Entrustment is an essential element of the crime of embezzlement. SCRA 1986, 14–1641 (Recomp.1986). Entrust means "to 'commit or surrender to another with a certain confidence regarding his care, use, or disposal' 'of that which has been committed or surrendered.'" State v. Moss, 83 N.M. 42, 44, 487 P.2d 1347, 1349 (Ct.App.1971) (quoting Webster's Third New International Dictionary (1966)).

Here, the evidence was that Defendant was responsible for the money after it was received and placed in the desk drawer. The fact that Defendant did not personally take money from the tenants is not dispositive. All the money received from tenants was to be deposited in the bank. Defendant took the money from the drawer and prepared the deposit slips. He was also responsible for making sure that the books balanced. This is sufficient to show that Defendant was entrusted with the rental money.

Defendant contends that the jury should have been specially instructed on the meaning of the word "entrust," citing State v. Franklin, 78 N.M. 127, 428 P.2d 982 (1967). In addition, under Jackson v. State, 100 N.M. 487, 672 P.2d 660 (1983), Defendant argues that the trial court has the duty to properly instruct the jury on all essential questions of law. However, Moss, 83 N.M. at 44, 487 P.2d at 1349, holds that, absent clearly expressed legislative intent to modify the ordinary meaning of "entrust," no special instruction need be given on the meaning of the word. Therefore, the defendant is not entitled to have the jury specially instructed on the meaning of the word "entrust."

. . .

V. CONCLUSION

Defendant's conviction of seven counts of embezzlement and his sentence requiring the payment of restitution to the insurance company of RMS are affirmed.

IT IS SO ORDERED.

■ FLORES, J., concurs.

■ BIVINS, J., dissents and files opinion.[16]

Morgan v. Commonwealth

Court of Appeals of Kentucky, 1932.
242 Ky. 713, 47 S.W.2d 543.

■ DIETZMAN, C.J. Appellant was convicted of the offense of grand larceny, sentenced to serve two years in the penitentiary, and appeals.

The undisputed facts in this case are these: The Western Union Telegraph Company has for a number of years maintained a local office in Irving, Ky. In February, 1930, the appellant was put in full charge of this office. It is not clear how many employees were under him, but at least it is shown that there were a porter and a young lady employee who worked under his direction. The office was equipped with a safe. At the time appellant was put in charge of the office, the combination on the safe was reset and he was given a copy of it. Another copy of the combination was sealed in an envelope and sent to the main office of the company in Nashville, where it was placed among the archives not to be opened unless the appellant severed his connection with the company and it became necessary to ascertain what the combination was in order to get into the safe. Thus although the company could, by opening this sealed envelope, apprise itself of what the combination was, yet so long as appellant continued in its employ it remained in actual ignorance of the combination to the safe and the appellant was the only one who had actual access to the safe. Inside of the safe was a small portable steel vault or box, the keys to which were intrusted to appellant. In this steel vault or box appellant placed at night the funds which came into the office during the day, and in the morning took them out either for use as change, for deposit in bank, or to be forwarded to the company. On the morning of July 5, 1930, the safe

---

16. "The distinction between larceny by fraud and embezzlement is some times very close. Whether larceny is committed by fraud or whether the taker is guilty of embezzlement is determined with reference to the time when the fraudulent intent to convert the property to the taker's own use arises. If the criminal intent exists at the time of the taking of the property, it is 'larceny' but if the intent does not arise until after the defendant received possession, then it is 'embezzlement.' " Lovick v. State, 646 P.2d 1296, 1297–98 (Okl.Cr.App. 1982).

Where defendant never had control over money taken although he was in charge of the store. Money was in a drop box handled exclusively by the store manager. The offense is larceny not embezzlement. State v. Stahl, 93 N.M. 62, 596 P.2d 275 (1979).

Where shift supervisor at a detention facility took money from incoming prisoner accounts which had been "entrusted" to him, he was properly convicted of embezzlement. State v. Eder, 103 N.M. 211, 704 P.2d 465 (App.1985).

See also Commonwealth v. Ryan, 155 Mass. 523, 30 N.E. 364 (1892).

was discovered open. Its handle and dial were broken off, and the steel vault or box which had in it approximately $90 of the funds of the company was missing. It was later discovered empty in a field near by appellant's boarding house. We shall assume for the purpose of the decision of this case, and without detailing the facts at length, that the commonwealth's proof made out a case to go to the jury that the abstraction of the steel vault from the safe and the conversion of the funds that it contained were done by the appellant. Appellant was indicted, as stated, for the offense of grand larceny, and he insists on this appeal that his motion for a peremptory instruction should have been sustained because the proof shows that if any offense was committed it was that of embezzlement and not larceny.

The main distinction between embezzlement and larceny in cases like the instant one turns on the distinction between custody and possession. We quote from the case of Warmoth v. Commonwealth, 81 Ky. 135:

"A distinction exists where a servant has merely the custody and where he has the possession of the goods. In the former case the felonious appropriation of the goods is larceny; in the latter it is not larceny, but embezzlement...."

In 20 C.J. 410, it is said: "Embezzlement differs from larceny in that it is the wrongful appropriation or conversion of property where the original taking was lawful, or with the consent of the owner, while in larceny the taking involves a trespass, and the felonious intent must exist at the time of such taking. Thus, a bailee who obtains possession of property without fraudulent intent is not guilty of larceny where he subsequently converts it. So long as he has lawful possession he cannot commit a trespass with respect to the property. But where a person enters into a contract of bailment and obtains possession of the property with felonious intent, existing at the time, to appropriate or apply the property to his own use, he is guilty of a trespass and larceny, and not embezzlement, and if one enters into a contract of bailment fraudulently, but without felonious intent, and afterward converts the property, his offense is larceny and not embezzlement.... Since, therefore, larceny at common law involves the element of an original wrongful taking or trespass, it cannot apply to the stealing or wrongful conversion of property by an agent or bailee, or by a servant having the possession, as distinguished from the mere custody, or by anyone else intrusted with the possession of the property; and to remedy this defect and prevent an evasion of justice in such cases, statutes of embezzlement were passed."

Under the peculiar facts of this case, we are constrained to the view that at the time the appellant converted the funds here involved (as we have assumed the evidence so establishes) he had the possession as distinguished from the custody of such funds. They were in the safe, the combination of which was known actually only by him. It was intended, in the absence of some untoward circumstance, that at least until he forwarded these funds to the company they should be in his possession. They came into his possession as the servant of the Western Union. He was in full charge of the office. It was he who locked the safe at night and it was only he who could open it in the morning. Although the company had the right to demand the funds of him at any time, and although the company could potentially enter the safe by opening the sealed envelope and apprising itself of the combination, yet it was not intended by the company that it should interfere with appellant's control and possession of the contents of this safe and the funds of the company unless and until some condition which had not occurred in this case at the time of the conversion had come to pass. It is quite manifest that the possession of these funds at the time they were converted was in the appellant and that it had not yet become that of the Western Union. This being true, the conversion amounted to an embezzlement and not larceny. *Warmoth v. Commonwealth, supra.* The two offenses are not degrees of one another. They are distinct offenses. Hence appellant could not be convicted of the offense of larceny when it was shown that what he did constituted embezzlement and not larceny. It follows that appellant's motion for a peremptory instruction should have been sustained. Judgment reversed, with instructions to grant the appellant a new trial in conformity with this opinion.

Whole court sitting.[17]

United States v. Bowser

United States Circuit Court of Appeals, Ninth Circuit, 1976.
532 F.2d 1318.

OPINION

■ Before BROWNING and DUNIWAY, CIRCUIT JUDGES, and CHRISTENSEN,[18] DISTRICT JUDGE.

■ CHRISTENSEN, DISTRICT JUDGE.

The larceny from the bank may have been a fake as far as the appellant and a coconspirator teller were concerned; it was very real as to the bank from which more than $5,000 of its money was taken and carried away without its consent by a third conspirator according to the proofs of the government. This distinction leads to our rejection of the primary contention on this appeal: that there was fatal variance between the allegations of the indictment based on a theory of larceny and the proof which established no more than that appellant was associated with the teller in the commission of embezzlement.

A three count indictment jointly charged Sharon Held, Robert P. Farrelly and appellant Curtis Bowser with the offenses of entering a bank with intent to commit a felony, to-wit: bank larceny, in violation of 18 U.S.C.A. § 2113(a),[19] bank larceny in violation of 18 U.S.C. § 2113(b),[20] and

---

17. The manager of a service station who wrongfully appropriated the cash "bank" of the station was guilty of embezzlement. Reynolds v. People, 172 Colo. 137, 471 P.2d 417 (1970).

18. Honorable A. Sherman Christensen, Senior United States District Judge for the District of Utah, sitting by designation.

19. Whoever enters . . . any bank . . . with intent to commit in such bank . . . any felony affecting such bank . . . and in violation of any statute of the United States, or any larceny—

Shall be fined not more than $5,000 or imprisoned not more than twenty years, or both.

20. Whoever takes and carries away, with intent to steal or purloin, any property or money . . . exceeding $100 belonging to, or in the care, custody, control, management, or

conspiracy to commit bank larceny in violation of 18 U.S.C. § 371.[21] Upon arraignment each defendant entered a plea of not guilty. Thereafter, Farrelly and Held withdrew such pleas and entered pleas of guilty to count three of the indictment, the other counts being dismissed as to them. Appellant stood trial before a jury and was convicted and sentenced on all three counts.

The evidence adduced by the government, in the light of appellant's testimony and the other evidence he presented as to his claimed alibi, was ample to prove that he, Held and Farrelly conspired to take money from the Crocker Bank, 1 Montgomery Street, San Francisco, California, through feigned intimidation of Held as teller of the bank; that pursuant to their plan appellant waited outside in a getaway car and Farrelly entered the bank and handed Held a note demanding money under threat of bodily harm;[22] that Held delivered the sum of $5,158.37 of the bank's funds to Farrelly, who placed the money into a dark attache case he had carried with him into the bank; that Farrelly then joined appellant in the getaway car, and that Held waited moments after Farrelly left her window, then told a superior in the bank that she had been robbed and produced the note.

Appellant claims here, as he maintained below, that he was charged under the wrong statutes; that the basis of the indictment should have been embezzlement by an employee of an insured bank in violation of 18 U.S.C. § 656,[23] and for this reason his conviction must be reversed.

There would be a certain poetic justice in rejecting this contention out of hand by taking the conspirators at their word that this was, indeed, a trespassory taking under threat of violence, as documented by the note handed to the teller. But we have looked deeper to assure ourselves that the substance of the circumstances as well as their form warranted the charges as laid.

As we view it, it is much less realistic to think that appellant and Farrelly aided and abetted Held in embezzlement than that Held's cooperative compliance made it easier for them to accomplish larceny. It may be conceded that up to a point Held was lawfully in possession of the funds as a trusted employee of the bank. But in turning over the bank's money to one obviously entitled to neither its benefits nor its possession, Held was not representing the bank but was acting adversely to it by aiding in accomplishing a trespassory taking and carrying away of bank property.

possession of any bank ... shall be fined not more than $5,000 or imprisoned not more than ten years, or both....

21. If two or more persons conspire either to commit any offense against the United States, or to defraud the United States, or any agency thereof in any manner or for any purpose, and one or more of such persons do any act to effect the object of the conspiracy, each shall be fined not more than $10,000 or imprisoned not more than five years, or both.

22. "This is a robbery, give me large bills only. I am not alone, cooperate or I will shoot."

23. Whoever, being an ... employee of ... any ... national bank or insured bank ... embezzles, abstracts, purloins or willfully misapplies any of the moneys ... of such bank ... shall be fined not more than $5,000 or imprisoned not more than five years, or both....

Perhaps from as early as *The Carrier's Case* in 1473,[24] most common law courts would have thought the circumstances sufficient to establish the offense of larceny. We need not be troubled by the idea of feigned or sham crimes which have been of concern in other contexts[25] since, as we observed at the beginning, the offense of larceny was real and unconsented to as far as the bank was concerned. To establish that the gist of the present case is bank larceny pure and simple, resort need not be had to any expansion of the statute in question by reference to legislative history or general purpose.[26] The authorities primarily relied upon by appellant, LeMasters v. United States, 378 F.2d 262 (9th Cir.1967), and Bennett v. United States, 399 F.2d 740 (9th Cir.1968), demonstrate the significant distinctions.

In *LeMasters* the defendant was charged with bank larceny in claimed violation of § 2113(b) and with related offenses, as in the present case. However, in that case the facts in no way suggested a trespassory taking.[27] In *Bennett* a similar conclusion was reached because the bank intended to part with its funds and there was no taking or carrying away with intent to steal or purloin.[28]

United States v. Brown, 455 F.2d 1201 (9th Cir.), cert. denied, 406 U.S. 960, 92 S.Ct. 2069, 32 L.Ed.2d 347 (1972), is more in point. Wells Fargo Bank in Oakland, California, had been robbed of approximately $6500. Mrs. Hoff, the victimized teller, reported the incident and furnished a description of the robber to the FBI. After further investigation and questioning, Mrs. Hoff admitted her involvement in the crime, contending that she was forced to take part. She was indicted, but the charges against her were dismissed in exchange for her testimony against the codefendants who were convicted of bank larceny. At the trial and on appeal, among other things, the latter contended that the evidence did not support the crime of larceny; they argued that because of Mrs. Hoff's position as a trusted employee of the bank, the most they were guilty of was embezzlement. This court held

---

24. Y.B. Pasch., 13 Edw. 4, f. 9, pl. 5 (1473), 64 Selden Soc'y 30 (1945), see Fletcher, The Metamorphosis of Larceny, 89 Harv.L.Rev. 469, 481 (1976).

25. *Fletcher, The Metamorphosis of Larceny, supra*, note 6, at 491–96.

26. Cf. United States v. Turley, 352 U.S. 407, 77 S.Ct. 397, 1 L.Ed.2d 430 (1957), which deals with the Dyer Act. The rationale of *Turley* which interpreted the word "stolen" so as not to limit it to situations which at common law would be considered larceny was considered in reference to the statute here in question and rejected in LeMasters v. United States, 378 F.2d 262 (9th Cir.1967).

27. In *LeMasters*, "... the appellant succeeded in persuading a teller, acting as such, at the bank that he was Tournour, that he had lost his savings account pass book, that the bank should issue him a new pass book, of course in the name of Tournour." 378 F.2d at 263. Tournour had not given the appellant any authority to withdraw any money, but appellant succeeded in obtaining the money by signing Tournour's name to a withdrawal slip and thus duping the bank. There was no federal law against obtaining money under false pretenses. A judgment of conviction was reversed by this court because a trespassory taking had not been shown.

28. The defendant as an intermediary in procuring a loan, obtained a check from a borrower for $8,000 which he presented to the bank in which he was an officer for a cashier's check made out to himself. Then he deposited the check to his own account and wrongfully converted the proceeds. This court held that he was not guilty of bank larceny, although the money was obtained unlawfully either through employees of the bank or by acts of the defendant constituting the taking of property by false pretenses.

that "[r]egardless of Mrs. Hoff's status, the evidence establishes the requisite intent coupled with a trespassory taking sufficient to constitute larceny." *Id.* at 1204.

The appellant here attempts to draw some significant distinctions by pointing out that in *Brown* the teller cooperated with the robbers out of fear of exposure of her indiscretions to her husband if she did not participate while Sharon Held in this case admitted that she was a willing participant. Subjective motivations of a conspirator cannot carry such decisive consequences in the present context. Whether through fear, blackmail, intimidation, persuasion, love, avarice, hunger, or complex combinations of other forces to which the human mind may be subjected, the fact remains that in both cases there was a trespassory taking as against the bank whose consent could not be constructed out of the adverse conduct of the teller, however, motivated. There was no variance between allegations and proof in this case any more than in *Brown* . . . .

Affirmed.[29]

(C) TAKING

Thompson v. State

Supreme Court of Alabama, 1891.
94 Ala. 535, 10 So. 520.

Indictment for larceny from the person. The opinion states the material facts. Charge No. 1, asked and refused, was in these words: "The jury must believe, beyond a reasonable doubt, that the defendant got the money into his hand, or actual possession of it, before they can convict him of larceny."

■ WALKER, J. The witness for the State testified that he held out his open hand with two silver dollars therein, showing the money to the defendant; that the defendant struck witness' hand, and the money was either knocked out of his hand or was taken by the defendant, he could not tell positively which. It was after twelve o'clock at night, and the witness did not see the money, either in defendant's possession or on the ground. The court charged the jury: "If the jury find from the evidence that the defendant, with a felonious intent, grabbed for the money, but did not get it, but only knocked it from the owner's hand with a felonious intent, this would be a sufficient carrying away of the money, although defendant never got possession at any time of said money." This charge was erroneous. To constitute larceny, there must be a felonious taking and carrying away of personal property. There must be such a caption that the accused acquires dominion over the property, followed by such an asportation or carrying away as to supersede the possession of the owner for an apprecia-

---

29. The federal bank robbery statute, 18 U.S.C. § 2113(b), which imposes a criminal sanction on anyone who "takes and carries away" bank property with intent to steal, applies to common law larcenies as well as obtaining by false pretenses if there is a "carrying away." Bell v. United States, 462 U.S. 356, 103 S.Ct. 2398 (1983).

Verb "steal" in federal statute is the taking away from one in lawful possession without right. United States v. Hill, 835 F.2d 759 (10th Cir.1987).

ble period of time. Though the owner's possession is disturbed, yet the offense is not complete if the accused fails to acquire such dominion over the property as to enable him to take actual custody or control. It is not enough that the money was knocked out of the owner's hand, if it fell to the ground and the defendant never got possession of it. The defendant was not guilty of larceny, if he did not get the money under his control. If the attempt merely caused the money to fall from the owner's hand to the ground, and the defendant ran off without getting it, the larceny was not consummated, as the dominion of the trespasser was not complete. Charge No. 1 was a proper statement of the law as applicable to the evidence above referred to, and it should have been given.

Reversed and remanded.

Cummings v. Commonwealth

Kentucky Court of Appeals, 1883.
5 Ky.L.Rep. 200.

The appellant, Cummings, according to the evidence, told Sweet he wished to sell him a sow and pigs, and after agreement on the price, went to where a sow and pigs were lying down on the commons and pointed them out as his, and Sweet paid him $7 in money for them and then drove them off. The sow and pigs belonged to John Flauher, who lived near by.

The appellant seems to have been out of money and resorted to this means of obtaining some to supply his wants, and then proceeded to the fair.

Having been convicted of the offense of larceny or hog stealing under the statute, the appellant has appealed, and his counsel contend that his offense was not larceny because there was no asportation *by him*, but it was obtaining money by false pretenses if anything.

He was not indicted for obtaining the $7 for the sow and pigs, but for stealing the sow and pigs. Whether his acts constituted both offenses of larceny of the hogs and obtaining money by false pretenses, for which he might be punished, need not be determined, as there has been no attempt to try him twice for the same acts.

The owner of the sow and pigs never parted with the possession or the property in them. The asportation was by the hand or physical act of Sweet, but the act of felonious taking was that of the appellant committed through Sweet, who was his instrument in committing the trespass upon the property of Flauher.

East, Hale and Hawkins, who are approved by Archbold, say that if the taking be by the hand of another, it is the same as if by the hand of the thief himself. For instance, if the thief procure a child within the age of discretion, or an idiot, to steal goods for him, such taking must be charged to him....

The judgment is therefore affirmed.[30]

---

30. Accord: Smith v. State, 11 Ga.App. 197, 74 S.E. 1093 (1912); State v. Hunt, 45 Iowa 673 (1877); State v. Patton, 364 Mo. 1044, 271 S.W.2d 560 (1954).

(D) NECESSITY OF TRESPASS

(1) Cases of Fraud

Another gap that appeared during the development of the law of larceny was due to the rule that no larceny could be recognized in a transaction in which the wrongdoer acquired title to the property in question. This led to the enactment of an English statute, old enough to be common law in this country, which created the offense of obtaining property by false pretenses—often abbreviated to "false pretenses". This offense and larceny were also interpreted to be mutually exclusive.[31] Modern codes often encompass false pretenses and larceny under a general theft statute.

The King v. Pear

Court for Crown Cases Reserved, 1779.
1 Leach 212, 168 Eng.Rep. 208.

The prisoner was indicted for stealing a black horse, the property of Samuel Finch. It appeared in evidence that Samuel Finch was a Livery–Stable–keeper in the Borough; and that the prisoner, on the 2d of July 1779, hired the horse of him to go to Sutton, in the county of Surry, and back again, saying on being asked where he lived, that he lodged at No. 25 in King-street, and should return about eight o'clock the same evening. He did not return; and it was proved that he had sold the horse on the very day he had hired it, to one William Hollist, in Smithfield Market; and that he had no lodging at the place to which he had given the prosecutor directions.

The learned Judge said: There had been different opinions on the law of this class of cases; ... that in the present case the horse was hired to take a journey into Surry, and the prisoner sold him the same day, without taking any such journey; that there were also other circumstances which imported that at the time of the hiring the prisoner had it in intention to sell the horse, as his saying that he lodged at a place where in fact he was not known. He therefore left it with the Jury to consider, Whether the

---

Contra: State v. Laborde, 202 La. 59, 11 So.2d 404 (1942). The court said "Since the defendant at no time had the actual or constructive possession of the animal, the act of the purchaser in carrying it away for his own account cannot be said in legal contemplation to have been the act of the seller. The facts of the case repel any idea of implied agency, because Jeansonne unquestionably acted as a bona fide purchaser for himself."

Shooting and butchering a cow was sufficient asportation for larceny. Grooms v. State, 673 P.2d 162 (Okl.Cr.1983). The least removal of an item is sufficient asportation for theft even if the property is not removed from the owner's possession or returned by the defendant. State v. Williams, 16 Ohio App.3d 232, 475 N.E.2d 168 (1984).

31. "The subtle distinction which the statute was intended to remedy was this: that if a person, by fraud, induced another to part with the possession only of goods and converted them to his own use, this was larceny; while if he induced another by fraud to part with the property in [i.e., ownership of] the goods as well as the possession, this was not larceny." The Queen v. Killiam, L.R. 1 C.C. 261 (1870).

See Graham Ferris, The Origins of "Larceny by a Trick" and "Constructive Possession," Crim. Law Rev. p. 175 [1998] (Eng.).

prisoner meant at the time of the hiring to take such journey, but was afterwards tempted to sell the horse? for if so he must be acquitted; but that if they were of opinion that at the time of the hiring the journey was a mere pretence to get the horse into his possession, and he had no intention to take such journey but intended to sell the horse, they would find that fact specially for the opinion of the Judges.

The Jury found that the facts above stated were true; and also that the prisoner had hired the horse with a fraudulent view and intention of selling it immediately.

The question was referred to the Judges, Whether the delivery of the horse by the prosecutor to the prisoner, had so far changed the possession of the property, as to render the subsequent conversion of it a mere breach of trust, or whether the conversion was felonious? (see the case of Sharpless and Another, ante, page 92, case 52).

The Judges differed greatly in opinion on this case; and delivered their opinions *seriatim* upon it at Lord Chief Justice De Gray's house on 4th February 1780 and on the 22nd of the same month Mr. Baron Perryn delivered their opinion on it. The majority of them thought, That the question, as to the original intention of the prisoner in hiring the horse, had been properly left to the jury; and as they had found, that his view in so doing was fraudulent, the parting with the property had not changed the nature of the possession, but that it remained unaltered in the prosecutor at the time of the conversion; and that the prisoner was therefore guilty of felony.[32]

The Queen v. Prince

Court for Crown Cases Reserved, 1868.
L.R. 1 C.C. 150.

(Mrs. Allen forged her husband's signature and thereby obtained money equal to his entire deposit in the bank. She then left Allen and ran away with Prince. She gave some of this money to Prince who was convicted of knowingly receiving money stolen from the bank.)

■ BOVILL, C.J. I am of opinion that this conviction cannot be sustained. The distinction between larceny and false pretences is material. In larceny the taking must be against the will of the owner. That is of the essence of the offence. The cases cited by Mr. Collins on behalf of the prisoner are clear and distinct upon this point, shewing that the obtaining of property from its owner, or his servant absolutely authorized to deal with it, by false pretences will not amount to larceny. The cases cited on the other side are cases where the servant had only a limited authority from his master. Here, however, it seems to me that the bank clerk had a general authority to part

---

32. The majority held that this was "such a taking as would have made the prisoner liable to an action of trespass at the suit of the owner, . . ." 2 East P.C. 688.

In this jurisdiction the crime of larceny remains as it was at common law. Hence it requires that the taking of the property be by trespass. If the taking was fraudulent it was by trespass and the subsequent appropriation was larceny. Farlow v. State, 9 Md.App. 515, 265 A.2d 578 (1970).

with both the property in and possession of his master's money on receiving what he believed to be a genuine order, and that as he did so part with both the property in and possession of the note in question the offence committed by Mrs. Allen falls within the cases which make it a false pretence, and not a larceny, and therefore the prisoner cannot be convicted of knowingly receiving a stolen note.

■ CHANNEL, B. I am of the same opinion. . . .

■ BYLES, J. I am of the same opinion. I would merely say that I ground my judgment purely on authority.

■ BLACKBURN, J. I also am of the same opinion. I must say I cannot but lament that the law now stands as it does. The distinction drawn between larceny and false pretences, one being made a felony and the other a misdemeanor—and yet the same punishment attached to each—seems to me, I must confess, unmeaning and mischievous. The distinction arose in former times, and I take it that it was then held in favour of life that in larceny the taking must be against the will of the owner, larceny then being a capital offence. However, as the law now stands, if the owner intended the property to pass, though he would not so have intended had he known the real facts, that is sufficient to prevent the offence of obtaining another's property from amounting to larceny; and where the servant has an authority co-equal with his master's, and parts with his master's property, such property cannot be said to be stolen, inasmuch as the servant intends to part with the property in it. If, however, the servant's authority is limited, then he can only part with the possession, and not with the property; if he is tricked out of the possession, the offence so committed will be larceny. In Reg. v. Longstreeth,[33] the carrier's servant had no authority to part with the goods, except to the right consignee. His authority was not generally to act in his master's business, but limited in that way. The offence was in that case held to be larceny on that ground, and this distinguishes it from the pawnbroker's case,[34] which the same judges, or at any rate some of them, had shortly before decided. There the servant, from whom the goods were obtained, had a general authority to act for his master, and the person who obtained the goods was held not to be guilty of larceny. So, in the present case, the cashier holds the money of the bank with a general authority from the bank to deal with it. He has authority to part with it on receiving what he believes to be a genuine order. Of the genuineness he is the judge; and if under a mistake he parts with money, he none the less intends to part with the property in it, and thus the offence is not, according to the cases, larceny, but an obtaining by false pretences. The distinction is inscrutable to my mind, but it exists in the cases. There is no statute enabling a count for larceny to be joined with one for false pretences; and as the prisoner was indicted for the felony, the conviction must be quashed.

■ LUSH, J. I also agree that the conviction must be quashed. . . . [35]

---

33. [Numbered footnotes by the Court.] 1 Mood.C.C. 137.

34. Reg. v. Jackson, 1 Mood.C.C. 119.

35. *See* Anderson v. State, 33 Ala.App. 531, 36 So.2d 242 (1948).

Wilkinson v. State

Supreme Court of Mississippi, 1952.
215 Miss. 327, 60 So.2d 786.

[Three head of cattle belonging to Leonard had strayed and were picked up by Ferguson who was holding them for the owner, without knowing who the owner was. Some of Whittington's cattle had strayed and he went to Ferguson's farm to see the strays being held there. He ascertained that the strays were not his, but his hired hand, Wilkinson, persuaded him to claim them which he did. Ferguson delivered the cattle to Whittington and Wilkinson, believing that they belonged to Whittington. Whittington sold the cattle and gave part of the purchase money to Wilkinson.]

■ ETHRIDGE, JUSTICE. Appellant, Fred Wilkinson, was indicted and convicted at the January 1952 term of the Circuit Court of Franklin County of grand larceny, consisting of the theft of three head of cattle. He argues here that the conviction was against the great weight of the evidence, was based upon the uncorroborated testimony of an accomplice, and that he was indicted and convicted under the wrong statute. . . .

Secondly, the indictment was properly found under the grand larceny statute, Sec. 2240. The general rule is set forth in 32 Am.Jur., Larceny, Sec. 33: "Although there is some authority to the contrary, the better rule is that one who falsely personates another and in such assumed character receives property intended for such other person is guilty of larceny if he does so with the requisite felonious intent, provided the transaction does not involve the passing of title to the property from the owner to him. Although express statutes to this effect exist in some jurisdictions, it is larceny at common law for a person to pretend that he is the owner or person entitled to personal property in order to obtain possession thereof with the felonious intent of converting it to his own use and depriving the owner of it. Subject to this rule, one who fraudulently claims an estray from the person taking it up or lost property from the finder may be convicted of larceny."

The distinction, a rather fine one, between the crimes of obtaining property by false pretenses and that of larceny through obtaining possession by fraud seems to rest in the intention with which the owner parts with possession. Thus if the possession is obtained by fraud and the owner intends to part with his title as well as his possession, the crime is that of obtaining property by false pretenses, provided the means by which it is acquired comply therewith. But if the possession is fraudulently obtained with a present intent on the part of the person obtaining it to convert the

It was held to be larceny if the title did not actually pass although the intention had been to pass both title and possession. English v. State, 80 Fla. 70, 85 So. 150 (1920). Contra: Rex v. Adams, Russ. & Ry. 225, 168 Eng.Rep. 773 (1812); Rex v. Atkinson, 2 East P.C. 673 (1799).

A check payable to D(1) was sent by mistake to D(2), a different person but having the same name. D(2), knowing it was not intended for him, indorsed his name on the back and cashed it.

This was held not to be larceny but a different crime—false pretenses. Hinman v. State, 179 Miss. 503, 176 So. 264 (1937).

property to his own use, and the owner intends to part with his possession merely and not with the title, the offense is larceny. . . .

At common law, for a person to pretend that he was the owner of the property in order to get possession of it with the felonious intent of converting it to his own use constituted larceny. Accordingly convictions of larceny have been sustained where a person has fraudulently claimed an estray from the person taking it up, and where a person has claimed to be the owner of lost property from the finder. . . .

The foregoing authorities support the conviction under the general grand larceny statute, Sec. 2240. The distinction rests upon the intention with which the owner or possessor parts with possession. Here the possessor of the estrays, Ferguson, obviously had no intent to part with any title to the estrays. Like Sims in the Atterberry case, Ferguson thought he was transferring simply the possession back to the true owner. This accords with the principle that if possession is fraudulently obtained, with present intent on the part of the person obtaining it, to convert the property to his own use, and the owner or possessor intends to part with his possession merely and not with the title, the offense is larceny. The crime for which appellant was convicted constitutes grand larceny both at common law and under Code Sec. 2240. . . .

■ McGehee, C.J., and Lee, Kyle and Arrington, JJ., concur.[36]

Regina v. Hands

Court for Crown Cases Reserved, 1887.
16 Cox C.C. 188, 56 L.T. 370.

■ Lord Coleridge, C.J. In this case a person was indicted for committing a larceny from what is known as an "automatic box," which was so constructed that, if you put a penny into it and pushed a knob in accordance with the directions on the box, a cigarette was ejected on to a bracket and presented to the giver of the penny. Under these circumstances there is no doubt that the prisoners put in the box a piece of metal which was of no value, but which produced the same effect as the placing a penny in the box produced. A cigarette was ejected which the prisoners appropriated; and in

---

36. "Although the crimes of larceny by trick and obtaining property under false pretenses are very similar, there is a distinction which the statutes and case law clearly draw between the two crimes."

The distinction turns on the intent of the victim in parting with the property. . . .

The absence of an intent on the part of the cashiers to knowingly and voluntarily transfer possession or title to any money in excess of that received places the defendant's conduct within the ambit of larceny rather than the ambit of obtaining property under false pretenses. People v. Long, 93 Mich.App. 579, 286 N.W.2d 909, 910–911 (1979). The Michigan Supreme Court reversed on the application of the facts to the law observing:

"The creation of the offense of false pretenses by statute had its historical origins in the lawmaker's need to fill a void in the common law which existed by virtue of the fact that common-law larceny did not extend to punish the party who, without taking and carrying away, had obtained both possession and title to another's property. Against this historical background, our Legislature early chose to recognize the offense. The conduct charged against defendant falls within the legislatively recognized category; thus marked, it is distinct from larceny." People v. Long, 409 Mich. 346, 294 N.W.2d 197, 200 (Mich.1980).

a case of that class it appears to me there clearly was larceny. The means [*Issue*] by which the cigarette was made to come out of the box were fraudulent, [*Rule*] and the cigarette so made to come out was appropriated.... [37]

(2) Lost Property

Regina v. Thurborn

Court for Crown Cases Reserved, 1848.
1 Den. 387, 169 Eng.Rep. 293.

The prisoner was tried before PARKE, B., at the Summer Assizes for Huntingdon, 1848, for stealing a bank note.

He found the note, which had been accidentally dropped on the high road. There was no name or mark on it, indicating who was the owner, nor were there any circumstances attending the finding which would enable him to discover to whom the note belonged when he picked it up; nor had he any reason to believe that the owner knew where to find it again. The prisoner meant to appropriate it to his own use, when he picked it up. The [*Facts*] day after, and before he had disposed of it, he was informed that the prosecutor was the owner, and had dropped it accidentally; he then changed it, and appropriated the money taken to his own use. The jury found that he had reason to believe, and did believe it to be the prosecutor's property, before he thus changed the note.

The learned Baron directed a verdict of guilty, intimating that he should reserve the case for further consideration. Upon conferring with Maule J., the learned Baron was of opinion that the original taking was not felonious, and that in the subsequent disposal of it, there was no taking, and he therefore declined to pass sentence, and ordered the prisoner to be discharged, on entering into his own recognizance to appear when called upon.

On the 30th of April, A.D. 1849, the following judgment was read by Parke B.

A case was reserved by Parke B. at the last Huntingdon Assizes. It was not argued by counsel, but the Judges who attended the sitting of the Court after Michaelmas Term, 1848, namely, the L.C. Baron, Patteson J., Rolfe B., Cresswell J., Williams J., Coltman J., and Parke B., gave it much consideration on account of its importance, and the frequency of the occurrence of cases in some degree similar, in the administration of the criminal law, and the somewhat obscure state of the authorities upon it. [The learned Baron here stated the case.] ...

---

37. Defendant's acceptance of natural gas service without payment did not constitute theft. Defendant made no verbal or physical act of deception, fraud, or threat. Defendant did not use a false token or mechanical or electrical device to avoid payment. Defendant was never billed for a gas meter on the premises. State v. Kocen, 222 N.J.Super. 517, 537 A.2d 731 (1988).

18 U.S.C. § 1029(a)(1) makes it an offense to "knowingly and with intent to defraud" produce, use or traffic in one or more "counterfeit access devices." "Access device" is defined in § 1029(e)(1).

The result of these authorities is, that the rule of law on this subject seems to be, that if a man find goods that have been actually lost, or are reasonably supposed by him to have been lost, and appropriates them, with intent to take the entire dominion over them, really believing when he takes them, that the owner cannot be found, it is not larceny. But if he takes them with the like intent, though lost, or reasonably supposed to be lost, but reasonably believing that the owner can be found, it is larceny.

In applying this rule, as indeed in the application of all fixed rules, questions of some nicety may arise, but it will generally be ascertained whether the person accused had reasonable belief that the owner could be found, by evidence of his previous acquaintance with the ownership of the particular chattel, the place where it is found, or the nature of the marks upon it. In some cases it would be apparent, in others appear only after examination.

It would probably be presumed that the taker would examine the chattel as an honest man ought to do, at the time of taking it, and if he did not restore it to the owner, the jury might conclude that he took it, when he took complete possession of it, *animo furandi.* The mere taking it up to look at it, would not be a taking possession of the chattel.

To apply these rules to the present case; the first taking did not amount to larceny, because the note was really lost, and there was no mark on it or other circumstance to indicate then who was the owner, or that he might be found, nor any evidence to rebut the presumption that would arise from the finding of the note as proved, that he believed the owner could not be found, and therefore the original taking was not felonious; and if the prisoner had changed the note or otherwise disposed of it, before notice of the title of the real owner, he clearly would not have been punishable; but after the prisoner was in possession of the note, the owner became known to him, and he then appropriated it, *animo furandi,* and the point to be decided is whether that was a felony.

Upon this question we have felt considerable doubt.

If he had taken the chattel innocently, and afterwards appropriated it without knowledge of the ownership, it would not have been larceny, nor would it, we think, if he had done so, knowing who was the owner, for he had the lawful possession in both cases, and the conversion would not have been a trespass in either. But here the original taking was not innocent in one sense, and the question is, does that make a difference? We think not, it was dispunishable as we have already decided, and though the possession was accompanied by a dishonest intent, it was still a lawful possession and good against all but the real owner, and the subsequent conversion was not therefore a trespass in this case more than the others, and consequently no larceny.

We therefore think that the conviction was wrong.[38]

---

38. One who appropriated a coat he found on a bench is not guilty of larceny if the original taking was with intent to restore it to the owner. Milburne's Case, 1 Lewin 251, 168 Eng.Rep. 1030 (1829).

Brooks v. State

Supreme Court of Ohio, 1878.
35 Ohio St. 46.

(Charles B. Newton lost a $200 roll of bank bills. Notice of the loss was published in a newspaper. Nearly a month later George Brooks found the money in the street. There is no evidence that he had seen the published notice or knew of Newton's loss, but he was with other workmen at the time and took pains not to let them know of his find. He appropriated the money shortly thereafter. He was convicted of larceny.)

■ WHITE, J. We find no ground in the record for reversing the judgment.

The first instruction asked was properly refused. It was not necessary to the conviction of the accused that he should, at the time of taking possession of the property, have known, or have had reason to believe he knew, the *particular person* who owned it, or have had the means of identifying him *instanter*. The charge asked was liable to this construction, and there was no error in its refusal.

The second instruction asked was substantially given in the general charge.

Larceny may be committed of property that is casually lost as well as of that which is not. The title to the property, and its constructive possession, still remains in the owner; and the finder, if he takes possession of it for his own use, and not for the benefit of the owner, would be guilty of trespass, unless the circumstances were such as to show that it had been abandoned by the owner.

The question is, under what circumstances does such property become the subject of larceny by the finder?

In Baker v. The State, 29 Ohio St. 184, the rule stated by Baron Parke, in Thurborn's case, was adopted. It was there laid down, that "when a person finds goods that have actually been lost, and takes possession with intent to appropriate them to his own use, really believing, at the time, or having good ground to believe, that the owner can be found, it is larceny."

It must not be understood from the rule, as thus stated, that the finder is bound to use diligence or to take pains in making search for the owner.[39] His belief, or grounds of belief, in regard to finding the owner, is not to be determined by the degree of diligence that he might be able to use to accomplish that purpose, but by the circumstances apparent to him at the time of finding the property. If the property has not been abandoned by the owner, it is the subject of larceny by the finder, when, at the time he finds it, he has reasonable ground to believe, from the nature of the property, or the circumstances under which it is found, that if he does not conceal but deals honestly with it, the owner will appear or be ascertained. But before

---

"Under the common law, the person last in possession of property retains constructive possession until he abandons it, gives it to another person, or until another person otherwise acquires actual possession." United States v. Sellers, 670 F.2d 853, 854 (9th Cir.1982).

39. Some of the statutes require diligence on the part of the finder if the circumstances of the finding suggest a means of inquiry. *See* West's Ann.Cal.Pen.Code § 485 (1970).

the finder can be guilty of larceny, the intent to steal the property must have existed at the time he took it into his possession. . . . [40]

Judgment affirmed.

■ OKEY, J. I do not think the plaintiff was properly convicted. A scavenger, while in the performance of his duties in cleaning the streets, picked up from the mud and water in the gutter, a roll of money, consisting of bank bills of the denominations of five, ten, and twenty dollars, and amounting, in the aggregate, to two hundred dollars. It had lain there several weeks, and the owner had ceased to make search for it. The evidence fails to show that the plaintiff had any information of a loss previous to the finding, and in his testimony he denied such notice. There was no mark on the money to indicate the owner, nor was there any thing in the attending circumstances pointing to one owner more than another. He put the money in his pocket, without calling the attention of his fellow-workmen to the discovery, and afterward, on the same day, commenced applying it to his own use.

No doubt the plaintiff was morally bound to take steps to find the owner. An honest man would not thus appropriate money, before he had made the finding public, and endeavored to find the owner. But in violating the moral obligation, I do not think the plaintiff incurred criminal liability. . . .

■ GILMORE, C.J., concurs in the dissenting opinion.

State v. Kaufman

Supreme Court of North Dakota, 1981.
310 N.W.2d 709.

■ PAULSON, JUSTICE. Frank Kaufman was convicted in the Stutsman County Court of Increased Jurisdiction of theft of property lost, mislaid, or delivered by mistake, under § 12.1–23–04 of the North Dakota Century Code, and was sentenced to serve six months in the Stutsman County jail with 2½ months suspended, pay a $100 fine and $79.75 in restitution. Kaufman appeals his conviction and sentence. We affirm.

In November and December, 1980, the Jamestown West End Hide and Fur Company, a junk dealership, purchased several large rolls of scrap copper wire from Otter Tail Power Company. This wire was stored in the hide and fur company's open yard. In early December, 1980, Mr. Archie Oster, a partner in the company, noticed that several rolls of wire were missing. In checking with the manager of Porter Brothers, another junk dealership in the area, Oster learned that a similar roll of wire had been purchased by Porter Brothers on December 4, 1980, from Frank Kaufman.

---

40.   Regina v. Shea, 7 Cox C.C. 147 (1856).

"For a person to be guilty of the common law offense of misappropriation of lost property, two elements must coexist at the time the finder discovers the lost property. The finder must intend to convert the property absolutely to his own use. Secondly, the circumstances surrounding the finding must afford some reasonable clues for determining the identity of the rightful owner." State v. Campbell, 536 P.2d 105, 110 (Alaska, 1975).

Defendant committed the crime of theft when he found a forged check and presented it for payment. State v. Skorpen, 57 Wash. App. 144, 787 P.2d 54 (1990).

At trial, Oster identified the wire that Porter Brothers had purchased from Kaufman as the same wire which had been missing from the hide and fur company's yard.

Jack Miller, Deputy Sheriff of Stutsman County, testified that he had contacted Kaufman during his investigation of the theft and that Kaufman had stated that he found the wire "out by Windsor". The trial judge found Kaufman guilty of theft of property "lost, mislaid, or delivered by mistake", § 12.1–23–04, N.D.C.C., and sentenced him to six months in the Stutsman County jail, with 2½ months suspended, and that he pay a $100 fine and $79.75 in restitution. Kaufman appeals his conviction and sentence.

Three issues are presented on appeal:

1. Is property which is stolen and later abandoned by the thief "lost" for the purpose of § 12.1–23–04, N.D.C.C., which makes appropriation of "lost" property unlawful?

2. Was the evidence sufficient to support the conviction? . . .

I

Kaufman's first contention is that the copper wire was stolen from the hide and fur company's yard, and, therefore, was not "lost" and could not be the basis of a prosecution under § 12.1–23–04, N.D.C.C., which provides:

"*12.1–23–04. Theft of property lost, mislaid, or delivered by mistake.*—A person is guilty of theft if he:

"1. Retains or disposes of property of another when he knows it has been lost or mislaid; or

"2. Retains or disposes of property of another when he knows it has been delivered under a mistake as to the identity of the recipient or as to the nature or amount of the property,

and with intent to deprive the owner of it, he fails to take readily available and reasonable measures to restore the property to a person entitled to have it."

Although this court has never previously been presented with this issue, courts in other jurisdictions have indicated that property which is stolen and abandoned by the thief is indeed "lost" to the original owner. For example, in Automobile Insurance Co. of Hartford v. Kirby, 25 Ala.App. 245, 144 So. 123 (1932), that Court stated that "when property is stolen and is afterwards abandoned by the thief at a place unknown to the owner, such property is lost within the meaning of our statute". *Id.* 144 So. at 124.

Although Title 12.1, N.D.C.C., does not provide a definition of "lost", this court has previously discussed the term. In State v. Brewster, 72 N.D. 409, 7 N.W.2d 742 (1943), the court, in discussing a predecessor to § 12.1–23–04, N.D.C.C., noted that "The term 'lost' is concerned with *the involuntary change of location or inability to find*". *Brewster, supra* 7 N.W.2d at 744 (emphasis added). Applying this definition to the evidence in the instant case, it is clear that the location of the hide and fur company's wire had been changed and it could not be found by the company at the time that Kaufman found it. We therefore conclude that the stolen wire was "lost" when Kaufman found it.

Support is lent to this conclusion by the anomalous result which would follow from the interpretation of the statute urged by Kaufman. Kaufman would have this court hold that stolen property abandoned by the thief is not lost and, therefore, cannot be the basis for prosecution under § 12.1–2304, N.D.C.C. If this interpretation were adopted, a person who found property, believing it to be lost or mislaid, and who thereafter sold it or otherwise deprived the owner of possession might escape prosecution merely because, unbeknownst to him, the property had previously been stolen from the true owner. ✗ *delivery by mistake*

Such a result would be contrary to the purpose of Chapter 12.1–23, N.D.C.C. Section 12.1–23–04 was adopted verbatim from § 1734 of the Final Report of the National Commission on Reform of Federal Criminal Laws. This court has previously indicated that the Commission's Working Papers may be considered when construing provisions of North Dakota's Criminal Code. The Comment to § 1734 indicates that the intent behind such section is to make the appropriation of found or discovered property constitute theft:

"The point, of course, is that the actor is just as culpable if he intends to appropriate property he knows to belong to another whether he takes it, finds it, or discovers it as it is being mistakenly delivered to him. And it is just as clear that the extent of his criminal liability should not turn on technical differences between whether the money was lost, mislaid, or simply placed somewhere for safekeeping. This, in any event, is the premise of the proposal to make appropriation of found or discovered property theft just like any other kind of theft." [Working Papers of the National Commission on Reform of Federal Criminal Laws, Vol. II, p. 939 (1970)].

A result which would relieve a person from criminal liability simply because of the occurrence of a fortuitous act such as an unknown prior theft of the property would defeat the purpose of the statute.

We hold that property which is stolen and later abandoned by the thief is "lost" for the purposes of § 12.1–23–04, N.D.C.C., making appropriation of lost property unlawful.

II

Kaufman also contends that the evidence at trial was insufficient to support a verdict of guilty of the crime charged. Specifically, he contends that the State failed to prove that the copper wire which he sold to Porter Brothers was the "property of another", and that the State failed to prove that he knew the property was lost or mislaid.

We have consistently held that a verdict based upon circumstantial evidence is accorded the same presumption of correctness as other verdicts and will not be disturbed on appeal unless the verdict is unwarranted. The role of the Supreme Court on appeal is to merely review the record to determine if there is competent evidence which allowed the factfinder to draw an inference reasonably tending to prove guilt and fairly warranting a conviction. . . .

Affirmed.[41]

(3) Delivery by Mistake

Cooper v. Commonwealth

Court of Appeals of Kentucky, 1901.
110 Ky. 123, 60 S.W. 938.

■ Opinion of the Court by JUDGE O'REAR. Reversing.

Appellants, Grant Cooper, Fred Cooper, Thomas Harris and Sandy Waggener, were convicted in the Union Circuit Court of the crime of grand larceny, under the following state of facts: The four named had been shucking corn, and were paid $6 for their services. In order to divide the money equally among themselves, they went to the Bank of Uniontown to have $2 of the money changed into smaller denominations. Appellant, Sandy Waggener, went into the bank and to the cashier's counter, handed him the $2 and asked for the change. The cashier handed him two half dollars and a roll of small-sized coin wrapped in paper saying, "There are twenty nickels." Waggener, without unwrapping the coins, and not knowing what was in the paper, except from the statement of the cashier, rejoined his companions; and the four together went a distance of some four squares, to a more secluded spot, to divide their money. On opening the package they discovered it contained twenty 5–dollar gold coins, instead of nickels. Waggener remarked, "Boys, banks don't correct mistakes," and the money was divided among the four and appropriated by them. Upon this evidence the court gave the jury the following instruction: "If you believe from the evidence, to the exclusion of a reasonable doubt, that in this county, and prior to the finding of the indictment herein, the defendants, Grant Cooper, Fred Cooper and Thos. Harris and Sandy Waggener, sought to have some money changed at the Bank of Uniontown in order to get twenty nickels, or some small change, and that Chas. Kelleners, the assistant cashier of said bank, in making said change delivered by mistake to the defendants twenty five-dollar gold pieces, wrapped in a paper, believing at the time that he was giving them twenty nickels, and that the defendants, sharing in that belief, shortly thereafter opened said paper, and found therein twenty five-dollar gold pieces, and failed to return said gold pieces to said bank—now, if you further believe from the evidence, to the exclusion of a reasonable doubt, that when said defendants unwrapped said paper, and found therein, and in their possession, the said five-dollar gold pieces, they knew that same had been delivered to them by said Kelleners through mistake, and knew or had the means of ascertaining that the bank was the owner of said gold pieces, but thereupon nevertheless feloniously converted the same to their own use, intending to premanently [sic] deprive the owner thereof, you will find them guilty as charged; and in your verdict

---

41. *See* Harris v. State, 207 Miss. 241, 42 So.2d 183 (1949); Long v. State, 33 Ala.App. 334, 33 So.2d 382 (1948).

Defendant cannot be convicted of theft of lost or mislaid property unless the finder failed to take reasonable measures to return the property to its true owner. State v. Evans, 119 Idaho 383, 807 P.2d 62 (App. 1991).

you will fix their punishment at confinement in the penitentiary for not less than one nor more than five years." Appellants objected to the foregoing, and asked the court to give the jury these instructions: "(a) The court instructs the jury that, to find the defendants guilty of larceny, they must believe that at the time they received the money from Chas. Kelleners they must have then had the purpose and intent to convert the excess which they received over and above what was justly due them as change to their own use and benefit, and to deprive the bank of its money feloniously; that, unless the felonious intent was proven at the time of receiving the money, the law is for the defendants, and the jury will so find. (b) The court instructs the jury that the felonious intent must exist at the time of receiving the money, and that no felonious intent, subsequent or wrongful conversion, will amount to a felony"—which were rejected by the court.

It was held in Elliott v. Com., 12 Bush 176, that where the possession of the goods was obtained by the accused for a particular purpose, with the intent then, however, on the part of the accused, to convert them to his own use, which he subsequently did, it would constitute larceny. In Snapp v. Com., 82 Ky. 173, we held that, where money came into the hands of the accused lawfully, his subsequent felonious conversion would not be larceny. In the last-named case the court said it devolved upon the Commonwealth to show an unlawful taking of this money from the city (the owner) by the accused with a felonious intent, and that "the money had been received without fraud and as a matter of right, and in such a case, although he may have the *animus furandi* afterwards, and convert it to his own use, he was not guilty of larceny." In Smith v. Com., 96 Ky. 85, 87, 27 S.W. 852, this court announced, "The general and common-law rule is that when property comes lawfully into the possession of a person, either as agent, bailee, part owner, or otherwise, a subsequent appropriation of it is not larceny, unless the intent to appropriate it existed in the mind of the taker at the time it came into his hands." Whart.Cr.Law, section 958, says, "To constitute larceny in receiving an overpayment, the defendant must know at the time of the overpayment, and must intend to steal." The authorities seem to be agreed that, to constitute the crime of larceny, there must be a simultaneous combination of an unlawful taking, an asportation, and a felonious intent.

We conclude that the instructions asked by appellants should have been given to the jury, and that the idea expressed in the first instruction given—that if appellants received the money under a mutual mistake, and after discovering it feloniously converted it—should not have been given. Judgment reversed and cause remanded for a new trial, and for proceedings consistent herewith.[42]

---

42. The purchaser of a supposedly empty trunk converted a coat and vest which he found therein. This was held to be larceny. Robinson v. State, 11 Tex.App. 403 (1882). The court said: "The owner, or rather his clerk, whilst selling and delivering the trunk never intended to convey and did not convey either the title or possession of its contents; for he was wholly ignorant of its contents. So was defendant, when he purchased and became possessed of the trunk. The goods, so far as these parties were concerned, were lost, because they neither knew anything of their existence or their whereabouts. When defendant opened, examined and came across them in the trunk, they were in every sense lost goods which he found; as much so as if he had come across them upon the public highway or any other place where the owner

State v. Langford

Court of Appeal of Louisiana, 1985.
467 So.2d 41.

■ SCHOTT, JUDGE.

After a bench trial, defendant was convicted of theft of $848,879.39 from Hibernia National Bank between April 1, 1981 and September 24, 1981 and sentenced to eight years at hard labor.

On March 18, 1981 defendant opened a NOW account, i.e., an interest-earning checking account, at the Hibernia National Bank in New Orleans with a deposit of $5,362.21. When the account was processed into the bank's computer it was erroneously assigned a code which provided for unlimited overdrafts without charge to the customer. On September 24 the bank was contacted to verify that a check defendant was offering to deposit at a savings and loan association was good. Upon checking the account, the bank discovered it was overdrawn by $848,879.39. Further investigation revealed that the account had become overdrawn a few weeks after it was opened, no additional deposits were ever made, and defendant had written over two hundred checks on the account. The bank immediately demanded payment of the overdrafts by defendant who responded with an offer to execute a note in the bank's favor.

A week before defendant opened his NOW account he had applied for a $225,000 loan from the bank, but he was turned down because of his credit standing.

Defendant's NOW account was processed almost exclusively by computer. Each day defendant was notified of additional overdrafts and the current negative balance was shown. At the end of each month he was sent a statement showing the negative balance in his account and returning the checks he wrote during the month. Because of the erroneous classification assigned to the account initially as one eligible for unlimited overdrafts they would not automatically come to the attention of anyone on a day to day basis. Unfortunately for the bank, daily computer printouts which were supposed to be reviewed by a manager supervising defendant's account on a daily basis were routinely thrown in the trash by some clerk and never reviewed by the manager.

Assignments of Error 1 and 3.

By these assignments defendant argues that there was no evidence of a non-consensual taking or an intent to permanently deprive. He contends that the bank had a choice between dishonoring each check or creating an overdraft and that an overdraft is simply a loan to the customer.

In order to convit defendant of theft the state had to prove the taking of the money from Hibernia without its consent and with the intent to deprive it permanently of the money. . . .

The evidence absolutely precludes the possibility that the bank consented to defendant's conduct. The bank was a victim of its own mistakes,

---

had dropped, mislaid, left them by mistake, or lost them." Accord: Merry v. Green, 7 Mees. and W. 623, 151 Eng.Rep. 916 (1841).

one in the erroneous coding of the account when it was first opened, and the other in the destruction of the computer printouts before they could be reviewed by a responsible official. The bank's intention was to allow no overdrafts on NOW accounts but this was frustrated by its unfortunate errors. That the bank consented to defendant's taking $848,000 as some sort of loan is not a reasonable hypothesis when its refusal to loan defendant $225,000 one week before the account was opened is considered.

In State v. Johnson, 408 So.2d 1280 (La.1982) the following appears at page 1283:

"In order to consent to the theft of his property, an owner must do more than passively assent to the taking. Where the criminal intent of design is neither suggested nor ratified by the owner, he may even facilitate the taking of the goods in order to detect the thief."

Defendant's argument on this assignment is that the bank did suggest criminal intent to defendant by sending him overdraft notices which failed to request repayment of the account. However the first answer to this argument is that the bank suggested no such thing to defendant. These notices were not being consciously sent to defendant but were automatically generated by a computer as a result of an error in the initial coding of the account. Defendant had to know a mistake was being made and could not believe these notices were an invitation to keep the money. It would be unreasonable to hypothesize otherwise.

The only reasonable hypothesis for defendant who found himself getting to spend an unlimited amount of the bank's money shortly after he was denied a loan of $225,000 is that he knew he was the beneficiary of a mistake on the bank's part. We find the following from La Fave & Scott Crim.Law HB, Section 85, page 629 to be applicable and correct:

"... It is well settled that the recipient of the mistaken delivery who appropriates the property commits a trespass in the taking, and so is guilty of larceny, if, realizing the mistake at the moment he takes delivery, he then forms an intent to steal the property...."

Perhaps it is arguable that defendant did not realize the mistake and did not form an intent to steal when the first overdrafts were written, but at some point when he had continued to receive the notices along with statements showing his huge negative balance he had to realize the mistake. At this point his failure to notify the bank or take some action to refund the money proved his intent to deprive to the exclusion of any reasonable hypothesis of innocence....

Turning to the proof that defendant intended to deprive Hibernia permanently of the money R.S. 15:445 states that though intent is a question of fact, it need not be proven as a fact, but may be inferred from the circumstances.... The only reasonable hypothesis flowing from this pattern is that defendant intended to deprive the bank permanently. It stands to reason that his criminal intent was present even if he had some vague, indefinite intention to pay the money back. Significantly, when the bank caught its mistake and called on defendant to pay the money back he could not. These assignments have no merit.

The conviction and sentence are affirmed.

(4) Appropriation By Wife or Husband

At common law neither spouse could commit larceny of the other's property. The marital relation was held to be such that possession of either was possession by both and hence neither could take possession from the other. That premise no longer prevails. It has been abrogated by the Married Women's Acts as interpreted in some of the states. There is no accord in the very few states in which the problem is directly controlled by statute. Illinois law provides "where the property involved is that of the offender's spouse, no prosecution for theft may be maintained unless the parties were not living together as man and wife and were living in separate abodes at the time of the alleged theft.[43]" It is no defense that the theft was from the actor's spouse, except that misappropriation of household and personal effects or other property normally accessible to both spouses is theft only if it involves the property of the other spouse and only if it occurs after the parties have ceased living together.[44]

(5) Appropriation by Bailee[45]

Rex v. Banks

Court for Crown Cases Reserved, 1821.
Russ. & Ry. 441, 168 Eng.Rep. 887.

The prisoner was tried and convicted before Mr. Justice Baylay, at the Lancaster Lent assizes, in the year 1821, for horse-stealing.

It appeared that the prisoner borrowed a horse, under pretence of carrying a child to a neighbouring surgeon. Whether he carried the child thither did not appear; but the day following, after the purpose for which he borrowed the horse was over, he took the horse in a different direction and sold it.

The prisoner did not offer the horse for sale, but was applied to sell it, so that it was possible he might have had no felonious intention till that application was made.

The jury thought the prisoner had no felonious intention when he took the horse; but as it was borrowed for a special purpose, and that purpose was over when the prisoner took the horse to the place where he sold it, the learned judge thought it right upon the authority of 2 East, P.C. 690, 694, and 2 Russ. 1089, 1090,[46] to submit to the consideration of the judges,

---

43. 720 ILCS 516–4(b) (1993).

44. E.g. Ky.Rev.Stat. 514.020(2) (1985).

45. A bailee who intends to appropriate the chattel at the time he first receives it from the bailor is guilty of larceny. Cunningham v. District Court, 432 P.2d 992 (Okl.Cr.1967).

46. In 2 Russ. 1089, it is said that, "In the case of a delivery of a horse upon hire or loan, if such delivery were obtained *bona fide,* no subsequent wrongful conversion pending the contract will amount to felony; and so of other goods. But when the purpose of the hiring, or loan, for which the delivery was made, has been ended, felony may be committed by a conversion of the goods."

whether the subsequent disposing of the horse, when the purpose for which it was borrowed was no longer in view, did not in law include in it a felonious taking?

In Easter term, 1821, the judges met and considered this case. They were of opinion that the doctrine laid down on this subject in 2 East, P.C. 690 & 694, and 2 Russell, 1089 & 1090 was not correct. They held that if the prisoner had not a felonious intention when he originally took the horse, his subsequent withholding and disposing of it did not constitute a new felonious taking, or make him guilty of felony; consequently the conviction could not be supported.[47]

The Breaking Bulk Doctrine

In 1473 one who had bargained to take certain bales to Southampton wrongfully took them to another place where he broke open the bales and appropriated the contents. Whether or not this was larceny was debated in the Star Chamber. A motion to transfer the case to the common-law court was rejected because "the complainant was a merchant stranger, whose case ought to be judged by the law of nature in Chancery, and without the delay of a trial by jury". Hence it was disposed of in the Exchequer Chamber where most of the judges held that it was larceny, but for different reasons.[48] The reason offered by one was that the carrier had possession of the bales but not the contents so that he committed trespass by removing the contents from the bales. This was later adopted as the holding of the case and resulted in this anomalous rule: If a bailee having lawful possession of a bale wrongfully appropriates it, bale and all, it is not larceny; but if he wrongfully breaks it open and appropriates part or all[49] of the contents this is larceny. In the course of time the doctrine of "breaking bale" seems to have changed to one of "breaking bulk", which was even more peculiar. Under this notion if property such as wheat was delivered in bulk to the bailee's own vehicle it was not larceny if the bailee converted it all, but was larceny if he separated a portion from the mass and converted only that portion.[50] The whole doctrine has been largely, if not entirely, wiped out by legislation.

---

47. [Note by Compiler.] This case repudiates the theory of the trial court in Tunnard's Case, 1 Leach 214 note, 168 Eng.Rep. 209 note (1729).

If possession of the property was acquired innocently, but later there was a change of mind resulting in appropriation, there was no larceny because there was no trespass. Farlow v. State, 9 Md.App. 515, 265 A.2d 578 (1970).

48. Carrier's Case, Year Book, 13 Ed. IV, 9, pl. 5 (1473).

49. A bailee who wrongfully opens up a bag and takes all of the contents is just as much guilty of larceny as if he had taken only a part. Rex v. Brazier, Russ. and Ry. 337, 168 Eng.Rep. 833 (1817).

Armored car employee who opened money bags could be convicted of "stealing" under 18 U.S.C.A. § 2113(a) on a theory of breaking the bulk. United States v. Mafnas, 701 F.2d 83 (9th Cir.1983).

50. Commonwealth v. Brown, 4 Mass. 580 (1808); Nichols v. People, 17 N.Y. 114 (1858); Rex v. Howell, 7 Car. and P. 325, 173 Eng.Rep. 145 (1836); Rex v. Pratley, 5 Car. and P. 533, 172 Eng.Rep. 1086 (1833). Contra: Rex v. Madox, Russ. and Ry. 92, 168 Eng.Rep. 700 (1805).

(6) Continuing Trespass

Regina v. Riley

Court of Criminal Appeal, 1853.
6 Cox C.C. 88, Dearsly 149, 169 Eng.Rep. 674.

At the General Quarter Sessions of the Peace for the county of Durham, held at the city of Durham (before Rowland Burdon, Esq., Chairman), on the 18th of October, in the year of our Lord 1852, the prisoner was indicted for having, on the 5th day of October, 1852, stolen a lamb, the property of John Burnside. The prisoner pleaded Not Guilty. On the trial it was proved that on Friday, the 1st day of October, in the year of our Lord 1852, John Burnside, the prosecutor, put ten white-faced lambs into a field in the occupation of John Clarke, situated near to the town of Darlington. On Monday, the 4th day of October, the prisoner went with a flock of twenty-nine black-faced lambs to John Clarke, and asked if he might put them into Clarke's field for a night's keep, and upon Clarke agreeing to allow him to do so for one penny per head, the prisoner put his twenty-nine lambs into the same field with the prosecutor's lambs. At half-past seven o'clock in the morning of Tuesday, the 5th of October, the prosecutor went to Clarke's field, and in counting his lambs he missed one, and the prisoner's lambs were gone from the field also. Between eight and nine o'clock in the morning of the same day, the prisoner came to the farm of John Calvert, at Middleton St. George, six miles east from Darlington, and asked him to buy twenty-nine lambs. Calvert agreed to do so, and to give 8s. a-piece for them. Calvert then proceeded to count the lambs, and informed the prisoner that there were thirty instead of twenty-nine in the flock, and pointed out to him a white-faced lamb; upon which the prisoner said, "If you object to take thirty, I will draw one." Calvert however bought the whole, and paid the prisoner 12l. for them. One of the lambs sold to Calvert was identified by the prosecutor as his property, and as the lamb missed by him from Clarke's field. It was a half-bred white-faced lamb, marked with the letter "T.," and similar to the other nine of the prosecutor's lambs. The twenty-nine lambs belonging to the prisoner were black-faced lambs. On the 5th October, in the afternoon, the prisoner stated to two of the witnesses that he never had put his lambs into Clarke's field, and had sold them on the previous afternoon, for 11l. 12s., to a person on the Barnard Castle-road, which road leads west from Darlington.

There was evidence in the case to show that the prisoner must have taken the lambs from Clarke's field early in the morning, which was thick and rainy.

It was argued by the counsel for the prisoner, in his address to the jury, that the facts showed that the original taking from Clarke's field was by mistake; and if the jury were of that opinion, then, as the original taking was not done *animo furandi,* the subsequent appropriation would not make it a larceny, and the prisoner must be acquitted. The chairman, in summing up, told the jury that though they might be of opinion that the prisoner did not know that the lamb was in his flock, until it was pointed out to him by Calvert, he should rule that, in point of law, the taking occurred when it was so pointed out to the prisoner and sold by him to Calvert, and not at the time of leaving the field. The jury returned the following verdict: The jury say that at the time of leaving the field the prisoner did not know that the lamb was in his flock, and that he was guilty of felony at the time it was pointed out to him.

The prisoner was then sentenced to six months' hard labour in the house of correction at Durham; and being unable to find bail, was thereupon committed to prison until the opinion of this court could be taken upon the question, whether Charles Riley was properly convicted of larceny. . . .

■ POLLOCK, C.B. We are all of opinion that the conviction is right. The case is distinguishable from those cited. R. v. Thristle decides only that if a man once gets into rightful possession, he cannot, by a subsequent fraudulent appropriation, convert it into a felony. So in R. v. Thurborn, in the elaborate judgment delivered by my brother Parke on behalf of the court of which I was a member, the same rule is laid down. It is there said that the mere taking up of a lost chattel to look at it, would not be a taking possession of it; and no doubt that may be done without violating any social duty. A man may take up a lost chattel and carry it home, with the proper object of endeavouring to find the owner; and then afterwards, if he yields to the temptation of appropriating it to his own use, he is not guilty of felony. In Leigh's Case, also, the original taking was rightful, but here the original taking was wrongful. I am not desirous of calling in aid the technicality of a continuing trespass; and I think this case may be decided upon the ground either that there was no taking at all by the prisoner in the first instance, or a wrongful taking, and, in either case, as soon as he appropriates the property, the evidence of felony is complete.

■ PARKE, B. I think that this case may be disposed of on a short ground. The original taking was not lawful, but a trespass, upon which an action in that form might have been founded; but it was not felony, because there was no intention to appropriate. There was, however, a continuing trespass up to the time of appropriation, and at that time, therefore, the felony was committed. Where goods are carried from one county to another, they may be laid as taken in the second county, and the difference between this and Leigh's Case, as well as the others cited, is that the original taking was no trespass. It was by the implied license of the owner, and the same thing as if he had been entrusted by the prosecutor with the possession of the goods.

■ WILLIAMS, TALFOURD, and CROMPTON, JJ., concurred.

Conviction affirmed.[51]

State v. Coombs

Supreme Judicial Court of Maine, 1868.
55 Me. 477.

■ DICKERSON, J. Exceptions. The prisoner was indicted for the larceny of a horse, sleigh and buffalo robes. The jury were instructed that, if the

---

51. One who took another's bull from the range, thinking it was his own, and sold it under such claim, was not guilty of larceny even if the owner had laid claim to the bull before the sale was made. Wilson v. State, 96 Ark. 148, 131 S.W. 336 (1910).

prisoner obtained possession of the team by falsely and fraudulently pretending that he wanted it to drive to a certain place, and to be gone a specified time, when in fact he did not intend to go to such place, but to a more distant one, and to be absent a longer time, without intending at the time to steal the property, the team was not lawfully in his possession, and that a subsequent conversion of it to his own use, with a felonious intent while thus using it, would be larceny.

It is well settled that where one comes lawfully into possession of the goods of another, with his consent, a subsequent felonious conversion of them to his own use, without the owner's consent, does not constitute larceny, because the felonious intent is wanting at the time of the taking.

But how is it when the taking is fraudulent or tortious, and the property is subsequently converted to the use of the taker with a felonious intent? Suppose one takes his neighbor's horse from the stable, without consent, to ride him to a neighboring town, with the intention to return him, but subsequently sells him and converts the money to his own use, without his neighbor's consent, is he a mere trespasser, or is he guilty of larceny? In other words, must the felonious intent exist at the time of the original taking, when that is fraudulent or tortious, to constitute larceny?

When property is thus obtained, the taking or trespass is continuous. The wrongdoer holds it all the while without right, and against the right and without the consent of the owner. If at this point no other element is added, there is no larceny. But, if to such taking there be subsequently superadded a felonious intent, that is, an intent to deprive the owner of his property permanently without color of right, or excuse, and to make it the property of the taker without the owner's consent, the crime of larceny is complete.... [52]

Exceptions overruled.

Judgment for the State.

(E) CARRYING AWAY

People v. Khoury

Appellate Department, Superior Court, Los Angeles County, 1980.
108 Cal.App.3d Supp. 1, 166 Cal.Rptr. 705.

■ FAINER, JUDGE. Defendant appeals his conviction, by jury trial, for violation of Penal Code section 487, subdivision 1 (grand theft). The pertinent facts of this case were that defendant, after being observed for several hours pushing a shopping cart around a Fed Mart Store, was seen pushing a cart, with a large cardboard chandelier box on it, up to a check stand in the store. An alert cashier at the check stand, noticing that the box was loosely taped, stated that he would have to open and check the contents of the box before he would allow defendant to pay the price marked and remove the box from the store. Defendant then walked back

---

52. Accord: Commonwealth v. White, 11 Cush. 483 (Mass.1853).

Defendant, a salesman, who received a check from a purchaser as a down payment and then converted the funds to his own use was properly convicted of larceny by conversion. People v. O'Shea, 149 Mich.App. 268, 385 N.W.2d 768 (1986).

through the check stand and into the store, leaving the box with the cashier. Defendant was arrested by store security after the box was opened, disclosing in excessing of $900.00 worth of store items, consisting of batteries, tools, and chain saws, but no chandelier.

Defendant contends that these facts were insufficient evidence to convict him of grand theft. More specifically, defendant contends that the evidence was insufficient to show an asportation or carrying away of the personal property of the Fed Mart Store and therefore was, at most, an attempt to commit grand theft.

Our function on appeal in this case is to determine first the applicable law of theft by larceny, which is the theft for which defendant was specifically charged, and then to examine the record to ascertain whether there was substantial evidence of the disputed element of the crime to support the judgment of conviction.

The crime of larceny is the stealing or taking of the property of another. (Pen.Code, § 484.) The completed crime of larceny—as distinguished from attempted larceny—requires *asportation* or carrying away, in addition to the taking.

"The element of asportation is not satisfied unless it is shown that 'the goods were severed from the possession or custody of the owner, and in the possession of the thief, though it be but for a moment.' "

The other element of theft by larceny is the specific intent in the mind of the perpetrator "... to deprive the owner permanently of his property...."

The sufficiency of the evidence to support a finding of intent is not a claim of error on this appeal but is important in reviewing the jury's determination of the existence of the element of asportation or carrying away, a question of fact. The jury was instructed that "[I]n order to constitute a carrying away, the property need not be ... actually removed from the premises of the owner. Any removal of the property from the place where it was kept or placed by the owner, done with the specific intent to deprive the owner permanently of his property ..., whereby the perpetrator obtains possession and control of the property for any period of time, is sufficient to constitute the element of carrying away."

The cases make a distinction between fact patterns in which the defendant takes possession of the owner's property and moves it with the intent to carry it away, so that it is not attached to any other property of the owner and those cases in which a thief is frustrated in his attempt to carry the property away. All of the cases cited above make it clear that the property does not have to be actually removed from the premises of the owner. The jury was properly instructed as to the necessary elements of the crime of theft by larceny. They were not told that there could be no taking or carrying away or asportation unless defendant was able to get the chandelier box containing other store property past the cashier. This was a factor to be considered by the jury, as the trier of fact, in determining whether there was or was not an asportation.

The defendant was seen pushing a shopping cart carrying a carton or container for packaging a chandelier; the chandelier had been removed from the carton and the items already described, of a value of $900, were in the carton. The carton was taped. It was the recent taping of the carton that prompted the cashier not to permit the defendant to go through the check stand until the contents of the carton were checked. The defendant, on being informed of this, walked back into the store, leaving the carton behind. These facts, and the reasonable inferences which can be drawn therefrom support the jury's finding of asportation by substantial evidence.

The intent to permanently deprive the store of its merchandise was clear. The defendant in this appeal does not even attempt to negate the element of intent by proof of innocent though careless mistake.

The judgment of conviction is affirmed.

■ IBANEZ, P.J., concurs.

■ BIGELOW, JUDGE. I respectfully dissent.

In my opinion, as a matter of law, the facts fail to show sufficient asportation of the items to constitute a completed theft. The defendant is only guilty of *attempted* grand theft in violation of Penal Code sections 664, 484, and 487, subdivision (1).

In People v. Thompson (1958) 158 Cal.App.2d 320, 322 P.2d 489, the defendant entered a Thrifty Drug Store, concealed several records under his coat and went through the check stand without paying for the records. He was arrested 10 feet beyond the check stand, but before he left the store.

The physical layout of the store in our case at bench was similar to that of the store in the *Thompson* case, *supra*. In each case there was a check stand where the items selected for purchase are to be paid for by the customer. The *Thompson* case, *supra*, at page 323, 322 P.2d at page 490, stated, "The carrying of the records through the check stand constituted an asportation of the goods, as the act effectively removed them from the store's possession and control, even if only for a moment."

In this case, an alert clerk at the check stand prevented defendant from removing the items from the store's possession and control, even for a moment. All the other facts of placing the items in a box, taping it, etc., are proof of his intent to permanently deprive the owner-store of its property without paying the proper marked prices for them. Defendant's attempted theft was frustrated and he did not asportate the goods past the check stand.

I would modify the verdict and judgment to provide that the defendant is guilty of the offense of attempted grand theft (Pen.Code, §§ 664, 484, 487, subd. 1), affirm the judgment as modified and remand the matter to the trial court for resentencing of the defendant.

(F) WITH INTENT TO STEAL

People v. Brown
Supreme Court of California, 1894.
105 Cal. 66, 38 P. 518.

■ GAROUTTE, J. The appellant was convicted of the crime of burglary, alleged by the information to have been committed in entering a certain house with intent to commit grand larceny. The entry is conceded, and also it is conceded that appellant took therefrom a certain bicycle, the property of the party named in the information, and of such a value as to constitute grand larceny. The appellant is a boy of 17 years of age, and, for a few days immediately prior to the taking of the bicycle, was staying at the place from which the machine was taken, working for his board. He took the stand as a witness, and testified: "I took the wheel to get even with the boy, and, of course, I didn't intend to keep it. I just wanted to get even with him. The boy was throwing oranges at me in the evening, and he would not stop when I told him to, and it made me mad, and I left Yount's house Saturday morning. I thought I would go back and take the boy's wheel. He had a wheel, the one I had the fuss with. Instead of getting hold of his, I got Frank's, but I intended to take it back Sunday night; but, before I got back, they caught me. I took it down by the grove, and put it on the ground, and covered it with brush, and crawled in, and Frank came and hauled off the brush, and said: 'What are you doing here?' Then I told him ... I covered myself up in the brush so that they could not find me until evening, until I could take it back. I did not want them to find me. I expected to remain there during the day, and not go back until evening." Upon the foregoing state of facts, the court gave the jury the following instruction: "I think it is not necessary to say very much to you in this case. I may say, generally, that I think counsel for the defense here stated to you in his argument very fairly the principles of law governing this case, except in one particular. In defining to you the crime of grand larceny, he says it is essential that the taking of it must be felonious. That is true; the taking with the intent to deprive the owner of it; but he adds the conclusion that you must find that the taker intended to deprive him of it permanently. I do not think that is the law. I think in this case, for example, if the defendant took this bicycle, we will say for the purpose of riding twenty-five miles, for the purpose of enabling him to get away, and then left it for another to get it, and intended to do nothing else except to help himself away for a certain distance, it would be larceny, just as much as though he intended to take it all the while. A man may take a horse, for instance, not with the intent to convert it wholly and permanently to his own use, but to ride it to a certain distance, for a certain purpose he may have, and then leave it. He converts it to that extent to his own use and purpose feloniously." This instruction is erroneous, and demands a reversal of the judgment. If the boy's story be true, he is not guilty of larceny in taking the machine; yet, under the instruction of the court, the words from his own mouth convicted him. The court told the jury that larceny may be committed, even though it was only the intent of the party taking the property to deprive the owner of it temporarily. We think the authorities form an unbroken line to the effect that the felonious intent must be to deprive the owner of the property permanently. The illustration contained in the instruction as to the man taking the horse is too broad in its terms as stating a correct principle of law. Under the circumstances depicted by the illustration, the man might, and again he might not, be guilty of larceny. It would be a pure question of fact for the jury, and dependent for its true solution upon all the circumstances surrounding the transaction. But the test of law to be applied to these circumstances for the purpose of determining the ultimate fact as to the man's guilt or innocence is, did he intend to permanently deprive the owner of his property? If he did not intend so to do, there is no felonious intent, and his acts constitute but a trespass. While the felonious intent of the party taking need not necessarily be an intention to convert the property to his own use, still it must in all cases be an intent to wholly and permanently deprive the owner thereof.... For the foregoing reasons, it is ordered that the judgment and order be reversed, and the cause remanded for a new trial.

■ We concur: McFarland, J.; Harrison, J.; Van Fleet, J.; Fitzgerald, J.; De Haven, J.

State v. Savage

Court of General Sessions for Sussex County, Delaware, 1936.
37 Del. 509, 186 A. 738.

■ Layton, C.J., sitting. The indictment was for larceny. The evidence on the part of the State was that the defendant took from the unattended automobile of the prosecuting witness a metal can and three gallons of gasoline contained therein; that after taking the property he drove away and at a place about one mile distant he poured the gasoline into the tank of his car and threw the can into a nearby branch, and that he made no effort to inform the owner of his act, or to restore the property or pay for it.

The defendant was allowed to testify that while driving his automobile he ran out of gasoline and seeing the car of the prosecuting witness nearby, went to it and there found the can and gasoline; that he then and there poured the gasoline in his own car and drove off; that he left the can near the branch instructing a companion to return the can to the prosecuting witness and to inform him that he would return a like amount of gasoline. This was denied by the companion.

■ Layton, C.J., charged the jury, in part, as follows:

Larceny has been defined to be the taking and carrying away of the personal property of another with felonious intent to convert it to his own use without the owner's consent.

It is incumbent upon the State to prove to the satisfaction of the jury beyond a reasonable doubt every material element of the crime charged. So, the State must prove that the taking of the property occurred in Sussex County; that the property was of some value; that the person alleged to be the owner had a general or special property in the goods taken; that the defendant took and carried away the property, or some part of it, against the consent of the owner; and that the taker at the time of the taking had the felonious intent to convert the property to his own use.

The word "felonious," as applied to an act, simply means wrongful, in that there was no color of right or excuse for the act.[53]

The issue in this case is within a narrow compass. The defendant admits the taking in Sussex County. There is no denial that the property was of some value. It is not pretended that the taking was with the consent of the owner. That the person named in the indictment as the owner had such a special property in the goods as would support the indictment was sufficiently proved.

---

53. West's California Penal Code § 484 (1996) defines theft in part, to "feloniously steal, take, carry, lead, or drive away the personal property of another...."

The defendant does deny that he took the property with felonious intent to convert it to his own use. He contends that he took it for a temporary purpose, then and there intending to restore that property which was capable of being restored in specie, and a like quantity of gasoline.

It is not every taking of the property of another without his knowledge or consent that amounts to larceny. To constitute the crime the intent must be wholly to deprive the owner of the property. The general rule may be said to be that a taking of property for a temporary purpose with the bona fide intention to return the property to the owner does not amount to larceny, however liable the taker may be in a civil action of trespass. So, a borrowing of property, even though it be wrongful as being without the owner's knowledge or consent, with the intention of returning the property to its owner, is not larceny.

The property here is of two kinds, the can which could be restored, and the gasoline which admittedly was consumed, but exactly the same thing in quantity and quality could be restored, and, on principle, it would seem that if the defendant took the gasoline intending then and there to return a like quantity, the taking would not amount to larceny. It would be a different matter, perhaps, if the property taken were of some particular kind or quality which the owner reasonably might desire to be returned in specie.

It must be kept in mind, however, another principle, that if the defendant, at the time he took the property, had no intention of restoring it to the owner, but took it with the intention of converting it to his own use, the fact that he later repented, and desired or attempted to restore the goods would not purge him of guilt. The taking in such circumstances would be larceny.

You must find the intent with which the defendant took the property from all the facts and circumstances. You, of course, may and should, consider the testimony of the defendant, and, like all other testimony, you should give to it that degree of credit which you think it ought to have. You may also consider the manner and place of the taking, the conduct of the defendant thereafter, and his effort or attempt, if any, to restore the property or to account to the owner for it.

If you shall find from the evidence that the defendant took the property for a temporary purpose, and with the intention, then and there, to restore the can to the owner, and to account to the owner for the gasoline taken, or if you shall entertain a reasonable doubt of the felonious intent with which the defendant is charged, your verdict should be not guilty.

State v. Langis

Supreme Court of Oregon, Department 1, 1968.
251 Or. 130, 444 P.2d 959.

■ DENECKE, JUSTICE. The defendant was convicted of larceny of a motor vehicle. He appeals, contending that the court improperly instructed the jury.

The defendant and one Richard Carrier were traveling from Vancouver, B.C., to San Francisco and had gone as far as Eugene by bus and hitchhiking. The car was taken in Eugene. The State Police stopped the car south of Eugene and north of Roseburg, Oregon. Roseburg is the next principal city south of Eugene on the interstate freeway. They are 70 miles apart. Carrier testified that he actually took the car in Eugene and was driving at the time of apprehension. (This testimony was verified by the officer.) Carrier testified that he intended to leave the car in Roseburg in "perfect condition."

In order to prove larceny there must be proof that the defendant had " ... the intent to deprive such other of such property permanently...." § ORS 164.310.

At the prosecution's request the trial court instructed the jury as follows:

"You are further instructed that if you find that the defendant took the automobile with the intent to appropriate it to his own use and with intent to abandon later the automobile in such circumstances as would render its recovery by the owner difficult or unlikely, then you may find that the taking was with the intent to permanently deprive the owner of the property."

The defendant excepted to the instruction upon the ground that there was no evidence of an intent to abandon in circumstances that would render recovery by the owner difficult or unlikely, and even if there were, such intent does not amount to an intent to deprive the owner of the property permanently.

There was evidence from which the jury could have found that the defendant intended to abandon the vehicle under circumstances that would render recovery difficult or unlikely. The defendant's witness, Carrier, said they were going to abandon the car in Roseburg. However, in view of the evidence that their destination was San Francisco, about 500 miles to the south, the jury reasonably could have believed that defendant intended to abandon it in San Francisco.

The substance of the instruction is also correct. Intent to deprive the owner of the property permanently can be inferred from abandonment under certain circumstances:

" ... An intent to take the property of another by trespass, use it for a temporary purpose and then abandon it, *may* be an intent to steal. An intent of the latter type is not an intent to steal if the intended abandonment is under such circumstances that the property will in all probability be restored to the owner; but it is an intent to steal if the intended abandonment will create a considerable risk of permanent loss to the owner. To take a horse from the owner's pasture on a farm, ride it a mile or two, and then turn it loose does not create any considerable risk of permanent loss to the owner; but such risk is created if a traveler, caught in an unexpected rain, takes an umbrella in one city and abandons it in another city some miles away...." Perkins, Criminal Law, 225 (1957).

The crux of the instruction is the phrase that the circumstances of the abandonment make recovery "difficult or unlikely." "Unlikely" accurately describe [sic] the concept that the circumstances of the abandonment are such that there is considerable risk that the owner will suffer a permanent deprivation of his property. "Difficult" is not as accurate in describing this concept and we do not encourage its use. Nevertheless, we conclude that its use in this context was not error. It is true that there is some degree of difficulty in recovering any car that has been abandoned any appreciable distance from the location of the owner; however, we find that the jury could reasonably have understood that "difficult" means so arduous that the chances were substantial that the owner would be permanently deprived of his property.

Affirmed.

State v. Komok

Supreme Court of Washington, 1989.
113 Wash.2d 810, 783 P.2d 1061.

■ SMITH, JUSTICE.

This case involves the simple question whether Washington's theft statute, RCW 9A.56.020(1), retains the common law requirement of "intent to permanently deprive," although the language of the statute merely states "intent to deprive." We answer that it does not.

Petitioner Joseph A. Komok, age 16, was convicted in the Juvenile Department of the King County Superior Court under an information charging him with theft in the third degree. The trial court . . . found him "guilty" of aiding and abetting his 14–year-old sister in taking a baseball cap, girls' stretch leggings, and a T-shirt belonging to Lamonts, a department store, without permission.

In his findings, [the trial judge], after reciting details of the taking, stated that "in doing so, the respondent [Petitioner Komok] intended to deprive Lamonts of the property."

. . .

The Court of Appeals . . . affirmed the conviction. That court held that intent to "permanently deprive" is not an element of theft under our statute; that the information properly alleged facts on each element of the offense stated in the statute; and that the trial court made sufficient findings on each element of the offense.

Petitioner Komok claims the information under which he was charged was defective because it did not include the common law language of "intent to permanently deprive," and that the findings of fact made by the trial court were insufficient because they did not specifically include the language indicating that common law element.

On August 24, 1987, Petitioner Joseph A. Komok entered a Lamonts store in West Seattle with his 14–year-old sister. They proceeded to the men's department and looked at merchandise. They did not have any money with them. The security manager, Phil Wineinger, observed their actions.

Petitioner Komok picked up a baseball cap and handed it to his sister. She left the men's department with the cap and proceeded to the girls' department. She picked up leggings and rejoined her brother in the men's department. The security manager observed them standing about a foot apart and "looking around as if to see if there was someone watching them." While petitioner stood facing his sister, she concealed the baseball cap, the leggings, and a T-shirt under the sweatshirt she was wearing.

Petitioner's sister then left the store without paying for the concealed items. Petitioner remained in the men's department. After the sister left the store, Mr. Wineinger stopped her, identified himself as the store security manager, and asked her to come back into the store. Upon reentering the store, the security manager observed petitioner leaving and stopped him. Petitioner and his sister returned to the security office with the manager.

According to Mr. Wineinger, Petitioner Komok said that he and his sister "had come in for school clothes and this was how they got them and just give them a break." Mr. Wineinger advised Mr. Komok that his sister was being detained for "shoplifting." He then notified the police.

The security manager testified for the State at the fact finding hearing for Petitioner Komok. Petitioner and his sister testified that she took the merchandise on her own, even though petitioner told her not to take it.

Petitioner relies on State v. Burnham, 19 Wash.App. 442, 576 P.2d 917, *review denied*, 90 Wash.2d 1020 (1978) to support his argument that the theft statute requires intent to permanently deprive. In *Burnham*, the Court of Appeals ... stated that "enactment of RCW 9A.56 did not abrogate the common-law requirement" and concluded that "the intent to permanently deprive remains an element of the crime of theft as defined in RCW 9A.56.020(1)(a)." This is not necessarily so. *Burnham* principally relied on secondary authority for its conclusion.

The legislature may define crimes. Where it does so, its statutory definition may supersede common law.

The theft statute states:

"Theft" means: ~~TAKING OF PERSONAL PROPERTY OF ANOTHER~~ [handwritten annotation]

(a) To wrongfully obtain or exert unauthorized control over the property or services of another or the value thereof, with intent to deprive him of such property or services;

IPD → IS NOT NEEDED [handwritten annotation]

RCW 9A.56.020(1)(a).

Under the statute, "wrongfully obtain or exert unauthorized control" means: "(a) To take the property or services of another;" RCW 9A.56.010(7).

In the statutory definition of "deprive,"[54] the legislature made no reference to the common law requirement of intent to "permanently

54. The only definition of "deprive" is in RCW 9A.56.010(5). After acknowledging the word as including its "common meaning," the statute states that the word also means "to make unauthorized use or an unauthorized copy of records, information, data, trade secrets, or

deprive," but acknowledged that the word retains its common meaning in cases not involving theft of intellectual property. RCW 9A.56.010(5)....
Under the statute, then, "deprive" retains its common meaning.

The present theft statute, RCW 9A.56.020, was included in revision of the criminal code in 1975, the first major revision since 1909.

As originally introduced, the statute included the common law language "intent permanently to deprive." Senate Bill 384, 42d Legislature (1971). As finally enacted, however, the statute used merely the language "intent to deprive." Based on this history, the Court of Appeals concluded in this case that the statute, RCW 9A.56.020(1)(a), does not incorporate the element of "intent to permanently deprive."

. . .

The legislative history indicates an intent to omit the common law concept of intent to "permanently" deprive. The Court of Appeals correctly concluded that it was thus not an element of the theft statute, RCW 9A.56.020. We agree.

Petitioner claims the information which charged him in the language of the statute was constitutionally defective because it omits the common law element of intent to "permanently deprive" the owner of property, even though it is not included in the statute. He claims this omission violates Const. art. 1, § 22, which provides that an accused has the right to "demand the nature and cause of the accusation against him," and the sixth amendment to the United States Constitution which states that an accused has the right "to be informed of the nature and cause of the accusation."

We need not consider this claim because of the conclusion we have reached on the principal issue.

Petitioner further claims the trial court erred in failing to state in its written findings whether petitioner intended to permanently deprive the owner of goods, and thus judgment should be vacated and the case remanded to the trial court for a finding on the element of intent to "permanently deprive."

We need not consider this claim either because of the conclusion we have reached on the principal issue.

We therefore affirm the decision of the Court of Appeals. The language of our theft statute, RCW 9A.56.020, and the legislative history indicate that the legislature, in its 1975 revision of the criminal code, did not intend to retain the common law requirement of intent to "permanently deprive" in the offense of theft by taking.

Affirmed.

(G) GRAND LARCENY

Larceny was a capital crime under the common law of England but an early statute divided the offense into two grades—grand larceny if the

---

computer programs". RCW 9A.56.010(5). This is apparently a legislative device to incorporate intellectual property into our concept of theft.

value of the stolen property exceeded twelve pence, and petit (or petty) larceny if it did not. Both were felonies under this statute, but whipping was substituted for death as the penalty for petit larceny. This statute is old enough to be common law in this country but under modern statutes petit larceny is usually a misdemeanor. At one time the dividing line between the two was generally $10. Several jurisdictions set the value at $100 and under some statutes it is much higher.[55]

State v. Delmarter

Supreme Court of Washington, 1980.
94 Wn.2d 634, 618 P.2d 99.

■ DOLLIVER, JUSTICE. Defendant, Rodney Guy Delmarter, was charged with simple assault and attempted theft in the first degree of property in Warren's Drug Store. None of the witnesses who testified at trial saw defendant enter the store, nor noticed him until he was near the prescription counter at the back of the store.

Defendant testified that he went to the drugstore to purchase some cough syrup, placed his change on the pharmacy counter, and some of it rolled off the counter to the floor inside the pharmacy area. Defendant stated he then went behind the counter, which is off limits to customers, to pick up his change. He further testified that he was looking for the pharmacist at that time. Entry to the pharmacy area is through a swinging door and a step up about 8 inches onto the raised floor.

The pharmacist testified that he first observed defendant in the area near the prescription counter walking around among the shelves and magazine racks, and that he saw defendant weaving and looking behind the counter to see if anybody was there. Later, he found defendant inside the pharmacy area crouched down on the floor in front of but facing away from a camouflaged cash drawer. The pharmacist also testified that, shortly before the incident, a clerk had obtained change from the cash drawer; that it was used to make change many times a day; and that the requests for change were sometimes shouted by clerks at the other end of the store. When the pharmacist confronted defendant, a struggle ensued which resulted in the assault conviction. Defendant broke away and fled from the store with his two companions.

Testimony at trial established that a camouflaged cash drawer, which appeared to be nothing more than a shelf containing medications, was situated behind the prescription counter approximately 17 feet from the swinging door used to enter the pharmacy area and that employees using the cash drawer could be seen from various parts of the store. Approximately $1,800 in cash was in the drawer at the time of this incident along with certain controlled substances. The drugs concealed in the cash drawer

---

55. California has set the value for grand theft of general personal property at $400. West's Cal. Penal Code § 487(a) (1996).

Grand larceny includes petit larceny as a necessarily included offense. Theriault v. United States, 434 F.2d 212 (5th Cir.1970).

were valued at approximately $100 acquisition cost while the retail value of all the drugs in the store was around $15,000.

Defendant was convicted of simple assault and attempted theft in the first degree. After the jury returned its verdict, defendant moved for a new trial and, in the alternative, asked the court to reduce the conviction to attempted theft in the third degree to conform with the evidence. Both motions were denied.

Defendant appealed only the conviction of attempted theft in the first degree. The Court of Appeals affirmed. We granted defendant's petition for review in which defendant seeks a remand of the case with instructions to reduce the grade of the conviction to attempted theft in the third degree.

Defendant was convicted of attempted theft in the first degree under RCW 9A.28.020(1), which provides:

A person is guilty of an attempt to commit crime if, *with intent to commit a specific crime,* he does any act which is a substantial step toward the commission of that crime.

(Italics ours.) Theft is defined in RCW 9A.56.020 as follows:

(1) "Theft" means:

(a) To wrongfully obtain or exert unauthorized control over the property or services of another or the value thereof, with intent to deprive him of such property or services; ...

RCW 9A.56.030 establishes the elements of theft in the first degree:

(1) A person is guilty of theft in the first degree if he commits theft of:

(a) Property or services which exceed(s) one thousand five hundred dollars in value; ...

While defendant concedes there is sufficient evidence to convict him of attempted theft, he asserts the evidence is insufficient to prove he had the specific intent to take property valued in excess of $1,500.

Initially, defendant contends that to be convicted of attempted first-degree theft, the state must prove he knew the property he attempted to steal had a value in excess of $1,500. Defendant confuses knowledge with intent. RCW 9A.56.020.–030(1)(a) does not include as an element of the crime that defendant must have knowledge of the value of the property. Defendant cites no case authority for his position other than State v. Leach, 36 Wash.2d 641, 219 P.2d 972 (1950), which concerns intent, not knowledge, and is not in point.

The crucial question is whether there is sufficient evidence that defendant intended to steal from the camouflaged cash drawer. Defendant claims that since there is no evidence he knew of the existence of the cash drawer there is insufficient evidence to convict.

The rule applied in this state by an appellate court in determining the sufficiency of the evidence in a criminal case has been altered recently by the United States Supreme Court in Jackson v. Virginia, 443 U.S. 307, 99 S.Ct. 2781, 61 L.Ed.2d 560 (1979). Prior to *Jackson,* it was necessary for the court, to be satisfied that there [was] "substantial evidence" to support either the state's case, or the particular element in question. When that quantum of evidence has been presented, there is *some proof* of the element or crime in question and the motion in arrest of judgment must be denied.

State v. Randecker, 79 Wash.2d 512, 518, 487 P.2d 1295 (1971). The standard of review enunciated in *Jackson,* however, now requires us to determine:

> whether, after viewing the evidence in the light most favorable to the prosecution, *any* rational trier of fact could have found the essential elements of the crime *beyond a reasonable doubt.*

Jackson v. Virginia, *supra*, 443 U.S. at 319, 99 S.Ct. at 2789. We have recently applied the *Jackson* test in analyzing the sufficiency of the evidence in a criminal case.

[handwritten margin note: Was D Aware of the value of the property]

Upon reviewing the evidence in the light most favorable to the State, we conclude that any rational trier of fact could have found the essential elements of attempted theft in the first degree. In determining the sufficiency of the evidence, circumstantial evidence is not to be considered any less reliable than direct evidence. Furthermore, the specific criminal intent of the accused may be inferred from the conduct where it is plainly indicated as a matter of logical probability.

The following evidence and inferences to be drawn therefrom support our holding that any rational trier of fact could have found the essential elements of the crime beyond a reasonable doubt:

(1) The defendant was in a restricted access area without authorization; (2) the restricted character of the area was obvious, indicating a lack of the possibility of mistake; (3) the defendant was crouching in front of the cash drawer well inside the pharmacy, indicating knowledge of the existence of the drawer; (4) the cash drawer is some 17 feet inside the pharmacy area, indicating a lack of unintentional or mistaken entry into the area; (5) the cash drawer is 9 feet past the cash register, indicating that the defendant's actions were directed at the acquisition of the contents of the drawer; (6) patrons of Warren's Drug could, by observing the actions of store employees, learn of the existence and function of the drawer; and (7) immediately prior to the incident, store employees had obtained money from the cash drawer.

The Court of Appeals is affirmed.

■ ROSELLINI, STAFFORD, WRIGHT and BRACHTENBACH, JJ., concur.

■ WILLIAMS, JUSTICE (dissenting).

Although the majority opinion correctly states the applicable test for analyzing a challenge to the sufficiency of the evidence, I believe the majority has misapplied the test and reached the wrong result. I would remand the case with instructions to reduce the conviction to attempted theft in the third degree.

In my view, our task is to determine whether, after viewing the evidence in the light most favorable to the State, any rational trier of fact could have found the elements of attempted first-degree theft.

Applying this doctrine, there is no question, and indeed the defendant concedes, that a rational trier of fact could have found beyond a reasonable doubt the elements of attempted theft in the third degree. The statute provides, in pertinent part:

(1) A person is guilty of theft in the third degree if he commits theft of property or services which does not exceed two hundred and fifty dollars in value.

RCW 9A.56.050(1).

There was substantial evidence in the record to establish the elements of attempted third-degree theft. *See* Majority Opinion, at 101. A reasonable trier of fact could find beyond a reasonable doubt that all the elements of attempted third-degree theft were present, from the following evidence: (1) defendant was in a restricted access area without authorization; (2) the restricted character of the area was obvious to customers; (3) the defendant was crouching down well inside the restricted area of the pharmacy; and (4) there was property of value within easy reach of defendant.

The entire record evidence fails, however, to rise to the level required for a rational trier of fact to find the elements of attempted *first-degree* theft beyond a reasonable doubt. The record contains *no* evidence establishing which property defendant intended to take. There is no evidence that he had seen a store employer use the drawer, either immediately before the incident in question or at any time. The suggestion that defendant knew of the location of the camouflaged cash drawer is speculation at best. The existence of an intent to wrongfully obtain the contents of the drawer may be plausible but more likely is an inference that defendant intended to take controlled substances from shelves adjoining the hidden cash drawer. The pharmacist testified that such drugs were in clear view on nearby shelves. In my opinion, no reasonable trier of fact, on the evidence adduced in this case, could find beyond a reasonable doubt that defendant intended to commit theft of the contents of the cash drawer.

Accordingly, I am compelled to dissent.

■ UTTER, C.J., and HOROWITZ and HICKS, JJ., concur.[56]

---

56. It is larceny to steal the clothing from a buried corpse. Haynes Case, 12 Co.Rep. 113, 77 Eng.Rep. 1389 (1614).

A series of acts may be aggregated to establish the level of theft involved in a single criminal impulse. In appropriate circumstances, the question of whether aggregation is proper is to be left to the jury as a question of fact. State v. Amsden, 300 N.W.2d 882 (Iowa 1981). *See also*, State v. Johnson, 86 Or.App. 430, 739 P.2d 1048 (1987).

D was apprehended in an alley near three partially stripped cars. **D**'s fingerprints were found on the steering wheel of one of the cars and on car-parts located on the ground. He was charged with grand theft-auto and found guilty. The trial judge entered judgment of guilty of the statutory offense of "tampering" with a vehicle. This was upheld on the ground that "tampering" with a vehicle is necessarily included as a lesser offense of the charge of theft of the vehicle. People v. Anderson, 15 Cal.3d 806, 126 Cal.Rptr. 235, 543 P.2d 603 (1975).

Where **D**, charged with larceny of a car, testified that he moved the car in question to tow another car, he was entitled to an instruction on the lesser-included offense of operating a motor vehicle without consent. State v. Walker, 218 N.W.2d 915 (Iowa 1974).

SECTION 2. ROBBERY

At common law robbery was larceny from, or in the presence of, the person by force or threat. American jurisdictions recognize the offense with modest statutory variations. In addition, many jurisdictions have adopted specific statutes to deal with types of robbery that for one reason or another call for special legal treatment. The federal car-jacking statute, discussed in Holloway v. United States, 526 U.S. 1, 119 S.Ct. 966, 143 L.Ed.2d 1 (1999), *infra* Chapter VII, is a prominent example.

People v. Butler

Supreme Court of California, In Bank, 1967.
65 Cal.2d 569, 55 Cal.Rptr. 511, 421 P.2d 703.

[**B** shot and killed **A** (and also wounded **L**). **B** testified that **A** owed him money and that **A** admitted owing it but kept postponing the payment. He testified that he threatened **A** in order to compel **A** to pay what he owed, and that the gun went off when **A** grabbed for it.]

■ TRAYNOR, CHIEF JUSTICE. Defendant was charged by information with the murder of Joseph H. Anderson and with assault with intent to murder William Russell Locklear. A jury convicted defendant of first degree felony murder and of assault with a deadly weapon; it fixed the penalty for the murder at death. This appeal is automatic. (Pen.Code, § 1239, subd. (b).)

We have determined that error in the guilt phase of the trial deprived defendant of his primary defense to the charge of first degree felony murder. The judgment of conviction of murder must therefore be reversed....

No evidence of premeditation or deliberation was adduced by the prosecution. The court instructed the jury that since these elements were not present, it could find first degree murder only if defendant committed the killing in the perpetration of a robbery.

Defendant testified that he did not intend to rob Anderson when he went to the house, but intended only to recover money owed to him. Over his objection, the prosecutor argued to the jury, "If you think a man owes you a hundred dollars, or fifty dollars, or five dollars, or a dollar, and you go over with a gun to try to get his money, it's robbery." And, "If you go into a man's home and merely because he's supposed to owe you some money, you take money from him at gunpoint, you have robbed him." Again objecting to further argument by the prosecutor that a robbery was committed even if defendant believed Anderson owed him money, defendant suggested that a necessary element of theft, the intent to steal, was requisite to robbery, but was overruled by the court.

Defendant's objection was well taken. "Robbery is a felonious taking of personal property in the possession of another, from his person or immediate presence, and against his will, accomplished by means of force or fear." (Pen.Code, § 211.) An essential element of robbery is the felonious intent or *animus furandi* that accompanies the taking. Since robbery is but larceny aggravated by the use of force or fear to accomplish the taking of property from the person or presence of the possessor, the felonious intent requisite to robbery is the same intent common to those offenses that, like larceny, are grouped in the Penal Code designation of "theft."[57] The taking of property is not theft in the absence of an intent to steal, and a specific intent to steal, i.e., an intent to deprive an owner permanently of his property, is an essential element of robbery.

Although an intent to steal may ordinarily be inferred when one person takes the property of another, particularly if he takes it by force, proof of the existence of a state of mind incompatible with an intent to steal precludes a finding of either theft or robbery. It has long been the rule in this state and generally throughout the country that a bona fide belief, even though mistakenly held, that one has a right or claim to the property negates felonious intent. A belief that the property taken belongs to the taker, or that he had a right to retake goods sold is sufficient to preclude felonious intent. Felonious intent exists only if the actor intends to take the property of another without believing in good faith that he has a right or claim to it.[58]

Defendant testified that in going to Anderson's home "my sole intention was to try to get my money; and that was all." The jury was properly instructed that if the intent to take the money from Anderson did not arise until after Anderson had been fatally wounded, the killing could not be murder in the perpetration of robbery. Since the jury returned a verdict of first degree murder it believed defendant intended to take money from Anderson by force before the shooting occurred. Accordingly, defendant's only defense to robbery-murder was the existence of an honest belief that he was entitled to the money. The trial court's approval of the prosecutor's argument that no such defense exists removed completely from the consideration of the jury a material issue raised by credible, substantial evidence. It precluded any finding that an intent to steal was absent. Defendant has a constitutional right to have every significant issue determined by a jury. The denial of that right was a miscarriage of justice within the meaning of article VI, section 13[59] of the California Constitution and requires reversal.

The judgment of conviction of murder is reversed. In all other respects the judgment is affirmed.

---

57. "Every person who shall feloniously steal, take, carry, lead, or drive away the personal property of another, or who shall fraudulently appropriate property which has been entrusted to him, or who shall knowingly and designedly, by any false or fraudulent representation or pretense, defraud any other person of money, labor or real or personal property, or who causes or procures others to report falsely of his wealth or mercantile character and by thus imposing upon any person, obtains credit and thereby fraudulently gets or obtains possession of money, or property or obtains the labor or service of another, is guilty of theft. . . ." (Pen.Code, § 484.)

58. Defendant concedes, as he must, that although the offense could not constitute robbery absent an intent to steal, an unprovoked assault accompanying an attempt to collect a debt may be a crime other than robbery. Among the range of offenses that might have been committed are: assault (Pen.Code, § 240), assault with a deadly weapon (Pen.Code, § 245), assault with intent to commit murder (Pen.Code, § 217).

59. Amendment adopted Nov. 8, 1966. [By the Compiler.]

■ PETERS, TOBRINER, BURKE and PEEK, JJ., concur.

■ McCOMB, JUSTICE. In my opinion there was no prejudicial error. Therefore, under the provisions of article VI, section 13, of the California Constitution, I would affirm the judgment in its entirety.

■ MOSK, JUSTICE. I dissent.

Penal Code section 211 defines robbery as "the felonious taking of personal property in the possession of another, from his person or immediate presence, and against his will, accomplished by means of force or fear." This code section was enacted in 1872 and has remained unchanged since that date.

It is significant that the section requires the taking be from the *possession* of another, and makes no reference whatever to *ownership* of the property.

The question here, then, is whether the defendant may assert *ipse dixit* his belief that he was entitled to an unpaid debt taken from another by force or fear as a defense to a charge of robbery, and by extrapolation as a defense to a charge of murder committed in the course of a robbery. While there is some authority suggesting this query be answered in the affirmative (People v. Devine (1892) 95 Cal. 227, 30 P. 378; People v. Vice (1863) 21 Cal. 344; People v. Stone (1860) 16 Cal. 369), there has been no explicit holding of this court on the issue.

Thus, the question is ultimately one of basic public policy, which unequivocally dictates that the proper forum for resolving debt disputes is a court of law, pursuant to legal process—not the street, at the business end of a lethal weapon. . . .

I would rely upon the specific provisions of Penal Code section 211, which raise no issue of ownership of property forcibly taken, but only its possession. Here, possession of the money was in the deceased, and when it was taken from him by means of force, the crime of robbery was committed.

State v. Skaggs

Court of Appeals of Oregon, 1979.
42 Or.App. 763, 601 P.2d 862.

■ JOSEPH, PRESIDING JUDGE. Defendant was convicted in a jury trial of theft in the first degree, assault in the second degree, robbery in the third degree and unauthorized use of a vehicle. He appeals, assigning as error (1) denial of his motion for a directed verdict of acquittal for robbery, (2) entering of a separate conviction for robbery, and (3) entering of a separate conviction for unauthorized use of a vehicle.[60]

---

60. Defendant was charged under two indictments. The first was for theft in the first degree. The second contained counts of attempted murder, assault in the second degree, robbery in the first degree and unauthorized use of a vehicle. The cases were consolidated for trial. The trial court merged the convictions for robbery, assault and unauthorized use in sentencing defendant on the assault charge.

Late in the evening of October 25, 1976, defendant and another person were accosted by a Clackamas County deputy sheriff while they were apparently in the act of stealing a vehicle. The officer engaged in a scuffle with the other person over possession of the officer's service revolver. During the struggle defendant stabbed the officer twice and then grabbed him by the hair, held an object to his throat and said, "Let go of the gun or I'll cut it," or "I'll slit it." After being struck a third time, the officer lost control of the revolver. The two assailants made their escape from the scene in the officer's patrol car, taking the gun with them.

On the first assignment of error defendant argues that there was insufficient evidence to show intent to commit theft of the revolver, which was the theft element in the robbery charge, because the evidence suggested that defendant's original and continuing intent was to steal a car. He asserts that his actions were intended only to disarm the officer and to escape and that the intent to disarm excluded intent to commit theft of the gun.

The crime of robbery does not require an actual taking of property, but only intent to commit theft, for "repression of violence is the principal reason for being guilty of robbery." Commentary, Oregon Criminal Code of 1971, 190 (1975 ed.). The requisite intent under the robbery statute[61] is derived from the theft statute[62] and the definitions of theft.[63] Intent to commit theft is present where there is intent to dispose of property "under such circumstances as to render it unlikely that an owner will recover such property." ORS 164.005(2)(b).

As stated in State v. Gibson, 36 Or.App. 111, 115, 583 P.2d 584, rev. den. 285 Or. 319 (1978),

"[T]he issue is not whether we believe defendant guilty beyond a reasonable doubt, but whether the evidence was sufficient for the trier of fact so to find."

---

61.   ORS 164.395 provides in pertinent part:

"(1) A person commits the crime of robbery in the third degree if in the course of committing or attempting to commit theft he uses or threatens the immediate use of physical force upon another person with the intent of:

"(a) Preventing or overcoming resistance to his taking of the property or to his retention thereof immediately after the taking; or...."

62.   ORS 164.015 provides in pertinent part:

"A person commits theft when, with intent to deprive another of property or to appropriate property to himself or to a third person, he:

"(1) Takes, appropriates, obtains or withholds such property from an owner thereof; or...."

63.   ORS 164.005(2):

" 'Deprive another of property' or 'deprive' means to:

"(a) Withhold property of another or cause property of another to be withheld from him permanently or for so extended a period or under such circumstances that the major portion of its economic value or benefit is lost to him; or

"(b) dispose of the property in such manner or under such circumstances as to render it unlikely that an owner will recover such property."

In State v. Mack, 31 Or.App. 59, 569 P.2d 624 (1977), we held that for purposes of determining commission of theft, intent permanently to deprive the owner of possession of property could be inferred from the circumstances surrounding the act.

From the circumstances of the episode, an inference could reasonably have been drawn by the jury that the deputy sheriff was unlikely to recover his revolver after the violent attempt to disarm him and the escape. The revolver was not left behind at the scene of the incident, and a witness testified that he saw the gun later that evening when defendant and a co-defendant were trying to operate the jammed mechanism. Next morning the witness brought the gun to the police and assisted in the arrest of defendant. The question was properly submitted to the jury.

Affirmed in part.

SECTION 3. EMBEZZLEMENT

There is no English common-law crime known as embezzlement.[64] If an employee received, for his employer, property which was delivered to him by a third party, and appropriated this property before it had come into the possession of his employer, this was held not to constitute larceny; and the first statute on embezzlement was enacted to provide a punishment for this kind of misconduct.

Additional statutes, under the name of embezzlement, were enacted to provide a penalty for the wrongful appropriation of property by such persons as brokers, bankers, attorneys, agents and trustees, who may have title to, as well as possession of, what has been entrusted to them.

This still left an important "gap" due to the rule that the appropriation by an ordinary bailee was not larceny if he had had no wrongful intent at the time he took possession of the property bailed to him. By statute this also was punished as embezzlement.

As the statutes on embezzlement were enacted to fill "gaps" which had appeared in the development of the law of larceny, the two offenses were held to be mutually exclusive. The same evidence which would prove guilt of one would disprove guilt of the other.[65] For this reason it is more

---

64. A.T.N. Smith, Property Offenses, 1–14 (1994).

65. "There is a difference between the crimes of embezzlement and stealing. The crimes are inconsistent. Embezzlement presupposes lawful possession and theft does not." United States v. Trevino, 491 F.2d 74, 75 (5th Cir.1974).

"The elements necessary to establish embezzlement are a trust relation, possession or control of property by virtue of the trust relation, and a fraudulent appropriation of the property to a use or purpose not in the due and lawful execution of the trust." State v. Gomez, 27 Ariz.App. 248, 553 P.2d 1233, 1237 (1976).

In this jurisdiction the crime of larceny remains as it was at common law. Hence it requires that the taking of the property be by trespass. If the taking was fraudulent it was by trespass and the subsequent appropriation is larceny. But if the original taking was without trespass the subsequent wrongful appropriation is embezzlement and not larceny. Farlow v. State, 9 Md.App. 515, 265 A.2d 578 (1970).

effective to deal with them together than separately, and for the most part they were included in the cases on larceny.

Today embezzlement remains a separate offense in some jurisdictions. Most progressive jurisdictions have joined the offense in a consolidated theft statute.

State v. Stahl

Court of Appeals of New Mexico, 1979.
93 N.M. 62, 596 P.2d 275.

OPINION

■ WOOD, CHIEF JUDGE. Defendant was convicted of embezzling over $100. To have embezzled the money, defendant must have been entrusted with the money. Section 30–16–8, N.M.S.A.1978. Defendant contends there is no evidence that he was entrusted with over $100. We agree.

Defendant was a clerk at a store. The store had two cash registers and a drop-box. There was a slit in the counter; money pushed through this slit went into the drop-box. The drop-box was locked with two padlocks, the keys to which were retained by the manager. When money accumulated in the registers, portions of the accumulation were placed in the drop-box through the slit in the counter.

About 7:30 p.m. on the night in question, the manager removed the money from the drop-box. About 11:00 p.m. the clerk on duty closed down one of the registers, placing the money from that register into the drop-box. When defendant went on duty at midnight, the one register being used contained $50 to $75. Defendant's shift was from midnight to 8:00 a.m. At 3:00 a.m., defendant was absent from the store. The drop-box had been pried open and its money removed. There is evidence that defendant took a total of $612 from the drop-box and the register being used.

Defendant was the only clerk on duty when the money was taken; he was "in charge of the whole store" and "responsible for the entire store." The register being used, and its contents, were for defendant's use in performing his duties. Defendant does not claim that he was not entrusted

---

Where the defendant employee did not receive the property taken in any special capacity as an employee the offense was larceny not embezzlement. State v. Keyes, 64 N.C.App. 529, 307 S.E.2d 820 (1983).

Property involuntarily entrusted may be embezzled. Property which should have been sent to the bank was inadvertently sent to defendant, who converted it with knowledge of the situation. A conviction of embezzlement was affirmed. People v. Newman, 49 Cal.App.3d 426, 122 Cal.Rptr. 455 (1975).

Where one, in good faith, believes he is authorized to appropriate property which he is accused of embezzling, the fraudulent intent which is a necessary element of that crime is lacking. People v. Stewart, 16 Cal.3d 133, 127 Cal.Rptr. 117, 544 P.2d 1317 (1976).

Since the statute in this state provides that part ownership is no defense to larceny, it is held that it is also no defense to embezzlement. Babcock v. State, 91 Nev. 312, 535 P.2d 786 (1975).

If **D** altered a $22 check to make it read $2200 he could be convicted of embezzlement of the $22 check despite his guilt of forgery. State v. Vanderlinden, 21 Ariz.App. 358, 519 P.2d 211 (1974).

with the money in this register and does not contend that the money he took from this register was not embezzlement. However, there is no proof that the money taken from the register was over $100, and no proof that the amount of money in the register, plus money from sales after defendant went on duty, ever amounted to $100.

The State asserts that defendant was also entrusted with money which defendant took from the register and placed in the drop-box. We need not answer this contention because there is no evidence that defendant placed any money into the drop-box.

To reach a monetary amount over $100, the money taken from the drop-box must be included. Under the evidence, the money in the drop-box was put there by another clerk, and before defendant was on duty. Defendant did not have the keys to the drop-box, he had no permission or authority to get any money out of the box, he had no permission to have possession of the money in the drop-box, or "use it for change or anything...." The only one supposed to take money from the drop-box was the manager. These facts are not disputed.

The trial court denied defendant's motion for a directed verdict on the charge of embezzlement over $100. Because defendant was in charge of the store, the trial court was of the view that defendant had been entrusted with "everything there on the premises" including the drop-box. We disagree; defendant had not been entrusted with the contents of the drop-box.

"Entrust" means to commit or surrender to another with a certain confidence regarding his care, use or disposal of that which has been committed or surrendered. The money in the drop-box would not have been entrusted to defendant unless the money came into defendant's possession by reason of his employment.

2 Wharton's Criminal Law and Procedure, § 468 (1957) states:

A clerk taking money or goods from his employer's safe, till or shelves is guilty of larceny unless he is authorized to dispose of such money or goods at his discretion. An employee who feloniously appropriates to his own use property of his master or employer to which he has access only by reason of a mere physical propinquity as an incident of the employment, and not by reason of any charge, care, or oversight of the property entrusted to him, may be guilty of larceny by such act the same as any stranger.

Although defendant was in charge of the entire store, the undisputed facts show that the money in the drop-box was not committed or surrendered to defendant's care, use or disposal; that money was to be handled exclusively by the manager. Defendant was excluded from having anything to do with that money. Defendant's offense, as to the money in the drop-box, was larceny, not embezzlement, because he had not been entrusted with that money.

Because of an absence of evidence showing that defendant was entrusted with over $100 of the money he took, his embezzlement conviction is reversed.

It is so ordered.[66]

■ LOPEZ and WALTERS, JJ., concur.

United States v. Faulkner

United States Court of Appeals, Ninth Circuit, 1981.
638 F.2d 129.

■Before SKOPIL, ALARCON and BOOCHEVER, CIRCUIT JUDGES.

■ SKOPIL, CIRCUIT JUDGE:

INTRODUCTION

Faulkner appeals his conviction of violation of 18 U.S.C. § 659, which prohibits embezzlement or theft from an interstate shipment. He contends that the evidence was insufficient to establish his guilt, because he never physically removed goods from the truck, and never sold the goods. We affirm.

FACTS

Faulkner was a truck driver for North American Van Lines. He picked up 105 refrigerators in San Diego, which he was to transport to Hartford, Connecticut. Faulkner stopped in Las Vegas, Nevada. He called Richard Urbauer, the owner of an appliance store, and offered to sell the refrigerators. Urbauer informed the police.

Faulkner and Urbauer discussed the sale of the refrigerators. Faulkner left the store and returned with his truck. He broke the truck's seals, entered the rear, and opened two cartons to show Urbauer the refrigerators. Urbauer examined the two refrigerators while Faulkner rearranged the boxes in the truck.

Faulkner and Urbauer went back to the store and tried to consummate a deal. They were unable to reach an agreement. Faulkner started to leave the store and was arrested.

Faulkner was convicted by a jury of embezzlement or theft from an interstate shipment, in violation of 18 U.S.C. § 659. He appeals.

---

66. Defendant holding an electronic monitoring device under an assumption of trust who converted it to personal use is guilty of embezzlement. State v. Archie, 123 N.M. 503, 943 P.2d 537 (App.1997).

Whether a bailee who converts property bailed to him is guilty of larceny or embezzlement depends upon the time of his intent. "If the criminal intent exists at the time of the taking of the property, it is 'larceny,' but if the intent does not arise until after the defendant receives possession, then it is 'embezzlement.'" Lovick v. State, 646 P.2d 1296, 1297–98 (Okl.Cr.App. 1982).

An employee who embezzles property cannot defend on the ground that the employer did not have title to the property. State v. Boueri, 99 Nev. 790, 672 P.2d 33 (1983).

Embezzlement builds on conversion but requires the property to have been in the lawful possession of the defendant at the time of its appropriation and knowledge that the appropriation is contrary to the wishes of the owner. United States v. Stockton, 788 F.2d 210 (4th Cir.1986).

ISSUE

Faulkner contends that the evidence was insufficient to support his conviction.

DISCUSSION

I.   Standard of Review.

This court must uphold the verdict if the evidence, considered in the light most favorable to the government as prevailing party, would permit a rational conclusion by the jury that the accused was guilty beyond a reasonable doubt.

18 U.S.C. § 659 provides, in pertinent part: "Whoever embezzles, steals, or unlawfully takes, carries away, or conceals, or by fraud or deception obtains from any ... motor-truck ... with intent to convert to his own use any goods ... which are a part of ... an interstate or foreign shipment" shall be guilty of an offense.

In enacting section 659 Congress sought to protect the channels of interstate commerce from interference. The statute must be construed broadly to accomplish this purpose. It is not limited in its application to the strictly defined offense of common law larceny.

The stealing or unlawful taking contemplated by the statute consists of taking over possession and control with intent to convert to the use of the taker. The statute does not require physical removal of the goods, nor even asportation in the common law larceny sense.

The felonious intent required by the statute consists of the intent to appropriate or convert the property of the owner. An intent to return the property does not exculpate the defendant.

We hold that there was sufficient evidence establishing the requisite act and intent. Faulkner exercised dominion and control over the refrigerators by leaving his assigned route to go to Urbauer's store and negotiate a sale. There was competent evidence that Faulkner broke the truck's seals, opened the cartons and moved the goods to exhibit them to Urbauer, in furtherance of his attempt to sell them. The jury could therefore find that Faulkner had assumed possession and control of the goods. These facts also permitted the jury to conclude that Faulkner intended to convert the goods to his own use. It was not necessary that Faulkner remove the goods from the truck, nor complete the sale.

CONCLUSION

The evidence was sufficient to support Faulkner's conviction of violating section 659. The judgment appealed from is affirmed.

SECTION 4.   FALSE PRETENSES

In addition to those "gaps" in the criminal law which were due to the rule that there is no larceny without trespass de bonis (which have been largely, though not entirely, closed by statutes on embezzlement and now general theft), a very important hiatus resulted from the holding that no larceny was committed by a transaction in which the wrongdoer obtained the title or ownership of the property in question.

One who cheated another in a sale or trade was guilty of a misdemeanor known as a common-law cheat if he made use of some false token, as it was called, such as a false weight or false measure; but guilty of no crime at all under the English common law if the deceit was merely by spoken words, no matter how wilful and extreme the deceit might be. This called forth the English statute which made it an offense to obtain the property of another by false pretenses. This statute, enacted in 1757, was generally accepted in the Colonies and is a part of our common law.

The result again is two offenses that were mutually exclusive, the familiar statement being that if the wrongdoer, by his fraud, obtained possession only, his appropriation of the property was larceny by trick; whereas if he obtained both title and possession the crime was false pretenses.

Modern codes combine false pretenses with other forms of theft. Many jurisdictions have adopted a wide variety of special statutes to deal with various forms of false pretenses and deception.

People v. Ashley

Supreme Court of California, In Bank, 1954.
42 Cal.2d 246, 267 P.2d 271.

■ TRAYNOR, JUSTICE. Defendant was convicted of four counts of grand theft under section 484 of the Penal Code. He "appeals from the verdicts and judgments as to each count," and from the order denying his motion for a new trial. . . .

Although the crimes of larceny by trick and device and obtaining property by false pretenses are much alike, they are aimed at different criminal acquisitive techniques. Larceny by trick and device is the appropriation of property, the possession of which was fraudulently acquired; obtaining property by false pretenses is the fraudulent or deceitful acquisition of both title and possession. In this state these two offenses, with other larcenous crimes, have been consolidated into the single crime of theft, Pen.Code, § 484, but their elements have not been changed thereby. The purpose of the consolidation was to remove the technicalities that existed in the pleading and proof of these crimes at common law. Indictments and informations charging the crime of "theft" can now simply allege an "unlawful taking." Pen.Code, §§ 951, 952. Juries need no longer be concerned with the technical differences between the several types of theft, and can return a general verdict of guilty if they find that an "unlawful taking" has been proved. The elements of the several types of theft included within section 484 have not been changed, however, and a judgment of conviction of theft, based on a general verdict of guilty, can be sustained only if the evidence discloses the elements of one of the consolidated offenses. In the present case, it is clear from the record that each of the prosecuting witnesses intended to pass both title and possession, and that the type of theft, if any, in each case, was that of obtaining property by false pretenses. Defendant was not prejudiced by the instruction to the jury relating to larceny by trick and device. Indeed, he requested instructions relating to both larceny by trick and device and obtaining property by false pretenses. Moreover, his defense was not based on distinctions between title and possession, but rather he contends that there was no unlawful taking of any sort.

To support a conviction of theft for obtaining property by false pretenses, it must be shown that the defendant made a false pretense or representation with intent to defraud the owner of his property, and that the owner was in fact defrauded. It is unnecessary to prove that the defendant benefitted personally from the fraudulent acquisition. The false pretense or representation must have materially influenced the owner to part with his property, but the false pretense need not be the sole inducing cause. If the conviction rests primarily on the testimony of a single witness that the false pretense was made, the making of the pretense must be corroborated. Pen.Code, § 1110.

The crime of obtaining property by false pretenses was unknown in the early common law, see Young v. The King, 3 T.R. 98, 102 [1789], and our statute, like those of most American states, is directly traceable to 30 Geo. II, ch. 24, section 1 (22 Statutes-at-Large 114 [1757]). In an early Crown Case Reserved, Rex v. Goodhall, Russ. & Ry. 461 (1821), the defendant obtained a quantity of meat from a merchant by promising to pay at a future day. The jury found that the promise was made without intention to perform. The judges concluded, however, that the defendant's conviction was erroneous because the pretense "was merely a promise of future conduct, and common prudence and caution would have prevented any injury arising from it." Russ. & Ry. at 463. The correctness of this decision is questionable in light of the reasoning in an earlier decision of the King's Bench, *Young v. The King, supra*—not mentioned in *Rex v. Goodhall*. By stating that the "promise of future conduct" was such that "common prudence and caution" could prevent any injury arising therefrom, the new offense was confused with the old common law "cheat." The decision also seems contrary to the plain meaning of the statute, and was so interpreted by two English writers on the law of crimes. Archbold, Pleading and Evidence in Criminal Cases 183 [3rd ed., 1828]; Roscoe, Digest of the Law of Evidence in Criminal Cases 418 [2d Amer. ed., 1840]. The opinion in *Rex v. Goodhall, supra*, was completely misinterpreted in the case of Commonwealth v. Drew, 1837, 19 Pick. 179, at page 185, 36 Mass. 179, at page 185, in which the Supreme Judicial Court of Massachusetts declared by way of dictum, that under the statute "naked lies" could not be regarded as "false pretenses." On the basis of these two questionable decisions, Wharton formulated the following generalization: "... the false pretense to be within the statute, must relate to a state of things averred to be at the time existing, and not to a state of things thereafter to exist." Wharton, American Criminal Law 542 [1st ed., 1846]. This generalization has been followed in the majority of American cases, almost all of which can be traced to reliance on Wharton or the two cases mentioned above....

In California, the precedents are conflicting. Early decisions of the district courts of appeal follow the general rule as originally formulated by Wharton, ... but more recently it has been held, and the holdings were approved by this court in People v. Jones, 36 Cal.2d 373, 377, 224 P.2d 353 that a promise made without intention to perform is a misrepresentation of a state of mind, and thus a misrepresentation of existing fact, and is a false pretense within the meaning of section 484 of the Penal Code.... These decisions, like those following the majority rule, were made with little explanation of the reasons for the rule. The Court of Appeals for the District of Columbia has, however, advanced the following reasons in defense of the majority rule: "It is of course true that then, [at the time of the early English cases cited by *Wharton, supra*] as now, the intention to commit certain crimes was ascertained by looking backward from the act and finding that the accused intended to do what he did do. However, where, as here, the act complained of—namely, failure to repay money or use it as specified at the time of borrowing—is as consonant with ordinary commercial default as with criminal conduct, the danger of applying this technique to prove the crime is quite apparent. Business affairs would be materially incumbered by the ever present threat that a debtor might be subjected to criminal penalties if the prosecutor and jury were of the view that at the time of borrowing he was mentally a cheat. The risk of prosecuting one who is guilty of nothing more than a failure or inability to pay his debts is a very real consideration....

"If we were to accept the government's position the way would be open for every victim of a bad bargain to resort to criminal proceedings to even the score with a judgment proof adversary. No doubt in the development of our criminal law the zeal with which the innocent are protected has provided a measure of shelter for the guilty. However, we do not think it wise to increase the possibility of conviction by broadening the accepted theory of the weight to be attached to the mental attitude of the accused." Chaplin v. United States, 81 U.S.App.D.C. 80, 157 F.2d 697, 698–699, 168 A.L.R. 828; but see the dissenting opinion of Edgerton, J., 157 F.2d at pages 699–701. We do not find this reasoning persuasive. In this state, and in the majority of American states as well as in England, false promises can provide the foundation of a civil action for deceit. Civ.Code, § 1572, subd. 4, 1710, subd. 4; see 125 A.L.R. 881–882. In such actions something more than nonperformance is required to prove the defendant's intent not to perform his promise. Nor is proof of nonperformance alone sufficient in criminal prosecutions based on false promises.... In such prosecutions the People must, as in all criminal prosecutions, prove their case beyond a reasonable doubt. Any danger, through the instigation of criminal proceedings by disgruntled creditors, to those who have blamelessly encountered "commercial defaults" must, therefore, be predicated upon the idea that trial juries are incapable of weighing the evidence and understanding the instruction that they must be convinced of the defendant's fraudulent intent beyond a reasonable doubt, or that appellate courts will be derelict in discharging their duty to ascertain that there is sufficient evidence to support a conviction.

The problem of proving intent when the false pretense is a false promise is no more difficult than when the false pretense is a misrepresentation of existing fact, and the intent not to perform a promise is regularly proved in civil actions for deceit. Specific intent is also an essential element of many crimes. Moreover, in cases of obtaining property by false pretenses, it must be proved that any misrepresentations of fact alleged by the People were made knowingly and with intent to deceive. If such misrepresentations are made innocently or inadvertently, they can no more form the basis for a prosecution for obtaining property by false pretenses than can an innocent breach of contract. Whether the pretense is a false promise or a misrepresentation of fact, the defendant's intent must be proved in both instances by something more than mere proof of nonperformance or actual falsity. Cf. U.S. v. Ballard, 322 U.S. 78, 64 S.Ct. 882, 88 L.Ed. 1148, and the defendant is entitled to have the jury instructed to that effect. "[T]he accepted theory of the weight to be attached to the mental attitude of the accused" is, therefore, not "broadened," but remains substantially the same. Cf. Chaplin v. United States, *supra*, 157 F.2d 697, 699. . . .

The purported appeals from the verdicts are dismissed as nonappealable. The judgment and the order denying the motion for a new trial are affirmed.[67]

■ GIBSON, C.J., and SHENK, EDMONDS and SPENCE, JJ., concur.

■ SCHAUER, JUSTICE. I concur in the judgment solely on the ground that the evidence establishes, with ample corroboration, the making by the defendant of false representations as to existing facts. On that evidence the convictions should be sustained pursuant to long accepted theories of law.

It is unnecessary on the record to make of this rather simple case a vehicle for the revolutionary holding, contrary to the weight of authority in this state and elsewhere, that a promise to pay or perform at a future date, if unfulfilled, can become the basis for a criminal prosecution on the theory that it was a promise made without a present intention to perform it and that, therefore, whatever of value was received for the promise was property procured by a false representation. Accordingly, I dissent from all that portion of the opinion which discusses and pronounces upon the theories which in my view are extraneous to the proper disposition of any issue actually before us. . . .

■ CARTER, J., concurs.

■ Rehearing denied; CARTER and SCHAUER, JJ., dissenting.

State v. Duncan

Supreme Court of Montana, 1979.
181 Mont. 382, 593 P.2d 1026.

■ SHEEHY, JUSTICE. Defendant Norman Duncan appeals from his conviction following a nonjury trial in the District Court, Gallatin County, of deceptive practices and the sale of unregistered securities.

---

67. California Penal Code sec. 476a makes it an offense to issue a check with intent to defraud, without sufficient funds or credit with the bank. D issued a check without sufficient funds. He told the payee that his account was insufficient but promised to make the necessary deposit, which he did not do. It was held that a false promise is not sufficient for conviction under this statute. People v. Poyet, 6 Cal.3d 530, 99 Cal.Rptr. 758, 492 P.2d 1150 (1972).

Defendant was president of Smart Pak, Inc., of Montana, which produced and marketed a dry granulated charcoal lighter (Smart Start) and a combination package of Smart Start and charcoal briquettes (Smart Pak). Smart Pak, Inc., was one of five corporations set up by defendant in different states to produce and market these products. The parent corporation was Survival Heat Products, Inc., of Idaho Falls.

In the fall of 1975 and spring of 1976, defendant discovered that automated packaging machines could not properly seal the special "child-proof" paper used to package his products. Thereafter, he and other company employees began selling "package sealer agreements" in Gallatin County. The buyers of these contracts paid from $500 to $5000 to become package sealers for Smart Pak. The company supplied them with manual sealing machines and rolls of package paper depending on the amount paid by the sealer. After the sealers sealed the bags on three sides, they sold all properly sealed bags back to the company for 5per bag.

The operation worked smoothly for a short time, but then, due to a series of mix-ups, the sealers did not receive their quota of bags to be sealed. These mix-ups, as asserted by defendant, included a paper shortage and errors in printing the bags.

In March 1976 Smart Pak came under investigation by both the Federal Securities Exchange Commission and the State Auditor's Office in which securities sold in Montana are to be registered. At that point, the focus of these investigations concerned only whether the package sealer agreements were in fact investment contracts which defendant had failed to register.

Although neither agency told defendant to cease operations beyond ceasing to advertise and sell the questioned package sealer agreements, defendant did in fact close down his entire operation and refused to accept or pay for any sealed bags from the sealers or to send any more bags to be sealed. The reason defendant gave for his action was that the adverse publicity concerning the investigations had dried up the sales of these products.

In June 1976 defendant filed a receivership petition for Smart Pak. The sealers were thus left holding the "bags." After the initial few months, they did not receive payment for their work or recoupment of their investment.

On July 9, 1976, the State filed an information against defendant. The information consisted of four counts: Count I charged deceptive practices in violation of section 94–6–307, R.C.M.1947, now section 45–6–317 MCA; Count II charged fraudulent securities practices in violation of section 15–2005(1), R.C.M.1947, now section 30–10–301 MCA; Count III charged failure to register securities violation of section 15–2007, R.C.M.1947, now section 30–10–202 MCA; and Count IV charged issuing a bad check in violation of section 94–6–309(1), R.C.M.1947, now section 45–6–316 MCA. Defendant filed a motion to dismiss the information. On February 22, 1977, the court dismissed Count IV and defendant pleaded "not guilty" to the remaining three counts. On that same day, defendant signed a written waiver of his right to trial by jury.

The case then came on for a hearing, on February 23, 1977, to the court sitting without a jury. On April 4, 1977, the District Court, in open court, found defendant guilty of Counts I and III. The court dismissed Count II. On May 6, 1977, the court entered written findings of fact and imposed sentence of five years imprisonment on Count I and three years imprisonment on Count III, the sentences to run concurrently. Defendant, thereafter, brings this appeal.

Additional facts are discussed as they become pertinent.

The issues presented for our consideration are:

1.   Whether the evidence is sufficient to sustain defendant's conviction of deceptive practices? . . .

Defendant was convicted of violating section 94–6–307, R.C.M.1947, now section 45–6–317 MCA. This Court has not construed this statute since its enactment in 1973. Defendant would have us apply the same elements to this statute as we found in its predecessor, "Obtaining money, property or services by false pretenses", section 94–1805, R.C.M.1947. Under the former statute, we held it was necessary to prove four elements for a conviction:

". . . (1) The making by the accused to the person injured, of one or more representations of past events or existing facts; (2) that such injured party believed such representations to be true and, relying thereon, parted with money or property, which was received by the accused; (3) that such representations were false; and (4) were made knowingly and designedly, with the intent to defraud such other person." State v. Bratton (1919), 56 Mont. 563, 566, 186 P. 327, 328.

The new statute clearly modifies the elements of proof necessary for conviction and for that reason the cases cited by defendant are inapplicable. Breaking the new statute down into its elements, we determine the State need prove only that:

(1) the defendant acted "purposely or knowingly" in

(2) making or directing another to make a false or deceptive statement

(3) addressed to the public or any person

(4) for the purpose of promoting or procuring the sale of property or services.

Gone are any requirements that the statements relate to past events or existing facts or that the injured party relied thereon in parting with money or property. In addition, "[s]ection 94–6–307 is designed to cover a greater variety of deceptive practices than were formerly proscribed by Montana law." Commission Comment, section 94–6–307, R.C.M.1947. The legislative intent to expand the spectrum of criminal activities in the area of false pretenses previously punishable under Montana law is obvious. It is against these guidelines that we measure defendant's actions.

Initially we note that no real challenge is made by defendant to elements 1, 3, and 4 listed above. Defendant concedes he deliberately sought people to enter into these contracts at specified costs (elements 1 and 4) and that in so doing he caused to be broadcast and published various advertisements asking people to contact him or his employees (element 3). The only question concerns whether his statements to potential sealers were false or deceptive.

The State in its information alleged that defendant or defendant's employees acting at his direction repeatedly made five false statements with the purpose to induce persons to enter into the package sealer contracts at a cost of between $500 and $5000. Proof beyond a reasonable doubt of any one of these five false statements is sufficient to sustain defendant's conviction.

The State alleged that in the package sealer contract itself defendant promised that 5 percent of each sealer's deposit was "to be held in trust for the purpose of guaranteeing repayment of deposit made by Package Sealer at the execution of this Agreement." The contract further stated that the trust fund was to be established at a specified bank in Bozeman.

The evidence presented at trial showed, however, that defendant made only nominal deposits to an escrow, not trust, account until the day before his meeting on March 30, 1976, with State and federal officials concerning possible securities registration violations. At that time, he suddenly deposited $15,000 to this account on advice of counsel. Thereafter, defendant withdrew virtually the entire amount between April 26 and May 6, 1976. Clearly, defendant had no intention of honoring his contractual promise regarding the 5 percent trust reserve.

The other allegations by the State were also supported by sufficient evidence. For example defendant told or implied by means of a prominent wall chart to those persons entering contracts that only 55 such contracts would be sold in the Bozeman area. In fact, 82 contracts were sold in Bozeman and approximately 275 were sold throughout Montana.

Defendant guaranteed each sealer a set quota of bags and a regular income depending on the amount of deposit. Yet as early as January 1976 many sealers were receiving less than their guaranteed quota of bags. Later the corporation office refused to accept or pay for sealed bags from the sealers. Indeed, as defendant himself testified, he needed monthly income of approximately $360,000 to buy the unsealed bags from the supplier and to pay his sealers for sealing them, without taking into account any other expenses or profits. When this figure is compared to the actual monthly income from sales of the products of $2,700, one is compelled to conclude that defendant knew his contractual promises would fail at the time they were made.

As a final example, defendant repeatedly represented that he had secured large contracts for the purchase of his products with Safeway Stores and the Coleman Company, among others. In fact, Safeway had agreed to only a trial contract and the Coleman Company formally demanded that defendant cease misrepresenting the existence of *any* contracts between them.

In sum defendant sold $417,000 worth of package sealer contracts on behalf of his company which had capital stock of only $3,100 and total income from product sales of only $13,500 over five months. The financial obligation under these contracts exceeded $500,000 per month. The inescapable conclusion is that defendant deliberately made false statements to induce others to enter these contracts. His conviction on this count is affirmed.

The judgment of the District Court convicting defendant of deceptive practices and of selling unregistered securities is affirmed.[68]

■ HASWELL, C.J., and HARRISON, J., concur.

■ DALY, JUSTICE, concurring in part and dissenting in part:

I concur in the majority decision on Issue Nos. 1, 3, 4, 5, and 6. I further concur in the adoption of the broadened flexible definition of "investment contract" as that term is used in the Securities Act of Montana.

---

68.   Accord: Chaplin v. United States, 81 U.S.App.D.C. 80, 157 F.2d 697 (1946); Commonwealth v. Althause, 207 Mass. 32, 93 N.E. 202 (1910); State v. Allison, 186 S.W. 958 (Mo.App.1916); People v. Karp, 298 N.Y. 213, 81 N.E.2d 817 (1948); Linne v. State, 674 P.2d 1345 (Alaska App.1983).

In reversing a conviction of false pretenses based upon promissory fraud the court said: "We recognize there is authority for the view contended for by appellee that misrepresentation of intention is a misrepresentation of an existing fact. We are not persuaded by that argument and hold with the majority opinion that such is not the correct construction. Many cases could be cited. . . ." Bonney v. United States, 254 F.2d 392, 393 (9th Cir.1958).

A selection from the whole truth so partial and fragmentary as to give a misleading impression may be ground for criminal liability despite the literal truth of every statement made. Rex v. Kylsant, 48 T.L.R. 62 (1931).

The Model Penal Code takes the position that a false promise (made without the intention of performance) should be sufficient for conviction but adds that "a majority of the American states adhere to a rule of nonliability in false pretense prosecutions". Tentative Draft No. 2, § 206.2(2), and comment 7 (1954).

A false promise is not sufficient for guilt of false pretenses. Dean v. State, 258 Ark. 32, 522 S.W.2d 421 (1975). It "cannot amount to a statutory false pretense." Id. at 423.

False promise alone is insufficient to uphold theft by deception conviction. State v. Hamilton, 6 Kan. App.2d 646, 631 P.2d 1255 (1981).

Where defendants obtained money on representation they would place their baby for adoption with victims and defendants did not intend to do so, "deception" was committed. State v. Vigil, 922 P.2d 15 (Utah App.1996).

A false pretense conviction may not be had in Michigan upon a misrepresentation of the present intent to do a future act. People v. Cage, 410 Mich. 401, 301 N.W.2d 819 (1981).

Reliance on a false representation is required in many jurisdictions. See State v. Johnson, 179 Ariz. 375, 880 P.2d 132 (1994); State v. Eppens, 30 Wn.App. 119, 633 P.2d 92 (1981). Recently, some jurisdictions have abandoned the reliance requirement. A Maryland court has held that under its theft consolidation statute, theft by deception does not require reliance. Cardin v. State, 73 Md.App. 200, 533 A.2d 928 (1987).

Accord, Kellogg v. State, 551 P.2d 301 (Okl.Cr.1976).

The Kansas "statute does not equate a false promise with a false pretense." State v. Hamilton, 6 Kan.App.2d 646, 631 P.2d 1255 (1981).

Materiality of a false statement to a federally insured bank is not an element of knowingly making a false statement for the purpose of influencing the bank's action. United States v. Wells, 519 U.S. 482, 117 S.Ct. 921 (1997).

It is to the majority's application to defendant of this newly broadened definition, not before adopted in Montana, that I respectfully dissent.

Allen v. State

Court of Appeals of Ohio, Lucas County, 1926.
21 Ohio App. 403, 153 N.E. 218.

■ RICHARDS, J. The plaintiff in error was convicted of obtaining $400 in money by false pretenses. . . .

On Application for Rehearing

■ RICHARDS, J. The judgment finding the plaintiff in error guilty of obtaining money under false pretenses was affirmed on February 23, 1926. The money which he was convicted of obtaining under false pretenses was in his possession as agent of the owner. It is now urged that the trial court erred in charging the jury as follows:

"It is not a matter of concern as to whether she paid him the money out of her own pocket, or whether it was money which he had collected and held for her as her agent."

As the statute provides for punishing whoever "obtains" anything of value by false and fraudulent pretenses, it is insisted that the conviction could not be had for obtaining money of which the accused already had the possession, and, no doubt, as a general proposition, that is true; but the rule can have no application where the delivery of the money is not necessary in order to obtain dominion over it. If the defendant had possession of the money as agent, and obtained the title to it by false and fraudulent pretenses, that would be sufficient obtaining of the property within the meaning of the statute. The principal [sic] was directly decided in Commonwealth v. Schwartz, 92 Ky. 510, 18 S.W. 775, 36 Am.St.Rep. 609. I quote the third proposition of the syllabus:

"Where one who is in possession of money belonging to another obtains the title by false pretenses, he is guilty of the statutory offense of obtaining money by false pretenses. In such a case it is not necessary to constitute the offense that the possession should have been obtained by false pretenses."

In that case a banker had the money in his possession, which he had collected for the owner, and he thereafter obtained the title to it by false and fraudulent pretenses. He was held to be rightly convicted; the court deciding that the general rule requiring that both the property and the title should be obtained by false pretenses only applies where it takes delivery of the possession to complete the transfer of the title.

Rehearing denied.[69]

■ WILLIAMS and YOUNG, JJ., concur.

---

69. One who obtained title to property by false pretenses, but did not have possession and never succeeded in getting possession away from the other, was not guilty of false pretenses. Commonwealth v. Randle, 119 Pa.Super. 217, 180 A. 720 (1935).

Barker v. State

Supreme Court of Wyoming, 1979.
599 P.2d 1349.

■ ROSE, JUSTICE. This appeal by appellant-Kenneth L. Barker from a conviction of obtaining property by false pretenses under § 6–3–106, W.S. 1977[70], presents only one issue which we need resolve, namely:

Was § 6–3–106, W.S.1977 (the false-pretenses statute, fn. 1, *supra*), repealed by § 6–3–110, W.S.1977[71] (the insufficient-funds-check law), insofar as the use of a check with insufficient funds is concerned, thereby precluding a conviction under § 6–3–106?

We will hold that it was not, and affirm the trial court.

We parse the aforementioned statutes as follows:

The *insufficient-funds* statute—§ 6–3–110 (later statute) provides:

(1) Whoever writes an insufficient-funds check with intent to defraud *by obtaining property* or

(2) whoever writes an insufficient-funds check with intent to defraud *in the payment of any obligation*

is guilty of a crime.

The *false-pretenses* statute—§ 6–3–106 (earlier statute) says:

Whoever by *false pretenses obtains property* ... is guilty of a crime.

The essential facts are that Barker opened a checking account with the First Wyoming Bank of Rawlins on April 25, 1978. At the same time, he had the bank prepare a "customer's draft" directing a Montana bank to transfer by wire $30,000.00 to the Rawlins Bank, while representing that he had sufficient funds in the Montana bank to cover the draft. In point of fact, appellant had no current account with the Montana Bank. The following day, Barker returned to the First Wyoming Bank of Rawlins and cashed a $500.00 check against his new checking account. The Rawlins bank cashed Barker's check without ascertaining whether or not the

[handwritten margin note: FALSE PRETENSE? NOT YET]

---

70. Section 6–3–106, W.S. 1977, provides, in relevant part:

"If any person or persons shall knowingly and designedly, by false pretense or pretenses, obtain from any other person or persons any choses in action, money, goods, wares, chattels, effects, or other valuable thing whatever, with intent to cheat or defraud any such person or persons of the same, every person so offending shall be deemed a cheat, and upon conviction, where the value of such chose in action, money, goods, wares, chattels, effects or other valuable thing shall be twenty-five dollars ($25.00) or more, shall be imprisoned in the penitentiary for a period not more than 10 (10) years...."

71. Section 6–3–110, W.S.1977, provides, in relevant part:

"(a) Whoever, with intent to defraud by obtaining money, merchandise, property, credit, or other thing of value, although no express representation is made in reference thereto, or who, in the payment of any obligation, shall make, draw, utter or deliver any check, draft or order for the payment of money in the sum of fifty dollars ($50.00) or upwards upon any bank, depository, person, firm or corporation, knowing at the time of such making, drawing, uttering or delivering that the maker or drawer has not sufficient funds in such bank, depository, person, firm or corporation for the payment of such check, draft or order in full upon its presentation, shall be guilty of a misdemeanor and upon conviction thereof shall be fined not more than one thousand dollars ($1,000.00) or imprisoned in the county jail for not more than one (1) year or both...."

Montana bank had wired the money as he had requested. The Montana bank returned the "customer's draft" unpaid, and the check drawn against the new Rawlins account was without funds.

Appellant seems to concede that the State has proved all of the elements of the crime of obtaining property by false pretenses (§ 6–3–106, *supra*). Driver v. State, Wyo., 589 P.2d 391, 393 (1979), reh. den. It is, however, his contention that § 6–3–110, *supra*, was the statute that was violated and that § 6–3–110 repeals § 6–3–106, *supra*, by implication; therefore he was not subject to trial and conviction under § 6–3–106.

Appellant observes that the false-pretenses statute (§ 6–3–106, *supra*) was enacted earlier than the insufficient-funds statute (§ 6–3–110, *supra*), and since the violation of the earlier statute is a felony if the value of the property wrongfully obtained is $25.00 or greater, and since both statutes prohibit the same, identical act, he, therefore, is entitled to be charged with and tried for violation of § 6–3–110, the later insufficient-funds statute (violation of which is a misdemeanor) instead of the more stringent statute making it a crime to obtain property under false pretenses.

The State responded by urging that §§ 6–3–106 and 6–3–110 are calculated to govern different categories of criminal conduct and, therefore, require proof of distinct and different material or essential elements. They do not, it is therefore contended, conflict in the factual setting of this case and no repeal by implication is required.

Our inquiry leads us to the conclusions that obtaining property is never a necessary element of violating the insufficient-funds statute, while the obtaining of property is always a necessary element of the false-pretenses enactment. The insufficient-funds statute prohibits two types of conduct: (1) The mere issuance of a bad check with *intent to defraud by obtaining property* is a violation of the statute, and we do not read in a requirement that property must actually be obtained. (2) Giving a bad check in payment of an obligation is also a violation of the statute, in which case the crime may be committed even though property is not obtained as a result of writing the bad check.[72]

There is authority from other jurisdictions to the effect that, if an insufficient-funds statute does not require as an element for its violation the actual obtaining of property, a prosecution for a more serious theft offense is proper where an insufficient-funds check is issued and property is obtained. State v. Roderick, 85 Idaho 80, 375 P.2d 1005, 1007 (1962); Christiansen v. State, Tex.Cr.App., 575 S.W.2d 42, 44 (1979); State v. Covington, 59 N.J. 536, 284 A.2d 532, 533 (1971); and State v. Culver, 103 Ariz. 505, 446 P.2d 234, 236 (1968).

The State also urges that where the deceit extends beyond the mere passing of an insufficient-funds check, an insufficient-funds statute should not serve to provide protection against a greater theft offense. Authority for this proposition is found in State v. Hodge, 266 Minn. 193, 123 N.W.2d 323 (1963). In that case the Supreme Court of Minnesota stated that the mere passing of an insufficient-funds check would not suffice for prosecution of

---

72. *See*, Bailey v. State, Wyo., 408 P.2d 244 (1965), in which defendant was convicted of writing a bad check to settle an account for a series of meals previously received.

the felony of swindling—as opposed to prosecution for the gross misdemeanor of issuing checks with knowledge of insufficient funds to back them. However, the court found that additional misrepresentations—defendant's use of his wife's maiden name, a driver's license in that name, the wearing of post office insignia—sufficed to support a felony conviction. Additional authority for this point is found in the discussion in People v. LaRose, 87 Mich.App. 298, 274 N.W.2d 45, 47 (1978), reh. den., of People v. Vida, 2 Mich.App. 409, 140 N.W.2d 559 (1966), aff'd 381 Mich. 595, 166 N.W.2d 465 (1969).

We also find instructive the following thoughts on legislative intent from the Supreme Court of Iowa on the difference between the then-existing misdemeanor bad-check statute and the felony of cheating by false pretenses:

"... It may have been thought that the drawing of checks upon depleted bank accounts was a sin so nearly universal, and which carried so many graduations of moral turpitude, that, even though fraudulent, a seven-year term in the penitentiary was too severe a punishment therefor ... Section 13047 [the bad-check statute] seems to cover completely those cases of false pretense *wherein the pretense consists in presenting a check upon a bank where knowingly sufficient funds are not on deposit....*" [Emphasis supplied] State v. Marshall, 202 Iowa 954, 211 N.W. 252, 253 (1926).

In our case, it is clear that the appellant's deceitful scheme extended beyond the mere writing of a bad check and a simple express or implied assurance that the check was good.

The combination of these two arguments for affirmance persuades us to affirm this conviction, with the holding that the crime of obtaining property by false pretenses has been and can be committed, notwithstanding the fact that the property was obtained by writing a bad check where, as in this case, (1) the accused actually obtains property by writing a bad check, and (2) the false representation is more than a simple express or implied statement that the check is good, and (3) all of the other elements of the crime of obtaining property by false pretenses are met.

Affirmed.

Bell v. United States

Supreme Court of the United States, 1983.
462 U.S. 356, 103 S.Ct. 2398, 76 L.Ed.2d 638.

■ JUSTICE POWELL delivered the opinion of the Court.

The issue presented is whether 18 U.S.C. § 2113(b), a provision of the Federal Bank Robbery Act, proscribes the crime of obtaining money under false pretenses.

I

On October 13, 1978, a Cincinnati man wrote a check for $10,000 drawn on a Cincinnati bank. He endorsed the check for deposit to his account at Dade Federal Savings & Loan of Miami and mailed the check to an agent there. The agent never received the check. On October 17, petitioner Nelson Bell opened an account at a Dade Federal branch and deposited $50—the minimum amount necessary for new accounts. He used his own name, but gave a false address, birth date, and social security number. Later that day, at another branch, he deposited the Cincinnati man's $10,000 check into this new account. The endorsement had been altered to show Bell's account number. Dade Federal accepted the deposit, but put a 20-day hold on the funds. On November 7, as soon as the hold had expired, Bell returned to the branch at which he had opened the account. The total balance, with accrued interest, was then slightly over $10,080. Bell closed the account and was paid the total balance in cash.

Bell was apprehended and charged with violating 18 U.S.C. § 2113(b). The statute provides, in relevant part:

"Whoever takes and carries away, with intent to steal or purloin, any property or money or any other thing of value exceeding $100 belonging to, or in the care, custody, control, management, or possession of any bank, credit union, or any savings and loan association, shall be fined not more than $5,000 or imprisoned not more than ten years, or both. . . ."

Bell was convicted after a jury trial. . . .

We now affirm.

II

In the 13th century, larceny was limited to trespassory taking: a thief committed larceny only if he feloniously "took and carried away" another's personal property *from his possession*. The goal was more to prevent breaches of the peace than losses of property, and violence was more likely when property was taken from the owner's actual possession.

As the common law developed, protection of property also became an important goal. The definition of larceny accordingly was expanded by judicial interpretation to include cases where the owner merely was deemed to be in possession. Thus when a bailee of packaged goods broke open the packages and misappropriated the contents, he committed larceny. The Carrier's Case, Y.B.Pasch. 13 Edw. IV, f. 9, pl. 5 (Star Ch. and Exch. Ch. 1473), reprinted in 64 Selden Society 30 (1945). The bailor was deemed to be in possession of the contents of the packages, at least by the time of the misappropriation. Similarly, a thief committed "larceny by trick" when he obtained custody of a horse by telling the owner that he intended to use it for one purpose when he in fact intended to sell it and to keep the proceeds. King v. Pear, 1 Leach 212, 168 Eng.Rep. 208 (Cr.Cas.Res.1779). The judges accepted the fiction that the owner retained possession of the horse until it was sold, on the theory that the thief had custody only for a limited purpose.

By the late 18th century, courts were less willing to expand common-law definitions. Thus when a bank clerk retained money given to him by a customer rather than depositing it in the bank, he was not guilty of larceny, for the bank had not been in possession of the money. King v. Bazeley, 2 Leach 835, 168 Eng.Rep. 517 (Cr.Cas.Res.1799). Statutory crimes such as embezzlement and obtaining property by false pretenses therefore were created to fill this gap.

The theoretical distinction between false pretenses and larceny by trick may be stated simply. If a thief, through his trickery, acquired *title* to the property from the owner, he has obtained property by false pretenses; but if he merely acquired *possession* from the owner, he has committed larceny by trick. In this case the parties agree that Bell is guilty of obtaining money by false pretenses. When the teller at Dade Federal handed him $10,080 in cash Bell acquired title to the money. The only dispute is whether 18 U.S.C. § 2113(b) proscribes the crime of false pretenses, or whether the statute is instead limited to common-law larceny.

III

A

Bell's argument in favor of the narrower reading of § 2113(b) relies principally on the statute's use of the traditional common-law language "takes and carries away." He cites the rule of statutory construction that when a federal criminal statute uses a common-law term without defining it, Congress is presumed to intend the common-law meaning. In § 2113(b), however, Congress has not adopted the elements of larceny in common-law terms. The language "takes and carries away" is but one part of the statute and represents only one element of common-law larceny. Other language in § 2113(b), such as "with intent to steal or purloin," has no established meaning at common law. *See Turley, supra*, at 411–412, 77 S.Ct., at 399–400. Moreover, "taking and carrying away," although not a necessary element of the crime, is entirely consistent with false pretenses.

Two other aspects of § 2113(b) show an intention to go beyond the common-law definition of larceny. First, common-law larceny was limited to thefts of tangible personal property. This limitation excluded, for example, the theft of a written instrument embodying a chose in action. Section 2113(b) is thus broader than common-law larceny, for it covers "any property or money or any other thing of value exceeding $100." Second, and of particular relevance to the distinction at issue here, common-law larceny required a theft from the possession of the owner. When the definition was expanded, it still applied only when the owner was deemed to be in possession. Section 2113(b), however, goes well beyond even this expanded definition. It applies when the property "belong[s] to," or is "in the care, custody, control, management, or possession of," a covered institution.

In sum, the statutory language does not suggest that it covers only common-law larceny. Although § 2113(b) does not apply to a case of false pretenses in which there is not a taking and carrying away, it proscribes Bell's conduct here. The evidence is clear that he "t[ook] and carrie[d] away, with intent to steal or purloin, [over $10,000 that was] in the care, custody, control, management, or possession of" Dade Federal Savings & Loan.

B

The legislative history of § 2113(b) also suggests that Congress intended the statute to reach Bell's conduct. As originally enacted in 1934, the Federal Bank Robbery Act, ch. 304, 48 Stat. 783, governed only robbery—a crime requiring a forcible taking. Congress apparently was concerned with " 'gangsters who operate habitually from one State to another in robbing banks.' "

By 1937 the concern was broader, for the limited nature of the original Act " 'ha[d] led to some incongruous results.' " It was possible for a thief to steal a large amount from a bank " 'without displaying any force or violence and without putting any one in fear,' " and he would not violate any federal law. Congress amended the Act to fill this gap, adding language now found at § 2113(a) and (b). Although the term "larceny" appears in the legislative reports, the congressional purpose plainly was to protect banks from those who wished to steal banks' assets—even if they used no force in doing so.

The congressional goal of protecting bank assets is entirely independent of the traditional distinction on which Bell relies. To the extent that a bank needs protection against larceny by trick, it also needs protection from false pretenses. We cannot believe that Congress wished to limit the scope of the amended Act's coverage, and thus limit its remedial purpose, on the basis of an arcane and artificial distinction more suited to the social conditions of 18th century England than the needs of 20th century America. Such an interpretation would signal a return to the "incongruous results" that the 1937 amendment was designed to eliminate.

IV

We conclude that 18 U.S.C. § 2113(b) is not limited to common-law larceny. Although § 2113(b) may not cover the full range of theft offenses, it covers Bell's conduct here. His conviction therefore was proper, and the judgment of the Court of Appeals accordingly is

Affirmed.

State v. Moses

Court of Appeals of Arizona, Division 1, Department B, 1979.
123 Ariz. 296, 599 P.2d 252.

OPINION

■ SCHROEDER, PRESIDING JUDGE. Appellant, Willie Joe Moses, was convicted after a jury trial of obtaining money by a confidence game in violation of former A.R.S. § 13–312, and of obtaining money by means of a scheme or artifice to defraud in violation of former A.R.S. § 13–320.01.[73] He appeals only from his conviction under the latter section and the sentence imposed on that conviction of not less than five nor more than ten years.

---

73. With some modifications, these statutes have been enacted in the present Criminal Code as A.R.S. § 13–2310.

Appellant's conviction under A.R.S. § 13–320.01 was based upon his participation in a scam known as the "Jamaican Switch." The appellant approached the victim and, in an assumed foreign accent, asked directions to a boarding house. The appellant's accomplice, Patricia Hard, then approached appellant and offered to show him to a boarding house. Appellant then showed the victim that he had a large amount of cash and stated that he did not trust the woman. He prevailed upon the victim to hold the cash for him, and to indicate his good faith by placing the victim's own money in the same handkerchief with that of the appellant. The handkerchief was then deposited in the trunk of the victim's automobile. Unknown to the victim, however, the appellant switched the handkerchiefs. When the victim later opened the handkerchief, he found only folded paper. He was unable to relocate either the appellant or Hard.

The sole issue raised in this appeal is whether the state must prove that the victim intended to transfer title of the property to the appellant in order to support a conviction under § 13–320.01. The appellant argues that this essential element is missing because the victim merely intended to part with his money temporarily as a display of good faith.

A.R.S. § 13–320.01 provides as follows:

Any person who, pursuant to a scheme or artifice to defraud, knowingly and intentionally obtains or attempts to obtain money, property or any other thing of value by means of false or fraudulent pretenses, representations or promises is guilty of a felony punishable by imprisonment in the state prison for not more than twenty years, by a fine not to exceed twenty thousand dollars, or both.

Appellant argues that this provision is a codification of the common law crime of false pretenses, and that even though the statute itself makes no reference to any requirement of intent to transfer title or ownership, that element is nevertheless embodied in it. Appellant relies upon cases in other jurisdictions holding that proof of an intent to pass to the victim only temporary possession of the property is not sufficient to sustain a conviction under the statutes of those states. That view is succinctly stated in Perkins on Criminal Law, ch. 4 § 4(C)(1) 2nd ed. 1969, p. 306:

.... [T]he generally accepted view is that the crime of false pretenses has not been committed unless the wrongdoer, by his fraudulent scheme, has obtained the title or ownership—or whatever property interest the victim had in the chattel if it was less than title.

Appellant's entire argument is premised on the assumption that in enacting A.R.S. § 13–320.01 the legislature intended to codify a common law crime of false pretenses. We disagree. The State correctly recognizes that the section was derived from the Federal Mail Fraud Statute, 18 U.S.C. §§ 1341–1343. It was not enacted until 1976 and encompasses a very broad range of fraudulent activities.

We hold that the State offered sufficient evidence to support the appellant's conviction of fraudulently obtaining money pursuant to a scheme or artifice, in violation of former A.R.S. § 13–320.01.

Affirmed.

■ OGG, C.J., concurring.

■ JACOBSON, J., concurs in the result.[74]

SECTION 5.   THEFT[75]

The technical distinctions between larceny, embezzlement and false pretenses serve no useful purpose in the criminal law but are useless handicaps from the standpoint of the administration of criminal justice. One solution has been to combine all three in one section of the code, under some such name as "larceny" or "theft". Some of the penal codes include these three offenses and others under the name of "theft" but with definitions that include much that had not been included before. A more sweeping provision, adopted in a few states, provides that the offense of theft shall include the offenses previously known as larceny, embezzlement, false pretenses, extortion, blackmail and receiving stolen property, and is also worded so as to provide punishment for conduct not previously punishable.

State v. McCartney

Supreme Court of Montana, 1978.
179 Mont. 49, 585 P.2d 1321.

■ HASWELL, CHIEF JUSTICE. Defendant appeals from his conviction by the District Court, Fergus County, after a nonjury trial before Judge LeRoy L. McKinnon. Defendant was charged with one count of felony theft and one count of felony forgery. The trial court found defendant guilty of both crimes and sentenced him to five years in the state penitentiary, with four years suspended. On appeal, defendant contends that the state failed to prove the elements of felony theft and forgery, that the evidence was insufficient to sustain the judgment of conviction, and that he was tried by the District Court without properly having waived his right to trial by jury.

The facts, essentially undisputed, are as follows:

In April 1970, defendant and James T. Johnson entered into a cattle sharing agreement which provided that defendant was to receive 60 percent and Johnson 40 percent of the yearly calf production from cows owned by Johnson which were to be pastured on land leased by defendant. The calves were to be branded in the spring with Johnson's 3–Lazy T brand and the 60–40 split was to be made when the calves were sold in the fall.

The agreement ended in 1974 and the remaining calves were apparently sold at that time. Defendant thereafter sold his ranch. In 1975, a cow

---

74. Former employee department store managers could not be convicted of theft by deception in using bogus refund vouchers to cover up their thefts of store funds. There was no deception in the defendants obtaining their positions and the vouchers were not used to get anything from the employer but to cover thefts. Defendants should have been charged with embezzlement. State v. Rios, 246 Kan. 517, 792 P.2d 1065 (1990).

75. "One charged with theft will not be heard to raise nice and delicate questions as to the title of" a stolen vehicle. Abrams v. State, 229 Ga.App. 152, 493 S.E.2d 561, 563 (1997).

was found on property owned by the Ayers Hutterite colony, which bordered the land defendant had leased. The cow carried Johnson's brand. The president of the Ayers colony, John Stahl, believing the stray belonged to defendant, approached defendant about purchasing the cow. Defendant agreed to sell, and made out a bill of sale on November 26, 1976. Defendant signed Johnson's name as "seller" and his own name as "witness" on the bill of sale. Defendant also drew a Lazy T in the middle of a 3, as the brand of the cow to be sold, on the bill of sale. That brand was similar to Johnson's 3–Lazy T brand. The Ayers colony promised defendant some beef as consideration for the sale.

On March 1, 1977, Stahl checked with the brand office in Lewistown about the Lazy T in the middle of a 3 brand. He had noticed the cow's brand did not match that brand as drawn by defendant on the bill of sale. Stahl was told the brand on the bill of sale was not Johnson's brand and he then called defendant who told him to "put on the other brand." Stahl assumed defendant meant Johnson's 3–Lazy T brand.

On March 2, 1977, Stahl sold the cow at the Central Montana Livestock Market for $241. The brand office thereafter contacted Johnson, and upon learning he had not sold the cow, began an investigation of the transaction. Defendant was charged and arrested for theft and forgery, both felonies, as a result of that investigation.

Defendant first contends he had neither actual nor constructive possession of the cow prior to its sale and did not deliver the cow to anyone and therefore cannot be guilty of theft. Under the old criminal code provisions and cases interpreting them, the State had to prove a defendant took possession of another's property and carried it away to secure a larceny conviction. Defendant cites cases to that effect and Am.Jur.2d comments concerning the classic elements of larceny. The classic taking and carrying away, however, has not been continued in the criminal codes under which defendant was convicted.

Section 94–6–302, R.C.M.1947, provides in pertinent part:

"*Theft.* (1) A person commits the offense of theft when he purposely or knowingly obtains or exerts unauthorized control over property of the owner and:

"(a) has the purpose of depriving the owner of the property;

"(b) purposely or knowingly uses, conceals, or abandons the property in such manner as to deprive the owner of the property . . ."

Section 94–2–101(32), R.C.M.1947, defines "obtain" as:

"(a) in relation to property, to bring about a transfer of interest or possession whether to the offender or to another."

Section 94–2–101(33), R.C.M.1947, provides:

" 'Obtains or exerts control' includes but is not limited to the taking, carrying away, or sale, conveyance, transfer of title to, interest in, or possession of property."

The Commission comment to section 94–6–302, provides in part:

"After extended and exhaustive study and consideration by the commission, matching various combinations of the subsections to cover every type of conduct proscribed by the old law, and extending such matching to conduct covered by statutes in other states, it is believed this section will cover any conceivable form of theft.

" . . .

" . . . the method by which unauthorized control is obtained or exerted is immaterial in subsection (1) . . ."

It is clear that these statutes encompass more than the actual taking and asportation of another's property. This state has adopted its code provisions from Illinois. The precursor of section 94–6–302, is Chapter 38, § 16–1 of the Illinois Criminal Code. In discussing the scope of "theft" under this statute, the Illinois Court stated in People v. Nunn (1965), 63 Ill.App.2d 465, 212 N.E.2d 342, 344:

"Section 16–1(a)(1) is not limited to the theft of property in which only the actor who initiates the wrongful asportation is guilty of the offense. A person who 'knowingly obtains or exerts unauthorized control over property of the owner' is the statutory description of a thief, provided only that his act is accompanied by the requisite mental state. As expressly pointed out in section 15–8, the phrase 'obtains or exerts control' over property includes, but is not limited to, the taking or carrying away of the property. It also includes (though still not exclusively) the bringing about of a transfer of possession of the property."

In People v. Petitjean (1972), 7 Ill.App.3d 231, 287 N.E.2d 137, the court held the theft statute included the wrongful sale or conveyance of property and was not limited to theft of property in which only the actor who institutes the wrongful asportation is guilty of the offense.

In the present case, the State proved that defendant brought about a transfer of title and possession of James E. Johnson's cow to one other than the owner through a wrongful sale which resulted in depriving James E. Johnson of his property. If the requisite mental state is proven along with this, no more is required under section 94–6–302.

Defendant's next contention is that the State did not prove he acted knowingly or purposely with respect to obtaining or exerting unauthorized control over Johnson's cow. He contends in essence the District Court was required to accept his testimony which was plausible, and therefore the testimony negated any finding by the District Court that he had the requisite mental state. There was however, sufficient circumstantial evidence for the trial court to conclude otherwise.

Defendant testified that in the spring of 1970 or 1971, he branded a calf with the 3–Lazy T brand believing the calf was from one of Johnson's cows. Two weeks later he saw that calf following one of his own cows. Realizing he had been mistaken as to the calf's origin, defendant branded it again, this time with one of his own brands. When Stahl called him about the stray in 1976, defendant thought it was the twice-branded cow. He further testified he signed Johnson's name as "seller" on the bill of sale because he thought the 3–Lazy T would "show up better" than his own brand when the cow was examined. He wanted the seller's name to conform to the most legible brand. Defendant also asserts that when he told Stahl to "put the other brand" on the bill of sale, he meant his own brand, not Johnson's. The entire episode, according to defendant, was a mistake compounded by misunderstanding.

On the other hand, the circumstantial evidence negating this misunderstanding, includes: defendant's failure to ask Stahl whether the stray had two brands when he was told of the cow's discovery; defendant's failure to mention the twice-branded cow story when Stahl called him about the brand discrepancy; defendant's drawing of a brand similar to Johnson's rather than his own on the bill of sale; defendant's signing of Johnson's name on the "seller" line and his own name on the "witness" line on the bill of sale; and defendant's failure to apprise Johnson of the situation at any time before or after the sale. We note moreover, that defendant had experience as a brand inspector and knew that the brand drawn on the bill of sale must be that of the animal's seller as listed on the bill of sale.

Clearly, under these circumstances, the determination of intent was to be made by the trial court as the trier of fact. As we stated in State v. Farnes (1976), 171 Mont. 368, 558 P.2d 472, 475, 33 St.Rep. 1270.

"The element of felonious intent in every contested criminal case must necessarily be determined from facts and circumstances of the particular case—this for the reason that criminal intent, being a state of mind, is rarely susceptible of direct or positive proof and therefore must usually be inferred from the facts testified to by witnesses and the circumstances as developed by the evidence . . ."

Here, the District Court resolved the question of intent against defendant.

The Judgment is affirmed.[76]

State v. Saylor

Supreme Court of Kansas, 1980.
228 Kan. 498, 618 P.2d 1166.

■ PRAGER, JUSTICE. This is a direct appeal from a conviction of theft by deception (K.S.A.1979 Supp. 21–3701[b]). The Court of Appeals in a published opinion, State v. Saylor, 4 Kan.App.2d 563, 608 P.2d 421 (1980), reversed and remanded with directions to grant the defendant a new trial on the lesser included offense of attempt to commit theft by deception. We granted review on petition of the State.

---

76. Theft statute defines a single crime and sets forth alternative means of committing the offense. State v. Southard, 49 Wn.App. 59, 741 P.2d 78 (1987).

Theft by receiving is properly charged under the general theft statute. State v. Taylor, 570 P.2d 697 (Utah 1977). For another broad consolidation statute punishing several forms of unauthorized control over the property of another, see State v. Bourbeau, 250 N.W.2d 259 (N.D.1977). The specific theory of theft need not be alleged in the indictment. Williams v. State, 648 P.2d 603 (Alaska App.1982).

Jury unanimity as to the manner of committing theft is not required and in the consolidated theft statute only a single crime "theft" is involved. Rice v. State, 311 Md. 116, 532 A.2d 1357 (1987).

The facts in the case are well summarized in the opinion of the Court of Appeals. On September 27, 1978, in the city of Lawrence, a K–Mart store security officer observed the defendant, Glenn Lee Saylor, as he made numerous trips through the store placing items in his shopping cart. He would go to the hardware department with items in the cart, but would leave that department with an empty cart. The security officer observed the defendant move about in one particular area, but was unable to see exactly what he was doing. She saw him take a bottle of glue to the area, use it, and then return it to a counter. The defendant then made a minor purchase and left the store. The security officer notified her supervisor. On investigation, she found in the hardware department a cardboard box which should have been located in the toy department and which ordinarily would contain a $13.97 plastic pig toy chest. The cover of the box had recently been resealed with glue. The security officer did not move or otherwise touch the box. When the defendant returned to the store later that evening, the security officer and the police were on hand. The defendant went to the hardware department where he placed the box in a shopping cart. He proceeded to the checkout counter and paid for two items—a quart of oil and a plastic pig toy chest priced at $13.97. The checkout cashier did not suspect there was anything wrong. The defendant was arrested outside the store in the parking lot. There the box was opened and found to contain several chainsaws, metal rules, cigarettes, heavy duty staple guns, and record albums, with a total value in excess of $500. The defendant was arrested for theft. He was charged with and convicted of theft by deception under K.S.A.1979 Supp. 21–3701(*b*).

The defendant appealed raising several points of alleged error. The Court of Appeals reversed the conviction, finding error in the trial court's failure to instruct the jury on *attempted* theft by deception. Noting this court's decision in State v. Finch, 223 Kan. 398, 573 P.2d 1048 (1978), the Court of Appeals held that, since there had been no actual reliance by or actual deception of the corporate victim, K–Mart, the defendant could only be guilty of attempted theft by deception. The Court of Appeals reversed the conviction and directed a new trial on attempted theft by deception.

On petition for review, the State of Kansas urges this court to reconsider the elements of theft by deception as enumerated by *Finch,* claiming that by interpreting 21–3701(*b*) to require reliance by or actual deception of the owner, the court added to the offense of theft an element not contained in the statutory definition. Alternatively, the State argues that the present case is distinguishable from *Finch,* claiming that there was actual deception in this case, at least in part, since the checkout cashier was totally unaware of defendant's larcenous intent and no one within the employment of K–Mart had more than a suspicion of defendant's scheme at the time defendant purchased the merchandise and left the store with the box. The State finally argues that, under the consolidated theft statute, a conviction of theft should be sustained, even though the burden of proof is not met as to the offense specified in the indictment or information, if the evidence supports conviction of theft under any other subsection of K.S.A. 1979 Supp. 21–3701.

We have reconsidered the rule announced in State v. Finch, and have concluded that it is a correct statement of the law. The syllabus in *Finch* states the rule which is consistent with prior decisions of this court and with the rule generally accepted throughout the United States:

"In order to convict a defendant of theft by deception under K.S.A. 21–3701(*b*) the state must prove that the defendant with the required intent obtained control over another's property *by means* of a false statement or representation. To do so the state must prove that the victim was actually deceived and relied in whole or in part upon the false representation."

The rationale of the rule and the reasons why it was adopted by this court are discussed in depth in that opinion. We have concluded, however, that, under its particular facts, the present case is distinguishable from *Finch,* in that the K–Mart checkout cashier, who permitted the defendant to leave the store premises with the box, was completely unaware of the true contents hidden in the box and relied upon the deception practiced by the defendant at that time.

The State argues that the defendant could have properly been charged under section (*a*) of K.S.A.1979 Supp. 21–3701, since the evidence established that the defendant, with intent to deprive the owner permanently of the possession, use, or ownership of the owner's property, exerted unauthorized control over the property by concealing the articles in the cardboard box. We agree with the State. It is clear to us that where a customer in a self-service store conceals on his person, or in a box or receptacle, property of the store and has the requisite specific criminal intent, that customer has committed a theft under subsection (*a*) of K.S.A.1979 Supp. 21–3701. The specific criminal intent is difficult to prove, however, unless the customer actually fails to make proper payment for the property at the cashier's desk and leaves the store with the same remaining concealed. In this case, the defendant was not specifically charged under subsection (*a*) of K.S.A.1979 Supp. 21–3701. The State did not seek to amend the information to include that subsection, nor was an appropriate instruction on that subsection given to the jury. The State thus relied only on proving theft by *deception* under subsection (*b*). The conviction of the defendant must stand or fall on the sufficiency of the evidence to show that the defendant, with the required specific intent, obtained control over the property by deception. We have concluded that the evidence was sufficient and that an instruction on attempted theft was not required.

In concluding that the evidence established a completed theft by deception, the trial court pointed out that the security employees of K–Mart had only a suspicion that the defendant was planning to steal articles of merchandise from the store. The actual merchandise taken was not determined until the box was opened following the defendant's arrest in the parking lot. We think it also important to note that the act of deception and false representation did not actually occur until the defendant deceived the cashier into believing that the box contained a plastic pig toy chest of a value of $13.97.

The rule of *Finch* simply requires the State to prove that the victim was actually deceived and relied wholly or *in part* upon the false representation made by the defendant. We note that this same result was reached under similar factual circumstances in Lambert v. State, 55 Ala.App. 242, 314 So.2d 318, cert. denied 294 Ala. 763, 314 So.2d 322 (1975). In *Lambert,* it was held that *reliance* upon a misrepresentation was proved in a prosecution for false pretense, although the evidence showed that numerous persons in the store knew of defendant's scheme to change price tags on merchandise, where the checkout girl to whom defendant took the falsely priced merchandise relied upon the false representation as to those prices and parted with the merchandise, having no knowledge of the defendant's scheme. Since the undisputed evidence in this case showed the cashier at the checkout counter at K–Mart relied upon the false representation made by the defendant as to the contents of the box and permitted defendant to take control of the box and its contents outside the confines of the store, we hold that the trial court did not err in concluding that there was the required reliance and thus an instruction on the lesser offense of attempted theft by deception was not required.

We now address the contention of the State that, under the consolidated statute, K.S.A.1979 Supp. 21–3701, a conviction of theft may be upheld even though the burden of proof is not sustained as to the particular subsection specified in the information, if the evidence supports the conviction of theft under any one of the other subsections. We agree with the State that the primary purpose of the consolidated theft statute was to eliminate the complexities of pleading and proving the vague historical distinctions in the various types of theft. See comment, Judicial Council, 21–3701 (1968). Professor Paul E. Wilson, in his article, Thou Shalt Not Steal: Ruminations on the New Kansas Theft Law, 20 Kan.L.Rev. 385 (1972), makes the following observation:

"[C]onsolidation should eliminate the procedural difficulties that sometimes result from the fact that boundaries between the traditional theft crimes are obscure and the defendant who is charged with one crime cannot be convicted by proving another. An inexperienced—or even an experienced—prosecutor may have difficulty in determining whether a given set of facts indicates larceny, false pretense, or embezzlement. And even though the right charge is selected, a conviction based on borderline facts is more likely to be challenged on appeal. The objective, then, has been to define the crime broadly enough to include all vaguely separated theft offenses, so that evidence of appropriation by any of the forbidden methods will support the charge." p. 393.

Likewise, the Model Penal Code, § 223.1 (Proposed Off. Draft, May 4, 1962), provides:

"(1) *Consolidation of Theft Offenses.* Conduct denominated theft in this Article constitutes a single offense embracing the separate offenses heretofore known as larceny, embezzlement, false pretense, extortion, blackmail, fraudulent conversion, receiving stolen property, and the like. An accusation of theft may be supported by evidence that it was committed in any manner that would be theft under this Article, notwithstanding the specification of a different manner in the indictment or information, subject only to the power of the Court to ensure fair trial by granting a continuance or other appropriate relief where the conduct of the defense would be prejudiced by lack of fair notice or by surprise."

Under the former Kansas code as it existed prior to the adoption of the present code, effective July 1, 1970, the crime of false pretenses was covered by K.S.A. 21–551 and 21–552 (Corrick 1964). The legislature recognized the difficulties of proof in this area by enacting K.S.A. 21–553 (Corrick 1964):

"21–553. Conviction of larceny under 21–551, 21–552. If upon the trial of any person indicted for any offense prohibited in the last two sections, it should be proved that he obtained the money or other thing in question in such manner as to amount in law to a larceny, he shall not by reason thereof be entitled to an acquittal, but he shall be convicted and punished as if the offense had been proved as charged."

In Talbot v. Wulf, 122 Kan. 1, 5, 251 P. 438 (1926), this court stated that G.S. 21–553 was designed to prevent a failure of justice on account of a variance between pleading and proof dependent on the distinction between the crime of larceny and the crime of obtaining property by false pretense.

It is obvious to us that one of the purposes of the enactment of the consolidated theft statute, K.S.A. 21–3701, was to avoid the pitfalls of pleading where a defendant might escape a conviction for one type of theft by proof that he had committed another type of theft. There is now only the single crime of theft which is complete when a man takes property not his own with the intent to take it and deprive the owner thereof. A defendant may be convicted of theft upon proof of facts establishing either embezzlement, larceny, receiving stolen property, or obtaining property by false pretense. It has long been the law of Kansas that an accusatory pleading in a criminal action may, in order to meet the exigencies of proof, charge the commission of the same offense in different ways. In such a situation, a conviction can be upheld only on one count, the function of the added counts in the pleading being to anticipate and obviate fatal variance between allegations and proof. Thus, it has been held proper to charge by several counts of an information the same offense committed in different ways or by different means to the extent necessary to provide for every possible contingency in the evidence.

Where there is a question in the mind of the prosecutor as to what the evidence will disclose at trial, the correct procedure is to charge the defendant in the alternative under those subsections to K.S.A.1979 Supp. 21–3701 which may possibly be established by the evidence. This may properly be done under Kansas law by charging several counts in the information to provide for every possible contingency in the evidence. By so doing, the jury may properly be instructed on the elements necessary to establish the crime of theft under any of the subsections charged and the defendant will have no basis to complain that he has been prejudiced in his defense.

It should also be noted that, under K.S.A.1979 Supp. 22–3201(4), a trial court may permit a complaint or information to be amended at any time before verdict or finding if no additional crime is charged and if substantial rights of the defendant are not prejudiced. Following that statute, we have a number of decisions which hold that it is proper for the State to amend the information during trial by adding words which change the method by which the particular crime was committed in the particular case. For example in State v. Lamb, 215 Kan. 795, 798, 530 P.2d 20 (1974), the State was permitted to amend a charge of kidnapping by adding the words "or deception" to the allegation "by means of force," since there was evidence presented in the case that the kidnapping was accomplished both through force and deception. In State v. Bell, 224 Kan. 105, 106, 577 P.2d 1186 (1978), the State was permitted to amend certain counts in the information, charging kidnapping, to add the words "by force and deception" to make the information conform to the evidence presented. *See also* State v. Rives, 220 Kan. 141, 144–45, 551 P.2d 788 (1976) (where the information was amended to charge that the defendant took the purloined property "from the presence of" a named individual rather than "from the person of" the same individual); State v. Ferguson, 221 Kan. 103, 105, 558 P.2d 1092 (1976) (where the State was permitted to amend the *date* of the violation originally charged in the information). In this case, as mentioned above, the State did not seek to amend the charge of theft contained in the information to include an allegation of theft under subsection (*a*) of K.S.A.1979 Supp. 21–3701 and the jury was not instructed on that charge. Thus, the jury could not properly consider the question of defendant's guilt or innocence of the crime of theft under subsection (*a*).

In closing, it should be noted that we have considered the other point of complained error raised in defendant's brief that the district court erred in allowing the State to introduce certain rebuttal testimony. We find this point to be without merit.

For the reasons set forth above, we hold that the judgment of the district court upholding the conviction of the defendant for theft by deception (K.S.A.1979 Supp. 21–370[*b*]) is affirmed. It is further ordered that the judgment of the Court of Appeals is reversed for the reasons set forth in the opinion.

People v. Home Insurance Co.

Supreme Court of Colorado, En Banc, 1979.
197 Colo. 260, 591 P.2d 1036.

■ Lee, Justice. The People appeal from the dismissal of theft and theft-related charges by the trial court at the close of the prosecution's case. The charges arose from the surreptitious procurement by agents of the insurance company defendants of confidential medical information concerning two patients of a Denver hospital. The trial court granted the dismissal because the medical information obtained was not a "thing of value" as defined in the pertinent statute and therefore was not subject to theft. We affirm.

The defendants hired an injury claims investigative service to obtain medical information reports on two claimants. Through the use of the telephone, an investigator for the service obtained a verbatim reading of the medical reports which he later transcribed and sent to the defendants. The actual medical records themselves never left the hospital file room; rather, only the medical information contained in the records was thus acquired.

The theft statute, section 18–4–401(1)(a), C.R.S.1973 (1978 Repl.Vol. 8), reads in pertinent part:

"A person commits theft when he knowingly obtains or exercises control over anything of value of another without authorization, or by threat or deception, and:

"(a) Intends to deprive the other person permanently of the use or benefit of the thing of value . . . ."

Crucial to our determination of this case is the definition of "thing of value" contained in section 18–1–901(3)(r), C.R.S.1973 (1978 Repl.Vol. 8):

" 'Thing of value' includes real property, tangible and intangible personal property, contract rights, choses in action, services, and any rights or use or enjoyment connected therewith."

The People argue that the confidentiality inherent in one's personal medical information is a "thing of value" within the meaning of the theft statute inasmuch as the confidentiality is intangible personal property. We do not agree with this expansive interpretation of the theft statute.

In determining the meaning of criminal statutes, we are guided by the principle that such statutes must be strictly construed in favor of the accused and they cannot be extended either by implication or construction.

As far as we have been able to determine, and no cases have been cited by the People to the contrary, confidentiality has never been considered as intangible personal property. Rather, the term intangible personal property has been held to be property which is merely representative of value, such as certificates of stock, bonds, promissory notes, patents, copyrights, tradebrands and franchises. We, therefore, would have to expand unduly the traditional concept of intangible property if we were to accept the People's contention.

Furthermore, the General Assembly has specifically addressed the violation of analogous privacy interests in the criminal code. Thus, it has authorized criminal sanctions for the theft of trade secrets, section 18–4–408, C.R.S.1973 (1978 Repl.Vol. 8),[77] unauthorized wiretapping of telephone or telegraph communication, section 18–9–303, C.R.S.1973 (1978 Repl.Vol. 8); eavesdropping, section 18–9–304, C.R.S.1973 (1978 Repl.Vol. 8); and unauthorized reading, learning or disclosure of telephone, telegraph or mail messages, section 18–9–306, C.R.S.1973 (1978 Repl.Vol. 8). The foregoing amply demonstrates that the General Assembly has the legislative competence, if inclined to do so, to make illegal the invasion of privacy or confidentiality. The legislature, however, has not chosen to apply criminal sanctions to the invasion of the confidentiality of medical information. We will not now do so by an unwarranted interpretation of the meaning of intangible personal property as it is used in the statutory definition of "thing of value."

In the civil context the legislature has considered the importance of confidentiality of medical information. Section 25–1–802, C.R.S.1973 (1978

---

77. Although traditionally there has been a civil remedy for appropriation of trade secrets, see Trade Secret Litigation: Injunctions and Other Equitable Remedies, 48 U.Colo. L.Rev. 189 (1977), the legislature considered the increasing encroachment on this type of confidentiality as warranting criminal penalties.

Supp.) concerns confidentiality of patient records in the custody of health care facilities. Section 27–10–120, C.R.S.1973, provides that all information obtained in the course of providing services to the mentally ill in state institutions shall be confidential and privileged. Section 25–1–312, C.R.S. 1973, makes records of alcoholics compiled at treatment facilities confidential and privileged. Section 24–72–204(3), C.R.S.1973, provides that public records containing medical and psychological data shall not be available for public inspection except in certain prescribed circumstances. The legislature, therefore, has taken specific steps to protect the confidentiality of medical information by creating statutory duties, the breach of which could serve as the basis for a civil remedy. However, the legislature has not imposed criminal penalties for violations of the confidentiality or privilege.

Finally, the acceptance of the People's contention that invasion of the confidentiality of one's medical records constitutes theft would have far-reaching ramifications. Conceivably, a person who committed one of the four recognized torts for the invasion of privacy[78] could be tried for theft. Also, the breach of one of the recognized privileges (e.g., husband-wife, attorney-client, clergyman-penitent, doctor-patient, accountant-client and psychologist-client, *see* section 13–90–107, C.R.S.1973) might possibly be construed as theft. In our view, such an expansion of criminal liability could not have been intended by the legislature when it adopted the theft statute. Although we agree with the trial court that the defendants' conduct was "reprehensible and outrageous," that conduct simply was not made criminal under the theft statute. Proof of moral turpitude is not alone sufficient to authorize a criminal conviction.

Because of our disposition, it is unnecessary to address the issue of how to calculate the monetary worth of the medical information or the issue of whether the evidence established the element of permanent deprivation.

The judgment is affirmed.

■ CARRIGAN, J., does not participate.

SECTION 6.   RECEIVING (OR CONCEALING) STOLEN PROPERTY

Under the common law and early statutes of England one who received stolen property, knowing it was stolen, was punishable although not always under the same theory. Under one of these statutes he was guilty of a separate substantive offense known as receiving stolen property, and most of the penal codes in this country have taken that position. Some of the statutes extend the coverage to include one who "aids in concealing" such property.

In the early English cases the "receiver" was guilty of a misdemeanor except that under one of the statutes he was declared to be guilty as accessory after the fact to the larceny by which the goods had originally been taken. This, of course, made him a felon. Under most of the modern

---

78. According to W. Prosser, Torts § 117 (4th ed. 1971), the common law tort of invasion of privacy contains four distinct kinds of invasion of four different interests: (1) intrusion upon physical solitude; (2) public disclosure of private facts; (3) false light in the public eye; and (4) appropriation of name or likeness.

American statutes the offense is either a felony or a misdemeanor depending upon the value of the property received—or sometimes upon the kind of property. It is often incorporated in consolidated theft statutes.

SECTION 7. COMPUTER CRIME

With the significant use of computers in society to perform many essential commercial and private functions, most jurisdictions have enacted statutes sanctioning various forms of misuse of computers or computer information. Statutes are often comprehensive and directed toward protecting a variety of interests that could be affected by computer misuse. The statutes prohibit access of computer data without permission, the damaging, destruction, deletion, or misuse of computer data, including printing computer data. Theft of computer services is often prohibited as well as contamination of computer data.[79]

SECTION 8. MALICIOUS MISCHIEF

Malicious mischief, sometimes called malicious trespass, is the malicious destruction of, or damage to, the property of another, whether real or personal. It is a misdemeanor at common law but an occasional statute has provided that it may be a felony depending upon either the nature of the property or the value thereof.

SECTION 9. FORGERY AND UTTERING A FORGED INSTRUMENT

Forgery is the fraudulent making of a false writing having apparent legal significance. It may be accomplished by starting with blank paper or a blank form and doing all the writing which results in the false instrument; or by starting with a genuine writing and fraudulently altering it so as to make it false.

Uttering a forged instrument is knowingly offering, as genuine, one known to be false. The offer itself completes the uttering even if promptly rejected.

Both forgery and uttering were misdemeanors at common law but are almost universally felonies under modern statutes.

United States v. McGovern

United States Court of Appeals, Third Circuit, 1981.
661 F.2d 27.

OPINION OF THE COURT

■ ALDISERT, CIRCUIT JUDGE. The question for decision is whether the appellants' conduct constituted a violation of paragraph four of 18 U.S.C. § 2314:

---

79. West's Cal. Penal Code § 502 (1997).

Whoever, with unlawful or fraudulent intent, transports in interstate or foreign commerce any traveler's checks bearing a forged countersignature . . . shall be fined . . . or imprisoned . . . or both.

Convicted in a bench trial, McGovern and Scull argue in this appeal that the government failed to prove the predicate of the federal statutory offense: common law forgery. Appellants contend that the existence of authority to sign another's name to an instrument defeats a forgery charge, and that here appellant McGovern, purchaser of the traveler's checks, authorized appellant Scull to sign McGovern's name to the checks. We will affirm essentially for the reasons set forth by Chief Judge Weber.

I.

In the modern idiom, the appellants' fascinating plan could be dubbed "CITISCAM," because the participants devised a novel method of defrauding Citibank Corporation and certain businesses. The motive for the operation was the existence of an $1,800 debt McGovern owed an increasingly impatient Scull. The scheme was obvious: McGovern would buy $2,400 (for good measure) in traveler's checks from a bank; Scull would sign McGovern's name to the checks and cash them and McGovern would claim to the bank that he had lost the checks, knowing that according to highly advertised traveler's check policy the issuer would promptly "refund" his "lost" checks. If the scheme was successful, either the businesses or the issuer of the checks would bear the loss.

Citibank, one of the planned victims under the scheme, issued the checks to McGovern through a Niagara Falls, New York, bank. The purchase agreement that McGovern signed stated:

The purchaser agrees to sign each check in the upper left corner at the time of purchase with the same signature used in signing this agreement; and to countersign each check in the lower left corner when cashed, in the presence of the person cashing it.

Not attuned to the consequences of crossing state lines, McGovern then proceeded to Erie, Pennsylvania, thereby vesting the federal authorities with jurisdiction over the conspirators' activities. There, tutored by McGovern, Scull practiced imitating McGovern's signature, and then, armed with his co-conspirator's driver's license as identification, Scull entered two Erie banks and a GTE store where he cashed the checks and collected $2,400. Playing out the scenario, McGovern then reported to the New York police that his checks had been stolen from his automobile while in Buffalo; one day later he reported the loss to Citibank and, not surprisingly, Citibank issued McGovern $2,400 in replacement checks.

II.

As explained in detail by Chief Judge Weber, forgery in § 2314 means what the term meant under common law in 1823. Common law forgery has three elements: (a) The false making or material alteration (b) with intent to defraud (c) of a writing which, if genuine, might be of legal efficacy.

McGovern and Scull contend that under the facts, the first element cannot be established. They rely on the common law precept that authority to sign another's name to a written instrument negates a charge of forgery regardless of fraud or falsehood in the transaction. Whatever validity this argument may have in other contexts, we do not believe that those cases control a traveler's check transaction.

The purchaser's agreement to sign each traveler's check at the time of purchase and to counter-sign the checks only in the presence of the person cashing them, in our view, invalidates his attempt to authorize another to sign his name. As the fifth circuit observed in Berry v. United States, 271 F.2d 775, 777 (5th Cir.1959), cert. denied, 362 U.S. 903, 80 S.Ct. 612, 4 L.Ed.2d 555 (1960), traveler's checks are unique. Unlike other negotiable instruments, they are cashed not on the credit of the negotiator, but on the credit of the issuer together with the conformity of the negotiator's signature with that on the face of the instrument. These instruments are negotiated freely because of the assured credit of the check issuer and relative ease of determining signature validity. The traveler's check contract clearly denies the purchaser the right to authorize another to sign for him and the reason seems clear: a representative signature complicates the negotiation process and thereby dilutes the advantage of ready acceptance. Without authority to delegate the check-cashing power to another, a purported delegation is of no effect under the law of agency. Thus, the decisions holding that authority to sign another's name negates a charge of "false making" are *a fortiori* inapplicable to this case.

Moreover, under the facts presented here, the businesses cashing the checks were deliberately deceived into believing that the person signing the checks was the purchaser. They, as much as Citibank, were defrauded in the transaction because Scull was impersonating McGovern. This case, therefore, differs from cases in which the person accepting the instrument was informed of the purported authorization. If the authorization was valid, there would be no forgery and no defrauding of the cashing person. Of course, a person who cashes a traveler's check in those circumstances is on notice that the issuer of the check may refuse to honor the instrument because of an invalid signature. But the knowledge of the cashing person that the person signing is acting in a representative capacity negates a charge of forgery. When the person signing the traveler's checks is an imposter, however, his unauthorized signature on a traveler's check, when accompanied by an intent to defraud, constitutes common law forgery.

McGovern, the purchaser of the traveler's checks, knew the effect his actions would have on Citibank and on the business cashing them—indeed, appellants conceded that this was the sole purpose of having Scull sign the checks. Scull was an imposter and possessed no authority to sign the checks because McGovern could not grant him this authority. When coupled with the appellants' intent to defraud, the unauthorized signature on the otherwise legally sufficient instruments constituted common law forgery. The elements of the offense having been established we conclude that the convictions must stand.

III.

Accordingly, for the foregoing reasons and as more elaborately set forth by the district court, the judgment of the district court will be affirmed.[80]

SECTION 10.   COUNTERFEITING

Counterfeiting is the unlawful making of false money in the similitude of the genuine. As a federal crime it belongs in a different category—offenses affecting sovereignty or the administration of governmental functions (Chapter 5, Section 3). But since counterfeiting is for the purpose of defrauding others, both counterfeiting and knowingly uttering counterfeit money are offenses against property and punishable as felonies under many of the state statutes. The offense is defined under state and federal statutes.

SECTION 11.   EXTORTION

Common-law extortion is the corrupt collection of an unlawful fee by an officer under color of his office.[81] At common law, and for the most part under statutes, it is a misdemeanor.

Statutory extortion, including blackmail, is either (1) the unlawful extraction of money or other value by means of a threat not sufficient for robbery, or (2) a communication for the purpose of such extraction. It is usually a felony.

MODEL PENAL CODE

Article 223.   Theft and Related Offenses[82]

"Theft is any of the following acts done with intent to deprive the owner permanently of the possession, use or benefit of his property.

"1. Obtaining or exerting unauthorized control over property;

"2. Obtaining by deception control over property;

"3. Obtaining by threat control over property; or

"4. Obtaining control over stolen property knowing the property to have been stolen...."

This was held "in its entirety, to be unconstitutional" (void for vagueness). Rowell v. Smith, 534 P.2d 689 (Okl.Cr.1975).

Section 223.0   Definitions.

In this Article, unless a different meaning plainly is required:

(1) "deprive" means: (a) to withhold property of another permanently or for so extended a period as to appropriate a major portion of its economic value, or with intent to restore only upon payment of reward or other compensation;

---

80. 18 U.S.C.A. § 2314 prohibiting interstate transportation of a forged security did not require proof of forgery before the item is taken across state lines. McElroy v. United States, 455 U.S. 642, 102 S.Ct. 1332 (1982).

81. *See* 18 U.S.C. § 1951; People v. Norris, 40 Cal.3d 51, 219 Cal.Rptr. 7, 706 P.2d 1141 (1985); Evans v. United States, 504 U.S. 255, 112 S.Ct. 1881, 119 L.Ed.2d 57 (1992).

82. The Oklahoma statute on theft (21 O.S.Supp.1974, § 1733) read as follows:

or (b) to dispose of the property so as to make it unlikely that the owner will recover it.

(2) "financial institution" means ...

(3) "government" means ...

(4) "movable property" means property the location of which can be changed, including things growing on, affixed to, or found in land, and documents although the rights represented thereby have no physical location. "Immovable property" is all other property.

(5) "obtain" means: (a) in relation to property, to bring about a transfer or purported transfer of a legal interest in the property, whether to the obtainer or another; or (b) in relation to labor or service, to secure performance thereof.

(6) "property" means anything of value, including real estate, tangible and intangible personal property, contract rights, choses-in-action and other interests in or claims to wealth, admission or transportation tickets, captured or domestic animals, food and drink, electric or other power.

(7) "property of another" includes property in which any person other than the actor has an interest which the actor is not privileged to infringe, regardless of the fact that the actor also has an interest in the property and regardless of the fact that the other person might be precluded from civil recovery because the property was used in an unlawful transaction or was subject to forfeiture as contraband. Property in possession of the actor shall not be deemed property of another who has only a security interest therein, even if legal title is in the creditor pursuant to a conditional sales contract or other security agreement.

Section 223.1 Consolidation of Theft Offenses; Grading; Provisions Applicable to Theft Generally.

(1) Consolidation of Theft Offenses. Conduct denominated theft in this Article constitutes a single offense. An accusation of theft may be supported by evidence that it was committed in any manner that would be theft under this Article, notwithstanding the specification of a different manner in the indictment or information, subject only to the power of the Court to ensure fair trial by granting a continuance or other appropriate relief where the conduct of the defense would be prejudiced by lack of fair notice or by surprise.

(2) Grading of Theft Offenses.

(a) Theft constitutes a felony of the third degree if the amount involved exceeds $500, or if the property stolen is a firearm, automobile, airplane, motor cycle, motor boat or other motor-propelled vehicle, or in the case of theft by receiving stolen property, if the receiver is in the business of buying or selling stolen property.

(b) Theft not within the preceding paragraph constitutes a misdemeanor, except that if the property was not taken from the person or by threat, or in breach of a fiduciary obligation, and the actor proves by a preponderance of the evidence that the amount involved was less than $50, the offense constitutes a petty misdemeanor.

(c) The amount involved in a theft shall be deemed to be the highest value, by any reasonable standard, of the property or services which the actor stole or attempted to steal. Amounts involved in thefts committed pursuant to one scheme or course of conduct, whether from the same person or several persons, may be aggregated in determining the grade of the offense.

(3) Claim of Right. It is an affirmative defense to prosecution for theft that the actor:

(a) was unaware that the property or service was that of another; or

(b) acted under an honest claim of right to the property or service involved or that he had a right to acquire or dispose of it as he did; or

(c) took property exposed for sale, intending to purchase and pay for it promptly, or reasonably believing that the owner, if present, would have consented.

(4) Theft from Spouse. It is no defense that theft was from the actor's spouse, except that misappropriation of household and personal effects, or other property normally accessible to both spouses, is theft only if it occurs after the parties have ceased living together.

Section 223.2   Theft by Unlawful Taking or Disposition.

(1) Movable Property. A person is guilty of theft if he unlawfully takes, or exercises unlawful control over, movable property of another with purpose to deprive him thereof.

(2) Immovable Property. A person is guilty of theft if he unlawfully transfers immovable property of another or any interest therein with purpose to benefit himself or another not entitled thereto.

Section 223.3   Theft by Deception.

A person is guilty of theft if he purposely obtains property of another by deception. A person deceives if he purposely:

(1) creates or reinforces a false impression, including false impressions as to law, value, intention or other state of mind; but deception as to a person's intention to perform a promise shall not be inferred from the fact alone that he did not subsequently perform the promise; or

(2) prevents another from acquiring information which would affect his judgment of a transaction; or

(3) fails to correct a false impression which the deceiver previously created or reinforced, or which the deceiver knows to be influencing another to whom he stands in a fiduciary or confidential relationship; or

(4) fails to disclose a known lien, adverse claim or other legal impediment to the enjoyment of property which he transfers or encumbers in consideration for the property obtained, whether such impediment is or is not valid, or is or is not a matter of official record.

The term "deceive" does not, however, include falsity as to matters having no pecuniary significance, or puffing by statements unlikely to deceive ordinary persons in the group addressed.

Section 223.4   Theft by Extortion.

A person is guilty of theft if he purposely obtains property of another by threatening to:

(1) inflict bodily injury on anyone or commit any other criminal offense; or

(2) accuse anyone of a criminal offense; or

(3) expose any secret tending to subject any person to hatred, contempt or ridicule, or to impair his credit or business repute; or

(4) take or withhold action as an official, or cause an official to take or withhold action; or

(5) bring about or continue a strike, boycott or other collective unofficial action, if the property is not demanded or received for the benefit of the group in whose interest the actor purports to act; or

(6) testify or provide information or withhold testimony or information with respect to another's legal claim or defense; or

(7) inflict any other harm which would not benefit the actor.

It is an affirmative defense to prosecution based on paragraphs (2), (3) or (4) that the property obtained by threat of accusation, exposure, lawsuit or other invocation of official action was honestly claimed as restitution or indemnification for harm done in the circumstances to which such accusation, exposure, lawsuit or other official action relates, or as compensation for property or lawful services.

Section 223.5   Theft of Property Lost, Mislaid, or Delivered by Mistake.

A person who comes into control of property of another that he knows to have been lost, mislaid, or delivered under a mistake as to the nature or amount of the property or the identity of the recipient is guilty of theft if, with purpose to deprive the owner thereof, he fails to take reasonable measures to restore the property to a person entitled to have it.

Section 223.6   Receiving Stolen Property.

(1) Receiving. A person is guilty of theft if he purposely receives, retains, or disposes of movable property of another knowing that it has been stolen, or believing that it has probably been stolen, unless the property is received, retained, or disposes with purpose to restore it to the owner. "Receiving" means acquiring possession, control or title, or lending on the security of the property.

(2) Presumption of Knowledge. The requisite knowledge or belief is presumed in the case of a dealer who:

(a) is found in possession or control of property stolen from two or more persons on separate occasions; or

(b) has received stolen property in another transaction within the year preceding the transaction charged; or

(c) being a dealer in property of the sort received, acquires it for a consideration which he knows is far below its reasonable value.

"Dealer" means a person in the business of buying or selling goods, or a pawnbroker.

Section 223.7   Theft of Services.

(1) A person is guilty of theft if he purposely obtains services which he knows are available only for compensation, by deception or threat, or by false token or other means to avoid payment for the service. "Services" includes labor, professional service, transportation, telephone or other public service, accommodation in hotels, restaurants or elsewhere, admission to exhibitions, use of vehicles or other movable property. Where compensation for service is ordinarily paid immediately upon the rendering of such service, as in the case of hotels and restaurants, refusal to pay or absconding without payment or offer to pay gives rise to a presumption that the service was obtained by deception as to intention to pay.

(2) A person commits theft if, having control over the disposition of services of others, to which he is not entitled, he knowingly diverts such services to his own benefit or to the benefit of another not entitled thereto.

Section 223.8   Theft by Failure to Make Required Disposition of Funds Received.

A person who purposely obtains property upon agreement, or subject to a known legal obligation, to make specified payment or other disposition, whether from such property or its proceeds or from his own property to be reserved in equivalent amount, is guilty of theft if he deals with the property obtained as his own and fails to make the required payment or disposition. The foregoing applies notwithstanding that it may be impossible to identify particular property as belonging to the victim at the time of the actor's failure to make the required payment or disposition. An officer or employee of the government or of a financial institution is presumed: (i) to know any legal obligation relevant to his criminal liability under this Section, and (ii) to have dealt with the property as his own if he fails to pay or account upon lawful demand, or if an audit reveals a shortage or falsification of accounts.

Section 223.9   Unauthorized Use of Automobiles and Other Vehicles.

A person commits a misdemeanor if he operates another's automobile, airplane, motorcycle, motorboat, or other motor-propelled vehicle without consent of the owner. It is an affirmative defense to prosecution under this Section that the actor reasonably believed that the owner would have consented to the operation had he known of it.[83]

---

83.   Copyright © 1962 by the American Law Institute. Reprinted with the permission of the American Law Institute.

CHAPTER 5

OTHER OFFENSES

SECTION 1.   OFFENSES AGAINST MORALITY

The whole field of substantive criminal law const
moral code. It is not exhaustive in this respect but rep
which conduct is deemed so offensive to the mor
community as to call for punishment. This frequently leads to the question.
Why are certain crimes spoken of as offenses against morality?

There is reason to believe that at a very early day in the English law
the Church preempted jurisdiction over certain types of misconduct. It is
known that the starting point of benefit of clergy was the Church's refusal
to permit members of the clergy to be tried for crime in lay courts. The
time came when benefit of clergy could be claimed only after guilt had been
established, by verdict or plea, but this was after a very substantial change
in the relative power of Church and State. Much earlier the Church had
said to the common-law judges, in effect: "If a charge of misconduct is
brought against a clergyman, that is none of your business. That is our
business; send him to us and we shall handle the matter." And for
generations this is exactly what happened.

In like manner it is more than probable that at the peak of its power
the Church made it known to the common-law judges that jurisdiction over
certain types of misconduct belonged exclusively to the ecclesiastical court.
In any event the Church did take jurisdiction over those offenses and the
common-law judges did not do so for many years—not in fact until they had
been made punishable by acts of Parliament. Prior to that time they were
no doubt referred to as "offenses only against morality".

(A) ADULTERY, FORNICATION AND ILLICIT COHABITATION

Adultery is punished as a crime under several state statutes, some of
which provide that both parties to the illicit intercourse are guilty of this
offense if either is married to a third person. Many jurisdictions have
repealed their adultery statutes.

Fornication—illicit intercourse which is not adultery—is punished in a
few states.

Illicit cohabitation is living together in a relation of either adultery or
fornication. At one time this was an offense under many of the statutes,
but has been abandoned in most jurisdictions.

None of the three was a common-law crime except that if illicit
cohabitation was so open and notorious as to create a public scandal it was
punishable.

(B) BIGAMY

Bigamy is contracting a second marriage during the existence of a prior marital relation or the marrying of more than one spouse at the same time. It was not a common-law crime but is punished under modern statutes. A few states punish the offense as polygamy.

(C) INCEST

In its broadest scope, incest is either marriage, or sexual intercourse without marriage, between persons related within the degrees in which marriage is prohibited by law. Originally it was only an ecclesiastical offense but has very generally been made a crime by statute.

(D) SEDUCTION

Although a statutory crime in some states, seduction was not punished by the common law. The statutes are not uniform, but in general seduction may be said to be illicit sexual intercourse obtained by a man with a woman whom he has induced to surrender her chastity by a promise of marriage, or in some states either by such a promise or some other seductive art.

(E) SODOMY

Sodomy is a generic term which includes both "bestiality" and "buggery".

Bestiality is carnal copulation with a beast.

Buggery is copulation *per anum*—sometimes enlarged by statute to include the case where the act is in the mouth *per os*.

Sodomy was not a crime according to the common law of England, being left to the jurisdiction of the ecclesiastical courts. It was made a felony there by early statutes generally assumed to be part of the American common law.

In *Lawrence v. Texas, infra* Chapter 1, the Supreme Court overruled *Bowers v. Hardwick* and struck down the Texas sodomy statute. The Texas statute proscribed oral and anal sex between persons of the same gender. Five justices, however, joined an opinion invalidating the law on a substantive due-process theory, which logically applies to sodomy laws that are not limited to same-gender couples. Beyond that, the implications of *Lawrence* remain open to speculation and debate.

(F) PROSTITUTION AND INDECENCY

Prostitution is the common lewdness of a person for gain. It was only an ecclesiastical offense in itself but the keeping of a bawdy house, or house of prostitution, was a common-law nuisance. Pandering is the paid procurement of a person as an inmate of a house of prostitution. The procurer is often referred to as a "pimp".

The Mann Act, or white slave traffic law, is a federal statute which provides a penalty for the interstate transportation of a person for prostitution or other illegal sexual purpose. Congress has also prohibited the transportation of minors for prostitution or prohibited sexual conduct.[1]

Salaiscooper v. Eighth Judicial District Court

Supreme Court of Nevada, 2001.
117 Nev. 892, 34 P.3d 509.

■ PER CURIAM.

INTRODUCTION

Petitioner Virginia Anchond Salaiscooper contends that, in prosecuting her for solicitation of prostitution, Clark County District Attorney Stewart Bell is engaging in impermissible unconstitutional selective prosecution that violates her right to equal protection under the law. More specifically, Salaiscooper contends that the district attorney intended to discriminate against females by implementing a policy that prohibited his deputies from entering into plea negotiations with female defendants charged with solicitation of prostitution, thereby foreclosing any possibility that they could attend a diversion class in order to avoid solicitation convictions.

Had the district attorney done as Salaiscooper alleges and, in exercising his prosecutorial discretion, intended to discriminate against women, we would agree with Salaiscooper. However, the unrefuted evidence in this matter demonstrates that the district attorney's prosecution policy differentiates between buyers of sex and sellers of sex, not between males and females. We cannot say that a prosecutor intends to discriminate against females by allowing all buyers of sex, regardless of gender, to attend a successful diversion program, which is designed solely for buyers of sex. We also cannot say that a prosecutor intends to discriminate against females by implementing a policy treating sellers of sex differently in order to deter acts of prostitution committed by those who work in the adult entertainment industry. Because we conclude that this is a case of prosecutorial discretion and not unconstitutional selective prosecution, we deny Salaiscooper's petition. . . .

Salaiscooper argues that, in enacting the policy, the district attorney engaged in impermissible and unconstitutional selective prosecution that violated her right to equal protection under the law. Specifically, Salaiscooper argues that the policy's distinction between buyers and sellers of sex is "nothing more than a facade" concealing "conscious, intentional discrimination" against women, and thereby violates the Equal Protection Clauses of the United States and Nevada Constitutions. We conclude that Salaiscooper's argument lacks merit.

"The government's decision to deny an arrestee admission into a diversion program is a decision to prosecute and [on review is treated] as a claim of selective prosecution." A defendant alleging unconstitutional selective prosecution has an onerous burden. Indeed, a district attorney is vested with immense discretion in deciding whether to prosecute a particu-

---

1.   18 U.S.C.A. § 2423 (1978).

lar defendant that "necessarily involves a degree of selectivity."[2] In exercising this discretion, the district attorney is clothed with the presumption that he acted in good faith and properly discharged his duty to enforce the laws. Although the district attorney's prosecutorial discretion is broad, it is not without limitation. The Equal Protection Clause constrains the district attorney from basing a decision to prosecute upon an unjustifiable classification, such as race, religion or gender.

The requisite analysis for a claim of unconstitutional selective prosecution is two-fold. First, the defendant has the burden to prove a prima facie case of discriminatory prosecution.[3] To establish a prima facie case, the defendant must show that a public officer enforced a law or policy in a manner that had a discriminatory effect, and that such enforcement was motivated by a discriminatory purpose.[4] A discriminatory effect is proven where a defendant shows that other persons similarly situated "are generally not prosecuted for the same conduct."[5] A discriminatory purpose or "evil eye" is established where a defendant shows that a public administrator chose a particular course of action, at least in part, because of its adverse effects upon a particular group.[6] If a defendant proves a prima facie case, the burden then shifts to the State to establish that there was a reasonable basis to justify the unequal classification.[7] Where the classification is based on gender, the court applies an intermediate standard of scrutiny; in other words, the court must conclude the unequal classification in the policy is " 'reasonable, not arbitrary, and [rests] upon some ground of difference having a fair and substantial relation to the object of the legislation.' "

In the instant case, the justice court found that the district attorney had a valid, gender-neutral motivation for creating the policy classification—to draw a distinction between buyers and sellers of sex in order to deter acts of prostitution. More specifically, the justice court found that it was reasonable for the district attorney to prohibit sellers of sex from attending the one-day diversion program because it would have no deterrent effect. The justice court opined that the classification was therefore necessary because buyers of sex should not be precluded from participating in a successful diversion program merely because such treatment would be

---

2. State v. Barman, 183 Wis.2d 180, 515 N.W.2d 493, 497 (Ct.App.1994); *see also* U.S. v. Armstrong, 517 U.S. 456, 464, 116 S.Ct. 1480, 134 L.Ed.2d 687 (1996) (" 'so long as the prosecutor has probable cause to believe that the accused committed an offense defined by statute, the decision whether or not to prosecute, and what charge to file or bring before a grand jury, generally rests entirely in his discretion' " (quoting Bordenkircher v. Hayes, 434 U.S. 357, 364, 98 S.Ct. 663, 54 L.Ed.2d 604 (1978))).

3. Yick Wo v. Hopkins, 118 U.S. 356, 373–74, 6 S.Ct. 1064, 30 L.Ed. 220 (1886) (holding that laws that are administered with an "unequal hand" and an "evil eye" are unconstitutional); *see also* Armstrong, 517 U.S. at 464–65, 116 S.Ct. 1480.

4. *See* Armstrong, 517 U.S. at 464–65, 116 S.Ct. 1480.

5. U.S. v. Aguilar, 883 F.2d 662, 706 (9th Cir.1989) (citing U.S. v. Wilson, 639 F.2d 500, 503 (9th Cir.1981)).

6. Wayte v. U.S., 470 U.S. 598, 610, 105 S.Ct. 1524, 84 L.Ed.2d 547 (1985); State v. McCollum, 159 Wis.2d 184, 464 N.W.2d 44 (Wis.Ct.App.1990); *Armstrong,* 517 U.S. at 465, 116 S.Ct. 1480.

7. Minneapolis v. Buschette, 307 Minn. 60, 240 N.W.2d 500, 505 (1976).

ineffective in rehabilitating the sellers. Finally, the justice court found that there was "nothing sinister" about the district attorney's primary goal of obtaining solicitation of prostitution convictions against sellers of sex so that he could revoke their work cards and, ultimately, stop prostitutes from working in the adult entertainment industry.

The lower court's findings with respect to the district attorney's motivation and intent underlying the policy are findings of fact to be given deference, and they should not be reversed if supported by substantial evidence. The district court correctly concluded that there is substantial evidence in support of the justice court's factual findings. In particular, Dr. Murphy testified that the diversion class would not be an effective deterrent for sex sellers because they would need a one-year rehabilitation program in light of the deeply-entrenched culture of drug abuse, psychological abuse, and violence associated with prostitution. Moreover, Officer Davis testified that the district attorney needed solicitation convictions against sellers of sex so that Metro could revoke their work cards and eradicate prostitution from the strip clubs. Because the State presented evidence that the purpose of the policy's buyer/seller distinction was to deter acts of prostitution, the justice court's findings that the policy did not run afoul of the Equal Protection Clause is supported by substantial evidence.

Other jurisdictions have reached an analogous conclusion, holding that it is constitutionally permissible to treat prostitutes differently than the customers who patronize them. In *People v. Superior Court of Alameda County*,[8] the Supreme Court of California, sitting en banc, held that it was permissible for law enforcement officials to target sellers of sex, because the "sexually unbiased policy of concentrating its enforcement effort on the 'profiteer'" was not initiated by an intent to discriminate. The court reasoned that the policy was created because of the belief that focusing criminal prosecution on the sellers of sex had the most deterrent effect: "Prostitutes, the municipal court found, average five customers per night; the average customer does not patronize prostitutes five times a year. Because of an effective grapevine, arrest of one prostitute by an undercover officer will deter others, at least for a time."[9]

Like the law enforcement officials in *Alameda*, the law enforcement officials in Clark County believed that targeting sex sellers would deter

---

8. 138 Cal.Rptr. 66 (1977). Sellers of sex were "targeted": (1) by utilizing male police officer "decoys"; (2) where no decoy was used, by arresting only the prostitute and letting the buyer go free; and (3) even in instances where both were arrested, the prostitute would be subject to custodial arrest and quarantine, where the male customer would be released on his own recognizance.

9. *Id.* This identical reasoning was also set forth in *Buschette*, 240 N.W.2d at 505, which held that it was permissible for the police to arrest prostitutes, and not their customers, because "the arrest of one seller will prevent more occurrences of the behavior proscribed by the ordinance in question than the arrest of a number of buyers." In so holding, the *Buschette* court emphasized that: " '[p]lainly, it is outside the province of a trial court to direct a police department, whose manpower is already severely strained in coping with the increase in such major felonies as murder, robbery, rape, and other assaults, how best to utilize its personnel in the enforcement of a relatively minor misdemeanor statute.' " *Id.* at 505–06 (quoting U.S. v. Wilson, 342 A.2d 27, 32–33 (D.C.App.1975) (Reilly, C.J., concurring)).

future acts of prostitution. The State presented evidence in support of its belief that a one-day class would not stop a prostitute from selling sex. . . .

CONCLUSION

In light of our conclusion that the policy does not violate the Equal Protection Clauses of the United States and Nevada Constitutions, we conclude that extraordinary relief is not warranted in this matter. The legislature has vested the district attorney with prosecutorial discretion, and we conclude it is within the purview of the district attorney's prosecution powers to treat buyers of sex differently than sellers of sex. After all, the decision to prosecute, including the offer of a plea bargain, is a complex decision involving multiple considerations, including prior criminal history, the gravity of the offense, the need to punish, the possibility of rehabilitation, and the goal to deter future crime. Unless a defendant can prove that a district attorney's decision to prosecute arose from an impermissible desire to discriminate on the basis of race, gender or other protected class, our federal and state constitutions do not compel our intervention. Because there is no evidence of a discriminatory motive in the case before us, we deny Salaiscooper's petition.

(G) OBSCENITY

Obscenity is that which is offensive to public sensibilities about sexual conduct. It is material which deals with sex in a manner appealing to prurient interest, portrays sex in a patently offensive way, and which, taken as a whole, does not have serious literary, artistic, political or scientific value.[10]

Indecency is often used with the same meaning, but may also include anything which is outrageously disgusting. These were not the names of common-law crimes, but were words used in describing or identifying certain deeds which were.

An obscene libel is a writing, book or picture of such an obscene nature as to shock the public sense of decency. It was a misdemeanor at common law to publish such a libel. Today the offense is virtually unknown.

Indecent exposure of the person in public is a common-law nuisance, as is also the public utterance of obscene or profane language in such a manner as to seriously annoy the public and constitute obscene expression.[11]

The Model Penal Code suggests something of a return to the original position. It does not penalize nonviolent, uncommercialized sexual sins—fornication, adultery, sodomy or other consensual illicit sexual activity not involving imposition upon children, mental incompetents, wards or other dependents. The position taken is that such matters are best left to religious, educational or other social influences. It does penalize open lewdness, by which others are likely to be affronted or alarmed (Section

---

10.   Miller v. California, 413 U.S. 15, 23, 93 S.Ct. 2607, 2614, 37 L.Ed.2d 419 (1973). A reasonable person standard applies. Pope v. Illinois, 481 U.S. 497, 107 S.Ct. 1918, 95 L.Ed.2d 439 (1987). A less exacting standard applies to child pornography. New York v. Ferber, 458 U.S. 747, 102 S.Ct. 3348, 73 L.Ed.2d 1113 (1982).

11.   Baker v. Glover, 776 F.Supp. 1511 (M.D.Ala. 1991).

251.1), professional prostitution (Section 251.2), and commercialized obscenity (Section 251.4). Also forbidden under penalty are bigamy and polygamy (Section 230.1), incest (Section 230.2) and unjustified abortion (Section 230.3).[12] What is said above gives the traditional definition of prostitution, but modern criminal law has been forced to recognize the male prostitute, particularly in regard to homosexual and other deviate sexual relations. This suggests the following definition:

The California court held that the public nuisance statutes may properly regulate the exhibition of obscene material to consenting adults.[13] It was mentioned that the Supreme Court had categorically disapproved the theory "that obscene, pornographic films acquire constitutional immunity from state regulation simply because they are exhibited for consenting adults only."[14] However, a nuisance ordinance directed at controlling obscene material may be so broadly drawn as to constitute an invalid prior restraint.[15]

SECTION 2.   OFFENSES AGAINST THE PUBLIC PEACE

(A) BREACH OF THE PEACE

Misconduct which disturbs the peace and tranquillity of the community may have a special name, such as affray. If not, it is called "breach of the peace", "disturbing the peace," "public disturbance", or "disorderly conduct". Statutes often describe specific conduct as disorderly conduct.[16]

(B) FIGHTING

There is no common-law crime known as "fighting" but a fight (other than a friendly contest of strength or skill) usually constitutes a crime. It may be only an assault and battery—by one, if the other is not exceeding his privilege of self-defense—otherwise by both.

An *affray* is a mutual fight in a public place to the terror or alarm of the public. It is a common-law misdemeanor. Prize-fighting was not punishable at common law unless held in a public place. In some states it is prohibited, in some it is an offense unless licensed by public authority.

(C) UNLAWFUL ASSEMBLY, ROUT AND RIOT

Each of these was a misdemeanor at common law.

---

12. For presentations of the Code's position on these matters see the Model Penal Code, Tent. Draft No. 4 pp. 204–238; Tent. Draft No. 6 pp. 5–95; Tent. Draft No. 9 pp. 146–162. And for a scholarly discussion see Schwartz, Morals Offenses and the Model Penal Code, 63 Colum.L.Rev. 669 (1963).

13. People ex rel. Busch v. Projection Room Theater, 17 Cal.3d 42, 130 Cal.Rptr. 328, 550 P.2d 600 (1976).

14. Paris Adult Theatre I v. Slaton, 413 U.S. 49, 57, 93 S.Ct. 2628, 2635, 37 L.Ed.2d 446 (1973).

15. Vance v. Universal Amusement Co., Inc., 445 U.S. 308, 100 S.Ct. 1156, 63 L.Ed.2d 413 (1980); Arcara v. Cloud Books, Inc., 478 U.S. 697, 106 S.Ct. 3172, 92 L.Ed.2d 568 (1986).

16. West's Cal. Penal Code § 647 (1996).

An *unlawful assembly* is a meeting of three or more persons with intent to—

(a) commit a crime by force or violence, or

(b) execute a common design, lawful or unlawful, in a manner likely to cause courageous persons to apprehend a breach of the peace.

A *rout* is the movement of unlawful assemblers on the way to carry out their common design.

A *riot* is a tumultuous disturbance by unlawful assemblers in the execution of their plan.[17]

Three or more persons who happen to be together for some other purpose could suddenly engage in a riot. On the other hand they might gather at one place to make plans, go to another place and there accomplish their purpose. If so, they have committed three offenses at common law. Under some statutes a riot may be a felony, and under some no more than two persons are required for any of these three offenses. Rout has frequently been omitted from the codes.

(D) DISTURBANCE OF PUBLIC ASSEMBLY

Any unauthorized disturbance of a public assembly is a misdemeanor at common law, except that it would be excused if quite unintentional.

(E) DISORDERLY HOUSE

Any house in which disorderly persons are permitted to congregate, and to disturb the tranquility of the neighborhood by fighting, quarreling, swearing or other type of disorder, is a disorderly house; and the keeping thereof is a misdemeanor at common law. Statutes often encompass keeping or operating a house of prostitution.

(F) FORCIBLE ENTRY AND DETAINER

A mere trespass upon the land of another is not a crime, but if an entry is accomplished by force or intimidation; or if such methods are employed for detention after peaceable entry, there is a crime according to English law known as forcible entry and detainer. Whether it was punishable by the English common law or not it was made a crime by English statutes old enough to be common law in this country.

Any unlawful act of forcible entry or detainer will involve some other crime, such as an assault. For this reason it is omitted from some penal codes. Modern codes often refer to the offense as trespass but require some conduct beyond that which would be required for civil liability.[18]

---

17. Illegal conduct is not protected merely because it is in part carried out by language. When clear and present danger of riot appears, the power of the state to prevent or punish is clear. People v. Davis, 68 Cal.2d 481, 67 Cal.Rptr. 547, 439 P.2d 651 (1968).

18. Defendant who attended classes after her application for admission to a university was refused and temporary permission to attend classes was revoked committed a trespass. City of Kansas City v. Estill, 717 S.W.2d 258 (Mo.App.1986).

(G) LIBEL

Libel is the malicious publication of durable defamation. A common explanation is that the malicious publication of defamation is slander if oral and libel if written. This gives the idea in a general way but libel may be committed without writing, as by hanging a man in effigy. In law "publication" means to make known, and showing the defamatory matter is sufficient. Any intentional publication of defamation is malicious in the absence of some justification or excuse.

Most of the libel cases in modern times have been tort cases and there is substantial support for the view that this is an area properly left to control by civil sanctions. It is not included in the Model Penal Code.[19]

(H) CARRYING WEAPONS

Because of its tendency to stir up breaches of the peace, "terrifying the good people of the land by *riding or going armed* with dangerous or unusual weapons" was a common-law misdemeanor. Apparently the wearing of a sword in the customary manner by a person "of quality" was not deemed alarming, for this was not an offense; but the position of one of lower degree was less fortunate.

Unlike the theory of the ancient law which regarded the display of arms in a manner calculated to cause alarm as the harm to be prevented, the modern basic statute has been directed against the carrying of *concealed* weapons. Some of the provisions do not go beyond this but some do—such as the clause forbidding the carrying of a pistol or revolver "whether concealed or otherwise" in a vehicle, without a license therefor.

Many modern statutes prohibit carrying a weapon in connection with another offense or increase the punishment when a weapon is used.[20]

(I) VAGRANCY

The Statute of Labourers, enacted in 1349, provided for the imprisonment of an able-bodied male under sixty, without means of support, who refused to work. It was preventive rather than punitive because incarceration could be avoided by giving assurance that work would be undertaken, supported by a bond with acceptable surety. The primary purpose was to require the man without means to work for a living rather than to gain subsistence by begging, but this was not all. If the man without means found it difficult to satisfy all his desires by begging he might be tempted to try other methods even more antisocial in their nature, hence the enforcement of this statute may well have had a tendency to prevent crime.

Modern vagrancy statutes include proscriptions against living in idleness without visible means of support; roaming, wandering or loitering; begging; being a common prostitute, drunkard, beggar or gambler; and sleeping outdoors or in a non-residential building without permission.

---

19. Illinois defamation statute is limited to fighting words. People v. Heinrich, 104 Ill.2d 137, 83 Ill.Dec. 546, 470 N.E.2d 966 (1984).

20. 18 U.S.C. § 924(c).

Many of the provisions of the vagrancy statutes have been held to be unconstitutional either because of vagueness or because of imposing a punishment for conduct that is not properly punishable.

The Model Penal Code (Sec. 250.6) would omit the provisions of the present vagrancy statutes and substitute a section on "loitering or prowling". It would authorize the arrest of one loitering or prowling in a place, time or manner unusual for law-abiding individuals and under circumstances that warrant alarm for the safety of persons or property. This would constitute what the Code calls a "violation", meaning that it would be punishable only by fine, not by a jail sentence. It is not entirely certain that it could withstand a constitutional attack.

SECTION 3. OFFENSES AFFECTING SOVEREIGNTY OR THE ADMINISTRATION OF GOVERNMENTAL FUNCTIONS

(A) TREASON

Treason against the United States is defined by the Constitution and consists only "in levying war against them, or in adhering to their enemies, giving them aid and comfort". Breach of allegiance is the essence of treason and hence this offense cannot be committed by a non-resident foreigner.

(B) PERJURY AND SUBORNATION

The common law had two similar offenses, both misdemeanors. Perjury is a false oath in a judicial proceeding in regard to a material matter.[21] A false oath is a wilful and corrupt sworn statement without sincere belief in its truthfulness. False swearing is what would be perjury except that it is not in a judicial proceeding but in some other proceeding or matter in which an oath is required by law. Many of the statutes combine the two under the name of perjury, which is now usually a felony. An affirmation is now generally recognized as the legal equivalent of an oath. And constructive perjury does not require either oath or affirmation, being a signature attached "under the penalties of perjury".

Subornation of perjury is the procurement of perjury by another.

(C) BRIBERY

Bribery is the corrupt conveyance or receipt of a private price for official action.[22] It was a common-law misdemeanor and is frequently a felony under modern statutes. There has been a tendency for legislation to extend the offense beyond the original field of official bribery. Such enactments may provide a penalty for quasi-official bribery (such as bribery of employees of public institutions), commercial bribery (as where a wholesaler bribes an agent of a retailer), or bribery in sports.

---

21. Perjury is committed when a defendant takes a lawful oath in a judicial proceeding and swears willfully and falsely to a material matter in issue. Smith v. State, 51 Md.App. 408, 443 A.2d 985 (1982).

22. *See* People v. Diedrich, 31 Cal.3d 263, 182 Cal.Rptr. 354, 643 P.2d 971 (1982).

(D) MISCONDUCT IN OFFICE (OFFICIAL MISCONDUCT)

Misconduct in office is corrupt misbehavior by an officer in the exercise of the duties of his office or while acting under color of his office.

Common-law extortion is the corrupt collection of an unlawful fee by an officer under color of his office. (Statutory extortion is what is popularly known as blackmail.)[23]

If the illegal act of the officer, done corruptly to the harm of another and under color of his office, takes some form other than extortion the offense is known as oppression. If the illegal and corrupt act of the officer takes the form of a fraud or breach of trust affecting the public it is known as fraud by an officer or breach of trust by an officer. If it takes the form of wilful forbearance to perform a duty of his office it is called neglect of official duty.

Many jurisdictions prohibit public official conflicts of interest or impose restrictions on "ethics" of public officials and employees.

(E) EMBRACERY

Embracery is an attempt, by corrupt and wrongful means, to influence a juror in regard to a verdict to be found.

(F) COUNTERFEITING

Counterfeiting is the unlawful making of false money in the similitude of the genuine.

(G) OBSTRUCTION OF JUSTICE

Any wilful act of corruption, intimidation or force which tends to distort or impede the administration of law, either civil or criminal, is an offense usually known as obstruction of justice, unless it has been given a special name, such as bribery or embracery. One of the common forms of this offense involves an interference with a public officer in the discharge of his official duty.[24]

(H) ESCAPE AND KINDRED OFFENSES

Escape is unauthorized departure of a prisoner from legal custody without the use of force. If the escape is by use of force the offense is *prison breach,* or breach of prison. These two common-law offenses are frequently combined under the name of "escape" in modern statutes.[25]

---

23. The Hobbs Antiracketeering Act, 18 U.S.C.A. § 1951 (1970) makes it a federal crime to obstruct commerce by extortion and reaches actions done under color of official right. United States v. Rabbitt, 583 F.2d 1014 (8th Cir.1978).

24. Defendant who destroyed documents subpoenaed in connection with a grand jury investigation could be convicted of obstruction of justice. United States v. McKnight, 799 F.2d 443 (8th Cir.1986).

25. **D**'s claim that he had been improperly convicted of attempted burglary is no defense to the charge of attempted escape. Self-help is not an acceptable method of challenging the legality of a conviction. United States v. Haley, 417 F.2d 625 (4th Cir.1969).

If the officer in charge of a prisoner permits him to escape the officer is guilty of the offense of *permitting escape,* which is usually punishable more severely if intentional than if merely negligent.

Rescue is forcibly freeing a prisoner from lawful custody.

Violation of parole is commonly made an offense by statute.

(I) MISPRISION OF FELONY

Misprision of felony is concealment and (or) nondisclosure of the known felony of another. In ancient times when the Hue and Cry was at the peak point of its importance, the private person, who was required to join in the chase in the effort to track down the felon, may have had a duty to report any known felony in order that the Hue and Cry might be started. It is said that in 1314 those present when *murder* was committed, and did not report it, were fined.[26] If there was ever a duty to report every known felony it tended to disappear at a very early day and years ago. Judge Stephen referred to the "practically obsolete offense of misprision."[27] However, it is not entirely obsolete in England, and one who failed to disclose knowledge of the theft of 100 pistols, 4 submachine guns and 1960 rounds of ammunition was convicted of misprision of felony.[28] But it seems that the use of this offense in England is limited to crimes of an "aggravated complexion."[29]

In this country, misprision of felony in the form of mere non-disclosure of a known felony, is rare indeed. The federal Code of Crimes has a section entitled "misprision of felony."[30] It is not violated, however, by mere nondisclosure of a known felony. Something in the way of concealment is required.[31] It was held that the section does not violate the privilege against self-incrimination because it requires concealment in addition to nondisclosure.[32] Most of the states do not recognize misprision of felony in any form, and it is not included in the Model Penal Code.

---

26. Year Books of Edward II, 24 Seldon Society 152–53.

27. 2 Stephen History of the Criminal Law of England 238 (1883).

28. Sykes v. Director of Public Prosecutions, [1961] 3 All.Eng.L.Rep. 33.

29. Williams, Criminal Law, 423 (2d ed. 1961).

30. 18 U.S.C. sec. 4 (1973).

31. Neal v. United States, 102 F.2d 643, 649 (8th Cir.1939).

Misprision of felony under 18 U.S.C. § 4, requires some act of concealment. Mere failure to report a known felony is not sufficient. United States v. Johnson, 546 F.2d 1225 (5th Cir.1977).

32. United States v. Daddano, 432 F.2d 1119 (7th Cir.1970).

Misprision of felony under the federal statute requires more than mere nondisclosure of a known federal felony. And even if this element is found **D** could not be convicted of misprision if his disclosure of the felony might tend to cause him to be charged with complicity therein. United States v. King, 402 F.2d 694 (9th Cir.1968).

The statute relating to harboring and concealing a person from arrest proscribes acts calculated to obstruct efforts of authorities to effect the arrest of a fugitive, but it does not impose a duty on one who is aware of the whereabouts of a fugitive to reveal this information on pain of criminal prosecution. United States v. Foy, 416 F.2d 940 (7th Cir.1969).

(J) COMPOUNDING CRIME

Following the lead of an English statute in the 1500s it has been common to authorize the compromise of certain crimes, usually with the court's consent as a requirement. It is an offense known as compounding crime to accept anything of value under an agreement not to prosecute a known offender for any offense unless the compromise is authorized by law.[33]

(K) CONTEMPT

Misconduct adversely affecting the administration of a governmental function may take the form of improper interference with the work of the legislative body or of the court. In England either house of Parliament could commit for contempt of itself, and in this country the power to commit for contempt extends to the Senate and House of Representatives of the United States and to the corresponding bodies of the respective states. Such contempt includes any insult to the legislative body in the form of disrespectful or disorderly conduct in its presence and also any wilful obstruction of the performance of a legislative function. Such misconduct, it is to be noted, is not indictable but is punished by the legislative body itself. Contempt of Congress, or its committees, has been made a misdemeanor by statute and hence such misbehavior may now be dealt with the same as any other offense of corresponding grade.

Under the common law of England courts had the inherent power to punish for contempt and this has been accepted as a part of our common law at least so far as courts of record are concerned. Contempt of court has been classified in two different ways: (a) depending upon the purpose of the proceeding, into (1) civil contempt and (2) criminal contempt, and (b) depending upon the factor of proximity or remoteness, into (1) direct contempt and (2) constructive (indirect or consequential) contempt. Civil contempt is misconduct in the form of disobedience to an order or direction of the court by one party to a judicial proceeding to the prejudice of the other litigant. The harm is to the injured litigant rather than to the public and the "penalty" imposed, being purely coercive in purpose, can be avoided by compliance with the court's order. Thus a person who had wrongfully taken a child from its lawful guardian and disobeyed the order of the judge to bring the child into court or disclose its whereabouts was ordered committed to jail until she should obey the court's order.

A criminal contempt[34] on the other hand is misconduct which is disrespectful to the court, calculated to bring the court into disrepute, or of

---

33. Statutes sometimes require that certain persons report evidence that may indicate crime, such as requiring medical personnel to report wounds apparently resulting from violence, or requiring certain persons such as social workers or teachers to report evidence of child-abuse. See a Note, Compounding Crimes, 27 Hastings L.J. 175, 181–187 (1975). *See also* West's Cal. Penal Code § 153 (1996).

34. It had been held repeatedly that a "criminal contempt", though resembling a crime, was not a crime and hence the proceedings for the punishment thereof were not subject to the requirements of a criminal trial. For example, it was held that the contemner was not entitled to a jury trial. United States v. Barnett, 376 U.S. 681, 84 S.Ct. 984, 12 L.Ed.2d 23 (1964).

a nature which tends to obstruct the administration of justice, and the purpose of convicting for such contempt is vindication of the public interest by punishment of contemptuous conduct.[35] The same misdeed may constitute both a civil contempt and a criminal contempt and in one such case the judgment was that the contemnor be imprisoned for one day (punishment for his criminal contempt) and that after the expiration of the first day he remain in prison until he complied with the order of the court (coercive and avoidable by prompt compliance).

A direct contempt is one committed in the presence of the court, or of a judge at chambers, or so near thereto as to interrupt or hinder judicial proceedings. Illustrations include an assault on the marshal in open court or a vindictive and uncalled for remark to the court. A constructive, or indirect contempt is an act done, not in the presence of the court or a judge acting judicially, but at a distance under circumstances that reasonably tend to degrade the court or the judge as a judicial officer, or to obstruct, prevent, or embarrass the administration of justice by the court or judge.[36]

Overruling all such holdings it has now been held that a "criminal contempt" is a crime and hence if the punishment is to be more than imprisonment for six months a jury trial may be demanded. Bloom v. Illinois, 391 U.S. 194, 88 S.Ct. 1477, 20 L.Ed.2d 522 (1968). ("Any misdemeanor, the penalty for which does not exceed imprisonment for a period of six months or a fine of not more than $500, or both, is a petty offense." 18 U.S.C. § 1(3) (1968).)

During **M**'s trial in a state court, **M** acted as his own counsel and on eleven different occasions he vilified the judge in extreme fashion. After the conclusion of the trial the judge sentenced **M** to one-to-two years on each of eleven counts, or a total of 11 to 22 years. The conviction was vacated and remanded on the ground that the contempt trial should have been before a separate judge. The Court said that the judge "could, with propriety, have instantly acted, holding petitioner in contempt,...." But since he waited until the trial was over the contempt proceeding should have been before another judge. Mayberry v. Pennsylvania, 400 U.S. 455, 91 S.Ct. 499, 27 L.Ed.2d 532 (1971). *See also*, United States v. Dixon, 509 U.S. 688, 113 S.Ct. 2849, 125 L.Ed.2d 556 (1993).

Spitting on the judge in open court constitutes direct contempt of court. Knox v. Municipal Court, 185 N.W.2d 705 (Iowa 1971).

35. "[T]he critical features are the substance of the proceeding and the character of the relief that the proceeding will afford. 'If it is for civil contempt the punishment is remedial, and for the benefit of the complainant. But if it is for criminal contempt the sentence is punitive, to vindicate the authority of the court.' The character of the relief imposed is thus ascertainable by applying a few straightforward rules. If the relief provided is a sentence of imprisonment, it is remedial if 'the defendant stands committed unless and until he performs the affirmative act required by the court's order,' and is punitive if 'the sentence is limited to imprisonment for a definite period.' If the relief provided is a fine, it is remedial when it is paid to the complainant, and punitive when it is paid to the court, though a fine that would be payable to the court is also remedial when the defendant can avoid paying the fine simply by performing the affirmative act required by the court's order. These distinctions lead up to the fundamental proposition that criminal penalties may not be imposed on someone who has not been afforded the protections that the Constitution requires of such criminal proceedings, including the requirement that the offense be proved beyond a reasonable doubt." Hicks on Behalf of Feiock v. Feiock, 485 U.S. 624, 630, 632, 108 S.Ct. 1423, 1429, 1430, 99 L.Ed.2d 721 (1988).

Criminal contempt requires the defendant be afforded the protection of the constitution applicable in criminal cases. International Union, United Mine Workers of America v. Bagwell, 512 U.S. 821, 114 S.Ct. 2552, 129 L.Ed.2d 642 (1994).

36. The power to punish for contempts, inherent in all courts, reaches conduct before the court and that beyond the court's confines. Chambers v. NASCO, Inc., 501 U.S. 32, 111 S.Ct. 2123, 115 L.Ed.2d 27 (1991).

It may be committed in many ways, such for example, as by violating the judge's instructions to jurors not to separate or make contact with outsiders during trial, or by published criticism of the judicial proceedings of a nature tending to "scandalize the court" to use the familiar phrase. Insofar as a constructive contempt is in the form of a wilful violation of an order of the court, or other direct obstruction of the judicial proceedings, no difficulty is encountered; but so great and so important is the public interest in a public trial that out-of-court discussions and publications in regard to such a proceeding are protected by constitutional privilege even if they tend to cast discredit upon the court or the judge unless carried to such an extreme as to create a "clear and present danger" to the administration of justice.

(L) OTHER OFFENSES

If space permitted, numerous other offenses might be considered in this connection. An important governmental function of a democracy is the holding of elections to fill public offices and to determine certain public questions; hence penalties are provided for unlawful registration as a voter, illegal voting, and various other election offenses. Another such function is the raising of public funds; wherefore penalties are provided for failure to file a required income tax return and various other taxation offenses. Most of the states have undertaken to regulate the manufacture and sale of intoxicating liquor, and the results are certain liquor offenses. To this list might be added countless offenses connected with the regulations of trades, occupations, monopolies, banking and finance, the sale of securities and other matters of a similar nature. Only one sample will be used from this list.

Fraudulent banking. This phrase, which might be applied to other misdeeds in the banking field, is usually used only to refer to the following offense. In many states it is made a crime for an officer of a bank to accept a deposit when his bank is insolvent, to his knowledge. A few jurisdictions have made a more severe requirement, making it an offense for the officer of a bank, which is in fact insolvent, to accept a deposit when he knows *or has reason to believe* that it is insolvent. Although the distinction between these two types of legislation was overlooked in one case, the proper interpretation is this: Under the first type the banker who accepts a deposit while his bank is insolvent is excused from guilt if he believes in good faith that his bank is solvent, even if he is at fault in not being aware of the insolvency. Under the second type, the banker is not excused unless the insolvency has occurred under such unusual circumstances that he not only does not know of this fact, but is free from criminal negligence in not knowing. Some of the banking laws do not include any such provision, on the ground that whether a bank is or is not insolvent at a certain critical moment in a depression may be difficult to ascertain, and thus the threat of such a penalty may force the closing of banks which it would be in the public interest to have kept open. Many jurisdictions punish the making of false reports by business or other financial institutions in order to insure proper regulation of banking practices.

Recently, Congress has enacted extensive banking legislation covering banking fraud,[37] money laundering,[38] and bribery.[39]

---

37. 18 U.S.C.A. §§ 1344–1346 (1993).

38. 18 U.S.C.A. § 1956(a)(1) et seq. (1993); 31 U.S.C. §§ 5311–5328 (1993).

39. 18 U.S.C.A. § 215 (1993).

CHAPTER 6

IMPUTABILITY

SECTION 1. THE NECESSITY OF AN ACT

4 Blackstone, Commentaries on the Laws of England, 78–79. Let us next see what is a *compassing* or *imagining* of the death of the king & c. These are synonymous terms, the word *compass* signifying the purpose or design of the mind or will, and not, as in common speech, the carrying such design to effect.... But, as this compassing or imagining is an act of the mind, it cannot possibly fall under any judicial cognizance, unless it be demonstrated by some open or *overt* act.... There is no question, also, but that taking any measures to render such treasonable purposes effectual, as assembling and consulting on the means to kill the king, is a sufficient overt act of high treason.[1] The act necessary to be cognizable as criminal must be that required for the actus reus of the offense.

State v. Quick

Supreme Court of South Carolina, 1942.
199 S.C. 256, 19 S.E.2d 101.

■ FISHBURNE, JUSTICE. The defendant was convicted of the unlawful manufacture of intoxicating liquor under Section 1829, Code 1932, and amendments thereto. The main question in the case, as we see it, is whether the lower Court erred in refusing to direct a verdict of acquittal, a motion therefor having been made at the close of the evidence offered by the State....

We think there can be no doubt but that the evidence overwhelmingly tends to show an intention on the part of the appellant to manufacture liquor; certainly such inference may reasonably be drawn. But intent alone, not coupled with some overt act toward putting the intent into effect, is not cognizable by the Courts. The law does not concern itself with mere guilty intention, unconnected with any overt act. State v. Kelly, 114 S.C. 336, 103 S.E. 511; 14 Am.Jur., Sec. 25, Page 786....

In our opinion the defendant is entitled to a new trial in any event. But because of the error in overruling his motion for a directed verdict the judgment is reversed, with direction to enter a verdict of not guilty.

■ BONHAM, C.J., BAKER and STUKES, JJ., and WM. H. GRIMBALL, A.A.J., concur.

---

1. 18 U.S.C.A. § 871 (1976) punishes knowingly and willfully making a threat against the President. It requires proof of a true threat but it need not be communicated to the President. United States v. Frederickson, 601 F.2d 1358 (8th Cir.1979).

Mere political rhetoric is insufficient. A true threat is required. Watts v. United States, 394 U.S. 705, 89 S.Ct. 1399, 22 L.Ed.2d 664 (1969).

State v. Rider

Supreme Court of Missouri, 1886.
90 Mo. 54, 1 S.W. 825.

■ HENRY, C.J. At the September term, 1885, of the Saline criminal court the defendant was indicted for murder for killing one R.P. Tallent, and was tried at the November term of said court, 1885, and convicted of murder in the first degree. From that judgment he has appealed to this court.

The evidence for the state proved that he killed the deceased, and of that fact there is no question. It also tended to prove that he armed himself with a gun, and sought the deceased with the intent to kill him. The evidence tended to prove that the relations between the defendant and his wife were not of the most agreeable character, and that the deceased was criminally intimate with her, and on the day of the homicide had taken her off in a skiff to Brunswick. That defendant went in search of his wife to the residence of the deceased, armed with a shot gun, and met the latter near his residence. What then occurred no one witnessed, except the parties engaged, but defendant testified as follows: "Well, me and Mr. Merrill went to this path that was leading toward the river. When we come to that path Mr. Merrill stopped, and I went on in the direction of Mr. Tallent's house, to see if I could learn anything about where my wife was, and I discovered no sign of her there, and I started back north on this path, going down on the slough bank; after going down some distance from the bank I meets Mr. Tallent; I spoke to Mr. Tallent and asked him if he knew where my wife was, and he made this remark: 'I have taken her where you won't find her;' and he says, 'God damn you, we will settle this right here.' He started at me with his axe in a striking position, and I bid Mr. Tallent to stop; then he advanced a few feet, and I fired. I fired one time." The axe of deceased, found on the ground, had a shot in the handle near the end farthest from the blade, and on the same side as the blade, and this evidence had a tendency to corroborate the testimony of the accused, showing that the axe was pointing in the direction from which the shot came, and was held in an upright position.

The court, for the state, instructed the jury as follows:

"The court instructs the jury, that if they believe from the evidence that prior to the killing of the deceased, the defendant prepared and armed himself with a gun, and went in search of, and sought out, deceased, with the intention of killing him, or shooting him, or doing him some great bodily harm, and that he did find, overtake, or intercept, deceased, and did shoot and kill deceased while he was returning from the river to his home, then it makes no difference who commenced the assault, and the jury shall not acquit the defendant; and the jury are further instructed that in such case they shall disregard any and all testimony tending to show that the character or reputation of deceased for turbulency, violence, peace and quiet was bad, and they shall further disregard any and all evidence of threats made by deceased against the defendant."

The mere intent to commit a crime is not a crime. An attempt to perpetrate it is necessary to constitute guilt in law. One may arm himself with the purpose of seeking and killing an adversary, and may seek and find him, yet, if guilty of no overt act, commits no crime. It has been repeatedly held in this and nearly every state in the Union, that one against whom threats have been made by another is not justifiable in assaulting him unless the threatener makes some attempt to execute his threats. A threat to kill but indicates an intent or purpose to kill; and the unexpressed purpose or intent certainly affords no better excuse for an assault by the person against whom it exists than such an intent accompanied with a threat to accomplish it. The above instruction authorized the jury to convict the defendant even though he had abandoned the purpose to kill the deceased when he met him, and was assaulted by deceased and had to kill him to save his own life. . . .

For the errors above noted the judgment is reversed and cause remanded. All concur.[2]

SECTION 2. WHAT CONSTITUTES AN ACT

State v. Taft

Supreme Court of Appeals of West Virginia, 1958.
143 W.Va. 365, 102 S.E.2d 152.

■ GIVEN, JUDGE. . . . The indictment in the instant case is in two counts. The first count charges defendant with having driven an automobile while "under the influence of intoxicating liquor". . . . On the verdict of the jury, the judgment was that defendant serve six months in the county jail, the sentence to run consecutively to the sentence mentioned in case No. 10907. . . .

After the jury had considered of a verdict for some time, the foreman requested the trial court to answer the question, "Is there a legal definition for what constitutes driving a car?" Whereupon, over objection of defendant, the court instructed the jury "that the term 'driving' has been defined and construed as requiring that a vehicle be in motion in order for the offense to be committed." Defendant then offered, in writing, an instruction which would have told the jury "that if they believe from the evidence that defendant got in his parked car for the purpose of waiting for someone else, and that the brakes of his car accidentally released and the car drifted some two to three feet into the rear end of a car parked in front of said Taft car, and that the movement of said car was accidental, and not the act and intent of the defendant, then you are authorized to find and determine that the defendant was not then and there driving his said car, and if you so find that the defendant was not then and there driving his said car, you may find the defendant not guilty."

The statute on which the indictment is based makes it a criminal offense for a person "to drive any vehicle on any highway of this state"

---

2. Rider was tried again under proper instructions and again convicted. This conviction was affirmed. State v. Rider, 95 Mo. 474, 8 S.W. 723 (1888).

"In every crime or public offense, there must exist a union, or joint operation of act and intent, or criminal negligence." West's Cal. Penal Code § 20 (1996).

while "under the influence of intoxicating liquor"; or "under the influence of any narcotic drug." The question posed by the action of the court, as related to the instructions mentioned above, is whether the mere motion of the vehicle constituted "driving" of the vehicle, within the meaning of the statute. We think that it does not.

Though movement of a vehicle is an essential element of the statutory requirement, the mere movement of a vehicle does not necessarily, in every circumstance, constitute a "driving" of the vehicle. To "drive" a vehicle necessarily implies a driver or operator and an affirmative or positive action on the part of the driver. A mere movement of the vehicle might occur without any affirmative act by a driver, or, in fact by any person. If a vehicle is moved by some power beyond the control of the driver, or by accident, it is not such an affirmative or positive action on the part of the driver as will constitute a driving of a vehicle within the meaning of the statute. This being true, the instruction telling the jury that the vehicle must "be in motion in order for an offense to be committed" necessarily, in view of the evidence before the jury, had the effect of telling them that any accidental movement of the vehicle was sufficient to constitute a driving of the vehicle within the meaning of the statute, and constituted prejudicial error. What is said in this respect also indicates prejudicial error in the refusal to give to the jury the instruction offered by defendant, quoted above, after the giving of the instruction first mentioned. . . .

For the reasons indicated, the judgment of the circuit court is reversed, the verdict of the jury set aside, and defendant is awarded a new trial.[3]

Reversed; verdict set aside; new trial awarded.

People v. Decina

Court of Appeals of New York, 1956.
2 N.Y.2d 133, 157 N.Y.S.2d 558, 138 N.E.2d 799.

[Defendant was convicted of the statutory offense known as "criminal negligence in the operation of a vehicle resulting in death." He appealed, insisting that the court erred (1) in overruling his demurrer to the indictment and (2) in the admission of incompetent testimony. The Appellate Division held that the demurrer was properly overruled but reversed and granted a new trial on the second ground. From this determination both parties appealed.]

■ FROESSEL, JUDGE. . . . We turn first to the subject of defendant's cross appeal, namely, that his demurrer should have been sustained, since the *indictment* here does not charge a crime. The indictment states essentially

---

3. The statute makes it an offense to be in "actual physical control of a motor vehicle while under the influence of intoxicating liquor." One may be in "actual physical control" of a motor vehicle without actually driving it. Hughes v. State, 535 P.2d 1023 (Okl.Cr.1975).

A person who is asleep and whose vehicle is off the road and not running is not in actual physical control of the vehicle. State v. Bugger, 25 Utah 2d 404, 483 P.2d 442 (1971).

Defendant was in actual physical control of a vehicle where he was asleep behind the steering wheel of a vehicle stuck in a borrow pit. State v. Taylor, 203 Mont. 284, 661 P.2d 33 (1983).

that defendant, *knowing* "that he was subject to epileptic attacks or other disorder rendering him likely to lose consciousness for a considerable period of time", was culpably negligent "in that he *consciously* undertook to and *did operate* his Buick sedan on a public highway" (emphasis supplied) and "while so doing" suffered such an attack which caused said automobile "to travel at a fast and reckless rate of speed, jumping the curb and driving over the sidewalk" causing the death of 4 persons. In our opinion, this clearly states a violation of section 1053—a of the Penal Law. The statute does not require that a defendant must deliberately intend to kill a human being, for that would be murder. Nor does the statute require that he knowingly and consciously follow the precise path that leads to death and destruction. It is sufficient, we have said, when his conduct manifests a "disregard of the consequences which may ensue from the act, and indifference to the rights of others. No clearer definition, applicable to the hundreds of varying circumstances that may arise, can be given. Under a given state of facts, whether negligence is culpable is a question of judgment." People v. Angelo, 246 N.Y. 451, 457, 159 N.E. 394, 396.

Assuming the truth of the indictment, as we must on a demurrer, this defendant knew he was subject to epileptic attacks and seizures that might strike *at any time.* He also knew that a moving motor vehicle uncontrolled on a public highway is a highly dangerous instrumentality capable of unrestrained destruction. With this *knowledge,* and without anyone accompanying him, he deliberately took a chance by making a conscious choice of a course of action, in disregard of the consequences which he knew might follow from his conscious act, and which in this case did ensue. How can we say as a matter of law that this did not amount to culpable negligence within the meaning of section 1053–a?

To hold otherwise would be to say that a man may freely indulge himself in liquor in the same hope that it will not affect his driving, and if it later develops that ensuing intoxication causes dangerous and reckless driving resulting in death, his unconsciousness or involuntariness at that time would relieve him from prosecution under the statute. His awareness of a condition which he knows may produce such consequences as here, and his disregard of the consequences, renders him liable for culpable negligence, as the courts below have properly held. To have a sudden sleeping spell, an unexpected heart or other disabling attack, without any prior knowledge or warning thereof, is an altogether different situation, and there is simply no basis for comparing such cases with the flagrant disregard manifested here....

Accordingly, the Appellate Division properly sustained the lower court's order overruling the demurrer, as well as its denial of the motion in arrest of judgment on the same ground....

[The court agreed with the Appellate Division that reversible error had been committed in the admission of evidence.]

Accordingly, the order of the Appellate Division should be affirmed.[4]

---

4. A driver of a vehicle who had an epileptic seizure while driving when he knew he was subject to a seizure was responsible for the resulting homicide when defendant's vehicle struck a child. The defendant's conduct was gross negligence. Commonwealth v. Cheatham, 419 Pa.

■ DESMOND, JUDGE (concurring in part and dissenting in part).

I agree that the judgment of conviction cannot stand but I think the indictment should be dismissed because it alleges no crime. Defendant's demurrer should have been sustained. . . .

Just what is the court holding here? No less than this: that a driver whose brief blackout lets his car run amuck and kill another has killed that other by reckless driving. But any such "recklessness" consists necessarily not of the erratic behavior of the automobile while its driver is unconscious, but of his driving at all when he knew he was subject to such attacks. Thus, it must be that such a black-out-prone driver is guilty of reckless driving. Vehicle and Traffic Law, Consol.Laws, c. 71, § 58, whenever and as soon as he steps into the driver's seat of a vehicle. Every time he drives, accident or no accident, he is subject to criminal prosecution for reckless driving or to revocation of his operator's license, Vehicle and Traffic Law, § 71, subd. 3. And how many of this State's 5,000,000 licensed operators are subject to such penalties for merely driving the cars they are licensed to drive? No one knows how many citizens or how many or what kind of physical conditions will be gathered in under this practically limitless coverage of section 1053–a of the Penal Law and section 58 and subdivision 3 of section 71 of the Vehicle and Traffic Law. It is no answer that prosecutors and juries will be reasonable or compassionate. A criminal statute whose reach is so unpredictable violates constitutional rights, as we shall now show. . . .

■ CONWAY, CH. J., DYE and BURKE, JJ., concur with FROESSEL, J.; DESMOND, J., concurs in part and dissents in part in an opinion in which FULD and VAN VOORHIS, JJ., concur.

Order affirmed.

State v. Kimbrell

Supreme Court of South Carolina, 1987.
294 S.C. 51, 362 S.E.2d 630.

■ CHANDLER, JUSTICE:

Appellant Vicki Kimbrell (Kimbrell) was convicted of trafficking in cocaine and sentenced to twenty-five years imprisonment. We reverse and remand for a new trial.

FACTS

On March 31, 1986, a confidential informant (Roberts) arranged a meeting between an undercover police officer (O'Donald) and Kimbrell's ex-husband, Gene Kimbrell (Gene), a suspected drug dealer. At 5:00 that afternoon, Roberts and O'Donald went to Gene's mobile home where O'Donald bought an ounce of cocaine from Gene and agreed to purchase

Super. 603, 615 A.2d 802 (1992). *See* Forbes v. Commonwealth, 498 S.E.2d 457 (Va.App.1998) (diabetic did not act with criminal negligence in driving when he only had slight warning of a problem).

cocaine every two weeks. Although Kimbrell was present during these discussions, she did not participate in the drug transaction.

Based upon the information O'Donald had acquired during the March 31 meeting, narcotics officers obtained a warrant to search Gene's mobile home. They then planned a "buy-bust" operation. Thereafter, O'Donald called Gene and arranged for a buy of both cocaine and marijuana.

O'Donald, wearing a hidden transmitter, arrived at Gene's mobile home on the afternoon of April 3. When he and Gene went into the kitchen, O'Donald saw a small amount of cocaine on a plate and a zip-lock bag of cocaine on the kitchen counter. A set of scales was on the kitchen table.

When O'Donald asked to see the marijuana, Gene led him down the hallway towards the back door. Gene stopped at the bedroom door, knocked, and told Kimbrell "the toot (cocaine) is laying on the table, we're going outside, watch it." Kimbrell, carrying a beige pocketbook, then walked out of the bedroom and into the kitchen.

Gene and O'Donald proceeded outside and viewed the marijuana in Gene's pickup truck. When they reentered the mobile home, Kimbrell returned to the bedroom and closed the door.

O'Donald then transmitted a signal to the other officers that they should commence the bust. Kimbrell ran out from the bedroom shouting that a car had just pulled up, after which she ran back into the bedroom and closed the door. Upon their arrival, the other officers found Kimbrell sitting on the bed, the butt of a pistol protruding from her beige pocketbook.

DIRECTED VERDICT

In reviewing the denial of a motion for directed verdict in a criminal case, the evidence must be viewed in the light most favorable to the State. A jury issue is created when there is any direct or circumstantial evidence which reasonably tends to prove the guilt of the accused.

A person who is *knowingly* in actual or constructive possession of ten or more grams of cocaine is guilty of trafficking in cocaine. The thrust of Kimbrell's directed verdict motion is that the State failed to present sufficient evidence of her *knowing possession* of the cocaine seized.

An accused person has possession of contraband when he has both the power and intent to control its disposition or use. Here, the State produced evidence that Kimbrell had actual knowledge of the presence of the cocaine. Because actual knowledge of the presence of the drug is strong evidence of intent to control its disposition or use, knowledge may be equated with or substituted for the intent element. Possession may be inferred from circumstances.

From the evidence in this case it can be inferred that Kimbrell had both the power and intent to control the cocaine during the time Gene and the undercover agent were outside the mobile home.

From the record, it is patent that the State presented sufficient evidence to submit the case to the jury. While Gene's testimony as to what transpired is at variance with that of the State's witnesses, it was for the jury to resolve the disputed evidence.

. . .

MERE PRESENCE

Kimbrell argues the trial judge erred in refusing her request to charge that "mere presence, where the drugs are present, would not be sufficient to convict, without more." We agree.

It is error to refuse a requested charge on an issue raised by the indictment and the evidence presented at trial. The charge requested by Kimbrell is a correct statement of the law. The judge's charge, as given, did not adequately cover the substance of Kimbrell's request. Failure to charge on *mere presence* constitutes reversible error.[5]

Reversed and Remanded.

MODEL PENAL CODE
Article 2. General Principles of Liability

Section 2.01 Requirement of Voluntary Act; (Omission as Basis of Liability;) Possession as an Act.

(1) A person is not guilty of an offense unless his liability is based on conduct which includes a voluntary act or the omission to perform an act of which he is physically capable.

(2) The following are not voluntary acts within the meaning of this Section:

   (a) a reflex or convulsion;

   (b) a bodily movement during unconsciousness or sleep;

   (c) conduct during hypnosis or resulting from hypnotic suggestion;

   (d) a bodily movement that otherwise is not a product of the effort or determination of the actor, either conscious or habitual.

(4) Possession is an act, within the meaning of this Section, if the possessor knowingly procured or received the thing possessed or was aware of his control thereof for a sufficient period to have been able to terminate his possession.[6]

SECTION 3.   ATTEMPT AND KINDRED PROBLEMS

(A) ATTEMPT

(i) In General

Moffett v. State

Supreme Court of Nevada, 1980.
96 Nev. 822, 618 P.2d 1223.

■ PER CURIAM. Although appellant makes several assignments of error, we recognize only one as meriting discussion, namely, whether there is sufficient evidence to support the attempted murder conviction.

---

5. [Added by compiler]. Mere presence of a controlled substance in defendant's urine did not constitute possession under a statute prohibiting unlawful possession of a controlled substance. State v. Lewis, 394 N.W.2d 212 (Minn.App.1986).

Attempted possession with intent to distribute is a crime. State v. Curry, 107 N.M. 133, 753 P.2d 1321 (App.1988).

6. Copyright © 1962 by the American Law Institute. Reprinted with the permission of the American Law Institute.

In the early morning hours of August 29, 1978, the victim, Linda Exner, was asleep alone in her apartment. She was awakened by appellant, Deanna Moffett, who had begun to tie her up. Deanna was accompanied by Bobby McPherson, age 14, who held a knife to the throat of the victim. Appellant then threatened Linda and untied her hands to enable Linda to write in her own handwriting, her "suicide note" appellant had written earlier. The note provided:

Dear Ed, you might think I'm happy seeing you like this, but I'm not. I know that I will never really have you and I can't bear that. You're always looking at other girls when I'm with you, and when you don't spend the night with me, I know you are making love to someone else so I'm ending it. I love you, Linda.

Thereafter, Moffett instructed the victim to write the above message and told her that afterwards she would give her some pills to make her sleep for 48 hours.

The victim wrote approximately one line of the letter before she escaped following a struggle. The appellant and her accomplice then fled and returned to the residence of Ed McPherson where they were apprehended. Upon their arrival at Linda's apartment, the police found the following incriminating evidence: a bottle of wine, a switchblade knife, a flashlight, a bottle of pills, another knife, a short length of hemp rope, and the note.

Dr. Green, a board certified pathologist and toxicologist, testified that the pills found at the victim's apartment were sleeping pills. He stated that a high dosage was dangerous and would be fatal absent immediate and adequate medical intervention. He further testified that if alcohol was ingested in conjunction with the pills, the effect would be even more extreme.

Found guilty of both attempted murder and burglary, felonies, appellant appeals.

To prove an attempt to commit a crime, the prosecution must establish (1) the intent to commit the crime; (2) performance of some act towards its commission; and (3) failure to consummate its commission. Appellant alleges that there was insufficient evidence presented to establish the performance of some act, beyond mere preparation, toward the commission of murder. We disagree.

The preparation for a crime consists in "devising or arranging the means or measures necessary for the commission of the offense; the attempt is the direct movement towards the commission after the preparations are made." In interpreting NRS 208.070,[7] we stated in Darnell v. State, 92 Nev. at 682, 558 P.2d at 625, that a "direct but ineffectual act toward the commission of the crime" is the required *actus reus* for an attempted crime. The act need not be, as appellant herein asserts, actual commencement of the potentially death producing action.

---

7. NRS 208.070 provides in part: "An act done with intent to commit a crime, and tending but failing to accomplish it, is an attempt to commit that crime...."

Here, appellant's own testimony showed, *inter alia,* that she obtained the keys to the victim's apartment without the victim's or Ed McPherson's knowledge or consent; that she made a list of the instruments she was taking to Linda's apartment; and the night before she went to Linda's apartment she wrote the note she wanted Linda to write to Ed. After entering Linda's apartment, the appellant tied the victim's hands, woke the victim up, and started to dictate to the victim the note that appellant had previously written. Appellant further testified that she had planned the incident about two days in advance of her going to the victim's apartment. She acquired the necessary materials prior to entering the victim's apartment, then pursuant to her plan, entered the victim's apartment and exercised sufficient control over the victim to begin to effectuate her plan. Had it not been for Linda's fortuitous escape, appellant would have effectuated her purpose.

We will "not destroy the practical and common sense administration of the law with subtleties as to what constitutes preparation and [acts] done toward the commission of a crime." Appellant clearly took sufficient steps beyond mere preparation, to support the attempted murder conviction.

Other assignments of error are either not supported by persuasive authority or are without merit and we need not consider them.

Accordingly, we affirm both judgments of conviction.

(ii) Mens Rea

People v. Collie

Supreme Court of California, 1981.
30 Cal.3d 43, 177 Cal.Rptr. 458, 634 P.2d 534.

■ Mock, Justice.

I

On the evening of July 6, 1978, defendant Bertram Collie visited his estranged wife at her residence, as he had often done before. She and her daughter were in the bedroom watching television and, as defendant entered, the daughter retired to her own room, where she remained for the evening.

Defendant invited his wife to drink and to have sexual intercourse with him, but she refused. He subsequently bound her feet and hands and forcibly sodmized her. He then taped her mouth, ransacked the bedroom, left the room, and locked the door behind him. His wife heard him leave the house at about midnight.

Mrs. Collie then detected the odor of gas. She managed to free herself and unlock the door, and found that the stove burners were turned on, unlit. She turned them off. In the dining room she discovered and extinguished a lighted candle surrounded by combustible material. She then awakened her daughter, who was safe in her own bedroom and oblivious to all that had occurred. . . .

The jury found defendant guilty of attempted first degree murder of his wife, attempted second degree murder of his daughter, and forcible sodomy.

III

Defendant correctly contends that the trial court erred in instructing the jury that it could convict of attempted second degree murder despite the absence of a specific intent to kill. The court instructed the jury in the language of CALJIC No. 8.31 (1974 rev.) which, as modified by the court in the language we have italicized, reads as follows: "Murder of the second degree is (also) the unlawful killing of a human being as the direct causal result of an act involving a high degree of probability that it will result in death, which act is done for a base, antisocial purpose and with wanton disregard for human life by which is meant an awareness of a duty imposed by law not to commit such acts followed by the commission of the forbidden act despite that awareness. (P) When the killing, or the attempted killing in this case, is the direct result of such an act, it is not necessary to establish that the defendant intended that his act would result in the death of a human being."

In People v. Murtishaw (1981) 29 Cal.3d 733, 175 Cal.Rptr. 738, 631 P.2d 446, we held that an assault with intent to commit murder required express malice, and could not be founded on the malice implied from reckless conduct with wanton disregard for human life. Relying on a line of authority originating in People v. Mize (1889) 80 Cal. 41, 22 P. 80, we observed, "once a defendant intends to kill, any malice he may harbor is necessarily express malice. Implied malice, as defined in CALJIC No. 8.11 (and CALJIC No. 8.31), cannot coexist with a specific intent to kill. To instruct on implied malice in that setting, therefore, may confuse the jury by suggesting that they can convict without finding a specific intent to kill." (Murtishaw, supra, 29 Cal.3d at pp. 764–765, 175 Cal.Rptr. 738, 631 P.2d 446.)

The same reasoning applies to attempted murder. "Specific intent to kill is a necessary element of attempted murder. It must be proved, and it cannot be inferred merely from the commission of another dangerous crime." (People v. Belton (1980) 105 Cal.App.3d 376, 380, 164 Cal.Rptr. 340.) Hence the trial court erred in instructing the jury that it need not find a specific intent to kill in order to convict of attempted murder.

The instructional error was harmless regarding the conviction for the attempted first degree murder of Mrs. Collie, because the jury was properly instructed that the verdict required findings of premeditation and deliberation, which entail a specific intent to kill. But the verdict of guilt on the attempted second degree murder charge was not insulated from error. Although the jury was properly instructed that a specific intent to kill would satisfy the intent requirement of an attempted second degree murder charge, it is impossible to determine whether the verdict rested on that ground, for which there was little evidence, or on the impermissible basis of defendant's wanton conduct, which was more clearly supported by the record. Because we cannot know on which instruction the jury relied, the conviction for attempted second degree murder of defendant's daughter must be reversed. (*See*, People v. Rhoden (1972) 6 Cal.3d 519, 526, 99 Cal.Rptr. 751, 492 P.2d 1143; People v. Dail (1943) 22 Cal.2d 642, 653, 140 P.2d 828.). . . .

The judgment is reversed as to the conviction of attempted second degree murder. In all other respects the judgment is affirmed.

■ BIRD, C.J., and TOBRINER and ABBE, JJ., concur.

[The separate opinions of NEWMAN, J., concurring, and RICHARDSON, J., dissenting, are omitted.]

People v. Van Ronk

Court of Appeal, Third District, California, 1985.
171 Cal.App.3d 818, 217 Cal.Rptr. 581.

■ SPARKS, ASSOCIATE JUSTICE.

In this appeal we consider whether attempted voluntary manslaughter is such a logical and legal absurdity that it cannot exist as a crime. We conclude that it is not an absurdity and consequently reaffirm that it constitutes a crime in California.

FACTS

On the night of November 3, 1983, James Gravelle stayed overnight with his sister, Ruth. Defendant telephoned him there and asked whether he could obtain "a pound of pot" for him. Although James agreed to try to locate a pound of pot, he claimed that he would not profit in the deal and that he was only doing it as a friend. On the next morning, defendant went to Ruth's apartment and asked James if he had obtained the pound of pot. James said "nothing was up," meaning that he could not get it then. Defendant said he would return at noon.

Shortly after noon defendant returned to the apartment, this time accompanied by a young woman named Cindy. Defendant and Cindy remained about two hours during which time James attempted to locate some marijuana. At some point James and Cindy went to the store and while they were gone defendant told Ruth he thought he was being cheated. When James and Cindy returned defendant said he wanted to leave but Cindy refused to go with him. Defendant told her that she was his responsibility and that he would not leave her. She replied that he was not her "daddy," and refused to leave. James interjected: "The lady don't want to go. She don't want to go." At that point defendant asked James to go for a ride. He also suggested that he was getting cheated. James declined to depart with defendant, explaining that he refuses to get in a car with someone who is angry with him.

Defendant then asked James to step outside, acting as though he wanted to fight. James agreed, and added, "I'll break every bone in your body." As James stood and began walking to the door, defendant pulled out a pistol and said, "I should kill you." James raised his hands and said, "Get off." Defendant responded by shooting. James was hit three times. Defendant then shot at Cindy but missed, and also fired an errant shot at Ruth as she jumped into the kitchen. Defendant then commanded: "Ruth, come out here. I'm going to shoot you." She begged him not to shoot her, and he agreed if she would give him time to leave. Defendant then argued with Cindy over "the money" and left after she told him where it was.

After defendant left Ruth looked outside and saw her friend, Debbie Jones, drive up. Ruth and Debbie helped James to Debbie's car, and Debbie drove him to the hospital. The treating physician testified that James' wounds were critical and would have been fatal in the absence of immediate treatment. Meanwhile, Ruth returned to her apartment. Cindy wanted to use the telephone but was afraid to stay at the apartment, so Ruth took her to the Shortstop Market. There by chance they encountered defendant, who ran into some apartments. Ruth then gave Cindy a ride to where she wanted to go, and she has not seen her since.

The defendant did not testify and presented no evidence. Instead the defense constructed a theory of self-defense from the prosecution's case in chief. Essentially the defense argued that it was obvious that the incident arose over a drug deal, and that it was likely that James and Ruth were cheating defendant in the deal. Defendant also argued that James probably had a weapon, and that defendant shot in self-defense. Although James and Ruth denied that James had a weapon, defendant pointed out that Ruth did not immediately call the police and did not accompany James to the hospital. She also told a false story to the police in the initial stages of investigation. From this diaphanous evidence defense counsel argued that she probably stayed to dispose of unfavorable evidence before the police arrived.

DISCUSSION

I

Defendant contends that the crime of attempted voluntary manslaughter is a logical and legal absurdity. This issue has been resolved contrary to defendant in prior appellate court decisions. (People v. Williams (1980) 102 Cal.App.3d 1018, 1025, 162 Cal.Rptr. 748. *See also* People v. Tucciarone (1982) 137 Cal.App.3d 701, 705, 187 Cal.Rptr. 159; People v. Ibarra (1982) 134 Cal.App.3d 413, 184 Cal.Rptr. 639; People v. Kozel (1982) 133 Cal. App.3d 507, 525, 184 Cal.Rptr. 208; People v. Heffington (1973) 32 Cal. App.3d 1, 11–12, 107 Cal.Rptr. 859.) We reject defendant's argument under the authority of those decisions and for the additional reason that our independent consideration compels the conclusion that defendant's argument is unsound.

Murder is an unlawful homicide with malice aforethought. (Pen.Code, § 187, subd. (a).) In the absence of other statutory circumstances, first degree murder is distinguished from second degree murder by the presence or absence of premeditation and deliberation. (Pen.Code, § 189.) Premeditation and deliberation are not to be confused with a deliberate intent to kill. Premeditation and deliberation require "substantially more reflection; i.e., more understanding and comprehension of the character of the act than the mere amount of thought necessary to form the intention to kill." (People v. Wolff (1964) 61 Cal.2d 795, 822, 40 Cal.Rptr. 271, 394 P.2d 959.) It is therefore "obvious that the mere intent to kill is not the equivalent of a deliberate and premeditated intent to kill." (People v. Bender (1945) 27

Cal.2d 164, 181, 163 P.2d 8.) Consequently, an intentional killing is not first degree murder unless the intent to kill was formed upon a preexisting reflection and was the subject of actual deliberation.[8]

In the same way that premeditation and deliberation will elevate an intentional killing to first degree murder, mitigating factors may reduce an intentional killing to manslaughter. Thus "[h]omicide itself is not a crime, but a class of crimes, graduated according to the mental state and personal turpitude of the offender." (People v. Horn (1974) 12 Cal.3d 290, 295, 115 Cal.Rptr. 516, 524 P.2d 1300.) As explained in People v. Elmore (1914) 167 Cal. 205, at page 210, 138 P. 989, the law acts out of forebearance for the weakness of human nature and, where sufficient facts are shown, will disregard the actual deliberate and malicious intent and reduce the crime to manslaughter. "[A]ccording to common law tradition, the malice is presumed to be wanting in such a situation [involving a killing in the heat of passion upon adequate provocation], the act 'being rather imputed to the infirmity of human nature.' " (Pike, *What is Second Degree Murder in California?* (1936) 9 So.Cal.L.Rev. 112, 113, quoting 1 Mitchie, Homicide (1914), 130, § 21.) In addition to an intentional killing upon a sudden quarrel or heat of passion induced by adequate provocation, an honest but unreasonable belief that it is necessary to act in self-defense will also serve to mitigate an intentional killing to manslaughter. (People v. Flannel (1979) 25 Cal.3d 668, 674–680, 160 Cal.Rptr. 84, 603 P.2d 1.) Yet a specific intent to kill remains implicit in the statutory definition of voluntary manslaughter. (People v. Gorshen (1959) 51 Cal.2d 716, 732, 336 P.2d 492. People v. Bridgehouse (1956) 47 Cal.2d 406, 413, 303 P.2d 1018. People v. Welborn (1966) 242 Cal.App.2d 668, 673, 51 Cal.Rptr. 644.).

An attempt to commit a crime requires an intention to commit the crime and an overt act towards its completion. (People v. Miller (1935) 2 Cal.2d 527, 530, 42 P.2d 308. People v. Goldstein (1956) 146 Cal.App.2d 268, 275, 303 P.2d 892. *See also* § 664.) Where a person intends to kill another person and makes an unsuccessful attempt to do so, his intention may be accompanied by any of the aggravating or mitigating circumstances which can accompany the completed crimes. In other words, the intent to kill may have been formed after premeditation or deliberation, it may have been formed upon a sudden explosion of violence, or it may have been brought about by a heat of passion or an unreasonable but good faith belief in the necessity of self-defense. If the law acts out of forebearance for the weakness of human nature and mitigates an intentional killing where mitigating circumstances appear, then we can discern no plausible reason why the law should not also mitigate an intentional attempt to kill under similar circumstances.

Defendant argues that the crime of attempted voluntary manslaughter is impossible because it would require the perpetrator to kill in a planned heat of passion or under a planned honest but unreasonable belief in the necessity of self-defense. This argument confuses planning with intent. The requisite intent for first degree murder on a premeditation and deliberation

---

8. Nonetheless, "[t]o prove the killing was 'deliberate and premeditated,' it shall not be necessary to prove the defendant maturely and meaningfully reflected upon the gravity of his or her act." (§ 189.)

theory and the intent necessary for voluntary manslaughter are identical: both crimes require the specific intent to kill. (*See* People v. Gorshen, *supra*, 51 Cal.2d at pp. 732–733, 336 P.2d 492.) Although the law distinguishes between completed intentional homicides on the basis of the manner in which the intent to kill was formed, the intent remains the same.

It is true that a person cannot plot in advance to kill in the heat of passion. Such a calculated plan is logically inconsistent with a spontaneous act committed in a moment of passion. But an assailant can form an intent to kill even under a paroxysm of passion. And this is true regardless of whether he is successful or unsuccessful in carrying out his intent. There is nothing illogical or absurd in a finding that a person who unsuccessfully attempted to kill another did so with the intent to kill which was formed in a heat of passion or which arose out of an honest but unreasonable belief in the necessity of self-defense. Under those circumstances, the less culpable person is guilty of attempted voluntary manslaughter rather than attempted murder.

The judgment is affirmed.

■ PUGLIA, P.J., and CARR, J., concur.

(iii) Perpetrating Act

People v. Rizzo

Court of Appeals of New York, 1927.
246 N.Y. 334, 158 N.E. 888.

■ CRANE, J. The police of the city of New York did excellent work in this case by preventing the commission of a serious crime. It is a great satisfaction to realize that we have such wide-awake guardians of our peace. Whether or not the steps which the defendant had taken up to the time of his arrest amounted to the commission of a crime, as defined by our law, is, however, another matter. He has been convicted of an attempt to commit the crime of robbery in the first degree and sentenced to State's prison. There is no doubt that he had the intention to commit robbery if he got the chance. An examination, however, of the facts is necessary to determine whether his acts were in preparation to commit the crime if the opportunity offered, or constituted a crime in itself, known to our law as an attempt to commit robbery in the first degree. Charles Rizzo, the defendant, appellant, with three others, Anthony J. Dorio, Thomas Milo and John Thomasello, on January 14th planned to rob one Charles Rao of a payroll valued at about $1,200 which he was to carry from the bank for the United Lathing Company. These defendants, two of whom had firearms, started out in an automobile, looking for Rao or the man who had the payroll on that day. Rizzo claimed to be able to identify the man and was to point him out to the others who were to do the actual holding up. The four rode about in their car looking for Rao. They went to the bank from which he was supposed to get the money and to various buildings being constructed by the United Lathing Company. At last they came to One Hundred Eightieth street and Morris Park avenue. By this time they were watched and followed by two police officers. As Rizzo jumped out of the car and ran into the building all four were arrested. The defendant was taken out of from the building in which he was hiding. Neither Rao nor a man named Previti, who was also supposed to carry a payroll, were at the place at the time of the arrest. The defendants had not found or seen the man they intended to rob; no person with a payroll was at any of the places where they had stopped and no one had been pointed out or identified by Rizzo. The four men intended to rob the payroll man, whoever he was; they were looking for him, but they had not seen or discovered him up to the time they were arrested.

Does this constitute the crime of an attempt to commit robbery in the first degree? The Penal Law, section 2, prescribes, "An act, done with intent to commit a crime, and tending but failing to effect its commission, is 'an attempt to commit that crime.'" The word *"tending"* is very indefinite. It is perfectly evident that there will arise differences of opinion as to whether an act in a given case is one *tending* to commit a crime. "Tending" means to exert activity in a particular direction. Any act in preparation to commit a crime may be said to have a tendency towards its accomplishment. The procuring of the automobile, searching the streets looking for the desired victim, were in reality acts tending toward the commission of the proposed crime. The law, however, has recognized that many acts in the way of preparation are too remote to constitute the crime of attempt. The line has been drawn between those acts which are remote and those which are proximate and near to the consummation. The law must be practical, and, therefore, considers those acts only as tending to the commission of the crime which are so near to its accomplishment that in all reasonable probability the crime itself would have been committed but for timely interference. The cases which have been before the courts express this idea in different language, but the idea remains the same. The act or acts must come or advance very near to the accomplishment of the intended crime. In People v. Mills, 178 N.Y. 274, 284, 70 N.E. 786, it was said: "Felonious intent alone is not enough, but there must be an overt act shown in order to establish even an attempt. An overt act is one done to carry out the intention, and it must be such as would naturally effect that result, unless prevented by some extraneous cause." In Hyde v. U.S., 225 U.S. 347, 32 S.Ct. 793, 56 L.Ed. 1114, it was stated that the act amounts to an attempt when it is so near to the result that the danger of success is very great. "There must be dangerous proximity to success." Halsbury in his "Laws of England" (Vol. IX, p. 259) says: "An act, in order to be a criminal attempt, must be immediately, and not remotely, connected with and directly tending to the commission of an offence." Commonwealth v. Peaslee, 177 Mass. 267, 59 N.E. 55, refers to the acts constituting an attempt as coming *very near* to the accomplishment of the crime.

The method of committing or attempting crime varies in each case so that the difficulty, if any, is not with this rule of law regarding an attempt, which is well understood, but with its application to the facts. As I have said before, minds differ over proximity and the nearness of the approach.

How shall we apply this rule of immediate nearness to this case? The defendants were looking for the payroll man to rob him of his money. This is the charge in the indictment. Robbery is defined in section 2120 of the

Penal Law as "the unlawful taking of personal property, from the person or in the presence of another against his will, by means of force, or violence, or fear of injury, immediate or future, to his person;" and it is made robbery in the first degree by section 2124 when committed by a person aided by accomplices actually present. To constitute the crime of robbery the money must have been taken from Rao by means of force or violence, or through fear. The crime of attempt to commit robbery was committed if these defendants did an act tending to the commission of this robbery. Did the acts above described come dangerously near to the taking of Rao's property? Did the acts come so near the commission of robbery that there was reasonable likelihood of its accomplishment but for the interference? Rao was not found; the defendants were still looking for him; no attempt to rob him could be made, at least until he came in sight; he was not in the building at One Hundred and Eightieth street and Morris Park avenue. There was no man there with the payroll for the United Lathing Company whom these defendants could rob. Apparently no money had been drawn from the bank for the payroll by anybody at the time of the arrest. In a word, these defendants had planned to commit a crime and were looking around the city for an opportunity to commit it, but the opportunity fortunately never came. Men would not be guilty of an attempt at burglary if they had planned to break into a building and were arrested while they were hunting about the streets for the building not knowing where it was. Neither would a man be guilty of an attempt to commit murder if he armed himself and started out to find the person whom he had planned to kill but could not find him. So here these defendants were not guilty of an attempt to commit robbery in the first degree when they had not found or reached the presence of the person they intended to rob.

For these reasons, the judgment of conviction of this defendant, appellant, must be reversed and a new trial granted. . . .

Young v. State

Court of Appeals of Maryland, 1985.
303 Md. 298, 493 A.2d 352.

Usually a criminal conviction is predicated upon the completion of the crime; the conduct of the accused has satisfied the elements necessary to establish the offense and he has actually committed the act as proscribed. But what if the conduct of the accused has not progressed to the point where a crime has been committed, that is, he has tried to commit the offense but for some reason he has not been successful?

[T]here is just as much need to stop, deter and reform a person who has unsuccessfully attempted or is attempting to commit a crime than one who has already committed such an offense.

This is why the law of attempts exists.

The notion that an attempt to commit a crime is itself a crime came relatively late into Anglo–American jurisprudence. The Court of Special Appeals set out its history in Gray v. State, 43 Md.App. 238, 403 A.2d 853, cert. denied, 286 Md. 747 (1979):

[The crime of attempt] had its origins in the Court of Star Chamber, during Tudor and early Stuart times. Its crystallization into its present form, however, is generally traced to the case of Rex v. Scofield, Cald. 397, in 1784.... The doctrine was locked into its modern mold by 1801 with the case of Rex v. Higgins, 2 East 5.... In the wake of *Scofield* and *Higgins,* it was clear that *an attempt to commit any felony or misdemeanor, of common law origin or created by statute, was itself a misdemeanor. Id.* at 239 (emphasis added; footnotes omitted).

The offense of criminal attempt has long been accepted as a part of the criminal law of Maryland.[9] We recognized a criminal attempt as a common law misdemeanor....

Our opinions leave much unanswered. The application of particular facts to the law of criminal attempts frequently gives rise to problems in one or more of three aspects:

(1) The determination of the overt act which is beyond mere preparation in furtherance of the commission of the crime.

(2) At what point may the attempt to commit the intended crime be abandoned so as to escape liability.

(3) What is the effect on culpability of impossibility to commit the intended crime.

. . .

Such was the posture of the law of Maryland regarding criminal attempts when Raymond Alexander Young, also known as Morris Prince Cunningham and Prince Alexander Love, was found guilty by a jury in the Circuit Court for Prince George's County of two crimes: (1) the attempted armed robbery of the manager of the Fort Washington, Md. branch of the First National Bank of Southern Maryland (the Bank) ...

There is no dispute as to the circumstances which led to the indictment of Young. Several banks in the Oxon Hill–Fort Washington section of Prince George's County had been held up. The Special Operations Division of the Prince George's Police Department set up a surveillance of banks in the area. In the early afternoon of 26 November 1982 the police team observed Young driving an automobile in such a manner as to give rise to a reasonable belief that he was casing several banks. They followed him in his reconnoitering. At one point when he left his car to enter a store, he was seen to clip a scanner onto his belt. The scanner later proved to contain an operable crystal number frequency that would receive Prince George's County uniform patrol transmissions. At that time Young was dressed in a brown waist-length jacket and wore sunglasses.

Around 2:00 p.m. Young came to rest at the rear of the Fort Washington branch of the First National Bank of Southern Maryland. Shortly before, he had driven past the front of the Bank and parked in the rear of it for a brief time. He got out of his car and walked hurriedly beside the Bank toward the front door. He was still wearing the brown waist-length jacket

---

9. Maryland has not enacted a general attempt statute. It has, however, provided by way of legislation that an attempt to commit certain specified crimes is an offense.

and sunglasses, but he had added a blue knit stocking cap pulled down to the top of the sunglasses, white gloves and a black eyepatch. His jacket collar was turned up. His right hand was in his jacket pocket and his left hand was in front of his face. As one of the police officers observing him put it, he was "sort of duck[ing] his head."

It was shortly after 2:00 p.m. and the Bank had just closed. Through the windows of his office the Bank Manager saw Young walking on the "landscape" by the side of the Bank toward the front door. Young had his right hand in his jacket pocket and tried to open the front door with his left hand. When he realized that the door was locked and the Bank was closed, he retraced his steps, running past the windows with his left hand covering his face. The Bank Manager had an employee call the police.

Young ran back to his car, yanked open the door, got in, and put the car in drive "all in one movement almost," and drove away. The police stopped the car and ordered Young to get out. . . .

. . . Young concedes that "evidence is present . . . from which it is possible to infer that [he] may have intended to commit a crime inside the bank. . . ." He suggests, however, that this evidence is not "compelling. . . ." We think that it is most compelling. We believe that it is more than legally sufficient to establish beyond a reasonable doubt that Young had the specific intent to commit an armed robbery as charged.

. . . Of course, if the person's conduct has not progressed beyond mere preparation, in other words, he has not performed the requisite overt act, he would not be culpable in any event. . . . The determination of the overt act which is beyond mere preparation in furtherance of the commission of the intended crime is a most significant aspect of criminal attempts. If an attempt is to be a culpable offense serving as the basis for the furtherance of the important societal interests of crime prevention and the correction of those persons who have sufficiently manifested their dangerousness, the police must be able to ascertain with reasonable assurance when it is proper for them to intervene. It is not enough to say merely that there must be "some overt act beyond mere preparation in furtherance of the crime" as the general definition puts it. . . .

. . . What act will suffice to show that an attempt itself has reached the stage of a completed crime has persistently troubled the courts. They have applied a number of approaches in order to determine when preparation for the commission of a crime has ceased and the actual attempt to commit it has begun. . . .

"The Model Penal Code Approach" looks to § 5.01 of the Model Penal Code (Proposed Official Draft 1962) to solve the problem. Under subsection (1)(c) a person is guilty of an attempt to commit a crime if, acting with the kind of culpability otherwise required for commission of the crime, he

> purposely does or omits to do anything which, under the circumstances as he believes them to be, is an act or omission constituting a *substantial step* in a course of conduct planned to culminate in his commission of the crime. (emphasis added).

Each of these approaches is not without advantages and disadvantages in theory and in application, as is readily apparent from a perusal of the comments of various text writers and of the courts.

We believe that the preferable approach is one bottomed on the "substantial step" test as is that of Model Penal Code. We think that using a "substantial step" as the criterion in determining whether an overt act is more than mere preparation to commit a crime is clearer, sounder, more practical and easier to apply to the multitude of differing fact situations which may occur. Therefore, in formulating a test to fix the point in the development of events at which a person goes further than mere unindictable preparation and becomes guilty of attempt, we eliminate from consideration the "Proximity Approach," the "Probable Desistance Approach" and the "Equivocality Approach."

We are by no means alone in the belief that an approach based on the substantial step test is superior. This belief was shared by the Commission which drafted a proposed criminal code for this State following the Model Penal Code approach with respect to criminal attempts. . . .

When the facts and circumstances of the case *sub judice* are considered in the light of the overt act standard which we have adopted, it is perfectly clear that the evidence was sufficient to prove that Young attempted the crime of armed robbery as charged. As we have seen, the police did not arrive on the scene after the fact. They had the advantage of having Young under observation for some time before his apprehension. They watched his preparations. They were with him when he reconnoitered or cased the banks. His observations of the banks were in a manner not usual for law-abiding individuals and were under circumstances that warranted alarm for the safety of persons or property. Young manifestly endeavored to conceal his presence by parking behind the Bank which he had apparently selected to rob. He disguised himself with an eyepatch and made an identification of him difficult by turning up his jacket collar and by donning sunglasses and a knit cap which he pulled down over his forehead. He put on rubber surgical gloves. Clipped on his belt was a scanner with a police bank frequency. Except for the scanner, which he had placed on his belt while casing the Bank, all this was done immediately before he left his car and approached the door of the Bank. As he walked towards the Bank he partially hid his face behind his left hand and ducked his head. He kept his right hand in the pocket of his jacket in which, as subsequent events established, he was carrying, concealed, a loaded handgun, for which he had no lawful use or right to transport. He walked to the front door of the Bank and tried to enter the premises. When he discovered that the door was locked, he ran back to his car, again partially concealing his face with his left hand. He got in his car and immediately drove away. He removed the knit hat, sunglasses, eyepatch and gloves, and placed the scanner over the sun visor of the car. When apprehended, he was trying to take off his jacket. His question as to how much time he could get for attempted bank robbery was not without significance.

It is clear that the evidence which showed Young's conduct leading to his apprehension established that he performed the necessary overt act towards the commission of armed robbery, which was more than mere preparation. . . .

. . . Therefore, the evidence was sufficient in law to sustain the conviction. We so hold.

Judgments of the Court of Special Appeals Affirmed.[10]

(iv) Impossibility

State v. Mitchell

Supreme Court of Missouri, Division Two, 1902.
170 Mo. 633, 71 S.W. 175.

■ GANTT, J. Defendant was tried upon an information filed by the prosecuting attorney of Clinton county at the May term, 1901, and convicted of an attempt to murder John O. Warren. His punishment was assessed at five years in the penitentiary. . . .

I. The first insistence is that the first count in the information is so defective that it will not sustain the sentence. Whether the objection is well taken or not, depends upon what constitutes the offense and what is essential to be proven. The statute provides that "every person who shall attempt to commit an offense prohibited by law, and in such an attempt shall do any act towards the commission of such offense, but shall fail in the perpetration thereof, or be intercepted or prevented from executing the same," etc., shall be punished as therein provided. Murder is an offense prohibited. When the defendant armed himself with a loaded revolver and went to the window of the room in which he believed John O. Warren was sleeping, from his knowledge acquired by visiting his family, and fired his pistol at the place where he thought Warren was lying, he was attempting to assassinate and murder him. The fact that Warren was not there as he believed him to be, did not make it any the less an attempt to murder. Our statute on this subject is substantially like that of Massachusetts, construed in Com. v. McDonald, 5 Cush. 365, and Com. v. Sherman, 105 Mass. 169, in which it was held "that neither allegation nor proof was necessary, that there was any property, capable of being stolen, in the pocket or upon the person of the one against whom the attempt to commit larceny was made."
. . . [11]

So in this case the intent evidenced by the firing into the bedroom with a deadly weapon accompanied by a present capacity in defendant to murder Warren if he were in the room, and the failure to do so only because Warren haply retired upstairs instead of in the bed into which defendant

---

10. "The majority of jurisdictions considering the issue have also held that solicitation is not an attempt." State v. Otto, 102 Idaho 250, 629 P.2d 646 (1981).

Solicitation of another to commit murder may constitute an attempt if it constitutes a "substantial step toward the commission" of murder. State v. Kilgus, 128 N.H. 577, 519 A.2d 231 (1986).

11. Accord: People v. Moran, 123 N.Y. 254, 25 N.E. 412 (1890).

An English case held, contra, that larceny cannot be attempted by reaching into an empty pocket. Regina v. Collins, 9 Cox C.C. 497 (1864). This case was later overruled. *See* Regina v. Ring, 17 Cox C.C. 491 (1892).

fired, made out a perfect case of an attempt within the meaning of the statute, and the information is sufficient. The evidence conclusively supported the information. It discloses a deliberate and dastardly attempt at assassination, which was only averted by the intended victim's going upstairs to bed that night. . . .

We find no error in the record, and affirm the judgment. All concur.

People v. Rojas

Supreme Court of California, In Bank, 1961.
55 Cal.2d 252, 10 Cal.Rptr. 465, 358 P.2d 921.

[Hall, who had stolen $4,500 worth of electrical conduit, was arrested while in possession of the stolen property and taken to the police station. He said he had an arrangement with one of the defendants to sell him any and all electrical materials obtained. From the police station Hall made three phone calls, monitored by the police, which resulted in a plan by which Hall left a truck, containing the conduit, at a place designated by the defendants. Later one of the defendants came and drove away the truck to a lot near his place of business. He was arrested the next morning when he began to unload the truck.]

■ SCHAUER, JUSTICE. In a trial by the court, after proper waiver of jury, defendants Rojas and Hidalgo were found guilty of a charge of receiving stolen property. Defendants' motions for new trial were denied. Rojas was granted probation without imposition of sentence and Hidalgo was sentenced to state prison. They appeal, respectively, from the order granting probation, the judgment, and the orders denying the motions for new trial.

Defendants urge that they were guilty of no crime (or, at most, of an attempt to receive stolen property) because when they received the property it had been recovered by the police and was no longer in a stolen condition. The attorney general argues that because the thief stole the property pursuant to prearrangement with defendants he took it as their agent, and the crime of receiving stolen property was complete when the thief began its asportation toward defendants and before the police intercepted him and recovered the property. We have concluded that defendants are guilty of attempting to receive stolen goods; that other matters of which they complain do not require a new trial; and that the appeal should be disposed of by modifying the finding that defendants are guilty as charged to a determination that they are guilty of attempting to receive stolen property, and by reversing with directions to the trial court to enter such judgments or probation orders as it deems appropriate based upon the modified finding. . . .

The offense with which defendants were charged and of which they were convicted was receiving "property which has been *stolen* . . ., *knowing the same to be so stolen.*" Pen.Code, § 496, subd. 1; italics added. Defendants, relying particularly upon People v. Jaffe (1906), 185 N.Y. 497, 501 [78 N.E. 169, 9 L.R.A., N.S., 263, 266], urge that they neither received stolen goods nor criminally attempted to do so because the conduit, when defendants received it, was not in a stolen condition but had been recovered by the police. In the Jaffe case the stolen property was recovered by the owner while it was en route to the would-be receiver and, by arrangement with the police, was delivered to such receiver as a decoy, not as property in a stolen condition. The New York Court of Appeals held that there was no attempt to receive stolen goods "because neither [defendant] nor anyone else in the world could know that the property was stolen property inasmuch as it was not in fact stolen property.... If all which an accused person intends to do would if done constitute no crime it cannot be a crime to attempt to do with the same purpose a part of the thing intended."

Defendants also cite People v. Zimmerman (1909), 11 Cal.App. 115, 118, 104 P. 590, which contains the following dictum concerning a state of facts like that in the Jaffe case: "The circumstances of the transaction ... did not constitute an offense, as the goods were taken to the defendant's house with the consent and at the request of the owner."

As pointed out by the District Court of Appeal in Faustina v. Superior Court (1959), 174 Cal.App.2d 830, 833[1], 345 P.2d 543, "The rule of the Jaffe case has been the subject of much criticism and discussion." ...

In the case at bench the criminality of the attempt is not destroyed by the fact that the goods, having been recovered by the commendably alert and efficient action of the Los Angeles police, had, unknown to defendants, lost their "stolen" status, any more than the criminality of the attempt in the case of In re Magidson (1917), 32 Cal.App. 566, 568, 163 P. 689, was destroyed by impossibility caused by the fact that the police had recovered the goods and taken them from the place where the would-be receiver went to get them. In our opinion the consequences of intent and acts such as those of defendants here should be more serious than pleased amazement that because of the timeliness of the police the projected criminality was not merely detected but also wiped out....

The orders denying defendants' motions for new trial are affirmed. The trial court's finding that defendants are guilty as charged is modified to find them guilty of the offense of attempting to receive stolen property. The judgment and probation order are reversed and the cause is remanded to the trial court for further proceedings not inconsistent with the views hereinabove expressed, and with directions to enter such lawful judgment or order against each defendant, based on the modified finding, as the court deems appropriate.[12]

---

12. One who receives what he believes to be stolen property may be convicted of an attempt to receive stolen property even if the property was not in fact stolen. State v. Carner, Ariz.App., 541 P.2d 947 (1975); People v. Moss, 55 Cal.App.3d 179, 127 Cal.Rptr. 454 (1976); People v. Darr, 193 Colo. 445, 568 P.2d 32 (1977).

Where property stolen by burglars was recovered by police, who had an undercover agent sell it to D, D could not properly be convicted of receiving stolen property, because it had lost its character of stolen property. But D could be convicted of an attempt to receive stolen property if he believed it was stolen. State v. Niehuser, 21 Or.App. 33, 533 P.2d 834 (1975).

"Does stolen property lose its identity as stolen property when it is recovered by law enforcement officers? We conclude that it does." State v. Sterling, 230 Kan. 790, 640 P.2d 1264 (1982). Contra: State v. Pappas, 705 P.2d 1169 (Utah 1985). Defendant could be convicted of receiving stolen property where property was not stolen based on wording of the statute.

■ GIBSON, C.J., and TRAYNOR, McCOMB, PETERS, WHITE and DOOLING, JJ., concur.

Booth v. State

Court of Criminal Appeals of Oklahoma, 1964.
398 P.2d 863.

[Having stolen a coat, the thief telephoned to Booth saying he had it and would let Booth have it for $20.00. It was arranged that Booth would meet the thief at the latter's house at 11:00 A.M. to effect the transfer. In the meantime the thief was arrested and confessed. The police recovered the coat and called in the owner who identified it. It was then returned to the thief to carry out the original plan which was done, after which Booth was arrested. From a conviction of attempting to receive stolen property an appeal was taken.]

■ NIX, JUDGE. . . . In People v. Finkelstein, 21 Misc.2d 723, 197 N.Y.S.2d 31 (1960) the court said:

"A defendant may not be convicted for receiving stolen property if property is no longer in category of stolen property when he receives it."

The law seems to be clear on this point, leaving the only question to be decided as whether or not the defendant could be convicted of an attempt to receive stolen property in such cases. It is the defendant's contention that if he could not be convicted of the substantive charge, because the coat had lost its character as stolen property; neither could he be convicted of an attempt because the coat was not in the category of stolen property at the time he received it.

The briefs filed in the case, and extensive research has revealed that two states have passed squarely on the question—New York and California. It is definitely one of first impression in Oklahoma.

The New York Court, in passing upon the question, laid down the following rule in the case of People v. Jaffe, 185 N.Y. 497, 78 N.E. 169, 6 L.R.A., N.S., 263, on the following facts:

"A clerk stole goods from his employer under an agreement to sell them to accused, but before delivery of the goods the theft was discovered and the goods were recovered. Later the employer redelivered the goods to the clerk to sell to accused, who purchased them for about one-half of their value, believing them to have been stolen.

"Held, that the goods had lost their character as stolen goods at the time defendant purchased them, and that his criminal intent was insufficient to sustain a conviction for an attempt to receive stolen property, knowing it to have been stolen."

The *Jaffe* case, *supra*, was handed down in 1906, and has prevailed as the law in New York state 58 years without modification—being affirmed in People v. Finklestein [sic] *supra*; . . . and finally in the case of People v. Rollino (1962), 37 Misc.2d 14, 233 N.Y.S.2d 580.

The State of California has passed upon the question several times and up until 1959, they followed the rule laid down in the *Jaffe* case, *supra*.

In 1959, in the case of People v. Camodeca, 52 Cal.2d 142, 338 P.2d 903, the California Court abandoned the *Jaffe* rationale that a person accepting goods which he believes to have been stolen, but which was not in fact stolen goods, is not guilty of an attempt to receive stolen goods, and imposed a liability for the attempt, overruling its previous holding to the contrary in the above cited cases. The *Camodeca* case, *supra*, was affirmed in People v. Rojas, 55 Cal.2d 252, 10 Cal.Rptr. 465, 358 P.2d 921, 85 A.L.R.2d 252, 1961.

Though the instant case, insofar as it pertains to the specific crime of attempting to receive stolen property is one of first impression in Oklahoma. This Court held in the Nemecek v. State, 72 Okl.Cr. 195, 114 P.2d 492, 135 A.L.R. 1149, involving attempting to receive money by false pretenses:

"An accused cannot be convicted of an attempt to commit a crime unless he could have been convicted of the crime itself if his attempt had been successful. Where the act, if accomplished, would not constitute the crime intended, there is no indictable attempt."

In the *Nemecek* case, *supra*, the Court quotes with approval, In re Schurman, 40 Kan. 533, 20 P. 277; wherein the Kansas Court said:

"With reference to attempt, it has also been said that 'if all which the accused person intended would, had it been done, constitute no substantive crime, it cannot be a crime, under the name "attempt," to do, with the same purpose, a part of this thing.' "

The two paramount cases of latest date; *Rojas* of Calif.1961, *supra*, and *Rollino* of New York 1962, *supra*; present two rationales directly contrary to each other relative to an attempt to receive stolen property after it had been recovered by the police....

The authorities in the various states and the text-writers are in general agreement that where there is a "legal impossibility" of completing the substantive crime, the accused cannot be successfully charged with an attempt, whereas in those cases in which the "factual impossibility" situation is involved, the accused may be convicted of an attempt. Detailed discussion of the subject is unnecessary to make it clear that it is frequently most difficult to compartmentalize a particular set of facts as coming within one of the categories rather than the other.... Your writer is of the opinion that the confusion that exists as a result of the two diverse rationales laid down in the *Rollino* case (NY) *supra*, and the *Rojas* case (Calif.) *supra*, was brought about by the failure to recognize the distinction between a factual and a legal impossibility to accomplish the crime. In the *Camodeca* case (Calif.) *supra*, the facts revealed a prevention of the crime because of a factual situation as stated on page 906, 338 P.2d:

"In the present case there was not a legal but only a factual impossibility of consummating the intended offense...."

In the *Rojas* case, *supra*, wherein was adopted the departure from the *Jaffe* case, by saying:

"The situation here is materially like those considered in People v. Camodeca."

The *Rojas* case was definitely not materially the same. In the *Rojas* case the facts reveal a legal and not factual impossibility.

In the case at bar the stolen coat had been recovered by the police for the owner and consequently had, according to the well-established law in this country, lost its character as stolen property. Therefore, a legal impossibility precluded defendant from being prosecuted for the crime of Knowingly Receiving Stolen Property.... Sayre, 41 Harvard Law Review 821, 853–54 (1928) states the rationale in this manner:

"It seems clear that cases (where none of the intended consequences is in fact criminal) cannot constitute criminal attempts. If none of the consequences which the defendant sought to achieve constitute a crime, surely his unsuccessful efforts to achieve his object cannot constitute a criminal attempt. The partial fulfillment of an object not criminal cannot itself be criminal. If the whole is not criminal, the part cannot be."

The defendant in the instant case leaves little doubt as to his moral guilt. The evidence, as related by the self-admitted and perpetual law violator indicates defendant fully intended to do the act with which he was charged. However, it is fundamental to our law that a man is not punished merely because he has a criminal mind. It must be shown that he has, with that criminal mind, done an act which is forbidden by the criminal law.

Adhering to this principle, the following example would further illustrate the point.

A fine horse is offered to A at a ridiculously low price by B, who is a known horse thief. A, believing the horse to be stolen buys the same without inquiry. In fact, the horse had been raised from a colt by B and was not stolen. It would be bordering on absurdity to suggest that A's frame of mind, if proven, would support a conviction of an attempt. It would be a "legal impossibility"....

In view of our statutory law, and the decisions herein related, it is our duty to Reverse this case, with orders to Dismiss, and it is so ordered. However, there are other avenues open to the County Attorney which should be explored.[13]

■ JOHNSON, P.J., and BUSSEY, J., concur.

[Rehearing denied Feb. 17, 1965.]

United States v. Oviedo

United States Court of Appeals, Fifth Circuit, 1976.
525 F.2d 881.

■ Before GODBOLD, DYER and MORGAN, CIRCUIT JUDGES.

■ DYER, CIRCUIT JUDGE.

---

13. "In sum, to be convicted of attempt the defendant's objective actions, taken as a whole, must strongly corroborate the required culpability." United States v. Innella, 690 F.2d 834 (11th Cir.1982).

Oviedo appeals from a judgment of conviction for the attempted distribution of heroin, in violation of 21 U.S.C.A. § 846.[14] Oviedo contends that under the facts of this case, he is not guilty of any criminal offense. We agree and reverse.

Oviedo was contacted by an undercover agent, who desired to purchase narcotics. Arrangements were made for the sale of one pound of heroin. The agent met Oviedo at the appointed time and place. Oviedo transferred the substance to the agent, and asked for his money in return. However, the agent informed Oviedo that he would first have to test the substance. A field test was performed with a positive result. Oviedo was placed under arrest.

Subsequent to the arrest, a search warrant was issued for Oviedo's residence. When the search was executed, two pounds of a similar substance was found hidden in a television set. Up to this point, the case appeared unexceptional.

A chemical analysis was performed upon the substances seized, revealing that the substances were not in fact heroin, but rather procaine hydrochloride, an uncontrolled substance.[15] Since any attempt to prosecute for distribution of heroin would have been futile, the defendant was charged with an attempt to distribute heroin.

At trial, Oviedo took the stand and stated that he knew the substance was not heroin, and that he, upon suggestion of his cohorts, was merely attempting to "rip off" the agent. It was, in his view, an easy way to pocket a few thousand dollars.

The court instructed the jury that they could find Oviedo guilty of attempted distribution if he delivered the substance thinking it to be heroin.[16] The jury rejected Oviedo's claimed knowledge of the true nature of the substance, and returned a verdict of guilty. Although Oviedo argues on appeal that there was insufficient evidence to establish that he thought the substance was heroin, this contention is without merit.[17] We thus take as fact Oviedo's belief that the substance was heroin.

---

14. 21 U.S.C.A. § 846 (1981) provides:

Any person who attempts or conspired to commit any offense defined in this subchapter is punishable by imprisonment or fine or both which may not exceed the maximum punishment prescribed for the offense, the commission of which was the object of the attempt or conspiracy.

15. Although not an opium derivative, procaine hydrochloride will give a positive reaction to the Marquis Reagent Field Test.

16. The court charged the jury on this issue:

In other words, if you find beyond a reasonable doubt that Mr. Oviedo did knowingly and unlawfully and intentionally attempt to distribute what you have found beyond a reasonable doubt . . . he believed to be one pound of heroin . . . it would be no defense that the substance involved was not actually heroin. On the other hand, if you do not find beyond a reasonable doubt that the Defendant believed the substance involved to be heroin, even though you might find all of the other elements of the offense present beyond a reasonable doubt, then it would be your duty to acquit the Defendant.

17. The fact that the procaine was secreted inside a television set, together with the discussions between Oviedo and the undercover agent, lead to the reasonable inference that Oviedo thought the substance to be heroin, and support the jury's conclusion.

The facts before us are therefore simple—Oviedo sold a substance he thought to be heroin, which in reality was an uncontrolled substance. The legal question before us is likewise simple—are these combined acts and intent cognizable as a criminal attempt under 21 U.S.C.A. § 846. The answer, however, is not so simple.

Oviedo and the government both agree the resolution of this case rests in an analysis of the doctrines of legal and factual impossibility as defenses to a criminal attempt. Legal impossibility occurs when the actions which the defendant performs or sets in motion, even if fully carried out as he desires, would not constitute a crime. U.S. v. Conway, 5 Cir.1975, 507 F.2d 1047. Factual impossibility occurs when the objective of the defendant is proscribed by the criminal law but a circumstance unknown to the actor prevents him from bringing about that objective. *Id*. at 1050. The traditional analysis recognizes legal impossibility as a valid defense, but refuses to so recognize factual impossibility. U.S. v. Berrigan, 3 Cir.1973, 482 F.2d 171.

These definitions are not particularly helpful here, for they do nothing more than provide a different focus for the analysis. In one sense, the impossibility involved here might be deemed legal, for those *acts* which Oviedo set in motion, the transfer of the substance in his possession, were not a crime. In another sense, the impossibility is factual, for the *objective* of Oviedo, the sale of heroin, was proscribed by law, and failed only because of a circumstance unknown to Oviedo.[18]

Although this issue has been the subject of numerous legal commentaries,[19] federal cases reaching this question are few, and no consensus can be found.[20] United States v. Berrigan, 3 Cir.1973, 482 F.2d 171; United States v. Heng Awkak Roman, S.D.N.Y.1973, 356 F.Supp. 434, aff'd 2 Cir.1973,

---

18. At least one writer has recognized that legal impossibility is logically indistinguishable from factual impossibility. See Hall, Criminal Attempt—A Study of Foundations of Criminal Liability, 49 Yale L.J. 789, 836 (1940).

19. *See* articles listed in United States v. Berrigan, 3 Cir.1973, 482 F.2d 171, 187, fn. 29.

20. State court cases are similarly divergent. State courts have labelled the following situations as involving legal impossibility, and concluded that there could be no attempt: (1) A person who accepts goods which he believes to be stolen, but which are not in fact stolen, is not guilty of attempting to receive stolen goods. People v. Jaffe, 1906, 185 N.Y. 497, 78 N.E. 169. (2) A person who offers a bribe to one whom he believes to be a juror, but who was not a juror, is not guilty of attempting to bribe a juror. State v. Taylor, 1939, 345 Mo. 325, 133 S.W.2d 336. (3) A hunter who shoots a stuffed deer, believing it to be alive, is not guilty of attempting to shoot a deer out of season. State v. Guffey, Mo.App.1953, 262 S.W.2d 152.

In other apparently analogous situations, courts have concluded that the impossibility is factual, and therefore no defense to a charge of attempt: (1) A person who fires a gun at a bed, thinking it to be occupied by a man, is guilty of attempted murder, even though the bed is empty. State v. Mitchell, 1902, 170 Mo. 633, 71 S.W. 175. (2) A person who possesses a substance thinking it is narcotics, is guilty of attempted possession, notwithstanding that the substance is in fact talcum powder. People v. Siu, 1954, 126 Cal.App.2d 41, 271 P.2d 575. (3) A person who introduces instruments into a woman for the purpose of producing an abortion is guilty of attempting an abortion, even though the woman is not pregnant. People v. Cummings, 1956, 141 Cal.App.2d 193, 296 P.3d 610.

Other impossibility cases are collected in Annot., 37 A.L.R.3d 375. We list these cases not to offer support to our conclusions, but rather to illustrate the inconsistency of approach which plagues this area of legal theory.

484 F.2d 1271; Rosado v. Martinez, D.P.R., 1974, 369 F.Supp. 477; United States v. Hair, D.C.1973, 356 F.Supp. 339; *see also* United States v. Marin, 2 Cir.1975, 513 F.2d 974.

In *Roman,* the defendants were transporting a suitcase containing heroin. Through the aid of an informer and unknown to the defendants, the contents of the suitcase were replaced with soap powder. The defendants were arrested when they attempted to sell the contents of the suitcase, and were subsequently charged with *attempted* possession with intent to distribute. The court rejected defendants' contention that they could not be charged with attempted possession, since it was impossible for them to possess heroin. Recognizing the difficulty in distinguishing between legal and factual impossibility, the court never so categorized the case. Nevertheless, the court concluded that since the objective of the defendants was criminal, impossibility would not be recognized as a defense.

The defendants in *Berrigan* were charged with attempting to violate 18 U.S.C.A. § 1791, prohibiting the smuggling of objects into or out of a federal correctional institution. Since the evidence established that the warden had knowledge of the smuggling plan, and since lack of knowledge was a necessary element of the offense, the defendants could not be found guilty of violating the statute. The court held that such knowledge by the warden would also preclude conviction for the attempt, since "attempting to do that which is not a crime is not attempting to commit a crime." *Berrigan,* at 190.

The *Berrigan* court rested its determination on a strict view of legal impossibility. According to the court, such impossibility exists when there is an intention to perform a physical act, the intended physical act is performed, but the consequence resulting from the intended act does not amount to a crime. In this analysis, the intent to perform a physical act is to be distinguished from the motive, desire or expectation to violate the law.[21]

The application of the principles underlying these cases leads to no clearer result than the application of our previous definitions of legal and factual impossibility. Applying *Roman,* we would not concern ourselves with any theoretical distinction between legal and factual impossibility, but would affirm the conviction, since the objective of Oviedo was criminal. Applying *Berrigan,* we would look solely to the physical act which Oviedo "intended", the transfer of the procaine in his possession, and we would conclude that since the transfer of procaine is not criminal, no offense is stated. The choice is between punishing criminal intent without regard to objective acts, and punishing objective acts, regarding intent as immaterial.

In our view, both *Roman* and *Berrigan* miss the mark, but in opposite directions. A strict application of the *Berrigan* approach would eliminate any distinction between factual and legal impossibility, and such impossibil-

---

21. This distinction is easily illustrated. If A takes a book which he thinks belongs to B, his desire or expectation is criminal. However, if the book turns out to belong to A, A does not have the requisite intent to be guilty of a criminal attempt, for his intent is to take the book, and it is not criminal to take one's own book. *See Berrigan, supra,* at 188, fn. 35.

ity would *always* be a valid defense, since the "intended" physical acts are never criminal.[22] The *Roman* approach turns the attempt statute into a new substantive criminal statute where the critical element to be proved is *mens rea simpliciter*. It would allow us to punish one's thoughts, desires, or motives, through indirect evidence, without reference to any objective fact. *See Berrigan, supra* at 189, fn. 39. The danger is evident.

We reject the notion of *Roman,* adopted by the district court, that the conviction in the present case can be sustained since there is sufficient proof of intent, not because of any doubt as to the sufficiency of the evidence in that regard, but because of the inherent dangers such a precedent would pose in the future.

When the question before the court is whether certain conduct constitutes mere preparation which is not punishable, or an attempt which is, the possibility of error is mitigated by the requirement that the objective acts of the defendant evidence commitment to the criminal venture and corroborate the *mens rea.* United States v. Mandujano, 5 Cir.1974, 499 F.2d 370. To the extent this requirement is preserved it prevents the conviction of persons engaged in innocent acts on the basis of a *mens rea* proved through speculative inferences, unreliable forms of testimony, and past criminal conduct.

Courts could have approached the preparation/attempt determination in another fashion, eliminating any notion of particular objective facts, and simply could have asked whether the evidence at hand was sufficient to prove the necessary intent. But this approach has been rejected for precisely the reasons set out above, for conviction upon proof of mere intent provides too great a possibility of speculation and abuse.

In urging us to follow *Roman,* which found determinative the criminal intent of the defendants, the government at least implicitly argues that we should reject any requirement demanding the same objective evidentiary facts required in the preparation—attempt determination. We refuse to follow that suggestion.

When the defendant sells a substance which is actually heroin, it is reasonable to infer that he knew the physical nature of the substance, and to place on him the burden of dispelling that inference. United States v. Moser, 7 Cir.1975, 509 F.2d 1089, 1092; United States v. Joly, 2 Cir.1974, 493 F.2d 672, 676.[23] However, if we convict the defendant of attempting to sell heroin for the sale of a non-narcotic substance, we eliminate an objective element that has major evidentiary significance and we increase the risk of mistaken conclusions that the defendant believed the goods were narcotics.[24]

---

22. If the "intended" physical acts were criminal, the defendant would be guilty of the completed crime, rather than the attempt.

23. A similar inference obtains when possession is established, but the defendant contends that he did not know of the presence of the controlled substance. *See, e.g.,* U.S. v. Squella–Avendano, 5 Cir.1973, 478 F.2d 433, 438; U.S. v. Dixon, 9 Cir.1972, 460 F.2d 309; U.S. v. Hood, 9 Cir.1974, 493 F.2d 677, 681.

24. Enker, Impossibility in Criminal Attempts—Legality and the Legal Process, 53 Minn.L.R. 665, 680 (1969).

Thus, we demand that in order for a defendant to be guilty of a criminal attempt, the objective acts performed, without any reliance on the accompanying *mens rea,* mark the defendant's conduct as criminal in nature. The acts should be unique rather than so commonplace that they are engaged in by persons not in violation of the law.

Here we have only two objective facts. First, Oviedo told the agent that the substance he was selling was heroin, and second, portions of the substance were concealed in a television set. If another objective fact were present, if the substance were heroin, we would have a strong objective basis for the determination of criminal intent and conduct consistent and supportive of that intent. The test set out above would be met, and, absent a delivery, the criminal attempt would be established. But when this objective basis for the determination of intent is removed, when the substance is not heroin, the conduct becomes ambivalent, and we are left with a sufficiency-of-the-evidence determination of intent rejected in the preparation—attempt dichotomy. We cannot conclude that the objective acts of Oviedo apart from any indirect evidence of intent mark his conduct as criminal in nature. Rather, those acts are consistent with a noncriminal enterprise. Therefore, we will not allow the jury's determination of Oviedo's intent to form the sole basis of a criminal offense. . . .

Reversed.[25]

Mens rea is within one's control but, as already seen, it is not subject to direct proof. More importantly perhaps, it is not subject to direct refutation either. It is the subject of inference and speculation. The act requirement with its relative fixedness, its greater visibility and difficulty of fabrication, serves to provide additional security and predictability by limiting the scope of the criminal law to those who have engaged in conduct that is itself objectively forbidden and objectively verifiable. Security from officially imposed harm comes not only from the knowledge that one's thoughts are pure but that one's acts are similarly pure. So long as a citizen does not engage in forbidden conduct, he has little need to worry about possible erroneous official conclusions about his guilty mind.

Id. at 688.

25. [Added by Compilers.] To clarify *Oviedo* the court held in another case that where D's intent to sell cocaine was not disputed (he admitted it), he may be convicted of an intent to sell cocaine although it was actually a simulated substance. United States v. Hough, 561 F.2d 594 (5th Cir.1977).

"We are convinced that Congress intended to eliminate the defense of impossibility when it enacted [21 U.S.C. § 846] . . . When Congress enacted section 846 the doctrine of impossibility had become enmeshed in unworkable distinctions and was no longer widely accepted as part of the meaning of 'attempt' at common law." United States v. Everett, 700 F.2d 900, 904 (3d Cir.1983).

In upholding a conviction for attempted possession of cocaine, the court said that, "Impossibility of commission of the underlying crime . . . is not a defense . . . if such crime could have been committed had the attendant circumstances been as the accused believed them to be." Guzman v. State, 424 S.E.2d 849 (Ga.App.1992).

The enactment of KSA 21–3301(2) eliminated both legal and factual impossibility as a defense to an attempt charge. State v. Logan, 232 Kan. 646, 656 P.2d 777 (1983). Accord, U.C.A. 1953, § 76–4–101(3)(b); State v. Johnson, 821 P.2d 1150 (Utah 1991); State v. Hale, 65 Wash. App. 752, 829 P.2d 802 (1992).

Under the New York Revised Penal Code it is not a defense to a charge of attempted murder that the victim was already dead when the attempt was made. If it cannot be shown beyond a reasonable doubt that the victim was alive at the time, there can be no conviction of murder, but the defendant can be convicted of attempted murder if he thought the victim was

(B) AGGRAVATED ASSAULT

State v. Wilson

Supreme Court of Oregon, 1959.
218 Or. 575, 346 P.2d 115.

■ O'CONNELL, JUSTICE. The defendant appeals from a judgment of the circuit court for Multnomah county entered on a verdict pronouncing him guilty of the crime of attempted assault with a dangerous weapon under Count I of the indictment, . . .

[The evidence showed that defendant had confronted and threatened his estranged wife in her place of employment, after which he procured a loaded shotgun from his car just outside to carry out his threat. He was unable to reach his wife the second time, however, because she was then safely behind locked doors.]

The crime of assault with a dangerous weapon is defined in ORS 163.250 as follows:

"Any person, who is armed with a dangerous weapon and assaults another with such weapon, shall be punished upon conviction by imprisonment in the penitentiary for not more than 10 years, or by imprisonment in the county jail not less than one month nor more than one year, or by a fine of not less than $100 nor more than $1,000."

There is no statute dealing specifically with an attempt to commit assault with a dangerous weapon. The state relies upon the general attempt statute, ORS 161.090, which reads in part as follows:

"Any person who attempts to commit a crime, and in the attempt does any act towards the commission of the crime but fails or is prevented or intercepted in the perpetration thereof, shall be punished upon conviction, when no other provision is made by law for the punishment of such attempt, as follows: . . ."

The defendant attacks Count I of the indictment on the ground that it does not state a crime under the laws of this state. Defendant argues that there is no such crime as an attempted assault with a dangerous weapon. In stating his grounds for objecting to the introduction of evidence in proof of the first count counsel for defendant said ". . . it is the contention of the defendant that there is no such thing as an attempted assault; it is no more than an attempt to inflict an injury or battery, . . . If then, there is such a crime as attempted assault, the one so attempting must have intent to commit an assault. Does he then intend to commit a battery?" To answer this rhetorical question defendant relies upon the following language in Wilson v. State, 1874, 53 Ga. 205, 206:

". . . Plainly and in terms, they say they find him guilty of attempt to make an assault. The question is, can any judgment be entered upon such a verdict? Is it a legal verdict? Is there any such crime? . . . As an assault is itself an attempt to commit a crime, an attempt to make an assault can

alive when he shot him. People v. Dlugash, 395 N.Y.S.2d 419, 41 N.Y.2d 725, 363 N.E.2d 1155 (1977).

only be an attempt to attempt to do it, or to state the matter still more definitely, it is to do any act towards doing an act towards the commission of the offense. This is simply absurd...."

The charge that an attempt to attempt to do an act is beyond understanding, seems at first blush to be justified. It could be interpreted to be the equivalent of a statement that one is guilty of a crime if he proceeds to act in such a way that, if not interrupted, his conduct would result in the commission of an act which if not interrupted would result in a substantive crime.

The bulk of the Oregon cases defining criminal assault, however, do so in terms of attempted battery and limit the crime to acts which are intended to cause corporal injury under circumstances in which the actor has the present ability to carry out his intent. Typical of such definitions is that found in Smallman v. Gladden, 1956, 206 Or. 262, 272, 291 P.2d 749, 754, where the court said:

"... An assault is an intentional attempt by one person by force or violence to do an injury to the person of another, coupled with present ability to carry the intention into effect...."

Under the latter definition, apprehension of injury on the part of the victim need not be shown to make out the crime. Further, it seems clear that an act done with the intention to place one in apprehension of injury only and not to inflict corporal injury would not constitute the crime of assault in this state. And too, according to the definition, an act done with the intention to inflict corporal injury, but where the actor did not have the present ability to inflict corporal injury would not be a criminal assault ... We are of the opinion that criminal assault, even as defined by this court, should be regarded as a distinct crime rather than as an uncompleted battery.

If we should regard assault as an attempted battery, is it reasonable to recognize the crime of attempted assault? It has been categorically asserted that there can be no attempt to commit a crime which is itself merely an attempt. 1 Wharton, Criminal Law & Procedure (Anderson ed.). Upon the basis of this premise it is said that there can be no such offense as an attempted assault. 1 Wharton, *op. cit. supra*, § 72 at 154, states that "as an assault is an attempt to commit a battery there can be no attempt to commit an assault." The same idea is found in Clark & Marshall, Crimes (6th ed.) § 4.07, p. 218, where it is said:

"Since a simple assault is nothing more than attempt to commit a battery, and aggravated assaults are nothing more than attempts to commit murder, rape, or robbery, an attempt to commit an assault, whether simple or aggravated is not a crime."

... The mere fact that assault is viewed as preceding a battery should not preclude us from drawing a line on one side of which we require the present ability to inflict corporal injury, denominating this an assault, and on the other side conduct which falls short of a present ability, yet so advanced toward the assault that it is more than mere preparation and which we denominate an attempt.... The acts of the defendant after obtaining the gun from his automobile may not have been sufficient to establish that he had the present ability to inflict corporal injury upon his wife who was behind a locked door, but he had proceeded far beyond the stage of preparation and it is reasonable to treat his conduct as an attempt within the meaning of ORS 161.090. It is the function of the law of criminal attempt to permit the courts to adjust the penalty in cases where the conduct falls short of a completed crime. 40 Yale L.J. 53, 74, 75. Our legislature has provided that assault with a dangerous weapon is a crime. ORS 161.090 permits the courts of this state to treat conduct which is short of statutory crimes as a crime, and we regard an attempt to commit an assault as within the intendment of this statute....

The judgment of the lower court is affirmed.[26]

■ McALLISTER, C.J., dissents.

(C) SOLICITATION

State v. Blechman

New Jersey Supreme Court, 1946.
135 N.J.L. 99, 50 A.2d 152.

■ HEHER, J.... Although we have but a meager description of the content of the indictment, it would seem, as said, that it accuses plaintiff in error merely of counseling another to set fire to the dwelling house; and it is urged at the outset that such is not an offense denounced by the cited statute unless the wrongful act thus counseled is done, and the injured

---

26. The crime of attempted felonious assault is a crime in Michigan and is not precluded by the language of the attempt statute. People v. Jones, 443 Mich. 88, 504 N.W.2d 158 (1993).

There is no such crime as attempted simple battery. "An attempted simple battery is a simple assault." State v. Nazar, 675 So.2d 780 (La.App.1996).

Although an attempt to do an act placing another in apprehension of receiving an immediate battery would be an attempt to assault, there is no such offense as an attempt to assault with intent to murder. People v. Etchison, 123 Mich.App. 448, 333 N.W.2d 309 (1983). There is no offense of attempted assault and battery. Joplin v. State, 663 P.2d 746 (Okl.Cr. 1983).

D was convicted of an attempt to commit conspiracy to commit first-degree murder. This conviction was reversed on the ground that there is no such crime as an attempt to commit conspiracy. It was held that D could have been convicted of solicitation to commit murder. Hutchinson v. State, 315 So.2d 546 (Fla.App.1975).

A conviction of attempted assault was reversed for lack of evidence. The court assumed that there was such an offense, but did not expressly pass upon the point. State v. Merseal, 167 Mont. 412, 538 P.2d 1366 (1975).

It was error to instruct the jury on the theory of attempted reckless murder. There is no crime of attempt to act recklessly. State v. Smith, 21 Or.App. 270, 534 P.2d 1180 (1975): ... "one cannot attempt to act recklessly." Id. at 1184.

Attempt to commit aggravated assault is not recognized in Tennessee. State v. Jackson, 697 S.W.2d 366 (Tenn.Crim.App.1985).

Attempt to commit aggravated assault requires proof of defendant's specific intent. Commonwealth v. Rosado, 454 Pa.Super. 17, 684 A.2d 605 (1996).

Maine recognizes the offense of aggravated assault by inflicting bodily harm under circumstances manifesting extreme indifference to the value of human life. The serious impairment of life as a value must have been reasonably likely from the circumstances. State v. Porter, 693 A.2d 743 (Me.1997).

property is actually burned. We do not so read the statute. It plainly classifies as a high misdemeanor the counseling or solicitation of another to set fire to or burn any insured building, ship or vessel, or goods, wares, merchandise or other chattels, with intent to prejudice or defraud the insurer; and in this regard the statute is primarily declaratory of the common law.

At common law, it is a misdemeanor for one to counsel, incite or solicit another to commit either a felony or a misdemeanor, certainly so if the misdemeanor is of an aggravated character, even though the solicitation is of no effect, and the crime counseled is not in fact committed. The gist of the offense is the solicitation. It is not requisite that some act should be laid to have been done in pursuance of the incitement. While the bare intention to commit evil is not indictable, without an act done, the solicitation, itself, is an act done toward the execution of the evil intent and therefore indictable. An act done with a criminal intent is punishable by indictment. It was said by an eminent common law judge (Lawrence, J., in *Rex v. Higgins, infra*) that under the common law all offenses of a public nature, i.e., "all such acts or attempts as tend to the prejudice of the community," are indictable; and it goes without saying that an attempt to incite another to commit arson or a kindred offense is prejudicial to the community and public in its nature.... In the case of State v. Brand, 76 N.J.L. 267, 69 A. 1092, affirmed 77 N.J.L. 486, 72 A. 131, this court construed the statute as denouncing two separate and distinct offenses, i.e., the willful or malicious setting fire to or burning of insured property, with intent to prejudice the underwriter, and aiding, counseling, procuring or consenting to the setting fire to or burning of such property; but our court of last resort found it unnecessary to consider the question, for there the indictment used the statutory terms in the conjunctive and thus charged that the merchandise was in fact burned.

The solicitation constitutes a substantive crime in itself,[27] and not an abortive attempt to perpetrate the crime solicited. It falls short of an attempt, in the legal sense, to commit the offense solicited.[28] An attempt to commit a crime consists of a direct ineffectual overt act toward the consummation of the crime, done with an intent to commit the crime. Neither intention alone nor acts in mere preparation will suffice. There must be an overt act directly moving toward the commission of the designed offense—such as will apparently result, in the usual and natural course of events, if not hindered by extraneous causes, in the commission of the crime itself.

Of course, at common law one who counsels, incites or solicits another to commit a felony, is indictable as a principal or an accessory before the

---

27. "The solicitation itself is a distinct offense, and is punishable irrespective of the reaction of the person solicited; i.e. the solicitor is guilty even though that person immediately rejects the request or proposal." Hutchins v. Municipal Court of Los Angeles, 61 Cal.App.3d 77, 88, 132 Cal.Rptr. 158, 165 (1976).

28. "Therefore in conformity with the weight of authority, we hold that merely soliciting one to commit a crime does not constitute an attempt." State v. Davis, 319 Mo. 1222, 1229, 6 S.W.2d 609, 612 (1928).

fact, if the designed felony is accomplished, depending upon his presence and participation or absence at the time of its commission.

Plaintiff in error sets great store upon the case of Wimpling v. State, 171 Md. 362, 189 A. 248. But it is not in point. The statute there under review was substantially different; it defined the offense of "arson" in terms that clearly signified an actual burning of the property as an indispensible [sic] ingredient of the crime.

We think that, apart from the statutory recognition of a subsisting common law offense, the prime, if not the exclusive, purpose of the legislative act in question was the classification as a high misdemeanor of what would otherwise be a misdemeanor. . . .

Let the judgment be affirmed.

(D) Abandonment

Stewart v. State

Supreme Court of Nevada, 1969.
85 Nev. 388, 455 P.2d 914.

■ Mowbray, Justice. A jury found Ernest Stewart guilty of attempted robbery. He has appealed to this court, seeking a reversal, on the sole ground that the evidence received during his trial was insufficient to support the jury's verdict.

Marvin Luedtke, who was the victim of the crime, and two police officers appeared for the State. Their testimony stands uncontroverted. It shows that the appellant, Stewart, approached Luedtke, a service station operator, and after brandishing a loaded .32 caliber automatic pistol, said, "I want all of your money." When Luedtke told him that the money was kept in a cash box located near the fuel pumps in front of the station, Stewart demanded the contents of Luedtke's wallet, which Luedtke promptly produced. It was at this juncture that the two police officers drove into the station. One of the officers actually saw the pistol in Stewart's hand. When Stewart saw the officers, he directed Luedtke to bring him two cans of oil and to act as though he, Stewart, were purchasing the oil. Luedtke gave him the oil. Stewart took one can, put his pistol in Luedtke's desk drawer, and attempted to leave the station. He was immediately apprehended by the officers.

Stewart argues that the attempted robbery was not proved because the evidence shows that he had abandoned his intent to commit the crime when he put down the pistol and left the station. We do not agree. The attempted robbery of Luedtke was completed when Stewart produced his pistol and demanded the money. The fact that Luedtke was apprehended on the spot does not lessen his guilt. As the court said in People v. Robinson, 180 Cal.App.2d 745, 4 Cal.Rptr. 679, 682 (1960), ". . . once an intent to commit a crime has been formed and overt acts toward the commission of that crime have been committed by a defendant he is then guilty of an attempt, whether he abandoned that attempt because of the approach of other persons or because of a change in his intentions due to a stricken conscience."

Affirmed.[29]

■ COLLINS, ZENOFF, BATJER and THOMPSON, JJ., concur.

State v. Peterson

Supreme Court of Minnesota, 1942.
213 Minn. 56, 4 N.W.2d 826.

■ PETERSON, JUSTICE. Defendant was convicted of arson in the second degree, and appeals.

The indictment charges her with burning her dwelling house on October 30, 1940. The house was at Lake Minnetonka in Hennepin county.

The state claimed, and its evidence was to the effect, that she did not personally set the fire, but caused it to be set by an accomplice, one August Anderson. There was no dispute as to Anderson's having set the fire. Defendant stoutly maintained that she did not have anything to do with the burning of her house and that she not only direct Anderson not to go to the house on the occasion when the fire was set, but that she tried to persuade him before he set the fire to leave the premises to which he had gone contrary to her directions. . . .

Numerous errors are assigned to the effect . . . and (4) that, assuming the truth of the state's evidence that Anderson and defendant were accomplices, defendant is not liable because she withdrew before the fire was set. Since it is decisive, only the last point need be discussed.

It is important to bear in mind that defendant is not charged with the crime of conspiracy.[30] A conspiracy to commit arson is a misdemeanor. Mason St.1927, §§ 10055, 10056. Arson is a felony. *Id.* §§ 10309–10310; *Id.* 1940 Supp. § 10311. A conspiracy to commit a crime is a separate offense from the crime which is the object of the conspiracy.

One who has procured, counseled, or commanded another to commit a crime may withdraw before the act is done and avoid criminal responsibili-

---

29. "[A]bandonment is not a defense to the commission of the crime of criminal attempt under Nebraska law. . . ." State v. Manchester, 213 Neb. 670, 331 N.W.2d 776, 781 (1983); State v. Fredenburg, 441 So.2d 443 (La.App.1983) (there can be no withdrawal from a completed attempt).

"We are persuaded by the trend of modern authority and hold that voluntary abandonment is an affirmative defense to a prosecution for criminal attempt. . . . Abandonment is not 'voluntary' when the defendant fails to complete the attempted crime because of unanticipated difficulties, unexpected resistance, or circumstances which increase the probability of detention or apprehension." People v. Kimball, 109 Mich.App. 273, 311 N.W.2d 343, 349 (1981).

"By the specific terms of the statute, § 18–2–101(3), C.R.S.1973, abandonment is an affirmative defense to an attempt crime." People v. Johnson, 41 Colo.App. 220, 585 P.2d 306, 308 (1978).

30. An affirmative defense of voluntary abandonment must be recognized against a charge of attempted commission of a crime. United States v. Byrd, 24 M.J. 286 (CMA 1987).

"In the Bridgewater Case [unreported], referred to at the bar, and in which I was counsel, nothing was done in fact; yet a gentleman was convicted because he had entered into an unlawful combination from which almost on the spot he withdrew altogether. No one was harmed, but the public offence was complete." Per Lord Coleridge in Mogul S.S. Co. v. McGregor, Gow & Co., 21 Q.B.D. 544, 549 (1888).

ty by communicating the fact of his withdrawal to the party who is to commit the crime....

By her efforts through Carlson to induce Anderson to leave the premises before he set the fire and to go immediately to her in the hospital where she was then confined, the defendant in the instant case took the most effective measures within her power to arrest the execution of the plan, if there was one, to burn the house. Anderson must have known that if she wanted him to comply with her request to leave the premises before he set the fire she did not want him to burn the house. She not only withdrew in ample time from any plan to burn the house, but made that fact known to Anderson in an unmistakable manner. By withdrawing, defendant avoided criminal responsibility. Anderson was solely criminally responsible for the fire which he set. The facts being undisputed on this point, the verdict cannot stand.

Reversed.[31]

■ MR. JUSTICE STONE, absent because of illness, took no part in the consideration or decision of this case.

MODEL PENAL CODE

Article 5. Inchoate Crimes

Section 5.01 Criminal Attempt.

(1) Definition of Attempt. A person is guilty of an attempt to commit a crime if, acting with the kind of culpability otherwise required for commission of the crime, he:

    (a) purposely engages in conduct which would constitute the crime if the attendant circumstances were as he believes them to be; or

    (b) when causing a particular result is an element of the crime, does or omits to do anything with the purpose of causing or with the belief that it will cause such result without further conduct on his part; or

    (c) purposely does or omits to do anything which, under the circumstances as he believes them to be, is an act or omission constituting a substantial step in a course of conduct planned to culminate in his commission of the crime.

(2) Conduct Which May Be Held Substantial Step Under Subsection (1)(c). Conduct shall not be held to constitute a substantial step under Subsection (1)(c) of this Section unless it is strongly corroborative of the actor's criminal purpose. Without negativing the sufficiency of other conduct, the following, if strongly corroborative of the actor's criminal purpose, shall not be held insufficient as a matter of law:

    (a) lying in wait, searching for or following the contemplated victim of the crime;

    (b) enticing or seeking to entice the contemplated victim of the crime to go to the place contemplated for its commission;

    (c) reconnoitering the place contemplated for the commission of the crime;

    (d) unlawful entry of a structure, vehicle or enclosure in which it is contemplated that the crime will be committed;

---

31. The effect of this judgment was that the case was remanded for a new trial. State v. Peterson, 214 Minn. 204, 7 N.W.2d 408 (1943).

(e) possession of materials to be employed in the commission of the crime, which are specially designed for such unlawful use or which can serve no lawful purpose of the actor under the circumstances;

(f) possession, collection or fabrication of materials to be employed in the commission of the crime, at or near the place contemplated for its commission, where such possession, collection or fabrication serves no lawful purpose of the actor under the circumstances;

(g) soliciting an innocent agent to engage in conduct constituting an element of the crime.

(3) Conduct Designed to Aid Another in Commission of a Crime. A person who engages in conduct designed to aid another to commit a crime which would establish his complicity under Section 2.06 if the crime were committed by such other person, is guilty of an attempt to commit the crime, although the crime is not committed or attempted by such other person.

(4) Renunciation of Criminal Purpose. When the actor's conduct would otherwise constitute an attempt under Subsection (1)(b) or (1)(c) of this Section, it is an affirmative defense that he abandoned his effort to commit the crime or otherwise prevented its commission, under circumstances manifesting a complete and voluntary renunciation of his criminal purpose. The establishment of such defense does not, however, affect the liability of an accomplice who did not join in such abandonment or prevention.

Within the meaning of this Article, renunciation of criminal purpose is not voluntary if it is motivated, in whole or in part, by circumstances, not present or apparent at the inception of the actor's course of conduct, which increase the probability of detection or apprehension or which make more difficult the accomplishment of the criminal purpose. Renunciation is not complete if it is motivated by a decision to postpone the criminal conduct until a more advantageous time or to transfer the criminal effort to another but similar objective or victim.

Section 5.02 Criminal Solicitation.

(1) Definition of Solicitation. A person is guilty of solicitation to commit a crime if with the purpose of promoting or facilitating its commission he commands, encourages or requests another person to engage in specific conduct which would constitute such crime or an attempt to commit such crime or which would establish his complicity in its commission or attempted commission.

(2) Uncommunicated Solicitation. It is immaterial under Subsection (1) of this Section that the actor fails to communicate with the person he solicits to commit a crime if his conduct was designed to effect such communication.

(3) Renunciation of Criminal Purpose. It is an affirmative defense that the actor, after soliciting another person to commit a crime, persuaded him not to do so or otherwise prevented the commission of the crime, under circumstances manifesting a complete and voluntary renunciation of his criminal purpose.

Section 5.04 Incapacity, Irresponsibility or Immunity of Party to Solicitation or Conspiracy.

(1) Except as provided in Subsection (2) of this Section, it is immaterial to the liability of a person who solicits or conspires with another to commit a crime that:

(a) he or the person whom he solicits or with whom he conspires does not occupy a particular position or have a particular characteristic which is an element of such crime, if he believes that one of them does; or

(b) the person whom he solicits or with whom he conspires is irresponsible or has an immunity to prosecution or conviction for the commission of the crime.

(2) It is a defense to a charge of solicitation or conspiracy to commit a crime that if the criminal object were achieved, the actor would not be guilty of a crime under the law defining the offense or as an accomplice under Section 2.06(5) or 2.06(6)(a) or (b).

Section 5.05 Grading of Criminal Attempt, Solicitation and Conspiracy; Mitigation in Cases of Lesser Danger; Multiple Convictions Barred.

(1) Grading. Except as otherwise provided in this Section, attempt, solicitation and conspiracy are crimes of the same grade and degree as the most serious offense which is attempted or solicited or is an object of the conspiracy. An attempt, solicitation or conspiracy to commit a [capital crime or a] felony of the first degree is a felony of the second degree.

(2) Mitigation. If the particular conduct charged to constitute a criminal attempt, solicitation or conspiracy is so inherently unlikely to result or culminate in the commission of a crime that neither such conduct nor the actor presents a public danger warranting the grading of such offense under this Section, the Court shall exercise its power under Section 6.12[32] to enter judgment and impose sentence for a crime of lower grade or degree or, in extreme cases, may dismiss the prosecution.

(3) Multiple Convictions. A person may not be convicted of more than one offense defined by this Article for conduct designed to commit or to culminate in the commission of the same crime.[33]

SECTION 4. NEGATIVE ACTS

Biddle v. Commonwealth

Supreme Court of Appeals of Virginia, 1965.
206 Va. 14, 141 S.E.2d 710.

■ I'ANSON, JUSTICE. Defendant, Shirley Mae Biddle, having waived a jury trial, was tried by the court on an indictment charging her with the murder of her three-month-old baby girl and found guilty of murder in the first degree. After receiving a report from the probation officer, the trial court fixed her punishment and sentenced her to the State penitentiary for a period of twenty years. We granted her a writ of error.

Defendant contends that the trial court erred ... and (2) in holding that the evidence was sufficient to sustain a conviction of first degree murder....

The defendant says that the evidence is sufficient to sustain a conviction of manslaughter but it fails to support her conviction of murder in the

---

32. Section 6.12 provides: "If, when a person, having been convicted of a felony, the Court having regard to the nature and circumstances of the crime and to the history and character of the defendant, is of the view that it would be unduly harsh to sentence the offender in accordance with the Code, the Court may enter judgment of conviction for a lesser degree of felony or for a misdemeanor and impose sentence accordingly."

33. Copyright © 1962 by the American Law Institute. Reprinted with the permission of the American Law Institute.

first degree, because the death of the baby resulted from negligence and not from a malicious omission of duty.

When the detectives visited defendant's home on the night of January 22, 1964, Henley observed the deceased baby's body in an extreme condition of malnutrition, and when he unpinned her diaper he found blood spots on it and on her private parts from diaper rash. He observed another infant lying on newspapers in a bassinet, with a leather jacket over her, and her diapers were wet and dirty and there was a rash on her buttocks. In the kitchen, the detectives saw a large, open can of Pet milk, with a saucer covering the top, and food on the stove which appeared to have been there for several days.

Medical testimony shows that when the baby was born on October 18, 1963, she "seemed to be perfectly healthy." There was also evidence that the baby weighed 5 pounds 8 ounces at birth.

Testimony of the medical examiner reveals that he made a post-mortem examination of the baby's body two days after her death; that she weighed 4 pounds 5½ ounces; that the intestinal tract and stomach were entirely empty, and that the body was dehydrated. It was his opinion that the child had not been fed for several days.

The defendant ... testified that she fed the baby every day but she was small and sometimes would not drink all the milk she gave her; that she fed her three times on the day she died; that she ate very little pablum and fruit; that she never cried because she was hungry; that she loved the baby and did not treat her any differently from the rest of her children; that she had the means to buy food for the children and had milk and other baby food on hand at all times; that she knew the baby had lost weight but had not taken her to a doctor; that her husband had accused her of having the baby by her stepfather and her other children by other men, and she stayed upset most of the time over his untrue accusations.

Defendant's mother said that the baby had been in her home during the day she died and that she had fed her a small amount of fruit and pablum twice on that day, but that she did not appear to be very well.

Section 18.1–21, Code of 1950, as amended, 1960 Repl.Vol., 1964 Cum.Supp., distinguishes the degrees of murder, but it does not define murder itself. . . .

Murder at common law is a homicide committed with malice afore-thought, either express or implied.

The precise question presented here seems never to have been decided by this Court. The general rule, supported by numerous authorities in England and the United States, is that if death is the direct consequence of the malicious omission of the performance of a duty, such as of a mother to feed her child, this is a case of murder; but if the omission is not wilful, and arose out of neglect only, it is manslaughter. . . .

Thus, from the authorities heretofore quoted, whether the defendant was guilty of manslaughter or murder depends upon the nature and character of the act or acts which resulted in the child's death.

Here the defendant was harassed by her husband's accusations that none of her children was his, and the baby's feedings appeared to depend upon how she and her husband got along. When the relationship between them was pleasant she fed the baby, but when it was not she neglected her. She had milk in the house to feed the baby the night it died, but it is apparent from the medical examiner's testimony that she had not fed her for several days. The conditions found when the detectives first went to the apartment and the statements contained in the second signed paper writing made by the defendant to Henley at police headquarters show that she neglected the baby and was careless and indifferent in the performance of her duties not only to the baby, but to other members of her family as well. But, from a consideration of all the facts and circumstances of the case, the Commonwealth has not proved beyond a reasonable doubt that defendant wilfully or maliciously withheld food and liquids from the baby. Hence the conviction of first degree murder is not supported by the evidence, and for this reason the judgment is reversed and the case is remanded for a new trial.

Defendant's court-appointed counsel is allowed a fee of $200, plus expenses, for representing her on the appeal in this Court.

Reversed and remanded.[34]

Commonwealth v. Teixera

Supreme Judicial Court of Massachusetts, 1986.
396 Mass. 746, 488 N.E.2d 775.

■ HENNESSEY, CHIEF JUSTICE.

The defendant appeals from his conviction by a six-person jury in the District Court of neglecting to support an illegitimate child (G.L. c. 273, § 15).[35] On appeal, the defendant argues that the judge erred in denying his motion for a required finding of not guilty, contending that the evidence was insufficient to establish certain elements of the crime. Among these insufficiencies, the defendant contends, is the Commonwealth's failure to establish his financial ability to support the allegedly illegitimate child. Additionally, the defendant argues that the judge's charge that failure to provide support is prima facie evidence that the neglect is wilful and without cause impermissibly shifted the burden of proof to the defendant.... We conclude that a judgment of not guilty must be entered

---

34. "The question thus posed to the jury was whether defendant's omission to provide food for his child was 'aggravated, culpable, gross, or reckless' neglect 'incompatible with a proper regard for human life' (involuntary manslaughter) or involved such a high degree of probability that it would result in death that it constituted 'a wanton disregard for human life' making it second degree murder." People v. Burden, 72 Cal.App.3d 603, 140 Cal.Rptr. 282, 289 (1977).

The elements that support murder by omission and murder by commission are the same. Defendant must act intentionally or knowingly. State v. Tucker, 10 Haw.App. 43, 861 P.2d 24 (1993) remanded other ground and second opinion, 10 Haw.App. 73, 861 P.2d 37 (1993).

35. The defendant was placed on probation with support payments to be determined by probation officers.

because the Commonwealth failed to establish the defendant's financial ability to support the child....

The mother of the child for whom support is sought met the defendant in August, 1979, while hitchhiking. The mother testified that she dated the defendant approximately once a week from August, 1979, to January, 1980. According to her testimony, she became sexually intimate with the defendant at the end of August and continued relations through December, 1979. Near the end of November, 1979, she stated, she discovered that she was pregnant. She testified that she informed the defendant of the pregnancy, and that he suggested that she have an abortion, although he did not offer to pay for the procedure. On another occasion, she testified, the defendant suggested that she place the child for adoption. Her testimony indicates that she did not see the defendant after March, 1980, until November, 1983, when the nonsupport action was pending.

The child was born on June 30, 1980.... [T]he mother testified that in July, 1980, she informed the defendant by telephone that he had a son. The mother applied for welfare benefits for the child in September, 1980, and in August, 1981, a complaint issued against the defendant for nonsupport of an illegitimate child.

At trial, no direct evidence was presented regarding the mother's marital status, and no evidence was introduced as to the defendant's financial circumstances. The defendant, who claims to be indigent, did not testify in his own defense....

The defendant contends that the judge erred in denying the defendant's motion for a required finding of not guilty because the Commonwealth failed to produce evidence regarding the defendant's financial ability to support the child during the period for which the defendant was charged with nonsupport. Section 15 of G.L. c. 273 (1984 ed.) is designed to provide criminal penalties for a parent who "neglects or wilfully refuses to support." In proceedings under § 15, therefore, the Commonwealth must prove each element of the offense beyond a reasonable doubt....

To find a defendant guilty of a violation of § 15, the Commonwealth must prove the following elements beyond a reasonable doubt: (1) the defendant is the parent of the illegitimate child; (2) the defendant, if male, knew or should have known of the existence of a valid claim of his parentage prior to the service of the complaint; and (3) the defendant neglected or wilfully refused to contribute reasonably to the child's support and maintenance.

The statutory requirement that the parents contribute reasonably to the child's support and that the failure to do so be wilful or neglectful before a conviction can be sustained requires the Commonwealth to prove that the defendant was financially able or had the earning capacity to contribute to the support of the child.... Because there was no such proof in the instant case, the defendant was entitled to a required finding of not guilty.[36]

Reversed.

---

36. Financial ability or earning capacity of the defendant may be established by inference drawn from the testimony of the mother or by other direct evidence....

Jones v. United States

United States Court of Appeals, District of Columbia Circuit, 1962.
113 U.S.App.D.C. 352, 308 F.2d 307.

[Shirley Green was the mother of the two children mentioned. Because she was not married and was living with her parents at the time, she arranged to have appellant take Robert from the hospital to appellant's home and agreed to pay appellant $72 a month for his care. There was a dispute in the evidence as to whether these payments were continued beyond five months. When Anthony was born, and was ready to leave the hospital, he also was taken to appellant's home. There seems to have been no specific monetary agreement covering his support, but he remained at appellant's home. Shirley also lived there for at least three weeks, there was a dispute in the evidence as to where she was living later.]

■ WRIGHT, CIRCUIT JUDGE. Appellant, together with one Shirley Green, was tried on a three-count indictment charging them jointly with (1) abusing and maltreating Robert Lee Green, (2) abusing and maltreating Anthony Lee Green, and (3) involuntary manslaughter through failure to perform their legal duty of care for Anthony Lee Green, which failure resulted in his death. At the close of evidence, after trial to a jury, the first two counts were dismissed as to both defendants. On the third count, appellant was convicted of involuntary manslaughter. Shirley Green was found not guilty....

Appellant also takes exception to the failure of the trial court to charge that the jury must find beyond a reasonable doubt, as an element of the crime, that appellant was under a legal duty to supply food and necessities to Anthony Lee. Appellant's attorney did not object to the failure to give this instruction, but urges here the application of Rule 52(b).

The problem of establishing the duty to take action which would preserve the life of another has not often arisen in the case law of this country. The most commonly cited statement of the rule is found in People v. Beardsley, 150 Mich. 206, 113 N.W. 1128, 1129, 13 L.R.A., N.S., 1020:

"The law recognizes that under some circumstances the omission of a duty owed by one individual to another, where such omission results in the death of the one to whom the duty is owing, will make the other chargeable with manslaughter.... This rule of law is always based upon the proposition that the duty neglected must be a legal duty, and not a mere moral obligation. It must be a duty imposed by law or by contract, and the omission to perform the duty must be the immediate and direct cause of death...."

There are at least four situations in which the failure to act may constitute breach of a legal duty. One can be held criminally liable: first, where a statute imposes a duty to care for another; second, where one stands in a certain status relationship to another; third, where one has assumed a contractual duty to care for another; and fourth, where one has voluntarily assumed the care of another and so secluded the helpless person as to prevent others from rendering aid.

It is the contention of the Government that either the third or the fourth ground is applicable here. However, it is obvious that in any of the four situations, there are critical issues of fact which must be passed on by the jury—specifically in this case, whether appellant had entered into a contract with the mother for the care of Anthony Lee or, alternatively, whether she assumed the care of the child and secluded him from the care of his mother, his natural protector. On both of these issues, the evidence is in direct conflict, appellant insisting that the mother was actually living with appellant and Anthony Lee, and hence should have been taking care of the child herself, while Shirley Green testified she was living with her parents and was paying appellant to care for both children.

In spite of this conflict, the instructions given in the case failed even to suggest the necessity for finding a legal duty of care. The only reference to duty in the instructions was the reading of the indictment which charged, inter alia, that the defendants "failed to perform their legal duty." A finding of legal duty is the critical element of the crime charged and failure to instruct the jury concerning it was plain error. . . .

Reversed and remanded.[37]

Davis v. Commonwealth

Supreme Court of Virginia, 1985.
230 Va. 201, 335 S.E.2d 375.

■ STEPHENSON, JUSTICE.

In a bench trial, Mary B. Davis was convicted of involuntary manslaughter of her mother, Emily B. Carter, . . . The trial court found that

---

37. A woman, entrusted with her grandchild, who became so intoxicated that she allowed it to be suffocated although its screams could be heard throughout the neighborhood, is guilty of manslaughter. Cornell v. State, 159 Fla. 687, 32 So.2d 610 (1947). A guard at a railroad crossing, who did not see an approaching train because he was looking the other way and hence did not operate the safety devices, with the result that a motorist was killed, is guilty of manslaughter. State v. Benton, 38 Del. 1, 187 A. 609 (1936). Compare Regina v. Smith, 11 Cox C.C. 210 (1869) with Rex v. Pittwood, 19 Times Law Rep. 37 (1902) and State v. Harrison, 107 N.J.L. 213, 152 A. 867 (1930).

Some early English cases held the failure to provide medical care for a child could result in a manslaughter conviction. Regina v. Downes, 18 Cox CC III (Cr.App. 1875); Regina v. Senior, however, in Regina v. Lowe [1973] 1 All ER 805, the Court of Appeal held the cases were no longer good law for the purposes of constructive manslaughter.

Where husband, a diabetic, made a choice to forego insulin treatment, wife was under no duty to seek medical aid for the husband who died of diabetic ketoacidosis. Commonwealth v. Konz, 450 A.2d 638 (Pa.1982).

A parent who, sincerely motivated by religious faith, failed to secure medical treatment for child, can be convicted of negligent homicide notwithstanding Free Exercise Clause of the First Amendment. Walker v. Superior Court, 763 P.2d 852 (1988).

Good faith belief of parent in spiritual means alone to treat child may be a defense to misdemeanor offense of failing to provide medical care for the child and therefore to manslaughter. State v. Lockhart, 664 P.2d 1059 (Okla.Cr.1983).

Carter's death resulted from Davis' criminal negligence in failing to provide her mother with heat, food, liquids, and other necessaries.

The principal issues in this appeal are: (1) whether Davis had a legal duty to care for Carter, and if so, (2) whether she breached the duty by conduct constituting criminal negligence....

On November 29, 1983, a paramedic with the Lynchburg Fire Department responded to a call at a house located at 1716 Monroe Street in the City of Lynchburg. The house was occupied by Davis and Carter. The paramedic arrived about 5:35 p.m. and found Carter lying on a bed. It was a cold day, and there was no heat in Carter's room. The only source of heat was a tin heater, and it was not being used. The only food in the house was two cans of soup, a can of juice, and an open box of macaroni and cheese. Two trash cans were found behind the house. One contained 11 or 12 empty vegetable cans, and the other was full of empty beer cans. An operable stove, a supply of firewood and a color television were found in Davis' upstairs bedroom.

Carter was admitted to a hospital that evening....

A forensic pathologist with the Chief Medical Examiner's Office conducted an autopsy on Carter's body. He concluded that the causes of death were "pneumonia and freezing to death due to exposure to cold with a chronic state of starvation." He stated that any one of these conditions alone could have caused her death.

Additionally, the pathologist testified that a body temperature of 80 degrees was extremely low and that, except in rare, isolated cases involving children or young people, "no one survives" such a low body temperature....

The pathologist further testified that when a person's dehydration reaches a five to seven percent range, it suggests that she has received no liquids for at least two days. He described Carter's condition as "bone dry." He also testified that Carter's physical condition at the time of the autopsy indicated that she had eaten "no food whatsoever" for at least 30 days.

For a number of years, Carter had been senile and totally disabled. The attending physician testified that Davis said her mother was "not able to feed herself at all; that she was not able to care for her personal needs and that she had to wear diapers and had to have total care." Moreover, Davis informed a number of people that she was responsible for the total care of Carter.

Carter signed a writing naming Davis her authorized representative to apply for, receive, and use her food stamps. Relying on this document, the Department of Social Services awarded Davis additional food stamp benefits of $75 per month and exempted her from the requirement of registering for outside employment as a requisite to receiving these benefits.

Davis also was the representative payee of Carter's social security benefits in the amount of $310 per month. Davis' household expenses were paid exclusively from Carter's social security. Davis also received $23 per month in food stamps for her mother.

Next, we determine whether, under the facts and circumstances presented, Davis was under a legal duty to care for her mother. This presents an issue which we have not addressed previously.

A legal duty is one either "imposed by law, or by contract." When a death results from an omission to perform a legal duty, the person obligated to perform the duty may be guilty of culpable homicide. Biddle v. Commonwealth, 206 Va. 14, 20, 141 S.E.2d 710, 714 (1965). If the death results from a malicious omission of the performance of a duty, the offense is murder. On the other hand, although no malice is shown, if a person is criminally negligent in omitting to perform a duty, he is guilty of involuntary manslaughter.

Davis acknowledges the accuracy of the foregoing legal principles. She contends, however, that the evidence fails to establish that she had a legal duty to care for her mother, asserting that the evidence proved at most a moral duty. We do not agree.

The evidence makes clear that Davis accepted sole responsibility for the total care of Carter. This became her full-time occupation. In return, Carter allowed Davis to live in her home expense free and shared with Davis her income from social security. Additionally, Carter authorized Davis to act as her food stamp representative, and for this Davis received food stamp benefits in her own right. From this uncontroverted evidence, the trial court reasonably could find the existence of an implied contract. Clearly, Davis was more than a mere volunteer; she had a legal duty, not merely a moral one, to care for her mother.

Finally, we consider whether the evidence is sufficient to support the trial court's finding of criminal negligence. . . .

When the proximate cause of a death is simply ordinary negligence, i.e., the failure to exercise reasonable care, the negligent party cannot be convicted of involuntary manslaughter. To constitute criminal negligence essential to a conviction of involuntary manslaughter, an accused's conduct "must be of such reckless, wanton or flagrant nature as to indicate a callous disregard for human life and of the probable consequences of the act."

Davis contends that she cared for her mother as best she could under the circumstances. She points to the testimony of her four sisters and her boyfriend who stated that everything seemed normal and that they observed nothing to suggest that Carter was being neglected. These witnesses stated that the house always was heated properly and that sufficient food was available at all times.

Against this testimony, however, was the scientific evidence that Carter died of starvation and freezing. The evidence indicates that Carter had received no food for at least 30 days. She lay helpless in bed in an unheated room during cold weather. The trial court, as the trier of fact, determines the weight of the evidence and the credibility of the witnesses. Obviously, the court, as it had the right to do, accepted the Commonwealth's evidence and gave little or no weight to the testimony of the defendant and her witnesses. The court reasonably could conclude that

Carter could not have starved or frozen to death unless she had been neglected completely for a protracted period of time.

We hold, therefore, that the evidence supports the trial court's finding that Davis' breach of duty was so gross and wanton as to show a callous and reckless disregard of Carter's life and that Davis' criminal negligence proximately caused Carter's death. Accordingly, we will affirm the judgment of the trial court.

Affirmed.

Van Buskirk v. State

Court of Criminal Appeals of Oklahoma, 1980.
611 P.2d 271.

■ CORNISH, PRESIDING JUDGE. On July 9, 1977, during an argument between the appellant and her boyfriend, Robert Rose, the pair stopped in a low place between two hills on the road from Allen to Ada, Oklahoma. Rose was ordered to get out of the car, and he was thereafter struck by the appellant's vehicle. The appellant then drove away, leaving Rose in the roadway. Subsequently, Rose was struck by another car moving at a high speed. The appellant was charged with Murder in the Second Degree in Pontotoc County District Court. She was convicted of Manslaughter, Second Degree, and sentenced to two (2) years' imprisonment.

I

The first question for determination is whether the trial court erred in instructing the jury on Manslaughter in the Second Degree. The appellant's position is that the manslaughter in the second degree statute, 21 O.S. 1971, § 716, was impliedly repealed when the negligent homicide statute, 47 O.S.1971, § 11–903, was passed. The appellant's assertion is correct to the extent that motor vehicles are involved. Atchley v. State, Okl.Cr., 473 P.2d 286 (1970). However, the negligent homicide statute applies only when death is caused "by the driving of any vehicle in reckless disregard of the safety of others." Section 11–903(a). A review of the facts indicates that § 11–903(a) is not applicable here.

According to the appellant's testimony, she was driving when Rose slapped her, knocking her eyeglasses off her face. She stopped the car, ordered Rose to get out and searched for her glasses. Rose left the passenger's side of the car and started to walk in front of the vehicle around to the driver's side. The appellant said that as she leaned over to look for her eyeglasses she accidentally pressed the gas pedal. The result was that the car lurched forward, lifting Rose onto the hood. Rose pounded on the windshield, cursing, and the appellant then hit the brake pedal, throwing Rose to the ground. The appellant testified that Rose was starting to get up as she put the vehicle in reverse, swerved around him and drove away.

A passing motorist saw Rose lying in the roadway. He stopped his car and attempted to signal to a rapidly approaching car. The motorist said that Rose was "sort of moaning." The motorist's efforts to stop the approaching car were to no avail. The automobile struck Rose and dragged him a short distance down the highway. Having ascertained that Rose was dead, he pulled the body from the road.

Under these facts, we do not believe that Rose was the victim of negligent homicide. The crime was committed, not when the appellant struck Rose, but when she abandoned him in a position of peril. At that time she could reasonably have anticipated that another vehicle might strike Rose. The foreseeability of such a consequence—where the victim lay helpless in a lane of traffic, in a low place between two hills—is apparent. It places the appellant squarely within the scope of 21 O.S.1971, § 716:

"Every killing of one human being by the act, procurement *or culpable negligence* of another, which, under the provisions of this chapter, is not murder, nor manslaughter in the first degree, nor excusable nor justifiable homicide, is manslaughter in the second degree." (Emphasis added)

Thus, the trial court correctly instructed the jury on Manslaughter in the Second Degree.

II

In the fourth, fifth, and sixth assignments of error the appellant complains that the trial court failed to give instructions on proximate cause, justifiable homicide and/or self-defense, and circumstantial evidence. The record indicates that at the time of the trial the appellant neither objected to the instructions given by the trial court nor requested that any particular instruction be given. In such a situation, this Court will generally limit itself to an examination of the instructions which were given, to see whether they fairly covered the issues raised during the trial. We have carefully examined the trial court's instructions and find that they adequately cover the subject matter of inquiry.

III

The next alleged error also relates to the jury instructions. The fourth instruction defines murder in the second degree, but the ninth instruction informs the jury that the trial judge made a judicial determination that the facts of the case would not support a conviction for murder in the second degree, and that they should not consider that charge. The appellant argues that the combination of instructions must have prejudiced the jury against her. Although we are uncertain why the trial court chose to proceed in this manner, we fail to see how the appellant suffered any prejudice thereby. The appellant raises no more than speculation as to the effect of the instructions. Where, as here, the appellant has been deprived of no fundamental right, this Court will not search the books for authorities to support the mere assertion that the trial court has erred.

IV

The remaining allegations of error relate to the sufficiency of the evidence. The appellant argues that her demurrer to the evidence should have been sustained, that the trial court erred in failing to direct a verdict in her favor, and that the verdict is contrary to the evidence. When an appellant challenges the sufficiency of the evidence presented at the trial, the function of this Court is to determine whether the State presented a prima facie case. If so, then all questions of fact were properly submitted to the jury. In the case before us, the State did present a prima facie case, and these assignments of error are without merit. The judgment and sentence is AFFIRMED.

■ BRETT and BUSSEY, JJ., concur.[38]

MODEL PENAL CODE

Section 2.01 (Requirement of Voluntary Act;) Omission as Basis of Liability; (Possession as an Act.)

. . .

(3) Liability for the commission of an offense may not be based on an omission unaccompanied by action unless:

(a) the omission is expressly made sufficient by the law defining the offense; or

(b) a duty to perform the omitted act is otherwise imposed by law.[39]

SECTION 5. PARTIES TO CRIME

State v. Sowell

Court of Appeals of Maryland, 1999.
353 Md. 713, 728 A.2d 712.

Respondent Brian Lamont Sowell was convicted by a jury in the Circuit Court for Prince George's County of armed robbery, robbery, two counts of use of a handgun in the commission of a crime of violence, and first degree assault for his involvement along with three other men in the robbery of his employer, Recycling Incorporated.[1] He appealed to the Court of Special Appeals. That court reversed respondent's convictions, holding that the evidence presented to the jury was not sufficient to support a finding that respondent was present at the scene of the crime, either constructively or actually. Therefore, under the common law rules relating

---

38. A defendant who provided victim with an overdose of cocaine and then failed to promptly summon medical assistance was properly convicted of manslaughter. Herman v. State, 472 So.2d 770 (Fla.App.1985).

Hawaii statute requiring a person at the scene of a crime, who knows that a victim of a crime is suffering from serious physical harm, to obtain aid if the person can do so without danger, applies to the perpetrators of crime as well as others and a perpetrator who abused a child could be guilty of homicide for failure to aid. State v. Cabral, 8 Haw.App. 506, 810 P.2d 672 (1991).

39. Copyright © 1962 by the American Law Institute. Reprinted with the permission of the American Law Institute.

1. Terrell Roshsay Pinkney was tried with respondent as a co-defendant and convicted of armed robbery, robbery, two counts of use of a handgun, false imprisonment, and first degree assault for his participation in the robbery at Recycling Incorporated. Mr. Pinkney and respondent both appealed to the Court of Special Appeals. That court affirmed the judgments as to Mr. Pinkney. Mr. Pinkney takes no part in the present appeal.

to principals and accessories, that court held that the respondent should not have been convicted as a principal in the second degree.

We granted a writ of certiorari to consider whether the common law distinction between principals and accessories remains viable in Maryland. We hold that it does. Accordingly, we shall affirm.

I. Facts

On the date of the underlying crimes, October 17, 1995, respondent was employed by Recycling Incorporated. The company paid its employees' wages in cash, and the money normally was distributed by DeLisa Holmes, the office manager. Around 11:30 a.m., respondent called Recycling Incorporated's office to inquire when the payroll would be ready. Ms. Holmes told respondent the payroll would be ready at 12:00 p.m. Respondent then asked how the employees were going to be paid. Ms. Holmes replied that they would be paid in cash, to which respondent replied, "good." Respondent picked up his pay in cash at around 12:30 p.m.

About an hour later, three men wearing dark clothing and carrying guns entered the Recycling Incorporated office. One man walked directly to Brian Fowler, the vice-president of the company, and held a gun on him. A second man put a gun to Ms. Holmes' head and told her to get the cash. She placed all of the cash, $14,600, in a bag provided by one of the men and the three men left. Ms. Holmes testified that the man who held the gun to her head seemed familiar with the office and knew where the money was located.

Testimony by other witnesses indicated that respondent was the mastermind behind the robbery. Anthony Williams testified that prior to the robbery, respondent told Williams he knew where they could get some easy money and that he had it "all planned out." Respondent targeted the recycling company because it paid its employees in cash and he knew how someone could get in and out quickly. Williams further testified that respondent had a map of the recycling center detailing where the employees would be standing, who should be grabbed, and who might have a gun. Respondent told the others that the robbery should occur between 11:30 a.m. and 12:30 p.m. and that while the robbery was in process, he would be on his route for the recycling company. The men arranged to meet later to split up the money. Williams further testified that he saw the men involved in the robbery the next day. Respondent said that "it was easy, just like he had planned."

II. Discussion and Analysis

A. Common Law Doctrine of Accessoryship

The question for which we issued the writ of certiorari and as phrased in the State's brief is: "Was the evidence sufficient to establish that [respondent] was an accomplice either because constructive presence is not required to establish accomplice liability or because he was constructively present?"

The underlying issue argued by both parties is whether Maryland should retain the common law distinction between principals and accessories before the fact. The Court of Special Appeals, although criticizing the long-standing Maryland common law rule that distinguishes an accessory before the fact from a principal in the second degree by the requirement that the principal be actually or constructively present, nonetheless reversed respondent's convictions as a principal in the second degree. That court held:

> There is, of course, a major legal hurdle regarding the State's request [to dispense with the distinction between accessories before the fact and principals]. The argument, in *Lewis* [*v. State*, 285 Md. 705, 404 A.2d 1073 (1979)], to change the rule mandating that an accessory cannot be tried before the principal is sentenced, was presented to the Maryland Court of Appeals, the State court of last resort authorized to set policy. It may well be that that Court would be favorably disposed to dispense with the distinction between accessories and principals, particularly principals in the second degree. Until and unless the Court of Appeals effectuates such a change, we hold that the evidence before the jury neither directly nor inferentially permitted a finding that [respondent] was constructively or actually present at the scene of the crime. Therefore, he could have been convicted only of being an accessory before the fact, rather than a principal in the second degree. Accordingly, we must reverse the judgements of conviction of [respondent] Sowell.

This Court described the common law distinction between principals and accessories in *State v. Ward*, 284 Md. 189, 197, 396 A.2d 1041, 1046–47 (1978):

> A *principal in the first degree* is one who actually commits a crime, either by his own hand, or by an inanimate agency, or by an innocent human agent. A *principal in the second degree* is one who is guilty of felony by reason of having aided, counseled, commanded or encouraged the commission thereof in his presence, either actual or constructive. An *accessory before the fact* is one who is guilty of felony by reason of having aided, counseled, commanded or encouraged the commission thereof, without having been present either actually or constructively at the moment of perpetration. An *accessory after the fact* is one who, with knowledge of the other's guilt, renders assistance to a felon in the effort to hinder his detection, arrest, trial or punishment.

The main difference between an accessory before the fact and a principal in the second degree is that the latter must be actually or constructively present at the scene of the crime.

As noted by the Court of Special Appeals in its opinion below, the distinction has not been without criticism. In *State v. Williamson*, 282 Md. 100, 112–14, 382 A.2d 588, 594–95 (1978), Judge Levine, concurring, took issue with the majority's failure to abandon the accessory before the fact distinction:

> Since accessories and principals at common law were deemed to be equally culpable and therefore subject to the same punishment, *Agresti v. State*, 2 Md.App. at 281, [234 A.2d 284]; 1 J. Chitty, *A Practical Treatise on the Criminal Law* (1819); Clark & Marshall, *A Treatise on*

the Law of Crimes § 8.05, at 522 (7th ed.1967), the classification of parties as principals and accessories had little, if any, substantive significance.

On the other hand, the common law doctrines of accessoryship did give rise to several highly technical procedural rules which, as one recent commentator has stated, "tended to shield accessories from punishment notwithstanding overwhelming evidence of their criminal assistance." W. LaFave & A. Scott, *Handbook on Criminal Law* § 63, at 498–99 (1972)....

. . . .

The reason for the development of these rules is obscure at best. Professor Perkins has speculated that they were devised by 14th and 15th century English common law courts as a means of alleviating the harshness of the death penalty in felony cases. R. Perkins, *Criminal Law* 669 (2d ed.1969); *and see* W. LaFave & A. Scott, *Handbook on Criminal Law* § 63, at 499 (1972). If this theory of the historical provenience of the common law categories and procedures be correct, it is now beyond question that the rules have outlived their purpose, in light of the universal rejection of capital punishment for any but the most heinous felonies and the manifold constitutional restrictions placed upon application of the death penalty in recent years. *See, e.g., Gregg v. Georgia,* 428 U.S. 153, 96 S.Ct. 2909, 49 L.Ed.2d 859 (1976); *Furman v. Georgia,* 408 U.S. 238, 92 S.Ct. 2726, 33 L.Ed.2d 346 (1972).[2]

The common law principles of accomplicity and their procedural counterparts, in my opinion, have injected a most undesirable hypertechnicality into the law of accomplice responsibility, which not infrequently operates to thwart justice and reduce judicial efficiency. *See* Note, 19 Wash. & Lee L.Rev. 96 (1962). As this Court candidly stated in *Watson v. State,* 208 Md. at 218, [117 A.2d 549]:

    " 'This distinguishing of the accessory before the fact from the principal is a pure technicality. It has no existence either in natural reason or the ordinary doctrines of the law. For in natural reason the procurer of a crime is not chargeable differently from the doer; and a familiar rule of the common law is that what one does through another's agency is regarded as done by himself.... Likewise in morals, there are circumstances wherein we attach more blame to the accessory before the fact than to his principal;....' " (Quoting 1 J. Bishop, *Criminal Law* § 673, at 486–87 (9th ed.1923)).

The time has come in my opinion to discard the common law distinction between principals and accessories before the fact and to replace these categories with an all-encompassing doctrine which would treat all those who knowingly procure, command, counsel, encourage, aid or abet a felon in the commission of a crime as principals regardless of whether the aider or abettor was actually or constructively present at the scene of the crime.

---

    2. Many of these restrictions on the application of the death penalty subsequently have been modified.

Similar sentiments have been expressed by this Court, but only with regard to the technical procedural rules accompanying the common law doctrine of accessoryship. *See, e.g., Jones v. State,* 302 Md. 153, 160–61, 486 A.2d 184, 188 (1985) (criticizing as illogical and unreasonable the common law rules that the principal must be convicted before the accessory and that the accessory cannot be convicted of a higher crime than the principal); *Lewis,* 285 Md. at 715, 404 A.2d at 1079 (recognizing as unsound "the common law rule precluding trial of an accessory until the principal is sentenced"); *Ward,* 284 Md. at 192, 396 A.2d at 1043–44 (pointing out that the technical procedural rules accompanying the common law doctrine of accessoryship are illogical and "shield accessories from punishment notwithstanding overwhelming evidence of their criminal assistance").

Even though in Maryland the common law may be modified by legislative act, Maryland Declaration of Rights, Article 5(a), or by judicial decision, *see State v. Hawkins,* 326 Md. 270, 291–92, 604 A.2d 489, 500–01 (1992), we commented in *Ward* that "Maryland is one of the few, if not the only state, which has retained this doctrine in virtually the same form as it existed at the time of William Blackstone in the 18th century, and it represents the law of Maryland at the present time." *Ward,* 284 Md. at 191, 396 A.2d at 1043.

All of the states substantively modifying the common law rule appear to have done so legislatively. The states that have legislatively modified the common law by explicit statutory language abolishing the distinction or language legislatively nullifying the distinction, albeit retaining some of the common law terminology, are Alabama, Alaska, Arizona, Arkansas, California, Colorado, Connecticut, Delaware, Florida, Georgia, Hawaii, Idaho, Illinois, Indiana, Iowa, Kansas, Kentucky, Louisiana, Maine, Massachusetts, Michigan, Minnesota, Mississippi, Missouri, Montana, Nebraska, Nevada, New Hampshire, New Jersey, New Mexico, New York, North Carolina, North Dakota, Ohio, Oklahoma, Oregon, Pennsylvania, Rhode Island, South Carolina, South Dakota, Tennessee, Texas, Utah, Vermont, Virginia, Washington, West Virginia, Wisconsin, and Wyoming. *See* MODEL PENAL CODE § 2.04, App. at 40–41 (Tentative Draft No. 1, 1956) ("Every American jurisdiction except Maryland has also legislated on the subject."); MODEL PENAL CODE § 2.06 cmt. 1, n. 3 (1985) (Official Draft and Revised Comments). *See also* WAYNE R. LaFAVE & AUSTIN W. SCOTT, JR., CRIMINAL LAW § 6.6(e), at 574–75 (2d ed.1986).[3] Even the birthplace of the common law, England, abrogated some of the technicalities of the doctrine of accessoryship, albeit by legislative reform. *See id.* (citing The Accessories and Abettors Act, 1861, 24 & 25 Viced. ch. 94 (Eng.)). . . .

---

3. California, for example, expressly abrogated the common law distinction and the need to indict an accused specifically as a principal or an accessory in 1872. *See* CAL.PENAL CODE, § 971 (West 1985). That statute provides:

The distinction between an accessory before the fact and a principal, and between principals in the first and second degree is abrogated; and all persons concerned in the commission of a crime, who by the operation of other provisions of this code are principals therein, shall hereafter be prosecuted, tried and punished as principals and no other facts need be alleged in any accusatory pleading against any such person than are required in an accusatory pleading against a principal.

This Court has abrogated judicially some aspects of the common law of accessoryship. For instance, in *Hawkins,* 326 Md. at 294, 604 A.2d at 501, we abolished the common law limitation that an accessory after the fact may not be a principal in either degree in the commission of a substantive felony. In *Jones,* 302 Md. at 159–61, 486 A.2d at 188, we held that an accessory before the fact may be convicted of a greater crime than the principal. *Lewis,* 285 Md. at 715–16, 404 A.2d at 1077–78, abrogated the common law requirement that a principal must be convicted before the accessory. Finally, in *Ward,* 284 Md. at 207, 396 A.2d at 1048, we held that there may be an accessory before the fact for murder in the second degree. Nonetheless, this Court has yet to address expressly the specific issue at hand of whether Maryland should abandon the common law doctrine of accessoryship. *See Ward,* 284 Md. at 191 n. 3, 396 A.2d at 1043 n. 3; *Williamson,* 282 Md. at 110, 382 A.2d at 593. This Court is not precluded from altering a common law rule in situations in which "in light of changed conditions or increased knowledge, ... the rule has become unsound in the circumstances of modern life, a vestige of the past, no longer suitable to our people." *State v. Wiegmann,* 350 Md. 585, 604, 714 A.2d 841, 850 (1998) (quoting *Harrison,* 295 Md. at 459, 456 A.2d at 903).

"[I]n considering whether a long-established common law rule-unchanged by the legislature and thus reflective of this state's public policy-is unsound in the circumstances of modern life, we have always recognized that declaration of the public policy of Maryland is normally the function of the General Assembly." *Gaver,* 316 Md. at 28–29, 557 A.2d at 216 (quoting *Harrison,* 295 Md. at 460, 456 A.2d at 903). We have recognized that the General Assembly's failure to amend or abrogate a common law rule sometimes reflects its desired public policy. *See Wiegmann,* 350 Md. at 605, 714 A.2d at 850–51....

[A]lthough Maryland apparently is the only jurisdiction that has not rejected the common law distinctions between principals and accessories, the majority of the other jurisdictions rejecting the distinctions have done so legislatively. Given the relative importance in completely abrogating an ancient and historic common law doctrine such as accessoryship, we believe such a task is generally better left to the legislative body of this State. *See, e.g., Wiegmann,* 350 Md. at 607, 714 A.2d at 851–52 (declining to abolish the common law rule permitting persons to resist illegal arrests). We decline, at this time, to abrogate the doctrine by judicial action.

B. Constructive Presence

Because we decline to abolish the common law distinctions between principals and accessories, we must address whether the Court of Special Appeals erred in holding "the evidence before the jury neither directly nor inferentially permitted a finding that [respondent] was constructively or actually present at the scene of the crime." *Sowell,* 122 Md.App. at 238, 712 A.2d at 104....

The indictment, as relevant to the issue before the Court, provided in the first count: "The Grand Jurors ... do present that Brian Lamont Sowell ... feloniously with a dangerous and deadly weapon did rob ... and violently did steal." The second count provided that respondent "feloniously did rob ... and violently did steal." In the third and sixth count, the indictment provided: "The Grand Jurors ... do present that Brian Lamont Sowell ... did unlawfully use a handgun in the commission of a crime of violence." In the seventh count, the indictment provided: "The Grand Jurors ... do present that Brian Lamont Sowell ... did unlawfully assault." As is evident, the language of the indictment fails to charge respondent specifically as a principal or as an accessory. There is no indication in the record, however, that respondent moved to dismiss this indictment.

The Court of Special Appeals long has recognized that the State must charge a defendant correctly as a principal or accessory. For example, that court explained in great detail in *Agresti v. State*, 2 Md.App. 278, 281, 234 A.2d 284, 286 (1967):

> Although at common law an accessory before the fact is liable to the same punishment as the principal, the distinction between them is important in practice unless the distinction has been changed by statute. At common law, an indictment must charge a person correctly as principal or accessory according to the facts and on an indictment charging a person as principal there could be no conviction on evidence showing that he was merely an accessory and vice versa. *Clark and Marshall, Crimes, supra,* § 8.05, p. 462; *Sanders v. State,* 1 Md.App. 630, 232 A.2d 555. It is stated in *Perkins on Criminal Law* (1957), ch. 6, § 8, D, 1 b, page 583:

> "The case may be lost in advance either by carelessness in the pleading or by a mistaken notion as to whether the particular defendant was or was not present at the time the crime was committed. One charged with felony as a principal cannot be convicted if the evidence established assessorial guilt, and one charged as an accessory cannot be convicted if the evidence shows him to have been a principal. One may be charged as a principal and as an accessory in separate counts of the same indictment, but the prosecution can be required to elect upon which count it will rely before the case is finally submitted to the jury."

In *Williamson,* 282 Md. at 107–08, 382 A.2d at 592, this Court, after discussing the Court of Special Appeals' holdings, *supra,* described the modern tendency of courts to shy away from the "strict requirements" for common law indictments. We then went on to hold that the defendant in that case need not have been indicted specifically as an accessory or principal because the General Assembly by legislative enactment relaxed the formal indictment requirements for accomplices in cases of homicide. 1906 Md. Laws, Chap. 248. No such legislative acts have relaxed the requirements for specifically charging defendants as an accessory or principal to robbery or robbery with a deadly weapon.

The State evidently proceeded under the theory that respondent was charged as a principal, as that is what the judge instructed the jury to consider:

> I also instruct you at this time, folks, on the doctrine of aiding and abetting. The Defendants are charged with the crimes of robbery with

a dangerous weapon, robbery, use of a handgun in the commission of a crime of violence, two times, and first degree assault.

A person who aids and abets in the commission of a crime is as guilty as the actual perpetrator, even though he did not personally commit each of the acts that constitutes the crime.

A person aids and abets the commission of a crime by knowingly associating with the criminal venture with the intent to help commit the crime, *being present when the crime is committed,* and seeking by some act to make the act succeed.

In order to prove that the Defendants aided and abetted the commission of a crime, the State must prove that the Defendants were *present when the crime was committed,* and that the Defendants willfully participated with the intent to make the crime succeed.

Presence means being at the scene or close enough to render assistance to other perpetrators.

Willful participation means voluntary and intentional participation in the criminal act.

Some conduct by the Defendants in furtherance of the crime is necessary. The mere presence of the Defendants at the time and place of the commission of the crime is not enough to prove that they aided and abetted. But if presence is proven, it is a fact that may be considered along with all of the surrounding circumstances.

However, *presence at the scene of a crime can be sufficient, if it was intended to and does aid the primary actor;* for example, standing by as a lookout to warn the primary actor of danger. [Emphasis added.]

From the record, it appears the State made no objection to this instruction. We therefore must proceed on the assumption that it intended to charge respondent as a principal in the second degree because the jury never was instructed on the law as to accessories before the fact.

Before this Court, the parties do not dispute that respondent was not actually present during the commission of the robbery and concede the only issue is whether he was constructively present. In *Ward,* 284 Md. at 197, 396 A.2d at 1046–47, we explained that

[a] *principal in the second degree* is one who is guilty of felony by reason of having aided, counseled, commanded or encouraged the commission thereof in his presence, either actual or constructive. An *accessory before the fact* is one who is guilty of felony by reason of having aided, counseled, commanded or encouraged the commission thereof, without having been present either actually or constructively at the moment of perpetration.

We further described in detail the distinction between principals in the second degree and accessories before the fact in *Williamson,* 282 Md. at 103–04, 382 A.2d at 590 (quoting 4 W. Blackstone, *Commentaries*):

"A principal in the ... second degree ... is who is present, aiding and abetting the fact to be done. Which *presence* need not always be an actual immediate standing by, within sight or hearing of the fact; but there may be also a constructive presence, as when one commits a robbery or murder and another keeps watch or guard at some convenient distance." *Id.* 282 Md. at 103, 382 A.2d at 590. (Emphasis in original.) (Footnotes omitted.)

"As to the second point, who may be an accessary *before* the fact; Sir Matthew Hale defines him to be one who, being absent at the time of the crime committed, doth yet procure, counsel, or command another to commit a crime. Herein absence is necessary to make him an accessary; for if such procurer, or the like, be present, he is guilty of the crime as principal."

The concept of constructive presence is fairly broad, as one need not be in sight or hearing of the crime being committed to be a principal in the second degree. The test is not whether the alleged principal in the second degree could see the scene of the crime, but whether he or she could render assistance to the actual perpetrator. *See Williamson,* 282 Md. at 105, 382 A.2d at 591 ("A person is regarded as constructively present, within the rules relating to parties in criminal cases, whenever he is cooperating with the perpetrator and is so situated as to be able to aid him, with a view known to the other, to insure success in the accomplishment of the common purpose." (quotations and citation omitted)); *McBryde,* 30 Md. App. at 360, 352 A.2d at 326 ("A person is constructively present, hence guilty as a principal, if he is acting with the person who actually commits the deed in pursuance of a common design, and is aiding his associate, either by keeping watch or otherwise or is so situated as to be able to aid him, with a view, known to the other, to insure success in the accomplishment of the common enterprise." (citation omitted)). In *Williamson,* for example, even though the defendant was physically close enough to the scene of her husband's murder to render assistance to the killer, there was no evidence that she in fact was present in order to render aid of any kind; thus she could not, even though nearby, be convicted as a principal in the second degree.[8] *Williamson,* 282 Md. at 105, 382 A.2d at 591. By contrast, the defendants in *McBryde,* although not within sight of the scene of the crime, were waiting nearby to aid the principal in the first degree in his escape after he robbed a convenience store and thus were principals in the second degree. *McBryde,* 30 Md.App. at 360, 352 A.2d at 326–27. The common element in constructive presence for the purpose of proving a defendant was a principal in the second degree, therefore, is the ability, desire, and design to render any necessary aid to the principal in the first degree during the commission of the crime.

One commentator is in accord with this interpretation:

A person is constructively present when he is physically absent from the situs of the crime but aids and abets the principal in the first degree at the time of the offense from some distance. This may happen when one stands watch for the primary actor, signals to the principal from a distance that the victim is coming, or stands ready (though out

---

8. The defendant was asleep in the house when her husband was killed inside a car in their driveway.

of sight) to render aid to the principal if needed. However, one must be close enough to render aid if needed.

LaFave & Scott, *supra,* § 6.6(b), at 571 (footnotes omitted). . . .

Turning to the case at hand, the evidence tended to show that respondent went to Recycling Incorporated to pick up his wages at approximately 12:30 p.m. About an hour later, the three men who ultimately committed the robbery and other crimes entered Recycling Incorporated's offices and took the cash. Respondent was not present on the premises or nearby when the crimes took place. One witness testified that prior to the commission of the crimes, respondent drove to the area where the actors were waiting in parked cars and told them to go ahead. The witness testified:

A. He pulls up to the car, his side of the car in the front.

Q. And then drives off?

A. He says go ahead.

Q. You drive off and [respondent] drives off?

A. Yes.

Q. Their car is there, your car is there, Smoot's car is there, and [respondent] goes off in a different direction?

A. Yes.

Q. *He drives his car off, and he's out of sight, right?*

A. Yes. [Emphasis added.]

Another witness testified as to the following:

Q. . . . [W]hat, if anything, did [respondent] say about where he would be when the robbery took place?

. . . .

THE WITNESS: *He said he was going to go out on his route so it wouldn't look like he had anything to do with it,* and that he would meet them back around Tuley Street right after everything happened, and then they would split the money up. [Emphasis added.]

There was no evidence presented that respondent waited as a lookout or in a getaway car during the robbery. In fact, the evidence showed that respondent purposefully absented himself from the scene of the crime to avoid suspicion about his involvement. That he "scouted out" the situation *before* the robbery and signaled to the actors to "go ahead" with their plan, although making him an accessory before the fact, does not render respondent actually or constructively present during the crime for purposes of principal in the second degree liability. There was no evidence that respondent had the ability to render aid to the principals during the actual commission of the crimes. Although the evidence tended to show that respondent was the mastermind of the robbery and planned the crimes from beginning to end, the simple fact is that he was not present, either actually or constructively, during the commission of these crimes. Accordingly, we hold there was not sufficient evidence from which to convict respondent as a principal in the second degree.

III. Conclusion

We hold that until the Legislature provides otherwise, Maryland retains the common law distinction between principals and accessories. Respondent was tried only as a principal in the second degree, which requires presence, not as an accessory before the fact, which does not require presence. Accordingly, we must affirm the Court of Special Appeals and reverse respondent's convictions because there was not sufficient evidence to find that he was present, actually or constructively, at the scene of the crime.

■ RAKER, Judge, concurring.

I concur only in the judgment of the Court. I agree with the majority that the evidence was insufficient to establish that Sowell was a principal in the first or second degree and that, under the current state of the law in Maryland, his conviction must be reversed. I part company with the majority, however, because I believe that the time has come for this Court to abolish the common law distinction in charging between principals and accessories.

Writing for the Court of Special Appeals in *Williamson,* 36 Md.App. at 413, 374 A.2d at 914, Judge Thomas Hunter Lowe, in his perfervid dissent, noted the futility in awaiting a legislative change of the common law distinction between accessories before the fact and principals. He wrote:

> It is hardly conceivable that in the 20th Century, a court of last resort could so clearly recognize the utter purposelessness of so horrendously harmful a semantic distinction, yet must still recognize its viability. Worse yet is the fact that more than two decades have passed since this 'pure technicality ... [which] has no existence either in natural reason or the ordinary doctrines of the law ...' was held up to ridicule in that case, and the Legislature has done nothing to correct it. Nor did our own attempt at flagging this fictional foolishness in *Agresti v. State,* 2 Md.App. 278, 281, 234 A.2d 284, elicit a statutory erasure of that common law blot upon jurisdictional reasoning, as has been accomplished in many, if not most common law jurisdictions. See 40 Am. Jur.2d, *Homicide* §§ 28, 29; 21 Am.Jur.2d, *Criminal Law* §§ 120–124; 22 C.J.S. *Criminal Law* § 82; see also 95 A.L.R.2d 175, 178, 187.

(Alteration and omissions in original) (footnote omitted).

The judicial system and the common law created the doctrine in question, and thus, it is appropriate for the judicial branch of government to correct the anomaly when we recognize that the distinction is not practical, useful, or fair. As Judge Lowe noted:

> This has caused us factually to distinguish and interpretatively whittle away at the rule, but such intellectual exercises hardly do justice to the judicial system. Because it was not the legislative branch but the common law judicial system that created the technical monster, I would no longer await the action of a Legislature which may well be too occupied with matters of state to clean up the jurisprudential cobwebs we have accumulated. The common law is a growing thing and when it outgrows old garments not only of no further use but of potential harm, they should be discarded.

Id. at 413–14, 374 A.2d at 914.

This Court, in this case, should change the law, to be applied prospectively, and should no longer cling to a common law rule that has been rejected by *every* state in the nation. Whatever may have been the reason for the rule governing the indictment of the actor as a principal or accessory before the fact, that reason, as we noted in *Lewis* regarding the 7 sequence of the principal's and accessory's trials, has long since disappeared. As observed by Judge Levine in *Williamson,* and Judge Eldridge in *Lewis,* the procedural rules probably were devised by 14th and 15th century English courts as a means of alleviating the harshness of the death penalty in all felony cases. *Williamson,* 282 Md. at 113, 382 A.2d at 595; *Lewis,* 285 Md. at 715, 404 A.2d at 1079; *see also Watson v. State,* 208 Md. at 219, 117 A.2d at 553; 1 J. BISHOP, CRIMINAL LAW § 673, at 486–87 (9th ed.1923). Today, the death penalty in Maryland, with two exceptions, is reserved for principals in the first degree, and thus, the original purpose of the distinction-to restrict excessive executions when all felonies were punishable by death-no longer exists. *See* PERKINS & BOYCE, CRIMINAL LAW, *Parties to Crime* at 759 (3d ed. 1982) ("Since the reason for the principal-accessory distinction ceased to exist when most felonies were removed from the category of capital crimes, the distinction itself should be abrogated ...."). Further, the punishment for accessories before the fact in Maryland is the same as for principals. *See Ward,* 284 Md. at 210, 396 A.2d at 1053 ("As an accessory before the fact he is punished as a partaker of the guilt of the principal and is liable to the same punishment as the principal."). The distinction has outlived its purpose....

MD Code, Criminal Procedure, 4–204

4–204. Accessory before the fact

(a) In this section, the words accessory before the fact and principal have their judicially determined meanings.

(b) Except for a sentencing proceeding under 2–303 or 2–304 of the Criminal Law Article:

(1) the distinction between an accessory before the fact and a principal is abrogated; and (2) an accessory before the fact may be charged, tried, convicted, and sentenced as a principal.

(c) An accessory before the fact may be charged, tried, convicted, and sentenced for a crime regardless of whether a principal in the crime has been:

(1) charged with the crime;

(2) acquitted of the crime; or

(3) convicted of a lesser or different crime.

(d) If a crime is committed in the State, an accessory before the fact may be charged, tried and convicted, and sentenced in a county where:

(1) an act of accessoryship was committed; or

(2) a principal in the crime may be charged, tried and convicted, and sentenced.

Added by Acts 2001, c. 10, § 2, eff. Oct. 1, 2001. Amended by Acts 2001, c. 35, § 1, eff. Oct. 1, 2001; Acts 2002, c. 213, 6, eff. Oct. 1, 2002.

People v. Beeman

Supreme Court of California, 1984.
35 Cal.3d 547, 199 Cal.Rptr. 60, 674 P.2d 1318.

■ REYNOSO, JUSTICE.

Timothy Mark Beeman appeals from a judgment of conviction of robbery, burglary, false imprisonment, destruction of telephone equipment and assault with intent to commit a felony (Pen.Code, §§ 211, 459, 236, 591, 221). Appellant was not present during commission of the offenses. His conviction rested on the theory that he aided and abetted his acquaintances James Gray and Michael Burk.

The primary issue before us is whether the standard California Jury Instructions (CALJIC Nos. 3.00 and 3.01) adequately inform the jury of the criminal intent required to convict a defendant as an aider and abettor of the crime.

We hold that instruction No. 3.01 is erroneous. Sound law, embodied in a long line of California decisions, requires proof that an aider and abettor rendered aid with an intent or purpose of either committing, or of encouraging or facilitating commission of, the target offense. It was, therefore, error for the trial court to refuse the modified instruction requested by appellant. Our examination of the record convinces us that the error in this case was prejudicial and we therefore reverse appellant's convictions.

.   .   .

Burk, Gray and appellant were jointly charged. After the trial court severed the trials, Burk and Gray pled guilty to robbery. At appellant's trial they testified that he had been extensively involved in planning the crime.

According to Gray appellant had been present at a discussion three days before the robbery when it was mentioned that appellant could not go because his 6 foot 5 inch, 310 pound frame could be too easily recognized. Two days before the offense, however, appellant told Gray that he wanted nothing to do with the robbery of his relatives. On the day preceding the incident appellant and Gray spoke on the telephone. At that time appellant repeated he wanted nothing to do with the robbery, but confirmed that he had told Burk that he would not say anything if the others went ahead.

Gray confirmed that appellant was upset when he saw that his friends had gone through with the robbery and had taken all of the victim's jewelry. He was angered further when he discovered that Burk might easily be recognized because he had not disguised himself. . . .

Appellant Beeman's testimony contradicted that of Burk and Gray as to nearly every material element of his own involvement. Appellant testified that he did not participate in the robbery or its planning. . . . He claimed that he had sketched a floor plan of the house some nine months prior to the robbery, only for the purpose of comparing it with the layout of a house belonging to another brother. He at first denied and then admitted describing the Beeman family cars, but insisted this never occurred in the context of planning a robbery.

. . .

Appellant requested that the jury be instructed in accord with People v. Yarber (1979) 90 Cal.App.3d 895, 153 Cal.Rptr. 875 that aiding and abetting liability requires proof of intent to aid. The request was denied.

After three hours of deliberation, the jury submitted two written questions to the court: "We would like to hear again how one is determined to be an accessory and by what actions can he absolve himself"; and "Does inaction mean the party is guilty?" ... The court denied appellant's renewed request that the instructions be modified as suggested in *Yarber*, explaining that giving another, slightly different instruction at this point would further complicate matters. The jury returned its verdicts of guilty on all counts two hours later.

Penal Code section 31 provides in pertinent part: "All persons concerned in the commission of a crime, ... whether they directly commit the act constituting the offense, or aid and abet in its commission, or, not being present, have advised and encouraged its commission, ... are principals in any crime so committed." Thus, those persons who at common law would have been termed accessories before the fact and principals in the second degree as well as those who actually perpetrate the offense, are to be prosecuted, tried and punished as principals in California. (See Pen.Code, § 971.)[121] The term "aider and abettor" is now often used to refer to principals other than the perpetrator, whether or not they are present at the commission of the offense.

CALJIC No. 3.00 defines principals to a crime to include "Those who, with knowledge of the unlawful purpose of the one who does directly and actively commit or attempt to commit the crime, aid and abet in its commission ..., or ... Those who, whether present or not at the commission or attempted commission of the crime, advise and encourage its commission...." CALJIC No. 3.01 defines aiding and abetting as follows: "A person aids and abets the commission of a crime if, with knowledge of the unlawful purpose of the perpetrator of the crime, he aids, promotes, encourages or instigates by act or advice the commission of such crime."

. . .

Appellant asserts that the current instructions, in particular CALJIC No. 3.01, substitute an element of knowledge of the perpetrator's intent for

---

121. The major purpose and effect of this abrogation of the common law distinction between parties to crime apparently has been to alleviate certain procedural difficulties. For instance, at common law an accessory before the fact was punishable where the incitement occurred while the principals were punishable where the offense occurred; one could not be convicted as an accessory if charged as a principal and vice versa; an accessory could not be tried before the principal had been found guilty. (See generally, Perkins, Criminal Law (1982) pp. 751–757.) Now, as at common law, one who is found guilty of the same offense on a theory of aiding and abetting while present at the scene of the crime, or conspiring with the perpetrator beforehand or instigating, encouraging, or advising commission of the crime, is subject to the same punishment as the one who with the requisite criminal intent commits the crime by his or her own acts.

the element of criminal intent of the accomplice, in contravention of common law principles and California case law. He argues that the instruction given permitted the jury to convict him of the same offenses as the perpetrators without finding that he harbored either the same criminal intent as they, or the specific intent to assist them, thus depriving him of his constitutional rights to due process and equal protection of the law. . . .

The People argue that the standard instruction properly reflects California law, which requires no more than that the aider and abettor have knowledge of the perpetrator's criminal purpose and do a voluntary act which in fact aids the perpetrator. . . .

There is no question that an aider and abettor must have criminal intent in order to be convicted of a criminal offense. Decisions of this court dating back to 1898 hold that "the word 'abet' includes knowledge of the wrongful purpose of the perpetrator *and* counsel and encouragement in the crime" and that it is therefore error to instruct a jury that one may be found guilty as a principal if one aided *or* abetted. The act of encouraging or counseling itself implies a purpose or goal of furthering the encouraged result. "An aider and abettor's fundamental purpose, motive and intent is to aid and assist the perpetrator in the latter's commission of the crime."

The essential conflict in current appellate opinions is between those cases which state that an aider and abettor must have an intent or purpose to commit or assist in the commission of the criminal offenses, and those finding it sufficient that the aider and abettor engage in the required acts with knowledge of the perpetrator's criminal purpose.

. . .

We agree with the *Yarber* court that the facts from which a mental state may be inferred must not be confused with the mental state that the prosecution is required to prove. Direct evidence of the mental state of the accused is rarely available except through his or her testimony. The trier of fact is and must be free to disbelieve the testimony and to infer that the truth is otherwise when such an inference is supported by circumstantial evidence regarding the actions of the accused. Thus, an act which has the effect of giving aid and encouragement, and which is done with knowledge of the criminal purpose of the person aided, may indicate that the actor intended to assist in fulfillment of the known criminal purpose. However, as illustrated by Hicks v. U.S. (1893) 150 U.S. 442, 14 S.Ct. 144, 37 L.Ed. 1137 (conviction reversed because jury not instructed that words of encouragement must have been used with the intention of encouraging and abetting crime in a case where ambiguous gesture and remark may have been acts of desperation) and People v. Bollinger (1886) 71 Cal. 17, 11 P. 799 (feigned accomplice not guilty because lacks common intent with the perpetrator to unite in the commission of the crime), the act may be done with some other purpose which precludes criminal liability.

. . .

Thus, we conclude that the weight of authority and sound law require proof that an aider and abettor act with knowledge of the criminal purpose of the perpetrator *and* with an intent or purpose either of committing, or of encouraging or facilitating commission of, the offense.

When the definition of the offense includes the intent to do some act or achieve some consequence beyond the *actus reus* of the crime, the aider and abettor must share the specific intent of the perpetrator.... The liability of an aider and abettor extends also to the natural and reasonable consequences of the acts he knowingly and intentionally aids and encourages.

CALJIC No. 3.01 inadequately defines aiding and abetting because it fails to insure that an aider and abettor will be found to have the required mental state with regard to his or her own act. While the instruction does include the word "abet," which encompasses the intent required by law, the word is arcane and its full import unlikely to be recognized by modern jurors. Moreover, even if jurors were made aware that "abet" means to encourage or facilitate, and implicitly to harbor an intent to further the crime encouraged, the instruction does not *require* them to find that intent because it defines an aider and abettor as one who "aids, promotes, encourages or instigates"....

Reversed.

People v. Keefer

Supreme Court of California, Department One, 1884.
65 Cal. 232, 3 P. 818.

■ MCKINSTRY, J. Counsel for defendant asked the court to charge the jury:

"If you believe from the evidence that the defendant James Keefer was not present when the [*victim*] *Lee Yuen* was killed by *Chapman,* and did not aid and abet in the killing, and that defendant, at the time or prior to the killing, had not conspired with *Chapman* to commit the act, and that he had not advised and encouraged *Chapman* therein, and that the killing was not done in pursuance of any conspiracy between this defendant and *Chapman* to rob said [*victim*], and that this defendant only assisted in throwing the dead body of the [*victim*] into the creek, then you are instructed that, under the indictment, you must find the defendant not guilty."

It is to be regretted that the foregoing instruction was not given to the jury. Of course, if defendant had done no act which made him responsible for the murder, the mere fact that he aided in concealing the dead body would render him liable only as accessory after the fact—an offense of which he could not be found guilty under an indictment for murder. However incredible the testimony of defendant he was undoubtedly entitled to an instruction based upon the hypothesis that his testimony was entirely true.

Assuming the testimony of defendant to be true, there was evidence tending to show that no robbery was committed or attempted. In robbery, as in larceny, it must appear that the goods were taken *animo furandi;* and there was evidence tending to prove that his property was not taken from deceased *lucri causa,* or with intent to deprive him of it permanently. So also there was evidence tending to prove that defendant was not personally present at the killing, and that the killing was not done in pursuance of any agreement or understanding to which defendant was a party, but that it was done by Chapman without the knowledge, assent, or connivance of the defendant.

The testimony of defendant was to the effect that he did not advise or encourage Chapman to follow and *tie* the deceased. But even if we could be supposed to be justified in deciding the *fact,* in holding that his conduct conclusively proved—notwithstanding his testimony to the contrary—that he did encourage Chapman in his purpose to follow and tie the deceased, such encouragement would not of itself, make him accessory to the killing. An accessory before the fact to a robbery (or any other of the felonies mentioned in section 198 of the Penal Code), although not present when the felony is perpetrated or attempted, is guilty of a murder committed in the perpetration or attempt to perpetrate the felony. This is by reason of the statute, and because the law super-adds the intent to kill to the original felonious intent. One who has only advised or encouraged a misdemeanor, however, is not *necessarily* responsible for a murder committed by his co-conspirator, not in furtherance, but independent of the common design.

In the case at bar, if defendant simply encouraged the *tying* of the deceased—a misdemeanor which did not and probably could not cause death or any serious injury—as the killing by Chapman was neither necessarily nor probably involved in the battery or false imprisonment, nor incidental to it, but was an independent and malicious act with which defendant had no connection, the jury were not authorized to find defendant guilty of the murder, or of manslaughter. If the deceased had been strangled by the cords with which he had been carelessly or recklessly bound by Chapman, or had died in consequence of exposure to the elements while tied, defendant might have been held liable. But, if the testimony of defendant was true—and as we have said, he was entitled to an instruction based upon the assumption that the facts were as he stated them to be—the killing of deceased was an independent act of Chapman, neither aided, advised, nor encouraged by him, and not involved in nor incidental to any act by him aided, advised, or encouraged. The court erred in refusing the instruction....

Judgment and order reversed and cause remanded for a new trial.

■ Ross, J., concurring. As there was testimony tending to show that defendant was not personally present at the killing, and that the killing was not done in pursuance of any agreement or undertaking to which defendant was a party, I agree that the court below erred in refusing to give the instruction first set out in the opinion of Mr. Justice McKinstry, and therefore concur in the judgment. I also agree with what is said in the opinion upon the last point discussed.

■ McKee, J., concurred in the opinion of Mr. Justice Ross.

People v. Brown

2005 WL 1899400 (unreported) (Cal.App. 6 Dist.).

■ Duffy, J.

Michael G. and his friend were sitting in Michael's automobile after finishing their day of high school and before they were to attend football practice. They were approached by defendant Robert Fitzgerald Brown and an accomplice. After forcing the two youths out of the vehicle, defendant robbed Michael of $50.00 located inside the car. Defendant was convicted after a trial by jury of second degree robbery and false imprisonment (violations of Pen.Code, §§ 211–212.5, and 236, respectively). The jury also found true the allegation charged as to each crime that defendant personally used a firearm (§ 12022.53, subd. (b), and § 12022.5, subd. (a)). Including the enhancements for each offense, defendant received a 12–year prison sentence for the robbery conviction, and a concurrent prison sentence of four years and four months for the false imprisonment conviction.

Defendant challenges the judgment, claiming instructional error. . . .

FACTS

At approximately 2:45 p.m. on September 8, 2003, Michael (then 17) was sitting in his car outside of a San Jose gas station with his friend, Mohammad M. They were having a snack before attending their high school football practice. Two individuals approached on bicycles. Defendant (who bore arm tattoos with the name "Little Rob") approached the driver's side of Michael's vehicle; codefendant Jacob Dinino approached the passenger's side and "was mugging, giving dirty looks." Michael had never seen defendant or Dinino before this incident.

Defendant told Michael to get out of his car and instructed him to act as if he knew defendant. At that time, defendant put his left arm through the window opening while he was holding what Michael believed to be a gun. Mohammad also observed that defendant was holding a gun. Both Michael and Mohammad testified that the gun was mostly covered by a blue bandanna; only one and one-half inches (or less) of the gun barrel were exposed. Defendant pointed the gun at Michael's chest, and he felt "slight pressure" from the gun. Michael was scared by having the gun pointed at his chest.

Michael initially refused defendant's demand that he get out of the car. Defendant then took the keys out of the ignition (breaking the horn doing so) and threatened to throw them on the gas station's roof; Michael then got out of the car because he was afraid that he would be shot. At that point, Dinino opened the passenger door and pulled Mohammad forcefully out of the car by his shirt. Dinino intimidated Mohammad and challenged him to a fight, saying, " 'What, bitch, what are you going to do?' " Mohammad felt threatened by Dinino and did not feel that he was free to leave.

After Michael backed away from the vehicle, defendant searched the center console of the car where Michael had stored $50.00. He took the money against Michael's will. Defendant threw Michael's keys away from the car. Defendant and Dinino then returned to their bicycles and rode off with defendant yelling, " 'Little Rob just robbed your ass, bitches.' " Defendant also mentioned the name of a gang, "Seven Trees Crips."

PROCEDURAL BACKGROUND

Defendant was charged by information filed November 20, 2003, with two counts: (1) second degree robbery of Michael (violation of §§ 211–212.5, subd. (c)); and (2) false imprisonment of Mohammad (violation of § 236). The information also alleged that defendant personally used a handgun in the commission of the offenses (under § 12022.53, subd. (b), and § 12022.5, subd. (a)).

After a jury trial, defendant was convicted on January 27, 2004, of both counts, i.e., second degree robbery and false imprisonment.[6] The jury also found true the firearms allegations applicable to count 1 and count 2 (violations of § 12022.53, subd. (b), and § 12022.5, subd. (a), respectively). Defendant thereafter filed a motion for new trial, which the court denied on June 4, 2004. The court sentenced defendant to 12 years in prison on count 1 (with the firearms enhancement). Defendant was sentenced to four years and four months in prison on count 2 (with the firearms enhancement), said sentence running concurrent to the 12–year prison sentence for the count 1 conviction. Defendant filed a timely notice of appeal on June 28, 2004.

Claimed Instructional Error In Giving CALJIC No. 3.02 (Aiding and Abetting)

A. *Contentions of the Parties*

Defendant contends that the court erred by instructing the jury under CALJIC No. 3.02. Under that instruction, the jury was advised that defendant could be held criminally liable for Dinino's false imprisonment of Mohammad (Count 2) as an aider and abettor of the crime under the natural and probable consequences doctrine.[15] Defendant asserts that the instruction should not have been given because (1) there was no evidence that he intended to encourage or assist Dinino in committing a target offense, and (2) Dinino's false imprisonment was not a natural and proba-

---

6. Dinino was likewise charged with second degree robbery and false imprisonment. Defendant and codefendant Dinino were tried together. Dinino was also convicted as to both counts. Only defendant appealed from the judgment entered in the case.

15. The court instructed the jury (using CALJIC No. 3.02) as follows: "One who aids and abets another in the commission of a crime or crimes is not only guilty of that crime but is also guilty of any other crime committed by a principal which is a natural and probable consequence of the crimes originally aided and abetted. In order to find the defendant guilty of the crime charged in Count 1, you must be satisfied beyond a reasonable doubt that: [¶] 1. The crime charged in Count 1 was committed; [¶] 2. That the defendant aided and abetted that crime; [¶] 3. That a co-principal in that crime committed the crime charged in Count 1; and [¶] 4. The crime charged in Count 2 was a natural and probable consequence of the commission of the crime charged in Count 1.[¶] In determining whether a consequence is 'natural and probable,' you must apply an objective test, based not on what the defendant actually intended, but on what a person of reasonable and ordinary prudence would have expected likely to occur. The issue is to be decided in light of all the circumstances surrounding the incident. A 'natural' consequence is one which is within the normal range of outcomes that may be reasonably expected to occur if nothing unusual has intervened. 'Probable' means likely to happen. [¶] You are not required to unanimously agree as to which originally contemplated crime the defendant aided and abetted, so long as you are satisfied beyond a reasonable doubt and unanimously agree that the defendant aided and abetted the commission of an identified and defined target crime and that the crime charged in Count 2 was a natural and probable consequence of the commission of that target crime."

ble consequence of the target offense of robbery. The Attorney General responds that CALJIC No. 3.02 was properly given, or, alternatively, if there was instructional error, it was harmless. We reject defendant's claim of instructional error.

B. *Natural and Probable Consequences Doctrine*

One who aids and abets in the commission of a crime—just as the person who directly commits the act constituting an offense—is a "principal" in the crime committed. (§ 31.)[16] An aider and abettor's liability for the criminal act is thus "vicarious" (*People v. Croy* (1985) 41 Cal.3d 1, 12, fn. 5) and " 'derivative' " (*People v. Prettyman* (1996) 14 Cal.4th 248, 259 (*Prettyman*)).

"[A] person aids and abets the commission of a crime when he or she, acting with (1) knowledge of the unlawful purpose of the perpetrator; and (2) the intent or purpose of committing, encouraging, or facilitating the commission of the offense, (3) by act or advice aids, promotes, encourages or instigates, the commission of the crime." (*People v. Beeman* (1984) 35 Cal.3d 547, 561 (*Beeman*).) An aider and abettor, however, " 'is not only guilty of the particular crime that to his knowledge his confederates are contemplating committing, but he is also liable for the natural and reasonable consequences of any act that he knowingly aided or encouraged.' " (*People v. Croy, supra,* 41 Cal.3d at p. 12, fn. 5, quoting *People v. Durham* (1969) 70 Cal.2d 171, 181, italics omitted; see also *People v. Coffman* (2004) 34 Cal.4th 1, 107.)

Thus, under the natural and probable consequences doctrine, the defendant may be criminally liable as an aider and abettor although he "need not have intended to encourage or facilitate the particular offense ultimately committed by the perpetrator. His knowledge that an act which is criminal was intended, and his action taken with the intent that the act be encouraged or facilitated, are sufficient to impose liability on him for any reasonably foreseeable offense committed as a consequence by the perpetrator." (*People v. Croy, supra,* 41 Cal.3d at p. 12, fn. 5.) As our Supreme Court has explained, in instances in which the prosecution invokes the natural and probable consequences doctrine to impose criminal liability as an aider and abettor for an offense other than a target crime, the jury must find not only each of the three *Beeman* elements noted, *ante,* it must "must also find that (4) the defendant's confederate committed an offense *other than* the target crime; and (5) the offense committed by the confederate was a natural and probable consequence of the target crime that the defendant aided and abetted." (*Prettyman, supra,* 14 Cal.4th at p. 262, fn. omitted; see also *id.* at p. 271.)

The court may instruct the jury on this natural and probable consequences issue "only when (1) the record contains substantial evidence that the defendant intended to encourage or assist a confederate in committing a target offense, and (2) the jury could reasonably find that the crime actually committed by the defendant's confederate was a 'natural and

---

16. "All persons concerned in the commission of a crime, whether it be felony or misdemeanor, and whether they directly commit the act constituting the offense, or aid and abet in its commission, ... are principals in any crime so committed." (§ 31.)

probable consequence' of the specifically contemplated target offense." (*Prettyman, supra,* 14 Cal.4th at p. 269.) And where such an instruction is necessary, the court is *required* to identify for the jury the target crime in order to "facilitate the jury's task of determining whether the charged crime allegedly committed by the aider and abettor's confederate was indeed a natural and probable consequence of any uncharged target crime that, the prosecution contends, the defendant knowingly and intentionally aided and abetted." (*Id.* at p. 267.)

"The test for an aider and abettor's liability for collateral criminal offenses is ... case specific, that is, it depends upon all of the facts and circumstances surrounding the particular defendant's conduct." (*People v. Nguyen* (1993) 21 Cal.App.4th 518, 535.) The factors that may be considered to determine whether a person may have aided and abetted a crime include, inter alia, " 'presence at the scene of the crime, companionship, and conduct before and after the offense. [Citations.]' " (*People v. Chagolla* (1983) 144 Cal.App.3d 422, 429.)

C.   *Trial Court's Giving of CALJIC No. 3.02*

Here, defendant does not contend that the court failed to identify the target offense as required under *Prettyman.* Indeed, the court did identify the target offense. Instead, defendant argues that the instruction (CALJIC No. 3.02) should not have been given at all. We disagree.

Applying the five-factor test enunciated in *Prettyman* discussed, *ante,* the natural and probable consequences doctrine was clearly applicable to this case. By virtue of the evidence that defendant and Dinino arrived at the scene, coordinated their efforts in the commission of the robbery, and left the scene together, it may be readily concluded that defendant had "knowledge of the unlawful purpose of the perpetrator" (*Prettyman, supra,* 14 Cal.4th at p. 262), defendant's confederate, Dinino. (See *People v. Chagolla, supra,* 144 Cal.App.3d at p. 429 [factors concerning aiding and abetting liability include presence at crime scene, companionship, and conduct before and after offense]; see also *People v. Fagalilo* (1981) 123 Cal.App.3d 524, 532 [where defendant and confederates entered store together, defendant robbed store, and they then escaped store together after commission of crimes, "jury could reasonably infer that they were jointly engaged in a robbery"].)

Second, the actions of defendant evidenced his "intent or purpose of committing, encouraging, or facilitating the commission of a predicate or target offense" (*Prettyman, supra,* 14 Cal.4th at p. 262), i.e., the robbery of Michael.

Third, there is ample record—indeed, there was no evidence refuting the robbery—that defendant, "by act or advice aided, promoted, encouraged or instigated the commission of the target crime [robbery]." (*Prettyman, supra,* 14 Cal.4th at p. 262.)

Applying the fourth *Prettyman* factor, the evidence clearly supported the conclusion that "defendant's confederate committed an offense *other than* the target crime" (*Prettyman, supra,* 14 Cal.4th at p. 262, fn. omitted): Dinino committed the criminal act of false imprisonment upon Mohammad, which was a crime different from the target crime of robbery.

Fifth and finally, defendant's contention notwithstanding, we have no trouble finding that "the offense committed by the confederate [i.e., the false imprisonment] was a natural and probable consequence of the target crime(s) [i.e., robbery] that the defendant encouraged or facilitated." (*Prettyman, supra,* 14 Cal.4th at p. 267.) Numerous cases have held the defendant criminally responsible as an aider and abettor of the offense committed by his confederate under circumstances warranting a finding that the offense was a natural and probable consequence of the target crime of robbery. (See, e.g., *People v. Bishop* (1996) 44 Cal.App.4th 220, 228–235 [murder held as natural and probable consequence of robbery]; *People v. Hammond* (1986) 181 Cal.App.3d 463, 468 [defendant's act of driving getaway car was ample evidence of assistance of accomplice in robbery of jewelry store, and murder of store worker was natural and probable consequence of robbery]; *People v. George* (1968) 259 Cal.App.2d 424, 429 [accomplice's assault with deadly weapon upon witness during escape after store robbery was natural and probable consequence of robbery in which defendant participated].)

Here, in the course of the commission of the robbery by defendant and Dinino, the detention of the victims, including Mohammad's false imprisonment, was a natural and probable consequence of the robbery. Indeed, the false imprisonment of Dinino—temporarily occupying him and getting him away from the vehicle while defendant rummaged through the vehicle to locate any contents he deemed worth stealing—directly facilitated the commission of the target crime of robbery. Thus, defendant could have properly been found criminally responsible as aiding and abetting the crime of false imprisonment, consistent with the view that "aiders and abettors should be responsible for the criminal harms they have naturally, probably and foreseeably put in motion." (*People v. Luparello* (1986) 187 Cal.App.3d 410, 439.)

We thus conclude that there was substantial evidence that defendant and Dinino committed the target crime of robbery, and that Dinino's false imprisonment of Mohammad was a natural and probable consequence of that target offense. Accordingly, the court properly advised the jury on this issue by giving CALJIC No. 3.02.

DISPOSITION

The judgment is affirmed.

United States v. Roberson

474 F.3d 432 (7th Cir. 2007).

■ POSNER, J.

The defendant, with three accomplices, committed an armed bank robbery, netting $133,000, of which the defendant's share was $50,000. He was charged with both bank robbery, 18 U.S.C. §§ 2113(a), (d), and using a firearm in a crime of violence (which bank robbery is). 18 U.S.C. § 924(c)(1)(A). It is unclear, but also irrelevant, whether he was carrying a gun. One of his accomplices brandished a gun, and a defendant is liable for the reasonably foreseeable crimes committed by his accomplices in the course of the conspiracy, *Pinkerton v. United States,* 328 U.S. 640, 646–48 (1946); *United States v. McLee,* 436 F.3d 751, 758 (7th Cir.2006); *United States v. Rawlings,* 341 F.3d 657, 660 (7th Cir.2003), whether or not a conspiracy is charged. *United States v. Chairez,* 33 F.3d 823, 827 (7th Cir.1994); *United States v. Lopez,* 271 F.3d 472, 480–81 (3d Cir.2001).

State v. Williams

Supreme Court of North Carolina, 1948.
229 N.C. 348, 49 S.E.2d 617.

The defendants were indicted for being accessories after the fact to the felony of the murder of Thompson Hooker by Bud Hicks. The indictment contained the specific allegation that the aid rendered to the principal offender, Bud Hicks, by the defendants consisted in transporting him from the scene of his crime for the purpose of enabling him to escape apprehension and punishment.

Testimony was presented at the trial by both the prosecution and the defense. This evidence is stated below in the light most favorable to the State.

On the afternoon of Sunday, June 6, 1948, Bud Hicks deliberately shot and wounded Thompson Hooker without provocation while the latter was standing before his doorstep at 404 Ramseur Street in Sanford. Immediately after the shooting, Hicks fled from Sanford to a rural section of Lee County in an automobile owned by himself and driven by the defendant, Prentiss Watson. Hicks and Watson were accompanied on this flight by the defendants, Annie Williams and Elizabeth Badgett. Peace officers found Hicks and his companions at the home of Annie Williams in a country neighborhood in Lee County at a later hour of the afternoon. Hicks, Watson, and Annie Williams thereupon sought unsuccessfully to dissuade the officers from arresting Hicks by falsely representing that Hicks had not been in Sanford any time that day. After all these events had transpired, namely, on Monday, June 7, 1948, Thompson Hooker died in consequence of his gun-shot wound.

Elizabeth Badgett was acquitted, but the jury found Annie Williams and Prentiss Watson guilty as charged in the bill of indictment. Judgment was pronounced against both of these parties. Watson accepted his sentence, and Annie Williams appealed to this Court, assigning as error the denial of her motion for judgment of nonsuit made when the State rested its case and renewed when all the evidence was concluded.

■ ERVIN, JUSTICE. When the State prosecutes one upon the charge of being an accessory after the fact to the felony of murder, it assumes the burden of proving the three essential elements of the offense, namely: (1) That the principal felon had actually committed the felony of murder; (2) that the accused knew that such felony had been committed by the principal felon; and (3) that the accused received, relieved, comforted, or assisted the principal felon in some way in order to help him escape, or to hinder his arrest, trial, or punishment. . . .

In the nature of things, one cannot become an accessory after the fact to a felony until such felony has become an accomplished fact. Consequently, it is well established in law that "one cannot be convicted as an accessory after the fact unless the felony be complete, and until such felony has been consummated, any aid or assistance rendered to a party in order to enable him to escape the consequences of his crime will not make the person affording the assistance an accessory after the fact." . . .

Thus, it is held that a person cannot be convicted as an accessory after the fact to a murder because he aided the murderer to escape, when the aid was rendered after the mortal wound was given, but before death ensued, as a murder is not complete until the death results. . . .

Such is the instant case. The evidence disclosed that the assistance, which was alleged to have been rendered by the appellant, Annie Williams, with intent to enable the principal felon, Bud Hicks, to escape, was given after Thompson Hooker had been mortally wounded, but before he died. Hence, the testimony showed that the felony of murder was not an accomplished fact when the assistance was given, and the Court erred in denying the appellant's motion for judgment of involuntary nonsuit. G.S. § 15–173.

The statute provides for punishment for any person becoming an accessory after the fact to any felony, "whether the same be a felony at common law or by virtue of any statute made, or to be made." G.S. § 14–7. Since no such charge is laid in the present indictment, we refrain from expressing any opinion as to whether the evidence made out a case for the jury against the appellant as an accessory after the fact to the statutory felony of a secret assault under G.S. § 14–31 or the statutory felony of an assault with intent to kill under G.S. § 14–32. But it is noted that there are at least two interesting decisions in other States in which similar problems are considered. . . .

For the reasons stated, the judgment pronounced against the appellant, Annie Williams, in the court below is

Reversed.[11]

State v. Truesdell

Court of Criminal Appeals of Oklahoma, 1980.
620 P.2d 427.

■ BUSSEY, JUDGE. The State has appealed to this Court from a ruling of the District Court in Nowata County, dismissing Case No. CRF § 79–41. In

---

11. Accessory after the fact under Cal. Penal Code § 32 must lend assistance to the principal after the commission of the offense with the intent of helping the principal escape capture, trial or punishment. People v. Nguyen, 21 Cal.App.4th 518, 26 Cal.Rptr.2d 323 (1993).

A defendant charged with only one offense of being an accessory after the fact may be convicted if the defendant knew the principal had committed some felony and it was not necessary for the jury to agree which felony the defendant was aware the principal had committed. People v. Perryman, 188 Cal.App.3d 1546, 234 Cal.Rptr. 181(1987). Aid to the felon in the form of supplying him with a false alibi is sufficient to make the aider guilty of the felony as accessory after the fact. People v. Duty, 269 Cal.App.2d 97, 74 Cal.Rptr. 606 (1969).

D, having seen the murder committed, concealed the murder weapon and gave the officers false evidence as to the killing, intending to throw suspicion away from the killer. D's conviction of being "an accessory after the fact to murder" was affirmed. Self v. People, 167 Colo. 292, 448 P.2d 619 (1968). (Rehearing denied Jan. 13, 1969).

that case Zola v. Truesdell was charged with being an accessory to the crime of Shooting With the Intent to Kill after her ex-husband was shot ten times by their twelve-year-old son. There was a preliminary hearing and she was ordered to be held for trial, but at a subsequent motion hearing a district judge ruled that a juvenile cannot commit a felony and that therefore there was no crime to which Ms. Truesdell could have been an accessory. . . .

In Oklahoma, all parties to a crime are either principals or accessories after the fact. The elements of the crime of accessory after the fact are that the predicate felony be completed, that the offender have knowledge that the person she's aiding (the principal) committed the crime, and that the accessory conceal or aid the principal. Title 21 O.S.1971, § 173. This Court has held that an accessory is not connected with the offender after the original offense has been committed. Thus, the crime of accessory after the fact is a separate and distinct crime, standing on its own particular elements. And because accessory after the fact is a separate and distinct crime, a conviction of the principal is not a condition precedent to the conviction of an accessory after the fact.

Accordingly, the fact that the principal, the Truesdell child, was not charged with the assault has no bearing on whether Ms. Truesdell has committed the crime of accessory after the fact. The fact that the principal is a minor goes to his legal status, not his factual status, and it is immaterial as to the guilt or innocence of the defendant on the charge of accessory after the fact. A conviction of accessory after the fact depends on whether there is sufficient evidence presented to show that there was a principal who was guilty of the crime charged, regardless of whether or not the principal was ever charged with the criminal offense. *Britto v. People, supra.* Thus it was error for the District Court to dismiss the case.

■ CORNISH, P.J., and BRETT, J., concur in results.

■ BRETT, JUDGE: concurring in results.

I concur that the trial court order be reversed and this matter be remanded for further proceedings. It is clear that the trial court sustained defendant's motion to quash the information. That order has been properly appealed under the provisions of 22 O.S.1971, § 1053. Clearly Laws 1977, c. 42, § 1, 21 O.S.Supp.1977, § 652, now, 21 O.S.Supp.1979, § 652, defines the offense of Shooting With Intent to Kill. 21 O.S.1971, § 173, defines the offense of being an Accessory. The Juvenile Code in Title 10, is a procedural statute describing treatment of a juvenile who commits an offense that would be a felony if committed by an adult.

Therefore, insofar as the reason given for sustaining defendant's motion ("the Court finds that the commission by a juvenile of a felony cannot be the predicate act for accessory to commit said felony as set out in the instant information") was in error, I agree that this matter be reversed and remanded for further proceedings.[123]

---

123. A person not a state official may be guilty of the crime of embezzling public funds if he aids and abets an official in this act. People v. Hess, 104 Cal.App.2d 642, 234 P.2d 65 (1951).

MODEL PENAL CODE

Section 2.06 Liability for Conduct of Another; Complicity.

(1) A person is guilty of an offense if it is committed by his own conduct or by the conduct of another person for which he is legally accountable, or both.

(2) A person is legally accountable for the conduct of another person when:

(a) acting with the kind of culpability that is sufficient for the commission of the offense, he causes an innocent or irresponsible person to engage in such conduct; or

(b) he is made accountable for the conduct of such other person by the Code or by the law defining the offense; or

(c) he is an accomplice of such other person in the commission of the offense.

(3) A person is an accomplice of another person in the commission of an offense if:

(a) with the purpose of promoting or facilitating the commission of the offense, he

(i) solicits such other person to commit it; or

(ii) aids or agrees or attempts to aid such other person in planning or committing it; or

(iii) having a legal duty to prevent the commission of the offense, fails to make proper effort so to do; or

(b) his conduct is expressly declared by law to establish his complicity.

(4) When causing a particular result is an element of an offense, an accomplice in the conduct causing such result is an accomplice in the commission of that offense, if he acts with the kind of culpability, if any, with respect to that result that is sufficient for the commission of the offense.

(5) A person who is legally incapable of committing a particular offense himself may be guilty thereof if it is committed by the conduct of another person for which he is legally accountable, unless such liability is inconsistent with the purpose of the provision establishing his incapacity.

(6) Unless otherwise provided by the Code or by the law defining the offense, a person is not an accomplice in an offense committed by another person if:

(a) he is a victim of that offense; or

(b) the offense is so defined that his conduct is inevitably incident to its commission; or

(c) he terminates his complicity prior to the commission of the offense and

(i) wholly deprives it of effectiveness in the commission of the offense; or

(ii) gives timely warning to the law enforcement authorities or otherwise makes proper effort to prevent the commission of the offense.

(7) An accomplice may be convicted on proof of the commission of the offense and of his complicity therein, though the person claimed to have committed the offense has not been prosecuted or convicted or has been convicted of a different

---

Although only a minor can be guilty of the offense of being a minor in possession of alcoholic liquor, one not a minor may be guilty of aiding and abetting a minor in the commission of that offense. State v. Norman, 193 Neb. 719, 229 N.W.2d 55 (1975).

offense or degree of offense or has an immunity to prosecution or conviction or has been acquitted.

Section 242.3 Hindering Apprehension or Prosecution.

A person commits an offense if, with purpose to hinder the apprehension, prosecution, conviction or punishment of another for crime, he:

(1) harbors or conceals the other; or

(2) provides or aids in providing a weapon, transportation, disguise or other means of avoiding apprehension or effecting escape; or

(3) conceals or destroys evidence of the crime, or tampers with a witness, informant, document or other source of information, regardless of its admissibility in evidence; or

(4) warns the other of impending discovery or apprehension, except that this paragraph does not apply to a warning given in connection with an effort to bring another into compliance with law; or

(5) volunteers false information to a law enforcement officer.

The offense is a felony of the third degree if the conduct which the actor knows has been charged or is liable to be charged against the person aided would constitute a felony of the first or second degree. Otherwise it is a misdemeanor.

Section 242.4 Aiding Consummation of Crime.

A person commits an offense if he purposely aids another to accomplish an unlawful object of a crime, as by safeguarding the proceeds thereof or converting the proceeds into negotiable funds. The offense is a felony of the third degree if the principal offense was a felony of the first or second degree. Otherwise it is a misdemeanor.

Section 242.5 Compounding.

A person commits a misdemeanor if he accepts or agrees to accept any pecuniary benefit in consideration of refraining from reporting to law enforcement authorities the commission or suspected commission of any offense or information relating to an offense. It is an affirmative defense to prosecution under this Section that the pecuniary benefit did not exceed an amount which the actor believed to be due as restitution or indemnification for harm caused by the offense.[124]

SECTION 6.   CONSPIRACY[40]

Traditionally, a conspiracy is an agreement or combination for an unlawful purpose but the purpose could be unlawful even if it would not be punishable if perpetrated by one alone. The classic illustration of a punishable conspiracy to do a non-criminal act is the combination to defraud another without the use of a false token. Such a fraud is punishable today,

---

124.   Copyright © 1962 by the American Law Institute. Reprinted with the permission of the American Law Institute.

40.   Conspiracy is a separate offense, distinct from the substantive crime which was the object of the conspiracy, and there may be a valid conviction of both the substantive offense and the conspiracy to commit it. Wright v. United States, 519 F.2d 13 (7th Cir.1975); United States v. Smith, 46 F.3d 1223 (1st Cir.1995).

Defining conspiracy as "co-operating" to aid in doing an unlawful act, was sufficient. Goddard v. People, 172 Colo. 498, 474 P.2d 210 (1970).

even if perpetrated by one alone, but before the English statute on false pretenses it was punishable for two or more to combine to perpetrate such a fraud. More recently a combination of three persons whereby they lent small sums of money to poor people and charged them exorbitant rates of interest was held to be a punishable conspiracy although usury was not a crime.[41]

The rule of the common law that the purpose of an agreement may be sufficiently "unlawful" to make the combination a conspiracy, even if what is agreed upon is not in itself punishable as a crime, has been abandoned by most of the new codes. Under them a conspiracy is a combination for the commission of a crime. For the most part, harms deemed sufficiently "unlawful" to make the combination therefor a conspiracy, have since been made punishable as crimes, if they were not so at common law, and the original rule is no longer necessary.

State v. Hanks

Appellate Court of Connecticut, 1995.
39 Conn.App. 333, 665 A.2d 102.

■ SCHALLER, JUDGE.

The defendants appeal from the judgments of conviction, rendered after a jury trial, of assault in the first degree, ... assault of an employee of the department of correction, ... attempted escape in the first degree.... The defendant Jose Roque also appeals from the judgment of conviction, rendered after a jury trial, of conspiracy to commit assault in the first degree and escape in the first degree....[42]

---

41. Commonwealth v. Donoghue, 250 Ky. 343, 63 S.W.2d 3 (1933).

The term "unlawful" in relation to conspiracy, includes situations where the purpose of a group plan or the proposed means of accomplishing that plan, "even if not criminal, involve 'an evil intent to oppress and injure the public' (or, perhaps, third persons) by activity, which is 'illegal, void and against public policy.'" Commonwealth v. Bessette, 351 Mass. 148, 154, 217 N.E.2d 893 (1966).

A conspiracy may be between two or more officers or employees of a corporation, or two or more corporations acting through an officer or employee representing each corporation, or between a person and a corporation acting through a separate person. *See* United States v. Santa Rita Store Co., 16 N.M. 3, 113 P. 620 (1911). Where defendant was the only person to defraud the government, no conspiracy could be claimed because the corporation must be represented by another person. One corporate employee is not enough. United States v. Stevens, 909 F.2d 431 (11th Cir.1990). A corporation may be convicted of conspiracy based solely on a conspiracy between its officers and employees. Dussouy v. Gulf Coast Inv. Corp., 660 F.2d 594 (5th Cir.1981). Welling, Intra–Corporate Plurality in Criminal Conspiracy Law, 33 Hast.L.J. 1155, 1174–1199 (1982); Shaun P. Martin, Intracorporate Conspiracies, 50 Stan. L. Rev. 399 (1998).

The common-law theory, that husband and wife are one, made it impossible for them to be guilty of conspiracy if no third person was involved. Dawson v. United States, 10 F.2d 106 (9th Cir.1926); People v. Miller, 82 Cal. 107, 22 P. 934 (1889). But the tendency is to abandon this theory and hold that they can be guilty of conspiracy even without the cooperation of anyone else. For example, Dawson and Miller have both been overruled. United States v. Dege, 364 U.S. 51, 80 S.Ct. 1589, 4 L.Ed.2d 1563 (1960); People v. Pierce, 61 Cal.2d 879, 40 Cal.Rptr. 845, 395 P.2d 893 (1964).

42. General Statutes § 53a–48(a) provides: "A person is guilty of conspiracy when, with intent that conduct constituting a crime be performed, he agrees with one or more persons to

... We affirm the judgment of the trial court.

The jury reasonably could have found the following facts. On January 16, 1993, Correction Officer Gary DuBois was working the midnight to 8 a.m. shift in block 39A at the community correctional center in Bridgeport. The block consisted of three corridors, A7, A8 and A10. Each corridor contained twelve cells. A guard bubble was located in the middle of the block allowing the guard to observe all three corridors. The bubble contained controls for all of the corridors and cell doors in the bubble. A dayroom was located at the end of each corridor next to the guard bubble.

At 12:30 a.m., DuBois let certain inmates out of their cells to clean the block. The inmates had a mop, a mop wringer and a bucket with which to clean. At some point, an inmate, John Baldwin, called DuBois over to the cell of another inmate, Emile King, in the A8 corridor. As DuBois spoke with King, DuBois was hit from behind. Inmates Baldwin and Curtis Davis then jumped DuBois, hit him in the face and took his keys and body alarm.

Baldwin, Davis, another inmate, Patrick Nemhart, and the defendant Roque all struck DuBois. Davis hit DuBois with the mop wringer that weighed about ten pounds. Roque took a swing at DuBois and then went to the bubble. The defendant Ronell Hanks kicked DuBois and was then told by Davis and Baldwin that he should go to the front of the bubble and look out for other correction officers. Baldwin and Curtis dragged DuBois into a cell.

Officer Anthony Wilson was on duty in block 38A. He noticed a plastic bag over a corridor door and the door sliding back and forth in block 39A. He called DuBois on the telephone, but did not get an answer. Other correction officers responded when DuBois did not answer his telephone. The corridor door leading to the block had butter smeared on it, but the officers still were able to see into the block. The officers then noticed that the defendant Roque was in the guard bubble and that almost all the lights in block 39A had been turned off. The officers also heard loud booming noises.

One of the responding officers, William Jackson, saw Roque in the bubble. Jackson and Officer Orlando McGee entered block 39A. McGee saw three inmates including Hanks in the corridor. Jackson found DuBois in a cell with blood on his mouth and the left side of his jaw swollen. Jackson and McGee found Roque in another inmate's cell.

When the officers inspected the A10 dayroom they found the screen bent up on a window leading to an outside yard and two fire extinguishers that were generally kept in the bubble.

I

The defendants claim that there was insufficient evidence to sustain their convictions of first degree assault as accessories and attempted escape, and Roque's conviction of conspiracy.

. . .

---

engage in or cause the performance of such conduct, and any one of them commits an overt act in pursuance of such conspiracy.''

C

The defendants claim that the evidence was insufficient to convict the defendant Roque of conspiracy to commit assault and to escape. " 'To prove the crime of conspiracy, in violation of § 53a–48, the state must establish beyond a reasonable doubt that an agreement existed between two or more persons to engage in conduct constituting a crime and that subsequent to the agreement one of the conspirators performed an overt act in further-ance of the conspiracy.... The state is also obligated to prove that the accused intended that conduct constituting a crime be performed.' " (Cita-tions omitted.) State v. Jones, 35 Conn.App. 839, 846, 647 A.2d 43 (1994).

"The existence of a formal agreement between the parties, however, need not be proved; it is sufficient to show that they are knowingly engaged in a mutual plan to do a forbidden act. Because of the secret nature of conspiracies, a conviction is usually based on circumstantial evidence. Consequently, it is not necessary to establish that the defendant and his coconspirators signed papers, shook hands, or uttered the words 'we have an agreement.' Indeed, a conspiracy can be inferred from the conduct of the accused."

Here, the jury reasonably could have found that Roque participated in all acts of the assault and attempt to escape. From his actions the jury could infer that these activities were planned in advance in order to facilitate an escape. "Participation in a single act in furtherance of the conspiracy is enough to sustain a finding of knowing participation." The four inmates attacked DuBois, disabled him, and took his keys. Roque used the keys to enter the bubble and proceeded to open and close various doors, which allowed Baldwin and Davis to place DuBois in a cell and to gain access to the dayroom. From this evidence the jury could infer that a conspiracy existed among these inmates and that Roque was a participant in the conspiracy.

Affirmed.

United States v. Payan

United States Court of Appeals, Fifth Circuit, 1993.
992 F.2d 1387.

■ WIENER, CIRCUIT JUDGE:

Pedro Carrillo Payan appeals several aspects of his criminal convictions relating to the transportation in interstate and foreign commerce of stolen property. He also appeals his resulting sentence. Finding no reversible error, we affirm.

I

FACTS AND PROCEEDINGS

Between October, 1990 and June 1991, farm equipment began disap-pearing from the Texas panhandle and northeastern New Mexico. During this same period, a relative of one of the dispossessed tractor owners noticed similar tractors appearing in Mexico. Law enforcement officers also received information that Payan was exporting stolen tractors from the

United States and selling them in Mexico. An arrest warrant was issued for Payan, and federal and state authorities at the United States Customs port of entry at Columbus, New Mexico were alerted to watch for stolen farm equipment.

In June, 1991, Mark Ancira was arrested while attempting to transport into Mexico two tractors that had been stolen in Texas. At the time of his arrest, Ancira was in possession of fraudulent invoices for the tractors made out to Payan as purchaser. Payan was arrested the next day when he entered the United States from Mexico.

Payan was indicted subsequently on one count of conspiracy to transport stolen goods in interstate and foreign commerce, and fifteen counts of transportation of stolen goods in interstate and foreign commerce.

At trial, the government introduced credible evidence that Payan and Ancira cooperated in the transportation and disposal of substantially all of the farm equipment stolen from this geographic area during the period in question. Payan was subsequently convicted on the conspiracy count and on eleven of the substantive counts. Consequently, Payan was sentenced to serve a prison term followed by supervised release; and to pay a fine, restitution, and a special assessment. Payan timely appealed.

II

ANALYSIS

. . .

A. Wharton's Rule . . .

Payan insists that, under the circumstances of the instant case, his convictions for both transportation of stolen property and conspiracy to transport stolen property cannot stand. Two related principles underlie this claim. First, Wharton's Rule generally prohibits convictions for both a substantive offense and conspiracy to commit that offense if the substantive offense necessarily requires the participation and cooperation of two persons.[43] "[W]here it is impossible under any circumstances to commit the substantive offense without cooperative action, the preliminary agreement between the same parties to commit the offense is not an indictable conspiracy."[44] . . .

1. Wharton's Rule

Payan acknowledges that as a general rule a person can be convicted of both transportation of stolen goods and conspiracy to commit that same offense. Nonetheless, he argues that the instant case is distinguishable because the government relied on both the statute prohibiting the transportation of stolen goods[45] and the statute providing for aider and abettor responsibility[46] in obtaining convictions against him on the substantive counts. This latter statute provides:

---

43. *See generally* Iannelli v. United States, 420 U.S. 770, 95 S.Ct. 1284, 43 L.Ed.2d 616 (1975).

44. Gebardi v. United States, 287 U.S. 112, 122, 53 S.Ct. 35, 37, 77 L.Ed. 206 (1932).

45. 18 U.S.C. § 2313.

46. 18 U.S.C. § 2.

(a) Whoever commits an offense against the United States or aids, abets, counsels, commands, induces or procures its commission, is punishable as a principal.

(b) Whoever willfully causes an act to be done which if directly performed by him or another would be an offense against the United States, is punishable as a principal.

Payan argues that, by definition, a conviction based solely on aider and abettor responsibility requires the involvement of at least two persons in the criminal activity; one cannot aid and abet himself. Likewise, he continues, a conspiracy requires at least two persons. Payan next observes that the evidence introduced at trial established that two and only two persons (Payan and Ancira) were involved in the conspiracy and in the substantive offenses. Further, he asserts, the evidence established that he only "aided and abetted or caused [Ancira] to violate the law." Consequently, Payan's argument concludes, his convictions on the substantive offenses were based solely on aider and abettor responsibility, so that under the facts of the instant case both his substantive convictions and his conviction for conspiracy cannot stand.

Although Payan's argument initially sounds appealing, it cannot withstand scrutiny. First, Payan improperly treats 18 U.S.C. § 2 (aiding and abetting) as the target offense. Instead, 18 U.S.C. § 2313 (transportation of stolen goods) was the basis of Payan's indictment and his convictions. 18 U.S.C. § 2 does not define a crime, but rather simply allows one who aids or abets the commission of a substantive offense to be punished as a principal.[47] Additionally, 18 U.S.C. § 2 "is an alternative charge in every count, whether explicit or implicit."[48] Under Payan's reasoning, no defendant could ever be convicted for both conspiracy to commit a substantive offense and the substantive offense itself, as 18 U.S.C. § 2 is implicit in every criminal charge. Such a result, however, would be contrary to well established law. "[I]t is well recognized that in most cases separate sentences can be imposed for the conspiracy to do an act and for the subsequent accomplishment of that end."[49]

Second, "Wharton's Rule applies only to offenses that *require* concerted criminal activity, a plurality of criminal agents."[50] Only when it is impossible under any circumstances to commit the substantive offense without cooperative action, does Wharton's Rule bar convictions for both the substantive offense and conspiracy to commit that same offense.[51] For example, Wharton's Rule has traditionally been applied to crimes such as adultery and dueling, offenses that are impossible to commit absent the participation of at least two persons. In contrast, it is quite possible for one person, acting alone, to transport stolen goods.

---

47. United States v. Walker, 621 F.2d 163, 166 (5th Cir.1980), cert. denied, 450 U.S. 1000, 101 S.Ct. 1707, 68 L.Ed.2d 202 (1981).

48. Id.; United States v. Bullock, 451 F.2d 884, 888 (5th Cir.1971).

49. Iannelli, 420 U.S. at 777–78, 95 S.Ct. at 1290.

50. Iannelli, 420 U.S. at 785, 95 S.Ct. at 1293.

51. Gebardi, 287 U.S. at 122, 53 S.Ct. at 37.

Third, the Supreme Court has instructed that a Wharton inquiry should focus on the statutory elements of the substantive offense rather than the evidence used to prove those elements at trial.[52] As the statutory elements of transporting stolen goods do not include a multiplicity of actors, Wharton's Rule is not made viable by the fact that the evidence adduced at trial may have focused on actions of two defendants in connection with transporting the stolen tractors.

Fourth, the principles underlying the creation of Wharton's Rule do not support its application in the instant situation. Conspiracies generally pose dangers that are distinct from those of the immediate underlying substantive crime. Collective criminal activity increases the chances that the criminal objective will be attained, decreases the chances that the involved individuals will abandon the criminal path, makes larger criminal objective attainable, and increases the probability that crimes unrelated to the original purpose for which the group was formed will be committed.

The major premise underlying Wharton's Rule, however, is that agreements to commit certain crimes do not appear to present these distinct dangers. These crimes, such as the classic examples of adultery and dueling, "are characterized by the general congruence of the agreement and the completed substantive offense." In such offenses, the parties to the agreement are the only persons who participate in the commission of the substantive offense, and are the only persons who bear the immediate consequences of the crime.

As the Supreme Court instructs us, "a legal principle commands less respect when extended beyond the logic that supports it." Unlike the traditional Wharton's Rule offenses, the transportation of stolen goods has immediate consequences for persons who are not parties to the criminal agreement. The significant differences in the characteristics and consequences of the instant offense and the kinds of offenses that gave rise to Wharton's Rule "counsel against attributing significant weight to the presumption that the Rule erects."

Fifth, Wharton's Rule "has continued vitality only as a judicial presumption, to be applied in the absence of legislative intent to the contrary." The legislative history of the federal statutes regarding aiding and abetting and conspiracy indicates that Congress found no duplication or conflict between these and their predicate crimes, but instead intended that each be treated as an independent offense or basis of responsibility....

We find that under these circumstances Wharton's Rule does not preclude conviction for both the interstate transportation of stolen goods (even when obtained in conjunction with an instruction on aiding-and-abetting) and conspiracy to commit that same substantive offense.

. . . .

Affirmed.[53]

---

52. Iannelli, 420 U.S. at 780, 95 S.Ct. at 1291.

53. [Added by the Compiler.] In Iannelli v. United States, 420 U.S. 770, 95 S.Ct. 1284, 43 L.Ed.2d 616 (1975), the Supreme Court rejected the traditional application of Wharton's Rule as a substantive limitation on the law of conspiracy and held that the rule should be viewed as

Gebardi v. United States

Supreme Court of the United States, 1932.
287 U.S. 112, 53 S.Ct. 35, 77 L.Ed. 206.

■ MR. JUSTICE STONE delivered the opinion of the Court.

This case is here on certiorari, 286 U.S. 539, 52 S.Ct. 648, 76 L.Ed. 1278, to review a judgment of conviction for conspiracy to violate the Mann Act (36 Stat. 825; 18 U.S.C. § 397 et seq.). Petitioners, a man and a woman, not then husband and wife, were indicted in the District Court for Northern Illinois, for conspiring together, and with others not named, to transport the woman from one state to another for the purpose of engaging in sexual intercourse with the man. At the trial without a jury there was evidence from which the court could have found that the petitioners had engaged in illicit sexual relations in the course of each of the journeys alleged; that the man purchased the railway tickets for both petitioners for at least one journey, and that in each instance the woman, in advance of the purchase of the tickets, consented to go on the journey and did go on it voluntarily for the specified immoral purpose. There was no evidence supporting the allegation that any other person had conspired. The trial court overruled motions for a finding for the defendants, and in arrest of judgment, and gave judgment of conviction, which the Court of Appeals for the Seventh Circuit affirmed 57 F.2d 617, on the authority of United States v. Holte, 236 U.S. 140, 35 S.Ct. 271, 59 L.Ed. 504....

Section 2 of the Mann Act (18 U.S.C. § 398), violation of which is charged by the indictment here as the object of the conspiracy, imposes the penalty upon "Any person who shall knowingly transport or cause to be transported, or aid or assist in obtaining transportation for, or in transporting in interstate or foreign commerce ... any woman or girl for the purpose of prostitution or debauchery or for any other immoral purpose ..." Transportation of a woman or girl whether with or without her consent, or causing or aiding it, or furthering it in any of the specified

---

a judicial presumption of the legislative intent in the absence of evidence to the contrary. The Court found a legislative intent contrary to Wharton's Rule as to the federal anti-gambling law, 18 U.S.C.A. § 1955.

The federal drug abuse act (21 U.S.C.A. § 841 et seq.) does not prohibit conviction for both the substantive crime of distribution and conspiracy to distribute where more than the seller and distributor are involved. United States v. Bommarito, 524 F.2d 140 (2d Cir.1975); United States v. Rueter, 536 F.2d 296 (9th Cir.1976).

"The widely recognized rule of construction known as Wharton's Rule states that when a substantive offense necessarily requires the participation of two persons, and where no more than two persons are alleged to have been involved in the agreement to commit the offense, the charge of conspiracy will not lie.... If a third person does participate so as to enlarge the scope of the agreement, however, all three may be charged with conspiracy." State v. Langworthy, 92 Wn.2d 148, 594 P.2d 908, 910 (1979).

Extortion and conspiracy to commit extortion are not effected by Wharton's Rule. "In practice, Wharton's Rule generally operates as a judicial presumption to proscribe a conspiracy charge in the absence of legislative intent to the contrary." People v. Carter, 415 Mich. 558, 330 N.W.2d 314, 321 (1982).

Wharton's Rule does not apply where more persons than are necessary to complete the substantive offense are involved in the conspiracy. United States v. Phillips, 959 F.2d 1187 (3d Cir.1992). Accord State v. Jacobson, 74 Wash. App. 715, 876 P.2d 916 (1994).

ways, are the acts punished, when done with a purpose which is immoral within the meaning of the law.

The Act does not punish the woman for transporting herself; it contemplates two persons—one to transport and the woman or girl to be transported. For the woman to fall within the ban of the statute she must, at the least, "aid or assist" someone else in transporting or in procuring transportation for herself. But such aid and assistance must, as in the case supposed in United States v. Holte,[54] *supra* 236 U.S. 145, 35 S.Ct. 271, 59 L.Ed. 504, be more active than mere agreement on her part to the transportation and its immoral purpose. For the statute is drawn to include those cases in which the woman consents to her own transportation. Yet it does not specifically impose any penalty upon her, although it deals in detail with the person by whom she is transported. In applying this criminal statute we cannot infer that the mere acquiescence of the woman transported was intended to be condemned by the general language punishing those who aid and assist the transporter, any more than it has been inferred that the purchaser of liquor was to be regarded as an abettor of the illegal sale. The penalties of the statute are too clearly directed against the acts of the transporter as distinguished from the consent of the subject of the transportation. So it was intimated in *United States v. Holte, supra*, and this conclusion is not disputed by the Government here, which contends only that the conspiracy charge will lie though the woman could not commit the substantive offense.

We come thus to the main question in the case, whether, admitting that the woman, by consenting, has not violated the Mann Act, she may be convicted of a conspiracy with the man to violate it. Section 37 of the Criminal Code (18 U.S.C., § 88), punishes a conspiracy by two or more persons "to commit any offense against the United States." The offense which she is charged with conspiring to commit is that perpetrated by the man, for it is not questioned that in transporting her he contravened § 2 of the Mann Act. Hence we must decide whether her concurrence, which was not criminal before the Mann Act, nor punished by it, may, without more, support a conviction under the conspiracy section, enacted many years before.

As we said in the Holte Case (p. 144 of 236 U.S., 35 S.Ct. 271, 272), an agreement to commit an offense may be criminal, though its purpose is to do what some of the conspirators may be free to do alone. Incapacity of one to commit the substantive offense does not necessarily imply that he may with impunity conspire with others who are able to commit it. For it is the collective planning of criminal conduct at which the statute aims.[55] The plan is itself a wrong which, if any act be done to effect its object, the state has elected to treat as criminal, Clune v. United States, 159 U.S. 590, 595,

---

54. *Holte* held that an indictment charging the man and woman with a conspiracy to have her transported across state lines for the purpose of prostitution was not demurrable because she would be guilty of conspiracy if the plan called for her to do much more than merely acquiesce in the transportation.

55. "The government's ability to deter and punish those who increase the likelihood of crime by concerted action has long been established." United States v. Spock, 416 F.2d 165, 171 (1st Cir.1969).

16 S.Ct. 125, 40 L.Ed. 269. And one may plan that others shall do what he cannot do himself.

But in this case we are concerned with something more than an agreement between two persons for one of them to commit an offense which the other cannot commit. There is the added element that the offense planned, the criminal object of the conspiracy, involves the agreement of the woman to her transportation by the man, which is the very conspiracy charged.

Congress set out in the Mann Act to deal with cases which frequently, if not normally, involve consent and agreement on the part of the woman to the forbidden transportation. In every case in which she is not intimidated or forced into the transportation, the statute necessarily contemplates her acquiescence. Yet this acquiescence, though an incident of a type of transportation specifically dealt with by the statute, was not made a crime under the Mann Act itself. Of this class of cases we say that the substantive offense contemplated by the statute itself involves the same combination or community of purpose of two persons only which is prosecuted here as conspiracy. If this were the only case covered by the Act, it would be within those decisions which hold, consistently with the theory upon which conspiracies are punished, that where it is impossible under any circumstances to commit the substantive offense without cooperative action, the preliminary agreement between the same parties to commit the offense is not an indictable conspiracy either at common law, or under the federal statute. But criminal transportation under the Mann Act may be effected without the woman's consent, as in cases of intimidation or force (with which we are not now concerned). We assume therefore, for present purposes, as was suggested in the Holte case, *supra*, 145 of 236 U.S., 35 S.Ct. 271, 272, that the decisions last mentioned do not in all strictness apply. We do not rest our decision upon the theory of those cases, nor upon the related one that the attempt is to prosecute as conspiracy acts identical with the substantive offense. United States v. Dietrich, 126 F. 664. We place it rather upon the ground that we perceive in the failure of the Mann Act to condemn the woman's participation in those transportations which are effected with her mere consent, evidence of an affirmative legislative policy to leave her acquiescence unpunished. We think it a necessary implication of that policy that when the Mann Act and the conspiracy statute came to be construed together, as they necessarily would be, the same participation which the former contemplates as an inseparable incident of all cases in which the woman is a voluntary agent at all, but does not punish, was not automatically to be made punishable under the latter. It would contravene that policy to hold that the very passage of the Mann Act effected a withdrawal by the conspiracy statute of that immunity which the Mann Act itself confers.

It is not to be supposed that the consent of an unmarried person to adultery with a married person, where the latter alone is guilty of the substantive offense, would render the former an abettor or a conspirator, compare In re Cooper, 162 Cal. 81, 85, 121 P. 318, or that the acquiescence of a woman under the age of consent would make her a co-conspirator with the man to commit statutory rape upon herself. The principle, determinative of this case, is the same.

On the evidence before us the woman petitioner has not violated the Mann Act and, we hold, is not guilty of a conspiracy to do so. As there is no proof that the man conspired with anyone else to bring about the transportation, the convictions of both petitioners must be

Reversed.[56]

■ MR. JUSTICE CARDOZO concurs in the result.

People v. Swain

Supreme Court of California, 1996.
12 Cal.4th 593, 49 Cal.Rptr.2d 390, 909 P.2d 994.

■ BAXTER, ASSOCIATE JUSTICE.

Defendants Jamal K. Swain and David Chatman were each convicted of conspiracy to commit murder and other crimes, stemming from the drive-by shooting death of a 15–year-old boy. As we shall explain, we hold that intent to kill is a required element of the crime of conspiracy to commit murder. In light of the jury instructions given, and general verdicts returned, we cannot determine beyond a reasonable doubt whether the jury found that the defendants conspired with an intent to kill. That conclusion requires us to reverse defendants' conspiracy convictions.

FACTS AND PROCEDURAL BACKGROUND

The question before us is one of law; the facts found by the Court of Appeal, summarized below, are not disputed.

---

56. Accord: Regina v. Murphy & Bieneck, 60 CCC 2d 1 (Albt.1981).

The status of prostitution under state law has no bearing on the legality of an agreement under the Mann Act. A conspiracy conviction was upheld for transporting a prostitute to Nevada where prostitution is not illegal. United States v. Pelton, 578 F.2d 701, 712 (8th Cir.1978).

The current federal statute prohibiting interstate transportation for prostitution is applicable to the transportation of "any individual." 18 U.S.C. § 2421 (1996).

At one time the California law did not make it an offense for one serving a sentence of life imprisonment to escape from prison, although it did make it an offense for one serving less than a life sentence to escape. At that time C, serving a life sentence and P, serving a term less than life, agreed to escape from prison with whatever force was required. In this escape P killed a guard. C was convicted of first-degree murder, and the conviction was affirmed although there was no evidence that he had ever touched the deceased. People v. Creeks, 170 Cal. 368, 149 P. 821 (1915).

"Under Minn.St. 609.175, subd. 2, defendant was properly convicted of conspiracy to commit a crime even though the person with whom he conspired feigned agreement and at no time intended to go through with the plan." (Syllabus by the Court). State v. St. Christopher, 305 Minn. 226, 232 N.W.2d 798, 799 (1975). Arizona conspiracy statute mandates a unilateral conspiracy standard. State v. Felkins, 156 Ariz. 37, 749 P.2d 946 (App.1988).

N.B. This is under a statute which expressly provides for "unilateral" conspiracy. See Model Penal Code § 5.04. A similar approach has been taken in Iowa Code Ann. § 706.1 (1987) but the statute is much more specific that a unilateral conspiracy is within the law. Many jurisdictions adopting the Model Penal Code approach recognize a unilateral conspiracy offense. State v. John, 328 N.W.2d 181 (Neb.1982); State v. LaForge, 183 N.J.Super. 118, 443 A.2d 269 (1981); State v. Welty, 729 S.W.2d 594 (Mo.App.1987). However, see People v. Foster, 457 N.E.2d 405 (Ill.1983).

Prosecution evidence established that a brown van passed through the Hunter's Point neighborhood of San Francisco about 2:00 a.m. on January 13, 1991. It slowed down near the spot where the young victim, who was of *facts* Samoan descent, and his friends were listening to music on the street.

A young Black male who appeared to have no hair was driving the van. Suddenly several shots were fired from the front of the van. Defendant Chatman and another young man also fired guns from the rear of the van. One of the intended victims had yelled out "drive-by" as a warning of the impending shooting, so most of the people on the street ducked down. The 15–year-old victim, Hagbom Saileele, who was holding the radio from which music was playing, was shot twice from behind. He later died in surgery.

Afterward, defendant Swain was in jail and boasted to jailmates about what good aim he had with a gun: "He was talking about what a good shot he was. [¶] ... [¶] He was saying he had shot that Samoan kid when they were in the van going about 30 miles an hour up a hill." The area where the shooting occurred is hilly; the van would have had to have been traveling uphill as it passed by the scene of the shooting.

. . .

The abandoned brown van was recovered by police; in the van and nearby were found surgical gloves, expended cartridges, a hooded ski mask, and two handguns: a .380–caliber semi-automatic and a .25–caliber automatic. Defendant Swain's fingerprint was on the inside of the driver's side window. The forensic evidence established that whoever had used the .380–caliber semi-automatic handgun, from which the fatal shots were fired, had been sitting in the driver's side front seat of the van.

The .380–caliber gun was traced, through a series of owners and transactions involving narcotics, to defendant Chatman. Chatman was interrogated by police; he denied any knowledge of the van and claimed he had not purchased the gun. When this story proved false, Chatman admitted he had bought the gun, but claimed it had been stolen from him. Still later, he claimed he had sold it to someone else.

A warrant was obtained for Chatman's arrest. After waiving his rights, Chatman told police he and two other people, not including Swain, had driven the van to the crime scene in order to get revenge for a car theft by a rival gang. Chatman insisted, to the police and at trial, that Swain had not been in the van. He could not, however, explain Swain's fingerprint inside the van.

The owner of the van testified Swain had never been inside his van prior to the incident, but that Swain had intimidated him into telling police he (Swain) had previously been inside the vehicle, since otherwise "he was going to have something done to him."

At trial, Chatman admitted he had been in the van, which was driven to Hunter's Point to retaliate for a car theft attributed to a neighborhood youth who was not the victim of the shooting. The original plan was allegedly to steal the car of the thief. Chatman admitted he had fired shots, but claimed he fired wildly and only in self-defense. In support of this self-defense theory, he testified he heard an initial shot and thought it was fired by someone outside the van shooting at him, so he returned the fire. As noted, Chatman claimed Swain was not in the van.

Swain testified he was not in the van during the shooting and did not do any shooting. He claimed he had entered the van earlier in the evening, but had left because "the smell of marijuana bothered him." He claimed he took BART (Bay Area Rapid Transit) to Berkeley, where he spent the evening at a relative's home. He denied boasting about shooting the victim and denied having threatened any witnesses.

The jury first returned a verdict finding defendant Chatman guilty of second degree murder and conspiracy. As instructed, the jury also made a finding that the target offense of the conspiracy was murder in the second degree. Several days later, the jury returned verdicts against defendant Swain, finding him not guilty of murder or its lesser included offenses, but guilty of conspiracy and of attempting to dissuade a witness from testifying by threats. Once again, the jury made a finding under the conspiracy count that the target offense of the conspiracy was murder in the second degree.

. . . .

Both defendants appealed on several grounds, including the question of whether intent to kill is a required element of the crime of conspiracy to commit murder. More particularly, where, as here, the target offense is determined to be murder in the second degree, does conviction of conspiracy to commit murder necessarily require proof of express malice—the functional equivalent of intent to kill—or can one conspire to commit implied malice murder? . . .

Defendants contend the jury should have been instructed that proof of intent to kill is required to support a conviction of conspiracy to commit murder, whether the target offense of the conspiracy—murder—is determined to be in the first or second degree. More particularly, defendants assert it was error to instruct the jury on the principles of implied malice second degree murder in connection with the determination of whether they could be found guilty of conspiracy to commit murder, since implied malice does not require a finding of intent to kill. As we shall explain, we agree.

Conspiracy is an inchoate crime. (*See* United States v. Feola (1975) 420 U.S. 671, 694, 95 S.Ct. 1255, 1268–69, 43 L.Ed.2d 541.) It does not require the commission of the substantive offense that is the object of the conspiracy. "As an inchoate crime, conspiracy fixes the point of legal intervention at [the time of] agreement to commit a crime," and "thus reaches further back into preparatory conduct than attempt. . . ." (Model Pen.Code & Commentaries (1985) com. 1 to § 5.03, pp. 387–388.)

The crime of conspiracy is defined in the Penal Code as "two or more persons conspir[ing]" "[t]o commit any crime," together with proof of the commission of an overt act "by one or more of the parties to such agreement" in furtherance thereof. (Pen.Code, § 182, subd. (a)(1), 184.) "Conspiracy is a 'specific intent' crime. . . . The specific intent required divides logically into two elements: (a) the intent to agree, or conspire, and (b) the intent to commit the offense which is the object of the conspiracy. . . . To sustain a conviction for conspiracy to commit a particular offense, the prosecution must show not only that the conspirators intended to agree *but also that they intended to commit the elements of that offense."* In some instances, the object of the conspiracy "is defined in terms of proscribed conduct." (Model Pen.Code & Commentaries, *supra*, com. 2(c) to § 5.03, p. 402.) In other instances, it "is defined in terms of ... a proscribed result under specified attendant circumstances."

. . .

Turning next to the elements of the target offense of the conspiracy here in issue, Penal Code section 187 defines the crime of murder as the "unlawful killing of a human being ... with malice aforethought." (Pen. Code, § 187, subd. (a).) Malice aforethought "may be express or implied." (Pen.Code, § 188.) "It is express when there is manifested a deliberate intention unlawfully to take away the life of a fellow creature. It is implied, when no considerable provocation appears, or when the circumstances attending the killing show an abandoned and malignant heart." (Ibid.)

This court has observed that proof of unlawful "intent to kill" is the functional equivalent of express malice. (*See* People v. Saille (1991) 54 Cal.3d 1103, 1114, 2 Cal.Rptr.2d 364, 820 P.2d 588 ["Pursuant to the language of [Penal Code] section 188, when an intentional killing is shown, malice aforethought is established."].)[57]

Penal Code section 189 distinguishes between murders in the first degree and murders in the second degree. "All murder which is perpetrated by means of a destructive device or explosive ... , poison, lying in wait, torture, *or by any other kind of willful, deliberate, and premeditated killing,* or which is committed in the perpetration of, or attempt to perpetrate, [certain enumerated felonies], or any murder which is perpetrated by means of discharging a firearm from a motor vehicle, intentionally at another person outside of the vehicle with the intent to inflict death, is murder of the first degree. All other kinds of murders are of the second degree."

California law, in turn, recognizes three theories of *second degree* murder.

The first is unpremeditated murder with express malice. (["Murder of the second degree is [also] the unlawful killing of a human being with malice aforethought when there is manifested an intention unlawfully to kill a human being but the evidence is insufficient to establish deliberation and premeditation."].)

The second, of particular concern here, is implied malice murder. (["Murder of the second degree is [also] the unlawful killing of a human being when: 1. The killing resulted from an intentional act, 2. The natural consequences of the act are dangerous to human life, and 3. The act was deliberately performed with knowledge of the danger to, and with conscious disregard for, human life. When the killing is the direct result of such an act, it is not necessary to establish that the defendant intended that his act would result in the death of a human being."].)

---

57. Of course unreasonable self-defense or a heat of passion defense can further reduce an intentional killing to voluntary manslaughter.

The third theory is second degree felony murder. ["The unlawful killing of a human being, whether intentional, unintentional or accidental, which occurs [during] [as the direct causal result of] the commission or attempted commission of [certain crimes] is murder of the second degree when the perpetrator had the specific intent to commit such crime."].

As noted, the jury in this case was instructed on the elements of murder, including principles of implied malice second degree murder. Under the instructions given, the jury could have based its verdicts finding defendants guilty of conspiracy to commit murder in the second degree on a theory of implied malice murder. . . .

We have noted that conspiracy is a specific intent crime requiring an intent to agree or conspire, and a further intent to commit the target crime, here murder, the object of the conspiracy. Since murder committed with intent to kill is the functional equivalent of *express malice* murder, conceptually speaking, no conflict arises between the specific intent element of conspiracy and the specific intent requirement for such category of murders. Simply put, where the conspirators agree or conspire with specific intent to kill and commit an overt act in furtherance of such agreement, they are guilty of conspiracy to commit express malice murder. The conceptual difficulty arises when the target offense of murder is founded on a theory of implied malice, which requires no intent to kill.

Implied malice murder, in contrast to express malice, requires instead an intent to do some act, the natural consequences of which are dangerous to human life. "*When the killing is the direct result of such an act,*" the requisite mental state for murder—malice aforethought—is implied. In such circumstances, " . . . it is not necessary to establish that the defendant intended that his act would result in the death of a human being." Hence, under an *implied malice* theory of second degree murder, the requisite mental state for murder—malice aforethought—is by definition "implied," as a matter of law, from the specific intent to do some act dangerous to human life *together with the circumstance that a killing has resulted from the doing of such act.*

. . .

The element of malice aforethought in implied malice murder cases is therefore derived or "implied," in part through hindsight so to speak, from (i) proof of the specific intent to do some act dangerous to human life and (ii) the circumstance that a killing has resulted therefrom. It is precisely due to this nature of *implied malice* murder that it would be *illogical* to conclude one can be found guilty of conspiring to commit murder where the requisite element of malice is implied. Such a construction would be at odds with the very nature of the crime of conspiracy—an "inchoate" crime that "fixes the point of legal intervention at [the time of] agreement to commit a crime," and indeed "reaches further back into preparatory conduct than [the crime of] attempt" (Model Pen.Code & Commentaries, *supra*, com. 1 to § 5.03, pp. 387–388)—precisely because commission of the crime could never be established, or deemed complete, unless and until a killing actually occurred.

We conclude that a conviction of conspiracy to commit murder requires a finding of intent to kill, and cannot be based on a theory of implied malice.

Affirmed in part, reversed in part.

United States v. Loscalzo

United States Court of Appeals, Seventh Circuit, 1994.
18 F.3d 374.

■ Bauer, Circuit Judge.

Anthony Loscalzo, Andrew Loscalzo, Merry Stumpf, David Siegel, and Albert Boemo were convicted of conspiracy to defraud the United States and several counts of mail fraud. Their convictions stem from fraudulent representations made in connection with obtaining a contract procured by the United States Postal Service ("Postal Service")....

On May 8, 1991, the grand jury returned an indictment charging the defendants with one count of conspiracy to defraud the United States and thirty-one counts of mail fraud. The indictment alleged that the defendants conspired to impair and obstruct the Postal Service in its awarding of minority enterprise contracts by establishing corporations with a nonparticipating minority person listed as a figurehead president.

Upon the jury verdict finding all the defendants guilty of conspiracy and mail fraud, the court entered judgment and sentenced each defendant to various terms of imprisonment and supervised release. Anthony Loscalzo was sentenced to thirty-seven months imprisonment and two years of supervised release....

Albert Boemo and Merry Stumpf offer alternative challenges. Each argues that even if the two corporations were involved in fraudulent activity, their own respective roles were insignificant and, therefore, the evidence supporting their convictions was insufficient to prove beyond a reasonable doubt that they had the requisite specific intent to commit the crimes. We note as a preliminary matter that the government offered, in addition to the substantive conspiracy theory, an aiding and abetting theory. This permitted the jury to convict the defendants of conspiracy if they found either that the defendants were parties to the original agreement and committed an overt act in furtherance of the conspiracy or, alternatively, that the defendants performed some act which they knew would further the conspiracy. The evidence need only have supported one of the two theories.

.   .   .

Stumpf claims that her duties were purely clerical and her participation in any conspiracy could not be "knowing and affirmative." In support of her argument, Stumpf cites United States v. Casperson, 773 F.2d 216 (8th Cir.1985), in which the Eighth Circuit overturned on sufficiency grounds, the conviction of a coconspirator charged in connection with a fraudulent investment scheme. The defendant's responsibilities in *Casperson* were limited to taking notes at meetings and keeping track of potential investors. Id. at 220. He made no decisions and on at least one occasion, his conduct had been completely inconsistent with the aims of the scheme. Because the defendant's role in the scheme did not rise to the level of knowing and affirmative participation, the conviction was overturned.

Unlike the defendant in *Casperson*, Merry Stumpf's involvement in Martinez Manufacturing and Soltech was substantial. In her capacity as the only true officer of Martinez Manufacturing, she filed annual reports with the state. All of these reports, filed after Martinez's participation had ceased, affirmed that Martinez was president of the corporation and one of these reports contained what purported to be Martinez's signature. Having determined that Martinez Manufacturing's status as a minority business was the product of fraud, the jury could plausibly have found that Stumpf's actions were designed to deliberately conceal the fact that no minority person was involved with Martinez Manufacturing.

Stumpf's participation in the affairs of Soltech were also more substantial than that of the defendant in *Casperson*. Not only was she a director of Soltech and thus responsible for replacing Solis with Phillips but she was also responsible for arranging financing for Soltech after it was awarded the contract. Stumpf's duties were not of the sort normally entrusted to a clerical employee. The evidence suggests a level of knowledge and responsibility consistent with the jury's finding.

Our review of the record leads us to conclude that there was substantial evidence supporting the jury's finding that Martinez Manufacturing's and Soltech's minority classifications were the product of fraudulent actions on the part of the defendant. The evidence also supports the jury's conclusion that Albert Boemo and Merry Stumpf were knowing participants in the scheme.

Jury Instructions

Stumpf alleges that the trial court made three errors in charging the jury. Our review of the record assures us, however, that the trial judge's instructions were intelligible and faithful to the law.

. . .

First, Stumpf argues that the trial court's instruction on aiding and abetting[58] created confusion of constitutional dimension. Far from lucid, Stumpf's contention appears to be that an instruction on aiding and abetting, in addition to the instructions on the elements of conspiracy, misled the jury into believing that Stumpf could be convicted of conspiracy without a finding that she was a knowing party to the agreement. She adds that the confusion was enhanced because aiding and abetting was not charged in the indictment.

Aiding and abetting is not a separate crime. An aider or abettor of a substantive offense may be treated as a principal. 18 U.S.C. § 2. Since conspiracy is a substantive offense, a defendant may be found to have aided

---

58. Instruction #11 reads as follows:

Any person who knowingly aids, abets, counsels, commands, induces or procures the commission of a crime is guilty of that crime. However, that person must knowingly associate himself or herself with the criminal venture, participate in it, and try to make it work.

or abetted a conspiracy. United States v. Galiffa, 734 F.2d 306 (7th Cir.1984).

Stumpf's argument recognizes the distinction between aiding and abetting a conspiracy and participating in a conspiracy, but she contends that this distinction is somehow improper. We disagree. The aiding and abetting statute serves to complement the substantive offense of conspiracy. Recognizing that conspirators often employ assistants in carrying out their plans, the statute enables the government to prosecute those who have knowingly furthered the aims of the conspiracy but who were not members of the conspiracy. The charge of aiding and abetting does not exempt the government from proving the defendant had the requisite criminal intent because the jury must still find that the aider or abettor knowingly acted to make the venture succeed.

Taken as a whole, the charge informed the jury that there were two alternate means of finding Stumpf guilty of the substantive offense and that they had to consider both. The government was not required to charge Stumpf with aiding and abetting in the indictment. Aiding and abetting need not be specifically pleaded, and an aider or abettor still may be convicted of the substantive offense as long as no unfair surprise exists. United States v. Tucker, 552 F.2d 202, 204 (7th Cir.1977). Stumpf does not claim that any unfair surprise was created here, and we, therefore, do not reach that issue.

. . .

Affirmed.[59]

Pinkerton v. United States

Supreme Court of the United States, 1946.
328 U.S. 640, 66 S.Ct. 1180, 90 L.Ed. 1489.

■ Mr. Justice Douglas delivered the opinion of the Court.

Walter and Daniel Pinkerton are brothers who live a short distance from each other on Daniel's farm. They were indicted for violations of the

---

59. In United States v. Falcone, 109 F.2d 579 (2d Cir.1940), aff'd 311 U.S. 205 (1940), it was held defendants who supplied ordinary commercial food items to persons who used the items in the manufacture of illicit liquor could not be convicted of aiding and abetting a conspiracy absent a showing of a stake in the conspiracy.

If the commodities involved in the sale are not articles of free commerce such as sugar and cans, but restricted commodities such as narcotic drugs which can be sold only by compliance with order forms and registration and are incapable of further legal use without compliance with rigid regulations, the seller's knowledge of the buyer's extensive illegal use of the drugs over an extended period of time may be sufficient to establish a conspiracy. Direct Sales Co. v. United States, 319 U.S. 703, 63 S.Ct. 1265, 87 L.Ed. 1674 (1943).

C sold a gun to D under such circumstances that it was criminally negligent for him to do so because of the likelihood that D would use it to kill X, which D did. D was convicted of first-degree murder and C was convicted of involuntary manslaughter. People v. Howk, 56 Cal.2d 687, 16 Cal.Rptr. 370, 365 P.2d 426 (1961).

"One who sells a gun to another knowing that he is buying it to commit a murder, would hardly escape conviction as an accessory to the murder by showing that he received full price for the gun." Backun v. United States, 112 F.2d 635, 637 (4th Cir.1940).

Internal Revenue Code. The indictment contained ten substantive counts and one conspiracy count. The jury found Walter guilty on nine of the substantive counts and on the conspiracy count. It found Daniel guilty on six of the substantive counts and on the conspiracy count. Walter was fined $500 and sentenced generally on the substantive counts to imprisonment for thirty months. On the conspiracy count he was given a two year sentence to run concurrently with the other sentence. Daniel was fined $1,000 and sentenced generally on the substantive counts to imprisonment for thirty months. On the conspiracy count he was fined $500 and given a two year sentence to run concurrently with the other sentence. The judgments of conviction were affirmed by the Circuit Court of Appeals. 151 F.2d 499. The case is here on a petition for a writ of certiorari which we granted, 66 S.Ct. 702, because one of the questions presented involved a conflict between the decision below and United States v. Sall, 116 F.2d 745, decided by the Circuit Court of Appeals for the Third Circuit.

A single conspiracy was charged and proved. Some of the overt acts charged in the conspiracy count were the same acts charged in the substantive counts. Each of the substantive offenses found was committed pursuant to the conspiracy. . . .

It is contended that there was insufficient evidence to implicate Daniel in the conspiracy. But we think there was enough evidence for submission of the issue to the jury.

There is, however, no evidence to show that Daniel participated directly in the commission of the substantive offenses on which his conviction has been sustained, although there was evidence to show that these substantive offenses were in fact committed by Walter in furtherance of the unlawful agreement or conspiracy existing between the brothers. The question was submitted to the jury on the theory that each petitioner could be found guilty of the substantive offenses, if it was found at the time those offenses were committed petitioners were parties to an unlawful conspiracy and the substantive offenses charged were in fact committed in furtherance of it.

Daniel relies on *United States v. Sall, supra.* That case held that participation in the conspiracy was not itself enough to sustain a conviction for the substantive offense even though it was committed in furtherance of the conspiracy. The court held that, in addition to evidence that the offense was in fact committed in furtherance of the conspiracy, evidence of direct participation in the commission of the substantive offense or other evidence from which participation might fairly be inferred was necessary.

We take a different view. We have here a continuous conspiracy. There is here no evidence of the affirmative action on the part of Daniel which is necessary to establish his withdrawal from it. Hyde v. United States, 225 U.S. 347, 369, 32 S.Ct. 793, 803, 56 L.Ed. 1114, Ann.Cas. 1914A, 614. As stated in that case, "Having joined in an unlawful scheme, having constituted agents for its performance, scheme and agency to be continuous until full fruition be secured, until he does some act to disavow or defeat the purpose he is in no situation to claim the delay of the law. As the offense has not been terminated or accomplished, he is still offending. And we think, consciously offending,—offending as certainly, as we have said, as at the first moment of his confederation, and consciously through every moment of its existence." And so long as the partnership in crime continues, the partners act for each other in carrying it forward. It is settled that "an overt act of one partner may be the act of all without any new agreement specifically directed to that act." United States v. Kissel, 218 U.S. 601, 608, 31 S.Ct. 124, 126, 54 L.Ed. 1168. Motive or intent may be proved by the acts or declarations of some of the conspirators in furtherance of the common objective. A scheme to use the mails to defraud, which is joined in by more than one person, is a conspiracy. Yet all members are responsible, though only one did the mailing. The governing principle is the same when the substantive offense is committed by one of the conspirators in furtherance of the unlawful project. The criminal intent to do the act is established by the formation of the conspiracy. Each conspirator instigated the commission of the crime. The unlawful agreement contemplated precisely what was done. It was formed for the purpose. The act done was in execution of the enterprise. The rule which holds responsible one who counsels, procures, or commands another to commit a crime is founded on the same principle. That principle is recognized in the law of conspiracy when the overt act of one partner in crime is attributable to all. An overt act is an essential ingredient of the crime of conspiracy under § 37 of the Criminal Code, 18 U.S.C. § 88, 18 U.S.C.A. § 88. If that can be supplied by the act of one conspirator, we fail to see why the same or other acts in furtherance of the conspiracy are likewise not attributable to the others for the purpose of holding them responsible for the substantive offense.

A different case would arise if the substantive offense committed by one of the conspirators was not in fact done in furtherance of the conspiracy, did not fall within the scope of the unlawful project, or was merely a part of the ramifications of the plan which could not be reasonably foreseen as a necessary or natural consequence of the unlawful agreement. But as we read this record, that is not this case.

Affirmed.

■ MR. JUSTICE JACKSON took no part in the consideration or decision of this case.

■ MR. JUSTICE RUTLEDGE, dissenting in part....

United States v. Rosado–Fernandez

United States Court of Appeals, Fifth Circuit, 1980.
614 F.2d 50.

■ AINSWORTH, CIRCUIT JUDGE: Appellants Jose Eligio Borges and Angel Oscar Rosado–Fernandez, along with two other defendants, were convicted of conspiracy to possess with intent to distribute cocaine, 21 U.S.C. § 846, and possession with intent to distribute cocaine, 21 U.S.C. § 841(a)(1), 18 U.S.C. § 2. Rosado was also convicted of use of a communication facility during the course of and in the commission of a felony, in violation of 21 U.S.C. §§ 841(a)(1), 846, 843(b). On appeal, Borges contends that there is insufficient evidence to convict him of the conspiracy charge, and also contends that he cannot be found guilty of the possession charge since he never had actual possession of the cocaine in question. Rosado contends that the Government failed to prove that the cocaine involved in the attempted drug transaction was "L" cocaine rather than purportedly legal "D" cocaine. The contentions of both appellants are meritless and we affirm.

On January 3, 1979, Agent John Lawler of the Drug Enforcement Agency (DEA), acting in an undercover capacity as a New York cocaine buyer, went to the residence of appellant Borges. Lawler informed Borges that he wanted to buy three kilos of cocaine. Borges quoted a price, and stated that delivery could be arranged. During the conversation Borges was sifting a white powder on his kitchen table. He stated the cocaine would be better than that on the table. Borges then made a phone call in Spanish and told Lawler to return later that evening. When Lawler returned the parties agreed to meet still later at a nearby restaurant. Borges indicated he would bring his supplier to the restaurant.

Later that evening, Borges came to the restaurant accompanied by appellant Rosado, and Rosado's stepfather. Borges introduced Rosado to Lawler, and Lawler stated he was interested in purchasing three kilos of cocaine. Rosado stated it would be no problem as he had 40 kilos in the area. Borges was present during this entire conversation. Rosado then made a phone call and told Lawler the cocaine would be delivered to an apartment. Rosado and Lawler discussed delivery and agreed that they would be the only ones present during the actual transaction. Borges concurred in this arrangement. No actual delivery took place that evening.

The next day Lawler and Rosado had a series of telephone conversations, which were recorded and played for the jury. During the conversations, Rosado apologized for the delay and stated the price would be $46,000 per kilo. Lawler and Rosado later met at the home of the third codefendant Nelson Garcia. A quantity of white powder was produced, and Lawler tested it. The test indicated that the powder was cocaine. Shortly thereafter arrests were made. While Garcia and Rosado were being arrested, the fourth codefendant Zayas took the cocaine and dumped it into the swimming pool. Agent Lawler dove in the pool and recovered samples of the water and the cocaine, as well as a sample from the table inside. All samples were found to contain cocaine.

Borges does not deny that he introduced Agent Lawler to codefendant Rosado, but he contends that he had no part of the final drug transaction involving Rosado and codefendant Garcia. He argues that the Rosado–Garcia drug transaction is a separate conspiracy, as the purchase arranged by him was to involve Rosado and a drug source other than Garcia. The fact that Rosado eventually obtained the cocaine from a source not originally contemplated by Borges, however, is not sufficient to exonerate Borges.

To be convicted of conspiracy, a defendant must have knowledge of the conspiracy, and must intend to join or associate himself with the objectives of the conspiracy. Knowledge, actual participation and criminal intent must be proved by the Government. Participation, however, need not be proved by direct evidence; a common purpose and plan may be inferred from a pattern of circumstantial evidence. The essential elements of a criminal conspiracy are an agreement among the conspirators to commit an offense attended by an overt act by one of them in furtherance of the agreement. However, under the provisions of the drug conspiracy statute involved here, it is not necessary that an overt act be alleged or proved.

The facts at trial established a conspiracy between Borges and Rosado to sell cocaine to Lawler. They agreed to commit an offense against the United States. Borges was the organizer of the venture. He set up the meeting, and was present during the negotiations for the sale of the cocaine. The conspirators need not know each other nor be privy to the details of each enterprise comprising the conspiracy as long as the evidence is sufficient to show that each defendant possessed full knowledge of the conspiracy's general purpose and scope. Borges knew that Lawler wanted to buy cocaine. Borges knew that Rosado would obtain the cocaine for Lawler from one of Rosado's several sources. Under these circumstances the conspiracy was proved.

Borges next contends that he cannot be convicted of possession since the evidence shows he never had physical control of the cocaine involved in the transaction. It is undisputed, however, that Rosado had possession of the drug. A party to a continuing conspiracy may be responsible for a substantive offense committed by a coconspirator in furtherance of the conspiracy even though that party does not participate in the substantive offense or have any knowledge of it. As we stated recently in United States v. Michel, 588 F.2d 986, 999 (5th Cir.1979):

Once the conspiracy and a particular defendant's knowing participation in it has been established beyond a reasonable doubt, the defendant is deemed guilty of substantive acts committed in furtherance of the conspiracy by any of his criminal partners. This principle has been repeatedly applied by this circuit in cases involving drug conspiracies and substantive drug violations.

Affirmed.

Marquiz v. People

Supreme Court of Colorado, 1986.
726 P.2d 1105.

■ LOHR, JUSTICE.

We granted certiorari to review the decision of the Colorado Court of Appeals in People v. Marquiz, 685 P.2d 242 (Colo.App.1984), sustaining the defendant's convictions for first-degree murder and conspiracy to commit first-degree murder. We limited our review, however, to the issue of whether the defendant, Steven Richard Marquiz, could be convicted of conspiracy to commit first-degree murder after his two alleged coconspirators had previously been acquitted of conspiracy at separate trials.... We affirm the judgment of the court of appeals and hold that the rule of consistency is not applicable to situations where all alleged coconspirators are not tried in the same proceeding.

The defendant's convictions stem from the slaying of seventeen-year-old Debra Terhorst early in January of 1981. According to evidence presented at trial, Marquiz believed that the victim had stolen some property from his apartment, and he resolved to kill her. Marquiz enlisted the cooperation of Rudy Gallegos and Antonio Laroza in this endeavor. The three men induced the victim to accompany them to a location on Lookout Mountain, where they stabbed her several times and cut her throat, resulting in her death.

Shortly after the killing, Marquiz, Gallegos and Laroza were arrested and charged with first-degree murder and conspiracy to commit first-degree murder. §§ 18–3–102 and 18–2–201, 8B C.R.S. (1986). The cases against the three defendants were severed for trial. A jury found Gallegos guilty of first-degree murder but not guilty of conspiracy to commit first-degree murder. A separate jury acquitted Laroza of both the murder charge and the conspiracy charge. The trial of Marquiz did not begin until May 17, 1982, well after the trials of the other two defendants had been completed.

A jury found Marquiz guilty of both first-degree murder and conspiracy to commit first-degree murder. . . .

The rule of consistency, simply stated, is that where all alleged coconspirators but one are acquitted of conspiracy, the remaining alleged coconspirator may not be convicted of conspiracy. When alleged coconspirators are tried in separate proceedings, however, the majority of courts that have considered the issue have held that the rule of consistency is inapplicable. *E.g.,* United States v. Sangmeister, 685 F.2d 1124 (9th Cir.1982); United States v. Espinosa–Cerpa, 630 F.2d 328 (5th Cir.1980); People v. Superior Court, 44 Cal.App.3d 494, 118 Cal.Rptr. 702 (1975); Smith v. State, 250 Ga. 264, 297 S.E.2d 273 (1982); Gardner v. State, 286 Md. 520, 408 A.2d 1317 (1979); Commonwealth v. Cerveny, 387 Mass. 280, 439 N.E.2d 754 (1982); People v. Anderson, 418 Mich. 31, 340 N.W.2d 634 (1983); Platt v. State, 143 Neb. 131, 8 N.W.2d 849 (1943); Commonwealth v. Byrd, 490 Pa. 544, 417 A.2d 173 (1980). A few courts have held, without extensive examination of the validity of the rationale for the rule in the context of separate trials, that the rule of consistency applies even when alleged coconspirators are tried in separate proceedings. Romontio v. United States, 400 F.2d 618 (10th Cir.1968), cert. granted, 400 U.S. 901, 91 S.Ct. 144, 27 L.Ed.2d 137 (1970), cert. dismissed, 402 U.S. 903, 91 S.Ct. 1384, 28 L.Ed.2d 644 (1971); . . . We adopt the position of the majority of jurisdictions and hold that the rule of consistency is inapplicable where all alleged coconspirators are not tried in the same proceeding.

The rule of consistency has its origins in a time when all alleged coconspirators were routinely charged in the same proceeding. In such cases the evidence against the defendants commonly would be identical and the composition of the jury would be the same as to each defendant. Were the jury to convict one defendant of conspiracy while acquitting the others "[t]he effect analytically [*would be*] that the fact-finder in such cases found simultaneously that 'an agreement between two or more persons' existed and that it did not exist with regard to the same alleged conspirators." The rule of consistency therefore serves as a check upon the jury in two ways:

First, it insures that the jury will adhere to the conspiracy requirement of the concurrence of at least two guilty minds; and second, it prevents the jury from weighing the same pieces of evidence differently in regard to each of the alleged conspirators.

When alleged coconspirators are tried in separate proceedings, however, the reasons for the rule lose much if not all of their force.[60]

There is no inherent inconsistency when different juries return different verdicts in separate trials, because the acquittal of one of the conspirators " 'could [result] from a multiplicity of factors completely unrelated to the actual existence of a conspiracy.' " The evidence presented to the juries and the manner in which that evidence is presented may be significantly different and certainly will never be identical. Certain witnesses or other evidence may be available for one trial and not the other, the prosecution may not present all of the available evidence in each trial, new evidence may be discovered between trials, and the prosecution may not present its case as effectively in one trial as it does in the other. In some instances, evidence may be admissible at the trial of one defendant but not at that of another.

Different verdicts may also result simply from the different compositions of the juries. Separate juries may reasonably take different views of the same evidence. "Moreover, the jury may assume the power to acquit out of compassion or prejudice, and the prosecution is then powerless to seek a judgment notwithstanding the verdict or a new trial on the ground that the verdict is against the weight of the evidence." Public policy dictates that we guard against compounding the effect of a possibly erroneous or irrational acquittal. . . .

The value of the rule of consistency as a check upon the jury also disappears in the context of separate trials.

Application of the consistency rule in this situation neither insures that the two juries understand the crime of conspiracy nor that they evaluated the facts of the case consistently in regard to each conspirator.

We conclude that the policies sought to be furthered by the rule of consistency are not served by application of the rule to situations in which all alleged coconspirators are not tried in the same proceeding.

The judgment of the court of appeals is affirmed.[61]

ENTERPRISE LIABILITY

Recently, legislative innovation has produced a new concept similar to conspiracy but not the same. This is enterprise liability. Congress and

---

60.   It has been suggested that the rule may not retain its validity in any context because of the "true nature of an acquittal in the American criminal justice system." United States v. Espinosa–Cerpa, 630 F.2d 328, 331–32 (5th Cir.1980); *see* Government of Virgin Islands v. Hoheb, 777 F.2d 138, 142 n. 6 (3d Cir.1985) ("[Recent cases decided by the United States Supreme Court] suggest that the rule of consistency may be a vestige of the past."). We are not faced with a case involving a traditional application of the rule of consistency, and we therefore decline to express any view as to whether the rule retains its validity in the context of a joint trial of all alleged coconspirators.

61.   Where A and B were separately tried on a conspiracy charge and A was acquitted B could still be tried and convicted. DPP v. Shannon, [1975] A.C. 717. Accord: Commonwealth v. Byrd, 490 Pa. 544, 417 A.2d 173 (1980). Where both A and B were tried together and convicted but A's conviction is set aside on appeal B's conviction was upheld. Queen v. Darby, 56 Aust.L.J.Rpts. 688 (Aust.H.C.1982).

Contra, State v. Jackson, 7 S.C. 283 (1876).

several states have enacted legislation in the area of racketeering[62] and drugs[63] to get at persons who engage in continuing criminal activity that often is broadly based and diverse in the criminal objective. These statutes frequently carry severe sanctions. The RICO Act provides a strong federal supplement to the traditional conspiracy prosecution. Although the statute is aimed at racketeering activity, it is not limited to organized crime activities.[64]

United States v. Turkette

Supreme Court of the United States, 1981.
452 U.S. 576, 101 S.Ct. 2524, 69 L.Ed.2d 246.

■ JUSTICE WHITE delivered the opinion of the Court.

Chapter 96 of Title 18 of the United States Code, 18 U.S.C. §§ 1961–1968 (1976 ed. and Supp. III), entitled Racketeer Influenced and Corrupt Organizations (RICO), was added to Title 18 by Title IX of the Organized Crime Control Act of 1970, Pub.L. 91–452, 84 Stat. 941. The question in this case is whether the term "enterprise" as used in RICO encompasses both legitimate and illegitimate enterprises or is limited in application to the former. The Court of Appeals for the First Circuit held that Congress did not intend to include within the definition of "enterprise" those organizations which are exclusively criminal. . . .

Count Nine of a nine-count indictment charged respondent and 12 others with conspiracy to conduct and participate in the affairs of an enterprise[65] engaged in interstate commerce through a pattern of racketeering activities, in violation of 18 U.S.C. § 1962(d).[66] The indictment described the enterprise as "a group of individuals associated in fact for the purpose of illegally trafficking in narcotics and other dangerous drugs, committing arsons, utilizing the United States mails to defraud insurance companies, bribing and attempting to bribe local police officers, and corruptly influencing and attempting to corruptly influence the outcome of state court proceedings. . . ." The other eight counts of the indictment charged the commission of various substantive criminal acts by those engaged in and associated with the criminal enterprise, including possession with intent to distribute and distribution of controlled substances, and

---

62. 18 U.S.C.A. § 1961 et seq. (RICO).

63. 21 U.S.C.A. § 848 (continuing criminal enterprise).

64. See Lynch, RICO: The Crime of Being a Criminal, Parts I, II, III, & IV, 87 Columbia L.Rev. 661, 920 (1987).

65. Title 18 U.S.C. § 1961(4) provides:

" 'enterprise' includes any individual, partnership, corporation, association, or other legal entity, and any union or group of individuals associated in fact although not a legal entity."

66. Title 18 U.S.C. § 1962(d) provides that "(i)t shall be unlawful for any person to conspire to violate any of the provisions of subsections (a), (b), or (c) of this section." Pertinent to these charges, subsection (c) provides:

"It shall be unlawful for any person employed by or associated with any enterprise engaged in, or the activities of which affect, interstate or foreign commerce, to conduct or participate, directly or indirectly, in the conduct of such enterprise's affairs through a pattern of racketeering activity or collection of unlawful debt."

several counts of insurance fraud by arson and other means. The common thread to all counts was respondent's alleged leadership of this criminal organization through which he orchestrated and participated in the commission of the various crimes delineated in the RICO count or charged in the eight preceding counts.

. . .

On appeal, respondent argued that RICO was intended solely to protect legitimate business enterprises from infiltration by racketeers and that RICO does not make criminal the participation in an association which performs only illegal acts and which has not infiltrated as attempted to infiltrate a legitimate enterprise. The Court of Appeals agreed. We reverse.

In determining the scope of a statute, we look first to its language....

Section 1962(c) makes it unlawful "for any person employed by or associated with any enterprise engaged in, or the activities of which affect, interstate or foreign commerce, to conduct or participate, directly or indirectly, in the conduct of such enterprise's affairs through a pattern of racketeering activity or collection of unlawful debt." The term "enterprise" is defined as including "any individual, partnership, corporation, association, or other legal entity, and any union or group of individuals associated in fact although not a legal entity." § 1961(4). There is no restriction upon the associations embraced by the definition: an enterprise includes any union or group of individuals associated in fact. On its face, the definition appears to include both legitimate and illegitimate enterprises within its scope; it no more excludes criminal enterprises than it does legitimate ones. Had Congress not intended to reach criminal associations, it could easily have narrowed the sweep of the definition by inserting a single word, "legitimate." But it did nothing to indicate that an enterprise consisting of a group of individuals was not covered by RICO if the purpose of the enterprise was exclusively criminal.

... Considering the language and structure of § 1961(4), however, we not only perceive no uncertainty in the meaning to be attributed to the phrase, "any union or group of individuals associated in fact" but we are convinced for another reason that *ejusdem generis* is wholly inapplicable in this context.

Section 1961(4) describes two categories of associations that come within the purview of the "enterprise" definition. The first encompasses organizations such as corporations and partnerships, and other "legal entities." The second covers "any union or group of individuals associated in fact although not a legal entity." ... Each category describes a separate type of enterprise to be covered by the statute—those that are recognized as legal entities and those that are not. The latter is not a more general description of the former. The second category itself not containing any specific enumeration that is followed by a general description, ejusdem generis has no bearing on the meaning to be attributed to that part of § 1961(4).

... That a wholly criminal enterprise comes within the ambit of the statute does not mean that a "pattern of racketeering activity" is an "enterprise." In order to secure a conviction under RICO, the Government must prove both the existence of an "enterprise" and the connected "pattern of racketeering activity." The enterprise is an entity, for present purposes a group of persons associated together for a common purpose of engaging in a course of conduct. The pattern of racketeering activity is, on the other hand, a series of criminal acts as defined by the statute. 18 U.S.C. § 1961(1) (1976 ed., Supp. III). The former is proved by evidence of an ongoing organization, formal or informal, and by evidence that the various associates function as a continuing unit. The latter is proved by evidence of the requisite number of acts of racketeering committed by the participants in the enterprise. While the proof used to establish these separate elements may in particular cases coalesce, proof of one does not necessarily establish the other. The "enterprise" is not the "pattern of racketeering activity"; it is an entity separate and apart from the pattern of activity in which it engages. The existence of an enterprise at all times remains a separate element which must be proved by the Government.

Apart from § 1962(c)'s proscription against participating in an enterprise through a pattern of racketeering activities, RICO also proscribes the investment of income derived from racketeering activity in an enterprise engaged in or which affects interstate commerce as well as the acquisition of an interest in or control of any such enterprise through a pattern of racketeering activity. 18 U.S.C. §§ 1962(a) and (b).[67] The Court of Appeals concluded that these provisions of RICO should be interpreted so as to apply only to legitimate enterprises. If these two sections are so limited, the Court of Appeals held that the proscription in § 1962(c), at issue here, must be similarly limited. Again, we do not accept the premise from which the Court of Appeals derived its conclusion. It is obvious that § 1962(a) and (b) address the infiltration by organized crime of legitimate businesses, but we cannot agree that these sections were not also aimed at preventing racketeers from investing or reinvesting in wholly illegal enterprises and from acquiring through a pattern of racketeering activity wholly illegitimate enterprises such as an illegal gambling business or a loan-sharking operation. There is no inconsistency or anomaly in recognizing that § 1962 applies to both legitimate and illegitimate enterprises. . . .

---

67. Title 18 U.S.C. §§ 1962(a) and (b) provide:

"(a) It shall be unlawful for any person who has received any income derived, directly or indirectly, from a pattern of racketeering activity or through collection of an unlawful debt in which such person has participated as a principal within the meaning of section 2, title 18, United States Code, to use or invest, directly or indirectly, any part of such income, or the proceeds of such income, in acquisition of any interest in, or the establishment or operation of, any enterprise which is engaged in, or the activities of which affect, interstate or foreign commerce. A purchase of securities on the open market for purposes of investment, and without the intention of controlling or participating in the control of the issuer, or of assisting another to do so, shall not be unlawful under this subsection if the securities of the issuer held by the purchaser, the members of his immediate family, and his or their accomplices in any pattern or racketeering activity or the collection of an unlawful debt after such purchase do not amount in the aggregate to one percent of the outstanding securities of any one class, and do not confer, either in law or in fact, the power to elect one or more directors of the issuer.

"(b) It shall be unlawful for any person through a pattern of racketeering activity or through collection of an unlawful debt to acquire or maintain, directly or indirectly, any interest in or control of any enterprise which is engaged in, or the activities of which affect, interstate or foreign commerce."

Similarly, the Court of Appeals noted that various civil remedies were provided by § 1964,[68] including divestiture, dissolution, reorganization, restrictions on future activities by violators of RICO, and treble damages. These remedies it thought would have utility only with respect to legitimate enterprises. As a general proposition, however, the civil remedies could be useful in eradicating organized crime from the social fabric, whether the enterprise be ostensibly legitimate or admittedly criminal. The aim is to divest the association of the fruits of its ill-gotten gains. Even if one or more of the civil remedies might be inapplicable to a particular illegitimate enterprise, this fact would not serve to limit the enterprise concept. Congress has provided civil remedies for use when the circumstances so warrant. It is untenable to argue that their existence limits the scope of the criminal provisions.

Finally, it is urged that the interpretation of RICO to include both legitimate and illegitimate enterprises will substantially alter the balance between federal and state enforcement of criminal law. This is particularly true, so the argument goes, since included within the definition of racketeering activity are a significant number of acts made criminal under state law. But even assuming that the more inclusive definition of enterprise will have the effect suggested, the language of the statute and its legislative history indicate that Congress was well aware that it was entering a new domain of federal involvement through the enactment of this measure. Indeed, the very purpose of the Organized Crime Control Act of 1970 was to enable the Federal Government to address a large and seemingly neglected problem. The view was that existing law, state and federal, was not adequate to address the problem, which was of national dimensions. . . .

Contrary to the judgment below, neither the language nor structure of RICO limits its application to legitimate "enterprises." . . .

The statement of findings that prefaces the Organized Crime Control Act of 1970 reveals the pervasiveness of the problem that Congress was addressing by this enactment:

"The Congress finds that (1) organized crime in the United States is a highly sophisticated, diversified, and widespread activity that annually drains billions of dollars from America's economy by unlawful conduct and the illegal use of force, fraud, and corruption; (2) organized crime derives a

---

68. Title 18 U.S.C. §§ 1964(a) and (c) provide:

"(a) The district courts of the United States shall have jurisdiction to prevent and restrain violations of section 1962 of this chapter by issuing appropriate orders, including, but not limited to: ordering any person to divest himself of any interest, direct or indirect, in any enterprise; imposing reasonable restrictions on the future activities or investments of any person, including, but not limited to, prohibiting any person from engaging in the same type of endeavor as the enterprise engaged in, the activities of which affect interstate or foreign commerce; or ordering dissolution or reorganization of any enterprise, making due provision for the rights of innocent persons.

. . .

"(c) Any person injured in his business or property by reason of a violation of section 1962 of this chapter may sue therefore in any appropriate United States district court and shall recover threefold the damages he sustains and the cost of the suit, including a reasonable attorney's fee."

major portion of its power through money obtained from such illegal endeavors as syndicated gambling, loan sharking, the theft and fencing of property, the importation and distribution of narcotics and other dangerous drugs, and other forms of social exploitation; (3) this money and power are increasingly used to infiltrate and corrupt legitimate business and labor unions and to subvert and corrupt our democratic processes; (4) organized crime activities in the United States weaken the stability of the Nation's economic system, harm innocent investors and competing organizations, interfere with free competition, seriously burden interstate and foreign commerce, threaten the domestic security, and undermine the general welfare of the Nation and its citizens; and (5) organized crime continues to grow because of defects in the evidence-gathering process of the law inhibiting the development of the legally admissible evidence necessary to bring criminal and other sanctions or remedies to bear on the unlawful activities of those engaged in organized crime and because the sanctions and remedies available to the Government are unnecessarily limited in scope and impact." 84 Stat. 922–923.

In light of the above findings, it was the declared purpose of Congress "to seek the eradication of organized crime in the United States by strengthening the legal tools in the evidence-gathering process, by establishing new penal prohibitions, and by providing enhanced sanctions and new remedies to deal with the unlawful activities of those engaged in organized crime." *Id.,* at 923.[69] The various Titles of the Act provide the tools through which this goal is to be accomplished. . . .

Considering this statement of the Act's broad purposes, the construction of RICO suggested by respondent and the court below is unacceptable. Whole areas of organized criminal activity would be placed beyond the substantive reach of the enactment. For example, associations of persons engaged solely in "loan sharking, the theft and fencing of property, the importation and distribution of narcotics and other dangerous drugs," *id.,* at 922–923, would be immune from prosecution under RICO so long as the association did not deviate from the criminal path. . . . In view of the purposes and goals of the Act, as well as the language of the statute, we are unpersuaded that Congress nevertheless confined the reach of the law to only narrow aspects of organized crime, and, in particular, under RICO, *only* the infiltration of legitimate business.

.   .   .

As a measure to deal with the infiltration of legitimate businesses by organized crime, RICO was both preventive and remedial. Respondent's view would ignore the preventive function of the statute. If Congress had intended the more circumscribed approach espoused by the Court of Appeals, there would have been some positive sign that the law was not to reach organized criminal activities that give rise to the concerns about

---

69.   *See also* 116 Cong.Rec. 602 (1970) (remarks of Sen. Yarborough) ("a full scale attack on organized crime"); *id.,* at 819 (remarks of Sen. Scott) ("purpose is to eradicate organized crime in the United States"); *id.,* at 35199 (remarks of Rep. Rodino) ("a truly full-scale commitment to destroy the insidious power of organized crime groups"); *id.,* at 35300 (remarks of Rep. Mayne) (organized crime "must be sternly and irrevocably eradicated").

infiltration. The language of the statute, however—the most reliable evidence of its intent—reveals that Congress opted for a far broader definition of the word "enterprise," and we are unconvinced by anything in the legislative history that this definition should be given less than its full effect.

The judgment of the Court of Appeals is accordingly Reversed.[70]

MODEL PENAL CODE

Section 5.03 Criminal Conspiracy.

(1) Definition of Conspiracy. A person is guilty of conspiracy with another person or persons to commit a crime if with the purpose of promoting or facilitating its commission he:

(a) agrees with such other person or persons that they or one or more of them will engage in conduct which constitutes such crime or an attempt or solicitation to commit such crime; or

(b) agrees to aid such other person or persons in the planning or commission of such crime or of an attempt or solicitation to commit such crime.

(2) Scope of Conspiratorial Relationship. If a person guilty of conspiracy, as defined by Subsection (1) of this Section, knows that a person with whom he conspires to commit a crime has conspired with another person or persons to commit the same crime, he is guilty of conspiring with such other person or persons, whether or not he knows their identity, to commit such crime.

(3) Conspiracy With Multiple Criminal Objectives. If a person conspires to commit a number of crimes, he is guilty of only one conspiracy so long as such multiple crimes are the object of the same agreement or continuous conspiratorial relationship.

(4) Joinder and Venue in Conspiracy Prosecutions.

(a) Subject to the provisions of paragraph (b) of this Subsection, two or more persons charged with criminal conspiracy may be prosecuted jointly if:

(i) they are charged with conspiring with one another; or

(ii) the conspiracies alleged, whether they have the same or different parties, are so related that they constitute different aspects of a scheme of organized criminal conduct.

(b) In any joint prosecution under paragraph (a) of this Subsection:

---

70. In order to make out a pattern of racketeering, the two predicate acts must show "continuity plus relationship." Merely showing two predicate acts is insufficient. There must be a threat of continued criminal activity. Separate schemes are not required. H.J. Inc. v. Northwestern Bell Telephone Co., 492 U.S. 229, 109 S.Ct. 2893, 106 L.Ed.2d 195 (1989).

Isolated predicate acts do not constitute a RICO pattern. S.P.R.L. v. Imrex Co., 473 U.S. 479, 105 S.Ct. 3275, 87 L.Ed.2d 346 (1985).

RICO's "liberal construction" clause is designed to ensure that Congress's intent is not frustrated by an overly narrow reading of RICO. It is not intended to apply to new purposes. Reves v. Ernst & Young, 507 U.S. 170, 113 S.Ct. 1163, 122 L.Ed.2d 525 (1993).

RICO is not unconstitutionally vague. United States v. Freeman, 6 F.3d 586 (9th Cir.1993).

Rico does not require an underlying economic motive. National Organization for Women, Inc. v. Scheidler, 510 U.S. 249, 114 S.Ct. 798, 127 L.Ed.2d 99 (1994).

(i) no defendant shall be charged with a conspiracy in any county [parish or district] other than one in which he entered into such conspiracy or in which an overt act pursuant to such conspiracy was done by him or by a person with whom he conspired; and

(ii) neither the liability of any defendant nor the admissibility against him of evidence of acts or declarations of another shall be enlarged by such joinder; and

(iii) the Court shall order a severance or take a special verdict as to any defendant who so requests, if it deems it necessary or appropriate to promote the fair determination of his guilt or innocence, and shall take any other proper measures to protect the fairness of the trial.

(5) Overt Act. No person may be convicted of conspiracy to commit a crime, other than a felony of the first or second degree, unless an overt act in pursuance of such conspiracy is alleged and proved to have been done by him or by a person with whom he conspired.

(6) Renunciation of Criminal Purpose. It is an affirmative defense that the actor, after conspiring to commit a crime, thwarted the success of the conspiracy, under circumstances manifesting a complete and voluntary renunciation of his criminal purpose.

(7) Duration of Conspiracy. For purposes of Section 1.06(4):

(a) conspiracy is a continuing course of conduct which terminates when the crime or crimes which are its object are committed or the agreement that they be committed is abandoned by the defendant and by those with whom he conspired; and

(b) such abandonment is presumed if neither the defendant nor anyone with whom he conspired does any overt act in pursuance of the conspiracy during the applicable period of limitation; and

(c) if an individual abandons the agreement, the conspiracy is terminated as to him only if and when he advises those with whom he conspired of his abandonment or he informs the law enforcement authorities of the existence of the conspiracy and of his participation therein.

Section 5.05 Grading of Criminal Attempt, Solicitation and Conspiracy; Mitigation in Cases of Lesser Danger; Multiple Convictions Barred.

(1) Grading. Except as otherwise provided in this Section, attempt, solicitation and conspiracy are crimes of the same grade and degree as the most serious offense which is attempted or solicited or is an object of the conspiracy. An attempt, solicitation or conspiracy to commit a [capital crime or a] felony of the first degree is a felony of the second degree.

(2) Mitigation. If the particular conduct charged to constitute a criminal attempt, solicitation or conspiracy is so inherently unlikely to result or culminate in the commission of a crime that neither such conduct nor the actor presents a public danger warranting the grading of such offense under this Section, the Court shall exercise its power under Section 6.12 to enter judgment and impose sentence for a crime of lower grade or degree or, in extreme cases, may dismiss the prosecution.

(3) Multiple Convictions. A person may not be convicted of more than one offense defined by this Article for conduct designed to commit or to culminate in the commission of the same crime.[71]

---

71. Copyright © 1962 by the American Law Institute. Reprinted with the permission of the American Law Institute.

[Section 5.04 Incapacity, Irresponsibility or Immunity of Party to Solicitation or Conspiracy, was quoted at the end of Section 3.]

SECTION 7. AGENCY

Rex v. Huggins

King's Bench, 1730.
2 Ld.Raym. 1574, 92 Eng.Rep. 518.

[An indictment charged the warden of a prison, and his deputy, with the murder of a prisoner, by keeping him in an unwholesome place, and so forth, until he died. The jury returned a special verdict. The LORD CHIEF JUSTICE—RAYMOND—delivered the opinion of the justices.]

In this case two questions have been made. 1. What crime the facts found upon Barnes in the special verdict will amount to? 2. Whether the prisoner at the Bar is found guilty of the same offence with Barnes?

1. As to the first question, it is very plain that the facts found upon Barnes do amount to murder in him. Murder may be committed without any stroke. The law has not confined the offence to any particular circumstances or manner of killing; but there are as many ways to commit murder, as there are to destroy a man, provided the act be done with malice, either express or implied. Hale P.C. 46. 3 Inst. 52. Murder is, where a person kills another of malice, so he dies within a year and a day. Hale P.C. 43. And malice may be either expressed or implied. In this case the jury have found the malice express: for the facts charged on Barnes are laid in the indictment to be ex malitia sua praecogitata, to wit, that he having the custody of Arne assaulted him, and carried him to this unwholesome room, and confined him there by force against his will, and without his consent, and without proper support, ex malitia sua praecogitata; by means of which he languished and died. And the jury have found that Barnes did all these facts, modo et forma prout in indictamento praedicto specificatur. . . .

The Judges are all unanimously of opinion, that the facts found in this special verdict do not amount to murder in the prisoner at the Bar; but as this special verdict is found, they are of opinion, that he is not guilty. Though he was warden, yet it being found, that there was a deputy; he is not, as warden, guilty of the facts committed under the authority of his deputy. He shall answer as superior for his deputy civilly,[72] but not criminally. It has been settled, that though a sheriff must answer for the offences of his gaoler civilly, that is, he is subject in an action, to make satisfaction to the party injured; yet he is not to answer criminally for the offences of his under-officer. He only is criminally punishable, who immediately does the act, or permits it to be done.[73] Hale's P.C. 114. So that if an act be done by an under-officer, unless it is done by the command or

---

72. *But see* Oppenheimer v. Los Angeles, 104 Cal.App.2d 545, 232 P.2d 26 (1951).

73. "The civil doctrine of respondeat superior was not conceived, nor is it to be applied, to include the responsibility of a master to the state for the independent acts of the servant." Lovelace v. State, 191 Miss. 62, 2 So.2d 796 (1941).

direction, or with the consent of the principal, the principal is not criminally punishable for it. In this case the fact was done by Barnes; and it no where appears in the special verdict, that the prisoner at the Bar ever commanded, or directed, or consented to this duress of imprisonment, which was the cause of Arne's death. 1. No command or direction is found. And 2. It is not found, that Huggins knew of it. That which made the duress in this case was, 1. Barnes's carrying, and putting, and confining Arne in this room by force and against his consent. 2. The situation and condition of this room. Now it is not found that Huggins knew these several circumstances, which made the duress. 1. It is not found, that he knew any thing of Barnes's carrying Arne thither. 2. Nor that he was there without his consent, or without proper support. 3. As to the room, it is found by the verdict, 1. That the room was built of brick and mortar. 2. That the walls were valde humidae. 3. That the room was situate on the common sewer of the prison, and near the place where the filth of the prison and excrement of the prisoners were usually laid, ratione quorum the room was very unwholesome, and the life of any man kept there was in great danger. But all that is found with respect to the prisoner's knowledge is, that for fifteen days before Arne's death he knew that the room was then lately built, recenter, that the walls were made of brick and mortar, and were then damp. But it is not found, nor does it appear, that he knew, they were dangerous to a man's life, or that there was a want of necessary support. Nor is it found, that he directed, or consented, that Arne should be kept or continued there. . . .

Upon the whole, there is no authority against the Court's giving judgment of acquittal, upon a verdict that is not sufficient to convict; and therefore this verdict, not finding facts sufficient to make the prisoner guilty of murder, he must be adjudged not guilty. And he was discharged.[74]

MODEL PENAL CODE

Section 2.06 Liability for Conduct of Another; Complicity.

(1) A person is guilty of an offense if it is committed by his own conduct or by the conduct of another person for which he is legally accountable, or both.[75]

SECTION 8.   INCORPORATION

"A corporation is not indictable, but the particular members are." This statement of Chief Justice Holt[76] represents the original position of the common law which held firm for many years. It was repeated in substance by Blackstone[77] and in early judicial opinion in this country.[78] Now,

---

74. Defendant could be convicted of rape on a complicity theory based on defendant having coerced a ten-year-old boy to commit the offense. The boy was not guilty of the offense because of defendant's duress. Parnell v. State, 323 Ark. 34, 912 S.W.2d 422 (1996).

75. Copyright © 1962 by the American Law Institute. Reprinted with the permission of the American Law Institute.

76. Anonymous, 12 Mod. 559, 88 Eng.Rep. 1518 (K.B.1706).

77. 1 Bl.Comm. *476.

78. State v. Great Works Milling & Manufacturing Co., 20 Me. 41 (1841).

however, it represents little more than an echo from a bygone day. The change from this position originated in the area where the proceeding is criminal in form but civil in substance,—the so-called "civil offense." And the first step was unavoidable. To insure proper maintenance of roads and bridges a statutory fine was provided for those who, having the duty to make needed repairs thereof, failed to do so. If a corporation had such a duty, which it neglected to perform, no sound reason against its conviction was available. And it was but a short step from recognition of corporate guilt of a civil offense based on nonfeasance to such guilt based on misfeasance. Since such an offense does not have the normal mens rea requirement for criminal guilt, and conviction may be supported on the basis of *respondeat superior,* the possibility of convicting a corporation of a civil offense became firmly established.[79] For years it seemed that the change from the original position would stop at this point and that a corporation would be held incapable of committing a true crime on the ground that the corporation could not have mens rea. "[C]orporations are not properly indictable for crimes involving a criminal state of mind, ..." said a writer[80] in 1914. And ten years later another writer pointed out that the numerous statements in regard to convicting a corporation were chiefly *dicta* except in the civil offense field.[81] Gradually, however, the change moved forward into the area of true crime. On the one hand it was urged that the punishment,—a fine imposed on the corporation, falls upon those who are entirely free from fault as well as upon others who are blameworthy, and hence is unjust.[82] Others urged that nothing less would suffice to keep corporate activities in proper hands.[83] No one seriously urged that it would withhold the hand of the law from the guilty individuals because conviction of the corporation would be no bar to a prosecution of those persons who actually caused the harm.

If a truck driver has a fatal traffic accident, as a result of his criminal negligence in driving the vehicle, he is guilty of manslaughter. This will not of itself be sufficient to taint his employer with criminal guilt, but the employer might have sent out the driver with such instructions as to speed, or with a vehicle known to him to be so unsafe, that the employer also acted with criminal negligence. If so, the employer also is guilty of manslaughter if he is an individual. Would a corporate employer be guilty of manslaughter in such a case? A New Jersey court has said yes[84] and Texas has also agreed.[85] The New York court said no.[86] In the latter case,

---

79. Overland Cotton Mill Co. v. People, 32 Colo. 263, 75 P. 924 (1904).

80. Canfield, Corporate Responsibility for Crime, 14 Col.L.Rev. 469, 480 (1914).

81. Francis, Criminal Responsibility of the Corporation, 18 Ill.L.Rev. 305 (1924). "Punishment falls on the individual members alone. Such being the case, the punishment is awkward, unscientific, and uncertain." *Id.* at 322.

82. See the articles in notes 6 and 7.

83. Edgerton, Corporate Criminal Responsibility, 36 Yale L.Jour. 827 (1927).

84. State v. Lehigh Valley R. Co., 90 N.J.L. 372, 103 A. 685 (1917).

A corporation may be charged with and convicted of homicide by negligent operation of a vehicle. State v. Steenberg Homes, Inc., 223 Wis.2d 511, 589 N.W.2d 668 (App.1998).

85. Vaughan and Sons, Inc. v. State, 737 S.W.2d 805 (Tex.Cr.App.1987).

86. People v. Rochester Railway & Light Co., 195 N.Y. 102, 88 N.E. 22 (1909).

however, it was recognized that a corporation can be guilty of a true crime and the reversal of this conviction was based entirely upon the definition of the particular offense. The court pointed out that manslaughter requires homicide and that homicide is defined by its statute (as at common law) as the killing of one human being "by another." This was held, quite properly, to mean the killing by another human being. The court then concluded that a corporation cannot be guilty of manslaughter, overlooking entirely that the corporation can do nothing except by aid of human beings. There could never be a case in which a corporation has killed a human being who was not killed by a human being. However, the corporate cumulative liability could be greater than that of any one individual. Under certain circumstances the act of the employee is imputed to the employer. The difficult problem is to determine whose criminal negligence (or knowledge or intent and so forth) shall be held to be the criminal negligence of the corporation as distinguished from that of an agent of the corporation.[87] Recently, a few courts have held corporations to be subject to homicide prosecutions. The conclusion has been supported by a statutory definition defining homicide in terms of a killing by a "person" and including corporations within the definition of the term person.[88]

The Model Penal Code imposes criminal liability on a corporation; however, the legislative purpose must be clear or a specific duty imposed on the corporation or the conduct of the board of directors or a high managerial agent acting for the corporation and within the scope of the office. This standard provides a specific standard and imposes corporate liability for activity properly attributable to the corporation.

United States v. George F. Fish, Inc.

United States Circuit Court of Appeals, Second Circuit, 1946.
154 F.2d 798.

■ CLARK, CIRCUIT JUDGE. An information filed in the District Court charged the defendants George F. Fish, Inc., a wholesale dealer in fruits and vegetables, and Michael Simon, its salesman, with "unlawfully, wilfully and knowingly" evading the provisions of Revised Maximum Price Regulation No. 426, issued under the authority of § 2, Emergency Price Control Act of 1942, 50 U.S.C.A. Appendix, § 902. After a jury verdict of guilt, the court entered judgment of a fine against the corporate defendant, and imprisonment against the individual defendant. 50 U.S.C.A. Appendix, §§ 904, 925(b). Defendants appeal from the conviction, urging the invalidity of the regulation, the failure of the information to allege a crime, the insufficiency

---

87. "In all cases where a corporation is convicted of an offense for the commission of which a natural person would be punishable with imprisonment, as for a felony, such corporation is punishable by a fine of not more than five thousand dollars." N.Y.Pen.Laws 1932.

88. *See* State v. Ford Motor Co., 47 L.W. 2515 (Ind.Super.1979). Vaughan and Sons, Inc. v. State, 737 S.W.2d 805 (Tex.Cr.App.1987). See, Corporate Criminal Liability for Employee–Endangering Activities, 18 Colum.J.L. & Soc.Probs. 39 (1983).

For a position raising the question of whether corporate criminal liability has value over and above a civil sanction, see V.S. Khanna, Corporate Criminal Liability: What Purpose Does It Serve?, 109 Harv. L. Rev. 1477 (1996).

of the evidence to support the verdict, and the nonliability of the corporate defendant to criminal prosecution for the acts charged....

The corporate defendant makes a separate contention that the guilt of its salesman is not to be attributed to it. But the Supreme Court has long ago determined that the corporation may be held criminally liable for the acts of an agent within the scope of his employment, and the state and lower federal courts have been consistent in their application of that doctrine....

No distinctions are made in these cases between officers and agents, or between persons holding positions involving varying degrees of responsibility. And this seems the only practical conclusion in any case, but particularly here where the sales proscribed by the Act will almost invariably be performed by subordinate salesmen, rather than by corporate chiefs, and where the corporate hierarchy does not contemplate separate layers of official dignity, each with separate degrees of responsibility. The purpose of the Act is a deterrent one; and to deny the possibility of corporate responsibility for the acts of minor employees is to immunize the offender who really benefits, and open wide the door for evasion. Here Simon acted knowingly and deliberately and hence "wilfully" within the meaning of the Act, and his wilful act is also that of the corporation....

Judgment affirmed.[89]

(Certiorari denied 328 U.S. 869, 66 S.Ct. 1377, 90 L.Ed. 1639.)

People v. Canadian Fur Trappers' Corp.

Court of Appeals of New York, 1928.
248 N.Y. 159, 161 N.E. 455.

■ CRANE, J. The defendant, a corporation, has been found guilty of grand larceny, second degree, and fined $5,000. The argument presented here is that a corporation cannot commit the crime of larceny as it is impossible for a corporation as such to have intent to steal or misappropriate property.

We think this question has been fairly well settled to the contrary....

It has long been the law that a corporation may be liable criminally for the acts of its agents in doing things prohibited by statute....

This is the law for corporations whose servants violate positive prohibitions or commands of statutes regarding corporate acts. Such offenses do not necessarily embody the element of intent to commit a crime. The corporation would be guilty of the violation in many instances irrespective of intent or knowledge.

When it comes, however, to such crimes as larceny, there enters as a necessary element the intent accompanying the act. There must be the intent to steal, to misappropriate, to apply the property of another to the use of the corporation to constitute the crime. The mere knowledge and intent of the agent of [or] the servant to steal would not be sufficient in

---

89. A corporation acts only by and through its agents, a corporate agent is culpable and cannot defend on the basis that the act was performed on behalf of the corporate enterprise. Compton v. Commonwealth, 22 Va.App. 751, 473 S.E.2d 95 (1996).

and of itself to make the corporation guilty. While a corporation may be guilty of larceny, may be guilty of the intent to steal, the evidence must go further than in the cases involving solely the violation of prohibitive statutes. The intent must be the intent of the corporation and not merely that of the agent. How this intent may be proved or in what cases it becomes evident depends entirely upon the circumstances of each case. Probably no general rule applicable to all situations could be stated. It has been said that the same evidence which in a civil case would be sufficient to prove a specific or malicious intention upon the part of a corporation defendant would be sufficient to show a like intention upon the part of a corporation charged criminally with the doing of an act prohibited by law (U.S. v. Kelso Co., 86 F. 304), and Judge Hough in U.S. v. New York Herald Co., 159 F. 296, said: "To fasten this species of knowledge upon a corporation requires no other or different kind of legal inference than has long been used to justify punitive damages in cases of tort against an incorporated defendant." *See, also*, People v. Star Co., 135 App.Div. 517, 120 N.Y.S. 498, where the malicious intent of the agents in writing a libel was attributable to the corporation. *See, also*, Grant Bros. Construction Co. v. U.S., 13 Ariz. 388, 114 P. 955, and State v. Salisbury Ice & Fuel Co., 166 N.C. 366, 81 S.E. 737, involving false pretenses. Also Standard Oil Co. v. State, 117 Tenn. 618, 100 S.W. 705, where the intent of the officers became the intent of the corporation. Sufficient to say that in this case the law was correctly laid down to the jury by the trial judge when he said: "The defendant is liable in a prosecution for larceny only for acts which it authorizes through action of its officers or which is done with the acquiescence of its officers, and unless the jury find beyond a reasonable doubt such authority or acquiescence, there must be an acquittal." This in my judgment was a correct statement of the law for this case. . . .

In this case the able assistant district attorney, Mr. Marcy, recognized the rule and attempted to bring his evidence within it. He sought to prove that one of the officers of the corporation had given instructions to do the acts constituting larceny and he also sought to prove that there had been such a long-continued user of felonious practices as to prove knowledge or intent upon the part of the corporation. In his attempt to substantiate these elements of the crime, he was largely frustrated by the rulings of the trial judge.

At this point it may be well to state the facts in order to elucidate our meaning. The defendant was a domestic corporation known as Canadian Fur Trappers Corporation, carrying on the business of selling fur coats on the installment plan in Buffalo, N.Y., under the name of "Fields." Four brothers, named Dornfeldt, constituted the corporation and were its only officers. It advertised attractive sales during the summer of 1926. The prosecuting witness, Mrs. Ella Stanley, bought a coat at one of these sales for $295, paying a deposit of $25, the coat to be delivered to her upon payment of the balance. There was no time fixed in which the balance was to be paid. The evidence fairly shows that the defendant agreed to keep the coat in storage or on deposit for Mrs. Stanley until the balance was paid. Later in the fall when she paid the balance the coat was gone. It had been disposed of and there was evidence which would justify the jury in believing that some one in the defendant's employ had resold the coat. The defendant's employees and officers attempted to deliver to Mrs. Stanley another coat which they said was the one she had selected. In this they were evidently mistaken, if not willfully falsifying, as the coat was of a different size and make. The evidence is quite conclusive upon this point. There is also evidence to show that the coat which this defendant through its employees attempted to deliver to Mrs. Stanley as the one purchased had been theretofore sold to Vera M. Owen. Whatever became of Mrs. Stanley's coat no one apparently knows. The fact is she did not receive it when she paid the balance of her money, and the coat which was offered to her was not the one she had selected. The evidence sustains this conclusion. Of course upon these facts alone, these two transactions, the defendant could not be found guilty of larceny as defined by our penal law. It is at this point the People, therefore, attempted to prove that the officers of the corporation had instructed the employees to resell the coats held on deposit and that this was the method of doing business. When a coat was purchased and the deposit paid, instead of keeping the coat for the purchaser, as the defendant promised to do, until the balance was paid, the course of business was to resell the coat many times and deliver it to whomever first paid the full purchase price. Such facts, if proved, would no doubt establish larceny by the corporation. The difficulty arises over the failure of this proof....

This leaves the charge against the defendant resting upon the sale to Mrs. Stanley and the evidence of the resale or attempted resale later of Mrs. Owen's coat to Mrs. Stanley. The defendant's officers and employees denied that they had resold Mrs. Stanley's coat or that such was their method of doing business.

Under the law as correctly charged in this case by the trial judge, the defendant corporation was criminally liable only for such felonious acts as it had authorized through the Dornfeldts, the officers of the corporation, or for such acts as through a course of business must have been known to the corporation and its officers, and thus authorized by them. The People failed to prove that the officers or any one acting as manager of the Buffalo store, in the place and stead of the officers had authorized a resale of the complainant's coat; and further, that if the complainant's coat was resold, the resale of purchased coats was a continuous and established practice in the defendant's establishment....

There are other rulings which we think were not quite correct, but it is unnecessary to refer to them, as in view of what is here said the judgment of the Appellate Division and that of the County Court should be reversed and a new trial ordered.

■ CARDOZO, C.J., POUND, ANDREWS, LEHMAN, KELLOGG and O'BRIEN, JJ., concur.

Judgments reversed, etc.[90]

---

90. For an excellent discussion of the law in this area see, Canadian Dredge & Dock Co. Ltd. v. Queen, 19 CCC 3d 1 (S.C.C.1985).

Corporation liability for offering a false instrument for filing could be based on the actions of a "high managerial agent." People v. Guido, 132 A.D.2d 707, 518 N.Y.S.2d 188 (1987).

A corporation is not guilty of the crime of extortion unless the act was authorized, requested, commanded, performed or recklessly tolerated by the board of directors or a high

MODEL PENAL CODE

Section 2.07 Liability of Corporations, Unincorporated Associations and Persons Acting, or Under a Duty to Act, in Their Behalf.

(1) A corporation may be convicted of the commission of an offense if:

(a) the offense is a violation or the offense is defined by a statute other than the Code in which a legislative purpose to impose liability on corporations plainly appears and the conduct is performed by an agent of the corporation acting in behalf of the corporation within the scope of his office or employment, except that if the law defining the offense designates the agents for whose conduct the corporation is accountable or the circumstances under which it is accountable, such provisions shall apply; or

(b) the offense consists of an omission to discharge a specific duty of affirmative performance imposed on corporations by law; or

(c) the commission of the offense was authorized, requested, commanded, performed or recklessly tolerated by the board of directors or by a high managerial agent acting in behalf of the corporation within the scope of his office or employment.

(2) When absolute liability is imposed for the commission of an offense, a legislative purpose to impose liability on a corporation shall be assumed, unless the contrary plainly appears.

(3) An unincorporated association may be convicted of the commission of an offense if:

(a) the offense is defined by a statute other than the Code which expressly provides for the liability of such an association and the conduct is performed by an agent of the association acting in behalf of the association within the scope of his office or employment, except that if the law defining the offense designates the agents for whose conduct the association is accountable or the circumstances under which it is accountable, such provisions shall apply; or

(b) the offense consists of an omission to discharge a specific duty of affirmative performance imposed on associations by law.

(4) As used in this Section:

(a) "corporation" does not include an entity organized as or by a governmental agency for the execution of a governmental program;

(b) "agent" means any director, officer, servant, employee or other person authorized to act in behalf of the corporation or association and, in the case of an unincorporated association, a member of such association;

---

managerial agent acting on its behalf. State v. Adjustment Department Credit Bureau, 94 Idaho 156, 483 P.2d 687 (1971).

A corporation can be held liable for a corporate agent's wrongdoing only if the agent was within the scope of the agent's employment and intended to benefit the corporation. United States v. Cincotta, 689 F.2d 238 (1st Cir.1982).

The president of a corporation is not criminally liable for the acts of his subordinate unless they are authorized or consented to by him. State v. Carmean, 126 Iowa 291, 102 N.W. 97 (1905). But the president of a corporation can be convicted, on proof by circumstantial evidence, that he aided and abetted his subordinates in their criminal activities. Nye & Nissen v. United States, 336 U.S. 613, 69 S.Ct. 766, 93 L.Ed. 919 (1949).

Brickey, Rethinking Corporate Liability Under The Model Penal Code, 19 Rutgers L.Rev. 593 (1988). Ellen Hochstedler, ed., Corporations as Criminals (1984).

(c) "high managerial agent" means an officer of a corporation or an unincorporated association, or, in the case of a partnership, a partner, or any other agent of a corporation or association having duties of such responsibility that his conduct may fairly be assumed to represent the policy of the corporation or association.

(5) In any prosecution of a corporation or an unincorporated association for the commission of an offense included within the terms of Subsection (1)(a) or Subsection (3)(a) of this Section, other than an offense for which absolute liability has been imposed, it shall be a defense if the defendant proves by a preponderance of evidence that the high managerial agent having supervisory responsibility over the subject matter of the offense employed due diligence to prevent its commission. This paragraph shall not apply if it is plainly inconsistent with the legislative purpose in defining the particular offense.

(6)(a) A person is legally accountable for any conduct he performs or causes to be performed in the name of the corporation or an unincorporated association or in its behalf to the same extent as if it were performed in his own name or behalf.

(b) Whenever a duty to act is imposed by law upon a corporation or an unincorporated association, any agent of the corporation or association having primary responsibility for the discharge of the duty is legally accountable for a reckless omission to perform the required act to the same extent as if the duty were imposed by law directly upon himself.

(c) When a person is convicted of an offense by reason of his legal accountability for the conduct of a corporation or an unincorporated association, he is subject to the sentence authorized by law when a natural person is convicted of an offense of the grade and the degree involved.[91]

Section 9. Causation

"Starting with a human act, we must next find a causal relation between the act and the harmful result; for in our law—and, it is believed, in any civilized law—liability cannot be imputed to a man unless it is in some degree a result of his act." Beale, The Proximate Consequences of An Act, 33 Harv.L.Rev. 633, 637 (1920).

"As the law of evidence excludes much that is evidential, the law of causation excludes much that is consequential." Edgerton, Legal Cause, 72 U. of Pa.Law Rev. 343, 344 (1924).

"John Stuart Mill, in his work on logic 9th Eng.Ed. 378–383 says, in substance, that the cause of an event is the sum of all the antecedents, and that we have no right to single out one antecedent and call that the cause. . . . The question is not what philosophers or logicians will say is the cause. The question is what the courts will regard as the cause." Jeremiah Smith, Legal Cause in Actions of Tort, 25 Harv.Law Rev. 103, 104 (1911).

"It would seem too clear for argument that considerations of fairness or justice have a bearing." McLaughlin, Proximate Cause, 39 Harv.Law Rev. 149, 155 (1925).

---

91. Copyright © 1962 by the American Law Institute. Reprinted with the permission of the American Law Institute.

"It has been said that an act which in no way contributed to the result in question cannot be a cause of it; but this, of course, does not mean that an event which *might* have happened in the same way though the defendant's act or omission had not occurred, is not a result of it. The question is not what would have happened, but what did happen." Beale, The Proximate Consequences of An Act, 33 Harv.Law Rev. 633, 638 (1920).

"Here is the key to the juridical treatment of the problems of causation. We pick out the cause which in our judgment ought to be treated as the dominant one with reference, not merely to the event itself, but to the jural consequences that ought to attach to the event." Cardozo, The Parodoxes of Legal Science, 83 (1928).

The line of demarkation between causes which will be recognized as "proximate" and those disregarded as "remote" "is really a flexible line." I Street, Foundations of Legal Liability, 111 (1906).

"There are no cases where it can be truthfully said that legal cause exists where cause in fact does not though it may happen by reason of relaxation of proof that liability will be imposed in cases where cause in fact is not by the ordinary rules of proof shown to exist." Carpenter, Workable Rules for Determining Proximate Cause, 20 Cal.Law Rev. 396, 407 (1932).

"A primary requisite to either criminal or civil liability is that the act of the defendant be the cause in fact of the injury. This requirement is embodied in the familiar *causa sine qua non* rule, generally called the 'but for' rule. This test generally is satisfactory when applied in negative form, and it is a basic principle that a defendant is not liable unless the injury would not have resulted but for his wrongful act. But as an affirmative test the 'but for' rule provides no infallible standard and does not constitute a fair test of liability in the absence of further qualifications. . . .

"The modern authorities, while agreed that the 'but for' test is inadequate differ materially in their concepts of proximate causation. The theories conveniently may be placed into two groups. One group seeks the necessary connection between the result and the act; the other, between the result and the actor's mind." Focht, Proximate Cause In the Law of Homicide With Special Reference To California Cases, 12 So.Cal.L.Rev. 19, 20–21 (1938).

"There are three, and only three, tests of proximateness, namely, intention, probability and the non-intervention of an independent cause.

"Any intended consequence of an act is proximate. It would plainly be absurd that a person should be allowed to act with an intention to produce a certain consequence, and then when that very consequence in fact follows his act, to escape liability for it on the plea that it was not proximate.

"Probability . . . is a name for some one's opinion or guess as to whether a consequence will result. . . .

"The person whose opinion is taken is a reasonable and prudent man in the situation of the actor. . . .

"The third test of proximateness is the non-intervention of an independent cause between the original cause and the consequence in question. . . . Therefore it will be convenient to call it an isolating cause." Terry,

Proximate Consequences in the Law of Torts, 28 Harv.L.Rev. 10, 17–20 (1914).[125]

State v. Hallett

Supreme Court of Utah, 1980.
619 P.2d 335.

■ CROCKETT, CHIEF JUSTICE: Defendant Kelly K. Hallett appeals his conviction of negligent homicide, in that he caused the death of Betty Jean Carley.

On the evening of September 24, 1977, a number of young people gathered at the defendant's home in Kearns. During the evening, some of them engaged in drinking alcoholic beverages. At about 10:30 p.m., they left the home, apparently bent on revelry and mischief. When they got to the intersection of 5215 South and 4620 West, defendant and the codefendant Richard Felsch (not a party to this appeal) bent over a stop sign, which faced northbound traffic on 4620 West, until it was in a position parallel to the ground. The group then proceeded north from the intersection, uprooted another stop sign and placed it in the backyard of a Mr. Arlund Pope, one of the state's witnesses. Traveling further on, defendant and his friends bent a bus stop sign over in a similar manner.

The following morning, Sunday, September 25, 1977, at approximately 9:00 a.m., one Krista Limacher was driving east on 5215 South with her husband and children, en route to church. As she reached the intersection of 4620 West, the deceased, Betty Jean Carley, drove to the intersection from the south. The stop sign was not visible, since the defendant had bent it over, and Ms. Carley continued into the intersection. The result was that Mrs. Limacher's vehicle struck the deceased's car broadside causing her massive injuries which resulted in her death in the hospital a few hours later.

Defendant was charged with manslaughter on the ground that his unlawful act was the cause of the death of Ms. Carley. Upon a trial to the court, he was found guilty of the lesser offense of negligent homicide, a class A misdemeanor. . . .

Defendant next argues that the pulling down of a stop sign does not show the requisite intent to constitute negligent homicide. It is recognized that one should not be so convicted unless he acts with some degree of culpable intent.[126] Our statute provides that a person is guilty of negligent homicide if he causes the death of another:

---

125. "A cause must be the efficient, commonly called the proximate, cause or it is not a cause at all in law." State v. Osmus, 73 Wyo. 183, 276 P.2d 469, 474 (1954). Kenneth J. Arenson, Causation in the Criminal Law: A Search for Doctrinal Consistency, 20 Crim. L. J. 189 (1996) (Aust.).

If **D** intentionally pointed a loaded and cocked gun at deceased who was killed by a discharge thereof, **D** is the legally-recognized cause of the death even if the discharge resulted when the other grabbed for the gun. State v. Madden, 104 Ariz. 111, 449 P.2d 39 (1969).

126. U.C.A. 1953, Sec. 76–2–101 provides:

(4) With criminal negligence or is criminally negligent with respect to circumstances surrounding his conduct or the result of his conduct when he ought to be aware of a substantial and unjustifiable risk that the circumstances exist or the result will occur. The risk must be of such a nature and degree that the failure to perceive it constitutes a gross deviation from the standard of care that an ordinary person would exercise in all the circumstances as viewed from the actor's standpoint.[127]

As to the issue of the defendant's intent: The inquiry is whether from the evidence and the reasonable inferences to be drawn therefrom, the trial court could believe beyond a reasonable doubt that the defendant's conduct met the elements of that statute. In his analysis of the evidence, the trial court was justified in viewing the situation thus: The defendant could not fail to know that stop signs are placed at particular intersections where they are deemed to be necessary because of special hazards; and that without the stop sign, the hazards which caused it to be placed there would exist; and that he should have foreseen that its removal would result in setting a trap fraught with danger and possible fatal consequences to others.

From what has been delineated above, the trial judge expressly found that the defendant should have foreseen that his removal of the stop sign created a substantial risk of injury or death to others; and that his doing so constituted a gross deviation from the standard of care that an ordinary person would exercise in all the circumstances.

Defendant makes a separate argument that the evidence does not support the conclusion that his acts were the proximate cause of Ms. Carley's death. He starts with a uniformly recognized definition: that proximate cause is the cause which through its natural and foreseeable consequence, unbroken by any sufficient intervening cause, produces the injury which would not have occurred but for that cause. His urgence here is that there was evidence that as the deceased approached from the south, she was exceeding the speed limit of 25 mph; and that this was the subsequent intervening and proximate cause of her own death. This is based upon the fact that a motorist, who was also coming from the south, testified that he was going 25 mph and that Ms. Carley passed him some distance to the south as she approached the intersection.

In regard to that contention, there are three observations to be made: The first is that the evidence just referred to would not necessarily compel the trial court to believe that the deceased was exceeding 25 mph as she got close to and entered the intersection, nor did the trial court make any such finding. Second, even if it be assumed that she was so exceeding the speed limit, the reasonable and proper assumption is that if the stop sign had

---

Requirements of criminal conduct and criminal responsibility.—No person is guilty of an offense unless his conduct is prohibited by law and:

(1) He acts intentionally, knowingly, recklessly or with criminal negligence with respect to each element of the offense as the definition of the offense requires; or

(2) His acts constitute an offense involving strict liability.

127.   See U.C.A. 1953, Sec. 76–2–103.

been there, she would have heeded it and there would have been no collision.

The foregoing provides sufficient justification for the trial court's rejection of the defendant's contentions. But there is yet a third proposition to be considered. It is also held that where a party by his wrongful conduct creates a condition of peril, his action can properly be found to be the proximate cause of a resulting injury, even though later events which combined to cause the injury may also be classified as negligent, so long as the later act is something which can reasonably be expected to follow in the natural sequence of events. Moreover, when reasonable minds might differ as to whether it was the creation of the dangerous condition (defendant's conduct) which was the proximate cause, or whether it was some subsequent act (such as Ms. Carley's driving), the question is for the trier of the fact to determine.

Reflecting upon what has been said above, we are not persuaded to disagree with the view taken by the trial court: that whether the defendant's act of removing the stop sign was done in merely callous and thoughtless disregard of the safety of others, or with malicious intent, the result, which he should have foreseen, was the same: that it created a situation of peril; and that nothing that transpired thereafter should afford him relief from responsibility for the tragic consequences that did occur.

Affirmed. No costs awarded.

■ MAUGHAN, WILKINS and STEWART, JJ., concur.

■ HALL, JUSTICE (dissenting).

I respectfully dissent.

The offense of negligent homicide is consummated where "the actor, acting with criminal negligence, causes the death of another."[128] The language of the statute punctuates the necessity of a substantial causal relationship between the act of defendant and the death of the victim, which relationship constitutes a necessary element of the offense. To this end, criminal law adopts the notion of proximate cause—the defendant's conduct must proximately result in the victim's injury. As in other areas of the law, a defendant's criminal liability is cut off where the injury in question arose from the operation of an unforeseeable, independent intervening force. Under such circumstances, the defendant's conduct becomes a remote cause, which gives rise to no legal responsibility. This holds true even where the defendant, by negligent action, creates a condition which is subsequently acted upon by another unforeseeable, independent and distinct agency to produce the injury, even though the injury would not have occurred except for defendant's act. It is, moreover, noteworthy that proximate causation, like any other element of a crime, must be proven beyond a reasonable doubt. Where, on appeal, it appears from the evidence (viewed in a light most favorable to the state) that reasonable minds must have entertained a reasonable doubt regarding the causal relationship in question, reversal and dismissal are in order.

---

128. U.C.A., 1953, 76–5–206.

The evidence produced at trial does not discount beyond a reasonable doubt the possibility that the actions of the decedent on the morning of September 25, 1977, constituted an independent, unforeseeable intervening cause. In this regard, it is to be noted that the evidence produced at trial clearly established that the accident occurred in broad daylight and that the stop sign in question had not been removed from the intersection, but merely bent over into a position where it was still marginally visible. Moreover, the word "Stop" was clearly printed in large block letters on the pavement leading into the intersection. Even if we were to assume, however, that defendant's action in bending the stop sign over erased all indication that vehicles proceeding north on 4620 West were obliged to yield right-of-way, such would render the location of the accident an unmarked intersection. The law requires due care in approaching such intersections, with such reasonable precautions as may be necessary under the circumstances.

Evidence also appearing in the record indicates that decedent was moving at an imprudent speed when she entered the intersection. Although the exact rate of speed is disputed, it is unchallenged that she had, less than a block behind, passed a truck which, itself, was doing the legal speed limit. All parties testified that she made no attempt to slow or brake upon entering the intersection. Under such circumstances, reasonable minds must entertain a reasonable doubt that the defendant's conduct was the sole efficient legal cause of her death.

I would reverse the trial court and dismiss the charge of negligent homicide.

People v. Roberts

Supreme Court of California, In Bank, 1992.
2 Cal.4th 271, 6 Cal.Rptr.2d 276, 826 P.2d 274.

■ Mosk, Justice.

Defendant was charged with, and found guilty by a jury of, the following offenses: the first degree murders of Charles Gardner, a fellow prison inmate, and Albert Patch, a correctional officer (Pen.Code, § 187); conspiracy to commit murder (§ 182); assault by a life prisoner resulting in death (§ 4500); and possession of a weapon by an inmate (§ 4502). The jury also found true special circumstance allegations that defendant had previously been convicted of first degree murder (§ 190.2, subd. (a)(2)), that he had committed multiple murders (§ 190.2, subd. (a)(3)), and that he had lain in wait to kill Gardner (§ 190.2, subd. (a)(15)). He was sentenced to death for the murder of Gardner and for the violation of section 4500, and to life imprisonment without possibility of parole for Patch's killing. . . .

For reasons that will appear, the judgment is reversed with regard to the murder of Patch. The multiple-murder special-circumstance finding is set aside. In all other respects, the judgment is affirmed.

THE GUILT PHASE.

Early on the morning of August 17, 1980, Charles Gardner, an inmate at the California Medical Facility, Vacaville, walked down a first-floor corridor as his fellow inmates lounged against the walls on both sides. He emerged with 11 stab wounds that would shortly prove to be fatal. Nevertheless, he was able to grab a knife that an assailant had left on the floor. In pursuit of Menefield, Gardner ran or staggered some distance up a flight of stairs to the second floor, where he plunged the knife into the chest of a prison guard, Officer Patch. Patch died within the hour at the prison clinic, Gardner shortly afterward.

Two issues dominated the trial: the identity of Gardner's murderer or murderers, and Gardner's mental state when he attacked Patch.

The prosecution sought to prove defendant killed Gardner. It offered evidence to support two scenarios, both based on a theory that Gardner was killed in a gang dispute. One possibility was that defendant and Menefield planned to kill Gardner as part of a conflict among members of the Black Guerrilla Family (BGF), a prison gang. Gardner was the protege of Ruben Williams, the Vacaville BGF leader, with whom defendant disagreed over gang tactics. However, there was evidence that cast doubt on this possibility: defendant may have obtained the prison-made knife with which he stabbed Gardner from Williams himself. The other possibility was that defendant stabbed Gardner because he had called him a "punk nigger" in the prison yard and thereby showed disrespect to a fellow BGF member. "Punk" is prison jargon for a passive homosexual. There was testimony that the term is a serious insult to many inmates, and was intolerable to defendant.

Inmates testified they saw defendant stab Gardner repeatedly and saw Menefield restrain Gardner when he tried to escape. . . .

In response, defendant introduced evidence that the prosecution's key witnesses—inmates Long, Hayes, Cade, and Rooks—had won benefits from the state that gave them a motive to lie. Defendant also contended that witnesses had been housed together and had had a chance to reconcile their testimony.

Defendant did not testify at the guilt phase. He sought to prove that he was on the third floor when Gardner was stabbed. There was evidence that he had been seen at that location just after an alarm had sounded as a result of the attack and that it was impossible for him to have made his way there from the first floor in time. For its part, the prosecution introduced evidence that an agile person could run from the first floor to certain key locations in seconds and walk briskly to defendant's cell in less than one minute, and that defendant could have done so unseen.

Defendant also sought to prove that the stabbing of Gardner was not the proximate cause of his death: there was evidence that Gardner was relatively well physically on arrival at the prison clinic and died as a result of incompetent medical care.

As for Patch's killing, there was evidence that Gardner, though failing rapidly, pursued Menefield up the stairs to the second floor. Prison guards hearing the commotion rushed toward the two, seizing Menefield and, in the case of Patch, trying to secure Gardner. Gardner then stabbed Patch.

The prosecution presented expert testimony to support its theory that Gardner fell rapidly into shock from loss of blood after his stabbing and became an unconscious agent of defendant.... Defendant introduced evidence that Gardner intended to stab Patch to exact revenge on his keepers, whom he hated, and that when he attacked Patch he was physically capable of thinking for himself and merely took advantage of the opportunity presented by having a knife in hand.

. . .

2.   Proximate Cause.

Defendant contends the court erred when it refused to give his modified jury instruction that if the medical care Gardner received after the assault was so inadequate that it amounted to the sole cause of his death, then he was not the proximate cause of Gardner's killing and was not liable for it.

The question of the quality of the medical care given Gardner was barely explored during the evidentiary phase of the trial; discussion of the point appears to have been limited to a few comments by Dr. Donald Trunkey, chief of surgery at San Francisco General Hospital. A fair reading of Dr. Trunkey's testimony is that Gardner was very close to death minutes after the stabbing. He testified that a medical technician did all he could with limited resources at the scene, but that the prison clinic could have done more to try to save Gardner, who was "salvageable." The clinic tried to resuscitate Gardner by the wrong means.

The court gave an instruction based on a modified version of CALJIC Nos. 8.55 and 8.57 (4th ed. 1979 rev.). Saying "That's all we are interested in," the court stated that the important language was CALJIC No. 8.57's advice that "the fact that the immediate cause of death was the medical or surgical treatment administered or that such treatment was a factor contributing to the cause of death will not relieve the person who inflicted the original injury from responsibility." The jury heard that language, together with other material from CALJIC Nos. 8.55 and 8.57: "The word 'proximate cause of a death' is a cause which, in natural and continuous sequence, produces the death, and without which the death would not have occurred," and when "the original injury is not a proximate cause of the death and the death was proximately caused by ... medical or surgical treatment or some other cause, then the defendant is not guilty of an unlawful homicide."

Defendant contends the instructions failed to alert the jury that it must decide whether the possibly substandard treatment of Gardner was foreseeable. We disagree: in our view, the court adequately explained the law in light of the evidence.

If a person inflicts a dangerous wound on another, it is ordinarily no defense that inadequate medical treatment contributed to the victim's death. To be sure, when medical treatment is grossly improper, it may discharge liability for homicide if the maltreatment is the sole cause of death and hence an unforeseeable intervening cause. Annot., Homicide:

Liability Where Death Immediately Results From Treatment or Mistreatment of Injury Inflicted by Defendant (1965) (100 A.L.R.2d 769, 786.) But here the record is devoid of any evidence of grossly improper treatment.... As a matter of law, the treatment regimen shown by the record fails to constitute a supervening cause of Gardner's death. The jury need not be instructed on a theory for which no evidence has been presented. (People v. Carter (1957) 48 Cal.2d 737, 758, 312 P.2d 665.)

. . .

LIABILITY FOR THE KILLING OF OFFICER PATCH.

At trial, defendant moved for a judgment of acquittal on the charge of the murder of Officer Patch, on the ground there was insufficient evidence of his criminal liability for that death. The court denied the motion. Defendant now contends there was insufficient evidence to find him liable for the first degree murder of Patch. He also contends the jury was incorrectly instructed on the issue.

As will appear, we conclude there was sufficient evidence for the jury to find that defendant's act was the proximate cause of the murder of Patch. But the instruction removed the element of proximate cause from the jury's consideration, an error of constitutional magnitude that requires reversal under United States Supreme Court precedent. We therefore reverse defendant's conviction for that murder.

. . . [T]he prosecution persuaded the court that if defendant caused Gardner to lose his faculties and stab Patch impulsively or unreasoningly, Gardner's blow was a dependent intervening act for which foreseeability was not required. (See also Perkins & Boyce, Criminal Law (3d ed. 1982) pp. 796–797 (hereafter Perkins & Boyce); Focht, Proximate Cause in the Law of Homicide—With Special Reference to California Cases (1938) 12 So.Cal.L.Rev. 19, 33 (hereafter Focht).) The court read the following instruction: "A defendant is the proximate cause of the death of another even though the immediate cause of the death is the act of a third person, if the third person is no longer a free moral agent as the direct result of the defendant's unlawful act. A defendant who, in conscious and reckless disregard for human life, intentionally and unlawfully inflicts an injury upon a third person is criminally responsible for the acts of that person while in delirium or a similar state of unconsciousness where such condition is the direct result of the defendant's unlawful act. *It is immaterial that the defendant could not reasonably have foreseen the harmful result....* If the evidence establishes that, at the time of the assault upon Albert Patch, Charles Gardner was unconscious due to hypovolemic shock caused by the unlawful act of a defendant, he was not a free moral agent and the defendant is responsible for his act."

The precise causation question may be posed as follows: what is the liability of A for an assault on B that deprives B of his reason and causes him to attack C, who lies some distance away? The authorities cited above do not consider this situation. Nor has our own or the parties' research divulged any case that does.

. . .

Of course, moral culpability is found in homicide cases when, despite the lack of any intent to kill, the consequences of the evil act are so natural or probable that liability is established as a matter of policy. Thus, for example, the Legislature has chosen to designate certain felonies as so inherently dangerous that death in the course of their commission or completion constitutes first degree murder. Or, under the common law doctrine of transferred intent, if A shoots at B with malice aforethought but instead kills C, who is standing nearby, A is deemed liable for murder notwithstanding lack of intent to kill C. (*See Perkins & Boyce, supra,* at p. 924.) . . .

Likewise, principles of proximate cause may sometimes assign homicide liability when, foreseeable or not, the consequences of a dangerous act directed at a second person cause an impulsive reaction that so naturally leads to a third person's death that the evil actor is deemed worthy of punishment. The few cases on point find their foundation in the famous intentional tort case of Scott v. Shepherd (1773) 96 Eng.Rep. 525. Young Shepherd threw a lighted gunpowder squib into a crowded marketplace. The recipient threw it to another, who threw it to another, who threw it to Scott, another minor. Scott was partially blinded when the device exploded. The jury awarded Scott $100 and the court affirmed, holding that the chain of causation was not broken.

Our research discloses a few cases in the annals of American law that, following *Scott v. Shepherd, supra,* have found criminal liability for the death of a third party from the second party's impulsive reaction to the dangerous act. In those cases, physical proximity allowed the trier of fact to find the victim's death to be the natural and probable consequence of the defendant's violence and hence proximately caused by the defendant's act.

. . .

The criminal law thus is clear that for liability to be found, the cause of the harm not only must be direct, but also not so remote as to fail to constitute the natural and probable consequence of the defendant's act. Commentators and drafters have made this conclusion explicit. (Perkins & Boyce, *supra,* at p. 774; LaFave & Scott, Criminal Law (2d ed. 1986) Causation, p. 284 [the doctrine of transferred intent should not apply when A, standing in a lonely desert with B, shoots to kill B but instead kills C, who lies unseen behind some sagebrush]; Model Pen.Code, § 2.03, subd. (2)(b) [when purpose or knowledge of a result is an element of an offense, the actor is not liable for an unintended or uncontemplated result unless, as relevant here, "the actual result involves the same kind of injury or harm as that designed or contemplated and is not too remote or accidental in its occurrence to have a . . . bearing on the actor's liability or on the gravity of his offense."].) Moreover, if one aim of the criminal law is to punish in proportion to moral culpability, little purpose is served by imposing the same punishment for direct but remote consequences of a violent act as for natural and probable direct consequences. . . .

Here, following an instruction that foreseeability was not to be considered, the jury found defendant guilty of murder in the first degree for Gardner's killing of Patch. The questions are threefold: was there sufficient evidence to confer liability for first degree murder; was there sufficient evidence of proximate cause for any criminal liability to attach to defendant for Patch's death; and does the instruction regarding foreseeability require reversal of defendant's conviction?

The first question need not long detain us. Liability for first degree murder cannot attach absent evidence of premeditation and deliberation or of other acts irrelevant to this discussion. (§ 189.) There is no evidence whatever that defendant contemplated the murder of Patch, much less premeditated and deliberated it. On that ground, the first degree murder conviction cannot stand, for we discern no other doctrine, such as felony murder or transferred intent, that would suffice to confer liability for that degree of murder in this case.

The next question is whether the evidence permitted the jury to determine that defendant's acts were the proximate cause of Patch's death. We hold there was sufficient evidence of proximate cause for the jury to decide that liability attached for defendant's acts.

. . .

After considerable reflection, however, we conclude that the evidence sufficed to permit the jury to conclude that Patch's death was the natural and probable consequence of defendant's act. This is so because Patch was in the area in which harm could foreseeably occur as a result of a prison stabbing. Defendant mortally wounded Gardner, but the latter nevertheless was able to seize a knife that an assailant had left on the floor. As the jury found, the attack left Gardner in a daze, without the ability to reason or calculate. In that condition he staggered up a flight of stairs to the second floor in pursuit of defendant's accomplice Menefield. There he engaged in a purely reflexive struggle with Patch and plunged the knife into him. It is foreseeable that a wounded inmate might try to arm himself with a weapon abandoned at the scene of a prison melee and pursue his attackers a short distance. The jury was entitled to find that the distance Gardner pursued Menefield was not so great as to break the chain of causation.

As stated above, however, our inquiry does not end here. Because the jurors found that Gardner was unconscious when he attacked Patch, the instruction directed them not to consider whether the attack on Patch was foreseeable. Under that instruction, whether Patch was standing next to Gardner or half a mile away was not to be taken into account, as long as Patch's killing was the "direct result" of defendant's act.

As we have explained, the instruction incorrectly stated the law of proximate cause. A result cannot be the natural and probable cause of an act if the act was unforeseeable. (*See* Perkins & Boyce, *supra*, at p. 824 [the abnormality of a response is an element to be considered in evaluating proximate cause].) An instruction that told the jury to disregard foreseeability would inevitably lead it to ignore the nature of Gardner's response to defendant's attack, and hence would substantially distract the jury from considering the causation element of the offense—an element that was very much at issue in the case. The instructional error thus cannot be said to have been harmless beyond a reasonable doubt (Chapman v. California, *supra*, 386 U.S. 18, 87 S.Ct. 824) and defendant's conviction of the murder of Patch must be reversed.

Affirmed in part, Reversed in part.

People v. Lewis

Supreme Court of California, Department Two, 1899.
124 Cal. 551, 57 P. 470.

■ TEMPLE, J. The defendant was convicted of manslaughter and appeals from the judgment and from an order refusing a new trial. It is his second appeal. The main facts are stated in the decision of the former appeal, People v. Lewis, 117 Cal. 186, 48 P. 1088, 59 Am.St.Rep. 167. . . .

Defendant and deceased were brothers-in-law, and not altogether friendly, although they were on speaking and visiting terms. On the morning of the homicide the deceased visited the residence of the defendant, was received in a friendly manner, but after a while an altercation arose, as a result of which defendant shot deceased in the abdomen, inflicting a wound that was necessarily mortal. Farrell fell to the ground, stunned for an instant, but soon got up and went into the house, saying: "Shoot me again; I shall die anyway." His strength soon failed him and he was put to bed. Soon afterwards, about how long does not appear, but within a very few minutes, when no other person was present except a lad about nine years of age, nephew of the deceased and son of the defendant, the deceased procured a knife and cut his throat, inflicting a ghastly wound, from the effect of which, according to the medical evidence, he must necessarily have died in five minutes. The wound inflicted by the defendant severed the mesenteric artery, and medical witnesses testified that under the circumstances it was necessarily mortal, and death would ensue within one hour from the effects of the wound alone. Indeed, the evidence was that usually the effect of such a wound would be to cause death in less time than that, but possibly the omentum may have filled the wound, and thus, by preventing the flow of the blood from the body, have stayed its certain effect for a short period. Internal hemorrhage was still occurring, and, with other effects of the gunshot wound, produced intense pain. The medical witnesses thought that death was accelerated by the knife wound. Perhaps some of them considered it the immediate cause of death.

Now, it is contended that this is a case where one languishing from a mortal wound is killed by an intervening cause, and, therefore, deceased was not killed by Lewis. To constitute manslaughter, the defendant must have killed some one, and if, though mortally wounded by the defendant, Farrell actually died from an independent intervening cause, Lewis, at the most, could only be guilty of a felonious attempt. He was as effectually prevented from killing as he would have been if some obstacle had turned aside the bullet from its course and left Farrell unwounded. And they contend that the intervening act was the cause of death, if it shortened the life of Farrell for any period whatever.

The attorney general does not controvert the general proposition here contended for, but argues that the wound inflicted by the defendant was the direct cause of the throat cutting, and, therefore, defendant is criminally responsible for the death. He illustrates his position by supposing a case of one dangerously wounded and whose wounds had been bandaged by a surgeon. He says, suppose through the fever and pain consequent upon the wound the patient becomes frenzied and tears away the bandage and thus accelerates his own death. Would not the defendant be responsible for a homicide? Undoubtedly he would be, for in the case supposed the deceased died from the wound, aggravated, it is true, by the restlessness of the deceased, but still the wound inflicted by the defendant produced death. Whether such is the case here is the question.

The attorney general seems to admit a fact which I do not concede, that the gunshot wound was not, when Farrell died, then itself directly contributory to the death. I think the jury were warranted in finding that it was. But if the deceased did die from the effect of the knife wound alone, no doubt the defendant would be responsible, if it was made to appear, and the jury could have found from the evidence, that the knife wound was caused by the wound inflicted by the defendant in the natural course of events. If the relation was causal, and the wounded condition of the deceased was not merely the occasion upon which another cause intervened, not produced by the first wound or related to it in other than a casual way, then defendant is guilty of a homicide. But, if the wounded condition only afforded an opportunity for another unconnected person to kill, defendant would not be guilty of a homicide, even though he had inflicted a mortal wound. In such case, I think, it would be true that the defendant was thus prevented from killing.

The case, considered under this view, is further complicated from the fact that it is impossible to determine whether deceased was induced to cut his throat through pain produced by the wound. May it not have been from remorse, or from a desire to shield his brother-in-law? In either case the causal relation between the knife wound and the gunshot wound would seem to be the same. In either case, if defendant had not shot the deceased, the knife wound would not have been inflicted.

Suppose one assaults and wounds another intending to take life, but the wound, though painful, is not even dangerous, and the wounded man knows that it is not mortal, and yet takes his own life to escape pain, would it not be suicide only? Yet, the wound inflicted by the assailant would have the same relation to death which the original wound in this case has to the knife wound. The wound induced the suicide, but the wound was not, in the usual course of things, the cause of the suicide. . . .

This case differs from that in this, that here the intervening cause, which it is alleged hastened the death, was not medical treatment, designed to be helpful, and which the deceased was compelled to procure because of the wound, but was an act intended to produce death, and did not result from the first wound in the natural course of events. But we have reached the conclusion by a course of argument unnecessarily prolix, except from a desire to fully consider the earnest and able argument of the defendant, that the test is—or at least one test—whether, when the death occurred, the wound inflicted by the defendant, did contribute to the event. If it did, although other independent causes also contributed, the causal relation between the unlawful acts of the defendant and the death has been made out. Here, when the throat was cut, Farrell was not merely languishing from a mortal wound. He was actually dying—and after the throat was cut he continued to languish from both wounds. Drop by drop the life current went out from both wounds, and at the very instant of death the gunshot wound was contributing to the event. If the throat cutting had been by a third person, unconnected with the defendant, he might be guilty; for although a man cannot be killed twice, two persons, acting independently, may contribute to his death and each be guilty of a homicide. A person dying is still in life, and may be killed, but if he is dying from a wound given by another both may properly be said to have contributed to his death. . . .

The court refused to instruct the jury as follows: "If you believe from the evidence that it is impossible to tell whether Will Farrell died from the wound in the throat, or the wound in the abdomen, you are bound to acquit." The instruction was properly refused. It assumed that death must have resulted wholly from one wound or the other, and ignored the proposition that both might have contributed—as the jury could have found from the evidence.

The other points are relatively trivial. I have examined them and cannot see how injury could have resulted, supposing the rulings to have been erroneous.

The judgment is affirmed.[129]

---

129.   **D** inflicted a knife wound on **X** after which **D**'s son shot **X**. It was held that if the knife wound contributed to the death of **X**, **D** may be convicted of murder even if there was no preconcert between D and his son, and the knife wound was not necessarily fatal. Henderson v. State, 11 Ala.App. 37, 65 So. 721 (1913).

One who inflicted a mortal wound by a shot fired in privileged self defense, and later fired another shot after all danger to himself had obviously come to an end is guilty of murder if the second shot contributed to the death. People v. Brown, 62 Cal.App. 96, 216 P. 411 (1923).

Where the conduct of two or more persons contributes concurrently as proximate causes of a death, the conduct of each of said persons is a proximate cause of the death regardless of the extent to which each contributes to the death. A cause is concurrent if it was operative at the moment of death and acted with another cause to produce the death.

"The evidence establishes that the two body wounds, the one in the abdomen and the one in the chest were fired by defendant Batiste from his position to the left of Holmes. The shot to the head was fired by Bolden. Either the chest wound or the head wound and possibly the abdominal wound would have caused the victim's death. . . .

"Bolden and Batiste jointly participated in the killing. Each was a principal in the crime. LSA–R.S. 14:24. Although there is no evidence of conspiracy, they were acting together. Holmes was fatally injured by Batiste and Bolden responded by inflicting another fatal wound while aiding Batiste. Bolden accelerated Holmes' death, but Batiste had independently fired a fatal shot.

"Bolden's act cannot be insulated from Batiste's, because the two were acting in concert. Holmes was sandwiched between them when the last 'immediately fatal' shot was fired. Batiste's actions caused Bolden's intervention. Holmes' death would have resulted from Batiste's shots regardless of this intervention, and the intervention was also caused by Batiste's actions. Batiste is responsible, because Bolden's interposition resulted from Batiste's initial wrongful acts. Both are guilty." State v. Batiste, 410 So.2d 1055, 1056, 1057–58 (La.1982).

■ McFARLAND, J., and HENSHAW, J., concurred.

Hearing in Bank denied.

Ex Parte Heigho

Supreme Court of Idaho, 1910.
18 Idaho 566, 110 P. 1029.

■ AILSHIE, J. Petitioner was held by the probate judge of Washington county to answer the charge of manslaughter, and has applied to this court for his discharge on the ground that the facts of the case do not disclose the commission of a public offense. The evidence produced at the preliminary examination has been attached to the petition. This court cannot weigh the evidence on habeas corpus, but, if it wholly fails to disclose a public offense for which a prisoner may be held on preliminary examination, then the petitioner would be entitled to his discharge. In re Knudtson, 10 Idaho 676, 79 P. 641.

The facts disclosed by the evidence are in substance as follows: On the 4th day of August, 1910, at Weiser, Washington county, the petitioner, Edgar M. Heigho, hearing that one J.W. Barton had made remarks derogatory to petitioner's character, called one of his employes, Frank Miller, and requested him to accompany petitioner to the residence of Barton. Heigho and Miller went to Barton's residence about 7 o'clock in the evening,

---

Where a group of persons, including defendant, beat the victim in a brawl, the defendant is responsible for the injuries caused to the victim. State v. Thomas, 210 Neb. 298, 314 N.W.2d 15 (1981).

Liability of one of several defendants as a contributing cause of a victim's death did not need to be related to any theory of joint liability if a person inflicts a wound in such a manner as to put life in jeopardy. Commonwealth v. McLeod, 394 Mass. 727, 477 N.E.2d 972 (1985).

An instruction to a jury in a homicide case that there may be more than one cause of death and defendant may cause the death of a person even though there are other direct causes of the victim's death is proper. Commonwealth v. Paolello, 542 Pa. 47, 665 A.2d 439 (1995).

Where abortion protesters arguably acted independently in charging through U.S. Marshals protecting an abortion clinic, conviction for obstruction of a judicial decree was proper under 18 U.S.C. § 1509 without proof of conspiracy or of aiding and abetting though no single individual's act was sufficient to interfere with or block access to the abortion clinic. Culpability was properly based on contributory causes. United States v. Cooley, 1 F.3d 985 (10th Cir.1993).

A gunshot wound to the head of the victim in October was a sufficient direct cause of death in December to establish responsibility for homicide of the victim even though he pulled off his feeding tube, refused food and ingested only liquids. Victim's acts were a suicide attempt resulting from the gunshot and malnutrition. People v. Velez, 159 Misc.2d 38, 602 N.Y.S.2d 758 (1993).

A conscious decision of a 97–year-old victim, whose neck had been broken and spinal cord severed by defendant's assault where the victim was kept alive on a ventilator, to remove the life support rather than live paralyzed, was not a superseding cause of the victim's death. Defendant was properly convicted of homicide. People v. Caldwell, 295 Ill. App.3d 172, 229 Ill.Dec. 675, 692 N.E.2d 448 (1998).

Concurrent shots, even if from independent sources, will not excuse one shooter whose shot was a contributing factor to the victim's death. McFarland v. State, 928 S.W.2d 482, 516 (Tex.Cr.App.1996).

ascended the front porch, and Heigho rang the doorbell. Mrs. Sylvia Riegleman, the mother-in-law of Barton, was living at the Barton residence, and was in a bedroom at the front of the house, and immediately off from and adjoining the reception room or hallway, at the time the doorbell rang. Barton responded to the call, and, as he passed through the front room and was about to open the front door, Mrs. Riegleman, who was then near him, exclaimed, "Oh, he has a gun." Barton stepped out at the door and found Heigho standing on the front porch with a gun, commonly called a revolver or pistol, hanging in a holster or scabbard which was strapped about his body. Miller stood by the side of Heigho. Heigho asked Barton some questions as to the statements Barton had been making about him, and, upon Barton asserting that he had not told anything that was not true or not common talk in the town, Heigho struck him in the face with his fist, and Barton staggered back, and fell into the wire netting on the screen door. Barton did not rise for a few seconds, and in the meanwhile his wife came and assisted him to arise. Heigho and Miller backed off the porch and stood in front of the doorway. Barton advanced on Heigho and struck him a couple of blows, whereupon they clinched, and the wife interfered and separated them, and ordered Heigho and Miller off the premises. Mrs. Riegleman was at this time at the door crying, and had been heard to say a time or two, "He will kill you," or "He has a gun." Barton and wife immediately mounted the porch where Mrs. Riegleman was on her knees, resting against or over the banister, apparently unable to rise. She remarked to Barton that she was dying, and again repeated something about "him having a gun." She began spitting a bloody froth and rattling in the chest. A physician was called, and was unable to give her any relief, and she died inside of about 30 minutes from the time of the appearance of Heigho on the front porch. The physician who attended her made a post mortem examination, and testified that she had an aneurism of the ascending aorta, and this had ruptured into the superior vena cava and caused her death. He said that excitement was one of three principal causes that will produce such a result. Heigho was thereafter arrested on the charge of manslaughter in causing the death of Mrs. Riegleman by terror and fright while he was engaged in the commission of an unlawful act not amounting to felony.

We are now asked to determine whether under the statute of this state a person can be held for manslaughter where death was caused by fright, fear, or nervous shock, and where the prisoner made no assault or demonstration against the deceased, and neither offered nor threatened any physical force or violence toward the person of the deceased. In the early history of the common law a homicide to be criminal must have resulted from corporal injury. Fright, fear, nervous shock, or producing mental disturbance, it was said, could never be the basis of a prosecution for homicide. East in his Pleas of the Crown, c. 5, § 13, says: "Working upon the fancy of another or treating him harshly or unkindly, by which he dies of grief or fear, is not such a killing as the law takes notice of." An examination of the ancient English authorities fully corroborates and establishes this to have been the early English rule. 1 Hale P.C. 425–29; Steph.Dig.Cr.Law, art. 221. This rule appears, however, to have been gradually modified and greatly relaxed in modern times by most of the English courts. So in later years we find the court holding a prisoner for manslaughter where his conduct toward his wife caused her death from shock to her nervous system. Reg. v. Murton, 3 F. & F. 492. And in Reg. v. Dugal, 4 Quebec, 492, the Canadian court held the prisoner guilty of manslaughter where with violent words and menaces he had brandished a table knife over his father, and the latter became greatly agitated and weakened from the fright, and died in 20 minutes thereafter of syncope. . . .

As to whether a death caused from fright, grief, or terror, or other mental or nervous shock, can be made the basis for a criminal prosecution, has been touched upon but lightly by the text-writers, and none have ventured to enunciate a modern rule on the subject. Such comments and observations as the text-writers have made are valuable as indicating the personal views of the writers touching this matter. Sir James Stephen in his note to article 221 of his Digest of Criminal Law, commenting on the old rule, says: "Suppose a man were intentionally killed by being kept awake till the nervous irritation of sleeplessness killed him; might not this be murder? Suppose a man kills a sick man, intentionally, by making a loud noise which wakes him when sleep gives him a chance of life, or suppose, knowing that a man has aneurism of the heart, his heir rushes into his room and roars in his ear, 'Your wife is dead,' intending to kill and killing him, why are not these acts murder? They are no more 'secret things belonging to God' than the operation of arsenic. As to the fear that by admitting that such acts are murder people might be rendered liable to prosecution for breaking the hearts of their fathers or wives by bad conduct, the answer is that such an event could never be proved. A long course of conduct gradually 'breaking a man's heart' could never be the 'direct or immediate' cause of death. If it was, and it was intended to have that effect, why should it not be murder?" The author of the text in 21 Am. & Eng.Ency. of Law (2d Ed.) p. 98, speaking of the reason for the old rule and the modern trend of authority, says: "A hint of the reason for this exclusion may be gathered from Lord Hale's assertion that 'secret things belong to God,' upon which Sir James Stephen comments that he suspects the fear of encouraging prosecutions for witchcraft was the real reason. In default of a better explanation it would seem, therefore, that the rule has no firmer foundation than the ignorance and superstition of the time in which it was formulated. Hence the courts have in some later cases shown a tendency to break away from the old rule where substantial justice required it. It will be observed, however, that in all these cases the death has been caused by shock of terror produced by an assault, so that the question in many of its aspects may still be regarded as unsettled. Yet on principle there is no reason why a death from nervous irritation or shock should not be as criminal as any other. It certainly entails greater difficulty in the matter of proof, but this is purely a question of fact, and, if the prosecution is able to establish its case by evidence satisfactory to a jury, there seems to be no sufficient reason why the law should forbid a conviction." Clark & Marshall on the Law of Crimes (2d Ed.) p. 314, says: "It is no doubt very true that the law cannot undertake to punish as for homicide when it is claimed that the death was caused solely by grief or terror, for the death could not be traced to such causes with any degree of certainty. Working upon the feelings and fears of another, however, may be the direct cause of physical or corporeal injury resulting in death, and in such a case the person causing the injury may be as clearly responsible for the death as if he had used a knife." The statute of this state (section 6565, Rev.Codes) defines manslaughter as follows: "Manslaughter is the unlawful killing of a human being without malice. It is of two kinds: (1) Voluntary—upon a sudden quarrel or heat of passion; (2) involuntary—in the commission of an unlawful act, not amounting to felony, or in the commission of a lawful act which might produce death, in an unlawful manner, or without due caution and circumspection." Manslaughter has perhaps in the variety of its circumstances no equal in the catalogue of crimes. An unlawful killing, though unintentional and involuntary, if accomplished by one while engaged in the commission of an unlawful act, is defined by the statute as manslaughter, and this statute does not circumscribe the means or agency causing the death. The law clearly covers and includes any and all means and mediums by or through which a death is caused by one engaged in an unlawful act. The statute has the effect of raising the grade of the offense in which the party is engaged to the rank of manslaughter where it results in the death of a human being.

With such aid as we get from the foregoing authorities and the independent consideration we have been able to give the matter, we reach the conclusion that it would be unsafe, unreasonable, and often unjust for a court to hold as a matter of law that under no state of facts should a prosecution for manslaughter be sustained where death was caused by fright, fear or terror alone, even though no hostile demonstration or overt act was directed at the person of the deceased. Many examples might be called to mind where it would be possible for the death of a person to be accomplished through fright, nervous shock, or terror as effectually as the same could be done with a knife or gun. If the proof in such a case be clear and undoubted, there can be no good reason for denying a conviction. If A. in a spirit of recklessness shoot through B.'s house in which a sick wife or child is confined, and the shock and excitement to the patient cause death, the mere fact that he did not shoot at or hit any one and that he did not intend to shoot any one should not excuse him. It should be enough that he was at the time doing an unlawful act or was acting "without due caution and circumspection." It would seem that in some instances force or violence may be applied to the mind or nervous system as effectually as to the body (1 Russel on Crimes, p. 489). Indeed, it is a well-recognized fact, especially among physicians and metaphysicians, that the application of corporal force or violence often intensifies mentally and nervously the physical effects that flow from the use and application of such force or violence.[130]

---

130. Defendant's negligently-parked car on a hillside crashed into a house in which Victim's death occurred when she heard a noise at night and became frightened on finding a door had been pried open. The victim suffered a heart attack due to a previously damaged heart and the excitement. An involuntary manslaughter conviction was upheld. State v. Losey, 23 Ohio App.3d 93, 491 N.E.2d 379 (1985).

Defendant threw a stone at the victim's house. The victim did not hear it but suffered a heart attack when told of the incident by her son. An involuntary manslaughter conviction was quashed. Commonwealth v. Colvin, 340 Pa.Super. 278, 489 A.2d 1378 (1985).

We express no opinion whatever and refrain from any comment on the evidence in this case. That is a matter to be passed on by a jury. They should determine from all the facts and circumstances whether the accused was the direct and actual cause of the death of the deceased. As was said by Justice Denman in the Towers Case, it would be "laying down a dangerous precedent for the future" for us to hold as a conclusion of law that manslaughter could not be committed by fright, terror, or nervous shock. The fair and deliberate judgment of a jury of 12 men can generally be relied upon as an ample safeguard for the protection of one who should in fact be acquitted. The dangers of unwarranted prosecutions for such causes are no greater or more imminent than from any other cause, while, on the other hand, the proofs will generally be more difficult. The difficulty of making proofs, however, should never be considered as an argument against the application of a rule of law.

The writ is quashed, and the prisoner is remanded to the custody of the sheriff of Washington county.[131]

■ SULLIVAN, C.J., concurs.

People v. Stamp

Court of Appeal of California, Second District, Division 3, 1969.
2 Cal.App.3d 203, 82 Cal.Rptr. 598.

■ COBEY, ASSOCIATE JUSTICE. These are appeals by Jonathan Earl Stamp, Michael John Koory and Billy Dean Lehman, following jury verdicts of guilty of robbery and murder, both in the first degree. Each man was given a life sentence on the murder charge together with the time prescribed by law on the robbery count.

Defendants appeal their conviction of the murder of Carl Honeyman who, suffering from a heart disease, died between 15 and 20 minutes after Koory and Stamp held up his business, the General Amusement Company, on October 26, 1965, at 10:45 a.m. Lehman, the driver of the getaway car, was apprehended a few minutes after the robbery; several weeks later Stamp was arrested in Ohio and Koory in Nebraska.

Broadly stated, the grounds of this appeal are: (1) insufficiency of the evidence on the causation of Honeyman's death; (2) inapplicability of the felony-murder rule to this case; . . . .

---

131. **D** placed his hand, or hands, around **X**'s throat and choked him. Within seconds **D** released his grip whereupon **X** slumped to the ground. **X** died two months and seventeen days later without having recovered consciousness for any substantial period, if at all. A doctor testified that **X** had had high blood pressure and expressed the opinion that death was caused by cerebral hemorrhage, resulting from excitement. There had been no autopsy but the death certificate gave pneumonia as the primary cause of death with cerebral hemorrhage as a secondary cause. A conviction of manslaughter was reversed on the ground that it cannot be said with any degree of certainty that X died as a result of any criminal agency. Fine v. State, 193 Tenn. 422, 246 S.W.2d 70 (1952).

D unlawfully struck **B** who had a child in her arms at the time, the infant became frightened and went into convulsions and thereafter died. **D**'s guilt on manslaughter was held to be a jury question. Verdict: Not guilty. R. v. Towers, 12 Cox C.C. 530 (1874).

On this appeal appellants primarily rely upon their position that the felony-murder doctrine should not have been applied in this case due to the unforeseeability of Honeyman's death.

THE FACTS

Defendants Koory and Stamp, armed with a gun and a blackjack, entered the rear of the building housing the offices of General Amusement Company, ordered the employees they found there to go to the front of the premises, where the two secretaries were working. Stamp, the one with the gun, then went into the office of Carl Honeyman, the owner and manager. Thereupon Honeyman, looking very frightened and pale, emerged from the office in a "kind of hurry." He was apparently propelled by Stamp who had hold of him by an elbow.

The robbery victims were required to lie down on the floor while the robbers took the money and fled out the back door. As the robbers, who had been on the premises 10 to 15 minutes, were leaving, they told the victims to remain on the floor for five minutes so that no one would "get hurt."

Honeyman, who had been lying next to the counter, had to use it to steady himself in getting up off the floor. Still pale, he was short of breath, sucking air, and pounding and rubbing his chest. As he walked down the hall, in an unsteady manner, still breathing hard and rubbing his chest, he said he was having trouble "keeping the pounding down inside" and that his heart was "pumping too fast for him." A few minutes later, although still looking very upset, shaking, wiping his forehead and rubbing his chest, he was able to walk in a steady manner into an employee's office. When the police arrived, almost immediately thereafter, he told them he was not feeling very well and that he had a pain in his chest. About two minutes later, which was 15 to 20 minutes after the robbery had occurred, he collapsed on the floor. At 11:25 he was pronounced dead on arrival at the hospital. The coroner's report listed the immediate cause of death as heart attack.

The employees noted that during the hours before the robbery Honeyman had appeared to be in normal health and good spirits. The victim was an obese, sixty-year-old man, with a history of heart disease, who was under a great deal of pressure due to the intensely competitive nature of his business. Additionally, he did not take good care of his heart.

Three doctors, including the autopsy surgeon, Honeyman's physician, and a professor of cardiology from U.C.L.A., testified that although Honeyman had an advanced case of atherosclerosis, a progressive and ultimately fatal disease, there must have been some immediate upset to his system which precipitated the attack. It was their conclusion in response to a hypothetical question that but for the robbery there would have been no fatal seizure at that time. The fright induced by the robbery was too much of a shock to Honeyman's system. There was opposing expert testimony to the effect that it could not be said with reasonable medical certainty that fright could ever be fatal.

SUFFICIENCY OF THE EVIDENCE RE CAUSATION

Appellants' contention that the evidence was insufficient to prove that the robbery factually caused Honeyman's death is without merit. The test on review is whether there is substantial evidence to uphold the judgment of the trial court, and in so deciding this court must assume in the case of a jury trial the existence of every fact in favor of the verdict which the jury could reasonably have deduced from the evidence. A review of the facts as outlined above shows that there was substantial evidence of the robbery itself, that appellants were the robbers, and that but for the robbery the victim would not have experienced the fright which brought on the fatal heart attack.[132]

APPLICATION OF THE FELONY–MURDER RULE

Appellants' contention that the felony-murder rule is inapplicable to the facts of this case is also without merit. Under the felony-murder rule of section 189 of the Penal Code, a killing committed in either the perpetration of or an attempt to perpetrate robbery is murder of the first degree. This is true whether the killing is willful, deliberate and premeditated, or merely accidental or unintentional, and whether or not the killing is planned as a part of the commission of the robbery. People v. Washington, 62 Cal.2d 777, 783, 44 Cal.Rptr. 442, 402 P.2d 130, merely limits the rule to situations where the killing was committed by the felon or his accomplice acting in furtherance of their common design. (*See* People v. Gilbert, 63 Cal.2d 690, 705, 47 Cal.Rptr. 909, 408 P.2d 365.)

The doctrine presumes malice aforethought on the basis of the commission of a felony inherently dangerous to human life.[133] This rule is a rule of substantive law in California and not merely an evidentiary shortcut to finding malice as it withdraws from the jury the requirement that they find either express malice or the implied malice which is manifested in an intent to kill. Under this rule no intentional act is necessary other than the attempt to or the actual commission of the robbery itself. When a robber

---

132. Appellants' position that the medical evidence was insufficient to prove the causal link between the robbery and the death because the physicians testifying to the result did so solely in response to a hypothetical question which was erroneous and misleading, and because the doctors answered in terms of "medical probability rather than actual certainty" is not well taken. A conviction on the basis of expert medical testimony, couched in terms of "reasonable medical certainty" rather than of "beyond a reasonable doubt" is valid (People v. Phillips, 64 Cal.2d 574, 579, fn. 2, 51 Cal.Rptr. 225, 414 P.2d 353, 357) and a hypothetical question need not state all the evidence in a case so long as it does not omit essential facts and issues. This did not occur here. (*See* McCullough v. Langer, 23 Cal.App.2d 510, 521, 73 P.2d 649, hear.den.) Furthermore, an appellate court will not overrule a trial court on the matter of the sufficiency of the qualifications of expert witnesses in the absence of a manifest abuse of such discretion. (People v. Phillips, 64 Cal.2d at 578–579, fn. 1, 51 Cal.Rptr. 225, 414 P.2d 353.) An examination of the record shows that there was no such abuse by the trial court in permitting the prosecution's expert medical witnesses to testify as to the cause of the heart attack.

133. In view of the fact that the Legislature has not seen fit to change the language of Penal Code section 189 since the decisions holding that the requisite malice aforethought is to be implied from the commission of those felonies inherently dangerous to human life, it must be presumed that these cases accurately state the law. (People v. Hallner, 43 Cal.2d 715, 720, 277 P.2d 393.)

enters a place with a deadly weapon with the intent to commit robbery, malice is shown by the nature of the crime.

There is no requirement that the killing occur, "while committing" or "while engaged in" the felony, or that the killing be "a part of" the felony, other than that the few acts be a part of one continuous transaction. (People v. Chavez, 37 Cal.2d 656, 670, 234 P.2d 632.) Thus the homicide need not have been committed "to perpetrate" the felony. There need be no technical inquiry as to whether there has been a completion or abandonment of or desistence from the robbery before the homicide itself was completed.

The doctrine is not limited to those deaths which are foreseeable. Rather a felon is held strictly liable for *all* killings committed by him or his accomplices in the course of the felony. (People v. Talbot, 64 Cal.2d 691, 704, 51 Cal.Rptr. 417, 414 P.2d 633.) As long as the homicide is the direct causal result of the robbery the felony-murder rule applies whether or not the death was a natural or probable consequence of the robbery. So long as a victim's predisposing physical condition, regardless of its cause, is not the *only* substantial factor bringing about his death, that condition, and the robber's ignorance of it, in no way destroys the robber's criminal responsibility for the death. So long as life is shortened as a result of the felonious act, it does not matter that the victim might have died soon anyway. In this respect, the robber takes his victim as he finds him. . . .

The judgment is affirmed.[134]

■ SCHWEITZER and ALLPORT, JJ., concur.

State v. Sauter

Supreme Court of Arizona, In Banc, 1978.
120 Ariz. 222, 585 P.2d 242.

■ STRUCKMEYER, VICE CHIEF JUSTICE.

Appellant, Richard Robert Sauter, was convicted after trial by jury of voluntary manslaughter, and appeals. Jurisdiction is pursuant to Rule 47(e)(5), Rules of the Supreme Court. Judgment affirmed.

---

134. [Added by the Compiler.] Elderly victim's death due to heart failure which would not have occurred "but for" a robbery, the pursuit of the attackers, and recounting the episode to the police, supported a conviction for felony murder. State v. Reardon, 486 A.2d 112 (Me.1984).

Victim had a prior heart condition and died from myocardial infarction after confronting a burglar in the victim's house. Conviction of felony murder was proper. People v. Ingram, 67 N.Y.2d 897, 501 N.Y.S.2d 804, 492 N.E.2d 1220 (1986).

F struck **G** on the jaw once with his fist. Under other circumstances the moderate blow might well have been forgotten, but **G** was a hemophiliac and a slight laceration resulted on the inside of the mouth. At the time and place there was no medical skill competent to stop the bleeding and G died ten days later as a result of the uninterrupted hemorrhage. A conviction of manslaughter was affirmed although **F** did not know **G** was a hemophiliac and had no reason to expect serious consequences from the relatively mild battery. State v. Frazier, 339 Mo. 966, 98 S.W.2d 707 (1936).

Defendant struck **V** several blows to the head. **V** died from a pulmonary embolism resulting from a leg vein thrombosis due to immobility as a result of the blows. A murder conviction was affirmed. State v. Hall, 129 Ariz. 589, 633 P.2d 398 (1981).

The record in the court below established that appellant, while intoxicated and during the course of an altercation, stabbed Matt Charles Lines. Lines was taken to the emergency room of a hospital in Phoenix, Arizona, where he was attended by a general surgeon. The surgeon opened the abdominal cavity and repaired lacerations to both the anterior and posterior stomach walls, the main stomach artery, the superior pancreatic artery and pancreatic tissue. The surgeon also palpitated the abdominal aorta, but did not observe bleeding in the area. After the surgery, Lines continued to lose large amounts of blood. An autopsy revealed that he died from the loss of blood, principally through a one-inch, unrepaired laceration in the abdominal aorta.

Appellant's position is that he was guilty of assault rather than homicide because of the intervening malpractice of the surgeon who did not discover the laceration in Lines' aorta, and he urges that error occurred when the trial court refused to allow evidence of the surgeon's failure to discover the wound to Lines' aorta. We, however, do not think so.

In State v. Myers, 59 Ariz. 200, 125 P.2d 441 (1942), we quoted with approval from State v. Baruth, 47 Wash. 283, 91 P. 977, to the effect that where one unlawfully inflicts a wound upon another calculated to endanger his life, it is no defense to a charge of murder to show that the wounded person might have recovered if the wound had been more skillfully treated. We said in State v. Ulin, 113 Ariz. 141, 143, 548 P.2d 19 (1976), that medical malpractice will break the chain of causation and become the proximate cause of death only if it constitutes the sole cause of death. We think these cases correctly summarize the law relative to intervening acts arising out of medical treatment in the United States. See 100 A.L.R.2d 769, anno. "Homicide; liability where death immediately results from treatment or mistreatment of injury inflicted by defendant." *See also* the cases cited supporting the basic rule, commencing at page 783 and running through page 784. For example, in People v. Stamps, 8 Ill.App.3d 896, 291 N.E.2d 274, 279 (1972), the court held:

"* * * it is the generally recognized principle that where a person inflicts upon another a wound which is dangerous, that is, calculated to endanger or destroy life, it is no defense to a charge of homicide that the alleged victim's death was contributed to by, or immediately resulted from, unskillful or improper treatment of the wound or injury by attending physicians or surgeons."

See also People v. Stewart, 40 N.Y.2d 692, 389 N.Y.S.2d 804, 358 N.E.2d 487, 491 (1976), where the court said:

"Neither does 'direct' mean 'unaided' for the defendant will be held liable for the death although other factors, entering after the injury, have contributed to the fatal result. Thus if 'felonious assault is operative as a cause of death, the causal co-operation of erroneous surgical or medical treatment does not relieve the assailant from liability for homicide.' "

Rule

Only if the death is attributable to the medical malpractice and not induced at all by the original wound does the intervention of the medical malpractice constitute a defense. Such is not the case here.

Judgment affirmed.[135]

---

135. If a gun-shot wound inflicted by **D** on a pregnant woman caused a miscarriage, and the miscarriage caused septic peritonitis which in turn resulted in death, **D** has caused the death even if the medical treatment received by the woman in the hospital was not of the best. People v. Kane, 213 N.Y. 260, 107 N.E. 655 (1915).

Death of a 91–year-old victim from pneumonia and sepsis 17 days following a beating supported a felony-murder conviction where the pneumonia was connected to the assault. State v. Barnes, 703 S.W.2d 611 (Tenn.1985).

H and **S** had an argument which resulted in a fight. During the fight **H** knocked **S** down and in a fit of rage jumped on his face and kicked him in the head. **S** was taken to the hospital in semi-comatose condition. He was violent and in shock. After receiving a blood transfusion S had tubes inserted into his nasal passages and trachea in order to maintain the normal breathing process. It was necessary to restrain his violence by fastening leather handcuffs on him. When it became desirable to change the bed clothes, the restraints were removed and were not put back because he was no longer violent. Early the following morning **S** had a convulsion and immediately thereafter pulled out the tubes with his own hands. He died an hour later of asphyxiation.

Being tried for the murder of **S**, **H** claimed that S had killed himself by pulling out the tubes which were necessary for his breathing because of his injured condition. It was not clear whether the pulling out of the tubes was a reflex action, or was a conscious deliberate act. Under either possibility it was held that **H** was the proximate cause of **S**'s death and he was convicted of manslaughter. United States v. Hamilton, 182 F.Supp. 548 (D.D.C.1960).

Even if physicians were negligent in believing the victim was dead before they performed a nephrectomy and even if such negligence was a contributing factor to the victim's death, the physicians' negligence does not break the chain of causation and death is still attributable to the victim being shot by the defendant. Cranmore v. State, 85 Wis.2d 722, 271 N.W.2d 402 (1978).

Defendant draped a rattlesnake around the neck of a three-year-old child and the snake bit and killed the child. Defendant's claim of medical malpractice was not an intervening cause and the conviction for manslaughter was affirmed. State v. Wessendorf, 777 P.2d 523 (Utah App.1989).

Removal of life support systems where the original need was due to the wrongful conduct of the defendant renders the defendant liable for homicide even if the doctors failed to follow acceptable procedures in terminating a life support system. R v. Malcherek [1981] All E.R. 422 (Ct.App.)

Defendant beat a 71–year-old man who died two days later in the hospital. Defendant contended there was medical malpractice in failing to provide oxygen. The victim died of bronchopneumonia. As long as the prosecution establishes the defendant's conduct was a significant cause of death, causation for a murder conviction was established. Reg. V. Mellor, [1996] 2 Cr.App.B 245

Someone's erroneous removal of a tracheotomy tube, where victim died one day later, did not preclude a finding of defendant's criminal culpability for manslaughter for causing the victim's death attributable to an accident two months before in an automobile/motorcycle collision. State v. Baker, 87 Or.App. 285, 742 P.2d 633 (1987).

Removal of life support systems on medical determination by physicians of victim's brain death did not break the chain of causation. Clay v. State, 256 Ga. 797, 353 S.E.2d 517 (1987); also, Eby v. State, 702 P.2d 1047 (Okl.Cr.1985).

From the evidence the jury might have found that **D**'s reckless conduct left the victim in the street where she was run over and killed by a second car. Even so **D**'s reckless conduct was the cause of the death. The second car did not constitute a supervening cause but was an intermediate cause reasonably foreseeable by **D**. People v. Parra, 35 Ill.App.3d 240, 340 N.E.2d 636 (1975). *See also* People v. Kibbe, 35 N.Y.2d 407, 362 N.Y.S.2d 848, 321 N.E.2d 773 (1974); State v. Baggett, 836 S.W.2d 593 (Tenn.Cr.App.1992) (fact that driver in second car striking the victim was intoxicated did not preclude defendant's conviction).

Letner v. State

Supreme Court of Tennessee, 1927.
156 Tenn. 68, 299 S.W. 1049.

■ MR. JUSTICE MCKINNEY delivered the opinion of the Court.

Plaintiff in error, referred to herein as the defendant, was indicted for murder of Alfred Johnson. The jury found him guilty of involuntary manslaughter and fixed his punishment at two years in the penitentiary.

Alfred Johnson, nineteen years of age, his older brother, Walter Johnson, and Jesse Letner, seventeen years of age, half brother of the defendant, were crossing Emory River in a boat from the west to the east side, at a point known as "Devil's Race Track," this being a dangerous place, of unknown depth, where the water circles and eddies continuously. When in the middle of the river some man on the high bluff above the west bank shot into the water about six feet east of the boat, which caused the water to splash up. A second shot was fired, which hit the water nearer the boat; thereupon Walter Johnson, who was steering the boat, jumped out of same into the river, resulting in its being capsized, and Alfred and Walter were drowned.

The only question of fact is were either of these shots fired by defendant? He did not testify, and offered no evidence in his behalf....

(4) It is also assigned for error that the court improperly charged the jury as follows:

"If you should believe from the evidence, and that beyond a reasonable doubt, that this defendant saw the deceased and other boys in a canoe or boat, and shot into the river near them without any purpose of hitting the deceased, but to play a prank on the deceased, and if the deceased became frightened and jumped into the river and was drowned, then in that event, the defendant would be guilty of involuntary manslaughter."

This was a correct statement of the law, but was inaccurate so far as the facts of this case are concerned. The uncontroverted testimony shows that deceased did not jump out of the boat, but that his brother, Walter, jumped out and, in doing so, capsized the boat and precipitated the deceased into the water. No criticism, however, is made with respect to this feature of the charge.

The act of the defendant, whether he was shooting to kill or only to frighten these boys, was an unlawful one, and comes within the universal rule that every person will be held to contemplate and be responsible for the natural consequences of his own act; but he will not be held criminally responsible for a homicide unless his act can be said to be the cause of death.

(5) When a person unintentionally or accidentally kills another, while engaged in an unlawful act, the authorities all hold that he is guilty of some degree of homicide.

In this case if defendant had accidentally struck the deceased, causing his death, or had capsized the boat and deceased had drowned, unquestionably he would have been guilty of some grade of homicide....

From the foregoing it appears that the defendant is liable even where his act was not the immediate cause of the death, if he was connected with the intervening cause, or if the act or intervention was the natural result of his act.

(7) In other words, the defendant cannot escape the consequences of his wrongful act by relying upon a supervening cause when such cause naturally resulted from his wrongful act.

By firing the gun the defendant caused Walter Johnson to take to the water, resulting in the overturn of the boat and the drowning of Alfred. . . .

The judgment should also provide that the defendant undergo confinement in the penitentiary (in this case) not less than one nor more than two years. As thus modified, the judgment of the trial court will be affirmed.[136]

State v. Leopold

Supreme Court of Errors of Connecticut, 1929.
110 Conn. 55, 147 A. 118.

■ BANKS, J. In the early morning of February 5, 1928, an explosion followed by a fire occurred in a building on Baldwin street in Waterbury, and two boys, the sons of a tenant of the building, were burned to death. The fee of the property was in the name of the wife of the accused, and a portion of the building was used for the storage of furniture by the Waterbury Furniture Company, a corporation of which the accused was a majority stockholder. The accused, jointly with one Shellnitz, was indicted upon a charge of murder in the first degree, and of having caused the death of the two boys by willfully burning the building. The charge against the accused was that he employed Weiss to set fire to the building, for the purpose of collecting insurance upon the building and the furniture stored in it. Weiss was burned to death in the fire. . . .

Error is predicated upon the refusal of the court to charge as requested, upon the charge as given, and upon numerous rulings upon evidence. The accused claimed that the two boys who were burned to death were awake after the fire, and were on their way out of the building, and would not have met their death if they had continued on their way, but that of their own will they remained in the building, or were sent back into a room of the building by their father to recover some money or other property there deposited, and requested the court to charge that, if they had a reasonable opportunity to escape from the burning building, and would have escaped but for their own conduct, or the act of their father in

---

136. D made improper advances to a girl in a moving automobile. To avoid him she jumped from the car and was killed by the fall. A conviction of murder was reversed because the judge's charge to the jury permitted conviction of murder without requiring a finding (a) that deceased's fear of a felonious assault was a reasonable one, or (b) that her act in jumping was an act of a reasonably prudent person under the circumstances, or (c) that her act in jumping was one which in its consequences naturally tended to destroy the life of a human being. Patterson v. State, 181 Ga. 698, 184 S.E. 309 (1936). Cf. State v. Myers, 7 N.J. 465, 81 A.2d 710 (1951); State v. Selby, 183 N.J.Super. 273, 443 A.2d 1076 (1981); State v. Lassiter, 197 N.J.Super. 2, 484 A.2d 13 (1984).

directing them to return, the accused could not be found guilty of causing their death. The court did not so charge, but told the jury that the negligence of the victims of a crime did not diminish or nullify the crime, and that, even if they found the claim as to the conduct of these boys to be true, the accused would not thereby be excused. This was a correct statement of the law.... Every person is held to be responsible for the natural consequences of his acts, and if he commits a felonious act and death follows, it does not alter its nature or diminish its criminality to prove that other causes co-operated to produce that result. The act of the accused need not be the immediate cause of the death; he is responsible, though the direct cause is an act of the deceased, if such act, not being itself an independent and efficient cause, results naturally from, and is reasonably due to, the unlawful act of the accused. If the death of these boys resulted in a natural sequence from the setting of the building on fire, even though their conduct contributed to, or was the immediate cause of it, the accused would be responsible, and the effort of a person to save property of value which is liable to destruction by fire is such a natural and ordinary course of conduct that it cannot be said to break the sequence of cause and effect....

A careful examination of the entire record fails to disclose any error prejudicial to the accused, and makes it clear that he had a fair trial.

There is no error.

All the Judges concur.[137]

State v. Iten

Court of Appeals of Minnesota, 1987.
401 N.W.2d 127.

■ NIERENGARTEN, JUDGE.

Raymond Iten appeals from judgment entered pursuant to a jury verdict convicting him of criminal vehicular operation resulting in death, Minn.Stat. § 609.21, subd. 1(1) (1984). We affirm.

FACTS

Iten was headed east on Highway 55. When he was approximately 600 feet west of the intersection with South Shore Drive, Iten saw the light turn yellow, and then saw the light turn red when he was approximately 320 feet from the intersection.

Iten decided he would not be able to make a safe stop and honked his horn to alert other cars at the intersection. As he neared the intersection, he saw Marna Quarnstrom's car entering the intersection from the south. He downshifted and moved into the left lane to avoid hitting Quarnstrom, but the truck's right front bumper hit her car. She was thrown from the car onto the road where the truck's rear dual wheels ran over her, killing

---

137. **D** maliciously set fire to a store building and a fireman lost his life while fighting the fire. A conviction of first degree murder was affirmed. State v. Glover, 330 Mo. 709, 50 S.W.2d 1049 (1932).

her instantly. Iten stopped the truck immediately and remained at the scene.

. . .

Evidence at trial also showed that Iten's brakes were operating at 50% effectiveness due to rust and oil deposits. Even with this impairment, however, the evidence showed that Iten had time to bring the truck to a safe stop had he chosen to do so. Iten did not check the brakes on the truck prior to driving it, although this is required by federal and state regulations, because he was in a hurry.

Iten further testified he did not stop at the intersection because he was afraid the load would shift, the brakes would lock or catch fire, or that the truck would jack-knife.

. . .

A person is guilty of criminal vehicular operation resulting in death if he or she caused the death of another person by operating a vehicle in a grossly negligent manner. Minn.Stat. § 609.21, subd. 1(1) (1984). Gross negligence is "the want of even scant care." State v. Bolsinger, 221 Minn. 154, 158, 21 N.W.2d 480, 485 (1946). Iten's claim of insufficient evidence requires us to view the evidence in the light most favorable to the prosecution and assume that the jury believed the state's witnesses and disbelieved any contrary evidence.

Iten contends the evidence is insufficient to support the jury's verdict because he believed he did the best he could to avoid the accident under the circumstances. No excessive speed was involved. Iten sounded his horn before entering the intersection. Iten swerved and executed other maneuvers to avoid hitting Quarnstrom's car. He admits his negligence, but contends he exercised much more than "scant care." At the time of Iten's evasive action, however, he had already displayed "want of even scant care" by failing to inspect the truck as required by law and by failing to stop when he had more than sufficient time to do so.

Iten's only defense is his sincere belief that he did not have sufficient time to stop safely. The facts indicate otherwise. Iten admitted the light changed first to yellow and then to red before he reached the intersection. He did not brake at any time before impact. An accident reconstructionist concluded Iten received the yellow light 598 feet back from the point of impact and received the red light 321 feet back from that point.

Viewed in the light most favorable to the State, and without disturbing the jury's right to believe the State's witnesses and to disbelieve any contrary witnesses, the evidence was sufficient to support the verdict.

Iten argues that evidence on whether Quarnstrom was wearing a seatbelt is relevant because of its bearing on proximate cause. Trial courts have broad discretion to exclude evidence on the basis of relevancy. The evidence Iten offered concerned only whether Quarnstrom would have been thrown from the car had she been wearing a seatbelt.

However, no law required the wearing of seatbelts at the time the accident occurred. Even if a seatbelt would have prevented Quarnstrom's death, any negligence on her part is relevant only if it constituted a superseding intervening cause of the accident. Contributory negligence is not a defense to a criminal prosecution.

[handwritten: ✶ NOT A CRIMINAL DEFENSE]

The trial court instructed the jury on the elements of criminal vehicular operation resulting in death, including the definition of gross negligence. The court further instructed the jury on the effect of any negligence by the victim, including the statement that her negligence was relevant "only insofar as it may tend to show that the Defendant was not negligent or that his actions did not constitute the proximate cause of the victim's death."

Appellant contends the trial court erred by refusing to instruct the jury on the definition of proximate cause. Trial courts have broad discretion in determining the propriety of a specific jury instruction. Proximate cause has no application to criminal law. State v. King, 367 N.W.2d 599, 602 (Minn.Ct.App.1985). Instruction on proximate cause could only serve to confuse the jury into believing that Quarnstrom's negligence could have caused the accident whereas proximate cause here is relevant only to Iten's own negligence. The trial court's refusal of additional instructions on causation was not an abuse of discretion.

DECISION

... Neither evidence concerning the victim's seatbelt nor jury instructions on proximate cause are relevant to this criminal prosecution.

Affirmed.[138]

Regina v. Benge and Another

Maidstone Crown Court, Kent Summer Assizes, 1865.
4 F. & F. 504, 176 Eng.Rep. 665.

[Benge and Gallimore were indicted for manslaughter, but it was admitted that there was no case against Gallimore and the case proceeded only against Benge. He was foreman of a crew employed to repair rails on a certain portion of the track. He had a book telling exactly when trains were due but looked at the wrong date and as a result ordered certain rails removed from a bridge shortly before a train was due. As was usual he sent

---

138. [Added by the Compiler.] Three men engaged in target practice under circumstances of extreme negligence. Using a rifle that was sighted for 900 yards and would probably be fatal at a mile, they fired across three highways and intervening territory, with no precautions. One shot killed a boy who was playing in his garden. There was no evidence as to which one fired the fatal shot. All three were convicted of manslaughter. The court took the position, in substance, that as they had joined in a criminally-negligent enterprise, each shot was, in legal effect, the shot of all. Regina v. Salmon, 14 Cox C.C. (1880).

N.B. Had careful shooting at the target been safe, and only the fatal shot fired with criminal negligence, it would not have imputed to the others.

Victim's failure to wear seatbelt is irrelevant to a prosecution for vehicular manslaughter. People v. Wattier, 51 Cal.App.4th 948, 59 Cal.Rptr.2d 483 (1996).

Absence of an attenuator truck to protect construction workers was not an intervening cause or superseding cause of death. People v. Autry, 37 Cal.App.4th 351, 43 Cal.Rptr.2d 135 (1995).

one of the crew with a flag to signal if any train should approach while the rails were not in place. This man was to go at least 1000 yards in the direction from which a train would come, but he went only 540 yards. The flag signal could be seen by the engineer at a distance of 500 yards or more but he was inattentive and did not see it until abreast of the flagman. He did all he could to stop the train but it was then too late and a wreck resulted in which many lives were lost. There was evidence showing that the train could easily have been stopped within 1000 yards at any speed.]

■ PIGOTT, B., said, that assuming culpable negligence on the part of the prisoner which materially contributed to the accident, it would not be material that others also by their negligence contributed to cause it. Therefore he must leave it to the jury whether there was negligence of the prisoner which had been the substantial cause of the accident. In summing up the case to the jury, he said, their verdict must depend upon whether the death was mainly caused by the culpable negligence of the prisoner. Was the accident caused by the taking up of the rails at a time when an express train was about to arrive, was that the act of the prisoner, and was it owing to culpable negligence on his part? ... Now, here the primary cause was certainly the taking up of the rails at a time when the train was about to arrive, and when it would be impossible to replace them in time to avoid the accident. And this the prisoner admitted was owing to his own mistake. Was that mistake culpable negligence, and did it mainly or substantially cause the accident? Then as to its being the main cause of the accident, it is true that the company had provided other precautions to avoid any impending catastrophe, and that these were not observed upon this particular occasion; but was it not owing to the prisoner's culpable negligence that the accident was impending, and if so, did his negligence the less cause it, because if other persons had not been negligent it might possibly have been avoided?[139]

Verdict—Guilty.

---

139. **D** shot **X** who was taken to a hospital promptly and in time to have been saved by proper surgical treatment. But he died from hemorrhage because the surgeon neglected for more than ten hours to control the bleeding. A conviction of manslaughter was affirmed on the ground that the surgeon's gross neglect was not superseding. "The factual situation is in legal effect the same, whether the victim bleeds to death because surgical attention is not available, or because, although available, it is delayed by reason of the surgeon's gross neglect or incompetence." People v. McGee, 31 Cal.2d 229, 243, 187 P.2d 706, 715 (1947).

"The fact that a third person might have, but did not, rescue the victims cannot lessen defendant's responsibility for the consequences of his acts." People v. Nichols, 3 Cal.3d 150, 89 Cal.Rptr. 721, 725, 474 P.2d 673, 677 (1970).

If death would not have resulted had it not been for the gross negligence of the attendant physician, the one who caused the original injury cannot be said to have caused the death. Gross negligence is abnormal human conduct which is not foreseeable, and is superseding. People v. Calvaresi, 188 Colo. 277, 534 P.2d 316 (1975). *See also* People v. Saavedra–Rodriguez, 971 P.2d 223 (Colo.1998).

Drinking of liquor by a victim killed in vehicular collision is only contributory negligence and will not defeat the causation from defendant's gross negligence. Wilson v. State, 74 Md.App. 204, 536 A.2d 1192 (1988).

Failure to properly transport victim to the hospital did not relieve defendant for death of victim who could only be saved from gunshot wound by immediate surgery. People v. Weir, 112 A.D.2d 594, 492 N.Y.S.2d 119 (1985).

Lewis v. State

Court of Criminal Appeals of Alabama, 1985.
474 So.2d 766.

■ TYSON, JUDGE.

Alvin Ronald Lewis was indicted for murder in violation of § 13A–6–2, Code of Alabama 1975. At the conclusion of the State's evidence, the trial judge granted the appellant's motion for judgment of acquittal as to the offenses of murder and manslaughter. The case was then submitted to the jury on the charge of criminally negligent homicide. The jury found the appellant "guilty" and he was sentenced to twelve months' imprisonment in the county jail.

Linda Sanders testified that on May 30, 1983, she and her four children lived in London Village Mobile Home Park. Her son, Damon Sanders, is the victim in this case and was fifteen years old at the time of his death. Sanders said her son knew the appellant because he lived in London Village with one of her son's friends, Paul Schmuch.

Jo Ann Kennedy stated that, on the day in question, she lived at Spring Lake Manor Apartments and was dating the appellant....

Around 8:00 p.m., the appellant and the victim came over to her apartment in the appellant's truck. The appellant told Kennedy that he and the victim had been playing Russian Roulette. He demonstrated to her how they were playing this infamous "game." The appellant said that the victim was upset because he had broken up with his girl friend.

Kennedy and the appellant then spoke on the phone about an hour later. The appellant again said something about playing Russian Roulette. She heard a clicking noise over the phone. The appellant told her there was only one bullet and it wasn't in the gun. Kennedy told the appellant to put the gun up. The conversation ended at this point because Kennedy went to the store.

When Kennedy returned from the store around 9:30, she called the appellant. The two talked for a while and the appellant changed phones and went into the bedroom. A few minutes later the appellant said, "I've got to go, I've got to go, I've got to go, something's happened." (R. 33)....

A while later, the appellant came to her apartment and she would not let him in. The appellant told her that the victim "had blew his brains out" (R. 30). She told him to call an ambulance and the appellant left.

Joyce Harper stated that on May 30, 1983, she also lived in London Village. At approximately 10:00 on this night, she and her husband were walking by Paul Schmuch's trailer. Harper looked in and saw the victim sitting on the sofa holding a gun in his hand. She saw the victim spin the chamber and heard a "whirr." When Harper and her husband were past Schmuch's trailer, Harper thought she heard a shot. Her husband told her it was a firecracker.

. . .

Nelson Byess, an investigator with the Trussville Police Department, testified that, when he arrived at Schmuch's trailer on the night in question, he saw a body lying in the back yard. The victim had suffered a gunshot wound to the temple and there was a gun in his hand. Byess then went into the living room and gave the appellant his *Miranda* rights. The appellant then waived those rights and made a statement. The following excerpt from the transcript is the statement that the appellant gave that night:

"A 'Okay. Approximately 1:30 a.m., May 30th, Alvin Ronald Lewis made out the following statement at his residence, 1917 London Village Drive in Birmingham. Or Birmingham mailing route. I had been riding my bike, shooting my gun and drinking beer with Damon. Went by Jo Ann's house and came back to the trailer. I put the gun back into Paul's closet and was talking to Jo Ann on the phone in my bedroom. I heard a crack noise and walked into the living room.' I said 'I have got to go, something terrible has happened.' I hung up, I went to pieces. Damon was sitting on the couch with his head slumped against his chest, blood was running down his face into his shirt. His arms was across his lap, he was holding the gun. I took the gun and laid it on the table, then I got a towel and wrapped it around his head...."

Jerome Lift, the Assistant Coronor Medical Examiner for Jefferson County, testified that he performed an autopsy on the victim. His examination revealed that the victim had sustained a gunshot wound to the right side of the head at the level of his ear. Due to the disposition of gunpowder particles and smoke stain, he concluded that the gun was in close contact to the victim's head when it was fired. Lift stated that the cause of death was a gunshot wound to the head but he was unable to determine the manner of death. He testified that the wound was absolutely characteristic of a self-inflicted wound and that it was not consistent with any homicide wound he had ever seen.

. . .

The appellant urges this court to reverse his conviction on the ground that his motion for judgment of acquittal should have been granted because there was not sufficient evidence presented at trial to sustain his conviction of criminally negligent homicide. He further contends that his acts were not the proximate cause of the victim's death. Since these issues are so closely related, we will consider them together.

. . .

The relevant evidence to this problem can be stated briefly. The victim had been present when the appellant and his brother played Russian Roulette with a loaded gun some time during the week prior to the victim's death. The appellant and the victim had played Russian Roulette on the day of the victim's death. It is unclear whether the gun was loaded or not during this time but there was some evidence that it was not. After the two finished playing the game, the appellant put the gun away. Later, the victim was seen alone holding a gun and spinning the chamber. A few minutes later, a noise which sounded like a gunshot was heard. At approximately the same time, the appellant ended a phone conversation because "something's happened." The coroner testified that the victim's wound was typical of a self-inflicted gunshot wound.

The evidence is clear that the deceased either committed suicide or fell victim to an unfortunate misadventure. Therefore, this Court is faced with a different question. "When may one human being be held criminally liable for the self-destruction of another?" Brenner, Undue Influence in the Criminal Law: A Proposed Analysis of the Criminal Offense of "Causing Suicide" 47 Albany L.Rev. 62, 63 (1982). "The problem lies, of course, in determining when, and if, an accused did in fact cause his alleged victim to commit suicide. This difficult determination requires proof that the suicide was caused by the accused's actions and was not the result of the victim's own free will." *Brenner, supra* at 63.

In Alabama, "[a] person is criminally liable if the result would not have occurred but for his conduct, operating either alone or concurrently with another cause, unless the concurrent cause was sufficient to produce the result and the conduct of the actor clearly insufficient." Ala.Code, § 13A–2–5(a) (1975).

Clearly, the problem encountered in this case is causation. The State contends that the appellant's acts were the proximate cause and the cause in fact of the victim's death. The basis of the State's contention is that the victim would not have killed himself playing Russian Roulette if the appellant had not "directed, instructed and influenced" him to play the game and that the appellant should have been aware of the risk that the victim might be killed playing Russian Roulette by himself when he directed, instructed and influenced the victim to play the game.

If the victim had shot himself while he and the appellant were playing Russian Roulette, or if the appellant was present when the victim was playing the game by himself, the appellant's conduct of influencing the victim to play would have been the cause-in-fact and the proximate cause of the victim's death. However, the key is the appellant's presence at the time the victim shot himself. However, the evidence in the case at bar indicates the appellant was not present when the victim shot himself.

It also seems clear that the appellant would be responsible for the victim's death if he had left the room while the victim was still playing the game because he should have perceived the result. But, the evidence reveals that the appellant had put the gun away after they finished playing the "game."

A determination as to whether the conduct of a person caused the suicide of another must necessarily include an examination of the victim's free will. Cases have consistently held that the "free will of the victim is seen as an intervening cause which ... breaks the chain of causation." Therefore, the crux of this issue is whether the victim exercised his own free will when he got the gun, loaded it and shot himself. We hold that the victim's conduct was a supervening, intervening cause sufficient to break the chain of causation.

Even though the victim might never have shot himself in this manner if the appellant had not taught him to play Russian Roulette, we cannot say that the appellant should have perceived the risk that the victim would play the game by himself or that he intended for him to do this.

This case presents a tragic situation and we do not condone the appellant's conduct, in any manner. However, the causal link between the appellant's conduct and the victim's death was severed when the victim exercised his own free will.

. . .

Reversed and Rendered.

Green v. State

Supreme Court of Georgia, 1996.
266 Ga. 758, 470 S.E.2d 884.

■ FLETCHER, PRESIDING JUSTICE.

Bernard William Green was convicted of felony murder in the death of his wife Cynthia Grant, who died of a stress ulcer in the hospital a week after Green stabbed her. There was conflicting expert testimony at trial concerning whether the stab wound or the drug Toradol caused the stress ulcer. Green alleges that his trial counsel was ineffective in failing to request the proper charge on secondary causation of death and to object to improper charges. Since the jury charge as a whole was sufficient, we affirm.

Grant's three teenage children testified at trial that Green and their mother were fussing one Friday night when the oldest daughter hit the defendant on the head with a mop, Grant threw an empty barbecue bottle at him, and Green stabbed Grant in the back with a knife. While lying on a bed waiting for police, Grant told a neighbor, "Bernard hurt me bad. He stabbed me in front of my two babies." She died suddenly a week later after being approved for release from the hospital. The state's pathologist testified that there was a direct relationship between the stabbing and its treatment and Grant's death from the bleeding ulcer. He stated that the stab wound caused the stress and that Grant would not have been given the pain killer Toradol if she had not been stabbed. Green's defense was that he did not stab his wife and the stab wound did not cause her death. His expert testified that the victim died from an ulcer inspired by Toradol.

In considering whether there was sufficient evidence to convict, we review the evidence in the light most favorable to the jury's determination of guilt. Applying this standard, we conclude that a rational trier of fact could have found Green guilty of felony murder.

. . .

The trial court gave the pattern charge on causation, instructing the jury that an unlawful injury may be the cause of death if "the injury directly and materially contributed to the happening of a secondary or consequential cause of death." After the jury asked a question about drugs as a secondary factor in the victim's death, the trial court repeated the pattern charge. It later responded further by instructing the jury: "if some intervening cause not set in motion by said wound caused the death of the deceased, then the defendant would not be criminally [liable] for the death."

These charges were a correct statement of the law, consistent with each other, and sufficient without any additional charge on causation. Although the experts at trial disputed the primary cause of death, they agreed that stress caused the ulcer. The evidence at trial was sufficient for the jury to find that Green stabbed his wife, thus setting in motion a series of events that resulted in her death, and that the hospital's treatment of her wound was a secondary, rather than intervening, cause of death.

Therefore, we conclude that the trial court did not err in its charges on felony murder, voluntary manslaughter, and causation. Since the jury charge taken as a whole was sufficient, we hold that Green has failed to show that his trial counsel's failure to object or request certain charges fell outside the range of reasonable professional conduct.

Judgment affirmed.

All the Justices concur.[140]

MODEL PENAL CODE[141]

Section 2.03 Causal Relationship Between Conduct and Result; Divergence Between Result Designed or Contemplated and Actual Result or Between Probable and Actual Result.

(1) Conduct is the cause of a result when:

(a) it is an antecedent but for which the result in question would not have occurred; and

(b) the relationship between the conduct and result satisfies any additional causal requirements imposed by the Code or by the law defining the offense.

(2) When purposely or knowingly causing a particular result is an element of an offense, the element is not established if the actual result is not within the purpose or the contemplation of the actor unless:

(a) the actual result differs from the designed or contemplated, as the case may be, only in the respect that a different person or different property is injured or affected or that the injury or harm designed or contemplated would have been more serious or more extensive than that caused; or

(b) the actual result involves the same kind of injury or harm as that designed or contemplated and is not too remote or accidental in its occurrence to have a [just] bearing on the actor's liability or on the gravity of his offense.

(3) When recklessly or negligently causing a particular result is an element of an offense, the element is not established if the actual result is not within the risk

---

140. Beating victim's fatal staph infection was not an extraordinary intervening cause to preclude defendant's murder conviction where the staph infection developed after surgery required because of a beating. Gibson v. State, 515 N.E.2d 492 (Ind.1987).

A felony-murder conviction was allowed where an 85–year-old rape victim died five weeks after assault of asphyxiation while being fed by staff at a nursing home. The need for feeding was attributable to defendant's criminal acts. People v. Brackett, 117 Ill.2d 170, 109 Ill.Dec. 809, 510 N.E.2d 877 (1987).

The claim that a person without defendant's medical history might not have died from the trauma inflicted by the defendant is no basis for a defense. People v. Wilks, 124 Ill.Dec. 709, 175 Ill.App.3d 68, 529 N.E.2d 690 (1988).

141. See Causation in the Model Penal Code, 78 Col.L.Rev. 1249 (1978).

of which the actor is aware or, in the case of negligence, of which he should be aware unless:

(a) the actual result differs from the probable result only in the respect that a different person or different property is injured or affected or that the probable injury or harm would have been more serious or more extensive than that caused; or

(b) the actual result involves the same kind of injury or harm as the probable result and is not too remote or accidental in its occurrence to have a [just] bearing on the actor's liability or on the gravity of his offense.

(4) When causing a particular result is a material element of an offense for which absolute liability is imposed by law, the element is not established unless the actual result is a probable consequence of the actor's conduct.[143]

---

143. Copyright © 1962 by the American Law Institute. Reprinted with the permission of the American Law Institute.

CHAPTER 7

RESPONSIBILITY: IN GENERAL

SECTION 1. MENS REA

Responsibility means answerability or accountability. It is used in the criminal law in the sense of "criminal responsibility" and hence means answerability to the criminal law. No one is answerable to the criminal law for consequences not legally imputable to him. The present problem does not arise except in connection with consequences attributable to the one accused within the rules of imputability. On the other hand, consequences properly imputable to a certain person may be very harmful and yet not under such circumstances as to require him to answer criminally for what he has done. Whether they do or do not require him so to answer presents the problem of "responsibility."

Crime is frequently said to require both act and intent. As so used the word "intent" has quite a different meaning than "intention." An effort to avoid this variant use of the word has led to this suggestion: For guilt of crime there must be the union or joint operation of act and intent, or criminal negligence. This is not an improvement. It implies the use of "intent" in the strict sense of "intention," and with this limitation the mere addition of "criminal negligence" is inadequate to give full scope to the mental element involved in crime. Either form of expression, however, emphasizes the existence of the mental element. Leaving aside for the moment (1) the so-called "civil offenses" which are beyond the periphery of true crime, (2) the possibility of change by statute, and (3) difficulties of interpretation in certain situations, we find blameworthiness essential to criminal guilt.

The phrase "criminal intent" often has been used to express this requirement of blameworthiness. At other times "general criminal intent" has been employed to emphasize that the mental element so designated is not limited to actual intention.[1] Hence it is necessary to draw a very sharp line between actual intent (in the strict sense) and the various states of mind included within the very loose label of "general criminal intent." The term "criminal intent" is collective of various states of mind.

The requirement of blameworthiness frequently has been couched in law Latin: "*Actus non facit reum, nisi mens sit rea.*" And it has been common to pick two words from this sentence and substitute "*mens rea*" for "guilty mind" or "mind at fault." Hence *mens rea* is essential to

---

1. "Criminal intent" in its narrow and proper sense is "nothing more than the intentional doing of 'that which the law declares to be a crime,' ..." People v. Zerillo, 36 Cal.2d 222, 232, 223 P.2d 223, 230 (1950). "It is the criminal mind and purpose going with the act which distinguishes a criminal trespass from a mere civil injury." State v. Smith, 135 Mont. 18, 334 P.2d 1099, 1102 (1959).

criminal guilt (with the qualifications mentioned above as to blameworthiness, which will receive attention under the head of "strict liability" and will be assumed here without further repetition).

Stated in other words, every crime is made up of two constituent parts: (1) the physical part and (2) the mental part. These may be described quite adequately as "the physical part of the crime" and "the mental part of the crime." Shorter labels are needed, however, for discussion purposes. The terms "guilty deed" and "guilty mind" are not entirely satisfactory because the former may be thought to be sufficient for punishment, whereas the union of both parts is required for conviction of crime. Hence it may be well to substitute Latin phrases which have the same meaning. These phrases are *actus reus* and *mens rea*.

If we can prove the existence of the physical part of the crime charged, and that this happening is attributable to the defendant within the legal rules of imputability, we have established his *actus reus*. And if we can prove that in doing what he did the defendant's state of mind was one which satisfies the requirements of the mental element of the crime charged we have established his *mens rea*. Neither one alone is sufficient for conviction; it is the combination of the two which constitutes criminal guilt.

The general mens rea. The mental element of crime is sometimes regarded as a state of mind common to all offenses, and sufficient for some, although an additional mental element may be required for others. Stated as a formula: "State-of-mind-X is common to all crimes and is sufficient for conviction unless the particular offense requires some additional mental element such as state-of-mind-Y or state-of-mind-Z."

Such a formula may have some value if care is taken to limit its application rather narrowly. A person may be so young that nothing can exist in his mind which will meet the juridical requirement of *mens rea;* hence it may be said that for *mens rea* the mind of the person must not be too young. Again, for *mens rea* the mental faculties must not be too greatly disturbed by mental disease; and under many circumstances a sane mind must not be too greatly diverted by a misunderstanding of the relevant facts or constrained by certain types of compulsion. Without going further into detail it is sufficient to point out the need of excluding every mental pattern which contains any factor sufficient in law to exculpate one who has done the particular deed in question. If every such factor is excluded and there is present an intent to do the deed which constitutes the *actus reus* of a certain offense, the result may be said to be the "general *mens rea.*" It is necessary to add, however, that for certain crimes it is possible to substitute some other mental factor (such as criminal negligence) for the actual intent to do the *actus reus*.

In brief, while *mens rea* has certain factors which remain constant, these have to do with the general outlines of the mental pattern rather than with the minute details. For *mens rea:* (1) on the negative side there must not be found any factor which is sufficient for exculpation; (2) on the positive side there must be found an intent to do the deed which constitutes the *actus reus* of the offense charged (or some other mental element recognized as a substitute as, for example, criminal negligence in prosecutions for certain crimes). This is the so-called "general *mens rea*" or "general criminal intent" which is common to all true crime. It is indispensable, and is sufficient for guilt of some offenses although some additional mental element is required for others.

The *actus reus* may be the same in two crimes as in murder and manslaughter. For the most part, however, it differs from crime to crime. In burglary the *actus reus* is the nocturnal breaking into the dwelling house of another; in murder it is homicide; in battery it is the unlawful application of force to the person of another. The other constituent part also differs from crime to crime. In common-law burglary the *mens rea* is the intent to commit a felony or later theft; in murder it is malice aforethought; in battery no more is needed than the so-called "general criminal intent" which in a particular case may be criminal negligence. Hence in considering whether or not the actual *mens rea* has been established in a particular case, it is necessary to direct attention, not only to the state of mind with which the defendant acted, but also to the particular offense with which he is charged.

The cases in this section establish two important premises. First, courts presume the legislature intended to require some culpable mental state before imposing criminal liability. Second, establishing the particular mental state the legislature intended to demand poses difficult and pervasive problems of statutory interpretation.

Morissette v. United States

Supreme Court of the United States, 1952.
342 U.S. 246, 72 S.Ct. 240, 96 L.Ed. 288.

■ MR. JUSTICE JACKSON delivered the opinion of the Court.

This would have remained a profoundly insignificant case to all except its immediate parties had it not been so tried and submitted to the jury as to raise questions both fundamental and far-reaching in federal criminal law, for which reason we granted certiorari.

On a large tract of uninhabited and untilled land in a wooded and sparsely populated area of Michigan, the Government established a practice bombing range over which the Air Force dropped simulated bombs at ground targets. These bombs consisted of a metal cylinder about forty inches long and eight inches across, filled with sand and enough black powder to cause a smoke puff by which the strike could be located. At various places about the range signs read "Danger—Keep Out—Bombing Range." Nevertheless, the range was known as good deer country and was extensively hunted.

Spent bomb casings were cleared from the targets and thrown into piles "so that they will be out of the way." They were not sacked or piled in any order but were dumped in heaps, some of which had been accumulating for four years or upwards, were exposed to the weather and rusting away.

Morissette, in December of 1948, went hunting in this area but did not get a deer. He thought to meet expenses of the trip by salvaging some of these casings. He loaded three tons of them on his truck and took them to a nearby farm, where they were flattened by driving a tractor over them. After expending this labor and trucking them to market in Flint, he realized $84.

Morissette, by occupation, is a fruit stand operator in summer and a trucker and scrap iron collector in winter. An honorably discharged veteran of World War II, he enjoys a good name among his neighbors and has had no blemish on his record more disreputable than a conviction for reckless driving.

The loading, crushing and transporting of these casings were all in broad daylight, in full view of passers-by, without the slightest effort at concealment. When an investigation was started, Morissette voluntarily, promptly and candidly told the whole story to the authorities, saying that he had no intention of stealing but thought the property was abandoned, unwanted and considered of no value to the Government. He was indicted, however, on the charge that he "did unlawfully, wilfully and knowingly steal and convert" property of the United States of the value of $84, in violation of 18 U.S.C. § 641, 18 U.S.C.A. § 641, which provides that "whoever embezzles, steals, purloins, or knowingly converts" government property is punishable by fine and imprisonment.[2] Morissette was convicted and sentenced to imprisonment for two months or to pay a fine of $200. The Court of Appeals affirmed, one judge dissenting.

On his trial, Morissette, as he had at all times told investigating officers, testified that from appearances he believed the casings were cast-off and abandoned, that he did not intend to steal the property, and took it with no wrongful or criminal intent. The trial court, however, was unimpressed, and ruled: "[H]e took it because he thought it was abandoned and he knew he was on government property. * * * That is no defense. * * * I don't think anybody can have the defense they thought the property was abandoned on another man's piece of property." The court stated: "I will not permit you to show this man thought it was abandoned. * * * I hold in this case that there is no question of abandoned property." The court refused to submit or to allow counsel to argue to the jury whether Morissette acted with innocent intention. It charged: "And I instruct you that if you believe the testimony of the government in this case, he intended to take it. * * * He had no right to take this property. * * * [A]nd it is no defense to claim that it was abandoned, because it was on private property. * * * And I instruct you to this effect: That if this young man took this property (and he says he did), without any permission (he says he did), that was on the property of the United States Government (he says it was), that it was of the value of one cent or more (and evidently it

---

2. 18 U.S.C. § 641, 18 U.S.C.A. § 641, so far as pertinent, reads:

"Whoever embezzles, steals, purloins, or knowingly converts to his use or the use of another, or without authority, sells, conveys or disposes of any record, voucher, money, or thing of value of the United States or of any department or agency thereof, or any property made or being made under contract for the United States or any department or agency thereof;

"Shall be fined not more than $10,000 or imprisoned not more than ten years, or both; but if the value of such property does not exceed the sum of $100, he shall be fined not more than $1,000 or imprisoned not more than one year, or both."

was), that he is guilty of the offense charged here. If you believe the government, he is guilty. * * * The question on intent is whether or not he intended to take the property. He says he did. Therefore, if you believe either side, he is guilty." Petitioner's counsel contended, "But the taking must have been with a felonious intent." The court ruled, however: "That is presumed by his own act."

The Court of Appeals suggested that "greater restraint in expression should have been exercised", but affirmed the conviction because, "As we have interpreted the statute, appellant was guilty of its violation beyond a shadow of doubt, as evidenced even by his own admissions." Its construction of the statute is that it creates several separate and distinct offenses, one being knowing conversion of government property. The court ruled that this particular offense requires no element of criminal intent. This conclusion was thought to be required by the failure of Congress to express such a requisite and this Court's decisions in United States v. Behrman, 258 U.S. 280, 42 S.Ct. 303, 66 L.Ed. 619, and United States v. Balint, 258 U.S. 250, 42 S.Ct. 301, 66 L.Ed. 604.

I.

In those cases this Court did construe mere omission from a criminal enactment of any mention of criminal intent as dispensing with it. If they be deemed precedents for principles of construction generally applicable to federal penal statutes, they authorize this conviction. Indeed, such adoption of the literal reasoning announced in those cases would do this and more— it would sweep out of all federal crimes, except when expressly preserved, the ancient requirement of a culpable state of mind. We think a resume of their historical background is convincing that an effect has been ascribed to them more comprehensive than was contemplated and one inconsistent with our philosophy of criminal law.

The contention that an injury can amount to a crime only when inflicted by intention is no provincial or transient notion. It is as universal and persistent in mature systems of law as belief in freedom of the human will and a consequent ability and duty of the normal individual to choose between good and evil.[3] A relation between some mental element and punishment for a harmful act is almost as instinctive as the child's familiar exculpatory "But I didn't mean to," and has afforded the rational basis for a tardy and unfinished substitution of deterrence and reformation in place of retaliation and vengeance as the motivation for public prosecution. Unqualified acceptance of this doctrine by English common law in the Eighteenth Century was indicated by Blackstone's sweeping statement that to constitute any crime there must first be a "vicious will."[4] Common-law commentators of the Nineteenth Century early pronounced the same

---

3. For a brief history and philosophy of this concept in Biblical, Greek, Roman, Continental and Anglo–American law see Radin, Intent, Criminal, 8 Encyc.Soc.Sci. 126. For more extensive treatment of the development in English Law, see 2 Pollock and Maitland, History of English Law, 448–511. "Historically, our substantive criminal law is based upon a theory of punishing the vicious will. It postulates a free agent confronted with a choice between doing right and doing wrong and choosing freely to do wrong." Pound, Introduction to Sayre, Cases on Criminal Law (1927).

4. 4 Bl.Comm. 21.

principle,[5] although a few exceptions not relevant to our present problem came to be recognized.[6]

Crime, as a compound concept, generally constituted only from concurrence of an evil-meaning mind with an evil-doing hand, was congenial to an intense individualism and took deep and early root in American soil.[7] As the state codified the common law of crimes, even if their enactments were silent on the subject, their courts assumed that the omission did not signify disapproval of the principle but merely recognized that intent was so inherent in the idea of the offense that it required no statutory affirmation. Courts, with little hesitation or division, found an implication of the requirement as to offenses that were taken over from the common law. The unanimity with which they have adhered to the central thought that wrongdoing must be conscious to be criminal is emphasized by the variety, disparity and confusion of their definitions of the requisite but elusive mental element. However, courts of various jurisdictions, and for the purposes of different offenses, have devised working formulae, if not scientific ones, for the instruction of juries around such terms as "felonious intent," "criminal intent," "malice aforethought," "guilty knowledge," "fraudulent intent," "wilfulness," "scienter," to denote guilty knowledge, or "mens rea," to signify an evil purpose or mental culpability. By use or combination of these various tokens, they have sought to protect those who were not blameworthy in mind from conviction of infamous common-law crimes.

However, the Balint and Behrman offenses belong to a category of another character, with very different antecedents and origins. The crimes there involved depend on no mental element but consist only of forbidden acts or omissions. This, while not expressed by the Court, is made clear from examination of a century-old but accelerating tendency, discernible both here and in England, to call into existence new duties and crimes which disregard any ingredient of intent. The industrial revolution multiplied the number of workmen exposed to injury from increasingly powerful and complex mechanisms, driven by freshly discovered sources of energy, requiring higher precautions by employers. Traffic of velocities, volumes and varieties unheard of came to subject the wayfarer to intolerable casualty risks if owners and drivers were not to observe new cares and uniformities of conduct. Congestion of cities and crowding of quarters

---

5. Examples of these texts and their alterations in successive editions in consequence of evolution in the law of "public welfare offenses," as hereinafter recited, are traced in Sayre, Public Welfare Offenses, 33 Col.L.Rev. 55, 66.

6. Exceptions came to include sex offenses, such as rape, in which the victim's actual age was determinative despite defendant's reasonable belief that the girl had reached age of consent. Absence of intent also involves such considerations as lack of understanding because of insanity, subnormal mentality, or infancy, lack of volition due to some actual compulsion, or that inferred from doctrines of coverture. Most extensive inroads upon the requirement of intention, however, are offenses of negligence, such as involuntary manslaughter or criminal negligence and the whole range of crimes arising from omission of duty. Cf. Commonwealth v. Welansky, 1944, 316 Mass. 383, 55 N.E.2d 902.

7. Holmes, The Common Law, considers intent in the chapter on The Criminal Law, and earlier makes the pithy observation: "Even a dog distinguishes between being stumbled over and being kicked." P. 3. Radin, Intent, Criminal, 8 Encyc.Soc.Sci. 126, 127, points out that in American law "mens rea is not so readily constituted from any wrongful act" as elsewhere.

called for health and welfare regulations undreamed of in simpler times. Wide distribution of goods became an instrument of wide distribution of harm when those who dispersed food, drink, drugs, and even securities, did not comply with reasonable standards of quality, integrity, disclosure and care. Such dangers have engendered increasingly numerous and detailed regulations which heighten the duties of those in control of particular industries, trades, properties or activities that affect public health, safety or welfare.

While many of these duties are sanctioned by a more strict civil liability, lawmakers, whether wisely or not, have sought to make such regulations more effective by invoking criminal sanctions to be applied by the familiar technique of criminal prosecutions and convictions. This has confronted the courts with a multitude of prosecutions, based on statutes or administrative regulations, for what have been aptly called "public welfare offenses." These cases do not fit neatly into any of such accepted classifications of common-law offenses, such as those against the state, the person, property, or public morals. Many of these offenses are not in the nature of positive aggressions or invasions, with which the common law so often dealt, but are in the nature of neglect where the law requires care, or inaction where it imposes a duty. Many violations of such regulations result in no direct or immediate injury to person or property but merely create the danger or probability of it which the law seeks to minimize. While such offenses do not threaten the security of the state in the manner of treason, they may be regarded as offenses against its authority, for their occurrence impairs the efficiency of controls deemed essential to the social order as presently constituted. In this respect, whatever the intent of the violator, the injury is the same, and the consequences are injurious or not according to fortuity. Hence, legislation applicable to such offenses, as a matter of policy, does not specify intent as a necessary element. The accused, if he does not will the violation, usually is in a position to prevent it with no more care than society might reasonably expect and no more exertion than it might reasonably exact from one who assumed his responsibilities. Also, penalties commonly are relatively small, and conviction does not grave damage to an offender's reputation. Under such considerations, courts have turned to construing statutes and regulations which make no mention of intent as dispensing with it and holding that the guilty act alone makes out the crime. This has not, however, been without expressions of misgiving.

The pilot of the movement in this country appears to be a holding that a tavernkeeper could be convicted for selling liquor to an habitual drunkard even if he did not know the buyer to be such. Barnes v. State, 1849, 19 Conn. 398. Later came Massachusetts holdings that convictions for selling adulterated milk in violation of statutes forbidding such sales require no allegation or proof that defendant knew of the adulteration. Commonwealth v. Farren, 1864, 9 Allen 489; Commonwealth v. Nichols, 1865, 10 Allen 199; Commonwealth v. Waite, 1865, 11 Allen 264. Departures from the common-law tradition, mainly of these general classes, were reviewed and their rationale appraised by Chief Justice Cooley, as follows: "I agree that as a rule there can be no crime without a criminal intent, but this is not by any means a universal rule. * * * Many statutes which are in the nature of police regulations, as this is, impose criminal penalties irrespective of any intent to violate them, the purpose being to require a degree of diligence for the protection of the public which shall render violation impossible." People v. Roby, 1884, 52 Mich. 577, 579, 18 N.W. 365, 366.

After the turn of the Century, a new use for crimes without intent appeared when New York enacted numerous and novel regulations of tenement houses, sanctioned by money penalties. Landlords contended that a guilty intent was essential to establish a violation. Judge Cardozo wrote the answer: "The defendant asks us to test the meaning of this statute by standards applicable to statutes that govern infamous crimes. The analogy, however, is deceptive. The element of conscious wrongdoing, the guilty mind accompanying the guilty act, is associated with the concept of crimes that are punished as infamous. * * * Even there it is not an invariable element. * * * But in the prosecution of minor offenses there is a wider range of practice and of power. Prosecutions for petty penalties have always constituted in our law a class by themselves. * * * That is true, though the prosecution is criminal in form." Tenement House Department of City of New York v. McDevitt, 1915, 215 N.Y. 160, 168, 109 N.E. 88, 90.

Soon, employers advanced the same contention as to violations of regulations prescribed by a new labor law. Judge Cardozo, again for the court, pointed out, as a basis for penalizing violations whether intentional or not, that they were punishable only by fine "moderate in amount", but cautiously added that in sustaining the power so to fine unintended violations "we are not to be understood as sustaining to a like length the power to imprison. We leave that question open." People ex rel. Price v. Sheffield Farms–Slawson–Decker Co., 1918, 225 N.Y. 25, 32–33, 121 N.E. 474, 476, 477.

Thus, for diverse but reconcilable reasons, state courts converged on the same result, discontinuing inquiry into intent in a limited class of offenses against such statutory regulations.

Before long, similar questions growing out of federal legislation reached this Court. Its judgments were in harmony with this consensus of state judicial opinion, the existence of which may have led the Court to overlook the need for full exposition of their rationale in the context of federal law. In overruling a contention that there can be no conviction on an indictment which makes no charge of criminal intent but alleges only making of a sale of a narcotic forbidden by law, Chief Justice Taft, wrote: "While the general rule at common law was that the scienter was a necessary element in the indictment and proof of every crime, and this was followed in regard to statutory crimes even where the statutory definition did not in terms include it * * *, there has been a modification of this view in respect to prosecutions under statutes the purpose of which would be obstructed by such a requirement. It is a question of legislative intent to be construed by the court. * * * "United States v. Balint, *supra*, 258 U.S. 251–252, 42 S.Ct. 302.

He referred, however, to "regulatory measures in the exercise of what is called the police power where the emphasis of the statute is evidently upon achievement of some social betterment rather than the punishment of the crimes as in cases of mala in se," and drew his citation of supporting authority chiefly from state court cases dealing with regulatory offenses. Id., 258 U.S. at page 252, 42 S.Ct. at page 302.

On the same day, the Court determined that an offense under the Narcotic Drug Act does not require intent, saying, "If the offense be a statutory one, and intent or knowledge is not made an element of it, the indictment need not charge such knowledge or intent." United States v. Behrman, *supra*, 258 U.S. at page 288, 42 S.Ct. at page 304.

Of course, the purpose of every statute would be "obstructed" by requiring a finding of intent, if we assume that it had a purpose to convict without it. Therefore, the obstruction rationale does not help us to learn the purpose of the omission by Congress. And since no federal crime can exist except by force of statute, the reasoning of the Behrman opinion, if read literally, would work far-reaching changes in the composition of all federal crimes. Had such a result been contemplated, it could hardly have escaped mention. . . .

It was not until recently that the Court took occasion more explicitly to relate abandonment of the ingredient of intent, not merely with considerations of expediency in obtaining convictions, nor with the malum prohibitum classification of the crime, but with the peculiar nature and quality of the offense. We referred to " * * * a now familiar type of legislation whereby penalties serve as effective means of regulation", and continued, "such legislation dispenses with the conventional requirement for criminal conduct—awareness of some wrongdoing. In the interest of the larger good it puts the burden of acting at hazard upon a person otherwise innocent but standing in responsible relation to a public danger." But we warned: "Hardship there doubtless may be under a statute which thus penalizes the transaction though consciousness of wrongdoing be totally wanting."

Neither this Court nor, so far as we are aware, any other has undertaken to delineate a precise line or set forth comprehensive criteria for distinguishing between crimes that require a mental element and crimes that do not. We attempt no closed definition, for the law on the subject is neither settled nor static. The conclusion reached in the Balint and Behrman cases has our approval and adherence for the circumstances to which it was there applied. A quite different question here is whether we will expand the doctrine of crimes without intent to include those charged here.

Stealing, larceny, and its variants and equivalents, were among the earliest offenses known to the law that existed before legislation; they are invasions of rights of property which stir a sense of insecurity in the whole community and arouse public demand for retribution, the penalty is high and, when a sufficient amount is involved, the infamy is that of a felony, which, says Maitland, is " * * * as bad a word as you can give to man or thing."[8] State courts of last resort, on whom fall the heaviest burden of interpreting criminal law in this country, have consistently retained the requirement of intent in larceny-type offenses.[9] If any state has deviated,

---

8. 2 Pollock & Maitland, History of English Law, 465.

9. Examples of decision in diverse jurisdictions may be culled from any digest. Most nearly in point are Johnson v. State, 36 Tex. 375, holding that to take a horse running at large on the range is not larceny in the absence of an intent to deprive an owner of his property;

the exception has neither been called to our attention nor disclosed by our research.

Congress, therefore, omitted any express prescription of criminal intent from the enactment before us in the light of an unbroken course of judicial decision in all constituent states of the Union holding intent inherent in this class of offense, even when not expressed in a statute. Congressional silence as to mental elements in an Act merely adopting into federal statutory law a concept of crime already so well defined in common law and statutory interpretation by the states may warrant quite contrary inferences than the same silence in creating an offense new to general law, for whose definition the courts have no guidance except the Act. Because the offenses before this Court in the Balint and Behrman cases were of this latter class, we cannot accept them as authority for eliminating intent from offenses incorporated from the common law. Nor do exhaustive studies of state court cases disclose any well-considered decisions applying the doctrine of crime without intent to such enacted common-law offenses,[10] although a few deviations are notable as illustrative of the danger inherent in the Government's contentions here.[11]

The Government asks us by a feat of construction radically to change the weights and balances in the scales of justice. The purpose and obvious effect of doing away with the requirement of a guilty intent is to ease the prosecution's path to conviction, to strip the defendant of such benefit as he derived at common law from innocence of evil purpose, and to circumscribe the freedom heretofore allowed juries. Such a manifest impairment of the immunities of the individual should not be extended to common-law crimes on judicial initiative.

The spirit of the doctrine which denies to the federal judiciary power to create crimes forthrightly admonishes that we should not enlarge the reach of enacted crimes by constituting them from anything less than the incriminating components contemplated by the words used in the statute.

Jordan v. State, 107 Tex.Cr.R. 414, 296 S.W. 585, that, if at the time of taking parts from an automobile the accused believed that the car had been abandoned by its owner, he should be acquitted; Fetkenhauer v. State, 112 Wis. 491, 88 N.W. 294, that an honest, although mistaken, belief by defendant that he had permission to take property should be considered by the jury; and Devine v. People, 20 Hun., N.Y., 98, holding that a claim that an act was only a practical joke must be weighed against an admitted taking of property. . . .

10. Sayre, Public Welfare Offenses, 33 Col.L.Rev. 55, 73, 84, cites and classifies a large number of cases and concludes that they fall roughly into subdivisions of (1) illegal sales of intoxicating liquor, (2) sales of impure or adulterated food or drugs, (3) sales of misbranded articles, (4) violations of antinarcotic Acts, (5) criminal nuisances, (6) violations of traffic regulations, (7) violations of motor-vehicle laws, and (8) violations of general police regulations, passed for the safety, health or well-being of the community.

11. Sayre points out that in criminal syndicalism or sedition cases, where the pressure to convict is strong, it has been accomplished by dispensing with the element of intent, in some instances by analogy with the public welfare offense. Examples are State v. Hennessy, 114 Wash. 351, 195 P. 211; People v. Ruthenberg, 229 Mich. 315, 201 N.W. 358; State v. Kahn, 56 Mont. 108, 182 P. 107; State v. Smith, 57 Mont. 563, 190 P. 107. Compare People v. McClennegen, 195 Cal. 445, 234 P. 91. This although intent is of the very essence of offenses based on disloyalty. Cf. Cramer v. United States, 325 U.S. 1, 65 S.Ct. 918, 89 L.Ed. 1441; Haupt v. United States, 330 U.S. 631, 67 S.Ct. 874, 91 L.Ed. 1145, where innocence of intention will defeat a charge even of treason.

And where Congress borrows terms of art in which are accumulated the legal tradition and meaning of centuries of practice, it presumably knows and adopts the cluster of ideas that were attached to each borrowed word in the body of learning from which it was taken and the meaning its use will convey to the judicial mind unless otherwise instructed. In such case, absence of contrary direction may be taken as satisfaction with widely accepted definitions, not as a departure from them.

We hold that mere omission from § 641 of any mention of intent will not be construed as eliminating that element from the crimes denounced.

II.

It is suggested, however, that the history and purposes of § 641 imply something more affirmative as to elimination of intent from at least one of the offenses charged under it in this case. The argument does not contest that criminal intent is retained in the offenses of embezzlement, stealing and purloining, as incorporated into this section. But it is urged that Congress joined with those, as a new, separate and distinct offense, knowingly to convert government property, under circumstances which imply that it is an offense in which the mental element of intent is not necessary. . . .

Congress has been alert to what often is a decisive function of some mental element in crime. It has seen fit to prescribe that an evil state of mind, described variously in one or more such terms as "intentional," "wilful," "knowing," "fraudulent" or "malicious," will make criminal an otherwise indifferent act, or increase the degree of the offense or its punishment. Also, it has at times required a specific intent or purpose which will require some specialized knowledge or design for some evil beyond the common-law intent to do injury. The law under some circumstances recognizes good faith or blameless intent as a defense, partial defense, or as an element to be considered in mitigation of punishment. And treason—the one crime deemed grave enough for definition in our Constitution itself—requires not only the duly witnessed overt act of aid and comfort to the enemy but also the mental element of disloyalty or adherence to the enemy. In view of the care that has been bestowed upon the subject, it is significant that we have not found, nor has our attention been directed to, any instance in which Congress has expressly eliminated the mental element from a crime taken over from the common law. . . .

Had the statute applied to conversions without qualification, it would have made crimes of all unwitting, inadvertent and unintended conversions. Knowledge, of course, is not identical with intent and may not have been the most apt words of limitation. But knowing conversion requires more than knowledge that defendant was taking the property into his possession. He must have had knowledge of the facts, though not necessarily the law, that made the taking a conversion. In the case before us, whether the mental element that Congress required be spoken of as knowledge or as intent, would not seem to alter its bearing on guilt. for it is not apparent how Morissette could have knowingly or intentionally converted property that he did not know could be converted, as would be the case if it was in fact abandoned or if he truly believed it to be abandoned and unwanted property. . . .

We find no grounds for inferring any affirmative instruction from Congress to eliminate intent from any offense with which this defendant was charged.

III.

As we read the record, this case was tried on the theory that even if criminal intent were essential its presence (a) should be decided by the court (b) as a presumption of law, apparently conclusive, (c) predicated upon the isolated act of taking rather than upon all of the circumstances. In each of these respects we believe the trial court was in error.

Where intent of the accused is an ingredient of the crime charged, its existence is a question of fact which must be submitted to the jury. State court authorities cited to the effect that intent is relevant in larcenous crimes are equally emphatic and uniform that it is a jury issue. The settled practice and its reason are well stated by Judge Andrews in People v. Flack, 125 N.Y. 324, 334, 26 N.E. 267, 270, 11 L.R.A. 807: "It is alike the general rule of law, and the dictate of natural justice, that to constitute guilt there must be not only a wrongful act, but a criminal intention. Under our system, (unless in exceptional cases,) both must be found by the jury to justify a conviction for crime. However clear the proof may be, or however incontrovertible may seem to the judge to be the inference of a criminal intention, the question of intent can never be ruled as a question of law, but must always be submitted to the jury. Jurors may be perverse, the ends of justice may be defeated by unrighteous verdicts; but so long as the functions of the judge and jury are distinct, the one responding to the law, the other to the facts, neither can invade the province of the other without destroying the significance of trial by court and jury. * * * "

It follows that the trial court may not withdraw or prejudge the issue by instruction that the law raises a presumption of intent from an act. It often is tempting to cast in terms of a "presumption" a conclusion which a court thinks probable from given facts. The Supreme Court of Florida, for example, in a larceny case, from selected circumstances which are present in this case, has declared a presumption of exactly opposite effect from the one announced by the trial court here: "But where the taking is open and there is no subsequent attempt to conceal the property, and no denial, but an avowal, of the taking, a strong presumption arises that there was no felonious intent, which must be repelled by clear and convincing evidence before a conviction is authorized. * * * " Kemp v. State, 146 Fla. 101, 104, 200 So. 368, 369. . . .

Of course, the jury, considering Morissette's awareness that these casings were on government property, his failure to seek any permission for their removal and his self-interest as a witness, might have disbelieved his profession of innocent intent and concluded that his assertion of a belief that the casings were abandoned was an afterthought. Had the jury convicted on proper instructions it would be the end of the matter. But juries are not bound by what seems inescapable logic to judges. They might have concluded that the heaps of spent casings left in the hinterland to rust away presented an appearance of unwanted and abandoned junk, and that lack of any conscious deprivation of property or intentional injury was indicated by Morissette's good character, the openness of the taking, crushing and transporting of the casings, and the candor with which it was all admitted. They might have refused to brand Morissette as a thief. Had they done so, that too would have been the end of the matter.

Reversed.

■ MR. JUSTICE DOUGLAS concurs in the result.

■ MR. JUSTICE MINTON took no part in the consideration or decision of this case.

United States v. Bailey

Supreme Court of the United States, 1980.
444 U.S. 394, 100 S.Ct. 624, 62 L.Ed.2d 575.

■ MR. JUSTICE REHNQUIST delivered the opinion of the Court.

In the early morning hours of August 26, 1976, respondents Clifford Bailey, James T. Cogdell, Ronald C. Cooley, and Ralph Walker, federal prisoners at the District of Columbia jail, crawled through a window from which a bar had been removed, slid down a knotted bedsheet, and escaped from custody. Federal authorities recaptured them after they had remained at large for a period of time ranging from one month to three and one-half months. Upon their apprehension, they were charged with violating 18 U.S.C. § 751(a), which governs escape from federal custody.[1] At their trials, each of the respondents adduced or offered to adduce evidence as to various conditions and events at the District of Columbia jail, but each was convicted by the jury. The Court of Appeals for the District of Columbia Circuit reversed the convictions by a divided vote, holding that the District Court had improperly precluded consideration by the respective juries of respondents' tendered evidence. We granted certiorari, 440 U.S. 957, 99 S.Ct. 1497, 59 L.Ed.2d 770, and now reverse the judgments of the Court of Appeals. . . .

In reaching our conclusion, we must decide the state of mind necessary for violation of § 751(a) and the elements that constitute defenses such as duress and necessity. In explaining the reasons for our decision, we find ourselves in a position akin to that of the mother crab who is trying to teach her progeny to walk in a straight line, and finally in desperation exclaims: "Don't do as I do, do as I say." The Act of Congress we construe

---

1. Title 18 U.S.C. § 751(a) provides:

"Whoever escapes or attempts to escape from the custody of the Attorney General or his authorized representative, or from any institution or facility in which he is confined by direction of the Attorney General, or from any custody under or by virtue of any process issued under the laws of the United States by any court, judge or magistrate, or from the custody of an officer or employee of the United States pursuant to lawful arrest, shall, if the custody or confinement is by virtue of an arrest on a charge of felony, or conviction of any offense, be fined not more than $5,000 or imprisoned not more than five years, or both; or if the custody or confinement is for extradition or by virtue of an arrest or charge of or for a misdemeanor, and prior to conviction, be fined not more than $1,000 or imprisoned not more than one year, or both."

consists of one sentence set forth in the margin, n. 1, *supra*; our own pragmatic estimate, expressed *infra*, at 637, is that "in general, trials for violations of § 751(a) should be simple affairs." Yet we have written, reluctantly but we believe necessarily, a somewhat lengthy opinion supporting our conclusion, because in enacting the Federal Criminal Code Congress legislated in the light of a long history of case law that is frequently relevant in fleshing out the bare bones of a crime that Congress may have proscribed in a single sentence. See *Morissette v. United States*, 342 U.S. 246, 72 S.Ct. 240, 96 L.Ed. 288 (1952).

I

All respondents requested jury trials and were initially scheduled to be tried jointly. At the last minute, however, respondent Cogdell secured a severance. Because the District Court refused to submit to the jury any instructions on respondents' defense of duress or necessity and did not charge the jury that escape was a continuing offense, we must examine in some detail the evidence brought out at trial.

The prosecution's case in chief against Bailey, Cooley, and Walker was brief. The Government introduced evidence that each of the respondents was in federal custody on August 26, 1976, that they had disappeared, apparently through a cell window, at approximately 5:35 a. m. on that date, and that they had been apprehended individually between September 27 and December 13, 1976.

Respondents' defense of duress or necessity centered on the conditions in the jail during the months of June, July, and August 1976, and on various threats and beatings directed at them during that period. In describing the conditions at the jail, they introduced evidence of frequent fires in "Northeast One," the maximum-security cellblock occupied by respondents prior to their escape. Construed in the light most favorable to them, this evidence demonstrated that the inmates of Northeast One, and on occasion the guards in that unit, set fire to trash, bedding, and other objects thrown from the cells. According to the inmates, the guards simply allowed the fires to burn until they went out. Although the fires apparently were confined to small areas and posed no substantial threat of spreading through the complex, poor ventilation caused smoke to collect and linger in the cellblock.

Respondents Cooley and Bailey also introduced testimony that the guards at the jail had subjected them to beatings and to threats of death. Walker attempted to prove that he was an epileptic and had received inadequate medical attention for his seizures.

Consistently during the trial, the District Court stressed that, to sustain their defenses, respondents would have to introduce some evidence that they attempted to surrender or engaged in equivalent conduct once they had freed themselves from the conditions they described. But the court waited for such evidence in vain. Respondent Cooley, who had eluded the authorities for one month, testified that his "people" had tried to contact the authorities, but "never got in touch with anybody." App. 119. He also suggested that someone had told his sister that the Federal Bureau of Investigation would kill him when he was apprehended.

Respondent Bailey, who was apprehended on November 19, 1976, told a similar story. He stated that he "had the jail officials called several times," but did not turn himself in because "I would still be under the threats of death." Like Cooley, Bailey testified that "the FBI was telling my people that they was going to shoot me." *Id.*, at 169, 175–176.

Only respondent Walker suggested that he had attempted to negotiate a surrender. Like Cooley and Bailey, Walker testified that the FBI had told his "people" that they would kill him when they recaptured him. Nevertheless, according to Walker, he called the FBI three times and spoke with an agent whose name he could not remember. That agent allegedly assured him that the FBI would not harm him, but was unable to promise that Walker would not be returned to the D.C. jail. *Id.*, at 195–200.[2] Walker testified that he last called the FBI in mid-October. He was finally apprehended on December 13, 1976.

At the close of all the evidence, the District Court rejected respondents' proffered instruction on duress as a defense to prison escape. The court ruled that respondents had failed as a matter of law to present evidence sufficient to support such a defense because they had not turned themselves in after they had escaped the allegedly coercive conditions. After receiving instructions to disregard the evidence of the conditions in the jail, the jury convicted Bailey, Cooley, and Walker of violating § 751(a).

Two months later, respondent Cogdell came to trial before the same District Judge who had presided over the trial of his co-respondents. When Cogdell attempted to offer testimony concerning the allegedly inhumane conditions at the D.C. jail, the District Judge inquired into Cogdell's conduct between his escape on August 26 and his apprehension on September 28. In response to Cogdell's assertion that he "may have written letters," the District Court specified that Cogdell could testify only as to "what he did ... [n]ot what he may have done." App. 230. Absent such testimony, however, the District Court ruled that Cogdell could not present evidence of conditions at the jail. Cogdell subsequently chose not to testify on his own behalf, and was convicted by the jury of violating § 751(a).

By a divided vote, the Court of Appeals reversed each respondent's conviction and remanded for new trials. See 190 U.S.App.D.C. 142, 585 F.2d 1087 (1978); 190 U.S.App.D.C. 185, 585 F.2d 1130 (1978). The majority concluded that the District Court should have allowed the jury to consider the evidence of coercive conditions in determining whether the respondents had formulated the requisite intent to sustain a conviction under § 751(a). According to the majority, § 751(a) required the prosecution to prove that a particular defendant left federal custody voluntarily, without permission, and "with an intent to avoid confinement." 190 U.S.App.D.C., at 148, 585 F.2d, at 1093. The majority then defined the word "confinement" as encompassing only the "normal aspects" of punishment prescribed by our legal system. Thus, where a prisoner escapes in order to avoid "non-confinement" conditions such as beatings or homosex-

---

2. On rebuttal, the prosecution called Joel Dean, the FBI agent who had been assigned to investigate Walker's escape in August 1976. He testified that, under standard Bureau practice, he would have been notified of any contact made by Walker with the FBI. According to Dean, he never was informed of any such contact. App. 203–204.

ual attacks, he would not necessarily have the requisite intent to sustain a conviction under § 751(a). According to the majority:

> "When a defendant introduces evidence that he was subject to such 'non-confinement' conditions, the crucial factual determination on the intent issue is . . . whether the defendant left custody only to avoid these conditions or whether, in addition, the defendant *also* intended to avoid confinement. In making this determination the jury is to be guided by the trial court's instructions pointing out those factors that are most indicative of the presence or absence of an intent to avoid confinement." 190 U.S.App.D.C., at 148, n. 17, 585 F.2d, at 1093, n. 17 (emphasis in original).

Turning to the applicability of the defense of duress or necessity, the majority assumed that escape as defined by § 751(a) was a "continuing offense" as long as the escapee was at large. Given this assumption, the majority agreed with the District Court that, under normal circumstances, an escapee must present evidence of coercion to justify his continued absence from custody as well as his initial departure. Here, however, respondents had been indicted for "flee[ing] and escap[ing]" "[o]n or about August 26, 1976," and not for "leaving *and staying away from* custody." 190 U.S.App.D.C., at 155, 585 F.2d, at 1100 (emphasis in original). Similarly, "[t]he trial court's instructions when read as a whole clearly give the impression that [respondents] were being tried only for leaving the jail on August 26, and not for failing to return at some later date." *Id.*, at 155, n. 50, 585 F.2d, at 1100, n. 50. Under these circumstances, the majority believed that neither respondents nor the juries were acquainted with the proposition that the escapes in question were continuing offenses. This failure, according to the majority, constituted "an obvious violation of [respondents'] constitutional right to jury trial." *Id.*, at 156, 585 F.2d, at 1101.

The dissenting judge objected to what he characterized as a revolutionary reinterpretation of criminal law by the majority. He argued that the common-law crime of escape had traditionally required only "general intent," a mental state no more sophisticated than an "intent to go beyond permitted limits." *Id.*, at 177, 585 F.2d, at 1122 (emphasis deleted). The dissent concluded that the District Court had properly removed from consideration each respondent's contention that conditions and events at the D.C. jail justified his escape, because each respondent had introduced no evidence whatsoever justifying his continued absence from jail following that escape.

II

Criminal liability is normally based upon the concurrence of two factors, "an evil-meaning mind [and] an evil-doing hand. . . ." *Morissette v. United States*, 342 U.S., at 251, 72 S.Ct., at 244. In the present case, we must examine both the mental element, or *mens rea*, required for conviction under § 751(a) and the circumstances under which the "evil-doing hand" can avoid liability under that section because coercive conditions or necessity negates a conclusion of guilt even though the necessary *mens rea* was present.

A

Few areas of criminal law pose more difficulty than the proper definition of the *mens rea* required for any particular crime. In 1970, the National Commission on Reform of Federal Criminal Laws decried the "confused and inconsistent ad hoc approach" of the federal courts to this issue and called for "a new departure." See 1 Working Papers of the National Commission on Reform of Federal Criminal Laws 123 (hereinafter Working Papers). Although the central focus of this and other reform movements has been the codification of workable principles for determining criminal culpability, see, *e. g.*, American Law Institute, Model Penal Code §§ 2.01–2.13 (Prop. Off. Draft 1962) (hereinafter Model Penal Code); S. 1, 94th Cong., 2d Sess., §§ 301–303 (1976), a byproduct has been a general rethinking of traditional *mens-rea* analysis.

At common law, crimes generally were classified as requiring either "general intent" or "specific intent." This venerable distinction, however, has been the source of a good deal of confusion. As one treatise explained:

"Sometimes 'general intent' is used in the same way as 'criminal intent' to mean the general notion of *mens rea*, while 'specific intent' is taken to mean the mental state required for a particular crime. Or, 'general intent' may be used to encompass all forms of the mental state requirement, while 'specific intent' is limited to the one mental state of intent. Another possibility is that 'general intent' will be used to characterize an intent to do something on an undetermined occasion, and 'specific intent' to denote an intent to do that thing at a particular time and place." W. LaFave & A. Scott, Handbook on Criminal Law § 28, pp. 201–202 (1972) (footnotes omitted) (hereinafter LaFave & Scott).

This ambiguity has led to a movement away from the traditional dichotomy of intent and toward an alternative analysis of *mens rea*. See *id.*, at 202. This new approach, exemplified in the American Law Institute's Model Penal Code, is based on two principles. First, the ambiguous and elastic term "intent" is replaced with a hierarchy of culpable states of mind. The different levels in this hierarchy are commonly identified, in descending order of culpability, as purpose, knowledge, recklessness, and negligence.[4] See LaFave & Scott 194; Model Penal Code § 2.02. Perhaps the most significant, and most esoteric, distinction drawn by this analysis is that between the mental states of "purpose" and "knowledge." As we pointed out in *United States v. United States Gypsum Co.*, 438 U.S. 422, 445, 98 S.Ct. 2864, 2877, 57 L.Ed.2d 854 (1978), a person who causes a particular result is said to act purposefully if " 'he consciously desires that result, whatever the likelihood of that result happening from his conduct,' " while he is said to act knowingly if he is aware " 'that that result is

---

4. This hierarchy does not attempt to cover those offenses where criminal liability is imposed in the absence of any *mens rea* whatsoever. Such "strict liability" crimes are exceptions to the general rule that criminal liability requires an "evil-meaning mind." Compare *Morissette v. United States*, 342 U.S. 246, 250–263, 72 S.Ct. 240, 243–250, 96 L.Ed. 288 (1952), with *United States v. Dotterweich*, 320 U.S. 277, 280–281, 284, 64 S.Ct. 134, 136–137, 138, 88 L.Ed. 48 (1943). Under the Model Penal Code, the only offenses based on strict liability are "violations," actions punishable by a fine, forfeiture, or other civil penalty rather than imprisonment. See Model Penal Code § 2.05(1)(a). See also LaFave & Scott 218–223.

practically certain to follow from his conduct, whatever his desire may be as to that result.' "

In the case of most crimes, "the limited distinction between knowledge and purpose has not been considered important since 'there is good reason for imposing liability whether the defendant desired or merely knew of the practical certainty of the result[s].' " *United States v. United States Gypsum Co., supra,* at 445, 98 S.Ct., at 2877, quoting LaFave & Scott 197. Thus in *Gypsum* we held that a person could be held criminally liable under § 1 of the Sherman Act if that person exchanged price information with a competitor either with the knowledge that the exchange would have unreasonable anticompetitive effects or with the purpose of producing those effects. 438 U.S., at 444–445, and n. 21, 98 S.Ct., at 2877–2878.

In certain narrow classes of crimes, however, heightened culpability has been thought to merit special attention. Thus, the statutory and common law of homicide often distinguishes, either in setting the "degree" of the crime or in imposing punishment, between a person who knows that another person will be killed as the result of his conduct and a person who acts with the specific purpose of taking another's life. See LaFave & Scott 196–197. Similarly, where a defendant is charged with treason, this Court has stated that the Government must demonstrate that the defendant acted with a purpose to aid the enemy. See *Haupt v. United States,* 330 U.S. 631, 641, 67 S.Ct. 874, 878, 91 L.Ed. 1145 (1947). Another such example is the law of inchoate offenses such as attempt and conspiracy, where a heightened mental state separates criminality itself from otherwise innocuous behavior. See Model Penal Code § 2.02, Comments, p. 125 (Tent. Draft No. 4, 1955) (hereinafter MPC Comments).

In a general sense, "purpose" corresponds loosely with the common-law concept of specific intent, while "knowledge" corresponds loosely with the concept of general intent. See *ibid.*; LaFave & Scott 201–202. Were this substitution of terms the only innovation offered by the reformers, it would hardly be dramatic. But there is another ambiguity inherent in the traditional distinction between specific intent and general intent. Generally, even time-honored common-law crimes consist of several elements, and complex statutorily defined crimes exhibit this characteristic to an even greater degree. Is the same state of mind required of the actor for each element of the crime, or may some elements require one state of mind and some another? In *United States v. Feola,* 420 U.S. 671, 95 S.Ct. 1255, 43 L.Ed.2d 541 (1975), for example, we were asked to decide whether the Government, to sustain a conviction for assaulting a federal officer under 18 U.S.C. § 111, had to prove that the defendant knew that his victim was a federal officer. After looking to the legislative history of § 111, we concluded that Congress intended to require only "an intent to assault, not an intent to assault a federal officer." 420 U.S., at 684, 95 S.Ct., at 1264. What *Feola* implied, the American Law Institute stated: "[C]lear analysis requires that the question of the kind of culpability required to establish the commission of an offense be faced separately with respect to each material element of the crime[.]" MPC Comments 123. See also Working Papers 131; LaFave & Scott 194.

Before dissecting § 751(a) and assigning a level of culpability to each element, we believe that two observations are in order. First, in performing such analysis courts obviously must follow Congress' intent as to the required level of mental culpability for any particular offense. Principles derived from common law as well as precepts suggested by the American Law Institute must bow to legislative mandates. In the case of § 751(a), however, neither the language of the statute nor the legislative history mentions the *mens rea* required for conviction.[6]

Second, while the suggested element-by-element analysis is a useful tool for making sense of an otherwise opaque concept, it is not the only principle to be considered. The administration of the federal system of criminal justice is confided to ordinary mortals, whether they be lawyers, judges, or jurors. This system could easily fall of its own weight if courts or scholars become obsessed with hair-splitting distinctions, either traditional or novel, that Congress neither stated nor implied when it made the conduct criminal.

As relevant to the charges against Bailey, Cooley, and Walker, § 751(a) required the prosecution to prove (1) that they had been in the custody of the Attorney General, (2) as the result of a conviction, and (3) that they had escaped from that custody. As for the charges against respondent Cogdell, § 751(a) required the same proof, with the exception that his confinement was based upon an arrest for a felony rather than a prior conviction. Although § 751(a) does not define the term "escape," courts and commentators are in general agreement that it means absenting oneself from custody without permission. See, *e. g.*, 190 U.S.App.D.C., at 148, 585 F.2d, at 1093; *id.*, at 177, 585 F.2d, at 1122 (Wilkey, J., dissenting); *United States v. Wilke*, 450 F.2d 877 (CA9 1971), cert. denied, 409 U.S. 918, 93 S.Ct. 250, 34 L.Ed.2d 180 (1972). See also 2 J. Bishop, Criminal Law § 1103, p. 819 (9th ed. 1923); 1 W. Burdick, Law of Crime, 462–463 (1946); R. Perkins, Criminal Law 429 (1957); 3 F. Wharton, Criminal Law § 2003, p. 2178 (11th ed. 1912).

Respondents have not challenged the District Court's instructions on the first two elements of the crime defined by § 751(a). It is undisputed that, on August 26, 1976, respondents were in the custody of the Attorney General as the result of either arrest on charges of felony or conviction. As for the element of "escape," we need not decide whether a person could be convicted on evidence of recklessness or negligence with respect to the limits on his freedom. A court may someday confront a case where an escapee did not know, but should have known, that he was exceeding the bounds of his confinement or that he was leaving without permission. Here, the District Court clearly instructed the juries that the prosecution bore the burden of proving that respondents "knowingly committed an act which the law makes a crime" and that they acted "knowingly, intentional-

---

6. This omission does not mean, of course, that § 751(a) defines a "strict liability" crime for which punishment can be imposed without proof of any *mens rea* at all. As we held in *Morissette v. United States, supra,* 342 U.S., at 263, 72 S.Ct., at 250, "mere omission [from the statute] of any mention of intent will not be construed as eliminating that element from the crimes denounced." See also *United States v. United States Gypsum Co.*, 438 U.S. 422, 437, 98 S.Ct. 2864, 2873, 57 L.Ed.2d 854 (1978).

ly, and deliberately...." App. 221–223, 231–233. At a minimum, the juries had to find that respondents knew they were leaving the jail and that they knew they were doing so without authorization. The sufficiency of the evidence to support the juries' verdicts under this charge has never seriously been questioned, nor could it be.

The majority of the Court of Appeals, however, imposed the added burden on the prosecution to prove as a part of its case in chief that respondents acted "with an intent to avoid confinement." While, for the reasons noted above, the word "intent" is quite ambiguous, the majority left little doubt that it was requiring the Government to prove that the respondents acted with the purpose—that is, the conscious objective—of leaving the jail without authorization. In a footnote explaining their holding, for example, the majority specified that an escapee did not act with the requisite intent if he escaped in order to avoid " 'non-confinement' conditions" as opposed to "normal aspects of 'confinement.' " 190 U.S.App.D.C., at 148, n. 17, 585 F.2d, at 1093, n. 17.

We find the majority's position quite unsupportable. Nothing in the language or legislative history of § 751(a) indicates that Congress intended to require either such a heightened standard of culpability or such a narrow definition of confinement. As we stated earlier, the cases have generally held that, except in narrow classes of offenses, proof that the defendant acted knowingly is sufficient to support a conviction. Accordingly, we hold that the prosecution fulfills its burden under § 751(a) if it demonstrates that an escapee knew his actions would result in his leaving physical confinement without permission. Our holding in this respect comports with parallel definitions of the crime of escape both in the Model Penal Code and in a proposed revision of the Federal Criminal Code. See Model Penal Code §§ 2.02(3), 242.6(1); Report of Senate Committee on the Judiciary to Accompany S. 1, S. Rep. No. 94–00, pp. 333–334 (Comm.Print 1976).[7] Moreover, comments accompanying the proposed revision of the Federal Criminal Code specified that the new provision covering escape "substantially carrie[d] forward existing law...." *Id.*, at 332. [The Court goes on to reject respondents' claim that they are entitled to a new trial on grounds of the affirmative defenses of duress and necessity].

Because the juries below were properly instructed on the *mens rea* required by § 751(a), and because the respondents failed to introduce evidence sufficient to submit their defenses of duress and necessity to the juries, we reverse the judgments of the Court of Appeals.

Reversed.

---

7. Under the Model Code, a defendant is guilty of escape if he acts even recklessly toward the material elements of the offense, since § 2.02(3) provides that, unless otherwise provided in the definition of the offense, an element of any offense "is established if a person acts purposely, knowingly or recklessly with respect thereto." S. 1, a proposed revision of the Federal Criminal Code, would have imposed liability on an escapee "if (1) he is reckless as to the fact that he is subject to official detention, that is, he is aware that he may be in official detention ... but disregards the risk that he is in fact in official detention, and (2) knowingly leaves the detention area or breaks from custody." As noted earlier, we do not have to decide whether or under what circumstances an escapee can be held liable under § 751(a) if he acted only recklessly with respect to the material elements of the offense. See *supra*, at 633.

[The separate opinions of Justice Stevens, concurring, and Justice Blackmun, dissenting, are omitted.]

United States v. Feola

Supreme Court of the United States, 1975.
420 U.S. 671, 95 S.Ct. 1255, 43 L.Ed.2d 541.

■ JUSTICE BLACKMUN delivered the opinion of the Court.

This case presents the issue whether knowledge that the intended victim is a federal officer is a requisite for the crime of conspiracy, under 18 U.S.C. § 371, to commit an offense violative of 18 U.S.C. § 111,[12] that is, an assault upon a federal officer while engaged in the performance of his official duties.

Respondent Feola and three others (Alsondo, Rosa, and Farr) were indicted for violations of §§ 371 and 111. A jury found all four defendants guilty of both charges. Feola received a sentence of four years for the conspiracy and one of three years, plus a $3,000 fine, for the assault. The three-year sentence, however, was suspended and he was given three years' probation "to commence at the expiration of confinement" for the conspiracy. The respective appeals of Feola, Alsondo, and Rosa were considered by the United States Court of Appeals for the Second Circuit in a single opinion. After an initial ruling partially to the contrary, that court affirmed the judgment of conviction on the substantive charges, but reversed the conspiracy convictions. United States v. Alsondo, 486 F.2d 1339, 1346 (1973). Because of a conflict among the federal Circuits on the scienter issue with respect to a conspiracy charge, we granted the Government's petition for a writ of certiorari in Feola's case.

I

The facts reveal a classic narcotics "rip-off." The details are not particularly important for our present purposes. We need note only that the evidence shows that Feola and his confederates arranged for a sale of heroin to buyers who turned out to be undercover agents for the Bureau of Narcotics and Dangerous Drugs. The group planned to palm off on the purchasers, for a substantial sum, a form of sugar in place of heroin and, should that ruse fail, simply to surprise their unwitting buyers and relieve them of the cash they had brought along for payment. The plan failed when one agent, his suspicions being aroused,[13] drew his revolver in time to

---

12. "§ 111. Assaulting, resisting, or impeding certain officers or employees.

"Whoever forcibly assaults, resists, opposes, impedes, intimidates, or interferes with any person designated in section 1114 of this title while engaged in or on account of the performance of his official duties, shall be fined not more than $5,000 or imprisoned not more than three years, or both.

"Whoever, in the commission of any such acts uses a deadly or dangerous weapon, shall be fined not more than $10,000 or imprisoned not more than ten years, or both."

Among the persons "designated in section 1114" of 18 U.S.C. is "any officer or employee ... of the Bureau of Narcotics and Dangerous Drugs."

13. The agent opened a closet door in the Manhattan apartment where the sale was to have taken place and observed a man on the floor, bound and gagged. App. 11–12.

Facts

counter an assault upon another agent from the rear. Instead of enjoying the rich benefits of a successful swindle, Feola and his associates found themselves charged, to their undoubted surprise, with conspiring to assault, and with assaulting, federal officers.

Issue

At the trial, the District Court, without objection from the defense, charged the jurors that, in order to find any of the defendants guilty on either the conspiracy count or the substantive one, they were not required to conclude that the defendants were aware that their quarry were federal officers.

The Court of Appeals reversed the conspiracy convictions on a ground not advanced by any of the defendants. Although it approved the trial court's instructions to the jury on the substantive charge of assaulting a federal officer, it nonetheless concluded that the failure to charge that knowledge of the victim's official identity must be proved in order to convict on the conspiracy charge amounted to plain error. 486 F.2d, at 1344. The court perceived itself bound by a line of cases, commencing with Judge Learned Hand's opinion in United States v. Crimmins, 123 F.2d 271 (CA2 1941), all holding that scienter of a factual element that confers federal jurisdiction, while unnecessary for conviction of the substantive offense, is required in order to sustain a conviction for conspiracy to commit the substantive offense. Although the court noted that the Crimins rationale "has been criticized," 486 F.2d, at 1343, and, indeed, offered no argument in support of it, it accepted "the controlling precedents somewhat reluctantly." Id., at 1344.

II

The Government's plea is for symmetry. It urges that since criminal liability for the offense described in 18 U.S.C. § 111 does not depend on whether the assailant harbored the specific intent to assault a federal officer, no greater scienter requirement can be engrafted upon the conspiracy offense, which is merely an agreement to commit the act proscribed by § 111. Consideration of the Government's contention requires us preliminarily to pass upon its premise, the proposition that responsibility for assault upon a federal officer does not depend upon whether the assailant was aware of the official identity of his victim at the time he acted.

That the "federal officer" requirement is anything other than jurisdictional is not seriously urged upon us; indeed, both Feola and the Court of Appeals, 486 F.2d at 1342, concede that scienter is not a necessary element of the substantive offense under § 111. Although some early cases were to the contrary, the concession recognizes what is now the practical unanimity of the Courts of Appeals. Nevertheless, we are not always guided by concessions of the parties, and the very considerations of symmetry urged by the Government suggest that we first turn our attention to the substantive offense.

The Court has considered § 111 before. In Ladner v. United States, 358 U.S. 169, 79 S.Ct. 209, 3 L.Ed.2d 199 (1958), the issue was whether a single shotgun blast which wounded two federal agents effected multiple assaults, within the meaning of 18 U.S.C. § 254 (1940 ed.), one of the statutory predecessors to the present § 111.[14] The Government urged that § 254 had been intended not only to deter interference with federal law enforcement activities but, as well, to forestall injury to individual officers, as 'wards' of the United States. Given the latter formulation of legislative intent, argued the Government, a single blast wounding two officers would constitute two offenses. The Court disagreed because it found an equally plausible reading of the legislative intent to be that "the congressional aim was to prevent hindrance to the execution of official duty ... and was not to protect federal officers except as incident to that aim," 358 U.S., at 175–176, 79 S.Ct. at 213. Under that view of legislative purpose, to have punishment depend upon the number of officers impeded would be incongruous. With no clear choice between these alternative formulations of congressional intent, in light of the statutory language and sparse legislative history, the Court applied a policy of lenity and, for purposes of the case, adopted the less harsh reading. Id., at 177–178, 79 S.Ct., at 213–214. It therefore held that the single discharge of a shotgun constituted only a single violation of § 254.

In the present case, we see again the possible consequences of an interpretation of § 111 that focuses on only one of the statute's apparent aims. If the primary purpose is to protect federal law enforcement personnel, that purpose could well be frustrated by the imposition of a strict scienter requirement. On the other hand, if § 111 is seen primarily as an anti-obstruction statute, it is likely that Congress intended criminal liability to be imposed only when a person acted with the specific intent to impede enforcement activities. Otherwise, it has been said: "Were knowledge not required in obstruction of justice offenses described by these terms, wholly innocent (or even socially desirable) behavior could be transformed into a felony by the wholly fortuitous circumstance of the concealed identity of the person resisted."[15] Although we adhere to the conclusion in Ladner that either view of legislative intent is "plausible," we think it plain that Congress intended to protect both federal officers and federal functions, and that, indeed, furtherance of the one policy advances the other. The rejection of a strict scienter requirement is consistent with both purposes.

Section 111 has its origin in § 2 of the Act of May 18, 1934, c. 299, 48 Stat. 781. Section 1 of that Act, in which the present 18 U.S.C. § 1114 has its roots, made it a federal crime to kill certain federal law enforcement personnel while engaged in, or on account of, the performance of official duties,[16] and § 2 forbade forcible resistance or interference with, or assault

---

14. Section 111 assumed its present form in 1948, 62 Stat. 688, when it replaced both § 118 and § 254 of 18 U.S.C. (1940 ed.). The Reviser's Note states that this was done "with changes in phraseology and substance necessary to effect the consolidation." H.R.Rep.No.304, 80th Cong., 1st Sess., A12 (1947).

15. United States v. Fernandez, 497 F.2d, at 744 (Hufstedler, J., concurring).

16. Section 1 provided:

"That whoever shall kill, as defined in sections 273 and 274 of the Criminal Code, any United States marshal or deputy United States marshal, special agent of the Division of Investigation of the Department of Justice, post-office inspector, Secret Service operative, any officer or enlisted man of the Coast Guard, any employee of any United States penal or correctional institution, any officer of the customs or of the internal revenue, any immigrant

upon, any officer designated in § 1 while so engaged. The history of the 1934 Act, though scanty, offers insight into its multiple purposes. The pertinent committee reports consist, almost in their entirety, of a letter dated January 3, 1934, from Attorney General Cummings urging the passage of the legislation. In that letter the Attorney General states that this was needed "for the protection of Federal officers and employees." Compelled reliance upon state courts, "however respectable and well disposed, for the protection of (federal) investigative and law-enforcement personnel" was inadequate, and there was need for resort to a federal forum.

Although the letter refers only to the need to protect federal personnel, Congress clearly was concerned with the safety of federal officers insofar as it was tied to the efficacy of law enforcement activities. This concern is implicit in the decision to list those officers protected rather than merely to forbid assault on any federal employee. Indeed, the statute as originally formulated would have prohibited attack on "any civil official, inspector, agent, or other officer or employee of the United States." See H.R.Rep.No. 1455, 73d Cong., 2d Sess., 1 (1934). The House rejected this and insisted on the version that was ultimately enacted. Although the reason for the insistence is unexplained, it is fair to assume that the House was of the view that the bill as originally drafted strayed too far from the purpose of insuring the integrity of law enforcement pursuits.[17]

In resolving the question whether Congress intended to condition responsibility for violation of § 111 on the actor's awareness of the identity of his victim, we give weight to both purposes of the statute, but here again, as in Ladner, we need not make a choice between them. Rather, regardless of which purpose we would emphasize, we must take note of the means Congress chose for its achievement.

Attorney General Cummings, in his letter, emphasized the importance of providing a federal forum in which attacks upon named federal officers could be prosecuted. This, standing alone, would not indicate a congressional conclusion to dispense with a requirement of specific intent to assault a federal officer, for the locus of the forum does not of itself define the reach

---

inspector or any immigration patrol inspector, while engaged in the performance of his official duties, or on account of the performance of his official duties, shall be punished as provided under section 275 of the Criminal Code." C. 299, 48 Stat. 780.

A glance at the present § 1114 reveals how the list of protected federal officers has been greatly expanded. Plainly, some of those now named, viz., "employee of the Postal Service" and "employee of the National Park Service," are not necessarily engaged in the execution of federal law.

17. This conclusion is supported by the wording of § 2 of the 1934 Act (and of the present § 111), for that section outlawed more than assaults. It made it a criminal offense "forcibly (to) resist, oppose, impede, intimidate, or interfere with" the named officials while in the performance of their duty. Statutory language of this type had appeared as early as 1866, in § 6 of the Act of July 18 of that year, 14 Stat. 179, embracing a comprehensive scheme for the prevention of smuggling. The bulk of that statute, to be sure, was concerned with essentially regulatory matters; § 6, however, proscribed a broad range of actions—beyond simple forcible resistance—that would frustrate effective enforcement of the body of the statute. In employing a similar formulation in 1934, Congress could be presumed to be going beyond mere protection of the safety of federal officers without regard to the integrity of their official functions.

of the substantive offense. But the view that § 111 requires knowledge of the victim's office rests on the proposition that the reference to the federal forum was merely a shorthand expression of the need for a statute to fill a gap in the substantive law of the States. *See* United States v. Fernandez, 497 F.2d 730, 745 (CA9 1974) (concurring opinion), cert. pending, No. 73–6868. In that view § 111 is seen merely as a federal aggravated assault statute, necessary solely because some state laws mandate increased punishment only for assaults on state peace officers; assaults on federal personnel would be punishable, under state law, only for simple assault. As a federal aggravated assault statute, § 111 would be read as requiring the same degree of knowledge as its state-law counterparts. *See* Morissette v. United States, 342 U.S. 246, 263, 72 S.Ct. 240, 249, 96 L.Ed. 288 (1952). The argument fails, however, because it is fairly certain that Congress was not enacting § 111 as a federal counterpart to state proscriptions of aggravated assault.

The Attorney General's call for a federal forum in which to prosecute an attacker of a federal officer was directed at both sections of the proposed bill that became the 1934 Act. The letter concerned not only the section prohibiting assaults but also the section prohibiting killings. The latter, § 1, was not needed to fill a gap in existing substantive state law. The States proscribed murder, and, until recently, with the enactment of certain statutes in response to the successful attack on capital punishment, murder of a peace officer has not been deemed an aggravated form of murder, for all States usually have punished murderers with the most severe sanction the law allows. Clearly, then, Congress understood that it was not only filling one gap in state substantive law but in large part was duplicating state proscriptions in order to insure a federal forum for the trial of offenses involving federal officers. Fulfillment of the congressional goal to protect federal officers required then, as it does now, the highest possible degree of certainty that those who killed or assaulted federal officers were brought to justice. In the congressional mind, with the reliance upon the Attorney General's letter, certainty required that these cases be tried in the federal courts, for no matter how "respectable and well disposed," it would not be unreasonable to suppose that state officials would not always or necessarily share congressional feelings of urgency as to the necessity of prompt and vigorous prosecutions of those who violate the safety of the federal officer. From the days of prohibition to the days of the modern civil rights movement, the statutes federal agents have sworn to uphold and enforce have not always been popular in every corner of the Nation. Congress may well have concluded that § 111 was necessary in order to insure uniformly vigorous protection of federal personnel, including those engaged in locally unpopular activity.

We conclude, from all this, that in order to effectuate the congressional purpose of according maximum protection to federal officers by making prosecution for assaults upon them cognizable in the federal courts, § 111 cannot be construed as embodying an unexpressed requirement that an assailant be aware that his victim is a federal officer. All the statute requires is an intent to assault, not an intent to assault a federal officer. A contrary conclusion would give insufficient protection to the agent enforcing an unpopular law, and none to the agent acting under cover.[18]

This interpretation poses no risk of unfairness to defendants. It is no snare for the unsuspecting. Although the perpetrator of a narcotics "rip-off," such as the one involved here, may be surprised to find that his intended victim is a federal officer in civilian apparel, he nonetheless knows from the very outset that his planned course of conduct is wrongful. The situation is not one where legitimate conduct becomes unlawful solely because of the identity of the individual or agency affected. In a case of this kind the offender takes his victim as he finds him. The concept of criminal intent does not extend so far as to require that the actor understand not only the nature of his act but also its consequence for the choice of a judicial forum.

We are not to be understood as implying that the defendant's state of knowledge is never a relevant consideration under § 111. The statute does require a criminal intent, and there may well be circumstances in which ignorance of the official status of the person assaulted or resisted negates the very existence of mens rea. For example, where an officer fails to identify himself or his purpose, his conduct in certain circumstances might reasonably be interpreted as the unlawful use of force directed either at the defendant or his property. In a situation of that kind, one might be justified in exerting an element of resistance, and an honest mistake of fact would not be consistent with criminal intent.

We hold, therefore, that in order to incur criminal liability under § 111 an actor must entertain merely the criminal intent to do the acts therein specified. We now consider whether the rule should be different where persons conspire to commit those acts.

■ MR. JUSTICE STEWART, with whom MR. JUSTICE DOUGLAS joins, dissenting.

.   .   .

---

18. Some indication that Congress did not intend to exclude undercover agents from the protection of the statute comes from the inclusion of the term "Secret Service operative" in the list of protected officials in the 1934 Act. In the 1948 revision, that term was replaced by "any officer, or employee of the secret service or of the Bureau of Narcotics." 62 Stat. 756. That Bureau, in 1948 part of the Treasury, has since been abolished and its functions transferred to the Bureau of Narcotics and Dangerous Drugs, the predecessor agency to the present Drug Enforcement Administration. See Reorganization Plan No. 2 of 1973, 38 Fed.Reg. 15932.

Our Brother STEWART in dissent asserts, that since only state prohibitions of simple assault deter attack on the undercover agent, it is "nonsense" to hold that Congress concluded that a strict scienter requirement would have given insufficient protection to undercover agents. This argument conveniently ignores § 1 of the 1934 Act, the homicide prohibition. Certainly prior to 1934 all States outlawed murder, and if the congressional judgment that there was need to prosecute in federal courts assaults upon federal officers regardless of the reach of state law was "nonsense," enactment of the homicide prohibition—completely duplicating the coverage of state statutes—was legislative fatuity. It is more plausible, we think, to conclude that Congress chose not to entrust to the States sole responsibility for the interdiction of attacks, fatal or not, upon federal law enforcement officials—a matter essential to the morale of all federal law enforcement personnel and central to the efficacy of federal law enforcement activities. The dissent would have us conclude that Congress silently chose to treat assaults and homicides differently; but we have before us one bill with a single legislative history, and we decline to bifurcate our interpretation.

The Court recognizes that "(t)he question ... is not whether the ('federal officer') requirement is jurisdictional, but whether it is jurisdictional only." Put otherwise, the question is whether Congress intended to write an aggravated assault statute, analogous to the many state statutes which protect the persons and functions of state officers against assault, or whether Congress intended merely to federalize every assault which happens to have a federal officer as its victim. The Court chooses the latter interpretation, reading the federal-officer requirement to be jurisdictional only. This conclusion is inconsistent with the pertinent legislative history, the verbal structure of § 111, accepted canons of statutory construction, and the dictates of common sense.

Many States provide an aggravated penalty for assaults upon state law enforcement officers; typically the victim-status element transforms the assault from a misdemeanor to a felony. These statutes have a twofold purpose: to reflect the societal gravity associated with assaulting a public officer and, by providing an enhanced deterrent against such assault, to accord to public officers and their functions a protection greater than that which the law of assault otherwise provides to private citizens and their private activities. Consonant with these purposes, the accused's knowledge that his victim had an official status or function is invariably recognized by the States as an essential element of the aggravated offense. Where an assailant had no such knowledge, he could not of course be deterred by the statutory threat of enhanced punishment, and it makes no sense to regard the unknowing assault as being any more reprehensible, in a moral or retributive sense, than if the victim had been, as the assailant supposed, a private citizen.

The state statutes protect only state officers. I would read § 111 as filling the gap and supplying analogous protection for federal officers and their functions. An aggravated penalty should apply only where an assailant knew, or had reason to know, that his victim had some official status or function. It is immaterial whether the assailant knew the victim was employed by the federal, as opposed to a state or local, government. That is a matter of "jurisdiction only," for it does not affect the moral gravity of the act. If the victim was a federal officer, § 111 applies; if he was a state or local officer, an analogous state statute or local ordinance will generally apply. But where the assailant reasonably thought his victim a common citizen or, indeed, a confederate in crime, aggravation is simply out of place, and the case should be tried in the appropriate forum under the general law of assault, as are unknowing assaults on state officers.

The history of § 111 permits no doubt that this is an aggravated assault statute, requiring proof of scienter. . . .

Rummaging through the spare legislative history of the 1934 law, the Court manages to persuade itself that Congress intended to reach unknowing assaults on federal officers. But if that was the congressional intention, which I seriously doubt, it found no expression in the legislative product. The fact is that the 1934 statute expressly required scienter for an assault conviction. An assault on a federal officer was proscribed only if perpetrated "on account of the performance of his official duties." That is, it was necessary not only that the assailant have notice that his victim possessed official status or duties but also that the assailant's motive be retaliation against the exercise of those duties.

It was not until the 1948 recodification that the proscription was expanded to cover assaults on federal officers "while engaged in," as well as "on account of," the performance of official duties. This was, as the Reviser observed, a technical alteration; it produced no instructive legislative history. As presently written, the statute does clearly reach knowing assaults regardless of motive. But to suggest that it also reaches wholly unknowing assaults is to convert the 1948 alteration into one of major substantive importance, which it concededly was not.

The Court has also managed to convince itself that § 254 was not an aggravated assault statute. The surest evidence that § 254 was an aggravated assault statute may be found in its penalty provision. A single unarmed assault was made, and remains, punishable by a sentence of three years' imprisonment and a $5,000 fine. One need not make an exhaustive survey of state law to appreciate that this is a harsher penalty than is typically imposed for an unarmed assault on a private citizen. In 1934, federal law already defined and proscribed all varieties of assault occurring within the admiralty, maritime, and territorial jurisdiction of the United States: The penalty structure extended in graded steps, turning on the intent and methods of the assailant, from three months' to 20 years' imprisonment. If Congress had intended the victim-status element in § 254 to be "jurisdictional only"—to provide merely another jurisdictional basis for trying assaults in the federal courts—there would have been no need to append a new and unique penalty provision to § 254. Instead, Congress could simply have made cross-reference to the pre-existing penalty structure for assaults within federal jurisdiction. This is not idle speculation. It was precisely the solution adopted, in the same 1934 Act, for the new offense of killing a federal officer: Congress provided that that new offense be defined and punished according to the pre-existing, graded, penalty structure for homicides within the maritime, admiralty, and territorial jurisdiction of the United States.

This deliberated difference in definition and penalty treatment between the homicide and the assault statutes has an obvious significance. Congress gave to the new assault statute a unique and substantively novel definition and penalty. Unless we wish to assume that Congress was scatterbrained, we must conclude that it regarded the victim-status element as of substantive—and not merely jurisdictional—importance. That element was seen as an aggravating circumstance, just as is true in the state statutes, and not merely as a factor giving federal prosecutors and judges jurisdiction to deal with the offense.

The Court reasons otherwise. Positing that the victim-status element in the homicide statute is jurisdictional only, the Court concludes that the same must be true of the assault statute. Even assuming the premise, the conclusion does not follow. Quite apart from the radically different ways in which the two statutes provide for offense-definition and penalties, it requires little imagination to appreciate how Congress could regard the victim status element as "jurisdictional only" in the homicide case but substantively significant in the assault case. The Court itself supplies a possible reason:

"(The homicide statute) was not needed to fill a gap in existing substantive state law. The States proscribed murder, and, until recently, with the enactment of certain statutes in response to the successful attack on capital punishment, murder of a peace officer has not been deemed an aggravated form of murder, for all States usually have punished murderers with the most severe sanction the law allows."

In other words, the Court suggests that the widely perceived distinction, in morality and social policy, between assaults, depending upon the assailant's knowledge of the identity of the victim, found little or no echo in the law of homicide. From this, the natural conclusion—fortified by the penalty provisions—would be that Congress discriminated between the two statutes, recognizing the substantive distinction in the one and not in the other. For reasons I cannot fathom, the Court instead assumes that Congress was unable to discriminate in this fashion—that what had been self-evident to state legislatures was beyond the capacity of the National Legislature to comprehend. The Court says it cannot believe "Congress silently chose to treat assaults and homicides differently. . . . (W)e have before us one bill with a single legislative history, and we decline to bifurcate our interpretation." Ante, n. 18. But it was Congress itself that "bifurcated" the 1934 statute—by treating homicides and assaults differently as regards penalty and offense definition, and by proscribing only those assaults that were "on account of the performance of official duties." What the Court "declines" to do is to read the statute that Congress wrote.

While the legislative history of the 1934 law is "scant," Ladner v. United States, 358 U.S., at 174, 79 S.Ct., at 212, it is sufficient to locate a congressional purpose consistent only with implication of a scienter requirement. As the Court said in Ladner: "(T)he congressional aim was to prevent hindrance to the execution of official duty, and thus to assure the carrying out of federal purposes and interests, and was not to protect federal officers except as incident to that aim." Id., at 175–176, 79 S.Ct., at 213. This purpose is, of course, exactly analogous to the purposes supporting the state statutes which provide enhanced punishment for assault on state officers. A statute proscribing interference with official duty does not "prevent hindrance" with that duty where the assailant thinks his victim is a mere private citizen, or indeed, a confederate in his criminal activity.

To avoid this self-evident proposition, the Court effectively overrules Ladner and concludes that the assault statute aims as much at protecting individual officers as it does at protecting the functions they execute. If the Ladner Court had shared this opinion, it would not have held, as it did, that a single shotgun blast wounding two federal agents was to be considered a single assault. But in any event, even today's revisionist treatment of Ladner does not succeed in getting the Court where it wants to go. So far as the scienter requirement is concerned, it makes no difference whether the statute aims to protect individuals, or functions, or both. The Court appears to think that extending § 111 to unknowing assaults will deter such assaults—will "give ... protection ... to the agent acting under cover." This, of course, is nonsense. The federal statute "protects" an officer from assault only when the assailant knows that the victim is an officer. Absent such knowledge, the only "protection" is that provided by the general law of assault, for that is the only law which the potential assailant reasonably, if erroneously, believes applicable in the circumstances.

The Court also suggests that implication of a scienter requirement "would give insufficient protection to the agent enforcing an unpopular law." This is to repeat the same error. Whatever the "popularity" of the laws he is executing, and whatever the construction placed on § 111, a federal officer is "protected" from assault by that statute only where the assailant has some indication from the circumstances that his victim is other than a private citizen. Assuming, arguendo, that Congress thought that local prosecutors and judges were insufficiently enthusiastic about trying cases involving assaults on federal officers, it remains the fact that a federal statute proscribing knowing assaults meets this concern in every case where local attitudes might conceivably embolden the populace to interfere with federal officers enforcing an "unpopular" law.

The fact is that there is absolutely no indication that before 1934 local prosecutors and judges were lax in trying cases involving assaults on federal officers, that Congress thought so, or—and this is the major point—that Congress was so obsessed by the esoteric "problem" of unknowing assaults on officers who, if known, would be unpopular, as to enact a statute severely aggravated in penalty but blind to the commonsense distinction between knowing and unknowing assaults. The list of covered officers was long and varied in 1934; it has since become even more so. I can perceive no design to single out officers charged with the execution of "unpopular" laws or given to using undercover techniques. The Attorney General's letter in support of the 1934 enactment disavowed any criticism of the integrity or good faith of local law enforcement authorities. He was at pains to stress that the "Federal Government should not be compelled to rely upon the courts of the states, however respectable and well disposed...." His particular concern was that "(i)n these cases resort must usually be had to the local police court, which affords but little relief to us, under the circumstances, in our effort to further the legitimate purposes of the Federal Government." This is most reasonably read as a reference to the fact that, absent some statute aggravating the offense, assault was and is merely a misdemeanor—a "police court" offense—in many States. To deal with this problem, the Attorney General sought enactment of a federal aggravated assault statute, Congress obliged, and this Court should give the statute its natural interpretation.

Turning from the history of the statute to its structure, the propriety of implying a scienter requirement becomes manifest. The statute proscribes not only assault but also a whole series of related acts. It applies to any person who "forcibly assaults, resists, opposes, impedes, intimidates, or interferes with (a federal officer) ... while engaged in or on account of the performance of his official duties." (Emphasis added.) It can hardly be denied that the emphasized words imply a scienter requirement. Generally speaking, these acts are legal and moral wrongs only if the actor knows that his "victim" enjoys a moral or legal privilege to detain him or order him about. . . .

If the words grouped in the statute with "assaults" require scienter, it follows that scienter is also required for an assault conviction. One need hardly rely on such Latin Phrases as ejusdem generis and noscitur a sociis to reach this obvious conclusion. The Court suggests that assault may be treated differently, "with no risk of unfairness," because an assailant—unlike one who merely "opposes" or "resists"—"knows from the very outset that his planned course of conduct is wrongful" even though he "may be surprised to find that his intended victim is a federal officer in civilian apparel." This argument will not do, either as a matter of statutory construction or as a matter of elementary justice.

The Court is saying that because all assaults are wrong, it is "fair" to regard them all as equally wrong. This is a strange theory of justice. As the States recognize, an unknowing assault on an officer is less reprehensible than a knowing assault; to provide that the former may be punished as harshly as the latter is to create a very real "risk of unfairness." It is not unprecedented for Congress to enact stringent legislation, but today it is the Court that rewrites a statute so as to create an inequity which Congress itself had no intention of inflicting.

To treat assaults differently from the other acts associated with it in the statute is a pure exercise in judicial legislation. In Ladner v. United States, 358 U.S., at 176, 79 S.Ct., at 213, the Court noted that the "Government frankly conceded on the oral argument that assault can be treated no differently from the other outlawed activities." The Court characterized this concession as "necessary in view of the lack of any indication that assault was to be treated differently, and in light of 18 U.S.C. § 111, the present recodification of § 254, which lumps assault in with the rest of the offensive actions," id., at 176 n. 4, 79 S.Ct. 213. This analysis was not mere dictum but strictly necessary to the result reached in Ladner. No contrary analysis can be squared with the statutory history.

The implication of scienter here is as necessary and proper as it was in Morissette v. United States, 342 U.S. 246, 72 S.Ct. 240, 96 L.Ed. 288. The Court there read a scienter requirement into a federal larceny statute over the government's objection that the need for scienter should not be implied for a federal offense when the statute that created the offense was silent on the subject. The Court said:

"Congressional silence as to mental elements in an Act merely adopting into federal statutory law a concept of crime already so well defined in common law and statutory interpretation by the states may warrant quite contrary inferences than the same silence in creating an offense new to general law, for whose definition the courts have no guidance except the Act. . . .

". . . (W)here Congress borrows terms of art in which are accumulated the legal tradition and meaning of centuries of practice, it presumably knows and adopts the cluster of ideas that were attached to each borrowed word in the body of learning from which it was taken and the meaning its use will convey to the judicial mind unless otherwise instructed." Id., at 262–263, 72 S.Ct. at 249–250.

The same principle applies here. The terms and purposes of § 111 flow from well-defined and familiar law proscribing obstructions of justice, and the provision complements a pattern of state aggravated assault statutes which are uniform and unambiguous in requiring scienter.

We see today the unfortunate consequences of deciding an important question without the benefit of the adversary process. In this rush to judgment, settled precedents, such as *Ladner v. United States, supra,* are subverted. Legislative history is ignored or imaginatively reconstructed. Statutory terms are broken from their context and given unnatural readings. On top of it all, the Court disregards two firmly established cannons of statutory construction—"two wise principles this Court has long followed":

"First, as we have recently reaffirmed, 'ambiguity concerning the ambit of criminal statutes should be resolved in favor of lenity.' Rewis v. United States, 401 U.S. 808, 812, 91 S.Ct. 1056, 1059, 28 L.Ed.2d 493 (1971). *See also* Ladner v. United States, 358 U.S. 169, 177, 79 S.Ct. 209, 213, 3 L.Ed.2d 199 (1958); Bell v. United States, 349 U.S. 81, 75 S.Ct. 620, 99 L.Ed. 905 (1955); United States v. Five Gambling Devices etc., 346 U.S. 441, 74 S.Ct. 190, 98 L.Ed. 179 (1953) (plurality opinion for affirmance) . . .

". . . (S)econd . . .: unless Congress conveys its purpose clearly, it will not be deemed to have significantly changed the federal-state balance. Congress has traditionally been reluctant to define as a federal crime conduct readily denounced as criminal by the States. . . . In traditionally sensitive areas, such as legislation affecting the federal balance, the requirement of clear statement assures that the legislature has in fact faced, and intended to bring into issue, the critical matters involved in the judicial decision." United States v. Bass, 404 U.S. 336, 347, 92 S.Ct. 515, 522, 30 L.Ed.2d 488.

If the Congress desires to sweep all assaults upon federal employees into the federal courts, a suitable statute could be easily enacted. I should hope that in so doing the Congress, like every State which has dealt with the matter, would make a distinction in penalty between an assailant who knows the official identity of the victim and one who does not. That result would have a double advantage over the result reached by the Court today. It would be a fair law, and it would be the product of the lawmaking branch of our Government.

For the reasons stated, I believe that before there can be a violation of 18 U.S.C. § 111, an assailant must know or have reason to know that the person he assaults is an officer. It follows a fortiori that there can be no criminal conspiracy to violate the statute in the absence of at least equivalent knowledge. Accordingly, I respectfully dissent from the opinion and judgment of the Court.

Flores–Figueroa v. United States

Supreme Court of the United States, 2009.
___ U.S. ___, 129 S.Ct. 1886, 173 L.Ed.2d 853.

■ JUSTICE BREYER delivered the opinion of the Court.

A federal criminal statute forbidding "[a]ggravated identity theft" imposes a mandatory consecutive 2–year prison term upon individuals

convicted of certain other crimes *if,* during (or in relation to) the commission of those other crimes, the offender "*knowingly* transfers, possesses, or uses, without lawful authority, *a means of identification of another person.*" 18 U.S.C. § 1028A(a)(1) (emphasis added). The question is whether the
statute requires the Government to show that the defendant *knew* that the "means of identification" he or she unlawfully transferred, possessed, or used, in fact, belonged to "another person." We conclude that it does.

I

A

The statutory provision in question references a set of predicate crimes, including, for example, theft of government property, fraud, or engaging in various unlawful activities related to passports, visas, and immigration. § 1028A(c). It then provides that if any person who commits any of those other crimes (in doing so) "knowingly transfers, possesses, or uses, without lawful authority, a means of identification of another person," the judge must add two years' imprisonment to the offender's underlying sentence. § 1028A(a)(1). All parties agree that the provision applies only where the offender knows that he is transferring, possessing, or using *something.* And the Government reluctantly concedes that the offender likely must know that he is transferring, possessing, or using that *something* without lawful authority. But they do not agree whether the provision requires that a defendant also know that the *something* he has unlawfully transferred is, for example, a real ID belonging to another person rather than, say, a fake ID (*i.e.,* a group of numbers that does not correspond to any real Social Security number).

Petitioner Ignacio Flores–Figueroa argues that the statute requires that the Government prove that he *knew* that the "means of identification" belonged to someone else, *i.e.,* was "a means of identification *of another person.*" The Government argues that the statute does not impose this particular knowledge requirement. The Government concedes that the statute uses the word "knowingly," but that word, the Government claims, does not modify the statute's last phrase ("a means of identification of another person") or, at the least, it does not modify the last three words of that phrase ("of another person").

B

The facts of this case illustrate the legal problem. Ignacio Flores–Figueroa is a citizen of Mexico. In 2000, to secure employment, Flores gave his employer a false name, birth date, and Social Security number, along with a counterfeit alien registration card. The Social Security number and the number on the alien registration card were not those of a real person. In 2006, Flores presented his employer with new counterfeit Social Security and alien registration cards; these cards (unlike Flores' old alien registration card) used his real name. But this time the numbers on both cards were in fact numbers assigned to other people.

Flores' employer reported his request to U.S. Immigration and Customs Enforcement. Customs discovered that the numbers on Flores' new documents belonged to other people. The United States then charged Flores with two predicate crimes, namely, entering the United States without inspection, 8 U.S.C. § 1325(a), and misusing immigration documents, 18 U.S.C. § 1546(a). And it charged him with aggravated identity theft, 18 U.S.C. § 1028A(a)(1), the crime at issue here.

Flores moved for a judgment of acquittal on the "aggravated identity theft" counts. He claimed that the Government could not prove that he *knew* that the numbers on the counterfeit documents were numbers assigned to other people. The Government replied that it need not prove that knowledge, and the District Court accepted the Government's argument. After a bench trial, the court found Flores guilty of the predicate crimes and aggravated identity theft. The Court of Appeals upheld the District Court's determination. 274 Fed.Appx. 501 (C.A.8 2008) *(per curiam)*. And we granted certiorari to consider the "knowledge" issue-a matter about which the Circuits have disagreed. Compare *United States v. Godin,* 534 F.3d 51 (C.A.1 2008) (knowledge requirement applies to "of another person"); *United States v. Miranda–Lopez,* 532 F.3d 1034 (C.A.9 2008) (same); *United States v. Villanueva–Sotelo,* 515 F.3d 1234 (C.A.D.C. 2008) (same), with *United States v. Mendoza–Gonzalez,* 520 F.3d 912 (C.A.8 2008) (knowledge requirement does not apply to "of another person"); *United States v. Hurtado,* 508 F.3d 603 (C.A.11 2007) (per curiam) (same); *United States v. Montejo,* 442 F.3d 213 (C.A.4 2006) (same).

II

There are strong textual reasons for rejecting the Government's position. As a matter of ordinary English grammar, it seems natural to read the statute's word "knowingly" as applying to all the subsequently listed elements of the crime. The Government cannot easily claim that the word "knowingly" applies only to the statutes first four words, or even its first seven. It makes little sense to read the provision's language as heavily penalizing a person who "transfers, possesses, or uses, without lawful authority" a *something,* but does not know, at the very least, that the "something" (perhaps inside a box) is a "means of identification." Would we apply a statute that makes it unlawful *"knowingly* to possess drugs" to a person who steals a passenger's bag without knowing that the bag has drugs inside?

The Government claims more forcefully that the word "knowingly" applies to all but the statute's last three words, *i.e.,* "of another person." The statute, the Government says, does not require a prosecutor to show that the defendant *knows* that the means of identification the defendant has unlawfully used in fact belongs to another person. But how are we to square this reading with the statute's language?

In ordinary English, where a transitive verb has an object, listeners in most contexts assume that an adverb (such as knowingly) that modifies the transitive verb tells the listener how the subject performed the entire action, including the object as set forth in the sentence. Thus, if a bank official says, "Smith knowingly transferred the funds to his brother's account," we would normally understand the bank official's statement as telling us that Smith knew the account was his brother's. Nor would it matter if the bank official said "Smith knowingly transferred the funds to the account of his brother." In either instance, if the bank official later told us that Smith did not know the account belonged to Smith's brother, we should be surprised.

Of course, a statement that does *not* use the word "knowingly" may be unclear about just what Smith knows. Suppose Smith mails his bank draft to Tegucigalpa, which (perhaps unbeknownst to Smith) is the capital of Honduras. If the bank official says, "Smith sent a bank draft to the capital of Honduras," he has expressed next to nothing about Smith's knowledge of that geographic identity. But if the official were to say, "Smith *knowingly* sent a bank draft to the capital of Honduras," then the official has suggested that Smith knows his geography.

Similar examples abound. If a child knowingly takes a toy that belongs to his sibling, we assume that the child not only knows that he is taking something, but that he also knows that what he is taking is a toy *and* that the toy belongs to his sibling. If we say that someone knowingly ate a sandwich with cheese, we normally assume that the person knew both that he was eating a sandwich and that it contained cheese. Or consider the Government's own example, " 'John knowingly discarded the homework of his sister.' " Brief for United States 9. The Government rightly points out that this sentence "does not *necessarily*" imply that John knew whom the homework belonged to. *Ibid.* (emphasis added). But that is what the sentence, as *ordinarily* used, does imply.

At the same time, dissimilar examples are not easy to find. The Government says that "knowingly" modifies only the verbs in the statute, while remaining indifferent to the subject's knowledge of at least part of the transitive verb's object. In certain contexts, a listener might understand the word "knowingly" to be used in that way. But the Government has not provided us with a single example of a sentence that, when used in typical fashion, would lead the hearer to believe that the word "knowingly" modifies only a transitive verb without the full object, *i.e.,* that it leaves the hearer gravely uncertain about the subject's state of mind in respect to the full object of the transitive verb in the sentence. The likely reason is that such sentences typically involve special contexts or themselves provide a more detailed explanation of background circumstances that call for such a reading. As Justice ALITO notes, the inquiry into a sentence's meaning is a contextual one. No special context is present here.

The manner in which the courts ordinarily interpret criminal statutes is fully consistent with this ordinary English usage. That is to say courts ordinarily read a phrase in a criminal statute that introduces the elements of a crime with the word "knowingly" as applying that word to each element. *United States v. X–Citement Video, Inc.,* 513 U.S. 64, 79, 115 S.Ct. 464, 130 L.Ed.2d 372 (1994) (STEVENS, J., concurring). For example, in *Liparota v. United States,* 471 U.S. 419, 105 S.Ct. 2084, 85 L.Ed.2d 434 (1985), this Court interpreted a federal food stamp statute that said, " 'whoever knowingly uses, transfers, acquires, alters, or possesses coupons or authorization cards *in any manner not authorized by [law]* ' " is subject to imprisonment. *Id.,* at 420, n. 1, 105 S.Ct. 2084. The question was whether the word "knowingly" applied to the phrase "in any manner not authorized by [law]." *Id.,* at 423, 105 S.Ct. 2084. The Court held that it did, *id.,* at 433, 105 S.Ct. 2084, despite the legal cliche "ignorance of the law is no excuse."

More recently, we had to interpret a statute that penalizes "[a]ny person who-(1) knowingly transports or ships using any means or facility of interstate or foreign commerce by any means including by computer or mails, any visual depiction, if-(A) the producing of such visual depiction involves the use of a minor engaging in sexually explicit conduct." 18 U.S.C. § 2252(a)(1)(A); *X-Citement Video, supra.* In issue was whether the term "knowingly" in paragraph (1) modified the phrase "the use of a minor" in subparagraph (A). *Id.,* at 69, 115 S.Ct. 464. The language in issue in *X-Citement Video* (like the language in *Liparota*) was more ambiguous than the language here not only because the phrase "the use of a minor" was not the direct object of the verbs modified by "knowingly," but also because it appeared in a different subsection. 513 U.S., at 68–69, 115 S.Ct. 464. Moreover, the fact that many sex crimes involving minors do not ordinarily require that a perpetrator know that his victim is a minor supported the Government's position. Nonetheless, we again found that the intent element applied to "the use of a minor." *Id.,* at 72, and n. 2, 115 S.Ct. 464. Again the Government, while pointing to what it believes are special features of each of these cases, provides us with no convincing counterexample, although there may be such statutory instances.

The Government correctly points out that in these cases more was at issue than proper use of the English language. But if more is at issue here, what is it? The Government makes a further textual argument, a complex argument based upon a related provision of the statute. That provision applies "[a]ggravated identity theft" where the predicate crime is terrorism. See § 1028A(a)(2). The provision uses the same language as the provision before us up to the end, where it adds the words "or a false identification document." Thus, it penalizes anyone who "knowingly transfers, possesses, or uses, without lawful authority, a means of identification of another person or a false identification document." § 1028A(a)(2).

The Government's argument has four steps. Step One: We should not interpret a statute in a manner that makes some of its language superfluous. See, *e.g., TRW Inc. v. Andrews,* 534 U.S. 19, 31, 122 S.Ct. 441, 151 L.Ed.2d 339 (2001). Step Two: A person who knows that he is transferring, possessing, or using a " 'means of identification' " " 'without lawful authority,' " must know that the document either (a) belongs " 'to another person' " or (b) is a " 'false identification document' " because " '*there are no other choices.*' " Brief for United States 14 (emphasis added). Step Three: Requiring the offender to *know* that the "means of identification" belongs to another person would consequently be superfluous in this terrorism provision. Step Four: We should not interpret the same phrase ("of another person") in the two related sections differently.

If we understand the argument correctly, it seems to suffer two serious flaws. If the two listed circumstances (where the ID belongs to another person; where the ID is false) are the only two circumstances possibly present when a defendant (in this particular context) unlawfully uses a "means of identification," then why list them at all? Why not just stop after criminalizing the knowing unlawful use of a "means of identification"? (Why specify that Congress does not mean the statute to cover, say, the use of dog tags?) The fact is, however, that the Government's reasoning at Step Two is faulty. The two listed circumstances are *not* the only two circumstances possibly present when a defendant unlawfully uses a "means of identification." One could, for example, verbally provide a seller or an employer with a made-up Social Security number, not an "identification *document*," and the number verbally transmitted to the seller or employer might, or might not, turn out to belong to another person. The word "knowingly" applied to the "other person" requirement (even in a statute that similarly penalizes use of a "false identification *document*") would not be surplus.

The Government also considers the statute's purpose to be a circumstance showing that the linguistic context here is special. It describes that purpose as "provid[ing] enhanced protection for individuals whose identifying information is used to facilitate the commission of crimes." *Id.,* at 5. And it points out that without the knowledge requirement, potential offenders will take great care to avoid wrongly using IDs that belong to others, thereby enhancing the protection that the statute offers.

The question, however, is whether Congress intended to achieve this enhanced protection by permitting conviction of those who do not *know* the ID they unlawfully use refers to a real person, *i.e.,* those who do not *intend* to cause this further harm. And, in respect to this latter point, the statute's history (outside of the statute's language) is inconclusive.

On the one hand, some statements in the legislative history offer the Government a degree of support. The relevant House Report refers, for example, both to "identity*1893 theft" (use of an ID belonging to someone else) and to "identity fraud" (use of a false ID), often without distinguishing between the two. See, *e.g.,* H.R.Rep. No. 108–528, p. 25 (2004), U.S.Code Cong. & Admin.News 2004, pp. 779, 788 (statement of Rep. Coble). And, in equating fraud and theft, Congress might have meant the statute to cover both-at least where the fraud takes the form of using an ID that (without the offender's knowledge) belongs to someone else.

On the other hand, Congress separated the fraud crime from the theft crime in the statute itself. The title of one provision (not here at issue) is "Fraud and related activity in connection with identification documents, authentication features, and information." 18 U.S.C. § 1028. The title of another provision (the provision here at issue) uses the words "identity *theft*." § 1028A (emphasis added). Moreover, the examples of theft that Congress gives in the legislative history all involve instances where the offender would know that what he has taken identifies a different real person. H.R.Rep. No. 108–528, at 4–5, U.S.Code Cong. & Admin.News 2004, pp. 779, 780–81 (identifying as examples of "identity theft" " 'dumpster diving,' " "accessing information that was originally collected for an authorized purpose," "hack[ing] into computers," and "steal[ing] paperwork likely to contain personal information").

Finally, and perhaps of greatest practical importance, there is the difficulty in many circumstances of proving beyond a reasonable doubt that a defendant has the necessary knowledge. Take an instance in which an alien who unlawfully entered the United States gives an employer identification documents that *in fact* belong to others. How is the Government to prove that the defendant *knew* that this was so? The Government may be able to show that such a defendant knew the papers were not his. But perhaps the defendant did not care whether the papers (1) were real papers belonging to another person or (2) were simply counterfeit papers. The difficulties of proof along with the defendant's necessary guilt of a predicate crime and the defendant's necessary knowledge that he has acted "without lawful authority," make it reasonable, in the Government's view, to read the statute's language as dispensing with the knowledge requirement.

We do not find this argument sufficient, however, to turn the tide in the Government's favor. For one thing, in the classic case of identity theft, intent is generally not difficult to prove. For example, where a defendant has used another person's identification information to get access to that person's bank account, the Government can prove knowledge with little difficulty. The same is true when the defendant has gone through someone else's trash to find discarded credit card and bank statements, or pretends to be from the victim's bank and requests personal identifying information. Indeed, the examples of identity theft in the legislative history (dumpster diving, computer hacking, and the like) are all examples of the types of classic identity theft where intent should be relatively easy to prove, and there will be no practical enforcement problem. For another thing, to the extent that Congress may have been concerned about criminalizing the conduct of a broader class of individuals, the concerns about practical enforceability are insufficient to outweigh the clarity of the text. Similar interpretations that we have given other similarly phrased statutes also created practical enforcement problems. See, *e.g., X–Citement Video,* 513 U.S. 64, 115 S.Ct. 464, 130 L.Ed.2d 372; *Liparota,* 471 U.S. 419, 105 S.Ct. 2084, 85 L.Ed.2d 434. But had Congress placed conclusive weight upon practical enforcement, the statute would likely not read the way it now reads. Instead, Congress used the word "knowingly" followed by a list of offense elements. And we cannot find indications in statements of its purpose or in the practical problems of enforcement sufficient to overcome the ordinary meaning, in English or through ordinary interpretive practice, of the words that it wrote.

We conclude that § 1028A(a)(1) requires the Government to show that the defendant knew that the means of identification at issue belonged to another person. The judgment of the Court of Appeals is reversed, and the case is remanded for further proceedings consistent with this opinion.

It is so ordered.

■ JUSTICE SCALIA, with whom JUSTICE THOMAS joins, concurring in part and concurring in the judgment.

I agree with the Court that to convict petitioner for "knowingly transfer [ring], possess[ing], or us[ing], without lawful authority, a means of identification of another person," 18 U.S.C. § 1028A(a)(1), the Government must prove that he "*knew* that the 'means of identification' he . . .

unlawfully transferred, possessed, or used, in fact, belonged to 'another person.'" "Knowingly" is not limited to the statute's verbs, *ante,* at 1890. Even the Government must concede that. See *United States v. Villanueva-Sotelo,* 515 F.3d 1234, 1237 (C.A.D.C.2008) ("According to the government, this text is unambiguous: the statute's knowledge requirement extends only so far as 'means of identification'"). But once it is understood to modify the object of those verbs, there is no reason to believe it does not extend to the phrase which limits that object ("of another person"). Ordinary English usage supports this reading, as the Court's numerous sample sentences amply demonstrate. See *ante,* at 1890.

But the Court is not content to stop at the statute's text, and I do not join that further portion of the Court's opinion. First, the Court relies in part on the principle that "courts ordinarily read a phrase in a criminal statute that introduces the elements of a crime with the word 'knowingly' as applying that word to each element." If that is meant purely as a description of what most cases do, it is perhaps true, and perhaps not. I have not canvassed all the cases and am hence agnostic. If it is meant, however, as a normative description of what courts *should* ordinarily do when interpreting such statutes-and the reference to Justice STEVENS' concurring opinion in *United States v. X–Citement Video, Inc.,* 513 U.S. 64, 79, 115 S.Ct. 464, 130 L.Ed.2d 372 (1994), suggests as much-then I surely do not agree. The structure of the text in *X-Citement Video* plainly separated the "use of a minor" element from the "knowingly" requirement, wherefore I thought (and think) that case was wrongly decided. See *id.,* at 80–81, 115 S.Ct. 464 (SCALIA, J., dissenting). It is one thing to infer the common-law tradition of a *mens rea* requirement where Congress has not addressed the mental element of a crime. See *Staples v. United States,* 511 U.S. 600, 605, 114 S.Ct. 1793, 128 L.Ed.2d 608 (1994); *United States v. United States Gypsum Co.,* 438 U.S. 422, 437–438, 98 S.Ct. 2864, 57 L.Ed.2d 854 (1978). It is something else to expand a *mens rea* requirement that the statutory text has carefully limited.

I likewise cannot join the Court's discussion of the (as usual, inconclusive) legislative history. Relying on the statement of a single Member of Congress or an unvoted-upon (and for all we know unread) Committee Report to expand a statute beyond the limits its text suggests is always a dubious enterprise. And consulting those incunabula with an eye to making criminal what the text would otherwise permit is even more suspect. See *United States v. R.L.C.,* 503 U.S. 291, 307–309, 112 S.Ct. 1329, 117 L.Ed.2d 559 (1992) (SCALIA, J., concurring in part and concurring in judgment). Indeed, it is not unlike the practice of Caligula, who reportedly "wrote his laws in a very small character, and hung them up upon high pillars, the more effectually to ensnare the people," 1 W. Blackstone, Commentaries on the Laws of England 46 (1765).

The statute's text is clear, and I would reverse the judgment of the Court of Appeals on that ground alone.

■ JUSTICE ALITO, concurring in part and concurring in the judgment.

While I am in general agreement with the opinion of the Court, I write separately because I am concerned that the Court's opinion may be read by some as adopting an overly rigid rule of statutory construction. The Court says that "[i]n ordinary English, where a transitive verb has an object, listeners in most contexts assume that an adverb (such as knowingly) that modifies the transitive verb tells the listener how the subject performed the entire action, including the object as set forth in the sentence." The Court adds that counterexamples are "not easy to find," and I suspect that the Court's opinion will be cited for the proposition that the *mens rea* of a federal criminal statute nearly always applies to every element of the offense.

I think that the Court's point about ordinary English usage is overstated. Examples of sentences that do not conform to the Court's rule are not hard to imagine. For example: "The mugger knowingly assaulted two people in the park-an employee of company X and a jogger from town Y." A person hearing this sentence would not likely assume that the mugger knew about the first victim's employer or the second victim's home town. What matters in this example, and the Court's, is context.

More to the point, ordinary writers do not often construct the particular kind of sentence at issue here, *i.e.*, a complex sentence in which it is important to determine from the sentence itself whether the adverb denoting the actor's intent applies to every characteristic of the sentence's direct object. Such sentences are a staple of criminal codes, but in ordinary speech, a different formulation is almost always used when the speaker wants to be clear on the point. For example, a speaker might say: "Flores–Figueroa used a Social Security number that he knew belonged to someone else" or "Flores–Figueroa used a Social Security number that just happened to belong to a real person." But it is difficult to say with the confidence the Court conveys that there is an "ordinary" understanding of the usage of the phrase at issue in this case.

In interpreting a criminal statute such as the one before us, I think it is fair to begin with a general presumption that the specified *mens rea* applies to all the elements of an offense, but it must be recognized that there are instances in which context may well rebut that presumption. For example, 18 U.S.C. § 2423(a) makes it unlawful to "knowingly transpor[t] an individual who has not attained the age of 18 years in interstate or foreign commerce ... with intent that the individual engage in prostitution, or in any sexual activity for which any person can be charged with a criminal offense." The Courts of Appeals have uniformly held that a defendant need not know the victim's age to be guilty under this statute. See, *e.g.*, *United States v. Griffith*, 284 F.3d 338, 350–351 (C.A.2 2002); *United States v. Taylor*, 239 F.3d 994, 997 (C.A.9 2001); cf. *United States v. Chin*, 981 F.2d 1275, 1280 (C.A.D.C.1992) (Ginsburg, J.) (holding that 21 U.S.C. § 861(a)(1), which makes it unlawful to "knowingly and intentionally ... employ, hire, use, persuade, induce, entice, or coerce, a person under eighteen years of age to violate" drug laws, does not require the defendant to have knowledge of the minor's age). Similarly, 8 U.S.C. § 1327 makes it unlawful to "knowingly ai[d] or assis[t] any alien inadmissible under section 1182(a)(2) (insofar as an alien inadmissible under such section has been convicted of an aggravated felony) ... to enter the United States." The Courts of Appeals have held that the term "knowingly" in this context does not require the defendant to know that the alien had been convicted of an aggravated felony. See, *e.g., United States v. Flores–Garcia,* 198 F.3d 1119, 1121–1123 (C.A.9 2000); *United States v. Figueroa,* 165 F.3d 111, 118–119 (C.A.2 1998).

In the present case, however, the Government has not pointed to contextual features that warrant interpreting 18 U.S.C. § 1028A(a)(1) in a similar way. Indeed, the Government's interpretation leads to exceedingly odd results. Under that interpretation, if a defendant uses a made-up Social Security number without having any reason to know whether it belongs to a real person, the defendant's liability under § 1028A(a)(1) depends on chance: If it turns out that the number belongs to a real person, two years will be added to the defendant's sentence, but if the defendant is lucky and the number does not belong to another person, the statute is not violated.

I therefore concur in the judgment and join the opinion of the Court except insofar as it may be read to adopt an inflexible rule of construction that can rarely be overcome by contextual features pointing to a contrary reading.

SECTION 2.   NEGLIGENCE AND RECKLESSNESS

Statements can be found to the effect that "negligence is a state of mind" or on the other hand that it is "not a state of mind." The difference is largely in the use of terms. Thus if negligence is said to be a state of mind it is conceded that to have juridical consequences it must be "manifested." If it is said not to be a state of mind, this is to emphasize that "the state of mind, which is the cause, must be distinguished from the actual negligence, which is its effect." The tendency is to use the word "negligence" as a synonym for "negligent conduct." This implies something done (or not done under circumstances involving a breach of duty to perform) with a state of mind involving this type of blameworthiness.

Intentional harm falls into quite a different category; and an act may be done with such a wanton and wilful disregard of a socially-harmful consequence known to be likely to result, that the attitude of mind will be more blameworthy than is imported by the word "negligence." Hence attention must be directed to risks of harm created by a state of mind different from either of these. Since some element of risk is involved in many kinds of useful conduct, socially-acceptable conduct cannot be limited to acts which involve no risk at all. To distinguish risks not socially acceptable from those regarded as fairly incident to our mode of life, the former are spoken of as "unreasonable." Even an unreasonable risk, (from the standpoint of the one endangered), may have been created without social fault, if the one who created the risk did not know or have reason to know of the existence of such risk under the circumstances. Hence a distinction is made between risks that are "realizable" and those that are not. Conduct, therefore, may be said to fall below the line of social acceptability if it involves a realizable and unreasonable risk of social harm. With this preface the following definition may be offered: Negligence is any conduct, except conduct intentionally harmful or recklessly disregardful of an interest of others, which falls below the standard established by law for the protection of others against unreasonable risk of harm.[19]

The social purpose underlying the requirement of compensation to the person harmed is not identical with that which forms the basis of punishment. Conceivably, therefore, the standard adopted in the criminal law of negligence might be entirely different from that used in civil cases. This is not exactly the answer since the "measuring stick" here is the conduct of a reasonable person under like circumstances. But whereas the civil law requires conformity to this standard, a very substantial deviation is normally essential to criminal guilt according to the common law. To express this greater degree of deviational behavior it has been common to modify the word "negligence" with some such epithet as "criminal," "culpable," "gross" or "wicked." Needless to say this is a field not subject to exact measurement. What it amounts to as a practical matter is a caution to the jury not to convict of crime, where other elements of culpability are lacking, except where the conduct causing the harm represents a rather extreme case of negligence. The format in some states is to recognize as criminal a standard of negligent conduct denominated as "criminal negligence" and to also punish more severely under a standard of recklessness.[20]

Under some of the statutes guilt may be established by proof of negligence without showing that the conduct fell so far short of social acceptability as to merit the label "criminal" negligence. And a few jurisdictions seem to have taken this position as a matter of common law. Recently, several jurisdictions have accepted a simple negligence standard for criminal liability where the risk of harm is significant or there is a special matter of public safety involved.[21] On the other side of the picture, many offenses require something more than negligence of any degree in order to establish the *mens rea*.

Gian–Cursio v. State

District Court of Appeal of Florida, Third District, 1965.
180 So.2d 396.

■ CARROLL, JUDGE. The appellants, who are chiropractic physicians, were informed against in Dade County, charged with manslaughter by having caused the death of one Roger Mozian through culpable negligence.[22] The

---

19. This follows rather closely the definition adopted for torts by the American Law Institute: "In the Restatement of this Subject, negligence is any conduct, which falls below the standard established by law for the protection of others against unreasonable risk of harm. It does not include conduct recklessly disregardful of an interest of others." Restatement, Second, Torts § 282 (1965).

The torts definition does not include intentional harm. Id. at comment d. For our purposes it seems better to express this exclusion than to leave it to inference.

20. Model Penal Code § 2.02(2)(c) and (d) (1962).

21. West's Cal. Penal Code § 192(c).

22. § 782.07, Fla.Stat., F.S.A., provides as follows: "The killing of a human being by the act, procurement or culpable negligence of another, in cases where such killing shall not be justifiable or excusable homicide nor murder, according to the provisions of this chapter, shall be deemed manslaughter, and shall be punished by imprisonment in the state prison not

defendants were tried together and convicted. Dr. Gian–Cursio was sentenced to confinement for a period of five years, and sentence was suspended as to Dr. Epstein. Motions for new trial filed by defendants were denied, and they appealed. The two appeals were consolidated for presentation in this court.

Appellants contend the evidence was insufficient to support the verdicts and judgments of conviction. In addition, appellant Gian–Cursio, in a second point in his brief, claims errors at trial which he lists as allowing introduction of certain inadmissible evidence and improper impeachment of a witness, and prejudicial remarks by the prosecutor in argument. We have examined the voluminous record of the proceedings on the trial, and on consideration thereof and of the briefs and arguments we conclude that the contentions of the appellants are without merit. In our view the evidence adequately supports the verdicts and judgments against the appellants, and we find no reversible error in the rulings or action of the trial court as referred to in the second point in the brief of appellant Gian–Cursio.

The record discloses that one Roger Mozian died of pulmonary tuberculosis in May of 1963. His disease had been diagnosed in 1951 by Dr. Matis, a New York medical doctor in whose charge he remained for some ten years, during which his tuberculosis continued dormant or arrested. An X-ray examination of Mozian by Dr. Matis in January of 1962 showed his disease had become active. Dr. Matis recommended hospitalization and drug treatment, which Mozian refused. Mozian went under the care of Dr. Gian–Cursio, a licensed chiropractic physician in the State of New York, who practiced Natural Hygiene. Dr. Gian–Cursio was advised that Mozian was suffering from tuberculosis. His treatment of the patient was without drugs and by a vegetarian diet, interspersed with fasting periods. Evidence was in conflict as to length of fasting. There was testimony that on occasion the fasting continued 14 days. Dr. Epstein was a licensed chiropractic physician of Florida. Acting with Dr. Gian–Cursio and under his direction, Dr. Epstein operated a home or establishment for patients in Dade County, Florida. Beginning in the winter of 1962, on the advice of Dr. Gian–Cursio, Mozian went there and was treated by the appellant doctors, in the manner stated above. Eventually, in May of 1963 he was hospitalized, where through other doctors he was given drugs and other approved treatment for the disease but within a matter of days he died, on May 16, 1963. There was testimony that the treatment given Mozian was not approved medical treatment for one with active tuberculosis, and that had he been treated by approved medical methods and given available drugs his disease could have been arrested or controlled. From the evidence the jury could, and no doubt did, conclude that the treatment afforded by the appellants advanced rather than retarded the patient's tuberculosis infection and caused his death, and that their method of treatment of this tuberculosis patient amounted to culpable negligence as it has been defined in the decisions of the Supreme Court of this State. In State v. Heines, 144 Fla. 272, 197 So. 787, 788 the Florida Supreme Court reversed an order quashing a manslaughter information which charged a chiropractic physician with causing

---

exceeding twenty years, or imprisonment in the county jail not exceeding one year, or by fine not exceeding five thousand dollars."

the death of a patient who suffered from diabetes, by culpable negligence through treatment which included taking him off insulin. After citing and discussing the earlier Florida decision, the Florida Supreme Court said:

"We need add little more to what has been written in the three cases cited to show how one who is proven to have offended as detailed in the information has violated the law against manslaughter. If a person undertakes to cure those who search for health and who are, because of their plight, more or less susceptible of following the advice of any one who claims the knowledge and means to heal, he cannot escape the consequence of his gross ignorance of accepted and established remedies and methods for the treatment of diseases, from which he knows his patients suffer and if his wrongful acts, positive or negative, reach the degree of grossness he will be answerable to the State."

In the earlier case of Hampton v. State, the Florida Court went into the matter at greater length, and what they held there is applicable to the situation presented by this record. In that case the Court said (39 So. at 424):

"We do not agree with this contention of the able counsel for the defendant. The law seems to be fairly well settled, both in England and America, that where the death of a person results from the criminal negligence of the medical practitioner in the treatment of the case the latter is guilty of manslaughter, and that this criminal liability is not dependent on whether or not the party undertaking the treatment of the case is a duly licensed practitioner, or merely assumes to act as such, acted with good intent in administering the treatment, and did so with the expectation that the result would prove beneficial, and that the real question upon which the criminal liability depends in such cases is whether there was criminal negligence; that criminal negligence is largely a matter of degree, incapable of precise definition, and whether or not it exists to such a degree as to involve criminal liability is to be determined by the jury; that criminal negligence exists where the physician or surgeon, or person assuming to act as such, exhibits gross lack of competency, or gross inattention, or criminal indifference to the patient's safety, and that this may arise from his gross ignorance of the science of medicine or surgery and of the effect of the remedies employed, through his gross negligence in the application and selection of remedies and his lack of proper skill in the use of instruments, or through his failure to give proper instructions to the patient as to the use of the medicines; that where the person treating the case does nothing that a skillful person might not do, and death results merely from an error of judgment on his part, or an inadvertent mistake, he is not criminally liable."

We reject as unsound the arguments of appellants that because their treatment conformed to generally accepted practice of drugless healers and was rendered in good faith in an effort to help Mozian, it was proper and could not be found to constitute criminal negligence. That, and appellants' further argument that their treatment of Mozian could not have been tested through testimony of medical doctors, is answered adversely to appellants by *Hampton v. State, supra.* In Hampton it was held to be immaterial "whether or not the party undertaking the treatment of the case is a duly licensed practitioner, or merely assumes to act as such, acted with good intent in administering the treatment and did so with the expectation that the results would prove beneficial." Additionally, appellants argue that proximate cause was not established. The issue of proximate cause was one for the jury, and the record furnished substantial evidence upon which that issue was submitted for jury determination.

Under the applicable law as enunciated in the cited Florida cases, the trial court was eminently correct in denying defendants' motions for directed verdict and in submitting the issue of their alleged culpable negligence to the jury. No reversible error having been made to appear, the judgments in appeals numbered 64–514 and 64–561 should be and hereby are affirmed.

Affirmed.[23]

State v. Petersen

Court of Appeals of Oregon, 1974.
17 Or.App. 478, 522 P.2d 912. Affirmed in part, reversed in part, 270 Or. 166, 526 P.2d 1008 (1974).

[This is the case, reported in part in the section on Causation, in which a drag-race which reached speeds of 60–80 miles an hour in a 35–mile zone resulted in the collision of one of the cars, causing the death of the passenger in that vehicle. It was there pointed out that the driver of the other competing vehicle was a proximate cause of the death of the deceased.]

■ Before SCHWAB, C.J., and FORT and TANZER, JJ.

■ TANZER, JUDGE. . . .

A person commits criminal homicide if without justification or excuse, he intentionally, knowingly, recklessly or with criminal negligence causes the death of another human being. ORS 163.005. Criminal homicide constitutes manslaughter when it is committed "recklessly," ORS 163.125(1)(a), which is defined in ORS 161.085(9) as follows:

" 'Recklessly,' when used with respect to a result or to a circumstance described by a statute defining an offense, means that a person is aware of and consciously disregards a substantial and unjustifiable risk that the

---

23.   Accord, Commonwealth v. Pierce, 138 Mass. 165 (1884).

It must be culpable or criminal negligence to support a conviction of manslaughter. Frey v. State, 97 Okl.Cr. 410, 265 P.2d 502 (1953).

To prove criminal negligence the state must prove that defendant's conduct, viewed objectively, constituted a gross deviation from the standard that a reasonable prudent person would have observed. State v. Gorman, 648 A.2d 967 (Me.1994).

The defendant, an anesthetist, was validly convicted of manslaughter during an eye operation when the oxygen ventilator tube became disconnected for six minutes. Gross negligence was enough for conviction. Reg. v. Adomako, [1994] 3 All Engl. R. 79 (HL).

Conviction of midwives for criminal negligence of an infant during delivery was proper. Midwives were under a duty to have and use reasonable knowledge, skill and care. Defendants had no formal training as midwives. Reg. v. Sullivan & Lemay, 31 CCC 3d 62 (B.C. Sup. Ct. 1986).

result will occur or that the circumstance exists. The risk must be of such nature and degree that disregard thereof constitutes a gross deviation from the standard of care that a reasonable person would observe in the situation.''

Thus, in order for defendant's conviction to be upheld, there must be proof from which the fact-finder can infer that defendant acted "recklessly" and that defendant's reckless conduct "caused" Warren's death.

There can be no question that the risk created by the race at its inception was "substantial and unjustifiable" and that disregard of such a risk would constitute a "gross deviation from the standard of care that a reasonable person would observe in the situation." The testimony indicated that defendant's pickup truck reached a speed of 70–80 miles per hour before decelerating, and that the decedents' car was only slightly behind defendant. The posted speed limit on the street was 35 miles per hour. The area through which the drivers raced was a residential area, and in the course of the race they passed a number of houses, three intersections with cross-streets (Clinton, Taggart and Woodrow), a school and a playground. The risk to the lives of other motorists, pedestrians, bystanders, and even residents of the houses along the route was obvious.

There is also evidence in the record that defendant was aware of the risk to human life which his conduct created and consciously disregarded it. The testimony indicated that defendant was familiar with automobiles and automobile racing, and defendant himself acknowledged that he knew at the time of the race that he should not have engaged in the race. Thus, defendant acted recklessly in entering into the race and in racing with Wille down the street.

Defendant contends that even if he was reckless while actively engaged in racing with Wille, his act of slowing down and stopping prior to reaching the intersection where the collision occurred was an act of prudence which terminated his recklessness. A similar contention was rejected by the Supreme Court in Lemons v. Kelly, 239 Or. 354, 360, 397 P.2d 784, 787 (1964):

"... One who does participate in setting in motion such hazardous conduct cannot thereafter turn his liability off like a light switch. From the authorities cited we conclude that one who participates in setting such hazardous conduct in motion cannot later be heard to say: 'Oh! I withdrew before harm resulted even though no one else was aware of my withdrawal.' It would be a reasonable probability that the excitement and stimulus created by this race of several miles had not dissipated nor, in fact, terminated at all, in the fraction of a minute in time between the act of passing and the accident. The state of mind of the participants was material. We cannot gauge that state of mind to the point of saying that the stimulus or intent had ended...."

While *Lemons* was a civil case, its factual analysis is equally applicable to the case at bar. The fact-finder was not required to find that the defendant's unilateral and uncommunicated act of slowing and stopping was such an act of termination as would purge his earlier initiation of the race of its quality of recklessness. The evidence authorized a finding that defendant's setting the race in motion was reckless or that there was no effective withdrawal so long as the acts which defendant helped impel had not yet ceased. The substantial and unjustifiable risk to the lives of other motorists and pedestrians created in part by his conduct could be found to have continued unabated up to and including the time of the collision....

Affirmed....[24]

Conroy v. State

Court of Appeals of Texas, 1992.
843 S.W.2d 67.

■ MIRABAL, JUSTICE.

Appellant, Edward Patrick Conroy, was charged with murder and entered a plea of not guilty. A jury found appellant guilty of the lesser included offense of involuntary manslaughter, found he had used a deadly weapon in the commission of the offense, and assessed punishment at three years confinement. We reverse and remand.

In his first point of error, appellant asserts there was insufficient evidence to establish the element of reckless mental state to support his conviction.

In reviewing the sufficiency of the evidence to support a conviction, the evidence is viewed in the light most favorable to the judgment....

The evidence at appellant's trial, viewed in the light most favorable to the verdict, was as follows:

On February 5, 1985, at 3:00 a.m., after drinking at a bar for several hours, appellant and three friends returned to appellant's house, where appellant's wife, niece and nephew, and two other friends were sleeping. Appellant called an escort service, and four women came to the house. One of the women who arrived was Elissa Anne Roberts, using the name Michelle.

Appellant paid the four women $220 each, and directed the men and women to different rooms in his house. Appellant remained in the living room, drinking beer. At some point, appellant decided it would be funny if he burst into the various rooms, with his passport and his handgun, saying that he was a vice officer and that everyone was under arrest. Appellant removed two bullets from the gun "for safety reasons," but left three bullets in the revolver's chambers.

---

24. Defendant's simple negligence in making an illegal left hand turn in front of an oncoming motorcycle did not justify a conviction for vehicle homicide. Recklessness or criminal negligence is required. Commonwealth v. Heck, 517 Pa. 192, 535 A.2d 575 (1987).

Defendant, a psychiatric nurse in a psychiatric unit, killed a patient by the use of a choke hold when the patient, a violent person, was harassing an elderly patient. It was held that "criminal negligence" had not been shown since the defendant's action occurred during an emergency with little time for reflection or the opportunity to weigh alternatives. People v. Futterman, 86 A.D.2d 70, 449 N.Y.S.2d 108 (1982). See Treiman, Recklessness and the Model Penal Code, 9 Am.Jnl. of Crim.L. 281 (1981).

At trial, one of the women who came to the house, Brenda Merritt, testified that at about 5:50 a.m., appellant burst into the bedroom she was in, holding the gun and the passport, saying he was a vice cop. She said appellant told her she was "busted." Merritt said she stood up to get dressed, and appellant pushed her down. Merritt slapped appellant, and he got very angry. Appellant pushed her down again, hit her on the leg and groin area with the gun, and said he would shove the gun up her vagina and shoot her if she did not do as he said. Appellant then told the man Merritt was with to sit on her so she could not get dressed. Appellant left the room, and Merritt was able to talk the man into allowing her to dress.

Appellant burst into another bedroom, where his brother, Chris, and two of the women were, again saying he was a vice officer and the women were under arrest. One of the women, Penelope Lagerstrom, realized that appellant was holding a passport and not a badge, and began laughing at appellant. Appellant put the gun against Lagerstrom's head, just above her ear, and told the women to get on the floor. Appellant called Lagerstrom a bitch and told her if she did not do as he said he would blow her away. Appellant left that room, telling his brother Chris he would return with Chris' gun. Appellant reentered Merritt's room, again telling the man she was with not to let her dress.

Appellant then went into another room in the house, where the third man and Elissa were. He opened the door to the room, holding the gun at waist level and cocked. A shot was fired, and Elissa was hit in the head. Merritt and the other women heard the shot and began calling to Elissa, but got no answer. Merritt testified she heard appellant call out, "That's a warning shot to the rest of you ... in there." ... Once the police arrived, Merritt and Lagerstrom went to the room Elissa was in and saw that she had been shot and killed.

Appellant testified that he had not intended to shoot anyone that night, he did not see Elissa when he entered the room, and the gun just went off accidentally. Appellant said he remembered cocking the gun at some point, but he did not remember hitting anyone, pointing the gun at anyone, or pulling the trigger.

Appellant had been in the military, had been trained in the use of firearms, and had previously fired pistols on a firing range. Appellant testified he had owned the pistol for a year, and he knew the gun was loaded. He knew the gun was cocked, he knew he had his finger on the trigger when he entered the room where he shot Elissa, and he entered the room holding the gun loosely about waist high. He said he did not intend to fire the gun or to shoot anyone, let alone shoot Elissa. Appellant testified that, after the gun went off, he said it was just a warning shot so that the other people would not get scared ... Appellant said the pistol had not gone off accidentally in the time he had owned it. Both appellant and appellant's father testified that the first thing anyone handling a gun is taught, is to always point a loaded gun at the ground, due to the danger of accidental firing. Appellant called the police and reported what had happened as an accident. The 911 tape was played for the jury.

A weapons expert testified that the gun would not go off accidentally, but only if the trigger was pulled. He said the pistol required three and a half pounds of pressure to fire in the single action mode (with the gun cocked), and 13 pounds of pressure in the double action mode (with the hammer down). He also testified that the cylinder would rotate whenever the gun was cocked, in either direction. The gun had no safety button because it was designed to go off only when the trigger was pulled. This was described as a "mechanical safety." The gun was in good working condition.

Appellant was tried for murder, but the jury was also charged on the lesser-included offense of involuntary manslaughter. The jury charge read:

A person commits the offense of involuntary manslaughter if he recklessly causes the death of an individual.

A person acts recklessly, or is reckless, with respect to circumstances surrounding his conduct or the result of his conduct when he is aware of but consciously disregards a substantial and unjustifiable risk that the circumstances exist or the result will occur. The risk must be of such a nature and degree that its disregard constitutes a gross deviation from the standard of care that an ordinary person would exercise under all the circumstances as viewed from the defendant's standpoint.

Before a person is deemed to be "reckless," there must actually be both a substantial and an unjustifiable risk that the circumstances exist or that the result will occur, and that the person acting was actually aware of such risk and consciously disregarded it, and if you have a reasonable doubt as to any of such matters, then you would be bound to acquit the defendant of involuntary manslaughter.

Now, if you believe from the evidence beyond a reasonable doubt that on or about the 5th day of February, 1985, in Harris County, Texas, the defendant, Edward Patrick Conroy, did recklessly, as that term is herein above defined, cause the death of Elissa Anne Roberts by shooting Elissa Anne Roberts with a deadly weapon, namely, a firearm, then you will find the defendant guilty of involuntary manslaughter.

The jury charge tracked the statutes defining recklessness and involuntary manslaughter. Tex.Penal Code Ann. § 6.03(c) (Vernon 1974); Tex.Penal Code Ann. § 19.05(a)(1) (Vernon 1989).

Appellant objected to the charge and requested an instruction to the jury on negligent homicide, submitting his requested wording. Appellant's request was denied.

. . .

To be guilty of involuntary manslaughter, the actor must be aware of the substantial and unjustifiable risk surrounding his conduct or the results thereof, but consciously disregard that risk. The specific intent to kill is not an element of the offense of involuntary manslaughter.

Appellant, who had some knowledge of firearms, entered a darkened room he knew was occupied, holding a gun he knew was loaded and cocked. Appellant, knowing a loaded gun should always be pointed at the ground, entered the room with the gun at waist level, not pointing it at the ground or at the ceiling, with his finger on the trigger. He had previously entered two other rooms and pointed the loaded gun at other people. Appellant knew the only way the gun would fire was by pulling the trigger.

Evidence that a defendant knows a gun is loaded, that he is familiar with guns and their potential injury, and that he points a gun at another, indicates a person who is aware of a risk created by that conduct and disregards that risk.

We find that a jury could have rationally found that appellant was aware of the risk of death associated with his actions, that the risk was substantial and unjustifiable, and that he consciously disregarded that risk.

We overrule appellant's first point of error.

In point of error two, appellant asserts the trial court erred in denying his requested jury charge on negligent homicide. In point of error three, appellant asserts the trial court erred in overruling appellant's objections to the jury charge for failing to include a charge on negligent homicide.

When evidence from any source raises an issue and a jury charge is properly requested, the issue must be submitted to the jury. A charge on a lesser included offense should be given to the jury if the lesser included offense is within the proof of the charged offense, and there is evidence that if the appellant is guilty, he is guilty of only the lesser included offense. The credibility of the evidence and whether it is controverted or conflicts with other evidence may not be considered in determining whether the charge on the lesser offense should be given.

Criminally negligent homicide is a lesser included offense of murder. Criminal negligence, as a culpable mental state, is defined in § 6.03(d) of the penal code:

> A person acts with criminal negligence, or is criminally negligent, with respect to circumstances surrounding his conduct or the result of his conduct when he ought to be aware of a substantial and unjustifiable risk that the circumstances exist or the result will occur. The risk must be of such a nature and degree that the failure to perceive it constitutes a gross deviation from the standard of care that an ordinary person would exercise under all the circumstances as viewed from the actor's standpoint.

Tex.Penal Code Ann. § 6.03(d) (Vernon 1989). Appellant's requested jury instruction tracked the statutory language.

Criminal negligence is a lesser culpable mental state than recklessness. The key to criminal negligence is that the actor failed to perceive the risk. The mental states of recklessness and criminal negligence cannot co-exist.

Appellant testified that he was aware there were three bullets in the gun because he opened the chamber and checked the location of the bullets. Appellant gave the following explanation for having three rounds in the gun:

> [By Defense Counsel] Q: And can you explain to the jury why there's only three rounds in the pistol?

> [By appellant] A: For safety reasons.

Q: Explain that to them. Why only three. I don't understand. You say safety reasons. I don't understand. Tell me.

A. On the pistol I thought if I put the empty chamber where the trigger was and then another chamber that was empty next to the trigger, that if the trigger had ever gone off, the pistol would not fire because there was two empty chambers.

Appellant said he did not know how the gun went off; he did not intend to shoot anybody that night, but was only intending to play a joke.

We find this evidence raised the issue of whether appellant was criminally negligent. The trial court, therefore, erred in failing to include appellant's requested instruction on criminally negligent homicide in the jury charge. We find the error was harmful.

We sustain points of error two and three.

In his fourth point of error, appellant asserts the trial court erred in refusing to submit his requested jury charge on involuntary conduct.

Under Tex.Penal Code Ann. § 6.01(a) (Vernon Supp.1992), a person commits an act only if he engages in voluntary conduct, including an act, an omission, or possession. A person voluntarily engages in conduct when the conduct includes a voluntary act and its accompanying mental state, and the fact that such conduct also includes an involuntary act does not render engaging in that conduct involuntary.

Appellant has not contested that his conduct leading up to the shooting was intentional. He merely argues that his act of shooting the deceased was unintentional. Even assuming that the discharge of the weapon was unintended, the intentional pointing of a weapon is a voluntary act and the resulting death is imputable to the appellant.

We find the trial court did not err in refusing to submit appellant's requested instruction on involuntary conduct.

We overrule appellant's fourth point of error.

We reverse the judgment and remand the case to the trial court.

State v. Howard

Supreme Court of Utah, 1979.
597 P.2d 878.

■ MAUGHAN, JUSTICE. Defendant was convicted in a jury trial of two counts of criminal homicide, viz., second degree murder and manslaughter. His sole contention before us is the district court erred by refusing his requested instruction on the lesser included offense of negligent homicide. We affirm. All statutory references are to Utah Code Ann., 1953, as amended.

The facts are essentially undisputed. In late summer of 1977, animosity developed between two former friends, Marilyn Rust and Tammy Johnson. The feud between the girls involved their friends, including the defendant, who was a friend of Marilyn Rust.

In November of 1977, Marilyn found two threatening notes on her automobile. Defendant thereafter brought a 30–06 rifle and a .22 pistol to Marilyn's apartment, leaving them there fully loaded.

Late in November, defendant slashed the tires on Tammy Johnson's car; subsequently, the tires on Marilyn's car were slashed. On January 13, 1978, defendant slashed tires on various automobiles belonging to Tammy and her husband, Danny Johnson.

The next day defendant, expecting trouble, brought a loaded 12–gauge shotgun to Marilyn's apartment. Defendant and a friend, Paul Onstadt, remained at the apartment with Marilyn throughout the evening of January 14. At approximately midnight, Tammy and Danny Johnson, Decie Johnson, and Eddy Foy came to the apartment to see Marilyn. An argument over the tire slashing ensued which lasted approximately one hour. During the argument, two friends of Marilyn and defendant, Liz Stoker and Stan Crager, arrived at the apartment. During the entire argument, defendant stood by the couch in the living room holding the shotgun in plain view at his side, indicating at one point that it was loaded.

After the argument, as Tammy, Danny, Decie, and Eddy were leaving, Tammy made an obscene remark to defendant. He in turn made an obscene suggestion to her which was heard by her husband, Danny, as he was walking downstairs. Danny ran back to the apartment door and told Marilyn to open it, which she did. Danny stood in the doorway and demanded that defendant come out and fight; defendant, however, had no intention of fighting Danny since Danny was larger than defendant. Danny then stated he would count to five and if defendant did not come out in the hall, Danny would come in and get him. When Danny reached the count of five, he lunged through the door toward defendant, who in turn aimed the shotgun toward Danny and fired. At that second, Stan Crager, who had been standing in the room in front of defendant, jumped in front of Danny in an effort to prevent a fight, and was hit in the back by the shotgun blast. Danny, knocked off balance when Stan fell against him, veered in the direction of the kitchen door on the other side of the room by which stood the 30–06 rifle. As he did so, defendant pumped the shotgun and fired again, hitting Danny in the back. Both Stan and Danny subsequently died from their wounds.

Defendant was charged with first degree murder on two counts in the amended information. He pleaded not guilty to both counts, contending at trial he acted in self-defense.

In its instructions to the jury, the court included the definitions of the lesser included offenses of second degree murder and manslaughter, but refused to include defendant's requested instruction on negligent homicide. The relevant definitional provisions of the code are as follows:

76–5–203. Murder in the second degree.—(1) Criminal homicide constitutes murder in the second degree if the actor:

(a) Intentionally or knowingly causes the death of another; or

(b) Intending to cause serious bodily injury to another, he commits an act clearly dangerous to human life that causes the death of another; or

(c) Acting under circumstances evidencing a depraved indifference to human life, he recklessly engaged in conduct which creates a grave risk of death to another and thereby causes the death of another; or

(d) . . .

76–5–205. Manslaughter.—(1) Criminal homicide constitutes manslaughter if the actor:

(a) Recklessly causes the death of another; or

(b) Causes the death of another under the influence of extreme mental or emotional disturbance for which there is a reasonable explanation or excuse;

(c) Causes the death of another under circumstances where the actor reasonably believes the circumstances provide a moral or legal justification or extenuation for his conduct although the conduct is not legally justifiable or excusable under the existing circumstances.

76–5–206. Negligent homicide.—(1) Criminal homicide constitutes negligent homicide if the actor, acting with criminal negligence, causes the death of another.

76–2–103. Definitions of "intentionally, or with intent or willfully"; "knowingly, or with knowledge"; "recklessly, or maliciously"; and "criminal negligence or criminally negligent."—A person engages in conduct:

(1) Intentionally, or with intent or willfully with respect to the nature of his conduct or to a result of his conduct, when it is his conscious objective or desire to engage in the conduct or cause the result.

(2) Knowingly, or with knowledge, with respect to his conduct or to circumstances surrounding his conduct when he is aware of the nature of his conduct or the existing circumstances. A person acts knowingly, or with knowledge, with respect to a result of his conduct when he is aware that his conduct is reasonably certain to cause the result.

(3) Recklessly, or maliciously, with respect to circumstances surrounding his conduct when he is aware of but consciously disregards a substantial and unjustifiable risk that the circumstances exist or the result will occur. The risk must be of such a nature and degree that its disregard constitutes a gross deviation from the standard of care that an ordinary person would exercise under all the circumstances as viewed from the actor's standpoint.

(4) With criminal negligence or is criminally negligent with respect to circumstances surrounding his conduct or the result of his conduct when he ought to be aware of a substantial and unjustifiable risk that the circumstances exist or the result will occur. The risk must be of such a nature and degree that the failure to perceive it constitutes a gross deviation from the standard of care that an ordinary person would exercise in all the circumstances as viewed from the actor's standpoint.

Also relevant is the following provision:

76–5–204. Death of other than intended victim no defense.—In any prosecution for criminal homicide, evidence that the actor caused the death of a person other than the intended victim shall not constitute a defense for any purpose to criminal homicide.

We have often stated our position where the contention is that an instruction on a lesser included offense should have been given. In State v. Dougherty, Utah, 550 P.2d 175, 176 (1976), we stated:

When an appellant makes an issue of a refusal to instruct on included offenses, we will survey the evidence, and the inferences which admit of rational deduction, to determine if there exists reasonable basis upon which a conviction of the lesser offense could rest.

In State v. Hendricks, 596 P.2d 633 (1979), we noted:

It is a basic legal premise that a defendant in a criminal case is entitled to have his theory of the case presented to the jury. However, the right is not absolute, and a defense theory must be supported by a certain quantum of evidence before an instruction as to an included offense need be given.

Applying these principles to the case at hand, we believe there is no reasonable basis under the facts in this case which would justify a conviction of negligent homicide. As to Count I, defendant's conviction for second degree murder, the facts leave no room to suggest that, according to a reasonable view of the evidence, defendant negligently fired the shotgun when he pumped the gun, aimed at Danny Johnson, and fired as Johnson was heading toward the kitchen door of the apartment. Defendant himself presented no evidence tending to show he was unaware of a "substantial and unjustifiable risk" that the death of Johnson would occur by firing the shotgun at him. The evidence clearly does not support a negligent homicide instruction as to Count I.

Regarding Count II, defendant contends evidence presented established that the jury reasonably could have concluded defendant was unaware of a substantial and unjustifiable risk that Stan Crager would be killed in the affray. Specifically, defendant contends he was solely concerned with defending himself for an expected attack by Danny Johnson, as Johnson stood at the apartment door and counted to five. Defendant testified he knew Crager was in the room when he fired at Johnson, but he did not know where.

Thus, he asserts, since he testified he was unaware at the time he shot at Johnson that Crager would jump in the line of fire, the jury could have reasonably come to the conclusion he ought to have been, but in fact was unaware of a substantial and unjustifiable risk that Crager would be killed.

We must reject defendant's argument for the following reason: The difference between the minimum required *mens rea* of recklessness for manslaughter and criminal negligence for negligent homicide is simply whether the defendant was *aware, but consciously disregarded* a substantial risk the result would happen, or was *unaware but ought to have been aware* of a substantial risk the result would happen. This distinction is purely one of subjective intent in the mind of the actor; and, as we have noted a question of fact to be decided by the jury if any reasonable view of the evidence supports the lesser included offense. However, the question before us is not defendant's state of mind as to Crager, whom he accidentally shot, but as to Johnson at whom defendant admits he aimed the shotgun when he fired the first time. Section 76–5–204, given above, requires the focus of the intent question not upon the actual victim, but upon the *intended* victim, who in this case was Danny Johnson. Thus, the question before us is whether under any reasonable view of the evidence, defendant was unaware, but ought to have been aware, of a substantial risk that Danny Johnson, the intended victim, would be killed by the shotgun blast.

We believe that question must be answered in the negative, since no evidence supports the conclusion that the defendant was unaware of a substantial risk of death to Johnson, if he fired the shotgun at him. Indeed, it is consistent with defendant's assertion of self-defense that he intended to shoot Johnson, believing he was justified in so doing to protect his own life. No evidence was presented which would warrant an instruction of negligent homicide, especially since defendant himself admitted at trial he aimed at Johnson, and that "I usually hit what I aim at."

The jury could have reasonably come to the conclusion that defendant was at least reckless in shooting at Johnson and hitting Crager, or that defendant intentionally or knowingly shot at Johnson and hit Crager in the mistaken belief he was justified, according to the definition of manslaughter. Applying § 76–5–204, the fact that Crager instead of Johnson was shot becomes irrelevant. The court instructed the jury regarding § 76–5–204 and properly refused the requested instruction on negligent homicide.

■ CROCKETT, C.J., and WILKINS, HALL and STEWART, JJ., concur.[25]

SECTION 3. INTENT: GENERAL, SPECIFIC, AND CONDITIONAL

Despite the loose phrases "criminal intent" and "general criminal intent" courts have not lost sight of the fact that the word "intent" in its strict sense has the same meaning as "intention." Hence we find them reiterating that intent means purpose or design. The effort to assign the exact meaning has not been free from difficulty. "Intention then," writes Markby, "is the attitude of mind in which the doer of an act adverts to a consequence of the act and desires it to follow. But the doer of an act may advert to a consequence and not desire it: and therefore not intend it."[26] At the other extreme, Austin says that a result is intended if it is contemplated as a probable consequence, whether it is desired or not.[27] Salmond

---

25. It was held that the statute which defines manslaughter in terms of a person who "recklessly causes the death of another person" constitutes a distinction without a sufficiently pragmatic difference from the less culpable counterpart, criminally negligent homicide, and hence is unconstitutional. The conviction of manslaughter was reversed and the case remanded with directions to resentence defendant for violation of the lesser offense. People v. Webb, 189 Colo. 400, 542 P.2d 77 (1975).

"... recklessness and knowledge are mutually inconsistent culpable mental states." People v. Fornear, 176 Ill.2d 523, 680 N.E.2d 1383, 1387 (1997).

The instruction that malice might be found if defendant showed "a reckless disregard for human life" was not improper in a murder trial. This was not equivalent to an instruction that gross negligence equalled malice. State v. Kelly, 112 Ariz. 468, 543 P.2d 780 (1975).

26. Markby, Elements of Law, § 220 (4th ed. 1889).

27. 1 Austin, Jurisprudence 424 (5th ed. 1885).

requires the element of desire but gives this word a somewhat forced construction. He says that a man desires not only the end but also the means to the end, and hence desires, although he may "deeply regret" the necessity for, the means.[28]

So far as actual intention is concerned, more is required than an expectation that the consequence is likely to result from the act. On the other hand it is not necessary that the consequence should be "desired" in the usual sense of the word, although this element may become important. If one acts for the purpose of causing a certain result he intends that result whether it is likely to happen or not. On the other hand he intends a consequence which he knows is bound to result from his act whether he desires it, regrets it or is quite indifferent as to it. And to avoid philosophical imponderables as to what is or is not "bound to happen" it is customary to speak of consequences "substantially certain to be produced." Stated in terms of a formula: Intended consequences are those which (a) represent the very purpose for which an act is done (regardless of likelihood of occurrence), or (b) are known to be substantially certain to result (regardless of desire).[29]

Use of the phrases "criminal intent" and "general criminal intent," in the broad sense of blameworthiness, has caused some confusion when actual intention was the idea to be expressed. At times the phrase "specific intent" has been employed for this purpose. In this sense "specific intent" indicates actual intention as distinguished from "general criminal intent" which includes the whole field of blameworthiness. Actual intention, however, can be expressed without the use of this phrase and there is a more important meaning for which "specific intent" should be reserved.

Some crimes require a specified intention in addition to an intended act. For example, the physical part of the crime of larceny is the trespassory taking and carrying away of the personal goods of another. But this may be done intentionally, deliberately, with full knowledge of all the facts and complete understanding of the wrongfulness of the act without constituting larceny. If this wilful misuse of another's property is done with the intention of returning it (with no change of mind in this regard) the state of mind needed for larceny is lacking. Such a wrongdoer is answerable in a civil suit, and may be guilty of some special statutory offense, such as operating a motor vehicle without the owner's consent. For guilt of common-law larceny, however, he must not only intentionally take the other's

---

28.   Salmond, Jurisprudence 395 (8th ed. 1930).

29.   "The word 'intent' is used throughout the Restatement of this Subject to denote that the actor desires to cause the consequences of his act, or that he believes that the consequences are substantially certain to result from it". Restatement, Second, Torts § 8A (1965).

X handed money to **D** in payment for a mattress. **D** refused to deliver the mattress and applied the money to a pre-existing debt owed by **X** to **D**. This was held not to prove an intent to defraud. City of Cincinnati v. Young, 20 Ohio App.2d 92, 252 N.E.2d 173 (1969).

There are three essential elements of forgery: a false writing or material alteration of an instrument; the instrument as made must be apparently capable of defrauding, and there must be an intent to defraud.

To intend means to have in mind as a purpose or goal. People v. Osband, 13 Cal.4th 622, 55 Cal.Rptr.2d 26, 919 P.2d 640 (1996).

property by trespass, and carry it away; he must also have an additional intention in mind—the intent to steal. Burglary, moreover, cannot be defined as "intentionally breaking and entering the dwelling house of another in the nighttime," because this may be done without committing this felony. For common-law burglary there is required, not only the intentional breaking and entering of the dwelling house of another in the nighttime, but also an additional intent,—which is to commit a felony. This additional requirement is a "specific intent." It is an additional intent specifically required for guilt of the particular offense.

In recent years there has been dissatisfaction expressed with the term "specific intent." The Model Penal Code does not employ the term and uses a hierarchy of definitions, i.e. purposely, knowingly, recklessly and negligently as the standards for the mental element of crime.[30] However, the term specific intent still has descriptive utility and some jurisdictions that have adopted the Model Penal Code still approve the reference to specific intent.[31]

State v. Wickstrom

Court of Appeals of Minnesota, 1987.
405 N.W.2d 1.

■ MULALLY, JUDGE.

Appellant Donald Wickstrom was convicted of first-degree assault, criminal abortion and fifth-degree assault, following a trial to the court. He appeals from the judgment of conviction, . . .

The charges against appellant Donald Wickstrom arose out of an incident occurring August 26, 1985 at the home of his mother Gayle Gonsoir. Wickstrom assaulted Gonsoir and his former girlfriend, Cynthia Hall, who was eight-months pregnant with his child.

The assaults followed an argument with Hall over money Wickstrom owed her. Wickstrom hit each of the women, pulled their hair, and kicked Hall with hard-toed boots, some of the kicks landing on her abdomen.

---

30.   Model Penal Code § 2.01.

31.   "We are aware that the Model Penal Code has abandoned use of the terms 'specific intent' and 'general intent.'" See Model Penal Code § 2.02 comment 1, at 230–32 (Official Draft and Revised Comments 1985); W. LaFave & A. Scott, Handbook on Criminal Law § 28, at 202 (1972). We also recognize that the terms "general intent" and "specific intent" have not been altogether free of difficulty in the criminal law. But we do not believe that total abandonment of the terms will serve to clarify this vital corner of the law. . . . For want of a better term, and because of its historic use in the criminal law, we continue to use the term "specific intent" to refer to such mind sets, even though the term "specific intent" is sometimes confused with general intent (or volitional act) and implies an actual intent, when in reality its meaning, as a term of art, also includes mental states that are not intentional. Because the term "specific intent" has an accepted meaning as a term of art and because that term also has special significance in connection with the diminished capacity defense, we decline to abandon it totally. State v. Standiford, 769 P.2d 254, 260 (Utah 1988).

For bribery "there must be a *quid pro quo*—a specific intent to give or receive something of value in *exchange* for an official act." United States v. Sun–Diamond Growers of California, 526 U.S. 398, 119 S.Ct. 1402, 1406, 143 L.Ed.2d 576 (1999).

Hall's three-year-old son, Jason, witnessed the assault, at one point being shielded by his mother. Hall did not fight back.

. . . Wickstrom persisted despite the pleas of both women. At one point, Hall told him she was having cramps and was going to go to the hospital. He then stopped and asked her if she was okay, but began beating her again when she tried to get to her car.

Wickstrom testified he had had six to eight beers at a bar that afternoon, and eight more beers and two shots of whiskey at a restaurant before going to his mother's. Wickstrom testified he was drunk, and did not intend to hit either Hall or his mother, but "might have" kicked and struck both women, and pulled their hair. Hall and Gonsoir disagreed on whether Wickstrom showed signs of intoxication. The police officers who later arrested and interviewed Wickstrom saw no signs of intoxication.

. . .

The emergency room physician twice noted a fetal heart rate of about 160 beats per minute, which is in the normal range, within an hour of Hall's arrival. He noted multiple abrasions and contusions on Hall's arms, temple, abdomen, back and feet. At 9:30 he called Hall's personal physician, who ordered her taken to the labor and delivery room for continuous monitoring of fetal heart tones. Hall was taken to labor and delivery at 10:15. At that time, the fetal heart rate was measured at 60 to 80 beats per minute, which signifies severe fetal distress. An obstetrician was called and a Cesarean section performed at 11:25 p.m. A female child was delivered with no signs of life and resuscitation efforts were unsuccessful.

Wickstrom testified he did not intend to abort the pregnancy. He stated he was happy about the pregnancy, and had attended prenatal classes with Hall. Both Hall and Gonsoir agreed that Wickstrom wanted the child. Hall stated Wickstrom was happy she was pregnant and wanted to get back together with her. She confirmed he had attended prenatal classes. She thought Wickstrom was trying to hurt her, but not the baby.

The grand jury indicted Wickstrom for second-degree felony murder, first-degree assault, and criminal abortion under Minn.Stat. § 145.412, subd. 3 (1986). . . .

Wickstrom was found guilty of all counts. The court found that Wickstrom "wilfully performed an abortion" on Hall, as required by the criminal abortion statute, that the alleged negligence of the hospital was not an intervening cause of the death of the fetus, and that Wickstrom was not so intoxicated as to prevent him from forming the intent to assault Hall and Gonsoir.

. . .

The offense of criminal abortion

Wickstrom contends his conduct does not fit within the terms of the statute because the statute was intended to apply only to clinical, consensual abortions. We disagree.

Wickstrom's argument focuses not on the language of Minn.Stat. § 145.412, subd. 1, but on its presumed intent. . . . Wickstrom's conduct was the conduct most plainly proscribed by the statute because it violated all the conditions required to make abortions lawful.

. . .

Specific intent

Wickstrom contends the phrase "wilfully perform an abortion" introduces as an element of the offense a specific intent to terminate the pregnancy.

The term "wilfully" is not among those used to denote specific intent as an element of a crime. The supreme court stated in State v. Bowers, 178 Minn. 589, 591, 228 N.W. 164, 165 (1929):

The most common definition of the word "wilfully" as used in a penal statute, is that it means with a bad purpose or an evil intent.

. . .

The statute defines "abortion" as follows:

"Abortion" includes an act, procedure or use of any instrument, medicine or drug which is supplied or prescribed for or administered to a pregnant woman which results in the termination of pregnancy.

This definition is broad enough to include an assault committed upon the pregnant woman. Moreover, the statute proscribes an act which *results* in termination of pregnancy, rather than one which is designed to produce a termination of pregnancy.

Had the legislature intended to make specific intent an element of the offense, it would have used language denoting that mental state, such as "with intent to," or so defined "abortion" as to include intent. We read the statute as requiring only the general intent "to do the act which is prohibited by the statute," under the conditions under which it is prohibited.

Affirmed.

Dobbs' Case

Buckingham Assizes, 1770.
2 East, P.C. 513.

Joseph Dobbs was indicted for burglary in breaking and entering the stable of James Bayley, part of his dwelling-house, in the night, with a felonious intent to kill and destroy a gelding of one A.B. there being. It appeared that the gelding was to have run for 40 guineas, and that the prisoner cut the sinews of his fore-leg to prevent his running, in consequence of which he died.

■ PARKER, CH. B., ordered him to be acquitted; for his intention was not to commit the felony by killing and destroying the horse, but a trespass only to prevent his running; and therefore no burglary. But the prisoner was again indicted for killing the horse, and capitally convicted.[32]

---

32. "Specific intent exists where from the circumstances the offender must have subjectively desired the prohibited result. General intent exists when the prohibited result

Thacker v. Commonwealth

Supreme Court of Appeals of Virginia, 1922.
134 Va. 767, 114 S.E. 504.

■ WEST, J., delivered the opinion of the court.

This writ of error is to a judgment upon the verdict of a jury finding John Thacker, the accused, guilty of attempting to murder Mrs. J.A. Ratrie, and fixing his punishment at two years in the penitentiary.

The only assignment of error is the refusal of the trial court to set aside the verdict as contrary to the law and the evidence.

The accused, in company with two other young men, Doc Campbell and Paul Kelly, was attending a church festival in Alleghany county, at which all three became intoxicated. They left the church between ten and eleven o'clock at night, and walked down the county road about one and one-half miles, when they came to a sharp curve. Located in this curve was a tent in which the said Mrs. J.A. Ratrie, her husband, four children and a servant were camping for the summer. The husband, though absent, was expected home that night, and Mrs. Ratrie, upon retiring, had placed a lighted lamp on a trunk by the head of her bed. After eleven o'clock she was awakened by the shots of a pistol and loud talking in the road near by, and heard a man say, "I am going to shoot that God-damned light out;" and another voice said, "Don't shoot the light out." The accused and his friends then appeared at the back of the tent, where the flaps of the tent were open, and said they were from Bath county and had lost their way, and asked Mrs. Ratrie if she could take care of them all night. She informed them she was camping for the summer and had no room for them. One of the three thanked her, and they turned away, but after passing around the tent the accused used some vulgar language and did some cursing and singing. When they got back in the road, the accused said again he was going to shoot the light out, and fired three shots, two of which went through the tent, one passing through the head of the bed in which Mrs. Ratrie was lying, just missing her head and head of her baby, who was sleeping with her. The accused did not know Mrs. Ratrie and had never seen her before. He testified he did not know any of the parties in the tent and had no ill will against either of them; that he simply shot at the light, without any intent to harm Mrs. Ratrie or anyone else; that he would not have shot had he been sober, and regretted his action.

The foregoing are the admitted facts in the case.

An attempt to commit a crime is composed of two elements: (1) The intent to commit it; and (2) a direct, ineffectual act done towards its commission. The act must reach far enough towards the accomplishment of the desired result to amount to the commencement of the consummation.

The law can presume the intention so far as realized in the act, but not an intention beyond what was so realized. The law does not presume, because an assault was made with a weapon likely to produce death, that it

may reasonably be expected to follow from the offender's voluntary act even without any specific intent by the offender." People v. Garland, 254 Ill.App.3d 827, 194 Ill.Dec. 261, 627 N.E.2d 377, 380–381 (1993).

was an assault with the intent to murder. And where it takes a particular intent to constitute a crime, that particular intent must be proved either by direct or circumstantial evidence, which would warrant the inference of the intent with which the act was done.

When a statute makes an offense to consist of an act combined with a particular intent, that intent is just as necessary to be proved as the act itself, and must be found as a matter of fact before a conviction can be had; and no intent in law or mere legal presumption, differing from the intent in fact, can be allowed to supply the place of the latter.

In discussing the law of attempts, Mr. Clark, in his work on criminal law, says, at p. 111: "The act must be done with the specific intent to commit a particular crime. This specific intent at the time the act is done is essential. To do an act from general malevolence is not an attempt to commit a crime, because there is no specific intent, though the act according to its consequences may amount to a substantive crime. To do an act with intent to commit one crime cannot be an attempt to commit another crime though it might result in such other crime. To set fire to a house and burn a human being who is in it, but not to the offender's knowledge, would be murder, though the intent was to burn the house only; but to attempt to set fire to the house under such circumstances would be an attempt to commit arson only and not an attempt to murder. A man actuated by general malevolence may commit murder though there is no actual intention to kill; to be guilty of an attempt to murder there must be a specific intent to kill."

Mr. Bishop, in his Criminal Law, Vol. 1 (8th ed.), at section 729, says: "When the law makes an act, whether more or less evil in itself, punishable, though done simply from general malevolence, if one takes what, were all accomplished, would be a step towards it, yet if he does not mean to do the whole, no court can justly hold him answerable for more than he does. And when the thing done does not constitute a substantive crime, there is no ground for treating it as an attempt. So that necessarily an act prompted by general malevolence, or by a specific design to do something else, is not an attempt to commit a crime not intended.... When we say that a man attempted to do a given wrong, we mean that he intended to do, specifically, it; and proceeded a certain way in the doing. The intent in the mind covers the thing in full; the act covers it only in part. Thus (section 730) to commit murder, one need not intend to take life, but to be guilty of an attempt to murder, he must so intend. It is not sufficient that his act, had it proved fatal, would have been murder (section 736). We have seen that the unintended taking of life may be murder, yet there can be no attempt to murder without the specific intent to commit it—a rule the latter branch whereof appears probably in a few of the States to have been interfered with by statutes (citing Texas cases). For example, if one from a housetop recklessly throws down a billet of wood upon the sidewalk where persons are constantly passing, and it falls upon a person passing by and kills him, this would be the common law murder, but if, instead of killing, it inflicts only a slight injury, the party could not be convicted of an assault with attempt to commit murder, since, in fact, the murder was not intended."

The application of the foregoing principals to the facts of the instant case shows clearly, as we think that the judgment complained of is erroneous. While it might possibly be said that the firing of the shot into the head of Mrs. Ratrie's bed was an act done towards the commission of the offense charged, the evidence falls far short of proving that it was fired with the intent to murder her.

However averse we may be to disturb the verdict of the jury, our obligation to the law compels us to do so.

The judgment complained of will be reversed, the verdict of the jury set aside, and the case remanded for a new trial therein, if the Commonwealth shall be so advised.[33]

Reversed.

Commonwealth v. Shea

Supreme Judicial Court of Massachusetts, 1986.
398 Mass. 264, 496 N.E.2d 631.

■ O'CONNOR, JUSTICE.

After a jury trial, the defendant was convicted of armed assault with intent to murder, assault and battery by means of a dangerous weapon, and disorderly conduct. The judge sentenced the defendant to two concurrent six to ten year terms on the armed assault with intent to murder conviction and the conviction of assault and battery by means of a dangerous weapon.... The defendant appealed. The Appeals Court issued an order reversing the judgment on the armed assault with intent to murder indictment and affirming the judgment on the assault and battery by means of a dangerous weapon indictment....

We summarize the evidence presented at trial. In the early morning hours of November 7, 1982, Jeffrey Thyng went to the Thunderbird Country Club in Tyngsborough where he socialized with friends until the club closed at approximately 2 A.M. As Thyng was leaving the club, he was approached by the defendant and Bradford Couronis. Couronis made a derogatory remark to Thyng and Thyng made a similar statement in reply. After this brief exchange, Thyng walked into the parking lot to catch up with Susan Landry and Cindy Schalk, who earlier had agreed to give Thyng a ride home. The defendant and Couronis followed Thyng across the

---

33. The common-law rule "differentiates between the intent requirements for attempted and a completed crime only where the completed crime may be committed without an intent to commit that crime in particular, as in the case of felony murder." State v. Maestas, 652 P.2d 903, 905 (Utah 1982).

"Established California authority ... demonstrates that the concept of implied malice, insofar as it permits a conviction without proof of intent to kill, is also inapplicable to a charge of assault with intent to commit murder." People v. Johnson, 30 Cal.3d 444, 179 Cal.Rptr. 209, 637 P.2d 676, 678 (1981).

See Enker, Mens Rea and Criminal Attempt, 1977 Am.B. Foundation Research J. 845. *See also* People v. Avena, 13 Cal.4th 394, 53 Cal.Rptr. 2d 301, 916 P.2d 1000 (1996). The former West's Cal. Penal Code § 217 has been repealed.

Specific intent that would give rise to an attempt to commit a certain crime is the intent to commit that particular crime. State v. Schmitz, 559 N.W.2d 701 (Minn.App.1997).

parking lot and, as Thyng, Landry and Schalk reached the crest of a hill, the defendant and Couronis confronted Thyng.

Indicating displeasure with Thyng's earlier statement, Couronis and the defendant began shoving Thyng. Thyng tried to retreat and protect himself but the altercation continued. Couronis pushed Thyng in the chest and Thyng fell to the ground, breaking his right hand. While Thyng was on the ground, the defendant and Couronis kicked him. During the ensuing scuffle, Thyng felt two or three thumps on his chest after which he blindly reached up and grabbed the full beard of a man to his right. There was testimony that the defendant had a full beard on the night of the fight. Couronis was described as having facial hair of about a week's growth. Thyng testified that it was the defendant's beard that he grabbed, and that the thumps he felt prior to grabbing the defendant's beard were the only applications of force to his chest other than Couronis's initial push that sent him to the ground. Some two minutes after he felt the thumps to his chest, Thyng stood up, discovered he was bleeding from the chest and that his yellow sweater was completely red, and fell to the ground, where he "played dead." Later it was discovered that Thyng had been stabbed once in the chest. Neither Thyng nor any other witness, however, could identify which of the two men stabbed him.

At some point during the altercation, Schalk ran to find a police officer, and Tyngsborough police officer Michael Coulter, who had been on duty that night at the club, responded. After Officer Coulter observed Thyng lying on the ground with "blood pumping from his chest . . . four to five inches," he and another officer pursued the defendant and Couronis as they ran away from the scene of the fight. As the two men approached a red pickup truck, Officer Coulter observed the defendant throw a very small object to Couronis. Coulter testified that he did not observe Couronis discard anything during the pursuit. Couronis was apprehended attempting to enter the driver's side of the truck and the defendant was taken into custody on the opposite side of the vehicle. The officers then searched the two men. They discovered no weapons on Couronis, but the officers found an unbuckled sheath on the defendant's belt which contained a knife. The knife was covered with blood.

. . . At the police station, the defendant was advised of his Miranda rights. After he was informed of his rights, the defendant pointed to an object on a desk and stated, "That's my knife. What are you doing with it?" When asked why there was blood all over the knife, the defendant replied, "I don't know." Blood was observed all over the insides of the defendant's hands, inside the right sleeve of his coat, on his right arm, and on his belt. Blood was also detected on Couronis's jersey, undershirt, jeans, and sweatshirt. He had no blood on his hands or arms. At a hospital that night, Thyng identified the defendant and Couronis as his attackers.

The defendant argued in the Appeals Court that reversal of the assault with intent to murder conviction was required because the judge incorrectly instructed the jury with respect to the intent required for that crime and because the judge's explanation of circumstantial evidence unfairly assisted the Commonwealth's case. The defendant did not object to either aspect of the judge's charge. In its unpublished memorandum, the Appeals Court, viewing the judge's charge on intent to murder in light of Commonwealth v. Henson, 394 Mass. 584, 590–592, 476 N.E.2d 947 (1985), and Commonwealth v. Ennis, 20 Mass.App.Ct. 263, 264–269, 479 N.E.2d 733 (1985), held that the judge's instruction was erroneous because it "did not make clear that a necessary element to be proved on a charge of assault with intent to murder is 'an actual, subjective intent ... of the defendant to kill,' an intent 'far more specific than that implied by the general concept of malice,' " ...

We agree with the Appeals Court that the judge's instruction on intent to murder was erroneous. Although, at the outset of the case the judge explained to the jury that the Commonwealth must prove that the assault was "with the formed mental idea not merely of doing harm, but of murdering, of killing," in his final instructions to the jury the judge impermissibly equated the concepts of malice aforethought and specific intent to kill. The relevant portion of the judge's charge is set forth in the margin.[34] Viewed as a whole, the judge's charge inadequately conveyed to the jury that a conviction for armed assault with intent to murder requires a finding of actual, subjective intent to kill.

The Commonwealth argues that, even if the judge's instruction was erroneous, the defendant's conviction for armed assault with intent to murder should be affirmed because the judge's error did not create a substantial risk of a miscarriage of justice. We agree. Contrary to the defendant's present assertion that his mental state on the night of the attack was a "central feature" of his defense at trial, and that therefore the erroneous instruction on that issue created a substantial risk of a miscarriage of justice, a review of the record clearly demonstrates that the theory of the defendant's case was that it was Couronis, not he, who stabbed Thyng. Thus, identification of the man who stabbed the victim was the only live issue at trial. We are aware that a defendant's theory of his case cannot relieve the Commonwealth of its burden of proving every element of a crime beyond a reasonable doubt. Nevertheless, whether the issue of intent was contested at trial is highly relevant to our determination whether the error in the judge's charge prejudiced the defendant.

---

34. "Now if the threat is made with a dangerous weapon, ... then that's an assault with a dangerous weapon, an assault while armed. If the assault while armed is made with the intent to commit murder, then the offense is complete; that is to say, if the Government proves ... not only the assault with the dangerous weapon, but the assault with intent to murder, then the Government will have proved its case.

"There are three elements, the assault, the dangerous weapon and the intent to murder. 'Intent' means a mental decision to commit murder. Not a mental decision just to wound somebody, not a mental decision just to scare somebody, but a mental decision to commit murder, which is defined—murder is defined *as the killing of a human being with malice aforethought. What the crime of murder encompasses is the killing of a human being without justification or excuse with the intent to inflict injury, and the death then resulting from the infliction of the injury.*

"So that if the Government proves, in addition to the assault and the dangerous weapon, that there was in ... [Shea's] mind ... *an intent to inflict an injury, the sort that a reasonable person would or should understand would result in serious injury* or death, then in that case, the Government, if ... [it has] proved those things beyond a reasonable doubt, has proved the offense of assault, armed with a dangerous weapon with intent to murder." (Emphasis added.)

INADEQUATE INSTRUCTION - HARMLESS ERROR
Δ DID _NOT_ HAVE SPECIFIC INTENT TO KILL

Not only did the defendant refrain from contending at trial that the assailant lacked any intention to kill, but also the evidence fully supports a conclusion that whoever stabbed Thyng intended to kill him. The seriousness of the wound disclosed by the evidence was inconsistent with any intent other than an intent to kill. Officer Coulter, who administered first aid to Thyng at the scene, described the wound as an inch long and as "opened up . . . sucking air into the chest cavity." He described blood "pumping from [Thyng's] chest . . . four to five inches." Thyng had bled from the chest, a vital area, profusely.

Therefore, no harm accrued to the defendant from the jury charge on the mental state required for assault with intent to murder.

Judgment affirmed.

Holloway v. United States

Supreme Court of the United States, 1999.
526 U.S. 1, 119 S.Ct. 966, 143 L.Ed.2d 1.

■ STEVENS, J., delivered the opinion of the court, in which REHNQUIST, C.J., and O'CONNOR, KENNEDY, SOUTER, GINSBURG, and BREYER, JJ., joined. SCALIA, J., *post,* p. 972, and THOMAS, J., *post,* p. 977, filed dissenting opinions.

■ JUSTICE STEVENS delivered the opinion of the Court.

Carjacking "with the intent to cause death or serious bodily harm" is a federal crime.[35] The question presented in this case is whether that phrase requires the Government to prove that the defendant had an unconditional intent to kill or harm in all events, or whether it merely requires proof of an intent to kill or harm if necessary to effect a carjacking. Most of the judges who have considered the question have concluded, as do we, that Congress intended to criminalize the more typical carjacking carried out by means of a deliberate threat of violence, rather than just the rare case in which the defendant has an unconditional intent to use violence regardless of how the driver responds to his threat.

I

A jury found petitioner guilty on three counts of carjacking, as well as several other offenses related to stealing cars. In each of the carjackings,

---

35. As amended by the Violent Crime Control and Law Enforcement Act of 1994, § 60003(a)(14), 108 Stat.1970, and by the Carjacking Correction Act of 1996, § 2, 110 Stat. 3020, the statute provides: "Whoever, *with the intent to cause death or serious bodily harm* takes a motor vehicle that has been transported, shipped, or received in interstate or foreign commerce from the person or presence of another by force and violence or by intimidation, or attempts to do so, shall—

"(1) be fined under this title or imprisoned not more than 15 years, or both,

"(2) if serious bodily injury (as defined in section 1365 of this title, including any conduct that, if the conduct occurred in the special maritime and territorial jurisdiction of the United States, would violate section 2241 or 2242 of this title) results, be fined under this title or imprisoned not more than 25 years, or both, and

"(3) if death results, be fined under this title or imprisoned for any number of years up to life, or both, or sentenced to death." 18 U.S.C. § 2119 (1994 ed. and Supp. III) (emphasis added).

petitioner and an armed accomplice identified a car that they wanted and followed it until it was parked. The accomplice then approached the driver, produced a gun, and threatened to shoot unless the driver handed over the car keys. The accomplice testified that the plan was to steal the cars without harming the victims, but that he would have used his gun if any of the drivers had given him a "hard time." When one victim hesitated, petitioner punched him in the face, but there was no other actual violence.

The District Judge instructed the jury that the Government was required to prove beyond a reasonable doubt that the taking of a motor vehicle was committed with the intent "to cause death or serious bodily harm to the person from whom the car was taken." After explaining that merely using a gun to frighten a victim was not sufficient to prove such intent, he added the following statement over petitioner's objection:

"In some cases, intent is conditional. That is, a defendant may intend to engage in certain conduct only if a certain event occurs.

"In this case, the government contends that the defendant intended to cause death or serious bodily harm if the alleged victims had refused to turn over their cars. If you find beyond a reasonable doubt that the defendant had such an intent, the government has satisfied this element of the offense. . . . "

In his post-verdict motion for a new trial, petitioner contended that this instruction was inconsistent with the text of the statute. The District Judge denied the motion, stating that there "is no question that the conduct at issue in this case is precisely what Congress and the general public would describe as carjacking, and that Congress intended to prohibit it in § 2119." 921 F.Supp. 155, 156 (E.D.N.Y.1996). He noted that the statute as originally enacted in 1992 contained no intent element but covered all carjackings committed by a person "possessing a firearm." A 1994 amendment had omitted the firearm limitation, thus broadening the coverage of the statute to encompass the use of other weapons, and also had inserted the intent requirement at issue in this case. The judge thought that an "odd result" would flow from a construction of the amendment that "would no longer prohibit the very crime it was enacted to address except in those unusual circumstances when carjackers also intended to commit another crime—murder or a serious assault." *Id.*, at 159. Moreover, the judge determined that even though the issue of conditional intent has not been discussed very often, at least in the federal courts, it was a concept that scholars and state courts had long recognized.

Over a dissent that accused the majority of "a clear judicial usurpation of congressional authority," United States v. Arnold, 126 F.3d 82, 92 (C.A.2 1997) (opinion of Miner, J.), the Court of Appeals affirmed. The majority was satisfied that "the inclusion of a conditional intent to harm within the definition of specific intent to harm" was not only "a well-established principle of criminal common law," but also, and "most importantly," comported "with a reasonable interpretation of the legislative purpose of the statute." *Id.*, at 88. The alternative interpretation, which would cover "only those carjackings in which the carjacker's sole and unconditional purpose at the time he committed the carjacking was to kill or maim the victim," the court concluded, was clearly at odds with the intent of the statute's drafters. *Ibid.*

To resolve an apparent conflict with a decision of the Ninth Circuit, United States v. Randolph, 93 F.3d 656 (1996), we granted certiorari. 523 U.S. 1093, 118 S.Ct. 1558, 140 L.Ed.2d 791 (1998).

II

Writing for the Court in United States v. Turkette, 452 U.S. 576, 593, 101 S.Ct. 2524, 69 L.Ed.2d 246 (1981), Justice White reminded us that the language of the statutes that Congress enacts provides "the most reliable evidence of its intent." For that reason, we typically begin the task of statutory construction by focusing on the words that the drafters have chosen. In interpreting the statute at issue, "[w]e consider not only the bare meaning" of the critical word or phrase "but also its placement and purpose in the statutory scheme." Bailey v. United States, 516 U.S. 137, 145, 116 S.Ct. 501, 133 L.Ed.2d 472 (1995).

The specific issue in this case is what sort of evil motive Congress intended to describe when it used the words "with the intent to cause death or serious bodily harm" in the 1994 amendment to the carjacking statute. More precisely, the question is whether a person who points a gun at a driver, having decided to pull the trigger if the driver does not comply with a demand for the car keys, possesses the intent, at that moment, to seriously harm the driver. In our view, the answer to that question does not depend on whether the driver immediately hands over the keys or what the offender decides to do after he gains control over the car. At the relevant moment, the offender plainly does have the forbidden intent.

The opinions that have addressed this issue accurately point out that a carjacker's intent to harm his victim may be either "conditional" or "unconditional." The statutory phrase at issue theoretically might describe (1) the former, (2) the latter, or (3) both species of intent. Petitioner argues that the "plain text" of the statute "unequivocally" describes only the latter: that the defendant must possess a specific and unconditional intent to kill or harm in order to complete the proscribed offense. To that end, he insists that Congress would have had to insert the words "if necessary" into the disputed text in order to include the conditional species of intent within the scope of the statute. See Reply Brief for Petitioner 2. Because Congress did not include those words, petitioner contends that we must assume that Congress meant to provide a federal penalty for only those carjackings in which the offender actually attempted to harm or kill the driver (or at least intended to do so whether or not the driver resisted).

We believe, however, that a commonsense reading of the carjacking statute counsels that Congress intended to criminalize a broader scope of conduct than attempts to assault or kill in the course of automobile robberies. As we have repeatedly stated, " 'the meaning of statutory language, plain or not, depends on context.' " Brown v. Gardner, 513 U.S. 115, 118, 115 S.Ct. 552, 130 L.Ed.2d 462 (1994) (quoting King v. St. Vincent's Hospital, 502 U.S. 215, 221, 112 S.Ct. 570, 116 L.Ed.2d 578 (1991)). When petitioner's argument is considered in the context of the statute, it becomes apparent that his proffered construction of the intent element overlooks the significance of the placement of that element in the statute. The carjacking statute essentially is aimed at providing a federal penalty for a particular type of robbery. The statute's *mens rea* component thus modifies the act of "tak[ing]" the motor vehicle. It directs the factfinder's attention to the defendant's state of mind at the precise moment he demanded or took control over the car "by force and violence or by intimidation." If the defendant has the proscribed state of mind at that moment, the statute's scienter element is satisfied.

Petitioner's reading of the intent element, in contrast, would improperly transform the *mens rea* element from a modifier into an additional *actus reus* component of the carjacking statute; it would alter the statute into one that focuses on attempting to harm or kill a person in the course of the robbery of a motor vehicle.[36] Indeed, if we accepted petitioner's view of the statute's intent element, even Congress' insertion of the qualifying words "if necessary," by themselves, would not have solved the deficiency that he believes exists in the statute. The inclusion of those words after the intent phrase would have excluded the unconditional species of intent—the intent to harm or kill even if not necessary to complete a carjacking. Accordingly, if Congress had used words such as "if necessary" to describe the conditional species of intent, it would also have needed to add something like "or even if not necessary" in order to cover both species of intent to harm. Given the fact that the actual text does not mention either species separately—and thus does not expressly exclude either—that text is most naturally read to encompass the *mens rea* of both conditional and unconditional intent, and *not* to limit the statute's reach to crimes involving the additional *actus reus* of an attempt to kill or harm.

Two considerations strongly support the conclusion that a natural reading of the text is fully consistent with a congressional decision to cover both species of intent. First, the statute as a whole reflects an intent to authorize federal prosecutions as a significant deterrent to a type of criminal activity that was a matter of national concern.[37] Because that purpose is better served by construing the statute to cover both the conditional and the unconditional species of wrongful intent, the entire statute is consistent with a normal interpretation of the specific language that Congress chose. *See* John Hancock Mut. Life Ins. Co. v. Harris Trust and Sav. Bank, 510 U.S. 86, 94–95, 114 S.Ct. 517, 126 L.Ed.2d 524 (1993) (statutory language should be interpreted consonant with "the provisions

---

36. Although subsections (2) and (3) of the carjacking statute envision harm or death resulting from the crime, subsection (1), under petitioner's reading, would have to cover attempts to harm or kill when no serious bodily harm resulted.

37. Although the legislative history relating to the carjacking amendment is sparse, those members of Congress who recorded comments made statements reflecting the statute's broad deterrent purpose. See 139 Cong. Rec. 27867 (1993) (statement of Sen. Lieberman) ("Th[e 1994] amendment will broaden and strengthen th[e] [carjacking] law so our U.S. attorneys will have every possible tool available to them to attack the problem"); 140 Cong. Rec. E858 (May 5, 1994) (extension of remarks by Rep. Franks) ("We must send a message to [carjackers] that committing a violent crime will carry a severe penalty"). There is nothing in the 1994 amendment's legislative history to suggest that Congress meant to create a federal crime for only the unique and unusual subset of carjackings in which the offender intends to harm or kill the driver regardless of whether the driver accedes to the offender's threat of violence.

of the whole law, and . . . its object and policy" (internal quotation marks omitted)). Indeed, petitioner's interpretation would exclude from the coverage of the statute most of the conduct that Congress obviously intended to prohibit.

Second, it is reasonable to presume that Congress was familiar with the cases and the scholarly writing that have recognized that the "specific intent" to commit a wrongful act may be conditional. *See* Cannon v. University of Chicago, 441 U.S. 677, 696–698, 99 S.Ct. 1946, 60 L.Ed.2d 560 (1979). The facts of the leading case on the point are strikingly similar to the facts of this case. In People v. Connors, 253 Ill. 266, 97 N.E. 643 (1912), the Illinois Supreme Court affirmed the conviction of a union organizer who had pointed a gun at a worker and threatened to kill him forthwith if he did not take off his overalls and quit work. The court held that the jury had been properly instructed that the "specific intent to kill" could be found even though that intent was "coupled with a condition" that the defendant would not fire if the victim complied with his demand.[38] That holding has been repeatedly cited with approval by other courts and by scholars. Moreover, it reflects the views endorsed by the authors of the Model Criminal Code.[39] The core principle that emerges from these sources is that a defendant may not negate a proscribed intent by requiring the victim to comply with a condition the defendant has no right to impose; "[a]n intent to kill, in the alternative, is nevertheless an intent to kill."[40]

This interpretation of the statute's specific intent element does not, as petitioner suggests, render superfluous the statute's "by force and violence or by intimidation" element. While an empty threat, or intimidating bluff, would be sufficient to satisfy the latter element, such conduct, standing on its own, is not enough to satisfy § 2119's specific intent element. In a carjacking case in which the driver surrendered or otherwise lost control over his car without the defendant attempting to inflict, or actually inflicting, serious bodily harm, Congress' inclusion of the intent element

---

38. The trial judge had given this instruction to the jury:

" 'The court instructs you as to the intent to kill alleged in the indictment that though you must find that there was a specific intent to kill the prosecuting witness, Morgan H. Bell, still, if you believe from the evidence beyond a reasonable doubt that the intention of the defendants was only in the alternative—that is, if the defendants, or any of them, acting for and with the others, then and there pointed a revolver at the said Bell with the intention of compelling him to take off his overalls and quit work, or to kill him if he did not—and if that specific intent was formed in the minds of the defendants and the shooting of the said Bell with intent to kill was only prevented by the happening of the alternative—that is, the compliance of the said Bell with the demand that he take off his overalls and quit work—then the requirement of the law as to the specific intent is met.' " 253 Ill., at 272–273, 97 N.E., at 645.

39. Section 2.02(6) of the Model Penal Code provides:

"Requirement of Purpose Satisfied if Purpose is Conditional.

"When a particular purpose is an element of an offense, the element is established although such purpose is conditional, unless the condition negatives the harm or evil sought to be prevented by the law defining the offense." American Law Institute, Model Penal Code (1985).

Of course, in this case the condition that the driver surrender the car was the precise evil that Congress wanted to prevent.

40. Perkins & Boyce, Criminal Law, at 647.

requires the Government to prove beyond a reasonable doubt that the defendant would have at least attempted to seriously harm or kill the driver if that action had been necessary to complete the taking of the car.

In short, we disagree with petitioner's reading of the text of the Act and think it unreasonable to assume that Congress intended to enact such a truncated version of an important criminal statute.[41] The intent requirement of § 2119 is satisfied when the Government proves that at the moment the defendant demanded or took control over the driver's automobile the defendant possessed the intent to seriously harm or kill the driver if necessary to steal the car (or, alternatively, if unnecessary to steal the car). Accordingly, we affirm the judgment of the Court of Appeals.

■ JUSTICE SCALIA, dissenting.

The issue in this case is the meaning of the phrase, in 18 U.S.C. § 2119, "with the intent to cause death or serious bodily harm." (For convenience' sake, I shall refer to it in this opinion as simply intent to kill.) As recounted by the Court, petitioner's accomplice, Vernon Lennon, "testified that the plan was to steal the cars without harming the victims, but that he would have used his gun if any of the drivers had given him a 'hard time.' " *Ante,* at 968. The District Court instructed the jury that the intent element would be satisfied if petitioner possessed this "conditional" intent. Today's judgment holds that instruction to have been correct.

I dissent from that holding because I disagree with the following, utterly central, passage of the opinion:

> "[A] carjacker's intent to harm his victim may be either 'conditional' or 'unconditional.' The statutory phrase at issue theoretically might describe (1) the former, (2) the latter, or (3) both species of intent."
> *Ante,* at 970 (footnote omitted).

I think, to the contrary, that in customary English usage the unqualified word "intent" does not usually connote a purpose that is subject to any conditions precedent except those so remote in the speaker's estimation as to be effectively nonexistent—and it *never* connotes a purpose that is subject to a condition which the speaker hopes will not occur. (It is this last sort of "conditional intent" that is at issue in this case, and that I refer to in my subsequent use of the term.) "Intent" is "[a] state of mind in which a person seeks to accomplish a given result through a course of action." Black's Law Dictionary 810 (6th ed.1990). One can hardly "seek to accomplish" a result he hopes will not ensue.

The Court's division of intent into two categories, conditional and unconditional, makes the unreasonable seem logical. But Aristotelian classification says nothing about linguistic usage. Instead of identifying *two*

---

41. We also reject petitioner's argument that the rule of lenity should apply in this case. We have repeatedly stated that " '[t]he rule of lenity applies only if, after seizing everything from which aid can be derived, . . . we can make no more than a guess as to what Congress intended.' " Muscarello v. United States, 524 U.S. 125, 138, 118 S.Ct. 1911, 141 L.Ed.2d 111 (1998) (quoting United States v. Wells, 519 U.S. 482, 499, 117 S.Ct. 921, 137 L.Ed.2d 107 (1997)) (additional quotations and citations omitted). Accord, Ladner v. United States, 358 U.S. 169, 178, 79 S.Ct. 209, 3 L.Ed.2d 199 (1958). The result of our preceding analysis requires us to make no such guess in this case.

categories, the Court might just as readily have identified *three:* unconditional intent, conditional intent, and feigned intent. But the second category, like the third, is simply not conveyed by the word "intent" alone. There is intent, conditional intent, and feigned intent, just as there is agreement, conditional agreement, and feigned agreement—but to say that in either case the noun alone, without qualification, "theoretically might describe" all three phenomena is simply false. Conditional intent is no more embraced by the unmodified word "intent" than a sea lion is embraced by the unmodified word "lion."

If I have made a categorical determination to go to Louisiana for the Christmas holidays, it is accurate for me to say that I "intend" to go to Louisiana. And that is so even though I realize that there are some remote and unlikely contingencies—"acts of God," for example—that might prevent me. (The fact that these remote contingencies are always implicit in the expression of intent accounts for the humorousness of spelling them out in such expressions as "if I should live so long," or "the Good Lord willing and the creek don't rise.") It is less precise, though tolerable usage, to say that I "intend" to go if my purpose is conditional upon an event which, though not virtually certain to happen (such as my continuing to live), is reasonably likely to happen, and which I hope will happen. I might, for example, say that I "intend" to go even if my plans depend upon receipt of my usual and hoped-for end-of-year bonus.

But it is *not* common usage—indeed, it is an unheard-of usage—to speak of my having an "intent" to do something, when my plans are contingent upon an event that is not virtually certain, and that I hope will not occur. When a friend is seriously ill, for example, I would not say that "I intend to go to his funeral next week." I would have to make it clear that the intent is a conditional one: "I intend to go to his funeral next week if he dies." The carjacker who intends to kill if he is met with resistance is in the same position: He has an "intent to kill if resisted"; he does not have an "intent to kill." No amount of rationalization can change the reality of this normal (and as far as I know exclusive) English usage. The word in the statute simply will not bear the meaning that the Court assigns.

The Government makes two contextual arguments to which I should respond. First, it points out that the statute criminalizes not only carjackings accomplished by "force and violence" but also those accomplished by mere "intimidation." Requiring an unconditional intent, it asserts, would make the number of covered carjackings accomplished by intimidation "implausibly small." Brief for United States 22. That seems to me not so. It is surely not an unusual carjacking in which the criminal jumps into the passenger seat and forces the person behind the wheel to drive off at gunpoint. A carjacker who intends to kill may well use this *modus operandi,* planning to kill the driver in a more secluded location. Second, the Government asserts that it would be hard to imagine an unconditional-intent-to-kill case in which the first penalty provision of § 2119 would apply, *i.e.,* the provision governing cases in which no death or bodily harm has occurred. *Id.,* at 23. That is rather like saying that the crime of attempted murder should not exist, because someone who intends to kill always succeeds. . . .

It is so utterly clear in normal usage that "intent" does *not* include conditional intent, that only an accepted convention in the criminal law could give the word a different meaning. And an accepted convention is not established by the fact that some courts have thought so some times. One must decide, I think, which line of cases is correct, and in my judgment it is that which rejects the conditional-intent rule. . . .

Suppose that a person acquires and possesses a small quantity of cocaine for his own use, and that he in fact consumes it entirely himself. But assume further that, at the time he acquired the drug, he told his wife not to worry about the expense because, if they had an emergency need for money, he could always resell it. If conditional intent suffices, this person, who has never sold drugs and has never "intended" to sell drugs in any normal sense, has been guilty of possession with intent to distribute. . . . The course selected by the Court, of course—"intent" is sometimes conditional and sometimes not—would require us to sift through these many statutes one-by-one, making our decision on the basis of such ephemeral indications of "congressional purpose" as the Court has used in this case, to which I now turn.

Ultimately, the Court rests its decision upon the fact that the purpose of the statute—which it says is deterring carjacking—"is better served by construing the statute to cover both the conditional and the unconditional species of wrongful intent." It supports this statement, both premise and conclusion, by two unusually uninformative statements from the legislative history (to stand out in that respect in that realm is quite an accomplishment) that speak generally about strengthening and broadening the carjacking statute and punishing carjackers severely. *Ante,* n. 7. But every statute intends not only to achieve certain policy objectives, but to achieve them by the means specified. Limitations upon the means employed to achieve the policy goal are no less a "purpose" of the statute than the policy goal itself. *See* Director, Office of Workers' Compensation Programs v. Newport News Shipbuilding & Dry Dock Co., 514 U.S. 122, 135–136, 115 S.Ct. 1278, 131 L.Ed.2d 160 (1995). Under the Court's analysis, any interpretation of the statute that would broaden its reach would further the purpose the Court has found. Such reasoning is limitless and illogical.

The Court confidently asserts that "petitioner's interpretation would exclude from the coverage of the statute most of the conduct that Congress obviously intended to prohibit." It seems to me that one can best judge what Congress "obviously intended" not by intuition, but by the words that Congress enacted, which in this case require intent (not conditional intent) to kill. Is it implausible that Congress intended to define such a narrow federal crime? Not at all. The era when this statute was passed contained well publicized instances of not only carjackings, and not only carjackings involving violence or the threat of violence (as, of course, most of them do); but also of carjackings in which the perpetrators senselessly harmed the car owners when that was entirely unnecessary to the crime. I have a friend whose father was killed, and whose mother was nearly killed, in just such an incident—after the car had already been handed over. It is not at all implausible that Congress should direct its attention to this particularly savage sort of carjacking—where killing the driver is part of the intended crime.[42]

Indeed, it seems to me much more implausible that Congress would have focused upon the ineffable "conditional intent" that the Court reads into the statute, sending courts and juries off to wander through "would-a, could-a, should-a" land. It is difficult enough to determine a defendant's actual intent; it is infinitely more difficult to determine what the defendant planned to do upon the happening of an event that the defendant hoped would not happen, and that he himself may not have come to focus upon. There will not often be the accomplice's convenient confirmation of conditional intent that exists in the present case. Presumably it will be up to each jury whether to take the carjacker ("Your car or your life") at his word. Such a system of justice seems to me so arbitrary that it is difficult to believe Congress intended it. Had Congress meant to cast its carjacking net so broadly, it could have achieved that result—and eliminated the arbitrariness—by defining the crime as "carjacking under threat of death or serious bodily injury." Given the language here, I find it much more plausible that Congress meant to reach—as it said—the carjacker who intended to kill.

In sum, I find the statute entirely unambiguous as to whether the carjacker who hopes to obtain the car without inflicting harm is covered. Even if ambiguity existed, however, the rule of lenity would require it to be resolved in the defendant's favor. *See generally* United States v. Wiltberger, 5 Wheat. 76, 95, 5 L.Ed. 37 (1820). The Government's statement that the rule of lenity "has its *primary* application in cases in which there is some doubt whether the legislature intended to criminalize conduct that might otherwise appear to be innocent," Brief for United States 31 (emphasis added), is carefully crafted to conceal the fact that we have repeatedly applied the rule to situations just like this. For example, in Ladner v. United States, 358 U.S. 169, 79 S.Ct. 209, 3 L.Ed.2d 199 (1958), the statute at issue made it a crime to assault a federal officer with a deadly weapon. The defendant, who fired one shotgun blast that wounded two federal officers, contended that under this statute he was guilty of only one, and not two, assaults. The Court said, in an opinion joined by all eight Justices who reached the merits of the case:

---

42. Note that I am discussing what was a *plausible* congressional purpose in enacting this language—not what I necessarily think was the real one. I search for a plausible purpose because a text without one may represent a "scrivener's error" that we may properly correct. *See* Green v. Bock Laundry Machine Co., 490 U.S. 504, 528–529, 109 S.Ct. 1981, 104 L.Ed.2d 557 (1989) (SCALIA, J., concurring in judgment); *see also* United States v. X–Citement Video, Inc., 513 U.S. 64, 82, 115 S.Ct. 464, 130 L.Ed.2d 372 (1994) (SCALIA, J., dissenting). There is no need for such correction here; the text as it reads, unamended by a meaning of "intent" that contradicts normal usage, makes total sense. If I *were* to speculate as to the *real* reason the "intent" requirement was added by those who drafted it, I think I would select neither the Court's attribution of purpose nor the one I have hypothesized. Like the District Court, *see* 921 F.Supp. 155, 158 (E.D.N.Y.1996), and the Court of Appeals for the Third Circuit, *see* United States v. Anderson, 108 F.3d 478, 482–483 (1997), I suspect the "intent" requirement was inadvertently expanded beyond the new subsection 2119(3), which imposed the death penalty—where it was thought necessary to ensure the constitutionality of that provision. Of course the actual intent of the draftsmen is irrelevant; we are governed by what Congress enacted.

"This policy of lenity means that the Court will not interpret a federal criminal statute so as to increase the penalty that it places on an individual when such an interpretation can be based on no more than a guess as to what Congress intended. If Congress desires to create multiple offenses from a single act affecting more than one federal officer, Congress can make that meaning clear. We thus hold that the single discharge of a shotgun alleged by the petitioner in this case would constitute only a single violation of § 254." *Id.*, at 178, 79 S.Ct. 209.

. . .

If that is no longer the presupposition of our law, the Court should say so, and reduce the rule of lenity to a historical curiosity. But if it remains the presupposition, the rule has undeniable application in the present case. If the statute is not, as I think, clear in the defendant's favor, it is at the very least ambiguous and the defendant must be given the benefit of the doubt.

* * *

This seems to me not a difficult case. The issue before us is not whether the "intent" element of some common-law crime developed by the courts themselves—or even the "intent" element of a statute that replicates the common-law definition—includes, or should include, conditional intent. Rather, it is whether the English term "intent" used in a statute defining a brand new crime bears a meaning that contradicts normal usage. Since it is quite impossible to say that longstanding, agreed-upon legal usage has converted this word into a term of art, the answer has to be no. And it would be no even if the question were doubtful. I think it particularly inadvisable to introduce the new possibility of "conditional-intent" prosecutions into a modern federal criminal-law system characterized by plea bargaining, where they will predictably be used for *in terrorem* effect. I respectfully dissent.

■ JUSTICE THOMAS, dissenting.

I cannot accept the majority's interpretation of the term "intent" in 18 U.S.C. § 2119 (1994 ed. and Supp. III) to include the concept of conditional intent. The central difficulty in this case is that the text is silent as to the meaning of "intent"—the carjacking statute does not define that word, and Title 18 of the United States Code, unlike some state codes, lacks a general section defining intent to include conditional intent. *See, e.g.,* Del.Code Ann., Tit. 11, § 254 (1995); Haw.Rev.Stat. § 702–209 (1993); 18 Pa. Cons. Stat. § 302(f) (1998). As the majority notes, there is some authority to support its view that the specific intent to commit an act may be conditional. In my view, that authority does not demonstrate that such a usage was part of a well-established historical tradition. Absent a more settled tradition, it cannot be presumed that Congress was familiar with this usage when it enacted the statute. For these reasons, I agree with Justice SCALIA the statute cannot be read to include the concept of conditional intent and, therefore, respectfully dissent.

SECTION 4. OTHER PARTICULAR STATES OF MIND

The phrase "specific intent" has been used, at times, to refer to any special state of mind required for the *mens rea* of a particular offense. The underlying thought is this: Some crimes require only the general *mens rea;* others require a specific intent. Unfortunately, this adds to the confusion attaching to the use of the word "intent." This usage is too common to be ignored. It is well to emphasize, however, that many offenses require some particular state of mind other than a "specific intent" in the strict sense of the phrase.

If guilt of a certain offense requires that an act be done "fraudulently," this means it must be done with an intent to defraud. This is a specific intent in the strict sense of the phrase, but other factors are involved if the *mens rea* requirement is "malice," "knowledge" or "wilfulness."

(A) MALICE

Many statements are to be found to the effect that malice, as it is used in the law, does not imply any feeling of hatred, grudge, anger or ill-will, but requires only an intent to do harm without lawful justification or excuse. The last clause requires some modification in the homicide cases where the term has taken on a meaning distinct to murder. An intent to kill may be in such sudden heat of passion engendered by adequate provocation as to fall outside of the "malice" label. On the other side, an act may be done with such wanton and wilful disregard of an obvious and extreme risk of causing death that it will be said to be done with malice aforethought (if there was no justification, excuse or mitigation) even if there was no actual intent to kill. To say that the law will "imply" an intent to kill in such a case, or that such a wanton and wilful disregard of an obvious hazard is "equivalent" to an intent to kill, is to indulge in "doubletalk." It is quite proper to bring such a killing within the category of murder. The preferable explanation, however, is a frank recognition of the possibility of malice aforethought without an actual intent to kill. This may be illustrated by the case of one who intentionally blows up a building, without justification, excuse or mitigation, hoping the place to be empty but having no way of knowing whether this is the fact or not. The wrongdoer is guilty of murder if there were people in the building who were killed by the explosion. To say he "intended" to take human life is to misuse the word, but to speak of his state of mind as "malicious" is entirely unobjectionable.

If the word as it is used in the phrase "malice aforethought" gives a reasonable clue to its meaning in other than homicide cases, it would seem to be this: "Malice" means an intent to do the very harm done, or harm of a similar nature, or a wanton and wilful disregard of an obvious likelihood of causing such harm, with an implied negation of any justification, excuse or mitigation.

Because of the artful nature of the term malice at the common law and in earlier American statutory law, the Model Penal Code does not use the term.

State v. Lauglin

Supreme Court of North Carolina, 1861.
53 N.C. 354.

Indictment for felonious burning, tried before SAUNDERS, JUDGE, at the spring term, 1861, of Robeson Superior Court.

The indictment charged that the defendant "feloniously, wilfully, and maliciously did set fire to, and burn a certain barn then having corn in the same." The proof was that the prisoner maliciously and wilfully did set fire to a stable with fodder in it, and that a crib with corn and peas in it, which stood within twenty-six feet of the stable, was partially consumed, but by great exertion was saved from total destruction.

The Court charged as to the crib (which he sometimes in the alternative calls a barn), "that if satisfied of the burning of the stable by the prisoner, as it was an unlawful act, the prisoner was responsible for the consequences; and if they (the jury) were satisfied, beyond a reasonable doubt, that the stable was likely to and did communicate to the crib, and it was thereby burnt, they should convict; but they were to be satisfied that by the burning of the stable, the burning of the crib was a reasonable probability to follow; in which case the prisoner would be answerable." The defendant's counsel excepted.

Verdict, "guilty." Sentence was pronounced, and defendant appealed.

■ BATTLE, JUDGE. The bill of exceptions presents for consideration two questions, both of which are of great importance to the community, as well as to the prisoner. The first is, whether the wilful and malicious setting fire to the house of another, the burning of which is only a misdemeanor, will become a capital felony, if a dwelling-house or barn with grain in it, be thereby burnt, where such burning is the probable consequence of the first illegal act. Upon this question we concur in the opinion given in the Court below: that in such a case, the prisoner is guilty of the felonious burning of the dwelling-house or barn, upon the principle that he is to be held responsible for the natural and probable consequence of his first criminal act. In support of this proposition, the burning of one's own dwelling-house with a malicious and unlawful intent, furnishes a strong argument from analogy. Such burning is, of itself, only a high misdemeanor; but if the dwellings of other persons be situated so near to the one burnt, that they take fire and are consumed, as an immediate and necessary consequence of the first illegal act, it will amount to a felony....[43]

---

43. Malice required for a conviction of simple arson need not be directed to a particular being or entity. Defendant's burning of an insured's motor vehicle in agreement with the insured constituted a willful and malicious act. United States v. Banta, 26 M.J. 109 (CMA 1988).

Malicious arson under a statute requiring a willful act must be done intentionally. Batt v. State, 111 Nev. 1127, 901 P.2d 664, 666 (1995).

(For other reasons the judgment was reversed.)

Terrell v. State

Supreme Court of Tennessee, 1888.
86 Tenn. 523, 8 S.W. 212.

■ CALDWELL, J. The plaintiff in error, Ned Terrell, stands convicted of the crime of mayhem, and is under sentence of two years' confinement in the penitentiary. The indictment charges him with having unlawfully, feloniously, willfully, and maliciously made an assault upon the prosecutor, James Wilson, and struck him in one eye with a stone, or some other hard substance, whereby the eye was put out, and the prosecutor was maimed and disfigured. It is shown in the proof, and admitted by the prisoner, that he struck the prosecutor in one eye with "a half of a brick," and that the prosecutor was thereby rendered entirely blind, having previously lost the other eye. On the trial of the case his honor, the circuit judge, quoted to the jury the statute under which the prisoner is presented, and then charged them further, and among other things, that "in order to convict the defendant in this case, it must be shown by the proof that he did put out the eye of the prosecutor, as alleged in the indictment, by willfully and maliciously striking him in the eye with the brick or other hard substance and that it was done unlawfully,—that is, without lawful excuse, . . ." and that if he did this "from feelings of malice toward the prosecutor . . . he would be guilty as charged." The prisoner's counsel requested the court to instruct the jury, in addition, that unless "the defendant did of his malice aforethought inflict the blow, with purpose or intent to put out the eye, or inflict some other mayhem on the prosecutor, then the defendant would not be guilty of mayhem." This request was refused by the court, and that refusal is assigned as error.

Upon this action arises the inquiry, is a specific intent to maim a necessary element of the crime of mayhem? This precise question never having been decided in this state, its solution can be best arrived at by a brief review of some of the authorities and statutes upon the general subject. "Mayhem, at common law," says Mr. East, "is such a bodily hurt as renders a man less able, in fighting, to defend himself or annoy his adversary; but if the injury be such as disfigures him only, without diminishing his corporal abilities, it does not fall within the crime of mayhem." 1 Whart.Crim.Law, (8th Ed.) § 581. . . .

The words characterizing the forbidden acts are "unlawfully and maliciously." They are used alike with respect to every offense mentioned in the section, and must be given the same significance as applied to each of

---

Words "willfully and maliciously" in an arson statute describe the act to be committed rather than the desire to produce a specific result and do not require an instruction on specific intent. Dean v. State, 668 P.2d 639 (Wyo.1983).

In a prosecution for statutory extortion, based upon a threat to accuse X of arson with intent to extort money from X, evidence that X did in fact burn the building was excluded as immaterial. Commonwealth v. Buckley, 148 Mass. 27, 18 N.E. 577 (1888). One who threatens a thief with criminal prosecution unless he returns the stolen property is guilty of extortion. People v. Beggs, 178 Cal. 79, 172 P. 152 (1918).

them. They mean the same thing when applied to mayhem that they do when applied to malicious shooting or stabbing. "Unlawfully" always means without legal justification; but "maliciously" has different meanings, which it is not important now to give in detail. Its signification as used in the fifty-fifth section of the act of 1829 is well stated and illustrated in Wright v. State, 9 Yerg. 343, 344. Wright was indicted and convicted for malicious stabbing under that section, and on appeal in error to this court it was insisted, in his behalf, that the proof did not show that degree of malice necessary to constitute the offense charged. JUDGE TURLEY, delivering the opinion of the court, said: "It is true that the statute requires that this offense shall be committed with malice aforethought, by which is not meant such malice as is required by the third section of the same act to constitute the crime of murder in the first degree, but malice according to its common law signification, which is not confined to a particular animosity to the person injured, but extends to an evil design in general, a wicked and corrupt nature, an intention to do evil." . . . "The question then arises, is the proof in this case of a character to justify the jury in having found the existence of malice according to the definition given? We consider it unnecessary to go into a minute investigation of the testimony on this point. It shows beyond a doubt that the prisoner stabbed Lewis Underwood, the prosecutor. Upon this proof the law presumes malice." With this approved interpolation, applied, as it must be, in reference to each of the offenses enumerated, the use of the word "maliciously" in the statutes is shown to afford no justification for the contention that the crime of mayhem can be committed only when the blow is stricken for the purpose of inflicting that particular injury upon the sufferer. The character of malice necessary to the crime of mayhem has in fact been held by this court to be the same as that defined in the case of malicious stabbing just quoted. Werley v. State, 11 Humph. 175. Werley was convicted for the castration of his slave. In his defense it was shown that the slave was of very lewd character, and that his master's purpose was to reform him. Upon the facts it was argued that the necessary malice was wanting. The decision was that the act was unlawful, and, that being so, malice would be implied unless circumstances of provocation be shown to remove the legal presumption. The conviction was affirmed. . . .

It is next insisted that, even under the charge of the law as given to the jury, the verdict is not supported by the evidence. Upon this contention, the whole of the evidence has been given a very careful consideration by this court, but it is not deemed necessary to enter into a minute statement or discussion of it in this opinion. It is sufficient to say that the prosecutor's testimony makes a strong case of an unexpected, unprovoked, and violent assault upon him in the nighttime, resulting, as already stated, in the destruction of his only eye, and rendering him totally blind. The only countervailing testimony is that of the defendant himself, introduced for the purpose of showing provocation and apprehension of danger from the prosecutor when the blow was stricken. The other testimony in the record is in conflict with his statements, and corroboration of those of the prosecutor.

We are well satisfied with the verdict. Let the judgment be affirmed.[44]

■ TURNEY, C.J., and SNODGRASS, J., dissent.

State v. Nastoff

Court of Appeals, Idaho, 1993.
124 Idaho 667, 862 P.2d 1089.

■ LANSING, JUDGE.

By this appeal we are called upon to determine the state of mind or *"mens rea"* necessary to establish criminal culpability for malicious injury to property under I.C. § 18–7001. James P. Nastoff appeals from an order withholding judgment upon a jury's verdict finding him guilty of felony malicious injury to property. He challenges the sufficiency of the evidence to support the verdict, the district court's denial of his motion for acquittal. . . . Because we conclude the state did not meet its burden to prove that Nastoff acted "maliciously," as is necessary for conviction under I.C. § 18–7001, we reverse.

This case stems from a five-acre timber fire that burned on state and private land on August 9, 1991, near Paddy Flat Summit in Valley County. In connection with the fire, Nastoff was arrested and charged with one felony, malicious injury to property, I.C. § 18–7001; and three misdemeanors, operation of an engine without adequate protection, I.C. § 38–121; firing timber, I.C. § 18–7004; and destruction of timber on state lands, I.C. § 18–7009. The felony count was tried separately in district court and is the sole focus of this appeal. . . .

At the jury trial, the state introduced the following evidence. Nastoff and two associates had been woodcutting in the area two days prior to the fire.[45] During fire suppression efforts, a chain saw was found approximately twenty yards from the asserted origin of the fire. The saw had been pushed for an unknown distance and run over by a bulldozer before the bulldozer operator observed it. The chain saw spark arrester had been removed, and holes had been punched in the muffler cover. These modifications, which were allegedly in violation of I.C. § 38–121, caused the saw to emit carbon when idling. Nastoff admitted that he owned the saw and had been operating it. He indicated to one witness that he knew of the modifications to the saw, though they had been made before he acquired it. The state's theory at trial was that Nastoff's operation of the saw resulted in emission of carbon, which smoldered for two days before igniting the fire. The value of timber destroyed in the fire was established to be over $1,000. The state did not contend that Nastoff intended to start a fire by his operation of the chain saw.

This case turns upon interpretation of the word "maliciously" as used in I.C. § 18–7001. That section states in part:

---

44. Specific intent to disfigure is not a required element of the statutory offense of mayhem. Crawford v. State, 100 Nev. 617, 691 P.2d 433 (1984).

45. The state does not contend that the woodcutting, itself, was illegal or wrongful.

Malicious injury to property.—Every person who maliciously injures or destroys any real or personal property not his own, in cases otherwise than such as are specified in this code, is guilty of a misdemeanor, unless the damages caused by a violation of this section exceed one thousand dollars ($1,000) in value, in which case such person is guilty of a felony. . . .

By clear terms of this statute, one may be guilty of the proscribed offense only if the injury to property was carried out "maliciously."

A definition of "malice" is provided by I.C. § 18–101, which states:

18–101 Definition of terms—The following words have in this code the signification attached to them in this section, unless otherwise apparent from the context:

* * *

4.   The words "malice," and "maliciously" import a wish to vex, annoy, or injure another person, or an intent to do a wrongful act, established either by proof or presumption of law.

Under that definition, malice may take either of two quite distinct forms—it may constitute (1) a purpose or desire to vex, annoy or injure another; or (2) an intent to do a wrongful act, regardless of the presence or absence of any desire to inflict harm on another.

The state does not contend that Nastoff started the fire to vex, annoy or injure another person but, rather, focuses on the second alternative definition of malice—the "intent to do a wrongful act." Consequently, for our analysis, we also consider only that second definition, which defines "maliciously" to be essentially synonymous with "intentionally." Nastoff urges that because the record is devoid of any evidence that he intended to burn the timber, he cannot be convicted of malicious injury to property under that definition.

The state, however, asserts that Nastoff was acting "maliciously" within the meaning of the statute by intentionally operating the chain saw while knowing it was illegally modified. Nastoff intended the "wrongful act" of operating a chain saw in violation of I.C. § 38–121, says the state, and the intent to perform that act constitutes the requisite malice, as defined by I.C. § 18–101(4). Thus, according to the state, the intent to do any wrongful act will constitute the "malice" supporting a conviction for malicious injury to property. It need not be an intent to damage property, but may be an intent to do some other wrongful act that ultimately (even accidentally) results in injury to property. The state finds support for this argument in the fact that the definition of malice in I.C. § 18–101(4) refers to intent to do a wrongful act, not the wrongful act.

Thus, the issue presented is whether the intent to do a wrongful act that is required to establish malice for purposes of criminal liability under I.C. § 18–7001 must be an intent to injure or destroy property, or whether intent to engage in other wrongful conduct will suffice so long as the conduct ultimately leads to property damage. As the introductory clause of I.C. § 18–101 acknowledges, the definitions given in that section must be utilized with consideration of the contexts within which the defined terms are used in other sections of the penal code. Here, we must apply the I.C.

§ 18–101(4) definition of "maliciously" in light of the context of its use in I.C. § 18–7001.

.   .   .

Accordingly, to determine the requisite *mens rea* for a violation of I.C. § 18–7001, we begin our analysis with the language of that statute. Section 18–7001 establishes two components for commission of the crime of malicious injury to property—a culpable act or result (injury to the property of another) and a harmful state of mind (malice). The statute states that one is guilty of the offense who "maliciously injures or destroys . . . property. . . ." The use of "maliciously" to modify the verbs "injures or destroys," indicates that the act that must be performed with intent is the injuring or destroying of property. We do not perceive from the plain language of the statute any implication that an intent to do a *different* wrongful act may be engrafted upon the proscribed conduct of damaging property to provide the requisite malice for criminal liability under I.C. § 18–7001. The words of the statute do not imply a legislative intent to create criminal liability under this section where the injury to property was an unintended consequence of conduct that may have violated some other statute. Hence, we conclude by its plain language, I.C. § 18–7001 creates culpability for malicious injury to property only where the defendant's conduct causing the injury is accompanied by an intent to injure property of another.[46]

This conclusion is bolstered by the provisions of I.C. § 18–114 which provides:

In every crime or public offense there must exist a union, or joint operation, of act and intent, or criminal negligence.

Section 18–114 appears to be a legislative adoption of a common law rule that guilt of a crime generally requires a concurrence of the requisite mental fault (whether it be intent, knowledge, negligence or some other formulation) with the prohibited act or result. . . .

If the state's statutory construction were adopted, enabling criminal liability under I.C. § 18–7001 to be predicated upon Nastoff's intentional use of an illegally modified chain saw, without any accompanying intent to cause a fire, then culpability under that statute would be based upon mere negligence. We recognize that Nastoff may have been negligent in operating the saw, and his negligence may have caused the fire. Such negligence might give rise to criminal liability under other statutes, including I.C. §§ 18–7004 and 18–7005 as well as § 38–121, and it might create civil liability for damage to the timber. We cannot conclude, however, that the legislature, in using the term "maliciously," intended to proscribe and punish merely negligent conduct under I.C. § 18–7001. If that were the legislative intent, it is probable that the legislature would have used the words "negligently," "recklessly," or "carelessly" to describe the requisite *mens rea* as it has in other criminal statutes, e.g., I.C. §§ 18–7004, 18–3312 and 18–6001, rather than the term "maliciously," which was used in I.C.

---

46. We intimate no opinion that the intent must be to injure precisely the same property that is in fact injured. See, 1 LaFave and Scott, SUBSTANTIVE CRIMINAL LAW, § 3.12(d) at 399–400 (1986).

§ 18–7001. The definition of "malice" in I.C. § 18–101(4) leaves no room for an interpretation of the term to include negligence.

For the foregoing reasons, we hold that Nastoff could not properly be found guilty of violating I.C. § 18–7001 absent evidence that he intended to burn the timber.[47]

. . .

The order withholding judgment is reversed with directions to enter an order of acquittal.

■ WALTERS, C.J., and PERRY, J., concur.[48]

(B) KNOWLEDGE (SCIENTER)

The relation of knowledge to convictability is a variable factor within a wide range. At one extreme is found the type of offense for which knowledge of some particular matter is required for guilt by the very definition of the crime itself; as, uttering a forged instrument with knowledge of the forgery, receipt of deposit by a banker knowing that his bank is insolvent, or transportation of a vehicle in interstate commerce, knowing it to have been stolen.[49] At the other extreme is found the type (which should be restricted to the so-called public torts or civil offenses) in connection with which the element of knowledge or lack of knowledge is so immaterial that conviction may result although the defendant acted under such a mistake

---

47. We reiterate that proof of malice under the alternative definition given by I.C. § 18–7001, a "wish to vex, annoy, or injure another person," would have also sufficed if supported by facts in evidence, but the state makes no claim that Nastoff harbored such desire or intent.

48. A veterinarian caused a swelling in a mare's shoulders in order to get money by pretending to cure the animal of a disease. This intentional harm to the animal was held to constitute malicious mischief although inflicted without ill will toward either the owner or the mare. Brown v. State, 26 Ohio St. 176 (1875).

It was error to instruct the jury in a malicious destruction of property case that an intentional injury without legal justification was adequate for conviction. Malice requires hostility, revenge or cruelty. Commonwealth v. Peruzzi, 15 Mass.App.Ct. 437, 446 N.E.2d 117 (1983).

The killing of a mare by a forest ranger, in good faith discharge of his duties and in compliance with a regulation of the Secretary of Agriculture, was not malicious mischief even if the regulation was invalid. Fears v. State, 33 Ariz. 432, 265 P. 600 (1928).

During the early days of prohibition in Kansas a militant reformer wrecked a saloon with an ax. Being charged with malicious trespass she insisted that she was merely putting an unlawful establishment out of business, and had "no ill will against the owner or possessor of the property, or design to destroy property merely for the purpose of its destruction", and hence had acted without malice. In upholding her conviction the court held the word "malicious" as found in this statute is employed in "the usual sense in which it is used in criminal statutes". State v. Boies, 68 Kan. 167, 74 P. 630 (1903).

49. See Ratzlaf v. United States, 510 U.S. 135, 114 S.Ct. 655, 126 L.Ed.2d 615 (1994). Generally, the government must prove that the defendant had knowledge of facts which would make the conduct illegal, but ordinarily is not required to prove defendant's awareness of the legal consequences of the conduct, i.e., that the conduct was illegal. United States v. Hilliard, 31 F.3d 1509 (10th Cir.1994).

The early American malicious mischief statutes were taken from England. A bad intent or evil mind was required for criminal liability for damage to property. State v. Johnson, 7 Wyo. 512, 54 P. 502 (1898).

that, had the facts been as he reasonably supposed them to be, his conduct would have been acceptable in every respect. Such "offenses" are considered under "strict liability."

Between these two extremes are found offenses, for guilt of which the matter of knowledge cannot be ignored although the definitions themselves contain no specific requirement thereof. This is because knowledge or lack of knowledge may be among the determining factors of some other attitude of mind, which is required, such as intent, wilfulness, malice or criminal negligence.

From the standpoint of the prosecution (leaving out of consideration those "offenses" which have no normal *mens-rea* requirement) knowledge may be a positive factor or the want of knowledge may be a negative factor. In some prosecutions the state must prove defendant's knowledge of some particular matter to make out even a *prima facie* case of guilt. Such knowledge may be proven, like any other fact, by circumstantial evidence. It may be established from all the facts and circumstances of the case, although denied by the defendant. But the burden is on the State. In other prosecutions the want of knowledge may be peculiarly a matter of defense.

"Absolute knowledge can be had of but few things," said the Massachusetts court, and the philosopher might add "if any." For most practical purposes "knowledge" is not confined to what we have personally observed or to what we have evolved by our own cognitive faculties. Even within the domain of the law itself the word is not always employed with exactly the same signification. Suppose a man has been told that a certain bill of exchange is a forgery and he believes the statement to be true. Does he have *knowledge* of this? Obviously not if the purpose of the inquiry is to determine whether he is qualified to take the witness stand and swear that the instrument is false. But if he passes the bill as genuine he will be uttering a forged instrument with "knowledge" of the forgery if his belief and the fact correspond.

The need, therefore, is to search for the state of mind, or states of mind, which the courts have spoken of as "knowledge" for the purpose of a particular case.[50]

Modern statutes in many jurisdictions have specific statutes defining knowledge or knowingly, which are often based on the Model Penal Code Section 2.03(2).

State v. Beale

Supreme Judicial Court of Maine, 1973.
299 A.2d 921.

■ Before DUFRESNE, C.J., and WEBBER, WEATHERBEE, POMEROY, WERNICK and ARCHIBALD, JJ.

---

50. When knowledge of the existence of a particular fact is an element of an offense, such knowledge is established if the person is aware of a high probability of its existence, unless he actually believes that it does not exist. Leary v. United States, 395 U.S. 6, 46, 89 S.Ct. 1532, 1553, 23 L.Ed.2d 57 (note 93) (1969).

A defendant charged with refusing registration in the armed forces must have knowledge of the duty to register. United States v. Kerley, 838 F.2d 932 (7th Cir.1988).

■ WEATHERBEE, JUSTICE.

The Defendant, who operates an antique shop in Hallowell, was convicted under 17 M.R.S.A. § 3551 of the offense of knowingly concealing stolen property. His appeal presents us for the first time with the opportunity to construe the phrase "knowing it to be stolen" found in this statute.

One Saturday during the summer of 1971, when the Defendant was absent and his store was in Mrs. Beale's care, a prospective customer, a Mrs. Johnson, noticed that some of the displayed merchandise looked familiar. On examining it further she became convinced that several items were in fact pieces of silverware and glass which had been stolen from her several months earlier.

She left and returned after a short interval with a Hallowell police officer. She then pointed out to Mrs. Beale the items which she believed to have been stolen from her. The officer told Mrs. Beale that these items were "possibly stolen" and that they should be placed aside and not displayed or sold. She then gathered these items and put them on a shelf. The officer testified that he told Mrs. Beale to tell her husband to "contact me as soon as he got back". He later testified that he said that she "would be contacted, probably, later on that day".

There was no further contact between the Beales and the police during the weekend. The following Monday morning the investigation was apparently taken over by a deputy sheriff from the county where the theft had occurred. When he called at Defendant's store Defendant informed him that he had put the articles back in the counter for sale Sunday morning and that he had sold many of these items that day in spite of knowing that the police officer had requested that they be withdrawn from sale. Among those which the Defendant said he had sold were all the articles which bore the distinctive initials by which the owner had identified them as hers.

The Defendant testified that he had purchased these items at different times from people whom he considered to be reliable, that he had receipts for many of them and that he was entitled to sell them regardless of the officer's warning. The only testimony as to the details of the complaint by Mrs. Johnson and the officer's admonitions to Mrs. Beale which were in fact related to Mr. Beale was given by Mrs. Beale (called by the State) and the Defendant himself. The Defendant and Mrs. Beale testified that Mrs. Beale told the Defendant that Mrs. Johnson claimed that these items had been stolen from her home, and that the officer had asked Mrs. Beale to put the items aside saying that he would be back later.

The statute creating this offense—17 M.R.S.A. § 3551—reads, in pertinent part:

"Whoever buys, receives or aids in concealing stolen property, knowing it to be stolen, shall be punished . . .".

At the close of the testimony, Defendant's counsel made several timely requests for instructions. One of them, number 3, was not given and the issue raised by it, together with counsel's related objection, prove decisive of this appeal. It reads:

"(3) The fact that the Defendant was notified that the goods were stolen after they had been purchased and received and yet went ahead and sold them does not of itself make him guilty of the crime charged, if the Defendant in truth believed that he had a valid receipt for the goods and that he had lawful possession of them."

. . .

The jury found the Defendant guilty.

Although the Defendant's requested instruction failed to focus clearly upon the issue, his objection to the Justice's charge adequately presents the issue for our review. The issue is one of statutory interpretation of the words "knowing it to be stolen". Did the Legislature intend that the jury be satisfied as to the knowledge of the Defendant by testing it subjectively or objectively? To put it another way, must the State satisfy the jury that the Defendant himself actually had knowledge that the goods were stolen or is it enough that a reasonable person, with the information that was available to the Defendant, would have known that the goods were stolen?

We find a split of authority among the jurisdictions which have had the occasion to examine this issue, with the majority requiring that the State's proof should meet the subjective test. A representative summary of the reasoning of the majority is found in the language of Von Sprecken v. State, 70 Ga.App. 222, 225, 28 S.E.2d 341, 343 (1943):

"... The gist of the offense is the actual state of the *defendant's* mind ... and not what, under like circumstances, might be the state of mind of some other person ...". (Emphasis added.)

The Massachusetts Supreme Judicial Court took a similar position in reversing a conviction for receiving stolen property which was based upon a finding of knowledge under the reasonable man standard, saying:

"... The infraction of this statute is not proved by negligence nor by failure to exercise as much intelligence as the ordinarily prudent man. The statute does not punish one too dull to realize that the goods which he bought honestly and in good faith had been stolen.

. . .

The knowledge or belief of the defendant must be personal to him and our statute furnishes no substitute or equivalent." Commonwealth v. Boris, 317 Mass. 309, 58 N.E.2d 8, 12 (1944).

The issue has also been before the Vermont Supreme Court. The Vermont statute did not define the offense of receiving stolen goods and the Court found that the elements were those defined by the common law. The Court rejected the State's contention that reasonable notice was sufficient to supply the common law requirement of knowledge that the goods were in fact stolen. The Court said:

"If he did not have actual or positive knowledge, the question is whether from the circumstances he—not some other person—believed they had been stolen. The circumstances must have that effect upon his mind, to constitute knowledge by him." State v. Alpert, 88 Vt. 191, 92 A. 32, 37 (1914).

A minority of jurisdictions apply the so-called objective test as to knowledge, being impressed, perhaps, by the difficulties of proof as to the actual state of a defendant's mind. The position of these courts appears to be represented by the statement of the Mississippi Court in Pettus v. State, 200 Miss. 397, 410, 27 So.2d 536, 540 (1946)—a position recently reaffirmed by that Court in Bennett v. State, Miss., 211 So.2d 520, 526 (1968):

"[T]he word, 'knowing': in its relation to receiving stolen goods means that, if a person has information from facts and circumstances which should convince him that property had been stolen, or which would lead a reasonable man to believe that property had been stolen, then in a legal sense he knew it."[51]

We consider that the distinction between the bases of the two points of view[52] was clarified by an opinion from the Circuit Court of Appeals, 2nd Circuit, written by Judge Learned Hand. He wrote:

"The defendants ask us to distinguish between 'knowing' that goods are stolen and merely being put upon an inquiry which would have led to discovery; but they have misconceived the distinction which the decisions have made. The receivers of stolen goods almost never 'know' that they have been stolen, in the sense that they could testify to it in a court room. The business could not be so conducted, for those who sell the goods—the "fences"—must keep up a more respectable front than is generally possible for the thieves. Nor are we to suppose that the thieves will ordinarily admit their theft to the receivers: that would much impair their bargaining power. For this reason, some decisions even go so far as to hold that it is enough, if a reasonable man in the receiver's position would have supposed that the goods were stolen. That we think is wrong; and the better law is otherwise, although of course the fact that a reasonable man would have thought that they had been stolen, is some basis for finding that the accused actually did think so. But that the jury must find that the receiver did more than infer the theft from the circumstances has never been demanded, so far as we know; and to demand more would emasculate the

---

51. In some states the statutes define the offense as being committed by one who knows or who has reasonable cause to believe that the property received had been stolen. See, e.g., 21 O.S.1971, § 1713(1); McMillan v. State, 720 P.2d 1274 (Okl.Cr.1986). Reckless disregard of knowledge that property is stolen was adequate. Elerson v. State, 732 P.2d 192 (Alaska App.1987).

52. Theft by receiving under Utah Code Ann. 1953, § 7–6–408(1) requires only that the actor believe property of another to be stolen when received. The property need not actually be stolen. Reckless disregard that the property stolen is sufficient for the mens rea element of receiving. State v. Pappas, 705 P.2d 1169 (Utah 1985).

In order to be found guilty of receiving stolen property, the defendant must know or have reason to know the property is stolen. State v. Tharpe, 726 S.W.2d 896 (Tenn.1987).

720 Illinois Compiled Stat. 5/16–1(4) (1994) provides: "A person commits theft when he knowingly: . . . Obtains control over stolen property knowing the property to have been stolen or under circumstances as would reasonably induce him to believe that the property was stolen."

To establish the offense of theft of stolen property, the state must prove that property was stolen and that defendant knew that the property was stolen by another person. State v. Smith, 276 Mont. 434, 916 P.2d 773 (1996).

[Added by the Compiler.]

statute, for the evil against which it is directed is exactly that: i.e., making a market for stolen goods which the purchaser believes to have probably been stolen." United States v. Werner, 160 F.2d 438, 441–442 (2d Cir. 1947)....

It appears to us that the minority jurisdictions which follow the "ordinary reasonable man" test are failing to stress sufficiently the distinction between civil and criminal responsibility. In civil cases the failure of the defendant to act with the degree of care which a person of ordinary prudence would have used may be the test of his responsibility without any determination that the defendant, himself, was a person of ordinary prudence or that he had any wrongful intent. On the other hand, the very essence of his criminal offense is the intentional wrongdoing of the defendant.

Such was the case at common law (*State v. Alpert, supra*) and if the Legislature had intended something less than actual knowledge, more appropriate language could easily have been chosen.

The distinction is more than one of semantics. It is made necessary by the fact that while a defendant may have received information which would have convinced a person of ordinary intelligence and average capacity to comprehend and evaluate facts, a defendant may be a person of less than average intelligence, comprehension and reasoning powers. The true test is, did the *defendant* know the goods were stolen.

This is not to say that the defendant must have direct knowledge or positive proof that the goods were stolen, such as he would have gained by actually witnessing the theft or hearing the admission of the thief. It is enough if he was made aware of circumstances which caused him to believe that they were stolen.

The fact that the jury must be satisfied as to the state of the defendant's personal belief does not present the State with an insurmountable task when direct proof of his belief is absent. Juries have been instructed from time immemorial as to other offenses that they may draw rational inferences as to intent from a defendant's speech and conduct in relation to the subject matter and from evidence showing the information of which a defendant was aware. The state of a defendant's belief may be resolved by inference in the same manner.

While the objective test of what an ordinary intelligent man would have believed cannot serve as the absolute standard which determines the defendant's guilt or innocence, the jury, in making its determination as to the state of a defendant's belief, may properly take into consideration, among other things, the belief which the jury concludes a person of ordinary intellectual capacity would have formed from such facts and circumstances. The jury may consider this in the light of its evaluation of a defendant as an intelligent person, based upon what the jury has learned about the defendant from testimony and observation.

The Presiding Justice several times presented the issue to the jury in the alternative—that is, that the requirement of guilty knowledge was satisfied if the jury found *either* that the Defendant believed the goods had been stolen *or* that a reasonable man under those circumstances would have believed that they had been stolen.

Since we are convinced that the statute must be construed to require proof that the Defendant himself believed that the goods were stolen, the verdict must be set aside.

Appeal sustained. Remanded for new trial.[53]

All Justices concurring.

People v. Kanan

Supreme Court of Colorado, In Department, 1974.
186 Colo. 255, 526 P.2d 1339.

■ Erickson, Justice. The defendant, John E. Kanan, was convicted of passing short checks, a felony under 1967 Perm.Supp., C.R.S.1963, 40–14–20. He contends that his conviction should be reversed because the trial court did not properly instruct the jury. We agree and, therefore, reverse and remand for a new trial.

Kanan wrote three separate checks totaling seventy-five dollars to the ABC Liquor Store during the course of one week in February 1972. The manager of the store deposited the checks, which were returned with the notation that Kanan's account was closed for insufficient funds in January.

---

53. "A finding of either actual knowledge or a belief by the defendant that the property was stolen is essential to a conviction for theft by receiving. In the absence of direct evidence, the jury may draw reasonable inferences from the facts and circumstances of the case that the defendant either knew or believed that the property was stolen." State v. Korelis, 273 Or. 427, 541 P.2d 468, 469 (1975).

Equating "reasonably should be aware" with "knowingly" was error in an instruction on a charge of knowingly introducing contraband. People v. Etchells, 646 P.2d 950 (Colo.App. 1982).

In a perjury case the state is not required to allege and prove that **D** knew the statement he made under oath was false. But **D** may exculpate himself by proving that he believed he was testifying in a truthful manner. Gauthier v. State, 496 S.W.2d 584 (Tex.Cr.App.1973).

[Some statutes are broader.]

Because the statute on receiving stolen property is worded in terms of "knowing or having reasonable cause to believe the same to have been stolen," the state need not prove actual knowledge that the property was stolen but only that **D** had reasonable cause so to believe. Richardson v. State, 545 P.2d 1292 (Okl.Cr.App.1976).

The Utah statute is worded in terms of receiving stolen property "knowing that it has been stolen, or believing that it probably has been stolen." State v. Plum, 552 P.2d 124 (Utah 1976).

A defendant was properly convicted of receiving stolen property by circumstantial knowledge that the property was probably stolen. State v. Hankerson, 70 Ohio St.2d 87, 434 N.E.2d 1362 (1982).

"Knowingly" as used in a statute making it a crime to knowingly traffic in stolen vehicles or parts is not unconstitutionally vague. Knowingly requires that a defendant be cognizant of facts which should have caused him to believe that vehicles or parts were stolen. State v. Blakey, 399 N.W.2d 317 (S.D.1987).

Evidence that defendant paid five to ten dollars for stolen statues valued between $111 and $164 would aid in supporting the conclusion that defendant knowingly received stolen property. State v. Priesmeyer, 719 S.W.2d 873 (Mo.App.1986).

There is conflicting evidence as to whether Kanan had knowledge that his checking account was overdrawn. The bank sent Kanan's monthly bank statements to Kanan's address in October, November, December and January, and each statement showed that Kanan's account was overdrawn. The bank also mailed the notice of closure of the account to the same location. The evidence established that the December and January statements were returned to the bank and were not delivered to Kanan.

The jury found Kanan guilty, and he was sentenced to the penitentiary. Defense counsel contends that the trial court committed error and deprived Kanan of the presumption of innocence when the following instruction was given:

"You are instructed that a check drawn and delivered by a person carries with it a representation that such person knows the status of his account and that there are sufficient funds on deposit to pay the check upon its presentation for payment at the bank named as drawee on such check."

We agree. The presumption of innocence, coupled with proof of each element of the charge beyond a reasonable doubt, provides the foundation for our system of criminal justice. People v. Hill, Colo., 512 P.2d 257 (1973).

Under the provisions of the Short Check Statute, the prosecution must prove that the drawer of the check knew that there were insufficient funds in his account to pay the check. 1967 Perm.Supp., C.R.S.1963, 40–14–20(6). The instruction dispensed with the prosecution's obligation to prove knowledge and reversed the burden of proof.

We will not permit the prosecution to utilize a presumption of guilt as a basis for obtaining a conviction in a bad check case. People v. Vinnola, 177 Colo. 405, 494 P.2d 826 (1972); Moore v. People, 124 Colo. 197, 235 P.2d 798 (1951). We stated in *Moore* that the law does not allow an intent to defraud to be presumed whenever a bank refuses to honor a check.

Bank operations, although efficient, are subject to ordinary mistakes which fallible employees make. To conclude that whenever a check was returned to the payee, the drawer must have known the state of his account, would be "a result [which] strikes at the very foundation of our system of criminal justice." *People v. Vinnola, supra.* The trial court committed reversible error by submitting an instruction which forced the defendant to meet and rebut a presumption that he had knowledge of the state of his account. . . .

The prosecution contends that even if the court improperly instructed the jury, the error was harmless. We disagree. Prejudice to the defendant is inevitable when the court instructs the jury in such a way as to reduce the prosecution's obligation to prove each element of its case beyond a reasonable doubt. Gonzales v. People, 166 Colo. 557, 445 P.2d 74 (1968).

Accordingly, we reverse and remand for a new trial.

■ KELLEY, GROVES and LEE, JJ., concur.[54]

---

54. A defendant cannot be convicted of check fraud if the person had a reasonable expectation the check would be paid as a result of some arrangement or understanding with

United States v. Jewell

United States Court of Appeals, Ninth Circuit, 1976.
532 F.2d 697.

OPINION

■ Before CHAMBERS, KOELSCH, BROWNING, DUNIWAY, ELY, HUFSTEDLER, WRIGHT, TRASK, CHOY, GOODWIN, WALLACE, SNEED and KENNEDY, CIRCUIT JUDGES.

■ BROWNING, CIRCUIT JUDGE: . . .

In the course of in banc consideration of this case, we have encountered another problem that divides us.

Appellant defines "knowingly" in 21 U.S.C. §§ 841 and 960 to require that positive knowledge that a controlled substance is involved be established as an element of each offense. On the basis of this interpretation, appellant argues that it was reversible error to instruct the jury that the defendant could be convicted upon proof beyond a reasonable doubt that if he did not have positive knowledge that a controlled substance was concealed in the automobile he drove over the border, it was solely and entirely because of the conscious purpose on his part to avoid learning the truth. The majority concludes that this contention is wrong in principle, and has no support in authority or in the language or legislative history of the statute.

It is undisputed that appellant entered the United States driving an automobile in which 110 pounds of marihuana worth $6,250 had been concealed in a secret compartment between the trunk and rear seat. Appellant testified that he did not know the marihuana was present. There was circumstantial evidence from which the jury could infer that appellant had positive knowledge of the presence of the marihuana, and that his contrary testimony was false.[55] On the other hand there was evidence from

---

bank, or because defendant intended to deposit sufficient funds to cover it before its presentation for payment. Cox v. State, 964 P.2d 1235 (Wyo.1998).

An instruction presuming an intent to defraud and knowledge of insufficient funds upon dishonor and non-payment of a check was held to be error in the absence of a further explanation. State v. Merriweather, 625 S.W.2d 256 (Tenn.1981). Accord: Hunter v. State, 740 P.2d 1206 (Okl.Cr.1987).

In order to avoid a constitutional issue, a statutory presumption must be presented to the jury as an inference. Brackhan v. State, 839 P.2d 414 (Alaska App.1992).

Under either a charge of theft by deception or theft by check, a post-dated check can be evidence of deception even though both parties knew the check was not good at the time defendant issued it if defendant never had the intention to pay the check or knew he or she would not be able to pay it. State v. Hogrefe, 557 N.W.2d 871 (Iowa 1996).

Missouri insufficient funds check statute that sanctions the person passing a check with intent to defraud does not require the check to be given to procure something of value or in payment of a past due debt, it only requires the person act with purpose to defraud, knowing that the check will not be paid by the drawee. State v. Madani, 910 S.W.2d 362 (Mo.App.1995).

For a person to commit the crime of passing a bad check, intent to defraud must be present at the time the check is issued. State v. Wyman, 945 S.W.2d 74 (Mo.App.1997).

55. Appellant testified that a week before the incident in question he sold his car for $100 to obtain funds "to have a good time." He then rented a car for about $100, and he and a friend drove the rented car to Mexico. Appellant and his friend were unable to adequately

which the jury could conclude that appellant spoke the truth—that although appellant knew of the presence of the secret compartment and had knowledge of facts indicating that it contained marihuana, he deliberately avoided positive knowledge of the presence of the contraband to avoid responsibility in the event of discovery.[56] If the jury concluded the latter was indeed the situation, and if positive knowledge is required to convict, the jury would have no choice consistent with its oath but to find appellant not guilty even though he deliberately contrived his lack of positive knowledge. Appellant urges this view. The trial court rejected the premise that only positive knowledge would suffice, and properly so.

Appellant tendered an instruction that to return a guilty verdict the jury must find that the defendant knew he was in possession of marihuana. The trial judge rejected the instruction because it suggested that "absolutely, positively, he has to know that it's there." The court said, "I think, in this case, it's not too sound an instruction because we have evidence that if the jury believes it, they'd be justified in finding he actually didn't know what it was—he didn't because he didn't want to find it."

The court instructed the jury that "knowingly" meant voluntarily and

---

explain their whereabouts during the period of about 11 hours between the time they left Los Angeles and the time they admitted arriving in Mexico.

Their testimony regarding acquisition of the load car follows a pattern common in these cases: they were approached in a Tijuana bar by a stranger who identified himself only by his first name—"Ray." He asked them if they wanted to buy marihuana, and offered to pay them $100 for driving a car north across the border. Appellant accepted the offer and drove the load car back, alone. Appellant's friend drove appellant's rented car back to Los Angeles.

Appellant testified that the stranger instructed him to leave the load car at the address on the car registration slip with the keys in the ashtray. The person living at that address testified that he had sold the car a year earlier and had not seen it since. When the Customs agent asked appellant about the secret compartment in the car, appellant did not deny knowledge of its existence, but stated that it was in the car when he got it.

There were many discrepancies and inconsistencies in the evidence reflecting upon appellant's credibility. Taking the record as a whole, the jury could have concluded that the evidence established an abortive scheme, concocted and carried out by appellant from the beginning, to acquire a load of marihuana in Mexico and return it to Los Angeles for distribution for profit.

56. Both appellant and his companion testified that the stranger identified as "Ray" offered to sell them marihuana and, when they declined, asked if they wanted to drive a car back to Los Angeles for $100. Appellant's companion "wanted no part of driving the vehicle." He testified, "It didn't sound right to me." Appellant accepted the offer. The Drug Enforcement Administration agent testified that appellant stated "he thought there was probably something wrong and something illegal in the vehicle, but that he checked it over. He looked in the glove box and under the front seat and in the trunk, prior to driving it. *He didn't find anything, and, therefore, he assumed that the people at the border wouldn't find anything either*"—(emphasis added). Appellant was asked at trial whether he had seen the special compartment when he opened the trunk. He responded, "Well, you know, I saw a void there, but I didn't know what it was." He testified that he did not investigate further. The Customs agent testified that when he opened the trunk and saw the partition he asked appellant "when he had that put in." Appellant told the agent "that it was in the car when he got it."

The jury would have been justified in accepting all of the testimony as true and concluding that although appellant was aware of facts making it virtually certain that the secret compartment concealed marihuana, he deliberately refrained from acquiring positive knowledge of the fact.

intentionally and not by accident or mistake.[57] The court told the jury that the government must prove beyond a reasonable doubt that the defendant "knowingly" brought the marihuana into the United States (count 1: 21 U.S.C. § 952(a)), and that he "knowingly" possessed the marihuana (count 2: 21 U.S.C. § 841(a)(1)). The court continued:

"The Government can complete their burden of proof by proving, beyond a reasonable doubt, that if the defendant was not actually aware that there was marihuana in the vehicle he was driving when he entered the United States his ignorance in that regard was solely and entirely a result of his having made a conscious purpose to disregard the nature of that which was in the vehicle, with a conscious purpose to avoid learning the truth."

The legal premise of these instructions is firmly supported by leading commentators here and in England. Professor Rollin M. Perkins writes, "One with a deliberate anti-social purpose in mind ... may deliberately 'shut his eyes' to avoid knowing what would otherwise be obvious to view. In such cases, so far as criminal law is concerned, the person acts at his peril in this regard, and is treated as having 'knowledge' of the facts as they are ultimately discovered to be."[58] J.Ll.J. Edwards, writing in 1954, introduced a survey of English cases with the statement, "For well-nigh a hundred years, it has been clear from the authorities that a person who deliberately shuts his eyes to an obvious means of knowledge has sufficient *mens rea* for an offence based on such words as ... 'knowingly.' "[59] Professor Glanville Williams states, on the basis both English and American authorities, "To the requirement of actual knowledge there is one strictly limited exception.... [T]he rule is that if a party has his suspicion aroused but then deliberately omits to make further enquiries, because he wishes to remain in ignorance, he is deemed to have knowledge."[60] Professor Williams concludes, "The rule that wilful blindness is equivalent to knowledge is essential, and is found throughout the criminal law."

The substantive justification for the rule is that deliberate ignorance and positive knowledge are equally culpable. The textual justification is that in common understanding one "knows" facts of which he is less than absolutely certain. To act "knowingly," therefore, is not necessarily to act only with positive knowledge, but also to act with an awareness of the high

---

57.   The court said:

An act is done knowingly if it's done voluntarily and intentionally and not because of mistake or accident or other innocent reason.

The purpose of adding the word "knowingly" was to insure that no one would be convicted for acts done because of an omission or failure to act due to mistake or accident or other innocent reason.

58.   R. Perkins, Criminal Law 776 (2d ed. 1969).

59.   Edwards, The Criminal Degrees of Knowledge, 17 Modern L.Rev. 294, 298 (1954). Later in his discussion Mr. Edwards writes, "[N]o real doubt has been cast on the proposition that connivance is as culpable as actual knowledge. We have already seen the diverse fashions in which this state of mind has been defined, ranging from the original expression 'wilful shutting of the eyes' and its closest counterpart 'wilful blindness,' to the less forceful but equally satisfactory formulae 'purposely abstaining from ascertaining' and 'wilfully abstaining from knowing.' " Id. at 302.

60.   G. Williams, Criminal Law: The General Part, § 57 at 157 (2d ed. 1961).

probability of the existence of the fact in question. When such awareness is present, "positive" knowledge is not required. . . .

"Deliberate ignorance" instructions have been approved in prosecutions under criminal statutes prohibiting "knowing" conduct by the Courts of Appeals of the Second, Sixth, Seventh, and Tenth Circuits. In many other cases, Courts of Appeals reviewing the sufficiency of evidence have approved the premise that "knowingly" in criminal statutes is not limited to positive knowledge, but includes the state of mind of one who does not possess positive knowledge only because he consciously avoided it. These lines of authority appear unbroken. Neither the dissent nor the briefs of either party has cited a case holding that such an instruction is error or that such evidence is not sufficient to establish "knowledge."

There is no reason to reach a different result under the statute involved in this case. Doing so would put this court in direct conflict with Courts of Appeals in two other circuits that have approved "deliberate ignorance" instructions in prosecutions under 21 U.S.C. § 841(a), or its predecessor, 21 U.S.C. § 174. Nothing is cited from the legislative history of the Drug Control Act indicating that Congress used the term "knowingly" in a sense at odds with prior authority. Rather, Congress is presumed to have known and adopted the "cluster of ideas" attached to such a familiar term of art. Congress was aware of *Leary* and *Turner,* and expressed no dissatisfaction with their definition of the term.

Appellant's narrow interpretation of "knowingly" is inconsistent with the Drug Control Act's general purpose to deal more effectively "with the growing menace of drug abuse in the United States." Holding that this term introduces a requirement of positive knowledge would make deliberate ignorance a defense. It cannot be doubted that those who traffic in drugs would make the most of it. This is evident from the number of appellate decisions reflecting conscious avoidance of positive knowledge of the presence of contraband—in the car driven by the defendant or in which he is a passenger, in the suitcase or package he carries, in the parcel concealed in his clothing.

It is no answer to say that in such cases the fact finder may infer positive knowledge. It is probable that many who performed the transportation function, essential to the drug traffic, can truthfully testify that they have no *positive* knowledge of the load they carry. Under appellant's interpretation of the statute, such persons will be convicted only if the fact finder errs in evaluating the credibility of the witness or deliberately disregards the law.

It begs the question to assert that a "deliberate ignorance" instruction permits the jury to convict without finding that the accused possessed the knowledge required by the statute. Such an assertion assumes that the statute requires positive knowledge. But the question is the meaning of the term "knowingly" in the statute. If it means positive knowledge, then, of course, nothing less will do. But if "knowingly" includes a mental state in which the defendant is aware that the fact in question is highly probable but consciously avoids enlightenment, the statute is satisfied by such proof. . . . In the language of the instruction in this case, the government must prove, "beyond a reasonable doubt, that if the defendant was not actually aware . . . his ignorance in that regard was *solely* and *entirely* a result of . . . a conscious purpose to avoid learning the truth.''

No legitimate interest of an accused is prejudiced by such a standard, and society's interest in a system of criminal law that is enforceable and that imposes sanctions upon all who are equally culpable requires it.

The conviction is affirmed.[61]

■ ANTHONY M. KENNEDY, CIRCUIT JUDGE, with whom ELY, HUFSTEDLER and WALLACE, CIRCUIT JUDGES, join (dissenting).

Jewell was convicted and received concurrent sentences on two counts: (1) knowingly or intentionally importing a controlled substance, 21 U.S.C. §§ 952(a), 960(a)(1); (2) knowingly or intentionally possessing, with intent to distribute, a controlled substance, id. § 841(a)(1). We agree with the majority that the jury was not required to find, as to count one, that the defendant knew *which* controlled substance he possessed. We further agree that the additional state of mind required by count two—intent to distribute the substance—must be specifically proven as an element of a section 841(a)(1) violation. . . .

The majority opinion justifies the conscious purpose jury instruction as an application of the wilful blindness doctrine recognized primarily by English authorities. A classic illustration of this doctrine is the connivance of an innkeeper who deliberately arranges not to go into his back room and thus avoids visual confirmation of the gambling he believes is taking place. The doctrine is commonly said to apply in deciding whether one who acquires property under suspicious circumstances should be charged with knowledge that it was stolen.

One problem with the wilful blindness doctrine is its bias towards visual means of acquiring knowledge. We may know facts from direct impressions of the other senses or by deduction from circumstantial evidence, and such knowledge is nonetheless "actual." Moreover, visual sense impressions do not consistently provide complete certainty.

Another problem is that the English authorities seem to consider wilful blindness a state of mind distinct from, but equally culpable, as "actual" knowledge. When a statute specifically requires knowledge as an element of a crime, however, the substitution of some other state of mind cannot be justified even if the court deems that both are equally blameworthy.

---

61. "A deliberate avoidance of knowledge is culpable only when coupled with a subjective awareness of high probability." United States v. Valle–Valdez, 554 F.2d 911, 914 (9th Cir.1977).

The giving of a *Jewell* instruction was error where there was no evidence "that the defendant tried to close his eyes or ears to what was happening." United States v. Beckett, 724 F.2d 855, 856 (9th Cir.1984).

Mere "reckless avoidance of knowledge" is insufficient to justify a *Jewell* instruction. United States v. Fulbright, 105 F.3d 443, 447 (9th Cir.1997).

Instructions adequately distinguished "deliberate ignorance" which goes to defendant's knowledge and "mere presence" which is concerned with culpability for aiding and abetting. United States v. Guerrero, 114 F.3d 332 (1st Cir.1997).

Note, Model Penal Code Section 2.02(7) and Willful Blindness, 102 Yale L.J. 2231 (1993).

Finally, the wilful blindness doctrine is uncertain in scope. There is disagreement as to whether reckless disregard for the existence of a fact constitutes wilful blindness or some lesser degree of culpability. Some cases have held that a statute's scienter requirement is satisfied by the constructive knowledge imputed to one who simply fails to discharge a duty to inform himself. There is also the question of whether to use an "objective" test based on the reasonable man, or to consider the defendant's subjective belief as dispositive.

The approach adopted in section 2.02(7) of the Model Penal Code clarifies, and, in important ways restricts,[62] the English doctrine:

When knowledge of the existence of a particular fact is an element of an offense, such knowledge is established if a person is aware of a high probability of its existence, unless he actually believes that it does not exist.

This provision requires an awareness of a high probability that a fact exists, not merely a reckless disregard, or a suspicion followed by a failure to make further inquiry. It also establishes knowledge as a matter of subjective belief, an important safeguard against diluting the guilty state of mind required for conviction. It is important to note that section 2.02(7) is a *definition* of knowledge, not a substitute for it; as such, it has been cited with approval by the Supreme Court.

In light of the Model Penal Code's definition, the "conscious purpose" jury instruction is defective in three respects. First, it fails to mention the requirement that Jewell have been aware of a high probability that a controlled substance was in the car. It is not culpable to form "a conscious purpose to avoid learning the truth" unless one is aware of facts indicating a high probability of that truth. To illustrate, a child given a gift-wrapped package by his mother while on vacation in Mexico may form a conscious purpose to take it home without learning what is inside; yet his state of mind is totally innocent unless he is aware of a high probability that the package contains a controlled substance. Thus, a conscious purpose instruction is only proper when coupled with a requirement that one be aware of a high probability of the truth.

The second defect in the instruction as given is that it did not alert the jury that Jewell could not be convicted if he "actually believed" there was no controlled substance in the car. The failure to emphasize, as does the Model Penal Code, that subjective belief is the determinative factor, may allow a jury to convict on an objective theory of knowledge—that a reasonable man should have inspected the car and would have discovered what was hidden inside. . . .

We do not question the sufficiency of the evidence in this case to support conviction by a properly-instructed jury. As with all states of mind, knowledge must normally be proven by circumstantial evidence. There is

---

62. Professor Perkins observes that section 2.02(7) of the Model Penal Code "covers must [much] less than 'knowledge' as it has been interpreted as a mens-rea requirement in the common law." With regard to the receipt of stolen property, he criticizes the Code for not imposing liability in "the case of the man who has no belief one way or the other, but has been put on notice that it may be stolen and 'shuts his eyes' in order not to find out." R. Perkins, supra note 1 at 799 [779].

evidence which could support a conclusion that Jewell was aware of a high probability that the car contained a controlled substance and that he had no belief to the contrary. However, we cannot say that the evidence was so overwhelming that the erroneous jury instruction was harmless. Accordingly, we would reverse the judgment on this appeal.[63]

(C) WILFULNESS

The adverb "wilfully" has such extreme differences of meaning that it gives no clue to the *mens rea* requirement to which it refers if it is considered alone. It must be studied with its context and in the light of the particular offense or statute.[64] With reference to its meaning the Supreme Court of the United States has had this to say: "The word often denotes an act which is intentional, or knowing, or voluntary, as distinguished from accidental. But when used in a criminal statute it generally means an act done [1] with a bad purpose ...; [2] without justifiable excuse ...; [or 3] stubbornly, obstinately, perversely.... The word is also employed [4] to characterize a thing done without ground for believing it is lawful ..., or [5] conduct marked by careless disregard whether or not one has the right so to act, ..."[65]

---

63. In a prosecution for willfully causing false claims to be made against the United States the failure to include "balancing language" instructing the jurors that willful blindness constitutes knowledge "only where the individual is aware of a high probability that fact exists and does not subjectively disbelieve the fact" was held not to be error. The court did, however, indicate such language may provide "useful clarification." United States v. Cincotta, 689 F.2d 238, 243–244 (1st Cir.1982).

Failure to give an instruction on "high probability" and "actual belief" in a deliberate ignorance instruction was not plain error. United States v. Glick, 710 F.2d 639 (10th Cir.1983).

"Willful blindness" instruction was properly given in a mail fraud prosecution of an attorney for a scheme to defraud insurance companies. An instruction does not have to distinguish between willful blindness and conscious avoidance. United States v. Krowen, 809 F.2d 144 (1st Cir.1987).

64. The term "willful" as used in criminal statutes is a word of many meanings and its construction is often influenced by its context. Ratzlaf v. United States, 510 U.S. 135, 114 S.Ct. 655, 126 L.Ed.2d 615 (1994).

Sharon L. Davies, The Jurisprudence of Willfulness: An Evolving Theory of Excusable Ignorance, 48 Duke L.J. 341 (1998).

65. United States v. Murdock, 290 U.S. 389, 394–5, 54 S.Ct. 223, 225, 78 L.Ed. 381 (1933). Brackets added. And *see* Nabob Oil Co. v. United States, 190 F.2d 478 (10th Cir.1951).

The word "wilful" in a criminal statute means no more than that the forbidden act was done deliberately and with knowledge. It does not require an evil intent. McBride v. United States, 225 F.2d 249 (5th Cir.1955).

"Wilfulness", as used in the statute proscribing the wilful failure to make timely payment of income taxes, requires a specific wrongful intent. United States v. Palermo, 259 F.2d 872 (3d Cir.1958). Even gross negligence in the failure to pay the tax does not warrant conviction under this statute. Ibid.

A deliberate ignorance instruction was warranted in importation of heroin prosecution when defendant claimed complete ignorance of the contents of luggage she walked through Customs on her return from Japan. Evidence indicated no reasonable person would believe the trip to Japan was for anything than an illicit purpose. United States v. Withers, 100 F.3d 1142 (4th Cir.1996).

Fields v. United States

United States Court of Appeals, District of Columbia, 1947.
164 F.2d 97.

■ CLARK, ASSOCIATE JUSTICE. Appellant was convicted by the verdict of a jury in the District Court of the United States for the District of Columbia under an indictment charging him with violation of 52 Stat. 942, Act June 22, 1938, 2 U.S.C.A. § 192 which reads as follows: "Every person who having been summoned as a witness by the authority of either House of Congress to give testimony or to produce papers upon any matter under inquiry before either House, or any joint committee established by a joint or concurrent resolution of the two Houses of Congress, or any committee of either House of Congress, willfully makes default, or who, having appeared, refuses to answer any question pertinent to the question under inquiry, shall be deemed guilty of a misdemeanor, punishable by a fine of not more than $1,000 nor less than $100 and imprisoned in a common jail for not less than one month nor more than twelve months." He appeals from the judgment of conviction. . . .

For his failure to produce the records called for by the subpoena appellant was cited by the House of Representatives, upon the recommendation of the committee, for contempt. The indictment returned by the grand jury contained two counts of alleged contempt, similar in substance but referring to the separate days of August 14 and 15, 1946. The lower court granted a motion for acquittal as to the first count but appellant was convicted on the second count. He was sentenced to be confined for a term of three months and to pay a fine of two hundred and fifty dollars.

The Government charged there were at least three documents pertinent to the transaction under investigation by the committee which were available to the appellant at the time of the committee hearing. These documents were produced at the trial. The jury found that one or more of these documents had been willfully withheld from the committee by the appellant.

The principal issues raised on appeal are whether or not the court below erred in failing to direct a judgment of acquittal as to the second count; whether or not the word "willfully", as used in the statute, implies an evil or bad purpose; and the related question of whether or not good faith has any bearing on the issue of willfulness. The last two issues arise from the court's charge to the jury that an evil or bad purpose is immaterial, and the court's refusal to charge that appellant's acts assertedly constituting good faith had a bearing on the issue of willfulness.

As to the first issue we are of the opinion that the evidence presented by the Government was clearly sufficient to warrant submission of the case to the jury.

Appellant contends that the word "willful" has a meaning which includes an evil or bad purpose when used in a criminal statute. We think the term has acquired no such fixed meaning according to the type of statute in which it is employed. The Supreme Court has said, long ago, "In construing a statute, penal as well as others, we must look to the object in view, and never adopt an interpretation that will defeat its own purpose, if it will admit of any other reasonable construction." The Emily and The Caroline, 1824, 9 Wheat. 381, 6 L.Ed. 116. . . .

The apparent objective of the statute involved here would be largely defeated if, as appellant contends, a person could appear before a congressional investigating committee and by professing willingness to comply with its requests for information escape the penalty for subsequent default. This court said, in Townsend v. United States, 1938, 68 App.D.C. 223, 229, 95 F.2d 352, 358: "The meaning of the word [willful] depends in large measure upon the nature of the criminal act and the facts of the particular case. It is only in very few criminal cases that 'willful' means 'done with a bad purpose.' Generally, it means 'no more than that the person charged with the duty knows what he is doing. It does not mean that, in addition, he must suppose that he is breaking the law.' " (Quoting Learned Hand, J., in American Surety Co. v. Sullivan, 2 Cir., 1925, 7 F.2d 605, 606.) At the trial of this case the court said, in its charge to the jury:

"The word 'willful' does not mean that the failure or refusal to comply with the order of the committee must necessarily be for an evil or a bad purpose. The reason or the purpose of failure to comply or refusal to comply is immaterial, so long as the refusal was deliberate and intentional and was not a mere inadvertence or an accident." We uphold that differentiation in our view of the purpose of the statute.

Closely related to the issue of willfulness is appellant's assertion of error in the trial court's refusal to charge that appellant's voluntary production of certain records constituted evidence that he acted in good faith and did not "willfully" default. Such an assertion does not penetrate the question whether or not appellant was guilty of deliberately failing to produce subpoenaed records subject to his control, and it was the alleged failure to do so that served as the basis for the contempt citation. That question of fact was properly referred to the jury in the trial below, and the jury returned a verdict against the appellant. . . .

In conclusion, we have carefully examined the record on appeal and find in it no reversible error. Accordingly, the judgment of the trial court is

Affirmed.[66]

(Certiorari denied 332 U.S. 851, 68 S.Ct. 355, 92 L.Ed. 421. Rehearing denied 333 U.S. 839, 68 S.Ct. 607, 92 L.Ed. 1123.)

Bryan v. United States

Supreme Court of the United States, 1998.
524 U.S. 184, 118 S.Ct. 1939, 141 L.Ed.2d 197.

■ JUSTICE STEVENS delivered the opinion of the Court.

Petitioner was convicted of "willfully" dealing in firearms without a federal license. The question presented is whether the term "willfully" in 18 U.S.C. § 924(a)(1)(D) requires proof that the defendant knew that his

---

66. In a regulatory statute the word "wilful" means intentional but does not imply fraud or malice. Department of Transportation v. Transportation Commission, 111 Wis.2d 80, 330 N.W.2d 159 (1983).

conduct was unlawful, or whether it also requires proof that he knew of the federal licensing requirement.

I

In 1968 Congress enacted the Omnibus Crime Control and Safe Streets Act. 82 Stat. 197–239. In Title IV of that Act Congress made findings concerning the impact of the traffic in firearms on the prevalence of lawlessness and violent crime in the United States and amended the Criminal Code to include detailed provisions regulating the use and sale of firearms. As amended, 18 U.S.C. § 922 defined a number of "unlawful acts;" subsection (a)(1) made it unlawful for any person except a licensed dealer to engage in the business of dealing in firearms. Section 923 established the federal licensing program and repeated the prohibition against dealing in firearms without a license, and § 924 specified the penalties for violating "any provision of this chapter." Read literally, § 924 authorized the imposition of a fine of up to $5,000 or a prison sentence of not more than five years, "or both," on any person who dealt in firearms without a license even if that person believed that he or she was acting lawfully. As enacted in 1968, §§ 922(a)(1) and 924 omitted an express scienter requirement and therefore arguably imposed strict criminal liability on every unlicensed dealer in firearms. The 1968 Act also omitted any definition of the term "engaged in the business" even though that conduct was an element of the unlawful act prohibited by § 922(a)(1).

In 1986 Congress enacted the Firearms Owners' Protection Act (FOPA), in part, to cure these omissions. The findings in that statute explained that additional legislation was necessary to protect law-abiding citizens with respect to the acquisition, possession, or use of firearms for lawful purposes. FOPA therefore amended § 921 to include a definition of the term "engaged in the business," and amended § 924 to add a scienter requirement as a condition to the imposition of penalties for most of the unlawful acts defined in § 922. For three categories of offenses the intent required is that the defendant acted "knowingly;" for the fourth category, which includes "any other provision of this chapter," the required intent is that the defendant acted "willfully." The § 922(a)(1)(A) offense at issue in this case is an "other provision" in the "willfully" category.

II

The jury having found petitioner guilty, we accept the Government's version of the evidence. That evidence proved that petitioner did not have a federal license to deal in firearms; that he used so-called "straw purchasers" in Ohio to acquire pistols that he could not have purchased himself; that the straw purchasers made false statements when purchasing the guns; that petitioner assured the straw purchasers that he would file the serial numbers off the guns; and that he resold the guns on Brooklyn street corners known for drug dealing. The evidence was unquestionably adequate to prove that petitioner was dealing in firearms, and that he knew that his conduct was unlawful. There was, however, no evidence that he was aware of the federal law that prohibits dealing in firearms without a federal license.

Petitioner was charged with a conspiracy to violate 18 U.S.C. § 922(a)(1)(A), by willfully engaging in the business of dealing in firearms, and with a substantive violation of that provision. After the close of evidence, petitioner requested that the trial judge instruct the jury that petitioner could be convicted only if he knew of the federal licensing requirement, but the judge rejected this request. Instead, the trial judge gave this explanation of the term "willfully:"

"A person acts willfully if he acts intentionally and purposely and with the intent to do something the law forbids, that is, with the bad purpose to disobey or to disregard the law. Now, the person need not be aware of the specific law or rule that his conduct may be violating. But he must act with the intent to do something that the law forbids."

Petitioner was found guilty on both counts. On appeal he argued that the evidence was insufficient because there was no proof that he had knowledge of the federal licensing requirement, and that the trial judge had erred by failing to instruct the jury that such knowledge was an essential element of the offense. The Court of Appeals affirmed ...

Because the Eleventh Circuit has held that it is necessary for the Government to prove that the defendant acted with knowledge of the licensing requirement, United States v. Sanchez–Corcino, 85 F.3d 549, 553–554 (C.A.11 1996), we granted certiorari to resolve the conflict.

III

The word "willfully" is sometimes said to be "a word of many meanings" whose construction is often dependent on the context in which it appears. *See, e.g.,* Spies v. United States, 317 U.S. 492, 497, 63 S.Ct. 364, 367, 87 L.Ed. 418 (1943). Most obviously it differentiates between deliberate and unwitting conduct, but in the criminal law it also typically refers to a culpable state of mind. As we explained in United States v. Murdock, 290 U.S. 389, 54 S.Ct. 223, 78 L.Ed. 381 (1933), a variety of phrases have been used to describe that concept.[67] As a general matter, when used in the criminal context, a "willful" act is one undertaken with a "bad purpose."[68]

---

67. "The word often denotes an act which is intentional, or knowing, or voluntary, as distinguished from accidental. But when used in a criminal statute it generally means an act done with a bad purpose (Felton v. United States, 96 U.S. 699 [24 L.Ed. 875]; Potter v. United States, 155 U.S. 438 [15 S.Ct. 144, 39 L.Ed. 214]; Spurr v. United States, 174 U.S. 728 [19 S.Ct. 812, 43 L.Ed. 1150]); without *justifiable* excuse (Felton v. United States, *supra*; Williams v. People, 26 Colo. 272, 57 P. 701; People v. Jewell, 138 Mich. 620, 101 N.W. 835; St. Louis, I.M. & S. Ry. Co. v. Batesville & W. Tel. Co., 80 Ark. 499, 97 S.W. 660; Clay v. State, 52 Tex.Cr. 555, 107 S.W. 1129); stubbornly, obstinately, perversely, Wales v. Miner, 89 Ind. 118, 127; Lynch v. Commonwealth, 131 Va. 762, 109 S.E. 427; Claus v. Chicago Gt. W. Ry. Co., 136 Iowa 7, 111 N.W. 15; State v. Harwell, 129 N.C. 550, 40 S.E. 48. The word is also employed to characterize a thing done without ground for believing it is lawful (Roby v. Newton, 121 Ga. 679, 49 S.E. 694), or conduct marked by careless disregard whether or not one has the right so to act, United States v. Philadelphia & R. Ry. Co., 223 Fed. 207, 210; State v. Savre, 129 Iowa 122, 105 N.W. 387; State v. Morgan, 136 N.C. 628, 48 S.E. 670." 290 U.S., at 394–395, 54 S.Ct., at 225.

68. *See, e.g.,* Heikkinen v. United States, 355 U.S. 273, 279, 78 S.Ct. 299, 303, 2 L.Ed.2d 264 (1958) ("There can be no *willful* failure by a deportee, in the sense of § 20(c), to apply to, and identify, a country willing to receive him in the absence of evidence ... of a 'bad purpose' or '[non-]justifiable excuse,' or the like.... [I]t cannot be said that he acted 'willfully'—*i.e.,*

In other words, in order to establish a "willful" violation of a statute, "the Government must prove that the defendant acted with knowledge that his conduct was unlawful." Ratzlaf v. United States, 510 U.S. 135, 137, 114 S.Ct. 655, 657, 126 L.Ed.2d 615 (1994).

Petitioner argues that a more particularized showing is required in this case for two principal reasons. First, he argues that the fact that Congress used the adverb "knowingly" to authorize punishment of three categories of acts made unlawful by § 922 and the word "willfully" when it referred to unlicensed dealing in firearms demonstrates that the Government must shoulder a special burden in cases like this. This argument is not persuasive because the term "knowingly" does not necessarily have any reference to a culpable state of mind or to knowledge of the law. As Justice Jackson correctly observed, "the knowledge requisite to knowing violation of a statute is factual knowledge as distinguished from knowledge of the law." Thus, in United States v. Bailey, 444 U.S. 394, 100 S.Ct. 624, 62 L.Ed.2d 575 (1980), we held that the prosecution fulfills its burden of proving a knowing violation of the escape statute "if it demonstrates that an escapee knew his actions would result in his leaving physical confinement without permission." *Id.*, at 408, 100 S.Ct., at 634. And in Staples v. United States, 511 U.S. 600, 114 S.Ct. 1793, 128 L.Ed.2d 608 (1994), we held that a charge that the defendant's possession of an unregistered machinegun was unlawful required proof "that he knew the weapon he possessed had the characteristics that brought it within the statutory definition of a machinegun." *Id.*, at 602, 114 S.Ct., at 1795. It was not, however, necessary to prove that the defendant knew that his possession was unlawful. *See* Rogers v. United States, 522 U.S. 252, 254–255, 118 S.Ct. 673, 674–676, 139 L.Ed.2d 686 (1998) (plurality opinion). Thus, unless the text of the statute dictates a different result,[69] the term "knowingly" merely requires proof of knowledge of the facts that constitute the offense.

With respect to the three categories of conduct that are made punishable by § 924 if performed "knowingly," the background presumption that every citizen knows the law makes it unnecessary to adduce specific evidence to prove that "an evil-meaning mind" directed the "evil-doing hand." More is required, however, with respect to the conduct in the fourth category that is only criminal when done "willfully." The jury must find

---

with a 'bad purpose' or without 'justifiable excuse' "); United States v. Murdock, 290 U.S. 389, 394, 54 S.Ct. 223, 225, 78 L.Ed. 381 (1933) ("[W]hen used in a criminal statute [willfully] generally means an act done with a bad purpose"); Felton v. United States, 96 U.S. 699, 702, 24 L.Ed. 875 (1877) ("Doing or omitting to do a thing knowingly and wilfully, implies not only a knowledge of the thing, but a determination with a bad intent to do it or to omit doing it. "The word 'wilfully,' says Chief Justice Shaw, in the ordinary sense in which it is used in statutes, means not merely 'voluntarily,' but with a bad purpose." 20 Pick. (Mass.) 220. "It is frequently understood," says Bishop, "as signifying an evil intent without justifiable excuse." Crim. Law, vol. i. sect. 428); 1 L. Sand, J. Siffert, W. Loughlin, & S. Reiss, Modern Federal Jury Instructions & para; 3A.01, p. 3A–18 (1997) (" 'Willfully' means to act with knowledge that one's conduct is unlawful and with the intent to do something the law forbids, that is to say with the bad purpose to disobey or to disregard the law").

69. Liparota v. United States, 471 U.S. 419, 105 S.Ct. 2084, 85 L.Ed.2d 434 (1985), was such a case. We there concluded that both the term "knowing" in 7 U.S.C. § 2024(c) and the term "knowingly" in § 2024(b)(1) literally referred to knowledge of the law as well as knowledge of the relevant facts. *See id.*, at 428–430, 105 S.Ct., at 2089–2091.

that the defendant acted with an evil-meaning mind, that is to say, that he acted with knowledge that his conduct was unlawful.

Petitioner next argues that we must read § 924(a)(1)(D) to require knowledge of the law because of our interpretation of "willfully" in two other contexts. In certain cases involving willful violations of the tax laws, we have concluded that the jury must find that the defendant was aware of the specific provision of the tax code that he was charged with violating. *See, e.g.*, Cheek v. United States, 498 U.S. 192, 201, 111 S.Ct. 604, 610, 112 L.Ed.2d 617 (1991). Similarly, in order to satisfy a willful violation in *Ratzlaf,* we concluded that the jury had to find that the defendant knew that his structuring of cash transactions to avoid a reporting requirement was unlawful. *See* 510 U.S., at 138, 149, 114 S.Ct., at 657–658, 663. Those cases, however, are readily distinguishable. Both the tax cases and *Ratzlaf* involved highly technical statutes that presented the danger of ensnaring individuals engaged in apparently innocent conduct. As a result, we held that these statutes "carv[e] out an exception to the traditional rule" that ignorance of the law is no excuse and require that the defendant have knowledge of the law. The danger of convicting individuals engaged in apparently innocent activity that motivated our decisions in the tax cases and *Ratzlaf* is not present here because the jury found that this petitioner knew that his conduct was unlawful

Thus, the willfulness requirement of § 924(a)(1)(D) does not carve out an exception to the traditional rule that ignorance of the law is no excuse; knowledge that the conduct is unlawful is all that is required.

IV

Petitioner advances a number of additional arguments based on his reading of congressional intent. Petitioner first points to the legislative history of FOPA, but that history is too ambiguous to offer petitioner much assistance. Petitioner's main support lies in statements made by opponents of the bill.[70] As we have stated, however, "[t]he fears and doubts of the opposition are no authoritative guide to the construction of legislation." Schwegmann Brothers v. Calvert Distillers Corp., 341 U.S. 384, 394, 71 S.Ct. 745, 750, 95 L.Ed. 1035 (1951). "In their zeal to defeat a bill, they understandably tend to overstate its reach." NLRB v. Fruit Packers, 377 U.S. 58, 66, 84 S.Ct. 1063, 1068, 12 L.Ed.2d 129 (1964).

Petitioner next argues that, at the time FOPA was passed, the "willfulness" requirements in other subsections of the statute—§§ 923(d)(1)(C)–(D)—had uniformly been interpreted by lower courts to require knowledge of the law; petitioner argues that Congress intended that "willfully" should have the same meaning in § 924(a)(1)(D). As an initial matter, the lower courts had come to no such agreement. While some courts had stated that

---

70. For example, Representative Hughes, a staunch opponent of the bill, stated that the willfulness requirement would "make it next to impossible to convict dealers, particularly those who engage in business without acquiring a license, because the prosecution would have to show that the dealer was personally aware of every detail of the law, and that he made a conscious decision to violate the law." 132 Cong.Rec. 6875 (1986). Even petitioner's *amicus* acknowledges that this statement was "undoubtedly an exaggeration." Brief for National Association of Criminal Defense Lawyers as *Amicus Curiae* 14.

willfulness in § 923(d)(1) is satisfied by a disregard of a known legal obligation, willful was also interpreted variously to refer to "purposeful, intentional conduct," "indifferen[ce] to the requirements of the law," or merely a "conscious, intentional, deliberate, voluntary decision." Moreover, in each of the cases in which disregard of a known legal obligation was held to be sufficient to establish willfulness, it was perfectly clear from the record that the licensee had knowledge of the law; thus, while these cases support the notion that disregard of a known legal obligation is sufficient to establish a willful violation, they in no way stand for the proposition that it is required.

Finally, petitioner argues that § 922(b)(3), which is governed by § 924(a)(1)(D)'s willfulness standard, indicates that Congress intended "willfully" to include knowledge of the law. Section 922(b)(3) prohibits licensees from selling firearms to any person who the licensee knows or has reasonable cause to believe does not reside in the licensee's State, except where, *inter alia*, the transaction fully complies with the laws of both the seller's and buyer's State. The subsection further states that the licensee "shall be presumed, . . . in the absence of evidence to the contrary, to have had actual knowledge of the State laws and published ordinances of both States." Although petitioner argues that the presumption in § 922(b)(3) indicates that Congress intended willfulness to require knowledge of the law for all offenses covered by § 924(a)(1)(D), petitioner is mistaken. As noted above, while disregard of a known legal obligation is certainly sufficient to establish a willful violation, it is not necessary—and nothing in § 922(b)(3) contradicts this basic distinction.[71]

V

One sentence in the trial court's instructions to the jury, read by itself, contained a misstatement of the law. In a portion of the instructions that were given after the correct statement that we have already quoted, the judge stated: "In this case, the government is not required to prove that the defendant knew that a license was required, *nor is the government required to prove that he had knowledge that he was breaking the law.*" (emphasis added). If the judge had added the words "that required a license," the sentence would have been accurate, but as given it was not.

Nevertheless, that error does not provide a basis for reversal for four reasons. First, petitioner did not object to that sentence, except insofar as he had argued that the jury should have been instructed that the Government had the burden of proving that he had knowledge of the federal licensing requirement. Second, in the context of the entire instructions, it

---

71. Petitioner also argues that the statutory language—"willfully violates any other provision of this chapter"—indicates a congressional intent to attach liability only when a defendant possesses specific knowledge of the "provision[s] of [the] chapter." We rejected a similar argument in United States v. International Minerals & Chemical Corp., 402 U.S. 558, 91 S.Ct. 1697, 29 L.Ed.2d 178 (1971). Although that case involved the word "knowingly" (in the phrase "knowingly violates any such regulation"), the response is the same:

"We . . . see no reason why the word 'regulations' [or the phrase 'any other provision of this chapter'] should not be construed as a shorthand designation for specific acts or omissions which violate the Act. The Act, so viewed, does not signal an exception to the rule that ignorance of the law is no excuse . . . ." *Id.*, at 562, 91 S.Ct., at 1700.

seems unlikely that the jury was misled. *See, e.g.,* United States v. Park, 421 U.S. 658, 674–675, 95 S.Ct. 1903, 1912–1913, 44 L.Ed.2d 489 (1975). Third, petitioner failed to raise this argument in the Court of Appeals. Finally, our grant of certiorari was limited to the narrow legal question whether knowledge of the licensing requirement is an essential element of the offense.

Accordingly, the judgment of the Court of Appeals is affirmed.

■ JUSTICE SOUTER, concurring.

I join in the Court's opinion with the caveat that if petitioner had raised and preserved a specific objection to the erroneous statement in the jury instructions, see Part V, *ante,* at 1949, I would vote to vacate the conviction.

■ JUSTICE SCALIA, with whom THE CHIEF JUSTICE and JUSTICE GINSBURG join, dissenting.

Petitioner Sillasse Bryan was convicted of "willfully" violating the federal licensing requirement for firearms dealers. The jury apparently found, and the evidence clearly shows, that Bryan was aware in a general way that some aspect of his conduct was unlawful. *See ante,* at 1944, and n. 8. The issue is whether that general knowledge of illegality is enough to sustain the conviction, or whether a "willful" violation of the licensing provision requires proof that the defendant knew that his conduct was unlawful specifically because he lacked the necessary license. On that point the statute is, in my view, genuinely ambiguous. Most of the Court's opinion is devoted to confirming half of that ambiguity by refuting Bryan's various arguments that the statute clearly requires specific knowledge of the licensing requirement. The Court offers no real justification for its implicit conclusion that either (1) the statute unambiguously requires only general knowledge of illegality, or (2) ambiguously requiring only general knowledge is enough. Instead, the Court curiously falls back on "the traditional rule that ignorance of the law is no excuse" to conclude that "knowledge that the conduct is unlawful is all that is required." In my view, this case calls for the application of a different canon—"the familiar rule that, 'where there is ambiguity in a criminal statute, doubts are resolved in favor of the defendant.'" Adamo Wrecking Co. v. United States, 434 U.S. 275, 285, 98 S.Ct. 566, 572–573, 54 L.Ed.2d 538 (1978), quoting United States v. Bass, 404 U.S. 336, 348, 92 S.Ct. 515, 523, 30 L.Ed.2d 488 (1971).

Title 18 U.S.C. § 922(a)(1)(A) makes it unlawful for any person to engage in the business of dealing in firearms without a federal license. That provision is enforced criminally through § 924(a)(1)(D), which imposes criminal penalties on whoever "willfully violates any other provision of this chapter." The word "willfully" has a wide range of meanings, and "'its construction [is] often ... influenced by its context.'" Ratzlaf v. United States, 510 U.S. 135, 141, 114 S.Ct. 655, 659, 126 L.Ed.2d 615 (1994), quoting Spies v. United States, 317 U.S. 492, 497, 63 S.Ct. 364, 367, 87 L.Ed. 418 (1943). In some contexts it connotes nothing more than "an act which is intentional, or knowing, or voluntary, as distinguished from accidental." United States v. Murdock, 290 U.S. 389, 394, 54 S.Ct. 223, 225,

78 L.Ed. 381 (1933). In the present context, however, inasmuch as the preceding three subparagraphs of § 924 specify a *mens rea* of "knowingly" for *other* firearms offenses, see § § 924(a)(1)(A)–(C), a "willful" violation under § 924(a)(1)(D) must require some mental state more culpable than mere intent to perform the forbidden act. The United States concedes (and the Court apparently agrees) that the violation is not "willful" unless the defendant knows in a general way that his conduct is unlawful. Brief for United States 7–9; [majority opinion] *ante* ("The jury must find that the defendant acted with an evil-meaning mind, that is to say, that he acted with knowledge that his conduct was unlawful").

That concession takes this case beyond any useful application of the maxim that ignorance of the law is no excuse. Everyone agrees that § 924(a)(1)(D) requires some knowledge of the law; the only real question is *which* law? The Court's answer is that knowledge of *any* law is enough— or, put another way, that the defendant must be ignorant of *every* law violated by his course of conduct to be innocent of willfully violating the licensing requirement. The Court points to no textual basis for that conclusion other than the notoriously malleable word "willfully" itself. Instead, it seems to fall back on a presumption (apparently derived from the rule that ignorance of the law is no excuse) that even where ignorance of the law *is* an excuse, that excuse should be construed as narrowly as the statutory language permits.

I do not believe that the Court's approach makes sense of the statute that Congress enacted. I have no quarrel with the Court's assertion that "willfully" in § 924(a)(1)(D) requires only "general" knowledge of illegality—in the sense that the defendant need not be able to recite chapter and verse from Title 18 of the United States Code. It is enough, in my view, if the defendant is generally aware that the *actus reus* punished by the statute—dealing in firearms without a license—is illegal. But the Court is willing to accept a *mens rea* so "general" that it is entirely divorced from the *actus reus* this statute was enacted to punish. That approach turns § 924(a)(1)(D) into a strange and unlikely creature. Bryan would be guilty of "willfully" dealing in firearms without a federal license even if, for example, he had never heard of the licensing requirement but was aware that he had violated the law by using straw purchasers or filing the serial numbers off the pistols. *Ante,* at 1944, n. 8. The Court does not even limit (for there is no rational basis to limit) the universe of relevant laws to federal *firearms* statutes. Bryan would also be "act[ing] with an evil-meaning mind," and hence presumably be guilty of "willfully" dealing in firearms without a license, if he knew that his street-corner transactions violated New York City's business licensing or sales tax ordinances. (For that matter, it ought to suffice if Bryan knew that the car out of which he sold the guns was illegally double-parked, or if, in order to meet the appointed time for the sale, he intentionally violated Pennsylvania's speed limit on the drive back from the gun purchase in Ohio.) Once we stop focusing on the conduct the defendant is actually charged with (*i.e.,* selling guns without a license), I see no principled way to determine *what* law the defendant must be conscious of violating. *See, e.g.*, Lewis v. United States, 523 U.S. 155, 174–175, 118 S.Ct. 1135, 1146, 140 L.Ed.2d 271 (1998)

(SCALIA, J., concurring in judgment) (pointing out a similar interpretive problem potentially raised by the Assimilative Crimes Act).

Congress is free, of course, to make criminal liability under one statute turn on knowledge of another, to use its firearms dealer statutes to encourage compliance with New York City's tax collection efforts, and to put judges and juries through the kind of mental gymnastics described above. But these are strange results, and I would not lightly assume that Congress intended to make liability under a federal criminal statute depend so heavily upon the vagaries of local law—particularly local law dealing with completely unrelated subjects. If we must have a presumption in cases like this one, I think it would be more reasonable to presume that, when Congress makes ignorance of the law a defense to a criminal prohibition, it ordinarily means ignorance of the unlawfulness of the specific conduct punished *by that criminal prohibition.*

That is the meaning we have given the word "willfully" in other contexts where we have concluded it requires knowledge of the law. *See, e.g., Ratzlaf, supra,* at 149, 114 S.Ct., at 663 ("To convict Ratzlaf of the crime with which he was charged, . . . the jury had to find he knew the structuring in which he engaged was unlawful"); Cheek v. United States, 498 U.S. 192, 201, 111 S.Ct. 604, 610, 112 L.Ed.2d 617 (1991) ("[T]he standard for the statutory willfulness requirement is the 'voluntary, intentional violation of a known legal duty.' . . . [T]he issue is whether the defendant knew of the duty purportedly imposed by the provision of the statute or regulation he is accused of violating"). The Court explains these cases on the ground that they involved "highly technical statutes that presented the danger of ensnaring individuals engaged in apparently innocent conduct." *Ante,* at 1947. That is no explanation at all. The complexity of the tax and currency laws may explain why the Court interpreted "willful" to require some awareness of illegality, as opposed to merely "an act which is intentional, or knowing, or voluntary, as distinguished from accidental." *Murdock,* 290 U.S., at 394, 54 S.Ct., at 225. But it *in no way* justifies the distinction the Court seeks to draw today between knowledge of the law the defendant is actually charged with violating and knowledge of *any* law the defendant could conceivably be charged with violating. To protect the pure of heart, it is not necessary to forgive someone whose surreptitious laundering of drug money violates, unbeknownst to him, a technical currency statute. There, as here, regardless of how "complex" the violated statute may be, the defendant would have acted "with an evil-meaning mind." . . . .

SECTION 5.   STRICT LIABILITY

It has been necessary to recognize that some *offenses* are not *true crimes* in the common law sense of opprobrious conduct. The offense is regulatory and *mala prohibitia.* Parking overtime in a restricted zone is an extreme illustration. In the absence of legislation a properly parked car could be left where it is for three hours as justifiably as for ten minutes. In the exercise of the police power, zones have been established in moderately congested areas in which parking is permitted, but for limited periods only.

The length of the period depends upon needs of the particular situation. If the limit established for a certain zone is thirty minutes this is not for the reason that it would be inherently wrong for a car to be left there for a longer period. Nothing but expediency is involved. Penalties are provided as a means of enforcement but no one considers the driver who has parked overtime a criminal. His violation differs from murder or theft by more than degree. It is a different kind of a breach.

To express this difference there has been a tendency to speak of such violations as "civil offenses," "public torts," "public welfare offenses," or "administrative misdemeanors." Since they are not true crimes the normal *mens rea* requirement of crime does not attach.[72] They are enforced on the basis of "strict liability" unless the particular statute or ordinance adds some limitation. In recent years there has been an increase in the use of this type of offense.[73]

It is necessary to give special attention to three problems: (1) Is the particular offense under consideration a "civil offense" or a true crime? (2) If it is a "civil offense," has the wording of the enactment added a *mens rea* requirement of some nature? (3) If it is a true crime, has the wording of a statute eliminated the *mens rea* requirement (and if so what is the effect)?

Strict liability is most frequently employed in the area of food and drug control, traffic regulation, restrictions on pollution and navigation, animal cruelty, regulation of alcohol and liquor, and explosives and hazardous chemicals.

Commonwealth v. Olshefski

Pennsylvania District and County Court, 1948.
64 Pa. D. & C. 343.

■ KREISHER, P.J., September 9, 1948. On February 6, 1948, John Fisher, a driver for above-named defendant, at the direction of defendant, purchased a load of coal at the Gilberton Coal Company colliery and had the same loaded upon a truck owned by defendant, which had a "U" tag on it, and which, under The Vehicle Code of May 1, 1929, P.L. 905, is permitted to weigh 15,000 pounds plus five percent, or a gross weight of 15,750 pounds. The load was weighed by a licensed weighmaster at the colliery and the weight was given at 15,200 pounds. Fisher drove the truck to the home of defendant, who was out of town at the time and then placed the weigh slip from the colliery in the compartment of the truck. The following day defendant went to the Danville National Bank to do some banking business and observed the Pennsylvania State Police at the Northern end of the river bridge checking on trucks. He then returned to his home and drove

---

72. Kenny, Outlines of Criminal Law 44–45 (18th ed. by Turner, 1962).

"However when the sanction is regulatory, rather than punitive, it does not support the characterization of the statute as criminal." State v. Rhoades, 54 Or.App. 254, 634 P.2d 806, 808 (1981).

73. Strict liability has been distinguished from absolute liability. In the former, some defenses are recognized. In the latter situation, the only real defense is that there is no *actus reus.* For an interesting discussion of the differences between strict liability and absolute liability, *see* Regina v. City of Sault Ste. Marie, 40 CCC 2d 353, 362–374 (SCC 1978).

his truck with the load of coal to the northern end of the river bridge on his way to the borough water department scales for the purpose of having it weighed. He states that he was selling the coal in Danville, and pursuant to the requirements of an ordinance in Danville, he had to have a Danville weigh slip. Before reaching the water department's scales a State policeman stopped him and he was directed to the scales where his load was weighed by the officer and the weigh slip was signed by a licensed weighmaster, showing that his gross weight was 16,015, and that he was, therefore, overloaded 265 pounds. The officer lodged an information for his violation of The Vehicle Code. Defendant waived a hearing and the matter is now before us for disposition. . . .

It is also contended by counsel for defendant that this prosecution should be dismissed for the reason that defendant had in his possession a weigh bill for this particular load by a duly licensed weighmaster, which was weighed the day before, showing that the gross weight of the truck and the load was within the load allowed by law for this particular truck, and that defendant, relying upon this weigh bill, voluntarily drove to where he knew the police were weighing trucks, and was of the belief that his load was a legal load, and therefore, because of this belief, he is not guilty of the crime charged.

In criminal law we have two distinct types of crimes: The one type of crime being the common-law crimes, which are designated as crimes mala in se, which means that they are crimes because the act is bad in and of itself. The other type of crime which did not exist at common law covers those acts which are made criminal by statute, and are termed crimes mala prohibita, and simply means that they are crimes not because they are bad in and of themselves, but merely because the legislative authority makes the act criminal and penal.

In crimes that are mala in se, two elements are necessary for the commission of the crime, viz., the mental element and the physical element. In this type of crime intent is a necessary element, but in statutory crimes, which are simply mala prohibita, the mental element is not necessary for the commission of the crime, and one who does an act in violation of the statute and is caught and prosecuted, is guilty of the crime irrespective of his intent or belief. The power of the legislature to punish an act as a crime, even though it is not bad in and of itself, is an absolute power of the legislature, the only restriction being the constitutional restrictions, and it is the duty of the court to enforce these enactments irrespective of what the court might personally think about the prosecution or the wisdom of the act.

Except for constitutional limitations, the power of the State legislature is absolute. It may punish any act which in its judgment requires punishment, provided it violates no constitutional restriction, and its enactments must be enforced by the courts. The courts cannot review the discretion of the legislature, or pass upon the expediency, wisdom, or propriety of legislative action in matters within its powers. Neither can the courts pass upon the action of a prosecuting officer who prosecutes a person for the violation of a statute which is violated by that person, even though the court might be of the opinion that the officer should have not instituted the prosecution.

If the testimony shows, as in this case, that defendant violated the law, and is prosecuted for that violation, then the court is bound to enforce the legislative enactments, and cannot in good conscience set itself up as the legislature and excuse one person who has violated the law and find another person guilty for the same violation. It is true that this rule of law may seem harsh and unjustifiable, but the court is powerless to correct it, and, therefore, under our duty as judge, we are obliged to hold that this defendant violated The Vehicle Code by having his truck overloaded, and that he is guilty as charged. To this end we make the following

Rule

Order

And now, to wit, September 9, 1948, it is ordered, adjudged and decreed that Felix Olshefski is guilty as charged, and the sentence of the court is that he pay the costs of prosecution, and that he pay a fine of $25 to the Commonwealth of Pennsylvania for the use of the County of Montour, and in default of payment thereof, shall undergo imprisonment in the Montour County Jail for an indeterminate period of not less than one day nor more than two days. Said sentence to be complied with on or before September 15, 1948.

Staples v. United States

Supreme Court of the United States, 1994.
511 U.S. 600, 114 S.Ct. 1793, 128 L.Ed.2d 608.

■ JUSTICE THOMAS delivered the opinion of the Court.

The National Firearms Act makes it unlawful for any person to possess a machinegun that is not properly registered with the Federal Government. Petitioner contends that, to convict him under the Act, the Government should have been required to prove beyond a reasonable doubt that he knew the weapon he possessed had the characteristics that brought it within the statutory definition of a machinegun. We agree and accordingly reverse the judgment of the Court of Appeals.

Issue

I

The National Firearms Act (Act), 26 U.S.C. §§ 5801–5872, imposes strict registration requirements on statutorily defined "firearms." The Act includes within the term "firearm" a machinegun, § 5845(a)(6), and further defines a machinegun as "any weapon which shoots ... or can be readily restored to shoot, automatically more than one shot, without manual reloading, by a single function of the trigger." § 5845(b). Thus, any fully automatic weapon is a "firearm" within the meaning of the Act. Under the Act, all firearms must be registered in the National Firearms Registration and Transfer Record maintained by the Secretary of the Treasury. § 5841. Section 5861(d) makes it a crime, punishable by up to 10 years in prison, see § 5871, for any person to possess a firearm that is not properly registered.

Upon executing a search warrant at petitioner's home, local police and agents of the Bureau of Alcohol, Tobacco and Firearms (BATF) recovered, among other things, an AR–15 assault rifle. The AR–15 is the civilian version of the military's M–16 rifle, and is, unless modified, a semiautomatic weapon. The M–16, in contrast, is a selective fire rifle that allows the operator, by rotating a selector switch, to choose semiautomatic or automatic fire. Many M–16 parts are interchangeable with those in the AR–15 and can be used to convert the AR–15 into an automatic weapon. No doubt to inhibit such conversions, the AR–15 is manufactured with a metal stop on its receiver that will prevent an M–16 selector switch, if installed, from rotating to the fully automatic position. The metal stop on petitioner's rifle, however, had been filed away, and the rifle had been assembled with an M–16 selector switch and several other M–16 internal parts, including a hammer, disconnector, and trigger. Suspecting that the AR–15 had been modified to be capable of fully automatic fire, BATF agents seized the weapon. Petitioner subsequently was indicted for unlawful possession of an unregistered machinegun in violation of § 5861(d).

At trial, BATF agents testified that when the AR–15 was tested, it fired more than one shot with a single pull of the trigger. It was undisputed that the weapon was not registered as required by § 5861(d). Petitioner testified that the rifle had never fired automatically when it was in his possession. He insisted that the AR–15 had operated only semiautomatically, and even then imperfectly, often requiring manual ejection of the spent casing and chambering of the next round. According to petitioner, his alleged ignorance of any automatic firing capability should have shielded him from criminal liability for his failure to register the weapon. He requested the District Court to instruct the jury that, to establish a violation of § 5861(d), the Government must prove beyond a reasonable doubt that the defendant "knew that the gun would fire fully automatically." 1 App. to Brief for Appellant in No. 91–5033 (CA10), p. 42.

The District Court rejected petitioner's proposed instruction and instead charged the jury as follows:

"The Government need not prove the defendant knows he's dealing with a weapon possessing every last characteristic [which subjects it] to the regulation. It would be enough to prove he knows that he is dealing with a dangerous device of a type as would alert one to the likelihood of regulation."

Petitioner was convicted and sentenced to five years' probation and a $5,000 fine.

The Court of Appeals affirmed. . . .

II

A

Whether or not § 5861(d) requires proof that a defendant knew of the characteristics of his weapon that made it a "firearm" under the Act is a question of statutory construction. . . . Thus, we have long recognized that determining the mental state required for commission of a federal crime requires "construction of the statute and . . . inference of the intent of

Congress." United States v. Balint, 258 U.S. 250, 253, 42 S.Ct. 301, 302, 66 L.Ed. 604 (1922).

The language of the statute, the starting place in our inquiry, provides little explicit guidance in this case. Section 5861(d) is silent concerning the *mens rea* required for a violation. It states simply that "[i]t shall be unlawful for any person ... to receive or possess a firearm which is not registered to him in the National Firearms Registration and Transfer Record." 26 U.S.C. § 5861(d). Nevertheless, silence on this point by itself does not necessarily suggest that Congress intended to dispense with a conventional *mens rea* element, which would require that the defendant know the facts that make his conduct illegal. (Traditionally, "scienter" was a necessary element in every crime). On the contrary, we must construe the statute in light of the background rules of the common law, in which the requirement of some *mens rea* for a crime is firmly embedded. As we have observed, "[t]he existence of a *mens rea* is the rule of, rather than the exception to, the principles of Anglo–American criminal jurisprudence." *See* Morissette v. United States, 342 U.S. 246, 250, 72 S.Ct. 240, 243, 96 L.Ed. 288 (1952) ("The contention that an injury can amount to a crime only when inflicted by intention is no provincial or transient notion. It is as universal and persistent in mature systems of law as belief in freedom of the human will and a consequent ability and duty of the normal individual to choose between good and evil").

There can be no doubt that this established concept has influenced our interpretation of criminal statutes. Indeed, we have noted that the common law rule requiring *mens rea* has been "followed in regard to statutory crimes even where the statutory definition did not in terms include it." Relying on the strength of the traditional rule, we have stated that offenses that require no *mens rea* generally are disfavored, and have suggested that some indication of congressional intent, express or implied, is required to dispense with *mens rea* as an element of a crime.

According to the Government, however, the nature and purpose of the National Firearms Act suggest that the presumption favoring *mens rea* does not apply to this case. The Government argues that Congress intended the Act to regulate and restrict the circulation of dangerous weapons. Consequently, in the Government's view, this case fits in a line of precedent concerning what we have termed "public welfare" or "regulatory" offenses, in which we have understood Congress to impose a form of strict criminal liability through statutes that do not require the defendant to know the facts that make his conduct illegal. In construing such statutes, we have inferred from silence that Congress did not intend to require proof of *mens rea* to establish an offense.

For example, in *Balint, supra*, we concluded that the Narcotic Act of 1914, which was intended in part to minimize the spread of addictive drugs by criminalizing undocumented sales of certain narcotics, required proof only that the defendant knew that he was selling drugs, not that he knew the specific items he had sold were "narcotics" within the ambit of the statute. *See Balint, supra*, at 254, 42 S.Ct., at 303. Cf. United States v. Dotterweich, 320 U.S. 277, 281, 64 S.Ct. 134, 136, 88 L.Ed. 48 (1943) (stating in dicta that a statute criminalizing the shipment of adulterated or misbranded drugs did not require knowledge that the items were misbranded or adulterated). As we explained in *Dotterweich, Balint* dealt with "a now familiar type of legislation whereby penalties serve as effective means of regulation. Such legislation dispenses with the conventional requirement for criminal conduct—awareness of some wrongdoing."

Such public welfare offenses have been created by Congress, and recognized by this Court, in "limited circumstances." United States Gypsum, 438 U.S., at 437, 98 S.Ct., at 2873. Typically, our cases recognizing such offenses involve statutes that regulate potentially harmful or injurious items. Cf. United States v. International Minerals & Chemical Corp., 402 U.S. 558, 564–565, 91 S.Ct. 1697, 1701–1702, 29 L.Ed.2d 178 (1971) (characterizing Balint and similar cases as involving statutes regulating "dangerous or deleterious devices or products or obnoxious waste materials"). In such situations, we have reasoned that as long as a defendant knows that he is dealing with a dangerous device of a character that places him "in responsible relation to a public danger," *Dotterweich, supra*, at 281, 64 S.Ct., at 136, he should be alerted to the probability of strict regulation, and we have assumed that in such cases Congress intended to place the burden on the defendant to "ascertain at his peril whether [his conduct] comes within the inhibition of the statute." Thus, we essentially have relied on the nature of the statute and the particular character of the items regulated to determine whether congressional silence concerning the mental element of the offense should be interpreted as dispensing with conventional *mens rea* requirements. *See generally Morissette, supra*, at 252–260, 72 S.Ct., at 244–248.[74]

B

The Government argues that § 5861(d) defines precisely the sort of regulatory offense described in *Balint*. In this view, all guns, whether or not they are statutory "firearms," are dangerous devices that put gun

---

74. By interpreting such public welfare offenses to require at least that the defendant know that he is dealing with some dangerous or deleterious substance, we have avoided construing criminal statutes to impose a rigorous form of strict liability. *See, e.g.,* United States v. International Minerals & Chemical Corp., 402 U.S. 558, 563–564, 91 S.Ct. 1697, 1700–1701, 29 L.Ed.2d 178 (1971) (suggesting that if a person shipping acid mistakenly thought that he was shipping distilled water, he would not violate a statute criminalizing undocumented shipping of acids). True strict liability might suggest that the defendant need not know even that he was dealing with a dangerous item. Nevertheless, we have referred to public welfare offenses as "dispensing with" or "eliminating" a *mens rea* requirement or "mental element," see, e.g., Morissette, 342 U.S., at 250, 263, 72 S.Ct. at 249–250; United States v. Dotterweich, 320 U.S. 277, 281, 64 S.Ct. 134, 136–137, 88 L.Ed. 48 (1943), and have described them as strict liability crimes, United States v. United States Gypsum Co., 438 U.S. 422, 437, 98 S.Ct. 2864, 2873, 57 L.Ed.2d 854 (1978). While use of the term "strict liability" is really a misnomer, we have interpreted statutes defining public welfare offenses to eliminate the requirement of *mens rea*; that is, the requirement of a "guilty mind" with respect to an element of a crime. Under such statutes we have not required that the defendant know the facts that make his conduct fit the definition of the offense. Generally speaking, such knowledge is necessary to establish *mens rea*, as is reflected in the maxim *ignorantia facti excusat*. *See generally* J. Hawley & M. McGregor, Criminal Law 26–30 (1899); R. Perkins, Criminal Law 785–786 (2d ed. 1969); G. Williams, Criminal Law: The General Part 113–174 (1953). Cf. Regina v. Tolson, 23 Q.B. 168, 187 (1889) (Stephen, J.) ("[I]t may, I think, be maintained that in every case knowledge of fact [when not appearing in the statute] is to some extent an element of criminality as much as competent age and sanity").

owners on notice that they must determine at their hazard whether their weapons come within the scope of the Act. . . .

The Government seeks support for its position from our decision in United States v. Freed, 401 U.S. 601, 91 S.Ct. 1112, 28 L.Ed.2d 356 (1971), which involved a prosecution for possession of unregistered grenades under § 5861(d). The defendant knew that the items in his possession were grenades, and we concluded that § 5861(d) did not require the Government to prove the defendant also knew that the grenades were unregistered. To be sure, in deciding that *mens rea* was not required with respect to that element of the offense, we suggested that the Act "is a regulatory measure in the interest of the public safety, which may well be premised on the theory that one would hardly be surprised to learn that possession of hand grenades is not an innocent act." Grenades, we explained, "are highly dangerous offensive weapons, no less dangerous than the narcotics involved in United States v. Balint." But that reasoning provides little support for dispensing with *mens rea* in this case.

. . . Moreover, our analysis in *Freed* likening the Act to the public welfare statute in Balint rested entirely on the assumption that the defendant knew that he was dealing with hand grenades—that is, that he knew he possessed a particularly dangerous type of weapon (one within the statutory definition of a "firearm"), possession of which was not entirely "innocent" in and of itself. The predicate for that analysis is eliminated when, as in this case, the very question to be decided is whether the defendant must know of the particular characteristics that make his weapon a statutory firearm.

. . .

Neither, in our view, can all guns be compared to hand grenades. . . . [T]he fact remains that there is a long tradition of widespread lawful gun ownership by private individuals in this country. Such a tradition did not apply to the possession of hand grenades in Freed or to the selling of dangerous drugs that we considered in *Balint*. In fact, in *Freed* we construed § 5861(d) under the assumption that "one would hardly be surprised to learn that possession of hand grenades is not an innocent act." Here, the Government essentially suggests that we should interpret the section under the altogether different assumption that "one would hardly be surprised to learn that owning a gun is not an innocent act." That proposition is simply not supported by common experience. Guns in general are not "deleterious devices or products or obnoxious waste materials, . . ."

The Government protests that guns, unlike food stamps, but like grenades and narcotics, are potentially harmful devices. . . . But that an item is "dangerous," in some general sense, does not necessarily suggest, as the Government seems to assume, that it is not also entirely innocent. Even dangerous items can, in some cases, be so commonplace and generally available that we would not consider them to alert individuals to the likelihood of strict regulation. As suggested above, despite their potential for harm, guns generally can be owned in perfect innocence. Of course, we might surely classify certain categories of guns—no doubt including the machineguns, sawed-off shotguns, and artillery pieces that Congress has subjected to regulation—as items the ownership of which would have the same quasi-suspect character we attributed to owning hand grenades in Freed. But precisely because guns falling outside those categories traditionally have been widely accepted as lawful possessions, their destructive potential, while perhaps even greater than that of some items we would classify along with narcotics and hand grenades, cannot be said to put gun owners sufficiently on notice of the likelihood of regulation to justify interpreting § 5861(d) as not requiring proof of knowledge of a weapon's characteristics.

. . .

If we were to accept as a general rule the Government's suggestion that dangerous and regulated items place their owners under an obligation to inquire at their peril into compliance with regulations, we would undoubtedly reach some untoward results. Automobiles, for example, might also be termed "dangerous" devices and are highly regulated at both the state and federal levels. Congress might see fit to criminalize the violation of certain regulations concerning automobiles, and thus might make it a crime to operate a vehicle without a properly functioning emission control system. But we probably would hesitate to conclude on the basis of silence that Congress intended a prison term to apply to a car owner whose vehicle's emissions levels, wholly unbeknownst to him, began to exceed legal limits between regular inspection dates.

. . .

C

The potentially harsh penalty attached to violation of § 5861(d)—up to 10 years' imprisonment—confirms our reading of the Act. Historically, the penalty imposed under a statute has been a significant consideration in determining whether the statute should be construed as dispensing with *mens rea*. Certainly, the cases that first defined the concept of the public welfare offense almost uniformly involved statutes that provided for only light penalties such as fines or short jail sentences, not imprisonment in the state penitentiary.

As commentators have pointed out, the small penalties attached to such offenses logically complemented the absence of a *mens rea* requirement: in a system that generally requires a "vicious will" to establish a crime, 4 W. Blackstone, Commentaries *21, imposing severe punishments for offenses that require no *mens rea* would seem incongruous. See Sayre, Public Welfare Offenses, 33 Colum.L.Rev. 55, 70 (1933). Indeed, some courts justified the absence of *mens rea* in part on the basis that the offenses did not bear the same punishments as "infamous crimes," and questioned whether imprisonment was compatible with the reduced culpability required for such regulatory offenses. Similarly, commentators collecting the early cases have argued that offenses punishable by imprisonment cannot be understood to be public welfare offenses, but must require *mens rea*. See R. Perkins, Criminal Law 793–798 (2d ed. 1969) (suggesting that the penalty should be the starting point in determining whether a statute describes a public welfare offense).[75]

In rehearsing the characteristics of the public welfare offense, we, too, have included in our consideration the punishments imposed and have noted that "penalties commonly are relatively small, and conviction does no grave damage to an offender's reputation." *Morissette*, 342 U.S., at 256, 72 S.Ct., at 246.[76] We have even recognized that it was "[u]nder such considerations" that courts have construed statutes to dispense with *mens rea*.

Our characterization of the public welfare offense in *Morissette* hardly seems apt, however, for a crime that is a felony, as is violation of § 5861(d). After all, "felony" is, as we noted in distinguishing certain common law crimes from public welfare offenses, " 'as bad a word as you can give to man or thing.' " . . .

We need not adopt such a definitive rule of construction to decide this case, however. Instead, we note only that where, as here, dispensing with *mens rea* would require the defendant to have knowledge only of traditionally lawful conduct, a severe penalty is a further factor tending to suggest that Congress did not intend to eliminate a *mens rea* requirement. In such a case, the usual presumption that a defendant must know the facts that make his conduct illegal should apply.

III

In short, we conclude that the background rule of the common law favoring *mens rea* should govern interpretation of § 5861(d) in this case. Silence does not suggest that Congress dispensed with *mens rea* for the element of § 5861(d) at issue here. Thus, to obtain a conviction, the Government should have been required to prove that petitioner knew of the features of his AR–15 that brought it within the scope of the Act.

. . . .

For the foregoing reasons, the judgment of the Court of Appeals is reversed and the case remanded for further proceedings consistent with this opinion.

So ordered.[77]

---

75. *But see, e.g.*, State v. Lindberg, 125 Wash. 51, 215 P. 41 (1923) (applying the public welfare offense rationale to a felony).

76. See also United States Gypsum, 438 U.S., at 442, n. 18, 98 S.Ct., at 2876, n. 18 (noting that an individual violation of the Sherman Antitrust Act is a felony punishable by three years in prison or a fine not exceeding $100,000 and stating that "[t]he severity of these sanctions provides further support for our conclusion that the [Act] should not be construed as creating strict-liability crimes"). Cf. Holdridge v. United States, 282 F.2d 302, 310 (C.A.8 1960) (Blackmun, J.) ("[W]here a federal criminal statute omits mention of intent and ... where the penalty is relatively small, where conviction does not gravely besmirch, [and] where the statutory crime is not one taken over from the common law, ... the statute can be construed as one not requiring criminal intent").

77. A burglary-type statute, providing for punishment without a requirement of any unlawful intent, was held to be unconstitutional. State v. Stern, 526 P.2d 344 (Wyo.1974).

"At common law, criminal intent was an essential element of proof of every crime. It remains an essential element, today, in crimes *mala in se,* particularly ones involving the

Stepniewski v. Gagnon

United States Court of Appeals, Seventh Circuit, 1984.
732 F.2d 567.

■ BAUER, CIRCUIT JUDGE.

Petitioner–Appellee Richard Stepniewski filed a petition for a writ of habeas corpus in the district court claiming that his conviction without proof of criminal intent violates his constitutional right to due process of law. The district court agreed and granted the writ. Stepniewski v. Gagnon, 562 F.Supp. 329 (E.D.Wis.1983). We reverse.

On February 15, 1980, Stepniewski was convicted in Milwaukee County Circuit Court of twelve counts of home improvement trade practice violations, contrary to Wis.Stats. §§ 100.20(2) and 100.26(3) (1972). The court sentenced Stepniewski to one year incarceration plus six consecutive and five concurrent one year sentences, stayed by probation, for each of the twelve convictions. Upon a showing by the prosecution that Stepniewski was on probation for a felony theft by contractor conviction involving misappropriation of $24,000, the trial court imposed an additional six-month period of incarceration, to be served consecutively, . . . Both the Wisconsin Court of Appeals, and the Wisconsin Supreme Court affirmed the convictions.

. . .

Section 100.20(2) of the Trade Practices Act grants the Wisconsin Department of Agriculture authority to "issue general orders forbidding methods of competition in business or trade practices in business which are determined by the department to be unfair." Stepniewski was convicted under Section 100.26(3) of the Act for violating home improvement contractor regulations. Section 100.26(3) states in part:

Any person . . . who intentionally refuses, neglects or fails to obey any regulation made under section . . . 100.20 shall, for each offense, be punished by a fine of not less than twenty-five nor more than five

---

taking of another's property" (citations omitted). And where necessary it "would be read into" the statute by the courts. United States v. Parker, 522 F.2d 801 (4th Cir.1975).

Parker, 522 F.2d 801 (4th Cir.1975).

Securities law provisions are not strict liability offenses under Illinois law. People v. Whitlow, 89 Ill.2d 322, 60 Ill.Dec. 587, 433 N.E.2d 629 (1982). Accord: Hentzner v. State, 613 P.2d 821 (Alaska 1980).

Delivery of a controlled substance offense does not require knowledge that substance delivered was heroin. People v. Delgado, 404 Mich. 76, 273 N.W.2d 395 (1978).

"[W]e hold that a defendant's state of mind or intent is an element of a criminal antitrust offense which must be established by evidence and inferences drawn therefrom and cannot be taken from the trier of fact through reliance on a legal presumption of wrongful intent from proof of an effect on prices." United States v. United States Gypsum Co., 438 U.S. 422, 435, 98 S.Ct. 2864, 2872, 57 L.Ed.2d 854 (1978).

Criminal offenses requiring no *mens rea* have a generally disfavored status, and courts are reluctant to conclude that Congress intended to dispense with *mens rea* as an element of a crime absent some indication of Congressional intent. United States v. Nguyen, 73 F.3d 887 (9th Cir. 1995).

thousand dollars, or by imprisonment in the county jail for not more than one year, or by both such fine and imprisonment.

Wis.Admin.Code, Chapter AG 110, issued pursuant to section 100.20(2), states in part:

AG 110.02 Prohibited trade practices. No seller shall engage in the following unfair methods of competition or unfair trade practices:

. . .

(7) PERFORMANCE. . . .

(b) Fail to begin or complete work on the dates or within the time period specified in the home improvement contract, or as otherwise represented, unless the delay is for reason of labor stoppage, unavailability of supplies or materials, unavoidable casualties, or any other case beyond the seller's control. Any changes in the dates or time periods stated in a written contract shall be agreed to in writing.

AG 110.05 Home improvement contract requirements. . . .

. . .

(2) Home improvement contracts and all changes in the terms and conditions thereof, required under this section to be in writing, shall be signed by all parties thereto, and shall clearly and accurately set forth in legible form all terms and conditions of the contract, and particularly the following:

. . .

(d) The dates or time period on or within which the work is to begin and to be completed by the seller.

The Wisconsin Supreme Court interpreted the word "intentionally" in section 100.26(3) as modifying only "refuses," and not "neglects" or "fails." The court thus concluded that mere failure to obey the regulation can result in conviction. This court is bound to accept the construction of the Act by the Wisconsin Supreme Court. Our task is to determine whether that construction violates the due process clause of the United States Constitution.

In his petition for a writ of habeas corpus, Stepniewski claimed that he could not constitutionally be convicted and sentenced under the Act without any finding of criminal intent. The district court agreed and held that, on the basis of Morissette v. United States, 342 U.S. 246, 72 S.Ct. 240, 96 L.Ed. 288 (1952), a strict liability crime can be valid under the due process clause of the fifth and fourteenth amendments only if "the 'nature and quality' of the crime [is] more heinous than the proscribed conduct in the case at bar." The district court read *Morissette* to establish, as a matter of constitutional law, three factors for determining whether the "nature and quality" of an offense precludes application of strict liability. The district court set those factors as: (1) whether the defendant is in a position to avoid transgressions by the exercise of reasonable care; (2) whether the penalty is relatively small; and (3) whether a conviction would result in no grave damage to the defendant's reputation.

The district court incorrectly interprets *Morissette*. Although the *Morissette* court enunciated various factors, including those used by the district court, for federal courts to consider when reviewing statutes that arguably impose strict liability, the Court did not establish those factors as principles of constitutional law. Rather, the Court discusses the factors as general policy concerns which in part explain the historical development of strict liability crimes. This discussion assisted the Court in ultimately concluding that when

> Congress borrows terms of art in which are accumulated the legal tradition and meaning of centuries of practice, it presumably knows and adopts the cluster of ideas that were attached to each borrowed word.... [Therefore] absence of contrary direction may be taken as satisfaction with widely accepted definitions, not as departure from them.

> The Court thus held that Congress' mere omission of intent from a statute punishing conversion of United States property would not be interpreted as the removal of the intent element of the crime. Federal courts have applied these various factors when interpreting federal criminal statutes which the government sought to apply as strict liability offenses.

A state or the federal government does not violate due process protections each time it chooses not to include intent to violate a regulation as an element of the crime. "The power of the legislature to declare an offense, and to exclude the elements of knowledge and due diligence from any inquiry as to its commission, cannot, we think, be questioned." Chicago, B. & Q. Ry. v. United States, 220 U.S. 559, 578, 31 S.Ct. 612, 617, 55 L.Ed. 582 (1911). Similarly, "(t)he objection that punishment of a person for an act as a crime when ignorant of the facts making it so, involves a denial of due process of law has more than once been overruled." Williams v. North Carolina, 325 U.S. 226, 238, 65 S.Ct. 1092, 1099, 89 L.Ed. 1577 (1945). Moreover, "public policy may require that in the prohibition or punishment of particular acts it may be provided that he who shall do them shall do them at his peril and will not be heard to plead in defense good faith or ignorance." Shevlin–Carpenter Co. v. Minnesota, 218 U.S. 57, 70, 30 S.Ct. 663, 666, 54 L.Ed. 930 (1910).

The United States Supreme Court has not ruled specifically when, if ever, the imposition of strict liability in a criminal statute by itself violates the due process clause of the fourteenth amendment. The Supreme Court has recognized, however, that strict liability criminal offenses are not necessarily unconstitutional, Lambert v. California, 355 U.S. 225, 228, 78 S.Ct. 240, 242, 2 L.Ed.2d 228 (1957), and that the federal courts should interpret a law as one of strict liability only when Congress clearly so intends. In addition, the Court has stated that no single rule resolves whether a crime must require intent to be valid, "for the law on the subject is neither settled nor static."

The petitioner offers Supreme Court dicta to the effect that "[p]encils, dental floss, paper clips may also be regulated. But they may be the type of products which might raise substantial due process questions if Congress did not require '*mens rea*' as to each ingredient of the offense." United

States v. International Minerals & Chemical Corp., 402 U.S. 558, 564–65, 91 S.Ct. 1697, 1701–02, 29 L.Ed.2d 178 (1971). That analysis, although instructive, does not compel the result in the district court.

Traditional common law offenses, such as murder and assault, usually require some showing of intent before they are punished. Regulatory measures dealing with the possession or transportation of drugs, explosives, or dangerous chemicals, for example, often do not require any showing of intent to violate the regulation by the actor before a conviction can be obtained. *See* United States v. Balint, 258 U.S. 250, 42 S.Ct. 301, 66 L.Ed. 604 (1922); United States v. Freed, 401 U.S. 601, 91 S.Ct. 1112, 28 L.Ed.2d 356 (1971); United States v. International Minerals & Chemical Corp., 402 U.S. 558, 91 S.Ct. 1697, 29 L.Ed.2d 178 (1971). A state's decisions regarding which actions or activities will give rise to strict criminal liability rest within that state's sound legislative discretion.

To determine the constitutionality of Section 100.26(3), we apply basically the same standards applicable to criminal statutes which do not impose strict liability. Due process prohibits such statutes from shifting burdens of proof onto the defendant, prohibits punishment of wholly passive conduct, protects against vague or overbroad statutes, and requires that statutes must give fair warning of prohibited conduct. The due process clause imposes little other restraint on the state's power to define criminal acts.

The regulation before us does not threaten the first due process consideration. A state cannot require a defendant to prove the absence of a fact necessary to constitute the crime. Mullaney v. Wilbur, 421 U.S. 684, 697, 95 S.Ct. 1881, 1888, 44 L.Ed.2d 508 (1975). The government must prove each element of the charged crime beyond a reasonable doubt. In re Winship, 397 U.S. 358, 362, 90 S.Ct. 1068, 1071, 25 L.Ed.2d 368 (1970). The petitioner does not argue that the state failed to prove each element, save of course intent, beyond a reasonable doubt. The petitioner instead contends that the element of intent should have been part of the state's burden of proof. But, removing the element of intent for the offense does not amount to shifting the burden of proof; rather, the state has chosen to redefine what conduct violates the statute. The state still must prove each element of the strict liability crime beyond a reasonable doubt.

Nor does the crime here punish wholly passive conduct. The petitioner actively solicited the contracts at issue, and usually initiated the contacts between the petitioner and his victims. The petitioner's conduct thus is quite unlike the defendant's conduct in Lambert v. California, 355 U.S. 225, 78 S.Ct. 240, 2 L.Ed.2d 228 (1957), where the defendant was convicted for mere failure to register upon arrival in Los Angeles as a convicted felon. The Supreme Court concluded that the wholly passive conduct there could not properly form the basis for criminal liability.[78]

---

78. In Ingraham v. Wright, 430 U.S. 651, 667, 97 S.Ct. 1401, 1410, 51 L.Ed.2d 711 (1977), the Supreme Court stated that the Cruel and Unusual Punishments Clause circumscribes the criminal process in three ways: First, it limits the kinds of punishment that can be imposed on those convicted of crimes, ... second, it proscribes punishment grossly disproportionate to the severity of the crime, ... and third, it imposes substantive limits on what can be

A longstanding principle of constitutional law is that a statute can be neither vague nor overbroad. [The Court determined the statute was not vague nor overbroad.]

The Supreme Court has upheld similarly rigorous laws. In United States v. Dotterweich, 320 U.S. 277, 64 S.Ct. 134, 88 L.Ed. 48 (1943), for example, the Court recognized the reasonableness of imposing strict liability under the Federal Food, Drug, and Cosmetic Act, which restricts, among other things, sales of adulterated or misbranded drugs and punishes "persons whose failure to exercise the authority and supervisory responsibility reposed in them by the business organization resulted in the violation complained of." United States v. Park, 421 U.S. 658, 671, 95 S.Ct. 1903, 1911, 44 L.Ed.2d 489 (1975). The Court also has sustained, on due process grounds, convictions under regulatory measures dealing with the possession or transportation of drugs, unregistered handguns, and sulphuric acid without proof of intent to violate the regulations. United States v. Balint, 258 U.S. 250, 42 S.Ct. 301, 66 L.Ed. 604 (1922); United States v. Freed, 401 U.S. 601, 91 S.Ct. 1112, 28 L.Ed.2d 356 (1971); United States v. International Minerals & Chemical Corp., 402 U.S. 558, 91 S.Ct. 1697, 29 L.Ed.2d 178 (1971). In these cases the regulations concerned conduct which the defendants could "reasonably understand to be proscribed." . . .

Section 100.26(3) infringes none of the due process clause protections. Principally, Section 100.26(3) gives fair warning of the proscribed conduct largely because the petitioner reasonably could have expected his conduct, in that regulated business, to be illegal. Therefore, the grant of the writ of habeas corpus is reversed.

Reversed.

Commonwealth v. Koczwara

Supreme Court of Pennsylvania, 1959.
397 Pa. 575, 155 A.2d 825.

■ COHEN, JUSTICE. This is an appeal from the judgment of the Court of Quarter Sessions of Lackawanna County sentencing the defendant to three months in the Lackawanna County Jail, a fine of five hundred dollars and the costs of prosecution, in a case involving violations of the Pennsylvania Liquor Code. . . .

Defendant raises two contentions, both of which, in effect, question whether the undisputed facts of this case support the judgment and

---

made criminal and punished as such. We have recognized the last limitation as one to be applied sparingly.

Section 100.26(3) is not one of those narrow classifications of offenses upon which the eighth amendment places substantive limitations. The petitioner has raised neither of the other two classifications of eighth amendment proscriptions in his petition, and we will not decide them now. We note, however, that the eighth amendment gives the states great latitude in punishing non-capital offenses. E.g., Rummel v. Estelle, 445 U.S. 263, 100 S.Ct. 1133, 63 L.Ed.2d 382 (1980). Although the eighth amendment places some proportionality limitations on imprisonment as punishment, this case is a far cry from the life-imprisonment-without-parole sentence found unconstitutional in Solem v. Helm, 463 U.S. 277, 103 S.Ct. 3001, 77 L.Ed.2d 637 (1983).

sentence imposed by the Quarter Sessions Court. Judge Hoban found as fact that "in every instance the purchase [by minors] was made from a bartender, not identified by name, and service to the boys was made by the bartender. There was *no* evidence that the defendant was present on any one of the occasions testified to by these witnesses, nor that he had any personal knowledge of the sales to them or to other persons on the premises." We, therefore, must determine the criminal responsibility of a licensee of the Liquor Control Board for acts committed by his employees upon his premises, without his personal knowledge, participation, or presence, which acts violate a valid regulatory statute passed under the Commonwealth's police power.

While an employer in almost all cases is not criminally responsible for the unlawful acts of his employees, unless he consents to, approves, or participates in such acts, courts all over the nation have struggled for years in applying this rule within the framework of "controlling the sale of intoxicating liquor." At common law, any attempt to invoke the doctrine of *respondeat superior* in a criminal case would have run afoul of our deeply ingrained notions of criminal jurisprudence that guilt must be personal and individual.[79] In recent decades, however, many states have enacted detailed regulatory provisions in fields which are essentially noncriminal, e.g., pure food and drug acts, speeding ordinances, building regulations, and child labor, minimum wage and maximum hour legislation. Such statutes are generally enforceable by light penalties, and although violations are labelled crimes, the considerations applicable to them are totally different from those applicable to true crimes, which involve moral delinquency and which are punishable by imprisonment or another serious penalty. Such so-called statutory crimes are in reality an attempt to utilize the machinery of criminal administration as an enforcing arm for social regulations of a purely civil nature, with the punishment totally unrelated to questions of moral wrongdoing or guilt. It is here that the social interest in the general well-being and security of the populace has been held to outweigh the individual interest of the particular defendant. The penalty is imposed despite the defendant's lack of a criminal intent or mens rea. . . .

In the Liquor Code, Section 493, the legislature has set forth twenty-five specific acts which are condemned as unlawful, and for which penalties are provided in Section 494. Subsections (1) and (14) of Section 493 contain the two offenses charged here. In neither of these subsections is there any language which would require the prohibited acts to have been done either knowingly, wilfully or intentionally, there being a significant absence of such words as "knowingly, wilfully, etc." That the legislature intended such a requirement in other related sections of the same Code is shown by examining Section 492(15), wherein it is made unlawful to *knowingly* sell

---

79. The distinction between *respondeat superior* in tort law and its application to the criminal law is obvious. In tort law, the doctrine is employed for the purpose of settling the incidence of loss upon the party who can best bear such loss. But the criminal law is supported by totally different concepts. We impose penal treatment upon those who injure or menace social interests, partly in order to reform, partly to prevent the continuation of the anti-social activity and partly to deter others. If a defendant has personally lived up to the social standards of the criminal law and has not menaced or injured anyone, why impose penal treatment?

any malt beverages to a person engaged in the business of illegally selling such beverages. The omission of any such word in the subsections of Section 494 is highly significant. It indicates a legislative intent to eliminate both knowledge and criminal intent as necessary ingredients of such offenses. To bolster this conclusion, we refer back to Section 491 wherein the Code states, "It shall be unlawful (1) For any person, by himself *or by an employe or agent,* to expose or keep for sale, or directly or *indirectly* . . . to sell or offer to sell any liquor within this Commonwealth, except in accordance with the provisions of this act and the regulations of the board." The Superior Court has long placed such an interpretation on the statute.

As the defendant has pointed out, there is a distinction between the requirement of a mens rea and the imposition of vicarious absolute liability for the acts of another. It may be that the courts below, in relying on prior authority, have failed to make such a distinction. In any case, we fully recognize it. Moreover, we find that the intent of the legislature in enacting this Code was not only to eliminate the common law requirement of a mens rea, but also to place a very high degree of responsibility upon the holder of a liquor license to make certain that neither he nor anyone in his employ commit any of the prohibited acts upon the licensed premises. Such a burden of care is imposed upon the licensee in order to protect the public from the potentially noxious effects of an inherently dangerous business. We, of course, express no opinion as to the *wisdom* of the legislature's imposing vicarious responsibility under certain sections of the Liquor Code. There may or may not be an economic-sociological justification for such liability on a theory of deterrence. Such determination is for the legislature to make, so long as the constitutional requirements are met.

Can the legislature, consistent with the requirements of due process, thus establish absolute criminal liability? Were this the defendant's first violation of the Code, and the penalty solely a minor fine of from $100–$300, we would have no hesitation in upholding such a judgment. Defendant, by accepting a liquor license, must bear this financial risk. Because of a prior conviction for violations of the Code, however, the trial judge felt compelled under the mandatory language of the statute, Section 494(a), to impose not only an increased fine of five hundred dollars, but also a three month sentence of imprisonment. Such sentence of imprisonment in a case where liability is imposed vicariously cannot be sanctioned by this Court consistently with the law of the land clause of Section 9, Article I of the Constitution of the Commonwealth of Pennsylvania, P.S.

The Courts of the Commonwealth have already strained to permit the legislature to carry over the civil doctrine of *respondeat superior* and to apply it as a means of enforcing the regulatory scheme that covers the liquor trade. We have done so on the theory that the Code established petty misdemeanors involving only light monetary fines. It would be unthinkable to impose vicarious criminal responsibility in cases involving true crimes. Although to hold a principal criminally liable might possibly be an effective means of enforcing law and order, it would do violence to our more sophisticated modern-day concepts of justice. Liability for all true crimes, wherein an offense carries with it a jail sentence, must be based exclusively upon personal causation. It can be readily imagined that even a licensee who is meticulously careful in the choice of his employees cannot supervise every single act of the subordinates. A man's liberty cannot rest on so frail a reed as whether his employee will commit a mistake in judgment. See Sayre, Criminal Responsibility For Acts of Another, 43 Harv.L.Rev. 689 (1930).... Therefore, we are only holding that so much of the judgment as calls for imprisonment is invalid, and we are leaving intact the five hundred dollar fine imposed by Judge Hoban under the subsequent offense section....

Judgment, as modified, is affirmed.

■ BELL, MUSMANNO and McBRIDE, JJ., file separate dissenting opinions.

■ BELL, JUSTICE (dissenting)....

I would affirm the judgment and the sentence on the opinion of JUDGE HIRT, speaking for a unanimous Superior Court.

■ MUSMANNO, JUSTICE (dissenting)....

I conclude by saying that the Majority has been so remiss in affirming the conviction in this case that I myself would be remiss if I did not dissent against a decision which flouts the Constitution, ignores the Bill of Rights and introduces into the temple of the law the Asiatic rite of "vicarious criminal liability."

■ McBRIDE, JUSTICE (dissenting). I would agree that a man who sells liquor to a minor may be punished even if he did not know that the person to whom he sold was a minor. But in my opinion, the statute does not and cannot validly create an indictable misdemeanor under which a liquor licensee is punished by a fine or imprisonment, or both, for the act of an employee in selling to a minor, where, as here, the act itself is done without the licensee's knowledge, consent, or acquiescence. I would reverse the judgment and discharge the defendant.

SECTION 6. UNLAWFUL CONDUCT

It is frequently said that one who is committing an unlawful act has "general *mens rea*—or a general criminal intent." Care must be taken not to infer too much from such a statement. In the first place the phrase "unlawful act," as used in this connection, has a very restricted meaning. The state of mind of one who is committing such an "unlawful act" may be substituted for criminal negligence in establishing the *mens rea* needed for guilt of certain crimes. This is true of manslaughter and of battery but it is not true of offenses which require a specific intent or other special mental element.

Commonwealth v. Mink

Supreme Judicial Court of Massachusetts, 1877.
123 Mass. 422.

INDICTMENT for the murder of Charles Ricker at Lowell, in the county of Middlesex, on August 31, 1876. Trial before Ames and Morton, JJ., who allowed a bill of exceptions in substance as follows:

It was proved that Charles Ricker came to his death by a shot from a pistol in the hand of the defendant. The defendant introduced evidence tending to show that she had been engaged to be married to Ricker; that an interview was had between them at her room, in the course of which he expressed his intention to break off the engagement and abandon her entirely; that she thereupon went to her trunk, took a pistol from it, and attempted to use it upon herself, with the intention of taking her own life; that Ricker then seized her to prevent her from accomplishing that purpose, and a struggle ensued between them; and that in the struggle the pistol was accidentally discharged, and in that way the fatal wound inflicted upon him.

The jury were instructed on this point as follows: "If you believe the defendant's story, and that she did put the pistol to her head with the intention of committing suicide, she was about to do a criminal and unlawful act, and that which she had no right to do. It is true, undoubtedly, that suicide cannot be punished by any proceeding of the courts, for the reason that the person who kills himself has placed himself beyond the reach of justice, and nothing can be done. But the law, nevertheless, recognizes suicide as a criminal act, and the attempt at suicide is also criminal. It would be the duty of any bystander who saw such an attempt about to be made, as a matter of mere humanity, to interfere and try to prevent it. And the rule is, that if a homicide is produced by the doing of an unlawful act, although the killing was the last thing that the person about to do it had in his mind, it would be an unlawful killing, and the person would incur the responsibility which attaches to the crime of manslaughter."

■ GRAY, C.J. The life of every human being is under the protection of the law, and cannot be lawfully taken by himself, or by another with his consent, except by legal authority. By the common law of England, suicide was considered a crime against the laws of God and man, the goods and chattels of the criminal were forfeited to the King, his body had an ignominious burial in the highway, and he was deemed a murderer of himself and a felon, *felo de se* . . . .

Suicide has not ceased to be unlawful and criminal in this Commonwealth by the simple repeal of the Colony Act of 1660 by the St. of 1823, c. 143, which (like the corresponding St. of 4 G. IV c. 52, enacted by the British Parliament within a year before) may well have had its origin in consideration for the feelings of innocent surviving relatives; nor by the briefer directions as to the form of coroner's inquests in the Rev.Sts. c. 140, § 8, and the Gen.Sts. c. 175, § 9, which in this, as in most other matters, have not repeated at length the forms of legal proceedings set forth in the statutes codified; nor by the fact that the Legislature, having in the general revisions of the statutes measured the degree of punishment for attempts to commit offences by the punishment prescribed for each offence if actually committed, has, intentionally or inadvertently, left the attempt to commit suicide without punishment, because the completed act would not be punished in any manner. Rev.Sts. c. 133, § 12. Gen.Sts. c. 168, § 8. Commonwealth v. Dennis, 105 Mass. 162. After all these changes in the statutes, the point decided in Bowen's case was ruled in the same way by

Chief Justice Bigelow and Justices Dewey, Metcalf and Chapman, in a case which has not been reported.

Since it has been provided by statute that "any crime punishable by death or imprisonment in the state prison is a felony, and no other crime shall be so considered," it may well be that suicide is not technically a felony in this Commonwealth. Gen.Sts. c. 168, § 1. St. 1852, c. 37, § 1. But being unlawful and criminal as *malum in se*, any attempt to commit it is likewise unlawful and criminal. Every one has the same right and duty to interpose to save a life from being so unlawfully and criminally taken, that he would have to defeat an attempt unlawfully to take the life of a third person. And it is not disputed that any person who, in doing or attempting to do an act which is unlawful and criminal, kills another, though not intending his death, is guilty of criminal homicide, and, at the least, of manslaughter.

The only doubt that we have entertained in this case is, whether the act of the defendant, in attempting to kill herself, was not so malicious, in the legal sense, as to make the killing of another person, in the attempt to carry out her purpose, murder, and whether the instructions given to the jury were not therefore too favorable to the defendant.

Exceptions overruled.[80]

State v. Horton

Supreme Court of North Carolina, 1905.
139 N.C. 588, 51 S.E. 945.

■ HOKE, J., after stating the case: It will be noted that the finding of the jury declares that the act of the defendant was not in itself dangerous to human life and excludes every element of criminal negligence, and rests the guilt or innocence of the defendant on the fact alone that at the time of the homicide the defendant was hunting on another's land without written permission from the owner. The act which applies only in the counties of Orange, Franklin and Scotland, makes the conduct a misdemeanor, and imposes a punishment on conviction, of not less than five nor more than ten dollars.

The statement sometimes appears in works of approved excellence to the effect that an unintentional homicide is a criminal offense when occasioned by a person engaged at the time in an unlawful act. In nearly every instance, however, will be found the qualification that if the act in question is free from negligence, and not in itself of dangerous tendency, and the criminality must arise, if at all, entirely from the fact that it is

---

80. "We affirm the holding that driving a car on the public roads or highways while in an intoxicated condition is an unlawful act; therefore it was entirely proper for the court to give the instruction defining manslaughter as: '. . . being that which is done in the commission of an unlawful act, not amounting to a felony. . . .' " State v. Medicine Bull Jr., 152 Mont. 34, 445 P.2d 916 (1968).

Since the ordinance forbidding the discharge of a firearm within the city has for its purpose the protection of human life or safety, unintentional death resulting from such a discharge is involuntary manslaughter. State v. Thomas, 6 Kan.App.2d 925, 636 P.2d 807 (1981).

unlawful, in such case, the unlawful act must be one that is *malum in se* and not merely *malum prohibitum,* and this we hold to be the correct doctrine. In Foster's Crown Law, it is thus stated at page 258: "In order to bring a case within this description (excusable homicide) the act upon which death ensueth must be lawful. For if the act be unlawful, I mean if it be *malum in se,* the case will amount to felony, either murder or manslaughter, as circumstances may vary the nature of it. If it be done in prosecution of a felonious intent, it will be murder; but if the intent went no further than to commit a bare trespass, it will be manslaughter." At page 259, the same author puts an instance with his comments thereon as follows: "A shooteth at the poultry of B and by accident killeth a man; if his intention was to steal the poultry, which must be collected from circumstances, it will be murder by reason of that felonious intent, but if it was done wantonly and without that intention, it will be barely manslaughter. The rule I have laid down supposeth that the act from which death ensued was *malum in se.* For if it was barely *malum prohibitum,* as shooting at game by a person not qualified by statute law to keep or use a gun for that purpose, the case of a person so offending will fall under the same rule as that of a qualified man. For the statutes prohibiting the destruction of the game under certain penalties will not, in a question of this kind, enhance the accident beyond its intrinsic moment."

One of these disqualifying statutes here referred to as an instance of *malum prohibitum* was an act passed (13 Richard II, chap. 13), to prevent certain classes of persons from keeping dogs, nets or engines to destroy game, etc., and the punishment imposed on conviction was one year's imprisonment. There were others imposing a lesser penalty.

1 Bishop, New Criminal Law, sec. 332, treats of the matter as follows: "In these cases of an unintended evil result, the intent whence the act accidentally sprang must probably be, if specific, to do a thing which is *malum in se* and not merely *malum prohibitum.*" Thus Archbold says: "When a man in the execution of one act, by misfortune or chance and not designedly, does another act for which if he had willfully committed it, he would be liable to be punished—in that case, if the act he were doing were lawful or merely *malum prohibitum,* he shall not be punishable for the act arising from misfortune or chance, but if it be *malum in se,* it is otherwise. To illustrate: since it is *malum prohibitum,* not *malum in se,* for an unauthorized person to kill game in England contrary to the statutes, if, in unlawfully shooting at game, he accidently kills a man, it is no more criminal in him than if he were authorized. But, to shoot at another's fowls, wantonly or in sport, an act which is *malum in se,* though a civil trespass, and thereby accidentally to kill a human being is manslaughter. If the intent in the shooting were to commit larceny of the fowls, we have seen that it would be murder."

An offense *malum in se* is properly defined as one which is naturally evil as adjudged by the sense of a civilized community, whereas an act *malum prohibitum* is wrong only because made so by statute. For the reason that acts *mala in se* have, as a rule, become criminal offenses by the course and development of the common law, an impression has sometimes obtained that only acts can be so classified which the common law makes criminal, but this is not at all the test. An act can be, and frequently is, *malum in se,* when it amounts only to a civil trespass, provided it has a malicious element or manifests an evil nature, or wrongful disposition to harm or injure another in his person or property.

The distinction between the two classes of acts is well stated in 19 Am. & Eng.Enc. (2d Ed.) at p. 705: "An offense *malum in se* is one which is naturally evil, as murder, theft, and the like. Offenses at common law are generally *malum in se.* An offense *malum prohibitum,* on the contrary, is not naturally an evil, but becomes so in consequence of being forbidden."

We do not hesitate to declare that the offense of the defendant in hunting on the land without written permission of the owner was *malum prohibitum,* and the special verdict having found that the act in which the defendant was engaged was not in itself dangerous to human life, and negatived all idea of negligence, we hold that the case is one of excusable homicide, and the defendant should be declared not guilty. . . .

There was error in holding the defendant guilty, and, on the facts declared, a verdict of not guilty should be directed and the defendant discharged.

Reversed.

■ WALKER, J., concurs in result only.

State v. Sealy

Supreme Court of North Carolina, 1961.
253 N.C. 802, 117 S.E.2d 793.

■ DENNY, JUSTICE. The defendant assigns as error those portions of the court's charge to the jury hereinafter set out. The court, after having read to the jury G.S. § 20–158 (the statute which requires the driver of a motor vehicle to stop before entering or crossing certain through highways), and G.S. § 20–140 (the statute defining reckless driving), charged: "If you find from the evidence in this case, . . . beyond a reasonable doubt that the defendant intentionally violated one or more of the statutes read to you, designed and intended to protect human life, and . . . that such intentional violation thereof was the proximate cause of the death of the deceased, then it would be your duty to return a verdict of guilty of involuntary manslaughter."

". . . (I)f you are satisfied from the testimony beyond a reasonable doubt that the driver of this car, the defendant in this case, Mr. Howard Franklin Sealy, was operating his motor vehicle in violation of the statute, in respect to stopping at the stop sign, . . . and that such action on his part was the proximate cause of the death of these two men, you would find him guilty of involuntary manslaughter."

The above instructions are conflicting and the State concedes error in the latter. According to the provisions of G.S. § 20–158, a violation thereof is not negligence *per se* in any action at law for injury to person or property, but the failure to stop at a stop sign before entering an intersection with a dominant highway may be considered with other facts in the case in determining whether or not under all the facts and circumstances involved, such driver was guilty of negligence or contributory negligence.

"Culpable negligence in the law of crimes necessarily implies something more than actionable negligence in the law of torts." . . .

"An intentional, wilful or wanton violation of a statute or ordinance, designed for the protection of human life or limb, which proximately results in injury or death, is culpable negligence." State v. Cope, supra [204 N.C. 28, 167 S.E. 456]. But, where there is an unintentional or inadvertent violation of the statute, such violation standing alone does not constitute culpable negligence. The inadvertent or unintentional violation of the statute must be accompanied by recklessness of probable consequences of a dangerous nature, when tested by the rule of reasonable prevision, amounting altogether to a thoughtless disregard of consequences or of a heedless indifference to the safety of others.

Other assignments of error need not be considered or discussed since they may not arise on another hearing.

The defendant is entitled to a new trial and it is so ordered.

New trial.

Section 7.   "Transferred Intent"

A tort concept, which serves a useful purpose in that field[81] but has no proper place in criminal law, because it tends more to confusion than to clarity of thought, is the so-called "doctrine of the transfer of the intent to the unintended act." This is frequently stated in some such form as this: Whenever a man meaning one wrong does another unmeant, he is punishable unless some specific intent is required. The reason sometimes offered is that "the thing done, having proceeded from a corrupt mind, is to be viewed the same whether the corruption was of one particular form or another."[82]

Such a notion results from an imperfect analysis of the case law. Common law burglary is the breaking and entering of the dwelling house of another in the nighttime with intent to commit a felony, petty larceny or assault. In other words the intent to commit some *other* crime (which must be a felony at common law) is the very state of mind which constitutes the *mens rea* for burglary. For certain offenses the intent to commit some other offense is not essential to the *mens rea* but may suffice for this purpose. Murder is an excellent example. Certain crimes such as arson, rape, robbery and burglary have been found to involve such an unreasonable element of human risk that he who is perpetrating or attempting one of them is held to have a state of mind which falls within the label "malice aforethought." Hence if homicide is caused thereby it is murder however

---

81.   If defendant shoots at A and hits B instead, the "intent is said to be 'transferred' to the victim—which is obviously a fiction, or a legal conclusion, to accomplish the desired result of liability". Prosser and Keeton, Torts p. 37 (5th ed. 1984).

82.   Bishop, Criminal Law § 327 (8th ed. 1892).

unintended the killing may be. This is due to the law of homicide and not to any doctrine of "transferred intent."

To test the soundness of such a doctrine it is necessary to consider offenses other than burglary (which requires an intent to commit some other crime) or murder (for which an intent to commit certain other crimes will be sufficient for the *mens rea* requirement). A person who has in his pocket a weapon he has no authority to carry is not guilty of the crime of carrying a concealed weapon if it was put there secretly by others without his knowing or having any reason to know of its presence. And a man who marries a second wife, after the death of the first, is not guilty of bigamy even if he does not know of the death and thinks the first wife is still alive. In the first case we find the *actus reus* but no *mens rea*. In the second, the *mens rea* but no *actus reus*. And if the man who contracted such a marriage happened to be wearing a coat with an unsuspected weapon concealed therein, the intent to commit bigamy could not be coupled with the unintentional carrying of the concealed weapon so as to establish guilt of either offense. If he borrowed the coat for the sole purpose of wearing it during the wedding ceremony there would be some connection between the two but the *actus reus* and the *mens rea* still would not match in such a manner as to constitute criminal guilt.

It was stated by Lord Hale, and repeated in substance by Blackstone, that "if *A.* by malice aforethought strikes at *B.* and missing him strikes *C.* whereof he dies, though he never bore any malice to *C.* yet it is murder, and the law transfers the malice to the party slain."[83] Unquestionably the slayer is guilty of murder in such a case, and if any resort is to be made to a theory of transferred intent it should be limited to this general type of situation. The general mental pattern is the same whether the malicious endeavor was to kill B or to kill C. If the word "malicious" is omitted the statement might not be true. An intent to kill B might represent a very different mental pattern than an intent to kill C. For example, B at the time might be a murderer, fleeing from lawful arrest under such circumstances that A was privileged to kill him. If such was the fact an intent by A to kill B would not be a guilty state of mind. It would not constitute *mens rea*. If at the same time C was obviously an innocent bystander an intent by A to kill C would amount to malice aforethought. Under such circumstances, if A should shoot at B in the proper and prudent exercise of his privilege and should happen quite unexpectedly, by a glance of the bullet, to cause the death of C, A would be free from criminal guilt. This seems to lend support to the theory of "transferred intent." The intent to kill B did not constitute *mens rea* and this innocent intent *seems* to be transferred to the unintended victim.

The hypothetical situation, however, supposes not only the privilege to direct deadly force against B, but also the proper and prudent exercise of this privilege. If, on the other hand, he exercised this privilege so imprudently and improperly as to constitute a criminally negligent disregard of the life of the innocent bystander, C, the killing of C would be manslaugh-

---

83. 1 Hale P.C. *466; 4 Bl.Comm. *201.

ter. The intent is given due consideration, but it is not "transferred." However, the term transferred intent is used very frequently by the courts.

Harrod v. State

Court of Special Appeals of Maryland, 1985.
65 Md.App. 128, 499 A.2d 959.

■ ALPERT, JUDGE.

We are called upon in this appeal to decide, *inter alia,* whether a person can be convicted of assaulting another who has suffered no harm and was never aware of the alleged assault. Appellant John G. Harrod was charged with two counts of assault and two counts of carrying a deadly weapon openly with intent to injure. He was convicted of these offenses on December 11, 1984, following a trial without a jury. . . . On appeal to this court, appellant presents three questions:

I. Was the evidence sufficient to sustain the charge of assault upon James Christopher Harrod?

.   .   .

The common law crime of assault encompasses two definitions: (1) an attempt to commit a battery or (2) an unlawful intentional act which places another in reasonable apprehension of receiving an immediate battery. . . . R. Perkins and R. Boyce, Criminal Law 159 (3d ed. 1982). . . .

The assault charges arose out of a confrontation among appellant, his wife Cheryl, and her friend Calvin Crigger. The only two witnesses at trial were appellant and Cheryl Harrod.

Cheryl testified that on September 15, 1983, Calvin Crigger came over to visit when she thought appellant had gone to work; that "all of a sudden [appellant] came out of the bedroom with a hammer in his hand, swinging it around, coming after me and my friend [Calvin]"; that Calvin ran out of the house and down the steps; that appellant "had thrown the hammer over top of [Christopher's] port-a-crib in the living room, and it went into the wall"; that appellant then reentered the bedroom and returned with a five-inch blade hunting knife; that appellant told Cheryl that he was going to kill her and that, if she took his daughter away from him, he was going to kill Christopher; that appellant put the knife into the bannister near Cheryl's arm; that appellant followed Cheryl out to Calvin's car and "went after Calvin, going around and around the car."

.   .   .

In rendering its verdict, the court stated:

And, the Court finds beyond a reasonable doubt and to a moral certainty that Mr. Harrod . . . came after [Cheryl] and . . . Calvin; and that Mr. Harrod came out of his room swinging a . . . hammer, and ultimately threw it, not too far from the child, Christopher, and that he went after both Cheryl and Calvin, down the steps with a knife, with a blade of about four to five inches. The Court finds that he is guilty of two counts of Carrying a Deadly Weapon; that is the knife and the hammer; and, also two counts of Assault; one against Cheryl and one against the minor child.

Defense counsel inquired of the court: "On the second count of the Information, is the Court finding specific intent on behalf of the Defendant to injure his child?" The court responded, "Yes. Threw that hammer within a very short distance—sticking it—it was still sticking in the wall."

. . .

The facts in the case *sub judice* do not support a finding that appellant committed an attempted battery towards the infant, Christopher. An attempt to commit any crime requires a specific intent to commit that crime. Perkins and Boyce, Criminal Law 637; W. LaFave & A. Scott, Criminal Law § 59 (1972). An attempted battery-type assault thus requires that the accused harbor a specific intent to cause physical injury to the victim, and take a substantial step towards causing that injury.

Nowhere does the record indicate that appellant threw the hammer with the specific intent to injure Christopher. . . .

Transferred Intent

An additional question raised by the parties in the briefs is whether the necessary specific intent as against Christopher could derive from the specific intent toward Calvin; in other words, did the intent to injure Calvin *transfer* to Christopher? This doctrine of "transferred intent" was explained by the Court of Appeals in Gladden v. State, 273 Md. 383, 330 A.2d 176 (1974):

"[I]f one intends injury to the person of another under circumstances in which such a mental element constitutes mens rea, and in the effort to accomplish this end he inflicts harm upon a person other than the one intended, he is guilty of the same kind of crime as if his aim had been more accurate." In such cases all the components of the crime are present. The psychical element which consists of a certain general mental pattern is not varied by the particular person who may be actually harmed.

Gladden, as well as all of the cases cited in that opinion, involved an attempt to kill one person, but resulted in the death or injury of another, unintended victim. In every case cited in *Gladden,* the third party to whom the intent was "transferred" was in fact injured. The Court of Appeals expressly held that, under the doctrine, "the *mens rea* of a defendant as to his intended victim will carry over and affix his culpability *when such criminal conduct causes the death of an unintended victim.*" 273 Md. at 405, 330 A.2d 176 (emphasis added).

By illustration, Professor Perkins explains the logic underlying the limited application of this doctrine:

If, without justification, excuse or mitigation D with intent to kill A fires a shot which misses A but unexpectedly inflicts a non-fatal injury upon B, D is guilty of an attempt to commit murder—but the attempt was to murder A whom D was trying to kill and not B who was hit quite accidentally. And so far as the criminal law is concerned there is no transfer of this intent from one to the other so as to make D guilty of an attempt to murder B. Hence, an indictment or information charging an attempt to murder B, or (under statute) an assault with intent to murder B, will not support a conviction if the evidence shows that the injury to B was accidental and the only intent was to murder A.

Perkins, Criminal Law 826 (2d ed. 1969) (footnote omitted).

The closest case we have found to support the rule that the doctrine does not apply absent actual injury is State v. Martin, 342 Mo. 1089, 119 S.W.2d 298 (1938). In *Martin,* the defendants were charged with assault upon Lloyd DeCasnett, with the intent to maim. The evidence in that case showed that the defendants threw a sulphuric acid-filled light bulb at a vehicle in which DeCasnett was a passenger. However, there was no evidence that the defendants knew that DeCasnett was in fact there, while there was ample evidence that they were aware of other persons in the target vehicle. The Missouri court considered the common law notion in homicide cases "that a constructive intent follows the bullet," but stated, "it cannot be the law in a case like this *where no one was hurt,* and the State's case rests solely on the overt act of throwing the acid-filled bulb and the felonious intent to be deduced therefrom." *Martin, supra,* at 302 (emphasis added). The court went on to reverse the conviction for assault with intent to maim DeCasnett, because, although the record evidence demonstrated a felonious intent to injure a passenger in the car, it did not appear that DeCasnett was the object of that intent.

To extend the doctrine of transferred intent to cases where the intended victim is not harmed would be untenable. The absurd result would be to make one criminally culpable for each unintended victim who, although in harm's way, was in fact not harmed by a missed attempt towards a specific person. We refuse, therefore, to extend the doctrine of transferred intent to cases where a third person is not in fact harmed.

This is the situation before us in the instant case. The record indicates that appellant swung a hammer which struck the wall "not too far from" Christopher. Significantly, there is no evidence that Christopher was harmed. Further, the weight of the evidence shows that appellant's specific intent, if any, was to injure Calvin, not Christopher. Why the State charged appellant with assaulting Christopher, rather than Calvin, we will not speculate. There is clearly insufficient evidence to find that appellant committed an attempted battery-type assault upon Christopher.

. . .

Reversed in part.

Regina v. Smith

Court of Criminal Appeal, 1855.
Dears. 560, 169 Eng.Rep. 845.

■ The following case was stated for the opinion of the Court of Criminal Appeal by MR. JUSTICE CROMPTON.

The prisoner was convicted before me at the Winchester Summer Assizes, 1855, on an indictment charging him with wounding William Taylor, with intent to murder him.

On the night in question the prisoner was posted as a sentry at Parkhurst, and the prosecutor, Taylor, was posted as a sentry at a neighbouring post.

The prisoner intended to murder one Maloney, and supposing Taylor to be Maloney, shot at and wounded Taylor.

The jury found that the prisoner intended to murder Maloney, not knowing that the party he shot at was Taylor, but supposing him to be Maloney, and the jury found that he intended to murder the individual he shot at supposing him to be Maloney.

I directed sentence of death to be recorded, reserving the question, whether the prisoner could be properly convicted on this state of facts of wounding Taylor with intent to murder him?

Charles Crompton

■ This case was considered on 24th November 1855, by JERVIS, C.J., and PARKE, B., WIGHTMAN, J., CROMPTON, J., and WILLES, J.

No Counsel appeared either for the Crown or for the prisoner.

■ JERVIS, C.J. There is nothing in the objection. The conviction is good.

■ PARKE, B. The prisoner did not intend to kill the particular person, but he meant to murder the man at whom he shot.

The other learned Judges concurred.

Conviction affirmed.

Regina v. Faulkner

Court of Crown Cases Reserved, Ireland, 1877.
13 Cox C.C. 550.

Case reserved by Lawson, J., at the Cork Summer Assizes, 1876, the prisoner was indicted for setting fire to the ship *Zemindar,* on the high seas, on the 26th day of June, 1876.... It was proved that the *Zemindar* was on her voyage home with a cargo of rum, sugar, and cotton, worth 50,000*l.* That the prisoner was a seaman on board, that he went into the forecastle hold, opened the sliding door in the bulk head, and so got into the hold where the rum was stored; he had no business there, and no authority to go there, and went for the purpose of stealing some rum, that he bored a hole in the cask with the gimlet, that the rum ran out, that when trying to put a spile in the hole out of which the rum was running, he had a lighted match in his hand; that the rum caught fire; that the prisoner himself was burned on the arms and neck; and that the ship caught fire and was completely destroyed. At the close of the case for the Crown, counsel for the prisoner asked for a direction of an acquittal on the ground that on the facts proved the indictment was not sustained, nor the allegation that the prisoner had unlawfully and maliciously set fire to the ship proved. The Crown contended that, inasmuch as the prisoner was at the time engaged in the commission of a felony, the indictment was sustained, and the allegation of the intent was immaterial.

At the second hearing of the case before the Court for Crown Cases Reserved, the learned judge made the addition of the following paragraph to the case stated by him for the court.

"It was conceded that the prisoner had no actual intention of burning the vessel, and I was not asked to leave any question to the jury as to the prisoner's knowing the probable consequences of his act, or as to his reckless conduct."

The learned judge told the jury that, although the prisoner had no actual intention of burning the vessel, still if they found he was engaged in stealing the rum, and that the fire took place in the manner above stated, they ought to find him guilty. The jury found the prisoner guilty on both counts, and he was sentenced to seven years' penal servitude. The question for the court was whether the direction of the learned judge was right, if not, the conviction should be quashed. . . .

■ FITZGERALD, J. I concur in opinion with my brother Barry, and for the reasons he has given, that the direction of the learned judge cannot be sustained in law, and that therefore the conviction should be quashed. I am further of opinion that in order to establish the charge of felony under sect. 42, the intention of the accused forms an element in the crime to the extent that it should appear that the defendant intended to do the very act with which he was charged, or that it was the necessary consequence of some other felonious or criminal act in which he was engaged, or that having a probable result which the defendant foresaw, or ought to have foreseen, he, nevertheless, persevered in such other felonious or criminal act. The prisoner did not intend to set fire to the ship—the fire was not the necessary result of the felony he was attempting; and if it was a probable result, which he ought to have foreseen, of the felonious transaction on which he was engaged, and from which a malicious design to commit the injurious act with which he is charged might have been fairly imputed to him, that view of the case was not submitted to the jury. On the contrary, it was excluded from their consideration on the requisition of the counsel for the prosecution. Counsel for the prosecution in effect insisted that the defendant, being engaged in the commission of, or in an attempt to commit a felony, was criminally responsible for every result that was occasioned thereby, even though it was not a probable consequence of his act or such as he could have reasonably foreseen or intended. No authority has been cited for a proposition so extensive, and I am of opinion that it is not warranted by law. Referring to the statute on which the prisoner is charged, it is to be observed that in several instances the sections creating substantive felonies are followed by others making an attempt to do the same thing also a felony. Now, it is obvious that an attempt to do a particular thing necessarily involves the intention to commit the act. If, in the case before us, the burning rum had been extinguished before the ship took fire, could it be contended that an indictment for a wilful and malicious attempt to set fire to the ship could have been maintained?

■ FITZGERALD, B. I am of opinion that the direction of the learned judge at the trial was wrong, and that the conviction cannot be sustained. There can, I think, be no doubt that malice or malicious intent (which seems to me to mean the same thing) is an essential part of the character of the felony charged in the indictment....

■ O'BRIEN, J. I am also of opinion that the conviction should be quashed, ...

■ KEOGH, J. I have the misfortune to differ from the other members of the Court.... I am, therefore, of opinion, that the conviction should stand, as I consider all questions of intention and malice are closed by the finding of the jury, that the prisoner committed the act with which he was charged whilst engaged in the commission of a substantive felony....

■ PALLES, C.B. I concur in the opinion of the majority of the Court, and I do so for the reasons already stated by my brother Fitzgerald. I agree with my brother Keogh that from the facts proved the inference might have legitimately drawn that the setting fire to the ship was malicious within the meaning of the 24 & 25 Vict. c. 97. I am of opinion that that inference was one of fact for the jury, and not a conclusion of law at which we can arrive upon the case before us....

■ DEASY, B., and LAWSON, J., concurred.

Conviction quashed.

SECTION 8. MOTIVE

Although sometimes confused, motive and intent and are not synonymous terms. Motive has been said to be "that something in the mind, or that condition of the mind, which incites to the action," or the "moving power which impels to action," "induces action," or "gives birth to a purpose." The difference between intent and motive may be emphasized by illustration. If one person has caused the death of another by a pistol shot, his *intent* may have been any one of a number, such as (a) to kill the deceased, (b) to frighten the deceased by shooting near him without hitting him, (c) to intimidate the deceased by pointing the weapon at him without shooting (the trigger having been pulled by accident), (d) to shoot at a target (perhaps without realizing that any other person was present), or (e) to test the "pull" of a trigger of a gun supposed to be unloaded. If in the particular case the intent was to kill the deceased, the *motive* of the shooter may also have been one (or more) of a number of possible motives, such as (a) hatred, (b) revenge, (c) jealousy, (d) avarice, (e) fear or even (f) love (as where a loved one is slain to end the suffering from an incurable disease).

Some writers have advanced the notion that when an act is committed with more than one object in view, only the most immediate intent is called "intent" and any "ulterior intent is called the motive of the act." For example, some would say that if a burglar breaks and enters the dwelling of another in the nighttime with intent to steal, the mental attitude in regard to the contemplated larceny is not (at the time of breaking into the building) an *intent* but a *motive*.[84] *This, however, is quite at variance with*

---

84. Stroud, Mens Rea 114 (1914).

juridical usage of these terms. The burglar's design to steal is so far from being no intent at all that it is called a "specific intent." The search for the distinction must go much deeper than this. If in the supposed case the burglar's purpose was to steal food which he wished to eat, his intent to eat would also be an intent although one more step removed from his immediate intent at the time of the breaking. But his urge to satisfy his appetite would be, not an *intent,* but a *motive.* This urge might come from the immediate pangs of hunger or from the recollection of such pangs on previous occasions. The burglarious act of another may be prompted by the urge for the feeling of power which money may give, or by any other impulse which may prompt a person to desire that which he does not have.[85]

An emotional urge, unless counteracted by other urges, "leads the mind to desire" a particular result. This desire in turn may—or may not—prompt an intent to bring about that end. If the mental activity continues until such an intent is developed (all of which might occur with lightning speed) the desire is coupled with the intention and may in a sense be a part thereof. Nevertheless it is important to distinguish between the basic urge itself and the intent which resulted in the mind of the particular person, but which might not have been generated in the mind of another. When, for example, it is said that a legatee, who was aware of a large bequest in his favor, had a motive for killing his deceased testator, it is not meant that this fact is sufficient to establish an intent to kill. No more is meant than that this fact was sufficient to generate a primitive urge in that direction, although it might be completely checked by more social impulses.

It is frequently said that "motive is not an essential element of crime."[86] Sometimes the statement is even more positive in form: "Motive is never an essential element of a crime."[87] Such broad generalizations cannot be accepted without some reservation, but with complete assurance we may say: "Proof of motive is never necessary to support a conclusion of guilt otherwise sufficiently established."[88] To this we must add the further qualification, that some statutes by express terms require proof of some particular motive before a conviction may be had. An example is the Mann Act, which prohibits interstate transportation of women for the purpose of prostitution.

The motive with which an *actus reus* was committed is always relevant. The presence or absence of a motive on the part of the defendant which might tend to the commission of such a deed may always be considered by the jury on the question of whether the Defendant did commit it. But whenever it is clearly established that he committed it, with whatever state of mind is required for the *mens rea* of the particular

---

85. "Motive in criminal law means that which tempts the mind to indulge in a criminal act." Sandy v. State, 870 P.2d 352 (Wyo.1994).

86. United States v. Hirschberg, 988 F.2d 1509 (7th Cir.1993); State v. Radabaugh, 93 Idaho 727, 471 P.2d 582 (1970).

87. People ex rel. Hegeman v. Corrigan, 195 N.Y. 1, 12, 87 N.E. 792, 796 (1909).

88. People v. Daly, 8 Cal.App.4th 47, 10 Cal.Rptr.2d 21 (1992); State v. Guilfoyle, 109 Conn. 124, 140, 145 A. 761, 767 (1929).

offense, all the requisites of criminal guilt are present, even if no possible motive for the deed can be shown.

SECTION 9.   CONCURRENCE OF MENS REA AND ACTUS REUS

The *mens rea* and the *actus reus* must concur to constitute a crime. The doctrine of trespass *ab initio* does not apply in criminal jurisprudence. The doctrine of continuing trespass is altogether different. *Trespass de bonis asportatis* is deemed to continue, so far as the law of larceny is concerned, as long as the trespasser keeps possession of the property so obtained. But this assumes an original trespass. It does not make a trespass out of what was not a trespass when done by any theory of "relation." And the familiar maxim *"omnis ratihabitio retrotrahitur, et mandato priori equiparatur"* (every ratification relates back, and is equivalent to a prior authorization), does not apply to criminal cases.

Concurrence, it should be emphasized, is something other than mere coincidence. The two elements of the crime must be "brought together" in the sense that the *actus reus* must be attributable to the *mens rea*.

It should be mentioned that some courts describe some offenses as ongoing and continuing in nature such as conspiracy or criminal enterprise.[89]

People v. Jeffers

Court of Appeal, Fifth District, California, 1996.
41 Cal.App.4th 917, 49 Cal.Rptr.2d 86.

■ STONE, ACTING PRESIDING JUDGE.

A jury convicted defendant, Bronico D. Jeffers, of violating Penal Code section 12021 which makes possession of a firearm by a felon a crime. . . .

On appeal, defendant claims the trial court committed instructional error. . . .

FACTS

On June 7, 1993, defendant entered Chuck's Gun Works in Porterville and asked to talk to Richard Maness. Charles Bodoh, a gunsmith and owner of the gun shop, told defendant Richard was busy but he could help defendant. Defendant handed Bodoh a box wrapped in a paper bag and said he was making a delivery for a friend. Bodoh unwrapped and opened the box in which he found a .380 caliber handgun. Bodoh was looking at the pistol to determine whether it was loaded when he noticed defendant was walking out the door. Bodoh called to defendant to return because he required more information to enter the gun into the log. Defendant provided his name, address and telephone number before leaving the gun shop.

---

89.   United States v. Maull, 806 F.2d 1340 (8th Cir.1986).

Bodoh gave Maness the gun to log in while Bodoh took a telephone call. Maness noticed the serial numbers on the gun had been ground off. Bodoh contacted the Bureau of Alcohol, Tobacco and Firearms to report tampering with the serial numbers. Richard Beaudreaux, a detective with the Tulare County Sheriff's Department later confiscated the gun and contacted defendant.

Defendant told Detective Beaudreaux that he had taken the gun to the gun shop for a friend. He said a pin was missing from the trigger. His friend's name was Kent Johnson, but defendant could not tell Detective Beaudreaux how to find Johnson. He later told Detective Beaudreaux that Johnson's full name was Richard Kent Johnson. Defendant described Johnson to Beaudreaux as White, slender, six feet two inches tall and in his early twenties. Defendant said Johnson had been a roommate of another friend, Kent Rowell.

Detective Beaudreaux spoke with Rowell who corroborated defendant's story, but said the friend's name was Richard Johnson and they had never been roommates. Johnson was visiting Rowell's apartment when Rowell overheard him ask defendant to deliver something.

Detective Beaudreaux was unable to locate Richard Kent Johnson in the Porterville area and a check of Department of Motor Vehicle records revealed no such person.

DISCUSSION

I. Instructional Error

Defendant does not challenge the sufficiency of the evidence to support the verdict. He claims evidence also supports the defense theory that defendant did not know what was in the package until he arrived at the gun shop and that he immediately got rid of the gun. According to defendant, had the jury been instructed properly, it is reasonably probable they could have found him not guilty of violating section 12021, subdivision (a).

Defendant alleges two instances of instructional error. First, the court failed to instruct regarding the required criminal intent. (CALJIC No. 3.30.) Second, the court refused defendant's pinpoint instruction which provides:

> "When an ex-felon comes into possession of a firearm, without knowing that he has a firearm, and he later learns that he has a firearm, he does not automatically violate Penal Code section 12021(a) upon acquiring knowledge. The ex-felon violates the law only if he continues to possess the firearm for an unreasonable time, without taking steps to rid himself of the firearm."

Defendant contends there is an evidentiary basis for the instruction. We agree there is evidence to support the defense theory and the trial court committed reversible instructional error.

We begin with a summary of the testimony which supports the defense theory.

Kent Rowell testified defendant delivered a pizza to Rowell's apartment on the day in question. Rowell had several visitors that day, including Richard Johnson. Rowell overheard Johnson ask defendant if he would do Johnson a favor and drop a package off for him. He heard no mention of a gun. He saw defendant leave with a shoe-box-sized parcel.

Richard Maness testified he received a telephone call at the gun shop from a man who asked if he could send in a gun to have either the barrel or the firing pin repaired. The call was before defendant brought in the gun. The voice did not sound like defendant's. Maness saw defendant enter the shop with a box wrapped in a paper bag. He overheard defendant tell the shop owner, Charles Bodoh that he was delivering the package for someone. Defendant did not say what was in the package, nor did he say it needed repair. He merely brought it to the counter, said it was a delivery and started to leave when Bodoh asked him to come back to give more information.

Bodoh testified defendant entered the shop and asked for "Richard." When Bodoh said Richard was busy, defendant said, "I deliver pizza. I'm delivering this to the shop for somebody." He then turned to leave. Defendant said nothing about a gun being in the package. Bodoh unwrapped and checked to see if the gun was loaded. He testified he may also have observed a broken firing pin and said something to defendant about the problem with the gun. Bodoh called to defendant as he was leaving and said he needed to give defendant a receipt and to log in the gun. At Bodoh's request, defendant gave his name, address and telephone number before leaving.

Detective Boudreaux testified that when he spoke with defendant the following day defendant stated he received the gun from Richard Kent Johnson in a bag; he did not look in the bag and did not know what was in the bag until he arrived at the gun shop.

The following day Bodoh received a telephone call regarding the gun. The caller sounded like an older White man. Bodoh was certain it was not defendant's voice. The man was very upset that the gun had been confiscated. Bodoh asked the man if he was aware it was illegal to possess a gun without a serial number. The man said he didn't know it was illegal; he bought the gun "some time ago" to carry on his job as a truck driver. He told Bodoh he gave the gun to defendant to bring to the shop to be repaired. The caller gave his name, but Bodoh could only recall it was a very short, single syllable name like Joe, Kent or Sam.

. . .

The elements of the offense proscribed by section 12021 are conviction of a felony and ownership, possession, custody or control of a firearm.

As with any crime or public offense, in order to prove a violation of section 12021, subdivision (a), the prosecution must prove, beyond a reasonable doubt, a union, or joint operation of act and intent. No specific criminal intent is required for this crime; general intent to commit the proscribed act is sufficient to sustain a conviction. The act proscribed by section 12022, subdivision (a) is possession of a firearm. Therefore, whether possession is actual or constructive, it must be intentional.

Wrongful intent must be shown with regard to the possession and custody elements of the crime of being a felon in possession of a firearm. A person who commits a prohibited act "through misfortune or by accident, when it appears that there was no evil design, intention or culpable negligence" has not committed a crime. Thus, a felon who acquires possession of a firearm through misfortune or accident, but who has no intent to exercise control or to have custody, commits the prohibited act without the required wrongful intent.

Respondent argues the general intent requirement is satisfied by proof of knowledge. We agree knowledge plus physical possession may ordinarily demonstrate an intent to exercise dominion and control, but knowledge does not conclusively demonstrate such intent as a matter of law. Otherwise, a felon would be strictly liable for the crime immediately upon finding a firearm, even if found under innocent circumstances.

Although the clerk's transcript reflects the court agreed, upon the prosecution's request, to instruct the jury regarding general intent, for some undisclosed reason the court failed to do so. The offered instruction read:

> "In the crime[s] charged in the information there must exist a union or joint operation of act or conduct and general criminal intent. To constitute general criminal intent it is not necessary that there should exist an intent to violate the law. When a person intentionally does that which the law declares to be a crime, [he] is acting with general criminal intent, even though [he] [she] [sic] may not know [his] act or conduct is unlawful." (Emphasis added.)

The failure to read the instruction was not harmless. Defendant's theory was that the prosecution failed to prove a joint union of possession and intent, i.e., a knowing, intentional exercise of control over the gun. The general intent instruction was critical to the jury's understanding of the defense.

The problem was compounded by the trial court's response to a question from the jury during deliberations.

. . .

Whether defendant had actual knowledge of the gun was not the only issue. The issue of whether defendant intentionally exercised control over the gun was very much in dispute under defendant's theory of the case. His knowledge was merely a part of the equation. Without the general intent instruction and in light of the court's response to the inquiry, the jury reasonably could have believed the only issue to be decided was whether defendant had knowledge a gun was in the package even if that knowledge was not acquired until he arrived at the gun shop and even if possession was not intentional.

This brings us to defendant's claim that the court should have instructed the jury with the . . . special instruction:

. . .

We agree with respondent that the final sentence appears to introduce the elements of time and reasonableness of possession which are not legally required to establish a violation of section 12022, subdivision (a). However, the instruction appears to be an attempt to focus upon the defendant's conduct and what that conduct suggests with regard to his intent to exercise dominion and control over the gun. If the jury believed he did not know or have reason to suspect he was delivering a gun until he arrived at the gun shop, evidence he took immediate steps to relinquish possession supports his claim that he did not intend to exercise control over the weapon, i.e., his temporary possession was unintentional.

A defendant, upon proper request therefor, has a right to an instruction to direct the jury's attention to evidence from which a reasonable doubt of his guilt could be inferred. Disbelief is no justification for refusing a requested instruction if there is evidence to support defendant's theory. Although the instruction may be flawed in some respects, it was a reasonable attempt to articulate a valid legal principle supported by the evidence. Had the jury been instructed properly regarding general intent, we would have confidence this legal principle was considered by the jury in reaching its verdict. However, the failure to so instruct compels reversal.

The judgment is reversed.

■ VARTABEDIAN and HARRIS, JJ., concur.[90]

Thabo Meli and Others v. Reginam

[1954] 1 All. Eng. Rep. 373.

Jan. 13. LORD REID: The four appellants in this case were convicted of murder after a trial before Sir Walter Harragin, judge of the High Court of Basutoland, in March, 1953. The appeal which has been heard by this Board dealt with two matters: first, whether the conclusions of the learned judge on questions of fact were warranted: and, secondly, whether, on a point of law, the accused are entitled to have the verdict quashed.

On the first matter, there really is no ground for criticising the learned judge's treatment of the facts. It is established by evidence, which was believed and which is apparently credible, that there was a preconceived plot on the part of the four accused to bring the deceased man to a hut and there to kill him, and then to fake an accident, so that the accused should escape the penalty for their act. The deceased man was brought to the hut. He was there treated to beer and was at least partially intoxicated; and he was then struck over the head in accordance with the plan of the accused. Witnesses say that while the deceased was seated and bending forward he was struck a heavy blow on the back of the head with a piece of iron like the instrument produced at trial. But a post-mortem examination showed that his skull had not been fractured and medical evidence was to the effect that a blow such as the witnesses described would have produced more severe injuries than those found at the post-mortem examination. There is at least doubt whether the weapon which was produced as being like the

---

90. See West's California Penal Code § 20; State v. Hassard, 9 Haw.App. 368, 842 P.2d 267 (1992).

weapon which was used could have produced the injuries that were found, but it may be that this weapon is not exactly similar to the one which was used, or it may be that the blow was a glancing blow and produced less severe injuries than those which one might expect. In any event, the man was unconscious after receiving the blow, but he was not then dead. There is no evidence that the accused then believed that he was dead, but their Lordships are prepared to assume from their subsequent conduct that they did so believe; and it is only on that assumption that any statable case can be made for this appeal. The accused took out the body, rolled it over a low krantz or cliff, and dressed up the scene to make it look like an accident. Obviously, they believed at that time that the man was dead, but it appears form the medical evidence that the injuries which he received in the hut were not sufficient to cause the death and that the final cause of his death was exposure when he was left unconscious at the foot of the krantz.

The point of law which was raised in this case can be simply stated. It is said that two acts were done:—first, the attack in the hut; and, secondly, the placing of the body outside afterwards—and that they were separate acts. It is said that, while the first act was accompanied by mens rea, it was not the cause of death; but that the second act, while it was the cause of death, was not accompanied by mens rea; and on that ground, it is said that the accused are not guilty of murder, though they may have been guilty of culpable homicide. It is said that the mens rea necessary to establish murder is an intention to kill, and that there could be no intention to kill when the accused thought that the man was already dead, so their original intention to kill had ceased before they did the act which caused the man's death. It appears to their Lordships impossible to divide up what was really one series of acts in this way. There is no doubt that the accused set out to do all these acts in order to achieve their plan, and as parts of their plan; and it is much too refined a ground of judgment to say that, because they were under a misapprehension at one stage and thought that their guilty purpose had been achieved before, in act, it was achieved, therefore they are to escape the penalties of the law. Their Lordships do not think that this is a matter which is susceptible of elaboration. There appears to be no case, either in South Africa or England, or for that matter elsewhere, which resembles the present. Their Lordships can find no difference relevant to the present case between the law of South Africa and the law of England; and they are of opinion that by both laws there can be no separation such as that for which the accused contend. Their crime is not reduced from murder to a lesser crime merely because the accused were under some misapprehension for a time during the completion of their criminal plot.

Their Lordships must, therefore, humbly advise Her Majesty that this appeal should be dismissed.

Appeal dismissed.

MODEL PENAL CODE

Section 2.02 General Requirements of Culpability.

(1) Minimum Requirements of Culpability. Except as provided in Section 2.05, a person is not guilty of an offense unless he acted purposely, knowingly, recklessly

or negligently, as the law may require, with respect to each material element of the offense.

(2) Kinds of Culpability Defined.

(a) Purposely.

A person acts purposely with respect to a material element of an offense when:

(i) if the element involves the nature of his conduct or a result thereof, it is his conscious object to engage in conduct of that nature or to cause such a result; and

(ii) if the element involves the attendant circumstances, he is aware of the existence of such circumstances or he believes or hopes that they exist.

(b) Knowingly.

A person acts knowingly with respect to a material element of an offense when:

(i) if the element involves the nature of his conduct or the attendant circumstances, he is aware that his conduct is of that nature or that such circumstances exist; and

(ii) if the element involves a result of his conduct, he is aware that it is practically certain that his conduct will cause such a result.

(c) Recklessly.

A person acts recklessly with respect to a material element of an offense when he consciously disregards a substantial and unjustifiable risk that the material element exists or will result from his conduct. The risk must be of such a nature and degree that, considering the nature and purpose of the actor's conduct and the circumstances known to him, its disregard involves a gross deviation from the standard of conduct that a law-abiding person would observe in the actor's situation.

(d) Negligently.

A person acts negligently with respect to a material element of an offense when he should be aware of a substantial and unjustifiable risk that the material element exists or will result from his conduct. The risk must be of such a nature and degree that the actor's failure to perceive it, considering the nature and purpose of his conduct and the circumstances known to him, involves a gross deviation from the standard of care that a reasonable person would observe in the actor's situation.

(3) Culpability Required Unless Otherwise Provided. When the culpability sufficient to establish a material element of an offense is not prescribed by law, such element is established if a person acts purposely, knowingly or recklessly with respect thereto.

(4) Prescribed Culpability Requirement Applies to All Material Elements. When the law defining an offense prescribes the kind of culpability that is sufficient for the commission of an offense, without distinguishing among the material elements thereof, such provision shall apply to all the material elements of the offense, unless a contrary purpose plainly appears.

(5) Substitutes for Negligence, Recklessness and Knowledge. When the law provides that negligence suffices to establish an element of an offense, such element also is established if a person acts purposely, knowingly or recklessly. When recklessness suffices to establish an element, such element also is established if a person acts purposely or knowingly. When acting knowingly suffices to establish an element, such element also is established if a person acts purposely.

(6) Requirement of Purpose Satisfied if Purpose Is Conditional. When a particular purpose is an element of an offense, the element is established although such

purpose is conditional, unless the condition negatives the harm or evil sought to be prevented by the law defining the offense.

(7) Requirement of Knowledge Satisfied by Knowledge of High Probability. When knowledge of the existence of a particular fact is an element of an offense, such knowledge is established if a person is aware of a high probability of its existence, unless he actually believes that it does not exist.

(8) Requirement of Wilfulness Satisfied by Acting Knowingly. A requirement that an offense be committed wilfully is satisfied if a person acts knowingly with respect to the material elements of the offense, unless a purpose to impose further requirements appears.

(9) Culpability as to Illegality of Conduct. Neither knowledge nor recklessness or negligence as to whether conduct constitutes an offense or as to the existence, meaning or application of the law determining the elements of an offense is an element of such offense, unless the definition of the offense or the Code so provides.

(10) Culpability as Determinant of Grade of Offense. When the grade or degree of an offense depends on whether the offense is committed purposely, knowingly, recklessly or negligently, its grade or degree shall be the lowest for which the determinative kind of culpability is established with respect to any material element of the offense.

Section 2.05 When Culpability Requirements Are Inapplicable to Violations and to Offenses Defined by Other Statutes; Effect of Absolute Liability in Reducing Grade of Offense to Violation.

(1) The requirements of culpability prescribed by Sections 2.01 and 2.02 do not apply to:

(a) offenses which constitute violations, unless the requirement involved is included in the definition of the offense or the Court determines that its application is consistent with effective enforcement of the law defining the offense; or

(b) offenses defined by statutes other than the Code, insofar as a legislative purpose to impose absolute liability for such offenses or with respect to any material element thereof plainly appears.

(2) Notwithstanding any other provision of existing law and unless a subsequent statute otherwise provides:

(a) when absolute liability is imposed with respect to any material element of an offense defined by a statute other than the Code and a conviction is based upon such liability, the offense constitutes a violation; and

(b) although absolute liability is imposed by law with respect to one or more of the material elements of an offense defined by a statute other than the Code, the culpable commission of the offense may be charged and proved, in which event negligence with respect to such elements constitutes sufficient culpability and the classification of the offense and the sentence that may be imposed therefor upon conviction are determined by Section 1.04 and Article 6 of the Code.[91]

---

91. Copyright © 1962 by the American Law Institute. Reprinted with the permission of the American Law Institute.

CHAPTER 8

RESPONSIBILITY: LIMITATIONS ON CRIMINAL CAPACITY

SECTION 1.   IMMATURITY (INFANCY)

Every civilized society must recognize criminal incapacity based upon extreme immaturity. No matter what harm is caused by one of very tender years the situation must be dealt with by some means other than the machinery established for the administration of criminal justice. This is too clear for any possibility of doubt, although there are differences of opinion as to just what should be regarded as such immaturity as to preclude criminal guilt.

While failing to develop techniques comparable to modern juvenile court and youth correction authority acts, the common law made a very reasonable approach to this problem. Because of wide differences in individuals two ages were emphasized. A child under the age of seven has no criminal capacity. At common law there is an "irrebuttable presumption of incapacity" on the part of one so young,—to use the familiar explanation of the judges. Fourteen is the other age. One who has reached the age of fourteen has criminal capacity unless incapacity is established on some entirely different basis, such as insanity. Furthermore, this means physical age and not so-called "mental age." Between the ages of seven and fourteen there is a rebuttable presumption of criminal incapacity. The common law permits the criminal conviction of a child between these ages, but only upon clear proof of such precocity as to establish a real appreciation of the wrongfulness of the thing done. This presumption is extremely strong at the age of seven and diminishes gradually until it disappears entirely at the age of fourteen.

The words of Blackstone are significant: "The law of England does in some cases privilege an infant under the age of twenty-one, as to common misdemeanors, so as to escape fine, imprisonment, and the like: and particularly in cases of omission, as not repairing a bridge, or a highway, and other similar offences; for, not having the command of his fortune till twenty-one he wants the capacity to do those things which the law requires. But where there is any notorious breach of the peace, a riot, battery, or the like (which infants, when full grown, are at least as liable as others to commit) for these an infant, above the age of fourteen, is equally liable to suffer as a person at the full age of twenty-one.

"With regard to capital crimes, the law is still more minute and circumspect; distinguishing with greater nicety the several degrees of age and discretion.... Thus a girl of thirteen has been burned for killing her mistress; and one boy of ten, and another of nine years old, who had killed their companions, have been sentenced to death, and he of ten years actually hanged; because it appeared, upon their trials, that the one hid himself, and the other hid the body he had killed, which hiding manifested a consciousness of guilt, and a discretion to discern between good and evil. And there was an instance in the last century where a boy of eight years old was tried at Abingdon for firing two barns; and, it appearing that he had malice, revenge, and cunning, he was found guilty, condemned, and hanged accordingly. Thus, also, in very modern times, a boy of ten years old was convicted on his own confession of murdering his bedfellow, there appearing in his whole behaviour plain tokens of a mischievous discretion; and, as the sparing this boy merely on account of his tender years might be of dangerous consequence to the public by propagating a notion that children might commit such atrocious crimes with impunity, it was unanimously agreed by all the judges that he was a proper subject of capital punishment. But, in all such cases, the evidence of that malice which is to supply age ought to be strong and clear beyond all doubt and contradiction" (4 Bl.Comm. 22–24).

The age, below which there is complete criminal incapacity, has been raised by statute in some jurisdictions. Thus it has been placed at ten in England, at fifteen in Texas, at sixteen in Colorado and at thirteen in Georgia. Furthermore, the net result of some of the juvenile delinquency statutes is to raise it much higher, although recently there has been a trend to lower the age and prosecute a child as an adult for serious crime.

Such age is omitted entirely from some of the statutes as, for example, the California section which provides in substance that children under the age of fourteen are incapable of crime "in the absence of clear proof that at the time of committing the act charged against them, they knew its wrongfulness" (Cal.Pen.Code § 26). Any provision of this nature should be read in the light of the common law. It clearly recognizes the existence of a presumption although the word is not used. And it is more logical to assume this means the established presumption of the common law than any other: that is, a presumption which is conclusive below the age of seven, extremely strong at that age, and does not disappear entirely until the age of fourteen.

Whether such a statute does or does not abolish the conclusive part of the common-law presumption is largely academic. This presumption applies only to one *under* the age of seven. Except where the age has been raised by statute it has always been possible, in legal theory, to rebut the presumption of incapacity of a seven-year-old child,—but it has never yet been done.

What has been said has reference to mental incapacity. An additional presumption applies in the rape cases. Under English common law a boy under the age of fourteen is conclusively presumed to be incapable of committing this offense. If two indictments were found against a thirteen-year-old boy, one charging rape and the other charging murder, the prosecution of the rape case would be stopped the moment his age was established. The murder case would be permitted to go to the jury with an instruction emphasizing the prima-facie presumption of incapacity. Some of the states in this country have adopted the same view. In others the presumption of physical incapacity of a boy under fourteen to commit rape is rebuttable.

What amounts to a limitation of criminal capacity has been established in a few jurisdictions at a much higher age. This is in the form of a provision that no one shall be deprived of life by reason of any act done before attaining a specified age. The age so specified in Texas, for example, is seventeen, and that in California is eighteen.[1] In Stanford v. Kentucky, 492 U.S. 361, 109 S.Ct. 2969, 106 L.Ed.2d 306 (1989), the Supreme Court upheld the constitutionality of executing murderers who were as young as sixteen at the time of the crime. *Stanford* divided the justices five to four, the Court's membership has changed since, and the recent decision in Atkins v. Virginia, 536 U.S. 304, 122 S.Ct. 2242, 153 L.Ed.2d 335 (2002) (reversing prior precedent, and holding the execution of mentally retarded offender unconstitutionally disproportionate in light of society's evolving standards of decency) suggests that the Court might be willing to reconsider the question resolved in *Stanford*.

The problem of criminal incapacity by reason of immaturity has been disguised to some extent by the juvenile delinquency statutes, with particular emphasis upon procedure. These enactments differ widely from state to state. Some of the earlier acts merely provided an alternative procedure which might be used, in the discretion of the judge, in cases of children below a specified age. The more progressive statutes provide that what would be a crime, if committed by an older person, is not a crime but an entirely different type of misbehavior, called "juvenile delinquency," if committed by a "juvenile." Some of these statutes do not remove from the category of crime any act punishable by death or by life imprisonment. One development is to enlarge the scope of "juvenile delinquency" to include even a misdeed which would be capital on the part of an older person.[2] The net result of such a provision is to raise the age of total criminal incapacity. However, several states have enacted legislation that provides that certain crimes are excluded from delinquency treatment or that after hearing a juvenile may be certified to stand trial as an adult for a criminal act.[3] In recent years several states have expanded the offenses for which a juvenile may be certified as an adult, reduced the age for certification, or allowed direct filing of a serious adult charge against a juvenile.

State v. Q.D.

Supreme Court of Washington, 1984.
102 Wn.2d 19, 685 P.2d 557.

■ DIMMICK, JUSTICE.

Two juveniles appeal from separate adjudications which found that they had committed offenses which if committed by an adult would be

1. West's Ann.Cal.Pen.Code, § 190.5 (1988). See also Vernon's Texas Penal Code § 8.07 (1997).

2. "No person shall be convicted of any offense unless he had attained his 13th birthday at the time the offense was committed." 720 Ill. Comp. Statutes 5/6–1.

Under the New York Penal Code, McKinney's Consol. Laws of N.Y. (1987):

"§ 30.00 Infancy

"1. ...a person less than sixteen years old is not criminally responsible for conduct."

Subsection 2 provides that for certain crimes persons thirteen, fourteen and fifteen are responsible.

3. Feld, The Juvenile Court Meets the Principle Offense: Legislative Changes in Juvenile Waiver Statutes, 78 Jnl.Crim.L. & Criminology 471 (1987).

crimes. The Court of Appeals, in these consolidated appeals, certified to this court the questions whether the statutory presumption of infant incapacity, RCW 9A.04.050,[4] applies to juvenile adjudications,
and if it does, what
standard of proof is required to rebut the presumption. Each defendant argues that the trial court's determinations of capacity were erroneous under any standard. Appellant Q.D. additionally argues that there was insufficient evidence to convict him of trespass in the first degree. . . .

We hold that (1) RCW 9A.04.050 applies to juvenile adjudications, (2) the standard of proof necessary to rebut the presumption of incapacity is clear and convincing proof, . . .

Appellant Q.D. was found to have capacity per RCW 9A.04.050 in a pretrial hearing. He was 11½ years old at the time of the alleged offense. At trial a different judge determined he had committed trespass in the first degree. The evidence introduced to show capacity consisted of testimony from a case worker and a detective who had worked with him in connection with his plea of guilty to a burglary committed at age 10 years. The case worker testified that Q.D. was familiar with the justice system, was street wise, and that he used his age as a shield. The detective told the court that Q.D. was cooperative in the burglary investigation, and he appeared to know his rights. The evidence in the guilt phase consisted of testimony from the principal and a custodial engineer of the school in which Q.D. was charged with trespass. . . .

Counsel for both the State and the defendants urge us to hold that the infant incapacity defense in RCW 9A.04.050 applies to juvenile proceedings. We so hold.

At common law, children below the age of 7 were conclusively presumed to be incapable of committing crime, and children over the age of 14 were presumed capable and treated as adults. Children between these ages were rebuttably presumed incapable of committing crime. Washington codified these presumptions amending the age of conclusive incapacity to 7, and presumed capacity to 12 years of age. As recently as 1975, the Legislature again included the infancy defense in the criminal code. The purpose of the presumption is to protect from the criminal justice system those individuals of tender years who are less capable than adults of appreciating the wrongfulness of their behavior.

The infancy defense fell into disuse during the early part of the century with the advent of reforms intended to substitute treatment and rehabilitation for punishment of juvenile offenders. This parens patriae system, believed not to be a criminal one, had no need of the infancy defense.

---

4. RCW 9A.04.050 provides in part:

"Children under the age of eight years are incapable of committing crime. Children of eight and under twelve years of age are presumed to be incapable of committing crime, but this presumption may be removed by proof that they have sufficient capacity to understand the act or neglect, and to know that it was wrong."

The juvenile justice system in recent years has evolved from parens patriae scheme to one more akin to adult criminal proceedings. The United States Supreme Court has been critical of the parens patriae scheme as failing to provide safeguards due an adult criminal defendant, while subjecting the juvenile defendant to similar stigma, and possible loss of liberty. *See* In re Gault, 387 U.S. 1, 87 S.Ct. 1428, 18 L.Ed.2d 527 (1967); and In re Winship, 397 U.S. 358, 90 S.Ct. 1068, 25 L.Ed.2d 368 (1970). This court has acknowledged Washington's departure from a strictly parens patriae scheme to a more criminal one, involving both rehabilitation and punishment. Being a criminal defense, RCW 9A.04.050 should be available to juvenile proceedings that are criminal in nature.

. . .

A finding that RCW 9A.04.050 does not apply to juvenile courts would render that statute meaningless or superfluous contrary to rules of construction. Juvenile courts have exclusive jurisdiction over all individuals under the chronological age of 18 who have committed acts designated criminal if committed by an adult. Declination of jurisdiction and transfer to adult court is limited to instances where it is in the best interest of the juvenile or the public. State v. Holland, 98 Wash.2d 507, 656 P.2d 1056 (1983). Thus, all juveniles who can avail themselves of the infancy defense will come under the jurisdiction of the juvenile court, and most will remain there.... Goals of the Juvenile Justice Act of 1977 include accountability for criminal behavior and punishment commensurate with age and crime. A goal of the criminal code is to safeguard conduct that is not culpable. RCW 9A.04.020. The infancy defense which excludes from criminal condemnation persons not capable of culpable, criminal acts, is consistent with the overlapping goals of the Juvenile Justice Act of 1977 and the Washington Criminal Code.

The State has the burden of rebutting the statutory presumption of incapacity of juveniles age 8 and less than 12 years. Capacity must be found to exist separate from the specific mental element of the crime charged. While capacity is similar to the mental element of a specific crime or offense, it is not an element of the offense, but is rather a general determination that the individual understood the act and its wrongfulness. Both defendants liken the incapacity presumption to a jurisdictional presumption. Were capacity an element of the crime, proof beyond a reasonable doubt would be required. But capacity, not being an element of the crime, does not require as stringent a standard of proof.

. . .

The Legislature, by requiring the State to rebut the presumption of incapacity, has assumed a greater burden than the minimal proof imposed by the preponderance of the evidence standard. On the other hand, to require the State to prove capacity beyond a reasonable doubt when the State must also prove the specific mental element of the charged offense by the same standard, is unnecessarily duplicative. Frequently, the same facts required to prove mens rea will be probative of capacity, yet the overlap is not complete. Capacity to be culpable must exist in order to maintain the specific mental element of the charged offense. Once the generalized determination of capacity is found, the State must prove beyond a reasonable doubt that the juvenile defendant possessed the specific mental element. The clear and convincing standard reflects the State's assumption of a greater burden than does the preponderance of the evidence standard. At the same time, the liberty interest of the juvenile is fully protected by the requirement of proof beyond a reasonable doubt of the specific mental element. We therefore require the State to rebut the presumption of incapacity by clear and convincing evidence.

We do not need to reach the question of whether there was substantial evidence to show that Q.D. understood the act of trespass or understood it to be wrong, as we reverse on other grounds. Nevertheless, a discussion of capacity in this case may prove instructive to trial courts. Q.D. argues that the evidence showed only that he was familiar with the juvenile system through his previous plea of guilty to a burglary charge, but did not show he understood the act and wrongfulness of trespass. The language of RCW 9A.04.050 clearly indicates that a capacity determination must be made in reference to the specific act charged: "understand *the act* . . . and to know that it was wrong." (Italics ours.) If Q.D. is correct that the evidence showed no more than a general understanding of the justice system, he would be correct in concluding that the State did not show an understanding and knowing wrongfulness of trespass. In addition, an understanding of the wrongfulness of burglary does not alone establish capacity in regard to trespass. While both offenses include entry or unlawfully remaining in a building, burglary also requires an intent to commit a crime against a person or property therein. Defendant may well understand that it is wrong to enter a locked building with the intention of committing a crime, but not know that entering an unlocked school building is wrong.

Reversed.

Corder v. Rogerson

United States Court of Appeals, Eighth Circuit, 1999.
192 F.3d 1165.

■ LOKEN, CIRCUIT JUDGE.

Iowa inmate James Steven Corder is serving a life sentence for killing his stepmother and burning their family residence when he was sixteen years old. Corder was tried as an adult and convicted of murder and arson after an Iowa juvenile court granted the State's motion to waive jurisdiction. On March 22, 1997, Corder delivered a petition for a federal writ of habeas corpus to prison officials for mailing to the district court. . . . Corder now appeals the district court's denial of that petition, arguing that the juvenile court denied him due process in waiving its jurisdiction. We affirm.

I.

The crime occurred on March 25, 1987. On April 13, the State filed a Petition Alleging Delinquent Act against Corder in the Juvenile Division of the Jackson County District Court. The Court issued a warrant for Corder's arrest after finding probable cause to believe that he had committed murder and arson based upon an affidavit by an Iowa criminal investigator describing incriminating evidence and witness statements. On April 15, the juvenile court issued a detention order pursuant to Iowa Code § 232.44, making the findings required by Iowa Code § 232.22(1)(d). The detention order recited that the court "has heretofore made a probable cause finding in approving the State's complaint and issuing a warrant." On April 16, the State filed a motion asking the juvenile court to waive its jurisdiction so that Corder could be tried as an adult. *See* Iowa Code § 232.45. After a hearing at which Corder was represented by appointed counsel, the juvenile court granted that motion. In making the probable cause determination required by § 232.45, the court relied upon the probable cause determination in its previous detention order. Use of that procedure is the principal due process issue raised in this appeal.

Corder was then tried as an adult, and a jury convicted him of first degree murder and second degree arson. He appealed, contending that the juvenile court denied him due process in waiving jurisdiction because it found probable cause on the basis of the State's complaint and affidavit, without hearing any witnesses. The Iowa Court of Appeals affirmed. In February 1995, the Iowa Court of Appeals also affirmed the trial court's denial of Corder's application for state post-conviction relief, an application that did not revisit the juvenile court's proceedings. Corder then filed this federal habeas petition. The district court denied relief but granted a certificate of appealability on the question whether Corder's "due process rights were violated in the waiver process by which [he] was transferred from juvenile to district court."

II.

"There is no doubt that the Due Process Clause is applicable in juvenile proceedings." Schall v. Martin, 467 U.S. 253, 263, 104 S.Ct. 2403, 81 L.Ed.2d 207 (1984). The problem is to determine how much process is due in a particular type of juvenile proceeding. In Kent v. United States, 383 U.S. 541, 556, 86 S.Ct. 1045, 16 L.Ed.2d 84 (1966), the Supreme Court observed that a juvenile court's decision to waive its jurisdiction so that a youthful offender may be tried as an adult, though civil rather than criminal in nature, "is a 'critically important' action determining vitally important statutory rights of the juvenile." Therefore, the Court concluded that, while a juvenile is not entitled to all the constitutional guarantees that attend a criminal trial, "as a condition to a valid waiver order, petitioner was entitled to a hearing, including access by his counsel to the social records and probation or similar reports which presumably are considered by the court, and to a statement of reasons for the Juvenile Court's decision." *Kent,* 383 U.S. at 557, 86 S.Ct. 1045. *Kent* was based upon the Court's construction of a District of Columbia statute, but the Court has since referred to *Kent* as a Due Process Clause decision. *See Schall,* 467 U.S. at 277, 104 S.Ct. 2403. Consistent with *Kent,* Iowa Code § 232.45 requires a waiver hearing, provides that the juvenile's counsel must have timely access to the probation officer's report and to "all written material to be considered by the court," prescribes statutory factors upon which the waiver decision must be based, and requires that a juvenile court waiving jurisdiction must "file written findings as to its reasons." It is undisputed that the Jackson County juvenile court complied with these statutory procedures in deciding to waive its jurisdiction over Corder.

On appeal, Corder ... contends the juvenile court lacked a proper evidentiary basis for the probable cause determination that must be made under state law. The Iowa statute provides that a juvenile court may waive its jurisdiction only if "[t]he court determines, *or has previously determined in a detention hearing under section 232.44,* that there is probable cause to believe that the child has committed a delinquent act which would constitute" an offense warranting trial as an adult. Iowa Code § 232.45(6)(b) (emphasis added). At Corder's waiver hearing, the court based this determination on the probable cause determination made at the prior detention hearing, which in turn was based upon the probable cause found in issuing a warrant for Corder's arrest. Corder argues this procedure denied him due process because he was not afforded an opportunity to confront and cross-examine the State's probable cause witnesses at the waiver hearing.

In rejecting this argument, the Iowa Court of Appeals analyzed the Supreme Court's decision in *Kent* and Breed v. Jones, 421 U.S. 519, 537, 95 S.Ct. 1779, 44 L.Ed.2d 346 (1975),[5] and concluded that confrontation is not one of the "panoply of trial rights" that is applicable to juvenile waiver proceedings. Under the recent amendments to the federal habeas corpus statute, our review of this iowa Court of Appeals decision is limited to determining whether its conclusion "resulted in a decision that was contrary to, or involved an unreasonable application of, clearly established Federal law, as determined by the Supreme Court of the United States." 28 U.S.C. § 2254(d)(1). Applying that standard, we must reject Corder's contention.

The Iowa statute and Corder's waiver hearing complied with the requirements of *Kent,* where the Supreme Court emphasized that a waiver hearing need not "conform with all of the requirements of a criminal trial or even of the usual administrative hearing." *Kent,* 383 U.S. at 562, 86 S.Ct. 1045. Corder relies upon *In re Gault,* 387 U.S. 1, 56–57, 87 S.Ct. 1428, 18 L.Ed.2d 527 (1967), a Due Process Clause case in which the Court held that "confrontation and sworn testimony by witnesses available for cross-examination [are] essential for a finding of 'delinquency.'" But the determination of delinquency is the juvenile court equivalent of a criminal conviction, "with the consequence that [the juvenile] may be committed to a state institution." *Gault,* 387 U.S. at 13, 87 S.Ct. 1428. By contrast, probable cause is a preliminary determination, usually made in deciding whether to issue a warrant or to detain a defendant prior to trial. In those contexts, "the full panoply of adversary safeguards," such as confrontation and cross-examination, "are not essential for the probable cause determina-

---

5. In *Breed,* the Court held that if a waiver hearing is adjudicatory in nature, jeopardy will attach and bar a subsequent criminal prosecution of the juvenile as an adult. In thus concluding that a prior waiver hearing must be non-adjudicatory, the Court observed, "nothing decided today forecloses States from requiring, as a prerequisite to the transfer of a juvenile [to adult court], substantial evidence that he committed the offense charged, so long as the showing required is not made in an adjudicatory proceeding." *Breed,* 421 U.S. at 538 n. 18, 95 S.Ct. 1779. Of course, requiring confrontation and cross examination of the State's probable cause witnesses, as Corder urges, would make the waiver hearing adjudicatory, or come dangerously close to doing so.

tion required by the Fourth Amendment." Instead, probable cause "traditionally has been decided by a magistrate in a nonadversary proceeding on hearsay and written testimony, and the Court has approved these informal modes of proof." Gerstein v. Pugh, 420 U.S. 103, 119–20, 95 S.Ct. 854, 43 L.Ed.2d 54 (1975).

Although *Gerstein* concerned the determination of probable cause in adult rather than juvenile proceedings, we have no reason to believe the Supreme Court would impose a different constitutional standard for juvenile waiver hearings, particularly in light of the double jeopardy hazard defined in *Breed*. *See generally* Government of Virgin Islands ex rel. A.M., 34 F.3d 153, 161 (3d Cir.1994). Therefore, we conclude that the Iowa Court of Appeals decision was neither "contrary to" nor "an unreasonable application of" the Supreme Court's juvenile court due process decisions. *See* Long v. Humphrey, 184 F.3d 758, 760 (8th Cir.1999) (standard of review). Indeed, we agree with the state court that the Iowa procedure for determining probable cause in a juvenile court waiver proceeding is constitutionally permissible....

The judgment of the district court is affirmed.

McKeiver v. Pennsylvania

Supreme Court of the United States, 1971.
403 U.S. 528, 91 S.Ct. 1976, 29 L.Ed.2d 647.

[Joseph McKeiver, age 16, was accused of robbery, larceny and receiving stolen goods. Although these are felonies under Pennsylvania law, they were not charged as such but as acts of juvenile delinquency in a juvenile court proceeding. Another boy, age 15, was charged with acts of juvenile delinquency in the form of assault and battery and conspiracy (misdemeanors). In separate proceedings, in each of which counsel's request for a jury trial had been denied, the boys were found to be juvenile delinquents. The Supreme Court of Pennsylvania consolidated the cases for the purpose of appeal, the sole question being "whether there is a constitutional right to a jury trial in juvenile court." The answer was "no" and the Supreme Court noted probable jurisdiction. This was case No. 322.

Case No. 128 was a North Carolina case in which children ranging in age from 11 to 15 had been declared to be delinquent by the juvenile court which placed them on probation for one or two years. The juvenile court had excluded the public from these proceedings, over counsel's objection, and had denied counsel's request for a jury trial. The judgment of the juvenile court was affirmed by the Supreme Court of North Carolina and the Supreme Court granted certiorari and considered the two cases together.]

■ MR. JUSTICE BLACKMUN announced the judgment of the Court and an opinion in which THE CHIEF JUSTICE, MR. JUSTICE STEWART, and MR. JUSTICE WHITE join.

These cases present the narrow but precise issue whether the Due Process Clause of the Fourteenth Amendment assures the right to trial by jury in the adjudicative phase of a state juvenile court delinquency proceeding. . . .

1. Some of the constitutional requirements attendant upon the state criminal trial have equal application to that part of the state juvenile proceeding that is adjudicative in nature. Among these are the rights to appropriate notice, to counsel, to confrontation and to cross-examination, and the privilege against self-incrimination. Included, also, is the standard of proof beyond a reasonable doubt.

2. The Court, however, has not yet said that *all* rights constitutionally assured to an adult accused of crime also are to be enforced or made available to the juvenile in his delinquency proceeding. Indeed, the Court specifically has refrained from going that far:

"We do not mean by this to indicate that the hearing to be held must conform with all of the requirements of a criminal trial or even of the usual administrative hearing; but we do hold that the hearing must measure up to the essentials of due process and fair treatment."

3. The Court, although recognizing the high hopes and aspirations of JUDGE JULIAN MACK, the leaders of the Jane Addams School and the other supporters of the juvenile court concept, has also noted the disappointments of the system's performance and experience and the resulting widespread disaffection. *Kent*, 383 U.S., at 555–556, 86 S.Ct., at 1054–1055; *Gault*, 387 U.S., at 17–19, 87 S.Ct., at 1438–1439. There have been, at one and the same time, both an appreciation for the juvenile court judge who is devoted, sympathetic, and conscientious, and a disturbed concern about the judge who is untrained and less than fully imbued with an understanding approach to the complex problems of childhood and adolescence. There has been praise for the system and its purposes, and there has been alarm over its defects.

4. The Court has insisted that these successive decisions do not spell the doom of the juvenile court system or even deprive it of its "informality, flexibility or speed." *Winship*, 397 U.S., at 366–367, 90 S.Ct., at 1073–1074. On the other hand, a concern precisely to the opposite effect was expressed by two dissenters in *Winship*. 397 U.S., at 375–376, 90 S.Ct., at 1078–1079. . . .

We must recognize, as the Court has recognized before, that the fond and idealistic hopes of the juvenile court proponents and early reformers of three generations ago have not been realized. The devastating commentary upon the system's failures as a whole, contained in the Task Force Report: Juvenile Delinquency and Youth Crime (President's Commission on Law Enforcement and the Administration of Justice (1967)), pp. 7–9, reveals the depth of disappointment in what has been accomplished. Too often the juvenile court judge falls far short of that stalwart, protective and communicating figure the system envisaged.[6] The community's unwillingness to provide people and facilities and to be concerned, the insufficiency of time devoted, the scarcity of professional help, the inadequacy of dispositional

---

6. "A recent study of juvenile court judges ... revealed that half had not received undergraduate degrees; a fifth had received no college education at all; a fifth were not members of the bar." Task Force Report, p. 7.

alternatives, and our general lack of knowledge all contribute to dissatisfaction with the experiment.[7]

The Task Force Report, however, also said, page 7, "To say that juvenile courts have failed to achieve their goals is to say no more than what is true of criminal courts in the United States. But failure is most striking when hopes are highest."

Despite all these disappointments, all these failures, and all these shortcomings, we conclude that trial by jury in the juvenile court's adjudicative stage is not a constitutional requirement. We so conclude for a number of reasons:

1. The Court has refrained, in the cases heretofore decided, from taking the easy way with a flat holding that all rights constitutionally assured for the adult accused are to be imposed upon the state juvenile proceeding. . . .

2. There is a possibility, at least, that the jury trial, if required as a matter of constitutional precept, will remake the juvenile proceeding into a fully adversary process and will put an effective end to what has been the idealistic prospect of an intimate, informal protective proceeding.

3. The Task Force Report, . . . expressly recommends against abandonment of the system and against the return of the juvenile to the criminal courts.[8]

---

7. "What emerges, then, is this: In theory the juvenile court was to be helpful and rehabilitative rather than punitive. In fact the distinction often disappears, not only because of the absence of facilities and personnel but also because of the limits of knowledge and technique. In theory the court's action was to affix no stigmatizing label. In fact a delinquent is generally viewed by employers, schools, the armed services—by society generally—as a criminal. In theory the court was to treat children guilty of criminal acts in noncriminal ways. In fact it labels truants and runaways as junior criminals.

"In theory the court's operations could justifiably be informal, its findings and decisions made without observing ordinary procedural safeguards, because it would act only in the best interest of the child. In fact it frequently does nothing more nor less than deprive a child of liberty without due process of law—knowing not what else to do and needing, whether admittedly or not, to act in the community's interest even more imperatively than the child's. In theory it was to exercise its protective powers to bring an errant child back into the fold. In fact there is increasing reason to believe that its intervention reinforces the juvenile's unlawful impulses. In theory it was to concentrate on each case the best of current social science learning. In fact it has often become a vested interest in its turn, loathe to cooperate with innovative programs or avail itself of forward-looking methods." Task Force Report, p. 9.

8. "Nevertheless, study of the juvenile courts does not necessarily lead to the conclusion that the time has come to jettison the experiment and remand the disposition of children charged with crime to the criminal courts of the country. As trying as are the problems of the juvenile courts, the problems of the criminal courts, particularly those of the lower courts, which would fall heir to much of the juvenile court jurisdiction, are even graver; and the ideal of separate treatment of children is still worth pursuing. What is required is rather a revised philosophy of the juvenile court based on the recognition that in the past our reach exceeded our grasp. The spirit that animated the juvenile court movement was fed in part by a humanitarian compassion for offenders who were children. That willingness to understand and treat people who threaten public safety and security should be nurtured, not turned aside as hopeless sentimentality, both because it is civilized and because social protection itself demands constant search for alternatives to the crude and limited expedient of condemnation and punishment. But neither should it be allowed to outrun reality. The juvenile court is a court of law charged like other agencies of criminal justice with protecting the community

4. The Court specifically has recognized by dictum that a jury is not a necessary part even of every criminal process that is fair and equitable.

5. The imposition of the jury trial on the juvenile court system would not strengthen greatly, if at all, the fact-finding function, and would, contrarily, provide an attrition of the juvenile court's assumed ability to function in a unique manner. It would not remedy the defects of the system. Meager as has been the hoped-for advance in the juvenile field, the alternative would be regressive, would lose what has been gained, and would tend once again to place the juvenile squarely in the routine of the criminal process.

6. The juvenile concept held high promise. We are reluctant to say that, despite disappointments of grave dimensions, it still does not hold promise, and we are particularly reluctant to say, as do the Pennsylvania petitioners here, that the system cannot accomplish its rehabilitative goals. So much depends on the availability of resources, on the interest and commitment of the public, on willingness to learn, and on understanding as to cause and effect and cure. In this field, as in so many others, one perhaps learns best by doing. We are reluctant to disallow the States further to experiment and to seek in new and different ways the elusive answers to the problems of the young, and we feel that we would be impeding that experimentation by imposing the jury trial. The States, indeed, must go forward. If, in its wisdom, any State feels the jury trial is desirable in all cases, or in certain kinds, there appears to be no impediment to its installing a system embracing that feature. That, however, is the State's privilege and not its obligation.

7. Of course there have been abuses. The Task Force Report has noted them. We refrain from saying at this point that those abuses are of constitutional dimension. They relate to the lack of resources and of dedication rather than to inherent unfairness.

8. There is, of course, nothing to prevent a juvenile court judge, in a particular case where he feels the need, or when the need is demonstrated, from using an advisory jury.

9. "The fact that a practice is followed by a large number of states is not conclusive in a decision as to whether that practice accords with due process, but it is plainly worth considering in determining whether the practice 'offends some principle of justice so rooted in the traditions and conscience of our people as to be ranked as fundamental.' " It therefore is of more than passing interest that at least 29 States and the District of Columbia by statute deny the juvenile a right to a jury trial in cases such as these. The same result is achieved in other States by judicial decision. In 10 States statutes provide for a jury trial under certain circumstances.

---

against threatening conduct. Rehabilitating offenders through individualized handling is one way of providing protection, and appropriately the primary way in dealing with children. But the guiding consideration for a court of law that deals with threatening conduct is nonetheless protection of the community. The juvenile court, like other courts, is therefore obliged to employ all the means at hand, not excluding incapacitation, for achieving that protection. What should distinguish the juvenile from the criminal courts is greater emphasis on rehabilitation, not exclusive preoccupation with it." Task Force Report, p. 9.

10. Since *Gault* and since *Duncan* the great majority of States, in addition to Pennsylvania and North Carolina, that have faced the issue have concluded that the considerations that led to the result in those two cases do not compel trial by jury in the juvenile court. . . .

12. If the jury trial were to be injected into the juvenile court system as a matter of right, it would bring with it into that system the traditional delay, the formality and the clamor of the adversary system and, possibly, the public trial. . . .

If the formalities of the criminal adjudicative process are to be superimposed upon the juvenile court system, there is little need for its separate existence. Perhaps that ultimate disillusionment will come one day, but for the moment we are disinclined to give impetus to it.

Affirmed.

■ [MR. JUSTICE HARLAN concurred in the judgments in these cases because he disagrees with the theory that the constitution requires a jury in any state criminal trial in which a jury would be required in a comparable federal case. In his opinion jury trials are not required in a state criminal case either by the Sixth Amendment or by due process.

■ MR. JUSTICE BRENNAN seems to be of opinion that a juvenile in a juvenile court proceeding may be denied either a jury or a public hearing, but not both. Hence he concurred in the judgment in No. 322 but dissented in No. 128.

■ JUSTICES DOUGLAS, BLACK and MARSHALL dissented in both on the theory that appellants should have been entitled to a jury trial in both cases.][9]

MODEL PENAL CODE[10]

Section 4.10 Immaturity Excluding Criminal Conviction; Transfer of Proceedings to Juvenile Court.

(1) A person shall not be tried for or convicted of an offense if:

(a) at the time of the conduct charged to constitute the offense he was less than sixteen years of age [, in which case the Juvenile Court shall have exclusive jurisdiction[11]]; or

(b) at the time of the conduct charged to constitute the offense he was sixteen or seventeen years of age, unless:

(i) the Juvenile Court has no jurisdiction over him, or,

(ii) the Juvenile Court has entered an order waiving jurisdiction and consenting to the institution of criminal proceedings against him.

---

9. The issue has recently arisen again, as courts asked whether a juvenile adjudication rendered without jury trial may be used to enhance the sentence for a future felony conviction rendered in the regular courts. *See* Barry Feld, *The Constitutional Tension Between* Apprendi *and* McKeiver: *Sentence Enhancements Based on Delinquency Convictions and the Quality of the Juvenile Courts*, 38 Wake Forest L. Rev. 1111 (2003).

10. Copyright © 1962 by the American Law Institute. Reprinted with the permission of the American Law Institute.

11. The bracketed words are unnecessary if the Juvenile Court Act so provides or is amended accordingly.

(2) No court shall have jurisdiction to try or convict a person of an offense if criminal proceedings against him are barred by subsection (1) of this section. When it appears that a person charged with the commission of an offense may be of such an age that criminal proceedings may be barred under subsection (1) of this section, the Court shall hold a hearing thereon, and the burden shall be on the prosecution to establish to the satisfaction of the Court that the criminal proceeding is not barred upon such grounds. If the Court determines that the proceeding is barred, custody of the person charged shall be surrendered to the Juvenile Court, and the case, including all papers and processes relating thereto, shall be transferred.

Section 6.05 Young Adult Offenders.

(1) Specialized Correctional Treatment. A young adult offender is a person convicted of a crime who, at the time of sentencing, is sixteen but less than twenty-two years of age. A young adult offender who is sentenced to a term of imprisonment which may exceed thirty days [alternatives: (1) ninety days; (2) one year] shall be committed to the custody of the Division of Young Adult Correction of the Department of Correction, and shall receive, as far as practicable, such special and individualized correctional and rehabilitative treatment as may be appropriate to his needs.

(2) Special Term. A young adult offender convicted of a felony may, in lieu of any other sentence of imprisonment authorized by this Article, be sentenced to a special term of imprisonment without a minimum and with a maximum of four years, regardless of the degree of the felony involved, if the Court is of the opinion that such special term is adequate for his correction and rehabilitation and will not jeopardize the protection of the public.

[(3) Removal of Disabilities; Vacation of Conviction.

(a) In sentencing a young adult offender to the special term provided by this Section or to any sentence other than one of imprisonment, the Court may order that so long as he is not convicted of another felony, the judgment shall not constitute a conviction for the purposes of any disqualification or disability imposed by law upon conviction of a crime.

(b) When any young adult offender is unconditionally discharged from probation or parole before the expiration of the maximum term thereof, the Court may enter an order vacating the judgment of conviction.]

[(4) Commitment for Observation. If, after presentence investigation, the Court desires additional information concerning a young adult offender before imposing sentence, it may order that he be committed, for a period not exceeding ninety days, to the custody of the Division of Young Adult Correction of the Department of Correction for observation and study at an appropriate reception or classification center. Such Division of the Department of Correction and the [Young Adult Division of the] Board of Parole shall advise the Court of their findings and recommendations on or before the expiration of such ninety-day period.]

SECTION 2. MENTAL DISEASE OR DEFECT (INSANITY)

The problem of insanity may become important at various points in a criminal case. The *first* is at the time of the alleged crime. Insanity of the defendant at the time of the *actus reus,* if of such character and degree as to negative criminal responsibility, will entitle him to an acquittal. The *second* point is at the time set for arraignment. If the mind of one accused of crime by indictment or information is so disordered by mental disease that he is unable to understand the charge against him, and to plead intelligently thereto, he should not be permitted to plead until his reason is restored. This problem is similar to the next and can be considered therewith. The *third* point is at the time set for trial,—or during the trial.[12] Mental disorder at this time has nothing to do with the issue of guilt or innocence (except to the extent that it may have some tendency to indicate what his mental condition was at the time of the harmful deed). But one whose mental condition is now so disordered that he is unable to understand the charge against him, and possible defenses thereto, or unable rationally to advise with his counsel in regard to the conduct of the trial, ought not to be tried now,—whatever his mental condition may have been at the time of the alleged crime. Upon such a finding the defendant is committed to a proper hospital. He is to remain there until his reason is restored, at which time he is to be returned to the court for trial. If he is to be committed beyond a reasonable time, it is necessary to resort to regular commitment procedure.[13]

The *fourth* point is at the time of allocution (when the defendant is asked by the judge, after a verdict or plea of guilty, if he knows of any reason why judgment should not be pronounced against him). In the words of Blackstone: "If, after he be tried and found guilty, he loses his senses before judgment, judgment shall not be pronounced . . .: for peradventure,

---

12. An insane person cannot plead to an indictment, be subjected to trial, have judgment pronounced against him or undergo punishment, but a valid indictment may be found against him although no further proceedings can be had at the time. Frye v. Settle, 168 F.Supp. 7 (W.D.Mo.1958).

Amnesia does not per se render a defendant unable to stand trial or receive a fair trial. State v. Gilder, 223 Kan. 220, 574 P.2d 196 (1977); Commonwealth v. Barky, 476 Pa. 602, 383 A.2d 526 (1978); United States v. Mota, 598 F.2d 995 (5th Cir.1979); State v. Gilbert, 229 Conn. 228, 640 A.2d 61 (1994); State v. Forsyth, 547 N.W.2d 833 (Iowa App.1996); State v. Dixon, 668 So.2d 388 (La.App.1996).

A criminal defendant may not plead guilty unless he is competent and the same standards of competency apply to pleas of guilty as are applicable to a defendant's competency to stand trial. Godinez v. Moran, 509 U.S. 389, 113 S.Ct. 2680, 125 L.Ed.2d 321 (1993).

The standard for competence to stand trial is whether the defendant has "sufficient present ability to consult with his lawyer with a reasonable degree of rational understanding" and has "a rational as well as factual understanding of the proceedings against him." Dusky v. United States, 362 U.S. 402, 80 S.Ct. 788, 4 L.Ed.2d 824 (1960).

A state may presume that the defendant is competent and require the defendant to prove incompetence by a preponderance of the evidence. Medina v. California, 505 U.S. 437, 449, 112 S.Ct. 2572, 2579, 120 L.Ed.2d 353 (1992).

13. Jackson v. Indiana, 406 U.S. 715, 92 S.Ct. 1845, 32 L.Ed.2d 435 (1972).

Where a defendant is acquitted on the grounds of insanity he may be committed pending a determination that he has regained his sanity and may be kept beyond the period for which defendant may have been kept had the defendant been convicted. The defendant's insanity must be established by a preponderance of evidence and due process standards must be satisfied in determining the need for commitment. Jones v. United States, 463 U.S. 354, 103 S.Ct. 3043, 77 L.Ed.2d 694 (1983). *See* Harris v. Oklahoma County Dist. Court, 750 P.2d 1129 (Okl.Cr.1988).

A finding of not guilty by reason of insanity is sufficient foundation to hold the insanity acquittee to determine whether the person is a danger to the community or to the person. Automatic commitment for 180 days does not violate due process. Glatz v. Kort, 807 F.2d 1514 (10th Cir.1986) (consideration of Colorado law).

says the humanity of the English law, had the prisoner been of sound memory, he might have alleged something in stay of judgment...." (4 Bl.Comm. 24–25). A finding of insanity at this point requires a commitment of the defendant to a proper hospital until he regains his reason. He is then to be returned for sentence.

The *fifth* point is at the time of execution.[14] At common law this probably was limited to the execution of a sentence of death, but it is to be remembered that all felonies were capital at common law. In any event the person must not be put to death while unable to understand the punishment, for if a defendant had reason the person might be able to allege something in stay of execution.

Quite apart from a criminal case, it may be added, one who is mentally disordered to such an extent as to be a menace to himself or herself, or to others, may be committed to a proper hospital until and unless his reason is restored. This, however, is not a criminal problem. As a matter of logic this section is concerned only with the first point mentioned although it will be convenient to extend the inquiry somewhat beyond this.

The nature and extent of mental disorder which will entitle the defendant to an acquittal, constitutes the outstanding problem in this branch of the law of insanity. No distinction is made, in this inquiry, between *dementia* and *amentia*. The point here is not whether the person once had a sound mind which has deteriorated as a result of disease or injury, or was mentally deficient from birth. The sole determinant is the nature and extent of the mental abnormality. It must be emphasized that the phrase "mental disease" is employed in a very broad sense in the criminal law.[15] Any serious mental disorder or abnormality resulting from

---

14. The Eighth Amendment prohibits a state from inflicting the death penalty upon a prisoner who is insane. Such punishment has questionable retributive value, presents no example to others and has no deterrent value, and offends humanity. Ford v. Wainwright, 477 U.S. 399, 106 S.Ct. 2595, 91 L.Ed.2d 335 (1986).

A plurality of the Court also held that a panel of psychiatrists appointed by the Governor was an inadequate process to determine sanity. Id.

Powell, J., concluded a prisoner is insane for Eighth Amendment purposes if the prisoner is unaware of his impending execution and the reason for it. Id. p. 2609.

Louisiana statute which allowed the continued confinement of an insanity acquitee on the basis of antisocial personality, after a hospital review committee had reported no evidence of mental illness and recommended conditional discharge violated due process. Foucha v. Louisiana, 504 U.S. 71, 112 S.Ct. 1780, 118 L.Ed.2d 437 (1992).

15. Arteriosclerosis affecting the defendant's mental functions raises a M'Naghten issue. R. v. Kemp, [1957] 1 Q.B. 399. Compulsive gambling isn't a mental disease for insanity defense purposes. United States v. Lewellyn, 723 F.2d 615 (8th Cir.1983). Testimony on the effects of television in support of defendant's claim of "involuntary subliminal television intoxication" is not relevant on the issue of insanity. Zamora v. State, 361 So.2d 776 (Fla.App.1978).

Transient ischemic attack (TIA), a small stroke, was not a mental disease or defect within the meaning of the insanity defense. The evidence could still be used on whether defendant had the required "knowing" state of mind. Reed v. State, 693 N.E.2d 988 (Ind.App.1998).

Consider Utah Code Ann. § 76–2–305(4) (1990): "Mental illness means a mental disease or defect that substantially impairs a person's mental, emotional, or behavior functioning. A mental defect may be a congenital condition, the result of injury, or a residual effect of a physical or mental disease and includes, but is not limited to mental retardation. Mental

mental disease, physical disease, physical injury or congenital deficiency often will be placed loosely under the label "mental disease." This is because the consequences of all are the same, so far as the law of crimes is concerned. At times some other phrase has been used such as "mental disease or defect." This is more precise, but it is important to keep in mind that the term "mental disease" often is used in the cases to cover the entire field.

One interesting question in this general field is this: Can evidence of some kind or grade of mental disorder, insufficient for an acquittal, be sufficient to call for conviction of a lower grade or degree of crime than would otherwise be proper? There is some authority for a negative answer. Thus it has been held that mental disorder not amounting to "legal insanity" cannot negative deliberation and premeditation and thus reduce the homicide from first to second-degree murder.[16] The rule in several jurisdictions, however, is that such mental disorder may negative deliberation and premeditation,[17] leaving the question whether it may be sufficient to rule out malice aforethought. Several jurisdictions apply a rule that a mental disorder short of insanity that precludes the defendant from entertaining the required state of mind will reduce a charge to a lesser offense requiring a less demanding state of mind.[18]

Clark v. Arizona

Supreme Court of the United States, 2006.
548 U.S. 735, 126 S.Ct. 2709, 165 L.Ed.2d 842.

■ SOUTER, J., delivered the opinion of the Court, in which ROBERTS, C. J., and SCALIA, THOMAS, AND ALITO, JJ., joined, and in which BREYER, J., joined except as to Parts III–B and III–C and the ultimate disposition. BREYER, J., filed an opinion concurring in part and dissenting in part KENNEDY, J., filed a dissenting opinion, in which STEVENS and GINSBURG, JJ., joined.

■ JUSTICE SOUTER delivered the opinion of the Court.

---

illness does not mean a personality or character disorder or abnormality manifested only by repeated criminal conduct."

16. Fisher v. United States, 328 U.S. 463, 66 S.Ct. 1318, 90 L.Ed. 1382 (1946).

"[U]nless psychiatric testimony is introduced for the purpose of showing insanity under the M'Naghten Rule, (a) *it is admissible only after guilt has been determined by a jury or Court, and (b) is relevant and admissible thereafter only for the limited purpose of aiding the jury or Court in fixing the penalty.*" Commonwealth v. Rightnour, 435 Pa. 104, 253 A.2d 644, 649 (1969).

"We hold, therefore, that the partial defense of diminished capacity is not recognized in Ohio and consequently, a defendant may not offer expert psychiatric testimony, unrelated to the insanity defense...." State v. Wilcox, 70 Ohio St.2d 182, 436 N.E.2d 523, 533 (1982).

17. Disease of the mind, insufficient for acquittal, can prevent one from truly deliberating and from being capable of a deliberate premeditation necessary for guilt of first-degree murder. State v. Padilla, 66 N.M. 289, 347 P.2d 312 (1959).

18. "Therefore, although the State did not adopt Section 4.02 of the Model Penal Code, basic rules of evidence require that a defendant have the right to adduce evidence which would tend to disprove the existence of specific intent." State v. Sessions, 645 P.2d 643 (Utah 1982).

The case presents two questions: whether due process prohibits Arizona's use of an insanity test stated solely in terms of the capacity to tell whether an act charged as a crime was right or wrong; and whether Arizona violates due process in restricting consideration of defense evidence of mental illness and incapacity to its bearing on a claim of insanity, thus eliminating its significance directly on the issue of the mental element of the crime charged (known in legal shorthand as the *mens rea,* or guilty mind). We hold that there is no violation of due process in either instance.

I

In the early hours of June 21, 2000, Officer Jeffrey Moritz of the Flagstaff Police responded in uniform to complaints that a pickup truck with loud music blaring was circling a residential block. When he located the truck, the officer turned on the emergency lights and siren of his marked patrol car, which prompted petitioner Eric Clark, the truck's driver (then 17), to pull over. Officer Moritz got out of the patrol car and told Clark to stay where he was. Less than a minute later, Clark shot the officer, who died soon after but not before calling the police dispatcher for help. Clark ran away on foot but was arrested later that day with gunpowder residue on his hands; the gun that killed the officer was found nearby, stuffed into a knit cap.

Clark was charged with first-degree murder under Ariz.Rev.Stat. Ann. § 13–1105(A)(3) (West Supp.2005) for intentionally or knowingly killing a law enforcement officer in the line of duty.[1] In March 2001, Clark was found incompetent to stand trial and was committed to a state hospital for treatment, but two years later the same trial court found his competence restored and ordered him to be tried. Clark waived his right to a jury, and the case was heard by the court.

At trial, Clark did not contest the shooting and death, but relied on his undisputed paranoid schizophrenia at the time of the incident in denying that he had the specific intent to shoot a law enforcement officer or knowledge that he was doing so, as required by the statute. Accordingly, the prosecutor offered circumstantial evidence that Clark knew Officer Moritz was a law enforcement officer. The evidence showed that the officer was in uniform at the time, that he caught up with Clark in a marked police car with emergency lights and siren going, and that Clark acknowledged the symbols of police authority and stopped. The testimony for the prosecution indicated that Clark had intentionally lured an officer to the scene to kill him, having told some people a few weeks before the incident that he wanted to shoot police officers. At the close of the State's evidence, the trial court denied Clark's motion for judgment of acquittal for failure to prove intent to kill a law enforcement officer or knowledge that Officer Moritz was a law enforcement officer.

In presenting the defense case, Clark claimed mental illness, which he sought to introduce for two purposes. First, he raised the affirmative defense of insanity, putting the burden on himself to prove by clear and

---

1. Section 13–1105(A)(3) provides that "[a] person commits first degree murder if . . . [i]ntending or knowing that the person's conduct will cause death to a law enforcement officer, the person causes the death of a law enforcement officer who is in the line of duty."

convincing evidence, § 13–502(C) (West 2001), that "at the time of the commission of the criminal act [he] was afflicted with a mental disease or defect of such severity that [he] did not know the criminal act was wrong," § 13–502(A). Second, he aimed to rebut the prosecution's evidence of the requisite *mens rea,* that he had acted intentionally or knowingly to kill a law enforcement officer. See, *e.g.,* Record in No. CR 2000–538 (Ariz.Super.Ct.), Doc. 374 (hereinafter Record).

A defendant found "guilty except insane" is committed to a state mental-health facility for treatment. See § 13–502(D).

The trial court ruled that Clark could not rely on evidence bearing on insanity to dispute the *mens rea.* The court cited *State v. Mott,* 187 Ariz. 536, 931 P.2d 1046, cert. denied, 520 U.S. 1234, 117 S.Ct. 1832, 137 L.Ed.2d 1038 (1997), which "refused to allow psychiatric testimony to negate specific intent," 187 Ariz., at 541, 931 P.2d, at 1051, and held that "Arizona does not allow evidence of a defendant's mental disorder short of insanity . . . to negate the *mens rea* element of a crime," *ibid.*[3]

As to his insanity, then, Clark presented testimony from classmates, school officials, and his family describing his increasingly bizarre behavior over the year before the shooting. Witnesses testified, for example, that paranoid delusions led Clark to rig a fishing line with beads and wind chimes at home to alert him to intrusion by invaders, and to keep a bird in his automobile to warn of airborne poison. There was lay and expert testimony that Clark thought Flagstaff was populated with "aliens" (some impersonating government agents), the "aliens" were trying to kill him, and bullets were the only way to stop them. A psychiatrist testified that Clark was suffering from paranoid schizophrenia with delusions about "aliens" when he killed Officer Moritz, and he concluded that Clark was incapable of luring the officer or understanding right from wrong and that he was thus insane at the time of the killing. In rebuttal, a psychiatrist for the State gave his opinion that Clark's paranoid schizophrenia did not keep him from appreciating the wrongfulness of his conduct, as shown by his actions before and after the shooting (such as circling the residential block with music blaring as if to lure the police to intervene, evading the police after the shooting, and hiding the gun).

At the close of the defense case consisting of this evidence bearing on mental illness, the trial court denied Clark's renewed motion for a directed verdict grounded on failure of the prosecution to show that Clark knew the victim was a police officer.[4] The judge then issued a special verdict of first-degree murder, expressly finding that Clark shot and caused the death of Officer Moritz beyond a reasonable doubt and that Clark had not shown that he was insane at the time. The judge noted that though Clark was indisputably afflicted with paranoid schizophrenia at the time of the

3. The trial court permitted Clark to introduce this evidence, whether primarily going to insanity or lack of intent, "because it goes to the insanity issue and because we're not in front of a jury." App. 9. It also allowed him to make an offer of proof as to intent to preserve the issue on appeal. *Ibid.*

4. Clark did not at this time make an additional offer of proof, as contemplated by the trial court when it ruled that it would consider evidence bearing on insanity as to insanity but not as to *mens rea.* See n. 3, *supra.*

shooting, the mental illness "did not . . . distort his perception of reality so severely that he did not know his actions were wrong." For this conclusion, the judge expressly relied on "the facts of the crime, the evaluations of the experts, [Clark's] actions and behavior both before and after the shooting, and the observations of those that knew [Clark]." *Id.,* at 333. The sentence was life imprisonment without the possibility of release for 25 years.

Clark moved to vacate the judgment and sentence, arguing, among other things, that Arizona's insanity test and its *Mott* rule each violate due process. As to the insanity standard, Clark claimed (as he had argued earlier) that the Arizona Legislature had impermissibly narrowed its standard in 1993 when it eliminated the first part of the two-part insanity test announced in *M'Naghten's Case,* 10 Cl. & Fin. 200, 8 Eng. Rep. 718 (1843). The court denied the motion.

The Court of Appeals of Arizona affirmed Clark's conviction, treating the conclusion on sanity as supported by enough evidence to withstand review for abuse of discretion, and holding the State's insanity scheme consistent with due process. As to the latter, the Court of Appeals reasoned that there is no constitutional requirement to recognize an insanity defense at all, the bounds of which are left to the State's discretion. Beyond that, the appellate court followed *Mott,* reading it as barring the trial court's consideration of evidence of Clark's mental illness and capacity directly on the element of *mens rea.* The Supreme Court of Arizona denied further review.

We granted certiorari to decide whether due process prohibits Arizona from thus narrowing its insanity test or from excluding evidence of mental illness and incapacity due to mental illness to rebut evidence of the requisite criminal intent. We now affirm.

II

Clark first says that Arizona's definition of insanity, being only a fragment of the Victorian standard from which it derives, violates due process. The landmark English rule in *M'Naghten's Case, supra,* states that

> "the jurors ought to be told . . . that to establish a defence on the ground of insanity, it must be clearly proved that, at the time of the committing of the act, the party accused was laboring under such a defect of reason, from disease of the mind, as not to know the nature and quality of the act he was doing; or, if he did know it, that he did not know he was doing what was wrong." *Id.,* at 210, 8 Eng. Rep., at 722.

The first part asks about cognitive capacity: whether a mental defect leaves a defendant unable to understand what he is doing. The second part presents an ostensibly alternative basis for recognizing a defense of insanity understood as a lack of moral capacity: whether a mental disease or defect leaves a defendant unable to understand that his action is wrong.

When the Arizona Legislature first codified an insanity rule, it adopted the full *M'Naghten* statement (subject to modifications in details that do not matter here):

"A person is not responsible for criminal conduct if at the time of such conduct the person was suffering from such a mental disease or defect as not to know the nature and quality of the act or, if such person did know, that such person did not know that what he was doing was wrong." Ariz.Rev.Stat. Ann. § 13–502 (West 1978).

In 1993, the legislature dropped the cognitive incapacity part, leaving only moral incapacity as the nub of the stated definition. See 1993 Ariz. Sess. Laws ch. 256, §§ 2–3.[6] Under current Arizona law, a defendant will not be adjudged insane unless he demonstrates that "at the time of the commission of the criminal act [he] was afflicted with a mental disease or defect of such severity that [he] did not know the criminal act was wrong," Ariz.Rev.Stat. Ann. § 13–502(A) (West 2001).

A

Clark challenges the 1993 amendment excising the express reference to the cognitive incapacity element. He insists that the side-by-side *M'Naghten* test represents the minimum that a government must provide in recognizing an alternative to criminal responsibility on grounds of mental illness or defect, and he argues that elimination of the *M'Naghten* reference to nature and quality " 'offends [a] principle of justice so rooted in the traditions and conscience of our people as to be ranked as fundamental,' " *Patterson v. New York,* 432 U.S. 197, 202, 97 S.Ct. 2319, 53 L.Ed.2d 281 (1977) (quoting *Speiser v. Randall,* 357 U.S. 513, 523, 78 S.Ct. 1332, 2 L.Ed.2d 1460 (1958)); see also *Leland v. Oregon,* 343 U.S. 790, 798, 72 S.Ct. 1002, 96 L.Ed. 1302 (1952).

The claim entails no light burden, see*Montana v.Egelhoff,* 518 U.S. 37, 43, 116 S.Ct. 2013, 135 L.Ed.2d 361 (1996) (plurality opinion), and Clark does not carry it. History shows no deference to *M'Naghten* that could elevate its formula to the level of fundamental principle, so as to limit the traditional recognition of a State's capacity to define crimes and defenses, see *Patterson, supra,* at 210, 97 S.Ct. 2319; see also *Foucha v. Louisiana,* 504 U.S. 71, 96, 112 S.Ct. 1780, 118 L.Ed.2d 437 (1992) (KENNEDY, J., dissenting).

Even a cursory examination of the traditional Anglo–American approaches to insanity reveals significant differences among them, with four traditional strains variously combined to yield a diversity of American standards. The main variants are the cognitive incapacity, the moral incapacity, the volitional incapacity, and the product-of-mental-illness tests.[7] The first two emanate from the alternatives stated in the *M'Naghten* rule. The volitional incapacity or irresistible-impulse test, which surfaced

---

6. This change was accompanied by others, principally an enumeration of mental states excluded from the category of "mental disease or defect," such as voluntary intoxication and other conditions, and a change of the insanity verdict from "not responsible for criminal conduct" by reason of insanity to "guilty except insane." See 1993 Ariz. Sess. Laws ch. 256, §§ 2–3. The 1993 amendments were prompted, at least in part, by an acquittal by reason of insanity in a murder case. See Note, Arizona's Insane Response to Insanity, 40 Ariz. L.Rev. 287, 290 (1998).

7. "Capacity" is understood to mean the ability to form a certain state of mind or motive, understand or evaluate one's actions, or control them.

over two centuries ago (first in England,[8] then in this country[9]), asks whether a person was so lacking in volition due to a mental defect or illness that he could not have controlled his actions. And the product-of-mental-illness test was used as early as 1870,[10] and simply asks whether a person's action was a product of a mental disease or defect.[11] Seventeen States and the Federal Government have adopted a recognizable version of the *M'Naghten* test with both its cognitive incapacity and moral incapacity components. One State [Alaska] has adopted only *M'Naghten's* cognitive incapacity test, and 10 (including Arizona) have adopted the moral incapacity test alone. Fourteen jurisdictions, inspired by the Model Penal Code,[15] have in place an amalgam of the volitional incapacity test and some variant of the moral incapacity test, satisfaction of either (generally by showing a defendant's substantial lack of capacity) being enough to excuse. Three States combine a full *M'Naghten* test with a volitional incapacity formula. And New Hampshire alone stands by the product-of-mental-illness test. The alternatives are multiplied further by variations in the prescribed insanity verdict: a significant number of these jurisdictions supplement the traditional "not guilty by reason of insanity" verdict with an alternative of "guilty but mentally ill." Finally, four States have no affirmative insanity defense,[20] though one provides for a "guilty and mentally ill" verdict. These four, like a number of others that recognize an affirmative insanity defense, allow consideration of evidence of mental illness directly on the element of *mens rea* defining the offense.

With this varied background, it is clear that no particular formulation has evolved into a baseline for due process, and that the insanity rule, like

---

8. See *Queen v. Oxford,* 9 Car. & P. 525, 546, 173 Eng. Rep. 941, 950 (1840) ("If some controlling disease was, in truth, the acting power within [the defendant] which he could not resist, then he will not be responsible"); *Hadfield's Case,* 27 How. St. Tr. 1281, 1314–1315, 1354–1355 (K.B.1800). But cf. *Queen v. Burton,* 3 F. & F. 772, 780, 176 Eng. Rep. 354, 357 (1863) (rejecting the irresistible-impulse test as "a most dangerous doctrine").

9. *E.g., Parsons v. State,* 81 Ala. 577, 2 So. 854 (1887); *State v. Thompson,* Wright's Ohio Rep. 617 (1834).

10. *State v. Jones,* 50 N.H. 369 (1871); *State v. Pike,* 49 N.H. 399 (1870).

11. This distillation of the Anglo–American insanity standards into combinations of four building blocks should not be read to signify that no other components contribute to these insanity standards or that there are no material distinctions between jurisdictions testing insanity with the same building blocks. For example, the jurisdictions limit, in varying degrees, which sorts of mental illness or defect can give rise to a successful insanity defense. Compare, *e.g.,* Ariz.Rev.Stat. Ann. § 13–502(A) (West 2001) (excluding from definition of "mental disease or defect" acute voluntary intoxication, withdrawal from alcohol or drugs, character defects, psychosexual disorders, and impulse control disorders) with, *e.g.,*Ind.Code § 35–41–3–6(b) (West 2004) (excluding from definition of "mental disease or defect" "abnormality manifested only by repeated unlawful or antisocial conduct"). We need not compare the standards under a finer lens because our coarser analysis shows that the standards vary significantly.

15. ALI, Model Penal Code § 4.01(1), p. 66 (Proposed Official Draft 1962) ("A person is not responsible for criminal conduct if at the time of such conduct as a result of mental disease or defect he lacks substantial capacity either to appreciate the criminality [wrongfulness] of his conduct or to conform his conduct to the requirements of law").

20. Idaho Code § 18–207 (Lexis 2004); Kan. Stat. Ann. § 22–3220 (1995); Mont.Code Ann. §§ 46–14–102, 46–14–311 (2005); Utah Code Ann. § 76–2–305 (Lexis 2003). We have never held that the Constitution mandates an insanity defense, nor have we held that the Constitution does not so require. This case does not call upon us to decide the matter.

the conceptualization of criminal offenses, is substantially open to state choice. Indeed, the legitimacy of such choice is the more obvious when one considers the interplay of legal concepts of mental illness or deficiency required for an insanity defense, with the medical concepts of mental abnormality that influence the expert opinion testimony by psychologists and psychiatrists commonly introduced to support or contest insanity claims. For medical definitions devised to justify treatment, like legal ones devised to excuse from conventional criminal responsibility, are subject to flux and disagreement. See *infra;* cf. *Leland,* 343 U.S., at 800–801, 72 S.Ct. 1002 (no due process violation for adopting the *M'Naghten* standard rather than the irresistible-impulse test because scientific knowledge does not require otherwise and choice of test is a matter of policy). There being such fodder for reasonable debate about what the cognate legal and medical tests should be, due process imposes no single canonical formulation of legal insanity.

B

Nor does Arizona's abbreviation of the *M'Naghten* statement raise a proper claim that some constitutional minimum has been shortchanged. Clark's argument of course assumes that Arizona's former statement of the *M'Naghten* rule, with its express alternative of cognitive incapacity, was constitutionally adequate (as we agree). That being so, the abbreviated rule is no less so, for cognitive incapacity is relevant under that statement, just as it was under the more extended formulation, and evidence going to cognitive incapacity has the same significance under the short form as it had under the long.

Though Clark is correct that the application of the moral incapacity test (telling right from wrong) does not necessarily require evaluation of a defendant's cognitive capacity to appreciate the nature and quality of the acts charged against him, his argument fails to recognize that cognitive incapacity is itself enough to demonstrate moral incapacity. Cognitive incapacity, in other words, is a sufficient condition for establishing a defense of insanity, albeit not a necessary one. As a defendant can therefore make out moral incapacity by demonstrating cognitive incapacity, evidence bearing on whether the defendant knew the nature and quality of his actions is both relevant and admissible. In practical terms, if a defendant did not know what he was doing when he acted, he could not have known that he was performing the wrongful act charged as a crime.[23] Indeed, when the two-part rule was still in effect, the Supreme Court of Arizona held that a jury instruction on insanity containing the moral incapacity part but not a full recitation of the cognitive incapacity part was fine, as the cognitive incapacity part might be " 'treated as adding nothing to the requirement that the accused know his act was wrong.' " *State v. Chavez,*

---

23. He might, of course, have thought delusively he was doing something just as wrongful as the act charged against him, but this is not the test: he must have understood that he was committing the act charged and that it was wrongful, see Ariz.Rev.Stat. Ann. § 13–502(A) (West 2001) ("A person may be found guilty except insane if at the time of the commission of the criminal act the person was afflicted with a mental disease or defect of such severity that the person did not know the criminal act was wrong").

143 Ariz. 238, 239, 693 P.2d 893, 894 (1984) (quoting A. Goldstein, The Insanity Defense 50 (1967)).

The Court of Appeals of Arizona acknowledged as much in this case, too ("It is difficult to imagine that a defendant who did not appreciate the 'nature and quality' of the act he committed would reasonably be able to perceive that the act was 'wrong' "), and thus aligned itself with the long-accepted understanding that the cognitively incapacitated are a subset of the morally incapacitated within the meaning of the standard *M'Naghten* rule, see, *e.g.,* Goldstein, *supra,* at 51 ("In those situations where the accused does not know the nature and quality of his act, in the broad sense, he will not know that it was wrong, no matter what construction 'wrong' is given"); 1 W. LaFave, Substantive Criminal Law § 7.2(b)(3), p. 536 (2d ed. 2003) ("Many courts feel that knowledge of 'the nature and quality of the act' is the mere equivalent of the ability to know that the act was wrong" (citing cases)); *id.,* § 7.2(b)(4), at 537 ("If the defendant does not know the nature and quality of his act, then quite obviously he does not know that his act is 'wrong,' and this is true without regard to the interpretation given to the word 'wrong' "); cf. 1 R. Gerber, Criminal Law of Arizona 502–7, n. 1 (2d ed.1993).[24]

Clark, indeed, adopted this very analysis himself in the trial court: "[I]f [Clark] did not know he was shooting at a police officer, or believed he had to shoot or be shot, even though his belief was not based in reality, this would establish that he did not know what he was doing was wrong.". The trial court apparently agreed, for the judge admitted Clark's evidence of cognitive incapacity for consideration under the State's moral incapacity formulation. And Clark can point to no evidence bearing on insanity that was excluded. His psychiatric expert and a number of lay witnesses testified to his delusions, and this evidence tended to support a description of Clark as lacking the capacity to understand that the police officer was a human

---

24. We think this logic holds true in the face of the usual rule of statutory construction of " ' "giv[ing] effect, if possible, to every clause and word of a statute," ' " *Duncan v. Walker,* 533 U.S. 167, 174, 121 S.Ct. 2120, 150 L.Ed.2d 251 (2001) (quoting *United States v. Menasche,* 348 U.S. 528, 538–539, 75 S.Ct. 513, 99 L.Ed. 615 (1955)); see also 2 J. Sutherland, Statutes and Statutory Construction § 4705 (3d ed.1943). Insanity standards are formulated to guide the factfinder to determine the blameworthiness of a mentally ill defendant. See, *e.g., Jones v. United States,* 463 U.S. 354, 373, n. 4, 103 S.Ct. 3043, 77 L.Ed.2d 694 (1983) (Brennan, J., dissenting). The *M'Naghten* test is a sequential test, first asking the factfinder to conduct the easier enquiry whether a defendant knew the nature and quality of his actions. If not, the defendant is to be considered insane and there is no need to pass to the harder and broader enquiry whether the defendant knew his actions were wrong. And, because, owing to this sequence, the factfinder is to ask whether a defendant lacks moral capacity only when he possesses cognitive capacity, the only defendants who will be found to lack moral capacity are those possessing cognitive capacity. Cf. 2 C. Torcia, Wharton's Criminal Law § 101 (15th ed.1994). Though, before 1993, Arizona had in place the full *M'Naghten* test with this sequential enquiry, see, *e.g., Schantz,* 98 Ariz., at 207, 403 P.2d, at 525, it would appear that the legislature eliminated the cognitive capacity part not to change the meaning of the insanity standard but to implement its judgment that a streamlined standard with only the moral capacity part would be easier for the jury to apply, see Arizona House of Representatives, Judiciary Committee Notes 3 (Mar. 18, 1993); 1 R. Gerber, Criminal Law of Arizona 502–6, 502–11 (2d ed.1993 and Supp.2000). This is corroborated by the State's choice for many years against revising the applicable recommended jury instruction (enumerating the complete *M'Naghten* test) in order to match the amended statutory standard. See 1 Gerber, *supra,* at 502–6 (2d ed.1993 and Supp.2000).

being. There is no doubt that the trial judge considered the evidence as going to an issue of cognitive capacity, for in finding insanity not proven he said that Clark's mental illness "did not . . . distort his perception of reality so severely that he did not know his actions were wrong,"

We are satisfied that neither in theory nor in practice did Arizona's 1993 abridgment of the insanity formulation deprive Clark of due process.

III

Clark's second claim of a due process violation challenges the rule adopted by the Supreme Court of Arizona in *State v. Mott,* 187 Ariz. 536, 931 P.2d 1046, cert. denied, 520 U.S. 1234, 117 S.Ct. 1832, 137 L.Ed.2d 1038 (1997). This case ruled on the admissibility of testimony from a psychologist offered to show that the defendant suffered from battered women's syndrome and therefore lacked the capacity to form the *mens rea* of the crime charged against her. The opinion variously referred to the testimony in issue as "psychological testimony," 187 Ariz., at 541, 931 P.2d, at 1051, and "expert testimony," *ibid.,* and implicitly equated it with "expert psychiatric evidence," *id.,* at 540, 931 P.2d, at 1050 (internal quotation marks omitted), and "psychiatric testimony," *id.,* at 541, 931 P.2d, at 1051.[25] The state court held that testimony of a professional psychologist or psychiatrist about a defendant's mental incapacity owing to mental disease or defect was admissible, and could be considered, only for its bearing on an insanity defense; such evidence could not be considered on the element of *mens rea,* that is, what the State must show about a defendant's mental state (such as intent or understanding) when he performed the act charged against him. See *id.,* at 541, 544, 931 P.2d, at 1051, 1054.[26]

A

Understanding Clark's claim requires attention to the categories of evidence with a potential bearing on *mens rea*. First, there is "observation evidence" in the everyday sense, testimony from those who observed what Clark did and heard what he said; this category would also include testimony that an expert witness might give about Clark's tendency to think in a certain way and his behavioral characteristics. This evidence may support a professional diagnosis of mental disease and in any event is the kind of evidence that can be relevant to show what in fact was on Clark's mind when he fired the gun. Observation evidence in the record covers Clark's behavior at home and with friends, his expressions of belief around the time of the killing that "aliens" were inhabiting the bodies of local people (including government agents),[27] his driving around the neigh-

---

25. We thus think the dissent reads *Mott* too broadly. See *post,* (opinion of KENNEDY, J.) (no distinction between observation and mental-disease testimony, or lay and expert).

26. The more natural reading of *Mott* suggests to us that this evidence cannot be considered as to *mens rea* even if the defendant establishes his insanity, though one might read *Mott* otherwise.

27. Clark's parents testified that, in the months before the shooting and even days beforehand, Clark called them "aliens" and thought that "aliens" were out to get him. See, *e.g.,* Tr. of Bench Trial in No. CR 2000–538, pp. 110–112, 136, 226–228 (Aug. 20, 2003). One

borhood before the police arrived, and so on. Contrary to the dissent's characterization, see (opinion of KENNEDY, J.), observation evidence can be presented by either lay or expert witnesses.

Second, there is "mental-disease evidence" in the form of opinion testimony that Clark suffered from a mental disease with features described by the witness. As was true here, this evidence characteristically but not always comes from professional psychologists or psychiatrists who testify as expert witnesses and base their opinions in part on examination of a defendant, usually conducted after the events in question. The thrust of this evidence was that, based on factual reports, professional observations, and tests, Clark was psychotic at the time in question, with a condition that fell within the category of schizophrenia.

Third, there is evidence we will refer to as "capacity evidence" about a defendant's capacity for cognition and moral judgment (and ultimately also his capacity to form *mens rea*). This, too, is opinion evidence. Here, as it usually does,[29] this testimony came from the same experts and concentrated on those specific details of the mental condition that make the difference between sanity and insanity under the Arizona definition.[30] In their respective testimony on these details the experts disagreed: the defense expert gave his opinion that the symptoms or effects of the disease in Clark's case included inability to appreciate the nature of his action and to tell that it was wrong, whereas the State's psychiatrist was of the view that Clark was a schizophrenic who was still sufficiently able to appreciate the reality of shooting the officer and to know that it was wrong to do that.[31]

night before the shooting, according to Clark's mother, Clark repeatedly viewed a popular film characterized by her as telling a story about "aliens" masquerading as government agents, a story Clark insisted was real despite his mother's protestations to the contrary. See *id.,* at 59–60 (Aug. 21, 2003). And two months after the shooting, Clark purportedly told his parents that his hometown, Flagstaff, was inhabited principally by "aliens," who had to be stopped, and that the only way to stop them was with bullets. See, *e.g., id.,* at 131–132 (Aug. 20, 2003); *id.,* at 24–25 (Aug. 21, 2003).

29. In conflict with the dissent's characterization, see *post,* (opinion of KENNEDY, J.), it does not always, however, come from experts.

30. Arizona permits capacity evidence, see, *e.g., State v. Sanchez,* 117 Ariz. 369, 373, 573 P.2d 60, 64 (1977); see also Ariz. Rule Evid. 704 (2006) (allowing otherwise admissible evidence on testimony "embrac[ing] an ultimate issue to be decided by the trier of fact"), though not every jurisdiction permits such evidence on the ultimate issue of insanity. See, *e.g.,* Fed. Rule Evid. 704(b) ("No expert witness testifying with respect to the mental state or condition of a defendant in a criminal case may state an opinion or inference as to whether the defendant did or did not have the mental state or condition constituting an element of the crime charged or of a defense thereto. Such ultimate issues are matters for the trier of fact alone"); *United States v. Dixon,* 185 F.3d 393, 400 (C.A.5 1999) (in the face of mental-disease evidence, Rule 704(b) prohibits an expert "from testifying that [the mental-disease evidence] does or does not prevent the defendant from appreciating the wrongfulness of his actions").

31. Arizona permits evidence bearing on insanity to be presented by either lay or expert witnesses. See *State v. Bay,* 150 Ariz. 112, 116, 722 P.2d 280, 284 (1986). According to *Bay,* "[f]oundationally, a lay witness must have had an opportunity to observe the past conduct and history of a defendant; the fact that he is a lay witness goes not to the admissibility of the testimony but rather to its weight." *Ibid.* (citation omitted); see also *State v. Hughes,* 193 Ariz. 72, 83, 969 P.2d 1184, 1195 (1998). In fact, a defendant can theoretically establish insanity solely via lay testimony. See *Bay, supra,* at 116, 722 P.2d, at 284. But cf. *State v. McMurtrey,* 136 Ariz. 93, 100, 664 P.2d 637, 644 (1983) ("[I]t is difficult to imagine how a defendant could place his or her sanity in issue ... without expert testimony as to the defendant's state of mind at the time of the crime").

A caveat about these categories is in order. They attempt to identify different kinds of testimony offered in this case in terms of explicit and implicit distinctions made in *Mott*. What we can say about these categories goes to their cores, however, not their margins. Exact limits have thus not been worked out in any Arizona law that has come to our attention, and in this case, neither the courts in their rulings nor counsel in objections invoked or required precision in applying the *Mott* rule's evidentiary treatment, as we explain below. Necessarily, then, our own decision can address only core issues, leaving for other cases any due process claims that may be raised about the treatment of evidence whose categorization is subject to dispute.

B

It is clear that *Mott* itself imposed no restriction on considering evidence of the first sort, the observation evidence. We read the *Mott* restriction to apply, rather, to evidence addressing the two issues in testimony that characteristically comes only from psychologists or psychiatrists qualified to give opinions as expert witnesses: mental-disease evidence (whether at the time of the crime a defendant suffered from a mental disease or defect, such as schizophrenia) and capacity evidence (whether the disease or defect left him incapable of performing or experiencing a mental process defined as necessary for sanity such as appreciating the nature and quality of his act and knowing that it was wrong).

Mott was careful to distinguish this kind of opinion evidence from observation evidence generally and even from observation evidence that an expert witness might offer, such as descriptions of a defendant's tendency to think in a certain way or his behavioral characteristics; the Arizona court made it clear that this sort of testimony was perfectly admissible to rebut the prosecution's evidence of *mens rea,* 187 Ariz., at 544, 931 P.2d, at 1054. Thus, only opinion testimony going to mental defect or disease, and its effect on the cognitive or moral capacities on which sanity depends under the Arizona rule, is restricted.

In this case, the trial court seems to have applied the *Mott* restriction to all evidence offered by Clark for the purpose of showing what he called his inability to form the required *mens rea,* see, *e.g.,* Record, Doc. 406, at 7–10 (that is, an intent to kill a police officer on duty, or an understanding that he was engaging in the act of killing such an officer, see Ariz.Rev.Stat. Ann. § 13–1105(A)(3) (West Supp.2005)). Thus, the trial court's restriction may have covered not only mental-disease and capacity evidence as just defined, but also observation evidence offered by lay (and expert) witnesses who described Clark's unusual behavior. Clark's objection to the application of the *Mott* rule does not, however, turn on the distinction between lay and expert witnesses or the kinds of testimony they were competent to present.[32]

---

32. With respect to "the limited factual issues the trial court held it could consider under [Ariz.Rev.Stat. Ann.] § 13–502 and *Mott,* defense counsel made no additional 'offer of proof' at the conclusion of the case but preserved [Clark's] legal contentions by asking the court to consider all of the evidence presented in determining whether the state had proved its case." Brief for Petitioner 10, n. 20 (citation omitted).

C

There is some, albeit limited, disagreement between the dissent and ourselves about the scope of the claim of error properly before us. To start with matters of agreement, all Members of the Court agree that Clark's general attack on the *Mott* rule covers its application in confining consideration of capacity evidence to the insanity defense.

In practical terms, our agreement on issues presented extends to a second point. JUSTICE KENNEDY understands that Clark raised an objection to confining mental-disease evidence to the insanity issue. As he sees it, Clark in effect claimed that in dealing with the issue of *mens rea* the trial judge should have considered expert testimony on what may characteristically go through the mind of a schizophrenic, when the judge considered what in fact was in Clark's mind at the time of the shooting. See *post,* (dissenting opinion) ("[T]he opinion that Clark had paranoid schizophrenia-an opinion shared by experts for both the prosecution and defense-bears on efforts to determine, as a factual matter, whether he knew he was killing a police officer"). He thus understands that defense counsel claimed a right to rebut the State's *mens rea* demonstration with testimony about how schizophrenics may hallucinate voices and other sounds, about their characteristic failure to distinguish the content of their imagination from what most people perceive as exterior reality, and so on. It is important to be clear that this supposed objection was not about dealing with testimony based on observation of Clark showing that he had auditory hallucinations when he was driving around, or failed in fact to appreciate objective reality when he shot; this objection went to use of testimony about schizophrenics, not about Clark in particular. While we might dispute how clearly Clark raised this objection, we have no doubt that the objection falls within a general challenge to the *Mott* rule; we understand that *Mott* is meant to confine to the insanity defense any consideration of characteristic behavior associated with mental disease, see 187 Ariz., at 544, 931 P.2d, at 1054 (contrasting *State v. Christensen,* 129 Ariz. 32, 628 P.2d 580 (1981), and *State v. Gonzales,* 140 Ariz. 349, 681 P.2d 1368 (1984)). We will therefore assume for argument that Clark raised this claim, as we consider the due process challenge to the *Mott* rule.

The point on which we disagree with the dissent, however, is this: did Clark apprise the Arizona courts that he believed the trial judge had erroneously limited the consideration of observation evidence, whether from lay witnesses like Clark's mother or (possibly) the expert witnesses who observed him? This sort of evidence was not covered by the *Mott* restriction, and confining it to the insanity issue would have been an erroneous application of *Mott* as a matter of Arizona law. For the following reasons we think no such objection was made in a way the Arizona courts could have understood it, and that no such issue is before us now. We think the only issue properly before us is the challenge to *Mott* on due process grounds, comprising objections to limits on the use of mental-disease and capacity evidence.

It is clear that the trial judge intended to apply *Mott:*

"[R]ecognizing that much of the evidence that [the defense is] going to be submitting, in fact all of it, as far as I know ... that has to do with the insanity could also arguably be made along the lines of the Mott issues as to form and intent and his capacity for the intent. I'm going to let you go ahead and get all that stuff in because it goes to the insanity issue and because we're not in front of a jury. At the end, I'll let you make an offer of proof as to the intent, the Mott issues, but I still think the supreme court decision is the law of the land in this state."

At no point did the trial judge specify any particular evidence that he refused to consider on the *mens rea* issue. Nor did defense counsel specify any observation or other particular evidence that he claimed was admissible but wrongly excluded on the issue of *mens rea,* so as to produce a clearer ruling on what evidence was being restricted on the authority of *Mott* and what was not. He made no "offer of proof" in the trial court; [33] and although his brief in the Arizona Court of Appeals stated at one point that it was not inconsistent with *Mott* to consider nonexpert evidence indicating mental illness on the issue of *mens rea,* and argued that the trial judge had failed to do so, Appellant's Opening Brief in No. 1CA–CR–03–0851 etc., pp. 48–49 (hereinafter Appellant's Opening Brief), he was no more specific than that, see, *e.g., id.,* at 52 ("The Court's ruling in *Mott* and the trial court's refusal to consider whether as a result of suffering from paranoid schizophrenia [Clark] could not formulate the *mens rea* necessary for first degree murder violated his right to due process"). Similarly, we read the Arizona Court of Appeals to have done nothing more than rely on *Mott* to reject the claim that due process forbids restricting evidence bearing on "*[a]bility to [f]orm [m]ens [r]ea,*" (emphasis in original), (*i.e.,* mental-disease and capacity evidence) to the insanity determination.

This failure in the state courts to raise any clear claim about observation evidence, see Appellant's Opening Brief 46–52, is reflected in the material addressed to us, see Brief for Petitioner 13–32. In this Court both the question presented and the following statement of his position were couched in similarly worded general terms:

"I. ERIC WAS DENIED DUE PROCESS WHEN THE TRIAL COURT REFUSED TO CONSIDER EVIDENCE OF HIS SEVERE MENTAL ILLNESS IN DETERMINING FACTUALLY WHETHER THE PROSECUTION PROVED THE MENTAL ELEMENTS OF THE CRIME CHARGED." *Id.,* at 13.

But as his counsel made certain beyond doubt in his reply brief,

"Eric's Point I is and always has been an attack on the rule of *State v. Mott,* which both courts below held applicable and binding. *Mott* announced a categorical 'rejection of the use of psychological testimony to challenge the *mens rea* element of a crime,' and upheld this rule against federal due process challenge." Reply Brief for Petitioner 2 (citations omitted).

---

33. We do not agree with the State's argument that the failure to make an offer of proof, see n. 4, *supra,* is a bar to pressing Clark's claim about the admissibility of mental-illness or capacity evidence as to *mens rea,* see Brief for Respondent 27–29, especially when the Arizona Court of Appeals rejected Clark's argument on the merits rather than clearly on this ground, see App. 351–353; see also *Michigan v. Long,* 463 U.S. 1032, 1042, 103 S.Ct. 3469, 77 L.Ed.2d 1201 (1983) ("[I]t is not clear from the opinion itself that the state court relied upon an adequate and independent state ground and ... it fairly appears that the state court rested its decision primarily on federal law").

This explanation is supported by other statements in Clark's briefs in both the State Court of Appeals and this Court, replete with the consistently maintained claim that it was error to limit evidence of mental illness and incapacity to its bearing on the insanity defense, excluding it from consideration on the element of *mens rea.* See, *e.g.,* Appellant's Opening Brief 46, 47, 51; Brief for Petitioner 11, 13, 16, 20–23.

In sum, the trial court's ruling, with its uncertain edges, may have restricted observation evidence admissible on *mens rea* to the insanity defense alone, but we cannot be sure.[34] But because a due process challenge to such a restriction of observation evidence was, by our measure, neither pressed nor passed upon in the Arizona Court of Appeals, we do not consider it. See, *e.g., Kentucky v. Stincer,* 482 U.S. 730, 747, n. 22, 107 S.Ct. 2658, 96 L.Ed.2d 631 (1987); *Illinois v. Gates,* 462 U.S. 213, 217–224, 103 S.Ct. 2317, 76 L.Ed.2d 527 (1983). What we do know, and now consider, is Clark's claim that *Mott* denied due process because it *"preclude[d] Eric from contending that ... factual inferences"* of the "mental states which were necessary elements of the crime charged" *"should not be drawn* because the behavior was explainable, instead, as a manifestation of his chronic paranoid schizophrenia." Brief for Petitioner 13 (emphasis in original). We consider the claim, as Clark otherwise puts it, that "Arizona's prohibition of 'diminished capacity' evidence by criminal defendants violates" due process, *ibid.*

D

Clark's argument that the *Mott* rule violates the Fourteenth Amendment guarantee of due process turns on the application of the presumption of innocence in criminal cases, the presumption of sanity, and the principle that a criminal defendant is entitled to present relevant and favorable evidence on an element of the offense charged against him.

1

The first presumption is that a defendant is innocent unless and until the government proves beyond a reasonable doubt each element of the offense charged, see *Patterson,* 432 U.S., at 210–211, 97 S.Ct. 2319; *In re Winship,* 397 U.S. 358, 361–364, 90 S.Ct. 1068, 25 L.Ed.2d 368 (1970), including the mental element or *mens rea.* Before the last century, the *mens rea* required to be proven for particular offenses was often described in general terms like "malice," see, *e.g., In re Eckart,* 166 U.S. 481, 17 S.Ct. 638, 41 L.Ed. 1085 (1897); 4 W. Blackstone, Commentaries *21 ("[A]n unwarrantable act without a vicious will is no crime at all"), but the

---

34. We therefore have no reason to believe that the courts of Arizona would have failed to restrict their application of *Mott* to the professional testimony the *Mott* opinion was stated to cover, if Clark's counsel had specified any observation evidence he claimed to be generally admissible and relevant to *mens rea.* Nothing that we hold here is authority for restricting a factfinder's consideration of observation evidence indicating state of mind at the time of a criminal offense (conventional *mens rea* evidence) as distinct from professional mental-disease or capacity evidence going to ability to form a certain state of mind during a period that includes the time of the offense charged. And, of course, nothing held here prevents Clark from raising this discrete claim when the case returns to the courts of Arizona, if consistent with the State's procedural rules.

modern tendency has been toward more specific descriptions, as shown in the Arizona statute defining the murder charged against Clark: the State had to prove that in acting to kill the victim, Clark intended to kill a law enforcement officer on duty or knew that the victim was such an officer on duty. See generally Gardner, The *Mens Rea* Enigma: Observations on the Role of Motive in the Criminal Law Past and Present, 1993 Utah L.Rev. 635. As applied to *mens rea* (and every other element), the force of the presumption of innocence is measured by the force of the showing needed to overcome it, which is proof beyond a reasonable doubt that a defendant's state of mind was in fact what the charge states. See *Winship, supra,* at 361–363, 90 S.Ct. 1068.

2

The presumption of sanity is equally universal in some variety or other, being (at least) a presumption that a defendant has the capacity to form the *mens rea* necessary for a verdict of guilt and the consequent criminal responsibility. See *Leland,* 343 U.S., at 799, 72 S.Ct. 1002; *Davis v. United States,* 160 U.S. 469, 486–487, 16 S.Ct. 353, 40 L.Ed. 499 (1895); *M'Naghten's Case,* 10 Cl. & Fin., at 210, 8 Eng. Rep., at 722; see generally 1 LaFave, Substantive Criminal Law § 8.3(a), at 598–599, and n. 1. This presumption dispenses with a requirement on the government's part to include as an element of every criminal charge an allegation that the defendant had such a capacity. The force of this presumption, like the presumption of innocence, is measured by the quantum of evidence necessary to overcome it; unlike the presumption of innocence, however, the force of the presumption of sanity varies across the many state and federal jurisdictions, and prior law has recognized considerable leeway on the part of the legislative branch in defining the presumption's strength through the kind of evidence and degree of persuasiveness necessary to overcome it, see *Fisher v. United States,* 328 U.S. 463, 466–476, 66 S.Ct. 1318, 90 L.Ed. 1382 (1946).[36]

There are two points where the sanity or capacity presumption may be placed in issue. First, a State may allow a defendant to introduce (and a factfinder to consider) evidence of mental disease or incapacity for the bearing it can have on the government's burden to show *mens rea.* See, *e.g., State v. Perez,* 882 A.2d 574, 584 (R.I.2005).[37] In such States the evidence showing incapacity to form the guilty state of mind, for example, qualifies the probative force of other evidence, which considered alone indicates that the defendant actually formed the guilty state of mind. If it is shown that a defendant with mental disease thinks all blond people are robots, he could not have intended to kill a person when he shot a man with blond hair,

---

36. Although a desired evidentiary use is restricted, that is not equivalent to a *Sandstrom* presumption. See *Sandstrom v. Montana,* 442 U.S. 510, 514–524, 99 S.Ct. 2450, 61 L.Ed.2d 39 (1979) (due process forbids use of presumption that relieves the prosecution of burden of proving mental state by inference of intent from an act).

37. In fact, Oregon had this scheme in place when we decided *Leland v. Oregon,* 343 U.S. 790, 794–796, 72 S.Ct. 1002, 96 L.Ed. 1302 (1952). We do not, however, read any part of *Leland* to require as a matter of due process that evidence of incapacity be considered to rebut the *mens rea* element of a crime.

even though he seemed to act like a man shooting another man.[38] In jurisdictions that allow mental-disease and capacity evidence to be considered on par with any other relevant evidence when deciding whether the prosecution has proven *mens rea* beyond a reasonable doubt, the evidence of mental disease or incapacity need only support what the factfinder regards as a reasonable doubt about the capacity to form (or the actual formation of) the *mens rea,* in order to require acquittal of the charge. Thus, in these States the strength of the presumption of sanity is no greater than the strength of the evidence of abnormal mental state that the factfinder thinks is enough to raise a reasonable doubt.

The second point where the force of the presumption of sanity may be tested is in the consideration of a defense of insanity raised by a defendant. Insanity rules like *M'Naghten* and the variants discussed in Part II, *supra,* are attempts to define, or at least to indicate, the kinds of mental differences that overcome the presumption of sanity or capacity and therefore excuse a defendant from customary criminal responsibility, see *Jones v. United States,* 463 U.S. 354, 373, n. 4, 103 S.Ct. 3043, 77 L.Ed.2d 694 (1983) (Brennan, J., dissenting); D. Hermann, The Insanity Defense: Philosophical, Historical and Legal Perspectives 4 (1983) ("A central significance of the insanity defense . . . is the separation of nonblameworthy from blameworthy offenders"), even if the prosecution has otherwise overcome the presumption of innocence by convincing the factfinder of all the elements charged beyond a reasonable doubt. The burden that must be carried by a defendant who raises the insanity issue, again, defines the strength of the sanity presumption. A State may provide, for example, that whenever the defendant raises a claim of insanity by some quantum of credible evidence, the presumption disappears and the government must prove sanity to a specified degree of certainty (whether beyond reasonable doubt or something less). See, *e.g., Commonwealth v. Keita,* 429 Mass. 843, 846, 712 N.E.2d 65, 68 (1999). Or a jurisdiction may place the burden of persuasion on a defendant to prove insanity as the applicable law defines it, whether by a preponderance of the evidence or to some more convincing degree, see Ariz.Rev.Stat. Ann. § 13–502(C) (West 2001); *Leland,* 343 U.S., at 798, 72 S.Ct. 1002. In any case, the defendant's burden defines the presumption of sanity, whether that burden be to burst a bubble or to show something more.

3

The third principle implicated by Clark's argument is a defendant's right as a matter of simple due process to present evidence favorable to

---

38. We reject the State's argument that *mens rea* and insanity, as currently understood, are entirely distinguishable, so that mental-disease and capacity evidence relevant to insanity is simply irrelevant to *mens rea.* Not only does evidence accepted as showing insanity trump *mens rea,* but evidence of behavior close to the time of the act charged may indicate both the actual state of mind at that time and also an enduring incapacity to form the criminal state of mind necessary to the offense charged. See Brief for American Psychiatric Association et al. as *Amici Curiae* 12–13; Arenella, The Diminished Capacity and Diminished Responsibility Defenses: Two Children of a Doomed Marriage, 77 Colum. L.Rev. 827, 834–835 (1977); cf. *Powell v. Texas,* 392 U.S. 514, 535–536, 88 S.Ct. 2145, 20 L.Ed.2d 1254 (1968) (plurality opinion) (the "doctrines of *actus reus, mens rea,* insanity, mistake, justification, and duress" are a "collection of interlocking and overlapping concepts which the common law has utilized to assess the moral accountability of an individual for his antisocial deeds").

himself on an element that must be proven to convict him.[39] As already noted, evidence tending to show that a defendant suffers from mental disease and lacks capacity to form *mens rea* is relevant to rebut evidence that he did in fact form the required *mens rea* at the time in question; this is the reason that Clark claims a right to require the factfinder in this case to consider testimony about his mental illness and his incapacity directly, when weighing the persuasiveness of other evidence tending to show *mens rea*, which the prosecution has the burden to prove.

As Clark recognizes, however, the right to introduce relevant evidence can be curtailed if there is a good reason for doing that. "While the Constitution ... prohibits the exclusion of defense evidence under rules that serve no legitimate purpose or that are disproportionate to the ends that they are asserted to promote, well-established rules of evidence permit trial judges to exclude evidence if its probative value is outweighed by certain other factors such as unfair prejudice, confusion of the issues, or potential to mislead the jury." *Holmes v. South Carolina,* 547 U.S. 319, 326, 126 S.Ct. 1727, 1732, 164 L.Ed.2d 503 (2006); see *Crane v. Kentucky,* 476 U.S. 683, 689–690, 106 S.Ct. 2142, 90 L.Ed.2d 636 (1986) (permitting exclusion of evidence that "poses an undue risk of 'harassment, prejudice, [or] confusion of the issues' " (quoting *Delaware v. Van Arsdall,* 475 U.S. 673, 679, 106 S.Ct. 1431, 89 L.Ed.2d 674 (1986))); see also *Egelhoff,*518 U.S. 37, 116 S.Ct. 2013, 135 L.Ed.2d 361; *Chambers v. Mississippi,* 410 U.S. 284, 302, 93 S.Ct. 1038, 35 L.Ed.2d 297 (1973). And if evidence may be kept out entirely, its consideration may be subject to limitation, which Arizona claims the power to impose here. State law says that evidence of mental disease and incapacity may be introduced and considered, and if sufficiently forceful to satisfy the defendant's burden of proof under the insanity rule it will displace the presumption of sanity and excuse from criminal responsibility. But mental-disease and capacity evidence may be considered only for its bearing on the insanity defense, and it will avail a defendant only if it is persuasive enough to satisfy the defendant's burden as defined by the terms of that defense. The mental-disease and capacity evidence is thus being channeled or restricted to one issue and given effect only if the defendant carries the burden to convince the factfinder of insanity; the evidence is not being excluded entirely, and the question is whether reasons for requiring it to be channeled and restricted are good enough to satisfy the standard of fundamental fairness that due process requires. We think they are.

E

1

The first reason supporting the *Mott* rule is Arizona's authority to define its presumption of sanity (or capacity or responsibility) by choosing an insanity definition, as discussed in Part II, *supra,* and by placing the

---

39. Clark's argument assumes that Arizona's rule is a rule of evidence, rather than a redefinition of *mens rea,* see *Montana v. Egelhoff,* 518 U.S. 37, 58–59, 116 S.Ct. 2013, 135 L.Ed.2d 361 (1996) (GINSBURG, J., concurring in judgment); *id.,* at 71, 116 S.Ct. 2013 (O'Connor, J., dissenting). We have no reason to view the rule otherwise, and on this assumption, it does not violate due process, see *infra,* at 2733–2737.

burden of persuasion on defendants who claim incapacity as an excuse from customary criminal responsibility. No one, certainly not Clark here, denies that a State may place a burden of persuasion on a defendant claiming insanity, see *Leland, supra,* at 797–799, 72 S.Ct. 1002 (permitting a State, consistent with due process, to require the defendant to bear this burden). And Clark presses no objection to Arizona's decision to require persuasion to a clear and convincing degree before the presumption of sanity and normal responsibility is overcome.

But if a State is to have this authority in practice as well as in theory, it must be able to deny a defendant the opportunity to displace the presumption of sanity more easily when addressing a different issue in the course of the criminal trial. Yet, as we have explained, just such an opportunity would be available if expert testimony of mental disease and incapacity could be considered for whatever a factfinder might think it was worth on the issue of *mens rea.* As we mentioned, the presumption of sanity would then be only as strong as the evidence a factfinder would accept as enough to raise a reasonable doubt about *mens rea* for the crime charged; once reasonable doubt was found, acquittal would be required, and the standards established for the defense of insanity would go by the boards.

Now, a State is of course free to accept such a possibility in its law. After all, it is free to define the insanity defense by treating the presumption of sanity as a bursting bubble, whose disappearance shifts the burden to the prosecution to prove sanity whenever a defendant presents any credible evidence of mental disease or incapacity. In States with this kind of insanity rule, the legislature may well be willing to allow such evidence to be considered on the *mens rea* element for whatever the factfinder thinks it is worth. What counts for due process, however, is simply that a State that wishes to avoid a second avenue for exploring capacity, less stringent for a defendant, has a good reason for confining the consideration of evidence of mental disease and incapacity to the insanity defense.

It is obvious that Arizona's *Mott* rule reflects such a choice. The State Supreme Court pointed out that the State had declined to adopt a defense of diminished capacity (allowing a jury to decide when to excuse a defendant because of greater than normal difficulty in conforming to the law). The court reasoned that the State's choice would be undercut if evidence of incapacity could be considered for whatever a jury might think sufficient to raise a reasonable doubt about *mens rea,* even if it did not show insanity. 187 Ariz., at 541, 931 P.2d, at 1051. In other words, if a jury were free to decide how much evidence of mental disease and incapacity was enough to counter evidence of *mens rea* to the point of creating a reasonable doubt, that would in functional terms be analogous to allowing jurors to decide upon some degree of diminished capacity to obey the law, a degree set by them, that would prevail as a stand-alone defense.[42]

---

42. It is beyond question that Arizona may preclude such a defense, see *Fisher v. United States,* 328 U.S. 463, 466–476, 66 S.Ct. 1318, 90 L.Ed. 1382 (1946), and there is no doubt that the Arizona Legislature meant to do so, see Ariz.Rev.Stat. Ann. § 13–502(A) (West 2001) ("Mental disease or defect does not include disorders that result from acute voluntary intoxication or withdrawal from alcohol or drugs, character defects, psychosexual disorders or

2

A State's insistence on preserving its chosen standard of legal insanity cannot be the sole reason for a rule like *Mott,* however, for it fails to answer an objection the dissent makes in this case. An insanity rule gives a defendant already found guilty the opportunity to excuse his conduct by showing he was insane when he acted, that is, that he did not have the mental capacity for conventional guilt and criminal responsibility. But, as the dissent argues, if the same evidence that affirmatively shows he was not guilty by reason of insanity (or "guilty except insane" under Arizona law, Ariz.Rev.Stat. Ann. § 13–502(A) (West 2001)) also shows it was at least doubtful that he could form *mens rea,* then he should not be found guilty in the first place; it thus violates due process when the State impedes him from using mental-disease and capacity evidence directly to rebut the prosecution's evidence that he did form *mens rea.*

Are there, then, characteristics of mental-disease and capacity evidence giving rise to risks that may reasonably be hedged by channeling the consideration of such evidence to the insanity issue on which, in States like Arizona, a defendant has the burden of persuasion? We think there are: in the controversial character of some categories of mental disease, in the potential of mental-disease evidence to mislead, and in the danger of according greater certainty to capacity evidence than experts claim for it.

To begin with, the diagnosis may mask vigorous debate within the profession about the very contours of the mental disease itself. See, *e.g.,* American Psychiatric Association, Diagnostic and Statistical Manual of Mental Disorders xxxiii (4th ed. text rev.2000) (hereinafter DSM–IV–TR) ("DSM–IV reflects a consensus about the classification and diagnosis of mental disorders derived at the time of its initial publication. New knowledge generated by research or clinical experience will undoubtedly lead to an increased understanding of the disorders included in DSM–IV, to the identification of new disorders, and to the removal of some disorders in future classifications. The text and criteria sets included in DSM–IV will require reconsideration in light of evolving new information"); P. Caplan, They Say You're Crazy: How the World's Most Powerful Psychiatrists Decide Who's Normal (1995) (criticism by former consultant to the DSM against some of the DSM's categories). And Members of this Court have previously recognized that the end of such debate is not imminent. See *Jones,* 463 U.S., at 365, n. 13, 103 S.Ct. 3043 (" 'The only certain thing that can be said about the present state of knowledge and therapy regarding mental disease is that science has not reached finality of judgment' " (quoting *Greenwood v. United States,* 350 U.S. 366, 375, 76 S.Ct. 410, 100 L.Ed. 412 (1956))); *Powell v. Texas,* 392 U.S. 514, 537, 88 S.Ct. 2145, 20 L.Ed.2d 1254 (1968) (plurality opinion) ("It is simply not yet the time to write into the Constitution formulas cast in terms whose meaning, let alone relevance, is not yet clear ... to doctors"). Though we certainly do not

---

impulse control disorders. Conditions that do not constitute legal insanity include but are not limited to momentary, temporary conditions arising from the pressure of the circumstances, moral decadence, depravity or passion growing out of anger, jealousy, revenge, hatred or other motives in a person who does not suffer from a mental disease or defect or an abnormality that is manifested only by criminal conduct").

"condem[n mental-disease evidence] wholesale," Brief for American Psychiatric Association et al. as *Amici Curiae* 15, the consequence of this professional ferment is a general caution in treating psychological classifications as predicates for excusing otherwise criminal conduct.

Next, there is the potential of mental-disease evidence to mislead jurors (when they are the factfinders) through the power of this kind of evidence to suggest that a defendant suffering from a recognized mental disease lacks cognitive, moral, volitional, or other capacity, when that may not be a sound conclusion at all. Even when a category of mental disease is broadly accepted and the assignment of a defendant's behavior to that category is uncontroversial, the classification may suggest something very significant about a defendant's capacity, when in fact the classification tells us little or nothing about the ability of the defendant to form *mens rea* or to exercise the cognitive, moral, or volitional capacities that define legal sanity.[43] See DSM–IV–TR xxxii-xxxiii ("When the DSM–IV categories, criteria, and textual descriptions are employed for forensic purposes, there are significant risks that diagnostic information will be misused or misunderstood. These dangers arise because of the imperfect fit between the questions of ultimate concern to the law and the information contained in a clinical diagnosis. In most situations, the clinical diagnosis of a DSM–IV mental disorder is not sufficient to establish the existence for legal purposes of ... 'mental diseas[e]' or 'mental defect.' In determining whether an individual meets a specified legal standard (e.g., for ... criminal responsibility ...), additional information is usually required beyond that contained in the DSM–IV diagnosis"). The limits of the utility of a professional disease diagnosis are evident in the dispute between the two testifying experts in this case; they agree that Clark was schizophrenic, but they come to opposite conclusions on whether the mental disease in his particular case left him bereft of cognitive or moral capacity. Evidence of mental disease, then, can easily mislead; it is very easy to slide from evidence that an individual with a professionally recognized mental disease is very different, into doubting that he has the capacity to form *mens rea,* whereas that doubt may not be justified. And of course, in the cases mentioned before, in which the categorization is doubtful or the category of mental disease is itself subject to controversy, the risks are even greater that opinions about mental disease may confuse a jury into thinking the opinions show more than they do. Because allowing mental-disease evidence on *mens rea* can thus easily mislead, it is not unreasonable to address that tendency by confining consideration of this kind of evidence to insanity, on which a defendant may be assigned the burden of persuasion.

There are, finally, particular risks inherent in the opinions of the experts who supplement the mental-disease classifications with opinions on incapacity: on whether the mental disease rendered a particular defendant incapable of the cognition necessary for moral judgment or *mens rea* or

---

43. Our observation about the impact of mental-disease evidence on understandings of capacity in no way undermines the assertion by the American Psychiatric Association, the American Psychological Association, and the American Academy of Psychiatry in this case that "[e]xpert evidence of mental disorders ... is ... relevant to the mental-state issues raised by *mens rea* requirements," Brief for American Psychiatric Association et al. as *Amici Curiae* 15.

otherwise incapable of understanding the wrongfulness of the conduct charged. Unlike observational evidence bearing on *mens rea,* capacity evidence consists of judgment, and judgment fraught with multiple perils: a defendant's state of mind at the crucial moment can be elusive no matter how conscientious the enquiry, and the law's categories that set the terms of the capacity judgment are not the categories of psychology that govern the expert's professional thinking. Although such capacity judgments may be given in the utmost good faith, their potentially tenuous character is indicated by the candor of the defense expert in this very case. Contrary to the State's expert, he testified that Clark lacked the capacity to appreciate the circumstances realistically and to understand the wrongfulness of what he was doing, but he said that "no one knows exactly what was on [his] mind" at the time of the shooting. And even when an expert is confident that his understanding of the mind is reliable, judgment addressing the basic categories of capacity requires a leap from the concepts of psychology, which are devised for thinking about treatment, to the concepts of legal sanity, which are devised for thinking about criminal responsibility. See Insanity Defense Work Group, American Psychiatric Association Statement on the Insanity Defense, 140 Am. J. Psychiatry 681, 686 (1983), reprinted in 2 The Role of Mental Illness in Criminal Trials 117, 122 (J. Moriarty ed. 2001) ("The American Psychiatric Association is not opposed to legislatures restricting psychiatric testimony about the ... ultimate legal issues concerning the insanity defense.... When ... 'ultimate issue' questions are formulated by the law and put to the expert witness who must then say 'yea' or 'nay,' then the expert witness is required to make a leap in logic. He no longer addresses himself to medical concepts but instead must infer or intuit what is in fact unspeakable, namely, the *probable relationship* between medical concepts and legal or moral constructs such as free will. These impermissible leaps in logic made by expert witnesses confuse the jury.... This state of affairs does considerable injustice to psychiatry and, we believe, possibly to criminal defendants. These psychiatric disagreements ... cause less than fully understanding juries or the public to conclude that psychiatrists cannot agree. In fact, in many criminal insanity trials both prosecution and defense psychiatrists do agree about the nature and even the extent of mental disorder exhibited by the defendant at the time of the act" (emphasis in original; footnote omitted)); DSM–IV–TR xxxii-xxxiii; P. Giannelli & E. Imwinkelried, Scientific Evidence § 9–3(B), p. 286 (1986) ("[N]o matter how the test for insanity is phrased, a psychiatrist or psychologist is no more qualified than any other person to give an opinion about whether a particular defendant's mental condition satisfies the legal test for insanity"); cf. R. Slovenko, Psychiatry and Criminal Culpability 55 (1995) ("The scope of the DSM is wide-ranging and includes 'conduct disorders' but 'evil' is not mentioned"). In sum, these empirical and conceptual problems add up to a real risk that an expert's judgment in giving capacity evidence will come with an apparent authority that psychologists and psychiatrists do not claim to have. We think that this risk, like the difficulty in assessing the significance of mental-disease evidence, supports the State's decision to channel such expert testimony to consideration on the insanity defense, on which the party seeking the benefit of this evidence has the burden of persuasion.

It bears repeating that not every State will find it worthwhile to make the judgment Arizona has made, and the choices the States do make about dealing with the risks posed by mental-disease and capacity evidence will reflect their varying assessments about the presumption of sanity as expressed in choices of insanity rules.[44] The point here simply is that Arizona has sensible reasons to assign the risks as it has done by channeling the evidence.[46]

F

Arizona's rule serves to preserve the State's chosen standard for recognizing insanity as a defense and to avoid confusion and misunderstanding on the part of jurors. For these reasons, there is no violation of due process under *Chambers* and its progeny, and no cause to claim that channeling evidence on mental disease and capacity offends any " 'principle of justice so rooted in the traditions and conscience of our people as to be ranked as fundamental,' " *Patterson*, 432 U.S., at 202, 97 S.Ct. 2319 (quoting *Speiser*, 357 U.S., at 523, 78 S.Ct. 1332).

* * *

The judgment of the Court of Appeals of Arizona is, accordingly, affirmed.

It is so ordered.

■ JUSTICE BREYER, concurring part and dissenting in part.

As I understand the Court's opinion, it distinguishes among three categories of evidence related to insanity: (1) fact-related evidence as to the defendant's specific state of mind at the time of the crime, *e.g.*, evidence that shows he thought the policeman was not a human being; (2) expert opinion evidence that the defendant suffered from a mental disease that would have affected his capacity to form an intent to kill a policeman, *e.g.*, that he suffers from a disease of a kind where powerful voices command the sufferer to kill; and (3) expert opinion evidence that the defendant was legally insane, *e.g.*, evidence that he did not know right from wrong.

---

44. A State in which the burden of persuasion as to a defendant's sanity lies with the prosecution might also be justified in restricting mental-disease and capacity evidence to insanity determinations owing to the potential of mental-disease evidence to mislead and the risk of misjudgment inherent in capacity evidence. We need not, in the context of this case, address that issue.

46. Arizona's rule is supported by a further practical reason, though not as weighty as those just considered. As mentioned before, if substantial mental-disease and capacity evidence is accepted as rebutting *mens rea* in a given case, the affirmative defense of insanity will probably not be reached or ruled upon; the defendant will simply be acquitted (or perhaps convicted of a lesser included offense). If an acquitted defendant suffers from a mental disease or defect that makes him dangerous, he will neither be confined nor treated psychiatrically unless a judge so orders after some independent commitment proceeding. But if a defendant succeeds in showing himself insane, Arizona law (and presumably that of every other State with an insanity rule) will require commitment and treatment as a consequence of that finding without more. It makes sense, then, to channel capacity evidence to the issue structured to deal with mental incapacity when such a claim is raised successfully. See, *e.g.*, *Jones*, 463 U.S., at 368, 103 S.Ct. 3043 ("The purpose of commitment following an insanity acquittal ... is to treat the individual's mental illness and protect him and society from his potential dangerousness").

I agree with the Court's basic categorization. I also agree that the Constitution permits a State to provide for consideration of the second and third types of evidence solely in conjunction with the insanity defense. A State might reasonably fear that, without such a rule, the types of evidence as to intent would become confused in the jury's mind, indeed that in some cases the insanity question would displace the intent question as the parties litigate both simultaneously.

Nonetheless, I believe the distinction among these kinds of evidence will be unclear in some cases. And though I accept the majority's reading of the record, I remain concerned as to whether the lower courts, in setting forth and applying *State v. Mott*, 187 Ariz. 536, 931 P.2d 1046, cert. denied, 520 U.S. 1234, 117 S.Ct. 1832, 137 L.Ed.2d 1038 (1997), focused with sufficient directness and precision upon the distinction.

Consequently, I would remand this case so that Arizona's courts can determine whether Arizona law, as set forth in *Mott* and other cases, is consistent with the distinction the Court draws and whether the trial court so applied Arizona law here. I would also reserve the question (as I believe the Court has done) as to the burden of persuasion in a case where the defendant produces sufficient evidence of the second kind as to raise a reasonable doubt that he suffered from a mental illness so severe as to prevent him from forming any relevant intent at all.

For this reason, I dissent only from Parts III–B and III–C of the Court's opinion and the ultimate disposition of this case, and I join the remainder.

■ JUSTICE KENNEDY, with whom JUSTICE STEVENS and JUSTICE GINSBURG join, dissenting.

In my submission the Court is incorrect in holding that Arizona may convict petitioner Eric Clark of first-degree murder for the intentional or knowing killing of a police officer when Clark was not permitted to introduce critical and reliable evidence showing he did not have that intent or knowledge. The Court is wrong, too, when it concludes the issue cannot be reached because of an error by Clark's counsel. Its reasons and conclusions lead me to file this respectful dissent.

Since I would reverse the judgment of the Arizona Court of Appeals on this ground, and the Arizona courts might well alter their interpretation of the State's criminal responsibility statute were my rationale to prevail, it is unnecessary for me to address the argument that Arizona's definition of insanity violates due process.

I

Clark claims that the trial court erred in refusing to consider evidence of his chronic paranoid schizophrenia in deciding whether he possessed the knowledge or intent required for first-degree murder. Seizing upon a theory invented here by the Court itself, the Court narrows Clark's claim so he cannot raise the point everyone else thought was involved in the case. The Court says the only issue before us is whether there is a right to introduce mental-disease evidence or capacity evidence, not a right to introduce observation evidence. This restructured evidentiary universe, with no convincing authority to support it, is unworkable on its own terms. Even were that not so, however, the Court's tripartite structure is something not addressed by the state trial court, the state appellate court, counsel on either side in those proceedings, or the briefs the parties filed with us. The Court refuses to consider the key part of Clark's claim because his counsel did not predict the Court's own invention. It is unrealistic, and most unfair, to hold that Clark's counsel erred in failing to anticipate so novel an approach. If the Court is to insist on its approach, at a minimum the case should be remanded to determine whether Clark is bound by his counsel's purported waiver.

The Court's error, of course, has significance beyond this case. It adopts an evidentiary framework that, in my view, will be unworkable in many cases. The Court classifies Clark's behavior and expressed beliefs as observation evidence but insists that its description by experts must be mental-disease evidence or capacity evidence. These categories break down quickly when it is understood how the testimony would apply to the question of intent and knowledge at issue here. The most common type of schizophrenia, and the one Clark suffered from, is paranoid schizophrenia. See P. Berner et al., Diagnostic Criteria for Functional Psychoses 37 (2d ed.1992). The existence of this functional psychosis is beyond dispute, but that does not mean the lay witness understands it or that a disputed issue of fact concerning its effect in a particular instance is not something for the expert to address. Common symptoms of the condition are delusions accompanied by hallucinations, often of the auditory type, which can cause disturbances of perception. *Ibid.* Clark's expert testified that people with schizophrenia often play radios loudly to drown out the voices in their heads. Clark's attorney argued to the trial court that this, rather than a desire to lure a policeman to the scene, explained Clark's behavior just before the killing. *Id.,* at 294–295. The observation that schizophrenics play radios loudly is a fact regarding behavior, but it is only a relevant fact if Clark has schizophrenia.

Even if this evidence were, to use the Court's term, mental-disease evidence, because it relies on an expert opinion, what would happen if the expert simply were to testify, without mentioning schizophrenia, that people with Clark's symptoms often play the radio loudly? This seems to be factual evidence, as the term is defined by the Court, yet it differs from mental-disease evidence only in forcing the witness to pretend that no one has yet come up with a way to classify the set of symptoms being described. More generally, the opinion that Clark had paranoid schizophrenia-an opinion shared by experts for both the prosecution and defense-bears on efforts to determine, as a factual matter, whether he knew he was killing a police officer. The psychiatrist's explanation of Clark's condition was essential to understanding how he processes sensory data and therefore to deciding what information was in his mind at the time of the shooting. Simply put, knowledge relies on cognition, and cognition can be affected by schizophrenia. See American Psychiatric Association, Diagnostic and Statistical Manual of Mental Disorders 299 (4th ed. text rev. 2000) ("The characteristic symptoms of Schizophrenia involve a range of cognitive and emotional dysfunctions that include perception"); *ibid.* (Symptoms include delusions, which are "erroneous beliefs that usually involve a misinterpretation of perceptions or experiences"). The mental-disease evidence at trial was also intertwined with the observation evidence because it lent needed credibility. Clark's parents and friends testified Clark thought the people in his town were aliens trying to kill him. These claims might not be believable without a psychiatrist confirming the story based on his experience with people who have exhibited similar behaviors. It makes little sense to divorce the observation evidence from the explanation that makes it comprehensible.

Assuming the Court's tripartite structure were feasible, the Court is incorrect when it narrows Clark's claim to exclude any concern about observation evidence. In deciding Clark's counsel failed to raise this issue, the Court relies on a series of perceived ambiguities regarding how the claim fits within the Court's own categories. The Court cites no precedent for construing these ambiguities against the claimant and no prudential reason for ignoring the breadth of Clark's claim. It is particularly surprising that the Court does so to the detriment of a criminal defendant asserting the fundamental challenge that the trier of fact refused to consider critical evidence showing he is innocent of the crime charged.

The alleged ambiguities are, in any event, illusory. The evidence at trial addressed more than the question of general incapacity or opinions regarding mental illness; it went further, as it included so-called observation evidence relevant to Clark's mental state at the moment he shot the officer. There was testimony, for example, that Clark thought the people in his town, particularly government officials, were not human beings but aliens who were trying to kill him. See App. 119–121, 131–132, 192–197, 249–256; Tr. of Bench Trial in No. CR 2000–538, pp. 110–112, 131–132, 136, 226–228 (Aug. 20, 2003); *id.*, at 24–25, 59–60 (Aug. 21, 2003). The Court recognizes the existence of this essential observation evidence.

The Court holds, nonetheless, that "we cannot be sure" whether the trial court failed to consider this evidence. It is true the trial court ruling was not perfectly clear. Its language does strongly suggest, though, that it did not consider any of this testimony in deciding whether Clark had the knowledge or intent required for first-degree murder. After recognizing that "much of the evidence that [the defense is] going to be submitting, in fact all of it, as far as I know . . . that has to do with the insanity could also arguably be made . . . as to form and intent and his capacity for the intent," the court concluded "we will be focusing, as far as I'm concerned, strictly on the insanity defense." In announcing its verdict, the trial court did not mention any of the mental-illness evidence, observation or otherwise, in deciding Clark's guilt. The most reasonable assumption, then, would seem to be that the trial court did not consider it, and the Court does not hold otherwise.

Clark's objection to this refusal by the trier of fact to consider the evidence as it bore on his key defense was made at all stages of the proceeding. In his post-trial motion to vacate the judgment, Clark argued that "prohibiting consideration of *any* evidence reflecting upon a mentally ill criminal defendant's ability to form the necessary *mens rea* violates due process." Record, Doc. 406, p. 8. Clark pressed the same argument in the Arizona Court of Appeals. See Appellant's Opening Brief in No. 1CA–CR–

03–0851 etc., pp. 46–52 (hereinafter Appellant's Opening Brief). He also noted that the trial judge had erred in refusing to consider nonexpert testimony-presumably what the Court would call observation evidence-on Clark's mental illness. *Id., at* 47–48 ("The trial court therefore violated [Clark's] right to present a defense because [the] court refused to consider *any evidence,* including the multiple testimonials of *lay* witnesses . . . in deciding whether he could form the requisite *mens rea*"). The appeals court decided the issue on the merits, holding that the trial court was correct not to consider the evidence of mental illness in determining whether Clark had the *mens rea* for first-degree murder. It offered no distinction at all between observation or mental-disease evidence. . . .

Clark seeks resolution of issues that can be complex and somewhat overlapping. In the end, however, we must decide whether he had the right to introduce evidence showing he lacked the intent or knowledge the statute itself sets forth in describing a basic element of the crime. Clark has preserved this issue at all stages, including in this Court.

II

Clark was charged with first-degree murder for the shooting of Officer Jeffrey Moritz. "A person commits first-degree murder if," as relevant here, "[i]ntending or knowing that the person's conduct will cause death to a law enforcement officer, the person causes the death of a law enforcement officer who is in the line of duty." Ariz.Rev.Stat. Ann. § 13–1105(A)(3) (West Supp.2005). Clark challenges the trial court's refusal to consider any evidence of mental illness, from lay or expert testimony, in determining whether he acted with the knowledge or intent element of the crime.

States have substantial latitude under the Constitution to define rules for the exclusion of evidence and to apply those rules to criminal defendants. See *United States v. Scheffer,* 523 U.S. 303, 308, 118 S.Ct. 1261, 140 L.Ed.2d 413 (1998). This authority, however, has constitutional limits. " 'Whether rooted directly in the Due Process Clause of the Fourteenth Amendment or in the Compulsory Process or Confrontation Clauses of the Sixth Amendment, the Constitution guarantees criminal defendants "a meaningful opportunity to present a complete defense.' " *Holmes v. South Carolina,* 547 U.S. 319, 324, 126 S.Ct. 1727, 1731, 164 L.Ed.2d 503 (2006) (quoting *Crane v. Kentucky,* 476 U.S. 683, 690, 106 S.Ct. 2142, 90 L.Ed.2d 636 (1986), in turn quoting *California v. Trombetta,* 467 U.S. 479, 485, 104 S.Ct. 2528, 81 L.Ed.2d 413 (1984)). "This right is abridged by evidence rules that 'infring[e] upon a weighty interest of the accused' and are 'arbitrary' or 'disproportionate to the purposes they are designed to serve.' " " *Holmes, supra,* at 324, 126 S.Ct., at 1731 (quoting *Scheffer, supra,* at 308, 118 S.Ct. 1261, in turn citing and quoting *Rock v. Arkansas,* 483 U.S. 44, 58, 56, 107 S.Ct. 2704, 97 L.Ed.2d 37 (1987)).

The central theory of Clark's defense was that his schizophrenia made him delusional. He lived in a universe where the delusions were so dominant, the theory was, that he had no intent to shoot a police officer or knowledge he was doing so. It is one thing to say he acted with intent or knowledge to pull the trigger. It is quite another to say he pulled the trigger to kill someone he knew to be a human being and a police officer. If the trier of fact were to find Clark's evidence sufficient to discount the case made by the State, which has the burden to prove knowledge or intent as an element of the offense, Clark would not be guilty of first-degree murder under Arizona law. . . .

This is not to suggest all general rules on the exclusion of certain types of evidence are invalid. If the rule does not substantially burden the defense, then it is likely permissible. See *Scheffer,* 523 U.S., at 316–317, 118 S.Ct. 1261 (upholding exclusion of polygraph evidence in part because this rule "does not implicate any significant interest of the accused"); *id.,* at 318, 118 S.Ct. 1261 (KENNEDY, J., concurring in part and concurring in judgment) ("[S]ome later case might present a more compelling case for introduction of the testimony than this one does"). Where, however, the burden is substantial, the State must present a valid reason for its *per se* evidentiary rule.

In the instant case Arizona's proposed reasons are insufficient to support its categorical exclusion. While the State contends that testimony regarding mental illness may be too incredible or speculative for the jury to consider, this does not explain why the exclusion applies in all cases to all evidence of mental illness. "A State's legitimate interest in barring unreliable evidence does not extend to *per se* exclusions that may be reliable in an individual case." *Rock, supra,* at 61, 107 S.Ct. 2704. States have certain discretion to bar unreliable or speculative testimony and to adopt rules to ensure the reliability of expert testimony. Arizona has done so, and there is no reason to believe its rules are insufficient to avoid speculative evidence of mental illness. See Ariz. Rules Evid. 403, 702 (2006). This is particularly true because Arizona applies its usual case-by-case approach to permit admission of evidence of mental illness for a variety of other purposes. See, *e.g., State v. Lindsey,* 149 Ariz. 472, 474–475, 720 P.2d 73, 75–76 (1986) (en banc) (psychological characteristics of molestation victims); *State v. Hamilton,* 177 Ariz. 403, 408–410, 868 P.2d 986, 991–993 (App.1993) (psychological evidence of child abuse accommodation syndrome); *Horan v. Industrial Comm'n, of Ariz.,* 167 Ariz. 322, 325–326, 806 P.2d 911, 914–915 (App. 1991) (psychiatric testimony regarding neurological deficits).

The risk of jury confusion also fails to justify the rule. The State defends its rule as a means to avoid the complexities of determining how and to what degree a mental illness affects a person's mental state. The difficulty of resolving a factual issue, though, does not present a sufficient reason to take evidence away from the jury even when it is crucial for the defense. "We have always trusted juries to sort through complex facts in various areas of law." *United States v. Booker,* 543 U.S. 220, 289, 125 S.Ct. 738, 160 L.Ed.2d 621 (2005) (STEVENS, J., dissenting in part). Even were the risk of jury confusion real enough to justify excluding evidence in most cases, this would provide little basis for prohibiting all evidence of mental illness without any inquiry into its likely effect on the jury or its role in deciding the linchpin issue of knowledge and intent. Indeed, Arizona has a rule in place to serve this very purpose. See Rule 403.

Even assuming the reliability and jury-confusion justifications were persuasive in some cases, they would not suffice here. It does not overcome the constitutional objection to say that an evidentiary rule that is reasonable on its face can be applied as well to bar significant defense evidence without any rational basis for doing so. . . .

The Court undertakes little analysis of the interests particular to this case. By proceeding in this way it devalues Clark's constitutional rights. The reliability rationale has minimal applicability here. The Court is correct that many mental diseases are difficult to define and the subject of great debate. Schizophrenia, however, is a well-documented mental illness, and no one seriously disputes either its definition or its most prominent clinical manifestations. The State's own expert conceded that Clark had paranoid schizophrenia and was actively psychotic at the time of the killing. The jury-confusion rationale, if it is at all applicable here, is the result of the Court's own insistence on conflating the insanity defense and the question of intent. Considered on its own terms, the issue of intent and knowledge is a straightforward factual question. A trier of fact is quite capable of weighing defense testimony and then determining whether the accused did or did not intend to kill or knowingly kill a human being who was a police officer. True, the issue can be difficult to decide in particular instances, but no more so than many matters juries must confront.

The State attempts to sidestep the evidentiary issue entirely by claiming that its mental-illness exclusion simply alters one element of the crime. The evidentiary rule at issue here, however, cannot be considered a valid redefinition of the offense. Under the State's logic, a person would be guilty of first-degree murder if he knowingly or intentionally killed a police officer or committed the killing under circumstances that would show knowledge or intent but for the defendant's mental illness. To begin with, Arizona law does not say this. And if it did, it would be impermissible. States have substantial discretion in defining criminal offenses. In some instances they may provide that the accused has the burden of persuasion with respect to affirmative defenses. See *Patterson v. New York,* 432 U.S. 197, 210, 97 S.Ct. 2319, 53 L.Ed.2d 281 (1977). "But there are obviously constitutional limits beyond which the States may not go in this regard." *Ibid.* If it were otherwise, States could label all evidentiary exclusions as redefinitions and so evade constitutional requirements. There is no rational basis, furthermore, for criminally punishing a person who commits a killing without knowledge or intent only if that person has a mental illness. Cf. *Robinson v. California,* 370 U.S. 660, 666, 82 S.Ct. 1417, 8 L.Ed.2d 758 (1962). The State attempts to bring the instant case within the ambit of *Montana v. Egelhoff,* 518 U.S. 37, 116 S.Ct. 2013, 135 L.Ed.2d 361 (1996); but in *Egelhoff* the excluded evidence concerned voluntary intoxication, for which a person can be held responsible. Viewed either as an evidentiary rule or a redefinition of the offense, it was upheld because it "comports with and implements society's moral perception that one who has voluntarily impaired his own faculties should be responsible for the consequences." *Id.,* at 50, 116 S.Ct. 2013 (plurality opinion). An involuntary mental illness does not implicate this justification.

Future dangerousness is not, as the Court appears to conclude, see *ante,* at 2737, n. 45, a rational basis for convicting mentally ill individuals of crimes they did not commit. Civil commitment proceedings can ensure that individuals who present a danger to themselves or others receive proper treatment without unfairly treating them as criminals. The State presents no evidence to the contrary, and the Court ought not to imply otherwise. . . .

Putting aside the lack of any legitimate state interest for application of the rule in this case, its irrationality is apparent when considering the evidence that is allowed. See *Washington, supra,* at 22, 87 S.Ct. 1920 ("The absurdity of the rule is amply demonstrated by the exceptions that have been made to it"). Arizona permits the defendant to introduce, for example, evidence of "behavioral tendencies" to show he did not have the required mental state. See *Mott,* 187 Ariz., at 544, 931 P.2d, at 1054; *Christensen,* 129 Ariz., at 35–36, 628 P.2d, at 583–584. While defining mental illness is a difficult matter, the State seems to exclude the evidence one would think most reliable by allowing unexplained and uncategorized tendencies to be introduced while excluding relatively well-understood psychiatric testimony regarding well-documented mental illnesses. It is unclear, moreover, what would have happened in this case had the defendant wanted to testify that he thought Officer Moritz was an alien. If disallowed, it would be tantamount to barring Clark from testifying on his behalf to explain his own actions. If allowed, then Arizona's rule would simply prohibit the corroboration necessary to make sense of Clark's explanation. In sum, the rule forces the jury to decide guilt in a fictional world with undefined and unexplained behaviors but without mental illness. This rule has no rational justification and imposes a significant burden upon a straightforward defense: He did not commit the crime with which he was charged.

These are the reasons for my respectful dissent.

State v. Fetters

Court of Appeals of Iowa, 1997.
562 N.W.2d 770.

■ HABHAB, CHIEF JUDGE.

Kristina Joy Fetters appeals from the judgment and sentence entered following her conviction of first-degree murder. She challenges (1) the sufficiency of evidence to support her conviction; (2) the district court's exclusion of her proposed jury instruction to inform the jury of the consequences of a not guilty by reason of insanity or diminished capacity verdict; . . .

The State filed a trial information charging defendant with first-degree murder with malice aforethought and premeditation and/or while participating in the forcible felony of robbery of Arlene Klehm. Jurisdiction had been transferred from juvenile court to district court on February 17, 1995. Defendant admitted to the murder but asserted insanity and diminished capacity defenses.

On December 18, 1995, a jury found defendant guilty of the first-degree murder of Arlene Klehm. Klehm was defendant's seventy-three-year-old great aunt. Defendant was fifteen years old at the time of the conviction. The district court denied defendant's motions for judgment of acquittal. Defendant was sentenced to life imprisonment.

Defendant appeals.

. . .

The facts reveal that in January 1994 defendant became a resident of Orchard Place, a residential facility for the psychological and emotional treatment of children, located in Des Moines. At trial, the State presented the testimony of three residents of Orchard Place who testified they had discussions with defendant about running away. The record reveals defendant began planning to elope from Orchard Place in mid-October. Jessica Wilhite testified that during her conversations with defendant she explained Klehm had a lot of money and she (defendant) and Tisha Versendaal planned to kill her and take her truck and money.

Tisha Versendaal was also a resident of Orchard Place. She testified she also had conversations with defendant about eloping. She explained defendant planned to kill Klehm by stabbing her and cutting her throat while she was sitting in a chair. Further, defendant had informed her Klehm had money kept in a safe. She explained that in the days just before defendant eloped, she noticed defendant appeared more and more volatile and upset.

Jeanie Fox was defendant's suite mate at Orchard Place and accompanied her at the time of the homicide. She testified she and defendant each packed a bag and left Orchard Place together. As they were leaving, defendant mentioned to her that she was going to kill her aunt. That afternoon the two stopped at three different places before proceeding to the aunt's home. One of the home's occupants testified, after being asked to describe defendant's demeanor that afternoon, "She seemed to know what she was doing. She seemed to have it all down just what she was going to say and how she was going to do it." One of the residents of another home testified that defendant joined in conversation, appeared to understand, and appropriately responded to questions. The two girls eventually made their way to the home of a friend of defendant and there obtained a small paring knife. Defendant joked about killing Klehm before leaving the apartment.

The two girls were dropped off on the east side of Des Moines near Klehm's home. Fox explained that when the two arrived at Klehm's home, a van was parked outside. The two concealed themselves outside the house near a fence and waited for the owners of the van to leave. While waiting, defendant repeated her plan to kill her aunt and explained Satan had given her the power to do so.

After the van left, the two girls went up to the house and Klehm let them in. At some point, defendant pulled Fox into a side room and again informed her that she was going to kill her aunt. Defendant then returned to the kitchen area where Klehm was sitting. Thereafter, defendant struck Klehm on the head from behind with a kettle while Klehm was seated in the kitchen. Klehm got up and asked her what happened. Defendant then struck her in the head again with a frying pan. Defendant then asked Fox for the paring knife. She got on top of Klehm and attempted to slit her throat. Defendant then got a bigger kitchen knife and proceeded to stab Klehm in the back.

During the attack, Klehm was screaming and asked Fox for help. Klehm also attempted to reach for a phone in the kitchen area. Defendant told her "no" and removed the phone from the hook.

After the attack, defendant removed her bloody clothing. She then took some necklaces and began looking for the keys to her aunt's safe and truck but was unable to locate them. Defendant and Fox then left the scene. Once outside, defendant thought she heard sirens. The two girls started running. Defendant began to cry. The two girls then started pounding on neighborhood doors until they found someone who called the police. After police arrived, defendant cried and stated repeatedly she had killed her aunt.

a) Insanity Defense. Iowa Code section 701.4 (1993) provides, in part:

> A person shall not be convicted of a crime if at the time the crime is committed the person suffers from such a disease or deranged condition of the mind as to render the person incapable of knowing the nature and quality of the act the person is committing or incapable of distinguishing between right and wrong in relation to that act. Insanity need not exist for any specific length of time before or after the commission of the alleged criminal act.

When a defendant raises a defense of insanity, her burden of proof is by a preponderance of the evidence. Iowa Code § 701.4. Defendant argues she has produced sufficient evidence to establish she was either incapable of knowing the nature and quality of her actions in killing Klehm or that she could not distinguish right from wrong in relation to that act.

As it relates to defendant's insanity defense, the State presented the testimony of psychiatrist Michael Taylor. Dr. Taylor examined defendant and opined she was fully capable of understanding the nature and quality of her acts and was fully capable of distinguishing right from wrong on October 25. He explained that he found no evidence of any diagnosable psychiatric disorder and he believed she suffered from only a personality disorder. Dr. Taylor noted defendant's precise planning and deception in the execution of her plan and statements she made after the killing which reflected she understood what she had done.

In support of her defense of insanity, defendant directs us to the trial testimony of psychiatrist Gaylord Nordine. Dr. Nordine testified defendant did not know the difference between right and wrong and was incapable of understanding the nature of her acts on October 25 because she was in a psychotic state. He opined she had a physical disorder involving the brain's limbic system. He also believed Prozac prescribed to defendant and her treatment at Orchard Place may have had a "toxic" effect on her.

However, Dr. Taylor noted the various medications defendant was then receiving, including Prozac, would not have had any adverse consequences for her. It was also noted by Dr. Taylor that defendant was receiving Thorazine at the time, which has the effect of making one less inclined to be aggressive.

Dr. Nordine additionally testified as to his belief that defendant was in a sustained affectively-centered psychotic state by approximately the first few days of October 1994. He explained he believed defendant experienced an "affective storm" which totally overwhelmed all other operations of her brain, leaving her in a dangerous limbic psychotic state before murdering Klehm. He testified defendant's ability to carry out ministerial tasks just prior to the killing of her aunt did not alter his opinion that she was not sane when killing Klehm. He also explained it was not inconsistent with defendant's mental condition that she would have understood the nature and consequences of her actions one hour after the killing.

Defendant also directs us to the trial testimony of Jeanie Fox. Fox testified defendant was repeating the word "Anthony" while killing Klehm. There was also stipulated testimony at trial that shortly thereafter defendant was experiencing hallucinations. Defendant argues this evidence established she was legally insane at the time of the murder.

Dr. Taylor, however, testified he was skeptical of defendant's claims of hallucinations. Two other professionals who had contact with defendant had also indicated skepticism of defendant's reports of symptoms of mental disturbances, with one noting a concern that defendant's reports might be made "to gain some particular objective."

In explaining his opinions, Dr. Taylor noted the facts regarding defendant's planning, deception, exercise of her plan with precision, and the statements she made after which reflected she knew what had been done. Dr. Taylor further testified the most important information he received that formed the basis of his opinion was the information he received from defendant. He testified:

> In talking with her I found absolutely no evidence of any type of psychiatric disorder, and in talking with her I found absolutely no indication that she was doing anything on October 25, 1994, other than killing her aunt.

b) Insanity Defense–Jury Question. A defendant may not be acquitted by reason of insanity unless the evidence shows defendant suffered from a disease or deranged condition of the mind which rendered defendant either: (1) "incapable of knowing the nature and quality of the act"; or (2) "incapable of distinguishing between right and wrong in relation to that act." Iowa Code § 701.4 (1993). The first prong concerns whether at the time of a crime a defendant "knew what he [or she] was doing;" the second prong concerns whether a defendant knew the act was wrong despite awareness of what he [or she] was doing. State v. Thomas, 219 N.W.2d 3, 6 (Iowa 1974). The jury was instructed consistent with these principles.

The defense called witnesses who testified favorably on those questions. Likewise, the State called expert witnesses who gave testimony directly rebutting the defense's evidence. When conflicting psychiatric testimony is presented to the fact finder, sanity is "clearly an issue for the jury to decide." When the psychiatric testimony is conflicting, the reviewing court will "not determine anew the weight to be given trial testimony."

We find there is substantial evidence in the record to uphold the conviction of first-degree murder. In addition, we find there is substantial evidence to support the jury's conclusion that defendant failed to show by a preponderance of evidence she was incapable of knowing the nature and quality of her actions or that she was incapable of distinguishing between right and wrong in relation to her actions at the time she killed Klehm.

. . .

We have carefully considered all of the evidentiary concerns raised by defendant and find there is substantial evidence to support defendant's conviction of first-degree murder.

. . .

Affirmed.[26]

State v. Smith

Supreme Court of Vermont, 1978.
136 Vt. 520, 396 A.2d 126.

■ Before BARNEY, C.J., and DALEY, LARROW, BILLINGS, and HILL, JJ.

■ BARNEY, CHIEF JUDGE.

This is a prosecution for the rape of a sixteen year old babysitter and the murder of her charge, her eight year old cousin. As is so frequent in cases involving serious criminal violence, sanity is a critical issue. It is the principal concern of the appeal.

The killing is conceded, both below and here, and no issues separately contesting the rape conviction are urged here. No extended recital of facts is required. The defendant was twenty-one years old at the time of these events. The evidence disclosed that the defendant, after finding out that the babysitter was alone with her charge, went to the apartment and was admitted by the little boy while the babysitter was on the telephone. He explained his presence by claiming he had permission to borrow some records from the little boy's mother. Shortly thereafter he assaulted the babysitter and the rape occurred. Afterwards the defendant attempted to strangle the boy with a cord, then finally killed him by stabbing him with a large knife he got from the kitchen. When that happened the babysitter grabbed for the knife, cutting her hand, succeeding in knocking the defendant down, and escaped. As she ran into the street he apparently threw the knife at her but missed. The babysitter fled to a neighbor's and when the police arrived the defendant was gone. When the identity of the defendant became known, the foster family with whom he was living was contacted. He was later brought by one of them to the police station.

Almost simultaneously with the issuance of the warrant and before arraignment, the State moved for a mental examination in anticipation of a plea of insanity. That motion asserted that the defendant had a history of treatment for personality disorders at Metropolitan State Hospital in Waltham, Massachusetts; New Hampshire Hospital in Concord, New

---

26. Right from wrong means societal standard of morality, not the defendant's personal belief. "Deific decree" may render a defendant legally insane. People v. Serravo, 823 P.2d 128 (Colo.1992).

A defendant's ability to know the wrongfulness of his conduct refers to a standard of social morality. State v. Wilson, 700 A.2d 633 (Conn.1997).

Hampshire; and Waterbury State Hospital in Waterbury, Vermont. The motion was granted at the arraignment and the examination undertaken.

The test of responsibility for criminal conduct is set out in 13 V.S.A. § 4801:

The test when used as a defense in criminal cases shall be as follows:

(1) A person is not responsible for criminal conduct if at the time of such conduct as a result of mental disease or defect he lacks adequate capacity either to appreciate the criminality of his conduct or to conform his conduct to the requirements of law.

(2) The terms "mental disease or defect" do not include an abnormality manifested only by repeated criminal or otherwise anti-social conduct. The terms "mental disease or defect" shall include congenital and traumatic mental conditions as well as disease. . . .

There remains only the claim that the trial court should have charged on what is coming to be known as "diminished capacity." This issue was before the trial court and may occur on retrial, therefore it is appropriate for review on this appeal.

Contrary to the position taken by the State, our cases do not limit the application of the "diminished capacity" doctrine to the use of intoxicants. Rather, the matter of intoxication has been noted as one area of its application, where supported by appropriate facts.

The concept is directed at the evidentiary duty of the State to establish those elements of the crime charged requiring a conscious mental ingredient. There is no question that it may overlap the insanity defense in that insanity itself is concerned with mental conditions so incapacitating as to totally bar criminal responsibility. The distinction is that diminished capacity is legally applicable to disabilities not amounting to insanity, and its consequences, in homicide cases, operate to reduce the degree of the crime rather than to excuse its commission. Evidence offered under this rubric is relevant to prove the existence of a mental defect or obstacle to the presence of a state of mind which is an element of the crime, for example: premeditation or deliberation.

Since these states of mind are neither complex nor difficult to achieve, aside from special instances involving drugs, alcohol, injury or emotional frenzy, the issue frequently tends to reduce itself to situations involving lack of mental capacity itself.

For the purposes of the matter before us it is sufficient to say that where the evidence in any form supports it, a request to charge on the jury's duty to determine the existence of the states of mind required to establish the particular crime at issue in the light of any diminished capacity should be carefully reviewed by the trial court, and if appropriate, given.[27]

---

27. Concept of diminished capacity requires presence of a mental disease or defect not amounting to legal insanity which may be considered in determining whether defendant had the specific intent for the crime charged. State v. Friberg, 252 Kan. 141, 843 P.2d 218 (1992).

The California court apparently took the lead in developing the concept of diminished capacity. Thus it held "that evidence of mental infirmity, not amounting to legal insanity, is

Reversed and remanded.

People v. Ramsey

Supreme Court of Michigan, 1985.
422 Mich. 500, 375 N.W.2d 297.

■ BRICKLEY, JUSTICE.

These cases involve the constitutionality of M.C.L. § 768.36; M.S.A. § 28.1059, the statute which introduced the verdict of guilty but mentally ill to this state. In both cases, it is asserted that the guilty but mentally ill verdict violates principles of due process of law. We hold the statute to be constitutional.

Defendant Bruce Ramsey was charged with first-degree murder, M.C.L. § 750.316; M.S.A. § 28.548, as a result of the death of his wife. Ramsey had first choked her, and then stabbed her thirty-two times. At trial, he raised the defense of insanity, claiming he believed that he was exorcising a demon from his wife by stabbing her and that she would return to life once the demon was removed.

In the trial court, defendant moved that the verdict of guilty but mentally ill be held unconstitutional and that the jury not be instructed on that verdict. According to defendant, he opted for a bench trial because his motion was denied.

. . .

The day of the killing, Ramsey, after a full day of work, called his mother in Kentucky. He was excited; his mother described him as exuberant over his "return to God."

---

admissible and should be considered by the jury on the questions of premeditation and deliberation." People v. Baker, 42 Cal.2d 550, 569, 268 P.2d 705, 716 (1954). This means that even if defendant is not entitled to an acquittal, he may be guilty of only second-degree murder. Later it was held that by reason of diminished capacity defendant might have been unable to harbor malice aforethought, and hence be guilty of manslaughter rather than murder. People v. Henderson, 60 Cal.2d 482, 35 Cal.Rptr. 77, 386 P.2d 677 (1963). Still later this was carefully explained. "Even intentional killings can be mitigated to voluntary manslaughter if the killing occurred with sufficient provocation to arouse a reasonable man to a fit of passion or sudden quarrel or if the defendant did not attain the mental state of malice due to mental illness, mental defect or intoxication." People v. Burton, 6 Cal.3d 375, 385, 99 Cal.Rptr. 1, 7, 491 P.2d 793 (1971).

This did not meet the approval of the California legislature which enacted section 28 to the Penal Code, which provides:

"(b) As a matter of public policy there shall be no defense of diminished capacity, diminished responsibility, or irresistible impulse in a criminal action...." West's Cal.Penal Code 28(b) (1988).

§ 25(a) provides:

"The defense of diminished capacity is hereby abolished. In a criminal action ... evidence concerning an accused person's intoxication, trauma, mental illness, disease or defect shall not be admissible to show or negate capacity to form the particular purpose, intent, motive, malice aforethought, knowledge or other mental state required for the commission of the crime charged."

This does not preclude evidence of the actual absence of the required mens rea of the crime. See West's Cal.Penal Code § 28(a).

As for the killing itself, which was witnessed by Ramsey's children, who testified at trial, the victim and Ramsey had apparently argued. One of Ramsey's children testified that the victim came to the child's room crying. Ramsey entered the room and said, "Walk." The victim left the room and locked herself in the bathroom. Ramsey broke down the bathroom door.

Ramsey testified that he had attempted to choke, and then to stab, the demon out of his wife. Ramsey's son testified that he heard Ramsey say, "Die demon, die." When Ramsey realized that the victim was dead and was not returning to life, he placed her body in bed, crawled in next to her, and stabbed himself in the chest. Found in that position by the police (the children had fled to a neighbor's home), Ramsey was taken to a hospital. There, he made statements to family and friends to the effect that he was "screwed up" and that his wife "wasn't supposed to die." Hospital psychiatrists diagnosed Ramsey as acutely psychotic upon admission.

Psychiatrists called by the prosecution and the defense differed over whether Ramsey was mentally ill or insane at the time of the killing....

... Ramsey contend[s] that the guilty but mentally ill verdict denied [him] the due process of law guaranteed by the Fourteenth Amendment to the United States Constitution....

... Our concern here is only whether the statute is invalid because it denies criminal defendants a fair trial.

M.C.L. § 768.36(1); M.S.A. § 28.1059(1) provides:

"If the defendant asserts a defense of insanity in compliance with section 20a [MCL 768.20a; MSA 28.1043(1)], the defendant may be found 'guilty but mentally ill' if, after trial, the trier of fact finds all of the following beyond a reasonable doubt:

"(a) That the defendant is guilty of an offense.

"(b) That the defendant was mentally ill at the time of the commission of that offense.

"(c) That the defendant was not legally insane at the time of the commission of that offense."

M.C.L. § 768.21a; M.S.A. § 28.1044(1) defines insanity:

"A person is legally insane if, as a result of mental illness ... that person lacks substantial capacity either to appreciate the wrongfulness of his conduct or to conform his conduct to the requirements of the law."

Finally, mental illness is defined in M.C.L. § 330.1400a; M.S.A. § 14.800(400a) as:

"[A] substantial disorder of thought or mood which significantly impairs judgment, behavior, capacity to recognize reality, or ability to cope with the ordinary demands of life."

The history of the guilty but mentally ill verdict is well set forth in Smith & Hall, *Evaluating Michigan's guilty but mentally ill verdict: An empirical study,* 16 U. of Mich.J.L.Ref. 77 (1982). For our purposes here, it suffices to state that the statute was a reaction to this Court's decision in People v. McQuillan, 392 Mich. 511, 221 N.W.2d 569 (1974). Following that decision, a large number of persons found not guilty by reason of insanity, whom professionals had determined to be presently sane, were released from institutions, with tragic results. Two of the released persons soon committed violent crimes. See Comment, Guilty but mentally ill: An historical and constitutional analysis, 53 U. of Det.J.Urban L. 471, 471–472 (1976); Robey, Guilty but mentally ill, 6 Bull of Am.Ass'n of Psychiatry 374–375. Amid public outcry, the Legislature responded with the guilty but mentally ill verdict.

The major purpose in creating the guilty but mentally ill verdict is obvious. It was to limit the number of persons who, in the eyes of the Legislature, were *improperly* being relieved of all criminal responsibility by way of the insanity verdict. . . .

There is nothing impermissible about such a purpose. It is well within the power of the Legislature to attempt to cure what it sees to be a misuse of the law. What we must decide, however, is whether the verdict acts to deny defendants a fair trial.

It is claimed that the guilty but mentally ill verdict introduces a confusing irrelevancy into jury deliberations. Therefore, the first question we must face is whether the inclusion of the guilty but mentally ill verdict is so confusing to the jury that it denies a defendant a fair trial.

. . .

[W]e reject the claim that a jury is unable to comprehend the distinctions made by the Legislature between the concepts of mental illness and insanity. Our statutory scheme recognizes a continuum of mental functioning. A person is mentally ill if suffering from "a substantial disorder of thought or mood which significantly impairs judgment, behavior, capacity to recognize reality, or ability to cope with the ordinary demands of life." M.C.L. § 330.1400a; M.S.A. § 14.800(400a). A person is insane, however, only if that substantial impairment results in the lack of "substantial capacity either to appreciate the wrongfulness of his conduct or to conform his conduct to the requirements of law." M.C.L. § 768.21a; M.S.A. § 28.1044(1). Under these definitions, one must be mentally ill before he can be found insane, but the converse is not true. . . .

Also, M.C.L. § 768.36(1); M.S.A. § 28.1059(1) requires the jury to find that the defendant is not insane, that is, that the defendant does not lack the substantial capacity to appreciate the wrongfulness of his conduct or the ability to conform his conduct to the law, before it can conclude that the defendant is guilty but mentally ill.

We conclude that the Legislature has created a clear distinction between mental illness and insanity. Of course, in particular cases, this distinction may be very subtle and difficult for the jury to apply. But, it is no more subtle or difficult than the distinction between the intent to do great bodily harm and the intent to kill, a distinction we allow juries to make which often determines whether a defendant is guilty of first-or second-degree murder. In short, we cannot say that the legislative distinctions between mental illness and insanity deny the right to a fair trial.

[Defendant] also contend[s] that the inclusion of the guilty but mentally ill verdict infringed on [his] right to a fair trial by creating an unjustifiable risk of a compromise verdict. We find this claim to be wholly speculative, and must reject it.

. . .

Malice aforethought, or stated otherwise, the mental state necessary for the crime of murder, requires the intent to kill, the intent to do great bodily harm, and the intentional creation of a great risk of death or great bodily harm with the knowledge that death is the probable result. People v. Aaron, 409 Mich. 672, 299 N.W.2d 304 (1980). A finding of mental illness, even when defined as a substantial disorder of thought or mood, does not inexorably lead to the conclusion that the defendant did not entertain the requisite malice aforethought for murder. As explained in LaFave & Scott, Criminal Law, § 42, p. 326:

"A defendant in a criminal case, at the time he engaged in the conduct giving rise to the charges against him, may have been suffering from an abnormal mental condition which was not of a kind or character to afford him a successful insanity defense under the right-wrong test or other standard applicable in that jurisdiction. But, while this defendant is therefore ineligible for a finding of not guilty by reason of insanity, his mental abnormality may nonetheless be a most relevant consideration in the determination of whether he is guilty of the crime charged. Under the doctrine referred to as partial responsibility, diminished responsibility, or (somewhat less accurately) partial insanity, evidence concerning the defendant's mental condition is admissible on the question of whether the defendant had the mental state which is an element of the offense with which he is charged."

Thus, while his mental illness may be a consideration in evaluating the requisite state of mind for the crime charged, we decline to accept Ramsey's invitation to hold that a finding of mental illness negates malice aforethought as a matter of law.[28]

The trial court in this case found that *Ramsey* entertained the malice aforethought necessary to support a conviction of second-degree murder. Defendant would have us require that the trial judge affirmatively state that the mental illness did not affect the defendant's ability to form the requisite intent.

Had the trial judge indicated a refusal to consider the defendant's mental illness as a diminishing factor in his decision of whether defendant possessed the requisite malice aforethought, we would find it necessary to address the question of the extent to which mental illness could diminish the intent requirement for second-degree murder. But he did not. We therefore are faced with a statement by the judge that defendant possessed the requisite intent.

We are disinclined, under the circumstances of this case, to place a further burden on the fact-finding of a judge in a bench trial which would

---

28. Of course, if we were to hold that mental illness negates malice aforethought as a matter of law, a jury would have to be instructed that if they found the defendant mentally ill they could not find him guilty of murder. Considering the history of the guilty but mentally ill verdict, we doubt that such a result would comport with the intent of the Legislature.

require, in addition to a finding of guilt on the elements of the crime, an affirmative statement that all potential mitigating factors have been considered and rejected.

Boyd raises one matter which requires additional consideration.[29] He claims that error which requires reversal occurred when the trial court, over objection, instructed the jury on the disposition of a defendant found not guilty by reason of insanity and on the disposition of a defendant found guilty but mentally ill. The Court of Appeals rejected Boyd's claim on the strength of authorities now questionable in light of our recent decision in People v. Goad, 421 Mich. 20, 364 N.W.2d 584 (1984).

■ WILLIAMS, C.J., and RYAN, J., concur.

■ BOYLE, JUSTICE (concur[s]).

. . .

■ LEVIN, JUSTICE dissents.

Fulcher v. State

Supreme Court of Wyoming, 1981.
633 P.2d 142.

■ Before ROSE, C.J., and RAPER, THOMAS, ROONEY and BROWN, JJ.

■ BROWN, JUSTICE.

Appellant-defendant was found guilty of aggravated assault without dangerous weapon in violation of § 6–4–506(a), W.S.1977, by the district court sitting without a jury. While appellant characterizes the issues on appeal differently, we believe the issues to be:

(1) Is it necessary for a defendant to plead "not guilty by reason of mental illness or deficiency" before evidence of unconsciousness can be presented?

(2) Was there sufficient evidence to sustain appellant's conviction?

We will affirm.

On November 17, 1979, the appellant consumed seven or eight shots of whiskey over a period of four hours in a Torrington bar, and had previously had a drink at home.

Appellant claims he got in a fight in the bar restroom, then left the bar to find a friend. According to his testimony, the last thing he remembers until awakening in jail, is going out of the door at the bar.

Appellant and his friend were found lying in the alley behind the bar by a police officer who noted abrasions on their fists and faces. Appellant and his friend swore, were uncooperative, and combative. They were subsequently booked for public intoxication and disturbing the peace. During booking appellant continued to swear, and said he and his friend were jumped by a "bunch of Mexicans." Although his speech was slurred,

---

29. Boyd also finds error in the trial court's failure to reopen the proofs sua sponte. We find no clear error in the conclusion of the Court of Appeals that the trial court did not err.

he was able to verbally count his money, roughly $500 to $600 in increments of $20, and was able to walk to his cell without assistance.

Appellant was placed in a cell with one Martin Hernandez who was lying unconscious on the floor of the cell. After the jailer left the cell, he heard something that sounded like someone being kicked. He ran back to the cell and saw appellant standing by Hernandez. When the jailer started to leave again, the kicking sound resumed, and he observed appellant kicking and stomping on Hernandez's head. Appellant told the officer Hernandez had fallen out of bed. Hernandez was bleeding profusely and was taken to the hospital for some 52 stitches in his head and mouth. He had lost two or three teeth as a result of the kicking. . . .

At his arraignment in district court, appellant first entered a plea of "not guilty by reason of temporary mental illness." Upon being advised by the trial judge that he would have to be committed for examination pursuant to § 7–11–304, W.S.1977, he withdrew that plea and entered a plea of not guilty. . . .

At the trial Dr. LeBegue testified that in his expert medical opinion appellant suffered brain injury and was in a state of traumatic automatism at the time of his attack on Hernandez. Dr. LeBegue defined traumatic automatism as the state of mind in which a person does not have conscious and willful control over his actions, and lacks the ability to be aware of and to perceive his external environment. Dr. LeBegue further testified that another possible symptom is an inability to remember what occurred while in a state of traumatic automatism. . . .

We hold that the trial court properly received and considered evidence of unconsciousness absent a plea of "not guilty by reason of mental illness or deficiency."

The defense of unconsciousness perhaps should be more precisely denominated as the defense of automatism. Automatism is the state of a person who, though capable of action, is not conscious of what he is doing. While in an automatistic state, an individual performs complex actions without an exercise of will. Because these actions are performed in a state of unconsciousness, they are involuntary. Automatistic behavior may be followed by complete or partial inability to recall the actions performed while unconscious. Thus, a person who acts automatically does so without intent, exercise of free will, or knowledge of the act.

Automatism may be caused by an abnormal condition of the mind capable of being designated a mental illness or deficiency. Automatism may also be manifest in a person with a perfectly healthy mind. In this opinion we are only concerned with the defense of automatism occurring in a person with a healthy mind. To further narrow the issue to be decided in this case, we are concerned with alleged automatism caused by concussion.

The defense of automatism, while not an entirely new development in the criminal law, has been discussed in relatively few decisions by American appellate courts, most of these being in California where the defense is statutory. Some courts have held that insanity and automatism are separate and distinct defenses, and that evidence of automatism may be presented under a plea of not guilty. Some states have made this distinction by statute. In other states the distinction is made by case law. . . .

"The defenses of insanity and unconsciousness are not the same in nature, for unconsciousness at the time of the alleged criminal act need not be the result of a disease or defect of the mind. As a consequence, the two defenses are not the same in effect, for a defendant found not guilty by reason of unconsciousness, as distinct from insanity, is not subject to commitment to a hospital for the mentally ill." State v. Caddell, 287 N.C. 266, 215 S.E.2d 348, 360 (1975).

The principal reason for making a distinction between the defense of unconsciousness and insanity is that the consequences which follow an acquittal will differ. The defense of unconsciousness is usually a complete defense.[30] That is, there are no follow-up consequences after an acquittal; all action against a defendant is concluded.

However, in the case of a finding of not guilty by reason of insanity, the defendant is ordinarily committed to a mental institution. . . .

In some states the commitment is automatic after a finding of not guilty by reason of insanity. In Wyoming the trial judge may commit a defendant based on evidence produced at trial or the commitment may be by separate proceedings.

The mental illness or deficiency plea does not adequately cover automatic behavior. Unless the plea of automatism, separate and apart from the plea of mental illness or deficiency is allowed, certain anomalies will result. For example, if the court determines that the automatistic defendant is sane, but refuses to recognize automatism, the defendant has no defense to the crime with which he is charged. If found guilty, he faces a prison term. The rehabilitative value of imprisonment for the automatistic offender who has committed the offense unconsciously is nonexistent. The cause of the act was an uncontrollable physical disorder that may never recur and is not a moral deficiency.

If, however, the court treats automatism as insanity and then determines that the defendant is insane, he will be found not guilty. He then will be committed to a mental institution for an indefinite period. The commitment of an automatistic individual to a mental institution for rehabilitation has absolutely no value. Mental hospitals generally treat people with psychiatric or psychological problems. This form of treatment is not suited to unconscious behavior resulting from a bump on the head.

---

30. Unconsciousness is not a complete defense under all circumstances. An incomplete list of situations will illustrate. In California, "unconsciousness produced by voluntary intoxication does not render a defendant incapable of committing a crime." People v. Cox, 67 Cal.App.2d 166, 153 P.2d 362 (1944), and cases cited. In Colorado a person who participates in a fracas and as a result is hit on the head and rendered semi-conscious or unconscious cannot maintain that he is not criminally responsible. Watkins v. People, 158 Colo. 485, 408 P.2d 425 (1965). In Oklahoma a motorist is guilty of manslaughter if he drives an automobile with knowledge that he is subject to frequent blackouts. Carter v. State, Okl.Cr., 376 P.2d 351 (1962). *See also*, Smith v. Commonwealth, Ky., 268 S.W.2d 937 (1954). As to somnambulism, see Fain v. Commonwealth, 78 Ky. 183, 39 Am.Rep. 213 (1879); and Lewis v. State, 196 Ga. 755, 27 S.E.2d 659 (1943). See also § 6–1–116, W.S.1977.

It may be argued that evidence of unconsciousness cannot be received unless a plea of not guilty by reason of mental illness or deficiency is made pursuant to Rule 15, W.R.Cr.P. We believe this approach to be illogical.

"... Insanity is incapacity from disease of the mind, to know the nature and quality of one's act or to distinguish between right and wrong in relation thereto. In contrast, a person who is completely unconscious when he commits an act otherwise punishable as a crime cannot know the nature and quality thereof or whether it is right or wrong...." State v. Mercer, *supra*, 165 S.E.2d at 335.

It does not seem that the definition of "mental deficiency" in § 7–11–301(a)(iii),[31] W.S.1977, which includes "brain damage," encompasses simple brain trauma with no permanent after effects. It is our view that the "brain damage" contemplated in the statute is some serious and irreversible condition having an impact upon the ability of the person to function. It is undoubtedly something far more significant than a temporary and transitory condition. The two defenses are merged, in effect, if a plea of "not guilty by reason of mental illness or deficiency" is a prerequisite for using the defense of unconsciousness....

Although courts hold that unconsciousness and insanity are separate and distinct defenses, there has been some uncertainty concerning the burden of proof. We believe the better rule to be that stated in State v. Caddell, *supra*, 215 S.E.2d at 363:[32]

"We now hold that, under the law of this state, unconsciousness, or automatism, is a complete defense to the criminal charge, separate and apart from the defense of insanity; that *it is an affirmative defense; and that the burden rests upon the defendant to establish this defense, unless it arises out of the State's own evidence,* to the satisfaction of the jury." (Emphasis added.)

The rationale for this rule is that the defendant is the only person who knows his actual state of consciousness. Hill v. Baxter, 1 All E.R. 193 (1958), 1 Q.B. 277.

Our ruling on the facts of this case is that the defense of unconsciousness resulting from a concussion with no permanent brain damage is an affirmative defense and is a defense separate from the defense of not guilty by reason of mental illness or deficiency.

The appellant's conviction must, nevertheless, be affirmed. Dr. LeBegue was unable to state positively whether or not appellant had the requisite mental state for aggravated assault. He could not state that the character of the act was devoid of criminal intent because of the mind alteration. The presumption of mental competency was never overcome by appellant and the evidence presented formed a reasonable basis on which

---

31. Section 7–11–301(a)(iii):

" 'Mental deficiency' means a defect attributable to mental retardation, brain damage and learning disabilities."

32. State v. Mercer, 275 N.C. 108, 165 S.E.2d 328, 335 (1969), held that "unconsciousness is never an affirmative defense." State v. Caddell, 287 N.C. 266, 215 S.E.2d 348, 363 (1975), overruled *Mercer, supra,* and stated that "it [unconsciousness] is an affirmative defense."

the trial judge could find and did find that the State had met the required burden of proof. . . .

■ RAPER, JUSTICE, specially concurring, with whom ROONEY, JUSTICE, joins.[33]

I concur only in the result reached by the majority, except to the extent I otherwise herein indicate.

The reasoning of the majority with respect to the defense of unconsciousness in this case is contrary to clear legislative will and has judicially amended the statutes of this state pertaining to mental illness or deficiency excluding criminal responsibility. . . .

I am not concerned with the fact that unconsciousness may be a defense in this case but am distressed that the procedure for taking advantage of it has been cast aside. In order to reach the conclusion of the majority that it is not necessary to plead mental deficiency as a defense in the case of unconsciousness, it is indispensable that it be pretended that § 7–11–301, *supra*, does not exist. The appellant's disorder, if it existed, was caused by "brain damage" according to the appellant's own testimony. That is "mental deficiency" by statutory definition. The majority has feebly attempted to jump the hurdle of a statutory definition by saying "unconsciousness" is not "insanity," but we no longer use that term. It must be pointed out that under the old statutes and before adoption of the current law pertaining to mental deficiency, "insanity" was not legislatively defined. The majority is attempting to adopt the law of an era gone by-by, rather than what the authors of the new legislation considered a more informed and modern concept. . . .

MODEL PENAL CODE

Article 4. Responsibility

Section 4.01 Mental Disease or Defect Excluding Responsibility.

(1) A person is not responsible for criminal conduct if at the time of such conduct as a result of mental disease or defect he lacks substantial capacity either to appreciate the criminality [wrongfulness] of his conduct or to conform his conduct to the requirements of law.

(2) As used in this Article, the terms "mental disease or defect" do not include an abnormality manifested only by repeated criminal or otherwise anti-social conduct.

---

33. See also Polston v. State, 685 P.2d 1 (Wyo.1984).

The defense of unconsciousness negates the necessary mens rea for the offense. State v. Massey, 242 Kan. 252, 747 P.2d 802 (1987).

A claim of automatism based on sleep deprivation was independent of the insanity defense. It bore on the voluntariness of the defendant's conduct in striking police. Automatism is not a disease or defect, but an aspect of voluntariness. McClain v. State, 678 N.E.2d 104 (Ind. 1997).

The defense of automatism is independent from the defense of insanity and the prosecution bears the burden of proof beyond a reasonable doubt to overcome the automatism claim. State v. Hinkle, 489 S.E.2d 257 (W.Va.1996).

Evidence of retardation and brain damage did not warrant an instruction on automatism. Smith v. State, 932 P.2d 521 (Okl.Cr.1996).

Section 4.02 Evidence of Mental Disease or Defect Admissible When Relevant to Element of the Offense; [Mental Disease or Defect Impairing Capacity as Ground for Mitigation of Punishment in Capital Cases].

(1) Evidence that the defendant suffered from a mental disease or defect is admissible whenever it is relevant to prove that the defendant did or did not have a state of mind which is an element of the offense.

[(2) Whenever the jury or the Court is authorized to determine or to recommend whether or not the defendant shall be sentenced to death or imprisonment upon conviction, evidence that the capacity of the defendant to appreciate the criminality [wrongfulness] of his conduct or to conform his conduct to the requirements of law was impaired as a result of mental disease or defect is admissible in favor of sentence of imprisonment.]

Section 4.03 Mental Disease or Defect Excluding Responsibility Is Affirmative Defense; Requirement of Notice; Form of Verdict and Judgment When Finding of Irresponsibility is Made.

(1) Mental disease or defect excluding responsibility is an affirmative defense.

(2) Evidence of mental disease or defect excluding responsibility is not admissible unless the defendant, at the time of entering his plea of not guilty or within ten days thereafter or at such later time as the Court may for good cause permit, files a written notice of his purpose to rely on such defense.

(3) When the defendant is acquitted on the ground of mental disease or defect excluding responsibility, the verdict and the judgment shall so state.[34]

SECTION 3.   DRUNKENNESS (INTOXICATION)

The early common law seems to have ignored the problem of intoxication at the time of the *actus reus*.[35] Coke and Blackstone, in fact, were inclined to urge that intoxication of one who committed a harmful deed should be regarded as a circumstance of aggravation. This suggestion was not adopted, but prior to the nineteenth century intoxication, to whatever extent, was no defense in a criminal case. Since then there have been some modifications of that strict rule. Three modifications usually are mentioned: (1) Involuntary (innocent) intoxication may be so extreme as to be

---

34. Copyright © 1962 by the American Law Institute. Reprinted with the permission of the American Law Institute.

35. Under the law of England until the early 19th Century voluntary intoxication was never an excuse for criminal misconduct. Director of Public Prosecutions v. Beard, [1920] App.Cas. 479.

"Intoxication" includes excitement or stupefaction induced by drugs as well as by liquor. People v. Lim Dum Dong, 26 Cal.App.2d 135, 78 P.2d 1026 (1938). A drunken frenzy is not insanity despite the fact that it has sometimes been referred to loosely as "delirium tremens." Cheadle v. State, 11 Okl.Cr. 566, 149 P. 919 (1915); State v. Kidwell, 62 W.Va. 466, 59 S.E. 494 (1907). Delirium tremens proper is a form of mental disease and is treated on the same basis as any other form of insanity. State v. Alexander, 215 La. 245, 40 So.2d 232 (1949). The person suffering from delirium tremens is not free from fault, it is true, but the law takes notice only of the *immediate condition which is a mental disease, and not of the excessive drinking which is* remote. United States v. Drew, 25 Fed.Cas. 913, No. 14,993 (C.C.D.Mass.1828).

Voluntary intoxication is not an excuse but may be taken into consideration in determining the existence or nonexistence of malice aforethought which distinguishes murder from manslaughter. State v. Hudson, 85 Ariz. 77, 331 P.2d 1092 (1958).

exculpating; (2) voluntary (culpable) intoxication may entitle the defendant to an acquittal if the crime charged requires a specific intent or special state of mind and he was too drunk to have such intent or state of mind; (3) alcoholic-induced mental illness is treated the same as other types of insanity although it results from overindulgence in liquor.

Firmly entrenched in the common law, although the wisdom thereof has been questioned by some, is the rule that voluntary intoxication is never exculpating. It is necessary, however, to draw a clear distinction between lack of excuse, on one hand, and disproof of some essential element of the crime charged, on the other. If the offense charged requires a specific intent, the defendant is not guilty if he was too intoxicated at the time to have any such intent, and had not entertained such an intent prior to his intoxication.[36] In such a case, proof of extreme intoxication (although "voluntary") may result in an acquittal, but it is not on any theory of exculpation. Suppose **D** has been indicted for burglary, for example. The indictment charges that **D** broke and entered the dwelling house of **X** at night with intent to steal. The evidence shows that **D** opened the front door of **X's** house late at night, went in and was found in a drunken stupor on the floor. **D** was searched and it was learned that nothing was taken. And when **D** is tried the jury is satisfied that while **D** managed to stumble into **X's** house before he lost consciousness, **D's** mind was too befogged with drink to be capable of entertaining any intent. Such a finding will not support a conviction of burglary.[37] This is not on any theory of excusing **D's** conduct. One of the essential elements of the crime charged is missing. If **D** broke and entered the dwelling house of another at night (however wrongfully), **D** is still not guilty of burglary unless **D** did so with the intention of committing some crime therein (which crime must amount to felony at common law). Any evidence which proves the absence of such intent will disprove the charge of burglary.

A person should not be convicted of larceny upon proof that the person drank until the individual's mind was so blank that the person staggered away from the bar still clutching the glass from which the person had been drinking, but unable to realize this fact or to entertain any intent. A man who rapes a woman while intoxicated cannot invoke the defense of intoxication. But if the charge were an attempt to rape, intoxication could be asserted as a defense since the attempt requires a specific intent.[38] A drunkard (voluntarily drunk) walking with an axe on his shoulder who

---

36. One who drinks to "nerve" himself to commit a crime already decided upon, and who thereupon does commit that crime, is not in a position to maintain that he was too drunk at the time to entertain the intent which he executed. State v. Butner, 66 Nev. 127, 206 P.2d 253 (1949); State v. Robinson, 20 W.Va. 713 (1882).

37. State v. Phillips, 80 W.Va. 748, 93 S.E. 828 (1917). And a fumbling effort to get into a building by one too drunk to be capable of entertaining any intent is not an attempt to commit burglary. People v. Jones, 263 Ill. 564, 105 N.E. 744 (1914).

38. In a prosecution for attempted suicide intoxication of the prisoner at the time of the alleged attempt "is a material fact in order to arrive at the conclusion whether or not the prisoner really intended to destroy his life." Regina v. Doody, 6 Cox C.C. 463 (1854).

In a robbery trial there was evidence tending to show that D was too drunk at the time to form an intent to rob. It was reversible error for the judge to refuse to let this issue go to the jury. Womack v. United States, 336 F.2d 959 (D.C.Cir.1964).

staggers in such a manner as to bump another with the axe is guilty of battery. This is true however intoxicated the person may be because battery requires no more than criminal negligence. But the person is not guilty of assault with intent to murder if the person had no such intention. And proof that the defendant was too dazed at the time to be capable of entertaining any intent will disprove the aggravated charge.

In jurisdictions following the Model Penal Code[39] intoxication is a defense if it prevents an accused from having the required state of mind for the offense. However, intoxication is not always a complete defense and if the mental element required for the offense is recklessness or criminal negligence, then intoxication is no defense.[40] Other jurisdictions allow intoxication to be considered on the defendant's ability to entertain the mental state for the offense.[41]

Provocation. Voluntary homicide is manslaughter rather than murder if it results from heat of passion engendered by adequate provocation and before the lapse of the "cooling time." Whether the provocation received was adequate or inadequate, and whether the time between the provocation and the fatal blow was sufficient or insufficient for passion once inflamed to subside, are both measured by an objective test,—the ordinary reasonable person. Hence the fact of intoxication has no bearing on the adequacy of the provocation or the sufficiency of the time for "cooling."[42] But whether the killing was actually in hot blood or cold blood depends upon the frame of mind of the killer himself. And if the fact of intoxication tends to throw any light upon the frame of mind of the defendant at the moment of the killing, the jury should have the benefit of this evidence with an instruction to consider it on this point only.[43]

State v. Cooper

Supreme Court of Arizona, In Division, 1974.
111 Ariz. 332, 529 P.2d 231.

■ HOLOHAN, JUSTICE. The appellant, Eugene Raymond Cooper, was convicted of kidnapping and assault with a deadly weapon for which he was sentenced to confinement for concurrent terms of 30 years to life for each

---

39. Model Penal Code § 2.8 (1962).

40. McGuire v. Commonwealth, 885 S.W.2d 931 (Ky.1994); State v. Trieb, 315 N.W.2d 649 (N.D.1982); State v. Glidden, 122 N.H. 41, 441 A.2d 728 (1982); State v. Royball, 710 P.2d 168 (Utah 1985).

41. See State v. Coates, 107 Wn.2d 882, 735 P.2d 64 (1987).

42. Bishop v. United States, 71 App.D.C. 132, 107 F.2d 297 (1939); Commonwealth v. Bridge, 495 Pa. 568, 435 A.2d 151 (1981); Willis v. Commonwealth, 73 Va. 929 (1879); Rex v. Carroll, 7 Car. & P. 145, 173 Eng.Rep. 64 (1835).

Some courts have repeated Bishop's suggestion that an intent to drink may supply the malice aforethought needed for guilt of murder. *See,* for example, Newsome v. State, 214 Ark. 48, 50, 214 S.W.2d 778, 779 (1948); Weakley v. State, 168 Ark. 1087, 1089, 273 S.W. 374, 376 (1925).

43. Rex v. Thomas, 7 Car. & P. 817, 173 Eng.Rep. 356 (1837); Regina v. Olbey, 30 N.R. 152, 50 CCC2d 257 (S.C.Can.1979).

offense. He appeals, raising the single issue of whether it was error for the trial court to refuse to submit the issue of insanity to the jury.

The appellant had been reported to the police as driving recklessly on the street and around a shopping center parking lot. A patrolman pursued appellant at high speed through rush-hour traffic. The appellant shot at and wounded the pursuing police officer. Shortly thereafter appellant kidnapped a man from a parking lot at gunpoint. The kidnap victim eventually wrestled the gun away from appellant, and the auto crashed into the divider on a freeway. Appellant fled on foot and was soon apprehended.

Pursuant to the request of the defense, an examination of the defendant's mental condition was ordered by the trial court. The court-appointed psychiatrists reported that the defendant was competent to assist his counsel and that the defendant understood the nature of the proceedings. A hearing was held, and the trial court found that the defendant was competent to stand trial.

The defendant gave timely notice of his intention to raise the defense of insanity at the trial.

During the trial the defense offered testimony by a psychiatrist and a psychologist as to the defendant's mental condition at the time of the offense. After hearing the evidence the trial court ruled that the evidence presented did not raise an issue as to the defendant's sanity, and the trial court refused all instructions submitted by the defense on the issue of sanity. The trial court did instruct the jury on the effect of voluntary intoxication in terms substantially the same as stated in the statute. A.R.S. § 13–132.

There is a presumption of sanity in every criminal case. To rebut that presumption and cause sanity to become an issue in the case, the defendant must introduce sufficient evidence to generate a doubt as to his sanity. If the evidence generates a reasonable doubt as to sanity, the burden falls upon the state to prove sanity beyond a reasonable doubt. Arizona has long adhered to the rule that the test of insanity is the M'Naghten rule.

The defense argues that not only did the evidence presented generate a reasonable doubt of the defendant's sanity but it would fully support a finding that the defendant was insane at the time of the commission of the criminal acts charged. The defense points out that both the psychiatrist and psychologist testified that the defendant was insane under the M'Naghten standard.

The state concedes that each of the defense experts testified that the defendant did not know the nature and quality of his acts and that he did not know he was doing wrong at the time of the acts charged, but the state points out that the condition of the defendant's mind was caused by his use of drugs and this does not constitute the defense of insanity. We agree.

The record shows that both of the defense experts testified that without the use of the drugs during the time in question the defendant would have been sane. They agreed that it was the use of drugs which induced his mental incapacity. The psychiatrist described the condition of the defendant as toxic psychosis, and the psychologist labeled it as "acute drug induced psychotic episode."

The authorities have distinguished between an existing state of mental illness and a temporary episode of mental incapacity caused by the voluntary use of liquor or drugs. In the first instance the defense of insanity is available even though the state of mental illness may have been brought about by excessive or prolonged use of liquor or drugs, but in the latter instance the defense is not available. While the cases usually deal with excessive use of liquor, the same principles are applicable to drugs. Voluntary intoxication, whether by alcohol or drugs, is not a defense to crime, but evidence of such intoxication is admissible to show lack of specific intent.

It is not contested that the defendant had been voluntarily taking amphetamines for several days prior to the conduct at issue. Prior to that time the experts for the defense state that the defendant was sane. His subsequent condition, leading to his bizarre actions, was a result of an artificially produced state of mind brought on by his own hand at his own choice. The voluntary actions of the defendant do not provide an excuse in law for his subsequent, irrational conduct.

The defendant's burden to overcome the presumption of sanity was not met; therefore, the refusal of the trial court to instruct on insanity was correct.

Affirmed.

■ CAMERON, V.C.J., and STRUCKMEYER, J., concur.

Harris v. State

Court of Appeals of Maryland, 1999.
353 Md. 596, 728 A.2d 180.

■ RAKER, JUDGE.

Appellant was convicted of the offense of carjacking, in violation of Maryland Code (1957, 1996 Repl.Vol., 1997 Supp.), Article 27 § 348A. The issue we must decide in this case is whether the trial court erred in instructing the jury that carjacking is not a specific intent crime. We conclude that carjacking is not a specific intent crime, and accordingly, we shall affirm the trial court.

I

We shall briefly state the facts. On November 26, 1996, Timothy Harris, Jack Tipton and several other friends were playing cards and drinking alcohol at a friend's house. Tipton offered to drive Harris home. Tipton testified that Harris became angry when Tipton refused to go to the District of Columbia, and that Harris forcibly removed Tipton from the car and drove away. Tipton reported the car as stolen.

Appellant was indicted by the Grand Jury for Prince George's County with the crimes of carjacking in violation of Art. 27, § 348A, unlawful taking of a motor vehicle in violation of Art. 27, § 342A, and second degree assault in violation of Art. 27, § 12A. At trial, Harris's defense was voluntary intoxication. He testified that he had consumed alcohol and smoked marijuana throughout the evening, and that he "blacked out" after leaving the get-together.

Appellant requested a jury instruction on voluntary intoxication, arguing that he was too intoxicated from drugs and alcohol to form the specific intent required for the offenses of carjacking and unlawful taking of a motor vehicle. The court declined to instruct the jury that carjacking required specific intent. The trial court instructed the jury that when charged with an offense requiring specific intent, a defendant cannot be guilty if he was so intoxicated by drugs and/or alcohol that he was unable to form the necessary intent. The court further instructed the jury that the unlawful taking of a motor vehicle was the only offense that required specific intent. As to the offense of carjacking, the trial court instructed the jury as follows:

An individual is guilty of carjacking when that individual obtains unauthorized possession or control of a motor vehicle from another individual in actual possession by force or violence, or by putting that individual in fear through intimidation or threat of force or violence.

The jury found Harris not guilty of the crime of unauthorized taking of a motor vehicle, and guilty of carjacking and assault.

Appellant noted a timely appeal to the Court of Special Appeals. We granted certiorari on our own motion to address the issue of whether specific intent is an element of the crime of carjacking.

II

Maryland's carjacking statute, Art. 27, § 348A reads in pertinent part:

(b) *Elements of offense.*—(1) An individual commits the offense of carjacking when the individual obtains unauthorized possession or control of a motor vehicle from another individual in actual possession by force or violence, or by putting that individual in fear through intimidation or threat of force or violence.

* * *

(c) *Penalty—In general.*—An individual convicted of carjacking ... is guilty of a felony and shall be sentenced to imprisonment for not more than 30 years.

(d) *Same—Additional to other offenses.*—The sentence imposed under this section may be imposed separate from and consecutive to a sentence for any other offense arising from the conduct underlying the offenses of carjacking or armed carjacking.

(e) *Defenses.*—It is not a defense to the offense of carjacking or armed carjacking that the defendant did not intend to permanently deprive the owner of the motor vehicle.

The State argues that the plain language of § 348A clearly establishes that carjacking is not a specific intent crime. The State observes that the trial court's carjacking instruction tracked the language of § 348A(b)(1). According to the State, the Legislature's failure to include language which would ordinarily indicate a specific intent requirement refutes Harris's claim that carjacking requires a specific intent to deprive without regard to duration. Rather, the Legislature clearly intended that the offense is committed without any additional deliberate and conscious purpose or design to accomplish a specific and more remote result.

Appellant argues that carjacking requires specific intent "without regard to the intended duration of the deprivation." He argues that carjacking is a type of robbery without the need to prove a specific intent to deprive permanently. Alternatively, he argues that carjacking is the equivalent of an unauthorized use of a motor vehicle, preceded by an assault, battery, or an aggravated assault, and as such, requires the State to prove a specific intent to deprive, without regard to the duration of the intended deprivation. In particular, Appellant argues that carjacking is little more than robbery without the need to prove specific intent to *permanently* deprive, and the equivalent of unauthorized use preceded by an assault, battery, or an aggravated assault. Appellant maintains that the intent requirement of carjacking is like that of unauthorized use—that an intent to deprive *temporarily* is the specific intent requirement. Noting that the standard for specific intent is "whether, in addition to the general intent to do the immediate act, it embraces some additional purpose or design to be accomplished beyond that immediate act," Appellant reasons that "[c]arjacking requires that, through force or violence, or a threat of force or violence (the immediate act), a person obtains unauthorized possession or control of a motor vehicle (the purpose beyond the immediate act)."

III

Generally there are two aspects of every crime—the *actus reus* or guilty act and the *mens rea* or the culpable mental state accompanying the forbidden act. Garnett v. State, 332 Md. 571, 577–78, 632 A.2d 797, 800 (1993). Maryland continues to observe the distinction between general and specific intent crimes. Shell v. State, 307 Md. 46, 65, 512 A.2d 358, 366–67 (1986). The distinction is particularly significant when a defendant claims that his voluntary intoxication prevents him from forming the requisite intent to commit a crime. *See id.* at 65, 512 A.2d at 367 (noting that the distinction "does serve to reconcile fairness to the accused with the need to protect the public from intoxicated offenders and to deter such persons"); Wieland v. State, 101 Md.App. 1, 35, 643 A.2d 446, 463 (1994) ("It is a distinction that takes on critical importance most frequently in assessing the effect of voluntary intoxication on a defendant's capacity to entertain a certain *mens rea*."). It has long been the law in Maryland that while voluntary intoxication is a defense to a specific intent crime, it is not a defense to a general intent crime. *See Shell*, 307 Md. at 58, 512 A.2d at 367 (conducting extensive review of Maryland cases addressing asserted defense of voluntary intoxication and specific intent generally).

Specific intent has been defined as not simply the intent to do an immediate act, but the "additional deliberate and conscious purpose or design of accomplishing a very specific and more remote result." *Shell*, 307 Md. at 63, 512 A.2d at 366 (quoting Smith v. State, 41 Md.App. 277, 305, 398 A.2d 426, 443 (1979)); *see also* In re Taka C., 331 Md. 80, 84, 626 A.2d 366, 368–69 (1993); Ford v. State, 330 Md. 682, 702, 625 A.2d 984, 993

(1993); State v. Gover, 267 Md. 602, 606, 298 A.2d 378, 381 (1973). In Shell, we quoted with approval the explanation of specific intent by JUDGE MOYLAN, writing for the Court of Special Appeals in Smith v. State, 41 Md.App. at 305–06, 398 A.2d at 442–43:

A specific intent is not simply the intent to do the immediate act but embraces the requirement that the mind be conscious of a more remote purpose or design which shall eventuate from the doing of the immediate act. Though assault implies only the general intent to strike the blow, assault with intent to murder, rob, rape, or maim requires a fully formed and conscious purpose that those further consequences shall flow from the doing of the immediate act. To break and enter requires a mere general intent but to commit burglary requires the additional specific intent of committing a felony after the entry has been made. A trespassory taking requires a mere general intent but larceny (or robbery) requires the specific *animus furandi* or deliberate purpose of depriving the owner permanently of the stolen goods. *This is why even voluntary intoxication may negate a specific intent though it will not negate a mere general intent.*

* * *

The larger class "specific intent" includes such other members as 1) assault with intent to murder, 2) assault with intent to rape, 3) assault with intent to rob, 4) assault with intent to maim, 5) burglary, 6) larceny, 7) robbery and 8) the specific-intent-to-inflict-grievous-bodily-harm variety of murder. h of these requires not simply the general intent to do the immediate act with no particular, clear or undifferentiated end in mind, but the additional deliberate and conscious purpose or design of accomplishing a very specific and more remote result.

307 Md. at 62–63, 512 A.2d at 366 (emphasis added). . . .

By way of example, the Court of Special Appeals has held that the common law crime of assault of the intent to frighten variety is a specific intent crime. *Wieland,* 101 Md.App. at 38, 643 A.2d at 464. That crime has been defined as "the doing of an act that places the victim in apprehension of immediate bodily harm *with the intent to cause such apprehension." Id.,* 643 A.2d at 464.

The general intent is the intent to commit the immediate act, i.e., the intent to make the threatening gesture. *Id.,* 643 A.2d at 464. An additional requirement is that there be a specific intent for that immediate act to place the victim in fear of imminent bodily harm. *Id.,* 643 A.2d at 464. The court noted, by way of contrast, that an assault of the attempted battery type is a general intent crime requiring no specific intent. *Id.,* 643 A.2d at 464. JUDGE MOYLAN, writing for the court, noted:

Accurately employed, the term "specific intent" designates some specific mental element or intended purpose above and beyond the mental state required for the mere *actus reus* of the crime itself. Were it not so, every intentional crime would be deemed a specific intent crime and there would no longer even be such a category as that of general intent crimes.

Id. at 39, 643 A.2d at 464–65. Each crime must be reviewed on an *ad hoc* basis. *Id.* at 37–38, 643 A.2d at 464. Distilled to its essence, to determine whether a particular crime requires a necessary specific intent, "we must inquire whether, in addition to the general intent to do the immediate act, it embraces some additional purpose or design to be accomplished beyond that immediate act." *Id.*, 643 A.2d at 464. . . .

IV

We have consistently stated that the cardinal rule in statutory construction is to effectuate the Legislature's broad goal or purpose. Gargliano v. State, 334 Md. 428, 435 639 A.2d 675, 678 (1994). The primary source of legislative intent is the text of the statute itself. Rose v. Fox Pool Corp., 335 Md. 351, 359, 643 A.2d 906, 909 (1994). To determine if a criminal statute requires specific intent, we look first to the language of the statute. *See* Richmond v. State, 326 Md. 257, 262, 604 A.2d 483, 485 (1992); *Shell*, 307 Md. at 69, 512 A.2d at 370 (stating that particular language and purpose of each statute must be considered). If the language alone does not provide sufficient information as to the Legislature's intent, we look to other sources to discern the Legislature's purpose. *See* Jones v. State, 336 Md. 255, 261, 647 A.2d 1204, 1206–07 (1994). In determining legislative intent, the key is the purpose of the legislation, determined in the light of the statute's language and context. "[W]e look at statutory language in context; we consider legislative history when it is available. . . . Our endeavor always is to construe a statute so as to implement the legislative goal, not to frustrate it."

Warfield v. State, 315 Md. 474, 499, 554 A.2d 1238, 1251 (1989) (alteration in original) (citation omitted) (quoting NCR Corp. v. Comptroller, 313 Md. 118, 145–46, 544 A.2d 764, 777 (1988)).

Viewing the statute as a whole, the language of the carjacking statute does not evidence an intent on the part of the General Assembly to create a specific intent crime. Words such as "with intent to" are conspicuously absent from the statute.[44] "When a statute does not contain any reference to intent, general intent is ordinarily implied." United States v. Martinez, 49 F.3d 1398, 1401 (9th Cir.1995).

The legislative history as well as the plain language of the statute make clear that the General Assembly intended to create a new criminal offense known as carjacking. *See* Senate Judicial Proceedings Committee, Floor Report for Senate Bill 339, at 1 (1993) ("This bill creates and defines the crimes of carjacking and armed carjacking."); *cf.* Pixley v. United States, 692 A.2d 438, 439 (D.C.1997) (carjacking is a new criminal offense). The Legislature created a new offense that does not require any additional

---

44. The General Assembly has created specific intent crimes, using explicit language to indicate the required specific intent. It is evident that when the Legislature desires to create a specific intent crime, it knows how to do so. *See, e.g.,* Burglary in first degree, Art. 27, § 29(a) (A person may not break and enter the dwelling of another with the intent to commit theft or a crime of violence); Burglary in second degree, Art. 27, § 30(a) (A person may not break and enter the storehouse of another with the intent to commit theft, a crime of violence, or arson in the second degree); Burglary in third degree, Art. 27, § 31 (A person may not break and enter the dwelling of another with the intent to commit any crime). These offenses are specific intent crimes. *Cf.* Warfield v. State, 315 Md. 474, 554 A.2d 1238 (1989) (examining the predecessors to these crimes and concluding that they were specific intent crimes).

deliberate or conscious purpose beyond that of obtaining unauthorized possession or control of a motor vehicle.

We look initially to the plain language of the statute. First, the Legislature clearly and unequivocally provided that any sentence imposed for carjacking may be separate from and consecutive to a sentence for any other offense arising from the conduct underlying the offenses of carjacking or armed carjacking. Art. 27, § 348A(d). Second, the Legislature clearly focused on specific intent when it explicitly provided that it is not a defense that the defendant did not intend to permanently deprive the owner of the motor vehicle, and failed to substitute an intent requirement. *See* Art. 27, § 348A(e). In eliminating the specific intent to permanently deprive, the Legislature could have included a different intent if it chose to do so. All that the statute requires is the intent to do the proscribed act; no further purpose or intent to achieve some additional consequence is necessary.

We turn next to the legislative history. In 1991, a new offense, coined "carjacking", was on the rise nationally. *See* G. Wing, *Putting the Brakes on Carjacking or Accelerating It? The Anti Car Theft Act of 1992*, 28 U. RICH L.REV. 385 (1994). In response, Congress passed the Anti Car Theft Act of 1992, and many state legislatures, sparked by the violent death of Dr. Pamela Basu in Howard County, Maryland, followed the federal lead and enacted legislation to address this new twist to car thefts. *See infra* statutes cited p. 187.

In response to the Basu carjacking, Senate Bill 339 and House Bill 415 were introduced in the Maryland General Assembly as emergency measures by Governor William Donald Schaefer in January, 1993. As emergency legislation, the Maryland General Assembly enacted Art. 27, § 348A, chapter 69, Acts of 1993, on April 26, 1993, effective upon enactment. *See* Bill File for House Bill 415 (1993); Bill File for Senate Bill 339 (1993) (reflecting that emergency legislation was necessary for the immediate preservation of the public health and safety). The intent of the Legislature "was to proscribe actions which although already crimes, i.e., robbery, were deemed to be of such an aggravated nature as to require specific legislation and punishment." Price v. State, 111 Md.App. 487, 497, 681 A.2d 1206, 1211 (1996). Testifying before the Senate Judicial Proceeding Committee on Senate Bill 339, Steven B. Larsen of the Governor's Legislative Office said:

While the separate acts that constitute a carjacking technically fall within current chargeable offenses, the existing penalties are wholly inadequate for the gravity of the offense. This legislation provides prosecutors with additional tools needed to place carjackers behind bars, and sends a strong signal to carjackers that the penalties for carjacking are severe.

See Bill File for Senate Bill 339 (1993).

It is clear that the broad aim of the statute was to enhance the penalties applicable to individuals who use force or threat of force or intimidation to obtain possession or control of a motor vehicle and to make it easier for prosecutors to obtain convictions for carjacking. By looking at the statute as a whole, including the enhanced penalties applicable to carjackers over and above those penalties for the underlying conduct, as well as the explicit rejection of the specific intent to permanently deprive, it is clear that the Legislature did not intend to require a specific intent to achieve some additional consequence beyond the immediate act of taking the vehicle.

Finally, we find no support in the nature of carjacking itself to indicate that it is a specific intent crime. Carjacking requires the general intent to commit the act of obtaining unauthorized possession or control of a motor vehicle from another individual in actual possession by force or violence, or by putting that individual in fear through intimidation or threat of force or violence. The temporary deprivation of the property is substantially certain to result, regardless of the desire of the actor. The General Assembly gave no indication that "the mind [of the perpetrator] be conscious of a more remote purpose or design which shall eventuate from the doing of the immediate act." *Shell,* 307 Md. at 62, 512 A.2d at 366 (quoting *Smith,* 41 Md.App. at 305, 398 A.2d at 442). We agree with the State that the Legislature's clear intent was that, without any additional deliberate and conscious purpose or design of accomplishing a very specific and more remote result, the offense is committed. Simply stated, "[t]he mens rea . . . is implicit in the intentional doing of the act." State v. Yanez, 716 A.2d 759, 767 (R.I.1998).

We hold that the intent element of carjacking is satisfied by proof that the defendant possessed the general criminal intent to commit the act, *i.e.,* general intent to obtain unauthorized possession or control from a person in actual possession by force, intimidation or threat of force. Thus, the trial court properly refused to instruct the jury on voluntary intoxication as requested by Appellant. . . .

■ BELL, CHIEF JUDGE, dissenting:

The majority holds that the offense of carjacking, see Maryland Code (1957, 1996 Repl.Vol., 1997 Cum.Supp.) Article 27 § 348A, is not a specific intent crime. I do not agree and, so, dissent.

Carjacking is nothing more than a "particular type of robbery," Holloway v. United States, 526 U.S. 1, ___, 119 S.Ct. 966, 971–72, 143 L.Ed.2d 1 (1999), one in which the thing taken is an automobile. *See also* Price v. State, 111 Md.App. 487, 497, 681 A.2d 1206, 1210–11 (1996), in which the Court of Special Appeals stated, "[t]he intent of the legislature [in enacting the carjacking statute] was to proscribe actions which although already crimes, *i.e.* robbery, were deemed to be of such an aggravated nature as to require specific legislation and punishment" and, thus, carjacking "is little more than robbery without the need to prove specific intent to permanently deprive the owner of his property." That is, in truth, also all that the legislative history shows. . . .

To be sure, the General Assembly did address, to some extent, the intent element of carjacking; by providing that proof of an intent permanently to deprive the owner of the vehicle is not a defense to carjacking, § 348A (e), the Legislature did not define carjacking to be the identical offense as robbery or theft. That is the only indication of the Legislature's awareness of the intent issue. As we have seen, by contrast, the Legislature spent a considerable amount of time debating the proper penalty and collateral impact of enacting a carjacking statute.

But negating the intent permanently to deprive as a defense does not equate to eliminating altogether the requirement to prove the specific intent to deprive the owner temporarily of the vehicle. In point of fact, the opposite would appear to be the case—by specifying the specific intent that is not a defense, the Legislature inferentially recognized that another, lesser specific intent may be a defense. The fact that the Legislature specifically noted that the State was not required to prove intent to deprive *permanently* implies that some proof of intent to deprive, even if the intended deprivation is temporary, is necessary. Had the Legislature intended to relieve the State of the burden of proving intent to deprive for any period of time, it could have, and I submit would have, refrained from using the qualifying word, "permanently," in subsection (e). To interpret the statute, on that basis, as not requiring proof of any specific intent to deprive, would render the word "permanently" superfluous. It is well settled that, "absent a clear intent to the contrary, a statute is to be read so that no word, clause, sentence or phrase is rendered surplusage, superfluous, meaningless, or nugatory." Montgomery County v. Buckman, 333 Md. 516, 523–24, 636 A.2d 448, 452 (1994)....

In any event, subsection (e) is at best ambiguous; it certainly is not clear and unambiguous. When dealing with a criminal statute that is ambiguous, the Rule of Lenity applies, entitling the defendant to the benefit of the ambiguity. *See* Gardner v. State, 344 Md. 642, 651, 689 A.2d 610, 614 (1997), in which this Court stated: "Lenity expressly prohibits a court from interpreting a criminal statute to increase the penalty it places on a defendant 'when such an interpretation can be based on no more than a guess as to what [the Legislature] intended,'" quoting Monoker v. State, 321 Md. 214, 222, 582 A.2d 525, 529 (1990), which in turn quotes Ladner v. United States, 358 U.S. 169, 178, 79 S.Ct. 209, 214, 3 L.Ed.2d 199, 205 (1958).

When looking at the carjacking statute's intent and penalty element, together with those crimes related to carjacking, the majority's interpretation of the intent requirement produces an anomalous result. Unauthorized use of an automobile is a specific intent offense. Under the statute, in order to be convicted of unauthorized use of an automobile, the State is required to prove that the car was taken with the specific intent to deprive the owner of the automobile, although not permanently. *See* In Re Lakeysha P. 106 Md.App. 401, 425, 665 A.2d 264, 275 (1995), *cert. granted,* 341 Md. 522, 671 A.2d 500, *dismissed as improvidently granted,* 343 Md. 627, 684 A.2d 5 (1996). Unauthorized use carries a minimum penalty of six months and a maximum penalty of four years.

Theft, as defined in Art. 27, § 342, may be committed in several different ways. *See* Cicoria v. State, 332 Md. 21, 30, 629 A.2d 742, 746 (1993) ("The theft statute prescribes five ways in which the crime of theft can be committed.") However it is committed, it is a specific intent crime. § 341; *See* Jones v. State, 303 Md. 323, 493 A.2d 1062 (1985); Brown v. State, 236 Md. 505, 204 A.2d 532 (1964); Fletcher v. State, 231 Md. 190, 189 A.2d 641 (1963); Putinski v. State, 223 Md. 1, 161 A.2d 117 (1960). A person convicted of theft where the value of the goods or services is under $300.00, may be imprisoned for up to 18 months, § 342(f)(2), while if the conviction is for felony theft, where the value of the property or services is greater than $300, he or she may be imprisoned for up to 15 years. § 342(f)(1).

The crime of theft, coupled with the use of violence or intimidation, creates the offense of robbery. Once again, for conviction, the State is required to prove that the defendant had a specific intent, the intent to steal. State v. Gover, 267 Md. 602, 606, 298 A.2d 378, 381 (1973). A person convicted of robbery may be sentenced to imprisonment for up to fifteen years. § 486. A person convicted of armed robbery may be sentenced to imprisonment for up to twenty years. § 488.

Carjacking obviously has been deemed by the Legislature to be the most serious of the offenses. Accordingly and logically, it is punishable by up to 30 years. Under the majority's interpretation, however, the state is required only to prove general intent, without the Legislature clearly evidencing its intention that it be so; it is also much easier to prove.

This statutory scheme evidences that the majority's decision produces an anomalous result. A defendant prosecuted for unauthorized use, theft, or robbery faces a less severe punishment than a defendant charged with carjacking and, in those cases, the State must prove, in addition to the act itself, the intent with which the defendant acted, *i.e.* to deprive the owner of the property either temporarily or permanently. The result of the majority's decision is to require the prosecutor to prove less even though the potential punishment and other consequences are greater, when there is no clear intent expressed by the Legislature that it desired that result. This result is fundamentally unfair, defies logic and common sense, and is violative of the Rule of Lenity. Since we have adopted the principle that "unreasonableness of the result produced by one among alternative possible interpretations of the statute is reason for rejecting that interpretation in favor of another which would produce a reasonable result," D & Y, Inc. v. Winston, 320 Md. 534, 538, 578 A.2d 1177, 1179–80, (quoting 2 A *Sutherland Statutory Construction,* § 45.12 (4th Ed.1984)), carjacking should be interpreted as requiring proof of the specific intent, at least temporarily, to deprive the owner of the car.

■ JUDGES ELDRIDGE and CHASONOW share the views expressed herein.

Commonwealth v. Hathaway

Superior Court of Pennsylvania, 1985.
347 Pa.Super. 134, 500 A.2d 443

■ BECK, JUDGE.

After a five day jury trial appellant Byron Hathaway was convicted on December 11, 1981 of the first degree murder of his wife, Bernadette, and possession of firearms without a license. Appellant timely filed motions for a New Trial and in Arrest of Judgment which the trial court overruled. Appellant subsequently filed a writ of Habeas Corpus alleging ineffectiveness of counsel and the trial court deferred the holding of a hearing on the Writ until the appellate court disposed of appellant's direct appeal. Upon review of appellant's post-verdict motions and the record, we find that the trial court properly denied his motions and that appellant's allegations of ineffectiveness of counsel are meritless. We deny his request to remand for a hearing.

After a brief description of the facts, we will turn to the discussion of appellant's post-verdict motions, and then his allegations of ineffectiveness of counsel.

On April 28, 1981, at approximately 8:45 a.m. at the Church of the Holy Apostle on Remington Road in Haverford Township, appellant met his estranged wife as she was leaving the Martessan School, conducted by the Church, having dropped off her and the defendant's son. After appellant and his wife talked for a short period of time appellant pulled out a .32 caliber pistol. Mrs. Hathaway attempted to run away, but the defendant pursued her and fired several shots at her, causing her to fall to the ground. Appellant walked over to the wife's body, reloaded the gun, placed the gun at her head and fired several more shots. Appellant returned to his car and drove several blocks until the police apprehended him.

At trial the issue of whether appellant shot his estranged wife was not in dispute. Rather, the issue of appellant's mental state at the time of the killing was contested. Appellant presented extensive psychiatric testimony to support his defense that as a result of intoxication and mental disturbances, he had a diminished capacity and thus, the inability to form the specific intent to commit first degree murder. The jury rejected his defense, and found him guilty of first degree murder.

Appellant's post-verdict motions consist of six trial court errors. We find them all to be baseless.

Appellant's third contention is that the trial court erred in refusing to allow defense counsel to question Dr. Gerald Cooke, a psychiatrist and defense witness, about appellant's ability to control his actions at the time of the crime. We find the trial court properly excluded the following question which the defense asked Dr. Cooke:

> Based upon your interviews, observations and tests are you able to say with reasonable medical certainty whether or not Byron Hathaway was able to control his actions on April 28, 1981 at about 8:45 a.m. while he was with this weapon at the Holy Apostles Church? (emphasis added)

The question clearly relates to the irresistible impulse defense, a species of the insanity defense, *Commonwealth v. Walzack*, 468 Pa. 210, 360 A.2d 914 (1976), which is not recognized in Pennsylvania.

Appellant was attempting to prove the diminished capacity defense and the question was not relevant to that defense. The diminished capacity defense assumes the defendant is sane but lacks the ability to form a specific intent to kill, and thus reduces the charge of first degree murder to third degree murder. *Commonwealth v. Walzack*, supra. The irresistible impulse defense is an insanity defense and involves considerations distinct from the diminished capacity doctrine. Therefore the judge properly found the question not to be relevant, *Commonwealth v. Walzack*, supra, and excluded it.

We now turn to appellant's allegations on the effectiveness of counsel. Appellant requests that we remand this case for a hearing on this issue. Since we can fully rule on appellant's allegations of ineffectiveness of counsel from the record in its present state, we deny his request for an evidentiary hearing. Furthermore, counsel will not be deemed ineffective for failing to raise baseless or frivolous issues. It is only when the claim which has been foregone is of arguable merit that further inquiry is made into the basis for counsel's decision not to pursue the matter. *Commonwealth v. Anderson,* 501 Pa. 275, 461 A.2d 208 (1983). In addition, appellant must show he was prejudiced by trial counsel's action or inaction. *Commonwealth v. Litzenberger,* 333 Pa.Super. 471, 482 A.2d 968 (1984). The appellant's allegations of ineffectiveness of counsel are plentiful. The purported instances of ineffectiveness are listed "A"-"R". We find the allegations meritless.

(A) Appellant contends that his counsel was ineffective in failing to introduce a medical doctor to explain to the jurors the meaning of the defense's stipulation that eight hours after the killing, appellant had a blood alcohol level (BAC) between .16 and .28. As a result, appellant argues the jury could not properly consider appellant's defense of diminished capacity. Appellant's trial counsel introduced a medical doctor, Dr. Harvey Bartle, Jr., who testified as to the effect of BAC between .16 and .28 on appellant. (N.T.Vol. I p. 190a). Further, Dr. Morgenstern testified that appellant could not have formed the specific intent at the time of the shooting because appellant was quite inebriated (N.T.Vol. I 163a through 164a). Thus, his counsel did introduce evidence of the meaning of BAC and this contention is baseless. . . .

Montana v. Egelhoff

Supreme Court of the United States, 1996.
518 U.S. 37, 116 S.Ct. 2013, 135 L.Ed.2d 361.

■ JUSTICE SCALIA announced the judgment of the Court and delivered an opinion, in which THE CHIEF JUSTICE, JUSTICE KENNEDY, and JUSTICE THOMAS join.

We consider in this case whether the Due Process Clause is violated by Montana Code Annotated § 45–2–203, which provides, in relevant part, that voluntary intoxication "may not be taken into consideration in determining the existence of a mental state which is an element of [a criminal] offense."

I

In July 1992, while camping out in the Yaak region of northwestern Montana to pick mushrooms, respondent made friends with Roberta Pavola and John Christenson, who were doing the same. On Sunday, July 12, the three sold the mushrooms they had collected and spent the rest of the day and evening drinking, in bars and at a private party in Troy, Montana. Some time after 9 p.m., they left the party in Christenson's 1974 Ford Galaxy station wagon. The drinking binge apparently continued, as respondent was seen buying beer at 9:20 p.m. and recalled "sitting on a hill or a bank passing a bottle of Black Velvet back and forth" with Christenson.

At about midnight that night, officers of the Lincoln County, Montana, sheriff's department, responding to reports of a possible drunk driver, discovered Christenson's station wagon stuck in a ditch along U.S. Highway 2. In the front seat were Pavola and Christenson, each dead from a single gunshot to the head. In the rear of the car lay respondent, alive and yelling obscenities. His blood-alcohol content measured .36 percent over one hour later. On the floor of the car, near the brake pedal, lay respondent's .38 caliber handgun, with four loaded rounds and two empty casings; respondent had gunshot residue on his hands.

Respondent was charged with two counts of deliberate homicide, a crime defined by Montana law as "purposely" or "knowingly" causing the death of another human being. . . . Respondent's defense at trial was that an unidentified fourth person must have committed the murders; his own extreme intoxication, he claimed, had rendered him physically incapable of committing the murders, and accounted for his inability to recall the events of the night of July 12. Although respondent was allowed to make this use of the evidence that he was intoxicated, the jury was instructed, pursuant to Mont.Code Ann. § 45–2–203 (1995), that it could not consider respondent's "intoxicated condition . . . in determining the existence of a mental state which is an element of the offense." The jury found respondent guilty on both counts, and the court sentenced him to 84 years' imprisonment.

The Supreme Court of Montana reversed. It reasoned (1) that respondent "had a due process right to present and have considered by the jury all relevant evidence to rebut the State's evidence on all elements of the offense charged," and (2) that evidence of respondent's voluntary intoxication was "clear[ly] . . . relevant to the issue of whether [respondent] acted knowingly and purposely". Because § 45–2–203 prevented the jury from considering that evidence with regard to that issue, the court concluded that the State had been "relieved of part of its burden to prove beyond a reasonable doubt every fact necessary to constitute the crime charged," and that respondent had therefore been denied due process. . . .

II

The cornerstone of the Montana Supreme Court's judgment was the proposition that the Due Process Clause guarantees a defendant the right to present and have considered by the jury "all relevant evidence to rebut the State's evidence on all elements of the offense charged." Respondent does not defend this categorical rule; he acknowledges that the right to present relevant evidence "has not been viewed as absolute." That is a wise concession, since the proposition that the Due Process Clause guarantees the right to introduce all relevant evidence is simply indefensible. As we have said: "The accused does not have an unfettered right to offer [evidence] that is incompetent, privileged, or otherwise inadmissible under standard rules of evidence." . . . And any number of familiar and unquestionably constitutional evidentiary rules also authorize the exclusion of relevant evidence. . . . Of course, to say that the right to introduce relevant evidence is not absolute is not to say that the Due Process Clause places no limits upon restriction of that right. But it is to say that the defendant asserting such a limit must sustain the usual heavy burden that a due process claim entails:

"[P]reventing and dealing with crime is much more the business of the States than it is of the Federal Government, and . . . we should not lightly construe the Constitution so as to intrude upon the administration of justice by the individual States. Among other things, it is normally 'within the power of the State to regulate procedures under which its laws are carried out,' . . . and its decision in this regard is not subject to proscription under the Due Process Clause unless 'it offends some principle of justice so rooted in the traditions and conscience of our people as to be ranked as fundamental.'" Patterson v. New York, 432 U.S. 197, 201–202, 97 S.Ct. 2319, 2322, 53 L.Ed.2d 281 (1977).

. . . Respondent's task, then, is to establish that a defendant's right to have a jury consider evidence of his voluntary intoxication in determining whether he possesses the requisite mental state is a "fundamental principle of justice."

Our primary guide in determining whether the principle in question is fundamental is, of course, historical practice. Here that gives respondent little support. By the laws of England, wrote Hale, the intoxicated defendant "shall have no privilege by this voluntarily contracted madness, but shall have the same judgment as if he were in his right senses." 1 M. Hale, Pleas of the Crown *32–33. According to Blackstone and Coke, the law's condemnation of those suffering from dementia affectata was harsher still: Blackstone, citing Coke, explained that the law viewed intoxication "as an aggravation of the offence, rather than an excuse for any criminal misbehaviour." 4 W. Blackstone, Commentaries *25–26. This stern rejection of inebriation as a defense became a fixture of early American law as well. The American editors of the 1847 edition of Hale wrote:

"Drunkenness, it was said in an early case, can never be received as a ground to excuse or palliate an offence: this is not merely the opinion of a speculative philosopher, the argument of counsel, or the obiter dictum of a single judge, but it is a sound and long established maxim of judicial policy, from which perhaps a single dissenting voice cannot be found. But if no other authority could be adduced, the uniform decisions of our own Courts from the first establishment of the government, would constitute it now a part of the common law of the land." Hale, supra, at *32, n. 3. . . .

The historical record does not leave room for the view that the common law's rejection of intoxication as an "excuse" or "justification" for crime would nonetheless permit the defendant to show that intoxication prevented the requisite mens rea. . . .

Against this extensive evidence of a lengthy common-law tradition decidedly against him, the best argument available to respondent is the one made by his amicus and conceded by the State: Over the course of the 19th century, courts carved out an exception to the common law's traditional across-the-board condemnation of the drunken offender, allowing a jury to consider a defendant's intoxication when assessing whether he possessed the mental state needed to commit the crime charged, where the crime was one requiring a "specific intent." The emergence of this new rule is often traced to an 1819 English case, in which Justice Holroyd is reported to have held that "though voluntary drunkenness cannot excuse from the commission of crime, yet where, as on a charge of murder, the material question is, whether an act was premeditated or done only with sudden heat and impulse, the fact of the party being intoxicated [is] a circumstance proper to be taken into consideration." 1 W. Russell, Crimes and Misdemeanors *8 (citing King v. Grindley, Worcester Sum. Assizes 1819, MS). This exception was "slow to take root," however, Hall, Intoxication and Criminal Responsibility, 57 Harv. L.Rev. 1045, 1049 (1944), even in England. . . .

. . . Eventually, however, the new view won out, and by the end of the 19th century, in most American jurisdictions, intoxication could be considered in determining whether a defendant was capable of forming the specific intent necessary to commit the crime charged.

On the basis of this historical record, respondent's *amicus* argues that "[t]he old common-law rule . . . was no longer deeply rooted at the time the Fourteenth Amendment was ratified." That conclusion is questionable, but we need not pursue the point, since the argument of *amicus* mistakes the nature of our inquiry. It is not the State which bears the burden of demonstrating that its rule is "deeply rooted," but rather respondent who must show that the principle of procedure *violated* by the rule (and allegedly required by due process) is " 'so rooted in the traditions and conscience of our people as to be ranked as fundamental.' " Patterson v. New York, 432 U.S., at 202, 97 S.Ct., at 2322. . . . The burden remains upon respondent to show that the "new common law" rule—that intoxication may be considered on the question of intent—was so deeply rooted at the time of the Fourteenth Amendment (or perhaps has become so deeply rooted since) as to be a fundamental principle which that Amendment enshrined.

That showing has not been made. . . . [O]ne-fifth of the States either never adopted the "new common-law" rule at issue here or have recently abandoned it.[45] . . .

It is not surprising that many States have held fast to or resurrected the common-law rule prohibiting consideration of voluntary intoxication in

---

45. Besides Montana, those States are Arizona, *see* State v. Ramos, 133 Ariz. 4, 6, 648 P.2d 119, 121 (1982) (upholding statute precluding jury consideration of intoxication for purposes of determining whether defendant acted "knowingly"); Ariz.Rev.Stat. Ann. § 13–503 (Supp.1995–1996) (voluntary intoxication "is not a defense for any criminal act or requisite state of mind"); Arkansas, *see* White v. State, 290 Ark. 130, 134–137, 717 S.W.2d 784, 786–788 (1986) (interpreting Ark.Code Ann. § 5–2–207 (1993)); Delaware, *see* Wyant v. State, 519 A.2d 649, 651 (1986) (interpreting Del.Code Ann., Tit. 11, § 421 (1995)); Georgia, *see* Foster v. State, 258 Ga. 736, 742–745, 374 S.E.2d 188, 194–196 (1988) (interpreting Ga.Code Ann. § 16–3–4 (1992)), *cert. denied*, 490 U.S. 1085, 109 S.Ct. 2110, 104 L.Ed.2d 671 (1989); Hawaii, see Haw.Rev.Stat. § 702–230(2) (1993), State v. Souza, 72 Haw. 246, 248, 813 P.2d 1384, 1386 (1991) (§§ 702–230(2) is constitutional); Mississippi, see Lanier v. State, 533 So.2d 473, 478–479 (1988); Missouri, see Mo.Rev.Stat. § 562.076 (1994), State v. Erwin, 848 S.W.2d 476, 482 (§ 562.076 is constitutional), cert. denied, 510 U.S. 826, 114 S.Ct. 88, 126 L.Ed.2d 56 (1993); South Carolina, *see* State v. Vaughn, 268 S.C. 119, 124–126, 232 S.E.2d 328, 330–331 (1977); and Texas, *see* Hawkins v. State, 605 S.W.2d 586, 589 (Tex.Crim.App.1980) (interpreting Tex. Penal Code Ann. § 8.04).

the determination of mens rea, because that rule has considerable justification—which alone casts doubt upon the proposition that the opposite rule is a "fundamental principle." A large number of crimes, especially violent crimes, are committed by intoxicated offenders; modern studies put the numbers as high as half of all homicides, for example. Disallowing consideration of voluntary intoxication has the effect of increasing the punishment for all unlawful acts committed in that state, and thereby deters drunkenness or irresponsible behavior while drunk. The rule also serves as a specific deterrent, ensuring that those who prove incapable of controlling violent impulses while voluntarily intoxicated go to prison. And finally, the rule comports with and implements society's moral perception that one who has voluntarily impaired his own faculties should be responsible for the consequences.

. . .

In sum, not every widespread experiment with a procedural rule favorable to criminal defendants establishes a fundamental principle of justice. Although the rule allowing a jury to consider evidence of a defendant's voluntary intoxication where relevant to mens rea has gained considerable acceptance, it is of too recent vintage, and has not received sufficiently uniform and permanent allegiance to qualify as fundamental, especially since it displaces a lengthy common-law tradition which remains supported by valid justifications today.

. . .

"The doctrines of *actus reus*, *mens rea*, insanity, mistake, justification, and duress have historically provided the tools for a constantly shifting adjustment of the tension between the evolving aims of the criminal law and changing religious, moral, philosophical, and medical views of the nature of man. This process of adjustment has always been thought to be the province of the States." (plurality opinion). The people of Montana have decided to resurrect the rule of an earlier era, disallowing consideration of voluntary intoxication when a defendant's state of mind is at issue. Nothing in the Due Process Clause prevents them from doing so, and the judgment of the Supreme Court of Montana to the contrary must be reversed.

It is so ordered.

■ Justice Ginsburg, concurring in the judgment.

The Court divides in this case on a question of characterization. The State's law, Mont.Code Ann. § 45–2–203 (1995), prescribes that voluntary intoxication "may not be taken into consideration in determining the existence of a mental state which is an element of [a criminal] offense." For measurement against federal restraints on state action, how should we type that prescription? If § 45–2–203 is simply a rule designed to keep out "relevant, exculpatory evidence," Justice O'Connor maintains, Montana's law offends due process. If it is, instead, a redefinition of the mental-state element of the offense, on the other hand, Justice O'Connor's due process concern "would not be at issue," for "[a] state legislature certainly has the authority to identify the elements of the offenses it wishes to punish," and to exclude evidence irrelevant to the crime it has defined.

Beneath the labels (rule excluding evidence or redefinition of the offense) lies the essential question: Can a State, without offense to the Federal Constitution, make the judgment that two people are equally culpable where one commits an act stone sober, and the other engages in the same conduct after his voluntary intoxication has reduced his capacity for self-control? For the reasons that follow, I resist categorizing § 45–2–203 as merely an evidentiary prescription, but join the Court's judgment refusing to condemn the Montana statute as an unconstitutional enactment.

Section 45–2–203 does not appear in the portion of Montana's Code containing evidentiary rules (Title 26), the expected placement of a provision regulating solely the admissibility of evidence at trial. Instead, Montana's intoxication statute appears in Title 45 ("Crimes"), as part of a chapter entitled "General Principles of Liability." Mont.Code Ann., Tit. 45, ch. 2 (1995). No less than adjacent provisions governing duress and entrapment, § 45–2–203 embodies a legislative judgment regarding the circumstances under which individuals may be held criminally responsible for their actions.

As urged by Montana and its *amici*, § 45–2–203 "extract[s] the entire subject of voluntary intoxication from the mens rea inquiry," thereby rendering evidence of voluntary intoxication logically irrelevant to proof of the requisite mental state. Thus, in a prosecution for deliberate homicide, the State need not prove that the defendant "purposely or knowingly cause[d] the death of another," Mont.Code Ann. § 45–5–102(a) (1995), in a purely subjective sense. To obtain a conviction, the prosecution must prove only that (1) the defendant caused the death of another with actual knowledge or purpose, *or* (2) that the defendant killed "under circumstances that would otherwise establish knowledge or purpose 'but for' [the defendant's] voluntary intoxication." Brief for American Alliance for Rights and Responsibilities et al. as *Amici Curiae* 6. See also Brief for Petitioner 35–36; Brief for United States as *Amicus Curiae* 10–12. Accordingly, § 45–2–203 does not "lighte[n] the prosecution's burden to prove [the] mental-state element beyond a reasonable doubt," as JUSTICE O'CONNOR suggests, for "[t]he applicability of the reasonable-doubt standard ... has always been dependent on how a State defines the offense that is charged," *Patterson v. New York,* 432 U.S. 197, 211, n. 12, 97 S.Ct. 2319, 2327, n. 12, 53 L.Ed.2d 281 (1977).

Comprehended as a measure redefining *mens rea,* § 45–2–203 encounters no constitutional shoal. States enjoy wide latitude in defining the elements of criminal offenses, see, *e.g., Martin v. Ohio,* 480 U.S. 228, 232, 107 S.Ct. 1098, 1101, 94 L.Ed.2d 267 (1987); *Patterson,* 432 U.S., at 201–202, 97 S.Ct., at 2322–2323, particularly when determining "the extent to which moral culpability should be a prerequisite to conviction of a crime," *Powell v. Texas,* 392 U.S. 514, 545, 88 S.Ct. 2145, 2160, 20 L.Ed.2d 1254 (1968) (Black, J., concurring). When a State's power to define criminal conduct is challenged under the Due Process Clause, we inquire only whether the law "offends some principle of justice so rooted in the traditions and conscience of our people as to be ranked as fundamental." *Patterson,* 432 U.S., at 202, 97 S.Ct., at 2322 (internal quotation marks omitted). Defining *mens rea* to eliminate the exculpatory value of voluntary intoxication does not offend a "fundamental principle of justice," given the lengthy common-law tradition, and the adherence of a significant minority of the States to that position today. See *ante,* at 2017–2020; see also *post* (SOUTER, J., dissenting) ("[A] State may so define the mental element of an offense that evidence of a defendant's voluntary intoxication at the time of commission does not have exculpatory relevance and, to that extent, may be excluded without raising any issue of due process.").

Other state courts have upheld statutes similar to § 45–2–203, not simply as evidentiary rules, but as legislative redefinitions of the mental-state element. See *State v. Souza,* 72 Haw. 246, 249, 813 P.2d 1384, 1386 (1991) ("legislature was entitled to redefine the mens rea element of crimes and to exclude evidence of voluntary intoxication to negate state of mind"); *State v. Ramos,* 133 Ariz. 4, 6, 648 P.2d 119, 121 (1982) ("Perhaps the state of mind which needs to be proven here is a watered down *mens rea;* however, this is the prerogative of the legislature."); *Commonwealth v. Rumsey,* 309 Pa.Super. 137, 139, 454 A.2d 1121, 1122 (1983) (quoting *Powell,* 392 U.S., at 536, 88 S.Ct., at 2156 (plurality opinion)) ("Redefinition of the kind and quality of mental activity that constitutes the *mens rea* element of crimes is a permissible part of the legislature's role in the 'constantly shifting adjustment between the evolving aims of the criminal law and changing religious, moral, philosophical, and medical views of the nature of man.' "). Legislation of this order, if constitutional in Arizona, Hawaii, and Pennsylvania, ought not be declared unconstitutional by this Court when enacted in Montana.

If, as the plurality, JUSTICE O'CONNOR, and JUSTICE SOUTER agree, it is within the legislature's province to instruct courts to treat a sober person and a voluntarily intoxicated person as equally responsible for conduct-to place a voluntarily intoxicated person on a level with a sober person-then the Montana law is no less tenable under the Federal Constitution than are the laws, with no significant difference in wording, upheld in sister States. The Montana Supreme Court did not disagree with the courts of other States; it simply did not undertake an analysis in line with the principle that legislative enactments plainly capable of a constitutional construction ordinarily should be given that construction. See *Edward J. DeBartolo Corp. v. Florida Gulf Coast Building & Constr. Trades Council,* 485 U.S. 568, 575, 108 S.Ct. 1392, 1397–1398, 99 L.Ed.2d 645 (1988); *State v. Lilburn,* 265 Mont. 258, 266, 875 P.2d 1036, 1041 (1994).

The Montana Supreme Court's judgment, in sum, strikes down a statute whose text displays no constitutional infirmity. If the Montana court considered its analysis forced by this Court's precedent, it is proper for this Court to say what prescriptions federal law leaves to the States, and thereby dispel confusion to which we may have contributed, and attendant state-court misperception.

■ JUSTICE O'CONNOR, with whom JUSTICE STEVENS, JUSTICE SOUTER, and JUSTICE BREYER join, dissenting.

The Montana Supreme Court unanimously held that Mont.Code Ann. § 45–2–203 (1995) violates due process. I agree. Our cases establish that due process sets an outer limit on the restrictions that may be placed on a defendant's ability to raise an effective defense to the State's accusations. Here, to impede the defendant's ability to throw doubt on the State's case, Montana has removed from the jury's consideration a category of evidence relevant to determination of mental state where that mental state is an essential element of the offense that must be proved beyond a reasonable doubt. Because this disallowance eliminates evidence with which the defense might negate an essential element, the State's burden to prove its case is made correspondingly easier. The justification for this disallowance is the State's desire to increase the likelihood of conviction of a certain class of defendants who might otherwise be able to prove that they did not satisfy a requisite element of the offense. In my view, the statute's effect on the criminal proceeding violates due process. . . .

A state legislature certainly has the authority to identify the elements of the offenses it wishes to punish, but once its laws are written, a defendant has the right to insist that the State prove beyond a reasonable doubt every element of an offense charged. See *McMillan v. Pennsylvania,* 477 U.S. 79, 85, 106 S.Ct. 2411, 2415–2416, 91 L.Ed.2d 67 (1986); *Patterson v. New York,* 432 U.S. 197, 211, n. 12, 97 S.Ct. 2319, 2327, n. 12, 53 L.Ed.2d 281 (1977) ("The applicability of the reasonable-doubt standard, however, has always been dependent on how a State defines the offense that is charged"). "[T]he Due Process Clause protects the accused against conviction except upon proof beyond a reasonable doubt of every fact necessary to constitute the crime with which he is charged." *In re Winship,* 397 U.S. 358, 364, 90 S.Ct. 1068, 1073, 25 L.Ed.2d 368 (1970); *Patterson, supra,* at 210, 97 S.Ct., at 2327. Because the Montana Legislature has specified that a person commits "deliberate homicide" only if he "purposely or knowingly causes the death of another human being," Mont.Code Ann. § 45–5–102(1)(a) (1995), the prosecution must prove the existence of such mental state in order to convict. That is, unless the defendant is shown to have acted purposely or knowingly, *he is not guilty of the offense of deliberate homicide.* The Montana Supreme Court found that it was inconsistent with the legislature's requirement of the mental state of "purposely" or "knowingly" to prevent the jury from considering evidence of voluntary intoxication, where that category of evidence was relevant to establishment of that mental-state element. 272 Mont., at 122–123, 900 P.2d, at 265–266.

Where the defendant may introduce evidence to negate a subjective mental-state element, the prosecution must work to overcome whatever doubts the defense has raised about the existence of the required mental state. On the other hand, if the defendant may *not* introduce evidence that might create doubt in the factfinder's mind as to whether that element was met, the prosecution will find its job so much the easier. A subjective mental state is generally proved only circumstantially. If a jury may not consider the defendant's evidence of his mental state, the jury may impute to the defendant the culpability of a mental state he did not possess.

In *Martin v. Ohio,* 480 U.S. 228, 107 S.Ct. 1098, 94 L.Ed.2d 267 (1987), the Court considered an Ohio statute providing that a defendant bore the burden of proving, by a preponderance of the evidence, an affirmative defense such as self-defense. We held that placing that burden on the defendant did not violate due process. The Court noted in explanation that it would nevertheless have been error to instruct the jury that "self-defense evidence could not be considered in determining whether there was a reasonable doubt about the State's case" where Ohio's definition of the intent element made self-defense evidence relevant to the State's burden. *Id.,* at 233–234, 107 S.Ct., at 1101–1102. "Such an instruction would relieve the State of its burden and plainly run afoul of *Winship*'s mandate." *Id.,* at 234, 107 S.Ct., at 1102. In other words, the State's right to shift the burden of proving an affirmative defense did not include the power to prevent the defendant from attempting to prove self-defense in an effort to cast doubt on the State's case. Dictum or not, this observation explained our reasoning and is similarly applicable here, where the State has benefited from the defendant's inability to make an argument which, if accepted, could throw reasonable doubt on the State's proof. The placement of the burden of proof for affirmative defenses should not be confused with the use of evidence to negate elements of the offense charged. . . .

The Due Process Clause protects those " 'principle[s] of justice so rooted in the traditions and conscience of our people as to be ranked as fundamental.' " *Patterson v. New York,* 432 U.S., at 202, 97 S.Ct., at 2322–2031 (citations omitted). At the time the Fourteenth Amendment was ratified, the common-law rule on consideration of intoxication evidence was in flux. The plurality argues that rejection of the historical rule in the 19th century simply does not establish that the " 'new common-law' " rule is a principle of procedure so "deeply rooted" as to be ranked "fundamental." *Ante,* at 2018–2019. But to determine whether a fundamental principle of justice has been violated here, we cannot consider only the historical disallowance of intoxication evidence, but must also consider the "fundamental principle" that a defendant has a right to a fair opportunity to put forward his defense, in adversarial testing where the State must prove the elements of the offense beyond a reasonable doubt. As concepts of *mens rea* and burden of proof developed, these principles came into conflict, as the shift in the common law in the 19th century reflects. . . .

A state legislature certainly possesses the authority to define the offenses it wishes to punish. If the Montana Legislature chose to redefine this offense so as to alter the requisite mental-state element, the due process problem presented in this case would not be at issue.

There is, however, no indication that such a "redefinition" occurred. JUSTICE GINSBURG's reading of Montana law is plainly inconsistent with that given by the Montana Supreme Court, and therefore cannot provide a valid basis to uphold § 45–2–203's operation. "We are, of course, bound to accept the interpretation of [state] law by the highest court of the State." *Hortonville Joint School Dist. No. 1 v. Hortonville Ed. Assn.,* 426 U.S. 482, 488, 96 S.Ct. 2308, 2312, 49 L.Ed.2d 1 (1976); accord, *Groppi v. Wisconsin,* 400 U.S. 505, 507, 91 S.Ct. 490, 491, 27 L.Ed.2d 571 (1971); *Kingsley Int'l*

Pictures Corp. v. Regents of Univ. of N.Y., 360 U.S. 684, 688, 79 S.Ct. 1362, 1365, 3 L.Ed.2d 1512 (1959)....

Because the management of criminal justice is within the province of the States, *Patterson, supra,* at 201–202, 97 S.Ct., at 2322–2323, this Court is properly reluctant to interfere in the States' authority in these matters. Nevertheless, the Court must invalidate those rules that violate the requirements of due process. The plurality acknowledges that a reduction of the State's burden through disallowance of exculpatory evidence is unconstitutional if it violates a principle of fairness. I believe that such a violation is present here. Montana's disallowance of consideration of voluntary-intoxication evidence removes too critical a category of relevant, exculpatory evidence from the adversarial process by prohibiting the defendant from making an essential argument and permitting the prosecution to benefit from its suppression. Montana's purpose is to increase the likelihood of conviction of a certain class of defendants, who might otherwise be able to prove that they did not satisfy a requisite element of the offense. The historical fact that this disallowance once existed at common law is not sufficient to save the statute today. I would affirm the judgment of the Montana Supreme Court....

■ JUSTICE SOUTER, dissenting.

I have no doubt that a State may so define the mental element of an offense that evidence of a defendant's voluntary intoxication at the time of commission does not have exculpatory relevance and, to that extent, may be excluded without raising any issue of due process. I would have thought the statute at issue here (Mont.Code Ann. § 45–2–203 (1995)) had implicitly accomplished such a redefinition, but I read the opinion of the Supreme Court of Montana as indicating that it had no such effect, and I am bound by the state court's statement of its domestic law.

Even on the assumption that Montana's definitions of the purposeful and knowing culpable mental states were untouched by § 45–2–203, so that voluntary intoxication remains relevant to each, it is not a foregone conclusion that our cases preclude the State from declaring such intoxication evidence inadmissible. A State may typically exclude even relevant and exculpatory evidence if it presents a valid justification for doing so. There may (or may not) be a valid justification to support a State's decision to exclude, rather than render irrelevant, evidence of a defendant's voluntary intoxication. Montana has not endeavored, however, to advance an argument to that effect. Rather, the State has effectively restricted itself to advancing undoubtedly sound reasons for defining the mental state element so as to make voluntary intoxication generally irrelevant (though its own Supreme Court has apparently said the legislature failed to do that) and to demonstrating that evidence of voluntary intoxication was irrelevant at common law (a fact that goes part way, but not all the way, to answering the due process objection). In short, I read the State Supreme Court opinion as barring one interpretation that would leave the statutory scheme constitutional, while the State's failure to offer a justification for excluding relevant evidence leaves us unable to discern whether there may be a valid reason to support the statute as the State Supreme Court appears to view it. I therefore respectfully dissent from the Court's judgment. . . .

People v. Saille

Supreme Court of California, In Bank, 1991.
54 Cal.3d 1103, 2 Cal.Rptr.2d 364, 820 P.2d 588.

■ P ANELLI, J USTICE.

We granted review in this case to resolve a conflict among the Courts of Appeal regarding the impact of legislation abolishing diminished capacity on the crime of voluntary manslaughter. Specifically, the issue is whether the law of this state still permits a reduction of what would otherwise be murder to nonstatutory voluntary manslaughter due to voluntary intoxication and/or mental disorder. In this case, the Court of Appeal held that it does not. After careful examination of the relevant statutes and legislative history, we agree.

[D]efendant was convicted of the first degree murder of Guadalupe Borba (Pen.Code, § 187) and the attempted murder of David Ballagh. . . .

Facts

On November 30, 1985, defendant started drinking at a friend's house shortly before noon. He had drunk 15 to 18 beers by about 6 o'clock that evening; he then went to a bar and drank about 3 or 4 more beers. He was noticeably drunk when he went to Eva's Cafe about 9 p.m. The bartender signalled the security guard, David Ballagh, to ask defendant to leave. Ballagh told defendant he could not drink there because he appeared intoxicated and asked defendant to leave; defendant did so. Defendant returned about an hour later, but was reminded by Ballagh that he could not come in. Defendant left but returned again around 11 p.m. and was rebuffed once again by Ballagh. As he left he said to Ballagh, "I'm going to get a gun and kill you."

Defendant went home around 1 a.m., got his rifle (a semiautomatic assault rifle), and returned to the bar. As he entered the bar, defendant said to Ballagh, "I told you I would be back." Ballagh tried to grab the rifle; it discharged and killed a patron. Defendant was eventually subdued outside the bar; both he and Ballagh were shot during the struggle.

A blood sample taken from defendant about two hours later showed a blood-alcohol level of .14 percent. Expert testimony at trial established that the level would have been about .19 percent at the time of the shooting.

Contentions

Defendant contends the court's instructions on the effect of voluntary intoxication were inadequate. The court gave CALJIC No. 4.21, stating that voluntary intoxication could be considered in determining whether defendant *had the specific intent to kill*. The court instructed on first and second degree murder and voluntary and involuntary manslaughter. It did not, however, relate voluntary intoxication to anything other than the specific intent to kill. Defendant contends the instructions were insufficient because they did not tell the jury that voluntary intoxication, like heat of passion upon adequate provocation, could negate express malice and reduce what would otherwise be murder to voluntary manslaughter. Defendant also contends that the court should have instructed sua sponte that the jury could consider his voluntary intoxication in determining whether he had premeditated and deliberated the murder. Defendant further contends that the instructions on involuntary manslaughter improperly required a showing of unconsciousness.

. . .

[I]n People v. Gorshen (1959) 51 Cal.2d 716, 336 P.2d 492. Gorshen, a longshoreman, reported to work intoxicated and was told by his foreman to go home. After Gorshen refused to leave, the two men fought briefly. The fight ended when the foreman knocked Gorshen to the ground. Gorshen announced that he was going to go home, get his gun, return, and kill the foreman. Gorshen went home, cleaned and loaded his gun, returned to the docks, and killed the foreman. In addition to introducing evidence of his intoxication, Gorshen introduced psychiatric testimony that he was suffering from a mental disease at the time of the killing. The psychiatrist described the effect of the disease and concluded that Gorshen did " 'not have the mental state which is required for malice aforethought or premeditation or anything which implies intention, deliberation or premeditation.' " (Id., at p. 723, 336 P.2d 492.) The trial court found Gorshen guilty of second degree murder. The court relied on the psychiatrist's testimony to reduce the murder to second degree, but found there was malice aforethought.

. . .

In response to our request, the Joint Committee for Revision of the Penal Code held two public hearings on the subject of psychiatric evidence and the defenses of diminished capacity and insanity. . . .

Senate Bill No. 54 added to the Penal Code sections 28 and 29, which abolished diminished capacity and limited psychiatric testimony. It amended section 22 on the admissibility of evidence of voluntary intoxication, section 188 on the definition of malice aforethought, and section 189 on the definition of premeditation and deliberation. Other sections not relevant here were also amended.

. . .

Section 22 was amended to reflect the abolition of diminished capacity. It provides that evidence of voluntary intoxication is not admissible to negate the capacity to form any mental state, but it is admissible "solely on the issue of whether or not the defendant actually formed a required specific intent, premeditated, deliberated, or harbored malice aforethought, when a specific intent crime is charged."

A provision abolishing the defense of diminished capacity was also included in the initiative measure adopted in June 1982 and known as Proposition 8. Section 25 was added to the Penal Code as part of Proposition 8. Subdivision (a) of section 25 provides: "The defense of diminished capacity is hereby abolished. In a criminal action, as well as any juvenile court proceeding, evidence concerning an accused person's intoxication, trauma, mental illness, disease, or defect shall not be admissible to show or negate capacity to form the particular purpose, intent, motive, malice aforethought, knowledge, or other mental state required for the commission of the crime charged."

. . .

Scope of Voluntary Manslaughter

Defendant argues that the new legislation did not limit the ability of an accused to reduce an intentional killing to voluntary manslaughter as a result of mental illness or involuntary intoxication. . . .

Pursuant to the language of section 188, when an intentional killing is shown, malice aforethought is established. Accordingly, the concept of "diminished capacity voluntary manslaughter" (nonstatutory manslaughter) is no longer valid as a defense.

. . .

We still must reconcile the narrowed definition of malice aforethought in section 188 with the language of sections 22, subdivision (b) and 28, subdivision (a). These latter sections make evidence of voluntary intoxication and mental illness admissible solely on the issue of whether the accused "actually formed a required specific intent, premeditated, deliberated, or harbored malice aforethought, when a specific intent crime is charged."

. . .

Sections 22 and 28 state that voluntary intoxication or mental condition may be considered in deciding whether the defendant actually had the required mental state, including malice. These sections relate to any crime, and make no attempt to define what mental state is required. Section 188, on the other hand, defines malice for purposes of murder. In combination, the statutes provide that voluntary intoxication or mental condition may be considered in deciding whether there was malice as defined in section 188. Contrary to defendant's contention, we see no conflict in these provisions.

Defendant further argues that, the Legislature's narrowing of the definition of express malice and the resulting restriction of the scope of voluntary manslaughter presents a due process problem. We disagree. The Legislature can limit the mental elements included in the statutory definition of a crime and thereby curtail use of mens rea defenses. (See Patterson v. New York (1977) 432 U.S. 197, 210–211, 97 S.Ct. 2319, 2327, 53 L.Ed.2d 281.) If, however, a crime requires a particular mental state the Legislature may not deny a defendant the opportunity to prove he did not possess that state. The abolition of the diminished capacity defense and limitation of admissible evidence to actual formation of various mental states has been held not to violate the due process right to present a defense. If there is no due process impediment to the deletion of malice as an element of the crime of felony murder, there is likewise no problem here. In amending section 188 in 1981, the Legislature equated express malice with an intent unlawfully to kill. Since two distinct concepts no longer exist, there has been some narrowing of the mental element included in the statutory definition of express malice. A defendant, however, is still free to show that because of his mental illness or voluntary intoxication, he did not in fact form the intent unlawfully to kill (i.e., did not have malice aforethought). In a murder case, if this evidence is believed, the only supportable verdict would be involuntary manslaughter or an acquittal. If such a showing gives rise to a reasonable doubt, the killing (assuming there is no implied malice) can be no greater than involuntary manslaughter.

It follows from the foregoing analysis that the trial court did not err in failing to instruct that voluntary intoxication could negate express malice so as to reduce a murder to voluntary manslaughter.

Duty to Instruct Sua Sponte

Defendant contends that the trial court erred in failing to instruct sua sponte that the jury should consider his voluntary intoxication in determining whether he had premeditated and deliberated the murder. As previously mentioned, the instructions given related voluntary intoxication only to the question of whether defendant had the specific intent to kill.

The Court of Appeal held that the abolition of the defense of diminished capacity had eliminated the need for a sua sponte instruction relating mental illness or voluntary intoxication to the required mental states....

Thus, even if there were a duty on the trial court to instruct sua sponte on voluntary intoxication when the defense of diminished capacity existed, we do not believe that it is reasonable for such a duty to continue after abolition of the diminished capacity defense.

In our view, under the law relating to mental capacity as it exists today, it makes more sense to place on the defendant the duty to request an instruction which relates the evidence of his intoxication to an element of a crime, such as premeditation and deliberation. This is so because the defendant's evidence of intoxication can no longer be proffered as a defense to a crime but rather is proffered in an attempt to raise a doubt on an element of a crime which the prosecution must prove beyond a reasonable doubt. In such a case the defendant is attempting to relate his evidence of intoxication to an element of the crime. Accordingly, he may seek a "pinpoint" instruction that must be requested by him, but such a pinpoint instruction does not involve a "general principle of law" as that term is used in the cases that have imposed a sua sponte duty of instruction on the trial court. The court did not err, therefore, in failing to instruct sua sponte.

. . .

The judgment of the Court of Appeal is affirmed.

Burrows v. State

Supreme Court of Arizona, 1931.
38 Ariz. 99, 297 P. 1029.

■ LOCKWOOD, J. Richard N. Burrows, hereinafter called defendant, on the 7th day of June, 1929, was informed against by the county attorney of

Maricopa county for the crime of murder, alleged to have been committed April 26th of that year. He was duly tried on such information, and the jury returned a verdict finding defendant guilty of murder in the first degree, fixing the penalty at death, and, from the judgment rendered on the verdict and the order overruling the motion for a new trial, this appeal has been taken. With the exception of two points, which we shall refer to in the course of this opinion, there is singularly little conflict in the evidence, and we therefor [sic] state the facts as follows:

Defendant, whose home was in Chicago, was a boy of eighteen or nineteen, and during the spring of 1929 was at a military school in Delafield, Wis. His closest friend there was one Milton Drucker. The two boys apparently came to the conclusion they would leave school for the purpose of seeing the country, and, taking a car belonging to the Drucker boy's parents, started west. They were at that time in the possession of some $55 in cash, while Drucker had a small amount of money in bank. After some days' travel they reached Phoenix, and were there detained by the police at the request of Drucker's parents. The latter's mother came on from San Diego, where she had been staying, and took her son back to Chicago. Defendant asked permission to go back with them, but was informed by Mrs. Drucker that his adopted parents had decided it would be a good lesson for him if he had to shift for himself and go to work, and for that reason she would not take him. He was alone in Phoenix, unacquainted with any one except the police who had had him in charge for a few days, and substantially, if not entirely, without money. He determined to try to get back to Chicago, and beat his way by railroad as far as Aguila, Ariz., where he discovered that he was on the way to Los Angeles instead of Chicago. He then decided to try to get back to Phoenix, where he had left a suitcase containing personal effects, and make a new start for Chicago, and seeing one Jack Martin, whom we shall hereafter call deceased, at a filling station in Aguila, and discovering the latter was going to Phoenix, asked if he might ride with him. Deceased answered affirmatively, and the two started to Phoenix in the latter's car.

Deceased was either carrying intoxicating liquor in his car, or secured some along the road, for by the time they reached Morristown, a small town some fifty miles northwest of Phoenix, he was so obviously intoxicated that the service station proprietor there suggested to the two that defendant had better drive, to which deceased assented. They left Morristown, and some few miles beyond it defendant shot and killed deceased, who was at that time sitting slumped down in the car in a drunken stupor. Defendant drove the car off the road to a small arroyo, and after taking what money deceased had on his person, placed the body in the arroyo and partially covered it with dirt, took the car, and went onto Phoenix, where he stopped at the police station and secured his personal effects. He then drove on to Denver, Colo., where he was apprehended and brought back to Phoenix. This statement of the facts is based on defendant's own testimony, and in the absence of anything further unquestionably establishes beyond the peradventure of a doubt a case of murder in the first degree.

The only defense offered at the trial was one of involuntary intoxication. Defendant testified that shortly after they left Aguila deceased began urging him to drink some beer which he was carrying in the car. Defendant had never tasted intoxicating liquor and objected most strenuously, whereupon deceased became very abusive, stating that, if defendant would not drink he would put him out of the car. Defendant, being alone, penniless, and fearing that he might be ejected and left on the desert, did drink three or four bottles of the beer, and since he was unused to intoxicating liquor, and had had little to eat in the preceding twenty-four hours, began to feel very queer.

When the parties reached Wickenburg, deceased procured some whisky, and with increasing vehemence urged defendant to partake of that. At first the latter remonstrated, but finally, as he states, through fear of what deceased might do to him, did drink some whisky. He claimed that its effect was to make him sick at the stomach and dizzy, until he had very little idea of what was happening, and that at the time the shooting occurred he was so dazed that he was unable to realize what was happening until after the fatal shot was fired, when his mind cleared up and he did realize what he had done, and that his conduct thereafter was due to panic at realizing his situation, and an effort to escape from the consequences thereof....

The real issue involved is as to the manner in which involuntary intoxication must be induced, and the extent to which it must go. So far as the last point is concerned, we are of the opinion that the intoxication must be sufficient to affect the reason of a defendant to the extent that he does not understand and appreciate the nature and consequences of his act, or, as is commonly said, that he does not know right from wrong.

The other point is more difficult. It is the contention of defendant that any suggestion or influence which induces another to become intoxicated, when, if he had been left entirely to himself, he would have remained sober, excuses him from the consequences of a crime. It is the theory of the state that the influence must go to the extent of actual coercion and abuse. While this precise point has never been decided by any court, so far as the matter has been called to our attention, we are of the opinion that the true rule is that the influence exercised on the mind of a defendant must be such as to amount to duress or fraud. The law has always jealously guarded the effect of drunkenness as a defense in criminal cases, and, even with all the restrictions surrounding it, the doctrine is a dangerous one, and liable to be abused. In this case there is no suggestion of fraud, and it was for the jury to decide whether or not there was coercion and abuse to the extent of duress. While the instruction was not, perhaps as happily worded as it might have been, we are of the opinion that the jury was correctly informed as to the true rule in regard to a defense of involuntary intoxication; that (1) it must be induced by acts amounting in effect to duress; and that (2) it must go to such an extent that the mind of the defendant was incapable of understanding the criminal nature of his act....

Because of the necessarily prejudicial remarks of the county attorney above discussed, the judgment is reversed, and the case remanded to the superior court of Maricopa county for a new trial.

■ McALISTER, C.J., and ROSS, J., concur.[47]

---

47. If, having been given cocaine tablets with the statement that they were "breath fresheners", D took them with no notion that they were intoxicating and as a result became so

Powell v. Texas

Supreme Court of the United States, 1968.
392 U.S. 514, 88 S.Ct. 2145, 20 L.Ed.2d 1254.

■ MR. JUSTICE MARSHALL announced the judgment of the Court and delivered an opinion in which THE CHIEF JUSTICE, MR. JUSTICE BLACK, and MR. JUSTICE HARLAN join.

In late December 1966, appellant was arrested and charged with being found in a state of intoxication in a public place, in violation of Vernon's Ann.Texas Penal Code, Art. 477 (1952), which reads as follows:

"Whoever shall get drunk or be found in a state of intoxication in any public place, or at any private house except his own, shall be fined not exceeding one hundred dollars."

Appellant was tried in the Corporation Court of Austin, Texas, found guilty, and fined $20. He appealed to the County Court at Law No. 1 of Travis County, Texas, where a trial *de novo* was held. His counsel urged that appellant was "afflicted with the disease of chronic alcoholism," that "his appearance in public [while drunk was] ... not of his own volition," and therefore that to punish him criminally for that conduct would be cruel and unusual, in violation of the Eighth and Fourteenth Amendments to the United States Constitution.

The trial judge in the county court, sitting without a jury, made certain findings of fact, but ruled as a matter of law that chronic alcoholism was not a defense to the charge. He found appellant guilty, and fined him $50. There being no further right to appeal within the Texas judicial system, appellant appealed to this Court; we noted probable jurisdiction....

Following this abbreviated exposition of the problem before it, the trial court indicated its intention to disallow appellant's claimed defense of "chronic alcoholism." Thereupon defense counsel submitted, and the trial court entered, the following "findings of fact":

"(1) That chronic alcoholism is a disease which destroys the afflicted person's will power to resist the constant, excessive consumption of alcohol.

---

intoxicated he did not know what he was doing and caused the death of another while in that condition, he is not guilty of crime. People v. Penman, 271 Ill. 82, 110 N.E. 894 (1915).

An "involuntarily intoxicated defendant's mental state must be measured by the test of legal insanity...." State v. Mriglot, 15 Wash.App. 446, 448, 550 P.2d 17, 18 (1976).

Involuntary intoxicated person is not criminally responsible for his conduct if, at the time of the alleged offense, the defendant "lacks capacity to conform his conduct to the requirements of the law." People v. Low, 732 P.2d 622, 627 (Colo.1987).

If defendant can prove he was temporarily so intoxicated during involuntary ingestion of drugs that he lacked the culpable mental state necessary for the crime, defendant will be acquitted. State v. Gardner, 870 P.2d 900 (Utah 1993).

"Involuntary intoxication is a defense to criminal culpability when it is shown that: (1) the accused has exercised no independent judgment or volition in taking the intoxicant; and (2) as a result of his intoxication, the accused did not know that his conduct was wrong or was incapable of conforming his conduct to the requirement of the law" allegedly violated. Aliff v. State, 955 S.W.2d 891, 893 (Tex.App.1997).

"(2) That a chronic alcoholic does not appear in public by his own volition but under a compulsion symptomatic of the disease of chronic alcoholism.

"(3) That Leroy Powell, defendant herein, is a chronic alcoholic who is afflicted with the disease of chronic alcoholism."

Whatever else may be said of them, these are not "findings of fact" in any recognizable, traditional sense in which that term has been used in a court of law; they are the premises of a syllogism transparently designed to bring this case within the scope of this Court's opinion in Robinson v. State of California, 370 U.S. 660, 82 S.Ct. 1417, 8 L.Ed.2d 758 (1962). Nonetheless, the dissent would have us adopt these "findings" without critical examination; it would use them as the basis for a constitutional holding that "a person may not be punished if the condition essential to constitute the defined crime is part of the pattern of his disease and is occasioned by a compulsion symptomatic of the disease."

The difficulty with that position, as we shall show, is that it goes much too far on the basis of too little knowledge. In the first place, the record in this case is utterly inadequate to permit the sort of informed and responsible adjudication which alone can support the announcement of an important and wide-ranging new constitutional principle. We know very little about the circumstances surrounding the drinking bout which resulted in this conviction, or about Leroy Powell's drinking problem, or indeed about alcoholism itself. The trial hardly reflects the sharp legal and evidentiary clash between fully prepared adversary litigants which is traditionally expected in major constitutional cases. The State put on only one witness, the arresting officer. The defense put on three—a policeman who testified to appellant's long history of arrests for public drunkenness, the psychiatrist, and appellant himself.

Furthermore, the inescapable fact is that there is no agreement among members of the medical profession about what it means to say that "alcoholism" is a "disease." One of the principal works in this field states that the major difficulty in articulating a "disease concept of alcoholism" is that "alcoholism has too many definitions and disease has practically none."[48] This same author concludes that *a disease is what the medical profession recognizes as such.*[49] In other words, there is widespread agreement today that "alcoholism" is a "disease," for the simple reason that the medical profession has concluded that it should attempt to treat those who have drinking problems. There the agreement stops. Debate rages within the medical profession as to whether "alcoholism" is a separate "disease" in any meaningful biochemical, physiological or psychological sense, or whether it represents one peculiar manifestation in some individuals of underlying psychiatric disorders.[50]

---

48. E. Jellinek, The Disease Concept of Alcoholism 11 (1960).

49. Id., at 12 (emphasis in original).

50. See, e.g., Joint Information Serv. of the Am. Psychiatric Assn. & the Nat. Assn. for Mental Health, The Treatment of Alcoholism—A Study of Programs and Problems 6–8 (1967) (hereafter cited as Treatment of Alcoholism).

Nor is there any substantial consensus as to the "manifestations of alcoholism." . . .

The trial court's "finding" that Powell "is afflicted with the disease of chronic alcoholism," which "destroys the afflicted person's will power to resist the constant, excessive consumption of alcohol" covers a multitude of sins. Dr. Wade's testimony that appellant suffered from a compulsion which was an "exceedingly strong influence," but which was "not completely overpowering" is at least more carefully stated, if no less mystifying. Jellinek insists that conceptual clarity can only be achieved by distinguishing carefully between "loss of control" once an individual has commenced to drink and "inability to abstain" from drinking in the first place. Presumably a person would have to display both characteristics in order to make out a constitutional defense, should one be recognized. Yet the "findings" of the trial court utterly fail to make this crucial distinction, and there is serious question whether the record can be read to support a finding of either loss of control or inability to abstain. . . . But just as there is no agreement among doctors and social workers with respect to the causes of alcoholism, there is no consensus as to why particular treatments have been effective in particular cases and there is no generally agreed-upon approach to the problem of treatment on a large scale.[51] Most psychiatrists are apparently of the opinion that alcoholism is far more difficult to treat than other forms of behavioral disorders, and some believe it is impossible to cure by means of psychotherapy; indeed, the medical profession as a whole, and psychiatrists in particular, have been severely criticized for the prevailing reluctance to undertake the treatment of drinking problems.[52] Thus it is entirely possible that, even were the manpower and facilities available for a full-scale attack upon chronic alcoholism, we would find ourselves unable to help the vast bulk of our "visible"—let alone our "invisible"—alcoholic population.

However, facilities for the attempted treatment of indigent alcoholics are woefully lacking throughout the country.[53] It would be tragic to return large numbers of helpless, sometimes dangerous and frequently unsanitary inebriates to the streets of our cities without even the opportunity to sober up adequately which a brief jail term provides. Presumably no State or city

---

51.   See Treatment of Alcoholism 13–17.

52.   Id., at 18–26.

53.   Encouraging pilot projects do exist. See President's Commission on Law Enforcement and Administration of Justice, Task Force Report: Drunkenness 50–64, 82–108 (1967). But the President's Commission concluded that the "strongest barrier" to the abandonment of the current use of the criminal process to deal with public intoxication "is that there presently are no clear alternatives for taking into custody and treating those who are now arrested as drunks." President's Commission on Law Enforcement and Administration of Justice, The Challenge of Crime in a Free Society 235 (1967). Moreover, even if massive expenditures for physical plants were forthcoming, there is a woeful shortage of trained personnel to man them. One study has concluded that:

"[T]here is little likelihood that the number of workers in these fields could be sufficiently increased to treat even a large minority of problem drinkers. In California, for instance, according to the best estimate available, providing all problem drinkers with weekly contact with a psychiatrist and once-a-month contact with a social worker would require the full time work of *every* psychiatrist and *every* trained social worker in the United States." Cooperative Commission on Study of Alcoholism, Alcohol Problems 120 (1967) (emphasis in original).

will tolerate such a state of affairs. Yet the medical profession cannot, and does not, tell us with any assurance that, even if the buildings, equipment and trained personnel were made available, it could provide anything more than slightly higher-class jails for our indigent habitual inebriates. Thus we run the grave risk that nothing will be accomplished beyond the hanging of a new sign—reading "hospital"—over one wing of the jailhouse.[54]

One virtue of the criminal process is, at least, that the duration of penal incarceration typically has some outside statutory limit; this is universally true in the case of petty offenses, such as public drunkenness, where jail terms are quite short on the whole. "Therapeutic civil commitment" lacks this feature; one is typically committed until one is "cured." Thus, to do otherwise than affirm might subject indigent alcoholics to the risk that they may be locked up for an indefinite period of time under the same conditions as before, with no more hope than before of receiving effective treatment and no prospect of periodic "freedom."[55]

Faced with this unpleasant reality, we are unable to assert that the use of the criminal process as a means of dealing with the public aspects of problem drinking can never be defended as rational. The picture of the penniless drunk propelled aimlessly and endlessly through the law's "revolving door" of arrest, incarceration, release and re-arrest is not a pretty one. But before we condemn the present practice across-the-board, perhaps we ought to be able to point to some clear promise of a better world for these unfortunate people. Unfortunately, no such promise has yet been forthcoming. If, in addition to the absence of a coherent approach to the problem of treatment, we consider the almost complete absence of facilities and manpower for the implementation of a rehabilitation program, it is difficult to say in the present context that the criminal process is utterly lacking in social value. This Court has never held that anything in the Constitution requires that penal sanctions be designed solely to achieve therapeutic or rehabilitative effects, and it can hardly be said with assurance that incarceration serves such purposes any better for the general run of criminals than it does for public drunks.

---

54. For the inadequate response in the District of Columbia following Easter v. District of Columbia, 124 U.S.App.D.C. 33, 361 F.2d 50 (1966), which held on constitutional and statutory grounds that a chronic alcoholic could not be punished for public drunkenness, see President's Commission on Crime in the District of Columbia, Report 486–490 (1966).

55. Counsel for *amici curiae* ACLU et al., who has been extremely active in the recent spate of litigation dealing with public intoxication statutes and the chronic inebriate, recently told an annual meeting of the National Council on Alcoholism:

"We have not found for two years to extract DeWitt Easter, Joe Driver, and their colleagues from jail, only to have them involuntarily committed for an even longer period of time, with no assurance of appropriate rehabilitative help and treatment.... The euphemistic name 'civil commitment' can easily hide nothing more than permanent incarceration.... I would caution those who might rush headlong to adopt civil commitment procedures and remind them that just as difficult legal problems exist there as with the ordinary jail sentence."

Quoted in Robitscher, Psychiatry and Changing Concepts of Criminal Responsibility, 31 Fed.Prob. 44, 49 (No. 3 Sept. 1967). Cf. Note, The Nascent Right to Treatment, 53 Va.L.Rev. 1134 (1967).

Ignorance likewise impedes our assessment of the deterrent effect of criminal sanctions for public drunkenness. The fact that a high percentage of American alcoholics conceal their drinking problems, not merely by avoiding public displays of intoxication but also by shunning all forms of treatment, is indicative that some powerful deterrent operates to inhibit the public revelation of the existence of alcoholism. Quite probably this deterrent effect can be largely attributed to the harsh moral attitude which our society has traditionally taken toward intoxication and the shame which we have associated with alcoholism. Criminal conviction represents the degrading public revelation of what Anglo–American society has long condemned as a moral defect, and the existence of criminal sanctions may serve to reinforce this cultural taboo, just as we presume it serves to reinforce other, stronger feelings against murder, rape, theft, and other forms of antisocial conduct.

Obviously, chronic alcoholics have not been deterred from drinking to excess by the existence of criminal sanctions against public drunkenness. But all those who violate penal laws of any kind are by definition undeterred. The long-standing and still raging debate over the validity of the deterrence justification for penal sanctions has not reached any sufficiently clear conclusions to permit it to be said that such sanctions are ineffective in any particular context or for any particular group of people who are able to appreciate the consequences of their acts. Certainly no effort was made at the trial of this case, beyond a monosyllabic answer to a perfunctory one-line question, to determine the effectiveness of penal sanctions in deterring Leroy Powell in particular or chronic alcoholics in general from drinking at all or from getting drunk in particular places or at particular times.

III.

Appellant claims that his conviction on the facts of this case would violate the Cruel and Unusual Punishment Clause of the Eighth Amendment as applied to the States through the Fourteenth Amendment. The primary purpose of that clause has always been considered, and properly so, to be directed at the method or kind of punishment imposed for the violation of criminal statutes; the nature of the conduct made criminal is ordinarily relevant only to the fitness of the punishment imposed.[56]

Appellant, however, seeks to come within the application of the Cruel and Unusual Punishment Clause announced in Robinson v. State of California, 370 U.S. 660, 82 S.Ct. 1417, 8 L.Ed.2d 758 (1962), which involved a state statute making it a crime to "be addicted to the use of narcotics." This Court held there that "a state law which imprisons a person thus afflicted [with narcotic addiction] as a criminal, even though he has never touched any narcotic drug within the State or been guilty of any irregular behavior there, inflicts a cruel and unusual punishment...." Id., at 667, 82 S.Ct., at 1420–1421.

On its face the present case does not fall within that holding, since appellant was convicted, not for being a chronic alcoholic, but for being in

---

56. See generally Note, The Cruel and Unusual Punishment Clause and the Substantive Criminal Law, 79 Harv.L.Rev. 635 (1966).

public while drunk on a particular occasion. The State of Texas thus has not sought to punish a mere status, as California did in *Robinson;* nor has it attempted to regulate appellant's behavior in the privacy of his own home. Rather, it has imposed upon appellant a criminal sanction for public behavior which may create substantial health and safety hazards, both for appellant and for members of the general public, and which offends the moral and esthetic sensibilities of a large segment of the community. This seems a far cry from convicting one for being an addict, being a chronic alcoholic, being "mentally ill, or a leper...." Id., at 666, 82 S.Ct., at 1420.

Robinson so viewed brings this Court but a very small way into the substantive criminal law. And unless *Robinson* is so viewed it is difficult to see any limiting principle that would serve to prevent this Court from becoming, under the aegis of the Cruel and Unusual Punishment Clause, the ultimate arbiter of the standards of criminal responsibility, in diverse areas of the criminal law, throughout the country....

Traditional common-law concepts of personal accountability and essential considerations of federalism lead us to disagree with appellant. We are unable to conclude, on the state of this record or on the current state of medical knowledge, that chronic alcoholics in general, and Leroy Powell in particular, suffer from such an irresistible compulsion to drink and to get drunk in public that they are utterly unable to control their performance of either or both of these acts and thus cannot be deterred at all from public intoxication. And in any event this Court has never articulated a general constitutional doctrine of *mens rea.*[57]

We cannot cast aside the centuries-long evolution of the collection of interlocking and overlapping concepts which the common law has utilized to assess the moral accountability of an individual for his antisocial deeds.[58] The doctrines of *actus reus, mens rea,* insanity, mistake, justification, and duress have historically provided the tools for a constantly shifting adjustment of the tension between the evolving aims of the criminal law and changing religious, moral, philosophical, and medical views of the nature of man. This process of adjustment has always been thought to be the province of the States.

Nothing could be less fruitful than for this Court to be impelled into defining some sort of insanity test in constitutional terms. Yet, that task would seem to follow inexorably from an extension of *Robinson* to this case. If a person in the "condition" of being a chronic alcoholic cannot be criminally punished as a constitutional matter for being drunk in public, it would seem to follow that a person who contends that, in terms of one test, "his unlawful act was the product of mental disease or mental defect," Durham v. United States, 94 U.S.App.D.C. 228, 241, 214 F.2d 862, 875, 45

---

57. The Court did hold in Lambert v. People of State of California, 355 U.S. 225, 78 S.Ct. 240, 2 L.Ed.2d 228 (1957), that a person could not be punished for a "crime" of omission, if that person did not know, and the State had taken no reasonable steps to inform him, of his duty to act and of the criminal penalty for failure to do so. It is not suggested either that *Lambert* established a constitutional doctrine of *mens rea,* see generally Packer, Mens Rea and the Supreme Court, 1962 Sup.Ct.Rev. 107, or that appellant in this case was not fully aware of the prohibited nature of his conduct and of the consequences of taking his first drink.

58. See generally Sayre, Mens Rea, 45 Harv.L.Rev. 974 (1932).

A.L.R.2d 1430 (1954), would state an issue of constitutional dimension with regard to his criminal responsibility had he been tried under some different and perhaps lesser standard, e.g., the right-wrong test of *M'Naghten's Case*.[59] The experimentation of one jurisdiction in that field alone indicates the magnitude of the problem. But formulating a constitutional rule would reduce, if not eliminate, that fruitful experimentation, and freeze the developing productive dialogue between law and psychiatry into a rigid constitutional mold. It is simply not yet the time to write the Constitutional formulas cast in terms whose meaning, let alone relevance, is not yet clear either to doctors or to lawyers.

Affirmed.

■ [MR. JUSTICE BLACK and MR. JUSTICE HARLAN, who joined in the opinion of MR. JUSTICE MARSHALL, also wrote a concurring opinion, and MR. JUSTICE WHITE wrote an opinion concurring in the result. MR. JUSTICE FORTAS, with whom MR. JUSTICE DOUGLAS, MR. JUSTICE BRENNAN and MR. JUSTICE STEWART joined, wrote a dissenting opinion.][60]

MODEL PENAL CODE

Section 2.08 Intoxication.

(1) Except as provided in Subsection (4) of this Section, intoxication of the actor is not a defense unless it negatives an element of the offense.

(2) When recklessness establishes an element of the offense, if the actor, due to self-induced intoxication, is unaware of a risk of which he would have been aware had he been sober, such unawareness is immaterial.

(3) Intoxication does not, in itself, constitute mental disease within the meaning of Section 4.01.

(4) Intoxication which (a) is not self-induced or (b) is pathological is an affirmative defense if by reason of such intoxication the actor at the time of his conduct lacks substantial capacity either to appreciate its criminality [wrongfulness] or to conform his conduct to the requirements of law.

(5) Definitions. In this Section unless a different meaning plainly is required:

(a) "intoxication" means a disturbance of mental or physical capacities resulting from the introduction of substances into the body;

(b) "self-induced intoxication" means intoxication caused by substances which the actor knowingly introduces into his body, the tendency of which to cause intoxication he knows or ought to know, unless he introduces them pursuant to medical advice or under such circumstances as would afford a defense to a charge of crime;

(c) "pathological intoxication" means intoxication grossly excessive in degree, given the amount of the intoxicant, to which the actor does not know he is susceptible.[61]

---

59. 10 Cl. & Fin. 200, 8 Eng.Rep. 718 (1843).

60. The dissenting justices admit that they would distinguish between a chronic alcoholic who gets drunk, and one who commits a crime such as robbery or assault while drunk, because such "offenses require independent acts or conduct and do not typically flow from and are not part of the syndrome of the disease of chronic alcoholism". (392 U.S. at 559, 88 S.Ct. at 2167, note 2.)

61. Copyright © 1962 by the American Law Institute. Reprinted with the permission of the American Law Institute.

SECTION 4.   COVERTURE

Under rather narrow limitations, to be considered in a subsequent chapter, a harmful deed which would otherwise be a crime will be excused if done under compulsion. Under the common-law "doctrine of coercion" a married woman was excused for an *actus reus* perpetrated by her under the command or coercion of her husband, without being subject to the ordinary limitations of compulsion. In fact, under the "doctrine of coercion," coverture involved a limitation of criminal capacity. The wife "cannot be guilty", says Lord Hale, if her husband is guilty of the same larceny or burglary (1 Hale P.C. * 46).

The "doctrine of coercion" did not apply in cases of treason or murder, or in offenses such as keeping a brothel which are assumed to be "generally conducted by the intrigues of the female sex." Except for these offenses (and perhaps robbery) a married woman was entitled to an acquittal if the *actus reus* was perpetrated by her under the coercion, or even the bare command, of her husband. Furthermore, the mere presence of the husband at the time of the harmful deed was sufficient to give rise to a presumption of coercion on his part. This presumption could be rebutted by evidence showing clearly the absence of coercion, but it was a powerful shield in her defense.

There may have been some reason for this doctrine in the ancient law, but there is none today. And it is not recognized in American jurisdictions. It is no longer true that a married woman cannot be guilty of the very same larceny or burglary of which her husband is convicted. It is a mistake, however, to assume that the "doctrine of coercion" has no utility as it may have some application in *fact* in the context of specific cases.

MODEL PENAL CODE

Section 2.09 Duress. . . .

(3) It is not a defense that a woman acted on the command of her husband, unless she acted under such coercion as would establish a defense under this Section. [The presumption that a woman, acting in the presence of her husband, is coerced is abolished.][62]

---

62. Copyright © 1962 by the American Law Institute. Reprinted with the permission of the American Law Institute.

CHAPTER 9

RESPONSIBILITY: MODIFYING CIRCUMSTANCES

SECTION 1. IGNORANCE OR MISTAKE

(A) IGNORANCE OR MISTAKE OF LAW

"Ignorance of the law is no excuse," is one of the most familiar phrases in this branch of jurisprudence. It is not entirely without exception, although the exceptions are rare. What is intended to convey the same general idea in other words is this: "Every person is presumed to know the law." In order to understand either the rule itself, or the exceptions thereto, it is necessary to know what is meant by the word "presumed." And this is complicated by the fact that the words "presumed" and "presumption" are used in three different senses in the law.

One of the senses is to signify a mere inference of fact. If two persons are in a small well-lighted room at the same time when no one else is there, and if both are there, fully conscious, for a substantial period of time, it can be inferred ("presumed") that each knew of the other's presence. This is not a rule of law. It is merely a common sense conclusion based upon ordinary experience. It is unfortunate that the words "presumed" and "presumption" were ever used in this sense, and such usage can be ignored for the purposes of this subsection. Nothing could be more absurd than to suggest as a common sense conclusion, based upon ordinary experience, that everyone knows all of the criminal law.[1] The fair inference is that nobody does. Hence attention here may be concentrated upon the other two meanings.

A true presumption is a rule of law which calls for a certain result unless the party adversely affected comes forward with evidence to overcome it. This (although it is the true presumption) often is referred to as a "prima facie presumption" to distinguish it from the so-called "conclusive presumption" which is a legal device in the form of a postulate used for the determination of a particular case whether it represents the actual facts or not. A typical example is the conclusive presumption of delivery by all prior parties to a negotiable instrument which has reached the hands of a holder in due course. The net result of this "conclusive presumption" is that such a holder in due course can enforce the instrument as effectively against a

---

[1]. A judge thinking of this presumption in terms of an inference of fact would be bound to reject it. "There is no presumption in this country that every person knows the law: it would be contrary to common sense and reason if it were so." Per Maule, J. in Martindale v. Falkner, 2 C.B. 720, 135 Eng.Rep. 1124 (1846). Quoted in Ryan v. State, 104 Ga. 78, 82, 30 S.E. 678, 680 (1898).

prior party who did not deliver it as against one who did. It merely disguises a rule of substantive law in the language of a rule of evidence.

If "everyone is presumed to know the law" in this sense, it means that a particular case will be disposed of exactly as if the defendant actually did know the law whether such is the fact or not.[2] And this is exactly the sense in which this word is used ordinarily in this phrase. This is the sense in which it is used in all of those cases in which "ignorance of the law is no excuse." In those rare and exceptional cases in which ignorance of the law is recognized as an excuse in a criminal case the presumption is rebuttable. In other words, while there are exceptions to the rule that "ignorance of the law is no excuse" there are none to the statement that "everyone is presumed to know the law"—except to the extent that the presumption may be overcome by evidence where this is permissible. Stated differently, knowledge of the law is presumed; in most cases this presumption is conclusive but under exceptional circumstances it is disputable.

The most obvious instance in which the presumption of knowledge of the law is rebuttable is in a prosecution for an offense requiring a specific intent. One does not commit larceny, for example, by a trespassory taking and carrying away of the chattel of another if it is done without an intent to steal. Hence one does not commit larceny by such an asportation of another's chattel if he does so under the honest belief that it belongs to him and he has the right to immediate possession of it. And under such circumstances it is immaterial whether the error which led to this bona-fide belief was due to a mistake of fact or a mistake of law. It is to be observed, however, that the ignorance or mistake in such a case concerns some other law and not the law violated. In a larceny case it may be shown that a misunderstanding of property law led to a bona-fide belief that the particular chattel belonged to the defendant and that he had a lawful right to immediate possession thereof, but not that he never heard of the law of larceny or that he mistakenly believed he could take away and appropriate another's property wrongfully without subjecting himself to the penalty of that law under the particular circumstances of the taking. To illustrate further: In a prosecution for malicious trespass based upon removing a fence from a certain path, it could be shown that a mistaken belief with reference to the law of right of way led to the opinion that the fence should not be there, but not that the defendant did not know there was a penalty for wrongfully tearing down another's property.

Problems of particular difficulty in this field are: (1) To what extent does the rule permitting evidence of a misunderstanding of some law, other than the one violated, apply to offenses requiring some particular state of mind which is not "specific intent?" and (2) may circumstances ever be so exceptional as to permit an excuse based upon ignorance or mistake of law (a) in prosecutions for offenses requiring only the "general mens rea," or (b) in prosecutions for a violation of the very law which is claimed to have been misunderstood?

---

2. Lack of knowledge that the law prescribes an act is not a defense to its commission. People v. Barrett, 52 Cal.App.4th 1495, 61 Cal.Rptr.2d 482 (Order not published) (1997).

State v. Cude

Supreme Court of Utah, 1963.
14 Utah 2d 287, 383 P.2d 399.

■ CALLISTER, JUSTICE. Defendant appeals from his conviction and judgment of grand larceny. It appears from the record that the defendant left his automobile at a garage in Ogden, Utah with the request that the same be repaired. The garage owner initially estimated the cost of the necessary work to be in the neighborhood of $180.00. There was evidence, however, that the defendant authorized the garage owner to fix the car, irrespective of the cost. After leaving his automobile at the garage, defendant left the state and returned a few days later. At that time he was presented with a repair bill in the amount of $345.00. Unable to pay this charge (or, for that matter, the estimate of $180.00) the defendant was refused possession of the car by the garageman. Several hours thereafter (after the garage had closed for the night) defendant returned and, using a duplicate key, drove the automobile away.

The automobile was recovered by the police a day or so later while in the possession of a friend of the defendant. It was the contention of the latter that he had taken the car for the purpose of selling the same to realize enough cash to pay off the garage bill.

This court has previously ruled that an owner of personalty in the possession of another by virtue of some special right or title, as bailee or otherwise, is guilty of larceny, if he takes such property from the person in possession *with the fraudulent intention of depriving such person of his rights.*

The defendant requested an instruction regarding his defense, namely, that he could not be found guilty if, at the time of the taking, he honestly believed that he had a right to the possession of the automobile. We are of the opinion that the lower court erred in refusing to give such an instruction.

It is fundamental that an essential element of larceny is the intent to steal the property of another. Consequently, if there is any reasonable basis in the evidence upon which the jury could believe that the accused thought he had a right to take possession of his automobile, or if the evidence in that regard is such that it might raise a reasonable doubt that he had the intent to steal, then that issue should be presented to the jury. The principle is correctly stated in 52 C.J.S. Larceny § 150, p. 999, that if the property was taken under any "... circumstances from which the jury might infer that the taking was under a claim of right, [the] accused is entitled to an appropriate charge distinguishing larceny from a mere trespass." ...

It is held, and we think correctly so, that the general charge that the accused must have the intent to steal does not meet the request to have this particular theory of defense presented to the jury. In a prosecution for stealing sheep, the trial court had given such a general instruction but refused to give the defendant's request, similar to the one submitted here, that if the defendant believed he had a right to take the sheep, he would not be guilty of larceny. Defendant assigned the refusal to give his request as error. After discussing a number of authorities on the subject the court reversed on that ground stating:

"The foregoing authorities would seem to clearly establish that the defendant's requested instruction ... [as to belief of right to possession] ... or one similar to it should have been given by the district court, and that it was prejudicial error to refuse it."

It is suggested that the defendant's own evidence shows he had the necessary intent to steal at the time he took the car. This seems to argue the weight of the evidence; that the defense was not made in good faith; and that it could not be believed. This is a jury question. The defendant's position was exactly to the contrary. The testimony of the garageman is that the defendant requested permission to leave his car on the lot while he went to Salt Lake to get money. Defendant gave an explanation of his return to the lot and the removal of the car which could be considered as consistent with his theory of defense. He also testified that, "But since that I was the owner of the automobile I had never in my life believed I was committing any felony by taking the car for just a day or two, and that is what I did." That he thought he had a right to take his own car was the only avenue of defense open to the defendant and the only one he asserted. It is consistent with the testimony just quoted and with his request for the instruction referred to above. We think it inescapable that the refusal of the trial court to submit the case to the jury upon his theory deprived defendant of a fair trial, and for that reason the judgment should be reversed on that ground.

We find no merit to defendant's assignment of error relating to the cross-examination with respect to his felony record.

Reversed and remanded for a new trial.

■ McDonough, Crockett and Wade, JJ., concur.

■ Henriod, Chief Justice (dissenting)....

People v. Marrero

Court of Appeals of New York, 1987.
69 N.Y.2d 382, 515 N.Y.S.2d 212, 507 N.E.2d 1068.

OPINION OF THE COURT

■ Bellacosa, Judge.

The defense of mistake of law (Penal Law § 15.20(2)(a), (d)) is not available to a Federal corrections officer arrested in a Manhattan social club for possession of a loaded .38 caliber automatic pistol who claimed he mistakenly believed he was entitled, pursuant to the interplay of CPL 2.10, 1.20 and Penal Law § 265.20, to carry a handgun without a permit as a peace officer.

. . .

On the trial of the case, the court rejected the defendant's argument that his personal misunderstanding of the statutory definition of a peace officer is enough to excuse him from criminal liability under New York's mistake of law statute. The court refused to charge the jury on this issue and defendant was convicted of criminal possession of a weapon in the third degree. We affirm....

Defendant was a Federal corrections officer in Danbury, Connecticut, and asserted that status at the time of his arrest in 1977. He claimed at trial that there were various interpretations of fellow officers and teachers, as well as the peace officer statute itself, upon which he relied for his mistaken belief that he could carry a weapon with legal impunity.

The starting point for our analysis is the New York mistake statute as an outgrowth of the dogmatic common-law maxim that ignorance of the law is no excuse. The central issue is whether defendant's personal misreading or misunderstanding of a statute may excuse criminal conduct in the circumstances of this case.

The common-law rule on mistake of law was clearly articulated in *Gardner v. People,* 62 N.Y. 299. In *Gardner,* the defendants misread a statute and mistakenly believed that their conduct was legal. The court insisted, however, that the "mistake of law" did not relieve the defendants of criminal liability. The statute at issue, relating to the removal of election officers, required that prior to removal, written notice must be given to the officer sought to be removed. The statute provided one exception to the notice requirement: "removal ... shall only be made after notice in writing ... unless made while the inspector is actually on duty on a day of registration, revision of registration, or election, and for improper conduct" (L.1872, ch. 675, § 13). The defendants construed the statute to mean that an election officer could be removed without notice for improper conduct at any time. The court ruled that removal without notice could only occur for improper conduct on a day of registration, revision of registration or election.

In ruling that the defendant's misinterpretation of the statute was no defense, the court said: "The defendants made a mistake of law. Such mistakes do not excuse the commission of prohibited acts. 'The rule on the subject appears to be, that in acts *mala in se,* the intent governs, but in those *mala prohibita,* the only inquiry is, has the law been violated?' (3 Den., 403). The act prohibited must be intentionally done. A mistake as to the fact of doing the act will excuse the party, but if the act is intentionally done, the statute declares it a misdemeanor, irrespective of the motive or intent ... The evidence offered [showed] that the defendants were of [the] opinion that the statute did not require notice to be given before removal. This opinion, if entertained in good faith, mitigated the character of the act, but was not a defence [sic]" (Gardner v. People, 62 N.Y. 299, 304, *supra*)....

The desirability of the *Gardner*-type outcome, which was to encourage the societal benefit of individuals' knowledge of and respect for the law, is underscored by Justice Holmes' statement: "It is no doubt true that there are many cases in which the criminal could not have known that he was breaking the law, but to admit the excuse at all would be to encourage ignorance where the law-maker has determined to make men know and obey, and justice to the individual is rightly outweighed by the larger interests on the other side of the scales" (Holmes, The Common Law, at 48 [1881]).

The revisors of New York's Penal Law intended no fundamental departure from this common-law rule in Penal Law § 15.20, which provides in pertinent part:

"§ 15.20. *Effect of ignorance or mistake upon liability.*

. . .

"2. A person is not relieved of criminal liability for conduct because he engages in such conduct under a mistaken belief that it does not, as a matter of law, constitute an offense, unless such mistaken belief is founded upon an official statement of the law contained in (a) a statute or other enactment . . . (d) an interpretation of the statute or law relating to the offense, officially made or issued by a public servant, agency, or body legally charged or empowered with the responsibility or privilege of administering, enforcing or interpreting such statute or law."

. . .

The defendant claims as a first prong of his defense that he is entitled to raise the defense of mistake of law under section 15.20(2)(a) because his mistaken belief that his conduct was legal was founded upon an official statement of the law contained in the statute itself. Defendant argues that his mistaken interpretation of the statute was reasonable in view of the alleged ambiguous wording of the peace officer exemption statute, and that his "reasonable" interpretation of an "official statement" is enough to satisfy the requirements of subdivision (2)(a). However, the whole thrust of this exceptional exculpatory concept, in derogation of the traditional and common-law principle, was intended to be a very narrow escape valve. Application in this case would invert that thrust and make mistake of law a generally applied or available defense instead of an unusual exception which the very opening words of the mistake statute make so clear, i.e., "A person is not relieved of criminal liability for conduct . . . unless" (Penal Law § 15.20). . . .

The prosecution further counters defendant's argument by asserting that one cannot claim the protection of mistake of law under section 15.20(2)(a) simply by misconstruing the meaning of a statute but must instead establish that the statute relied on actually permitted the conduct in question and was only later found to be erroneous. To buttress that argument, the People analogize New York's official statement defense to the approach taken by the Model Penal Code (MPC). Section 2.04 of the MPC provides:

"Section 2.04. *Ignorance or Mistake.*

. . .

"(3) A belief that conduct does not legally constitute an offense is a defense to a prosecution for that offense based upon such conduct when . . . (b) he acts in reasonable reliance upon an official statement of the law, *afterward determined to be invalid or erroneous,* contained in (i) a statute or other enactment" (emphasis added).

Although the drafters of the New York statute did not adopt the precise language of the Model Penal Code provision with the emphasized clause, it is evident and has long been believed that the Legislature intended the New York statute to be similarly construed....

In the case before us, the underlying statute never *in fact authorized* the defendant's conduct; the defendant only thought that the statutory exemptions permitted his conduct when, in fact, the primary statute clearly forbade his conduct. Moreover, by adjudication of the final court to speak on the subject in this very case, it turned out that even the exemption statute did not permit this defendant to possess the weapon. It would be ironic at best and an odd perversion at worst for this court now to declare that the same defendant is nevertheless free of criminal responsibility.

The "official statement" component in the mistake of law defense in both paragraphs (a) and (d) adds yet another element of support for our interpretation and holding.... We agree with the People that the trial court also properly rejected the defense under Penal Law § 15.20(2)(d) since none of the interpretations which defendant proffered meets the requirements of the statute. The fact that there are various complementing exceptions to section 15.20, none of which defendant could bring himself under, further emphasizes the correctness of our view which decides this case under particular statutes with appropriate precedential awareness.

It must also be emphasized that, while our construction of Penal Law § 15.20 provides for narrow application of the mistake of law defense, it does not, as the dissenters contend, "rule out *any* defense based on mistake of law." To the contrary, mistake of law is a viable exemption in those instances where an individual demonstrates an effort to learn what the law is, relies on the validity of that law and, later, it is determined that there was a *mistake in the law itself.*

The modern availability of this defense is based on the theory that where the government has affirmatively, albeit unintentionally, misled an individual as to what may or may not be legally permissible conduct, the individual should not be punished as a result. This is salutary and enlightened and should be firmly supported in appropriate cases. However, it also follows that where, as here, the government is not responsible for the error (for there is none except in the defendant's own mind), mistake of law should not be available as an excuse.

We recognize that some legal scholars urge that the mistake of law defense should be available more broadly where a defendant misinterprets a potentially ambiguous statute not previously clarified by judicial decision and reasonably believes in good faith that the acts were legal. Professor Perkins, a leading supporter of this view, has said: "[i]f the meaning of a statute is not clear, and has not been judicially determined, one who has acted 'in good faith' should not be held guilty of crime if his conduct would have been proper had the statute meant what he 'reasonably believed' it to mean, even if the court should decide later that the proper construction is otherwise." (Perkins, Ignorance and Mistake in Criminal Law, 88 U.Pa. L.Rev. 35, 45.) In support of this conclusion Professor Perkins cites two cases: State v. Cutter, 36 N.J.Law. 125 and Burns v. State, 123 Tex.Cr.R. 611, 61 S.W.2d 512. In both these cases mistake of law was viewed as a valid defense to offenses where a specific intent (i.e., willfully, knowingly, etc.) was an element of the crime charged. In *Burns,* the court recognized mistake of law as a defense to extortion. The statute defining "extortion" made the "willful" doing of the prohibited act an essential ingredient of the offense. The court, holding that mistake of law is a defense only where the mistake negates the specific intent required for conviction, borrowed language from the *Cutter* case: "In State v. Cutter ... the court said: 'The argument goes upon the legal maxim ignorantia legis neminem excusat. But this rule, in its application to the law of crimes, is subject ... to certain important exceptions. Where the act done is malum in se, or where the law which has been infringed was settled and plain, the maxim, in its rigor, will be applied; but where the law is not settled, or is obscure, *and where the guilty intention, being a necessary constituent of the particular offence, is dependent on a knowledge of the law, this rule, if enforced, would be misapplied'*" (Burns v. State, 123 Tex.Cr.R. at 613, 61 S.W.2d at 513, *supra* (emphasis added)). Thus, while Professor Perkins states that the defense should be available in cases where the defendant claims mistaken reliance on an ambiguous statute, the cases he cites recognize the defense only where the law was ambiguous and the ignorance or mistake of law negated the requisite intent. In this case, the forbidden act of possessing a weapon is clear and unambiguous, and only by the interplay of a double exemption does defendant seek to escape criminal responsibility, i.e., the peace officer statute and the mistake statute.

We conclude that the better and correctly construed view is that the defense should not be recognized, except where specific intent is an element of the offense or where the misrelied-upon law has later been properly adjudicated as wrong. Any broader view fosters lawlessness....

Strong public policy reasons underlie the legislative mandate and intent which we perceive in rejecting defendant's construction of New York's mistake of law defense statute. If defendant's argument were accepted, the exception would swallow the rule. Mistakes about the law would be encouraged, rather than respect for and adherence to law. There would be an infinite number of mistake of law defenses which could be devised from a good-faith, perhaps reasonable but mistaken, interpretation of criminal statutes, many of which are concededly complex. Even more troublesome are the opportunities for wrongminded individuals to contrive in bad faith solely to get an exculpatory notion before the jury. These are not in terrorem arguments disrespectful of appropriate adjudicative procedures; rather, they are the realistic and practical consequences were the dissenters' views to prevail. Our holding comports with a statutory scheme which was not designed to allow false and diversionary stratagems to be provided for many more cases than the statutes contemplated. This would not serve the ends of justice but rather would serve game playing and evasion from properly imposed criminal responsibility.

Accordingly, the order of the Appellate Division should be affirmed.

■ HANCOCK, JUDGE (dissenting).

The rule adopted by the majority prohibiting the defense of mistake of law under Penal Law § 15.20(2)(a) in the circumstances here is directly contrary to the plain dictates of the statute and a rejection of the jurisprudential reforms and legislative policies underlying its enactment. For these reasons, as more fully explained herein, we cannot agree with this decision.

The basic difference which divides the court may be simply put. Suppose the case of a man who has committed an act which is criminal not because it is inherently wrong or immoral but solely because it violates a criminal statute. He has committed the act in complete good faith under the mistaken but entirely reasonable assumption that the act does not constitute an offense because it is permitted by the wording of the statute. Does the law require that this man be punished? The majority says that it does and holds that (1) Penal Law § 15.20(2)(a) must be construed so that the man is precluded from offering a defense based on his mistake of law and (2) such construction is compelled by prevailing considerations of public policy and criminal jurisprudence. We take issue with the majority on both propositions.

... Since he has not knowingly committed a wrong there can be no reason for society to exact retribution. Because the man is law-abiding and would not have acted but for his mistaken assumption as to the law, there is no need for punishment to deter him from further unlawful conduct. Traditionally, however, under the ancient rule of Anglo–American common law that ignorance or mistake of law is no excuse, our supposed man would be punished.

The maxim "*ignorantia legis neminem excusat*" finds its roots in Medieval law when the "actor's intent was irrelevant since the law punished the *act itself*".... Various justifications have been offered for the rule, but all are frankly pragmatic and utilitarian—preferring the interests of society (e.g., in deterring criminal conduct, fostering orderly judicial administration, and preserving the primacy of the rule of law) to the interest of the individual in being free from punishment except for intentionally engaging in conduct which he knows is criminal.

Today there is widespread criticism of the common-law rule mandating categorical preclusion of the mistake of law defense. The utilitarian arguments for retaining the rule have been drawn into serious question but the fundamental objection is that it is simply wrong to punish someone who, in good-faith reliance on the wording of a statute, believed that what he was doing was lawful. It is contrary to "the notion that punishment should be conditioned on a showing of subjective moral blameworthiness". This basic objection to the maxim "*ignorantia legis neminem excusat*" may have had less force in ancient times when most crimes consisted of acts which by their very nature were recognized as evil (*malum in se*). In modern times, however, with the profusion of legislation making otherwise lawful conduct criminal (*malum prohibitum*), the "common law fiction that every man is presumed to know the law has become indefensible in fact or logic".

People v. Weiss

Court of Appeals of New York, 1938.
276 N.Y. 384, 12 N.E.2d 514.

[During the investigation of the kidnaping and murder of the Lindbergh baby in New Jersey, one of the suspects was Wendel. In the effort to solve the case, defendants assisted a New Jersey detective in seizing Wendel in New York and there confining him in an effort to extort a confession from him. They offered evidence to show that before they assisted in the arrest they were assured by the detective that he had authority to make the arrest, and power to authorize their assistance, and they believed they were authorized and were doing police work. Most of this evidence was excluded by the trial judge.]

■ O'BRIEN, JUDGE.... Counsel for defendants requested: "That if the defendants, or either of them, acted in the honest belief that his act in seizing and confining Wendel was done with authority of law, even if they were mistaken in such belief, that they cannot be convicted of seizing, confining or kidnapping Wendel, with intent, to cause him without authority of law to be confined or imprisoned within the State, and the jury must acquit such defendants or defendant." To this request the court replied: "I not only decline to charge that but I repeat that the question of good faith is no defense." The jury was also instructed that "even if they [defendants] did believe it, it is no defense in this case." If such interpretation is to prevail, then it must follow that in every instance where a defendant admits the fact that he intended to make the arrest and the courts later declare the arrest to have been made without authority of law, he must necessarily be convicted as a kidnapper, irrespective of his belief or his intentions to conform with the law. A peace officer, in the mistaken belief that he is acting with authority of law, makes an illegal arrest and later, in an effort to extort a confession, puts his prisoner through the third degree. He is guilty of the crime of assault, or of official oppression, but he is certainly not a kidnapper. The question of assault is not in this case. So the trial judge charged.

The intent of defendants to seize and confine Wendel cannot be doubted, but their intent to perform these acts without authority of law depends upon the state of mind of the actors. If in good faith they believed that they were acting within the law, there could have been no intent to act "without authority of law." Their belief or disbelief indicates intent or lack of it, and they were entitled to testify in respect to their intent based upon their belief.

No matter how doubtful the credibility of these defendants may be or how suspicious the circumstances may appear, we cannot say as matter of law that, even in so strong a case as this for the prosecution, the jury was not entitled to consider the question whether defendants in good faith believed that they were acting with authority of law. We are, therefore, constrained to reverse the judgment of conviction and order a new trial for the purpose of submitting that question of fact to the jury.

The judgments should be reversed and a new trial ordered.[3]

---

3. An alien's alleged reasonable belief that he had the consent of the Attorney General to reenter the United States is a viable mistake of law defense to a charge of unlawful reentry of a deported alien. United States v. Anton, 683 F.2d 1011 (7th Cir.1982).

The so-called 007 defense is not available to a defendant to claim reliance on the apparent authority of officials of United States intelligence agencies to authorize criminal conduct. United States v. Berg, 643 F.Supp. 1472 (E.D.N.Y.1986). *See also,* United States v. Barker, 546 F.2d 940 (D.C.Cir.1976) (mistake of law defense available to minor Watergate defendant);

■ CRANE, CHIEF JUDGE (dissenting). I must dissent from the conclusions of JUDGE O'BRIEN in this case, upon three grounds:

First. I believe that the charge and rulings of the court were correct, and that the law has been well stated by Judge Johnston in the prevailing opinion. The fact that the defendants may have thought they had authority to confine Wendel is no excuse for the criminal act and no defense. The crime of kidnapping is committed when a person seizes and confines another with intent to cause him to be confined or imprisoned within the state, and the act is done without lawful authority. The fact that the person thought he had lawful authority has nothing to do with the matter. The intent applies to the seizing and to the confining. The defendants in this case intended to seize Wendel and to confine him within the state. In fact they confined him, bound, in Schlossman's home. Whether they thought they were acting according to law or not, or had legal authority, is no defense. They had no legal authority, and the judge so charged as matter of law. In this he was correct, for such is the law. In fact, no one claims they had any legal authority. Where, therefore, one is seized, taken away, and secretly confined, and it turns out that the person doing it had no legal authority to do it, the crime of kidnapping is committed. Of course, if there be legal authority, there is no crime, but the fact that the person mistakenly thought that they had authority does not lessen the crime. . . .

■ LEHMAN, LOUGHRAN, and RIPPEY, JJ., concur with O'BRIEN, J.

■ CRANE, C.J., dissents in opinion, in which HUBBS and FINCH, JJ., concur.

Judgments reversed, etc.

Lambert v. California

Supreme Court of the United States, 1957.
355 U.S. 225, 78 S.Ct. 240, 2 L.Ed.2d 228.

■ MR. JUSTICE DOUGLAS delivered the opinion of the Court.

Section 52.38(a) of the Los Angeles Municipal Code defines "convicted person" as follows:

"Any person who, subsequent to January 1, 1921, has been or hereafter is convicted of an offense punishable as a felony in the State of California, or who has been or who is hereafter convicted of any offense in any place other than the State of California, which offense, if committed in the State of California, would have been punishable as a felony."

Section 52.39 provides that it shall be unlawful for "any convicted person" to be or remain in Los Angeles for a period of more than five days without registering; it requires any person having a place of abode outside the city to register if he comes into the city on five occasions or more during a 30–day period; and it prescribes the information to be furnished the Chief of Police on registering.

_____

United States v. Duggan, 743 F.2d 59 (2d Cir.1984) (defendant's belief that he thought person was a CIA agent who had authority to authorize a weapons shipment to Northern Ireland did not provide a mistake of law defense).

Section 52.43(b) makes the failure to register a continuing offense, each day's failure constituting a separate offense.

Appellant, arrested on suspicion of another offense, was charged with a violation of this registration law. The evidence showed that she had been at the time of her arrest a resident of Los Angeles for over seven years. Within that period she had been convicted in Los Angeles of the crime of forgery, an offense which California punishes as a felony. Though convicted of a crime punishable as a felony, she had not at the time of her arrest registered under the Municipal Code. At the trial, appellant asserted that § 52.39 of the Code denies her due process of law and other rights under the Federal Constitution, unnecessary to enumerate. The trial court denied this objection. The case was tried to a jury which found appellant guilty. The court fined her $250 and placed her on probation for three years. Appellant, renewing her constitutional objection, moved for arrest of judgment and a new trial. This motion was denied. On appeal the constitutionality of the Code was again challenged. The Appellate Department of the Superior Court affirmed the judgment, holding there was no merit to the claim that the ordinance was unconstitutional. The case is here on appeal. 28 U.S.C. § 1257(2), 28 U.S.C.A. § 1257(2). We noted probable jurisdiction, 352 U.S. 914, 77 S.Ct. 218, 1 L.Ed.2d 121, and designated *amicus curiae* to appear in support of appellant. The case, having been argued and reargued, we now hold that the registration provisions of the Code as sought to be applied here violate the Due Process requirement of the Fourteenth Amendment.

The registration provision, carrying criminal penalties, applies if a person has been convicted "of an offense punishable as a felony in the State of California" or, in case he has been convicted in another State, if the offense "would have been punishable as a felony" had it been committed in California. No element of willfulness is by terms included in the ordinance nor read into it by the California court as a condition necessary for a conviction.

We must assume that appellant had no actual knowledge of the requirement that she register under this ordinance, as she offered proof of this defense which was refused. The question is whether a registration act of this character violates Due Process where it is applied to a person who has no actual knowledge of his duty to register, and where no showing is made of the probability of such knowledge.

We do not go with Blackstone in saying that "a vicious will" is necessary to constitute a crime, 4 Bl.Comm. * 21, for conduct alone without regard to the intent of the doer is often sufficient. There is wide latitude on the law-makers to declare an offense and to exclude elements of knowledge and diligence from its definition. But we deal here with conduct that is wholly passive—mere failure to register. It is unlike the commission of acts, or the failure to act under circumstances that should alert the doer to the consequences of his deed. The rule that "ignorance of the law will not excuse" is deep in our law, as is the principle that of all the powers of local government, the police power is "one of the least limitable." On the other hand, Due Process places some limits on its exercise. Engrained in our concept of Due Process is the requirement of notice. Notice is sometimes essential so that the citizen has the chance to defend charges. Notice is required before property interests are disturbed, before assessments are made, before penalties are assessed. Notice is required in a myriad of situations where a penalty or forfeiture might be suffered for mere failure to act.... These cases involved only property interests in civil litigation. But the principle is equally appropriate where a person, wholly passive and unaware of any wrongdoing, is brought to the bar of justice for condemnation in a criminal case.

Registration laws are common and their range is wide. Many such laws are akin to licensing statutes in that they pertain to the regulation of business activities. But the present ordinance is entirely different. Violation of its provisions is unaccompanied by any activity whatever, mere presence in the city being the test. Moreover, circumstances which might move one to inquire as to the necessity of registration are completely lacking. At most the ordinance is but a law enforcement technique designed for the convenience of law enforcement agencies through which a list of the names and addresses of felons then residing in a given community is compiled. The disclosure is merely a compilation of former convictions already publicly recorded in the jurisdiction where obtained. Nevertheless, this registrant on first becoming aware of her duty to register was given no opportunity to comply with the law and avoid its penalty, even though her default was entirely innocent. She could but suffer the consequences of the ordinance, namely, conviction with the imposition of heavy criminal penalties thereunder. We believe that actual knowledge of the duty to register or proof of the probability of such knowledge and subsequent failure to comply are necessary before a conviction under the ordinance can stand. As Holmes wrote in The Common Law, "A law which punished conduct which would not be blameworthy in the average member of the community would be too severe for the community to bear." Id., at 50. Its severity lies in the absence of an opportunity either to avoid the consequences of the law or to defend any prosecution brought under it. Where a person did not know of the duty to register and where there was no proof of the probability of such knowledge, he may not be convicted consistently with Due Process. Were it otherwise, the evil would be as great as it is when the law is written in print too fine to read or in a language foreign to the community.

Reversed.[4]

■ MR. JUSTICE BURTON dissents because he believes that, as applied to this appellant, the ordinance does not violate her constitutional rights.

■ MR. JUSTICE FRANKFURTER, with whom MR. JUSTICE HARLAN and MR. JUSTICE WHITTAKER join, dissenting....[5]

---

4. On remand the Municipal Court ordered a new trial. On petition the California Supreme Court issued a writ of prohibition on the ground that the Los Angeles ordinance violated the state constitution, Art. XI, sec. 1, since it is in conflict with state legislation which has preempted this field. Lambert v. Municipal Court, 53 Cal.2d 690, 3 Cal.Rptr. 168, 349 P.2d 984 (1960).

5. Most jurisdictions have some form of sexual offender registration law. See West's Cal.Penal Code § 290 (1997). The willful violation of the registration law is punishable as either a felony or a misdemeanor depending on the circumstances. Id. Subsection (g). The

MODEL PENAL CODE

Section 2.04   Ignorance or Mistake.

(1) Ignorance or mistake as to a matter of fact or law is a defense if:

(a) the ignorance or mistake negatives the purpose, knowledge, belief, recklessness or negligence required to establish a material element of the offense; or

(b) the law provides that the state of mind established by such ignorance or mistake constitutes a defense.

(2) Although ignorance or mistake would otherwise afford a defense to the offense charged, the defense is not available if the defendant would be guilty of another offense had the situation been as he supposed. In such case, however, the ignorance or mistake of the defendant shall reduce the grade and degree of the offense of which he may be convicted to those of the offense of which he would be guilty had the situation been as he supposed.

(3) A belief that conduct does not legally constitute an offense is a defense to a prosecution for that offense based upon such conduct when:

(a) the statute or other enactment defining the offense is not known to the actor and has not been published or otherwise reasonably made available prior to the conduct alleged; or

(b) he acts in reasonable reliance upon an official statement of the law, afterward determined to be invalid or erroneous, contained in (i) a statute or other enactment; (ii) a judicial decision, opinion or judgment; (iii) an administrative order or grant of permission; or (iv) an official interpretation of the public officer or body charged by law with responsibility for the interpretation, administration or enforcement of the law defining the offense.

(4) The defendant must prove a defense arising under Subsection (3) of this Section by a preponderance of evidence.

Section 2.02(9)   Culpability as to Illegality of Conduct.

Neither knowledge nor recklessness or negligence as to whether conduct constitutes an offense or as to the existence, meaning or application of the law determining the elements of an offense is an element of such offense, unless the definition of the offense or the Code so provides.[6]

(B) IGNORANCE OR MISTAKE OF FACT

Ignorance or mistake of fact is very often an excuse for what would otherwise be a crime. An airline attendant, for example, who ejects a passenger from the plane (without the use of unreasonable force) under the honest and reasonable, though mistaken, belief that the passenger's fare has not been paid, is liable to the passenger in a civil action but not guilty

---

statute has been held to be constitutional. People v. King, 16 Cal.App.4th 567, 20 Cal.Rptr.2d 220 (1993). See Survey, 6 Bost.U.Pub.Int.L.J. 321 (1996).

Several states have enacted so-called "Megan's laws" requiring that notice be given of a sex offender's presence in a community. *See* E.B. v. Verniero, 119 F.3d 1077 (3d Cir.1997); Kathleen v. Heaphy, Megan's Law: Protecting the Vulnerable or Unconstitutionally Punishing Sex Offenders?, 7 Seton Hall Const.L.J. 913 (1997); Note, 85 Geo.L.J. 2039 (1977).

6. Copyright © 1962 by the American Law Institute. Reprinted with the permission of the American Law Institute.

of criminal assault and battery. *"Ignorantia facti excusat,"* however, is too sweeping even for a general statement of law, because it is clear (to mention only one point for the moment) that if a certain deed would constitute exactly the same crime under either of two factual situations, it will be no excuse that one was mistaken for the other.

A general statement which will apply to the ordinary situation, although it is subject to important qualifications, is this: Mistake of fact will disprove a criminal charge if the mistaken belief is (a) honestly entertained, (b) based upon reasonable grounds, and (c) of such a nature that the conduct would have been lawful had the facts been as they were reasonably supposed to be.[7] This general rule is subject to many exceptions and these exceptions may cut in either direction, so to speak. (1) At times an honest mistake of fact may be exculpating although not based upon reasonable grounds. (2) In other prosecutions a well-grounded belief of a fact which would entitle the defendant to an acquittal if true may not save the person from conviction if erroneous. Mistake of fact may be stated by statute in the jurisdiction and contain variable standards.

Typical instances of the first kind of exception are found in prosecutions of those offenses, such as larceny, requiring a specific intent. There is no such thing in the common law as larceny by negligence. One does not commit this crime by carrying away the chattel of another in the mistaken belief that it is his own, no matter how great may have been the fault leading to this belief, if the belief itself is genuine. And the defendant is entitled to an acquittal in the prosecution for any crime requiring a specific intent or other special mental element, if such intent or other element is lacking,—even if the reason for its absence is a mistaken belief as to some fact. Such a belief must be genuine and sincere but is not necessary for it to be based upon due care.[8]

Offenses enforced on the basis of strict liability give opportunity for exceptions of the second type. Cases holding that a mistake of fact can never be a defense to a prosecution for a strict liability offense go too far, but even a well-grounded mistake of fact is not exculpating if the mistake

---

7. Defense of mistake of fact is comprised of three elements: (1) mistake must be honest and reasonable; (2) mistake must be about a matter of fact; and (3) the mistake must serve to negate the culpability required for the offense. Nordstrom v. State, 627 N.E.2d 1380 (Ind.App. 1994).

8. The Texas statute (Vernon's Ann.Pen.Code art. 41) provided that for an act, otherwise criminal, to be excusable because of mistake of fact, it had to be a mistake that "does not arise from a want of proper care on the part of the person so acting." Even under this statute one who takes what he honestly believes to be his is not guilty of theft whether this belief did or did not result from want of due care. Green v. State, 153 Tex.Cr.R. 442, 221 S.W.2d 612 (1949).

"There is, of course, no question about the proposition: if the defendant took the property under an honest but mistaken belief that he was entitled to do so, that would negative his intent to steal; and he would not be guilty of theft; ... ." State v. Kazda, 545 P.2d 190, 192 (Utah 1976).

"As a general principle of law a person is not guilty of robbery in forcibly taking property from the person of another, if he does so under a bona fide belief that he is the owner of the property. The reason for this rule is that one who takes his own property or that which he believes to be his own property lacks the felonious intent required for larceny or robbery." United States v. Mack, 6 M.J. 598, 599 (ACMR 1978).

could have been discovered by the use of greater care which it is not unreasonable to require of one in such a situation.

People v. Hernandez

Supreme Court of California, In Bank, 1964.
61 Cal.2d 529, 39 Cal.Rptr. 361, 393 P.2d 673.

■ PEEK, JUSTICE. By information defendant was charged with statutory rape. (Pen.Code, § 261, subd. 1.) Following his plea of not guilty he was convicted as charged by the court sitting without a jury and the offense determined to be a misdemeanor.

Section 261 of the Penal Code provides in part as follows: "Rape is an act of sexual intercourse, accomplished with a female not the wife of the perpetrator, under either of the following circumstances: 1. Where the female is under the age of 18 years; . . . ."

The sole contention raised on appeal is that the trial court erred in refusing to permit defendant to present evidence going to his guilt for the purpose of showing that he had in good faith a reasonable belief that the prosecutrix was 18 years or more of age.

The undisputed facts show that the defendant and the prosecuting witness were not married, and had been companions for several months prior to January 3, 1961—the date of the commission of the alleged offense. Upon that date the prosecutrix was 17 years and 9 months of age and voluntarily engaged in an act of sexual intercourse with defendant.

In support of his contention defendant relies upon Penal Code, § 20, which provides that "there must exist a union, or joint operation of act and intent, or criminal negligence" to constitute the commission of a crime. He further relies upon section 26 of that code which provides that one is not capable of committing a crime who commits an act under an ignorance or mistake of fact which disproves any criminal intent.

Thus the sole issue relates to the question of intent and knowledge entertained by the defendant at the time of the commission of the crime charged.

Consent of the female is often an unrealistic and unfortunate standard for branding sexual intercourse a crime as serious as forcible rape. Yet the consent standard has been deemed to be required by important policy goals. We are dealing here, of course, with statutory rape where, in one sense, the lack of consent of the female is not an element of the offense. In a broader sense, however, the lack of consent is deemed to remain an element but the law makes a conclusive presumption of the lack thereof because she is presumed too innocent and naive to understand the implications and nature of her act. The law's concern with her capacity or lack thereof to so understand is explained in part by a popular conception of the social, moral and personal values which are preserved by the abstinence from sexual indulgence on the part of a young woman. An unwise disposition of her sexual favor is deemed to do harm both to herself and the social mores by which the community's conduct patterns are established. Hence the law of statutory rape intervenes in an effort to avoid such a disposition. This goal, moreover, is not accomplished by penalizing the naive female but by imposing criminal sanctions against the male, who is conclusively presumed to be responsible for the occurrence.

The assumption that age alone will bring an understanding of the sexual act to a young woman is of doubtful validity. Both learning from the cultural group to which she is a member and her actual sexual experiences will determine her level of comprehension. The sexually experienced 15–year old may be far more acutely aware of the implications of sexual intercourse than her sheltered cousin who is beyond the age of consent. A girl who belongs to a group whose members indulge in sexual intercourse at an early age is likely to rapidly acquire an insight into the rewards and penalties of sexual indulgence. Nevertheless, even in circumstances where a girl's actual comprehension contradicts the law's presumption, the male is deemed criminally responsible for the act, although himself young and naive and responding to advances which may have been made to him.

The law as presently constituted does not concern itself with the relative culpability of the male and female participants in the prohibited sexual act. Even where the young woman is knowledgeable it does not impose sanctions upon her. The knowledgeable young man, on the other hand, is penalized and there are none who would claim that under any construction of the law this should be otherwise. However, the issue raised by the rejected offer of proof in the instant case goes to the culpability of the young man who acts *without* knowledge that an essential factual element exists and has, on the other hand, a positive, reasonable belief that it does not exist.

The primordial concept of *mens rea,* the guilty mind, expresses the principle that it is not conduct alone but conduct accompanied by certain specific mental states which concerns or should concern the law. In a broad sense the concept may be said to relate to such important doctrines as justification, excuse, mistake, necessity and mental capacity, but in the final analysis it means simply that there must be a "joint operation of act and intent," as expressed in section 20 of the Penal Code, to constitute the commission of a criminal offense. The statutory law, however, furnishes no assistance to the courts beyond that, and the casebooks are filled to overflowing with the courts' struggles to determine just what state of mind should be considered relevant in particular contexts. In numerous instances culpability has been completely eliminated as a necessary element of criminal conduct in spite of the admonition of section 20 to the contrary. More recently, however, this court has moved away from the imposition of criminal sanctions in the absence of culpability where the governing statute, by implication or otherwise, expresses no legislative intent or policy to be served by imposing strict liability. (People v. Stuart, 47 Cal.2d 167, 302 P.2d 5, 55 A.L.R.2d 705; People v. Vogel, 46 Cal.2d 798, 299 P.2d 850; People v. Winston, 46 Cal.2d 151, 293 P.2d 40.)

Statutory rape has long furnished a fertile battleground upon which to argue that the lack of knowledgeable conduct is a proper defense. The law in this state now rests, as it did in 1896, with this court's decision in People v. Ratz, 115 Cal. 132, at pages 134 and 135, 46 P. 915, at page 916, where it is stated: "The claim here made is not a new one. It has frequently been pressed upon the attention of courts, but in no case, so far as our examination goes, has it met with favor. The object and purpose of the law are too plain to need comment, the crime too infamous to bear discussion. The protection of society, of the family, and of the infant, demand that one who has carnal intercourse under such circumstances shall do so in peril of the fact, and he will not be heard against the evidence to urge his belief that the victim of his outrage had passed the period which would make his act a crime." The age of consent at the time of the Ratz decision was 14 years, and it is noteworthy that the purpose of the rule, as there announced, was to afford protection to young females therein described as "infants." The decision on which the court in Ratz relied was The Queen v. Prince, L.R. 2 Crown Cas. 154. However England has now, by statute, departed from the strict rule, and excludes as a crime an act of sexual intercourse with a female between the ages of 13 and 16 years if the perpetrator is under the age of 24 years, has not previously been charged with a like offense, and believes the female "to be of the age of sixteen or over and has reasonable cause for the belief." (Halsburg's Statutes of England, 2d Ed., Vol. 36, Continuation Volume 1956, at page 219.)

The rationale of the Ratz decision, rather than purporting to eliminate intent as an element of the crime, holds that the wrongdoer must assume the risk; that, subjectively, when the act is committed, he consciously intends to proceed regardless of the age of the female and the consequences of his act, and that the circumstances involving the female, whether she be a day or a decade less than the statutory age, are irrelevant. There can be no dispute that a criminal intent exists when the perpetrator proceeds with utter disregard of, or in the lack of grounds for, belief that the female has reached the age of consent. But if he participates in a mutual act of sexual intercourse, believing his partner to be beyond the age of consent, with reasonable grounds for such belief, where is his criminal intent? In such circumstances he has not consciously taken any risk. Instead he has subjectively eliminated the risk by satisfying himself on reasonable evidence that the crime cannot be committed. If it occurs that he has been misled, we cannot realistically conclude that for such reason alone the intent with which he undertook the act suddenly becomes more heinous.

While the specific contentions herein made have been dealt with and rejected both within and without this state, the courts have uniformly failed to satisfactorily explain the nature of the criminal intent present in the mind of one who in good faith believes he has obtained a lawful consent before engaging in the prohibited act. As in the Ratz case the courts often justify convictions on policy reasons which, in effect, eliminate the element of intent. The Legislature, of course, by making intent an element of the crime, has established the prevailing policy from which it alone can properly advise us to depart.

We have recently given recognition to the legislative declarations in sections 20 and 26 of the Penal Code, and departed from prior decisional law which had failed to accord full effect to those sections as applied to charges of bigamy. (People v. Vogel, *supra*, 46 Cal.2d 798, 299 P.2d 850.)

. . .

We are persuaded that the reluctance to accord to a charge of statutory rape the defense of a lack of criminal intent has no greater justification than in the case of other statutory crimes, where the Legislature has made identical provision with respect to intent. " 'At common law an honest and reasonable belief in the existence of circumstances, which, if true, would make the act for which the person is indicted an innocent act, has always been held to be a good defense. . . . So far as I am aware it has never been suggested that these exceptions do not equally apply to the case of statutory offenses unless they are excluded expressly or by necessary implication.' " (Matter of Application of Ahart, 172 Cal. 762, 764–765, 159 P. 160, 161–162, quoting from Regina v. Tolson, [1889] 23 Q.B.D. 168, s.c., 40 Alb.L.J. 250.) Our departure from the views expressed in Ratz is in no manner indicative of a withdrawal from the sound policy that it is in the public interest to protect the sexually naive female from exploitation. No responsible person would hesitate to condemn as untenable a claimed good faith belief in the age of consent of an "infant" female whose obviously tender years preclude the existence of reasonable grounds for that belief. However, the prosecutrix in the instant case was but three months short of 18 years of age and there is nothing in the record to indicate that the purposes of the law as stated in Ratz can be better served by foreclosing the defense of a lack of intent. This is not to say that the granting of consent by even a sexually sophisticated girl known to be less than the statutory age is a defense. We hold only that in the absence of a legislative direction otherwise, a charge of statutory rape is defensible wherein a criminal intent is lacking.[9]

For the foregoing reasons People v. Ratz, *supra*, 115 Cal. 132, 46 P. 915, and People v. Griffin, *supra*, 117 Cal. 583, 49 P. 711 are overruled, and People v. Sheffield, 9 Cal.App. 130, 98 P. 67, is disapproved to the extent that such decisions are inconsistent with the views expressed herein.

Some question has been raised that the offer of proof of defendant's reasonable belief in the age of the prosecutrix was insufficient to justify the pleading of such belief as a defense to the act. It is not our purpose here to make a determination that the defendant entertained a reasonable belief. Suffice to state that the offer demonstrated a sufficient basis upon which, when fully developed, the trier of fact might have found in defendant's favor. We conclude that it was reversible error to reject the offer.

The judgment is reversed.

■ GIBSON, C.J., and TRAYNOR, SCHAUER, McCOMB, PETERS and TOBRINER, JJ., concur.[10]

---

9. Those engaged in commercialized vice must determine the age of the females at their peril. People v. Zeihm, 40 Cal.App.3d 1085, 1089, 115 Cal.Rptr. 528, 531 (1974).

Where defendant was charged with inducing a minor to use marijuana he was entitled to a jury instruction on the defense issue of a reasonable belief that the victims were adults. People v. Goldstein, 130 Cal.App.3d 1024, 182 Cal.Rptr. 207 (1982).

Reasonable mistake as to the victim's age is not a defense to a charge of lewd or lascivious conduct with a child under the age of 14 years. People v. Olsen, 36 Cal.3d 638, 205 Cal.Rptr. 492, 685 P.2d 52 (1984).

10. A mistake of fact instruction is proper on the question of whether the defendant in a forcible rape and kidnaping case reasonably believed the victim consented to the defendant's

People v. Cash

Supreme Court of Michigan, 1984.
419 Mich. 230, 351 N.W.2d 822.

■ WILLIAMS, CHIEF JUSTICE.

The main issue presented in this case requires us to reconsider whether a reasonable mistake of fact as to a complainant's age is a defense to a statutory rape charge. Over 61 years ago, this Court enunciated a rule rejecting such a defense in People v. Gengels, 218 Mich. 632, 188 N.W. 398 (1922), which involved a similar charge under the former statutory rape statute. We reaffirm the *Gengels* rule and likewise reject this defense in cases brought under § 520d(1)(a) of the third-degree criminal sexual conduct statute.

. . .

On the evening of September 23, 1979, the complainant, who was one month shy of her 16th birthday, met the defendant at a Greyhound bus station in Detroit. The complainant was running away from home at the time. After talking with complainant for a couple of hours and gaining her trust, defendant persuaded complainant to accompany him on a drive in his car. They drove to a motel in Marshall, Michigan, where two separate acts of sexual intercourse took place. The complainant managed to leave the motel room undetected after defendant fell asleep, and awakened the person in charge of the motel, who in turn called the police. The defendant was charged with two counts of third-degree criminal sexual conduct,

---

acts. People v. Mayberry, 15 Cal.3d 143, 125 Cal.Rptr. 745, 542 P.2d 1337 (1975). However, *see* People v. Williams, 4 Cal.4th 354, 14 Cal. Rptr.2d 441, 841 P.2d 961 (1992) (mistake instruction is not required unless the mistake was reasonable and in good faith).

Mistake of age is a defense to a charge of committing indecent acts with a child under age sixteen if the mistake is honest and reasonable. United States v. Strode, 43 M.J. 29 (CAAF 1995). See also 18 U.S.C. 2243(c)(1) recognizing mistake of age as a defense to sexual abuse of a minor. The burden of proof is on the defendant.

Defendant charged with producing a pornographic film involving a 16–year–old actress was entitled to present a mistake of age defense that he believed the girl to be 18 or older. United States v. Kantor, 677 F.Supp. 1421 (C.D.Cal.1987).

Most states have rejected the *Hernandez* position. State v. Searles, 159 Vt. 525, 621 A.2d 1281 (1993); State v. Randolph, 12 Wn.App. 138, 528 P.2d 1008 (1974); State v. Vicars, 186 Neb. 311, 183 N.W.2d 241 (1971).

"It has long been the law of this Commonwealth that it is no defense that the defendant did not know that the victim was under the statutory age of consent. Further, it is immaterial that the defendant reasonably believed that the victim was sixteen years of age or older or that he may have attempted to ascertain her age." Commonwealth v. Miller, 385 Mass. 521, 432 N.E.2d 463 (1982).

Alaska has ruled that a defendant has a constitutional right under the Alaska Constitution to submit a defense of reasonable mistake of age to a charge of sexual abuse of a minor. State v. Fremgen, 889 P.2d 1083 (Alaska App.1995).

Mistake of age is no defense to lewd and lascivious conduct with a child under 14. People v. Olsen, 36 Cal.3d 638, 205 Cal.Rptr. 492, 685 P.2d 52 (1984); In re Donald R., 14 Cal.App.4th 1627, 18 Cal.Rptr.2d 442 (1993).

Mistake of age is not a defense, as to the age of a person to whom defendant sold cocaine, to sale to a minor merely provides a greater punishment. People v. Williams, 233 Cal.App.3d 407, 284 Cal.Rptr. 454 (1991).

namely, engaging in sexual penetration with a person between the ages of 13 and 16 years. Documents found in the court file indicate that at the time of the offense, the defendant was 30 years old.

At the preliminary examination, complainant admitted that she told defendant that she was 17 years old. The defendant had also indicated to the police at the time of his arrest that the complainant told him she was 17. The complainant was described by defendant as being 5' 8" tall and weighing about 165 pounds.

Prior to trial, defendant brought a motion requesting that the jury be instructed that a reasonable mistake as to the complainant's age is a defense, . . .

During the course of jury voir dire, defendant asserted his right to represent himself. The trial court permitted defendant to proceed in his own defense with his attorney remaining present to assist defendant. At trial, the complainant testified that she had voluntarily, though reluctantly, engaged in sexual intercourse with defendant out of fear that defendant would otherwise harm her. Defendant tried to impeach the complainant with questions about her lifestyle to show that she was "street-wise", but the trial court prohibited this cross-examination. Defendant was also prohibited from questioning complainant's mother as to her daughter's life-style.

. . .

. . . Over defendant's objection, the court later instructed the jury that "[i]t is no defense that the defendant believed that [the complainant] was 16 years old or older at the time of the alleged act".

The defendant was found guilty by the jury of third-degree criminal sexual conduct, and was sentenced to a term of from 5 to 15 years in prison. . . .

REASONABLE–MISTAKE–OF–AGE DEFENSE

The Gengels Decision

This Court first stated that a good-faith or reasonable mistake as to the complainant's age is not a defense to a statutory rape charge in People v. Gengels, nearly 61 years ago. In that case, the defendant was convicted under the predecessor to the current criminal sexual conduct statute of carnally knowing a female child under 16 years of age. The defendant testified that the complainant told him that she was 18 years old. . . . While recognizing that such evidence may be admissible where guilt of a particular crime depends on intent, the Court noted:

"But in the crime charged here proof of the intent goes with proof of the act of sexual intercourse with a girl under the age of consent. It is not necessary for the prosecution to prove want of consent. Proof of consent is no defense, for a female child under the statutory age is legally incapable of consenting. Neither is it any defense that the accused believed from the statement of his victim or others that she had reached the age of consent."

. . .

Is Gengels Still Viable?

This Court for the first time has the opportunity to review the rule announced in *Gengels* and determine whether it is still viable under the successor provision of the third-degree criminal sexual conduct statute and, if so, whether it comports with a defendant's right to due process.

The statute reads, in relevant part:

"(1) A person is guilty of criminal sexual conduct in the third degree if the person engages in sexual penetration with another person and if any of the following circumstances exists:

"(a) That other person is at least 13 years of age and under 16 years of age." M.C.L. § 750.520d; M.S.A. § 28.788(4).

. . .

In the present case, defendant directly attacks the constitutionality of the above statute on due process grounds for imposing criminal liability without requiring proof of specific criminal intent, *i.e.,* that the accused know that the victim is below the statutory age of consent. In particular, he argues that the crime of statutory rape is rooted in the common law and, as with other common-law offenses, the element of intent must be implied within the statutory definition of a crime, absent clear legislative language to the contrary. We are urged by defendant to construe the statute's silence with respect to the element of intent as not negating the defense of a reasonable mistake of fact as to the complainant's age.

In support of his argument, defendant relies primarily on two out-of-state cases which represent the minority view that, in a statutory rape prosecution, an accused's reasonable, though mistaken, belief that the complainant was of the age of consent is a valid defense.[11] People v. Hernandez, 61 Cal.2d 529, 39 Cal.Rptr. 361, 393 P.2d 673 (1964); State v. Guest, 583 P.2d 836 (Alas., 1978). In both these cases, the Court engrafted a *mens rea* element onto the statutes in question where they were otherwise silent as to any requisite criminal intent.

The vast majority of states, as well as the federal courts, which have considered this identical issue have rejected defendant's arguments and do not recognize the defense of a reasonable mistake of age to a statutory rape charge. For the reasons discussed below, we agree with the majority's position.

---

11. See generally Anno: Mistake or Lack of Information as to Victim's Age as Defense to Statutory Rape, 8 A.L.R.3d 1100.

A few states have adopted, by statute, the reasonable-mistake-of-age defense in statutory rape cases. See, e.g., Alas.Rev.Stat. § 11.41.445(b); Ariz.Rev.Stat.Ann. § 13–1407(B); Ark.Stat. Ann. § 41–1802(3); Ill.Ann.Stat. ch. 38, § 11–4(c) (Smith–Hurd); Ky.Rev.Stat. § 510.030; Mont.Rev.Codes Ann. § 45–5–506(1); Wash.Rev.Code § 9A.44.030(2).

This defense has also been adopted in limited fashion in the 1962 Proposed Draft of the Model Penal Code § 213.6(1), which reads:

"(1) Mistake as to Age. Whenever in this Article the criminality of conduct depends on a child's being below the age of 10, it is no defense that the actor did not know the child's age, or reasonably believed the child to be older than 10. When criminality depends on the child's being below a critical age other than 10, it is a defense for the actor to prove that he reasonably believed the child to be above the critical age."

After careful examination of the statute in the instant case and its legislative history, we are persuaded that the Legislature, in enacting the new criminal sexual conduct code, 1974 P.A. 266, intended to omit the defense of a reasonable mistake of age from its definition of third-degree criminal sexual conduct involving a 13– to 16–year–old, and we follow the legislative intention.

. . . Had the Legislature desired to revise the existing law by allowing for a reasonable-mistake-of-age defense, it could have done so, but it did not do so. This is further supported by the fact that under another provision of the same section of the statute, concerning the mentally ill or physically helpless rape victim, the Legislature specifically provided for the defense of a reasonable mistake of fact by adding the language that the actor "knows or has reason to know" of the victim's condition where the prior statute contained no requirement of intent. The Legislature's failure to include similar language under the section of the statute in question indicates to us the Legislature's intent to adhere to the *Gengels* rule that the actual, and not the apparent, age of the complainant governs in statutory rape offenses.

Second, while the crime of statutory rape has its origins in the English common law, Michigan's new criminal sexual conduct statute represents a major attempt by the Legislature to redefine the law of sexually assaultive crimes, including that of statutory rape. It is well established that the Legislature may, pursuant to its police powers, define criminal offenses without requiring proof of a specific criminal intent and so provide that the perpetrator proceed at his own peril regardless of his defense of ignorance or an honest mistake of fact. In the case of statutory rape, such legislation, in the nature of "strict liability" offenses, has been upheld as a matter of public policy because of the need to protect children below a specified age from sexual intercourse on the presumption that their immaturity and innocence prevents them from appreciating the full magnitude and consequences of their conduct.

. . . .

These discrete choices made by the Legislature evidence careful consideration of age and a deliberate determination to retain the law of statutory rape where the prohibited conduct occurred and the victim was within the protected age group.

One critic has argued that the exclusion of a reasonable-mistake-of-age defense in statutory rape cases is no longer justified given the increased age of consent, the realities of modern society that young teens are more sexually mature, and the seriousness of the penalty as compared with other strict liability offenses. We are not convinced that the policy behind the statutory rape laws of protecting children from sexual exploitation and possible physical or psychological harm from engaging in sexual intercourse is outmoded. Indeed, the United States Supreme Court recently acknowledged the state's authority to regulate the sexual behavior of minors in order to promote their physical and mental well-being, even under a gender-based statutory rape law.[12]

---

12. See Michael M. v. Superior Court of Sonoma County, 450 U.S. 464, 472, fn. 8, 101 S.Ct. 1200, 1209, fn. 8, 67 L.Ed.2d 437 (1981), wherein the court upheld, against an equal protection challenge, California's statutory rape law which exclusively punished male perpetrators.

Is the Defense of a Reasonable Mistake of Age Constitutionally Mandated?

Contrary to defendant's contention, the mistake-of-age defense, at least with regard to statutory rape crimes, is not constitutionally mandated. We quote with approval the following language from Nelson v. Moriarty, 484 F.2d 1034, 1035–1036 (C.A.1, 1973):

"Petitioner claims that his honest belief that the prosecutrix of the statutory rape charge was over sixteen years of age should constitute a defense, of constitutional dimensions, to statutory rape. The effect of *mens rea* and mistake on state criminal law has generally been left to the discretion of the states. * * * The Supreme Court has never held that an honest mistake as to the age of the prosecutrix is a constitutional defense to statutory rape, * * * and nothing in the Court's recent decisions clarifying the scope of procreative privacy, * * * suggests that a state may no longer place the risk of mistake as to the prosecutrix's age on the person engaging in sexual intercourse with a partner who may be young enough to fall within the protection of the statute. Petitioner's argument is without merit."

Moreover, given the already highly emotional setting of a statutory rape trial, the allowance of a mistake-of-age defense would only cause additional undue focus on the complainant by the jury's scrutinizing her appearance and any other visible signs of maturity. The obvious problem is that because early adolescents tend to grow at a rapid rate, by the time of trial a relatively undeveloped young girl or boy may have transformed into a young woman or man. A better procedure would be to permit any mitigating and ameliorating evidence in support of a defendant's mistaken belief as to the complainant's age to be considered by the trial judge at the time of sentencing.

We again note that our decision is in line with the preponderant majority of jurisdictions, both state and federal, which do not recognize the reasonable-mistake-of-age defense for statutory rape offenses and have likewise upheld against due process challenges their respective statutes' imposition of criminal liability without the necessity of proving the defendant's knowledge that the victim was below the designated age. Accordingly, we reaffirm our earlier opinion in *Gengels* and reject the reasonable-mistake-of-age defense for cases brought under the third-degree criminal sexual conduct statute.

Affirmed.

People v. Crane

Supreme Court of Illinois, 1991.
145 Ill.2d 520, 165 Ill.Dec. 703, 585 N.E.2d 99.

■ JUSTICE HEIPLE:

Following a jury trial in the circuit court of Winnebago County, defendant, David Crane, was found guilty of the beating and burning murder of Robert Gahan, and sentenced to a 40–year term of imprisonment. Defendant appealed to the appellate court, which reversed and remanded defendant's conviction. 196 Ill.App.3d 264, 144 Ill.Dec. 78, 554 N.E.2d 1117. We affirm the appellate court.

FACTS

On April 21, 1986, Robert Gahan was killed by being beaten and burned. As a result of a police investigation, defendant was determined to be the prime suspect. Defendant was arrested by New Mexico police on December 23, 1986, on misdemeanor traffic charges, and, due to an Illinois parole violation and an outstanding warrant, he was held as a fugitive from justice. While being held in Las Cruces, New Mexico, defendant, on January 7, 1987, was interviewed by Illinois Detectives Roger Costello and Larry Schultz.

Defendant told the Illinois detectives that Gahan gave him a ride while he was hitchhiking. Gahan asked defendant if he wanted to smoke marijuana, and defendant responded that he did. Defendant directed Gahan to a secluded area, and while they were smoking the marijuana, Gahan grabbed defendant by the neck and began to choke him. Defendant responded by repeatedly striking Gahan with numchucks (martial arts weapons) until he fell to the ground. Defendant, thinking that Gahan was dead, took Gahan's car to a friend's house, Brian Carlson, and related what had just occurred. At Carlson's suggestion, defendant decided to destroy the evidence by burning Gahan's body. Defendant poured gasoline over Gahan and lit him on fire. Defendant also stated that a few days later he heard that Gahan was alive at the time of the burning, and that upon hearing this news he started to cry. After giving his statement, defendant was asked to put it in writing. At this point defendant requested an attorney, and all questioning stopped.

. . .

MISTAKE OF FACT JURY INSTRUCTION

Defendant was charged with two counts of murder. Both charges stated that he beat and burned and thereby caused the death of Gahan. Count I charged that defendant acted "with intent to kill or do great bodily harm," and count II charged defendant acted "knowing such acts created a strong probability of death or great bodily harm." (Ill.Rev.Stat.1987, ch. 38, pars. 9–1(a)(1), (a)(2).) Defendant argues that in regard to the beating, the action taken by him, in repeatedly striking Gahan with numchucks, was in self-defense. In regard to the burning, defendant argues that he is not guilty of murder because at the time of the burning, he believed that Gahan was already dead. The trial court instructed the jury on self-defense, but refused to give defendant's mistake of fact instruction.

Defendant argues that the appellate court correctly determined that he was denied a fair trial by the trial court's refusal to instruct the jury on mistake of fact. We agree. A defendant is entitled to an instruction on his theory of the case if there is some foundation for the instruction in the evidence, and if there is such evidence, it is an abuse of discretion for the trial court to refuse to so instruct the jury. Defendant's mistake of fact defense was supported by the evidence. Detectives Costello and Schultz both testified that while defendant was giving his statement, he said that he believed Gahan was dead prior to the burning. The State's experts who testified on Gahan's cause of death were unable to conclusively determine that Gahan was alive at the time of burning. While Doctor Powers testified that Gahan was probably alive at the time of the burning, he acknowledged that it was possible that he was already dead. Doctor Blum testified that a lay person seeing an unconscious body with injuries like Gahan's might reasonably conclude that the person was dead. This evidence satisfies the requirement of some foundation to entitle defendant to an instruction on mistake of fact.

Mistake of fact is a valid defense if the mistake negates "the existence of the mental state which the statute prescribes with respect to an element of the offense." (Ill.Rev.Stat.1987, ch. 38, par. 4–8.) In the present case, the trial court, while acknowledging that defendant's tendered mistake of fact instruction was an accurate statement of the law, refused to give it to the jury on the basis that the standard jury instructions adequately covered the mental state requirement. In the instant case, the jury was instructed:

"To sustain the charge of murder, the State must prove the following propositions: first, that the defendant performed the acts which caused the death of Robert P. Gahan; and second, that when the defendant did so, he intended to kill or do great bodily harm to Robert P. Gahan or he knew that his acts created a strong probability of death or great bodily harm to Robert P. Gahan; and third, that the defendant was not justified in using the force which he used. If you find from your consideration of all the evidence that each one of these propositions has been proved beyond a reasonable doubt, you should find the defendant guilty. If you find from your consideration of all the evidence that any one of these propositions has not been proved beyond a reasonable doubt, you should find the defendant not guilty."

This instruction, while sufficiently informing the jury of the mental state requirements, does not expressly draw to the jury's attention the concept of mistake of fact. Since Illinois recognizes the defense of mistake of fact, when this defense is supported by the evidence it is not sufficient to merely inform the jury of the mental state requirements, but it must also be informed of the validity of the mistake of fact defense. Since (1) defendant's whole case rested upon the concepts of self-defense and mistake of fact, and (2) there exists some evidence upon which a jury could reasonably conclude that defendant burned Gahan under the mistaken belief that he was dead, the failure to give the mistake of fact instruction to the jury cannot be considered harmless.

. . .

Affirmed.

MODEL PENAL CODE

Section 213.6   Provisions Generally Applicable to Article 213. [Sexual Offenses.]

(1) Mistake as to Age. Whenever in this Article the criminality of conduct depends on a child's being below the age of 10, it is no defense that the actor

did not know the child's age, or reasonably believed the child to be older than 10. When criminality depends on the child's being below a critical age other than 10, it is a defense for the actor to prove by a preponderance of the evidence that he reasonably believed the child to be above the critical age.

. . .

Section 230.1   Bigamy and Polygamy.

(1) Bigamy. A married person is guilty of bigamy, a misdemeanor, if he contracts or purports to contract another marriage, unless at the time of the subsequent marriage:

(a) the actor believes that the prior spouse is dead; or

(b) the actor and the prior spouse have been living apart for five consecutive years throughout which the prior spouse was not known by the actor to be alive; or

(c) a Court has entered a judgment purporting to terminate or annul any prior disqualifying marriage, and the actor does not know that judgment to be invalid; or

(d) the actor reasonably believes that he is legally eligible to remarry.

(2) Polygamy. A person is guilty of polygamy, a felony of the third degree, if he marries or cohabits with more than one spouse at a time in purported exercise of the right of plural marriage. The offense is a continuing one until all cohabitation and claim of marriage with more than one spouse terminates. This section does not apply to parties to a polygamous marriage, lawful in the country of which they are residents or nationals, while they are in transit through or temporarily visiting this State.

(3) Other Party to Bigamous or Polygamous Marriage. A person is guilty of bigamy or polygamy, as the case may be, if he contracts or purports to contract marriage with another knowing that the other is thereby committing bigamy or polygamy.[13]

SECTION 2.   IMPELLED PERPETRATION

A command or order, not backed by public authority, will not excuse a deed which would otherwise be a crime. Under certain circumstances one who has carried out a private command or order may be free from guilt although the criminal law was violated, but the excuse will be based upon some other ground such as lack of a necessary mental element for criminal culpability. If, for example, the thing commanded is not obviously wrongful, and the order is carried out in innocence of the criminal purpose intended, the "innocent agent" is not guilty of crime. This may happen in various ways, such as where an employer commits larceny by directing an employee to take a certain chattel (which actually belongs to another) and place it in the employer's house or store. The employee is not guilty of crime if he carries out this order in the innocent belief that the chattel belongs to his employer. In such cases, however, it is the mistake of fact, and not the command, which constitutes the excuse.

If a command or order is accompanied by violence or threat of violence, the real problem is not the command but the compulsion. An "act" is a

---

willed movement. Hence if one's body is propelled against his will, this is not his act. The classic example is this: **A, B** and **C** are standing near the edge of a precipice. Suddenly **A** shoves **B** violently against **C,** causing **C** to fall to his death. **A** has caused the death of **C,** but **B** whose body was used as a tool by **A,** so to speak, has not caused this death. **B** did not act, he was acted upon.

Such a situation is mentioned to avoid any possible misunderstanding, but "compulsion" has quite a different meaning. "Compulsion," as used in this connection, applies where it is the *will* rather than the *body* which is coerced. If, in a case similar to the one mentioned, **A** had not touched **B,** but had pointed a loaded pistol at **B** and threatened to kill **B** unless **B** pushed **C** over the edge, and **B** had done this to save **B**'s own life, it would have been a case of compulsion. In this case **B** had a choice. It was not an easy choice, to be sure, but when **B** decided to push **C** causing **C**'s death rather than risk **B**'s own life, this was a willed movement and hence an "act." And the resulting death is legally imputable to **B** as well as to **A.** Whether **B** is criminally responsible for the death **B** has caused depends upon whether or not this compulsion will be recognized as an excuse.

Statements can be found by some of the early writers indicating that no person is ever criminally answerable for what the person was compelled to do in order to save the person's own life. And unquestionably such compulsion or necessity will be recognized as an excuse for most deeds which would otherwise be criminal. But Blackstone asserted: "... though a man be violently assaulted, and hath no other possible means of escaping death but by killing an innocent person, this fear and force shall not acquit him of murder; for he ought rather to die himself than escape by the murder of an innocent."[14] No sound analogy can be drawn from the "self defense" cases because that defense does not involve the killing of an *innocent* person. And the very few cases of this nature which have reached the courtroom show that the common law does not justify or excuse such a killing.[15] Strangely enough the possibility of manslaughter rather than

---

14. 4 Bl.Comm. 30.

"[C]oercion is not a defense to murder." United States v. Buchanan, 529 F.2d 1148, 1153 (7th Cir.1975).

Duress was held to be a possible defense to murder where defendant, who was not quite 15 at the time of the killing, was compelled by a 25–year–old co-defendant, who had shot defendant when he was 12, threatened to shoot defendant again if he did not participate in the offense. People v. Jenkins, 214 A.D.2d 584, 625 N.Y.S.2d 70 (1995).

The House of Lords has ruled that the defense of compulsion or duress was available to a principal in the second degree to homicide although not necessarily to a principal in the first degree. In Regina v. Gotts, [1992] 1 All ER 832 (H.L.), a divided court held duress was not an available defense to attempted murder. The court acknowledged the American courts have held to the contrary. However, in Regina v. Howe, [1987] 1 All E.R. 771 (H.L.), the House of Lords overruled *Lynch* and held duress was not available to a charge of murder whether the actor was a principal in the first or second degree. D.P.P. v. Lynch [1975] 1 All E.R. 913 (H.L.). The Canadian Supreme Court has taken the same position as the *Lynch* case. Regina v. Paquette, 30 CCC 2d 417 (S.C.Can.1976). *See also* Regina v. Hibbert, 99 CCC 3d 193 (S.C.Can. 1995).

15. The leading case is Brewer v. State, 72 Ark. 145, 78 S.W. 773 (1904). An Alabama opinion goes into the subject rather thoroughly although the actual decision turns on another point. Arp v. State, 97 Ala. 5, 12 So. 301 (1893).

murder in such cases seems not to have been adopted as another approach. The killing is intentional to be sure, and there is no legally recognized *provocation.*[16] But the circumstances are extremely *mitigating.* The mitigation in such a case is entitled to greater recognition than that in most instances of voluntary manslaughter committed in the sudden heat of passion. The state of mind of one who reluctantly takes the life of an innocent person as the only means of saving his own, while not guiltless, is certainly not malice aforethought.

The statement above refers to the common law. In some of the new penal codes it is provided that such a killing is manslaughter.[17] In other codes following the Model Penal Code § 2.09 the defense of duress is available in homicide cases.[18]

For most offenses, however, a well-grounded fear of immediate death or great bodily injury is recognized as an excuse. One is not punishable for robbery because of having driven the get-away car for robbers if it is done at the point of a pistol and under the threat of immediate death.[19] And one who damaged a threshing machine with a sledge hammer was held not guilty of crime when it was found that he had been compelled to do so by a violent mob.[20] It was even recognized that one who joins the enemy forces in time of war is not guilty of treason if he does so in fear of death or great bodily injury, and escapes at the first reasonable opportunity[21]—provided he has not caused death in the meantime.[22]

In Axtell's Case, J. Kelyng, 13, 84 Eng.Rep. 1060 (1660), arising out of the conviction and execution of Charles I, it was held that Axtell, the soldier "who commanded the guards at the King's tryal, and at his murder" was guilty although he claimed "that all he did was as a soldier, by the command of his superiour officer, whom he must obey or die" because "where the command is traiterous, there the obedience to that command is also traiterous".

16. State v. Ivey, 325 S.C. 137, 481 S.E.2d 125, 127 (1997).

17. E.g. Wis.Stat.Ann. § 940.05, 940.01(d), 939.45(1), 939.46 (1996).

18. ALI, Model Penal Code and Commentaries § 2.09 Comment 3. Duress is not a defense to first degree murder. State v. Rumble, 680 S.W.2d 939 (Mo.1984); Tully v. State, 730 P.2d 1206 (Okl.Cr.1986); People v. Dittis, 157 Mich.App. 38, 403 N.W.2d 94 (1987). However, the defense of duress may apply to felony murder if duress precludes conviction of the underlying felony. Tully v. State, *supra*; contra, State v. Ng, 110 Wn.2d 32, 750 P.2d 632 (1988) (based on statute).

19. People v. Merhige, 212 Mich. 601, 180 N.W. 418 (1920); Regina v. Mena, 34 CCC 3d 304, 57 C.R.3d 172 (Ont.C.A.1987).

Standard for duress defense is objective, reasonable, ordinary person is the test. R. v. Bowen, [1996] 2 Cr.App.R. (1996).

20. Rex v. Crutchley, 5 Car. & P. 133, 172 Eng.Rep. 909 (1831).

21. Oldcastle's Case, 3 Co.Inst. *10, 1 Hale, P.C. 50, 1 East, P.C. 70. "An American . . . charged with playing the role of the traitor may defend by showing that force or coercion compelled such conduct". Kawakita v. United States, 343 U.S. 717, 736, 72 S.Ct. 950, 962, 96 L.Ed. 1249 (1952). As to what constitutes compulsion see D'Aquino v. United States, 192 F.2d 338 (9th Cir.1951).

Respublica v. McCarty, 2 U.S. (2 Dall.) 86, 1 L.Ed. 300 (Pa.1781). In this case defendant was not excused because he was still with the British forces eleven months after he claimed to have been compelled to join them.

22. The soldier "who commanded the guards at the king's tryal, and at his murder" had no defense although "all that he did was as a soldier, by the command of his superior officer, whom he must obey or die." Axtell's Case, Kelyng 13, 84 Eng.Rep. 1060 (1660).

It has been argued that if such compulsion will excuse treason it should excuse any crime, and therefore murder.[23] The answer, however, is obvious. Joining enemy forces, with mental reservation, and leaving at the earliest opportunity causes no lasting harm. Homicide does.

The word "compulsion," as it is used in the criminal law, is limited usually to situations in which the unwilling action is compelled by some other person. Quite similar emergencies may arise in which the pressure is exerted by some other agency, and the result is the same. Here also it is necessary to distinguish between forcing the body and forcing the will. Treating physical impossibility and extreme pressure of circumstances as if they were identical "is one of the oldest fallacies of the law."[24] If a tornado hurls the body of **A** against **B**, with fatal results to **B**, this death is not caused by the act of **A**. But if **A** and **B** are adrift in a small boat 1000 miles from land and without food, and **A** kills **B** and eats his flesh as the only means of saving his own life, this death is caused by **A**. Traditionally, no matter how great the necessity, the law will not excuse the intentional killing of an *innocent* person on the plea that it was necessary to save the life of the slayer. In the boat case mentioned the English court insisted that the crime was murder and pronounced sentence of death,[25] but the sentence was afterward commuted by the crown to six months' imprisonment. It would seem that circumstances so obviously and extremely mitigating as to cause such a reduction by the pardoning power should have been recognized by the court as reducing the grade of the crime itself. In the famous case of "human jettison," the actual verdict was guilty of manslaughter. In this case a leaking boat loaded with survivors after a shipwreck was in grave danger of sinking in a storm. It was not a modern lifeboat and all would have been lost if it had gone down. The sailors threw some passengers overboard to lighten the load. As thus lightened the boat was kept afloat during the storm and the survivors were picked up by a passing vessel the following day. The judge charged the jury that the sailors had no privilege to sacrifice passengers even in such extreme peril.[26] He intimated, although it was quite beside the point, that if several are in such peril that some must be sacrificed in order for any to be saved—and none of the group owes any duty to others in this emergency—choice by lot would be proper.

What seems to be the traditionally accepted view, among the few cases, is that no one is privileged to choose the death of some other innocent person in order to preserve one's own life. In extreme emergencies, however, the field of legally-recognized causation may be somewhat narrow. One may not wilfully plunge a knife into an obviously guiltless breast, but it

---

Compulsion, as a defense to a charge of crime, must involve a threat of "imminent" infliction of death or great bodily harm. Such a threat directed at some indefinite time in the future is not a defense. State v. Milum, 213 Kan. 581, 516 P.2d 984 (1973).

23.   1 East, Pleas of the Crown 294 (1803).

24.   Per Mr. Justice Holmes in the Eliza Lines, 199 U.S. 119, 130, 26 S.Ct. 8, 10, 50 L.Ed. 115 (1905).

25.   Regina v. Dudley and Stephens, 14 Q.B.D. 273 (1884).

26.   United States v. Holmes, 1 Wall.Jr. 1, 26 Fed.Cas. No. 15,383 (1842). The judge emphasized the duty owed by sailors to passengers.

does not follow that in a race, or even a struggle, for means of safety, adequate to preserve the life of only one, the winner shall under all circumstances be said to have killed the loser.

On the other hand, where the *necessity* is great, a deed not involving death or great bodily harm may be excused, even if otherwise it would be a crime. For example, if merchant vessels are forbidden to enter a certain port, and such a ship is forced to take refuge there during a violent storm, for the safety of the vessel and those on board, there has been no violation of the embargo.[27] And what might otherwise constitute attempted revolt by sailors on the high seas may be excused by the unseaworthiness of the vessel.[28] Where a prisoner is confined in immediate life threatening circumstances, the person may be privileged to escape from the situation until the threat has subsided.[29] However, general bad prison conditions will not provide a defense to a charge of escape.[30]

The problem that seems to have aroused the most discussion and the least litigation is that of taking food to avoid starvation. Although Lord Bacon said that "if a man steals viands to satisfy a present hunger, this is no felony nor larceny,"[31] the books are full of statements indicating that "economic necessity" is no defense to a criminal charge. And it has been so held.[32] But "economic necessity," as this phrase has been used, falls far short of an actual need to prevent starvation. And mere convenience will not excuse the intentional deprivation of another's property. Under ordinary circumstances in the modern community it is not *necessary* to take another's food, without his consent, because an appeal may be made to the public authorities. But if a ship should be disabled on the high seas and its communications destroyed, and those on board, after exhausting the ship's provisions, should find that part of the cargo was food and should break open boxes of freight and eat the contents as the only means of saving themselves from starvation, they would not be guilty of larceny. Doubtless the lack of any case holding such an appropriation not to be larceny (or *contra*) is because the result is too obvious to have resulted in prosecution. The necessity is determined by an objective standard.[33]

The bank cashier who hands over money to an armed bandit, under threat of immediate death if the cashier refuses, thereby appropriates the bank's money to save the cashier's own life. But this is not theft.[34]

The Model Penal Code[35] and statutes of some states[36] have adopted a standard for duress that is more liberal than the traditional rule. The

---

27. The William Gray, 1 Paine 16, Fed.Cas. No. 17,694 (1810). Compare Commonwealth v. Brooks, 99 Mass. 434 (1868).

28. United States v. Ashton, 2 Sumn. 13, Fed.Cas. No. 14,470 (1834).

29. People v. Lovercamp, 43 Cal.App.3d 823, 118 Cal.Rptr. 110 (1974); State v. Tuttle, 730 P.2d 630 (Utah 1986).

30. Damron v. Commonwealth, 687 S.W.2d 138 (Ky.1985).

31. Bacon: Maxims, reg. 5.

32. State v. Moe, 174 Wash. 303, 24 P.2d 638 (1933).

33. State v. Mills, 117 Idaho 534, 789 P.2d 530 (App. 1990).

34. State v. McGuire, 107 Mont. 341, 88 P.2d 35 (1938).

35. 2.09.

36. Ariz.Rev.Stat.Ann. § 13–412 (1978); Utah Code Ann.1953, § 76–2–302.

standard recognizes a defense to any crime if the actor was coerced to commit the offense by use or threat to use unlawful force against him or another, "which a person of reasonable firmness in his situation would have been unable to resist." The Model Penal Code[37] also recognizes that conduct may be justifiable if the actor believes it to be necessary to avoid a harm or evil to himself or another and the harm or evil to be avoided is greater than the conduct sought to be prevented. This embodies a *choice of evils* for the actor and a defense so long as the actor has not made an inappropriate choice. The concept of choice of evils does not necessarily rule out the alternative defense of duress. Some courts have recognized the availability of a defense of choice of evils or necessity in proper circumstances but a real emergency must be shown, not merely a choice of courses of action, before the defense is available.[38]

People v. Anderson

Supreme Court of California, 2002.
28 Cal.4th 767, 122 Cal.Rptr.2d 587, 50 P.3d 368.

■ CHIN, J.

Over two centuries ago, William Blackstone, the great commentator on the common law, said that duress is no excuse for killing an innocent person: "And, therefore, though a man be violently assaulted, and hath no other possible means of escaping death, but by killing an innocent person, this fear and force shall not acquit him of murder; for he ought rather to die himself than escape by the murder of an innocent." (2 Jones's Blackstone (1916) p. 2197.)

We granted review to decide whether these words apply in California. We conclude that, as in Blackstone's England, so today in California: fear for one's own life does not justify killing an innocent person. Duress is not a defense to murder. We also conclude that duress cannot reduce murder to manslaughter. Although one may debate whether a killing under duress should be manslaughter rather than murder, if a new form of manslaughter is to be created, the Legislature, not this court, should do it.

---

37. 3.02.

38. In proving that there were no legal alternatives available to assist him so as to establish a defense of necessity, a defendant must show he was confronted with a crisis which did not permit selection from among several solutions some of which did not involve criminal acts. United States v. Meraz–Valeta, 26 F.3d 992 (10th Cir. 1994).

A defendant cannot claim the defense of duress when defendant had, but passed, an opportunity to seek aid of law enforcement officials. United States v. Rawlings, 982 F.2d 590 (D.C.Cir.1993).

Choice of evils or necessity defense is available against a charge of possession of marijuana allegedly needed for relief from spasticity associated with quadraplegia. State v. Tate, 102 N.J. 64, 505 A.2d 941 (1986).

"[W]here a criminal defendant is charged with escape and claims that he is entitled to an instruction on the theory of duress or necessity, he must proffer evidence of a bona fide effort to surrender or return to custody as soon as the claimed duress or necessity had lost its coercive force." United States v. Bailey, 444 U.S. 394, 100 S.Ct. 624, 637, 62 L.Ed.2d 575 (1980).

I. THE FACTS AND PROCEDURAL HISTORY

Defendant was charged with kidnapping and murdering Margaret Armstrong in a camp area near Eureka called the South Jetty. Defendant and others apparently suspected the victim of molesting two girls who resided in the camp. Ron Kiern, the father of one of the girls, pleaded guilty to Armstrong's second degree murder and testified at defendant's trial.

The prosecution evidence showed that a group of people, including defendant and Kiern, confronted Armstrong at the camp. Members of the group dragged Armstrong to a nearby field, beat her, put duct tape over her mouth, tied her naked to a bush, and abandoned her. Later, defendant and Kiern, in Kiern's car, saw Armstrong going naked down the street away from the jetty. The two grabbed Armstrong, forced her into the car, and drove away. They then put Armstrong into a sleeping bag, wrapped the bag with duct tape, and placed her, screaming, into the trunk of Kiern's car.

Witnesses testified that defendant picked up a large rock, brought it to the trunk, and handed it to Kiern. Kiern appeared to hit Armstrong with the rock, silencing her. Kiern testified that defendant said Armstrong had to die. After they put her into the trunk, defendant dropped a small boulder onto her head. Kiern also said that defendant picked up the rock again, handed it to Kiern, and told him to drop it on Armstrong or something would happen to his family. Kiern dropped the rock but believed it missed Armstrong. Kiern and defendant later commented to others that Armstrong was dead.

The evidence indicated that defendant and Kiern disposed of Armstrong's body by rolling it down a ravine. One witness testified that Kiern stated he had stepped on her neck until it crunched to ensure she was dead before putting her in the ravine. The body was never found.

Defendant testified on his own behalf. He said he had tried to convince Kiern to take Armstrong to the hospital after she had been beaten. When he and Kiern saw her going down the road beaten and naked, Kiern grabbed her and put her in the backseat of the car. Back at camp, Kiern put Armstrong in the sleeping bag and bound it with duct tape. At Kiern's instruction, defendant opened the trunk and Kiern put Armstrong inside. Kiern told defendant to retrieve a certain rock the size of a cantaloupe. Defendant said, "Man, you are out of your mind for something like that." Kiern responded, "Give me the rock or I'll beat the shit out of you." Defendant gave him the rock because Kiern was bigger than he and he was "not in shape" to fight. When asked what he thought Kiern would have done if he had said no, defendant replied: "Punch me out, break my back, break my neck. Who knows." Kiern hit Armstrong over the head with the rock two or three times. Kiern's wife was standing there yelling, "Kill the bitch."

Defendant testified that later they left in Kiern's car. They pulled over and Kiern opened the trunk. Armstrong was still moaning and moving around. Defendant tried to convince Kiern to take her to a hospital, but Kiern refused. Defendant got back into the car. A few minutes later, Kiern closed the trunk, got in the car, and said, "She's dead now. I stomped on her neck and broke it."

A jury convicted defendant of first degree murder and kidnapping. Based primarily on his testimony that Kiern threatened to "beat the shit out of" him, defendant contended on appeal that the trial court erred in refusing to instruct the jury on duress as a defense to the murder charge. The Court of Appeal concluded that duress is not a defense to first degree murder and affirmed the judgment. We granted defendant's petition for review to decide to what extent, if any, duress is a defense to a homicide-related crime, and, if it is a defense, whether the trial court prejudicially erred in refusing a duress instruction.

II. DISCUSSION

A. Whether Duress Is a Defense to Murder

At common law, the general rule was, and still is today, what Blackstone stated: duress is no defense to killing an innocent person.[39] "Stemming from antiquity, the nearly 'unbroken tradition' of Anglo–American common law is that duress never excuses murder, that the person threatened with his own demise 'ought rather to die himself, than escape by the murder of an innocent.'" (Dressler, *Exegesis of the Law of Duress: Justifying the Excuse and Searching for Its Proper Limits* (1989) 62 So.Cal. L.Rev. 1331, 1370, fns. omitted; *see also id.* at p. 1343 & fn. 83, and cases cited.)[40]

The basic rationale behind allowing the defense of duress for other crimes "is that, for reasons of social policy, it is better that the defendant, faced with a choice of evils, choose to do the lesser evil (violate the criminal law) in order to avoid the greater evil threatened by the other person." (LaFave, Criminal Law, *supra,* § 5.3, p. 467.) This rationale, however, "is strained when a defendant is confronted with taking the life of an innocent third person in the face of a threat on his own life.... When the defendant commits murder under duress, the resulting harm—i.e. the death of an innocent person—is at least as great as the threatened harm—i.e. the death of the defendant." (U.S. v. LaFleur, *supra,* 971 F.2d at p. 205.) We might add that, when confronted with an apparent kill-an-innocent-person-or-be-killed situation, a person can always choose to resist. As a practical matter, death will rarely, if ever, inevitably result from a choice not to kill. The law should require people to choose to resist rather than kill an innocent person.

A state may, of course, modify the common law rule by statute. The Model Penal Code, for example, does not exclude murder from the duress defense. (See LaFave, Criminal Law, *supra,* § 5.3(b), p. 469, fn. 13.) Defendant contends the California Legislature modified the rule in the 19th century and made duress a defense to some murders.

---

39. By "innocent," we mean merely that the person did not cause the duress, not that the person has never committed a crime.

40. See also Perkins and Boyce, Criminal Law (3d ed.1982) chapter 9, section 2, page 1058 ("For the most part today, as at common law, one is not excused for the intentional killing of an obviously innocent person, even if it was necessary to save oneself from death."); LaFave, Criminal Law (3d ed.2000) section 5.3(b), pages 468–469; Annotation, Coercion, Compulsion, or Duress as Defense to Criminal Prosecution (1955) 40 A.L.R.2d 908, 909 ("[I]t appears to be generally accepted that coercion or duress may be a defense to all crimes except taking the life of an innocent person"); U.S. v. LaFleur (9th Cir.1991) 971 F.2d 200, 205, and cases cited.

Since its adoption in 1872, Penal Code section 26 has provided: "All persons are capable of committing crimes except those belonging to the following classes: [¶] ... [¶] ... Persons (unless the crime be punishable with death) who committed the act or made the omission charged under threats of menaces sufficient to show that they had reasonable cause to and did believe their lives would be endangered if they refused." Defendant contends the reference to a "crime ... punishable with death" means that the crimes to which duress is not a defense include only those forms of murder that are punishable with death, and that these forms change with changes in death penalty law. In 1872, when the current Penal Code was adopted, all first degree murder was punishable with death. (People v. Green (1956) 47 Cal.2d 209, 218, 302 P.2d 307.) Today only first degree murder with special circumstances is so punishable. (§§ 190, subd. (a), 190.2, subd. (a).) Accordingly, defendant contends that today, duress is a defense to all murder except first degree murder with special circumstances. In effect, he argues that a killing under duress is either first degree murder with special circumstances or no crime at all. Because the prosecution did not allege special circumstances in this case, he continues, duress provides a full defense....

In this case, the Court of Appeal concluded that, because all first degree murders were punishable with death in 1872, when section 26 was enacted, duress is not a defense to any first degree murder. In effect, the court concluded that section 26's exception for a "crime ... punishable with death" includes any crime punishable with death as of 1872 unaffected by later changes in death penalty law. As we explain, we agree, except that the Court of Appeal did not go back far enough in time. The exception for a crime punishable with death refers to a crime punishable with death as of 1850, not 1872. Section 26 derives from section 10 of the original 1850 Act Concerning Crimes and Punishments, which similarly excepted a crime "punishable with death" from the duress defense. Section 5, enacted as part of the original Penal Code in 1872 and unchanged since, provides: "The provisions of this Code, so far as they are substantially the same as existing statutes, must be construed as continuations thereof, and not as new enactments." As relevant, section 26 was merely a continuation of the then existing 1850 statute. For this reason, we must "begin ... by inquiring into the intent of the Legislature in 1850...." (Keeler v. Superior Court (1970) 2 Cal.3d 619, 625, 87 Cal.Rptr. 481, 470 P.2d 617 [applying § 5 to § 187].)

In 1850, all murder was punishable with death. (Stats.1850, ch. 99, § 21, p. 231.) Not until 1856 was murder divided into degrees, with death the punishment for first degree but not second degree murder. (Stats.1856, ch. 139, § 2, p. 219.) This means that in 1850, duress was no defense to any murder. Thus, like many of California's early penal statutes (see, e.g., People v. Davis (1998) 19 Cal.4th 301, 304, fn. 1, 79 Cal.Rptr.2d 295, 965 P.2d 1165 [theft]; Keeler v. Superior Court, *supra,* 2 Cal.3d at pp. 624–625, 87 Cal.Rptr. 481, 470 P.2d 617 [murder]), section 26 effectively adopted the common law, although the Legislature used a problematic method in which to do so. The question before us is whether the exception for a crime punishable with death changes with every change in death penalty law, which would mean that by 1872, the exception included only first degree murder and today it includes only first degree murder with special circumstances. We think not, for several reasons.

We see no suggestion that the 1850, or any, Legislature intended the substantive law of duress to fluctuate with every change in death penalty law. That interpretation would create strange anomalies. For example, special circumstances were added to the murder laws in the 1970's to conform California's death penalty law to the requirements of the United States Constitution. (People v. Frierson (1979) 25 Cal.3d 142, 173–175, 158 Cal.Rptr. 281, 599 P.2d 587.) Defendant's position would mean that constitutional death penalty jurisprudence would control the substantive law of duress, something we doubt the Legislature intended. Even more anomalously, defendant's position would mean that when the Legislature created special circumstances to give California a valid death penalty law, it simultaneously *expanded* the circumstances in which someone may kill an innocent person.

The presence or absence of special circumstances has no relationship to whether duress should be a defense to killing an innocent person. For example, because a prior murder conviction is a special circumstance (§ 190.2, subd. (a)(2)), defendant's position would mean that a person with a prior murder conviction who intentionally kills an innocent person under duress without premeditating commits no crime, but if the person premeditates, the killing is a capital crime. A person without the prior conviction committing the same premeditated killing would commit no crime unless some other special circumstance happened to attach, in which case the killing would be a capital crime. The Legislature can hardly have intended such random results.

Defendant's interpretation would also force prosecutors to charge special circumstances to prevent duress from becoming a defense. As the Court of Appeal said in this case, "a rule making the availability of the duress defense turn on the manner in which prosecutorial discretion is exercised is potentially pernicious, and may do an unnecessary disservice to criminal defendants. The decision of whether to seek the death penalty ... should not be encumbered by tactical considerations, such as blocking anticipated defenses. The charging decision must be governed by more sagacious considerations than whether the punishment charged will deprive a defendant of a defense to the crime."

Other statutory provisions lead to the conclusion that, like the common law, section 26 excludes all murder from the duress defense. By itself, section 26 (or its 1850 predecessor) is not clear whether the reference to a "crime" punishable with death means the crime of murder in all its forms or only those forms of murder punishable with death. But section 26 does not exist by itself. A court does not determine the meaning of a statute from a single word or sentence but in context; provisions relating to the same subject must be harmonized to the extent possible. (Lungren v. Deukmejian (1988) 45 Cal.3d 727, 735, 248 Cal.Rptr. 115, 755 P.2d 299.) Accordingly, a statute should be construed with reference to the whole system of law of which it is a part. (Landrum v. Superior Court (1981) 30 Cal.3d 1, 14, 177 Cal.Rptr. 325, 634 P.2d 352.) When read in conjunction with other statutes, it becomes clear that section 26's reference to a "crime" means the crime of murder in general and not just those forms of murder punishable with death at any given time.

The original 1850 statute defining murder provided that the "punishment of any person convicted of the *crime of murder* shall be death." (Stats. 1850, ch. 99, § 21, p. 231, italics added.) The 1856 statute that divided murder into degrees, with death the punishment only for first degree murder—and thus, under defendant's position, the statute that first abrogated the common law of duress—referred to determining "the degree of the crime." (Stats. 1856, ch. 139, § 2, p. 219.) These statutes thus indicate that the "crime" was and remained "murder" even after it was divided into degrees.

Other statutes also indicate that the "crime" is "murder." Section 951 provides guidelines as to how to charge a crime in an information or indictment. It states the pleading may simply "giv[e] the name of the *crime,* as murder, burglary, etc...." (Italics added.) An accusatory pleading charging simply murder, without specifying the degree, is sufficient to charge any degree of murder. (*In re Walker* (1974) 10 Cal.3d 764, 781, 112 Cal.Rptr. 177, 518 P.2d 1129; People v. Mendez (1945) 27 Cal.2d 20, 23, 161 P.2d 929.)

Moreover, section 1157 provides that when "a defendant is convicted of a *crime* ... which is distinguished into degrees," the jury or court must find the degree of the crime. (Italics added.) Both sections 951 and 1157 were substantially identical in relevant respects in 1872, when section 26 was enacted. Section 1157 apparently has no antecedent before the 1872 Penal Code (but compare the 1856 law dividing murder into degrees, cited in the preceding paragraph [Stats. 1856, ch. 139, § 2, p. 219]), but section 951 derives from the 1850 law, which was similar as relevant here. In * * * accordance with these statutes, the information in this case charged defendant simply with the crime of "murder." The jury then found the crime to be first degree.

Thus, sections 951 and 1157 provide that the "crime" is "murder." In light of those provisions, it is apparent that section 26 also refers to the "crime" of murder, not a particular form of murder. Indeed, we have explained that when, in 1856, the Legislature created the degrees of murder, it merely "divide[d] the crime of murder into two degrees...." (People v. Dillon (1983) 34 Cal.3d 441, 466, 194 Cal.Rptr. 390, 668 P.2d 697.) Moreover, we have explained that a special circumstance, today necessary to permit the death penalty, is itself "not a 'crime,' and an element of a special circumstance thus is not an 'element of a crime.'" (People v. Garcia (1984) 36 Cal.3d 539, 552, 205 Cal.Rptr. 265, 684 P.2d 826.) Even when special circumstances are alleged, the substantive crime remains murder. Murder is punishable with death, although not all forms of murder are so punishable. Here, defendant was properly charged simply with murder. Hence, duress was no defense to that charge.

Other provisions of the Penal Code bolster this conclusion. Sections 195 and 197, both enacted in 1872, describe those situations in which homicide is excusable or justifiable. If the homicide is excusable or justifiable under these provisions, the person must be acquitted. (§ 199.) The original 1850 law had provisions comparable to, although somewhat different from, sections 195 and 197. (Stats.1850, ch. 99, §§ 29–36, p. 232.) None of these provisions mentions duress as excusing or justifying homicide. It is unreasonable to suppose the Legislature carefully described the situations in which homicide is excusable or justifiable in those provisions, but also intended to create by oblique implication in section 26 (or any other statute) yet another form of excusable or justifiable homicide, especially when doing so would abrogate the settled common law rule that duress is no defense to killing an innocent person.

Moreover, no reason appears for the Legislature to have silently abrogated the common law rule. The reasons for the rule applied as well to 19th-century California as to Blackstone's England. They apply, if anything, with greater force in California today. A person can always choose to resist rather than kill an innocent person. The law must encourage, even require, everyone to seek an alternative to killing. Crimes are often committed by more than one person; the criminal law must also, perhaps especially, deter those crimes. California today is tormented by gang violence. If duress is recognized as a defense to the killing of innocents, then a street or prison gang need only create an internal reign of terror and murder can be justified, at least by the actual killer. Persons who know they can claim duress will be more likely to follow a gang order to kill instead of resisting than would those who know they must face the consequences of their acts. Accepting the duress defense for any form of murder would thus encourage killing. Absent a stronger indication than the language of section 26, we do not believe the Legislature intended to remove the sanctions of the criminal law from the killing of an innocent even under duress. . . .

The concurring and dissenting opinion also argues that duress especially should be a defense to implied malice second degree murder. It evokes the image of an innocent person who is forced at gunpoint by fleeing armed robbers to drive recklessly, and who is then charged with murder when a fatal accident ensues. In reality, the situation is not so grim. Although duress is not an affirmative defense to murder, the circumstances of duress would certainly be relevant to whether the evidence establishes the elements of implied malice murder. The reasons a person acted in a certain way, including threats of death, are highly relevant to whether the person acted with a conscious or wanton disregard for human life. (People v. Watson (1981) 30 Cal.3d 290, 300, 179 Cal.Rptr. 43, 637 P.2d 279.) This is not due to a special doctrine of duress but to the requirements of implied malice murder.

Defendant argues that the rule of lenity compels a different result. (See People v. Avery (2002) 27 Cal.4th 49, 57–58, 115 Cal.Rptr.2d 403, 38 P.3d 1.)

We disagree. As explained in *Avery,* the rule of lenity compels courts to resolve true statutory ambiguities in a defendant's favor, but this rule applies only if two reasonable interpretations of the statute stand in relative equipoise. Courts should not strain to interpret a penal statute in a defendant's favor if they can fairly discern a contrary legislative intent.

Here, for the reasons stated, the possible interpretations of section 26 do not stand in relative equipoise. Reasonably construed, section 26 preserves the common law rule that duress is not a defense to murder.

Defendant also cites legislative inaction in support of his position. The Legislature amended section 26 in 1976 and again in 1981, both times to delete a class of persons that the original statute had made incapable of committing crimes. (Stats.1976, ch. 1181, § 1, p. 5285 [deleting the class of married women acting under threats by their husbands]; Stats.1981, ch. 404, § 3, p. 1592 [deleting the class of "lunatics and insane persons"].) Defendant argues that because the Legislature did not also amend the provision relating to duress, it "made the decision that not only should not all murderers be eligible for the penalty of death, but not all should be deprived of the defense of duress." Again, we disagree. "To be sure, where the Legislature amends a statute without altering a consistent and long-standing judicial interpretation of its operative language, courts generally indulge in a presumption that the Legislature has ratified that interpretation." (People v. Escobar (1992) 3 Cal.4th 740, 750–751, 12 Cal.Rptr.2d 586, 837 P.2d 1100.)

But legislative inaction is a weak indication of intent at best; it is generally more fruitful to examine what the Legislature has done rather than not done. (*Id.* at p. 751, 12 Cal.Rptr.2d 586, 837 P.2d 1100.) Here, there is no indication the Legislature even considered duress when it amended section 26 in other areas. Moreover, when it did amend the section, there was no long-standing and consistent judicial interpretation that duress was a defense to some but not all murder, only fleeting dicta in a single intermediate appellate court decision that duress was a defense to all murder when there was no death penalty.

Accordingly, we conclude that duress is not a defense to any form of murder.

B.   Whether Duress Can Reduce Murder to a Lesser Crime

Defendant also argues that even if duress is not a complete defense to murder, at least it reduces the crime to manslaughter by negating malice.

"Manslaughter is 'the unlawful killing of a human being without malice.' (§ 192.) A defendant lacks malice and is guilty of voluntary manslaughter in 'limited, explicitly defined circumstances: either when the defendant acts in a "sudden quarrel or heat of passion" (§ 192, subd. (a)), or when the defendant kills in "unreasonable self-defense"—the unreasonable but good faith belief in having to act in self-defense (*see In re Christian S.* (1994) 7 Cal.4th 768, [30 Cal.Rptr.2d 33, 872 P.2d 574]; People v. Flannel [(1979)] 25 Cal.3d 668, [160 Cal.Rptr. 84, 603 P.2d 1]).' " (People v. Blakeley (2000) 23 Cal.4th 82, 87–88, 96 Cal.Rptr.2d 451, 999 P.2d 675.) Neither of these two circumstances describes the killing of an innocent person under duress. Nevertheless, defendant argues that we should make duress a third way in which a defendant lacks malice.

No California case has recognized the killing of an innocent person under duress as a form of manslaughter. Some states have provided by statute that a killing under duress is manslaughter. (See Perkins & Boyce,

Criminal Law, *supra*, ch. 9, § 2, p. 1058 & fn. 18; LaFave, Criminal Law, *supra*, § 7.11(c), pp. 719–720.) But California has not done so. The cases that have considered the question absent a statute have generally rejected the argument that duress can reduce murder to manslaughter. (*E.g.*, U.S. v. LaFleur, *supra*, 971 F.2d at p. 206; State v. Nargashian (1904) 26 R.I. 299, 58 A. 953, 955 [often cited as a leading case on the subject]; contra, Wentworth v. State (1975) 29 Md.App. 110, 349 A.2d 421, 428.) Relying heavily on People v. Flannel, *supra*, 25 Cal.3d 668, 160 Cal.Rptr. 84, 603 P.2d 1, and legal commentators, defendant argues that this court should do what the Legislature has not done: recognize a killing under duress as a form of manslaughter.

Some commentators do, indeed, argue that fear for one's own life, although not justifying the killing of an innocent, should at least mitigate murder to manslaughter. "[T]he holding that a killing in such an extremity is necessarily murder has not been adequately considered. While moral considerations require the rejection of any claim of excuse, they do not require that the mitigation of the circumstances be overlooked. A killing in such an extremity is far removed from cold-blooded murder, and should be held to be manslaughter." (Perkins & Boyce, Criminal Law, *supra*, ch. 9, § 2, p. 1058.) "[I]t is arguable that [a defendant's] crime should be manslaughter rather than murder, on the theory that the pressure upon him, although not enough to justify his act, should serve at least to mitigate it to something less than murder." (LaFave, Criminal Law, *supra*, § 7.11(c), p. 719.)

This court has never decided the question. (*See* People v. Bacigalupo (1991) 1 Cal.4th 103, 124–125, 2 Cal.Rptr.2d 335, 820 P.2d 559 [concluding only that any error in not giving duress instructions was harmless]; People v. Beardslee (1991) 53 Cal.3d 68, 86, 279 Cal.Rptr. 276, 806 P.2d 1311 [not deciding "what relevance, if any," People v. Flannel, *supra*, 25 Cal.3d 668, 160 Cal.Rptr. 84, 603 P.2d 1, has in the duress context].) The problem with making a killing under duress a form of manslaughter is that no statute so provides. The difference between murder and manslaughter "is that murder includes, but manslaughter lacks, the element of malice." (People v. Rios (2000) 23 Cal.4th 450, 460, 97 Cal.Rptr.2d 512, 2 P.3d 1066.) Both forms of voluntary manslaughter currently recognized—provocation and imperfect self-defense—are grounded in statutory language. The provocation form of manslaughter is obviously based on statute. Section 192 "specif[ies] that an unlawful killing that lacks malice because committed 'upon a sudden quarrel or heat of passion' is voluntary manslaughter." (People v. Rios, *supra*, 23 Cal.4th at p. 461, 97 Cal.Rptr.2d 512, 2 P.3d 1066; *see also* § 188 [malice is "implied, when no considerable provocation appears"].)

Although less obvious, the imperfect self-defense form of manslaughter is also based on statute. People v. Flannel, *supra*, 25 Cal.3d 668, 160 Cal.Rptr. 84, 603 P.2d 1, the leading case developing the doctrine, "had two *independent* premises: (1) the notion of mental capacity . . . and (2) a grounding in both well-developed common law and in the statutory requirement of malice (Pen.Code, § 187)." (*In re Christian S., supra*, 7 Cal.4th at p. 777, 30 Cal.Rptr.2d 33, 872 P.2d 574.) In 1981, the Legislature abolished diminished capacity, thus making the first premise no longer valid. (*Ibid.*) But the second premise remains valid. (*Ibid.*) Express malice exists "when there is manifested a deliberate intention *unlawfully* to take away the life of a fellow creature." (§ 188, italics added.) A killing in self-defense is *lawful*. Hence, a person who actually, albeit unreasonably, believes it is necessary to kill in self-defense intends to kill lawfully, not unlawfully. "A person who actually believes in the need for self-defense necessarily believes he is acting lawfully." (*In re Christian S., supra,* 7 Cal.4th at p. 778, 30 Cal.Rptr.2d 33, 872 P.2d 574.) Because express malice requires an intent to kill unlawfully, a killing in the belief that one is acting lawfully is not malicious. The statutory definition of implied malice does not contain similar language, but we have extended the imperfect self-defense rationale to any killing that would otherwise have malice, whether express or implied. "[T]here is no valid reason to distinguish between those killings that, absent unreasonable self-defense, would be murder with express malice, and those killings that, absent unreasonable self-defense, would be murder with implied malice." (People v. Blakeley, *supra,* 23 Cal.4th at p. 89, 96 Cal.Rptr.2d 451, 999 P.2d 675.)

Defendant's reliance on People v. Flannel, *supra,* 25 Cal.3d 668, 160 Cal.Rptr. 84, 603 P.2d 1, and its recognition of unreasonable self-defense as a form of manslaughter, is thus misplaced. A killing in self-defense is lawful, but a killing of an innocent person under duress is unlawful. In contrast to a person killing in imperfect self-defense, a person who kills an innocent believing it necessary to save the killer's own life intends to kill unlawfully, not lawfully. Nothing in the statutes negates malice in that situation. Recognizing killing under duress as manslaughter would create a new form of manslaughter, which is for the Legislature, not courts, to do.

When this court developed the doctrine of diminished capacity as a form of manslaughter, we rejected the argument that we were improperly creating a nonstatutory crime: "In People v. Conley [(1966)] 64 Cal.2d 310, [49 Cal.Rptr. 815, 411 P.2d 911], we pointed out that section 192 had been adopted before the concept of diminished capacity had been developed and therefore that section's enumeration of nonmalicious criminal homicides could not be considered exclusive. We did not thereby create a 'non statutory crime,' nor could we do so consistently with Penal Code section 6. Rather we gave effect to the *statutory* definition of manslaughter by recognizing that factors other than sudden quarrel or heat of passion may render a person incapable of harboring malice." (People v. Mosher (1969) 1 Cal.3d 379, 385, fn. 1, 82 Cal.Rptr. 379, 461 P.2d 659.) This justification of diminished capacity does not apply to duress. Sections 26, 187, and 192, all enacted in 1872 and unchanged since as far as duress is concerned, postdate the development of the law that duress does not justify killing an innocent person. Moreover, the Legislature has now abolished the doctrine of diminished capacity. (*In re Christian S., supra,* 7 Cal.4th at p. 774, 30 Cal.Rptr.2d 33, 872 P.2d 574; People v. Saille (1991) 54 Cal.3d 1103, 2 Cal.Rptr.2d 364, 820 P.2d 588.) Thus, we see no basis on which to create a new, nonstatutory, form of voluntary manslaughter.

Two other circumstances also point to this conclusion. First, section 190.3 lists factors a jury should consider in deciding whether to impose the death penalty when the defendant has been convicted of first degree murder with special circumstances. Among the factors is whether the defendant "acted under extreme duress. . . ." (§ 190.3, factor (g).) This provision implies that a person acting even "under extreme duress" may be convicted of first degree murder with special circumstances, an implication inconsistent with the notion that duress reduces what would otherwise be murder to manslaughter. Second, recognizing that duress could reduce murder to manslaughter would create a conundrum with no obvious solution. Manslaughter has always been a separate crime from murder. Both section 187, defining murder, and section 192, defining manslaughter, were enacted in 1872. They derive from the 1850 law. (Stats.1850, ch. 99, §§ 19–26, p. 231.) But manslaughter has never been punishable by death. If a killing under duress were a form of manslaughter, it would seem that the same duress would then provide a *defense* to manslaughter. Thus, duress would become a complete defense to murder by a two-step process: first, duress would reduce murder to manslaughter; second, duress would supply a defense to that manslaughter. These problems are for the Legislature to sort out if it should choose to do so.

We recognize that policy arguments can be made that a killing out of fear for one's own life, although not justified, should be a crime less than the same killing without such fear. On the other hand, because duress can often arise in a criminal gang context, the Legislature might be reluctant to do anything to reduce the current law's deterrent effect on gang violence. These policy questions are for the Legislature, not a court, to decide. Accordingly, we reject defendant's argument that we should create a new form of voluntary manslaughter. His arguments are better directed to the Legislature.

Defendant also argues that, at least, duress can negate premeditation and deliberation, thus resulting in second degree and not first degree murder. We agree that a killing under duress, like any killing, may or may not be premeditated, depending on the circumstances. If a person obeys an order to kill without reflection, the jury might find no premeditation and thus convict of second degree murder. As with implied malice murder, this circumstance is not due to a special doctrine of duress but to the legal requirements of first degree murder. The trial court instructed the jury on the requirements for first degree murder. It specifically instructed that a killing "upon a sudden heat of passion or *other condition precluding the idea of deliberation*" would not be premeditated first degree murder." (Italics added.) Here, the jury found premeditation. In some other case, it might not. It is for the jury to decide. But, unless and until the Legislature decides otherwise, a malicious, premeditated killing, even under duress, is first degree murder.

On a final point, we note, contrary to the Attorney General's argument, that duress can, in effect, provide a defense to murder on a felony-murder theory by negating the underlying felony. (*See* People v. Anderson (1991) 233 Cal.App.3d 1646, 1666–1667, fn. 18, 285 Cal.Rptr. 523; Perkins & Boyce, Criminal Law, *supra*, ch. 9, § 2, pp. 1058–1059; LaFave, Criminal Law, *supra*, § 5.3(b), pp. 468–469.) If one is not guilty of the underlying felony due to duress, one cannot be guilty of felony murder based on that felony. Here, for example, the court instructed the jury that duress could be a defense to the kidnapping charge. It also instructed on felony murder with kidnapping as the underlying felony. If the jury had found defendant not guilty of kidnapping due to duress (it did not), it could not have found that he killed during the commission of that kidnapping. Defendant could not have killed during the perpetration of a crime of which he was innocent.

Our conclusion that duress is no defense to murder makes it unnecessary to decide whether the evidence would have warranted duress instructions in this case.

III. CONCLUSION

We affirm the judgment of the Court of Appeal.

■ WE CONCUR: GEORGE, C.J., BAXTER, WERDEGAR, BROWN and MORENO, JJ.

■ Concurring and Dissenting Opinion by KENNARD, J.

Under California law, the death penalty may be imposed for the crime of murder only if the murder is of the first degree and committed with one or more of the statutorily defined special circumstances. (Pen.Code, §§ 190, 190.2.) California law allows a person accused of crime to defend against any criminal charge on the ground that the defendant acted under duress "unless the crime be punishable with death." (*Id.*, § 26, subd. Six.) Here, defendant contends that, because the death penalty may not be imposed for second degree murder, the trial court erred in not instructing the jury that duress, if proven, was a complete defense to second degree murder.

The majority concludes that the trial court did not err because, under California law, duress is not a defense to second degree murder, or to any form of murder, whether or not the particular form of murder is punishable by death. I disagree. Applying established rules of statutory construction, I would hold that duress is unavailable as a defense only when the offense is capital murder—that is, first degree murder with a special circumstance—and that duress is available as a defense to all noncapital forms of murder, including murder in the second degree. Because no substantial evidence of duress was presented here, however, I agree with the majority that defendant was not entitled to have the trial court instruct the jury on that defense....

III

The majority appears to argue that this court *must* construe section 26 as not permitting the defense of duress to any form of murder because sound considerations of public policy require that no amount of threats or menaces can justify the taking of innocent human life. In my view, such public policy considerations have a very limited role to play in the process of statutory construction. In general, this court may not substitute its public policy views for those of the Legislature under the guise of statutory construction. When the language of a statute is ambiguous, however, this court may prefer a resolution of the ambiguity that avoids absurd consequences or that no reasonable legislative body could have intended. (People v. Rubalcava (2000) 23 Cal.4th 322, 328, 96 Cal.Rptr.2d 735, 1 P.3d 52.)

Here, a construction of section 26 that makes the defense of duress unavailable as to capital murder but available as to noncapital murder does not produce results that are absurd or that no reasonable legislative body could have intended. On the contrary, the question of the proper boundaries or limits on the defense of duress is one on which reasonable minds can differ and have differed, and the construction of section 26 that I have arrived at by applying well-established rules of statutory construction represents a moderate approach in line with mainstream legal thinking.

For example, the Model Penal Code allows the defense of duress to be asserted against *all* criminal charges, including murder. (Model Pen.Code, § 2.09.) Under the Model Penal Code's formulation of the defense, duress is a defense whenever "a person of reasonable firmness in [the defendant's] situation would have been unable to resist." (*Id.,* § 209, subd. (1).) In the official comment to this provision, the American Law Institute explains that "persons of reasonable firmness surely break at different points depending on the stakes that are involved"; it further observes "that even homicide may sometimes be the product of coercion that is truly irresistible, that danger to a loved one may have greater impact on a person of reasonable firmness than a danger to himself, and, finally, that long and wasting pressure may break down resistance more effectively than a threat of immediate destruction." (Model Pen.Code & Commentaries, com. 3 to § 209, p. 376.)

The states of Connecticut, New York, North Dakota, Tennessee, Texas, and Utah have adopted statutes similar to the Model Penal Code allowing duress as a defense to homicide. (See Rutkowski, *A Coercion Defense for the Street Gang Criminal: Plugging the Moral Gap in Existing Law* (1996) 10 Notre Dame J.L. Ethics and Pub. Pol'y 137, 205, fn. 332.) Also, the laws of most civil law countries—including Belgium, Greece, the Netherlands, Germany, Switzerland and Sweden—recognize duress as a defense to any crime, including murder. (Swaak–Goldman, *International Decision: Prosecutor v. Erdemovic, Judgement* (1998) 92 Am. J. Int'l L. 282, 284, fn. 14.)

As a leading commentator on the law of duress has stated, "[d]uress always is a matter of line drawing about which reasonable minds can differ" (Dressler, *Exegesis of the Law of Duress: Justifying the Excuse and Searching for Its Proper Limits* (1989) 62 So.Cal. L.Rev. 1331, 1367). Indeed, the weight of scholarly commentary favors the Model Penal Code's definition of duress and its abolition of the common law murder exception to the duress defense. . . .

I do not here suggest that the Legislature should adopt the Model Penal Code approach, under which duress is available as a defense to any crime, including capital murder. I suggest only that a construction of section 26 under which duress is a defense to noncapital murder, but not to capital murder, represents a moderate, middle-of-the road approach that a legislative body plausibly could have adopted to resolve a difficult and complex issue on which reasonable minds may differ.

The majority's discussion appears to assume that murder necessarily involves a *choice* to take an innocent life. Second degree murder, however, does not require an intent to kill. A person who engages in a provocative act (*see* People v. Nieto Benitez (1992) 4 Cal.4th 91, 107–108, 13 Cal.

Rptr.2d 864, 840 P.2d 969) or who drives with great recklessness (*see* People v. Watson (1981) 30 Cal.3d 290, 297–299, 179 Cal.Rptr. 43, 637 P.2d 279) may be convicted of second degree murder under an implied malice theory. Yet, under the majority's construction, section 26 does not allow a duress defense even in situations of unintentional implied malice killings.

Imagine, for example, this scenario: Two armed robbers fleeing the scene of a store robbery force their way into a car that is leaving the parking lot. One robber holds a gun to the driver's head, while the other places a gun against the head of the driver's wife. They order the driver to take off at high speed and not to stop or slow down for stop signs or signal lights, threatening immediate death to the driver and his wife. If the driver complies, and an accident ensues resulting in the death of an innocent person, the driver could be prosecuted for second degree murder on an implied malice theory, and, under the majority's construction of section 26, the driver could not assert duress as a defense. I doubt that our Legislature intended to withhold the defense of duress under these or similar circumstances.

The majority expresses concern that if defendants can assert a duress defense to noncapital murder, the defense may be used to excuse killings by gang members. But most if not all gang-motivated killings are capital murder because it is a special circumstance that "the defendant intentionally killed the victim while the defendant was an active participant in a criminal street gang ... and the murder was carried out to further the activities of the criminal street gang." (Pen.Code, § 190.2, subd. (a)(22).) Moreover, the defense of duress is not available to a defendant who recklessly or intentionally placed himself in a situation where coercion to commit criminal acts could reasonably be anticipated. Because persons who join criminal street gangs or terrorist organizations can anticipate pressure to commit crimes, the defense would usually be unavailable to those individuals. (*See* State v. Scott (1992) 250 Kan. 350, 827 P.2d 733, 739–740 [defendant who voluntarily joined drug-selling organization barred from asserting duress when coerced into torturing fellow gang member]; Rutkowski, *A Coercion Defense for the Street Gang Criminal: Plugging the Moral Gap in Existing Law, supra,* 10 Notre Dame J., L. Ethics & Pub. Pol'y. at p. 186, fn. 239 ["Most jurisdictions hold that intentionally placing oneself in the position where one would likely be the subject of coercion will defeat a duress defense."].)

IV

Because, as I have concluded, duress is a defense to noncapital murder, a defendant charged with noncapital murder is entitled to a jury instruction on the defense if there is substantial evidence to support it. This means " 'evidence from which a jury composed of reasonable [people] could have concluded that there was [duress] sufficient to negate the requisite criminal intent.' " (People v. Flannel (1979) 25 Cal.3d 668, 685, 160 Cal.Rptr. 84, 603 P.2d 1, quoting People v. Carr (1972) 8 Cal.3d 287, 294, 104 Cal.Rptr. 705, 502 P.2d 513.) Under section 26, the defense of duress is only available to defendants who present evidence of threats or menace sufficient to show a reasonable and actual belief that their life was presently and immediately endangered if participation was refused. (People v. Perez (1973) 9 Cal.3d 651, 657, 108 Cal.Rptr. 474, 510 P.2d 1026; People v. Quinlan (1970) 8 Cal.App.3d 1063, 1068, 88 Cal.Rptr. 125.)

Here, defendant failed to present substantial evidence of duress. He testified that Ron Kiern told him, "Give me the rock or I'll beat the shit out of you" and that he complied because he feared that Kiern, a stronger and bigger man, would beat him severely. Yet, Kiern did not threaten him with death, and there was no history of violence between the two men despite their long acquaintance. In addition, defendant voluntarily joined Kiern in the initial attack on the victim, thereby placing himself in the situation where he should have anticipated that Kiern would pressure him to commit further acts of violence. Throughout the day, defendant made no use of opportunities to leave Kiern and to obtain help for the victim.

Because defendant presented insufficient evidence of duress to warrant a jury instruction on that defense, I agree with the majority that the Court of Appeal properly affirmed defendant's conviction.

CONCLUSION

Under California law, duress is a defense to any criminal charge "unless the crime be punishable with death." (§ 26.) According to the majority, this means that duress is never a defense to murder, even though California law restricts the death penalty to first degree murders with special circumstances. The majority reaches its result largely by applying a maxim—no amount of duress excuses the taking of innocent human life— that it treats as an infallible solution to a profound moral quandary. I cannot agree, not only because the majority's maxim is not a fair reading of the far different statutory language, but also because the majority oversimplifies a highly complex issue. I would adopt a statutory construction more consistent with the ordinary meaning of the statutory text, barring the defense of duress only as to capital murder and other capital crimes, and leaving to the jury in all other situations the question whether duress excuses an otherwise criminal act.

Tyner v. State

Court of Appeals of Texas, Dallas.
2001 WL 683638 (not designated for publication).

■ BRIDGES, J.

Rayland Ladon Tyner appeals his aggravated robbery conviction. The jury convicted appellant and sentenced him to fifty-five years' confinement and a $1645.50 fine. In a single point of error, appellant argues the trial court erred in denying his request for an instruction on the law of duress. We reverse the trial court's judgment and remand for further proceedings.

We note appellant does not challenge the sufficiency of the evidence to support his conviction. Thus, only a brief recitation of the facts is necessary. On September 27, 1998, appellant robbed a Sonic restaurant at gunpoint. At trial, appellant testified and admitted committing the robbery but claimed he did so under duress. Specifically, appellant testified he was at an apartment complex prior to the robbery when three men, members of a rival gang, drove up and confronted him. The driver of the car pointed a gun at appellant and told him to get in the car. Appellant refused. The driver told appellant "we got your baby mama around the corner pregnant and she can deliver any time, any time." At the time, appellant's wife was pregnant, and he testified he got in the car because he was afraid for her. Appellant had seen his wife earlier that day but had not seen her since. In the car, appellant told the men they had him, but he asked them to leave his wife alone. Appellant testified he had been selling drugs in some apartments on the men's turf, and they said he had caused a shortage in their money. Appellant thought the men were going to kill him, so to help himself survive, appellant took out a mirror and snorted $200 to $300 worth of cocaine that he had. Appellant believed the cocaine would make his heart keep pumping and allow him to live longer if the men shot him.

The men drove appellant around Dallas and finally stopped and told appellant to give them everything in his pockets. The driver of the car pointed at a Sonic restaurant and told appellant, "I want you to bring me the money." Appellant understood this to mean they wanted him to rob the Sonic. One of the men threw appellant a black hat, but appellant stayed in the car. Appellant asked for a gun, and one of the men hit him in the back of the head with a gun. One of the men asked appellant if he thought it was a game and said, "didn't you buy that pistol from Kevin the other day?" In fact, appellant had a pistol tucked in his waistband under his shirt. Appellant got out of the car and approached the Sonic. One of the men told appellant to "think about your baby mama while you're in there. She can still go into labor at any time." Appellant pulled the hat over his face and went into the Sonic and told a woman, "I need your money." The Sonic employees put money in a bag that appellant took outside. The men who had brought appellant to the Sonic drove away, and police arrived and arrested appellant.

In his sole point of error, appellant argues the trial court erred in failing to include his requested instruction on the law of duress. It is an affirmative defense to prosecution that a person engaged in proscribed conduct because he was compelled to do so by threat of imminent death or serious bodily injury to himself or another. Tex.Pen.Code Ann. § 8.05(a) (Vernon 1994). An accused is entitled to an affirmative defense instruction on every issue raised by the evidence, regardless of whether such evidence is strong, feeble, unimpeached or contradicted, and even if the trial court is of the opinion that the testimony is not entitled to belief. Brown v. State, 955 S.W.2d 276, 279 (Tex.Crim.App.1997) (emphasis added). However, the claim of duress must have an objective, reasonable basis. Cameron v. State, 925 S.W.2d 246, 250 (Tex.App.—El Paso 1995, no pet.); see Bernal v. State, 647 S.W.2d 699, 706 (Tex.App.—San Antonio 1982, no pet.). Compulsion within the meaning of section 8.05 exists only if the force or threat of force would render a person of reasonable firmness incapable of resisting the pressure. Tex.Pen.Code Ann. § 8.05(c) (Vernon 1994). The defense of duress is unavailable if the actor intentionally, knowingly, or recklessly placed himself in a situation in which it was probable that he would be subjected to compulsion. Id. § 8.05(d).

At trial, appellant requested that the trial court charge the jury on the defense of duress. The trial court refused, stating the defense of duress is not available if the actor intentionally, knowingly, or recklessly placed himself in a situation in which it was probable that he would be subjected to compulsion. The trial court explained the evidence showed appellant engaged in drug selling activities in an area controlled by a gang of which he was not a member. For that reason, appellant testified, he was taken in a vehicle and forced to commit a robbery. The trial court concluded appellant's testimony effectively took away the defense of duress. We disagree.

Follow the trial court's rationale in denying appellant's request, no defendant would ever be entitled to a charge on duress if the defendant placed himself in a situation where it was probable he would be subjected to *any* compulsion. In this case, appellant was aware he was selling drugs in an area controlled by a rival gang, and he also testified he was aware his activity could put him and his wife in danger. However, we cannot conclude appellant thereby placed himself in a situation in which it was *probable* that he would be subject to being taken by armed men, who threatened his pregnant wife's safety, and compelled to rob a restaurant. *Id.* Accordingly, the trial court erred refusing to charge the jury on this issue.

Having so concluded, we determine whether sufficient harm resulted from the error to require reversal. Payne v. State, 11 S.W.3d 231, 232–33 (Tex.Crim.App.2000). Because appellant timely objected to the charge error in this case, reversal is required if the error is "calculated to injure the rights of defendant," which means that there must be *some* harm to the accused from the error. Almanza v. State, 686 S.W.2d 157, 171 (Tex.Crim. App.1984). Here, if the jury had been charged on the issue of duress and found appellant committed the underlying robbery only because he was compelled to do so by threat of imminent death or bodily injury to his wife, he would have been entitled to acquittal. *See* Tex.Pen.Code Ann. § 8.05(a) (Vernon 1994). Thus, we conclude the charge error in this case resulted in some harm to appellant. *See Almanza,* 686 S.W.2d at 171. We sustain appellant's sole point of error.

We reverse the trial court's judgment and remand for further proceedings.

State v. Burney

Court of Appeals of Oregon, 1980.
49 Or.App. 529, 619 P.2d 1336.

■ GILLETTE, PRESIDING JUDGE. This is a criminal case in which the defendant was charged with the offense of being an ex-convict in possession of a firearm. ORS 166.270.[41] He was found guilty after a trial to the court. The

---

41. ORS 166.270 provides that

"(1) Any person who has been convicted of a felony under the law of this state or any other state, or who has been convicted of a felony under the laws of the Government of the United States, who owns, or has in his possession or under his custody or control any

sole issue on his appeal is whether the trial court erred in refusing to consider the "choice of evils" defense, ORS 161.200, in assessing the evidence presented at trial. We reverse and remand.

The principal facts are not in dispute. Defendant, who is an ex-convict, moved from Boise, Idaho, to Portland on November 6, 1979. The weekend prior to moving, he had been fishing with a friend. That friend left a pistol in defendant's pickup, without defendant's knowledge. Several weeks later, on the evening of the incident in question, the defendant found the pistol. The circumstances surrounding its discovery led to the crime charged in this case.

Shortly after midnight on December 2, 1979, defendant was returning home from a birthday celebration. He pulled into the lot behind the Burger King, at Broadway and Burnside in Portland, to have a hamburger. The Burger King was closed. When defendant went back to his pickup, it would not start.

Thinking the pickup would start again if he let it sit for awhile, defendant went to call his wife to let her know what was happening. While waiting, he had a glass of wine and played a few games of pool for money in Mary's Club, a nearby establishment. Defendant won ten to sixteen dollars and decided to leave. He had just left Mary's when he noticed Griffin, one of the persons from whom he had won money, coming out of the club with a broken-down cue stick. Because Griffin had been belligerent and was acting strangely, defendant was afraid of him. Specifically, defendant feared Griffin would try to take his money back.

Defendant stopped and asked what Griffin wanted. He walked beside Griffin for a short distance. Griffin became involved in an altercation with an unknown person who bumped into him on the sidewalk. Another unknown person intervened. Defendant left as Griffin and the other two were straightening things out.

Defendant had crossed Burnside and was in the parking lot where his pickup was parked when he heard running footsteps behind him. He turned as he reached his truck and saw Griffin "coming out" at him. Defendant

pistol, revolver, or other firearms capable of being concealed upon the person, or machine gun, commits the crime of exconvict in possession of a firearm.

"(2) For the purposes of this section, a person 'has been convicted of a felony' if, at the time of his conviction for an offense, that offense was a felony under the law of the jurisdiction in which it was committed. Provided, however, that such conviction shall not be deemed a conviction of a felony if:

"(a) At the time of conviction, and pursuant to the law of the jurisdiction in which the offense occurred, the offense was made a misdemeanor by the type or manner of sentence actually imposed; or

"(b) The offense was for possession of marijuana.

"(3) Subsection (1) of this section shall not apply to any person who has been convicted of only one felony under the law of this state or any other state, or who has been convicted of only one felony under the laws of the United States, which felony did not involve the possession or use of a firearm, and who has been discharged from imprisonment, parole or probation for said offense for a period of 15 years prior to the date of alleged violation of subsection (1) of this section.

"(4) Exconvict in possession of a firearm is Class C felony."

reached under the seat of the pickup for a tire iron to protect himself from what he feared was an impending attack. Instead of the tire iron, he felt his friend's pistol. He had not known until that moment that the pistol was there. Defendant pointed the pistol at Griffin's legs and told him to get away. Griffin left. Defendant tossed the pistol back under the seat and tried to restart his truck. Before he could start it the police arrived.

James Powell, a Portland police officer, testified that on December 2, 1979, at 2:40 a.m. he received a radio call to go to the Sealander Restaurant. When Officer Powell arrived he observed Patrick Griffin, who had a cue stick in his hand, pointing to the defendant's vehicle and saying the defendant had a gun on his person. The police immediately approached the defendant's vehicle and ordered him out of his truck. Once outside the defendant denied having a gun.[42] The police searched the vehicle and found the handgun under the passenger seat. The defendant was then advised of his rights, whereupon he admitted he pointed the gun at Griffin because Griffin was threatening him with a cue stick. He also admitted to the officers at the scene that he had been convicted of rape in Utah.

After considering all of the evidence, and indicating that he believed the defendant's story with respect to the circumstances under which the incident occurred, the trial judge found the defendant guilty of the charge. He specifically ruled that the defense of "choice of evils" was not available in a case in which the defendant is charged with being an ex-convict in possession of a firearm. The defendant argues that, because the evidence showed (and the trial judge apparently believed) that the defendant feared for his safety, the defense was applicable.

The "choice of evils" defense is set out in ORS 161.200 as follows:

"(1) Unless inconsistent with other provisions of chapter 743, Oregon Laws 1971, defining justifiable use of physical force, or with some other provision of law, conduct which would otherwise constitute an offense is justifiable and not criminal when:

"(a) That conduct is necessary as an emergency measure to avoid an imminent public or private injury; and

"(b) The threatened injury is of such gravity that, according to ordinary standards of intelligence and morality, the desirability and urgency of avoiding the injury clearly outweigh the desirability of avoiding the injury sought to be prevented by the statute defining the offense in issue.

"(2) The necessity and justifiability of conduct under subsection (1) of this section shall not rest upon considerations pertaining only to the morality and advisability of the statute, either in its general application or with respect to its application to a particular class of cases arising thereunder."

We think that the trial judge's conclusion that ORS 161.200 is inapplicable to the offense of being an ex-convict in possession of a firearm is

---

42. The police testified that defendant denied having a gun. Defendant testified that he denied having a gun *on his person,* because he understood the officer's question to be directed at that possibility. The trial judge specifically stated that he believed defendant's testimony.

incorrect. The statute contains no such express exception, and we see no justification for implying one. To the contrary, one who has been previously convicted of a felony is just as entitled to defend himself from an imminent threat of injury as is any other private citizen. We hold that the defense is available to those who have been previously convicted of a felony and, in appropriate circumstances, may justify their resort to a weapon which it would otherwise be unlawful for them to possess.[43]

We have previously stated that a defendant is entitled to the choice of evils defense if there is evidence that

"(1) ... [H]is conduct was necessary to avoid a threatened injury; (2) ... the threatened injury was imminent; and (3) ... it was reasonable for defendant to believe that the need to avoid the injury was greater than the need to avoid the injury which the [other statute] seeks to prevent." State v. Matthews, 30 Or.App. 1133, 1136, 569 P.2d 662 (1977); State v. Lawson, 37 Or.App. 739, 588 P.2d 110 (1978).

The trial judge apparently found all of those elements present in this case, but declined to apply the defense solely because he believed it was unavailable in this kind of charge. Inasmuch as he was mistaken in this premise, his rationale in convicting the defendant was erroneous.

A question remains as to whether or not this error requires reversal. The state argues that, even if we decide that the choice of evils defense was available to the defendant, all of the testimony establishes that the defendant maintained control of the gun far beyond the time it was necessary to do so in order to protect himself. In fact, the gun was hidden away in the defendant's pickup and was only discovered after a police search. In light of this evidence, the state argues, the defendant is guilty in any event, and we should affirm.

We agree with the state that there was sufficient evidence from which the trial court could find that the defendant was guilty of being an ex-convict in possession of a firearm for the period of time during which, by his own admission, he retained the gun after the threat to his person had ended. However, the evidence was not such as to *require* the trial court to find the defendant guilty. The reason for defendant's hiding of the gun is not established. He may have intended to return it to its owner in Idaho. On the other hand, he may have intended to turn it over to a policeman as soon as possible. If the former was his intent, he is guilty. If the latter was, he may not be; it would be unconscionable to hold defendant guilty for continuing to possess a gun which came into his possession rightfully, unless and until he thereafter had a reasonable opportunity to divest himself of it in a manner which would not create a public peril.

---

43. Defense of necessity will rarely lie in a felon-in-possession of a firearm case, unless the ex felon, not being engaged in criminal activity, does nothing more than grab a gun with which he or another is being threatened or when another might be a possessor of a gun threatening suicide. United States v. Perez, 86 F.3d 735 (7th Cir.1996). *See also* United States v. Schulte, 7 F.3d 698 (7th Cir.1993). However, *see* United States v. Paul, 110 F.3d 869 (2d Cir.1997) (duress is defense to felon in possession of ammunition).

Defendant was never asked what his intent was. There are permissible inferences both ways. The question is one for a trier of fact.

Reversed and remanded for a new trial.[44]

Commonwealth v. Capitolo

Supreme Court of Pennsylvania, 1985.
508 Pa. 372, 498 A.2d 806.

■ PAPADAKOS, JUSTICE.

This case raises the sole issue of whether the defense of justification as defined in Section 503 of our Crimes Code is available to Appellees who were charged with criminal trespass.

On July 15, 1979, Appellees, violating a clearly visible "No Trespass" sign, crawled under a fence surrounding the Shippingsport Power Plant in Beaver County and sat down holding hands. Told to leave by a plant security guard and a deputy sheriff, or face arrest for trespassing, Appellees remained seated. They were then bodily removed by Deputy Sheriffs from the property and each charged with criminal trespass. No injuries or property damage resulted from the trespass at the plant, which was in a two-week shutdown at the time.

. . . Appellees attempted to defend their actions, relying on Section 503 of the Crimes Code which provides:

§ 503.   Justification generally.

(a) General rule—Conduct which the actor believes to be necessary to avoid a harm or evil to himself or to another is justifiable if:

---

44. To establish a prima facie case of duress the defendant must show that he acted under immediate threat of death or serious bodily injury, that his fear was well grounded, and that he had no reasonable opportunity to avoid or escape the threatened harm. United States v. Joelson, 7 F.3d 174 (9th Cir.1993).

The defense of duress fails if defendant recklessly places himself in a position in which it was probable that he would be subject to duress. United States v. Paul, 110 F.3d 869 (2d Cir.1997).

Evidence that defendant suffered from battered woman's syndrome is irrelevant to duress defense which must be based on objective test. United States v. Willis, 38 F.3d 170 (5th Cir.1994).

A seventeen-year-old boy in an Industrial School who submitted to an act of sodomy with a guard, under threats that the guard would "slap him down" every time he saw him, acted under compulsion. Perryman v. State, 63 Ga.App. 819, 12 S.E.2d 388 (1940).

One is not guilty of killing moose without a license and out of season if this was reasonably necessary to protect his property. Cross v. State, 370 P.2d 371 (Wyo.1962). However, *see* State v. Webber, 85 Or.App. 347, 736 P.2d 220 (1987), upholding a requirement that an individual obtain a permit to kill deer damaging a person's property.

In defense against a charge of sale of amphetamine tablets, D claimed duress in that his friends had been threatened with death if he did not sell. The court apparently would have recognized this threat to D's friends as a defense except that: "Avenues of escape were always available, . . ." United States v. Gordon, 526 F.2d 406, 408 (9th Cir.1975). However, *see* People v. Pegram, 152 Ill.App.3d 656, 105 Ill.Dec. 673, 504 N.E.2d 958 (1987). However, see State v. Spalding, 247 Mont. 317, 806 P.2d 1029 (1991).

"We hold that the duress defense is available in Michigan whenever a defendant offers evidence that his escape was necessitated by an immediate threat of death or seriously bodily injury, including a threat of homosexual attack." People v. Mendoza, 108 Mich.App. 733, 310 N.W.2d 860, 864 (1981).

(1) the harm or evil sought to be avoided by such conduct is greater than that sought to be prevented by the law defining the offense charged;

(2) neither this title nor other law defining the offense provides exceptions or defenses dealing with the specific situation involved; and

(3) a legislative purpose to exclude the justification claimed does not otherwise plainly appear.

(b) Choice of evils—When the actor was reckless or negligent in bringing about the situation requiring a choice of harms or evils or in appraising the necessity for his conduct, the justification afforded by this section is unavailable in a prosecution for any offense for which recklessness or negligence, as the case may be, suffices to establish culpability.

Appellees demanded to present evidence from experts which they believed would show:

(1) that there were various activities aimed at shutting down the power plant;

(2) that pursuing other means would not eliminate the danger generated by the plant;

(3) that this type of trespass has been used in the past to stop construction of a power plant;

(4) that the low level radiation emanating from a power plant is a risk and danger.

The trial court rejected this offer ruling, as a matter of law, that the justification defense as defined by Section 503 was not available because Appellees' criminal trespass was neither a necessary nor an effective means by which to avoid their anticipated danger from radioactivity. Appellees were permitted to testify as to their own beliefs concerning the dangers inherent in nuclear power plants, these beliefs being relevant to the issue of motivation, but the jury was given no charge on justification as a defense. Guilty verdicts against Appellees were returned on November 30, 1979, . . .

Our statute (18 Pa.C.S. § 503) adopts the view that a principle of necessity, properly conceived, affords a general justification for conduct that otherwise would constitute an offense; and that such a qualification, like the requirements of culpability, is essential to the rationality and justice of all penal prohibitions. (See Model Penal Code Comment T.D. No. 8, pp. 5–10.) The defense of necessity, however, does not arise from a "choice" of several courses of actions; instead it is based on a real emergency. It can be asserted only by an actor who is confronted with such a crisis as a personal danger (to oneself or others), a crisis which does not permit a selection from among several solutions, some of which do not involve criminal acts. U.S. v. Seward, 687 F.2d 1270 (1982) Court of Appeals (10th Cir., Colo.); U.S. v. Kroncke, 459 F.2d 697 (1972) Court of Appeals (8th Cir., Minn.). Accordingly, the defense can be raised only in situations that deal with harms or evils that are readily apparent and recognizable to reasonable persons. The defense cannot be permitted to justify acts taken to foreclose speculative and uncertain dangers, and is therefore limited in application to acts directed at the avoidance of harm that is reasonably certain to occur.

Furthermore, the actor must reasonably believe that the conduct chosen was necessary to avoid the greater threatened harm or evil. Because the harm must be real, and not an imagined, speculative, or non-imminent harm, the actions taken to avoid the harm must support a reasonable belief or inference that the actions would be effective in avoiding or alleviating the impending harm.

In order, then, to be entitled to an instruction on justification as a defense to a crime charged, the actor must first offer evidence that will show:

> (1) that the actor was faced with a clear and imminent harm, not one which is debatable or speculative;

> (2) that the actor could reasonably expect that the actor's actions would be effective in avoiding this greater harm;

> (3) that there is no legal alternative which will be effective in abating the harm; and

> (4) that the Legislature has not acted to preclude the defense by a clear and deliberate choice regarding the values at issue.

. . .

The trial court was correct in ruling that, as a matter of law, justification was not an available defense to Appellees. Furthermore, the record is clear that the nuclear power plant was shutdown for two-weeks at the time Appellees chose to trespass. Even if low-level radiation and nuclear waste were emanating from the shut-down plant (as Appellees believed), we do not find this to be the type of danger classified as an emergency sufficient to justify criminal activity. To be imminent, the danger must be, or must reasonably appear to be, threatening to occur immediately, near at hand, and impending.

Reviewing the record in this light, it is abundantly clear that Appellees could not establish that their criminal conduct was *necessary* to avoid harm or evil to themselves or others. Their conduct neither terminated nor reduced the danger which they claimed was posed by the presence of the radioactive fuel in the plant, nor could their conduct have done so. Their act of criminal trespass was a deliberate and calculated choice, not an act that was urgently necessary to avoid a clear and imminent danger.

. . .

Having concluded from our review of the record that the trial court was correct in refusing to charge on justification or to admit evidence on that defense, we find no abuse of discretion or error of law was committed in so ruling. Because we so conclude, it is unnecessary to determine whether the common law should be read into Section 503(a), or whether federal or state legislation regulating nuclear power preempts the availability of the justification defense.

A number of our sister states have unanimously held that trespassing on private property of nuclear power plants may not be justified by the presence of dangerous materials or activities and further, is not legally justified by philosophical disagreement.[45] Section 503 does not condone this type of ad hoc self help which forebodes legal chaos.

. . .

Reversed and judgments of sentence reinstated.

MODEL PENAL CODE

Section 2.09   Duress.

(1) It is an affirmative defense that the actor engaged in the conduct charged to constitute an offense because he was coerced to do so by the use of, or a threat to use, unlawful force against his person or the person of another, which a person of reasonable firmness in his situation would have been unable to resist.

(2) The defense provided by this Section is unavailable if the actor recklessly placed himself in a situation in which it was probable that he would be subjected to duress. The defense is also unavailable if he was negligent in placing himself in such a situation, whenever negligence suffices to establish culpability for the offense charged.

(4) When the conduct of the actor would otherwise be justifiable under Section 3.02, this Section does not preclude such defense.

Section 3.02   Justification Generally: Choice of Evils.

(1) Conduct which the actor believes to be necessary to avoid a harm or evil to himself or to another is justifiable, provided that:

(a) the harm or evil sought to be avoided by such conduct is greater than that sought to be prevented by the law defining the offense charged; and

(b) neither the Code nor other law defining the offense provides exceptions or defenses dealing with the specific situation involved; and

(c) a legislative purpose to exclude the justification claimed does not otherwise plainly appear.

(2) When the actor was reckless or negligent in bringing about the situation requiring a choice of harms or evils or in appraising the necessity for his conduct, the justification afforded by this Section is unavailable in a prosecution for any offense for which recklessness or negligence, as the case may be, suffices to establish culpability.[46]

---

45. U.S. v. Cassidy, 616 F.2d 101, 4th Circuit (1979); U.S. v. Kroncke, 459 F.2d 697, 8th Circuit (1972); U.S. v. Seward, 687 F.2d 1270, 10th Circuit (1982); State v. Marley, 54 Haw. 450, 509 P.2d 1095 (1973); State v. Greene, 5 Kan.App.2d 698, 623 P.2d 933 (1981); Commonwealth v. Brugmann, 13 Mass.App. 373, 433 N.E.2d 457 (1982); State v. Kee, 398 A.2d 384 (1979) (Me.); State v. Dorsey, 118 N.H. 844, 395 A.2d 855 (1978); State v. Warshow, 138 Vt. 22, 410 A.2d 1000 (1979); State v. Olsen, 99 Wis.2d 572, 299 N.W.2d 632 (1980).

46. Copyright © 1962 by the American Law Institute. Reprinted with the permission of the American Law Institute.

SECTION 3. CONSENT OF THE OTHER PARTY

The problem of consent in the criminal law requires particular attention to two different matters: (1) What is the legal effect of consent or non-consent? (2) What will be regarded as consent within the legal meaning of the term?

In studying the legal effect of consent or non-consent it is important to recognize three different categories of crime.

(1) In certain offenses the *want* of consent of the person harmed is an essential ingredient of the crime by the very words of the definition, or the necessary implication of other terms. Thus in common law rape the phrase "without her consent" (or "against her will") is found in the definition itself. The finding of consent on the part of the person alleged to have been harmed completely disproves the commission of such a crime. Consent by a person whose property was taken absolves the person who took it of theft.[47]

(2) At the other extreme will be found those offenses which can be committed even with the consent of the person harmed, such as "statutory rape" (carnal knowledge of a child) or murder. Furthermore, touching a child under the age of consent with intent to have intercourse with her is an assault with intent to commit rape,[48] or an attempt to commit rape[49] or sexual abuse[50] although no force or violence is intended and the child is entirely willing. And the sound view is that a child is just as incapable of giving a legally-recognized permission to an indecent fondling of the person as the child is of giving such license to the act of intercourse itself, and hence the child's consent to such liberties is no defense.[51] A person under the age of consent is frequently said to be incapable of giving consent to such actions. What is meant, of course, is that the person's consent is incapable of giving a legally-recognized permission.

(3) Between these two extremes is a third category in which consent or non-consent will determine whether the conduct was lawful or unlawful within certain limits,—but not beyond. The typical example is battery. What is called "fond embrace" when gladly accepted by a companion is called "assault and battery" when perpetrated upon another without their consent. And the act of one who grabs another by the ankles and causes the person to fall violently to the ground may

---

47. See Kellett v. State, 577 So.2d 915 (Ala.Cr.App.1990).

48. People v. Babcock, 160 Cal. 537, 117 P. 549 (1911); Commonwealth v. Murphy, 165 Mass. 66, 42 N.E. 504 (1896); Fannin v. State, 65 Okl.Cr. 444, 88 P.2d 671 (1939); Steptoe v. State, 134 Tex.Cr.R. 320, 115 S.W.2d 916 (1938). Contra: State v. Pickett, 11 Nev. 255 (1876).

49. Alford v. State, 132 Fla. 624, 181 So. 839 (1938); Rainey v. Commonwealth, 169 Va. 892, 193 S.E. 501 (1937); Regina v. Martin, 9 Car. & P. 213, 169 Eng.Rep. 49 (1840).

50. State v. Landino, 38 Or.App. 447, 590 P.2d 737 (1979).

51. People v. Gibson, 232 N.Y. 458, 134 N.E. 531 (1922); Carter v. State, 121 Tex.Cr. 493, 51 S.W.2d 316 (1932).

result in a substantial jail sentence under some circumstances, but receive thunderous applause if it stops a ball carrier on the gridiron. The difference is because one who engages in a game such as football consents to such physical contact as is normally and properly to be expected in playing the game.[52]

There are limits, however, to the extent to which the law will recognize a license based on such consent. Just as there can be no legally-valid permission to be killed, so the law will not recognize a license unnecessarily to be maimed. One may permit an amputation made necessary by accident or disease. But he who struck off the hand of a "lustie rogue" to enable him to beg more effectively was guilty despite the other's request.[53] A wrongdoer effectively may give consent to moderate chastisement and a person who inflicts such permitted punishment is not guilty of assault and battery although the person would be guilty without consent.[54] On the other hand, if two engage in a fist fight, by mutual consent, exchanging blows intended or likely to cause great bodily injury, both are guilty of assault and battery.[55]

In a prosecution for any offense falling within the second category, or one beyond the permitted limits in the third category, it is futile to talk of consent because this will not be exculpating even if established. If the crime falls within the first category the prosecution must negative consent to make out even a prima-facie case. A prima-facie case does not necessarily require positive evidence of non-consent, if the offense is within the third category, but within the limits permitted by law proof of consent will disprove the charge. This invites inquiry as to just what will be regarded as consent within the legal meaning of the term.

It has been said: "A 'compelled consent' is in law no consent at all."[56] And this is beyond question if the duress employed was sufficient. Submission under extreme pain or fear is not that positive concurrence with the desire of another which is implied by the word "consent" as it is used in the law. What is claimed to have been duress in a particular case may be inadequate for this purpose. This will depend upon all the circumstances including the offense alleged to have been committed. In no case, however, will "consent" be recognized if it was induced by threats of immediate death or great bodily harm imposed by one apparently able and willing to enforce his threats if frustrated.

---

52. Sadomasochistic activity is not a sport, social or other activity under Iowa C.Ann. § 708.1 and participant could not consent to such assault. State v. Collier, 372 N.W.2d 303 (Iowa App.1985).

53. Wright's Case, Co.Litt. 127a (1604).

54. State v. Beck, 19 S.C.L. (1 Hill) 363 (1833).

55. People v. Lucky, 45 Cal.3d 259, 247 Cal.Rptr. 1, 753 P.2d 1052 (1988); State v. Newland, 27 Kan. 764 (1882); Commonwealth v. Collberg, 119 Mass. 350 (1876); King v. Donovan, [1934] 2 K.B. 498. See 2.11(2)(a) Model Penal Code; A.G.'s Reference [1981] 2 All E.R. 1057 (C.A.).

56. Shehany v. Lowry, 170 Ga. 70, 72, 152 S.E. 114, 115 (1930). Agreement by a warden not to seek reprisals against prisoners who took hostages is void and unenforceable as against public policy. Wagner v. State, 364 N.W.2d 246, 250 (Iowa 1985).

Certain of the statutory additions to the crime of extortion are enlightening on this point. They provide a punishment for the obtaining of property from another "with his consent, induced by a wrongful use of force or fear."[57] The fear may be induced by a threat to harm the person or a relative or member of the person's family, by injury to person or property, accusation of crime, imputation of deformity or disgrace, exposure of a secret,[58] or kidnaping. If the force or fear generates a well-grounded belief that the property must be handed over to avoid immediate death or great bodily injury, the submission thereto is not "consent," in the legal view, and the obtaining of the property by such means is robbery,—not extortion. If the property is freely and voluntarily handed over without any coercion it is a gift,—not extortion. Only between these extremes is the other's property obtained "with his consent by a wrongful use of force and fear."

Conditional consent is no consent beyond the terms of the condition. If one places an article in the hands of another for inspection with the understanding that he will either return it or pay for it now, there is no consent for him to run off with it without payment.[59] And the proprietor of a store who placed a large box of matches on the counter, for the convenience of customers in lighting pipes and cigars in the store, did not consent that the whole box of matches should be carried away.[60] Consent to one thing, moreover, is not consent to a different or additional thing. The girl who willingly ate a fig did not consent to eat a deleterious drug added without her knowledge.[61] Nor would her consent have included some entirely different article if it had been substituted by sleight of hand undetected by her.

Consent obtained by fraud has given rise to some of the most difficult problems in this field.

Rex v. Turvey

Court of Criminal Appeal, 1946.
[1946] 2 All E.R. 60.

■ LORD GODDARD, L.C.J. [delivering the judgment of the court]: In this case the court is of the opinion that the conviction must be quashed. The appellant appeals against his conviction on count 1 of the indictment only.

The circumstances were these: The appellant was charged that on Dec. 12, 1945, being a servant of His Majesty's Minister of Works, he stole from the Minister a considerable number of table knives, spoons, and so forth. He had got into touch with some foreigner living at Newton Abbot, and found that he would be a ready receiver of goods which could be stolen from the Ministry of Works. Then, being in charge at that time of a depot of the Ministry of Works at Torquay, he approached one Ward, who was in

---

57. West's Ann.Cal.Pen.Code § 518 (1997).

58. Id. at § 519.

59. Anonymous, T.Raym. 275, 83 Eng.Rep. 142 (1678).

60. Mitchum v. State, 45 Ala. 29 (1871).

61. Commonwealth v. Stratton, 114 Mass. 303 (1873).

charge of a depot at Exeter. Ward was tempted to steal the property of the Ministry of Works and hand it to the appellant, who would in turn hand it to the man at Newton Abbot. Ward at once communicated with his superiors at Bristol, the people who were really in control of the property, and told them of this plan which had been suggested to him. The officials of the Ministry of Works said it would be a good thing to let this plan go on and catch them at a suitable time, which would enable them to prosecute this appellant for stealing. What they did was this: They told Ward to hand over the property to the appellant, and Ward handed over the property to the appellant. He intended to hand it to the appellant and did hand it to the appellant.

That being so, the question arose whether or not the appellant could be charged with stealing. He could have been charged with conspiracy that he was inciting to commit a felony and other charges, there is no doubt, but could he be charged with the felony of stealing? In this case it is perfectly clear that if he stole the goods, he stole them at Exeter, but he did not take them there against the will of the owner because the owner handed them to him and meant to hand them to him. The chairman in his ruling, when counsel submitted no case, set out his findings, and it appears that he decided principally on the authority of R. v. Eggington [sic] (1), an old case, but perfectly good law, and also because he took a certain view with regard to the control the owner was exercising over the goods.

R. v. Egginton[62] was a case in which a servant told his master that someone was going to rob the premises. "Very well," said the master, "let them rob the premises and we will catch them"; in other words, to put a homely illustration, a man, knowing that somebody is going to break into his house, leaves the bolts drawn and so makes it easy for the man to come into the house, and when he comes in he catches him and a crime has been committed; he commits the crime none the less that the servant has been told to make things easy.[63] In this case, if Ward had been told by the person who really had control of these matters, "Let the appellant come in and take the goods," that would have been one thing, but he told him to take the goods and hand them to the appellant, and that makes all the difference.

One matter to which the chairman seems to have attached considerable importance was this, that Ward said to the appellant at the time when he was handing over the goods: "You must give me a receipt, I must have a receipt for these goods," and the appellant said he quite understood that and he would give a receipt for the goods. Thereupon, a perfectly fictitious document is made out, which both parties knew and intended to be fictitious, under which it is made to look as though the goods were handed over to the appellant to take to the Palace Hotel at Torquay, but, of course, that was not an authority by Ward to the appellant to take the goods to Torquay because everybody knew that the appellant was meaning to steal these goods and they were to go to the receiver at Newton Abbot. No one intended that they were to go to Torquay, and this document was simply

---

62. [By the Compiler.] R. v. Egginton (1801), 2 Bos. & P. 508; 15 Digest 883, 9693.

63. But it is otherwise if the servant opened the door for D at the master's direction. Smith v. State, 362 P.2d 1071 (Alaska 1961).

manufactured as a blind, or whatever word you like to use; it is not a genuine document, and therefore it is as if it did not exist.

The other point on which the chairman in his direction to the jury, as we think, went wrong was that he told the jury that these goods always remained under the control of the Ministry, because apparently the police had been warned, and the police were to follow the prisoner once he had stolen them, either to follow him or go immediately to Newton Abbot and find them in the possession of the receiver. But that will not do. Once the goods were handed over to the appellant the goods were under his control and nobody else's. What was to happen supposing, while he was driving along being followed by the police, the police car broke down? Of course, he would cheerfully drive away with these goods. Of course the goods were under the appellant's control as soon as he went away with the goods.

The charge that was put against the appellant was the wrong charge, a charge of which he could not have been convicted because there was no evidence here of what, to use a technical expression, is termed asportation. He did not carry away the goods against the will of the owner but because the owner was willing that he should have the goods and gave them to him. In those circumstances, the conviction will be quashed, so far as this charge is concerned, and the appeal allowed on count 1.

Appeal allowed.[64]

People v. Cook

District Court of Appeal, Second District, Division 4, California, 1964.
228 Cal.App.2d 716, 39 Cal.Rptr. 802.

■ BURKE, PRESIDING JUSTICE. Frank Billy Ray Cook, defendant, was charged by information with violation of section 487, subd. 3 of the Penal Code (Grand Theft Auto) and Vehicle Code, section 10851. He was acquitted by a jury of Grand Theft Auto, but found guilty of violating Vehicle Code, section 10851. A new trial was denied, probation was denied, and defendant was sentenced to the state prison for the term prescribed by law. . . .

The first ground of appeal is that the Mercury was taken with the consent of Frahm Pontiac, and even though such consent be deemed to have been induced by trick and device and under false pretenses, nevertheless, it constituted consent. The arrangements were made to register the Mercury in the buyer's name which would entitle him to possession and use of the vehicle. Frahm Pontiac acquired defendant's Buick as a trade-in and part consideration for the Mercury. Having acquired the Mercury with Frahm's consent, possession cannot be held to have been obtained in violation of section 10851 of the Vehicle Code.[65] The point appears to be

---

64. Resident's struggle with defendant after admitting defendant into an apartment was withdrawal of consent allowing a conviction for burglary. Ray v. State, 522 So.2d 963 (Fla.App.1988).

65. Section 10851 of the Vehicle Code reads in part as follows:

"Any person who drives or takes a vehicle not his own, without the consent of the owner thereof, and with intent either permanently or temporarily to deprive the owner thereof of this title to or possession of the vehicle, whether with or without intent to steal the same, or

novel in California but defendant offers persuasive authority from other jurisdictions to the effect that fraudulent inducement does not vitiate the consent given to the extent of creating the crime of auto theft.

In Perkins on Criminal Law, p. 859, it is stated:

"It has been held, it may be emphasized, that one who obtains the owner's consent to drive his car by fraudulently misrepresenting the use to be made of it, is not guilty of operating a car without the consent of the owner although the owner would not have consented to the use actually made."

One of the earliest cases holding that fraudulently induced consent is consent nonetheless and that such consent prevents a violation of a vehicle joy ride statute is State v. Boggs, 181 Iowa 358, 164 N.W. 759 (1917), the court stating: "The gist of the offense charged is taking and driving of the motor car in question without the consent of the owner."

The court then noted: "It is contended on behalf of appellant that consent obtained by trick, deceit, or misrepresentation is not consent in fact." In rejecting this contention, the court concluded: "The statute was not designed to punish one who [by misrepresentation or for a fraudulent purpose], obtains consent of the owner to take and operate his motor vehicle...."

In State v. Mularkey, 195 Wis. 549, 218 N.W. 809 (1928), State v. Boggs, supra, was discussed with approval, and the court there held that consent, however obtained, presented a violation of the Wisconsin Joy Ride Statute.

In United States v. One 1941 Chrysler, 74 F.Supp. 970 (E.D.Mich. 1947), the court was called upon to construe sections 413 and 414 of the Michigan Penal Statutes. These two sections are the equivalent of California's Penal Code, section 499b (the Misdemeanor Joy Ride Statute) and Vehicle Code, section 10851, the court holding:

"The provisions of such statutes as Sections 413 and 414 are not designed to punish one who obtains consent of the owner to take and operate his motor vehicle by misrepresentations or for a fraudulent purpose. They are directed against one who takes possession of such a vehicle without the consent of the owner." (See also People v. Smith, 213 Mich. 351, 182 N.W. 64.)

The above mentioned cases constitute specific applications of the basic common law rule that, unless there is statutory language to the contrary, whenever lack of consent is a necessary element of a crime, the fact that consent is obtained through misrepresentation will not supply the essential element of non-consent.

Perkins on Criminal Law, at page 859, states:

"Except for this, (larceny by trick) if it is truly an exception, and except where the result has been changed by statute, an offense which requires

---

any person who is a party or accessory to or an accomplice in the driving or unauthorized taking or stealing is guilty of a felony, ..." (Stats.1959, c. 3, p. 1597, § 10851.)

"If [defendant] was privileged to exchange his family's printer for the school's printer by virtue of the school board's consent then [he] would have a complete defense to the crime of theft." State v. Fahlk, 246 Neb. 834, 524 N.W.2d 39, 49 (1994).

the absence of consent is not committed if there was consent to exactly what was done, even if such consent was induced by fraud." . . .

People v. Perez, 203 Cal.App.2d 397, 21 Cal.Rptr. 422, has been cited as supporting defendant's conviction of a violation of Vehicle Code, § 10851. In that case, the defendant attained possession of an automobile under the false representation that he had a buyer for it. He was given permission by the owner to keep the car for three days to make the sale to his buyer. Defendant never returned the car. The court stated (p. 399, 21 Cal.Rptr. p. 424): "Even though his original possession had been lawful, he had no authority to keep [the automobile] more than three days and then only for the purpose of consummating a sale to [his purported buyer.] . . . Actually, his original possession, his keeping the car beyond three days, his driving the car to Arizona . . . were all unlawful and, . . . if believed, could not be construed in any other way than intentionally taking and depriving the owner of possession, to say the least. Intent to deprive the owner may be established from the circumstances of the case, [citation] and is a question for the trier of fact. [Citations.] Each time defendant drove the car without the consent of the owner it was a violation of the statute. [Citation.]"

There is a generally recognized distinction, however, between *fraud in the factum,* which gives rise to no consent at all, and *fraud in the inducement,* which does not vitiate consent. *Perez, supra,* is an example of *fraud in the factum,* since the owner never intended that the defendant would acquire possession of the car for his own use.

Here, there was *fraud in the inducement;* the owner intended to sell defendant the car and consented to the taking of possession of it by him and, unlike Perez, the fraud did not vitiate consent.

No authorities are cited in opposition to defendant's contentions that consent, albeit falsely induced, bars prosecution under such section 10851 of the Vehicle Code. Respondent argues only that the facts conclusively establish an intent on defendant's part, defendant having been an accomplice, to deprive Frahm Pontiac of its title or possession of the 1959 Mercury, which is the essence of the charge; that the fraud in obtaining consent vitiates the consent and does not excuse the criminal act.

Fraud, vitiating consent, as indicated, is a completely tenable principle in contract law, and when specifically incorporated in a penal statute determines the operation of the section, as in the case of Penal Code, section 484. However, section 10851 of the Vehicle Code makes no reference to fraud, false pretense or trick and device but is specifically based upon the taking without consent. . . .

The judgment of conviction is reversed and the cause remanded to the trial court with directions to dismiss.[66]

■ JEFFERSON and KINGSLEY, JJ., concur.

---

66. *Cook* was reaffirmed in People v. Donell, 32 Cal.App.3d 613, 108 Cal.Rptr. 232 (1973). *See* however, People v. Harris, 93 Cal.App.3d 103, 155 Cal.Rptr. 472 (1979) (consent is defense to kidnapping even if some fraud involved).

United States v. Bygrave

U.S. Court of Appeals for the Armed Forces, 1997.
46 M.J. 491.

■ ARTERTON, DISTRICT JUDGE:[67]

Appellant was tried by a general court-martial, military judge alone, on March 23 and 25, 1992, and was convicted of two specifications of assault with a means likely to cause death or grievous bodily harm, in violation of Article 128(b)(1), Uniform Code of Military Justice, 10 USC § 928(b)(1).... The Navy–Marine Corps Court of Military Review (now the Court of Criminal Appeals initially ordered a new convening authority's action), 40 MJ 839 (NMCMR 1994), subsequent to which the Court of Criminal Appeals affirmed the findings and the approved sentence.... We granted review of the following issue:

WHETHER THE FINDING OF GUILTY TO AGGRAVATED ASSAULT CAN STAND IN LIGHT OF THE FACT THAT THE ALLEGED VICTIM CONSENTED TO HAVING SEXUAL INTERCOURSE WITH APPEL-LANT DESPITE ACTUAL KNOWLEDGE THAT APPELLANT WAS HIV-POSITIVE.

FACTS

In 1986, appellant tested positive for the Human Immunodeficiency Virus (HIV), resulting in treatment at the HIV Ward of the Naval Hospital in San Diego. Despite warnings of the risk of spreading the virus through sexual intercourse, appellant maintained a sexually active lifestyle involving at least two partners. The first partner, Petty Officer J, engaged in heterosexual sex with appellant over a year-long period, including acts of unprotected sex. Appellant did not warn Petty Officer J that he was HIV-positive. In June 1988, Petty Officer J herself tested positive for the virus.

Appellant's second partner, beginning in January 1990, was Boat-swain's Mate Third Class (BM3) C. Prior to commencing sexual relations, appellant informed BM3 C of his HIV-positive status. Thereafter, appellant and BM3 C engaged in consensual sexual intercourse on a regular basis, using a condom on most, but not all, occasions. In July 1991, BM3 C tested positive for HIV. Six months later, BM3 C and appellant were married.

After a trial in March of 1992, a general court-martial convicted appellant on two specifications of aggravated assault, one arising from his sexual relationship with Petty Officer J; the other from his sexual relation-ship with BM3 C. Appellant has not challenged his conviction on the first specification. The only issue before us on the present appeal is whether BM3 C's informed consent constitutes a valid defense to the second specification.

---

67. Judge Janet Bond Arterton of the United States District Court for the District of Connecticut, sitting by designation pursuant to Article 142(f), Uniform Code of Military Justice, 10 USC § 942(f). We heard oral argument in this case at the United States Coast Guard Academy, Groton, Connecticut, without objection from the parties involved. See 34 MJ 228, 229 n. 1 (1992).

DISCUSSION

This Court has made clear on numerous occasions that an HIV-positive service member commits an aggravated assault by having unprotected sexual intercourse with an uninformed partner.[68] United States v. Schoolfield, 40 MJ 132 (CMA 1994); United States v. Joseph, 37 MJ 392 (CMA 1993); United States v. Johnson, 30 MJ 53 (CMA 1990). We have concluded that "under many circumstances, AIDS [Acquired Immune Deficiency Syndrome] is 'the natural and probable consequence' of exposure to HIV." Accordingly, we have held that any time a service member "willfully or deliberately" exposes another person to HIV, that service member may be found to have acted in a manner "likely to produce death or grievous bodily harm."

While appellant obviously can make no claim that informed consent by itself eliminates the risk of HIV transmission—indeed, the infection of appellant's wife would persuasively belie any argument to that effect—he offers a number of other reasons why he believes that informed consent either removes this case from the ambit of Article 128 or renders his prosecution under Article 128 unconstitutional.

Appellant correctly notes that none of our prior HIV decisions squarely address whether informed consent provides a defense to a prosecution for aggravated assault under Article 128. However, the relevance of the victim's state of mind is not readily apparent on the face of the statute. We note that aggravated assault is not a crime like rape, in which lack of consent is an element of the offense. Moreover, the very nature of the offense invalidates, as a matter of law, any consent that has been given. Aggravated assault, of course, differs from simple assault in that the perpetrator has used a "means or force likely to produce death or grievous bodily harm." Art. 128(b)(1). As this Court has previously observed, "[O]ne cannot consent to an act which is likely to produce grievous bodily harm or death." United States v. Outhier, 45 MJ 326, 330 (1996). Thus, while under certain circumstances consent may be a defense to simple assault, Joseph, 37 MJ at 396 n. 5, consent is generally not a valid defense to aggravated assault. See, e.g., United States v. Outhier, supra; United States v. Brantner, 28 MJ 941, 944 (NMCMR 1989); R. Perkins & R. Boyce, Criminal Law 155 (3d ed.1982).

At oral argument, appellant suggested that consent negates one of the required elements of aggravated assault, namely, that the act be perpetrated with "unlawful force or violence." However, our prior decisions make clear that an act of sexual intercourse may in some circumstances be an "offensive touching" subject to prosecution under Article 128, even in the

---

68. The elements of aggravated assault are as follows:

(i) That the accused attempted to do, offered to do, or did bodily harm to a certain person;

(ii) That the accused did so with a certain weapon, means, or force;

(iii) That the attempt, offer, or bodily harm was done with unlawful force or violence; and

(iv) That the weapon, means, or force was used in a manner likely to produce death or grievous bodily harm.

Para. 54b (4)(a), Part IV, Manual for Courts–Martial, United States (1995 ed.).

absence of overt coercion or violence. See, e.g., Joseph, 37 MJ at 395 n. 4. In order for consent to be relevant to the "unlawful force or violence" element, the consent must be legally cognizable. For that reason, consent to sex secured without disclosure of HIV-positive status does not remove the act from the ambit of Article 128, for the consent has been improperly obtained. By similar reasoning, even informed consent cannot save an accused in a case such as this one, for, as we have just noted, assault law does not recognize the validity of consent to an act that is likely to result in grievous injury or death, such as unprotected sex with an HIV-positive partner.[69] Given that appellant's unprotected sex acts with BM3 C were performed without legally valid consent, we must conclude that they amount to "unlawful force or violence" within the meaning of Article 128.[70]

Next, appellant points to the numerous states that have adopted specific criminal statutes addressing HIV transmission, including some that provide for a defense of informed consent. Appellant contends that the criminalization of HIV transmission, particularly in the context of informed consent, requires us to balance a number of highly sensitive public-policy concerns. Appellant argues that Congress should follow the lead of many state legislatures in passing a law to address this issue directly, and that this Court should refrain from holding that Article 128 encompasses informed, consensual sex until after Congress decides how to balance the competing interests. The problem with appellant's argument is that Congress has already established a mechanism for balancing the competing interests: Article 128. The Uniform Code of Military Justice provides for the prosecution of individuals who commit assault by "means or force likely to produce death or grievous bodily harm." Congress created no exceptions for cases in which the act likely to produce grievous bodily harm is sexual intercourse involving a person who is HIV-positive. Congress is certainly

---

69. Because appellant was only prosecuted for having unprotected sex, we need not, and do not, address whether one may validly consent to protected sex with an HIV-positive partner. Although we have previously held that, in certain circumstances, a court may find that protected sex is an act likely to result in grievous bodily harm or death, *see* United States v. Joseph, 37 MJ 392, 397 (CMA 1993), we have never held that protected sex with an HIV-positive partner must be so found as a matter of law.

70. Because there is no dispute that BM3 C was HIV-free prior to her relationship with appellant, we need not address the question of whether, or under what circumstances, one who is already HIV-positive may provide valid consent to sexual intercourse with another HIV-positive individual. If the added health risk of sexual intercourse between people who are already HIV-positive was shown to be minimal, then we might be more inclined to view informed consent as relevant to the Article 128 analysis. However, appellant has not argued that these circumstances are present in his case; nor have we been provided with an evidentiary record as to current medical knowledge of any increased health risks under these circumstances. *See* Gruca v. Alpha Therapeutic Corp., 51 F.3d 638, 641–43 (7th Cir.1995) (noting expert testimony offered at trial as to "antigenic stimulation" theory, under which additional exposure to HIV increases speed with which HIV-positive individuals begin to show symptoms of full-blown AIDS, and remanding case to trial court to determine whether testimony on this theory comported with requirements of Daubert v. Merrell Dow Pharmaceuticals, Inc., 509 U.S. 579, 113 S.Ct. 2786, 125 L.Ed.2d 469 (1993)).

In a similar vein, we note that appellant does not challenge the medical conclusions underlying our prior holdings that exposure to HIV is likely to produce grievous bodily harm or death. However, continued progress in the treatment of HIV patients may some day necessitate a reconsideration of those conclusions.

entitled to carve out exceptions for this class of cases, or subcategories thereof, and appellant has offered valid public-policy reasons in support of such legislation; however, until Congress acts to remove HIV transmission from the ambit of Article 128, the precedents of this Court clearly establish that conduct like appellant's, with or without the sex partner's informed consent, falls within the statutory meaning of "aggravated assault" under the UCMJ.

Having concluded that appellant could be found to have committed aggravated assault in violation of Article 128, the Court may now address the question of whether appellant's conviction violated his constitutional rights. . . .

. . . We do conclude, however, that the Government has sufficiently compelling interests to proscribe unprotected sexual intercourse between HIV-positive servicemembers and uninfected, unmarried, noncivilian partners, even assuming that some sort of constitutional right to private heterosexual intercourse exists.

The decision of the United States Navy–Marine Corps Court of Criminal Appeals is affirmed.

■ CHIEF JUDGE COX and JUDGES SULLIVAN, GIERKE, and EFFRON concur.[71]

R. v. Brown

House of Lords [1993].
2 All ER.

■ LORD TEMPLEMAN. My Lords, the appellants were convicted of assaults occasioning actual bodily harm contrary to § 47 of the Offences against the Person Act 186 1. Three of the appellants were also convicted of wounding contrary to § 20 of the 1861 Act. The incidents which led to each conviction occurred in the course of consensual sado-masochistic homosexual encounters. The Court of Appeal upheld the convictions and certified the following point of law of general public importance:

---

71. Consensual intercourse did not support an aggravated assault charge where defendant did not inform his partners that he was HIV positive. Regina v. Cuerrier, 111 CCC 3d 261 (B.C. App. 1996).

"If a woman be beguiled into her consent by marrying a man who had another wife living, or by causing the nuptials to be illegally celebrated, and persuading her that the directions of the law had been observed; in neither case will the pretended husband be guilty of a rape." State v. Murphy, 6 Ala. 765, 770 (1844).

Procuring sexual intercourse with a single woman by the device of a sham marriage is rape by fraud under the Texas statute. Lee v. State, 44 Tex.Cr. 354, 72 S.W. 1005 (1902). Oklahoma held otherwise on the ground that the artifice meant by the statute is such as deceives the woman as to the identity of the man with whom she is having intercourse. Draughn v. State, 12 Okl.Cr. 479, 158 P. 890 (1916).

A defendant who procured intercourse with a prostitute on the false promise to pay $100 was not guilty of rape. Regina v. Petrozzi, 35 CCC3d 528 (B.C.App.1987).

Fraud in the inducement is not rape, but fraud in fact as to the nature of the act or the identity of the participant is fraud in factum supporting a finding of rape. United States v. Booker, 25 M.J. 114 (CMA 1987).

Where A wounds or assaults B occasioning him actual bodily harm in the course of a sado-masochistic encounter, does the prosecution have to prove lack of consent on the part of B before they can establish A's guilt under section 20 and section 47 of the 1861, Offences Against the Person Act?

. . .

At common law, an assault is an act by which a person intentionally recklessly causes another to apprehend immediate and unlawful person violence and a battery is an act by which a person intentionally or recklessly inflicts personal violence upon another. However, the term "assault" is now in both ordinary legal usage and in statutes, regularly used to cover both assault and battery.

There are now three types of assault in ascending order of gravity: first, common assault, secondly, assault which occasions actual bodily harm and, thirdly, assault which inflicts grievous bodily harm. . . .

In the present case each of the appellants intentionally inflicted violence upon another (to whom I shall refer as "the victim") with the consent of the victim and thereby occasioned actual bodily harm or in some cases wounding or grievous bodily harm. Each appellant was therefore guilty of an offence under § 47 or § 20 of the 1861 Act unless the consent of the victim was effective to prevent the commission of the offence or effective to constitute a defence to the charge.

In some circumstances violence is not punishable under the criminal law. When no actual bodily harm is caused, the consent of the person affected precludes him from complaining. There can be no conviction for the summary offence of common assault if the victim has consented to the assault. Even when violence is intentionally inflicted and results in actual bodily harm, wounding or serious bodily harm the accused is entitled to be acquitted if the injury was a foreseeable incident of a lawful activity in which the person injured was participating. Surgery involves intentional violence resulting in actual or sometimes serious bodily harm but surgery is a lawful activity. Other activities carried on with consent by or on behalf of the injured person have been accepted as lawful, notwithstanding that they involve actual bodily harm or may cause serious bodily, harm. Ritual circumcision, tattooing, ear-piercing and violent sports including boxing are lawful activities.

In earlier days some other forms of violence were lawful and when they ceased to be lawful they were tolerated until well into the nineteenth century. Duelling and fighting were at first lawful and then tolerated provided the protagonists were voluntary participants. But, where the results of these activities was the maiming of one of the participants, the defence of consent never availed the aggressor: see I Hawkins' Pleas of the Crown (8th edn., 1824) ch. 15. A maim was bodily harm whereby a man was deprived of the use of any member of his body which he needed to use in order to fight but a bodily injury was not a maim merely because it was a disfigurement. The act of maim was unlawful because, the King was deprived of the services of an able-bodied citizen for the defence of the realm. Violence which maimed was unlawful despite consent to the activity which produced the maiming. In these days there is no difference between maiming on the one hand and wounding or causing grievous bodily harm on the other hand except with regard to sentence.

When duelling became unlawful, juries remained unwilling to convict but the judges insisted that persons guilty of causing death or bodily injury should be convicted despite the consent of the victim.

Similarly, in the old days, fighting was lawful provided the protagonists consented because it was thought that fighting inculcated bravery and skill and physical fitness. The brutality of knuckle fighting however caused the courts to declare that such fights were unlawful even if the protagonists consented. Rightly or wrongly the courts accepted that boxing is a lawful activity.

. . .

Stephen J said (at 549):

When one person is indicted for inflicting personal injury upon another, the consent of the person who sustains the injury is no defence to the person who inflicts the injury, if the injury is of such a nature, or is inflicted under such circumstances, that its infliction is injurious to the public as well as to the person injured. But the injuries given and received in prize-fights are injurious to the public, both because it is against the public interest that the lives and the health of the combatants should be endangered by blows and because prize-fights are disorderly exhibitions, mischievous on many obvious grounds. Therefore the consent of the parties to the blows which they mutually receive does not prevent those blows from being assaults . . . In cases where life and limb are exposed to no serious danger in the common course of things, I think that consent is a defence to a charge of assault, even when considerable force is used, as, for instance, in cases of wrestling, singlestick, sparring with gloves, football and the like; but in all cases the question whether consent does or does not take from the application of force to another its illegal character, is a question of degree depending upon circumstances.

In R v. Donovan [1934] 2 KB 498, [1934] All ER Rep 207 the appellant in private beat a girl of 17 for purposes of sexual gratification, it was said with her consent. Swift J said ([1934] 2 KB 4–8 at 507, [1934] All ER Rep 207 at 210):

. . . it is an unlawful act to beat another person with such a degree of violence that the infliction of bodily harm is a probable consequence, and when such an act is proved, consent is immaterial.

In A–G's Reference (No 6 of 1980) [1981] 2 All ER 1057 at 1059, [1981] QB 715 at 719 where two men quarrelled and fought with bare fists Lord Lane CJ, delivering the judgment of the Court of Appeal, said:

. . . it is not in the public interest that people should try to cause or should cause each other bodily harm for no good reason. Minor struggles are another matter. So, in our judgment, it is immaterial whether the act occurs in private or in public; it is an assault if actual bodily harm is intended and/or caused. This means that most fights will be unlawful regardless of consent. Nothing which we have said is intended to cast doubt on the accepted legality of properly conducted games and sports, lawful chastisement or correction, reasonable surgical interference, dangerous exhibitions etc. These apparent exceptions can be justified as involving the exercise of a legal right, in the case of chastisement or correction, or as needed in the public interest, in the other cases.

Duelling and fighting are both unlawful and the consent of the protagonists, affords no defence to charges of causing actual bodily harm, wounding or grievous bodily harm in the course of an unlawful activity.

The appellants and their victims in the present case were engaged in consensual homosexual activities. The attitude of the public towards homosexual practices changed in the second half of this century. Change in public attitudes led to change in the law.

The *Report of the Committee on Homosexual Offences and Prostitution* (the Wolfenden Report) (Cmnd. 247 (1957)) ch. 2 para. 13, declared that the function the criminal law in relation to homosexual behaviour—

is to preserve public order and decency, to protect the citizen from what is offensive or injurious, and to provide sufficient safeguards against., exploitation and corruption of others, particularly those who are especially vulnerable because they are young, weak in body or mind, inexperienced, or in a state of special, physical, official or economic dependence.

In response to the Wolfenden Report and consistently with its recommendations, Parliament enacted § I of the Sexual Offences Act 1967, which provided:

. . .

(6) It is hereby declared that where in any proceedings it is charged that a homosexual act is an offence the prosecutor shall have the burden of proving that the act was done otherwise than in private or otherwise than with the consent of the parties or that any of the parties had not attained the age of twenty-one years.

. . .

By the 1967 Act Parliament recognised and accepted the practice of homosexuality. Subject to exceptions not here relevant, sexual activities conducted in private between not more than two consenting adults of the same sex or different sexes are now lawful. Homosexual activities performed in circumstances which do not fall within § I(I) of the 1967 Act remain unlawful....

My Lords, the authorities dealing with the intentional infliction of bodily harm do not establish that consent is a defence to a charge under the 186 1 Act. They establish that the courts have accepted that consent is a defence to the infliction of bodily harm in the course of some lawful activities. The question is whether the defence should be extended to the infliction of bodily harm in the course of sado-masochistic encounters. The Wolfenden Committee did not make any recommendations about sado-masochism and Parliament did not deal with violence in 1967. The 1967 Act is of no assistance for present purposes because b the present problem was not under consideration.

The question whether the defence of consent should be extended to the consequences of sado-masochistic encounters can only be decided by consideration of policy and public interest. Parliament can call on the advice of doctors, psychiatrists, criminologists, sociologists and other experts and can also sound and take into account public opinion. But the question must at this stage be decided by this House in its judicial capacity in order to determine whether the convictions of the appellants should be upheld or quashed.

. . .

The assertion was made on behalf of the appellants that the sexual appetites of sadists and masochists can only be satisfied by the infliction of bodily harm and that the law should not punish the consensual achievement of sexual satisfaction. There was no evidence to support the assertion that sado-masochist activities are essential to the happiness of the appellants or any other participants but the argument would be acceptable if sado-masochism were only concerned with sex, as the appellants contend. In my opinion sado-masochism is not only concerned with sex. Sado-masochism is also concerned with violence. The evidence discloses that the practices of the appellants were unpredictably dangerous and degrading to body and, mind and were developed with increasing barbarity and taught to persons whose consents were dubious or worthless.

A sadist draws pleasure from inflicting or watching cruelty. A masochist derives pleasure from his own pain or humiliation. The appellants are middle-aged men. The victims were youths some of whom were introduced to sado-masochism before they attained the age of 21. . . .

The evidence disclosed that drink and drugs were employed to obtain consent and increase enthusiasm. The victim was usually manacled so that the sadist could enjoy the thrill of power and the victim could enjoy the thrill of helplessness. The victim had no control over the harm which the sadist, also stimulated by J drink and drugs, might inflict. In one case a victim was branded twice on the thigh and there was some doubt as to whether he consented to or protested against the second branding. The dangers involved in administering violence must have d been appreciated by the appellants because, so it was said by their counsel, each victim was given a code word which he could pronounce when excessive harm or pain was caused. The efficiency of this precaution, when taken, depends on the circumstances and on the personalities involved. No one can feel the pain of another. The charges against the appellants were based on genital torture and violence to the buttocks, anus, penis, testicles and nipples. The victims were degraded and humiliated, sometimes beaten, sometimes wounded with instruments and sometimes branded. Bloodletting and the smearing of human blood produced excitement. There were obvious dangers of serious personal injury and blood infection. Prosecuting counsel informed the trial judge against the protests of defence counsel that, although the appellants had not contracted AIDS, two members of the group had died from AIDS and one other had contracted an HIV infection although not necessarily from the practices of the group. Some activities involved excrement. The assertion that the instruments employed by the sadists were clean and sterilised could not have removed the danger of infection, and the assertion that care was taken demonstrates the possibility of infection. Cruelty to human beings was on occasions supplemented by cruelty to animals in the form of bestiality. it is fortunate that there were no permanent injuries to a victim though no one knows the extent of harm inflicted in other cases. . . .

In principle there is a difference between violence which is incidental and violence which is inflicted for the indulgence of cruelty. The violence of sado-masochistic encounters involves the indulgence of cruelty by sadists and the degradation of victims. Such violence is injurious to the participants and unpredictably dangerous. I am not prepared to invent a defence of consent for sado-masochistic encounters which breed and glorify cruelty and result in offences under §§ 47 and 20 of the 1861 Act.

.   .   .

The appellants' counsel relied, somewhat faintly, on art 7 of the European Convention on Human Rights (see the Convention for the Protection of Human Rights and Fundamental Freedoms (Rome, 4 November 1950; TS 71 (1953); Cmd. 8969)). That article, so far as material, provides:

I.   No one shall be guilty of any criminal offence on account of any act or omission which did not constitute a criminal offence under national or international law at the time when it was committed . . .

At the relevant time it was a criminal offence under English law to inflict actual bodily harm or worse. Counsel submitted that the appellants reasonably believed that consent was a defence. This was an ingenious argument for which there was no foundation in fact or principle and which in any event does not seem to me to provide a defence under art 7.

The appellants' counsel relied on art 8 of the convention, which is in these terms:

1.   Everyone has the right to respect for his private and family life, his home and his correspondence.

2.   There shall be no interference by a public authority with the exercise of this right except such as is in accordance with the law and is necessary in a democratic society in the interests of natural security, public safety or the economic well-being of the country, for the prevention of disorder or crime, for the protection of health or morals, or for the protection of the rights and freedoms of others.

It is not clear to me that the activities of the appellants were exercises of rights. in respect of private and family life. But assuming that the appellants are claiming to exercise those rights I do not consider that art 8 invalidates a law which forbids violence which is intentionally harmful to body and mind. Society is entitled and bound to protect itself against a cult of violence. Pleasure derived from the infliction of pain is an evil thing. Cruelty is uncivilised. I would answer the certified question in the negative and dismiss the appeals of the appellants against conviction.

Affirmed. Other opinions omitted.[72]

---

72. Where the victim of a homosexual assault arranged for, aided, and encouraged the assailant to use force against the victim the victim's consent prevented the assailant's conviction for forcible sexual assault. State v. Booher, 305 N.C. 554, 290 S.E.2d 561 (1982).

MODEL PENAL CODE

Section 2.11   Consent.

(1) In General. The consent of the victim to conduct charged to constitute an offense or to the result thereof is a defense if such consent negatives an element of the offense or precludes the infliction of the harm or evil sought to be prevented by the law defining the offense.

(2) Consent to Bodily Harm. When conduct is charged to constitute an offense because it causes or threatens bodily harm, consent to such conduct or to the infliction of such harm is a defense if:

(a) the bodily harm consented to or threatened by the conduct consented to is not serious; or

(b) the conduct and the harm are reasonably foreseeable hazards of joint participation in any concerted activity of a kind not forbidden by law; or

(c) the consent establishes a justification for the conduct under Article 3 of the Code.

(3) Ineffective Consent. Unless otherwise provided by the Code or by the law defining the offense, assent does not constitute consent if:

(a) it is given by a person who is legally incompetent to authorize the conduct charged to constitute the offense; or

(b) it is given by a person who by reason of youth, mental disease or defect or intoxication is manifestly unable or known by the actor to be unable to make a reasonable judgment as to the nature or harmfulness of the conduct charged to constitute the offense; or

(c) it is given by a person whose improvident consent is sought to be prevented by the law defining the offense; or

(d) it is induced by force, duress or deception of a kind sought to be prevented by the law defining the offense.

Section 3.08   Use of Force by Persons with Special Responsibility for Care, Discipline or Safety of Others.

The use of force upon or toward the person of another is justifiable if: . . .

(4) the actor is a doctor or other therapist or a person assisting him at his direction, and:

(a) the force is used for the purpose of administering a recognized form of treatment which the actor believes to be adapted to promoting the physical or mental health of the patient; and

(b) the treatment is administered with the consent of the patient or, if the patient is a minor or an incompetent person, with the consent of his parent or guardian or other person legally competent to consent in his behalf, or the treatment is administered in an emergency when the actor believes that no one competent to consent can be consulted and that a reasonable person, wishing to safeguard the welfare of the patient, would consent; or . . . .

Section 213.1   Rape and Related Offenses. . . .

(2) Gross Sexual Imposition. A male who has sexual intercourse with a female not his wife commits a felony of the third degree if: . . .

(c) he knows that she is unaware that a sexual act is being committed upon her or that she submits because she falsely supposes that he is her husband.[73]

SECTION 4.   GUILT OF THE INJURED PARTY

Guilt of the injured party will be a complete defense as to acts, which would otherwise be criminal, if such acts were committed in self-defense or otherwise to prevent crime and did not exceed the privilege recognized by law for such a purpose. In such a case the person has no wrongful purpose in mind but is merely seeking to frustrate a crime attempted by another. On the other hand it is an established principle of law that one crime is no excuse for another. The fact that the person killed was himself a murderer is no defense to a charge of murder. And it is just as much larceny to steal from a thief as to steal from anyone else,?[74] although needless to say the recapture of stolen property from the thief, by or for the lawful owner, is not stealing. It is also larceny to steal liquor or drugs from one who violated the law by possessing it.[75] And the fact that counterfeit coin was paid to a prostitute for unlawful intercourse is no defense to a charge of uttering counterfeit coin.[76]

United States v. Dykes

United States Court of Appeals, Ninth Circuit, 2001.
24 Fed. Appx. 718.

[memorandum opinion] Defendant Isabel Dykes appeals her conviction, after a jury trial, for blackmail, claiming that the conviction was not supported by sufficient evidence. We affirm.

The French–American International School (FAIS) in San Francisco hired Defendant, a British citizen, to teach mathematics. The school gave her the necessary paperwork to fill out so that she could obtain a J–1 visa.

Shortly after Defendant arrived in the United States, her relationship with her new employer began to deteriorate. FAIS decided to fire her. It wrote a letter terminating Defendant's employment and advising her to return to England because her J–1 visa "becomes null and void at this time."

Defendant and her boyfriend responded with a long letter, which became the subject of this prosecution. The heading of Defendant's letter

---

73. Copyright © 1962 by the American Law Institute. Reprinted with the permission of the American Law Institute.

74. Ward v. People, 3 Hill 395 (N.Y.1842). And it is no defense to a charge of embezzling money from a city that the city acquired the money illegally. State v. Patterson, 66 Kan. 447, 71 P. 860 (1903).

75. State v. Donovan, 108 Wash. 276, 183 P. 127 (1919). And it is malicious mischief wilfully to destroy liquor so held by another. State v. Stark, 63 Kan. 529, 66 P. 243 (1901).

Robbery by taking contraband is subject to a criminal sanction. People v. Dillon, 34 Cal.3d 441, 194 Cal.Rptr. 390, 668 P.2d 697 (1983); Guy v. State, 108 Nev. 770, 839 P.2d 578 (1992) (drugs).

76. The Queen v. ___, 1 Cox C.C. 250 (1845).

said that it would detail "[t]he *illegal methods* systematically used by FAIS to damage those teachers hired from abroad." (Emphasis in original.) Defendant's letter referred to the *"illegal"* manner in which FAIS tried to harm Defendant and the *"illegal extremes* to which [FAIS is] prepared to go to achieve this." (Emphasis in original.) After describing the termination letter's discussion of the J–1 visa as a legally unjustified attempt to "terrorize [Defendant] into leaving the USA," Defendant's letter continued:

The fact however that you at FAIS *readily abuse U.S. laws to illegally get rid of those teachers* who refuse to be intimidated and forced into submission by you clearly exposes not only your trap and racket but also *what criminal elements you all are.*

. . .

... As a first step *I will send this letter* not just *to* the British and French Counsuls [sic] and Ambassadors and *relevant authorities* here but also to all the newspapers and TV stations. I hope you are aware that the Internet, of which I am knowledgeable, offers unlimited possibilities to make you and your school famous world-wide....

. . .

The only way I can see for you and FAIS to get off the hook is for you to provide Ms. Dykes with an apology for your inferior behavior. However since I know what crooks you are, *your apology can be truthful only if you immediately pay Ms. Dykes her full salary of $40,000 plus $20,000 for the damages you have caused* to her. You have her bank account number here in San Francisco, so deposit this money there at the latest by Friday 14:00. *This opportunity given to you and FAIS is neither negotiable or revocable.*

(Underlined emphasis in original; italics added.)

The statute that Defendant was convicted of violating provides:

Whoever, under a threat of informing, or as a consideration for not informing, against any violation of any law of the United States, demands or receives any money or other valuable thing, shall be fined under this title or imprisoned not more than one year, or both.

18 U.S.C. § 873.

The elements of the statute are simple. Under § 873, a threat to expose a violation of federal law unless a thing of value is given is blackmail. A rational trier of fact could have found that Defendant's letter threatened to inform the public and the authorities of alleged violations of federal immigration laws if FAIS did not pay Defendant $60,000. That is all that § 873 requires.

AFFIRMED.

SECTION 5. CONDUCT OF THE INJURED PARTY

The rules of law concerning negligence as a defense in civil actions for personal injuries have no application to criminal prosecutions.[77] "It is

---

77. Bowen v. State, 100 Ark. 232, 140 S.W. 28 (1911); People v. McKee, 80 Cal.App. 200, 251 P. 675 (1926); State v. Campbell, 82 Conn. 671, 74 A. 927 (1910); State v. Medlin, 355 Mo. 564, 197 S.W.2d 626 (1946); Click v. State, 144 Tex.Cr.R. 468, 164 S.W.2d 664 (1942).

enough to say that contributory negligence, if shown, is never a defense or excuse for crime, nor can it in any degree serve to purge an act otherwise constituting a public offense of its criminal character."[78] In one case a man threw a handful of blasting powder into an open fireplace. A resulting explosion set fire to the building and the wife and 19 year old son of the host were burned to death. Several others, some of them younger and less able to take care of themselves than those who were killed, were able to get out of the house in safety. But this did not entitle defendant to an instruction that he was excused if those who did not reach safety had failed to use due care in the effort.[79] In another case defendants had run over and killed a pedestrian while they were driving a horse and carriage at an excessive rate and were somewhat intoxicated. They thought they should be excused because deceased, who was deaf, had the habit of walking in the middle of the road at various times of the day and night. But the court held otherwise.[80]

It does not follow, however, that the conduct of the injured party must be ignored. His conduct may have a bearing on whether or not the one who caused the injury was culpably negligent.[81] Or it may be found that the negligence of the injured party was the *sole* cause of his injury.[82] "If the decedents were negligent," said the Washington court, "and such negligence was the sole cause of their death, then the appellant would not be guilty of manslaughter."[83]

State v. Munnell

Court of Appeals of Minnesota, 1984.
344 N.W.2d 883.

■ FOLEY, JUDGE.

Appellant Marion Munnell was charged with criminal vehicular operation in violation of Minn.Stat. § 609.21, subd. 1. At an omnibus hearing she moved for dismissal, contending the statute is vague and overbroad and

---

78. Contributory negligence of the victim is not a defense in a criminal prosecution. Buckles v. State, 830 P.2d 702 (Wyo.1992). State v. Moore, 129 Iowa 514, 519, 106 N.W. 16, 17 (1906). Accord: Penix v. Commonwealth, 313 Ky. 587, 233 S.W.2d 89 (1950). See Wis.Stat.Ann. 939.14 (1982).

79. Embry v. Commonwealth, 236 Ky. 204, 32 S.W.2d 979 (1930).

80. Regina v. Longbottom and Another, 3 Cox C.C. 439 (1849). *See also* Regina v. Kew, 12 Cox C.C. 355 (1872).

81. Held v. Commonwealth, 183 Ky. 209, 208 S.W. 772 (1919); People v. Campbell, 237 Mich. 424, 212 N.W. 97 (1927).

82. In some instances the decedent's negligence may have intervened between the conduct of D and the fatal result so as to have been the sole proximate cause of the death. State v. Gordon, 219 Kan. 643, 549 P.2d 886 (1976).

83. State v. Ramser, 17 Wash.2d 581, 590, 136 P.2d 1013, 1017 (1943). And see Commonwealth v. Aurick, 138 Pa.Super. 180, 10 A.2d 22 (1939).

that its failure to distinguish between drivers under the influence who are more and less negligent than the victims whose deaths they cause violates the equal protection clause.... The trial court denied both motions but, pursuant to Minn.R.Crim.P. 28.03, certified four questions raised by the motions for consideration by the Court of Appeals. We affirm the trial court's position on all four questions certified.

FACTS

Early on the morning of August 20, 1983, Munnell was traveling south on Itasca County Highway #39. She swerved across the yellow double center line and struck Kenneth Cloud, who was lying unconscious on the road. Her right front and rear tires ran over Cloud and killed him. Blood alcohol tests showed that defendant had an alcohol concentration of .11 percent, and the victim had an alcohol concentration of at least .24 percent.

ISSUES

The trial court certified the following questions for our consideration:

. . .

Is being less at fault than the deceased victim a defense to a prosecution under Minn.Stat. § 609.21, subd. 1?

Fault of Defendant as a Defense

Finally, the trial court properly refused to instruct the jury that fault of the victim is a defense to Minn.Stat. § 609.21, subd. 1. The Minnesota Supreme Court has repeatedly held that contributory negligence of the victim is not a defense in a criminal prosecution. Courts of other states have likewise rejected victim negligence as a defense in vehicular negligent homicide cases. Wren v. State, 577 P.2d 235 (Alaska 1978); Hart v. State, 75 Wis.2d 371, 249 N.W.2d 810 (1977); State v. Pope, 6 Conn.Cir.Ct. 712, 313 A.2d 84 (1972).

However, a victim's negligence is relevant on the question of whether the defendant was negligent, and, if so, whether that negligence was the proximate cause of the victim's injuries.

DECISION

Minn.Stat. § 609.21, subd. 1 is constitutional, both on its face and as applied to drivers under the influence less negligent than the victims whose deaths they cause. Fault of the victim is not a defense to the statute.

Affirmed and remanded for trial.

Regina v. Holland

Liverpool Assizes, 1841.
2 Moody & R. 351, 174 Eng.Rep. 313.

Indictment for murder. The prisoner was charged with inflicting divers mortal blows and wounds upon one Thomas Garland, and (amongst others) a cut upon one of his fingers.

It appeared by the evidence that the deceased had been waylaid and assaulted by the prisoner, and that, amongst other wounds, he was severely cut across one of his fingers by an iron instrument. On being brought to the infirmary, the surgeon urged him to submit to the amputation of the finger, telling him, unless it were amputated, he considered that his life would be in great hazard. The deceased refused to allow the finger to be amputated. It was thereupon dressed by the surgeon, and the deceased attended at the infirmary from day to day to have his wounds dressed; at the end of a fortnight, however, lockjaw came on, induced by the wound on the finger; the finger was then amputated, but too late, and the lockjaw ultimately caused death. The surgeon deposed, that if the finger had been amputated in the first instance, he thought it most probable that the life of the deceased would have been preserved.

For the prisoner, it was contended that the cause of death was not the wound inflicted by the prisoner, but the obstinate refusal of the deceased to submit to proper surgical treatment, by which the fatal result would, according to the evidence, have been prevented.

■ MAULE, J., however, was clearly of opinion that this was no defence, and told the jury that if the prisoner wilfully, and without any justifiable cause, inflicted the wound on the party, which wound was ultimately the cause of death, the prisoner was guilty of murder; that for this purpose it made no difference whether the wound was in its own nature instantly mortal, or whether it became the cause of death by reason of the deceased not having adopted the best mode of treatment; the real question is, whether in the end the wound inflicted by the prisoner was the cause of death?

Guilty.[84]

SECTION 6. CONDONATION BY INJURED PARTY

"Of a nature somewhat similar to the two last is the offence of *theft bote,* which is where the party robbed not only knows the felon, but also takes his goods again, or other amends, upon agreement not to prosecute. This is frequently called compounding of felony, and formerly was held to make a man an accessory; but is now punished only with fine and imprisonment.... By statute 25 Geo. II, c. 36, even to advertise a reward for the return of things stolen, with no questions asked, or words to the same purport, subjects the advertiser and the printer to a forfeiture of 50*l.* each." 4 Bl.Comm. 133–4.

---

84. After a violent attack by **D, X** was in bed in a prison hospital in a semiconscious condition. He fell out of bed several times and died five days after the attack. **D**'s conviction of second-degree murder was affirmed. He was the cause of the death even if it was the falls out of bed that proved fatal. State v. Little, 57 Wn.2d 516, 358 P.2d 120 (1961).

The victim of a criminally negligent traffic accident was moved from the hospital, by his mother, contrary to the doctor's orders. There was no evidence that this actually hastened the death but the court indicates that it would not have been superseding had it done so. People v. Clark, 106 Cal.App.2d 271, 235 P.2d 56 (1951).

For the rule under a Texas statute *see* Noble v. State, 54 Tex.Cr.R. 436, 113 S.W. 281 (1908).

The owner's reacquisition of a chattel previously stolen from him is not of itself sufficient to taint him with criminal guilt. It is his act of obtaining it under agreement or understanding to abstain from prosecution or to withhold evidence of the larceny that is illegal. This is merely a particular instance of a general crime. For anyone to obtain anything of value, or a promise thereof, upon such an agreement or understanding in regard to any felony is a common-law offense known as compounding a felony. The ancient classification of such an offender as an accessory to the crime after the fact suggests that it was limited to cases of felony in the early days. But that limitation has tended to disappear. It has been said that to take a reward to forbear or stifle a criminal prosecution for a misdemeanor is also indictable at common law, except for offenses largely of the nature of private injuries or of low grade.[85] The chief exception to the rule has been in the category of the so-called minor or petty offenses. And it has not been uncommon for statutes to forbid the compounding of any criminal offense.[86]

Discussions of the subject often suggest that an attempt by the offender and the offended to settle the offense outside of the criminal court room is usually a crime and always quite ineffective. This is far from the true picture.[87] To begin with, a multitude of offenses, including a substantial number of serious crimes, are not prosecuted because they are settled between the two persons involved and never reach the attention of the prosecuting authorities. This, of course, is merely a factual matter and does not dispute the statement as to the law. The law itself, however, has taken definite strides in this direction. The most sweeping provision of this nature is a statute expressly authorizing the compromise of a misdemeanor for which the injured person has a civil action (unless there are special circumstances of aggravation).[88] The court may have discretion to permit the prosecution to proceed notwithstanding such a compromise,[89] but it will be exercised rarely and only under unusual circumstances.

There are also certain specific provisions to be considered. Some statutes invite a settlement by the parties, such as a bad check act providing a penalty for the issuance of such an instrument unless it is paid within five days after written notice;[90] or a statute making the refusal of an officer, clerk or agent to hand over money or property in his care, on demand, prima-facie evidence of embezzlement.[91]

Any such provision gives to the person harmed by a crime more or less power to control whether prosecution shall or shall not be brought. Beyond any of the foregoing in this regard is the enactment found in some states

---

85. State v. Carver, 69 N.H. 216, 39 A. 973 (1898).

86. Murphy v. Rochford, 55 Ill.App.3d 695, 13 Ill.Dec. 543, 371 N.E.2d 260 (1977); West's Cal. Pen. Code § 153 (1997).

87. For an elaborate consideration of the field see Miller, The Compromise of Criminal Cases, 1 So.Cal.L.Rev. 1 (1927).

88. For example, West's Ann.Cal.Pen.Code, §§ 1377–1379 (1997).

89. Id. at § 1378. See also, § 8.11 (1996).

90. Tenn.Code Ann. § 39–1960 (1975). Under some of the statutes payment on written notice does not bar the prosecution but merely negatives the presumption of fraudulent intent. Cook v. Commonwealth, 178 Va. 251, 16 S.E.2d 635 (1941). *See also* 10 U.S.C.A. § 923a.

91. Id. at § 39–4233 (1955).

providing that no prosecution for adultery shall be brought except upon complaint of the aggrieved spouse.[92]

These exceptions have been mentioned not because of their importance, but because they are exceptions. A criminal offense is a public wrong. The act which constitutes a crime may *also* be a private wrong, such as larceny or battery, or be a public wrong only, such as joining enemy forces in time of war or making fraudulent misstatements in an income tax return. Insofar as an act constitutes a private wrong (tort) the injured individual is free to make a settlement with the wrongdoer, or to forgive him entirely without any reparation. However, even an offense that is against a person's individual interest is also a crime and a subsequent ratification or reparation is no defense.[93] But the general rule is that a private individual has no power to ratify, settle or condone a public wrong even if it was a wrong which injured his person or harmed his property.[94] If he is able to do so it is only because of some exception to the general rule and in the exact manner provided.[95] In the absence of such exception the victim of rape cannot excuse the ravisher by ratifying or forgiving the act.[96] The owner of money or property, even after complete restitution has been made, cannot forgive the crime of embezzlement[97] or larceny.[98] It is even beyond the power of a mother's love to wipe out the criminal guilt of a son who maliciously burned her barn.[99]

MODEL PENAL CODE

Section 213.3   Corruption of Minors and Seduction.

(1) Offense Defined. A male who has sexual intercourse with a female not his wife, or any person who engages in deviate sexual intercourse or causes another to engage in deviate sexual intercourse, is guilty of an offense if: . . .

---

92. For example, Iowa Code Ann. § 702.1. Whether or not consent given by filing the complaint can be withdrawn later, so as to stop the prosecution, is discussed in State v. Allison, 175 Minn. 218, 220 N.W. 563 (1928).

93. People v. Lucero, 623 P.2d 424 (Colo.App.1980). Private parties cannot agree to waive application of a criminal statute. United States v. Savoie, 985 F.2d 612 (1st Cir.1993).

94. Victim cannot ratify criminal conduct after the crime has been committed. State v. Martinez, 188 Mont. 271, 613 P.2d 974 (1980).

95. Commonwealth v. Heckman, 113 Pa.Super. 70, 172 A. 28 (1934).

The "misdemeanor compromise statute" A.R.S. § 13–3981 (1978) does not apply. The damage to another vehicle was only incidental to the crime of leaving the scene of an accident. Hence the fact that defendant reached a settlement with the driver of the other vehicle does not bar a prosecution for leaving the scene of an accident. State ex rel. Baumert v. Municipal Court, 125 Ariz. 429, 610 P.2d 63 (1980).

"A.R.S. § 13–3981 applies only when a misdemeanor offense invariably creates a civil cause of action." As this is not true of indecent exposure, it cannot be compromised. State ex rel. Baumert v. Superior Court, 130 Ariz. 256, 635 P.2d 849, 850 (1981).

96. Commonwealth v. Slattery, 147 Mass. 423, 18 N.E. 399 (1888).

97. Fleener v. State, 58 Ark. 98, 23 S.W. 1 (1893).

98. Breaker v. State, 103 Ohio St. 670, 134 N.E. 479 (1921).

99. State v. Craig, 124 Kan. 340, 259 P. 802 (1927).

(d) the other person is a female who is induced to participate by promise of marriage which the actor does not mean to perform.[100]

---

100. Copyright 1962 by the American Law Institute. Reprinted with the permission of the American Law Institute.

CHAPTER 10

SPECIAL DEFENSES

SECTION 1.   PUBLIC AUTHORITY

Nothing done under valid public authority is a crime if such authority is in no way exceeded or abused. Deeds which would otherwise be crimes, such as taking or destroying property, taking hold of a person by force and against one's will, placing a person in confinement, or even taking life, are not criminal if done with proper public authority. The typical instances in which even the extreme act of taking human life is done by public authority are (1) the killing of an enemy as an act of war and within the rules of war, and (2) the execution of a sentence of death pronounced by a competent tribunal.

Any unauthorized departure from the authority given destroys the privilege which would otherwise be present. Even in time of war an alien enemy may not be killed needlessly after he has been disarmed and securely imprisoned.[1] No one other than the proper officer or his duly appointed deputy may lawfully execute the sentence of death.[2] And that officer may not substitute one method of execution for another.[3] Suppose, for example, in a state in which the electric chair is used for capital punishment, the officer in charge should discover that no electric current was available at the time set for execution. The sentence of the court would specify that particular means of carrying out the sentence, and if the officer should shoot the prisoner, or hang him, the officer would be guilty of criminal homicide.

"And, further, if judgment of death be given by a judge not authorized by lawful commission, and execution is done accordingly, the judge is guilty of murder. And upon this account Sir Matthew Hale himself, though he accepted the place of a judge of the common pleas under Cromwell's government, (since it is necessary to decide the disputes of civil property in the worst of times,) yet declined to sit on the crown side at the assizes and try prisoners, having very strong objections to the legality of the usurper's commission; a distinction perhaps rather too refined, since the punishment

---

1. "That it is legal to kill an alien enemy in the heat and exercise of war, is undeniable; but to kill such an enemy after he has laid down his arms, and especially when he is confined in prison, is murder." State v. Gut, 13 Minn. (Gil.) 315, 330 (1868).

"... an order to kill unresisting Vietnamese would be an illegal order, and that if Calley knew the order was illegal or should have known it was illegal, obedience to an order was not a valid defense." Calley v. Callaway, 519 F.2d 184, 193 (5th Cir.1975), *cert. denied* 425 U.S. 911, 96 S.Ct. 1505, 47 L.Ed.2d 760.

2. "... even though it be the judge himself." 4 Bl.Comm. 179.

3. "If an officer beheads one who is adjudged to be hanged, or *vice versa*, it is murder, ..." Ibid.

886

of crimes is at least as necessary to society as maintaining the boundaries of property."[4]

Wilful abuse of authority will also destroy the privilege. Thus obviously excessive physical force against a disobedient convict, by a guard, constituted criminal assault and battery.[5] It may also violate federal civil right statutes.[6]

The exercise of public authority most commonly resulting in an application of force to the person is the making of an arrest, or the detention of one already in custody. A peace officer, or even a private person, may have authority to arrest a certain individual. This authority is sometimes under a warrant and at other times without a warrant.[7] The amount of force that may lawfully be used in the apprehension depends upon all of the facts in the particular case, including the conduct of the arrestee and the nature of the offense for which the arrest is being made. If the arrest itself is authorized, and the force used in making it is not excessive, there is no assault, battery or false imprisonment.[8] On the other hand, a battery results from any laying on of hands to make an unauthorized arrest,[9] or

---

4. Id. at 178.

5. State v. Mincher, 172 N.C. 895, 90 S.E. 429 (1916).

6. 18 U.S.C. § 241–242 (1997).

7. Professor Wilgus, in his very scholarly analysis, has reached this conclusion: At common law either officer or private person was privileged to arrest without a warrant for treason, felony or breach of the peace committed in his presence,—except that the arrest for breach of the peace was not privileged without a warrant unless it was effected while the breach was being committed or on immediate and continuous pursuit thereafter. Wilgus, Arrest Without a Warrant, 22 Mich.L.Rev. 673 (1924). Compare Restatement, Second, Torts, §§ 119, 121 (1965).

At common law, moreover, either officer or private person is privileged, without a warrant, to arrest one who is reasonably believed to be guilty of felony, with one important distinction: The officer is protected if he believes upon reasonable grounds (1) that a felony has been committed and (2) that the arrestee is the guilty person; whereas for the protection of a private person it is necessary (1) that a felony has in fact been committed and (2) that he has reasonable grounds for believing the arrestee guilty of committing it. Ibid.; A.L.I. Code of Criminal Procedure, 236–40 (official draft with commentaries, 1931).

Changes have been made by statutes, usually enlarging the scope of the privilege to arrest without a warrant, especially in cases involving misdemeanors. McKinney's Consol.L.N.Y. § 140–10 (1971).

8. State v. Fuller, 96 Mo. 165, 168, 9 S.W. 583, 584 (1888).

9. Restatement, Second, Torts § 118, comment b (1965).

West's Ann.Cal.Pen.Code § 196 (1988). "Homicide is justifiable when committed by public officers and those acting by their command in their aid and assistance, either ... When necessarily committed in retaking felons who have been rescued or have escaped, or when necessarily committed in arresting persons charged with felony, and who are fleeing from justice or resisting such arrest." § 197. "Homicide is also justifiable when committed by any person in any of the following cases: ...

"4. When necessarily committed in attempting, by lawful ways and means, to apprehend any person for any felony committed, ...".

People v. Curtis, 70 Cal.2d 347, 74 Cal.Rptr. 713, 450 P.2d 33 (1969), involved one who injured a police officer while resisting an unlawful arrest. One statute prohibits forceful resistance to an arrest by a known officer even if unlawful. Another statute provides that a battery on a police officer "engaged in the performance of his duties" is a felony. It was held that forceful resistance to a known officer who was attempting an unlawful arrest was a

from the use of excessive force in making an arrest that would otherwise be lawful.[10]

United States v. Burrows

United States Court of Appeals, Ninth Circuit, 1994.
36 F.3d 875.

■ FLETCHER, CIRCUIT JUDGE:

Ronald Olen Burrows appeals from his conviction for drug trafficking crimes, arguing that two of the district court's jury instructions were erroneous. . . .

BACKGROUND

In early December 1991, "Bugsy," an informant working for the DEA, had a series of consensually monitored telephone conversations with Burrows. Bugsy offered to put Burrows in contact with a prospective buyer who, Bugsy said, wished to purchase five pounds of methamphetamine. Unbeknownst to Burrows, the prospective buyer was an undercover DEA agent. Bugsy and Burrows arranged to meet at a liquor store on December 5, 1991, and thereafter to meet the supposed purchaser.

Burrows testified that on December 4, 1991, the day before the meeting with Bugsy and the buyer, he contacted his source, codefendant Rodriguez. On December 5, before the scheduled meeting, Burrows and Rodriguez drove to a hotel room in Oceanside, where Rodriguez retrieved the methamphetamine and gave it to Burrows. Burrows then drove back to the San Fernando Valley, joined up with Bugsy, and went with him to a shopping center parking lot. Bugsy and Burrows were met there by DEA agent Steve Youngblood, posing as a buyer. Burrows was arrested after he produced the five pounds of methamphetamine.

Burrows immediately waived his *Miranda* rights and attempted to convince the agents that he too was working undercover, helping Riverside County Deputy Sheriff Kenneth Vann to arrest Rodriguez. Burrows agreed to assist the DEA agents by placing a call to Rodriguez, his supplier. Burrows was eventually able to summon Rodriguez by telling him the deal was in danger of unravelling because the buyers had not brought enough money. Rodriguez arrived at the shopping center with two companions and prepared to negotiate. He and his companions were arrested.

Burrows continued to cooperate with the government, twice meeting with the U.S. Attorney's Office and the DEA and inculpating Rodriguez and his two companions, Paez and Rivas. Burrows also continued to maintain, however, that at the time of his arrest he was working undercover for Deputy Vann. Not believing this story, the government prosecuted Burrows along with Rodriguez and Paez.

---

battery because of the first statute, but it was a misdemeanor rather than a felony because an officer attempting an unlawful arrest is not "engaged in the performance of his duties."

10.   Moody v. State, 120 Ga. 868, 48 S.E. 340 (1904); Reynolds v. Griffith, 126 W.Va. 766, 30 S.E.2d 81 (1944).

The three were tried together. At trial, Burrows testified that he was or believed himself to have been working undercover in an attempt to help Deputy Vann. Vann testified that he had visited Burrows in jail at Burrows's request and had asked him to target Rodriguez, but that Burrows had never worked as an informant for him, never paged him during the events giving rise to this case, and was not working for him at the time of those events.

The district court instructed the jury on the defense of public authority. The jury rejected Burrows's defense, and convicted him of possession with intent to distribute methamphetamine and conspiracy to distribute methamphetamine. On appeal, Burrows argues that the district court erred by instructing the jury that he could make out a defense of public authority only if he reasonably believed that he was acting pursuant to police authority. Burrows also contends that the district court erred by instructing the jury, at the behest of Rodriguez, that the testimony of a drug addict—which Burrows at one time had been—should be regarded with special scrutiny.

. . .

Public Authority Instruction

Burrows's defense at trial was that he was working as an informant, under the direction of the Riverside County Sheriff's Department and Deputy Vann. The district court instructed the jury as follows:

If you find that defendant Burrows was acting or reasonably believed he was acting on behalf of a law enforcement agency or officer when he engaged in the narcotics transaction charged in counts one and two of the indictment, then you must acquit him of these charges.

Burrows contends that the district court erred by including the word "reasonably" in the instruction. According to Burrows, the public authority defense turns solely on a defendant's subjective beliefs. . . .

Burrows relies heavily on Fed.R.Crim.P. 12.3, which requires defendants to give pre-trial notice if they intend to raise a defense of "actual or believed exercise of public authority." Burrows argues that because Rule 12.3 refers only to belief, and not to reasonable belief, reasonableness is not an element of the public authority defense. This argument, however, misapprehends the nature and purpose of Rule 12.3. Rule 12.3 prescribes procedures which both the defense and the prosecution must follow whenever a defendant considers raising a public authority defense. The Advisory Committee Note to Rule 12.3 makes clear that the rule's purpose is to avoid unfair surprise to the government because the defense "remains an unusual defense" and "the government rarely will have reason to anticipate it." The Note further provides that Rule 12.3 embodies the same rationale as Rules 12.1 (Notice of Alibi) and 12.2 (Notice of Defense Based Upon Mental Condition).

We have never found that Rules 12.1 or 12.2 affect the substantive law of the insanity and alibi defenses, which of course were recognized long before the adoption of the Federal Rules of Criminal Procedure. Instead, we have noted that Rule 12.1 was intended to avoid unfair surprise and prevent trial delays due to an unexpected witness or alibi defense.... Just as Rules 12.1 and 12.2 embody notice requirements but do not alter the substance of the alibi and insanity defenses, Rule 12.3 sets forth a notice requirement but does not limit or expand the public authority defense. See also Fed.R.Crim.P. 1 ("These rules govern the *procedure* in all criminal proceedings in the courts of the United States") (emphasis added); Fed. R.Crim.P. 2 (purpose of the Federal Rules of Criminal Procedure is "to secure simplicity in procedure, fairness in administration and the elimination of unjustifiable expense and delay"). To determine what the elements of the public authority defense are, we must look not to procedural rules but rather to the federal common law dealing with the substance of the defense.

We find considerable assistance in negotiating our way through this area from the roadmap recently provided by the Eleventh Circuit in United States v. Baptista–Rodriguez, 17 F.3d 1354 (11th Cir.1994):

Several defenses may apply when a defendant claims he performed the acts for which he was charged in response to a request from an agency of the government....

First, the defendant may allege that he lacked criminal intent because he honestly believed he was performing the otherwise-criminal acts in cooperation with the government. "Innocent intent" is not a defense *per se*, but a defense strategy aimed at negating the *mens rea* for the crime, an essential element of the prosecution's case....

A second possible defense is "public authority." With this affirmative defense, the defendant seeks exoneration based on the fact that he reasonably relied on the authority of a government official to engage him in a covert activity. The validity of this defense depends upon whether the government agent in fact had the authority to empower the defendant to perform the acts in question. If the agent had no such power, then the defendant may not rest on the "public authority" [defense]....

A third possible defense ... is "entrapment by estoppel." This defense applies when a government official tells a defendant that certain conduct is legal and the defendant commits what would otherwise be a crime in reasonable reliance on the official's representation.

Id. at 1368 n. 18 (citations omitted).

. . .

We conclude that the reasoning of Lansing applies no less to the defense of public authority than it does to the defense of entrapment by estoppel. Lansing held that "uniform enforcement of law" dictates a reasonableness limitation when the defendant purports to have relied on a government official who mistakenly misled him into committing an offense. The difference between the entrapment by estoppel defense and the public authority defense is not great. In the first, a government official commits an error and the defendant relies on it and thereby violates the law. In the second, a government official makes some statement or performs some act and the defendant relies on it, possibly mistakenly, and commits an offense in so doing. If we hold defendants to a reasonableness standard even where the government has erred—and under Lansing, we do—there is no reason why defendants should be treated any more leniently when *their* mistakes are the source of error. Since under Lansing we do not require the government to pay for its mistake by losing a conviction, *a fortiori* we will not exact that price when the mistake is the defendant's. We adopt the standard set forth in Lansing, and hold that a defendant makes out a defense of public authority only when he has shown that his reliance on governmental authority was reasonable as well as sincere. This result makes our law internally consistent, and at the same time brings it into harmony with that of other courts which have addressed the issue.

. . . The district court's instruction was correct.

Affirmed in Part, Remanded in Part.[11]

State v. Mantelli

Court of Appeals of New Mexico, 2002.
131 N.M. 692, 42 P.3d 272.

■ BUSTAMANTE, JUDGE.

Joseph Mantelli (Defendant), a police officer, appeals his conviction for voluntary manslaughter, aggravated assault with a deadly weapon (a firearm), and shooting at a motor vehicle resulting in injury. . . .

Concluding that Defendant was entitled to have the jury instructed on justifiable homicide by a police officer in accordance with NMSA 1978, § 30–2–6 (1989), we reverse Defendant's convictions and take this opportunity to discuss the use of deadly force by police officers in New Mexico. . . .

I.   FACTS

Defendant, a uniformed officer with the Las Vegas, New Mexico Police Department (LVPD), shot and killed Abelino Montoya, an eighteen-year-old Robertson High School senior, in the early morning hours of February 14, 1998. At trial Defendant testified that while on duty, wearing his uniform and patrolling in a marked police unit with Sergeant Steve Marquez (Sgt. Marquez), the officers spotted a white Toyota truck near the Las Vegas City Plaza. They believed this was the same vehicle that earlier that night was going the wrong way on a one-way street, causing Sgt. Marquez to swerve to avoid a collision. The truck, driven by Montoya, had in fact eluded Sgt. Marquez after a brief chase that ended when Sgt. Marquez's marked police unit became disabled.

Defendant activated the overhead lights and wig-wag lights on the police unit and moved to get behind the truck. Defendant testified that Montoya reacted to the lights by increasing his speed, and proceeding through an intersection without stopping for a stop signal. During the course of the pursuit, Montoya ran through six or seven stop signs, eventually reaching a dead-end at Valley and Chavez Streets.

---

11. International law does not provide a valid defense to a violation of state criminal laws where no treaty is applicable. Yoos v. State, 522 So.2d 898 (Fla.App.1988).

What occurred next was disputed at trial. Gabriel Rubio, a passenger in Montoya's truck throughout the evening, testified for the State. Rubio testified that Montoya, in an attempt to avoid being stopped, drove north on Valley Street, which dead-ends at Chavez Street. Montoya apparently was not aware that Valley Street came to a dead-end until he was in the intersection of Valley and Chavez Streets. Once in the intersection Montoya slammed on his brakes and the truck skidded at least a car length past the intersection. Rubio was watching the police car coming at them. Meanwhile, Montoya had put the truck in reverse and was backing up trying to position the truck to avoid a rock wall at the intersection as he attempted to turn the truck onto Chavez Street. Rubio testified the two vehicles collided in the middle of the intersection of Valley and Chavez.

Once the two vehicles collided, Rubio testified that Defendant seemed to immediately be at the driver's side window trying to break the window with the butt of his handgun. At the same time Montoya was shifting the manual transmission of the truck out of reverse and turning the wheel to the right in a continuing attempt to turn down Chavez Street. While they were still in the middle of the intersection, Defendant succeeded in breaking the driver's side window. Montoya put the truck into first gear and began to drive away, going up and over the curb. He had to drive slowly as he turned right down Chavez Street to avoid the rock wall at the intersection. After clearing the wall, Montoya drove the truck fast down Chavez Street. As they were driving away, Rubio heard two shots. With one shot Rubio felt something graze his head and he ducked. He also told Montoya to stop. Rubio described the shots as coming one right after the other. After the shots rang out, the truck went out of control and hit the side of a house some distance down Chavez Street. Montoya suffered one shot in the back and a second in the head, killing him almost instantly. Rubio testified that he did not think that he and Montoya had ever put any officer's life in danger.

The dispatcher tape-recorded Sgt. Marquez's calls as the second chase proceeded. The tape included the sound of the crash at the intersection of Valley and Chavez, and fifteen seconds later Sgt. Marquez saying "shots fired," and forty-one seconds from the crash Sgt. Marquez announcing that there was a death.

The State's theory at trial was that Defendant shot Montoya to prevent him from escaping. The State also presented testimony from Defendant's roommate, Adrian Crispin, a fellow LVPD officer, that Defendant told him right after the shooting that he had shot at the truck as it was moving away because it was about to get away.

At trial Defendant testified to a different reason for the shooting. Defendant testified he believed at the time of the shooting that the truck was being used as a deadly weapon to attack him and Sgt. Marquez, that their lives were in danger, and that he was therefore justified in using deadly force in self-defense and defense of another.

Defendant testified that he positioned his police car to try to "block-in" the truck so that it could not escape. On cross-examination, Defendant also admitted that he was aware of department policy that an officer was not to use his patrol car as a roadblock without ensuring the pursued vehicle had a way out of the roadblock. Defendant testified that he was shocked and scared when Montoya began to back up the truck. Defendant believed that Sgt. Marquez had exited the police car and then had been knocked down and possibly run over and killed or injured. Thus, standing an arm's length away from the truck, Defendant fired one round into the truck because he believed that his partner was in danger. He fired two more shots to the back of the truck because he thought the truck was backing up a second time to ram them again, and not because Montoya was trying to escape by negotiating the rock wall at the corner of Chavez and Valley. Sgt. Marquez also fired a single shot at the truck.

II. JURY INSTRUCTION ON JUSTIFIABLE HOMICIDE BY A POLICE OFFICER

a. Background

Defendant argues that it was reversible error for the trial court to refuse to instruct the jury on justifiable homicide by a police officer in accordance with Section 30–2–6. Defendant requested one modified uniform jury instruction, based on UJI 14–5173 NMRA 2001, and three non-uniform instructions premised upon the United States Supreme Court decision in Tennessee v. Garner, 471 U.S. 1, 105 S.Ct. 1694, 85 L.Ed.2d 1 (1985), which related to justifiable homicide by a police officer. The State does not argue that the requested instructions were incorrect statements of the law.

Defendant asserted that as a commissioned police officer in the line of duty for the LVPD, he was authorized to use deadly force under Section 30–2–6 to apprehend a fleeing felon who had threatened him and Sgt. Marquez with serious harm or deadly force and the jury should have been allowed to consider this defense under proper instructions. Defendant asserts that instructions on this theory specifically applicable to police officers would have allowed him to argue additional and alternative theories of justification for the shooting which went beyond the normal self-defense and defense-of-others theories applicable to the public at large.

The State has never disputed that Defendant was a commissioned police officer and on-duty for the LVPD at the time of the shooting, and that he was justified in pursuing and attempting to apprehend Montoya. However, it argues that State v. Johnson, 1998–NMCA–019, 124 N.M. 647, 954 P.2d 79, requires a defendant requesting a justifiable homicide instruction to establish that his conduct satisfied a standard of "objective reasonableness" for the use of the deadly force prior to receiving such an instruction. *Id.* ¶ 13. The State contends that Defendant's actions in shooting at Montoya as he fled, exceeded Defendant's authority under Section 30–2–6 to use deadly force and cannot be considered reasonable as a matter of law. The State dramatized this point to the jury in its closing argument by repeatedly stating that police officers in New Mexico are not allowed to "shoot at a fleeing suspect."

The State also argues that Defendant did not present evidence that he shot Montoya in an attempt to arrest him for committing a felony per Section 30–2–6. Instead, it argues that under Defendant's version of events, the proper instruction was that the killing was justified as occurring in self-defense or defense of another and not "necessarily committed" in order to prevent the escape of a felon. Defendant was granted the UJI 14–5171 NMRA 2001 self-defense instruction.

The trial judge, persuaded by the State's arguments, refused to instruct the jury on justifiable homicide because sufficient evidence was not presented by Defendant for the court to believe that Defendant's actions could be considered objectively reasonable. At the hearing on Defendant's motion for a new trial, the trial judge also explained that he believed Defendant's theory was self-defense and defense of another and that he had not argued that the killing of Montoya was justifiable homicide.

b. Standard of Review

The trial court's rejection of Defendant's submitted jury instructions is reviewed by this Court de novo. State v. Lucero, 1998–NMSC–044, ¶ 5, 126 N.M. 552, 972 P.2d 1143. A "defendant is entitled to a jury instruction on the theory of his case as long as the evidence exists to support it" which is sufficient to allow reasonable minds to differ with respect to all elements of the defense. State v. Arias, 115 N.M. 93, 96, 847 P.2d 327, 330 (Ct.App. 1993). This is true whether the evidence raising the defense is adduced by the State or by defendant. State v. Akin, 75 N.M. 308, 310, 404 P.2d 134, 136 (1965); State v. Heisler, 58 N.M. 446, 454, 272 P.2d 660, 665 (1954). "The adequacy of a jury instruction is evaluated in the context of all the instructions given to the jury, in order to determine whether the instruction accurately states the law." State v. Sosa, 1997–NMSC–032, ¶ 25, 123 N.M. 564, 943 P.2d 1017.

c. Use of Deadly Force and *Tennessee v. Garner*

The use of deadly force by police officers to prevent the escape of a felony suspect originated in the common law. The common law rule "allowed the use of whatever force was necessary to effect the arrest of a fleeing felon, though not a misdemeanant." *Garner,* 471 U.S. at 12, 105 S.Ct. 1694. Under the common law rule, which New Mexico accepted for much of its history, the reasonableness and necessity of the officer's resort to deadly force was frequently judged solely on the basis of whether the officer could have arrested the suspect without shooting him. Alaniz v. Funk, 69 N.M. 164, 166–67, 364 P.2d 1033, 1034 (1961). Under this approach, it made no difference that the felon was nonviolent or that the felon posed no danger to the safety of others.

In *Garner,* the father of Edward Garner, a fifteen-year-old boy who was shot and killed by a police officer while fleeing from the burglary of an unoccupied house, brought a wrongful death action under the Federal Civil Rights Act, 42 U.S.C. § 1983, against the police officer who fired the shot, the police department, as well as others. *Garner,* 471 U.S. at 5, 105 S.Ct. 1694. The shooting occurred after the officer responded to a report of a nighttime burglary and saw Garner running across the backyard of the house to a six-foot-high chain-link fence. *Id.* at 3, 105 S.Ct. 1694. The officer, using a flashlight, saw Garner's face and hands, but saw no sign of a weapon. *Id.* When Garner began to climb over the fence after the officer's warning to halt, the officer shot and mortally wounded him. *Id.* at 4, 105 S.Ct. 1694. The officer testified that if Garner would have successfully scaled the fence he would have escaped capture. *Id.* at 4 n. 3, 105 S.Ct. 1694.

In using deadly force, the officer acted in accordance with a Tennessee statute permitting the use of deadly force to effect the arrest of a felon fleeing from or resisting arrest. *Id.* at 4, 105 S.Ct. 1694. The statute reflected the common law fleeing-felon doctrine. However, the Supreme Court in *Garner* held that a police officer may not use deadly force to apprehend a fleeing felon who does not pose a "significant threat of death or serious physical injury to the officer or others." *Id.* at 3, 105 S.Ct. 1694. The Supreme Court reasoned that apprehension using deadly force is a "seizure" subject to the reasonableness requirement of the Fourth Amendment of the United States Constitution, and that the indiscriminate use of deadly force to prevent escape of all felony suspects is constitutionally impermissible. *Id.* at 7, 105 S.Ct. 1694. Almost all of the states have modified their police deadly force laws and policies in response to *Garner*. *See generally* "Police Use of Deadly Force: How Courts and Policy–Makers Have Misapplied Tennessee v. Garner." 7 Kan. J.L. & Pub. Pol'y 100 (1998).

The Court explained that in determining whether a deadly-force seizure is reasonable, the suspect's rights under the Fourth Amendment had to be balanced against the government's interests in effective law enforcement. *Garner*, 471 U.S. at 9, 105 S.Ct. 1694. The factors that weigh heavily against the use of deadly force are "[t]he suspect's fundamental interest in his own life," the unmatched "intrusiveness of a seizure by means of deadly force," and "the interest of the individual, and of society, in judicial determination of guilt and punishment," which is frustrated by the use of deadly force. *Id.* The Supreme Court found that these factors outweigh the government's interest in the use or threat of use of deadly force to encourage suspects to submit peacefully to arrest. Thus, "[t]he use of deadly force to prevent the escape of all felony suspects, whatever the circumstances, is constitutionally unreasonable." *Id.* at 11, 105 S.Ct. 1694. The Court framed the inquiry as one designed to determine "whether the totality of the circumstances justified a particular sort of search or seizure." *Id.* at 8–9, 105 S.Ct. 1694.

While the Court held that "[t]he Tennessee statute is unconstitutional insofar as it authorizes the use of deadly force against such [unarmed and non-dangerous] fleeing suspects," the Court also held that the statute was not unconstitutional on its face. *Id.* at 11, 105 S.Ct. 1694. The Court stated "[w]here the officer has probable cause to believe that the suspect poses a threat of serious physical harm, either to the officer or to others, it is not unconstitutionally unreasonable to prevent escape by using deadly force." *Id.* Thus, it should be clear that under *Garner* the constitutionality of deadly force statutes should not be considered in the abstract; instead, courts should focus on the constitutionality of specific applications of a challenged statute to specific factual circumstances. Finally, *Garner* rejected the felony-misdemeanor distinction as a guide for deciding when deadly force may be used.

In Graham v. Connor, 490 U.S. 386, 396, 109 S.Ct. 1865, 104 L.Ed.2d 443 (1989), the Court clarified its holding in *Garner* and ruled that excessive force claims brought against police officers are to be analyzed under the "objective reasonableness" standard of the Fourth Amendment. The Court cautioned that the "proper application" of this reasonableness standard "requires careful attention to the facts and circumstances of each particular case, including the severity of the crime at issue, whether the suspect poses an immediate threat to the safety of the officers or others, and whether he is actively resisting arrest or attempting to evade arrest by flight." *Graham*, 490 U.S. at 396, 109 S.Ct. 1865. With these facts and circumstances in mind, "[t]he 'reasonableness' of a particular use of force must be judged from the perspective of a reasonable officer on the scene, rather than with the 20/20 vision of hindsight." *Id.* The Court emphasized that this is an objective standard "without regard to [the actual officer's] underlying intent or motivation." *Id.* at 387, 109 S.Ct. 1865.

d.   Section 30–2–6

Section 30–2–6, "Justifiable homicide by public officer or public employee," has evolved in response to the Supreme Court's pronouncements on the use of deadly force by law enforcement officers. (Emphasis omitted.) Specifically, the Legislature added Section 30–2–6(B), in response to *Garner. Johnson*, 1998–NMCA–019, ¶ 11, 124 N.M. 647, 954 P.2d 79. Section 30–2–6 provides in pertinent part:

A.   Homicide is justifiable when committed by a public officer or public employee or those acting by their command and in their aid and assistance:

. . .

(2) when necessarily committed in overcoming actual resistance to the execution of some legal process or to the discharge of any other legal duty;

(3) when necessarily committed in retaking felons who have been rescued or who have escaped or when necessarily committed in arresting felons fleeing from justice; or

(4) when necessarily committed in order to prevent the escape of a felon from any place of lawful custody or confinement.

B.   For the purposes of this section, homicide is necessarily committed when a public officer or public employee has probable cause to believe he or another is threatened with serious harm or deadly force while performing those lawful duties described in this section. Whenever feasible, a public officer or employee should give warning prior to using deadly force.

Section 30–2–6(B)['s] requirement that a homicide be "necessarily committed" places a limit on the use of deadly force by law enforcement officers in New Mexico that was envisioned in *Garner*.[12]

In remarkably similar language, the *Garner* court stated:

---

12.   While Section 30–2–6 speaks of justifiable homicide, we read it as authorizing the use of deadly force by law enforcement officers whether or not the suspect is ultimately killed. *Graham*, 490 U.S. at 395, 109 S.Ct. 1865 ("All claims that law enforcement officers have used excessive force—deadly or not—in the course of an arrest ... of a free citizen should be analyzed under the Fourth Amendment and its '[objective] reasonableness' standard.") (emphasis omitted).

Thus, if the suspect threatens the officer with a weapon or there is probable cause to believe that he has committed a crime involving the infliction or threatened infliction of serious physical harm, deadly force may be used if necessary to prevent escape, and if, where feasible, some warning has been given.

Garner, 471 U.S. at 11–12, 105 S.Ct. 1694.

Under Section 30–2–6, the crucial consideration is the conduct and dangerousness of the suspect, not the classification of the crime that he or she has committed or is alleged to have committed. It is also apparent, through the inclusion of "probable cause" in Section 30–2–6(B), that the reasonableness of an individual police officer's actions is an objective analysis evaluated from his perspective at the time of the incident and is necessarily a factual inquiry.

We discussed extensively the use of deadly force under Section 30–2–6 in *Johnson,* even though *Johnson* itself involved New Mexico's statute on justifiable homicide by a private citizen, NMSA 1978, § 30–2–7(C) (1963). In *Johnson,* the defendant—a private citizen—shot and killed a man he had observed fleeing from a parking lot where a vehicle had just been burglarized. The defendant never asserted he acted in self-defense. *Johnson,* 1998–NMCA–019, ¶ 2, 124 N.M. 647, 954 P.2d 79. The defendant pled guilty to involuntary manslaughter reserving the right to appeal the district court's refusal to give a justifiable homicide instruction. The instruction would have permitted the jury to consider whether the death of the victim was justified if the defendant was attempting to make a citizen's arrest of a fleeing felon. *Id.* ¶ 3.

This Court upheld the trial judge's denial of the jury instruction on justifiable homicide on the grounds that there was no evidence the defendant could have satisfied the reasonableness standard for use of deadly force by a citizen in the apprehension of a fleeing felon. *Id.* ¶ 28. We noted that the "reasonableness in the use of force is generally, [but not always], a matter for the jury," *id.* ¶ 16, by analogizing the statute in question with Section 30–2–6, and stated that "Defendant's actions, if performed by a police officer, would never be tolerated." *Id.* ¶ 12. We observed that the *Garner* decision had wrought a change in New Mexico law on the use of deadly force, noting that the Supreme Court "required that officers have probable cause to believe that they or others are threatened with serious harm before the use of deadly force could be constitutionally reasonable under the Fourth Amendment." *Johnson,* 1998–NMCA–019, ¶ 8, 124 N.M. 647, 954 P.2d 79.

Similarly, in Archuleta v. LaCuesta, 1999–NMCA–113, 128 N.M. 13, 988 P.2d 883, we discussed the issue of the use of deadly force by police officers in the context of a tort action. The case involved a suit for wrongful death, brought under 42 U.S.C. § 1983 (1994) and the State Tort Claims Act, NMSA 1978, §§ 41–4–1 to–27 (1976 as amended through 2001), by the estate of a domestic violence suspect who was shot and killed by a state police officer. *Archuleta,* 1999–NMCA–113, ¶ 2, 128 N.M. 13, 988 P.2d 883.

In *Archuleta,* this Court stated:

Whether an officer's [use of deadly force] was reasonable is heavily fact dependent. The reasonableness of the use of deadly force in any particular situation is an objective test from the perspective of the officer on the scene, with the understanding that officers must often make split-second decisions in difficult situations about what force is necessary.

Id. ¶ 8 (citations omitted). We held that the "reasonableness" of the force used in the case involved a factual dispute "surrounding the circumstances immediately connected to the shooting which includes passing on the credibility of witnesses," and should therefore be decided by the jury. *Id.* ¶ 14.

The *Johnson* Court's discussion of Section 30–2–6, despite being dicta, and the *Archuleta* Court's announcements on the use of deadly force provide a framework to evaluate the issue presented in this case.

    e. Discussion

The crux of this issue is whether a jury could find that Defendant had probable cause to believe Montoya posed a threat of serious harm or deadly force to him or Sgt. Marquez, and that the use of deadly force was necessary to avert the threat. In order to be entitled to a jury instruction on justifiable homicide, Defendant was required to introduce or identify evidence that would support an argument that he reasonably and objectively believed that Montoya threatened him or Sgt. Marquez with serious physical harm or deadly force. If such evidence was present it was for the jury to decide if Defendant's use of deadly force was reasonable, considering the totality of the circumstances, and therefore constituted justifiable homicide. *See Johnson,* 1998–NMCA–019, ¶ 16, 124 N.M. 647, 954 P.2d 79.

In State v. Lopez, 2000–NMSC–003, ¶ 23, 128 N.M. 410, 993 P.2d 727, (quoting State v. Duarte, 121 N.M. 553, 556, 915 P.2d 309, 312 (Ct.App. 1996)), our Supreme Court clearly stated the standard to be applied by the trial court in ruling whether a request for an instruction on a claim of self-defense or defense of another should be granted. The Court stated:

"[W]here self-defense is involved in a criminal case and there is any evidence, although slight, to establish [such defense], it is not only proper for the court, but its duty as well, to instruct the jury fully and clearly on all phases of the law on [that] issue." ... However, we interpret this standard to require evidence that is "sufficient to allow reasonable minds to differ as to all elements of the defense." We affirm [*State v.*] *Branchal* [101 N.M. 498, 684 P.2d 1163 (Ct.App.1984)]: a self defense instruction is required "whenever a defendant presents evidence sufficient to allow reasonable minds to differ as to all elements of the defense."

Id. (citations omitted). This is also the standard that should be applied when determining if the jury should be instructed on justifiable homicide by a police officer in accordance with Section 30–2–6. We also note that the identity of the party introducing the evidence, Defendant or the State, is irrelevant. *Akin,* 75 N.M. at 310, 404 P.2d at 136; *Heisler,* 58 N.M. at 454, 272 P.2d at 665. What is important is that the evidence was presented to the jury.

Defendant, a commissioned police officer on duty for the LVPD, was pursuing Montoya with Sgt. Marquez. The prosecution's case, as discussed above, was premised on the theory that Montoya was fleeing the scene in order to evade capture. In fact, the State's closing argument began with the assertion that "[w]e do not shoot at a fleeing suspect" because to do so would be against the law. The State argued that if the physical evidence showed Montoya was not in the process of backing up the Toyota in the direction of Defendant and Sgt. Marquez at the time of the shooting, the jury must convict because under such a scenario Defendant could not have acted in self-defense or defense of another. The State characterized Defendant's theory of self-defense and defense of another as a "backward attack theory" which was not supported by the physical evidence that suggested that Montoya had cleared the rock wall and had begun to flee down Chavez Street.

Defendant testified that, upon arrival at the intersection of Valley and Chavez Streets, he positioned his police cruiser to execute a "felony stop." He also testified that the Toyota truck began to accelerate in reverse toward the officers and that there was an impact between the two vehicles.

Defendant testified that he was shocked and scared by the driver's actions. Defendant then testified that he drew his weapon, ran up to the side of the truck on the driver's side door, planning to pull the driver out of the truck. Sgt. Marquez instructed Defendant to "stop him, stop him" multiple times. Defendant testified that during this time he lost sight of Sgt. Marquez and that he thought Marquez had exited the police cruiser, had been knocked down and possibly run over and killed or injured. In response, standing an arm's length away from the truck, Defendant testified he fired one round into the truck. After he fired the first round, believing that the truck was coming back to ram them again, he testified he fired two more rounds into the back of the truck. Sgt. Marquez also fired a single shot at the truck.

Defendant testified his belief at the time was that the truck was being used as a deadly weapon to attack him and Sgt. Marquez, that their lives were in danger, and that he was therefore justified in using deadly force. He also testified that his training taught him to use deadly force if necessary in this situation. Sgt. Marquez testified similarly.

Tom Gillespie testified on behalf of Defendant and was qualified as an expert witness in the area of police training, procedures, and the use of deadly force. Mr. Gillespie testified that Defendant's actions in firing his weapon to stop the alleged attack was consistent with his training and the policies and procedures of the LVPD. He also opined that the ramming of the police cruiser by Montoya constituted an aggravated battery on the police officers, a felony under New Mexico law. NMSA 1978, § 30–22–25 (1971).

We hold that Defendant submitted sufficient evidence to warrant a jury instruction on justifiable homicide by a police officer. A reasonable jury, if it believed Defendant's version of the facts, could have concluded that Defendant was justified in using deadly force to protect himself and his partner. It is important to note that this entire incident began and ended very rapidly and the testimony contains many factual disputes that turn on the credibility accorded the witnesses. In our view, the reasonableness of Defendant's actions in using deadly force was for the jury to decide under instructions reflecting the provision of Section 30–2–6(B). *Archuleta,* 1999 NMCA 113, ¶ 14, 128 N.M. 13, 988 P.2d 883.

The State reminds us that the jury was given UJI 14–5171, the general self-defense instruction and argues that it adequately addressed Defendant's concerns, so that refusing the justifiable homicide instruction was harmless error. We believe that Section 30–2–6(B) is intended to provide police officers a wider scope of privilege than the general public with regard to the use of deadly force. *Garner* and Section 30–2–6(B) do not work to make police officer justifiable homicide equal to or indistinguishable from normal self-defense. As detailed in Section 30–2–6(A), a police officer may be legally justified in using deadly force in a variety of situations that would not apply to self-defense and the ordinary citizen. Police officer justifiable homicide is sufficiently different from self-defense or defense of others that giving UJI 14–5171 does not render harmless the refusal to give Defendant's instruction.

To support an instruction on ordinary self-defense, there must be evidence that defendant was put in fear by an apparent danger of immediate death or great bodily harm, that the killing resulted from that fear, and that defendant acted as a reasonable person would act under those circumstances. UJI 14–5171. The requirement for the immediacy of the threat that is necessary for self-defense or defense of others does not appear in Section 30–2–6. Further, Section 30–2–6(B) states that the public officer may use deadly force if he has "probable cause to believe he or another is threatened with serious harm" and differs from the requirement under UJI 14–5171 that an individual face "apparent danger of immediate death or great bodily harm." It is unclear how temporally proximate and severe the suspect's threatening actions must be to justify the use of deadly force by a police officer. And, as previously stated, this factual and situational inquiry explores the definition of "reasonableness" under the Fourth Amendment and is generally, but not always, a matter for the jury. *Johnson,* 1998–NMCA–019, ¶ 16, 124 N.M. 647, 954 P.2d 79.

For example, one could foresee situations in which a police officer, even though not himself in immediate danger, might be justified in using deadly force to prevent a dangerous felon from evading capture and threatening serious harm to others outside the immediate scope of activity. A police officer shoulders that responsibility as part of his duty to protect the public. A private citizen's privilege, on the other hand, would be more narrowly contained to the immediate threat posed to the citizen and others in the immediate vicinity. This is one way in which the ordinary self-defense instruction simply does not convey the breadth of the use-of-deadly-force privilege that accompanies a police officer.

Another example lies in Instruction 17 given by the Court at the request of the State. It states,

Self-defense is not available to the defendant if he was the aggressor unless;

(1) The defendant was using force which would not ordinarily create a substantial risk of death or great bodily harm; and

(2) Abelino Montoya responded with force which would ordinarily create a substantial risk of death or great bodily harm.

Private citizens ordinarily may not be the aggressor and then claim self-defense. Police officers, however, sometimes may have a lawful duty to be aggressors in the course of fulfilling their responsibilities to the public. It very much depends on the facts and circumstances of a given case. Instruction 17, while appropriate to ordinary self-defense, creates a fatal inconsistency as applied to the privilege of police officers. That is one more reason why the instruction on self-defense falls short of defining the privilege available under law to police officers.

Given these differences, we find it curious that the trial court could conclude that there was sufficient evidence to support a jury instruction on self-defense and defense of another, with its heightened requirements that the danger being threatened be grievous and immediate, but not enough to support an instruction on justifiable homicide. To the contrary, there may be situations of justifiable homicide applicable to a police officer that would not fit comfortably within the confines of ordinary self-defense and defense of another as applied to the public at large.

We recognize that in this particular case the *only* harm allegedly threatened to Defendant and his partner was "immediate." That is, Defendant was not claiming a privilege to use deadly force to defend against any later, non-immediate threat. Thus, it might be argued that in this particular case the justifiable homicide instruction, as applied, was no broader than the ordinary self-defense instruction.

We are not persuaded, however, that the error in rejecting Defendant's instruction can be so easily explained away. Either expressly or tacitly, rejection of the justifiable homicide instruction stripped Defendant of a defense uniquely applicable to police officers and others similarly situated. That rejection placed Defendant in the smaller shoes of an ordinary citizen. Yet the circumstances in which Defendant found himself and which provoked his shooting of Montoya, were anything but the circumstances of an ordinary citizen.

Whether reversal is required is a close question. The error was preserved and the Court as a whole agrees that there is evidence supporting the justifiable homicide instruction. Thus, Defendant was entitled to the instruction. State v. Rubio, 1999–NMCA–018, ¶ 18, 126 N.M. 579, 973 P.2d 256. There is also an arguable view of the evidence which supports the argument that in this particular case the correct instruction would not add anything material to the defense. However, we cannot say as a matter of law that the evidence could not support a jury finding of justifiable homicide. *See* State v. Orosco, 113 N.M. 780, 783–84, 833 P.2d 1146, 1149–51 (1992) (failing to instruct on an element of a case is not reversible error if there was no dispute that the element was established by the evidence). Thus, we cannot say the error was harmless beyond a reasonable doubt. *Cf.* State v. Pettigrew, 116 N.M. 135, 142, 860 P.2d 777, 784 (Ct.App.1993) (even constitutional error does not require reversal if it was harmless beyond a reasonable doubt). In such close circumstances, where the error involves the central issue in the case, it is the better policy to require a new trial under the correct instruction. Requiring a new trial obviates any need or opportunity for us to speculate as to how the jury might have resolved— or will resolve—the case under the correct instruction. Reversal also honors prior authorities requiring reversal for error in jury instructions where there is the slightest evidence of prejudice. Kennedy v. Dexter Consol. Sch., 2000–NMSC–025, ¶ 27, 129 N.M. 436, 10 P.3d 115; Bachicha v. Lewis, 105 N.M. 726, 729, 737 P.2d 85, 88 (Ct.App.1987).

In reaching our conclusion, we do not retreat from our holding in *Johnson*. In *Johnson*, the defendant submitted no evidence that he acted in self-defense or that he or anyone else was in any way physically threatened by the victim in that case. The circumstances in *Johnson* would not have supported an instruction on justifiable homicide if the shooting had been done by a police officer. *Id.* ¶ 2. Defendant has presented evidence that at a certain point the suspect presented a real threat to him and others. Whether that threat had dissipated sufficiently by the time he fired the fatal rounds to make his use of deadly force unreasonable was for the jury to decide.

Finally, we note that UJI 14–5173 has not been modified to meet the requirements of Section 30–2–6(B) as amended in 1989, and does not reflect the current law of New Mexico on justifiable homicide by a public officer or public employee. State v. Wilson, 116 N.M. 793, 796, 867 P.2d 1175, 1178 (1994) (holding that this Court "has authority to question uniform jury instructions" that have been adopted by the Supreme Court, and may "amend, modify, or abolish [an erroneous] instruction" if the instruction has not been previously challenged). As a service to the bar and a suggestion to the parties, UJI 14–5173 could be modified as follows:

14–5173.   Justifiable homicide; public officer or employee.

Evidence has been presented that the killing of _____ (name of victim) was justifiable homicide. A homicide is justifiable when it is necessarily committed by a public officer or public employee while

[overcoming the actual resistance of _____ (name of victim) to the execution of _____ (describe legal process)]

[overcoming the actual resistance of _____ (name of victim) to the discharge of _____ (describe other legal duty)]

[retaking _____ (name of victim) (name of person), who committed _____ (name felony) and who had (been rescued) (escaped)]

[arresting _____ (name of victim) (name of person) who committed _____ (name felony) and was fleeing from justice]

[attempting to prevent the escape from _____ (name place of lawful custody or confinement) by _____ (name of victim) (name of person) who committed _____ (name felony)].

Homicide is necessarily committed when a public officer or public employee has probable cause to believe he or another is threatened with serious harm or deadly force while performing those lawful duties described above. For there to be probable cause, the facts must be such as would warrant a belief by a reasonable officer based upon the expertise and experience of the officer. [When feasible, a public officer or employee should give warning prior to using deadly force.]

The burden is on the state to prove beyond a reasonable doubt that the killing was not justifiable. If you have reasonable doubt as to whether the killing was justifiable, you must find the defendant not guilty.

■ WECHSLER, JUDGE (concurring in part and dissenting in part).

I agree that there is a view of the evidence such that Defendant could construct a defense of justifiable homicide. However, I do not believe that a jury instruction on justifiable homicide would have made a material difference in this case. With that belief, I respectfully dissent from the majority's holding reversing and remanding for a new trial on the voluntary manslaughter and aggravated assault with a deadly weapon charges....

Defendant fairly raised the question of whether he acted to protect Sergeant Marquez or himself. He testified at trial that he placed his car in a position to block Mr. Montoya's truck so that he could execute a "felony-stop." He was very clear in his testimony that the truck reversed twice toward his car. He testified that he believed that the truck was coming back to hit him once again when he fired his second and third shots to the back of the truck. He was specific in his testimony that he believed at the time that Mr. Montoya was attacking both Sergeant Marquez and him with the truck such that his use of deadly force was justified. Sergeant Marquez testified that he fell out of the car as the truck pushed the car backward. He said that he saw the truck's tires coming at him and he fired because he feared his life was in danger.

Defendant's testimony supported instructions on self-defense and defense of another, which the jury received. With these instructions, the jury was instructed that if Defendant believed that he or Sergeant Marquez was in immediate danger of death or great bodily harm, and that Defendant shot Mr. Montoya to prevent the death or great bodily harm and acted as a reasonable person in the same circumstances would have, the jury should find Defendant not guilty. UJI 14–5171, UJI 14–5172 NMRA 2001. Defendant does not contend that there is any significant difference in this case between these requirements and the requirements of justifiable homicide that an officer have probable cause to believe the officer or another is threatened with serious harm or deadly force. Faced squarely with this determination, the jury concluded that Defendant did not act in self-defense or defense of another.

I agree with the majority that the defense of justifiable homicide is broader in the general sense than self-defense or defense of another. It is uniquely available to law enforcement officers who may have to be aggressors in their protection of the public and whom we do not want to handicap in the performance of their lawful duties.

As the majority points out, a justifiable homicide defense embraces more than the immediate situation addressed by self-defense or defense of another. In justifiable homicide, an officer may indeed use deadly force to prevent the escape of a fleeing felon who is a threat of serious harm or deadly force to other persons who are not at the flight scene. But, most significantly, there were no material issues of such threats of harm in this case. Defendant testified that he acted to prevent the immediate harm to himself or Sergeant Marquez. Tom Gillespie, who testified on Defendant's behalf as an expert on police training, procedure, and the use of force, presented testimony that Defendant acted in accordance with his training when Defendant thought the truck was going to come back to him. But, Mr. Gillespie did not testify that the circumstances justified the use of deadly force to avoid harm to unidentified persons or any person other than Defendant or Sergeant Marquez. Thus, although I agree that the defense of justifiable homicide could, under certain circumstances, permit the use of deadly force for the protection of the public even if an officer was not acting under an immediate threat of harm that could justify self-defense or defense of another, such issues were not material ones in this case. . . .

MODEL PENAL CODE

Section 2.10   Military Orders.

It is an affirmative defense that the actor, in engaging in the conduct charged to constitute an offense, does no more than execute an order of his superior in the armed services which he does not know to be unlawful.

Section 3.03   Execution of Public Duty.

(1) Except as provided in Subsection (2) of this Section, conduct is justifiable when it is required or authorized by:

(a) the law defining the duties or functions of a public officer or the assistance to be rendered to such officer in the performance of his duties; or

(b) the law governing the execution of legal process; or

(c) the judgment or order of a competent court or tribunal; or

(d) the law governing the armed services or the lawful conduct of war; or

(e) any other provision of law imposing a public duty.

(2) The other sections of this Article apply to:

(a) the use of force upon or toward the person of another for any of the purposes dealt with in such sections; and

(b) the use of deadly force for any purpose, unless the use of such force is otherwise expressly authorized by law or occurs in the lawful conduct of war.

(3) The justification afforded by Subsection (1) of this Section applies:

(a) when the actor believes his conduct to be required or authorized by the judgment or direction of a competent court or tribunal or in the lawful execution of legal process, notwithstanding lack of jurisdiction of the court or defect in the legal process; and

(b) when the actor believes his conduct to be required or authorized to assist a public officer in the performance of his duties, notwithstanding that the officer exceeded his legal authority.

Section 3.07   Use of Force in Law Enforcement.

(1) Use of Force Justifiable to Effect an Arrest. Subject to the provisions of this Section and of Section 3.09, the use of force upon or toward the person of another is justifiable when the actor is making or assisting in making an arrest and the actor believes that such force is immediately necessary to effect a lawful arrest.

(2) Limitations on the Use of Force.

(a) The use of force is not justifiable under this Section unless:

(i) the actor makes known the purpose of the arrest or believes that it is otherwise known by or cannot reasonably be made known to the person to be arrested; and

(ii) when the arrest is made under a warrant, the warrant is valid or believed by the actor to be valid.

(b) The use of deadly force is not justifiable under this Section unless:

(i) the arrest is for a felony; and

(ii) the person effecting the arrest is authorized to act as a peace officer or is assisting a person whom he believes to be authorized to act as a peace officer; and

(iii) the actor believes that the force employed creates no substantial risk of injury to innocent persons; and

(iv) the actor believes that:

(1) the crime for which the arrest is made involved conduct including the use or threatened use of deadly force; or

(2) there is a substantial risk that the person to be arrested will cause death or serious bodily harm if his apprehension is delayed.

(3) Use of Force to Prevent Escape from Custody. The use of force to prevent the escape of an arrested person from custody is justifiable when the force could justifiably have been employed to effect the arrest under which the person is in custody, except that a guard or other person authorized to act as a peace officer is justified in using any force, including deadly force, which he believes to be immediately necessary to prevent the escape of a person from a jail, prison, or other institution for the detention of persons charged with or convicted of a crime.

(4) Use of Force by Private Person Assisting an Unlawful Arrest.

(a) A private person who is summoned by a peace officer to assist in effecting an unlawful arrest, is justified in using any force which he would be justified in using if the arrest were lawful, provided that he does not believe the arrest is unlawful.

(b) A private person who assists another private person in effecting an unlawful arrest, or who, not being summoned, assists a peace officer in effecting an unlawful arrest, is justified in using any force which he would be justified in using if the arrest were lawful, provided that (i) he believes the arrest is lawful, and (ii) the arrest would be lawful if the facts were as he believes them to be.

Section 3.09 Mistake of Law as to Unlawfulness of Force or Legality of Arrest; Reckless or Negligent Use of Otherwise Justifiable Force; Reckless or Negligent Injury or Risk of Injury to Innocent Persons.

(1) The justification afforded by Sections 3.04 to 3.07, inclusive, is unavailable when:

(a) the actor's belief in the unlawfulness of the force or conduct against which he employs protective force or his belief in the lawfulness of an arrest which he endeavors to effect by force is erroneous; and

(b) his error is due to ignorance or mistake as to the provisions of the Code, any other provision of the criminal law or the law governing the legality of an arrest or search.

(2) When the actor believes that the use of force upon or toward the person of another is necessary for any of the purposes for which such belief would establish a

justification under Sections 3.03 to 3.08 but the actor is reckless or negligent in having such belief or in acquiring or failing to acquire any knowledge or belief which is material to the justifiability of his use of force, the justification afforded by those Sections is unavailable in a prosecution for an offense for which recklessness or negligence, as the case may be, suffices to establish culpability.

(3) When the actor is justified under Sections 3.03 to 3.08 in using force upon or toward the person of another but he recklessly or negligently injures or creates a risk of injury to innocent persons, the justification afforded by those Sections is unavailable in a prosecution for such recklessness or negligence towards innocent persons.[13]

SECTION 2. DOMESTIC AUTHORITY

References may be found to an ancient authority of a husband to chastise his wife[14] with a "whip or rattan no bigger than my thumb, in order to inforce the salutary restraints of domestic discipline."[15] This was doubted in Blackstone's time,[16] and is definitely not recognized in the modern common law. Hence a husband who strikes his wife, even to enforce obedience to his commands, is guilty of battery,[17] and most states now have domestic abuse statutes prohibiting domestic violence.[18] Spouse beating is frequently made punishable by express statutory provision and there are many special statutes which address various forms of domestic abuse.[19]

Firmly recognized in the law, however, is the right of the parent to discipline his minor child by means of moderate chastisement.[20] The right to correct an adopted child is the same as the right of a natural parent in this regard;[21] and this authority has been extended even to one who has taken a child into one's home to be brought up as a member of the family without formal adoption.[22] Similarly, a guardian may lawfully administer moderate chastisement for the correction of a ward.[23]

The common law authorized a master to punish an apprentice in the same manner; but true apprenticeship is a special relation. An employer has no authority to administer corporal punishment to a servant merely

---

13. Copyright © 1962 by the American Law Institute. Reprinted with the permission of the American Law Institute.

14. "They refuse to bind him to keep the peace at her suit unless her life be in danger, because by the law he hath the power of castigation; . . ." Bradley v. His Wife, 1 Keb. 637, 83 Eng.Rep. 1157 (1663).

15. Bradley v. State, Walker 156, 157 (Miss.1824).

16. 1 Bl.Comm. 444–5.

17. Fulgham v. State, 46 Ala. 143 (1871).

18. Cal. Family Code § 6200, etc., specifically § 6211.

19. West's Ann.Cal.Pen.Code, § 273.5 (1997); Mass.Gen.Laws Ann., c. 208 § 34c (1978).

20. State v. Russell, 69 Wash.App. 237, 848 P.2d 743 (1993); Richardson v. State Board, 98 N.J.L. 690, 121 A. 457 (1923); People v. Taggart, 621 P.2d 1375 (Colo.1981).

21. State v. Koonse, 123 Mo.App. 655, 101 S.W. 139 (1907).

22. See the instruction in State v. Gillett, 56 Iowa 459, 9 N.W. 362 (1881).

23. Stanfield v. State, 43 Tex. 167 (1875).

because the particular employee happens to be a minor.[24] The parent's authority to punish a minor child may be delegated to an employer or teacher; but the employer has no such privilege unless he has received permission from the parent.[25] A school teacher, unless prohibited by statute, ordinance, or rule, may use reasonable force to maintain discipline of a student.

"By law as well as immemorial usage, a schoolmaster is regarded as standing in loco parentis, and, like the parent, has the authority to moderately chastise pupils under his care."[26] A statute, ordinance, or school-board regulation may restrict the privilege of the teacher in this regard, or may forbid the teacher to resort to corporal punishment in any form, but in the absence of such restriction the ordinary corporal punishment of a pupil, for wilful disobedience of lawful rules, is not an assault and battery by the teacher, if administered for discipline and not in anger or with undue severity.[27]

The authority of a parent or teacher to punish a child will not justify immoderate punishment, and any excess of this nature will constitute an assault and battery or a violation of civil rights;[28] but the test of unreasonableness in this regard should be found, not in some slight error of judgment as to the force to be used, but in the substitution of a malicious desire to inflict pain in place of a genuine effort to correct the child by proper means.[29]

Those in charge of airplanes, trains, boats, theaters, stadia and similar places, while without authority to punish members of the public for misbehavior, may use reasonable and moderate force to expel a person who refuses to pay a fare or admission,[30] or is guilty of serious misconduct even after he has paid. But even one with authority to remove such a person will be guilty of assault and battery if he does so improperly as by ejecting a passenger from a moving vehicle.[31]

Cleary v. Booth

Queen's Bench Division, 1893.
[1893] 1 Q.B. 465.

■ LAWRENCE, J. The question in this case is not an easy one; there is no authority, and it is a case of first impression. The question for us is

---

24. Tinkle v. Dunivant, 84 Tenn. 503 (1886). "The rule obtaining in this state is that a master has no authority to chastise his servant, no matter how flagrant his violation of duty may be." Cook v. Cook, 232 Mo.App. 994, 996, 124 S.W.2d 675, 676 (1939).

25. Cooper v. State, 67 Tenn. 324 (1874).

26. Roberson v. State, 22 Ala.App. 413, 414, 116 So. 317, 318 (1928). See discussion Ingraham v. Wright, 430 U.S. 651, 664, 97 S.Ct. 1401, 1408–1409, 51 L.Ed.2d 711 (1977).

27. Danenhoffer v. State, 69 Ind. 295 (1879).

28. State v. Mizner, 50 Iowa 145 (1878); Clasen v. Pruhs, 69 Neb. 278, 95 N.W. 640 (1903); Garcia by Garcia v. Miera, 817 F.2d 650 (10th Cir.1987).

29. See Boyd v. State, 88 Ala. 169, 172, 7 So. 268, 269 (1890).

30. Carpenter v. Washington & G.R. Co., 121 U.S. 474, 7 S.Ct. 1002, 30 L.Ed. 1015 (1887).

31. State v. Kinney, 34 Minn. 311, 25 N.W. 705 (1885).

whether the head master of a board school is justified in inflicting corporal punishment upon one of his scholars for an act done outside the limits of the school, and the appellant's counsel has in his argument relied on what might happen if a boy were not punished by the master for such acts. The facts seem to be that a boy while coming to the appellant's school was assaulted by another boy belonging to the same school; that complaint was made to the appellant, who then and there punished the boy who had committed the assault and also the respondent, who was in his company. The first observation that occurs to one to make is that one of the greatest advantages of any punishment is that it should follow quickly on the offence. The cases cited to us shew that the schoolmaster is in the position of the parent. What is to become of a boy between his school and his home? Is he not under the authority of his parent or of the schoolmaster? It cannot be doubted that he is; and in my opinion among the powers delegated by the parent to the schoolmaster, such a power as was exercised by the appellant in this case would be freely delegated. If we turn to the Code we find that there are several things for which a grant may be given, including discipline and organization, and that the children are to be brought up in habits of good manners and language, and of consideration for others. Can it be reasonably argued that the only right of a schoolmaster to inflict punishment is in respect of acts done in the school, and that it is only while the boys are there that he is to see that they are well-mannered, but that he has exceeded all the authority delegated to him by the parent if he punishes a boy who within a yard of the school is guilty of gross misbehaviour? It is difficult to express in words the extent of the schoolmaster's authority in respect to the punishment of his pupils; but in my opinion his authority extends, not only to acts done in school, but also to cases where a complaint of acts done out of school, at any rate while going to and from school, is made to the schoolmaster. In the present case I think that weight may properly be placed on the fact that the act for which the boy was punished was done to another pupil of the same school. I think, therefore, that the justices were wrong in convicting the appellant as they did, and that the case must be sent back to them to find as a fact whether the punishment was excessive.

■ Collins, J. I am of the same opinion. It is clear law that a father has the right to inflict reasonable personal chastisement on his son. It is equally the law, and it is in accordance with very ancient practice, that he may delegate this right to the schoolmaster. Such a right has always commended itself to the common sense of mankind. It is clear that the relation of master and pupil carries with it the right of reasonable corporal chastisement. As a matter of common sense, how far is this power delegated by the parent to the schoolmaster? Is it limited to the time during which the boy is within the four walls of the school, or does it extend in any sense beyond that limit? In my opinion the purpose with which the parental authority is delegated to the schoolmaster, who is entrusted with the bringing up and discipline of the child, must to some extent include an authority over the child while he is outside the four walls. It may be a question of fact in each case whether the conduct of the master in inflicting corporal punishment is right. Very grave consequences would result if it were held that the parent's authority was exclusive up to the door of the school, and that then, and only then, the master's authority commenced; it would be a most anomalous result to hold that in such a case as the present the boy who had been assaulted had no remedy by complaint to his master, who could punish the assailant by a thrashing, but must go before the magistrate to enforce a remedy between them as citizens. Not only would such a position be unworkable in itself, but the Code, which has the force of an Act of Parliament, clearly contemplates that the duties of the master to his pupils are not limited to teaching. A grant may be made for discipline and organization, and it is clear that he is entrusted with the moral training and conduct of his pupils. It cannot be that such a duty or power ceases the moment that the pupil leaves school for home; There is not much opportunity for a boy to exhibit his moral conduct while in school under the eye of the master: the opportunity is while he is at play or outside the school; and if the schoolmaster has no control over the boys in their relation to each other except when they are within the school walls, this object of the Code would be defeated. In such a case as the present, it is obvious that the desired impression is best brought about by a summary and immediate punishment. In my opinion parents do contemplate such an exercise of authority by the schoolmaster. I should be sorry if I felt myself driven to come to the opposite conclusion, and am glad to be able to say that the principle shews that the authority delegated to the schoolmaster is not limited to the four walls of the school. It is always a question of fact whether the act was done outside the delegated authority; but in the present case I am satisfied, on the facts, that it was obviously within it. The question of excess is one for the magistrates.

State v. Crouser

Supreme Court of Hawaii, 1996.
81 Hawai'i 5, 911 P.2d 725.

■ Moon, Chief Justice.

Following a bench trial, defendant-appellant Delbert L. Crouser was convicted of abuse of a family and household member, in violation of Hawai'i Revised Statutes (HRS) § 709–906 (1993). On appeal, Crouser contends that: (1) the court's finding that his conduct was not justified under HRS § 703–309 (1993)[32] is clearly erroneous; (2) there was insufficient evidence to support the conviction; . . .

---

32. HRS § 703–309 provides in relevant part that:

The use of force upon or toward the person of another is justifiable under the following circumstances:

(1) The actor is the parent or guardian or other person similarly responsible for the general care and supervision of a minor, or a person acting at the request of the parent, guardian, or other responsible person, and:

(a) The force is employed with due regard for the age and size of the minor and is reasonably related to the purpose of safeguarding or promoting the welfare of the minor, including the prevention or punishment of the minor's misconduct; and

(b) The force used is not designed to cause or known to create a risk of causing substantial bodily injury, disfigurement, extreme pain or mental distress, or neurological damage.

I. BACKGROUND

In May 1993, the victim, a fourteen-year-old special education student at Kealakehe Intermediate School (Minor), moved from her father's home into the home of her mother and her mother's boyfriend, Crouser. By all accounts, Minor was prone to untruths. Her school counselor, the school health aide, and her foster mother characterized Minor as a pleasant, cooperative girl, who would sometimes make up stories to get attention, or lie to agree with adults and not make waves, but never to hurt others.

Minor was required by her mother and Crouser to bring home a daily progress report signed by her teachers. On May 19, 1993, Minor forgot to pick up the report from her counselor for her teachers to sign. She therefore filled the report out herself, changing some of the grades and her attendance record. Minor testified that she changed her perfect attendance record to reflect some absences because she believed that Crouser would not believe the reported perfect attendance and that Crouser would therefore discipline her for lying.

Crouser somehow learned that Minor had made changes to the report and went to Minor's room, where she was doing her homework. Minor testified that Crouser called her a liar and hit her across both sides of her face, knocking her to the floor. As she was trying to get up, Crouser grabbed her and threw her face down on the bed. According to Minor's testimony, Crouser put his knee on Minor's back, pulled her pants and underwear down to her knees, and started "whacking" her bare buttocks. When Crouser left the room, Minor pulled up her underwear and pants, but Crouser returned with a plastic bat and closed the door. He again pulled down Minor's pants and underwear and struck her with the bat on the buttocks, arm, thighs, and torso until the bat broke. Minor could not remember the number of times that she had been struck, but testified that the incident lasted approximately thirty minutes. Although Minor testified on direct examination that her mother was not home at the time, she admitted on cross-examination that her mother could have been home, but Minor had not seen her. Minor opined that, if her mother had been home at the time, her mother would have "do[ne] something." After being disciplined, Minor had a hard time sitting and felt dizzy for an hour or so. Minor testified that her bottom hurt for a couple of weeks after the incident. She also testified that, while in school on the day following the incident, she could not sit on the hard student chairs, that one of her teachers let her use the padded teacher's chair, and that, in her other classes, she just stood.

On the day following the incident, May 20, 1993, Minor was sent by a teacher to the office of the school health aide, Shirley Yamaguchi, because she complained of being unable to sit down. Yamaguchi observed that Minor waddled stiffly as though she was in extreme pain, was very emotional, and was unable to sit at the desk, where she customarily talked with students. Minor told Yamaguchi that she got a spanking from her "stepfather," Crouser, because of her grades. Yamaguchi called the school counselor, Diane McCary, into the office, and Yamaguchi and McCary observed that Minor's buttocks were bruised and colored a deep reddish-purple. They also observed bruising to Minor's arm, thigh, and torso, which

Minor explained had occurred when she was moving around to try to block the blows from the bat. . . . [Yamaguchi] further testified that, when Minor began describing what had happened to her, she cried uncontrollably, "a deep sobbing hurt kind of cry like a cry that's been held in for a while." At trial, McCary similarly testified.

Marilyn Hagoes . . . testified that she interviewed Crouser on May 27, 1993. She showed Crouser the photographs of Minor and asked him how the bruising got there. According to Hagoes, Crouser told her that he "worked [Minor's] butt," explaining that he hit her about twenty-five times on the buttocks, mostly with his hand and some with a plastic bat. Crouser also advised Hagoes that he wanted to make it hard for her to sit down, but, when asked about the bruising to Minor's arm, torso, and leg, Crouser stated that those bruises were self-inflicted. Hagoes also testified that, in her ten years of experience, she had never seen such extensive bruising in a parental discipline case and that she considered the discipline excessive and not reasonably related to the purpose of safeguarding or promoting the welfare of a minor, including the punishment of misconduct.

. . .

The prosecution also elicited testimony from Detective Bradley Ballesteros, Sr., who testified that he had interviewed Crouser on May 28, 1993. According to Ballesteros, Crouser admitted that the photos of Minor's injuries looked "pretty serious" but that he did not feel that he had gone beyond reasonable discipline, and the incident had been blown out of proportion.

Attorney Darl Gleed, guardian *ad litem* for Minor in family court, testified that Crouser had told him, prior to a court hearing, that Minor's punishment was twenty-five swats on one side of her buttocks and thirty-five on the other. According to Gleed, Crouser later clarified his statement by saying that he only spanked Minor twenty-five times on one side, leaving the other side untouched so that she could sit down, and meant to get around to the other thirty-five swats later.

. . .

The only witness called by the defense was Minor's mother (Mother). Mother testified that she had arrived home from work early on the afternoon of May 19, 1993 and was sitting about fifteen feet from Minor's room on an outside deck, with a clear view of the incident. She testified that Crouser did not hit Minor in the face and that Minor was not knocked to the floor. According to Mother, Minor got on the bed herself. She admitted that Crouser spanked Minor, but testified that he did not remove Minor's pants or put his knee into her back. She also testified that Crouser spanked only the right side of Minor's buttocks, but not excessively, and, if it had been excessive, that she "would have stopped it immediately." In Mother's view, "[Crouser] wasn't using any force on Minor that day." When shown the prosecution's exhibits depicting the extensive bruising of Minor's buttocks, Mother testified that she did not think that Crouser's spanking of Minor caused the bruises.

. . .

II. DISCUSSION

1. *The trial court's conclusion was not clearly erroneous.*

Crouser argues that the trial court clearly erred in finding that the force used was not reasonably related to the purpose of safeguarding or promoting Minor's welfare, including the prevention or punishment of her misconduct, and that the use of force was designed to cause or known to create the risk of causing substantial bodily injury, extreme pain or mental distress. . . .

Crouser was charged with abuse of a family or household member, in violation of HRS § 709–906. His conviction required proof beyond a reasonable doubt of each of the following three elements: (1) that he physically abused Minor; (2) that he did so intentionally, knowingly or recklessly;[33] and (3) that Minor was a present or former family or household member of Crouser's. To invoke the defense of justification under HRS § 703–309, Crouser was required to make a showing that the record contained evidence supporting the following elements: (1) he was a parent, guardian, or other person as described in HRS § 703–309(1); (2) he used force against a minor for whose care and supervision he was responsible; (3) his use of force was with due regard to the age and size of the recipient and reasonably related to the purpose of safeguarding or promoting the welfare of the minor, including the prevention or punishment of misconduct; and (4) the force used was not designed to cause, or known to create a risk of causing, substantial bodily injury, disfigurement, extreme pain or mental distress, or neurological damage. In turn, the prosecution had the burden of disproving beyond a reasonable doubt the justification evidence that was adduced, or proving beyond a reasonable doubt facts negativing the justification defense. *Id.* at 350, 841 P.2d at 1079. Because the requirements of HRS § 703–309(1) are set out in the conjunctive, rather than the disjunctive, the prosecution needed only to disprove one element beyond a reasonable doubt to defeat the justification defense.

a. **The use of force was not reasonably related to the purpose of safeguarding Minor's welfare.**

As previously indicated, the trial court found that

the State has proven each element of the charge beyond a reasonable doubt and has proven beyond a reasonable doubt that the force used was not reasonably related to the purpose of safeguarding the welfare of the minor and it was designed to cause or known to create a risk of causing substantial bodily injury or mental distress.

. . . Crouser argues that the family court's conclusion that his use of force was not reasonably related to the purpose of safeguarding or promoting Minor's welfare was clearly erroneous. . . .

Crouser claims that . . . there is no evidence in the present case that his use of force was for any other purpose than punishment. . . . In 1992

---

33. HRS § 709–906 does not specify the requisite state of mind for the commission of the offense. HRS § 702–204 (1993), however, provides in relevant part that, "[w]hen the state of mind required to establish an element of an offense is not specified by the law, that element is established if, with respect thereto, a person acts intentionally, knowingly, or recklessly."

... the statute was amended to require that, "[i]n determining whether or not the level of force used is permitted under law, a court must consider the age and size of the recipient and whether a reasonable relationship exists between the force used and a legitimate purpose as specified in the statute."

Crouser contends that the amendment "liberalized the purpose requirement." According to Crouser, "[i]nstead of requiring that the force used [be] for punishment, the 1992 amendment only requires that the force used [be] reasonably related to the purpose of punishment." Therefore, he argues, the court's conclusion that Crouser's use of force was not reasonably related to protecting Minor's welfare was clearly erroneous. Crouser's interpretation of the effect of the amendment is specious.

HRS § 703–309(1) (1985) was adopted verbatim from section 3.08(1) of the Model Penal Code, the commentary [states]:

The formulation is in some respects less stringent than that in Section 147 of the Restatement of Torts, which speaks of "such reasonable force" and "such reasonable confinement" as the parent "reasonably believes to be necessary for" the "proper control, training, or education" of the child....[34]

The formulation also differs from the Restatement in not explicitly demanding that the force be reasonable. It was believed that so long as a parent uses moderate force for permissible purposes, the criminal law should not provide for review of the reasonableness of the parent's judgment.

The 1992 amendments significantly altered this formulation. It is no longer enough that the use of force be for the purpose of discipline; it must be reasonably related to that purpose. The present version of HRS § 703–309(1) ... provides for objective review of the parent's judgment, bringing the statute much closer to the formulation found in the Restatement (Second) of Torts § 147 and that used by a substantial majority of other jurisdictions. See Annotation, Criminal Liability for Excessive or Improper Punishment Inflicted on Child by Parent, Teacher, or One in Loco Parentis, 89 A.L.R.2d 396 (1963 & Supp.1995).

Although we have found no other statute employing the identical language, it seems clear that to be "reasonably related" to the purpose of punishing misconduct, use of force must be both reasonably proportional to the misconduct being punished and reasonably believed necessary to protect the welfare of the recipient. Subsection (b) of HRS § 703–309(1) defines the maximum degree of force that is justifiable under the statute.

---

34. Restatement (Second) of Torts § 147 (1965) provides that:

(1) A parent is privileged to apply such reasonable force or to impose such reasonable confinement upon his child as he reasonably believes to be necessary for its proper control, training, or education.

(2) One other than a parent who has been given by law or has voluntarily assumed in whole or in part the function of controlling, training, or educating a child, is privileged to apply such reasonable force or to impose such reasonable confinement as he reasonably believes to be necessary for its proper control, training, or education, except in so far as the parent has restricted the privilege of one to whom he has entrusted the child.

Subsection (a), as amended, makes clear that physical discipline may be so excessive that it is no longer reasonably related to safeguarding the welfare of the minor, even if it does not exceed the bounds set in subsection (b).

In this case, the family court noted that it "must judge the action based upon the reasonable hand standard or reasonable person standard." Considering (1) Minor's age and her size relative to Crouser's, (2) the testimony that the force was excessive and caused her to be unable to sit in her classes, (3) the nature of the injuries as depicted by the photos, (4) the medical testimony, and, in particular, (5) Pond's testimony that she was able to help Minor improve her grades significantly and stop lying without resort to physical force, the court concluded that the physical discipline Minor endured was not reasonably related to the purpose of protecting her welfare. There is nothing in the record that leads us to a "definite and firm conviction that a mistake has been made." Therefore, we hold that the trial court's conclusion that the force used was not reasonably related to protecting Minor's welfare was not clearly erroneous. Consequently, Crouser's contention that "[t]here was insufficient evidence to support the verdict in the instant case because the Prosecution failed to negative the justification defense of parental discipline" is without merit.

> ### b. **Crouser's beating of Minor was designed to cause, or known to create a risk of causing, substantial bodily injury, extreme pain, or mental distress.**

Crouser asserts that, because the force he used on Minor did not exceed the level applied in State v. Deleon, 72 Haw. 241, 813 P.2d 1382 (1991) ... it was justifiable under HRS § 703–309(1)(b). In *Deleon*, the trial court convicted the defendant based upon its finding that he was guilty of causing "extreme pain" when he struck his fourteen-year-old daughter six to ten times with a folded belt above the knee and over her pants. The daughter had testified that "she felt a little pain, that the spanking stung her, and that the pain lasted an hour and a half. She had bruises for about a week. She cried for half an hour." Because the phrase "extreme pain" was not defined in the statute, this court employed "an ancient canon of construction," *noscitur a sociis*,[35] and reasoned that the pain inflicted did not come anywhere near, in degree, the other statutorily forbidden results. Thus, we held that the defendant's conduct was justified under HRS § 703–309(1) and reversed the conviction. *Id.* at 244–45, 813 P.2d at 1383–84. We note that, at the time *Deleon* was decided, the other prohibited results were death, serious bodily injury, disfigurement, extreme mental distress, or gross degradation. *Id.*

. . .

As previously stated, HRS § 703–309(1) was amended in 1992 for the express purpose of "reduc[ing] the permitted level of force that a person responsible for the care of a minor ... may use." In order to accomplish the purpose, "the standard of harm [was] lowered by lowering the level of

---

35. "Noscitur a sociis" is Latin for "it is known from its associates." Black's Law Dictionary 1060 (6th ed. 1990). Under the doctrine of noscitur a sociis, the meaning of words or phrases in a statute may be determined by reference to the meaning of words or phrases associated with it.

risk, and reducing the permissible level of injury to that which is less than 'substantial' as defined in section 707–700 of the Hawaii Penal Code." The changes made reflect the legislature's concern with results of the *noscitur a sociis* analysis employed in *Deleon*. "Death" and "gross degradation" were removed from the enumerated prohibited results because "the lower threshold makes [them] surplusage and [their] elimination removes the risk of other words in that paragraph being interpreted '*noscitur a sociis*' with ... term[s] that [are] not pertinent to the lower threshold. As a result of these changes, the terms retained from the prior law must be reinterpreted by the courts, since the changes affect the application of the rule of construction applied in State v. Deleon, 72 Haw. 241, 813 P.2d 1382 (1991)."

Reinterpreting "extreme pain" in light of the reduced level of force permitted by the amendments, we cannot say that the trial court clearly erred when it found that the use of force caused Minor extreme pain. The permissible level of injury was reduced to that which is less than "substantial bodily injury," which is defined as:

bodily injury which causes:

(1) a major avulsion, laceration, or penetration of the skin;

(2) a chemical, electrical, friction, or scalding burn of second degree severity;

(3) a bone fracture;

(4) a serious concussion; or

(5) a tearing, rupture, or corrosive damage to the esophagus, viscera, or other internal organs.

HRS § 707–700 (1993). Interpreting "extreme pain" *noscitur a sociis* with substantial bodily injury, we believe Minor's pain was comparable in degree to the other statutorily forbidden results, such as a laceration of the skin or a burn of second degree severity. Unlike *Deleon*, where the testimony was that there was "a little pain" for about an hour and a half, or *Kaimimoku*, where the pain was of unknown degree or duration, the testimony in this case was that Minor was in extreme pain for days and unable to sit without pain for weeks. Therefore, we hold that the court's conclusion that "the injuries inflicted by the defendant [were] designed to cause or ...—known to create a risk of substantial bodily injury, extreme pain or mental distress" was not clearly erroneous.

. . .

III. CONCLUSION

Based on the foregoing, we hold that: (1) the family court's conclusion that Crouser's conduct was not justified under HRS § 703–309 was not clearly erroneous; (2) there was sufficient evidence to support Crouser's conviction; and (3) HRS § 703–309(1) is not unconstitutionally vague or overbroad. Consequently, we affirm the trial court's judgment convicting Crouser of abuse of a household member, in violation of HRS § 709–906.[36]

---

36. Defendant father could not claim discipline of a child as a defense where the defendant beat his son with a stick two feet long and one inch in diameter. The conduct was not "reasonable discipline." State v. Bell, 647 So.2d 498 (La.App.1994).

MODEL PENAL CODE

Section 3.08 Use of Force by Persons with Special Responsibility for Care, Discipline or Safety of Others.

The use of force upon or toward the person of another is justifiable if:

(1) the actor is the parent or guardian or other person similarly responsible for the general care and supervision of a minor or a person acting at the request of such parent, guardian or other responsible person and:

(a) the force is used for the purpose of safeguarding or promoting the welfare of the minor, including the prevention or punishment of his misconduct; and

(b) the force used is not designed to cause or known to create a substantial risk of causing death, serious bodily harm, disfigurement, extreme pain or mental distress or gross degradation; or

(2) the actor is a teacher or a person otherwise entrusted with the care or supervision for a special purpose of a minor and:

(a) the actor believes that the force used is necessary to further such special purpose, including the maintenance of reasonable discipline in a school, class or other group, and that the use of such force is consistent with the welfare of the minor; and

(b) the degree of force, if it had been used by the parent or guardian of the minor, would not be unjustifiable under Subsection (1)(b) of this Section; or ... [37]

[There are also provisions for certain other persons such as guardians, doctors, wardens, and persons responsible for the safety of vessels or aircraft, or authorized to maintain order or decorum in a train or in a place where others are assembled.]

Section 3. Prevention of Crime

Two important privileges overlap. They are the privilege (1) to intervene for the purpose of preventing the perpetration of crime and (2) to defend person or property. To the extent of the overlap both privileges are available to the one thus benefited. "It is not necessary that he should intervene solely for the purpose of protecting the public order or of protecting the private interests imperiled. His act, though a single one, may well be done for both purposes. If so, either privilege is available to him."[38]

Perhaps it should be said that any unoffending person may intervene for the purpose of preventing the commission or consummation of any crime if the person does so without resorting to measures which are excessive under all of the facts of the particular case. This kind of force must be distinguished from the authority to use force by a peace officer or citizen to make a lawful arrest, although the concepts are similar and may overlap in some circumstances.

---

37. Copyright © 1962 by the American Law Institute. Reprinted with the permission of the American Law Institute.

38. Restatement, Second, Torts, Scope Note to c. 5, Topic 2 (1965).

In the absence of legislative authority, the privilege to intervene for the purpose of preventing the commission or consummation of a crime does not authorize the use of force in case of a misdemeanor which is not a breach of the peace.[39] In considering statutory enlargements of this field it is important to bear in mind that the "privilege to use force to prevent the commission of crime is usually co-extensive with the privilege to make an arrest therefor without a warrant."[40] It is not uncommon for current statutes to authorize either a peace officer[41] or a private person[42] to arrest without a warrant for any public offense committed or attempted in his presence, and such an enactment *may* be held to make a corresponding enlargement in the field of crime prevention.

No legislative authority is needed for the privilege other than that indicated above. The common law recognizes the privilege to use force to prevent the commission or consummation, not only of a felony, but also of a misdemeanor amounting to a breach of the peace.[43] As to all such offenses the question is not whether force may be used but only under what circumstances and to what extent.

The use of deadly force for crime prevention is limited. Restricting attention for the moment to force neither intended nor likely to cause death or serious bodily harm, and to offenses within the general scope of the preventive privilege (whether by common law or by legislative enlargement), the following generalization may be offered: Any amount of non-deadly force is privileged to prevent the commission or consummation of such an offense if it is reasonably believed to be necessary for this purpose.[44] The use of force, although not intended or likely to cause death or serious bodily harm, constitutes a battery if it is clearly in excess of that reasonably believed necessary for the prevention.

This takes us to the most difficult part of the field, which is the use of deadly force for crime prevention.[45]

---

39.   Id. at § 140.

40.   Id. at § 140, comment *a*.

41.   For example, West's Ann.Cal.Pen.Code, § 836(2) (1997).

42.   Id. at § 837.

43.   Ward v. De Martini, 108 Cal.App. 745, 292 P. 192 (1930); Spicer v. People, 11 Ill.App. 294 (1882). As so used a "breach of the peace" means a public offense done by violence or one causing or likely to cause an immediate disturbance of public order. Restatement, Second, Torts § 116 and § 140, comment *a* (1965).

44.   Restatement, Second, Torts §§ 141–143 (1965).

45.   Statutes on this point differ widely. For example, compare the following:

West's Ann.Cal.Pen.Code, § 197 (1997). "Homicide is also justifiable when committed by any person in either of the following cases:

"1. When resisting any attempt to murder any person or to commit a felony, or to do some great bodily injury upon any person; or,

"2. When committed in defense of habitation, property or person, against one who manifestly intends or endeavors, by violence or surprise, to commit a felony, or against one who manifestly intends and endeavors, in a violent, riotous or tumultuous manner, to enter the habitation of another for the purpose of offering violence to any person therein; . . ."

Commonwealth v. Emmons

Superior Court of Pennsylvania, 1945.
157 Pa.Super. 495, 43 A.2d 568.

■ Opinion by ARNOLD, J., July 19, 1945:

The defendant, Mildred E. Emmons, on September 21, 1943 shot one Edward Gray with a rifle and seriously injured him. She was indicted in three counts,—assault and battery with intent to murder, aggravated assault and battery and simple assault and battery. The jury found her guilty of aggravated assault and battery. The court overruled defendant's motion for new trial and sentenced, and this appeal followed.

The defendant lived in a second floor apartment of a house in Sacone, Upper Darby, Delaware County, Pa. The apartment house fronted on a forty foot wide improved street known as Broadway Avenue. On the side of the house was an unopened street known as Beechwood Avenue, which was a cul-de-sac ending at the rear of the apartment house premises, and was used by the defendant as a way to a garage on the premises.

The defendant had purchased under a bailment lease a Chevrolet Sedan automobile, and on September 21, 1943 was in default thereunder in the amount of $115.66, being two monthly installments. The bailment lease gave the bailor the right to repossess upon default. The lease had been assigned by the seller-bailor to a finance company, which determined to repossess. Its representative came to defendant's second floor apartment on September 21, 1943 at about 11:00 o'clock A.M., knocked on the door and also rang the door bell. There was no response, the defendant later claiming she was asleep.

Defendant's automobile was at this time parked on the unopened cul-de-sac street called Beechwood Avenue. With the aid of Gray (an employee of a commercial garage) defendant's automobile was pushed backwards onto Broadway Avenue and parked near the curb, and the hood of the automobile was raised in order to check the serial numbers. Two shots were fired and the left femur bone in the leg of Edward Gray was badly shattered.

Circumstances led the police officers to interview the defendant who stated that she had fired with a .22 rifle, but did not recall how many shots. She said that she believed the men were stealing her automobile, and that she fired at a point near the intersection of the unopened street and

---

This statute would have to be construed in light of the constitutional limitation addressed in Tennessee v. Garner, 471 U.S. 1, 105 S.Ct. 1694, 85 L.Ed.2d 1 (1985) at least if a state actor were involved.

"But the right to kill is based upon the law of necessity or apparent necessity.... The doctrine of the right to protect one's habitation gives no moral right to kill another, unless necessity or apparent necessity, for purposes countenanced by law, exists.... after the deceased had entered, though burglariously, and after he was in the house, the defendant had no right to kill him for the act of entry already committed.... The right of defendant, in other words, was limited (1) to the protection of himself, (2) to prevent a felony in the bedroom and, probably, (3) to prevent the deceased from entering that room at all." State v. Sorrentino, 31 Wyo. 129, 137–8, 224 P. 420, 422 (1924).

See Kadish, Respect for Live and Regard for Rights in the Criminal Law, 64 Cal.L.Rev. 871 (1976).

Broadway Avenue, and did not aim at or intend to shoot anyone. There was, however, evidence on the part of the Commonwealth upon which the jury may well have found that the defendant intentionally shot Gray.

The various assignments of error raise but one question, viz.:

Where in good faith and upon reasonable grounds, one believes her automobile is being stolen from where it was parked in broad daylight on an unopened street (or private way), may one shoot the person believed to be the thief in order to prevent the supposed larceny? The learned court below answered this question in the negative, and so do we.

While it has been asserted that some rule of law exists which justifies killing in order to prevent *any* felony. To justify the killing it must be to prevent the commission of a felony which is either an atrocious crime or one attempted to be committed by force (or surprise) such as murder, arson, burglary, rape, kidnapping, sodomy or the like.

While we are unable to discover any Pennsylvania cases on the subject, all writers seem to be in accord, both where the death of the supposed felon results, and where some form of assault and battery is committed.

40 C.J.S., Homicide, Section 101, states the rule: "The taking of human life is justifiable when done for the prevention of any *atrocious* crime attempted to be committed with force.... A homicide is justifiable when committed by necessity and in good faith in order to prevent a felony attempted by *force* or surprise, such as murder, robbery, burglary, arson, rape, sodomy and the like.... Killing to prevent a felony is not justifiable if the felony is a secret one, or *unaccompanied by force,* or if it *does not involve the security of the person or home....*" (Emphasis supplied.)

26 Am.Jur., Homicide, Section 172, states the rule: "In general, it may be said that the law countenances the taking of human life in connection with the defense of property *only where an element of danger to the person of the slayer* is present...." (Emphasis supplied.) "The mere fact that such (personal) property is being wrongfully taken ... does not justify a homicide committed in an attempt to prevent the taking or detention."

1 Bishop Criminal Law, 9th Ed., Section 876, states the rule: "A felonious homicide is committed by one who inflicts death in opposing an unlawful endeavor to carry away his property. There is here the right to resist, but not to the taking of life."

The rule is the same where the supposed felon does not die and the indictment is for some form of assault and battery: 6 C.J.S., Assault and Battery, Section 94, "It is only in extreme cases that a person is entitled to inflict great bodily harm or endanger human life in protecting (personal) property, although *where the defense of person or of a dwelling, is involved, it would seem that the use of a deadly weapon may sometimes be justified.*" (Emphasis supplied.)

Likewise in 4 Am.Jur., Assault and Battery, Section 63: "While a man may use as much force as is necessary in the defense of his property, it is generally held *that in the absence of the use of force on the part of the intruder,* he is not justified in inflicting great bodily harm or endangering life." (Emphasis supplied.) "The preservation of human life and limb from grievous harm is of more importance to society than the protection of property." . . .

In the present case the defendant was not defending her person, or her home or "castle". There was no felony by force or any atrocious crime to be prevented. There was no danger to her or her habitation. There was no force by an intruder for her to repel. There was no justification in law for her infliction of grievous bodily harm.

The assignments of error are overruled, the judgment of the court below is affirmed, and defendant is directed to appear in the court below at such time as she may be there called, and that she be by that court committed until she has complied with her sentence or any part of it that had not been performed at the time the appeal was made a supersedeas.[46]

■ RHODES, DITHRICH and ROSS, JJ., dissent.

State v. Barr

Court of Appeals of Arizona, 1977.
115 Ariz. 346, 565 P.2d 526.

■ HOWARD, CHIEF JUDGE.

Appellant appeals from his conviction of voluntary manslaughter while armed with a gun. The conviction arose out of the fatal shooting of Timothy Tylutki as he and several companions left appellant's yard after attempting to steal some wooden chairs valued at less than $5.00.

At trial, appellant testified that on December 21, 1970, he was living in a small house in back of an antique store in the area of the University of Arizona. Because of a number of thefts and burglaries in the neighborhood, the owner of the antique business, Thomas Koenen, had asked appellant some months before "to keep an eye" on the yard where Koenen kept old chairs and dressers which he used for parts in preparing other furniture for sale. On the night of December 21, appellant went to bed at approximately 9:00 p.m. but was later awakened by noises and voices coming from all around his house. He looked out a window and saw two men standing and talking nearby, one of whom was urinating on his wall. He then looked out another window and saw what he believed to be three more men milling back and forth in the yard.

---

46. Originally the common law rule was that the use of deadly force was justifiable whenever the use of such force was necessary to prevent or terminate the commission of any felony. State v. Sundberg, 611 P.2d 44 (Alaska 1980). Compare State v. Metcalfe, 206 N.W. 620 (Iowa 1925), superseded by the opinion in State v. Metcalfe, 203 Iowa 155, 212 N.W. 382 (1927).

"The use of force or the imposition of a confinement intended or likely to cause death or serious bodily harm is privileged if the felony for the prevention of which the actor is intervening is of a type threatening death or serious bodily harm or involving the breaking and entry of a dwelling place." Restatement, Second, Torts § 143(2) (1965).

To be within the privilege the force must be used for the purpose of preventing a felony. One who actually prevented the consummation of a felony by shooting the felon was not protected in a case in which the fact of the intended felony was unknown to the shooter at the time. Regina v. Dadson, 4 Cox C.C. 360 (1850).

Appellant testified he became frightened and believed that the men were stealing something. He found his pistol, left the house, and confronted two young men near the back wall, telling them he did not appreciate what they were doing on his wall. According to appellant, they acted "snooty" and walked away to the northeast across a nearby parking lot. Appellant then saw the other men in the yard. He asked them to come out and to drop what they were carrying. Appellant testified that two young men emerged, dropped a couple of chairs, and then walked on up the alley to the west, ignoring his orders to stop.

As the young men walked away, appellant fired a couple of warning shots straight up in the air. Appellant testified he then heard something like a rock whiz by him and felt the air rush by. When the men continued to walk away, he lowered the gun and fired at a height he thought was still over their heads, "but close enough so that they were certain that they were real bullets rather than a cap gun." One of the two men, Timothy Tylutki, age 19, was struck in the head and leg and died.

John Caid, the young man accompanying the victim, gave the following account of the incident which differs in some respects from appellant's version. Caid testified that on December 21, he, Tom Sloyan, Pat Brady and Tim Tylutki were at a party at a house which Caid and Sloyan rented with several other students. All but Sloyan had been drinking. In the course of the evening, they decided they needed more chairs. They walked to the antique store where one of them had seen some old chairs hanging on nails on a wall in the back yard. Pat Brady and Tom Sloyan were the men appellant first encountered. John Caid and Tim Tylutki were the people appellant saw carrying chairs in the yard area.

Caid testified that he and Tim took the chairs from the wall but could not see the condition of the chairs because of the darkness. When they got to the alley where there was some light they decided the chairs were not worth keeping so they left them and started off down the alley. Caid testified that during this time they had neither seen appellant nor heard him say anything to them. As they walked away, however, they heard a yell and a "crack". They then saw appellant standing in the yard and heard another shot. Caid testified that they kept on walking, but that as they walked Caid turned slightly, made a motion with his hand and went "swoosh". He said that neither he nor Tim threw a rock at appellant. He then heard a third shot and Tylutki fell to the ground. He heard one more shot and felt Tylutki's body jerk. Appellant was questioned at the scene, charged with manslaughter, tried and convicted.

Appellant presents six arguments on appeal. The first three relate to the trial court's refusal to allow his defense that the killing was justified under A.R.S. § 13–462(4) because he was attempting to apprehend a fleeing felon. In this regard, appellant contends the trial court erred in refusing (1) to give certain instructions dealing with the justifiable homicide defense. . . .

The theory of appellant's proposed justifiable homicide defense was embodied in his requested instructions numbers 13 and 19. Instruction No. 13 which derives from dicta in Viliborghi v. State, 45 Ariz. 275, 43 P.2d 210 (1935), reads:

"After a burglary has been completed and the burglar is withdrawing from the scene of the crime, if the burglar attempts to flee from arrest a citizen may use such force as is reasonably necessary for the apprehension of the offender, even to the taking of life. And in all such cases the question of the necessity of the killing depends upon the reasonable apprehension and belief of the defendant, and not whether such apprehension and belief was justified by the facts as they actually existed."

Instruction No. 19 reflects the wording of A.R.S. § 13–462(4):

"Homicide is justifiable when committed by a person necessarily in attempting, by lawful ways and means, to apprehend a person for any felony committed."

The trial court refused these instructions for basically two reasons: (1) no felony was in fact committed because the yard was neither "enclosed" nor "commercial" within the meaning of A.R.S. § 13–302 which defines burglary; and (2) the court believed that the law set forth in *Viliborghi* had been modified by State v. McIntyre, 106 Ariz. 439, 477 P.2d 529 (1970).

Appellant argues that the court erred in rejecting the defense and the instructions because the justification of a homicide committed while attempting to apprehend a fleeing felon depends not on whether there has been a felony in fact but rather on whether appellant reasonably believed a felony was being committed. He points to the following language in *Viliborghi* :

". . . in all of such cases the question of the necessity of the killing depends upon the reasonable apprehension and belief of the defendant, and not whether such apprehension and belief was justified by the facts as they actually existed." (Emphasis added) 45 Ariz. at 291, 43 P.2d at 217.

This language, however, does not support appellant's contention. It explains the requirement that once a felony has been committed, the use of deadly force must be or appear to be reasonably necessary for the apprehension of the felon. It does not mean that the use of deadly force is justified upon a reasonable belief that a felony has been committed. The law has always been that the authority of a private person to make arrests is much more limited than the right of a police officer. While a police officer may arrest with impunity upon probable cause to believe a crime has been committed, a private person may arrest only where a felony has in fact been committed. If no felony was committed, an arrest by a private person is illegal. Therefore, since a homicide is justified under A.R.S. § 13–462(4) only where the arrest is attempted by "lawful ways and means", a private person is not authorized to shoot or kill another in an attempt to arrest merely on suspicion that a felony has been committed. Commonwealth v. Chermansky, 430 Pa. 170, 242 A.2d 237 (1968). In order to invoke the defense of justifiable homicide in apprehending a fleeing felon, the defendant at a minimum must show that: (1) the overt elements of a felony were in fact present and (2) the taking of life was (or appeared to be) reasonably necessary in order to apprehend the fleeing felon. *Cf.* People v. Walker, 32 Cal.App.3d 897, 108 Cal.Rptr. 548 (1973).

Here the trial court found as a matter of law that the elements of a burglary were not present and therefore appellant could not invoke the defense. We agree with the trial court. A.R.S. § 13–302(A) defines burglary, in part, as:

"A person entering ... a fenced or otherwise enclosed commercial yard used for storing equipment or supplies, including but not limited to scrap metals, steel or construction materials, with intent to commit grand or petty theft, or any felony...."

The trial court found that the yard appellant shared with the antique business was not "fenced" or "enclosed" within the meaning of the statute. Evidence at trial indicated that the wall "just kind of tapered off" and that there were pathways leading out which were blocked in some places only by plywood boards to keep appellant's puppies from escaping. Appellant himself described the wall at one point as consisting of two bricks which he could just step over.

The general concept of burglary reflected in the statute is an unauthorized entry into an area protected against intrusion. A "commercial yard" is not within the burglary statute unless it is fully enclosed and its wall, fence, or other enclosing structure is erected mainly for the purpose of protecting property and not merely as a boundary or for aesthetic considerations. We thus hold that the trial court did not err in finding that a felony was not in fact committed and the defense of justifiable homicide under A.R.S. § 13–462(4) was therefore properly rejected.

We note, however, that we also agree with the trial court's second reason for rejecting the defense. We find, as did the trial court, that serious inroads have been made in the authority of private persons to use deadly force to effect an arrest and that the law no longer allows a private person to use deadly force to arrest for every felony. *See e. g.,* People v. Piorkowski, 41 Cal.App.3d 324, 115 Cal.Rptr. 830 (1974); Commonwealth v. Chermansky, supra. In State v. Copley, 101 Ariz. 242, 418 P.2d 579 (1966) which involved the defense of justifiable homicide in resisting an attempt to commit a felony, A.R.S. § 13–462(1), our Supreme Court held that the felony must be one which reasonably creates a fear of great bodily injury. The same standard was applied in *State v. McIntyre, supra,* to justifiable homicide in defense of habitation against one who intends to commit a felony, A.R.S. § 13–462(2). The court stated:

"... (I)t is our opinion that the statute does not give a person carte blanche to shoot another simply because that other person is committing an act which under the statutes might be considered a felony. Rather, it is necessary that the act 'reasonably creates a fear of great bodily injury.' " 106 Ariz. at 445, 477 P.2d at 535.

As the court explained in *Copley,* the statutes on justifiable homicide are a codification of the common law principles which developed at a time when all felonies were capital offenses. With the modern statutory expansion of the classes of felonies, the common law rule is no longer adequate. We find no reason to distinguish the defense of justifiable homicide in arresting a fleeing felon under A.R.S. § 13–462(4) from the defense in *Copley* and *McIntyre,* nor any rationale to support the justification of a homicide committed while attempting to arrest a person guilty of bribing a livestock inspector, A.R.S. § 24–109(B); of breaking into a coin-operated vending machine, § 13–676; of a second offense of publicly displaying explicit sexual materials, § 13–537(C); or of stealing a horse or any neat or horned animal, § 13–663(A)(3).

Affirmed.[47]

People v. Ceballos

Supreme Court of California, In Bank, 1974.
12 Cal.3d 470, 116 Cal.Rptr. 233, 526 P.2d 241.

■ BURKE, JUSTICE.

Don Ceballos was found guilty by a jury of assault with a deadly weapon (Pen.Code, § 245). Imposition of sentence was suspended and he

---

47. It is reversible error to instruct that in order to establish a defense the defendant's act must have been to prevent a felony and the force used by him no more than necessary to prevent the felony. He might have been mistaken as to a felony actually impending, or as to the force needed to repel it. Spicer v. People, 11 Ill.App. 294 (1882).

X proposed sexual intercourse to Mrs. D which she refused. X said he would be back next morning to compel her. She told D. D pretended to leave for work next morning but returned and concealed himself near the bedroom. X came, found Mrs. D in the kitchen, led her to the bedroom; whereupon D stabbed X to death. D was indicted for murder and convicted of manslaughter. The conviction was affirmed because a killing to prevent a felony cannot be justified unless there was reason to believe it was necessary for that purpose. Luttrell v. State, 178 Miss. 877, 174 So. 53 (1937).

A defendant may use deadly force if necessary to repel a sexual assault involving forced penetration. People v. Landrum, 160 Mich.App. 159, 407 N.W.2d 614 (1986).

Mrs. Moore found deceased with his arm around her daughter and his other hand under her clothes. She shot and killed him. The daughter was under the age of consent and Mrs. Moore's defense was that she shot to prevent the crime of rape. A conviction of murder was reversed because the judge failed to instruct the jury that defendant was privileged to kill if necessary to prevent statutory rape. Moore v. State, 91 Tex.Cr.R. 118, 237 S.W. 931 (1922).

Defendant charged with manslaughter was entitled to an instruction that the killing could be justified to prevent robbery. Defendant had been working alone and shot victim as victim was leaving the store without paying for beer. The defendant had heard the victim and his brother discussing robbing the defendant. Laney v. State, 184 Ga.App. 463, 361 S.E.2d 841 (1987).

Defendant is entitled to an instruction on the justifiable use of deadly force to protect against a forcible act of deviate sexual intercourse. Rasmussen v. Commonwealth, 705 S.W.2d 914 (Ky.1986).

A woman is not privileged to kill a man who is attempting to rape her if she is obviously and safely able to prevent the rape without the use of deadly force. Tolbert v. State, 31 Ala.App. 301, 15 So.2d 745 (1943).

The statute which provides that a homicide is justifiable when committed by a person "in defense of habitation or property, against one who manifestly intends and endeavors, by violence or surprise, to commit a felony", does not give carte blanche to shoot another simply because the other is committing an act which might be considered a felony. "Rather, it is necessary that the act 'reasonably creates a fear of great bodily injury.' " State v. McIntyre, 106 Ariz. 439, 445, 477 P.2d 529, 535 (1970).

Defendant was entitled to an instruction in an aggravated assault prosecution on use of force to prevent burglary of defendant's motel room when defendant found the victim in the room armed with a knife. State v. Hussain, 942 P.2d 1168 (Ariz.App.1997).

Where defendant shot victim who had been invited into defendant's apartment to physically settle a dispute, defendant was not entitled to an instruction on the right to use force to terminate a burglary. People v. Godfrey, 80 N.Y.2d 860, 600 N.E.2d 225 (1992).

was placed on probation. He appeals from the judgment, contending primarily that his conduct was not unlawful because the alleged victim was attempting to commit burglary when hit by a trap gun mounted in the garage of defendant's dwelling and that the court erred in instructing the jury. We have concluded that the former argument lacks merit, that the court did not commit prejudicial error in instructing the jury, and that the judgment should be affirmed.

Defendant lived alone in a home in San Anselmo. The regular living quarters were above the garage, but defendant sometimes slept in the garage and had about $2,000 worth of property there.

In March 1970 some tools were stolen from defendant's home. On May 12, 1970, he noticed the lock on his garage doors was bent and pry marks were on one of the doors. The next day he mounted a loaded .22 caliber pistol in the garage. The pistol was aimed at the center of the garage doors and was connected by a wire to one of the doors so that the pistol would discharge if the door was opened several inches.

The damage to defendant's lock had been done by a 16–year–old boy named Stephen and a 15–year–old boy named Robert. On the afternoon of May 15, 1970, the boys returned to defendant's house while he was away. Neither boy was armed with a gun or knife. After looking in the windows and seeing no one, Stephen succeeded in removing the lock on the garage doors with a crowbar, and, as he pulled the door outward, he was hit in the face with a bullet from the pistol.

Stephen testified: He intended to go into the garage "[f]or musical equipment" because he had a debt to pay to a friend. His "way of paying that debt would be to take [defendant's] property and sell it" and use the proceeds to pay the debt. He "wasn't going to do it [i.e., steal] for sure, necessarily." He was there "to look around," and "getting in, I don't know if I would have actually stolen."

Defendant, testifying in his own behalf, admitted having set up the trap gun. He stated that after noticing the pry marks on his garage door on May 12, he felt he should "set up some kind of a trap, something to keep the burglar out of my home." When asked why he was trying to keep the burglar out, he replied, "... Because somebody was trying to steal my property ... and I don't want to come home some night and have the thief in there ... usually a thief is pretty desperate ... and ... they just pick up a weapon ... if they don't have one ... and do the best they can."

When asked by the police shortly after the shooting why he assembled the trap gun, defendant stated that "he didn't have much and he wanted to protect what he did have."

As heretofore appears, the jury found defendant guilty of assault with a deadly weapon. (Pen.Code, § 245.) An assault is "an unlawful attempt, coupled with a present ability, to commit a violent injury on the person of another." (Pen.Code, § 240.)

Defendant contends that had he been present he would have been justified in shooting Stephen since Stephen was attempting to commit burglary (Pen.Code, § 459), that under cases such as United States v. Gilliam, 25 Fed.Cas. p. 1319, No. 15,205A, defendant had a right to do indirectly what he could have done directly, and that therefore any attempt by him to commit a violent injury upon Stephen was not "unlawful" and hence not an assault. The People argue that the rule in *Gilliam* is unsound, that as matter of law a trap gun constitutes excessive force, and that in any event the circumstances were not in fact such as to warrant the use of deadly force.

The issue of criminal liability under statutes such as Penal Code section 245 where the instrument employed is a trap gun or other deadly mechanical device appears to be one of first impression in this state, but in other jurisdictions courts have considered the question of criminal and civil liability for death or injuries inflicted by such a device. . . .

In the United States, courts have concluded that a person may be held criminally liable under statutes proscribing homicides and shooting with intent to injure, or civilly liable, if he sets upon his premises a deadly mechanical device and that device kills or injures another. However, an exception to the rule that there may be criminal and civil liability for death or injuries caused by such a device has been recognized where the intrusion is, in fact, such that the person, were he present, would be justified in taking the life or inflicting the bodily harm with his own hands. The phrase "were he present" does not hypothesize the actual presence of the person (see Rest.2d Torts, § 85, coms. (a), (c) & (d)), but is used in setting forth in an indirect manner the principle that a person may do indirectly that which he is privileged to do directly.

Allowing persons, at their own risk, to employ deadly mechanical devices imperils the lives of children, firemen and policemen acting within the scope of their employment, and others. Where the actor is present, there is always the possibility he will realize that deadly force is not necessary, but deadly mechanical devices are without mercy or discretion. Such devices "are silent instrumentalities of death. They deal death and destruction to the innocent as well as the criminal intruder without the slightest warning. The taking of human life [or infliction of great bodily injury] by such means is brutally savage and inhuman."

It seems clear that the use of such devices should not be encouraged. . . .

. . . Penal Code section 197 provides: "Homicide is . . . justifiable . . . 1. When resisting any attempt to murder any person, or to commit a felony, or to do some great bodily injury upon any person; or, 2. When committed in defense of habitation, property, or person, against one who manifestly intends or endeavors, by violence or surprise, to commit a felony. . . ." (See also Pen.Code, § 198.) Since a homicide is justifiable under the circumstances specified in section 197, *a fortiori* an attempt to commit a violent injury upon another under those circumstances is justifiable.

By its terms subdivision 1 of Penal Code section 197 appears to permit killing to prevent any "felony," but in view of the large number of felonies today and the inclusion of many that do not involve a danger of serious bodily harm, a literal reading of the section is undesirable. People v. Jones, 191 Cal.App.2d 478, 481, 12 Cal.Rptr. 777, in rejecting the defendant's theory that her husband was about to commit the felony of beating her

(Pen.Code, § 273d) and that therefore her killing him to prevent him from doing so was justifiable, stated that Penal Code section 197 "does no more than codify the common law and should be read in light of it." *Jones* read into section 197, subdivision 1, the limitation that the felony be "some atrocious crime attempted to be committed by force." *Jones* (at p. 482, 12 Cal.Rptr. at p. 780) further stated, "the punishment provided by a statute is not necessarily an adequate test as to whether life may be taken for in some situations it is too artificial and unrealistic. We must look further into the character of the crime, and the manner of its perpetration (see Storey v. State [71 Ala. 329]). *When these do not reasonably create a fear of great bodily harm,* as they could not if defendant apprehended only a misdemeanor assault, *there is no cause for the exaction of a human life.*" (Italics added.)

Jones involved subdivision 1 of Penal Code section 197, but subdivision 2 of that section is likewise so limited. The term "violence of [sic] surprise" in subdivision 2 is found in common law authorities and, whatever may have been the very early common law the rule developed at common law that killing or use of deadly force to prevent a felony was justified only if the offense was a forcible and atrocious crime. (*See Storey v. State, supra*; II Cooley's Blackstone, p. 1349; Perkins on Criminal Law, supra, pp. 989–993; 1 Hale, Pleas of the Crown (1847), p. 487.) "Surprise" means an unexpected attack—which includes force and violence (see Perkins, supra, p. 1026, fn. 3), and the word thus appears redundant.

Examples of forcible and atrocious crimes are murder, mayhem, rape and robbery. In such crimes "from their atrocity and violence human life [or personal safety from great harm] either is, or is presumed to be, in peril".

Burglary has been included in the list of such crimes. However, in view of the wide scope of burglary under Penal Code section 459, as compared with the common law definition of that offense, in our opinion it cannot be said that under all circumstances burglary under section 459 constitutes a forcible and atrocious crime.[48]

Where the character and manner of the burglary do not reasonably create a fear of great bodily harm, there is no cause for exaction of human life or for the use of deadly force. The character and manner of the burglary could not reasonably create such a fear unless the burglary threatened, or was reasonably believed to threaten, death or serious bodily harm.

---

48.   At common law burglary was the breaking and entering of a mansion house in the night with the intent to commit a felony. (People v. Barry, 94 Cal. 481, 482, 29 P. 1026 (1892); see 1 Cooley's Blackstone, pp. 223–228; comment, 25 So.Cal.L.Rev. 75.) Burglary under Penal Code section 459 differs from common law burglary in that the entry may be in the daytime and of numerous places other than a mansion house (see 1 Witkin, supra, pp. 416–418), and breaking is not required (see People v. Allison, 200 Cal. 404, 408, 253 P. 318). For example, under section 459 a person who enters a store with the intent of committing theft is guilty of burglary. (See People v. Corral, 60 Cal.App.2d 66, 140 P.2d 172.) It would seem absurd to hold that a store detective could kill that person if necessary to prevent him from committing that offense. (See 13 Stan.L.Rev. 566, 579.)

In the instant case the asserted burglary did not threaten death or serious bodily harm, since no one but Stephen and Robert was then on the premises. . . .

We thus conclude that defendant was not justified under Penal Code section 197, subdivisions 1 or 2, in shooting Stephen to prevent him from committing burglary. . . .

We recognize that our position regarding justification for killing under Penal Code section 197, subdivisions 1 and 2, differs from the position of section 143, subdivision (2), of the Restatement Second of Torts, regarding the use of deadly force to prevent a "felony . . . of a type . . . involving the breaking and entry of a dwelling place"[49] (see also Perkins on Criminal Law, supra, p. 1030, which is in accord with the foregoing section of the Rest.2d Torts) but in view of the supreme value of human life we do not believe deadly force can be justified to prevent all felonies of the foregoing type, including ones in which no person is, or is reasonably believed to be, on the premises except the would-be burglar. . . .

We conclude that as a matter of law the exception to the rule of liability for injuries inflicted by a deadly mechanical device does not apply under the circumstances here appearing. . . .

The judgment is affirmed.[50]

■ Wright, C.J., and McComb, Tobriner, Mosk, Sullivan and Clark, JJ., concur.

MODEL PENAL CODE

Section 3.07 . . .

(5) Use of Force to Prevent Suicide or the Commission of a Crime.

(a) The use of force upon or toward the person of another is justifiable when the actor believes that such force is immediately necessary to prevent such other person from committing suicide, inflicting serious bodily harm upon himself, committing or consummating the commission of a crime involving or threatening bodily harm, damage to or loss of property or a breach of the peace, except that:

---

49. Section 143, subdivision (2), of Restatement Second of Torts, reads, "The use of force . . . intended or likely to cause death or serious bodily harm is privileged if the actor reasonably believes that the commission or consummation of the felony cannot otherwise be prevented and the felony for the prevention of which the actor is intervening is of a type threatening death or serious bodily harm or *involving the breaking and entry of a dwelling place.*" (Italics added.)

The comment to that subsection states:

"The Statement in this Subsection permits the use of means intended or likely to cause death or serious bodily harm for the purpose of preventing such crimes as murder, voluntary manslaughter, mayhem, robbery, common law rape, kidnapping, and *burglary.*" (Italics added.)

50. A Spring gun erected at the front door of a trailer which caused a death could not be justified to protect the habitation when defendant was absent at the time of the shooting. The defendant could not reasonably have believed the force was necessary at the time. Bishop v. State, 257 Ga. 136, 356 S.E.2d 503 (Ga.1987). See also, State v. Britt, 510 So.2d 670 (La.App.1987).

(i) any limitations imposed by the other provisions of this Article on the justifiable use of force in self-protection, for the protection of others, the protection of property, the effectuation of an arrest or the prevention of an escape from custody shall apply notwithstanding the criminality of the conduct against which such force is used; and

(ii) the use of deadly force is not in any event justifiable under this Subsection unless:

(1) the actor believes that there is a substantial risk that the person whom he seeks to prevent from committing a crime will cause death or serious bodily harm to another unless the commission or the consummation of the crime is prevented and that the use of such force presents no substantial risk of injury to innocent persons; or

(2) the actor believes that the use of such force is necessary to suppress a riot or mutiny after the rioters or mutineers have been ordered to disperse and warned, in any particular manner that the law may require, that such force will be used if they do not obey.

(b) The justification afforded by this Subsection extends to the use of confinement as preventive force only if the actor takes all reasonable measures to terminate the confinement as soon as he knows that he safely can, unless the person confined has been arrested on a charge of crime.

Section 3.06   Use of Force for the Protection of Property....

(3) Limitations on Justifiable Use of Force....

(d) Use of Deadly Force. The use of deadly force is not justifiable under this Section unless the actor believes that: ...

(ii) the person against whom the force is used is attempting to commit or consummate arson, burglary, robbery or other felonious theft or property destruction and either:

(1) has employed or threatened deadly force against or in the presence of the actor; or

(2) the use of force other than deadly force to prevent the commission or the consummation of the crime would expose the actor or another in his presence to substantial danger of serious bodily harm.[51]

SECTION 4.   SELF-DEFENSE

It is convenient to discuss problems of self-defense in terms of deadly force (force either intended or likely to cause death or great bodily injury) and nondeadly force (force neither intended nor likely to cause death or great bodily injury). It is important also to distinguish between reasonable force and unreasonable force, these being complex concepts dependent upon the nature of the force itself and the circumstances under which it is employed. It is misleading to speak of a division of the field into (1) deadly force and (2) reasonable force because these terms are neither mutually exclusive nor collectively exhaustive. Either deadly force or nondeadly force may be either reasonable or unreasonable, depending upon the circum-

---

51. Copyright © 1962 by the American Law Institute. Reprinted with the permission of the American Law Institute.

stances of its use. Deadly force is unreasonable if nondeadly force is obviously sufficient to prevent the threatened harm.[52] And nondeadly force is unreasonable if it is obviously and substantially in excess of what is needed for the particular defense.[53]

There are some indications of an original requirement of actual necessity[54] but they do not represent the modern common law of self-defense. The privilege to use force in the effort to avert harm threatened (actually or apparently) by the wrongful act of another is based upon the reasonable belief of the defender under the circumstances as they appear at the moment.[55] One is neither limited by, nor entitled to the benefit of, secret intentions or other unknown factors. One who has knocked down another, in the reasonable belief that this was necessary to prevent being stabbed, is not guilty of battery because it is learned later that the other intended no harm but was merely playing too realistic a joke with a rubber dagger.[56] On the other hand, proof that a fatal shot actually saved the life of the slayer is no defense if the actor fired in cold blood while utterly unaware of the impending danger.[57] One caution should be added. A bona-fide belief which is correct will not be held to be unreasonable merely because the defender is unable to paint a word-picture explaining exactly how he knew what the real facts were.[58]

---

52. Etter v. State, 185 Tenn. 218, 205 S.W.2d 1 (1947).

53. United States v. Hawk Wing, 694 F.2d 1115 (8th Cir.1982); People v. Moody, 62 Cal.App.2d 18, 143 P.2d 978 (1943); Restatement, Second, Torts § 70 (1965). A kick is not a justifiable method of turning a trespasser out of the house. Wild's Case, 2 Lewin C.C. 214, 168 Eng.Rep. 1132 (1837).

"Use of excessive force constitutes battery." Coleman v. State, 320 A.2d 740 (Del.1974).

54. Scott v. State, 203 Miss. 349, 34 So.2d 718 (1948); Regina v. Smith, 8 Car. and P. 160, 173 Eng.Rep. 441 (1837); Regina v. Bull, 9 Car. and P. 22, 173 Eng.Rep. 723 (1939).

Force may be used commensurate with the harm faced. State v. Stone, 266 Mont. 345, 880 P.2d 1296 (1994).

55. State ex rel. Romley v. Superior Court, 172 Ariz. 232, 836 P.2d 445 (App. 1992); State v. Bush, 307 N.C. 152, 297 S.E.2d 563 (1982); People v. Anderson, 44 Cal. 65 (1872); People v. Toledo, 85 Cal.App.2d 577, 193 P.2d 953 (1948); Territory v. Yadao, 35 Hawaii 198 (1939); Weston v. State, 167 Ind. 324, 78 N.E. 1014 (1906); State v. Anderson, 230 N.C. 54, 51 S.E.2d 895 (1949). One whose life has been threatened by another, and who sees that other apparently reaching for a weapon, may shoot in self-defense although the other does not have a weapon in hand or in sight at the moment. Lomax v. State, 205 Miss. 635, 39 So.2d 267 (1949). As to the rule under the Texas statute see Brown v. State, 152 Tex.Cr.R. 440, 214 S.W.2d 792 (1948).

56. Restatement, Second, Torts § 63, Illustrations 5, 9 (1965). See State v. Hundley, 236 Kan. 461, 693 P.2d 475, 479 (1985).

57. Trogdon v. State, 133 Ind. 1, 32 N.E. 725 (1892); Josey v. United States, 77 U.S.App.D.C. 321, 135 F.2d 809 (1943); Restatement, Second, Torts § 63, Comment f (1965).

58. The American Law Institute has stated this result in other words:

"... correctly or reasonably believes ..."

Restatement, Second, Torts §§ 63(2), 70(1) (1965).

"It would be absurd to anticipate that a defendant could calculate a mathematically accurate quantity of force essential to do no more than repel an attack, at the moment of the attack. It is equally unrealistic to acknowledge the jury's responsibility to judge the appropriateness of the force used by the defendant under the circumstances and simultaneously pretend that there is no responsibility on the part of the defendant to measure the force

One who is free from fault is privileged to use whatever nondeadly force reasonably seems to the actor to be necessary to prevent being harmed by the wrongful act of another.[59] This is true whether the threatened harm is deadly or nondeadly. And he may use this force without yielding ground unless the endangering conduct of the other is negligent rather than intentional.[60] Deadly force is not privileged in defense against nondeadly force.[61] One, for example, must submit to a box on the ear and seek redress in the courts if the person is unable to prevent it by means other than resort to deadly force.[62] One who is at fault in bringing on the encounter, or in engaging in it, is not privileged to use any force to defend oneself against nondeadly force.

There is a sharp split with reference to the privilege of using deadly force in self-defense. Some states follow the "retreat rule" and others the "no retreat rule." These labels are not precise because no jurisdiction either requires retreat, or permits a standing of ground, under all circumstances. To understand the difference between the two rules it is necessary to think in terms of three situations. (1) One, entirely free from fault, is the victim of an assault which was murderous from the beginning. (2) One who was the aggressor in an ordinary fist fight, or other nondeadly encounter, or who willingly engaged therein, finds that the adversary has suddenly and unexpectedly changed the nature of the contest and is resorting to deadly force. (3) One who started an encounter with a murderous assault upon another, or who willingly engaged in mutual combat of a deadly nature, has a change of mind in the midst of the fight and would like to stop. According to Sir Michael Foster the common law made a different provision for each of the three.[63] Under his analysis the person identified above as "one" is in situation—(1) entitled to stand the ground and defend oneself with deadly force if this reasonably seems necessary for the person's protection there; (2) required to retreat rather than to use deadly force in his defense if a reasonably safe retreat is available, unless in one's "castle" at the time; (3) required to "withdraw" before resorting to deadly force. As to (3) there seems to be little disagreement. The murderous assailant has not lost the privilege of self-defense forever,[64] but has forfeited it for the

---

necessary at the time of the attack. The jury is required to determine whether '... a reasonable person, in the circumstances and from the viewpoint of the defendant, would reasonably have believed that he/she was in imminent danger ... [and further] ... The amount of force used may not exceed the amount of force a reasonable person, in the circumstances and from the viewpoint of the defendant, would have used ...' The measurement of force sufficient to repel an attack must be made by the defendant on the scene; he will be judged subsequently by the jury on the reasonableness of his reaction under the circumstances." Hommer v. State, 657 P.2d 172 (Okl.Cr.1983).

59. State v. Gough, 187 Iowa 363, 174 N.W. 279 (1919); People v. Katz, 263 App.Div. 883, 32 N.Y.S.2d 157 (1942); State v. Sherman, 16 R.I. 631, 18 A. 1040 (1889).

60. Restatement, Second, Torts § 64 (1965).

61. State v. Doherty, 52 Or. 591, 98 P. 152 (1908); United States v. Hawk Wing, 694 F.2d 1115 (8th Cir.1982). Compare State v. Bartlett, 170 Mo. 658, 71 S.W. 148 (1902). As to the rule under a particular statute see Witty v. State, 150 Tex.Cr.R. 555, 203 S.W.2d 212 (1947).

62. Restatement, Second, Torts § 65, Illustration 1 (1965).

63. Foster, Crown Law 273–277 (1762).

64. State v. Goode, 271 Mo. 43, 195 S.W. 1006 (1917).

moment. The actor cannot reacquire it by "retreat to the wall." The person must bring the attack to an end.[65] And if one is unable to get entirely away from the adversary, the person must in some manner convey to the adversary the information that the fight is over.[66] If circumstances do not permit the person to do so this is the person's own misfortune for beginning such a predicament.[67]

The chief controversy has been in regard to situation (1). Professor Joseph H. Beale took the position that the innocent victim of a murderous assault is always required to take advantage of an obviously safe retreat, rather than to resort to deadly force unless he is (a) the victim of attempted robbery, (b) attacked by a person he is lawfully attempting to arrest, or (c) in his "castle" at the time.[68]

The so-called "no retreat rule" jurisdictions tend to follow the analysis of Foster.[69] The "retreat rule" jurisdictions tend to accept Beale's position with reference to situation (1). This has tended to cause confusion in regard to situation (2). Foster thought of one in this situation as having an "imperfect" right of self-defense because required to retreat rather than use deadly force if a safe retreat was available. Some courts have interpreted this "imperfect" right of self-defense to mean that it is only partly exculpatory. One killing under an "imperfect" right of self-defense is not guilty of murder, but is guilty of manslaughter, under this analysis.[70] However, there are courts that express the no retreat rule in almost absolute terms where the person attacked is where the person has a right to be.[71]

A murderous assailant who had abandoned his purpose, withdrawn from the conflict, and fled into his house had regained the privilege of self-defense and could use deadly force when the other broke into the house to kill him. Stoffer v. State, 15 Ohio St. 47 (1864). It is an assault for the victim of an attack to hunt up his assailant and strike him after he has withdrawn completely. Wendler v. State, 128 Fla. 618, 175 So. 255 (1937).

West's Ann.Cal.Pen.Code, § 197 (1997). "Homicide is also justifiable when committed by any person in any of the following cases: . . .

"(3) When committed in the lawful defense of such person . . . ; but such person . . . if he was the assailant or engaged in mutual combat, must really and in good faith have endeavored to decline any further struggle before such homicide was committed; . . .".

65. People v. Button, 106 Cal. 628, 39 P. 1073 (1895). For the distinction between "retreat" and "withdrawal" see State v. Mayberry, 360 Mo. 35, 226 S.W.2d 725 (1950); Allen v. State, 871 P.2d 79 (Okl.Cr.1994).

66. State v. Smith, 10 Nev. 106 (1875); State v. Jones, 56 N.C.App. 259, 289 S.E.2d 383 (1982).

Defendant who was initial aggressor effectively withdrew and was entitled to a self-defense instruction. State v. Moore, 711 S.W.2d 533 (Mo.App.1986).

67. People v. Button, 106 Cal. 628, 39 P. 1073 (1895).

68. Beale, Retreat from a Murderous Assault, 16 Harv.L.Rev. 567 (1903).

69. "We conclude the no duty to retreat rule as recognized in our earlier cases remains the law in Kansas." State v. Scobee, 242 Kan. 421, 748 P.2d 862, 867 (1988); State v. Ricks, 257 Kan. 435, 894 P.2d 191 (1995).

70. People v. Renteria, 190 Cal.App.3d 1016, 235 Cal.Rptr. 807 (1987); State v. Partlow, 90 Mo. 608, 4 S.W. 14 (1887); People v. Filippelli, 173 N.Y. 509, 66 N.E. 402 (1903).

71. People v. Willner, 879 P.2d 19 (Colo.1994); Bechtel v. State, 840 P.2d 1 (Okl.Cr. 1992); State in Interest of M.S., 584 P.2d 914 (Utah 1978); State v. Williams, 81 Wash.App. 738, 916 P.2d 445 (1996).

The phrase "retreat to the wall," although derived from the facts of an ancient case,[72] is used strictly as a metaphor. One who is subject to this requirement is bound to elect an obviously safe retreat in preference to the use of deadly force, if such an avenue of escape is available. Whenever the circumstances are such that no obviously safe retreat is available the person is "at the wall" and no retreat (or further retreat) is required.

State v. Realina

Intermediate Court of Appeals of Hawaii, 1980.
1 Hawaii App. 167, 616 P.2d 229.

■ Before HAYASHI, C.J., and PADGETT and BURNS, JJ.

■ BURNS, JUDGE.

Defendant Marcelino Realina appeals from a district court judgment convicting him of the offense of terroristic threatening in violation of HRS § 707–715(a).[73]

At the time of the alleged offense, complainant Steve Hardisty was 24 years old, approximately 5 feet 6 inches to 5 feet 9 inches and 200 pounds. Defendant Realina was 44 years old. The record fails to indicate his height and weight. Realina sometimes testified through an Ilocano dialect interpreter and sometimes directly in English.

The relationship between Hardisty and Realina preceded the evening of the alleged offense.

Hardisty testified that during a period when he was still living with his wife, he found Realina at his home and told Realina "if I ever catch you again, you better watch out. . . . You better stay out of my way."

Realina testified that in July or August 1977 Hardisty telephoned Realina and twice said, "Y__ F__. You fool around with my wife. I'm going to kill you." Realina reported these threats to the police and was told that he did not have to worry because they would talk to Hardisty.

Thereafter, but prior to the alleged offense, Hardisty separated from his wife in contemplation of eventual divorce.

On December 8, 1977, just prior to 7 p.m., while driving in Hilo, Hardisty saw Realina also driving. Hardisty concluded that Realina was going to visit Hardisty's wife and got upset. Hardisty followed Realina, who, seeing Hardisty following him, drove to the Hilo police station.[74]

When they reached the police station parking lot, they stopped their cars. Hardisty got out of his car and approached Realina, telling Realina, "You come out you f__ Filipino. I'll kill you." The situation continued with Realina silent in his car and Hardisty outside repeating his threats.

---

72. Anonymous, Fitzh.Abr.Corone, pl. 284 (1328).

73. This section was substantially amended by Act 184, Session Laws 1979. For purposes of this appeal, we refer only to the offense as it was defined at the time of arrest and trial.

74. [DEFENSE COUNSEL:] Q . . . . If you have any idea, could you tell us why Mr. Realina drove to the police station?

[HARDISTY:] A. I guess maybe he was afraid or something.

After a while Realina started his car's engine, preparing to drive away. To prevent Realina from leaving, Hardisty reached in the car and grabbed Realina by the shirt. Realina turned off his car's engine and Hardisty let go of his shirt. Realina looked in his car for a weapon, found a cane knife, and came out of the car with it in his hand. Hardisty turned and ran to the police station, approximately 100 yards away. Realina ran after him, about 30 yards behind. Hardisty entered the police station and in a very excited state reported that he was being chased by a man who was trying to kill him. A police officer listened to Hardisty's story and then went to the doorway and saw Realina running toward the police station, still at least 30 feet away, with the cane knife held in an upward position. As Realina approached, the officer placed his hand on his gun and ordered Realina to drop the cane knife. Realina immediately complied.

The Police Lieutenant in the station then instructed the officer to arrest Realina for terroristic threatening, which he did.

Although he had no prior record, Realina was sentenced to 30 days confinement.

Our standard of review is prescribed in State v. Hernandez, 61 Haw. 475, 605 P.2d 75.

On appeal, the test to ascertain the legal sufficiency of the evidence is whether, viewing the evidence in the light most favorable to the State, there is substantial evidence to support the conclusion of the trier of fact. [Citations omitted.]

To determine whether there is substantial evidence to support the conviction, we must first determine the elements of the crime of which Realina was convicted and the available defenses. To do that, we have to wind our way through the penal code's statutory maze.

§ 707–715[75] *Terroristic threatening.*

(1) A person commits the offense of terroristic threatening if he threatens, by word or conduct, to cause bodily injury to another person . . .:

(a) With the intent to terrorize, or in reckless disregard of the risk of terrorizing, another person; . . .

. . .

§ 703–300. *Definitions relating to justification.* In this chapter, unless a different meaning is plainly required:

(1) "Believes" means reasonably believes.

(2) "Force" means any bodily impact, restraint, or confinement, or the threat thereof.

(3) "Unlawful force" means force which is employed without the consent of the person against whom it is directed and the employment of which constitutes an offense or would constitute an offense except for a defense not amounting to a justification to use the force. . . .

---

75. See n. 1, supra.

(4) "Deadly force" means force which the actor uses with the intent of causing or which he knows to create a substantial risk of causing death or serious bodily harm.... A threat to cause death or serious bodily injury, by the production of a weapon or otherwise, so long as the actor's intent is limited to creating an apprehension that he will use deadly force if necessary, does not constitute deadly force.

. . .

§ 703–301 *Justification a defense; civil remedies unaffected.* (1) In any prosecution for an offense, justification, as defined in sections 703–302 through 703–309, is a defense.

. . .

COMMENTARY ON § 703–301

... Subsection (1) merely establishes that justification is a defense. This places the burden of producing some credible evidence of the existence of justification on the defendant. If he produces such evidence, or if it appears as part of the prosecution's case, the defendant is entitled to have the defense considered by the jury. The prosecution, however, must prove beyond a reasonable doubt, facts which negative the defense.

. . .

§ 703–304 *Use of force in self-protection.* (1) ... [T]he use of force upon or toward another person is justifiable when the actor believes that such force is immediately necessary for the purpose of protecting himself against the use of unlawful force by the other person on the present occasion.

(2) The use of deadly force is justifiable under this section if the actor believes that deadly force is necessary to protect himself against death, serious bodily injury, kidnapping ...

. . .

§ 701–115 *Defenses.* (1) A defense is a fact or set of facts which negatives penal liability.

(2) No defense may be considered by the trier of fact unless evidence of the specified fact or facts has been presented. If such evidence has been presented, then:

> (a) If the defense is not an affirmative defense, the defendant is entitled to an acquittal if the trier of fact finds that the evidence, when considered in the light of any contrary prosecution evidence, raises a reasonable doubt as to the defendant's guilt ...

. . .

Since, by definition, "force", as enumerated in HRS § 703–300, includes "the threat" of force and since the essence of terroristic threatening is a threat, it follows that the authorization to use force or deadly force contained in HRS §§ 703–304(1) and (2) may be available in a justification defense to a charge of terroristic threatening. Whether deadly force may be used depends upon whether the defendant reasonably believed such force was necessary to protect him from certain dangers enumerated in HRS § 703–304(2). Whether nondeadly force may be used depends upon whether the defendant reasonably believed it necessary to prevent unlawful force from being used against him. Those conclusions lead to the following inquiry.

What kind of force did Realina use? With respect to deadly force, certainly Realina's cane knife could have been used to cause serious bodily harm. Whether his use of it in this case created a substantial risk of causing serious bodily harm is not so certain. Further, if Realina's intent in wielding the knife was limited to creating an *apprehension* that he would use deadly force if necessary,[76] his conduct would not have constituted "deadly force" within the meaning of HRS § 703–300(4).

According to HRS § 703–304(2), the use of deadly force was justifiable if Realina believed it necessary to protect himself against kidnapping. According to HRS § 707–720, "... A person commits the offense of kidnapping if he intentionally restrains another person with intent to: ... (d) Inflict bodily injury upon him ...; or (e) Terrorize him ..." In the present case, the testimony seems to establish a *prima facie* showing that Hardisty violated HRS § 707–720 before Realina reached for the knife. Therefore, the record contains sufficient evidence to initially justify Realina's resort to deadly force. It, of course, follows that if Realina used only nondeadly force, justification was available as a defense, since the force previously used by Hardisty was clearly unlawful, and Realina could reasonably have believed force was immediately necessary to protect himself.

Thus, whether the force he used was deadly or nondeadly, Realina clearly met the burden imposed on him by HRS § 701–115 to come forward with evidence of justification. Justification is not an affirmative defense under the Penal Code. The burden was on the prosecution to prove facts negativing the justification defense beyond a reasonable doubt. See HRS § 701–115(2)(a) and Commentary to HRS § 703–301, supra. On review, the question is whether there is substantial evidence negativing the defense.

The State contends that Realina's justification defense "evaporated in the long chase of the victim." In other words, the State concedes that Realina's actions were lawful until some point between his car and the police station, at which point the State contends his actions became unlawful. In view of the special and unusual facts of this case, and especially in view of the facts that it was Realina who drove to the police

---

76. [REALINA:] A .... So, in order to defend myself, I look at the knife—just to defend myself in case.

[DEFENSE COUNSEL:] Q. So you?

[REALINA:] A. I came out of my car and then he run away and just as (inaudible) I know that he going reach by the police station.

[DEFENSE COUNSEL:] Q. So you followed him because you knew he was going to reach the police station.

[REALINA:] A. Yeah.

[DEFENSE COUNSEL:] Q. Did you ever threaten him?

[REALINA:] A. No.

[DEFENSE COUNSEL:] Q. Did you intend to hurt him with the knife?

[REALINA:] A. No. In fact, as I said I was only trying to defend myself just in case.

station and that the chase was into the police station from the police station parking lot, we do not think the length of the chase is substantial evidence negativing Realina's justification defense.

We hold that the record lacks substantial evidence to support the trier of facts' conclusion of guilt.

Reversed.[77]

People v. La Voie

Supreme Court of Colorado, 1964.
155 Colo. 551, 395 P.2d 1001.

■ MOORE, JUSTICE. The defendant in error, to whom we will refer as defendant, was accused of the crime of murder in an information filed in the district court of Jefferson county. He entered a plea of not guilty and a jury was selected to try the case. At the conclusion of the evidence, the trial court, on motion of counsel for defendant, directed the jury to return a verdict of not guilty. It was the opinion of the trial court that the evidence was insufficient to warrant submission of any issue to the jury in that the sum total thereof established a clear case of justifiable homicide. The district attorney objected, and the case is here on writ of error requesting this court to render an opinion expressing its disapproval of the action of the trial court in directing the verdict of not guilty.

Eighteen witnesses testified during the trial; thirteen were called as witnesses for the prosecution and five for the defense, including the defendant himself. We have read the record and have found nothing therein which would warrant the submission of any issue to the jury for determination.

For purposes of focus and clarity we will summarize the pertinent facts leading up to the homicide. The defendant was employed as a pharmacist at the Kincaid Pharmacy, 7024 West Colfax Avenue, Lakewood, Colorado. His day's work ended at about 12:30 A.M. After leaving his place of employment, he obtained something to eat at a nearby restaurant and started on his way home. He was driving east on West Colfax Avenue, toward the city of Denver, at about 1:30 A.M. An automobile approached his car from the rear. The driver of this auto made contact with the rear bumper of defendant's car and thereupon forcibly, unlawfully, and deliberately accelerated his motor, precipitating the defendant forward for a substantial distance and through a red traffic light. There were four men in the automobile who were under the influence of intoxicating liquor in varying degrees. Prior to ramming the car of the defendant they had agreed to shove him along just for "kicks." The defendant applied his brakes to the full; but the continuing force from behind precipitated him forward, caus-

---

77. Conviction of assault in the third degree was affirmed although the initial attack was by the other against defendant. The evidence showed that after defendant knocked his assailant down, he kicked him three times in the face while he was down. It was held that the evidence supported the conclusion that defendant did not reasonably believe these kicks were necessary in his defense. State v. Sanchez, 2 Hawaii App. 577, 636 P.2d 1365 (1981). Accord, Hickman v. State, 186 Ga.App. 118, 366 S.E.2d 426 (1988).

ing all four wheels to leave a trail of skid marks. When defendant's car ultimately came to a stop the auto containing the four men backed away a few feet. The defendant got out of his car and as he did so he placed a revolver beneath his belt. He had a permit to carry the gun. The four men got out of their auto and advanced toward the defendant threatening to "make you eat that damn gun," to "mop up the street with you," and also directed vile, profane and obscene language at him. The man who was in advance of his three companions kept moving toward defendant in a menacing manner. At this point the defendant shot him. As a result, he died at the scene of the affray.

In upholding the action of the trial court we think it sufficient to direct attention to the opinion of this court in People v. Urso, 129 Colo. 292, 269 P.2d 709, where we find, inter alia, the following pertinent language:

"... It is our opinion, and we so state, that if it is within the power of a trial court to set aside a verdict, not supported by competent legal evidence, then it is equally within the province and power of the court to prevent such a verdict ever coming into existence. In either position, before or after the verdict, the trial court is compelled to survey and analyze the evidence, and from the same evidence, his analysis would undoubtedly be the same before or after a verdict. If it is to the end that the evidence is insufficient or incompetent, and no part of it is convincing beyond a reasonable doubt, then he should be courageous enough to prevent a miscarriage of justice by a jury...."

The law of justifiable homicide is well set forth by this court in the case of Young v. People, 47 Colo. 352, 107 P. 274:

"... When a person has reasonable grounds for believing, and does in fact actually believe, that danger of his being killed, or of receiving great bodily harm, is imminent, he may act on such appearances and defend himself, even to the extent of taking human life when necessary, although it may turn out that the appearances were false, or although he may have been mistaken as to the extent of the real or actual danger...."

The defendant was a stranger to all four occupants of the auto. He was peaceably on his way home from work, which terminated after midnight. Under the law and the circumstances disclosed by the record, defendant had the right to defend himself against the threatened assault of those whose lawlessness and utter disregard of his rights resulted in the justifiable killing of one of their number.

The judgment is affirmed.[78]

■ SUTTON and HALL, JJ., concur.

---

78. Under the law of self-defense the totality of the circumstances, including the number of persons reasonably appearing to be threatening the accused, must be considered by the trier of fact. People v. Jones, 675 P.2d 9 (Colo.1984); People v. Cuevas, 740 P.2d 25 (Colo.App.1987).

Dwyer was partially disabled by arthritis. He was hemmed in by a wall at his back and a bar at his side. In this helpless position he was approached by an alleged karate expert who invited Dwyer to fight. As the assailant continued his charge upon Dwyer, Dwyer cut the other several times with a knife, inflicting injuries which resulted in death. A conviction of manslaughter was reversed on the ground that this was justifiable self-defense. State v. Dwyer, 317 So.2d 149 (Fla.App.1975).

People v. Goetz

Court of Appeals of New York, 1986.
68 N.Y.2d 96, 506 N.Y.S.2d 18, 497 N.E.2d 41.

■ CHIEF JUDGE WACHTLER.

A Grand Jury has indicted defendant on attempted murder, assault, and other charges for having shot and wounded four youths on a New York City subway train after one or two of the youths approached him and asked for $5. The lower courts, concluding that the prosecutor's charge to the Grand Jury on the defense of justification was erroneous, have dismissed the attempted murder, assault and weapons possession charges. We now reverse and reinstate all counts of the indictment.

The precise circumstances of the incident giving rise to the charges against defendant are disputed, and ultimately it will be for a trial jury to determine what occurred. We feel it necessary, however, to provide some factual background to properly frame the legal issues before us. Accordingly, we have summarized the facts as they appear from the evidence before the Grand Jury. . . .

On Saturday afternoon, December 22, 1984, Troy Canty, Darryl Cabey, James Ramseur, and Barry Allen boarded an IRT express subway train in The Bronx and headed south toward lower Manhattan. The four youths rode together in the rear portion of the seventh car of the train. Two of the four, Ramseur and Cabey, had screwdrivers inside their coats, which they said were to be used to break into the coin boxes of video machines.

Defendant Bernhard Goetz boarded this subway train at 14th Street in Manhattan and sat down on a bench towards the rear section of the same car occupied by the four youths. Goetz was carrying an unlicensed .38 caliber pistol loaded with five rounds of ammunition in a waistband holster. The train left the 14th Street station and headed towards Chambers Street.

"Perfect self-defense excuses a killing altogether and is established when it is shown that, at the time of the killing:

(1) it appeared to defendant and he believed it to be necessary to kill the deceased in order to save himself from death or great bodily harm; and

(2) defendant's belief was reasonable in that the circumstances as they appeared to him at the time were sufficient to create such a belief in the mind of a person of ordinary firmness; and

(3) defendant was not the aggressor in bringing on the affray, i.e., he did not aggressively and willingly enter into the fight without legal excuse or provocation; and

(4) defendant did not use excessive force, i.e., did not use more force than was necessary under the circumstances to protect himself from death or great bodily harm."

State v. Bush, 307 N.C. 152, 297 S.E.2d 563, 568 (1982).

Defendant claimed the victim had controlled him by voodoo for the past ten to twenty years and that defendant shot the victim after a lengthy period of fear and intimidation. Since there was no evidence that defendant believed that deadly force was imminent, an instruction on self-defense was not warranted. McDaniel v. State, 257 Ga. 345, 359 S.E.2d 642 (1987).

It appears from the evidence before the Grand Jury that Canty approached Goetz, possibly with Allen beside him, and stated "give me five dollars". Neither Canty nor any of the other youths displayed a weapon. Goetz responded by standing up, pulling out his handgun and firing four shots in rapid succession. The first shot hit Canty in the chest; the second struck Allen in the back; the third went through Ramseur's arm and into his left side; the fourth was fired at Cabey, who apparently was then standing in the corner of the car, but missed, deflecting instead off of a wall of the conductor's cab. After Goetz briefly surveyed the scene around him, he fired another shot at Cabey, who then was sitting on the end bench of the car. The bullet entered the rear of Cabey's side and severed his spinal cord.

. . . The conductor, who had been in the next car, heard the shots and instructed the motorman to radio for emergency assistance. The conductor then went into the car where the shooting occurred and saw Goetz sitting on a bench, the injured youths lying on the floor or slumped against a seat, and two women who had apparently taken cover, also lying on the floor. Goetz told the conductor that the four youths had tried to rob him.

. . .

On December 31, 1984, Goetz surrendered to police in Concord, New Hampshire, identifying himself as the gunman being sought for the subway shootings in New York nine days earlier. Later that day, after receiving *Miranda* warnings, he made two lengthy statements, both of which were tape recorded with his permission. In the statements, which are substantially similar, Goetz admitted that he had been illegally carrying a handgun in New York City for three years. He stated that he had first purchased a gun in 1981 after he had been injured in a mugging. Goetz also revealed that twice between 1981 and 1984 he had successfully warded off assailants simply by displaying the pistol.

According to Goetz's statement, the first contact he had with the four youths came when Canty, sitting or lying on the bench across from him, asked "how are you," to which he replied "fine". Shortly thereafter, Canty, followed by one of the other youths, walked over to the defendant and stood to his left, while the other two youths remained to his right, in the corner of the subway car. Canty then said "give me five dollars". Goetz stated that he knew from the smile on Canty's face that they wanted to "play with me". Although he was certain that none of the youths had a gun, he had a fear, based on prior experiences, of being "maimed".

Goetz then established "a pattern of fire," deciding specifically to fire from left to right. His stated intention at that point was to "murder [the four youths], to hurt them, to make them suffer as much as possible". When Canty again requested money, Goetz stood up, drew his weapon, and began firing, aiming for the center of the body of each of the four. Goetz recalled that the first two he shot "tried to run through the crowd (but) they had nowhere to run". Goetz then turned to his right to "go after the other two". One of these two "tried to run through the wall of the train, but * * * he had nowhere to go". The other youth (Cabey) "tried pretending that he wasn't with [the others]" by standing still, holding on to one of the subway hand straps, and not looking at Goetz. Goetz nonetheless fired his fourth shot at him. He then ran back to the first two youths to make sure they had been "taken care of". Seeing that they had both been shot, he spun back to check on the latter two. Goetz noticed that the youth who had been standing still was now sitting on a bench and seemed unhurt. As Goetz told the police, "I said '[y]ou seem to be all right, here's another'", and he then fired the shot which severed Cabey's spinal cord. Goetz added that "if I was a little more under self-control * * * I would have put the barrel against his forehead and fired." He also admitted that "if I had had more [bullets], I would have shot them again, and again, and again."

. . .

On March 27, 1985, the second Grand Jury filed a 10–count indictment, containing four charges of attempted murder (Penal Law §§ 110.00, 125.25(1)), four charges of assault in the first degree (Penal Law § 120.10(1)), one charge of reckless endangerment in the first degree (Penal Law § 120.25), and one charge of criminal possession of a weapon in the second degree (Penal Law § 265.03 (possession of loaded firearm with intent to use it unlawfully against another)). Goetz was arraigned on this indictment on March 28, 1985, and it was consolidated with the earlier three-count indictment.

On October 14, 1985, Goetz moved to dismiss the charges contained in the second indictment alleging, among other things, that the evidence before the second Grand Jury was not legally sufficient to establish the offenses charged, and that the prosecutor's instructions to that Grand Jury on the defense of justification were erroneous and prejudicial to the defendant so as to render its proceedings defective.

. . .

In an order dated January 21, 1986, Criminal Term 131 Misc.2d 1, 502 N.Y.S.2d 577, granted Goetz's motion to the extent that it dismissed all counts of the second indictment, other than the reckless endangerment charge, with leave to resubmit these charges to a third Grand Jury. The court, after inspection of the Grand Jury minutes, first rejected Goetz's contention that there was not legally sufficient evidence to support the charges. It held, however, that the prosecutor, in a supplemental charge elaborating upon the justification defense, had erroneously introduced an objective element into this defense by instructing the grand jurors to consider whether Goetz's conduct was that of a "reasonable man in [Goetz's] situation". The court, citing prior decisions from both the First and Second Departments (see, e.g., People v. Santiago, 110 A.D.2d 569, 488 N.Y.S.2d 4 [1st Dept.]; People v. Wagman, 99 A.D.2d 519, 471 N.Y.S.2d 147 [2d Dept.]), concluded that the statutory test for whether the use of deadly force is justified to protect a person should be wholly subjective, focusing entirely on the defendant's state of mind when he used such force. It concluded that dismissal was required for this error because the justification issue was at the heart of the case.

. . .

On appeal by the People, a divided Appellate Division, 116 A.D.2d 316, 501 N.Y.S.2d 326, affirmed Criminal Term's dismissal of the charges. . . .

Penal Law article 35 recognizes the defense of justification, which "permits the use of force under certain circumstances". One such set of circumstances pertains to the use of force in defense of a person, encompassing both self-defense and defense of a third person. Penal Law § 35.15(1) sets forth the general principles governing all such uses of force: "[a] person may * * * use physical force upon another person when and to the extent he *reasonably believes* such to be necessary to defend himself or a third person from what he *reasonably believes* to be the use or imminent use of unlawful physical force by such other person" (emphasis added).

Section 35.15(2) sets forth further limitations on these general principles with respect to the use of "deadly physical force": "A person may not use deadly physical force upon another person under circumstances specified in subdivision one unless (a) He *reasonably believes* that such other person is using or about to use deadly physical force * * *[79] or (b) He *reasonably believes* that such other person is committing or attempting to commit a kidnapping, forcible rape, forcible sodomy or robbery" (emphasis added).

Thus, consistent with most justification provisions, Penal Law § 35.15 permits the use of deadly physical force only where requirements as to triggering conditions and the necessity of a particular response are met. As to the triggering conditions, the statute requires that the actor "reasonably believes" that another person either is using or about to use deadly physical force or is committing or attempting to commit one of certain enumerated felonies, including robbery. As to the need for the use of deadly physical force as a response, the statute requires that the actor "reasonably believes" that such force is necessary to avert the perceived threat.

Because the evidence before the second Grand Jury included statements by Goetz that he acted to protect himself from being maimed or to avert a robbery, the prosecutor correctly chose to charge the justification defense in section 35.15 to the Grand Jury. The prosecutor properly instructed the grand jurors to consider whether the use of deadly physical force was justified to prevent either serious physical injury or a robbery, and, in doing so, to separately analyze the defense with respect to each of the charges. He elaborated upon the prerequisites for the use of deadly physical force essentially by reading or paraphrasing the language in Penal Law § 35.15. The defense does not contend that he committed any error in this portion of the charge.

When the prosecutor had completed his charge, one of the grand jurors asked for clarification of the term "reasonably believes". The prosecutor responded by instructing the grand jurors that they were to consider the circumstances of the incident and determine "whether the defendant's conduct was that of a reasonable man in the defendant's situation". It is this response by the prosecutor—and specifically his use of "a reasonable

---

79. Section 35.15(2)(a) further provides, however, that even under these circumstances a person ordinarily must retreat "if he knows that he can with complete safety as to himself and others avoid the necessity of (using deadly physical force) by retreating".

man"—which is the basis for the dismissal of the charges by the lower courts....

Penal statutes in New York have long codified the right recognized at common law to use deadly physical force, under appropriate circumstances, in self-defense. These provisions have never required that an actor's belief as to the intention of another person to inflict serious injury be correct in order for the use of deadly force to be justified, but they have uniformly required that the belief comport with an objective notion of reasonableness. The 1829 statute, using language which was followed almost in its entirety until the 1965 recodification of the Penal Law, provided that the use of deadly force was justified in self-defense or in the defense of specified third persons "when there shall be a reasonable ground to apprehend a design to commit a felony, or to do some great personal injury, and there shall be imminent danger of such design being accomplished".

. . .

In 1961 the Legislature established a Commission to undertake a complete revision of the Penal Law and the Criminal Code. The impetus for the decision to update the Penal Law came in part from the drafting of the Model Penal Code by the American Law Institute, as well as from the fact that the existing law was poorly organized and in many aspects antiquated. Following the submission by the Commission of several reports and proposals, the Legislature approved the present Penal Law in 1965 (L.1965, ch. 1030), and it became effective on September 1, 1967. The drafting of the general provisions of the new Penal Law, including the article on justification, was particularly influenced by the Model Penal Code. While using the Model Penal Code provisions on justification as general guidelines, however, the drafters of the new Penal Law did not simply adopt them verbatim.

The provisions of the Model Penal Code with respect to the use of deadly force in self-defense reflect the position of its drafters that any culpability which arises from a mistaken belief in the need to use such force should be no greater than the culpability such a mistake would give rise to if it were made with respect to an element of a crime (*see,* ALI, Model Penal Code and Commentaries, part I, at 32, 34....) Accordingly, under Model Penal Code § 3.04(2)(b), a defendant charged with murder (or attempted murder) need only show that he "*believe[d]* that (the use of deadly force) was necessary to protect himself against death, serious bodily injury, kidnapping or [forcible] sexual intercourse" to prevail on a self-defense claim (emphasis added). If the defendant's belief was wrong, and was recklessly, or negligently formed, however, he may be convicted of the type of homicide charge requiring only a reckless or negligent, as the case may be, criminal intent.

The drafters of the Model Penal Code recognized that the wholly subjective test set forth in section 3.04 differed from the existing law in most States by its omission of any requirement of reasonableness. The drafters were also keenly aware that requiring that the actor have a "reasonable belief" rather than just a "belief" would alter the wholly subjective test....

New York did not follow the Model Penal Code's equation of a mistake as to the need to use deadly force with a mistake negating an element of a crime, choosing instead to use a single statutory section which would provide either a complete defense or no defense at all to a defendant charged with any crime involving the use of deadly force. The drafters of the new Penal Law adopted in large part the structure and content of Model Penal Code § 3.04, but, crucially, inserted the word "reasonably" before "believes".

The plurality below agreed with defendant's argument that the change in the statutory language from "reasonable ground," used prior to 1965, to "he reasonably believes" in Penal Law § 35.15 evinced a legislative intent to conform to the subjective standard contained in Model Penal Code § 3.04. This argument, however, ignores the plain significance of the insertion of "reasonably". Had the drafters of section 35.15 wanted to adopt a subjective standard, they could have simply used the language of section 3.04. "Believes" by itself requires an honest or genuine belief by a defendant as to the need to use deadly force. Interpreting the statute to require only that the defendant's belief was "reasonable to *him*," as done by the plurality below, would hardly be different from requiring only a genuine belief; in either case, the defendant's own perceptions could completely exonerate him from any criminal liability.

. . .

We can only conclude that the Legislature retained a reasonableness requirement to avoid giving a license for such actions. The plurality's interpretation, as the dissenters below recognized, excises the impact of the word "reasonably". . . .

. . . Following the example of the Model Penal Code, the drafters of section 35.15 eliminated this sharp dichotomy between the use of ordinary force and deadly force in defense of a person. Not surprisingly then, the integrated section reflects the wording of Model Penal Code § 3.04, with the addition of "reasonably" to incorporate the long-standing requirement of "reasonable ground" for the use of deadly force and apply it to the use of ordinary force as well.

. . .

Goetz also argues that the introduction of an objective element will preclude a jury from considering factors such as the prior experiences of a given actor and thus, require it to make a determination of "reasonableness" without regard to the actual circumstances of a particular incident. This argument, however, falsely presupposes that an objective standard means that the background and other relevant characteristics of a particular actor must be ignored. To the contrary, we have frequently noted that a determination of reasonableness must be based on the "circumstances" facing a defendant or his "situation" (*see, e.g.,* People v. Ligouri, 284 N.Y. 309, 316, 31 N.E.2d 37.) Such terms encompass more than the physical movements of the potential assailant. As just discussed, these terms include any relevant knowledge the defendant had about that person. They also necessarily bring in the physical attributes of all persons involved, including the defendant. Furthermore, the defendant's circumstances encompass any prior experiences he had which could provide a reasonable basis for a belief that another person's intentions were to injure or rob him or that the use of deadly force was necessary under the circumstances.

Accordingly, a jury should be instructed to consider this type of evidence in weighing the defendant's actions. The jury must first determine whether the defendant had the requisite beliefs under section 35.15, that is, whether he believed deadly force was necessary to avert the imminent use of deadly force or the commission of one of the felonies enumerated therein. If the People do not prove beyond a reasonable doubt that he did not have such beliefs, then the jury must also consider whether these beliefs were reasonable. The jury would have to determine, in light of all the "circumstances", as explicated above, if a reasonable person could have had these beliefs.

The prosecutor's instruction to the second Grand Jury that it had to determine whether, under the circumstances, Goetz's conduct was that of a reasonable man in his situation was thus essentially an accurate charge. . . .

. . . The prosecutor more than adequately fulfilled this obligation here. His instructions were not as complete as the court's charge on justification should be, but they sufficiently apprised the Grand Jury of the existence and requirements of that defense to allow it to intelligently decide that there is sufficient evidence tending to disprove justification and necessitating a trial. The Grand Jury has indicted Goetz. It will now be for the petit jury to decide whether the prosecutor can prove beyond a reasonable doubt that Goetz's reactions were unreasonable and therefore excessive.

Reversed.[80]

People v. Humphrey

Supreme Court of California, 1996.
13 Cal.4th 1073, 56 Cal.Rptr.2d 142, 921 P.2d 1.

■ CHIN, JUSTICE.

The Legislature has decreed that, when relevant, expert testimony regarding "battered woman's syndrome" is generally admissible in a criminal action. (Evid. Code, § 1107.) We must determine the purposes for which a jury may consider this evidence when offered to support a claim of self-defense to a murder charge.

The trial court instructed that the jury could consider the evidence in deciding whether the defendant actually believed it was necessary to kill in self-defense, but not in deciding whether that belief was reasonable. The instruction was erroneous. Because evidence of battered woman's syndrome may help the jury understand the circumstances in which the defendant found herself at the time of the killing, it is relevant to the reasonableness of her belief. Moreover, because defendant testified, the evidence was relevant to her credibility. The trial court should have allowed the jury to

---

80. For a critical consideration of this case see George P. Fletcher, A Crime of Self Defense (1988).

consider this testimony in deciding the reasonableness as well as the existence of defendant's belief that killing was necessary.

Finding the error prejudicial, we reverse the judgment of the Court of Appeal.

I. THE FACTS

A. Prosecution Evidence

During the evening of March 28, 1992, defendant shot and killed Albert Hampton in their Fresno home. Officer Reagan was the first on the scene. A neighbor told Reagan that the couple in the house had been arguing all day. Defendant soon came outside appearing upset and with her hands raised as if surrendering. She told Officer Reagan, "I shot him. That's right, I shot him. I just couldn't take him beating on me no more." She led the officer into the house, showed him a .357 magnum revolver on a table, and said, "There's the gun." Hampton was on the kitchen floor, wounded but alive.

A short time later, defendant told Officer Reagan, "He deserved it. I just couldn't take it anymore. I told him to stop beating on me." "He was beating on me, so I shot him. I told him I'd shoot him if he ever beat on me again." A paramedic heard her say that she wanted to teach Hampton "a lesson." Defendant told another officer at the scene, Officer Terry, "I'm fed up. Yeah, I shot him. I'm just tired of him hitting me. He said, 'You're not going to do nothing about it.' I showed him, didn't I? I shot him good. He won't hit anybody else again. Hit me again; I shoot him again. I don't care if I go to jail. Push come to shove, I guess people gave it to him, and, kept hitting me. I warned him. I warned him not to hit me. He wouldn't listen."

Officer Terry took defendant to the police station, where she told the following story. The day before the shooting, Hampton had been drinking. He hit defendant while they were driving home in their truck and continued hitting her when they arrived. He told her, "I'll kill you," and shot at her. The bullet went through a bedroom window and struck a tree outside. The day of the shooting, Hampton "got drunk," swore at her, and started hitting her again. He walked into the kitchen. Defendant saw the gun in the living room and picked it up. Her jaw hurt, and she was in pain. She pointed the gun at Hampton and said, "You're not going to hit me anymore." Hampton said, "What are you doing?" Believing that Hampton was about to pick something up to hit her with, she shot him. She then put the gun down and went outside to wait for the police.

Hampton later died of a gunshot wound to his chest. The neighbor who spoke with Officer Reagan testified that shortly before the shooting, she heard defendant, but not Hampton, shouting. The evening before, the neighbor had heard a gunshot. Defendant's blood contained no drugs but had a blood-alcohol level of .17 percent. Hampton's blood contained no drugs or alcohol.

B. Defense Evidence

Defendant claimed she shot Hampton in self-defense. To support the claim, the defense presented first expert testimony and then nonexpert testimony, including that of defendant herself.

1. Expert Testimony

Dr. Lee Bowker testified as an expert on battered woman's syndrome. The syndrome, he testified, "is not just a psychological construction, but it's a term for a wide variety of controlling mechanisms that the man or it can be a woman, but in general for this syndrome it's a man, uses against the woman, and for the effect that those control mechanisms have."

Dr. Bowker had studied about 1,000 battered women and found them often inaccurately portrayed "as cardboard figures, paper-thin punching bags who merely absorb the violence but didn't do anything about it." He found that battered women often employ strategies to stop the beatings, including hiding, running away, counter-violence, seeking the help of friends and family, going to a shelter, and contacting police. Nevertheless, many battered women remain in the relationship because of lack of money, social isolation, lack of self-confidence, inadequate police response, and a fear (often justified) of reprisals by the batterer. "The battering man will make the battered woman depend on him and generally succeed at least for a time." A battered woman often feels responsible for the abusive relationship, and "she just can't figure out a way to please him better so he'll stop beating her." In sum, "It really is the physical control of the woman through economics and through relative social isolation combined with the psychological techniques that make her so dependent."

Many battered women go from one abusive relationship to another and seek a strong man to protect them from the previous abuser. "[W]ith each successful victimization, the person becomes less able to avoid the next one." The violence can gradually escalate, as the batterer keeps control using ever more severe actions, including rape, torture, violence against the woman's loved ones or pets, and death threats. Battered women sense this escalation. In Dr. Bowker's "experience with battered women who kill in self-defense their abusers, it's always related to their perceived change of what's going on in a relationship. They become very sensitive to what sets off batterers. They watch for this stuff very carefully. [¶] ... Anybody who is abused over a period of time becomes sensitive to the abuser's behavior and when she sees a change acceleration begin in that behavior, it tells them something is going to happen...."

Dr. Bowker interviewed defendant for a full day. He believed she suffered not only from battered woman's syndrome, but also from being the child of an alcoholic and an incest victim. He testified that all three of defendant's partners before Hampton were abusive and significantly older than she.

Dr. Bowker described defendant's relationship with Hampton. Hampton was a 49-year-old man who weighed almost twice as much as defendant. The two had a battering relationship that Dr. Bowker characterized as a "traditional cycle of violence." The cycle included phases of tension building, violence, and then forgiveness-seeking in which Hampton would promise not to batter defendant any more and she would believe him. During this period, there would be occasional good times. For example, defendant told Dr. Bowker that Hampton would give her a rose. "That's one of the things that hooks people in. Intermittent reinforcement is the key." But after a while, the violence would begin again. The violence would recur because "basically ... the woman doesn't perfectly obey. That's the bottom line." For example, defendant would talk to another man, or fail to clean house "just so."

The situation worsened over time, especially when Hampton got off parole shortly before his death. He became more physically and emotionally abusive, repeatedly threatened defendant's life, and even shot at her the night before his death. Hampton often allowed defendant to go out, but she was afraid to flee because she felt he would find her as he had in the past. "He enforced her belief that she can never escape him." Dr. Bowker testified that unless her injuries were so severe that "something absolutely had to be treated," he would not expect her to seek medical treatment. "That's the pattern of her life...."

Dr. Bowker believed defendant's description of her experiences. In his opinion, she suffered from battered woman's syndrome in "about as extreme a pattern as you could find."

2. Nonexpert Testimony

Defendant confirmed many of the details of her life and relationship with Hampton underlying Dr. Bowker's opinion. She testified that her father forcefully molested her from the time she was seven years old until she was fifteen. She described her relationship with another abusive man as being like "Nightmare on Elm Street." Regarding Hampton, she testified that they often argued and that he beat her regularly. Both were heavy drinkers. Hampton once threw a can of beer at her face, breaking her nose. Her dental plates hurt because Hampton hit her so often. He often kicked her, but usually hit her in the back of the head because, he told her, it "won't leave bruises." Hampton sometimes threatened to kill her, and often said she "would live to regret it." Matters got worse towards the end.

The evening before the shooting, March 27, 1992, Hampton arrived home "very drunk." He yelled at her and called her names. At one point when she was standing by the bedroom window, he fired his .357 Magnum revolver at her. She testified, "He didn't miss me by much either." She was "real scared."

The next day, the two drove into the mountains. They argued, and Hampton continually hit her. While returning, he said that their location would be a good place to kill her because "they wouldn't find [her] for a while." She took it as a joke, although she feared him. When they returned, the arguing continued. He hit her again, then entered the kitchen. He threatened, "This time, bitch, when I shoot at you, I won't miss." He came from the kitchen and reached for the gun on the living room table. She grabbed it first, pointed it at him, and told him "that he wasn't going to hit [her]." She backed Hampton into the kitchen. He was saying something, but she did not know what. He reached for her hand and she shot him. She believed he was reaching for the gun and was going to shoot her.

Several other witnesses testified about defendant's relationship with Hampton, his abusive conduct in general, and his physical abuse of, and threats to, defendant in particular.... A neighbor testified that the night before the shooting, she heard a gunshot. The next morning, defendant told the neighbor that Hampton had shot at her, and that she was afraid of him. After the shooting, investigators found a bullet hole through the frame of the bedroom window and a bullet embedded in a tree in line with the window. Another neighbor testified that shortly before hearing the shot that killed Hampton, she heard defendant say, "Stop it, Albert. Stop it."

C. Procedural History

Defendant was charged with murder with personal use of a firearm. At the end of the prosecution's case-in-chief, the court granted defendant's motion under Penal Code section 1118.1 for acquittal of first degree murder.

The court instructed the jury on second degree murder and both voluntary and involuntary manslaughter. It also instructed on self-defense, explaining that an actual and reasonable belief that the killing was necessary was a complete defense; an actual but unreasonable belief was a defense to murder, but not to voluntary manslaughter. In determining reasonableness, the jury was to consider what "would appear to be necessary to a reasonable person in a similar situation and with similar knowledge."

The court also instructed:

"Evidence regarding Battered Woman's Syndrome has been introduced in this case. Such evidence, if believed, may be considered by you only for the purpose of determining whether or not the defendant held the necessary subjective honest [belief] which is a requirement for both perfect and imperfect self-defense. However, that same evidence regarding Battered Woman's Syndrome may not be considered or used by you in evaluating the objective reasonableness requirement for perfect self-defense.

" . . . .

"Battered Woman's Syndrome seeks to describe and explain common reactions of women to that experience. Thus, you may consider the evidence concerning the syndrome and its effects only for the limited purpose of showing, if it does show, that the defendant's reactions, as demonstrated by the evidence, are not inconsistent with her having been physically abused or the beliefs, perceptions, or behavior of victims of domestic violence."

During deliberations, the jury asked for and received clarification of the terms "subjectively honest and objectively unreasonable." It found defendant guilty of voluntary manslaughter with personal use of a firearm. . . .

II. DISCUSSION

A. Background

With an exception not relevant here, Evidence Code section 1107, subdivision (a), makes admissible in a criminal action expert testimony regarding "battered woman's syndrome, including the physical, emotional, or mental effects upon the beliefs, perceptions, or behavior of victims of domestic violence. . . ." . . .

For killing to be in self-defense, the defendant must actually and reasonably believe in the need to defend. (People v. Flannel (1979) 25 Cal.3d 668, 674, 160 Cal.Rptr. 84, 603 P.2d 1.) If the belief subjectively exists but is objectively unreasonable, there is "imperfect self-defense," i.e., "the defendant is deemed to have acted without malice and cannot be convicted of murder," but can be convicted of manslaughter. (*In re Christian S.* (1994) 7 Cal.4th 768, 783, 30 Cal.Rptr.2d 33, 872 P.2d 574.) To constitute "perfect self-defense," i.e., to exonerate the person completely, the belief must also be objectively reasonable. As the Legislature has stated, "[T]he circumstances must be sufficient to excite the fears of a reasonable person...." (Pen. Code, § 198; see also § 197, subds. 2, 3.) Moreover, for either perfect or imperfect self-defense, the fear must be of imminent harm. "Fear of future harm—no matter how great the fear and no matter how great the likelihood of the harm—will not suffice. The defendant's fear must be of imminent danger to life or great bodily injury."

Although the belief in the need to defend must be objectively reasonable, a jury must consider what "would appear to be necessary to a reasonable person in a similar situation and with similar knowledge...." It judges reasonableness "from the point of view of a reasonable person in the position of defendant...." To do this, it must consider all the " 'facts and circumstances . . . in determining whether the defendant acted in a manner in which a reasonable man would act in protecting his own life or bodily safety.' " As we stated long ago, "... a defendant is entitled to have a jury take into consideration all the elements in the case which might be expected to operate on his mind...."

.   .   .

With these principles in mind, we now consider the relevance of evidence of battered woman's syndrome to the elements of self-defense.

B.   Battered Woman's Syndrome

Battered woman's syndrome "has been defined as 'a series of common characteristics that appear in women who are abused physically and psychologically over an extended period of time by the dominant male figure in their lives.' " (State v. Kelly (1984) 97 N.J. 178, 193 [478 A.2d 364, 371]; see also People v. Aris (1989) 215 Cal.App.3d 1178, 1194 [264 Cal.Rptr. 167] [" 'a pattern of psychological symptoms that develop after somebody has lived in a battering relationship' "]; Note, *Battered Women Who Kill Their Abusers* (1993) 106 Harv.L.Rev. 1574, 1578 ["a 'pattern of responses and perceptions presumed to be characteristic of women who have been subjected to continuous physical abuse by their mate[s]' "].)

The trial court allowed the jury to consider the battered woman's syndrome evidence in deciding whether defendant actually believed she needed to kill in self-defense. The question here is whether the evidence was also relevant on the reasonableness of that belief....

.   .   .

The Attorney General concedes that Hampton's behavior towards defendant, including prior threats and violence, was relevant to reasonableness, but distinguishes between evidence of this behavior—which the trial court fully admitted—and expert testimony about its effects on defendant. The distinction is untenable. "To effectively present the situation as perceived by the defendant, and the reasonableness of her fear, the defense has the option to explain her feelings to enable the jury to overcome stereotyped impressions about women who remain in abusive relationships." It is appropriate that the jury be given a professional explanation of the battering syndrome and its effects on the woman through the use of expert testimony.

The Attorney General also argues that allowing consideration of this testimony would result in an undesirable "battle of the experts" and raises the specter of other battles of experts regarding other syndromes. The Legislature, however, has decided that, if relevant, expert evidence on battered women's syndrome is admissible. (Evid. Code, § 1107.) We have found it relevant; it is therefore admissible. We express no opinion on the admissibility of expert testimony regarding other possible syndromes in support of a claim of self-defense, but we rest today's holding on Evidence Code section 1107.

... The jury must consider defendant's situation and knowledge, which makes the evidence relevant, but the ultimate question is whether a reasonable *person*, not a reasonable battered woman, would believe in the need to kill to prevent imminent harm. Moreover, it is the *jury*, not the expert, that determines whether defendant's belief and, ultimately, her actions, were objectively reasonable.

Battered woman's syndrome evidence was also relevant to defendant's credibility. It "would have assisted the jury in objectively analyzing [defendant's] claim of self-defense by dispelling many of the commonly held misconceptions about battered women." ...

The judgment of the Court of Appeal is reversed.[81]

People v. Ligouri

Court of Appeals of New York, 1940.
284 N.Y. 309, 31 N.E.2d 37.

■ SEARS, J. The defendants, Giro Ligouri and William Panaro, were indicted together for the crime of murder in the first degree. They have been found guilty by the verdict of a jury of the crime of murder in the second degree. Their convictions have been unanimously affirmed by the Appellate Divi-

---

81. "To claim self-defense, a defendant's belief about the necessity of defending himself must be based on reasonable grounds. A subjective belief of danger will not alone suffice; the defendant's belief of danger must also be reasonable." Scheikofsky v. State, 636 P.2d 1107, 1110 (Wyo.1981).

Defendant must show not only that he actually believed he was in danger of death or serious bodily harm, but that the belief was reasonable based on circumstances as perceived by the defendant, not as they actually existed. People v. Green, 113 Mich.App. 699, 318 N.W.2d 547 (1982).

In a murder prosecution, there is no unqualified duty to retreat, the possibility of escape is a recognized factor in determining whether or not defendant reasonably believed deadly force was necessary to avoid danger. State v. Carrier, 670 So.2d 794 (La.App.1996).

sion in the second department, and are brought before this court by an order granted by one of the judges of this court.

It is not disputed by either appellant that Ligouri, on October 24, 1938, shot and killed Nicholas Cosaluzzo. In fact, Ligouri, himself, sworn in his own behalf, testified to the shooting. The affair occurred about three o'clock in the afternoon in a public street in the borough of Brooklyn, New York City, at or near the corner of McDonald avenue and Avenue X. . . .

The defendant Ligouri urges that the trial court in its charge in respect to justification committed error. The court was requested on behalf of Ligouri to charge in this language: "If the defendant Ligouri was attacked feloniously by the deceased, Cosaluzzo, the defendant Ligouri had a right to shoot Cosaluzzo." The court declined to charge as requested, stating that it had already been covered. Defendant continued, "I ask Your Honor to charge the jury that a person who is feloniously attacked is under no obligation to retreat but may stand his ground, and if necessary, kill his opponent." This the court declined, saying, "If a person kills another whom he claims assaults him, he is under an obligation to retreat as far as possible, unless the circumstances are such that unless he acted as he did he would be the recipient of irreparable and grievous bodily harm." Exceptions were taken to the court's declining to charge as requested and to the charge. In the main charge the court had said on the subject of self-defense: "The defendant Ligouri claims that while he discharged these revolvers, what he did was done in self-defense. As I have already said, the law is that an act otherwise criminal is justified when done to protect the person committing it, or another whom he is bound to protect from inevitable and irreparable personal injury, and the injury could only have been prevented by the act, nothing more being done than is necessary to prevent the injury. A person who is attacked before he can resort to acts which result in death, is bound to retreat and to avoid the attack, unless the circumstances be such that he believes that he is in such imminent danger of irreparable injury, and the only thing he could do to protect himself and prevent that injury being inflicted upon him, would be to act as he did, and to do no more to prevent it than was necessary. If the circumstances justified the belief on his part that he is in danger of inevitable and irreparable injury, although it should turn out he was mistaken, an ordinarily prudent man under the same circumstances would be justified in doing what he did, if he thinks he is in danger of death. If you believe that Nick unexpectedly pulled this gun and snapped it on him, and under those circumstances he felt the only thing for him to do was to do what he did, discharge and empty both of his guns into him, even though death resulted, that would be justifiable under the law, but he could not do more than necessary, more than what an ordinarily prudent man under the same circumstances would be justified in doing. He does not have to satisfy you that the situation existed, but if, upon considering all the evidence in the case, there is a reasonable doubt, he must have the benefit of it, and your verdict will be not guilty, because the People must establish to your satisfaction beyond a reasonable doubt that this was a wilful, wanton killing, and was not excusable and not justifiable. That is their burden."

The applicable statute, Penal Law, section 1055, contains the following language:

"Homicide is also justifiable when committed:

"1. In the lawful defense of the slayer, or of his or her husband, wife, parent, child, brother, sister, master or servant, or of any other person in his presence or company, when there is reasonable ground to apprehend a design on the part of the person slain to commit a felony, or to do some great personal injury to the slayer, or to any such person, and there is imminent danger of such design being accomplished; or,

"2. In the actual resistance of an attempt to commit a felony upon the slayer, in his presence, or upon or in a dwelling or other place of abode in which he is."

The language employed by the court in the main charge is that applicable in the usual case of self-defense and falls within the first subdivision as above cited. This is not, however, the ordinary case. Here, on the assumption in the request, a felony was in process of being committed. So in substance the court charged. To avoid the felonious aggression against his person, if it occurred, Ligouri was justified under the second division of the section in standing his ground and, if necessary, destroying the person making the felonious attack....

We reach the conclusion that error occurred in the refusal of the trial court to charge as requested. It may be argued that the charge amounted to granting the request as no one could consider escape as reasonably possible from a pistol purposefully and directly aimed at the assailed. The charge, however, left this matter to deduction. The defendants were on trial for crimes punishable by death. They were entitled to have the judge charge the jury definitely and directly that if they found that the felonious assault, assumed in the request, was occurring, the defendant against whom it was being perpetrated was justified in killing the felonious aggressor if such were necessary in resisting the assault. This error goes to the very foundation of the defense, and necessitates a reversal of the conviction of Ligouri....

For these reasons the judgments should be reversed and a new trial ordered as to both defendants....[82]

■ LEHMAN, CH. J., LOUGHRAN and RIPPEY, JJ., concur with SEARS, J.; LEWIS, J., dissents in opinion in which FINCH, J., concurs as to Ligouri but concurs in the grant of a new trial to Panaro; CONWAY, J., concurs in the opinion of LEWIS, J., as to Ligouri but votes to affirm as to both defendants.

Judgments reversed, etc.

---

82. "We would further note the holding of this court in Gillaspy v. State, 96 Okl.Cr. 347, 255 P.2d 302 (1953), in which this court upheld the accuracy of an instruction which read in part as follows: 'It is the duty of a person so threatened with danger to his life or person to use at the time all reasonable means apparent to a reasonable person under the circumstances shown to avoid such danger before taking human life, except that he is not bound to retreat to avoid the necessity or apparent necessity of killing, if he is in a place where he has a right to be and has done no act on his part to bring about the necessity for killing.' 255 P.2d, at 309." Thompson v. State, 462 P.2d 299, 302 (Okl.Cr.1969).

Brown v. United States

Supreme Court of the United States, 1921.
256 U.S. 335, 41 S.Ct. 501, 65 L.Ed. 961.

■ MR. JUSTICE HOLMES delivered the opinion of the court.

The petitioner was convicted of murder in the second degree committed upon one Hermes at a place in Texas within the exclusive jurisdiction of the United States, and the judgment was affirmed by the Circuit Court of Appeals. 257 F.R. 46. A writ of certiorari was granted by this Court. 250 U.S. 637, 39 S.Ct. 494, 63 L.Ed. 1183....

The other question concerns the instructions at the trial. There had been trouble between Hermes and the defendant for a long time. There was evidence that Hermes had twice assaulted the defendant with a knife and had made threats communicated to the defendant that the next time one of them would go off in a black box. On the day in question the defendant was at the place above mentioned superintending excavation work for a post office. In view of Hermes's threats he had taken a pistol with him and had laid it in his coat upon a dump. Hermes was driven up by a witness, in a cart to be loaded, and the defendant said that certain earth was not to be removed, whereupon Hermes came toward him, the defendant says, with a knife. The defendant retreated some twenty or twenty-five feet to where his coat was and got his pistol. Hermes was striking at him and the defendant fired four shots and killed him. The judge instructed the jury among other things that "it is necessary to remember, in considering the question of self-defense, that the party assaulted is always under the obligation to retreat, so long as retreat is open to him, provided he can do so without subjecting himself to the danger of death or great bodily harm." The instruction was reinforced by the further intimation that unless "retreat would have appeared to a man of reasonable prudence, in the position of the defendant, as involving danger of death or serious bodily harm" the defendant was not entitled to stand his ground. An instruction to the effect that if the defendant had reasonable grounds of apprehension that he was in danger of losing his life or of suffering serious bodily harm from Hermes he was not bound to retreat was refused. So the question is brought out with sufficient clearness whether the formula laid down by the Court and often repeated by the ancient law is adequate to the protection of the defendant's rights.

It is useless to go into the developments of the law from the time when a man who had killed another no matter how innocently had to get his pardon, whether of grace or of course. Concrete cases or illustrations stated in the early law in conditions very different from the present, like the reference to retreat in Coke, Third Inst. 55, and elsewhere, have had a tendency to ossify into specific rules without much regard for reason. Other examples may be found in the law as to trespass *ab initio*. Rationally the failure to retreat is a circumstance to be considered with all the others in order to determine whether the defendant went farther than he was justified in doing; not a categorical proof of guilt. The law has grown, and even if historical mistakes have contributed to its growth it has tended in the direction of rules consistent with human nature. Many respectable writers agree that if a man reasonably believes that he is in immediate danger of death or grievous bodily harm from his assailant he may stand his ground and that if he kills him he has not exceeded the bounds of lawful self-defence. That has been the decision of this Court. Beard v. United States, 158 U.S. 550, 559, 15 S.Ct. 962, 39 L.Ed. 1086. Detached reflection cannot be demanded in the presence of an uplifted knife. Therefore in this Court, at least, it is not a condition of immunity that one in that situation should pause to consider whether a reasonable man might not think it possible to fly with safety or to disable his assailant rather than to kill him. Rowe v. United States, 164 U.S. 546, 558, 17 S.Ct. 172, 41 L.Ed. 547. The law of Texas very strongly adopts these views as is shown by many cases, of which it is enough to cite two. Cooper v. State, 49 Tex.Crim.Rep. 28, 38, 89 S.W. 1068. Baltrip v. State, 30 Tex.Ct.App. 545, 549, 17 S.W. 1106.

It is true that in the case of Beard he was upon his own land (not in his house), and in that of Rowe he was in the room of a hotel, but those facts, although mentioned by the Court, would not have bettered the defence by the old common law and were not appreciably more favorable than that the defendant here was at a place where he was called to be, in the discharge of his duty. There was evidence that the last shot was fired after Hermes was down. The jury might not believe the defendant's testimony that it was an accidental discharge, but the suggestion of the Government that this Court may disregard the considerable body of evidence that the shooting was in self-defence is based upon a misunderstanding of what was meant by some language in Battle v. United States, 209 U.S. 36, 38, 28 S.Ct. 422, 52 L.Ed. 670. Moreover if the last shot was intentional and may seem to have been unnecessary when considered in cold blood, the defendant would not necessarily lose his immunity if it followed close upon the others while the heat of the conflict was on, and if the defendant believed that he was fighting for his life.

The Government presents a different case. It denies that Hermes had a knife and even that Brown was acting in self-defence. Notwithstanding the repeated threats of Hermes and intimations that one of the two would die at the next encounter, which seem hardly to be denied, of course it was possible for the jury to find that Brown had not sufficient reason to think that his life was in danger at that time, that he exceeded the limits of reasonable self-defence or even that he was the attacking party. But upon the hypothesis to which the evidence gave much color, that Hermes began the attack, the instruction that we have stated was wrong.

Judgment reversed.[83]

■ Mr. Justice Pitney and Mr. Justice Clarke dissent.

---

83. "The doctrine of 'retreat to the wall' had its origin before the general introduction of guns. Justice demands that its application have due regard to the present general use and to the type of firearms. It would be good sense for the law to require, in many cases, an attempt to escape from a hand to hand encounter with fists, clubs, and even knives, as a condition of justification for killing in self-defense; while it would be rank folly to so require when experienced men, armed with repeating rifles, face each other in an open space, removed from shelter, with intent to kill or to do great bodily harm. What might be a reasonable chance for escape in the one situation might in the other be certain death. Self-defense has not, by statute nor by judicial opinion, been distorted by an unreasonable requirement of the duty to retreat, into self-destruction." State v. Gardner, 96 Minn. 318, 104 N.W. 971 (1905).

State v. Davis

Supreme Court of South Carolina, 1948.
214 S.C. 34, 51 S.E.2d 86.

■ OXNER, JUSTICE. Appellant, Mack Davis, was indicted and tried for the murder of Norman Gordon, Jr. He sought to excuse the homicide on the ground of self-defense. The trial resulted in a verdict of guilty with recommendation to the mercy of the Court and he was sentenced to imprisonment for life. The only question to be determined on this appeal is whether in establishing his plea of self-defense, appellant had the right to claim immunity from the law of retreat.

About 11 o'clock on Saturday night, August 2, 1947, appellant shot the deceased in a cornfield near a filling station and store operated by W.H. Hinds in a rural section of Florence County. Some time late that afternoon these two [men] had an argument at a tobacco barn where the deceased was working, as a result of which the deceased, apparently without much, if any, provocation, slapped or struck appellant and knocked him down. Appellant immediately left the scene. That night about 9 o'clock he came to the store of Mr. Hinds. About an hour and a half later the deceased arrived

---

"While one is not required to retreat, a person is not entitled to use a deadly weapon in order to pursue and ultimately stab and kill an unarmed person who, if he was ever engaged in a fray, had withdrawn from it." State v. Jordan, 250 Kan. 180, 825 P.2d 157 (1992).

Although there is no duty to retreat in this jurisdiction, "once having retreated from a place of danger, an act of voluntarily returning which is deliberately calculated to lead to further conflict deprives the defendant of his claim of self-defense." State v. Britson, 130 Ariz. 380, 636 P.2d 628, 634 (1981).

One who finds trouble by going out of his way to look for it does not have the privilege of self-defense. Valentine v. State, 108 Ark. 594, 159 S.W. 26 (1913). But the mere fact that a man has been threatened and has reason to expect an assault does not deprive him of the right to go about his business as usual, even if this will take him where he has reason to expect the other. People v. Gonzales, 71 Cal. 569, 12 P. 783 (1887). And if he does meet the other, and is attacked by him, he has the privilege of self-defense, in spite of the fact that he took the precaution of arming himself to be prepared for such an emergency. State v. Evans, 124 Mo. 397, 28 S.W. 8 (1894). A man cannot be said to be seeking a difficulty, in the sense of being deprived of the privilege of self-defense, merely because he is attempting to restrain a trespasser from unwarranted control over his property. And this is true even if he armed himself with a weapon to be prepared to defend himself if necessary. Ayers v. State, 60 Miss. 709 (1883). The fact that one is carrying a weapon unlawfully does not deprive him of the privilege of using it if necessary to defend himself from death or great bodily injury. State v. Doris, 51 Or. 136, 94 P. 44 (1908). The fact that a difficulty arose out of an unlawful gambling game does not deprive the innocent victim of a murderous assault of the privilege of self-defense. State v. Leaks, 114 S.C. 257, 103 S.E. 549 (1920). Compare Shack v. State, 236 Ala. 667, 184 So. 688 (1938).

A trespasser has the right of self-defense after he has availed himself of every means of retreat. Thompson v. State, 462 P.2d 299, 302 (Okl.Cr.1969).

The duty to retreat in a public street before engaging in self-defense applies only when deadly force is used. State v. Moore, 309 N.J.Super. 463, 707 A.2d 486 (1998).

Under the "true man doctrine," a person is not required to retreat from the threatened attack of another even though a person may safely do so and is not required to pause and consider whether a reasonable person might think it possible to safely flee rather than to attack and disable or kill an assailant. State v. Renner, 912 S.W.2d 701 (Tenn.1995).

and asked Hinds to lend him a gun, stating, according to Hinds, "I believe Mack (appellant) is going to shoot me." Hinds refused to do so and told the deceased that he didn't "want any shooting around here." The deceased replied that he had a gun at the tobacco barn which he could get and then left. About the same time or shortly thereafter, appellant went across the road in the direction of his home. Approximately a half hour later Hinds and several of those in the store heard the sound of a shotgun. They made an investigation and found the deceased lying fatally wounded in the cornfield at a point about 25 or 30 yards from the store and about 15 feet from the road, with a rifle near his body. He died shortly thereafter while being carried to the office of a physician.

Appellant testified that after hearing the conversation between the deceased and Hinds, he became alarmed and went home for the purpose of securing his shotgun, intending to return to the store where he had several matters to attend to. He said that he planned to approach the store from the rear through the cornfield because the deceased might see him first if he entered through the front. According to his testimony, while in the cornfield he saw the deceased approaching and squatted to escape observation but that the deceased when within close range recognized him and raised his rifle, whereupon he (appellant) shot in defense of his life. The theory of the State was that appellant concealed himself in the cornfield for the purpose of shooting the deceased as the latter returned to the store.

Appellant lived at the home of his sister and brother-in-law, a distance of about four-tenths of a mile from the scene of the homicide. The field in question was owned by Hinds and cultivated by appellant's brother-in-law as a sharecropper. Appellant worked for him and had assisted in cultivating this corn, which had been laid by at the time of the homicide, but the record does not disclose whether his compensation was in the form of wages or a share in the crop. The deceased also worked on some farm in the same community.

Counsel for appellant requested the Court "to charge the jury that the defendant was on the premises on which he was working and the law of retreat would not apply to him." The request was refused and the jury was instructed that it was incumbent upon appellant to establish all of the elements of self-defense, including that of retreating, which the Court then qualified as follows: "I charge you as a matter of law that if a person is threatened with a gun, any kind of firearms, within shooting range, why, obviously there is no duty to retreat; and it is only in cases where a person can with safety avoid a difficulty that he is required to retreat under the law to avoid committing murder." ...

It is now well established in this State that if a person is assaulted while on his own premises and is without fault in bringing on the difficulty, he is not bound to retreat in order to invoke the benefit of the doctrine of self-defense, but may stand his ground and repel the attack with as much force as is reasonably necessary.... This is true whether the attack occurs in defendant's home, place of business, or elsewhere on property owned or lawfully occupied by him. It was also held in State v. Marlowe, 120 S.C. 205, 112 S.E. 921, 922, that a member of a club, wrongfully attacked by another in the club rooms, was under no duty to retreat, the Court observing: "A man is no more bound to allow himself to be run out of his rest room than his workshop." In some jurisdictions the rule has been extended so as to relieve the defendant from the necessity of retreating if attacked in any place where he has a right to be, as when he is lawfully on a public street or highway. We have not gone that far. In State v. McGee, 185 S.C. 184, 193 S.E. 303, 306, the Court stated that "The fact that the defendant was on a public highway, where all men have equal rights, and in his automobile, did not constitute any one of those special privileges obviating the necessity of retreating before killing." It was held in State v. Gordon, *supra* [128 S.C. 422, 122 S.E. 503], that where a foreman on a farm was assaulted by one of the employees under him at the place where they were working, he was not required to retreat. The Court concluded that the place of work "was the defendant's place of business within the meaning of that term as employed in the law of retreat."

In the case at bar, we do not think under the circumstances that appellant is entitled to claim immunity from the law of retreat. The homicide did not occur at or within the curtilage of the home in which he resided. This house was located across the public road and at some distance from the scene of the shooting. Nor was appellant attacked while working at his "place of business". It is true that he had assisted during the year in cultivating the corn in this field but his presence there on the night in question was wholly unrelated to his employment. There is no showing that he even had any interest in the corn crop. Whether his brother-in-law, the sharecropper, would have been required to retreat if attacked in this cornfield under similar circumstances is a question that is not before us.

All exceptions are overruled and judgment affirmed.[84]

■ Baker, C.J., and Fishburne, Stukes and Taylor, JJ., concur.

---

84. Defendant on his own land acting in a legal manner need not retreat after being threatened before using deadly force. State v. Hendrix, 270 S.C. 653, 244 S.E.2d 503 (1978). Apartment was defendant's residence for purposes of the "castle doctrine" even though leased to victim's girlfriend where defendant had moved in with permission and had no other residence. State v. Stevenson, 81 N.C.App. 409, 344 S.E.2d 334 (1986).

Neither defendant or the victim who were in defendant's open driveway, 45–feet away from the defendant's home, were within the defendant's dwelling for purposes of "castle statute." Commonwealth v. Bennett, 41 Mass. App. Ct. 920, 671 N.E.2d 966 (1996).

Although retreat was not required by the occupant of a dwelling it did not apply to a tenant who only rented a second floor apartment where a shooting occurred on the front porch of the building where defendant's apartment was located. Commonwealth v. Fortini, 44 Mass.App.Ct. 562, 692 N.E.2d 110 (1998).

One who is attacked on his premises is immune from a duty to retreat. State v. Brown, 321 S.C. 184, 467 S.E.2d 922 (1996).

Minnesota imposes a duty to retreat before using lethal force even if the actor is in the person's own home. State v. Carothers, 585 N.W.2d 64 (Minn.App.1998).

The jury should have been instructed that since defendant was in her home she had no duty to retreat or escape but was entitled to stand her ground and take the life of the assailant if that became necessary. Jackson v. State, 31 Md.App. 518, 357 A.2d 845 (1976).

Where defendant was in his own home there was no duty to retreat. Collier v. State, 57 Ala.App. 375, 328 So.2d 626 (1975), *cert. denied* 295 Ala. 397, 328 So.2d 629 (1976).

A garage owner, attacked in the private driveway to his garage, was under no duty to retreat. State v. Sipes, 202 Iowa 173, 209 N.W. 458 (1926).

When a man is on his own premises other than his house or within the curtilage thereof the reasons for not retreating do not apply. Lee v. State, 92 Ala. 15, 9 So. 407 (1890).

Cooper v. United States

District of Columbia Court of Appeals, 1986.
512 A.2d 1002.

■ BELSON, ASSOCIATE JUDGE:

A jury convicted Leon D. Cooper of voluntary manslaughter while armed, D.C.Code §§ 22–2405 and–3202, and carrying a pistol without a license, *id*. § 3204. On appeal, Cooper asserts that the trial judge erred when he refused to instruct the jury that the appellant had an unqualified right to stand his ground in the face of an attack in his home, but instead instructed the jury in the language of Instruction 5.16B, Criminal Jury Instructions for the District of Columbia (3d ed. 1978), the standard instruction on the use of deadly force in self-defense. Finding no error, we affirm.

Leon Cooper and his brother Robert Parker lived with their mother, Alice Cooper. In the early part of August 1981, Parker unexpectedly left home for 10 days. Early on the morning of August 12th, he returned. He did not tell his mother or brother where he had been.

Parker stayed home for much of the day. Mrs. Cooper returned from work in the evening, and Cooper returned from his job shortly afterward. Cooper was carrying a pistol when he returned. The three were sitting in Mrs. Cooper's small living room when the two brothers began to quarrel after Cooper asked Parker where he had been during the past 10 days.

Suddenly, the quarrel escalated, and the two brothers found themselves standing in the middle of the living room, shouting at each other. Parker hit Cooper in the head with a small radio; Mrs. Cooper ran upstairs to call for help. She then heard a "pop." She went downstairs and saw Parker lying on the floor. Cooper said "I have shot my brother" and "Mama, I am so sorry. I mean?." Cooper later told the police that he had just shot his brother, that his brother was hitting him with the radio and "I couldn't take it anymore and I just shot him."

At trial, Cooper's counsel objected to instruction 5.16B, the standard instruction given when the defendant raises a claim of self-defense. The court instructed the jury, in pertinent part:

Now, if the defendant—If the defendant could have safely retreated but did not do so, his failure to retreat is a circumstance which you may consider together with all the other circumstances in determining whether he went further in repelling the danger, real or apparent, then he was justified in doing so under the circumstances.

The right to stand his ground applies to one while in his dwelling house, office, or place of business, or within the curtilage thereof. Bryant v. State, 252 Ala. 153, 39 So.2d 657 (1949).

The exception to the obligation to retreat in the case of a person attacked in their home does not apply to a person attacked in his own automobile. Baker v. State, 506 So.2d 1056 (Fla.App.1987).

Before a person can avail himself [of] the plea of self-defense against a charge of homicide, he must do everything in his power, consistent with his own safety, to avoid the danger and avoid the necessity of taking life. However, if the defendant actually believed that he was in imminent danger of death or serious bodily harm, and that deadly force was necessary to repel such danger, he was not required to retreat or consider whether he could safely retreat. He was entitled to stand his ground and use such force as was reasonably necessary under the circumstances to save his life or protect himself from serious bodily harm.

This instruction virtually tracks the language of Instruction 5.16B.[85]

Appellant took the position that the second sentence of the instruction which begins, "Before a person can avail himself [of] the plea of self-defense," inappropriately imposed a duty to retreat in the face of an attack. The trial court overruled counsel's objections. Defense counsel then asked the trial court for a "castle doctrine" instruction, i.e., that a person has no duty whatsoever to retreat when attacked in his own home. The trial judge denied the request, stating that, in his opinion, the castle doctrine applies when a person in his home is attacked by a stranger or one who comes onto the premises without permission, but not when a fight occurs between two co-occupants. The jury found Cooper guilty of voluntary manslaughter while armed and carrying a pistol without a license, . . .

We consider first whether, under the law of this jurisdiction, a person generally has the duty to retreat in the face of an assault by another, when retreat is a feasible alternative.

In Gillis v. United States, 400 A.2d 311 (D.C.1979), this court considered whether a person threatened with death or serious bodily harm has a duty to retreat, if it can be done safely, before using deadly force in defense. Gillis claimed that he had acted in self-defense when a man named Smith approached him on a deserted street late at night and accused him of being with Smith's girl friend. Gillis claimed that Smith reached in Smith's pocket, and pulled out a shiny object. Gillis then pulled out a pistol, shot, and mortally wounded Smith. Gillis was convicted of second-degree murder while armed.

On appeal, Gillis asserted that the trial court's jury instruction erroneously implied the existence of a duty to retreat, that instruction being essentially the instruction set out above except for its omission of the second sentence. . . . This formulation expressed an emphasis consistent

---

85. The text of Instruction 5.16B instructs the jury that the defendant must have actually believed and had reasonable grounds to believe that he was in imminent danger. We note that the trial court instructed the jury only that the defendant must have actually believed that he was in imminent danger. This omission does not give Cooper cause to complain, for it worked to his advantage. See Carter v. United States, 475 A.2d 1118, 1124 (D.C.1984), *cert. denied,* 469 U.S. 1226, 105 S.Ct. 1222, 84 L.Ed.2d 362 (1985) (noting that instruction requiring that defendant actually believe and have reasonable grounds for believing he is in imminent danger before invoking self-defense correctly stated the law), Gillis v. United States, 400 A.2d 311, 313 (D.C.1979) (same); see also United States v. Peterson, 157 U.S.App.D.C. 219, 227, 483 F.2d 1222, 1230, *cert. denied,* 414 U.S. 1007, 94 S.Ct. 367, 38 L.Ed.2d 244 (1973) (self-defense predicated on actual and reasonable belief); cf. Mitchell v. United States, 399 A.2d 866, 869 (D.C.1979) (finding no plain error in instruction focusing solely on reasonable person standard).

with the so-called "American rule," which holds that one is not required to retreat whether he is attacked in his home or elsewhere, but may stand his ground and defend himself.

We also noted in *Gillis,* however, that later in Laney v. United States, 54 App.D.C. 56, 294 F. 412 (1923), the Circuit Court of Appeals had written:

"It is a well-settled rule that, before a person can avail himself of the plea of self-defense against the charge of homicide, he must do everything in his power, consistent with his safety, to avoid the danger and avoid the necessity of taking life.... In other words, no necessity for killing an assailant can exist, so long as there is a safe way open to escape the conflict."

. . .

Faced with these apparently conflicting precedents, the *Gillis* court reconciled them in what it termed a "middle ground" approach to self-defense. The middle ground approach imposes no duty to retreat, but it "permit(s) the jury to consider whether a defendant, if he safely could have avoided further encounter by stepping back or walking away, was actually or apparently in imminent danger of bodily harm. In short, this rule permits the jury to determine if the defendant acted too hastily, was too quick to pull the trigger." We affirmed in Gillis, holding that the instruction given did not impose a duty to retreat, but allowed a failure to retreat, together with all the other circumstances, to be considered by the jury in determining whether the case was truly one of self-defense.

The unique question presented in this appeal is whether, when one is assaulted in one's home by a co-occupant, the availability of a means of retreat is as much a consideration as it otherwise is under the middle ground approach. No cases in this jurisdiction have been called to our attention which address the question regarding an occupant's duty or ability to retreat in the face of an assault by a co-occupant, nor have we been able to identify any. We look, then, to see how other courts have addressed this issue.

We begin by noting that the question whether an occupant has a duty to retreat when assaulted by a co-occupant will not arise in those jurisdictions which follow the American rule, for in those jurisdictions one can stand one's ground regardless of where one is assaulted, or by whom. Therefore, whatever guidance is available is provided by the courts of those jurisdictions which follow the common law, "retreat to the wall," rule.

Those jurisdictions following the common law rule have almost universally adopted the "castle doctrine" that one who through no fault of his own is attacked in one's own home is under no duty to retreat. While the status of the castle doctrine in the District of Columbia has never been squarely decided, we will assume for purposes of this discussion that appellant is correct in maintaining that the doctrine is applicable here.

Courts following the common law rule have split, however, regarding whether a defendant is entitled to a castle doctrine instruction when the defendant is assaulted by a co-occupant. An early case addressing this question was People v. Tomlins, 107 N.E. 496 (N.Y.1914). In *Tomlins,* a father shot and killed his son in their cottage. The New York Court of Appeals held that an instruction which informed the jury that the father had a duty to retreat was erroneous. The court first noted that if a man is assaulted in his home, "he may stand his ground and resist the attack. He is under no duty to take to the fields and the highways, a fugitive from his own home." The court then held that the rule is the same whether the attack is initiated by an intruder or a co-occupant; "why ... should one retreat from his own house, when assailed by a partner or co-tenant, any more than when assailed by a stranger who is lawfully on the premises? Whither shall he flee, and how far, and when may he be permitted to return?"

As other courts grappled with this question, they often returned to the questions posed by the *Tomlins* court, although frequently reaching a different result. A majority of courts favors giving a castle doctrine instruction when a defendant claims self-defense when attacked in his home by a co-occupant, *see, e.g.,* State v. Browning, 28 N.C.App. 376, 221 S.E.2d 375 (1976); People v. Lenkevich, 394 Mich. 117, 229 N.W.2d 298 (1975); State v. Grantham, 224 S.C. 41, 77 S.E.2d 291 (1953); State v. Phillips, 187 A. 721 (Del.1936), while a substantial minority holds that the castle doctrine does not apply in this special circumstance, *e.g.,* State v. Bobbitt, 415 So.2d 724 (Fla.1982); Commonwealth v. Walker, 447 Pa. 146, 288 A.2d 741 (1972); State v. Grierson, 96 N.H. 36, 69 A.2d 851 (1949). Those decisions which favor giving a castle doctrine instruction stress the occupant's interest in remaining in the home, *e.g., Tomlins,* 107 N.E. at 497, *Phillips,* 187 A. at 721, while those that oppose giving the instruction focus on the entitlement of both combatants to occupy the house and the fact that they usually are related, and reason that the parties have some obligation to attempt to defuse the situation.

Having examined these authorities, we are convinced that the reasoning of those jurisdictions holding that a castle doctrine instruction should *not* be given in instances of co-occupant attacks is the more compelling. As the Florida Supreme Court noted in *Bobbitt, supra,* both the decedent husband and accused wife in the case before it "had equal rights to be in the 'castle' and neither had the legal right to eject the other." The court further observed:

We see no reason why a mother should not retreat from her own son, even in her own kitchen. Such a view does not render her defenseless against a member of her family gone berserk, because ... a person placed in the position of imminent danger of death or great bodily harm to himself by the wrongful attack of another has no duty to retreat if to do so would increase his own danger of death or great bodily harm.

Although in *Bobbitt,* the Florida Supreme Court used the analogy of a mother attacked by her son, that court's reasoning is also applicable to situations where a daughter attacks her father, a husband attacks his wife, or as here, a brother attacks his brother. Indeed, all co-occupants, even those unrelated by blood or marriage, have a heightened obligation to treat each other with a degree of tolerance and respect. That obligation does not evaporate when one co-occupant disregards it and attacks another. We are satisfied, moreover, that an instruction that embraces the middle ground approach appropriately permits the jury to consider the truly relevant question, *i.e.*, whether a defendant, "if he safely could have avoided further encounter by stepping back or walking away, was actually or apparently in imminent danger of bodily harm." We hold that evidence that the defendant was attacked in his home by a co-occupant did not entitle him to an instruction that he had no duty whatsoever to retreat. The trial court did not err in refusing to give a castle doctrine instruction under the circumstances of this case.

Affirmed.

State v. Hanton

Supreme Court of Washington, En Bank, 1980.
94 Wn.2d 129, 614 P.2d 1280.

■ WILLIAMS, JUSTICE. Petitioner Solomon Hanton seeks review of a jury conviction of first-degree manslaughter while armed with a deadly weapon. The Court of Appeals affirmed the conviction in an unpublished opinion. We reverse the Court of Appeals and remand the case for a new trial.

Petitioner and the victim were driving their respective automobiles in Bellevue, Washington on February 25, 1977. While leaving an intersection, petitioner pulled in front of the victim's car in such a manner as to cut him off, causing him to apply his brakes to avoid an accident. This apparently made the victim quite angry, for he followed close behind petitioner's car until they stopped at the next stoplight. There the victim left his car, came up to petitioner's car, opened the door, and attempted to pull him out. Petitioner thereupon drew a pistol and shot him. He died several days later as a result of the wound.

Petitioner was charged with and convicted of first-degree manslaughter. RCW 9A.32.060(1)(a). At trial he requested the following instruction on self-defense:

When a defendant claims he killed another in defense of his person or property, the burden is upon that defendant only to produce some evidence, no matter how slight, tending to prove that the homicide was done in self-defense. It is not necessary for the defendant to prove this to you beyond a reasonable doubt, nor by a preponderance of the evidence. The defendant sustains this burden of proof, if from a consideration of the evidence in the case you have a reasonable doubt as to whether or not the killing was done in self-defense.

It is the duty of the State to prove beyond a reasonable doubt the lack of self-defense.

The court gave the following instruction:

When a defendant claims he killed another in defense of his person or property, the burden is upon that defendant only to produce some evidence tending to prove that the homicide was done in self-defense. It is not necessary for the defendant to prove this to you beyond a reasonable doubt, nor by a preponderance of the evidence. The defendant sustains this burden of proof, if from a consideration of the evidence in the case you have a reasonable doubt as to whether or not the killing was done in self-defense.

Instruction No. 13.

On appeal, petitioner argued that the instruction as given unconstitutionally placed on him the burden of proving self-defense and that such an allocation of the burden had been disapproved by this court in State v. Roberts, 88 Wash.2d 337, 562 P.2d 1259 (1977). The Court of Appeals rejected the applicability of this reasoning to homicide offenses under the new criminal code, RCW 9A.32, relying on State v. Bradley, 20 Wash.App. 340, 581 P.2d 1053 (1978).

We agree with petitioner that the effect of the challenged instruction was to shift to petitioner the burden of proof on self-defense. The instruction as given was substantially the same as the one at issue in *Roberts*. We found that instruction defective because it impermissibly shifted the burden to the accused. The same shift in the allocation of the burden occurred here. Therefore, the only question here is whether the burden may be allocated to an accused under the present statute.

We begin by noting that the due process clause of the fourteenth amendment to the United States Constitution requires the prosecution to prove beyond a reasonable doubt every fact necessary to constitute the crime with which an accused is charged. This principle has been reaffirmed recently by the United States Supreme Court in Sandstrom v. Montana, 442 U.S. 510, 99 S.Ct. 2450, 61 L.Ed.2d 39, 48 (1979). See also Patterson v. New York, 432 U.S. 197, 206–07, 97 S.Ct. 2319, 2324–25, 53 L.Ed.2d 281 (1977).

In order to determine which facts the prosecution must prove beyond a reasonable doubt, it is necessary to analyze each element of the crime charged. The Court of Appeals cited *State v. Bradley, supra*, in support of its holding that absence of self-defense is not an element of a *homicide offense* under the new criminal code and that the State may therefore impose on an accused the burden of proving it. But the court did not analyze the elements of the crime of manslaughter either in *Bradley* or in the present case. Since murder and manslaughter are clearly separate homicide offenses under the statutory scheme, we must analyze *each* element of first-degree manslaughter in our consideration of petitioner's claim.

RCW 9A.32.060(1)(a) states, in pertinent part:

> (1) A person is guilty of manslaughter in the first degree when:
>
> (a) He recklessly causes the death of another person . . .

Since recklessness is expressly made an element of the crime of first-degree manslaughter, the prosecution must prove it beyond a reasonable doubt. *State v. Roberts, supra*. The statute provides:

> (c) *Recklessness*. A person is reckless or acts recklessly when he knows of and disregards a substantial risk that a wrongful act may occur and his disregard of such substantial risk is a gross

deviation from conduct that a reasonable man would exercise in the same situation.

RCW 9A.08.010(1)(c).

Self-defense is explicitly made a lawful act by at least two provisions of the criminal code. First, homicide is justifiable when committed either:

> (1) In the lawful defense of the slayer, or his or her husband, wife, parent, child, brother, or sister, or of any other person in his presence or company, when there is reasonable ground to apprehend a design on the part of the person slain to commit a felony or to do some great personal injury to the slayer or to any such person, and there is imminent danger of such design being accomplished; or

> (2) In the actual resistance of an attempt to commit a felony upon the slayer, in his presence, or upon or in a dwelling, or other place of abode, in which he is.

RCW 9A.16.050(1) and (2). Moreover, use of force is not unlawful when used "by a party about to be injured ... in preventing or attempting to prevent an offense against his person." RCW 9A.16.020(3).

A person acting in self-defense cannot be acting recklessly as that term is defined in RCW 9A.08.010(1)(c). There can be no recklessness without disregard of risk of a wrongful act, and self-defense, as defined, is not "wrongful." Moreover, since self-defense is not wrongful, it cannot be "a gross deviation from conduct that a reasonable man would exercise in the same situation." RCW 9A.08.010(1)(c).

In short, an action taken in self-defense is inconsistent with the statutory definition of recklessness. Since proof of self-defense negates the element of recklessness in first-degree manslaughter, requiring an accused to prove self-defense places on him or her the burden of proving absence of recklessness. Such a result is proscribed by *Winship* and *Mullaney*. Accordingly, we hold that in a prosecution for first-degree manslaughter the State must bear the burden of proving absence of self-defense beyond a reasonable doubt. This conclusion makes it unnecessary to consider petitioner's statutory construction argument that the legislature intended to place the burden on the State.

It does not necessarily follow, however, that the court must instruct the jury that the burden of proof on self-defense rests on the prosecution. When recklessness is an element of the crime charged, and the court properly instructs the jury on the elements of recklessness, the jury must determine, before it may convict, that the accused knew of and disregarded a substantial risk that a wrongful act would occur and that such disregard was a gross deviation from the conduct of a reasonable person in the same situation. Such a finding is totally inconsistent with self-defense. A person acting in self-defense cannot be acting recklessly. Thus, if the jury is able to find that a defendant acted recklessly, it has already precluded a finding of self-defense. We hold, therefore, that an instruction allocating the burden of proof to the State to disprove self-defense is not necessary when there is adequate instruction on the elements of recklessness.

If a defendant presents sufficient evidence to raise an issue of self-defense, the court need only instruct on it without allocating the burden of proof. Such an instruction permits a defendant to fully argue his theory of the case. The jury may then consider the evidence of self-defense in determining whether a defendant was acting recklessly.

We reverse and remand for a new trial.[86]

■ UTTER, C.J., and ROSELLINI, STAFFORD, WRIGHT, BRACHTENBACH, HOROWITZ, DOLLIVER and HICKS, JJ., concur.

State v. Broadhurst

Supreme Court of Oregon, 1948.
184 Or. 178, 196 P.2d 407.

(Defendant, who had "married" Dr. Broadhurst although she was the wife of another, asked Williams to kill her "husband." Williams pretended to have car trouble at a spot on a lonely road where he knew Dr. Broadhurst would be driving. Dr. Broadhurst stopped to give help and Williams hit him over the head with a heavy wrench. At that point, according to Williams' testimony, he changed his mind and decided to leave without killing the other. But Dr. Broadhurst came at him and he was forced to kill to save his own life. Defendant was convicted of first degree murder and appeals.)

■ ROSSMAN, C.J. . . . Finally, under this contention the defendant argues that the testimony of Williams shows that he shot in self-defense and that Williams' testimony is binding upon the State. She, therefore, claims that the crime of murder was not committed.

In a preceding paragraph we showed that Williams swore that he struck Dr. Broadhurst only once with the wrench. He claimed that at that juncture he underwent a change of heart and decided to quit. His actual words were: "I had quit. . . . I decided I was going to leave the country right away." By reverting to the preceding paragraph, the testimony can be read upon which the defendant depends for a contention that two affrays occurred at the Succor Creek junction: (a) one in which Williams was the aggressor, and (b) a second in which Dr. Broadhurst was the aggressor. The defendant claims that Williams abandoned the first before the second purported affray was begun.

Dr. Joseph Beeman, whose qualifications are admitted, performed an autopsy upon Dr. Broadhurst's remains. He found three wounds upon the forehead. One was three-eights of an inch in diameter, another was an inch and a half in diameter. He said: "This wound had gone down to the skull."

---

86. This case states the majority position on the burden of proof in cases where self-defense is raised as an issue. State v. Richardson, 393 N.W.2d 657 (Minn.1986); Commonwealth v. Rodriguez, 370 Mass. 684, 352 N.E.2d 203 (1976); State v. Turner, 29 N.C.App. 33, 222 S.E.2d 745 (1976); State v. Parish, 118 N.M. 39, 878 P.2d 988 (1994). However, the United States Supreme Court has rejected a constitutional standard on whether the burden of proof may be placed on the defendant. "We are not moved by assertions that elements of aggravated murder and self-defense overlap in the sense that evidence to prove the latter will often tend to negate the former." A state may constitutionally shift the burden of proof of self defense to a defendant. Martin v. Ohio, 480 U.S. 228, 107 S.Ct. 1098, 1102 (1987).

The third wound "was one and five-eighths of an inch long and three-fourths of an inch wide." According to the witness it "had gone through the skull and had torn the frontal part ... had fractured the skull bone over the right eye." We call attention to the fact that two of the blows penetrated the skull and that one of them fractured the skull bone. Dr. Beeman testified that the shotgun wounds were in the right chest. We quote from him:

"He had the shotgun wounds in his right chest which was going from left to right, just slightly upwards and slightly backwards." ...

An aggressor, in a combat which led to the death of the assaulted party, can not claim that he struck the fatal blow in self-defense unless, before the blow, he withdrew in good faith from the combat, and, in addition, brought home to the assaulted man notice of his intention in such a way that the adversary, as a reasonable man, must have known that the assault was ended. Abandonment of the assault and reasonable notice thereof are essential to restore to the aggressor the right of self-defense. Vol. 40, C.J.S., Homicide, § 121, page 995, in stating the rule to which we are adverting says:

"... He must also in some manner make known his intention to his adversary; and if the circumstances are such that he cannot notify his adversary, as where the injuries inflicted by him are such as to deprive his adversary of his capacity to receive impressions concerning his assailant's design and endeavor to cease further combat, it is the assailant's fault and he must bear the consequences. As long as a person keeps his gun in his hand prepared to shoot, the person opposing him is not expected or required to accept any act or statement as indicative of an intent to discontinue the assault."

In 26 Am.Jur., Homicide, § 135, page 247, we find:

"... Nor is this all; the aggressor must inform his antagonist of his purpose to withdraw from the conflict. If the circumstances are such that he cannot do this, it is attributable to his own fault and he must abide by the consequences."

Both of the treatises from which we quoted cite in partial support of their statements People v. Button, 106 Cal. 628, 39 P. 1073, 28 L.R.A. 591, 46 Am.St.Rep. 259. That decision is carefully reasoned and fully supports the claims made for it.

If Williams had quit the combat before he shot Dr. Broadhurst, he did not manifest that fact in any way whatever, with the exception of walking a few steps to his automobile. But upon the seat of the car lay his gun ready to be fired. At the moment when he claims Dr. Broadhurst advanced upon him he still had the wrench in his hand. His own words are, "When he started after me I had the wrench in my hand." There is no evidence that Dr. Broadhurst, upon whose head three vicious blows had rained, one of which fractured his skull bone, had regained consciousness when he is said to have begun an attack upon his assailant. Unless Dr. Broadhurst in some miraculous manner had regained consciousness and had discovered the secret purpose of Williams to abandon the assault, the right of Williams to act in self-defense had not been restored. Williams was asked: "Was he pretty well recovered when you handed the shirt to him?'' He answered, ''No.'' The nearest he came to attributing consciousness to the battered, bloody victim of his brutal blows was made in the following answer: ''I had just got to the door and he started to come after me, so I imagine he was coming out of it.'' If Dr. Broadhurst advanced upon Williams, then we think that the following, taken from People v. Button, supra, is applicable:

''While the deceased had eyes to see and ears to hear, he had no mind to comprehend, for his mind was taken from him by the defendant at the first assault. Throughout the whole affray, it must be conceded that the deceased was guilty of no wrong, no violation of the law. When he attempted to kill the defendant, he thought he was acting in self-defense, and, according to his lights, he was acting in self-defense.''

We are certain that the fifth and sixth contentions are without merit. . . .

The judgment of the circuit court is affirmed.[87]

(Certiorari denied 337 U.S. 906, 69 S.Ct. 1046, 93 L.Ed. 1718.)

MODEL PENAL CODE

Section 3.04   Use of Force in Self–Protection.

(1) Use of Force Justifiable for Protection of the Person. Subject to the provisions of this Section and of Section 3.09, the use of force upon or toward another person is justifiable when the actor believes that such force is immediately necessary for the purpose of protecting himself against the use of unlawful force by such other person on the present occasion.

(2) Limitations on Justifying Necessity for Use of Force.

(a) The use of force is not justifiable under this Section:

(i) to resist an arrest which the actor knows is being made by a peace officer, although the arrest is unlawful; or

(ii) to resist force used by the occupier or possessor of property or by another person on his behalf, where the actor knows that the person using the force is doing so under a claim of right to protect the property, except that this limitation shall not apply if:

---

87. ''The right of self-defense is available only to one who is without fault. If a person voluntarily, i.e., aggressively and willingly, without legal provocation or excuse, enters into a fight, he cannot invoke the doctrine of self-defense unless he abandons the fight, withdraws from it, and gives notice to his adversary that he has done so.'' State v. Jones, 56 N.C.App. 259, 289 S.E.2d 383, 392 (1982).

''However, it is well settled ... that self-defense is not available to a person who is committing or attempting to commit a forcible felony.'' State v. Marks, 226 Kan. 704, 602 P.2d 1344, 1351 (1979).

Even if the victim were the original aggressor, once he withdrew from the encounter and the danger to defendant was no longer immediate, urgent and pressing the defendant was not justified in pursuing him to continue the fight. Girtman v. State, 285 Ark. 13, 684 S.W.2d 806 (1985). Accord, People v. Goedecke, 730 P.2d 900 (Colo.App.1986). See also Allen v. State, 871 P.2d 79 (Okl.Cr.1994).

Defendant who killed the victim in the course of a robbery could not claim self-defense in justification of the killing. State v. Bradley, 521 A.2d 289 (Me.1987).

Self-defense is not available where defendant is the aggressor or engages in mutual combat. State v. Pascual, 804 P.2d 553 (Utah App.1991).

(1) the actor is a public officer acting in the performance of his duties or a person lawfully assisting him therein or a person making or assisting in a lawful arrest; or

(2) the actor has been unlawfully dispossessed of the property and is making a re-entry or recaption justified by Section 3.06; or

(3) the actor believes that such force is necessary to protect himself against death or serious bodily harm.

(b) The use of deadly force is not justifiable under this Section unless the actor believes that such force is necessary to protect himself against death, serious bodily harm, kidnapping or sexual intercourse compelled by force or threat; nor is it justifiable if:

(i) the actor, with the purpose of causing death or serious bodily harm, provoked the use of force against himself in the same encounter; or

(ii) the actor knows that he can avoid the necessity of using such force with complete safety by retreating or by surrendering possession of a thing to a person asserting a claim of right thereto or by complying with a demand that he abstain from any action which he has no duty to take, except that:

(1) the actor is not obliged to retreat from his dwelling or place of work, unless he was the initial aggressor or is assailed in his place of work by another person whose place of work the actor knows it to be; and

(2) a public officer justified in using force in the performance of his duties or a person justified in using force in his assistance or a person justified in using force in making an arrest or preventing an escape is not obliged to desist from efforts to perform such duty, effect such arrest or prevent such escape because of resistance or threatened resistance by or on behalf of the person against whom such action is directed.

(c) Except as required by paragraphs (a) and (b) of this Subsection, a person employing protective force may estimate the necessity thereof under the circumstances as he believes them to be when the force is used, without retreating, surrendering possession, doing any other act which he has no legal duty to do or abstaining from any lawful action.

(3) Use of Confinement as Protective Force. The justification afforded by this Section extends to the use of confinement as protective force only if the actor takes all reasonable measures to terminate the confinement as soon as he knows that he safely can, unless the person confined has been arrested on a charge of crime.[88]

SECTION 5.   DEFENSE OF OTHERS

"Ordinarily,—if not always," says Bishop, "one may do in another's defence whatever the other might in the circumstances do for himself."[89] But while this has been repeated now and then[90] it is broader than the original special privilege granted to one to use force in the aid of another.[91]

---

88. Copyright © 1962 by the American Law Institute. Reprinted with the permission of the American Law Institute.

89. Bishop, Criminal Law § 877 (9th Ed.1923).

90. Stanley v. Commonwealth, 86 Ky. 440, 6 S.W. 155 (1887).

91. Morrison v. Commonwealth, 74 S.W. 277, 24 Ky.Law Rep. 2493 (1903); Restatement, Second, Torts § 76 (1965).

This special privilege seems to have had its roots in the law of property.[92] The privilege of one to protect what belongs to one was extended to include the protection of a spouse wife, children and servants. In the course of time this privilege outgrew the property analogy and came to be regarded as a "mutual and reciprocal defence."[93] The household was regarded as a group. Any member of the family had the privilege of defending another member; the master could defend the servant, or the servant defend the master.[94] Even this concept of the privilege has been outgrown. It now includes the members of one's immediate family or household and any other whom one is under a legal or socially-recognized duty to protect.[95] Thus a conductor is privileged to defend a passenger, and a person is privileged to defend a friend whom the person is with at the moment.[96] In recent years, these classifications became of less importance. The special privilege of using force for the defense of others has now generally been extended to include the protection of a stranger.[97]

The privilege to use force in defense of another is subject to the same general limitations and restrictions as the privilege to use force in self-defense. Hence deadly force may not be used to save another from non-deadly force,[98] and even non-deadly force must not be obviously in excess of what is needed for the purpose.[99]

This special privilege to use force in the defense of persons does not supersede the privilege to use force for the prevention of crime. It is in addition thereto.[100] One person may be in a position to claim both privileges.[101] Another may have the benefit of one only,—or of neither.

---

92.   Restatement, Second, Torts § 76, Comment *e* (1965).

93.   3 Bl.Comm. 3.

94.   "A man may defend his family, his servants or his master, whenever he may defend himself." Pond v. People, 8 Mich. 150, 176 (1860).

95.   Restatement, Second, Torts § 76, Comments *e, f* (1965).

96.   Ibid.

97.   "Nearly every American jurisdiction recognizes a justification for defense of other persons." Paul H.Robinson, Criminal Law Defenses § 133 (1984).

The defense of another is available to a defendant against a police officer using excessive force against another. Batson v. State, 113 Nev. 669, 941 P.2d 478 (Nev.1997).

98.   Id. at Comment *b*. People v. Jordan, 130 Ill.App.3d 810, 86 Ill.Dec. 86, 474 N.E.2d 1283 (1985).

99.   Ibid. State v. Pounders, 913 S.W.2d 904 (Mo.App.1996).

100.   In a case in which the relation between the parties was not emphasized the court said: "The law makes it the duty of every one, who sees a felony attempted by violence, to prevent it, if possible, and allows him to use the necessary means to make his resistance effectual. One may kill in defense of another under the same circumstances that he would have the right to kill in defense of himself." State v. Hennessy, 29 Nev. 320, 344, 90 P. 221, 227 (1907).

101.   "As to the defendant Wendell Reed, the court failed to charge the law with respect to both (a) his right to fight in the necessary defense of his step-father, and (b) his right and duty as a private citizen to interfere to prevent a felonious assault. Each right is recognized in the decisions of this court." State v. Robinson, 213 N.C. 273, 281, 195 S.E. 824, 829–30 (1938).

West's Ann.Cal.Pen.Code, § 197 (1996). "Homicide is also justifiable when committed by any person in any of the following cases: . . .

State v. Saunders

Supreme Court of Appeals of West Virginia, 1985.
175 W.Va. 16, 330 S.E.2d 674.

■ NEELY, CHIEF JUSTICE:

"The Hill" in downtown Beckley, West Virginia is a rough part of town. Its bars, poolrooms, speakeasies, and disco joints cater to an evening sub-culture that emerges at night to the dismay of the ordinary, law-abiding citizen. It was outside of one of "The Hill's" establishments, the Nite Flite, that ... the appellant, Robert Saunders, fatally shot Phillip Kincannon in the left buttocks, a wound from which Mr. Kincannon later bled to death on a pool table. Our appellant insists that by shooting Mr. Kincannon he was defending his brother, James Saunders. He argues that his conviction of first-degree murder and sentence of life imprisonment with a recommendation of mercy should be reversed because, inter alia, the circuit court refused an instruction on defense of another as an extension of the affirmative defense of self-defense.

Confusion and conflicting testimony surround the death of Mr. Kincannon. It appears, however, that the appellant's brother, James Saunders, was involved in a series of fights with the Kincannon brothers, Phillip and Brian. During one of these altercations, Brian Kincannon, assisted by his brother, wrestled James Saunders to the ground and pinned him in a full nelson.

Our appellant, while not directly involved in the melee between his brother and the Kincannons, had participated in much of the verbal foreplay that led to the fracas. That night, when Robert Saunders went to the Nite Flite his brother James and Phillip Kincannon were exchanging angry words.... Robert Saunders testified that when he intervened on his brother's behalf, Phillip Kincannon retreated to recruit his brother Brian to his aid. Fearing a brawl, the Nite Flite's owner escorted the Saunders brothers outside.

When the Saunders emerged from the bar the Kincannons confronted them. James was attacked and overwhelmed. Robert—a slight young man weighing under 130 pounds stood nervously aside. But when James was on the ground, tightly held by Phillip Kincannon, and being "frisked" for a weapon that he did not have, Robert Saunders panicked. The appellant and two other witnesses subsequently testified that Brian Kincannon was

---

"1. When resisting any attempt to murder any person ... or to do some great bodily injury upon any person; or ...

"3. When committed in the lawful defense of ... a wife or husband, parent, child, master, mistress, or servant of such person, when there is reasonable ground to apprehend a design to commit a felony or to do some great bodily injury, and imminent danger of such design being accomplished; but such person, or the person in whose behalf the defense was made, if he was the assailant or engaged in mutual combat must really and in good faith have endeavored to decline any further struggle before the homicide was committed; ...".

"The statutory justification for the use of deadly force in defense of a person as contained in K.S.A. 21–3211 is to be determined by the trier of fact using an objective standard, i.e., from the viewpoint of a reasonable man in accused's position." State v. Simon, 231 Kan. 572, 646 P.2d 1119 (1982) (Syllabus by the court).

exclaiming that he would kill James with James' own (non-existent) weapon.

The appellant at this time insists that he was afraid for his brother's life. He knew that one of the witnesses to the fight, Mr. Ronnie Campbell kept a gun in his automobile. Suddenly he darted over to Mr. Campbell's vehicle to extract the .357–calibre Magnum revolver. Mr. Campbell testified that although he snatched the gun from Mr. Saunders immediately and placed it under his belt, the appellant suddenly grabbed it from him and fired a shot over the heads of the combatants. The appellant testified that he then lowered the revolver, aimed at the deceased's leg and fired. He claims he did not realize that he hit the deceased but rather became frightened, dropped the revolver and fled. . . .

Over one hundred years ago this Court held that the right of self-defense may be exercised in behalf of a brother, or of a stranger. In 1883, this Court stated:

What one may lawfully do in defence of himself—when threatened with death or great bodily harm, he may do in behalf of a brother; but if the brother was in fault in provoking an assault, that brother must retreat as far as he safely can, before his brother would be justified in taking the life of his assailant in his defence of the brother. But if the brother was so drunk as not to be mentally able to know his duty to retreat, or was physically unable to retreat, a brother is not bound to stand by and see him killed or suffer great bodily harm, because he does not under such circumstances retreat. It is only the faultless, who are exempt from the necessity of retreating while acting in self-defence. Those in fault must retreat, if able to do so; if from the fierceness of the attack or for other reasons they are unable to retreat, they will be excused by the law for not doing so. State of W.Va. v. Greer, 22 W.Va. 800, at 819 (1883).

In the case before us the lower court refused any instructions on defense of another and apparently proceeded under the erroneous assumption that defense of another is not law in West Virginia. The court accordingly excluded the following defense instruction: "The court instructs you that if you believe from the evidence that Robert Saunders believed that his brother was about to be killed or in danger of great bodily harm, he had a right to use force to prevent his brother from being killed or injured."

The State counters that the court's refusal to give instructions in regard to the defense of another was harmless error. It notes that an unnumbered defendant's instruction, that was given, informed the jury that if the defendant's use of a dangerous and deadly weapon resulted from sudden passion brought about by his brother's being beaten, assaulted, and struck by the deceased and his brother without fault on the part of the defendant, then malice cannot be presumed. The State maintains that had the jury believed that the appellant was acting in defense of himself or his brother, a verdict of voluntary manslaughter would have been returned. Because the jury did not believe that contention, obviously the jury found that the appellant unlawfully, feloniously and maliciously, etc. murdered the deceased and thus the conviction of first-degree murder ought be affirmed by this Court.

The defense instruction to which the State refers is not improper but it is insufficient to explain to the jury the affirmative defense of defense of another, a defense available in this State and in many other jurisdictions. As such the instruction on which the State relies as an adequate statement of the right to defend another was misleading, confusing, and hence inadequate *on the issue of defense of another....*

Although this Court has not dealt directly in recent years with the defense of another defense, we are not bereft totally of collateral precedent. In State v. Collins, 154 W.Va. 771, 180 S.E.2d 54 (1971), this Court was presented with a situation in which a tavern owner fatally shot two patrons who were involved in a barroom brawl with a third customer. The Court failed to address directly the question of defense of another because it determined there was no necessity for the tavern owner to fire any shots other than his first two warning shots to end the disturbance. Although the tavern owner pleaded that he shot the patrons to protect, in addition to himself, the third party from injury or death, the evidence indicated that when he shot the fatal rounds the fight was over and "there was no necessity for him to act as he did to protect Marcum from danger of death or serious injury."

... The Court added, somewhat gratuitously, that:

"... it is unnecessary to consider or determine whether the (excluded) instruction correctly states the law as to the right of a person to intervene to protect another person whose life is in danger and as to the degree of force he may use to repel the attack of the assailant; and those questions are not discussed, considered or determined."

In discussing the use of deadly force by the occupant of a dwelling on an unlawful intruder who threatens imminent physical violence or the commission of a felony, this Court has stated that "[t]he taking of life to prevent the commission of a felony, however, is not limited to self-defense in the home, but is part of a more general rule relating to crime prevention." State v. W.J.B., 166 W.Va. 602, 276 S.E.2d 550, at 555 (1981). In *W.J.B.,* this Court opined that: "[w]e have recognized the accepted rule that the defendant may interpose the defense of self-defense in protecting a member of his family as well as in protecting himself."

Other jurisdictions grant that one has the right to intervene on behalf of another in certain situations. The right to defense of another usually falls under the rubric of self-defense. One simply steps into the shoes of the victim and is able to do only as much as the victim himself would lawfully be permitted to do. *See* State v. Barnes, 675 S.W.2d 195 (Tenn.Crim.App. 1984); State v. Matthews, 459 So.2d 40 (La.App. 1 Cir.1984), *cause remanded by* State v. Matthews, 464 So.2d 298 (1985); Commonwealth v. Gray, 441 Pa. 91, 271 A.2d 486, at 488 (1970); People v. Young, 12 A.D.2d 262, 210 N.Y.S.2d 358 (1961).

In the recent *Barnes* case, the Tennessee Court of Criminal Appeals dismissed a conviction for involuntary manslaughter where the appellant's defense was that he struck the deceased in defense of a lady who was being assaulted. The court stated: "A person can do whatever the person for whom he intervenes could have done in his own self-defense."

The validity of a claim of defense of another, like the question of self-defense, is properly a matter for the jury's determination. This Court has frequently stated, in cases of self-defense, that the prosecution must prove beyond a reasonable doubt that the defendant did not act in self-defense in order successfully to overcome the defendant's affirmative defense. In this case, the jury ought to have been provided with the proffered instruction on defense of another because the defense exists in West Virginia and because, in this case, there is sufficient evidence to allow the jury to consider whether the appellant believed the Kincannons were going to injure seriously or even kill his brother.

Accordingly we reverse the circuit court and remand this case for a new trial consistent with this opinion. Because the appellant will receive a new trial, it's unnecessary to address the appellant's other assignments of error.

Reversed and Remanded.[102]

Alexander v. State

Court of Special Appeals of Maryland, 1982.
52 Md.App. 171, 447 A.2d 880, affirmed 294 Md. 600, 451 A.2d 664 (1982).

■ LOWE, JUDGE.

In the decade that commenced with the assassination of President Kennedy, climaxed with the creation of this Court, and concluded with the marriage of Tiny Tim, violence proliferated, partly because police were constitutionally hobbled in controlling a rebellious reaction and partly because citizens were reluctant—or afraid—to become "involved" in deterring that violence. This reticence seemed to emanate less from fear of physical harm than from the potential consequences of a legal aftermath. Representative was the 1964 New York homicide of Catherine "Kitty" Genovese, who was viciously ravaged and repeatedly stabbed while onlookers turned their backs to avoid witnessing the butchery, and neighbors closed their doors and windows to shut out her screams of anguish until her suffering was finally ended by the murderer. Witnesses who were interviewed excused their indifference by noting that the law did not protect a protector from criminal assault charges if the one he aids was initially in the wrong, however misleading appearances may have been. See People v. Young, 11 N.Y.2d 274, 229 N.Y.S.2d 1, 183 N.E.2d 319 (1962). The onlookers hesitated to become involved in the fracas at their legal peril. Even if their hearts had been stout enough to enter the fray in defense of a stranger being violently assaulted, the fear of legal consequences chilled their better instincts.

---

102. "Although a person had the right to use deadly force to defend his spouse and children as well as himself from the infliction of great bodily injury, the exercise of that right must be grounded upon a reasonable apprehension of imminent harm, and a reasonable belief that the killing is necessary to protect against such injury. I.C. 18–4009 ..." State v. Carter, 103 Idaho 917, 655 P.2d 434 (1981).

The law of retreat does not apply to one coming to the defense of a third person. Hughes v. State, 721 S.W.2d 356 (Tex.App.1985), but see Henderson v. State, 906 S.W.2d 589 (Tex.App.1995).

At common law, the privilege of using force for crime prevention did not include authority for intervenors to protect third persons who were strangers to the intervenor. The privilege, even now in some jurisdictions, was limited to the protection of those closely related to, or associated with, the intervenor. See Guerriero v. State, 213 Md. 545, 132 A.2d 466 (1957). That restriction to family or close associates was imposed because the right evolved not from the right of self-defense, as most cases imply, but from the right to protect one's property. R. Perkins, Criminal Law (2nd ed. 1969) at 1018–1019. III W. Blackstone, Commentaries on the Law of England 3 (facsimile ed. 1979), described the right as only Blackstone could:

"In these cases, if the party himself, or any of these his relations, be forceably attacked on his person or property, it is lawful for him to repel force by force; and the breach of the peace which happens is chargeable upon him only who began the affray."

Although it was merely a defense, an excuse for breach of the peace (or even homicide), Blackstone put great emphasis upon the natural source of this legal right. He felt that it

"is justly called the primary law of nature, so it is not, neither can it be in fact, taken away by the law of society." *Id.* at 4.

Perhaps because the right to protect one's "property" (*i.e.,* his household, which included wife, children, servants, etc.) carried the same limitations upon the degree of force employed as did self-defense, many, if not most, of the courts in this country addressed the issue from the view that no force could be justifiably employed unless the protected person may have justifiably defended himself. That generally was the law espoused by the leading New York case of Young, *supra,* where the court affirmed the conviction for assault of a defendant who, in good faith, intervened in a struggle between a plain clothes police officer and a person whose arrest the police officer was attempting to effect.

The Maryland Court of Appeals has never directly addressed the issue, but inclined with the majority by strong dicta in 1957. . . .

"A third person, closely related to or associated with one attacked in such a manner that he could properly have defended himself by the use of force, has a right to go to the defense of the person attacked and to use the same degree and character of force that the one attacked could have used."

The care with which the Court chose to refrain from espousing any law beyond the narrow confines of the facts of that case is emphasized by the next sentence, in which the court hesitated to concede that a brother was a sufficiently close relative to warrant a right to that defense.

"The cases differ as to whether, and under what circumstances, one may so defend a brother in danger but we assume, without deciding, that he may, since the State concedes the point."

Early in this Court's judicial life, it carefully adhered to that narrow and restricted espousal of the right to aid third persons, limiting the beneficiaries of such right to relatives or close associates of the intervenor, but more significantly for our present purposes, by restricting the right to "such a manner that he (the victim) could properly have defended himself by the use of force...."

Although the reciprocal right limitation was not clearly or definitively expressed in either *Guerriero* or *Tipton,* both cases showed Maryland leaning toward the New York view that one goes to the aid of another at his peril, and his protection from criminal charges depends not on what appears to him when he intervenes, but rather upon the rights of the person whom he has succored. As Perkins, *supra,* points out,

"it has been common but quite unfortunate to say that the defender 'stands in the shoes' of the one defended with exactly the same privilege or lack of privilege as possessed by the latter."

Perkins finds fault with that theory because it forces a Good Samaritan to gamble not only his health but his freedom and reputation, and overlooks the likelihood that the intervenor might have acted entirely without mens rea, and perhaps even with the highest sense of duty. It deals with such a defender as the willing participant in a brawl; whereas, from his standpoint (with the facts as they reasonably appear to him), he may be seeking to defend an innocent victim from a felonious assault.

Perkins' preferred position better fulfills our contemporary social needs by merging the encouragement of crime prevention with the privilege of defending others.... Maryland abrogated its common law status in that regard in 1965 by broadly extending the right to intervene to aid an apparent victim of a violent assault. Md.Ann.Code (1982 Repl.Vol.), Art. 27, § 12A, provided that:

"*Any person witnessing a violent assault* upon the person of another *may lawfully aid the person being assaulted* by assisting in that person's defense. The force exerted upon the attacker or attackers by the person witnessing the assault may be that degree of force which the assaulted person is allowed to assert in defending himself."

. . .

When House Bill 139 (which became § 12A) was sponsored in 1965, it arose in the wake of the Genovese and other similar causes celebres publicizing the legal dangers of "involvement." As indicated by Pope [v. State, 284 Md. 309, 396 A.2d 1054 (1979)], the Act was clearly intended to encourage and to afford protection to "good samaritans" by removing their legal doubts, which might impede crime prevention and deter those who witness violent assaults upon persons, but who otherwise would aid an apparent victim of criminal violence....

Maryland thus appears to have been in the forefront in safeguarding the right which Blackstone recognized as a legal adjunct of natural instincts, and in adopting what Perkins recommends as the more "enlightened view."

"Subject to the familiar limitations as to the degree of force permitted, one who is himself free from fault may intervene and use force to protect an innocent victim of intended crime. And under the sound view he is protected by the usual mistake-of-fact doctrine and may act upon the situation as it reasonably seems to be."

The clear and unambiguous language of the statute is that the *witnessing* of the violent assault is that which affords protection for the intervenor. There is no reference at all in the Act indicating as a prerequisite to legal absolution that the apparent victim be faultless. To interpret the statute as limited by the common law restrictions would eliminate any purpose for its enactment.

—the factual setting—

The appellant, Ralph Alexander, a prisoner in the Maryland Penitentiary, was convicted by a jury in the Criminal Court of Baltimore (along with Bruce Shreeves, a fellow prisoner), of an assault on a correctional officer, Dale Tscheulin.... The State's witnesses contended that Officer Tscheulin was attacked by Shreeves, who was subsequently assisted in assaulting the officer by appellant Alexander. Appellant Alexander and his witnesses alleged that another officer, Samuel Stokes, Jr., had apparently grabbed prisoner Shreeves from behind, without provocation, and then Officer Tscheulin came to the scene and started hitting Shreeves. Although Shreeves implicitly acknowledged his initial aggression, he contended that Alexander had seen only the violent overreactions by the guards, and that Alexander's actions were therefore appropriate according to his limited view of the situation.

When Alexander approached Tscheulin to state that he didn't have to "beat on" Shreeves as he was doing (according to Alexander), Tscheulin turned around and struck him. Alexander stated that he then simply grabbed the bars and pinned Tscheulin between himself and the bars, but did not strike him; whereupon, he returned to his cell. The State's version did not vary substantially except as to the degree of force used by Alexander. Tscheulin and Stokes agreed that they were subduing Shreeves, who had approached them with a fighting pose on the catwalk of the third tier when the prisoners were ordered to "lock in" after exercise period. Alexander rushed upon the scene, leapt on Tscheulin, who was preoccupied with Shreeves, and struck the officer in the chest and head.

... The issue is whether the trial court erred when it instructed the jury in regard to the law applicable to the defense theory that appellant intervened to aid the apparent victim of an assault. The judge instructed the jurors on defendant Shreeves' right of self-defense as well as appellant's right of self-defense, if they chose to believe that right was raised by the facts or inferences available from the evidence. He then added:

"Now, as to the defendant Alexander there is an additional factor you have to consider. He has a right to go to the defense of Mr. Shreeves to the same extent that Mr. Shreeves has a right to defend himself. The defendant Alexander's right of self-defense is the same as that of the defendant Shreeves but no more, no less. In other words, if Shreeves had the right to defend himself, then Alexander had the right to go help him defend himself; if Shreeves did not have the right to defend himself, then Alexander didn't have the right to go help Shreeves defend himself. He stands in the same shoes as Shreeves when he elects to come to his assistance."

...

... The statute enacted by the Legislature in 1965 dealing with unrelated third persons aiding those under assault was not considered by the parties or the court below, or the parties on appeal. Under the facts of this case, however, the statute is particularly apposite if peculiarly not noted by anyone; ...

. . .

In light of appellant's singular defense and his counsel's pointed objection to the instructions, we believe the court erred in not correcting its instruction, which linked Alexander's fate to Shreeve's culpability. An intervenor's right to react is not strictly coterminous with a participant's right to self-defense. . . .

Under the statute, however, Alexander must be judged on his own conduct, based upon his own observation of the circumstances as they reasonably appeared to him. The reasonableness of his perceptions and the bona fides of his reactions are key elements of consideration by the factfinder, who must review the totality of the circumstances in their setting. . . .

Whatever the law may have been in Maryland prior to 1965, it is clear that the Legislature, motivated by increasing violence in society and the reluctance of citizens to "get involved," sought to afford protection to a defender who acts while injury may still be prevented, rather than awaiting judicial reprisals which are geared to provide punishment after the damage has been done. The probability of that having been appellant's motivation in this prison setting, however, remains a jury question under the proper instructions.

Reversed.

People v. Curtis

Supreme Court of Michigan, 1884.
52 Mich. 616, 18 N.W. 385.

■ CAMPBELL, J. Curtis was tried in the Cass county circuit court and convicted of murder in the second degree. Errors are assigned on rulings during the trial and in instructions to the jury. Macon Wilson was the person killed. . . .

The respondent was entitled and bound to take an interest in the life and safety of his brother. There was no difference in the testimony as to his being in danger, and all the instructions which confined the right of respondent to helping him only when he was entirely without fault were unwarranted. The court refused to charge that a brother might interpose against a felonious or serious bodily harm, unless the assailed party was entirely blameless, and this was contrary to the well-settled principle that a dangerous felony may be prevented by one who is not himself in the wrong, directly or by complicity. . . . [103]

---

103. One may kill if necessary to save his brother's life even if the latter started the difficulty unless he did so with felonious intent. Little v. State, 87 Miss. 512, 40 So. 165 (1906).

The judgment must be reversed and a new trial ordered. The prisoner must be remanded to the custody of the sheriff of Cass county, and must be allowed bail if he desires it, in a moderate amount.

The other Justices concurred.

MODEL PENAL CODE

Section 3.05   Use of Force for the Protection of Other Persons.

(1) Subject to the provisions of this Section and of Section 3.09, the use of force upon or toward the person of another is justifiable to protect a third person when:

(a) the actor would be justified under Section 3.04 in using such force to protect himself against the injury he believes to be threatened to the person whom he seeks to protect; and

(b) under the circumstances as the actor believes them to be, the person whom he seeks to protect would be justified in using such protective force; and

(c) the actor believes that his intervention is necessary for the protection of such other person.

(2) Notwithstanding Subsection (1) of this Section:

(a) when the actor would be obliged under Section 3.04 to retreat, to surrender the possession of a thing or to comply with a demand before using force in self-protection, he is not obliged to do so before using force for the protection of another person, unless he knows that he can thereby secure the complete safety of such other person; and

(b) when the person whom the actor seeks to protect would be obliged under Section 3.04 to retreat, to surrender the possession of a thing or to comply with a demand if he knew that he could obtain complete safety by so doing, the actor is obliged to try to cause him to do so before using force in his protection if the actor knows that he can obtain complete safety in that way; and

(c) neither the actor nor the person whom he seeks to protect is obliged to retreat when in the other's dwelling or place of work to any greater extent than in his own.[104]

SECTION 6.   DEFENSE OF THE HABITATION

The concept of a person's habitation as one's "castle" runs throughout the law and the privilege of defending the habitation must not be confused

---

"It is true, as a general proposition, that self-defense and the related defense of another are affirmative defenses to both murder and voluntary manslaughter. However, these general principles must accommodate a citizen's duty to accede to lawful government power and the special protection due federal officials discharging official duties.... 'We do not need citizen avengers who are authorized to respond to unlawful police conduct by gunning down the offending officers.' Other, non-violent remedies are available." United States v. Branch, 91 F.3d 699, 714 (5th Cir.1996).

A person may raise a "defense of others" in justification for injury other than the victim's actual assailant, but must show a reasonable belief that the person defended is in imminent danger of unlawful bodily harm, and a reasonable belief that another person is associating with and participating with the actual aggressor. Duckett v. State, 966 P.2d 941 (Wyo.1998).

104. Copyright © 1962 by the American Law Institute. Reprinted with the permission of the American Law Institute.

with the privilege of defending property which stands upon a much lower level. At common law the dweller is privileged to use deadly force if this reasonably seems necessary to prevent the commission or consummation of burglary. At this point no greater advantage is given than would be available under the privilege of crime prevention—the prevention of an atrocious felony or a so-called dangerous felony of which burglary is a typical example. And the same may be said of the dweller's privilege to use deadly force if this reasonably seems necessary to save one's habitation from arson.

The defense of the dwelling may be for the purpose of saving the house itself from damage or destruction,[105] or it may be to preserve its character as a place of refuge and repose by preventing the unlawful intrusion of outsiders. The dweller is privileged to use reasonable nondeadly force to prevent any unlawful harm or injury to one's place of abode, or to prevent any unlawful intrusion therein. The dweller is not privileged to use deadly force to prevent any and every trespass to the dwelling, but although there is limited authority otherwise,[106] the trend seems to be in the direction of holding that an unlawful entry of the dwelling for the purpose of an assault upon any person therein may be resisted by deadly force if this reasonably seems necessary for the purpose, "although the circumstances may not be such as to justify a belief that there was actual peril of life or great bodily harm."[107]

State v. Mitcheson

Supreme Court of Utah, 1977.
560 P.2d 1120.

■ Crockett, Justice. The defendant, Gary Alfred Mitcheson, was convicted of murder in the second degree for shooting Richard Herrera in the front yard of 432 South Fourth East, Price, Utah, at about 3:30 a.m. on February 7, 1976. He was sentenced to a term of five years to life in the state prison.

On his appeal the point of critical concern is his charge that the trial court erred in refusing his request to instruct the jury on the defense of using force in the protection of one's habitation.

The deceased, Richard Herrera, sold his car (a 1967 Chevrolet van) to Alfred Mitcheson, defendant's father, on December 15, 1975. The original wheels and tires had been changed for what are called "Mag Wheels" and tires, which have a wider tread. Some time after the father had taken possession of the van, a dispute arose between the parties over those wheels. The father, supported by the defendant, claimed that they had been included in the sale, but the deceased and his brother, Ernie Herrera, claimed they only agreed to loan the "Mag Wheels" and tires temporarily.

---

105. Where there was evidence that D acted in defense of his home, an instruction on his right to act in self-defense without an instruction also on his right to act in defense of his home was prejudicial error. State v. Edwards, 28 N.C.App. 196, 220 S.E.2d 158 (1975).

106. Carroll v. State, 23 Ala. 28 (1853).

107. People v. Eatman, 405 Ill. 491, 498, 91 N.E.2d 387, 390 (1950). Accord, Leverette v. State, 104 Ga.App. 743, 122 S.E.2d 745 (1961).

On several occasions in January, 1976, the two brothers requested that the wheels and tires be returned, but the defendant and his father did not comply. On one of those occasions the Herrera brothers and some friends went to the father's home to remove the wheels. The father protested and called the police. When they arrived they told the Herreras, the deceased and his brother, to leave the wheels alone and that any disagreement should be settled by going to court.

A few days thereafter, on February 6, 1976, the defendant was parked in the van at a drive-in restaurant when the deceased came up to the van, opened the door and hit the defendant on the jaw and eye; and made threats to the defendant to the effect that I will "put you under." A couple of hours later the defendant and some of his friends went to the home of Jerry Giraud, where they saw the deceased's car parked. There was a conversation in which the defendant offered to fight the deceased, which was then refused. But, they agreed to meet in the town park and fight at 2:00 o'clock the next afternoon.

Defendant and his friend, Wendell Johnson, drove to his father's house, where the defendant obtained a rifle. He and Johnson then arranged for a poker game to be held at the home of defendant's sister, Debbie, and went there in the van where they proceeded to play cards. Still later that night, at about 3:30 a.m., the deceased, Richard Herrera, and some of his friends drove up to this house for the stated purpose of removing the wheels from the van. When they entered upon her premises Debbie told them to leave. They did not comply. A considerable commotion ensued, including her screaming at them to get off her premises. Defendant came to the doorway of the house with the rifle. He fired a shot and Richard Herrera fell with a bullet wound in his neck from which he shortly expired.

The essence of the defense, and the basis for the requested instructions, was that the defendant was using the rifle as a backup resource in protection of the peace and security of his habitation and that its discharge and the striking of the deceased was an accident. The argument that the defendant was not entitled to that instruction is: (1) that the sister's home was not his habitation; . . .

Defense of Habitation

The pertinent statute is 76–2–405, U.C.A.1953, which provides in part:

A person is justified in using force against another when and to the extent that he reasonably believes . . . necessary to prevent . . . other's unlawful entry into or attack upon his habitation; however, he is justified in the use of force which is intended to cause death or serious bodily injury only if:

(1) The entry is made or attempted in a violent and tumultuous manner and he reasonably believes that the entry is attempted or made for the purpose of assaulting or offering personal violence to any person, dwelling or being therein. . . .

That statute has its roots in the ancient and honored doctrine of the common law that a man's home is his castle, and that even the peasant in his cottage, may peaceably abide within the protective cloak of the law, and no one, not even the king nor all his armies can enter to disturb him.[108]

In view of the salutary purpose of that statute, of preserving the peace and good order of society, it should be interpreted and applied in the broad sense to accomplish that purpose. Thus it would include not only a person's actual residence, but also whatever place he may be occupying peacefully as a substitute home or habitation, such as a hotel, motel, or even where he is a guest in the home of another;[109] and so would apply to the defendant in his sister's home....

In a criminal case the defendant need not specially plead his defenses. The entry of a plea of not guilty places upon the State the burden of proving every element of the offense beyond a reasonable doubt. This gives the defendant the benefit of every defense thereto which may cause a reasonable doubt to exist as to his guilt, arising either from the evidence, or lack of evidence, in the case; and this is true whether his defenses are consistent or not.

On the basis of what has been said herein, it is our opinion that if the requested instruction had been given and the jury had so considered the evidence, there is a reasonable likelihood that it may have had some effect upon the verdict rendered. Therefore the defendant's request should have been granted. Accordingly, it is necessary that the judgment be reversed.[110]

People v. McNeese

Supreme Court of Colorado, En Banc., 1995.
892 P.2d 304.

■ JUSTICE ERICKSON delivered the Opinion of the Court.

We granted certiorari to review People v. McNeese, 865 P.2d 881 (Colo.App.1993). We reverse and return this case to the court of appeals for

---

108. See Semayne's Case (1604) 5 Coke 91, 77 Eng.Reprint 194, where it was stated that "the house of everyone is to him his castle and fortress, as well for his defense against injury and violence, as for his repose; and although the life of a man is a thing precious and favored in law ... if thieves come to a man's house to rob him, or murder, and the owner or his servants kill any of the thieves in defense of himself and his house, it is not felony and he shall lose nothing ... (citing other older authorities)."

109. As to the guest in another's home, see State v. Osborne, 200 S.C. 504, 21 S.E.2d 178 (1942).

[Added by compiler] "The right of defendant, in other words, was limited (1) to the protection of himself, (2) to prevent a felony in the bedroom and, probably, (3) to prevent the deceased from entering that room at all." State v. Sorrentino, 31 Wyo. 129, 137–38, 224 P. 420, 422 (1924).

110. Consider the current Utah statute which authorizes the use of deadly force if the intruder's entry is made by violence, surreptitiously, or by stealth and the actor believes that the entry is for the purpose of assault or personal violence to any person or to prevent a felony. "The person using force or deadly force in defense of habitation is presumed for the purpose of both civil and criminal cases to have acted reasonably and had a reasonable fear of imminent peril of death or serious bodily harm if the entry or attempted entry is unlawful and is made or attempted by use of force, or in a violent or tumultuous manner, or surreptitiously or by stealth, or for the purpose of committing a felony." Utah Code Ann. § 76–2–405 (1997). See also, Okl.Stat.Ann. 21 § 1289.25 (1987).

remand to the district court to make findings of fact and conclusions of law consistent with this opinion or to conduct a further or new hearing.

The defendant, Robert Earl McNeese, was charged with first-degree murder, attempted first-degree murder, and first-degree assault. After a preliminary hearing, the county court bound the defendant over for trial on two counts of second-degree murder. The defendant was also bound over for trial on the attempted first-degree murder and first-degree assault charges arising out of the stabbing of Vivian Daniels. Defendant pleaded not guilty and filed a motion to dismiss in the district court, alleging that he was immune from prosecution under the "make-my-day" statute, section 18–1–704.5, 8B C.R.S. (1986). Section 18–1–704.5 provides:

Use of deadly physical force against an intruder.

(1) The general assembly hereby recognizes that the citizens of Colorado have a right to expect absolute safety within their own homes.

(2) Notwithstanding the provisions of section 18–1–704, any occupant of a dwelling is justified in using any degree of physical force, including deadly physical force, against another person when that other person has made an unlawful entry into the dwelling, and when the occupant has a reasonable belief that such other person has committed a crime in the dwelling in addition to the uninvited entry, or is committing or intends to commit a crime against a person or property in addition to the uninvited entry, and when the occupant reasonably believes that such other person might use any physical force, no matter how slight, against any occupant.

(3) Any occupant of a dwelling using physical force, including deadly physical force, in accordance with the provisions of subsection (2) of this section shall be immune from criminal prosecution for the use of such force.

(4) Any occupant of a dwelling using physical force, including deadly physical force, in accordance with the provisions of subsection (2) of this section shall be immune from any civil liability for injuries or death resulting from the use of such force.(Emphasis added.)

Following a pretrial hearing, the trial judge granted the defendant's motion to dismiss the second-degree murder charge for the stabbing death of John Daniels. The defendant's motion to dismiss the charges of second-degree murder of Wessels and attempted first-degree murder and first-degree assault of Vivian Daniels was denied.

I

Vivian Daniels testified that she was not getting along with John Daniels, her common-law husband, and was looking for a place to stay. She contacted the defendant and asked whether she could stay in his apartment and sleep on his couch. The apartment contained a small bedroom, a bathroom, and a combined living room and kitchen. Vivian Daniels moved into the defendant's apartment after agreeing to pay rent and on the condition that John Daniels was not to enter or come into the apartment under any circumstances. The defendant is an African–American, and the testimony established that John Daniels had a reputation for not liking African–Americans and was prone to violence, especially after he had been drinking. Vivian Daniels told the defendant that John Daniels had killed another man. John Daniels knew that the defendant did not want him in the apartment.

Vivian Daniels agreed to pay the defendant $50 a month for rent and to contribute funds for her share of the food. The defendant gave her a key shortly after she moved in, and she kept her clothes, television, art work, bedding, fan, and cat in the apartment. John Daniels never entered the apartment and would wave from across the street or knock on the window when he wanted to see his wife.

On November 15, 1991, approximately three months after moving into the apartment, Vivian Daniels and the defendant spent the day drinking at various bars. When they returned to the apartment, the defendant made sexual advances and Vivian Daniels decided to move. The defendant agreed that she should move out. She left the defendant's apartment at 11:30 p.m. on a cold, snowy night without a coat or any of her belongings. She went to John Daniels' apartment, which was about six blocks away.

Keith Tollefson, who shared the apartment with John Daniels, let her in, and she slept on a couch until John Daniels returned. John Daniels and David Wessels had both been drinking heavily at a number of bars and, when they returned to the apartment, they were told of the sexual advances made by the defendant. They decided to get Vivian Daniels' clothes and possessions from the defendant's apartment. John Daniels told Vivian Daniels there would be no violence. However, a defense witness testified he overheard John Daniels say to Wessels, in the presence of Vivian Daniels just before they left to go to the defendant's apartment, "let's go kill that fuckin' nigger." Vivian Daniels denied that John Daniels made such a statement to David Wessels. John Daniels had a blood alcohol level of .349, and Wessels had a blood alcohol level of .188. Vivian Daniels admitted that she was drunk. At approximately 2:30 a.m., John Daniels, Vivian Daniels, and Wessels entered the defendant's apartment using Vivian Daniels' key.

The defendant was in his bedroom asleep. When John Daniels went to get his wife's clothes out of the closet located immediately outside of the bedroom, he opened the defendant's door and talked to the defendant from the doorway. After Vivian Daniels asked her husband to help her collect her belongings, he returned to the living room and the defendant followed. Vivian Daniels went to the defendant's bedroom to get her pillow, and, when she returned to the living room, John Daniels was on the couch with his arm around the defendant's throat applying a chokehold and threatening to kill the defendant if he harmed Vivian Daniels.

The altercation ended after approximately two or three minutes. Vivian Daniels testified that neither the defendant nor John Daniels was hurt, and they were not arguing.

Vivian Daniels was gathering her possessions when she saw Wessels lying on the floor by the front door and John Daniels on the floor near the kitchen. The defendant confronted Vivian Daniels and stabbed her in the head. She ran from the apartment and called the police. Vivian Daniels could not recall anything else. She testified that she did not see, hear, or know what occurred when John Daniels and David Wessels were stabbed to death.

II

The trial judge centered his analysis on the oral lease agreement between the defendant and Vivian Daniels, and concluded that, since Vivian Daniels was entitled to a three-day notice of eviction, she was authorized to return to the apartment on November 16, 1991. The trial judge also held that she had the right to invite David Wessels into the apartment. However, allowing John Daniels to enter the apartment violated the oral lease agreement between Vivian Daniels and the defendant and made John Daniels' entry into the apartment unlawful.

The trial judge held John Daniels inflicted a third-degree assault on the defendant, and that the assault satisfied the requirement that John Daniels had committed or intended to commit a crime on the premises. See § 18–1–704.5(2) & (3). Also, because the physical contact may not have been over, the trial court held that the defendant was justified in fearing that John Daniels might use further physical force against him. The trial court found that the defendant established immunity from prosecution because he met the requirements of the "make-my-day" statute.

The prosecution appealed the trial judge's order of dismissal pursuant to section 16–12–102, 8A C.R.S. (1994 Supp.). The court of appeals affirmed the trial judge. . . .

The findings of fact and conclusions of law of the trial judge were based on an erroneous interpretation of the elements that must be proven to obtain immunity under section 18–1–704.5. Accordingly, the findings and conclusions were erroneous as a matter of law and are not binding on this court.

The court of appeals also erred in its analysis of the "make-my-day" statute. The General Assembly did not intend that the occupant of a dwelling be granted immunity from prosecution for the appearance of an unlawful entry by an intruder. The fact that John Daniels' entry may have been uninvited because the entry violated an oral agreement, does not establish that the entry was a knowing violation of the criminal law. John Daniels' entry does not satisfy the unlawful entry element in the "make-my-day" statute.

Section 18–1–704.5 contains two separate elements. In order to be granted immunity the defendant must first prove by a preponderance of the evidence that there was an unlawful entry. The second statutory requirement involves a determination of whether the occupant had a reasonable belief that the intruder intended to commit or committed a crime in the dwelling. When the legislature enacted 18–1–704.5 as part of the criminal code it did not define all of the terms used in the statute. We are guided by other provisions in the criminal code in determining the definition of unlawful entry and the elements that must be proven by a preponderance of the evidence.

III

Section 18–1–704.5 is part of the criminal code (Title 18).... The "make-my-day" statute lies in the criminal code along side [other] statutes. Section 18–1–704.5 is similar to self-defense and extends the justifications and exemptions formulated in part 7. The "make-my-day" statute justifies "deadly physical force," not just "physical force." However, the statute is not a license to commit homicide. The occupant of a dwelling is granted immunity from criminal prosecution for homicide, so safeguards must be imposed. Because the statute readily grants immunity for the taking of a life, the "knowingly" mens rea is required to carry out the principles of self-defense.

The specific provisions of the "make-my-day" statute permit an occupant of a dwelling to use physical force, including deadly physical force, against an intruder. Immunity from criminal prosecution is granted for acts and conduct that would be criminal but for the statute.... When section 18–1–704.5(3) is invoked prior to trial, the burden is on the defendant to establish by a preponderance of evidence, that:

(1) another person made an unlawful entry into the defendant's dwelling; (2) the defendant had a reasonable belief that such other person had committed a crime in the dwelling in addition to the uninvited entry, or was committing or intended to commit a crime against a person or property in addition to the uninvited entry; (3) the defendant reasonably believed that such other person might use physical force, no matter how slight, against any occupant of the dwelling; and (4) the defendant used force against the person who actually made the unlawful entry into the dwelling.

A prerequisite for immunity under the "make-my-day" statute is an unlawful entry into the dwelling. The explicit terms of the statute provide the occupant of a dwelling with immunity from prosecution only for force used against a person who has made an unlawful entry into the dwelling, but not against a person who remains unlawfully in the dwelling.

The ... reasonable belief standard relates only to the defendant's state of mind once the intruder is inside the dwelling:

There is nothing in section 18–1–704.5 suggesting that the General Assembly intended to broaden the conditions for statutory immunity to include a home occupant's right to use any degree of physical force against another person solely on the basis of an appearance, rather than the actuality, of an unlawful entry into the dwelling by that other person. The legislature adopted a "reasonable belief" or "appearance" standard in section 18–1–704.5 only with respect to those other statutory criteria for immunity relating to the intruder's conduct inside the dwelling. Under these circumstances, we are satisfied that the failure to include a similar "reasonable belief" or "appearance" standard with respect to the unlawful entry element of immunity was the result of deliberate legislative choice.

. . .

The General Assembly is vested with constitutional authority not only to define criminal conduct and to establish the legal components of criminal liability but also to delineate statutory defenses and bars to criminal prosecution. In *Guenther* we said "[s]ubsection (2) of the statute states that an occupant of a dwelling is justified in using physical force 'against *another person* when *that other person* has made an unlawful entry into the dwelling' (emphasis added) and when the additional statutory requirements are met." *Id.* at 979 (quoting § 18–1–704.5(2), 8B C.R.S. (1986)). The plain language of the statute, as we said in *Guenther*, requires proof of an actual unlawful entry and not merely a reasonable belief that the entry was unlawful. The statute does not require that the entry be both unlawful and uninvited, or that the entry be either unlawful or uninvited. The defendant must establish an unlawful entry to satisfy the threshold statutory requirement.

The most vexing question under the "make-my-day" statute is the proper definition of "unlawful entry." For purposes of section 18–1–704.5, the "unlawful entry" element requires an entry in knowing violation of the criminal law. The statutory language justifies an occupant's use of physical force against another person when the other person is knowingly engaging in criminal conduct. The statute provides that the occupant of the dwelling must reasonably believe that a crime has been, is being, or will be committed *in addition* to the threshold requirement of proof of an unlawful entry. By providing both objective[111] and subjective elements, the structure of section 18–1–704.5 contemplates that an unlawful entry means a knowing, criminal entry.

We recognize that the statute does not expressly describe a culpable mental state of "knowingly." However, if "no culpable mental state is expressly stated in a statute . . . a culpable mental state may nevertheless be required . . . with respect to some or all of the material elements thereof, if the proscribed conduct necessarily involves such a culpable mental state." § 18–1–503, 8B C.R.S. (1986). Under the "make-my-day" statute, an "unlawful entry" requires a "culpable mental state." Without a culpable mental state for the "unlawful entry" requirement, an occupant of a dwelling would be immune from criminal prosecution for the homicide of any unanticipated or unexpected "intruder." The statute was not intended to encourage arbitrary, casual killings.

. . .

---

111. Before assuming its present form, the "make-my-day" statute required that an occupant have "a reasonable belief that the intruder's entry was unlawful and forcible...." Dr. William Wilbanks, The Make My Day Law 326 (1990). However, the language of the enacted law protects an occupant "using deadly force only when he is correct that the entry was unlawful and uninvited—a reasonable belief is not good enough." *Id.* The objective language of the "unlawful entry" requirement permits "second-guessing" the reasonableness of an occupant's actions. *Id.* at 328. By failing to attach a reasonable belief standard to the "unlawful entry" element, the General Assembly may have eliminated its intent to remove the need for reflection by an occupant prior to taking protective action. *See id.* at 26; *see also id.* at 328 ("It thus appears that the failure to attach the reasonable belief standard to the nature of the entry was an [sic] mistake by the Legislature that should be corrected.").

The statute was enacted to immunize the occupant of a dwelling from prosecution for using physical force against another person who has committed, is committing, or intends to commit criminal acts in the dwelling. Immunity from criminal prosecution provides protection to the occupant of a dwelling who uses force against an intruder who has knowingly and unlawfully entered the dwelling to commit a crime. The immunity was not intended to justify use of physical force against persons who enter a dwelling accidently or in good faith.

. . .

The elements of first and second degree burglary established by the General Assembly may satisfy the "unlawful entry" requirement. See § 18–4–202(1), 8B C.R.S. (1986) . . . Where the elements of the crimes differ, the "make-my-day" statute does not extend to persons who unlawfully remain on property. The intruder's mental state must reflect an entry in knowing violation of the criminal code. Unlawfully remaining on property does not include a sufficient mens rea to satisfy the unlawful entry requirement of section 18–1–704.5.

. . .

Under the "make-my-day" statute, a person may be uninvited, but still may be lawfully on the premises. In People v. Malczewski, 744 P.2d 62 (Colo.1987), a police officer sought to enter the defendant's apartment to take the defendant's child into temporary custody, but the defendant would not allow him to enter. After the officer entered the apartment, over the defendant's objections, the defendant struck the officer numerous times. The officer suffered injuries on his head and throat, and the defendant was charged with second-degree assault for the beating of the officer.

. . .

We held that because the officer acted within his statutory authority by entering the apartment to take the child into temporary custody, there was "no evidence supporting the district court's determination that the officer's entry into the apartment was unlawful."

In addition to an unlawful entry, the "make-my-day" statute requires that the occupant have a reasonable belief that the intruder has committed, or intends to commit, a crime in the dwelling. § 18–1–704.5. Analysis of the subjective belief requirement is only undertaken after the threshold unlawful entry requirement has been satisfied.

. . .

To be immune from prosecution under the "make-my-day" statute, a defendant must establish by a preponderance of the evidence that he "had a reasonable belief that such other person had committed a crime in the dwelling in addition to the uninvited entry, or was committing or intended to commit a crime against a person or property in addition to the uninvited entry...." The inquiry for the second requirement focuses on the reasonable belief of the occupant. It does not center on the actual conduct of the intruder. The defendant failed to prove by a preponderance of the evidence that he had a reasonable belief that John Daniels committed or intended to commit a crime in the apartment. Vivian Daniels' testimony regarding the confrontation between John Daniels and the defendant in the apartment was insufficient to establish the second requirement of section 18–1–704.5.

First, the district court must determine whether John Daniels knowingly made an unlawful entry when he entered the defendant's apartment. Second, if the district court finds that John Daniels knowingly made an unlawful entry, the district court must then determine whether the defendant had a reasonable belief that John Daniels committed or intended to commit a crime in the defendant's apartment.

Accordingly, we return this case to the court of appeals with directions to remand to the district court to make findings of facts and conclusions of law consistent with this opinion or for a further or new hearing on the defendant's motion to dismiss.

■ ROVIRA, C.J., concurs in the result and dissents to part IV.

■ SCOTT, J., dissents.[112]

SECTION 7. DEFENSE OF PROPERTY

Criminal cases, in which defense of property has been relied upon as an exculpating circumstance, have seldom been entirely divorced from some other privilege, such as self-defense, crime prevention, or defense of habitation,[113] and the fact that the exercise of such other privilege may result incidentally in the protection of property, does not in any way narrow its scope. Hence property protection is usually overshadowed by self-defense, crime prevention or even the privilege of arrest. In fact, the chief impor-

---

112. West's Cal.Penal Code § 197.2 (1997) provides: "Homicide is also justifiable when committed by any person in any of the following cases: ... 2. When committed in defense of habitation, property, or person, against one who manifestly intends or endeavors, by violence or surprise, to commit a felony, or against one who manifestly intends and endeavors, in a violent, riotous or tumultuous manner, to enter the habitation of another for the purpose of offering violence to any person therein." and § 198.5 (1997) (Home Protection Bill of Rights): "Any person using force intended or likely to cause death or great bodily injury within his or her residence shall be presumed to have held a reasonable fear of imminent peril of death or great bodily injury to self, family, or a member of the household when that force is used against another person, not a member of the family or household, who unlawfully and forcibly enters or has unlawfully and forcibly entered the residence and the person using the force knew or had reason to believe that an unlawful and forcible entry occurred. As used in this section, great bodily injury means a significant or substantial physical injury."

The provisions of § 198.5 were not an available defense to a defendant who shot the victim standing on an unenclosed porch outside defendant's premises and was threatening defendant with a hammer. People v. Brown, 6 Cal.App.4th 1489, 8 Cal.Rptr.2d 513 (1992).

The Oklahoma "make my day" law applies to an invited guest. State v. Anderson, 972 P.2d 32 (Okl.Cr.1998).

Defendant could not claim a defense of habitation to a murder charge when the victim assailants were shot when fleeing and there was no longer any attempt of the victims to gain entry to the premises. People v. Torres, 269 Ill.App.3d 339, 206 Ill.Dec. 766, 645 N.E.2d 1018 (1995).

The burden of a pretrial claim of defense of habitation is on the defendant under § 18–1–704.5 Colo.Rev.Stat. (1986). See People v. Guenther, 740 P.2d 971 (Colo.1987).

113. For example, State v. Pollard, 139 Mo. 220, 40 S.W. 949 (1897).

tance of the privilege of protecting property is frequently that its exercise does not make one an "aggressor", or in any way at fault, and hence leaves all other privileges unimpaired.[114]

One is privileged to use nondeadly force when this reasonably appears to be necessary to protect one's property, real or personal, from unprivileged interference by another,—provided one does not employ more force than reasonably appears to be necessary for the purpose.[115] This privilege does not include the use of deadly force, at least if the habitation is not involved, even if the trespass cannot be otherwise prevented.[116] Bishop says, "it may now be deemed reasonably clear that, to prevent an unlawful entrance into a dwelling-house, the occupant may make defence to the taking of life, without being liable even for manslaughter."[117] But this seems not to be the accepted view where the defender has no reason to fear that the trespasser intends to commit a felony or to inflict personal harm upon the defender or some other person in the house.[118] Clearly, if the defender reasonably believes that the intruder intends to kill a person, or to inflict great bodily harm upon a person, the defender may make a defense at the threshold.[119] One is not bound to stay the use of deadly force until the other has gained the advantage of an entrance. But the accepted view does not permit the use of deadly force merely to prevent a relatively unimportant trespass, even if it takes the form of an entrance of the dwelling. The difference between this and Bishop's view is not so wide as might seem at first glance. When an intruder insists upon an unlawful entrance into the building with such violence that only deadly force can stop the person, the defender will usually have good reason to fear for one's safety or the safety of others. And no more than this is needed for the privilege to use deadly force. But one might know the facts to be otherwise. A householder who is on the outside, for example, and too far away at the moment to make use of nondeadly force would not be privileged to shoot to prevent the entrance of an intruder that the householder knew did not intend to commit a felony or to inflict personal harm.[120]

---

114. Ayers v. State, 60 Miss. 709 (1883).

115. Restatement, Second, Torts § 77 (1965). No force is privileged if a mere request would obviously be sufficient. Ibid.

116. Turpen v. State, 89 Okl.Cr. 6, 204 P.2d 298 (1949); State v. Patterson, 45 Vt. 308 (1873).

"But, in the absence of an attempt to commit a felony, he cannot defend his property, except his habitation, to the extent of killing the aggressor for the purpose of preventing the trespass; and if he should do so, he would be guilty of a felonious homicide." Carpenter v. State, 62 Ark. 286, 310, 36 S.W. 900, 907 (1896).

"Life being superior to property, no one has the right to kill in defence of the latter; yet by less extreme means, one may defend his own." 2 Bishop, Criminal Law § 706 (9th ed. 1923).

117. 2 Bishop, Criminal Law § 707 (9th ed. 1923).

118. Carroll v. State, 23 Ala. 28 (1853); People v. Young, 825 P.2d 1004 (Colo.App.1991); Miller v. Commonwealth, 188 Ky. 435, 222 S.W. 96 (1920); State v. Taylor, 143 Mo. 150, 44 S.W. 785 (1898); State v. Patterson, 45 Vt. 308 (1873).

119. Bailey v. People, 54 Colo. 337, 130 P. 832 (1913); Cooper's Case, Cro.Car. 554, 79 Eng.Rep. 1069 (K.B. 1639).

120. "A comes to B's premises during a severe storm and asks permission to take shelter in B's dwelling house. B refuses to permit him to do so, although he knows that A neither

Deadly force is privileged, if apparently necessary, not only to prevent a felonious intrusion of the dwelling house, but also to prevent a felonious attack upon the house itself, such as an attempt to commit arson or malicious mischief.[121] But in all such cases the privilege is rather that of crime prevention than property protection.[122] Deadly use of force is not proper just for the protection of uninhabited realty or personal property.[123]

Commonwealth v. Donahue

Supreme Judicial Court of Massachusetts, 1889.
148 Mass. 529, 20 N.E. 171.

■ HOLMES, J. This is an indictment for robbery, on which the defendant has been found guilty of an assault. The evidence for the Commonwealth was, that the defendant had bought clothes, amounting to twenty-one dollars and fifty-five cents, of one Mitchelman, who called at the defendant's house, by appointment, for his pay; that some discussion arose about the bill, and that the defendant went upstairs, brought down the clothes, placed them on a chair, and put twenty dollars on a table, and told Mitchelman that he could have the money or the clothes; that Mitchelman took the money and put it in his pocket, and told the defendant he owed him one dollar and fifty-five cents, whereupon the defendant demanded his money back, and, on Mitchelman refusing, attacked him, threw him on the floor, and choked him until Mitchelman gave him a pocket-book containing twenty-nine dollars. The defendant's counsel denied the receiving of the pocket-book, and said that he could show that the assault was justifiable, under the circumstances of the case, as the defendant believed that he had a right to recover his own money by force, if necessary. The presiding justice stated that he should be obliged to rule, that the defendant would not be justified in assaulting Mitchelman to get his own money, and that he should rule as follows: "If the jury are satisfied that the defendant choked and otherwise assaulted Mitchelman, they would be warranted in finding the defendant guilty, although the sole motive of the defendant was by this violence to get from Mitchelman by force money which the defendant honestly believed to be his own." Upon this the defendant saved his exceptions, and declined to introduce evidence; the jury were instructed as stated, and found the defendant guilty.

On the evidence for the Commonwealth, it appeared, or at the lowest the jury might have found, that the defendant offered the twenty dollars to Mitchelman only on condition that Mitchelman should accept that sum as full payment of his disputed bill, and that Mitchelman took the money, and at the same moment, or just afterwards, as part of the same transaction, repudiated the condition. If this was the case,—since Mitchelman, of

---

intends nor is likely to harm any person or thing in the house. A, a much larger man than B, attempts to overcome B's resistance by physical force which B is unable to resist except by shooting A. B is not privileged to do so to prevent A from entering his dwelling place." Restatement, Second, Torts § 79, Illustration 1 (1965).

121. State v. Couch, 52 N.M. 127, 193 P.2d 405 (1946).

122. Restatement, Second, Torts § 79, Comment *c* (1965).

123. State v. Clifton, 880 S.W.2d 737 (Tenn.Cr.App. 1994).

course, whatever the sum due him, had no right to that particular money except on the conditions on which it was offered, Commonwealth v. Stebbins, 8 Gray 492,—he took the money wrongfully from the possession of the defendant, or the jury might have found that he did, whether the true view be that the defendant did not give up possession, or that it was obtained from him by Mitchelman's fraud. . . .

It is settled by ancient and modern authority, that, under such circumstances, a man may defend or regain his momentarily interrupted possession by the use of reasonable force, short of wounding or the employment of a dangerous weapon. . . . To this extent the right to protect one's possession has been regarded as an extension of the right to protect one's person, with which it is generally mentioned. . . .

We need not consider whether this explanation is quite adequate. There are weighty decisions which go further than those above cited, and which hardly can stand on the right of self-defence, but involve other considerations of policy. It has been held, that, even where a considerable time had elapsed between the wrongful taking of the defendant's property and the assault, the defendant had a right to regain possession by reasonable force, after demand upon the third person in possession, in like manner as he might have protected it without civil liability. Whatever the true rule may be, probably there is no difference in this respect between the civil and the criminal law. The principle has been extended to a case where the defendant had yielded possession to the person assaulted, through the fraud of the latter. On the other hand, a distinction has been taken between the right to maintain possession and the right to regain it from another who is peaceably established in it, although the possession of the latter is wrongful. It is unnecessary to decide whether, in this case, if Mitchelman had taken the money with a fraudulent intent, but had not repudiated the condition until afterwards, the defendant would have had any other remedy than to hold him to his bargain if he could, even if he knew that Mitchelman still had the identical money upon his person.

If the force used by the defendant was excessive, the jury would have been warranted in finding him guilty. Whether it was excessive or not was a question for them; the judge could not rule that it was not, as matter of law. Therefore the instruction given to them, taken only literally, was correct. But the preliminary statement went further, and was erroneous; and coupling that statement with the defendant's offer of proof, and his course after the rulings, we think it fair to assume that the instruction was not understood to be limited, or, indeed, to be directed to the case of excessive force, which, so far as appears, had not been mentioned, but that it was intended and understood to mean that any assault to regain his own money would warrant finding the defendant guilty. Therefore the exceptions must be sustained.

It will be seen that our decision is irrespective of the defendant's belief as to what he had a right to do. . . . There is no question here of the effect of a reasonable but mistaken belief with regard to the facts. The facts were as defendant believed them to be.

Exceptions sustained.

People v. Ceballos

Supreme Court of California, In Bank, 1974.
12 Cal.3d 470, 116 Cal.Rptr. 233, 526 P.2d 241.

[This is the case, supra p. 924, in which a conviction of assault with a deadly weapon was affirmed. In the daytime, when no one else was near, two boys with larceny in mind, attempted to force open the door of a garage and one was shot in the face by a trap-gun that had been set by defendant to keep out intruders. Defendant's claim that the use of deadly force in this case was within the privilege of crime prevention, was rejected. The privilege of protecting property was not raised by defendant.]

■ BURKE, JUSTICE....

Defendant also does not, and could not properly, contend that the intrusion was in fact such that, were he present, he would be justified under Civil Code section 50 in using deadly force. That section provides, "Any necessary force may be used to protect from wrongful injury the person or property of oneself...." This section also should be read in the light of the common law, and at common law in general deadly force could not be used solely for the protection of property. (See Model Penal Code, supra, § 3.06, com. 8; Perkins on Criminal Law, supra, p. 1026, fn. 6; 13 Stan.L.Rev. 566, 575–576.) " 'The preservation of human life and limb from grievous harm is of more importance to society than the protection of property.' " Thus defendant was not warranted under Civil Code section 50 in using deadly force to protect his personal property.

The opinion of Justice McKee in Dinan v. Fitz Gibbon, 63 Cal. 387, contains language indicating that deadly force, if necessary, may be used to protect property against a trespasser. However, the other justices concurred in the judgment on the ground of an error in instructions and did not give their approval to that language. Thus Justice McKee's language has no controlling weight.

At common law an exception to the foregoing principle that deadly force could not be used solely for the protection of property was recognized where the property was a dwelling house in some circumstances. (See Simpson v. State, supra, 59 Ala. 1, 14; Perkins on Criminal Law, supra, pp. 1022–1025; Model Penal Code, supra, § 3.06, com. 8, pp. 38–41.) "According to the older interpretation of the common law, even extreme force may be used to prevent dispossession [of the dwelling house]." (See Model Penal Code, supra, com. 8.) Also at common law if another attempted to burn a dwelling the owner was privileged to use deadly force if this seemed necessary to defend his "castle" against the threatened harm. Further, deadly force was privileged if it was, or reasonably seemed, necessary to protect the dwelling against a burglar. (See Perkins on Criminal Law, supra, p. 1023.)

Here we are not concerned with dispossession or burning of a dwelling, and, as heretofore concluded, the asserted burglary in this case was not of such a character as to warrant the use of deadly force....[124]

---

124. Defendant set a spring gun in an unoccupied building with the intent to kill anyone who should force an entrance. This was done to protect his furniture. Two brothers went to

MODEL PENAL CODE

Section 3.06   Use of Force for the Protection of Property.

(1) Use of Force Justifiable for Protection of Property. Subject to the provisions of this Section and of Section 3.09, the use of force upon or toward the person of another is justifiable when the actor believes that such force is immediately necessary:

(a) to prevent or terminate an unlawful entry or other trespass upon land or a trespass against or the unlawful carrying away of tangible, movable property, provided that such land or movable property is, or is believed by the actor to be, in his possession or in the possession of another person for whose protection he acts; or

(b) to effect an entry or re-entry upon land or to retake tangible movable property, provided that the actor believes that he or the person by whose authority he acts or a person from whom he or such other person derives title was unlawfully dispossessed of such land or movable property and is entitled to possession, and provided, further, that:

(i) the force is used immediately or on fresh pursuit after such dispossession; or

(ii) the actor believes that the person against whom he uses force has no claim of right to the possession of the property and, in the case of land, the circumstances, as the actor believes them to be, are of such urgency that it would be an exceptional hardship to postpone the entry or re-entry until a court order is obtained.

(2) Meaning of Possession. . . .

(3) Limitations on Justifiable Use of Force.

(a) Request to Desist. The use of force is justifiable under this Section only if the actor first requests the person against whom such force is used to desist from his interference with the property, unless the actor believes that:

(i) such request would be useless; or

(ii) it would be dangerous to himself or another person to make the request; or

(iii) substantial harm will be done to the physical condition of the property which is sought to be protected before the request can effectively be made.

(b) Exclusion of Trespasser. The use of force to prevent or terminate a trespass is not justifiable under this Section if the actor knows that the

---

this building and one of them gained an entrance, merely to satisfy his curiosity, by breaking the lock. He was killed by the spring gun as he entered. A conviction of manslaughter was affirmed. State v. Green, 118 S.C. 279, 110 S.E. 145 (1921). See also Falco v. State, 407 So.2d 203 (Fla.1981).

The privilege to use deadly force by means of a spring gun, to protect property, is measured by the extent of the privilege the owner would have to use deadly force for this purpose, in person, if he were present. Restatement, Second, Torts, § 85 (1965).

A spring gun placed in a trunk in such a manner as to kill anyone who opened it, caused the death of a maid who looked in just as a matter of curiosity. A conviction of murder was reversed because the judge had approved the view of the prosecuting attorney that killing by means of a spring gun is privileged only to prevent the commission of a capital crime. State v. Marfaudille, 48 Wash. 117, 92 P. 939 (1907).

exclusion of the trespasser will expose him to substantial danger of serious bodily harm.

(c) Resistance of Lawful Re-entry or Recaption....

(d) Use of Deadly Force. The use of deadly force is not justifiable under this Section unless the actor believes that:

(i) the person against whom the force is used is attempting to dispossess him of his dwelling otherwise than under a claim of right to its possession; or

(ii) the person against whom the force is used is attempting to commit or consummate arson, burglary, robbery or other felonious theft or property destruction and either:

(1) has employed or threatened deadly force against or in the presence of the actor; or

(2) the use of force other than deadly force to prevent the commission or the consummation of the crime would expose the actor or another in his presence to substantial danger of serious bodily harm.

(4) Use of Confinement as Protective Force....

(5) Use of Device to Protect Property. The justification afforded by this Section extends to the use of a device for the purpose of protecting property only if:

(a) the device is not designed to cause or known to create a substantial risk of causing death or serious bodily harm; and

(b) the use of the particular device to protect the property from entry or trespass is reasonable under the circumstances, as the actor believes them to be; and

(c) the device is one customarily used for such a purpose or reasonable care is taken to make known to probable intruders the fact that it is used.

(6) Use of Force to Pass Wrongful Obstructor....[125]

SECTION 8.   ENTRAPMENT

Officers have sometimes gone too far in their zeal to secure convictions,—so far, in fact, as to defeat their own purpose. The most obvious cases are those in which the plot to trap an offender has been laid in a manner as to leave out some element essential to guilt. In one case, for example, officers planned to catch the person who had been aiding prisoners of war to escape. A prisoner, who was willing to cooperate with the officers, was directed what to do. The defendant took a prisoner, in her vehicle, beyond the ordinary prison limits to a point where she was arrested under the prearranged plan. A conviction of aiding a prisoner of war to escape was held to be improper because there had been no escape,—since the prisoner had gone only where he was directed to go by those in charge.[126] Under traditional American common law a detective who seemingly joins a criminal venture, not to promote its success but to secure evidence of the crime, is not a real conspirator and the detective's acts

---

125. Copyright © 1962 by the American Law Institute. Reprinted with the permission of the American Law Institute.

126. Rex v. Martin, Russ. and R.C.C. 196, 168 Eng.Rep. 757 (1811).

cannot be imputed to the others.[127] And if such a detective unlocks and opens the door through which the others enter there can be no conviction of common-law burglary. Since the intent was to frustrate the crime, the detective is not guilty. Since the detective is not guilty, the opening of the door cannot be imputed to the others and hence an essential element of common-law burglary may be lacking.[128] Or if a detective placed an obstruction on a railroad track, with authority from the company and with the intent to remove it before any harm was done, which was done, another could not properly be convicted on the theory that the offender was present aiding and abetting the commission of a crime.[129]

More difficult are those cases in which every element of the offense is present but it is claimed that there should be no conviction because of "entrapment" by a public officer. This is a separate affirmative defense. Providing an opportunity for those criminally inclined to perpetrate an offense in the presence of an officer will not bar conviction. It is no defense to an indictment for larceny, for example, that the money was stolen from a constable who feigned drunkenness with the intention of making an arrest if his money should be taken.[130]

The distinction is between detection and instigation. Traps may be laid or "decoys" employed to secure the conviction of those who intend to commit crime; but the zeal for enforcement must not induce officers to implant criminal ideas in an innocent mind.[131] The term entrapment generally refers to the inducement of an otherwise innocent person to commit a crime they otherwise would not commit. However, it may also refer to actions by police which are seen as so overzealous as to incite a law abiding citizen to commit an offense. The former is a subjective standard, the latter objective.[132]

---

127.   State v. Neely, 90 Mont. 199, 300 P. 561 (1931).

"The defendant is not to be charged with what was done by the detective, as the two were not acting together for a common purpose." State v. Currie, 13 N.D. 655, 661, 102 N.W. 875, 877 (1905).

In a jurisdiction that recognizes a unilateral conspiracy the result may be different. State v. La Forge, 183 N.J.Super. 118, 443 A.2d 269 (1981).

128.   Love v. People, 160 Ill. 501, 43 N.E. 710 (1896).

An even clearer case was the one where the "burglar" waited on the outside while a supposed accomplice, acting under directions of the sheriff, opened the door, went in, took some money, marked it so it could be identified, and then went out and delivered it. People v. Collins, 53 Cal. 185 (1878).

129.   State v. Douglass, 44 Kan. 618, 26 P. 476 (1891).

130.   People v. Hanselman, 76 Cal. 460, 18 P. 425 (1888). However, several cases have held it to be entrapment where a decoy feigns being a drunken bum with money protruding from a pocket. Moreland v. State, 101 Nev. 455, 705 P.2d 160 (Nev.1985); Cruz v. State, 465 So.2d 516 (Fla.1985); State v. Powell, 68 Haw. 635, 726 P.2d 266 (1986), *but see contra* State v. Long, 216 N.J.Super. 269, 523 A.2d 672 (1987).

131.   "Decoys are permissible to entrap criminals, but not to create them; ..." United States v. Healy, 202 Fed. 349 (D.C.Mont.1913).

132.   People v. Barraza, 23 Cal.3d 675, 153 Cal.Rptr. 459, 591 P.2d 947 (1979).

The mere fact that officers have led the defendant to furnish a specific instance of an habitual course of criminal conduct is not a defense.[133] Thus one may be convicted of using the United States mails to give information telling where obscene matter can be obtained, although his letter was in response to a request written by a post office inspector under a fictitious name.[134] And evidence of liquor purchased by officers may be used to convict the seller of a violation of the prohibition law.[135]

Recently, a number of courts have adopted a concept of entrapment that focuses on the conduct of the police rather than the predisposition of the offender.[136] If police employ methods of persuasion of inducement which create a substantial risk that an offense will be committed by persons other than those who are ready to commit it the defense of entrapment is available.[137]

There is no defense of private entrapment.[138]

People v. Barraza

Supreme Court of California, In Bank, 1979.
23 Cal.3d 675, 153 Cal.Rptr. 459, 591 P.2d 947.

■ MOSK, JUSTICE. We confront in this criminal appeal two separate issues: ... and (2) the proper test to be applied to the defense of entrapment.

Defendant appeals from his conviction on two counts of selling heroin (Health & Saf.Code, § 11352).

Count II charged a second sale of heroin on September 11, 1975; both the female agent and the defendant testified that the agent tried to contact defendant by telephoning the Golden State Mental Health Detoxification Center, where he worked as a patient care technician, several times during the three weeks between the dates of the two alleged heroin sale transactions. On September 11, the agent finally succeeded in speaking to defendant and asked him if he had "anything"; defendant asked her to come to the detoxification center. The two then met at the center and talked for some time—a few minutes according to the agent, more than an hour by the defendant's account.

The agent's version of this encounter described defendant as hesitant to deal because "he had done a lot of time in jail and he couldn't afford to go back to jail and ... he had to be careful about what he was doing." She further testified that after she convinced defendant she "wasn't a cop," he gave her a note, to present to a woman named Stella, which read: "Saw

133.   People v. Lindsey, 91 Cal.App.2d 914, 205 P.2d 1114 (1949); State v. Rodriguez, 107 N.M. 611, 762 P.2d 898 (App. 1988); State v. Walker, 185 Ariz. 228, 914 P.2d 1320 (App. 1995).

134.   Grimm v. United States, 156 U.S. 604, 15 S.Ct. 470, 39 L.Ed. 550 (1895).

135.   Moss v. State, 4 Okl.Cr. 247, 111 P. 950 (1910).

136.   People v. Barraza, 23 Cal.3d 675, 153 Cal.Rptr. 459, 591 P.2d 947 (1979); State v. Provard, 63 Hawaii 536, 631 P.2d 181 (1981); State v. Mullen, 216 N.W.2d 375 (Iowa 1974); People v. Turner, 390 Mich. 7, 210 N.W.2d 336 (1973); State v. Taylor, 599 P.2d 496 (Utah 1979). The New Jersey entrapment concept is both subjective and objective. State v. Rockholt, 96 N.J. 570, 476 A.2d 1236 (1984). See also State v. Sellers, 117 N.M. 644, 875 P.2d 400 (App.1994).

137.   Model Penal Code § 2.13(1)(b).

138.   United States v. Hollingsworth, 9 F.3d 593 (7th Cir. 1993).

Cheryl [the agent]. Give her a pair of pants [argot for heroin]. [signed] Cal." The agent concluded her testimony by stating that she then left defendant, used the note to introduce herself to the dealer Stella, and purchased an orange balloon containing heroin.

Defendant described a somewhat different pattern of interaction with the agent at their September 11th meeting. He related that he had asked her to come and see him because he was "fed up with her" and wanted her to quit calling him at the hospital where he worked because he was afraid she would cause him to lose his job. He insisted he told her during their conversation that he did not have anything; that he had spent more than 23 years in prison but now he had held a job at the detoxification center for four years, was on methadone and was clean, and wanted the agent to stop "bugging" him. He testified that the agent persisted in her efforts to enlist his aid in purchasing heroin, and that finally—after more than an hour of conversation—when the agent asked for a note to introduce her to a source of heroin he agreed to give her a note to "get her off . . . [his] back." According to the defendant, he told the agent that he did not know if Stella had anything, and gave her a note which read: "Saw Cheryl. If you have a pair of pants, let her have them." . . .

Defendant urges that his conviction on the second count must be reversed because the trial court erred in failing to instruct the jury sua sponte on the defense of entrapment. His contention requires that we reexamine the entrapment doctrine to determine the manner in which the defense must be raised.

Though long recognized by the courts of almost every United States jurisdiction,[139] the defense of entrapment has produced a deep schism concerning its proper theoretical basis and mode of application. The opposing views have been delineated in a series of United States Supreme Court decisions. The court first considered the entrapment defense in Sorrells v. United States (1932) 287 U.S. 435, 53 S.Ct. 210, 77 L.Ed. 413. The majority held that entrapment tended to establish innocence, reasoning that Congress in enacting the criminal statute there at issue could not have intended to punish persons otherwise innocent who were lured into committing the proscribed conduct by governmental instigation. This focus on whether persons were "otherwise innocent" let the majority to adopt what has become known as the subjective or origin-of-intent test under which entrapment is established only if (1) governmental instigation and inducement overstep the bounds of permissibility, and (2) the defendant did not harbor a preexisting criminal intent. Under the subjective test a finding that the defendant was predisposed to commit the offense would negate innocence and therefore defeat the defense. Finally, because entrapment was viewed as bearing on the guilt or innocence of the accused, the issue was deemed proper for submission to the jury.

---

139. The defense appears to have first been asserted by Eve, who complained, when charged with eating fruit of the tree of knowledge of good and evil: "The serpent beguiled me, and I did eat." (Genesis 3:13.) Though Eve was unsuccessful in asserting the defense, it has been suggested that the defense was unavailable to her because the entrapping party was not an agent of the punishing authority. Groot, The Serpent Beguiled Me and I (Without Scienter) Did Eat—Denial of Crime and the Entrapment Defense, (1973 U.Ill.L.F. 254.) See also, Marcus, The Development of Entrapment Law, 33 Wayne L.Rev. 5 (1986).

Justice Roberts wrote an eloquent concurring opinion, joined by Justices Brandeis and Stone, in which he argued that the purpose of the entrapment defense is to deter police misconduct. He emphatically rejected the notion that the defendant's conduct or predisposition had any relevance: "The applicable principle is that courts must be closed to the trial of a crime instigated by the government's own agents. No other issue, no comparison of equities as between the guilty official and the guilty defendant, has any place in the enforcement of this overruling principle of public policy." (Id. at p. 459, 53 S.Ct. at p. 219.) Because he viewed deterrence of impermissible law enforcement activity as the proper rationale for the entrapment defense, Justice Roberts concluded that the defense was inappropriate for jury consideration: "It is the province of the court and of the court alone to protect itself and the government from such prostitution of the criminal law." (Id. at p. 457, 53 S.Ct. at p. 218.)

In Sherman v. United States (1958) 356 U.S. 369, 78 S.Ct. 819, 2 L.Ed.2d 848, the majority refused to adopt the "objective" theory of entrapment urged by Justice Roberts, choosing rather to continue recognizing as relevant the defendant's own conduct and predisposition. The court held that "a line must be drawn between the trap for the unwary innocent and the trap for the unwary criminal." (Id. at p. 372, 78 S.Ct. at p. 821.) Justice Frankfurter, writing for four members of the court in a concurring opinion, argued forcefully for Justice Roberts' objective theory: "The courts refuse to convict an entrapped defendant, not because his conduct falls outside the proscription of the statute, but because, even if his guilt be admitted, the methods employed on behalf of the Government to bring about conviction cannot be countenanced." (Id. at p. 380, 78 S.Ct. at p. 824.) He reasoned that "a test that looks to the character and predisposition of the defendant rather than the conduct of the police loses sight of the underlying reason for the defense of entrapment. No matter what the defendant's past record and present inclinations to criminality, or the depths to which he has sunk in the estimation of society, certain police conduct to ensnare him into further crime is not to be tolerated by an advanced society.... Permissible police activity does not vary according to the particular defendant concerned...." (Id. at pp. 382–383, 78 S.Ct. at p. 826.) "Human nature is weak enough," he wrote, "and sufficiently beset by temptations without government adding to them and generating crime." (Id. at p. 384, 78 S.Ct. at p. 826.) Justice Frankfurter concluded that guidance as to appropriate official conduct could only be provided if the court reviewed police conduct and decided the entrapment issue.

The United States Supreme Court recently reviewed the theoretical basis of the entrapment defense in United States v. Russell (1973) 411 U.S. 423, 93 S.Ct. 1637, 36 L.Ed.2d 366, and once again the court split five votes to four in declining to overrule the subjective theory adopted in *Sorrells*. . . .

For all the foregoing reasons we hold that the proper test of entrapment in California is the following:[140] was the conduct of the law enforce-

---

140. The wording of this test is derived from the proposed new federal criminal code (Nat.Com. on Reform of Fed.Crim.Laws, Final Rep.—Proposed New Fed.Crim.Code (1971)

ment agent likely to induce a normally law-abiding person to commit the offense? For the purposes of this test, we presume that such a person would normally resist the temptation to commit a crime presented by the simple opportunity to act unlawfully. Official conduct that does no more than offer that opportunity to the suspect—for example, a decoy program—is therefore permissible; but it is impermissible for the police or their agents to pressure the suspect by overbearing conduct such as badgering, cajoling, importuning, or other affirmative acts likely to induce a normally law-abiding person to commit the crime.

Although the determination of what police conduct is impermissible must to some extent proceed on an ad hoc basis, guidance will generally be found in the application of one or both of two principles. First, if the actions of the law enforcement agent would generate in a normally law-abiding person a motive for the crime other than ordinary criminal intent, entrapment will be established. An example of such conduct would be an appeal by the police that would induce such a person to commit the act because of friendship or sympathy, instead of a desire for personal gain or other typical criminal purpose. Second, affirmative police conduct that would make commission of the crime unusually attractive to a normally law-abiding person will likewise constitute entrapment. Such conduct would include, for example, a guarantee that the act is not illegal or the offense will go undetected, an offer of exorbitant consideration, or any similar enticement.[141]

Finally, while the inquiry must focus primarily on the conduct of the law enforcement agent, that conduct is not to be viewed in a vacuum; it should also be judged by the effect it would have on a normally law-abiding person situated in the circumstances of the case at hand. Among the circumstances that may be relevant for this purpose, for example, are the transactions preceding the offense, the suspect's response to the inducements of the officer, the gravity of the crime, and the difficulty of detecting instances of its commission. (See Grossman v. State (Alaska 1969) supra, 457 P.2d 226, 230.) We reiterate, however, that under this test such matters as the character of the suspect, his predisposition to commit the offense, and his subjective intent are irrelevant.[142] . . .

The judgment is reversed.

■ BIRD, C.J., and TOBRINER, MANUEL and NEWMAN, JJ., concur.

■ RICHARDSON, JUSTICE, concurring and dissenting.

---

§ 702(2)) and Chief Justice Traynor's dissenting opinion in People v. Moran (1970) supra, 1 Cal.3d 755, 765, 83 Cal.Rptr. 411, 463 P.2d 763.

141. There will be no entrapment, however, when the official conduct is found to have gone no further than necessary to assure the suspect that he is not being "set-up." The police remain free to take reasonable, though restrained, steps to gain the confidence of suspects. A contrary rule would unduly hamper law enforcement; indeed, in the case of many of the so-called "victimless" crimes, it would tend to limit convictions to only the most gullible offenders.

142. Because the test of entrapment we adopt herein is designed primarily to deter impermissible police conduct, it will be applicable, except for the present defendant, only to trials that have not yet begun at the time this decision becomes final.

I concur in that portion of the majority's opinion which holds that defendant's conviction on count I should be reversed because of the prejudicial "mini-*Allen*" instruction erroneously given to the jury. . . .

■ CLARK, JUSTICE, dissenting.

The most significant question presented by this case is whether this court should adopt the "hypothetical-person" ("objective") test of entrapment.

The test now applied in California, in all but seven of the other states, and in the federal courts is the "origin-of-intent" ("subjective") standard. This test focuses, quite properly, upon the guilt of the particular defendant, asking whether he was predisposed to commit the crime charged. If he was ready and willing to commit the offense at any favorable opportunity, then the entrapment defense fails even if the police used an unduly persuasive inducement.

The guilt of the particular defendant is irrelevant under the hypothetical-person test. It focuses instead upon the conduct of the police. If the police use an inducement likely to cause a hypothetical person to commit the crime charged, then the fact that the particular defendant was ready and willing to commit it does not defeat the entrapment defense. The evil of the hypothetical-person test is apparent—it leads to acquittal of persons who are in fact guilty. By focusing on police conduct rather than the defendant's predisposition, it creates a risk of acquitting dangerous chronic offenders.

That risk is strikingly illustrated by the facts of this case. The evidence would support the conclusion that defendant is one of the most cynical manipulators of the criminal justice system imaginable, that he abused the trust placed in him as an employee of a drug detoxification program to sell heroin to the patients with whom he worked, nullifying the program's slight chances of success and wasting countless thousands of tax dollars, that he initially refused to sell heroin to the deputy solely because he suspected she was an undercover officer, and that, before finally agreeing to make the sale through his wife, he sought to immunize himself by "entrapping" the deputy into the conduct he now relies upon as the basis of his entrapment defense. If the factfinder takes this view of the evidence, but also concludes the officer's conduct would have induced a hypothetical person to commit the offense, defendant goes free. . . .

Jacobson v. United States

Supreme Court of the United States, 1992.
503 U.S. 540, 112 S.Ct. 1535, 118 L.Ed.2d 174.

■ JUSTICE WHITE.

On September 24, 1987, petitioner Keith Jacobson was indicted for violating a provision of the Child Protection Act of 1984 (Act), Pub.L. 98–292, 98 Stat. 204, which criminalizes the knowing receipt through the mails of a "visual depiction [that] involves the use of a minor engaging in sexually explicit conduct. . . ." 18 U.S.C. § 2252(a)(2)(A). Petitioner defended on the ground that the Government entrapped him into committing the crime through a series of communications from undercover agents that spanned the 26 months preceding his arrest. Petitioner was found guilty after a jury trial. The Court of Appeals affirmed his conviction, holding that the Government had carried its burden of proving beyond reasonable doubt that petitioner was predisposed to break the law and hence was not entrapped.

Because the Government overstepped the line between setting a trap for the "unwary innocent" and the "unwary criminal," Sherman v. United States, 356 U.S. 369, 372 (1958), and as a matter of law failed to establish that petitioner was independently predisposed to commit the crime for which he was arrested, we reverse the Court of Appeals' judgment affirming his conviction.

I

In February 1984, petitioner, a 56–year–old veteran-turned-farmer who supported his elderly father in Nebraska, ordered two magazines and a brochure from a California adult bookstore. The magazines, entitled Bare Boys I and Bare Boys II, contained photographs of nude preteen and teenage boys. The contents of the magazines startled petitioner, who testified that he had expected to receive photographs of "young men 18 years or older." On cross-examination, he explained his response to the magazines:

"[PROSECUTOR]: [Y]ou were shocked and surprised that there were pictures of very young boys without clothes on, is that correct?

"[JACOBSON]: Yes, I was.

"[PROSECUTOR]: Were you offended?

. . .

"[JACOBSON]: I was not offended because I thought these were a nudist type publication. Many of the pictures were out in a rural or outdoor setting. There was—I didn't draw any sexual connotation or connection with that."

The young men depicted in the magazines were not engaged in sexual activity, and petitioner's receipt of the magazines was legal under both federal and Nebraska law. Within three months, the law with respect to child pornography changed; Congress passed the Act illegalizing the receipt through the mails of sexually explicit depictions of children. In the very month that the new provision became law, postal inspectors found petitioner's name on the mailing list of the California bookstore that had mailed him Bare Boys I and II. There followed over the next 2 1/2 years repeated efforts by two Government agencies, through five fictitious organizations and a bogus pen pal, to explore petitioner's willingness to break the new law by ordering sexually explicit photographs of children through the mail.

[The Government sent letters to defendant from a fictitious organization expressing an interest in preteen sex and pedophilia].

Nevertheless, the Government's "prohibited mailing specialist" began writing to petitioner, using the pseudonym "Carl Long." The letters employed a tactic known as "mirroring," which the inspector described as "reflect[ing] whatever the interests are of the person we are writing to." Petitioner responded at first, indicating that his interest was primarily in "male-male items." Inspector "Long" wrote back:

"My interests too are primarily male-male items. Are you satisfied with the type of VCR tapes available? Personally, I like the amateur stuff better if its [sic] well produced as it can get more kinky and also seems more real. I think the actors enjoy it more."

Petitioner responded:

"As far as my likes are concerned, I like good looking young guys (in their late teens and early 20's) doing their thing together."

Petitioner's letters to "Long" made no reference to child pornography. After writing two letters, petitioner discontinued the correspondence.

By March 1987, 34 months had passed since the Government obtained petitioner's name from the mailing list of the California bookstore, and 26 months had passed since the Postal Service had commenced its mailings to petitioner. Although petitioner had responded to surveys and letters, the Government had no evidence that petitioner had ever intentionally possessed or been exposed to child pornography. The Postal Service had not checked petitioner's mail to determine whether he was receiving questionable mailings from persons—other than the Government—involved in the child pornography industry.

At this point, a second Government agency, the Customs Service, included petitioner in its own child pornography sting, "Operation Borderline," after receiving his name on lists submitted by the Postal Service. Using the name of a fictitious Canadian company called "Produit Outaouais," the Customs Service mailed petitioner a brochure advertising photographs of young boys engaging in sex. Petitioner placed an order that was never filled.

The Postal Service also continued its efforts in the Jacobson case, writing to petitioner as the "Far Eastern Trading Company Ltd." The letter began:

"As many of you know, much hysterical nonsense has appeared in the American media concerning 'pornography' and what must be done to stop it from coming across your borders. This brief letter does not allow us to give much comments; however, why is your government spending millions of dollars to exercise international censorship while tons of drugs, which makes yours the world's most crime ridden country are passed through easily."

The letter went on to say:

"[W]e have devised a method of getting these to you without prying eyes of U.S. Customs seizing your mail.... After consultations with American solicitors, we have been advised that once we have posted our material through your system, it cannot be opened for any inspection without authorization of a judge."

The letter invited petitioner to send for more information. It also asked petitioner to sign an affirmation that he was "not a law enforcement officer or agent of the U.S. Government acting in an undercover capacity for the purpose of entrapping Far Eastern Trading Company, its agents or customers." Petitioner responded. A catalog was sent, and petitioner ordered Boys Who Love Boys, a pornographic magazine depicting young boys engaged in various sexual activities. Petitioner was arrested after a controlled delivery of a photocopy of the magazine.

When petitioner was asked at trial why he placed such an order, he explained that the Government had succeeded in piquing his curiosity: "Well, the statement was made of all the trouble and the hysteria over pornography and I wanted to see what the material was. It didn't describe the—I didn't know for sure what kind of sexual action they were referring to in the Canadian letter."

In petitioner's home, the Government found the Bare Boys magazines and materials that the Government had sent to him in the course of its protracted investigation, but no other materials that would indicate that petitioner collected, or was actively interested in, child pornography.

Petitioner was indicted for violating 18 U.S.C. § 2252(a)(2)(A). The trial court instructed the jury on the petitioner's entrapment defense, petitioner was convicted. . . .

II

There can be no dispute about the evils of child pornography or the difficulties that laws and law enforcement have encountered in eliminating it. See generally Osborne v. Ohio, 495 U.S. 103, 110, 110 S.Ct. 1691, 1696, 109 L.Ed.2d 98 (1990); New York v. Ferber, 458 U.S. 747, 759–760, 102 S.Ct. 3348, 3355–3356, 73 L.Ed.2d 1113 (1982). Likewise, there can be no dispute that the Government may use undercover agents to enforce the law. It is well settled that the fact that officers or employees of the Government merely afford opportunities or facilities for the commission of the offense does not defeat the prosecution. Artifice and stratagem may be employed to catch those engaged in criminal enterprises.

In their zeal to enforce the law, however, Government agents may not originate a criminal design, implant in an innocent person's mind the disposition to commit a criminal act, and then induce commission of the crime so that the Government may prosecute. Where the Government has induced an individual to break the law and the defense of entrapment is at issue, as it was in this case, the prosecution must prove beyond reasonable doubt that the defendant was disposed to commit the criminal act prior to first being approached by Government agents.[143]

---

143. Inducement is not at issue in this case. The Government does not dispute that it induced petitioner to commit the crime. The sole issue is whether the Government carried its burden of proving that petitioner was predisposed to violate the law before the Government intervened. . . . Indeed, the proposition that the accused must be predisposed prior to contact with law enforcement officers is so firmly established that the Government conceded the point at oral argument, submitting that the evidence it developed during the course of its investigation was probative because it indicated petitioner's state of mind prior to the commencement of the Government's investigation.

This long-established standard in no way encroaches upon Government investigatory activities. Indeed, the Government's internal guidelines for undercover operations provide that an inducement to commit a crime should not be offered unless:

Thus, an agent deployed to stop the traffic in illegal drugs may offer the opportunity to buy or sell drugs and, if the offer is accepted, make an arrest on the spot or later. In such a typical case, or in a more elaborate "sting" operation involving government-sponsored fencing where the defendant is simply provided with the opportunity to commit a crime, the entrapment defense is of little use because the ready commission of the criminal act amply demonstrates the defendant's predisposition. Had the agents in this case simply offered petitioner the opportunity to order child pornography through the mails, and petitioner—who must be presumed to know the law—had promptly availed himself of this criminal opportunity, it is unlikely that his entrapment defense would have warranted a jury instruction.

But that is not what happened here. By the time petitioner finally placed his order, he had already been the target of 26 months of repeated mailings and communications from Government agents and fictitious organizations. Therefore, although he had become predisposed to break the law by May 1987, it is our view that the Government did not prove that this predisposition was independent and not the product of the attention that the Government had directed at petitioner since January 1985.

The prosecution's evidence of predisposition falls into two categories: evidence developed prior to the Postal Service's mail campaign, and that developed during the course of the investigation. The sole piece of preinvestigation evidence is petitioner's 1984 order and receipt of the Bare Boys magazines. But this is scant if any proof of petitioner's predisposition to commit an illegal act, the criminal character of which a defendant is presumed to know. It may indicate a predisposition to view sexually oriented photographs that are responsive to his sexual tastes; but evidence that merely indicates a generic inclination to act within a broad range, not all of which is criminal, is of little probative value in establishing predisposition.

Furthermore, petitioner was acting within the law at the time he received these magazines. Receipt through the mails of sexually explicit depictions of children for noncommercial use did not become illegal under federal law until May 1984, and Nebraska had no law that forbade petitioner's possession of such material until 1988. Evidence of predisposition to do what once was lawful is not, by itself, sufficient to show predisposition to do what is now illegal, for there is a common understanding that most people obey the law even when they disapprove of it. This obedience may reflect a generalized respect for legality or the fear of prosecution, but for whatever reason, the law's prohibitions are matters of consequence. Hence, the fact that petitioner legally ordered and received the Bare Boys magazines does little to further the Government's burden of

"(a) [T]here is a reasonable indication, based on information developed through informants or other means, that the subject is engaging, has engaged, or is likely to engage in illegal activity of a similar type; or

"(b) The opportunity for illegal activity has been structured so that there is reason for believing that persons drawn to the opportunity, or brought to it, are predisposed to engage in the contemplated illegal activity." Attorney General's Guidelines on FBI Undercover Operations (Dec. 31, 1980), reprinted in S.Rep. No. 97–682, p. 551 (1982).

proving that petitioner was predisposed to commit a criminal act. This is particularly true given petitioner's unchallenged testimony that he did not know until they arrived that the magazines would depict minors.

The prosecution's evidence gathered during the investigation also fails to carry the Government's burden. Petitioner's responses to the many communications prior to the ultimate criminal act were at most indicative of certain personal inclinations, including a predisposition to view photographs of preteen sex and a willingness to promote a given agenda by supporting lobbying organizations. Even so, petitioner's responses hardly support an inference that he would commit the crime of receiving child pornography through the mails. Furthermore, a person's inclinations and "fantasies ... are his own and beyond the reach of government...." Paris Adult Theatre I v. Slaton, 413 U.S. 49, 67, 93 S.Ct. 2628, 2641, 37 L.Ed.2d 446 (1973); Stanley v. Georgia, 394 U.S. 557, 565–566, 89 S.Ct. 1243, 1248, 22 L.Ed.2d 542 (1969).

On the other hand, the strong arguable inference is that, by waving the banner of individual rights and disparaging the legitimacy and constitutionality of efforts to restrict the availability of sexually explicit materials, the Government not only excited petitioner's interest in sexually explicit materials banned by law but also exerted substantial pressure on petitioner to obtain and read such material as part of a fight against censorship and the infringement of individual rights....

Petitioner's ready response to these solicitations cannot be enough to establish beyond reasonable doubt that he was predisposed, prior to the Government acts intended to create predisposition, to commit the crime of receiving child pornography through the mails. The evidence that petitioner was ready and willing to commit the offense came only after the Government had devoted 2 1/2 years to convincing him that he had or should have the right to engage in the very behavior proscribed by law. Rational jurors could not say beyond a reasonable doubt that petitioner possessed the requisite predisposition prior to the Government's investigation and that it existed independent of the Government's many and varied approaches to petitioner. As was explained in *Sherman* [Sherman v. United States, 356 U.S. 369 (1958)], where entrapment was found as a matter of law, "the Government [may not] pla[y] on the weaknesses of an innocent party and beguil[e] him into committing crimes which he otherwise would not have attempted."

Law enforcement officials go too far when they "implant in the mind of an innocent person the *disposition* to commit the alleged offense and induce its commission in order that they may prosecute." Like the *Sorrells* Court [Sorrells v. United States, 287 U.S. 435 (1932)], we are "unable to conclude that it was the intention of the Congress in enacting this statute that its processes of detection and enforcement should be abused by the instigation by government officials of an act on the part of persons otherwise innocent in order to lure them to its commission and to punish them." When the Government's quest for convictions leads to the apprehension of an otherwise law-abiding citizen who, if left to his own devices, likely would have never run afoul of the law, the courts should intervene.

Because we conclude that this is such a case and that the prosecution failed, as a matter of law, to adduce evidence to support the jury verdict that petitioner was predisposed, independent of the Government's acts and beyond a reasonable doubt, to violate the law by receiving child pornography through the mails, we reverse the Court of Appeals' judgment affirming the conviction of Keith Jacobson.

It is so ordered.[144]

MODEL PENAL CODE

Section 2.13   Entrapment.

(1) A public law enforcement official or a person acting in cooperation with such an official perpetrates an entrapment if for the purpose of obtaining evidence of the commission of an offense, he induces or encourages another person to engage in conduct constituting such offense by either:

(a) making knowingly false representations designed to induce the belief that such conduct is not prohibited; or

(b) employing methods of persuasion or inducement which create a substantial risk that such an offense will be committed by persons other than those who are ready to commit it.

(2) Except as provided in Subsection (3) of this Section, a person prosecuted for an offense shall be acquitted if he proves by a preponderance of evidence that his conduct occurred in response to an entrapment. The issue of entrapment shall be tried by the Court in the absence of the jury.

(3) The defense afforded by this Section is unavailable when causing or threatening bodily injury is an element of the offense charged and the prosecution is based on conduct causing or threatening such injury to a person other than the person perpetrating the entrapment.[145]

---

144. Derivative or vicarious entrapment is no defense; without direct government communication with defendant there is no basis for an entrapment defense. United States v. Martinez, 979 F.2d 1424 (10th Cir. 1992).

"Entrapment by estoppel" can apply when a law enforcement official assures a defendant that certain conduct is legal, and defendant reasonably relies on that advice and commits or continues the offense. United States v. Smith, 940 F.2d 710 (1st Cir.1991); United States v. Achter, 52 F.3d 753 (8th Cir.1995).

A defendant may raise entrapment defense even though defendant denies the commission of the offense. Mathews v. United States, 485 U.S. 58, 108 S.Ct.883, 99 L.Ed.2d 54 (1988).

145. Copyright © 1962 by the American Law Institute. Reprinted with the permission of the American Law Institute.

CHAPTER 11

SENTENCING

SECTION 1.   DISCRETIONARY SENTENCING

United States v. Bergman

United States District Court, S.D. New York, 1976.
416 F.Supp. 496.

SENTENCING MEMORANDUM

■ FRANKEL, DISTRICT JUDGE.

Defendant is being sentenced upon his plea of guilty to two counts of an 11–count indictment. The sentencing proceeding is unusual in some respects. It has been the subject of more extensive submissions, written and oral, than this court has ever received upon such an occasion. The court has studied some hundreds of pages of memoranda and exhibits, plus scores of volunteered letters. A broad array of issues has been addressed. Imaginative suggestions of law and penology have been tendered. A preliminary conversation with counsel, on the record, preceded the usual sentencing hearing. Having heard counsel again and the defendant speaking for himself, the court postponed the pronouncement of sentence for further reconsideration of thoughts generated during the days of studying the briefs and oral pleas. It seems fitting now to report in writing the reasons upon which the court concludes that defendant must be sentenced to a term of four months in prison.[1]

I.   Defendant and His Crimes

Defendant appeared until the last couple of years to be a man of unimpeachably high character, attainments, and distinction. A doctor of divinity and an ordained rabbi, he has been acclaimed by people around the world for his works of public philanthropy, private charity, and leadership in educational enterprises. Scores of letters have come to the court from across this and other countries reporting debts of personal gratitude to him for numerous acts of extraordinary generosity. (The court has also received a kind of petition, with fifty-odd signatures, in which the signers, based upon learning acquired as newspaper readers, denounce the defendant and urge a severe sentence. Unlike the pleas for mercy, which appear to reflect unquestioned facts inviting compassion, this document should and will be disregarded.) In addition to his good works, defendant has managed to

---

1. The court considered, and finally rejected, imposing a fine in addition to the prison term. Defendant seems destined to pay hundreds of thousands of dollars in restitution. The amount is being worked out in connection with a state criminal indictment. Apart from defendant's further liabilities for federal taxes, any additional money exaction is appropriately left for the state court.

amass considerable wealth in the ownership and operation of nursing homes, in real estate ventures, and in a course of substantial investments.

Beginning about two years ago, investigations of nursing homes in this area, including questions of fraudulent claims for Medicaid funds, drew to a focus upon this defendant among several others. The results that concern us were the present indictment and two state indictments. After extensive pretrial proceedings, defendant embarked upon elaborate plea negotiations with both state and federal prosecutors. A state guilty plea and the instant plea were entered in March of this year. (Another state indictment is expected to be dismissed after defendant is sentenced on those to which he has pled guilty.) As part of the detailed plea arrangements, it is expected that the prison sentence imposed by this court will comprise the total covering the state as well as the federal convictions.[2]

For purposes of the sentence now imposed, the precise details of the charges, and of defendant's carefully phrased admissions of guilt, are not matters of prime importance. Suffice it to say that the plea on Count One (carrying a maximum of five years in prison and a $10,000 fine) confesses defendant's knowing and wilful participation in a scheme to defraud the United States in various ways, including the presentation of wrongfully padded claims for payments under the Medicaid program to defendant's nursing homes. Count Three, for which the guilty plea carries a theoretical maximum of three more years in prison and another $5,000 fine, is a somewhat more "technical" charge. Here, defendant admits to having participated in the filing of a partnership return which was false and fraudulent in failing to list people who had bought partnership interests from him in one of his nursing homes, had paid for such interests, and had made certain capital withdrawals.

The conspiracy to defraud, as defendant has admitted it, is by no means the worst of its kind; it is by no means as flagrant or extensive as has been portrayed in the press; it is evidently less grave than other nursing-home wrongs for which others have been convicted or publicized. At the same time, the sentence, as defendant has acknowledged, is imposed for two federal felonies including, as the more important, a knowing and purposeful conspiracy to mislead and defraud the Federal Government.

II. The Guiding Principles of Sentencing

Proceeding through the short list of the supposed justifications for criminal sanctions, defense counsel urge that no licit purpose could be served by defendant's incarceration. Some of these arguments are plainly sound; others are not.

The court agrees that this defendant should not be sent to prison for "rehabilitation." Apart from the patent inappositeness of the concept to this individual, this court shares the growing understanding that no one should ever be sent to prison for rehabilitation. That is to say, nobody who would not otherwise be locked up should suffer that fate on the incongru-

---

2. This is not absolutely certain. Defendant has been told, however, that the imposition of any additional prison sentence by the state court will be an occasion for reconsidering today's judgment.

ous premise that it will be good for him or her. Imprisonment is punishment. Facing the simple reality should help us to be civilized. It is less agreeable to confine someone when we deem it an affliction rather than a benefaction. If someone must be imprisoned for other, valid reasons we should seek to make rehabilitative resources available to him or her. But the goal of rehabilitation cannot fairly serve in itself as grounds for the sentence to confinement.[3]

Equally clearly, this defendant should not be confined to incapacitate him. He is not dangerous. It is most improbable that he will commit similar, or any, offenses in the future. There is no need for "specific deterrence."

Contrary to counsel's submissions, however, two sentencing considerations demand a prison sentence in this case:

First, the aim of general deterrence, the effort to discourage similar wrongdoing by others through a reminder that the law's warnings are real and that the grim consequence of imprisonment is likely to follow from crimes of deception for gain like those defendant has admitted.

Second, the related, but not identical, concern that any lesser penalty would, in the words of the Model Penal Code, s 7.01(1)(c), "depreciate the seriousness of the defendant's crime."

Resisting the first of these propositions, defense counsel invoke Immanuel Kant's axiom that "one man ought never to be dealt with merely as a means subservient to the purposes of another."[4] In a more novel, but equally futile, effort, counsel urge that a sentence for general deterrence "would violate the Eighth Amendment proscription against cruel and unusual punishment." Treating the latter point first, because it is a short subject, it may be observed simply that if general deterrence as a sentencing purpose were now to be outlawed, as against a near unanimity of views among state and federal jurists, the bolt would have to come from a place higher than this.[5]

As for Dr. Kant, it may well be that defense counsel mistake his meaning in the present context.[6] Whether or not that is so, and without pretending to authority on that score, we take the widely accepted stance that a criminal punished in the interest of general deterrence is not being employed "merely as a means * * *." Reading Kant to mean that every man must be deemed more than the instrument of others, and must "always be treated as an end in himself,"[7] the humane principle is not offended here. Each of us is served by the enforcement of the law not least

---

3. This important point, correcting misconceptions still widely prevalent, is developed more fully by Dean Norval Morris in The Future of Imprisonment (1974).

4. Quoting from I. Kant, Philosophy of Law 1986 (Hastie Trans. 1887).

5. To a large extent the defendant's eighth amendment argument is that imprisoning him because he has been "newsworthy" would be cruelly wrong. This thought is accepted by the court without approaching the Constitution. (See below.) The reference at this point is meant to acknowledge, if only to reject, a seemingly broader submission.

6. See H. L. A. Hart, Punishment and Responsibility 243–44 (1968).

7. Andenaes, The Morality of Deterrence, 37 U.Chi.L.Rev. 649 (1970). See also O. Holmes, Common Law 43–44, 46–47 (1881).

a person like the defendant in this case, whose wealth and privileges, so long enjoyed, are so much founded upon law. More broadly, we are driven regularly in our ultimate interests as members of the community to use ourselves and each other, in war and in peace, for social ends. One who has transgressed against the criminal laws is certainly among the more fitting candidates for a role of this nature. This is no arbitrary selection. Warned in advance of the prospect, the transgressor has chosen, in the law's premises, "between keeping the law required for society's protection or paying the penalty."[8]

But the whole business, defendant argues further, is guesswork; we are by no means certain that deterrence "works." The position is somewhat overstated; there is, in fact, some reasonably "scientific" evidence for the efficacy of criminal sanctions as deterrents, at least as against some kinds of crimes.[9] Moreover, the time is not yet here when all we can "know" must be quantifiable and digestible by computers. The shared wisdom of generations teaches meaningfully, if somewhat amorphously, that the utilitarians have a point; we do, indeed, lapse often into rationality and act to seek pleasure and avoid pain.[10] It would be better, to be sure, if we had more certainty and precision. Lacking these comforts, we continue to include among our working hypotheses a belief (with some concrete evidence in its support) that crimes like those in this case deliberate, purposeful, continuing, non-impulsive, and committed for profit are among those most likely to be generally deterrable by sanctions most shunned by those exposed to temptation.[11]

The idea of avoiding depreciation of the seriousness of the offense implicates two or three thoughts, not always perfectly clear or universally agreed upon, beyond the idea of deterrence. It should be proclaimed by the court's judgment that the offenses are grave, not minor or purely technical. Some attention must be paid to the demand for equal justice; it will not do to leave the penalty of imprisonment a dead letter as against "privileged" violators while it is employed regularly, and with vigor, against others. There probably is in these conceptions an element of retributiveness, as counsel urge. And retribution, so denominated, is in some disfavor as a reason for punishment. It remains a factor, however, as Holmes perceived,[12] and as is known to anyone who talks to judges, lawyers, defendants, or people generally. It may become more palatable, and probably more humanely understood, under the rubric of "deserts" or "just deserts."[13] However the concept is formulated, we have not yet reached a state, supposing we ever should, in which the infliction of punishments for

---

8. H. L. A. Hart, supra note 6, at 23.

9. See, e.g., F. Zimring and G. Hawkins, Deterrence 168–71, 282 (1973).

10. See Andenaes, supra note 7, at 663–64.

11. For some supporting evidence that "white-collar" offenses are somewhat specially deterrable, see Chambliss, Types of Deviance and the Effectiveness of Legal Sanctions, 1967 Wis.L.Rev. 703, 708–10.

12. See O. Holmes, Common Law 41–42, 45 (1881).

13. See A. von Hirsch, Doing Justice 45–55 (1976); see also N. Morris, The Future of Imprisonment 73–77 (1974).

crime may be divorced generally from ideas of blameworthiness, recompense, and proportionality.

III.   An Alternative, "Behavioral Sanction"

Resisting prison above all else, defense counsel included in their thorough memorandum on sentencing two proposals for what they call a "constructive," and therefore a "preferable" form of "behavioral sanction." One is a plan for Dr. Bergman to create and run a program of Jewish vocational and religious high school training. The other is for him to take charge of a "Committee on Holocaust Studies," again concerned with education at the secondary school level....

... The seriousness of the crimes to which Dr. Bergman has pled guilty demands something more than "requiring" him to lend his talents and efforts to further philanthropic enterprises. It remains open to him, of course, to pursue the interesting suggestions later on as a matter of unforced personal choice.

IV.   "Measuring" the Sentence

In cases like this one, the decision of greatest moment is whether to imprison or not. As reflected in the eloquent submissions for defendant, the prospect of the closing prison doors is the most appalling concern; the feeling is that the length of the sojourn is a lesser question once that threshold is passed. Nevertheless, the setting of a term remains to be accomplished. And in some respects it is a subject even more perplexing, unregulated, and unprincipled.

Days and months and years are countable with a sound of exactitude. But there can be no exactitude in the deliberations from which a number emerges. Without pretending to a nonexistent precision, the court notes at least the major factors.

The criminal behavior, as has been noted, is blatant in character and unmitigated by any suggestion of necessitous circumstance or other pressures difficult to resist. However metaphysicians may conjure with issues about free will, it is a fundamental premise of our efforts to do criminal justice that competent people, possessed of their faculties, make choices and are accountable for them. In this sometimes harsh light, the case of the present defendant is among the clearest and least relieved. Viewed against the maxima Congress ordained, and against the run of sentences in other federal criminal cases, it calls for more than a token sentence.[14]

On the other side are factors that take longer to enumerate. Defendant's illustrious public life and works are in his favor, though diminished, of course, by what this case discloses. This is a first, probably a last, conviction. Defendant is 64 years old and in imperfect health, though by no means so ill, from what the court is told, that he could be expected to suffer inordinately more than many others of advanced years who go to prison.

---

14.   Despite Biblical teachings concerning what is expected from those to whom much is given, the court has not, as his counsel feared might happen, held Dr. Bergman to a higher standard of responsibility because of his position in the community. But he has not been judged under a lower standard either.

Defendant invokes an understandable, but somewhat unworkable, notion of "disparity." He says others involved in recent nursing home fraud cases have received relatively light sentences for behavior more culpable than his. He lays special emphasis upon one defendant whose frauds appear indeed to have involved larger amounts and who was sentenced to a maximum of six months' incarceration, to be confined for that time only on week nights, not on week days or weekends. This court has examined the minutes of that sentencing proceeding and finds the case distinguishable in material respects. But even if there were a threat of such disparity as defendant warns against, it could not be a major weight on the scales.

Our sentencing system, deeply flawed, is characterized by disparity. We are to seek to "individualize" sentences, but no clear or clearly agreed standards govern the individualization. The lack of meaningful criteria does indeed leave sentencing judges far too much at large. But the result, with its nagging burdens on conscience, cannot be meaningfully alleviated by allowing any handful of sentences in a short series to fetter later judgments. The point is easy, of course, where Sentence No. 1 or Sentences 1–5 are notably harsh. It cannot be that a later judge, disposed to more leniency, should feel in any degree "bound." The converse is not identical, but it is not totally different. The net of this is that this court has considered and has given some weight to the trend of the other cited sentences (though strict logic might call for none), but without treating them as forceful "precedents" in any familiar sense.

How, then, the particular sentence adjudged in this case? As has been mentioned, the case calls for a sentence that is more than nominal. Given the other circumstances, however including that this is a first offense, by a man no longer young and not perfectly well, where danger of recidivism is not a concern it verges on cruelty to think of confinement for a term of years. We sit, to be sure, in a nation where prison sentences of extravagant length are more common than they are almost anywhere else. By that light, the term imposed today is not notably long. For this sentencing court, however, for a nonviolent first offense involving no direct assaults or invasions of others' security (as in bank robbery, narcotics, etc.), it is a stern sentence. For people like Dr. Bergman, who might be disposed to engage in similar wrongdoing, it should be sufficiently frightening to serve the major end of general deterrence. For all but the profoundly vengeful, it should not depreciate the seriousness of his offenses. . . .

SECTION 2.   ADVISORY GUIDELINES

MINNESOTA SENTENCING GUIDELINES and COMMENTARY

Revised August 1, 2006.

I.   Statement of Purpose and Principles

The purpose of the sentencing guidelines is to establish rational and consistent sentencing standards which reduce sentencing disparity and ensure that sanctions following conviction of a felony are proportional to the severity of the offense of conviction and the extent of the offender's criminal history. Equity in sentencing requires (a) that convicted felons similar with respect to relevant sentencing criteria ought to receive similar sanctions, and (b) that convicted felons substantially different from a typical case with respect to relevant criteria ought to receive different sanctions.

The sentencing guidelines embody the following principles:

1. Sentencing should be neutral with respect to the race, gender, social, or economic status of convicted felons.

2. While commitment to the Commissioner of Corrections is the most severe sanction that can follow conviction of a felony, it is not the only significant sanction available to the sentencing judge. Development of a rational and consistent sentencing policy requires that the severity of sanctions increase in direct proportion to increases in the severity of criminal offenses and the severity of criminal histories of convicted felons.

3. Because the capacities of state and local correctional facilities are finite, use of incarcerative sanctions should be limited to those convicted of more serious offenses or those who have longer criminal histories. To ensure such usage of finite resources, sanctions used in sentencing convicted felons should be the least restrictive necessary to achieve the purposes of the sentence.

4. While the sentencing guidelines are advisory to the sentencing judge, departures from the presumptive sentences established in the guidelines should be made only when substantial and compelling circumstances exist.II. Determining Presumptive Sentences

The presumptive sentence for any offender convicted of a felony committed on or after May 1, 1980, is determined by locating the appropriate cell of the Sentencing Guidelines Grids. The grids represent the two dimensions most important in current sentencing and releasing decisions—offense severity and criminal history.

A. Offense Severity: The offense severity level is determined by the offense of conviction. When an offender is convicted of two or more felonies, the severity level is determined by the most severe offense of conviction. For persons convicted under Minn. Stat. §§ 609.2241—Knowing Transfer of Communicable Disease, 609.229, subd. 3 (a)—Crime Committed for Benefit of a Gang, 609.3453—Criminal Sexual Predatory Conduct, or 609.714—Offense in Furtherance of Terrorism, the severity level is the same as that for the underlying crime with the highest severity level.

Felony offenses, other than specified sex offenses, are arrayed into eleven levels of severity, ranging from low (Severity Level I) to high (Severity Level XI). Specified sex offenses are arrayed on a separate grid into eight severity levels labeled A thru H. First degree murder is excluded from the sentencing guidelines, because by law the sentence is mandatory imprisonment for life. Offenses listed within each level of severity are deemed to be generally equivalent in severity. The severity level for each felony offense is governed by Section V: Offense Severity Reference Table. Some offenses are designated as unranked offenses in the Offense Severity Reference Table. When unranked offenses are being sentenced, the sentencing judges shall exercise their discretion by assigning an appropriate severity level for that offense and specify on the record the reasons a particular level was assigned. If an offense is inadvertently omitted from the Offense Severity Reference Table, the offense shall be considered unranked and the above procedures followed.

B.   Criminal History: A criminal history index constitutes the horizontal axis of the Sentencing Guidelines Grids. The criminal history index is comprised of the following items: (1) prior felony record; (2) custody status at the time of the offense; (3) prior misdemeanor and gross misdemeanor record; and (4) prior juvenile record for young adult felons. . . .

Comment

II.B.01. The sentencing guidelines reduce the emphasis given to criminal history in sentencing decisions. Under past judicial practice, criminal history was the primary factor in dispositional decisions. Under sentencing guidelines, the offense of conviction is the primary factor, and criminal history is a secondary factor in dispositional decisions. In the past there were no uniform standards regarding what should be included in an offender's criminal history, no weighting format for different types of offenses, and no systematic process to check the accuracy of the information on criminal history.

II.B.02. The guidelines provide uniform standards for the inclusion and weighting of criminal history information. The sentencing hearing provides a process to assure the accuracy of the information in individual cases. These improvements will increase fairness and equity in the consideration of criminal history.

II.B.03. No system of criminal history record keeping ever will be totally accurate and complete, and any sentencing system will have to rely on the best available criminal history information.

The offender's criminal history index score is computed in the following manner:

1.   Subject to the conditions listed below, the offender is assigned a particular weight for every extended jurisdiction juvenile conviction and for every felony conviction for which a felony sentence was stayed or imposed before the current sentencing or for which a stay of imposition of sentence was given before the current sentencing. Multiple offenses are sentenced in the order in which they occurred. For purposes of this section, prior extended jurisdiction juvenile convictions are treated the same as prior felony sentences.

   a.   If the current offense is not a specified sex offense, the weight assigned to each prior felony sentence is determined according to its severity level, as follows:

Severity Level I–II = ½ point;

Severity Level III–V = 1 point;

Severity Level VI–VIII = 1 ½ points;

Severity Level IX–XI = 2 points;

Murder 1st Degree = 2 points;

Severity Level A = 2 points;

Severity Level B–E = 1 ½ points;

Severity Level F–G = 1 point; and

Severity Level H = ½ point for first offense

and 1 point for subsequent offenses.

    b. If the current offense is a specified sex offense, the weight assigned to each prior felony sentence is determined according to its severity level, as follows:

Severity Level I–II = ½ point;

Severity Level III–V = 1 point;

Severity Level VI–VIII = 1 ½ points;

Severity Level IX–XI = 2 points;

Murder 1st Degree = 2 points;

Severity Level A = 3 points;

Severity Level B–C = 2 points;

Severity Level D–E = 1 ½ points;

Severity Level F–G = 1 point; and

Severity Level H = ½ point for first offense

and 1 point for subsequent offenses.

Comment

II.B.101. The basic rule for computing the number of prior felony points in the criminal history score is that the offender is assigned a particular weight for every felony conviction for which a felony sentence was stayed or imposed before the current sentencing or for which a stay of imposition of sentence was given for a felony level offense, no matter what period of probation is pronounced, before the current sentencing. Prior felony convictions for an attempt or conspiracy for which a felony sentence was stayed or imposed before the current sentencing are weighted the same as completed offenses. The felony point total is the sum of these weights. No partial points are given—thus, a person with less than a full point is not given that point. For example, an offender with a total weight of 2½ would have 2 felony points.

The Commission determined that it was important to establish a weighting scheme for prior felony sentences to assure a greater degree of proportionality in the current sentencing. Offenders who have a history of serious felonies are considered more culpable than those offenders whose prior felonies consist primarily of low severity, nonviolent offenses . . . .

    2. One point is assigned if the offender:

        a. was on probation, parole, supervised release, conditional release, or confined in a jail, workhouse, or prison pending sentencing, following a guilty plea, guilty verdict, or extended jurisdiction juvenile conviction in a felony, non-traffic gross misdemeanor or gross misdemeanor driving while impaired or refusal to submit to a chemical test case; or

b. was released pending sentencing at the time the felony was committed for which he or she is being sentenced . . .

Comment

II.B.201. The basic rule assigns offenders one point if they were under some form of criminal justice custody when the offense was committed for which they are now being sentenced. The Commission believes that the potential for a custody status point should remain for the entire period of the initial length of stay pronounced by the sentencing judge. An offender who is discharged early but subsequently is convicted of a new felony within the period of the initial length of stay should still receive the consequence of a custody status point. If probation is revoked and the offender serves an executed sentence for the prior offense, eligibility for the custody status point ends with discharge from the sentence . . .

3. Subject to the conditions listed below, the offender is assigned one unit for each misdemeanor conviction and for each gross misdemeanor conviction included on the Misdemeanor and Gross Misdemeanor Offense List and for which a sentence was stayed or imposed before the current sentencing or for which a stay of imposition of sentence was given before the current sentencing. All felony convictions resulting in a misdemeanor or gross misdemeanor sentence shall also be used to compute units. Four such units shall equal one point on the criminal history score, and no offender shall receive more than one point for prior misdemeanor or gross misdemeanor convictions. . . .

Comment

II.B.301. The Commission established a measurement procedure based on units for misdemeanor and gross misdemeanor sentences which are totaled and then converted to a point value. The purpose of this procedure is to provide different weightings for convictions of felonies, gross misdemeanors, and misdemeanors. Under this procedure, misdemeanors and gross misdemeanors are assigned one unit. An offender must have a total of four units to receive one point on the criminal history score. No partial points are given—thus, a person with three units is assigned no point value.

As a general rule, the Commission eliminated traffic misdemeanors and gross misdemeanors from consideration. However, driving while impaired traffic offenses have particular relevance to the offenses of criminal vehicular homicide or injury and first degree (felony) driving while impaired. Therefore, prior misdemeanor and gross misdemeanor sentences for violations under 169A.20, 169A.31, 169.121, 169.1211, 169.129, or 360.0752 shall be used in the computation of the misdemeanor/gross misdemeanor point when the current conviction offense is criminal vehicular homicide or injury or first degree (felony) driving while impaired. . . .

4. [Subject to certain procedural requirements and other qualifications,] The offender is assigned one point for every two offenses committed and prosecuted as a juvenile that are felonies under Minnesota law....

Comment

II.B.401. The juvenile history item is included in the criminal history index to identify those young adult felons whose criminal careers were preceded by repeated felony-type offenses committed as a juvenile. The Commission held several public hearings devoted to the issue of using juvenile records in the criminal history index. Those hearings pointed out differences in legal procedures and safeguards between adult and juvenile courts, differing availability of juvenile records, and differing procedures among juvenile courts. As a result of these issues, the Commission originally decided to establish rigorous standards regulating the consideration of juvenile records in computing the criminal history score....

7. The criminal history score is the sum of points accrued under items one through four above.

C. Presumptive Sentence: The offense of conviction determines the appropriate severity level on the vertical axis of the appropriate grid. The offender's criminal history score, computed according to section B above, determines the appropriate location on the horizontal axis of the appropriate grid. The presumptive fixed sentence for a felony conviction is found in the Sentencing Guidelines Grid cell at the intersection of the column defined by the criminal history score and the row defined by the offense severity level. The offenses within the Sentencing Guidelines Grids are presumptive with respect to the duration of the sentence and whether imposition or execution of the felony sentence should be stayed.

The shaded areas on the Sentencing Guidelines Grids demarcate those cases for whom the presumptive sentence is stayed from those for whom the presumptive sentence is executed. For cases contained in cells outside of the shaded areas, the sentence should be executed. For cases contained in cells within the shaded areas, the sentence should be stayed, unless the conviction offense carries a mandatory minimum sentence....

D. Departures from the Guidelines: The sentence ranges provided in the Sentencing Guidelines Grids are presumed to be appropriate for the crimes to which they apply. Thus, the judge shall pronounce a sentence within the applicable range unless there exist identifiable, substantial, and compelling circumstances to support a sentence outside the range on the grids. A sentence outside the applicable range on the grids is a departure from the sentencing guidelines and is not controlled by the guidelines, but rather, is an exercise of judicial discretion constrained by case law and appellate review. However, in exercising the discretion to depart from a presumptive sentence, the judge must disclose in writing or on the record the particular substantial and compelling circumstances that make the departure more appropriate than the presumptive sentence.

Furthermore, if an aggravated departure is to be considered, the judge must afford the accused an opportunity to have a jury trial on the additional facts that support the departure and to have the facts proved beyond a reasonable doubt. If the departure facts are proved beyond a reasonable doubt, the judge may exercise the discretion to depart from the presumptive sentence. In exercising that discretion, it is recommended that the judge pronounce a sentence that is proportional to the severity of the crime for which the sentence is imposed and the offender's criminal history, and take into consideration the purposes and underlying principles of the sentencing guidelines. Because departures are by definition exceptions to the sentencing guidelines, the departure factors set forth in II.D are advisory only, except as otherwise established by settled case law. When the conviction is for a criminal sexual conduct offense or offense in which the victim was otherwise injured, and victim injury is established in proving the elements of the crime, an aggravated durational departure is possible without a jury determination of additional facts if the departure is based on the offender's prior history of a conviction for a prior criminal sexual conduct offense or an offense in which victim injury was established as an element of the offense.

1.   Factors that should not be used as reasons for departure: The following factors should not be used as reasons for departing from the presumptive sentences provided in the Sentencing Guidelines Grids:

    a.   Race

    b.   Sex

    c.   Employment factors, including:

        (1) occupation or impact of sentence on profession or occupation;

        (2) employment history;

        (3) employment at time of offense;

        (4) employment at time of sentencing.

    d.   Social factors, including:

        (1) educational attainment;

        (2) living arrangements at time of offense or sentencing;

        (3) length of residence;

        (4) marital status.

    e.   The exercise of constitutional rights by the defendant during the adjudication process.

2.   Factors that may be used as reasons for departure: The following is a nonexclusive list of factors which may be used as reasons for departure:

    a.   Mitigating Factors:

        (1) The victim was an aggressor in the incident.

        (2) The offender played a minor or passive role in the crime or participated under circumstances of coercion or duress.

        (3) The offender, because of physical or mental impairment, lacked substantial capacity for judgment when the offense was committed. The voluntary use of intoxicants (drugs or alcohol) does not fall within the purview of this factor.

(4) The offender's presumptive sentence is a commitment to the commissioner but not a mandatory minimum sentence, and either of the following exist:

(a) The current conviction offense is at severity level I or II and the offender received all of his or her prior felony sentences during less than three separate court appearances; or

(b) The current conviction offense is at severity level III or IV and the offender received all of his or her prior felony sentences during one court appearance.

(5) Other substantial grounds exist which tend to excuse or mitigate the offender's culpability, although not amounting to a defense.

(6) Alternative placement for offender with serious and persistent mental illness (See Minn. Stat. § 609.1055).

b. Aggravating Factors:

(1) The victim was particularly vulnerable due to age, infirmity, or reduced physical or mental capacity, which was known or should have been known to the offender.

(2) The victim was treated with particular cruelty for which the individual offender should be held responsible.

(3) The current conviction is for a Criminal Sexual Conduct offense or an offense in which the victim was otherwise injured and there is a prior felony conviction for a Criminal Sexual Conduct offense or an offense in which the victim was otherwise injured.

(4) The offense was a major economic offense, identified as an illegal act or series of illegal acts committed by other than physical means and by concealment or guile to obtain money or property, to avoid payment or loss of money or property, or to obtain business or professional advantage. The presence of two or more of the circumstances listed below are aggravating factors with respect to the offense:

(a) the offense involved multiple victims or multiple incidents per victim;

(b) the offense involved an attempted or actual monetary loss substantially greater than the usual offense or substantially greater than the minimum loss specified in the statutes;

(c) the offense involved a high degree of sophistication or planning or occurred over a lengthy period of time;

(d) the defendant used his or her position or status to facilitate the commission of the offense, including positions of trust, confidence, or fiduciary relationships; or

(e) the defendant has been involved in other conduct similar to the current offense as evidenced by the findings of civil or administrative law proceedings or the imposition of professional sanctions.

(5) The offense was a major controlled substance offense, identified as an offense or series of offenses related to trafficking in controlled

substances under circumstances more onerous than the usual offense. . . .

(6) The offender committed, for hire, a crime against the person.

(7) Offender is a "patterned sex offender" (See Minn. Stat. § 609.108).

(8) Offender is a "dangerous offender who commits a third violent crime" (See Minn. Stat. § 609.1095, subd. 2).

(9) Offender is a "career offender" (See Minn. Stat. § 609.1095, subd. 4).

(10) The offender committed the crime as part of a group of three or more persons who all actively participated in the crime.

(11) The offender intentionally selects the victim or the property against which the offense is committed, in whole or in part, because of the victim's, the property owner's or another's actual or perceived race, color, religion, sex, sexual orientation, disability, age or national origin.

(12) The offender's use of another's identity without authorization to commit a crime. This aggravating factor may not be used when the use of another's identity is an element of the offense.

IV. SENTENCING GUIDELINES GRID

Presumptive Sentence Lengths in Months

Italicized numbers within the grid denote the range within which a judge may sentence without the sentence being deemed a departure. Offenders with non-imprisonment felony sentences are subject to jail time according to law.

SEVERITY LEVEL OF CONVICTION OFFENSE (Common offenses listed in italics)		CRIMINAL HISTORY SCORE						
		0	1	2	3	4	5	6 or more
Murder, 2nd Degree (intentional murder; drive-by-shootings)	XI	306 *261–367*	326 *278–391*	346 *295–415*	366 *312–439*	386 *329–463*	406 *346–480²* 40 years, the range is capped at that number	426 *363–480²* 40 years, the range is capped at that number
Murder, 3rd Degree Murder, 2nd Degree (unintentional murder)	X	150 *128–180*	165 *141–198*	180 *153–216*	195 *166–234*	210 *179–252*	225 *192–270*	240 *204–288*
Assault, 1st Degree Controlled Substance Crime, 1st Degree	IX	86 *74–103*	98 *84–117*	110 *94–132*	122 *104–146*	134 *114–160*	146 *125–175*	158 *135–189*
Aggravated Robbery, 1st Degree Controlled Substance Crime 2nd Degree	VIII	48 *41–57*	58 *50–69*	68 *58–81*	78 *67–93*	88 *75–105*	98 *84–117*	108 *92–129*
Felony DWI	VII	36	42	48	54 *46–64*	60 *51–72*	66 *57–79*	72 *62–86*
Assault, 2nd Degree Felon in Possession of a Firearm	VI	21	27	33	39 *34–46*	45 *39–54*	51 *44–61*	57 *49–68*
Residential Burglary Simple Robbery	V	18	23	28	33 *29–39*	38 *33–45*	43 *37–51*	48 *41–57*
Nonresidential Burglary	IV	12¹	15	18	21	24 *21–28*	27 *23–32*	30 *26–36*
Theft Crimes (Over $2,500)	III	12¹	13	15	17	19 *17–22*	21 *18–25*	23 *20–27*
Theft Crimes ($2,500 or less) Check Forgery ($200–$2,500)	II	12¹	12¹	13	15	17	19	21 *18–25*
(Sales of Simulated Controlled Substance	I	12¹	12¹	12¹	13	15	17	19 *17–22*

☐ Presumptive commitment to state imprisonment. First Degree Murder is excluded from the guidelines by law and continues to have a mandatory life sentence. See section II.E. Mandatory Sentences for policy regarding those sentences controlled by law.

☐ Presumptive stayed sentence; at the discretion of the judge, up to a year in jail and/or other non-jail sanctions can be imposed as conditions of probation. However, certain offenses in this section of the grid always carry a presumptive commitment to state prison. See sections II.C. Presumptive Sentence and II.E. Mandatory Sentences.

¹ One year and one day

² M.S. § 244.09 requires the Sentencing Guidelines to provide a range of 15% downward and 20% upward from the presumptive sentence. However, because the statutory maximum sentence for these offenses is no more than 40 years, the range is capped at that number.

Effective August 1, 2006

Examples of Executed Sentences (Length in Months) Broken Down by:

Specified Minimum Term of Imprisonment and Specified Maximum Supervised Release Term

Offenders committed to the Commissioner of Corrections for crimes committed on or after August 1, 1993 will no longer earn good time. In accordance with Minn. Stat. § 244.101, offenders will receive an executed sentence pronounced by the court consisting of two parts: a specified minimum term of imprisonment equal to two-thirds of the total executed sentence and a supervised release term equal to the remaining one-third. This provision requires that the court pronounce the total executed sentence and explain the amount of time the offender will serve in prison and the amount of time the offender will serve on supervised release, assuming the offender commits no disciplinary offense in prison that results in the imposition of a disciplinary confinement period. The court shall also explain that the amount of time the offender actually serves in prison may be extended by the Commissioner if the offender violates disciplinary rules while in prison or violates conditions of supervised release. This extension period could result in the offender's serving the entire executed sentence in prison. The court's explanation is to be included in a written summary of the sentence.

Executed Sentence	Term of Imprisonment	Supervised Release Term	Executed Sentence	Term of Imprisonment	Supervised Release Term
12 and 1 day	8 and 1 day	4	78	52	26
13	8 2/3	4 1/3	86	57 1/3	28 2/3
15	10	5	88	58 2/3	29 1/3
17	11 1/3	5 2/3	98	65 1/3	32 2/3
18	12	6	108	72	36
19	12 2/3	6 1/3	110	73 1/3	36 2/3
21	14	7	122	81 1/3	40 2/3
23	15 1/3	7 2/3	134	89 1/3	44 2/3
24	16	8	146	97 1/3	48 2/3
27	18	9	150	100	50
28	18 2/3	9 1/3	158	105 1/3	52 2/3
30	20	10	165	110	55
33	22	11	180	120	60
36	24	12	190	126 2/3	63 1/3
38	25 1/3	12 2/3	195	130	65
39	26	13	200	133 1/3	66 2/3
42	28	14	210	140	70
43	28 2/3	14 1/3	220	146 2/3	73 1/3
45	30	15	225	150	75
48	32	16	230	153 1/3	76 2/3
51	34	17	240	160	80
54	36	18	306	204	102
57	38	19	326	217 1/3	108 2/3
58	38 2/3	19 1/3	346	230 2/3	115 1/3
60	40	20	366	244	122
66	44	22	386	257 1/3	128 2/3
68	45 1/3	22 2/3	406	270 2/3	135 1/3
72	48	24	426	284	142

State v. Spain

Supreme Court of Minnesota, 1999.
590 N.W.2d 85.

■ LANCASTER, J.

A Dakota County jury convicted appellant, Nancy Louise Spain, of first-degree arson The trial court sentenced appellant to 144 months, which constituted a triple durational departure from the presumptive sentence of 48 months set forth in the Minnesota Sentencing Guidelines. In an unpublished decision, the court of appeals affirmed. We granted appellant's petition for review for the limited purpose of reviewing the sentencing departure. We hold that the aggravating circumstances present in this case, while serious, do not justify a greater-than-double durational departure from the presumptive sentence and therefore reduce appellant's sentence to 96 months.

In July 1996, appellant's ex-husband, Eugene Letendre, allowed appellant to move into his South St. Paul home on a temporary basis after a rent increase forced her to move out of her apartment. While living in Letendre's home, appellant usually slept on the living room couch; when Letendre's and Spain's adult daughter was away, appellant would sometimes sleep in her bedroom. Letendre testified that during the few months that he allowed appellant to live in his home, he repeatedly rebuffed appellant's suggestions that he put her name on the deed to his house.

On the evening of October 5, 1996, Letendre drank beer with friends at a bar and then went to a restaurant for breakfast before returning home at about 2:40 a.m. When Letendre returned home, he did not see appellant sleeping on the living room couch, and he assumed that she was sleeping in their daughter's bedroom. Letendre retired to his bedroom and fell asleep.

A short time later, Letendre was awakened by his dog. He heard a "thud," as well as a "tinny" noise that sounded like tin cans falling on the floor. He immediately looked down the hallway and saw the appellant walking quickly toward the living room. Letendre also saw a 2–foot-high wall of flames that ran the length of his bed rising up from the hardwood floor.

Letendre attempted to smother the fire by throwing his bed comforter on the fire and stomping on it with his feet. As he tried unsuccessfully to extinguish the flames, he saw appellant standing in the living room, staring into his bedroom. Appellant then came running down the hallway, yelling that the house was on fire. Letendre told appellant to take his dog outside. He ran into the kitchen and dialed 911.

Firefighters subsequently arrived and extinguished the fire. Paramedics transported Letendre to a nearby hospital, where he was treated and then released the following day. In addition to experiencing some smoke inhalation, Letendre received burns to more than six percent of his body while trying to smother the fire. These "second degree, primarily superficial" burns were located on Letendre's feet, thighs, and the small finger of his left hand. These burns, described as "very painful" in the hospital's discharge summary, required the administration of morphine in the emergency room.

Fire investigators found a partially burned can of charcoal lighter fluid on Letendre's bedroom floor, and detected a burn pattern that ran along the side of Letendre's bed and along the foot of the bed. A forensic chemist from the Minnesota Bureau of Criminal Apprehension detected the presence of a chemical used in some charcoal lighter fluids after testing samples of the bedroom floor with a gas chromatograph.

A firefighter who saw appellant on the date of the fire noted that she was fully dressed, showed no signs of soot or smoke on her clothes, and was not coughing. The firefighter discovered that the living room couch was neatly made and did not look like it had been slept in. This conflicted with appellant's assertions to police and fire investigators that she had been asleep on the couch when the fire started and was awakened only after the presence of thick black smoke caused her to begin choking.

Appellant was subsequently arrested and charged with first-degree arson. Minn.Stat. § 609.561, subd. 1 (1998). The state argued at trial that appellant started the fire in Letendre's bedroom by pouring charcoal lighter fluid on the floor along his bed and then igniting it. Appellant asserted that Letendre caused the fire by falling asleep in bed with a lighted cigarette, thereby igniting some lighter fluid that he had previously spilled on the bedroom floor.

The state presented testimony from several witnesses who cast doubt on appellant's contention that Letendre accidentally started the fire. Letendre testified that the can of lighter fluid found in his bedroom was different than the brand he always bought, and that he did not keep lighter fluid inside his home. A fire investigator testified that he discovered a can of lighter fluid in Letendre's back yard near his barbecue.

South St. Paul firefighters and a private fire investigator testified that the burn pattern found on the bedroom floor indicated the fire had been set deliberately. A fire captain also testified that he was familiar with the brand of lighter fluid found in Letendre's bedroom, that its container would not empty if accidentally knocked over, and that a different pour pattern would have been found on the bedroom floor if the lighter fluid had accidentally spilled onto the floor.

The jury found appellant guilty of first-degree arson. In a victim impact statement presented to the court prior to sentencing, Letendre reported that the burns on his feet continued to affect his ability to work. Letendre stated that he is only able to stand for two or three hours before a "very bad burning feeling" in his feet forces him to sit down. Letendre also stated that he has been unable to get a full night's sleep since the fire, saying that he suffered from "flashbacks of [appellant] staring into my bedroom" while he struggled with the flames engulfing his bedroom. Letendre further stated that he suffered from "mental anguish" because he feared his ex-wife might still attempt to arrange for his murder.

The trial court sentenced appellant, who had no previous criminal history, to imprisonment of 144 months. This sentence constituted a triple durational departure from the 48–month presumptive sentence set forth in the sentencing guidelines. *See* Minnesota Sentencing Guidelines IV. (hereinafter MSG) (classifying first-degree arson a level VII offense); MSG V. (establishing presumptive sentence of 48 months for level VII offense committed by person with no criminal history). The trial court found the following aggravating circumstances justified this greater-than-double durational departure from the presumed sentence: (1) "[t]he offense was committed with premeditation and with a certain degree of stealth and planning"; (2) the offense was committed with "particular cruelty" to Letendre; (3) Letendre suffered serious physical injuries; (4) Letendre also suffered "significant emotional and psychological trauma"; (5) appellant's actions violated Letendre's zone of privacy and exploited the trust he had extended to her; and (6) Letendre's alcohol consumption had left him particularly vulnerable at the time of the offense.

In an unpublished decision, the court of appeals affirmed this sentence, concluding that the trial court did not abuse its discretion by finding these six aggravating factors and imposing a triple durational departure. *State v. Spain,* No. C0–97–1268, 1998 WL 217193 (Minn.App.1998). On appeal, Spain contends that the trial court abused its discretion by imposing a greater-than-double durational sentencing departure in the absence of severe aggravating circumstances.

We afford the trial court great discretion in the imposition of sentences and we cannot simply substitute our judgment for that of the trial court. *See State v. Murphy,* 545 N.W.2d 909, 916 (Minn.1996). A trial court's decision to depart from the presumptive sentence specified in the sentencing guidelines is reviewed for an abuse of discretion. *See Rairdon v. State,* 557 N.W.2d 318, 326 (Minn.1996).

The purposes of the sentencing guidelines will not be served if the trial courts generally fail to apply the presumptive sentences found in the guidelines. *See State v. Garcia,* 302 N.W.2d 643, 647 (Minn.1981). In fact, a sentencing court has no discretion to depart from the sentencing guidelines unless aggravating or mitigating factors are present. *See State v. Best,* 449 N.W.2d 426, 427 (Minn.1989).

The aggravating or mitigating circumstances justifying departure from the presumptive sentence must be present in the record. *See Rairdon,* 557 N.W.2d at 326. When considering whether these factors are present, the sentencing court "should consider whether the defendant's conduct was 'significantly more or less serious than that typically involved in the commission of the crime in question.' " *Id.* (quoting *State v. Back,* 341 N.W.2d 273, 276 (Minn.1983)). The list of potentially aggravating or mitigating factors is non-exclusive. *See* MSG Comment II.D.201.

When a sentencing court departs from the presumptive sentence, it must still strive to determine a sentence that is proportional to the severity of the offense. *See* MSG II.D. As a general rule, the maximum upward departure in sentence length that can be justified by aggravating circumstances is a double durational departure from the presumptive sentence. *See State v. Evans,* 311 N.W.2d 481, 483 (Minn.1981). However, if severe aggravating circumstances are present, the double durational departure limit does not apply. *See Murphy,* 545 N.W.2d at 917 (citing *Evans,* 311 N.W.2d at 483 (stating "there may well be rare cases in which the facts are so unusually compelling that an even greater degree of departure will be justified")).

Appellant does not contest that the factors cited by the court at sentencing can constitute aggravating circumstances. Instead, appellant argues that the magnitude of the durational departure imposed by the court is disproportional to the severity of her conduct.

When we review a sentencing court's imposition of a durational departure that more than doubles the presumptive sentence specified by the sentencing guidelines, we are mindful that no bright-line rule marks the boundary between the "aggravating circumstances" justifying a double durational departure and the "severe aggravating circumstances" justifying a greater-than-double durational departure. *See State v. Norton,* 328 N.W.2d 142, 146–47 (Minn.1982). Still, we also bear in mind that the circumstances justifying a departure that more than doubles a presumptive sentence are extremely rare. *See Rairdon,* 557 N.W.2d at 327. In addition, we are influenced by the knowledge that the aims of the sentencing guidelines, to achieve sentencing uniformity and to keep prison population levels manageable, might be defeated if sentencing departures which more than double the presumptive sentences set forth in the guidelines are allowed too liberally. *See Perkins v. State,* 559 N.W.2d 678, 692 (Minn.1997) (quoting *Norton,* 328 N.W.2d at 147).

In the end, our assessment of the severity of the aggravating circumstances present in this case "must be based on our collective, collegial experience in reviewing a large number of criminal appeals from all the judicial districts." *Murphy,* 545 N.W.2d at 917 (quoting *Norton,* 328 N.W.2d at 146–47). After carefully reviewing this case and comparing the sentence imposed with sentences imposed in other cases, we conclude that the extent of the sentencing departure imposed here was not justified.

We are particularly concerned that appellant's 144–month sentence approaches the 180–month presumptive sentence for defendants with a criminal history score of zero for first-degree attempted murder, and is nearly double the 75–month presumptive sentence for second-degree attempted murder.[1] *See* MSG V.; MSG II.G. The 144–month sentence also closely approximates the 150–month presumptive sentence available for offenders with no criminal history, such as appellant, who commit second-degree murder. *See* MSG V. Perhaps the state could successfully have prosecuted appellant for a more serious crime, such as first-degree attempted murder. However, it did not attempt to do so. Accordingly, we are troubled by a sentence that effectively punishes appellant as if she had been tried and convicted of first-degree attempted murder.

We do not wish to imply that the trial court in this case used the triple durational departure as a means of punishing appellant for attempting to

---

1. One of our first decisions reviewing the acceptable scope of durational departures under the sentencing guidelines was the 1981 case of *State v. Evans,* 311 N.W.2d 481, 483 (Minn.1981) (establishing general rule that the permissible upper limit on durational departures is double the presumptive sentence length). In *Evans,* our determination that a sentencing departure was excessive was based in part on our comparison of the defendant's sentence to the presumptive sentences available under the guidelines for other offenses. *Id.* at 483.

murder Letendre. *See State v. Simon,* 520 N.W.2d 393, 394 (Minn.1994) (stating "the state should not be able to use the fact that it might have been able to obtain a conviction of a greater offense—e.g., attempted murder—to support [a sentencing] departure"). Clearly, appellant's conduct was egregious, from the calculating manner with which she committed the crime, to the serious physical and psychological injuries she caused that continue to afflict the victim. Damage to a dwelling is an element of Minn.Stat. § 609.561, subd. 1, and first-degree arson is by definition the most serious type of arson. Even so, appellant committed the offense in a particularly serious way. Nonetheless, we conclude that imposition of a 144–month sentence in this matter would be inconsistent with the primary purpose of the sentencing guidelines, which is to ensure that sentences are "proportional to the severity of the offense of conviction and the extent of the offender's criminal history." MSG I.

We hold that a 144–month sentence is disproportional to the severity of appellant's conduct. We therefore modify appellant's sentence to 96 months, which constitutes a double durational departure from the presumptive sentence set forth in the sentencing guidelines.

Affirmed as modified.

State v. Dobbins

Minnesota Court of Appeals, 2006.
Not Reported in N.W.2d; 2006 WL 1320484.

In this sentencing appeal, appellant argues that the district court abused its discretion when it denied her motion for a downward dispositional departure and imposed the 43–month presumptive guidelines sentence for second-degree burglary because her mental impairment and the alternative treatment available to her supported a downward dispositional departure. Appellant also argues that the sentence is disproportional to the severity of the offense and her criminal history. We affirm.

FACTS

On January 29, 2004, appellant Ramona Dobbins approached 91–year–old John Postudensek at his home and asked him to help her start her car, which was nearby. While Postudensek was working on the vehicle, Dobbins left for a period of time. After approximately 20 minutes, Postudensek began walking back to his residence and saw Dobbins walking toward him with a battery charger. When Postudensek returned home, he discovered that his wallet containing approximately $49 in cash, along with money from his dresser and his battery charger, were missing from his residence. The following day, when Postudensek reported the incident to police, he advised that he suspected Dobbins had taken the items while he was working on her vehicle.

Police investigated the matter and charged Dobbins with second-degree burglary, a violation of Minn.Stat. § 609.582, subd. 2(a) (2002). Dobbins subsequently pleaded guilty to the charged offense. Dobbins moved for a downward dispositional departure from the presumptive guidelines sentence, citing her mental impairment and the opportunity to participate in a mental-health program if a probationary sentence were imposed. The district court denied the motion and sentenced Dobbins to the presumptive guidelines sentence of 43 months' imprisonment. This appeal followed.

DECISION

An appellate court "may review the sentence imposed or stayed to determine whether the sentence is inconsistent with statutory requirements, unreasonable, inappropriate, excessive, unjustifiably disparate, or not warranted by the findings of fact issued by the district court." Minn. Stat. § 244.11, subd. 2(b) (2004). The decision whether to depart from the sentencing guidelines rests within the district court's discretion, and we will not disturb the district court's decision "absent a clear abuse of that discretion." *State v. Oberg,* 627 N.W.2d 721, 724 (Minn.App.2001), *review denied* (Minn. Aug. 22, 2001). The district court's decision to impose the presumptive guidelines sentence rarely will be reversed on appeal. *State v. Kindem,* 313 N.W.2d 6, 7 (Minn.1981).

I.

Dobbins argues that the district court abused its discretion in denying her motion for a downward dispositional departure because she suffers from a mental impairment, mental-health treatment was available to her through an alternative placement, and she expressed a strong desire to rehabilitate herself. In support of her argument, Dobbins relies on the presentence investigation report (PSI) and the psychological evaluation, which establish a history of mental-health issues.

Under the Minnesota Sentencing Guidelines, the district court must order the presumptive guidelines sentence unless "substantial[ ] and compelling circumstances" warrant a downward departure. Minn. Sent. Guidelines II.D. A district court may depart if "[t]he offender, because of physical or mental impairment, lacked substantial capacity for judgment when the offense was committed." Minn. Sent. Guidelines II.D.2(a)(3). The district court also may depart from the presumptive sentence when an alternative placement exists for an offender with "serious and persistent mental illness." Minn. Sent. Guidelines II.D.2(a)(6).

When considering a dispositional departure, the district court "can focus more on the defendant as an individual and on whether the presumptive sentence would be best for [the defendant] and for society." *State v. Heywood,* 338 N.W.2d 243, 244 (Minn.1983). The district court may impose a downward dispositional departure and place a defendant on probation if the defendant is particularly amenable to probation or if mitigating circumstances regarding the offense are present. *State v. Donnay,* 600 N.W.2d 471, 473–74 (Minn.App.1999), *review denied* (Minn. Nov. 17, 1999).

Typically, the factors relevant to the district court in deciding whether to depart downward dispositionally are the defendant's age, prior record, remorse, cooperation, attitude while in court, and support from family or friends. *See State v. Trog,* 323 N.W.2d 28, 31 (Minn.1982) (holding that stay of execution of presumptive sentence may be justified when these factors indicate amenability to treatment in probationary setting). But even if the district court is presented with evidence of a defendant's mental impairment or amenability to probation, the district court is not required to grant a downward dispositional departure. *See State v. Wilson,* 539 N.W.2d 241, 247 (Minn.1995) (affirming consecutive sentences because defendant failed to establish extreme impairment or that his mental condition deprived him of control over his actions); *State v. Evenson,* 554 N.W.2d 409, 412–13 (Minn.App.1996) (holding that district court did not abuse its discretion in deciding against downward departure because even if defendant were amenable to treatment, that did not dictate result), *review denied* (Minn. Oct. 29, 1996); *State v. Stephani,* 369 N.W.2d 540, 550 (Minn.App.1985) (affirming upward departure in sentencing because evidence of mental impairment did not outweigh aggravating factors), *review denied* (Minn. Aug. 20, 1985).

The Minnesota Supreme Court has determined that "only *extreme* mental impairment justifies a mitigation of sentence." *Wilson,* 539 N.W.2d at 247. And only rarely will an appellate court reduce a sentence because of a defendant's mental impairment. *See State v. Hennum,* 441 N.W.2d 793, 801 (Minn.1989) (reducing presumptive guidelines sentence based on evidence of battered-woman syndrome and severe physical and mental abuse that victim had inflicted on defendant); *State v. Wall,* 343 N.W.2d 22, 25–26 (Minn.1984) (reducing upward departure in sentence to presumptive guidelines sentence because evidence of mental impairment was present and could not be ignored). As long as the record demonstrates that the district court considered all of the information presented before making its sentencing decision, we will not interfere with the district court's exercise of discretion. *State v. Van Ruler,* 378 N.W.2d 77, 80–81 (Minn.App.1985).

Here, the record establishes that, before imposing the sentence, the district court carefully considered the evidence and arguments presented regarding Dobbins's mental health and her request for treatment. The district court reviewed a psychological evaluation and the PSI report. These documents indicated that Dobbins had been diagnosed with bipolar disorder and antisocial personality disorder by a psychiatrist and that Dobbins was taking medication for the disorder. The district court also considered Dobbins's testimony in support of her motion.

The district court, however, was not persuaded that the evidence justified a downward dispositional departure. Specifically, the district court stated:

> I've had a chance to look at [the psychological evaluation], and I can't say that I necessarily take issue with anything in the report. It deals more with your employability, but it does also talk about the psychological struggles that you have had, but there is nothing in the report that tells me that—that in any way suggests why you're continually perpetrating offenses against many times vulnerable people.
>
> . . . .
>
> [Y]ou have regularly [taken] advantage of people and stolen from them. And maybe it is somewhat related to your mental illness, although I don't think there is anything in [the] report that would suggest that whatever you do is related to your criminal conduct or whatever you have in any way causes you to steal from people. And you choose to do

it again and again and again while you have been having these charges pending, and I guess I'm just not willing to subject the community to that and give you that chance that you have asked for.

As the district court noted, the psychological evaluation did not address how Dobbins's mental health affects her criminal behavior or choice of victim. And Dobbins presented no evidence that the *Trog* factors—her age, criminal record, remorse, cooperation, attitude, or support system—make her particularly amenable to treatment. Indeed, there is no evidence that any of these factors supports a determination that Dobbins is amenable to probation. Rather, Dobbins relies heavily on her testimony in support of her contention that she is amenable to treatment. But her testimony is contradicted by the PSI report, which concluded that Dobbins was not amenable to probation and recommended the presumptive guidelines sentence. Moreover, even if the district court credited the evidence of Dobbins's mental impairment and amenability to treatment, the district court would not be compelled to grant the motion for a downward dispositional departure. *Van Ruler,* 378 N .W.2d at 80–81. The district court is required only to consider all the information presented. *Id.*

Mindful of Dobbins's circumstances, the district court acknowledged that she was "struggling" with mental health, poverty, and family issues, and stated: "[T]hat's what makes this so difficult." In its careful consideration, however, the district court determined that, when weighed against public-safety concerns, Dobbins's mental health did not compel a downward dispositional departure. Based on this analysis, the district court determined that the presumptive guidelines sentence was appropriate. In doing so, the district court did not abuse its discretion in denying the motion for a downward dispositional departure.

II.

Dobbins next contends that, due to the nature of the offense and her criminal history, we should vacate the executed sentence of 43 months' imprisonment and modify it to a sentence more "proportional to the severity of the crime for which the sentence is imposed and [her] criminal history." Minn. Sent. Guidelines II.D.

A review of the motion for a downward departure and the sentencing transcript establishes that Dobbins failed to present her disproportionality argument to the district court. Arguments that were not raised before the district court ordinarily are waived. *Perkins v. State,* 559 N.W.2d 678, 691 (Minn.1997).

In deciding whether to grant a durational departure, the district court considers "whether the defendant's conduct was significantly more or less serious than that typically involved in the commission of the crime in question." *State v. Back,* 341 N.W.2d 273, 276 (Minn.1983). "[G]enerally it is proper for the sentencing court to consider the course of conduct underlying the charge for which the defendant is being sentenced." *Id.*

Dobbins argues that the district court failed to consider the mitigating fact that the conduct underlying the burglary offense was only a misdemeanor-level theft. *See* Minn.Stat. § 609.52, subd. 3(5) (2002) (providing that theft of property or services valued at $250 or less is misdemeanor); *Herme v. State,* 384 N.W.2d 205, 208–09 (Minn.App.1986) (holding that defendant's claim that his actions were more like a thief than a fence of stolen goods did not constitute a substantial and compelling reason for downward departure), *review denied* (Minn. May 22, 1986); *Back,* 341 N.W.2d at 276–77 (holding that despite defendant's argument that underlying offense in felony murder was only property crime, circumstances of crime justified upward durational departure). To the contrary, the record establishes that the district court considered the conduct underlying the burglary when imposing sentence and determined that the facts support imposing the presumptive guidelines sentence. The district court specifically noted that the victim in this case is an elderly man and Dobbins's criminal history shows that she has victimized the elderly on numerous occasions and that her behavior makes her "very, very dangerous to the community." *See* Minn. Sent. Guidelines II.D.2(b)(1) (providing that vulnerability of victim due to age is an aggravating factor that district court may consider as reason to depart); *State v. Norton,* 328 N.W.2d 142, 146 (Minn.1982) (noting that under sentencing guidelines, vulnerability of victim due to age is aggravating factor).

Dobbins relies on *State v. Curtiss,* 353 N.W.2d 262 (Minn.App.1984), in support of her argument that the misdemeanor nature of the burglary is a ground for downward departure. Her reliance on *Curtiss* is misplaced. We remanded for resentencing in *Curtiss* because the district court found no reasons to depart and failed to give any consideration to the legitimate reasons supporting departure. *Id.* at 263. We noted that we were not interfering with the district court's exercise of its discretion. *Id.* at 264. Rather, we were remanding because the district court had failed to exercise its discretion by considering both the valid reasons for departure and those against departure. *Id.* Unlike the district court in *Curtiss,* the district court exercised its discretion here. It properly addressed the reasons for departure that Dobbins presented—her mental impairment and the availability of an alternative placement—along with the reasons for imposing the presumptive guidelines sentence.

Dobbins also relies on our statement in *State v. Herrmann* that, when deciding whether to depart durationally, the district court "should not analyze the egregiousness of the act in and of itself, but must rather analyze the act as compared with other acts constituting the same offense." 479 N.W.2d 724, 728 (Minn.App.1992), *review denied* (Minn. Mar. 19, 1992). We held in *Herrmann* that the district court's reliance on the extent of the victim's injuries to justify an upward departure was improper because, with "great bodily harm" as an element of the offense, the seriousness of the victim's injuries was already factored into the presumptive sentence. *Id.* at 729–30. Thus, *Herrmann* also is inapposite here because the district court did not rely on elements of the burglary offense as a reason to depart from the presumptive sentence. Indeed, the district court imposed the presumptive sentence because it did not find substantial and compelling reasons to depart.

Dobbins also argues that the sentence imposed is disproportional to her criminal-history score because two of her prior convictions were almost

15 years old and part of the same behavioral incident and the others were nonviolent, theft-related convictions. But Dobbins does not challenge her criminal-history score under the sentencing guidelines. And, in addition to the two 1990 offenses, Dobbins's criminal history includes theft by swindle in 2000, state lottery fraud in 1999, wrongfully obtaining public assistance in 1998, theft by swindle in 1997, and escape in 1994. Our review of the record establishes that the district court properly considered Dobbins's criminal history, noting that Dobbins had been convicted of at least 16 theft-related offenses and had committed new offenses while the instant case was pending before the district court.

After weighing the aggravating and mitigating factors, the district court imposed the presumptive guidelines sentence because public safety warranted this disposition. In doing so, the district court's exercise of its discretion was sound.

Affirmed.

SECTION 3. THE FEDERAL SENTENCING GUIDELINES

(A) INTRODUCTION TO THE GUIDELINES

United States Sentencing Commission, **Guidelines Manual** 381 (2006)

SENTENCING TABLE
(in months of imprisonment)

Offense Level	Criminal History Category (Criminal History Points)					
	I (0 or 1)	II (2 or 3)	III (4, 5, 6)	IV (7, 8, 9)	V (10, 11, 12)	VI (13 or more)
Zone A 1	0-6	0-6	0-6	0-6	0-6	0-6
2	0-6	0-6	0-6	0-6	0-6	1-7
3	0-6	0-6	0-6	0-6	2-8	3-9
4	0-6	0-6	0-6	2-8	4-10	6-12
5	0-6	0-6	1-7	4-10	6-12	9-15
6	0-6	1-7	2-8	6-12	9-15	12-18
7	0-6	2-8	4-10	8-14	12-18	15-21
8	0-6	4-10	6-12	10-16	15-21	18-24
Zone B 9	4-10	6-12	8-14	12-18	18-24	21-27
Zone C 10	6-12	8-14	10-16	15-21	21-27	24-30
11	8-14	10-16	12-18	18-24	24-30	27-33
12	10-16	12-18	15-21	21-27	27-33	30-37
13	12-18	15-21	18-24	24-30	30-37	33-41
14	15-21	18-24	21-27	27-33	33-41	37-46
15	18-24	21-27	24-30	30-37	37-46	41-51
16	21-27	24-30	27-33	33-41	41-51	46-57
17	24-30	27-33	30-37	37-46	46-57	51-63
18	27-33	30-37	33-41	41-51	51-63	57-71
19	30-37	33-41	37-46	46-57	57-71	63-78
20	33-41	37-46	41-51	51-63	63-78	70-87
21	37-46	41-51	46-57	57-71	70-87	77-96
22	41-51	46-57	51-63	63-78	77-96	84-105
23	46-57	51-63	57-71	70-87	84-105	92-115
24	51-63	57-71	63-78	77-96	92-115	100-125
25	57-71	63-78	70-87	84-105	100-125	110-137
26	63-78	70-87	78-97	92-115	110-137	120-150
Zone D 27	70-87	78-97	87-108	100-125	120-150	130-162
28	78-97	87-108	97-121	110-137	130-162	140-175
29	87-108	97-121	108-135	121-151	140-175	151-188
30	97-121	108-135	121-151	135-168	151-188	168-210
31	108-135	121-151	135-168	151-188	168-210	188-235
32	121-151	135-168	151-188	168-210	188-235	210-262
33	135-168	151-188	168-210	188-235	210-262	235-293
34	151-188	168-210	188-235	210-262	235-293	262-327
35	168-210	188-235	210-262	235-293	262-327	292-365
36	188-235	210-262	235-293	262-327	292-365	324-405
37	210-262	235-293	262-327	292-365	324-405	360-life
38	235-293	262-327	292-365	324-405	360-life	360-life
39	262-327	292-365	324-405	360-life	360-life	360-life
40	292-365	324-405	360-life	360-life	360-life	360-life
41	324-405	360-life	360-life	360-life	360-life	360-life
42	360-life	360-life	360-life	360-life	360-life	360-life
43	life	life	life	life	life	life

U.S. Sentencing Commission, Sentencing Exercise, Robbery
(available online at http://www.ussc.gov/training/WS_Ex_rob.pdf)
(last visited November 8, 2006) (some slight modifications have been made
for clarity)

Conviction: Count 1

Offense: Armed Bank Robbery; violation of 18 U.S.C. § 2113(a) and (d)

Maximum Statutory Penalties: 25 years and/or $250,000; Class B Felony:
up to 5 years supervised release following imprisonment; up to 3 years
imprisonment upon subsequent revocation.

Note: an additional count of conviction for 18 U.S.C. § 924 (c) (use, carry,
possession of firearm in relation to a crime of violence) would have required
a consecutive sentence of at least 5 years imprisonment.

- committed robbery

- a federally insured bank

- carried a .38 caliber revolver (operational and loaded)

- pushed a teller, resulting in bodily injury (cut on forehead, bruises, contusions)

- restrained a customer (used packaging tape to bind and put into storage area)

- $18,000. in bank loot taken, $8000 recovered upon arrest 6 weeks after robbery

- within few days of apprehension defendant provided full information to the government and announced intentions to plead guilty

- defendant is a 23 year old male

- raised in broken family

- was sickly during childhood and missed a lot of school

- dropped out of school in the 9th grade and is functionally illiterate

- no job skills

- work history is that of construction laborer

- spotty employment record; currently unemployed and seeking work

- drinks 2 to 6 beers daily; occasional marijuana use

- lives with older sister

- never married

- has one child for which he is under a support order

- at time of robbery the defendant was in arrears in child support, had outstanding bills and had not contributed for some time to sister for living arrangements

- financial records show that within two weeks following the robbery, the defendant became current in his child support with a payment of $4000, paid off outstanding debts of $2000, gave his sister $1000 and made a $1000 down payment on a used car

- defendant has no noteworthy assets

- the defendant reports he was feeling pressure due to financial and family obligations and robbed the bank to get "out of the hole." In addition to the $8000 spent on financial obligations and the down payment for an automobile, the defendant states that he used the remaining $2000 to buy clothes and "party."

- the defendant has prior criminal record resulting from conduct committed after the defendant was 18 years old and disposed of in state court, as follows:

5 years ago auto theft 2 years probation

2 years ago grand larceny 6 months jail

Worksheet A (Offense Level)

Defendant SENTENCING EXERCISE District/Office _____ _____

Docket Number (Year–Sequence–Defendant No.) ____ ____-____ ____ ____

____ ____-____ _____

Count Number(s) 1 U.S. Code Title & Section 18 : 2113 (a) and (d)

____ : _____

Guidelines Manual Edition Used: 2002__(NOTE: *worksheets keyed to the Manual effective November 1, 2002)*

Instructions:

For each count of conviction (or stipulated offense), complete a separate Worksheet

A. Exception: Use only a single Worksheet A where the offense level for a group of closely related counts is based primarily on aggregate value or quantity

(see § 3D1.2(d)) or where a count of conspiracy, solicitation, or attempt is grouped with a substantive count that was the sole object of the conspiracy, solicitation, or attempt (see § 3D1.2(a) and (b)).

1. Offense Level (See Chapter Two)

Enter the applicable base offense level and any specific offense characteristics from Chapter Two and explain the bases for these determinations. Enter the sum in the box provided.

Guideline Description Level

§ 2B3.1(a) Base Offense Level **20**

§ 2B3.1(b)(1) Property of Financial Institution **2**

§ 2B3.1(b)(2)(C) Firearms (brandished or possessed) **5**

§ 2B3.1(b)(3)(A) Bodily Injury **2**

§ 2B3.1(b)(4)(B) Physical Restraint **2**

§ 2B3.1(b)(7)(B) Loss (more than $10,000) **1**

Sum: 32

2. Victim–Related Adjustments (See Chapter Three, Part A)

Enter the applicable section and adjustment. If more than one section is applicable,list each section and enter the combined adjustment. If no adjustment is applicable

enter"0." § _____

3. Role in the Offense Adjustments (See Chapter Three, Part B) Enter the applicable section and adjustment. If more than one section is applicable,list each section and enter the combined adjustment. If the adjustment reduces the offense level, enter a minus (-) sign in front of the adjustment. If no adjustment is applicable, enter "0." § _____

4. Obstruction Adjustments (See Chapter Three, Part C)

Enter the applicable section and adjustment. If more than one section is applicable, list each section and enter the combined adjustment. If no adjustment is applicable, enter "0." § _____

5. Adjusted Offense Level

Enter the sum of Items 1–4. If this worksheet does not cover all counts of conviction or stipulated offenses, complete Worksheet B. Otherwise, enter this result on Worksheet D, Item 1. **32**

_____

Check if the defendant is convicted of a single count. In such case, Worksheet B need not be completed.

If the defendant has no criminal history, enter criminal history "I" here and on Item 4, Worksheet D. In such case, Worksheet C need not be completed.

Worksheet B

(Multiple Counts or Stipulation to Additional Offenses)

Defendant: SENTENCING EXERCISE Docket Number _____

Instructions

Step 1: Determine if any of the counts group. (Note: All, some, or none of the counts may group. Some of the counts may have already been grouped in the application under Worksheet A, specifically, (1) counts grouped under § 3D1.2(d), or (2) a count charging conspiracy, solicitation, or attempt that is grouped with the substantive count of conviction (see § 3D1.2(a)).

Explain the reasons for grouping:

Step 2: Using the box(es) provided below, for each group of closely related counts, enter the highest adjusted offense level from the various "A" Worksheets (Item 5) that comprise the group (see § 3D1.3). (Note: A "group" may consist of a single count that has not grouped with any other count. In those instances, the offense level for the group will be the adjusted offense level for the single count.)

Step 3: Enter the number of units to be assigned to each group (see § 3D1.4) as follows:

• One unit (1) for the group of closely related counts with the highest offense level

• An additional unit (1) for each group that is equally serious or 1 to 4 levels less serious

• An additional half unit (1/2) for each group that is 5 to 8 levels less serious

• No increase in units for groups that are 9 or more levels less serious

1. Adjusted Offense Level for the First Group of Closely Related Counts

Count number(s):_____

2. Adjusted Offense Level for the Second Group of Closely Related Counts

Count number(s):_____

3. Adjusted Offense Level for the Third Group of Closely Related Counts

Count number(s):_____

4. Adjusted Offense Level for the Fourth Group of Closely Related Counts

Count number(s):_____

5. Adjusted Offense Level for the Fifth Group of Closely Related Counts

Count number(s):_____

6. Total Units

7. Increase in Offense Level Based on Total Units (See § 3D1.4)

1 unit: no increase 2 1/2–3 units: add 3 levels

1 1/2 units: add 1 level 3 1/2–5 units: add 4 levels

2 units: add 2 levels More than 5 units: add 5 levels

8. Highest of the Adjusted Offense Levels from Items 1–5 Above

9. Combined Adjusted Offense Level (See § 3D1.4)

Enter the sum of Items 7 and 8 here and on Worksheet D, Item 1.

Worksheet C (Criminal History)

Defendant: SENTENCING EXERCISE Docket Number_____

Enter the Date Defendant Commenced Participation in Instant Offense (Earliest Date of Relevant Conduct) 12/01/2002.

1. 3 Points for each prior ADULT sentence of imprisonment EXCEEDING ONE YEAR AND ONE MONTH imposed within 15 YEARS of the defendant's commencement of the instant offense OR resulting in incarceration during any part of that 15–YEAR period. (See §§ 4A1.1(a) and 4A1.2.)

2. 2 Points for each prior sentence of imprisonment of AT LEAST 60 DAYS resulting from an offense committed ON OR AFTER the defendant's 18th birthday not counted under § 4A1.1(a) imposed within 10 YEARS of the instant offense; and 2 Points for each prior sentence of imprisonment of AT LEAST 60 DAYS resulting from an offense committed BEFORE the defendant's 18th birthday not counted under § 4A1.1(a) from which the defendant was released from confinement within 5 YEARS of the instant offense. (See §§ 4A1.1(b) and 4A1.2.)

3. 1 Point for each prior sentence resulting from an offense committed ON OR AFTER the defendant's 18th birthday not counted under § 4A1.1(a) or § 4A1.1(b) imposed within 10 YEARS of the instant offense; and 1 Point for each prior sentence resulting from an offense committed BEFORE the defendant's 18th birthday not counted under § 4A1.1(a) or § 4A1.1(b) imposed within 5 YEARS of the instant offense. (See §§ 4A1.1(c) and 4A1.2.)

NOTE: A maximum sum of 4 Points may be given for the prior sentences in Item 3.

Date of Offense Sentence Release Guideline Criminal

Imposition Date** Section History Points

——————— ———————— ———————— ———————— ————————

12–01–96 Auto Theft 2 Yrs. Probation 4A1.1 (c): **1** point

12–01–99 Grand Larceny 6 Mos. Imprison. 4A1.1 (b): **2** points

* Indicate with an asterisk those offenses where defendant was sentenced as a juvenile.

** A release date is required in only three instances:

a. When a sentence covered under § 4A1.1(a) was imposed more than 15 years prior to the commencement of the instant offense but release from incarceration occurred within such 15–year period;

b. When a sentence counted under § 4A1.1(b) was imposed for an offense committed prior to age 18 and more than 5 years prior to the commencement of the instant offense, but release from incarceration occurred within such 5–year period; and

c. When § 4A1.1(e) applies because the defendant was released from custody on a sentence counted under 4A1.1(a) or 4A1.1 (b) within 2 years of the instant offense or was still in custody on such a sentence at the time of the instant offense (see Item 6).

4. Sum of Criminal History Points for prior sentences under §§ 4A1.1(a), 4A1.1(b), and 4A1.1(c)

(Items 1,2,3). 1 + 2 = **3** points

5. 2 Points if the defendant committed the instant offense while under any criminal justice sentence (e.g., probation, parole, supervised release, imprisonment, work release, escape status). (See §§ 4A1.1(d) and 4A1.2.) List the type of control and identify the sentence from which control resulted. Otherwise, enter 0 Points.

6. 2 Points if the defendant committed the instant offense LESS THAN 2 YEARS after release from imprisonment on a sentence counted under § 4A1.1(a) or (b), or while in imprisonment or escape status on such a sentence. However, enter only 1 Point for this item if 2 points were added at Item 5 under § 4A1.1(d). (See §§ 4A1.1(e) and 4A1.2.) List the date of release and identify the sentence from which release resulted. Otherwise, enter 0 Points.

Released on 6–1–00 from Sentence of 12–1–99: **Add 2 points.**

7. 1 Point for each prior sentence resulting from a conviction of a crime of violence that did not receive any points under § 4A1.1(a), (b), or (c) because such sentence was considered related to another sentence resulting from a conviction of a crime of violence. *Provided*, that this item does not apply where the sentences are considered related because the offenses occurred on the same occasion. (See §§ 4A1.1(f) and 4A1.2.) Identify the crimes of violence and briefly explain why the cases are considered related. Otherwise, enter 0 Points.

Note: A maximum sum of 3 Points may be given for Item 7.

8. Total Criminal History Points (Sum of Items 4–7)

3 + 2 = 5

9. Criminal History Category (Enter here and on Worksheet D, Item 4)

Total Points Criminal History Category

0–1 I

2–3 II

4–6 III

7–9 IV

10–12 V

13 or more VI

5 points puts the offender in Category III

Worksheet D (Guideline Worksheet)

Defendant: SENTENCING EXERCISE District _____

Docket Number _____

1.   Adjusted Offense Level (From Worksheet A or B) **32**

If Worksheet B is required, enter the result from Worksheet B, Item 9.

Otherwise, enter the result from Worksheet A, Item 5.

2.   Acceptance of Responsibility (See Chapter Three, Part E)

Enter the applicable reduction of 2 or 3 levels. If no adjustment is applicable, enter "0".: **–3 points** [recall that "within few days of apprehension defendant provided full information to the government and announced intentions to plead guilty"]

3.   Offense Level Total (Item 1 less Item 2): **32 – 3 = 29**

4.   Criminal History Category (From Worksheet C)

Enter the result from Worksheet C, Item 9: category III

5.   Terrorism/Career Offender/Criminal Livelihood/Armed

Career Criminal/Repeat and Dangerous Sex Offender

(see Chapter Three, Part A, and Chapter Four, Part B)

a.   Offense Level Total

If the provision for Career Offender (§ 4B1.1), Criminal Livelihood (§ 4B1.3), Armed Career Criminal (§ 4B1.4), or Repeat and Dangerous Sex Offender (§ 4B1.5) results in an offense level total higher than Item 3, enter the offense level total. Otherwise, enter "N/A."

b.   Criminal History Category

If the provision for Terrorism (§ 3A1.4), Career Offender (§ 4B1.1), Armed Career Criminal (§ 4B1.4), or Repeat and Dangerous Sex Offender (§ 4B1.5) results in a criminal history category higher than Item 4, enter the applicable criminal history category. Otherwise, enter "N/A."

6.   Guideline Range from Sentencing Table

Enter the applicable guideline range from Chapter Five, Part A.

108–135 months

7.   Restricted Guideline Range (See Chapter Five, Part G)

If the statutorily authorized maximum sentence or the statutorily required minimum sentence restricts the guideline range (Item 6) (see §§ 5G1.1 and 5G1.2), enter either the restricted guideline range or any statutory maximum or minimum penalty that would modify the guideline range. Otherwise, enter "N/A."

Check this box if § 5C1.2 (Limitation on Applicability of Statutory Minimum Penalties in Certain Cases) is applicable.

8.   Undischarged Term of Imprisonment (See § 5G1.3)

If the defendant is subject to an undischarged term of imprisonment, check this box and list the undischarged term(s) below.

9. Sentencing Options (Check the applicable box that corresponds to the Guideline Range entered in Item 6.)

(See Chapter Five, Sentencing Table)

Zone A If checked, the following options are available (see § 5B1.1):

C Fine (See § 5E1.2(a))

C "Straight" Probation

C Imprisonment

Zone B If checked, the minimum term may be satisfied by:

C Imprisonment

C Imprisonment of at least one month plus supervised release with a condition that substitutes community confinement or home detention for imprisonment (see § 5C1.1(c)(2))

C Probation with a condition that substitutes intermittent confinement, community confinement, or home detention for imprisonment (see § 5B1.1(a)(2) and § 5C1.1(c)(3))

Zone C If checked, the minimum term may be satisfied by:

C Imprisonment

C Imprisonment of at least one-half of the minimum term plus supervised release with a condition that substitutes community confinement or home detention for imprisonment (see § 5C1.1(d)(2))

C Zone D If checked, the minimum term shall be satisfied by a sentence of imprisonment (see § 5C1.1(f)): X

10. Length of Term of Probation (See § 5B1.2)

If probation is imposed, the guideline for the length of such term of probation is: (Check applicable box)

At least one year, but not more than five years if the offense level total is 6 or more

No more than three years if the offense level total is 5 or less

11. Conditions of Probation (See § 5B1.3)

List any mandatory conditions ((a)(1)-(9)), standard conditions ((c)(1)-(14)), and any other special conditions that maybe applicable:

12. Supervised Release (See §§ 5D1.1 and 5D1.2)

a. A term of supervised release is: (Check applicable box)

Required because a term of imprisonment of more than one year is to be imposed or if required by statute: X

Authorized but not required because a term of imprisonment of one year or less is to be imposed

b. Length of Term (Guideline Range of Supervised Release) (Check applicable box)

Class A or B Felony: Three to Five Year Term: X

Class C or D Felony: Two to Three Year Term

Class E Felony or Class A Misdemeanor: One Year

    c.   Restricted Guideline Range of Supervision Release

If a statutorily required term of supervised release impacts the guideline range, check this box and enter the required term. _____

13.   Conditions of Supervised Release (See § 5D1.3)

List any mandatory conditions ((a)(1)-(7)), standard conditions ((c)(1)-(15)), and any other special conditions that may be applicable: _____

14.   Restitution (See § 5E1.1)

a.   If restitution is applicable, enter the amount. Otherwise enter "N/A" and the reason: $10,000

b.   Enter whether restitution is statutorily mandatory or discretionary:

_____

c.   Enter whether restitution is by an order of restitution or solely as a condition of supervision. Enter the authorizing statute: _____

15.   Fines (Guideline Range of Fines for Individual Defendants) (See § 5E1.2)

a.   Special fine provisions Minimum Maximum

Check box if any of the counts of conviction is for a statute with a special fine provision. (This does not include the general fine provisions of 18 USC § 3571(b)(2), (d))

Enter the sum of statutory maximum fines for all such counts $_____

b.   Fine Table (§ 5E1.2(c)(3))

Enter the minimum and maximum fines $15,000 $150,000

c.   Guideline Range of Fines: $15,000 $150,000

(determined by the minimum of the fine table (Item 15(b))

and the greater maximum above (Item 15(a) or 15(b))

d.   Ability to Pay

Check this box if the defendant does not have an ability to pay.

16.   Special Assessments (See § 5E1.3)

Enter the total amount of special assessments required for all counts of conviction:

- $25 for each misdemeanor count of conviction

- Not less than $100 for each felony count of conviction

$100

17.   Additional Factors

List any additional applicable guidelines, policy statements, and statutory provisions. Also list any applicable aggravating and mitigating factors that may warrant a sentence at a particular point either within or outside the applicable guideline range. Attach additional sheets as necessary.

(B) RELEVANCE OF THE GUIDELINES AFTER *BOOKER* AND *FANFAN*

Kimbrough v. United States

Supreme Court of the United States, 2007.
552 U.S. 85, 128 S.Ct. 558, 169 L.Ed.2d 481.

■ GINSBURG, J., delivered the opinion of the Court, in which ROBERTS, C.J., and STEVEN, SCALIA, KENNEDY, SOUTER, and BREYER, JJ., joined. SCALIA, J., filed a concurring opinion. THOMAS, J., and ALITO, J., filed dissenting opinions.

■ JUSTICE GINSBURG delivered the opinion of the Court.

This Court's remedial opinion in *United States v. Booker,* 543 U.S. 220, 244, 125 S.Ct. 738, 160 L.Ed.2d 621 (2005), instructed district courts to read the United States Sentencing Guidelines as "effectively advisory," *id.,* at 245, 125 S.Ct. 738. In accord with 18 U.S.C. § 3553(a), the Guidelines, formerly mandatory, now serve as one factor among several courts must consider in determining an appropriate sentence. *Booker* further instructed that "reasonableness" is the standard controlling appellate review of the sentences district courts impose.

Under the statute criminalizing the manufacture and distribution of crack cocaine, 21 U.S.C. § 841, and the relevant Guidelines prescription, § 2D1.1, a drug trafficker dealing in crack cocaine is subject to the same sentence as one dealing in 100 times more powder cocaine. The question here presented is whether, as the Court of Appeals held in this case, "a sentence ... outside the guidelines range is per se unreasonable when it is based on a disagreement with the sentencing disparity for crack and powder cocaine offenses." 174 Fed.Appx. 798, 799 (C.A.4 2006) *(per curiam).* We hold that, under *Booker,* the cocaine Guidelines, like all other Guidelines, are advisory only, and that the Court of Appeals erred in holding the crack/powder disparity effectively mandatory. A district judge must include the Guidelines range in the array of factors warranting consideration. The judge may determine, however, that, in the particular case, a within-Guidelines sentence is "greater than necessary" to serve the objectives of sentencing. 18 U.S.C. § 3553(a) (2000 ed. and Supp. V). In making that determination, the judge may consider the disparity between the Guidelines' treatment of crack and powder cocaine offenses.

I

In September 2004, petitioner Derrick Kimbrough was indicted in the United States District Court for the Eastern District of Virginia and charged with four offenses: conspiracy to distribute crack and powder cocaine; possession with intent to distribute more than 50 grams of crack cocaine; possession with intent to distribute powder cocaine; and possession of a firearm in furtherance of a drug-trafficking offense. Kimbrough pleaded guilty to all four charges.

Under the relevant statutes, Kimbrough's plea subjected him to an aggregate sentence of 15 years to life in prison: 10 years to life for the three drug offenses, plus a consecutive term of 5 years to life for the firearm offense.[1] In order to determine the appropriate sentence within this statutory range, the District Court first calculated Kimbrough's sentence under the advisory Sentencing Guidelines.[2] Kimbrough's guilty plea acknowledged that he was accountable for 56 grams of crack cocaine and 92.1 grams of powder cocaine. This quantity of drugs yielded a base offense level of 32 for the three drug charges. See United States Sentencing Commission, Guidelines Manual § 2D1.1(c) (Nov.2004) (USSG). Finding that Kimbrough, by asserting sole culpability for the crime, had testified falsely at his codefendant's trial, the District Court increased his offense level to 34. See § 3C1.1. In accord with the presentence report, the court determined that Kimbrough's criminal history category was II. An offense level of 34 and a criminal history category of II yielded a Guidelines range of 168 to 210 months for the three drug charges. See *id.*, ch. 5, pt. A, Sentencing Table. The Guidelines sentence for the firearm offense was the statutory minimum, 60 months. See USSG § 2K2.4(b). Kimbrough's final advisory Guidelines range was thus 228 to 270 months, or 19 to 22.5 years.

A sentence in this range, in the District Court's judgment, would have been "greater than necessary" to accomplish the purposes of sentencing set forth in 18 U.S.C. § 3553(a). App. 72. As required by § 3553(a), the court took into account the "nature and circumstances" of the offense and Kimbrough's "history and characteristics." *Id.*, at 72–73. The court also commented that the case exemplified the "disproportionate and unjust effect that crack cocaine guidelines have in sentencing." *Id.*, at 72. In this regard, the court contrasted Kimbrough's Guidelines range of 228 to 270 months with the range that would have applied had he been accountable for an equivalent amount of powder cocaine: 97 to 106 months, inclusive of the 5–year mandatory minimum for the firearm charge, see USSG § 2D1.1(c); *id.*, ch. 5, pt. A, Sentencing Table. Concluding that the statutory minimum sentence was "clearly long enough" to accomplish the objectives listed in § 3553(a), the court sentenced Kimbrough to 15 years, or 180 months, in prison plus 5 years of supervised release. App. 74–75.[3]

In an unpublished *per curiam* opinion, the Fourth Circuit vacated the sentence. Under Circuit precedent, the Court of Appeals observed, a sentence "outside the guidelines range is per se unreasonable when it is based on a disagreement with the sentencing disparity for crack and powder

---

1. The statutory range for possession with intent to distribute more than 50 grams of crack is ten years to life. See 21 U.S.C. § 841(b)(1)(A)(iii) (2000 ed. and Supp. V). The same range applies to the conspiracy offense. See § 846 (2000 ed.). The statutory range for possession with intent to distribute powder cocaine is 0 to 20 years. See § 841(b)(1)(C) (Supp.V). Finally, the statutory range for possession of a firearm in furtherance of a drug-trafficking offense is five years to life. See 18 U.S.C. § 924(c)(1)(A)(i). The sentences for the three drug crimes may run concurrently, see § 3584(a), but the sentence for the firearm offense must be consecutive, see § 924(c)(1)(A).

2. Kimbrough was sentenced in April 2005, three months after our decision in *United States v. Booker*, 543 U.S. 220, 125 S.Ct. 738, 160 L.Ed.2d 621 (2005), rendered the Guidelines advisory. The District Court employed the version of the Guidelines effective November 1, 2004.

3. The prison sentence consisted of 120 months on each of the three drug counts, to be served concurrently, plus 60 months on the firearm count, to be served consecutively.

cocaine offenses." 174 Fed.Appx., at 799 (citing *United States v. Eura,* 440 F.3d 625, 633–634 (C.A.4 2006)).

We granted certiorari to determine whether the crack/powder disparity adopted in the United States Sentencing Guidelines has been rendered "advisory" by our decision in *Booker.*

II

We begin with some background on the different treatment of crack and powder cocaine under the federal sentencing laws. Crack and powder cocaine are two forms of the same drug. Powder cocaine, or cocaine hydrochloride, is generally inhaled through the nose; it may also be mixed with water and injected. See United States Sentencing Commission, Special Report to Congress: Cocaine and Federal Sentencing Policy 5, 12 (Feb. 1995), available at http://www.ussc.gov/crack/exec.htm (hereinafter 1995 Report). (All Internet materials as visited Dec. 7, 2007, and included in Clerk of Court's case file.) Crack cocaine, a type of cocaine base, is formed by dissolving powder cocaine and baking soda in boiling water. *Id.,* at 14. The resulting solid is divided into single-dose "rocks" that users smoke. *Ibid.* The active ingredient in powder and crack cocaine is the same. *Id.,* at 9. The two forms of the drug also have the same physiological and psychotropic effects, but smoking crack cocaine allows the body to absorb the drug much faster than inhaling powder cocaine, and thus produces a shorter, more intense high. *Id.,* at 15–19.[5]

Although chemically similar, crack and powder cocaine are handled very differently for sentencing purposes. The 100–to–1 ratio yields sentences for crack offenses three to six times longer than those for powder offenses involving equal amounts of drugs. See United States Sentencing Commission, Report to Congress: Cocaine and Federal Sentencing Policy iv (May 2002), available at http://www.ussc.gov/r_congress/02crack/2002crackrpt.pdf (hereinafter 2002 Report).[6] This disparity means that a major supplier of powder cocaine may receive a shorter sentence than a low-level dealer who buys powder from the supplier but then converts it to crack. See 1995 Report 193–194.

A

The crack/powder disparity originated in the Anti–Drug Abuse Act of 1986 (1986 Act), 100 Stat. 3207. The 1986 Act created a two-tiered scheme of five-and ten-year mandatory minimum sentences for drug manufacturing and distribution offenses. Congress sought "to link the ten-year mandatory minimum trafficking prison term to major drug dealers and to link the five-year minimum term to serious traffickers." 1995 Report 119. The 1986 Act uses the weight of the drugs involved in the offense as the sole proxy to identify "major" and "serious" dealers. For example, any defendant responsible for 100 grams of heroin is subject to the five-year mandatory

---

5. Injecting powder cocaine produces effects similar to smoking crack cocaine, but very few powder users inject the drug. See 1995 Report 18.

6. As explained in Part II–C, *infra,* the Sentencing Commission amended the Guidelines and reduced sentences for crack offenses effective November 1, 2007. Except as noted, this opinion refers to the 2004 Guidelines in effect at the time of Kimbrough's sentencing.

minimum, see 21 U.S.C. § 841(b)(1)(B)(i) (2000 ed. and Supp V), and any defendant responsible for 1,000 grams of heroin is subject to the ten-year mandatory minimum, see § 841(b)(1)(A)(i).

Crack cocaine was a relatively new drug when the 1986 Act was signed into law, but it was already a matter of great public concern: "Drug abuse in general, and crack cocaine in particular, had become in public opinion and in members' minds a problem of overwhelming dimensions." 1995 Report 121. Congress apparently believed that crack was significantly more dangerous than powder cocaine in that: (1) crack was highly addictive; (2) crack users and dealers were more likely to be violent than users and dealers of other drugs; (3) crack was more harmful to users than powder, particularly for children who had been exposed by their mothers' drug use during pregnancy; (4) crack use was especially prevalent among teenagers; and (5) crack's potency and low cost were making it increasingly popular. See 2002 Report 90.

Based on these assumptions, the 1986 Act adopted a "100–to–1 ratio" that treated every gram of crack cocaine as the equivalent of 100 grams of powder cocaine. The Act's five-year mandatory minimum applies to any defendant accountable for 5 grams of crack or 500 grams of powder, 21 U.S.C. § 841(b)(1)(B)(ii), (iii); its ten-year mandatory minimum applies to any defendant accountable for 50 grams of crack or 5,000 grams of powder, § 841(b)(1)(A)(ii), (iii).

While Congress was considering adoption of the 1986 Act, the Sentencing Commission was engaged in formulating the Sentencing Guidelines. In the main, the Commission developed Guidelines sentences using an empirical approach based on data about past sentencing practices, including 10,000 presentence investigation reports. See USSG § 1A.1, intro. comment., pt. A, ¶ 3. The Commission "modif[ied] and adjust[ed] past practice in the interests of greater rationality, avoiding inconsistency, complying with congressional instructions, and the like." *Rita v. United States,* 551 U.S. 338, ___, 127 S.Ct. 2456, 2464, 168 L.Ed.2d 203 (2007).

The Commission did not use this empirical approach in developing the Guidelines sentences for drug-trafficking offenses. Instead, it employed the 1986 Act's weight-driven scheme. The Guidelines use a drug quantity table based on drug type and weight to set base offense levels for drug trafficking offenses. See USSG § 2D1.1(c). In setting offense levels for crack and powder cocaine, the Commission, in line with the 1986 Act, adopted the 100–to–1 ratio. The statute itself specifies only two quantities of each drug, but the Guidelines "go further and set sentences for the full range of possible drug quantities using the same 100–to–1 quantity ratio." 1995 Report 1. The Guidelines' drug quantity table sets base offense levels ranging from 12, for offenses involving less than 250 milligrams of crack (or 25 grams of powder), to 38, for offenses involving more than 1.5 kilograms of crack (or 150 kilograms of powder). USSG § 2D1.1(c).[8]

---

8. An offense level of 12 results in a Guidelines range of 10 to 16 months for a first-time offender; an offense level of 38 results in a range of 235 to 293 months for the same offender. See USSG ch. 5, pt. A, Sentencing Table.

B

Although the Commission immediately used the 100–to–1 ratio to define base offense levels for all crack and powder offenses, it later determined that the crack/powder sentencing disparity is generally unwarranted. Based on additional research and experience with the 100–to–1 ratio, the Commission concluded that the disparity "fails to meet the sentencing objectives set forth by Congress in both the Sentencing Reform Act and the 1986 Act." 2002 Report 91. In a series of reports, the Commission identified three problems with the crack/powder disparity.

First, the Commission reported, the 100–to–1 ratio rested on assumptions about "the relative harmfulness of the two drugs and the relative prevalence of certain harmful conduct associated with their use and distribution that more recent research and data no longer support." *Ibid.;* see United States Sentencing Commission, Report to Congress: Cocaine and Federal Sentencing Policy 8 (May 2007), available at http://www.ussc.gov/r_congress/cocaine2007.pdf (hereinafter 2007 Report) (ratio Congress embedded in the statute far "overstate[s]" both "the relative harmfulness" of crack cocaine, and the "seriousness of most crack cocaine offenses"). For example, the Commission found that crack is associated with "significantly less trafficking-related violence . . . than previously assumed." 2002 Report 100. It also observed that "the negative effects of prenatal crack cocaine exposure are identical to the negative effects of prenatal powder cocaine exposure." *Id.,* at 94. The Commission furthermore noted that "the epidemic of crack cocaine use by youth never materialized to the extent feared." *Id.,* at 96.

Second, the Commission concluded that the crack/powder disparity is inconsistent with the 1986 Act's goal of punishing major drug traffickers more severely than low-level dealers. Drug importers and major traffickers generally deal in powder cocaine, which is then converted into crack by street-level sellers. See 1995 Report 66–67. But the 100–to–1 ratio can lead to the "anomalous" result that "retail crack dealers get longer sentences than the wholesale drug distributors who supply them the powder cocaine from which their crack is produced." *Id.,* at 174.

Finally, the Commission stated that the crack/powder sentencing differential "fosters disrespect for and lack of confidence in the criminal justice system" because of a "widely-held perception" that it "promotes unwarranted disparity based on race." 2002 Report 103. Approximately 85 percent of defendants convicted of crack offenses in federal court are black; thus the severe sentences required by the 100–to–1 ratio are imposed "primarily upon black offenders." *Ibid.*

Despite these observations, the Commission's most recent reports do not urge identical treatment of crack and powder cocaine. In the Commission's view, "some differential in the quantity-based penalties" for the two drugs is warranted, *id.,* at 102, because crack is more addictive than powder, crack offenses are more likely to involve weapons or bodily injury, and crack distribution is associated with higher levels of crime, see *id.,* at 93–94, 101–102. But the 100–to–1 crack/powder ratio, the Commission concluded, significantly overstates the differences between the two forms of the drug. Accordingly, the Commission recommended that the ratio be "substantially" reduced. *Id.,* at viii.

C

The Commission has several times sought to achieve a reduction in the crack/powder ratio. In 1995, it proposed amendments to the Guidelines that would have replaced the 100–to–1 ratio with a 1–to–1 ratio. Complementing that change, the Commission would have installed special enhancements for trafficking offenses involving weapons or bodily injury. See Amendments to the Sentencing Guidelines for United States Courts, 60 Fed.Reg. 25075–25077 (1995). Congress, acting pursuant to 28 U.S.C. § 994(p),[9] rejected the amendments. See Pub.L. 104–38, § 1, 109 Stat. 334. Simultaneously, however, Congress directed the Commission to "propose revision of the drug quantity ratio of crack cocaine to powder cocaine under the relevant statutes and guidelines." § 2(a)(2), *id.,* at 335.

In response to this directive, the Commission issued reports in 1997 and 2002 recommending that Congress change the 100–to–1 ratio prescribed in the 1986 Act. The 1997 Report proposed a 5–to–1 ratio. See United States Sentencing Commission, Special Report to Congress: Cocaine and Federal Sentencing Policy 2 (Apr.1997), http:// www.ussc.gov/r_ congress/newcrack.pdf. The 2002 Report recommended lowering the ratio "at least" to 20 to 1. 2002 Report viii. Neither proposal prompted congressional action.

The Commission's most recent report, issued in 2007, again urged Congress to amend the 1986 Act to reduce the 100–to–1 ratio. This time, however, the Commission did not simply await congressional action. Instead, the Commission adopted an ameliorating change in the Guidelines. See 2007 Report 9. The alteration, which became effective on November 1, 2007, reduces the base offense level associated with each quantity of crack by two levels. See Amendments to the Sentencing Guidelines for United States Courts, 72 Fed.Reg. 28571–28572 (2007).[10] This modest amendment yields sentences for crack offenses between two and five times longer than sentences for equal amounts of powder. See *ibid.*[11] Describing the amendment as "only ... a partial remedy" for the problems generated by the crack/powder disparity, the Commission noted that "[a]ny comprehensive

---

9. Subsection 994(p) requires the Commission to submit Guidelines amendments to Congress and provides that such amendments become effective unless "modified or disapproved by Act of Congress."

10. The amended Guidelines still produce sentencing ranges keyed to the mandatory minimums in the 1986 Act. Under the pre–2007 Guidelines, the 5- and 50–gram quantities that trigger the statutory minimums produced sentencing ranges that slightly *exceeded* those statutory minimums. Under the amended Guidelines, in contrast, the 5- and 50–gram quantities produce "base offense levels corresponding to guideline ranges that *include* the statutory mandatory minimum penalties." 2007 Report 9.

11. The Commission has not yet determined whether the amendment will be retroactive to cover defendants like Kimbrough. Even under the amendment, however, Kimbrough's Guidelines range would be 195 to 218 months-well above the 180–month sentence imposed by the District Court. See Amendments to the Sentencing Guidelines for United States Courts, 72 Fed.Reg. 28571–28572 (2007); USSG ch. 5, pt. A, Sentencing Table.

solution requires appropriate legislative action by Congress." 2007 Report 10.

III

With this history of the crack/powder sentencing ratio in mind, we next consider the status of the Guidelines tied to the ratio after our decision in *United States v. Booker,* 543 U.S. 220, 125 S.Ct. 738, 160 L.Ed.2d 621 (2005). In *Booker,* the Court held that the mandatory Sentencing Guidelines system violated the Sixth Amendment. See *id.,* at 226–227, 125 S.Ct. 738. The *Booker* remedial opinion determined that the appropriate cure was to sever and excise the provision of the statute that rendered the Guidelines mandatory, 18 U.S.C. § 3553(b)(1) (2000 ed., Supp. IV).[12] This modification of the federal sentencing statute, we explained, "makes the Guidelines effectively advisory." 543 U.S., at 245, 125 S.Ct. 738.

The statute, as modified by *Booker,* contains an overarching provision instructing district courts to "impose a sentence sufficient, but not greater than necessary" to accomplish the goals of sentencing, including "to reflect the seriousness of the offense," "to promote respect for the law," "to provide just punishment for the offense," "to afford adequate deterrence to criminal conduct," and "to protect the public from further crimes of the defendant." 18 U.S.C. § 3553(a) (2000 ed. and Supp. V). The statute further provides that, in determining the appropriate sentence, the court should consider a number of factors, including "the nature and circumstances of the offense," "the history and characteristics of the defendant," "the sentencing range established" by the Guidelines, "any pertinent policy statement" issued by the Sentencing Commission pursuant to its statutory authority, and "the need to avoid unwarranted sentence disparities among defendants with similar records who have been found guilty of similar conduct." *Ibid.* In sum, while the statute still requires a court to give respectful consideration to the Guidelines, see *Gall v. United States, ante,* 552 U.S., at ___, ___, 128 S.Ct. 586, at 594, 596, 2007 WL 4292116, *Booker* "permits the court to tailor the sentence in light of other statutory concerns as well," 543 U.S., at 245–246, 125 S.Ct. 738.

The Government acknowledges that the Guidelines "are now advisory" and that, as a general matter, "courts may vary [from Guidelines ranges] based solely on policy considerations, including disagreements with the Guidelines." Brief for United States 16; cf. *Rita v. United States,* 551 U.S. 338, ___, 127 S.Ct. 2456, 2465, 168 L.Ed.2d 203 (2007) (a district court may consider arguments that "the Guidelines sentence itself fails properly to reflect § 3553(a) considerations"). But the Government contends that the Guidelines adopting the 100–to–1 ratio are an exception to the "general freedom that sentencing courts have to apply the [§ 3553(a)] factors." Brief for United States 16. That is so, according to the Government, because the ratio is a "specific policy determinatio[n] that Congress has directed sentencing courts to observe." *Id.,* at 25. The Government offers three arguments in support of this position. We consider each in turn.

---

12. The remedial opinion also severed and excised the provision of the statute requiring *de novo* review of departures from the Guidelines, 18 U.S.C. § 3742(e), because that provision depended on the Guidelines' mandatory status. *Booker,* 543 U.S., at 245, 125 S.Ct. 738.

A

As its first and most heavily pressed argument, the Government urges that the 1986 Act itself prohibits the Sentencing Commission and sentencing courts from disagreeing with the 100–to–1 ratio.[13] The Government acknowledges that the "Congress did not *expressly* direct the Sentencing Commission to incorporate the 100:1 ratio in the Guidelines." Brief for United States 33 (brackets and internal quotation marks omitted). Nevertheless, it asserts that the Act "[i]mplicit[ly]" requires the Commission and sentencing courts to apply the 100–to–1 ratio. *Id.,* at 32. Any deviation, the Government urges, would be "logically incoherent" when combined with mandatory minimum sentences based on the 100–to–1 ratio. *Id.,* at 33.

This argument encounters a formidable obstacle: It lacks grounding in the text of the 1986 Act. The statute, by its terms, mandates only maximum and minimum sentences: A person convicted of possession with intent to distribute 5 grams or more of crack cocaine must be sentenced to a minimum of 5 years and the maximum term is 40 years. A person with 50 grams or more of crack cocaine must be sentenced to a minimum of 10 years and the maximum term is life. The statute says nothing about the appropriate sentences within these brackets, and we decline to read any implicit directive into that congressional silence. See *Jama v. Immigration and Customs Enforcement,* 543 U.S. 335, 341, 125 S.Ct. 694, 160 L.Ed.2d 708 (2005) ("We do not lightly assume that Congress has omitted from its adopted text requirements that it nonetheless intends to apply . . . ."). Drawing meaning from silence is particularly inappropriate here, for Congress has shown that it knows how to direct sentencing practices in express terms. For example, Congress has specifically required the Sentencing Commission to set Guidelines sentences for serious recidivist offenders "at or near" the statutory maximum. 28 U.S.C. § 994 (h). See also § 994(i) ("The Commission shall assure that the guidelines specify a sentence to a substantial term of imprisonment" for specified categories of offenders.).

Our cautious reading of the 1986 Act draws force from *Neal v. United States,* 516 U.S. 284, 116 S.Ct. 763, 133 L.Ed.2d 709 (1996). That case involved different methods of calculating lysergic acid diethylamide (LSD) weights, one applicable in determining statutory minimum sentences, the other controlling the calculation of Guidelines ranges. The 1986 Act sets mandatory minimum sentences based on the weight of "a mixture or substance containing a detectable amount" of LSD. 21 U.S.C. § 841(b)(1)(A)(v), (B)(v). Prior to *Neal,* we had interpreted that language to include the weight of the carrier medium (usually blotter paper) on which LSD is absorbed even though the carrier is usually far heavier than the LSD itself. See *Chapman v. United States,* 500 U.S. 453, 468, 111 S.Ct. 1919, 114 L.Ed.2d 524 (1991). Until 1993, the Sentencing Commission had interpreted the relevant Guidelines in the same way. That year, however, the Commission changed its approach and "instructed courts to give each

---

13. The Government concedes that a district court may vary from the 100–to–1 ratio if it does so "based on the individualized circumstance[s]" of a particular case. Brief for United States 45. But the Government maintains that the 100–to–1 ratio is binding in the sense that a court may not give any weight to its own view that the ratio itself is inconsistent with the § 3553(a) factors.

dose of LSD on a carrier medium a constructive or presumed weight of 0.4 milligrams." *Neal,* 516 U.S., at 287, 116 S.Ct. 763 (citing USSG § 2D1.1(c), n. (H) (Nov.1995)). The Commission's change significantly lowered the Guidelines range applicable to most LSD offenses, but defendants remained subject to higher statutory minimum sentences based on the combined weight of the pure drug and its carrier medium. The defendant in *Neal* argued that the revised Guidelines and the statute should be interpreted consistently and that the "presumptive-weight method of the Guidelines should also control the mandatory minimum calculation." 516 U.S., at 287, 116 S.Ct. 763. We rejected that argument, emphasizing that the Commission had not purported to interpret the statute and could not in any event overrule our decision in *Chapman.* See 516 U.S., at 293–295, 116 S.Ct. 763.

If the Government's current position were correct, then the Guidelines involved in *Neal* would be in serious jeopardy. We have just recounted the reasons alleged to justify reading into the 1986 Act an implicit command to the Commission and sentencing courts to apply the 100–to–1 ratio to all quantities of crack cocaine. Those same reasons could be urged in support of an argument that the 1986 Act requires the Commission to include the full weight of the carrier medium in calculating the weight of LSD for Guidelines purposes. Yet our opinion in *Neal* never questioned the validity of the altered Guidelines. To the contrary, we stated: "Entrusted within its sphere to make policy judgments, the Commission may abandon its old methods in favor of what it has deemed a more desirable 'approach' to calculating LSD quantities." *Id.,* at 295, 116 S.Ct. 763. If the 1986 Act does not require the Commission to adhere to the Act's method for determining LSD weights, it does not require the Commission-or, after *Booker,* sentencing courts-to adhere to the 100–to–1 ratio for crack cocaine quantities other than those that trigger the statutory mandatory minimum sentences.

B

In addition to the 1986 Act, the Government relies on Congress' disapproval of the Guidelines amendment that the Sentencing Commission proposed in 1995. Congress "not only disapproved of the 1:1 ratio," the Government urges; it also made clear "that the 1986 Act required the Commission (and sentencing courts) to take drug quantities into account, and to do so in a manner that respects the 100:1 ratio." Brief for United States 35.

It is true that Congress rejected the Commission's 1995 proposal to place a 1–to–1 ratio in the Guidelines, and that Congress also expressed the view that "the sentence imposed for trafficking in a quantity of crack cocaine should generally exceed the sentence imposed for trafficking in a like quantity of powder cocaine." Pub.L. 104–38, § 2(a)(1)(A), 109 Stat. 334. But nothing in Congress' 1995 reaction to the Commission-proposed 1–to–1 ratio suggested that crack sentences must exceed powder sentences by a ratio of 100 to 1. To the contrary, Congress' 1995 action required the Commission to recommend a "revision of the drug quantity ratio of crack cocaine to powder cocaine." § 2(a)(2), *id.,* at 335.

The Government emphasizes that Congress required the Commission to propose changes to the 100–to–1 ratio in the 1986 Act and the Guidelines. This requirement, the Government contends, implicitly foreclosed any deviation from the 100–to–1 ratio in the Guidelines (or by sentencing courts) in the absence of a corresponding change in the statute. See Brief for United States 35–36. But it does not follow as the night follows the day that, by calling for recommendations to change the statute, Congress meant to bar any Guidelines alteration in advance of congressional action. The more likely reading is that Congress sought proposals to amend both the statute and the Guidelines because the Commission's criticisms of the 100–to–1 ratio, see Part II–B, *supra,* concerned the exorbitance of the crack/powder disparity in both contexts.

Moreover, as a result of the 2007 amendment, the Guidelines now advance a crack/powder ratio that varies (at different offense levels) between 25 to 1 and 80 to 1. See Amendments to the Sentencing Guidelines for United States Courts, 72 Fed.Reg. 28571–28572. Adopting the Government's analysis, the amended Guidelines would conflict with Congress' 1995 action, and with the 1986 Act, because the current Guidelines ratios deviate from the 100–to–1 statutory ratio. Congress, however, did not disapprove or modify the Commission-initiated 2007 amendment. Ordinarily, we resist reading congressional intent into congressional inaction. See *Bob Jones Univ. v. United States,* 461 U.S. 574, 600, 103 S.Ct. 2017, 76 L.Ed.2d 157 (1983). But in this case, Congress failed to act on a proposed amendment to the Guidelines in a high-profile area in which it had previously exercised its disapproval authority under 28 U.S.C. § 994(p). If nothing else, this tacit acceptance of the 2007 amendment undermines the Government's position, which is itself based on implications drawn from congressional silence.

C

Finally, the Government argues that if district courts are free to deviate from the Guidelines based on disagreements with the crack/powder ratio, unwarranted disparities of two kinds will ensue. See 18 U.S.C. § 3553(a)(6) (sentencing courts shall consider "the need to avoid unwarranted sentence disparities"). First, because sentencing courts remain bound by the mandatory minimum sentences prescribed in the 1986 Act, deviations from the 100–to–1 ratio could result in sentencing "cliffs" around quantities that trigger the mandatory minimums. Brief for United States 33 (internal quotation marks omitted). For example, a district court could grant a sizable downward variance to a defendant convicted of distributing 49 grams of crack but would be required by the statutory minimum to impose a much higher sentence on a defendant responsible for only 1 additional gram. Second, the Government maintains that, if district courts are permitted to vary from the Guidelines based on their disagreement with the crack/powder disparity, "defendants with identical real conduct will receive markedly different sentences, depending on nothing more than the particular judge drawn for sentencing." *Id.,* at 40.

Neither of these arguments persuades us to hold the crack/powder ratio untouchable by sentencing courts. As to the first, the LSD Guidelines we approved in *Neal* create a similar risk of sentencing "cliffs." An offender who possesses LSD on a carrier medium weighing ten grams is subject to the ten-year mandatory minimum, see 21 U.S.C. § 841(b)(1)(A)(v), but an offender whose carrier medium weighs slightly less may receive a considerably lower sentence based on the Guidelines' presumptive-weight methodology. Concerning the second disparity, it is unquestioned that uniformity remains an important goal of sentencing. As we explained in *Booker,* however, advisory Guidelines combined with appellate review for reasonableness and ongoing revision of the Guidelines in response to sentencing practices will help to "avoid excessive sentencing disparities." 543 U.S., at 264, 125 S.Ct. 738. These measures will not eliminate variations between district courts, but our opinion in *Booker* recognized that some departures from uniformity were a necessary cost of the remedy we adopted. See *id.,* at 263, 125 S.Ct. 738 ("We cannot and do not claim that use of a 'reasonableness' standard will provide the uniformity that Congress originally sought to secure [through mandatory Guidelines]."). And as to crack cocaine sentences in particular, we note a congressional control on disparities: possible variations among district courts are constrained by the mandatory minimums Congress prescribed in the 1986 Act.[15]

Moreover, to the extent that the Government correctly identifies risks of "unwarranted sentence disparities" within the meaning of 18 U.S.C. § 3353(a)(6), the proper solution is not to treat the crack/powder ratio as mandatory. Section 3553(a)(6) directs *district courts* to consider the need to avoid unwarranted disparities-along with other § 3553(a) factors-when imposing sentences. See *Gall, ante,* 552 U.S., at ___, n. 6, ___, 128 S.Ct. 586, at 596—597, n. 6, 599, 2007 WL 4292116. Under this instruction, district courts must take account of sentencing practices in other courts and the "cliffs" resulting from the statutory mandatory minimum sentences. To reach an appropriate sentence, these disparities must be weighed against the other § 3553(a) factors and any unwarranted disparity created by the crack/powder ratio itself.

IV

While rendering the Sentencing Guidelines advisory, *United States v. Booker,* 543 U.S. 220, 245, 125 S.Ct. 738, 160 L.Ed.2d 621 (2005), we have nevertheless preserved a key role for the Sentencing Commission. As explained in *Rita* and *Gall,* district courts must treat the Guidelines as the "starting point and the initial benchmark," *Gall v. United States, ante,* 552 U.S., at ___, 128 S.Ct. 586, 2007 WL 4292116. Congress established the Commission to formulate and constantly refine national sentencing standards. See *Rita v. United States,* 551 U.S. 338, ___-___, 127 S.Ct. 2456, 2464–2465, 168 L.Ed.2d 203 (2007). Carrying out its charge, the Commission fills an important institutional role: It has the capacity courts lack to "base its determinations on empirical data and national experience, guided by a professional staff with appropriate expertise." *United States v. Pruitt,* 502 F.3d 1154, 1171 (C.A.10 2007) (McConnell, J., concurring); see *supra,* at 1171.

---

15. The Sentencing Commission reports that roughly 70% of crack offenders are responsible for drug quantities that yield base offense levels at or only two levels above those that correspond to the statutory minimums. See 2007 Report 25.

We have accordingly recognized that, in the ordinary case, the Commission's recommendation of a sentencing range will "reflect a rough approximation of sentences that might achieve § 3553(a)'s objectives." *Rita,* 551 U.S., at ___, 127 S.Ct., at 2465. The sentencing judge, on the other hand, has "greater familiarity with . . . the individual case and the individual defendant before him than the Commission or the appeals court." *Id.,* at ___, 127 S.Ct., at 2469. He is therefore "in a superior position to find facts and judge their import under § 3353(a)" in each particular case. *Gall, ante,* 552 U.S., at ___, 128 S.Ct. 586, 2007 WL 4292116 (internal quotation marks omitted) . In light of these discrete institutional strengths, a district court's decision to vary from the advisory Guidelines may attract greatest respect when the sentencing judge finds a particular case "outside the 'heartland' to which the Commission intends individual Guidelines to apply." *Rita,* 551 U.S., at ___, 127 S.Ct., at 2465. On the other hand, while the Guidelines are no longer binding, closer review may be in order when the sentencing judge varies from the Guidelines based solely on the judge's view that the Guidelines range "fails properly to reflect § 3553(a) considerations" even in a mine-run case. *Ibid.* Cf. Tr. of Oral Arg. in *Gall v. United States,* O.T.2007, No. 06–7949, pp. 38–39.

The crack cocaine Guidelines, however, present no occasion for elaborative discussion of this matter because those Guidelines do not exemplify the Commission's exercise of its characteristic institutional role. In formulating Guidelines ranges for crack cocaine offenses, as we earlier noted, the Commission looked to the mandatory minimum sentences set in the 1986 Act, and did not take account of "empirical data and national experience." See *Pruitt,* 502 F.3d, at 1171(McConnell, J., concurring). Indeed, the Commission itself has reported that the crack/powder disparity produces disproportionately harsh sanctions, *i.e.,* sentences for crack cocaine offenses "greater than necessary" in light of the purposes of sentencing set forth in § 3553(a). Given all this, it would not be an abuse of discretion for a district court to conclude when sentencing a particular defendant that the crack/powder disparity yields a sentence "greater than necessary" to achieve § 3553(a)'s purposes, even in a mine-run case.

V

Taking account of the foregoing discussion in appraising the District Court's disposition in this case, we conclude that the 180–month sentence imposed on Kimbrough should survive appellate inspection. The District Court began by properly calculating and considering the advisory Guidelines range. It then addressed the relevant § 3553(a) factors. First, the court considered "the nature and circumstances" of the crime, see 18 U.S.C. § 3553(a)(1), which was an unremarkable drug-trafficking offense. App. 72–73 ("[T]his defendant and another defendant were caught sitting in a car with some crack cocaine and powder by two police officers-that's the sum and substance of it—[and they also had] a firearm."). Second, the court considered Kimbrough's "history and characteristics." § 3553(a)(1). The court noted that Kimbrough had no prior felony convictions, that he had served in combat during Operation Desert Storm and received an honorable discharge from the Marine Corps, and that he had a steady history of employment.

Furthermore, the court alluded to the Sentencing Commission's reports criticizing the 100–to–1 ratio, cf. § 3553(a)(5) (Supp. V), noting that the Commission "recognizes that crack cocaine has not caused the damage that the Justice Department alleges it has." App. 72. Comparing the Guidelines range to the range that would have applied if Kimbrough had possessed an equal amount of powder, the court suggested that the 100–to–1 ratio itself created an unwarranted disparity within the meaning of § 3553(a). Finally, the court did not purport to establish a ratio of its own. Rather, it appropriately framed its final determination in line with § 3553(a)'s overarching instruction to "impose a sentence sufficient, but not greater than necessary" to accomplish the sentencing goals advanced in § 3553(a)(2). Concluding that "the crack cocaine guidelines [drove] the offense level to a point higher than is necessary to do justice in this case," App. 72, the District Court thus rested its sentence on the appropriate considerations and "committed no procedural error," *Gall v. United States, ante,* 552 U.S., at ___, 128 S.Ct. 586, at 600, 2007 WL 4292116.

The ultimate question in Kimbrough's case is "whether the sentence was reasonable-*i.e.,* whether the District Judge abused his discretion in determining that the § 3553(a) factors supported a sentence of [15 years] and justified a substantial deviation from the Guidelines range." *Ibid.* The sentence the District Court imposed on Kimbrough was 4.5 years below the bottom of the Guidelines range. But in determining that 15 years was the appropriate prison term, the District Court properly homed in on the particular circumstances of Kimbrough's case and accorded weight to the Sentencing Commission's consistent and emphatic position that the crack/powder disparity is at odds with § 3553(a). See Part II–B, *supra.* Indeed, aside from its claim that the 100–to–1 ratio is mandatory, the Government did not attack the District Court's downward variance as unsupported by § 3553(a). Giving due respect to the District Court's reasoned appraisal, a reviewing court could not rationally conclude that the 4.5–year sentence reduction Kimbrough received qualified as an abuse of discretion. See *Gall, ante,* at ___–___, 128 S.Ct. 586, at 601—602; *Rita v. United States,* 551 U.S. 338, ___, 127 S.Ct. 2456, 2469–2470, 168 L.Ed.2d 203 (2007).

* * *

For the reasons stated, the judgment of the United States Court of Appeals for the Fourth Circuit is reversed, and the case is remanded for further proceedings consistent with this opinion.

It is so ordered.

■ JUSTICE SCALIA concurring.

The Court says that "closer review may be in order when the sentencing judge varies from the Guidelines based solely on the judge's view that the Guidelines range 'fails properly to reflect § 3553(a) considerations' even in a mine-run case," but that this case "present[s] no occasion for elaborative discussion of this matter." *Ante,* at ___ (quoting *Rita v. United States,* 551 U.S. 338, ___, 127 S.Ct. 2456, 2465, 168 L.Ed.2d 203 (2007)). I join the opinion only because I do not take this to be an unannounced abandonment of the following clear statements in our recent opinions. . . .

These statements mean that the district court is free to make its own reasonable application of the § 3553(a) factors, and to reject (after due consideration) the advice of the Guidelines. If there is any thumb on the scales; if the Guidelines *must* be followed even where the district court's application of the § 3553(a) factors is entirely reasonable; then the "advisory" Guidelines would, over a large expanse of their application, *entitle* the defendant to a lesser sentence *but for* the presence of certain additional facts found by judge rather than jury. This, as we said in *Booker,* would violate the Sixth Amendment.

■ JUSTICE THOMAS, dissenting.

I continue to disagree with the remedy fashioned in *United States v. Booker,* 543 U.S. 220, 258–265, 125 S.Ct. 738, 160 L.Ed.2d 621 (2005). The Court's post-*Booker* sentencing cases illustrate why the remedial majority in *Booker* was mistaken to craft a remedy far broader than necessary to correct constitutional error. The Court is now confronted with a host of questions about how to administer a sentencing scheme that has no basis in the statute. Because the Court's decisions in this area are necessarily grounded in policy considerations rather than law, I respectfully dissent.

In *Booker,* the Court held that the Federal Sentencing Guidelines violate the Sixth Amendment insofar as they permit a judge to make findings that raise a sentence beyond the level justified by the " 'facts reflected in the jury verdict or admitted by the defendant.' " *Id.,* at 232, 125 S.Ct. 738 (quoting *Blakely v. Washington,* 542 U.S. 296, 303, 124 S.Ct. 2531, 159 L.Ed.2d 403 (2004) (emphasis deleted)). In my view, this violation was more suitably remedied by requiring any such facts to be submitted to the jury. . . . .

■ JUSTICE ALITO, dissenting.

For the reasons explained in my dissent in *Gall v. United States,* 552 U.S. 38, 128 S.Ct. 586, 169 L.Ed.2d 445, 2007 WL 4292116, I would hold that, under the remedial decision in *United States v. Booker,* 543 U.S. 220, 258–265, 125 S.Ct. 738, 160 L.Ed.2d 621 (2005), a district judge is still required to give significant weight to the policy decisions embodied in the Guidelines. The *Booker* remedial decision, however, does not permit a court of appeals to treat the Guidelines' policy decisions as binding. I would not draw a distinction between the Guideline at issue here and other Guidelines. Accordingly, I would vacate the decision of the Court of Appeals and remand for reconsideration.

SECTION 4.   PROCEDURAL ISSUES AT SENTENCING

United States v. McCaskill

United States Court of Appeals, Sixth Circuit, 2006.
202 Fed.Appx. 70.

■ STAFFORD, DISTRICT JUDGE.

The defendant, Luther McCaskill ("McCaskill"), appeals his conviction and sentence on charges of conspiracy, wire fraud, and possession of forged securities. We AFFIRM.

I. BACKGROUND

In 1997, Eric Hoberg ("Hoberg") sought private, unconventional financing to build a mill in North Dakota to grind organic grains into flour. He originally sought out the services of Richard Sclar ("Sclar"), in Florida, paying Sclar $2,500 to secure financing for a mill expected to cost about $3,500,000. When Sclar left the country having failed to procure the financing, Sclar's ex-wife, Sheila Greenspan ("Greenspan"), offered to help Hoberg obtain an insurance binder that could be used by Hoberg to obtain funding from a local bank or finance company. Hoberg acceded to Greenspan's offer of assistance.

In her effort to help Hoberg, Greenspan first contacted Jay Elbel ("Elbel") in Southern California. Describing himself as the attorney for Nigella Insurance Company ("Nigella"), whose president was Dan Cimini ("Cimini"), Elbel informed Greenspan that Nigella could handle the bonding, or insurance guarantee, for Hoberg's project. Because Nigella was not a double—or triple—A rated insurer, however, Greenspan was told that a major insurance company would have to reinsure, or provide an insurance wrap, for Nigella's policy. The initial binder price for the bond and the insurance wrap was $35,000, or 1% of the targeted financing amount. The ultimate cost of the bond was to be 10% percent of the loan.

Nigella, in fact, was a sham company created by McCaskill, an insurance businessman. When McCaskill learned that Greenspan was interested in obtaining financing for a multi-million dollar project, he contacted Ardeana Vance ("Vance") of A–Vance Insurance Agency in Detroit, Michigan. Vance was purportedly a licensed insurance broker who could write the policy and secure the necessary wrap from a major insurer such as Kemper or Western Surety Insurance Company. Greenspan thereafter received correspondence on A–Vance Insurance Agency's letterhead, informing her about efforts to obtain the insurance wrap and instructing her to send Hoberg's $35,000 binder to MC & D Service Company. On September 8, 1998, Hoberg wired the money as instructed. Hoberg's deposit was never returned to him even though no bond was ever issued and no financing was ever obtained. Instead, Hoberg's $35,000 was split between McCaskill ($10,000), Vance ($10,000), Cimini ($10,000) and Elbel ($5,000).

On March 20, 2002, McCaskill, Elbel, Vance, and Cimini were indicted in a 32–count indictment. The charges against Vance were dismissed before trial. Cimini entered into a plea agreement with the government, and Elbel was placed in a pretrial diversion program. Only McCaskill went to trial.

All but three counts of the indictment were dismissed by the government before trial. The surviving counts included: (1) Count One: conspiracy to execute a scheme to defraud, cause forged securities to be transported in interstate commerce, use interstate wire communications to execute the scheme to defraud, and engage in a monetary transaction in criminally derived property, all in violation of 18 U.S.C. § 371; (2) Count Twenty-

Five: wire fraud, in violation of 18 U.S.C. § 1343; and (3) Count Thirty–Two: possessing a forged security in violation of 18 U.S.C. § 513.

Trial began on April 13, 2004, and ended on April 16, 2004, with the jury's return of guilty verdicts on all three counts. McCaskill represented himself at trial, although an attorney was appointed to assist McCaskill as needed. McCaskill was sentenced to 60–month consecutive terms of imprisonment on Counts One and Twenty-five and a 68–month term of imprisonment on Count Thirty-two, for a total custodial sentence of 188 months, a bottom-of-the-guidelines sentence.

II. DISCUSSION

C. Sentencing

McCaskill was sentenced to 60–month consecutive terms of imprisonment on Counts One and Twenty-five and a 68–month term on Count Thirty-two, for a total custodial sentence of 188 months, a bottom-of-the-guidelines sentence. The statutory maximum sentence for Count One was 60 months; for Count Twenty–Five, 60 months; and for Count Thirty–Two, 120 months. Importantly, McCaskill's sentence did not exceed the statutory maximum.

McCaskill's sentence was based, in large part, on a pre-sentence report ("PSR") prepared by the probation office before the *Blakely v. Washington* decision was issued on June 24, 2004. In the PSR, it was noted that McCaskill "refused to participate in the presentence interview." Among other things, the PSR described as relevant conduct a pattern of criminal activity resembling the Hoberg scheme, but involving shell companies other than Nigella and victims other than Hoberg, that dated back several years. As noted in the PSR, these "related" swindles netted a total of $5,466,758.98 in fraudulent proceeds. The probation officer added eighteen points to McCaskill's base offense level for the described relevant conduct. The officer also added four points for McCaskill's role in the offense (he was a leader and/or organizer) and four points because the victims numbered fifty or more, resulting in a total offense level of thirty-three. The probation officer added three criminal history points for each of two prior criminal convictions, one for mail fraud in 1996, and one for conspiracy, forged security, bank fraud and other related offenses in 2001. In addition, the officer added two criminal history points because the instant offense occurred while McCaskill was on supervised release, and one criminal history point because the instant offense was committed less than two years after McCaskill was released from prison. Criminal history points totaled nine, placing McCaskill in a Criminal History Category IV. Based on a total offense level of thirty-three and a criminal history Category IV, McCaskill's guideline imprisonment range was 188 to 235 months.

McCaskill filed objections to the PSR, arguing, among other things, that under *Blakely,* no enhancements other than those proved to the jury could be assessed. After several postponements, McCaskill appeared for sentencing on February 14, 2005. At that hearing, which occurred after the Supreme Court decided *United States v. Booker,* 543 U.S. 220 (2005), the government presented the testimony of a certified fraud examiner from the

Florida Office of Financial Regulation. The examiner described her investigation into a scheme perpetrated by McCaskill and others that resulted in losses of $3,726,758.98 to victims. The hearing was rescheduled to allow the parties time to file supplemental memoranda regarding the impact of *Booker*. On March 4, 2005, at the resumed sentencing hearing, the government presented the testimony of an FBI agent who described additional frauds allegedly perpetrated by McCaskill and his co-conspirators, involving losses to victims of almost $9 million.

McCaskill responded to the government's evidence by denying that he was involved in the schemes described by the witnesses. He otherwise did not challenge the guideline computation set forth in the PSR. Imposing sentence, the district court stated on the record:

> With respect to the guidelines, as the Court has determined them, that range is 188 to 235 months. The sentencing factors that the Court ought to consider pursuant to the statute, I think call for a sentence on the same magnitude. We have a gentleman who is very, very bright, who is not understating his ability when he says he'd rather have himself speak for himself than anybody else because he believes he could do it better and I think I can just about accept [that] proposition no matter how highly trained an attorney might be. He has all the skills in the world and yet for his lifetime he has committed those skills to the pursuit of crime, victimizing a lot of people and depriving them of lot of their money, and he appears determined to pursue that life no matter how aggressively the justice system seeks to intervene to stop him, and the only appropriate sentence I'm afraid is a sentence which will hopefully incapacitate him from pursuing these violations for a substantial period. I think I do need to consider his age in making that determination, because of course among the sentencing factors is the length of confinement necessary to deter the Defendant himself from committing future offenses as well as general deterrent factors and a sentence that is proportionate to the violations committed. Here we have already described the enormous amount of money and large number of people who los[t] money as a consequence of his actions. . . . So, the Court, in weighing those factors, including the Defendant's age [61 years] and health find that a sentence at the low end of the range would be appropriate. J.A. at 505–07. Noting that the government did not object to the probation officer's calculation of losses attributable to relevant conduct ($5,466,758.98), the court limited the amount of relevant-conduct loss to the amount specified in the PSR and did not use the much higher figure offered by the government at the sentencing hearing. On appeal, McCaskill raises a number of issues regarding his sentence.

1. *Failure to Furnish Documents*

McCaskill first complains that his sentence was based on documents introduced as exhibits at his sentencing hearing, exhibits that he alleges he was never furnished beforehand. McCaskill's complaint, however, is meritless. The PSR described in detail the relevant conduct that the government sought to prove at the sentencing hearing; yet McCaskill submitted no objections to the probation officer's estimate of the losses attributed to relevant conduct. Instead, McCaskill objected, in a cursory manner, to the addition of *any* enhancements based on relevant conduct, stating that "there is, in reality, no need for McCaskill to argue relevant conduct ... [because] the U.S. Supreme Court put that to rest in *Blakely v. Washington.*" J.A. at 534. At the sentencing hearing, moreover, McCaskill did not complain that he had not seen or been given copies of the documents when the government moved to admit the challenged documents to prove the relevant fraud loss. Furthermore, although the documents were present in the courtroom and available for McCaskill's inspection, he never asked the court for time to review the documents. He simply objected to the introduction of hearsay evidence, then proceeded with his cross-examination, never suggesting that the documents were a surprise. Under the circumstances, the district court cannot be faulted for admitting the challenged documents.

2. *Crawford Claim*

Relying on *Crawford v. Washington,* 541 U.S. 36 (2004) (holding that the Confrontation Clause prohibits the admission of out-of-court statements that are testimonial in nature unless the declarant is unavailable and the defendant had a prior opportunity to cross-examine the declarant concerning the statements), McCaskill argues that the trial court erred in considering the hearsay testimony presented at his sentencing hearings. This court, however, has explicitly rejected such an argument. *See United States v. Katzopoulos,* 437 F.3d 569, 576 (6th Cir.2006) (explaining that "there is nothing specific in *Blakely, Booker or Crawford* that would cause this Court to reverse its long-settled rule of law that [the] Confrontation Clause permits the admission of testimonial hearsay evidence at sentencing proceedings"); *United States v. Stone,* 432 F.3d 651, 654 (6th Cir.2005) (holding that "*Crawford* does not change our long-settled rule that the confrontation clause does not apply in sentencing proceedings"), *cert. denied,* ___ S.Ct. ___, 2006 WL 1591782 (Oct. 2, 2006); *United States v. Silverman,* 976 F.2d 1502, 1510 (6th Cir.1992) (*en banc*) (holding that "confrontation rights do not apply in sentencing hearings as at a trial on the question of guilt or innocence"), *cert. denied,* 507 U.S. 990 (1993). Based on binding precedent, we find no error in the district court's admission of hearsay evidence.

3. *Rule 32 Claim*

McCaskill contends that the district court violated Rule 32 of the Federal Rules of Criminal Procedure by failing to explain both how it calculated the relevant conduct loss and why it enhanced McCaskill's sentence by four levels for his role in the offense. Rule 32 provides in relevant part:

(3) Court Determinations. At sentencing, the court:

(A) may accept any undisputed portion of the presentence report as a finding of fact;

(B) must—for any disputed portion of the presentence report or other controverted matter—rule on the dispute or determine that a ruling is unnecessary either because the matter will not affect sentencing, or because the court will not consider the matter in sentencing; and

(C) must append a copy of the court's determinations under this rule to any copy of the presentence report made available to the Bureau of Prisons.

Fed.R.Crim.P. 32.

McCaskill filed no written objections to that portion of the PSR recommending a four-level enhancement for his leadership/organizer role in the offense. At sentencing, having heard no objection to the leadership enhancement, the district court stated:

> I will also note that the presentence report also assigns points for Mr. McCaskill as a leader organizer of the fraud. I have heard ample testimony at the trial and in connection with the evidence assembled here to conclude that is a proper assignment of points as well, so I am adopting the factual findings and the application of the guideline range as it appears in the report.

J.A. at 492. After the judge made the above comments, McCaskill, for the first time, objected to the leadership enhancement by saying: "I take exception to the fact that if I would be a leader of something then believe me everyone involved would know who I am and no one would collect any money." J.A. at 495. He did not otherwise elaborate on his objection, and the district court did not thereafter revisit its conclusion that a four-level leadership enhancement was appropriate given the "ample" evidence presented at trial and at sentencing.

We find no Rule 32 violation in the district court's treatment of the leadership enhancement. McCaskill failed to submit an objection to the PSR in this regard, leading the district court—as permitted by Rule 32(3)(A)—to adopt the relevant, undisputed portion of the PSR as a factual finding. The court further explained that the enhancement was supported by "ample" record evidence. Although McCaskill thereafter objected to the enhancement, his objection was so perfunctory that it required no further elaboration by the district court. *See United States v. Brown,* 314 F.3d 1216, 1221 (10th Cir.2003) (explaining that unless "objections involve non-perfunctory specific allegations of factual inaccuracy, no controverted matter exists, and the district court's fact-finding obligation under Rule 32 ... is not implicated") (internal quotation marks and citation omitted), *cert. denied,* 537 U.S. 1223 (2003); *see also United States v. Pitts,* No. 96–2263, 1998 WL 165154, at *2 (6th Cir. Apr. 3, 1998) (explaining that a defendant who fails to object to the district court's lack of a sufficient explanation for imposing the particular sentence waives the issue) (citing *United States v. Tillman,* 25 F.3d 1052, 1994 WL 198165 (6th Cir. May 18, 1994)).

McCaskill did file a written objection to those portions of the PSR that outlined his relevant conduct. McCaskill explained his objection by stating that "[a]t this juncture there is, in reality, no need for McCaskill to argue the relevant conduct, [because] as of June 24, 2004, the U.S. Supreme Court, put that to rest, in *Blakely v. Washington.*" He provided no "specific allegations of factual inaccuracy." *Brown,* 314 F.3d at 1221. At sentencing, after the district court ruled that *Blakely/Booker* did not preclude enhancements based on judge-found facts, McCaskill again objected to the enhancement for relevant conduct, stating, in essence, that he had not received any money from anyone other than Hoberg. He also reiterated his argument that the Supreme Court had prohibited enhancements based on judge-found facts. Responding to McCaskill's objection, the district court stated: "I am satisfied given the evidence received that Mr. McCaskill was sufficiently involved in each of the fraudulent operations ... that he should be held accountable at least for the sum that is computed by [the probation officer]." J.A. at 491. Given the lack of specificity in McCaskill's objections, the district court's ruling was more than adequate to satisfy Rule 32(3)(B).

4. *Reasonableness Claim*

McCaskill claims that the sentence imposed by the district court was unreasonable. He supports his claim by stating: "There was a total lack of evidence to support his enhancement for relevant conduct, role in the offense and number of victims and thus his sentence was inherently unreasonable." Def.'s Br. at 77–78. Given the record evidence, including the district court's explanation for its choice of sentence, we find no merit to this claim.

5. *Booker/Blakely Claims*

In his remaining sentencing arguments, McCaskill challenges the trial court's enhancement of his guideline range by any factor that was not charged in the indictment and proved to the jury beyond a reasonable doubt—in essence, a *Blakely/Booker* argument.... In this case, the trial court made clear that it considered the Sentencing Guidelines to be advisory, not mandatory. As it was permitted to do, the court found, by a preponderance of the evidence, certain facts (none of which was specifically challenged by McCaskill either before or during sentencing) that resulted in points added to McCaskill's total offense level. *See United States v. Stafford,* 258 F.3d 465, 476 (6th Cir.2001) (finding that the defendant was deemed to have admitted facts contained in the PSR to which defendant failed to object). These judicially-found facts did not result in a sentence that was beyond the statutory maximum; they did not result in a sentence violative of McCaskill's Sixth Amendment rights; and they did not result in a violation of McCaskill's *ex post facto*-type due process rights.

III. CONCLUSION

For the reasons set forth above, we AFFIRM McCaskill's conviction and sentence.

SECTION 5. PLEA BARGAINING

Bordenkircher v. Hayes

Supreme Court of the United States, 1978.
434 U.S. 357, 98 S.Ct. 663, 54 L.Ed.2d 604.

■ MR. JUSTICE STEWART delivered the opinion of the Court.

The question in this case is whether the Due Process Clause of the Fourteenth Amendment is violated when a state prosecutor carries out a threat made during plea negotiations to reindict the accused on more serious charges if he does not plead guilty to the offense with which he was originally charged.

I

The respondent, Paul Lewis Hayes, was indicted by a Fayette County, Ky., grand jury on a charge of uttering a forged instrument in the amount of $88.30, an offense then punishable by a term of 2 to 10 years in prison. Ky.Rev.Stat. § 434.130 (1973) (repealed 1975). After arraignment, Hayes, his retained counsel, and the Commonwealth's Attorney met in the presence of the Clerk of the Court to discuss a possible plea agreement. During these conferences the prosecutor offered to recommend a sentence of five years in prison if Hayes would plead guilty to the indictment. He also said that if Hayes did not plead guilty and "save[d] the court the inconvenience and necessity of a trial," he would return to the grand jury to seek an indictment under the Kentucky Habitual Criminal Act,[1] then Ky.Rev.Stat. § 431.190 (1973) (repealed 1975), which would subject Hayes to a mandatory sentence of life imprisonment by reason of his two prior felony convictions.[2] Hayes chose not to plead guilty, and the prosecutor did obtain an indictment charging him under the Habitual Criminal Act. It is not disputed that the recidivist charge was fully justified by the evidence, that the prosecutor was in possession of this evidence at the time of the original indictment, and that Hayes' refusal to plead guilty to the original charge was what led to his indictment under the habitual criminal statute. That statute has been replaced by Ky.Rev.Stat. § 532.080 (Supp. 1977) under which Hayes would have been sentenced to, at most, an indeterminate term of 10 to 20 years. § 532.080(6)(b). In addition, under the new statute a previous conviction is a basis for enhanced sentencing only if a prison term of one year or more was imposed, the sentence or probation was completed within five years of the present offense, and the offender was over the age of 18 when the offense was committed. At least one of Hayes' prior convictions did not meet these conditions. See n. 3, *infra*.

A jury found Hayes guilty on the principal charge of uttering a forged instrument and, in a separate proceeding, further found that he had twice before been convicted of felonies. As required by the habitual offender statute, he was sentenced to a life term in the penitentiary. The Kentucky Court of Appeals rejected Hayes' constitutional objections to the enhanced sentence, holding in an unpublished opinion that imprisonment for life with the possibility of parole was constitutionally permissible in light of the previous felonies of which Hayes had been convicted,[3] and that the prosecu-

---

1. While cross-examining Hayes during the subsequent trial proceedings the prosecutor described the plea offer in the following language:

"Isn't it a fact that I told you at that time [the initial bargaining session] if you did not intend to plead guilty to five years for this charge and ... save the court the inconvenience and necessity of a trial and taking up this time that I intended to return to the grand jury and ask them to indict you based upon these prior felony convictions?" Tr. 194.

2. At the time of Hayes' trial the statute provided that "[a]ny person convicted a ... third time of felony ... shall be confined in the penitentiary during his life." Ky.Rev.Stat. § 431.190

3. According to his own testimony, Hayes had pleaded guilty in 1961, when he was 17 years old, to a charge of detaining a female, a lesser included offense of rape, and as a result

tor's decision to indict him as a habitual offender was a legitimate use of available leverage in the plea-bargaining process.

On Hayes' petition for a federal writ of habeas corpus, the United States District Court for the Eastern District of Kentucky agreed that there had been no constitutional violation in the sentence or the indictment procedure, and denied the writ. The Court of Appeals for the Sixth Circuit reversed the District Court's judgment. *Hayes v. Cowan*, 547 F.2d 42. While recognizing "that plea bargaining now plays an important role in our criminal justice system," *id.*, at 43, the appellate court thought that the prosecutor's conduct during the bargaining negotiations had violated the principles of *Blackledge v. Perry*, 417 U.S. 21, 94 S.Ct. 2098, 40 L.Ed.2d 628, which "protect[ed] defendants from the vindictive exercise of a prosecutor's discretion." 547 F.2d, at 44. Accordingly, the court ordered that Hayes be discharged "except for his confinement under a lawful sentence imposed solely for the crime of uttering a forged instrument." *Id.*, at 45. We granted certiorari to consider a constitutional question of importance in the administration of criminal justice. 431 U.S. 953, 97 S.Ct. 2672, 53 L.Ed.2d 269.

II

It may be helpful to clarify at the outset the nature of the issue in this case. While the prosecutor did not actually obtain the recidivist indictment until after the plea conferences had ended, his intention to do so was clearly expressed at the outset of the plea negotiations. Hayes was thus fully informed of the true terms of the offer when he made his decision to plead not guilty. This is not a situation, therefore, where the prosecutor without notice brought an additional and more serious charge after plea negotiations relating only to the original indictment had ended with the defendant's insistence on pleading not guilty. As a practical matter, in short, this case would be no different if the grand jury had indicted Hayes as a recidivist from the outset, and the prosecutor had offered to drop that charge as part of the plea bargain.

The Court of Appeals nonetheless drew a distinction between "concessions relating to prosecution under an existing indictment," and threats to bring more severe charges not contained in the original indictment—a line it thought necessary in order to establish a prophylactic rule to guard against the evil of prosecutorial vindictiveness.[6] Quite apart from this chronological distinction, however, the Court of Appeals found that the

---

had served five years in the state reformatory. In 1970 he had been convicted of robbery and sentenced to five years' imprisonment, but had been released on probation immediately.

6. "Although a prosecutor may in the course of plea negotiations offer a defendant concessions relating to prosecution under an existing indictment ... he may not threaten a defendant with the consequence that more severe charges may be brought if he insists on going to trial. When a prosecutor obtains an indictment less severe than the facts known to him at the time might permit, he makes a discretionary determination that the interests of the state are served by not seeking more serious charges.... Accordingly, if after plea negotiations fail, he then procures an indictment charging a more serious crime, a strong inference is created that the only reason for the more serious charges is vindictiveness. Under these circumstances, the prosecutor should be required to justify his action." 547 F.2d, at 44–45.

prosecutor had acted vindictively in the present case since he had conceded that the indictment was influenced by his desire to induce a guilty plea.[7] The ultimate conclusion of the Court of Appeals thus seems to have been that a prosecutor acts vindictively and in violation of due process of law whenever his charging decision is influenced by what he hopes to gain in the course of plea bargaining negotiations.

III

We have recently had occasion to observe: "[W]hatever might be the situation in an ideal world, the fact is that the guilty plea and the often concomitant plea bargain are important components of this country's criminal justice system. Properly administered, they can benefit all concerned." *Blackledge v. Allison,* 431 U.S. 63, 71, 97 S.Ct. 1621, 1627, 52 L.Ed.2d 136. The open acknowledgment of this previously clandestine practice has led this Court to recognize the importance of counsel during plea negotiations, *Brady v. United States,* 397 U.S. 742, 758, 90 S.Ct. 1463, 1474, 25 L.Ed.2d 747, the need for a public record indicating that a plea was knowingly and voluntarily made, *Boykin v. Alabama,* 395 U.S. 238, 242, 89 S.Ct. 1709, 1711, 23 L.Ed.2d 274, and the requirement that a prosecutor's plea-bargaining promise must be kept, *Santobello v. New York,* 404 U.S. 257, 262, 92 S.Ct. 495, 498, 30 L.Ed.2d 427. The decision of the Court of Appeals in the present case, however, did not deal with considerations such as these, but held that the substance of the plea offer itself violated the limitations imposed by the Due Process Clause of the Fourteenth Amendment. Cf. *Brady v. United States, supra,* 397 U.S., at 751 n. 8, 90 S.Ct., at 1470. For the reasons that follow, we have concluded that the Court of Appeals was mistaken in so ruling.

IV

This Court held in *North Carolina v. Pearce,* 395 U.S. 711, 725, 89 S.Ct. 2072, 2080, 23 L.Ed.2d 656, that the Due Process Clause of the Fourteenth Amendment "requires that vindictiveness against a defendant for having successfully attacked his first conviction must play no part in the sentence he receives after a new trial." The same principle was later applied to prohibit a prosecutor from reindicting a convicted misdemeanant on a felony charge after the defendant had invoked an appellate remedy, since in this situation there was also a "realistic likelihood of 'vindictiveness.' " *Blackledge v. Perry,* 417 U.S., at 27, 94 S.Ct., at 2102.

In those cases the Court was dealing with the State's unilateral imposition of a penalty upon a defendant who had chosen to exercise a legal right to attack his original conviction—a situation "very different from the give-and-take negotiation common in plea bargaining between the prosecution and defense, which arguably possess relatively equal bargaining power." *Parker v. North Carolina,* 397 U.S. 790, 809, 90 S.Ct. 1458, 1474, 1479, 25 L.Ed.2d 785 (opinion of Brennan, J.). The Court has emphasized that the due process violation in cases such as *Pearce* and *Perry* lay not in the possibility that a defendant might be deterred from the exercise of a legal

---

7.   "In this case, a vindictive motive need not be inferred. The prosecutor has admitted it." *Id.,* at 45.

right, see *Colten v. Kentucky*, 407 U.S. 104, 92 S.Ct. 1953, 32 L.Ed.2d 584; *Chaffin v. Stynchcombe*, 412 U.S. 17, 93 S.Ct. 1977, 36 L.Ed.2d 714, but rather in the danger that the State might be retaliating against the accused for lawfully attacking his conviction. See *Blackledge v. Perry, supra*, 417 U.S., at 26–28, 94 S.Ct., at 2101–02.

To punish a person because he has done what the law plainly allows him to do is a due process violation of the most basic sort, see *North Carolina v. Pearce, supra*, 395 U.S., at 738, 89 S.Ct., at 2082 (opinion of Black, J.), and for an agent of the State to pursue a course of action whose objective is to penalize a person's reliance on his legal rights is "patently unconstitutional." *Chaffin v. Stynchcombe, supra*, 412 U.S., at 32–33, n. 20, 93 S.Ct., at 1986. See *United States v. Jackson*, 390 U.S. 570, 88 S.Ct. 1209, 20 L.Ed.2d 138. But in the "give-and-take" of plea bargaining, there is no such element of punishment or retaliation so long as the accused is free to accept or reject the prosecution's offer.

Plea bargaining flows from "the mutuality of advantage" to defendants and prosecutors, each with his own reasons for wanting to avoid trial. *Brady v. United States, supra*, 397 U.S., at 752, 90 S.Ct., at 1471. Defendants advised by competent counsel and protected by other procedural safeguards are presumptively capable of intelligent choice in response to prosecutorial persuasion, and unlikely to be driven to false self-condemnation. 397 U.S., at 758, 90 S.Ct., at 1474. Indeed, acceptance of the basic legitimacy of plea bargaining necessarily implies rejection of any notion that a guilty plea is involuntary in a constitutional sense simply because it is the end result of the bargaining process. By hypothesis, the plea may have been induced by promises of a recommendation of a lenient sentence or a reduction of charges, and thus by fear of the possibility of a greater penalty upon conviction after a trial. See ABA Project on Standards for Criminal Justice, Pleas of Guilty § 3.1 (App. Draft 1968); Note, Plea Bargaining and the Transformation of the Criminal Process, 90 Harv. L.Rev. 564 (1977). Cf. *Brady v. United States, supra*, at 751, 90 S.Ct., at 1470; *North Carolina v. Alford*, 400 U.S. 25, 91 S.Ct. 160, 27 L.Ed.2d 162.

While confronting a defendant with the risk of more severe punishment clearly may have a "discouraging effect on the defendant's assertion of his trial rights, the imposition of these difficult choices [is] an inevitable"—and permissible—"attribute of any legitimate system which tolerates and encourages the negotiation of pleas." *Chaffin v. Stynchcombe, supra*, 412 U.S., at 31, 93 S.Ct., at 1985. It follows that, by tolerating and encouraging the negotiation of pleas, this Court has necessarily accepted as constitutionally legitimate the simple reality that the prosecutor's interest at the bargaining table is to persuade the defendant to forgo his right to plead not guilty.

It is not disputed here that Hayes was properly chargeable under the recidivist statute, since he had in fact been convicted of two previous felonies. In our system, so long as the prosecutor has probable cause to believe that the accused committed an offense defined by statute, the decision whether or not to prosecute, and what charge to file or bring before a grand jury, generally rests entirely in his discretion.[8] Within the limits set by the legislature's constitutionally valid definition of chargeable offenses, "the conscious exercise of some selectivity in enforcement is not in itself a federal constitutional violation" so long as "the selection was [not] deliberately based upon an unjustifiable standard such as race, religion, or other arbitrary classification." *Oyler v. Boles*, 368 U.S. 448, 456, 82 S.Ct. 501, 506, 7 L.Ed.2d 446. To hold that the prosecutor's desire to induce a guilty plea is an "unjustifiable standard," which, like race or religion, may play no part in his charging decision, would contradict the very premises that underlie the concept of plea bargaining itself. Moreover, a rigid constitutional rule that would prohibit a prosecutor from acting forthrightly in his dealings with the defense could only invite unhealthy subterfuge that would drive the practice of plea bargaining back into the shadows from which it has so recently emerged. See *Blackledge v. Allison*, 431 U.S., at 76, 97 S.Ct., at 1630.

There is no doubt that the breadth of discretion that our country's legal system vests in prosecuting attorneys carries with it the potential for both individual and institutional abuse.[9] And broad though that discretion may be, there are undoubtedly constitutional limits upon its exercise. We hold only that the course of conduct engaged in by the prosecutor in this case, which no more than openly presented the defendant with the unpleasant alternatives of forgoing trial or facing charges on which he was plainly subject to prosecution, did not violate the Due Process Clause of the Fourteenth Amendment.

Accordingly, the judgment of the Court of Appeals is *Reversed*.

■ Mr. Justice Blackmun, with whom Mr. Justice Brennan and Mr. Justice Marshall join, dissenting.

. . . . The Court now says, however, that this concern with vindictiveness is of no import in the present case, despite the difference between five years in prison and a life sentence, because we are here concerned with plea bargaining where there is give-and-take negotiation, and where, it is said, "there is no such element of punishment or retaliation so long as the accused is free to accept or reject the prosecution's offer." Yet in this case vindictiveness is present to the same extent as it was thought to be in *Pearce* and in *Perry*; the prosecutor here admitted that the sole reason for the new indictment was to discourage the respondent from exercising his right to a trial. Even had such an admission not been made, when plea negotiations, conducted in the face of the less serious charge under the first

---

8. This case does not involve the constitutional implications of a prosecutor's offer during plea bargaining of adverse or lenient treatment for some person *other* than the accused, see ALI Model Code of Pre–Arraignment Procedure, Commentary to § 350.3, pp. 614–615 (1975), which might pose a greater danger of inducing a false guilty plea by skewing the assessment of the risks a defendant must consider. Cf. *Brady v. United States*, 397 U.S. 742, 758, 90 S.Ct. 1463, 1474, 25 L.Ed.2d 747.

9. This potential has led to many recommendations that the prosecutor's discretion should be controlled by means of either internal or external guidelines. See ALI Model Code of Pre–Arraignment Procedure for Criminal Justice §§ 350.3(2)-(3) (1975); ABA Project on Standards for Criminal Justice, The Prosecution Function §§ 2.5, 3.9 (App. Draft 1971); Abrahms, Internal Policy: Guiding the Exercise of Prosecutorial Discretion, 19 UCLA L.Rev. 1 (1971).

indictment, fail, charging by a second indictment a more serious crime for the same conduct creates "a strong inference" of vindictiveness. As then Judge McCree aptly observed, in writing for a unanimous panel of the Sixth Circuit, the prosecutor initially "makes a discretionary determination that the interests of the state are served by not seeking more serious charges." *Hayes v. Cowan*, 547 F.2d 42, 44 (1976). I therefore do not understand why, as in *Pearce*, due process does not require that the prosecution justify its action on some basis other than discouraging respondent from the exercise of his right to a trial.

Prosecutorial vindictiveness, it seems to me, in the present narrow context, is the fact against which the Due Process Clause ought to protect. I perceive little difference between vindictiveness after what the Court describes, *ante*, at 667, as the exercise of a "legal right to attack his original conviction," and vindictiveness in the " 'give-and-take negotiation common in plea bargaining.' " Prosecutorial vindictiveness in any context is still prosecutorial vindictiveness. The Due Process Clause should protect an accused against it, however it asserts itself. The Court of Appeals rightly so held, and I would affirm the judgment.

It might be argued that it really makes little difference how this case, now that it is here, is decided. The Court's holding gives plea bargaining full sway despite vindictiveness. A contrary result, however, merely would prompt the aggressive prosecutor to bring the greater charge initially in every case, and only thereafter to bargain. The consequences to the accused would still be adverse, for then he would bargain against a greater charge, face the likelihood of increased bail, and run the risk that the court would be less inclined to accept a bargained plea. Nonetheless, it is far preferable to hold the prosecution to the charge it was originally content to bring and to justify in the eyes of its public.[2]

Even if overcharging is to be sanctioned, there are strong reasons of fairness why the charges should be presented at the beginning of the bargaining process, rather than as a filliped threat at the end. First, it means that a prosecutor is required to reach a charging decision without any knowledge of the particular defendant's willingness to plead guilty; hence the defendant who truly believes himself to be innocent, and wishes for that reason to go to trial, is not likely to be subject to quite such a devastating gamble since the prosecutor has fixed the incentives for the average case.

Second, it is healthful to keep charging practices visible to the general public, so that political bodies can judge whether the policy being followed is a fair one. Visibility is enhanced if the prosecutor is required to lay his

---

2. That prosecutors, without saying so, may sometimes bring charges more serious than they think appropriate for the ultimate disposition of a case, in order to gain bargaining leverage with a defendant, does not add support to today's decision, for this Court, in its approval of the advantages to be gained from plea negotiations, has never openly sanctioned such deliberate overcharging or taken such a cynical view of the bargaining process. See *North Carolina v. Alford*, 400 U.S. 25, 91 S.Ct. 160, 27 L.Ed.2d 162 (1970); *Santobello v. New York*, 404 U.S. 257, 92 S.Ct. 495, 30 L.Ed.2d 427 (1971). Normally, of course, it is impossible to show that this is what the prosecutor is doing, and the courts necessarily have deferred to the prosecutor's exercise of discretion in initial charging decisions.

cards on the table with an indictment of public record at the beginning of the bargaining process, rather than making use of unrecorded verbal warnings of more serious indictments yet to come. . . .

■ MR. JUSTICE POWELL, dissenting.

The prosecutor's initial assessment of respondent's case led him to forgo an indictment under the habitual criminal statute. The circumstances of respondent's prior convictions are relevant to this assessment and to my view of the case. Respondent was 17 years old when he committed his first offense. He was charged with rape but pleaded guilty to the lesser included offense of "detaining a female." One of the other participants in the incident was sentenced to life imprisonment. Respondent was sent not to prison but to a reformatory where he served five years. Respondent's second offense was robbery. This time he was found guilty by a jury and was sentenced to five years in prison, but he was placed on probation and served no time. Although respondent's prior convictions brought him within the terms of the Habitual Criminal Act, the offenses themselves did not result in imprisonment; yet the addition of a conviction on a charge involving $88.30 subjected respondent to a mandatory sentence of imprisonment for life.[1] Persons convicted of rape and murder often are not punished so severely . . .

It seems to me that the question to be asked under the circumstances is whether the prosecutor reasonably might have charged respondent under the Habitual Criminal Act in the first place. The deference that courts properly accord the exercise of a prosecutor's discretion perhaps would foreclose judicial criticism if the prosecutor originally had sought an indictment under that Act, as unreasonable as it would have seemed.[2] But here the prosecutor evidently made a reasonable, responsible judgment not to subject an individual to a mandatory life sentence when his only new offense had societal implications as limited as those accompanying the uttering of a single $88 forged check and when the circumstances of his prior convictions confirmed the inappropriateness of applying the habitual criminal statute.[3] I think it may be inferred that the prosecutor himself

1. It is suggested that respondent will be eligible for parole consideration after serving 15 years.

2. The majority suggests, *ante*, that this case cannot be distinguished from the case where the prosecutor initially obtains an indictment under an enhancement statute and later agrees to drop the enhancement charge in exchange for a guilty plea. I would agree that these two situations would be alike *only if* it were assumed that the hypothetical prosecutor's decision to charge under the enhancement statute was occasioned not by consideration of the public interest but by a strategy to discourage the defendant from exercising his constitutional rights. In theory, I would condemn both practices. In practice, the hypothetical situation is largely unreviewable. The majority's view confuses the propriety of a particular exercise of prosecutorial discretion with its unreviewability. In the instant case, however, we have no problem of proof. . . .

3. Indeed, the Kentucky Legislature subsequently determined that the habitual criminal statute under which respondent was convicted swept too broadly and did not identify adequately the kind of prior convictions that should trigger its application. At least one of respondent's two prior convictions would not satisfy the criteria of the revised statute; and the impact of the statute, when applied, has been reduced significantly in situations, like this one, where the third offense is relatively minor.

deemed it unreasonable and not in the public interest to put this defendant in jeopardy of a sentence of life imprisonment.

The plea-bargaining process, as recognized by this Court, is essential to the functioning of the criminal-justice system. It normally affords genuine benefits to defendants as well as to society. And if the system is to work effectively, prosecutors must be accorded the widest discretion, within constitutional limits, in conducting bargaining. Cf. n. 2, *supra*. This is especially true when a defendant is represented by counsel and presumably is fully advised of his rights. Only in the most exceptional case should a court conclude that the scales of the bargaining are so unevenly balanced as to arouse suspicion. In this case, the prosecutor's actions denied respondent due process because their admitted purpose was to discourage and then to penalize with unique severity his exercise of constitutional rights. Implementation of a strategy calculated solely to deter the exercise of constitutional rights is not a constitutionally permissible exercise of discretion. I would affirm the opinion of the Court of Appeals on the facts of this case.

SECTION 6. CAPITAL SENTENCING

Kansas v. Marsh

Supreme Court of the United States, 2006.
548 U.S. 163, 126 S.Ct. 2516, 165 L.Ed.2d 429.

■ JUSTICE THOMAS delivered the opinion of the Court.

Kansas law provides that if a unanimous jury finds that aggravating circumstances are not outweighed by mitigating circumstances, the death penalty shall be imposed. Kan. Stat. Ann. § 21–4624(e) (1995). We must decide whether this statute, which requires the imposition of the death penalty when the sentencing jury determines that aggravating evidence and mitigating evidence are in equipoise, violates the Constitution. We hold that it does not.

I

Respondent Michael Lee Marsh II broke into the home of Marry Ane Pusch and lay in wait for her to return. When Marry Ane entered her home with her 19–month–old daughter, M.P., Marsh repeatedly shot Marry Ane, stabbed her, and slashed her throat. The home was set on fire with the toddler inside, and M.P. burned to death.

The jury convicted Marsh of the capital murder of M.P., the first-degree premeditated murder of Marry Ane, aggravated arson, and aggravated burglary. The jury found beyond a reasonable doubt the existence of three aggravating circumstances, and that those circumstances were not outweighed by any mitigating circumstances. On the basis of those findings, the jury sentenced Marsh to death for the capital murder of M.P. The jury also sentenced Marsh to life imprisonment without possibility of parole for 40 years for the first-degree murder of Marry Ane, and consecutive sentences of 51 months' imprisonment for aggravated arson and 34 months' imprisonment for aggravated burglary.

On direct appeal, Marsh challenged § 21–4624(e), which reads:

"If, by unanimous vote, the jury finds beyond a reasonable doubt that one or more of the aggravating circumstances enumerated in K.S.A. 21–4625 ... exist and, further, that the existence of such aggravating circumstances is not outweighed by any mitigating circumstances which are found to exist, the defendant shall be sentenced to death; otherwise the defendant shall be sentenced as provided by law." Focusing on the phrase "shall be sentenced to death," Marsh argued that § 21–4624(e) establishes an unconstitutional presumption in favor of death because it directs imposition of the death penalty when aggravating and mitigating circumstances are in equipoise.

The Kansas Supreme Court agreed, and held that the Kansas death penalty statute, § 21–4624(e), is facially unconstitutional. 278 Kan. 520, 534–535, 102 P.3d 445, 458 (2004). The court concluded that the statute's weighing equation violated the Eighth and Fourteenth Amendments of the United States Constitution because, "[i]n the event of equipoise, *i.e.*, the jury's determination that the balance of any aggravating circumstances and any mitigating circumstances weighed equal, the death penalty would be required." *Id.*, at 534, 102 P.3d, at 457. The Kansas Supreme Court affirmed Marsh's conviction and sentence for aggravated burglary and premeditated murder of Marry Ane, and reversed and remanded for new trial Marsh's convictions for capital murder of M.P. and aggravated arson.[1] We granted certiorari, 544 U.S. 1060, 125 S.Ct. 2517, 161 L.Ed.2d 1109 (2005), and now reverse the Kansas Supreme Court's judgment that Kansas' capital sentencing statute, Kan. Stat. Ann. § 21–4624(e), is facially unconstitutional.

II

In addition to granting certiorari to review the constitutionality of Kansas' capital sentencing statute, we also directed the parties to brief and argue: (1) whether we have jurisdiction to review the judgment of the Kansas Supreme Court under 28 U.S.C. § 1257, as construed by *Cox Broadcasting Corp. v. Cohn*, 420 U.S. 469, 95 S.Ct. 1029, 43 L.Ed.2d 328 (1975); and (2) whether the Kansas Supreme Court's judgment is supported by adequate state grounds independent of federal law. 544 U.S. 1060, 125 S.Ct. 2517, 161 L.Ed.2d 1109. Having considered the parties' arguments, we conclude that we have jurisdiction in this case and that the constitutional issue is properly before the Court....

III

This case is controlled by *Walton v. Arizona*, 497 U.S. 639, 110 S.Ct. 3047, 111 L.Ed.2d 511 (1990), overruled on other grounds, *Ring v. Arizona*, 536 U.S. 584, 122 S.Ct. 2428, 153 L.Ed.2d 556 (2002). In that case, a jury had convicted Walton of a capital offense. At sentencing, the trial judge found the existence of two aggravating circumstances and that the mitigat-

---

1. The Kansas Supreme Court found that the trial court committed reversible error by excluding circumstantial evidence of third-party guilt connecting Eric Pusch, Marry Ane's husband, to the crimes, and, accordingly, ordered a new trial on this ground. 278 Kan., at 528–533, 102 P.3d, at 454–457.

ing circumstances did not call for leniency, and sentenced Walton to death. 497 U.S., at 645, 110 S.Ct. 3047. The Arizona Supreme Court affirmed, and this Court granted certiorari to resolve the conflict between the Arizona Supreme Court's decision in *State v. Walton,* 159 Ariz. 571, 769 P.2d 1017 (1989) (en banc) (holding the Arizona death penalty statute constitutional), and the Ninth Circuit's decision in *Adamson v. Ricketts,* 865 F.2d 1011, 1043–1044 (1988) (en banc) (finding the Arizona death penalty statute unconstitutional because, "in situations where the mitigating and aggravating circumstances are in balance, or, where the mitigating circumstances give the court reservation but still fall below the weight of the aggravating circumstances, the statute bars the court from imposing a sentence less than death"). See *Walton,* 497 U.S., at 647, 110 S.Ct. 3047. Consistent with the Ninth Circuit's conclusion in *Adamson,* Walton argued to this Court that the Arizona capital sentencing system created an unconstitutional presumption in favor of death because it "tells an Arizona sentencing judge who finds even a single aggravating factor, that death must be imposed, unless—as the Arizona Supreme Court put it in Petitioner's case—there are 'outweighing mitigating factors.'" Brief for Petitioner in *Walton v. Arizona,* O.T.1989, No. 88–7351, p. 33; see also *id.,* at 34 (arguing that the statute is unconstitutional because the defendant " 'must ... bear the risk of nonpersuasion that any mitigating circumstance will not outweigh the aggravating circumstance' " (alteration omitted)).

Rejecting Walton's argument, see 497 U.S., at 650, 651, 110 S.Ct. 3047, this Court stated: "So long as a State's method of allocating the burdens of proof does not lessen the State's burden to prove every element of the offense charged, or in this case to prove the existence of aggravating circumstances, a defendant's constitutional rights are not violated by placing on him the burden of proving mitigating circumstances sufficiently substantial to call for leniency." *Id.,* at 650, 110 S.Ct. 3047.

This Court noted that, as a requirement of individualized sentencing, a jury must have the opportunity to consider all evidence relevant to mitigation, and that a state statute that permits a jury to consider any mitigating evidence comports with that requirement. *Id.,* at 652, 110 S.Ct. 3047 (citing *Blystone v. Pennsylvania,* 494 U.S. 299, 307, 110 S.Ct. 1078, 108 L.Ed.2d 255 (1990)). The Court also pointedly observed that while the Constitution requires that a sentencing jury have discretion, it does not mandate that discretion be unfettered; the States are free to determine the manner in which a jury may consider mitigating evidence. 497 U.S., at 652, 110 S.Ct. 3047 (citing *Boyde v. California,* 494 U.S. 370, 374, 110 S.Ct. 1190, 108 L.Ed.2d 316 (1990)). So long as the sentencer is not precluded from considering relevant mitigating evidence, a capital sentencing statute cannot be said to impermissibly, much less automatically, impose death. 497 U.S., at 652, 110 S.Ct. 3047 (citing *Woodson v. North Carolina,* 428 U.S. 280, 96 S.Ct. 2978, 49 L.Ed.2d 944 (1976) (plurality opinion), and *Roberts v. Louisiana,* 428 U.S. 325, 96 S.Ct. 3001, 49 L.Ed.2d 974 (1976) (plurality opinion)). Indeed, *Walton* suggested that the only capital sentencing systems that would be impermissibly mandatory were those that would "automatically impose death upon conviction for certain types of murder." 497 U.S., at 652, 110 S.Ct. 3047.

Contrary to Marsh's contentions and the Kansas Supreme Court's conclusions, see 278 Kan., at 536–538, 102 P.3d, at 459, the question presented in the instant case was squarely before this Court in *Walton*. Though, as Marsh notes, the *Walton* Court did not employ the term "equipoise," that issue undeniably gave rise to the question this Court sought to resolve, and it was necessarily included in Walton's argument that the Arizona system was unconstitutional because it required the death penalty unless the mitigating circumstances *outweighed* the aggravating circumstances. See *supra,* at 2522. Moreover, the dissent in *Walton* reinforces what is evident from the opinion and the judgment of the Court— that the equipoise issue was before the Court, and that the Court resolved the issue in favor of the State. Indeed, the "equipoise" issue was, in large measure, the basis of the *Walton* dissent. See 497 U.S., at 687–688, 110 S.Ct. 3047 (opinion of Blackmun, J.) ("If the mitigating and aggravating circumstances are in equipoise, the [Arizona] statute requires that the trial judge impose capital punishment. The assertion that a sentence of death may be imposed in such a case runs directly counter to the Eighth Amendment requirement that a capital sentence must rest upon a 'determination that death is the appropriate punishment in a specific case'"). Thus, although *Walton* did not discuss the equipoise issue explicitly, that issue was resolved by its holding. Cf. *post,* at 2539 (STEVENS, J., dissenting); cf. also *post,* at 2541, n. 1 (SOUTER, J., dissenting). Our conclusion that *Walton* controls here is reinforced by the fact that the Arizona and Kansas statutes are comparable in important respects. Similar to the express language of the Kansas statute, the Arizona statute at issue in *Walton* has been consistently construed to mean that the death penalty will be imposed upon a finding that aggravating circumstances are not outweighed by mitigating circumstances.[2] See *State v. Ysea,* 191 Ariz. 372, 375, 956 P.2d 499, 502 (1998) (en banc); *State v. Gretzler,* 135 Ariz. 42, 55, 659 P.2d 1, 14 (1983) (in banc); *Adamson,* 865 F.2d, at 1041–1043. Like the Kansas statute, the Arizona statute places the burden of proving the existence of aggravating circumstances on the State, and both statutes require the defendant to proffer mitigating evidence.

The statutes are distinct in one respect. The Arizona statute, once the State has met its burden, tasks the defendant with the burden of proving sufficient mitigating circumstances to overcome the aggravating circumstances and that a sentence less than death is therefore warranted. In contrast, the Kansas statute requires the State to bear the burden of proving to the jury, beyond a reasonable doubt, that aggravators are not outweighed by mitigators and that a sentence of death is therefore appropriate; it places no additional evidentiary burden on the capital defendant. This distinction operates in favor of Kansas capital defendants. Otherwise the statutes function in substantially the same manner and are sufficiently

---

2. Ariz.Rev.Stat. Ann. § 13–703(E) (Supp.2005) provides:

"In determining whether to impose a sentence of death or life imprisonment, the trier of fact shall take into account the aggravating and mitigating circumstances that have been proven. The trier of fact shall impose a sentence of death if the trier of fact finds one or more of the aggravating circumstances enumerated in subsection F of this section and then determines that there are no mitigating circumstances sufficiently substantial to call for leniency."

analogous for our purposes. Thus, *Walton* is not distinguishable from the instant case.

Accordingly, the reasoning of *Walton* requires approval of the Kansas death penalty statute. At bottom, in *Walton,* the Court held that a state death penalty statute may place the burden on the defendant to prove that mitigating circumstances outweigh aggravating circumstances. *A fortiori,* Kansas' death penalty statute, consistent with the Constitution, may direct imposition of the death penalty when the State has proved beyond a reasonable doubt that mitigators do not outweigh aggravators, including where the aggravating circumstances and mitigating circumstances are in equipoise.

IV

A

Even if, as Marsh contends, *Walton* does not directly control, the general principles set forth in our death penalty jurisprudence would lead us to conclude that the Kansas capital sentencing system is constitutionally permissible. Together, our decisions in *Furman v. Georgia,* 408 U.S. 238, 92 S.Ct. 2726, 33 L.Ed.2d 346 (1972) *(per curiam),* and *Gregg v. Georgia,* 428 U.S. 153, 96 S.Ct. 2909, 49 L.Ed.2d 859 (1976) (joint opinion of Stewart, Powell, and Stevens, JJ.), establish that a state capital sentencing system must: (1) rationally narrow the class of death-eligible defendants; and (2) permit a jury to render a reasoned, individualized sentencing determination based on a death-eligible defendant's record, personal characteristics, and the circumstances of his crime. See *id.,* at 189, 96 S.Ct. 2909. So long as a state system satisfies these requirements, our precedents establish that a State enjoys a range of discretion in imposing the death penalty, including the manner in which aggravating and mitigating circumstances are to be weighed. See *Franklin v. Lynaugh,* 487 U.S. 164, 179, 108 S.Ct. 2320, 101 L.Ed.2d 155 (1988) (plurality opinion) (citing *Zant v. Stephens,* 462 U.S. 862, 875–876, n. 13, 103 S.Ct. 2733, 77 L.Ed.2d 235 (1983)).

The use of mitigation evidence is a product of the requirement of individualized sentencing. See *Graham v. Collins,* 506 U.S. 461, 484–489, 113 S.Ct. 892, 122 L.Ed.2d 260 (1993) (THOMAS, J., concurring) (discussing the development of mitigation precedent). In *Lockett v. Ohio,* 438 U.S. 586, 604, 98 S.Ct. 2954, 57 L.Ed.2d 973 (1978), a plurality of this Court held that "the Eighth and Fourteenth Amendments require that the sentencer . . . not be precluded from considering, *as a mitigating factor,* any aspect of a defendant's character or record and any of the circumstances of the offense that the defendant proffers as a basis for a sentence less than death." (Emphasis in original.) The Court has held that the sentencer must have full access to this " 'highly relevant' " information. *Id.,* at 603, 98 S.Ct. 2954 (alteration omitted) (quoting *Williams v. New York,* 337 U.S. 241, 247, 69 S.Ct. 1079, 93 L.Ed. 1337 (1949)). Thus, in *Lockett,* the Court struck down the Ohio death penalty statute as unconstitutional because, by limiting a jury's consideration of mitigation to three factors specified in the statute, it prevented sentencers in capital cases from giving independent weight to mitigating evidence militating in favor of a sentence other than death. 438 U.S., at 604–605, 98 S.Ct. 2954. Following *Lockett,* in *Eddings v.*

Oklahoma, 455 U.S. 104, 102 S.Ct. 869, 71 L.Ed.2d 1 (1982), a majority of the Court held that a sentencer may not categorically refuse to consider any relevant mitigating evidence. *Id.,* at 114, 102 S.Ct. 869; see also *Skipper v. South Carolina,* 476 U.S. 1, 3–4, 106 S.Ct. 1669, 90 L.Ed.2d 1 (1986) (discussing *Eddings*).

In aggregate, our precedents confer upon defendants the right to present sentencers with information relevant to the sentencing decision and oblige sentencers to consider that information in determining the appropriate sentence. The thrust of our mitigation jurisprudence ends here. "[W]e have never held that a specific method for balancing mitigating and aggravating factors in a capital sentencing proceeding is constitutionally required." *Franklin, supra,* at 179, 108 S.Ct. 2320 (citing *Zant, supra,* at 875–876, n. 13, 103 S.Ct. 2733). Rather, this Court has held that the States enjoy " 'a constitutionally permissible range of discretion in imposing the death penalty.' " *Blystone,* 494 U.S., at 308, 110 S.Ct. 1078 (quoting *McCleskey v. Kemp,* 481 U.S. 279, 305–306, 107 S.Ct. 1756, 95 L.Ed.2d 262 (1987)). See also 494 U.S., at 307, 110 S.Ct. 1078 (stating that "[t]he requirement of individualized sentencing in capital cases is satisfied by allowing the jury to consider all relevant mitigating evidence"); *Graham, supra,* at 490, 113 S.Ct. 892 (Thomas, J., concurring) (stating that "[o]ur early mitigating cases may thus be read as doing little more than safeguarding the adversary process in sentencing proceedings by conferring on the defendant an affirmative right to place his relevant evidence before the sentencer").

B

The Kansas death penalty statute satisfies the constitutional mandates of *Furman* and its progeny because it rationally narrows the class of death-eligible defendants and permits a jury to consider any mitigating evidence relevant to its sentencing determination. It does not interfere, in a constitutionally significant way, with a jury's ability to give independent weight to evidence offered in mitigation.

Kansas' procedure narrows the universe of death-eligible defendants consistent with Eighth Amendment requirements. Under Kansas law, imposition of the death penalty is an *option* only after a defendant is convicted of capital murder, which requires that one or more specific elements beyond intentional premeditated murder be found. See Kan. Stat. Ann. § 21–3439. Once convicted of capital murder, a defendant becomes *eligible* for the death penalty only if the State seeks a separate sentencing hearing, §§ 21–4706(c) (2003 Cum.Supp.), 21–4624(a); App. 23 (Instruction No. 2), and proves beyond a reasonable doubt the existence of one or more statutorily enumerated aggravating circumstances. Kan. Stat. Ann. §§ 21–4624(c), (e), and 21–4625; App. 24 (Instruction No. 3).

Consonant with the individualized sentencing requirement, a Kansas jury is permitted to consider *any* evidence relating to *any* mitigating circumstance in determining the appropriate sentence for a capital defendant, so long as that evidence is relevant. § 21–4624(c). Specifically, jurors are instructed: "A mitigating circumstance is that which in fairness or mercy may be considered as extenuating or reducing the degree of moral culpability or blame or which justify a sentence of less than death, although it does not justify or excuse the offense. The determination of what are mitigating circumstances is for you as jurors to resolve under the facts and circumstances of this case." The appropriateness of the exercise of mercy can itself be a mitigating factor you may consider in determining whether the State has proved beyond a reasonable doubt that the death penalty is warranted. *Id.,* at 24 (Instruction No. 4).[3]

Jurors are then apprised of, but not limited to, the factors that the defendant contends are mitigating. *Id.,* at 25–26. They are then instructed that "[e]ach juror must consider every mitigating factor that he or she individually finds to exist." *Id.,* at 26.

Kansas' weighing equation, *ibid.* (Instruction No. 5), merely channels a jury's discretion by providing it with criteria by which it may determine whether a sentence of life or death is appropriate. The system in Kansas provides the type of " 'guided discretion,' " *Walton,* 497 U.S., at 659, 110 S.Ct. 3047 (citing *Gregg,* 428 U.S., at 189, 96 S.Ct. 2909), we have sanctioned in *Walton, Boyde,* and *Blystone.*

Indeed, in *Boyde,* this Court sanctioned a weighing jury instruction that is analytically indistinguishable from the Kansas jury instruction under review today. The *Boyde* jury instruction read:

> " 'If you conclude that the aggravating circumstances outweigh the mitigating circumstances, you *shall impose* a sentence of death. However, if you determine that the mitigating circumstances outweigh the aggravating circumstances, you *shall impose* a sentence of confinement in the state prison for life without the possibility of parole.' " 494 U.S., at 374, 110 S.Ct. 1190 (emphasis in original). Boyde argued that the mandatory language of the instruction prevented the jury from rendering an individualized sentencing determination. This Court rejected that argument, concluding that it was foreclosed by *Blystone,* where the Court rejected a nearly identical challenge to the Pennsylvania death penalty statute. 494 U.S., at 307, 110 S.Ct. 1078.[4] In so holding, this Court noted that the mandatory language of the statute did not prevent the jury from *considering* all relevant mitigating evidence. *Boyde,* 494 U.S., at 374, 110 S.Ct. 1190. Similarly here, § 21–4624(e) does not prevent a Kansas jury from considering mitigating evidence. Marsh's argument that the Kansas provision is impermissibly mandatory is likewise foreclosed.[5]

---

3. The "mercy" jury instruction alone forecloses the possibility of *Furman*-type error as it "eliminate[s] the risk that a death sentence will be imposed in spite of facts calling for a lesser penalty." *Post,* at 2543 (Souter, J., dissenting).

4. In *Blystone,* the Pennsylvania statute authorized imposition of a death sentence if the jury concluded "that the aggravating circumstances outweigh[ed] the mitigating circumstances present in the particular crime committed by the particular defendant, or that there [were] no such mitigating circumstances." 494 U.S., at 305, 110 S.Ct. 1078.

5. Contrary to Justice Souter's assertion, the Court's decisions in *Boyde* and *Blystone* did not turn on the "predominance of the aggravators" in those cases. *Post,* at 2542 (dissenting opinion). Rather, those decisions plainly turned on the fact that the mandatory language of the respective statutes did not prevent the sentencing jury from "consider[ing] and giv[ing] effect to all relevant mitigating evidence." *Blystone, supra,* at 305, 110 S.Ct. 1078. See also *Boyde,*

Contrary to Marsh's argument, § 21–4624(e) does not create a general presumption in favor of the death penalty in the State of Kansas. Rather, the Kansas capital sentencing system is dominated by the presumption that life imprisonment is the appropriate sentence for a capital conviction. If the State fails to meet its burden to demonstrate the existence of an aggravating circumstance(s) beyond a reasonable doubt, a sentence of life imprisonment must be imposed. § 21–4624(e); App. 27 (Instruction No. 10). If the State overcomes this hurdle, then it bears the additional burden of proving beyond a reasonable doubt that aggravating circumstances are not outweighed by mitigating circumstances. *Ibid.* (Instruction No. 10); *id.*, at 26 (Instruction No. 5). Significantly, although the defendant appropriately bears the burden of proffering mitigating circumstances—a burden of production—he never bears the burden of demonstrating that mitigating circumstances outweigh aggravating circumstances. Instead, the State always has the burden of demonstrating that mitigating evidence does not outweigh aggravating evidence. Absent the State's ability to meet that burden, the default is life imprisonment. Moreover, if the jury is unable to reach a unanimous decision—in any respect—a sentence of life must be imposed. § 21–4624(c); App. 28 (Instruction No. 12). This system does not create a presumption that death is the appropriate sentence for capital murder.[6] Nor is there any force behind Marsh's contention that an equipoise determination reflects juror confusion or inability to decide between life and death, or that a jury may use equipoise as a loophole to shirk its constitutional duty to render a reasoned, moral decision, see *California v. Brown*, 479 U.S. 538, 545, 107 S.Ct. 837, 93 L.Ed.2d 934 (1987) (O'Connor, J., concurring), regarding whether death is an appropriate sentence for a particular defendant. Such an argument rests on an implausible characterization of the Kansas statute—that a jury's determination that aggravators and mitigators are in equipoise is not a *decision*, much less a decision *for death*—and thus misses the mark. Cf. *post*, at 2543—2544 (Souter, J., dissenting) (arguing that Kansas' weighing equation undermines individualized sentencing). Weighing is not an end; it is merely a means to reaching a decision. The decision the jury must reach is whether life or death is the appropriate punishment. The Kansas jury instructions clearly inform the

---

494 U.S., at 377, 110 S.Ct. 1190 ("[T]he legal principle we expounded in *Blystone* clearly requires rejection of Boyde's claim as well, because the mandatory language of [California jury instruction] 8.84.2 is not alleged to have interfered with the consideration of mitigating evidence"). The language of the Kansas statute at issue here no more "dictate[s] death," *post*, at 2542, than the mandatory language at issue in *Boyde* and *Blystone*. See *Blystone, supra*, at 305, 110 S.Ct. 1078 (explaining that the Pennsylvania statute is not " 'mandatory' as that term was understood in *Woodson* [*v. North Carolina*, 428 U.S. 280, 96 S.Ct. 2978, 49 L.Ed.2d 944 (1976)] or *Roberts* [*v. Louisiana*, 428 U.S. 325, 96 S.Ct. 3001, 49 L.Ed.2d 974 (1976)]" because "[d]eath is not automatically imposed upon conviction for certain types of murder").

6. Additionally, Marsh's argument turns on reading § 21–4624(e) in isolation. Such a reading, however, is contrary to " 'the well-established proposition that a single instruction to a jury may not be judged in artificial isolation, but must be viewed in the context of the overall charge.' " *Boyde v. California*, 494 U.S. 370, 378, 110 S.Ct. 1190, 108 L.Ed.2d 316 (1990) (citing *Boyd v. United States*, 271 U.S. 104, 107, 46 S.Ct. 442, 70 L.Ed. 857 (1926)). The constitutionality of a State's death penalty system turns on review of that system in context. We thus reject his disengaged interpretation of § 21–4624(e).

jury that a determination that the evidence is in equipoise is a decision for—not a presumption in favor of—death. Kansas jurors, presumed to follow their instructions, are made aware that: a determination that mitigators outweigh aggravators is a decision that a life sentence is appropriate; a determination that aggravators outweigh mitigators *or* a determination that mitigators do not outweigh aggravators—including a finding that aggravators and mitigators are in balance—is a decision that death is the appropriate sentence; and an inability to reach a unanimous decision will result in a sentence of life imprisonment. So informed, far from the abdication of duty or the inability to select an appropriate sentence depicted by Marsh and Justice Souter, a jury's conclusion that aggravating evidence and mitigating evidence are in equipoise is a *decision for death* and is indicative of the type of measured, normative process in which a jury is constitutionally tasked to engage when deciding the appropriate sentence for a capital defendant.

V

Justice Souter argues (hereinafter the dissent) that the advent of DNA testing has resulted in the "exoneratio[n]" of "innocent" persons "in numbers never imagined before the development of DNA tests." *Post,* at 2543–2544. Based upon this "new empirical demonstration of how 'death is different,'" *post,* at 2545, the dissent concludes that Kansas' sentencing system permits the imposition of the death penalty in the absence of reasoned moral judgment.

But the availability of DNA testing, and the questions it might raise about the accuracy of guilt-phase determinations in capital cases, is simply irrelevant to the question before the Court today, namely, the constitutionality of Kansas' capital *sentencing* system. Accordingly, the accuracy of the dissent's factual claim that DNA testing has established the "innocence" of numerous convicted persons under death sentences—and the incendiary debate it invokes—is beyond the scope of this opinion.[7]

The dissent's general criticisms against the death penalty are ultimately a call for resolving all legal disputes in capital cases by adopting the outcome that makes the death penalty more difficult to impose. While such a bright-line rule may be easily applied, it has no basis in law. Indeed, the logical consequence of the dissent's argument is that the death penalty can only be just in a system that does not permit error. Because the criminal justice system does not operate perfectly, abolition of the death penalty is the only answer to the moral dilemma the dissent poses. This Court,

---

7. But see The Penalty of Death, in Debating the Death Penalty: Should America Have Capital Punishment? The Experts on Both Sides Make Their Best Case, 117, 127–132, 134, (H. Bedau & P. Cassell eds. 2004). See also Comment, Protecting the Innocent: A Response to the Bedau–Radelet Study, 41 Stan. L.Rev. 121, 126–145 (1988) (examining accuracy in use of the term "innocent" in death penalty studies and literature); Marquis, The Myth of Innocence, 95 J.Crim. L. & C. 501, 508 (2005) ("[w]ords like 'innocence' convey enormous moral authority and are intended to drive the public debate by appealing to a deep and universal revulsion at the idea that someone who is genuinely blameless could wrongly suffer for a crime in which he had no involvement"); *People v. Smith,* 185 Ill.2d 532, 545, 236 Ill.Dec. 779, 708 N.E.2d 365, 371 (1999) ("[w]hile a not guilty finding is sometimes equated with a finding of innocence, that conclusion is erroneous. . . . Rather, [a reversal of conviction] indicates simply that the prosecution has failed to meet its burden of proof").

however, does not sit as a moral authority. Our precedents do not prohibit the States from authorizing the death penalty, even in our imperfect system. And those precedents do not empower this Court to chip away at the States' prerogatives to do so on the grounds the dissent invokes today.

* * *

We hold that the Kansas capital sentencing system, which directs imposition of the death penalty when a jury finds that aggravating and mitigating circumstances are in equipoise, is constitutional. Accordingly, we reverse the judgment of the Kansas Supreme Court, and remand the case for further proceedings not inconsistent with this opinion. *It is so ordered.*

■ JUSTICE SCALIA, concurring.

III

Finally, I must say a few words (indeed, more than a few) in response to Part III of Justice Souter's dissent. This contains the disclaimer that the dissenters are not (*yet*) ready to "generaliz[e] about the soundness of capital sentencing across the country," *post*, at 2545; but that is in fact precisely what they do. The dissent essentially argues that capital punishment is such an undesirable institution—it results in the condemnation of such a large number of innocents—that any legal rule which eliminates its pronouncement, including the one favored by the dissenters in the present case, should be embraced. See *ibid.*

As a general rule, I do not think it appropriate for judges to heap either praise or censure upon a legislative measure that comes before them, lest it be thought that their validation, invalidation, or interpretation of it is driven by their desire to expand or constrict what they personally approve or disapprove as a matter of policy. In the present case, for example, people might leap to the conclusion that the dissenters' views on whether Kansas's equipoise rule is constitutional are determined by their personal disapproval of an institution that has been democratically adopted by 38 States and the United States. But of course that requires no leap; just a willingness to take the dissenters at their word. For as I have described, the dissenters' very argument is that imposition of the death penalty should be minimized by invalidation of the equipoise rule because it is a bad, "risk[y]," and "hazard[ous]" idea, *ibid.* A broader conclusion that people should derive, however (and I would not consider this much of a leap either), is that the dissenters' encumbering of the death penalty in *other* cases, with unwarranted restrictions neither contained in the text of the Constitution nor reflected in two centuries of practice under it, will be the product of their policy views—views not shared by the vast majority of the American people. The dissenters' proclamation of their policy agenda in the present case is especially striking because it is nailed to the door of the wrong church—that is, set forth in a case litigating a rule that has nothing to do with the evaluation of guilt or innocence. There are, of course, many cases in which the rule at issue *does* serve that function, see, *e.g., House v. Bell,* 547 U.S. 518, 126 S.Ct. 2064, 165 L.Ed.2d 1 (2006). (Marsh himself has earned a remand by application of one such rule, see *ante,* at 2520–2521.) But as the Court observes, see *ante,* at 2528–2529, guilt or innocence is logically disconnected to the challenge in *this* case to *sentencing* standards. The *only* time the equipoise provision is relevant is when the State has proved a defendant guilty of a capital crime.[2]

There exists in some parts of the world sanctimonious criticism of America's death penalty, as somehow unworthy of a civilized society. (I say sanctimonious, because most of the countries to which these finger-waggers belong had the death penalty themselves until recently—and indeed, many of them would still have it if the democratic will prevailed.[3] It is a certainty that the opinion of a near-majority of the United States Supreme Court to the effect that our system condemns many innocent defendants to death will be trumpeted abroad as vindication of these criticisms. For that reason, I take the trouble to point out that the dissenting opinion has nothing substantial to support it.

It should be noted at the outset that the dissent does not discuss a single case—not one—in which it is clear that a person was executed for a crime he did not commit. If such an event had occurred in recent years, we would not have to hunt for it; the innocent's name would be shouted from the rooftops by the abolition lobby. The dissent makes much of the new-found capacity of DNA testing to establish innocence. But in every case of an executed defendant of which I am aware, that technology has *confirmed* guilt.This happened, for instance, only a few months ago in the case of Roger Coleman. Coleman was convicted of the gruesome rape and murder of his sister-in-law, but he persuaded many that he was actually innocent and became the poster-child for the abolitionist lobby. . . . But earlier this year, a DNA test ordered by a later Governor of Virginia proved that Coleman was guilty, see, *e.g.,* Glod & Shear, DNA Tests Confirm Guilt of

---

2. Not only are the dissent's views on the erroneous imposition of the death penalty irrelevant to the present case, but the dissent's proposed holding on the equipoise issue will not necessarily work to defendants' advantage. The equipoise provision of the Kansas statute imposes the death penalty only when the State proves *beyond a reasonable doubt* that mitigating factors do not outweigh the aggravators. See *ante,* at 2520. If we were to disallow Kansas's scheme, the State could, as Marsh freely admits, replace it with a scheme requiring the State to prove *by a mere preponderance of the evidence* that the aggravators outweigh the mitigators. See Tr. of Oral Rearg. 36. I doubt that any defense counsel would accept this trade. The "preponderance" rule, while it sounds better, would almost surely produce more death sentences than an "equipoise beyond a reasonable doubt" requirement.

3. It is commonly recognized that "[m]any European countries . . . abolished the death penalty in spite of public opinion rather than because of it." Bibas, Transparency and Participation in Criminal Procedure, 81 N.Y.U.L.Rev. 911, 931–932 (2006). See also *id.,* at 932, n. 88. Abolishing the death penalty has been made a condition of joining the Council of Europe, which is in turn a condition of obtaining the economic benefits of joining the European Union. See Waters, Mediating Norms and Identity: The Role of Transnational Judicial Dialogue in Creating and Enforcing International Law, 93 Geo. L.J. 487, 525 (2005); Demleitner, Is There a Future for Leniency in the U.S. Criminal Justice System? 103 Mich. L.Rev. 1231, 1256, and n. 88 (2005). The European Union advocates against the death-penalty even *in America;* there is a separate death-penalty page on the website of the Delegation of the European Commission to the U.S.A. See http://www.eurunion.org/legislat/deathpenalty/deathpenhome.htm (as visited June 17, 2006, and available in Clerk of Court's case file). The views of the European Union have been relied upon by Justices of this Court (including all four dissenters today) in narrowing the power of the American people to impose capital punishment. See, *e.g., Atkins v. Virginia,* 536 U.S. 304, 317, n. 21, 122 S.Ct. 2242, 153 L.Ed.2d 335 (2002) (citing, for the views of "the world community," the Brief for the European Union as *Amicus Curiae*).

Man Executed by Va., *supra,* at A1; Dao, *supra,* at A14, even though his defense team had "proved" his innocence and had even identified "the real killer" (with whom they eventually settled a defamation suit). See Frankel, *supra,* at W23. And Coleman's case is not unique. See Truth and Consequences: The Penalty of Death, in Debating the Death Penalty: Should America Have Capital Punishment? The Experts on Both Sides Make Their Best Case, 128–129 (H. Bedau & P. Cassell eds. 2004) (discussing the cases of supposed innocents Rick McGinn and Derek Barnabei, whose guilt was also confirmed by DNA tests).

Instead of identifying and discussing any particular case or cases of mistaken execution, the dissent simply cites a handful of studies that bemoan the alleged prevalence of wrongful death sentences. One study (by Lanier and Acker) is quoted by the dissent as claiming that " 'more than 110' death row prisoners have been released since 1973 upon findings that they were innocent of the crimes charged, and 'hundreds of additional wrongful convictions in potentially capital cases have been documented over the past century.' " *Post,* at 2545 (opinion of Souter, J.). For the first point, Lanier and Acker cite the work of the Death Penalty Information Center (more about that below) and an article in a law review jointly authored by Radelet, Lofquist, and Bedau (two professors of sociology and a professor of philosophy). For the second point, they cite only a 1987 article by Bedau and Radelet. See Miscarriages of Justice in Potentially Capital Cases, 40 Stan. L.Rev. 21. In the very same paragraph which the dissent quotes, Lanier and Acker also refer to that 1987 article as "hav[ing] identified 23 individuals who, in their judgment, were convicted and executed in this country during the 20th century notwithstanding their innocence." Lanier & Acker, Capital Punishment, the Moratorium Movement, and Empirical Questions, 10 Psychology, Public Policy & Law 577, 593 (2004). This 1987 article has been highly influential in the abolitionist world. Hundreds of academic articles, including those relied on by today's dissent, have cited it. It also makes its appearance in judicial decisions— cited recently in a six-judge dissent in *House v. Bell,* 386 F.3d 668, 708 (C.A.6 2004) (en banc) (Merritt, J., dissenting), for the proposition that "the system is allowing some innocent defendants to be executed." The article therefore warrants some further observations.

The 1987 article's obsolescence began at the moment of publication. The most recent executions it considered were in 1984, 1964, and 1951; the rest predate the Allied victory in World War II. (Two of the supposed innocents are Sacco and Vanzetti.) Bedau & Radelet, *supra,* at 73. Even if the innocence claims made in this study were true, all except (perhaps) the 1984 example would cast no light upon the functioning of our current system of capital adjudication. The legal community's general attitude toward criminal defendants, the legal protections States afford, the constitutional guarantees this Court enforces, and the scope of federal habeas review, are all vastly different from what they were in 1961. So are the scientific means of establishing guilt, and hence innocence—which are now so striking in their operation and effect that they are the subject of more than one popular TV series. (One of these new means, of course, is DNA testing—which the dissent seems to think is primarily a way to identify defendants erroneously convicted, rather than a highly effective way to avoid conviction of the innocent.)

But their current relevance aside, this study's conclusions are unverified. And if the support for its most significant conclusion—the execution of 23 innocents in the 20th century—is any indication of its accuracy, neither it, nor any study so careless as to rely upon it, is worthy of credence. The only execution of an innocent man it alleges to have occurred after the restoration of the death penalty in 1976—the Florida execution of James Adams in 1984—is the easiest case to verify. As evidence of Adams' innocence, it describes a hair that could not have been his as being "clutched in the victim's hand," Bedau & Radelet, *supra,* at 91. The hair was *not* in the victim's hand; "[i]t was a remnant of a sweeping of the ambulance and so could have come from another source." Markman & Cassell, Protecting the Innocent: A Response to the Bedau–Radelet Study, 41 Stan. L.Rev. 121, 131 (1988). The study also claims that a witness who "heard a voice inside the victim's home at the time of the crime" testified that the "voice was a woman's," Bedau & Radelet, *supra,* at 91. The witness's actual testimony was that the voice, which said " 'In the name of God, don't do it' " (and was hence unlikely to have been the voice of anyone but the male victim), " 'sounded kind of like a woman's voice, kind of like strangling or something....' " Markman & Cassell, Protecting the Innocent, at 130. Bedau and Radelet failed to mention that upon arrest on the afternoon of the murder Adams was found with some $200 in his pocket—one bill of which "was stained with type O blood. When Adams was asked about the blood on the money, he said that it came from a cut on his finger. His blood was type AB, however, while the victim's was type O." *Id.,* at 132. Among the other unmentioned, incriminating details: that the victim's *eyeglasses* were found in Adams' car, along with jewelry belonging to the victim, and clothing of Adams' stained with type O blood. *Ibid.* This is just a sample of the evidence arrayed against this "innocent." See *id.,* at 128–133, 148–150. . . .

Remarkably avoiding any claim of erroneous executions, the dissent focuses on the large numbers of *non*-executed "exonerees" paraded by various professors. It speaks as though exoneration came about through the operation of some outside force to correct the mistakes of our legal system, rather than *as a consequence of the functioning of our legal system.* Reversal of an erroneous conviction on appeal or on habeas, or the pardoning of an innocent condemnee through executive clemency, demonstrates not the failure of the system but its success. Those devices are part and parcel of the multiple assurances that are applied before a death sentence is carried out.

Of course even in identifying exonerees, the dissent is willing to accept anybody's say-so. It engages in no critical review, but merely parrots articles or reports that support its attack on the American criminal justice system. The dissent places significant weight, for instance, on the Illinois Report (compiled by the appointees of an Illinois Governor who had declared a moratorium upon the death penalty and who eventually commuted all death sentences in the State, see Warden, Illinois Death Penalty Reform: How It Happened, What It Promises, 95 J.Crim. L. & C. 381, 406–

407, 410 (2006)), which it claims shows that "false verdicts" are "remarkable in number." *Post,* at 2545 (opinion of Souter, J.). The dissent claims that this Report identifies 13 inmates released from death row after they were determined to be innocent. To take one of these cases, discussed by the dissent as an example of a judgment "as close to innocence as any judgments courts normally render," *post,* at 2544, n. 2: In *People v. Smith,* 185 Ill.2d 532, 236 Ill.Dec. 779, 708 N.E.2d 365 (1999) the defendant was twice convicted of murder. After his first trial, the Supreme Court of Illinois "reversed [his] conviction based upon certain evidentiary errors" and remanded his case for a new trial. *Id.,* at 534, 236 Ill.Dec. 779, 708 N.E.2d, at 366. The second jury convicted Smith again. The Supreme Court of Illinois again reversed the conviction because it found that the evidence was insufficient to establish guilt beyond a reasonable doubt. *Id.,* at 542–543, 236 Ill.Dec. 779, 708 N.E.2d, at 370–371. The court explained: "While a not guilty finding is sometimes equated with a finding of innocence, that conclusion is erroneous. Courts do not find people guilty or innocent.... A not guilty verdict expresses no view as to a defendant's innocence. Rather, [a reversal of conviction] indicates simply that the prosecution has failed to meet its burden of proof." *Id.,* at 545, 236 Ill.Dec. 779, 708 N.E.2d, at 371. This case alone suffices to refute the dissent's claim that the Illinois Report distinguishes between "exoneration of a convict because of actual innocence, and reversal of a judgment because of legal error affecting conviction or sentence but not inconsistent with guilt in fact," *post,* at 2544, n. 2. The broader point, however, is that it is utterly impossible to regard "exoneration"—however casually defined—as a failure of the capital justice system, rather than as a vindication of its effectiveness in releasing not only defendants who are innocent, but those whose guilt has not been established beyond a reasonable doubt.

Another of the dissent's leading authorities on exoneration of the innocent is Gross, Jacoby, Matheson, Montgomery, & Patil, Exonerations in the United States 1989 Through 2003, 95 J.Crim. L. & C. 523 (2006) (hereinafter Gross). The dissent quotes that study's self-congratulatory "criteria" of exoneration—seemingly so rigorous that no one could doubt the study's reliability. See *post,* at 2545, n. 3 (opinion of Souter, J.). But in fact that article, like the others cited, is notable not for its rigorous investigation and analysis, but for the fervor of its belief that the American justice system is condemning the innocent "in numbers," as the dissent puts it, "never imagined before the development of DNA tests." *Post,* at 2544 (opinion of Souter, J.). Among the article's list of 74 "exonerees," Gross 529, is Jay Smith of Pennsylvania. Smith—a school principal— earned three death sentences for slaying one of his teachers and her two young children. See *Smith v. Holtz,* 210 F.3d 186, 188 (C.A.3 2000). His retrial for triple murder was barred on double jeopardy grounds because of prosecutorial misconduct during the first trial. *Id.,* at 194. But Smith could not leave well enough alone. He had the gall to sue, under 42 U.S.C. § 1983, for false imprisonment. The Court of Appeals for the Third Circuit affirmed the jury verdict for the defendants, observing along the way that "our confidence in Smith's convictions is not diminished in the least. We remain firmly convinced of the integrity of those guilty verdicts." 210 F.3d, at 198....

In its inflation of the word "exoneration," the Gross article hardly stands alone; mischaracterization of reversible error as actual innocence is endemic in abolitionist rhetoric, and other prominent catalogues of "innocence" in the death-penalty context suffer from the same defect. Perhaps the best-known of them is the List of Those Freed From Death Row, maintained by the Death Penalty Information Center. See http://www.deathpenaltyinfo.org/article.php?scid=6&did=110. This includes the cases from the Gross article described above, but also enters some dubious candidates of its own. Delbert Tibbs is one of them. We considered his case in *Tibbs v. Florida,* 457 U.S. 31, 102 S.Ct. 2211, 72 L.Ed.2d 652 (1982), concluding that the Double Jeopardy Clause does not bar a retrial when a conviction is "revers[ed] based on the weight, rather than the sufficiency, of the evidence," *id.,* at 32, 102 S.Ct. 2211. The case involved a man and a woman hitchhiking together in Florida. A driver who picked them up sodomized and raped the woman, and killed her boyfriend. She eventually escaped and positively identified Tibbs. See *id.,* at 32–33, 102 S.Ct. 2211. The Florida Supreme Court reversed the conviction on a 4–to–3 vote. 337 So.2d 788 (Fla.1976). The Florida courts then grappled with whether Tibbs could be retried without violating the Double Jeopardy Clause. The Florida Supreme Court determined not only that there was no double-jeopardy problem, 397 So.2d 1120, 1127 (Fla.1981) *(per curiam),* but that the *very basis on which it had reversed the conviction was no longer valid law, id.,* at 1125, and that its action in "reweigh[ing] the evidence" in Tibbs' case had been "clearly improper," *id.,* at 1126. After we affirmed the Florida Supreme Court, however, the State felt compelled to drop the charges. The State Attorney explained this to the Florida Commission on Capital Cases: " 'By the time of the retrial, [the] witness/victim ... had progressed from a marijuana smoker to a crack user and I could not put her up on the stand, so I declined to prosecute. Tibbs, in my opinion, was never an innocent man wrongfully accused. He was a lucky human being. He was guilty, he was lucky and now he is free. His 1974 conviction was not a miscarriage of justice.' " Florida Commission on Capital Cases, Case Histories: A Review of 24 Individuals Released From Death Row 136–137 (rev. Sept. 10, 2002) http://www.floridacapitalcases.state.fl.us/Publications/innocentsproject.pdf. Other state officials involved made similar points. *Id.,* at 137. Of course, even with its distorted concept of what constitutes "exoneration," the claims of the Gross article are fairly modest: Between 1989 and 2003, the authors identify 340 "exonerations" *nationwide*—not just for capital cases, mind you, nor even just for murder convictions, but for various felonies. Gross 529. Joshua Marquis, a district attorney in Oregon, recently responded to this article as follows: "[L]et's give the professor the benefit of the doubt: let's assume that he understated the number of innocents by roughly a factor of 10, that instead of 340 there were 4,000 people in prison who weren't involved in the crime in any way. During that same 15 years, there were more than 15 million felony convictions across the country. That would make the error rate .027 percent—or, to put it another way, a success rate of 99.973 percent." The Innocent and the Shammed, N.Y. Times, Jan. 26, 2006, p. A23. The dissent's suggestion that capital defendants are *especially* liable to suffer from the lack of 100% perfection in our criminal justice system is implausible. Capital cases are given especially close scrutiny at every level, which is why in most cases many years elapse before the sentence is executed. And of course capital cases receive special attention in the application of executive clemency. Indeed, one of the arguments made by abolitionists is that the process of finally completing all the appeals and reexaminations of capital sentences is so lengthy, and thus so expensive for the State, that the game is not worth the candle. The proof of the pudding, of course, is that as far as anyone can determine (and many are looking), *none* of cases included in the .027% error rate for American verdicts involved a capital defendant erroneously executed.

Since 1976 there have been approximately a half million murders in the United States. In that time, 7,000 murderers have been sentenced to death; about 950 of them have been executed; and about 3,700 inmates are currently on death row. See Marquis, The Myth of Innocence, 95 J.Crim. L. & C. 501, 518 (2006). As a consequence of the sensitivity of the criminal justice system to the due-process rights of defendants sentenced to death, almost two-thirds of all death sentences are overturned. See *ibid.* "Virtually none" of these reversals, however, are attributable to a defendant's " 'actual innocence.' " *Ibid.* Most are based on legal errors that have little or nothing to do with guilt. See *id.,* at 519–520. The studies cited by the dissent demonstrate nothing more.

Like other human institutions, courts and juries are not perfect. One cannot have a system of criminal punishment without accepting the possibility that someone will be punished mistakenly. That is a truism, not a revelation. But with regard to the punishment of death in the current American system, that possibility has been reduced to an insignificant minimum. This explains why those ideologically driven to ferret out and proclaim a mistaken modern execution have not a single verifiable case to point to, whereas it is easy as pie to identify plainly guilty murderers who have been set free. The American people have determined that the good to be derived from capital punishment—in deterrence, and perhaps most of all in the meting out of condign justice for horrible crimes—outweighs the risk of error. It is no proper part of the business of this Court, or of its Justices, to second-guess that judgment, much less to impugn it before the world, and less still to frustrate it by imposing judicially invented obstacles to its execution.

■ Justice Souter, with whom Justice Stevens, Justice Ginsburg, and Justice Breyer join, dissenting.

I

Kansas's capital sentencing statute provides that a defendant "shall be sentenced to death" if, by unanimous vote, "the jury finds beyond a reasonable doubt that one or more aggravating circumstances ... exist and ... that the existence of such aggravating circumstances is not outweighed by any mitigating circumstances which are found to exist." Kan. Stat. Ann. § 21–4624(e) (1995). The Supreme Court of Kansas has read this provision to require imposition of the death penalty "[i]n the event of equipoise, [that is,] the jury's determination that the balance of any aggravating circumstances and any mitigating circumstances weighed equal." 278 Kan. 520, 534, 102 P.3d 445, 457 (2004) (case below); see also *State v. Kleypas,* 272

Kan. 894, 1016, 40 P.3d 139, 232 (2001) (stating that the language of § 21–4624(e) "provides that in doubtful cases the jury must return a sentence of death"). Given this construction, the state court held the law unconstitutional on the ground that the Eighth Amendment requires that a " 'tie g[o] to the defendant' when life or death is at issue." *Ibid.* Because I agree with the Kansas judges that the Constitution forbids a mandatory death penalty in what they describe as "doubtful cases," when aggravating and mitigating factors are of equal weight, I respectfully dissent.[1]

II

More than 30 years ago, this Court explained that the Eighth Amendment's guarantee against cruel and unusual punishment barred imposition of the death penalty under statutory schemes so inarticulate that sentencing discretion produced wanton and freakish results. See *Furman v. Georgia,* 408 U.S. 238, 309–310, 92 S.Ct. 2726, 33 L.Ed.2d 346 (1972) *(per curiam)* (Stewart, J., concurring) ("[T]he Eighth and Fourteenth Amendments cannot tolerate the infliction of a sentence of death under legal systems that permit this unique penalty to be ... wantonly and ... freakishly imposed" on a "capriciously selected random handful" of individuals). The Constitution was held to require, instead, a system structured to produce reliable, *Woodson v. North Carolina,* 428 U.S. 280, 305, 96 S.Ct. 2978, 49 L.Ed.2d 944 (1976) (plurality opinion), rational, *Jurek v. Texas,* 428 U.S. 262, 276, 96 S.Ct. 2950, 49 L.Ed.2d 929 (1976) (joint opinion of Stewart, Powell, and Stevens, JJ.), and rationally reviewable, *Woodson, supra,* at 303, 96 S.Ct. 2978, determinations of sentence. Decades of back-and-forth between legislative experiment and judicial review have made it plain that the constitutional demand for rationality goes beyond the minimal requirement to replace unbounded discretion with a sentencing structure; a State has much leeway in devising such a structure and in selecting the terms for measuring relative culpability, but a system must meet an ultimate test of constitutional reliability in producing " 'a reasoned moral response to the defendant's background, character, and crime,' " *Penry v. Lynaugh,* 492 U.S. 302, 319, 109 S.Ct. 2934, 106 L.Ed.2d 256 (1989) (quoting *California v. Brown,* 479 U.S. 538, 545, 107 S.Ct. 837, 93 L.Ed.2d 934 (1987) (O'Connor, J., concurring); emphasis deleted); cf. *Gregg v. Georgia,* 428 U.S. 153, 206, 96 S.Ct. 2909, 49 L.Ed.2d 859 (1976) (joint opinion of Stewart, Powell, and Stevens, JJ.) (sanctioning sentencing procedures that "focus the jury's attention on the particularized nature of the crime and the particularized characteristics of the individual defendant"). The Eighth Amendment, that is, demands both form and substance, both a system for decision and one geared to produce morally justifiable results.

---

1. The majority views *Walton v. Arizona,* 497 U.S. 639, 110 S.Ct. 3047, 111 L.Ed.2d 511 (1990), as having decided this issue. But *Walton* is ambiguous on this point; while the Court there approved Arizona's practice of placing the burden on capital defendants to prove, "by a preponderance of the evidence, the existence of mitigating circumstances sufficiently substantial to call for leniency," *id.,* at 649, 110 S.Ct. 3047 (plurality opinion), it did not quantify the phrase "sufficiently substantial." Justice Blackmun clearly thought otherwise, see *id.,* at 687, 110 S.Ct. 3047 (dissenting opinion), but he cried a greater foul than one can get from the majority opinion. *Stare decisis* does not control this case.

The State thinks its scheme is beyond questioning, whether as to form or substance, for it sees the tie-breaker law as equivalent to the provisions examined in *Blystone v. Pennsylvania,* 494 U.S. 299, 110 S.Ct. 1078, 108 L.Ed.2d 255 (1990), and *Boyde v. California,* 494 U.S. 370, 110 S.Ct. 1190, 108 L.Ed.2d 316 (1990), where we approved statutes that required a death sentence upon a jury finding that aggravating circumstances outweighed mitigating ones. But the crucial fact in those systems was the predominance of the aggravators, and our recognition of the moral rationality of a mandatory capital sentence based on that finding is no authority for giving States free rein to select a different conclusion that will dictate death. Instead, the constitutional demand for a reasoned moral response requires the state statute to satisfy two criteria that speak to the issue before us now, one governing the character of sentencing evidence, and one going to the substantive justification needed for a death sentence. As to the first, there is an obligation in each case to inform the jury's choice of sentence with evidence about the crime as actually committed and about the specific individual who committed it. See *Spaziano v. Florida,* 468 U.S. 447, 460, and n. 7, 104 S.Ct. 3154, 82 L.Ed.2d 340 (1984). Since the sentencing choice is, by definition, the attribution of particular culpability to a criminal act and defendant, as distinct from the general culpability necessarily implicated by committing a given offense, see *Penry, supra,* at 327–328, 109 S.Ct. 2934; *Spaziano, supra,* at 460, 104 S.Ct. 3154; *Zant v. Stephens,* 462 U.S. 862, 879, 103 S.Ct. 2733, 77 L.Ed.2d 235 (1983), the sentencing decision must turn on the uniqueness of the individual defendant and on the details of the crime, to which any resulting choice of death must be "directly" related. *Penry, supra,* at 319, 109 S.Ct. 2934

Second, there is the point to which the particulars of crime and criminal are relevant: within the category of capital crimes, the death penalty must be reserved for "the worst of the worst." See, *e.g., Roper v. Simmons,* 543 U.S. 551, 568, 125 S.Ct. 1183, 161 L.Ed.2d 1 (2005) ("Capital punishment must be limited to those offenders who commit 'a narrow category of the most serious crimes' and whose extreme culpability makes them 'the most deserving of execution'" (quoting *Atkins v. Virginia,* 536 U.S. 304, 319, 122 S.Ct. 2242, 153 L.Ed.2d 335 (2002)). One object of the structured sentencing proceeding required in the aftermath of *Furman* is to eliminate the risk that a death sentence will be imposed in spite of facts calling for a lesser penalty, *Penry, supra,* at 328–329, 109 S.Ct. 2934, and the essence of the sentencing authority's responsibility is to determine whether the response to the crime and defendant "must be death," *Spaziano, supra,* at 461, 104 S.Ct. 3154; cf. *Gregg, supra,* at 184, 96 S.Ct. 2909 (joint opinion of Stewart, Powell, and Stevens, JJ.). Of course, in the moral world of those who reject capital punishment in principle, a death sentence can never be a moral imperative. The point, however, is that within our legal and moral system, which allows a place for the death penalty, "must be death" does not mean "may be death." Since a valid capital sentence thus requires a choice based upon unique particulars identifying the crime and its perpetrator as heinous to the point of demanding death even within the class of potentially capital offenses, the State's provision for a tie breaker in favor of death fails on both counts. The dispositive fact under the tie breaker is not the details of the crime or the unique identity of the individual defendant. The determining fact is not directly linked to a particular crime or particular criminal at all; the law operates merely on a jury's finding of equipoise in the State's own selected considerations for and against death. Nor does the tie breaker identify the worst of the worst, or even purport to reflect any evidentiary showing that death must be the reasoned moral response; it does the opposite. The statute produces a death sentence exactly when a sentencing impasse demonstrates as a matter of law that the jury does not see the evidence as showing the worst sort of crime committed by the worst sort of criminal, in a combination heinous enough to demand death. It operates, that is, when a jury has applied the State's chosen standards of culpability and mitigation and reached nothing more than what the Supreme Court of Kansas calls a "tie," *Kleypas,* 272 Kan., at 1016, 40 P.3d, at 232 (internal quotation marks omitted). It mandates death in what that court identifies as "doubtful cases," *ibid.* The statute thus addresses the risk of a morally unjustifiable death sentence, not by minimizing it as precedent unmistakably requires, but by guaranteeing that in equipoise cases the risk will be realized, by "placing a 'thumb [on] death's side of the scale,'" *Sochor v. Florida,* 504 U.S. 527, 532, 112 S.Ct. 2114, 119 L.Ed.2d 326 (1992) (quoting *Stringer v. Black,* 503 U.S. 222, 232, 112 S.Ct. 1130, 117 L.Ed.2d 367 (1992); alteration in original).

In Kansas, when a jury applies the State's own standards of relative culpability and cannot decide that a defendant is among the most culpable, the state law says that equivocal evidence is good enough and the defendant must die. A law that requires execution when the case for aggravation has failed to convince the sentencing jury is morally absurd, and the Court's holding that the Constitution tolerates this moral irrationality defies decades of precedent aimed at eliminating freakish capital sentencing in the United States.

III

That precedent, demanding reasoned moral judgment, developed in response to facts that could not be ignored, the kaleidoscope of life and death verdicts that made no sense in fact or morality in the random sentencing before *Furman* was decided in 1972. See 408 U.S., at 309–310, 92 S.Ct. 2726 (Stewart, J., concurring). Today, a new body of fact must be accounted for in deciding what, in practical terms, the Eighth Amendment guarantees should tolerate, for the period starting in 1989 has seen repeated exonerations of convicts under death sentences, in numbers never imagined before the development of DNA tests. We cannot face up to these facts and still hold that the guarantee of morally justifiable sentencing is hollow enough to allow maximizing death sentences, by requiring them when juries fail to find the worst degree of culpability: when, by a State's own standards and a State's own characterization, the case for death is "doubtful."

A few numbers from a growing literature will give a sense of the reality that must be addressed. When the Governor of Illinois imposed a moratorium on executions in 2000, 13 prisoners under death sentences had been released since 1977 after a number of them were shown to be innocent, as described in a report which used their examples to illustrate a theme common to all 13, of "relatively little solid evidence connecting the charged defendants to the crimes." State of Illinois, G. Ryan, Governor, Report of the Governor's Commission on Capital Punishment: Recommendations Only 7 (Apr.2002) (hereinafter Report); see also *id.*, at 5–6, 7–9. During the same period, 12 condemned convicts had been executed. Subsequently the Governor determined that 4 more death row inmates were innocent. See *id.*, at 5–6; Warden, Illinois Death Penalty Reform, 95 J.Crim. L. & C. 381, 382, and n. 6 (2005).[2] Illinois had thus wrongly convicted and condemned even more capital defendants than it had executed, but it may well not have been otherwise unique; one recent study reports that between 1989 and 2003, 74 American prisoners condemned to death were exonerated, Gross, Jacoby, Matheson, Montgomery, & Patil, Exonerations in the United States 1989 Through 2003, 95 J.Crim. L. & C. 523, 531 (2006) (hereinafter Gross), many of them cleared by DNA evidence, *ibid.*[3] *Another report states that "more than 110" death row prisoners have been released since 1973 upon findings that they were innocent of the crimes charged, and "[h]undreds of additional wrongful convictions in potentially capital cases have been documented over the past century." Lanier & Acker, Capital Punishment, the Moratorium Movement, and Empirical Questions, 10 Psychology, Public Policy & Law 577, 593 (2004). Most of these wrongful convictions and sentences resulted from eyewitness misidentification, false confession, and (most frequently) perjury, Gross 544, 551–552, and the total shows that*

---

2. The Illinois Report emphasizes the difference between exoneration of a convict because of actual innocence, and reversal of a judgment because of legal error affecting conviction or sentence but not inconsistent with guilt in fact. See Report 9 (noting that, apart from the 13 released men, a "broader review" discloses that more than half of the State's death penalty cases "were reversed at some point in the process"). More importantly, it takes only a cursory reading of the Report to recognize that it describes men released who were demonstrably innocent or convicted on grossly unreliable evidence. Of one, the Report notes "two other persons were subsequently convicted in Wisconsin of" the murders. *Id.*, at 8. Of two others, the Report states that they were released after "DNA tests revealed that none of them were the source of the semen found in the victim. That same year, two other men confessed to the crime, pleaded guilty and were sentenced to life in prison, and a third was tried and convicted for the crime." *Ibid.* Of yet another, the Report says that "another man subsequently confessed to the crime for which [the released man] was convicted. He entered a plea of guilty and is currently serving a prison term for that crime." *Id.*, at 9.

3. The authors state the criteria for their study: "As we use the term, 'exoneration' is an official act declaring a defendant not guilty of a crime for which he or she had previously been convicted. The exonerations we have studied occurred in four ways: (1) In forty-two cases governors (or other appropriate executive officers) issued pardons based on evidence of the defendants' innocence. (2) In 263 cases criminal charges were dismissed by courts after new evidence of innocence emerged, such as DNA. (3) In thirty-one cases the defendants were acquitted at a retrial on the basis of evidence that they had no role in the crimes for which they were originally convicted. (4) In four cases, states posthumously acknowledged the innocence of defendants who had already died in prison...." Gross 524 (footnote omitted). The authors exclude from their list of exonerations "any case in which a dismissal or an acquittal appears to have been based on a decision that while the defendant was not guilty of the charges in the original conviction, he did play a role in the crime and may be guilty of some lesser crime that is based on the same conduct. For our purposes, a defendant who is acquitted of murder on retrial, but convicted of involuntary manslaughter, has not been exonerated. We have also excluded any case in which a dismissal was entered in the absence of strong evidence of factual innocence, or in which—despite such evidence—there was unexplained physical evidence of the defendant's guilt." *Ibid.*, n. 4.

among all prosecutions homicide cases suffer an unusually high incidence of false conviction, id., at 532, 552, probably owing to the combined difficulty of investigating without help from the victim, intense pressure to get convictions in homicide cases, and the corresponding incentive for the guilty to frame the innocent, *id.,* at 532.

A number were subject to judgments as close to innocence as any judgments courts normally render. In the case of one of the released men, the Supreme Court of Illinois found the evidence insufficient to support his conviction. See *People v. Smith,* 185 Ill.2d 532, 236 Ill.Dec. 779, 708 N.E.2d 365 (1999). Several others obtained acquittals, and still more simply had the charges against them dropped, after receiving orders for new trials.

At least 2 of the 13 were released at the initiative of the executive. We can reasonably assume that a State under no obligation to do so would not release into the public a person against whom it had a valid conviction and sentence unless it were certain beyond all doubt that the person in custody was not the perpetrator of the crime. The reason that the State would forgo even a judicial forum in which defendants would demonstrate grounds for vacating their convictions is a matter of common sense: evidence going to innocence was conclusive.

We are thus in a period of new empirical argument about how "death is different," *Gregg,* 428 U.S., at 188, 96 S.Ct. 2909 (joint opinion of Stewart, Powell, and Stevens, JJ.): not only would these false verdicts defy correction after the fatal moment, the Illinois experience shows them to be remarkable in number, and they are probably disproportionately high in capital cases. While it is far too soon for any generalization about the soundness of capital sentencing across the country, the cautionary lesson of recent experience addresses the tie-breaking potential of the Kansas statute: the same risks of falsity that infect proof of guilt raise questions about sentences, when the circumstances of the crime are aggravating factors and bear on predictions of future dangerousness.

In the face of evidence of the hazards of capital prosecution, maintaining a sentencing system mandating death when the sentencer finds the evidence pro and con to be in equipoise is obtuse by any moral or social measure. And unless application of the Eighth Amendment no longer calls for reasoned moral judgment in substance as well as form, the Kansas law is unconstitutional.

PART 2

PROCEDURE AND ENFORCEMENT

CHAPTER 12

THE LIMITATIONS OF PROSECUTION

SECTION 1. JURISDICTION

(A) THE EXTENT OF THE AUTHORITY OF THE STATE

Criminal prosecutions are subject to several limitations. Four distinct kinds, namely, jurisdiction, limitation of time, former jeopardy and the *ex post facto rule,* are entitled to special consideration.

"The power of a sovereign to affect the rights of persons, whether by legislation, by executive decree, or by the judgment of a court, is called *jurisdiction.*"[1] As relates to the power of a sovereign to affect the rights of persons by the judgment of a court, jurisdiction is the power to hear and determine a cause of action. Thus we use the word jurisdiction first, to mean the scope of authority of a state; and second, within the state, to signify the scope of authority of its various tribunals.[2] To have jurisdiction over a criminal prosecution means to have power, first, to inquire into the facts; second, to apply the law to the facts; and third, if the law as applied to these facts requires it, to pronounce the appropriate sentence. Any given court may lack these powers either because they are not within the judicial machinery of the state at all, or because they are lodged exclusively in some other part of this machinery. If any such question arises we have first to decide whether the state has the power to try the accused for the alleged crime. The different theories of criminal jurisdiction are entitled to first consideration.

---

1. Beale, The Jurisdiction of a Sovereign State, 36 Harv.L.Rev. 241 (1923).

2. In a criminal action, the trial court must not only have jurisdiction over the offense charged, but it must have jurisdiction over the question which its judgment assumes to decide. Carmichael v. State, 18 Kan.App.2d 435, 856 P.2d 934 (1993) reversed in part other grounds 255 Kan. 10, 872 P.2d 240 (1994).

TITLE 18–UNITED STATES CODE CRIMES AND CRIMINAL PROCEDURE

§ 1651. Piracy under law of nations[3]

Whoever, on the high seas, commits the crime of piracy as defined by the law of nations, and is afterwards brought into or found in the United States, shall be imprisoned for life.

§ 1652. Citizens as pirates

Whoever, being a citizen of the United States, commits any murder or robbery, or any act of hostility against the United States, or against any citizen thereof, on the high seas, under color of any commission from any foreign prince, or state, or on pretense of authority from any person, is a pirate, and shall be imprisoned for life.

§ 2381. Treason

Whoever, owing allegiance to the United States, levies war against them or adheres to their enemies, giving them aid and comfort within the United States or elsewhere, is guilty of treason and shall suffer death, or be imprisoned not less than five years and fined not less than $10,000; and shall be incapable of holding any office under the United States.

§ 953. Private correspondence with foreign governments

Any citizen of the United States, wherever he may be, who, without authority of the United States, directly or indirectly commences or carries on any correspondence or intercourse with any foreign government or any officer or agent thereof, with intent to influence the measures or conduct of any foreign government or of any officer or agent thereof, in relation to any disputes or controversies with the United States, or to defeat the measures of the United States, shall be fined not more than $5,000 or imprisoned not more than three years, or both.

This section shall not abridge the right of a citizen to apply, himself or his agent, to any foreign government or the agents thereof for redress of any injury which he may have sustained from such government or any of its agents or subjects.

§ 2112. Personal property of United States

Whoever robs another of any kind or description of personal property belonging to the United States, shall be imprisoned not more than fifteen years.

§ 471. Obligations or securities of United States

Whoever, with intent to defraud, falsely makes, forges, counterfeits, or alters any obligation or other security of the United States, shall be fined not more than $5,000 or imprisoned not more than fifteen years, or both.

---

3. Constitution of the United States, Art. I, § 8: 1. The Congress shall have power.... 10. To define and punish piracies and felonies committed on the high seas, and offenses against the law of nations.

TITLE 21–UNITED STATES CODE

§ 959. Possession, manufacture, or distribution of controlled substance or listed chemical

a) Manufacture or distribution for purpose of unlawful importation

It shall be unlawful for any person to manufacture or distribute a controlled substance in schedule I or II or flunitrazepam or listed chemical:

(1) intending that such substance or chemical will be unlawfully imported into the United States or into waters within a distance of 12 miles of the coast of the United States; or

(2) knowing that such substance or chemical will be unlawfully imported into the United States or into waters within a distance of 12 miles of the coast of the United States.

(b) Possession, manufacture, or distribution by person on board aircraft

It shall be unlawful for any United States citizen on board any aircraft, or any person on board an aircraft owned by a United States citizen or registered in the United States, to:

(1) manufacture or distribute a controlled substance or listed chemical; or

(2) possess a controlled substance or listed chemical with intent to distribute.

(c) Acts committed outside territorial jurisdiction of United States; venue

This section is intended to reach acts of manufacture or distribution committed outside the territorial jurisdiction of the United States. Any person who violates this section shall be tried in the United States district court at the point of entry where such person enters the United States, or in the United States District Court for the District of Columbia.

(i) In General

In re Carmen's Petition

United States District Court, N.D. California, S.D., 1958.
165 F.Supp. 942.

■ GOODMAN, CHIEF JUDGE. Petitioner is confined at the California State Penitentiary at San Quentin pursuant to a judgment of conviction of murder and a sentence of death imposed by the Superior Court of the State of California in and for the County of Madera, on October 30, 1951. By an application for the writ of habeas corpus, he seeks his discharge on the ground that the California Superior Court lacked jurisdiction to try him for the murder of which he was convicted because exclusive jurisdiction to try him for such offense was vested by federal statute in the United States District Court.

The statute relied upon by petitioner is often referred to as the Ten Major Crimes Act[4] and is now incorporated in Sections 1151, 1153, and 3242 of Title 18 of the United States Code. It provides in substance that an Indian who commits any of the ten listed crimes, among which is murder, in Indian Country shall be subject to the same laws and penalties and tried in the same courts as persons committing such crime within the exclusive jurisdiction of the United States. During petitioner's trial in the Superior Court apparently he and his counsel, the prosecution, and the court were all unaware of this statute. There was testimony at the trial indicating that both petitioner and his victim were Indians, but this testimony was given as background information and not for the purpose of questioning the court's jurisdiction. There was evidence that the scene of the crime was the victim's residence, but this evidence did not establish that his residence was in Indian Country. . . .

The testimony at petitioner's trial was that both he and his victim were Indians, and that the murder occurred at the victim's residence. Although these facts alone did not fully demonstrate the lack of jurisdiction in the trial court, they should have put the State Court on inquiry as to its own jurisdiction. The right to be tried in a Federal Court accorded petitioner by the Ten Major Crimes Act, was not a mere procedural right, waived unless asserted.[5] It could not have been waived even by express agreement. The Ten Major Crimes Act was enacted for the protection of the Indian wards of the United States. Both the trial court and the state's attorneys had a duty to uphold this federal statute. They had a responsibility to see to it that the court did not improperly assume jurisdiction over an Indian ward of the Federal government.

When the matter came to the attention of the United States, its representative promptly advised the California Supreme Court of the

---

4. As originally enacted in 1885, 23 Stat. 385, this Act dealt only with seven crimes and was then referred to as the Seven Major Crimes Act. In 1909, the crime of assault with a dangerous weapon was included. 35 Stat. 1151. And, in 1932, incest and robbery were added, 47 Stat. 337.

Currently see 18 U.S.C.A. § 1153 (1997). The present statute contains fourteen categories of offense.

5. [By the Compiler] Except for offenses enumerated in the Major Crimes Act, all crimes committed by enrolled Indians against other Indians in Indian Country are within the jurisdiction of the tribal courts, but a non-Indian charged with committing a crime against a non-Indian in Indian Country is subject to prosecution under state law. United States v. Antelope, 430 U.S. 641, 97 S.Ct. 1395, 51 L.Ed.2d 701 (1977).

Congress may punish a crime committed by a white person against an Indian. United States v. Kagama, 118 U.S. 375, 6 S.Ct. 1109, 30 L.Ed. 228 (1886).

Congress has plenary authority to alter jurisdictional guideposts with respect to offenses committed in "Indian country." Negonsott v. Samuels, 507 U.S. 99, 113 S.Ct. 1119, 122 L.Ed.2d 457 (1993).

Tribal courts do not have jurisdiction over non-Indians who violate a tribal law. Oliphant v. Suquamish Indian Tribe, 435 U.S. 191, 98 S.Ct. 1011, 55 L.Ed.2d 209 (1978).

"It has been repeatedly held in considering objections to the jurisdiction of the court in criminal prosecutions, a distinction must be made between those which involve jurisdiction of fundamental rights of the accused and those which involve mere personal privileges of the accused. The former cannot be waived, but the latter can." Ex parte Duty, 318 P.2d 900, 902 (Okl.Cr.1957).

jurisdictional question while the appeal was pending. The stipulation of the parties that petitioner was an Indian by blood, and that the locus of the crime was an Indian allotment, the title to which was held in trust, constituted at the least a prima facie showing of the lack of jurisdiction in the State court. If, in the opinion of the California Supreme Court, the exclusive federal jurisdiction also depended upon the fact that petitioner was a tribal Indian and had not received a fee patent to an allotment under the Dawes Act, these were facts which were a matter of public record and easily ascertainable. They were in fact ascertained by the Referee appointed by the California Supreme Court upon petitioner's application for the writ of habeas corpus, which was promptly presented to that court after his unsuccessful appeal. Yet the California Supreme Court deemed itself powerless to remedy an assumption of jurisdiction clearly in violation of a federal statute.

Under these circumstances, it becomes the plain duty of this Court to protect the jurisdiction vested in the Federal Courts by the Ten Major Crimes Act....

The writ of Habeas Corpus will issue and it is Ordered that petitioner be discharged from custody.[6]

Section 3231. District Courts.

(ii) Basis of Criminal Jurisdiction

United States v. Yunis

United States Court of Appeals, D.C. Circuit, 1991.
924 F.2d 1086.

■ MIKVA, CHIEF JUDGE:

Appellant Fawaz Yunis challenges his convictions on conspiracy, aircraft piracy, and hostage-taking charges stemming from the hijacking of a Jordanian passenger aircraft in Beirut, Lebanon. He appeals from orders of the district court denying his pretrial motions relating to jurisdiction....

Although this appeal raises novel issues of domestic and international law, we reject Yunis' objections and affirm the convictions.

---

6. The president of a national bank was charged with violation of a state statute which made it a felony for an officer of a bank to accept a deposit when his bank was insolvent and with knowledge of such insolvency. His conviction, affirmed by the state court, was reversed by the Supreme Court on the ground that Congress, having created a system of national banks, has the sole power to regulate and control the exercise of their operations. Easton v. Iowa, 188 U.S. 220, 23 S.Ct. 288, 47 L.Ed. 452 (1903).

Title 18 of the United States Code (Crimes and Criminal Procedure) has this provision:

The district courts of the United States shall have original jurisdiction, exclusive of the courts of the States, of all offenses against the laws of the United States.

Nothing in this title shall be held to take away or impair the jurisdiction of the courts of the several States under the laws thereof.

The fact that one is on probation under a federal conviction does not deprive the state, which has arrested him, of jurisdiction to try him for the state offense. Strand v. Schmittroth, 251 F.2d 590 (9th Cir.1957).

On June 11, 1985, appellant and four other men boarded Royal Jordanian Airlines Flight 402 ("Flight 402") shortly before its scheduled departure from Beirut, Lebanon. They wore civilian clothes and carried military assault rifles, ammunition bandoleers, and hand grenades. Appellant took control of the cockpit and forced the pilot to take off immediately. The remaining hijackers tied up Jordanian air marshals assigned to the flight and held the civilian passengers, including two American citizens, captive in their seats. The hijackers explained to the crew and passengers that they wanted the plane to fly to Tunis, where a conference of the Arab League was under way. The hijackers further explained that they wanted a meeting with delegates to the conference and that their ultimate goal was removal of all Palestinians from Lebanon.

After a refueling stop in Cyprus, the airplane headed for Tunis but turned away when authorities blocked the airport runway. Following a refueling stop at Palermo, Sicily, another attempt to land in Tunis, and a second stop in Cyprus, the plane returned to Beirut, where more hijackers came aboard. These reinforcements included an official of Lebanon's Amal Militia, the group at whose direction Yunis claims he acted. The plane then took off for Syria, but was turned away and went back to Beirut. There, the hijackers released the passengers, held a press conference reiterating their demand that Palestinians leave Lebanon, blew up the plane, and fled from the airport.

An American investigation identified Yunis as the probable leader of the hijackers and prompted U.S. civilian and military agencies, led by the Federal Bureau of Investigation (FBI), to plan Yunis' arrest. After obtaining an arrest warrant, the FBI put "Operation Goldenrod" into effect in September 1987. Undercover FBI agents lured Yunis onto a yacht in the eastern Mediterranean Sea with promises of a drug deal, and arrested him once the vessel entered international waters. The agents transferred Yunis to a United States Navy munitions ship and interrogated him for several days as the vessel steamed toward a second rendezvous, this time with a Navy aircraft carrier. Yunis was flown to Andrews Air Force Base from the aircraft carrier, and taken from there to Washington, D.C. In Washington, Yunis was arraigned on an original indictment charging him with conspiracy, hostage taking, and aircraft damage. A grand jury subsequently returned a superseding indictment adding additional aircraft damage counts and a charge of air piracy.

. . .

Yunis admitted participation in the hijacking at trial but denied parts of the government's account and offered the affirmative defense of obedience to military orders, asserting that he acted on instructions given by his superiors in Lebanon's Amal Militia. The jury convicted Yunis of conspiracy, 18 U.S.C. § 371 (1988), hostage taking, 18 U.S.C. § 1203 (1988), and air piracy, 49 U.S.C. App. § 1472(n) (1988). However, it acquitted him of three other charged offenses that went to trial: violence against people on board an aircraft, 18 U.S.C. § 32(b)(1) (1988), aircraft damage, 18 U.S.C. § 32(b)(2) (1988), and placing a destructive device aboard an aircraft, 18 U.S.C. § 32(b)(3) (1988). . . .

Yunis argues that the district court lacked subject matter and personal jurisdiction to try him on the charges of which he was convicted, that the indictment should have been dismissed because the government seized him in violation of the Posse Comitatus Act and withheld classified materials useful to his defense, and that the convictions should be reversed because of errors in the jury instructions. We consider these claims in turn.

A. *Jurisdictional Claims*

Yunis appeals first of all from the district court's denial of his motion to dismiss for lack of subject matter and personal jurisdiction. Appellant's principal claim is that, as a matter of domestic law, the federal hostage taking and air piracy statutes do not authorize assertion of federal jurisdiction over him. Yunis also suggests that a contrary construction of these statutes would conflict with established principles of international law, and so should be avoided by this court. Finally, appellant claims that the district court lacked personal jurisdiction because he was seized in violation of American law.

1. Hostage Taking Act

The Hostage Taking Act provides, in relevant part:

(a) [W]hoever, whether inside or outside the United States, seizes or detains and threatens to kill, to injure, or to continue to detain another person in order to compel a third person or a governmental organization to do or to abstain from any act ... shall be punished by imprisonment by any term of years or for life.

(b)(1) It is not an offense under this section if the conduct required for the offense occurred outside the United States unless—

(A) the offender or the person seized or detained is a national of the United States;

(B) the offender is found in the United States; or

(C) the governmental organization sought to be compelled is the Government of the United States.

18 U.S.C. § 1203. Yunis claims that this statute cannot apply to an individual who is brought to the United States by force, since those convicted under it must be "found in the United States." But this ignores the law's plain language. Subsections (A), (B), and (C) of section 1203(b)(1) offer *independent* bases for jurisdiction where "the offense occurred outside the United States." Since two of the passengers on Flight 402 were U.S. citizens, section 1203(b)(1)(A), authorizing assertion of U.S. jurisdiction where "the offender or the person seized or detained is a national of the United States," is satisfied. The statute's jurisdictional requirement has been met regardless of whether or not Yunis was "found" within the United States under section 1203(b)(1)(B).

Appellant's argument that we should read the Hostage Taking Act differently to avoid tension with international law falls flat. Yunis points to no treaty obligations of the United States that give us pause. Indeed, Congress intended through the Hostage Taking Act to execute the International Convention Against the Taking of Hostages, which authorizes any signatory state to exercise jurisdiction over persons who take its nationals hostage "if that State considers it appropriate."

Nor is jurisdiction precluded by norms of customary international law. The district court concluded that two jurisdictional theories of international law, the "universal principle" and the "passive personal principle," supported assertion of U.S. jurisdiction to prosecute Yunis on hijacking and hostage-taking charges. Under the universal principle, states may prescribe and prosecute "certain offenses recognized by the community of nations as of universal concern, such as piracy, slave trade, attacks on or hijacking of aircraft, genocide, war crimes, and perhaps certain acts of terrorism," even absent any special connection between the state and the offense. See RESTATEMENT (THIRD) OF THE FOREIGN RELATIONS LAW OF THE UNITED STATES §§ 404, 423 (1987) [hereinafter RESTATEMENT]. Under the passive personal principle, a state may punish non-nationals for crimes committed against its nationals outside of its territory, at least where the state has a particularly strong interest in the crime. *See id.* at § 402 comment *g*; United States v. Benitez, 741 F.2d 1312, 1316 (11th Cir.1984) (passive personal principle invoked to approve prosecution of Colombian citizen convicted of shooting U.S. drug agents in Colombia).

Relying primarily on the RESTATEMENT, Yunis argues that hostage taking has not been recognized as a universal crime and that the passive personal principle authorizes assertion of jurisdiction over alleged hostage takers only where the victims were seized because they were nationals of the prosecuting state. Whatever merit appellant's claims may have as a matter of international law, they cannot prevail before this court. Yunis seeks to portray international law as a self-executing code that trumps domestic law whenever the two conflict. That effort misconceives the role of judges as appliers of international law and as participants in the federal system. Our duty is to enforce the Constitution, laws, and treaties of the United States, not to conform the law of the land to norms of customary international law. See U.S. CONST. art. VI. As we said in *Committee of U.S. Citizens Living in Nicaragua v. Reagan*, 859 F.2d 929 (D.C.Cir.1988): "Statutes inconsistent with principles of customary international law may well lead to international law violations. But within the domestic legal realm, that inconsistent statute simply modifies or supersedes customary international law to the extent of the inconsistency."

To be sure, courts should hesitate to give penal statutes extraterritorial effect absent a clear congressional directive. *See* Foley Bros. v. Filardo, 336 U.S. 281, 285, 69 S.Ct. 575, 577, 93 L.Ed. 680 (1949); United States v. Bowman, 260 U.S. 94, 98, 43 S.Ct. 39, 41, 67 L.Ed. 149 (1922). Similarly, courts will not blind themselves to potential violations of international law where legislative intent is ambiguous. See Murray v. The Schooner Charming Betsy, 6 U.S. (2 Cranch) 64, 118, 2 L.Ed. 208 (1804) ("[A]n act of congress ought never to be construed to violate the law of nations, if any other possible construction remains...."). But the statute in question reflects an unmistakable congressional intent, consistent with treaty obligations of the United States, to authorize prosecution of those who take Americans hostage abroad no matter where the offense occurs or where the offender is found. Our inquiry can go no further.

2.   Antihijacking Act

The Antihijacking Act provides for criminal punishment of persons who hijack aircraft operating wholly outside the "special aircraft jurisdiction" of the United States, provided that the hijacker is later "found in the United States." 49 U.S.C.App. § 1472(n). Flight 402, a Jordanian aircraft operating outside of the United States, was not within this nation's special aircraft jurisdiction. Yunis urges this court to interpret the statutory requirement that persons prosecuted for air piracy must be "found" in the United States as precluding prosecution of alleged hijackers who are brought here to stand trial. But the issue before us is more fact-specific, since Yunis was indicted for air piracy while awaiting trial on hostage-taking and other charges; we must determine whether, once arrested and brought to this country on those other charges, Yunis was subject to prosecution under the Antihijacking Act as well.

The Antihijacking Act of 1974 was enacted to fulfill this nation's responsibilities under the Convention for the Suppression of Unlawful Seizure of Aircraft (the "Hague Convention"), which requires signatory nations to extradite or punish hijackers "present in" their territory. Convention for the Suppression of Unlawful Seizure of Aircraft, Dec. 16, 1970, art. 4, para. 2, Dec. 16, 1970, 22 U.S.T. 1643, 1645, T.I.A.S. No. 7192. This suggests that Congress intended the statutory term "found in the United States" to parallel the Hague Convention's "present in [a contracting state's] territory," a phrase which does not indicate the voluntariness limitation urged by Yunis. Moreover, Congress interpreted the Hague Convention as requiring the United States to extradite or prosecute "offenders in its custody," evidencing no concern as to how alleged hijackers came within U.S. territory....

The district court correctly found that international law does not restrict this statutory jurisdiction to try Yunis on charges of air piracy. Aircraft hijacking may well be one of the few crimes so clearly condemned under the law of nations that states may assert universal jurisdiction to bring offenders to justice, even when the state has no territorial connection to the hijacking and its citizens are not involved. But in any event we are satisfied that the Antihijacking Act authorizes assertion of federal jurisdiction to try Yunis regardless of hijacking's status vel non as a universal crime. Thus, we affirm the district court on this issue.

3.   Legality of Seizure

Yunis further argues that even if the district court had jurisdiction to try him, it should have declined to exercise that jurisdiction in light of the government's allegedly outrageous conduct in bringing him to the United States....

Principally, Yunis relies on United States v. Toscanino, 500 F.2d 267 (2d Cir.1974), in which the court held that due process requires courts to divest themselves of personal jurisdiction acquired through "the government's deliberate, unnecessary and unreasonable invasion of the accused's constitutional rights." *Id.* at 275. *Toscanino* establishes, at best, only a very limited exception to the general rule (known as the "*Ker–Frisbie* doctrine") that "the power of a court to try a person for crime is not impaired by the fact that he had been brought within the court's jurisdiction by reason of a 'forcible abduction.'" Frisbie v. Collins, 342 U.S. 519, 522, 72 S.Ct. 509, 511, 96 L.Ed. 541 (1952) (citing, *inter alia*, *Ker v. Illinois*, 119 U.S. 436, 7 S.Ct. 225, 30 L.Ed. 421 (1886)). *Toscanino's* rule has, moreover, been limited to cases of "torture, brutality, and similar outrageous conduct," United States ex rel. Lujan v. Gengler, 510 F.2d 62, 65 (2d Cir.), *cert. denied*, 421 U.S. 1001, 95 S.Ct. 2400, 44 L.Ed.2d 668 (1975), and the Supreme Court has since reaffirmed the *Ker–Frisbie* doctrine, see Immigration and Naturalization Serv. v. Lopez–Mendoza, 468 U.S. 1032, 1039, 104 S.Ct. 3479, 3483, 82 L.Ed.2d 778 (1984); United States v. Crews, 445 U.S. 463, 474, 100 S.Ct. 1244, 1251, 63 L.Ed.2d 537 (1980).

Even assuming, arguendo, that a district court could correctly dismiss a case otherwise properly before it for the reasons given in *Toscanino*, we find no merit in Yunis' claim. In *Yunis I*, we reviewed the facts of Operation Goldenrod in some detail, including the deception used to arrest Yunis, his injuries and hardships while in custody, and the delay between his arrest and arraignment in the United States. The court sought to determine whether or not these circumstances voided Yunis' waiver of Fifth and Sixth Amendment rights; we concluded that while the government's conduct was neither "picture perfect" nor "a model for law enforcement behavior," the "discomfort and surprise" to which appellant was subjected did not render his waiver invalid. *Yunis I*, 859 F.2d at 969. Similarly, we now find nothing in the record suggesting the sort of intentional, outrageous government conduct necessary to sustain appellant's jurisdictional argument.

Affirmed.[7]

United States v. Robinson

United States Court of Appeals, First Circuit, 1988.
843 F.2d 1.

■ BREYER, CIRCUIT JUDGE.

On June 3, 1986, the United States Coast Guard stopped a Panamanian ship, the M/V JUAN ROBINSON, as it sailed about 500 nautical miles east of North Carolina. Coast Guard officers, boarding with the master's consent, looked around the ship, became suspicious, obtained Panama's permission to proceed further, and eventually found about 20 tons of

---

7. "If it be committed on board of a foreign vessel by a citizen of the United States, or on board of a vessel of the United States by a foreigner, the offender is to be considered, *pro hac vice*, and in respect to this subject as belonging to the nation under whose flag he sails." United States v. Holmes, 18 U.S. 412, 417 (1820).

A ship is "floating territory" of the nation whose flag she flies. Skiriotes v. Florida, 313 U.S. 69, 78, 61 S.Ct. 924, 85 L.Ed. 1193 (1941).

United States courts had jurisdiction to prosecute United States citizens for drug offense committed on board a vessel in international waters. United States v. Reeh, 780 F.2d 1541 (11th Cir.1986).

marijuana hidden in a fake fuel tank. Subsequently, a jury convicted the appellants Hernando and Jorge Robinson of unlawfully possessing marijuana with intent to distribute it, 21 U.S.C. § 955a(c) (1982) (amended, recodified at 46 U.S.C. § 1903(a) and (c) (Supp. IV 1986)) and 18 U.S.C. § 2 (1982), and, along with appellant Roberto Robinson, of conspiring to do so. 21 U.S.C. § 955c (1982) (amended, recodified at 46 U.S.C. § 1903(j) (Supp. IV 1986)). All three appellants argue that principles of international, and of constitutional, law prevent the government from applying United States drug law to them; two appellants also question the sufficiency of the evidence. After examining the record and the relevant legal authorities, we conclude that their convictions are lawful.

Appellants' most important arguments focus upon 21 U.S.C. § 955a(c), a statute that, in part, forbids offshore drug possession. At first glance the statute does not seem to apply to the high seas, for it says that no "person on board any vessel within *the customs waters* of the United States" may knowingly "manufacture or distribute, or ... possess with intent to ... distribute, a controlled substance." (Emphasis added.) But a different statute, 19 U.S.C. § 1401(j) (1982), defines "customs waters" in a special way. With respect to any "foreign vessel" on the high seas, "customs waters" include "waters" within which "a foreign government" may "enabl[e] or permit[ ] the authorities of the United States to board, examine, search, seize, or otherwise to enforce ... the laws of the United States," as long as there is a "treaty or other arrangement" between the foreign government and the United States granting this permission. (See Appendix.) That is to say, if a foreign government "by treaty or other arrangement" permits the United States "to enforce [its laws] upon ... [a] vessel upon the high seas" the waters around the vessel become "customs waters," and 21 U.S.C. § 955a(c) then forbids drug possession.

Appellants claim that this effort to extend the United States' criminal jurisdiction outside the boundaries of the United States violates international law; they add that Congress did not intend to exceed the bounds of international law; and they conclude that we must interpret the statute so that it does not apply to them. . . .

Appellants' "international law" argument rests upon the fact that, so far, most courts have found jurisdictional authority for applying § 955a(c) on the high seas in international law's "protective principle," a principle that "permits a nation to assert jurisdiction over a person whose conduct outside the nation's territory threatens the nation's security or could potentially interfere with the operation of its governmental functions." United States v. Romero–Galue, 757 F.2d 1147, 1154 (11th Cir.1985) . . .

Appellants concede that the "protective principle" allows the United States to forbid extraterritorial conduct aimed at its "security" or "against other important state interests," such as "conspiracy to violate the ... customs laws." But, they ask, how can this principle justify prohibiting foreigners on foreign ships 500 miles offshore from possessing drugs that, as far as the statute (and clear proof here) are concerned, might be bound for Canada, South America, or Zanzibar? . . .

Moreover, any assertion of jurisdiction under the protective principle must be "reasonable." See Restatement (Revised) § 403; Brown, "Protective Jurisdiction," 34 Am.J.Int'l L. 112, 114 (1940). How is it reasonable, they ask, to assert jurisdiction under these circumstances, particularly once one realizes that the "protective principle," as interpreted by the courts, might allow the United States to act even *without* the consent of the flag state.

Appellants go on to point out that the Convention on the Territorial Sea and the Contiguous Zones, *opened for signature* April 29, 1958, art. 24, 15 U.S.T. 1606, T.I.A.S. No. 5639 (entered into force Sept. 10, 1964), which the United States has signed, allows states to assert customs and immigration interests in a contiguous zone 12 miles offshore, not 500 miles offshore. And, they add, recently codified international law does not consider drug dealers to be like pirates, slave traders, or pirate broadcasters, against whom that law says any nation can assert its laws wherever they are found.

In our view, however, appellants' arguments are beside the point, for there is another, different, but perfectly adequate basis in international law for the assertion of American jurisdiction. Panama *agreed* to permit the United States to apply its law on her ship. Panama's Director General of Consular and Shipping Affairs certified that on June 3, 1986, after the Coast Guard stopped the JUAN ROBINSON, the Panamanian government gave its "authorization" not only "to board, inspect, search, seize and escort the vessel to the United States," but also *"to prosecute the persons aboard the vessel."* It is clear, under international law's "territorial principle," that a "state has jurisdiction to prescribe and enforce a rule of law in the territory of another state to the extent provided by international agreement with the other state." Restatement (Second) § 25; Vermilya–Brown Co. v. Connell, 335 U.S. 377, 383–85, 69 S.Ct. 140, 143–45, 93 L.Ed. 76 (1948) (describing executive agreements transferring jurisdiction to United States); United States v. Shiroma, 123 F.Supp. 145 (D.Haw.1954) (American criminal jurisdiction over sovereign Japanese territory transferred by treaty); see also Ex Parte Crow Dog, 109 U.S. 556, 3 S.Ct. 396, 27 L.Ed. 1030 (1883) (United States can apply its pre-existing law to Indian nation by treaty without any further congressional action). Panama and the United States could agree to apply United States drug laws, say, in Panama City, should both nations wish to do so. See, e.g., Dizon v. Philippines–Ryukus Command, 81 Phil.Reports 286 (1948) (criminal jurisdiction over United States army base on Philippine territory can be ceded to United States by agreement); Miquiabas v. Philippines–Ryukus Command, 80 Phil.Reports 262 (1948) (same). Similarly, they can agree to apply American law on a Panamanian ship.

Of course, the "agreement" here does not take the form of a treaty. But, nations may agree through informal, as well as formal, means. In our view, the Panamanian statement giving the United States the right not only to board but "to prosecute" persons aboard the ship constitutes such an agreement. Panama, the only party who could object if the agreement was not so intended, see United States v. Hensel, 699 F.2d 18, 30 (1st Cir.), *cert. denied*, 461 U.S. 958, 103 S.Ct. 2431, 77 L.Ed.2d 1317 (1983), has not indicated otherwise. These well-established principles, together with Panama's statement of agreement, are a sufficient answer to appellants' "international law" objections.

Affirmed.[8]

Felton v. Hodges

United States Court of Appeals, Fifth Circuit, 1967.
374 F.2d 337.

[Felton brought a civil rights action[9] against Florida officials claiming that under color of Florida law they had deprived him of his constitutional rights. This was based upon the fact that he had been arrested, his personal property confiscated, and so forth, for activities of his beyond the territorial limits of Florida. The officials had acted under a Florida law which expressly undertook to regulate such activities of Florida fishermen "within or without the boundaries of such state waters". On defendant's motion the district court dismissed the suit. On appeal the question was whether this Florida law was valid.]

■ TUTTLE, CHIEF JUDGE. . . .

That critical question has been authoritatively answered, and the answer is affirmative. In Skiriotes v. State of Florida, 313 U.S. 69, 61 S.Ct. 924, 85 L.Ed. 1193 (1941), the issue was whether a Florida statute forbidding the use of diving equipment in the taking of commercial sponges had been unconstitutionally applied to convict the appellant, who claimed immunity from Florida regulation by reason of the fact that he was operating outside the territorial limits of the state. Florida contended that her boundaries did in fact encompass the territory in question. The Supreme Court found it unnecessary to decide this question. Instead, it said:

"Appellant's attack thus centers in the contention that the State has transcended its power simply because the statute has been applied to his operations inimical to its interests outside the territorial waters of Florida. The State denies this, pointing to its boundaries as defined by the state constitution of 1868, which the State insists had the approval of Congress and in which there has been acquiescence over a long period.

---

8. Federal law does not prohibit California's assertion of penal jurisdiction over its citizens even though at the time of their commission of the charged offenses they were outside of California's territorial limits. The state had a proper interest in controlling fishing near its limits, and its law was not in conflict with any federal rule. People v. Weeren, 26 Cal.3d 654, 163 Cal.Rptr. 255, 607 P.2d 1279 (1980).

9. Section 1983. Civil Action for Deprivation of Rights. Every person who, under color of any statute, ordinance, regulation, custom, or usage, of any State or Territory, subjects, or causes to be subjected, any citizen of the United States or other person within the jurisdiction thereof to the deprivation of any rights, privileges, or immunities secured by the Constitution and laws, shall be liable to the party injured in an action at law, suit in equity, or other proper proceeding for redress. R.S. § 1979. See currently 42 U.S.C.A. § 1983 (1981).

. . .

"[W]e do not find it necessary to resolve the contentions as to the interpretation and effect of the Act of Congress of 1868. *Even if it were assumed that the locus of the offense was outside the territorial waters of Florida, it would not follow that the State could not prohibit its own citizens from the use of the described divers' equipment at that place.* No question as to the authority of the United States over these waters, or over the sponge fishery, is here involved. No right of a citizen of any other State is here asserted. The question is solely between appellant and his own State. . . .

"If the United States may control the conduct of its citizens upon the high seas, we see no reason why the State of Florida may not likewise govern the conduct of its citizens upon the high seas with respect to matters in which the State has a legitimate interest and where there is no conflict with acts of Congress." *Id.* at 75–77, 61 S.Ct. at 929. (Emphasis added.)

Following the approach dictated by *Skiriotes,* we must inquire whether Florida has a legitimate interest in controlling the activities which it sought to regulate here. It appears from the complaint, and from the concessions made by appellant's counsel in oral argument, that appellant's crawfish traps were located in a group of reefs adjacent to the Florida Keys, and that the crawfish in this area move freely in and out of Florida's territorial waters, so that any taking of them would clearly have an effect upon the State's conservation efforts. Under these circumstances, we think it apparent that the State has an interest sufficient to enable it to subject appellant, one of its own citizens, to the conservation regulations which it sought to enforce here.

One further point requires discussion. As we read it, *Skiriotes* clearly holds that a state, given the requisite interest in a particular subject, may subject its citizens to extra-territorial regulation in order to protect that interest. It does not, however, explicitly hold that the state's officers may make arrests outside its boundaries in their efforts to effectuate such extra-territorial regulation. In his complaint, appellant has arguably, if inartfully, alleged that at least one of the arrests to which he was subjected took place beyond Florida's three mile seaward boundary. We must, therefore, consider the effect of such an allegation.

Obviously, no state is at liberty to abridge the rights of persons not subject to its jurisdiction by indiscriminate arrests effected beyond its territorial limits, under the guise of attempted exercise of the extra-territorial regulatory powers which it enjoys under the rule of *Skiriotes.* Here, however, as in *Skiriotes,* the question is solely between appellant and his own state. The arrests to which appellant alleges he was subjected were an integral part of the efforts of the State of Florida to regulate the conduct of one of its own citizens in a matter in which the State clearly had a legitimate interest. In our opinion, the added fact that one or more of these arrests may have taken place a few miles outside Florida's three mile seaward boundary line cannot transmute the otherwise proper efforts of these State officials into a violation of appellant's constitutional rights.

As we have noted, the predicate of appellant's complaint is simply that the State of Florida had no jurisdiction over his activities because his crawfish traps were set beyond the State's seaward boundary. This, in the light of *Skiriotes,* is untenable; and without that predicate, appellant's complaint fails, for its allegations demonstrate no deprivation of any right secured to him by the Constitution.

The judgment is affirmed.[10]

---

10. An English statute authorized the trial of any English subject charged in England with murder or manslaughter "whether committed within the King's dominions or without". Under this statute a conviction of murder was held to be proper, since the defendant was an English subject, although the crime was committed abroad. Regina v. Azzopardi, 1 Car. & K. 203, 174 Eng.Rep. 776 (1843).

In MacLeod v. Attorney General for New South Wales [1891] A.C. 455, the defendant, having first married in New South Wales and later married another wife in St. Louis, Missouri, was convicted of bigamy in the colony of New South Wales. The conviction was under this statute: "Whosoever being married marries another person during the life of the former husband or wife, wheresoever such second marriage takes place, shall be liable to penal servitude for seven years." This conviction was reversed by the Judicial Committee of the Privy Council. It was suggested that "whosoever" as here used means whosoever etc., "and who is amenable, at the time of the offence committed, to the jurisdiction of the colony of New South Wales," and that "wheresoever" as used in the statute means "wheresoever in this colony the offence is committed."

In other words, it is within the power of a nation to provide for the punishment of misconduct by its national wherever such misconduct may be committed, but since the common law limits criminal jurisdiction to that included within the territorial principle, any extension by statute must be clearly expressed.

The nature of the crime itself might be such as to indicate very clearly an intent to extend it beyond the territorial theory, such as the law making it an offense for a United States consul knowingly to certify a false invoice, which is used for illustration in United States v. Bowman, 43 S.Ct. 39, 260 U.S. 94, 99 (1922). See also the other illustrations given there and the statute actually involved in the case.

Jurisdiction was upheld over a defendant for federal crimes related to the killing of a United States Congressman in Guyana. The Court observed:

"Courts have generally inferred such jurisdiction for two types of statutes: (1) statutes which represent an effort by the government to protect itself against obstructions and frauds; and (2) statutes where the vulnerability of the United States outside its own territory to the occurrence of the prohibited conduct is sufficient because of the nature of the offense to infer reasonably that Congress meant to reach those extraterritorial offenses." United States v. Layton, 509 F.Supp. 212 (N.D.Cal.1981).

This interpretation was recently applied to a statute reading: "It is unlawful to use or operate or assist in using or operating any net, trap, line, spear, or appliance other than in connection with angling, in taking fish, except as provided in this chapter or Chapter 4 of this part." (Cal.Fish & Game Code, § 8603). People v. Foretich, 14 Cal.App.3d Supp. 6, 92 Cal.Rptr. 481 (1970). This very questionable application was assumed to be supported by *Skiriotes,* in which the Supreme Court made no attempt to interpret the Florida statute but held only that the statute, as interpreted by the state court did not "transcend the limits of" state power.

See Blakesley, United States Jurisdiction Over Extraterritorial Crime, 73 Jnl.Crim.L. & Crim. 1109 (1982).

Maritime Drug Enforcement Law giving United States jurisdiction over a vessel and crew where the secretary of state certifies the state of registration has consented is constitutional. United States v. Rojas, 53 F.3d 1212 (11th Cir.1995).

An American National can be convicted of violating child pornography statutes of the United States regardless of whether the acts on which the conviction was based occurred in the United States. United States v. Thomas, 893 F.2d 1066 (9th Cir.1990).

Hanks v. State

Texas Court of Appeals, 1882.
13 Tex.App. 289.

■ WHITE, P.J. There is but a single question which we think is involved in and requires discussion on this appeal.

Appellant and one P.F. Dillman were jointly indicted in the District Court of Travis county for the forgery of a transfer of a land certificate for a league and labor of land in the State of Texas. It is alleged in the indictment that the acts constituting the forgery were all committed in Caddo parish, in the State of Louisiana. No act or thing connected with the execution of the forgery is charged to have been done in Texas; but the crime and injury, so far as this State is concerned, are averred to consist in the fact that the said forgery in Louisiana "did then and there relate to and affect an interest in land in the State of Texas, ... and would, if the same were true and genuine, have transferred and affected certain property, to-wit, a certain land certificate, number 222, for one league and labor of land in the State of Texas," etc.

This indictment was brought under Article 451 of the Penal Code.

By Article 454 of the Code it is declared that "persons out of the State may commit and be liable to indictment and conviction for committing any of the offenses enumerated in this chapter which do not in their commission necessarily require a personal presence in this State, the object of this chapter being to reach and punish all persons offending against its provisions, whether within or without this State," etc.

It was made a ground both in the motion to quash the indictment and in arrest of judgment, and is again urgently insisted upon in the able brief of counsel for appellant, that the facts alleged, if true, would constitute an offense against the sovereign State of Louisiana alone, and one of which the courts of this State would have no jurisdiction.

If the position thus assumed in behalf of appellant be correct, then the Legislature had no authority to pass the act quoted, and the same is an absolute nullity. Can this proposition be maintained? It certainly cannot be found in any constitutional inhibition, State or Federal, depriving the Legislature of the authority, and unless there is some authority of law superior to the right of a State Legislature, which could and should control the action of the latter within the scope of its constitutional powers, we cannot well conceive how its enactments, if reasonable and consistent with that power, could be held inoperative and nugatory.

Two authorities, which are to the effect that "the Legislature of one State cannot define and punish crimes committed in another State," are mainly relied upon. The leading one is the case of The State v. Knight, taken from 2 Haywood, and reported in Taylor's North Carolina Reports, page 44. The other is People v. Merrill, 2 Park's Criminal Reports, 590. The defendant in the first case was indicted under a statute the words of which were: "And whereas there is reason to apprehend that wicked and ill disposed persons resident in the neighboring States make a practice of counterfeiting the current bills of credit of this State, and by themselves or emissaries utter or vend the same, with an intention to defraud the citizens of this State: Be it enacted, etc., that all such persons shall be subject to the same mode of trial, and on conviction liable to the same pains and penalties as if the offense had been committed within the limits of this State and prosecuted in the superior court of any district of this State." It was held that the jurisdiction to try in North Carolina was doubtful, and the prisoner was discharged.

Mr. Wharton, in his work on the Conflict of Laws, says: "The sturdiest advocates of the hypothesis that the *locus delicti* alone confers jurisdiction have admitted that there are cases in which a person whose residence is outside the territory may make himself, by conspiring extra-territorially to defeat its laws, infra-territorially responsible. If, for instance, a forger should establish on the Mexican side of the boundary between the United States and Mexico a manufactory for the forgery of United States securities, for us to hold that when the mischief is done he can take up his residence in the United States without even liability to arrest, would not merely expose our government to spoliation, but bring its authority into contempt. To say that in such a case the Mexican government can be relied upon to punish is no answer; because, first, in countries of such imperfect civilization, penal justice is uncertain; secondly, in cases where, in such country, the local community gains greatly by the fraud and suffers by it no loss, the chances of conviction and punishment would be peculiarly slight; and, thirdly, because all that the offender would have to do to escape justice in such a case would be to walk over the boundary line into the United States, where on this hypothesis he would go free." (Whart. Conflict of Laws, sec. 876.) Again he says: "Thus it has been held that the originator of a nuisance to a stream in one country which affects such stream in another country is liable to prosecution in the latter country; that the author of a libel uttered by him in one country and published by others in another country from which he is absent at the time is liable in the latter country; that he who on one side of a boundary shoots a person on the other side is amenable in the country where the blow is received; that he who in one State employs an innocent agent to obtain goods by false pretenses in another State is amenable in the latter State; and that he who sells through agents, guilty or innocent, lottery tickets in another State is amenable in the State of the sale, though he was absent from such State personally. In England we have the same principle affirmed by the highest judicial authority." And he quotes Lord Campbell as saying, "that a person may, by the employment as well of a conscious as of an unconscious agent, render himself amenable to the law of England when he comes within the jurisdiction of our courts;" and Cir.R. Phillimore as saying, "It is a monstrous thing that any technical rule of venue should prevent justice from being done in this country on a criminal for an offense which was perpetrated here but the execution of which was concocted in another country." (Whart. Conflict of Laws, sec. 877.)

Mr. Cooley, in his great work on Constitutional Limitations, treating of territorial limitation to legislative authority, says: "The legislative authority of every State must spend its force within the territorial limits of the State.... It cannot provide for the punishment as crimes of acts committed beyond the State boundary, because such acts, if offenses at all, must be offenses against the sovereignty within whose limits they have been done."

But, after laying down this doctrine, in the very next sentence he says: "But if the consequences of an unlawful act committed outside the State have reached their ultimate and injurious result within it, it seems that the perpetrator may be punished as an offender against such State." (Cooley's Const.Lim., 4 ed., pp. 154–5.) If this latter rule be the law, then it is a solecism to say that the Legislature cannot so declare it by express enactment.

Story, in his Conflict of Laws, says: "Although the penal laws of every country are in their nature local, yet an offense may be committed in one sovereignty in violation of the laws of another, and if the offender be afterwards found in the latter State, he may be punished according to the laws thereof, and the fact that he owes allegiance to another sovereignty is no bar to the indictment." (Story on the Conflict of Laws, 4 ed., section 625b.)

The offense charged in the indictment against appellant comes clearly within the terms of Article 454 of the Penal Code. Had it been committed by one of our own citizens within this State, there then could be no question as to his liability. Here, the defendant in effect says: "You may try and convict your own citizens for the same act I have committed, but you cannot try and punish me, because what I have done, though equally as violative of the spirit and letter of the law, is still not triable in your court because it was committed in another State, and your Legislature could not pass a law which could embrace me within its pains and penalties." We can see no valid reason why the Legislature of the State of Texas could not assert, as it has done in Article 454 supra, her jurisdiction over wrongs and crimes with regard to the land titles of the State, no matter whether the perpetrator of the crime was at the time of its consummation within or without her territorial limits. Such acts are offenses against the State of Texas and her citizens only, and can properly be tried only in her courts. It may in fact be no crime against the State in which it is perpetrated; and if it is under such circumstances as we are considering, that other State would have no interest in punishing it and would rarely, if ever, do so. When this forgery was committed in Louisiana, *eo instanti* a crime was committed against, and injury done to, the State of Texas, because it affected title to lands within her sovereignty.

Our conclusion is that the Legislature had authority to adopt the act in question; that the same is in violation of no law superior thereto; and that the jurisdiction thereby conferred can be rightly exercised by the courts of this State. The defendant appears to us to come clearly within the scope of that jurisdiction. He has been, as far as we can see, fairly and impartially tried under the law, and legally convicted according to the evidence exhibited in the record. We have found no error for which a reversal of the judgment should be had, and it is therefore affirmed.

Affirmed.[11]

---

11. Under the statute (18 U.S.C.A. § 1546) the United States District Court had jurisdiction to convict an alien of the crime of knowingly making a false statement under oath in a visa application to an American consular official located in a foreign country. The fact that the alien came into this country is no part of the offense. It was complete the moment he perjured himself in the foreign country. United States v. Pizzarusso, 388 F.2d 8 (2d Cir.1968).

(iii) The Situs of Crime

State v. Hall

Supreme Court of North Carolina, 1894.
114 N.C. 909, 19 S.E. 602.

■ Indictment for murder, tried at Spring Term, 1893, of Cherokee, before GRAVES, J., and a jury.

The defendants (Hall, as principal and Dockery, as accessory before the fact), were charged with the killing of Andrew Bryson on 11 July, 1892, in Cherokee County. The testimony tended to show that when the shooting occurred by which deceased was killed the defendants were in North Carolina and the deceased in Tennessee.

The defendants asked for the following instructions (among others):

"1. That it devolves upon the State to satisfy the jury beyond a reasonable doubt that the killing took place in the State of North Carolina; and if the State has failed to satisfy the jury beyond a reasonable doubt that the deceased received the wound from which he died whilst he was in the State of North Carolina, the defendants are not guilty.

"2. That if the prisoners were in North Carolina and the deceased was in Tennessee and the prisoners, or either of them, shot the deceased whilst he, the deceased, was in the State of Tennessee, and the deceased died from the effects of the wounds so received, the defendants are not guilty."

The instructions were refused, and after a verdict of guilty the defendants appealed from the judgment rendered thereon.

■ SHEPHERD, C.J. . . . . . It is a general principle of universal acceptation that one State or sovereignty can not enforce the penal or criminal laws of another, or punish crimes or offenses committed in and against another State or sovereignty. . . .

It seems to have been a matter of doubt in ancient times whether, if a blow was struck in one county and death ensued in another, the offender could be prosecuted in either, though according to Lord Hale (Pleas of the Crown, 426) "the more common opinion was that he might be indicted where the stroke was given." This difficulty, as stated by Mr. Starkie, was sought to be avoided by the legal device "of carrying the dead body back into the county where the blow was struck, and the jury might there," he adds, "inquire both of the stroke and death." 1 Starkie Cr.Pl., 2 Ed., 304; 1 Hawk, P.C., ch. 13; 1 East, 361. But to remove all doubt in respect to a matter of such grave importance, it was enacted by the statute 2 and 3 Edward VI that the murder might be tried in the county where the death occurred.[12] This statute, either as a part of the common law or by

---

If the elements of crime are committed in different jurisdictions, any state in which an essential part of the crime is committed may assert jurisdiction. Totemoff v. State, 905 P.2d 954 (Alaska 1995).

12. Missouri had no jurisdiction to prosecute a defendant for murder where the killing occurred in Illinois and the fatal blow was struck there even if the victim was kidnapped from Missouri to be killed. State v. Harvey, 730 S.W.2d 271 (Mo.App.1987).

reenactment, is in force in many of the States of the Union, and as applicable to counties within the same State its validity has never been questioned, but where its provisions have been extended so as to affect the jurisdiction of the different States its constitutionality has been vigorously assailed. Such legislation, however, has been very generally, if not indeed uniformly, sustained. . . .

Statutes of this character "are founded upon the general power of the Legislature, except so far as restrained by the Constitution of the Commonwealth and the United States to declare any willful or negligent act which causes an injury to person or property within its territory, to be a crime." Kerr on Homicide, 47. In many of the States there are also statutes substantially providing that where the death occurs outside of one State, by reason of a stroke given in another, the latter State may have jurisdiction. See our act, The Code, sec. 1197. The validity of these statutes seems to be undisputed, and indeed it has been held in many jurisdictions that such legislation is but in affirmance of the common law. It is manifest that statutes of this nature are only applicable to cases where the stroke and the death occur in different jurisdictions, and it is equally clear that where the stroke and the death occur in the same State the offense of murder at common law is there complete, and the courts of that State can alone try the offender for that specific common law crime.

The turning point, therefore, in this case is whether the stroke was, in legal contemplation, given in Tennessee, the alleged place of death; and upon this question the authorities all seem to point in one direction. . . .

In Simpson v. State, 92 Ga. 41, 17 S.E. 984, it was held by the Supreme Court of Georgia that one who, in the State of South Carolina, aims and fires a pistol at another who at the time is in the State of Georgia, is guilty of the offense of "shooting at another" although the ball did not take effect, but struck the water in the latter State. The Court said: "Of course the presence of the accused within this State is essential to make his act one which is done in this State, but the presence need not be actual; it may be constructive. The well-established theory of the law is that where one puts in force an agency for the commission of crime, he in legal contemplation accompanies the same to the point where it becomes effectual. . . . So, if a man in the State of South Carolina criminally fires a ball into the State of Georgia the law regards him as accompanying the ball and as being represented by it up to the point where it strikes. If an unlawful shooting occurred while both the parties were in this State the mere fact of missing

---

Where deceased died in Texas as a result of a blow struck by defendant in Quay County, New Mexico, venue of murder prosecution was properly laid in Quay County. State v. Justus, 65 N.M. 195, 334 P.2d 1104 (1959).

Under a statute providing: "If any such mortal wound shall be given, or other violence or injury shall be inflicted, or poison administered, on the high seas, or on any other navigable waters, or on land, either within or without the limits of this state, by means whereof death shall ensue in any county thereof, such offense may be prosecuted and punished in the county where such death may happen," defendant was convicted of murder, for inflicting, outside of Michigan, wounds of which the victim died within the state. Tyler v. People, 8 Mich. 320 (1860).

would not render the person who shot any the less guilty; consequently, if one shooting from another State goes, in a legal sense, where his bullet goes, the fact of his missing the object at which he aims can not alter the legal principle." ...

In view of the foregoing authorities it can not be doubted that the place of the assault or stroke in the present case was in Tennessee, and it is also clear that the offense of murder at common law was committed within the jurisdiction of that State. If this be so it must follow that unless we have some statute expressly conferring jurisdiction upon the courts of this State, or making the act of shooting under the circumstances a substantive murder, the offense with which the prisoners are charged can only be tried by the tribunals of Tennessee....

The fact that the prisoners and the deceased were citizens of the State of North Carolina can not affect the conclusion we have reached. If, as we have seen, the offense was committed in Tennessee, the personal jurisdiction generally, claimed by nations over their subjects who have committed offenses abroad or on the high seas can not be asserted by this State. Such jurisdiction does not exist as between the States of the Union under their peculiar relation to each other (Rorer Interstate Law, 308), and even if it could be rightfully claimed it could not in a case like the present be enforced in the absence of a statute providing that the offense should be tried in North Carolina. Even in England, where it seems the broadest claim to such jurisdiction is asserted, a statute (33 Hen. VIII) appears to have been necessary in order that the courts of that country could try a murder committed in Lisbon by one British subject upon another. In People v. Merrill, 2 Parker Cr. Cases, 600, it is said that by the common law offenses were local and the jurisdiction in such case depends upon statutory provisions. Granting, however, that in some instances the jurisdiction may exist without statute, it is not exercised in all cases. Dr. Wharton says: "It has already been stated that as to crimes committed by subjects in foreign civilized States, with the single exception in England of homicides, the Anglo–American practice is to take cognizance only of offenses directed against the sovereignty of the prosecuting State; perjury before consuls and forgery of government documents being included in this head." To the same effect is 3 A. & E. Enc., 539, in which it is said: "As to offenses committed in foreign civilized lands the country of arrest has jurisdiction only of offenses distinctively against its sovereignty." See also Dr. Wharton's article upon the subject in 1 Criminal Law Magazine, 715. As between the States the question is so clear to us that we forbear a general discussion of the subject. We may further remark that, while it is true that the criminal laws of a State can have no extra-territorial force, we are of the opinion that it is competent for the Legislature to determine what acts within the limits of the State shall be deemed criminal, and to provide for their punishment. Certainly, there could be no complaint where all the parties concerned in the homicide are citizens of North Carolina. It may also be observed that in addition to its common-law jurisdiction the State of Tennessee has provided by statute for the trial of an offender under the circumstances of this case.

For the reasons given we are constrained to say that the prisoners are entitled to a

New trial.[13]

---

13. Accord, State v. Carter, 27 N.J.L. 499 (1859).

A body of a victim found in Kentucky allows the Kentucky courts to consider the matter. Bedell v. Commonwealth, 870 S.W.2d 779 (Ky.1993).

New York had jurisdiction over felony murder where the killing was in New York while fleeing from the commission of a felony committed in another state. People v. Stokes, 88 N.Y.2d 618, 671 N.E.2d 1260 (1996).

New Jersey court lacked jurisdiction over a bigamy offense where the second marriage took place in Pakistan. Offense of bigamy was committed at the moment of the second marriage. State v. Ishaque, 312 N.J.Super. 207, 711 A.2d 416 (1997).

The same principle applies to other offenses. Thus the offense of obtaining property by false pretenses is committed where the property is obtained and not where the false pretense is made, Connor v. State, 29 Fla. 455, 10 So. 891 (1892); robbery is committed where the property is taken from the person, not where the person is first seized, if he is carried to another place before compelled to surrender his property, Sweat v. State, 90 Ga. 315, 17 S.E. 273 (1893), nor where the property is carried subsequently, 2 Hale P.C. *163; forgery is committed where the false instrument is made and the offense of uttering a forged instrument is committed where the instrument is uttered, State v. Hudson, 13 Mont. 112, 32 P. 413 (1893); the offense of receiving stolen goods is committed where they are received, State v. Rider, 46 Kan. 332, 26 P. 745 (1891); libel is committed at the place of publication, Commonwealth v. Blanding, 20 Mass. 304 (1825); contra: United States v. Smith, 173 F. 227 (D.Ind.1909); and bigamy is committed where the bigamous marriage is performed, 1 Hale P.C. *693.

The defendants were indicted for manslaughter of a man who died within the county in consequence of injuries inflicted by them upon him in a British merchant ship on the high seas. The statute provided "if a mortal wound is given, or other violence or injury inflicted, or poison is administered, on the high seas, or on land either within or without the limits of this state, by means whereof death ensues in any county thereof, such offence may be prosecuted and punished in the county where the death happens." This statute was upheld. Commonwealth v. Macloon, 101 Mass. 1 (1869).

The federal court had jurisdiction over a drug conspiracy case where the evidence indicated that the defendants intended to consummate the conspiracy within the territorial limits of the United States, even if no overt act of conspiracy had occurred within the territorial limits of the United States. Defendants had been arrested on the high seas. United States v. Gray, 659 F.2d 1296 (5th Cir.1981).

A "Ponzi" scheme involving oil wells in the United States was enough for federal court jurisdiction on mail fraud and securities violations for defrauding foreign investors. United States v. Cook, 573 F.2d 281 (5th Cir.1978).

Wyoming had jurisdiction to prosecute a father for failing or refusing to return a child to a custodial parent in Wyoming, even though at the time the crime was committed neither the father or the child had ever been in Wyoming. The criminal act had its effect in Wyoming. Rios v. State, 733 P.2d 242 (Wyo.1987).

Where Indians were charged with standing in Indian country and shooting at police officers who were outside of Indian country, the crime of assault with a dangerous weapon was consummated outside of Indian country and the South Dakota Court had jurisdiction. State v. Winckler, 260 N.W.2d 356 (S.D.1977).

Alabama had jurisdiction to try a capital murder defendant for the crime of murder/kidnaping where the murder occurred in Georgia, where the evidence showed the kidnaping began in Alabama. Heath v. Jones, 941 F.2d 1126 (11th Cir.1991).

Iowa had jurisdiction over murder of victim who lived in Illinois and was last seen there but whose body was found in Iowa. State v. Liggins, 557 N.W.2d 263 (Iowa 1996).

People v. Botkin

Supreme Court of California, In Bank, 1901.
132 Cal. 231, 64 P. 286.

■ GAROUTTE, J. Defendant has been convicted of the crime of murder, and prosecutes this appeal. The charge of the court given to the jury upon the law contained declarations which were held to be unsound in People v. Vereneseneckockockhoff, 129 Cal. 497, 58 P. 156. In view of the decision in that case, the attorney-general concedes that the judgment should be reversed and the cause remanded to the trial court for further proceedings. But defendant claims that she is not triable at all by the courts of this state, and this contention should now be passed upon. For if maintainable, a second trial becomes a useless expenditure of money, time, and labor, and necessarily should not be had.

For the purposes of testing the claim of lack of jurisdiction in the courts of California to try defendant, the facts of this case may be deemed as follows: Defendant, in the city and county of San Francisco, state of California, sent by the United States mail to Elizabeth Dunning, of Dover, Delaware, a box of poisoned candy, with intent that said Elizabeth Dunning should eat of the candy and her death be caused thereby. The candy was received by the party to whom addressed, she partook thereof, and her death was the result. Upon these facts may the defendant be charged and tried for the crime of murder in the courts of the state of California? We do not find it necessary to declare what the true rule may be at common law upon this state of facts, for, in our opinion, the statute of this state is broad enough to cover a case of the kind here disclosed. There can be no question but that the legislature of this state had the power to declare that the acts here pictured constitute the crime of murder in this state, and we now hold that the legislative body has made that declaration.

Section 27 of the Penal Code reads as follows:—

"The following persons are liable to punishment under the laws of this state:—

    "1. All persons who commit, in whole or in part, any crime within this state;

    "2. All who commit larceny or robbery out of this state, and bring to, or are found with the property stolen, in this state;

    "3. All who, being out of this state, cause or aid, advise or encourage, another person to commit a crime within this state, and are afterwards found therein."

Subdivision 1 covers the facts of this case. The acts of defendant constituted murder, and a part of those acts were done by her in this state. Preparing and sending the poisoned candy to Elizabeth Dunning, coupled with a murderous intent, constituted an attempt to commit murder, and defendant could have been prosecuted in this state for that crime, if, for any reason, the candy had failed to fulfill its deadly mission. That being so—those acts being sufficient, standing alone, to constitute a crime, and those acts resulting in the death of the person sought to be killed—nothing is plainer than that the crime of murder was in part committed within this state. The murder being committed *in part* in this state, the section of the law quoted declares that persons committing murder under those circumstances, "are liable to punishment under the laws of this state." The language quoted can have but one meaning, and that is: a person committing a murder in part in this state is punishable under the laws of this state, the same as though the murder was wholly committed in this state.

Counsel for defendant insist that this section contemplates only offenses committed by persons who, at the time, are without the state. This construction is not sound. For as to subdivision 1, it is not at all plain that a person without the state could commit, in whole, a crime within the state. Again, if the crime in whole is committed within the state by a person without the state, such a person could not be punished under the laws of this state, for the state has not possession of his body, and there appears to be no law by which it may secure that possession. Indeed, all of the subdivisions of the section necessarily contemplate a case where the person is, or comes, within the state. If the framers of the section had intended by subdivision 1 to cover the case of persons only who were without the state when the acts were committed which constitute the crime, they would have inserted in the section the contingency found in the remaining subdivisions, which subdivisions contemplate a return to the state of the person committing the crime. It is plain that the section, by its various provisions, was intended to embrace *all persons* punishable under the laws of the state of California. The defendant, having committed a murder in part in the state of California, is punishable under the laws of the state, exactly in the same way, in the same courts and under the same procedure, as if the crime was committed entirely within the state.

For the foregoing reasons the judgment and orders are reversed and the cause remanded.[14]

■ McFARLAND, J., VAN DYKE, J., HENSHAW, J., BEATTY, C.J., and TEMPLE, J., concurred.

---

14. Cf. People v. Licenziata, 199 App.Div. 106, 191 N.Y.S. 619 (2d Dep't 1921). In this case the defendant purchased a large quantity of wood alcohol in New York. This he put into mixtures called "whisky" and "brandy", which he sold for beverage purposes. A customer from Connecticut purchased part of it and this purchase found its way to a hotel at Chicopee Falls, Massachusetts, where a man died as a result of drinking it. It was shown that defendant knew of the poisonous nature of the mixture when he sold it in New York. A conviction of manslaughter in the first degree in New York was affirmed under the statutes of that state.

In People v. Zayas, 217 N.Y. 78, 111 N.E. 465 (1916), defendant was held triable in New York for there making false pretenses by means of which he obtained property which was delivered to him in Pennsylvania.

United States has jurisdiction over one who, while in a foreign country, conspires with persons within the United States, if an overt act in furtherance of the conspiracy is committed within the United States. Melia v. United States, 667 F.2d 300 (2d Cir.1981).

Michigan did not have jurisdiction over defendant who sold cocaine in Florida to a Michigan resident where defendant had not been advised that the drugs would be distributed in Michigan and where defendant had no interest in the cocaine beyond the original sale. People v. Blume, 443 Mich. 476, 505 N.W.2d 843 (1993). Contrast Commonwealth v. Snowdy, 412 Pa. Super. 493, 603 A.2d 1044 (1992).

People v. Utter

[California] Court of Appeal, Second District, Division 4, 1972.
24 Cal.App.3d 535, 101 Cal.Rptr. 214.

[The indictment against Utter had several counts but we are concerned here primarily with the first, which charged him with the murder of Norma Wilson. One of the other counts charged robbery. There was evidence which was intended to show that Utter, while in California and with intent to murder Mrs. Wilson, induced her to make a trip to Europe; that while still in California he purchased the tickets and the murder weapon; that he and Mrs. Wilson did make the trip to Europe; that he killed her in Spain; and returned to California bringing with him valuable jewelry she had been wearing when she left. He was convicted on several counts including those for murder and robbery.]

■ JEFFERSON, ACTING PRESIDING JUSTICE.

. . .

Defendant contends that the court lacked jurisdiction to conduct the trial with respect to the charges of murder and robbery. . . .

For the reasons set forth below we conclude that defendant is correct as to the lack of jurisdiction over the murder charge, but that the other contentions are without merit.

The defendant first contends that, because the physical acts relating to the murder and robbery took place outside the state of California, the courts of this state had no jurisdiction with respect to those charges. We conclude that, under the present state of decisional law in California, the trial court had jurisdiction over the robbery count, but not over the murder count.

Two sections of the Penal Code are applicable to the problem before us. They are sections 27 and 778a of the Penal Code, which read as follows:

Section 27: "The following persons are liable to punishment under the laws of this state:

"1. All persons who commit, in whole or in part, any crime within this state;

"2. All who commit any offense without this state which, if committed within this state, would be larceny, robbery, or embezzlement under the laws of this state, and bring the property stolen or embezzled, or any part of it, or are found with it, or any part of it, within this state;

"3. . . . "

Section 778a: "Whenever a person, with intent to commit a crime, does any act within this state in execution or part execution of such intent, which culminates in the commission of a crime, either within or without this state, such person is punishable for such crime in this state in the same manner as if the same had been committed entirely within this state."

The evidence shows that defendant brought the jewelry to California, where he turned it over to Forget. The express language of subdivision (2) of section 27 confers jurisdiction on the trial court over the robbery count. The case law so holds. (People v. Case (1957) 49 Cal.2d 24, 313 P.2d 840.)[15]

However, although a literal reading of subdivision (1) of section 27, and of section 778a, would seem to support jurisdiction over the murder count also, those sections have a history of judicial construction, binding on us in the case at bench, which requires us to read the statutory language in a manner more restrictive than a literal reading would suggest.

In People v. Muffum (*sic*) (1953) 40 Cal.2d 709, 256 P.2d 317, the Supreme Court construed the two sections above quoted and held that they required the doing, in California, of an act amounting to an "attempt" to commit the offense charged, within the definition of attempt in criminal cases generally—i.e., that there must be acts beyond mere preparation. Although there can be no doubt that there is no constitutional objection to a broader interpretation and although the *Buffum* decision has been strongly criticized, that case remains the law of California and we have no choice but to apply it in the case at bench.

The only acts of defendant which this record discloses which relate to the murder count are the act of inducing Mrs. Wilson to undertake the fatal trip, inferentially the act of purchasing the tickets, and the acquisition of the assumed murder weapon. The only direct evidence on the formation of the intent to kill is in Forget's testimony concerning a conversation in Spain, although from other things in the record it might be inferred that defendant had held that intent before the party left Los Angeles for Montreal. Giving the fullest possible effect to the whole record, clearly it falls short of an "attempt." It follows that, on the record before us, the trial court had no jurisdiction over the murder count. . . .

The judgment is modified, reversed in part and affirmed in part, as follows: (1) the judgment on count I is reversed; (2) the judgment on counts, II, IV and V is affirmed; (3) the judgment is modified by deleting the reference to count III; the sentence contained in said judgment is vacated and the case is remanded to the trial court for further proceedings consistent with this opinion.

---

15. [Compiler's note.] Without the aid of statute it was held that D, who stole a horse in Missouri and took it into Iowa, was guilty of larceny in Iowa as a matter of common law. State v. Bennett, 14 Iowa 479 (1863).

Kansas trial court had jurisdiction in theft case where property was stolen in another state and brought into Kansas. State v. Freitag, 247 Kan. 499, 802 P.2d 502 (1990).

Accord, State v. Ellis, 3 Conn. 185 (1819); Ferrill v. Commonwealth, 62 Ky. 153 (1864); Thomas v. Commonwealth, 15 S.W. 861, 12 Ky.L.Rep. 903 (1891); Cummings v. State, 1 Harr. & J. 340 (Md.Gen.1802); Worthington v. State, 58 Md. 403 (1882); Commonwealth v. Andrews, 2 Mass. 14 (1806); Commonwealth v. Holder, 75 Mass. 7 (1857); Hamilton v. State, 11 Ohio 435 (1842); State v. Johnson, 2 Or. 115 (1864); State v. Hill, 19 S.C. 435 (1883).

Whatever may be the rule at common law, it is clear that a state statute may make it a punishable offense, under the name of larceny, for a thief to bring into the state, goods stolen elsewhere by him. State v. Adams, 14 Ala. 486 (1848); La Vaul v. State, 40 Ala. 44 (1866); McFarland v. State, 4 Kan. 68 (1866); People v. Williams, 24 Mich. 156 (1871); State v. Butler, 67 Mo. 59 (1877); State v. Hickle, 268 N.W.2d 826 (S.D.1978).

■ KINGSLEY and DUNN, JJ., concur.

State v. Seekford

Supreme Court of Utah, 1981.
638 P.2d 525.

■ GOULD, DISTRICT JUDGE. Defendant appeals from his nonjury conviction of theft, a second degree felony.

Defendant rented a car on February 4, 1980, in Utah County, and immediately traveled with friends named Revoir to Price and Cleveland, Utah, and then to Las Vegas, Nevada, arriving in Las Vegas on February 5, 1980. They then traveled to Arizona and then Texas. During the course of their travel, defendant and Cary Revoir had several discussions regarding the rented car. During one of these conversations, Revoir said, "We ought to take the car back. We could get in trouble over it." Defendant's responses were that he would "handle it." Defendant and Revoirs then were separated, with defendant keeping the car. Revoirs located him a few days later by telephone, and asked if he was going to return the car, to which defendant replied he would "handle it." Defendant then indicated to Michelle Revoir that he had "some friends who could make him some license plates."

The vehicle was located and recovered several months later.

Defendant's attack is that the Utah court was without jurisdiction. U.C.A., 1953, 76–1–201 provides:

(1) A person is subject to prosecution in this state for an offense which he commits, while either within or outside the state, by his own conduct or that of another for which he is legally accountable, if:

(a) The offense is committed either wholly or partly within the state; or

(b) The conduct outside the state constitutes an attempt to commit an offense within the state; or

(c) The conduct outside the state constitutes a conspiracy to commit an offense within the state and an act in furtherance of the conspiracy occurs in the state; or

(d) The conduct within the state constitutes an attempt, solicitation, or conspiracy to commit in another jurisdiction an offense under the laws of both this state and such other jurisdiction.

(2) An offense is committed partly within this state if either the conduct which is an element of the offense, or the result which is such an element, occurs within this state. . . .

The court made no specific written finding that an element of the offense occurred in Utah, but did have the following exchange with counsel:

THE COURT: ... It may have been that at the time the Rental Agreement was made here, he knew very well he was never going to bring the car back.

MR. SCHUMACHER: But there is no evidence of that before the Court.

THE COURT: I don't know. Maybe there is. Maybe I could infer from what I heard of the entire chain of events, very reasonably, that he had that intent at the time he took it. I think there is stronger evidence along other lines. I think it's something that may be accumulated.

It is clear from this exchange that the court had in mind that the element of "intent" had to have existed in defendant's mind while he was in Utah.

Subsequently, the court found defendant guilty. In view of the exchange between the court and counsel as shown above, we must conclude that the court's finding of guilt encompassed a finding that defendant harbored an "intent to deprive the owner of his property" while in the State of Utah. The offense therefore was committed in this state, and the Utah courts have jurisdiction to try defendant for the offense. . . .

Defendant next contends that the state charged defendant improperly under the general theft statute when it had available a specific statute covering thefts pursuant to rental agreements. The present Utah theft statute consolidates the offenses known under prior law as larceny, embezzlement, extortion, receiving stolen property, and false pretenses into a single offense entitled "theft." All that is now required is simply to plead the general offense of theft and the accusation may be supported by evidence that it was committed in any manner specified in 404 through 410 of the Code.

The judgment of the trial court is affirmed.

■ HALL, C.J., HOWE and OAKS, JJ.

■ STEWART, J., concurs in the result.[16]

(iv) Jurisdiction Over Boundary Rivers

Nielsen v. Oregon

Supreme Court of the United States, 1909.
212 U.S. 315, 29 S.Ct. 383, 53 L.Ed. 528.

[Nielsen, a citizen of Washington, had a license from the Fish Commissioner of Washington to operate a purse net on the Columbia River and was on said river, within the limits of the State of Washington, operating a purse net when he was arrested by Oregon officers. An Oregon statute prohibited fishing with a purse net on the Columbia River and Nielson was convicted for a violation of that law. From that judgment the case was taken to the Supreme Court on error.

Before the territories had been admitted into the Union it had been provided by Act of Congress "that the Territory of Oregon and the Territory of Washington, shall have concurrent jurisdiction over all offenses

---

16. Montana had jurisdiction over a defendant when he left Montana in a truck with the owner's permission and then assumed unlawful control of the vehicle in another state and failed to return the truck to Montana. State v. White, 230 Mont. 356, 750 P.2d 440 (1988).

committed on the Columbia River, where said river forms the common boundary between said territories". And the Act of Congress admitting Oregon into the Union provides that it shall have "jurisdiction in civil and criminal cases upon the Columbia River and Snake River, concurrently with the states and territories of which those rivers form a boundary in common with this State".]

■ MR. JUSTICE BREWER.... Undoubtedly one purpose, perhaps the primary purpose, in the grant of concurrent jurisdiction was to avoid any nice question as to whether a criminal act sought to be prosecuted was committed on one side or the other of the exact boundary in the channel, that boundary sometimes changing by reason of the shifting of the channel. Where an act is *malum in se* prohibited and punishable by the laws of both States, the one first acquiring jurisdiction of the person may prosecute the offense, and its judgment is a finality in both States, so that one convicted or acquitted in the courts of the one State cannot be prosecuted for the same offense in the courts of the other. But, as appears from the quotation we have just made, it is not limited to this. It extends to civil as well as criminal matters, and is broadly a grant of jurisdiction to each of the States.

The present case is not one of the prosecution for an offense *malum in se,* but for one simply *malum prohibitum.* Doubtless the same rule would apply if the act was prohibited by each State separately, but where as here the act is prohibited by one State and in terms authorized by the other, can the one State which prohibits, prosecute and punish for the act done within the territorial limits of the other? Obviously, the grant of concurrent jurisdiction may bring up from time to time many and some curious and difficult questions, so we properly confine ourselves to the precise question presented. The plaintiff in error was within the limits of the State of Washington, doing an act which that State in terms authorized and gave him a license to do. Can the State of Oregon, by virtue of its concurrent jurisdiction, disregard that authority, practically override the legislation of Washington, and punish a man for doing within the territorial limits of Washington an act which that State had specially authorized him to do?[17] We are of opinion that it cannot. It is not at all impossible that in some instances the interests of the two States may be different. Certainly, as appears in the present case, the opinion of the legislatures of the two States is different, and the one State cannot enforce its opinion against that of the other, at least as to an act done within the limits of that other State. Whether, if the act of the plaintiff in error had been done within the territorial limits of the State of Oregon, it would make any difference we need not determine, nor whether, in the absence of any legislation by the State of Washington authorizing the act, Oregon could enforce its statute against the act done anywhere upon the waters of the Columbia. Neither is it necessary to consider whether the prosecution should be in the names of the two States jointly. It is enough to decide, as we do, that for an act done

---

17. *"[S]ubstantive law* is that which declares what acts are crimes and proscribes the punishment therefor; whereas *procedural law* is that which provides or regulates the steps by which one who violates the law is punished." State v. Augustine, 197 Kan. 207, 209, 416 P.2d 281, 283 (1966).

within the territorial limits of the State of Washington under authority and license from that State one cannot be prosecuted and punished by the State of Oregon. . . .

The judgment of the Supreme Court of the State of Oregon is reversed and the case remanded for further proceedings not inconsistent with this opinion.[18]

MODEL PENAL CODE

Section 1.03   Territorial Applicability.

(1) Except as otherwise provided in this Section, a person may be convicted under the law of this State of an offense committed by his own conduct or the conduct of another for which he is legally accountable if:

(a) either the conduct which is an element of the offense or the result which is such an element occurs within this State; or

(b) conduct occurring outside the State is sufficient under the law of this State to constitute an attempt to commit an offense within the State; or

(c) conduct occurring outside the State is sufficient under the law of this State to constitute a conspiracy to commit an offense within the State and an overt act in furtherance of such conspiracy occurs within the State; or

(d) conduct occurring within the State establishes complicity in the commission of, or an attempt, solicitation or conspiracy to commit, an offense in another jurisdiction which also is an offense under the law of this State; or

(e) the offense consists of the omission to perform a legal duty imposed by the law of this State with respect to domicile, residence or a relationship to a person, thing or transaction in the State; or

(f) the offense is based on a statute of this State which expressly prohibits conduct outside the State, when the conduct bears a reasonable relation to a legitimate interest of this State and the actor knows or should know that his conduct is likely to affect that interest.

---

18. In many cases the courts of one state have punished crimes committed upon that part of the river within the boundaries of another state: Carlisle v. State, 32 Ind. 55 (1869); Dougan v. State, 125 Ind. 130, 25 N.E. 171 (1890); Lemore v. Commonwealth, 127 Ky. 480, 105 S.W. 930 (1907); State v. Cunningham, 102 Miss. 237, 59 So. 76 (1912); State v. Metcalf, 65 Mo.App. 681 (1896); State v. Cameron, 2 Pin. 490 (Wis.1850); see Commonwealth v. Garner, 3 Grat. 655 (Va.1846). In Wiggins Ferry Co. v. Reddig, 24 Ill.App. 260 (1887), the court at page 265 said: "Undoubtedly it would be held that the judicial tribunal first taking cognizance of the cause would, under well established and understood principles, retain its jurisdiction to the end of the controversy, applying the law of the *forum* to the facts of the case in settling the rights of the parties."

Defendant was charged in Minnesota with larceny from the person. The evidence showed that the offense was committed on a bridge which spans the Mississippi River, at a point between Minnesota and Wisconsin, and was committed on a part of the bridge over an island which is on the Wisconsin side of the main channel of the river. It was held that the Minnesota court had jurisdiction. State v. George, 60 Minn. 503, 63 N.W. 100 (1895).

Where a river which forms a boundary line between two states suddenly leaves its old bed and forms a new one by the process of avulsion there is no change of the boundary line. State v. Jacobs, 93 Ariz. 336, 380 P.2d 998 (1963).

Indiana has concurrent jurisdiction over all parts of the Ohio River that are a part of its territorial jurisdiction. Benham v. State, 637 N.E.2d 133 (Ind.1994).

(2) Subsection (1)(a) does not apply when either causing a specified result or a purpose to cause or danger of causing such a result is an element of an offense and the result occurs or is designed or likely to occur only in another jurisdiction where the conduct charged would not constitute an offense, unless a legislative purpose plainly appears to declare the conduct criminal regardless of the place of the result.

(3) Subsection (1)(a) does not apply when causing a particular result is an element of an offense and the result is caused by conduct occurring outside the State which would not constitute an offense if the result had occurred there, unless the actor purposely or knowingly caused the result within the State.

(4) When the offense is homicide, either the death of the victim or the bodily impact causing death constitutes a "result," within the meaning of Subsection (1)(a) and if the body of a homicide victim is found within the State, it is presumed that such result occurred within the State.

(5) This State includes the land and water and the air space above such land and water with respect to which the State has legislative jurisdiction.[19]

(B) Venue

If an alleged offense is triable within a jurisdiction it is then necessary to determine which of the courts in the jurisdiction may try it. To decide this it is necessary to ascertain the particular area (or areas) of the jurisdiction within which it may be tried. This area will usually be a county or district, although in some states it may be some other subdivision such as a precinct. And the area appropriate for the trial is called the "venue." The word "venue" originally meant the neighborhood from which the jurors were to come. It still has that meaning except that the place of trial is the same whether it is to be by a jury or without a jury.

Statutory provisions with reference to venue differ from state to state. The American Law Institute included the following suggestions in its proposed Code of Criminal Procedure, after an exhaustive study of all of the existing statutes:

Section 238. Right to try where offense committed within state. Any person who commits within this state an offense against this state, whether he is within or without the state at the time of its commission, may be tried in this state.

Section 239. Offense in or against aircraft. Any person who commits an offense in or against any aircraft while it is in flight over this state may be tried in this state. The trial in such case may be in any county over which the aircraft passed in the course of such flight.

Section 240. Place of trial generally. In all criminal prosecutions the trial shall be in the county where the offense was committed unless otherwise provided in this Code.

Section 241. Where accessory in one county and offense committed in another. Where a person in one county aids, abets or procures the commission of an offense in another county he may be tried for the offense in either county.

---

19. Copyright © 1962 by the American Law Institute. Reprinted with the permission of the American Law Institute.

Section 242. Where offense committed partly in one and partly in another county. Where several acts are requisite to the commission of an offense, the trial may be in any county in which any of such acts occurs.

Section 243. Where offense committed on or near county boundary. Where an offense is committed on or within five hundred yards of the boundary of two or more counties the trial may be in any one of such counties.

Section 244. Where a person in one county commits offense in another. Where a person in one county commits an offense in another county the trial may be in either county.

Section 245. Where offense committed on railroad train or other vehicle. Where an offense is committed on a railroad train or other public or private vehicle while in the course of its trip the trial may be in any county through which such train or other vehicle passed during such trip.

Section 246. Where offense committed on vessel. Where an offense is committed on board a vessel in the course of its voyage, the trial may be in any county through which the vessel passed during such voyage.

Section 247. Where injury inflicted in one county and death occurs in another. Where a person inflicts an injury upon another person in one county from which the injured person dies in another county, the trial for the homicide may be in either county.

Section 248. Where stolen property brought into another county. Where a person obtains property by larceny, robbery, false pretenses or embezzlement in one county and brings the property so obtained into any other county or counties, he may be tried in the county in which he obtains the property or in any other county into which he brings it.

Section 249. Conviction or acquittal in one county bar to prosecution in another. Where a person may be tried for an offense in two or more counties, a conviction or acquittal of the offense in one county shall be a bar to a prosecution for the same offense in another county.

Where the evidence as to venue is disputed the jury should pass upon it as one of the issues of the case. If it is clear that the court has no jurisdiction over the offense the prosecution should be dismissed. But if the lack of jurisdiction is because the offense is within the exclusive jurisdiction of the court of some other area of the jurisdiction the usual procedure is not to discharge the defendant, but to have him committed, or admitted to bail, to await transfer to the proper venue for trial there.

State v. Favors

Supreme Court of Arizona, En Banc, 1962.
92 Ariz. 147, 375 P.2d 260.

■ UDALL, VICE CHIEF JUSTICE. Bobby Favors was convicted in the Superior Court of Pima County of the crime of wilfully and unlawfully robbing Jack Weylor on December 7, 1960. He appeals to this court.

With two other men Favors entered upon Weylor's property and with a 30–30 rifle forced him to give up his wallet along with its contents. The identity of Favors as one of the three men was established to the satisfaction of the jury, notwithstanding the fact that he claimed to have been elsewhere at the time of the commission of the crime.

The errors urged by the defendant relate to four different matters. First it is argued that the court erred in reopening the state's case to hear evidence on the question of venue, when the state failed to establish venue before the time that the court was to instruct the jury. When defendant had finished his own closing argument he asked the court to instruct the jury that there was no evidence in the trial that the crime had been committed in Pima County. Thereupon plaintiff moved the court for permission to reopen the case for the purpose of hearing evidence regarding the question of venue, which motion was granted. Deputy Sheriff Norman Ranger was recalled and he testified that the alleged robbery was committed in Pima County at the place specified in the information.

Such a ruling was within the sound discretion of the court. In State v. Cassady, 67 Ariz. 48, 190 P.2d 501, we said:

"Our rules of criminal procedure should be construed so as to promote justice—not to thwart it. To have refused to permit the state to reopen its case would have been an abuse of legal discretion and an 'assist' to the obstruction of justice." . . .

Judgment of conviction affirmed.[20]

---

20. Where defendant did not know that venue would not be proved he could move for an acquittal at the conclusion of the evidence. United States v. Brothman, 191 F.2d 70 (2d Cir.1951).

"The venue was a jurisdictional fact, . . ." People v. Adams, 300 Ill. 20, 24, 132 N.E. 765, 767 (1921). ". . . it has always been the law requiring the government or state, as the case might be, to prove the venue in order to show jurisdiction of the court to try and determine the issue." Jackson v. State, 187 Ind. 694, 699, 121 N.E. 114, 116 (1918). " 'It is a maxim in the law that consent can never confer jurisdiction; by which is meant that the consent of parties cannot empower a Court to act upon subjects which are not submitted to its determination and judgment by the law.' Cooley on Const.Lim. p. 575. . . . The general rule undoubtedly is that the objection that a court has no jurisdiction of the person of the accused may be waived. . . . This court holds that 'the right to object to the locality of trial is a personal privilege which the party may waive and thereby confer jurisdiction.' Brown v. Brown, 155 Tenn. 530, at page 537, 296 S.W. 356, 358, citing cases." State ex rel. Lea v. Brown, 166 Tenn. 669, 694–5, 64 S.W.2d 841, 849 (1933). Accord, Hilderbrand v. United States, 304 F.2d 716 (10th Cir.1962).

The federal statute provides (18 U.S.C.A. § 3231): "The district courts of the United States shall have original jurisdiction, exclusive of the courts of the States, of all offenses against the laws of the United States". Hence the question in regard to a particular court of the United States is one of venue rather than jurisdiction. Bickford v. Looney, 219 F.2d 555 (10th Cir.1955).

The right guaranteed by the Constitution to be tried in the county in which the crime is alleged to have been committed relates to venue rather than jurisdiction and is waived by a plea of guilty. Key v. Page, 424 P.2d 99 (Okl.Cr.1967).

D has a constitutional right to a trial by jury in the district in which the crime was committed. There is no constitutional guaranty that the accused has a right to be tried in the division of the district in which the crime was committed. Franklin v. United States, 384 F.2d 377 (5th Cir.1967).

Where the only reference from which venue might be inferred was testimony relating to certain named streets and business establishments the conviction was reversed. Morris v. State, 363 P.2d 377 (Okl.Cr.1961). The court said it would take judicial notice of the

■ BERNSTEIN, C.J., and STRUCKMEYER, JENNINGS and LOCKWOOD, JJ., concur.

State v. Zimmer

Supreme Court of Kansas, 1967.
198 Kan. 479, 426 P.2d 267.

■ HARMAN, COMMISSIONER. William Frederick Zimmer was convicted of the offenses of kidnaping in the first degree, with harm inflicted (K.S.A. 21–449) and of murder in the first degree (K.S.A. 21–401). As punishment the jury imposed the death penalty for the kidnaping charge and life imprisonment for the murder. The trial court denied appellant's motion for new trial, and adjudged sentences in accordance with the jury verdict, from which defendant Zimmer has appealed. . . .

Appellant urges as ground for reversal of his conviction that proper venue as to the murder offense was never established in Shawnee county, inasmuch as there was no evidence the killing occurred therein. He argues the state produced evidence the victim was last seen alive in Wamego in Pottawatomie county and her body was found in Pottawatomie county; therefore the murder offense could be prosecuted only in that county.

Section 10 of the bill of rights to our Kansas constitution provides in part:

"In all prosecutions, the accused shall be allowed to appear and defend in person, or by counsel . . . and a speedy public trial by an impartial jury of the county or district in which the offense is alleged to have been committed. . . ."

This is implemented by the following statutes:

"Offenses committed against the laws of this state shall be punished in the county in which the offense is committed, except as may be otherwise provided by law." (K.S.A. 62–401.)

"When a public offense has been committed, partly in one county and partly in another, or the act or effects constituting or requisite to the consummation of the offense occur in two or more counties, the jurisdiction is in either county." (K.S.A. 62–404.)

And our statute denouncing kidnaping provides:

---

boundaries of the counties and the geographical locations of the cities and towns of the state, but not of streets and buildings where there is no evidence as to the town or city in which they are located.

Permitting either trial or appellate court to decide venue from facts judicially noticed but not communicated to the jury would deprive defendant of trial by jury on the issue of fact alleged in the indictment. State v. Jones, 240 Or. 129, 400 P.2d 524 (1965).

Venue for the trial of a criminal case need not be proved beyond a reasonable doubt, but only by a preponderance of the evidence, and it may be established by circumstantial evidence. People v. Erb, 235 Cal.App.2d 650, 45 Cal.Rptr. 503 (1965). Contra, State v. Jones, 240 Or. 129, 400 P.2d 524 (1965).

Venue is not an element of the offense. United States v. Maldonado–Rivera, 922 F.2d 934 (2d Cir.1990). The government may prove venue by a preponderance of the evidence and need prove it beyond a reasonable doubt. United States v. Rosa, 17 F.3d 1531 (2d Cir.1994). Accord: United States v. Taylor, 828 F.2d 630 (10th Cir.1987).

"... Any person or persons charged with such offense may be tried in any county into or through which the person so seized, inveigled, decoyed, kidnaped, or otherwise taken shall have been carried or brought." (K.S.A. 21–449).

It is true as contended there was no evidence as to where the fatal blows were struck.

Appellant was charged in the information with felony murder, that is, killing while engaged in the perpetration of a felony, namely, kidnaping. The jury was instructed upon this type of murder and appellant stands convicted thereof. Hence the kidnaping was an essential element of the murder offense. Inasmuch as the initial abduction occurred in Shawnee county and the kidnaping was triable there, venue on the murder charge became permissible there under 62–404.

It may be noteworthy that the general area in Pottawatomie county where the victim was last seen alive other than by her killer and where her body was found, is so situated it lies within five or six minutes driving distance from three adjoining counties, including Shawnee, and no more than fifteen minutes from at least two others. A murderer should not escape punishment because the exact place of his crime is concealed.

The Supreme Court of Washington was confronted with an identical factual situation where the same legal contention was made as here in State v. Wilson, 38 Wash.2d 593, 231 P.2d 288, *cert. den.* 342 U.S. 855, 72 S.Ct. 81, 96 L.Ed. 644, *cert. den.* 343 U.S. 950, 72 S.Ct. 1044, 96 L.Ed. 1352. The defendants there were convicted of kidnaping in the first degree and murder in the first degree and the death penalty imposed. The facts were that the victim was kidnaped in Clark County, Washington, and a week later her body was found in Skamania County, Washington, fifty-five miles from the scene of the kidnaping. She had been brutally beaten, cut behind her ear and sexually violated. Death was caused by carbon monoxide poisoning. The evidence did not reveal where the cause of death occurred.

The state of Washington has a constitutional provision respecting place of trial essentially identical to that quoted from our own bill of rights and an implementing statute identical to our 62–404.

Under a statute similar to our own the defendants in Wilson were charged with felony murder. The court held the county wherein the kidnaping occurred had jurisdiction to try the murder charge, stating:

"Nor does the fact that no one can say with certainty whether the death occurred in Clark county, where the kidnaping occurred, or in Skamania county, where the body was found, present any bar to the prosecution for murder in Clark county."

We hold venue on the murder charge was properly established in Shawnee county.

At the conclusion of the prosecution evidence appellant moved for his discharge upon the venue issue already mentioned and upon the ground appellee had failed to prove the kidnaping charge. Denial of this motion is assigned as error. This contention is based upon the argument there was no evidence that the girl Gladys was confined against her will.

The child was taken under such circumstances as to cause crying and screaming in her younger brother and sister, she was crying when seen in appellant's company in the field northwest of Topeka and appellant admitted to officers he slapped her because she was crying. She was found brutally murdered. The contention is wholly without merit. Moreover, as a matter of law, a child of tender years may not consent to its seizure. At 1 Am.Jur., 2d Abduction and Kidnapping, § 16, the rule is stated:

"A child of tender years is ordinarily regarded as incapable of consenting to its seizure and abduction and, when taken from its rightful guardian, is deemed to have been taken without its consent as a matter of law."

The jury here was later instructed in accordance with the foregoing and properly so. The evidence was sufficient to support the charges, including the element of wilfulness, and the court committed no error in denying the motion to discharge.

The judgment and sentences are affirmed.

Approved by the court.[21]

State v. Reese

Supreme Court of Washington, Department One, 1920.
112 Wash. 507, 192 P. 934.

■ MAIN, J. The defendant was charged by information, by the prosecuting attorney of Spokane county, with the crime of grand larceny. The trial resulted in a verdict of guilty. A motion in arrest of judgment was made and sustained. The state appeals.

The information, omitting the formal parts, is as follows:

"That on or about August 31st, 1919, on a railway train of the Northern Pacific Railroad, arriving in, and passing through, Spokane county, Washington, the said defendant, Arthur Reese, whose other or true name is to the prosecuting attorney unknown, then and there being, did then and there, wilfully, unlawfully and feloniously, take, steal and carry away one certain gold watch of the value of $50 and one certain gold bougat [sic] watch fob of the value of $50, the property of, and belonging to, Chas. E. Roediger, with the intent to deprive and defraud the owner thereof."

It should be noted that, in this charge, it is not alleged that the offense was committed in Spokane county. Upon the trial it appeared from testimony that the respondent was a porter on the Northern Pacific train leaving

---

21. See also State v. Duvaul, 223 Kan. 718, 576 P.2d 653 (1978). Venue of an offense is jurisdictional and the state must prove the offense occurred in the county where it is prosecuted. State v. Myatt, 237 Kan. 17, 697 P.2d 836 (1985).

Venue is proper in any county where any element of the offense was committed. People v. Dixon, 161 Ill.Dec. 857, 219 Ill.App.3d 1, 579 N.E.2d 405 (1991).

"Locus delicti" is the statutory, not constitutional, concept of a right to be tried in the county in which the crime was committed. People v. Sering, 232 Cal.App. 3d 677, 283 Cal.Rptr. 507 (1991).

A defendant could be tried for murder in Humbolt County of a victim killed in Los Angeles where preparatory acts occurred in Humbolt County. People v. Price, 1 Cal.4th 324, 3 Cal.Rptr.2d 106, 821 P.2d 610 (1991).

Tacoma, Washington, on the evening of the 30th or 31st of August, 1919. The train arrived in Spokane the following morning. Among the passengers on the train was one C.E. Roediger, who occupied a berth in a sleeping car just in front of the car which was in charge of the respondent. Roediger retired about midnight, and at the time the train was near Yakima, Washington. At this time he had in his vest pocket a watch and fob. He awoke near Lind, Washington, and his watch and fob were missing. About a month later the respondent pawned the watch in the city of Spokane. Thereafter he was arrested, with the result as above indicated. The charge in this case is laid under § 2293 of Rem. & Bal.Code, which provides:

"The route traversed by any railway car, coach, train or other public conveyance, and the water traversed by any boat shall be criminal districts; and the jurisdiction of all public offenses committed on any such railway car, coach, train, boat or other public conveyance, or at any station or depot upon such route, shall be in any county through which said car, coach, train, boat or other public conveyance may pass during the trip or voyage, or in which the trip or voyage may begin or terminate."

By this statute, it is attempted to make the route traversed by a railway train a criminal district and to provide that the court in any county through which the train may pass during its trip shall have jurisdiction of any offense committed upon the train, regardless of whether, at the time the crime was committed, the train was in the county where the prosecution is attempted to be had. If this statute is constitutional, the judgment of the superior court cannot be sustained. On the other hand, if the statute is unconstitutional, the trial court ruled correctly on the motion in arrest of judgment. It should be kept in mind that this is not a case where property stolen in one county is carried by the thief into another, and in the latter county is charged with having committed an offense therein. As already pointed out, the information in this case does not charge that the offense was committed in Spokane county. Neither is it a case where an act done in one county contributes to the offense in another. The question is the constitutionality of the law under which the accused was tried and convicted. Const., art. 1, § 22, provides:

"In criminal prosecutions, the accused shall have the right to ... a speedy public trial by an impartial jury of the county in which the offense is alleged to have been committed...."

Under this section of the constitution one accused of crime has a right to be tried in the county in which the offense is alleged to have been committed. It requires no argument to show that the offense, being alleged in a particular county, the proof must show that it was committed in that county. Comparing the provisions of the statute with the requirements of the constitution, it appears that the statute goes beyond the constitutional limitation. Under the statute, the route traversed by a railway train is made a criminal district, and an offender may be prosecuted in any county in such district. Under the constitution, he can only be prosecuted in the county where the offense has been committed. In State v. Carroll, 55 Wash. 588, 104 Pac. 814, 133 Am.St. 1047, the court had before it a statute providing that, when property taken by burglary in one county had been brought into another county, the jurisdiction was in either county. It was there held that the statute violated Const., art. 1, § 22, which guaranteed to the accused a right to a trial in the county in which the offense was alleged to have been committed. While that case can hardly be said to be exactly in point upon the question presented upon this appeal, yet the analogy is very close.... In People v. Brock, 149 Mich. 464, 112 N.W. 1116, the question was before the supreme court of Michigan, and it was there held that such a statute cannot be sustained under a constitutional provision which guarantees to the accused the right to a trial in the county in which the offense has been committed. It was there said:

"It would be a startling innovation should we say that the legislature has power to subject a person charged with crime to prosecution in any one of several counties, covering a strip of territory coextensive with the length or breadth of the state, at the prosecutor's election, and yet that is what this statute authorizes if it is valid. It cannot be said that this offense was in 'contemplation of law' committed in each of said counties, as in a case where property stolen in one county is carried by the thief into another, or possibly where an act done in one county contributes to the commission of the offense in another."

In Watt v. People, 126 Ill. 9, 18 N.E. 340, the question was before the supreme court of Illinois and a different conclusion was there reached, though not by a unanimous court. The holding in that case seems to be influenced by the fact that the constitutional provision there being considered was less restrictive than were the similar provisions in either of the two earlier constitutions, and this fact led to the conclusion that it was the intention "to release in some degree the rigid rule formerly prevailing." As already stated, none of the other cases cited in the notes of Corpus Juris, or in the brief, discuss or decide the question here presented. Under this state of the authorities, we are constrained to disagree with the writer of the text upon where the weight of authority lies. It seems to us that reason and authority both support the view that the statute cannot take away from an accused a right guaranteed by the constitution.

The judgment will be affirmed.[22]

■ HOLCOMB, C.J., MITCHELL, PARKER, and MACKINTOSH, JJ., concur.

---

22. In 1922 the constitution of the State of Washington was amended as follows: "The route traversed by any railway coach, train or public conveyance, and the water traversed by any boat shall be criminal districts; and the jurisdiction of all public offenses committed on any such railway car, coach, train, boat or other public conveyance, or at any station or depot upon such route, shall be in any county through which the said car, coach, train, boat or other public conveyance may pass during the trip or voyage, or in which the trip or voyage may begin or terminate." Art. I, § 22. See now Amendment 10.

Accord, State v. Montgomery, 115 La. 155, 38 So. 949 (1905); State v. Hatch, 91 Mo. 568, 4 S.W. 502 (1887). A similar statute was held valid in Michigan, but the constitutional provisions were different. People v. Donaldson, 243 Mich. 104, 219 N.W. 602 (1928). In Oregon a statute authorizing trial in either county, if the offense is committed within a mile of the county line, was held not to violate defendant's right to be tried in the county in which the crime was committed. This statute was said merely to enlarge the boundaries of the county for judicial purposes. State v. Lehman, 130 Or. 132, 279 P. 283 (1929).

Where an offense is committed partly in one county and partly in another, a trial in either satisfies the constitutional provision which entitles the accused to be tried in the county in which the offense was committed. Kneefe v. Sullivan, 2 Or.App. 152, 465 P.2d 741 (1970).

In Commonwealth v. Macloon, 101 Mass. 1 (1869), it was held that death within the state, resulting from injuries inflicted elsewhere, was sufficient to authorize trial and conviction in

United States v. Cabrales

Supreme Court of the United States, 1998.
524 U.S. 1, 118 S.Ct. 1772, 141 L.Ed.2d 1.

■ JUSTICE GINGSBURG.

This case presents a question of venue, specifically, the place appropriate for trial on charges of money laundering in violation of 18 U.S.C. § 1956(a)(1)(B)(ii) (conducting a financial transaction to avoid a transaction-reporting requirement) and § 1957 (engaging in a monetary transaction in criminally derived property of a value greater than $10,000). The laundering alleged in the indictment occurred entirely in Florida. The currency purportedly laundered derived from the unlawful distribution of cocaine in Missouri. The defendant, respondent Vickie S. Cabrales, is not alleged to have transported funds from Missouri to Florida. Nor is she charged, in the counts before us, with participation in the Missouri cocaine distribution that generated the funds in question. In accord with the Court of Appeals for the Eighth Circuit, we hold that Missouri is not a proper place for trial of the money laundering offenses at issue.

I

In a three-count indictment returned in the United States District Court for the Western District of Missouri, Cabrales, as sole defendant, was

---

the state, under an express statutory provision to that effect. Accord, as to death in one county resulting from an injury inflicted in another county in the same state, under a statute expressly so providing. State v. Criqui, 105 Kan. 716, 185 P. 1063 (1919). In State v. Carter, 27 N.J.L. 499 (1859) it was held that an indictment charging a fatal assault committed in New York and resulting in death in New Jersey charged no crime in the latter state. Apparently New Jersey had a statute somewhat similar to the Massachusetts act, but the court held that it applied only to murder and not to manslaughter. The opinion indicates that it is beyond the power of the state to punish for acts done exclusively in another state, even if death results therefrom and occurs in New Jersey.

A prosecution for obtaining property by false pretenses could be maintained in the county in which the false and fraudulent representation was made, although the property was obtained in another county. State v. Knutson, 168 Wash. 633, 12 P.2d 923 (1932). The decision was under a statute allowing prosecution to be in either county if the offense was committed partly in each.

Theft under the venue statute is properly characterized as a "traveling offense." State v. Martinez, 255 Kan. 464, 874 P.2d 617 (1994).

Larceny could be prosecuted in either the county in which the theft occurred or in any county into which the thief later took the property. State v. Alvarez, 9 Kan.App.2d 371, 678 P.2d 1132 (1984).

The offense of filing a false income-tax return may be tried either in the district in which the return was prepared or in the district in which it was filed. United States v. United States District Court, 209 F.2d 575 (6th Cir.1954).

Although B's shooting of the witness occurred in the Middle District of Tennessee, venue for prosecution of obstruction of justice could lie in the Northern District of Alabama, where the case was pending in which the witness was scheduled to testify. United States v. Barham, 666 F.2d 521 (11th Cir.1982).

Venue of prosecution for making written threats is proper in either the county where the letters were written and mailed or in the county where the letters were received if an act constituting part of the offense occurred in both places. State v. Wise, 664 So.2d 1028 (Fla.App.1995).

charged with the following offenses: conspiracy to avoid a transaction-reporting requirement, in violation of 18 U.S.C. §§ 371, 1956(a)(1)(B)(ii) (Count I); conducting a financial transaction to avoid a transaction-reporting requirement, in violation of § 1956(a)(1)(B)(ii) (Count II); and engaging in a monetary transaction in criminally derived property of a value greater than $10,000, in violation of § 1957 (Count III). The indictment alleged that, in January 1991, Cabrales deposited $40,000 with the AmSouth Bank of Florida and, within a week's span, made four separate withdrawals of $9,500 each from that bank. The money deposited and withdrawn was traceable to illegal sales of cocaine in Missouri.

Cabrales moved to dismiss the indictment in its entirety for improper venue. On recommendation of the Magistrate, the District Court denied the motion as to Count I, the conspiracy count, based on the Government's assertions that Cabrales "was present in Missouri during the conspiracy, lived with a conspirator in Missouri, and participated in various activities in Missouri in furtherance of the conspiracy." App. to Pet. for Cert. 11a, 14a–15a. Also on the Magistrate's recommendation, the District Court granted the motion to dismiss Counts II and III, the money-laundering counts, because the deposit and withdrawals occurred in Florida and "[n]o activity of money laundering . . . occurred in Missouri."

On the Government's appeal, the Eighth Circuit affirmed the District Court's dismissal of the money-laundering counts. 109 F.3d 471, as amended, 115 F.3d 621 (C.A.8 1997). . . .

. . . Both Rule 18 of the Federal Rules of Criminal Procedure and the Constitution require that a person be tried for an offense where that offense is committed; also, the site of a charged offense " 'must be determined from the nature of the crime alleged and the location of the act or acts constituting it.' " "Continuing offenses," . . . those "begun in one district and completed in another," 18 U.S.C. § 3237(a), may be tried " 'in any district in which such [an] offense was begun, continued, or completed.' "

But "Cabrales was not accused of a 'continuing offense,' " the Eighth Circuit said, "[s]he was charged with money laundering, for transactions which began, continued, and were completed only in Florida. That the money came from Missouri is of no moment," the Court of Appeals next observed, for "Cabrales dealt with it only in Florida." The money laundering counts "include[d] no act committed by Cabrales in Missouri," the Eighth Circuit emphasized, nor did "the [G]overnment charge that Cabrales transported the money from Missouri to Florida."

The Government urges that, in conflict with the Eighth Circuit, other Courts of Appeals "have held that venue for money laundering offenses is proper in the district in which the funds were unlawfully generated, even if the financial transaction that constitutes the laundering occurred wholly within another district." We . . . now affirm the Eighth Circuit's judgment.

II

Proper venue in criminal proceedings was a matter of concern to the Nation's founders. Their complaints against the King of Great Britain, listed in the Declaration of Independence, included his transportation of colonists "beyond Seas to be tried." The Constitution twice safeguards the defendant's venue right: Article III, § 2, cl. 3 instructs that "Trial of all Crimes ... shall be held in the State where the said Crimes shall have been committed"; the Sixth Amendment calls for trial "by an impartial jury of the State and district wherein the crime shall have been committed." Rule 18 of the Federal Rules of Criminal Procedure, providing that "prosecution shall be had in a district in which the offense was committed," echoes the constitutional commands.

We adhere to the general guide invoked and applied by the Eighth Circuit: "[T]he locus delicti must be determined from the nature of the crime alleged and the location of the act or acts constituting it." Anderson, 328 U.S., at 703, 66 S.Ct., at 1216. Here, the crimes described in Counts II and III are defined in statutory proscriptions, 18 U.S.C. § 1956(a)(1)(B)(ii), 1957, that interdict only the financial transactions (acts located entirely in Florida), not the anterior criminal conduct that yielded the funds allegedly laundered.

Congress has provided by statute for offenses "begun in one district and completed in another"; such offenses may be "prosecuted in any district in which [the] offense was begun, continued, or completed." 18 U.S.C. § 3237(a). The Government urges that the money-laundering crimes described in Counts II and III of the indictment against Cabrales fit the § 3237(a) description. We therefore confront and decide this question: Do those counts charge crimes begun in Missouri and completed in Florida, rendering venue proper in Missouri, or do they delineate crimes that took place wholly within Florida?

Notably, the counts at issue do not charge Cabrales with conspiracy; they do not link her to, or assert her responsibility for, acts done by others. Nor do they charge her as an aider or abettor in the Missouri drug trafficking. See 18 U.S.C. § 2 (one who aids or abets an offense "is punishable as a principal"). Cabrales is charged in the money-laundering counts with criminal activity "after the fact" of an offense begun and completed by others. Cf. § 3 ("Whoever, knowing that an offense against the United States has been committed, ... assists the offender in order to hinder or prevent his ... punishment, is an accessory after the fact," punishable not as a principal, but by a term of imprisonment or fine generally "not more than one-half the maximum ... prescribed for the punishment of the principal[.]").

Whenever a defendant acts "after the fact" to conceal a crime, it might be said, as the Government urges in this case, that the first crime is an essential element of the second, and that the second facilitated the first or made it profitable by impeding its detection. But the question here is the place appropriate to try the "after the fact" actor. As the Government recognizes, it is immaterial whether that actor knew where the first crime was committed. The money launderer must know she is dealing with funds derived from "specified unlawful activity," here, drug trafficking, but the Missouri venue of that activity is, as the Eighth Circuit said, "of no moment." 109 F.3d, at 472.

Money laundering, the Court of Appeals acknowledged, arguably might rank as a "continuing offense," triable in more than one place, if the launderer acquired the funds in one district and transported them into another. But that is tellingly not this case. In the counts at issue, the Government indicted Cabrales "for transactions which began, continued, and were completed only in Florida." Under these circumstances, venue in Missouri is improper.

The Government identified Hyde v. United States, 225 U.S. 347, 32 S.Ct. 793, 56 L.Ed. 1114 (1912), and In re Palliser v. United States, 136 U.S. 257, 10 S.Ct. 1034, 34 L.Ed. 514 (1890), as the two best cases for its position that money launderers can in all cases be prosecuted at the place where the funds they handled were generated. Neither decision warrants the ruling the Government here seeks.

In Hyde, the defendants were convicted in the District of Columbia of conspiracy to defraud the United States. Although none of the defendants had entered the District as part of the conspiracy, venue was nevertheless appropriate, the Court ruled, based on the overt acts of a co-conspirator there. By contrast, the counts at issue in this case allege no conspiracy. They describe activity in which Cabrales alone, untied to others, engaged.

In re Palliser concerned a man who sent letters from New York to postmasters in Connecticut, attempting to gain postage on credit, in violation of then-applicable law. The Court held that the defendant could be prosecuted in Connecticut, where the mail he addressed and dispatched was received. The Palliser opinion simply recognizes that a mailing to Connecticut is properly ranked as an act completed in that State. See 18 U.S.C. § 3237(a) ("Any offense involving the use of the mails ... is a continuing offense and ... may be ... prosecuted in any district from, through, or into which such ... mail matter ... moves."); see also United States v. Johnson, 323 U.S. 273, 275, 65 S.Ct. 249, 250, 89 L.Ed. 236 (1944) (consistent with the Constitution "an illegal use of the mails ... may subject the user to prosecution in the district where he sent the goods, or in the district of their arrival, or in any intervening district"). Cabrales, however, dispatched no missive from one State into another. The counts before us portray her and the money she deposited and withdrew as moving inside Florida only.

Finally, the Government urges the efficiency of trying Cabrales in Missouri, because evidence in that State, and not in Florida, shows that the money Cabrales allegedly laundered derived from unlawful activity. Although recognizing that the venue requirement is principally a protection for the defendant, Reply Brief 10, the Government further maintains that its convenience, and the interests of the community victimized by drug dealers, merit consideration.

But if Cabrales is in fact linked to the drug-trafficking activity, the Government is not disarmed from showing that is the case. She can be, and indeed has been, charged with conspiring with the drug dealers in Missouri. If the Government can prove the agreement it has alleged, Cabrales can be prosecuted in Missouri for that confederacy, and her money laundering in Florida could be shown as overt acts in furtherance of the conspiracy. See 18 U.S.C. § 371 (requiring proof of an "act to effect the object of the conspiracy"). As the Government acknowledged, the difference in the end result "probably . . . would be negligible."

* * *

We hold that Missouri is not a place of proper venue for the money laundering offenses with which Cabrales is charged. For the reasons stated, the judgment of the Court of Appeals for the Eighth Circuit is

Affirmed.[23]

(C) Courts

Having determined the county (or other area) in which the accused may be tried, the final inquiry in the matter of jurisdiction is to ascertain which one of the tribunals sitting there is the proper one for this particular case. This is seldom a difficult problem although differences in the various jurisdictions tend to complicate any generalized statement.

To speak in very broad terms we may say that the ordinary criminal case will be tried in the court of general jurisdiction unless some other tribunal has been specifically provided for this purpose. The name will vary from state to state, the labels "circuit court", "district court" and "superior court" being the most common. In many of the large cities the trial will be in the "criminal court," which may be a separate tribunal, or may be merely the name applied to the division (or divisions), of the district, circuit or superior court to which the criminal cases are assigned.

If the prosecution is for the violation of a city ordinance it may be in a city tribunal which may be called a "police court" or "municipal court" or may have some other name. Such a court (or some other) may have

---

23. In cases involving a conspiracy offense under federal law, venue is proper in any district where the agreement was formed or an overt act occurred. United States v. Caldwell, 16 F.3d 623 (5th Cir.1994).

When an offense is begun in one district and completed in another one, venue is proper in any district in which the offense was begun, continued or completed. United States v. Fells, 78 F.3d 168 (5th Cir.1996).

Where two or more courts have concurrent jurisdiction of the same offense the established rule is that the court first acquiring jurisdiction of the prosecution, retains it to the end. State v. Parker, 234 N.C. 236, 66 S.E.2d 907 (1951), unless it voluntarily dismisses or abandons the prosecution, Rogers v. State, 101 Miss. 847, 58 So. 536 (1912), or the defendant waives his right to insist upon trial there, State v. Van Ness, 109 Vt. 392, 199 A. 759 (1938). Actual jurisdiction of the prosecution (as distinguished from potential jurisdiction of the offense) ordinarily requires jurisdiction of the person. Sherrod v. State, 197 Ala. 286, 72 So. 540 (1916). Hence if indictments for the same offense are found properly in two or more counties the case normally will be tried in the court first acquiring jurisdiction of the person by arrest. Smithey v. State, 93 Miss. 257, 46 So. 410 (1908). If, however, in the absence of any collusion on the part of the defendant, he is tried and acquitted in a court other than the one first acquiring jurisdiction, this is a complete bar to a subsequent trial in the first court. State v. Howell, 220 S.C. 178, 66 S.E.2d 701 (1951). On the other hand the state has a right to elect the forum in which it will proceed and is not to be deprived of this choice by the machinations of the defendant or his friends. McDaniel, Sheriff v. Sams, 259 Ky. 56, 82 S.W.2d 215 (1935).

Venue was proper in the Southern District of Alabama for an offense committed on the high seas where a joint offender with two other defendants was brought into the Southern District of Alabama even though the vessel and two other defendants were arrested and brought to Florida. United States v. Pearson, 791 F.2d 867 (11th Cir.1986).

concurrent jurisdiction with the circuit, district or superior court over part of the criminal field,—usually limited to misdemeanor cases.

If the accusation charges a petty offense it may be triable summarily before a magistrate, and in some states the magistrate may have exclusive jurisdiction over the case at this stage of the proceedings. Where this is true such a case can reach the court of general jurisdiction only on appeal,—although the provision may be for a trial *de novo* upon such appeal. It is important to distinguish the trial of a petty offense by a magistrate (which may or may not be appealed to the court of general jurisdiction) from a preliminary hearing by a magistrate which does not determine guilt or innocence but merely decides whether there is sufficient evidence of guilt to require that the accused be bound over to the other court.

If the defendant is a "juvenile" (a term having a special definition for this purpose which varies from state to state), and the misdeed charged is not expressly excluded by the statute authorizing this type of procedure, the case may be tried in the "juvenile court." Whether it *must* be tried there, or may be tried either there or in the ordinary courts, depends upon the legislation in the particular state. The more progressive statutes on the subject give the juvenile court exclusive jurisdiction over cases falling within its field.

State v. Shults

Supreme Court of Montana, 1976.
169 Mont. 33, 544 P.2d 817.

■ HASWELL, JUSTICE. The question in this case is whether a Montana district court retains jurisdiction of a criminal case in which the state amends an Information charging a single felony to one charging only a lesser included misdemeanor.

This appeal was submitted on an agreed statement of fact pursuant to section 95–2408(d), R.C.M.1947:

"On June 3, 1975, a one count Information was filed in the District Court of the First Judicial District of the State of Montana, in and for the County of Lewis and Clark, charging the defendant, Daniel Marcus Shults, with the offense of Theft, § 94–6–302(1)(a), R.C.M.1947, a felony. Arraignment was set for June 6, 1975. At the arraignment, upon motion of Deputy County Attorney Charles A. Graveley, the Information was amended to charge the Defendant with the offense of Unauthorized Use of a Motor Vehicle, § 94–6–305, R.C.M.1947, a misdemeanor. The Defendant was then arraigned in the District Court and plead guilty to the misdemeanor. Upon questioning by the Court, Defendant acknowledged his awareness that by entering such a plea he was risking the full punishment of imprisonment in the County Jail for a term not to exceed six (6) months, or a fine not to exceed Five Hundred Dollars ($500.00), or both. Whereupon the Court accepted Defendant's plea of guilty and sentenced him to serve a term of six (6) months in the Lewis and Clark County Jail.

"On June 9, 1975, the Defendant filed a motion in the District Court to set aside the judgment of conviction and to dismiss the amended Information on the grounds that the District Court lacked jurisdiction over the misdemeanor offense charged. The motion was briefed, a hearing was held and the District Court denied Defendant's motion on July 9, 1975. On July 17, 1975, Defendant filed a notice appealing the denial of said motion to the Supreme Court of the State of Montana."

The district court has original jurisdiction in all criminal cases amounting to a felony (Art. VII, Section 4, 1972 Montana Constitution) and ". . . of all public offenses not otherwise provided for" (section 95–301, R.C.M. 1947). The justice court has ". . . such original jurisdiction as may be provided by law" (Art. VII, Section 5, 1972 Montana Constitution) which jurisdiction includes ". . . all misdemeanors punishable by a fine not exceeding five hundred dollars ($500.00) or imprisonment not exceeding six (6) months, or both such fine and imprisonment . . ." (subject to exceptions not pertinent here). Section 95–302, R.C.M.1947.

Here the original charge carried a penalty of imprisonment up to ten years (section 94–6–302(4)) and was clearly a felony because of the potential sentence. Section 94–1–105(1), R.C.M.1947. The amended charge carried a penalty of a fine up to $500 or imprisonment in the county jail for a term not exceeding six months (section 94–6–305(2), R.C.M.1947) and was clearly a misdemeanor. Section 94–2–101(31), R.C.M.1947.

The misdemeanor here is a lesser included offense in the felony. Section 95–1711(1)(b)(i), R.C.M.1947. Unauthorized use of the automobile is the common element in both the original charge and the amended charge, the former requiring the additional element of an intent or purpose to deprive the owner of his property. Cf. section 94–6–302(1)(a), R.C.M. 1947, and section 94–6–305(1), R.C.M.1947.

In the instant case it is conceded that had the amended charge been filed originally, the district court would have had no subject matter jurisdiction over the crime. But because the original charge was a felony, the jurisdiction of the district court attached at the commencement of the action. Was the district court's jurisdiction divested when the state later amended the information to charge only a lesser included misdemeanor?

It has been held in a similar case from another jurisdiction that where the district court's jurisdiction is invoked by an indictment charging felony theft, it is not lost by the fact that the state subsequently reduces the charge to a lesser included misdemeanor theft. Bruce v. Texas (Tex.1967) 419 S.W.2d 646.

We consider this a sound rule. Here the parties concede that where a defendant is charged with a felony, tried by jury, and convicted of a lesser included misdemeanor, the district court does not lose jurisdiction. This conforms to the applicable general rule which has been stated in 22 C.J.S. Criminal Law § 169:

"As a general rule, where the court has jurisdiction of the crime for which accused is indicted, sometimes by reason of statute, it is not lost if on the evidence he is convicted of a crime of an inferior grade of which it would not have jurisdiction originally. . . ."

We see no difference in principle or result where the state amends the original charge prior to trial, and the defendant pleads guilty to the lesser included offense. If the rule were otherwise, the court of original jurisdiction would lose its ability to conclude the case with a just result.

The order of the district court refusing to set aside the conviction and dismiss the amended information is affirmed.[24]

■ JAMES T. HARRISON, C.J., and JOHN C. HARRISON, CASTLES and DALY, JJ., concur.

MODEL PENAL CODE

Section 1.03   Territorial Applicability.

(1) Except as otherwise provided in this Section, a person may be convicted under the law of this State of an offense committed by his own conduct or the conduct of another for which he is legally accountable if:

(a) either the conduct which is an element of the offense or the result which is such an element occurs within this State; or

(b) conduct occurring outside the State is sufficient under the law of this State to constitute an attempt to commit an offense within the State; or

(c) conduct occurring outside the State is sufficient under the law of this State to constitute a conspiracy to commit an offense within the State and an overt act in furtherance of such conspiracy occurs within the State; or

(d) conduct occurring within the State establishes complicity in the commission of, or an attempt, solicitation or conspiracy to commit, an offense in another jurisdiction which also is an offense under the law of this State; or

(e) the offense consists of the omission to perform a legal duty imposed by the law of this State with respect to domicile, residence or a relationship to a person, thing or transaction in the State; or

(f) the offense is based on a statute of this State which expressly prohibits conduct outside the State, when the conduct bears a reasonable relation to a legitimate interest of this State and the actor knows or should know that his conduct is likely to affect that interest.

(2) Subsection (1)(a) does not apply when either causing a specified result or a purpose to cause or danger of causing such a result is an element of an offense and

---

24. A conviction in the magistrate court must be reversed if the charge is one within the exclusive subject-matter jurisdiction of the district court. State v. Lynch, 82 N.M. 532, 484 P.2d 374 (1971).

A conviction in the superior court must be reversed if the offense charged was in the exclusive jurisdiction of an inferior court. People v. Fiene, 226 Cal.App.2d 305, 37 Cal.Rptr. 925 (1964).

On a trial for felonious assault in the district court the defendant may be convicted of a simple assault, although had the information charged only a simple assault the jurisdiction to try this misdemeanor would have been in an inferior court. People v. Spreckels, 125 Cal.App.2d 507, 270 P.2d 513 (1954); In re McKinney, 70 Cal.2d 8, 73 Cal.Rptr. 580, 447 P.2d 972 (1968).

As carrying a concealed firearm is now a felony the circuit court cannot refuse jurisdiction because the Civil and Criminal Court of Pinellas County has jurisdiction only of misdemeanors. State v. Hardy, 239 So.2d 279 (Fla.App.1970).

Cal.Penal Code, § 1462.1 (1997) provides: "The jurisdiction of the municipal and justice courts is the same and concurrent."

the result occurs or is designed or likely to occur only in another jurisdiction where the conduct charged would not constitute an offense, unless a legislative purpose plainly appears to declare the conduct criminal regardless of the place of the result.

(3) Subsection (1)(a) does not apply when causing a particular result is an element of an offense and the result is caused by conduct occurring outside the State which would not constitute an offense if the result had occurred there, unless the actor purposely or knowingly caused the result within the State.

(4) When the offense is homicide, either the death of the victim or the bodily impact causing death constitutes a "result", within the meaning of Subsection (1)(a) and if the body of a homicide victim is found within the State, it is presumed that such result occurred within the State.

(5) This State includes the land and water and the air space above such land and water with respect to which the State has legislative jurisdiction.[25]

SECTION 2. EXTRADITION

If the courts of the state in which the accused is found do not have the power to try him for the crime of which he is accused, the question arises whether the state or nation in which such person could be tried for the offense, has the right to ask the first state to arrest the accused and deliver him over to the second state for trial by it. The surrender of an accused person in this way is called "extradition;" and where it is between the states of the Union it is frequently referred to as "interstate rendition."[26] The demand for extradition is called a "requisition."[27] The "demanding state" makes the demand upon the "asylum state,"—in which the fugitive has taken refuge.

The Constitution of the United States provides (Art. IV, § 2, cl. 2) that "[a] person charged in any State with Treason, Felony or other Crime, who shall flee from Justice, and be found in another State, shall on Demand of the executive Authority of the State from which he fled, be delivered up, to be removed to the State having Jurisdiction of the Crime", and Congress has enacted (18 U.S.C.A. § 3182) that "Whenever the executive authority of any State or Territory demands any person as a fugitive from justice, of the executive authority of any State, District or Territory to which such person has fled, and produces a copy of an indictment found or an affidavit made before a magistrate of any State or Territory, charging the person demanded with having committed treason, felony, or other crime, certified as authentic by the governor or chief magistrate of the State or Territory from whence the person so charged has fled, the executive authority of the State, District or Territory to which such person has fled shall cause him to be arrested and secured, and notify the executive authority making such

---

25. Copyright © 1962 by the American Law Institute. Reprinted with the permission of the American Law Institute.

26. "Interstate rendition" was rejected in favor of the phrase "interstate extradition" in the uniform act on this subject.

27. "We hold that once the governor of the asylum state has acted on a requisition for extradition based on the demanding state's judicial determination that probable cause existed, no further judicial inquiry may be had on that issue in the asylum state." Michigan v. Doran, 439 U.S. 282, 290, 99 S.Ct. 530, 58 L.Ed.2d 521 (1978).

demand, . . ." (See also the following section.) In any case authorized by those provisions the governor of a state may appoint an agent to demand of the executive authority of another state or territory any fugitive from justice charged with any crime if its own statute is broad enough. The Tennessee statute, for example, authorizes the governor to "appoint an agent to demand and receive any fugitive from justice and return such person to this state."[28] The Iowa Code at one time, authorized the demand only in the case of a "fugitive from justice charged with treason or felony."[29] The Iowa statute authorized the governor to appoint agents to demand fugitives from justice, not only from the executive authority of another state or territory, but also "from the executive authority of a foreign government." But the clause just quoted was void. International extradition depends upon treaties and no state of the Union can enter into treaties with foreign nations. Furthermore international extradition is a matter of foreign relations, belonging exclusively to the national government.[30]

The Constitution and statutes of the United States authorize extradition of a fugitive from justice charged with "treason, felony or other crime," but this is only "on demand of the executive authority of the state from which he fled." The federal law imposes no duty upon the offended state to make a demand if it does not choose to do so. Hence a state statute limiting the authority of the governor, in his demand for the return of fugitives from other states, to those charged with treason or felony (as once did the Iowa statute) is entirely valid. The legislative body is free to

---

28. Tenn.Code Ann. § 40–9–121 (1982).

29. Iowa Code Ann. § 759.1 (1946). This has been changed by enactment of the Uniform Criminal Extradition Act. See Iowa Code Ann. Chap. 820.1 (1978).

30. "The laws of nations embrace no provision for the surrender of persons who are fugitives from the offended laws of one country to the territory of another. It is only by treaty that such surrender can take place." 4 Moore, Digest of International Law 245 (1906) quoting Mr. Rush, Sec. of State, to Mr. Hyde de Newville, Apr. 9, 1817. As the state of Iowa cannot enter into a treaty with a foreign government (U.S. Const. Art. I, § 10, cl. 1) it would never be in a position to demand the surrender of a fugitive as a matter of right from a foreign government. Clearly it could do no more than to request it as a matter of comity. But, "[a]lthough the question whether the several States of the United States possess the power to surrender fugitive criminals to foreign governments has never been actually decided by the Supreme Court, yet it may now be regarded as settled doctrine that they do not possess such power, but that it belongs exclusively to the National Government. The question has, however, been by no means free from controversy, and the present accepted view is the result of a gradual evolution of opinion and practice." 4 Moore, Digest of International Law 240 (1906). If Iowa cannot surrender a fugitive to a foreign government it would have little ground upon which to make requisition as a matter of comity. But more than that, if it lacks the power to make such a rendition it would seem equally to lack the power to make the demand. As said by Mr. Justice Miller in United States v. Rauscher, 119 U.S. 407, 414, 7 S.Ct. 234, 30 L.Ed. 425 (1886): "[I]t can hardly be admitted that, even in the absence of treaties or acts of Congress on the subject, the extradition of fugitives from justice can become the subject of negotiation between a state of this Union and a foreign government."

The truth is that as far as we are concerned with foreign countries, extradition is governed, exclusively by the treaties of the United States with such countries, and by Acts of Congress in furtherance of the provisions thereof. 18 U.S.C.A. §§ 752, 1502, 3051, 3181, 3185–6, 3188–93 (1985). As a matter of procedure all applications for requisitions should be addressed to the Secretary of State accompanied by the necessary papers. 18 U.S.C.A. § 3184 (1985).

establish a policy of not demanding the return of misdemeanants if it sees fit to do so. The mandate of the Constitution of the United States, however, does not permit a state legislature to establish a policy of not surrendering fugitive misdemeanants to other states. One part of the Texas Code purports to do this,[31] however, such a limitation would be unconstitutional. Texas has adopted the Uniform Extradition Act and extradition of a person charged with a misdemeanor is recognized under that provision.[32]

Pacileo v. Walker

Supreme Court of the United States, 1980.
449 U.S. 86, 101 S.Ct. 308, 66 L.Ed.2d 304.

■ PER CURIAM. The United States Constitution provides that "A person charged in any State with Treason, Felony or other Crime, who shall flee from Justice, and be found in another State, shall on Demand of the executive Authority of the State from which he fled, be delivered up, to be removed to the State having Jurisdiction of the Crime." Art. IV, § 2, cl. 2.

In this case, there is no dispute as to the facts necessary to resolve the legal question presented. In 1975, respondent James Dean Walker escaped from the Arkansas Department of Corrections and remained at large until he was apprehended in California in 1979. In December 1979, the Governor of Arkansas requested the arrest and rendition of respondent, alleging that respondent was a fugitive from justice. In February 1980, the Governor of California honored the request of the Governor of Arkansas and duly issued a warrant of arrest and rendition. This warrant was then served upon respondent by the Sheriff of El Dorado County, Cal. Respondent thereafter challenged the Governor's issuance of the warrant in both state and federal courts. He was unsuccessful until he reached the Supreme Court of California, which, on April 9, 1980, issued a writ of habeas corpus directing the Superior Court of El Dorado County to "conduct hearings to determine if the penitentiary in which Arkansas seeks to confine petitioner is presently operated in conformance with the Eighth Amendment of the United States Constitution and thereafter to decide the petition on its merits."

Petitioner Sheriff contends that Art. IV, § 2, cl. 2, and its implementing statute, 18 U.S.C. § 3182, do not give the courts of the "asylum" or "sending" state authority to inquire into the prison conditions of the "demanding" state. We agree. In Michigan v. Doran, 439 U.S. 282, 99 S.Ct. 530, 58 L.Ed.2d 521 (1978), our most recent pronouncement on the subject, we stated that "interstate extradition was intended to be a summary and mandatory executive proceeding derived from the language of Article IV, § 2, cl. 2 of the Constitution." *Id.* at 288, 99 S.Ct. at 535. We further stated that:

"A governor's grant of extradition is prima facie evidence that the constitutional and statutory requirements have been met.... Once the governor has granted extradition, a court considering release on habeas corpus can do no more than decide (a) whether the extradition documents on their face

---

31.   Vernon's Texas Code Crim.Proc. Art. 51.01 (1979).

32.   Id. Art. 51.13. See Ex parte Williams, 622 S.W.2d 482

(Tex.App.1981).

are in order; (b) whether the petitioner had been charged with a crime in the demanding state; (c) whether the petitioner is the person named in the request for extradition; and (d) whether the petitioner is a fugitive. These are historic facts readily verifiable." *Id.*, at 289, 99 S.Ct., at 535.

In Sweeney v. Woodall, 344 U.S. 86, 73 S.Ct. 139, 97 L.Ed. 114 (1952), this Court held that a fugitive from Alabama could not raise in the federal courts of Ohio, the asylum state, the constitutionality of his confinement in Alabama. We stated:

"Considerations fundamental to our federal system require that the prisoner test the claimed unconstitutionality of his treatment by Alabama in the courts of that State. Respondent should be required to initiate his suit in the courts of Alabama, where all parties may be heard, where all pertinent testimony will be readily available, and where suitable relief, if any is necessary, may be fashioned." *Id.*, at 90, 73 S.Ct., at 140.

We think that the Supreme Court of California ignored the teachings of these cases when it directed one of its own trial courts of general jurisdiction to conduct an inquiry into the present conditions of the Arkansas penal system. Once the Governor of California issued the warrant for arrest and rendition in response to the request of the Governor of Arkansas, claims as to constitutional defects in the Arkansas penal system should be heard in the courts of Arkansas, not those of California. "To allow plenary review in the asylum state of issues that can be fully litigated in the charging state would defeat the plain purposes of the summary and mandatory procedures authorized by Art. IV, § 2." Michigan v. Doran, 439 U.S., at 290, 99 S.Ct., at 536.

The petition for certiorari is granted, the judgment of the Supreme Court of California is reversed, and the case is remanded for further proceedings not inconsistent with this opinion.

Reversed and remanded.

■ JUSTICE MARSHALL, dissenting.

Because Michigan v. Doran, 439 U.S. 282, 99 S.Ct. 530, 58 L.Ed.2d 521 (1978) did not involve a claimed violation of the Eighth Amendment, and because Sweeney v. Woodall, 344 U.S. 86, 73 S.Ct. 139, 97 L.Ed. 114 (1952) did not involve a state court's decision to grant state habeas corpus relief, I do not believe that they control the question raised here, and I would set the case for plenary review.[33]

Puerto Rico v. Branstad

United States Supreme Court, 1987.
483 U.S. 219, 107 S.Ct. 2802, 97 L.Ed.2d 187.

■ JUSTICE MARSHALL delivered the opinion of the Court.

This case requires that we reconsider the holding of Kentucky v. Dennison, 24 How. 66, 16 L.Ed. 717 (1861), that federal courts have no

---

33. Four possible grounds for refusing to extradite a person are that the extradition documents facially are not in order, the person to be extradited has not been charged with a crime in the requesting state, the person is not the person named in the extradition documents, or the person is not a fugitive. State of Alabama ex rel Governor and Atty. Gen. v. Engler, 85 F.3d 1205 (6th Cir.1996).

power to order the Governor of a State to fulfill the State's obligation under the Extradition Clause of the Constitution, Art. IV, § 2, to deliver up fugitives from justice.

On January 25, 1981, respondent Ronald Calder, then a civilian air traffic controller employed by the Federal Aviation Administration in San Juan, Puerto Rico, struck two people with his automobile. . . .

. . . Calder was arrested, charged with homicide, arraigned before a municipal judge, and released on $5,000 bail. On February 4, 1981, Calder was arraigned before a District Court of the Commonwealth of Puerto Rico, charged with first degree murder and attempted murder. Calder failed to appear at a preliminary hearing on March 4, 1981, and bail was increased to $50,000. Despite representations by counsel that Calder would appear at a preliminary hearing on April 13, 1981, he did not do so. At that time Calder was declared a fugitive from justice, and bail was increased to $300,000. The Puerto Rican police, having reason to believe that Calder had left Puerto Rico and returned to his family's home in Iowa, notified local authorities in Iowa that Calder was a fugitive wanted in Puerto Rico on murder charges. On April 24, 1981, Calder surrendered to local authorities in Polk County, Iowa, . . . and was released.

On May 15, 1981, the Governor of Puerto Rico submitted to the Governor of Iowa a request for Calder's extradition. The requesting papers included the arrest warrant, the fugitive resolution, the charging documents, and three sworn statements of witnesses, including one in which the affiant identified a photograph of Calder as depicting the driver of the car. Counsel for Calder requested that the Governor of Iowa hold an extradition hearing, which was conducted by the Governor's counsel on June 17, 1981. . . .

After the extradition hearing in Iowa, discussions between and among Calder's counsel, the Governors of Iowa and Puerto Rico, and the prosecutorial authorities in Puerto Rico were held, apparently with a view to negotiating a reduction of the charges lodged against Calder. These discussions were unavailing, and on December 28, 1981, Iowa's Governor . . . formally notified the Governor of Puerto Rico that in the absence of a "change to a more realistic charge," the request for extradition was denied. . . .

On February 15, 1984, petitioner Commonwealth of Puerto Rico filed a complaint in the United States District Court for the Southern District of Iowa against respondents Governor . . . and the State of Iowa, seeking a declaration that failure to deliver Calder upon presentation of proper extradition papers violated the Extradition Clause and the Extradition Act, 18 U.S.C. § 3182 (Act).[34] The complaint further requested the issuance of a writ of mandamus directing respondent Branstad to perform the "ministe-

---

34. Section 3182 provides:

"Whenever the executive authority of any State or Territory demands any person as a fugitive from justice, of the executive authority of any State, District or Territory to which such person has fled, and produces a copy of an indictment found or an affidavit made before a magistrate of any State or Territory, charging the person demanded with having committed

rial duty" of extradition. . . . The District Court dismissed the complaint, agreeing with respondents that this Court's holding in Kentucky v. Dennison, 24 How. 66, 16 L.Ed. 717 (1861), absolutely barred any attempt to invoke federal judicial authority to compel compliance with the Clause or the Act. The Court of Appeals "[r]eluctantly" affirmed. . . . We reverse.

Kentucky v. Dennison was an action brought under this Court's original jurisdiction to compel by writ of mandamus the extradition of a fugitive felon. The grand jury of Woodford County, Kentucky, returned an indictment in October 1859 charging Willis Lago, a "free man of color," with the crime of assisting the escape of a slave. The defendant was a resident of Ohio, and papers requesting his extradition were served upon William Dennison, the Governor of that State. Dennison secured an opinion from Ohio's Attorney General, who took the view that the Extradition Clause[35] covered only those acts which were crimes under the law of the asylum State, or which were "regarded as *malum in se* by the general judgment and conscience of civilized nations." On this basis Dennison refused extradition, and Kentucky brought its mandamus action in this Court.

. . .

The Court firmly rejected the position taken by Dennison and the Governors of other free States that the Extradition Clause required only the delivery of fugitives charged with acts which would be criminal by the law of the asylum State. "Under such a vague and indefinite construction," the Court said, "the article would not be a bond of peace and union, but a constant source of controversy and irritating discussion." Interpreting for the first time the language of the Clause, the Court looked to the fundamental role of the right to request extradition in binding the individual States into a nation:

"Looking, therefore, to the words of the Constitution—to the obvious policy and necessity of this provision to preserve harmony between States, and order and law within their respective borders . . .—the conclusion is irresistible, that this compact engrafted in the Constitution included, and was intended to include, every offence made punishable by the law of the State in which it was committed, and that it gives the right to the Executive authority of the State to demand the fugitive from the Executive authority

---

treason, felony, or other crime, certified as authentic by the governor or chief magistrate of the State or Territory from whence the person so charged has fled, the executive authority of the State, District or Territory to which such person has fled shall cause him to be arrested and secured, and notify the executive authority making such demand, or the agent of such authority appointed to receive the fugitive, and shall cause the fugitive to be delivered to such agent when he shall appear. If no such agent appears within thirty days from the time of the arrest, the prisoner may be discharged."

The statute has remained substantially unchanged since its original enactment in the Extradition Act of 1793, 1 Stat. 302. See also 18 U.S.C. § 662 (1940 ed.); Rev.Stat. § 5278.

35. "A Person charged in any State with Treason, Felony, or other Crime, who shall flee from Justice, and be found in another State, shall on Demand of the executive Authority of the State from which he fled, be delivered up, to be removed to the State having Jurisdiction of the Crime." Art. IV, § 2, cl. 2.

of the State in which he is found; that the right given to 'demand' implies that it is an absolute right; and it follows that there must be a correlative obligation to deliver, without any reference to the character of the crime charged, or to the policy or laws of the State to which the fugitive has fled."

The Court then turned to the Extradition Act of 1793, 1 Stat. 302. In the procedures for the regulation of extradition established by that Act, the Court found the same absolute right to demand and correlative obligation to deliver. As to the Governor of the asylum State under the Act, the Court determined that "[t]he duty which he is to perform is ... merely ministerial—that is, to cause the party to be arrested, and delivered to the agent or authority of the State where the crime was committed." But the Court concluded that "the words 'it shall be the duty' were not used as mandatory and compulsory, but as declaratory of the moral duty" created by the Constitution. Such a construction was necessary, in the Court's view, to avoid constitutional infirmity.

"The act does not provide any means to compel the execution of this duty, nor inflict any punishment for neglect or refusal on the part of the Executive of the State; nor is there any clause or provision in the Constitution which arms the Government of the United States with this power. Indeed, such a power would place every State under the control and dominion of the General Government, even in the administration of its internal concerns and reserved rights. And we think it clear, that the Federal Government, under the Constitution, has no power to impose on a State officer, as such, any duty whatever, and compel him to perform it."

Thus, for over 125 years, Kentucky v. Dennison has stood for two propositions: first, that the Extradition Clause creates a mandatory duty to deliver up fugitives upon proper demand; and second, that the federal courts have no authority under the Constitution to compel performance of this ministerial duty of delivery. As to the first of these conclusions, the passage of time has revealed no occasion for doubt. The language of the Clause is "clear and explicit." Michigan v. Doran, 439 U.S. 282, 286, 99 S.Ct. 530, 534, 58 L.Ed.2d 521 (1978). Its mandatory language furthers its intended purposes: "to enable each state to bring offenders to trial as swiftly as possible in the state where the alleged offense was committed," and "to preclude any state from becoming a sanctuary for fugitives from justice of another state." ... We reaffirm the conclusion that the commands of the Extradition Clause are mandatory, and afford no discretion to the executive officers or courts of the asylum State.

The second, and dispositive, holding of Kentucky v. Dennison rests upon a foundation with which time and the currents of constitutional change have dealt much less favorably. . . .

Yet with respect to extradition the law has remained as it was more than a century ago. Considered *de novo,* there is no justification for distinguishing the duty to deliver fugitives from the many other species of constitutional duty enforceable in the federal courts. Indeed the nature of the obligation here is such as to avoid many of the problems with which federal courts must cope in other circumstances. That this is a ministerial duty precludes conflict with essentially discretionary elements of state governance, and eliminates the need for continuing federal supervision of state functions. The explicit and long-settled nature of the command, contained in a constitutional provision and a statute substantially unchanged for two hundred years, eliminates the possibility that state officers will be subjected to inconsistent direction. Because the duty is directly imposed upon the States by the Constitution itself, there can be no need to weigh the performance of the federal obligation against the powers reserved to the States under the Tenth Amendment.

Respondents contend, however, that an "executive common law" of extradition has developed through the efforts of governors to employ the discretion accorded them under *Dennison,* and that this "common law" provides a superior alternative to the "ministerial duty" to extradite provided for by the Constitution. Even assuming the existence of this tradition of "executive common law," no weight can be accorded to it. Long continuation of decisional law or administrative practice incompatible with the requirements of the Constitution cannot overcome our responsibility to enforce those requirements. . . .

Respondents further contend that even if the holding in Kentucky v. Dennison cannot withstand contemporary scrutiny, petitioner would not profit from its demise because Puerto Rico is not a State, and has no right to demand rendition of fugitives under the Extradition Clause. It is true that the words of the Clause apply only to "States," and we have never held that the Commonwealth of Puerto Rico is entitled to all the benefits conferred upon the States under the Constitution. We need not decide today what applicability the Extradition Clause may have to the Commonwealth of Puerto Rico, however, for the Extradition Act clearly applies. . . .

Kentucky v. Dennison is the product of another time. The conception of the relation between the States and the Federal Government there announced is fundamentally incompatible with more than a century of constitutional development. Yet this decision has stood while the world of which it was a part has passed away. We conclude that it may stand no longer. The decision of the Court of Appeals is Reversed.[36]

Hyatt v. People ex rel. Corkran

Supreme Court of the United States, 1903.
188 U.S. 691, 23 S.Ct. 456, 47 L.Ed. 657.

This proceeding by *habeas corpus* was commenced by the relator, defendant in error, to obtain his discharge from imprisonment by the plaintiff in error, the chief of police in the city of Albany, State of New York, who held the relator by means of a warrant issued in extradition proceedings by the governor of New York. The justice of the Supreme Court of New York, to whom the petition for the writ was addressed, and also upon appeal, the Appellate Division of the Supreme Court of New York, refused to grant the relator's discharge, but the Court of Appeals reversed

---

36. A state in comity with other states may provide by statute such as the Uniform Extradition Act, for the surrender of persons in another jurisdiction who are not fugitives from justice and who would not be extraditable under the federal extradition act. See Ex parte Cooper, 53 Cal.2d 772, 3 Cal.Rptr. 140, 349 P.2d 956 (1960); Ex parte Bledsoe, 93 Okl.Cr. 302, 227 P.2d 680 (1951).

their orders and discharged him. 172 N.Y. 176, 64 N.E. 825. A writ of error has been taken from this court to review the latter judgment.

The relator stated in his petition for the writ that he was arrested and detained by virtue of a warrant of the governor of New York, granted on a requisition from the governor of Tennessee, reciting that relator had been indicted in that State for the crime of grand larceny and false pretenses, and that he was a fugitive from the justice of that State; that the warrant under which he was held showed that the crimes with which he was charged were committed in Tennessee, and the relator stated that nowhere did it appear in the papers that he was personally present within the State of Tennessee at the time the alleged crimes were stated to have been committed; that the governor had no jurisdiction to issue his warrant in that it did not appear before him that the relator was a fugitive from the justice of the State of Tennessee, or had fled therefrom; that it did not appear that there was any evidence that relator was personally or continuously present in Tennessee when the crimes were alleged to have been committed; that it appeared on the face of the indictments accompanying the requisition that no crime under the laws of Tennessee was charged or had been committed. Upon this petition the writ was issued and served.

The return of the defendant in error, the chief of police, was to the effect that the relator was held by virtue of a warrant of the governor of New York, and a copy of it was annexed. . . .

Upon the hearing before the judge on March 17, 1902, the relator was sworn without objection, and testified that he had been living in the State of New York for the past fourteen months; that his residence when at home was in Lutherville, Maryland; that he was in the city of Nashville, in the State of Tennessee, on July 2, 1901, and (under objection as immaterial) had gone there on business connected with a lumber company in which he was a heavy stockholder; that he arrived in the city on July 2, in the morning, and left about half-past seven in the evening of the same day, and while there he notified the Union Bank and Trust Company (the subsequent prosecutor herein) that the resignation of the president of the lumber company had been demanded and would probably be accepted that day. That after such notification, and on the same day, the resignation was obtained, and the Union Bank and Trust Company was notified thereof by the relator before leaving the city on the evening of that day; that he passed through the city of Nashville on the 16th or 17th of July thereafter on his way to Chattanooga, but did not stop at Nashville at that time, and had not been in the State of Tennessee since the 16th day of July, 1901, at the time he went to Chattanooga; that he had never lived in the State of Tennessee, and had not been in that State between the 26th or 27th of May, 1899, and the 2d day of July, 1901.

Upon this state of facts the judge, before whom the hearing was had, dismissed the writ and remanded the relator to the custody of the defendant Hyatt, as chief of police. This order was affirmed without any opinion by the Appellate Division of the Supreme Court, 72 App.Div. 629, but, as stated, it was reversed by the Court of Appeals, 172 N.Y. 176, and the relator discharged. . . .

■ MR. JUSTICE PECKHAM, after making the foregoing statement of facts, delivered the opinion of the court. . . .

The subsequent presence for one day (under the circumstances stated above) of the relator in the State of Tennessee, eight days after the alleged commission of the act, did not, when he left the State, render him a fugitive from justice within the meaning of the statute. There is no evidence or claim that he then committed any act which brought him within the criminal law of the State of Tennessee, or that he was indicted for any act then committed. The proof is uncontradicted that he went there on business, transacted it and came away. The complaint was not made nor the indictments found until months after that time. His departure from the State after the conclusion of his business cannot be regarded as a fleeing from justice within the meaning of the statute. He must have been there when the crime was committed, as alleged, and if not, a subsequent going there and coming away is not a flight.

We are of opinion that as the relator showed without contradiction and upon conceded facts that he was not within the State of Tennessee at the times stated in the indictments found in the Tennessee court, nor at any time when the acts were, if ever committed, he was not a fugitive from justice within the meaning of the Federal statute upon that subject, and upon these facts the warrant of the governor of the State of New York was improperly issued, and the judgment of the Court of Appeals of the State of New York discharging the relator from imprisonment by reason of such warrant must be

Affirmed.[37]

---

37.   This rule does not prevail in international extradition. Rex v. Godfrey, 39 T.L.R. 5 (K.B.1922). For a discussion of the Godfrey case see 32 Yale L.J. 287 (1923).

"To be regarded as a fugitive from justice it is not necessary that one shall have left the State in which the crime is alleged to have been committed for the very purpose of avoiding prosecution." Hogan v. O'Neill, 255 U.S. 52, 56, 41 S.Ct. 222, 223, 65 L.Ed. 497, 500 (1921). Cf. Roberts v. Reilly, 116 U.S. 80, 97, 6 S.Ct. 291, 300, 29 L.Ed. 544, 549 (1885); Bassing v. Cady, 208 U.S. 386, 28 S.Ct. 392, 52 L.Ed. 540 (1907).

Ignorance of having violated the law does not prevent one who leaves the State from being a fugitive: Appleyard v. Massachusetts, 203 U.S. 222, 27 S.Ct. 122, 51 L.Ed. 161 (1906).

"It is upon the petitioner under such circumstances to prove that he is not in fact a fugitive from justice and the burden requires evidence which is practically conclusive." Seely v. Beardsley, 194 Iowa 863, 866, 190 N.W. 498, 500 (1922). The question of insanity will not be tried in such proceedings: Drew v. Thaw, 235 U.S. 432, 35 S.Ct. 137, 59 L.Ed. 302 (1914). Nor will the court pass on the statute of limitations. Biddinger v. Commissioner of Police of City of New York, 245 U.S. 128, 38 S.Ct. 41, 62 L.Ed. 193 (1917).

The court will not pass upon an alleged alibi of a fugitive who admits he was within the demanding state at the time of the alleged offense. Edmunds v. Griffin, 177 Iowa 389, 156 N.W. 353 (1916).

With the principal case, cf. Leonard v. Zweifel, 171 Iowa 522, 151 N.W. 1054 (1915); Taylor v. Wise, 172 Iowa 1, 126 N.W. 1126 (1910).

One, constructively present only at the time of the crime, who enters the jurisdiction voluntarily, gives bail and then departs, has waived his immunity. Kay v. State, 34 Ala.App. 8, 37 So.2d 525 (1948), rehearing denied 251 Ala. 419, 37 So.2d 529 (1948).

If **D** was within the state when he took steps which were intended to, and did, result in a crime his departure from the state makes him a "fugitive" in the constitutional sense even if he left the state before the crime was complete. Strassheim v. Daily, 221 U.S. 280, 31 S.Ct.

California v. Superior Court of California

Supreme Court of the United States, 1987.
482 U.S. 400, 107 S.Ct. 2433, 96 L.Ed.2d 332.

■ JUSTICE O'CONNOR delivered the opinion of the Court.

At issue in this case are the limits imposed by federal law upon state court habeas corpus proceedings challenging an extradition warrant.

Richard and Judith Smolin were divorced in California in 1978. Sole custody of their two children, Jennifer and Jamie, was awarded to Judith Smolin, subject to reasonable visitation rights for Richard. Until November 1979, all the parties remained in San Bernardino County, California, and Richard apparently paid his child support and exercised his visitation rights without serious incident. In August 1979, however, Judith married James Pope, and in November, Mr. Pope's work required that the family relocate to Oregon. When the Popes moved without informing Richard, the battle over the custody of the minor children began in earnest.

It is unnecessary to recite in detail all that ensued. Richard alleged, and the California courts later found, that the Popes deliberately attempted to defeat Richard's visitation rights and to preclude him from forming a meaningful relationship with his children in the course of their succeeding relocations from Oregon to Texas to Louisiana. On February 13, 1981, the Popes obtained a decree from a Texas court granting full faith and credit to the original California order awarding sole custody to Judith. Richard was served but did not appear in the Texas proceeding. Before the Texas decree was issued, however, Richard sought and obtained in California Superior Court modification of the underlying California decree, awarding joint custody to Richard and Judith. Though properly served, the Popes did not appear in these California proceedings; and, though served with the modification order, the Popes neither complied with its terms, nor notified the Texas court of its existence. On January 9, 1981, Richard instituted an action in California Superior Court to find Judith in contempt and to again modify the custody decree to give him sole custody. In February 1981, sole custody was granted to Richard by the California court, subject to reasonable visitation rights for Judith.

This order also was ignored by the Popes, apparently acting on the advice of counsel that the California courts no longer had jurisdiction over the matter. Richard did not in fact obtain physical custody for over two years. When he finally located the Popes in Louisiana, they began an adoption proceeding, later described by the California courts as "verging on the fraudulent," to sever Richard's legal tie to Jennifer and Jamie. After securing a California warrant to obtain custody of the children on February 27, 1984, Richard and his father, Gerard Smolin, resorted to self-help. On March 9, 1984, they picked up Jennifer and Jamie as they were waiting for

---

558, 55 L.Ed. 735 (1911). If **D** left the state after setting a bomb to murder **X**, although before the fatal explosion, he is a "fugitive".

Even though the accused or convicted defendant may leave a state with knowledge and consent of state officials, his or her fugitive status is not affected and he or she is not precluded from being subject to extradition. Gee v. State of Kansas, 912 F.2d 414 (10th Cir. 1990).

their school bus in Slidell, Louisiana, and brought them back to California. On April 11, 1984, the Popes submitted to the jurisdiction of the California Superior Court and instituted an action to modify the 1981 order granting Richard sole custody. Those proceedings are apparently still pending before the California courts.

Meanwhile, the Popes raised the stakes by instituting a criminal action against Richard and Gerard Smolin in Louisiana. On April 30, 1984, *after* the Popes instituted modification proceedings in California, Judith Pope swore out an affidavit charging Richard and Gerard Smolin with kidnaping Jennifer and Jamie from her custody and asserting that they had acted "without authority to remove children from (her) custody." On the basis of this affidavit, the assistant district attorney for the 22nd Judicial District of Louisiana, William Alford, Jr., filed an information charging Richard and Gerard Smolin each with two counts of violating La.Rev.Stat.Ann. § 14:45 (West 1986), the Louisiana kidnaping statute. On June 14, 1984, the Governor of Louisiana formally notified the Governor of California that Richard and Gerard Smolin were charged with "simple kidnaping" in Louisiana and demanded that they be delivered up for trial.

In early August 1984, the Smolins petitioned in the California Superior Court for a writ of habeas corpus to block the anticipated extradition warrants. On August 17, 1984, the anticipated warrants issued and on August 24, 1984, the Superior Court orally granted a writ of habeas corpus after taking judicial notice of the various custody orders that had been issued. The Court concluded "that the findings in the family law case adequately demonstrate that, in fact, the process initiated by Mrs. Pope in Louisiana and her declarations and affidavits were totally insufficient to establish any basis for rights of either herself personally or for the State ... of Louisiana." California then sought a writ of mandate in the California Court of Appeal on the ground that the Superior Court had abused its discretion in blocking extradition. The Court of Appeal reluctantly issued the writ:

"Although we abhor Judy's apparent willingness to take advantage of our federal system to further this custody battle, and are sympathetic to [the Smolins'] position, we must conclude that their arguments are irrelevant to the only issue a court in the asylum state may properly address: are the documents on their face in order."

A divided California Supreme Court reversed. The majority interpreted the Superior Court's finding to be that the Smolins were not substantially charged with a crime. It found that the California custody decrees were properly considered by the Superior Court, and that its conclusion that the Smolins were not substantially charged was correct. Under the full faith and credit provisions of the federal Parental Kidnaping Prevention Act of 1980, 28 U.S.C. § 1738A, the majority determined that those decrees conclusively established that Richard Smolin was the lawful custodian of the children at the time that they were taken from Louisiana to California. Finally, the court found that, under Louisiana law, the lawful custodian can not be guilty of kidnaping children in his custody. We granted certiorari to consider whether the Extradition Clause, Art. IV, § 2, cl. 2, and the

Extradition Act, 18 U.S.C. § 3182, prevent the California Supreme Court from refusing to permit extradition on these grounds.

The Federal Constitution places certain limits on the sovereign powers of the States, limits that are an essential part of the Framers' conception of national identity and Union. One such limit is found in Art. IV, § 2, cl. 2, the Extradition Clause:

"A person charged in any State with Treason, Felony, or other Crime, who shall flee from Justice, and be found in another State, shall on Demand of the executive Authority of the State from which he fled, be delivered up, to be removed to the State having Jurisdiction of the Crime."

The obvious objective of the Extradition Clause is that no State should become a safe haven for the fugitives from a sister State's criminal justice system....

The Extradition Clause, however, does not specifically establish a procedure by which interstate extradition is to take place, and, accordingly, has never been considered to be self-executing. Early in our history, the lack of an established procedure led to a bitter dispute between the States of Virginia and Pennsylvania.... Congress responded by enacting the Extradition Act of 1793, which provides in its current form:

"Whenever the executive authority of any State or Territory demands any person as a fugitive from justice, of the executive authority of any State, District or Territory to which such person has fled, and produces a copy of an indictment found or an affidavit made before a magistrate of any State or Territory, charging the person demanded with having committed treason, felony or other crime, certified as authentic by the governor or chief magistrate of the State or Territory from whence the person so charged has fled, the executive authority of the State, District or Territory to which such person has fled shall cause him to be arrested and secured, and notify the executive authority making such demand, or the agent of such authority appointed to receive the fugitive, and shall cause the fugitive to be delivered to such agent when he shall appear." 18 U.S.C. § 3182.

This Court has held the Extradition Act of 1793 to be a proper exercise of Congress' powers under the Extradition Clause and Art. IV, § 1 to "prescribe the manner in which acts, records and proceedings shall be proved, and the effect thereof." By the express terms of federal law, therefore, the asylum State is bound to deliver up to the demanding State's agent a fugitive against whom a properly certified indictment or affidavit charging a crime is lodged.

The language, history, and subsequent construction of the Extradition Act make clear that Congress intended extradition to be a summary procedure. As we have repeatedly held, extradition proceedings are "to be kept within narrow bounds"; they are "emphatically" not the appropriate time or place for entertaining defenses or determining the guilt or innocence of the charged party. Those inquiries are left to the prosecutorial authorities and courts of the demanding State, whose duty it is to justly enforce the demanding State's criminal law—subject, of course, to the limitations imposed by the Constitution and laws of the United States. The courts of asylum States may do no more than ascertain whether the requisites of the Extradition Act have been met. As the Court held in Michigan v. Doran, 439 U.S. 282 (1978), the Act leaves only four issues open for consideration before the fugitive is delivered up:

"(a) whether the extradition documents on their face are in order; (b) whether the petitioner has been charged with a crime in the demanding state; (c) whether the petitioner is the person named in the request for extradition; and (d) whether the petitioner is a fugitive." 439 U.S., at 289, 99 S.Ct., at 535. The parties argue at length about the propriety of the California courts taking judicial notice of their prior child custody decrees in this extradition proceeding. But even if taking judicial notice of the decrees is otherwise proper, the question remains whether the decrees noticed were relevant to one of these four inquiries. The Smolins do not dispute that the extradition documents are in order, that they are the persons named in the documents and that they meet the technical definition of a "fugitive." Their sole contention is that, in light of the earlier California custody decrees and the federal Parental Kidnaping Prevention Act, 28 U.S.C. § 1738A, they have not been properly charged with a violation of Louisiana's kidnaping statute, La.Rev.Stat.Ann. § 14:45 (West 1986).

. . .

The information is in proper form, and the Smolins do not dispute that the affidavit, and documents incorporated by reference therein, set forth facts that clearly satisfy each element of the crime of kidnaping as it is defined in La.Rev.Stat.Ann. § 14:45A(4) (West 1986). If we accept as true every fact alleged, the Smolins are properly charged with kidnaping under Louisiana law. In our view, this ends the inquiry into the issue of whether or not a crime is charged for purposes of the Extradition Act.

The Smolins argue, however, that more than a formal charge is required, citing the following language from Roberts v. Reilly, 116 U.S. 80, 95, 6 S.Ct. 291, 299–300, 29 L.Ed. 544 (1885):

"It must appear, therefore, to the governor of the State to whom such a demand is presented, before he can lawfully comply with it, first, that the person demanded is substantially charged with a crime against the laws of the State from whose justice he is alleged to have fled, by an indictment or an affidavit, certified as authentic by the governor of the State making the demand. . . .

"[This] is a question of law, and is always open upon the face of the papers to judicial inquiry, on an application for a discharge under a writ of *habeas corpus*."

The Smolins claim that this language in *Roberts* spawned a widespread practice of permitting the fugitive, upon a petition for writ of habeas corpus in the asylum State's courts, to show that the demanding State's charging instrument is so insufficient that it cannot withstand some generalized version of a motion to dismiss or common-law demurrer. . . .

To the contrary, our cases make clear that no such inquiry is permitted. . . .

This proceeding is neither the time nor place for the Smolins' arguments that Judith Pope's affidavit is fraudulent and that the California custody decrees establish Richard as the lawful custodian under the full faith and credit provision of the federal Parental Kidnaping Prevention Act of 1980.... Of course, the Parental Kidnaping Prevention Act of 1980 creates a uniform federal rule governing custody determinations, a rule to which the courts of Louisiana must adhere when they consider the Smolins' case on the merits. We are not informed by the record why it is that the States of California and Louisiana are so eager to force the Smolins halfway across the continent to face criminal charges that, at least to a majority of the California Supreme Court, appear meritless. If the Smolins are correct, they are not only innocent of the charges made against them, but also victims of a possible abuse of the criminal process. But, under the Extradition Act, it is for the Louisiana courts to do justice in this case, not the California courts: "surrender is not to be interfered with by the summary process of *habeas corpus* upon speculations as to what ought to be the result of a trial in the place where the Constitution provides for its taking place." The judgment of the California Supreme Court is

Reversed.[38]

Application of Robinson

Supreme Court of Nevada, 1958.
74 Nev. 58, 322 P.2d 304.

■ EATHER, JUSTICE.... Upon two grounds appellant asserts that the court below was in error in denying him discharge from custody under his writ.

First he contends that he was not a fugitive from justice of the state of Oregon.

In May, 1942 appellant was convicted of burglary in Oregon and sentenced to a term of five years in the state prison. In June, 1944 he was granted parole under the terms of which he was released to the custody of officers of Lincoln County, Nebraska, for the purpose of standing trial for felony. He was convicted in Nebraska and sentenced to serve 20 months in the state prison. He was released in August, 1945. On January 3, 1946, with a balance of his Oregon sentence remaining to be served, the Oregon parole board revoked his parole. The record before us is silent as to the

---

38. Defendant resisted extradition on the basis of a claim that he was not a fugitive because he had fled from Ohio under duress because of a fear Ohio authorities would revoke his parole without due process and cause defendant harm. The New Mexico Supreme Court denied extradition and based its decision in part on the New Mexico Constitution's right "of seeking and obtaining safety." The Supreme Court reversed, per curiam, ruling the action of new Mexico violated the federal Constitution, Article IV, and New Mexico went beyond any permissible inquiry for extradition. New Mexico ex rel. Ortiz v. Reed, 524 U.S. 151, 118 S.Ct. 1860, 141 L.Ed.2d 131 (1998).

Violation of a defendant's Fourth and Fifth Amendment rights because of an illegal search and interview does not entitle the defendant to dismissal of extradition proceedings. Romeo v. Roache, 820 F.2d 540 (1st Cir.1987).

Kansas court could not review probable cause determination for the demanding state where a judge or magistrate of the demanding state has issued a charge and warrant on a felony. Application of Danko, 240 Kan. 431, 731 P.2d 240 (1987).

basis for the revocation. We may assume it was for violation of the conditions of the parole. It was for the purpose of requiring him to serve the balance of his sentence that his return to Oregon was sought by the executive warrant here in question.

Appellant contends that in delivering him to Nebraska, Oregon has waived further service of sentence; that since he was compelled to leave Oregon under these circumstances he cannot be regarded as a fugitive from justice of that state. In support of his contention he relies upon In re Whittington, 34 Cal.App. 344, 167 P. 404.[39]

Authorities are divided upon this proposition. In our view the better rule and the weight of authority today is to the effect that the mode or manner of a person's departure from a demanding state generally does not affect his status as a fugitive from justice and that the fact that his departure was involuntary or under legal compulsion will not preclude his extradition. Brewer v. Goff, 10 Cir., 138 F.2d 710, holding that the Whittington decision is against the weight of authority.[40]

---

39. [By the Compiler.] The theory of implied waiver by sending a prisoner to another state was expressly disapproved. In re Patterson, 64 Cal.2d 357, 49 Cal.Rptr. 801, 411 P.2d 897 (1966).

Waiver of extradition is personal to a defendant and cannot be delegated. Gardner v. Gaubatz, 719 P.2d 329 (Colo.App.1985).

One may be a fugitive in the constitutional sense although he did not leave the demanding state voluntarily. Johnson v. Peterson, 1 Wn.App. 856, 466 P.2d 183 (1970).

The Oklahoma court held that if one in custody on a criminal charge was released to another jurisdiction, on extradition proceedings, this constituted a waiver of a demand that he be returned on extradition, but was not a waiver of a right to try the person if he was once more in the original jurisdiction. Peoples v. State, 523 P.2d 1123 (Okl.Cr.1974).

40. [Footnote by the Court.] California amendment of Penal Code, § 1549 (St.1937, p. 1583) destroyed the effect of the Whittington case by expressly giving authority to the Governor to surrender any person charged with crime in another state, even though such person left the demanding state involuntarily.

[Compiler's note]. A former inmate could be considered a fugitive, for purposes of extradition, at the time he left the state in which charges were pending against him, despite defendant's alleged lack of knowledge of the charges. White v. Armontrout, 29 F.3d 357 (8th Cir.1994).

Violation of the Uniform Criminal Extradition Act does not prevent the demanding state from trying the defendant after he has been extradited. Beachem v. Attorney General of Missouri, 808 F.2d 1303 (8th Cir.1987).

The Governor of Oregon honored a requisition made by the Governor of Texas for the delivery of the plaintiff in error for removal to Texas as a fugitive from the justice of that State. The accused was taken to Texas, tried for murder and a conspiracy to commit murder and acquitted. She was, however, not released from custody because she was ordered by the Governor of Texas under a requisition of the Governor of Georgia, to be held for delivery to an agent of the State of Georgia for removal to that State as a fugitive from justice. Held, that the failure of Congress when enacting the interstate extradition provisions to provide for the case of a fugitive from justice who has not fled into the state where he is found, but was brought into it involuntarily by a requisition from another state, does not take the matters within the unprovided area out of possible state action, but leaves the state free to deliver the accused to any state from whose justice he has fled. Innes v. Tobin, 240 U.S. 127, 36 S.Ct. 290, 60 L.Ed. 562 (1916). Accord: Hackney v. Welsh, 107 Ind. 253, 8 N.E. 141 (1886). Contra: In re Hope, 7 N.Y.Cr. 406, 10 N.Y.Supp. 28 (1889). See Spear, A Lawyer's Question, 13 Alb.L.Q. 230; Larremore, Inadequacy of the Present Federal Statute Regulating Interstate Rendition, 10 Col.L.Rev. 208 (1910).

The essential fact remains that having committed an act which the law of Oregon constitutes a crime and having been convicted and sentenced therefor, appellant departed from Oregon jurisdiction and, when sought for enforcement of his penal obligation to that state, was found in another state.

Nor do we feel that Oregon can be said to have waived its right to insist upon service of sentence. Delivery to Nebraska was under parole from Oregon. Under these circumstances appellant continued while in Nebraska and until revocation of parole to serve the Oregon sentence. It was for Oregon to fix the conditions under which its sentence might be served. Oregon's act was not a suspension of sentence or abandonment of the prisoner. The appellant was not prejudiced in any constitutional right by Oregon's action in aid of the administration of justice in a sister state.

Second: Appellant contends that Oregon's right of requisition is barred by res judicata. Following Oregon's revocation of parole in 1946, Oregon on two occasions (prior to the present proceeding) has laid claim to a right to take appellant into custody as a parole violator. On both occasions appellant has secured discharge through habeas corpus.

The first occasion was in Nebraska. Local authorities took appellant into custody at Oregon's request. Appellant sought habeas corpus. The writ was summarily denied. On appeal the Nebraska Supreme Court, Application of Robinson, 150 Neb. 443, 34 N.W.2d 887, directed the lower court to issue the writ and proceed to hearing. Oregon failed to press its rights. No hearing was had. Appellant was discharged, without hearing, on Oregon's default.

The second occasion was in Kansas. Appellant had been convicted of a federal offense and sentenced to the federal prison at Leavenworth. Oregon placed a detainer against him with the prison authorities. Appellant through habeas corpus attacked Oregon's right to custody. Oregon withdrew the detainer. No hearing was had.

It cannot be said that appellant's discharges under habeas corpus in these two occasions resulted from judicial determinations which now bar Oregon from asserting the right of requisition. Appellant's discharges resulted simply from Oregon's failure to press its rights. Although appellant contends that the failure of a state to assert or press its extradition rights at a given time would result in a waiver of these rights, no authority is cited in support of this contention, and none has come to the attention of the court. Never has any hearing been had upon the merits of appellant's contentions until the hearing before the court below. Never were those rights judicially determined until the present proceeding. Res judicata does not apply.[41]

On motion to dismiss: Motion denied.

On appeal: Affirmed.

See note, Fugitives from Justice under the Federal Rendition Clause, 18 Col.L.Rev. 70 (1918).

41. One who has been extradited from Florida to Connecticut can be brought back by extradition to serve the balance of a term for which he had received a conditional pardon that was later revoked. United States v. Matus, 218 F.2d 466 (2d Cir.1954).

■ Badt, C.J., and Merrill, J., concur.

In re Extradition of Adams

Court of Appeals of Ohio, 1989.
63 Ohio App.3d 638, 579 N.E.2d 752.

■ Brogan, Judge.

This is an appeal by Joanne S. Adams from the trial court's denial of her petition for a writ of habeas corpus challenging the legality of the warrant for her arrest and the extradition order issued by the Governor of Ohio.

The facts of this case relate to a custody dispute. On May 11, 1980, Adams gave birth to Russell Adams Young and on April 13, 1982, William M. Young acknowledged his paternity of Russell in the Superior Court of California, City and County of San Francisco. Physical custody of Russell was granted to Adams with visitation permitted to Young. Legal custody of Russell was to be shared by both parents.

Subsequently, Adams informed Young of her intent to relocate to Ohio and to take Russell with her. A hearing on the redetermination of custody, support and visitation resulted in an entry dated June 30, 1986, wherein Adams was granted full legal and physical custody of Russell. Young was granted visitation with Russell as follows:

"[T]he two week Christmas Holiday of 1986–1987, and the Easter week holidays in 1987. Father shall provide for the transportation and make the arrangements for the transportation. Mother shall contribute one-third of the cost of the transportation."

In December 1986, Young informed Adams of his intent to exercise visitation with Russell. To this end, Young purchased a round-trip ticket from Dayton to San Francisco. Russell was to depart from Dayton on December 20, 1986 and return on January 2, 1987. Adams, however, refused to permit the ordered visitation. Thereafter, on December 20, 1986, Adams was served with a motion for contempt for failure to permit visitation. The hearing upon this motion was scheduled in California on December 24, 1986.

The hearing, which Adams did not attend, resulted in an order whereby Adams was found in contempt for failure to permit Christmas visitation as ordered. Furthermore, the court changed custody of Russell from Adams to Young.

Young retained Ohio counsel for the purpose of enforcing the California court order. The California order was filed ... and Young moved for a contempt citation against Adams for failing to obey its provisions. Adams then challenged the jurisdiction of the California court to determine a change of custody. These proceedings culminated in a decision and order by the Greene County Common Pleas Court.... [T]he court found that the California court had properly exercised its jurisdiction over the parties and subject matter. The trial court found itself without jurisdiction to modify the order changing custody of Russell from Adams to Young.

Adams filed her appeal of the decision of the trial court with this court. On May 19, 1988, we determined that the California order was unenforceable in Ohio due to Adams' lack of adequate notice of the December 24, 1986 hearing.

Following our decision, Adams determined to relinquish custody of Russell to Young. We are unaware of the date of this occurrence.

On September 10, 1987, the Municipal Court of California, Santa Clara County, issued an arrest warrant for Adams. The warrant charges Adams with violating California Penal Code Section 278.5, which constitutes a felony. Section 278.5(b) states:

"Every person who has a right to physical custody of or visitation with a child pursuant to an order, judgment, or decree of any court which grants another person, guardian, or public agency right to physical custody of or visitation with that child, and who within or without the state detains, conceals, takes, or entices away that child with the intent to deprive the other person of that right to custody or visitation shall be punished by imprisonment in the state prison for 16 months, or two or three years, a fine of not more than ten thousand dollars ($10,000), or both; or by imprisonment in a county jail for a period of not more than one year, a fine of not more than one thousand dollars ($1,000), or both."

On July 8, 1988, the Governor of the state of Ohio issued a warrant of arrest for Adams, an "alleged fugitive from justice, who stands charged in Santa Clara County California with detention or concealment of a child in violation of a custody order." The warrant further instructed the Sheriff of Greene County to bring Adams before an Ohio court and, if directed by that court, to extradite Adams to California.

Adams filed her petition for a writ of habeas corpus on August 8, 1988. Following a hearing, the trial court denied Adams' petition in a judgment entry of October 11, 1988.

In its decision, the trial court relied upon R.C. 2963.06, an exception to the rule set forth in R.C. 2963.03, which requires that a suspect be a fugitive from justice before Ohio will permit extradition. R.C. 2963.03 states, in pertinent part:

"No demand for the extradition of a person charged with crime in another state shall be recognized by the governor unless the demand is in writing alleging, except in cases arising under section 2963.06 of the Revised Code, that the accused was present in the demanding state at the time of the commission of the alleged crime, and that thereafter he fled from the state * * * [.]"

R.C. 2963.06 states:

"The governor may surrender, on demand of the executive authority of any other state, any person in this state charged in such other state in the manner provided in section 2963.03 of the Revised Code with committing an act in this state, or in a third state, intentionally resulting in a crime in the state whose executive authority is making the demand, * * * even though the accused was not in that state at the time of the commission of the crime, and has not fled therefrom."

The trial court found that "[a]lthough Adams is not a fugitive [as defined in R.C. 2963.03], her actions in this case are within those defined by R.C. 2963.06. Adams' alleged affirmative act in this state was not allowing her son to visit his father in California." Further, the trial court found that Adams was charged with an offense under California law, that Adams was the individual named in the warrant, that extradition was not for the purpose of enforcing civil liability, and that the extradition documents were valid on their face.

It is from the denial of her petition for a writ of habeas corpus that Adams now appeals.

The first assignment of error sets forth the following:

"The trial court erred in determining that the extradition documents on their face are in order and that relator-appellant, Joanne S. Adams, is a fugitive, based upon the uncontroverted facts contained in the record."

Adams argues that R.C. 2963.06 has never before been applied to permit the extradition of an individual for failure to permit visitation. Rather, R.C. 2963.06 has been utilized to extradite individuals accused of aiding and abetting in the commission of out-of-state crimes, such as burglary or robbery. Further, Adams argues that Ohio statutes presently contain no criminal sanctions for the prevention of visitation and that they contain no exception to the requirement that an individual be a fugitive before he may be extradited. Adams' arguments are not well taken.

We first note that although there may exist no criminal sanctions in Ohio for prevention of visitation, it is not Ohio law, but California law, which concerns us here. R.C. 2963.06 specifically permits the extradition to another state of an individual who commits in Ohio an act which constitutes a crime in the other state. Additionally, R.C. 2963.06 contains an exception to the requirement of fugitivity set forth in R.C. 2963.03.

Finally, we find that R.C. 2963.06 has been applied to extradite an individual under circumstances analogous to those at bar. In In re Harris (1959), 170 Ohio St. 151, 10 O.O.2d 99, 163 N.E.2d 762, the Ohio Supreme Court decided whether, pursuant to R.C. 2963.06, a father in Ohio, who failed to support his child in Wisconsin, should be extradited to Wisconsin. In Wisconsin, failure to support a child constituted a criminal offense.

The Harris court discussed the fact that the father was not a fugitive from Wisconsin in that he was not present in that state when he committed a crime and did not flee from Wisconsin thereafter. Rather, at all pertinent times, the father was in Ohio. The Harris court explained:

"Prior to the adoption of the Uniform Extradition Act, it was possible to extradite only a criminal who could be said to be a 'fugitive,' i.e., one who had been physically present in the state in which he committed a crime and had fled therefrom. To remedy this situation, several of the states enacted what is generally known as Section 6 of the Uniform Extradition Act. The Ohio enactment is Section 2963.06, Revised Code. * * * *"

Adams, like the father in Harris, remained in Ohio when she committed the alleged crime of preventing visitation. Nonetheless, pursuant to

R.C. 2963.06, Adams' fugitivity is not at issue. The fact that she committed an act in Ohio which constitutes a crime in California is sufficient to permit her extradition.

The Harris court also discussed the issue of whether "one by failing to act in a particular regard commit[s] an act." In the instant case, the issue becomes whether, by failing to permit visitation, Adams committed a crime pursuant to R.C. 2963.06. We decide this issue in the affirmative.

The Harris court described a wilful and wrongful act as "one done by a person of his own mind and with the purpose of doing another some wrong, either by omission or commission." The Harris court then held:

"In our opinion, a person in Ohio who intentionally does nothing to support his child in another state, when under the laws of such other state he is required to do so, thereby 'commits an act' in Ohio which intentionally results in a crime in such other state, and he may be extradited therefor under Section 2963.06, Revised Code."

Likewise, we hold that Adams' intentional failure to permit Young visitation with their son constituted an act resulting in a crime in the state of California. Pursuant to R.C. 2963.06, Adams may therefore be extradited. Adams' first assignment of error is overruled.

Appellant's second assignment of error states:

"The trial court's judgment entry denying relator-appellant's writ of habeas corpus is against the manifest weight of the evidence."

Adams argues that because the state of Ohio failed to offer any evidence to rebut her evidence showing lack of fugitivity, she is entitled to a judgment in her favor.

We find this argument to be without merit and the Rowe case to be inapposite. This is so because in the case at bar, fugitivity is not an issue. See discussion of R.C. 2963.06, supra. In Rowe, however, fugitivity constituted a central issue. In that case, the court considered whether, in a habeas corpus proceeding, petitioner's evidence of lack of fugitivity was sufficient to rebut the prima facie evidence of fugitivity contained in the arrest warrant issued by the Governor of Ohio.

Pursuant to R.C. 2963.06, the fact that Adams was not a fugitive from California at the time when she prevented the visitation is irrelevant. The facts of this case show that Adams did commit an act in Ohio which constituted a crime in California despite the truth of Adams' contention that the state of Ohio presented no evidence against her.

Adams' second assignment of error is overruled. The judgment of the trial court will be affirmed.

Judgment affirmed.

■ WOLFF, P.J., and WILSON, J., concur.[42]

---

42. Although the federal constitution and statute require extradition only of one who has fled from the demanding state they do not prohibit the states from doing more. And the provision of the Uniform Extradition Act which authorizes the governor to issue his warrant of arrest and extradition of one who did an act intentionally resulting in a crime in the

United States v. Alvarez–Machain

Supreme Court of the United States, 1992.
504 U.S. 655, 112 S.Ct. 2188, 119 L.Ed.2d 441.

■ CHIEF JUSTICE REHNQUIST delivered the opinion of the Court.

The issue in this case is whether a criminal defendant, abducted to the United States from a nation with which it has an extradition treaty, thereby acquires a defense to the jurisdiction of this country's courts. We hold that he does not, and that he may be tried in federal district court for violations of the criminal law of the United States.

Respondent, Humberto Alvarez–Machain, is a citizen and resident of Mexico. He was indicted for participating in the kidnap and murder of United States Drug Enforcement Administration (DEA) special agent Enrique Camarena–Salazar and a Mexican pilot working with Camarena, Alfredo Zavala–Avelar. The DEA believes that respondent, a medical doctor, participated in the murder by prolonging Agent Camarena's life so that others could further torture and interrogate him. On April 2, 1990, respondent was forcibly kidnaped from his medical office in Guadalajara, Mexico, to be flown by private plane to El Paso, Texas, where he was arrested by DEA officials. The District Court concluded that DEA agents were responsible for respondent's abduction, although they were not personally involved in it.[43]

Respondent moved to dismiss the indictment, claiming that his abduction constituted outrageous governmental conduct, and that the District Court lacked jurisdiction to try him because he was abducted in violation of the extradition treaty between the United States and Mexico. Extradition

---

demanding state, although he was not therein, is constitutional and valid. Sheriff v. Thompson, 85 Nev. 211, 452 P.2d 911 (1969); Miller v. Decker, 411 F.2d 302 (1969).

All states have adopted this Uniform Act which has its own provisions for extradition. In re Morgan, 244 Cal.App.2d 903, 53 Cal.Rptr. 642 (1966).

K, who lived in Montana, was the father of two small children who lived with their mother in Washington. A Montana court had ordered **K** to pay $12.50 a month for the support of his children, which order had been almost completely ignored. **K** was extradited to Washington where he was convicted of criminal nonsupport. He was placed on probation conditioned on his support of his children until they reached the age of twenty-one. This conviction was affirmed. The situs of the crime of nonsupport is where the minor children are located. By his wilful failure to provide the required support, **K** did an act which intentionally resulted in the crime in Washington and hence was properly extraditable under the special provision of the statute. State v. Klein, 4 Wash.App. 736, 484 P.2d 455 (1971).

If **D** committed grand theft by embezzlement, having a duty to account for the money in Arizona, that state had jurisdiction over the crime. State v. Roderick, 9 Ariz.App. 19, 448 P.2d 891 (1968).

Even if defendants had not been in Louisiana, their extradition to Louisiana was proper where the offense was committed in Louisiana even though defendants were not physically present. A Mississippi statute, Miss. Code Ann. § 7–1–25 (1972 as amended) allowed extradition and defendants' claims that no offense was committed in Louisiana should be considered in that jurisdiction. State v. McCurley, 627 So.2d 339 (Miss.1993).

43. Apparently, DEA officials had attempted to gain respondent's presence in the United States through informal negotiations with Mexican officials, but were unsuccessful. DEA officials then, through a contact in Mexico, offered to pay a reward and expenses in return for the delivery of respondent to the United States. United States v. Caro–Quintero, 745 F.Supp., at 602–604.

Treaty, May 4, 1978, [1979] United States–United Mexican States, 31 U.S.T. 5059, T.I.A.S. No. 9656 (Extradition Treaty or Treaty). The District Court rejected the outrageous governmental conduct claim, but held that it lacked jurisdiction to try respondent because his abduction violated the Extradition Treaty. The District Court discharged respondent and ordered that he be repatriated to Mexico.

The Court of Appeals affirmed the dismissal of the indictment and the repatriation of respondent.... [T]he Court of Appeals [in *United States v. Verdugo Urquidez*] held that the forcible abduction of a Mexican national with the authorization or participation of the United States violated the Extradition Treaty between the United States and Mexico. Although the Treaty does not expressly prohibit such abductions, the Court of Appeals held that the "purpose" of the Treaty was violated by a forcible abduction, which, along with a formal protest by the offended nation, would give a defendant the right to invoke the Treaty violation to defeat jurisdiction of the District Court to try him. The Court of Appeals further held that the proper remedy for such a violation would be dismissal of the indictment and repatriation of the defendant to Mexico. [In this case the Court of Appeals ordered the indictment dismissed and the defendant repatriated.]

. . .

Although we have never before addressed the precise issue raised in the present case, we have previously considered proceedings in claimed violation of an extradition treaty and proceedings against a defendant brought before a court by means of a forcible abduction. We addressed the former issue in United States v. Rauscher, 119 U.S. 407 (1886); more precisely, the issue whether the Webster–Ashburton Treaty of 1842, 8 Stat. 572, 576, which governed extraditions between England and the United States, prohibited the prosecution of defendant Rauscher for a crime other than the crime for which he had been extradited. Whether this prohibition, known as the doctrine of specialty, was an intended part of the treaty had been disputed between the two nations for some time. Justice Miller delivered the opinion of the Court, which carefully examined the terms and history of the treaty; the practice of nations in regards to extradition treaties; the case law from the States; and the writings of commentators, and reached the following conclusion:

"[A] person who has been brought within the jurisdiction of the court *by virtue of proceedings under an extradition treaty*, can only be tried for one of the offences described in that treaty, and for the offence with which he is charged in the proceedings for his extradition, until a reasonable time and opportunity have been given him, after his release or trial upon such charge, to return to the country from whose asylum he had been forcibly taken under those proceedings."

. . .

In Ker v. Illinois, 119 U.S. 436, 7 S.Ct. 225, 30 L.Ed. 421 (1886), also written by Justice Miller and decided the same day as *Rauscher*, we addressed the issue of a defendant brought before the court by way of a forcible abduction. Frederick Ker had been tried and convicted in an Illinois court for larceny; his presence before the court was procured by means of forcible abduction from Peru. A messenger was sent to Lima with the proper warrant to demand Ker by virtue of the extradition treaty between Peru and the United States. The messenger, however, disdained reliance on the treaty processes, and instead forcibly kidnaped Ker and brought him to the United States. We distinguished Ker's case from *Rauscher*, on the basis that Ker was not brought into the United States by virtue of the extradition treaty between the United States and Peru, and rejected Ker's argument that he had a right under the extradition treaty to be returned to this country only in accordance with its terms.[44] We rejected Ker's due process argument more broadly, holding in line with "the highest authorities" that "such forcible abduction is no sufficient reason why the party should not answer when brought within the jurisdiction of the court which has the right to try him for such an offence, and presents no valid objection to his trial in such court."

In Frisbie v. Collins, 342 U.S. 519, rehearing denied, 343 U.S. 937 (1952), we applied the rule in *Ker* to a case in which the defendant had been kidnaped in Chicago by Michigan officers and brought to trial in Michigan. We upheld the conviction over objections based on the Due Process Clause and the federal Kidnaping Act and stated:

"This Court has never departed from the rule announced in [*Ker*] that the power of a court to try a person for crime is not impaired by the fact that he had been brought within the court's jurisdiction by reason of a 'forcible abduction.' No persuasive reasons are now presented to justify overruling this line of cases. They rest on the sound basis that due process of law is satisfied when one present in court is convicted of crime after having been fairly apprized of the charges against him and after a fair trial in accordance with constitutional procedural safeguards. There is nothing in the Constitution that requires a court to permit a guilty person rightfully convicted to escape justice because he was brought to trial against his will."[45]

The only differences between *Ker* and the present case are that *Ker* was decided on the premise that there was no governmental involvement in

---

44. In the words of Justice Miller, the "treaty was not called into operation, was not relied upon, was not made the pretext of arrest, and the facts show that it was a clear case of kidnapping within the dominions of Peru, without any pretence of authority under the treaty or from the government of the United States." Ker v. Illinois, 119 U.S., at 443, 7 S.Ct., at 229.

Two cases decided during the Prohibition Era in this country have dealt with seizures claimed to have been in violation of a treaty entered into between the United States and Great Britain to assist the United States in offshore enforcement of its prohibition laws, and to allow British passenger ships to carry liquor while in the waters of the United States. 43 Stat. 1761 (1924). The history of the negotiations leading to the treaty is set forth in Cook v. United States, 288 U.S. 102, 111–118, 53 S.Ct. 305, 308–311, 77 L.Ed. 641 (1933). In that case we held that the treaty provision for seizure of British vessels operating beyond the 3–mile limit was intended to be exclusive, and that therefore liquor seized from a British vessel in violation of the treaty could not form the basis of a conviction.

In Ford v. United States, 273 U.S. 593, 47 S.Ct. 531, 71 L.Ed. 793 (1927), the argument as to personal jurisdiction was deemed to have been waived.

45. We have applied Ker to numerous cases where the presence of the defendant was obtained by an interstate abduction. See, e.g., Mahon v. Justice, 127 U.S. 700, 8 S.Ct. 1204, 32 L.Ed. 283 (1888); Cook v. Hart, 146 U.S. 183, 13 S.Ct. 40, 36 L.Ed. 934 (1892); Pettibone v. Nichols, 203 U.S. 192, 215–216, 27 S.Ct. 111, 119, 51 L.Ed. 148 (1906).

the abduction; and Peru, from which Ker was abducted, did not object to his prosecution. Respondent finds these differences to be dispositive, as did the Court of Appeals in *Verdugo*, 939 F.2d, at 1346, contending that they show that respondent's prosecution, like the prosecution of *Rauscher*, violates the implied terms of a valid extradition treaty. The Government, on the other hand, argues that *Rauscher* stands as an "exception" to the rule in *Ker* only when an extradition treaty is invoked, and the terms of the treaty provide that its breach will limit the jurisdiction of a court. Therefore, our first inquiry must be whether the abduction of respondent from Mexico violated the Extradition Treaty between the United States and Mexico. If we conclude that the Treaty does not prohibit respondent's abduction, the rule in *Ker* applies, and the court need not inquire as to how respondent came before it.

. . .

[C]ritical to respondent's argument is Article 9 of the Treaty, which provides:

"1. Neither Contracting Party shall be bound to deliver up its own nationals, but the executive authority of the requested Party shall, if not prevented by the laws of that Party, have the power to deliver them up if, in its discretion, it be deemed proper to do so.

"2. If extradition is not granted pursuant to paragraph 1 of this Article, the requested Party shall submit the case to its competent authorities for the purpose of prosecution, provided that Party has jurisdiction over the offense."

According to respondent, Article 9 embodies the terms of the bargain which the United States struck: If the United States wishes to prosecute a Mexican national, it may request that individual's extradition. Upon a request from the United States, Mexico may either extradite the individual or submit the case to the proper authorities for prosecution in Mexico. In this way, respondent reasons, each nation preserved its right to choose whether its nationals would be tried in its own courts or by the courts of the other nation. This preservation of rights would be frustrated if either nation were free to abduct nationals of the other nation for the purposes of prosecution. More broadly, respondent reasons, as did the Court of Appeals, that all the processes and restrictions on the obligation to extradite established by the Treaty would make no sense if either nation were free to resort to forcible kidnaping to gain the presence of an individual for prosecution in a manner not contemplated by the Treaty.

We do not read the Treaty in such a fashion. Article 9 does not purport to specify the only way in which one country may gain custody of a national of the other country for the purposes of prosecution. In the absence of an extradition treaty, nations are under no obligation to surrender those in their country to foreign authorities for prosecution. (United States may not extradite a citizen in the absence of a statute or treaty obligation). Extradition treaties exist so as to impose mutual obligations to surrender individuals in certain defined sets of circumstances, following established procedures. The Treaty thus provides a mechanism which would not otherwise exist, requiring, under certain circumstances, the United States and Mexico to extradite individuals to the other country, and establishing the procedures to be followed when the Treaty is invoked.

The history of negotiation and practice under the Treaty also fails to show that abductions outside of the Treaty constitute a violation of the Treaty. . . .

Thus, the language of the Treaty, in the context of its history, does not support the proposition that the Treaty prohibits abductions outside of its terms. The remaining question, therefore, is whether the Treaty should be interpreted so as to include an implied term prohibiting prosecution where the defendant's presence is obtained by means other than those established by the Treaty. . . .

The Court of Appeals deemed it essential, in order for the individual defendant to assert a right under the Treaty, that the affected foreign government had registered a protest. ("[I]n the kidnapping case there must be a formal protest from the offended government after the kidnapping"). Respondent agrees that the right exercised by the individual is derivative of the nation's right under the Treaty, since nations are authorized, notwithstanding the terms of an extradition treaty, to voluntarily render an individual to the other country on terms completely outside of those provided in the treaty. The formal protest, therefore, ensures that the "offended" nation actually objects to the abduction and has not in some way voluntarily rendered the individual for prosecution. Thus the Extradition Treaty only prohibits gaining the defendant's presence by means other than those set forth in the Treaty when the nation from which the defendant was abducted objects.

This argument seems to us inconsistent with the remainder of respondent's argument. The Extradition Treaty has the force of law, and if, as respondent asserts, it is self-executing, it would appear that a court must enforce it on behalf of an individual regardless of the offensiveness of the practice of one nation to the other nation. In *Rauscher*, the Court noted that Great Britain had taken the position in other cases that the Webster–Ashburton Treaty included the doctrine of specialty, but no importance was attached to whether or not Great Britain had protested the prosecution of Rauscher for the crime of cruel and unusual punishment as opposed to murder.

More fundamentally, the difficulty with the support respondent garners from international law is that none of it relates to the practice of nations in relation to extradition treaties. . . . In the instant case, respondent would imply terms in the Extradition Treaty from the practice of nations with regards to international law more generally. Respondent would have us find that the Treaty acts as a prohibition against a violation of the general principle of international law that one government may not "exercise its police power in the territory of another state." There are many actions which could be taken by a nation that would violate this principle, including waging war, but it cannot seriously be contended that an invasion of the United States by Mexico would violate the terms of the Extradition Treaty between the two nations.

In sum, to infer from this Treaty and its terms that it prohibits all means of gaining the presence of an individual outside of its terms goes beyond established precedent and practice.... [T]o imply from the terms of this Treaty that it prohibits obtaining the presence of an individual by means outside of the procedures the Treaty establishes requires a much larger inferential leap, with only the most general of international law principles to support it. The general principles cited by respondent simply fail to persuade us that we should imply in the United States–Mexico Extradition Treaty a term prohibiting international abductions.

.   .   .

So ordered.[46]

■ JUSTICE STEVENS, with whom JUSTICE BLACKMUN and JUSTICE O'CONNOR dissent.

State v. Kealy

Supreme Court of Iowa, 1893.
89 Iowa 94, 56 N.W. 283.

■ ROTHROCK, J. The defendant was indicted for the crime of obtaining money under false pretenses. After the crime was committed, he left this state, and went to the state of New York. A requisition was made upon the governor of that state for the extradition of the defendant, upon the ground that he had been indicted in this state, and he was returned to this state in pursuance of the requisition. After he was brought to this state, and while he was in custody under that indictment, he was indicted for forging a promissory note. When he was brought into court on the last indictment, he made a motion to be discharged from restraint on the indictment for forgery, on the ground that he was not extradited on that charge, and that, being in restraint on the first charge, he could not be required to plead to the second indictment, nor could he be restrained of his liberty by reason thereof, he never having had an opportunity to return to the state of New York. The court overruled the motion, and required the defendant to plead to the indictment. A plea of guilty was entered, and the defendant was sentenced to imprisonment in the penitentiary for two years.

It appears from the abstract in the case that the two indictments were founded upon wholly different and distinct charges, and, as we understand

---

46. If **D** was assaulted by the officer of another state and brought here unlawfully, the state nevertheless had jurisdiction over him and his conviction is affirmed. State v. Crump, 82 N.M. 487, 484 P.2d 329 (1971). Accord State v. Anderson, 618 P.2d 42 (Utah 1980).

"[F]orcible return to the jurisdiction of the United States constitutes no bar to prosecution once the defendant is found within the United States." United States v. Lovato, 520 F.2d 1270, 1271 (9th Cir.1975).

"Once the defendant is before the court, the court will not inquire into the circumstances surrounding his presence there." United States v. Marzano, 537 F.2d 257, 271 (7th Cir.1976); Quiver v. State, 339 N.W.2d 303 (S.D.1983).

Where a person is unlawfully brought into the jurisdiction the court has jurisdiction to deal with him, but it also has discretion not to do so if the exercise of jurisdiction would constitute an abuse of process. Regina v. Levinge, 27 Aust.Crim.R. 163 (Ct. of App. NSW 1987).

it, they did not involve the same transaction. The record does not show what disposition was made of the indictment of obtaining money under false pretenses. It is stated in argument that the defendant was sentenced to imprisonment for one year on that charge.

The question presented for decision is stated by counsel for the appellant in the following language: "Can a party taken from one country or state to another, upon proceedings of extradition, legally be held to answer to another and different offense than that upon which he was so extradited, without being given an opportunity to return to the state of his asylum?"

This case does not involve any question of international extradition. The defendant's removal from the state of New York to this state was not procured by any fraudulent pretense or representation made to him for the purpose of bringing him within the jurisdiction of our courts. It is provided by section 2, article 4, of the constitution of the United States, that "a person charged in any state with treason, felony or other crime, who shall flee from justice and be found in another state, shall on demand of the executive authority of the state from which he fled be delivered up to be removed to the state having jurisdiction of the crime." There was no abuse of this constitutional provision in this case. Extradition was not resorted to as a means of procuring the presence of the defendant in this state for the purpose of serving him with process in a civil action. There can be no question that the grand jury of Jones county, in this state, had the power to find the second indictment against the defendant, and there was the same right of extradition upon that charge that there was on the first indictment. His counsel states in argument that he was sentenced to the penitentiary for one year on the first indictment, and the imprisonment of two years on the second indictment was to commence at the expiration of the imprisonment on the first. It will be observed that what the defendant demanded was that the second indictment should be held in abeyance until he was discharged from imprisonment on the first, and until a reasonable time and opportunity had been given him after his release on the first charge to return to New York, from which asylum he was forcibly taken on the first charge.

There is a conflict of authority upon this question. This court is committed to the doctrine that, when a person is properly charged with a crime, the courts will not inquire into the circumstances under which he was brought into this state, and within the jurisdiction of the court. State v. Ross, 21 Iowa 467. It is true that the defendants in that case were not brought to this state under a requisition upon the executive of another state. They were arrested in the state of Missouri without legal warrant, and after being forcibly brought to this state they were rearrested, and turned over to the civil authorities, and indicted. It is said in that case that, "the officers of the law take the requisite process, find the persons charged within the jurisdiction, and this, too, without force, wrong, fraud, or violence on the part of any agent of the state, or officer thereof. And it can make no difference whether the illegal arrest was made in another state or another government. The violation of the law of the other sovereignty, so far as entitled to weight, would be the same in principle in the one case as the other. That our own laws have been violated is sufficiently shown by the indictment. For this the state had a right to detain the prisoners, and it is of no importance how or where their capture was effected." In the case at bar the defendant was properly indicted, and when process was issued on the indictment, it is of no importance by what authority he was brought into this state. In support of this doctrine: State v. Stewart, 60 Wis. 587, 19 N.W. 429; Ham v. State, 4 Tex.App. 645; State v. Brewster, 7 Vt. 118; Dow's Case, 18 Pa.St. 37; State v. Wenzel, 77 Ind. 428; Ker v. People, 110 Ill. 627. The first two cases above cited are founded on facts substantially the same as the case at bar. As we have said, there is a conflict of authority upon the question. The cases will be found collected in 7 Am. and Eng. Encyclopedia of Law, 648. We have no disposition to depart from the rule adopted by this court in State v. Ross, supra, and the judgment of the district court is Affirmed.[47]

---

47. Accord that forcible removal to a jurisdiction does not preclude prosecution, Lascelles v. Georgia, 148 U.S. 537, 13 S.Ct. 687, 37 L.Ed. 549 (1893); State v. Rowe, 104 Iowa 323, 73 N.W. 833 (1898); Knox v. State, 164 Ind. 226, 73 N.E. 255 (1905); In re Flack, 88 Kan. 616, 129 P. 541 (1913), overruling State v. Hall, 40 Kan. 338, 19 P. 918 (1888); People v. Martin, 188 Cal. 281, 205 P. 121 (1922).

"In Knox v. State, at page 231, Montgomery, J., stated the following: 'The right of the person extradited to return to the country from which he has been surrendered is not a natural and inherent right of his own, but is based upon the right of his adopted sovereign to afford asylum to the fugitive, and to refuse to give him up to another except upon such terms as it is pleased to impose. The criminal himself never acquires a personal right of asylum or refuge anywhere, but all such rights as he may claim in this respect flow entirely out of the rights of the government to whose territory he has fled.' "

A defendant returned to the United States after being kidnapped in Uruguay and tortured in Brazil was held to be entitled to release if he could prove his charges. The court relied on due process grounds to find a divestiture of jurisdiction. United States v. Toscanino, 500 F.2d 267 (2d Cir.1974). The case has not been followed and was limited to its facts in United States ex rel. Lujan v. Gengler, 510 F.2d 62 (2d Cir.1975). In Gerstein v. Pugh, 420 U.S. 103, 95 S.Ct. 854 (1975), Supreme Court restated the rule that an illegal arrest or detention does not void a subsequent conviction.

"A long and almost unbroken line of authority holds that a state has jurisdiction to try a person for a crime if that person is within the state, even if his presence there was obtained by force, fraud, or violation of the laws of this or another state or country." Warmbo v. State, 578 P.2d 582, 584 (Alaska 1978); State v. Anderson, 618 P.2d 42 (Utah 1980).

"See note, Extradition—Prosecution for Other Offenses, 61 U. of Pa.Law Rev. 496 (1913)."

"See Ex parte Wilson, 63 Tex.Cr.R. 281, 140 S.W. 98 (1911); Dominguez v. State, 90 Tex.Cr.R. 92, 234 S.W. 79 (1921); In re Jones, 54 Cal.App. 423, 201 P. 944 (1921)." Keedy, Cases on the Administration of The Criminal Law, 272–3, n. 14 (1928).

In United States v. Rauscher, 119 U.S. 407, 7 S.Ct. 234, 30 L.Ed. 425 (1886), it was held that one extradited from England on an indictment for murder could not be put on trial for inflicting cruel and unusual punishment. Apparently it was assumed, when extradition was demanded, that the victim would die, but the death did not occur. Miller, J., said:

"That right, as we understand it, is that he shall be tried only for the offence with which he is charged in the extradition proceedings, and for which he was delivered up, and that if not tried for that, or after trial and acquittal, he shall have a reasonable time to leave the country before he is arrested upon the charge of any other crime committed previous to his extradition." *Id.* at 424.

"Therefore, international law recognizes that the asylum state may limit the trial of the fugitive in the demanding state to those crimes which have been found to be extraditable offenses in law and where probable cause to believe the petitioner committed the crime has

Carchman v. Nash

Supreme Court of the United States, 1985.
473 U.S. 716, 105 S.Ct. 3401, 87 L.Ed.2d 516.

■ JUSTICE BLACKMUN delivered the opinion of the Court.

Article III of the Interstate Agreement on Detainers gives a prisoner incarcerated in one State the right to demand the speedy disposition of "any untried indictment, information or complaint" that is the basis of a detainer lodged against him by another State. These cases present the issue whether Art. III applies to detainers based on probation-violation charges.

I

The Interstate Agreement on Detainers (Agreement) is a compact among 48 States, the District of Columbia, Puerto Rico, the Virgin Islands, and the United States. The Agreement was drafted in 1956 by the Council of State Governments and was adopted in 1958 by the State of New Jersey, where it is now codified as N.J.Stat.Ann. § 2A:159A–1 et seq. (West 1971). The Agreement is a congressionally sanctioned interstate compact within the Compact Clause, U.S.Const., Art. I, § 10, cl. 3, and thus is a federal law subject to federal construction.

A detainer is a request filed by a criminal justice agency with the institution in which a prisoner is incarcerated, asking the institution either to hold the prisoner for the agency or to notify the agency when release of the prisoner is imminent. Detainers generally are based on outstanding criminal charges, outstanding parole or probation-violation charges, or additional sentences already imposed against the prisoner.

The Agreement is based on a legislative finding that "charges outstanding against a prisoner, detainers based on untried indictments, informations or complaints, and difficulties in securing speedy trial of persons already incarcerated in other jurisdictions, produce uncertainties which obstruct programs of prisoner treatment and rehabilitation." Art. I. As has been explained:

"The inmate who has a detainer against him is filled with anxiety and apprehension and frequently does not respond to a training program. He often must be kept in close custody, which bars him from treatment such as trustyships, moderations of custody and opportunity for transfer to farms and work camps. In many jurisdictions he is not eligible for parole; there is little hope for his release after an optimum period of training and treatment, when he is ready for return to society with an excellent possibility that he will not offend again. Instead, he often becomes embittered with continued institutionalization and the objective of the correctional system is defeated." Council of State Governments, Suggested State Legislation, Program for 1957, p. 74 (1956).

Accordingly, the purpose of the Agreement is "to encourage the expeditious and orderly disposition of [outstanding] charges and determination of the

_____

been shown by the evidence." Freedman v. United States, 437 F.Supp. 1252, 1259 (D.C.N.D.Ga.1977).

proper status of any and all detainers based on untried indictments, informations or complaints." Art. I.

To achieve this purpose, Art. III of the Agreement establishes a procedure by which a prisoner incarcerated in one party State (the sending State) may demand the speedy disposition of "any untried indictment, information or complaint on the basis of which a detainer has been lodged against the prisoner"[48] by another party State (the receiving State). Specifically, Art. III requires the warden to inform the prisoner that a detainer has been lodged against him and that he may request final disposition of the indictment, information, or complaint upon which the detainer is based. If the prisoner makes such a request, the warden must forward it, together with a certificate providing certain information about the prisoner's terms of confinement, to the appropriate prosecuting official and court of the receiving State. The authorities in the receiving State then must bring the prisoner to trial within 180 days, absent good cause shown, or the court must dismiss the indictment, information, or complaint with prejudice, and the detainer will cease to be of any force or effect.

II

On June 21, 1976, respondent Richard Nash, in the Superior Court of New Jersey, Law Division, Mercer County, pleaded guilty to charges of breaking and entering with intent to rape, and of assault with intent to rape. On October 29, the Superior Court sentenced respondent to 18 months in prison on each count, with the sentences to run consecutively. The court suspended two years of the sentences and imposed a 2–year term of probation to follow respondent's imprisonment. On June 13, 1978, while on probation, respondent was arrested in Montgomery County, Pa., and charged with burglary, involuntary deviate sexual intercourse, and loitering. Respondent was tried and convicted on the Pennsylvania charges on March 14, 1979, and was sentenced on July 13 of that year.

While respondent was awaiting trial in Pennsylvania, the Mercer County Probation Department, on June 21, 1978, notified the Superior Court that respondent had violated his probation by committing offenses in Pennsylvania. At the Department's request, the Superior Court issued a bench warrant for respondent's arrest. The warrant was lodged as a detainer with the appropriate corrections officials in Pennsylvania.

Beginning on April 13, 1979, respondent sent a series of letters to New Jersey officials requesting final disposition of the probation-violation

---

48. Article III(a) provides in pertinent part:

"Whenever a person has entered upon a term of imprisonment in a penal or correctional institution of a party State, and whenever during the continuance of the term of imprisonment there is pending in any other party State any untried indictment, information or complaint on the basis of which a detainer has been lodged against the prisoner, he shall be brought to trial within 180 days after he shall have caused to be delivered to the prosecuting officer and the appropriate court of the prosecuting officer's jurisdiction written notice of the place of his imprisonment and his request for final disposition to be made of the indictment, information or complaint: provided that for good cause shown in open court, the prisoner or his counsel being present, the court having jurisdiction of the matter may grant any necessary or reasonable continuance."

charge. The State of New Jersey failed to bring respondent "to trial" on the probation-violation charge within 180 days after Art. III was invoked.

. . .

... On March 21, 1983, the District Court granted the petition for a writ of habeas corpus, vacated respondent's probation revocation, and ordered his release from state custody. Petitioner Philip S. Carchman, the Mercer County prosecutor, took an appeal to the United States Court of Appeals for the Third Circuit....

The Court of Appeals affirmed, holding that an outstanding probation-violation charge is an "untried indictment, information or complaint" within the meaning of Article III of the Agreement.

III

A

We begin by considering the language of the Agreement. Article III by its terms applies to detainers based on "any untried indictment, information or complaint." The most natural interpretation of the words "indictment," "information," and "complaint" is that they refer to documents charging an individual with having committed a criminal offense. See Fed.Rules Crim.Proc. 3 (complaint) and 7 (indictment and information). This interpretation is reinforced by the adjective "untried," which would seem to refer to matters that can be brought to full trial, and by Art. III's requirement that a prisoner who requests final disposition of the indictment, information, or complaint "shall be *brought to trial* within 180 days."

The language of Art. V also indicates that Art. III should be interpreted to apply solely to criminal charges. Article V(a) provides: "In response to a request made under Article III or Article IV hereof, the appropriate authority in a sending State shall offer to deliver temporary custody of such prisoner to the appropriate authority in the State where such indictment, information or complaint is pending against such person in order that speedy and efficient *prosecution* may be had." Article V(c) provides that "in the event that an action on the indictment, information or complaint on the basis of which the detainer has been lodged is not *brought to trial* within the period provided in Article III or Article IV hereof, the appropriate court of the jurisdiction where the indictment, information or complaint has been pending shall enter an order dismissing the same with prejudice, and any detainer based thereon shall cease to be of any force or effect." Finally, Art. V(d) provides: "The temporary custody referred to in this agreement shall be only for the purpose of permitting *prosecution* on the charge or charges contained in 1 or more untried indictments, informations or complaints which form the basis of the detainer or detainers or for *prosecution* on any other charge or charges arising out of the same transaction." (Emphasis added.)

The language of the Agreement therefore makes clear that the phrase "untried indictment, information or complaint" in Art. III refers to criminal charges pending against a prisoner. A probation-violation charge, which does not accuse an individual with having committed a criminal offense in the sense of initiating a prosecution, thus does not come within the terms of Art. III. Although the probation-violation charge might be based on the commission of a criminal offense, it does not result in the probationer's being "prosecuted" or "brought to trial" for that offense. Indeed, in the context of the Agreement, the probation-violation charge generally will be based on the criminal offense for which the probationer already was tried and convicted and is serving his sentence in the sending State.

Nor, of course, will the probationer be "prosecuted" or "brought to trial" on the criminal offense for which he initially was sentenced to probation, since he already will have been tried and convicted for that offense. Instead, the probation-violation charge results in a probation-revocation hearing, a proceeding to determine whether the conditions of probation should be modified or the probationer should be resentenced, at which the probationer is entitled to less than the full panoply of due process rights accorded a defendant at a criminal trial. *See* Gagnon v. Scarpelli, 411 U.S. 778, 93 S.Ct. 1756, 36 L.Ed.2d 656 (1973). *Cf.* Morrissey v. Brewer, 408 U.S. 471, 92 S.Ct. 2593, 33 L.Ed.2d 484 (1972) (parole-revocation hearing).

. . .

We therefore conclude from the language of the Agreement that a detainer based on a probation-violation charge is not a detainer based on "any untried indictment, information or complaint," within the meaning of Art. III.

. . .

The Agreement generally seeks "to encourage the expeditious and orderly disposition of [outstanding] charges," as well as the prompt "determination of the proper status of any and all detainers based on untried indictments, informations or complaints," in order to eliminate "uncertainties which obstruct programs of prisoner treatment and rehabilitation." Art. I. The uncertainties associated with probation-violation detainers, however, are less severe than the uncertainties associated with criminal-charge detainers. . . .

Indeed, it often may be desirable to delay rather than to expedite disposition of the probation-violation charge. As the Court explained in Moody v. Daggett, 429 U.S. 78, 97 S.Ct. 274, 50 L.Ed.2d 236 (1976), in the context of parole violations:

"[I]n cases such as this, in which the parolee admits or has been convicted of an offense plainly constituting a parole violation, the only remaining inquiry is whether continued release is justified notwithstanding the violation. This is uniquely a 'prediction as to the ability of the individual to live in society without committing antisocial acts.' *Morrissey, supra* [408 U.S.], at 480. In making this prophecy, a parolee's institutional record can be perhaps one of the most significant factors. Forcing decision immediately after imprisonment would not only deprive the parole authority of this vital information, but since the other most salient factor would be the parolee's recent convictions, . . . a decision to revoke parole would often be foreordained. Given the predictive nature of the hearing, it is appropriate that such hearing be held at the time at which prediction is both most relevant and most accurate—at the expiration of the parolee's intervening sentence." *Id.*, at 89.

Of course, the decision whether to request expeditious disposition lies with the prisoner, and there are circumstances under which the prisoner may have a legitimate interest in obtaining prompt disposition of a probation-violation charge underlying a detainer. For example, the prisoner may believe that he can present mitigating evidence that will lead to a decision not to revoke probation. Alternatively, he may hope for the imposition of a concurrent sentence. Finally, he simply may prefer the certainty of a known sentence to the relative uncertainty of a pending probation-violation charge.

Nevertheless, as discussed above, the purposes of the Agreement are significantly less advanced by application of Art. III to probation-violation detainers than by application of Art. III to criminal-charge detainers. Whether those purposes would be advanced sufficiently by application of Art. III to probation-violation detainers to outweigh the administrative costs, and, more generally, whether the procedures of Art. III are the most appropriate means of disposing of probation-violation detainers, are questions of legislative judgment that we must leave to the parties to the Agreement. Given the plain language of the Agreement and the relevant legislative history, we cannot conclude on the basis of the stated purposes of the Agreement alone that the parties to the Agreement intended Art. III to apply to probation-violation detainers. Accordingly, the judgment of the Court of Appeals is reversed.

It is so ordered.[49]

SECTION 3.   STATUTE OF LIMITATIONS

"With regard to limitations as to time, it is one of the peculiarities of English law that no general law of prescription in criminal cases exists among us. The maxim of our law has always been 'Nullum tempus occurrit regi,' and as a criminal trial is regarded as an action by the king, it follows that it may be brought at any time. This principle has been carried to great lengths in many well-known cases. In the middle of the last century Aram was convicted and executed for the murder of Clarke, fourteen years after his crime. Horne was executed for the murder of his bastard child (by his own sister) thirty-five years after his crime. In 1802 Governor Wall was executed for a murder committed in 1782. Not long ago a man named Sheward was executed at Norwich for the murder of his wife more than twenty years before; and I may add as a curiosity that, at the Derby Winter Assizes in 1863, I held a brief for the Crown in a case in which a man was

---

49.   Federal law governs interpretation of the Interstate Agreement on Detainers. New York v. Hill, 528 U.S. 110 (2000). Rights under the IAD may be waived through counsel. *Id.* Deviations from the procedures required by the IAD may not be excused; there is no *de minimis* exception. Alabama v. Bozeman, 533 U.S. 146 (2001).

charged with having stolen a leaf from a parish register in the year 1803. In this instance the grand jury threw out the bill.''[50]

Although the above observation was true at common law[51] statutory limitations of the time in which prosecutions may be instituted, are common and apply to most offenses.

Stogner v. California

Supreme Court of the United States, 2003.
539 U.S. 607, 123 S.Ct. 2446, 156 L.Ed.2d 544.

■ JUSTICE BREYER delivered the opinion of the Court.

California has brought a criminal prosecution after expiration of the time periods set forth in previously applicable statutes of limitations. California has done so under the authority of a new law that (1) permits resurrection of otherwise time-barred criminal prosecutions, and (2) was itself enacted *after* pre-existing limitations periods had expired. We conclude that the Constitution's *Ex Post Facto* Clause, Art. I, § 10, cl. 1, bars application of this new law to the present case.

In 1993, California enacted a new criminal statute of limitations governing sex-related child abuse crimes. The new statute permits prosecution for those crimes where "[t]he limitation period specified in [prior statutes of limitations] has expired"—provided that (1) a victim has reported an allegation of abuse to the police, (2) "there is independent evidence that clearly and convincingly corroborates the victim's allegation," and (3) the prosecution is begun within one year of the victim's report. 1993 Cal. Stats. ch. 390, § 1 (codified as amended at Cal.Penal Code Ann. § 803(g) (West Supp.2003)). A related provision, added to the statute in 1996, makes clear that a prosecution satisfying these three conditions "shall revive any cause of action barred by [prior statutes of limitations]." 1996 Cal. Stats. ch. 130, § 1 (codified at Cal.Penal Code Ann. § 803(g)(3)(A) (West Supp. 2003)). The statute thus authorizes prosecution for criminal acts committed many years beforehand—and where the original limitations period has expired—as long as prosecution begins within a year of a victim's first complaint to the police.

In 1998, a California grand jury indicted Marion Stogner, the petitioner, charging him with sex-related child abuse committed decades earlier—between 1955 and 1973. Without the new statute allowing revival of the State's cause of action, California could not have prosecuted Stogner. The statute of limitations governing prosecutions at the time the crimes were allegedly committed had set forth a 3–year limitations period. And that period had run 22 years or more before the present prosecution was brought.

Stogner moved for the complaint's dismissal. He argued that the Federal Constitution's *Ex Post Facto* Clause, Art. I, § 10, cl. 1, forbids

---

50. 2 Stephen, History of the Criminal Law of England 1–2 (1883).

51. See the statement in Brightman v. Hetzel, 183 Iowa 385, 395, 167 N.W. 89, 92 (1918).

revival of a previously time-barred prosecution. The trial court agreed that such a revival is unconstitutional. But the California Court of Appeal reversed, citing a recent, contrary decision by the California Supreme Court, People v. Frazer, 21 Cal.4th 737, 88 Cal.Rptr.2d 312, 982 P.2d 180 (1999), *cert. denied*, 529 U.S. 1108, 120 S.Ct. 1960, 146 L.Ed.2d 792 (2000). Stogner then moved to dismiss his indictment, arguing that his prosecution is unconstitutional under both the *Ex Post Facto* Clause and the Due Process Clause, Amdt. 14, § 1. The trial court denied Stogner's motion, and the Court of Appeal upheld that denial. Stogner v. Superior Court, 93 Cal.App.4th 1229, 114 Cal.Rptr.2d 37 (2001). We granted certiorari to consider Stogner's constitutional claims. 537 U.S. 1043, 123 S.Ct. 658, 154 L.Ed.2d 514 (2002).

II

The Constitution's two *Ex Post Facto* Clauses prohibit the Federal Government and the States from enacting laws with certain retroactive effects. See Art. I, § 9, cl. 3 (Federal Government); Art. I, § 10, cl. 1 (States). The law at issue here created a new criminal limitations period that extends the time in which prosecution is allowed. It authorized criminal prosecutions that the passage of time had previously barred. Moreover, it was enacted after prior limitations periods for Stogner's alleged offenses had expired. Do these features of the law, taken together, produce the kind of retroactivity that the Constitution forbids? We conclude that they do.

First, the new statute threatens the kinds of harm that, in this Court's view, the *Ex Post Facto* Clause seeks to avoid. Long ago the Court pointed out that the Clause protects liberty by preventing governments from enacting statutes with "manifestly *unjust and oppressive*" retroactive effects. Calder v. Bull, 3 Dall. 386, 391, 1 L.Ed. 648 (1798). Judge Learned Hand later wrote that extending a limitations period after the State has assured "a man that he has become safe from its pursuit ... seems to most of us unfair and dishonest." Falter v. United States, 23 F.2d 420, 426 (C.A.2), cert. denied, 277 U.S. 590, 48 S.Ct. 528, 72 L.Ed. 1003 (1928). In such a case, the government has refused "to play by its own rules," Carmell v. Texas, 529 U.S. 513, 533, 120 S.Ct. 1620, 146 L.Ed.2d 577 (2000). It has deprived the defendant of the "fair warning," Weaver v. Graham, 450 U.S. 24, 28, 101 S.Ct. 960, 67 L.Ed.2d 17 (1981), that might have led him to preserve exculpatory evidence. F. Wharton, Criminal Pleading and Practice § 316, p. 210 (8th ed. 1880) ("The statute [of limitations] is ... an amnesty, declaring that after a certain time ... the offender shall be at liberty to return to his country ... and ... may cease to preserve the proofs of his innocence"). And a Constitution that permits such an extension, by allowing legislatures to pick and choose when to act retroactively, risks both "arbitrary and potentially vindictive legislation," and erosion of the separation of powers, *Weaver, supra,* at 29, and n. 10, 101 S.Ct. 960. See Fletcher v. Peck, 6 Cranch 87, 137–138, 3 L.Ed. 162 (1810) (viewing the *Ex Post Facto* Clause as a protection against "violent acts which might grow out of the feelings of the moment").

Second, the kind of statute at issue falls literally within the categorical descriptions of *ex post facto* laws set forth by Justice Chase more than 200 years ago in *Calder v. Bull, supra*—a categorization that this Court has recognized as providing an authoritative account of the scope of the *Ex Post Facto* Clause. Collins v. Youngblood, 497 U.S. 37, 46, 110 S.Ct. 2715, 111 L.Ed.2d 30 (1990); *Carmell, supra,* at 539, 120 S.Ct. 1620. Drawing substantially on Richard Wooddeson's 18th-century commentary on the nature of *ex post facto* laws and past parliamentary abuses, Chase divided *ex post facto* laws into categories that he described in two alternative ways. See 529 U.S., at 522–524, and n. 9, 120 S.Ct. 1620. He wrote:

"I will state what laws I consider *ex post facto* laws, within the words and the intent of the prohibition. 1st. Every law that makes an action done before the passing of the law, and which was innocent when done, criminal; and punishes such action. *2d. Every law that aggravates a crime, or makes it greater than it was, when committed.* 3d. Every law that changes the punishment, and inflicts a greater punishment, than the law annexed to the crime, when committed. *4th. Every law that alters the legal rules of evidence, and receives less, or different, testimony, than the law required at the time of the commission of the offence, in order to convict the offender.* All these, and similar laws, are manifestly unjust and oppressive." *Calder, supra,* at 390–391, 1 L.Ed. 648 (emphasis altered from original).

In his alternative description, Chase traced these four categories back to Parliament's earlier abusive acts, as follows:

Category 1: "Sometimes they respected the crime, by declaring acts to be treason, which were not treason, when committed."

Category 2: *"[A]t other times they inflicted punishments, where the party was not, by law, liable to any punishment."*

Category 3: "[I]n other cases, they inflicted greater punishment, than the law annexed to the offence."

Category 4: *"[A]t other times, they violated the rules of evidence (to supply a deficiency of legal proof) by admitting one witness, when the existing law required two; by receiving evidence without oath; or the oath of the wife against the husband; or other testimony, which the courts of justice would not admit."* 3 Dall., at 389, 1 L.Ed. 648 (emphasis altered from original).

The second category—including any "law that *aggravates a crime,* or makes it *greater* than it was, when committed," *id.,* at 390, 1 L.Ed. 648— describes California's statute as long as those words are understood as Justice Chase understood them—*i.e.,* as referring to a statute that "inflict[s] *punishments,* where the party was not, by *law,* liable to *any punishment,*" *id.,* at 389, 1 L.Ed. 648. See also 2 R. Wooddeson, A Systematical View of the Laws of England 638 (1792) (hereinafter Wooddeson, Systematical View) (discussing the *ex post facto* status of a law that affects punishment by "making therein some innovation, *or creating some forfeiture or disability, not incurred in the ordinary course of law"* (emphasis added)). After (but not before) the original statute of limitations had expired, a party such as Stogner was not "liable to any punishment." California's new statute therefore "aggravated" Stogner's alleged crime, or made it "greater than it was, when committed," in the sense that, and to the extent that, it "inflicted punishment" for past criminal conduct that (when the new law was enacted) did not trigger any such liability. See also H. Black, American Constitutional Law § 266, p. 700 (4th ed.1927) (hereinafter Black, American Constitutional Law) ("[A]n act condoned by the expiration of the statute of limitations is no longer a punishable offense"). It is consequently not surprising that New Jersey's highest court long ago recognized that Chase's alternative description of second category laws *"exactly describes* the operation" of the kind of statute at issue here. Moore v. State, 43 N.J.L. 203, 217, 1881 WL 8329 (1881) (emphasis added). See also H. Black, Constitutional Prohibitions Against Legislation Impairing the Obligation of Contracts, and Against Retroactive and Ex Post Facto Laws § 235, p. 298 (1887) (hereinafter Black, Constitutional Prohibitions) ("Such a statute" "certainly makes that a punishable offense which was previously a condoned and obliterated offense").

So to understand the second category (as applying where a new law inflicts a punishment upon a person not then subject to that punishment, to any degree) explains why and how that category differs from both the first category (making criminal noncriminal behavior) and the third category (aggravating the punishment). And this understanding is consistent, in relevant part, with Chase's second category examples—examples specifically provided to illustrate Chase's *alternative* description of laws " 'inflict[ing] *punishments, where the party was not, by law, liable to any punishment,'* " *Calder, supra,* at 389, 1 L.Ed. 648.

Following Wooddeson, Chase cited as examples of such laws Acts of Parliament that banished certain individuals accused of treason. 3 Dall., at 389, and n. *, 1 L.Ed. 648; see also *Carmell,* 529 U.S., at 522–524, and n. 11, 120 S.Ct. 1620. Both Chase and Wooddeson explicitly referred to these laws as involving "banishment." *Calder, supra,* at 389 and n. *, 1 L.Ed. 648, ; 2 Wooddeson, Systematical View 638–639. This fact was significant because Parliament had enacted those laws not only after the crime's commission, but under circumstances where banishment "was simply not a form of penalty that could be imposed by the courts." *Carmell, supra,* at 523, n. 11, 120 S.Ct. 1620; see also 11 W. Holdsworth, A History of English Law 569 (1938). Thus, these laws, like the California law at issue here, enabled punishment where it was not otherwise available "in the ordinary course of law," 2 Wooddeson, Systematical View 638. As this Court previously recognized in *Carmell, supra,* at 523, and n. 11, 120 S.Ct. 1620, it was *this* vice that was relevant to Chase's purpose.

It is true, however, that Parliament's Acts of banishment, unlike the law in this case, involved a punishment (1) that the legislature imposed directly, and (2) that courts had *never* previously had the power to impose. But these differences are not determinative. The first describes not a retroactivity problem but an attainder problem that Justice Chase's language does not emphasize and with which the Constitution separately deals, Art. I, § 9, cl. 3; Art. I, § 10, cl. 1. The second difference seems beside the point. The example of Parliament's banishment laws points to concern that a legislature, knowing the accused and seeking to have the accused punished for a pre-existing crime, might enable punishment of the accused in ways that existing law forbids. That fundamental concern, related to basic concerns about retroactive penal laws and erosion of the separation of powers, applies with equal force to punishment like that enabled by California's law as applied to Stogner—punishment that courts lacked the power to impose at the time the legislature acted. See Black, Constitutional Prohibitions § 235, at 298 ("It would be superfluous to point out that such an act [reviving otherwise time-barred criminal liability] would fall within the evils intended to be guarded against by the prohibition in question"). Cf. 1 F. Wharton, Criminal Law § 444a, pp. 347–348, n. *b* (rev. 7th ed. 1874) (hereinafter Criminal Law).

In finding that California's law falls within the literal terms of Justice Chase's second category, we do not deny that it may fall within another category as well. Justice Chase's fourth category, for example, includes any "law that alters the *legal* rules of *evidence,* and receives less, or different, testimony, than the law required at the time of the commission of the offence, *in order to convict the offender.*" *Calder, supra,* at 390, 1 L.Ed. 648. This Court has described that category as including laws that diminish "the quantum of evidence required to convict." *Carmell, supra,* at 532, 120 S.Ct. 1620.

Significantly, a statute of limitations reflects a legislative judgment that, after a certain time, no quantum of evidence is sufficient to convict. See United States v. Marion, 404 U.S. 307, 322, 92 S.Ct. 455, 30 L.Ed.2d 468 (1971). And that judgment typically rests, in large part, upon evidentiary concerns—for example, concern that the passage of time has eroded memories or made witnesses or other evidence unavailable. United States v. Kubrick, 444 U.S. 111, 117, 100 S.Ct. 352, 62 L.Ed.2d 259 (1979); 4 W. LaFave, J. Israel, & N. King, Criminal Procedure § 18.5(a), p. 718 (1999); Wharton, Criminal Pleading and Practice § 316, at 210. Indeed, this Court once described statutes of limitations as creating "a presumption which renders proof unnecessary." Wood v. Carpenter, 101 U.S. 135, 139, 25 L.Ed. 807 (1879).

Consequently, to resurrect a prosecution after the relevant statute of limitations has expired is to eliminate a currently existing conclusive presumption forbidding prosecution, and thereby to permit conviction on a quantum of evidence where that quantum, at the time the new law is enacted, would have been legally insufficient. And, in that sense, the new law would "violate" previous evidence-related legal rules by authorizing the courts to " 'receiv[e] evidence ... which the courts of justice would not [previously have] admit[ted]' " as sufficient proof of a crime, *supra,* at 2450. Cf. *Collins,* 497 U.S., at 46, 110 S.Ct. 2715 ("Subtle *ex post facto* violations are no more permissible than overt ones"); Cummings v. Missouri, 4 Wall. 277, 329, 18 L.Ed. 356 (1867) (The *Ex Post Facto* Clause "cannot be evaded by the form in which the power of the State is exerted"). Nonetheless, given Justice Chase's description of the second category, we need not explore the fourth category, or other categories, further.

Third, likely for the reasons just stated, numerous legislators, courts, and commentators have long believed it well settled that the *Ex Post Facto* Clause forbids resurrection of a time-barred prosecution. Such sentiments appear already to have been widespread when the Reconstruction Congress of 1867—the Congress that drafted the Fourteenth Amendment—rejected a bill that would have revived time-barred prosecutions for treason that various Congressmen wanted brought against Jefferson Davis and "his coconspirators," Cong. Globe, 39th Cong., 2d Sess., 279 (1866–1867) (comments of Rep. Lawrence). Radical Republicans such as Roscoe Conkling and Thaddeus Stevens, no friends of the South, opposed the bill because, in their minds, it proposed an *"ex post facto* law," *id.,* at 68 (comments of Rep. Conkling), and threatened an injustice tantamount to "judicial murder," *id.,* at 69 (comments of Rep. Stevens). In this instance, Congress ultimately passed a law extending *unexpired* limitations periods, ch. 236, 15 Stat. 183—a tailored approach to extending limitations periods that has also been taken in modern statutes, *e.g.,* 18 U.S.C. § 3293 (notes on effective date of 1990 amendment and effect of 1989 amendment); Cal.Penal Code Ann. § 805.5 (West Supp.2003).

Further, Congressmen such as Conkling were not the only ones who believed that laws reviving time-barred prosecutions are *ex post facto.* That view was echoed in roughly contemporaneous opinions by State Supreme Courts. *E.g.,* State v. Sneed, 25 Tex. Supp. 66, 67, 1860 WL 5750 (1860); *Moore,* 43 N.J.L., at 216–217. *Cf.* State v. Keith, 63 N.C. 140, 145, 1869 WL 1378 (1869) (A State's repeal of an amnesty was "substantially an *ex post facto* law"). Courts, with apparent unanimity until California's decision in *Frazer,* have continued to state such views, and, when necessary, so to hold. *E.g.,* People ex rel. Reibman v. Warden, 242 A.D. 282, 285, 275 N.Y.S. 59, 62 (App.Div.1934); United States v. Fraidin, 63 F.Supp. 271, 276 (D.Md. 1945); People v. Shedd, 702 P.2d 267, 268 (Colo.1985) (en banc) *(per curiam);* State v. Hodgson, 108 Wash.2d 662, 667–669, 740 P.2d 848, 851–852 (1987) (en banc), *cert. denied,* 485 U.S. 938, 108 S.Ct. 1117, 99 L.Ed.2d 277 (1988); Commonwealth v. Rocheleau, 404 Mass. 129, 130–131, 533 N.E.2d 1333, 1334 (1989); State v. Nunn, 244 Kan. 207, 218, 768 P.2d 268, 277–278 (1989); State v. O'Neill, 118 Idaho 244, 247, 796 P.2d 121, 124 (1990); State v. Hirsch, 245 Neb. 31, 39–40, 511 N.W.2d 69, 76 (1994); State v. Schultzen, 522 N.W.2d 833, 835 (Iowa 1994); State v. Comeau, 142 N.H. 84, 88, 697 A.2d 497, 500 (1997) (citing State v. Hamel, 138 N.H. 392, 395–396, 643 A.2d 953, 955–956 (1994)); Santiago v. Commonwealth, 428 Mass. 39, 42, 697 N.E.2d 979, 981, *cert. denied,* 525 U.S. 1003, 119 S.Ct. 514, 142 L.Ed.2d 426 (1998). Cf. Thompson v. State, 54 Miss. 740, 743 (1877) (stating, without specifying further grounds, that a new law could not take away a vested statute-of-limitations defense); State v. Cookman, 127 Or.App. 283, 289, 873 P.2d 335, 338 (1994) (holding that a law resurrecting a time-barred criminal case "violates the Due Process Clause"), aff'd on state-law grounds, 324 Or. 19, 920 P.2d 1086 (1996); Commonwealth v. Guimento, 341 Pa.Super. 95, 97–98, 491 A.2d 166, 167–168 (1985) (enforcing a state ban on *ex post facto* laws apparently equivalent to the federal prohibition); People v. Chesebro, 185 Mich.App. 412, 416, 463 N.W.2d 134, 135–136 (1990) (reciting "the general rule" that, " 'where a complete defense has arisen under [a statute of limitations], it cannot be taken away by a subsequent repeal thereof' ").

Even where courts have upheld extensions of *unexpired* statutes of limitations (extensions that our holding today does not affect, see *supra,* at 2450–2451), they have consistently distinguished situations where limitations periods have *expired*. Further, they have often done so by saying that extension of existing limitations periods is not *ex post facto* "provided," "so long as," "because," or "if" the prior limitations periods have not expired—a manner of speaking that suggests a presumption that revival of time-barred criminal cases is *not* allowed. . . .

This Court itself has not previously spoken decisively on this matter. On the one hand, it has clearly stated that the Fifth Amendment's privilege against self-incrimination does not apply after the relevant limitations period has expired. Brown v. Walker, 161 U.S. 591, 597–598, 16 S.Ct. 644, 40 L.Ed. 819 (1896). And that rule may suggest that the expiration of a statute of limitations is irrevocable, for otherwise the passage of time would not have eliminated fear of prosecution.

On the other hand, in Stewart v. Kahn, 11 Wall. 493, 503–504, 20 L.Ed. 176 (1871), this Court upheld a statute, enacted during the Civil War, that retroactively tolled *all* civil and criminal limitations for periods during which the war had made service of process impossible or courts inaccessible. *Stewart*, however, involved a civil, not a criminal, limitations statute. *Id.*, at 500–501, 20 L.Ed. 176. Significantly, in reviewing this civil case, the Court upheld the statute as an exercise of Congress' war powers, *id.*, at 507, 20 L.Ed. 176, without explicit consideration of any potential collision with the *Ex Post Facto* Clause. Moreover, the Court already had held, independent of Congress' Act, that statutes of limitations were tolled for "the time during which the courts in the States lately in rebellion were closed to the citizens of the loyal States." *Id.*, at 503, 20 L.Ed. 176; see also Hanger v. Abbott, 6 Wall. 532, 539–542, 18 L.Ed. 939 (1868). Hence, the Court could have seen the relevant statute as ratifying a pre-existing expectation of tolling due to wartime exigencies, rather than as extending limitations periods that had truly expired. *See id.*, at 541, 18 L.Ed. 939; see also *Stewart, supra,* at 507, 20 L.Ed. 176. In our view, *Stewart* therefore no more dictates the outcome here than does seemingly contrary precedent regarding the Fifth Amendment privilege.

Instead, we believe that the outcome of this case is determined by the nature of the harms that California's law creates, by the fact that the law falls within Justice Chase's second category as Chase understood that category, and by a long line of authority holding that a law of this type violates the *Ex Post Facto* Clause. . . .

IV

The statute before us is unfairly retroactive as applied to Stogner. A long line of judicial authority supports characterization of this law as *ex post facto*. For the reasons stated, we believe the law falls within Justice Chase's second category of *ex post facto* laws. We conclude that a law enacted after expiration of a previously applicable limitations period violates the *Ex Post Facto* Clause when it is applied to revive a previously time-barred prosecution. The California court's judgment to the contrary is

Reversed.

■ JUSTICE KENNEDY, with whom THE CHIEF JUSTICE, JUSTICE SCALIA, and JUSTICE THOMAS join, dissenting.

California has enacted a retroactive extension of statutes of limitations for serious sexual offenses committed against minors. Cal.Penal Code Ann. § 803(g) (West Supp.2003). The new period includes cases where the limitations period has expired before the effective date of the legislation. To invalidate the statute in the latter circumstance, the Court tries to force it into the second category of *Calder v. Bull*, 3 Dall. 386, 1 L.Ed. 648 (1798), which prohibits a retroactive law " 'that *aggravates a crime,* or makes it *greater* than it was, when committed.' " *Ante,* at 2450 (quoting *Calder, supra,* at 390, 1 L.Ed. 648 (emphasis in original)). These words, in my view, do not permit the Court's holding, but indeed foreclose it. A law which does not alter the definition of the crime but only revives prosecution does not make the crime "greater than it was, when committed." Until today, a plea in bar has not been thought to form any part of the definition of the offense.

To overcome this principle, the Court invokes "a long line of authority holding that a law of this type violates the *Ex Post Facto* Clause." *Ante,* at 2455. The Court's list of precedents, *ante,* at 2452–2454, is less persuasive than it may appear at a first glance. Of the 22 cases cited by the Court, only 4 had to decide whether a revival of expired prosecutions was constitutional. *See* Moore v. State, 43 N.J.L. 203, 216–217 (1881); United States v. Fraidin, 63 F.Supp. 271, 276 (D.Md.1945); People v. Shedd, 702 P.2d 267, 268 (Colo.1985) (en banc) *(per curiam)*; Commonwealth v. Rocheleau, 404 Mass. 129, 130–131, 533 N.E.2d 1333, 1334 (1989), cited *ante,* at 2452–2453

. . . . .

In the remaining 17 cases, the question was not presented. As the Court itself concedes, eight of these cases considered only extensions of unexpired statutes of limitations, and upheld them. The Court does not mention that nine other cases have done so as well. *See* People ex rel. Reibman v. Warden, 242 App. Div. 282, 275 N.Y.S. 59 (1934); State v. Hodgson, 108 Wash.2d 662, 740 P.2d 848 (1987) (en banc); State v. Nunn, 244 Kan. 207, 768 P.2d 268 (1989); State v. O'Neill, 118 Idaho 244, 796 P.2d 121 (1990); State v. Schultzen, 522 N.W.2d 833 (Iowa 1994); State v. Comeau, 142 N.H. 84, 697 A.2d 497 (1997); State v. Hamel, 138 N.H. 392, 643 A.2d 953 (1994); Santiago v. Commonwealth, 428 Mass. 39, 697 N.E.2d 979 (1998), cited *ante,* at 2452–2453. Because these cases did not need to decide whether the *Ex Post Facto* Clause would bar the extension of expired limitations periods, the question did not receive the same amount of attention as if the courts were required to dispose of the issue.

The case law compiled by the Court is deficient, furthermore, at a more fundamental level. Our precedents hold that the reach of the *Ex Post Facto* Clause is strictly limited to the precise formulation of the *Calder* categories. We have made it clear that these categories provide "an exclusive definition of *ex post facto* laws," Collins v. Youngblood, 497 U.S. 37, 42, 110 S.Ct. 2715, 111 L.Ed.2d 30 (1990), and have admonished that it is "a mistake to stray *beyond Calder's* four categories," Carmell v. Texas, 529 U.S. 513, 539, 120 S.Ct. 1620, 146 L.Ed.2d 577 (2000). Justice Chase himself stressed that the categories must be construed with caution to avoid any unnecessary extension: "I am under a necessity to give a *construction,* or explanation of the words, '*ex post facto law,*' because they have not any certain meaning attached to them. But I will not go farther than I feel myself bound to do; and if I ever exercise the jurisdiction I will not decide *any law to be void, but in a very clear case.*" 3 Dall., at 395, 1 L.Ed. 648....

The majority seems to suggest that retroactive extension of expired limitations periods is " 'arbitrary and potentially vindictive legislation,' " *ante,* at 2450 (quoting Weaver v. Graham, 450 U.S. 24, 29, and n. 10, 101 S.Ct. 960, 67 L.Ed.2d 17 (1981)), but does not attempt to support this accusation. And it could not do so. The California statute can be explained as motivated by legitimate concerns about the continuing suffering endured by the victims of childhood abuse.

The California Legislature noted that "young victims often delay reporting sexual abuse because they are easily manipulated by offenders in positions of authority and trust, and because children have difficulty remembering the crime or facing the trauma it can cause." People v. Frazer, 21 Cal.4th 737, 744, 88 Cal.Rptr.2d 312, 982 P.2d 180, 183–184 (1999). The concern is amply supported by empirical studies. *See, e.g.,* Summit, Abuse of the Child Sexual Abuse Accommodation Syndrome, in 1 J. of Child Sexual Abuse 153, 156–163 (1992); Lyon, Scientific Support for Expert Testimony on Child Sexual Abuse Accommodation, in Critical Issues in Child Sexual Abuse 107, 114–120 (J. Conte ed.2002).

The problem the legislature sought to address is illustrated well by this case. Petitioner's older daughter testified she did not report the abuse because she was afraid of her father and did not believe anyone would help her. After she left petitioner's home, she tried to forget the abuse. Petitioner's younger daughter did not report the abuse because she was scared. He tried to convince her it was a normal way of life. Even after she moved out of petitioner's house, she was afraid to speak for fear she would not be believed. She tried to pretend she had a normal childhood. It was only her realization that the father continued to abuse other children in the family that led her to disclose the abuse, in order to protect them.

The Court tries to counter by saying the California statute is " 'unfair and dishonest' " because it violated the State's initial assurance to the offender that " 'he has become safe from its pursuit' " and deprived him of "the 'fair warning.' " *Ante,* at 2450 (quoting Falter v. United States, 23 F.2d, at 426; *Weaver, supra,* at 28, 101 S.Ct. 960). The fallacy of this rationale is apparent when we recall that the Court is careful to leave in place the uniform decisions by state and federal courts to uphold retroactive extension of unexpired statutes of limitations against an *ex post facto* challenge. *Ante,* at 2450–2451.

There are two rationales to explain the proposed dichotomy between unexpired and expired statutes, and neither works. The first rationale must be the assumption that if an expired statute is extended, the crime becomes more serious, thereby violating category two; but if an unexpired statute is extended, the crime does not increase in seriousness. There is no basis in logic, our cases, or in the legal literature to support this distinction. Both extensions signal, with equal force, the policy to prosecute offenders.

This leaves the second rationale, which must be that an extension of the expired statute destroys a reliance interest. We should consider whether it is warranted to presume that criminals keep calendars so they can mark the day to discard their records or to place a gloating phone call to the victim. The first expectation is minor and likely imaginary; the second is not, but there is no conceivable reason the law should honor it. And either expectation assumes, of course, the very result the Court reaches; for if the law were otherwise, there would be no legitimate expectation. The reliance exists, if at all, because of the circular reason that the Court today says so; it does not exist as part of our traditions or social understanding.

In contrast to the designation of the crime, which carries a certain measure of social opprobrium and presupposes a certain punishment, the statute of limitations has little or no deterrent effect. See Note, Retroactive Application of Legislatively Enlarged Statutes of Limitations for Child Abuse: Time's No Bar to Revival, 22 Ind. L.Rev. 989, 1014 (1989) ("The statute of limitations has no measurable impact on allegedly criminal behavior, neither encouraging nor deterring such conduct"); Note, Ex Post Facto Limitations on Legislative Power, 73 Mich. L.Rev. 1491, 1513 (1975) ("[W]hile many defendants rely on substantive definitions of proscribed conduct, few rely on many of the numerous laws regulating the enforcement processes"). The Court does not claim a sex offender would desist if he knew he would be liable to prosecution when his offenses were disclosed.

The law's approach to the analogous problem of reliance by wrongdoers in the civil sphere is instructive. We have held that expired statutes of limitations can be repealed to revive a civil action. *See, e.g.*, Chase Securities Corp., 325 U.S., at 314, 65 S.Ct. 1137; Plaut v. Spendthrift Farm, Inc., 514 U.S. 211, 229, 115 S.Ct. 1447, 131 L.Ed.2d 328 (1995). These holdings were made in the areas of contracts and investments where reliance does exist and does matter. We allow the civil wrong to be vindicated nonetheless. If we do so in the civil sphere where reliance is real, we should do so in the criminal sphere where it is, for the most part, a fictional construct.

When a child molester commits his offense, he is well aware the harm will plague the victim for a lifetime. See Briere & Runtz, Post Sexual Abuse Trauma: Data and Implications for Clinical Practice, 2 J. of Interpersonal Violence 367, 374–376 (1987); 1 J. Myers, Evidence in Child Abuse and Neglect Cases § 4.2, pp. 221–223 (2d ed.1992); Browne & Finkelhor, Initial and Long–Term Effects: A Review of the Research, in A Sourcebook on Child Sexual Abuse 143, 150–164 (D. Finkelhor et al. eds.1986). The victims whose interests § 803(g) takes into consideration have been subjected to sexual abuse within the confines of their own homes and by people they trusted and relied upon for protection. A familial figure of authority can use a confidential relation to conceal a crime. The violation of this trust inflicts deep and lasting hurt. Its only poor remedy is that the law will show its compassion and concern when the victim at last can find the strength, and know the necessity, to come forward. When the criminal has taken distinct advantage of the tender years and perilous position of a fearful victim, it is the victim's lasting hurt, not the perpetrator's fictional reliance, that the law should count the higher. The victims whose cause is now before the Court have at last overcome shame and the desire to repress these painful memories. They have reported the crimes so that the violators are brought to justice and harm to others is prevented. The Court now tells the victims their decision to come forward is in vain.

The gravity of the crime was known, and is being measured, by its wrongfulness when committed. It is a common policy for States to suspend statutes of limitations for civil harms against minors, in order to "protec[t] minors during the period when they are unable to protect themselves." 2 C. Corman, Limitation of Actions § 10.2.1, p. 104 (1991). Some States toll the limitations periods for minors even where a guardian is appointed, see *id.,* at 105–106, and even when the tolling conflicts with statutes of repose, *id.,* at 108. The difference between suspension and reactivation is so slight that it is fictional for the Court to say, in the given context, the new policy somehow alters the magnitude of the crime. The wrong was made clear by the law at the time of the crime's commission. The criminal actor knew it, even reveled in it. It is the commission of the then-unlawful act that the State now seeks to punish. The gravity of the crime is left unchanged by altering a statute of limitations of which the actor was likely not at all aware. . . .

People v. McGee

Supreme Court of California, In Bank, 1934.
1 Cal.2d 611, 36 P.2d 378.

■ Langdon, J. On November 3, 1930, an information was filed charging defendant with the crime of rape, and alleging the commission of the offense on or about March 30, 1926. A prior conviction of second degree burglary was also charged. Defendant appeared without counsel, pleaded guilty and was sentenced to imprisonment in the state prison. On March 18, 1933, defendant filed a motion to set aside the judgment, which was denied. This appeal is from the order denying the motion.

Section 800 of the Penal Code provides: "An indictment for any other felony than murder, the embezzlement of public money, or the falsification of public records, must be found, or an information filed, within three years after its commission." Section 802 of the same code provides: "If, when the offense is committed, the defendant is out of the state, indictment may be found or an information filed within the term herein limited after his coming within the state, and no time during which the defendant is not an inhabitant of, or usually resident within this state, is part of the limitation." On the face of the information herein it clearly appears that it was not filed within the period of the statute of limitations, and no allegations setting forth an exception to the running of the statute are made. If defendant had set up the bar of limitation, he would, so far as the record shows, have been entitled to a dismissal. But he failed to do so and raises the defense now for the first time after conviction and sentence. His contention is that the court lacked jurisdiction after the expiration of the three-year period, and that the judgment was therefore void.

Whether the statute of limitations in criminal cases is jurisdictional, or a matter of defense to be affirmatively pleaded by the defendant, is a question upon which there exists some diversity of opinion. In California the law is in a most confused state. This court, in Ex parte Blake, 155 Cal.

586 [102 P. 269, 18 Ann.Cas. 815], declared that the statute was a mere matter of defense, and not ground for discharge on habeas corpus. The District Court of Appeal, in Ex parte Vice, 5 Cal.App. 153 [89 P. 983], came to the opposite conclusion; and in People v. Hoffman, 132 Cal.App. 60 [22 P.2d 229], the court held that a motion to set aside a judgment would lie where the information showed on its face that the statute had run. A hearing in the Hoffman case was denied by this court. The early case of People v. Miller, 12 Cal. 291, also lends support to this conclusion.

It is necessary that this confusion be eliminated, and that the rule which shall govern prosecutions in this state be declared. In our view, the more desirable rule is that the statute is jurisdictional, and that an indictment or information which shows on its face that the prosecution is barred by limitations fails to state a public offense. The point may therefore be raised at any time, before or after judgment.[52]

This is, of course, a rule essentially different from that governing civil actions, and it results from the different character of the statute in the two kinds of proceedings. In civil actions the statute is a privilege which may be waived by the party. In criminal cases, the state, through its legislature, has declared that it will not prosecute crimes after the period has run, and hence has limited the power of the courts to proceed in the matter. It follows that where the pleading of the state shows that the period of the statute of limitations has run, and nothing is alleged to take the case out of the statute, for example, that the defendant has been absent from the state, the power to proceed in the case is gone. . . .

The order appealed from is reversed.[53]

■ SEAWELL, J., CURTIS, J., WASTE, C.J., SHENK, J., and PRESTON, J., concurred.

---

52. The statute of limitations in criminal cases is jurisdictional and hence may be raised at any time. It is not waived by failure to assert it. In re Demillo, 14 Cal.3d 598, 121 Cal.Rptr. 725, 535 P.2d 1181 (1975). People v. Garcia, 33 Cal.App. 4th 1119, 40 Cal.Rptr. 2d 12 (1995). Accord: Hunt v. State, 642 So.2d 999 (Ala.Cr.App.1993), affirmed Ex Parte Hunt, 642 So.2d 1060.

53. Criminal statute of limitations is not jurisdictional in nature and may be waived. United States v. Wilson, 26 F.3d 142 (D.C.Cir.1994). The statute of limitations is an affirmative defense which must be raised by defendant. United States v. Manning, 56 F.3d 1188 (9th Cir.1995). Accord, State v. Harrison, 34 Conn.App. 473, 642 A.2d 36 (1994); Hubbard v. State, 110 Nev. 671, 877 P.2d 519 (1994).

The statute of limitations is merely one of repose. It gives a right that is waived if not asserted. Hence the indictment need not negate the running of the period. People v. Brady, 257 App.Div. 1000, 13 N.Y.S.2d 789 (1939).

One may be a person "Fleeing from justice" so as to toll the federal statute of limitations although he was not within the federal district when the crime was committed. Brouse v. United States, 68 F.2d 294 (1st Cir.1933).

D was informed against for forceable rape. The information was later amended to charge statutory rape (intercourse with a female under 18). This amendment was at a time when the statute of limitations barred the prosecution. Since statutory rape was not an offense intended to be charged in the original information, nor necessarily included therein, the amendment could not relate back to the time of the original information. Prosecution for statutory rape was barred. People v. Chapman, 47 Cal.App.3d 597, 121 Cal.Rptr. 315 (1975).

The statute of limitations for intrafamilial sexual abuse was tolled during the period of coercion of a child by the father until the child moved to another state in the custody of the mother. State v. Johnson, 422 N.W.2d 14 (Minn.App.1988).

State v. Disbrow

Supreme Court of Iowa, 1906.
130 Iowa 19, 106 N.W. 263.

[D appealed from a conviction of embezzlement. The evidence had shown several acts of embezzlement over a period of six years. The conviction was under a second indictment after an earlier one found against **D** had been set aside as defective. The judge instructed the jury that **D** could be convicted of all his acts of embezzlement which had occurred within three years prior to the return of the first indictment. This ruling was assigned as error.]

■ WEAVER, J....

It is said, however, on the part of the State, that it is settled law that "the time during which an indictment which has been quashed or set aside was pending is not, in case a new indictment is found, computed as a part of the period of limitation, provided the same offense and the same offender are charged in both indictments." We find this general proposition stated in some of the text-books and cyclopedias; but reference to the cases relied upon, so far as we have been able to examine them, reveals in each instance that the decision turns upon a local statute expressly or impliedly providing that upon the setting aside of an indictment or the entry of a *nol. pros.* the right of the State to present a new indictment within a limited time shall not be prejudiced....

It seems to us a reasonable and just proposition that, in the absence of any statute saving such right to the State, the running of the statute of limitations ought not to be interrupted or suspended by the return and pendency of an indictment upon which no valid conviction or judgment can be founded. Such an indictment is no indictment. It is a nullity, and while it may serve as authority for the trial court to continue the defendant in custody and cause a resubmission of the case to the grand jury, such order is in effect the mere direction that the original inquiry shall be resumed as if the defective indictment had never been voted or returned into court. It is no more than a restoration of the case to the status it occupied at the time it was originally submitted. The grand jury takes it up anew, and may present or ignore the bill, without any reference whatever to the fact that one indictment has been presented and set aside. Cases are not wanting which tend to sustain this view.... But, without reference to the precedents from other States, our statute admits of no other conclusion than the one we have indicated....

Other questions argued are not likely to arise on a retrial and we need not discuss them. For the reasons stated, the case must be remanded to the district court for a new trial.

Reversed.[54]

---

54. Statute of limitations begins to run when the crime is complete, as soon as every element of the crime has taken place. United States v. Musacchio, 968 F.2d 782 (9th Cir.1991).

Return of a timely indictment tolls the limitations period as to the charges alleged. United States v. Davis, 953 F.2d 1482 (10th Cir.1992).

State v. Wilson

Supreme Court of Iowa, 1998.
573 N.W.2d 248.

■ LAVORATO, JUSTICE.

On January 29, 1996, the State charged the defendants, Keith Allen Wilson and Evelyn Louise Wilson, his wife, with theft by taking and theft by deception for an event the State alleged occurred "on or about the months of April through October, 1992." See Iowa Code § 714.1(1) (theft by taking), 714.1(3) (theft by deception) (1991). The Wilsons moved to dismiss the charges as untimely under Iowa's three-year statute of limitations for criminal actions. The State resisted and filed a motion to amend, alleging the one-year extension under Iowa Code section 802.5 for crimes of fraud saved the prosecution. The district court granted the Wilsons' motion and dismissed the prosecution. The State appealed. We affirm in part, reverse in part, and remand.

The District Court's Ruling.

The district court took evidence on the Wilsons' motion to dismiss. In its ruling the court noted that "[t]he essence of the charge is that [the Wilsons] staged a burglary at [their] home and then fraudulently collected monies from [their] household insurance carrier for the reported losses."

. . .

The Wilsons claimed their Story County home was burglarized on April 16, 1992. . . . The Wilsons filed a claim for their alleged losses with their insurer, Farm Bureau Insurance Company.

. . .

Bearden [a deputy sheriff] and the insurance company found [the] information [abut the burglary] perplexing but not indicative of the Wilsons' guilt. Thus, the company sent the Wilsons a check on October 5, 1992, which they cashed on October 9, 1992. . . .

Matters changed on September 26 and 29, 1995, when the Wilsons' son, Ryan, told Bearden his parents had staged the burglary to pay for a new front door. The Wilsons' daughter, Sonja, confirmed the plot on October 6, 1995.

The police obtained a search warrant for the Wilsons' property on December 15, 1995 and found some of the property that had been reported stolen in 1992.

The State filed the theft charges against the Wilsons on January 29, 1996.

The district court found that the crime of theft by taking was committed no later than October 9, 1992, the date the Wilsons cashed the

---

The statute is tolled while an indictment for the offense is pending, even if it is defective. Hickey v. State, 131 Tenn. 112, 174 S.W. 269 (1915).

A defective information lacking the prosecutor's signature tolled the statute of limitations until the information was dismissed. State v. Strand, 674 P.2d 109 (Utah 1983).

insurance check, and prosecution was therefore barred by the three-year statute of limitations in section 802.3(1).

The court also found that fraud is a material element of theft by deception; therefore, section 802.5 had to be considered. Section 802.5 extends the three-year statute of limitations by one year for crimes of fraud where the prosecution is commenced within one year after the discovery of the offense. The court interpreted section 802.5 to mean that it applies only to crimes of fraud discovered after expiration of the initial three-year limitations period. The court found that the State had discovered the Wilsons' alleged theft before the expiration of the three-year limitations period in section 802.3(1). For that reason, the court concluded, section 802.5 was not applicable and did not extend the statute of limitations. The court granted the motion to dismiss and the State appealed.

The Issues.

We consider three of the State's assignments of error. First, the State asserts fraud is a material element of both theft offenses. For that reason, the State insists the section 802.5 extension applies to both offenses. The district court ruled otherwise as to the theft by taking offense. The State contends this ruling was erroneous.

Second, the State asserts the section 802.5 extension applies regardless of when the crime is discovered. The district court ruled otherwise. The State contends this ruling was likewise erroneous.

Last, the State asserts discovery under section 802.5 does not occur until the victim or law enforcement is aware of both the loss and the crime associated with the loss. The State insists that, at the earliest, this was September 26, 1995, when Ryan Wilson first made revelations to [the sheriff]. But, the State argues, the most logical point would be December 15, 1995, when the police searched the Wilsons' home pursuant to a search warrant and discovered some of the property allegedly stolen in 1992. Under either date, the State contends, the prosecution was commenced in time and the district court's ruling to the contrary was also erroneous.

. . .

The district court ruled that the three-year statute of limitations applied to the theft by taking offense because the charge was filed more than three years after October 9, 1992. This was the date the insurance company paid the Wilsons the claim. The court simply concluded the theft by taking offense was committed no later than October 9, 1992 and made no reference to the one-year extension in section 802.5. Implicit in the court's ruling is that section 802.5 does not apply because fraud is not an element of theft by taking.

Iowa Code section 802.5 provides in part:

If the period prescribed in section 802.3 [statute of limitations for felonies and aggravated or serious misdemeanors] and 802.4 [statute of limitations for simple misdemeanors or ordinance violations] has expired, prosecution may nevertheless be commenced for any offense a material element of which is ... fraud ... within one year after discovery of the offense ... but in no case shall this provision extend the period of limitations otherwise applicable by more than three years.

Pennsylvania has a statute identical in language to section 802.5. It also has a theft by taking statute very similar to ours....

In Commonwealth v. Eackles, 286 Pa.Super. 146, 428 A.2d 614 (1981), the Pennsylvania Superior Court held that fraud is not a material element of theft by taking and therefore concluded its one-year extension statute did not apply to extend its two-year statute of limitations for a theft by taking. The court noted that "[f]raud is characterized by a false representation of a material matter made with knowledge of its falsity and with intent to deceive." The court reasoned that

if fraud is to be a material element of the offense charged, it would be necessary that it have some connection with the harm or evil sought to be prevented. The harm sought to be prevented by the language making theft a crime is clearly the unlawful taking of another's property. To convict of theft by unlawful taking, the Commonwealth is not required to prove that the taking was accompanied by fraud in the legal sense. Neither is fraud the harm or evil sought to be prevented by the language making theft by unlawful taking a crime....

When the legislature enacted the period of limitations within which to commence prosecution, the assumption was that offenses such as theft by unlawful taking were discoverable by the victim within a reasonable time thereafter. The same assumption could not be made where fraud was inherent in the offense and rendered discovery more difficult. Thus, the exception of [the one-year extension for fraud crimes] was created.

We think the same reasoning applies to our one-year extension for fraud crimes, and we adopt it. We hold that fraud is not a material element of theft by taking. See Iowa Code § 714.1(1). For that reason, section 802.5 does not apply to this offense.

The statute of limitations for a felony is found in Iowa Code section 802.3(1):

In all cases, except [murder and sexual abuse of a minor], an indictment or information for a felony ... shall be found within three years after its commission.

The trial information alleged that the theft by taking and theft by deception occurred on or about the months of April through October 1992. The information was filed on January 29, 1996, more than three years after October 1992. Thus, the district court correctly dismissed the theft by taking charge because it was time-barred by the three-year statute of limitations in section 802.3(1).

Neither party disputes the district court's conclusion that fraud is an element of theft by deception. Under the facts of this case, we have no quarrel with that ruling.

That brings us to the main issue in this case.

... As mentioned, the three-year period of limitations in section 802.3 may be extended as provided for in section 802.5:

If the period prescribed in section[ ] 802.3 . . . has expired, prosecution may nevertheless be commenced for any offense a material element of which is . . . fraud . . . within one year after discovery of the offense . . . but in no case shall this provision extend the period of limitation otherwise applicable by more than three years.

We have not had occasion to consider this statute before. The statute draws directly from the Model Penal Code. Model Penal Code and Commentaries § 1.06 at 91 n. 25 (1985).

Relying on the opening dependent clause—"If the period prescribed in section[] 802.3 has expired"—the district court reasoned that the legislature intended the extension in section 802.5 to apply only if the initial three-year period of limitations in section 802.3 had expired. Thus, the court considered the preposition "If" in the opening dependent clause of section 802.5 to be conditional.

We have a different view of the word "If" in the opening dependent clause of section 802.5. Another meaning of the word "if" is "in the event that"—a nonconditional meaning. We think the legislature used the word "If" in the opening dependent clause of section 802.5 to make clear that the extension would apply even though the three year statute of limitations had expired. This becomes more apparent when we consider the legislature used the word "nevertheless" in the main clause when talking about the commencement of prosecution. "Nevertheless" means "in spite of" or "notwithstanding." Thus, contrary to the district court, we think the gist of section 802.5 is this: In spite of the fact that the period of limitations in section 802.3 may have expired, prosecution may still be commenced. So we would read section 802.5 to mean that prosecution may commence despite the expiration of the three-year 802.3 limitations period, as long as the prosecution is within one year after discovery of the offense.

As the State points out, the district court's interpretation of section 802.5 would not allow prosecution for a crime discovered on the last day of the three-year statute of limitations but would allow prosecution for the same crime discovered the very next day. We doubt the legislature intended such a result.

Missouri and Ohio also have statutes containing language virtually identical to the language of section 802.5. Both states—like Iowa—drew language for their limitations extension statutes from the Model Penal Code. See Model Penal Code and Commentaries § 1.06 at 91 n. 25. Case authority in each state follows the interpretation we have given to section 802.5: prosecution may commence despite the expiration of the statute of limitations as long as the prosecution is commenced within one year after discovery of the offense. See State v. Holland, 781 S.W.2d 808, 811–12 (Mo.Ct.App.1989); State v. Lester, 111 Ohio App.3d 736, 676 N.E.2d 1270, 1271 (1996).

We conclude the district court erred when deciding that section 802.5 has no application when the fraud is discovered within three years of its commission.

Date of discovery. Applying a probable cause test, the district court found that the State discovered the fraud by at least September 29, 1995 (when [the deputy sheriff] interviewed the Wilsons' son), if not sooner. Thus, under the district court's interpretation, the section 802.5 extension would not apply because the fraud was discovered within the initial three-year statute of limitations, which the court held expired on October 9, 1995.

The district court made no finding about when the theft was discovered for the purposes of the one-year extension in section 802.5. We must therefore reverse and remand for a factual determination as to when the fraud was discovered for purposes of the section 802.5 extension.

To give the district court guidance concerning the factual determination on the discovery date, we proceed to consider what constitutes "discovery of the offense" for the purposes of extending the statute of limitations under section 802.5.

The State argues, and the Wilsons apparently agree, that defining discovery for purposes of section 802.5 as the point at which there is probable cause to believe the offense has been committed would provide district courts with a bright-line rule to measure the timeliness of criminal fraud actions. The Wilsons part company with the State by adding that we should impose a due or reasonable diligence requirement on the State, if it seeks to take advantage of section 802.5's one-year extension. Both parties want us to enunciate a discovery rule and to fix the date upon which the fraud was discovered and the limitations clock began to tick.

. . .

We are satisfied that the discovery rule here should include a probable cause element and a due or reasonable diligence requirement. We therefore hold that "discovery" for purposes of section 802.5 occurs when the authorities know or should know in the exercise of reasonable diligence that there is probable cause to believe a criminal fraud has been committed. The probable cause requirement fits well with the language of section 802.5, which requires "discovery of the offense." The due or reasonable diligence requirement is in harmony with our civil discovery rule. It also promotes one of the purposes of a criminal statute of limitations: to discourage inefficient or dilatory law enforcement.

As mentioned, the trial information was filed on January 29, 1996. Under our interpretation of section 802.5, if the district court finds the fraud was or should have been discovered anytime before January 29, 1995, the one-year extension would not apply and the prosecution would be barred. On the other hand, a finding that the discovery did occur or should have occurred any time after January 29, 1995, would trigger 802.5 and save the prosecution.

Affirmed in part, reversed in part, and remanded.

MODEL PENAL CODE

Section 1.06   Time Limitations.

(1) A prosecution for murder may be commenced at any time.

(2) Except as otherwise provided in this Section, prosecutions for other offenses are subject to the following periods of limitation:

(a) a prosecution for a felony of the first degree must be commenced within six years after it is committed;

(b) a prosecution for any other felony must be commenced within three years after it is committed;

(c) a prosecution for a misdemeanor must be commenced within two years after it is committed;

(d) a prosecution for a petty misdemeanor or a violation must be commenced within six months after it is committed.

(3) If the period prescribed in Subsection (2) has expired, a prosecution may nevertheless be commenced for:

(a) any offense a material element of which is either fraud or a breach of fiduciary obligation within one year after discovery of the offense by an aggrieved party or by a person who has legal duty to represent an aggrieved party and who is himself not a party to the offense, but in no case shall this provision extend the period of limitation otherwise applicable by more than three years; and

(b) any offense based upon misconduct in office by a public officer or employee at any time when the defendant is in public office or employment or within two years thereafter, but in no case shall this provision extend the period of limitation otherwise applicable by more than three years.

(4) An offense is committed either when every element occurs, or, if a legislative purpose to prohibit a continuing course of conduct plainly appears, at the time when the course of conduct or the defendant's complicity therein is terminated. Time starts to run on the day after the offense is committed.

(5) A prosecution is commenced either when an indictment is found [or an information filed] or when a warrant or other process is issued, provided that such warrant or process is executed without unreasonable delay.

(6) The period of limitation does not run:

(a) during any time when the accused is continuously absent from the State or has no reasonably ascertainable place of abode or work within the State, but in no case shall this provision extend the period of limitation otherwise applicable by more than three years; or

(b) during any time when a prosecution against the accused for the same conduct is pending in this State.[55]

SECTION 4. FORMER JEOPARDY

Litigation would never end if the issues determined in one action could be raised anew between the same parties by the mere commencement of another proceeding. In the words of the ancient maxim: *"Nemo debet bis vexari pro eadem causa"* (No one ought to be twice tried for the same cause). This found expression in the common law in the form of the plea of *res judicata* in civil suits and in the pleas of the *autrefois acquit* and *autrefois convict* in criminal prosecutions. Such a plea in a criminal case, in the words of Blackstone, "is grounded on this universal maxim of the common law of England, that no man is to brought into jeopardy of his life

---

55. Copyright © 1962 by the American Law Institute. Reprinted with the permission of the American Law Institute.

more than once for the same offence." 4 Bl.Comm. *335. The actual foundation is the broader maxim mentioned above, but it is from statements such as Blackstone's that we derive our phrases "former jeopardy," "double jeopardy" and "twice in jeopardy."

The Fifth Amendment says: ". . . nor shall any person be subject for the same offense to be twice put in jeopardy of life or limb; . . ." Similar language is to be found in the constitutions of many states, but it is important to keep in mind that there was no such common-law plea as "former jeopardy." The plea was either "former acquittal" (autrefois acquit) or "former conviction" (autrefois convict). There is no reason to believe that the phrase "twice put in jeopardy" was used in the Fifth Amendment for the purpose of introducing a change into this department of the law. In all likelihood the framers of the Constitution had no more in mind than embodiment of the common-law prohibition against placing a defendant in jeopardy a second time for the same offense after *acquittal* or *conviction*. However, an enlargement has resulted from judicial interpretation. The courts have held that a defendant is "in jeopardy" as soon as the jury has been impaneled and sworn (if the court has jurisdiction and the indictment is sufficient to support a conviction) and that the bar against a second trial begins at this point.[56] This position has tended to introduce new difficulties into this branch of the law. The common-law principle (to repeat) was that an accused person should not be prosecuted again for the same offense after the person had once been convicted or acquitted thereof.[57] The word "jeopardy" merely happened to be used by Blackstone and others in explanation of this principle. The principle itself was quite independent of the meaning of the word "jeopardy." And this word, apart from the meaning engrafted upon it by the courts, signifies danger or peril. It comes from the same source as the word "jeopardize" which means "to expose to loss or injury." In a very real sense a person is in jeopardy when the individual has been charged with crime by a valid indictment. Neither precedent nor policy forbids a second indictment for the same offense merely because of the finding of a prior one, and the bar of "former jeopardy" has never been carried to that extent.

The double jeopardy claim of the Fifth Amendment provides three separate restraints on prosecution authority. It prohibits reprosecution for the same offense after an acquittal, reprosecution for the same offense after conviction, and protection against multiple punishments for the same offense.[58] This may bar both civil and criminal sanctions for the same conduct.[59]

The bar known as "former jeopardy" is grounded partly upon expediency and partly upon "fair play." Expediency alone requires some device

---

56. Crist v. Bretz, 437 U.S. 28, 98 S.Ct. 2156, 57 L.Ed.2d 24 (1978).

57. Gun owner's acquittal on criminal charges does not preclude a subsequent in rem forfeiture proceeding against the same firearms. Forfeiture is not generally punishment and does not involve double jeopardy. United States v. One Assortment of 89 Firearms, 465 U.S. 354, 104 S.Ct. 1099, 79 L.Ed.2d 361 (1984).

58. Ohio v. Johnson, 467 U.S. 493, 104 S.Ct. 2536, 81 L.Ed.2d 425 (1984).

59. Department of Revenue of Montana v. Kurth Ranch, 511 U.S. 767, 114 S.Ct. 1937, 128 L.Ed.2d 767 (1994).

which will prevent the same issues being tried time and again by the same parties. "Fair play" may require more than this. It would be quite unfair to the defendant in a criminal case, for example, if either the prosecuting attorney or the judge could arbitrarily withdraw the case from the jury after the trial started, merely in the hope of obtaining another jury which might be more likely to find a verdict of guilty. Any such unfairness could have been prevented, without material change from the common-law concept by treating as the "equivalent of an acquittal" any disposition of a criminal case by which a jury which had been duly impaneled and sworn to try it was not permitted to bring in a verdict, by any improper act of the prosecuting attorney, or by any violation of judicial discretion on the part of the judge.

Another solution, however, was reached by many courts. This was grounded upon the premise that a defendant was "in jeopardy" when a jury was duly impaneled and sworn to try his case and that the trial of this same case by any other jury would be placing him "twice in jeopardy."[60] Such a position required certain exceptions to avoid obvious miscarriages of justice. The two views reach the same result in most cases but there are important shades of difference.

Because of these facts some of the problems in this field arise out of peculiarities in the proceedings themselves,—of which the following are merely examples. Was the case withdrawn from the jury after it had been duly impaneled and sworn but before it had rendered a verdict, and if so why? Has a retrial been ordered after a verdict was rendered, and if so what was the verdict and why was the retrial ordered?

---

60. Jeopardy attaches when the jury has been selected and sworn, even though no evidence has been taken. Downum v. United States, 372 U.S. 734, 83 S.Ct. 1033, 10 L.Ed.2d 100 (1963).

Although some state courts had held that more is required, the Supreme Court held that the Constitution requires the holding that jeopardy attaches in a state case when the jury is impaneled and sworn. Crist v. Bretz, 437 U.S. 28, 98 S.Ct. 2156, 57 L.Ed.2d 24 (1978).

In a case tried without a jury, jeopardy was held to attach when the court begins to hear evidence. Serfass v. United States, 420 U.S. 377, 95 S.Ct. 1055, 43 L.Ed.2d 265 (1975). United States v. Choate, 527 F.2d 748 (9th Cir.1975).

The evidence heard by a judge alone must be for the purpose of guilt or innocence for jeopardy to apply. United States v. Marchese, 46 F.3d 1020, 1022 (10th Cir.1995).

The double jeopardy clause does not prevent one who commits illegal acts while on probation from being accountable for those acts both through parole violation proceedings and by criminal prosecution. State v. Montgomery, 3 Or.App. 555, 474 P.2d 780 (1970).

The Court has distinguished between the pronouncement of sentence, which is not final, and an acquittal, which is, so that an enhanced penalty on appeal from the sentence is constitutionally permissible. United States v. DiFrancesco, 449 U.S. 117, 101 S.Ct. 426, 66 L.Ed.2d 328 (1980). It held that a sentence of life imprisonment imposed in the sentencing stage of a bifurcated trial under the Missouri statute, may not be increased to death upon retrial. Bullington v. Missouri, 451 U.S. 430, 101 S.Ct. 1852, 68 L.Ed.2d 270 (1981). See also, Arizona v. Rumsey, 467 U.S. 203, 104 S.Ct. 2305, 81 L.Ed.2d 164 (1984).

"Because probation is a form of punishment and a person cannot be placed twice in jeopardy of punishment, we now hold that the reimposition of a sentence after a defendant has been placed on probation, absent a violation of a condition of probation, is a violation of both the United States and Wisconsin Constitutions' double jeopardy clauses." State v. Dean, 111 Wis.2d 361, 330 N.W.2d 630, 632 (App.1983).

(A)   When Does "Jeopardy" Begin—and End?

United States v. Shinault

United States Court of Appeals, Tenth Circuit, 1998.
147 F.3d 1266.

■ Tacha, Circuit Judge.

At approximately 3:00 a.m. on July 11, 1995, Defendant Michael Shinault entered a Food–4–Less grocery store in Wichita, Kansas. Armed with a semi-automatic pistol, he robbed the store of $250. About an hour later, the defendant committed a similar armed robbery of a Total gas station, netting about $40. The defendant was charged with two counts of violating the Hobbs Act, 18 U.S.C. § 1951 (interfering with interstate commerce by robbery), two counts of violating 18 U.S.C. § 924(c) (using or carrying a weapon during a crime of violence), and one count of violating 18 U.S.C. § 922(g)(1) (being a felon in possession of a firearm). A jury returned a guilty verdict on all counts. . . .

The defendant went to trial in the Wichita–Hutchinson division of the District of Kansas. After voir dire, a jury with no alternates was sworn. At that point, one of the jurors noted that she had child-care responsibilities that would make it difficult for her to serve on the jury. The district court excused that juror and, without objection from either the government or the defense, swore in another juror. The jury found the defendant guilty of all the charged crimes. At the sentencing phase, the district court applied the Armed Career Criminal enhancement to the defendant's sentence, based on his previous criminal history. The defendant's term of imprisonment totaled 562 months.

The defendant [argues] . . . the unusual jury selection procedure used in this case violated the Double Jeopardy Clause of the Fifth Amendment . . . and . . . that the defendant's convictions under the Hobbs Act and 18 U.S.C. § 924(c) violated the Double Jeopardy Clause by imposing multiple punishments on the defendant for the same conduct.

II.   Double Jeopardy

The district court empaneled and swore in a complete jury. Then, after being advised that one of the jurors had child-care responsibilities that would not allow her to serve, the court excused that juror, replaced her with another, and swore in the new juror. This unusual procedure raises a tangle of double jeopardy issues. We review two different lines of cases in order to resolve those issues.

A.   The Terminating–Event Requirement

The Double Jeopardy Clause of the Fifth Amendment states that no person shall be "twice put in jeopardy of life or limb." U.S. CONST. amend. V. The clause protects criminal defendants against having to endure the risk of conviction twice. Thus, the first relevant line of cases expresses the logical principle that the Double Jeopardy Clause does not apply to situations in which the defendant has been placed in jeopardy only once. These cases have their origin in Ball v. United States, 163 U.S. 662,

672, 16 S.Ct. 1192, 41 L.Ed. 300 (1896), in which the Supreme Court held that the Double Jeopardy Clause does not prevent a second trial when the defendant's original conviction has been overturned on appeal. Ball rested on the notion that when a conviction is overturned, a new trial does not present the defendant with a new, or second risk of conviction. Ball "effectively formulated a concept of continuing jeopardy that has application where criminal proceedings against an accused have not run their full course." Price v. Georgia, 398 U.S. 323, 326, 90 S.Ct. 1757, 26 L.Ed.2d 300 (1970). The continuing jeopardy principle achieved its fullest expression in Richardson v. United States, 468 U.S. 317, 325, 104 S.Ct. 3081, 82 L.Ed.2d 242 (1984), in which the defendant challenged the prosecution's attempt to retry him after his original proceeding had ended in a mistrial because of a hung jury. The Supreme Court held "that the protection of the Double Jeopardy Clause by its terms applies only if there has been some event, such as an acquittal, which terminates the original jeopardy." Id.; see also Justices of Boston Mun. Court v. Lydon, 466 U.S. 294, 309, 104 S.Ct. 1805, 80 L.Ed.2d 311 (1984) (rejecting the defendant's double jeopardy argument because "he fails to identify any stage of the state proceedings that can be held to have terminated jeopardy"). The Court said that the declaration of a mistrial, in that instance, did not terminate his original jeopardy.

Only two other circuits have addressed the situation before us, the Ninth and the Sixth, and only the Ninth relied on the principle of continuing jeopardy to reject the defendant's argument (we discuss the Sixth Circuit's approach infra). In that case, a jury of twelve, with no alternates, was empaneled and sworn. See United States v. Trigg, 988 F.2d 1008, 1009 (9th Cir.1993). Before any testimony was given, the judge excused three jurors because of unavailability and replaced them with three jurors drawn from the venire. See id. The entire new jury was then sworn again. See id.

The Ninth Circuit concluded that the unusual procedure "cannot terminate jeopardy any more than a failure of a jury to reach a verdict." Id. at 1010. The court held that "jeopardy does not terminate during the process of jury selection merely because sworn jurors are excused during the process of selecting alternates." Id. The Trigg court apparently interpreted Richardson to mean that there could be no terminating event for Double Jeopardy purposes if the original jury had not, at the least, made a decision on the merits of the case. See also Richardson, 468 U.S. at 327, 104 S.Ct. 3081 (Brennan, J., concurring in part and dissenting in part) (interpreting Richardson to mean that "only an actual judgment of acquittal, or an unreversed conviction, would 'terminate' jeopardy and thereby bar retrial").

B. The Right to a Particular Tribunal

Trigg and Richardson seem to provide an easy answer here. In equipoise with those cases, however, is the long-standing principle that a defendant has a "valued right to have his trial completed by a particular tribunal." Illinois v. Somerville, 410 U.S. 458, 466, 93 S.Ct. 1066, 35 L.Ed.2d 425 (1973) (quoting Wade v. Hunter, 336 U.S. 684, 689, 69 S.Ct. 834, 93 L.Ed. 974 (1949)). As soon as the jury is sworn, the defendant acquires a constitutional interest in having that jury see his case through to a conclusion. See United States v. Martin Linen Supply Co., 430 U.S. 564, 569, 97 S.Ct. 1349, 51 L.Ed.2d 642 (1977). A proceeding judged by a tribunal other than the one originally selected "may be grossly unfair. It increases the financial and emotional burden on the accused, prolongs the period in which he is stigmatized by an unresolved accusation of wrongdoing, and may even enhance the risk that an innocent defendant may be convicted." Arizona v. Washington, 434 U.S. 497, 503–04, 98 S.Ct. 824, 54 L.Ed.2d 717 (1978).

The constitutional test derived from the defendant's right to have a trial completed by a particular tribunal is well established. Once a particular jury is sworn, the prosecutor may not try the defendant before another jury without demonstrating a "manifest necessity" for the new proceeding with a new tribunal. See id. at 505–06, 98 S.Ct. 824. The manifest necessity standard "has been quoted over and over again to provide guidance in the decision of a wide variety of cases." Id. at 506, 98 S.Ct. 824.

The cases protecting the right to a particular tribunal focus on the inception of the proceedings—that is, whether the jury was sworn—while Richardson asks whether there has been an end to those proceedings. We have noted the apparent inconsistency between Richardson and other strains of Double Jeopardy jurisprudence before. See United States v. Wood, 958 F.2d 963, 970 (10th Cir.1992) (noting that some of our cases are "inconsistent with the continuing jeopardy principle suggested in Richardson"). The different orientations could be read to create a conflict in a case such as this. On the one hand, because jeopardy attached after the swearing of the first jury, and that original tribunal did not ultimately decide the case, one might read the precedent to compel the government to prove a manifest necessity for trying the case before a new jury. The Sixth Circuit took this approach when faced with a situation similar to the one before us. It held that "[o]nce jeopardy attaches, prosecution of a defendant before a jury other than the original jury . . . is barred unless (1) there is a 'manifest necessity' for a mistrial or (2) the defendant either requests or consents to a mistrial." Watkins v. Kassulke, 90 F.3d 138, 141 (6th Cir.1996).[1]

On the other hand, under Richardson a terminating event must occur before the Double Jeopardy Clause even comes into play. Richardson found that a mistrial by virtue of a hung jury did not terminate jeopardy. Accordingly, the Ninth Circuit read Richardson to require no manifest necessity analysis at all, on the basis that jury selection procedures are

---

1. In *Watkins,* the defendant consented to the procedure, and therefore the court avoided the manifest necessity analysis. *See Watkins,* 90 F.3d at 142–43. In the instant case, counsel for the defendant did not object initially to the replacement of the juror. It is also true, however, that neither the court nor counsel made defendant aware of the constitutional right that he was forgoing so that he could make an informed, conscious waiver. Our cases may require such a conscious choice for there to be valid consent to a procedure implicating the Double Jeopardy clause. *See id.* at 141–42 (discussing *United States v. Rich,* 589 F.2d 1025 (10th Cir.1978)); *see also United States v. Broce,* 753 F.2d 811 (10th Cir.1985), *overruled on other grounds by* 488 U.S. 563, 109 S.Ct. 757, 102 L.Ed.2d 927 (1989) (finding that defendant does not relinquish right to contest conviction on grounds of Double Jeopardy unless he waived the right knowingly and voluntarily). Given the analysis that follows, however, we find it unnecessary to decide the consent issue here.

much less final than the hung jury at issue in Richardson. See Trigg, 988 F.2d at 1009–1011.

C.   Resolving the Two Principles

The precedent, however, does not conflict. Two points make this clear. First, it is mistaken to interpret Richardson to mean that nothing short of an acquittal or unreversed conviction implicates the Double Jeopardy Clause. Richardson used the doctrine of "continuing jeopardy" to find that a mistrial after a hung jury was not a terminating event, and therefore no double jeopardy violation occurred. The Richardson Court primarily relied, however, not on "continuing jeopardy" cases, but on the century and a half of jurisprudence that had already made clear that double jeopardy did not bar retrial in such a circumstance. Thus, the observation that " 'continuing jeopardy' describes both a concept and a conclusion" is appropriate. Breed v. Jones, 421 U.S. 519, 534, 95 S.Ct. 1779, 44 L.Ed.2d 346 (1975). In Richardson, the Court used "continuing jeopardy" to describe a conclusion. The Court's finding that jeopardy never terminated was, more than anything, a shorthand expression of a time-tested conclusion that the retrial procedure at issue did not violate the Double Jeopardy Clause. The Court did not revolutionize our understanding of "continuing jeopardy."

Second and more importantly, continuing jeopardy also "describes . . . a concept." Breed v. Jones, 421 U.S. 519, 534, 95 S.Ct. 1779, 44 L.Ed.2d 346 (1975) (emphasis added). All of the Supreme Court's double jeopardy cases, even those that seem to conflict with Richardson, "presuppose[ ] some identifiable point at which a first trial may be said to have ended." Lydon, 466 U.S. at 315, 104 S.Ct. 1805 (Brennan, J., concurring in part and concurring in the judgment). The Court has said, for instance, that the manifest necessity test should be used "when a criminal proceeding is terminated without finally resolving the merits." Arizona v. Washington, 434 U.S. 497, 505, 98 S.Ct. 824, 54 L.Ed.2d 717 (1978) (emphasis added); see also Somerville, 410 U.S. at 471, 93 S.Ct. 1066 (referring to the district court's decision to "abort" the proceedings) (emphasis added). Thus, even those cases that do not explicitly rely on the doctrine of "continuing jeopardy," implicitly recognize that the concept is pertinent when deciding double jeopardy questions. The relevant question in this case, then, is when does a defendant's "continuing jeopardy" terminate?

In order to determine whether the original proceeding ever "terminated," we look to the interests of the Double Jeopardy Clause. See Breed, 421 U.S. at 534, 95 S.Ct. 1779. "[T]he continuing jeopardy principle appears to rest on an amalgam of interests—e.g., fairness to society, lack of finality, and limited waiver, among others." Price v. Georgia, 398 U.S. 323, 329 n. 4, 90 S.Ct. 1757, 26 L.Ed.2d 300 (1970).

The question of whether jeopardy has objectively "terminated" should be analyzed in terms of the policies of the Double Jeopardy Clause, namely its concern that repeated trials may subject a defendant to embarrassment, expense and ordeal and compel him to live in a continuing state of anxiety and insecurity, as well as enhancing the possibility that even though innocent he may be found guilty. Jeopardy may be said to have terminated only when the posture of a trial in some objective sense leaves that defendant in such a position that resumption of proceedings would implicate those policies.

Lydon, 466 U.S. at 320, 104 S.Ct. 1805 (Brennan, J., concurring in part and concurring in the judgment) (emphasis added) (citations and internal quotation marks and alterations omitted); see also Lovato v. New Mexico, 242 U.S. 199, 201, 37 S.Ct. 107, 61 L.Ed. 244 (noting that mere irregularity of procedure does not implicate the Double Jeopardy Clause). Only if the trial before the new tribunal reasonably implicates the policies described above has the first proceeding terminated. Only then do we proceed to the manifest necessity analysis.

The procedure in this case did not threaten the defendant with any of the harms that the Double Jeopardy Clause was meant to prevent. The replacement of one juror before any witnesses had testified did not reasonably subject the defendant to "embarrassment, expense and ordeal," or force him to live in a "continuing state of anxiety," to any greater extent than that he would have experienced if the district court had sworn an alternate along with the original twelve jury members and thereby avoided the issue before us altogether. Furthermore, for us to hold that the trial terminated at such a preliminary stage, without any allegation that the replacement was attributable to prosecutorial tactics, would frustrate "society's interest in giving the prosecution one complete opportunity to convict those who have violated its laws." Arizona v. Washington, 434 U.S. 497, 509, 98 S.Ct. 824, 54 L.Ed.2d 717 (1978).

The defendant cannot point to any event that terminated the original jeopardy. That being the case, his Double Jeopardy challenge cannot succeed.

V. Commerce Clause and Multiple Punishment Challenges

The defendant raises two final arguments that this court has previously addressed and rejected. First, the defendant contends that Congress lacked the constitutional authority under the Commerce Clause to enact the Hobbs Act. We have held, however, that "[b]ecause the Hobbs Act regulates activities that in aggregate have a substantial effect on interstate commerce," the Act is a "permissible exercise of the authority granted to Congress under the Commerce Clause." United States v. Bolton, 68 F.3d 396, 399 (10th Cir.1995), cert. denied, 516 U.S. 1137, 116 S.Ct. 966, 133 L.Ed.2d 887 (1996); see also United States v. Romero, 122 F.3d 1334, 1340 (10th. Cir.1997), cert. denied, 523 U.S. 1025, 118 S.Ct. 1310, 140 L.Ed.2d 474 (1998).

The defendant also argues that his convictions violate his Fifth Amendment rights. For each of the defendant's acts of robbery, the jury convicted him of violating both the Hobbs Act (committing a robbery affecting interstate commerce) and 18 U.S.C. § 924(c) (using or carrying a weapon during a crime of violence). The crime of violence supporting the defendant's section 924(c) conviction was the Hobbs Act violation. The defendant contends that his convictions under both the Hobbs Act and section 924(c) violated the double jeopardy protection against receiving multiple punishment for the same conduct. See Blockburger v. United States, 284 U.S. 299, 52 S.Ct. 180, 76 L.Ed. 306 (1932). We have previously rejected this double jeopardy challenge, however, because "Congress may impose multiple punishment for the same conduct without violating the Double Jeopardy Clause if it clearly expresses its intent to do so," and Congress did so in section 924(c). United States v. Overstreet, 40 F.3d 1090, 1093, 1095 (10th Cir.1994). . . .

We AFFIRM.

■ McKay, Circuit Judge, dissenting:

I concur with everything that the court has said with one reservation. I cannot accept the court's disregard for clear and unmodified Supreme Court precedent that once a jury is empaneled and sworn, double jeopardy attaches and the defendant has a " 'valued right to have his trial completed by a particular tribunal.' " See Arizona v. Washington, 434 U.S. 497, 503, 98 S.Ct. 824, 54 L.Ed.2d 717 (1978) (quoting Wade v. Hunter, 336 U.S. 684, 689, 69 S.Ct. 834, 93 L.Ed. 974 (1949)); Downum v. United States, 372 U.S. 734, 736, 83 S.Ct. 1033, 10 L.Ed.2d 100 (1963); see also United States v. Rich, 589 F.2d 1025, 1030–31 (10th Cir.1978). A defendant's right to have his trial completed by the original jury is an independent and integral aspect of the Double Jeopardy Clause. See Crist v. Bretz, 437 U.S. 28, 35–36, 38, 98 S.Ct. 2156, 57 L.Ed.2d 24 (1978) (recognizing that a defendant's right to a particular jury is integral to the guarantee against double jeopardy because it "lies at the foundation of the federal rule that jeopardy attaches when the jury is empaneled and sworn").

The cases which articulate a defendant's right to a particular tribunal are easily harmonized with the line of cases requiring some event to terminate the original jeopardy. See Richardson v. United States, 468 U.S. 317, 325, 104 S.Ct. 3081, 82 L.Ed.2d 242 (1984); Justices of Boston Mun. Court v. Lydon, 466 U.S. 294, 309, 104 S.Ct. 1805, 80 L.Ed.2d 311 (1984). The harmony is simple: Once jeopardy attaches, the defendant's right to a particular tribunal may be overcome if there is manifest necessity for a mistrial or the defendant requests or consents to a mistrial. In other words, where manifest necessity is found or a defendant requests or consents to a mistrial, the loss of the right does not violate the Double Jeopardy Clause. See Arizona, 434 U.S. at 505, 98 S.Ct. 824; United States v. Dinitz, 424 U.S. 600, 606–07, 96 S.Ct. 1075, 47 L.Ed.2d 267 (1976); Wade, 336 U.S. at 689, 69 S.Ct. 834; Watkins v. Kassulke, 90 F.3d 138, 141 (6th Cir.1996); Rich, 589 F.2d at 1031–32; see also Illinois v. Somerville, 410 U.S. 458, 463, 468–71, 93 S.Ct. 1066, 35 L.Ed.2d 425 (1973) (holding that despite weighty interest of defendant in having his fate determined by the jury first empaneled, defendant's double jeopardy rights were not violated by court's declaration of mistrial which was required by "manifest necessity" or the "ends of public justice") (quoting United States v. Perez, 22 U.S. (9 Wheat.) 579, 580, 6 L.Ed. 165 (1824)). More importantly, the Supreme Court has found no conflict between the continuing jeopardy cases which require a terminating event and the cases which affirm a defendant's right to a particular tribunal.

Although Defendant does not appear to have objected initially to the replacement of the juror after the original jury was empaneled and sworn, I agree with the majority's footnote that "neither the court nor counsel made [D]efendant aware of the constitutional right that he was forgoing so that he could make an informed, conscious waiver." Ante, at ___ n. 1; see Rich, 589 F.2d at 1032–33. Thus because Defendant does not appear to have consented or requested a mistrial, and because the trial court made no finding of manifest necessity for a mistrial, I believe that the replacement of the juror and the subsequent trial with a jury different from the original sworn jury violated Defendant's right to a particular tribunal and his double jeopardy rights. See Rich, 589 F.2d at 1031–32. Had the trial court taken the simple measure of having an alternate juror sworn in the first place, we would not be confronted with this problem. Under these circumstances, however, I would reverse the judgment.

(B) WHEN IS THE ACCUSED IN JEOPARDY FOR "THE SAME OFFENSE"?

United States v. Turner & Kelly

United States Court of Appeals, Eighth Circuit, 1997.
130 F.3d 815.

■ MORRIS SHEPPARD ARNOLD, CIRCUIT JUDGE.

I

In January, 1995, Robert Turner and Guinn Kelly were indicted on various charges related to allegations that they submitted false time cards that showed more hours than they actually worked at a federal public housing project. Each count against Mr. Turner and Mr. Kelly specified a different pay period; each of the charges against them was brought under 18 U.S.C. § 641 (stealing money from a federal agency), 18 U.S.C. § 1001(a) (making a materially false statement to a federal agency), or 18 U.S.C. § 371 (conspiring with another person to do either or both of the above). A third defendant, Kenneth Givens, was also charged in the indictment.

By the time of trial, a superseding indictment against the three defendants (returned in February, 1995, and designated S1 by the parties) was in effect. On the fourth day of trial, when it appeared that the lawyer for Mr. Givens might have to testify on behalf of all three defendants to impeach a government witness, the trial court declared a mistrial with respect to all three defendants, over the objections of Mr. Turner and Mr. Kelly. The trial court, however, subsequently denied motions by Mr. Turner and Mr. Kelly to dismiss the indictment.

Mr. Turner and Mr. Kelly appealed the trial court's denial of their motions to dismiss. In United States v. Givens, 88 F.3d 608, 612 (8th Cir.1996), a panel of this court held that no "manifest necessity" existed for declaring a mistrial with respect to Mr. Turner and Mr. Kelly, since their cases could have been severed from that of Mr. Givens (and thus could have proceeded to verdict) without undue prejudice to the government, id. at 613, and without "offending the interests of justice," id. at 614. The panel therefore remanded the cases of Mr. Turner and Mr. Kelly "for further proceedings consistent with [its] opinion." Id.

Approximately four months later, the government returned another superseding indictment (designated S4 by the parties), this one against only Mr. Turner and Mr. Kelly (in the interim, Mr. Givens had pleaded guilty to one count of receiving money with the intent to defraud the federal Department of Housing and Urban Development, see 18 U.S.C. § 1012). Although the factual basis for the charges in S4 (submitting false time cards for pay periods from April, 1993, through March, 1994) is the same as the factual basis for the charges in S1 against Mr. Turner and Mr. Kelly, the individual allegations are different. In S4, some pay periods are added to or dropped from those in S1. With respect to the other pay periods, the charge against a particular defendant shifts from a violation of 18 U.S.C. § 641 (stealing money from a federal agency) in S1 to a violation of 18 U.S.C. § 1001(a) (making a materially false statement to a federal agency) in S4, or vice versa. Finally, in contrast to S1, no conspiracy charges are included in S4; charges of aiding and abetting, see 18 U.S.C. § 2(a), however, which do not appear anywhere in S1, are included in S4.

Mr. Turner and Mr. Kelly moved to dismiss S4 on the grounds of double jeopardy and res judicata. A magistrate judge recommended that the motions be denied. The trial court adopted the recommendations of the magistrate judge and denied the motions to dismiss. Mr. Turner and Mr. Kelly appeal the denial of their motions. With the exception of one count of S4 against Mr. Kelly, we affirm the ruling of the trial court.

I.

The Constitution provides that no person shall "be subject for the same offence to be twice put in jeopardy of life of limb." See U.S. Const. amend. V. Jeopardy under the Constitution is "the risk that is traditionally associated with criminal prosecution." Breed v. Jones, 421 U.S. 519, 528, 95 S.Ct. 1779, 1784, 44 L.Ed.2d 346 (1975). Because of the potentially serious consequences of criminal prosecution, such proceedings impose "heavy pressures and burdens—psychological, physical, and financial—on a person charged." Id. at 529–30, 95 S.Ct. at 1785–86. The purpose of the constitutional guarantee against double jeopardy, then, is to ensure that a person "be subject to the experience only once" for a particular crime. Id. at 530, 95 S.Ct. at 1785.

Since the indictment in effect at the time of trial was S1, the charges in it are the ones to which jeopardy attached for Mr. Turner and Mr. Kelly. They now argue that because the factual basis for the charges in S4 (submitting false time cards for pay periods from April, 1993, through March, 1994) is the same as the factual basis for the charges in S1, the constitutional guarantee against double jeopardy bars the government from bringing them to trial on the allegations in S4. Except for one count of S4 against Mr. Kelly, we disagree.

II.

We turn first to the counts in S4 related to pay periods that are not included in S1. The courts have regularly held that when a statute targets individual acts rather than a course of conduct as a whole, offenses charged with respect to separate dates, even though "of the same nature," United

States v. Banks, 10 F.3d 1044, 1050 (4th Cir.1993), cert. denied, 511 U.S. 1090, 114 S.Ct. 1850, 128 L.Ed.2d 475, 512 U.S. 1208, 114 S.Ct. 2681, 129 L.Ed.2d 814 (1994), are not the "same" offense for double jeopardy purposes. See, e.g., United States v. Gardner, 65 F.3d 82, 85–86 (8th Cir.1995), cert. denied, 516 U.S. 1064, ___, 116 S.Ct. 748, 1044, 133 L.Ed.2d 696, 134 L.Ed.2d 191 (1996) (mail fraud), and United States v. Lanier, 604 F.2d 1157, 1159 (8th Cir.1979) (per curiam) (false statements on bank deposit forms), dealing specifically with 18 U.S.C. § 1001(a); see also United States v. Banks, 10 F.3d at 1050 (drug charges), and United States v. Solomon, 726 F.2d 677, 678–79 (11th Cir.1984) (false statements on firearms sale forms). We hold, therefore, that the double jeopardy clause does not bar the government from prosecuting Mr. Turner on count 12 and Mr. Kelly on count 9, count 23, and count 25 of S4.

III.

There are 14 counts in S4 in which the charge against a particular defendant relative to a designated pay period shifts from a violation of 18 U.S.C. § 641 to a violation of 18 U.S.C. § 1001(a), or vice versa. Mr. Turner and Mr. Kelly contend that the charge of making a materially false statement to a federal agency under § 1001(a) is a lesser included offense of stealing money from a federal agency under § 641 and, therefore, that the double jeopardy clause bars the government from bringing them to trial on any of the counts in S4 that were shifted, relative to S1, from either statute to the other. See, e.g., Brown v. Ohio, 432 U.S. 161, 168–69, 97 S.Ct. 2221, 2226–27, 53 L.Ed.2d 187 (1977).

One offense is a lesser included offense of another only if "the elements of the lesser offense are a subset of the elements of the other offense." Schmuck v. United States, 489 U.S. 705, 716, 109 S.Ct. 1443, 1450, 103 L.Ed.2d 734 (1989); see also Illinois v. Vitale, 447 U.S. 410, 421, 100 S.Ct. 2260, 2267, 65 L.Ed.2d 228 (1980), and Brown, 432 U.S. at 168, 97 S.Ct. at 2226. In this case, therefore, we look to the statutory elements of § 641 to determine if it includes the statutory elements of § 1001(a). See Schmuck, 489 U.S. at 716–17, 109 S.Ct. at 1450–51; see also Vitale, 447 U.S. at 421, 100 S.Ct. at 2267 and Brown, 432 U.S. at 168, 97 S.Ct. at 2226.

As charged in both S1 and S4, the elements of the version of § 641 in effect at the relevant time are that the particular defendant, (1) knowingly and willfully, (2) stole (3) more than $100 (4) from a federal agency. See 18 U.S.C.A. § 641 (West 1976), amended by 18 U.S.C.A. § 641 (West supp. 1997); see also United States v. May, 625 F.2d 186, 189–90 (8th Cir.1980). "Stealing" under § 641 (as charged in this case) requires "the intent to appropriate [money] to a use inconsistent with the [federal agency's] rights and benefits." Ailsworth v. United States, 448 F.2d 439, 442 (9th Cir.1971); see also United States v. Wilson, 636 F.2d 225, 228 (8th Cir.1980).

As charged in both S1 and S4, the elements of § 1001(a) are that the particular defendant, (1) knowingly and willfully, (2) made a statement (3) that was materially false (4) to a federal agency. See 18 U.S.C. § 1001(a)(2); see also United States v. Johnson, 937 F.2d 392, 396 (8th Cir.1991). Even the most cursory comparison of the elements of the two statutes shows that § 1001(a) includes elements—specifically, at minimum, the requirement of a materially false statement—that are not necessary for proof of § 641; the elements of § 1001(a) cannot, therefore, be a subset of the elements of § 641. We thus reject the argument of Mr. Turner and Mr. Kelly that § 1001(a) is a lesser included offense of § 641.

Aside from the issue of lesser included offenses, however, Mr. Turner and Mr. Kelly further assert that because the government alleges that both the stealing under § 641 and the materially false statements under § 1001(a) were accomplished by means of submitting false time cards, the offenses as charged are the "same" for double jeopardy purposes. An analogous contention was the basis for the holding in Grady v. Corbin, 495 U.S. 508, 510, 110 S.Ct. 2084, 2087, 109 L.Ed.2d 548 (1990), where the Supreme Court declared that the double jeopardy clause bars a subsequent prosecution if, "to establish an essential element of [the] offense charged in [the second] prosecution, the government will prove conduct that constitutes an offense for which the defendant has already been prosecuted."

Unfortunately for Mr. Turner and Mr. Kelly, though, in United States v. Dixon, 509 U.S. 688, 704, 712, 113 S.Ct. 2849, 2860, 2864, 125 L.Ed.2d 556 (1993), the Supreme Court squarely overruled the principle announced in Grady. In an extended discussion, the Supreme Court established that the "only ... test," Dixon, 509 U.S. at 708, 113 S.Ct. at 2862 (emphasis in original), for double jeopardy purposes when the offenses are alleged to be the "same"—and no issue of lesser included charges is involved, id. at 705–07, 707 n. 11, 113 S.Ct. at 2860–61 n. 11—is the "same-elements test, ... [which] inquires whether each offense contains an element not contained in the other," id. at 696, 113 S.Ct. at 2855. See id. at 703–04, 706, 708–10, 113 S.Ct. at 2859–60, 2861, 2862–63; see also Blockburger v. United States, 284 U.S. 299, 304, 52 S.Ct. 180, 182, 76 L.Ed. 306 (1932), and Gavieres v. United States, 220 U.S. 338, 344–45, 31 S.Ct. 421, 423–24, 55 L.Ed. 489 (1911).

As noted above, the elements of § 1001(a) require proof of a materially false statement—a requirement not mandated for proof of § 641. Conversely, the elements of § 641 (as charged in this case) require proof of the theft of more than $100—a requirement not mandated for proof of § 1001(a). We conclude, therefore, that the double jeopardy clause does not bar the government from prosecuting Mr. Turner on counts 10–11 and counts 13–16 and Mr. Kelly on counts 1–4 and counts 6–8 of S4.

IV.

We turn, then, to the argument of Mr. Turner and Mr. Kelly that the aiding-and-abetting charges against them in S4 are lesser included offenses of crimes alleged in S1, see, e.g., United States v. Lincoln, 925 F.2d 255, 256 (8th Cir.1991), cert. denied, 501 U.S. 1222, 111 S.Ct. 2838, 115 L.Ed.2d 1006 (1991), and are therefore barred by the double jeopardy clause. That argument may be shortly dealt with.

For each relevant pay period, S1 charges that by submitting false time cards for himself, a particular defendant—specifically, Mr. Turner or Mr. Kelly—either stole more than $100 from a federal agency or made a materially false statement to a federal agency. Thus it is true that the double jeopardy clause protects Mr. Turner and Mr. Kelly, with respect to each one's own time cards for the specific pay periods designated in S1, from any subsequent prosecution for aiding and abetting the theft of more than $100 from a federal agency by means of his own time cards or for aiding and abetting the making of a materially false statement to a federal agency by means of his own time cards. See, e.g., id.

In S4, however, for each relevant pay period, the charges are that Mr. Turner and Mr. Kelly aided and abetted in the submission of false time cards by a third person and that that third person thereby made materially false statements to a federal agency. It is the third person's time cards for the relevant pay periods that are the basis for the aiding-and-abetting charges in S4, not Mr. Turner's and Mr. Kelly's own time cards for those pay periods. There are no charges in S1 of acts by Mr. Turner or Mr. Kelly relative to any third person's time cards. The double jeopardy clause therefore does not bar the government from prosecuting Mr. Turner or Mr. Kelly on counts 17–22 of S4. Cf. Standefer v. United States, 447 U.S. 10, 22 n. 16, 100 S.Ct. 1999, 2007 n. 16, 64 L.Ed.2d 689 (1980) (double jeopardy clause does not bar trial of defendant for aiding and abetting even though principal was acquitted of substantive charge in earlier trial).

V.

With respect to Mr. Kelly, count 5 in S4 is identical to count 18 in S1. Because those two charges are the same, the double jeopardy clause bars the government from prosecuting Mr. Kelly on count 5 of S4.

VI.

In addition to their arguments invoking double jeopardy, Mr. Turner and Mr. Kelly contend that the principle of res judicata protects them from further prosecution. They assert, first, that the purposes of the doctrine of res judicata are different from the purposes of the double jeopardy clause and that, for res judicata purposes, the charges in S1 and S4 are the "same," since they have the same factual basis (the submission of false time cards). Mr. Turner and Mr. Kelly then argue that this court's holding in their prior appeal—that no "manifest necessity" existed for a mistrial with respect to either of them, United States v. Givens, 88 F.3d 608, 612 (8th Cir.1996)—amounts to a ruling on the merits of the charges in S1 and therefore also to a judgment of acquittal for them on the charges in S1. Mr. Turner and Mr. Kelly thus urge that the doctrine of res judicata with respect to previous acquittals bars the government from prosecuting them on the charges in S4. See, e.g., Sealfon v. United States, 332 U.S. 575, 578, 580, 68 S.Ct. 237, 239, 92 L.Ed. 180 (1948).

The doctrine of res judicata in criminal proceedings "operates to conclude those matters in issue which the verdict determined though the offenses be different." Id. at 578 (emphasis supplied). There was no "verdict" in this case; there was only a mistrial.

By its own definition, then, the doctrine of res judicata is inapplicable.

The doctrine of collateral estoppel in criminal proceedings holds that "when an issue of ultimate fact has once been determined by a valid and final judgment, that issue cannot again be litigated." Ashe v. Swenson, 397 U.S. 436, 443, 90 S.Ct. 1189, 1193, 25 L.Ed.2d 469 (1970). The doctrine is a "component of the Double Jeopardy Clause." Dowling v. United States, 493 U.S. 342, 348, 110 S.Ct. 668, 672, 107 L.Ed.2d 708 (1990).

There is nothing in the record, however, that could reasonably be construed as a determination of whether the time cards at issue in the first trial were false—either in the transcript where the trial court declared a mistrial; in the trial court's order denying the defendants' motions, after the mistrial, to dismiss the indictment; in this court's opinion on the first appeal; or, for that matter, in the magistrate judge's report and recommendations with respect to the defendants' motions, after the first appeal, to dismiss the indictment or in the trial court's order adopting those recommendations. We therefore reject the argument of Mr. Turner and Mr. Kelly with respect to that issue.

VII.

For the reasons stated, we affirm the order of the trial court except as to count 5 of S4 against Mr. Kelly. We remand the cases for further proceedings consistent with this opinion.

State v. Carroll

Supreme Court of Hawaii, 1981.
63 Hawaii 345, 627 P.2d 776.

■ Before RICHARDSON, C.J., and OGATA, MENOR, LUM and NAKAMURA, JJ.

■ PER CURIAM. The State appeals from a circuit court order granting defendant-appellee Alfred Kapala Carroll's motion to dismiss an indictment charging him with a violation of HRS §§ 705–500 and 708–821(1)(b) (Attempted Criminal Property Damage in the Second Degree). In an earlier district court trial, defendant had been acquitted of the charge of violating Revised Ordinances of Honolulu (R.O.H.) § 13–21.3(a) (1969) (Possession of an Obnoxious Substance). The issue on appeal is whether the separate charges against defendant arose from the same "episode." If so, HRS §§ 701–109(2)[61] and 701–111(1)(b)[62] bar the State from bringing defendant to trial for Attempted Criminal Property Damage in the Second Degree

---

61. HRS § 701–109(2) provides as follows:

Except as provided in subsection (3) of this section, a defendant shall not be subject to separate trials for multiple offenses based on the same conduct or arising from the same episode, if such offenses are known to the appropriate prosecuting officer at the time of the commencement of the first trial and are within the jurisdiction of a single court.

62. HRS § 701–111(1)(b) provides:

When prosecution is barred by former prosecution for a different offense. Although a prosecution is for a violation of a different statutory provision or is based on different facts, it is barred by a former prosecution under any of the following circumstances:

(1) The former prosecution resulted in an acquittal which has not subsequently been set aside or in a conviction as defined in section 701–110(3) and the subsequent prosecution is for:

. . .

(b) Any offense for which the defendant should have been tried on the first prosecution under section 701–109 unless the court ordered a separate trial of the offense[.]

after prosecuting him on the possessory charge. We find that the two charges did not arise from the same episode and therefore, we reverse.

I.

Defendant was arrested on October 19, 1978 at 2:40 a.m. for starting a fire at Jefferson School. Police Officer Mossman, who was alerted to the scene by a private citizen, conducted a routine search of defendant for weapons and found a cannister. Believing it was a container of nasal spray, he returned it to defendant.

Defendant was then transported to the police station and booked for Attempted Criminal Property Damage in the Second Degree. During a custodial search by Police Officer Hee, the cannister was again recovered. This time, however, the police officer identified it as Mace. Defendant was subsequently charged at 3:20 a.m. for Possession of an Obnoxious Substance.

On December 26, 1978, defendant was brought to trial in the district court and acquitted of the misdemeanor charge of Possession of an Obnoxious Substance. On March 2, 1979, he was brought to trial in the circuit court on the felony charge of Attempted Criminal Property Damage in the Second Degree.[63] Defendant argued that the two offenses were part of a single "episode" within the context of HRS § 701–109(2), supra, and should have been prosecuted in the same proceeding.

Defendant moved to dismiss the indictment for Attempted Criminal Property Damage in the Second Degree on the ground that he had been prosecuted previously for Possession of an Obnoxious Substance, an offense arising from the same episode. He argued that the prosecution for Attempted Criminal Property Damage in the Second Degree was prohibited by HRS § 701–111(1)(b), supra.

The trial court concluded that the Attempted Criminal Property Damage offense was "closely related enough [to the possessory offense] so that it can be considered as part of a series and stemming from one incident or transaction that resulted in separate arrests." After finding that both charges were properly within its jurisdiction, the trial court granted defendant's motion to dismiss the indictment, based primarily on State v. Aiu, 59 Haw. 92, 576 P.2d 1044 (1978).

The question presented on appeal is whether HRS §§ 701–109(2) and 701–111(1)(b) prohibit the State from bringing defendant to trial for Attempted Criminal Property Damage in the Second Degree after defendant had been acquitted of the possessory charge.

II.

This court has previously addressed the issue of whether a subsequent prosecution must be barred by HRS § 701–109(2) in State v. Aiu, supra. However, in *Aiu,* it was conceded that the offenses charged arose from the

---

63. On October 24, 1978, this case was bound over to the circuit court from the district court. The indictment charging defendant with Attempted Criminal Property Damage in the Second Degree was filed on January 16, 1979.

same conduct or episode. *Id.*, 59 Haw. at 96, 576 P.2d at 1048. *Aiu* is therefore not precedential authority for the case at bar.

Section 701–109(2), HRS, prohibits the State from subjecting a defendant to separate trials for offenses arising from the same conduct or "episode," provided that the offenses are known to the prosecutor at the commencement of the first trial and are within the jurisdiction of a single court. Under HRS § 701–111(1)(b), the State is barred from subsequently prosecuting a defendant for any offense which should have been joined in a prior trial under HRS § 701–109(2). . . .

III.

All of the preconditions required for the application of HRS § 701–109(2) are satisfied in this case. It is uncontested that the appropriate prosecuting officer was aware of the existence of the Attempted Criminal Property Damage charge at the time that the possessory charge was prosecuted.[64] Furthermore, both charges are clearly within the jurisdiction of a single court.

We begin with consideration, and rejection, of the State's interpretation of the word "episode." First, the State contends erroneously that HRS § 701–109(2) was derived from Model Penal Code § 1.08(2) (Tent.Draft No. 5, 1956) and therefore assumes that the Model Penal Code does not use the word "episode." Thus, the State hypothesizes that the Legislature coined the word "episode" as a shorthand means of encompassing subsections (b) and (c) of Model Penal Code § 1.08(2).

We note that the provision upon which the State relies was amended and renumbered as Model Penal Code § 1.07(2) in the 1962 Proposed Official Draft and that the amended provision contained the word "episode." Model Penal Code § 1.07, status of section (Proposed Official Draft, 1962). Furthermore, the Table of Derivation accompanying the Hawaii Penal Code indicates that HRS §§ 701–109 was derived from Model Penal Code § 1.07 (Proposed Official Draft, 1962), rather than its predecessor. 7A HRS at 497, app. § 3. Model Penal Code § 1.07(2) provides:

(2) *Limitation on Separate Trials for Multiple Offenses.* Except as provided in Subsection (3) of this Section, a defendant shall not be subject to separate trials for multiple offenses based on the same conduct or arising from the same criminal episode, if such offenses are known to the appropriate prosecuting officer at the time of the commencement of the first trial and are within the jurisdiction of a single court.

Second, the comment accompanying Model Penal Code § 1.07(2) reveals that the drafters of the code did not intend "episode" to encompass the situations described in Model Penal Code § 1.08(2)(b) and (c) (Tent. Draft No. 5, 1956). Model Penal Code § 1.07(2), as originally drafted, was

---

64. Since the record on appeal does not contain a copy of the complaint charging defendant with Possession of an Obnoxious Substance, there is no evidence as to whether that complaint enumerated facts concerning the Attempted Criminal Property Damage charge. However, Officer Hee testified that the police report on the possessory charge mentioned that defendant had been initially arrested for Attempted Criminal Property Damage in the Second Degree.

considerably broader and would have required joinder of offenses where it is now merely permissible. Although the Model Penal Code Advisory Committee favored broadening the formulation to include offenses "based on a course of conduct having a common criminal purpose or plan or involving repeated commission of the same kind of offense," the Model Penal Code Council viewed both this and the original language in Model Penal Code § 1.08(2) (Tent.Draft No. 5, 1956) as too inclusive. Model Penal Code § 1.07, status of section (Proposed Official Draft, 1962). Model Penal Code § 1.07(2), limiting the requirement to "multiple offenses based on the same conduct or arising from the same criminal episode," was designed to meet the Council's view. *Id.* Thus, we can infer from the commentary to Model Penal Code § 1.07(2) that the Legislature, in formulating HRS § 701–109(2), did not intend a determination of a single criminal "episode" to be based solely upon a defendant's singular criminal objective or common purpose or plan.

Although we reject the State's interpretation of "episode," we acknowledge that evidence of one crime is admissible in the trial of another crime if it tends to prove motive, intent, common scheme or plan, or design involving the commission of two or more crimes so related that proof of one tends to prove the other. However, mere allegations of a defendant's subjective intent are insufficient to require joinder of offenses that are otherwise unrelated.

IV.

Section 701–109(2), HRS, reflects a policy that a defendant should not have to face the expense and uncertainties of multiple trials based on essentially the same conduct or episode. *Commentary* on HRS § 701–109. It is designed to prevent the State from harassing a defendant with successive prosecutions where the State is dissatisfied with the punishment previously ordered or where the State has previously failed to convict the defendant.

We agree with defendant that proximity in time, place and circumstances of the offenses will necessarily enter into the policy considerations underlying HRS § 701–109(2). Where the offenses occur at the same time and place and under the same circumstances, it is likely that the facts and issues involved in the charges will be similar. The witnesses to be used and the evidence to be offered will probably overlap to the extent that joinder of the charges would be justified. Compulsory joinder of offenses which share a proximity in time, place and circumstances would not only protect the defendant from successive prosecutions based on the same conduct or episode, but it would also save the defendant and the State time and money required in the presentation of repetitive evidence.

In view of the dual considerations of fairness to the defendant and society's interest in efficient law enforcement, we hold that the test for determining the singleness of a criminal episode should be based on whether the alleged conduct was so closely related in time, place and circumstances that a complete account of one charge cannot be related without referring to details of the other charge. We do not, of course, by our holding in this case, preclude a defendant from asserting his right to separate trials where joinder of the offenses would be unjust and prejudicial.

Applying the test to the facts before us, we reject defendant's contention that the offenses occurred concurrently. Defendant argues that it would be unreasonable to conclude that the possessory offense did not occur until the arrest at the police station. He points to the arresting officer's initial discovery of the cannister as evidence that he was in possession of the Mace at the schoolyard.

Defendant also attempts to draw an analogy between his predicament and the situation in State v. Matischeck, 20 Or.App. 332, 531 P.2d 737 (1975). In *Matischeck,* the defendant had been arrested for Driving Under the Influence of Intoxicating Liquor and a vial of tablets was recovered from his person during a routine search. Two days later, the tablets were identified as amphetamines and an information was filed charging the defendant with Criminal Activity in Drugs. *Id.* at 738. Defendant emphasizes that in *Matischeck,* the possessory charge was effective as of the arrest for Driving Under the Influence of Intoxicating Liquor, rather than at the time the substance was identified. Therefore, he argues that the possessory charge in the instant case should be effective as of the arrest for Attempted Criminal Property Damage in the Second Degree, rather than at the time the Mace was identified at the police station.

We find that defendant was charged with the commission of offenses which occurred at different times and places and under different circumstances. Our rationale is based primarily on the fact that the arresting officer failed to recognize the illegal nature of the cannister at the time of the search for weapons. As a result, defendant's possession of the Mace continued after his initial arrest, until the subsequent discovery and identification at the police station.

While it is true that the possessory offense can be traced to the time of the first arrest, we cannot say that the possessory charge should be deemed effective as of the time of that arrest. The point in time at which the Mace was identified is important because prior to the identification, the facts and circumstances within the first arresting officer's knowledge did not afford probable cause to believe that an offense other than Attempted Criminal Property Damage in the Second Degree had been committed. The facts can be distinguished from those in State v. Matischeck, 20 Or.App. 332, 531 P.2d 737 (1975), where the police officer's immediate seizure of the vial indicated that he had probable cause to suspect contraband. In contrast to the case at bar, the identification of the contraband in *Matischeck* served to verify the earlier suspicion.

Furthermore, under HRS § 701–108(4), an offense of a continuing nature such as the possession of Mace is deemed to be committed at the time when the course of conduct is terminated.

Not only did the offenses occur at different times and places, but they were discovered under different circumstances which resulted in arrests by different police officers. We therefore conclude that the offenses were so separate in time and place and so distinct in circumstances that the acquittal on the possessory charge did not bar prosecution for the Attempted Criminal Property Damage in the Second Degree.

Reversed and remanded for further proceedings not inconsistent with this opinion.[65]

(C) PLEA OF GUILTY

Ricketts v. Adamson

Supreme Court of the United States, 1987.
483 U.S. 1, 107 S.Ct. 2680, 97 L.Ed.2d 1.

Shortly after his trial for first-degree murder had commenced in an Arizona court, respondent and the prosecutor reached an agreement whereby respondent would plead guilty to second-degree murder and testify against other parties involved in the murder, in return for a specified prison term and a specified actual incarceration time. The agreement also provided that if respondent refused to testify "this entire agreement is null and void and the original charge will be automatically reinstated," and that "[i]n the event this agreement becomes null and void, then the parties shall be returned to the positions they were in before this agreement." The trial court accepted the plea agreement and proposed sentence, and respondent testified against the other individuals, who were convicted of first-degree murder. The Arizona Supreme Court reversed the latter convictions, remanding for retrial, and the prosecutor sought respondent's further cooperation but was informed that respondent believed his obligation to testify under the agreement terminated when he was sentenced. After the trial court refused to compel him to testify in pretrial proceedings, the State filed a new information charging him with first-degree murder. The trial court denied his motion to quash the information on double jeopardy grounds, and the Arizona Supreme Court, in special proceedings filed by respondent, vacated his second-degree murder conviction and reinstated the original charges, holding that the plea agreement contemplated availability of his testimony against the other individuals at both trial and retrial, that he had violated the agreement's terms, and that the agreement waived the defense of double jeopardy if it was violated. The State then declined his offer to testify at the other individuals' retrial, he was convicted of first-degree murder and sentenced to death, and the judgment was affirmed on appeal....

---

65. Citations for drunk driving, driving without a safety sticker, and driving without a registration certificate charged separate, independent offenses where they were committed at different times and were entirely unrelated to each other were not committed to accomplish a "single criminal objective" and a prosecution for drunk driving was not barred by guilty pleas to the other citations. Hupp v. Johnson, 606 P.2d 253 (Utah 1980).

Statute requiring all crimes arising from the same conduct to be prosecuted in a single prosecution if they are in the same jurisdiction and known to the prosecutor expands double jeopardy beyond the state or federal constitutions. Griffin v. State, 266 Ga. 115, 464 S.E.2d 371 (1995).

Even though forcible rape and incest are separate crimes for double jeopardy purposes, where they were a single act, conviction was barred under 21 Okl. Stat. Supp. 1987 § 11A authorizing only one punishment for a single act or omission. Hale v. State, 888 P.2d 1027 (Okl.Cr.1995).

■ JUSTICE WHITE delivered the opinion of the Court.

The question for decision is whether the Double Jeopardy Clause bars the prosecution of respondent for first-degree murder following his breach of a plea agreement under which he had pled guilty to a lesser offense, had been sentenced, and had begun serving a term of imprisonment. The Court of Appeals for the Ninth Circuit held that the prosecution of respondent violated double jeopardy principles and directed the issuance of a writ of habeas corpus. We reverse.

. . .

We may assume that jeopardy attached at least when respondent was sentenced in December 1978, on his plea of guilty to second-degree murder. Assuming also that under Arizona law second-degree murder is a lesser included offense of first-degree murder, the Double Jeopardy Clause, absent special circumstances, would have precluded prosecution of respondent for the greater charge on which he now stands convicted. Brown v. Ohio, 432 U.S. 161, 168, 97 S.Ct. 2221, 2226, 53 L.Ed.2d 187 (1977). The State submits, however, that respondent's breach of the plea arrangement to which the parties had agreed removed the double jeopardy bar to prosecution of respondent on the first-degree murder charge. We agree with the State.

Under the terms of the plea agreement, both parties bargained for and received substantial benefits. . . .

The agreement specifies in two separate paragraphs the consequences that would flow from respondent's breach of his promises. Paragraph 5 provides that if respondent refused to testify, "this entire agreement is null and void and the original charge will be *automatically* reinstated." (emphasis added). Similarly, Paragraph 15 of the agreement states that "[i]n the event this agreement becomes null and void, then the parties shall be returned to the positions they were in before this agreement." Respondent unquestionably understood the meaning of these provisions. At the plea hearing, the trial judge read the plea agreement to respondent, line by line, and pointedly asked respondent whether he understood the provisions in Paragraphs 5 and 15. Respondent replied "Yes, sir," to each question. On this score, we do not find it significant, as did the Court of Appeals, that "double jeopardy" was not specifically waived by name in the plea agreement. Nor are we persuaded by the court's assertion that "[a]greeing that charges may be reinstituted . . . is not equivalent to agreeing that if they are reinstituted a double jeopardy defense is waived." The terms of the agreement could not be clearer: in the event of respondent's breach occasioned by a refusal to testify, the parties would be returned to the *status quo ante,* in which case respondent would have *no* double jeopardy defense to waive. And, an agreement specifying that charges may be *reinstated* given certain circumstances is, at least under the provisions of this plea agreement, *precisely* equivalent to an agreement waiving a double jeopardy defense. . . .

We are also unimpressed by the Court of Appeals' holding that there was a good faith dispute about whether respondent was bound to testify a second time and that until the extent of his obligation was decided, there could be no knowing and intelligent waiver of his double jeopardy defense. But respondent knew that if he breached the agreement he could be retried, and it is incredible to believe that he did not anticipate that the extent of his obligation would be decided by a court. Here he sought a construction of the agreement in the Arizona Supreme Court, and that court found that he had failed to live up to his promise. The result was that respondent was returned to the position he occupied prior to execution of the plea bargain: he stood charged with first-degree murder. Trial on that charge did not violate the Double Jeopardy Clause. United States v. Scott, 437 U.S. 82, 98 S.Ct. 2187, 57 L.Ed.2d 65 (1978), supports this conclusion.

. . .

Respondent cannot escape the Arizona Supreme Court's interpretation of his obligations under the agreement. The State did not force the breach; respondent chose, perhaps for strategic reasons or as a gamble, to advance an interpretation of the agreement that proved erroneous. And, there is no indication that respondent did not fully understand the potential seriousness of the position he adopted. In the April 3 letter, respondent's counsel advised the prosecutor that respondent "is fully aware of the fact that your office may feel that he has not completed his obligations under the plea agreement . . . and, further, that your office may attempt to withdraw the plea agreement from him, [and] that he may be prosecuted for the killing of Donald Bolles on a first degree murder charge." This statement of respondent's awareness of the operative terms of the plea agreement only underscores that which respondent's plea hearing made evident: respondent clearly appreciated and understood the consequences were he found to be in breach of the agreement.

Finally, it is of no moment that following the Arizona Supreme Court's decision respondent offered to comply with the terms of the agreement. At this point, respondent's second-degree murder conviction had already been ordered vacated and the original charge reinstated. The parties did not agree that respondent would be relieved from the consequences of his refusal to testify if he were able to advance a colorable argument that a testimonial obligation was not owing. The parties could have struck a different bargain, but permitting the State to enforce the agreement the parties actually made does not violate the Double Jeopardy Clause.

The judgment of the Court of Appeals is reversed.

It is so ordered.[66]

MODEL PENAL CODE

Section 1.08   When Prosecution Barred by Former Prosecution for the Same Offense.

When a prosecution is for a violation of the same provision of the statutes and is based upon the same facts as a former prosecution, it is barred by such former prosecution under the following circumstances:

---

66. Defendants who voluntarily pled guilty to conspiracy charges without raising issue of double jeopardy, as to whether the same conduct was involved, waived such claim. United States v. Broce, 488 U.S. 563, 109 S.Ct. 757 (1989).

(1) The former prosecution resulted in an acquittal. There is an acquittal if the prosecution resulted in a finding of not guilty by the trier of fact or in a determination that there was insufficient evidence to warrant a conviction. A finding of guilty of a lesser included offense is an acquittal of the greater inclusive offense, although the conviction is subsequently set aside.

(2) The former prosecution was terminated, after the information had been filed or the indictment found, by a final order or judgment for the defendant, which has not been set aside, reversed, or vacated and which necessarily required a determination inconsistent with a fact or a legal proposition that must be established for conviction of the offense.

(3) The former prosecution resulted in a conviction. There is a conviction if the prosecution resulted in a judgment of conviction which has not been reversed or vacated, a verdict of guilty which has not been set aside and which is capable of supporting a judgment, or a plea of guilty accepted by the Court. In the latter two cases failure to enter judgment must be for a reason other than a motion of the defendant.

(4) The former prosecution was improperly terminated. Except as provided in this Subsection, there is an improper termination of a prosecution if the termination is for reasons not amounting to an acquittal, and it takes place after the first witness is sworn but before verdict. Termination under any of the following circumstances is not improper:

(a) The defendant consents to the termination or waives, by motion to dismiss or otherwise, his right to object to the termination.

(b) the trial court finds that the termination is necessary because:

(1) it is physically impossible to proceed with the trial in conformity with law; or

(2) there is a legal defect in the proceedings which would make any judgment entered upon a verdict reversible as a matter of law; or

(3) prejudicial conduct, in or outside the courtroom, makes it impossible to proceed with the trial without injustice to either the defendant or the State; or

(4) the jury is unable to agree upon a verdict; or

(5) false statements of a juror on voir dire prevent a fair trial.

Section 1.09 When Prosecution Barred by Former Prosecution for Different Offense.

Although a prosecution is for a violation of a different provision of the statutes than a former prosecution or is based on different facts, it is barred by such former prosecution under the following circumstances:

(1) The former prosecution resulted in an acquittal[67] or in a conviction as defined in Section 1.08 and the subsequent prosecution is for:

(a) any offense of which the defendant could have been convicted on the first prosecution; or

(b) any offense for which the defendant should have been tried on the first prosecution under Section 1.07, unless the Court ordered a separate trial of the charge of such offense; or

(c) the same conduct, unless (i) the offense of which the defendant was formerly convicted or acquitted and the offense for which he is subsequent-

---

67. See footnote, supra, Sec. 1.08(1).

ly prosecuted each requires proof of a fact not required by the other and the law defining each of such offenses is intended to prevent a substantially different harm or evil, or (ii) the second offense was not consummated when the former trial began.

(2) The former prosecution was terminated, after the information was filed or the indictment found, by an acquittal or by a final order or judgment for the defendant which has not been set aside, reversed or vacated and which acquittal, final order or judgment necessarily required a determination inconsistent with a fact which must be established for conviction of the second offense.

(3) The former prosecution was improperly terminated, as improper termination is defined in Section 1.08, and the subsequent prosecution is for an offense of which the defendant could have been convicted had the former prosecution not been improperly terminated.

Section 1.10   Former Prosecution in Another Jurisdiction: When a Bar.

When conduct constitutes an offense within the concurrent jurisdiction of this State and of the United States or another State, a prosecution in any such other jurisdiction is a bar to a subsequent prosecution in this State under the following circumstances:

(1) The first prosecution resulted in an acquittal or in a conviction as defined in Section 1.08 and the subsequent prosecution is based on the same conduct, unless (a) the offense for which the defendant was formerly convicted or acquitted and the offense for which he is subsequently prosecuted each requires proof of a fact not required by the other and the law defining each of such offenses is intended to prevent a substantially different harm or evil or (b) the second offense was not consummated when the former trial began; or

(2) The former prosecution was terminated, after the information was filed or the indictment found, by an acquittal or by a final order or judgment for the defendant which has not been set aside, reversed or vacated and which acquittal, final order or judgment necessarily required a determination inconsistent with a fact which must be established for conviction of the offense of which the defendant is subsequently prosecuted.

Section 1.11   Former Prosecution Before Court Lacking Jurisdiction or When Fraudulently Procured by the Defendant.

A prosecution is not a bar within the meaning of Sections 1.08, 1.09 and 1.10 under any of the following circumstances:

(1) The former prosecution was before a court which lacked jurisdiction over the defendant or the offense; or

(2) The former prosecution was procured by the defendant without the knowledge of the appropriate prosecuting officer and with the purpose of avoiding the sentence which might otherwise be imposed; or

(3) The former prosecution resulted in a judgment of conviction which was held invalid in a subsequent proceeding on a writ of habeas corpus, coram nobis or similar process.[68]

---

68. Copyright © 1962 by the American Law Institute. Reprinted with the permission of the American Law Institute.

SECTION 5.   EX POST FACTO LAWS

Another limitation placed upon criminal prosecutions is that a person shall not be punished on a criminal charge for an act which was no offense at the time it was performed. Such a law is known as an *ex post facto* law and is prohibited both by The Constitution of the United States and by State Constitutions.[69] The term *ex post facto* "applies only to criminal laws; such laws as make acts, innocent when done, criminal; or, if criminal when done, aggravate the crime, or increase the punishment. Every *ex post facto* law is necessarily retrospective; but the converse is not true.... Retrospective laws, as distinguished from *ex post facto* laws, are not in conflict with the United States Constitution, nor are they in conflict with our State Constitution."[70]

---

69. "No ... ex post facto Law shall be passed." U.S. Const. Art. I, § 9, cl. 3. "No State shall ... pass any ... ex post facto Law ..." U.S. Const. Art. I, § 10. "No ... ex post facto law ... shall ever be passed." Iowa Const. Art. I, § 21.

70. State v. Squires, 26 Iowa 340, 346–7 (1869). Cf. Polk Co. v. Hierb, 37 Iowa 361 (1873); Kring v. Missouri, 107 U.S. 221, 2 S.Ct. 443, 27 L.Ed. 506 (1883); In re Medley, 134 U.S. 160, 10 S.Ct. 384, 33 L.Ed. 835 (1890); Duncan v. Missouri, 152 U.S. 377, 14 S.Ct. 570, 38 L.Ed. 485 (1894). A statute which increases the punishment for an existing offense is not applicable to a violation occurring prior to the enactment of the punishment. State v. Marx, 200 Iowa 884, 205 N.W. 518 (1925). Hence a jail sentence on conviction of maintaining a liquor nuisance, at a time before the statute authorizing such jail sentence became effective, was erroneous. Ibid. A change from death to one year's imprisonment at hard labor, followed by death, or from death to death preceded by solitary confinement is *ex post facto* as to offenses committed prior to the statutory change. Hartung v. People, 22 N.Y. 95 (1860), 26 N.Y. 167 (1863); In re Petty, 22 Kan. 477 (1879); In re Medley, 134 U.S. 160, 10 S.Ct. 384, 33 L.Ed. 835 (1890).

Revision of presumptive sentencing guidelines to enhance the defendant's sentence for an offense subsequent to the time of its commission violates the Ex Post Facto Clause. The change was not merely procedural since it increased the quantum of punishment. The guidelines were legislatively enacted and had the force and effect of law. Miller v. Florida, 482 U.S. 423, 107 S.Ct. 2446, 96 L.Ed.2d 351 (1987).

Sentencing guidelines classification of defendant's three prior misdemeanors as a felony for criminal history purposes did not violate the prohibition against ex post facto laws. State v. Beard, 22 Kan.App.2d 877, 924 P.2d 1268 (1996).

Corrections in the method of calculating parole eligibility to conform to a correct interpretation of a state statute because of a decision by the state's highest court did not violate the ex post facto clause. Holguin v. Raines, 695 F.2d 372 (9th Cir.1982).

A statute reducing the punishment, which was enacted after the offense but prior to the conviction, applies to that conviction. People v. McGowan, 199 Misc. 1, 104 N.Y.S.2d 652 (1951).

A statute is not *ex post facto* because it attaches to a subsequent crime an increased punishment on account of former convictions, even though such former convictions were had prior to the enactment of the statute. State v. Williams, 309 N.J.Super. 117, 706 A.2d 795 (1998); State v. Pratt, 286 Mont. 156, 951 P.2d 37 (1997); People v. Mesce, 52 Cal.App.4th 618, 60 Cal.Rptr.2d 745 (1997); Bender v. State, 687 So.2d 219 (Ala.Cr.App.1996); McDonald v. Massachusetts, 180 U.S. 311, 21 S.Ct. 389, 45 L.Ed. 542 (1901); Ex parte Allen, 91 Ohio St. 315, 110 N.E. 535 (1915).

Statutes imposing additional punishments on persons previously convicted of crimes do not punish habitual criminals for their earlier offenses, but merely increase the penalty for

United States v. Ramirez

United States Court of Appeals, Ninth Circuit, 1973.
480 F.2d 76.

■ Before DUNIWAY and HUFSTEDLER, CIRCUIT JUDGES, and ANDERSON,[71] DISTRICT JUDGE.

■ PER CURIAM. In a single count indictment returned September 16, 1971, appellants Ballan and Ramirez and sixteen others were charged with conspiracy to import, receive, conceal and transport marijuana in violation of 21 U.S.C. § 176a. Defendants were found guilty by a jury on June 19, 1972, and sentence was pronounced the next morning, June 20, 1972. Ramirez received a sentence of seven years and a fine of $15,000.00. Ballan was sentenced for five years and a fine of $5,000.00. The sentences were imposed under Sec. 176a, which was repealed effective May 1, 1971. Comprehensive Drug Abuse Prevention and Control Act of 1970 (the Act), Pub.L. 91–513, 84 Stat. 1236, 21 U.S.C. Sec. 801 et seq. The acts charged against the appellants extended over a period of time from approximately March to November of 1970.

Appellants' main thrusts on this appeal are four-fold:

First: The government cannot initiate a prosecution after the effective date of repeal for alleged criminal acts occurring prior thereto;

Second: Assuming that the first proposition is answered adversely to appellants, they cannot be punished under the repealed provisions, but must be punished under the new and less severe penalty provisions;

Third: Sentencing under the harsher penalties of the repealed act amounts to cruel and unusual punishment proscribed by the Eighth Amendment. This point is raised only by Ramirez; . . .

FIRST ISSUE

The first issue was not raised in the recent case of Bradley v. United States, 410 U.S. 605, 93 S.Ct. 1151, 35 L.Ed.2d 528 (1973), affirming 455

---

repetition of further acts of criminal conduct, and do not violate the ex post facto clause. State v. Hall, 119 N.M. 707, 895 P.2d 229 (App. 1995).

A statute denying to convicts under sentence for a second offense the same reductions from their sentence for good behavior that are allowed to other convicts is not *ex post facto* as applied to the punishment of an offense subsequently committed, although the offender had been convicted of his first offense before the passage of the act. In re Miller, 110 Mich. 676, 68 N.W. 990 (1896).

A statute providing for a determination of guilt and then a separate determination as to penalty where the sentence may be death or imprisonment for life, is not *ex post facto* as to murder previously committed. People v. Ward, 50 Cal.2d 702, 328 P.2d 777 (1958).

Making the possession of a pistol, by one who has been convicted of robbery, a crime is not ex post facto as to such possession after the statute even if the robbery conviction was prior to its enactment. Salazar v. State, 423 S.W.2d 297 (Tex.Crim.App.1968).

Statutory amendment providing that if a plea of guilty is entered to a murder charge, without specification of the degree, a three-judge panel shall determine the degree of the crime and give sentence, replacing such determination by a single judge, is not ex post facto. Rainsberger v. Fogliani, 380 F.2d 783 (9th Cir.1967).

71. Honorable J. Blaine Anderson, United States District Judge, District of Idaho, sitting by designation.

F.2d 1181 (CA 1st Cir.), since the prosecution there was commenced before May 1, 1971. Nevertheless, this court has squarely ruled on the question and the reasoning is directly applicable to this case. United States v. Cummings, 468 F.2d 274 (9 Cir.1972). In *Cummings* as here, the interdicted acts took place before the repeal of the statute and the indictment was returned after the repeal. These prosecutions for violations of the law occurring before were saved by the general saving statute, 1 U.S.C. Sec. 109, and the special saving clauses of the Act, Sections 702 and 1103. *Cummings,* supra, pp. 276–77. It could not have been the intent of Congress to grant amnesty to the unapprehended as of May 1, 1971, while continuing interdiction and punishment for essentially the same conduct for violations occurring after May 1, 1971.

SECOND ISSUE

While it may be argued that if the prosecution had begun after May 1, 1971, punishment should be under the new Act, we do not believe the rationale of *Bradley* supports this notion, but on the contrary, supports the conclusion that the sentences were properly imposed under the provisions of the repealed Act, as saved. As stated in *Bradley* (93 S.Ct. p. 1155), "As we have said, sentencing is part of prosecution. The mandatory minimum sentence of five years must therefore be imposed on offenders who violated the law before May 1, 1971."

THIRD ISSUE

Ramirez alone raises the Eighth Amendment violation because of sentencing under the harsher provisions of the repealed Act. We conclude this is not cruel and unusual punishment. While United States v. Fithian, 452 F.2d 505, 506 (9th Cir.1971) does not speak in terms of cruel and unusual punishment, it unmistakably directs that sentencing under the repealed provision "was the only course available." Further, 1 U.S.C. § 109 provides that repeal "shall not have the effect to release or extinguish any penalty ..." and remains in force to sustain "the enforcement of such penalty". The sentence imposed on Ramirez was well within and below the maximum sentence which could have been imposed. He is in the same class as all persons convicted and sentenced under the repealed provisions. Sentences under Sec. 176a were not cruel and unusual punishment prior to repeal. They do not become so by the later promulgation of less severe penalties for similar prohibited conduct.

The district judge was correct in proceeding and sentencing appellants under 21 U.S.C. § 176a repealed effective May 1, 1971. . . .

After careful review we find nothing in appellants' other assignments of error justifying a reversal.

Appellants' bonds are revoked as of now.

Affirmed.[72]

---

72. [By the Compiler.] "We find it unnecessary to decide the question of the effective date of the indictment, since the general savings clause found in 1 U.S.C.A. § 109, coupled with judicial construction of that section, disposes of the issue in this case.

"The general savings clause provides in part:

■ HUFSTEDLER, CIRCUIT JUDGE (dissenting):

I dissent solely from the disposition of the second issue: Does the penalty provision under the new Act apply to a prosecution under section 176a initiated after the repeal of section 176a? In my view, the majority's negative response is contrary to the teaching of Bradley v. United States (1973) 410 U.S. 605, 93 S.Ct. 1151, 35 L.Ed.2d 528.

Section 1103(a) of the Comprehensive Drug Abuse Prevention and Control Act of 1970 provides in pertinent part: "Prosecutions for any violation of law occurring prior to the effective date of [the Act] shall not be affected by the repeals ... made by [it] or abated by reason thereof." The keystone of the *Bradley* rationale is its construction of the word "prosecutions" in section 1103(a) as "clearly imports a beginning and an end." The "end," as *Bradley* squarely held, is the conclusion of sentencing. The "beginning" of a prosecution is the return of an indictment. These indict-

---

" 'The repeal of any statute shall not have the effect to release or extinguish any penalty, forfeiture, or liability incurred under such statute, unless the repealing act shall so expressly provide, and such statute shall be treated as still remaining in force for the purpose of sustaining any proper action or prosecution for the enforcement of such penalty, forfeiture, or liability....' "

"Under this section, penalties accruing while a statute was in force may be prosecuted after its repeal, unless there is an express provision to the contrary in the repealing statute." United States v. Brown, 429 F.2d 566, 568 (5th Cir.1970).

Amendment lessening penalty did not apply to an offense being prosecuted at the time of the amendment by reason of 1 U.S.C. § 109. United States v. Jacobs, 919 F.2d 10 (3d Cir.1990). Accord, United States v. Johns, 15 F.3d 740 (8th Cir.1994).

When a penal statute is amended so as to lessen the punishment for the offense, the legislature could provide either that the old punishment or the new should apply to offenses already committed. If no provision is made either way this is a clear manifestation of legislative intent that the lighter punishment is the proper penalty for the prohibited act. This will prevail over a general saving clause and hence only the lighter sentence can be applied in any case in which the judgment had not become final before the amendment. In re Estrada, 63 Cal.2d 740, 48 Cal.Rptr. 172, 408 P.2d 948 (1965). See also In re Ring, 64 Cal.2d 450, 50 Cal.Rptr. 530, 413 P.2d 130 (1966).

A statute was amended so as to leave no penalty for the offense of which D had been convicted and sentenced for life. D's conviction had been affirmed by the state court but was being considered by the Supreme Court on a petition for certiorari at the time the amendment became effective. It was held that the conviction cannot stand. Webb v. Beto, 457 F.2d 346 (5th Cir.1972).

D was convicted of a narcotic offense which was repealed by a substitute statute with a saving clause saying prosecutions for prior violations were not affected by the change. Held, the mandatory sentence under the old law must be imposed. Bradley v. United States, 410 U.S. 605, 93 S.Ct. 1151 (1973).

"The purpose of the abatement and pardon doctrine is to prevent the injustice manifest in continuing to prosecute for an activity after the legislature has declared that activity to be lawful." United States v. Chiarizio, 525 F.2d 289, 295 (2d Cir.1975). The court held it did not apply to the case at bench because no outright repeal was involved. The old statute was replaced by another incorporating the same substantive offense. But there is no "abatement and pardon" doctrine so far as the repeal of a criminal statute is concerned. If a criminal statute is repealed with no saving clause, general or special, no sentence can be imposed for a prior violation for the simple reason that there is no law to authorize it. There is no manifest injustice in the punishment of one who has violated the law, even if the same act could be done now without transgressing the law. This is emphasized by the fact that many states have a general saving clause to the effect that the repeal of a criminal statute shall not bar prosecution for offenses already committed.

ments were returned after section 176a had been repealed. There was no prosecution to be saved by section 1103(a). *Bradley* means that any prosecution initiated before repeal of the statute carries with it the old section 176a penalty. Conversely, any prosecution under section 176a begun after repeal of section 176a for the substantive offense committed before repeal carries with it the milder penalties of the successor statute.

The substantive offense was specifically saved. Prosecutions initiated before repeal were "not ... affected" or "abated." Prosecutions begun after repeal of section 176a could be neither affected nor abated, because they were nonexistent when the old statute was repealed.

I would vacate the sentence and remand for resentencing under the new statute.

Collins v. Youngblood

United States Supreme Court, 1990.
497 U.S. 37, 110 S.Ct. 2715, 111 L.Ed.2d 30.

■ CHIEF JUSTICE REHNQUIST delivered the opinion of the Court.

The question presented in this case is whether the application of a Texas statute, which was passed after respondent's crime and which allowed the reformation of an improper jury verdict in respondent's case, violates the *Ex Post Facto* Clause of Art. I, § 10. We hold that it does not.

Respondent Carroll Youngblood was convicted in a Texas court of aggravated sexual abuse. The jury imposed punishment of life imprisonment and a fine of $10,000. After his conviction and sentence were affirmed by the Texas Court of Criminal Appeals, Youngblood applied for a writ of habeas corpus in the State District Court. He argued that the Texas Code of Criminal Procedure did not authorize a fine in addition to a term of imprisonment for his offense, and, thus, under the decision of the Court of Criminal Appeals in *Bogany v. State*, 661 S.W.2d 957 (1983), the judgment and sentence were void, and he was entitled to a new trial In April 1985, the District Court, feeling bound by *Bogany*, recommended that the writ be granted.

Before the habeas application was considered by the Texas Court of Criminal Appeals, ... a new Texas statute designed to modify the *Bogany* decision became effective. Article 37.10(b), as of June 11, 1985, allows an appellate court to reform an improper verdict that assesses a punishment not authorized by law. Relying on that statute, the Court of Criminal Appeals reformed the verdict in Youngblood's case by ordering deletion of the $10,000 fine and denied his request for a new trial.

. . .

The [United States] Court of Appeals reversed [a district court finding that the action did not violate the *Ex Post Facto* Clause]. It relied on the statement in this Court's decision in Thompson v. Utah, 170 U.S. 343, 18 S.Ct. 620, 42 L.Ed. 1061 (1898), that retroactive procedural statutes violate the *Ex Post Facto* Clause unless they " 'leave untouched all the substantial protections with which existing law surrounds the person accused of crime.'" It held that Youngblood's right to a new trial under the *Bogany* decision was such a "substantial protection," and therefore ordered that a writ of habeas corpus be issued. We granted certiorari.

. . .

. . . We granted certiorari to consider the merits of respondent's *ex post facto* claim, and we proceed to do so.

Although the Latin phrase "*ex post facto*" literally encompasses any law passed "after the fact," it has long been recognized by this Court that the constitutional prohibition on *ex post facto* laws applies only to penal statutes which disadvantage the offender affected by them. As early opinions in this Court explained, "*ex post facto law*" was a term of art with an established meaning at the time of the framing of the Constitution. Justice Chase's now familiar opinion in Calder expounded those legislative Acts which in his view implicated the core concern of the Ex Post Facto Clause:

"1st. Every law that makes an action done before the passing of the law, and which was *innocent* when done, criminal; and punishes such action. 2d. Every law that *aggravates a crime*, or makes it *greater* than it was, when committed. 3d. Every law that *changes the punishment*, and inflicts *a greater punishment*, than the law annexed to the crime, when committed. 4th. Every law that alters the *legal* rules of *evidence*, and receives less, or different, testimony, than the law required at the time of the commission of the offence, *in order to convict the offender*." *Id.*, at 390.

Early opinions of the Court portrayed this as an exclusive definition of *ex post facto* laws. ("This exposition of the nature of ex post facto laws has never been denied, nor has any court or any commentator on the Constitution added to the classes of laws here set forth, as coming within that clause"). . . .

The *Beazell* formulation is faithful to our best knowledge of the original understanding of the Ex Post Facto Clause: Legislatures may not retroactively alter the definition of crimes or increase the punishment for criminal acts. Several early State Constitutions employed this definition of the term, and they appear to have been a basis for the Framers' understanding of the provision. . . .

Another historical reference, Blackstone's Commentaries, which was discussed by the Framers during debates on the *Ex Post Facto* Clause, see 2 M. Farrand, Records of the Federal Convention of 1787, pp. 448–449 (1911), and deemed an authoritative source of the technical meaning of the term buttresses this understanding. According to Blackstone, a law is *ex post facto* "when after an action (indifferent in itself) is committed, the legislator then for the first time declares it to have been a crime, and inflicts a punishment upon the person who has committed it." 1 W. Blackstone, Commentaries *46. Although increased punishments are not mentioned explicitly in the historical sources, the Court has never questioned their prohibition, apparently on the theory that "[t]he enhancement of a crime, or penalty, seems to come within the same mischief as the creation of a crime or penalty." . . .

Respondent concedes that Tex.Code of Crim.Proc.Ann., Art. 37.10(b) (Vernon Supp.1990), does not fall within any of the *Beazell* categories and, under that definition, would not constitute an *ex post facto* law as applied to him. The new statute is a procedural change that allows reformation of improper verdicts. It does not alter the definition of the crime of aggravated sexual abuse, of which Youngblood was convicted, nor does it increase the punishment for which he is eligible as a result of that conviction. Nevertheless, respondent maintains that this Court's decisions have not limited the scope of the *Ex Post Facto* Clause to the finite *Beazell* categories, but have stated more broadly that retroactive legislation contravenes Art. I, § 10, if it deprives an accused of a "substantial protection" under law existing at the time of the crime. He argues that the new trial guaranteed him by former Texas law is such a protection.

Several of our cases have described as "procedural" those changes which, even though they work to the disadvantage of the accused, do not violate the *Ex Post Facto* Clause. *Dobbert v. Florida, supra,* at 292–293, and n. 6; Beazell v. Ohio, 269 U.S., at 171; Mallett v. North Carolina, 181 U.S. 589, 597 (1901). While these cases do not explicitly define what they mean by the word "procedural," it is logical to think that the term refers to changes in the procedures by which a criminal case is adjudicated, as opposed to changes in the substantive law of crimes. Respondent correctly notes, however, that we have said that a procedural change may constitute an *ex post facto* violation if it "affect[s] matters of substance," by depriving a defendant of "substantial protections with which the existing law surrounds the person accused of crime," Duncan v. Missouri, 152 U.S. 377, 382–383 (1894), or arbitrarily infringing upon "substantial personal rights."

We think this language from the cases cited has imported confusion into the interpretation of the Ex Post Facto Clause. The origin of the rather amorphous phrase, "substantial protections," appears to lie in a 19th-century treatise on constitutional law by Professor Thomas Cooley. According to Cooley, who notably assumed the *Calder* construction of the *Ex Post Facto* Clause to be correct, Constitutional Limitations *265, a legislature "may prescribe altogether different modes of procedure in its discretion, though it cannot lawfully, we think, in so doing, dispense with any of those substantial protections with which the existing law surrounds the person accused of crime."

This Court's decision in *Duncan v. Missouri,* subsequently adopted that phraseology:

"[A]n *ex post facto* law is one which imposes a punishment for an act which was not punishable at the time it was committed; or an additional punishment to that then prescribed; or changes the rules of evidence by which less or different testimony is sufficient to convict than was then required; or, in short, in relation to the offence or its consequences, alters the situation of a party to his disadvantage; but the prescribing of different modes or procedure and the abolition of courts and creation of new ones, *leaving untouched all the substantial protections with which the existing law surrounds the person accused of crime,* are not considered within the constitutional inhibition. Cooley Const.Lim. (5th ed.) 329." *Id.*, at 382–383 (other citations omitted) (emphasis added).

. . .

We think the best way to make sense out of this discussion in the cases is to say that by simply labeling a law "procedural," a legislature does not thereby immunize it from scrutiny under the *Ex Post Facto* Clause. Subtle ex post facto violations are no more permissible than overt ones....

Two decisions of this Court, relied upon by respondent, do not fit into this analytical framework. In Kring v. Missouri, 107 U.S. 221 (1883), the Court said "it is not to be supposed that the opinion in [*Calder v. Bull*] undertook to define, by way of exclusion, all the cases to which the constitutional provision would be applicable." It defined an *ex post facto* law, *inter alia*, as one which, " 'in relation to the offence or its consequences, alters the situation of a party to his disadvantage.' " And in Thompson v. Utah, 170 U.S. 343 (1898), the Court held that a change in Utah law reducing the size of juries in criminal cases from 12 persons to 8 deprived Thompson of "a substantial right involved in his liberty" and violated the *Ex Post Facto* Clause.

Neither of these decisions, in our view, is consistent with the understanding of the term "*ex post facto* law" at the time the Constitution was adopted. Nor has their reasoning been followed by this Court since *Thompson* was decided in 1898. These cases have caused confusion in state and lower federal courts about the scope of the *Ex Post Facto* Clause....

... A law that abolishes an affirmative defense of justification or excuse contravenes Art. I, § 10, because it expands the scope of a criminal prohibition after the act is done....

... We think such a reading of the Clause [in *Kring v. Missouri*] departs from the meaning of the Clause as it was understood at the time of the adoption of the Constitution, and is not supported by later cases. We accordingly overrule *Kring*.

The second case, *Thompson v. Utah*, must be viewed in historical context. Thompson was initially charged with his crime—grand larceny committed by stealing a calf—in 1895, when Utah was a Territory. He was tried by a jury of 12 persons and convicted. A new trial was subsequently granted, however, and in the meantime Utah was admitted into the Union as a State. The Constitution of the State of Utah provided that juries in noncapital cases would consist of 8 persons, not 12, and Thompson was retried and convicted by a panel of 8.

This Court reversed the conviction. It reasoned first that while Utah was a Territory, the Sixth Amendment applied to actions of the territorial government and guaranteed Thompson a right to a 12–person jury. 170 U.S., at 349–350. The Court then held that "the State did not acquire upon its admission into the Union the power to provide, in respect of felonies committed within its limits while it was a Territory, that they should be tried otherwise than by a jury such as is provided by the Constitution of the United States." *Id.*, at 350–351. Because the State Constitution "deprive[d] him of a substantial right involved in his liberty" and "materially alter[ed] the situation to his disadvantage," the Court concluded that Thompson's conviction was prohibited by the Ex Post Facto Clause. *Id.*, at 352–353.

The result in *Thompson v. Utah* foreshadowed our decision in Duncan v. Louisiana, 391 U.S. 145 (1968), which held that the Sixth Amendment right to trial by jury—then believed to mean a jury of 12—was incorporated and made applicable by the Fourteenth Amendment against the States. The Court held that since Utah was a Territory when Thompson's crime was committed, and therefore obligated to provide a 12–person jury by the Sixth Amendment, the *Ex Post Facto* Clause prevented the State from taking away that substantial right from him when it became a State and was no longer bound by the Sixth Amendment as then interpreted. The right to jury trial provided by the Sixth Amendment is obviously a "substantial" one, but it is not a right that has anything to do with the definition of crimes, defenses, or punishments, which is the concern of the *Ex Post Facto* Clause. To the extent that *Thompson v. Utah* rested on the *Ex Post Facto* Clause and not the Sixth Amendment, we overrule it.[73]

The Texas statute allowing reformation of improper verdicts does not punish as a crime an act previously committed, which was innocent when done; nor make more burdensome the punishment for a crime, after its commission; nor deprive one charged with crime of any defense available according to law at the time when the act was committed. Its application to respondent therefore is not prohibited by the *Ex Post Facto* Clause of Art. I, § 10.

The judgment of the Court of Appeals is reversed.[74]

---

73. The Court's holding in Thompson v. Utah, 170 U.S. 343, 18 S.Ct. 620, 42 L.Ed. 1061 (1898), that the Sixth Amendment requires a jury panel of 12 persons is also obsolete. Williams v. Florida, 399 U.S. 78, 90 S.Ct. 1893, 26 L.Ed.2d 446 (1970).

74. A law is not *ex post facto* which makes certain matters admissible in evidence. State v. Dowden, 137 Iowa 573, 115 N.W. 211 (1908). A law is not *ex post facto* which enlarges the class of persons who can testify. Hopt v. Utah, 110 U.S. 574, 4 S.Ct. 202, 28 L.Ed. 262 (1884). Cf. Mrous v. State, 31 Tex.Cr.R. 597, 21 S.W. 764 (1893); Wester v. State, 142 Ala. 56, 38 So. 1010 (1905).

The change in the federal evidence rule prohibiting expert testimony as to whether defendant had a mental condition constituting an element of the crime to conduct occurring prior to the rule change did not violate the *Ex Post Facto* Clause. United States v. Bartlett, 856 F.2d 1071 (8th Cir.1988). Changes in the Bail Reform Act 18 U.S.C.A. 3142, etc., do not constitute *ex post facto* violations. United States v. Kowalik, 765 F.2d 944 (10th Cir.1985). A statute authorizing an appeal by the State in proceedings for condemnation of liquors, relates only to procedure, and is not *ex post facto* as to such proceedings instituted before the act went into effect. State v. Taggart, 186 Iowa 247, 172 N.W. 299 (1919). It is not *ex post facto* to substitute proceedings by information for indictment. Lybarger v. State, 2 Wash. 552, 27 P. 449 (1891); In re Wright, 3 Wyo. 478, 27 P. 565 (1891).

Mere changes of prison discipline or penal administration are not *ex post facto*. People v. Bodjack, 210 Mich. 443, 178 N.W. 228 (1920); Commonwealth v. Kalck, 239 Pa. 533, 87 A. 61 (1913).

A change in the method of selecting grand jury lists is not unconstitutional as applied to a crime already committed. State v. Pell, 140 Iowa 655, 119 N.W. 154 (1909). Nor is a change in the number of grand jurors. State v. Ah Jim, 9 Mont. 167, 23 P. 76 (1890); Hallock v. United States, 185 F. 417 (8th Cir.1911). Nor is a law which changes the mode of summoning or impaneling the jury. Gibson v. Mississippi, 162 U.S. 565, 16 S.Ct. 904, 40 L.Ed. 1075 (1896); Stokes v. People, 53 N.Y. 164 (1873). Nor is one which limits the time for challenging the jurors. State v. Taylor, 134 Mo. 109, 35 S.W. 92 (1896). Nor is one which gives the state

■ JUSTICE STEVENS, with whom JUSTICE BRENNAN and JUSTICE MARSHALL join, concurred in the judgment.

Tapia v. Superior Court

Supreme Court of California, In Bank, 1991.
53 Cal.3d 282, 279 Cal.Rptr. 592, 807 P.2d 434.

■ PANELLI, JUSTICE.

Proposition 115, the "Crime Victims Justice Reform Act," changed criminal law in several respects on June 6, 1990. We granted review to determine whether the measure's provisions should be applied to prosecutions of crimes committed before its effective date. We conclude that certain provisions addressing the conduct of trials, and certain other provisions changing the law to the benefit of defendants, may be applied to such prosecutions. The remainder of the measure's provisions may not.

FACTS

The People have accused petitioner Robert Alan Tapia of committing first degree murder with special circumstances on February 12, 1989. The

---

additional peremptory challenges. State v. Ryan, 13 Minn. 370 (1868); Walston v. Commonwealth, 16 B.Mon. 15 (Ky.1855). Nor is one which gives the accused fewer peremptory challenges. South v. State, 86 Ala. 617, 6 So. 52 (1889); Mathis v. State, 31 Fla. 291, 12 So. 681 (1893). Nor is one which changes the grounds for challenge. Stokes v. People, 53 N.Y. 164 (1873). Nor is one which changes the requirements as to the pleadings. State v. Manning, 14 Tex. 402 (1855); Perry v. State, 87 Ala. 30, 6 So. 425 (1889). Nor is one which regulates the procedure on appeal. Jacquins v. Commonwealth, 63 Mass. 279 (1852).

Where at the time of defendant's conviction statute provided for a death penalty, which statute was declared unconstitutional, a new statute also applying a death penalty under proper procedures could be applied to prior crime for which defendant was again convicted without violating *ex post facto* provisions. Dobbert v. Florida, 432 U.S. 282, 97 S.Ct. 2290 (1977).

For a position distinguishing *Dobbert,* see People v. Harvey, 76 Cal.App.3d 441, 142 Cal.Rptr. 887 (1978).

A law which provides for separate trials of persons jointly indicted, only when granted by the court for good cause shown, is not *ex post facto* as to pending prosecutions, although the prior law authorized separate trials as a matter of right. Beazell v. Ohio, 269 U.S. 167, 46 S.Ct. 68, 70 L.Ed. 216 (1925).

The change in the mode of execution from hanging to electrocution, though after a verdict of guilty and before sentence does not come within the *ex post facto* rule. Ex parte Johnson, 96 Tex.Cr.R. 473, 258 S.W. 473 (1924).

A statute authorizing the admission of evidence of defendant's history and background, and other matters, in mitigation or aggravation may be applied to an offense committed prior to its enactment without violating the constitutional prohibition against *ex post facto* laws. People v. Feldkamp, 51 Cal.2d 237, 331 P.2d 632 (1958).

The statute provided that by good conduct a convict could earn "good time" and thereby advance the actual date of his release. This statute was amended by substantially reducing the amount of "good time" a convict could earn. In holding that the amended statute could not be applied to a convict whose offense was committed before the effective date of the statute, the Court said: "Thus, even if a statute merely alters penal provisions accorded by the grace of the legislature, it violates the Clause if it is both retrospective and more onerous than the law in effect on the date of the offense." Weaver v. Graham, 450 U.S. 24, 101 S.Ct. 960, 965 (1981).

prosecution is pending in the Superior Court of Tulare County. Voir dire has not yet commenced.

Proposition 115 took effect on June 6, 1990, the day after the voters approved the measure. Shortly thereafter, the superior court ruled that it would apply the measure's procedural provisions to the case before it and, accordingly, conduct voir dire under the new statute. The new voir dire statute provides that the court rather than the attorneys "shall conduct the examination of prospective jurors" and that the examination "shall be conducted only in aid of the exercise of challenges for cause." (Prop. 115, § 7, codified as Code Civ.Proc., § 223.) Seeking to have the superior court's order vacated, Tapia petitioned the Court of Appeal for a writ of mandate. The Court of Appeal summarily denied relief. We granted review and directed issuance of an alternative writ. We also stayed proceedings in the superior court pending our decision.

DISCUSSION

As stated, we granted review to determine whether the provisions of Proposition 115 should be applied to prosecutions of crimes committed before its effective date. To answer this question we must address two issues. The first is whether the presumption of prospectivity applies to this initiative. The second concerns the meaning of the terms "prospective" and "retrospective." We do not address any other issue concerning the applicability or validity of the measure's provisions.

I.

We may quickly dispose of the first issue. It is well settled that a new statute is presumed to operate prospectively absent an express declaration of retrospectivity or a clear indication that the electorate, or the Legislature, intended otherwise. Both the text of Proposition 115 and the related ballot arguments are entirely silent on the question of retrospectivity. Thus, as to most of Proposition 115's provisions we see no reason to depart from the ordinary rule of construction that new statutes are intended to operate prospectively.

II.

There remains the question of what the terms "prospective" and "retrospective" mean. Tapia argues that a law is being applied retrospectively if it is applied to the prosecution of a crime committed before the law's effective date. For some types of laws, the test which Tapia proposes is clearly appropriate. Certainly a law is retrospective if it defines past conduct as a crime, increases the punishment for such conduct, or eliminates a defense to a criminal charge based on such conduct. Such a law, as applied to a past crime, "change[s] the legal consequences of an act completed before [the law's] effective date," namely the defendant's criminal behavior. Application of such a law to past crimes would also violate the constitutional rule against ex post facto legislation. (U.S. Const., art. I, § 10, cl. 1; Cal. Const., art. I, § 9.)

Tapia's proposed test is not appropriate, however, for laws which address the conduct of trials which have yet to take place, rather than criminal behavior which has already taken place. Even though applied to the prosecution of a crime committed before the law's effective date, a law addressing the conduct of trials still addresses conduct in the future. This is a principle that courts in this state have consistently recognized. Such a statute " 'is not made retroactive merely because it draws upon facts existing prior to its enactment. . . .' [Instead,] [t]he effect of such statutes is actually prospective in nature since they relate to the procedure to be followed in the future." For this reason, we have said that "it is a misnomer to designate [such statutes] as having retrospective effect."

. . .

From . . . cases, it is evident that a law governing the conduct of trials is being applied "prospectively" when it is applied to a trial occurring after the law's effective date, regardless of when the underlying crime was committed or the underlying cause of action arose. Tapia challenges this conclusion, arguing that we previously rejected it in *Aetna Casualty,*, in *Evangelatos*, and in People v. Hayes, 49 Cal.3d 1260, 265 Cal.Rptr. 132, 783 P.2d 719. Those opinions, however, do not support his argument. In each opinion, we refused to apply a statute so as to change the legal consequences of the parties' past conduct. In determining whether such statutes changed "the legal effects of past events" we sometimes used the terms "substantive" and "procedural." *Evangelatos, supra,* 44 Cal.3d at p. 1226, fn. 26, 246 Cal.Rptr. 629, 753 P.2d 585. However, we also made it clear that it is the law's effect, not its form or label, which is important.

. . .

Thus, contrary to Tapia's argument, it is clear that neither *Aetna Casualty*, nor *Evangelatos*, repudiated the general rule that statutes addressing the conduct of trials are prospective. Instead, in each case we held the rule inapplicable to statutes which changed the legal consequences of past conduct by imposing new or different liabilities based upon such conduct.

Tapia also interprets our opinion in People v. Hayes, *supra*, 49 Cal.3d 1260, 265 Cal.Rptr. 132, 783 P.2d 719, as supporting his position. It does not. In *Hayes* we considered the effect of Evidence Code section 795, which requires the exclusion of prehypnotic testimony unless certain statutory procedures were followed at the time of hypnosis. As in our previous cases, we began by reaffirming the presumption that new statutes operate prospectively and proceeded to determine what "prospective" operation meant in the case before us. We did not hold that the statute would apply, or not, based upon the date the alleged crime was committed. Instead, we looked to the date of the conduct regulated by the statute. Because the prehypnotic evidence in question predated the statute, we held that "[t]o invoke section 795 to exclude such evidence . . . would be tantamount to giving the statute retroactive effect." The past conduct to which the statute attached legal consequences was the use of hypnosis; the date of the offense was irrelevant.

III.

Tapia next argues that a definition of "retrospective law" originally formulated in American States W.S. Co. v. Johnson (1939) 31 Cal.App.2d

606, 613, 88 P.2d 770 (*American States*), encompasses—and thus prohibits—the application of a new law to the prosecution of crimes committed before the law's effective date. In *American States*, the Court of Appeal defined a retrospective law "[as] one which affects rights, obligations, acts, transactions and conditions which are performed or exist prior to the adoption of the statute." We repeated the *American States* formulation in *Evangelatos*. Based upon this formulation, Tapia argues that a law addressing the conduct of trials, such as the new voir dire provision, "affects [a] right [ ] ... which ... exist[ed] prior to the adoption of the statute," the right in question being the supposed right to have voir dire conducted under the law existing at the time of the offense.

As the foregoing examination of our opinions demonstrates, however, we have not invoked the *American States* formulation to justify such a result. Tapia's argument appears to be an effort to incorporate into the definition of "retrospectivity" the now obsolete concept of "substantial protections." It was formerly held that a law violated the constitutional prohibition against ex post facto legislation if it eliminated a "substantial protection," whether substantive or procedural, existing at the time of the offense. However, the United States Supreme Court has repudiated that analysis. (Collins v. Youngblood (1990) 497 U.S. 37, 110 S.Ct. 2715, 2719, 111 L.Ed.2d 30 (*Collins*).) Although we have employed the federal concept of "substantial protections" in deciding questions under the ex post facto clause, the concept has never formed a part of the definition of "retrospectivity" in the context of statutory construction.

IV.

Finally, Tapia argues that our opinion in *People v. Smith, supra, 34 Cal.3d 251, 193 Cal.Rptr. 692, 667 P.2d 149 (Smith), dictates a contrary result. In* Smith *we held that the provisions of Proposition 8, the "Victims Bill of Rights," would apply only to prosecutions of offenses committed after the measure's effective date. We did not distinguish between provisions which addressed the defendant's criminal behavior and provisions which addressed the conduct of trials.*

The defendant in *Smith* was found guilty of robbery after the trial court denied his motion to suppress a confession. On appeal, defendant argued that his confession had been obtained in violation of the California Constitution. Proposition 8 took effect after we granted review and long after the defendant's crime and trial. One provision of that measure amended the California Constitution to provide that "relevant evidence shall not be excluded in any criminal proceeding." (Cal. Const., art. I, § 28, subd. (d).) We held that Proposition 8 could not be applied to validate the trial court's ruling, erroneous at the time it was made, denying the motion to suppress. Thus, the narrow question immediately before us in *Smith* was truly one of retrospectivity, that is, whether a new rule should be applied to change "the legal effects of past events."

In *Smith*, going beyond the facts of the case, we also held that Proposition 8 in its entirety would apply only to crimes committed after the measure's effective date. Because Proposition 115, like Proposition 8, includes various types of provisions, Tapia argues that we should follow the same approach in this case. However, the reasons supporting our decision in *Smith* do not dictate the same result in the case now before us.

The first reason we gave for our decision was that the "*primary* stated purpose of Proposition 8 [was] to deter the commission of crimes." Based on that purpose, we concluded that the electorate "must have intended the measure to apply only to offenses that *could* be deterred, i.e., that had not already been committed by the time Proposition 8 was adopted." In contrast, the voters in adopting Proposition 115 expressly declared that their purposes were to reduce the unnecessary "costs of criminal cases" and to "create a system in which justice is swift and fair...." (Prop. 115, § 1, subds. (b), (c).) We can best effectuate this purpose by giving the earliest possible application to reforms designed to accelerate the adjudication of criminal cases.

The second reason we gave for our decision in *Smith* was the desire to avoid resolving doubts about the initiative's constitutionality arising from the rule against ex post facto legislation. In 1983, when we decided *Smith*, some authorities suggested that even procedural reforms might violate the rule against ex post facto legislation unless they left "untouched all the *substantial protections* with which existing law surround[ed] the person accused of crime" at the time the crime was committed.

The United States Supreme Court has greatly simplified ex post facto law since *Smith*. In *Collins, supra,* the high court endorsed its earlier formulation of the law in Calder v. Bull (1798) 3 U.S. (3 Dall.) 386, 390, 1 L.Ed. 648 (*Calder*), and Beazell v. Ohio (1925) 269 U.S. 167, 169–170, 46 S.Ct. 68, 68–69, 70 L.Ed. 216 (Beazell), as "faithful to our best knowledge of the original understanding" of the ex post facto clause. (*Collins, supra,* 497 U.S. at p. 43, 110 S.Ct. at p. 2719.) Under that exclusive formulation, " 'any statute [1] which punishes as a crime an act previously committed, which was innocent when done; [2] which makes more burdensome the punishment for a crime, after its commission, or [3] which deprives one charged with crime of any defense available according to law at the time when the act was committed, is prohibited as *ex post facto*.' "[75] (*Collins, supra,* 497 U.S. at p. 43, 110 S.Ct. at p. 2719, quoting *Beazell, supra,* 269 U.S. at pp. 169–170, 46 S.Ct. at pp. 68–69.)

---

75. In Calder, the Supreme Court also suggested, as a fourth category of ex post facto law, that a legislative act would be ex post facto if it "alters the legal rules of evidence, and receives less, or different, testimony, than the law required at the time of the commission of the offense, in order to convict the offender." (Calder, supra, 3 U.S. at p. 391, italics in original; see Collins, supra, 497 U.S. at p. 43, 110 S.Ct. at p. 2719.) However, "[a]s cases subsequent to Calder make clear, this language was not intended to prohibit the application of new evidentiary rules in trials for crimes committed before the changes."

In People v. Bradford (1969) 70 Cal.2d 333, 74 Cal.Rptr. 726, 450 P.2d 46, we described the fourth Calder category as "dictum" and declined to give it literal effect. Relying on cases in which the high court had also declined to apply the fourth category (Hopt v. Utah (1884) 110 U.S. 574, 588–589, 4 S.Ct. 202, 209–210, 28 L.Ed. 262; Thompson v. Missouri (1898) 171 U.S. 380, 386, 18 S.Ct. 922, 924, 43 L.Ed. 204), we held it "unmistakably clear ... that changes in the rules of evidence which broaden the class of persons competent to testify are not deemed ex post facto in operation." (People v. Bradford, supra, 70 Cal.2d at p. 344, fn. 5, 74 Cal.Rptr. 726, 450 P.2d 46.)

In *Collins* the Supreme Court also rejected the proposition that a law violates the ex post facto clause simply because it eliminates a "substantial protection" existing at the time an offense was committed.[76] According to the high court, references in its earlier cases "to 'substantial protections' and 'personal rights' should not be read to adopt without explanation an undefined enlargement of the [ex post facto clause]." (Collins, supra, 497 U.S. at pp. 46–47, 110 S.Ct. at p. 2721.) While the Legislature, or the electorate, cannot immunize a law from scrutiny under the ex post facto clause simply by labelling it "procedural," "the prohibition which may not be evaded is the one defined by the *Calder* categories."

Accordingly, the United States Supreme Court has resolved the analytical difficulty which led us to conclude in Smith that it would be impractical to consider ex post facto challenges to Proposition 8's provisions on a case-by-case basis. After Collins, we need not determine "how substantial is the right that the statute impairs and how significant is that impairment." (Smith, supra, 34 Cal.3d at p. 260, 193 Cal.Rptr. 692, 667 P.2d 149.) Instead, we can resolve such challenges by applying the exclusive *Calder* categories.

Lastly on this point, Tapia argues that we should perpetuate "substantial protection" analysis by adopting it as a matter of state law. We decline to do so. While we unquestionably have the power to interpret a provision of the state Constitution differently than its federal counterpart (Cal. Const., art. I, § 24), neither the language nor the history of the state ex post facto clause supports a different interpretation.

. . .

As the high court's recent opinion in *Collins*, demonstrates, our apparent reluctance to employ "substantial protection" analysis was justified. Federal law had compelled us to follow that analysis, since we were never free to adopt an ex post facto rule less favorable to the defense than the federal rule. After Collins, there is no reason not to return to the original understanding of the scope of the rule against ex post facto laws expressed in both federal and state constitutions.

The third reason we gave for our decision in *Smith* was the desire to "avoid a number of practical consequences adverse to the administration of justice and the right of fair trial." As we have already discussed, the intervening simplification of ex post facto law eliminates the major administrative difficulty that we foresaw in *Smith*. Although we cannot altogether avoid further litigation concerning Proposition 115's application in particular cases, we must weigh that administrative burden against the substantial benefits that immediate application of the measure offers by reducing time spent in voir dire and preliminary hearings, among other things. On balance, considerations of administrative efficiency, as well as the electorate's stated goals of reducing delay and unnecessary cost, favor giving Proposition 115 the earliest possible application.

---

76. The high court overruled Kring v. Missouri (1883) 107 U.S. 221, 2 S.Ct. 443, 27 L.Ed. 506, and Thompson v. Utah, supra, 170 U.S. 343, 18 S.Ct. 620, 42 L.Ed. 1061, which had been cited as support for the proposition. (Collins, supra, 497 U.S. at pp. 50–53, 110 S.Ct. at pp. 2723–2724.)

V.

It remains to be determined which of Proposition 115's provisions may and may not be applied to the prosecution of crimes committed before the measure's effective date. The provisions fall into four categories: (A) provisions which change the legal consequences of criminal behavior to the detriment of defendants; (B) provisions which address the conduct of trials; (C) provisions which clearly benefit defendants; and (D) a single provision which codifies existing law.

A.

The first category of provisions, those which change the legal consequences of criminal behavior to the detriment of defendants, cannot be applied to crimes committed before the measure's effective date. These provisions include section 9 (amending Pen.Code, § 189), which adds crimes to the list of felonies supporting a conviction of first degree murder. . . .

Application of these provisions to crimes committed before the measure's effective date would be "retrospective" because each would change the legal consequences of the defendant's past conduct. Such application would also likely violate the rule against ex post facto legislation, since each of these provisions appears to define conduct as a crime, to increase punishment for a crime, or to eliminate a defense. Accordingly, these provisions may only be applied to prosecutions of crimes committed on or after June 6, 1990.

B.

Other provisions of Proposition 115 address the conduct of trials rather than the definition of, punishment for, or defenses to crimes. . . .

[T]he provisions . . . may be applied to pending cases regardless of when the charged offense is alleged to have occurred.

C.

The third category of new provisions consists of those which clearly benefit only defendants. . . .

Application of these provisions to trials of crimes committed before Proposition 115's operative date may change the legal consequences of a defendant's criminal conduct. Such application is permissible, however, because the provisions favor defendants. . . .

D.

Finally, section 10 also codifies the rule of People v. Anderson, *supra*, 43 Cal.3d 1104, 240 Cal.Rptr. 585, 742 P.2d 1306, to the effect that an actual killer, for a special circumstance to be found true, need not have had the intent to kill unless the applicable special circumstance specifically so requires. This provision, which does not change existing law, may be applied to crimes committed before Proposition 115's effective date.

DISPOSITION

The alternative writ is discharged. The judgment of the Court of Appeal is affirmed.

■ LUCAS, C.J., and KENNARD, ARABIAN and BAXTER, JJ., concur.[77]

■ MOSK, JUSTICE, dissents.

Bouie v. City of Columbia

Supreme Court of the United States, 1964.
378 U.S. 347, 84 S.Ct. 1697, 12 L.Ed.2d 894.

[A South Carolina statute provided: "Every entry upon the lands of another ... after notice from the owner or tenant prohibiting such entry, shall be a misdemeanor and punished...." Petitioners who had received no such notice entered a restaurant where they were not wanted and sat down at the counter. Having refused to leave when ordered to do so, they were arrested and charged with criminal trespass under the statute quoted above. On this charge they were convicted and this conviction was affirmed by the state court which construed the statute to cover not only "the act of entry on the premises of another after receiving notice not to enter, but also the act of remaining on the premises of another after receiving notice to leave." The Supreme Court granted certiorari.]

■ MR. JUSTICE BRENNAN delivered the opinion of the Court....

We think it clear that the South Carolina Supreme Court, in applying its new construction of the statute to affirm these convictions, has deprived petitioners of rights guaranteed to them by the Due Process Clause. If South Carolina had applied to this case its new statute prohibiting the act of remaining on the premises of another after being asked to leave, the constitutional proscription of *ex post facto* laws would clearly invalidate the convictions. The Due Process Clause compels the same result here, where the State has sought to achieve precisely the same effect by judicial construction of the statute. While such a construction is of course valid for the future, it may not be applied retroactively, any more than a legislative enactment may be, to impose criminal penalties for conduct committed at a time when it was not fairly stated to be criminal. Application of this rule is particularly compelling where, as here, the petitioners' conduct cannot be deemed improper or immoral....

---

77. California statute's alteration of parole procedures to decrease the frequency of parole suitability hearing in certain cases did not violate the ex post facto clause when applied to a person who was convicted prior to the amendment. California Dept. of Corrections v. Morales, 514 U.S. 499, 115 S.Ct. 1597 (1995).

If **D** was convicted of a crime that was then a felony, this conviction may be relied upon as a prior felony even if because of an amendment it is now a misdemeanor. Ibid.

Enhancement of defendant's sentence under California determinate sentence law was not in violation of bar against ex post facto laws where convictions which occurred prior to the new law were used to enhance the sentence. People v. Williams, 140 Cal.App.3d 445, 189 Cal.Rptr. 497 (1983).

In the last analysis the case is controlled, we think, by the principle which Chief Justice Marshall stated for the Court in United States v. Wiltberger, 5 Wheat. 76, 96, 5 L.Ed. 37:

"The case must be a strong one indeed, which would justify a Court in departing from the plain meaning of words, especially in a penal act, in search of an intention which the words themselves did not suggest. To determine that a case is within the intention of a statute, its language must authorise us to say so. It would be dangerous, indeed, to carry the principle, that a case which is within the reason or mischief of a statute, is within its provisions, so far as to punish a crime not enumerated in the statute, because it is of equal atrocity, or of kindred character, with those which are enumerated...."

The crime for which these petitioners stand convicted was "not enumerated in the statute" at the time of their conduct. It follows that they have been deprived of liberty and property without due process of law in contravention of the Fourteenth Amendment.

Reversed.[78]

---

78. Whether due process is violated by a judicial interpretation of a criminal statute depends on whether the interpretation was foreseeable. United States v. Capps, 77 F.3d 350 (10th Cir.1996). Ex post facto principles are applied to decide the due process issue. Lustgarden v. Gunter, 966 F.2d 552 (10th Cir.1992).

The principles of ex post facto prohibitions applies to judicial decisions in California. People v. King, 5 Cal.4th 59, 19 Cal.Rptr.2d 233, 851 P.2d 27 (1993). See also People v. Granados, 172 Ill.2d 358, 217 Ill.Dec. 253, 666 N.E.2d 1191 (1996).

Judicial decisions are not subject to ex post facto prohibition. Petersen v. Utah Bd. of Pardons, 907 P.2d 1148 (Utah 1995).

Ex post facto prohibitions of the State and Federal Constitutions apply only to penal and criminal actions, not civil actions, even where civil consequences are serious in nature. Hills v. Iowa Dept. Of Transp. and Motor Vehicle Div., 534 N.W.2d 640 (Iowa 1995). Accord Police Ass'n of New Orleans v. City of New Orleans, 649 So.2d 951 (La.1995).

A law may be ex post facto if the legislative purpose in adopting it was punitive rather than regulatory. State v. Ward, 123 Wash. 2d 488, 869 P.2d 1062 (1994).

CHAPTER 13

AN OVERVIEW OF CRIMINAL PROCEDURE: INVESTIGATION

Historical Introduction

When the United States ratified the Constitution of 1789, the criminal process closely resembled that in England. There was no paramilitary police force of the modern type. The military might be called out to suppress riots and insurrections. Detecting offenses and apprehending offenders, however, rested largely in private hands. Such law-enforcement offices as there were, such as the sheriff and the constable, were part-time posts, too few in number and too limited in force to overcome opposition without the assistance of volunteers, whether collected *ad hoc* or organized as the posse.

The key official in the process of this time was the justice of the peace. If citizens reported an offense, the jp could issue warrants to arrest and search. When private persons, or the sheriff or the constable, made an arrest, whether with or without a warrant, they presented the prisoner and the witnesses to the jp for examination. Under the so-called Marian commital statutes, the jp would take sworn statements, in writing, from the witnesses, and a written statement, unsworn, from the prisoner. In felony cases the prisoner would then be either jailed or bound over for the next term of court, and the witnesses would put under recognizances to appear at the same time.

When the felony court session came around, the grand jury would meet to consider the cases of prisoners either bailed by the jp or jailed for lack of sufficient sureties. Private persons could also tender accusations directly to the grand jury. A court clerk would draw up the bills of indictment in appropriate language and the grand jurors would prefer an indictment or return a no-true bill. Trial of those indicted followed promptly, with the prosecution conducted by the victim, the victim's family, or an attorney retained by them. The American colonies had ignored, or superseded by charter or other enactment, the English common-law rule prohibiting defense counsel at felony trials, but there was no universal practice of appointing counsel for the indigent. The rules of evidence focused on the competence of witnesses to be heard under oath in court; parties, including the criminal defendant, spouses of parties, heretics, and felons were all disqualified. Convicted defendants could move to arrest the judgment before sentence, but plenary appellate review of the trial for legal error was unknown.

During the nineteenth century the various American political subdivisions created professional police departments. Prosecution became an increasingly, and ultimately exclusively, public function. Defense lawyers became the norm, at least for those defendants who refused to plead guilty,

1233

even if not all jurisdictions made it official policy to appoint counsel for the indigent in all cases. The witness-incapacity rules were abolished. The penitentiary replaced the gallows as the standard punishment, facilitating the practice of plea bargaining. With the decline of the idea that juries should judge law as well as fact, review of criminal convictions for legal error became standard.

The law-enforcement bureaucracy that emerged from the nineteenth century reforms had vastly more capacity for effective social control than the eighteenth century arrangement. Police and prosecutors, however, operated without significant oversight or legal accountability. The Wickersham Commission, appointed by President Hoover to study various aspects of Prohibition-era criminal justice, famously documented "lawlessness in law enforcement" in a 1931 report. The situation in the South, where even grossly unfair investigations and trials struggled to displace open lynch law, was certainly no better than in the big cities studied by the commission.

During the 1930s the Supreme Court began to intervene in the process of criminal justice in the states. It did so under the authority of the Fourteenth Amendment's due process clause, rather than the more particular language of the Fourth, Fifth and Sixth Amendments. The Court articulated the due process test as requiring "fundamental fairness" judged by "the totality of the circumstances." "Involuntary confessions" and physical evidence obtained by "shocking" police methods were suppressed. Counsel was required for defendants facing capital charges or other "special circumstances."

The modern law of criminal procedure rests on a foundation laid between 1961 and 1970, when the Warren Court read the Fourteenth Amendment to apply the Fourth Amendment exclusionary rule, the Fifth Amendment privilege against self-incrimination, and the Sixth Amendment's counsel, confrontation, and jury-trial rights against the states. Statute law, important as it is, has grown up in response to perceived shortcomings or perceived excesses in the constitutional law; Title III of the 1968 Crime Control Act, authorizing and regulating electronic surveillance, is a leading illustration.

We begin, then, with a sample of the Warren Court's "criminal procedure revolution." We then look to some illustrative rulings by the Burger and Rehnquist courts—rulings that qualified, but did not overrule, the Warren Court landmarks. Finally, we turn to contemporary cases reflecting current doctrine.

SECTION 1. THE WARREN COURT LANDMARKS

Mapp v. Ohio

Supreme Court of the United States, 1961.
367 U.S. 643, 81 S.Ct. 1684, 6 L.Ed.2d 1081.

■ MR. JUSTICE CLARK delivered the opinion of the Court.

Appellant stands convicted of knowingly having had in her possession and under her control certain lewd and lascivious books, pictures, and photographs in violation of § 2905.34 of Ohio's Revised Code. As officially stated in the syllabus to its opinion, the Supreme Court of Ohio found that her conviction was valid though "based primarily upon the introduction in evidence of lewd and lascivious books and pictures unlawfully seized during an unlawful search of defendant's home * * *." 170 Ohio St. 427–428, 166 N.E.2d 387, 388.

On May 23, 1957, three Cleveland police officers arrived at appellant's residence in that city pursuant to information that "a person (was) hiding out in the home, who was wanted for questioning in connection with a recent bombing, and that there was a large amount of policy paraphernalia being hidden in the home." Miss Mapp and her daughter by a former marriage lived on the top floor of the two-family dwelling. Upon their arrival at that house, the officers knocked on the door and demanded entrance but appellant, after telephoning her attorney, refused to admit them without a search warrant. They advised their headquarters of the situation and undertook a surveillance of the house.

The officers again sought entrance some three hours later when four or more additional officers arrived on the scene. When Miss Mapp did not come to the door immediately, at least one of the several doors to the house was forcibly opened[2] and the policemen gained admittance. Meanwhile Miss Mapp's attorney arrived, but the officers, having secured their own entry, and continuing in their defiance of the law, would permit him neither to see Miss Mapp nor to enter the house. It appears that Miss Mapp was halfway down the stairs from the upper floor to the front door when the officers, in this highhanded manner, broke into the hall. She demanded to see the search warrant. A paper, claimed to be a warrant, was held up by one of the officers. She grabbed the "warrant" and placed it in her bosom. A struggle ensued in which the officers recovered the piece of paper and as a result of which they handcuffed appellant because she had been "belligerent" in resisting their official rescue of the "warrant" from her person. Running roughshod over appellant, a policeman "grabbed" her, "twisted (her) hand," and she "yelled (and) pleaded with him" because "it was hurting." Appellant, in handcuffs, was then forcibly taken upstairs to her bedroom where the officers searched a dresser, a chest of drawers, a closet and some suitcases. They also looked into a photo album and through personal papers belonging to the appellant. The search spread to the rest of the second floor including the child's bedroom, the living room, the kitchen and a dinette. The basement of the building and a trunk found therein were also searched. The obscene materials for possession of which she was ultimately convicted were discovered in the course of that widespread search.

At the trial no search warrant was produced by the prosecution, nor was the failure to produce one explained or accounted for. At best, "There

---

2. A police officer testified that "we did pry the screen door to gain entrance"; the attorney on the scene testified that a policeman "tried * * * to kick in the door" and then "broke the glass in the door and somebody reached in and opened the door and let them in"; the appellant testified that "The back door was broken."

is, in the record, considerable doubt as to whether there ever was any warrant for the search of defendant's home." 170 Ohio St. at page 430, 166 N.E.2d at page 389. The Ohio Supreme Court believed a "reasonable argument" could be made that the conviction should be reversed "because the 'methods' employed to obtain the (evidence) were such as to 'offend a sense of justice,'" but the court found determinative the fact that the evidence had not been taken "from defendant's person by the use of brutal or offensive physical force against defendant." 170 Ohio St. at page 431, 166 N.E.2d at pages 389–390.

The State says that even if the search were made without authority, or otherwise unreasonably, it is not prevented from using the unconstitutionally seized evidence at trial, citing Wolf v. People of State of Colorado, 1949, 338 U.S. 25, at page 33, 69 S.Ct. 1359. at page 1364, 93 L.Ed. 1782, in which this Court did indeed hold "that in a prosecution in a State court for a State crime the Fourteenth Amendment does not forbid the admission of evidence obtained by an unreasonable search and seizure." On this appeal, of which we have noted probable jurisdiction, 364 U.S. 868, 81 S.Ct. 111, 5 L.Ed.2d 90, it is urged once again that we review that holding.[3]

I.

Seventy-five years ago, in Boyd v. United States, 1886, 116 U.S. 616, 630, 6 S.Ct. 524, 532, 29 L.Ed. 746, considering the Fourth and Fifth Amendments as running "almost into each other"[5] on the facts before it, this Court held that the doctrines of those Amendments "apply to all invasions on the part of the government and its employes of the sanctity of a man's home and the privacies of life. It is not the breaking of his doors, and the rummaging of his drawers, that constitutes the essence of the offence; but it is the invasion of his indefeasible right of personal security, personal liberty and private property * * *. Breaking into a house and opening boxes and drawers are circumstances of aggravation; but any forcible and compulsory extortion of a man's own testimony or of his private papers to be used as evidence to convict him of crime or to forfeit his goods, is within the condemnation * * * (of those Amendments)."

The Court noted that "constitutional provisions for the security of person and property should be liberally construed. * * * It is the duty of courts to be watchful for the constitutional rights of the citizen, and against any stealthy encroachments thereon." In this jealous regard for

---

3. Other issues have been raised on this appeal but, in the view we have taken of the case, they need not be decided. Although appellant chose to urge what may have appeared to be the surer ground for favorable disposition and did not insist that Wolf be overruled, the amicus curiae, who was also permitted to participate in the oral argument, did urge the Court to overrule Wolf.

5. The close connection between the concepts later embodied in these two Amendments had been noted at least as early as 1765 by Lord Camden, on whose opinion in Entick v. Carrington, 19 Howell's State Trials 1029, the Boyd court drew heavily. Lord Camden had noted, at 1073:

"It is very certain, that the law obligeth no man to accuse himself; because the necessary means of compelling self-accusation, falling upon the innocent as well as the guilty, would be both cruel and unjust; and it should seem, that search for evidence is disallowed upon the same principle. There too the innocent would be confounded with the guilty."

maintaining the integrity of individual rights, the Court gave life to Madison's prediction that "independent tribunals of justice * * * will be naturally led to resist every encroachment upon rights expressly stipulated for in the Constitution by the declaration of rights." I Annals of Cong. 439 (1789). Concluding, the Court specifically referred to the use of the evidence there seized as "unconstitutional." At page 638 of 116 U.S., at page 536 of 6 S.Ct.

Less than 30 years after Boyd, this Court, in Weeks v. United States, 1914, 232 U.S. 383, at pages 391–392, 34 S.Ct. 341, at page 344, 58 L.Ed. 652, stated that

> "the 4th Amendment * * * put the courts of the United States and Federal officials, in the exercise of their power and authority, under limitations and restraints (and) * * * forever secure(d) the people, their persons, houses, papers, and effects, against all unreasonable searches and seizures under the guise of law * * * and the duty of giving to it force and effect is obligatory upon all entrusted under our Federal system with the enforcement of the laws."

Specifically dealing with the use of the evidence unconstitutionally seized, the Court concluded:

> "If letters and private documents can thus be seized and held and used in evidence against a citizen accused of an offense, the protection of the Fourth Amendment declaring his right to be secure against such searches and seizures is of no value, and, so far as those thus placed are concerned, might as well be stricken from the Constitution. The efforts of the courts and their officials to bring the guilty to punishment, praiseworthy as they are, are not to be aided by the sacrifice of those great principles established by years of endeavor and suffering which have resulted in their embodiment in the fundamental law of the land." At page 393 of 232 U.S., at page 344 of 34 S.Ct.

Finally, the Court in that case clearly stated that use of the seized evidence involved "a denial of the constitutional rights of the accused." At page 398 of 232 U.S., at page 346 of 34 S.Ct. Thus, in the year 1914, in the Weeks case, this Court "for the first time" held that "in a federal prosecution the Fourth Amendment barred the use of evidence secured through an illegal search and seizure." Wolf v. People of State of Colorado, supra, 338 U.S. at page 28, 69 S.Ct. at page 1361. This Court has ever since required of federal law officers a strict adherence to that command which this Court has held to be a clear, specific, and constitutionally required—even if judicially implied—deterrent safeguard without insistence upon which the Fourth Amendment would have been reduced to "a form of words." Holmes J., Silverthorne Lumber Co. v. United States, 1920, 251 U.S. 385, 392, 40 S.Ct. 182, 183, 64 L.Ed. 319. It meant, quite simply, that "conviction by means of unlawful seizures and enforced confessions * * * should find no sanction in the judgments of the courts * * *," Weeks v. United States, supra, 232 U.S. at page 392, 34 S.Ct. at page 344, and that such evidence "shall not be used at all." Silverthorne Lumber Co. v. United States, supra, 251 U.S. at page 392, 40 S.Ct. at page 183. . . .

II.

In 1949, 35 years after Weeks was announced, this Court, in Wolf v. People of State of Colorado, supra, again for the first time, discussed the effect of the Fourth Amendment upon the States through the operation of the Due Process Clause of the Fourteenth Amendment. [T]he Court decided that the Weeks exclusionary rule would not then be imposed upon the States as "an essential ingredient of the right."

... While in 1949, prior to the Wolf case, almost two-thirds of the States were opposed to the use of the exclusionary rule, now, despite the Wolf case, more than half of those since passing upon it, by their own legislative or judicial decision, have wholly or partly adopted or adhered to the Weeks rule. See Elkins v. United States, 1960, 364 U.S. 206, Appendix, at pages 224–232, 80 S.Ct. 1437, at pages 1448–1453, 4 L.Ed.2d 1669. Significantly, among those now following the rule is California, which, according to its highest court, was "compelled to reach that conclusion because other remedies have completely failed to secure compliance with the constitutional provisions * * *." People v. Cahan, 1955, 44 Cal.2d 434, 445, 282 P.2d 905, 911, 50 A.L.R.2d 513. In connection with this California case, we note that the second basis elaborated in Wolf in support of its failure to enforce the exclusionary doctrine against the States was that "other means of protection" have been afforded "the right to privacy."[7] The experience of California that such other remedies have been worthless and futile is buttressed by the experience of other States. The obvious futility of relegating the Fourth Amendment of the protection of other remedies has, moreover, been recognized by this Court since Wolf. See Irvine v. People of State of California, 1954, 347 U.S. 128, 137, 74 S.Ct. 381, 385, 98 L.Ed. 561....

It, therefore, plainly appears that the factual considerations supporting the failure of the *Wolf* Court to include the Weeks exclusionary rule when it recognized the enforceability of the right to privacy against the States in 1949, while not basically relevant to the constitutional consideration, could not, in any analysis, now be deemed controlling.

III.

... Today we once again examine Wolf's constitutional documentation of the right to privacy free from unreasonable state intrusion, and, after its dozen years on our books, are led by it to close the only courtroom door remaining open to evidence secured by official lawlessness in flagrant abuse of that basic right, reserved to all persons as a specific guarantee against that very same unlawful conduct. We hold that all evidence obtained by searches and seizures in violation of the Constitution is, by that same authority, inadmissible in a state court.

IV.

Since the Fourth Amendment's right of privacy has been declared enforceable against the States through the Due Process Clause of the

---

7. Less than half of the States have any criminal provisions relating directly to unreasonable searches and seizures. [The Court reviews the statutes of the 23 other states.]

Fourteenth, it is enforceable against them by the same sanction of exclusion as is used against the Federal Government. Were it otherwise, then just as without the Weeks rule the assurance against unreasonable federal searches and seizures would be "a form of words", valueless and undeserving of mention in a perpetual charter of inestimable human liberties, so too, without that rule the freedom from state invasions of privacy would be so ephemeral and so neatly severed from its conceptual nexus with the freedom from all brutish means of coercing evidence as not to merit this Court's high regard as a freedom "implicit in 'the concept of ordered liberty.'" At the time that the Court held in *Wolf* that the Amendment was applicable to the States through the Due Process Clause, the cases of this Court, as we have seen, had steadfastly held that as to federal officers the Fourth Amendment included the exclusion of the evidence seized in violation of its provisions. Even *Wolf* "stoutly adhered" to that proposition. The right to privacy, when conceded operatively enforceable against the States, was not susceptible of destruction by avulsion of the sanction upon which its protection and enjoyment had always been deemed dependent under the *Boyd, Weeks* and *Silverthorne* cases. Therefore, in extending the substantive protections of due process to all constitutionally unreasonable searches—state or federal—it was logically and constitutionally necessary that the exclusion doctrine—an essential part of the right to privacy—be also insisted upon as an essential ingredient of the right newly recognized by the Wolf case. In short, the admission of the new constitutional right by *Wolf* could not consistently tolerate denial of its most important constitutional privilege, namely, the exclusion of the evidence which an accused had been forced to give by reason of the unlawful seizure. To hold otherwise is to grant the right but in reality to withhold its privilege and enjoyment. Only last year the Court itself recognized that the purpose of the exclusionary rule "is to deter—to compel respect for the constitutional guaranty in the only effectively available way—by removing the incentive to disregard it." Elkins v. United States, supra, 364 U.S. at page 217, 80 S.Ct. at page 1444.

Indeed, we are aware of no restraint, similar to that rejected today, conditioning the enforcement of any other basic constitutional right. The right to privacy, no less important than any other right carefully and particularly reserved to the people, would stand in marked contrast to all other rights declared as "basic to a free society." Wolf v. People of State of Colorado, supra, 338 U.S. at page 27, 69 S.Ct. at page 1361. This Court has not hesitated to enforce as strictly against the States as it does against the Federal Government the rights of free speech and of a free press, the rights to notice and to a fair, public trial, including, as it does, the right not to be convicted by use of a coerced confession, however logically relevant it be, and without regard to its reliability. Rogers v. Richmond, 1961, 365 U.S. 534, 81 S.Ct. 735, 5 L.Ed.2d 760. And nothing could be more certain that when a coerced confession is involved, "the relevant rules of evidence" are overridden without regard to "the incidence of such conduct by the police," slight or frequent. Why should the same rule not apply to what is tantamount to coerced testimony by way of unconstitutional seizure of goods, papers, effect, documents, etc.? We find that, as to the Federal Government, the Fourth and Fifth Amendments and, as to the States, the freedom from unconscionable invasions of privacy and the freedom from convictions based upon coerced confessions do enjoy an "intimate relation" in their perpetuation of "principles of humanity and civil liberty (secured) * * * only after years of struggle." Bram v. United States, 1897, 168 U.S. 532, 543–544, 18 S.Ct. 183, 187, 42 L.Ed. 568. They express "supplementing phases of the same constitutional purpose—to maintain inviolate large areas of personal privacy." Feldman v. United States, 1944, 322 U.S. 487, 489–490, 64 S.Ct. 1082, 1083, 88 L.Ed. 1408. The philosophy of each Amendment and of each freedom is complementary to, although not dependent upon, that of the other in its sphere of influence—the very least that together they assure in either sphere is that no man is to be convicted on unconstitutional evidence.

V.

... There are those who say, as did Justice (then Judge) Cardozo, that under our constitutional exclusionary doctrine "(t)he criminal is to go free because the constable has blundered." People v. Defore, 242 N.Y. at page 21, 150 N.E. at page 587. In some cases this will undoubtedly be the result. But ... "there is another consideration—the imperative of judicial integrity." 364 U.S. at page 222, 80 S.Ct. at page 1447. The criminal goes free, if he must, but it is the law that sets him free. Nothing can destroy a government more quickly than its failure to observe its own laws, or worse, its disregard of the charter of its own existence. As Mr. Justice Brandeis, dissenting, said in Olmstead v. United States, 1928, 277 U.S. 438, 485, 48 S.Ct. 564, 575, 72 L.Ed. 944: "Our government is the potent, the omnipresent teacher. For good or for ill, it teaches the whole people by its example. * * * If the government becomes a lawbreaker, it breeds contempt for law; it invites every man to become a law unto himself; it invites anarchy." Nor can it lightly be assumed that, as a practical matter, adoption of the exclusionary rule fetters law enforcement. Only last year this Court expressly considered that contention and found that "pragmatic evidence of a sort" to the contrary was not wanting. Elkins v. United States, supra, 364 U.S. at page 218, 80 S.Ct. at page 1444. The Court noted that

> "The federal courts themselves have operated under the exclusionary rule of Weeks for almost half a century; yet it has not been suggested either that the Federal Bureau of Investigation has thereby been rendered ineffective, or that the administration of criminal justice in the federal courts has thereby been disrupted. Moreover, the experience of the states is impressive * * *. The movement towards the rule of exclusion has been halting but seemingly inexorable." Id., 364 U.S. at pages 218–219, 80 S.Ct. at pages 1444–1445.

... Our decision, founded on reason and truth, gives to the individual no more than that which the Constitution guarantees him, to the police officer no less than that to which honest law enforcement is entitled, and, to the courts, that judicial integrity so necessary in the true administration of justice.

The judgment of the Supreme Court of Ohio is reversed and the cause remanded for further proceedings not inconsistent with this opinion.

Reversed and remanded.

■ Mr. Justice Black, concurring.

... I am still not persuaded that the Fourth Amendment, standing alone, would be enough to bar the introduction into evidence against an accused of papers and effects seized from him in violation of its commands. For the Fourth Amendment does not itself contain any provision expressly precluding the use of such evidence, and I am extremely doubtful that such a provision could properly be inferred from nothing more than the basic command against unreasonable searches and seizures. Reflection on the problem, however, in the light of cases coming before the Court since *Wolf*, has led me to conclude that when the Fourth Amendment's ban against unreasonable searches and seizures is considered together with the Fifth Amendment's ban against compelled self-incrimination, a constitutional basis emerges which not only justifies but actually requires the exclusionary rule.

The close interrelationship between the Fourth and Fifth Amendments, as they apply to this problem, has long been recognized and, indeed, has expressly made the ground for this Court's holding in *Boyd v. United States*. There the Court fully discussed this relationship and declared itself "unable to perceive that the seizure of a man's private books and papers to be used in evidence against him is substantially different from compelling him to be a witness against himself." ...

■ Mr. Justice Harlan, with whom Mr. Justice Frankfurter and Mr. Justice Whittaker join, dissenting.

In overruling the *Wolf* case the Court, in my opinion, has forgotten the sense of judicial restraint which, with due regard for stare decisis, is one element that should enter into deciding whether a past decision of this Court should be overruled. Apart from that I also believe that the Wolf rule represents sounder Constitutional doctrine than the new rule which now replaces it. . . .

At the heart of the majority's opinion in this case is the following syllogism: (1) the rule excluding in federal criminal trials evidence which is the product of all illegal search and seizure is a "part and parcel" of the Fourth Amendment; (2) *Wolf* held that the "privacy" assured against federal action by the Fourth Amendment is also protected against state action by the Fourteenth Amendment; and (3) it is therefore "logically and constitutionally necessary" that the Weeks exclusionary rule should also be enforced against the States.[10]

This reasoning ultimately rests on the unsound premise that because *Wolf* carried into the States, as part of "the concept of ordered liberty" embodied in the Fourteenth Amendment, the principle of "privacy" underlying the Fourth Amendment (338 U.S. at page 27, 69 S.Ct. at page 1361), it must follow that whatever configurations of the Fourth Amendment have been developed in the particularizing federal precedents are likewise to be deemed a part of "ordered liberty," and as such are enforceable against the States. For me, this does not follow at all. . . .

[The concurring opinion of Justice Douglas is omitted]

---

10. Actually, only four members of the majority support this reasoning.

Gideon v. Wainwright

Supreme Court of the United States, 1963.
372 U.S. 335, 83 S.Ct. 792, 9 L.Ed.2d 799.

■ MR. JUSTICE BLACK delivered the opinion of the Court.

Petitioner was charged in a Florida state court with having broken and entered a poolroom with intent to commit a misdemeanor. This offense is a felony under Florida law. Appearing in court without funds and without a lawyer, petitioner asked the court to appoint counsel for him, whereupon the following colloquy took place:

"The COURT: Mr. Gideon, I am sorry, but I cannot appoint Counsel to represent you in this case. Under the laws of the State of Florida, the only time the Court can appoint Counsel to represent a Defendant is when that person is charged with a capital offense. I am sorry, but I will have to deny your request to appoint Counsel to defend you in this case.

"The DEFENDANT: The United States Supreme Court says I am entitled to be represented by Counsel."

Put to trial before a jury, Gideon conducted his defense about as well as could be expected from a layman. He made an opening statement to the jury, cross-examined the State's witnesses, presented witnesses in his own defense, declined to testify himself, and made a short argument "emphasizing his innocence to the charge contained in the Information filed in this case." The jury returned a verdict of guilty, and petitioner was sentenced to serve five years in the state prison. Later, petitioner filed in the Florida Supreme Court this habeas corpus petition attacking his conviction and sentence on the ground that the trial court's refusal to appoint counsel for him denied him rights "guaranteed by the Constitution and the Bill of Rights by the United States Government." Treating the petition for habeas corpus as properly before it, the State Supreme Court, "upon consideration thereof" but without an opinion, denied all relief. Since 1942, when Betts v. Brady, 316 U.S. 455, 62 S.Ct. 1252, 86 L.Ed. 1595, was decided by a divided Court, the problem of a defendant's federal constitutional right to counsel in a state court has been a continuing source of controversy and litigation in both state and federal courts. To give this problem another review here, we granted certiorari. Since Gideon was proceeding *in forma pauperis,* we appointed counsel to represent him and requested both sides to discuss in their briefs and oral arguments the following: "Should this Court's holding in Betts v. Brady, 316 U.S. 455, 62 S.Ct. 1252, 86 L.Ed. 1595, be reconsidered?" . . .

Treating due process as "a concept less rigid and more fluid than those envisaged in other specific and particular provisions of the Bill of Rights," the Court held that refusal to appoint counsel under the particular facts and circumstances in the *Betts* case was not so "offensive to the common and fundamental ideas of fairness" as to amount to a denial of due process. Since the facts and circumstances of the two cases are so nearly indistinguishable, we think the *Betts v. Brady* holding if left standing would require us to reject Gideon's claim that the Constitution guarantees him the assistance of counsel. Upon full reconsideration we conclude that *Betts v. Brady* should be overruled. . . .

We accept *Betts v. Brady's* assumption, based as it was on our prior cases, that a provision of the Bill of Rights which is "fundamental and essential to a fair trial" is made obligatory upon the States by the Fourteenth Amendment. We think the Court in *Betts* was wrong, however, in concluding that the Sixth Amendment's guarantee of counsel is not one of these fundamental rights. Ten years before *Betts v. Brady,* this Court, after full consideration of all the historical data examined in *Betts,* had unequivocally declared that "the right to the aid of counsel is of this fundamental character." Powell v. Alabama, 287 U.S. 45, 68, 53 S.Ct. 55, 63, 77 L.Ed. 158 (1932). While the Court at the close of its *Powell* opinion did by its language, as this Court frequently does, limit its holding to the particular facts and circumstances of that case, its conclusions about the fundamental nature of the right to counsel are unmistakable. . . .

Not only these precedents but also reason and reflection require us to recognize that in our adversary system of criminal justice, any person haled into court, who is too poor to hire a lawyer, cannot be assured a fair trial unless counsel is provided for him. This seems to us to be an obvious truth. Governments, both state and federal, quite properly spend vast sums of money to establish machinery to try defendants accused of crime. Lawyers to prosecute are everywhere deemed essential to protect the public's interest in an orderly society. Similarly, there are few defendants charged with crime, few indeed, who fail to hire the best lawyers they can get to prepare and present their defenses. That government hires lawyers to prosecute and defendants who have the money hire lawyers to defend are the strongest indications of the widespread belief that lawyers in criminal courts are necessities, not luxuries. The right of one charged with crime to counsel may not be deemed fundamental and essential to fair trials in some countries, but it is in ours. From the very beginning, our state and national constitutions and laws have laid great emphasis on procedural and substantive safeguards designed to assure fair trials before impartial tribunals in which every defendant stands equal before the law. This noble ideal cannot be realized if the poor man charged with crime has to face his accusers without a lawyer to assist him. A defendant's need for a lawyer is nowhere better stated than in the moving words of Mr. Justice Sutherland in *Powell v. Alabama:*

"The right to be heard would be, in many cases, of little avail if it did not comprehend the right to be heard by counsel. Even the intelligent and educated layman has small and sometimes no skill in the science of law. If charged with crime, he is incapable, generally, of determining for himself whether the indictment is good or bad. He is unfamiliar with the rules of evidence. Left without the aid of counsel he may be put on trial without a proper charge, and convicted upon incompetent evidence, or evidence irrelevant to the issue or otherwise inadmissible. He lacks both the skill and knowledge adequately to prepare his defense, even though he have a perfect one. He requires the guiding hand of counsel at every step in the proceedings against him. Without it, though he be not guilty, he faces the danger of conviction because he does not know how to establish his innocence." 287 U.S., at 68–69, 53 S.Ct., at 64, 77 L.Ed. 158.

The Court in *Betts v. Brady* departed from the sound wisdom upon which the Court's holding in *Powell v. Alabama* rested. Florida, supported by two other States, has asked that *Betts v. Brady* be left intact. Twenty-two States, as friends of the Court, argue that *Betts* was "an anachronism when handed down" and that it should now be overruled. We agree.

The judgment is reversed and the cause is remanded to the Supreme Court of Florida for further action not inconsistent with this opinion.

Reversed.

■ Mr. Justice Douglas.... My brother Harlan is of the view that a guarantee of the Bill of Rights that is made applicable to the States by reason of the Fourteenth Amendment is a lesser version of that same guarantee as applied to the Federal Government. Mr. Justice Jackson shared that view. But that view has not prevailed and rights protected against state invasion by the Due Process Clause of the Fourteenth Amendment are not watered-down versions of what the Bill of Rights guarantees.

[The separate opinions of Justice Clark and Justice Harlan are omitted]

Miranda v. Arizona[1]

Supreme Court of the United States, 1966.
384 U.S. 436, 10 Ohio Misc. 9, 86 S.Ct. 1602, 16 L.Ed.2d 694.

■ Mr. Chief Justice Warren delivered the opinion of the Court.

The cases before us raise questions which go to the roots of our concepts of American criminal jurisprudence: the restraints society must observe consistent with the Federal Constitution in prosecuting individuals for crime. More specifically, we deal with the admissibility of statements obtained from an individual who is subjected to custodial police interrogation and the necessity for procedures which assure that the individual is accorded his privilege under the Fifth Amendment to the Constitution not to be compelled to incriminate himself....

The constitutional issue we decide in each of these cases is the admissibility of statements obtained from a defendant questioned while in custody and deprived of his freedom of action. In each, the defendant was questioned by police officers, detectives, or a prosecuting attorney in a room in which he was cut off from the outside world. In none of these cases was the defendant given a full and effective warning of his rights at the outset of the interrogation process. In all the cases, the questioning elicited oral admissions, and in three of them, signed statements as well which were admitted at their trials. They all thus share salient features—incommunicado interrogation of individuals in a police-dominated atmosphere, resulting in self-incriminating statements without full warnings of constitutional rights....

---

1. The defendant was later killed in a barroom brawl. Miranda Slain; Main Figure in Landmark Suspects' Rights Case, N.Y. Times, Feb. 1, 1976, § 1, at 28, col. 4.

Our holding will be spelled out with some specificity in the pages which follow but briefly stated it is this: the prosecution may not use statements, whether exculpatory or inculpatory, stemming from custodial interrogation of the defendant unless it demonstrates the use of procedural safeguards effective to secure the privilege against self-incrimination. By custodial interrogation, we mean questioning initiated by law enforcement officers after a person has been taken into custody or otherwise deprived of his freedom of action in any significant way.[2] As for the procedural safeguards to be employed, unless other fully effective means are devised to inform accused persons of their right of silence and to assure a continuous opportunity to exercise it, the following measures are required. Prior to any questioning, the person must be warned that he has a right to remain silent, that any statement he does make may be used as evidence against him, and that he has a right to the presence of an attorney, either retained or appointed. The defendant may waive effectuation of these rights, provided the waiver is made voluntarily, knowingly and intelligently. If, however, he indicates in any manner and at any stage of the process that he wishes to consult with an attorney before speaking there can be no questioning. Likewise, if the individual is alone and indicates in any manner that he does not wish to be interrogated, the police may not question him. The mere fact that he may have answered some questions or volunteered some statements on his own does not deprive him of the right to refrain from answering any further inquiries until he has consulted with an attorney and thereafter consents to be questioned.

The presence of an attorney, and the warnings delivered to the individual, enable the defendant under otherwise compelling circumstances to tell his story without fear, effectively, and in a way that eliminates the evils in the interrogation process. Without the protections flowing from adequate warning and the rights of counsel, "all the careful safeguards erected around the giving of testimony, whether by an accused or any other witness, would become empty formalities in a procedure where the most compelling possible evidence of guilt, a confession, would have already been obtained at the unsupervised pleasure of the police." . . .

In order fully to apprise a person interrogated of the extent of his rights under this system then, it is necessary to warn him not only that he has the right to consult with an attorney, but also that if he is indigent a lawyer will be appointed to represent him. Without this additional warning, the admonition of the right to consult with counsel would often be understood as meaning only that he can consult with a lawyer if he has one or has the funds to obtain one. The warning of a right to counsel would be hollow if not couched in terms that would convey to the indigent—the person most often subjected to interrogation—the knowledge that he too has a right to have counsel present.[3] As with the warnings of the right to remain silent and of the general right to counsel, only by effective and

---

2. This is what we meant in *Escobedo* when we spoke of an investigation which had focused on an accused.

3. Cf. United States ex rel. Brown v. Fay, 242 F.Supp. 273, 277 (S.D.N.Y.1965); People v. Witenski, 15 N.Y.2d 392, 259 N.Y.S.2d 413, 207 N.E.2d 358 (1965).

express explanation to the indigent of this right can there be assurance that he was truly in a position to exercise it.[4]

Once warnings have been given, the subsequent procedure is clear. If the individual indicates in any manner, at any time prior to or during questioning, that he wishes to remain silent, the interrogation must cease.[5] At this point he has shown that he intends to exercise his Fifth Amendment privilege; any statement taken after the person invokes his privilege cannot be other than the product of compulsion, subtle or otherwise. Without the right to cut off questioning, the setting of in-custody interrogation operates on the individual to overcome free choice in producing a statement after the privilege has been once invoked. If the individual states that he wants an attorney, the interrogation must cease until an attorney is present. At that time, the individual must have an opportunity to confer with the attorney and to have him present during any subsequent questioning. . . .

This does not mean, as some have suggested, that each police station must have a "station house lawyer" present at all times to advise prisoners. It does mean, however, that if police propose to interrogate a person they must make known to him that he is entitled to a lawyer and that if he cannot afford one, a lawyer will be provided for him prior to any interrogation. If authorities conclude that they will not provide counsel during a reasonable period of time in which investigation in the field is carried out, they may do so without violating the person's Fifth Amendment privilege so long as they do not question him during that time. . . .

In dealing with statements obtained through interrogation, we do not purport to find all confessions inadmissible. Confessions remain a proper element in law enforcement. Any statement given freely and voluntarily without any compelling influences is, of course, admissible in evidence. The fundamental import of the privilege while an individual is in custody is not whether he is allowed to talk to the police without the benefit of warnings and counsel, but whether he can be interrogated. There is no requirement that police stop a person who enters a police station and states that he wishes to confess to a crime,[6] or a person who calls the police to offer a confession or any other statement he desires to make. Volunteered statements of any kind are not barred by the Fifth Amendment and their admissibility is not affected by our holding today.

---

4. While a warning that the indigent may have counsel appointed need not be given to the person who is known to have an attorney or is known to have ample funds to secure one, the expedient of giving a warning is too simple and the rights involved too important to engage in *ex post facto* inquiries into financial ability when there is any doubt at all on that score.

5. If an individual indicates his desire to remain silent, but has an attorney present, there may be some circumstances in which further questioning would be permissible. In the absence of evidence of overbearing, statements then made in the presence of counsel might be free of the compelling influence of the interrogation process and might fairly be construed as a waiver of the privilege for purposes of these statements.

6. See People v. Dorado, 62 Cal.2d 338, 354, 42 Cal.Rptr. 169, 179, 398 P.2d 361, 371 (1965).

To summarize, we hold that when an individual is taken into custody or otherwise deprived of his freedom by the authorities and is subjected to questioning, the privilege against self-incrimination is jeopardized. Procedural safeguards must be employed to protect the privilege, and unless other fully effective means are adopted to notify the person of his right of silence and to assure that the exercise of the right will be scrupulously honored, the following measures are required. He must be warned prior to any questioning that he has the right to remain silent, that anything he says can be used against him in a court of law, that he has the right to the presence of an attorney, and that if he cannot afford an attorney one will be appointed for him prior to any questioning if he so desires. Opportunity to exercise these rights must be afforded to him throughout the interrogation. After such warnings have been given, and such opportunity afforded him, the individual may knowingly and intelligently waive these rights and agree to answer questions or make a statement. But unless and until such warnings and waiver are demonstrated by the prosecution at trial, no evidence obtained as a result of interrogation can be used against him. . . .

If the individual desires to exercise his privilege, he has the right to do so. This is not for the authorities to decide. An attorney may advise his client not to talk to police until he has had an opportunity to investigate the case, or he may wish to be present with his client during any police questioning. In doing so an attorney is merely exercising the good professional judgment he has been taught. This is not cause for considering the attorney a menace to law enforcement. He is merely carrying out what he is sworn to do under his oath—to protect to the extent of his ability the rights of his client. In fulfilling this responsibility the attorney plays a vital role in the administration of criminal justice under our Constitution. . . .

Over the years the Federal Bureau of Investigation has compiled an exemplary record of effective law enforcement while advising any suspect or arrested person, at the outset of an interview, that he is not required to make a statement, that any statement may be used against him in court, that the individual may obtain the services of an attorney of his own choice and, more recently, that he has a right to free counsel if he is unable to pay. . . .

Because of the nature of the problem and because of its recurrent significance in numerous cases, we have to this point discussed the relationship of the Fifth Amendment privilege to police interrogation without specific concentration on the facts of the cases before us. We turn now to these facts to consider the application to these cases of the constitutional principles discussed above. In each instance, we have concluded that statements were obtained from the defendant under circumstances that did not meet constitutional standards for protection of the privilege.

No. 759. Miranda v. Arizona.

On March 13, 1963, petitioner, Ernesto Miranda, was arrested at his home and taken in custody to a Phoenix police station. He was there identified by the complaining witness. The police then took him to "Interrogation Room No. 2" of the detective bureau. There he was questioned by two police officers. The officers admitted at trial that Miranda was not advised that he had a right to have an attorney present. Two hours later, the officers emerged from the interrogation room with a written confession signed by Miranda. At the top of the statement was a typed paragraph stating that the confession was made voluntarily, without threats or promises of immunity and "with full knowledge of my legal rights, understanding any statement I make may be used against me."

At this trial before a jury, the written confession was admitted into evidence over the objection of defense counsel, and the officers testified to the prior oral confession made by Miranda during the interrogation. Miranda was found guilty of kidnapping and rape. He was sentenced to 20 to 30 years' imprisonment on each count, the sentences to run concurrently. On appeal, the Supreme Court of Arizona held that Miranda's constitutional rights were not violated in obtaining the confession and affirmed the conviction. In reaching its decision, the court emphasized heavily the fact that Miranda did not specifically request counsel.

We reverse. From the testimony of the officers and by the admission of respondent, it is clear that Miranda was not in any way apprised of his right to consult with an attorney and to have one present during the interrogation, nor was his right not to be compelled to incriminate himself effectively protected in any other manner. Without these warnings the statements were inadmissible. The mere fact that he signed a statement which contained a typed-in clause stating that he had "full knowledge" of his "legal rights" does not approach the knowing and intelligent waiver required to relinquish constitutional rights....

■ MR. JUSTICE WHITE, with whom MR. JUSTICE HARLAN and MR. JUSTICE STEWART join, dissenting.

I.

The proposition that the privilege against self-incrimination forbids in-custody interrogation without the warnings specified in the majority opinion and without a clear waiver of counsel has no significant support in the history of the privilege or in the language of the Fifth Amendment. As for the English authorities and the common-law history, the privilege, firmly established in the second half of the seventeenth century, was never applied except to prohibit compelled judicial interrogations. The rule excluding coerced confessions matured about 100 years later, "(b)ut there is nothing in the reports to suggest that the theory has its roots in the privilege against self-incrimination. And so far as the cases reveal, the privilege, as such, seems to have been given effect only in judicial proceedings, including the preliminary examinations by authorized magistrates." Morgan, The Privilege Against Self–Incrimination, 34 Minn.L.Rev. 1, 18 (1949).

Our own constitutional provision provides that no person "shall be compelled in any criminal case to be a witness against himself." These words, when "(c)onsidered in the light to be shed by grammar and the dictionary * * * appear to signify simply that nobody shall be compelled to give oral testimony against himself in a criminal proceeding under way in which he is defendant." Corwin, The Supreme Court's Construction of the Self–Incrimination Clause, 29 Mich.L.Rev. 1, 2. And there is very little in the surrounding circumstances of the adoption of the Fifth Amendment or in the provisions of the then existing state constitutions or in state practice which would give the constitutional provision any broader meaning. . . .

II.

That the Court's holding today is neither compelled nor even strongly suggested by the language of the Fifth Amendment, is at odds with American and English legal history, and involves a departure from a long line of precedent does not prove either that the Court has exceeded its powers or that the Court is wrong or unwise in its present reinterpretation of the Fifth Amendment. It does, however, underscore the obvious—that the Court has not discovered or found the law in making today's decision, nor has it derived it from some irrefutable sources; what it has done is to make new law and new public policy in much the same way that it has in the course of interpreting other great clauses of the Constitution.[1] This is what the Court historically has done. Indeed, it is what it must do and will continue to do until and unless there is some fundamental change in the constitutional distribution of governmental powers.

But if the Court is here and now to announce new and fundamental policy to govern certain aspects of our affairs, it is wholly legitimate to examine the mode of this or any other constitutional decision in this Court and to inquire into the advisability of its end product in terms of the long-range interest of the country. At the very least, the Court's text and reasoning should withstand analysis and be a fair exposition of the constitutional provision which its opinion interprets. Decisions like these cannot rest alone on syllogism, metaphysics or some ill-defined notions of natural justice, although each will perhaps play its part. In proceeding to such constructions as it now announces, the Court should also duly consider all the factors and interests bearing upon the cases, at least insofar as the relevant materials are available; and if the necessary considerations are not treated in the record or obtainable from some other reliable source, the Court should not proceed to formulate fundamental policies based on speculation alone.

III.

First, we may inquire what are the textual and factual bases of this new fundamental rule. To reach the result announced on the grounds it does, the Court must stay within the confines of the Fifth Amendment, which forbids self-incrimination only if compelled. Hence the core of the Court's opinion is that because of the "compulsion inherent in custodial surroundings, no statement obtained from (a) defendant (in custody) can truly be the product of his free choice," ante, at 1619, absent the use of adequate protective devices as described by the Court. However, the Court does not point to any sudden inrush of new knowledge requiring the rejection of 70 years' experience. Nor does it assert that its novel conclusion reflects a changing consensus among state courts, see Mapp v. Ohio, 367

---

1. Of course the Court does not deny that it is departing from prior precedent; it expressly overrules Crooker and Cicenia, ante, at 1630, n. 48, and it acknowledges that in the instant "cases we might not find the defendants' statements to have been involuntary in traditional terms," ante, at 1618.

U.S. 643, 81 S.Ct. 1684, 6 L.Ed.2d 1081, or that a succession of cases had steadily eroded the old rule and proved it unworkable, see Gideon v. Wainwright, 372 U.S. 335, 83 S.Ct. 792, 9 L.Ed.2d 799. Rather than asserting new knowledge, the Court concedes that it cannot truly know what occurs during custodial questioning, because of the innate secrecy of such proceedings. It extrapolates a picture of what it conceives to be the norm from police investigatorial manuals, published in 1959 and 1962 or earlier, without any attempt to allow for adjustments in police practices that may have occurred in the wake of more recent decisions of state appellate tribunals or this Court. But even if the relentless application of the described procedures could lead to involuntary confessions, it most assuredly does not follow that each and every case will disclose this kind of interrogation or this kind of consequence.[2] Insofar as appears from the Court's opinion, it has not examined a single transcript of any police interrogation, let alone the interrogation that took place in any one of these cases which it decides today. Judged by any of the standards for empirical investigation utilized in the social sciences the factual basis for the Court's premise is patently inadequate.

Although in the Court's view in-custody interrogation is inherently coercive, the Court says that the spontaneous product of the coercion of arrest and detention is still to be deemed voluntary. An accused, arrested on probable cause, may blurt out a confession which will be admissible despite the fact that he is alone and in custody, without any showing that he had any notion of his right to remain silent or of the consequences of his admission. Yet, under the Court's rule, if the police ask him a single question such as "Do you have anything to say?" or "Did you kill your wife?" his response, if there is one, has somehow been compelled, even if the accused has been clearly warned of his right to remain silent. Common sense informs us to the contrary. While one may say that the response was "involuntary" in the sense the question provoked or was the occasion for the response and thus the defendant was induced to speak out when he might have remained silent if not arrested and not questioned, it is patently unsound to say the response is compelled. . . .

On the other hand, even if one assumed that there was an adequate factual basis for the conclusion that all confessions obtained during in-custody interrogation are the product of compulsion, the rule propounded by the Court will still be irrational, for, apparently, it is only if the accused is also warned of his right to counsel and waives both that right and the right against self-incrimination that the inherent compulsiveness of interrogation disappears. But if the defendant may not answer without a warning a question such as "Where were you last night?" without having

---

2. In fact, the type of sustained interrogation described by the Court appears to be the exception rather than the rule. A survey of 399 cases in one city found that in almost half of the cases the interrogation lasted less than 30 minutes. Barrett, Police Practices and the Law—From Arrest to Release or Charge, 50 Calif.L.Rev. 11, 41–45 (1962). Questioning tends to be confused and sporadic and is usually concentrated on confrontations with witnesses or new items of evidence, as these are obtained by officers conducting the investigation. See generally LaFave, Arrest: The Decision to Take a Suspect into Custody 386 (1965); ALI, A Model Code of Pre–Arraignment Procedure, Commentary § 5.01, at 170, n. 4 (Tent.Draft No. 1, 1966).

his answer be a compelled one, how can the Court ever accept his negative answer to the question of whether he wants to consult his retained counsel or counsel whom the court will appoint? And why if counsel is present and the accused nevertheless confesses, or counsel tells the accused to tell the truth, and that is what the accused does, is the situation any less coercive insofar as the accused is concerned? The Court apparently realizes its dilemma of foreclosing questioning without the necessary warnings but at the same time permitting the accused, sitting in the same chair in front of the same policemen, to waive his right to consult an attorney. It expects, however, that the accused will not often waive the right; and if it is claimed that he has, the State faces a severe, if not impossible burden of proof.

All of this makes very little sense in terms of the compulsion which the Fifth Amendment proscribes. That amendment deals with compelling the accused himself. It is his free will that is involved. Confessions and incriminating admissions, as such, are not forbidden evidence; only those which are compelled are banned. I doubt that the Court observes these distinctions today. By considering any answers to any interrogation to be compelled regardless of the content and course of examination and by escalating the requirements to prove waiver, the Court not only prevents the use of compelled confessions but for all practical purposes forbids interrogation except in the presence of counsel. That is, instead of confining itself to protection of the right against compelled self-incrimination the Court has created a limited Fifth Amendment right to counsel—or, as the Court expresses it, a "need for counsel to protect the Fifth Amendment privilege * * *." Ante, at 1625. The focus then is not on the will of the accused but on the will of counsel and how much influence he can have on the accused. Obviously there is no warrant in the Fifth Amendment for thus installing counsel as the arbiter of the privilege.

In sum, for all the Court's expounding on the menacing atmosphere of police interrogation procedures, it has failed to supply any foundation for the conclusions it draws or the measures it adopts. . . .

In some unknown number of cases the Court's rule will return a killer, a rapist or other criminal to the streets and to the environment which produced him, to repeat his crime whenever it pleases him. As a consequence, there will not be a gain, but a loss, in human dignity.

[The separate opinions of Justices Harlan and Clark are omitted.]

SECTION 2.   THE WARREN COURT LANDMARKS IN THE BURGER AND REHNQUIST COURTS

United States v. Leon
Supreme Court of the United States, 1984.
468 U.S. 897, 104 S.Ct. 3405, 82 L.Ed.2d 677.

Acting on the basis of information from a confidential informant, officers of the Burbank, Cal., Police Department initiated a drug-trafficking investigation involving surveillance of respondents' activities. Based on an affidavit summarizing the police officers' observations, Officer Rombach prepared an application for a warrant to search three residences and respondents' automobiles for an extensive list of items. The application was reviewed by several Deputy District Attorneys, and a facially valid search warrant was issued by a state-court judge. Ensuing searches produced large quantities of drugs and other evidence. Respondents were indicted for federal drug offenses, and filed motions to suppress the evidence seized pursuant to the warrant. After an evidentiary hearing, the District Court granted the motions in part, concluding that the affidavit was insufficient to establish probable cause. Although recognizing that Officer Rombach had acted in good faith, the court rejected the Government's suggestion that the Fourth Amendment exclusionary rule should not apply where evidence is seized in reasonable, good-faith reliance on a search warrant. The Court of Appeals affirmed, also refusing the Government's invitation to recognize a good-faith exception to the rule. The Government's petition for certiorari presented only the question whether a good-faith exception to the exclusionary rule should be recognized.

Language in opinions of this Court and of individual Justices has sometimes implied that the exclusionary rule is a necessary corollary of the Fourth Amendment, Mapp v. Ohio, 367 U.S. 643, 651 (1961), or that the rule is required by the conjunction of the Fourth and Fifth Amendments. These implications need not detain us long. The Fifth Amendment theory has not withstood critical analysis or the test of time, and the Fourth Amendment "has never been interpreted to proscribe the introduction of illegally seized evidence in all proceedings or against all persons." Stone v. Powell, 428 U.S. 465, 486, 96 S.Ct. 3037, 3048 (1976).

The Fourth Amendment contains no provision expressly precluding the use of evidence obtained in violation of its commands, and an examination of its origin and purposes makes clear that the use of fruits of a past unlawful search or seizure "work[s] no new Fourth Amendment wrong." United States v. Calandra, 414 U.S. 338, 354, 94 S.Ct. 613, 623, 38 L.Ed.2d 561 (1974).... The rule thus operates as "a judicially created remedy designed to safeguard Fourth Amendment rights generally through its deterrent effect, rather than a personal constitutional right of the person aggrieved."

Whether the exclusionary sanction is appropriately imposed in a particular case, our decisions make clear, is "an issue separate from the question whether the Fourth Amendment rights of the party seeking to invoke the rule were violated by police conduct." Only the former question is currently before us, and it must be resolved by weighing the costs and benefits of preventing the use in the prosecution's case-in-chief of inherently trustworthy tangible evidence obtained in reliance on a search warrant issued by a detached and neutral magistrate that ultimately is found to be defective.

The substantial social costs exacted by the exclusionary rule for the vindication of Fourth Amendment rights have long been a source of concern.... An objectionable collateral consequence of this interference with the criminal justice system's truth-finding function is that some guilty defendants may go free or receive reduced sentences as a result of favorable plea bargains. Particularly when law enforcement officers have acted in objective good faith or their transgressions have been minor, the magnitude of the benefit conferred on such guilty defendants offends basic concepts of the criminal justice system. Indiscriminate application of the exclusionary rule, therefore, may well "generate[e] disrespect for the law and the administration of justice." Accordingly, "[a]s with any remedial device, the application of the rule has been restricted to those areas where its remedial objectives are thought most efficaciously served."

. . .

[T]he balancing approach that has evolved in various contexts—including criminal trials—"forcefully suggest[s] that the exclusionary rule be more generally modified to permit the introduction of evidence obtained in the reasonable good-faith belief that a search or seizure was in accord with the Fourth Amendment."

. . .

As cases considering the use of unlawfully obtained evidence in criminal trials themselves make clear, it does not follow from the emphasis on the exclusionary rule's deterrent value that "anything which deters illegal searches is thereby commanded by the Fourth Amendment." In determining whether persons aggrieved solely by the introduction of damaging evidence unlawfully obtained from their co-conspirators or co-defendants could seek suppression, for example, we found that the additional benefits of such an extension of the exclusionary rule would not outweigh its costs. Standing to invoke the rule has thus been limited to cases in which the prosecution seeks to use the fruits of an illegal search or seizure against the victim of police misconduct. Rakas v. Illinois, 439 U.S. 128, 99 S.Ct. 421, 58 L.Ed.2d 387 (1978)....

The same attention to the purposes underlying the exclusionary rule also has characterized decisions not involving the scope of the rule itself. We have not required suppression of the fruits of a search incident to an arrest made in good-faith reliance on a substantive criminal statute that subsequently is declared unconstitutional. Michigan v. DeFillippo, 443 U.S. 31, 99 S.Ct. 2627, 61 L.Ed.2d 343 (1979).[7]

. . .

As yet, we have not recognized any form of good-faith exception to the Fourth Amendment exclusionary rule.[8] But the balancing approach that

---

7. We have held, however, that the exclusionary rule requires suppression of evidence obtained in searches carried out pursuant to statutes, not yet declared unconstitutional, purporting to authorize searches and seizures without probable cause or search warrants. See, e.g., Ybarra v. Illinois, 444 U.S. 85, 100 S.Ct. 338, 62 L.Ed.2d 238 (1979); Torres v. Puerto Rico, 442 U.S. 465, 99 S.Ct. 2425, 61 L.Ed.2d 1 (1979); Almeida–Sanchez v. United States, 413 U.S. 266, 93 S.Ct. 2535, 37 L.Ed.2d 596 (1973); Sibron v. New York, 392 U.S. 40, 88 S.Ct. 1889, 20 L.Ed.2d 917 (1968); Berger v. New York, 388 U.S. 41, 87 S.Ct. 1873, 18 L.Ed.2d 1040 (1967). "Those decisions involved statutes which, by their own terms, authorized searches under circumstances which did not satisfy the traditional warrant and probable-cause requirements of the Fourth Amendment." Michigan v. DeFillippo, 443 U.S. 31, 39, 99 S.Ct. 2627, 2633, 61 L.Ed.2d 343 (1979). The substantive Fourth Amendment principles announced in those cases are fully consistent with our holding here.

8. One Court of Appeals, no doubt influenced by these individual urgings, has adopted a form of good-faith exception to the exclusionary rule. United States v. Williams, 622 F.2d 830 (C.A.5 1980) (en banc), *cert. denied,* 449 U.S. 1127, 101 S.Ct. 946, 67 L.Ed.2d 114 (1981).

has evolved during the years of experience with the rule provides strong support for the modification currently urged upon us. . . .

Because a search warrant "provides the detached scrutiny of a neutral magistrate, which is a more reliable safeguard against improper searches than the hurried judgment of a law enforcement officer 'engaged in the often competitive enterprise of ferreting out crime,' ". . .

Deference to the magistrate, however, is not boundless. It is clear, first, that the deference accorded to a magistrate's finding of probable cause does not preclude inquiry into the knowing or reckless falsity of the affidavit on which that determination was based. Franks v. Delaware, 438 U.S. 154, 98 S.Ct. 2674, 57 L.Ed.2d 667 (1978). Second, the courts must also insist that the magistrate purport to "perform his 'neutral and detached' function and not serve merely as a rubber stamp for the police." . . .

[R]eviewing courts will not defer to a warrant based on an affidavit that does not "provide the magistrate with a substantial basis for determining the existence of probable cause." Illinois v. Gates, supra, 462 U.S., at 239, 103 S.Ct., at 2332. "Sufficient information must be presented to the magistrate to allow that official to determine probable cause; his action cannot be a mere ratification of the bare conclusions of others." . . .

[W]e discern no basis, and are offered none, for believing that exclusion of evidence seized pursuant to a warrant will have a significant deterrent effect on the issuing judge or magistrate. Many of the factors that indicate that the exclusionary rule cannot provide an effective "special" or "general" deterrent for individual offending law enforcement officers apply as well to judges or magistrates. And, to the extent that the rule is thought to operate as a "systemic" deterrent on a wider audience, it clearly can have no such effect on individuals empowered to issue search warrants. Judges and magistrates are not adjuncts to the law enforcement team; as neutral judicial officers, they have no stake in the outcome of particular criminal prosecutions. The threat of exclusion thus cannot be expected significantly to deter them. Imposition of the exclusionary sanction is not necessary meaningfully to inform judicial officers of their errors, and we cannot conclude that admitting evidence obtained pursuant to a warrant while at the same time declaring that the warrant was somehow defective will in any way reduce judicial officers' professional incentives to comply with the Fourth Amendment, encourage them to repeat their mistakes, or lead to the granting of all colorable warrant requests.

If exclusion of evidence obtained pursuant to a subsequently invalidated warrant is to have any deterrent effect, therefore, it must alter the behavior of individual law enforcement officers or the policies of their departments. . . .

We have frequently questioned whether the exclusionary rule can have any deterrent effect when the offending officers acted in the objectively reasonable belief that their conduct did not violate the Fourth Amendment. "No empirical researcher, proponent or opponent of the rule, has yet been able to establish with any assurance whether the rule has a deterrent effect. . . ." But even assuming that the rule effectively deters some police misconduct and provides incentives for the law enforcement profession as a whole to conduct itself in accord with the Fourth Amendment, it cannot be expected, and should not be applied, to deter objectively reasonable law enforcement activity.

. . .

In short, where the officer's conduct is objectively reasonable,

"excluding the evidence will not further the ends of the exclusionary rule in any appreciable way; for it is painfully apparent that . . . the officer is acting as a reasonable officer would and should act under the circumstances. Excluding the evidence can in no way affect his future conduct unless it is to make him less willing to do his duty."

This is particularly true, we believe, when an officer acting with objective good faith has obtained a search warrant from a judge or magistrate and acted within its scope. In most such cases, there is no police illegality and nothing to deter. It is the magistrate's responsibility to determine whether the officer's allegations establish probable cause and, if so, to issue a warrant comporting in form with the requirements of the Fourth Amendment. In the ordinary case, an officer cannot be expected to question the magistrate's probable-cause determination or his judgment that the form of the warrant is technically sufficient. "[O]nce the warrant issues, there is literally nothing more the policeman can do in seeking to comply with the law." Penalizing the officer for the magistrate's error, rather than his own, cannot logically contribute to the deterrence of Fourth Amendment violations.

We conclude that the marginal or nonexistent benefits produced by suppressing evidence obtained in objectively reasonable reliance on a subsequently invalidated search warrant cannot justify the substantial costs of exclusion. We do not suggest, however, that exclusion is always inappropriate in cases where an officer has obtained a warrant and abided by its terms. "(S)earches pursuant to a warrant will rarely require any deep inquiry into reasonableness," for "a warrant issued by a magistrate normally suffices to establish" that a law enforcement officer has "acted in good faith in conducting the search." Nevertheless, the officer's reliance on the magistrate's probable-cause determination and on the technical sufficiency of the warrant he issues must be objectively reasonable, and it is clear that in some circumstances the officer will have no reasonable grounds for believing that the warrant was properly issued.

Suppression therefore remains an appropriate remedy if the magistrate or judge in issuing a warrant was misled by information in an affidavit that the affiant knew was false or would have known was false except for his reckless disregard of the truth. . . . Finally, depending on the circumstances of the particular case, a warrant may be so facially deficient—i.e., in failing to particularize the place to be searched or the things to be seized—that the executing officers cannot reasonably presume it to be valid. Cf. Massachusetts v. Sheppard, 468 U.S., at 988–991, 104 S.Ct., at 3428–3430.

In so limiting the suppression remedy, we leave untouched the probable-cause standard and the various requirements for a valid warrant. Other objections to the modification of the Fourth Amendment exclusionary rule we consider to be insubstantial. The good-faith exception for searches conducted pursuant to warrants is not intended to signal our unwillingness strictly to the requirements of the Fourth Amendment, and we do not believe that it will have this effect. . . .

If the resolution of a particular Fourth Amendment question is necessary to guide future action by law enforcement officers and magistrates, nothing will prevent reviewing courts from deciding that question before turning to the good-faith issue. . . .

When the principles we have enunciated today are applied to the facts of this case, it is apparent that the judgment of the Court of Appeals cannot stand. . . .

Accordingly, the judgment of the Court of Appeals is

Reversed.[9]

Strickland v. Washington

Supreme Court of the United States, 1984.
466 U.S. 668, 104 S.Ct. 2052, 80 L.Ed.2d 674.

■ JUSTICE O'CONNOR delivered the opinion of the Court.

This case requires us to consider the proper standards for judging a criminal defendant's contention that the Constitution requires a conviction or death sentence to be set aside because counsel's assistance at the trial or sentencing was ineffective.

Counsel actively pursued pretrial motions and discovery. He cut his efforts short, however, and he experienced a sense of hopelessness about the case, when he learned that, against his specific advice, respondent had also confessed to the first two murders. By the date set for trial, respondent was subject to indictment for three counts of first degree murder and multiple counts of robbery, kidnapping for ransom, breaking and entering and assault, attempted murder, and conspiracy to commit robbery. Respondent waived his right to a jury trial, again acting against counsel's advice, and pleaded guilty to all charges, including the three capital murder charges.

Counsel advised respondent to invoke his right under Florida law to an advisory jury at his capital sentencing hearing. Respondent rejected the

---

9. Where a warrant was issued but was invalid in part due to a technical error of the issuing judge, the Supreme Court applied the *Leon* standard and held evidence obtained by the warrant need not be excluded. An improper search warrant form was used. The judge issuing the warrant told the officer necessary changes in the warrant would be made, and proceeded to make inadequate changes. "... we refuse to rule that an officer is required to disbelieve a judge who has just advised him, by word and by action, that the warrant he possessed authorizes him to conduct the search he has requested." Massachusetts v. Sheppard, 468 U.S. 981, 104 S.Ct. 3424, 3429 (1984). *See also* Arizona v. Evans, 514 U.S. 1 (1995) (when illegal arrest is due to clerical error by employee of court, not police officers, fruits of unlawful arrest admitted, as exclusion would not deter police misconduct); Herring v. United States, 129 S.Ct. 695 (2009) (extending *Evans* to admit fruits of illegal arrests resulting from inaccurate records maintained by police, over a notable dissent joined by four justices taking issue with the deterrence-based balancing test of *Leon*).

advice and waived the right. He chose instead to be sentenced by the trial judge without a jury recommendation.

. . .

Counsel decided not to present and hence not to look further for evidence concerning respondent's character and emotional state. That decision reflected trial counsel's sense of hopelessness about overcoming the evidentiary effect of respondent's confessions to the gruesome crimes. It also reflected the judgment that it was advisable to rely on the plea colloquy for evidence about respondent's background and about his claim of emotional stress: the plea colloquy communicated sufficient information about these subjects, and by foregoing the opportunity to present new evidence on these subjects, counsel prevented the State from cross-examining respondent on his claim and from putting on psychiatric evidence of its own.

Counsel also excluded from the sentencing hearing other evidence he thought was potentially damaging. He successfully moved to exclude respondent's "rap sheet." Because he judged that a presentence report might prove more detrimental than helpful, as it would have included respondent's criminal history and thereby undermined the claim of no significant history of criminal activity, he did not request that one be prepared.

At the sentencing hearing, counsel's strategy was based primarily on the trial judge's remarks at the plea colloquy as well as on his reputation as a sentencing judge who thought it important for a convicted defendant to own up to his crime. Counsel argued that respondent's remorse and acceptance of responsibility justified sparing him from the death penalty. Counsel also argued that respondent had no history of criminal activity and that respondent committed the crimes under extreme mental or emotional disturbance, thus coming within the statutory list of mitigating circumstances. He further argued that respondent should be spared death because he had surrendered, confessed, and offered to testify against a co-defendant and because respondent was fundamentally a good person who had briefly gone badly wrong in extremely stressful circumstances. The State put on evidence and witnesses largely for the purpose of describing the details of the crimes. Counsel did not cross-examine the medical experts who testified about the manner of death of respondent's victims.

The trial judge found several aggravating circumstances with respect to each of the three murders.

In short, the trial judge found numerous aggravating circumstances and no (or a single comparatively insignificant) mitigating circumstance. With respect to each of the three convictions for capital murder, the trial judge concluded: "A careful consideration of all matters presented to the court impels the conclusion that there are insufficient mitigating circumstances ... to outweigh the aggravating circumstances...." He therefore sentenced respondent to death on each of the three counts of murder and to prison terms for the other crimes. The Florida Supreme Court upheld the convictions and sentences on direct appeal.

Respondent ... filed a petition for a writ of habeas corpus in the United States District Court for the Southern District of Florida.

* * *

The court ... denied the petition for a writ of habeas corpus.

* * *

The full Court of Appeals developed its own framework for analyzing ineffective assistance claims and reversed the judgment of the District Court and remanded the case for new factfinding under the newly announced standards.

Petitioners, who are officials of the State of Florida, filed a petition for a writ of certiorari seeking review of the decision of the Court of Appeals. The petition presents a type of Sixth Amendment claim that this Court has not previously considered in any generality. The Court has considered Sixth Amendment claims based on actual or constructive denial of the assistance of counsel altogether, as well as claims based on state interference with the ability of counsel to render effective assistance to the accused. *E.g.,* United States v. Cronic, *ante,* 466 U.S. 648, 104 S.Ct. 2039, 80 L.Ed.2d 657. With the exception of Cuyler v. Sullivan, 446 U.S. 335, 100 S.Ct. 1708, 64 L.Ed.2d 333 (1980), however, which involved a claim that counsel's assistance was rendered ineffective by a conflict of interest, the Court has never directly and fully addressed a claim of "actual ineffectiveness" of counsel's assistance in a case going to trial.

In assessing attorney performance, all the Federal Courts of Appeals and all but a few state courts have now adopted the "reasonably effective assistance" standard in one formulation or another. Yet this Court has not had occasion squarely to decide whether that is the proper standard.

In a long line of cases that includes Powell v. Alabama, 287 U.S. 45, 53 S.Ct. 55, 77 L.Ed. 158 (1932), Johnson v. Zerbst, 304 U.S. 458, 58 S.Ct. 1019, 82 L.Ed. 1461 (1938), and Gideon v. Wainwright, 372 U.S. 335, 83 S.Ct. 792, 9 L.Ed.2d 799 (1963), this Court has recognized that the Sixth Amendment right to counsel exists, and is needed, in order to protect the fundamental right to a fair trial.

Because of the vital importance of counsel's assistance, this Court has held that, with certain exceptions, a person accused of a federal or state crime has the right to have counsel appointed if retained counsel cannot be obtained. That a person who happens to be a lawyer is present at trial alongside the accused, however, is not enough to satisfy the constitutional command. The Sixth Amendment recognizes the right to the assistance of counsel because it envisions counsel's playing a role that is critical to the ability of the adversarial system to produce just results. An accused is entitled to be assisted by an attorney, whether retained or appointed, who plays the role necessary to ensure that the trial is fair.

For that reason, the Court has recognized that "the right to counsel is the right to the effective assistance of counsel." McMann v. Richardson, 397 U.S. 759, 771, n. 14, 90 S.Ct. 1441, 1449, n. 14, 25 L.Ed.2d 763 (1970). Government violates the right to effective assistance when it interferes in certain ways with the ability of counsel to make independent decisions about how to conduct the defense. *See, e.g.,* Geders v. United States, 425 U.S. 80, 96 S.Ct. 1330, 47 L.Ed.2d 592 (1976) (bar on attorney-client consultation during overnight recess); Herring v. New York, 422 U.S. 853, 95 S.Ct. 2550, 45 L.Ed.2d 593 (1975) (bar on summation at bench trial); Brooks v. Tennessee, 406 U.S. 605, 612–613, 92 S.Ct. 1891, 1895, 32 L.Ed.2d 358 (1972) (requirement that defendant be first defense witness); Ferguson v. Georgia, 365 U.S. 570, 593–596, 81 S.Ct. 756, 768–770, 5 L.Ed.2d 783 (1961) (bar on direct examination of defendant). Counsel, however, can also deprive a defendant of the right to effective assistance, simply by failing to render "adequate legal assistance".

A convicted defendant's claim that counsel's assistance was so defective as to require reversal of a conviction or death sentence has two components. First, the defendant must show that counsel's performance was deficient. This requires showing that counsel made errors so serious that counsel was not functioning as the "counsel" guaranteed the defendant by the Sixth Amendment. Second, the defendant must show that the deficient performance prejudiced the defense. This requires showing that counsel's errors were so serious as to deprive the defendant of a fair trial, a trial whose result is reliable. Unless a defendant makes both showings, it cannot be said that the conviction or death sentence resulted from a breakdown in the adversary process that renders the result unreliable.

As all the Federal Courts of Appeals have now held, the proper standard for attorney performance is that of reasonably effective assistance. The Court indirectly recognized as much when it stated in *McMann v. Richardson, supra,* that a guilty plea cannot be attacked as based on inadequate legal advice unless counsel was not "a reasonably competent attorney" and the advice was not "within the range of competence demanded of attorneys in criminal cases." When a convicted defendant complains of the ineffectiveness of counsel's assistance, the defendant must show that counsel's representation fell below an objective standard of reasonableness.

More specific guidelines are not appropriate. The Sixth Amendment refers simply to "counsel," not specifying particular requirements of effective assistance. It relies instead on the legal profession's maintenance of standards sufficient to justify the law's presumption that counsel will fulfill the role in the adversary process that the Amendment envisions. The proper measure of attorney performance remains simply reasonableness under prevailing professional norms.

These basic duties neither exhaustively define the obligations of counsel nor form a checklist for judicial evaluation of attorney performance. In any case presenting an ineffectiveness claim, the performance inquiry must be whether counsel's assistance was reasonable considering all the circumstances.... No particular set of detailed rules for counsel's conduct can satisfactorily take account of the variety of circumstances faced by defense counsel or the range of legitimate decisions regarding how best to represent a criminal defendant. Any such set of rules would interfere with the constitutionally protected independence of counsel and restrict the wide latitude counsel must have in making tactical decisions. Indeed, the existence of detailed guidelines for representation could distract counsel from the overriding mission of vigorous advocacy of the defendant's cause.

Moreover, the purpose of the effective assistance guarantee of the Sixth Amendment is not to improve the quality of legal representation, although that is a goal of considerable importance to the legal system. The purpose is simply to ensure that criminal defendants receive a fair trial.

Judicial scrutiny of counsel's performance must be highly deferential. It is all too tempting for a defendant to second-guess counsel's assistance after conviction or adverse sentence, and it is all too easy for a court, examining counsel's defense after it has proved unsuccessful, to conclude that a particular act or omission of counsel was unreasonable. A fair assessment of attorney performance requires that every effort be made to eliminate the distorting effects of hindsight, to reconstruct the circumstances of counsel's challenged conduct, and to evaluate the conduct from counsel's perspective at the time. Because of the difficulties inherent in making the evaluation, a court must indulge a strong presumption that counsel's conduct falls within the wide range of reasonable professional assistance; that is, the defendant must overcome the presumption that, under the circumstances, the challenged action "might be considered sound trial strategy." . . .

The availability of intrusive post-trial inquiry into attorney performance or of detailed guidelines for its evaluation would encourage the proliferation of ineffectiveness challenges. Criminal trials resolved unfavorably to the defendant would increasingly come to be followed by a second trial, this one of counsel's unsuccessful defense. Counsel's performance and even willingness to serve could be adversely affected. Intensive scrutiny of counsel and rigid requirements for acceptable assistance could dampen the ardor and impair the independence of defense counsel, discourage the acceptance of assigned cases, and undermine the trust between attorney and client.

Thus, a court deciding an actual ineffectiveness claim must judge the reasonableness of counsel's challenged conduct on the facts of the particular case, viewed as of the time of counsel's conduct. A convicted defendant making a claim of ineffective assistance must identify the acts or omissions of counsel that are alleged not to have been the result of reasonable professional judgment. The court must then determine whether, in light of all the circumstances, the identified acts or omissions were outside the wide range of professionally competent assistance. In making that determination, the court should keep in mind that counsel's function, as elaborated in prevailing professional norms, is to make the adversarial testing process work in the particular case. At the same time, the court should recognize that counsel is strongly presumed to have rendered adequate assistance and made all significant decisions in the exercise of reasonable professional judgment.

. . . As the Court of Appeals concluded, strategic choices made after thorough investigation of law and facts relevant to plausible options are virtually unchallengeable; and strategic choices made after less than complete investigation are reasonable precisely to the extent that reasonable professional judgments support the limitations on investigation. In other words, counsel has a duty to make reasonable investigations or to make a reasonable decision that makes particular investigations unnecessary. In any ineffectiveness case, a particular decision not to investigate must be directly assessed for reasonableness in all the circumstances, applying a heavy measure of deference to counsel's judgments.

The reasonableness of counsel's actions may be determined or substantially influenced by the defendant's own statements or actions. Counsel's actions are usually based, quite properly, on informed strategic choices made by the defendant and on information supplied by the defendant. In particular, what investigation decisions are reasonable depends critically on such information. For example, when the facts that support a certain potential line of defense are generally known to counsel because of what the defendant has said, the need for further investigation may be considerably diminished or eliminated altogether. And when a defendant has given counsel reason to believe that pursuing certain investigations would be fruitless or even harmful, counsel's failure to pursue those investigations may not later be challenged as unreasonable. In short, inquiry into counsel's conversations with the defendant may be critical to a proper assessment of counsel's investigation decisions, just as it may be critical to a proper assessment of counsel's other litigation decisions.

An error by counsel, even if professionally unreasonable, does not warrant setting aside the judgment of a criminal proceeding if the error had no effect on the judgment. . . .

In certain Sixth Amendment contexts, prejudice is presumed. Actual or constructive denial of the assistance of counsel altogether is legally presumed to result in prejudice. So are various kinds of state interference with counsel's assistance. See United States v. Cronic, 466 U.S., at 659, and n. 25, 104 S.Ct., at 2046–2047, and n. 25. Prejudice in these circumstances is so likely that case by case inquiry into prejudice is not worth the cost. *Id.,* at 658, 104 S.Ct., at 2046. Moreover, such circumstances involve impairments of the Sixth Amendment right that are easy to identify and, for that reason and because the prosecution is directly responsible, easy for the government to prevent.

Conflict of interest claims aside, actual ineffectiveness claims alleging a deficiency in attorney performance are subject to a general requirement that the defendant affirmatively prove prejudice. The government is not responsible for, and hence not able to prevent, attorney errors that will result in reversal of a conviction or sentence. Attorney errors come in an infinite variety and are as likely to be utterly harmless in a particular case as they are to be prejudicial. They cannot be classified according to likelihood of causing prejudice. Nor can they be defined with sufficient precision to inform defense attorneys correctly just what conduct to avoid. Representation is an art, and an act or omission that is unprofessional in one case may be sound or even brilliant in another. Even if a defendant shows that particular errors of counsel were unreasonable, therefore, the defendant must show that they actually had an adverse effect on the defense.

It is not enough for the defendant to show that the errors had some conceivable effect on the outcome of the proceeding. Virtually every act or omission of counsel would meet that test, and not every error that conceivably could have influenced the outcome undermines the reliability of the result of the proceeding. . . .

On the other hand, we believe that a defendant need not show that counsel's deficient conduct more likely than not altered the outcome in the case. This outcome-determinative standard has several strengths. It defines the relevant inquiry in a way familiar to courts, though the inquiry, as is inevitable, is anything but precise. The standard also reflects the profound importance of finality in criminal proceedings. Moreover, it comports with the widely used standard for assessing motions for new trial based on newly discovered evidence. Nevertheless, the standard is not quite appropriate.

Accordingly, the appropriate test for prejudice finds its roots in the test for materiality of exculpatory information not disclosed to the defense by the prosecution, United States v. Agurs, 427 U.S., at 104, 112–113, 96 S.Ct., at 2397, 2401–2402, and in the test for materiality of testimony made unavailable to the defense by Government deportation of a witness, United States v. Valenzuela–Bernal, 458 U.S., at 872–874, 102 S.Ct., at 3449–3450. The defendant must show that there is a reasonable probability that, but for counsel's unprofessional errors, the result of the proceeding would have been different. A reasonable probability is a probability sufficient to undermine confidence in the outcome.

In making the determination whether the specified errors resulted in the required prejudice, a court should presume, absent challenge to the judgment on grounds of evidentiary insufficiency, that the judge or jury acted according to law. . . . The assessment of prejudice should proceed on the assumption that the decisionmaker is reasonably, conscientiously, and impartially applying the standards that govern the decision. It should not depend on the idiosyncracies of the particular decisionmaker, such as unusual propensities toward harshness or leniency. Although these factors may actually have entered into counsel's selection of strategies and, to that limited extent, may thus affect the performance inquiry, they are irrelevant to the prejudice inquiry. Thus, evidence about the actual process of decision, if not part of the record of the proceeding under review, and evidence about, for example, a particular judge's sentencing practices, should not be considered in the prejudice determination.

In making this determination, a court hearing an ineffectiveness claim must consider the totality of the evidence before the judge or jury. Some of the factual findings will have been unaffected by the errors, and factual findings that were affected will have been affected in different ways. Some errors will have had a pervasive effect on the inferences to be drawn from the evidence, altering the entire evidentiary picture, and some will have had an isolated, trivial effect. Moreover, a verdict or conclusion only weakly supported by the record is more likely to have been affected by errors than one with overwhelming record support. Taking the unaffected findings as a given, and taking due account of the effect of the errors on the remaining findings, a court making the prejudice inquiry must ask if the defendant has met the burden of showing that the decision reached would reasonably likely have been different absent the errors.

A number of practical considerations are important for the application of the standards we have outlined. Most important, in adjudicating a claim of actual ineffectiveness of counsel, a court should keep in mind that the principles we have stated do not establish mechanical rules. Although those principles should guide the process of decision, the ultimate focus of inquiry must be on the fundamental fairness of the proceeding whose result is being challenged. In every case the court should be concerned with whether, despite the strong presumption of reliability, the result of the particular proceeding is unreliable because of a breakdown in the adversarial process that our system counts on to produce just results.

The principles governing ineffectiveness claims should apply in federal collateral proceedings as they do on direct appeal or in motions for a new trial. As indicated by the "cause and prejudice" test for overcoming procedural waivers of claims of error, the presumption that a criminal judgment is final is at its strongest in collateral attacks on that judgment.

Application of the governing principles is not difficult in this case. The facts as described above, see supra, at 1–8, make clear that the conduct of respondent's counsel at and before respondent's sentencing proceeding cannot be found unreasonable. They also make clear that, even assuming the challenged conduct of counsel was unreasonable, respondent suffered insufficient prejudice to warrant setting aside his death sentence.

Reversed.[10]

---

10. In United States v. Cronic, 466 U.S. 648, 104 S.Ct. 2039 (1984), an attorney who had never tried a criminal case and specialized in property law was given only 25 days to prepare for trial. The Court held the surrounding circumstances not to make it "unlikely" defendant could have received effective assistance of counsel.

Effectiveness of counsel at the plea process is to be determined by the same standard as *Strickland*. The defendant must show prejudice. This requires, at least, an allegation that but for the errors of counsel, the defendant would not have plead guilty. Hill v. Lockhart, 474 U.S. 52, 106 S.Ct. 366 (1985).

Due process requires effective counsel at the appellate stage. The failure to file proper papers to prosecute an appeal resulting in dismissal is a violation of a defendant's constitutional rights. Evitts v. Lucey, 469 U.S. 387, 105 S.Ct. 830 (1985).

The right to effective counsel under the Sixth Amendment does not extend to using perjury, and an attorney's duty to a client does not extend to assisting a client to commit perjury. Counsel's refusal to aid in presenting false testimony and advising the client of the possibility of disclosure of any perjury is not ineffective counsel. Nix v. Whiteside, 475 U.S. 157, 106 S.Ct. 988 (1986).

Defendant's right to effective counsel was not violated when a continuance was not granted to allow further preparation where counsel claimed to be sufficiently prepared. Defendant expressed unhappiness with counsel. The Sixth Amendment right to counsel does not guarantee a "meaningful attorney-client relationship." Morris v. Slappy, 461 U.S. 1, 103 S.Ct. 1610 (1983).

A defendant is entitled to representation by counsel who is free of conflicts of interest. Holloway v. Arkansas, 435 U.S. 475, 98 S.Ct. 1173 (1978); Cuyler v. Sullivan, 446 U.S. 335, 100 S.Ct. 1708 (1980). The defendant may waive a conflict of interest of counsel subject to the substantial latitude of the trial court to disallow representation if the conflict is of a serious nature. Wheat v. United States, 486 U.S. 153, 108 S.Ct. 1692 (1988).

Joint representation of two or more defendants by one attorney is not per se violative of the constitutional right to effective counsel. The failure to present some mitigating evidence in a capital case that was otherwise inconsistent with counsel's judgment as to the best

Dickerson v. United States

Supreme Court of the United States, 2000.
530 U.S. 428, 120 S.Ct. 2326, 147 L.Ed.2d 405.

■ CHIEF JUSTICE REHNQUIST delivered the opinion of the Court.

In Miranda v. Arizona, 384 U.S. 436, 86 S.Ct. 1602, 16 L.Ed.2d 694 (1966), we held that certain warnings must be given before a suspect's statement made during custodial interrogation could be admitted in evidence. In the wake of that decision, Congress enacted 18 U.S.C. § 3501, which in essence laid down a rule that the admissibility of such statements should turn only on whether or not they were voluntarily made. We hold that *Miranda,* being a constitutional decision of this Court, may not be in effect overruled by an Act of Congress, and we decline to overrule *Miranda* ourselves. We therefore hold that *Miranda* and its progeny in this Court govern the admissibility of statements made during custodial interrogation in both state and federal courts.

Petitioner Dickerson was indicted for bank robbery, conspiracy to commit bank robbery, and using a firearm in the course of committing a crime of violence, all in violation of the applicable provisions of Title 18 of the United States Code. Before trial, Dickerson moved to suppress a statement he had made at a Federal Bureau of Investigation field office, on the grounds that he had not received "*Miranda* warnings" before being interrogated. The District Court granted his motion to suppress, and the Government took an interlocutory appeal to the United States Court of Appeals for the Fourth Circuit. That court, by a divided vote, reversed the District Court's suppression order. It agreed with the District Court's conclusion that petitioner had not received *Miranda* warnings before making his statement. But it went on to hold that § 3501, which in effect makes the admissibility of statements such as Dickerson's turn solely on whether they were made voluntarily, was satisfied in this case. It then concluded that our decision in *Miranda* was not a constitutional holding, and that, therefore, Congress could by statute have the final say on the question of admissibility. 166 F.3d 667 (1999).

Because of the importance of the questions raised by the Court of Appeals' decision, we granted certiorari, 528 U.S. 1045, 120 S.Ct. 578, 145 L.Ed.2d 481 (1999), and now reverse.

In *Miranda,* we noted that the advent of modern custodial police interrogation brought with it an increased concern about confessions obtained by coercion. 384 U.S., at 445–458, 86 S.Ct. 1602. Because custodial police interrogation, by its very nature, isolates and pressures the individual, we stated that "[e]ven without employing brutality, the 'third degree' or [other] specific stratagems, . . . custodial interrogation exacts a heavy toll on individual liberty and trades on the weakness of individuals." *Id.,* at 455, 86 S.Ct. 1602. We concluded that the coercion inherent in custodial interrogation blurs the line between voluntary and involuntary statements, and thus heightens the risk that an individual will not be "accorded his privilege under the Fifth Amendment . . . not to be compelled to incrimi-

---

presentation of defendant's case was not ineffective representation. Burger v. Kemp, 483 U.S. 776, 107 S.Ct. 3114 (1987).

nate himself." *Id.*, at 439, 86 S.Ct. 1602. Accordingly, we laid down "concrete constitutional guidelines for law enforcement agencies and courts to follow." *Id.*, at 442, 86 S.Ct. 1602. Those guidelines established that the admissibility in evidence of any statement given during custodial interrogation of a suspect would depend on whether the police provided the suspect with four warnings. These warnings (which have come to be known colloquially as "*Miranda* rights") are: a suspect "has the right to remain silent, that anything he says can be used against him in a court of law, that he has the right to the presence of an attorney, and that if he cannot afford an attorney one will be appointed for him prior to any questioning if he so desires." *Id.*, at 479, 86 S.Ct. 1602.

Two years after *Miranda* was decided, Congress enacted § 3501. That section provides, in relevant part:

"(a) In any criminal prosecution brought by the United States or by the District of Columbia, a confession . . . shall be admissible in evidence if it is voluntarily given. Before such confession is received in evidence, the trial judge shall, out of the presence of the jury, determine any issue as to voluntariness. If the trial judge determines that the confession was voluntarily made it shall be admitted in evidence and the trial judge shall permit the jury to hear relevant evidence on the issue of voluntariness and shall instruct the jury to give such weight to the confession as the jury feels it deserves under all the circumstances.

"(b) The trial judge in determining the issue of voluntariness shall take into consideration all the circumstances surrounding the giving of the confession, including (1) the time elapsing between arrest and arraignment of the defendant making the confession, if it was made after arrest and before arraignment, (2) whether such defendant knew the nature of the offense with which he was charged or of which he was suspected at the time of making the confession, (3) whether or not such defendant was advised or knew that he was not required to make any statement and that any such statement could be used against him, (4) whether or not such defendant had been advised prior to questioning of his right to the assistance of counsel; and (5) whether or not such defendant was without the assistance of counsel when questioned and when giving such confession.

"The presence or absence of any of the above–mentioned factors to be taken into consideration by the judge need not be conclusive on the issue of voluntariness of the confession."

Given § 3501's express designation of voluntariness as the touchstone of admissibility, its omission of any warning requirement, and the instruction for trial courts to consider a nonexclusive list of factors relevant to the circumstances of a confession, we agree with the Court of Appeals that Congress intended by its enactment to overrule *Miranda. See also* Davis v. United States, 512 U.S. 452, 464, 114 S.Ct. 2350, 129 L.Ed.2d 362 (1994) (Scalia, J., concurring) (stating that, prior to *Miranda,* "voluntariness *vel non* was the touchstone of admissibility of confessions"). Because of the obvious conflict between our decision in *Miranda* and § 3501, we must address whether Congress has constitutional authority to thus supersede *Miranda.* If Congress has such authority, § 3501's totality-of-the-circumstances approach must prevail over *Miranda's* requirement of warnings; if not, that section must yield to *Miranda's* more specific requirements.

The law in this area is clear. This Court has supervisory authority over the federal courts, and we may use that authority to prescribe rules of evidence and procedure that are binding in those tribunals. Carlisle v. United States, 517 U.S. 416, 426, 116 S.Ct. 1460, 134 L.Ed.2d 613 (1996). However, the power to judicially create and enforce nonconstitutional "rules of procedure and evidence for the federal courts exists only in the absence of a relevant Act of Congress." Palermo v. United States, 360 U.S. 343, 353, n. 11, 79 S.Ct. 1217, 3 L.Ed.2d 1287 (1959) (citing Funk v. United States, 290 U.S. 371, 382, 54 S.Ct. 212, 78 L.Ed. 369 (1933), and Gordon v. United States, 344 U.S. 414, 418, 73 S.Ct. 369, 97 L.Ed. 447 (1953)). Congress retains the ultimate authority to modify or set aside any judicially created rules of evidence and procedure that are not required by the Constitution. *Palermo, supra,* at 345–348, 79 S.Ct. 1217; *Carlisle, supra,* at 426, 116 S.Ct. 1460; Vance v. Terrazas, 444 U.S. 252, 265, 100 S.Ct. 540, 62 L.Ed.2d 461 (1980).

But Congress may not legislatively supersede our decisions interpreting and applying the Constitution. *See, e.g.,* City of Boerne v. Flores, 521 U.S. 507, 517–521, 117 S.Ct. 2157, 138 L.Ed.2d 624 (1997). This case therefore turns on whether the *Miranda* Court announced a constitutional rule or merely exercised its supervisory authority to regulate evidence in the absence of congressional direction. Recognizing this point, the Court of Appeals surveyed *Miranda* and its progeny to determine the constitutional status of the *Miranda* decision. 166 F.3d, at 687–692. Relying on the fact that we have created several exceptions to *Miranda's* warnings requirement and that we have repeatedly referred to the *Miranda* warnings as "prophylactic," New York v. Quarles, 467 U.S. 649, 653, 104 S.Ct. 2626, 81 L.Ed.2d 550 (1984), and "not themselves rights protected by the Constitution," Michigan v. Tucker, 417 U.S. 433, 444, 94 S.Ct. 2357, 41 L.Ed.2d 182 (1974),[11] the Court of Appeals concluded that the protections announced in *Miranda* are not constitutionally required.

We disagree with the Court of Appeals' conclusion, although we concede that there is language in some of our opinions that supports the view taken by that court. But first and foremost of the factors on the other side—that *Miranda* is a constitutional decision—is that both *Miranda* and two of its companion cases applied the rule to proceedings in state courts—to wit, Arizona, California, and New York. See 384 U.S., at 491–494, 497–499. Since that time, we have consistently applied *Miranda's* rule to prosecutions arising in state courts. *See, e.g.,* Stansbury v. California, 511 U.S. 318, 114 S.Ct. 1526, 128 L.Ed.2d 293 (1994) (*per curiam*); Minnick v. Mississippi, 498 U.S. 146, 111 S.Ct. 486, 112 L.Ed.2d 489 (1990); Arizona v.

---

11. *See also* Davis v. United States, 512 U.S. 452, 457–458, 114 S.Ct. 2350, 129 L.Ed.2d 362 (1994); Withrow v. Williams, 507 U.S. 680, 690–691, 113 S.Ct. 1745, 123 L.Ed.2d 407 (1993) ("*Miranda's* safeguards are not constitutional in character"); Duckworth v. Eagan, 492 U.S. 195, 203, 109 S.Ct. 2875, 106 L.Ed.2d 166 (1989); Connecticut v. Barrett, 479 U.S. 523, 528, 107 S.Ct. 828, 93 L.Ed.2d 920 (1987) ("[T]he *Miranda* Court adopted prophylactic rules designed to insulate the exercise of Fifth Amendment rights"); Oregon v. Elstad, 470 U.S. 298, 306, 105 S.Ct. 1285, 84 L.Ed.2d 222 (1985); Edwards v. Arizona, 451 U.S. 477, 492, 101 S.Ct. 1880, 68 L.Ed.2d 378 (1981) (Powell, J., concurring in result).

Roberson, 486 U.S. 675, 108 S.Ct. 2093, 100 L.Ed.2d 704 (1988); Edwards v. Arizona, 451 U.S. 477, 481–482, 101 S.Ct. 1880, 68 L.Ed.2d 378 (1981). It is beyond dispute that we do not hold a supervisory power over the courts of the several States. Smith v. Phillips, 455 U.S. 209, 221, 102 S.Ct. 940, 71 L.Ed.2d 78 (1982) ("Federal courts hold no supervisory authority over state judicial proceedings and may intervene only to correct wrongs of constitutional dimension"); Cicenia v. La Gay, 357 U.S. 504, 508–509, 78 S.Ct. 1297, 2 L.Ed.2d 1523 (1958). With respect to proceedings in state courts, our "authority is limited to enforcing the commands of the United States Constitution." Mu'Min v. Virginia, 500 U.S. 415, 422, 111 S.Ct. 1899, 114 L.Ed.2d 493 (1991). *See also* Harris v. Rivera, 454 U.S. 339, 344–345, 102 S.Ct. 460, 70 L.Ed.2d 530 (1981) *(per curiam)* (stating that "[f]ederal judges ... may not require the observance of any special procedures" in state courts "except when necessary to assure compliance with the dictates of the Federal Constitution").[12]

The *Miranda* opinion itself begins by stating that the Court granted certiorari "to explore some facets of the problems ... of applying the privilege against self-incrimination to in-custody interrogation, *and to give concrete constitutional guidelines for law enforcement agencies and courts to follow.*" 384 U.S., at 441–442, 86 S.Ct. 1602 (emphasis added). In fact, the majority opinion is replete with statements indicating that the majority thought it was announcing a constitutional rule. Indeed, the Court's ultimate conclusion was that the unwarned confessions obtained in the four cases before the Court in *Miranda* "were obtained from the defendant under circumstances that did not meet constitutional standards for protection of the privilege."[13]

Additional support for our conclusion that *Miranda* is constitutionally based is found in the *Miranda* Court's invitation for legislative action to protect the constitutional right against coerced self-incrimination. After discussing the "compelling pressures" inherent in custodial police interrogation, the *Miranda* Court concluded that, "[i]n order to combat these

---

12. Our conclusion regarding *Miranda*'s constitutional basis is further buttressed by the fact that we have allowed prisoners to bring alleged *Miranda* violations before the federal courts in habeas corpus proceedings. See Thompson v. Keohane, 516 U.S. 99, 116 S.Ct. 457, 133 L.Ed.2d 383 (1995); *Withrow, supra,* at 690–695, 113 S.Ct. 1745. Habeas corpus proceedings are available only for claims that a person "is in custody in violation of the Constitution or laws or treaties of the United States." 28 U.S.C. § 2254(a). Since the *Miranda* rule is clearly not based on federal laws or treaties, our decision allowing habeas review for *Miranda* claims obviously assumes that *Miranda* is of constitutional origin.

13. Many of our subsequent cases have also referred to *Miranda*'s constitutional underpinnings. *See, e.g., Withrow, supra,* at 691, 113 S.Ct. 1745 (" 'Prophylactic' though it may be, in protecting a defendant's Fifth Amendment privilege against self-incrimination, *Miranda* safeguards a 'fundamental trial right' "); Illinois v. Perkins, 496 U.S. 292, 296, 110 S.Ct. 2394, 110 L.Ed.2d 243 (1990) (describing *Miranda*'s warning requirement as resting on "the Fifth Amendment privilege against self-incrimination"); Butler v. McKellar, 494 U.S. 407, 411, 110 S.Ct. 1212, 108 L.Ed.2d 347 (1990) ("[T]he Fifth Amendment bars police-initiated interrogation following a suspect's request for counsel in the context of a separate investigation"); Michigan v. Jackson, 475 U.S. 625, 629, 106 S.Ct. 1404, 89 L.Ed.2d 631 (1986) ("The Fifth Amendment protection against compelled self-incrimination provides the right to counsel at custodial interrogations"); Moran v. Burbine, 475 U.S. 412, 427, 106 S.Ct. 1135, 89 L.Ed.2d 410 (1986) (referring to *Miranda* as "our interpretation of the Federal Constitution"); *Edwards, supra,* at 481–482, 101 S.Ct. 1880.

pressures and to permit a full opportunity to exercise the privilege against self-incrimination, the accused must be adequately and effectively apprised of his rights and the exercise of those rights must be fully honored." *Id.,* at 467, 86 S.Ct. 1602. However, the Court emphasized that it could not foresee "the potential alternatives for protecting the privilege which might be devised by Congress or the States," and it accordingly opined that the Constitution would not preclude legislative solutions that differed from the prescribed *Miranda* warnings but which were "at least as effective in apprising accused persons of their right of silence and in assuring a continuous opportunity to exercise it."[14] *Ibid.*

The Court of Appeals also relied on the fact that we have, after our *Miranda* decision, made exceptions from its rule in cases such as New York v. Quarles, 467 U.S. 649, 104 S.Ct. 2626, 81 L.Ed.2d 550 (1984), and Harris v. New York, 401 U.S. 222, 91 S.Ct. 643, 28 L.Ed.2d 1 (1971). See 166 F.3d, at 672, 689–691. But we have also broadened the application of the *Miranda* doctrine in cases such as Doyle v. Ohio, 426 U.S. 610, 96 S.Ct. 2240, 49 L.Ed.2d 91 (1976), and Arizona v. Roberson, 486 U.S. 675, 108 S.Ct. 2093, 100 L.Ed.2d 704 (1988). These decisions illustrate the principle—not that *Miranda* is not a constitutional rule—but that no constitutional rule is immutable. No court laying down a general rule can possibly foresee the various circumstances in which counsel will seek to apply it, and the sort of modifications represented by these cases are as much a normal part of constitutional law as the original decision.

The Court of Appeals also noted that in Oregon v. Elstad, 470 U.S. 298, 105 S.Ct. 1285, 84 L.Ed.2d 222 (1985), we stated that " '[t]he *Miranda* exclusionary rule ... serves the Fifth Amendment and sweeps more broadly than the Fifth Amendment itself.' " 166 F.3d, at 690 (quoting *Elstad, supra,* at 306, 105 S.Ct. 1285). Our decision in that case—refusing to apply the traditional "fruits" doctrine developed in Fourth Amendment cases—does not prove that *Miranda* is a nonconstitutional decision, but simply recognizes the fact that unreasonable searches under the Fourth Amendment are different from unwarned interrogation under the Fifth Amendment.

As an alternative argument for sustaining the Court of Appeals' decision, the court-invited *amicus curiae*[15] contends that the section complies with the requirement that a legislative alternative to *Miranda* be equally as effective in preventing coerced confessions. See Brief for Paul G. Cassell as *Amicus Curiae* 28–39. We agree with the *amicus* "contention that there are more remedies available for abusive police conduct" than there were at the time *Miranda* was decided, *see, e.g.,* Wilkins v. May, 872 F.2d 190, 194 (C.A.7 1989) (applying Bivens v. Six Unknown Fed. Narcotics Agents, 403 U.S. 388, 91 S.Ct. 1999, 29 L.Ed.2d 619 (1971), to hold that a

---

14. The Court of Appeals relied in part on our statement that the *Miranda* decision in no way "creates a 'constitutional straightjacket.'" See 166 F.3d 667, 672 (C.A.4 1999) (quoting *Miranda,* 384 U.S., at 467, 86 S.Ct. 1602). However, a review of our opinion in *Miranda* clarifies that this disclaimer was intended to indicate that the Constitution does not require police to administer the particular *Miranda* warnings, not that the Constitution does not require a procedure that is effective in securing Fifth Amendment rights.

15. Because no party to the underlying litigation argued in favor of § 3501's constitutionality in this Court, we invited Professor Paul Cassell to assist our deliberations by arguing in support of the judgment below.

suspect may bring a federal cause of action under the Due Process Clause for police misconduct during custodial interrogation). But we do not agree that these additional measures supplement § 3501's protections sufficiently to meet the constitutional minimum. *Miranda* requires procedures that will warn a suspect in custody of his right to remain silent and which will assure the suspect that the exercise of that right will be honored. *See, e.g.,* 384 U.S., at 467, 86 S.Ct. 1602. As discussed above, § 3501 explicitly eschews a requirement of preinterrogation warnings in favor of an approach that looks to the administration of such warnings as only one factor in determining the voluntariness of a suspect's confession. The additional remedies cited by amicus do not, in our view, render them, together with § 3501, an adequate substitute for the warnings required by *Miranda.*

The dissent argues that it is judicial overreaching for this Court to hold § 3501 unconstitutional unless we hold that the *Miranda* warnings are required by the Constitution, in the sense that nothing else will suffice to satisfy constitutional requirements. *Post,* at 2341–2342, 2347–2348 (opinion of Scalia, J.). But we need not go further than *Miranda* to decide this case. In *Miranda,* the Court noted that reliance on the traditional totality-of-the-circumstances test raised a risk of overlooking an involuntary custodial confession, 384 U.S., at 457, 86 S.Ct. 1602, a risk that the Court found unacceptably great when the confession is offered in the case in chief to prove guilt. The Court therefore concluded that something more than the totality test was necessary. See *ibid.;* see also *id.,* at 467, 490–491, 86 S.Ct. 1602. As discussed above, § 3501 reinstates the totality test as sufficient. Section 3501 therefore cannot be sustained if *Miranda* is to remain the law.

Whether or not we would agree with *Miranda's* reasoning and its resulting rule, were we addressing the issue in the first instance, the principles of *stare decisis* weigh heavily against overruling it now. *See, e.g.,* Rhode Island v. Innis, 446 U.S. 291, 304, 100 S.Ct. 1682, 64 L.Ed.2d 297 (1980) (Burger, C. J., concurring in judgment) ("The meaning of *Miranda* has become reasonably clear and law enforcement practices have adjusted to its strictures; I would neither overrule *Miranda,* disparage it, nor extend it at this late date"). While " '*stare decisis* is not an inexorable command,' " State Oil Co. v. Khan, 522 U.S. 3, 20, 118 S.Ct. 275, 139 L.Ed.2d 199 (1997) (quoting Payne v. Tennessee, 501 U.S. 808, 828, 111 S.Ct. 2597, 115 L.Ed.2d 720 (1991)), particularly when we are interpreting the Constitution, Agostini v. Felton, 521 U.S. 203, 235, 117 S.Ct. 1997, 138 L.Ed.2d 391 (1997), "even in constitutional cases, the doctrine carries such persuasive force that we have always required a departure from precedent to be supported by some 'special justification.' "

We do not think there is such justification for overruling *Miranda.* *Miranda* has become embedded in routine police practice to the point where the warnings have become part of our national culture. *See* Mitchell v. United States, 526 U.S. 314, 331–332, 119 S.Ct. 1307, 143 L.Ed.2d 424 (1999) (Scalia, J., dissenting) (stating that the fact that a rule has found " 'wide acceptance in the legal culture' " is "adequate reason not to overrule" it). While we have overruled our precedents when subsequent cases have undermined their doctrinal underpinnings, *see, e.g.,* Patterson v. McLean Credit Union, 491 U.S. 164, 173, 109 S.Ct. 2363, 105 L.Ed.2d 132 (1989), we do not believe that this has happened to the *Miranda* decision. If anything, our subsequent cases have reduced the impact of the *Miranda* rule on legitimate law enforcement while reaffirming the decision's core ruling that unwarned statements may not be used as evidence in the prosecution's case in chief.

The disadvantage of the *Miranda* rule is that statements which may be by no means involuntary, made by a defendant who is aware of his "rights," may nonetheless be excluded and a guilty defendant go free as a result. But experience suggests that the totality-of-the-circumstances test which § 3501 seeks to revive is more difficult than *Miranda* for law enforcement officers to conform to, and for courts to apply in a consistent manner. *See, e.g.,* Haynes v. Washington, 373 U.S., at 515, 83 S.Ct. 1336 ("The line between proper and permissible police conduct and techniques and methods offensive to due process is, at best, a difficult one to draw"). The requirement that *Miranda* warnings be given does not, of course, dispense with the voluntariness inquiry. But as we said in Berkemer v. McCarty, 468 U.S. 420, 104 S.Ct. 3138, 82 L.Ed.2d 317 (1984), "[c]ases in which a defendant can make a colorable argument that a self-incriminating statement was 'compelled' despite the fact that the law enforcement authorities adhered to the dictates of *Miranda* are rare." *Id.,* at 433, n. 20, 104 S.Ct. 3138.

In sum, we conclude that *Miranda* announced a constitutional rule that Congress may not supersede legislatively. Following the rule of *stare decisis,* we decline to overrule *Miranda* ourselves.[16] The judgment of the Court of Appeals is therefore

Reversed.[17]

■ JUSTICE SCALIA, with whom JUSTICE THOMAS joins, dissenting.

Those to whom judicial decisions are an unconnected series of judgments that produce either favored or disfavored results will doubtless greet today's decision as a paragon of moderation, since it declines to overrule Miranda v. Arizona, 384 U.S. 436, 86 S.Ct. 1602, 16 L.Ed.2d 694 (1966). Those who understand the judicial process will appreciate that today's

---

16. Various other contentions and suggestions have been pressed by the numerous *amici,* but because of the procedural posture of this case we do not think it appropriate to consider them. *See* United Parcel Service, Inc. v. Mitchell, 451 U.S. 56, 60, n. 2, 101 S.Ct. 1559, 67 L.Ed.2d 732 (1981); Bell v. Wolfish, 441 U.S. 520, 531–532, n. 13, 99 S.Ct. 1861, 60 L.Ed.2d 447 (1979); Knetsch v. United States, 364 U.S. 361, 370, 81 S.Ct. 132, 5 L.Ed.2d 128 (1960).

17. In Chavez v. Martinez, 538 U.S. 760 (2003), the Court held that violations of *Miranda,* absent coercion in violation of due process, could not by themselves support an action for damages under 42 U.S.C. § 1983. Four justices joined a plurality opinion by Justice Thomas, rejecting the claim on the ground that there is no violation of the Fifth Amendment privilege against self-incrimination unless the compelled statements are actually used in evidence in a criminal case. The decisive votes for the result were provided in a concurrence by Justice Souter, joined by Justice Breyer, reasoning that recognizing a civil suit for damages for *Miranda* violations would extend the *Miranda* doctrine beyond the "core" of the Fifth Amendment.

In two recent cases, a closely divided Supreme Court held that evidence derived from statement voluntarily made but obtained in violation of the *Miranda* rules should be admitted, unless the police adopted a deliberate strategy of violating *Miranda* for the purpose of obtaining the derivative evidence. *See* Missouri v. Seibert, 542 U.S. 600 (2004); United States v. Patane, 542 U.S. 630 (2004). In these cases a majority of the justices treated such cases as *Elstad* and *Tucker* as remaining good law after *Dickerson.*

decision is not a reaffirmation of *Miranda,* but a radical revision of the most significant element of *Miranda* (as of all cases): the rationale that gives it a permanent place in our jurisprudence.

Marbury v. Madison, 1 Cranch 137, 2 L.Ed. 60 (1803), held that an Act of Congress will not be enforced by the courts if what it prescribes violates the Constitution of the United States. That was the basis on which *Miranda* was decided. One will search today's opinion in vain, however, for a statement (surely simple enough to make) that what 18 U.S.C. § 3501 prescribes—the use at trial of a voluntary confession, even when a *Miranda* warning or its equivalent has failed to be given—violates the Constitution. The reason the statement does not appear is not only (and perhaps not so much) that it would be absurd, inasmuch as § 3501 excludes from trial precisely what the Constitution excludes from trial, viz., compelled confessions; but also that Justices whose votes are needed to compose today's majority are on record as believing that a violation of *Miranda* is *not* a violation of the Constitution. *See* Davis v. United States, 512 U.S. 452, 457–458, 114 S.Ct. 2350, 129 L.Ed.2d 362 (1994) (opinion of the Court, in which KENNEDY, J., joined); Duckworth v. Eagan, 492 U.S. 195, 203, 109 S.Ct. 2875, 106 L.Ed.2d 166 (1989) (opinion of the Court, in which KENNEDY, J., joined); Oregon v. Elstad, 470 U.S. 298, 105 S.Ct. 1285, 84 L.Ed.2d 222 (1985) (opinion of the Court by O'CONNOR, J.); New York v. Quarles, 467 U.S. 649, 104 S.Ct. 2626, 81 L.Ed.2d 550 (1984) (opinion of the Court by REHNQUIST, J.). And so, to justify today's agreed-upon result, the Court must adopt a significant *new,* if not entirely comprehensible, principle of constitutional law. As the Court chooses to describe that principle, statutes of Congress can be disregarded, not only when what they prescribe violates the Constitution, but when what they prescribe contradicts a decision of this Court that "announced a constitutional rule," *ante,* at 2333. As I shall discuss in some detail, the only thing that can possibly mean in the context of this case is that this Court has the power, not merely to apply the Constitution but to expand it, imposing what it regards as useful "prophylactic" restrictions upon Congress and the States. That is an immense and frightening antidemocratic power, and it does not exist.

It takes only a small step to bring today's opinion out of the realm of power-judging and into the mainstream of legal reasoning: The Court need only go beyond its carefully couched iterations that "*Miranda* is a constitutional decision," *ante,* at 2333, that "*Miranda* is constitutionally based," *ante,* at 2334, that *Miranda* has "constitutional underpinnings," *ante,* at 2334, n. 5, and come out and say quite clearly: "We reaffirm today that custodial interrogation that is not preceded by *Miranda* warnings or their equivalent violates the Constitution of the United States." It cannot say that, because a majority of the Court does not believe it. The Court therefore acts in plain violation of the Constitution when it denies effect to this Act of Congress. . . .

SECTION 3.   CURRENT DOCTRINE: POLICE AUTHORITY TO SEARCH AND ARREST

The Supreme Court's generally increasing sympathy for the state in the criminal procedure cases, evident perhaps in *Miranda* and certainly by

Terry, accelerated during the tenures of Chief Justice Burger and Chief Justice Rehnquist. The Court, however, has not overruled the Warren Court's landmarks. As a result, modern doctrine reflects elaborate qualifications and exceptions on the basic framework erected in the 1960s. A thorough study in a volume devoted largely to the substantive criminal law is impossible. In what follows, we examine the most common categories of police search and arrest practices, working generally up the ladder of their intrusiveness.

(1) Undercover Agents

United States v. Hankins

United States Court of Appeals, Sixth Circuit, 2006.
195 Fed.Appx. 295.

■ PER CURIAM.

. . . . The evidence, viewed in the light most favorable to the Government as the prevailing party at trial, reveals that in July 2004, a confidential informant told the South Central Kentucky Drug Task Force that Mr. Hankins was growing marijuana on his property. On July 27, 2004, Detective Kevin Bibb of the South Central Kentucky Drug Task Force investigated the tip and discovered marijuana growing in a wooded area on a remote part of Mr. Hankins' property. A trail made by a four-wheel all-terrain vehicle led from the marijuana plants to Mr. Hankins' home. After discovering the marijuana, Detective Bibb obtained a warrant to search Mr. Hankins' home and surrounding property.

Officers from the South Central Kentucky Drug Task Force, the Bureau of Alcohol Tobacco and Firearms, the Kentucky State Police, and the Logan County Sheriff's Department jointly searched Mr. Hankins' home on July 27, 2004. Mr. Hankins was at home when the law enforcement officers arrived. He was arrested after Detective Bibb discovered a bag of marijuana and 1.5 papers used to form a marijuana joint in his kitchen cabinet. A subsequent search disclosed two plots of marijuana growing directly behind the home, one behind the garage, and another adjacent to a nearby horse shed. Plastic cups, Miracle–Gro, twine, and a spray bottle were discovered and seized next to the marijuana plots. Officers also seized weighing scales, plastic ziplock bags, a shotgun, a rifle, a revolver, ammunition, and Mr. Hankins' truck. In total, 212 marijuana plants were seized worth approximately $400,000.

Two days after the raid, Mr. Hankins went over to the South Central Kentucky Drug Task Force office to retrieve some items from his truck. Detective Bibb accompanied Mr. Hankins to the truck. Mr. Hankins' withdrew $2000 in cash hidden behind the backseat. Detective Bibb took the money and instructed Mr. Hankins to speak with Director Jim Devasher of the South Central Kentucky Drug Task Force about getting it back. Director Devasher asked Mr. Hankins about the source of the money. Mr. Hankins claimed that the cash was the proceeds from the sale of some farm equipment. Upon further questioning, Mr. Hankins could not remember the buyer's name. Mr. Hankins also admitted growing marijuana in the past. Director Devasher refused to return the money to Mr. Hankins.

Subsequently, Mr. Hankins contacted James Chick. Mr. Chick and Mr. Hankins had been friends for over twenty years, and Mr. Hankins frequently ate at Mr. Chick's restaurant. Unbeknownst to Mr. Hankins, Mr. Chick had been caught selling cocaine, and rather than serve jail time, agreed to work as an informant for Special Agent David Hayes of the Bureau of Alcohol, Tobacco, Firearms, and Explosives. Mr. Chick testified that he was approached by Mr. Hankins "[p]robably because of my reputation. Everybody thinks I'm—because I'm from Detroit, I was raised, you know, with Italians, and they thought I was affiliated with them, which I'm not. I'm just friends." Mr. Hankins said that "he had $20,000 to give to someone" if they were willing to come to Kentucky and kill Director Devasher. At first Mr. Chick "really didn't take him serious" but when Mr. Hankins appeared to be "very serious," Mr. Chick contacted Agent Hayes.

Agent Hayes asked Mr. Chick to get Mr. Hankins to repeat his threats on tape. Mr. Chick agreed and was outfitted with a concealed microphone transmitter. Mr. Chick wore the transmitter when he was a guest in Mr. Hankins' home on three separate occasions. His conversations with Mr. Hankins were secretly transmitted to Agent Hayes and recorded by him. Mr. Hankins threatened to kill and cripple Director Devasher during his conversation with Mr. Chick on November 9, 2004, and November 18, 2004. . . .

Mr. Hankins claims that his Fourth Amendment rights were violated when the prosecution introduced audio tape recordings that had been transmitted from his home without a warrant or his knowledge or consent. . . .

At the Fourth Amendment's core " 'stands the right of a man to retreat into his own home and there be free from unreasonable governmental intrusion.' " *Kyllo v. United States,* 533 U.S. 27, 31 (2001) (quoting *Silverman v. United States,* 365 U.S. 505, 511 (1961)). *See also Hoffa v. United States,* 385 U.S. 293, 301 (1966) ("[T]he Fourth Amendment protects ... the security a man relies upon when he places himself or his property within a constitutionally protected area, be it his home or his office, his hotel room or his automobile."). The Fourth Amendment, however, does not protect a person's "misplaced belief that a person to whom he voluntarily confides his wrongdoing will not reveal it." *Hoffa,* 385 U.S. at 302. *See also United States v. White,* 401 U.S. 745, 749 (1971) (plurality opinion) ("[H]owever strongly a defendant may trust an apparent colleague, his expectations in this respect are not protected by the Fourth Amendment when it turns out that the colleague is a government agent regularly communicating with the authorities.").

A person's Fourth Amendment rights are not infringed if he or she consents to the invasion. *See Schneckloth v. Bustamonte,* 412 U.S. 218, 227 (1973) ("In situations where the police have some evidence of illicit activity, but lack probable cause to arrest or search, a search authorized by a valid consent may be the only means of obtaining important and reliable evidence."); *United States v. Bramble,* 103 F.3d 1475, 1478 (9th Cir.1996) ("Once consent has been obtained from one with authority to give it, any expectation of privacy has been lost.") (quoting *United States v. Rubio,* 727 F.2d 786, 797 (9th Cir.1983)). A person may still validly consent to a guest's entry, even if the guest lies about his or her identity or the reasons for the entry. *Lewis v. United States,* 385 U.S. 206, 209 (1966) ("[I]n the detection of many types of crime, the Government is entitled to use decoys and to conceal the identity of its agents.") (*citing Grimm v. United States,* 156 U.S. 604, 610 (1895); *Andrews v. United States,* 162 U.S. 420, 423 (1896)).

The surreptitious transmission of a defendant's conversation in his home with an informant to monitoring Government agents does not violate the Fourth Amendment. *On Lee v. United States,* 343 U.S. 747, 751–53 (1952). "If the conduct and revelations of an agent operating without electronic equipment do not invade the defendant's constitutionally justifiable expectations of privacy, neither does a simultaneous recording of the same conversations made by the agent or by others from transmissions received from the agent to whom the defendant is talking and whose trustworthiness the defendant necessarily risks." *United States v. White,* 401 U.S. 745, 751 (1971) (plurality opinion). The District Court did not err in admitting the tape recordings.

(2) Detention for Investigation

In Terry v. Ohio, 392 U.S. 1, 88 S.Ct. 1868, 20 L.Ed.2d 889 (1968), a police officer observed three men reconnoitering a jewelry store in a suspicious manner. He could not arrest them, for the officer had nothing close to probable cause to believe that they had committed an offense. Does the Fourth Amendment permit the "seizure" of a citizen's "person" for purposes of investigation when the circumstances justify suspicion but fall short of probable cause? The *Terry* Court answered yes, and over the years a brief detention for purposes of investigation, called a *"Terry* stop," has become a standard police procedure and the subject of a significant body of doctrine defining the stop, the level of suspicion needed to justify one, and the scope of police authority to conduct a protective search during the process.

A. THE DISTINCTION BETWEEN A STOP AND A NONCOERCIVE ENCOUNTER

United States v. Duty

United States Court of Appeals, Fourth Circuit, 2006.
204 Fed.Appx. 236.

■ PER CURIAM.

Following the denial of his motion to suppress evidence, Jeremiah Duty was convicted of felon in possession of a firearm, in violation of 18 U.S.C. § 922(g)(1) (2000). Duty now appeals, arguing that the district court erred in denying his motion to suppress evidence. Duty asserts that he was improperly seized without reasonable suspicion of wrongdoing on his part. Because we conclude that the district court erred in denying the motion to suppress, we vacate and remand for further proceedings.

This court reviews the district court's factual findings underlying a motion to suppress ruling for clear error, and the district court's legal determinations de novo. *Ornelas v. United States,* 517 U.S. 690, 699 (1996); *United States v. Bush,* 404 F.3d 263, 275 (4th Cir.2005). When a suppression motion has been denied, this court reviews the evidence in the light most favorable to the Government. *United States v. Grossman,* 400 F.3d 212, 216 (4th Cir.2005).

On March 31, 2005, Richmond police officer Crystal Winston ("Winston") was on a routine patrol of the 1900 block of Raven Street, in Richmond, Virginia. This portion of Raven Street is managed by the Richmond Redevelopment and Housing Authority ("RRHA") and is privatized, restricted only to residents and authorized guests.

While on patrol, Winston saw a gray Chevrolet vehicle parked in the cul-de-sac of the street with its engine running. Winston testified that the two occupants of the vehicle, later identified as Duty and Jonathan Bish, looked at her as she passed. Winston circled around the cul-de-sac, activated her emergency lights,* and pulled behind the Chevrolet, stopping ten to fifteen feet behind the vehicle. Winston testified that she stopped "to see if they were ok, what their business was, and if they had a legitimate or social reason to be in the area." Bish and Duty made no move to leave when Winston pulled behind them.

Winston approached the driver's side of the Chevrolet, and asked Duty and Bish for identification to determine if either lived in the area. Winston ran the information, and learned that Duty had an outstanding arrest warrant. After confirming the warrant, Winston placed Duty under arrest. Winston conducted a search incident to arrest, during which she found several rounds of .22 caliber ammunition, a syringe, and several pills on Duty's person. Winston also searched the trunk of the Chevrolet, in which she found a .22 caliber rifle.

Duty filed a motion to suppress the evidence, alleging that it was obtained from an improper seizure. After a hearing, the district court denied the motion to suppress. The district court found that it was proper for Winston to approach Duty and ask for identification. Once Winston discovered Duty's outstanding warrant, the district court found that Winston acted properly by arresting Duty, and searching him incident to arrest. Although the search of the trunk exceeded the scope of the search incident to arrest, the district court found that the rifle inside of the trunk would have been inevitably discovered because the car was impounded and inventoried. Following his conviction, Duty filed a timely notice of appeal.

The issues on appeal are whether Duty was seized for purposes of the Fourth Amendment, and if so, whether the seizure violated Duty's Fourth Amendment rights. "The Fourth Amendment protects 'the people' against 'unreasonable searches and seizures.'" *United States v. Hylton,* 349 F.3d

---

* The district court made a factual determination that the emergency lights on top of Winston's vehicle were flashing when she pulled behind the parked car in which Duty and Bish were sitting. Both Duty and Bish unequivocally testified that the lights were flashing on top of the police car. Winston, on the other hand, could not affirmatively recall whether the lights were activated when she stopped behind the car in which Duty and Bish were sitting. Therefore, this factual determination was not clearly erroneous.

781, 785 (4th Cir.2003) (quoting U.S. Const. amend. IV), *cert. denied,* 541 U.S. 1065 (2004). A person is considered "seized" for Fourth Amendment purposes if, under the totality of the circumstances, a reasonable person in the position of the suspect would believe that he or she was not free to leave or to terminate the encounter. *Florida v. Bostick,* 501 U.S. 429, 436– 37 (1991). "Because the test [to determine whether a person has been seized for purposes of the Fourth Amendment] is an objective one, its proper application is a question of law." *United States v. Sullivan,* 138 F.3d 126, 133 (4th Cir.1998).

Winston seized Duty for purposes of the Fourth Amendment when she activated the emergency lights on top of her car and pulled behind the parked car in which Duty was sitting. Through this action, Winston displayed an unmistakable show of authority that would give a reasonable person the impression that he was not free to leave. *See Brower v. County of Inyo,* 489 U.S. 593, 597–98 (1989); *Michigan v. Chestnut,* 486 U.S. 567, 575 (1988). Thus, the district court erred in finding the initial encounter consensual.

Because Duty was seized for Fourth Amendment purposes, Winston was required to have reasonable suspicion. "[A]n officer may, consistent with the Fourth Amendment, conduct a brief, investigatory stop when the officer has a reasonable, articulable suspicion that criminal activity is afoot." *Illinois v. Wardlow,* 528 U.S. 119, 123 (2000); *see Terry v. Ohio,* 392 U.S. 1, 30 (1968). To conduct a *Terry* stop, there must be "at least a minimal level of objective justification for making the stop." *Wardlow,* 528 U.S. at 123; *see also United States v. Hensley,* 469 U.S. 221, 232 (1985). Reasonable suspicion requires more than a hunch but less than probable cause, and it may be based on the collective knowledge of officers involved in an investigation. *Id.*

In assessing police conduct in a *Terry* stop, courts must look to the totality of the circumstances. *United States v. Sokolow,* 490 U.S. 1, 8 (1989). Officers conducting a lawful *Terry* stop may take steps reasonably necessary to protect their personal safety, check for identification, and maintain the status quo. *Hensley,* 469 U.S. at 229, 235; *see also United States v. Moore,* 817 F.2d 1105, 1108 (4th Cir.1987) (brief but complete restriction of liberty is valid under *Terry*).

We find that Winston lacked the reasonable suspicion necessary to seize Duty. The only evidence presented was that Duty was sitting in an idle car on a private street, and looked at Winston when she drove by. Such evidence plainly does not provide a basis for reasonable suspicion.

Accordingly, the seizure was invalid because Winston did not possess articulable, reasonable suspicion that criminal activity was afoot when she pulled behind Duty with the emergency lights activated. Because the seizure was illegal, the district court erred in denying Duty's motion to suppress evidence.

The judgment of the district court is vacated and the case is remanded for further proceedings consistent with this opinion.

VACATED AND REMANDED.

C.A.4 (Va.), 2006.

B. *STANDARD OF JUSTIFICATION*

United States v. Muhammad

United States Court of Appeals, Second Circuit, 2006.
463 F.3d 115.

■ MINER, CIRCUIT JUDGE.

Defendant-appellant Abdul R. Muhammad appeals from a judgment of conviction and sentence for possession of a firearm as a convicted felon entered in the United States District Court for the Western District of New York (Skretny, J.) following a guilty plea. Prior to the plea, the District Court had denied a motion to suppress the assault rifle found in defendant's possession. That ruling was a consequence of the District Court's conclusion that the police had reasonable suspicion to stop Muhammad and that subsequent events justified the seizure of the rifle. On this appeal, Muhammad challenges the findings giving rise to the District Court's conclusion as well as the conclusion itself. We affirm for the reasons that follow.

The events giving rise to the apprehension of Muhammad began with an anonymous cell phone call to the Buffalo Police 911 Call Center at approximately 11:13 P.M. on August 31, 2003. The female caller reported that a black man, attired in a white sweat suit and carrying a gun, was riding a bicycle west on Stanislaus Street toward Fillmore Avenue in the City of Buffalo. According to the caller, who never was identified, the gun was "out in the open." At approximately 11:16 P.M., the information provided by the caller was relayed by radio transmission to Buffalo police officers Richard Cruz and Joseph Langdon, who were on duty in a marked patrol car. The transmission specifically advised the officers that a cell phone caller had reported that "a black male dressed in white on a bike had a gun in his hand on Stanislaus headed toward Fillmore."

After receiving the call, the officers made their way toward Stanislaus Street. Driving east on Stanislaus, the officers were approaching the intersection of Rother Avenue when Officer Cruz "noticed a black male on a bike dressed in white, traveling west on Stanislaus." Activating the patrol vehicle's spotlight and overhead lights, Officer Cruz "attempted to slow down the suspect by approaching him in a forty-five degree angle toward the curb." The suspect increased the speed of his bicycle and drove it between the curb and the patrol car. Officer Cruz considered that "the [suspect] was attempting to flee." At that time, there was no one else in the vicinity, which the officers knew to be a high crime area.

According to Officer Cruz, Officer Langdon got out of the patrol car, chased the suspect and yelled at him to stop while Cruz tried to cut off the suspect's departure by driving the patrol car in reverse. Officer Langdon, in his version of events, said that he did not leave the vehicle but yelled at the suspect through the window: "hey, hold up." According to Langdon, the suspect did not stop, continued to ride his bicycle, and "kept trying to pass our vehicle." As Officer Cruz drove a short distance in reverse, another marked patrol car arrived, pulled in front of the suspect, and blocked his passage.

The second patrol car was occupied by Buffalo police officers Ronald Clark and Thomas Moran. When these officers first came upon the scene, Officer Clark saw the bicyclist ride past the passenger side of the other patrol car. According to Officer Clark, the bicyclist was moving at a high rate of speed and "trying to get away from the vehicle that was trying to stop him." Officer Moran also observed Muhammad's attempt to drive around the other patrol car, which he characterized as "fleeing the scene." The suspect was "boxed in" when Officer Clark positioned the car he was driving in front of the suspect, and Officer Cruz, driving his vehicle in reverse, was able to narrow the space between the two vehicles so that any further movement of the bicycle was impossible. Accordingly, the bicycle was brought to what Officer Clark described as an "abrupt stop."

Exiting the patrol car, Officer Moran recognized the bicyclist as defendant Muhammad, with whom he had had a previous encounter and whom he described as a person who "gets very agitated" and is not cooperative. Officer Clark also had past experience with Muhammad and described him in similar terms and as one "likely to flee." Officer Langdon ran from his patrol car to the place where Muhammad had been stopped and was then "straddling his bike holding on to the handlebars." Muhammad dropped the bicycle as ordered, and Langdon grabbed one of Muhammad's arms and another officer took his other arm. The officers then escorted Muhammad to a patrol car, where he was constrained to stand with his hands on the trunk. It was at that point that Officer Cruz observed a black gym bag strapped to Muhammad's back.

In response to Officer Cruz's question as to the contents of the gym bag, Muhammad said that the bag contained a baseball bat. Aware of the time of night, the absence of baseball fields in the vicinity, and the fact that they were in a high crime area, the officers were concerned that the bag might contain a gun. The officers feared that even a baseball bat could be used against them. Accordingly, Officer Cruz "patted the bag down for officer safety," while Officer Langdon did a pat down of Muhammad's person. At the top of the closed bag, Cruz felt "some type of muzzle from some type of weapon." Opening the bag after removing it from Muhammad's back, Officer Cruz discovered within the bag an SKS 7.62 millimeter caliber assault rifle.

Approximately one minute and thirty seconds elapsed between the radio dispatch and the discovery of the rifle. . . . By motion filed on December 12, 2003, Muhammad sought suppression of the seized rifle on the ground that it was taken in violation of his Fourth Amendment rights. Muhammad contended that the police had no reasonable suspicion of the sort that would justify stopping him and that the consequent search of his gym bag and seizure of its contents were unlawful. . . .

ANALYSIS

Whenever an anonymous tip first alerts police to possible wrongdoing, the question to be answered is whether the "tip, suitably corroborated, exhibits 'sufficient indicia of reliability to provide reasonable suspicion to make the investigatory stop.' " *Florida v. J.L.*, 529 U.S. 266, 270, 120 S.Ct. 1375, 146 L.Ed.2d 254 (2000) (internal citation omitted). . . . The events leading to the investigatory stop in *J.L.* were succinctly stated by the Supreme Court as follows:

> On October 13, 1995, an anonymous caller reported to the Miami–Dade Police that a young black male standing at a particular bus stop and wearing a plaid shirt was carrying a gun. So far as the record reveals, there is no audio recording of the tip, and nothing is known about the informant. Sometime after the police received the tip—the record does not say how long—two officers were instructed to respond. They arrived at the bus stop about six minutes later and saw three black males "just hanging out [there]." One of the three, respondent J.L., was wearing a plaid shirt. Apart from the tip, the officers had no reason to suspect any of the three of illegal conduct. The officers did not see a firearm, and J.L. made no threatening or otherwise unusual movements. One of the officers approached J.L., told him to put his hands up on the bus stop, frisked him, and seized the gun from J.L.'s pocket. The second officer frisked the other two individuals, against whom no allegations had been made, and found nothing.

Id. at 268, 120 S.Ct. 1375 (internal citations omitted; alteration in original).

When charged under Florida law with carrying a concealed weapon without a license and possession of a firearm while under the age of eighteen, J.L. moved to suppress the gun as seized in violation of the Fourth Amendment. *Id.* at 269, 120 S.Ct. 1375. Ultimately, the Florida Supreme Court held that the search was invalid, and the Supreme Court agreed. *Id.* Critical to the Court's determination that reasonable suspicion for stopping and searching J.L. was lacking was the Court's observation that "[a]ll the police had to go on in this case was the bare report of an unknown, unaccountable informant who neither explained how he knew about the gun nor supplied any basis for believing he had inside information about J.L." *Id.* at 271, 120 S.Ct. 1375.

The Court rejected Florida's arguments that (1) the tip should have been considered reliable and therefore a basis for reasonable suspicion because the police actually found a young black male attired in a plaid shirt at the bus stop; and (2) that the *Terry* analysis should be modified by a "firearm exception" that would allow a stop and frisk whenever the tip alleged the possession of an illegal firearm. *Id.* at 271–73, 120 S.Ct. 1375. The first argument was rejected because a suspect's physical attributes do not demonstrate a tipster's knowledge of concealed criminal activity, and the second argument was rejected because a firearm exception would enable false anonymous calls for the purpose of harassment and would lead to an expansion of the categories of cases in which exceptions would be allowed. *Id.*

In the case before us, there also was an anonymous tip that lacked any indicia of reliability. Although the anonymous informant proffered that she had seen the gun in the bicyclist's hand, the responding police officers did not observe any gun. Indeed, the only aspects of the caller's information that were corroborated by their initial observations were that a black man in white clothing was riding a bicycle on a particular street. Absent any other information indicative of the caller's reliability, such as the provision of information predictive of activity suggesting criminal involvement, or prior experience with the particular informant, the information known to the police at the time of their initial observation of Muhammad was insufficient to justify stopping him. . . .

However, because reasonable suspicion is "measured by what the officers knew before they conducted the search," *id.*, personal observations made by the officers that corroborate information furnished by an unknown and unaccountable tipster may provide the basis for a reasonableness finding. *Cf. id.* at 270, 120 S.Ct. 1375. Such corroboration may come in the form of an officer's observation of flight in a high crime area. *See Illinois v. Wardlow*, 528 U.S. 119, 124, 120 S.Ct. 673, 145 L.Ed.2d 570 (2000). "[O]fficers are not required to ignore the relevant characteristics of a location in determining whether the circumstances are sufficiently suspicious to warrant further investigation." *Id.* Moreover, "[h]eadlong flight— whenever it occurs—is the consummate act of evasion: It is not necessarily indicative of wrongdoing, but it is certainly suggestive of such." *Id.* An individual approached by an officer who has no reasonable suspicion of wrongdoing may ignore the officer and go about his business, and his refusal to cooperate may not form the basis for his detention. *See Florida v. Royer*, 460 U.S. 491, 498, 103 S.Ct. 1319, 75 L.Ed.2d 229 (1983). "But unprovoked flight is simply not a mere refusal to cooperate. Flight, by its very nature, is not 'going about one's business'; in fact, it is just the opposite." *Wardlow*, 528 U.S. at 125, 120 S.Ct. 673.

Muhammad's detention was initiated when Officer Cruz activated the patrol vehicle's spotlight and overhead lights. While Cruz's conduct may be considered an unreasonable order to stop since reasonable suspicion was lacking at that point, it is the rule "that an unreasonable order to stop does not violate the Fourth Amendment and that the grounds for a stop may thus be based on events that occur after the order to stop is given." *United States v. Swindle*, 407 F.3d 562, 568 (2d Cir.2005) (citing *California v. Hodari D.*, 499 U.S. 621, 629, 111 S.Ct. 1547, 113 L.Ed.2d 690 (1991), as providing "strong impli[cation]" for this rule). In *Swindle*, the defendant was driving an automobile when he was ordered to stop by the activation of patrol car lights. He thereafter crossed a double yellow line, drove the wrong way on a one-way street, threw a bag of cocaine from the car, and was seized as he fled on foot. *Id.* at 564. We concluded that "Swindle was seized only when the police physically apprehended him" and that the discarded drugs, which he was charged with having possessed with intent to distribute, were "not the fruit of a Fourth Amendment seizure." *Id.* at 573.

Similarly, Muhammad was not seized until he was physically restrained when the patrol cars came together and the officers were able to take him by the arm as he straddled his bicycle . . . . . The officers' personal observation of Muhammad's evasive conduct was the additional factor, missing in *J.L.*, that corroborated the anonymous tip and provided the objective manifestation that criminal activity was afoot. The totality of the circumstances, which included the detailed description by the anonymous tipster, the rapid identification of the bicyclist as described in the tip, and the location of Muhammad in a high crime area, when combined with the officers' personal observations and their own experience and specialized training, provided a sufficient basis for the conclusion that the officers who stopped Muhammad did so on the basis of a reasonable suspicion that he was engaged in criminal activity.

C. INCIDENTAL SEARCH AUTHORITY

United States v. Muhammad, continued

Once the officers properly stopped Muhammad, they were entitled to conduct a patdown search following Muhammad's problematic response to their query as to the contents of the gym bag strapped to his back. Where an officer makes reasonable inquiries, and where nothing in the initial stages of the encounter serves to dispel his reasonable fear for his own or others' safety, he is entitled for the protection of himself and others in the area to conduct a carefully limited search of the outer clothing of such persons in an attempt to discover weapons which might be used to assault him.

Terry, 392 U.S. at 30, 88 S.Ct. 1868.

The officers here had a tip that the bicyclist had a gun, but even a baseball bat, which Muhammad said was in the bag, would be a danger to them. The patdown of the bag, of course, resulted in the seizure of the firearm sought to be suppressed. A patdown is reasonable to "allow the officer to pursue his investigation without fear of violence." *Adams v. Williams*, 407 U.S. 143, 146, 92 S.Ct. 1921, 32 L.Ed.2d 612 (1972). At the time they conducted the patdown, the officers also had identified Muhammad from previous encounters as one who "gets very agitated," is not cooperative, and is "likely to flee." These factors reinforced their determination to examine the bag's contents. *See Holeman v. City of New London*, 425 F.3d 184, 192 (2d Cir.2005) (holding that patdown was proper where police were in high crime area in middle of the night with convicted felon who was acting suspiciously). The District Court did not err in denying the motion to suppress the weapon....

D. LIMITS

Flowers v. Fiore

United States Court of Appeals, First Circuit, 2004.
359 F.3d 24.

■ STAHL, SENIOR CIRCUIT JUDGE.

Plaintiff-appellant Bernard Flowers appeals from the district court's grant of summary judgment in favor of defendant-appellees Darren Fiore, Michael Garafola, Lawrence Silvestri, and the Town of Westerly, Rhode Island ("Town"). Flowers' suit asserted violations of his constitutional rights under the Fourth and Fourteenth Amendments as well as pendent state law claims arising out of his stop and detention by members of the Westerly Police Department.

On September 24, 2001, at approximately 11:55 a.m., the Westerly Police received a telephone call from Nunzio Gaccione, a Westerly resident. Gaccione "guess[ed] there was a little fight there with Butch Corbin and a couple other people" and that he "just got word that Corbin is sending two colored people over here to start some trouble." The dispatcher then radioed for Officer Fiore to respond to the complaint at Gaccione's residence on Ashaway Road. Fiore arrived at the residence within four to five minutes and met with Gaccione. Gaccione related that he received a call from Maurice O'Rourke, who stated that another individual, Michael Corbin, was sending two African–American men to Gaccione's home with a gun. Gaccione said that he believed this was because his grandson, Jason Bolduc, "works with a guy that Corbin knows and they had some type of falling out." Fiore claims to be familiar with Corbin and Bolduc, as both in the past have been involved in several disturbances and possible drug activity.

Gaccione then told Fiore that he had seen two African–American men in a small gray or black vehicle drive by his home about five minutes prior to Fiore's arrival. Gaccione believed that these men may have been the ones to whom O'Rourke referred.

At 12:12 p.m., Fiore detailed Gaccione's complaint, including the description of the suspects, into his log. Fiore alerted on his radio that police should be looking for a small gray or black vehicle with two black men, possibly armed. He further stated that he was "not too sure what it is" and that "they made threats over here at the Gaccione complex."

Next, Fiore took a post at the intersection of Route 3 and Danielle Drive, which is about half a mile east of the Gaccione residence along Route 3. He chose this particular location upon a belief that the suspect vehicle would return to the Gaccione residence after having passed by the Gaccione residence the first time. Some twenty to thirty minutes later, Fiore noticed a small gray car moving through the intersection of Route 3 and Danielle Drive. Fiore thought that about twenty minutes had elapsed since he took his position on Route 3. He conceded, however, that the time interval may have been as long as thirty minutes, as radio logs indicated. He "caught a side view of [the occupant of the car] and saw that it was a black male." Prior to observing this particular vehicle, Fiore did not notice any other cars with African–American male occupants drive by his post.

Fiore decided to follow this vehicle because "it fit the description of the Gaccione complaint and it was heading in the direction of the Gaccione residence."[1] Although he noticed only one occupant, he believed that the other suspect either could have been dropped off at another location or was

---

1. The district court recounted that "Fiore followed [Flowers'] vehicle and used his onboard computer to perform a registration check" and that "[t]he information received by Fiore was that the license plate on Flowers' vehicle had been issued to a vehicle different from the one that Flowers was driving." *Flowers v. Fiore*, 239 F.Supp.2d 173, 176 (D.Mass.2003). The court continued, "Accordingly, Fiore radioed for help and signaled Flowers to pull over." *Id.* The record contains inconsistent statements by Fiore, however, as to when he conducted the check, whether it was before he pulled Flowers over or after Flowers had been released. Fiore's police report, written just after the incident, indicates that he "noticed a problem with Flowers' license plate *after* clearing the stop." In his affidavit, Fiore stated that before he pulled over Flowers, he "noticed really quick" that the plates did not match the vehicle. He attempted to reconcile his statement with the police report by suggesting that he "should have put 'remembered' in place of 'noticed' "in the police report because he "had noticed [the discrepancy] on the computer screen prior to the stop." Fiore now claims that the license plate discrepancy played no role in his decision to follow and stop the vehicle.

hiding in the vehicle. At 12:42 p.m., Fiore notified dispatchers that he was following a vehicle on Route 3. He based his "probable cause" to stop the vehicle on his belief that "the description of the vehicle fit the description by Mr. Gaccione, there was a black male that was operating the vehicle . . . the close proximity of the time of the call and the fact that it was heading toward Mr. Gaccione's residence."

After following the vehicle approximately one mile, Fiore activated his lights and signaled for Flowers to pull over. Both eventually stopped on High Street, approximately half a mile west of the Gaccione residence along Route 3. Fiore assumed that dispatch would send backup "because of the situation," and accordingly pulled Flowers over to a location near where he "knew backup was coming from a car stop." He instructed Flowers over the loudspeaker to remain in the vehicle. Next, two backup officers, Lawrence Silvestri and Michael Garafola, arrived in separate police cruisers. Garafola left his vehicle with a shotgun ready in hand. Fiore, again using the loudspeaker, directed Flowers to extend his arms out the window and then open the car door and exit the vehicle. Flowers complied. Fiore then directed Flowers to turn around with his hands in the air and walk backwards towards the officers. From the time they arrived and exited their vehicles, each officer had his weapon drawn.

Flowers contends that when he reached the officers, his "hands were forced behind [him], handcuffs were placed [on him] and [he] was dropped to [his knees]." Fiore claims that the officers directed Flowers to kneel on the road beside his car and lace his fingers behind his head, and that then Flowers was handcuffed, frisked, and placed in the back of Fiore's cruiser. All three officers also claim that they followed standard procedure for a high-risk (or felony) stop and that it was necessary to do so because they felt that there was a danger to their safety.[2]

While Flowers was in the back of the police cruiser, the backup officers searched Flowers' vehicle for weapons and a possible other suspect. Fiore claims that when nothing was recovered, he took Flowers out of the cruiser, removed his handcuffs, and explained why he was stopped. Flowers claims that Fiore first approached him and said, "Mr. Gaccione reported two black men threatened him and they had guns so you understand why I had to do what I had to do." Fiore then added that the two black men had a gray vehicle. With no apology, Flowers was ordered back to his car.

Fiore contends that he explained the situation to Flowers, at which time Flowers became very angry and accused him of racial profiling. Flowers then asked Fiore to use his phone so he could call his wife (who was working nearby and awaiting his arrival). Fiore responded that he did not have a phone. He suggested that Flowers use the phone at the gym across the street and then ordered Flowers to move his car. Flowers then went back to his car and drove to the local hospital, where his wife worked.

---

2. In his January 17, 2002 affidavit, Officer Fiore described a high risk motor vehicle stop as "a motor vehicle stop when there is a possibility of danger to the officer stopping the vehicle." In his March 12, 2002 affidavit, Officer Silvestri stated that upon his arrival at the scene, the officers decided to employ felony car stop tactics. He defined "felony car stop" to be the following: "Weapons drawn, have him walk to us, secure him, and then clear the car." Both affidavits are in the record on summary judgment.

By this time, both backup officers had driven away. Fiore proceeded to make "a couple passes by the Gaccione residence" until the end of his shift. Thereafter, he did not re-take a post to look for a suspect vehicle "because of the time that had gone by" and his belief that "the immediate threat had pretty much diminished."

Pursuant to 42 U.S.C. § 1983, Flowers brought this action against Officers Fiore, Silvestri, and Garafola, and the Town of Westerly, claiming (1) that the police officers detained him because of his race, in violation of the Equal Protection Clause of the Fourteenth Amendment, U.S. Const. amend. XIV, § 1; and (2) that the officers detained him without probable cause and used excessive force, and that the Town failed to properly train and supervise the officers, in violation of his right against unreasonable government search and seizure under the Fourth and Fourteenth Amendments of the federal Constitution. Flowers also asserted state law claims for assault and battery, false imprisonment, and intentional infliction of emotional distress, as well as for violations of his rights under Article 1, sections 2 and 6 of the Rhode Island Constitution. After the close of discovery, defendants moved for summary judgment, arguing that there were no constitutional violations, and that they were shielded from liability by the doctrine of qualified immunity. Upon determining that no constitutional rights had been violated, the court did not reach the issue of qualified immunity and granted summary judgment in favor of the defendants. This appeal followed.

. . . . For purposes of determining whether the stop and detention were constitutionally permissible, we must first decide whether the officers' actions amounted to an investigatory stop or was so intrusive as to constitute a *de facto* arrest. . . . Where police actions taken during the detention exceed what is necessary to dispel the suspicion that justified the stop, the detention may amount to an "arrest" and is lawful only if it is supported by probable cause. *United States v. Quinn,* 815 F.2d 153, 156 (1st Cir.1987). . . .

Generally, we say that an investigatory stop constitutes a *de facto* arrest "when a 'reasonable man in the suspect's position' would have understood his situation,' in the circumstances then obtaining, to be tantamount to being under arrest." *United States v. Zapata,* 18 F.3d 971, 975 (1st Cir.1994) (quoting *Berkemer v. McCarty,* 468 U.S. 420, 441, 104 S.Ct. 3138, 82 L.Ed.2d 317 (1984)). However, in a borderline case where the detention at issue has one or two arrest-like features but otherwise is consistent with a *Terry* stop, it will not be obvious just how the detention at issue ought reasonably to have been perceived. Such a case requires a fact-specific inquiry into whether the measures used by the police were reasonable in light of the circumstances that prompted the stop or that developed during the course of the stop. *See United States v. Young,* 105 F.3d 1, 8 (1st Cir.1997) ("our cases in this area evince the fact specific nature of the inquiry"). In the present case, we conclude that the actions of the police during the stop and detention did not go beyond an investigatory *Terry* stop and did not amount to an arrest.

While *Terry* stops generally are fairly unintrusive, we have repeatedly stressed that officers may take necessary steps to protect themselves if the circumstances reasonably warrant such measures. *See United States v. Lee,* 317 F.3d 26, 31–32 (1st Cir.2003); *Acosta-Colon,* 157 F.3d at 18; *United States v. Trullo,* 809 F.2d 108, 113 (1st Cir.1987). Similarly, other circuits have held that police officers may draw their weapons without transforming an otherwise valid *Terry* stop into an arrest. *See, e.g., United States v. Alvarez,* 899 F.2d 833, 838 (9th Cir.1990), *cert. denied,* 498 U.S. 1024, 111 S.Ct. 671, 112 L.Ed.2d 663 (1991); *United States v. Taylor,* 857 F.2d 210, 214 (4th Cir.1988); *United States v. Serna–Barreto,* 842 F.2d 965, 968 (7th Cir.1988); *United States v. Jones,* 759 F.2d 633, 638 (8th Cir.), *cert. denied,* 474 U.S. 837, 106 S.Ct. 113, 88 L.Ed.2d 92 (1985); *United States v. Jackson,* 652 F.2d 244, 249 (2d Cir.1981). Here, the officers drew their firearms because they were faced with a report of an armed threat. Moreover, upon restraining Flowers, they immediately holstered their weapons. It was not unreasonable under the circumstances for the officers to execute the *Terry* stop with their weapons drawn.

As for the officers' use of handcuffs during the stop, we in the past have required the government to point to "some specific fact or circumstance that could have supported a reasonable belief that the use of such restraints was necessary to carry out the legitimate purposes of the stop without exposing law enforcement officers, the public, or the suspect himself to an undue risk of harm." *Acosta–Colon,* 157 F.3d at 18–19. Where, as here, police officers have information that a suspect is currently armed and that a crime involving violence may soon occur, they are justified in using restraints such as handcuffs without causing an investigatory stop to cross over into an arrest. *See Washington v. Lambert,* 98 F.3d 1181, 1189 (9th Cir.1996).

The reasonable use of backup officers is also within the bounds of a *Terry* stop. "[M]ere numbers do not automatically convert a lawful *Terry* stop into something more forbidding." *Zapata,* 18 F.3d at 976. We have previously refused to hold that an investigative stop turned into a *de facto* arrest where five law enforcement officers were present at the scene of the stop. *United States v. Trueber,* 238 F.3d 79, 94 (1st Cir.2001). Here, Flowers was stopped and detained by only three officers, only one of whom—Fiore—was in direct proximity to him while he was detained in the police cruiser. Likewise, the fact that Flowers was placed in the back of a police cruiser does not elevate the detention beyond a *Terry* stop. *See Haynie v. County of Los Angeles,* 339 F.3d 1071, 1077 (9th Cir.2003); *United States v. Critton,* 43 F.3d 1089, 1092–94 (6th Cir.1995). Although there may be cases where individually reasonable police actions taken together go beyond the bounds of a *Terry* stop, such is not the case here where the circumstances justified the officers' overall handling of the situation.

As for the duration of the stop, we must examine whether the police "diligently pursued a means of investigation that was likely to confirm or dispel their suspicions quickly, during which time it was necessary to detain the defendant." *United States v. Sharpe,* 470 U.S. 675, 686, 105 S.Ct. 1568, 84 L.Ed.2d 605 (1985); *see also Royer,* 460 U.S. at 500, 103 S.Ct. 1319; *Summers,* 452 U.S. at 701 n. 14, 101 S.Ct. 2587. There is "no hard-and-fast time limit for a permissible *Terry* stop." *Sharpe,* 470 U.S. at 686, 105 S.Ct. 1568. Pursuant to Westerly Police Department standard procedure for high-risk (or felony) stops, the officers directed Flowers to kneel on the road next to his car, handcuffed, frisked, and placed him in the back seat of the police cruiser. Officers Silvestri and Garafola then searched Flowers' car for weapons and a possible other suspect. The entire detention took no more than fifteen minutes. Upon uncovering nothing, Officer Fiore promptly took Flowers out of the cruiser, removed his handcuffs, explained why he was stopped, and allowed him to return to his own car. We stress that the officers did not determine that Flowers was unarmed and that no weapon was hidden in the car until *after* he had been handcuffed and placed in the cruiser. Flowers presents no evidence that the officers were dilatory in their investigation and we see no way that the officers could have substantially shortened the detention if they were to dispel their suspicions meaningfully. . . .

It is also noteworthy that the officers never relocated Flowers to a station house or detention area. Nor did they read Flowers *Miranda* rights. In *Acosta–Colon,* we held that the detention of a suspect crossed over to a *de facto* arrest largely due to the fact that customs officers relocated the suspect from the place of the original stop—an airport gate—to an official interrogation room some distance from the gate. *See* 157 F.3d at 15; *see also Royer,* 460 U.S. at 494, 103 S.Ct. 1319. Similarly, the Supreme Court in *Dunaway* found a *de facto* arrest where police officers brought the defendant to the police station, read him his *Miranda* rights, and interrogated him. *See* 442 U.S. at 212–13, 99 S.Ct. 2248. At no point did Officers Fiore, Silvestri, or Garafola interrogate Flowers or remove him from the scene to an official holding area. The entire episode occurred in neutral surroundings—on a public street. Nor did the officers communicate verbally to Flowers that he was under arrest or that they wanted to arrest him.

The various incidents of the stop and detention—some arrest-like—ultimately add up to a situation where the officers responded in an urgent and reasonable fashion to a report of an armed threat that was substantially confirmed by Gaccione's firsthand observation. We stress again that we do not rely on any single factor as legally dispositive, but assess the cumulative impact of the various elements of the stop. We look at the total factual context of the stop, thereby following our directive to make fact-specific evaluations and inquiries of the situation as a whole. *See Young,* 105 F.3d at 8. Our conclusion is that the officers' stop and detention of Flowers did not go beyond the boundaries of a *Terry* stop. . . .

[T]his is a close case. However, against the proper standard and accounting for the district court's errors and elisions, we in the end conclude that the officers possessed sufficient and reasonable suspicion to stop Flowers and acted reasonably in dispelling that suspicion throughout the course of the detention.

[The concurring opinion of Chief Judge Boudin is omitted.]

(3) Arrest

A. *REQUIRED JUSTIFICATION*

Maryland v. Pringle

Supreme Court of the United States, 2003.
540 U.S. 366, 124 S.Ct. 795, 157 L.Ed.2d 769.

■ CHIEF JUSTICE REHNQUIST delivered the opinion of the Court.

In the early morning hours a passenger car occupied by three men was stopped for speeding by a police officer. The officer, upon searching the car, seized $763 of rolled-up cash from the glove compartment and five glassine baggies of cocaine from between the back-seat armrest and the back seat. After all three men denied ownership of the cocaine and money, the officer arrested each of them. We hold that the officer had probable cause to arrest Pringle—one of the three men.

At 3:16 a.m. on August 7, 1999, a Baltimore County Police officer stopped a Nissan Maxima for speeding. There were three occupants in the car: Donte Partlow, the driver and owner, respondent Pringle, the front-seat passenger, and Otis Smith, the back-seat passenger. The officer asked Partlow for his license and registration. When Partlow opened the glove compartment to retrieve the vehicle registration, the officer observed a large amount of rolled-up money in the glove compartment. The officer returned to his patrol car with Partlow's license and registration to check the computer system for outstanding violations. The computer check did not reveal any violations. The officer returned to the stopped car, had Partlow get out, and issued him an oral warning.

After a second patrol car arrived, the officer asked Partlow if he had any weapons or narcotics in the vehicle. Partlow indicated that he did not. Partlow then consented to a search of the vehicle. The search yielded $763 from the glove compartment and five plastic glassine baggies containing cocaine from behind the back-seat armrest. When the officer began the search the armrest was in the upright position flat against the rear seat. The officer pulled down the armrest and found the drugs, which had been placed between the armrest and the back seat of the car.

The officer questioned all three men about the ownership of the drugs and money, and told them that if no one admitted to ownership of the drugs he was going to arrest them all. The men offered no information regarding the ownership of the drugs or money. All three were placed under arrest and transported to the police station.

Later that morning, Pringle waived his rights under *Miranda v. Arizona,* 384 U.S. 436, 86 S.Ct. 1602, 16 L.Ed.2d 694 (1966), and gave an oral and written confession in which he acknowledged that the cocaine belonged to him, that he and his friends were going to a party, and that he intended to sell the cocaine or "[u]se it for sex." App. 26. Pringle maintained that the other occupants of the car did not know about the drugs, and they were released.

The trial court denied Pringle's motion to suppress his confession as the fruit of an illegal arrest, holding that the officer had probable cause to arrest Pringle. A jury convicted Pringle of possession with intent to distribute cocaine and possession of cocaine. He was sentenced to 10 years' incarceration without the possibility of parole. The Court of Special Appeals of Maryland affirmed. 141 Md.App. 292, 785 A.2d 790 (2001).

The Court of Appeals of Maryland, by divided vote, reversed, holding that, absent specific facts tending to show Pringle's knowledge and dominion or control over the drugs, "the mere finding of cocaine in the back armrest when [Pringle] was a front seat passenger in a car being driven by its owner is insufficient to establish probable cause for an arrest for possession." 370 Md. 525, 545, 805 A.2d 1016, 1027 (2002). We granted certiorari, 538 U.S. 921, 123 S.Ct. 1571, 155 L.Ed.2d 311 (2003), and now reverse.

Under the Fourth Amendment, made applicable to the States by the Fourteenth Amendment, *Mapp v. Ohio,* 367 U.S. 643, 81 S.Ct. 1684, 6 L.Ed.2d 1081 (1961), the people are "to be secure in their persons, houses, papers, and effects, against unreasonable searches and seizures, . . . and no Warrants shall issue, but upon probable cause. . . ." U.S. Const., Amdt. 4. Maryland law authorizes police officers to execute warrantless arrests, *inter alia,* for felonies committed in an officer's presence or where an officer has probable cause to believe that a felony has been committed or is being committed in the officer's presence. Md. Ann.Code, Art. 27, § 594B (1996) (repealed 2001). A warrantless arrest of an individual in a public place for a felony, or a misdemeanor committed in the officer's presence, is consistent with the Fourth Amendment if the arrest is supported by probable cause. *United States v. Watson,* 423 U.S. 411, 424, 96 S.Ct. 820, 46 L.Ed.2d 598 (1976); see *Atwater v. Lago Vista,* 532 U.S. 318, 354, 121 S.Ct. 1536, 149 L.Ed.2d 549 (2001) (stating that "[i]f an officer has probable cause to believe that an individual has committed even a very minor criminal offense in his presence, he may, without violating the Fourth Amendment, arrest the offender").

It is uncontested in the present case that the officer, upon recovering the five plastic glassine baggies containing suspected cocaine, had probable cause to believe a felony had been committed. Md. Ann.Code, Art. 27, § 287 (1996) (repealed 2002) (prohibiting possession of controlled dangerous substances). The sole question is whether the officer had probable cause to believe that Pringle committed that crime.[1]

The long-prevailing standard of probable cause protects "citizens from rash and unreasonable interferences with privacy and from unfounded charges of crime," while giving "fair leeway for enforcing the law in the community's protection." *Brinegar v. United States,* 338 U.S. 160, 176, 69 S.Ct. 1302, 93 L.Ed. 1879 (1949). On many occasions, we have reiterated that the probable-cause standard is a " 'practical, nontechnical conception' " that deals with " 'the factual and practical considerations of everyday life on which reasonable and prudent men, not legal technicians, act.' " *Illinois v. Gates,* 462 U.S. 213, 231, 103 S.Ct. 2317, 76 L.Ed.2d 527 (1983) (quoting *Brinegar, supra,* at 175–176, 69 S.Ct. 1302); see, *e.g., Ornelas v. United States,* 517 U.S. 690, 695, 116 S.Ct. 1657, 134 L.Ed.2d 911 (1996); *United States v. Sokolow,* 490 U.S. 1, 7–8, 109 S.Ct. 1581, 104 L.Ed.2d 1 (1989). "[P]robable cause is a fluid concept—turning on the assessment of probabilities in particular factual contexts—not readily, or even usefully, reduced to a neat set of legal rules." *Gates,* 462 U.S., at 232, 103 S.Ct. 2317.

The probable-cause standard is incapable of precise definition or quantification into percentages because it deals with probabilities and depends

---

1. Maryland law defines "possession" as "the exercise of actual or constructive dominion or control over a thing by one or more persons." Md. Ann.Code, Art. 27, § 277(s) (1996) (repealed 2002).

on the totality of the circumstances. See *ibid.; Brinegar,* 338 U.S., at 175, 69 S.Ct. 1302. We have stated, however, that "[t]he substance of all the definitions of probable cause is a reasonable ground for belief of guilt," *ibid.* (internal quotation marks and citations omitted), and that the belief of guilt must be particularized with respect to the person to be searched or seized, *Ybarra v. Illinois,* 444 U.S. 85, 91, 100 S.Ct. 338, 62 L.Ed.2d 238 (1979). In *Illinois v. Gates,* we noted:

> "As early as *Locke v. United States,* 7 Cranch 339, 348, 3 L.Ed. 364 (1813), Chief Justice Marshall observed, in a closely related context: '[T]he term "probable cause," according to its usual acceptation, means less than evidence which would justify condemnation.... It imports a seizure made under circumstances which warrant suspicion.' More recently, we said that 'the *quanta* ... of proof' appropriate in ordinary judicial proceedings are inapplicable to the decision to issue a warrant. *Brinegar,* 338 U.S., at 173, 69 S.Ct. 1302. Finely tuned standards such as proof beyond a reasonable doubt or by a preponderance of the evidence, useful in formal trials, have no place in the [probable-cause] decision." 462 U.S., at 235, 103 S.Ct. 2317.

To determine whether an officer had probable cause to arrest an individual, we examine the events leading up to the arrest, and then decide "whether these historical facts, viewed from the standpoint of an objectively reasonable police officer, amount to" probable cause, *Ornelas, supra,* at 696, 116 S.Ct. 1657.

In this case, Pringle was one of three men riding in a Nissan Maxima at 3:16 a.m. There was $763 of rolled-up cash in the glove compartment directly in front of Pringle.[2] Five plastic glassine baggies of cocaine were behind the back-seat armrest and accessible to all three men. Upon questioning, the three men failed to offer any information with respect to the ownership of the cocaine or the money.

We think it an entirely reasonable inference from these facts that any or all three of the occupants had knowledge of, and exercised dominion and control over, the cocaine. Thus, a reasonable officer could conclude that there was probable cause to believe Pringle committed the crime of possession of cocaine, either solely or jointly.

Pringle's attempt to characterize this case as a guilt-by-association case is unavailing. His reliance on *Ybarra v. Illinois, supra,* and *United States v. Di Re,* 332 U.S. 581, 68 S.Ct. 222, 92 L.Ed. 210 (1948), is misplaced. In *Ybarra,* police officers obtained a warrant to search a tavern and its

---

2. The Court of Appeals of Maryland dismissed the $763 seized from the glove compartment as a factor in the probable-cause determination, stating that "[m]oney, without more, is innocuous." 370 Md. 525, 546, 805 A.2d 1016, 1028 (2002). The court's consideration of the money in isolation, rather than as a factor in the totality of the circumstances, is mistaken in light of our precedents. See, *e.g., Illinois v. Gates,* 462 U.S. 213, 230–231, 103 S.Ct. 2317, 76 L.Ed.2d 527 (1983) (opining that the totality of the circumstances approach is consistent with our prior treatment of probable cause); *Brinegar v. United States,* 338 U.S. 160, 175–176, 69 S.Ct. 1302, 93 L.Ed. 1879 (1949) ("Probable cause exists where 'the facts and circumstances within their [the officers'] knowledge and of which they had reasonably trustworthy information [are] sufficient in themselves to warrant a man of reasonable caution in the belief that' an offense has been or is being committed"). We think it is abundantly clear from the facts that this case involves more than money alone.

bartender for evidence of possession of a controlled substance. Upon entering the tavern, the officers conducted patdown searches of the customers present in the tavern, including Ybarra. Inside a cigarette pack retrieved from Ybarra's pocket, an officer found six tinfoil packets containing heroin. We stated:

> "[A] person's mere propinquity to others independently suspected of criminal activity does not, without more, give rise to probable cause to search that person. *Sibron v. New York,* 392 U.S. 40, 62–63[, 88 S.Ct. 1889, 20 L.Ed.2d 917] (1968). Where the standard is probable cause, a search or seizure of a person must be supported by probable cause particularized with respect to that person. This requirement cannot be undercut or avoided by simply pointing to the fact that coincidentally there exists probable cause to search or seize another or to search the premises where the person may happen to be." 444 U.S., at 91, 100 S.Ct. 338.

We held that the search warrant did not permit body searches of all of the tavern's patrons and that the police could not pat down the patrons for weapons, absent individualized suspicion. *Id.,* at 92, 100 S.Ct. 338.

This case is quite different from *Ybarra.* Pringle and his two companions were in a relatively small automobile, not a public tavern. In *Wyoming v. Houghton,* 526 U.S. 295, 119 S.Ct. 1297, 143 L.Ed.2d 408 (1999), we noted that "a car passenger—unlike the unwitting tavern patron in *Ybarra*—will often be engaged in a common enterprise with the driver, and have the same interest in concealing the fruits or the evidence of their wrongdoing." *Id.,* at 304–305, 119 S.Ct. 1297. Here we think it was reasonable for the officer to infer a common enterprise among the three men. The quantity of drugs and cash in the car indicated the likelihood of drug dealing, an enterprise to which a dealer would be unlikely to admit an innocent person with the potential to furnish evidence against him.

In *Di Re,* a federal investigator had been told by an informant, Reed, that he was to receive counterfeit gasoline ration coupons from a certain Buttitta at a particular place. The investigator went to the appointed place and saw Reed, the sole occupant of the rear seat of the car, holding gasoline ration coupons. There were two other occupants in the car: Buttitta in the driver's seat and Di Re in the front passenger's seat. Reed informed the investigator that Buttitta had given him counterfeit coupons. Thereupon, all three men were arrested and searched. After noting that the officers had no information implicating Di Re and no information pointing to Di Re's possession of coupons, unless presence in the car warranted that inference, we concluded that the officer lacked probable cause to believe that Di Re was involved in the crime. 332 U.S., at 592–594, 68 S.Ct. 222. We said "[a]ny inference that everyone on the scene of a crime is a party to it must disappear if the Government informer singles out the guilty person." *Id.,* at 594, 68 S.Ct. 222. No such singling out occurred in this case; none of the three men provided information with respect to the ownership of the cocaine or money.

We hold that the officer had probable cause to believe that Pringle had committed the crime of possession of a controlled substance. Pringle's arrest therefore did not contravene the Fourth and Fourteenth Amendments. Accordingly, the judgment of the Court of Appeals of Maryland is reversed, and the case is remanded for further proceedings not inconsistent with this opinion.

B. JUDICIAL REVIEW

United States v. Stamper

United States Court of Appeals, Sixth Circuit, 2004.
91 Fed.Appx. 445.

■ KENNEDY, CIRCUIT JUDGE:

On September 16, 2000, defendant, [his lover], and their children were staying in room number 55 at the Sunset Motel in Grandview Plaza, Kansas, located in Geary County. In the early morning of September 17, 2000, Deputy John Thomas ("Deputy Thomas"), with the Geary County Sheriff's Department, was at the Sunset Motel, assisting Officer Rick Parsons ("Officer Parsons"), with the Grandview Plaza Police Department, in an unrelated investigation. Upon noticing the red Trans Am, which was parked directly outside room 55, Deputy Thomas ran a NCIC check on the license plate number through dispatch. According to the check, the license plate number was stolen and did not match the Trans Am. Deputy Thomas then ran a check on the Trans Am's Vehicle Identification Number. The check revealed that the Trans Am had been stolen in an armed robbery and, thus, that an occupant of the vehicle was probably armed. Deputy Thomas checked with the motel desk clerk to confirm that the Trans Am was associated with the individuals registered in room 55. The registration card for room 55 listed Bonapfel's name and home address. Deputy Thomas called dispatch for back-up assistance. Deputies Kratz and Wolfe of the Geary County Sheriff's Department arrived ten to fifteen minutes later. Deputy Thomas directed Deputy Kratz to go to the rear of the motel to secure a corridor connecting room 55–and other rooms at the front of the motel-with rooms at the back of the motel. While Deputies Thomas and Wolfe obtained the pass key for room 55 from the management office, Officer Parsons stood outside room 55 to secure it.

Without knocking, Officer Parsons opened the door with the pass key, breaking the chain lock that prevented him from fully opening the door. Identifying themselves as law enforcement, Officer Parsons and Deputies Wolfe and Thomas entered the motel room with their weapons drawn. Defendant, Bonapfel, and their two children had been sleeping. The officers took defendant into custody. Officer Parsons asked defendant about the Trans Am. Defendant admitted that the vehicle did not belong to him, but claimed that he had found it in Missouri with the keys inside of it. Officer Parsons then asked defendant whether he had any weapons in the room; responding in the affirmative, defendant directed Officer Parsons to a black fanny pack on the table next to the bed in which defendant had been sleeping. Officers seized a .25 caliber Raven Arms handgun from that fanny pack. The officers had not obtained a warrant to enter defendant's motel room.

While detained in the Geary County jail, defendant attempted to escape. Due to outstanding warrants, however, the Kansas officials transferred defendant to the custody of the FBI in Kentucky without prosecuting him on this charge. Sergeant Beth Gilmer–Jones ("Sergeant Gilmer–Jones") of the Geary County Sheriff's Department forwarded the disposable camera, which she had seized from the stolen Trans Am during a routine inventory, to the FBI in Kentucky. Sergeant Gilmer–Jones prepared a photographic line-up based upon defendant's arrest photograph, and also forwarded this line-up to the FBI. FBI Agent Steven Wight ("Agent Wight") separately presented the photographic line-up to Cochran [the salesman from whom defendant had taken the car by force during a test drive], and Steven Spitznagel ("Spitznagel"), a salesperson who was present when the Trans Am was taken for the test drive. From this photographic line-up, both Cochran and Spitznagel identified defendant as the perpetrator of the car-jacking. In addition to testifying to these out-of-court identifications of defendant, Cochran and Spitznagel also identified defendant as the perpetrator in open court at trial. . . .

Defendant filed a motion to suppress his arrest photograph and any identifications of defendant as the perpetrator based upon that photograph on the ground that such evidence was the fruit of defendant's unlawful arrest in his motel room. The district court denied this motion. Although it had previously held that the warrantless search of defendant's motel room was illegal because exigent circumstances did not exist, the district court held that defendant's arrest in the motel room was lawful. The district court reasoned that defendant had outstanding warrants for his arrest and, even if there had been no such warrants, the officers had probable cause to arrest defendant. Defendant appeals the denial of this suppression motion. To the extent that the district court's ruling suggests that only probable cause to arrest is necessary to render a warrantless arrest in a motel room lawful, such a suggestion is erroneous. In *Payton v. New York,* the Supreme Court held that the Fourth Amendment prohibits law enforcement officers from entering a home-whether to conduct a search or a seizure-absent either a warrant based upon probable cause or exigent circumstances. 445 U.S. 573, 583, 603, 100 S.Ct. 1371, 63 L.Ed.2d 639 (1980) (distinguishing *United States v. Watson,* 423 U.S. 411, 96 S.Ct. 820, 46 L.Ed.2d 598 (1976), which upheld a warrantless arrest in a *public place* solely on the basis of probable cause). The Supreme Court, in *Welsh v. Wisconsin,* affirmed that this Fourth Amendment protection of the home-known as the *Payton* rule-equally applies to a motel room; in addition, the Court clarified that, per the *Payton* rule, the Fourth Amendment requires that, absent a warrant, both probable cause *and* exigent circumstances exist. 466 U.S. 740, 749, 104 S.Ct. 2091, 80 L.Ed.2d 732 (1984) (involving a warrantless felony arrest in a motel room).

However, we need not determine whether defendant's arrest in his motel room violated the Fourth Amendment. Even assuming, *arguendo,* the unlawfulness of defendant's arrest, the exclusionary rule does not require the suppression of defendant's arrest photograph and any identifications of defendant based upon that photograph. *See United States Postal Serv. v. Nat'l Ass'n of Letter Carriers, AFL–CIO,* 330 F.3d 747, 750 (6th Cir.2003) ("We may affirm a decision of the district court if correct for any reason, including one not considered below."). In *New York v. Harris,* 495 U.S. 14, 21, 110 S.Ct. 1640, 109 L.Ed.2d 13 (1990), the Supreme Court held that, "where the police have probable cause to arrest a suspect, the exclusionary rule does not bar the . . . [government's] use of a statement made by the defendant outside of his home, even though the statement . . . [was] taken after an arrest made in the home in violation of *Payton.*" The Court reasoned that:

> [T]he rule in *Payton* was designed to protect the physical integrity of the home; it was not intended to grant criminal suspects . . . protection where the police have probable cause to arrest the suspect for committing a crime. . . . Nothing in the reasoning of that case suggests that an arrest in a home without a warrant but with probable cause somehow renders unlawful continued custody of the suspect once he is removed from the house. There could be no valid claim here that . . . [the defendant] was immune from prosecution because his person was the fruit of an illegal arrest. . . . Nor is there any claim that the warrantless arrest required the police to release . . . [the defendant] or that . . . [the defendant] could not be immediately rearrested if momentarily released. . . . For Fourth Amendment purposes, the legal issue is the same as it would be had the police arrested . . . [the defendant] on his doorstep, illegally entered his home to search for evidence, and later interrogated . . . [the defendant] at the station house.

Id. at 17–18. Thus, the Court held that, where a violation of the *Payton* rule exists, the exclusionary rule requires the suppression of only that incriminating evidence which is the fruit of the fact that the arrest occurred in the home, rather than in a public place. *Id.* at 20.

While *Harris* is somewhat factually distinguishable from the present case, its legal analysis is directly on-point. Following *Harris*, because the officers had probable cause to arrest defendant,[6] the exclusionary rule does not require the suppression of the photograph of defendant taken at the police station, even if that photograph was taken after defendant's arrest in his motel room in violation of *Payton. See United States v. Villa–Velzaquez,* 282 F.3d 553, (8th Cir.2002) (applying *Harris* to police officer's discovery of identity information); *United States v. Banister,* 956 F.2d 1168, 1992 WL 46695, at *1 (9th Cir.1992) (unpublished opinion) (applying *Harris* to police officers' discovery of incriminating evidence on defendant's person). Because the existence of probable cause to arrest defendant justified his continued custody following his removal from the motel room, defendant was in lawful custody at the time that his arrest photograph was taken at the police station. Thus, defendant's arrest photograph was neither the product of being in illegal custody nor the fruit of having been arrested in his motel room, rather than in a public place. *See id.* at 19. Because the exclusionary rule would not require the suppression of defendant's arrest photograph, it would likewise not require the suppression of any out-of-

---

6. Defendant does not dispute that the officers had probable cause to arrest him based upon both the NCIC dispatch that the Trans Am was stolen and had been used in an armed robbery and the vehicle's connection to the room in which defendant was staying. Thus, absent an arrest warrant, the lawfulness of defendant's arrest in his motel room hinges upon the existence of exigent circumstances. We express no opinion on whether the outstanding warrants for defendant's arrest on unrelated charges satisfy the Fourth Amendment's warrant requirement for this arrest of defendant.

court identifications of defendant based upon that photograph or any in-court testimony concerning such out-of-court identifications, as defendant contends. Thus, we affirm the district court's denial of defendant's motion to suppress his arrest photograph and any identifications based upon that photograph.

Lopez v. City of Chicago

United States Court of Appeals, Seventh Circuit, 2006.
464 F.3d 711.

■ SYKES, CIRCUIT JUDGE.

Joseph Lopez was arrested by Chicago police for a murder he did not commit. The murder victim was a twelve-year-old boy, an innocent by-stander hit by gunfire in a drive-by shooting. Lopez was arrested without a warrant, although with probable cause—an eyewitness identified him as the shooter.

Following his arrest, the individual defendants—all detectives with the Chicago Police Department—kept Lopez shackled to the wall of a window-less, nine-by-seven-foot interrogation room for four days and nights while they investigated the case. Lopez had nowhere to sleep but a four-foot-by-ten-inch metal bench or the dirty brick floor. The interrogation room had no toilet or sink; he had to "scream" for the detectives to let him out to use a bathroom. He was given only one bologna sandwich and one serving of juice as food and drink during the entire four days and nights he was kept in the interrogation room. The detectives questioned him from time to time and made him stand in two lineups.

After two-and-a-half days in these conditions, Lopez started to become disoriented and began hearing voices telling him to confess. He ultimately gave a statement containing a false confession that did not match the details of the crime. On the fifth day of his detention, Lopez was moved to the city lockup, charged, and finally taken to court. The following day, the police investigation led detectives to another individual who confessed to the murder. Lopez was released the next day.

Those were the facts the jury was entitled to believe based on evidence Lopez presented during a seven-day trial on his claim under 42 U.S.C. § 1983 for violation of his constitutional rights and his supplemental state law claim for intentional infliction of emotional distress. The detectives testified differently about their treatment of Lopez while he was in their custody, but there was no dispute that they detained him for five days after his warrantless arrest without taking him before a judge for a probable cause hearing. Remarkably, after hearing this evidence, the district court refused to submit the claims to the jury and instead granted the defendants' motion for judgment as a matter of law.

We reverse. Lopez was entitled to judgment as a matter of law on his claim that the detectives violated his Fourth Amendment right to a prompt judicial determination of probable cause. *See Gerstein v. Pugh*, 420 U.S. 103, 125, 95 S.Ct. 854, 43 L.Ed.2d 54 (1975). *County of Riverside v. McLaughlin*, 500 U.S. 44, 56–57, 111 S.Ct. 1661, 114 L.Ed.2d 49 (1991), holds that if a *Gerstein* probable cause hearing is not held within 48 hours of a warrantless arrest, the government must demonstrate the existence of an emergency or other extraordinary circumstance to justify its failure to promptly present the person arrested to a judicial officer for a probable cause determination. Here, the defendants offered no reason for the five-day delay other than the continuation of their investigation, but delays for the purpose of gathering additional evidence are per se unreasonable under *McLaughlin. Id.; see also Willis v. City of Chi.*, 999 F.2d 284, 288–89 (7th Cir.1993).

There was conflicting evidence at trial on Lopez's treatment while in the detectives' custody, raising a jury issue on his constitutional claim relating to the conditions of his warrantless detention and his state law claim for intentional infliction of emotional distress. The district judge should not have taken these claims from the jury and resolved the factual conflict himself; they are remanded for retrial. . . .

The district court should have analyzed the detectives' conduct under the Fourth Amendment and its "objectively unreasonable" standard. The Fourth Amendment protects against unreasonable seizures; an arrest is a seizure, and the Fourth Amendment affords persons who are arrested the further, distinct right to a judicial determination of probable cause "as a prerequisite to extended restraint of liberty following arrest." *Gerstein,* 420 U.S. at 114, 95 S.Ct. 854. The judicial determination of probable cause may be made before the arrest (in the form of an arrest warrant) or promptly after the arrest, at a probable cause hearing (sometimes called a *Gerstein* hearing). But whether the arresting officer opts to obtain a warrant in advance or present a person arrested without a warrant for a prompt after-the-fact *Gerstein* hearing, the Fourth Amendment requires a *judicial* determination of probable cause. *See Haywood v. City of Chi.*, 378 F.3d 714, 717 (7th Cir.2004) (even though warrantless arrest was "clearly" supported by probable cause, Fourth Amendment required a probable cause hearing before a judicial officer).

McLaughlin established a general rule that persons arrested without a warrant must receive a judicial determination of probable cause within 48 hours. *McLaughlin,* 500 U.S. at 56–57, 111 S.Ct. 1661. (We will have more to say on the *McLaughlin* issue later.) Because Lopez was arrested without a warrant and had not yet been presented for a probable cause hearing, the Fourth Amendment should have been applied to his claim relating to the treatment and conditions he endured during his four days and nights in warrantless detention. Although his claim does not challenge the existence of probable cause, our cases hold that the *Gerstein* probable cause hearing is the event that terminates the Fourth Amendment's applicability following a warrantless arrest.

Accordingly, we have held that "the Fourth Amendment governs the period of confinement between arrest without a warrant and the preliminary hearing at which a determination of probable cause is made, while due process regulates the period of confinement after the initial determination of probable cause." *Villanova v. Abrams,* 972 F.2d 792, 797 (7th Cir.1992); *see also Brokaw v. Mercer County,* 235 F.3d 1000, 1018 n. 14 (7th Cir.2000) (after a probable cause hearing the Fourth Amendment no longer applies);

Luck v. Rovenstine, 168 F.3d 323, 326 (7th Cir.1999) (Fourth Amendment applies before the probable cause hearing and Due Process Clause applies after); *Reed v. City of Chi.,* 77 F.3d 1049, 1052 (7th Cir.1996) (the "seizure" of an arrestee ends after the probable cause hearing). Our cases thus establish that the protections of the Fourth Amendment apply at arrest and through the *Gerstein* probable cause hearing, due process principles govern a pretrial detainee's conditions of confinement after the judicial determination of probable cause, and the Eighth Amendment applies following conviction.

Although the defendants agreed in the district court that the Fourth Amendment's "objectively unreasonable" standard should apply, they have changed their tune on appeal. They now agree with the district court and argue that the claim is governed by the due process analysis applicable to claims of pretrial detainees, which borrows from the Eighth Amendment's "deliberate indifference" standard, applicable to conditions-of-confinement claims by convicted prisoners. *See Cavalieri,* 321 F.3d at 620. They cite *Wilkins v. May,* 872 F.2d 190, 193–95 (7th Cir.1989), but their reliance on that case is misplaced. Although *Wilkins* held that the period between arrest and charge falls under the rubric of due process rather than the Fourth Amendment, later cases, cited above, have limited *Wilkins* in light of *Gerstein* and *McLaughlin.* In particular, *Villanova* specifically recognized the tension between this court's holding in *Wilkins* and the *Gerstein/McLaughlin* line of cases, which apply the Fourth Amendment's reasonableness standard to the deprivation of liberty suffered by a warrantless arrestee. *Villanova,* 972 F.2d at 797. *Villanova* held that the conflict in the cases "can be reconciled" by applying the Fourth Amendment to the period between a warrantless arrest and the judicial probable cause determination and the principles of due process to confinement after probable cause has been judicially determined. *Id.*

The defendants cite *Bell v. Wolfish,* 441 U.S. 520, 535, 99 S.Ct. 1861, 60 L.Ed.2d 447 (1979), for the proposition that the Fourth Amendment does not apply to pretrial detainees. But *Bell* concerned "persons who have been charged with a crime but who have not yet been tried on the charge"—that is, pretrial detainees for whom a judicial determination of probable cause has already been made. *Id.* at 523, 99 S.Ct. 1861. That the Fourth Amendment does not apply to postarraignment detention does not make its protections inapplicable to the period between Lopez's arrest and his probable cause hearing. *Bell* is inapposite. . . .

For the foregoing reasons, we REVERSE the judgment of the district court and REMAND this case to the district court for entry of judgment for Lopez on his duration-of-confinement claim and for a new trial on: (1) Lopez's unconstitutional conditions of confinement claim; (2) his intentional infliction of emotional distress claim; and (3) damages.

C. INCIDENTAL SEARCH AUTHORITY

United States v. Davis

United States Court of Appeals, Eighth Circuit, 2009.
569 F.3d 813.

■ SHEPHERD, CIRCUIT JUDGE.

Uneal Davis was charged with one count of possession of a firearm by a prohibited person in violation of 18 U.S.C. §§ 922(g)(1), 922(g)(3), and

924(a)(2). Davis entered a plea of guilty conditioned on his right to appeal the district court's denial of his motion to suppress. He appeals on the ground that the firearm was seized pursuant to a warrantless search of his vehicle in violation of the Fourth Amendment. We affirm.

I.

On May 4, 2007, Officer Shelby Howard of the Joplin, Missouri, police department stopped a 2007 Nissan Altima driven by Davis for speeding. John Hicks, a deputy with the Jasper County Sheriff's Department, assisted Officer Howard during the traffic stop. Because Officer Howard smelled the odor of marijuana as he approached the vehicle, he asked Davis to exit the vehicle so he could conduct a pat-down search.

During the pat-down, Officer Howard felt a lump that he believed to be a plastic bag in Davis's pocket. After Davis admitted that the lump was a bag of marijuana, Officer Howard arrested Davis and placed him in Deputy Hicks's patrol car. Officer Howard then ordered the three passengers riding with Davis out of the car so that he could search the vehicle. None of the passengers was secured in handcuffs while Officer Howard searched the vehicle. During the search, Officer Howard found a loaded Smith & Wesson 9mm handgun in the center console. Officer Howard also observed opened bottles of beer in the vehicle and arrested one of the passengers, Gregory Harlin, for being a minor in possession of alcohol. The two remaining passengers left in a taxi because they had been drinking.

After his indictment, Davis filed a motion to suppress the handgun on the ground that the search was impermissible under the decision by the Arizona Supreme Court in State v. Gant, 216 Ariz. 1, 162 P.3d 640 (2007), cert. granted in part, ___ U.S. ___, 128 S.Ct. 1443, 170 L.Ed.2d 274 (2008), which required that officers demonstrate a threat to their safety or a need to preserve evidence in order to justify a warrantless search incident to arrest. Id. at 643–44. The government opposed the motion on three alternative grounds: 1) that the search of the vehicle was a lawful search incident to arrest; 2) that under the "automobile exception" the odor and discovery of marijuana provided probable cause to search the vehicle without a warrant; and 3) that the firearm would have inevitably been discovered during an inventory search of the car after it was impounded. The district court denied Davis's motion on the grounds that both the search-incident-to-arrest and automobile exceptions obviated the need for a warrant. It declined to address the government's inevitable discovery argument. After Davis filed this appeal, the Supreme Court affirmed the Arizona Supreme Court's decision in State v. Gant limiting the search-incident-to-arrest exception to situations either threatening officer safety or the preservation of perishable evidence. Arizona v. Gant, ___ U.S. ___, 129 S.Ct. 1710, 1723, 173 L.Ed.2d 485 (2009).

II.

Davis does not challenge any of the district court's factual findings. Accordingly, we are faced with the purely legal question of whether the search of Davis's vehicle without a warrant was permissible under the Fourth Amendment.

It is now axiomatic that "searches conducted outside the judicial process, without prior approval by judge or magistrate, are per se unreasonable under the Fourth Amendment—subject only to a few specifically established and well-delineated exceptions." Katz v. United States, 389 U.S. 347, 357, 88 S.Ct. 507, 19 L.Ed.2d 576 (1967) (footnote omitted). "The exceptions are jealously and carefully drawn, and there must be a showing by those who seek exemption ... that the exigencies of the situation made that course imperative." Coolidge v. New Hampshire, 403 U.S. 443, 455, 91 S.Ct. 2022, 29 L.Ed.2d 564 (1971) (quotation and footnote omitted). "Among the exceptions to the warrant requirement is a search incident to a lawful arrest." Gant, 129 S.Ct. at 1716. Another "such exception is the so-called 'automobile exception,' which authorizes officers to search a vehicle without a warrant if they have probable cause to believe the vehicle contains evidence of criminal activity." United States v. Hill, 386 F.3d 855, 858 (8th Cir.2004).

Davis's primary argument is that the Gant decision requires suppression because the search of his vehicle was not a valid search incident to arrest. In Gant, police officers stopped the defendant's vehicle because he had an outstanding warrant for driving with a suspended license. 129 S.Ct. at 1714–15. The Supreme Court suppressed the evidence because the driver and two of his associates were "handcuffed and secured in separate patrol cars ..." before the search of his vehicle, and no evidence of the offense of arrest of driving with a suspended license could possibly be obtained by a search of his vehicle. Id. at 1715, 1719.

The Gant decision confined the applicability of the search-incident-to-arrest exception to two situations. First, police may "search a vehicle incident to a recent occupant's arrest only when the arrestee is unsecured and within reaching distance of the passenger compartment at the time of the search." Id. at 1719. The within-reach requirement places the search-incident-to-arrest exception within the boundaries set by the two underlying rationales for the rule set forth in Chimel v. California, 395 U.S. 752, 89 S.Ct. 2034, 23 L.Ed.2d 685 (1969)—ensuring officer safety and protecting perishable evidence. Id. at 762–63, 89 S.Ct. 2034.[4] In addition to the

---

4. Basing the exception on the twin rationales of officer safety and the preservation of perishable evidence, Chimel limited the scope of a search incident to arrest to "the arrestee's person and the area 'within his immediate control'—construing that phrase to mean the area from within which he might gain possession of a weapon or destructible evidence." 395 U.S at 763, 89 S.Ct. 2034. In New York v. Belton, 453 U.S. 454, 101 S.Ct. 2860, 69 L.Ed.2d 768 (1981), the Chimel rule was applied to vehicle searches to "hold that when a policeman has made a lawful custodial arrest of the occupant of an automobile, he may, as a contemporaneous incident of that arrest, search the passenger compartment of that automobile." Id. at 460, 101 S.Ct. 2860 (footnote omitted). After Belton, it was unclear whether Chimel's rationales limited the applicability of this exception to situations in which the arrestee actually posed such a threat. Subsequent courts disagreed as to whether Belton's seemingly bright-line rule removed the exception from its moorings in Chimel's rationales of protecting officer safety and preserving destructible evidence. Some courts continued to limit searches pursuant to traffic arrests to situations in which officers could show that the arrestee or undetained passengers were capable of accessing the passenger compartment. Most others took Belton at face value and permitted automobile searches even after the suspect had been handcuffed and safely

within-reach requirement, Gant also provided "that circumstances unique to the vehicle context justify a search incident to a lawful arrest when it is 'reasonable to believe evidence relevant to the crime of arrest might be found in the vehicle.'" Gant, 129 S.Ct. at 1719 (quoting Thornton v. United States, 541 U.S. 615, 632, 124 S.Ct. 2127, 158 L.Ed.2d 905 (2004) (Scalia, J., concurring in judgment)). Thus, police may validly search an automobile incident to an "arrest only if the arrestee is within reaching distance of the passenger compartment at the time of the search or it is reasonable to believe the vehicle contains evidence of the offense of arrest." Id. at 1723 (emphasis added).

Under the Gant decision, Officer Howard lawfully searched Davis's automobile. At the time of the search, Officer Howard had already discovered marijuana in Davis's pocket and placed Davis in custody. The odor of marijuana was wafting from the car. Empty beer bottles lay strewn in the back seat. Three passengers, all of whom had been drinking, were not in secure custody and outnumbered the two officers at the scene. Each of these facts comports with Gant's within-reach requirement and its two underlying rationales as articulated in Chimel. Although Davis had been detained, three unsecured and intoxicated passengers were standing around a vehicle redolent of recently smoked marijuana. These facts are textbook examples of "[t]he safety and evidentiary justifications underlying Chimel's reaching-distance rule...." Gant, 129 S.Ct. at 1714; see also id. at 1719 (distinguishing New York v. Belton, 453 U.S. 454, 101 S.Ct. 2860, 69 L.Ed.2d 768 (1981), on the grounds that there a single officer was confronted with four unsecured arrestees, whereas in Gant five officers had handcuffed and secured three arrestees in different patrol cars).[5]

In addition to his search-incident-to-arrest challenge, Davis also appeals the district court's ruling that the search was permissible under the "automobile exception" to the warrant requirement. "Under the automobile exception, officers may search a vehicle without a warrant if they have probable cause to believe the vehicle contains evidence of criminal activity." United States v. Cortez–Palomino, 438 F.3d 910, 913 (8th Cir.2006) (per curiam). In Cortez–Palomino, we held that the search of an automobile was supported by probable cause where officers observed packages wrapped in cellophane and detected the odor of masking agents commonly used to obscure the smell of narcotics. Id. If there had been any doubt about whether the smell of smoldering cannabis constituted probable cause to search the vehicle, such doubt was obviated by the discovery of a bag of marijuana in Davis's pocket. Consequently, Officer Howard was permitted

secured. See Gant, 129 S.Ct. at 1718 n. 2 (collecting and comparing cases). Gant settled the issue by limiting the applicability of vehicular searches incident to arrest within the confines of the two Chimel rationales of safety and evidence-preservation.

5. We also note that the discovery of marijuana in Davis's pocket combined with the smell of recently burned marijuana made it "reasonable to believe evidence relevant to the crime of arrest might be found in the vehicle." Gant, 129 S.Ct. at 1719 (quoting Thornton v. United States, 541 U.S. 615, 632, 124 S.Ct. 2127, 158 L.Ed.2d 905 (2004)). We do not decide the case on this basis, however, because the evidence-of-arresting-offense rule had not been established until after the filing of this appeal.

to search Davis's vehicle without a warrant under the automobile exception.[6]

III.

Accordingly, we affirm the district court's denial of Davis's motion to suppress.

(4) Search for Evidence

A. DEFINITION

Kyllo v. United States

Supreme Court of the United States, 2001.
533 U.S. 27, 121 S.Ct. 2038, 150 L.Ed.2d 94.

■ JUSTICE SCALIA delivered the opinion of the Court.

This case presents the question whether the use of a thermal-imaging device aimed at a private home from a public street to detect relative amounts of heat within the home constitutes a "search" within the meaning of the Fourth Amendment.

I

In 1991 Agent William Elliott of the United States Department of the Interior came to suspect that marijuana was being grown in the home belonging to petitioner Danny Kyllo, part of a triplex on Rhododendron Drive in Florence, Oregon. Indoor marijuana growth typically requires high-intensity lamps. In order to determine whether an amount of heat was emanating from petitioner's home consistent with the use of such lamps, at 3:20 a.m. on January 16, 1992, Agent Elliott and Dan Haas used an Agema Thermovision 210 thermal imager to scan the triplex. Thermal imagers detect infrared radiation, which virtually all objects emit but which is not visible to the naked eye. The imager converts radiation into images based on relative warmth—black is cool, white is hot, shades of gray connote relative differences; in that respect, it operates somewhat like a video camera showing heat images. The scan of Kyllo's home took only a few minutes and was performed from the passenger seat of Agent Elliott's vehicle across the street from the front of the house and also from the street in back of the house. The scan showed that the roof over the garage and a side wall of petitioner's home were relatively hot compared to the rest of the home and substantially warmer than neighboring homes in the triplex. Agent Elliott concluded that petitioner was using halide lights to grow marijuana in his house, which indeed he was. Based on tips from informants, utility bills, and the thermal imaging, a Federal Magistrate Judge issued a warrant authorizing a search of petitioner's home, and the agents found an indoor growing operation involving more than 100 plants. Petitioner was indicted on one count of manufacturing marijuana, in violation of 21 U.S.C. § 841(a)(1). He unsuccessfully moved to suppress the evidence seized from his home and then entered a conditional guilty plea.

---

6. It is unnecessary to address the government's argument that the firearm would have inevitably been discovered during an inventory search after the vehicle had been impounded.

The Court of Appeals for the Ninth Circuit remanded the case for an evidentiary hearing regarding the intrusiveness of thermal imaging. On remand the District Court found that the Agema 210 "is a non-intrusive device which emits no rays or beams and shows a crude visual image of the heat being radiated from the outside of the house"; it "did not show any people or activity within the walls of the structure"; "[t]he device used cannot penetrate walls or windows to reveal conversations or human activities"; and "[n]o intimate details of the home were observed." Supp. App. to Pet. for Cert. 39–40. Based on these findings, the District Court upheld the validity of the warrant that relied in part upon the thermal imaging, and reaffirmed its denial of the motion to suppress. A divided Court of Appeals initially reversed, 140 F.3d 1249 (1998), but that opinion was withdrawn and the panel (after a change in composition) affirmed, 190 F.3d 1041 (1999), with Judge Noonan dissenting. The court held that petitioner had shown no subjective expectation of privacy because he had made no attempt to conceal the heat escaping from his home, *id.,* at 1046, and even if he had, there was no objectively reasonable expectation of privacy because the imager "did not expose any intimate details of Kyllo's life," only "amorphous 'hot spots' on the roof and exterior wall," *id.,* at 1047. We granted certiorari. 530 U.S. 1305, 121 S.Ct. 29, 147 L.Ed.2d 1052 (2000).

II

The Fourth Amendment provides that "[t]he right of the people to be secure in their persons, houses, papers, and effects, against unreasonable searches and seizures, shall not be violated." "At the very core" of the Fourth Amendment "stands the right of a man to retreat into his own home and there be free from unreasonable governmental intrusion." Silverman v. United States, 365 U.S. 505, 511, 81 S.Ct. 679, 5 L.Ed.2d 734 (1961). With few exceptions, the question whether a warrantless search of a home is reasonable and hence constitutional must be answered no. *See* Illinois v. Rodriguez, 497 U.S. 177, 181, 110 S.Ct. 2793, 111 L.Ed.2d 148 (1990); Payton v. New York, 445 U.S. 573, 586, 100 S.Ct. 1371, 63 L.Ed.2d 639 (1980).

On the other hand, the antecedent question whether or not a Fourth Amendment "search" has occurred is not so simple under our precedent. The permissibility of ordinary visual surveillance of a home used to be clear because, well into the 20th century, our Fourth Amendment jurisprudence was tied to common-law trespass. *See, e.g.,* Goldman v. United States, 316 U.S. 129, 134–136, 62 S.Ct. 993, 86 L.Ed. 1322 (1942); Olmstead v. United States, 277 U.S. 438, 464–466, 48 S.Ct. 564, 72 L.Ed. 944 (1928). *Cf.* Silverman v. United States, *supra,* at 510–512, 81 S.Ct. 679 (technical trespass not necessary for Fourth Amendment violation; it suffices if there is "actual intrusion into a constitutionally protected area"). Visual surveillance was unquestionably lawful because " 'the eye cannot by the laws of England be guilty of a trespass.' " Boyd v. United States, 116 U.S. 616, 628, 6 S.Ct. 524, 29 L.Ed. 746 (1886) (quoting Entick v. Carrington, 19 How. St. Tr. 1029, 95 Eng. Rep. 807 (K.B.1765)). We have since decoupled violation of a person's Fourth Amendment rights from trespassory violation of his property, *see* Rakas v. Illinois, 439 U.S. 128, 143, 99 S.Ct. 421, 58 L.Ed.2d

387 (1978), but the lawfulness of warrantless visual surveillance of a home has still been preserved. As we observed in California v. Ciraolo, 476 U.S. 207, 213, 106 S.Ct. 1809, 90 L.Ed.2d 210 (1986), "[t]he Fourth Amendment protection of the home has never been extended to require law enforcement officers to shield their eyes when passing by a home on public thoroughfares."

One might think that the new validating rationale would be that examining the portion of a house that is in plain public view, while it is a "search" despite the absence of trespass, is not an "unreasonable" one under the Fourth Amendment. *See* Minnesota v. Carter, 525 U.S. 83, 104, 119 S.Ct. 469, 142 L.Ed.2d 373 (1998) (Breyer, J., concurring in judgment). But in fact we have held that visual observation is no "search" at all— perhaps in order to preserve somewhat more intact our doctrine that warrantless searches are presumptively unconstitutional. *See* Dow Chemical Co. v. United States, 476 U.S. 227, 234–235, 239, 106 S.Ct. 1819, 90 L.Ed.2d 226 (1986). In assessing when a search is not a search, we have applied somewhat in reverse the principle first enunciated in Katz v. United States, 389 U.S. 347, 88 S.Ct. 507, 19 L.Ed.2d 576 (1967). *Katz* involved eavesdropping by means of an electronic listening device placed on the outside of a telephone booth—a location not within the catalog ("persons, houses, papers, and effects") that the Fourth Amendment protects against unreasonable searches. We held that the Fourth Amendment nonetheless protected Katz from the warrantless eavesdropping because he "justifiably relied" upon the privacy of the telephone booth. *Id.,* at 353, 88 S.Ct. 507. As Justice Harlan's oft-quoted concurrence described it, a Fourth Amendment search occurs when the government violates a subjective expectation of privacy that society recognizes as reasonable. *See id.,* at 361, 88 S.Ct. 507. We have subsequently applied this principle to hold that a Fourth Amendment search does *not* occur—even when the explicitly protected location of a *house* is concerned—unless "the individual manifested a subjective expectation of privacy in the object of the challenged search," and "society [is] willing to recognize that expectation as reasonable." *Ciraolo, supra,* at 211, 106 S.Ct. 1809. We have applied this test in holding that it is not a search for the police to use a pen register at the phone company to determine what numbers were dialed in a private home, Smith v. Maryland, 442 U.S. 735, 743–744, 99 S.Ct. 2577, 61 L.Ed.2d 220 (1979), and we have applied the test on two different occasions in holding that aerial surveillance of private homes and surrounding areas does not constitute a search, *Ciraolo, supra*; Florida v. Riley, 488 U.S. 445, 109 S.Ct. 693, 102 L.Ed.2d 835 (1989).

The present case involves officers on a public street engaged in more than naked-eye surveillance of a home. We have previously reserved judgment as to how much technological enhancement of ordinary perception from such a vantage point, if any, is too much. While we upheld enhanced aerial photography of an industrial complex in *Dow Chemical,* we noted that we found "it important that this is *not* an area immediately adjacent to a private home, where privacy expectations are most heightened," 476 U.S., at 237, n. 4, 106 S.Ct. 1819 (emphasis in original).

III

It would be foolish to contend that the degree of privacy secured to citizens by the Fourth Amendment has been entirely unaffected by the advance of technology. For example, as the cases discussed above make clear, the technology enabling human flight has exposed to public view (and hence, we have said, to official observation) uncovered portions of the house and its curtilage that once were private. *See Ciraolo, supra,* at 215, 106 S.Ct. 1809. The question we confront today is what limits there are upon this power of technology to shrink the realm of guaranteed privacy.

The *Katz* test—whether the individual has an expectation of privacy that society is prepared to recognize as reasonable—has often been criticized as circular, and hence subjective and unpredictable. See 1 W. LaFave, Search and Seizure § 2.1(d), pp. 393–394 (3d ed.1996); Posner, The Uncertain Protection of Privacy by the Supreme Court, 1979 S.Ct. Rev. 173, 188; *Carter, supra,* at 97, 119 S.Ct. 469 (Scalia, J., concurring). But see *Rakas, supra,* at 143–144, n. 12, 99 S.Ct. 421. While it may be difficult to refine *Katz* when the search of areas such as telephone booths, automobiles, or even the curtilage and uncovered portions of residences is at issue, in the case of the search of the interior of homes—the prototypical and hence most commonly litigated area of protected privacy—there is a ready criterion, with roots deep in the common law, of the minimal expectation of privacy that *exists,* and that is acknowledged to be *reasonable.* To withdraw protection of this minimum expectation would be to permit police technology to erode the privacy guaranteed by the Fourth Amendment. We think that obtaining by sense-enhancing technology any information regarding the interior of the home that could not otherwise have been obtained without physical "intrusion into a constitutionally protected area," *Silverman,* 365 U.S., at 512, 81 S.Ct. 679, constitutes a search—at least where (as here) the technology in question is not in general public use. This assures preservation of that degree of privacy against government that existed when the Fourth Amendment was adopted. On the basis of this criterion, the information obtained by the thermal imager in this case was the product of a search.[18]

The Government maintains, however, that the thermal imaging must be upheld because it detected "only heat radiating from the external surface of the house," The dissent makes this its leading point, contending that there is a fundamental difference between what it calls "off-the-wall"

---

18. The dissent's repeated assertion that the thermal imaging did not obtain information regarding the interior of the home is simply inaccurate. A thermal imager reveals the relative heat of various rooms in the home. The dissent may not find that information particularly private or important, but there is no basis for saying it is not information regarding the interior of the home. The dissent's comparison of the thermal imaging to various circumstances in which outside observers might be able to perceive, without technology, the heat of the home—for example, by observing snowmelt on the roof,—is quite irrelevant. The fact that equivalent information could sometimes be obtained by other means does not make lawful the use of means that violate the Fourth Amendment. The police might, for example, learn how many people are in a particular house by setting up year-round surveillance; but that does not make breaking and entering to find out the same information lawful. In any event, on the night of January 16, 1992, no outside observer could have discerned the relative heat of Kyllo's home without thermal imaging.

observations and "through-the-wall surveillance." But just as a thermal imager captures only heat emanating from a house, so also a powerful directional microphone picks up only sound emanating from a house-and a satellite capable of scanning from many miles away would pick up only visible light emanating from a house. We rejected such a mechanical interpretation of the Fourth Amendment in *Katz,* where the eavesdropping device picked up only sound waves that reached the exterior of the phone booth. Reversing that approach would leave the homeowner at the mercy of advancing technology—including imaging technology that could discern all human activity in the home. While the technology used in the present case was relatively crude, the rule we adopt must take account of more sophisticated systems that are already in use or in development.[19] The dissent's reliance on the distinction between "off-the-wall" and "through-the-wall" observation is entirely incompatible with the dissent's belief, which we discuss below, that thermal-imaging observations of the intimate details of a home are impermissible. The most sophisticated thermal-imaging devices continue to measure heat "off-the-wall" rather than "through-the-wall"; the dissent's disapproval of those more sophisticated thermal-imaging devices is an acknowledgement that there is no substance to this distinction. As for the dissent's extraordinary assertion that anything learned through "an inference" cannot be a search that would validate even the "through-the-wall" technologies that the dissent purports to disapprove. Surely the dissent does not believe that the through-the-wall radar or ultrasound technology produces an 8–by–10 Kodak glossy that needs no analysis (*i.e.,* the making of inferences). And, of course, the novel proposition that inference insulates a search is blatantly contrary to United States v. Karo, 468 U.S. 705, 104 S.Ct. 3296, 82 L.Ed.2d 530 (1984), where the police "inferred" from the activation of a beeper that a certain can of ether was in the home. The police activity was held to be a search, and the search was held unlawful.

The Government also contends that the thermal imaging was constitutional because it did not "detect private activities occurring in private areas." It points out that in *Dow Chemical* we observed that the enhanced aerial photography did not reveal any "intimate details." 476 U.S., at 238, 106 S.Ct. 1819. *Dow Chemical,* however, involved enhanced aerial photography of an industrial complex, which does not share the Fourth Amendment sanctity of the home. The Fourth Amendment's protection of the home has never been tied to measurement of the quality or quantity of information obtained. In *Silverman,* for example, we made clear that any physical invasion of the structure of the home, "by even a fraction of an inch," was too much, 365 U.S., at 512, 81 S.Ct. 679, and there is certainly

---

19. The ability to "see" through walls and other opaque barriers is a clear, and scientifically feasible, goal of law enforcement research and development. The National Law Enforcement and Corrections Technology Center, a program within the United States Department of Justice, features on its Internet Website projects that include a "Radar–Based Through-the-Wall Surveillance System," "Handheld Ultrasound Through the Wall Surveillance," and a "Radar Flashlight" that "will enable law enforcement officers to detect individuals through interior building walls." www.nlectc.org/techproj/ (visited May 3, 2001). Some devices may emit low levels of radiation that travel "through-the-wall," but others, such as more sophisticated thermal-imaging devices, are entirely passive, or "off-the-wall" as the dissent puts it.

no exception to the warrant requirement for the officer who barely cracks open the front door and sees nothing but the nonintimate rug on the vestibule floor. In the home, our cases show, *all* details are intimate details, because the entire area is held safe from prying government eyes. Thus, in *Karo, supra,* the only thing detected was a can of ether in the home; and in Arizona v. Hicks, 480 U.S. 321, 107 S.Ct. 1149, 94 L.Ed.2d 347 (1987), the only thing detected by a physical search that went beyond what officers lawfully present could observe in "plain view" was the registration number of a phonograph turntable. These were intimate details because they were details of the home, just as was the detail of how warm—or even how relatively warm—Kyllo was heating his residence.

Limiting the prohibition of thermal imaging to "intimate details" would not only be wrong in principle; it would be impractical in application, failing to provide "a workable accommodation between the needs of law enforcement and the interests protected by the Fourth Amendment," Oliver v. United States, 466 U.S. 170, 181, 104 S.Ct. 1735, 80 L.Ed.2d 214 (1984). To begin with, there is no necessary connection between the sophistication of the surveillance equipment and the "intimacy" of the details that it observes—which means that one cannot say (and the police cannot be assured) that use of the relatively crude equipment at issue here will always be lawful. The Agema Thermovision 210 might disclose, for example, at what hour each night the lady of the house takes her daily sauna and bath—a detail that many would consider "intimate"; and a much more sophisticated system might detect nothing more intimate than the fact that someone left a closet light on. We could not, in other words, develop a rule approving only that through-the-wall surveillance which identifies objects no smaller than 36 by 36 inches, but would have to develop a jurisprudence specifying which home activities are "intimate" and which are not. And even when (if ever) that jurisprudence were fully developed, no police officer would be able to know *in advance* whether his through-the-wall surveillance picks up "intimate" details—and thus would be unable to know in advance whether it is constitutional.

The dissent's proposed standard—whether the technology offers the "functional equivalent of actual presence in the area being searched,"— would seem quite similar to our own at first blush. The dissent concludes that *Katz* was such a case, but then inexplicably asserts that if the same listening device only revealed the volume of the conversation, the surveillance would be permissible. Yet if, without technology, the police could not discern volume without being actually present in the phone booth, Justice Stevens should conclude a search has occurred. Cf. *Karo,* 468 U.S., at 735, 104 S.Ct. 3296 (Stevens, J., concurring in part and dissenting in part) ("I find little comfort in the Court's notion that no invasion of privacy occurs until a listener obtains some significant information by use of the de-vice.... A bathtub is a less private area when the plumber is present even if his back is turned"). The same should hold for the interior heat of the home if only a person present in the home could discern the heat. Thus the driving force of the dissent, despite its recitation of the above standard, appears to be a distinction among different types of information—whether the "homeowner would even care if anybody noticed." The dissent offers no practical guidance for the application of this standard, and for reasons already discussed, we believe there can be none. The people in their houses, as well as the police, deserve more precision.[20]

We have said that the Fourth Amendment draws "a firm line at the entrance to the house," *Payton,* 445 U.S., at 590, 100 S.Ct. 1371. That line, we think, must be not only firm but also bright—which requires clear specification of those methods of surveillance that require a warrant. While it is certainly possible to conclude from the videotape of the thermal imaging that occurred in this case that no "significant" compromise of the homeowner's privacy has occurred, we must take the long view, from the original meaning of the Fourth Amendment forward.

"The Fourth Amendment is to be construed in the light of what was deemed an unreasonable search and seizure when it was adopted, and in a manner which will conserve public interests as well as the interests and rights of individual citizens." Carroll v. United States, 267 U.S. 132, 149, 45 S.Ct. 280, 69 L.Ed. 543 (1925).

Where, as here, the Government uses a device that is not in general public use, to explore details of the home that would previously have been unknowable without physical intrusion, the surveillance is a "search" and is presumptively unreasonable without a warrant.

Since we hold the Thermovision imaging to have been an unlawful search, it will remain for the District Court to determine whether, without the evidence it provided, the search warrant issued in this case was supported by probable cause—and if not, whether there is any other basis for supporting admission of the evidence that the search pursuant to the warrant produced.

The judgment of the Court of Appeals is reversed; the case is remanded for further proceedings consistent with this opinion.

It is so ordered.

■ JUSTICE STEVENS, with whom THE CHIEF JUSTICE, JUSTICE O'CONNOR, and JUSTICE KENNEDY join, dissenting.

There is, in my judgment, a distinction of constitutional magnitude between "through-the-wall surveillance" that gives the observer or listener direct access to information in a private area, on the one hand, and the thought processes used to draw inferences from information in the public domain, on the other hand. The Court has crafted a rule that purports to deal with direct observations of the inside of the home, but the case before us merely involves indirect deductions from "off-the-wall" surveillance, that is, observations of the exterior of the home. Those observations were made with a fairly primitive thermal imager that gathered data exposed on the outside of petitioner's home but did not invade any constitutionally

---

20. The dissent argues that we have injected potential uncertainty into the constitutional analysis by noting that whether or not the technology is in general public use may be a factor. See *post,* at 2050. That quarrel, however, is not with us but with this Court's precedent. See *Ciraolo, supra,* at 215, 106 S.Ct. 1809 ("In an age where private and commercial flight in the public airways is routine, it is unreasonable for respondent to expect that his marijuana plants were constitutionally protected from being observed with the naked eye from an altitude of 1,000 feet"). Given that we can quite confidently say that thermal imaging is not "routine," we decline in this case to reexamine that factor.

protected interest in privacy. Moreover, I believe that the supposedly "bright-line" rule the Court has created in response to its concerns about future technological developments is unnecessary, unwise, and inconsistent with the Fourth Amendment. . . .

Since what was involved in this case was nothing more than drawing inferences from off-the-wall surveillance, rather than any "through-the-wall" surveillance, the officers' conduct did not amount to a search and was perfectly reasonable. . . .[21]

B. *REQUIRED JUSTIFICATION*

Illinois v. Gates

Supreme Court of the United States, 1983.
462 U.S. 213, 103 S.Ct. 2317, 76 L.Ed.2d 527.

■ JUSTICE REHNQUIST delivered the opinion of the Court.

Respondents Lance and Susan Gates were indicted for violation of state drug laws after police officers, executing a search warrant, discovered marijuana and other contraband in their automobile and home. Prior to trial the Gates' moved to suppress evidence seized during this search. The Illinois Supreme Court, 85 Ill.2d 376, 53 Ill.Dec. 218, 423 N.E.2d 887 (1981) affirmed the decisions of lower state courts, 82 Ill.App.3d 749, 38 Ill.Dec. 62, 403 N.E.2d 77 (1980) granting the motion. It held that the affidavit submitted in support of the State's application for a warrant to search the Gates' property was inadequate under this Court's decisions in Aguilar v. Texas, 378 U.S. 108, 84 S.Ct. 1509, 12 L.Ed.2d 723 (1964) and Spinelli v. United States, 393 U.S. 410, 89 S.Ct. 584, 21 L.Ed.2d 637 (1969).

We granted certiorari to consider the application of the Fourth Amendment to a magistrate's issuance of a search warrant on the basis of a partially corroborated anonymous informant's tip. . . .

We now turn to the question presented in the State's original petition for certiorari, which requires us to decide whether respondents' rights under the Fourth and Fourteenth Amendments were violated by the search of their car and house. A chronological statement of events usefully introduces the issues at stake. Bloomingdale, Ill., is a suburb of Chicago located in DuPage County. On May 3, 1978, the Bloomingdale Police Department received by mail an anonymous handwritten letter which read as follows:

"This letter is to inform you that you have a couple in your town who strictly make their living on selling drugs. They are Sue and Lance Gates, they live on Greenway, off Bloomingdale Rd. in the condominums. Most of their buys are done in Florida. Sue his wife drives their

---

21. When, however, a police technique enables officers to learn no facts beyond the commission of crimes, the Court has ruled that the police have not engaged in any "search" regulated by the Fourth Amendment. Thus, the detention of a suspect's luggage on reasonable suspicion it contained contraband and the use of a sniffer dog to determine if a prohibited substance was contained therein was proper, although the detention for a period of 90 minutes, under the circumstances, was improper. United States v. Place, 462 U.S. 696, 103 S.Ct. 2637 (1983).

car to Florida, where she leaves it to be loaded up with drugs, then
Lance flys down and drives it back. Sue flys back after she drops the
car off in Florida. May 3 she is driving down there again and Lance will
be flying down in a few days to drive it back. At the time Lance drives
the car back he has the trunk loaded with over $100,000.00 in drugs.
Presently they have over $100,000.00 worth of drugs in their base-
ment.

They brag about the fact they never have to work, and make their
entire living on pushers.

I guarantee if you watch them carefully you will make a big catch.
They are friends with some big drugs dealers, who visit their house
often.

Lance & Susan Gates Greenway In Condominiums"

The letter was referred by the Chief of Police of the Bloomingdale
Police Department to Detective Mader, who decided to pursue the tip.
Mader learned, from the office of the Illinois Secretary of State, that an
Illinois driver's license had been issued to one Lance Gates, residing at a
stated address in Bloomingdale. He contacted a confidential informant,
whose examination of certain financial records revealed a more recent
address for the Gates, and he also learned from a police officer assigned to
O'Hare Airport that "L. Gates" had made a reservation on Eastern
Airlines flight 245 to West Palm Beach, Fla., scheduled to depart from
Chicago on May 5 at 4:15 p.m.

Mader then made arrangements with an agent of the Drug Enforcement Administration for surveillance of the May 5 Eastern Airlines flight.
The agent later reported to Mader that Gates had boarded the flight, and
that federal agents in Florida had observed him arrive in West Palm Beach
and take a taxi to the nearby Holiday Inn. They also reported that Gates
went to a room registered to one Susan Gates and that, at 7:00 a.m. the
next morning, Gates and an unidentified woman left the motel in a
Mercury bearing Illinois license plates and drove northbound on an interstate frequently used by travelers to the Chicago area. In addition, the DEA
agent informed Mader that the license plate number on the Mercury
registered to a Hornet station wagon owned by Gates. The agent also
advised Mader that the driving time between West Palm Beach and
Bloomingdale was approximately 22 to 24 hours.

Mader signed an affidavit setting forth the foregoing facts, and submitted it to a judge of the Circuit Court of DuPage County, together with a
copy of the anonymous letter. The judge of that court thereupon issued a
search warrant for the Gates' residence and for their automobile. The
judge, in deciding to issue the warrant, could have determined that the
modus operandi of the Gates had been substantially corroborated. As the
anonymous letter predicted, Lance Gates had flown from Chicago to West
Palm Beach late in the afternoon of May 5th, had checked into a hotel
room registered in the name of his wife, and, at 7:00 a.m. the following
morning, had headed north, accompanied by an unidentified woman, out of
West Palm Beach on an interstate highway used by travelers from South
Florida to Chicago in an automobile bearing a license plate issued to him.

At 5:15 a.m. on March 7th, only 36 hours after he had flown out of Chicago, Lance Gates, and his wife, returned to their home in Blooming-dale, driving the car in which they had left West Palm Beach some 22 hours earlier. The Bloomingdale police were awaiting them, searched the trunk of the Mercury, and uncovered approximately 350 pounds of marijuana. A search of the Gates' home revealed marijuana, weapons, and other contra-band. The Illinois Circuit Court ordered suppression of all these items, on the ground that the affidavit submitted to the Circuit Judge failed to support the necessary determination of probable cause to believe that the Gates' automobile and home contained the contraband in question. This decision was affirmed in turn by the Illinois Appellate Court and by a divided vote of the Supreme Court of Illinois.

The Illinois Supreme Court concluded—and we are inclined to agree—that, standing alone, the anonymous letter sent to the Bloomingdale Police Department would not provide the basis for a magistrate's determination that there was probable cause to believe contraband would be found in the Gates' car and home. The letter provides virtually nothing from which one might conclude that its author is either honest or his information reliable; likewise, the letter gives absolutely no indication of the basis for the writer's predictions regarding the Gates' criminal activities. Something more was required, then, before a magistrate could conclude that there was probable cause to believe that contraband would be found in the Gates' home and car.

The Illinois Supreme Court also properly recognized that Detective Mader's affidavit might be capable of supplementing the anonymous letter with information sufficient to permit a determination of probable cause. In holding that the affidavit in fact did not contain sufficient additional information to sustain a determination of probable cause, the Illinois court applied a "two-pronged test," derived from our decision in Spinelli v. United States, 393 U.S. 410, 89 S.Ct. 584, 21 L.Ed.2d 637 (1969). The Illinois Supreme Court, like some others, apparently understood *Spinelli* as requiring that the anonymous letter satisfy each of two independent requirements before it could be relied on. J.A., at 5. According to this view, the letter, as supplemented by Mader's affidavit, first had to adequately reveal the "basis of knowledge" of the letter writer—the particular means by which he came by the information given in his report. Second, it had to provide facts sufficiently establishing either the "veracity" of the affiant's informant, or, alternatively, the "reliability" of the informant's report in this particular case.[22]

---

22. [Added by the Compiler.] A confidential informant who had frequently given the police information resulting in narcotics arrests, and whose information had always been reliable, telephoned L, a detective. The informant said that in approximately 15 minutes D would be driving to a specified parking lot, that he would be driving a black & gray Buick Riviera, license No. BB–6400 and would have several balloons of heroin with him. L went to the specified parking lot, saw D arrive there at the time indicated, driving a black & gray Buick Riviera, license No. BB–6400, and drive slowly from aisle to aisle as if looking for someone. L then arrested D and seized several balloons of heroin which were found in the car. It was held that the tip was so replete with detail as to be self-verifying. The court held the *Aguilar–Spinelli* test was satisfied relying upon *Draper*. People v. Williams, 189 Colo. 311, 541 P.2d 76 (1975).

The Illinois court, alluding to an elaborate set of legal rules that have developed among various lower courts to enforce the "two-pronged test," found that the test had not been satisfied. First, the "veracity" prong was not satisfied because, "there was simply no basis [for] . . . conclud[ing] that the anonymous person [who wrote the letter to the Bloomingdale Police Department] was credible." J.A., at 7a. The court indicated that corroboration by police of details contained in the letter might never satisfy the "veracity" prong, and in any event, could not do so if, as in the present case, only "innocent" details are corroborated. J.A., at 12a. In addition, the letter gave no indication of the basis of its writer's knowledge of the Gates' activities. The Illinois court understood *Spinelli* as permitting the detail contained in a tip to be used to infer that the informant had a reliable basis for his statements, but it thought that the anonymous letter failed to provide sufficient detail to permit such an inference. Thus, it concluded that no showing of probable cause had been made.

We agree with the Illinois Supreme Court that an informant's "veracity," "reliability" and "basis of knowledge" are all highly relevant in determining the value of his report. We do not agree, however, that these elements should be understood as entirely separate and independent requirements to be rigidly exacted in every case, which the opinion of the Supreme Court of Illinois would imply. Rather, as detailed below, they should be understood simply as closely intertwined issues that may usefully illuminate the commonsense, practical question whether there is "probable cause" to believe that contraband or evidence is located in a particular place.

This totality of the circumstances approach is far more consistent with our prior treatment of probable cause than is any rigid demand that specific "tests" be satisfied by every informant's tip. . . .

If, for example, a particular informant is known for the unusual reliability of his predictions of certain types of criminal activities in a locality, his failure, in a particular case, to thoroughly set forth the basis of his knowledge surely should not serve as an absolute bar to a finding of probable cause based on his tip. Likewise, if an unquestionably honest citizen comes forward with a report of criminal activity—which if fabricated would subject him to criminal liability—we have found rigorous scrutiny of the basis of his knowledge unnecessary. Conversely, even if we entertain some doubt as to an informant's motives, his explicit and detailed description of alleged wrongdoing, along with a statement that the event was observed first-hand, entitles his tip to greater weight than might otherwise be the case. Unlike a totality of circumstances analysis, which permits a balanced assessment of the relative weights of all the various indicia of

---

Where the informer was a witness to the crime it was reversible error to refuse to disclose his identity on demand at the trial. Roviaro v. United States, 353 U.S. 53, 77 S.Ct. 623, 1 L.Ed.2d 639 (1957). The identity of the informer must be disclosed (or the prosecution dismissed) if there is a reasonable possibility that he could give evidence on the issue of guilt which might exonerate D. Honore v. Superior Court, 70 Cal.2d 162, 74 Cal.Rptr. 233, 449 P.2d 169 (1969).

But where the informer was relied upon only to establish probable cause for the arrest of D his identity need not be disclosed. McCray v. Illinois, 386 U.S. 300, 87 S.Ct. 1056, 18 L.Ed.2d 62 (1967).

reliability (and unreliability) attending an informant's tip, the "two-pronged test" has encouraged an excessively technical dissection of informants' tips, with undue attention being focused on isolated issues that cannot sensibly be divorced from the other facts presented to the magistrate....

For all these reasons, we conclude that it is wiser to abandon the "two-pronged test" established by our decisions in *Aguilar* and *Spinelli*. In its place we reaffirm the totality of the circumstances analysis that traditionally has informed probable cause determinations. The task of the issuing magistrate is simply to make a practical, common-sense decision whether, given all the circumstances set forth in the affidavit before him, including the "veracity" and "basis of knowledge" of persons supplying hearsay information, there is a fair probability that contraband or evidence of a crime will be found in a particular place. And the duty of a reviewing court is simply to ensure that the magistrate had a "substantial basis for ... conclud[ing]" that probable cause existed. We are convinced that this flexible, easily applied standard will better achieve the accommodation of public and private interests that the Fourth Amendment requires than does the approach that has developed from *Aguilar* and *Spinelli*.

Our earlier cases illustrate the limits beyond which a magistrate may not venture in issuing a warrant. A sworn statement of an affiant that "he has cause to suspect and does believe that" liquor illegally brought into the United States is located on certain premises will not do. An affidavit must provide the magistrate with a substantial basis for determining the existence of probable cause, and the wholly conclusory statement at issue in *Nathanson* failed to meet this requirement. An officer's statement that "affiants have received reliable information from a credible person and believe" that heroin is stored in a home, is likewise inadequate. As in *Nathanson,* this is a mere conclusory statement that gives the magistrate virtually no basis at all for making a judgment regarding probable cause. Sufficient information must be presented to the magistrate to allow that official to determine probable cause; his action cannot be a mere ratification of the bare conclusions of others. In order to ensure that such an abdication of the magistrate's duty does not occur, courts must continue, to conscientiously review the sufficiency of affidavits on which warrants are issued. But when we move beyond the "bare bones" affidavits present in cases such as *Nathanson* and *Aguilar,* this area simply does not lend itself to a prescribed set of rules, like that which had developed from *Spinelli.* Instead, the flexible, common-sense standard articulated in *Jones, Ventresca,* and *Brinegar* better serves the purposes of the Fourth Amendment's probable cause requirement....

Our decision in Draper v. United States, 358 U.S. 307, 79 S.Ct. 329, 3 L.Ed.2d 327 (1959), however, is the classic case on the value of corroborative efforts of police officials. There, an informant named Hereford reported that Draper would arrive in Denver on a train for Chicago on one of two days, and that he would be carrying a quantity of heroin. The informant also supplied a fairly detailed physical description of Draper, and predicted that he would be wearing a light colored raincoat, brown slacks and black shoes, and would be walking "real fast". Hereford gave no indication of the basis for his information.

On one of the stated dates police officers observed a man matching this description exit a train arriving from Chicago; his attire and luggage matched Hereford's report and he was walking rapidly. We explained in *Draper* that, by this point in his investigation, the arresting officer "had personally verified every facet of the information given him by Hereford except whether petitioner had accomplished his mission and had the three ounces of heroin on his person or in his bag. And surely, with every other bit of Hereford's information being thus personally verified, [the officer] had 'reasonable grounds' to believe that the remaining unverified bit of Hereford's information—that Draper would have the heroin with him—was likewise true."

The showing of probable cause in the present case was fully as compelling as that in *Draper*. . . .

Finally, the anonymous letter contained a range of details relating not just to easily obtained facts and conditions existing at the time of the tip, but to future actions of third parties ordinarily not easily predicted. The letter writer's accurate information as to the travel plans of each of the Gates was of a character likely obtained only from the Gates themselves, or from someone familiar with their not entirely ordinary travel plans. If the informant had access to accurate information of this type a magistrate could properly conclude that it was not unlikely that he also had access to reliable information of the Gates' alleged illegal activities. Of course, the Gates' travel plans might have been learned from a talkative neighbor or travel agent; under the "two-pronged test" developed from *Spinelli,* the character of the details in the anonymous letter might well not permit a sufficiently clear inference regarding the letter writer's "basis of knowledge." But, as discussed previously, supra, 2332, probable cause does not demand the certainty we associate with formal trials. It is enough that there was a fair probability that the writer of the anonymous letter had obtained his entire story either from the Gates or someone they trusted. And corroboration of major portions of the letter's predictions provides just this probability. It is apparent, therefore, that the judge issuing the warrant had a "substantial basis for ... conclud[ing]" that probable cause to search the Gates' home and car existed. The judgment of the Supreme Court of Illinois therefore must be

Reversed.

■ [The separate opinions of JUSTICE WHITE, concurring, and

■ JUSTICE STEVENS, dissenting, are omitted]

c. *JUDICIAL REVIEW*

Arizona v. Hicks

Supreme Court of the United States, 1987.
480 U.S. 321, 107 S.Ct. 1149, 94 L.Ed.2d 347.

■ JUSTICE SCALIA delivered the opinion of the Court.

In *Coolidge v. New Hampshire,* 403 U.S. 443, 91 S.Ct. 2022, 29 L.Ed.2d 564 (1971), we said that in certain circumstances a warrantless seizure by police of an item that comes within plain view during their lawful search of a private area may be reasonable under the Fourth Amendment. See *id.,* at 465–471, 91 S.Ct. at 2037–2041 (plurality opinion); *id.,* at 505–506, 91 S.Ct. at 2057–2058 (Black, J., concurring and dissenting); *id.,* at 521–522, 91 S.Ct. at 2065–2066 (WHITE, J., concurring and dissenting). We granted certiorari, 475 U.S. 1107, 106 S.Ct. 1512, 89 L.Ed.2d 912 (1986), in the present case to decide whether this "plain view" doctrine may be invoked when the police have less than probable cause to believe that the item in question is evidence of a crime or is contraband.

I

On April 18, 1984, a bullet was fired through the floor of respondent's apartment, striking and injuring a man in the apartment below. Police officers arrived and entered respondent's apartment to search for the shooter, for other victims, and for weapons. They found and seized three weapons, including a sawed-off rifle, and in the course of their search also discovered a stocking-cap mask.

One of the policemen, Officer Nelson, noticed two sets of expensive stereo components, which seemed out of place in the squalid and otherwise ill-appointed four-room apartment. Suspecting that they were stolen, he read and recorded their serial numbers—moving some of the components, including a Bang and Olufsen turntable, in order to do so—which he then reported by phone to his headquarters. On being advised that the turntable had been taken in an armed robbery, he seized it immediately. It was later determined that some of the other serial numbers matched those on other stereo equipment taken in the same armed robbery, and a warrant was obtained and executed to seize that equipment as well. Respondent was subsequently indicted for the robbery.

The state trial court granted respondent's motion to suppress the evidence that had been seized. The Court of Appeals of Arizona affirmed. It was conceded that the initial entry and search, although warrantless, were justified by the exigent circumstance of the shooting. The Court of Appeals viewed the obtaining of the serial numbers, however, as an additional search, unrelated to that exigency. Relying upon a statement in *Mincey v. Arizona,* 437 U.S. 385, 98 S.Ct. 2408, 57 L.Ed.2d 290 (1978), that a "warrantless search must be 'strictly circumscribed by the exigencies which justify its initiation,' " *id.,* at 393, 98 S.Ct. at 2413 (citation omitted), the Court of Appeals held that the police conduct violated the Fourth Amendment, requiring the evidence derived from that conduct to be excluded. 146 Ariz. 533, 534–535, 707 P.2d 331, 332–333 (1985). Both courts—the trial court explicitly and the Court of Appeals by necessary implication—rejected the State's contention that Officer Nelson's actions were justified under the "plain view" doctrine of *Coolidge v. New Hampshire, supra.* The Arizona Supreme Court denied review, and the State filed this petition.

II

As an initial matter, the State argues that Officer Nelson's actions constituted neither a "search" nor a "seizure" within the meaning of the

Fourth Amendment. We agree that the mere recording of the serial numbers did not constitute a seizure. To be sure, that was the first step in a process by which respondent was eventually deprived of the stereo equipment. In and of itself, however, it did not "meaningfully interfere" with respondent's possessory interest in either the serial numbers or the equipment, and therefore did not amount to a seizure. See *Maryland v. Macon,* 472 U.S. 463, 469, 105 S.Ct. 2778, 2782, 86 L.Ed.2d 370 (1985).

Officer Nelson's moving of the equipment, however, did constitute a "search" separate and apart from the search for the shooter, victims, and weapons that was the lawful objective of his entry into the apartment. Merely inspecting those parts of the turntable that came into view during the latter search would not have constituted an independent search, because it would have produced no additional invasion of respondent's privacy interest. See *Illinois v. Andreas,* 463 U.S. 765, 771, 103 S.Ct. 3319, 3324, 77 L.Ed.2d 1003 (1983). But taking action, unrelated to the objectives of the authorized intrusion, which exposed to view concealed portions of the apartment or its contents, did produce a new invasion of respondent's privacy unjustified by the exigent circumstance that validated the entry. This is why, contrary to Justice Powell's suggestion, *post,* at 1156, the "distinction between 'looking' at a suspicious object in plain view and 'moving' it even a few inches" is much more than trivial for purposes of the Fourth Amendment. It matters not that the search uncovered nothing of any great personal value to respondent—serial numbers rather than (what might conceivably have been hidden behind or under the equipment) letters or photographs. A search is a search, even if it happens to disclose nothing but the bottom of a turntable.

III

The remaining question is whether the search was "reasonable" under the Fourth Amendment.

On this aspect of the case we reject, at the outset, the apparent position of the Arizona Court of Appeals that because the officers' action directed to the stereo equipment was unrelated to the justification for their entry into respondent's apartment, it was *ipso facto* unreasonable. That lack of relationship *always* exists with regard to action validated under the "plain view" doctrine; where action is taken for the purpose justifying the entry, invocation of the doctrine is superfluous. *Mincey v. Arizona, supra,* in saying that a warrantless search must be "strictly circumscribed by the exigencies which justify its initiation," 437 U.S., at 393, 98 S.Ct. at 2413 (citation omitted), was addressing only the scope of the primary search itself, and was not overruling by implication the many cases acknowledging that the "plain view" doctrine can legitimate action beyond that scope.

We turn, then, to application of the doctrine to the facts of this case. "It is well established that under certain circumstances the police may *seize* evidence in plain view without a warrant," *Coolidge v. New Hampshire,* 403 U.S., at 465, 91 S.Ct. at 2037 (plurality opinion) (emphasis added). Those circumstances include situations "[w]here the initial intrusion that brings the police within plain view of such [evidence] is supported ... by one of the recognized exceptions to the warrant requirement," *ibid.,* such as the exigent-circumstances intrusion here. It would be absurd to say that an object could lawfully be seized and taken from the premises, but could not be moved for closer examination. It is clear, therefore, that the search here was valid if the "plain view" doctrine would have sustained a seizure of the equipment.

There is no doubt it would have done so if Officer Nelson had probable cause to believe that the equipment was stolen. The State has conceded, however, that he had only a "reasonable suspicion," by which it means something less than probable cause. See Brief for Petitioner 18–19.* We have not ruled on the question whether probable cause is required in order to invoke the "plain view" doctrine. Dicta in *Payton v. New York,* 445 U.S. 573, 587, 100 S.Ct. 1371, 1380, 63 L.Ed.2d 639 (1980), suggested that the standard of probable cause must be met, but our later opinions in *Texas v. Brown,* 460 U.S. 730, 103 S.Ct. 1535, 75 L.Ed.2d 502 (1983), explicitly regarded the issue as unresolved, see *id.,* at 742, n. 7, 103 S.Ct. at 1543 n. 7 (plurality opinion); *id.,* at 746, 103 S.Ct. at 1545 (Stevens, J., concurring in judgment).

We now hold that probable cause is required. To say otherwise would be to cut the "plain view" doctrine loose from its theoretical and practical moorings. The theory of that doctrine consists of extending to nonpublic places such as the home, where searches and seizures without a warrant are presumptively unreasonable, the police's longstanding authority to make warrantless seizures in public places of such objects as weapons and contraband. See *Payton v. New York, supra,* at 586–587, 100 S.Ct. at 1380. And the practical justification for that extension is the desirability of sparing police, whose viewing of the object in the course of a lawful search is as legitimate as it would have been in a public place, the inconvenience and the risk—to themselves or to preservation of the evidence—of going to obtain a warrant. See *Coolidge v. New Hampshire, supra,* at 468, 91 S.Ct. at 2039 (plurality opinion). Dispensing with the need for a warrant is worlds apart from permitting a lesser standard of *cause* for the seizure than a warrant would require, *i.e.,* the standard of probable cause. No reason is apparent why an object should routinely be seizable on lesser grounds, during an unrelated search and seizure, than would have been needed to obtain a warrant for that same object if it had been known to be on the premises.

We do not say, of course, that a seizure can never be justified on less than probable cause. We have held that it can—where, for example, the seizure is minimally intrusive and operational necessities render it the only practicable means of detecting certain types of crime. See, *e.g., United States v. Cortez,* 449 U.S. 411, 101 S.Ct. 690, 66 L.Ed.2d 621 (1981) (investigative detention of vehicle suspected to be transporting illegal aliens); *United States v. Brignoni–Ponce,* 422 U.S. 873, 95 S.Ct. 2574, 45 L.Ed.2d 607 (1975) (same); *United States v. Place,* 462 U.S. 696, 709, and n. 9, 103 S.Ct. 2637, 2645 and n. 9, 77 L.Ed.2d 110 (1983) (dictum) (seizure of suspected drug dealer's luggage at airport to permit exposure to specially trained dog). No special operational necessities are relied on here, howev-

---

* Contrary to the suggestion in Justice O'CONNOR's dissent, this concession precludes our considering whether the probable-cause standard was satisfied in this case.

er—but rather the mere fact that the items in question came lawfully within the officer's plain view. That alone cannot supplant the requirement of probable cause.

The same considerations preclude us from holding that, even though probable cause would have been necessary for a *seizure,* the *search* of objects in plain view that occurred here could be sustained on lesser grounds. A dwelling-place search, no less than a dwelling-place seizure, requires probable cause, and there is no reason in theory or practicality why application of the "plain view" doctrine would supplant that requirement. Although the interest protected by the Fourth Amendment injunction against unreasonable searches is quite different from that protected by its injunction against unreasonable seizures, see *Texas v. Brown, supra,* 460 U.S., at 747–748, 103 S.Ct., at 1546 (Stevens, J., concurring in judgment), neither the one nor the other is of inferior worth or necessarily requires only lesser protection. We have not elsewhere drawn a categorical distinction between the two insofar as concerns the degree of justification needed to establish the reasonableness of police action, and we see no reason for a distinction in the particular circumstances before us here. Indeed, to treat searches more liberally would especially erode the plurality's warning in *Coolidge* that "the 'plain view' doctrine may not be used to extend a general exploratory search from one object to another until something incriminating at last emerges." 403 U.S., at 466, 91 S.Ct. at 2038. In short, whether legal authority to move the equipment could be found only as an inevitable concomitant of the authority to seize it, or also as a consequence of some independent power to search certain objects in plain view, probable cause to believe the equipment was stolen was required.

Justice O'CONNOR's dissent suggests that we uphold the action here on the ground that it was a "cursory inspection" rather than a "full-blown search," and could therefore be justified by reasonable suspicion instead of probable cause. As already noted, a truly cursory inspection—one that involves merely looking at what is already exposed to view, without disturbing it—is not a "search" for Fourth Amendment purposes, and therefore does not even require reasonable suspicion. We are unwilling to send police and judges into a new thicket of Fourth Amendment law, to seek a creature of uncertain description that is neither a "plain view" inspection nor yet a "full-blown search." Nothing in the prior opinions of this Court supports such a distinction, not even the dictum from Justice Stewart's concurrence in *Stanley v. Georgia,* 394 U.S. 557, 571, 89 S.Ct. 1243, 1251, 22 L.Ed.2d 542 (1969), whose reference to a "mere inspection" describes, in our view, close observation of what lies in plain sight.

Justice Powell's dissent reasonably asks what it is we would have had Officer Nelson do in these circumstances. *Post,* at ___. The answer depends, of course, upon whether he had probable cause to conduct a search, a question that was not preserved in this case. If he had, then he should have done precisely what he did. If not, then he should have followed up his suspicions, if possible, by means other than a search—just as he would have had to do if, while walking along the street, he had noticed the same suspicious stereo equipment sitting inside a house a few feet away from him, beneath an open window. It may well be that, in such circumstances, no effective means short of a search exist. But there is nothing new in the realization that the Constitution sometimes insulates the criminality of a few in order to protect the privacy of us all. Our disagreement with the dissenters pertains to where the proper balance should be struck; we choose to adhere to the textual and traditional standard of probable cause.

The State contends that, even if Officer Nelson's search violated the Fourth Amendment, the court below should have admitted the evidence thus obtained under the "good faith" exception to the exclusionary rule. That was not the question on which certiorari was granted, and we decline to consider it.

For the reasons stated, the judgment of the Court of Appeals of Arizona is

Affirmed.

■ [The separate opinions of JUSTICE WHITE, concurring, and JUSTICES POWELL and O'CONNOR, dissenting, are omitted]

United States v. Brown

United States Court of Appeals, Eleventh Circuit, 2006.
203 Fed.Appx. 997.

■ PER CURIAM:

Appellant Richard Owen Brown appeals his conviction for conspiracy to import cocaine, conspiracy to possess with intent to distribute cocaine, and attempt to possess with intent to distribute cocaine, in violation of 21 U.S.C. §§ 963 and 846. On appeal, Brown argues that the district court erred in denying his motion to suppress physical evidence seized from his girlfriend's car because the police lacked probable cause to search the car. Brown further argues that the police exceeded the scope of a valid inventory search when they read the contents of a document found in the car, thus converting it into an investigatory search.

"A district court's ruling on a motion to suppress presents a mixed question of law and fact. This Court reviews the district court's finding of facts under the clearly erroneous standard. The district court's application of the law to those facts is subject to de novo review." *United States v. Zapata,* 180 F.3d 1237, 1240 (11th Cir.1999) (citations omitted). "Further, when considering a ruling on a motion to suppress, all facts are construed in the light most favorable to the prevailing party below." *United States v. Bervaldi,* 226 F.3d 1256, 1262 (11th Cir.2000).

A party moving to suppress evidence must first show that he has standing, consisting of "a legitimate expectation of privacy" in the car being searched. *United States v. Miller,* 821 F.2d 546, 548 (11th Cir.1987). On appeal, the government does not dispute that Brown has standing to challenge the search of the car at issue, even though his girlfriend owned it. Furthermore, the record reflects that Brown had a reasonable expectation of privacy in the car because Brown had permission to drive it. *See United States v. Miller,* 821 F.2d 546, 548 (11th Cir.1987) (holding that a driver of a borrowed car had a legitimate expectation of privacy in it, and thus, had standing to challenge a search of the car).

In most circumstances, unless there is consent, police officers must obtain a warrant supported by probable cause to justify a search under the

Fourth Amendment. *United States v. Magluta,* 418 F.3d 1166, 1182 (11th Cir.2005), *cert. denied,* 126 S.Ct. 2966 (2006). There are, however, several exceptions to this rule, including "the automobile exception," which allows "officers [to] search any container in an operational car without a warrant as long as they have probable cause to believe that the container holds evidence of a crime." *Id.* (citing *California v. Acevedo, 500 U.S. 565, 579–80, 111 S.Ct. 1982, 1991, 114 L.Ed.2d 619 (1991)*). "Probable cause for a search exists when under the totality of the circumstances there is a fair probability that contraband or evidence of a crime will be found in a particular place." *Id.* (quotations and citations omitted). "In examining the totality of the circumstances, a reviewing court must give due weight to the officer's experience." *United States v. Briggman,* 931 F.2d 705, 709 (11th Cir.1991).

Furthermore, inventory searches, in accordance with reasonable police policy, are also permissible. *Colorado v. Bertine* 479 U.S. 367, 374, 107 S.Ct. 738, 742, 93 L.Ed.2d 739 (1987). An inventory search permits a thorough search of property lawfully in police custody, as long as that search is consistent with the police caretaking function. *United States v. O'Bryant,* 775 F.2d 1528, 1534 (11th Cir.1985). Probable cause is not required to conduct a valid inventory search. *Illinois v. Lafayette,* 462 U.S. 640, 643, 103 S.Ct. 2605, 2608, 77 L.Ed.2d 65 (1983). In this context, "the legitimacy of the search ... turns on its reasonableness in light of the community caretaking functions that allow inventory searches.... [T]he reasonableness of the inventory search depends on the particular facts and circumstances." *United States v. Laing,* 708 F.2d 1568, 1571 (11th Cir.1983). We have held that "the mere expectation of uncovering evidence will not vitiate an otherwise valid inventory search." *United States v. Roberson,* 897 F.2d 1092, 1096 (11th Cir.1990) (quotation and citation omitted).

Based on the totality of the evidence known at the time, we conclude from the record that authorities had a reasonable belief that Brown used the car to facilitate the drug transaction and a reasonable belief that they would find drugs or other evidence of criminal activity inside the car. Thus, authorities had probable cause to search the car and the search was permissible under the "automobile exception" to the Fourth Amendment's warrant requirement. *See Magluta,* 418 F.3d at 1182–83. We do not address whether authorities exceeded the scope of a valid inventory search by reading the contents of the seized documents because the warrantless search of Carlita's car was otherwise supported by probable cause, and thus, the district court did not err in denying Brown's motion to suppress. Accordingly, we affirm Brown's conviction.

AFFIRMED.

United States v. Williams

United States Court of Appeals, Fourth Circuit, 2005.
159 Fed.Appx. 500.

■ Per Curiam:

Bryant Williams entered a conditional guilty plea to possession with intent to distribute five kilograms or more of cocaine, in violation of 21

U.S.C. § 841 (2000). He reserved his right to challenge the district court's ruling on his motion to suppress. After the district court sentenced him to 120 months' imprisonment, Williams noted his appeal. . . .

At the hearing on Williams' motion to suppress, the Government and Williams stipulated to these facts. While conducting surveillance at an apartment complex in regard to suspected narcotics trafficking activities, Detective Peter Sullivan observed Williams enter the apartment building shortly after midnight. Some time later, he observed an unknown female, later identified as Tyra Tucker, arrive and enter the apartment building. Approximately ten minutes later, Williams and Tucker exited the building together and approached Tucker's vehicle. Williams was carrying a brown shoulder bag. Tucker opened the trunk of her vehicle and Williams placed the bag in the trunk. Williams then got into his vehicle and drove away from the apartment complex. Tucker, in her vehicle, followed closely behind Williams. The police officers then initiated a stop of both vehicles. The officers obtained from Tucker her consent to search her vehicle, and they recovered the bag from her trunk. Inside the bag, officers discovered ten kilograms of cocaine.

Williams asserted that he had—and at all times maintained—an ownership and possessory interest in the bag and its contents. He stated that, when he and Tucker left the apartment complex, he had instructed Tucker to "follow him and stay in close contact with him [so that] he could keep an eye on her and the bag at all times." Williams contends that he intended to retrieve the bag from Tucker once they reached their destination. Williams also asserted that Tucker did not know the contents of the bag.

Following the presentation of this evidence and argument on the issue, the district court denied the motion to suppress, finding that Williams lacked standing to contest the consent search. Williams appeals, arguing that the district court failed to recognize his supervisory role over the transportation of the bag and thus his expectation of privacy in the bag.

To succeed on a Fourth Amendment claim, an individual must have a legitimate expectation of privacy in the area searched or the item seized. *See Rawlings v. Kentucky,* 448 U.S. 98, 106, 100 S.Ct. 2556, 65 L.Ed.2d 633 (1980). A passenger in an automobile normally has no legitimate expectation of privacy in an automobile in which he asserts neither a property nor a possessory interest. *See Rakas v. Illinois,* 439 U.S. 128, 148–49, 99 S.Ct. 421, 58 L.Ed.2d 387 (1978); *United States v. Rusher,* 966 F.2d 868, 874 (4th Cir.1992). Here, Williams was never a passenger in the vehicle being searched. Thus, he could not have had an expectation of privacy in the *area being searched. See Rawlings,* 448 U.S. at 106, 100 S.Ct. 2556; *United States v. Washburn,* 383 F.3d 638 (7th Cir.2004) (finding defendant, who was not present during the search, lacked standing to challenge search of luggage he placed in a vehicle for delivery to another location), *cert. denied,* ___ U.S. ___, 125 S.Ct. 1746, 161 L.Ed.2d 605 (2005); *see also United States v. Wellons,* 32 F.3d 117, 119 (4th Cir.1994) (holding that unauthorized driver of rental car had no expectation of privacy in the car or any container found in the car, and denying standing to challenge search of luggage found in trunk of car).

Williams asserts, however, that he retained an expectation of privacy in the bag, which he placed in the trunk of Tucker's car. In *Florida v. Jimeno,*

500 U.S. 248, 251, 111 S.Ct. 1801, 114 L.Ed.2d 297 (1991), the Supreme Court held that a general consent to search an automobile authorized a search of any container within the vehicle that could contain contraband. The Court held that "it was objectively reasonable for the police to conclude that the general consent to search respondents' car [for narcotics] included consent to search containers within the car that might bear drugs." *Id.; see United States v. Gant,* 112 F.3d 239, 243 (6th Cir.1997) (explaining that " 'general consent [to a search] permits the opening of closed but unlocked containers found in the place as to which consent was given.' " (quoting Wayne R. LaFave, *Search and Seizure,* § 8.1(c) & n. 75 (1986))); *United States v. Zapata,* 18 F.3d 971, 977–78 (1st Cir.1994) ("Because the duffel bags were lying in the trunk, appellant's general consent to a search of the automobile constituted consent to a search of the duffel bags.").

Based on the above-cited authority, Tucker's consent to the search of her vehicle included consent to search the unlocked bag in the trunk of her vehicle. Williams' claim of a supervisory role over the transportation of the bag and its contents is insufficient to afford him standing to challenge the search of a vehicle belonging to another and the contents of that vehicle. *See United States v. Padilla,* 508 U.S. 77, 82, 113 S.Ct. 1936, 123 L.Ed.2d 635 (1993); *United States v. Al–Talib,* 55 F.3d 923, 930–31 (4th Cir.1995) ("No expectation of privacy is created simply because one has 'a supervisory role in the conspiracy or joint control over the place or property involved in the search or seizure.' " (quoting *Padilla,* 508 U.S. at 82, 113 S.Ct. 1936)).

Because Williams did not have an ownership interest in the vehicle searched, and because his co-conspirator/supervisor argument has been rejected by the Supreme Court, we find no error by the district court in determining that he lacked standing to challenge the search of Tucker's vehicle, including the bag in the vehicle. We therefore affirm the district court's order denying Williams' motion to suppress and affirm his conviction. We dispense with oral argument because the facts and legal contentions are adequately presented in the materials before the court and argument would not aid the decisional process.

AFFIRMED

D. "*Special Needs*"

United States v. Hartwell

United States Court of Appeals, Third Circuit, 2006.
436 F.3d 174.

■ Alito, Circuit Judge.

Christian Hartwell set off a metal detector at a security checkpoint in an airport. Transportation Security Administration ("TSA") agents then used a magnetic wand to pinpoint any metal on his person. They detected something in Hartwell's pocket and asked to see it. Ultimately, they discovered that the object was crack cocaine and placed Hartwell under arrest. Hartwell argues that the drugs should have been suppressed because the search offended the Fourth Amendment. We hold that it did not....

III.

Hartwell's search at the airport checkpoint was justified by the administrative search doctrine.[5] "A search or seizure is ordinarily unreasonable in the absence of individualized suspicion of wrongdoing. While such suspicion is not an 'irreducible' component of reasonableness, [the Supreme Court has] recognized only limited circumstances in which the usual rule does not apply." *City of Indianapolis v. Edmond,* 531 U.S. 32, 37, 121 S.Ct. 447, 148 L.Ed.2d 333 (2000) (citations omitted). These circumstances typically involve administrative searches of "closely regulated" businesses,[6] other so-called "special needs" cases, and suspicionless "checkpoint" searches.

Suspicionless checkpoint searches are permissible under the Fourth Amendment when a court finds a favorable balance between "the gravity of the public concerns served by the seizure, the degree to which the seizure advances the public interest, and the severity of the interference with individual liberty." *Illinois v. Lidster,* 540 U.S. 419, 427, 124 S.Ct. 885, 157 L.Ed.2d 843 (2004) (quoting *Brown v. Texas,* 443 U.S. 47, 51, 99 S.Ct. 2637, 61 L.Ed.2d 357 (1979)) (internal quotations omitted).[8]

Michigan Dept. of State Police v. Sitz, 496 U.S. 444, 110 S.Ct. 2481, 110 L.Ed.2d 412 (1990), provides an illustrative example of a permissible suspicionless checkpoint procedure. In that case, Michigan established a sobriety checkpoint along a state road, stopping every vehicle that passed by in order to question the driver and look for signs of intoxication. If the police observed indicia of impairment, they would pull drivers aside to

---

5. While the Supreme Court has not directly spoken on airport administrative searches, it has discussed them in dicta in two cases. In *Chandler v. Miller,* 520 U.S. 305, 323, 117 S.Ct. 1295, 137 L.Ed.2d 513 (1997), the Court mentioned that blanket suspicionless searches "may rank as 'reasonable'—for example, searches now routine at airports." And in *City of Indianapolis v. Edmond,* 531 U.S. 32, 47–48, 121 S.Ct. 447, 148 L.Ed.2d 333 (2000), it stated that "[o]ur holding also does not affect the validity of border searches or searches at places like airports and government buildings, where the need for such measures to ensure public safety can be particularly acute."

6. These searches are permissible without a warrant when: 1) a substantial government interest informs the regulatory scheme under which the search is made; 2) the search is necessary to further the regulatory scheme; and 3) the statute's inspection program is a "constitutionally adequate substitute for a warrant." *New York v. Burger,* 482 U.S. 691, 702–04, 107 S.Ct. 2636, 96 L.Ed.2d 601 (1987) (warrantless administrative inspection of premises of closely regulated business) (citing *Donovan v. Dewey,* 452 U.S. 594, 600–04, 101 S.Ct. 2534, 69 L.Ed.2d 262 (1981) and *United States v. Biswell,* 406 U.S. 311, 315, 92 S.Ct. 1593, 32 L.Ed.2d 87 (1972). *See also Michigan v. Tyler,* 436 U.S. 499, 507–12, 98 S.Ct. 1942, 56 L.Ed.2d 486 (1978) (administrative inspection of fire-damaged premises to determine cause of the fire); *Camara v. Municipal Court of City and County of San Francisco,* 387 U.S. 523, 534–39, 87 S.Ct. 1727, 18 L.Ed.2d 930 (1967) (administrative inspection to ensure compliance with city housing code is acceptable).

8. *See, e.g., Lidster,* 540 U.S. at 426–27, 124 S.Ct. 885 (2004) (checkpoint stop to find information about a "hit and run" one week before on the same road is permissible); *Edmond,* 531 U.S. at 44, 121 S.Ct. 447 (checkpoints aimed at finding drug offenders in order to advance an interest "ultimately indistinguishable" from a general interest in crime control, are impermissible); *Michigan Dept. of State Police v. Sitz,* 496 U.S. 444, 110 S.Ct. 2481, 110 L.Ed.2d 412 (1990) (sobriety checkpoint aimed to catch drunk drivers is acceptable); *Delaware v. Prouse,* 440 U.S. 648, 663, 99 S.Ct. 1391, 59 L.Ed.2d 660 (1979) (discretionary, suspicionless stop for a spot check of a motorist's driver's license and registration is illegal); *United States v.*

conduct additional tests. Applying the *Brown* balancing test, the Court found the system permissible because "the balance of the State's interest in preventing drunken driving, the extent to which this system can reasonably be said to advance that interest, and the degree of intrusion upon individual motorists who are briefly stopped, weighs in favor of the state program." *Sitz,* 496 U.S. at 455, 110 S.Ct. 2481. As to the State's interest, the Court wrote that "[n]o one can seriously dispute the magnitude of the drunken driving problem or the States' interest in eradicating it." *Id.* at 451, 110 S.Ct. 2481. The stop was deemed effective because some quantum of evidence showed that it furthered the purpose for which it was created. "Conversely," the Court stated, "the weight bearing on the other scale—the measure of the intrusion on motorists stopped briefly at sobriety checkpoints—is slight," because the stop lasted for only a short time and the investigation was of minimal intensity. *Id.*

In this case, the airport checkpoint passes the *Brown* test. First, there can be no doubt that preventing terrorist attacks on airplanes is of paramount importance.... Additionally, it is apparent that airport checkpoints have been effective.

Third, the procedures involved in Hartwell's search were minimally intrusive.... Only after Hartwell set off the metal detector was he screened with a wand—yet another less intrusive substitute for a physical pat-down. And only after the wand detected something solid on his person, and after repeated requests that he produce the item, did the TSA agents (according to Hartwell) reach into his pocket.

In addition to being tailored to protect personal privacy, other factors make airport screening procedures minimally intrusive in comparison to other kinds of searches. Since every air passenger is subjected to a search, there is virtually no "stigma attached to being subjected to search at a known, designated airport search point." *See United States v. Skipwith,* 482 F.2d 1272, 1275 (5th Cir.1973). Moreover, the possibility for abuse is minimized by the public nature of the search....

Lastly, the entire procedure is rendered less offensive—if not less intrusive—because air passengers are on notice that they will be searched.[11] Air passengers choose to fly, and screening procedures of this kind have existed in every airport in the country since at least 1974. The events of September 11, 2001, have only increased their prominence in the public's consciousness. It is inconceivable that Hartwell was unaware that he had to be searched before he could board a plane. Indeed, he admitted that he had previously been searched before flying. *Hartwell,* 296 F.Supp.2d at 605. *Cf. United States v. Pulido–Baquerizo,* 800 F.2d 899, 901 (9th Cir.1986) ("in

---

Martinez–Fuerte, 428 U.S. 543, 546–47, 96 S.Ct. 3074, 49 L.Ed.2d 1116 (1976) (border checkpoint to search for illegal aliens 100 miles from the border is legal).

11. Some courts, including the District Court in this case, have approved airport searches on consent-based rationales. *See, e.g., United States v. Henry,* 615 F.2d 1223, 1230–31 (9th Cir.1980); *United States v. Edwards,* 498 F.2d 496, 500–01 (2d Cir.1974); *United States v. Mather,* 465 F.2d 1035, 1036 (5th Cir.1972). Other courts, however, remain skeptical. *See, e.g., United States v. Albarado,* 495 F.2d 799, 806–07 (2d Cir.1974); *United States v. Kroll,* 481 F.2d 884, 886 (8th Cir.1973). *See also* Wayne R. LaFave, *Search and Seizure: A Treatise on the Fourth Amendment,* § 10.6(g) at 307–09 (4th ed.2004) (explaining that consent theories are "basically unsound" in the airport context because screening systems rarely meet the

light of the circumstances surrounding today's airport checkpoints," travelers who put their belongings on a conveyor belt "impliedly consent to a visual inspection and limited hand search of their luggage if the x-ray scan is inconclusive").

Hartwell argues that once the TSA agents identified the object in his pocket and he refused to reveal it, he should have had the right to leave rather than empty his pockets. We reject this theory. As several courts have noted, a right to leave once screening procedures begin "would constitute a one-way street for the benefit of a party planning airport mischief," *United States v. Herzbrun,* 723 F.2d 773, 776 (11th Cir.1984) (internal quotation marks and citation omitted), and "would 'encourage airline terrorism by providing a secure exit where detection was threatened,' " *People v. Heimel,* 812 P.2d 1177, 1182 (Colo.1991) (quoting *Pulido-Baquerizo,* 800 F.2d at 902).

In conclusion, Hartwell's search does not offend the Fourth Amendment even though it was initiated without individualized suspicion and was conducted without a warrant. It is permissible under the administrative search doctrine because the State has an overwhelming interest in preserving air travel safety, and the procedure is tailored to advance that interest while proving to be only minimally invasive, as that term is understood in *Brown.*[13]

SECTION 4.   CURRENT DOCTRINE: POLICE AUTHORITY TO INTERROGATE

(1)   Miranda doctrine

A.   CUSTODY

United States v. Beard
United States Court of Appeals, Fourth Circuit, 2005.
119 Fed.Appx. 462.

■ PER CURIAM.

The Government appeals the district court's order granting John Beard's motion to suppress statements he made to police officers. Because

---

requirements for express consent under *Schneckloth v. Bustamonte,* 412 U.S. 218, 222, 228, 93 S.Ct. 2041, 36 L.Ed.2d 854 (1973), and an implied consent analysis merely "diverts attention from the more fundamental question of whether the nature of the regulation undertaken by the government is in fact reasonable under the Fourth Amendment"). We find it unnecessary to reach this issue because we sustain the screening procedure under the administrative search doctrine.

13. Even assuming that the sole purpose of the checkpoint was to search only for weapons or explosives, the fruits of the search need not be suppressed so long as the search itself was permissible. *See Minnesota v. Dickerson,* 508 U.S. 366, 377, 113 S.Ct. 2130, 124 L.Ed.2d 334 (1993) ("The seizure of an item whose identity is already known occasions no further invasion of privacy.") (collecting cases); *United States v. Edwards,* 498 F.2d 496, 500 (2d Cir.1974) ("unless and until there should be evidence of abuse, we hold to the traditional rule that if the search is proper, it is of no moment that the object found was not what the officer was looking for") (citation omitted). Since the object in Hartwell's pocket could have been a small knife or bit of plastic explosives, the TSA agents were justified in examining it. *See also Marquez,* 410 F.3d at 617 ("The screening at issue here is not unreasonable simply because it revealed that Marquez was carrying cocaine rather than C–4 explosives.").

the district court applied the wrong legal test in determining that Beard was in custody, and because Beard was not in custody under the correct legal test, we reverse.

I.

On April 26, 2003, Richmond police received a report of a domestic disturbance at 1043 Barlen Drive. Two police officers, Officers Eugene J. Provost and Tim Degrauwe, responded to the report. Officer Provost interviewed Beard's mother, sister, and brother, while Officer Degrauwe went inside the house to speak with Beard.

Through his interviews, Officer Provost learned that Beard had threatened his sister with a shotgun. Officer Provost retrieved the shotgun from a van parked outside the house. After discovering that the barrel of the shotgun had been sawed off and was an illegal length, Officer Provost went inside to talk to Beard. Officer Provost found Officer Degrauwe and Beard, who was ironing clothes, in Beard's bedroom.

As Officer Provost entered the room, he signaled to Officer Degrauwe, "we [are] going to end up cuffing [Beard]." There is, however, no evidence that Beard either observed or understood this signal. Officer Provost then advised Beard of his "*Miranda* rights," but exactly what Officer Provost said is unclear. Officer Provost questioned Beard about the shotgun, and Beard confessed that he was a convicted felon, the gun was for home protection, and he had accidentally pointed the shotgun at his sister the night before. The officers handcuffed Beard and took him to the police station. The entire episode, from the time Officer Provost walked into Beard's bedroom to the time the officers handcuffed Beard, happened very quickly. At the police station, the officers gave Beard a Rights Waiver Form, but Beard refused to sign it or to cooperate further.

On July 22, 2003, a grand jury sitting in the Eastern District of Virginia charged Beard in a two-count indictment with being a felon in possession of a firearm ... and possessing an unregistered firearm.... Beard filed a motion to suppress his confession, arguing that it was taken in violation of *Miranda*....

Officer Provost was the only witness who testified at the hearing. On the stand, he recounted the events that lead up to Beard's arrest. When he discussed whether he informed Beard of his rights at the house, Officer Provost stated that he had advised Beard of his "constitutional rights," his "*Miranda* rights," or simply his "rights". The prosecutor did not ask Officer Provost to clarify exactly what he had said to Beard, and the district court closed the evidentiary portion of the hearing. At argument on the motion, Beard's attorney contended that Officer Provost's testimony was insufficient for the Government to carry its burden of showing it complied with *Miranda*. In response, the Government moved to reopen the record to allow Officer Provost to testify as to exactly what he said to Beard, but the district court denied the motion. The district court then granted the motion to suppress, finding that (1) the defendant was in custody for *Miranda* purposes, and (2) the Government had not shown that Officer Provost complied with *Miranda:*

> Now, the ... issue was whether or not Mr. Beard was under a custodial situation at the time that these questions were propounded to him, and it is clear to the Court, and I find, that he was not free to leave. And that's the test. As Officer Provost walks into the room and gives the signal to Degrauwe, the question you ask is at that point in time, [if] Mr. Beard says, "Adios, I'm taking off, I'll see you guys later," would they let him leave? And the answer is clearly no. So he was in custody at the time.

* * *

> Provost indicated that, and I'll use the exact wording from the testimony, he was advised of his constitutional rights and in later questioning, referred to advised of *Miranda* rights. There was an indication to Officer Provost that the defendant understood these rights, whatever they were. And then there was some discussion. And in the course of that discussion, the defendant made certain statements. Among them, that he did indeed aim the shotgun at his sister because he mistook her for someone trying to break into the house, and that the gun was for home protection. And I believe that he also indicated that he was a convicted felon....

> Now, the problem ... is that the burden is on the government to establish that the particular warnings given to the defendant were such that they would reasonably convey to a suspect what his actual rights are. And there is no way that I can come to any conclusion about that because I don't know what was said. The Court has been clear that you don't have to have some specific language. It doesn't have to be talismanic. But it is also clear that there must be enough for the Court to say that what was said was reasonably calculated to convey the message that needed to be conveyed. On this record, obviously, I can't do that.

The Government noted a timely appeal, and we have jurisdiction under 18 U.S.C.A. § 3731 (West 2002 & Supp.2004) (allowing interlocutory appeals from district court orders suppressing evidence if prosecutor makes appropriate certification).

II.

The Government argues that the district court erred in determining that Beard was in custody for *Miranda* purposes.[1] It contends that the district court applied the wrong legal test in determining that Beard was in custody, and that under the correct test, the facts show Beard was not in custody. We review a district court's factual findings on a motion to suppress for clear error and its legal conclusions de novo. *United States v. Parker,* 262 F.3d 415, 419 (4th Cir.2001). The Government does not challenge either the district court's denial of its motion to reopen the evidence or the district court's conclusion that the Government failed to

---

1. The Government does not challenge either the district court's denial of its motion to reopen the evidence or the district court's conclusion that the Government failed to carry its burden of proving that Beard had received the necessary warnings under *Miranda.*

carry its burden of proving that Beard had received the necessary warnings under *Miranda.*

In *Miranda,* the Supreme Court found that statements officers obtain by questioning a suspect in custody are presumptively compelled because of the inherently coercive nature of custodial interrogation. 384 U.S. at 457–58. To protect the Fifth Amendment right against self-incrimination, *see* U.S. Const. amend. V ("[n]o person . . . shall be compelled in any criminal case to be a witness against himself"), such statements are generally inadmissible in the prosecution's case-in-chief unless the government overcomes the presumption by showing that officers first (1) warned the suspect that (a) he has the right to remain silent, (b) anything he says can be used against him, (c) he has the right to an attorney, and (d) if he cannot afford an attorney, one will be appointed to him, and (2) obtained a waiver of these rights. *See Berkemer v. McCarty,* 468 U.S. 420, 429, 104 S.Ct. 3138, 82 L.Ed.2d 317 (1994) ("[I]f the police take a suspect into custody and then ask him questions without informing him of [his rights], his responses cannot be introduced into evidence to establish his guilt."); *Miranda,* 384 U.S. at 444 (listing warnings).

Miranda's exclusionary rule only applies, however, when officers elicit admissions by questioning a suspect who is "in custody." *Oregon v. Mathiason,* 429 U.S. 492, 495, 97 S.Ct. 711, 50 L.Ed.2d 714 (1977). In this context, custody is a flexible concept, which does not require a defendant actually be handcuffed or behind bars. *See Orozco v. Texas,* 394 U.S. 324, 326–27, 89 S.Ct. 1095, 22 L.Ed.2d 311 (1969) (holding that under certain circumstances, suspect can be in custody under *Miranda* in his own home). Rather, a suspect is in custody for *Miranda* purposes when, as in *Miranda* itself, the circumstances of the interrogation "exert[ ] upon a [suspect] pressures that . . . impair his free exercise of his privilege against self-incrimination." *Berkemer,* 468 U.S. at 437, or, in other words, when the "suspect's freedom of action is curtailed to a 'degree associated with formal arrest.' " *Id.* at 440 (quoting *California v. Beheler,* 463 U.S. 1121, 1125, 103 S.Ct. 3517, 77 L.Ed.2d 1275 (1983)).

Because the *Miranda* Court was concerned with coercion, a reviewing court determines whether a suspect is in "custody" by first examining the totality of the circumstances surrounding the limitations on the suspect's freedom as the suspect himself perceived them. *See Thompson v. Keohane,* 516 U.S. 99, 112, 116 S.Ct. 457, 133 L.Ed.2d 383 (1995); *Berkemer,* 468 U.S. at 437–38. Second, a reviewing court must focus not on how the suspect *actually* interpreted these facts, but rather on what a *reasonable person* in the suspect's position would have thought knowing the facts available to him. *See Thompson,* 516 U.S. at 112; *Stansbury v. California,* 511 U.S. 318, 323, 114 S.Ct. 1526, 128 L.Ed.2d 293 (1994). Therefore, "[a] policeman's unarticulated plan has no bearing on the question whether a suspect was 'in custody' at a particular time; the only relevant inquiry is how a reasonable man in the suspect's position would have understood his situation." *Berkemer,* 468 U.S. at 441.

In holding that Beard was in custody under *Miranda,* the district court found that [Beard] was not free to leave. . . . The district court's test asked what the officers would have done if Beard had attempted to leave his bedroom; it neither focused on the circumstances as Beard perceived them nor examined the conclusions a reasonable man would draw therefrom. *Cf. Thompson*, 516 U.S. at 112. The district court therefore erred.

Applying the correct test, we conclude that Beard was not in "custody."[2] The facts here are similar to those in *Parker*, 262 F.3d at 417. In *Parker*, federal officers came to Parker's home and met with her and her family for approximately 20 minutes in the kitchen of the house. The officers then requested to interview Parker in private, and her aunt pointed out a spare bedroom. During the 30–minute bedroom interview, Parker's aunt twice entered the room to speak with her. Parker did not leave the room during the interview, and at some point the officers informed her that she was not under arrest. The officers testified, however, they would not have allowed Parker to leave the house had she attempted to do so. On these facts, we found that the defendant was not in "custody":

> [Parker] was not handcuffed or otherwise restrained, and the agents did not draw their weapons in her presence. She was also in her own home during the questioning, and one of her relatives, at the relative's request, entered the interview room on two occasions during the questioning. She was not forced to enter the room with the officers, and she was never told that she was not free to leave.
>
> The fact that one of the agents testified at the suppression hearing that they likely would have arrested Parker had she attempted to end the interview and leave the house does not successfully undercut the holding of the district court that Parker was not under the functional equivalent of arrest during questioning. Custody determinations do not depend on the subjective views of . . . the interrogating law enforcement officers. . . . The agent's unarticulated views at the time [a suspect] was being questioned is of little weight. The relevant inquiry is how a reasonable man would have understood the suspect's position at the time.

Id. at 419 (citations omitted).

Like Parker, Beard was not handcuffed or otherwise restrained. In addition, there is no evidence that the officers drew their weapons in Beard's presence or were antagonistic toward him. Beard was in his own house, even his own room, and was never told that he was not free to leave. Finally, there is no evidence that Beard saw or understood Officer Provost's signal to Officer Degrauwe. Under these circumstances, we cannot conclude that a reasonable man in Beard's position would have believed his freedom of action was restrained to a "degree associated with formal arrest." *Beheler*, 463 U.S. at 1125.

Beard attempts to distinguish *Parker* by noting that (1) Beard was segregated from the other residents of the house, (2) Officer Provost was carrying the shotgun when he walked into Beard's bedroom, and (3) Beard was never allowed to associate with other household residents during the

---

2. The ultimate issue of whether Beard was in custody under *Miranda* is one that we may decide. *See Thompson v. Keohane*, 516 U.S. 99, 112, 116 S.Ct. 457, 133 L.Ed.2d 383 (1995) (holding that *Miranda* custodial determination is a legal question qualifying it for "mixed question of law and fact" review under 28 U.S.C. § 2254(d)).

interview.[3] These factual differences do not change the outcome in this case. First, there is no evidence that the officers affirmatively segregated Beard from the other residents of the house; in fact, the testimony indicates that Beard either was ironing clothes in his bedroom when the officers arrived or had enough freedom of movement after their arrival to go into his bedroom and begin ironing. These acts are simply inconsistent with a finding of custody under *Miranda.* Second, the fact that Officer Provost confronted Beard with the shotgun is not sufficient to put him into "custody." *Cf. Mathiason,* 429 U.S. at 495 (holding that interview at police station during which officers falsely told suspect that his fingerprints were found at crime scene was not custodial); *Beckwith v. United States,* 425 U.S. 341, 347, 96 S.Ct. 1612, 48 L.Ed.2d 1 (1976) (holding that interview with IRS investigators at home of suspect during which investigators informed suspect that they were investigating his tax records was not custodial); *Davis v. Allsbrooks,* 778 F.2d 168, 172 (4th Cir.1985) (holding that interview at police station where officers showed suspect pictures of crime scene was not custodial). Third, there is no suggestion that Beard asked to speak to his relatives, that his relatives attempted to enter the bedroom, or that the officers would have prevented such entry. Beard was not, therefore, in custody when he gave the incriminating statements.[4]

Beard does not focus on the fact that in *Parker* officers told the suspect that she was not under arrest. While this factual difference is not irrelevant, we do not find it significant given the totality of the circumstances, including the facts that, (1) like in *Parker,* the officers never told Beard he was under arrest, *see Davis v. Allsbrooks,* 778 F.2d 168, 171–72 (4th Cir.1985) ("Though informing a suspect that he is not under arrest is one factor frequently considered to show lack of custody, it is not a talismanic factor. Where, as here, the entire context establishes a lack of custody, failure to inform defendant of his status is not dispositive.") (citations

---

3. Beard also notes that the interview in *Parker* lasted 30 minutes, while here, the exchange between Beard and Officer Provost "happened very quickly." (Appellee's Br. at 9). But Beard does not point out, nor do we see, how this factual distinction helps him. In fact, common sense dictates that, all else being equal, a long interview is more likely than a short one to create a custodial situation.

4. In so holding, we do not discount the possibility that the giving of *Miranda* warnings itself can contribute with other circumstances to put a suspect into "custody." *See Sprosty v. Buchler,* 79 F.3d 635, 642 (7th Cir.1996) (noting that the giving of *Miranda* warnings can be a relevant circumstance in determining whether custody exists); *Davis,* 778 F.2d at 172 (holding that the giving of *Miranda* warnings "by itself" does not create custody). Even assuming, however, that Officer Provost gave Beard the full panoply of *Miranda* warnings, this fact would not, when combined with the other circumstances of Beard's confession, be sufficient to transform what was an otherwise non-custodial situation into a custodial one. *Cf. Sprosty,* 79 F.3d at 642 ("[I]n the context of a *prolonged* detention where there is *persistent, accusatory questioning* by several officers, the fact that the police observed certain formalities of a custodial arrest [such as giving the suspect *Miranda* warnings] without actually telling [the suspect] that he was not under arrest does provide some support for an inference that [the suspect] was in custody for purposes of *Miranda.*") (emphasis added); *Davis,* 778 F.2d at 172 (noting that giving of *Miranda* warnings could create custody where "a [subsequent] clash of wills over a suspect's desire to remain silent would create custody through overbearing police behavior."). On the facts of this case, Officer Provost's warnings, whatever they were, did not contribute with other circumstances to place Beard in custody.

omitted), and (2) here, unlike in *Parker,* the officers questioned Beard for only a short period of time.

III

We conclude that the district court applied the wrong legal test to decide whether Beard was in custody under *Miranda.* Applying the correct standard, we conclude that Beard was not in "custody" when he gave the incriminating statements. We therefore reverse the district court's order granting Beard's motion to suppress and remand for further proceedings.

REVERSED AND REMANDED

B. *INTERROGATION*

Caputo v. Nelson

United States Court of Appeals, First Circuit, 2006.
455 F.3d 45.

■ STAFFORD, SENIOR DISTRICT JUDGE.

In 1991, a Massachusetts Superior Court jury convicted Michael Caputo ("Caputo") on two counts of first-degree murder. Caputo appeals the district court's order denying his petition for writ of habeas corpus by a person in state custody. Because the state court decision affirming his conviction was neither contrary to, nor an unreasonable application of, clearly established federal law, we affirm.

I.

In the early morning hours of November 2, 1989, two Boston police officers were dispatched to a second-floor apartment in the Jamaica Plain neighborhood of Boston. In the apartment's bedroom, the police found the bodies of Caputo's estranged wife and mother-in-law. Caputo's wife had been stabbed twenty-two times, his mother-in-law seventeen times. Caputo's two young daughters, who were unharmed, were also found in the apartment.

Noting an open kitchen window that led to the back porch, the police discovered that the telephone wires to the apartment had been cut. There was no sign of forced entry. On the dining room table, the police found a protective order dated July 31, 1989, ordering Caputo to refrain from abusing his wife and to stay away from the Jamaica Plain apartment. The order contained Caputo's address in Plymouth, Massachusetts.

After the Boston police notified the Plymouth Police Department that Caputo was a suspect in a double homicide, six Plymouth police officers, including Sergeant Thornton Morse ("Morse") and Sergeant Richard Dorman ("Dorman"), arrived at Caputo's house. Caputo opened the front door after the officers repeatedly knocked on the front and rear doors. Morse and Dorman introduced themselves, then asked whether they could enter the house to speak with Caputo. Caputo acquiesced.

Once inside the house, Dorman informed Caputo that they were investigating a double homicide on behalf of the Boston Police Department. From a printed card, Dorman read Caputo his rights under *Miranda v.*

Arizona, 384 U.S. 436, 467–73, 86 S.Ct. 1602, 16 L.Ed.2d 694 (1966). When Dorman asked Caputo whether he understood his rights, Caputo initially replied: "No." Dorman then repeated each right, asking after each whether Caputo understood. Caputo replied affirmatively to each, then said that he thought it best if he said nothing further. The officers immediately stopped all questioning of Caputo. They were not, however, asked to leave the house.

After Dorman informed Caputo that they were investigating a double homicide, Caputo asked Dorman who had died. Dorman replied that he did not know. Soon thereafter, wanting to obtain more information about the investigation to pass along to Caputo, Morse asked whether he could use Caputo's telephone to call the Plymouth police station. Caputo agreed that Morse could use his phone. At the conclusion of his call to the station, Morse informed Caputo that the Plymouth police could not then supply any additional information about the double homicide.

Leaving some of the officers inside the house, Dorman went outside to examine the automobile parked in Caputo's driveway. The vehicle matched the description given to the Plymouth police. The hood was warm to the touch, and a registration plate with a number other than Caputo's registration number covered the automobile's assigned registration plate. It was later learned that the outer registration plate had been stolen from a vehicle in the Jamaica Plain section of Boston.

When he re-entered the house, Dorman asked whether he could use Caputo's telephone to again call the Plymouth police station. Caputo again agreed. Within Caputo's hearing, Dorman informed the lieutenant on the line that Caputo was at his residence, that the engine of Caputo's automobile was warm, and that there were two different registration plates on the automobile. Spontaneously, Caputo stated that he did not want to incriminate himself but that he had a story to tell. He then proceeded to tell the officers that two men kidnapped him after forcing their way into his home the night before and that he later awoke "in a daze" in the Braintree area wearing only his underwear. The officers did not ask any questions in response to Caputo's unelicited statements. . . .

On November 17, 1989, Caputo was charged in two indictments with the first-degree murders of his wife and mother-in-law. Before trial, Caputo moved to suppress the statements that he made at his home . . . After an evidentiary hearing, the motion judge denied Caputo's motions. The judge found that, on entering Caputo's house, the officers immediately informed Caputo of his *Miranda* rights, then ceased all questioning when Caputo indicated that he did not want to speak to them. . . .

On March 21, 1991, a jury found Caputo guilty of two counts of first-degree murder. He was sentenced that same day to two consecutive life sentences. The judgments were affirmed by the Supreme Judicial Court of Massachusetts ("SJC") on April 15, 2003.

In rejecting Caputo's claims on appeal, the SJC explained:

First, before he made any statement, [Caputo] received and acknowledged that he understood his Miranda rights. Second, when [Caputo] indicated a wish not to speak to the police, all questioning ceased. It was only after he overheard the police conversation that [Caputo] stated, unprovoked, that he had been kidnapped the previous night. We do not agree with [Caputo] that his statement should be suppressed because the police officer's request to use his telephone was "reasonably likely to elicit an incriminating response" from [Caputo], and therefore the "functional equivalent" of an interrogation. The telephone call was a report and request for further information, an action "normally attendant" to police procedures. [Caputo's] statement occurred only after and apparently because he had overheard the telephone conversation that tended to implicate him, not because of any "interrogation."

... [Caputo] gave his consent to the police to enter his home, he did not ask them to leave, and spoke to them only after he recognized that the police had seen potentially incriminating evidence outside. A defendant who is "nervous" because he is in the presence of police within hours of committing murder and who chooses to give false information to the police in an attempt, however clumsy, to throw them off the trail as he perceives their attention focusing on him as a suspect, cannot resort later to a claim of coercion.

. . .

Because we reject [Caputo's] claims that his statements to the police at his home should have been suppressed, we need not consider his argument that his later statements should have been suppressed as "fruit of the poisonous tree."

Commonwealth v. Caputo, 439 Mass. 153, 786 N.E.2d 352, 358–59 (2003) (footnote and citations omitted).

On April 12, 2004, Caputo filed a petition for writ of habeas corpus in federal court. The district court entered judgment for the respondent on December 5, 2005, and this timely appeal followed. The district court thereafter issued a certificate of appealability, limiting the appeal to Caputo's claim that his privilege against self-incrimination was violated when his statements were introduced at trial. . . .

III.

Caputo contends that his conviction was obtained through evidence that was obtained in violation of the Fifth Amendment privilege against self-incrimination. Specifically, he argues that the statements he gave to the police at his house were not the product of a voluntary waiver of his *Miranda* rights but were the product of police tactics intended to elicit an incriminating response from him. He also argues that the statements he made at the police station, after he signed a waiver form, were the "fruit of the poisonous tree," his earlier statements having been involuntarily made.

In *Miranda,* 384 U.S. at 467–73, 86 S.Ct. 1602, the Supreme Court held that a person in custody must be warned prior to interrogation that he has certain rights, including the right to remain silent. . . . The term "interrogation" under *Miranda* refers not only to express questioning but also "to any words or actions on the part of the police (other than those normally attendant to arrest and custody) that the police should know are reasonably likely to elicit an incriminating response from the suspect." *Rhode Island v. Innis*, 446 U.S. 291, 301, 100 S.Ct. 1682, 64 L.Ed.2d 297 (1980).

Here, Caputo contends that the police officer's use of Caputo's telephone, in Caputo's presence, to relay information about what the officers found at Caputo's residence was the functional equivalent of interrogation because it was "reasonably likely to elicit an incriminating response" from Caputo after he had claimed his right to remain silent. Citing *Miranda*, Caputo maintains that the story he blurted out upon hearing the officer's telephone conversation should have been suppressed as the product of that allegedly unlawful interrogation. Like the SJC, we are not persuaded.

In *Innis*, in the presence of a man arrested on suspicion of armed robbery, while conversing about the missing shotgun used in the robbery, two police officers expressed concern that a child might injure herself if, by chance, she found the missing weapon. This musing between the officers prompted the suspect to reveal the location of the weapon. In holding that the police officers did not engage in the functional equivalent of interrogation, the Supreme Court wrote:

> The case thus boils down to whether, in the context of a brief conversation, the officers should have known that the respondent would suddenly be moved to make a self-incriminating response. Given the fact that the entire conversation appears to have consisted of no more than a few off hand remarks, we cannot say that the officers should have known that it was reasonably likely that Innis would so respond. This is not a case where the police carried on a lengthy harangue in the presence of the suspect. Nor does the record support the respondent's contention that, under the circumstances, the officers' comments were particularly "evocative." It is our view, therefore, that the respondent was not subjected by the police to words or actions that the police should have known were reasonably likely to elicit an incriminating response from him.

Innis, 446 U.S. at 303, 100 S.Ct. 1682.

Since *Innis*, a number of courts have considered whether police may confront a suspect with evidence against him without engaging in the functional equivalent of interrogation. For example, in *United States v. Payne*, 954 F.2d 199 (4th Cir.1992), *cert. denied*, 503 U.S. 988, 112 S.Ct. 1680, 118 L.Ed.2d 396 (1992), the defendant made incriminating statements after a law enforcement officer informed the defendant that the FBI possessed inculpatory evidence against him. Rejecting the defendant's argument that the officer's statement constituted the functional equivalent of interrogation, the Fourth Circuit observed: "[T]he *Innis* definition of interrogation is not so broad as to capture within *Miranda's* reach all declaratory statements by police officers concerning the nature of the charges against the suspect and the evidence relating to those charges." *Id.* at 202. The court went on to explain:

> That no comment on the evidence in a case will ever issue in the presence of a criminal suspect seems to us neither realistic nor desirable as an absolute rule derived from the Fifth Amendment. Indeed, it

may even be in the interest of a defendant to be kept informed about matters relating to the charges against him.... Information about the evidence against a suspect may also contribute to the intelligent exercise of his judgment regarding what course of conduct to follow.

Id.; see also United States v. Thomas, 11 F.3d 1392, 1397 (7th Cir.1993) (finding no functional equivalent of interrogation where a police officer provided information about the results of his investigation to a suspect who had herself asked the officer to let her know such results).

Similarly, in *Plazinich v. Lynaugh,* 843 F.2d 836 (5th Cir.), *cert. denied,* 488 U.S. 1031, 109 S.Ct. 841, 102 L.Ed.2d 973 (1989), the Fifth Circuit rejected the defendant's argument that a policeman engaged in the functional equivalent of interrogation when he informed the defendant— after the defendant invoked his *Miranda* rights—that the defendant's accomplice had attempted suicide by slashing her wrists in the jail. Citing *Innis,* the court wrote:

[The officer's] information concerning [the defendant's accomplice] was not objectively likely to elicit an incriminating response from the suspect, who had just minutes before declined to be interrogated. In the brief and informal context in which it was made, the comment could at most be characterized as offering [the defendant] food for thought rather than seeking to provoke an incriminating response.

Id. at 840 (internal quotation marks omitted); *see also Enoch v. Gramley,* 70 F.3d 1490, 1500 (7th Cir.1995) (finding no functional equivalent of interrogation where the police identified the victim to the suspect and briefly stated the evidence against him), *cert. denied,* 519 U.S. 829, 117 S.Ct. 95, 136 L.Ed.2d 50 (1996).

In this case, Caputo volunteered false exculpatory information after hearing Dorman report to his shift commander that Caputo was at his residence, that the engine of Caputo's automobile was warm, and that there were two different registration plates on the automobile. Dorman did not pose any questions to Caputo, and he did not otherwise engage in subtle efforts to get Caputo to talk. Instead, he simply related to another law enforcement officer non-evocative facts about what he saw at Caputo's residence. Dorman had no reason to know or even suspect that, in response to his brief telephone call to the Plymouth police station, Caputo would spontaneously blurt out a fabricated story intended to be exculpatory and explanatory. Consistent with the case law set out above, the SJC determined that Caputo was *not* subjected to the functional equivalent of interrogation, and his Fifth Amendment right against compelled self-incrimination was *not* violated, when Dorman used Caputo's telephone, in Caputo's presence, to report what was found at Caputo's residence. Finding no Fifth Amendment violation when Caputo made his initial statements, the SJC determined that Caputo's later statements could not have been "fruit of the poisonous tree." The SJC thus upheld the trial court's denial of Caputo's motion to suppress.

When reviewing the SJC's decision upon Caputo's petition for federal habeas corpus relief, the district court concluded that the SJC properly applied the holdings of *Miranda* and *Innis* and, consequently, reached a decision that was neither contrary to, nor an unreasonable application of, Supreme Court precedent. We agree with the district court's conclusion and, accordingly, AFFIRM the judgment of the district court, denying Caputo's petition for writ of habeas corpus.

C. WAIVER AND INVOCATION

Freeman v. State

Court of Special Appeals of Maryland, 2004.
158 Md.App. 402, 857 A.2d 557.

■ HOLLANDER, JUDGE.

Kevin Gross was shot to death on March 30, 2000, by his girlfriend, Adele Florence Freeman, appellant. A jury in the Circuit Court for Calvert County subsequently convicted Freeman of first degree premeditated murder, as well as first degree assault and use of a firearm in the commission of a felony.... On appeal, Freeman claims that "the circuit court err[ed] by failing to suppress the statements [she] made ... during custodial interrogation."... First, appellant argues that the court erred in failing to suppress her statements because she had invoked her right to remain silent, and therefore her *Miranda* rights were violated.

I. FACTUAL SUMMARY—SUPPRESSION MOTION

Appellant moved to suppress various statements that she gave to the police during her interrogation on the evening of March 30, 2000. What follows is a summary of the evidence adduced at the suppression hearing in November 2001.

Sergeant Albert Paton of the Maryland State Police testified that he was the shift supervisor at the Prince Frederick Barrack on the evening of March 30, 2000. At about 8:00 p.m., appellant entered the barracks and announced: "I just shot someone." He recalled that a short time earlier, the police "had received a call for a shooting ... at 1255 Wilson Road. And ... that a female suspect had been involved in the shooting, that she had shot a black male subject, and that she had left the scene in a white Oldsmobile headed towards the Prince Frederick area."

Paton claimed that "before [he] could reply" to appellant's announcement that she shot someone, "she said I have the gun, it's here in my purse." Paton continued:

And as she is saying that she started to try to open the purse, and I told her just wait, I will get that from you, just as quickly as I could try to think of a way to approach her, you know, and maintain my safety. So I asked her to have a seat over by the door that comes into the barrack.

Paton then took appellant's purse and brought her into the "Trooper's Room where we put persons that are under arrest." At that time, Paton asked appellant which hand she used to shoot the victim, because he wanted to secure that hand in order to perform a gunshot residue test. After appellant responded that she had used her "left" hand, Paton handcuffed that hand to the bench.

Thereafter, Paton advised appellant of her "*Miranda* rights," reading "word for word" from a "card" provided to him by the State Police. The card was admitted into evidence. Appellant indicated that she understood her rights. However, when Paton asked appellant if she would "knowingly waive these rights," appellant "didn't say anything."

Paton then "retrieved the gun from [appellant's] purse . . . to make sure it didn't have any ammunition in it." He "examined" the weapon and noted "that all the shell casings that [he] could see were empty." Paton testified:

So in order so [sic] that I didn't have to keep handling it, I asked her how many shots she fired, and she said I don't remember. And then I asked her, well, did you fire all the bullets that were in the gun, and she said I don't know, it happened so fast.

Thereafter, Paton "opened the chambers just to see if there was any live ammunition in there." After Paton determined that no live ammunition was in the gun, he "left everything the way it was, closed it back up, and secured the gun." Paton then asked appellant "what happened tonight, and her reply was 'I don't want to talk about it right now.'" Accordingly, Paton "didn't ask [Freeman] anything else." He "got [appellant] a cup of water and just kept an eye on her, that was it." Paton described appellant's demeanor as "normal" and "calm."

On cross-examination, Paton testified that he sat at the front desk and greeted people who came in to the barracks. When appellant "first walked in the door," before she announced what she had done, he had no reason to believe she had committed the shooting. Paton also explained that, after he handcuffed appellant to the bench, he only questioned her "about the ammunition so that [he] could make the gun safe. [He] wasn't . . . investigating the case."

The following colloquy on redirect is pertinent:

[PROSECUTOR]: When Ms. Freeman walked in and told you she just shot someone, immediately in your mind what did you think based upon the information you had from dispatch?

[PATON]: That this was the woman that was at Wilson Road that had just shot this man.

[PROSECUTOR]: And so based upon that information and the fact that she told you she had a gun, you placed her under arrest?

[PATON]: Yes.

[PROSECUTOR]: When you were speaking with Ms. Freeman did you feel it was necessary to go over with her again the date, place, and nature of the event that she just turned herself in for?

[PATON]: No, ma'am.

[PROSECUTOR]: And when she asked—when she mentioned—when she said to you that she didn't want to talk about it right now, you scrupulously honored that request, did you not?

[PATON]: Yes, I did.

Corporal David Ruel was assigned to investigate the homicide. His "first contact" with appellant occurred in the Troopers' Room at "about 9:35, 9:45, somewhere in that area." At the time, Freeman was "seated on the prison bench handcuffed to the bench."

At the outset, Ruel asked Paton "to step out" of the room and "brief[] [him] on what had gone on up to that point...." Paton advised him that appellant did not want to talk. Ruel asked Ms. Freeman "if she wanted anything to eat or drink or if she needed anything, and she advised she wasn't hungry at the time, but she did need some medication" for blood pressure. Ruel instructed Corporal Delmar Smith to retrieve the medication. While Smith was gone, appellant remained in the Troopers' Room, and Ruel "would periodically just peek in to make sure that everything was okay in there and just let [appellant] sit for a while."

Appellant's medication arrived at about 10:20 p.m. At that time, Ruel asked appellant, who was still in the Troopers' Room, "if she needed the medication; she again said no." Ruel also "asked [appellant] if she wanted something to eat, and that time she said yes, she wanted something from McDonald's." So, Ruel "got her some food." When the food arrived at about 10:52 p.m., Ruel removed the handcuff so that appellant could eat. However, Ruel recalled that, "prior to ... eating" at about 10:55 p.m., he "read" appellant her *Miranda* rights from the form, and then they "sat down to eat, and ... just talked about her family, what her job was, what her aspirations were...." Ruel explained:

> I read the form in its entirety. Then after completing the last paragraph here, last sentence asking her if she is willing to talk, I have her sign the statement that [sic] where it said signature for her, and then I have her review it again just to make sure that she understands and place her initials by one, two, three, four, and five, each of her rights if she understands them.

According to Ruel, during his advisement appellant did not request a lawyer, nor did she have any questions. Moreover, her demeanor was "very calm and cooperative." Appellant, who was then forty-seven years old, had no difficulty understanding what Ruel said. Although Ruel did not ascertain appellant's educational level, he found her "very articulate", and he "figured she had at least graduated high school," because she "had mentioned earlier in [their] conversation that she had planned on going to college."

Appellant agreed to waive her rights, initialed each question in the waiver form, and signed it. Ruel denied threatening appellant or promising her anything to induce her to do so. Before appellant provided a statement, she told Ruel that she was diagnosed as "bipolar." After Freeman ate, she made an oral statement to Ruel, which he recounted:

> After finishing her dinner Ms. Freeman went on to advise that earlier that evening she had spoken with Mr. Gross on the phone for a few minutes. During the phone conversation they never argued. She just asked him if she could stop by, and he replied yes. A little later that same evening she drove herself over to Gross's house. At approxi-

mately 1930 hours she pulled into and parked in the Gross's driveway and never got out of her car.

Gross then came out of the house and sat in the passenger side front seat. The two sat in the car talking for a while about the upcoming weekend. Freeman advised she was kind of upset because Gross wouldn't take her out to dinner or the movies this Saturday. She then confronted him about the past few weekends that he hadn't taken her out and how he went to that dinner thing without asking her if she wanted to go.

Gross then told her he couldn't take her out this Saturday because he had to change the oil in his car. Ms. Freeman then confronted him again, advising him that it wouldn't take him all day to change the oil in his car. He then advised her he also had to tune his car up, but he would try to start working on his car a little earlier. Freeman then advised knowing that a tune-up and an oil change weren't the same thing she got upset and pulled her gun out from under the driver's side seat.

She then got out of the car through the driver's side door and with the gun in her left hand she pointed it at Gross and shot him. Gross then climbed out of the front passenger side door and fell to the ground. Freeman then got back in the car as Gross laid on the ground and shot him two more times. She then put the gun on the front passenger seat, closed the passenger side door, and drove to the barracks. When she arrived at the barracks she put the gun in her purse, walked into the ... lobby, and told them what she had done.

I then asked Freeman where she got the gun and why she had it, or why she had it with her that night. She advised that she bought the gun from somewhere in Wayson's Corner a while ago, but she couldn't recall the exact date. Freeman further advised that she normally keeps the gun under her front seat of her car for protection when she drives at night. I asked Freeman if she knew it was against the law to keep the gun in her car unless she had a permit to carry it. She advised that she knew this and that she had been meaning to apply for a permit, but she hadn't had the time.

* * *

I then asked Freeman to explain to me what caused this to happen so I could better understand why she did it. She advised me that it was hard for her to remember what happened because it all happened so fast, and she doesn't know why she did it. I then asked her if Gross had hit her or called her any kind of name that may have provoked her, and she advised, no, Kevin was a very nice—Kevin was very nice and never hit me.

I then asked Freeman about the statement witness Charles Gross[6] advised he had heard. She advised that she doesn't remember saying

---

6.   Charles Gross, Kevin Gross's brother, was a witness at trial. On January 14, 2002, he testified that he heard appellant say: "[Y]ou bastard, you, you don't have to worry about doing this to anybody else."

that. I then confronted Freeman with the possibility that Gross was cheating on her, and again she advised, no, Kevin was very nice.... [T]hat's basically all she advised at that point.

Upon completion of her oral statement, Ruel asked appellant if she would provide a written or taped statement. Freeman declined to do so and requested a lawyer. Therefore, Ruel "ended [his] questioning and re-secured [appellant] to the prisoner bench." Ruel denied that any questioning occurred after Freeman requested an attorney....

II. Discussion

A. The Right to Remain Silent

At trial, Paton testified that he advised appellant of her rights, and she did not have any questions. In Paton's direct testimony, he did not refer to his inquiry to appellant about whether she was willing to waive her rights, or her silence in response to the inquiry.[7] However, he stated that, after his advisement, he asked appellant, "what happened tonight...." Over defense objection, Paton testified as to appellant's reply: "I don't want to talk about it right now."

Appellant contends that the suppression court erred in finding that she did not invoke her Fifth Amendment privilege by remaining mute when Paton asked her if she was willing to waive her rights. Moreover, she insists that, because her silence was an invocation of her right to remain silent, "all questioning was required to cease." Consequently, Freeman asserts that her statement, "I don't want to talk about it right now," (which she designates as statement four), and her oral confession to Ruel (which she designates as statement five), were "erroneously admitted at trial in violation of *Miranda*," because both were obtained after she invoked her right to silence.

With regard to appellant's silence, the State maintains that appellant's "mere failure to answer a waiver question" did not constitute an invocation of the right to remain silent. Indeed, the State contends that it was apparent from the context that Freeman did not invoke her right to remain silent: she voluntarily "came to the police station to turn herself in and announced that she had shot someone, thereby plainly indicating to the police her willingness to accept responsibility for the crime."

The State argues that, at best, appellant's silence was an ambiguous invocation. Therefore, it urges us to apply the rationale of *Davis v. United States,* 512 U.S. 452, 114 S.Ct. 2350, 129 L.Ed.2d 362 (1994). *Davis* requires an unambiguous invocation of the right to counsel, so that police officers do not have "to make difficult judgment calls about whether the suspect in fact wants a lawyer...." *Id.* at 461, 114 S.Ct. 2350.

The State also insists that appellant's silence in regard to the waiver inquiry cannot "be divorced from her subsequent statement that she did not want to talk about the shooting 'right now.'" In effect, the State

---

7. It was defense counsel, on cross-examination, who elicited from Paton that appellant "remained silent" after the advisement. In closing argument, defense counsel also referred to appellant's silence to support her argument as to the involuntariness of appellant's statements.

disputes appellant's characterization of statement four as a statement. It claims that statement four "should not even be considered a 'statement' for purposes of *Miranda;* rather, it is itself an assertion of the right to silence." That assertion, says the State, "simply made clear that [appellant] did not waive her right to silence . . . ," and thus statement four "should not be deemed a 'statement' subject to suppression under *Miranda.*" The State adds:

Because Freeman's comment, which she designates as "statement 4," is fairly understood in conjunction with her earlier silence as an assertion of her Fifth Amendment right to silence, there is no need for this Court to address whether her mere silence, without more, would constitute an invocation of the right.

With regard to the confession to Ruel, the State maintains that the police "scrupulously honored" the invocation expressed in statement four, "I don't want to talk about it right now." Therefore, the State contends that the court properly admitted appellant's confession to Ruel.

For clarity in our discussion, we summarize, in chronological order, the various custodial statements and conduct identified by appellant, along with the court's rulings:

Statement No. 1: "I just shot someone." The court ruled that it constituted a "blurt" and was therefore admissible. It was introduced in evidence through the testimony of Paton. Appellant does not contest this ruling.

Statement No. 2: Before appellant was advised of her rights, she was asked which hand she used to shoot the victim. She responded, "left." The State conceded that this statement violated *Miranda,* and the court ruled that the statement was inadmissible. Therefore, it is not in issue.

Conduct: Paton advised appellant of her rights, and then asked her whether she would waive her rights. Appellant remained silent. The court ruled that the silence was not an invocation of the right to counsel, and appellant contests the court's finding.

Statement(s) No. 3: Paton asked appellant how many shots she fired, and she responded, "I don't remember." Paton then asked her, "Did you fire all the bullets that were in the gun?" Appellant replied, "I don't know, it happened so fast." These statements were not introduced at trial, and thus are not in issue.

Statement No. 4: Paton checked the gun and then asked, "What happened tonight?" Appellant responded, "I don't want to talk about it right now." The court ruled that this statement, made to Paton after appellant had been advised of her rights, was neither an invocation of the right to silence nor an invocation of the right to counsel. The court denied appellant's challenge to the statement, and the State introduced it at trial through the testimony of Sergeant Paton. Appellant challenges the admission of the statement.

Statement No. 5: A few hours after appellant said, "I don't want to talk about it right now," Corporel Ruel re-advised appellant of her rights, and appellant gave an oral statement, recounting the events of March 30, 2000. The court denied appellant's motion to suppress this statement, and it was introduced at trial through the testimony of Corporal Ruel. Appellant disputes the court's ruling.

Unlike the State, appellant focuses separately on her initial silence in response to Paton's waiver inquiry, claiming that, standing alone, it constituted an invocation of her *Miranda* rights. As the Supreme Court has observed, "[s]ilence in the wake of [*Miranda*] warnings may be nothing more than the arrestee's exercise of these *Miranda* rights. Thus, every post-arrest silence is insolubly ambiguous. . . ." *Doyle v. Ohio,* 426 U.S. 610, 617, 96 S.Ct. 2240, 49 L.Ed.2d 91 (1976); *see United States v. Hale,* 422 U.S. 171, 177, 95 S.Ct. 2133, 45 L.Ed.2d 99 (1975).

As we observed, the State relies on *Davis,* 512 U.S. 452, 114 S.Ct. 2350, to support its contention that appellant's silence was so ambiguous that the police were not required to regard it as an invocation of the right to remain silent. In the State's view, the *Davis* "requirement" for an unequivocal assertion of the right to counsel applies "with equal force to an invocation of the right to silence, where the need for a bright-line rule is equally compelling."

In *Davis,* Naval Investigative Service agents questioned Davis about a murder. *Id.* at 454, 114 S.Ct. 2350. After the agents advised Davis of his rights under military law, Davis agreed to waive his rights. *Id.* at 454–55, 114 S.Ct. 2350. During the interrogation, Davis said, " 'Maybe I should talk to a lawyer.' " *Id.* at 455, 114 S.Ct. 2350. One of the agents sought to clarify whether Davis was " 'asking for a lawyer or . . . just making a comment about a lawyer. . . .' " Davis responded that he was not requesting an attorney. *Id.* About an hour later, however, Davis said, " 'I think I want a lawyer before I say anything else.' " *Id.*

At that point, the questioning ended. *Id.*

Davis later moved to suppress his statements, claiming that the interrogators failed to honor his invocation of his right to counsel. The motion was denied, and Davis was convicted of murder. *Id.* On review, the Supreme Court sought to craft "a bright line" rule that could be "applied by officers in the real world of investigation and interrogation without unduly hampering the gathering of information." *Id.* at 461, 114 S.Ct. 2350. Insisting that the invocation of the right to counsel must be articulated with clarity, the Supreme Court said:

Invocation of the *Miranda* right to counsel "requires, at a minimum, some statement that can reasonably be construed to be an expression of a desire for the assistance of an attorney." But if a suspect makes a reference to an attorney that is ambiguous or equivocal in that a reasonable officer in light of the circumstances would have understood only that the suspect *might* be invoking the right to counsel, our precedents do not require the cessation of questioning.

* * *

Rather, *the suspect must unambiguously request counsel.* As we have observed, "a statement either is such an assertion of the right to counsel or it is not." *Id.* at 459, 114 S.Ct. 2350 (citations omitted) (Emphasis added).

Although the Supreme Court "declined to adopt a rule requiring officers to ask clarifying questions" when faced with an ambiguous assertion, it suggested that "it will often be good practice for the interviewing officers to clarify whether or not [the suspect] actually wants an attorney...." *Id.* at 461, 114 S.Ct. 2350. The Supreme Court reasoned: "Clarifying questions help protect the rights of the suspect by insuring that he gets an attorney if he wants one, and will minimize the chance of a confession being suppressed due to subsequent judicial second-guessing as to the meaning of the suspect's statement...." *Id.*

Freeman concedes that some jurisdictions "do not recognize silence as an invocation" of the right to remain silent, because of its ambiguity. In those jurisdictions, says appellant, "one's silence must be prefaced with an unequivocal statement that he or she is invoking his or her right to remain silent." However, she maintains that "[t]his line of reasoning" derives erroneously from the view "that the standard set forth for invoking one's right to counsel," articulated in *Davis,* 512 U.S. 452, 114 S.Ct. 2350, "is equally applicable to the invocation of silence." According to appellant, "[t]he United States Supreme Court ... has yet to determine whether the *Davis* invocation of counsel standard is in anyway [sic] appropriate to the invocation of silence." Moreover, she points out that "[a]t least six jurisdictions have ruled that a *Davis*-like standard is inappropriate to invocations of silence." With one exception, we are not persuaded to adopt Freeman's position based on the six foreign cases cited by her to support her claim that a *Davis*-like standard is inappropriate to invocations of silence.[10]

---

10. Appellant cites *United States v. Montana,* 958 F.2d 516 (2nd Cir.1992), but it was decided prior to *Davis.* She also cites *State v. Chew,* 150 N.J. 30, 695 A.2d 1301 (1997), which involved an ambiguous invocation of the right to counsel, not the right to silence. The Supreme Court of New Jersey acknowledged that, "in some circumstances," New Jersey law "affords greater protection of the right against self-incrimination than does federal law." *Id.* at 1316. Therefore, it considered "it prudent to continue to apply" its "precedent." *Id.* at 1318.

Similarly, in *State v. Hoey,* 77 Hawai'i 17, 881 P.2d 504 (1994), cited by appellant, the Supreme Court of Hawaii found error in the admission of the defendant's confession, but it relied on Hawaii's Constitution, *id.* at 523–24, "to afford [its] citizens broader protection ... than that recognized by the *Davis* majority under the United States Constitution...." *Id.* at 523. Nor does the decision of the West Virginia court in *State v. Farley,* 192 W.Va. 247, 452 S.E.2d 50 (1994), support appellant's position. The West Virginia court said, *id.* at 59 (citations omitted):

We believe that under *Davis* insubstantial and trivial doubt, reasonably caused by the defendant's ambiguous statements as to whether he wants the interrogation to end, should be resolved in favor of the police and that under these circumstances further interrogation by the police does not offend the West Virginia Constitution.... [W]e hold that to assert the *Miranda* right to terminate police interrogation, the words or conduct must be explicitly clear that the suspect wishes to terminate all questioning and not merely a desire not to comment on or answer a particular question.

We also regard *State v. Strayhand,* 184 Ariz. 571, 911 P.2d 577 (App.Div.1995), as factually inapposite. There, the court found that the police ignored the defendant's repeated invocation of his right to silence during interrogation. It then assumed, *arguendo,* that the invocation was ambiguous, and declined to apply *Davis. Id.* at 592. The court concluded that, under Arizona

Nevertheless, we agree with appellant that the *Davis* rationale does not apply to the analysis of appellant's silence, but for reasons not advanced by appellant.

Neither party has discussed whether the rationale of *Davis* applies to an ambiguous invocation made *prior* to a waiver of rights. In our view, in determining whether to apply the rationale of *Davis,* it is significant that appellant's alleged invocation of her right to silence occurred *prior* to a waiver of rights, and before interrogation ensued; unlike in *Davis,* it was not an ambiguous invocation that occurred *during* an interrogation and *after* a waiver of rights. While there may well be sound reason to apply the logic of *Davis* to the matter of an ambiguous invocation of the right to silence that follows a valid waiver of *Miranda* rights, that logic does not extend to an ambiguous invocation that occurs prior to the initial waiver of rights. We explain.

Davis involved an ambiguous invocation of the right to counsel that occurred *during* interrogation, and *after* the defendant had already waived his rights; the validity of Davis's *Miranda* waiver was not in issue. It was in that context, where the suspect had already waived his *Miranda* rights and later arguably sought to change his mind, that the Supreme Court ruled that a defendant must clearly articulate his request for counsel in order to invoke that right. Significantly, the Supreme Court said, 512 U.S. at 461, 114 S.Ct. 2350: "We therefore hold that, *after* a knowing and voluntary waiver of the *Miranda* rights, law enforcement officers may continue questioning until and unless the suspect clearly requests an attorney." (Emphasis added).

The issues of "[i]nvocation and waiver are entirely distinct inquiries, and the two must not be blurred...." *Smith v. Illinois,* 469 U.S. 91, 98, 105 S.Ct. 490, 83 L.Ed.2d 488 (1984) (per curiam). When a suspect "indicates in any manner" that he or she "wishes to remain silent," *Miranda* requires that "the interrogation must cease." *Miranda,* 384 U.S. at 473–74, 86 S.Ct. 1602. Moreover, there is no prescribed form or set way in which to waive *Miranda* rights. *See North Carolina v. Butler,* 441 U.S. 369, 373, 99 S.Ct. 1755, 60 L.Ed.2d 286 (1979) ("The question is not one of form, but rather whether the defendant in fact knowingly and voluntarily waived the rights delineated in the *Miranda* case."). If the State seeks to rely on a waiver of rights, however, it carries "a heavy burden" to show "that the defendant knowingly and intelligently waived his privilege against self-incrimination...." *Id.* at 475, 86 S.Ct. 1602. As the Supreme Court said in *Butler,* 441 U.S. at 373, 99 S.Ct. 1755:

> That does not mean that the defendant's silence, coupled with an understanding of his rights and a course of conduct indicating waiver, may never support a conclusion that a defendant has waived his rights. The courts must presume that a defendant did not waive his rights; the prosecution's burden is great; but in at least some cases waiver can

---

law, any interrogation had to " 'be for the sole purpose' " of clarification of the defendant's ambiguous assertion. *Id.* (Citation omitted).

Finally, appellant cites *State v. Leyva,* 906 P.2d 894 (Utah App.1995). But, it was reversed in part by *State v. Leyva,* 951 P.2d 738 (Utah 1997). As we shall see, *infra,* the 1997 decision in *Leyva* is helpful to our analysis, but not for the reason advanced by appellant.

be clearly inferred from the actions and words of the person interrogated.[]

Numerous jurisdictions, both federal and state, have applied the rationale of *Davis* to an ambiguous invocation of the right to silence, and have concluded that, as with an ambiguous invocation of the right to counsel, an equivocal invocation of the right to silence need not be honored by the police. Most of these cases, however, involve a defendant's ineffective attempt to invoke his or her constitutional rights *after* the defendant had previously waived *Miranda* rights. In this case, it is noteworthy that appellant's silence preceded a waiver of rights....

We are persuaded by the reasoning of the court in *State v. Leyva*, 951 P.2d 738 (Utah 1997), which distinguishes between an ambiguous response to an initial *Miranda* advisement and an equivocal post-waiver invocation. The Supreme Court of Utah declined to apply *Davis* to an ambiguous pre-waiver response, concluding that *Davis* was limited to a post-waiver ambiguous invocation of rights. *Id.* at 745. According to the Utah court, that scenario is an "entirely separate" issue from an ambiguous pre-waiver invocation. *Id.*

Noting that *Davis* did not "address" or "extend to prewaiver scenarios....", the Utah court said that "*Davis* made clear that its holding applied only to a suspect's attempt to *reinvoke* his *Miranda* rights 'after a knowing and voluntary waiver' of the same." *Id.* (quoting *Davis,* 512 U.S. at 461, 114 S.Ct. 2350). Therefore, the Utah court concluded that an officer faced with an ambiguous response to an initial advisement of *Miranda* rights, i.e., at the pre-waiver stage, is limited to posing questions designed to clarify the suspect's ambiguous response. *Id. Accord State v. Tuttle,* 650 N.W.2d 20, 28 (S.D.2002) (adopting *Leyva* and concluding that "[t]he *Davis* holding obviously applies to instances where suspects attempt to invoke *Miranda* rights after a knowing and voluntary waiver of those rights. *Davis,* in sum, applies to an equivocal postwaiver invocation of rights.").

We agree with the Utah court that a careful reading of *Davis* reveals that the Supreme Court's bright line rule, requiring an unequivocal assertion of the right to counsel, pertains to a situation in which the defendant had previously waived his right and then, during the interrogation, arguably sought to exercise his rights. Based on the foregoing, we decline to apply the rationale of *Davis* to our analysis of appellant's silence, because the silence occurred in a pre-waiver context.

Next, we consider whether the court erred in failing to recognize appellant's silence as an invocation. In support of appellant's claim that her silence constituted a separate invocation, from which "no legal penalty can flow," she relies on *Younie v. State*, 272 Md. 233, 322 A.2d 211 (1974), and *Crosby v. State*, 366 Md. 518, 784 A.2d 1102 (2001), *cert. denied,* 535 U.S. 941, 122 S.Ct. 1325, 152 L.Ed.2d 233 (2002).

In *Younie,* the defendant was convicted of armed robbery and murder. During a custodial interrogation, he waived his right to remain silent, in that he agreed to answer "some" questions about the crimes, but refused to answer all of them. *Id.* at 236–38, 322 A.2d 211. Nevertheless, he signed the bottom of each page of the interrogating officer's handwritten statement of the interview. *Id.* at 235, 322 A.2d 211. At trial, over objection, the court admitted the officer's handwritten record of the interview, in which Younie answered fifteen out of twenty-three questions. *Id.* at 236–38, 322 A.2d 211. During closing argument, the State was allowed to refer to Younie's refusals to respond to all of the questions. *Id.* at 238, 322 A.2d 211.

On appeal, Younie complained that "his silence was a permissible exercise of his [constitutional] privilege", and therefore the court should not have admitted in evidence the record of his refusals to answer. *Id.* The Court of Appeals agreed. It held that evidence that the defendant remained silent "creat[ed] the highly prejudicial inference that his failure to respond was motivated by guilt. . . ." *Id.* In the Court's view, the only reasonable inference to be drawn from the refusals to answer was that Younie elected to exercise his constitutional right to remain silent, but a jury might improperly regard his silence as a tacit admission. *Id.* at 244, 322 A.2d 211. The Court said: "[T]he Constitution . . . expressly permits [a suspect] to remain mute and not have this made known to [the jury]." *Id.* Further, it stated:

> Silence in the context of a custodial inquisition is presumed to be an exercise of the privilege against self-incrimination from which no legal penalty can flow, and the State has the heavy burden of demonstrating *by clear and convincing evidence that a failure to respond was not an invocation of this right.*

> *Id.* (Emphasis added). . . .

The tenor of the foregoing cases leads us to conclude that the court below erred in failing to construe appellant's pre-waiver silence as an invocation of her right to remain silent. Although the police could have sought to clarify whether appellant intended her silence as an invocation of her rights, with questions limited to the effort to clarify, Paton should not have ignored the silence by asking appellant "what happened." It follows that Freeman's response to that inquiry, "I don't want to talk about it right now," was erroneously admitted.

Nevertheless, we are satisfied, beyond a reasonable doubt, that, in the context of this case, any error was harmless. We explain.

First, the statement, "I don't want to talk about it right now," taken alone or in context, cannot be regarded as a tacit admission of guilt. The undisputed evidence showed that appellant came to the police station of her own accord and immediately announced that she had shot someone. In that light, her subsequent statement (statement four) is "fairly innocuous." *Hudson,* 152 Md.App. at 509, 832 A.2d 834. Indeed, the State certainly did not strengthen its case with the admission of statement four. Therefore, we are amply satisfied that "there is no reasonable possibility" that the admission of [statement four] contributed to the rendition of the guilty verdict.

Moreover, statement four was itself an invocation by Freeman of her right to remain silent. Yet, it does not necessarily follow that the court erred in admitting appellant's subsequent confession to Ruel. We explain.

Michigan v. Mosley, 423 U.S. 96, 96 S.Ct. 321, 46 L.Ed.2d 313 (1975), teaches that, even if a defendant invokes the right to silence, the police are not necessarily forever barred from attempting to question the suspect. Appellant concedes as much. Under certain circumstances, the "police may reinitiate discussion with a suspect who has invoked his or her right to remain silent if a significant period of time has elapsed and if the police have re-advised the suspect of his or her rights." *Raras v. State,* 140 Md.App. 132, 154, 780 A.2d 322 (discussing *Mosley*), *cert. denied,* 367 Md. 90, 785 A.2d 1292 (2001).

Mosley was arrested in connection with certain robberies. After he was advised of his rights, Mosley invoked his right to remain silent, and the detective "promptly ceased the interrogation." *Mosley,* 423 U.S. at 97, 96 S.Ct. 321. About two hours later, Mosley was again advised of his *Miranda* warnings by another detective who questioned Mosley about an unrelated murder. *Id.* at 97–98, 96 S.Ct. 321. Mosley did not ask to consult with a lawyer, nor did he "indicate that he did not want to discuss the homicide." *Id.* at 98, 96 S.Ct. 321. During the interrogation, which lasted approximately fifteen minutes, Mosley implicated himself in the homicide, and he was subsequently charged with first degree murder. *Id.* In his suppression motion, Mosley claimed that, under *Miranda,* "it was constitutionally impermissible" for the police to question him about the murder because he had previously asserted that "he did not want to answer any questions about the robberies." *Id.* at 98–99, 96 S.Ct. 321. The trial court denied the motion, and the statement was introduced at trial. *Id.* at 99, 96 S.Ct. 321. On appeal, the Supreme Court noted, *id.* at 104–05, 96 S.Ct. 321:

> A review of the circumstances leading to Mosley's confession reveals that his "right to cut off questioning" was fully respected in this case. Before his initial interrogation, Mosley was carefully advised that he was under no obligation to answer any questions and could remain silent if he wished. He orally acknowledged that he understood the *Miranda* warnings and then signed a printed notification-of-rights form. When Mosley stated that he did not want to discuss the robberies, Detective Cowie immediately ceased the interrogation and did not try either to resume the questioning or in any way to persuade Mosley to reconsider his position. After an interval of more than two hours, Mosley was questioned by another police officer at another location about an unrelated holdup murder. He was given full and complete *Miranda* warnings at the outset of the second interrogation. He was thus reminded again that he could remain silent and could consult with a lawyer, and was carefully given a full and fair opportunity to exercise these options. The subsequent questioning did not undercut Mosley's previous decision not to answer Detective Cowie's inquiries. Detective Hill did not resume the interrogation about the White Tower Restaurant robbery or inquire about the Blue Goose Bar robbery, but instead focused exclusively on the Leroy Williams homicide, a crime different in nature and in time and place of occurrence from the robberies for which Mosley had been arrested and interrogated by Detective Cowie. Although it is not clear from the record how much Detective Hill knew about the earlier interrogation, his questioning of Mosley about an unrelated homicide was quite consistent with a

reasonable interpretation of Mosley's earlier refusal to answer any questions about the robberies.

Recognizing that, under certain circumstances, the police may re-initiate an attempt to interrogate a suspect despite a prior invocation of the right to silence, the *Mosley* Court said, *id.* at 105–06, 96 S.Ct. 321:

> This is not a case ... where the police failed to honor a decision of a person in custody to cut off questioning, either by refusing to discontinue the interrogation upon request or by persisting in repeated efforts to wear down his resistance and make him change his mind. In contrast to such practices, the police here immediately ceased the interrogation, resumed questioning only after the passage of a significant period of time and the provision of a fresh set of warnings, and restricted the second interrogation to a crime that had not been a subject of the earlier interrogation.

Nevertheless, the Supreme Court underscored that the admissibility of an accused's statement, made after the invocation of his Fifth Amendment privilege, depends in part on whether the police "scrupulously honored" the accused's right to remain silent. It explained:

> A reasonable and faithful interpretation of the *Miranda* opinion must rest on the intention of the Court in that case to adopt "fully effective means ... to notify the person of his right of silence and to assure that the exercise of the right will be scrupulously honored...." [*Miranda,*] 384 U.S., at 479, [; 86 S.Ct. at 1630]. The critical safeguard identified in the passage at issue is a person's "right to cut off questioning." *Id.,* at 474 [86 S.Ct. at 1627]. Through the exercise of his option to terminate questioning he can control the time at which questioning occurs, the subjects discussed, and the duration of the interrogation. The requirement that law enforcement authorities must respect a person's exercise of that option counteracts the coercive pressures of the custodial setting. We therefore conclude that the admissibility of statements obtained after the person in custody has decided to remain silent depends under *Miranda* on whether his "right to cut off questioning" was "scrupulously honored."

Mosley, 423 U.S. at 103–04, 96 S.Ct. 321 (footnote omitted). *Compare Edwards v. Arizona,* 451 U.S. 477, 484–85, 101 S.Ct. 1880, 68 L.Ed.2d 378 (1981) (holding "that when an accused has invoked his right to have counsel present during custodial interrogation, a valid waiver of that right cannot be established by showing only that he responded to further police-initiated custodial interrogation even if he has been advised of his rights.... [A]n accused, ... having expressed his desire to deal with the police only through counsel, is not subject to further interrogation by the authorities until counsel has been made available to him, unless the accused himself initiates further communication, exchanges, or conversations with the police.").

Appellant maintains that *Mosley* is inapplicable here, because "the police did not 'scrupulously honor' appellant's invocation of her right to remain silent." She complains that Paton "continued to question appellant even though she refused to waive her *Miranda* rights by remaining silent." Freeman asserts that the police may reinitiate questioning only if: "(1) the police wait a significant period of time (per *Mosley,* at least two hours); (2) provide the suspect with a fresh set of *Miranda* warnings, and obtain a second *Miranda* waiver; (3) restrict the second interrogation to crimes not discussed prior to the original invocation; and, (4) conduct the interrogation in a different location with different interrogating officers." Appellant adds: "[A]lthough the interrogation was conducted by a different officer, approximately two hours later, and upon warning appellant a second time of her *Miranda* rights—the interrogation was conducted in the same location and concerned the same subject matter." Further, she contends: "Even if Sgt. Patton had scrupulously honored appellant's invocation of silence, Corporal Ruel did not comply with the holding of *Mosley* by conducting the interrogation in the same location and about the same subject matter." We disagree with appellant's analysis.

Latimer v. State, 49 Md.App. 586, 433 A.2d 1234 (1981), establishes that, even if appellant's silence was an invocation, further questioning was not forever barred. After Latimer was arrested, the police advised him of his *Miranda* rights. *Id.* at 587, 433 A.2d 1234. Because Latimer declined to waive his rights, the police did not question him. *Id.* However, when the police later sought a writing sample from Latimer, he was again advised of his rights on this occasion, he agreed to waive his rights and then gave a statement. *Id.* at 588, 433 A.2d 1234. Relying on *Edwards v. Arizona,* *supra,* 451 U.S. 477, 101 S.Ct. 1880, 68 L.Ed.2d 378, Latimer argued that his statement was inadmissible because he had initially availed himself of the right to remain silent, and he did not make an overture to police. *Id.* This Court opined that *Edwards* was "concerned specifically with a valid waiver of the right to counsel and does not encompass the specific request to remain silent." *Id.* The Court said, *id.:*

> [I]n the situation where the defendant has chosen to remain silent without more, he has not necessarily indicated a belief that he is unable to speak for himself and is in need of an attorney. Instead, he has chosen to remain silent for the present; that choice should not, in our opinion, destroy *all* lines of communication nor make a prelude by the defendant absolutely necessary before further questioning.

Guided by *Michigan v. Mosley,* 423 U.S. 96, 96 S.Ct. 321, 46 L.Ed.2d 313, we noted that: "there was an interval of more than two hours" before Latimer was questioned "by another police officer at another location." *Latimer,* 49 Md.App. at 589, 433 A.2d 1234. We said: "Although the questioning that resulted apparently included the same subject matter as was attempted at the first interrogation, the initial purpose of the second inquiry was for the extraction of handwriting exemplars." *Id.* Moreover, we recognized that *Miranda* "does not create a *per se* proscription of all further interrogation" after the suspect has invoked his right to silence. *Id.* at 59, 433 A.2d 1234.

The Court cited numerous cases for the proposition that, upon an invocation of the right to remain silent, police must cease their interrogation in order to "notify the defendant that all he needs to do to foreclose or halt questioning is to give a negative response when asked if he will submit thereto." *Id.* at 591, 433 A.2d 1234. The Court explained, *id.:*

> In order to communicate this message it is imperative that the interrogation stop for some period of time. By this stoppage the defendant is made aware that he need answer no further questions either then or

later unless he so desires. It seems then that the action that is condemned in *Miranda* is police refusal to take a defendant's "no" for an answer, that is, situations wherein the police continue to question and thereby harass and coerce the defendant so as to overcome his asseveration of his constitutional right to remain silent....

Here, Paton testified that, after appellant was non-responsive to his waiver inquiry, he secured her gun. Then, he asked appellant, "what happened tonight, and her reply was I don't want to talk about it right now." At that point, Paton claimed he "didn't ask [appellant] anything else." Thus, appellant's assertion was "scrupulously honored" for almost three hours, until a different investigator, Ruel, sought to question appellant after again advising her of her *Miranda* rights. At that time, Freeman agreed to waive her rights.

In sum, appellant's statement, "I don't want to talk about it *right now,*" did not "destroy *all* lines of communication nor make a prelude by the defendant absolutely necessary...." *Latimer,* 49 Md.App. at 588, 433 A.2d 1234. Consistent with *Mosley,* a reasonable period of time elapsed between appellant's invocation of her right to silence (Statement 4), and the interrogation conducted by Ruel. Although the locale and the topic were the same, the interrogator was different.

It was not until Ruel asked appellant if she would write out her statement, or allow it to be recorded, that appellant invoked her right to counsel. By then, she had already given an oral statement. There is no contention that, once appellant invoked her right to counsel, that right was violated. Accordingly, the court did not err in denying appellant's motion to suppress on the basis of a *Miranda* violation.

(2) Sixth Amendment Limits

United States v. Stewart & Delegal

United States Court of Appeals, Sixth Circuit, 1991.
951 F.2d 351.

■ Per Curiam.

Defendants Rodney Fred Delegal and Ronnie Lee Stewart were charged with and convicted of (1) conspiring to commit an offense against the United States in violation of 18 U.S.C. § 371 (1988), (2) committing a bank robbery in violation of 18 U.S.C. § 2113(a), (d) (1988), and (3) using a dangerous weapon in relation to a crime of violence in violation of 18 U.S.C. § 924(c) (1988). For the reasons that follow, we affirm the judgment below in all respects.

I

Sometime prior to November 28, 1989, Stewart and Beacher Drell Roach drove to Cleveland, Tennessee to survey a local bank. On the morning of November 28, Stewart and Roach returned to Cleveland, this time accompanied by Delegal and Benjamin Leavern Wells, intending to rob the bank. The defendants traveled in two cars, one of which was to be abandoned.

Stewart, Delegal, and Wells entered the bank disguised and armed while Roach waited outside. After collecting the loot, they fled the scene by car. As they made their escape, however, a "dye-pack" hidden in the bag of stolen money discharged, releasing dye and tear gas into the vehicle's passenger compartment. The car was quickly abandoned, and the defendants eventually made their way back to Georgia.

Soon thereafter, the FBI learned that Roach had been involved in the robbery and decided to confront him. Roach agreed to audio-record surreptitiously his accomplices discussing the incident. He later recorded a conversation with Stewart wherein Stewart implicated himself in the robbery. Stewart was subsequently arrested and held in detention.

On August 5, 1990, nine days before trial was scheduled to begin, Stewart made statements to Roderick Stafford, a fellow inmate at the Hamilton County (Ohio) Jail, in which he further implicated himself in the robbery. Stafford passed news of Stewart's disclosures on to government agents and later testified at trial. The United States claims, and Stewart does not contest, that Stafford's account came as a total surprise to the United States Attorney.

Meanwhile, on December 8, 1989, Kentucky police officers had arrested Delegal on state stolen vehicle charges. At the time of his arrest, and in the presence of FBI Agent Dan Brennan, Delegal was advised of his *Miranda* rights. The police detained Delegal as an escaped prisoner in Owensburo, Kentucky. On January 12, 1990, criminal complaints were filed against Delegal for unlawful possession of a handgun by a convicted felon and unlawful escape from the Florida State Penitentiary. On January 23, 1990, a Kentucky state grand jury indicted Delegal on the state charges.

On January 24, 1990, Brennan learned that Delegal was a suspect in the bank robbery. Brennan visited Delegal, presented the information implicating him in the bank robbery, readvised him of his *Miranda* rights, and left Delegal an advice of rights form, telling him that he would return in the morning. The next day, Brennan readvised Delegal of his rights, and Delegal executed a second advice of rights form. Delegal proceeded to describe his involvement in the bank robbery to Brennan. No witnesses were present, and Brennan did not tape the conversation.

On January 29, 1990, Delegal was arraigned on the state charges. On or about that time, Ben Hawes, Jr. was appointed to represent Delegal on charges arising out of the January 23, 1990 state court indictment.

On February 6, 1990, Stewart and Delegal were indicted on federal charges relating to the bank robbery. Also named in the indictment were Wells and Roach. At a suppression hearing on August 10, 1990, after Delegal was found competent to stand trial, the district court denied his motion to suppress his confession. Trial commenced on August 14, 1990, in which all of the above confessions were admitted. The court denied defense motions for acquittal at the close of the government's evidence. On August 17, 1990, the jury convicted Delegal and Stewart on all three counts ...

II

We begin our analysis with various challenges to the validity of defendants convictions. Delegal's sole claim alleges that the admission at trial of his January 25, 1990 confession to Agent Brennan violated his Sixth Amendment right to counsel.

The Sixth Amendment guarantees to criminal defendants the right to counsel in postindictment interviews with law enforcement authorities. *Massiah v. United States,* 377 U.S. 201, 205–07 (1964). Unlike the right to counsel secured under the Fifth Amendment, the Sixth Amendment right to counsel comes into existence regardless of whether the defendant is in custody, so long as adverse judicial proceedings have been initiated against him. *See Patterson v. Illinois,* 487 U.S. 285, 290, 298–99 (1988). Once a suspect against whom such proceedings have begun indicates his desire for the assistance of counsel, the authorities must cease interrogation, and any further questioning on the crime for which the defendant was indicted is forbidden unless counsel is present. *McNeil v. Wisconsin,* 111 S.Ct. 2204, 2207–08 (1991). As clarified in *Patterson,* however, the initiation of adverse judicial proceedings does not erect an absolute bar to postindictment police interrogation in the absence of counsel; rather, a defendant may be questioned where he knowingly and intelligently waives his right to counsel, thus establishing " 'an intentional relinquishment or abandonment of a known right or privilege.' " *Patterson,* 487 U.S. at 292 (quoting *Johnson v. Zerbst,* 304 U.S. 458, 464 (1938)). In *Patterson,* the Supreme Court further held that advising a defendant of his right to counsel by means of *Miranda* warnings establishes that the ensuing waiver is knowing and intelligent:

As a general matter, . . . an accused who is admonished with the warnings prescribed by this Court in *Miranda* has been sufficiently apprised of the nature of his Sixth Amendment rights, and of the consequences of abandoning those rights, so that his waiver on this basis will be considered a knowing and intelligent one. *Id.* at 296 (citation omitted).*

More recently, in *McNeil,* the Court held that, unlike the right to counsel embedded in the Fifth Amendment, an accused's invocation of his Sixth Amendment right to counsel is offense specific and, hence, does not extend to police interrogations of unrelated offenses. *McNeil,* 111 S.Ct. at 2207–08; *see also Maine v. Moulton,* 474 U.S. 159, 180 n. 16 (1985) ("Incriminating statements pertaining to other crimes, as to which the Sixth Amendment right has not yet attached, are . . . admissible at a trial of those offenses.").

In the case at bar, while an indictment against Delegal on state charges was handed down on January 23, 1990, formal proceedings on the federal charges at issue here did not commence until well after Delegal's January 25, 1989 confession to Agent Brennan. Thus, Brennan's interrogation could not have violated Delegal's as yet nonexistent Sixth Amendment rights

---

* [Editor's note] In Montejo v. Louisiana, 556 U.S. ___, 129 S.Ct. 2079 (2009), the Court held that a valid *Miranda* waiver also waives the Sixth Amendment, *Massiah* right, when the warning and waiver take place after an appointment of defense counsel in which the defendant acquiesced but did not affirmatively embrace, and before any actual consultation between defendant and defense counsel. The opinion abrogates Michigan v. Jackson, 475 U.S. 625 (1986).

predicated on the federal charges. Moreover, the district court found as a factual matter that Delegal never requested assistance of counsel and that he knowingly and intelligently waived any Sixth Amendment right to counsel he might conceivably have had, thus satisfying the requirements of *Patterson*. Although Delegal challenges both of these findings on appeal, our review of the record reveals no basis for disturbing the district court's finding. Accordingly, we conclude that the admission of Delegal's confession at trial did not constitute error.

Defendant Stewart likewise claims that the admission at trial of inmate Stafford's testimony regarding Stewart's incriminating statements violated the Sixth Amendment. The government responds that, because Stafford did not deliberately elicit the inculpatory remarks, his testimony did not transgress Stewart's Sixth Amendment rights.

In *Kuhlman v. Wilson,* 477 U.S. 436 (1986), the Court, drawing on its holdings in *Massiah* and *United States v. Henry,* 447 U.S. 264 (1980), reaffirmed that a secret government informant violates a defendant's Sixth Amendment right to counsel only where the informant acts in concert with law enforcement officials to deliberately elicit incriminating testimony from the defendant. The Court reasoned that such tactics constitute the " 'functional equivalent of interrogation.' " *Kuhlman,* 477 U.S. at 459 (quoting *Henry,* 447 U.S. at 277). Absent such deliberate elicitation, however, the defendant's Sixth Amendment rights remain unimpaired. As the *Kuhlman* majority explained,

> a defendant does not make out a violation of that right simply by showing that an informant, either through prior arrangement or voluntarily, reported his incriminating statements to the police. Rather, the defendant must demonstrate that the police and their informant took some action, beyond merely listening, that was designed deliberately to elicit incriminating remarks.

Id. In *Kuhlman,* the Court found no deliberate elicitation where the defendant made incriminating remarks to an inmate-informant instructed by government agents to report the defendant's remarks but not ask questions, despite the fact that the informant told the defendant that his original, non-incriminating account of the crime "didn't sound too good." *Id.* at 460. In *Moulton,* by contrast, the Court found a Sixth Amendment violation where the informant repeatedly asked the defendant about details of the crime and encouraged the defendant to describe his plan for killing witnesses, thereby encouraging the defendant to make incriminating statements. *Id.* at 165–66.

At trial of the instant case, Stafford recounted his version of the conversation with Stewart as follows:

> [Stewart] stated to me that he was a Federal prisoner, and I stated to him that I was a Federal prisoner, and we both discussed our charge and what we were locked up for....
>
> ... [H]e asked me how long had I been up at the Hamilton County jail on my charge. I told him ever since March the 8th, and then he mentioned how long he had been up at the Hamilton County jail, that he said ever since January [sic]. *And I said, man, I said, how come,*

why have you been, you know, in prison at this jail so long, why haven't you been to court or sent off yet.

And he said because the evidence that they had on him wasn't sufficient. He said when he got ready to go to court, they were going to drop all the evidence on him. I said what are you locked up for, he said bank robbery. I said bank robbery, and he said yeah.

* * *

And then I didn't ask him any questions, he just went on with the conversation and he started stating why, I mean, he started stating how they go about robbing the bank. . . .

J.A. at 190–91 (emphasis added). A number of incriminating statements followed.

Stewart points to the emphasized language as proving that Stafford deliberately elicited the incriminating statements. The district court found, however, and we agree, that Stafford's conduct did not rise to the level of deliberate elicitation found objectionable in *Moulton,* but rather falls closer to the unobjectionable passive listener upheld in *Kuhlman.* While Stewart would have us construe Stafford's query regarding Stewart's prolonged detention as seeking to elicit inculpatory statements, we find this interpretation unpersuasive. Stafford's question was most likely intended to elicit precisely the information it did: the reason for the delay in the government bringing its case. We note also that Stewart made the inculpatory statements long after the challenged comment and apparently on Stewart's initiation. In sum, we find that admission of Stafford's testimony did not deprive Stewart of his Sixth Amendment right to counsel.

For the reasons set forth above, we AFFIRM the judgment of the district court.[23]

(3) Due Process Limits

State v. Tuttle

Supreme Court of South Dakota, 2002.
650 N.W.2d 20.

■ KONENKAMP, JUSTICE.

The defendant was taken into police custody for questioning. During interrogation, the detective threatened that the defendant's failure to cooperate would be noted in the police report, suggesting that refusal to admit guilt might result in harsher treatment. Because a person cannot be coerced into foregoing a Fifth Amendment right, and because this threat plainly caused the defendant to confess, we conclude under the totality of

---

23. In Texas v. Cobb, 532 U.S. 162 (2001), the Supreme Court held that the test of the "same offense" for purposes of the Sixth Amendment right to counsel during pretrial questioning is the *Blockburger* same elements test used in double-jeopardy law. Thus if police obtain a statement from D in violation of the right to counsel on a pending burglary charge, the statement may not be used at trial of the burglary charge, but it may be used at the trial of an intent-to-kill murder charge alleging a homicide during the burglary.

circumstances that the confession was obtained involuntarily and should be suppressed. We reverse and remand for a new trial.

A.

Background

After having several drinks at a party on Monday, October 30, 2000, Thomas John Tuttle and his friend Bereket Emehezian drove to the residence of Tuttle's grandmother, a mobile home at the Park View Trailer Court, in Sioux Falls, South Dakota. Soon after arrival, Tuttle and Emehezian got into an argument. A shoving match ensued. Various residents of the trailer court came out to watch. One of them succeeded in separating the two, whereupon Emehezian got into his car and sped away. Tuttle chased him on foot as far as the entrance and then walked back to his grandmother's home.

Shortly afterwards, law enforcement officers arrived on the scene to investigate. Finding nothing unusual, they were preparing to leave when Tuttle's grandmother approached the officers and requested that they eject some people she did not want in her home. Upon entering her trailer, the officers found Terrance Yellow Earrings, leaning against the kitchen sink, bleeding profusely. There was a recently washed paring knife in the sink. In In addition to Yellow Earrings and Tuttle's grandmother, the officers found three other people in the trailer: Tuttle's mother (the girlfriend of Yellow Earrings), and Tuttle's two uncles. Tuttle himself was outside the trailer, leaning up against a vehicle, when the officers arrived. After Yellow Earrings received first aid from the officers, he was taken by ambulance to the hospital. A medical examination revealed that he had sustained eleven stab wounds.

None of the people found in the trailer claimed to know who had committed the stabbing. Accordingly, the police took them all, as well as Tuttle, in for questioning. Under interrogation by Detective Thaddeus Openhowski, Tuttle admitted to having stabbed Yellow Earrings three times. Tuttle was charged with aggravated assault in violation of SDCL 22–18–1.1(2). In the jury trial, Yellow Earrings was the only eyewitness who testified on the identity of his assailant. No one else present during the assault appeared as witnesses. During the course of his testimony, it emerged that Yellow Earrings was, at the time of trial, incarcerated on a charge of tampering with a witness involved in this case. The paring knife was admitted into evidence, over defense objection. The jury found Tuttle guilty. The court sentenced him to six years in the penitentiary, noting that this relatively light punishment was appropriate to Tuttle's age (eighteen) and his prospects of rehabilitation.

B.

Miranda Waiver

Tuttle moved to suppress statements he made during his interrogation on the grounds that (a) he did not waive his *Miranda* rights, and (b) his admissions were involuntary. The circuit court denied his motion. Tuttle argues that the court committed reversible error in so ruling. We give deference to pure fact findings on such questions as whether the proper warnings were actually given, but we review *de novo* a trial court's ruling on the question whether a defendant knowingly, intelligently, and voluntarily waived *Miranda* rights. *State v. Stanga,* 2000 SD 129, ¶ 8, 617 N.W.2d 486, 488. . . .

On the whole, we think the detective adequately clarified Tuttle's intent. Tuttle thereafter voluntarily and willingly agreed to waive his *Miranda* rights after indicating an understanding of those rights. To hold police officers to some higher requirement of providing an exhaustive explanation of the *Miranda* warnings would impose an unrealistic burden. During the interview, furthermore, Tuttle's responses to the detective's questions indicate that Tuttle well knew that any admission would be incriminating. Considering the totality of circumstances and applying the State's burden of showing waiver only by a preponderance of the evidence, we uphold the circuit court's conclusion that Tuttle knowingly, intelligently, and voluntarily waived his *Miranda* rights.

C.

Voluntariness of Confession

We turn to the question whether the confession itself was voluntary, keeping in mind that the validity of a *Miranda* waiver of rights and the voluntariness of an admission are separate but parallel inquiries.[4] Although there are often subsidiary factual questions deserving deference, the voluntariness of a confession is ultimately a legal question. *Miller v. Fenton,* 474 U.S. 104, 116, 106 S.Ct. 445, 452–53, 88 L.Ed.2d 405, 414–15 (1985). On appeal, we "examine the entire record and make an independent determination of the ultimate issue of voluntariness." *Beckwith v. United States,* 425 U.S. 341, 348, 96 S.Ct. 1612, 1617, 48 L.Ed.2d 1, 8 (1976) (quoting *Davis v. North Carolina,* 384 U.S. 737, 741–42, 86 S.Ct. 1761, 1764, 16 L.Ed.2d 895, 898 (1966)). The voluntariness of a confession depends on the absence of police overreaching. *Connelly,* 479 U.S. at 170, 107 S.Ct. at 523, 93 L.Ed.2d at 486. Confessions are not deemed voluntary if, in light of the totality of the circumstances, law enforcement officers have overborne the defendant's will. *Haynes v. Washington,* 373 U.S. 503, 513–14, 83 S.Ct. 1336, 1343, 10 L.Ed.2d 513, 520–21 (1963).

The burden of proving the voluntariness of a confession is the same as the burden for showing the voluntariness of a *Miranda* waiver. *Connelly,* 479 U.S. at 169–70, 107 S.Ct. at 523, 93 L.Ed.2d at 486. The State must establish the voluntariness of a confessant's admission by a preponderance of the evidence. *Nix v. Williams,* 467 U.S. 431, 444, 104 S.Ct. 2501, 81 L.Ed.2d 377, n.5, 467 U.S. 431, 104 S.Ct. 2501, 2509, 81 L.Ed.2d 377, n.5, 467 U.S. 431, 104 S.Ct. 2501, 81 L.Ed.2d 377, 387–88, n.5 (1984); *United States v. Matlock,* 415 U.S. 164, 178, 94 S.Ct. 988, 39 L.Ed.2d 242, n.14, 415

---

4. The *Supreme Court in Colorado v. Connelly* held that "[t]here is obviously no reason to require more in the way of a 'voluntariness' inquiry in the *Miranda* waiver context than in the Fourteenth Amendment confession context." 479 U.S. 157, 169–70, 107 S.Ct. 515, 523, 93 L.Ed.2d 473, 486 (1986). Thus, once a court concludes that a defendant's confession was voluntary under the Fourteenth Amendment, it follows that the defendant's waiver of *Miranda* rights was also voluntary. But the opposite is not necessarily true.

U.S. 164, 94 S.Ct. 988, 996, 39 L.Ed.2d 242, n.14, 415 U.S. 164, 94 S.Ct. 988, 39 L.Ed.2d 242, 253, n.14 (1974) ("[T]he controlling burden of proof at suppression hearings should impose no greater burden than proof by a preponderance of the evidence...."); *Lego v. Twomey,* 404 U.S. 477, 488, 92 S.Ct. 619, 626, 30 L.Ed.2d 618, 627 (1972). We now expressly abandon our prior standard holding the State to a higher burden in suppression hearings.[5] As the United States Supreme Court said in *Lego:*

> [E]xclusionary rules are very much aimed at deterring lawless conduct by police and prosecution, and it is very doubtful that escalating the prosecution's burden of proof in ... suppression hearings would be sufficiently productive in this respect to outweigh the public interest in placing probative evidence before juries for the purpose of arriving at truthful decisions about guilt or innocence.

> 404 U.S. at 489, 92 S.Ct. at 626, 30 L.Ed.2d at 627. Voluntariness determinations have "nothing to do with the reliability of jury verdicts; rather, [they are] designed to determine the presence of police coercion." *Connelly,* 479 U.S. at 168, 107 S.Ct. at 522, 93 L.Ed.2d at 485.

Once suspects in custody are properly advised of, and agree to waive, their *Miranda* rights, they may be freely questioned as long as interrogators do not obtain a confession through coercion. With coercive police conduct as a "necessary predicate" to finding a defendant's admission involuntary, we look at the totality of the circumstances under which the coercion was used. *See Connelly,* 479 U.S. at 167, 107 S.Ct. at 522, 93 L.Ed.2d at 484. The factual inquiry centers on (1) the conduct of law enforcement officials in creating pressure and (2) the suspect's capacity to resist that pressure. *Mincey v. Arizona,* 437 U.S. 385, 399–401, 98 S.Ct. 2408, 2417–18, 57 L.Ed.2d 290, 304–306 (1978). On the latter factor, we examine such concerns as the defendant's age; level of education and intelligence; the presence or absence of any advice to the defendant on constitutional rights; the length of detention; the repeated and prolonged nature of the questioning; the use of psychological pressure or physical punishment, such as deprivation of food or sleep; and the defendant's prior experience with law enforcement officers and the courts. Finally, "[d]eception or misrepresentation by the officer receiving the statement may also be factors for the trial court to consider; however, the police may use some psychological tactics in interrogating a suspect." *State v. Darby,* 1996 SD 127, ¶ 31, 556 N.W.2d 311, 320.

Tuttle ... argues that his confession was involuntary [because he received]an explicit threat that his failure to cooperate would be used against him. In particular, the detective told Tuttle that his report could be written to make things look good for Tuttle or that "I'm gonna have to write it up that you're not cooperating, you're being a real jerk about it." In this context, it is well to remember that an admission is not voluntary unless it is " 'the product of a rational intellect and a free will.' " *Black-*

---

5. The beyond a reasonable doubt standard still applies, of course, to the fact finder's determination at trial whether an admission or confession was made by the defendant and whether the statement is true or false, in whole or in part.

burn v. Alabama, 361 U.S. 199, 208, 80 S.Ct. 274, 280, 4 L.Ed.2d 242, 249 (1960).

The Fifth Amendment provides that "[n]o person ... shall be compelled in any criminal case to be a witness against himself." U.S. Const. amend. V. Involuntary confessions can encompass a broad range, including not only the familiar types of coerced statements obtained by actual or threatened violence, but also confessions extracted by psychological ploys or improper interrogation techniques deemed inconsistent with the right to be free from compelled self-incrimination. In some instances, however, "direct promises that officers would tell the prosecutor [whether] defendant cooperated are permissible, but promises that officers would see to it that a defendant would go to prison if he failed to cooperate are not." *State v. Tapia,* 159 Ariz. 284, 767 P.2d 5, 11 (1988) (citing *United States v. Tingle,* 658 F.2d 1332, 1336, n.n.4–5 (9th Cir.1981)). In *People v. Brommel,* the police told the suspect that unless he changed his story (he had denied injuring his daughter) they would write "liar" on their report to the judge. 56 Cal.2d 629, 633–34, 364 P.2d 845, 15 Cal.Rptr. 909 (1961) (overruled on other grounds by *People v. Cahill,* 5 Cal.4th 478, 494, 853 P.2d 1037, 1048, 20 Cal.Rptr.2d 582, 593 (1993)) (Cahill I). The court found that this conduct was both a threat and an implied promise of leniency, rendering the confession inadmissible. Other decisions have held likewise. In *U.S. v. Harrison,* 34 F.3d 886 (9th Cir.1994), the court wrote that "there are no circumstances in which law enforcement officers may suggest that a suspect's exercise of the right to remain silent may result in harsher treatment by a court or prosecutor." Applying this same principle, the Alabama Supreme Court in Ex parte Matthews, held that the following comments to a suspect were coercive threats: "You know there's two ways to go about things, either you go about it and you don't cooperate and the judge knows that you didn't and the district attorney knows you didn't or you turn around and you did cooperate, you know.... I can go back and tell the district attorney, [defendant] cooperated with me or I can go back and tell the district attorney that [defendant] did not cooperate with me." 601 So.2d 52, 52–53 (Ala.1992).

In *Tingle,* the court explained the distinction between encouraging cooperation and threatening for failure to cooperate:

> Although it is permissible for an interrogating officer to represent, under some circumstances that the fact that the defendant cooperates will be communicated to the proper authorities, the same cannot be said of a representation that a defendant's failure to cooperate will be communicated to a prosecutor. Refusal to cooperate is every defendant's right under the fifth amendment. Under our adversary system of criminal justice, a defendant may not be made to suffer for his silence. Because there is no legitimate purpose for the statement that failure to cooperate will be reported and because its only apparent objective is to coerce, we disapprove the making of such representations.

658 F.2d at 1336, n.5. Law enforcement agents told Tingle that if she refused to cooperate, they would inform the prosecutor that she was

"stubborn" and "hard headed."[10] We acknowledge, though, that the threats in *Tingle* were far more egregious than the one here. There, government agents preyed on "the maternal instinct and inculcate[d] fear in a [young] mother that she would not see her children in order to elicit cooperation." *Id.* at 1336. From the totality of the circumstances, the court concluded that the threats were "patently coercive," causing "Tingle to fear that, if she failed to cooperate, she would not see her young child for a long time." *Id.* . . . .

The line between making threats and simply informing suspects what the natural consequences of their acts are likely to be can sometimes be narrow, but that line must remain distinct. Merely telling suspects that they should think about the consequences of obstructing the investigation, or saying that if they do not cooperate the prosecutor will look upon their cases differently, or even suggesting that, unless they cooperate, the child victims of their sexual assaults would be forced to testify and would suffer great trauma, is not coercive. *State v. Deets,* 187 Wis.2d 630, 523 N.W.2d 180, 182, 183 (1994). These remarks are reasonable predictions, not coercive conduct. *Id.* at 183. Moreover, receiving threats from an interrogator should be distinguished from having a subjective fear that failure to confess will have adverse consequences. *See State v. P.Z.,* 152 N.J. 86, 703 A.2d 901, 916 (1997). A subjectively created state of mind is not dispositive of the question whether the will was overborne and the capacity for self-determination was critically impaired. *Schneckloth v. Bustamonte,* 412 U.S. 218, 225, 93 S.Ct. 2041, 2047, 36 L.Ed.2d 854, 862 (1973). . . .

Exactly what was the threat that the detective made? To quote again from the interview, the detective's second alternative was: "I'm gonna have to write it up that you're not cooperating, you're being a real jerk about it." The unmistakable message was, if Tuttle refused to confess, then the report to the authorities would be written to discourage any leniency, meaning Tuttle would likely suffer more severely for not confessing. This was coercive. The videotape of the interview reveals, without doubt, that the detective's threat occasioned Tuttle's admission of guilt: Tuttle, already weeping at that point, responded to it with these words: "OK. I stabbed him. Whatever. Shit." . . .

As we have said, it is not enough to show that threats were made to induce a confession. It must also be shown in the totality of circumstances that the suspect's will was overborne and that the overreaching police conduct was causally related to the confession. A suspect's will is overborne if the confession is not the product of a free and unconstrained choice. Tuttle's demeanor and response as we viewed it on the tape demonstrated that the threat found its mark. *See Culombe v. Connecticut,* 367 U.S. 568, 602, 81 S.Ct. 1860, 1879, 6 L.Ed.2d 1037, 1057–58 (1961). The message was

---

10. Unlike the defendants in *Tingle* and in *Lynumn v. Illinois,* 372 U.S. 528, 83 S.Ct. 917, 9 L.Ed.2d 922 (1963), another case in which a threat by interrogators rendered a confession involuntary, Tuttle had been charged with a felony previously (though the charges were later dropped), but his experience with the courts was not so extensive that he could be expected to know that the threat leveled against him could not be carried out. On the contrary, much of the interrogation involved Tuttle's worry that his brother was facing penitentiary time for a crime Tuttle did not believe his brother committed.

clear: if Tuttle failed to cooperate he would pay the consequences; he would be treated less favorably. Concededly, this was not the worst threat imaginable, but our Supreme Court has "held inadmissible even a confession secured by so mild a whip as the refusal, under certain circumstances, to allow a suspect to call his wife until he confessed." *Malloy v. Hogan,* 378 U.S. 1, 7, 84 S.Ct. 1489, 1493, 12 L.Ed.2d 653, 659 (1964) (citing *Haynes v. Washington,* 373 U.S. 503, 83 S.Ct. 1336, 10 L.Ed.2d 513 (1963)).

Reviewing the relevant facts, we conclude that the following weigh in favor of adjudging Tuttle's statement voluntary: there was no evidence that Tuttle lacked sufficient education or intelligence to understand the alternatives open to him; the length of his detention was less than an hour; the questioning, though somewhat repetitious, was not prolonged through several sessions; he did not suffer physical punishment or deprivation. On the other hand, we find that the following factors weigh against finding his statement voluntary: he was in custody and interrogated in a holding cell at 2:30 a.m.; he was under the influence of alcohol; he was eighteen at the time; he was deceived about statements of eyewitnesses; and, as explained earlier, he was subjected to an implied threat of more serious consequences if he refused to admit guilt. Weighing all these elements, the scale tilts toward holding the confession involuntary.

We conclude that the trial court erred in finding that Tuttle's statement was given voluntarily and, thus, we rule that, under the totality of circumstances in this case, the statement is inadmissible in evidence. Police may legitimately tell a suspect that cooperation will be passed on to the authorities and may increase the likelihood of leniency, but threatening to inform the prosecutor or the judge of a suspect's refusal to cooperate violates the Fifth Amendment right to remain silent. We must never forget that the reason courts suppress involuntary confessions is that the methods used to extract them offend an underlying principle in the enforcement of our criminal law: that ours is an accusatorial, and not an inquisitorial, system—a system in which the State must establish guilt by evidence independently and freely secured, and may not, by coercion, prove its charge against an accused out of his own mouth. *Rogers v. Richmond,* 365 U.S. 534, 541, 81 S.Ct. 735, 739–40, 5 L.Ed.2d 760 (1961).

Admission of unlawfully obtained, even coerced, confessions can sometimes be harmless error. An erroneously admitted involuntary confession will not mandate reversal if there is sufficient untainted evidence of guilt to prove the offense beyond a reasonable doubt. *Arizona v. Fulminante,* 499 U.S. 279, 296, 306–12, 111 S.Ct. 1246, 1257–58, 113 L.Ed.2d 302, 322–23 (1991). The admission of Tuttle's statement here was not harmless error because the other evidence, including testimony from the victim, was not overwhelming, and cannot, given the issues of credibility for the jury, be said to prove Tuttle's guilt beyond a reasonable doubt as a matter of law.

Since we conclude that the State has not met its burden of proving by a preponderance of the evidence that Tuttle's confession was voluntary, and the admission of his confession at trial was not harmless, we reverse and remand for a new trial. We need not reach the second and third appeal issues.

Reversed and remanded for a new trial.

■ GILBERTSON, CHIEF JUSTICE (concurring in part and dissenting in part).

I would not abandon this Court's traditional "totality of the circumstances" test in favor of a *per se* rule that would render all statements involuntary when they appear to result from what the defendant subjectively perceives to be a threat. There is a clear distinction between making threats or false promises to coerce a defendant's confession and simply apprising the defendant of all the facts so that he may make his decision of whether to cooperate in a knowing and intelligent manner. There is also a significant difference between remaining silent and lying to police to alleviate suspicion. Accordingly, I would affirm the trial court's admission of Tuttle's statement.

The essence of this inquiry is whether, under the totality of the circumstances, Tuttle's confession was coerced by the officer's statement. This Court claims the officer overcame Tuttle's will when he informed Tuttle "I'm gonna have to write it up that you're not cooperating, you're being a real jerk about it." However, the Court takes this statement out of context. The officer's entire comment, in response to Tuttle's repeated denials that he had anything to do with the stabbing, was as follows:

O: Here's the problem T.J., okay. Here's the problem. And this is—I can't make ya any deals. I can't make ya any promises. But this is the way it's gonna happen, okay. Everybody that's there—You know, I don't think there's a big conspiracy to get you in trouble, okay. But the facts are the facts as what happened. I can write it up one or two ways. I can say 'T.J. doesn't like this guy. He's beat up his mother, he's caused a lot of problems.' And for whatever reasons, ya accidentally stabbed this guy. Or I'm gonna have to write it up that you're not cooperating, you're being a real jerk about it.

T.J.: Okay, I stabbed him. Whatever. Shit.

The officer's statement was not a threat, which overcame Tuttle's free will to remain silent.[12] . . .

Finally, today's ruling will have a chilling effect upon the ability of law enforcement to elicit confessions. "It is a fact of life for law enforcement that suspected criminals do not often readily volunteer incriminating evidence." *State v. Frazier*, 2001 SD 19, ¶ 23, 622 N.W.2d 246, 256. Under this Court's ruling, law enforcement officers will be forbidden from uttering any words of consequences, for fear a defendant's confession will become involuntary. But they are also forbidden to withhold information that may cause a defendant's confession to be unknowing and, again, involuntary. This "catch 22" position will severely limit law enforcement capabilities in solving crimes. Indeed, if we are to take the Supreme Court's 1964 ruling in *Malloy* to its most literal conclusion, as this Court advocates today, even plea bargains would be unconstitutional.

---

12.   Moreover, this exchange took place only twelve minutes after the officer read Tuttle a *Miranda* warning.

SECTION 5. CURRENT DOCTRINE: IDENTIFICATION PROCEDURES

United States v. Montgomery

United States Court of Appeals, Ninth Circuit, 1998.
150 F.3d 983.

■ ALARCON, CIRCUIT JUDGE:

Bernard Vincent Montgomery ("Montgomery") was found guilty of conspiracy to manufacture methamphetamine, conspiracy to distribute methamphetamine, conspiracy to import methamphetamine, distribution of methamphetamine, and possession of ephedrine with intent to manufacture methamphetamine. Lloyd Ray Buxton ("Buxton") was found guilty of conspiracy to distribute methamphetamine.

Montgomery seeks reversal of the judgment of conviction on the ... grounds [inter alia, that] [t]he in-court identification of Montgomery by a prosecution witness was impermissibly tainted by improper identification procedures....

For the reasons stated below, we affirm the judgments of conviction on all counts.

III

Montgomery argues that he was deprived of his right to due process because the court admitted the in-court identification testimony of Lance Blondin ("Blondin"). Blondin, an employee of a Canadian chemical supply company, identified Montgomery at trial as the purchaser of a large quantity of red phosphorous—a key ingredient in the manufacture of methamphetamine. Montgomery contends that this in-court identification was tainted by impermissibly suggestive pretrial identification procedures employed by the Government. "Suggestive pretrial identification procedures may be so impermissibly suggestive as to taint subsequent in-court identifications and thereby deny a defendant due process of law." United States v. Bagley, 772 F.2d 482, 492 (9th Cir.1985).

We review de novo the constitutionality of pretrial identification procedures. United States v. Atcheson, 94 F.3d 1237, 1246 (9th Cir.1996), cert. denied, 519 U.S. 1156, 117 S.Ct. 1096, 137 L.Ed.2d 229 (1997). [C]onvictions based on eyewitness identification at trial following a pretrial identification ... will be set aside ... only if the [pretrial] identification procedure was so impermissibly suggestive as to give rise to a very substantial likelihood of irreparable misidentification. "Simmons v. U.S., 390 U.S. 377, 384, 88 S.Ct. 967, 19 L.Ed.2d 1247 (1968)." It is the likelihood of misidentification which violates a defendant's right to due process.... "Neil v. Biggers, 409 U.S. 188, 198, 93 S.Ct. 375, 34 L.Ed.2d 401 (1972)." "Suggestive confrontations are disapproved because they increase the likelihood of misidentification, and unnecessarily suggestive ones are condemned for the

further reason that the increased chance of misidentification is gratuitous."
Id.

A.   Were the pretrial identification procedures unnecessarily suggestive?

In August 1996, officers of the DEA and RCMP showed photos of Montgomery, Marks, and McClain to Blondin. He identified Montgomery as the person who, using the name "Jim Luna," had purchased a large quantity of red phosphorous on a rush basis. Several weeks prior to trial, Blondin requested that the DEA fax him a photograph of Montgomery, to "have it right in [his] mind that [he] could identify Montgomery." He later called an agent at the DEA to inform her that the man in the photograph was Montgomery. Blondin pinned this photograph to the wall of his office and looked at it several times prior to testifying.

The day before Blondin was scheduled to testify, he entered the courtroom with a DEA agent and looked at Montgomery, who was seated at the defense table. Blondin testified that he asked the DEA agent to bring him into the courtroom so that he could "have it straight in my mind that Montgomery was the fellow that had purchased the chemicals from us. . . ." Montgomery asserts that the combination of identification procedures—the initial photo-identification, the subsequent single photograph identification, and the one-on-one confrontation—was "unnecessarily suggestive and conducive to irreparable mistaken identification."

An identification procedure is suggestive when it "emphasize[s] the focus upon a single individual" thereby increasing the likelihood of misidentification. *Bagley,* 772 F.2d at 493 ("The repeated showing of the picture of an individual, for example, reinforces the image of the photograph in the mind of the viewer."); Stovall v. Denno, 388 U.S. 293, 302, 87 S.Ct. 1967, 18 L.Ed.2d 1199 (1967) ("The practice of showing suspects singly to persons for the purpose of identification, and not as part of a lineup, has been widely condemned."). We agree with Montgomery that showing Blondin the photographs of Marks, McClain, and Montgomery, granting Blondin's request for a photograph of Montgomery, and permitting Blondin to view Montgomery in the courtroom the day before the witness was scheduled to testify, were suggestive procedures that emphasized the focus of the investigation on Montgomery as the person who purchased the red phosphorous.

The Court in *Stovall* explained that a suggestive pretrial identification procedure does not violate due process when use of the procedure is "imperative." See *Stovall,* 388 U.S. at 301–02, 87 S.Ct. 1967 (holding that a one person show-up in a hospital room of critically wounded victim did not violate due process where the record revealed that the suggestive confrontation was "imperative"). The issue before the Court in *Stovall* was whether the pretrial identification procedure was "so unnecessarily suggestive and conducive to irreparable mistaken identification that [the defendant] was denied due process of law." Id. at 301, 87 S.Ct. 1967. We read *Stovall* to mean that an identification procedure is unnecessarily suggestive when its use is not imperative.

The record in the case before us is devoid of any indication that the Government's use of the suggestive identification procedures was imperative. The initial photo identification by Blondin took place one year after the purchase of red phosphorous by Montgomery. The Government had ample time to prepare a non-suggestive photographic array. The faxed photo identification and the in-court one-on-one confrontation were not compelled by any exigent circumstances. Accordingly, we conclude that the identification procedures employed by the Government were unnecessarily suggestive.

B. Was the in-court identification testimony sufficiently reliable under the totality of the circumstances?

"Should we find a pretrial procedure impermissibly suggestive, automatic exclusion of identification testimony is not required." *Bagley*, 772 F.2d at 492 (citing Manson v. Brathwaite, 432 U.S. 98, 113–14, 97 S.Ct. 2243, 53 L.Ed.2d 140 (1977); and *Biggers*, 409 U.S. at 198–99, 93 S.Ct. 375). "If under the totality of the circumstances the identification is sufficiently reliable, identification testimony may properly be allowed into evidence even if the identification was made pursuant to an unnecessarily suggestive procedure." Id.

The factors we consider in deciding whether in-court identification testimony is sufficiently reliable are: (1) the witness's opportunity to view the defendant at the time of the incident; (2) the witness's degree of attention; (3) the accuracy of the witness's prior description of the defendant; (4) the level of certainty demonstrated by the witness at the time of the identification procedure; and (5) the length of time between the incident and the identification. See *Biggers*, 409 U.S. at 199–200, 93 S.Ct. 375; United States v. Jones, 84 F.3d 1206, 1209–10 (9th Cir.), cert. denied, 519 U.S. 973, 117 S.Ct. 405, 136 L.Ed.2d 319 (1996).

Blondin had ample opportunity to view Montgomery at the time Montgomery purchased the red phosphorous. Furthermore, because the large order for a key methamphetamine ingredient raised Blondin's suspicions, he made a point of gaining a detailed description of the purchaser. This description was later recorded by Blondin and faxed to the RCMP. The district court found that this description was "accurate." One year later, when presented with photos of Marks, McClain, and Montgomery, Blondin was able to make a positive identification of Montgomery as the purchaser.

We conclude that Blondin's in-court identification of Montgomery was sufficiently reliable as a matter of law, based on the factors set out in *Biggers*. See 409 U.S. at 199–200, 93 S.Ct. 375. Thus, the admission of Blondin's in-court identification testimony was not a violation of due process. The unnecessarily suggestive pretrial identification procedures did not create a "substantial likelihood of irreparable misidentification." Simmons, 390 U.S. at 384, 88 S.Ct. 967.

IV

Montgomery also contends that the fact that the DEA agent granted Blondin's request to take him to the courtroom to confirm the witness's initial photo identification of Montgomery violated his right to counsel. He argues that the right to counsel at a post-indictment lineup also applies to the eyewitness's observation of Montgomery in the courtroom the day before the witness was scheduled to testify.

Montgomery's argument can be summarized in this syllogism:

A defendant is entitled to counsel at a post-indictment lineup or show up.

The police permitted an identification witness to see Montgomery in the courtroom without notifying his attorney the day before the witness testified.

Therefore, Montgomery was deprived of his right to counsel at a critical stage of the criminal proceedings against him.

Montgomery has confused the adversarial confrontation that occurs when a defendant is compelled to participate in a police lineup or show up with the surreptitious observation of the defendant in the court-room by an identification witness the day prior to his testimony.

In United States v. Ash, 413 U.S. 300, 93 S.Ct. 2568, 37 L.Ed.2d 619 (1973), the Supreme Court summarized the decisions interpreting the Sixth Amendment's guarantee of a right to counsel. The Court stated that "the core purpose of the counsel guarantee was to assure 'Assistance' at trial, when the accused was confronted with both the intricacies of the law and the advocacy of the public prosecutor." Id. at 309, 93 S.Ct. 2568. The Court instructed that the right to counsel applies to the formal trial, and to "pretrial events that might appropriately be considered to be parts of the trial itself." Id. at 310, 93 S.Ct. 2568. "The Court consistently has applied a historical interpretation of the guarantee, and has expanded the constitutional right to counsel only when new contexts appear presenting the same dangers that gave birth initially to the right itself." Id. at 311, 93 S.Ct. 2568.

The Court has recognized arraignment as "a critical stage in a criminal proceeding" requiring the guiding hand of counsel to prevent a waiver of available defenses. Hamilton v. Alabama, 368 U.S. 52, 53, 82 S.Ct. 157. In Coleman v. Alabama, 399 U.S. 1, 90 S.Ct. 1999, 26 L.Ed.2d 387 (1970), the Court held that a preliminary hearing to determine whether there is sufficient evidence to warrant presenting the accused's case to a grand jury is a critical stage of a state's criminal process because a "lawyer's skilled examination and cross-examination of witnesses may expose fatal weak-nesses in the State's case that may lead the magistrate to refuse to bind the accused over." Id. at 9, 90 S.Ct. 1999. Additionally, the Court reasoned that "[t]he inability of the . . . accused on his own to realize these advantages of a lawyer's assistance compels the conclusion that the Alabama preliminary hearing is a 'critical stage' of the State's criminal process at which the accused is 'as much entitled to such aid [of counsel] . . . as at the trial itself.' " Id. at 9–10, 90 S.Ct. 1999 (quoting Powell v. Alabama, 287 U.S. 45, 57, 53 S.Ct. 55, 77 L.Ed. 158 (1932)).

The right to counsel was extended to police lineups in United States v. Wade, 388 U.S. 218, 87 S.Ct. 1926, 18 L.Ed.2d 1149 (1967). In *Ash*, the Court explained the basis for its decision to extend the right to counsel at a lineup as follows:

The function of counsel in rendering "Assistance" continued at the lineup under consideration in *Wade* and its companion cases. Although the accused was not confronted there with legal questions, the lineup offered opportunities for prosecuting authorities to take advantage of the accused. Counsel was seen by the Court as being more sensitive to, and aware of, suggestive influences than the accused himself, and as better able to reconstruct the events at trial. Counsel present at lineup would be able to remove disabilities of the accused in precisely the same fashion that counsel compensated for the disabilities of the layman at trial. Thus, the Court mentioned that the accused's memory might be dimmed by "emotional tension," that the accused's credibility at trial would be diminished by his status as defendant, and that the accused might be unable to present his version effectively without giving up his privilege against compulsory self-incrimination. United States v. Wade, 388 U.S. at 230–231, 87 S.Ct. 1926. It was in order to compensate for these deficiencies that the Court found the need for the assistance of counsel. *Ash,* 413 U.S. at 312–13, 93 S.Ct. 2568.

The Court in *Ash* held that in determining whether an accused has the right to counsel, a court must examine "the event in order to determine whether the accused required aid in coping with legal problems or assistance in meeting his adversary." Id. at 313, 93 S.Ct. 2568. The Court concluded that the "Assistance of Counsel" is required at any trial-like confrontation "to preserve the adversary process by compensating for advantages of the prosecuting authorities." Id. at 314, 93 S.Ct. 2568. See also Moore v. Illinois, 434 U.S. 220, 231, 98 S.Ct. 458, 54 L.Ed.2d 424 (1977) (holding that an uncounseled identification conducted at a preliminary hearing violated the accused's Sixth Amendment right to counsel).

In *Ash,* the petitioner argued that "the Sixth Amendment grants an accused the right to have counsel present whenever the Government conducts a post-indictment photographic display, containing a picture of the accused, for the purpose of allowing a witness to attempt an identification of the offender." Id. at 301, 93 S.Ct. 2568. The Court declined to extend the right to counsel to this type of pretrial event because "the accused himself is not present at the time of the photographic display and asserts no right to be present ..., [therefore] no possibility arises that the accused might be misled by his lack of familiarity with the law or overpowered by his professional adversary." Id. at 317, 93 S.Ct. 2568 (internal citation omitted). The Court held that "[i]f accurate reconstruction of an event is possible" by an adversary confrontation with defense counsel during trial "the risks inherent in any confrontation still remain, but the opportunity to cure defects at trial causes the [pretrial] confrontation to cease to be 'critical.' " Id. at 316, 93 S.Ct. 2568. The Court thus recognized a distinction between adversarial confrontations at which the accused possesses the Sixth Amendment right to counsel, and non-adversarial confrontations at which the counsel guarantee is not implicated.

Relying on the Court's instruction in *Ash* and *Wade,* we held in Jordan v. Ducharme, 983 F.2d 933 (9th Cir.1993), that "[t]o determine whether a pretrial event implicates the right to counsel, a court must consider whether cross-examination can reveal any improper procedures that occur in counsel's absence." Id. at 937. Applying this test, we held that the appellant was not prejudiced when a police officer ordered defense counsel out of the witness preparation room while the identification witnesses were given preliminary instructions regarding the lineup procedures that followed. Id. at 937–38.

In *Jordan*, we rejected appellant's argument that counsel's presence is required while the police instruct identification witnesses prior to a lineup to avoid the risk of undue suggestion. We stated that this proposition "ignores the requirement that the pretrial event be a 'critical' stage where an accused may be overpowered by his professional adversary." Id. at 937.

Applying these principles to this matter, we conclude that the challenged event was not an adversarial confrontation. Montgomery was not confronted by a prosecutor with superior knowledge of the law. Nor was the accused placed in a position where he was threatened with a loss of an available defense because he did not have the guiding hand of counsel. Unlike a lineup where the accused is subject to emotional tension that might affect his or her memory regarding improper police suggestions or procedures, and thereby diminish his or her credibility as a witness, Montgomery was covertly observed sitting in the courtroom by an identification witness. Montgomery's counsel was not aware of this event until he elicited this information from Blondin during cross-examination. Montgomery was not faced with the choice of giving up his privilege against compulsory self-incrimination in order to present evidence of the unnecessarily suggestive nature of this identification procedure. Montgomery's counsel effectively reconstructed this event through cross-examination of the identification witness. Rather than losing an available defense, the possibility of an identification witness's unnecessarily suggestive confrontation with the defendant presented Montgomery's attorney with strong ammunition to attack the accuracy of Blondin's identification.

Under the circumstances presented in this record, the Government's failure to notify Montgomery's counsel prior to permitting Blondin to view Montgomery in the courtroom did not deprive him of his right to counsel. . . .

The judgment of conviction is AFFIRMED as to each appellant.

SECTION 6. CURRENT DOCTRINE: APPLICATION OF THE EXCLUSIONARY RULE

Mosby v. Seknowski

United States Court of Appeals, Second Circuit, 2006.
470 F.3d 515.

■ B.D. PARKER, JR., CIRCUIT JUDGE.

Marcus Mosby appeals from a judgment of the United States District Court for the Western District of New York (Richard J. Arcara, *Chief Judge*) denying his petition for a writ of habeas corpus. Mosby contends that he was denied his Sixth Amendment right to effective assistance of appellate counsel when, on direct appeal, his counsel failed to raise a suppression issue arising under the Fourth Amendment and the New York State Constitution. The state trial court ruled that Mosby lacked standing to challenge his warrantless arrest because he did not live in the house where he was arrested, and denied his motion to suppress a confession and photo identification that ultimately led to his murder conviction. Because the underlying suppression issue, when considered in accordance with the attenuation analysis of *Brown v. Illinois,* 422 U.S. 590, 95 S.Ct. 2254, 45 L.Ed.2d 416 (1975), lacks merit, we conclude that appellate counsel's omission did not prejudice Mosby. Consequently, we affirm.

BACKGROUND

On April 15, 1994, witnesses observed an assailant known only by the nickname "Florida" shoot and kill two men on Bloomingdale Street, in Rochester, New York. Five days later, Rochester police officers conducted an unrelated "buy and bust" operation, in which Mosby sold a $20 bag of crack cocaine to a police informant, with an undercover officer present. The drug deal took place through the window of a house at 46 Costar Street, two miles from the site of the homicides. Four uniformed police officers arrived shortly thereafter, without a warrant for Mosby's arrest. They knocked at the front door of the house, which was answered by Mosby's ten-year-old son. The child informed them that his father was upstairs, sleeping. After four or five attempts to coax him downstairs, the uniformed officers entered the house and took Mosby into custody. The undercover officer then identified Mosby as the person he had observed selling cocaine earlier, and Mosby was placed under arrest.

While Mosby was waiting in a police car outside the house, a passing neighbor, Lanna Pulley, noticed him in the car and asked an officer what was happening with "Florida." According to the arresting officers' report, Ms. Pulley told police that Mosby had been living at 46 Costar for the past two months.

On hearing the nickname "Florida" attributed to Mosby, the arresting officers contacted investigators working on the Bloomingdale Street homicides. Later that evening, the police presented a photo array including Mosby's photo to four different witnesses to the homicides. All four identified Mosby as the shooter. After being read *Miranda* warnings, Mosby declined an attorney, and the police questioned him about the homicides. Mosby ultimately confessed, and the police prepared a written statement which he reviewed and signed after midnight, on the same night as his arrest. He was subsequently indicted, tried, and convicted on homicide charges.

Prior to trial, Mosby moved to suppress the confession and photo identifications on the ground that his warrantless home arrest violated the Fourth Amendment. Mosby claimed that he had been living at 46 Costar Street for at least two months. The trial court held that Mosby did not have standing to assert a Fourth Amendment claim since he was merely a "casual visitor" with a "transient presence" at 46 Costar and thus had no "legitimate expectation of privacy" there. Accordingly, the court denied Mosby's suppression motion.

At trial, Mosby testified that he shot the two individuals in self-defense. The four eyewitnesses testified, identifying Mosby as the gunman. His confession was admitted during the state's rebuttal case. The jury convicted Mosby on two counts of murder in the second degree, and the court sentenced him to consecutive terms of twenty-five years to life.

On direct appeal, Mosby's attorney did not challenge the adverse suppression ruling. The only issue he raised was that, during cross-examination, the prosecutor improperly impeached Mosby by asking him about details in his trial testimony that did not appear in the statement he had given to the police. The Appellate Division rejected this argument, and the New York Court of Appeals denied Mosby leave to appeal. *People v. Mosby,* 239 A.D.2d 938, 659 N.Y.S.2d 610, 610–11 (1997); 90 N.Y.2d 942, 664 N.Y.S.2d 760, 687 N.E.2d 657 (1997).

Mosby then filed an application for a writ of *coram nobis* seeking to vacate his conviction on the ground of ineffective assistance of appellate counsel for failure to raise several issues, including the trial court's suppression ruling. The Appellate Division summarily denied the application. *See People v. Mosby,* 676 N.Y.S.2d 390 (1998). Subsequently, Mosby filed a habeas corpus petition asserting the same claim as his *coram nobis* petition, which the district court denied. We granted a certificate of appealability limited to the issue of whether failure to raise the suppression issue on direct appeal constituted ineffective assistance of appellate counsel. . . .

DISCUSSION

. . . . To establish ineffective assistance under *Strickland,* Mosby must show (1) that his appellate counsel's "representation fell below an objective standard of reasonableness" and (2) that he was prejudiced by the deficient representation. *Strickland,* 466 U.S. at 687–88, 104 S.Ct. 2052. To demonstrate prejudice, he "must show that there is a reasonable probability that, but for counsel's unprofessional errors, the result of the proceeding would have been different." *Id.* at 694, 104 S.Ct. 2052. Because Mosby's ineffective assistance claim is based on counsel's failure to raise Fourth Amendment issues, he must also show "that his Fourth Amendment claim is meritorious and that there is a reasonable probability that the verdict would have been different absent the excludable evidence." *Kimmelman v. Morrison,* 477 U.S. 365, 375, 106 S.Ct. 2574, 91 L.Ed.2d 305 (1986); *see also Laaman v. United States,* 973 F.2d 107, 113 (2d Cir.1992).

Under § 2254(d)(1), our inquiry is not whether the Appellate Division's rejection of Mosby's ineffective assistance claim was incorrect, but whether, in light of *Strickland,* it was "objectively unreasonable." *See Sellan,* 261 F.3d at 315; *Williams,* 529 U.S. at 410, 120 S.Ct. 1495 (O'Connor, J. for the Court, Pt. II) ("an *unreasonable* application of federal law is different from an *incorrect* application"). To be "objectively unreasonable," a state court's application of clearly established federal law must involve "[s]ome increment of incorrectness beyond error." *Sellan,* 261 F.3d at 315 (internal quotation marks omitted).

II. Mosby's Suppression Claim

A. *Warrantless Arrest*

To determine whether the Fourth Amendment claim underlying Mosby's ineffective assistance argument has merit, we begin with the state trial court's ruling that Mosby did not have standing to challenge his warrantless home arrest. This ruling turned on the factual determination that Mosby did not live at 46 Costar, and thus had no legitimate expectation of privacy there. In *Payton v. New York*, the Supreme Court observed that nowhere "is the zone of privacy more clearly defined than . . . [in] an individual's home," and held that, absent exigent circumstances or consent, the police must obtain a warrant before entering a suspect's home to make a routine felony arrest. 445 U.S. 573, 589, 100 S.Ct. 1371, 63 L.Ed.2d 639 (1980).

In cases subsequent to *Payton*, the Supreme Court has held that the zone of Fourth Amendment protection against warrantless arrests, despite probable cause, can extend beyond one's own home: for example, even an overnight guest in the home of another may have a "legitimate expectation of privacy" sufficient to invoke the protection. *Minnesota v. Olson*, 495 U.S. 91, 100, 110 S.Ct. 1684, 109 L.Ed.2d 85 (1990).

In ruling on the suppression motion, the trial court acknowledged that both *Payton* and *Olson* applied, but held that Mosby was a transient presence at 46 Costar, who had no legitimate expectation of privacy there. The trial court relied mainly on the testimony of Ms. Pulley, the neighbor who identified Mosby as "Florida." According to the court, Ms. Pulley "did not say that [Mosby] was an overnight guest at the apartment on the evening before his arrest." The court also noted that there was no evidence that Mosby had keys to the house, received mail there, or paid rent, and that, on the night of his arrest, Mosby told police that he lived at a different address.

The trial court ignored or mischaracterized evidence in the record that supported Mosby's assertion that he had a legitimate expectation of privacy at 46 Costar. The arresting officers' report, for example, included Ms. Pulley's statement that Mosby had been staying at 46 Costar for the past two months. This was confirmed during the suppression hearing, both on cross-examination of an officer and by Ms. Pulley herself. Mosby's aunt also testified that Mosby had been living at 46 Costar Street at the time of the arrest and that he kept his belongings there.

Regardless of whether 46 Costar was his permanent residence, the record before the trial court established that, at the time of his arrest, Mosby had a legitimate expectation of privacy there, and, at the very least, his suppression claim presented a highly compelling issue for appeal. Applying *Payton* and its progeny to facts in the record, we believe that the trial court had no reasonable basis to conclude that Mosby's presence at 46 Costar was more fleeting than even that of an overnight houseguest. *Cf. United States v. Fields*, 113 F.3d 313, 320 (2d Cir.1997) ("[S]ociety recognizes as legitimate the expectation of privacy possessed by an overnight guest—even though he has at best a fleeting connection to his host's home."). Concluding that Mosby had standing, however, is only a preliminary step toward establishing that the Fourth Amendment claim underlying his petition is meritorious. Mosby still must demonstrate that the subsequent confession and photo identification should have been suppressed.

B. *Attenuation*

Evidence obtained from an unlawful search or seizure is generally subject to exclusion as "fruit of the poisonous tree." *See Wong Sun v. United States,* 371 U.S. 471, 484–85, 488, 83 S.Ct. 407, 9 L.Ed.2d 441 (1963); *Townes v. City of New York,* 176 F.3d 138, 145 (2d Cir.1999). However, "[e]ven in situations where the exclusionary rule is plainly applicable," the Supreme Court has "declined to adopt a *'per se* or "but for' rule" that would make inadmissible any evidence . . . which somehow came to light through a chain of causation that began with an illegal arrest." *United States v. Ceccolini,* 435 U.S. 268, 276, 98 S.Ct. 1054, 55 L.Ed.2d 268 (1978) (quoting *Brown v. Illinois,* 422 U.S. 590, 603, 95 S.Ct. 2254, 45 L.Ed.2d 416 (1975)); *see also Wong Sun,* 371 U.S. at 487–88, 83 S.Ct. 407. The relevant constitutional question is "whether the connection between the lawless conduct of the police and the discovery of the challenged evidence has become so attenuated as to dissipate the taint." *Ceccolini,* 435 U.S. at 273–74.[3]

The attenuation doctrine allows introduction of evidence obtained after an unlawful arrest when "the causal link" between a Fourth Amendment violation and a subsequent confession, identification, or other form of evidence is "so long or tortuous that suppression of the evidence is unlikely to have the effect of deterring future violations of the same type." *United States v. Singh,* 811 F.2d 758, 767 (2d Cir.1987) (Kearse, J. dissenting). In *Brown v. Illinois,* the Supreme Court enumerated four factors relevant to an attenuation analysis: (1) the administration of *Miranda* warnings; (2) "[t]he temporal proximity of the arrest and the confession"; (3) "the presence of intervening circumstances"; and (4) "particularly, the purpose and flagrancy of the official misconduct." 422 U.S. at 603–04, 95 S.Ct. 2254; *see Kaupp v. Texas,* 538 U.S. 626, 633, 123 S.Ct. 1843, 155 L.Ed.2d 814 (2003) (per curiam); *Snype,* 441 F.3d at 134.

As a matter of federal law, Mosby's Fourth Amendment claim would almost certainly fail before even reaching a full attenuation analysis. In *New York v. Harris,* 495 U.S. 14, 21, 110 S.Ct. 1640, 109 L.Ed.2d 13 (1990), the Supreme Court held that, "where the police have probable cause to arrest a suspect, the exclusionary rule does not bar the State's use of a statement made by the defendant outside of his home, even though the statement is taken after an arrest made in the home in violation of *Payton.*" Such a statement is "not the product of being in unlawful custody. Neither [is] it the fruit of having been arrested in the home rather

---

3. Because we ultimately decide this case on attenuation grounds, we do not reach the issue of whether the warrantless arrest was justified because of consent or exigent circumstances, *see Georgia v. Randolph,* 547 U.S. 103, ___, 126 S.Ct. 1515, 1518, 164 L.Ed.2d 208 (2006) (consent); *Fields,* 113 F.3d at 322–23 (exigent circumstances). We also do not consider whether the confession and photo identifications need not have been suppressed based on the independent source and inevitable discovery doctrines. *See United States v. Singh,* 811 F.2d 758, 767 (2d Cir.1987) (Kearse, J. dissenting).

than someplace else." *Id.* at 19, 110 S.Ct. 1640. As a result, the Court found that it was not necessary to apply the *Brown* factors, since attenuation analysis "is only appropriate where, as a threshold matter, courts determine that 'the challenged evidence is in some sense the product of illegal government activity.'" *Id.* (citation omitted); *cf. Hudson v. Michigan,* 547 U.S. 586, ___–___, 126 S.Ct. 2159, 2164–65, 165 L.Ed.2d 56 (2006).

Applying this logic here, Mosby's confession at the station house cannot be deemed a product, for Fourth Amendment purposes, of any *Payton* violation that may have occurred.[4] However, ineffective assistance of counsel in violation of the Sixth Amendment is not limited to failures to raise meritorious federal claims. Failure to raise a valid state law claim on appeal may also constitute ineffective assistance, so long as the relevant standards under *Strickland* are met. *See Claudio v. Scully,* 982 F.2d 798, 803 n. 5 (2d Cir.1992); *cf. Sellan,* 261 F.3d at 306.

The Supreme Court's decision in *New York v. Harris ("Harris II")* reversed a prior decision of the New York Court of Appeals, *People v. Harris,* 72 N.Y.2d 614, 620–21, 536 N.Y.S.2d 1, 532 N.E.2d 1229 (1988) *("Harris I")*, on federal constitutional grounds—holding that the evidence at issue in the case need not be suppressed. The Supreme Court remanded the case to the Court of Appeals, which reinstated the prior outcome. *People v. Harris,* 77 N.Y.2d 434, 568 N.Y.S.2d 702, 570 N.E.2d 1051 (1991) *("Harris III")*. *Harris I* had applied *Brown* to a custodial confession by a suspect who had been arrested in violation of *Payton,* and found that the confession was not sufficiently attenuated from the illegal arrest. Despite the Supreme Court's disposition of the Fourth Amendment issue, the Court of Appeals on remand applied the New York State Constitution's right to counsel to find that custodial statements obtained following an arrest in violation of *Payton* "must be suppressed unless the taint resulting from the violation has been attenuated." *Harris III,* 77 N.Y.2d at 437, 568 N.Y.S.2d 702, 570 N.E.2d 1051. Re-applying the *Brown* attenuation analysis it had utilized in *Harris I,* the court concluded that "the causal connection between the illegal arrest and defendant's statement in the police station was not sufficiently attenuated from the *Payton* wrong because of the temporal proximity of the arrest and the statement, the absence of intervening circumstances and the purpose and flagrancy of the police misconduct." *Id.* at 440–41, 568 N.Y.S.2d 702, 570 N.E.2d 1051.

Thus, while Mosby's Fourth Amendment suppression claim appears to lack merit under *Harris II,* on direct appeal he might have been able to demonstrate that his confession and the photo identifications should have been suppressed under New York state law on the strength of *Harris III.*

1.   Mosby's Confession

Indeed, both parties concede that *Harris III* governs our analysis of Mosby's confession. Accordingly, to evaluate attenuation in the context of a

---

4. Although *Harris II* involved a confession, the Court's holding has been applied to other forms of evidence as well, including identifications. *See United States v. Villa–Velazquez,* 282 F.3d 553, 556 (8th Cir.2002); *Martin v. Mitchell,* 280 F.3d 594, 607 (6th Cir.2002); *see also United States v. Crawford,* 372 F.3d 1048, 1056 (9th Cir.2004) ("After [*Harris II*], the presence of probable cause to arrest has proved dispositive when deciding whether the exclusionary rule applies to evidence or statements obtained after the defendant is placed in custody.").

custodial confession following a warrantless home arrest, we apply the *Brown* factors. *See supra; Harris III,* 77 N.Y.2d at 434. All four factors—administration of *Miranda* warnings, temporal proximity of the arrest and statement, intervening circumstances, and the purpose and flagrancy of the official misconduct—suggest that the link between Mosby's arrest and confession was sufficiently attenuated so as not to require suppression.

The police did not begin questioning Mosby about the Bloomingdale Street homicides until approximately five hours after his arrest and following *Miranda* warnings. New York courts have found custodial statements given after *Miranda* warnings and similar passages of time sufficiently attenuated to break the causal chain from an unlawful arrest. *See, e.g., People v. Divine,* 21 A.D.3d 767, 800 N.Y.S.2d 545, 545 (2005) (four hours); *People v. Santos,* 3 A.D.3d 317, 770 N.Y.S.2d 314, 314 (2004) (six hours); *People v. Russell,* 269 A.D.2d 771, 704 N.Y.S.2d 395, 395–96 (2000) (five hours); *People v. Folks,* 246 A.D.2d 433, 668 N.Y.S.2d 179, 180 (1998) (seven or eight hours).

In addition, there were significant intervening circumstances between the warrantless arrest and the confession—most notably, Ms. Pulley's spontaneous appearance and reference to Mosby as "Florida." While his arrest might, in some sense, have been a but-for cause of his encounter with Ms. Pulley outside the house, this is not sufficient to justify exclusion. *See Hudson,* 126 S.Ct. at 2164 ("[B]ut-for causality is only a necessary, not a sufficient, condition for suppression."); *Ceccolini,* 435 U.S. at 274, 98 S.Ct. 1054. Ms. Pulley's appearance, in other respects, was entirely unrelated to Mosby's warrantless arrest, and was not a "product" of it for Fourth Amendment purposes. *Cf. Harris II,* 495 U.S. at 19, 110 S.Ct. 1640. Moreover, her unexpected statement connected Mosby to an entirely different crime from the one that prompted his arrest. *See* 6 WAYNE R. LAFAVE, ET AL., FOURTH AMENDMENT: SEARCH & SEIZURE, § 11.4 ("[O]ne kind of 'intervening circumstances' is the post-arrest discovery of information connecting defendant with another crime.").

The final *Brown* factor, flagrancy and purpose of police conduct, reflects the policies of deterrence and judicial integrity underlying the exclusionary rule. *See Dunaway v. New York,* 442 U.S. 200, 217, 99 S.Ct. 2248, 60 L.Ed.2d 824 (1979) ("When there is a close causal connection between the illegal seizure and the confession, not only is exclusion of the evidence more likely to deter similar police misconduct in the future, but also use of the evidence is more likely to compromise the integrity of the courts."). In *Brown,* the Supreme Court found that the arrest at issue, "both in design and execution, was investigatory," and that the police had embarked on an "expedition for evidence in the hope that something might turn up." 422 U.S. at 605, 95 S.Ct. 2254. The Court concluded that the illegal arrest therefore "had a quality of purposefulness" that tilted the balance toward exclusion of the defendant's subsequent confession. *Id.; see also Dunaway,* 442 U.S. at 218, 99 S.Ct. 2248. Here, the police could not have been trying to arrest Mosby for the purpose of linking him to the Bloomingdale Street homicides, since they had no idea he was involved in those homicides until after he was arrested and moved outside the house.

The arrest, moreover, cannot be characterized as "investigatory," since the police had already witnessed Mosby's involvement in a drug transaction.

Suppressing Mosby's confession would be unlikely to deter future police misconduct, since the police—at the time they entered 46 Costar to make a routine drug arrest—could not have anticipated the fortuitous chain of events that ultimately connected Mosby to the homicides. This is especially true because the catalyst for those events was the appearance of Ms. Pulley and her spontaneous comment to the police. *Cf. Ceccolini,* 435 U.S. at 276, 98 S.Ct. 1054 ("The greater the willingness of the witness to freely testify, the greater the likelihood that he or she will be discovered by legal means and, concomitantly, the smaller the incentive to conduct an illegal search to discover the witness."). In addition, the social costs of suppressing Mosby's voluntary confession to two homicides would have been considerable. *See Hudson,* 126 S.Ct. at 2165 ("Quite apart from the requirement of unattenuated causation, the exclusionary rule has never been applied except where its deterrence benefits outweigh its substantial social costs.") (internal quotation marks omitted). For these reasons we conclude that the New York courts would in all probability have found that Mosby's custodial confession was too attenuated from his warrantless arrest to require suppression. Consequently, the failure to raise this issue did not prejudice Mosby within the meaning of *Strickland.*

2. Identification Evidence

The New York Court of Appeals has held that the New York State Constitution "does not require the suppression of evidence of a lineup identification made after an arrest based on probable cause but in violation of *Payton.*" *People v. Jones,* 2 N.Y.3d 235, 244–45, 778 N.Y.S.2d 133, 810 N.E.2d 415 (2004). The *Jones* court distinguished *Harris III,* emphasizing the difference "between the role of counsel at a custodial interrogation compared to a lineup," and noting that "the identifications of defendant were not the 'product of' the *Payton* violation, but of the police having probable cause to believe that defendant was the perpetrator." *Id.* at 243–44, 778 N.Y.S.2d 133, 810 N.E.2d 415 (internal citation omitted).

Both parties agree that *Jones* controls, or at least is highly relevant to our analysis of whether the photo identifications should have been suppressed. Although *Jones* was decided after Mosby's direct appeal, the Supreme Court has held that current law should be applied retroactively for purposes of determining whether a party has demonstrated prejudice under *Strickland's* second prong. *Lockhart v. Fretwell,* 506 U.S. 364, 372, 113 S.Ct. 838, 122 L.Ed.2d 180 (1993). *Compare United States v. Gaskin,* 364 F.3d 438, 469 (2d Cir.2004) ("In evaluating the performance prong of an ineffective assistance claim, we do not view the challenged conduct through the 'distorting' lens of hindsight but 'from counsel's perspective at the time.'" (quoting *Strickland,* 466 U.S. at 689, 104 S.Ct. 2052)), *with Mayo v. Henderson,* 13 F.3d 528, 534 (2d Cir.1994) ("The outcome determination, unlike the performance determination, may be made with the benefit of hindsight." (citing *Lockhart,* 506 U.S. at 372–73, 113 S.Ct. 838)).

Here the trial court found that the police had probable cause to arrest Mosby for selling drugs. The photo array later presented to witnesses of the

Bloomingdale Street homicides was not prompted by the officers' warrantless arrest of Mosby at 46 Costar, or by anything they discovered while inside the house, but rather by Ms. Pulley's identification of Mosby as "Florida" when she saw him on the street. Here, as in *Jones,* application of the exclusionary rule is not warranted, since "the requisite connection between the violation of a constitutional right and the derivative evidence is absent." 2 N.Y.3d at 242, 778 N.Y.S.2d 133, 810 N.E.2d 415 (internal quotation marks omitted).

III.   Ineffective Assistance of Counsel

The district court did not explicitly endorse the trial court's conclusion that Mosby lacked standing to assert a Fourth Amendment claim, but emphasized the trial court's finding that the police had probable cause to arrest Mosby. The district court held that because Mosby could not demonstrate both that it was objectively unreasonable for his appellate counsel not to pursue the suppression issue, and that, had he done so, there was a reasonable probability that the appeal would have succeeded, he failed to establish ineffective assistance of counsel under *Strickland.* We agree. . . .

For the foregoing reasons, we affirm the district court's denial of Mosby's petition for a writ of habeas corpus.

CHAPTER 14

AN OVERVIEW OF CRIMINAL PROCEDURE: ADJUDICATION

SECTION 1. STEPS IN THE PROCESS

The line between *ex parte* investigation by the executive authority and adversary determination of a concrete accusation by judicial process is, like many other lines drawn by law, both important and indistinct. Most criminal cases come to court following an arrest, and most arrests are made without prior judicial authorization. There are a great number of arrests on warrants, and a smaller but still significant number of cases in which accusation by way of indictment or information precedes the arrest or surrender of the accused.

Moreover, as discussed in Chapter 1, section 3, the procedures for adjudicating misdemeanor and felony cases vary somewhat. In addition, each jurisdiction within the United States has its own rules of procedure, and these in turn may vary, either *de jure* or *de facto*, from one courthouse to the next.

In this section we walk through the steps of the criminal process following a warrantless arrest. An arrest warrant or a pre-arrest indictment obviate the necessity of a judicial probable cause determination, and the filing of a formal charge, even if the suspect has not been to court, triggers the Sixth Amendment right to counsel during interrogations and corporeal identification procedures. The last point is less significant than it might appear. The Supreme Court has held that a valid *Miranda* waiver by a suspect under indictment waives both the *Miranda* right to counsel and the Sixth Amendment right to counsel during the interrogation, Patterson v. Illinois, 487 U.S. 285, 108 S.Ct. 2389, 101 L.Ed.2d 261 (1988), that the Sixth Amendment does not require the presence of counsel at post-indictment photographic identification proceedings, United States v. Ash, 413 U.S. 300, 93 S.Ct. 2568, 37 L.Ed.2d 619 (1973), and that the Sixth Amendment right to counsel is "offense specific", meaning that evidence obtained in violation of the defendant's Sixth Amendment rights on a pending charge is admissible on any *nonpending* charge the prosecution can prove. Texas v. Cobb, 532 U.S. 162, 121 S.Ct. 1335, 149 L.Ed.2d 321 (2001).

Let us focus, then, on the typical felony suspect arrested by police acting without a warrant.

Step 1: Booking and Lock–Up

At the station house the police will record the suspect's name, age and address. The standard booking questions are exempt from *Miranda* under

Pennsylvania v. Muniz, 496 U.S. 582, 110 S.Ct. 2638, 110 L.Ed.2d 528 (1990). The police will also make a record of the suspected offense, impound the suspect's personal property, photograph the suspect, and take fingerprints. The suspect is traditionally allowed one phone call before being taken to the lock-up.

In a misdemeanor case some jurisdictions authorize the police to release the arrestee either with a citation or on modest bail. Juvenile suspects may be transferred to a separate facility. Adult felony suspects will be jailed pending presentment in court.

Step 2: Police Screening

While the suspect is detained pending a court appearance, the police may decide not to proceed further. They might choose to do so because the arrest was made for social control purposes that have been satisfied, as in separating combatants in a brawl or protecting a drunk on a cold night; or because the arresting officer's superiors regard the case as either unjustified or properly dealt with by citation.

Step 3: Judicial Determination of Probable Cause to Arrest

When the suspect has been arrested without a warrant, the Fourth Amendment requires a prompt judicial determination of probable cause. County of Riverside v. McLaughlin, 500 U.S. 44, 111 S.Ct. 1661, 114 L.Ed.2d 49 (1991), establishes a presumption that detention without a judicial probable cause finding longer than 48 hours is unreasonable. But the *McLaughlin* 48–hour window is satisfied by a probable cause finding, either before arrest by way of a warrant, or after arrest by an *ex parte* determination in which the judge hears only a police officer reciting hearsay. When a judge *has found* probable cause to hold the suspect, the need for prompt presentment is governed by local rules and, in extreme cases, by due process. *Compare* Baker v. McCollan, 443 U.S. 137, 99 S.Ct. 2689, 61 L.Ed.2d 433 (1979) (3 day delay does not violate due process) *with* Hayes v. Faulkner County, Arkansas, 388 F.3d 669 (8th Cir. 2004) (state rule provides that arrested persons be brought before a judge "without unnecessary delay" but suspect arrested on a warrant was held 38 days before court appearance; court affirms civil judgment against sheriff for due process violation). In many jurisdictions the probable cause determination will be made together with the first appearance, but this is not inevitable. We therefore treat the first appearance as a distinct step, although in practice it may coincide with the judicial probable cause finding.

Step 4: Complaint, First Appearance, and Ruling on Pretrial Release

If the police elect to pursue the case, the arresting officer will file a complaint—a sworn statement either by the victim, a witness, or the officer—stating the suspected offense and the place and time of its commission. The suspect will then be brought to court to advise the suspect of his rights, determine his eligibility for appointed counsel, and—practically speaking, most importantly—to set conditions of pretrial release.

Neither the filing of a complaint, nor a first appearance, triggers the Sixth Amendment right to counsel. *See, e.g.,* United States v. Moore, 122 F.3d 1154 (8th Cir. 1997) (complaint does not trigger right to counsel); Ross v. State, 254 Ga. 22, 326 S.E.2d 194 (1985) (first appearance did not trigger right to counsel). In Rothgery v. Gillespie County, ___ U.S. ___, 128 S.Ct. 2578, 171 L.Ed.2d 366 (2008), the Court held that a court appearance at which the arrested person is apprised of the formal charge, and has his liberty restricted by condition of release or pretrial detention, even if no prosecuting attorney appears for the state. The *Rothgery* Court carefully avoided the issue of what proceedings subsequent to such an arraignment-type appearance qualify as "critical stages" requiring the appearance, or waiver, of defense counsel.

The reticence of the *Rothgery* opinion reflects an important practical consideration. Two factors explain the reluctance of courts to insist on counsel at this stage. First, counsel for the state has not entered an appearance or filed a charge. Second, the object of the first appearance is to set conditions of pretrial release, and insisting on an appearance by defense counsel might needlessly prolong the suspect's time in jail. If the suspect cannot satisfy those conditions, or can but they are unduly onerous, counsel can move to revise the pretrial release decision in the near future.

The Supreme Court has upheld the constitutionality of preventive pretrial detention when the government can adduce strong evidence of the suspect's propensity to commit additional serious crimes. United States v. Salerno, 481 U.S. 739, 107 S.Ct. 2095, 95 L.Ed.2d 697 (1987). That proof will not often be available, and many states do not authorize preventive detention at all. When the government does not seek preventive detention, the pretrial release decision is premised on the presumption of innocence. Until convicted after a fair trial, the suspect is a free person, and limitations on his liberty can be justified only as means to the end of ensuring his appearance at that trial.

The factors listed in the federal Bail Reform Act are representative of the considerations judges take into account in making pretrial release decisions:

Factors to be considered.—The judicial officer shall, in determining whether there are conditions of release that will reasonably assure the appearance of the person as required and the safety of any other person and the community, take into account the available information concerning—

(1) the nature and circumstances of the offense charged, including whether the offense is a crime of violence, a Federal crime of terrorism, or involves a minor victim or a controlled substance, firearm, explosive, or destructive device;

(2) the weight of the evidence against the person;

(3) the history and characteristics of the person, including—

    (A) the person's character, physical and mental condition, family ties, employment, financial resources, length of residence in the community, community ties, past conduct, history relating to drug or alcohol abuse, criminal history, and record concerning appearance at court proceedings; and

    (B) whether, at the time of the current offense or arrest, the person was on probation, on parole, or on other release pending trial, sentencing, appeal, or completion of sentence for an offense under Federal, State, or local law; and

(4) the nature and seriousness of the danger to any person or the community that would be posed by the person's release. In considering the conditions of release described in subsection (c)(1)(B)(xi) or (c)(1)(B)(xii) of this section, the judicial officer may upon his own motion, or shall upon the motion of the Government, conduct an inquiry into the source of the property to be designated for potential forfeiture or offered as collateral to secure a bond, and shall decline to accept the designation, or the use as collateral, of property that, because of its source, will not reasonably assure the appearance of the person as required.

18 U.S.C. § 3160(g).

The court may release the suspect on his own recognizance or set any number of conditions for release pending trial. The most common condition is the posting of a bond to be forfeited if the suspect misses a court date, but other conditions are common, such as avoiding confrontations with the victim of the charged offense, or cooperating with substance-abuse or mental-health treatment.

At one time the suspect who could not post the entire amount of the bond in cash had to choose between languishing in jail or paying a percentage of the bond amount to a professional bondsman, who would then post the full amount with the court, thereby acquiring a strong incentive to ensure the suspect's appearance, by means fair or foul. While the professional bondsman remains in many places, many jurisdictions now permit the suspect to post either a "recognizance bond," *i.e.,* an unsecured promise to pay the bond amount in case of nonappearance, or a "ten percent bond," whereby the suspect pays the court ten percent of the bond amount, the remainder unsecured but enforceable against the suspect in case of nonappearance. If the suspect appears, the ten percent payment is returned.

Although the federal Eighth Amendment and state counterparts provide a constitutional right against "excessive bail," bail is not "excessive" simply because the suspect cannot raise the money. In *Salerno* the Court quoted the following passage from Carlson v. Landon, 342 U.S. 524, 545–546, 72 S.Ct. 525, 96 L.Ed. 547 (1952):

> The bail clause was lifted with slight changes from the English Bill of Rights Act. In England that clause has never been thought to accord a right to bail in all cases, but merely to provide that bail shall not be excessive in those cases where it is proper to grant bail. When this clause was carried over into our Bill of Rights, nothing was said that indicated any different concept. The Eighth Amendment has not prevented Congress from defining the classes of cases in which bail shall be allowed in this country. Thus, in criminal cases bail is not compulsory where the punishment may be death. Indeed, the very language of the Amendment fails to say all arrests must be bailable.

Where state constitutions are textually more explicit, the courts agree that bail beyond the suspect's reach is not unconstitutional, so long as the amount is proportionate to the risk of flight.

Step 5: Prosecutorial Screening

Under the common law any person could initiate and conduct a criminal prosecution by complaining to the grand jury or to a justice of the peace. If the grand jury indicted, the person who had brought the complaint would be responsible for conducting the trial on behalf of the government. That system was replaced during the nineteenth century by the present system of professional prosecutors holding a monopoly, whether *de facto* or *de jure*, on the authority to make charging decisions.

The prosecutor must first decide whether to proceed with the case at all. If she decides to go forward, she must then decide what charges to bring. Typical incidents of criminal behavior often can support either a multiplicity of counts and a variety of charges. An ex-con who robs a bank at gunpoint might be charged with armed robbery plus being a felon in possession, armed robbery alone, simple robbery, or even theft. If more than one bank teller was threatened, each victim can support a separate count of any of these offenses. The Supreme Court's decision in *Bordenkircher v. Hays, supra* Chapter 12, illustrates prosecutorial leverage over charging decisions in a dramatic way. The advent of sentencing guidelines that constrain *judicial* discretion over sentencing, a development discussed in Chapter 12 as well, has heightened the influence of the prosecutor still further.

As a statistical matter prosecutors decline to prosecute a significant number of arrests (the usual figure is between thirty and fifty percent). There can be many reasons for such a decision but the most common one is doubt about the prosecution's ability to meet its burden of proof; often the government does not have a witness who can testify that D actually committed the crime, or has such a witness but believes it unlikely that the witness will actually testify against the accused at trial.

Step 6: Grand Jury Review or Preliminary Hearing

In the common-law system of criminal justice, which relied on private prosecution, the risk of unfounded charges was significant. The ancient institution of the grand jury—traditionally a body of 23 reputable citizens—guarded against abuse of the criminal process. Before being tried for felony, a prisoner had to be indicted by the grand jury. The clerk of the court would help the prosecutor draw up the charge, and the grand jury would hear witnesses in secret. If the grand jurors believed the prisoner to be guilty they would return the charge, now an indictment, to the court with the endorsement "a true bill." If the grand jurors rejected the charge, they would write "ignoramus" on the bill and the prisoner would be freed. The Fifth Amendment to the federal Constitution provides: "No person shall be held to answer for a capital, or otherwise infamous crime, unless on a presentment or indictment of a Grand Jury, except in cases arising in the land or naval forces, or in the Militia, when in actual service in time of War or public danger[.]"

The Supreme Court has held that "infamous" crimes include any punishable by a term of imprisonment in a state prison or penitentiary, with or without hard labor, In re Claasen, 140 U.S. 200, 11 S.Ct. 735, 35 L.Ed. 409 (1891), as well as those punishable in other institutions if the penalty includes hard labor. United States v. Moreland, 258 U.S. 433, 42 S.Ct. 368, 66 L.Ed. 700 (1922). The constitution thus requires grand jury indictment, rather than charging by *ex parte* information, in federal felony prosecutions. The grand jury provision of the Fifth Amendment, however, is not binding on the states as a matter of Fourteenth Amendment due process. Hurtado v. California, 110 U.S. 516 (1884). About half the states permit prosecutions for felonies to be initiated by information.

As society became more populous, more urban, and more mobile, grand jurors ceased to have first-hand knowledge of the accusers and the accused. They became dependent on information supplied to them by police and prosecutors. As a result the grand jury has ceased to play a meaningful role in confining prosecutorial discretion.

The grand jury remains an important institution for the investigation of suspected offenses. The grand jury is a creature of the court, and grand-jury subpoenas are backed by the court's contempt power. Testimony before the grand jury is subject to the oath and the penalty for perjury. The grand jury proceeds in secrecy, and prosecutors may offer either immunity or lenient plea bargains to conspirators who turn on their fellows. The right to counsel does not attach until indictment, and so even when an individual knows himself to be a target of the grand jury investigation, counsel is not allowed inside the grand jury room during testimony. The federal practice allows counsel for the witness to sit just outside, and permits the witness to leave the chamber to consult with counsel before answering individual questions. The witness enjoys the protections of the Fifth Amendment privilege against self-incrimination under Counselman v. Hitchcock, 142 U.S. 547, 12 S.Ct. 195, 35 L.Ed. 1110 (1892), but must claim the privilege in response to a question. Answering the question waives the privilege. The Supreme Court has held that witnesses are not entitled to a *Miranda* warning before testifying before the grand jury. *See* United States v. Mandujano, 425 U.S. 564, 96 S.Ct. 1768, 48 L.Ed.2d 212 (1976). Federal prosecutors provide a warning to targets of the investigation as a matter of practice.

The government can overcome a claim of Fifth Amendment privilege by giving the witness immunity from prosecution. An immunity order is issued by the trial court, but only the prosecutor can initiate the immunity process. The current federal immunity statute authorizes both transactional immunity (a guarantee that the witness will not be prosecuted for the events about which he will be questioned) or use immunity (a guarantee that if the government prosecutes the witness it will base its case on evidence exclusive of the immunized testimony and any evidence derived from the immunized testimony). The Supreme Court has upheld the statute against Fifth Amendment challenge. Kastigar v. United States, 406 U.S. 441, 92 S.Ct. 1653, 32 L.Ed.2d 212 (1972).

The rise of the professional prosecutor, and the decline of the grand jury's capacity for independent review, led many states in the nineteenth century to adopt a different approach to reviewing prosecutorial charging decisions. While many of these states retain the grand jury for investigative purposes, they eliminated its screening role, permitting the prosecutor to initiate felony cases (even capital cases) by filing an information. The information contains the same description of the charge as an indictment, but it is filed solely in the discretion of the prosecutor with no review by the grand jury. To guard against prosecutorial excesses, the information states provided for an adversary preliminary hearing in open court. If the evidence against the accused does not show probable cause to proceed to trial, the court is authorized to dismiss the information. Sometimes the preliminary hearing takes place after the complaint and before the information; if the evidence shows no offense the court will discharge the suspect, and if the evidence shows probable cause to try an offense, the court will hold the suspect to answer the charges the prosecutor will file shortly. Even when the preliminary hearing takes place *before* the filing of an indictment or an information, the adversary court appearance, against a lawyer for the state, triggers the Sixth Amendment right to counsel under Coleman v. Alabama, 399 U.S. 1, 90 S.Ct. 1999, 26 L.Ed.2d 387 (1970).

The rigor of the preliminary hearing process is greatly diluted by the standard rule that probable cause to proceed may be shown by hearsay. Thus a police officer may take the stand and swear that the victim or some other witness, either orally or by affidavit, has accused the defendant. Moreover, because credibility questions are for the jury *at trial*, no weight of contrary testimony for the defendant can negative probable cause once the prosecution has identified witnesses who say he committed the offense charged. Perhaps most importantly, the court's only role is to judge the plausiblity of the state's evidentiary case, *not* the wisdom of the prosecutor's charging decision. The preliminary hearing's practical functions therefore have become those of discovery and preserving testimony rather than a serious pretrial check on prosecutorial discretion.

The indictment is a formal charge filed in court. Its primary purpose is to put the accused on notice of the charge he must prepare to defend at trial. During the eighteenth century, courts were sympathetic to defense claims of hypertechnical defects in the charging instrument. The cruelty of the prevailing penalty structure (all common-law felonies, larceny included, were capital), and the limited scope of review for other types of errors, led judges to nullify the substantive law with what means they had. Each ruling that the indictment was defective meant that future indictments had to include additional allegations, making the charging instrument the length of a judicial opinion.

The impetus in the direction of insisting upon technical perfection in criminal pleading—of "trying the record" instead of the defendant—not only outlived the original underlying purpose of serving as a safeguard against over-severity of punishment, but was carried to its most absurd extremes after the need for such manipulation had vanished. An outstanding example of justice being completely submerged in the formalism of the proceedings, is State v. Campbell, decided in 1907.[1] In this case a conviction of rape was reversed because the concluding sentence of the indictment was "against the peace and dignity of State" whereas the court held it should have been "against the peace and dignity of *the* State." Another verdict of guilty was overturned because the indictment concluded "against the peace

---

1.   210 Mo. 202, 109 S.W. 706.

and dignity of the State of W. Virginia," the court being of the opinion that the word *West* should have been written in full.[2] Another classic, this time in the field of technical variance, is the case in which a conviction of stealing a pair of shoes was reversed because the proof established the larceny of two shoes both for the right foot and hence not a pair.[3] A fourth illustration of what should be avoided in the administration of criminal justice is the decision which upset a conviction under a statute making it grand larceny to steal any "cow or animal of the cow kind." The evidence had disclosed the theft of a steer, which was not "of the cow kind," said the appellate court, because a steer is a male.[4] These cases illustrate the absurd application of a strict standard for indictments.

On the other hand, under statutes passed long ago it became possible to eliminate much of the needless verbosity and repetition with which common-law indictments were burdened. In fact the common legislative command was to use "ordinary and concise language, without repetition, and in such a manner as to enable a person of common understanding to know what is intended." But while the purpose was to simplify the wording of indictments to some extent, no change was made in the general plan, which required the indictment to include both the accusation of the offense itself and the particulars of the offense. The unfortunate result of retaining the same general plan was the retention of a large portion of the verbosity and archaism of expression, because prosecuting attorneys preferred to follow the old precedents rather than to venture the use of simpler language which was authorized by the legislature, without any guiding suggestions.

Today the direction is towards simplified indictments. The most progressive step in this direction reduces the indictment to a very simple and direct statement of the charge against the defendant, and entitles him to move for a bill of particulars if he wishes more information. This motion will be granted if additional information is needed.[5] The indictment, however, must allege every element of the charged offense, and this includes any fact that, if proved, increases the maximum sentence imposed upon conviction. The indictment need not allege facts that trigger a minimum sentence within the upper limit prescribed by the statute defin-

---

2. Lemons v. State, 4 W.Va. 755 (1870).

3. State v. Harris, 3 Har. 559 (Del.1841).

4. Marsh v. State, 3 Ala.App. 80, 57 So. 387 (1912).

Where the defendant was charged with prostitution but the information failed to specify the type of "sexual conduct" defendant was alleged to have offered or agreed to or engaged in the information was defective and the case dismissed. Kass v. State, 642 S.W.2d 463 (Tex.Cr.App.1981).

5. "In a number of cases the Court has emphasized two of the protections which an indictment is intended to guarantee, reflected by two of the criteria by which the sufficiency of an indictment is to be measured. These criteria are, first, whether the indictment 'contains the elements of the offense intended to be charged, and sufficiently apprises the defendant of what he must be prepared to meet, and, secondly, in case any other proceedings are taken against him for a similar offence, whether the record shows with accuracy to what extent he may plead a former acquittal or conviction.'" Russell v. United States, 369 U.S. 749, 763–764, 82 S.Ct. 1038, 8 L.Ed.2d 240 (1962).

ing the offense. Harris v. United States, 536 U.S. 545, 122 S.Ct. 2406, 153 L.Ed.2d 524 (2002).

Not all jurisdictions have simplified the indictment but most have departed from earlier technicality,[6] and it is desirable that it should be done. The defendant gets more information from such a direct statement (plus a bill of particulars if there is any reason therefor) than he ever received from the most verbose indictment drawn in "legalistic" language. Further, liberalized discovery makes the detailed indictment unnecessary.

The following example illustrates modern pleading practice:

IN THE UNITED STATES DISTRICT COURT

FOR THE EASTERN DISTRICT OF PENNSYLVANIA

UNITED STATES OF AMERICA

v.

ALESSANDRO TRAMO, a/k/a "Alex":

BRUCE ARMSTRONG

WILLIAM ANDERSON

VIOLATIONS:

18 U.S.C. § 371 (conspiracy to commit arson—1 count)

18 U.S.C. § 844(i) (arson—1 count)

18 U.S.C. § 2 (aiding and abetting)

CRIMINAL NO.:_____

DATE FILED:_____

I N D I C T M E N T

COUNT ONE

THE GRAND JURY CHARGES THAT:

At all times material to the indictment:

1. Ben's Deli and Cafeteria ("Ben's Deli"), located at 103 East Bridge Street, Morrisville, Bucks County, Pennsylvania, was a restaurant and business engaged in interstate commerce.

2. Defendant ALESSANDRO TRAMO was the owner of Anthony 4 Pizzeria, located at 44 Bridge Street, Morrisville, in close proximity to Ben's Deli.

3. Between in or about the summer of 2000 and in or about mid-December 2000, in Morrisville, Bucks County, in the Eastern District of Pennsylvania, and elsewhere, defendants

ALESSANDRO TRAMO,

a/k/a "Alex,"

BRUCE ARMSTRONG,

---

6. "The specificity formerly held necessary to charge an offense is no longer required or sanctioned." Hence it was not necessary for the indictment to mention that the officer was a "human being." Donnelly v. United States, 185 F.2d 559 (10th Cir.1950).

and

WILLIAM ANDERSON

conspired and agreed together and with another person known to the grand jury to commit arson, that is, to damage and destroy, by means of fire, Ben's Deli and Cafeteria, located at 103 East Bridge Street, Morrisville, Bucks County, Pennsylvania, in violation of Title 18, United States Code, Section 844(i).

MANNER AND MEANS

4.   It was part of the conspiracy that defendants ALESSANDRO TRAMO, WILLIAM ANDERSON, BRUCE ARMSTRONG, and another person known to the grand jury, agreed to burn down Ben's Deli to eliminate competition to defendant TRAMO's pizzeria.

It was a further part of the conspiracy that:

5.   Defendant ALESSANDRO TRAMO solicited defendant WILLIAM ANDERSON to burn down Ben's Deli for $10,000.

6.   Defendant WILLIAM ANDERSON, in turn, solicited defendant BRUCE ARMSTRONG and another person known to the grand jury to burn down Ben's Deli.

7.   Defendant WILLIAM ANDERSON provided Molotov cocktails to defendant BRUCE ARMSTRONG and the other person to set the fire.

8.   Defendant BRUCE ARMSTRONG and the other person set fire to Ben's Deli with the Molotov cocktails.

9.   Defendant ALESSANDRO TRAMO paid money to defendant WILLIAM ANDERSON for arranging the fire at Ben's Deli and to pay defendant BRUCE ARMSTRONG and the other person for setting the fire.

OVERT ACTS

In furtherance of the conspiracy, defendants and a person known to the grand jury committed the following overt acts in the Eastern District of Pennsylvania and elsewhere:

1.   In or about the summer of 2000, defendant ALESSANDRO TRAMO met with defendant WILLIAM ANDERSON and offered to pay $10,000 to have Ben's Deli burned down.

2.   In or about September 2000, defendant WILLIAM ANDERSON met with defendant BRUCE ARMSTRONG and a person known to the grand jury. ARMSTRONG and the other person agreed with defendant ANDERSON to burn down Ben's Deli for money.

3.   On or about December 1, 2000, defendant WILLIAM ANDERSON supplied two Molotov cocktails to defendant BRUCE ARMSTRONG and the other person.

4.   On or about December 2, 2000, defendant BRUCE ARMSTRONG and the other person set fire to Ben's Deli by throwing the Molotov cocktails into the business through the window.

5.   On or about December 2, 2000, defendant ALESSANDRO TRAMO paid $2,000 to defendant WILLIAM ANDERSON for disbursement to defendant BRUCE ARMSTRONG and the other person.

6. On or about December 2, 2000, defendant WILLIAM ANDERSON paid $2,000 to defendant BRUCE ARMSTRONG and the other person.

7. In or about mid-December 2000, defendant ALESSANDRO TRAMO paid $1,000 to defendant WILLIAM ANDERSON for arranging the fire at Ben's Deli.

All in violation of Title 18, United States Code, Section 371.

COUNT TWO

THE GRAND JURY FURTHER CHARGES THAT:

1. Paragraphs 1 and 2 and 4 through 9 of Count One are realleged.

2. On or about December 2, 2000, in Morrisville, Bucks County, in the Eastern District of Pennsylvania, defendants

ALESSANDRO TRAMO,

a/k/a "Alex,"

BRUCE ARMSTRONG,

and

WILLIAM ANDERSON

maliciously damaged and destroyed, attempted to damage and destroy, and aided, abetted, and procured the malicious damage and attempted destruction of, by means of fire, a building and equipment contained therein, used in interstate commerce and in activities affecting interstate commerce, that is, Ben's Deli and Cafeteria, located at 103 East Bridge Street, Morrisville, Bucks County, Pennsylvania. In violation of Title 18, United States Code, Section 844(i) and Section 2.

A TRUE BILL:

_____

FOREPERSON

_____

PATRICK L. MEEHAN

United States Attorney

Step 7: Arraignment and Plea

The arraignment is a court proceeding at which the accused is read and given a copy of the indictment and called upon to plead to the charge. A plea of not guilty may be changed to a plea of guilty or no contest subsequently, so unless a plea agreement has been reached at this point, a guilty plea is unusual.

Plea negotiations can take place at any stage of the process, whether before indictment or during trial itself. The more defense counsel can learn about the case through the discovery process, the more thoughtfully counsel can evaluate the case and advocate the client's interests with the prosecutor. On the other hand the further the case goes, the more it costs the government and the less the government stands to gain from a plea.

Defense counsel can of course learn about the case from the client (not always a reliable source). Quite apart from legally mandatory discovery, some prosecutors' offices maintain "open file" policies whereby defense counsel has access to police reports and witness statements. Defense access to the evidence facilitates plea bargaining, especially in the not uncommon case in which the defendant misrepresents the facts to defense counsel.

Plea bargaining involves two distinct exchanges between prosecutors and defense lawyers. One is a naked exchange of concessions for mutual advantage. Defense counsel can offer to spare the prosecutor the resources required to take the case to trial, as well as the risk of an acquittal. The defense may also be able to offer the prosecutor information and/or testimony about crimes by others. The prosecutor, in return, can reduce the charges or promise to make a generous sentence recommendation. By evidentiary rule (e.g., FRE 410), statements made in plea discussions with a prosecuting attorney are inadmissible at trial.

The second aspect of plea discussions does not really involve bargaining in the sense of a *quid pro quo*. Defense counsel simply argues that the prosecutor should exercise her discretion more leniently, either because the evidence does not support the charges or because the charges, although factually justified, are disproportionate to the guilt of the particular defendant. Most defendants whose cases are not dismissed by the court end up pleading guilty. Plea discussions with the prosecutor are, for practical purposes, the defendant's actual opportunity to be heard before sentencing.

Criminal procedure rules do not formalize the place, time, or content of plea discussions. They do, however, speak to some features of the process. For example, FRCP 11 *prohibits* judicial participation in plea discussions. It also identifies the possible pleas: not guilty, guilty, *nolo contendere*, and the conditional guilty plea. The no-contest plea is attractive to defendants who do not wish to admit guilt in a way that might expose them to collateral civil liabilities. The conditional guilty plea admits guilt but reserves the right to challenge on appeal the denial of a pretrial motion, typically a motion to suppress evidence.

Rule 11 also lays out the procedure for receiving a guilty plea:

(b) Considering and Accepting a Guilty or Nolo Contendere Plea.

(1) *Advising and Questioning the Defendant.*

Before the court accepts a plea of guilty or nolo contendere, the defendant may be placed under oath, and the court must address the defendant personally in open court. During this address, the court must inform the defendant of, and determine that the defendant understands, the following:

(A) the government's right, in a prosecution for perjury or false statement, to use against the defendant any statement that the defendant gives under oath;

(B) the right to plead not guilty, or having already so pleaded, to persist in that plea;

(C) the right to a jury trial;

(D) the right to be represented by counsel—and if necessary have the court appoint counsel—at trial and at every other stage of the proceeding;

(E) the right at trial to confront and cross-examine adverse witnesses, to be protected from compelled self-incrimination, to testify and present evidence, and to compel the attendance of witnesses;

(F) the defendant's waiver of these trial rights if the court accepts a plea of guilty or nolo contendere;

(G) the nature of each charge to which the defendant is pleading;

(H) any maximum possible penalty, including imprisonment, fine, and term of supervised release;

(I) any mandatory minimum penalty;

(J) any applicable forfeiture;

(K) the court's authority to order restitution;

(L) the court's obligation to impose a special assessment;

(M) the court's obligation to apply the Sentencing Guidelines, and the court's discretion to depart from those guidelines under some circumstances; and

(N) the terms of any plea-agreement provision waiving the right to appeal or to collaterally attack the sentence.

(2) *Ensuring That a Plea Is Voluntary.*

Before accepting a plea of guilty or nolo contendere, the court must address the defendant personally in open court and determine that the plea is voluntary and did not result from force, threats, or promises (other than promises in a plea agreement).

(3) *Determining the Factual Basis for a Plea.*

Before entering judgment on a guilty plea, the court must determine that there is a factual basis for the plea.

(c) Plea Agreement Procedure.

(1) *In General.*

An attorney for the government and the defendant's attorney, or the defendant when proceeding pro se, may discuss and reach a plea agreement. The court must not participate in these discussions. If the defendant pleads guilty or nolo contendere to either a charged offense or a lesser or related offense, the plea agreement may specify that an attorney for the government will:

(A) not bring, or will move to dismiss, other charges;

(B) recommend, or agree not to oppose the defendant's request, that a particular sentence or sentencing range is appropriate or that a particular provision of the Sentencing Guidelines, or policy statement, or sentencing factor does or does not apply (such a recommendation or request does not bind the court); or

(C) agree that a specific sentence or sentencing range is the appropriate disposition of the case, or that a particular provision of the Sentencing Guidelines, or policy statement, or sentencing factor does or does not apply (such a recommendation or request binds the court once the court accepts the plea agreement).

(2) *Disclosing a Plea Agreement.*

The parties must disclose the plea agreement in open court when the plea is offered, unless the court for good cause allows the parties to disclose the plea agreement in camera.

(3) *Judicial Consideration of a Plea Agreement.*

(A) To the extent the plea agreement is of the type specified in Rule 11(c)(1)(A) or (C), the court may accept the agreement, reject it, or defer a decision until the court has reviewed the presentence report.

(B) To the extent the plea agreement is of the type specified in Rule 11(c)(1)(B), the court must advise the defendant that the defendant has no right to withdraw the plea if the court does not follow the recommendation or request.

(4) *Accepting a Plea Agreement.*

If the court accepts the plea agreement, it must inform the defendant that to the extent the plea agreement is of the type specified in Rule 11(c)(1)(A) or (C), the agreed disposition will be included in the judgment.

(5) *Rejecting a Plea Agreement.*

If the court rejects a plea agreement containing provisions of the type specified in Rule 11(c)(1)(A) or (C), the court must do the following on the record and in open court (or, for good cause, in camera):

(A) inform the parties that the court rejects the plea agreement;

(B) advise the defendant personally that the court is not required to follow the plea agreement and give the defendant an opportunity to withdraw the plea; and

(C) advise the defendant personally that if the plea is not withdrawn, the court may dispose of the case less favorably toward the defendant than the plea agreement contemplated.

Frequently, disputes arise over whether the parties have *kept* a bargain once made. For example, the defendant may have agreed to cooperate with the government in the case against a coconspirator, and then not testify to the government's satisfaction at the coconspirator's trial. Santobello v. New York, 404 U.S. 257, 92 S.Ct. 495, 30 L.Ed.2d 427 (1971) held that when the government fails to perform its obligations, the constitution requires the state to either specifically perform its undertaking or permit the defendant to vacate his plea. *Santobello* has spawned a significant body of law concerning contract-type issues of interpreting plea agreements and remedying nonperformance. *See, e.g.,* Ricketts v. Adamson, 483 U.S. 1, 107 S.Ct. 2680, 97 L.Ed.2d 1 (1987) (D agreed to testify against accomplices and entered guilty plea to second-degree murder; D testified at trial of accomplices, who were convicted; the convictions of the accomplices were reversed on appeal; D refused to testify at the retrial; *held,* D's failure to perform justified the state in vacating the guilty plea and charging D with first-degree murder).

Step 8: Discovery

Discovery in criminal cases is more limited than in civil cases. The defendant enjoys the privilege against self-incrimination and therefore may not be questioned in a post-indictment judicial proceeding before trial. Some criminal defendants are also not above threatening, bribing, or even killing adverse witnesses. Courts and legislatures have feared that criminal discovery could become a one-way street for the defense, as well as a process that both through the burden of required pretrial testimony by witnesses and the assistance discovery might lend to witness tampering.

In the federal practice, FRCP 16(A) requires the government to disclose, upon request, any oral, written, or recorded statement of the defendant's, as well as any grand jury testimony given by the defendant. The rule also requires the government to disclose, upon request, the defendant's criminal record; and to make available for inspection physical evidence, and for inspection and copying, documents and lab reports. If the defendant requests disclosure of physical evidence or documents that the government expects to use at trial, Rule 16(B) obligates the defense to disclose material corresponding to the material it has requested. The Jencks Act, 18 U.S.C. § 3500, provides that the government need not disclose the grand jury transcripts of government witnesses until after they have testified at the trial.

Many states authorize somewhat broader defense discovery, as recommended by the American Bar Association's *Standards for Criminal Justice—Discovery* (3d ed. 1996). State provisions vary widely; the most contentious issue is prosecution disclosure of material the prosecution does *not* expect to use at trial, such as police reports or the identity of witnesses unsympathetic to the prosecution.

Many states require the prosecution to provide the names and addresses of the witnesses it intends to call at trial. Typically these jurisdictions impose a reciprocal obligation on the defense, and the Supreme Court has rejected constitutional challenges to such systems. *See* Taylor v. Illinois, 484 U.S. 400, 108 S.Ct. 646, 98 L.Ed.2d 798 (1988) (holding that, although a continuance is the preferred remedy for failure to list witness before trial, exclusion of unlisted defense witness's testimony is not *per se* unconstitutional); Williams v. Florida, 399 U.S. 78, 90 S.Ct. 1893, 26 L.Ed.2d 446 (1970) (rejecting self-incrimination challenge to state rule requiring pretrial disclosure of defense alibi witnesses). Moreover, most jurisdictions require advance notice of the intent to rely on certain defenses requiring unusual pretrial preparation by the government; alibi and insanity are the prime examples. *Williams* upheld prosecution discovery of evidence the defense intends to present at trial because the defense is only required to disclose evidence it plans on disclosing at trial anyway. Prosecution discovery therefore alters the timing of disclosure, but does not compel the defense to turn over any information it isn't planning on introducing at trial.

Under Brady v. Maryland, 373 U.S. 83, 83 S.Ct. 1194, 10 L.Ed.2d 215 (1963), due process requires the prosecution to disclose exculpatory evidence that is both material and requested by the defense. In United States v. Bagley, 473 U.S. 667, 105 S.Ct. 3375, 87 L.Ed.2d 481 (1985), the Court defined materiality by reference to the test for prejudice under *Strickland v. Washington*: "The evidence is material only if there is a reasonable probability that, had the evidence been disclosed to the defense, the result of the proceeding would have been different. A reasonable probability is a probability sufficient to undermine confidence in the outcome." The standard is said to be more easily met when the defense has made a more specific request for the material. Subsequent cases have fractured the Court without producing generalizable standards. *See, e.g.,* Banks v. Dretke, 540 U.S. 668, 124 S.Ct. 1256, 157 L.Ed.2d 1166 (2004).

Step 9: Pretrial Motions

Various issues may (and often must be) raised before trial by way of motion. These include motions to dismiss the charge, for a bill of particulars, for a change of venue, for a severance of parties or counts, to suppress evidence, and to rule *in limine* on the admissibility of evidence such as hearsay or prior crimes. When the facts bearing on a motion are disputed, the court will hold a hearing, typically using the preponderance of the evidence standard. *See* United States v. Matlock, 415 U.S. 164, 94 S.Ct. 988, 39 L.Ed.2d 242 (1974) (preponderance standard governs disputed facts pertinent to motion to suppress evidence on Fourth Amendment grounds).

Step 10: Trial

Article III and the Sixth Amendment guarantee the right to trial by jury. The defendant may waive this right but has no corresponding right to demand, over government objection, a bench trial. *See* Singer v. United States, 380 U.S. 24, 85 S.Ct. 783, 13 L.Ed.2d 630 (1965).

Trial by jury involves these discrete steps: (1) selecting the jury, (2) opening statements, (3) presentation of evidence, (4) the (optional but typical) defense motion for a directed verdict, (5) closing arguments, (6) the court's instructions to the jury, and, finally, (7) jury deliberations and the return of the verdict.

Jury selection procedures vary widely in their details but always involve questioning of prospective jurors (by the court, by counsel or by both, with or without a pretrial written questionaire), challenges for cause, and peremptory challenges. FRCP 24 is illustrative:

Rule 24. Trial Jurors

(a) Examination.

(1) *In General.*

The court may examine prospective jurors or may permit the attorneys for the parties to do so.

(2) *Court Examination.*

If the court examines the jurors, it must permit the attorneys for the parties to:

> (A) ask further questions that the court considers proper; or

> (B) submit further questions that the court may ask if it considers them proper.

(b) Peremptory Challenges.

Each side is entitled to the number of peremptory challenges to prospective jurors specified below. The court may allow additional peremptory challenges to multiple defendants, and may allow the defendants to exercise those challenges separately or jointly.

(1) *Capital Case.*

Each side has 20 peremptory challenges when the government seeks the death penalty.

(2) *Other Felony Case.*

The government has 6 peremptory challenges and the defendant or defendants jointly have 10 peremptory challenges when the defendant is charged with a crime punishable by imprisonment of more than one year.

(3) *Misdemeanor Case.*

Each side has 3 peremptory challenges when the defendant is charged with a crime punishable by fine, imprisonment of one year or less, or both.

(c) Alternate Jurors.

(1) *In General.*

The court may impanel up to 6 alternate jurors to replace any jurors who are unable to perform or who are disqualified from performing their duties.

(2) *Procedure.*

(A) Alternate jurors must have the same qualifications and be selected and sworn in the same manner as any other juror.

(B) Alternate jurors replace jurors in the same sequence in which the alternates were selected. An alternate juror who replaces a juror has the same authority as the other jurors.

(3) *Retaining Alternate Jurors.*

The court may retain alternate jurors after the jury retires to deliberate. The court must ensure that a retained alternate does not discuss the case with anyone until that alternate replaces a juror or is discharged. If an alternate replaces a juror after deliberations have begun, the court must instruct the jury to begin its deliberations anew.

(4) *Peremptory Challenges.*

Each side is entitled to the number of additional peremptory challenges to prospective alternate jurors specified below. These additional challenges may be used only to remove alternate jurors.

(A) *One or Two Alternates.*

One additional peremptory challenge is permitted when one or two alternates are impaneled.

(B) *Three or Four Alternates.*

Two additional peremptory challenges are permitted when three or four alternates are impaneled.

(C) *Five or Six Alternates.*

Three additional peremptory challenges are permitted when five or six alternates are impaneled.

The defendant has third-party standing to challenge the selection of the jury on grounds that the selection process violated the equal-protection rights of potential jurors. *See, e.g.,* Powers v. Ohio, 499 U.S. 400, 111 S.Ct. 1364, 113 L.Ed.2d 411 (1991) (white defendant has standing to raise equal-protection challenge to prosecution's use of peremptory challenges to excuse black members of venire).

Trial evidence is a law school course unto itself. Issues pertaining to the court's instructions appear throughout the treatment of the substantive criminal law. *See, e.g., Robinson v. California,* Chapter 1, *supra; State v. Dumlao,* Chapter 2, *supra.* We consider constitutional limits on evidence law in *Davis v. Washington, infra.*

Step 11: Sentencing

Sentencing, like Evidence, can be a law school course unto itself. Chapter 11, *supra,* offers an overview of the issues. In particular, *United States v. McCaskill,* Chapter 11, *supra,* reviews the procedural aspects of the sentencing hearing.

Step 12: Appeal

The common law made no provision for appellate review of criminal convictions in felony cases. The unjustly convicted could move in arrest of judgment on limited grounds, or petition the Crown for a pardon. Congress did not authorize review of federal criminal convictions by writ of error, the forerunner of the modern appeal, until 1879. Given this history, the Supreme Court has assumed that there is no constitutional right to appellate review. *See, e.g.,* Halbert v. Michigan, 545 U.S. 605, 125 S.Ct. 2582, 2586, 162 L.Ed.2d 552 (2005) ("The Federal Constitution imposes on the States no obligation to provide appellate review of criminal convictions.")

The Court has held, however, that when statutes do provide for an appeal, the federal constitution requires appointment of counsel for the indigent during the first appeal to which the defendant has an automatic right. *See* Douglas v. California, 372 U.S. 353, 83 S.Ct. 814, 9 L.Ed.2d 811 (1963). This right does not extend to discretionary review of an appellate court's ruling to the state Supreme Court, Ross v. Moffitt, 417 U.S. 600, 94 S.Ct. 2437, 41 L.Ed.2d 341 (1974), or to collateral attack proceedings, Pennsylvania v. Finley, 481 U.S. 551, 107 S.Ct. 1990, 95 L.Ed.2d 539 (1987).

The basis for this right, and the limitations thereon, is not the Sixth Amendment, but the equal protection, or perhaps due process, clause of the Fourteenth Amendment. As the Court stated in *Halbert, supra,* at 2587:

Cases on appeal barriers encountered by persons unable to pay their own way, we have observed, "cannot be resolved by resort to easy slogans or pigeonhole analysis." *M.L.B. v. S.L.J.,* 519 U.S. 102, 120, 117 S.Ct. 555, 136 L.Ed.2d 473 (1996) (internal quotation marks omitted). Our decisions in point reflect "both equal protection and due process concerns." *Ibid.* "The equal protection concern relates to the legitimacy of fencing out would-be appellants based solely on their inability to pay core costs," while "[t]he due process concern homes in on the essential fairness of the state-ordered proceedings." *Ibid.;* see also *Evitts v. Lucey,* 469 U.S. 387, 405, 105 S.Ct. 830, 83 L.Ed.2d 821 (1985).

Two considerations were key to our decision in *Douglas* that a State is required to appoint counsel for an indigent defendant's first-tier appeal as of right. First, such an appeal entails an adjudication on the "merits." 372 U.S., at 357, 83 S.Ct. 814. Second, first-tier review differs from subsequent appellate stages "at which the claims have once been presented by [appellate counsel] and passed upon by an appellate court." *Id.,* at 356, 83 S.Ct. 814. Under the California system at issue in *Douglas,* the first-tier appellate court independently examined the record to determine whether to appoint counsel. *Id.,* at 355, 83 S.Ct. 814. When a defendant able to retain counsel pursued an appeal, the *Douglas* Court observed, "the appellate court passe[d] on the merits of [the] case only after having the full benefit of written briefs and oral argument by counsel." *Id.,* at 356, 83 S.Ct. 814,. In contrast, when a poor person appealed, "the appellate court [wa]s forced to prejudge the merits [of the case] before it c[ould] even determine whether counsel should be provided." *Ibid.*

In *Ross,* we explained why the rationale of *Douglas* did not extend to the appointment of counsel for an indigent seeking to pursue a second-tier discretionary appeal to the North Carolina Supreme Court or, thereafter, certiorari review in this Court. The North Carolina Supreme Court, in common with this Court we perceived, does not sit as an error-correction instance. 417 U.S., at 615, 94 S.Ct. 2437. Principal criteria for state high court review, we noted, included "whether the subject matter of the appeal has significant public interest, whether the cause involves legal principles of major significance to the jurisprudence of the State, [and] whether the decision below is in probable conflict" with the court's precedent. *Ibid.* (internal quotation marks omitted). Further, we pointed out, a defendant who had already benefited from counsel's aid in a first-tier appeal as of right would have, "at the very least, a transcript or other record of trial proceedings, a brief on his behalf in the Court of Appeals setting forth his claims of error, and in many cases an opinion by the Court of Appeals disposing of his case." *Ibid.*

With modest modifications, defense appeals in criminal cases are subject to the familiar principles applicable in civil cases—the final judgment rule and its exceptions for collateral matters and supervisory writs, the requirement of contemporaneous objection and the plain error exception thereto, and the harmless error rule.

In criminal cases the harmless error rule is modified considerably from the civil version. Because the burden of proof on the prosecution is beyond-a-reasonable-doubt, the admission or exclusion of evidence can prejudice the criminal defendant more easily than a civil litigant. The nature of the criminal defendant's claims can also alter the analysis. In some types of cases, such as the actual or constructive denial of defense counsel, prejudice is presumed and reversal is automatic. Certain errors described as "structural"—i.e., a legal defect in the trial tribunal itself, such as improper venue or a grand jury selected in violation of the equal protection clause also call for automatic reversal.

On the other hand, some defense claims on appeal, such as those of ineffective assistance of trial counsel, or failure to disclose *Brady* material, can be established only by a showing of prejudice. *See* Strickland v. Washington, 466 U.S. 668, 104 S.Ct. 2052, 80 L.Ed.2d 674 (1984); United States v. Bagley, 473 U.S. 667, 105 S.Ct. 3375, 87 L.Ed.2d 481 (1985). The *Strickland–Bagley* showing of prejudice does not require the government to prove the error harmless beyond reasonable doubt, or the defense to prove that the outcome below was more likely than not to have been more favorable to the accused. Instead, this in-between standard imposes on the defense the burden of showing a substantial likelihood that the outcome would have differed, alternately defined as a showing that casts doubt on the reliability of the outcome below.

When constitutional error is not subject to the rule of automatic reversal or to a built-in standard of prejudice, the default standard is given by Chapman v. California, 386 U.S. 18, 87 S.Ct. 824, 17 L.Ed.2d 705 (1967). *Chapman* requires that, once the defense establishes constitutional error, the government can avoid reversal only by persuading the appellate court beyond a reasonable doubt that the error was harmless. The cases as a whole are less than fully satisfying; uncertainty and sharp divisions among the justices continue. *See, e.g.,* Neder v. United States, 527 U.S. 1, 119 S.Ct. 1827, 144 L.Ed.2d 35 (1999) (*Chapman* standard, not automatic reversal, applies to failure to instruct on essential element of charged offense; dissent argues denial of trial by jury on omitted element can never be harmless).

The double jeopardy clause does not bar the retrial of a defendant following the reversal of his conviction on appeal. Ball v. United States, 163 U.S. 662, 672, 16 S.Ct. 1192, 41 L.Ed. 300 (1896). For a further discussion of the "continuing jeopardy" theory and its implications, see United States v. Schinault, *supra* Chapter 12.

Step 13: Collateral Attack Proceedings

The "Great Writ" of habeas corpus probably originated as a device for securing the attendance of witnesses. It evolved in English law into a judicial process to test the legality of forcible detention. The petition asks the court to issue the writ, naming as the respondent the person holding the prisoner in custody. The writ orders the custodian to release the prisoner or to answer the writ with a legal justification for the detention.

The classic role of habeas corpus proceedings was to force the government to initiate the criminal process or release the prisoner. It was a good answer to the writ either that the prisoner faced a pending charge and had not made bail, or that the prisoner had been sentenced to prison after being convicted at trial. Habeas corpus could not be substituted for a writ of error. But if the trial court lacked jurisdiction to try the prisoner, or imposed a sentence not authorized by law, the judgment or sentence could be voided by way of habeas.

Article 1, § of the Constitution provides that "The Privilege of the Writ of Habeas Corpus shall not be suspended, unless when in Cases of Rebellion or Invasion the public Safety may require it." The Supreme Court has held that a statute will not be read as an implied suspension; congressional intent to suspend the writ must be unmistakably clear. *See* INS v. St. Cyr, 533 U.S. 289, 121 S.Ct. 2271, 150 L.Ed.2d 347 (2001).

During the nineteenth century habeas began to take on the role of an error-correction procedure akin to an appeal. The otherwise limited avenues of appellate review of criminal convictions then available led some courts to take an expansive view of when the trial court lost jurisdiction. Following the Civil War, congressional suspicions about the administration of justice in the states of the old confederacy led to the adoption of a statute now codified at 28 U.S.C. § 2254:

> The Supreme Court, a Justice thereof, a circuit judge, or a district court shall entertain an application for a writ of habeas corpus in behalf of a person in custody pursuant to the judgment of a State court only on the ground that he is in custody in violation of the Constitution or laws or treaties of the United States.

Over the years the Supreme Court expanded the notion of errors that oust the trial court of jurisdiction, eventually equating *any* constitutional error as cognizable on federal habeas. In Stone v. Powell, 428 U.S. 465, 96 S.Ct. 3037, 49 L.Ed.2d 1067 (1976), the Court held that state prisoners may not relitigate Fourth Amendment suppression motions on federal habeas, but subsequent cases have reaffirmed the cognizability of other claims, including claims that ineffective assistance of counsel caused the loss of a meritorious suppression motion, Kimmelman v. Morrison, 477 U.S. 365, 106 S.Ct. 2574, 91 L.Ed.2d 305 (1986), and *Miranda* claims, Withrow v. Williams, 507 U.S. 680, 113 S.Ct. 1745, 123 L.Ed.2d 407 (1993).

The use of habeas corpus to review criminal convictions has, however, been limited by both Court decisions and by the Ant–Terrorism and Effective Death Penalty Act of 1996. The three most important limitations are the exhaustion of remedies requirement, the procedural default doctrine, and the principle of deference to the state courts. The current statute, 28 U.S.C. § 2254(b)(1) requires the petitioner to exhaust state remedies, *i.e.,* pursue the appellate process through the state courts, including state post-conviction remedies. *See* O'Sullivan v. Boerckel, 526 U.S. 838, 119 S.Ct. 1728, 144 L.Ed.2d 1 (1999).

The Court explained the procedural default doctrine most recently in House v. Bell, 547 U.S. 518, 126 S.Ct. 2064, 165 L.Ed.2d 1 (2006):

> As a general rule, claims forfeited under state law may support federal habeas relief only if the prisoner demonstrates cause for the default and prejudice from the asserted error. See *Murray v. Carrier,* 477 U.S. 478, 485, 106 S.Ct. 2639, 91 L.Ed.2d 397 (1986); *Engle v. Isaac,* 456 U.S. 107, 129, 102 S.Ct. 1558, 71 L.Ed.2d 783 (1982); *Wainwright v. Sykes,* 433 U.S. 72, 87, 97 S.Ct. 2497, 53 L.Ed.2d 594 (1977). The rule is based on the comity and respect that must be accorded to state-court judgments. See, *e.g., Engle, supra,* at 126–129, 102 S.Ct. 1558; *Wainwright, supra,* at 89–90, 97 S.Ct. 2497. The bar is not, however,

unqualified. In an effort to "balance the societal interests in finality, comity, and conservation of scarce judicial resources with the individual interest in justice that arises in the extraordinary case," *Schlup,* 513 U.S., at 324, 115 S.Ct. 851, the Court has recognized a miscarriage-of-justice exception. " '[I]n appropriate cases,' " the Court has said, "the principles of comity and finality that inform the concepts of cause and prejudice 'must yield to the imperative of correcting a fundamentally unjust incarceration,' " *Carrier, supra,* at 495, 106 S.Ct. 2639, (quoting *Engle, supra,* at 135, 102 S.Ct. 1558).

Thus before the federal court will hear the prisoner's claim, the petitioner must show that the claim was presented to the state courts or explain why it was not and how the failure to press it in state court was prejudicial.

If the petitioner's claim was considered and rejected by the state courts, 28 U.S.C. § 2254(d) provides that:

> An application for a writ of habeas corpus on behalf of a person in custody pursuant to the judgment of a State court shall not be granted with respect to any claim that was adjudicated on the merits in State court proceedings unless the adjudication of the claim
>
> **(1)** resulted in a decision that was contrary to, or involved an unreasonable application of, clearly established Federal law, as determined by the Supreme Court of the United States; or
>
> **(2)** resulted in a decision that was based on an unreasonable determination of the facts in light of the evidence presented in the State court proceeding.

Put together, exhaustion, procedural default, and deference mean that the petitioner must first present the claim to the state courts and, if the state courts reject it, persuade the federal court that the state courts were not just wrong, but clearly wrong. The standard is demanding, but occasionally satisfied. *See* Wiggins v. Smith, 539 U.S. 510, 123 S.Ct. 2527, 156 L.Ed.2d 471 (2003) (state court unreasonably rejected petitioner's claim of ineffective assistance of counsel).

Controversy continues over the Great Writ's role in the war on terror. In Hamdan v. Rumsfeld, 548 U.S. 557, 126 S.Ct. 2749, 165 L.Ed.2d 723 (2006), a majority of the Court refused to apply a habeas-blocking provision of the Detainee Treatment Act of 2005 to the case at bar, as that case had been pending at the time of the Act. The Court went on to hold that, as then structured, the military commissions set up to try suspected terrorists failed to comply with both the Uniform Code of Military Justice and the Geneva Conventions. Congress responded by adopting the Military Commissions Act, which the President signed into law on October 16, 2006. The MCA authorizes trial by military commissions and provides that no one may raise the Geneva Conventions in a habeas corpus challenge to proceedings before the commissions. Because the MCA gives the President congressional authority for the commissions, the only remaining grounds for legal challenge would be constitutional.

Habeas corpus, then, remains the appropriate remedy for unlawful detention *outside* the regular course of criminal justice, *see, e.g.,* Clark v. Martinez, 543 U.S. 371, 125 S.Ct. 716, 160 L.Ed.2d 734 (2005) (issuing writ to release deportable aliens detained more than six months), as well as for detention that exceeds legal limits during the criminal process, as when there is a denial of speedy trial or failure to make a prompt judicial determination of probable cause. It also remains an important review mechanism within the criminal justice process, especially in capital cases, subject to the limitations previously noted.

Habeas litigation is technically civil rather than criminal. The petitioner is the prisoner, the respondent is the warden, jailer, or other custodian, and the action to test the legality of the prisoner's detention is an original action initiated by the filing of the petition. When the warden answers the writ by pleading the prisoner's prior criminal conviction, the petitioner argues that the conviction is invalid. The peculiar procedural posture explains why some important criminal law issues are settled in cases to which neither a state nor the United States is named as a party, and why habeas litigation and statutory post-conviction procedures based on habeas are referred to as "collateral attack proceedings."

SECTION 2.   SOME RIGHTS AND PRIVILEGES OF THE ACCUSED

(1)   The Right to Counsel

See *Gideon v. Wainwright* and *Strickland v. Washington, supra* Chapter 13.

(2)   The Privilege Against Self–Incrimination

The Fifth Amendment provides: "No person shall ... be compelled in any criminal case to be a witness against himself, ..." It seems that this provision was "originally intended only to prevent return to the hated practice of compelling a person, in a criminal proceeding directed at him, to swear against himself".[7] It has been extended by interpretation, however, to protect not only the defendant, but also a witness, in all methods of interrogation before a court, grand jury or coroner's inquest, in investigations by a legislative body or administrative official.[8] The Fifth Amendment applies not only in federal proceedings, but applies to the states through the Fourteenth Amendment.[9] Most states also have constitutional provi-

---

7. 8 Wigmore, Evidence, sec. 2252, p. 324 (McNaughton rev. 1961).

8. Id. at pp. 326–328. The classic contributions on the role of the oath ex officio in the development of the Fifth Amendment privilege are Wigmore, *supra*, and, Leonard W. Levy, Origins of the Fifth Amendment (Oxford U. Press, 1968). Recent historical scholarship has challenged the Wigmore–Levy view by (1) identifying European sources for the privilege and by (2) pointing out that the privilege was rarely honored in early American criminal practice, which was characterized by self-representation. These objections do not undermine the claim that the founders respected claims of privilege when they were raised, or that they did so in large measure because of hostility to the procedure before the Star Chamber and the High Commission. For the revisionist scholarship, see R.H. Helmholz, ed., The Privilege Against Self–Incrimination: Its Origins and Development (U. of Chicago Press, 1997). For a tart rejoinder, see Leonard W. Levy, *Origins of the Fifth Amendment and Its Critics,* 19 Cardozo L. Rev. 821 (1997).

9. **D** was held in contempt of court for refusing to answer certain questions in a state proceeding. He claimed that he was privileged not to answer because the questions called for

sions very similar to the federal constitution, although, occasionally a state provision will vary and a different interpretation of the self-incrimination standard will be reached.

We have considered the constitutional limits on police interrogation in Chapter 13, *supra*. Those limits include both the due process requirement that confessions be voluntary, and the *Miranda* rules that implement the Fifth Amendment privilege in the specific context of custodial interrogation. We turn no to consider Fifth Amendment privilege law generally, which differs from the *Miranda* rules in some ways.

To sustain a claim of Fifth Amendment privilege, the claimant must establish (1) compulsion to provide (2) testimonial evidence that (3) tends to incriminate him. The failure to claim the privilege works a waiver. *See* Garner v. United States, 424 U.S. 648, 96 S.Ct. 1178, 47 L.Ed.2d 370 (1976) (taxpayer failed to claim privilege when filing return required by law; failure to assert privilege results in its forfeiture). Thus Fifth Amendment law generally, unlike the *Miranda* rules, requires the individual to show actual, rather than presumed, compulsion, and does not require the government to take proactive steps, such as the *Miranda* warning, to ensure that the individual is aware of the right to refuse to answer.

A. COMPULSION

Griffin v. California

Supreme Court of the United States, 1965.
380 U.S. 609, 5 Ohio Misc. 127, 85 S.Ct. 1229, 14 L.Ed.2d 106.

[Griffin was convicted of first-degree murder in a jury trial during which his failure to testify was the subject of comment by the district attorney and an instruction by the judge. The conviction having been affirmed by the Supreme Court of California was carried to this Court by certiorari.]

■ MR. JUSTICE DOUGLAS delivered the opinion of the Court. . . .

If this were a federal trial, reversible error would have been committed. Wilson v. United States, 149 U.S. 60, 13 S.Ct. 765, 37 L.Ed. 650, so

---

answers that would tend to be incriminating. The state court upheld the conviction on a finding that the questions did not call for incriminating answers. The Supreme Court held that the questions did call for incriminating answers and reversed the conviction on the ground that the Fifth Amendment's exemption from self-incrimination is also protected by the Fourteenth against abridgment by the states. Malloy v. Hogan, 378 U.S. 1, 84 S.Ct. 1489, 12 L.Ed.2d 653 (1964).

The state may compel a witness to testify, notwithstanding the fact that such testimony might tend to incriminate him of a federal offense, but the federal government would not be permitted to make any use of the testimony thus compelled. Murphy v. Waterfront Commission of New York Harbor, 378 U.S. 52, 84 S.Ct. 1594, 12 L.Ed.2d 678 (1964). The Court held that the privilege protects either a state or a federal witness against incrimination under either state or federal law. It expressly overruled United States v. Murdock, 284 U.S. 141, 52 S.Ct. 63, 76 L.Ed. 210 (1931), which held that the federal government could compel a witness to give testimony that might incriminate him under state law. The implication is that the witness can be compelled to testify but that because of the privilege the state will not be permitted to make any use of compelled testimony. Compare Adams v. Maryland, 347 U.S. 179, 74 S.Ct. 442, 98 L.Ed. 608 (1954).

holds. It is said, however, that the Wilson decision rested not on the Fifth Amendment, but on an Act of Congress. 18 U.S.C. § 3481. That indeed is the fact, as the opinion of the Court in the Wilson case states. But that is the beginning, not the end of our inquiry. The question remains whether, statute or not, the comment rule, approved by California, violates the Fifth Amendment.

We think it does. It is in substance a rule of evidence that allows the State the privilege of tendering to the jury for its consideration the failure of the accused to testify. No formal offer of proof is made as in other situations; but the prosecutor's comment and the court's acquiescence are the equivalent of an offer of evidence and its acceptance. The Court in the Wilson case stated:

"... the Act was framed with a due regard also to those who might prefer to rely upon the presumption of innocence which the law gives to every one, and not wish to be witnesses. It is not every one who can safely venture on the witness stand, though entirely innocent of the charge against him. Excessive timidity, nervousness when facing others and attempting to explain transactions of a suspicious character, and offenses charged against him, will often confuse and embarrass him to such a degree as to increase rather than remove prejudices against him. It is not every one, however, honest, who would therefore willingly be placed on the witness stand. The statute, in tenderness to the weakness of those who from the causes mentioned might refuse to ask to be witnesses, particularly when they may have been in some degree compromised by their association with others, declares that the failure of a defendant in a criminal action to request to be a witness shall not create any presumption against him."

If the words "Fifth Amendment" are substituted for "Act" and for "statute" the spirit of the Self–Incrimination Clause is reflected. For comment on the refusal to testify is a remnant of the "inquisitorial system of criminal justice," which the Fifth Amendment outlaws.[10] It is a penalty imposed by courts for exercising a constitutional privilege. It cuts down on the privilege by making its assertion costly. It is said, however, that the inference of guilt for failure to testify as to facts peculiarly within the accused's knowledge is in any event natural and irresistible, and that comment on the failure does not magnify that inference into a penalty for asserting a constitutional privilege. People v. Modesto, 62 Cal.2d 452, 468–

---

10. Our decision today that the Fifth Amendment prohibits comment on the defendant's silence is no innovation, for on a previous occasion a majority of this Court indicated their acceptance of this proposition. In Adamson v. People of State of California, 332 U.S. 46, 67 S.Ct. 1672, the question was, as here, whether the Fifth Amendment proscribed California's comment practice. The four dissenters (Black, Douglas, Murphy and Rutledge, JJ.) would have answered this question in the affirmative. A fifth member of the Court, Justice Frankfurter, stated in a separate opinion: "For historical reasons a limited immunity from the common duty to testify was written into the Federal Bill of Rights, and I am prepared to agree that, as part of that immunity, comment on the failure of an accused to take the witness stand is forbidden in federal prosecutions." Id., at 61, 67 S.Ct. at 1680. But, though he agreed with the dissenters on this point, he also agreed with Justices Vinson, Reed, Jackson, and Burton that the Fourteenth Amendment did not make the Self–Incrimination Clause of the Fifth Amendment applicable to the States; thus he joined the opinion of the Court which so held (the Court's opinion assumed that the Fifth Amendment barred comment, but it expressly disclaimed any intention to decide the point. Id., at 50, 67 S.Ct. at 1674).

469, 42 Cal.Rptr. 417, 398 P.2d 753. What the jury may infer given no help from the court is one thing. What they may infer when the court solemnizes the silence of the accused into evidence against him is quite another. That the inference of guilt is not always so natural or irresistible is brought out in the Modesto opinion itself:

"Defendant contends that the reason a defendant refuses to testify is that his prior convictions will be introduced in evidence to impeach him ([Cal.] Code Civ.Proc. § 2051) and not that he is unable to deny the accusations. It is true that the defendant might fear that his prior convictions will prejudice the jury, and therefore another possible inference can be drawn from his refusal to take the stand."

We said in Malloy v. Hogan, supra, 378 U.S. p. 11, 84 S.Ct. p. 1495, that "the same standards must determine whether an accused's silence in either a federal or state proceeding is justified." We take that in its literal sense and hold that the Fifth Amendment, in its direct application to the federal government and its bearing on the States by reason of the Fourteenth Amendment, forbids either comment by the prosecution on the accused's silence or instructions by the court that such silence is evidence of guilt.[11]

Reversed.

■ THE CHIEF JUSTICE took no part in the decision of this case.

■ MR. JUSTICE HARLAN concurring.

I agree with the Court that within the federal judicial system the Fifth Amendment bars adverse comment by federal prosecutors and judges on a defendant's failure to take the stand in a criminal trial, a right accorded him by that amendment. And given last Term's decision in Malloy v. Hogan, 378 U.S. 1, 84 S.Ct. 1489, 12 L.Ed.2d 653, that the Fifth Amendment applies to the States in all its refinements, I see no legitimate escape from today's decision and therefore concur in it. I do so, however, with great reluctance, since for me the decision exemplifies the creeping paraly-

---

11. We reserve decision on whether an accused can require, as in Bruno v. United States, 308 U.S. 287, 60 S.Ct. 198, 84 L.Ed. 257, that the jury, be instructed that his silence must be disregarded.

[Added by compilers.]

The answer given later was affirmative. It is reversible error for the judge in a state case to refuse to give such an instruction. Carter v. Kentucky, 450 U.S. 288, 101 S.Ct. 1112 (1981). Earlier the Court had held that giving such an instruction over the objection of the defendant did not violate the federal constitution. Lakeside v. Oregon, 435 U.S. 333, 98 S.Ct. 1091 (1978). The Indiana Court held that giving a "no adverse inferences" instruction over defendant's objections was reversible error under state law. Hill v. State, 267 Ind. 480, 371 N.E.2d 1303, 1306 (1978). See also, James v. Kentucky, 466 U.S. 341, 104 S.Ct. 1830 (1984).

A prosecutor's argument constituting improper comment on an accused's silence is to be evaluated under the standard of harmless error beyond a reasonable doubt. United States v. Hasting, 461 U.S. 499, 103 S.Ct. 1974 (1983).

[By Mr. Justice Stewart.]

Evidence of a suspect's refusal to take a blood alcohol test does not violate the privilege against self-incrimination and the failure to warn a suspect of the potential use of such refusal does not change the result. South Dakota v. Neville, 459 U.S. 553, 103 S.Ct. 916 (1983).

sis with which this Court's recent adoption of the "incorporation" doctrine is infecting the operation of the federal system. . . .

■ MR. JUSTICE STEWART, with whom MR. JUSTICE WHITE joins, dissenting. . . .

Moreover, no one can say where the balance of advantage might lie as a result of counsels' discussion of the matter. No doubt the prosecution's argument will seek to encourage the drawing of inferences unfavorable to the defendant. However, the defendant's counsel equally has an opportunity to explain the various other reasons why a defendant may not wish to take the stand, and thus rebut the natural if uneducated assumption that it is because the defendant cannot truthfully deny the accusations made.

I think the California comment rule is not a coercive device which impairs the right against self-incrimination, but rather a means of articulating and bringing into the light of rational discussion a fact inescapably impressed on the jury's consciousness. The California procedure is not only designed to protect the defendant against unwarranted inferences which might be drawn by an uninformed jury; it is also an attempt by the State to recognize and articulate what it believes to be the natural probative force of certain facts. Surely no one would deny that the State has an important interest in throwing the light of rational discussion on that which transpires in the course of a trial, both to protect the defendant from the very real dangers of silence and to shape a legal process designed to ascertain the truth.

B. TESTIMONIAL EVIDENCE

Schmerber v. California

Supreme Court of the United States, 1966.
384 U.S. 757, 86 S.Ct. 1826, 16 L.Ed.2d 908.

■ MR. JUSTICE BRENNAN delivered the opinion of the Court.

Petitioner was convicted in Los Angeles Municipal Court of the criminal offense of driving an automobile while under the influence of intoxicating liquor. He had been arrested at a hospital while receiving treatment for injuries suffered in an accident involving the automobile that he had apparently been driving.[2] At the direction of a police officer, a blood sample was then withdrawn from petitioner's body by a physician at the hospital. The chemical analysis of this sample revealed a percent by weight of alcohol in his blood at the time of the offense which indicated intoxication, and the report of this analysis was admitted in evidence at the trial. Petitioner objected to receipt of this evidence of the analysis on the ground that the blood had been withdrawn despite his refusal, on the advice of his counsel, to consent to the test. He contended that in that circumstance the withdrawal of the blood and the admission of the analysis in evidence denied him due process of law under the Fourteenth Amendment, as well as specific guarantees of the Bill of Rights secured against the States by

---

2. Petitioner and a companion had been drinking at a tavern and bowling alley. There was evidence showing that petitioner was driving from the bowling alley about midnight November 12, 1964, when the car skidded, crossed the road and struck a tree. Both petitioner and his companion were injured and taken to a hospital for treatment.

that Amendment: his privilege against self-incrimination under the Fifth Amendment; his right to counsel under the Sixth Amendment; and his right not to be subjected to unreasonable searches and seizures in violation of the Fourth Amendment. The Appellate Department of the California Superior Court rejected these contentions and affirmed the conviction.[3] In view of constitutional decisions since we last considered these issues in Breithaupt v. Abram, 352 U.S. 432, 77 S.Ct. 408, 1 L.Ed.2d 448—see Escobedo v. State of Illinois, 378 U.S. 478, 84 S.Ct. 1758, 12 L.Ed.2d 977; Malloy v. Hogan, 378 U.S. 1, 84 S.Ct. 1489, 12 L.Ed.2d 653, and Mapp v. State of Ohio, 367 U.S. 643, 81 S.Ct. 1684, 6 L.Ed.2d 1081—we granted certiorari. 382 U.S. 971, 86 S.Ct. 542, 15 L.Ed.2d 464. We affirm....

II.

THE PRIVILEGE AGAINST SELF-INCRIMINATION CLAIM

Breithaupt summarily rejected an argument that the withdrawal of blood and the admission of the analysis report involved in that state case violated the Fifth Amendment privilege of any person not to "be compelled in any criminal case to be a witness against himself," citing Twining v. State of New Jersey, 211 U.S. 78, 29 S.Ct. 14, 53 L.Ed. 97. But that case, holding that the protections of the Fourteenth Amendment do not embrace this Fifth Amendment privilege, has been succeeded by Malloy v. Hogan, 378 U.S. 1, 8, 84 S.Ct. 1489, 1493, 12 L.Ed.2d 653. We there held that "(t)he Fourteenth Amendment secures against state invasion the same privilege that the Fifth Amendment guarantees against federal infringement—the right of a person to remain silent unless he chooses to speak in the unfettered exercise of his own will, and to suffer no penalty * * * for such silence." We therefore must now decide whether the withdrawal of the blood and admission in evidence of the analysis involved in this case violated petitioner's privilege. We hold that the privilege protects an accused only from being compelled to testify against himself, or otherwise provide the State with evidence of a testimonial or communicative nature,[5] and that the withdrawal of blood and use of the analysis in question in this case did not involve compulsion to these ends.

It could not be denied that in requiring petitioner to submit to the withdrawal and chemical analysis of his blood the State compelled him to submit to an attempt to discover evidence that might be used to prosecute him for a criminal offense. He submitted only after the police officer rejected his objection and directed the physician to proceed. The officer's

---

3. This was the judgment of the highest court of the State in this proceeding since certification to the California District Court of Appeal was denied. [The offense was at this time only a misdemeanor under California law.]

5. A dissent suggests that the report of the blood test was "testimonial" or "communicative," because the test was performed in order to obtain the testimony of others, communicating to the jury facts about petitioner's condition. Of course, all evidence received in court is "testimonial" or "communicative" if these words are thus used. But the Fifth Amendment relates only to acts on the part of the person to whom the privilege applies, and we use these words subject to the same limitations. A nod or headshake is as much a "testimonial" or "communicative" act in this sense as are spoken words. But the terms as we use them do not apply to evidence of acts noncommunicative in nature as to the person asserting the privilege, even though, as here, such acts are compelled to obtain the testimony of others.

direction to the physician to administer the test over petitioner's objection constituted compulsion for the purposes of the privilege. The critical question, then, is whether petitioner was thus compelled "to be a witness against himself."[6]

If the scope of the privilege coincided with the complex of values it helps to protect, we might be obliged to conclude that the privilege was violated. in Miranda v. Arizona, 384 U.S. 436, at 460, 86 S.Ct. 1602, at 1620, 16 L.Ed.2d 694, at 715, the Court said of the interests protected by the privilege: "All these policies point to one overriding thought: the constitutional foundation underlying the privilege is the respect a government—state or federal—must accord to the dignity and integrity of its citizens. To maintain a 'fair' state-individual balance," to require the government "to shoulder the entire load," * * * to respect the inviolability of the human personality, our accusatory system of criminal justice demands that the government seeking to punish an individual produce the evidence against him by its own independent labors, rather than by the cruel, simple expedient of compelling it from his own mouth. The withdrawal of blood necessarily involves puncturing the skin for extraction, and the percent by weight of alcohol in that blood, as established by chemical analysis, is evidence of criminal guilt. Compelled submission fails on one view to respect the "inviolability of the human personality." Moreover, since it enables the State to rely on evidence forced from the accused, the compulsion violates at least one meaning of the requirement that the State procure the evidence against an accused "by its own independent labors."

As the passage in *Miranda* implicitly recognizes, however, the privilege has never been given the full scope which the values it helps to protect suggest. History and a long line of authorities in lower courts have consistently limited its protection to situations in which the State seeks to submerge those values by obtaining the evidence against an accused through the cruel, simple expedient of compelling it from his own mouth. * * * In sum, the privilege is fulfilled only when the person is guaranteed the right "to remain silent unless he chooses to speak in the unfettered exercise of his own will." Ibid. The leading case in this Court is Holt v. United States, 218 U.S. 245, 31 S.Ct. 2, 54 L.Ed. 1021. There the question was whether evidence was admissible that the accused, prior to trial and over his protest, put on a blouse that fitted him. It was contended that compelling the accused to submit to the demand that he model the blouse violated the privilege. Mr. Justice Holmes, speaking for the Court, rejected the argument as "based upon an extravagant extension of the 5th Amendment," and went on to say: "(T)he prohibition of compelling a man in a

---

6. Many state constitutions, including those of most of the original Colonies, phrase the privilege in terms of compelling a person to give "evidence" against himself. But our decision cannot turn on the Fifth Amendment's use of the word "witness." "(A)s the manifest purpose of the constitutional provisions, both of the states and of the United States, is to prohibit the compelling of testimony of a self-incriminating kind from a party or a witness, the liberal construction which must be placed upon constitutional provisions for the protection of personal rights would seem to require that the constitutional guaranties, however differently worded, should have as far as possible the same interpretation * * *." Counselman v. Hitchcock, 142 U.S. 547, 584–585, 12 S.Ct. 195, 206, 35 L.Ed. 1110. 8 Wigmore, Evidence § 2252 (McNaughton rev. 1961).

criminal court to be witness against himself is a prohibition of the use of physical or moral compulsion to extort communications from him, not an exclusion of his body as evidence when it may be material. The objection in principle would forbid a jury to look at a prisoner and compare his features with a photograph in proof." 218 U.S., at 252–253, 31 S.Ct., at 6.[7]

It is clear that the protection of the privilege reaches an accused's communications, whatever form they might take, and the compulsion of responses which are also communications, for example, compliance with a subpoena to produce one's papers. Boyd v. United States, 116 U.S. 616, 6 S.Ct. 524, 29 L.Ed. 746. On the other hand, both federal and state courts have usually held that it offers no protection against compulsion to submit to fingerprinting, photographing, or measurements, to write or speak for identification, to appear in court, to stand, to assume a stance, to walk, or to make a particular gesture. The distinction which has emerged, often expressed in different ways, is that the privilege is a bar against compelling "communications" or "testimony," but that compulsion which makes a suspect or accused the source of "real or physical evidence" does not violate it.

Although we agree that this distinction is a helpful framework for analysis, we are not to be understood to agree with past applications in all instances. There will be many cases in which such a distinction is not readily drawn. Some tests seemingly directed to obtain "physical evidence," for example, lie detector tests measuring changes in body function during interrogation, may actually be directed to eliciting responses which are essentially testimonial. To compel a person to submit to testing in which an effort will be made to determine his guilt or innocence on the basis of physiological responses, whether willed or not, is to evoke the spirit and history of the Fifth Amendment. Such situations call to mind the principle that the protection of the privilege "is as broad as the mischief against which it seeks to guard." Counselman v. Hitchcock, 142 U.S. 547, 562, 12 S.Ct. 195, 198.

In the present case, however, no such problem of application is presented. Not even a shadow of testimonial compulsion upon or enforced communication by the accused was involved either in the extraction or in the chemical analysis. Petitioner's testimonial capacities were in no way implicated; indeed, his participation, except as a donor, was irrelevant to the results of the test, which depend on chemical analysis and on that alone.[9] Since the blood test evidence, although an incriminating product of

---

7. Compare Wigmore's view, "that the privilege is limited to testimonial disclosures. It was directed at the employment of legal process to extract from the person's own lips an admission of guilt, which would thus take the place of other evidence." 8 Wigmore, Evidence § 2263 (McNaughton rev. 1961). California adopted the Wigmore formulation in People v. Trujillo, 32 Cal.2d 105, 194 P.2d 681 (1948); with specific regard to blood tests, see People v. Haeussler, 41 Cal.2d 252, 260 P.2d 8 (1953); People v. Duroncelay, 48 Cal.2d 766, 312 P.2d 690 (1957). Our holding today, however, is not to be understood as adopting the Wigmore formulation.

9. This conclusion would not necessarily govern had the State tried to show that the accused had incriminated himself when told that he would have to be tested. Such incriminating evidence may be an unavoidable by-product of the compulsion to take the test, especially for an individual who fears the extraction or opposes it on religious grounds. If it wishes to

compulsion, was neither petitioner's testimony nor evidence relating to some communicative act or writing by the petitioner, it was not inadmissible on privilege grounds.

Petitioner has raised a similar issue in this case, in connection with a police request that he submit to a "breathalyzer" test of air expelled from his lungs for alcohol content. He refused the request, and evidence of his refusal was admitted in evidence without objection. He argues that the introduction of this evidence and a comment by the prosecutor in closing argument upon his refusal is ground for reversal under Griffin v. State of California, 380 U.S. 609, 85 S.Ct. 1229, 14 L.Ed.2d 106. We think general Fifth Amendment principles, rather than the particular holding of Griffin, would be applicable in these circumstances, see Miranda v. Arizona, 384 U.S. at p. 468, n. 37, 86 S.Ct. 1624. Since trial here was conducted after our decision in *Malloy v. Hogan, supra,* making those principles applicable to the States, we think petitioner's contention is foreclosed by his failure to object on this ground to the prosecutor's question and statements.

■ CHIEF JUSTICE WARREN, dissenting.

[The Court] concedes, as it must so long as Boyd v. United States, 116 U.S. 616, 6 S.Ct. 524, 29 L.Ed. 746, stands, that the Fifth Amendment bars a State from compelling a person to produce papers he has that might tend to incriminate him. It is a strange hierarchy of values that allows the State to extract a human being's blood to convict him of a crime because of the blood's content but proscribes compelled production of his lifeless papers. Certainly there could be few papers that would have any more "testimonial" value to convict a man of drunken driving than would an analysis of the alcoholic content of a human being's blood introduced in evidence at a trial for driving while under the influence of alcohol. In such a situation blood, of course, is not oral testimony given by an accused but it can certainly "communicate" to a court and jury the fact of guilt.

The Court itself expresses its own doubts, if not fears, of its own shadowy distinction between compelling "physical evidence" like blood which it holds does not amount to compelled self-incrimination, and "eliciting responses which are essentially testimonial." And in explanation of its fears the Court goes on to warn that

> "To compel a person to submit to testing (by lie detectors for example) in which an effort will be made to determine his guilt or innocence on the basis of physiological responses, whether willed or not, is to evoke the spirit and history of the Fifth Amendment. Such situations call to mind the principle that the protection of the privilege 'is as broad as the mischief against which it seeks to guard.' Counselman v. Hitchcock, 142 U.S. 547, 562, 12 S.Ct. 195, 198 (35 L.Ed. 1110)."

---

compel persons to submit to such attempts to discover evidence, the State may have to forgo the advantage of any testimonial products of administering the test—products which would fall within the privilege. Indeed, there may be circumstances in which the pain, danger, or severity of an operation would almost inevitably cause a person to prefer confession to undergoing the "search," and nothing we say today should be taken as establishing the permissibility of compulsion in that case. But no such situation is presented in this case. See text at n. 13 infra.

A basic error in the Court's holding and opinion is its failure to give the Fifth Amendment's protection against compulsory self-incrimination the broad and liberal construction that Counselman and other opinions of this Court have declared it ought to have. The liberal construction given the Bill of Rights' guarantee in *Boyd v. United States, supra,* which Professor Wigmore criticized severely, see 8 Wigmore, Evidence, s 2264 (3d ed. 1940), pp. 366–373, makes that one among the greatest constitutional decisions of this Court. In that case, 116 U.S. at 634–635, 6 S.Ct. at 534, all the members of the Court decided that civil suits for penalties and forfeitures incurred for commission of offenses against the law, " * * * are within the reason of criminal proceedings for all the purposes of * * * that portion of the fifth amendment which declares that no person shall be compelled in any criminal case to be a witness against himself; * * * within the meaning of the fifth amendment to the constitution * * *."*

Obviously the Court's interpretation was not completely supported by the literal language of the Fifth Amendment. Recognizing this, the Court announced a rule of constitutional interpretation that has been generally followed ever since, particularly in judicial construction of Bill of Rights guarantees:

> "A close and literal construction (of constitutional provisions for the security of persons and property) deprives them of half their efficacy, and leads to gradual depreciation of the right, as if it consisted more in sound than in substance. It is the duty of courts to be watchful for the constitutional rights of the citizen, and against any stealthy encroachments thereon." *Boyd v. United States, supra,* at 635, 6 S.Ct. at 535.

The Court went on to say, at 637, 6 S.Ct. at 536, that to require "an owner to produce his private books and papers, in order to prove his breach of the laws, and thus to establish the forfeiture of his property, is surely compelling him to furnish evidence against himself." The Court today departs from the teachings of *Boyd.* Petitioner Schmerber has undoubtedly been compelled to give his blood "to furnish evidence against himself," yet the Court holds that this is not forbidden by the Fifth Amendment. With all deference I must say that the Court here gives the Bill of Rights' safeguard against compulsory self-incrimination a construction that would generally be considered too narrow and technical even in the interpretation of an ordinary commercial contract.

The Court apparently, for a reason I cannot understand, finds some comfort for its narrow construction of the Fifth Amendment in this Court's decision in Miranda v. Arizona, 384 U.S. 436, 86 S.Ct. 1602, 16 L.Ed.2d 694. I find nothing whatever in the majority opinion in that case which either directly or indirectly supports the holding in this case. In fact I think the interpretive constitutional philosophy used in *Miranda,* unlike that used in this case, gives the Fifth Amendment's prohibition against compelled self-incrimination a broad and liberal construction in line with the wholesome admonitions in the Boyd case. The closing sentence in the Fifth

---

* A majority of the Court applied the same constitutional interpretation to the search and seizure provisions of the Fourth Amendment over the dissent of Mr. Justice Miller, concurred in by Chief Justice Waite.

Amendment section of the Court's opinion in the present case is enough by itself, I think, to expose the unsoundness of what the Court here holds. That sentence reads: "Since the blood test evidence, although an incriminating product of compulsion, was neither petitioner's testimony nor evidence relating to some communicative act or writing by the petitioner, it was not inadmissible on privilege grounds." How can it reasonably be doubted that the blood test evidence was not in all respects the actual equivalent of "testimony" taken from petitioner when the result of the test was offered as testimony, was considered by the jury as testimony, and the jury's verdict of guilt rests in part on that testimony? The refined, subtle reasoning and balancing process used here to narrow the scope of the Bill of Rights' safeguard against self-incrimination provides a handy instrument for further narrowing of that constitutional protection, as well as others, in the future. Believing with the Framers that these constitutional safeguards broadly construed by independent tribunals of justice provide our best hope for keeping our people free from governmental oppression, I deeply regret the Court's holding.[12]

C. Incrimination

Kastigar v. United States

Supreme Court of the United States, 1972.
406 U.S. 441, 92 S.Ct. 1653, 32 L.Ed.2d 212.

(In the effort to make needed evidence available without either being unfair to the individual or imposing unnecessary handicaps upon the Government, Congress enacted a new immunity statute (18 U.S.C. § 6002). This did not bar a subsequent prosecution for the offense involved, but provided that in any subsequent prosecution of one who had testified under grant of such immunity, there could be no use of the testimony given by him, or of any other evidence which had been made available because of such testimony (use or derivative use). Persons before the grand jury who had been granted such immunity refused to testify on the ground that the statute did not give them adequate protection and was hence unconstitutional. The District Court rejected this claim, found them in contempt, and ordered them imprisoned until either they testified or the term of the grand jury expired. This was affirmed by the Court of Appeals of the Ninth Circuit (440 F.2d 954), and the Supreme Court granted certiorari.)

■ Mr. Justice Powell delivered the opinion of the Court. . . .

---

12. In subsequent cases the Court indeed rejected *Boyd*'s special protection of private papers, holding that documents created prior to the issuance of a subpoena compelling their production enjoy no Fifth Amendment protection. United States v. Doe, 465 U.S. 605, 611–612 (1984) ("Respondent does not contend that he prepared the documents involuntarily or that the subpoena would force him to restate, repeat, or affirm the truth of their contents. The fact that the records are in respondent's possession is irrelevant to the determination of whether the creation of the records was compelled. We therefore hold that the contents of those records are not privileged."). More recently, however, the Court held that when the government first learns of the existence of a document through compliance with a subpoena demanding documents of a certain description, the act of production is testimonial. United States v. Hubbell, 530 U.S. 27 (2000).

Syllabus

The United States can compel testimony from an unwilling witness who invokes the Fifth Amendment privilege against compulsory self-incrimination by conferring immunity, as provided by 18 U.S.C. § 6002, from use of the compelled testimony and evidence derived therefrom in subsequent criminal proceedings, as such immunity from use and derivative use is coextensive with the scope of the privilege and is sufficient to compel testimony over a claim of the privilege. Transactional immunity would afford broader protection than the Fifth Amendment privilege, and is not constitutionally required. In a subsequent criminal prosecution, the prosecution has the burden of proving affirmatively that evidence proposed to be used is derived from a legitimate source wholly independent of the compelled testimony.[13]

(3)   *Rights as to the Time of Trial*

When the defendant has been indicted or informed against, has been arraigned and has entered his plea of not guilty (or had this plea entered by the court), the proceedings are in shape for trial. But although the proceedings are ready for trial the parties may not be. Two rights inhere in the defendant which protect him on both sides in this regard. The first of these is the right to a speedy trial; the other is the right not to be forced to trial until the defendant has had due time for preparation.

The right of a person charged with a public offense to demand a speedy trial dates back to Magna Carta. A "speedy trial" does not mean a trial forthwith.[14] The machinery of justice is not so adapted that every person accused of crime can be tried on the very day he is taken into custody under an indictment or information,—or on the day the formal charge is filed if he is in custody at that time. Due regard must be given to the terms of court and many other factors, in other than metropolitan areas. More

---

13.   See also Ullmann v. United States, 350 U.S. 422, 76 S.Ct. 497 (1956). See Strachan, Self–Incrimination, Immunity and Watergate, 56 Tex.L.Rev. 791 (1978). 18 U.S.C. § 6002 is the federal statute providing use immunity to overcome a claim of privilege against self-incrimination. The prosecution bears the burden of showing its use of immunized evidence has not tainted the defendant's case. United States v. North, 920 F.2d 940 (D.C.Cir.1990). If contested a *Kastigar* hearing must be held.

In Chavez v. Martinez, 538 U.S. 760 (2003), the Court held that violations of *Miranda*, absent coercion in violation of due process, could not by themselves support an action for damages under 42 U.S.C. § 1983. Four justices joined a plurality opinion by Justice Thomas, rejecting the claim on the ground that there is no violation of the Fifth Amendment privilege against self-incrimination unless the compelled statements are actually used in evidence in a criminal case. The decisive votes for the result were provided in a concurrence by Justice Souter, joined by Justice Breyer, reasoning that recognizing a civil suit for damages for *Miranda* violations would extend the *Miranda* doctrine beyond the "core" of the Fifth Amendment.

14.   For a note on the right to speedy trial see 21 L.Ed.2d 905 (1969).

An unexplained delay of 140 days between the filing of a misdemeanor complaint for a traffic violation and **D**'s arrest was an unreasonable deprivation of his right to a speedy trial, and a writ of prohibition was issued to bar the prosecution. Rost v. Municipal Court, 184 Cal.App.2d 507, 7 Cal.Rptr. 869, 85 A.L.R.2d 974 (1960). In California the right to a speedy trial attaches when a complaint is filed. People v. Hannon, 19 Cal.3d 588, 138 Cal.Rptr. 885, 564 P.2d 1203 (1977).

than this, the prosecution and defendant are entitled to a reasonable time to prepare and get ready for trial. The purpose of this right is not to embarrass the prosecuting officer in the performance of that duty, but only to prevent unreasonable imprisonment without trial, which was anciently a means of great oppression. The defendant cannot insist that the trial be set at a date too early to allow a reasonable opportunity to prepare the case against the defendant.[15] Even after the date is set if, without the fault of the prosecution, delay becomes necessary in order to procure the attendance of material witnesses, or for some other proper purpose, a reasonable continuance will be granted. But negligence or want of due diligence in the preparation of its case will not entitle the prosecution to a delay in the setting of the case for trial or for a postponement of the date after it has been set.

At common law there was nothing to prevent the prosecution from putting the defendant on trial immediately after arraignment unless sufficient cause for a continuance could be shown. Statutes frequently entitle a defendant to a certain period after the plea is entered (such as three, five or thirty days) without any showing on defendant's part. And with or without such a statutory provision the defendant will be given such reasonable time as can be shown is necessary for the preparation of a defense. Upon proper showing defendant will be entitled to a continuance even after the date for the trial has been set. Defendant is not entitled to a continuance just for the purpose of delay, but courts are reluctant to force a defendant to a criminal trial when it is insisted the defendant is not ready.

The first comprehensive analysis of the Sixth Amendment right to a speedy trial is found in Barker v. Wingo, 407 U.S. 514, 92 S.Ct. 2182, 33 L.Ed.2d 101 (1972). More than five years had elapsed between the arrest and the trial, but the Court held that under the circumstances of this case the right to a speedy trial had been waived or in any event did not result in prejudice. The Court's opinion made it clear that any detailed implementation of the right would need to be made by legislation rather than by judicial decision. This was followed by the Speedy Trial Act of 1974, 18 U.S.C. § 3161 et seq., 88 Stat. 2076 et seq. The time specified for the various steps of the prosecution, together with numerous periods of delay that are excluded in computing the time, are detailed at length in 18 U.S.C. § 3161.

(4) Right to Be Present During Trial

In all criminal prosecutions the defendant has a right to be present in person during the proceeding from arraignment to sentence unless the right has been waived or forfeited. A statute denying this right would be an unconstitutional violation of due process.

---

15. The Federal Speedy Trial Act, 18 U.S.C.A. § 1361 (1979) provides statutory standards within which a defendant must be brought to trial. The failure to meet the statutory time periods will result in the dismissal of the prosecution. The dismissal may be with or without prejudice. The statutory time frame is generally more demanding than federal constitutional requirements. See Frase, The Speedy Trial Act of 1974, 43 U.Chi.L.Rev. 667 (1976); Misner, The 1979 Amendments to the Speedy Trial Act, 32 Hast.L.J. 635 (1981).

Many variations are found in the statute dealing with this subject. Most of them provide that the defendant must be "personally present" if the prosecution is for a felony. A number of them authorize the defendant to appear by counsel for arraignment in a misdemeanor case and provide that the trial may be had in his absence. A few provide that if the defendant escapes after any trial has commenced it may continue to verdict. Rule 43 of the Federal Rules of Criminal Procedure reads:

Rule 43. Presence of the Defendant.

(a) Presence Required. The defendant shall be present at the arraignment, at the time of the plea, at every stage of the trial including the impaneling of the jury and the return of the verdict, and at the imposition of sentence, except as otherwise provided by this rule.

(b) Continued Presence Not Required. The further progress of the trial to and including the return of the verdict, and the imposition of sentence, will not be prevented and the defendant will be considered to have waived the right to be present whenever a defendant, initially present at trial, or having pleaded guilty or nolo contendere,

(1) is voluntarily absent after the trial has commenced (whether or not the defendant has been informed by the court of the obligation to remain during the trial),

(2) in a noncapital case, is voluntarily absent at the imposition of sentence, or

(3) after being warned by the court that disruptive conduct will cause the removal of the defendant from the courtroom, persists in conduct which is such as to justify exclusion from the courtroom.

(c) Presence Not Required. A defendant need not be present:

(1) when represented by counsel and the defendant is an organization, as defined in 18 U.S.C. § 18;

(2) when the offense is punishable by fine or by imprisonment for not more than one year or both, and the court, with the written consent of the defendant, permits arraignment, plea, trial, and imposition of sentence in the defendant's absence;

(3) when the proceeding involves only a conference or hearing upon a question of law; or

(4) when the proceeding involves a correction of sentence under Rule 35.

Illinois v. Allen, 397 U.S. 337 (1970), affirmed the bank robbery conviction of an accused who engaged in speech and conduct so noisy, disorderly and disruptive that it was was impossible to carry on the trial. After multiple warnings, the trial judge ordered the defendant removed, and defendant was absent during much of the trial. Upholding the conviction, the Court stated:

Although mindful that courts must indulge every reasonable presumption against the loss of constitutional rights, we explicitly hold today that a defendant can lose his right to be present at trial if, after he has been warned by the judge that he will be removed if he continues his disruptive behavior, he nevertheless insists on conducting himself in a manner so disorderly, disruptive, and disrespectful of the court that his trial cannot be carried on with him in the courtroom. Once lost, the right to be present can, of course, be reclaimed as soon as the defendant is willing to conduct himself consistently with the decorum and respect inherent in the concept of courts and judicial proceedings.[16]

The Supreme Court has held a defendant's right to be present at critical stages of the proceedings was not violated where defendant was excluded from a hearing to determine the competency of minor witnesses to testify. The defendant's presence would not have assisted in the defense at trial or the court in making a reliable determination of competency.[17]

(5) Right to a Public Trial

One accused of crime has a common-law right to a public trial[18] which has been embodied in the federal constitution and in the constitutions of most states. This means that the defendant has a right to a trial that is open to the public. If the trial is so open, there is no requirement that it must stop merely because no one the defendant regards as a member of the public happens to be present. It had been assumed at times that a public trial was not necessary if expressly waived by the defendant.[19] In any event it is clear that the defendant has no general right to a secret trial.[20]

Neither the defendant nor anyone else has a right to require the judge to admit to the courtroom any unneeded person whose presence will interfere with the due and orderly conduct of the trial. Overcrowding will result in such interference. Hence if members of the general public are admitted until the seating capacity of the courtroom is exhausted, the exclusion of others is entirely proper. Furthermore, if all available space is taken by witnesses and other persons necessary to the trial or having some special and proper interest therein, the exclusion of disinterested members of the public is unavoidable.[21] Disorderly persons may be evicted, and if all who are not necessary to the trial are disorderly, all may be required to

---

16. [Added by the Compiler.]

Rule 43, F.R.Cr.P. requires defendant's presence at trial but if the defendant absents himself from an ongoing trial the defendant may be tried in absentia. A defendant who absents prior to trial may not be tried in absentia. Crosby v. United States, 506 U.S. 255, 113 S.Ct. 748 (1993).

17. Kentucky v. Stincer, 482 U.S. 730, 107 S.Ct. 2658, 96 L.Ed.2d 631 (1987).

18. Radin, The Right to a Public Trial, 6 Temp.L.Q. 381 (1932).

The right to a public trial does not necessarily apply without request to a contempt proceeding associated with a grand jury investigation. Levine v. United States, 362 U.S. 610, 80 S.Ct. 1038, 4 L.Ed.2d 989 (1960).

For an exhaustive analysis of the leading cases on the subject of the right to public trial see State v. Lawrence, 167 N.W.2d 912 (Iowa 1969).

19. People v. Swafford, 65 Cal. 223, 3 P. 809 (1884); People v. Lang, 49 Cal.3d 991, 264 Cal.Rptr. 386, 782 P.2d 627 (1989). Land held that failure to object could constitute a waiver. There is authority contra on this point. Wade v. State, 207 Ala. 1, 92 So. 101 (1921).

20. Gannett Co. v. DePasquale, 443 U.S. 368, 99 S.Ct. 2898, 61 L.Ed.2d 608 (1979).

21. Kugadt v. State, 38 Tex.Cr.R. 681, 44 S.W. 989 (1898).

leave.[22] On the other hand it would be arbitrary and unreasonable if the judge, after having given such an order, should refuse to make any exceptions even upon a proper showing therefor. If defendant's parent or relative or some other relative or friend whose presence was desired by the defendant, could assure the judge that the person had not participated in the disorder and would not in any way interfere with the due and orderly conduct of the trial, it would be prejudicial error to compel such person to leave.

The Supreme Court reversed a conviction because the trial had been telecast despite **D**'s motion to prevent it.[23] There was no opinion of the Court and the six opinions left doubt as to the exact significance. Several states experimented with television. Televised trials are common today. The fact of television alone is not a basis for a claim of undue publicity. However, if the proceedings deteriorate to a "circus"-like atmosphere, a legitimate complaint may be made and restrictions imposed. Florida had a pilot program and in a case under it the Supreme Court held that with adequate safeguards a state may provide for television coverage of a criminal trial. Conviction in a televised trial was affirmed.[24]

An order "putting witnesses under the rule"[25] a restriction of communication does not necessarily violate defendant's right to a public trial.[26] There must be reasonable justification for a gag order, circumstances must show a likelihood of unjustly intruding on the fairness of the proceedings.[27]

Richmond Newspapers, Inc. v. Virginia

Supreme Court of the United States, 1980.
448 U.S. 555, 100 S.Ct. 2814, 65 L.Ed.2d 973.

Syllabus[28]

At the commencement of a fourth trial on a murder charge (the defendant's conviction after the first trial having been reversed on appeal,

---

22.   Grimmett v. State, 22 Tex.App. 36, 2 S.W. 631 (1886).

It was held that the exclusion of the public except for members of the press and the bar was not unreasonable where it was apparent that **D** and his sympathizers were attempting to prevent an orderly presentation of the case. United States v. Fay, 350 F.2d 967 (2d Cir.1965).

Excluding spectators for a short time to prevent escape or violence did not infringe on right to public trial. State v. Harding, 635 P.2d 33 (Utah 1981).

23.   Estes v. Texas, 381 U.S. 532, 85 S.Ct. 1628, 14 L.Ed.2d 543 (1965).

24.   Chandler v. Florida, 449 U.S. 560, 101 S.Ct. 802, 66 L.Ed.2d 740 (1981).

25.   This order excludes all other witnesses from the courtroom while any one of them is on the witness stand. See Rule 615, Federal Rules of Evidence.

26.   State v. Worthen, 124 Iowa 408, 100 N.W. 330 (1904). Putting witnesses "under the rule" is within the discretion of the judge but it is error for the court to refuse to do so without exercising discretion under the theory that he has abandoned the practice. Charles v. United States, 215 F.2d 825 (9th Cir.1954).

27.   See Gentile v. State Bar of Nevada, 501 U.S. 1030, 111 S.Ct. 2720, 115 L.Ed.2d 888 (1991).

28.   The syllabus constitutes no part of the opinion of the Court but has been prepared by the Reporter of Decisions for the convenience of the reader. See United States v. Detroit Lumber Co., 200 U.S. 321, 337, 26 S.Ct. 282, 287, 50 L.Ed. 499.

and two subsequent retrials having ended in mistrials), the Virginia trial court granted defense counsel's motion that the trial be closed to the public without any objections having been made by the prosecutor or by appellants, a newspaper and two of its reporters who were present in the courtroom, defense counsel having stated that he did not "want any information being shuffled back and forth when we have a recess as to . . . who testified to what." Later that same day, however, the trial judge granted appellant's request for a hearing on a motion to vacate the closure order, and appellants' counsel contended that constitutional considerations mandated that before ordering closure the court should first decide that the defendant's rights could be protected in no other way. But the trial judge denied the motion, saying that if he felt that the defendant's rights were infringed in any way and others' rights were not overridden he was inclined to order closure, and ordered the trial to continue "with the press and public excluded." The next day, the court granted defendant's motion to strike the prosecution's evidence, excused the jury, and found the defendant not guilty. Thereafter, the court granted appellants' motion to intervene *nunc pro tunc* in the case, and the Virginia Supreme Court dismissed their mandamus and prohibition petitions and, finding no reversible error, denied their petition for appeal from the closure order.

Held: The judgment is reversed.

Reversed.

■ MR. CHIEF JUSTICE BURGER, joined by MR. JUSTICE WHITE and MR. JUSTICE STEVENS, concluded that the right of the public and press to attend criminal trials is guaranteed under the First and Fourteenth Amendments. Absent an overriding interest articulated in findings, the trial of a criminal case must be open to the public.

(a) The historical evidence of the evolution of the criminal trial in Anglo–American justice demonstrates conclusively that at the time this Nation's organic laws were adopted, criminal trials both here and in England had long been presumptively open, thus giving assurance that the proceedings were conducted fairly to all concerned and discouraging perjury, the misconduct of participants, or decisions based on secret bias or partiality. In addition, the significant community therapeutic value of public trials was recognized: when a shocking crime occurs, a community reaction of outrage and public protect often follows, and thereafter the open processes of justice serve an important prophylactic purpose, providing an outlet for community concern, hostility, and emotion. To work effectively, it is important that society's criminal process "satisfy the appearance of justice," which can best be provided by allowing people to observe such process. From this unbroken, uncontradicted history, supported by reasons as valid today as in centuries past, it must be concluded that a presumption of openness inheres in the very nature of a criminal trial under this Nation's system of justice.

(b) The freedoms of speech, press, and assembly, expressly guaranteed by the First Amendment, share a common core purpose of assuring freedom of communication on matters relating to the functioning of government. In guaranteeing freedoms such as those of speech and press, the First Amendment can be read as protecting the right of everyone to attend trials so as to give meaning to those explicit guarantees; the First Amend-ment right to receive information and ideas means, in the context of trials, that the guarantees of speech and press, standing alone, prohibit govern-ment from summarily closing courtroom doors which had long been open to the public at the time the First Amendment was adopted. Moreover, the right of assembly is also relevant, having been regarded not only as an independent right but also as a catalyst to augment the free exercise of the other First Amendment rights with which it was deliberately linked by the draftsmen. A trial courtroom is a public place where the people generally—and representatives of the media—have a right to be present, and where their presence historically has been thought to enhance the integrity and quality of what takes place. Pp. 2826–2828.

(c) Even though the Constitution contains no provision which by its terms guarantees to the public the right to attend criminal trials, various fundamental rights, not expressly guaranteed, have been recognized as indispensable to the enjoyment of enumerated rights. The right to attend criminal trials is implicit in the guarantees of the First Amendment; without the freedom to attend such trials, which people have exercised for centuries, important aspects of freedom of speech and of the press could be eviscerated. Pp. 2828–2829.

(d) With respect to the closure order in this case, despite the fact that this was the accused's fourth trial, the trial judge made no findings to support closure; no inquiry was made as to whether alternative solutions would have met the need to ensure fairness; there was no recognition of any right under the Constitution for the public or press to attend the trial; and there was no suggestion that any problems with witnesses could not have been dealt with by exclusion from the courtroom or sequestration during the trial, or that sequestration of the jurors would not have guarded against their being subjected to any improper information. Pp. 2829–2830.

■ MR. JUSTICE BRENNAN, joined by MR. JUSTICE MARSHALL, concluded that the First Amendment—of itself and as applied to the States through the Fourteenth Amendment—secures the public a right of access to trial proceedings, and that, without more, agreement of the trial judge and the parties cannot constitutionally close a trial to the public. Historically and functionally, open trials have been closely associated with the development of the fundamental procedure of trial by jury, and trial access assumes structural importance in this Nation's government of laws by assuring the public that procedural rights are respected and that justice is afforded equally, by serving as an effective restraint on possible abuse of judicial power, and by aiding the accuracy of the trial factfinding process. It was further concluded that it was not necessary to consider in this case what countervailing interests might be sufficiently compelling to reverse the presumption of openness of trials, since the Virginia statute involved—authorizing trial closures at the unfettered discretion of the judge and parties—violated the First and Fourteenth Amendments.

■ MR. JUSTICE STEWART concluded that the First and Fourteenth Amend-ments clearly give the press and the public a right of access to trials, civil as well as criminal; that such right is not absolute, since various consider-ations may sometimes justify limitations upon the unrestricted presence of spectators in the courtroom; but that in the present case the trial judge apparently gave no recognition to the right of representatives of the press and members of the public to be present at the trial.

■ Mr. Justice Blackmun, while being of the view that *Gannett Co. v. DePasquale, supra,* was in error, both in its interpretation of the Sixth Amendment generally, and in its application to the suppression hearing involved there, and that the right to a public trial is to be found in the Sixth Amendment, concluded, as a secondary position, that the First Amendment must provide some measure of protection for public access to the trial, and that here, by closing the trial, the trial judge abridged these First Amendment interests of the public.[29]

(6) Right to a Trial by Jury

It has been said: "That the modern institution of trial by jury derives from Magna Carta is one of the most revered of legal fables."[30] "The 'judgment of his peers' there named is secured only to noblemen who are, by this provision, to be tried at the king's suit in the House of Lords."[31] But when we have shown that this protection was quite limited in its inception, and has since been broadened in its scope to include all people, we seem rather to have explained than to have contradicted the thought that this important benefit relates back to that great document. The right to trial by jury is still regarded by many as most important to liberty.

The usual common law classification of crimes recognizes three groups: (1) treason, (2) felony, and (3) misdemeanor. For certain important purposes of procedure, however, a different classification was employed. This emphasized the distinction between (1) indictable offenses and (2) petty offenses. Persons charged with very minor violations such as disorderly conduct, trivial breaches of the peace or infractions of municipal ordinances could be prosecuted without waiting for an indictment by the grand jury, and could be tried without the aid of a trial jury. Except for such petty offenses the common-law gives the defendant a right to a trial by jury in

---

29. A Massachusetts law requiring trial judges, for sexual offenses where the victim was under age 18, to exclude the press and public from the courtroom during the testimony of the victim was held to violate the First Amendment. "We emphasize that our holding is a narrow one: that a rule of mandatory closure respecting the testimony of minor sex victims is constitutionally infirm. In individual cases, and under appropriate circumstances, the First Amendment does not necessarily stand as a bar to the exclusion from the courtroom of the press and general public during the testimony of minor sex-offense victims. But a mandatory rule, requiring no particularized determination in individual cases, is unconstitutional." Globe Newspaper Co. v. Superior Court, 457 U.S. 596, 102 S.Ct. 2613, 2622 (1982).

The public cannot be denied the right to attend a preliminary hearing without a specific finding that there is a substantial probability that the defendant's right to a fair trial will be prejudiced and reasonable alternatives are not adequate. Press–Enterprise Co. v. Superior Court, 478 U.S. 1, 106 S.Ct. 2735 (1986). See also El Vocero de Puerto Ricio v. Puerto Rico, 508 U.S. 147, 113 S.Ct. 2004 (1993).

There is a presumption that the press should have access during the voir dire selection of jurors which may only be overcome by a finding of some overriding interest. Press–Enterprise Co. v. Superior Court, 464 U.S. 501, 104 S.Ct. 819 (1984).

30. Frankfurter and Corcoran, Petty Federal Offenses and the Constitutional Guaranty of Trial by Jury, 39 Harv.L.Rev. 917, 922 (1926).

31. Beale, Criminal Pleading and Practice 253, note 1 (1899).

every prosecution for crime. This right is guaranteed by most state constitutions as well as the Sixth Amendment. A few of the provisions seem to extend the right even beyond its common-law scope.[32]

Baldwin v. New York

Supreme Court of the United States, 1970.
399 U.S. 66, 90 S.Ct. 1886, 26 L.Ed.2d 437.

■ MR. JUSTICE WHITE announced the judgment of the Court and delivered an opinion in which MR. JUSTICE BRENNAN and MR. JUSTICE MARSHALL join.

Appellant was arrested and charged with "jostling"—a Class A misdemeanor in New York, punishable by a maximum term of imprisonment of one year.[33] He was brought to trial in the New York City Criminal Court. Section 40 of the New York City Criminal Court Act declares that all trials in that court shall be without a jury. Appellant's pretrial motion for jury trial was accordingly denied. He was convicted and sentenced to imprisonment for the maximum term. The New York Court of Appeals affirmed the conviction, rejecting appellant's argument that § 40 was unconstitutional insofar as it denied him an opportunity for jury trial. We noted probable jurisdiction. We reverse.

In Duncan v. Louisiana, 391 U.S. 145, 88 S.Ct. 1444, 20 L.Ed.2d 491 (1968), we held that the Sixth Amendment, as applied to the States through the Fourteenth, requires that defendants accused of serious crimes be afforded the right to trial by jury. We also reaffirmed the long-established view that so-called "petty offenses" may be tried without a jury. Thus the task before us in this case is the essential if not wholly satisfactory one, see *Duncan,* at 161, 88 S.Ct. at 1453, of determining the line between "petty" and "serious" for purposes of the Sixth Amendment right to jury trial.

---

32. The Sixth Amendment provides: "In all criminal prosecutions, the accused shall enjoy the right to a speedy and public trial, by an impartial jury...." Some of the state constitutions are similarly worded. But the phrase "criminal prosecutions," in such a constitutional clause, has been interpreted to include only what Blackstone refers to as "regular" proceedings as distinguished from the summary trial of petty offenses. 4 Bl.Comm. 280. In other words it is construed to preserve the right of trial by jury as it existed prior to the constitution and not to extend it to a broader field. Frankfurter and Corcoran, Petty Federal Offenses and the Constitutional Guaranty of Trial by Jury, 39 Harv.L.Rev. 917, 969 (1926).

But an occasional provision has an added phrase, such as that "In all criminal prosecutions, and in cases involving the life or liberty of an individual, the accused shall have the right to a speedy and public trial by an impartial jury." Iowa Const. Art. I, sec. 10. Since any imprisonment involves the liberty of an individual, and some of the petty offenses were punished by imprisonment for a short period, such a clause extends the right of trial by jury.

33. "Jostling" is one of the ways in which legislatures have attempted to deal with pickpocketing. See Denzer & McQuillan, Practice Commentary, N.Y.Penal Law § 165.25 (McKinney 1967); Pickpocketing: A Survey of the Crime and its Control, 104 U.Pa.L.Rev. 408, 419 (1955). The New York law provides:

"A person is guilty of jostling when, in a public place, he intentionally and unnecessarily:

1. Places his hand in the proximity of a person's pocket or handbag; or

2. Jostles or crowds another person at a time when a third person's hand is in the proximity of such person's pocket or handbag." N.Y.Penal Law § 165.25 (McKinney's Consol.Laws, c. 40, 1967).

Prior cases in this Court narrow our inquiry and furnish us with the standard to be used in resolving this issue. In deciding whether an offense is "petty," we have sought objective criteria reflecting the seriousness with which society regards the offense, District of Columbia v. Clawans, 300 U.S. 617, 628, 57 S.Ct. 660, 663, 81 L.Ed. 843 (1937), and we have found the most relevant such criteria in the severity of the maximum authorized penalty. Frank v. United States, 395 U.S. 147, 148, 89 S.Ct. 1503, 1505, 23 L.Ed.2d 162 (1969); Duncan v. Louisiana, supra, 391 U.S., at 159–161, 88 S.Ct., at 1452–1454; District of Columbia v. Clawans, supra, 300 U.S., at 628, 57 S.Ct., at 663. Applying these guidelines, we have held that a possible six-month penalty is short enough to permit classification of the offense as "petty," Dyke v. Taylor Implement Mfg. Co., 391 U.S. 216, 220, 88 S.Ct. 1472, 1475, 20 L.Ed.2d 538 (1968); Cheff v. Schnackenberg, 384 U.S. 373, 86 S.Ct. 1523, 16 L.Ed.2d 629 (1966), but that a two-year maximum is sufficiently "serious" to require an opportunity for jury trial, Duncan v. Louisiana, supra. The question in this case is whether the possibility of a one-year sentence is enough in itself to require the opportunity for a jury trial. We hold that it is. More specifically, we have concluded that no offense can be deemed "petty" for purposes of the right to trial by jury where imprisonment for more than six months is authorized.[34] . . .

Of necessity, the task of drawing a line "requires attaching different consequences to events which, when they lie near the line, actually differ very little." Duncan v. Louisiana, supra, at 161, 88 S.Ct., at 1453. One who is threatened with the possibility of imprisonment for six months may find little difference between the potential consequences which face him, and the consequences which faced appellant here. Indeed, the prospect of imprisonment for however short a time will seldom be viewed by the accused as a trivial or "petty" matter and may well result in quite serious repercussions affecting his career and his reputation. Where the accused cannot possibly face more than six months imprisonment, we have held that these disadvantages, onerous though they may be, may be outweighed by the benefits which result from speedy and inexpensive nonjury adjudications. We cannot, however, conclude that these administrative conveniences, in light of the practices which now exist in every one of the 50 States as well as in the federal courts, can similarly justify denying an accused the important right to trial by jury where the possible penalty exceeds six months' imprisonment. The conviction is

Reversed.[35]

---

34. Decisions of this Court have looked to both the nature of the offense itself, District of Columbia v. Colts, 282 U.S. 63, 51 S.Ct. 52, 75 L.Ed. 177, as well as the maximum potential sentence, Duncan v. Louisiana, 391 U.S. 145, 88 S.Ct. 1444, 20 L.Ed.2d 491 (1968), in determining whether a particular offense was so serious as to require a jury trial. In this case, we decide only that a potential sentence in excess of six-months imprisonment is sufficiently severe by itself to take the offense out of the category of "petty." None of our decisions involving this issue have ever held such an offense "petty."

35. [Added by the Compiler.] At the same time that this case was decided the Court held that the jury clause of the Sixth Amendment does not require twelve jurors. A panel of six was held to satisfy the requirement. Williams v. Florida, 399 U.S. 78, 90 S.Ct. 1893 (1970).

The Louisiana constitution authorized criminal trials by juries of six, and authorized convictions on the vote of five jurors. B was on trial for exhibiting obscene motion pictures, an

■ MR. JUSTICE BLACKMUN took no part in the consideration or decision of this case.

■ BLACK and DOUGLAS, JJ., concurred in the judgment reversing the conviction because of a belief that the defendant in any criminal prosecution is entitled to a jury trial.

■ BURGER, C.J., and HARLAN and STEWART, JJ., dissented because they disagree with the incorporation theory and conclude that the trial of Baldwin did not deprive him of due process.

At one time the jury trial of an indictable offense was considered by many to be a requirement rather than a mere right. As it was expressed by one author over a century ago, "the weight of authority, as well as the better opinion, is, that in prosecutions for crime other than minor misdemeanors and petty offenses, the defendant cannot waive his right to a trial by jury, or consent to a trial by a less number than twelve."[36] Some courts reversed convictions because the trial was without a full panel of twelve, although it was with the express consent of the defendant. The theory was that a common-law jury was essential to the jurisdiction of the court in criminal cases.

In *Patton*[37] the Supreme Court rejected this view, disposing of the jurisdiction theory as follows:

"In the absence of a valid consent, the District Court cannot proceed except with a jury, not because a jury is essential to its jurisdiction, but because the accused is entitled by the terms of the Constitution to that mode of trial".

---

offense for which the punishment could be more than six months imprisonment. He was found guilty by a vote of five of the six jurors and sentenced to two consecutive 7–month terms that were suspended. It was held that conviction of a nonpetty offense by a vote of five of a six-person jury deprived B of his constitutional right of trial by jury. Burch v. Louisiana, 441 U.S. 130, 99 S.Ct. 1623 (1979). In another case the Court had invalidated a statute allowing conviction by a unanimous five-person jury in nonpetty criminal cases. Ballew v. Georgia, 435 U.S. 223, 98 S.Ct. 1029 (1978). Thus the Court has held that the constitution does not require a jury of twelve for the trial of nonpetty criminal cases. A jury of six is constitutionally permissible, but a jury of fewer than six is invalid for such trials. And the Court has held that the constitution does not require unanimous verdicts in such trial if the jury is large enough. But in no case may conviction of such an offense be based upon the verdict of fewer than six jurors.

Conviction by a nonunanimous jury did not violate the Fourteenth Amendment. Johnson v. Louisiana, 406 U.S. 356, 92 S.Ct. 1620 (1972) (9 of 12 jurors); Apodaca v. Oregon, 406 U.S. 404, 92 S.Ct. 1628 (1972) (10 of 12 jurors). Of course, unanimity is required from a six-person jury.

In a state in which there is no provision for a nonunanimous verdict, the jury sent word that it was hopelessly deadlocked at 11 to 1, with no indication which way. When defendant was told this he said he would accept the nonunanimous verdict. The verdict was received and it was 11 to 1 for conviction. The court held that a defendant has the power to waive his right to a unanimous verdict, but that this conviction must be reversed because the judge accepted the waiver without properly informing the defendant. People v. Miller, 121 Mich.App. 691, 329 N.W.2d 460 (1982).

36. Rapalje, Criminal Procedure § 151 (1889).

37. Patton v. United States, 281 U.S. 276, 50 S.Ct. 253, 74 L.Ed. 854, 70 A.L.R. 263 (1930).

And Rule 23(a) of the Federal Rules of Criminal Procedure expressly authorizes the waiver. On the other hand the defendant has no absolute right to demand a trial without a jury. The provision of the rule requiring the court and government to consent to the waiver of jury trial is valid, at least unless defendant can show some impelling reason in a particular case why he should be entitled to a trial by the judge alone.[38]

Today, the power of the judge to try a criminal case without a jury, when the jury has been waived, is accepted without question unless some state statute or constitution provides otherwise.

Of late, the most hotly-contested issue regarding the right to trial by jury concerns the role of the jury at sentencing. In a series of decisions, consistently dividing five to four, the Supreme Court has held that when specific findings of fact trigger a mandatory enhancement of the defendant's sentence, the accused has a Sixth Amendment right to have the jury, rather than the judge, find those facts. United States v. Booker, 543 U.S. 220 (2005); Blakely v. Washington, 542 U.S. 296 (2004); Apprendi v. New Jersey, 530 U.S. 466 (2000). The Court has also held that the defendant has a constitutional right against capital punishment unless the jury determines that he is death-eligible. Ring v. Arizona, 536 U.S. 584 (2002). The issue is considered in somewhat greater detail in United States v. Crosby, *supra* Chapter 11, and Kansas v. Marsh, *supra* Chapter 11.

(7)   Right to a Fair and Impartial Trial

The rather common constitutional clause guaranteeing the defendant a "trial by an impartial jury" does not exhaust the right to impartiality. The requirement of due process of law entitles the defendant to a fair and impartial trial in every respect.[39] The case in which a violent mob moved into the courtroom and completely dominated the trial, intimidating witnesses, counsel, jurors and even the judge himself so that no one dared to do anything other than let the case proceed to a hasty conviction,[40] requires no discussion. Much less than this may be sufficient to deprive the

---

38.   Singer v. United States, 380 U.S. 24, 85 S.Ct. 783, 13 L.Ed.2d 630 (1965).

California constitution, Article 1, Section 16, provides: "... A jury may be waived in a criminal case, by the consent of both parties, expressed in open court by the defendant and his counsel, ...". See also West's Cal. Penal Code §§ 689, 1042. The consent of the trial judge is not necessary and he cannot overrule the decision of the parties. The consent of the prosecuting attorney is as essential as the consent of the defendant. People v. Terry, 2 Cal.3d 362, 85 Cal.Rptr. 409, 466 P.2d 961 (1970). The waiver must be express. People v. Ernst, 8 Cal.4th 441, 34 Cal.Rptr.2d 238, 881 P.2d 298 (1994).

39.   "He is also entitled to a fair trial, which has been well defined, as 'a trial before an impartial judge, an honest jury, and in an atmosphere of judicial calm' ". State v. Leland, 190 Or. 598, 608, 227 P.2d 785, 790 (1951). Cf. Robedeaux v. State, 94 Okl.Cr. 171, 232 P.2d 642 (1951). See Holtzoff, Relation Between the Right to a Fair Trial and the Right of Freedom of the Press. 1 Syracuse L.Rev. 369 (1950); Strauss, Why Its Not Free Speech Versus Fair Trial, 1998 U. Chi. Legal F. 109.

"Inconsistency in a verdict is not a sufficient reason for setting it aside." In holding that this is not limited to jury trials but applies also to a bench trial the Court, without finding more than "apparent inconsistency" in the case at bench, added: "The Constitution does not prohibit judges from being excessively lenient." Harris v. Rivera, 454 U.S. 339, 102 S.Ct. 460, 464, 465, 70 L.Ed.2d 530 (1981).

40.   Moore v. Dempsey, 261 U.S. 86, 43 S.Ct. 265, 67 L.Ed. 543 (1923).

defendant of a fair and impartial trial. The case of Tumey v. Ohio is illuminating.[41] The defendant was arrested and brought before a village mayor charged with unlawfully possessing intoxicating liquor. Ignoring a claim of disqualification, the mayor proceeded with a trial which resulted in a conviction. The judgment was reversed by the Court of Common Pleas on the ground that the mayor was disqualified as claimed, but this in turn was reversed by the Court of Appeals, and the State Supreme Court refused to disturb the conviction. The case was then taken to the Supreme Court of the United States upon a writ of error. The court discovered that under the relevant statutes and ordinances the mayor trying such a case was entitled to legal fees taxed in his favor in the event of a conviction but received nothing if an acquittal resulted. The court further found that the fees in this case amounted to $12.00 and that the mayor had been averaging about $100.00 a month from such fees in addition to his salary. In reversing the judgment the court said, speaking through Mr. Chief Justice Taft: "But it certainly violates the Fourteenth Amendment, and deprives a defendant in a criminal case of due process of law, to subject his liberty or property to the judgment of a court the judge of which has a direct, personal, substantial, pecuniary interest in reaching a conclusion against him in the case."

"As has often been stated, a defendant is entitled to a fair trial but not a perfect trial."[42] A judge is not disqualified because the judge is a layperson rather than a lawyer.[43]

(8)   Rights Relating to the Presentation of Evidence

A. THE RIGHT TO CONFRONT ADVERSE WITNESSES

Davis v. Washington

Supreme Court of the United States, 2006.
547 U.S. 813, 126 S.Ct. 2266, 165 L.Ed.2d 224.

■ JUSTICE SCALIA delivered the opinion of the Court.

These cases require us to determine when statements made to law enforcement personnel during a 911 call or at a crime scene are "testimonial" and thus subject to the requirements of the Sixth Amendment's Confrontation Clause.

I

A

The relevant statements in *Davis v. Washington*, No. 05–5224, were made to a 911 emergency operator on February 1, 2001. When the operator answered the initial call, the connection terminated before anyone spoke. She reversed the call, and Michelle McCottry answered. In the ensuing conversation, the operator ascertained that McCottry was involved in a

---

41.   273 U.S. 510, 47 S.Ct. 437, 71 L.Ed. 749 (1927). Accord: Ward v. Village of Monroeville, 409 U.S. 57, 93 S.Ct. 80, 34 L.Ed.2d 267 (1972).

42.   Moore v. United States, 375 F.2d 877, 882 (8th Cir.1967).

43.   North v. Russell, 427 U.S. 328, 96 S.Ct. 2709, 49 L.Ed.2d 534 (1976).

domestic disturbance with her former boyfriend Adrian Davis, the petitioner in this case:

"911 Operator: Hello.

"Complainant: Hello.

"911 Operator: What's going on?

"Complainant: He's here jumpin' on me again.

"911 Operator: Okay. Listen to me carefully. Are you in a house or an apartment?

"Complainant: I'm in a house.

"911 Operator: Are there any weapons?

"Complainant: No. He's usin' his fists.

"911 Operator: Okay. Has he been drinking?

"Complainant: No.

"911 Operator: Okay, sweetie. I've got help started. Stay on the line with me, okay? Complainant: I'm on the line.

"911 Operator: Listen to me carefully. Do you know his last name?

"Complainant: It's Davis.

"911 Operator: Davis? Okay, what's his first name?

"Complainant: Adrian

"911 Operator: What is it? Complainant: Adrian.

"911 Operator: Adrian?

"Complainant: Yeah.

"911 Operator: Okay. What's his middle initial?

"Complainant: Martell. He's runnin' now." App. in No. 05–5224, pp. 8–9.

As the conversation continued, the operator learned that Davis had "just r[un] out the door" after hitting McCottry, and that he was leaving in a car with someone else. *Id.,* at 9–10. McCottry started talking, but the operator cut her off, saying, "Stop talking and answer my questions." *Id.,* at 10. She then gathered more information about Davis (including his birthday), and learned that Davis had told McCottry that his purpose in coming to the house was "to get his stuff," since McCottry was moving. *Id.,* at 11–12. McCottry described the context of the assault, *id.,* at 12, after which the operator told her that the police were on their way. "They're gonna check the area for him first," the operator said, "and then they're gonna come talk to you." *Id.,* at 12–13.

The police arrived within four minutes of the 911 call and observed McCottry's shaken state, the "fresh injuries on her forearm and her face," and her "frantic efforts to gather her belongings and her children so that they could leave the residence." 154 Wash.2d 291, 296, 111 P.3d 844, 847 (2005) (en banc).

The State charged Davis with felony violation of a domestic no-contact order. "The State's only witnesses were the two police officers who responded to the 911 call. Both officers testified that McCottry exhibited injuries that appeared to be recent, but neither officer could testify as to the cause of the injuries." *Ibid.* McCottry presumably could have testified as to whether Davis was her assailant, but she did not appear. Over Davis's objection, based on the Confrontation Clause of the Sixth Amendment, the trial court admitted the recording of her exchange with the 911 operator, and the jury convicted him. The Washington Court of Appeals affirmed, 116 Wash.App. 81, 64 P.3d 661 (2003). The Supreme Court of Washington, with one dissenting justice, also affirmed, concluding that the portion of the 911 conversation in which McCottry identified Davis was not testimonial, and that if other portions of the conversation were testimonial, admitting them was harmless beyond a reasonable doubt. 154 Wash.2d, at 305, 111 P.3d, at 851. We granted certiorari. 546 U.S. 976, 126 S.Ct. 552, 163 L.Ed.2d 459 (2005).

B

In *Hammon v. Indiana,* No. 05–5705, police responded late on the night of February 26, 2003, to a "reported domestic disturbance" at the home of Hershel and Amy Hammon. 829 N.E.2d 444, 446 (Ind.2005). They found Amy alone on the front porch, appearing " 'somewhat frightened,' " but she told them that " 'nothing was the matter,' " *id.,* at 446, 447. She gave them permission to enter the house, where an officer saw "a gas heating unit in the corner of the living room" that had "flames coming out of the . . . partial glass front. There were pieces of glass on the ground in front of it and there was flame emitting from the front of the heating unit." App. in No. 05–5705, p. 16.

Hershel, meanwhile, was in the kitchen. He told the police "that he and his wife had 'been in an argument' but 'everything was fine now' and the argument 'never became physical.' " 829 N.E.2d, at 447. By this point Amy had come back inside. One of the officers remained with Hershel; the other went to the living room to talk with Amy, and "again asked [her] what had occurred." *Ibid.;* App. in No. 05–5705, at 17, 32. Hershel made several attempts to participate in Amy's conversation with the police, see *id.,* at 32, but was rebuffed. The officer later testified that Hershel "became angry when I insisted that [he] stay separated from Mrs. Hammon so that we can investigate what had happened." *Id.,* at 34. After hearing Amy's account, the officer "had her fill out and sign a battery affidavit." *Id.,* at 18. Amy handwrote the following: "Broke our Furnace & shoved me down on the floor into the broken glass. Hit me in the chest and threw me down. Broke our lamps & phone. Tore up my van where I couldn't leave the house. Attacked my daughter." *Id.,* at 2.

The State charged Hershel with domestic battery and with violating his probation. Amy was subpoenaed, but she did not appear at his subsequent bench trial. The State called the officer who had questioned Amy, and asked him to recount what Amy told him and to authenticate the affidavit. Hershel's counsel repeatedly objected to the admission of this evidence. See *id.,* at 11, 12, 13, 17, 19, 20, 21. At one point, after hearing the prosecutor defend the affidavit because it was made "under oath," defense counsel said, "That doesn't give us the opportunity to cross examine [the] person who allegedly drafted it. Makes me mad." *Id.,* at 19. Nonetheless, the trial court admitted the affidavit as a "present sense impression," *id.,* at 20, and Amy's statements as "excited utterances" that "are expressly permitted in these kinds of cases even if the declarant is not available to testify." *Id.,* at 40. The officer thus testified that Amy "informed me that she and Hershel had been in an argument. That he became irrate [sic] over the fact of their daughter going to a boyfriend's house. The argument became . . . physical after being verbal and she informed me that Mr. Hammon, during the verbal part of the argument was breaking things in the living room and I believe she stated he broke the phone, broke the lamp, broke the front of the heater. When it became physical he threw her down into the glass of the heater.

. . .

"She informed me Mr. Hammon had pushed her onto the ground, had shoved her head into the broken glass of the heater and that he had punched her in the chest twice I believe." *Id.,* at 17–18.

The trial judge found Hershel guilty on both charges, *id.,* at 40, and the Indiana Court of Appeals affirmed in relevant part, 809 N.E.2d 945 (2004). The Indiana Supreme Court also affirmed, concluding that Amy's statement was admissible for state-law purposes as an excited utterance, 829 N.E.2d, at 449; that "a 'testimonial' statement is one given or taken in significant part for purposes of preserving it for potential future use in legal proceedings," where "the motivations of the questioner and declarant are the central concerns," *id.,* at 456, 457; and that Amy's oral statement was not "testimonial" under these standards, *id.,* at 458. It also concluded that, although the affidavit was testimonial and thus wrongly admitted, it was harmless beyond a reasonable doubt, largely because the trial was to the bench. *Id.,* at 458–459. We granted certiorari. 546 U.S. 976, 126 S.Ct. 552, 163 L.Ed.2d 459 (2005).

II

The Confrontation Clause of the Sixth Amendment provides: "In all criminal prosecutions, the accused shall enjoy the right . . . to be confronted with the witnesses against him." In *Crawford v. Washington,* 541 U.S. 36, 53–54, 124 S.Ct. 1354, 158 L.Ed.2d 177 (2004), we held that this provision bars "admission of testimonial statements of a witness who did not appear at trial unless he was unavailable to testify, and the defendant had had a prior opportunity for cross-examination." A critical portion of this holding, and the portion central to resolution of the two cases now before us, is the phrase "testimonial statements." Only statements of this sort cause the declarant to be a "witness" within the meaning of the Confrontation Clause. See *id.,* at 51, 124 S.Ct. 1354. It is the testimonial character of the statement that separates it from other hearsay that, while subject to traditional limitations upon hearsay evidence, is not subject to the Confrontation Clause.

Our opinion in *Crawford* set forth "[v]arious formulations" of the core class of " 'testimonial' " statements, *ibid.,* but found it unnecessary to endorse any of them, because "some statements qualify under any definition," *id.,* at 52, 124 S.Ct. 1354. Among those, we said, were "[s]tatements taken by police officers in the course of interrogations," *ibid.;* see also *id.*, at 53, 124 S.Ct. 1354. The questioning that generated the deponent's statement in *Crawford*—which was made and recorded while she was in police custody, after having been given *Miranda* warnings as a possible suspect herself—"qualifies under any conceivable definition" of an " 'interrogation,'" 541 U.S., at 53, n. 4, 124 S.Ct. 1354. We therefore did not define that term, except to say that "[w]e use [it] ... in its colloquial, rather than any technical legal, sense," and that "one can imagine various definitions ..., and we need not select among them in this case." *Ibid.* The character of the statements in the present cases is not as clear, and these cases require us to determine more precisely which police interrogations produce testimony.

Without attempting to produce an exhaustive classification of all conceivable statements—or even all conceivable statements in response to police interrogation—as either testimonial or nontestimonial, it suffices to decide the present cases to hold as follows: Statements are nontestimonial when made in the course of police interrogation under circumstances objectively indicating that the primary purpose of the interrogation is to enable police assistance to meet an ongoing emergency. They are testimonial when the circumstances objectively indicate that there is no such ongoing emergency, and that the primary purpose of the interrogation is to establish or prove past events potentially relevant to later criminal prosecution.[1]

III

A

In *Crawford,* it sufficed for resolution of the case before us to determine that "even if the Sixth Amendment is not solely concerned with testimonial hearsay, that is its primary object, and interrogations by law enforcement officers fall squarely within that class." *Id.,* at 53, 124 S.Ct. 1354. Moreover, as we have just described, the facts of that case spared us the need to define what we meant by "interrogations." The *Davis* case today does not permit us this luxury of indecision. The inquiries of a police operator in the course of a 911 call[2] are an interrogation in one sense, but not in a sense that "qualifies under any conceivable definition." We must

---

1. Our holding refers to interrogations because, as explained below, the statements in the cases presently before us are the products of interrogations—which in some circumstances tend to generate testimonial responses. This is not to imply, however, that statements made in the absence of any interrogation are necessarily nontestimonial. The Framers were no more willing to exempt from cross-examination volunteered testimony or answers to open-ended questions than they were to exempt answers to detailed interrogation. (Part of the evidence against Sir Walter Raleigh was a letter from Lord Cobham that was plainly *not* the result of sustained questioning. *Raleigh's Case,* 2 How. St. Tr. 1, 27 (1603).) And of course even when interrogation exists, it is in the final analysis the declarant's statements, not the interrogator's questions, that the Confrontation Clause requires us to evaluate.

2. If 911 operators are not themselves law enforcement officers, they may at least be agents of law enforcement when they conduct interrogations of 911 callers. For purposes of this opinion (and without deciding the point), we consider their acts to be acts of the police. As in *Crawford v. Washington,* 541 U.S. 36, 124 S.Ct. 1354, 158 L.Ed.2d 177 (2004), therefore, our holding today makes it unnecessary to consider whether and when statements made to someone other than law enforcement personnel are "testimonial."

decide, therefore, whether the Confrontation Clause applies only to testimonial hearsay; and, if so, whether the recording of a 911 call qualifies.

The answer to the first question was suggested in *Crawford,* even if not explicitly held:

> "The text of the Confrontation Clause reflects this focus [on testimonial hearsay]. It applies to 'witnesses' against the accused—in other words, those who 'bear testimony.' 1 N. Webster, An American Dictionary of the English Language (1828). 'Testimony,' in turn, is typically 'a solemn declaration or affirmation made for the purpose of establishing or proving some fact.' *Ibid.* An accuser who makes a formal statement to government officers bears testimony in a sense that a person who makes a casual remark to an acquaintance does not." 541 U.S., at 51, 124 S.Ct. 1354.

A limitation so clearly reflected in the text of the constitutional provision must fairly be said to mark out not merely its "core," but its perimeter.

We are not aware of any early American case invoking the Confrontation Clause or the common-law right to confrontation that did not clearly involve testimony as thus defined. Well into the 20th century, our own Confrontation Clause jurisprudence was carefully applied only in the testimonial context. See, *e.g., Reynolds v. United States,* 98 U.S. 145, 158, 25 L.Ed. 244 (1879) (testimony at prior trial was subject to the Confrontation Clause, but petitioner had forfeited that right by procuring witness's absence); *Mattox v. United States,* 156 U.S. 237, 240–244, 15 S.Ct. 337, 39 L.Ed. 409 (1895) (prior trial testimony of deceased witnesses admitted because subject to cross-examination); *Kirby v. United States,* 174 U.S. 47, 55–56, 19 S.Ct. 574, 43 L.Ed. 890 (1899) (guilty pleas and jury conviction of others could not be admitted to show that property defendant received from them was stolen); *Motes v. United States,* 178 U.S. 458, 467, 470–471, 20 S.Ct. 993, 44 L.Ed. 1150 (1900) (written deposition subject to cross-examination was not admissible because witness was available); *Dowdell v. United States,* 221 U.S. 325, 330–331, 31 S.Ct. 590, 55 L.Ed. 753 (1911) (facts regarding conduct of prior trial certified to by the judge, the clerk of court, and the official reporter did not relate to defendants' guilt or innocence and hence were not statements of "witnesses" under the Confrontation Clause)....

Most of the American cases applying the Confrontation Clause or its state constitutional or common-law counterparts involved testimonial statements of the most formal sort—sworn testimony in prior judicial proceedings or formal depositions under oath—which invites the argument that the scope of the Clause is limited to that very formal category. But the English cases that were the progenitors of the Confrontation Clause did not limit the exclusionary rule to prior court testimony and formal depositions, see *Crawford, supra,* at 52, and n. 3, 124 S.Ct. 1354. In any event, we do not think it conceivable that the protections of the Confrontation Clause can readily be evaded by having a note-taking policeman *recite* the unsworn hearsay testimony of the declarant, instead of having the declarant sign a deposition. Indeed, if there is one point for which no case—English or early American, state or federal—can be cited, that is it.

The question before us in *Davis,* then, is whether, objectively considered, the interrogation that took place in the course of the 911 call produced testimonial statements. When we said in *Crawford, supra,* at 53, 124 S.Ct. 1354, that "interrogations by law enforcement officers fall squarely within [the] class" of testimonial hearsay, we had immediately in mind (for that was the case before us) interrogations solely directed at establishing the facts of a past crime, in order to identify (or provide evidence to convict) the perpetrator. The product of such interrogation, whether reduced to a writing signed by the declarant or embedded in the memory (and perhaps notes) of the interrogating officer, is testimonial. It is, in the terms of the 1828 American dictionary quoted in *Crawford,* " '[a] solemn declaration or affirmation made for the purpose of establishing or proving some fact.' " 541 U.S., at 51, 124 S.Ct. 1354. (The solemnity of even an oral declaration of relevant past fact to an investigating officer is well enough established by the severe consequences that can attend a deliberate falsehood. See, *e.g., United States v. Stewart,* 433 F.3d 273, 288 (C.A.2 2006) (false statements made to federal investigators violate 18 U.S.C. § 1001); *State v. Reed,* 2005 WI 53, ¶ 30, 280 Wis.2d 68, 695 N.W.2d 315, 323 (state criminal offense to "knowingly giv[e] false information to [an] officer with [the] intent to mislead the officer in the performance of his or her duty").) A 911 call, on the other hand, and at least the initial interrogation conducted in connection with a 911 call, is ordinarily not designed primarily to "establis[h] or prov[e]" some past fact, but to describe current circumstances requiring police assistance.

The difference between the interrogation in *Davis* and the one in *Crawford* is apparent on the face of things. In *Davis,* McCottry was speaking about events *as they were actually happening,* rather than "describ[ing] past events," *Lilly v. Virginia,* 527 U.S. 116, 137, 119 S.Ct. 1887, 144 L.Ed.2d 117 (1999) (plurality opinion). Sylvia Crawford's interrogation, on the other hand, took place hours after the events she described had occurred. Moreover, any reasonable listener would recognize that McCottry (unlike Sylvia Crawford) was facing an ongoing emergency. Although one *might* call 911 to provide a narrative report of a crime absent any imminent danger, McCottry's call was plainly a call for help against bona fide physical threat. Third, the nature of what was asked and answered in *Davis,* again viewed objectively, was such that the elicited statements were necessary to be able to *resolve* the present emergency, rather than simply to learn (as in *Crawford*) what had happened in the past. That is true even of the operator's effort to establish the identity of the assailant, so that the dispatched officers might know whether they would be encountering a violent felon. See, *e.g., Hiibel v. Sixth Judicial Dist. Court of Nev., Humboldt Cty.,* 542 U.S. 177, 186, 124 S.Ct. 2451, 159 L.Ed.2d 292 (2004). And finally, the difference in the level of formality between the two interviews is striking. Crawford was responding calmly, at the station house, to a series of questions, with the officer-interrogator taping and making notes of her answers; McCottry's frantic answers were provided over the phone, in an environment that was not tranquil, or even (as far as any reasonable 911 operator could make out) safe.

We conclude from all this that the circumstances of McCottry's interrogation objectively indicate its primary purpose was to enable police assistance to meet an ongoing emergency. She simply was not acting as a *witness;* she was not *testifying.* What she said was not "a weaker substitute for live testimony" at trial, *United States v. Inadi,* 475 U.S. 387, 394, 106 S.Ct. 1121, 89 L.Ed.2d 390 (1986), like Lord Cobham's statements in *Raleigh's Case,* 2 How. St. Tr. 1 (1603), or Jane Dingler's *ex parte* statements against her husband in *King v. Dingler,* 2 Leach 561, 168 Eng. Rep. 383 (1791), or Sylvia Crawford's statement in *Crawford.* In each of those cases, the *ex parte* actors and the evidentiary products of the *ex parte* communication aligned perfectly with their courtroom analogues. McCottry's emergency statement does not. No "witness" goes into court to proclaim an emergency and seek help.

Davis seeks to cast McCottry in the unlikely role of a witness by pointing to English cases. None of them involves statements made during an ongoing emergency. In *King v. Brasier,* 1 Leach 199, 168 Eng. Rep. 202 (1779), for example, a young rape victim, "immediately on her coming home, told all the circumstances of the injury" to her mother. *Id.,* at 200, 168 Eng. Rep., at 202. The case would be helpful to Davis if the relevant statement had been the girl's screams for aid as she was being chased by her assailant. But by the time the victim got home, her story was an account of past events.

This is not to say that a conversation which begins as an interrogation to determine the need for emergency assistance cannot, as the Indiana Supreme Court put it, "evolve into testimonial statements," 829 N.E.2d, at 457, once that purpose has been achieved. In this case, for example, after the operator gained the information needed to address the exigency of the moment, the emergency appears to have ended (when Davis drove away from the premises). The operator then told McCottry to be quiet, and proceeded to pose a battery of questions. It could readily be maintained that, from that point on, McCottry's statements were testimonial, not unlike the "structured police questioning" that occurred in *Crawford,* 541 U.S., at 53, n. 4, 124 S.Ct. 1354. This presents no great problem. Just as, for Fifth Amendment purposes, "police officers can and will distinguish almost instinctively between questions necessary to secure their own safety or the safety of the public and questions designed solely to elicit testimonial evidence from a suspect," *New York v. Quarles,* 467 U.S. 649, 658–659, 104 S.Ct. 2626, 81 L.Ed.2d 550 (1984), trial courts will recognize the point at which, for Sixth Amendment purposes, statements in response to interrogations become testimonial. Through *in limine* procedure, they should redact or exclude the portions of any statement that have become testimonial, as they do, for example, with unduly prejudicial portions of otherwise admissible evidence. Davis's jury did not hear the *complete* 911 call, although it may well have heard some testimonial portions. We were asked to classify only McCottry's early statements identifying Davis as her assailant, and we agree with the Washington Supreme Court that they were not testimonial. That court also concluded that, even if later parts of the call were testimonial, their admission was harmless beyond a reasonable doubt. Davis does not challenge that holding, and we therefore assume it to be correct.

B

Determining the testimonial or nontestimonial character of the statements that were the product of the interrogation in *Hammon* is a much easier task, since they were not much different from the statements we found to be testimonial in *Crawford*. It is entirely clear from the circumstances that the interrogation was part of an investigation into possibly criminal past conduct—as, indeed, the testifying officer expressly acknowledged, App. in No. 05–5705, at 25, 32, 34. There was no emergency in progress; the interrogating officer testified that he had heard no arguments or crashing and saw no one throw or break anything, *id.*, at 25. When the officers first arrived, Amy told them that things were fine, *id.*, at 14, and there was no immediate threat to her person. When the officer questioned Amy for the second time, and elicited the challenged statements, he was not seeking to determine (as in *Davis*) "what is happening," but rather "what happened." Objectively viewed, the primary, if not indeed the sole, purpose of the interrogation was to investigate a possible crime—which is, of course, precisely what the officer *should* have done.

It is true that the *Crawford* interrogation was more formal. It followed a *Miranda* warning, was tape-recorded, and took place at the station house, see 541 U.S., at 53, n. 4, 124 S.Ct. 1354. While these features certainly strengthened the statements' testimonial aspect—made it more objectively apparent, that is, that the purpose of the exercise was to nail down the truth about past criminal events—none was essential to the point. It was formal enough that Amy's interrogation was conducted in a separate room, away from her husband (who tried to intervene), with the officer receiving her replies for use in his "investigat[ion]." App. in No. 05–5705, at 34. What we called the "striking resemblance" of the *Crawford* statement to civil-law *ex parte* examinations, 541 U.S., at 52, 124 S.Ct. 1354, is shared by Amy's statement here. Both declarants were actively separated from the defendant—officers forcibly prevented Hershel from participating in the interrogation. Both statements deliberately recounted, in response to police questioning, how potentially criminal past events began and progressed. And both took place some time after the events described were over. Such statements under official interrogation are an obvious substitute for live testimony, because they do precisely *what a witness does* on direct examination; they are inherently testimonial.

Both Indiana and the United States as *amicus curiae* argue that this case should be resolved much like *Davis*. For the reasons we find the comparison to *Crawford* compelling, we find the comparison to *Davis* unpersuasive. The statements in *Davis* were taken when McCottry was alone, not only unprotected by police (as Amy Hammon was protected), but apparently in immediate danger from Davis. She was seeking aid, not telling a story about the past. McCottry's present-tense statements showed immediacy; Amy's narrative of past events was delivered at some remove in time from the danger she described. And after Amy answered the officer's questions, he had her execute an affidavit, in order, he testified, "[t]o establish events that have occurred previously." App. in No. 05–5705, at 18.

Although we necessarily reject the Indiana Supreme Court's implication that virtually any "initial inquiries" at the crime scene will not be testimonial, see 829 N.E.2d, at 453, 457, we do not hold the opposite—that *no* questions at the scene will yield nontestimonial answers. We have already observed of domestic disputes that "[o]fficers called to investigate ... need to know whom they are dealing with in order to assess the situation, the threat to their own safety, and possible danger to the potential victim." *Hiibel*, 542 U.S., at 186, 124 S.Ct. 2451. Such exigencies may *often* mean that "initial inquiries" produce nontestimonial statements. But in cases like this one, where Amy's statements were neither a cry for help nor the provision of information enabling officers immediately to end a threatening situation, the fact that they were given at an alleged crime scene and were "initial inquiries" is immaterial. Cf. *Crawford, supra,* at 52, n. 3, 124 S.Ct. 1354.

IV

Respondents in both cases, joined by a number of their *amici,* contend that the nature of the offenses charged in these two cases—domestic violence—requires greater flexibility in the use of testimonial evidence. This particular type of crime is notoriously susceptible to intimidation or coercion of the victim to ensure that she does not testify at trial. When this occurs, the Confrontation Clause gives the criminal a windfall. We may not, however, vitiate constitutional guarantees when they have the effect of allowing the guilty to go free. Cf. *Kyllo v. United States*, 533 U.S. 27, 121 S.Ct. 2038, 150 L.Ed.2d 94 (2001) (suppressing evidence from an illegal search). But when defendants seek to undermine the judicial process by procuring or coercing silence from witnesses and victims, the Sixth Amendment does not require courts to acquiesce. While defendants have no duty to assist the State in proving their guilt, they *do* have the duty to refrain from acting in ways that destroy the integrity of the criminal-trial system. We reiterate what we said in *Crawford:* that "the rule of forfeiture by wrongdoing ... extinguishes confrontation claims on essentially equitable grounds." 541 U.S., at 62, 124 S.Ct. 1354 (citing *Reynolds,* 98 U.S., at 158–159). That is, one who obtains the absence of a witness by wrongdoing forfeits the constitutional right to confrontation.

We take no position on the standards necessary to demonstrate such forfeiture, but federal courts using Federal Rule of Evidence 804(b)(6), which codifies the forfeiture doctrine, have generally held the Government to the preponderance-of-the-evidence standard, see, *e.g., United States v. Scott,* 284 F.3d 758, 762 (C.A.7 2002). State courts tend to follow the same practice, see, *e.g., Commonwealth v. Edwards,* 444 Mass. 526, 542, 830 N.E.2d 158, 172 (2005). Moreover, if a hearing on forfeiture is required, *Edwards,* for instance, observed that "hearsay evidence, including the unavailable witness's out-of-court statements, may be considered." *Id.,* at 545, 830 N.E.2d, at 174. The *Roberts* approach to the Confrontation Clause undoubtedly made recourse to this doctrine less necessary, because prosecutors could show the "reliability" of *ex parte* statements more easily than they could show the defendant's procurement of the witness's absence. *Crawford,* in overruling *Roberts,* did not destroy the ability of courts to protect the integrity of their proceedings.

We have determined that, absent a finding of forfeiture by wrongdoing, the Sixth Amendment operates to exclude Amy Hammon's affidavit. The Indiana courts may (if they are asked) determine on remand whether such a claim of forfeiture is properly raised and, if so, whether it is meritorious.

* * *

We affirm the judgment of the Supreme Court of Washington in No. 05–5224. We reverse the judgment of the Supreme Court of Indiana in No. 05–5705, and remand the case to that Court for proceedings not inconsistent with this opinion.

It is so ordered.

[The dissenting opinion of Justice Thomas is omitted]*

B. THE RIGHT TO PUT ON A DEFENSE

Due process requires a fair trial, and the Sixth Amendment confers on the accused the right to compulsory process to secure the attendance of witnesses in his favor. Based on due process, the Supreme Court has held that the criminal defendant has the right to give sworn testimony in his own defense. Ferguson v. Georgia, 365 U.S. 570 (1961). Relying on both due process and the Sixth Amendment, the Court has held unconstitutional state evidence rules that have the effect of excluding the out-of-court confession of another suspect.

The criminal defendant, however, does not have a right of free proof. Exclusionary rules of evidence that apply even-handedly to all litigants are constitutional when applied to the criminal defendant, so long as these rules are not "arbitrary or disproportionate" to some legitimate state interest, such as reliability (*see* United States v. Scheffer, 523 U.S. 303 (1998) (military rule of evidence barring evidence of polygraph examination held constitutional) or ensuring defense compliance with reasonable discovery rules (*see* Michigan v. Lucas, 500 U.S. 145 (1991) (upholding exclusion from trial of rape charge defense evidence of prior consensual sex between **D** and **V** because defense did not notify state before trial of intent to introduce such evidence as required by disclosure provision of rape shield law).

C. THE RIGHT TO PROOF BEYOND A REASONABLE DOUBT

On the due process requirement of proof beyond a reasonable doubt, see *In re Winship, supra* Chapter 1, and *Patterson v. New York, supra* Chapter 2.

---

* In Giles v. California, 128 S.Ct. 2678 (2008), the Court rejected the theory of "reflexive forfeiture" by holding that wrongdoing by the accused forfeits the confrontation clause objection only when the proof shows a motive to silence, as well as a wrongdoing that causes the unavailability of the declarant. In Melendez–Diaz v. Massachusetts, 129 S.Ct. 2527 (2009), the Court held that lab reports prepared by state forensic analysts are "testimonial" under the *Crawford* formula.

INDEX